£19-99

D1463956

Broadcasting It

The Cassell Lesbian and Gay Studies list offers a broad-based platform to lesbian, gay and bisexual writers for the discussion of contemporary issues and for the promotion of new ideas and research.

COMMISSIONING:
Steve Cook

CONSULTANTS:
Liz Gibbs
Christina Ruse
Peter Tatchell

Keith Howes

Broadcasting It

An Encyclopaedia of Homosexuality
on Film, Radio and TV in the UK 1923–1993

Foreword by Ned Sherrin

CASSELL

Cassell
Villiers House
41/47 Strand
London WC2N 5JE

387 Park Avenue South
New York
NY 10016–8810

First published 1993

British Library Cataloguing-in-Publication Data
A catalogue entry for this book is available from the British Library.

Library of Congress Cataloging-in-Publication Data
Applied for.

ISBN 0–304–32700–X (hardback)
      0–304–32702–6 (paperback)

Printed and bound in Great Britain by
Mackays of Chatham PLC, Chatham, Kent

Users' Guide

The encyclopaedia uses an A–Z arrangement. Entry terms appear in bold and individually are usually arranged letter by letter. Definite and indefinite articles appearing at the beginning of entry terms are ignored for filing purposes, while Mc is treated as Mac. Fictional characters have their form of address or initial name appearing at the beginning of an entry term (not in bold), but they are filed as though the surname appeared first.

In the text of an entry, titles of films, plays, documentaries, serials, series etc are displayed in italics, as are titles of books and stage plays. Titles of individual works within a series, of episodes within a serial and of broadcast short stories are given single quotation marks. In round brackets beside the relevant titles can be found the date of first broadcast (screening if it relates to a cinema presentation together with a code letter to denote whether the work is cinema, radio, television or – very occasionally – video; these categories may sometimes overlap because of different productions and near-simultaneous television and cinema showings). The citation of dates for cinema films, television and radio programmes relates, wherever possible, to the first public showing of each production in its country of origin. In some cases, however, when precise dates are either unavailable or difficult to assess, the work has been assigned a date which is the one most generally given in relevant reference works. Titles of songs are given quotation marks.

As well as listing all the milestones of television and radio's presentation of homosexuality and related issues over the past 70 years, *Broadcasting It* attempts to map some of the secret passages which broadcasting has allowed homosexuals or which homosexuals have created for themselves, even during the years where words, acts and identities were officially prohibited, those times when homosexuality did not exist as a topic for polite conversation, when people who were 'that way' laid low.

Context was everything. If certain words or phrases occurred in conjunction with a profession or a costume that regularly connoted deviance, it is tempting to believe, in the absence of concrete evidence, that the author, director, actor or costume designer is trying 'to tell us something'. Not all the characters or items listed in *Broadcasting It* can be 'read' as homosexual, or even sexually ambiguous. Sometimes there is a mood created by or around these people or objects, a feeling, a trace element. I have erred on the side of comprehensiveness in this area, helped by the use of small capitals for names, words, subjects and titles which are given their own entry elsewhere in the text. In this way the book can achieve a much greater depth in what must always remain, especially in its pre-liberation clothing, a very elusive pattern of voice, gesture, behaviour and interplay.

The entries themselves number over 3,000. They vary from a few lines to several pages. They can be grouped roughly in the following ways:

Characters in fiction or in legend. These are cited with their full name and/or nickname followed by information on the name of the actor(s) playing him or her and the title of the play, serial or series. Length of entry varies according to the significance of the role from a dramatic or historical viewpoint, or in terms of audience reaction.

Real-life people. These are cited surname first, followed by first name(s) and date of birth (if known) and, where relevant, of death (if known). Their inclusion reflects my judgement of their significance for, and impact upon, gay and lesbian culture and is not intended to suggest that any individual is specifically homosexually orientated. Some of the entries include extensive credits in – where appropriate – cinema, radio and television. Others indicate major highlights of a career, always giving prominence to gay or lesbian material. If someone's acknowledged homosexuality is a significant attribute of his or her contribution to gay and lesbian culture, I have made that clear in the entry.

Groups of people. A small number of entries relate to ethnic or national groups (Aborigines, Australians, black gay men and lesbians) or to generic groups (transvestites, transsexuals, young gay and lesbian people) etc.

Professions and jobs. These are cited under the most common term and usually relate only to the occupations of fictional characters in radio or television comedy or drama as well as films shown on television.

Names (of individual characters). I have attached considerable importance to the bestowing of certain names on fictional characters. Sometimes individual names are consistently applied to explicitly and implicitly gay or lesbian characters. Sometimes a first name appears regularly only in Britain or sometimes it is more noticeable in American productions. Often certain time periods throw a name into greater relief than others. These names are given individual entries with substantial examples of usage.

Similarly, first names with a special significance to gay men or lesbians are singled out, even if none or few relevant characters bear the name. There are also entries under first names and surnames which discuss the most frequent or the more intriguing examples. Names are featured in other entries, eg 'Gay' and 'penises', and are also to be found in abuse/slang terms.

Abstract subjects. These are roughly grouped as:

Domestic activities, eg bed, housework, housing, sewing and washing up.

Meeting places for homosexual people, eg bathhouse, bars and cinemas.

Politics, eg ACT UP and gay liberation.

Types of activity, eg dancing and drinking.

Titles of films and radio and television programmes. An entry carries the most commonly used English-language title followed by country or countries of production and the date of first release (with alternative date if sporadic screenings over a period of years). Wherever possible the title has been taken from the on-screen credit titles or from listings in *Radio Times* or *TV Times*. A brief description of the work is followed by production details.

Titles of songs and pieces of music.

Words. These are roughly grouped into:

Abuse: words intended to demean, belittle or intimidate gay or lesbian people – sometimes coined by themselves – and used in an aggressive way.

Catch-phrases: phrases or questions used on a regular basis by characters in series.

Euphemisms: words used by and about homosexual people which are or were intended to replace 'offensive' or 'embarrassing' ones.

Psycho-legal: words used in law or by the medical profession to define certain kinds of homosexual or homosexual behaviour.

Slang: this overlaps considerably with abuse and includes the homosexual 'secret language' polari.

Most of these words are not given a 'dictionary' definition. The aim of an entry is purely to show the development of the word(s) in fictional dialogue or everyday speech as heard on radio or television.

Cross-referencing is extensive. In addition to the use of small capitals for cross-references within an entry, numerous *see also* references appear at the end of entries.

Wherever possible, comments on material are derived from the actual works as broadcast or transmitted. However, because the book covers such a wide time period and so much material has not been preserved – especially that produced between 1923 and 1956 – reasonable use has been made of scripts and contemporary reviews in the *Listener* and selected national and regional newspapers. Nevertheless, the book is not intended to be a comprehensive critical analysis, merely a dip into a vast ocean.

I was enormously encouraged by Stephen Bourne, creator of the first lesbian and gay television season, 'Out of the Archives', which has now happily become an annual event under the auspices of the British Film Institute at the Museum of the Moving Image. Much gratitude also to Oliver Keen and to Hock Tin who checked and assimilated material for me in London. Invaluable was the generous and thoughtful provision of an airmail subscription to *Radio Times* from Valerie Blackborn, Barbie Boxall and Carolyn Keen which obliterated my isolation more than somewhat from Britain since 1986, as well as alerting me to relevant current material.

Salutations, too, to Mary Tinegate for her help with material, and to my sister Joy, whose valiant, long-suffering recording of programmes has ensured a measure of comprehensiveness in matters audio and televisual right up to the present moment.

In a warm sea of people who have kept up my morale through the years of research, I must particularly thank Colin Thurlow who has been a vigilant spotter of relevant matters in the US and, in Australia, Adrian Clarke, David Clarke, Cyrus Dumasia, Paul Knobel, Cedric Lee and Bruce Winn.

The book would not have been possible without the active faith, hope and (almost) charity of Steve Cook at Cassell, who, spurred on by the recommendation of Michael Mason, then of *Capital Gay*, was prepared to give the green light on the strength of one chapter.

The true angel and bringer of light in many hours of gloom and darkness (who would ever be interested in a book about 'gays and television'?) is my lover, friend, defender and counsellor who has had to live amid oceans of scraps of paper, drafts, drafts of drafts, video and audio tape for more years than anyone should have to care to remember.

Peter, I'm finally Broadcasting It.

Over the years, particularly when I grazed wild and free, untrammelled by being a reviewer or an activist or the compiler of a broadcasting encyclopaedia of a very particular kind, I have amassed a whole gallery of loves and hates on television and radio. In my searches through my memories, those of other people, the archives and the airwaves themselves, I have discarded a lot of material which, for one reason or another, I found unappealing. It is a selective rather than a comprehensive collection of sight and sound. Therefore, if your favourite programme (with that – very subtle – gay or lesbian message) is not to be found anywhere inside this book, you can write to me, via the publishers, with as many details as possible, and I'll move heaven and earth to track down the relevant work for possible inclusion in a follow-up volume.

But, for now, rejoice! This is homosexuality run amok through Britain's lounges, parlours and dining-rooms. Often unannounced, very often unrecognized (and therefore allowed its head). Through the miraculous technology available in the 20th century, a despised, threatened, disempowered minority group has been audible and visible, in a quite remarkable number of guises, for the past 70 years. The relative lack of inhibition granted to those who wish homosexuals not to be seen, if possible, and, most definitely, not to be heard enables mean-spirited condescension, untested hypotheses and jagged abuse to be highlighted in a way that, in the past as well as in the present day, would not have been allowed to be used against almost any other group in British society. The enormous constraints on the projection of positive characteristics by homosexuals also offer the delicious spectacle of much clever zigging and zagging, through the use of ambiguous phrases, gesture, nuance and context.

Broadcasting It, for all its bulk, is only one part of the long march of humanity as brought to us by mainstream home entertainment. Even something as detailed as this can only hint at the enormous battles fought, compromises made and courage needed (and often lacked) by the women and men who created the thousands of hours (out of thousands of thousands) of radio and television that have been specifically monitored – wherever possible by myself – for this project.

Specific thanks go to Irene Basterfield and her staff at the BBCTV Script Unit, and to Neil Sutcliffe and his colleagues at the BBC Written Archives Centre. Their assistance in preserving and then making accessible, through scripts, many hours of radio and television that are lost forever has been invaluable. In a different but similar vein,

Given the common language, a considerable number of quotations and examples are from the US, but television only since American radio, with a few exceptions, has not travelled to British shores. The inclusion of cinema films pays tribute both to their ubiquity on all four British channels and to television's role in making available film culture from many nations and across the whole talkie, and occasionally the silent, era.

Cinema's inclusion also brings lesbians and gays – and their parents, friends and workmates – sometimes grittier, often more erotic portrayals than can be managed in the present state of television, with its reliance upon 'family audience' time slots, ratings, advertising, sexual restraint and co-production finance. The other side of the celluloid coin is the undifferentiated nature of television, fuzzed even further by the advent of the remote control button and the fast forward. Films made years ago and with antediluvian attitudes towards homosexuals pop up without contextualization, and often with the full complement of biased baggage including streams of invective, suicide, murder and impenetrable gloom or ridicule.

The increasingly blurred line between cinema and video is almost entirely skirted in this work which is intended solely to represent works broadcast by a central body at appointed times. Videos for hire which can be played once or many times at whim have, except for one or two important examples, been left for a separate listing in someone else's compilation.

No schema can be entirely cut and dried. I have given due note to a few regional or local mainstream programmes where they illustrated particular subject areas better than or in addition to their more widespread counterparts. For better or worse, the viewpoint is generally South of Watford – or mid-Manhattan, uptown LA.

Because it is English-speaking and because it's been my country since the mid-1980s, a limited number of Australian radio and television programmes not available outside their country of origin are discussed. Another book – by a native of longer-standing – is needed to do justice to the work of the Australian Broadcasting Corporation (ABC) and to its much younger cousin, Special Broadcasting Services (SBS).

Biases and prejudices are at the heart of so many items in *Broadcasting It*. As well then to declare my own. I'm a gay man, middle-class British (of working-class parents and grandparents), raised on BBC radio and television, recently decanted to middle-class, white suburban Australia.

Television and radio throw out irreconcilable differences at us all the time; controversy and name-calling, shock tactics, daggers drawn. But essentially they aim for consensus, and letting sleeping dogs lie. Less airtime is made available for gradations of opinion, subtleties of emotion and feeling, crossovers of sense and sensibility. Perhaps this explains why, among not a few lesbians and gay people, broadcasting (by which most mean television) is viewed with the weary suspicion of the oft-seduced and oft-abandoned.

The huge spaces of time broadcasting needs to fill – coupled with the extreme potency of a section of society whose lives and behaviour are (or were until very recently) secret, off limits and condemned – mean that, per head of the gay population at least, certain aspects of the homosexual's lot are rarely off the sound and vision channels. The picture, so runs the litany, is skewed. Even the best intended programmes emerge as partial, defended by clauses and asterisks, unrepresentative of the 'normal', 'ordinary' lesbian woman or gay man living in Basildon, Essex or Swansea, Wales or, for that matter, Peoria, Illinois or Dubbo, Australia.

From this base – namely that television and radio are unwilling to show the Truth or a number of the Truths – homosexual viewers and listeners append all kinds of wild assertions and disgruntled beliefs to the motives of broadcasting companies, their employees and, in some cases, the strands of big business that indirectly pay the wages. However, the pros and cons of licensed national corporations versus commercial concerns, local as distinct from homogenized central programming, regulated and deregulated listening and watching are not the concern of this already fat book.

As far as possible the aim of *Broadcasting It* is to dip into the many subjects which are of specific interest to lesbian women, gay men and others who have been marginalized because of their sexual preferences. Some elements of homosexuality are dealt with in entries that are chock-a-block with examples, others are very short and sparsely represented.

In keeping with the title, I have mainly concentrated on material which has been available nationally inside Britain since the British Broadcasting Corporation (then Company) began its service in 1923, concentrating on drama, comedy, documentary and feature films. News bulletins, current affairs, sport and pop videos must wait for another day.

and ushered in, alternately roaring and bleating, the (mainly Western) phenomenon of Gay Liberation and its language of rights and freedom, of sexism and homophobia. The patchy gains were then threatened with obliteration by the arrival of AIDS in the early 1980s. A fifth time span would now appear to be upon us: post-AIDS hysteria, together with the dawn of the lesbian or gay citizen, seeking equality in employment, child-rearing, conjugality and service in the armed forces.

An encyclopaedia, rather than a history, seemed a better method of charting the choppy, 2 steps forward, 4, 5, 6 and 7 steps back or sideways progress of lesbian and gay people as projected, inhibited or propelled by the massive velocity of mainstream, national broadcasting.

The words that we use, many of the concepts and visual conceits that pertain to homosexuality either began or were nurtured in our living rooms or those of our parents or grandparents . The catch-phrases, the awful warnings, the dress and colour codings, even the first names and surnames of fictional characters were often selected and refined by radio and television to present a particular image of those who could not or would not obey. Not all these daubings were necessarily hostile in intent; indeed many flowed upwards from the subculture itself.

I have concentrated for the most part on sounds and images from the airwaves to the exclusion of the most usual reference work bundles of quotations from books, newspapers, magazines and official reports, although these have been included where they illustrate a particularly juicy flurry of opinion by individuals or groups. In general, however, I have tried to let the pervasive national home entertainments speak for themselves: a narrative form which will become more common as the colossal relevance of broadcasting seeps through the traditional bounds of general knowledge, history, science, language, art and religion.

The words recorded here emanate from ephemeral 'stars', fictional characters and caricatures, from pundits and from activists. Each quote aims to flesh out a particular production, topic or prejudice: the cliché, the punchline, the philosophical, the erotic, the subtle, the crude. They are the croûtons in this alphabet soup of electronic feelings and opinions from and about the world as they especially, but far from entirely, impact on those who are deemed to live on its periphery.

Strange bedfellows: Rock Hudson and Professor Jacob Bronowski; Margaret Thatcher and Greta Garbo; Dixon of Dock Green and Ian McKellen; Mr Humphries and Colin from Albert Square; police and perfume; ACT UP and Ambridge.

Preface

Catch-phrases, songs, household names. Sitcoms, drama, documentaries, dramatized documentaries. Stereotypes and role models. Villainy and heroism. Witches and vampires. Love and kisses. Nudity. Things cut and uncut. Family favourites, children's favourites and things seen only after 11 o'clock.

That's obviously the broadcasting part. But what about the 'It'?

Put simply, *Broadcasting It* is a collection of lists and essays on areas in nationwide radio and (terrestrial) television which describe – or fail to describe – people who are homosexual, bisexual, transvestite, transsexual or otherwise outside the *cordon sanitaire* of 100 per cent heterosexual normality as enshrined most recently by the Thatcher government's Clause 28 (now Section 28 of the Local Government Act 1988).

The title derives from the commonly heard cry: 'Yes, I'm homosexual/gay/lesbian/bisexual/queer/a dyke. But I don't broadcast it.'

Although not in any way a linear history of the 20th century as it has affected lesbians, gays and other sexual minorities, this encyclopaedia – a kind of archaeological dig through the airwaves – inevitably stratifies much of its contents into years and decades.

Some of the pieces forcefully demonstrate the four eras of 20th-century British homosexual history beginning with the post-Oscar Wilde trial paranoia blending into the Red Queens under the bed scares of the post-Second World War period; then the bluer skies but still blustery winds of the Wolfenden Committee and its 1957 Report leading to much greater discussion and political lobbying for repeal of the 'Blackmailer's Charter' which had done for Wilde, destroyed the lives of so many other men (and by association and legal penalty harmed the careers of lesbians like Maud Allen and Radclyffe Hall).

This second epoch ended in good old British compromise (the 1967 Sexual Offences Act) and Manhattan tumult (the 1969 Stonewall riots) revealed that, at the opening night of Commercial TV's Birmingham studio, Tyrone Power tried to seduce him in the bathroom. Monkhouse resisted and Power told him that he 'had blown it'! Silently Monkhouse begged to differ.

One vital pre-reform TV sketch, *But My Dear* by Peter Shaffer, deserves a mention in the next edition. He was inspired to write it for *That Was the Week That Was* by the trial of John Vassall, the homosexual spy, and the courtroom examination of his correspondence with his Minister, Thomas Galbraith. Lance Percival and David Kernan played it. A senior civil servant quizzes his junior about a letter he has drafted full of compromising phrases; 'Dear', 'favour of an early reply' and 'thanking you in anticipation' are all found to conceal blatant *double entendres*. The senior finally hits the roof when he reads the sign-off 'Your obedient servant' and discovers that his junior's name is 'Fairy'. His last word on the subject is: 'The only way to stop a homosexual being blackmailed is to stop him being a homosexual. And the only way you can do that is to lock him up in a building with 500 other men. That way he can see how unattractive they really are.'

I look forward to welcoming new editions of *Broadcasting It* as more and more material becomes available to the indefatigable Keith Howes.

NED SHERRIN

Foreword

I shudder in awe at the amount of time and scholarship Keith Howes has lavished on this mammoth, invaluable and timely book – ranging far wider than the United Kingdom to which he limits himself in his subtitle. Perhaps he feels that only in this area can he claim to be fully comprehensive. He is too modest.

The encyclopaedia does not appear a moment too soon; but I suppose Mr Howes needed the passing of a few decades to throw up enough screen and airwave evidence after the loosening up of the Wolfenden Report (1957) and the change in the law (1967). Certainly the effect of the Labouchere amendment in the nineteenth century was to inhibit discussion for the next 80 years as certainly as it contained gay behaviour behind the closet doors.

I am not sure why, apart from the boundaries set by his title, Mr Howes has largely ignored the theatre, where the missionary stance of the late 1950s and 1960s was a more potent instrument towards changes in the law than in any other performance medium. Perhaps it would have made an already huge work too long; but, after all, Sir Ian McKellen has said that one key reason why he became an actor was 'because I thought I would meet a lot of queers'; and Mr Howes could also have included Dame Judi Dench's account of a rehearsal of *The Gay Lord Quex* in the crypt of St James's Church, Piccadilly, in London. It was interrupted by a man who rushed out of a loo holding aloft a pair of trousers, mysteriously pursued by another man who was wearing no trousers at all. Dame Judi, her director, Sir John Gielgud and the rest of the cast laughed so much that they could not continue and rehearsals were cancelled for the day.

Another equally conscientious and scholarly writer will have to take up the torch for the stage. Meanwhile Mr Howes will be fully occupied in keeping his witty and comprehensive researches up to date. Bob Monkhouse, in his autobiography *Crying with Laughter*, has recently

Contents

Main Published Sources

Books

Box of Delights: The Golden Years of Television by Hilary Kingsley and Geoff Tibballs. Macmillan, London, 1989. 314 pp.

British Film Actors' Credits, 1895–1987 by Scott Palmer. St James Press, Chicago and London, 1988. xviii, 917 pp.

The Celluloid Closet: Homosexuality in the Movies by Vito Russo. Harper & Row, New York, 1981; 2nd ed 1987. xii, 368 pp.

Encyclopaedia of Homosexuality, ed Wayne R. Dynes. Garland, New York and London, 2 vols, 1990. xxxviii, 1484 pp.

Gays and Film, ed Richard Dyer. Zoetrope, New York, rev. ed 1984. 110 pp.

Halliwell's Filmgoer's Companion by Leslie Halliwell. Grafton Books, London, 9th ed 1988. xiv, 786 pp.

Halliwell's Television Companion by Leslie Halliwell with Philip Purser. Grafton Books, London, 3rd ed 1986. xv, 941 pp.

The Lavender Screen by Boze Hadleigh. Citadel Press, New York, 1993. 254 pp.

Leonard Maltin's Movie and Video Guide. Signet Books, 1992. xxv, 1487 pp.

Now You See It. Studies on Lesbian and Gay Film by Richard Dyer. Routledge, London and New York, 1990. xi, 328 pp.

The Oxford Companion to English Literature, ed Margaret Drabble. Oxford University Press, Oxford, 1985. xii, 1155 pp.

The Radio Companion: The A–Z Guide to Radio – from Its Inception to the Present Day by Paul Donovan. HarperCollins, London, 1991. xii, 301 pp.

The Story of Cinema: An Illustrated History by David Shipman. Hodder & Stoughton, London, 2 vols, 1982 & 1984. 1280 pp.

Total Television: A Comprehensive Guide to Programming from 1948 to the Present by Alex McNeil. Penguin Books, New York and London, 1980; rev. ed 1984. vii, 1027 pp.

Vampires and Violets: Lesbians in the Cinema by Andrea Weiss. Jonathan Cape, London, 1992. 184 pp.

We Can Always Call Them Bulgarians: The Emergence of Lesbians and Gay Men on the American Stage by Kaier Curtin. Alyson, Boston, 1987. 342 pp.

Who's Who: An Annual Biographical Dictionary. Black, London, 1849– Annual. (Also *Who Was Who* from the same publisher.)

Newspapers, Magazines and Journals
Gay News, 1972–83. GN Publications Ltd. Fortnightly.

The Listener, 1929–91. Listener Publications Ltd. Weekly.

Monthly Film Bulletin, 1934–91. British Film Institute. (Now part of *Sight and Sound*.)

Radio Times, 1923–   . BBC Magazines. Weekly.

TV Times, 1955–   . Independent Television Publications/IPC magazines. Weekly.

Variety, 1905–   . Variety Inc. Weekly.

Together with personal viewings of or listenings to over 3,000 broadcast programmes, and sightings of over 700 scripts of plays, serials, series episodes and comedy shows.

Of great help over the years of gestation and preparation have been informal talks as well as formal interviews with many actors, writers, directors and producers. Among the most significant have been the late Jonquil Antony, actor–writer Neil Bartlett, Glyn Dearman of BBC Radio 4 Drama, writer–producer W. Stephen Gilbert, writer Jill Hyem, writer David Sale and the late Lord (Ted) Willis.

Abbreviations

Aust	Australia
C	Cinema films
c	*circa*
Can	Canada
Ch	Choreographer
co-D, co-W etc	co-Director, co-Writer etc
Cr	Creator
D	Director
E	Editor
EP	Executive Producer
Fr	France
Ger	Germany
It	Italy
L	Lyrics
M	Music
Narr	Narrator
Neth	Netherlands
NZ	New Zealand
P	Producer
R	Radio
Sc	Scotland
Sp	Spain
Sw	Sweden
T	Television
V	Video
W	Writer/Adaptor

Aboriginal people/Aborigines Possibly the world's smallest, most important minority, caretakers of AUSTRALIA for 40,000 years. Often presented as no-hopers, criminals and/or drunks. NUMBER 96 was unusual for its time (mid-1970s) for including Justine Sanders as a hairdresser. Gay and lesbian Aborigines were seen and heard for the first time in OUT 'Double Trouble' (1991 T).

abortion There was an allusion to one in *I Am a Camera* (1955 C) and the aftermath of one shown in the musical version CABARET (1972 C); there was intense discussion about a termination (between Dr Dale and a colleague) in THE DALES in 1967. Michelle had one (Lofty's impregnation) in EASTENDERS (1986 T); and so did Elizabeth Archer in THE ARCHERS (1992 R). Discussed now in relation to gay/lesbian embryos: THE GAY AND LESBIAN WORLD and *Equinox* (1992 T); and Brian was devastated when his girlfriend insisted on an abortion, partly after learning he was gay, in TOGETHER ALONE.

About Men A trio of 1983 documentaries enquiring into men's expectations, feelings and relationships. A group of 10 men from Coventry was featured. The producer/director Paul Morrison commented: 'These particular films grew out of 12 years of wondering and talking about my own upbringing and role as a man. The women I have been close to have all been feminists who supported attempts that I and other men around me were making to make sense of our lives and purposes in gender terms' (CHANNEL 4 press release).

One of the three, *About Men ... And Men* explored 'the sensitive issue of men's relationships with other men and with friendship between men. ... As gay men and women have become more open about their rights over the past 50 years, and particularly in the last decade, so it seems men's anxieties have come more to the surface, leading on the one hand to brutal attacks on gay people, both physically and legislatively, and on the other hand attempts by some men to question their own sexuality. In our society it seems that not only homosexuality, but any expression of affection of one man for one another must be regarded with extreme caution' (from the booklet accompanying the series).

Two 'STRAIGHT' men from the group volunteered to confront two gays in a club, and find out who and what they were. Barry Johnston, a carpenter, reported back his findings: 'Maybe I was expecting three eyes, but once I got talking to them ... I could see their side of it which I never seen before. They're all right. It's a lot of codswallop that's been dinned into me by a lot of bloody idiots.'

About Men SBS Television in Australia presented 30 special documentaries, films, comedies and dramas solely devoted to the diverse, rich and colourful subject of the male during July 1992. A number dealt specifically with gay men and included showings of PARTING GLANCES, LAW OF DESIRE and *L'Homme Blessé*.

Abse, Leo (1917–) MP. Chief among those responsible in the House of Commons for pushing through changes to the law under which male homosexuals could be sent to prison – and for the Divorce Reform Bill.

On *Talkabout* (1980 R) he extolled the benefits of fatherhood and father figures. 'The committed homosexual, the whole homosexual has the disadvantage – and serious disadvantage – of not being likely to become a father.' It was the absence of a father figure, he said, that led to children growing up gay – no, not gay, homo-sex-u-al. ROSE ROBERTSON, from Parents Enquiry, was on the panel. In her non-threateningly chiding way, she asked Abse for clarification: 'If [what you say] were true, how can you explain that during the last world war many young boys were left in the care of their mother for the best part of six years and yet the incidence of homosexuality has shown no increase?'

Abse was the subject of a 1979 radio *Profile*, and was featured, deploring gay liberation and all its acts, in HOMOSEXU-ALITY – THE YEARS OF CHANGE (1977 R).

Absolute Hell! (UK 1991 T) Alcoholic NYMPHOMANIAC Christine Foskett (Judi Dench) runs a seedy drinking club for American servicemen and 'no-hopers', including her on–off BISEXUAL lover (William Nigh). Set in the weeks leading up to the 1945 election and condemned as a 'libel on the British people' (and that was with the gay scenes omitted). The play, lively and depressing by turns, contained various gay characters and two lesbians, one of whom has a heart attack and dies.
W: Rodney ACKLAND (1951 play *The Pink Room*); P: Simon Curtis; D: Anthony Page; 5.10.91; BBC2.

Absolutely Positive (US 1990 T) A look at the lives of some of the estimated 1.5 million Americans who are infected with HIV but do not yet have AIDS. Men and women from 17 to 60 across America reveal themselves.
D: Peter Adair, Janet Cole and Veronica Silver; 90 mins.

abuse Quentin CRISP was a recipient of much verbal as well as physical pummelling in London for three decades ('You effing PANSY, you ought to be locked up' in THE NAKED CIVIL SERVANT). Gay people abusing each other (affectionately?) included Charlie DYER in STAIRCASE who showers his Harry with anti-endearments such as 'ramshackle old QUEEN', and 'mean, slutfaced puff'.

Army drill instructors have long used anti-gay language to exhort their men to greater heights of buttressed masculinity. In *The Wild Geese* (1978 C) the mercenary Whitty (Kenneth GRIFFITH) is jumped on from a great height by a massive sergeant-major: 'You bleeding, screaming FAGGOT. Get up before I ... up your arse!'

By the 1970s 'QUEER' and 'POOF' were so much part of the accepted national argot that the beleaguered black hero Bill (Rudolph Walker) of *Love Thy Neighbour* (1971–74 T) fights back against his white oppressor (Jack Smethurst) by calling him a 'racialist poof'. In a kindlier vein, the BROTHERS in ACCOUNTS rough each other up physically to the accompaniment of cries of 'queer' and 'poof'. In America, teenage comedies and tough guy movies used and continue to use such epithets as 'faggot' and 'FAIRY' with the same concentrated vehemence as 'mugger', 'rapist' and 'CHILD MOLESTER'.
See also SLANG WORDS FOR HOMOSEXUALS.

Academy Awards Known as Oscars. After a number of nominations (Al Pacino in DOG DAY AFTERNOON etc), an actor (William Hurt) finally won an Oscar (in 1985) for starring as an openly gay man (the prisoner who uses his imagination to escape in KISS OF THE SPIDER WOMAN).

Winners include THE TIMES OF HARVEY MILK (1984 Best Documentary); RAY'S HETEROSEXUAL DANCE HALL (1987 Best Short); COMMON THREADS: STORIES FROM THE QUILT (1990 Best Documentary); Callie Khouri for the original script for THELMA AND LOUISE (1991). Recent nominees include: Robert Preston in VICTOR/VICTORIA (1982 Supporting Actor); Bruce Davison in LONGTIME COMPANION (1990 Supporting Actor); Tommy Lee Jones as Clay Shaw in *JFK* (1991 Supporting Actor); Fanni Flagg and Carol Sobieski for Best Adapted Screenplay for FRIED GREEN TOMATOES AT THE WHISTLE STOP CAFE (1991).

In 1992, the 3-hour show was watched by one billion people in 86 countries.

Access 'Offensive to Some' (UK 1973 R) A talk on BBC Radio 3 by John Chesterman in which he tried, in 20 minutes, to widen the narrowed worldview into which gay people were being squeezed. Why should the sexual spectrum be weighted at the extremities instead of balanced in the centre? Why should anyone be denied even the possibility of communication in such a natural way with half the human race? 'We have been taught to hate ourselves and the guilt and cynicism run so deep that it has taken until now for even a handful of us to question the process to honestly assess our nature and identity, and realize, with growing anger, that we're not the criminals, but the victims, that we're not the sickness but may be part of the cure.' 'Victims' and 'sickness' were familiar and comforting. It was the concept of actively helping to cure the whole society that could be neither swallowed nor countenanced.

This was the listening public's first introduction to gay liberation: spells equal, spells balance, spells justice.

access programmes The chance for viewers and listeners to express their views to a national audience. R: *Any Answers?* which began in 1955, the companion to ANY QUESTIONS? T: POINTS OF VIEW from 1962, presented first by Robert Robinson and more recently by Anne Robinson on BBC1; CHANNEL 4's RIGHT TO REPLY from 1983. Individuals or groups could make themselves heard, with a significant degree of technical and editorial help, in BBC2's *Open Door* and *Open Space*. VIDEO DIARIES 'written' by one person in the privacy of their lives began in the 1980s, including 'Diary of a Frontliner' in the 40 MINUTES series in 1988 (Peter, who had AIDS, recording his personal reflections). A degree of access was afforded by the programmes made by the London Minorities Unit such as GAYLIFE and *Skin*.

In Australia, viewers can have their say about ABC programmes on *BackChat* and about those presented by SBS on *Hot Line*. For gays and lesbians, no national access exists through broadcast media although there are now local radio programmes like Sydney's GAYWAVES and *Wild Gals* which are volunteer run and encourage listeners to ring in with views and requests.

See also PHONE-INS.

Accolade (UK 1957 T) A public figure, Will Trenting MP (James Donald), is exposed as an orgy-goer.
D: Desmond Davies; 15.5.57; Associated Rediffusion.

Emlyn WILLIAMS' stage play preceded SEPARATE TABLES in disguising homosexuality and prodding society's double standards. The *TV Times* synopsis spoke of the protagonist being 'threatened by the strange forces in his own nature.' Variants of this phrase would become increasingly familiar in capsule descriptions of television and radio plays in the post-WOLFENDEN REPORT decade.

Williams wrote a much shorter story of entrapment, crackling with forbidden undertones, in the portmanteau film *Friday the Thirteenth* (1933), in which he played the blackmailer 'William Blake' who told his victim (Frank Lawton) that he was 'awfully active'.

accountants Mouse-like creatures: Carmen, Madame Irma's book-keeper and lover in *The Balcony* (Lee Grant 1963 C; June Tobin 1964 R); George with young lover under threat in *Target* 'The Run' (1978 T); James Ridley-Bowes, the family friend who lusts after one of the brothers in ACCOUNTS (George Pensiotti, 1982 R; Jonathan Newth, 1983 T); Antoine (Francis Frappat) in NOIR ET BLANC (1986 C) who tells his newfound friend, the black masseur, that he had been too shy to explore what he really wanted: 'Like everything in my life it was no choice of mine. Now that it's there, all I want is to satisfy it.'

Accounts (UK 1983 T) Fighting fluctuating markets and skyrocketing interest rates, the dairy and sheep farming Mawson brothers Andy (Robert Smeaton) and Donald (Michael McNally) still have some energy for a cuddle in the night. Donald takes the initiative with an older man (Jonathan Newth) while eating fish and chips after a Young Farmers' music hall – and is politely rebuffed. He then tells his experienced elder brother that he's more into 'taps' than 'ewes'.
W: Michael Wilcox; P: Tom Sachs; D: Michael Darlow; 22.12.83; Channel 4; 90 mins.

Underneath the simple season-by-season sheep and dairy farming calendar is a searching story of buried feelings. The decision of the younger brother to seek love from men emerges only obliquely. And in the final minutes, a stray line of dialogue begs more questions, intriguing ones, about the family ram.

> Donald: 'Maybe you could sleep in your own bed from now on.'
> Andy: 'It's cold ... there's no need for rules.'

Achilles God-hero of the Greeks. He is given a lover, Patroclus, in the Trojan War plays of Aeschylus, the surviving fragments of which were performed during Kenneth Dover's series *The Greeks* (1980 T). Achilles is usually depicted as mean, moody and magnificent: Stanley Baker in *Helen of Troy* (1956 C, with Terence Longdon, a colourless Patroclus) and Robert Hardy in *The Anger of Achilles* (1964 R) being typical. Exceptions were Kenneth Haigh in the wall-to-wall camp interpretation of *Troilus and Cressida* (1981 T) and Alick ROWE's wicked rerouting of the mythical character via Glasgow and gay liberation (Henry Stamper, OPERATION LIGHTNING PEGASUS 1981 R).

Achilles and Patroclus. 'Lovers in war', 'bonded' but not necessarily 'homosexual'. They are the narrators of ALEXANDER (1993 R). In VALMOUTH, the two chums liken themselves to the Greek war buddies as they launch into 'It's Fine to Have a Friend'.

Ackerley, J[oseph] R[andolph] (1896–1967) British writer and literary editor of the *Listener*. His play *The Prisoners of War* (1924) produced on radio in 1953 as THE INTERNED. Henry REED's flustered young pup in the Richard SHEWIN radio dramas of the 1950s is supposedly one-quarter based on Reed's friend, who liked picking up working lads on a number of continents.

Ackerley is depicted as callow young Joe in SECRET ORCHARDS (Joseph Blatchley 1980 T) lusting after FOOTBALLERS, having sex in a train toilet and trying to discover the truth about his FATHER; in WE THINK THE WORLD OF YOU (1980 T) he is the older, much respected J. R. Ackerley living with his beloved Alsatian, QUEENIE, and having companionable affairs with young, heterosexually identified working men. Benjamin WHITROW played him in the latter, bringing off one of the most difficult tasks given to an actor: suggesting literary taste, intellectual curiosity, warm friendship, compulsive cruising and mild bestiality. Alan BATES was Ackerley (but called 'Frank') in the 1988 film version of *We Think the World of You.*

Ackland, Rodney (1908–91) English playwright and screenwriter whose best work is crafted with great passion and insight. His *The Pink Room* was televised (with all cuts, mainly relating to its many gay and lesbian characters, restored) as ABSOLUTE HELL! Other plays include: *Before the Party* (1930 R); *A Dead Secret* (1959 T); *The Dark River* (1986 R, with Ackland himself as Mr Veness). Hilary Spurling called the latter 'perhaps the one indisputably great play of the past half century in English'. He worked with Alfred HITCHCOCK in the 1930s, adapted Hugh WALPOLE's THE OLD LADIES for the stage, and wrote the screenplays for *Bank Holiday* (1938), *49th Parallel* (1941) and *The Queen of Spades* (1948).

acting The sharp division between an actor's search for truth and the encroachment of social conditioning is particularly acute with gay or lesbian, or even bisexual, roles. The combination of social unacceptability with the unlocking of inner doors causes many actors and actresses to shun any hint of sexual ambivalence in their professional lives. This was especially true in the 1960s and early 1970s in America. Angela Lansbury, for example, turned down the leading role in THE KILLING OF SISTER GEORGE. When casting for the TV movie THAT CERTAIN SUMMER in 1972, the producers approached a leading actor at a party and asked him to play the main role. He refused point-blank, saying that his fans would never accept him as a homosexual. When asked if he would consider playing Hitler he replied, 'Of course.'

The climate has changed radically since then, with the range of acting talent willing to essay such roles now expanded fourfold. However, projects like THE FRONT RUNNER and RUBYFRUIT JUNGLE remain unrealised because no actors with any kind of box office pull are willing to commit themselves to playing a gay hero or lesbian heroine.

'Don't play no faggots,' Sylvester Stallone is supposed to have counselled Perry King – who ignored the advice and played the lead in A DIFFERENT STORY.

In 1991, Harry Hamlin still saw MAKING LOVE as his major career disaster which left him, 9 years later and after 5 years as a TV star in L.A. LAW, virtually blacklisted from major film-making. 'It closed off certain avenues that, had I been able to exploit them, would probably mean that I would now be making my choices about feature films, good ones, rather than television and not-so-good feature films. A lot of people responded very negatively to that picture' (*Radio Times*, 24–30.8.91).

Hamlin had told the *Washington Post* in 1986: 'A guy can play an ax murderer and still be considered sexy and still get another role as leading man. But if you play a homosexual, suddenly you're not in contention anymore for the ax murderers.' And *Time* magazine noted: 'Though Hamlin's credentials as a heterosexual were beyond dispute – he was living at the time with sexy Ursula Andress – his realistic characterization cast his career into a gloom that was lifted only by TV's L.A. LAW' (4.7.88).

Acton, Sir Harold (1904–   ) Historian, novelist and Oxford contemporary of Evelyn WAUGH. He wrote *Memoirs of an Aesthete* in 1948. Partly the inspiration for Anthony BLANCHE. Very visible (on programmes like AQUARIUS) from the late 1960s onwards: *Contrasts* (1968 T); *Evelyn Waugh* (1967 R); *Portrait of Brian Howard* (1968 R); *Aquarius* 'Sir Harold in Italy' (1971 T); *The Faces of* MAUGHAM (1974 R); *Russell* HARTY

(1976 T); *Lord* BERNERS (1983 R); *Norman* DOUGLAS*: Looking Back* (1987 R); ARENA 'The Waugh Trilogy – Bright Young Thing' (1987 T).

actors Cecil 'Tiny' Calloway, 'Cherry-blossom in Chelsea'-style matinée idol in VICTIM; David Dane (James Villiers), TV flavour of the month in *Girl in the Headlines* (1963 C); Alfred 'Alfie' Knight (Clinton Greyn), Shakespearian actor with despised COCKNEY roots (*The Love Machine* 1971 C); Martin Kurath (Jurgen Prochnow), imprisoned in THE CONSEQUENCE; Randy Brent (Tony Curtis), Hollywood idol in *The Users* (1978 T); Sparger (Michael Deacon), an off-off Broadway performer in KENNEDY'S CHILDREN; Jimmy Perino (James COCO), perennial young hopeful in *Only When I Laugh* (1981 C); George Banks (Peter WOODTHORPE 1976 R, Tom Courtenay 1985 T), ageing *jeune premier* with a marshmallow heart in Noel COWARD's *Me and the Girls*; Howard Palin (Patrick Cassidy), beefy and beautiful in LONGTIME COMPANION: 'He rents with another guy. They both have fabulous bodies. *You tell me*,' exclaims Willy's sister; Rock HUDSON (Thomas Ian Griffith) in *Rock Hudson* (1990 T).

actors playing female characters C: Silent era – John Bunny; Fatty Arbuckle in *Miss Fatty's Seaside Lovers*; Wallace Beery as Sweedie; Charlie Chaplin as *A Woman*. Talkies – Julian ELTINGE; LAUREL AND HARDY as their wives; Arthur Lucan as Old Mother Riley; Alec Guinness (as Lady Agatha D'Ascoyne) in *Kind Hearts and Coronets* (1949); Alastair Sim in *The Belles of St Trinians* (as headmistress Millicent Fritton and her crooked brother 1954); Peter SELLERS in *The Mouse That Roared* (as the Grand Duchess 1959), and as Queen Victoria in *The Great McGonagall* (1974); Peter BULL (as Queen ANNE in *Yellowbeard* 1983); DIVINE in *Pink Flamingos, Female Trouble, Lust in the Dust, Hairspray*; Dorothy Richards aka Michael Dorsey (Dustin Hoffman) in *Tootsie* (1983); Dom de Luise as Auntie in *Haunted Honeymoon* (1986); Dabney

Coleman as Aunt Bea in *Meet the Applegates* (1991).

R: Harry GORDON from Aberdeen portrayed 'wifies' (fish wives) during 1920s and 1930s in such sketches as 'Fish', 'The Dentist's Chair', 'Stung' and 'Mrs McIntyre Visits the Sick'; Arthur MARSHALL as Nurse DUGDALE; Al Reid; Dan Agar as MRS 'OBBS (1950s).

T: Norman Evans in *Over the Garden Wall*; Rex JAMESON as Mrs SHUFFLEWICK; Hylda Baker's stooge Cynthia; Dick Emery as Mandy; Barry HUMPHRIES as Dame Edna EVERAGE; John INMAN in ARE YOU BEING SERVED? (as his mother); George Logan and Patrick Fyffe as HINGE AND BRACKET; Kenny EVERETT as Venus; Les Dawson as a gluttonous centenarian in *Nona* (1991).

actresses Ambitious and ruthless Eve HARRINGTON in ALL ABOUT EVE; June Buckridge alias district nurse in THE KILLING OF SISTER GEORGE; ambitious and sexually accommodating Shirley Rose in YOU'RE NOT WATCHING ME, MUMMY; Carla Romanelli, predatory and deceptive (*The Lonely Lady* 1983 C); Melanie Adams, conniving superstar, careless of her public image (*Scruples* 1980 T).

actresses playing boy characters A common practice on BBC radio, giving chirpy employment to a number of versatile actresses, notably Patricia Hayes, Marjorie Westbury and Billie Whitelaw, in the 1950s and 1960s. Praising the use of *real* boys in the *Jennings* school series in 1962, the Rev. Andrew Hodgson wrote in *Radio Times*: 'How refreshingly natural the voices of Jennings and his friends always sound! Why, in other programmes, do we so often have to make do with females painfully overacting in their attempts to portray the "fine manly little chap"?'

actresses playing male characters C: Asta Nielsen as *Hamlet* (1920); Mathilde Comont (billed as Mat) in *The Thief of Bagdad* (1924) as the Persian Prince (with moustache); Elspeth Dudgeon ('John Dudgeon') in *The Old Dark House* (1932); Jessie Matthews in *First a Girl* (1935); Julie Andrews in VICTOR/VICTORIA; Sena Jurinac as Octavian in *Der Rosenkavalier* (1960); Jean Arless as Warren in *Homicidal* (1961); Debbie Reynolds in *Goodbye Charlie* (1964); Ivy Ling Po as the hero Chang in *The Mermaid* (1966); Caroline Johnson as the Prince of Denmark in *Hamlet* (Can 1971); Anne Heywood as Roy in *I Want What I Want* (1972); Victoria Abril in *I Want To Be A Woman* (1977); Li Chinghsia as effeminate young man, Pao Yu in *Dream of the Red Chamber* (Hong Kong 1977); Anne Carlisle in *Liquid Sky* (1982); Eva Mattes in *A Man Like Eva* (1983); Gillian Jones as SEBASTIAN in *Twelfth Night* (Aust 1986); Debra Winger as archangel Emmett in *Made in Heaven* (1987); Theresa Russell as King Zog in the Nicolas Roeg portion of *Aria* (1987); the four schoolboys in *Summer Vacation 1999* (1989); Cathy Moriarty as Montana in *Soapdish* (1991); Ellen Barkin as Amanda/Steve in SWITCH (1991); Tilda Swinton as ORLANDO (1992).

R: Jennie Stoller as ORLANDO (1984 R); Samantha Bond as James Gray (alias Hannah Snell) in *Against the Wind* (1987).

T: Vanessa REDGRAVE as Richard Radley in SECOND SERVE (1986 T); Nancy Cartwright as the voice of Bart in THE SIMPSONS – sarcastic, quippy (a lot of them ad libbed); 'Boys go catatonic when they discover the truth about their idol,' says Bart's creator.

One of the more extraordinary impersonations was Linda Hunt's Billy Kwan in *The Year of Living Dangerously* (1983 C). A male actor was cast, but found to be unsuitable. Joel Grey, Bob Balaban and even Wallace Shawn were then seriously considered. The book's author David Atkins claimed (in *Books and Writing*, Aust 1991 R): 'Billy is quite malignant in the book. But Peter [Weir] made him saint-like – the moral core of the film.'

See also MALE IMPERSONATORS; PANTOMIME; TRANSVESTISM.

actors' agents Burly Shelley Winters in *S.O.B.* (1981 C); waistcoated and one of the guys: Joella Smith in *The Lonely Lady* (1983 C); Henry Willson (Andrew Robinson), mentor of *Rock Hudson* (1990 T).

An Actor's Life For Me Sung by the two gay villains in *Pinocchio* (1940 C); dusted down for the 1991 comedy series of the same name, sung by Nick Curtis – but without the key line 'An actor's life is gay'.

An Actor's Revenge (Japan 1963 C) FEMALE IMPERSONATOR Yukinojo (Kazuo Husegawa) plots revenge on the three nobles who forced his parents to commit suicide. As a man trained as a woman, he must reassert his manhood for the sake of family honour. The actor played the same role in KINUGASA's version made nearly 30 years before.
W/D: Kon Ichikawa; based on a story by Otokichi Mikami; 114 mins.
James KIRKUP wrote the libretto to Minoru Miki's music for the opera version, broadcast on BBC Radio 3 in 1979 with Kenneth Bowen as the wistful, driven Yukinojo.

ACT UP (Aids Coalition to Unleash Power) Activist organization. The aims and confrontational tactics of the New York branch to wake up institutions and vested interests to the need to release drugs and money are shown in the documentaries VOICES FROM THE FRONT, OVER OUR DEAD BODIES and STOP THE CHURCH! Members of ACT UP are presented as heroes in the feature film *Acceptable Risks* (1993 C).

Adam and Yves An attempt by ABC to bring the fizz water of LA CAGE AUX FOLLES to television. *Adam and Yves* was to have starred Danny Arnold from *Barney Miller* as a straight-looking banker with a flamboyant, failed drag-queen lover. The network cooled on the project after receiving more than 100,000 letters, mostly generated by the American Christian Cause. The organization's director, the Rev. Robert G. Grant had warned its members: 'MILITANT HOMOSEXUALS may score a terrifying breakthrough in their war against the Christian family.' ABC then announced that this was not 'the right time' for such a show. The same fearfulness clobbered Tony RANDALL's intention to play a middle-aged JEWISH homosexual living in New York, sharing his apartment with a young mother and her daughter. LOVE, SIDNEY, an offshoot of SIDNEY SHORR – A GIRL'S BEST FRIEND (1981 T), emerged as a gentle comedy series about a lonely bachelor, no longer particularly Jewish and with no sexual urges in any direction.

Adam's Rib (US 1949 C) Much loved, much analysed Tracy-HEPBURN comedy about spikey spouses fighting on opposite sides of the courtroom. Amanda/Hepburn's friend, Kip Kipple (David Wayne) is an early example of Feminist Man and there's a brief fantasy role-reversal scene involving husband (Tom Ewell), deceived wife (Judy Holliday) and mistress (Jean Hagen). A television series of the same name appeared in 1972 with Kipple's name changed to Lurie and his character substantially de-wimped.
W: Ruth Gordon and Garson Kanin; P: Lawrence Weingarten; D: George CUKOR; 101 mins.

adolescents Joe Cassidy in A HARD GOD; ERNESTO (Martin Halm), spoilt 17-year-old (1979 C); GERALD (Justin Kelly) in *Findings on a Late Afternoon* (1981 T); 16-year-old BOBBY (Timothy Williams) in WELCOME HOME, BOBBY; ASHLEY Light (Dominic Rickhards) in OCTOBER SCARS THE SKIN (1989 R); David (Eddie Castrodad) in TORCH SONG TRILOGY (1988 C); Jess (Charlotte Coleman) in ORANGES ARE NOT THE ONLY FRUIT (1990 T); etc.
In Britain, 'James' appeared first on OPEN TO QUESTION: 'Where There's Life' (1986 T) and then on BRASS TACKS: 'Good As You?', both times with his parents; Stephen trying to come out to his Pentecostal parents in one of the VIDEO DIARIES (1991 T).
See also YOUNG GAY/LESBIAN PEOPLE.

adoptive parents Two men bring up

Robert MOORE in TELL ME THAT YOU LOVE ME, JUNIE MOON (1970 C); Arnold is David's mother and father in TORCH SONG TRILOGY; Geoffrey and Derek were Eliot's role-models in THE LOST LANGUAGE OF CRANES; single man tries to adopt boy in *Second Best* (1993 C); Graham CHAPMAN and his adolescent son were featured in GAY LIFE 'Adoption' (1980 T); adoption and fostering by lesbians and gays discussed in OUT ON TUESDAY (1989 T).

Adrian Boy's name long associated with gay characters, mainly in Britain. Latin = of Adria; originally from *ater*, 'black'. 'Man from the dark sea.' The name was 22nd in the Top Fifty British First Names list in 1965; 36th in 1975; and by 1981 it was tying 48th with Scott and Damien. Could any of the following have had anything to do with its fall?

UK: Adrian Lomax (Jeremy Spenser), one of the children affected by his parents' estrangement in *Background/ Edge of Divorce* (1953 C); Adrian Lee (Alan WHEATLEY), suede shoe-wearing television set designer in *Simon and Laura* (1955 C); Adrian Miller (Geoffrey Wearing) in *Joyous Errand* (1957 T); David Oxley as Sir Adrian in *The Adventures of Robin Hood* (1957–8 T); Steve Temple sums up a suspect, Adrian Frost (Simon LACK) as 'actorish' in PAUL TEMPLE *and the Spencer Affair* (1958 R) – Paul responds with steady emphasis: 'I know what you mean'; Adrian (John Fiedler), Broadway actor in *Stage Struck* (1958 C); Adrian (Anthony Viccars), an artist with a 'friend' in THE CRIME AT BLOSSOMS (1958 R); Keith Baxter was a selfish and egotistical playwright who ruins the life of two women in *Square Dance* (1960 T); the copywriter played by Nicholas Phipps in *Something to Shout About* (1960–1 R); Adrian (Dennis PRICE), smoothie Harley Street psychiatrist in *The Millionairess* (1960 C); barman Adrian (Lockwood West) who 'can't stand scenes' in *Unwieldy Elephant* (1962 R); women's magazine art assistant Adrian Coombs (Robert Desmond) in COMPACT (1962–5 T): 'A bachelor with

a flair for interior design; a clown on the surface, a bit irresponsible, perhaps even a bit pathetic at times, but underneath there's a more serious side' (*Radio Times*, 6.6.63), and one of the few characters to remain 'unscathed in the perpetual battle of the sexes waged in the Compact offices'; a dead man reaching out from the grave in *The List of Adrian Messenger* (1963 C); the Rev. Adrian Tenterden (Michael Goodliffe), a teacher is accused of bringing 'bent' children (his son) into the world in THE CONNOISSEUR (1966 T); Adrien (Trader FAULKNER) ordered to be guillotined in *A Man Condemned* (1963 R); Adrian Hartley (Harold Reese), servant and friend of the hero in *The Ordeal of Richard Feverel* (1968 R); Michael WARD was Morecambe and Wise's gay acquaintance in 1970; Adrian White (John Le Mesurier), the *Traitor* based on Kim Philby (1970 R; 1971 T); Adrian (William Relton) wrongly thought to be offering very personal services in *Young Guy Seeks Part-time Work* (1973 T); Adrian (Julian Holloway) in *Carry On Loving* (1970 C); Adrian (Peter STRAKER) is one of the gayer members of a touring ballet company in *Village Hall* 'Dancing in the Dark' (1975 T); Roman soldier Adrian (Ken Hicks) in SEBASTIANE (1976 C) – he of the contentious erection; Adrian (Oswald Bullock), an unsuccessful accountant in *Jubilee* 'Plain Jane' (1977 T), and in *An Englishman's Castle* (1978 T); Adrian (Valentine DYALL) is 'an effeminate old man' in *The Losers* 'The Naming Part' (1978 T); Adrian Castallack (Gene Foad), jealous half-brother, sexually ambiguous in PENMARRIC (1979 T); Hugh Paddick as ultrasensitive Adrian, poet in black and yellow with GREEN CARNATION, encouraging Ernie's artistic bent in *The Morecambe and Wise Show* (1980 T); Adrian (Trevor Nichols), DJ with empathy for MEN'S LIBERATION in *Men!* (1984 R); artist Adrian (Charles Grant) in THE WEATHER IN THE STREETS (1984 T) thrower of wild parties; actor Aidan (Greg Hicks) in *Fortunes of War* (1987 T) also in *The Levant Tragedy* (1981 R) – unrequitedly in love with

Guy, changed his name from Adrian; Lord Adrian (Hugh[ie] Grant) in *Privileged* (1982 C) – handsome but melancholy, he challenges the hero to a duel; Adrian (Jon Finch), ambitious musician who makes a diabolical pact in *Doctor Faustus* (1982 T); Mr Adrian (Roland CURRAM) in *Bird Of Prey 2* (1984 T); Adrian Horowitz (Patrick Drury) is a milliner in *Shine On Harvey Moon* 'Spring Will Be A Little Late This Year' (1984 T); Jewish bachelor art dealer Adrian Avigdor (Ian Richardson) in *Mistral's Daughter* (1984 T); West End director Adrian Gurney (Aubrey WOODS) in *Star Quality* (1985 T); Adrian Mole, aged 13¾ (Gian Sanmarco in *The Secret Diary of Adrian Mole* (1985 T): he was called NIGEL in the 1982 radio version; dreamy, gentle Adrian (Jonathon Morris), the quiet, sensitive son in *Bread* (1987 T): 'He may have more CSEs than the rest of the Boswells, but that doesn't stop him from being the thickest. He can't keep a job or a girlfriend'; Adrian (Richard Pasco), reclusive widower in *The Crossing-keeper's House* (1986 R); Adrian (Richard Heffer) in *Just Good Friends* (1986 T); Adrian Chapple (John GIELGUD), a smug and condescending pillar of British intelligence, who is also a Russian spy (in *The Whistle Blower* 1987 C); Adrian LeDuc (Colin Firth) living in *Apartment Zero* (1988 C); literary pundit (Graham Harley) in *Inside Stories* 'The Twin' (Can 1988 T); Adrian Vowchurch (Robert Daws) in *Dead Lucky* (1988 T); Adrian the dentist (Bob Peck) in *Shades of Blue* (1990 R), who, on his daughter's wedding day, discovers that his mistress is pregnant, his wife has fallen in love with his best friend, and his hoped-for political career is fast evaporating; Adrian (Gerard Thoolen), one of the washed-up courtiers in *Prospero's Books* (1991 C); Adrian Cherrell (John Moffatt) in *The Forsyte Chronicles* (1991 R); Adrian (Michael Tudor-Barnes), sexually ambivalent husband in *Making It Better* (1991 R); 'Mr Adrian' in the Margery Sharp story *Vicarage Picnic* (1992 R), a circumspect BACHELOR who 'had been in prison'; Adrian Deschelles

(David Foxxe) and JEREMY Molyneaux (Christopher Good) in *Lovejoy* 'Highland Fling' (1992 T), guests at a wedding in a Scottish castle; Adrian (Peter WOODTHORPE) who compromises with the repressive new regime in *When the Barbarians Came* (1992 R): 'Theatre is its own justification, dear boy ... the theatre has no politics ... Find out what they want and give it to them.'

US: Adrians are rare in American media. When they do appear, either they are cameo appearances: William Shatner in *Testimony of Two Men* (1977 T); Adrian Benson (Ed Prentiss), a spy for Them in *Man on a String* (1960 C); or they are demented (or heading that way): Adrian (Jan-Michael Vincent), the hippy who refuses to adapt to military life in *Tribes* (1970 T); Adrian Vico (David Janssen) in *Night Chase* (1970 T), a wealthy businessman on the run to the Mexican border after his wife is murdered; Adrian aka Andrew (Stephen McHattie), demon child now grown to manhood in *Look What's Happened to Rosemary's Baby* (1976 T); Adrian Harcomb (Robert Walker), a blind psychic, suspiciously adept at finding kidnap victims in *Matt Houston* 'The Outsider' (1986 T). And, most memorably: Adrian Cronauer (Robin Williams), the very idiosyncratic disc jockey in *Good Morning Vietnam* (1987 C). Just one American dizzy gay man: Mark Neely in BROTHERS 'Lay the Points' (1986).

Adrian, Max (1903–1973) Irish-born, barnstorming, big-boned, curvilinear, gluggy voiced, lots-of-teeth actor with brilliant ear for accents. A 40-year career.

C: *The Primrose Path* (1930); *Why Pick on Me?* (1938); as Chester Coote in *Kipps* (1941); as Sheridan in *The Young Mr Pitt* (1942); the Dauphin in *Henry V* (1944); fifth billed as Catoni with Jean Kent in *Her Favourite Husband* (1947) as Lambert; as Vernon in *Pool of London* (1950); Professor in *Uncle Vanya* (1963); *Dr Terror's House of Horrors* (1965); *Julius Caesar* (1970); Father Barré in *The Devils* (1971); the harassed actor-director in *The Boy Friend* (1971).

R: Piers Gaveston in EDWARD II (1943); Pandarus in *Troilus and Cressida* (1946); *He Was Born Gay* (1946) with Alec Guinness; *Iris* by Pinero (1947); *The Millionairess* (1952); Tristan, lackey to Peter Coke in de Vega's *The Dog in the Manger* (1954); *The Player King* as Henry VIII (1954); 'his voice a slinky swagger' as Parolles, 'a light nut without a kernel' (*Listener*) in *All's Well That Ends Well* (1952); DE CHARLUS in *Saint Loup* (1956) – 'magnificent malevolence of his voice' (*Listener*); 'extraordinarily versatile' as the Dauphin in *Ordeal By Fire* (about JOAN OF ARC, 1956); in *Exercises in Style* (about Raymond Queneau, 1959); one of the brothers in *The Wrong Box* (1959); George Arthur Rose in *Hadrian VII* (1959); Old Lucifer in *The Salvation of Faust* (1960) to Frank Duncan's young one; Bolingbroke in *A Glass of Water* with Jessie Evans as Queen ANNE (about Marlborough, 1960); *The Love of the Three Colonels* (1961) as the Wicked Fairy (with June Tobin as the good one); Ferdinand co-starring with Edith Evans in *Time Revisited* (1961); starring as Paul Southman in *Saints Day* (1961); Oscar WILDE 'dying of his disgrace' in *Echo de Paris* (1961); Isaac Mendoza in Sheridan's *The Duenna* (1962) with Marjorie Westbury in title role; the Baron in *You Can't Think of Everything* (1962); Sir August Thwaites, the owner of a stately home in *August for the People* (1962); Father Barré in *The Devils* (1963) with Dorothy Tutin and Derek Godfrey; The Marquis of Forlipopoli in Goldoni's *Mine Hostess* (*La Locandiera*) (1963); Noah in John Mortimer's *Education of an Englishman* (1964); SOCRATES in *Triad* (1965–8) 'The Melos Affair' (1965), 'The Last Expedition' (1967) and 'The Prisoners in the Cave' (1968) – Athens during the Peloponnesian War of the 5th Century BC; Polonius to Kenneth GRIFFITH'S *Hamlet* (1966); Crabtree in *The School for Scandal* (1967); Bernard Shaw in *The First Night of Pygmalion* (1970).

T: *Sunday Afternoon* 'What Would Aunt Matilda Have Said?' (1955); as 'the madonna of the expresso bar' in *The Show Parade* (1956); *Alfred Hitchcock*

Presents 'Banquo's Chair' (1958); PERRY MASON 'The Case of the Deadly Toy' (1959) as Ralph (married with all-American kid); as Hans Frick in *The Pets* 'The Hiding Place' (1960) with Robert Shaw and Sean Connery; Fagin in *Oliver Twist* (1962); Jaques in *As You Like It* (1963); Eli de Coetqurch, the cynical old tramp in *The Bachelors* (1964); Disraeli in *Victoria Regina* (1964); *Doctor Who* 'House of Destruction' (1965) as Priam; unforgettable as Delius in *Song of Summer* (1968); Ludicrus in *Up Pompeii* (1969–70) – Michael Hordern played him in the film; Rubenstein in *Somerset Maugham* 'The Alien Corn' (1970); with Peter PEARS, Laurence Olivier etc marking Britain's entry to the EC at Covent Garden (3.1.73).

Also: DESERT ISLAND DISCS (1969); *Soundings* (Arts and ideas in Australia) interviewed by Tony Morpeth; *Max Adrian – A Memoir* with Eric Porter 'remembering the actor and revue artist' (1973).

adultery In 1963 at the height of the Profumo affair, on ANY QUESTIONS? a Mr C. J. Hudson of Ditcheat asked the panel consisting of Isobel Barnett, Marghanita Laski, Malcolm Muggeridge and Clifford Selly (farmer and agricultural correspondent of the Observer): 'To what extent should the private life of men in the public eye affect their position and career?'

Marghanita Laski followed Malcolm Muggeridge (who was very tolerant of adultery) with a surprising – and – to the fans of this institution – unsettling proposition:

I think we should judge ... that we should judge adultery harshly and that we should judge homosexuality kindly ... adultery is a matter of choice ... and I think it must be judged, except in the most exceptional cases, wrong. But when there was a case a little while back where another Minister was merely accused of homosexuality which might, in certain cases, have affected no one but himself ... we all immediately as a public thought it right to judge and judge harshly. I say if we're going to refrain from judging, let's refrain from judging all sexual misdemeanours. But I think we should judge adultery harshly and that we should judge homosexuality kindly.

Symptomatic of a massive social change in the last 30 years, KALEIDOSCOPE (1990 R) looked at misconduct among consenting adults in 'The Adultery Novel': extramarital affairs, real (63 per cent of spouses unfaithful) and fictional, remain hugely popular, with BRIEF ENCOUNTER maintaining its position in British hearts and minds as *the* adultery romance.

The Adventures of Barry McKenzie
(Aust 1972)
W: Barry Humphries and Bruce Beresford based on *Private Eye* comic strip; P: Phillip Adams; D: Bruce Beresford; 114 mins.

Antipodean taste: putrefaction and expectoration are uppermost. The film début of Edna EVERAGE. Said Barry HUMPHRIES on *Film '72*: 'One of the things that worries Australians in AUSTRALIA is that when English people visit Australia they describe us as latent homosexuals. It's very worrying to such a virile race. But I think Barry Mackenzie proves that they're not latent homosexuals, but LATENT HETEROSEXUALS.' There was a sequel, *Barry McKenzie Holds His Own* (1974).

advertising/advertisements Gay and lesbian people are noticeable by their almost complete absence from television commercials. In 1962, a HORLICKS ad (directed by Joseph Losey) featured two women motor rally drivers, one comfortable in short, styled hair, in sheepskin jackets winning the trophy before cosying up with the famous milk and barley hot drink. Gay men had to be content with 'YOU'RE NEVER ALONE WITH A STRAND' and the much chortled-over jingle 'Omo adds bright, bright brightness'. In the 1980s a Swedish advertisement for nylons showed two women playing footsie under a dinner table, while in Australia men's underpants were brazenly promoted in a plethora of

crotch shots with the slogan 'Everyone's getting into them' as men of various shapes and sizes raced towards another group of men wearing pink knickers (1987). THE GOODIES guyed the hypermasculine ethos of British beer ads with a pay-off that has the two hunks lispingly disputing whose drink is whose: 'It's my beer, *cheeky cat!*' (1973). A breakthrough of sorts was achieved in various promotions for jeans, one brand featuring well muscled youths stripping off in public places.

In general, though, advertising by its very nature has to exclude anything problematic, awkward, ill-fitting, unacceptable. Sven Linquist, writing four decades ago (in *Advertising Is Dangerous*), maintained that 'industry and business ... have no intention of solving anybody's sexual conflicts for the benefit of mankind. These conflicts must be transformed into needs for consumption.'

Increasingly, the fragmentation of markets does allow for considerable latitude in more specialized advertising. MAKING LOVE, the 1982 'daring' mainstream movie, was given two distinct marketing campaigns. Richard Avedon photographed the two heroes looking desirable, and touching each other. This was directed at the gay media. Elsewhere, the image was of a rapt husband and wife in tender, if tentative contact, with the other man an almost androgynous outsider. Two years later, the British group BRONSKI BEAT's debut album *The Age of Consent* was put across (on CHANNEL 4) via the record's cover, a PINK TRIANGLE. Hardly a blanket campaign, the ad appeared only sporadically, for example during breaks in the lesbian TV movie A QUESTION OF LOVE.

Such visibility continues patchily. Writing in the *Los Angeles TV News* in 1981, Steve Schulte, the director of the Gay and Lesbian Service Center of LA, observed: 'Blacks, Hispanics, women, Asians and old people are now permitted to hawk products, but not gays. No lean cowpoke kisses his buddy as he hands over a pizza, no woman tells her lover what shampoo will leave her hair shinier and more appealing to other women; no handsome young executive compliments his boyfriend on how white he got the shirt collar this week. Probably no group looks out on a vaster wasteland than gays.'

advertising revenue THIRTYSOMETHING lost $500,000 with its 1989 segment showing two men in bed. ABC's *Rock Hudson* did not rate too well either and some advertisers became resistant to gay and/or AIDS themes. The highly praised *Lifestyle Stories* episode about the gay newscaster with AIDS lost $500,000 on ads for NBC in December 1990.

Advise and Consent (US 1962 C)
Young senator (Don Murray) driven to SUICIDE by BLACKMAIL threats and stalking by HOMOPHOBIC Southern senator (Charles LAUGHTON in his final role).
W: Wendell Mayes from the novel by Allen Drury; P/D: Otto Preminger; 139 mins.
   Critic Robin Wood wrote: 'I remember going to see *The Trials of Oscar Wilde* and VICTIM when they came out and they both seemed to confirm the idea that marriage is the right thing. *Advise and Consent* ... shock, horror, consternation! The character was in the same situation (as I was): happily married, with three children but with a gay past. And he killed himself by cutting his throat ... The scene where he visits a gay BAR helped establish an image I had of the gay world when I was supposedly a happily married man with three children' (*Gay News*, 1977).

Africa Made up of 27 countries and, according to the few programmes that have even considered the subject since 1960, none of them contains any homosexual or bisexual citizens. Dr Tom Lambo, a Nigerian psychiatrist, told Stephen Black in *A Matter of Mind* (1965 T): 'After 15 years of practice in Nigeria, we have never encountered a single case of homosexuality.' However, one or two slipped through: one of the slave traders in *Ashanti* (1979 C); acti-vist Simon Nkoli in *A Moffie Called Simon* (1989 T); and OUT ON TUESDAY (1989 T). The first admission that some African people were homosexual came in THE GAY AND LESBIAN WORLD.

African Queen The name of the increasingly battered boat in the 1951 John Huston film. Used affectionately(?) by EMORY to Bernard in THE BOYS IN THE BAND. The massively cut American TV version of the film retains this epithet, but expunges Harold's *self*-definition as a 'Jew fairy'.

Afro-American people *See* BLACK GAY MEN; BLACK LESBIANS.

After Henry (1985–8 R; 1988–92 T)
Enormously popular, reassuring light comedy series written by Simon Brett, starring Prunella Scales as a widow trying to adjust to life without a mate. She receives much calm consideration from her boss, Russell (Benjamin WHITROW, R), who lives with a chap. Simple, characterful comedy with a cast of four or five, which was so popular that as soon as the first series ended a repeat began. The only radio series since the early 1960s to transfer to television (with Jonathan Newth rendering Russell unthreatening, almost non-gay – and whose bookshop never seems to attract a single customer). The CHRISTMAS 1985 episode had one line that could be considered mildly critical of the exclusion of homosexuals from humankind during the season of goodwill, but this was expunged from the television redo of the script.

Afternoon of a Nymph (UK 1962 T)
According to John Russell Taylor's *Anatomy of a Television Play* (1962), it was director Philip Saville's plan to have Jackie Lane (as Ginger) touch the arm of Janet Munro (as Elaine) and KISS the nape of her neck as she delivered the line 'I don't even *like* men' in Robert Muller's play about a show-business hopeful. The producer, Sydney Newman, demanded that this action and the accompanying line be cut. A few hours of volatility ensued with the result that

the line and the squeeze was transmitted but the kiss wasn't.

afternoon programmes The derestriction of broadcasting hours in 1972 led to the introduction of a number of series/serials with a social conscience. These included CROWN COURT, *Rooms*, COUPLES, TOGETHER and GEMS. Nearly all featured gay men, and there were one or two worthwhile lesbians popping up now and then. On radio, gay relevance was to be found, from the late 1960s, in such favourites as THE DALES, WAGGONERS' WALK and 'Afternoon Theatre'. The afternoons (outside of school holiday periods) were deemed 'safe' for minority issues, if not opinions. Even so, Mary WHITEHOUSE of the National Viewers and Listeners' Association (National VALA) was driven to protest about nice gay Paul who held hands with a boyfriend across a kitchen table in *Gems* (1985 T).

aftershave lotion The heavy scent around the chin of ASSASSIN Wint (Bruce Glover) alerts James BOND to his lethal chicanery in the final scene of DIAMONDS ARE FOREVER (1971 C): 'I smell a rat' he says deductively. All-American Mr Cleaver uses it in LEAVE IT TO BEAVER 'Wally's Dream Girl' (1961 T). Still problematic for men, especially in country areas: the one BROTHER mocks the other for using Brut in ACCOUNTS; and Tony Archer sneers at his son John (THE ARCHERS 1992): 'Oh, cologne! Pardon me, Duchess.' – John retaliates: 'Dad is jealous because I'm young and all the girls fancy me.' *See also* DEODORANT; PERFUME.

After You – Who? In COUNTRY MATTERS 'Breeze Anstey', Fred Astaire sings as the women paint walls, beat carpets and burn off wood in preparation for life on the farm – with a close-up of Breeze admiring Lorna. The Cole PORTER song is heard again in the final minutes as Breeze, realizing that Lorn can never return her love, packs up and drives off into the night.

Agate, James (1877–1947) The leading British drama critic between the two world wars, and presenter of *Agate on Theatre* on radio during the 1920s and early 1930s. His autobiography *Ego* was read by Carleton HOBBS in 1975, with a footnote by the writer and critic Alan Dent who was Agate's secretary for many years: 'He was extravagant in all ways and did not pretend to be anything else' (STORY TIME).

Agatha Girl's name often given to dominant, aggressive characters: Agatha Payne in THE OLD LADIES (Edith Evans 1968 R; Katina Paxinou 1968 T; Fabia Drake 1984 R: 'a large, stout, shapeless woman with deep black hair and highly coloured cheeks').

Other strong, stand-over Agathas include: Hattie Jacques as battle-ready Agatha Potter in *Watch Your Stern* (1960); Aunt Agatha (Fabia Drake) in *P. G. Wodehouse's The World of Wooster* (1965 T); matriarch Mary MORRIS as Agatha in *The Family Reunion* (1966 R); Agatha Poldark (Eileen Way) in *Poldark* (1977 T); and one unattractive spinster: Barbara Murray as Agatha Purvis in *The Bright One* (1959 T) who goes for a swim in the Mediterranean and emerges as the beautiful Phaea; else she's a viper: Agnes Gregory (Veronica Rose), a model who poisons her rival in *Death in High Heels* (1947 C).

The marginally more amenable ones include: glamorous Agatha Caraway (Mae Murray) in *Bachelor Apartment* (1931 C); Lady Agatha Hewitt (Margaret Halstan) in *The Middle Watch* (1930 C); Agatha Poskett (Iris Hooey) in *Those Were The Days* (1934 C, a version of Pinero's *The Magistrate*); Agatha (Lucille Ball), wildcat daughter of *nouveau riche* mother in *Fancy Pants* (1950 C); liberal congresswoman Agatha Reid (Joan Crawford) in *Goodbye My Fancy* (1951 C) – 'aggressive ... adamantine ... frigid ... humourless ... acrimonious ...'; Aggie (Lee Patrick) in *Boss Lady* (1952 T); Aggie (Molly Weir) in *Life with the Lyons* (1950–6 R); missionary Agatha Andrews (Margaret Leighton) in *Seven Women* (1966 C); Sister Agatha (Lila Skala) in *Ironside*

(1967 T); Agatha Murphy (Shelley Winters) in *The Sex Symbol* (1974 T); Agatha Spanner (Renée Houston) in *Carry On at Your Convenience* (1973 C); Agatha Christie (Vanessa REDGRAVE), shy and distracted crime author in *Agatha* (1979 C); Agatha (Mary Wimbush), spy in *Skorpion* (1983 T); Agatha, lover of Jo in *She Must Be Seeing Things* (1987 C); Lady Agatha Shawcross (Angela Scoular) in *You Rang, M'Lud* (1990–1 T).

age difference Colin and Graham have a post-coital discussion on the gay age of consent, and the discrimination against 'old' people in the gay world in ONLY CONNECT (1979 T): little do either of them realize that Graham will have sex with a man in his seventies the next day. Ralph is naturally open and honest, but as a SOCIAL WORKER he has to be careful – doubly so because his boyfriend is a boy (one year below the heterosexual AGE OF CONSENT and six years below the gay one) (TWO PEOPLE 1979 T). Other couples where the age gap yawns are in THE CONSEQUENCE, EASTENDERS and in THE KILLING OF SISTER GEORGE (but CHILDIE is older than she looks and acts).

ageing Said Quentin CRISP: 'It was 1948. I was 40. I started forcing red out and forcing blue in.' Michael's lover in AN EARLY FROST plucks a grey hair from his head ('Time's running out'), not realizing that Michael will only have a year to live.

Between these two images lie a whole huge bed of anguish, rumpled by the ageing queen, the fairy nobody loves after she's 40. Charles DYER, never lost for words in STAIRCASE, tries to cheer up his pudgy, completely bald lover, Harry: 'We're all depreciating, mate. What about varicose veins? My legs are like fouled parrots' perches. Can hardly get my wind and I haven't seen my kneecaps since 1953.' (This dialogue was not transferred from stage to screen for Rex Harrison to deliver.) Harry cannot be placated: 'I'm finished ... even though I'm the same inside. I'm wearing tiddly

briefs inside, Charlie, and my heart can still dance; but who knows it? Who'd want me on a beach? ... a yellowing sow's ear ... a curled-at-the-edges *passé* phallic symbol.'

Oliver, the evil sybarite in David Mercer's A SUPERSTITION, does go swimming but 'the skin is getting terribly like old parchment. One seems to shed more and more – it's revolting. In the pool I felt like an old rug.' DIAGHILEV alias *Chinchilla* (1981 R) says: 'We'd save ourselves a lot of trouble if we all died at 30', which would seem to echo Marlon Brando's speech (written by himself) in *Last Tango in Paris* (1972 C): 'Only a certain desperate melancholy. A gloomy regret. A hatred for oneself. All men when they reach my age, unless they are absolute idiots, must feel a sort of emptiness inside, a sense of anguish, of uselessness.'

The loneliness that can often accompany physical deterioration is frequently expressed by gay characters themselves (Toddy in *Rooms* 1975: 'Do you know what it's like to have nowhere to turn?') or by interested observers of their fate (Cassie in *My Father's House* (1981 T), who protects the sensitive Raymond Bell (Steve Mann) but has no doubts about his eventual destination: 'He'll go on picking up pretty little boys and playing the big spender, buying affection. Then, one day, either he'll grow up as most of us have to do, or else he'll do a better job with the gas fire').

A welcome relief from the gloom came in ONLY CONNECT: a man of 70 plus is asked by a man of 25 if he would care to share his bed for the night. An agreeable time is had by both; this occurrence parallels the night when the older man, as a boy of 18, had sex with an 80-year-old, Edward CARPENTER.

With the advent of AIDS, a new perspective opened up for dramatists – premature decay and change. The image of OLDER GAY MEN remains firmly etched in MISS HAVISHAM-like bile, confirming what one of THE BOYS IN THE BAND asserted two decades ago: 'FAGGOTS are worse than women about their age.'

agents provocateurs Policemen who proposition men in public places (usually parks or LAVATORIES) and, upon eliciting a flicker of response, arrest them: first portrayed in *The New Centurions* (1972 C) wherein Stacy Keach is encouraged to 'swish a little' and by so doing ends up in a lake, with his colleagues, when a muscular pickup gets stroppy. The use of police in this way was delineated in MORE LIVES THAN ONE and *For the Greater Good*. *Spitting Image* had a field-day when a Tory MP was arrested in a gay CLUB in 1984: showing a deportment course for cops who had to 'act gay'. *See also* COTTAGING; GROSS INDECENCY; POLICE.

age of consent Five yawning, all-important years separate gay British men from their heterosexual counterparts as far as achieving sexual majority is concerned. A whole generation has grown up under this edict (since the 1967 decriminalization) and men under the age of 21 (but over 16) can be prosecuted (and jailed) for this sexual offence (as, of course, can their post-21 partners). BRONSKI BEAT drew this to the attention of many young people with their debut album *The Age of Consent* in 1984.

The discrepancy was alluded to by Per in TWO PEOPLE: 'The Trouble with a Kitten': 'I'm four years away from the Great Divide.' It was trumpeted by a very merry Barry celebrating his liberating 21st in EASTENDERS: 'TWENTY-ONE TODAY, twenty-one today. I've got the key of the door. Never felt so flippin' legal before.' This earned a rebuke from Mary Kenny in the *Daily Mail*: 'Recently, an underage homosexual man ... was bemoaning the fact that he had to wait until his 21st birthday to have anal intercourse legally' (9.4.87). In TWO OF US (1988 T) Matthew (Jason Rush) looks longingly across the Channel and dreams of living in a country where 'it's legal at 16'.

On *Tonight* 'Age of Consent' (1977 T) the value of the change was minimized by someone scoffing that the move towards reform was a device of the Hampstead humanists and the Highgate high-

brows. The subject resurfaced in OUT 'Huntley and Palmer' (1990 T) included the Labour Party Shadow Minister Barry Sheerman; and in 1992 Edwina Currie MP was very vocal about the damage young gay men suffered in this area, and the fear it aroused in them and their older lovers.

Agnes Woman's name, usually reserved for plain, pure women (for example Agnes Wickfield in DAVID COPPERFIELD) in strong contrast to AGATHA. Two lesbian Agnes's: (Doreen Hepburn) who does a little night work on the side in *Phonefun Ltd* (1982 T); and the murdered stockbroker in *Killing Orders* (1991 R).

Agony (UK 1979–81 T) Robust comedy series in which radio agony aunt, Jane Lucas (Maureen Lipman) wrestles with a wayward husband (in-principle liberated male/psychiatrist/nitwit), a domineering (Jewish stereotype) mother, various clients (including a bald black lesbian mother and a would-be TRANSSEXUAL, Mr Mince), and nice gay NEIGHBOURS, Rob and Michael (Jeremy Bulloch and Peter Denyer).

P: John Reardon; London Weekend Television.

In the second batch, Michael is 'OUTED' on a radio phone-in which loses him his teaching job. His subsequent unemployment and deep depression head to his SUICIDE half-way through series three. His DOCTOR lover goes through a short, though touching BEREAVEMENT. In the final episode, he meets an AUSTRALIAN who likes CRICKET too and just happens to be a blond version of the late Michael.

The 1979 series was created and written by Len RICHMOND, an American gay activist, and by Anna Raeburn, a well-respected magazine and radio advice-giver, on whom Jane is based. After disagreements, the 1980 and 1981 scripts were penned by Andrew Nickolds and Stan Hey, with Len Richmond returning home to work on the American version, which – minus gays – became *The Lucie Arnaz Show* which soon went phffft in 1985.

'The homosexual lovers are involved in the show's humour as both makers and butts of jokes.' (Bruce Crowther and Mike Pinfold, *Bring Me Laughter: Four Decades of TV Comedy*, 1987).

agony aunts *See* PSYCHOLOGISTS; Claire RAYNER.

Sir Andrew **Aguecheek** Silly-billy companion of Sir Toby Belch in TWELFTH NIGHT, often played as effete ninny: Donald Layne-Smith (1947 R); Heron CARVIC (1956 & 1962 R); Richard Johnson (1958 T); John Moffatt (1970 T); Ronnie Stevens (1978 T).

AID (artificial insemination by donor) Shock-horror subject that interests the broadcast media only fitfully: *A Blessing or a Sin?* (1958 T); TONIGHT (1978 T); GAY LIFE (1980 T); G.P. 'More than Friends' (1991 T); *Sixty Minutes* 'Women In Love' (Aust 1991 T); *The Coming Out Show* 'Baby Hunger' (Aust 1991 R); while HEART OF THE MATTER 'And Donor Makes Three' (1991 T) and OUT: 'Oy Gay' (1992 T) both featured lesbian families with a daughter born through artificial insemination.

AIDS (acquired immune deficiency syndrome) A viral disease without a cure, often passed on through sexual intercourse; western victims tended at first to be male gays. One of the most talked about subjects in the media since 1985–6. Highly controversial because linked to a deviant group.

AIDS – a draining experience for many: flotillas of statistics, scare tactics, conflicting information on an area hitherto impaled on politeness. Above all, it introduced disturbing insights into male–male sexuality, allowed previously taboo words to be spoken, and looked death and dying straight in the eye.

Approach ranged from shock-horror (fears of heterosexual epidemic), friendly distance, jolly practicality, self-conscious jargoneering, HOMOPHOBIA disguised as medical opinion – and occasional empathy. Among the most memorable programmes were *The Visit*

'Living with AIDS', *Remembering Terry* and some TV VIDEO DIARIES.

The pandemic allowed people – from gay men and lesbians to government ministers – to use words that were rarely or never used on television before 1986. However, it was claimed (on THE CUTTING EDGE 'The Silent War' 1991) that the 'general population is unaware of the scope of the epidemic or how to prevent it' – despite the onslaught of AIDS programmes (from talk shows to music bonanzas to speeches at the ACADEMY AWARDS ceremony).

In drama, AIDS was first referred to by celebate villain Steve Rideaux in Howard SCHUMAN's VIDEOSTARS in late 1983: 'You can't be too careful these days.'

Casual, inaccurate or just plain callous references began appearing in mainstream movies in 1985–86, for example *Power* and *Hannah and Her Sisters*. There was the gay man with straight friends who likes 12-year-old boys and has blood in his urine in the Canadian *The Decline of the American Empire*.

Within a year, HIV/AIDS would be packaged for episodes in every 'adult' North American TV show including: THIRTYSOMETHING; *Designing Women*; *Miami Vice*; MIDNIGHT CALLER; *21 Jump Street*; *Beverly Hills 90210*; DEGRASSI HIGH; *Mama's Boy*; HOOPERMAN; *Doogie Howser MD*.

Mark Harmon's randy doctor was making jokes about the disease in ST ELSEWHERE at the same time, before he himself had to confront the results of the virus (transmitted by a female PROSTITUTE). On the same show, in 1985, a married city councillor (Michael Brandon) was found to have AIDS, a fact which played havoc with the hospital's blood donor drive.

HOTEL dealt with both AIDS and HOMOPHOBIA in one of its 1986 segments: an anti-gay barman who was given infected blood during a gall bladder operation. In the generally light-hearted MR BELVEDERE, a young haemophiliac 'Wesley's Friend' (1986 T) is ostracized at school because he has contracted the virus through blood transfusion. In the main, of course, it was gay men who held centre stage in these programmes: trying to commit SUICIDE with an electric carving knife (CASUALTY 'Blood Brothers' 1987 T); committing euthanasia (L.A. LAW 1987 T); or being warned by a parent (Steven in the last episode of the 1985–6 season of DYNASTY). Sometimes the gay victim gives advice and comfort to heterosexuals – as in *Intimate Contact* (1987 T), while strenuously working out and eating well to strengthen his immune system.

Occasionally, the organizations that gay men, lesbians and some heterosexual people set up (usually in response to establishment foot-dragging, hostility or indifference) merited a mention. More often than not, the full-scale AIDS dramas documented families (nuclear) giving support (after initially rejecting), or lovers/ex-lovers facing the harsh facts together in the light of pain, terror and a bit of humour. AN EARLY FROST is an example of the former, *As Is* of the latter, with A DEATH IN THE FAMILY and PARTING GLANCES representing a more balanced, less hysterical middle way: people coping with a life crisis integrated into everyday doings for a foreseeable future.

In mainstream cinema, AIDS was initially ignored, being left to one or two documentaries or a few timid one-liners, beginning with Bette MIDLER's character in *Down and Out in Beverly Hills* (1986 C) screaming: 'Don't touch him, he may have AIDS!' A British short, *Sleepwalker*, made early in 1984, takes its place in social history for being the first home with an AIDS joke. Fulton McKay asks his gay waiter colleague (Michael Medwin): 'Do you know what "gay" means?' The reply to the answer 'no' is: 'Got-AIDS-Yet?'

Honest, liberating satire on and around the epidemic and its gathering hysteria was to be found only in *The AIDS Show* (1986 T) and Rosa VON PRAUNHEIM's *A Virus Has No Morals* (1986 C/T).

The multi-million pound public awareness campaign launched in Britain at the beginning of 1987 (its TV arm

featuring a doom-laden John HURT voice-over and an iceberg) drew a response from the inhabitants of that East End square: the reactionary Dot Cotton shunning the two gay men whenever she meets them – in street, pub or launderette. The secular but traditional Pete Beale was pugnacious over it all, but his wife Kathy was sympathetic to the victims, about the disease itself, and wary of the media ravings that accompanied it. Publican Den was worried about the effect the gay couple drinking in his establishment would have on takings. And Gran Beale thought it was all due to them Russians.

A year later, the series gained dramatic mileage from Colin's fears about his health (it was multiple sclerosis); heterosexual Mark was later discovered to be HIV positive, and his girlfriend developed full-blown AIDS, dying just after their wedding day (1992).

The ultimate British bigot, Alf Garnett, devoted part of a 1987 episode of IN SICKNESS AND IN HEALTH to slagging off gays. It was *they*, after all, who had forced Mrs THATCHER's government to talk about smutty things so openly on television, radio and billboards: comment directed at Alf's home-help WINSTON, dubbed 'Marigold'.

At the same time, Kenneth Branagh was playing Oswald in Ibsen's GHOSTS (1987 T). He told *Radio Times* that, like young people in the era of AIDS, 'Oswald suffers from a barrage of conflicting information' (on syphilis).

Swirling around in the information and misinformation were various plague motifs. The film *Fatal Attraction* was tagged 'the movie that helped kill off the ONE-NIGHT STAND', as though it was part of an information campaign rather than a slam-bang thriller about a vicious, sex-crazed independent woman who boiled up a pet bunny and worse. And there was a compelling episode of DYNASTY, filmed after Rock HUDSON was diagnosed, wherein the entire cast kissed each other anywhere but on the parted lips.

It was left to the gutsy granny (Sylvia Sidney) in AN EARLY FROST, a moving

and, within the limits of the TV movie
format, honest piece of work, to encapsulate what all the conflicting statistics,
projects and fear-makers couldn't: a
simple comparison. Talking to her terminally ill grandson while cutting roses,
she recalls her husband's illness of
cancer: 'People thought if they breathed
the same air as him they'd develop a
tumour. It's a disease, not a disgrace.
Now give your grandma a kiss.'

C: Usually oblique rather than dealt
with directly: *Rustler's Rhapsody* (1985);
Betty Blue (1986); *Les Patterson Saves the
World* (1987); etc. Occasionally, minor
characters are seen coping with
immuno-suppression, eg in *Close Your
Eyes* (1991). LONGTIME COMPANION
(1990) was the only mainstream film to
deal head-on with the crisis, until a
spate of 1993–4 Hollywood projects
including AND THE BAND PLAYED ON.

R: *File on 4* (1986); *A Perfect Pest* (1987);
Play Safe Special 'AIDS and You' (presented by Janice Long on BBC Radio 1,
1987); *Anatomy of an Epidemic* (1988);
AIDS in Africa (BBC WORLD SERVICE
1989); COMPROMISED IMMUNITY
(1991); THE GAY AND LESBIAN WORLD
'AIDS' (BBC WORLD SERVICE 1992); etc.

T: Drama: *As Is* (1987); *Intimate Con-
tact* (1987); *Sweet as You Are* (1988);
EASTENDERS (1992); *Diana: Her True
Story* (1993); *The Volunteer* (1993); etc.
Documentary/current affairs: HORIZON
'Killer in the Village' (1983); *The Ele-
venth Hour* 'Bright Eyes' (1984); HORI-
ZON 'Sex and Gay Men' (1986, not
shown); *Horizon* 'AIDS: A Strange and
Deadly Virus' (1986); PANORAMA 'AIDS
– The Race for a Cure' (1986); *Horizon*
'Can AIDS Be Stopped?' (1987); QED
'Your Biological Guide to AIDS'
(1987); *Panorama* 'AIDS – The Fight
For Control' (1987); *AIDS: The Facts*
(1987); SCENE 'AIDS – What is the Real
Risk and Relevance?' (1987); QED
'Suzi's Story' (1988); *Bodymatters*
'AIDS' (1988): 'Bodymatters team of
qualified doctors guide you through the
biological facts clearly and simply so that
you can decide for yourselves how likely
it is that you personally will be affected
by AIDS: the disease that's now killing

two Britons every day'; *Panorama* 'Heterosexual AIDS, the Myths and the
Menace' (1992); etc.

See also HOMOPHOBIA; PLAGUE; SEX-
UALLY TRANSMITTED DISEASES.

AIDS Coalition to Unleash Power *See*
ACT UP.

AIDS line helpers Gordon COLLINS
'secretly' in BROOKSIDE (1989 T).

AIDS Memorial Quilt Project *See* THE
QUILT.

**Ain't Nothing Bad About Feelin'
Good** Raunchy chorus number from
James Ivory's *The Wild Party* (1974 C).
It is preluded by the seduction of the
simple, disabled Bertha by predatory
movie queen Madeline True. As the
chorus sing 'Let me hold you/Like a
lover man would', Madeline begins to
KISS Bertha – passionately, hungrily.
The camera moves across the house to
reveal combinations of half-naked
people whose love-making becomes
more frenzied as does the tempo of the
song.

Their lust-crazed thirsts slaked, the
revellers greet the dawn and the viewer
is returned to Madeline and the now
ecstatic Bertha in each other's arms.
Bertha's former dancing partner, Jackie
(a 'half-caste'!) – now her pimp – has
previously been seen being pleasured by
another man and by a woman, as he
snorts cocaine. It is Jackie, rather than
upfront Madeline, who will lead the
three heterosexual characters into
violence which ends the party and the
film. In true Hollywood style, this musical erotica is offered up, garnished and
then denounced, carrying down with it
the genuine enjoyment the two women
discovered in one another.

air force Mutual support and affection
between two of the escapees (James
Garner and Donald Pleasence) in *The
Great Escape* (1963 C). During the Battle
of Britain, Fitz loves Mac, who is blown
to pieces in A MOMENT IN TIME (1979
T). The female impersonator Lorri Lee
recalls the glorious euphoria of the

demob train when, still dressed in smart RAF grey, he tells his mate 'Crystal' that he's queer – and Crystal says, 'Snap!' (40 MINUTES 'Lol – A Bona Queen of Fabularity' 1981 T). Sergeant Leonard Matlovich drummed out of the force, despite a flawless service record in SERGEANT MATLOVICH VS THE US AIR FORCE; the prosecutor sums up the attitude: '"Anything Goes" may be acceptable to civilians, but it's not acceptable to the Air Force.' Which isn't to say that 'it' doesn't go on: if *Top Gun* (1986 C) is to be believed, homoeroticism keeps the guys in the skies.

Noel **Airman** (Gene Kelly in *Marjorie Morningstar* 1958 C) The slightly tarnished hero of the stage-struck Jewish heroine (Natalie Wood). He is first encountered as the social director at her summer camp, but he shrinks in stature once the romantic glow of the holiday dies. In Herman Wouk's novel, Noel is compared to 'pixies' and 'fauns'. The weak film version features Marjorie's javelin-tongued mother (Claire Trevor) who infers Noel is a PETER PAN, which is, she emphasizes, 'a FAIRY story'. Because Gene Kelly plays the role in such a blah manner, no further layers are visible. Yet the film retains Wouk's dialogue in which Airman consistently alludes to himself in the passive role: 'I'm tired of playing horse to your rider ... You have ridden me mercilessly.' A strong indication of Airman's superficiality and childish temperament (disguising a tiny talent, it is inferred) is his passing for Aryan. His real name is Saul Erhmann. He chose his first name as a tribute to Noel COWARD. In the novel Airman becomes a third-rate television writer. The film ends with Noel back at the summer camp: singing, dancing, composing and directing, surrounded by adulatory young men and women.

Airplane! (US 1980 C) Parody of the *Airport* series of disaster dramas from the creators of *The Kentucky Fried Movie*. W/D: Jim Abrahams, David Zucker and Jerry Zucker; P: Jon Davison; 87 mins.
Gay sensibility at work here! Not only

discernible in the craggy he-man pilot (Peter Graves) with a penchant for gladiator movies and little boys, but also in the assistant flight controller who's a quivering mass of movie lore and dinky quips.

Albee, Edward (1928–) American playwright. *The Death of Bessie Smith* (T); *A Delicate Balance* (1975 T); *The American Dream* (1965 T; 1987 R); *The Zoo Story* (T); WHO'S AFRAID OF VIRGINIA WOOLF? (1966 C; 1975 R).
Interviewed on *Release*: 'I will show you fear in a handful of dust' (1969 T); *P.M. Reports* (1972 R); *Release* (1977 T); *The Playwright vs The Theatre* (1980); *Albee Directs* (1984 T).

Albin aka Zaza Napoli (Michel Serrault in LA CAGE AUX FOLLES 1978; *La Cage aux Folles II* 1980; *La Cage aux Folles III: The Wedding* 1985 C) The star of the all-male Riviera revue, co-owned with his lover, Renato (Ugo Tognazzi). Somewhat prone to fits of hysteria, hyperventilation and hypochondria, Albin/Zaza is forced to 'pass' as a heterosexual male when Renato's son decides to marry the daughter of the local moral rearmer. Albin fails miserably and has to hastily improvise another, more comfortable guise: that of Renato's prim 'wife'. In the 1980 sequel Albin, on the run from the Mafia – quite contentedly (at least at first) – works in the fields as a typical Siciliana. In the third and final instalment, Albin is forced to marry (a woman) in order to claim a legacy.
There are many people all over the world (the first film was a major box office hit) who regard Albin, and Michel Serrault's rendition of him, as a pinnacle of comic timing and neat observation; good taste tightrope walking. Others regard the bizarre primping and squealing as hand-me-down and hostile. The musical version (by Jerry Herman and Harvey FIERSTEIN) gave Albin one of the great gay anthems: I AM WHAT I AM.

alcohol The most dangerous of all drugs. For gay men and for lesbians one of the problems of avoiding excessive intake is the restricted number of meeting places. Most of them offer alcohol and positively discriminate in its favour. Gisela the terse German with a mysterious past in SILENT WING courts social ostracism and even physical violence when she both refuses to drink alcohol and starts to inveigh against its ubiquity at a women's disco: 'Anyone who has to drink to free themselves can't ever do it. Your bloodstream is in bondage to beer.' An overbearing woman BARTENDER tells Gisela that she'd do well to change her attitude 'or it can be changed for you. We'll see you later.' *See also* DRINKING/ DRINK.

alcoholics Notably Sebastian FLYTE in BRIDESHEAD REVISITED; Gerald Haxton (Barry Dennen), Maugham's lover (WEEKEND WITH WILLIE 1981 R) who died in the alcoholics' ward of a New York hospital in 1944; Alain (Maurice Ronet) who leaves the clinic in search of people who will give him a reason for living in LE FEU FOLLET (1963 C); Sparger (Michael Deacon) in KENNEDY'S CHILDREN (1978 R): 'I try to keep busy. If I don't, my liver is going to wind up inflammable-like a plum pudding.'

Alexander/Alex Boy's name which, in the early 1960s, was often attached to 'weak' or co-dependent American men; later US TV's first male prostitute – *Alexander: The Other Side of Dawn*. Rare in Britain, except for Graham's full name in ONLY CONNECT – Alexander Graham after the inventor of the telephone (impersonated with successful flamboyance by Alec MCCOWEN in 1965 T).

Alexander (UK 1993 R) David Wade's 6-part radio portrait leaves his relationships with men 'open': 'We leave it as open as history leaves it,' says the director, Glyn DEARMAN. 'We now know he was an alcoholic and we know he went into a decline after Hephaestion's death. ... We are not going to shirk it ... they were incredibly close.'

Alexander the Great aka Alexander of Macedon (356–323 BC) Conqueror of Asia, dead at 33, he heads, with MICHELANGELO, the list of great gays. Lovers included Bagoas, Hephaestion and Medius. Alexander's complex personality (mirroring the culture in which he lived) has never been fully portrayed in mainstream drama, though Richard Burton looked properly god-like in the 1956 film and Sean Connery was imposing with a suggestion of wrack and ruin in Terence RATTIGAN's *Adventure Story* (1961 T). Rattigan took some pains to delve into the lustrous ruler's sexuality: despised by his father as weak and effeminate, the young Alexander is told by Pythia at Delphi to 'know yourself'. His beloved Hephaestion appears, but the intriguing resonances were more successfully worked upon in the novels of Mary RENAULT, none of which has yet been filmed. BBC Radio recently tackled ALEXANDER taking into account post-Renault findings (which seem to suggest no concrete evidence for homosexuality).

Alfie One of the very few songs directly addressed to a man. Others are DANNY BOY, and 'Bill' from *Show Boat*; while 'Ben' was sung to a rat (by Michael Jackson) for the 1972 film.

Algy Friend of Biggles (John Leyton in the 1960 series), decried as gay in a MONTY PYTHON sketch, and very much relegated to the sidelines in *Biggles* (1986 C played by Michael Siberry).

Alice (Randee Heller in SOAP 1979 T) Jodie's flatmate and soulmate in a handful of episodes. Says the show's announcer: 'They both find out they have a lot in common – they're both depressed and gay.' US sitcom's first regular lesbian, or rather semi-regular, who was then erased. She was a friendly, lolloping creature who left for Alaska just when the actress was developing a salty style. As Jodie's brother Danny (Ted Wass) put it: 'She's cute. How could she be gay? Boys are gay. Not girls. If girls were gay and boys were gay they...'

alien/aliens creatures of paranoia: sexually lawless women (for example *Cat People*); gangster fops controlling government; the Red Menace; body-snatchers; witches; Martians; blacks; gays; lesbians; serial killers; etc. Harold PINTER discussed minorities in general in Britain, but specifically lesbians and gays in the light of the passing of SECTION 28 (1988 T): 'It is quite clear', he told Anna Ford, 'that the homosexual is being seen as an alien force, something to be feared and therefore to be rejected and repressed.' Quentin CRISP was the *Resident Alien* in New York (1990 T). Stella (Carole Boyd) talks to ASHLEY about her dead and only son, Vincent in OCTOBER SCARS THE SKIN (1989 R): 'I felt he was alien to me ... a creature from another planet, a monster almost. It's true he was my own flesh and blood and I could barely believe him human. Does that shock you?'

All About Eve (US 1950 C) The quintessential Broadway tragicomedy: neurosis, fear of ageing, despair, the fickleness of fame, ruthlessness, elation. The cutting edge of show business at its most jagged as a she-wolf in sheep's clothing dethrones a star who has begun to tarnish. Eve Harrington, with her ambiguous clothes, hairstyle and body language, has an uneasy intimacy with an acerbic theatre critic and we witness a seduction of a young fan at her apartment. George Sanders was never more jaded, never more astringent, never more appealing as Addison De Witt. With a starlet (Marilyn MONROE) on his arm he appears to be a womanizer, but his dressing-room confrontation with the equally scheming Eve indicates that they share a similar secret life. 'We deserve each other,' he tells her through hooded eyes. 'Neither of us has the ability to love or be loved.'
W/D: Joseph L. Mankiewicz; P: Darryl F. ZANUCK; 138 mins.

Allen, Peter [Peter Woolnough] (1944–92) Australo-American cabaret singer, songwriter. As one of the Allen Brothers (with Chris Bell) he appeared on *The Johnny Carson Show* (1966–8). Much US and Australian television since. Songs include: 'Quiet Please, There's A Lady On Stage'; 'I Go To Rio'; 'I Honestly Love You' (recorded by Olivia Newton-John); 'I'd Rather Leave While I'm In Love' (Rita Coolidge); 'Don't Cry Out Loud' (Melissa Manchester); 'You and Me' (aka 'We Wanted It All' – Frank Sinatra); 'Arthur's Theme' (with Carol Bayer Sager, sung by Chris Cross in *Arthur*: Academy Award Best Song 1981).

Allen, Woody [Allen Stewart Konigsberg] (1935–) Almost a fictional character in his own autobiographical films (or vice versa). Allen's worried, self-analytical New York Jewish heterosexual has carried audiences with him for over two decades – not always the same audiences as his style has developed or retarded according to taste, taking in a couple of Ingmar BERGMAN homages along the way which sorely tried the patience of many. What has remained constant through his madcap farces, through his yuppie romances and back again is his fascination/obsession with the surface of male homosexuality. In his Tolstoy meets Marx Brothers' *Love and Death* (1975 C) our hero ponders human existence and considers why he has persistent dreams of waiters stepping out of coffins and waltzing together. 'All those Greeks were homosexual. My, they must have had some wild parties.' He assures us that he is not homosexual, though once some cossacks whistled at him. Naturally enough. 'I have the kind of body that excites both persuasions.'
Two films later, Allen's alter ego (named Isaac Davis) has an estranged wife, Jill (Meryl Streep) who not only leaves him for another woman but writes a (best-selling) book about their marriage (*Manhattan* 1979). One of the most widely disliked movies in the canon, *Stardust Memories* (1980) sees Allen as the much feted film artist whose fans include many a slithersome quean and whose young friend appears to have had a recent lesbian affair.

Unconsciously perhaps, Allen crystallized the unbudgeability of the stereotype in his 1977 *Annie Hall*. Diane Keaton has invited him to meet her family, including 'Grammy' of whom she talks incessantly. Allen sits uncomfortably at the daintily laid dinner table, surrounded by WASPs, trying to be totally himself but not too Jewish. This doesn't fool flinty Grammy. Momentarily, taking her point of view, we see Allen in full Rabbinical rig: black hat, black coat, locks and beard – the very embodiment of Jesus Christ's personal executioner, the purveyor of everything ethnic and alien. Substitute lavender shirt, limp wrist, molesting hands and you have the homophobe's perfect target.

All for Love (UK 1982–3) Drama series based on short stories by people like Francis KING and Elizabeth Taylor. Two had homosexual themes. In 'Combat' the mother (Joyce Redman) tries to discomfort her son's boyfriend Clement (Nigel HAVERS). She compares her boy's passing interest in market gardening to the likely (short) duration of their cohabitation ('a PHASE'). 'He was always one for phases. Phases never last.' In 'Miss A and Miss M' Miss Alliott (Kika Markham) and Miss Martin (Jennifer Hilary) fascinate young Lizzie Coles (Colette Barker). Granada; 60 mins each.

All Gone Sepentine music from Johnny (now John) Dankworth and swooning delivery by Cleo Laine of Harold PINTER's lyrics perfectly embody the dark, fetid relationship between master Tony and man Barrett in *The Servant*. The song is featured on half-a-dozen occasions. The message remains the same whether it's up-tempo and inconsequential (for the male–female coupling) or sinister and morose (the two men): 'Leave it alone, it's all gone.' But Tony is a prisoner who cannot resist whatever it is that Barrett holds out to him on the silver tray: 'Can't live without you, can't love without you.' 'All Gone' is the musical equivalent of Dorian GRAY's portrait. It begins as pleasant

background music; moves on to be an upper-class heterosexual love lyric; then becomes a backdrop for heterosexual ROUGH TRADE, before turning into a dirge for male mutual dependence; and is finally a symbol of moral and physical collapse as the servant achieves total domination over his erstwhile master.

all in the best possible taste Kenny EVERETT as an overdressed, bosomy Hollywood actress, Venus, crossing and recrossing her legs and adjusting her bosom: in *The Kenny Everett Video Show* (1982 T) all part of the rudimentary craziness. The bearded lovely made her final appearance in 1986. She was replaced by Verity Treacle, calm, soothing, relentlessly motherly.

All in the Family (US 1971–8 T) Archie Bunker (Carroll O'Connor) was a more loveable free-style bigot than his British equivalent, Alf Garnett, but he aroused the same sort of ire. In 1973, President Nixon, formerly a fan, was mighty sore that Archie's bar crony turned out to be a gay man (and him a FOOTBALLER!). A couple of years later, Archie's long-long-long suffering wife Edith (Jean Stapleton) reveals that her dear sweet, unmarried 'Cousin Liz' was a dear, sweet, 'married' lesbian. Worse, the sexy Beverley LA SALLE, whom Archie aided when she was injured in a pedestrian accident, turned out to be a he not a she. On this occasion, Archie had time to chew on his prejudices as Beverley made two return visits to the Bunker household. In the late 1970s, Archie went it alone and opened *Archie Bunker's Place* (1979–83). On the payroll was a waiter, Fred: genus swish. In one episode, Archie gives Fred basic lessons in straight-acting (school of LA CAGE AUX FOLLES).

All My Children (US 1976– T) The first daily American soap opera to bring on a lesbian character: LYNN Carson, sympathetic for as long as she lasted (a couple of months in 1977).

'Allo, 'Allo (1984/1985–92 T) Fitfully rollicking Jeremy Lloyd and David Croft comedy serial set in Occupied France and making mock of English, French and German stereotypes – a sure-fire recipe for commercial success. One of the Germans is a long-faced, timid gay (Lieutenant GRUBER) while the dreaded Herr Flick of the SS (Richard Gibson) enjoys slipping into something sheer and rustling. The first British sitcom to be nationally syndicated in the US, so no surprises whatsoever. Very trad, but directed, designed and played to the hilt with cunning disguises and contrivances.

P/D: David Croft; BBC1.

all she needs/all he needs is a good ... A well-endowed man is the answer to a gay maiden's prayer. Thus was Pussy Galore put on the correct path by Connery/Bond in *Goldfinger* (1964 C); the sexually experimental wife, Suzanne (Melinda Dillon) given the once-over by interventionary force Paul Newman ('I can get you straight') in *Slap Shot* (1977 C); and student Felicity wooed away from her girlfriend by Antony SHER's *History Man* (1981 T).

Sometimes a gal reaches safe harbour with the help of a rich patroness (LAKEY in THE GROUP), but usually she'll have to fight the marauding male – often unsuccessfully – to preserve her womanhood and sometimes her woman: 'Breeze Anstey' in COUNTRY MATTERS, Jill in THE FOX. Not all are as tough as Kim in THE OTHER WOMAN. Her lover, Robin hopes that a session of love-making will divert her from her onslaught upon the young secretary, Nikki. But Kim spikes his guns by telling him that she doesn't enjoy the during or the after ('lying here in your pool of muck'). His response ('Queer bitch!') is the signal for Kim to get out of bed, mount her motorbike and go zooming back to Nikki.

For men, there is an insistent pressure, a force-feeding, but it is not as violently enforced. There's a persistent staking out of the male (by Romola de Pulasky) in NIJINSKY and *Chinchilla* (1981 R) and by Carol of Jodie in SOAP: 'For 25 years I'm gay. Suddenly, a girl comes on a little bit and I'm in bed with her ... It

wasn't even unpleasant. What does this make me? Imagine how confused my hormones are.' The spirit of enthusiastic over-optimism is to be found in one of the women at the village cocktail party in *Goodbye, Darling* (1981 T) surveying antique dealer, Malcolm Penney (Neville Jason):

First woman: 'What pretty girl do you think he's got his eye on?'
Second woman: 'For heaven's sake, the man's a queer.'
First woman: 'I'm sure he's not. There are so many nice girls around. He's waiting for Miss Right.'
Second woman: 'On the contrary, dear. He *is* Miss Right.'

The mystery of why so many homosexual men and women end up frustrated, deceitful and sometimes violent in marriages might be solved by listening to the barrage of almost subliminal messages and directives issued to men who remain 'eligible' and to women who 'wait' that worrying fraction of a second too long before taking the plunge.

Michael's splendidly understanding mother in AN EARLY FROST says, almost in passing: 'If there's anyone you want to bring home, I just want you to know that she's always welcome.' Given the constant tom-tomming of prejudice and the blandishments of the family life package, some people – guilt-ridden, embarrassed, confused or unaligned with a partner or close circle of friends – may be persuaded to 'give it a try'. For the sake of the neighbours or Great Aunt Fanny (strange she never married). The hope is that the marriage Mrs Durham pushes Clive into in MAURICE will soon be a thing of the past (understandable though, given the need to carry on the family name/line). Down the class pole, the plight of someone like Ronald Merrick (Tim Pigott-Smith) in THE JEWEL IN THE CROWN (1984 T) is also acute. Merrick, in his clumsy arid way, tries to woo Daphne Manners: 'I've never found the right kind of girl. I kept pretty much to myself.' On their first date, he asks her if she'd like to be engaged to him. She delicately if rather too rapidly refuses. Merrick says: 'I thought I'd ask.' To which she replies: 'Yes, it was very kind.' He eventually marries the young widow of his adored friend, soon thereafter recognizing his true nature in a way that leads to his death in grotesque circumstances. But society is served. He is an army officer, and he is a married man. It is put about that he died in a riding accident – an unconscious sexual reference.

Whether it is Laura Reynolds unbuttoning her blouse to initiate effeminate Tom Lee in the ways of 'real' sex in TEA AND SYMPATHY, or any one of the scores of Emmanuelle clones given the good-malekeeping seal of approval after a bout of lesbian passion, the drive to heterosexualize grinds on remorselessly. In the final scene of the 'Solution' episode of THE GENTLE TOUCH (1982), a young policeman and a middle-aged police doctor watch as a lesbian woman walks away from them down a corridor:

> Policeman: 'Shame. Nice-looking bird.'
> Doctor: 'Yes. We all know what they need, women like that.'
> Policeman: 'Yeah! (slight smile). Come back to my place!'

Doctor double-takes.

Madge **Allsop** (Madeleine Orr 1976–80; Emily Perry *c*1985–) The much abused, silent bridesmaid of Dame Edna EVERAGE seen in her TV shows and always referred to with terrifying vehemence by her bosom friend. She was discovered – under a mound of bedclothes – next to Dame Edna in her broadcast to the world from the 'Saveloy Hotel' on the occasion of Australia's bicentennial (*Australia Live* 1988 T). Edna says she gives Madge a 'hand up', as well as help with her 'tonguing and grooving' (1987).

all that fuss over such a little thing Sister Joan Sims giving Kenneth Connor a blanket bath in CARRY ON *Nurse* (1959 C) and looking down at an angle relative to the base of his abdomen. This squib has appeared in various guises ever since but it was considered very cheeky, dirty even, in those pre-Lady Chatterley/Profumo days.

All the Queen's Men GRANADA project about an all-gay army unit. Brian Armstrong, head of comedy, told GAY NEWS in November 1976: 'There won't be anything crude – no outrageous prancing types.' But the idea was quietly scrapped before a pilot could be made.

All Things Bright and Beautiful Traditional hymn, sung by choirboy (Jake Kavanagh) in the opening scene of STAIRCASE while Harry (Richard Burton) gazes over the fence into the graveyard. With his bandaged head and white barber's tunic, he is an ALIEN form desperately seeking normality (wife, kids, neighbourly approval, religious sanction).

Also rendered – lustily – by Breeze and Lorn as they plant herbs in COUNTRY MATTERS 'Breeze Anstey', only to be interrupted by the postman bearing a letter from Lorn's lover Vernon announcing his arrival – and sounding the death-knell on Breeze's secret desires.

Almodóvar, Pedro (1951–) Spanish film director whose scattershot approach effectively blurs the borders between hetero-, homo-, bi- and transsexual without alienating majority or minority audiences. When he's at full throttle, he makes entertainments of great fluency, tenderness and perfectly judged stylistics, though always with a tough undertow. Interviewed by Jonathan Ross (1991); profiled in *Pedro Almodóvar* (1991 T). He plays small parts in some of his movies, like *Women on the Edge of a Nervous Breakdown*; briefly seen in IN BED WITH MADONNA.

The Alternative Miss World (UK 1980) Bizarre and fascinating film record (1978) of an annual beauty pageant held before an audience of fashion followers and the *avant garde* of the London art world. Among those on parade: Nigel Adey (Miss Wolverhampton Municipal Baths); Ricardo de Velasco (Miss Perm); John Thomas

(Miss Little Egypt); John Maybury (Miss Winscale Nuclear Reactor); William Waldron (Miss Cruella Cardinale); James Birch (Miss Consumer Products); Miss Linda Carrage, who was 'just a normal boy from Liverpool, someone you pass on the street.' Judges included Lionel Bart, Duggie Fields, Joan Bakewell, Molly Parkin, Zandra Rhodes, Eric Roberts and Michael Roberts. *And* DIVINE.

D: Richard Gayor; 90 mins.

Altman, Dennis (1943–) Australian writer and activist. Much television from early 1970s, during which time he was Australia's most visible homosexual, apart from Patrick WHITE. Author of *AIDS and the New Puritanism*, he always appears confident and glowing whether on *Hypotherical* 'Does Dracula Have AIDS?' (1986 T) or discussing stamps on *Late Night Live* (1991 R); etc.

Amazons Mad (Toyah Willcox), Bod (Jenny Runacre), Amyl Nitrate (Jordan) and Crabs (Little Nell) suffocate, stab, shoot, castrate, cover in tomato ketchup, fire-bomb and flay their (mainly male) victims while leading lives of sedate domesticity playing monopoly, boxing and fencing in JUBILEE. Other Amazons can be found in *A Midsummer Night's Dream* (Queen Hippolyta), *Penthesilea* (Queen of the Amazons played by Barbara Jefford, 1971 R); DIAMONDS ARE FOREVER (Bambi and Thumper, the wrestlers); Vanessa REDGRAVE as Amelia in *The Ballad of the Sad Café* (1991 C); Laurene Landon as the last of her tribe who has to conceive before it's too late in *Amazons* (1984 T); while Tarzan, Hercules, the STAR TREK team and many other he-men have encountered these she-men, whose Queen is nearly always looking for male sperm to repopulate.

ambidextrous Carol GREY describes herself thus, in THE ARCHERS (1954 R); as does Tom Vermeer (Peter WHITMAN), explaining why he has sex with Claudia as well as young men in *Slipping Away* (1984 R).

Ambridge The fictional Midlands village created by Godfrey Baseley, which is home to THE ARCHERS and 350 other souls, none of whom appears to be out of the closet yet. However, the ghost of a drummer boy can sometimes be heard tapping on a bedroom window at the Bull Inn ...

For millions a safe place of pig noises, swill buckets, bleats, squawks of hens, the jingling approach of horses, the rustle of sheaves ... Not to mention the smell of the manure and of Doris' hot pot, Irish stew (with dumplings) and stuffed heart. Ah! the unalloyed pleasures of digging heels into wet, lush pastures and soaking up the seasonal doings and dramas. During its first year (1951), Dan discovers his low-fat milk content and sterilizes the ground for early tomatoes, Doris burns the custard, and so on.

The Archers were described (in episode 22) as 'children of the soil' and, from the very earliest episodes, sex was very much a part of the picture. Rita Flynn, it was strongly hinted in episode 7, sleeps not only with married men (like Jack Archer) but also with young men (like his brother Phil). Grace Fairbrother asks Phil breathlessly: 'Did you ... *were* you?'; but he declines to answer. Married Basil nearly leads Christine off the straight and narrow, and LADY HYLBEROW, who has another go, offering to take her away from the peaceful village to foreign climes.

Two other contrastedly sexy souls, Nelson GABRIEL, the perennial bad boy with a mysterious past, and his curmudgeonly old Dad, Walter display their various idiosyncracies while, around them, the village and farming undergo radical change because of new-fangled ways and economic necessity, emerging as the thoroughly modern Ambridge of the 1990s where sex and love are firmly on the dramatic agenda.

An American Family (US 1973 T) Living in Santa Barbara – with 5 children, 3 dogs, 2 cats and a bowl of goldfish, palm trees in the garden and a pool – is easy. But behind the cloudless facade the Louds' 20-year-old marriage is collapsing. The parents discover 'to their uncomprehending amazement' that their eldest son, Lance, is gay. In one scene Mrs Loud visits him in New York where he is living in a gay commune in a hotel. Presented by the Public Broadcasting Service (PBS), this series, one of the first to subject 'ordinary' people to prolonged exposure in front of the camera, had huge impact and made Lance LOUD the most famous gay person in the US ... for a few months. He became a journalist, and his contribution as a role-model was recalled in THE GAY AND LESBIAN WORLD in 1992.

American Playhouse One of the Public Broadcasting Service's flagships which has presented, during the 1980s and 1990s, a number of dramas featuring homosexual relationships. These include: LONGTIME COMPANION; *Lemon Sky*; *The Fifth of July*; *Tidy Endings*; *André's Mother*; and *Waiting for the Moon*.

Amnesty International Until very recently, victimized homosexuals were not regarded as political prisoners anywhere in the world. Neither the United Nations nor Amnesty recognized sexual preference as grounds for unfair arrest, torture, trial, imprisonment or execution. Amnesty's conflict over the homosexual issue was delineated in OUT ON TUESDAY in 1990.

Amsterdam Netherlands city renowned for its tolerance and social/sexual mingling. As a gay mecca it has been featured in *Encounter* 'Sex and Religion' (1990 T) and *Rough Guide to Europe* (1988 T). The latter encapsulated its flavour as: 'Canals, controversy, squatters, football, rock music, clubs, pirate radio and ... homosexuals.' The programme also included a visit to the Homo-Monument commemorating 'those hundreds of thousands forced to wear the PINK TRIANGLE, as well as those among them who wore yellow stars'.

anal crease One of the topics of discourse on DONAHUE's piquantly titled 'Banning Butts on the Beach Is Definitely In' (1990 T). For 50 minutes, the audience was asked to consider: was the visibility or non-visibility of the upper part of the mid-buttock region suitable for public display? Although a young man appeared in revealing swimming attire, all the attention was paid to the female sunbather, who had also been arrested for wearing a minute piece of cloth separating the two buttocks, and uncovering that which is rarely seen. *See also* ANAL OBSESSION; ANAL SEX.

anal obsession *Days of Thunder*, *Three Fugitives* and *Men at Work* form just a small sample of 1980s and 1990s American films whose dialogue, supposed to be joshingly funny, is anally obsessed, as in 'up your ass, asshole'. The true connoisseur of the anal passage ('I'm not interested in balls') is Bob in TENUE DE SOIREE/EVENING DRESS who tells terrified (and hitherto heterosexual) Antoine: 'Your asshole will quiver with joy.'

anal sex Says Gerard to Valerie in THE LAST WOMAN: 'We've both got shit for memories' as he begins his rhythmic thrusts (inspired by a photograph of a lion mounting his mate). It is the last sexual act he performs before taking the electric carving knife to himself. Probably the most famous heterosexual example was that of Marlon Brando using butter on Maria SCHNEIDER in *Last Tango in Paris* (1972 C). But it was also intimated seen between Charles Swann (Jeremy Irons) and a female prostitute in *Swann in Love* (1984 C); between Nola Rae and one of her three suitors in *She's Gotta Have It* (1986 C); and, against her will, between Mariel Hemingway and Eric Roberts in *Star '80* (1983 C). It was also seen briefly between two members of the audience (standing up) in *Cinema Paradiso* (1988 C); and it is suggested by the drunk would-be rapist in the car park in THELMA AND LOUISE.

Male–male sodomy is usually very discreetly handled or shown as a brutal act of power and domination, as in prison movies like FORTUNE AND MEN'S EYES, or in epics like EXODUS (Nazis), LAW-

RENCE OF ARABIA (Arabs), and *The Black Robe* (North American Indians 1991 C). However, outside the mainstream, especially since the AIDS crisis, anal intercourse between men is quite often depicted or discussed: Walt and Roberto in MALA NOCHE; the film director and his fan in LAW OF DESIRE; Brian and Bryan in TOGETHER ALONE; the two HIV-positive men in THE LIVING END and, very briefly, Philip and Eliot in THE LOST LANGUAGE OF CRANES.

British radio has only extensively depicted anal sex once, courtesy of Roger CASEMENT's diaries in CRIES FROM CASEMENT AS HIS BONES ARE BROUGHT TO DUBLIN: 'Denis, Pierre the Yid, Lofty, Jock of Sloane Square ... Jamie McAllister's is growing nicely ... I take it up for him. Fully 8 inches he had at extension and the red head of it huge: it was good.'

One of the most graphic discussions of the impact of (unwanted?) anal intercourse took place in the sonnets of William SHAKESPEARE. Gore VIDAL saw Sonnet 35, 'No more be grieved at that which thou hast done' as Shakespeare's apology for a particularly violent or unsuccessful anal penetration of a young man: 'loathsome canker lives in sweetest bud.'

Andersen, Hans Christian (1805–75) Danish writer of children's stories, 168 of them, all of which have been translated into more than 100 languages and transformed into plays, ballets and cartoons. Andersen played with DOLLS as a child, was kept by a male lover, and wanted to be a BALLET DANCER – though not in the Sam Goldwyn version of his life (1952 C with Danny KAYE). He was also portrayed by Esmé PERCY in *My Life is a Lovely Adventure* (1947 R), and by Murray MELVIN in *Adventures of a Flying Trunk* (1979 C). His stories continue to delight: versions of 'The King's New Clothes' are numerous, and Walt Disney rendered *The Little Mermaid* (Andersen's most deeply felt, autobiographical and homoemotional story) as a heterosexual teen romance to popular and critical acclaim in 1988. The teen idol Jason Donovan was due to star as Andersen ('fictionalized', the makers declared almost redundantly) in a 1993 television musical.

Andrea Girl's name (meaning strong and masculine) bestowed on a significant number of strong, spiky or dyky characters: beginning with Andrea Spedding (Gale Sondergaard) in *Sherlock* HOLMES *and the Spider Woman* (1944 C) and continuing with Andrea (Marla English), possessed by a former life as she rises from the sea as *The She Creature* (1956 C) creating havoc and killing people; Andrea Thomas (JoAnna Cameron), taken over by the spirit of Egypt's fertility goddess in *ISIS* (1975 T); Andrea, who hates all men after being raped in the shower, in *Stand Up and Be Counted* (1971 C) aka *Everybody's at It* aka *The Female Response*; Odette Laurent as *Andrea* (1977 C), a porn film set on the island of Lesbos; Andrea Fleming (Susan Blakely), a promiscuous woman driven by her sexual fantasies in *Secrets* (1977 T).

Then there is the very tough Andrea Calman (Carolyn Seymour) in one of the *Tales from the Darkside* 'Dream Girl' (1985 T). Embattled and bossy in life, she is transformed into a Playboyish cream puff by a dreaming male: 'The nerve of that creep. I don't even own a mini-skirt!' More worrying was Andrea (Elizabeth Ashley) in *Windows* (1980 C). She hates men. Assaulted by her father, she kills her psychiatrist, the neighbours *and* the cat before trying to force her female beloved (Talia Shire) – whom she has previously had raped by two men – to have sex with her at knife point.

Less endangering Andreas have included: Andrea Whiting (Virginia Gilmore), ex-wife of Sam in *Search for Tomorrow* (1950s T); Andrea Lemaine (Hope Lange), sweet and pregnant in *In Love and War* (1958 C); Andrea (Annie) Cooper (Quinn Cummings), an orphan in *Family* (1978–80 T); Andrea (Luisa Maneri), daughter of French cabinet minister in charge of morals in LA CAGE AUX FOLLES; Andrea Korackes (Patricia Mauceri) in *As the World Turns* (1983

T); the unmarried and pregnant (by Terry Duckworth) Andrea Clayton in CORONATION STREET; Andrea (Phyllis Logan), former nightclub singer, tough and cynical, mother of three, in cancer ward in *And the Cow Jumped over the Moon* (1991 T); Andrea (Moir Leslie) running an NHS health education unit threatened by a marketing director in *Add Life to Years* (1992 R).

There is an increasing trend towards Andreas who are known as Andi or Andy: the unresponding love object of a male teenager who commits suicide in *Silence of the Heart* (1984 T), described as 'an airhead'; Andie Walsh (Molly Ringwald) in *Pretty in Pink* (1986 C); Andy (Sheila McCarthy), a slave to fitness, the mousy one who has an affair with the only man in the group, Geoff in *Stepping Out* (1991 C).

The classic female outsider: Andrea Zuckerman (Gabrielle Carteris) the nerdette, the bright kid from the wrong side of the tracks, bespectacled, intellectual in *Beverly Hills 90210* (1990– T) who went on a voyage of sexual discovery at the end of the first series.

Commented Gabrielle Carteris in an interview with Peter Holmes: 'Andrea is someone who is different from the norm, and sometimes doesn't fit in, but in the end she's friends with all of them … Even the most popular kids who write me letters say they always felt a little bit on the outside. Even the most popular people, you see them as being one thing, but sometimes they see themselves as being someone else. So Andrea is a character people really relate to' (*Sydney Morning Herald*, 2.1.91).

Andrews, Harry (1911–87) British actor usually in abrupt, commanding roles who was memorably queer in ENTERTAINING MR SLOANE and, more subtly, in LENT. His long relationship with a man was not referred to in THIS IS YOUR LIFE (1985). His last role was as FitzGeorge in Vita SACKVILLE-WEST's *All Passion Spent* (1986 T).

Andromeda Leader of one of the famous Lesbos 'girls' colleges' where an all-round education was guaranteed. The only prominent example is the robotic nymphet, partly created by a woman, played by Julie Christie in *A for Andromeda* (1961 T) and then by Susan Hampshire in *The Andromeda Breakthrough*. Bringer of a message to a world gone out of control.

And the Band Played On Highly controversial 1989 book by journalist Randy Shilts about the early days of the AIDS crisis in the US. Roger Spottiswoode directed the TV version (for Home Box Office) for showing in 1993 after two of the major networks passed on the project three years earlier. Steve Martin, Richard Gere and Lily TOMLIN were among the big name actors playing small parts. Matthew Modine starred as the gay doctor who tries to alert the medical profession to the threat of the disease.

Andy Pandy Boy doll in the BBC Children's TV series (1950–3; repeated until 1970) who lived with Teddy and Looby Loo in a menage that was always rumour-ridden. 'Andy's attire was always somewhat effeminate with his blue and white striped jogging suit and matching floppy hat. Indeed there is a school of thought that believes he inspired Quentin CRISP' (Hilary Kingsley and Geoff Tibballs, *Box of Delights: The Golden Years of Television*, 1990).

It was Marty FELDMAN who first demolished Andy's pristine image in *It's Marty* (1969 T) when, dressed as Punch, he sneered: 'You know what it's like in this business. It's not who you are but whose hand you've got up your back that counts. Look at Andy. Handy Andy all right – he's a good performer, but you know how he got there, don't you, smarmy little POOF.' (He also had a go at FLOWERPOT MEN and Basil Brush.)

The Angelic Conversation (UK 1985 C/T) Super-8 images of a young male couple in slow motion counterpoint 14 SHAKESPEARE sonnets, read by Judi Dench. The lovers, wearing incongruous black swimming trunks, are played (or, rather photographed as is) by Paul Reynolds and Phillip Williamson. This is Derek JARMAN's homage to Shakespeare's male love poetry that he was not allowed to make in CHANNEL 4's the sonnets of William Shakespeare which he was originally going to co-direct. Shots of playfulness in a rock pool with a wondrous shell have a magic about them, but the annointing scene is one of the most risible ever committed to film. For once in a Jarman film the words are almost everything. The film lasts 78 minutes. 'It was a very simple film. It dispenses with narrative more than any of my others. Time is suspended in it ... The camera falls in love with the actors; it's my most romantic film.'

Angels (UK 1976–82 T) Early evening hospital series about nurses, most of them female and none gay or lesbian. It wasn't until 1979 that nursing tutor Ken HASTINGS entered the picture, promoting new teaching methods which 'just might drag this profession into the 1980s' and protesting about the government cuts. He is at first presented as a footloose soul in his private life, but a regular lover, Paul (Michael Troughton) materializes in a couple of 1980 episodes to belabour him for his workaholism: 'You worry in Cinemascope ... you spend too much time trying to see the other guy's point of view. Fight back or pack up. There's plenty of other jobs you could do. And another thing ... you're getting to be a right pain to live with.' This scene comes so late in the series that we never know whether Ken takes Paul's advice to stop carrying the death agonies of the nation's health service on his shoulders. The battle, if not the war, is won. St Angela's casualty department is saved. At the celebration party, Ken is dressed as St George.

angels When they're male they're usually soft and malleable; heavenly, one might say: CLARENCE (Henry Travers) in *It's a Wonderful Life* (1946 C); Cary GRANT as DUDLEY in *The Bishop's Wife* (1947 C); Edward Everett HORTON as

Messenger 7013 in *Here Comes Mr Jordan* (1941 C); and again in *Down to Earth* (1947 C); occasionally suave and sexy (but English): James Mason in *Forever Darling* (1956 C). A couple of butch angelics: Michael Landon as Jonathan in *Highway to Heaven* (1984–8 T); Paul Hogan in *Almost an Angel* (1990 C). Jimmy SOMERVILLE, whose voice has been described as angelic, appeared as an angel in ORLANDO.

animals don't do it 'Even the animals in the field don't fornicate with their own sex,' says a Rugby city councillor in *Diverse Reports* 'What a Difference a Gay Makes' (1984 T). This tightly held belief is often used by anti-homosexual fundamentalists, although its tenability is being challenged by pair-bonding revelations about male stump-tailed macaques, female rhesus monkeys, female sheep, male greylag geese, male lizards, female mountain goats ... If the statement *is* true, it may be useful to ponder the other things animals can't or don't do, like commit suicide or cook food or shave or wear earrings or sit in chairs or have their hair dyed and permed or make jokes or feel pity and compassion.

ankh An Egyptian symbol of eternal life, worn by Catherine Deneuve and David Bowie in THE HUNGER (1983 C) – the sharp end accidentally causes Susan Sarandon's death, apparently releasing her from the threat of that eternal life known as vampirism.

Anne (1665–1714) Queen of Great Britain and Ireland. Played by Margaret Tyzack in THE FIRST CHURCHILLS and shown to be emotionally drawn towards Sarah Churchill and Abigail Hill; also portrayed *in travesti* by Peter BULL in *Yellowbeard* (1983 C).

Another Country (UK 1984 C) Gangling, scruffy schoolboy, Guy Bennett (Rupert Everett) who, passed over as a prefect, throws in his lot with the Communist Tommy Judd (Colin Firth) whose portrait is in his Moscow flat 30 years later.
W: Julian MITCHELL from his play; P:

David Puttnam; D: Marek Kanievska; 90 mins.

Rejected and denied the glamour and privilege he sees as his right, Bennett does not cut a very sympathetic figure. In the film, most of the appealing scruffiness has gone. Firth's studious Communist lacks the essential charisma to convince us that Bennett would be attracted to Marxism purely because of his ostracism at school. One of the added scenes which 'open up' the claustrophobic play, Guy and James Harcourt (Cary Elwes) lie together in a punt at night with their arms around one another. However, their lips could not touch because, according to the director: 'The sight of two men kissing might have alienated the audience. I thought that by stressing the longing between them it would be much more poignant.' The most damaging departure from the play was one of the irreparable idiocies of British cinema: Kenneth Branagh was not asked to repeat his stage role. His extraordinary complicity with Rupert Everett (and also with Daniel Day-Lewis who replaced him) gave much needed dramatic balance, as well as political sinew.

Another Way (Hungary 1982 C) Hungarian journalist Eva Szylansky (Jadwiga Janowska-Cieslak), who works on *The Truth*, shares an office with Lina (Grazyna Szapolowska). When Eva's girlfriend is released from prison, she doesn't continue the affair. Incapable of compromise Eva pursues her stories and her relationship with Lina equally. W/D: Karoly Makk; 109 mins.

Based on a true story of a heroic woman journalist whose lesbianism made her an easy target in the Hungary of 1958. An arresting and honest film about a rarely shown subject: the working and sexual relationship of two women colleagues. Few punches are pulled and it is a much needed example to western film makers on how to make lesbian lovers come alive, and not just in the bedroom.

antique dealers Much featured in background detail and usually camp or mildly eccentric; occasionally sexy and vigorous: *Lovejoy* (1985– T). The swishy ones include: Alan BENNETT in *On the Margin* (1966–7); Teddy, the man who is murdered and castrated in THE DETECTIVE (1968 C); Terence Huntley (Hurd HATFIELD) who has the collected works of De Sade in *The Boston Strangler* (1968 C); Colin Bartley (Roger Hammond) in WAGGONERS' WALK (1971 R); the pair (Ted Harris and Rick Metzler) who admire a coffin and end up in it (*Blacula* 1972 C); the lover of the unfortunate, dumbfounded Fox in FOX AND HIS FRIENDS; two of the inhabitants of THE CREZZ, Terry and Denny, 'husband and wife' who dabbled in antiques too, although Denny prefers pottering around in the garden – with the gardener; murderous Michael (Paul Shenar) in 'Night Horrors' (1979 T), a segment of *Hart to Hart*; David Daker as the friend of Arthur Daley, now gay and running a Chelsea antique emporium with his boyfriend (who Terry, reluctantly, has to watch over) in MINDER: 'Whose Wife Is It Anyway?' (1980 T); the celibate leading character (Alec MCCOWEN) in *The Reason of Things* (1981 T); Malcolm Penney (Neville Jason), friend of beautiful older women in *Goodbye, Darling* (1981 T); Ian (Iain Agnew) in *Quintet in October* (1984 R), who runs Queen's Elm Curios with his lover: 'Good prices paid on silver ... Uniform to buy or rent'; the clonish ex-husband (Robert Kingswell) of Julie Walters threatened by a fiendish telephone exchange in *Unfair Exchanges* (1985 T); Arnie (Harold INNOCENT) in *Hideaway* (1986 T), a crook with a muscle-bound young lover; Brian (Jeremy Brett) in *Deceptions* (1985 T); Derek JACOBI as Franklyn Madson, guilty of a murderous childhood action in *Dead Again* (1991 C).

While not exactly butch, an interest in antiques has become okay for men from the early 1970s onwards because of inflation and Arthur Negus's *Talking about Antiques* and *The Antiques Travelling Roadshow*. Before, it had been very much the province of the little old lady or the confirmed bachelor. Anybody else who praised something beautiful and well-crafted was given a sidelong glance; as for example the housemaster George Stoupe in THE CONNOISSEUR (1966 T) who loved fine china ornaments – and left his boys to indulge their passions undisturbed; *The Baron* (Steve Forrest 1965 T; this was a blind: he was really a secret agent); the trio of outsiders who, at various times, ran an antique shop: John TREGORRAN, Nelson GABRIEL and Kenton ARCHER in THE ARCHERS; much married Patrick Woodford (Patrick Cargill) in *Father, Dear Father* (1968–73 T); Derek Waring in *Moody and Peg* (1974 T); Tom Conti as Mark in *Full Circle* (1978 C); the ageing but virile pair in *Never the Twain* (Windsor Davies and Donald Sinden 1981 T); Eric Pollard (Christopher Chittell) who was lined up for gaydom in EMMERDALE in 1992 – but was 'reprieved'.

Antonio Bassanio's older friend in *The Merchant of Venice*, often given a same-sexual propulsion. Played by, among others, Raymond Westwell (with Denis QUILLEY 1955 R); Jack May (with Tony Britton 1958 R); Charles GRAY (with Christopher Gable 1973 T).

Antony, Jonquil (1911–77) Radio scriptwriter, creator (with Ted WILLIS) of MRS DALE'S DIARY in 1947. Stalwart of BBC radio from 1936 (over 2,500 features, biographies and serial episodes), for example HAMPSTEAD HEATH (1937); *Edward Lear* (1939); GORDON *of Khartoum* (1940); *Emily Brontë* (1941); *Burne-Jones* (1948); *The Robinson Family* (1946). Adapted her friend Patrick WHITE'S A CHEERY SOUL for television in 1966.

Anyone Can Fall In Love The theme from EASTENDERS given words by Leslie Osborne and Brian May, and sung by Anita Dobson who played Angie. Notably genderless and promoting love for all persuasions. The song reached no. 4 in the British charts in 1986.

Anyone Here For Love? Jane Russell tries, without success, to arouse the American Olympic male swimming team in and around the pool in *Gentlemen Prefer Blondes* (1953 C). She and Marilyn MONROE end up getting married (to men) but the framing of the final last shot suggests that it is *their* love that is here to stay.
M/L: Jule Styne and Leo Robin.

Any Questions? (UK 1947– R) Fiery radio it was, and still is! Instead of the many chaperoned interviews by well-meaning pod-people, it brings politicians, economists, industrialists, writers and actors face to face in British cities and towns with audiences who ask 'spontaneous' questions about matters of the day. Almost every subject has been 'debated' under the careful and egregious chairmanship of Freddy Grisewood, David Jacobs and others. *Any Questions?* does occasionally allow people like Chris Smith MP and Lynda Bellos airtime, the first in 1988, the second in 1990. But usually, homosexuals are the subject of discussion rather than the discussers. Among the highlights: John Junor, Eric Heffer, Anna Raeburn and Malcolm Muggeridge heatedly debating child sexuality laws in Mrs THATCHER's seat (Finchley, London) in 1979; equality for homosexuals shot down by Jean Rook and Sir Ray Pennock, trivialized by David Bellamy and stoutly upheld by former Communist union leader and journalist, Jimmy Reid (1980); Jean Rook (again), Baroness Phillips and Dennis Healey MP on AGENTS PROVOCATEURS (1984); Donald Soper complaining about footballers kissing one another (1981). '... the type of radio programme most loathed by dictators who have to suffer live, uncensored opinion. Economic errors are pinpointed and, occasionally, someone makes us laugh' (*Radio Times*, 1986).

Anything Goes Written by Cole PORTER, performed by Harpers Bizarre over the opening credits of THE BOYS IN THE BAND.

Appointment with Fear Radio anthology of the chilling, perverse and supernatural introduced by Valentine DYALL as the 'Man in Black' during the 1940s. One of the half-hour plays, 'A Mind in Shadow' (1946) about two young writers living together in the country derived in part from the love affair of Terence RATTIGAN and actor Kenneth MORGAN – who later committed suicide. Morgan played John (who goes mad and tries to strangle his friend) and Lewis Stringer was Richard (who tries to stop John from doing in the cleaning woman, Grizelda Hervey). The series was restored to life as *Fear on 4* in the 1980s with Edward De Souza as the host with the mist-at-midnight voice.

aprons Unless calf-length and made of sturdy cloth, an apron is not acceptable as male apparel – if it flops, frills, pleats or enfolds. Aprons are used as shorthand for weakness or effeminacy ... Or 'worse'. But it was not always so. In *The Last Trail* (1927 C) cowboy hero Tom Mix has to be father and mother to the kids in an orphanage, and has to dress appropriately with check apron, scarf and high-heeled boots. This unselfconsciousness did not progress into the talkie era, despite the fact that during the depression of the 1930s many men had to become house-husbands. No film chronicles this role change, except as a source of fantasy or brief snidery. Men were not usually shown wearing that most potent symbol of male humiliation: the apron. Ian Hunter was an exception – but he's divorced *and* English – in *The Devil Is a Sissy* (1936 C), and he is not seen cooking. The first men seen in aprons were usually elderly dads (Lewis Stone in *Judge Hardy and Son* 1939 C), or the occasional elderly, widowed professor like the one played by Edgar Stehli, who cooks dinner for a young colleague from the university (Kevin McCarthy), the title character in THE TWILIGHT ZONE's 'Long Live, Walter Jameson' (1960 T).

Perry Como turns up in a white frilly concoction (left over from Judy Garland's *The Harvey Girls*?) for his 'Mountain Greenery' number in WORDS AND MUSIC (1947 C). He doesn't appear

embarrassed by it, even though there is no context for his being so dressed and no reference in the lyric, unless it's contained in the phrase 'just two crazy people together'.

James DEAN's ineffectual father (Jim Backus) wears one in REBEL WITHOUT A CAUSE (1955 C), driving his son to rage: 'I don't ever want to be like him.'

In Britain, David (Peter Byrne) wore one in the privacy of his own home in the second episode of THE PATTERN OF MARRIAGE (1953 T). The same actor, now playing DIXON OF DOCK GREEN's son-in-law PC Andy Crawford, wore his wife's bouncy number in 'A Happ'orth Of all Sorts' (1957 T); Dixon himself cooks an omelette for his sergeant togged up in one in 'The Salvation of Duffy' (1958 T). In *Sykes ... And a Job* (1961 T) Eric Sykes is at home all day while sister Hattie (Jacques) goes out to work in a factory; he is attired in mob cap and fussy apron before deciding to rebel. Henry Thurston (Tony Steedman) strains vegetables through a colander in *Are You Ready for the Music?* (1965 T); his 'nephew' Simon (John CARLIN) insists he take off his apron before a party in case the guests get 'ideas'; Mr Joyboy (Rod Steiger) in *The Loved One* (1965 C) lives with his mother, but has a beautiful fiancée who says he looks 'undistinguished in an apron'. Apron-clad Arnold Plum (Dick Shawn) rustles up a salad for his virgin fiancée Leslie Caron in *A Very Special Favour* (1965 C).

An apron denotes submission – man tamed and cowed. An example is Ranson Stoddard (James Stewart) who is upbraided by his wife (Vera Miles) in *The Man Who Shot Liberty Valance* (1962 C): 'What good has reading and writing done you. Look at you – sat in an *apron*!' In Woody ALLEN's *Sleeper* (1973 C) the robot owned by a gay couple manifests all their swishy qualities and wears a lavender apron as does Tim's in a 1974 THE GOODIES (T) show. As an indication of how firmly stamped with the image of 'woman not man in the kitchen' the apron is, the distraught bachelor son in *Melancholy* (1981 R) manifests his dislocation by putting on his mother's apron and tidying the room immediately after she dies.

To be totally untainted, a man's apron should be tailored in a strong colour and, if possible, have a cheeky design or slogan. Thus Robin (Richard O'Sullivan) in *Man about the House* 'When the Cat's Away' (1975 T). One of his female flatmates' friends is discovered wearing a blue pinny in another 1975 episode of the same show (but this is acceptable because he's just helped produce twins); a plastic one with 'Come and get it' in red written upon it is worn by henpecked George (Brian Murphy) with chef's hat in *George and Mildred* (1979 T) while his wife does the 'man's work' of preparing the sausages; Robert Wagner's in *Hart to Hart* (1982 T) is royal blue and announces 'Don't expect too much'; former great actor Sir Ben Farrant (Ralph Michael) wears his wife's in *Love and Marriage* 'Sweet Echo' (1984 T), but although it is frilled chintz it doesn't jar with his attire of flowery kerchief and pinky ring; vet Siegfried (Robert Hardy) in *All Creatures Great and Small* 'The Rough and the Smooth' has a green brocade one (1989 T); psychiatrist Dad (Alan Thicke) is clad in one in *Growing Pains* (1989 T); Phil Archer and Bert are forced into 'very floral' pinnies during the AMBRIDGE fête of August 1992.

Aquarius 'Down There on a Visit' (UK 1977 T) A profile of Christopher ISHERWOOD and his life in California with his lover Don Bachardy. Isherwood talks about working for gay liberation, probably the first celebrity to do so. He expressed his undying gratitude to the young man at Cambridge in the 1930s who locked the door and got him into bed for the first time. The only advice he can give to young gays is: 'Well, it didn't do me any harm.' 'To maintain the essential individuality of a person is almost impossible with the commentary insisting on the usual formula of ordinariness and glamour, droning on about how Christopher and Don have a weekly woman in to clean and to cook for their dinner parties ... that – just fancy! – they own a collection of pictures ... While the narrator spoke primly about his "companion", Isherwood recounted laconically that some people observed in shocked tones that when he first met Don Bachardy there was a difference of thirty years between them. "I replied, 'There still is'"' (Peter Bennett, GAY NEWS, 1977).

Aramis One of the Three Musketeers – aesthetic, spiritual and sometimes performed with a gay lilt – Allan MCCLELLAND (1946 R) and Paul Hansard (in very camp blond wig) in the 1954 television production. Richard Chamberlain played him sweet and sensitive in the two Musketeer films of 1974 and 1975.

Christine **Archer** (Pamela Mant 1951–3; Lesley Saweard 1954–) Daughter of Dan and Doris, sister of Phil. Reckoned to be either 'going through a PHASE' or 'FRIGID' during the first decade of THE ARCHERS. In the first episode it was stated that Christine was not interested in 'sparkin''. She did have affairs – or close friendships – with a number of men. These included Basil, her married boss at the dairy, whose daughter, Meryl – 'blonde, attractive' – seemed sexually inclined towards her father and towards Christine: 'It would be rather nice to have a really intimate friend, someone like yourself, for instance' (1951). But the major controversy arose over being invited to go abroad with LADY HYLBEROW, as her 'companion'. Again, in a 1951 episode Christine rounded on her dad and brother: 'I'm nineteen ... And I'm quite capable of distinguishing between right and wrong and black and white. I'm intelligent ... I'm not a fool ... What do you think I am?'

Christine's boyfriends tried everything to thaw her, including cave man tactics to which she retorts: 'Loose me, you idiot – if that's the type of boy you are' (1951). Significantly she begins to respond 'as a woman' on a date with Nelson GABRIEL, a fellow vacillator in sexual matters. There were lots of nudges towards marriage (Peggy: 'You'll get married sometime, Christine, the same as I did'; Christine: 'Wouldn't be surprised if I didn't.' 1951). She took the plunge in 1956, with Paul Johnson, but not without considerable misgivings, changing her mind back and forth the day before: 'Nerves, or something.' There were problems – she either couldn't or wouldn't conceive and Paul intimated that she didn't have the right stuff in bed. Poor Christine worried Dan and Doris (and the listeners) for years. But she is now seemingly content as the wife of George Barford.

Kenton Archer (Graham Seed; followed by Graeme Kirk 1989–) The twin of Shula, son of Philip and Jill, in THE ARCHERS. He's an ANTIQUE DEALER whom Nelson GABRIEL describes in typically acerbic fashion: 'Always the bridesmaid never the bride ... tough as old boots and half as sensitive ... childish but will redeem himself' (July 1992). Kenton, selfish and insensitive though he undoubtedly is, sees himself as 'a social worker'. Was at sea, remains unmarried and sexually noncommittal. Mark Hebden says Kenton never thinks about anything 'unless it's about making a fast buck'.

Archer, Robyn (1948–) Australian singer, songwriter. One of her specialties is interpreting Bertolt Brecht (in the musical biography *Songs for the Bad Times* 1983 T); another is portraying women luscious and victimized, lusty and powerful: *A Star is Torn* (1983 R); *Pack of Women* (1986 T). British appearances include *No Place Quite Like It – Writers at the ICA* (1987 T), and *A Colonial Cabaret* (1988 R): 'part history, part autobiography, part comment, part satire.' A rare openly non-heterosexually identified Australian in the entertainment industry, she is a frequent guest on television chat shows. Her address to the Australian Press Club was televised in 1991.

The Archers (UK 1951– R) An everyday story of country folk, set in AMBRIDGE, broadcast each weekday at 1.40 pm and 7.05 pm with an omnibus edition on Sunday mornings (BBC Radio 4). *The Archers* began 1 January 1951 as a Light Programme replacement for *Dick Barton, Special Agent*, which was axed by the Head of Drama, Val Gielgud because it was a bad influence on the youth of Britain. Very few of the early days are represented on BBC Archive discs, although two compilations called *Vintage Archers* were successfully sold on tape in 1989. Nothing seems to remain of the extraordinary banter between Simon and Walter GABRIEL or between John TREGORRAN and Carol GREY, and Lady HYLBEROW is only referred to in passing by Christine. Sadly, most of the days before *The Archers* became more tense and fearful (and therefore more rigid and less sensitive in the way it portrays its characters) have melted into the ether.

architects Anna Tarrant (Joanne Storer) in *South of the Border* (1990 T) fighting her husband for custody. MILES Cooper (David Cameron) in *Chances* 'Bite the Golden Bullet' (1991 T): 'architect to the stars', now on the slide, rumoured to have AIDS. His life is characterized as essentially friendless (except for the young woman in the flat opposite and his poodle) and closeted ('I've been hiding ... for 20 years').

Arena Imaginative and sensible 1970s BBC2 arts series, edited by Alan Yentob, followed by Nigel Finch and Anthony Wall. Generous time allocation (occasionally up to 75 minutes), daring choice of subjects, honest about sexuality of same. Notable were:

'The Chelsea Hotel' (3.1.81). A look at New York's haunt of the famous and the infamous. Past and present residents interviewed include Quentin CRISP, William BURROUGHS (seen having dinner with Andy WARHOL), Jobriath Boone, and a very etiolated tour guide who invokes the memories of Behan, WILDE, Twain and Tennessee WILLIAMS.

'A Genius Like Us' (9.11.82). About Joe ORTON and Kenneth Halliwell.

'The Strange Case of Yukio MISHIMA' (3.12.85): 'An intellectual and a right-wing militarist and ferociously western. Committed suicide by ritual hara-kiri.'

'Hair' (1.2.83): 'Blue rinse, quiff, mohican, short back and sides, dreadlocks or just shaved off altogether. By your choice of hairstyle you tell the world about yourself. You can blend in with the crowd or stand out from it.' Includes a gay barber, and a TRANSSEXUAL bank worker with a hennaed 'trojan'.

'Francis BACON' (10.11.84): '... amid the spectacular disorder of his Chelsea studio, Bacon talks with great candour to his friend of many years, the distinguished writer and critic David Sylvester.'

'The Spirit of LORCA' (28.11.86): 'Recollections of friends and fellow poets.'

'Saint Genet' (12.11.85): 'Now 75, GENET remains a self-declared outcast ... still questioning society's expectations ... he denounces even the interview itself as a "piece of bad theatre" and asks the crew some uncomfortable questions.'

Are We Being Served? The title of a report published in 1986 by the Lesbian and Gay Broadcasting Project. One week of British radio and television (12–18 August 1985) was closely monitored for any mention at all of homosexual people or issues. The findings were even worse than anyone could have envisaged. Gays and lesbians accounted for 3.38 per cent of the total time – 9 hours 4 minutes out of 268 hours. On radio the percentage was 0.32 per cent (1 hour 21 minutes out of 420 hours). Of the representations, hardly any were positive, inspiring, dynamic or effectual. 'From the evidence found from the monitoring week, it is clear that the broadcasting media are reinforcing prejudice and perpetuating ignorance.'

are you a man or a mouse? Shirley Temple shrieks at a curly-topped boy child in *Just Around the Corner* (1937 C). She later removes his glasses and has his curls cut off. Forty-three years later, Jim Hacker's parliamentary agent asks him which one he is in *Yes Minister* 'Big Brother' (1980 T). Captain Bertorelli (Gavin Richards) asked his craven crew if they were 'a men-a or de mice-a' in 'ALLO, 'ALLO (1989 T), and there was a Man or Mouse? competition in *Telethon 90*.

Are You Being Served? (UK 1973–84 T) Unsophisticated, familiar, lively, smutty bounce around a department store's ladies- and menswear department with, among others, Mr HUMPHRIES and Mrs SLOCOMBE whose PUSSY gave her so many problems.
W: Jeremy Lloyd and David Croft; P/D: David Croft and others; 30 mins.

Was this the BBC going downmarket (and promoting one of the direst homosexual STEREOTYPES in television history) or an overdue homage to the innocent halcyon days of the English seaside postcard? The jury is still out, but the series was consistently popular all over the world, spawning an Australian version in 1980 and a film. It made John INMAN a family favourite. Many of the characters returned in 1992 with GRACE AND FAVOUR, which is more of the same in a country house.

are you courtin'? Each week, on *Have a Go!* (UK 1950s R) Wilfred Pickles would put this question, in a fruity nudging voice, to any man or woman between the ages of 15 and 100. He meant, of course, are you heterosexually active? There is no recorded example of anyone deviating from the standard answers: 'Yes, I am' and 'No, I'm not'. Neither is there a case of a person answering Pickles' second question 'Have you ever had an embarrassing moment?' with 'Yes. You asking me whether I'm involved with anybody' before an audience of millions. The Pickles' touch ('presenting the people to the people') was celebrated in *'Ow Do, 'Ow Are You?*, a 3-part biography (1988 R).

aristocrats Single-sex schools, nannies and over-refined tastes lead many an aristo into the thorny thickets of gay love: wildly experimental Lord George BYRON; Algernon MONCRIEFF; Baron DE CHARLUS, seeker after beautiful boys and beatings; Sebastiane FLYTE decanting himself into premature obsolescence; Crassus (Laurence Olivier), lover of snails as well as oysters (SPARTACUS 1960 C); Lord Fullbrook, blackmailed peer in VICTIM; Tony, weak young pup in *The Servant*; Lord DARNLEY, husband of *Mary, Queen of Scots* (1972 C); Baron Von Rimmer (Horst Janson) caught with his valet in UPSTAIRS, DOWNSTAIRS 'A Suitable Marriage' (1971 T); Prince Yussoupof (Martin Potter), assassin of Rasputin in *Nicholas and Alexandra* (1971 C); the accommodating baron (Helmut Griem) in CABARET, friend and bed-mate of both Sally and Brian; the readily seducible son (Anthony Corlan) of the Baroness in *Something for Everyone/Black Flowers for the Bride* (1971 C); the elderly earl (Harry ANDREWS) in *The Ruling Class* (1972 C) hanging himself in a tutu; Lord Stambleton hosting very private parties at his seat in Hampshire in CROWN COURT 'Such A Charming Man' (1977 T); Count De Gunzberg (Alan BADEL) who would like to take DIAGHILEV's place as the patron/lover of NIJINSKY; the Comte de Vaudreil whose exotic junketings may be the answer to the mystery of *Miss Morrison's Ghosts* at Versailles (1981 T); André Raffalovich (Sandor Eles) turning to the church after a variegated life (*Aubrey* 1982 T); Bobbie Shaw (Nigel HAVERS) jailed for GROSS INDECENCY in *Nancy Astor* (1982 T); the Grand Duke of Harzock travelling in style with a pretty retinue in *And the Ship Sails On* (1986 C); the Prussian baron (Joseph Fuerst), one of 2,000 Jewish refugees from Europe interned in Australia as possible spies in *The Dunera Boys* (1985 T). A ripe parody of the rapacious aristo can be found in Hercule GRYTPYPE-THYNNE and his partner in crime Count Jim MORIARTY, in decline after ravishing the armed forces of the world (THE GOON SHOW).

A blessing there are so few blue bloods in the world to prevent more debauchery. In Jeffrey Archer's *First among Equals* (1986 T) one of a quartet of MPs (Jeremy Child) is openly contemptuous of his brother, Rupert (Pavel Douglas) who has inherited the family seat under primogeniture even though he is unlikely to have any heirs, dallying as he is with a tousled cupid as hippies frolic on his lawns. Jamie (Michael Grandage) is called a raving NANCY in *Chelworth* (1989 T).

Armchair Theatre Rediffusion's prestigious series of adult drama was a flagship for quality and 'adult themes' in the 1950s and early 1960s. GIDE's *Symphonie Pastorale* was adapted as *Tears in the Wind* ('Tares in the Wheat') to open the series in September 1956. Relevant productions included: THE PICTURE OF DORIAN GRAY (1957); *Please Murder Me*, based very loosely on Gore VIDAL's novel *The Judgement of Paris* (1958); *Death of Satan* (WILDE and BYRON are giving HELL too good a name, 1958); *Girl in a Birdcage* (1960 with a lesbian prisoner, called Toni, played by Judy Parfitt). There were supporting deviants also in *The Photographer* (1960), *My Representative* (1960), THE ROSE AFFAIR (1961) and AFTERNOON OF A NYMPH.

armed forces British and American forces still maintain the bar on, and witchhunt, gay/lesbian/bisexual personnel whether or not they have relationships with comrades, superiors or civilians. Documentaries usually with ousted people plus one or two dissenting voices of authority: SEX IN OUR TIME (RAF officer in the 'For Queer Read Gay' segment 1976); GAY LIFE (1980 T); WORLD IN ACTION 'The Death of Private Dakin' (1982 T); HEART OF THE MATTER 'Falling Out' (1991 T); OPEN SPACE 'Straight and Narrow-Minded' (1988 T). In Australia FOUR CORNERS (1992 T); lesbians cut out of WOMEN AT ARMS (1979 T) and marginal in *Soldier Girls* (1990 T). Changes caused controversy in Australia late in 1992 (heated phone-ins, discussions, newspaper correspondence) and more raged in the US on the heels of President Clinton's post-election action to lift the ban on homosexual military personnel.

The difficulties faced by homosexual people in various ranks were dramatized in: *The Strange One/End as a Man* (1957 C); *Redcap* (1966 T); *The Other Man* (1964 T); REFLECTIONS IN A GOLDEN EYE (1967 C); *Young Torless* (1968 C); *The Parachute* (1968 R; 1986 T); *The Sergeant* (1969 C); GIRL; *It Ain't Half Hot, Mum* (1974–82); SERGEANT MATLOVICH VS THE US AIR FORCE (1978 T); PEARL; PRIVATES ON PARADE (1982 C); DRESS GRAY; *Walking on Sticks* (Aust 1991 R).

Arms and Legs (UK 1972 R) Sarah (Barbara Mitchell) is a painter. Her friend, Milly (Julia Foster) is married to Rob (Nigel Lambert), who watches football on the telly and is a male chauvinist. Sarah wants Milly so she has Rob model for her, reducing him on canvas to his anatomical parts. At the play's climax, Sarah has persuaded fluffy Milly to live with her: 'And it seems to me we have a perfect relationship ... I mean, in that it is very honest. Surely, we're more honest with each other than we ever could be with men.'
W: Jennifer Phillips; P: Charles Lefeaux; 27.2.72; BBC Radio 3; 55 mins.

One of the first 'women fight back' plays of the 1970s.

Army of Lovers or Revolt of the Perverts (US/Ger 1978 C/T)
P/D: Rosa VON PRAUNHEIM; *c* 90 mins.
The sad message of *Army of Lovers* is articulated by a member of the Pink Satin Bombers troupe who says 'when we fought this revolution 10 years ago, I didn't know that the benefit would be 700 leather bars and the right to join the army ... that isn't what I had in mind.' *Army of Lovers*, with few exceptions, examines the stridencies of political and social extremes. The history of political activism in the United States is told through institutions, newsreel footage, still photographers, marches, rallies and excerpts from gay theatre including the Pink Satin Bombers and the US Gay

Sweatshop. The resultant visual mixture has an inherent fascination for any movement historian and is sufficiently exciting to hold the interest of gay activity presently concerned with 'where we're going.' (Vito RUSSO, *Gay News* 167, 1978).

Arne, Peter (1922–83) British character actor, mainly sinister or sleazy. His murder was discussed in *A Shred of Evidence* (1984 T).
C: *Time Slip* (1955); *The Purple Plain* (1955); *The Moonraker* (1957); *Danger Within* (1959); *Conspiracy of Hearts* (1960); *A Story of David* (1960); *Scent of Mystery* (1960); *Straw Dogs* (1971); *Providence* (1977); *Agatha* (1978); VICTOR/VICTORIA (as the gay nightclub owner, 1982). He made the most of his tiny role as KITCHENER in *Khartoum* (1966).
T: Joe Griggs in *The Hero* (1953); as Peter Kendall who doesn't care whether he lives or dies in *Joyous Errand* (1957); in episodes of *The Mask of Janus*, *The Champions*, *The Shattered Eye*, *The Stallion*; *Task Force*; *The Venturers*; etc.

Artemis '81 (UK 1981 T) David Rudkin's long, dense phantasmagoria involving satanic and angelic forces featured Hywel Bennett, as Gideon becoming enraptured by a man from another world (played by Sting), which possibly makes him re-evaluate his own role in the life of a friend, Jed, a film lecturer (Ian Redford). Jed is a sad, haunted man, disturbed by the daily degradations of the planet and by his inability to connect with feelings outside those on celluloid. Gideon tries to calm his anxieties: 'Jed, being gay isn't the end of the world these days ... You see the world too much as an image of yourself.' Jed makes one desperate effort to reach Gideon – he kisses him and receives the expected polite rebuff. Jed later commits SUICIDE.
P: David Rose; D: Alistair Reid; 29.12.81; BBC 1; 185 mins.

artists The link with the artist and the sexual outsider has remained strong since the early part of the 20th century,

tragic at first, frisky in DESIGN FOR LIV-
ING, then back to stressful. The two
halves were probably best displayed in
the documentary *A Bigger Splash* (1974
C) wherein, amidst a great deal of
inconsequential chat, David HOCKNEY's
creative and emotional break-up with
Peter Schlesinger is obliquely charted.
Few shreds of comfort for the artist
from a friend of Meriel in THE TINKER'S
DAUGHTER: 'Artists are lonely. That is
the price you have to pay ... You are
creating something that wasn't there
before so you live in a continual state of
anxiety.'

Zoret (Benjamin Christensen) in *Mikael* (1924 C) based on Auguste Rodin;
the Clark Gable character in *It Happened
One Night* (1934 C), who was originally
to have been a GREENWICH VILLAGE
painter – no one liked the character and
the writer Myles Connolly said, 'He
must be one of us. Forget the PANTY-
WAIST painter and make him a guy we all
know and like' (*The Name above the Title*,
1972); Countess Anna GESCHWITZ in
PANDORA'S BOX; Michael Fane (Brian
Aherne), admirer of Sylvester who is
really SYLVIA SCARLETT; Christine Gilbert (Alexis Smith) who seems to have a
certain empathy with bachelor George
Gershwin (Robert Alda) in *Rhapsody in
Blue* (1945 C); Basil Hallward who
paints THE PICTURE OF DORIAN GRAY;
Finch Whiteoak in WHITEOAKS; Amy
North (Lauren Bacall), socialite and
dabbler in *Young Man with A Horn* (1950
C); Vincent VAN GOGH (Kirk Douglas)
turbulently tied to Paul Gauguin
(Anthony Quinn) in *Lust for Life* (1956
C); ADRIAN (Anthony Viccars) accompanied by his 'friend' in THE CRIME
AT BLOSSOMS (1958 R); Lisa who,
according to Marcello, paints just so she
can make out with her female models in
LA DOLCE VITA (1960 C); Frank Leeson
(Harold INNOCENT), a Francis BACON
lookalike in THE AVENGERS 'The Medi-
cine Men' (1963 T); Stellan, specialist
in gratifying elderly women in *Loving
Couples* (1964 C); Peter Young (Alfred
Lynch), commercial artist haunted by a
man from his student days in HORROR OF
DARKNESS; Sir Francis Hinsley (John

GIELGUD) in *The Loved One* (1965 C);
Johan Borg (Max Von Sydow) dream-
ridden on a Swedish island in *The Hour
of the Wolf* (1966 C); CEDRIC Malmsley
(John STRATTON) in *Artists in Crime*
(1968 T); Loerke (Vladek Sheybal),
fantastical and demonic, encountered by
Gudrun in the Alps in WOMEN IN LOVE
(1969 C); Kim, motor-bike riding barbarian in THE OTHER WOMAN; Augus-
tine, the one fulfilling liaison for Koo
Stark in (*The Awakening of*) *Emily* (1977
C); Gunnar Wedelman (Michael
Byrne) having a fling with his subject in
COMING OUT (1979 T); Bill HAYDON
amateur painter and full-time Russian
spy in TINKER, TAILOR, SOLDIER, SPY;
Mico (Paul Herzberg), catalyst for a fellow artist's jealousy in FACING THE SUN;
Stephen Grain (Ian Hogg), friend of the
anti-hero in *Very Like a Whale* (1980 T);
Vivienne (Camilla Sparv), saviour of the
down-and-out Jennifer North in VALLEY
OF THE DOLLS (1981 T); Charles Ryder,
Sebastian's inamorato in BRIDESHEAD
REVISITED; the 18th-century artist
Winckelmann whose art and murder by
a cook he picked up piques the life-long
interest of a closeted don Gilbert Sage
(Norman Rodway) in *Death in Trieste*
(1981 R); James King in *King's Royal*
(1983 T); Gwen John (Anna MASSEY) in
Journey into the Shadows (1984 T);
Quaint Irene (Cicely Hobbs) with a big
pash on Lucia in MAPP AND LUCIA; the
eponymous *Anne Trister*, growing closer,
ever closer to a child psychologist while
tackling a huge painting (1986 C); Meriel Baigent defying convention with a
below stairs lover of the same sex in THE
TINKER'S DAUGHTER; Michelangelo
CARAVAGGIO (Nigel Terry), base of an
emotional triangle which leads to
murder, exile and his death (1986 C);
Fiona ridiculed by her family for her artistic vocation, non-meat-eating and
love of a woman (A HORSE CALLED GER-
TRUDE STEIN); Doogie who helps an
artist with AIDS in *Doogie Howser MD*
'Vinnie, Video, Vici' (1991 T based on
Keith Haring).

art gallery owners The divinely decadent Una Marberry (Cherie Lunghi) in

Ellis Island (1984 T); Kim Basinger's twee boss in *Nine and a Half Weeks* (1986 C) counterpointing a scene where she and Mickey Rourke are pursued by queerbashers; Gabrielle St Peres (Paule Baillargeon), Polly's discreet object of desire and admiration in I'VE HEARD THE MERMAIDS SINGING (1987 C); Colin Fitzroy-Langham-Browne in *Figure with Meat* (1991 R).

art historians/professors A Russian picked up within minutes by a CIA agent (George SANDERS) who needs an entrée to Moscow's gay scene in *The Kremlin Letter* (1970 C); married but artistic Professor Rollo Verdew (Roddy MCDOWALL) who sets up patronage for a young composer (Barry Evans) in *Journey to the Unknown* 'The Killing Bottle' (1971 T); ageing bachelor Burt Lancaster who finds himself attracted to a sexually and politically dangerous young man (Helmut Berger) in CONVERSATION PIECE (1974 C); Anthony BLUNT (Ian RICHARDSON) in *Blunt* (1987 T); James FOX in A QUESTION OF ATTRIBUTION (1991 T).

artist's models Sometimes more than solid flesh in a studio, the model in most fiction is there to suggest Art in action, or a sexual dalliance in progress. This character was also a neat way of suggesting or showing nudity. Countess Alesca (Gloria Holden) tempted young girls by offering a chance to pose for her. She – DRACULA'S DAUGHTER (1936 C) – then sucked their blood. Fates were kinder to Countess Liz's lissome blonde (Ava Noring) in *The Snows Of Kilimanjaro* (1952 C); Quentin CRISP as THE NAKED CIVIL SERVANT; the young boy in *The Devil's Advocate* (1977 C) taught 'interesting things' by the English painter; the girl with the itch that sculptress Gertrude Whitney Vanderbilt (Angela Lansbury) was most happy to scratch for her in *Little Gloria ... Happy at Last* (1982 T); Amy Wallace whose nude bathing inspires Meriel (Deborah Makepeace) to immortalize her on canvas and to fall deeply in love with her in THE TINKER'S DAUGHTER; Rose

(Rosalind Adams), the prostitute-lover of the truculent Kim in THE OTHER WOMAN, the only person who truly cares for her and understands her thought processes. Of the real-life models there has not yet been a gay/lesbian version of *Camille Claudel*. There was a fascinating keyhole sketch of artist and model in *A Bigger Splash* (1974 C): Peter Schlesinger as Hockney's primary human inspiration for five years and during the aftermath of their breakup. How such passion could have ended was surmised in CARAVAGGIO (1986 C).

art students GEOFFREY Ingham in A TASTE OF HONEY; Martin Ingram (Michael Johnson), murder suspect in THE EXPERT 'The Visitor' (1969 T); Sonia Potkin used as a pawn in *The Kremlin Letter* (1970 C).

Arthur, George K. (1899–) British actor who played the hero in silents, before playing kerfuffly men.

C: *Kipps* (1921); *A Dear Fool* (1922). In Hollywood thereafter: *Madness of Youth* (1923); *Lights of Old Broadway* (1925); *The Salvation Hunters* (1925); Roger Van Horn in *Pretty Ladies* (1925); as Madame Lucy in *Irene* (1926); *The Boob* (1926); Adolphe in *Kiki* (1926); *When the Wife's Away* (1926); as Mr Winthrop posing as a butler and as a woman; as Bob Blake in *Almost a Lady* (3rd billed, 1926); as Eustace Tewksbury in *Spring Fever* (1927); Johnny Cousins, village boy in *The Gingham Girl* (1927); LESLIE in *Wickedness Preferred* (1928); *The Boy Friend* (1926); *Rookies* (1927, first of a series); *Baby Mine* (1928); *The Last of Mrs Cheyney* (1929); *Chasing Rainbows* (1930); *Oliver Twist* (1933); *Riptide* (1934) as Bertie dressed as a giant insect in the opening costume ball; *Vanessa* (1935).

Became a financier and distributor of art shorts, including Wendy Toye's malevolent *The Stranger Left No Card* (1952) and her other classic, the mauvey-pink *On the Twelfth Day* (1953).

Arthur or Martha? The young Irish builder recalls why he came to London in *Byline* 'A Kiss Is Still A Kiss' (1991 T): 'I didn't know whether I was Arthur or Martha.'

arty 'His friends are so arty and well dressed' comments SEBASTIAN's malicious aunt (Mercedes McCambridge) with fizzing venom in SUDDENLY LAST SUMMER; Macool (Geoffrey Lumsden), an accusatory parent in *Yorky* 'The New Teacher' (1961 T) is described as 'a big, rather handsome chap who looks a bit arty'; Mrs Felicity Smallgood (Margot Boyd), the one-woman moral-waste disposal unit in SWIZZLEWICK (1964 T) has no time for difference: 'I have always found much iniquity among the arty-crafty.'

The Ascent of F6 (UK 1937 R) 'A conflict between a contemplative life and personal ambition ... the short-term embrace of fame versus the eternal search for meaning.' Beneath the surface of the tale of a mountaineering party and its charismatic leader (based on T. E. LAWRENCE) there lies a mystic-satiric exploration of the self and its slow squeezing by the British class system. Among the venturers is a botanist, Edward Lamp who adores his leader Michael Ransom and who dies trying to pick a rare flower. AUDEN and ISHERWOOD's play with music by Benjamin BRITTEN was performed on radio three times altogether (1937, 1950 and 1988), and there was a television production in 1938. Mick Ford was Michael Ransom, David Learner Edward Lamp and Robert EDDISON the Abbot in Glyn DEARMAN and John Evans' 1988 production.

The Ascent of Man (UK 1973–4 T) Dr Jacob BRONOWSKI's series about the development of human skills, talents, abilities, trials and errors over thousands of exultant, painful years.
P: Dick Gilling; BBC 1; 13 parts; 50 mins.

In his summing up, our enthusiastic guide saw severe drawbacks in the present system, whether in the developed or the undeveloped world: 'The girls are little mothers in the making; the boys are little herdsmen in a static and minority culture. The child is told to conform to the adult.'
Bronowski believed that until human beings throw off this heritage and tradition, they will continue to live in 'The Long Childhood'.

Instead of retreating from knowledge into Zen Buddhism, ESP, transcendentalism and the rest, we should, he urged, be aiming for self-knowledge, bringing together experience of the arts and of the sciences. Knowledge and its integration are crucial. 'It is not the business of science to inherit the earth, but to inherit the moral imagination ... without that we will perish together.'

Ashley 'Oh, Ash-ley, Ash-ley!' Boy's name, forever associated with Ashley Wilkes (Leslie Howard), representative of an honourable, unrealistic South that's *Gone with the Wind* (1939 C); now increasingly used for women – and for semi-gay characters: from Ashley Weston (Raymond Young) in MRS DALE'S DIARY (1952) to Ashley Light in OCTOBER SCARS THE SKIN. The name is Old English, meaning 'from the ash-tree lea or nearby'. It was never fashionable in America, but enjoyed popularity in Britain and Australia during the 1970s as a result of GWTW revivals.

Richard Burton as artist Ashley having an affair with nymphet in *Circle of Two* (1980 C); Ashley (Nicholas Lyndhurst), the feckless male cohabitee in *The Two of Us* (1986–90 T); artist Ashley Wilkes in *Lovejoy* 'One Born Every Minute' (1991 T); Ashley Brown (David Ryall) in *Minder* 'Three Cons Make a Mountain' (1991 T). HOOPERMAN freaks out when his lover Susan (Deborah Farentino) gets a set on Ashley – 'if it's a boy' – as the name for their unborn child: 'He'll be beaten up by all the boys – and the girls' (1988 T). No such inhibitions in the documentary *Loveless in Letchworth* (1990 T): baby Ashley was born from a brief and finite liaison between a North Herts maiden and a British soldier serving in Germany.

Examples of the increasing use as a

female name: Ashley St Ives (Edy Williams), Juno in a bikini, driving a red convertible and laying waste young male virgins in *Beyond the Valley of the Dolls* (1970 C); Ashley Abbott, cosmetician king's daughter in *The Young and the Restless* (1973– T); Lady Ashley Mitchell (Ali MacGraw), before being killed in the Moldavia massacre, had an affair with Jeff and a chaste one with Blake in DYNASTY (1984); 12-year-old, already dating Ashley Banks (Tatyana M. Ali) in *The Fresh Prince of Bel-Air* (1990 T); Ashley, self-possessed young woman in *Days of Our Lives*.

Ashton, Sir Frederick (1904–88) English dancer and choreographer whose best known work on film is probably *Tales from Beatrix Potter*; his renowned Ugly Sister (partnered by Robert HELPMANN) was seen on television in 1970. Involved in early transmissions: *The Vic-Wells Ballet Company* (1937); *Les Rendezvous* (1938). DESERT ISLAND DISCS in 1959; OMNIBUS 'Sir Fred: A Celebration' including Margot Fonteyn, Hans Werner Henze, Peter Schaufuss and Lynn Seymour with excerpts from *La Fille Mal Gardée*, *The Two Pigeons*, *A Month in the Country*, and *Cinderella* (1988 R); *Story of Three Loves* (1953).

Asian people Still rarely seen in a homosexual context except for exotic heroines or villainesses (*Confessions of a Chinese Courtesan* 1973; *The Last Emperor* 1987); female impersonators (*M. Butterfly*); male impersonators (*Summer Vacation 1999*); or victimized boys (*Manila: In the Claws of Darkness*; *The Outsiders*). Interesting exceptions are now coming from Japan, China and Taiwan.

In documentaries, young Asians are surfacing very quietly: WORD IS OUT; THE TIMES OF HARVEY MILK; *On the Train to New Zealand*, part 4 (1980 R); *Network East* 'Lesbian and Gay Men's Group SHAKTI' (1989 T); THE GAY AND LESBIAN WORLD 'Life in the East'. 'Should one explain … that Chinese women get together in lesbian sorori-

ties? I think not' (Anthony Burgess in *The Corruption of the Exotic* 1963 R).

assassins Wint and Kidd have James BOND in their squinty, squelchy sights in DIAMONDS ARE FOREVER (1971 C); Rohl (Bob Peck) and boyfriend (Simon Rouse) are in *Parker* (1984 C); Julie Newmar wears a suit in *Hart to Hart* 'Change of Hart' (1983 T); bald, blue-eyed Australian Edward Sheppick (Clive Merrison) in *Call Me Mister*: Long Shot (1986 T) has a Siamese CAT, wears a shortie dressing gown, is callous and cold, doesn't say 'bloody' (but does drink Fosters lager).

As the World Turns (US 1956– T) In 1988 Douglas Marland was given the approval of producers and the sponsors 'to do it right, not to hold back, not to worry about stepping on the toes of middle America'. 'It' materialized in the person of FASHION DESIGNER Hank ELLIOTT who became the first regular gay character in a daytime TV soap opera since the genre's inception in the late 1940s. Although Hank has had a lover for five years (in New York), he was not in the series.

As Time Goes By Played and warbled by 'Sam' (Dooley Wilson) in *Casablanca* (1942 C). The archetypal 1940s heterosexual love song, already a standard (M/L: Herman Hupfeld; written for a 1931 show) when used in what was to become one of the world's most beloved movies. Its appeal, of course, crosses sexual categories. Two women dining in front of open French windows enjoy its 'fundamental things' in *Pictures of Women* 'Who Do You Love?' (1983 T), as do the disco patrons in THE ONLY ONE SOUTH OF THE RIVER (1980 R). The cast of GAY SWEATSHOP's *As Time Goes By* sing the number in ARMY OF LOVERS (1978 C). It was played in Michael CASHMAN's *Byline* 'A Kiss Is Just a Kiss' (1991 T).

astrology 'I'm a Virgo,' says Ron in SHARE AND SHARE ALIKE; other sexual innuendoes attached to the zodiac are Aries the Ram and Taurus the Bull. Rikki is looking for a gorgeous, butch

Taurean in PLAYMATES. The suspicious wife discovers that her husband's English friend Peter is a Scorpio in FACING THE SUN: 'Scorpios are dangerous, they sting. We must be careful.' (She is Taurus, her husband is Cancer.)

As You Like It SHAKESPEARE's comedy about a girl, ROSALIND, (originally played by a boy) pretending to be a boy who gives another boy lessons in how to make love to a girl. Notable productions for television starred Margaret Leighton (1953), Vanessa REDGRAVE (1963) and Helen Mirren (1978). They all left VICTOR/VICTORIA dead in the water.

athletes PERSONAL BEST (1982 C); Wieland (Wieland Samolak) in *Der Sprinter* (1984 C), who has taken up running and heterosexuality to please his parents, becomes involved with a 'mannish' woman; Glenn Oates (James Noble) who falls heavily for Bob Buzzard in A VERY PRIVATE PRACTICE (1988 T).

at least he had a sense of humour Comment made by women about gay men: in *Sons of the Sea* (1939 C) about 'Mr Hull' (later revealed to be a Nazi spy) and in THE DETECTIVE about Teddy, the murdered ANTIQUE DEALER.

Auberjonois, René (1940–) American actor. As Howie in *Lilith* (1964 C); *N.E.T. Playhouse* 'Ofoenti' (1966 T); *The Birdmen* (1971 T); as Jimmy Twitchell in *Pete 'n' Tillie* (1972 C); CHARLIE'S ANGELS 'The Seance' (1976 T); starred in *Panache* (1976 T); as a FASHION DESIGNER in *The Rockford Files* 'With the French Heel back, can the Nehru Jacket be far behind?' (1978 T); CHARLIE'S ANGELS 'Angels on Skates' (1978 T); as Clayton Endicott, governor's officious aide in *Benson* (1979–83 T); as film director Edward Dmytryk in *Are You Now or Have You Ever Been?* (1988 R); *Ashenden* (1991 T); as Geoffrey in THE LOST LANGUAGE OF CRANES.

Aubrey Boy's name: Aubrey Tanqueray in *The Second Mrs Tanqueray*; spendthrift Aubrey Piper (Ford Sterling 1926; Spencer Tracy 1934 C) in *The Show Off*;

Franklyn PANGBORN as Aubrey Weems, a comic Harvard graduate in *Someone to Love* (1927 C); Aubrey Hacker (Roland Winters) in *Naked City* 'Take and Put' (1961 T), who spends $12 m in a few years, has a gayish son and a flighty wife.

In UK: friend of LESLIE in YOU'RE NOT WATCHING ME, MUMMY (1980 T); Aubrey Mandrake (Steven Pacey), physically and morally twisted writer in *Death and the Dancing Footman* (1986 R); Aubrey (Peter Blake), lorry driver in *Dogfood Dan and the Camarthen Cowboy* (1987 T); Aubrey Bellweather in *4-Play* 'Goodbye and I Hope We Meet Again' (1989 T); Aubrey Nash (Alwyn Kurts), long-lost love of Hettie McGlashan (Yvonne Lawley) in CHANCES (1991 T); Aubrey Harrington (Richard Pearce) in *The Mystery of the Butcher's Shop* (1991 R).

Auden, W[ystan] H[ugh] (1907–73) English poet. With Christopher ISHERWOOD, he wrote THE ASCENT OF F6. Interviewed during the 1950s on MONITOR and sporadically until his death. Ten years later came *The Auden Landscape* (1983 T); Margaret Gardiner spoke about 'his homosexuality, friendship and his relationship with Chester Kallman' (1982 R). Also: *And So to Ned* (Major Donald Neville-Whiting in 1982 R); 2-part biography, *The Double Man* (1984 R); *A Christian Ought to Write in Prose* (1991 R) looks at the complicated relationship between life and art in his work. Alan BENNETT discussed his work in *Poetry in Motion* (1990 T). 'I suggest ... that all are primarily concerned with the praise and affirmation of personal being: I am that I am; or of personal becoming. I shall become that which I choose to be or ought to become.' (*On Writing Poetry Today* 'The Dyer's Art' 1955 R).

audiences Spot the gays in *Barbra Streisand: A Happening in Central Park* (1969 T); in the front rows in *The Marlene* DIETRICH *Show* (1972 T); in the DISCO finale of CAN'T STOP THE MUSIC (1980 C); in Bette MIDLER's *Divine Madness* (1980 C); in the *Stand by Me* concert on

AIDS Day 1987; and in the 'Opera In The Park' sequence of *Clive James's Postcard from Sydney* (1991 T). In all six cases, the gay fans have been tweezered out in the editing process; in Clive James' case he has turned a gay mecca into 'a butch outdoor activity' along with CRICKET and surfing. Only a quick eye can locate a spotlighted clump of ecstatic men hugging the stage in the penultimate shot of *A Happening in Central Park*. Elsewhere the camera manages to elbow them out in favour of opposite-sexed couples. The 'People' number is especially diligent in illuminating anything normal that moves in the audience, though with a bias towards the multi-ethnic. The editors seem to have worked overtime to ensure that gays would not intrude.

auntie A camp name either used by gay men ('"Auntie" Gerald, she knows of what she speaks' in COMING OUT 1979 T) or used in a CAMP way by HETERO-SEXUALS (Phil Archer to his sister: 'Tell Auntie Phil all about it' 1952 R).

aunt/aunty John INMAN maintains that Mr HUMPHRIES is not homosexual: 'I play him as an auntie.' This remark, made in 1983, recalls Reginald BECK-WITH, playing his second out-front 'queer', in *Doctor in Love* (1960 C). He was a busy little body called Wildwinde, the surgery's receptionist. His boss describes him as 'a universal aunt ... I took him over with the furniture ... He's rather dreadful but he cleans leather well.' Even more evasively, Simon GRAY painted the gurgling ACCOUNTANT Wyecroft (Will Leighton) in SPOILED as an uncle: 'He's been very good to me, really. He's got to uncle everybody or he wouldn't know he existed.' The teenage boy interviewed by Ray GOSLING in an episode in his series *On the Train to New Zealand* 'Pakistan' (1980 R) has an active sex life with European men. It is not expressed directly, either by boy or reporter: 'He has lots of uncles.'

A female version of this armchair sexuality was 'Aunt Lucy', a woman who picked up an innocent (or so the inno-

cent maintained) waif and made her a love-slave or, as the script of WITHIN THESE WALLS 'Invasion Of Privacy' (1976 T) put it, 'secretary'. 'I loved her. I thought that was how everyone lived. She wrote books, too, and I was to type them.' Soon the girl is wearing a maid's uniform and forced to read 'salacious' books to her mistress.

Finally, there is an auntie who is the mother's lover: a coverall title for children to use so they won't be ragged at school for having two mothers, Diana Graham (Rachel Davies) and Beth James (Dorothy White) in CROWN COURT 'A Friend of the Family' (1979 T).

aunts When prominently designated as such they tend to be benign and sexless or NYMPHOMANIACAL and panting. Occasionally prone to smothering sensitive young men in lieu of mother or sussing out sensitive young man's secret before the rest of the family (Doreen Mantle in SECRET ORCHARDS; Pauline Delaney in *The Mourning Thief* 1984). Once in a blue moon they can display the remote possibility of physical feelings for a niece, eg Aunt Lydia (Agnes Moorhead) in 'The Jealous Lover' segment of *The Story of Three Loves* (1953 C). She tells her ballet-dancer niece to go up to bed ('I'll be up soon ... but not to talk'); Ashley's Aunt Sally admits she once squeezed the nipple of a lesbian from Newport Pagnell: 'It was the least I could do' (OCTOBER SCARS THE SKIN). Other aunts of gays who have given them support and even a bit of sparkle include Don FINLAYSON's Amanda von Pappenberg (Carol Raye) in NUMBER 96. *See also* UNCLES.

Aunty Jack Australian children's television character of the early 1970s, played by Grahame Bond in wig, long skirts and moustache; rough as guts. Introduced to Britain in *The Little Big Show* (1978 T).

aunty-man Used in the West Indies and in West Indian communities to describe a man who does not come up to the sexual mark. Coupled with 'BATTIE-BOY' in YOUNG SOUL REBELS.

Australia/Australian people No POOF-TERS in God's Own Country! A few slipped through the net – notably Joe Cassidy in A HARD GOD, caught between his catholicism and the more than matey vibes his older friend throws off. Also his uncle may have had a gay past so anxious is his wife to burn his letters when he dies. The big butch OCKER shell sometimes acts as a mask: the scientist Frank Marsh (Allan Lander) in *The Deep Concern* (1979 T); the Vietnam war hero (Grant Kennedy) in THE FLY-ING DOCTORS 'Return of the Hero' (1986 T). But a queen is a queen no matter the birthplace or current domi-cile: Eric Dancer ('from Brisbane') uses a video to blackmail his shady LAWYER ex-lover in VIDEOSTARS; 'Matilda', the passport-forging HAIRDRESSER in *Call Me Mister* 'Long Shot' (1986 T); and a dead man's LANDLORD, Ritchie Richardson in THE GENTLE TOUCH story 'Blade' (1980 T), who tells the unsym-pathetic policeman: 'In Australia, you're either an Olympic athlete or you're a poof.' Mr HUMPHRIES had to dress as an Ocker to try to fool the immigration people in the Australian retread of ARE YOU BEING SERVED? (an episode called 'Undesirable Alien' 1981 T). By the mid-1980s the Ocker image, guyed mercilessly by Barry McKenzie, Dame Edna EVERAGE (whose son KENNY used to be a member of Gaiety Liberation) and Sir Les Patterson (*The Adventures of Barry Mackenzie* 1972 C; *Sir Les Patter-son Saves the World* 1987 C), had been rendered in iron with the advent of *The Paul Hogan Show*. Hogan's alter ego Mick Dundee alias *Crocodile Dundee* (1986 C) had no time for poofters, par-ticularly if he's about to root one in the mistaken belief that she's a (New York) sheila. The harsher undergrowth of this mentality was revealed in *Outback* (aka *Wake in Fright* 1970 C), and it is fully understandable why the majority of gay Australians would make for the cities or go overseas. Examples are Graham Simpson (Peter Denyer) in the final epi-sode of AGONY (1981 T) ('Not all Aus-sies are into beer and women'), who achieves the near impossible within days of landing in Earl's Court by meeting a handsome young English DOCTOR who is into art, music and cricket; Wally Sul-livan (Noel Ferrier), a fair dinkum Aus-sie with an Indonesian boyfriend in *The Year of Living Dangerously* (1983 C); powder-blue-suited Leslie Kendall (Peter Whitford) in STRICTLY BALL-ROOM (1992 C).

Real-life homosexuals began appearing on Australian television from the early 1970s: they included activists Dennis ALTMAN and Lex Watson, and the couples interviewed in their homes on CHEQUERBOARD in 1972. There is still no equivalent of GAY LIFE or OUT in Australia, but attitudes have softened considerably over recent decades, helped particularly by the participation of a nice guy, semi-regular bloke character in NUMBER 96; through some fairly hard-hitting discussion pro-grammes on the ABC as well as good – though fast-fading – story lines on its soap G.P. In addition, the consistent showing of good lesbian and gay films and documentaries on SBS, appearances by performers like Robyn ARCHER, and last, but not least, the rough and ready but essentially good-hearted and sup-portive women of Wentworth Detention Centre in PRISONER. There has certainly been a huge shift since that Alan WHICKER programme of 1971 entitled *This Is the Problem – Women Are Not People.*

Australian cinema – with the exception of mateship sagas like *Gallipoli* and melodramas like THE EVERLASTING SECRET FAMILY – has generally steered clear of male homosexuality (lesbianism – of the more lyrical kind – did receive the nod in *Picnic at Hanging Rock* and THE GETTING OF WISDOM). Lawrence Johnston's projected film *Forever Young*, 'if it is produced', will be the first gay-themed feature to be produced in this country by a gay film-maker.

Australian lesbians are likely to be found in sedate ladies' academies (*Picnic at Hanging Rock*; *The Getting of Wisdom*) or rollicking around the world with a pack on their back and gruff put-downs to advancing men (Judy COOLIBAH in ROUND THE HORNE 1968 R, predating Germaine GREER by five years). Or they're in prison (PRISONER 1979–87). Or they're on television (Judy Nunn in *The Box*). Or they're witches (Toni Lamond in NUMBER 96 1973 T). Last but never, never least Dame Edna EVERAGE came out to a vast audience in *Australia Live*, in bed with the faithful Madge ALLSOP, to celebrate the 1988 bicentennial. It's a long way from Shirley Abicair and her zither.

aversion therapy The psychiatrist Hodge (Anthony Hill) gives nausea drugs followed by pictures of women in Caryl Churchill's satire LOVESICK (1967 R). The result is 'fuzzy, hazy, cloudy reactions and an inability to relate to anyone sexually'.

It wasn't until WORLD IN ACTION 'Joe' in 1973 that the subject was taken seriously and full details of aversion therapy were made public. The programme included interviews with patients whose sexual and emotional lives had been destroyed by the treatment, which had bad side-effects. A 33-year-old man, Joe had undergone a course of therapy administered by a psychologist. As a result Joe said he had never been able to fall in love with other men – or with women. No qualified PSYCHIATRIST or PSYCHOLOGIST was on hand to put the case against. Members of the Merseyside Campaign for Homosexual Equality (*see* CHE) did question the practice, but none of its members had any personal experience. Far from hiding from public view, the psychologist told WORLD IN ACTION she believed that what she was doing was beneficial. In one scene, Joe had electrodes attached to his legs while being shown a picture of a naked man with a moustache riding a horse. Electric current was then switched on. Then a picture of a naked woman was shown. Without electrical accompaniment. GAY NEWS called the programme 'nothing more than a free advertisement for aversion therapy', allowing only its 'professional advocates to speak about it'.

A female victim in WORD IS OUT spoke about the effects aversion therapy had on her life (1978 C); electric shock also features in WITCHES, POOFTERS, FAGGOTS AND DYKES: 'We could castrate you but let's try some healing first.' Albert slams down the piano lid onto Harold's hands to deter him from his 'musical leanings'; Harold, caustically recalling this, says, 'Aversion therapy, they call it now' (STEPTOE AND SON 'Steptoe and Sons' 1968 T).

awards *see* ACADEMY AWARDS; EMMY AWARDS; TONY AWARDS.

B

Babuscio, Jack (1937–90) American-born, British-based film lecturer, counsellor, writer and film critic for GAY NEWS (1974–83) and GAY TIMES (1986–90). Leading character based on him in Kevin ELYOT's stage play *Coming Clean* (1982).

T: GAY LIFE 'Gays in the Media' (1980); ONE IN FIVE (1983).

babysitters Lynn BELVEDERE (Clifton Webb) in *Sitting Pretty* (1948 C); the estranged husband of *Helen – A Woman of Today* (1973 T) reacts adversely when he discovers that 'a poof' is minding 'his' baby; Joanna Redwine (Stephanie Zimbalist) appears in *The Babysitter* (1980 T) and seduces the alcoholic wife (Patty Duke) after causing her car to crash; Harvey (Peter John) is mother's little helper in *That Beryl Marston ...!* (1981 T); Joey (Leigh McCloskey) is accused of 'interfering' with one of his charges in a 1985 episode of HOTEL (T); the youth (Mark Lee) in THE EVERLASTING SECRET FAMILY (1988 C) initiates an affair with his lover's 18-year-old son, thus closing the circle which began with his 'seduction' by the father when he was a schoolboy; Barry and Colin look after Pauline's baby son in EASTENDERS (1987 T).

bachelor boy Cyril (Melvyn Hayes) with dyed blond hair calls Don (Cliff Richard) one in *Summer Holiday* (1963). Cliff sings a song of this title which has haunted him ever since: when the film was shown in 1976, the continuity announcer gushed: 'And now BBC2 invites you to take a "Summer Holiday" with Bachelor Boy Cliff Richard.' The singer at that time was in his mid-thirties.

bachelor girl In the world from the 1920s to the 1960s, this was a well-used term for unmarried women of independent attitudes (and 'boyish' mien). *Joanna Builds a Nest* was a 1928 book, 'a sparkling comedy of a bachelor girl's life'. The term was gratefully employed by the English distributors of Jacqueline Audry's *La Garconne* (1958 C); the title

is translatable as 'The Boy-Girl', but it was released in Britain as *The Bachelor Girl*. The singer Alma COGAN was dubbed a bachelor girl: '... known as Cogie, [she] paints and lives a happy, busy bachelor-girl existence in a streamlined flat in High Street Kensington' (*Radio Times*, 19.5.57).

The public is less easily put off today, and 'bachelor girl' as a concept and even as an evasion has almost ceased to exist. A lightweight Jane Fonda comedy, *Any Wednesday* appeared in Britain as *Bachelor Girl Apartment* in 1966. In the few years between its cinema showings and its first television airings, the title had become either antiquated or too suggestively lesbian, and it reverted to the original. The term was used in Hugh Leonard's play *The Egg on the Face of the Tiger* (1968 T) 'about two bachelor girls' and then seems to have disappeared, although two decades later it turned up as the title of an Australian film about a Jewish maiden lady, Dot Bloom (Lyn Pierse) in 1987.

bachelors Alec Hamm (Ronald Reagan), a bachelor more or less gay in *Dark Victory* (1939 C); Stephen LYNN (Valentine DYALL), Trevor Howard's doctor friend who gives out a key to his flat in BRIEF ENCOUNTER and then petulantly demands it back; George Sanders who designs rose-covered wallpaper and lives with his sisters in *The Strange Affair of Uncle Harry* (1945 C); cop Dana Andrews constantly being nagged about getting married in *Where the Sidewalk Ends* (1949 C); Charles Coutray (James Mason) coldly rejecting Moira Shearer for his (and her) Art in *The Story of Three Loves* 'The Jealous Lover' (1953 C); Jeff (James Stewart), the photographer with a strong aversion to marriage, even to Grace Kelly in *Rear Window* (1954 C); KENNY, a cheeky exterior hiding what? (Francis Matthews in *My Friend Charles* 1956 T; Derek Farr in *The Vicious Circle* 1957 C); almost tearful, certainly scared Albert (Philip Abbott) out on the town on his last night of freedom (THE BACHELOR PARTY); the two sillies (Bob Monkhouse and Alfred Marks) trying to marry and then bump off their heiress cousin in *She'll Have to Go* (1961 C); Tab Hunter as a cartoonist hunting for nubility in *Bachelor at Large* (1960–1 T); Terry Scott lodging with Hugh Lloyd and his dear old Mum in *Hugh and I* (1962–6 T); Bill Kerr idling his life away in the company of Tony Hancock in HANCOCK'S HALF HOUR (1954–8 R); George Webster (John Meillon) whose nakedly unmarried state gives cause for family concern in *A Girl for George* (1960 T); Mr Brown (Richard WATTIS), the interfering supercilious neighbour of Eric and Hattie in *Sykes* (1960); Percy Windrush (Harry H. Corbett) confessing his fears to PROSTITUTE Diane Cilento that he might be one of them in *Rattle of a Simple Man* (1964 C); Henry Higgins (Rex Harrison) who would prefer a woman to be more like a man in *My Fair Lady* (1964 C); Sherlock HOLMES (Robert STEPHENS) seemingly unconcerned by the whispers about himself and Watson (*The Private Life of Sherlock Holmes* 1970 C); Robert Stephens again as 'the Confirmed Bachelor' in *Vienna 1900* (1973 T); and many, many more.

From the mid-1970s bachelorhood beyond a certain age, say 30, was not to be encouraged. There was usually some heavily signposted reason as to why the unmarried hero was thus: wife's early death; a bad experience. More analytical studies were to be found in *Love and Marriage* 'Lucifer' (1984 T) about a pianist (William Gaunt) reluctantly brought to heel by his dog; *Morgan's Boy* (1984 T) where the taciturn farmer is forced to unlock his emotions when his city-bred nephew comes to stay; and *Shadowlands* (1985 T) which found the writer C. S. Lewis (Joss Ackland) entertaining late flowering love.

In the age of gay liberation and AIDS, the bachelor gay has to be more circumspect. Better that they occupy themselves with a baby (*Three Men and a Baby* 1987 C) if they haven't made it down the aisle by 30. An old-style fussy, AUNTIE kind of bachelor surfaced in the adaptation of Jeffrey Archer's *First Among Equals* (1986 T) in which Alec

Pimkin (Clive Swift) was a BOW-TIED little terrier, much prized at Tory dinner parties. The most recent long-term bachelors are *Inspector Morse* (John Thaw) who tells a woman that he is very happy to remain so (1987 T), and the young pups, semi-dysfunctional, in *Gone to the Dogs*, *Men Behaving Badly* and *Bottom!* (1991– T). And Mr HUMPHRIES shows no sign of getting wed.

A Bachelor Gay Am I Words and music by James W. Tate, Clifford G. Harris and Arthur Valentine, written in 1917. Used as the signature tune for George Cole's radio series *A Life of Bliss* (1953–9; 1961 T) Peter Dawson's classic recording was listened to with rapt attention by John Osborne (THE SOUTH BANK SHOW 1991 T) as he recalls the many women he encountered in a life 'overwhelmed by passion'.

The Bachelor Party (US 1957 C) Strong, subtle study of the bonds that bind a group of married men and how the impending wedding of the only bachelor forces all of them to look in the mirror. Bridegroom-to-be Philip Abbott communicates panic and feels much safer with buddy Don Murray and his mother. The GREENWICH VILLAGE setting enables a lesbian (Karen Norris) to make a couple of appearances (eyeing Carolyn Jones) at a party.

W: Paddy Chayevsky from his TV play; P: Harold Hecht; D: Delbert Mann; 93 mins.

Bacon, Sir Francis (1561–1626) English statesman, philosopher and writer who said, prior to HAMLET, 'be so true to thyself as thou be not false to others'. Portrayed as smooth and devious by Donald Crisp in *The Private Lives of Elizabeth and Essex* (1939 C), and at more length by Alexander Archdale in QUALITY STREET's 'A Wise, Sinuous, Dangerous Creature' (Aust 1967 R). However, nowhere has there been a proper sound or visual portrait of the man who wrote 'love maketh mankind/ friendly lovers perfect it.' *The Yankee Seeress and the Stratford Booby* was a portrait of Delia Bacon (1811–59) who declared Shakespeare a fake and Francis Bacon the true author of his works (1987 R).

Bacon, Francis (1909–92) Irish-born painter whose twisted, violent imagery was powerful and repellent. Many of the interviews with him were conducted by David Sylvester (1963 R; *Fragments of a Portrait* 1966 T; ARENA 1984 T). Bacon became a little more forthcoming in the mid-1980s, saying that his sexuality was a major difference in his life, but was not encouraged to elaborate. He influenced the character of Frank Leeson, played by Harold INNOCENT in THE AVENGERS 'The Medicine Men' (1963 T), and Oswald, the artist friend of Richard FULTON in MRS DALE'S DIARY (1955 R). Bacon's paintings were used in the opening credits of *Last Tango in Paris* (1972 C) and one inspired the title of the 1991 radio play *Figure with Meat*, about the art world, the Moral Majority and the hereafter. He also made a short but striking contribution to ARENA's William BURROUGHS (1983 T).

Badel, Alan (1923–82) Stylish British actor, especially persuasive as men contemptuous of anything prosaic in life.
C: Tiny role, billed as 'Allan Burdell' in *The Young Mr Pitt* (1942); the conjurer murderer in *The Stranger Left No Card* (1952); John the Baptist in *Salome* (1953); mesmerist Mendoza in *Will Any Gentleman?* (1953); *Three Cases of Murder* (1955); Richard Wagner in *Magic Fire* (1956); *This Sporting Life* (1963); Karl Denny in *Bitter Harvest* (1963); David Neville in *Children of the Damned* (1964); Sophia Loren's Arab husband, Beshraavi in *Arabesque* (1966); *Otley* (1969); *Where's Jack?* (1969); playboy dictator Rojo in *The Adventurers* (1970); barrister in *The Medusa Touch* (1978); newspaper proprietor in *Agatha* (1978); Colonel Malchenko in *Telefon* (1980); Baron Dimitri De Gunzberg in NIJINSKY (1980).
R: Romeo to Claire Bloom's Juliet in 1952; Shelley in *The Summer by the Sea* (1953); *Chastelard* (by Algernon Charles

Swinburne) with Rachel Gurney (1954); Christopher in *'Pincher' Martin* (1958); Roger Webb in *The Substitute* as a hopeless schoolmaster and would-be author (1961); Sampson ('polite though sinister') in *Unlawful Occasions* (1962); the Marquis de Valberg in *You Can't Think Of Everybody* (1963); read *Le Grand Meaulnes* in WOMAN'S HOUR (1966); August STRINDBERG in *Lunatic and Lover* (1977); opposite daughter Sarah Badel in *Caesar and Cleopatra* (1975); Shylock in *The Merchant of Venice* (1977).
T: Fouquier-Tinville in *The Public Prosecutor* (with Laurence Payne as Tallien, 1957); Mr Darcy (with Jane Downs as Elizabeth) in *Pride and Prejudice* (1958); Clive Root in *The Complaisant Lover* (1961); husband in *The Lover* (1963); the Cardinal in *The Prisoner* (1963) with Patrick McGoohan; Edmund Dantes in *The Count of Monte Cristo* (1964); Oscar WILDE as 'M. Sebastien Melmoth' in *Famous Gossips* (1965); General GORDON in *Gordon of Khartoum* (1966); David De Beaudrigue Capitoul (Magistrate of Toulouse) in *The Fanatics* (1968) about Voltaire (Leonard Rossiter); Von Reger in THE PARACHUTE (1968); Edward Kimberley in *The Creeper* (1970); Tom Simpkins in *A Raging Calm* (1974); Sir Robert Morton ('delightfully fey', *Listener*) in *The Winslow Boy* (1976); Cabinet Minister David Last, the only one *Bill Brand* respects (1976); *Svengali* (1976); *The One and Only Buster Barnes*, ex-MP, ex-tycoon, ex-convict (1978); in *Shogun* (1980); Count FOSCO in *The Woman in White* (1982).

badges Condensing a thousand invigorating ideas, articulating social concerns, making public political thought, badges flourished throughout the 1970s, first visible – to a GAY NEWS reviewer – on two women in the audience of a 1973 BBC2 talk show. During this period no self-respecting gay or lesbian-feminist activist would be seen without one, especially when facing television cameras. In the short film made by the Campaign for Homosexual Equality (CHE) DAVID IS

A HOMOSEXUAL, there's a squally confrontation in a pub between customers and a man wearing a badge proclaiming 'Gay Is Beautiful'. Ten of the gay liberation badges were featured in a *Radio Times* photograph coincidental with HOMOSEXUALITY – THE YEARS OF CHANGE (1977 R), including 'GLAD TO BE GAY', 'HOW DARE YOU PRESUME I'M HETEROSEXUAL', 'Gay Liberation Front', 'Gay Power', 'Gay Is Good', 'Lesbians Ignite' and 'Avenge Oscar WILDE'.

The politics of badge-wearing in those better blatant than latent days were mulled over by COLIN (Karl Johnson), the bus conductor activist in ONLY CONNECT (1979), which was set in the mid-1970s: 'I take it off when I go on the buses, but someday, someday ... I won't have to take it off ... And the next someday after that I won't have to wear it at all. And on that someday, the Golden Era will have really arrived.' The battery of slogans disappeared almost completely except for a discreet PINK TRIANGLE or a 'SILENCE = DEATH' badge. In Britain, the wearing of badges began to decline after 1982 – the front-row audience members of *Bennett Bites Back* were almost the last gasp (31 December 1982).

Baker, Josephine (1906–75) American singer. Tamed and partially neutered in the 1991 'rags-to-riches' filmed-in-Budapest TV movie with Lynn Whitfield.

Bailey, Paul (1937–) Writer and regular broadcaster on radio arts programmes such as CRITICS' FORUM and *Third Ear*. Appeared on the 1991 television tribute to Sir Angus WILSON. Writes biographical radio features on such people as Karen Blixen (*The Tale Bearer* 'The Life of Karen Blixen and the Art of Isak Dinesen' 1980); Wyndham Lewis (*The Enemy* 1983); Pier Paolo PASOLINI (*A Desperate Vitality* 1984). Plays and screenplays include *At Cousin Harry's* (1964 R); WE THINK THE WORLD OF YOU (1980 T); PERSONAL SERVICES (1987 C).

Balch, Anthony (1937–80) Film producer, director and distributor who also edited and directed TV commercials and shorts. Producer and director of *Secrets of Sex* (1964 C); *Towers Open Fire* (about William BURROUGHS 1964 C); *Horror Hospital* (1973 C). Distributed films like *Truck Stop Women* and *Slaves*. Between 1967 and 1972 ran the Baker Street and Piccadilly cinemas in London. Black and white scenes by Balch are included in *Burroughs* (1983 T).

Baldwin, James (1924–87) American black writer and civil rights activist. Plays include: *Blues for Mister Charlie* (1988 R). Autobiography: GO TELL IT ON THE MOUNTAIN (1984 T). Sporadic television appearances from 1964 (*Bookstand*), notably in *I Heard It Through the Grapevine* in 1983 (returning to the American South) and *Ebony* (1987, on the Rev. Jesse Jackson).

No Complaints was a 60th birthday sound portrait by the British black writer Caryl Phillips in 1984: 'We chatted over the course of 4 days at his home in France, where he's been based for the last 15 years. At one time he was an *enfant terrible*, a radical champion of civil and gay rights, but though he has fallen out of the spotlight lately he is still addressing himself to these issues. Times haven't changed that much, he says. Being black and homosexual in America in the 1960s was quite a cross to bear' (*Radio Times*, 3.11.84). A shorter but equally revealing interview was Baldwin's meeting with Mavis Nicholson on afternoon television in 1987 in which he said HOMOPHOBIA was indivisible from RACISM.

The Ballad of Reading Gaol Oscar WILDE poem, written in France in 1897 and published under the pseudonym of his prison number C33, about the execution of a young man who killed 'the thing he loved' (his wife). Set to music in *In the Gold Room* (1984 R) and in *Vicious Circle* (1985 T, aka HUIS CLOS); the poignant words are sung by lesbian Ines (Jeanne Moreau) who is in another kind of prison. Perversely, it was not this poem but 'THE LOVE THAT DARES NOT SPEAK ITS NAME' that Quentin CRISP recited in *The Ballad of Reading Gaol* (1988 T).

ballet dancers Despite their necessary stamina and muscularity, men who dance for a living are usually presented as weak and soppy (*Designing Woman*; *Summer Wishes, Winter Dreams*) or petulant and arrogant (*Not Now Comrade*). More realistic images in NIJINSKY (1980 C); *Chinchilla* (1981 R); *Dancers* 'The Benefit' (1983 T).

ballet dancer's bulge *See* CODPIECES.

ballroom dancing Usually treated with sly contempt, whether by Benny HILL and Stanley BAXTER, by WORLD IN ACTION 'Ballroom Dancing' (1964 T); by *Hi-de-Hi* (Yvonne and Barry 1980–3 T) or by the play MIDNIGHT AT THE STARLIGHT (1980 T) where the wives of two drippy males run off together after the last waltz. The frocks and sequins have been given a fresh coat of varnish in STRICTLY BALLROOM (1992 C) where satire and sentiment seamlessly entwine, but wickeder imaginations may still prefer JULIAN AND SANDY's Bona Academy of Ballroom Dancing in ROUND THE HORNE (1967). Here the boys 'troll the gamut of yer terpsichore' going one step beyond with the military, namely the 'Military Three Step'. Unfortunately, Jule had to give up competition dancing because 'all the judges had his number' and there was also the matter of his queuing up for the Ladies' Powder Room (he thought it was a conga line).

banana The banana owes its present popularity in Britain to Roger Ackerley, father of Joe. He was appointed chief salesman of Elders and Fyffes banana importers in 1898. The fruit became part of the national consciousness when 'Have a banana' was interpolated into the song 'Let's All Go Down The Strand'. The firm also benefitted from 'Yes, We Have No Bananas' in 1922 and 'I've Never Seen A Straight Banana'.

'BURLINGTON BERTIE FROM BOW' had a banana 'with Lady Di-ana' and bananas dangled as a skirt for a bare-breasted Josephine BAKER (*The Josephine Baker Story* 1991 T).

It became the phallic symbol for all the family to munch on, coming fully into its own in the oral 1960s: the hero/ine of Andy WARHOL's *Harlot* (Mario Montez) advises, 'Eat the banana . . . peel it slowly . . . slowly' (1965 C). It appears regularly thereafter: in *The Sunday Woman*, the lecher in restaurant uses one as a pick-up technique (1974 C); Bo Derek's in *Tarzan, the Ape Man* (1981 C); in *The Summer of Miss Forbes* (1988 T) the formidable governess (Hanna Schygulla) slits hers decisively down the middle – in this adaptation of a García Márquez story, phallic symbols abound: from shark knives to a spatula dripping with chocolate; a large man munches significantly on one in an effort to arouse exorcist Leslie Nielsen in *Repossessed* (1990 C); and heavily moustached Aunt Bea (Dabney Coleman) in *Meet the Applegates* (1991 C) brings one across the border into America which is immediately confiscated by a HOMO-PHOBIC customs officer: 'If as much as one strange fruit fly crosses the border, it could cause an ecological disaster'.

Bananas have found a new and striking role as safe-sex tools: condoms are fitted on them in DI ANA'S HAIR EGO (1990 V/C), *Sex with Sophie Lee* (Aust 1992 T) and *Sex and the Sandinistas* (1991 T).

The most blatant bananas of all time were the gigantic ones that chorus girls raised and lowered during the Carmen Miranda number 'The Lady in the Tutti Frutti Hat' in *The Gang's All Here* (1943 C).

Bankhead, Tallulah (1902–68) American actress with brimstone voice whose film career was mainly disappointing with the exception of Hitchcock's *Lifeboat* in 1944. Was popular on American radio with *The Big Show* in the early 1950s. She appeared in *Main Street to Broadway* (1953 C) as herself, desperately in search of a new play that would show her as she really is – a simple housewife; but she was her more familiar louche self, harassed by star-struck Lucille Ball in *The Lucy–Desi Comedy Hour* 'The Celebrity Next Door.' In the 1960s, she was castaway on DESERT ISLAND DISCS (1964), went berserk as a religious zealot in *Fanatic/Die, Die, My Darling* (1965 C), and bowed out with a semblance of her old style as Black Widow in a 1966 BATMAN episode. Neither cinema nor television has been game enough to produce her biography, and the one made for BBC Radio 4 in 1980 (with Elaine Stritch) was never broadcast because of legal problems completely unrelated to the subject's way of life or bisexuality.

banned songs The BBC never used words like 'banned'; material deemed unsuitable was removed from the playlist. Among the musical outcasts were Cole PORTER's LOVE FOR SALE and 'The Physician' and, amazingly, in the early 1950s 'He's Got The Whole World in His Hands'. In the 1980s, RELAX was the most famous casualty of corporate displeasure. Among those not deemed suggestive were 'I'd Like To Dunk You In My Coffee' ('Spread You On Bread, Smother You With Mushrooms', etc then into cannibalism) and Ambrose's 1929 'That Old Feeling': 'When you came inside, I got that old feeling.'

Barber, Peter (194?–) English television editor/director: responsible for many HORIZON and ARENA programmes, as well as 40 MINUTES 'Something for the Ladies' (1983), *Real Lives* 'Phantom Ladies' (1984), TWO OF US (1988) and Michael CASHMAN's BYLINE 'A Kiss Is Still a Kiss' (1991). Directed *Inside Stories* 'COMING OUT' in 1980.

bare buttocks *See* BUTTOCKS.

Barney, Natalie Clifford (1877–1972) American writer and patron of the arts. Her friends included COLETTE, Ezra Pound and Ford Madox Ford. Interviewed on the BBC2 arts programme *Release* in 1966, with suitable asterisks for most of the interesting bits of her life – which included a love affair with Liane De Pougy for 40 years, and sleeping with 39 other women including Romaine Brooks and the Duchesse De Clermont-Tonerre. She was the inspiration for lesbian poetry by Renée Vivien and was the subject of a chapter in COLETTE's *Le Pur et l'Impur*. She featured as Miss Flossie in the Claudine stories (1900–3) and as Flossie in Liane De Pougy's *Idylle Saphique* (1901).

Barrie, Sir J[ames] M[atthew] (1860–1937) Scottish writer. His plays were popular until the early 1960s when their whimsy became unfashionable, with the exception of PETER PAN.
A Kiss for Cinderella (1925 C); *Seven Days Leave* (based on *The Old Lady Shows Her Medals*); *Peter Pan* (1926 C; 1952 C; 1960 T; 1974 T/C; 1987 R; *Hook* 1991 C); *Darling, How Could You* (from *Alice-Sit-by-the-Fire* 1952 C); *The Admirable Crichton* (1957 C); *The Professor's Love Story* (1960 T); etc.
Barrie's relationship with the Llewellyn-Davies boys was first scrutinized in *The Sexless Sensibility* (1960 R), in which David Daiches said Peter Pan made him uncomfortable. 'For those who want to explain rather than evaluate his work, there is much more to say.' Reviewing the programme for the *Listener*, Joanna Richardson called it 'devastating ... far from the hagiography we may have expected'. A fuller version, THE LOST BOYS, appeared in 1978.

Barry Boy's name, which is often used for tearaways and over-aged brats.
US: Barry Conrad (James Stacy) spoilt, treacherous TV star in PERRY MASON 'The Case of the Final Fade-Out' (1966 T) – no girlfriend and called 'baby' by his male colleagues; Barry Corwin (Rich Little), reluctant FEMALE IMPERSONATOR in *The Love Boat* 'A Rose Is Not a Rose' (1984 T); Barry Allen (John Wesley Shipp), police chemist struck by lightning and consequently becoming the fastest man alive, known as *The Flash* (1990 T).
UK: Barry Black (Clive Francis), spoilt pop star alias *The Man Who Had Power Over Women* (1970 C); a monument to

Australian OCKERISM: 'Bazza' (Barry Crocker) in *The Adventures of Barry McKenzie* (1972 C) and *Barry McKenzie Holds His Own* (1974 C); Barry Strap (Roland CURRAM) in 'Harry Sebrof's Story' (1973 T); Barry Gems (Gerry Sundquist) in CROWN COURT 'Meeting Place' (1978 T), QUEER BASHER; prissy ballroom dancer Barry STUART-HAR-GREAVES (Barry Howard) in *Hi-de-Hi!* (1980–3 T) always deferring to his lady partner; Barry CLARK (Gary Hailes), lover of Colin before he is panicked into finding a girlfriend in EASTENDERS (1986–8 T); Barry (Bill Nighy) in *Bergerac* 'All for Love' (1991), conniving lover of fellow antique-dealer's wife.

bars The first full-scale look came in ADVISE AND CONSENT when Don Murray stands transfixed with horror at the sight of men chatting amicably at candlelit tables, listening to Frank Sinatra on the juke box. Six years later in *The Detective* (1968 C, which starred Sinatra) the theme music (minus lyric) from *Laura* is heard in L'Harlequin as two men DANCE.

By the beginning of the 1970s, gay bars were open everywhere for business in films: in San Francisco – George SANDERS, wearing blonde wig and feather boa and playing 'Love Is A Many Splendored Thing' on the piano (*The Kremlin Letter* 1970 C); in Rome – James Franciscus on the track of a killer in *Cat o'Nine Tails* (1971 C); in Tokyo – the violent love story *Funeral Parade of Roses* (1970 C) was set in and around the GENET Bar. The entire action of SOME OF MY BEST FRIENDS ARE ... (1971 C) was set one Christmas Eve in the Blue Jay. The owner confides to a cop: 'These fags paid for my daughter's first communion party.' Bowling on through the decade, audiences were taken to gay bars in *The Laughing Policeman/An Investigation of Murder* (1973 C) where leather guys toast drag queens with champagne; *Busting* (1973 C) a 'real' bar with 'real' extras yet the usual homophobic action: 'That greasy faggot' – try substituting Jew – 'took a chunk out of my leg!'; Craig RUSSELL made a big hit

at the Jack Rabbit in New York in OUT-RAGEOUS! (1977); Diane Keaton enters a *grand guignol* dive in *Looking for Mr Goodbar* (1977) to clock sad-faced gays slobbering over their beer; a German one 'full of camp jealousy and disposable promiscuity' featured in THE CONSEQUENCE (1977 T/C).

Probably American television's first 'alternative' bars were to be found in *NYPD* (1967) and other dramatic shows. Comedy followed: an entire episode of *Sanford and Son* in 1973 ('Lamont ... Is That You?') was built around events in one, with no STEREOTYPE being allowed to escape, according to GAY NEWS. The trendy Maude Findlay (Bea Arthur) and her conservative neighbour, Arthur fall out over a hostelry opening round the corner from their home in *Maude* 'The Gay Bar' (1975).

Usually these places were a mite Dante-esque: Pinocchio's (red wall hangings, three black dancers ogled by men in leather) in the TV movie *Kiss Me ... Kill Me* (1976); the Astor Bar on Times Square in the 1950s where William Bast (Michael Brandon) is sent by his friend James DEAN (Stephen McHattie 1977) to report back; the half-empty Green Parrot where Charles Pierce imitates Bette DAVIS and other camp favourites in STARSKY AND HUTCH 'Death in a Different Place' (1977). Occasionally, eg SERGEANT MATLOVICH VS THE US AIR FORCE (1978), they were as apple pie and beeswax as a church hall (called the Wilde Place, its patrons chit-chatted about everyday matters like the state of sociology in the world today). And there was a not unpleasing one in *Police Story* 'The Ripper' (1974), with women dancing together too. Lesbian places began to surface with the eponymous IN THE GLITTER PALACE (1977) and in A QUESTION OF LOVE (1978) a watering hole called the Rendezvous is mentioned disparagingly but not seen. On radio, the first such locale was the setting for part of NOW SHE LAUGHS, NOW SHE CRIES (1975).

In cinema films, Al Pacino scours leather haunts (filmed mainly at the

Ramrod) for local colour and a ruthless killer in CRUISING; the Blue Oyster is a leather and check-shirt bar regularly visited by the comic cops of *Police Academy* (1984 etc) where leather guys dance the TANGO; Bart spends most of his time, when he's not watching video movies, in Los Angeles bars in MAKING LOVE (1982); in the Taiwanese *The Outsiders* (1986), the camp photographer who shelters waifs and strays (male) opens a bar/CLUB/DISCO called the Blue Angel (1986), which remains one of the most glamorous and yet welcoming gay establishments to date.

By the 1980s, television was recognizing the huge diversity of gay establishments in large American cities. In HOTEL 'Hornet's Nest' (1986) the STONEWALL in San Francisco has yuppies swanning in and out, all vicuña sweaters and white trousers, one couple with their arms tenderly enfolding one another.

In *Trapper John* 'Straight and Narrow' (1982) Gonzo Gates (Gregory Harrison) takes an uptight colleague to a huge western bar, the Corrall. Stan notes the complete absence of women: 'Guys hang out and no chicks to fight over', but quickly dons dark glasses when the true nature of the place is revealed. Gonzo tries to reassure him. 'No one's going to make a pass at you.' A stricken look. 'Why, am I that ugly?'

Kirk Douglas in *Tough Guys* (1987 C) revisits a favourite hang-out in LA after 20 years in jail, Mickies. Glenn Miller's smoochy 'Moonlight Serenade' pours from the jukebox, but the joint's full of men. Douglas doesn't suspect anything until a middle-aged man (Matthew Farson) asks him to dance. The BARTENDER winks and Douglas bolts. He then tells his pal (Burt Lancaster) that perhaps Mickies is no longer the place for him.

The male bar scene is viewed as either icily elegant (the Velvet Spike in BROTHERS) or dark and airless (*Tough Guys*). A third strain portrays it as little different from a circle of HELL (CRUISING). Only in *Some Of My Best Friends Are …* and *Siege* (1983 C) are they viewed as essential meeting places

where people have a chance to be themselves. In *Siege*, rowdies enter the Crypt to 'correct' the supposed perversion, egged on by a right-wing group called the New Order. Witnesses to the killing of the BARTENDER are bound and gagged and then executed. Daniel (Terry Despres) escapes and the New Order is repelled. This time …

In transposing THE LOST LANGUAGE OF CRANES to an English milieu, New York's Boy Bar became London's L.A. The capital's other bars have been seen in series as different as MINDER ('Whose Wife Is It, Anyway?' 1980) and *The Fear* (1986). The Royal Hotel in Sydney was the location for the QUEER-BASHING episode of G.P. 'Tests of Conscience' (1992 T).

bartenders Scared rabbit Louis Orde (George Chandler) in *Dead Reckoning* (1947 C) patronized, in both senses of the word, by Humphrey Bogart; John CARLIN in *Man About the House* (1974–5 T); Arnold Soboloff, frilly-shirted with chains around his neck, looking after the Mardi Gras bar in *Kiss Me … Kill Me* (1976 T); Jeff Rawle dressed as a matelot, doing drugs on the side in *Wilde Alliance* 'Game for Two Players' (1978 T): 'I'm looking for a woman,' says the hero. 'Well, you won't find one in *here*'; Ron Rifkin playing a similar, though nastier cove (called Sailor) in *Flareup* (1969 C). Ron Rifkin was behind a bar again (a gay one this time) in IN THE GLITTER PALACE as Roger, mixed up with the BLACKMAILERS and thrown off a roof by one of them.

Rikki (Angus Lennie), one of gay liberation's greatest critics and lover of extra-rough trade, the mainstay of a Manchester sanctuary in PLAYMATES; the hatchet-faced Mary WORONOV giving Chad Everett a frostbite welcome ('Can I do something for you?') when he invades the basement Carousel club for women only in *In the Glitter Palace*; Nino (Richard Harradine), the Italian boyfriend of a charity kingpin's secretary, who knows how the man met his end in *Bergerac* 'Nice People Die in Bed' (1981 T); Christopher Godwin, ready with the philosophical turn of phrase for two women (Victoria Wood and Julie Walters) out on the town in *Nearly a Happy Ending* (1980 T); Ellen McIntosh telling Gisela (Diana QUICK) where to get off when the latter begins a diatribe against the evils of alcohol in SILENT WING (1984 R); Robin (Ben Daniels) who becomes Philip's crutch after his abandonment by Eliot in THE LOST LANGUAGE OF CRANES (1992 T).

In a number of HOTEL episodes, pretty, saint-like Joey (Leigh McCloskey) works as a barman to help him through college. In 'Passports' (1986), his colleague Frank's anti-gay remarks go in one ear and out the other: 'I've got my own little Archie Bunker.' He accompanies Frank (Ken Kercheval) to the hospital (where he is diagnosed as having AIDS), buys him a plant, visits his wife (she's anti-gay too), and is still around at the family reunion – at which he is virtually ignored. But he keeps on smiling and giving – poor, lonely Joey.

Bartlett, Neil (1958–   ) English writer, actor and film-maker whose short personal–political vignettes pack a knockout punch, beginning with *Alter Image* 'THAT'S WHAT FRIENDS ARE FOR' (codirected with Robin Whitmore 1988) through to *Now That It's Morning* (1992 T).

Basil Boy's name, often given to unappealing characters like Basil Fawlty and Basil Brush. Also DORIAN GRAY's patron Basil Hallward; Christine ARCHER's married suitor (1952 R); the inhibited intellectual (Alan BATES) prised out of his shell by *Zorba the Greek* (1964 C); the 'male' half (Alan Rowe) of the gay couple in WANTED: SINGLE GENTLEMAN (1967 T); and the estranged son (Gareth Forwood) used as sexual bait in *Man and Boy* (1971 T).

Bastards! The final line spoken by Franky DOYLE (Carol Burns) in PRISONER (1979 T) after she has been shot by the police. Typical of Franky's terse speech and attitude towards authority.

Bates, Alan (1930–   ) English actor of insight and charisma whose vein of shaggy, appealing cynicism has been expertly mined by Simon GRAY in plays like BUTLEY and TWO SUNDAYS. Is equally adept at calculating, egotistical characters (DIAGHILEV in NIJINSKY; the social climber in *Nothing But the Best* (1964 C); the misogynistic villain in *Royal Flash* (1975 C)) and clumsy, soul-searching men (the young man propelled into a hollow marriage in *A Kind of Loving* (1962 C); the idealistic Rupert Birkin in WOMEN IN LOVE; the repressed Basil in *Zorba the Greek* (1964 C)). One of the roles he was offered but turned down was that of TCHAIKOVSKY in *The Music Lovers*.

He first attracted attention as Jimmy Porter's soul-mate Cliff in the Royal Court production of LOOK BACK IN ANGER (1956 T) and made his film debut as Laurence Olivier's son in THE ENTERTAINER (1960). His television play that year, *Three on a Gas Ring*, was banned after intervention from the Church, because of its seeming endorsement of cohabitation outside marriage.

Recent work includes playing an Irish crime boss who is also a mortician in *A Prayer for the Dying* (1987 C); a thinly disguised Joe ACKERLEY in WE THINK THE WORLD OF YOU (1988 C); the master criminal Mabuse in *Dr M* (1990 C); a bluff colonial civil servant confronting grief and pain with his 12-year-old son in *Losing Track* (1992 T); playwright Hamish Partt in *Unnatural Pursuits* (1992 T).

Norman **Bates** Character played by Anthony Perkins in *Psycho* (1960 C) and three 1980s sequels. On the surface a calm, shy man, Norman's personality is braided with that of his dead mother, whom he has stuffed. It is 'she' who encourages him to stab young women 'she' judges to be 'immoral', thus releasing his scary potential for sudden evil. The character is based upon Ed Gein, a Wisconsin farmhand and handyman who killed two women (neither of whom was his mother) and who skinned the dug up corpses of thirteen more. Gein died in a mental institution in 1984, aged 77.

baths Roman governor Crassus (Laurence Olivier) propositions his slave (Tony Curtis) as he is helped out of his marble tub in SPARTACUS (1960 C); Lawrence Kirkbridge (Ian Ogilvy) is lathered by his seductive, calculating MANSERVANT Thomas (John Alderton) in UPSTAIRS, DOWNSTAIRS 'The New Man' (1973 T): 'You may scrub harder', 'I aim to give satisfaction'; Frank (RIPPLOH) and Bernd (Broaderup) share the suds in TAXI ZUM KLO; producer's wife Joanne Castella (Kendal Kaldwell) invites Gerri (Pia Zadora) to share her jacuzzi in *The Lonely Lady* (1983 C); one guy is soaping another's back in the documentary COMING OUT (1980 T). Communal baths, with exhilirated, muddy lads splashing about together after the match, feature in *The Loneliness of the Long Distance Runner* (1962 C) and *This Sporting Life* (1963 C).

Raymond Bell (Steve Mann) goes to a London Turkish bath every Tuesday in *My Father's House* (1981 T), set in the 1950s. Across the Atlantic and 30 years on, Michael (Aidan Quinn) recalls his visits to the baths in AN EARLY FROST (1984 T), with the strong suggestion that he contracted AIDS there. A bathhouse was the background for the comedy of errors in THE RITZ (1976 C) – all manner of madcappery went on amid luxurious surroundings (sauna, restaurant, pool, bridge, amateur nights and free blood tests every Wednesday). The legendary Continental Baths provided the backdrop for a bisexual man's coming-out story in *Saturday Night at the Baths* (1976 C).

The bath-house as a source of relaxation and renewal for women was posited in STEAMING (1984 C), but the sensual effect the place has on two of its customers (Vanessa REDGRAVE and Sarah Miles) was played down in Joseph Losey's wrecking of Nell Dunn's play. *See also* SHOWERS.

Batman and Robin The Dynamic Duo, comprising the bicepted Caped Cru-

sader and the cute Boy Wonder; otherwise known as millionaire Bruce Wayne and his ward, Dick Grayson. Created in 1939 by Bob Kane, they stepped out of comic books to make radio appearances on *Superman* before being featured in film serials between 1943 and 1949 (Lewis Wilson, Robert Lowry etc as Batman; Douglas Croft, Johnny Duncan etc as Robin).

Recycled in colour, the pair leapt into the top ten American programmes (and became merchandising catnip) for most of 1966 with a 'CAMP' TV series full of 'Pow!' and 'Splat!' The Duo departed the airwaves in March 1968 only to return, in cartoon form, a few months later and throughout the next decade in *The Batman/Superman Hour* (Bud Collyer and Casey Kasem providing voices); *Batman and the Super 7* (1968–70/ 1970–1); then, with new voices, as part of the 1970s cartoon series *Superfriends*; and, finally, TV's live pair Adam West and Burt Ward contributing vocally to *The New Adventures of Batman and Robin* as part of *The Batman/Tarzan Adventure Hour* (1977–8). The Duo was finally split up when the blockbuster 1989 film version unapologetically dropped Robin and made Bruce irrevocably non-pederastic, if still a tad eccentric and exhibitionistic.

On the Australian comedy show *Fast Forward* in 1991, Batman and Robin were shown climbing up a skyscraper in very close, near indecent proximity before Robin launches into an attack on his guardian's 'ridiculous homoerotic fantasies'; calling him a 'pantomime ponce', 'a pathetic, poncing pantomime pouf', 'a simpering SISSY in stockings' and a 'limp-wristed loser in Lycra leotards'.

battie/batty man; battie/batty boy Denigrating term used in West Indian communities: heard in YOUNG SOUL REBELS. 'Batty Boy' in *Hollywood Shuffle* (1987 C). *See also* AUNTY MAN.

The Battle for Tuntenhaus (UK 1991 T) A settlement of 30 DRAG queens in BERLIN is evicted by police, one of the actions which sparked off what has been called Germany's STONEWALL: riots lasting three days in November 1990, at one stage involving 3,000 police.

D: Juliet Bashore; 24 mins.

A follow-up showing the disintegration of the community was televised in 1992, again in the OUT series.

Baxt, George (1923–90?) American screenwriter, playwright and novelist who began as a radio announcer and actor's agent. Scripted the British *Sword of Freedom* (1957 T); adapted *Meet Me in St Louis* with Jane Powell and Tab Hunter for US television in 1959; scripted a number of bluntly effective, sensationalist flicks: *Circus of Horrors* (1960); *Payroll* (1960); *Night of the Eagle/Burn Witch, Burn* (1961); *City of the Dead* (1961); *Shadow of the Cat* (1961); also provided the story for *Tower of Evil* (1972) and the script for the Danish–British *Male-Bait* (1971 unreleased) about three gay men and a hitch-hiker in an English village. His short story 'What Have You Been Up To Lately?' was dramatized by Denis Cannan as one of the *Tales of the Unexpected* in 1982: two failed actors (Benjamin WHITROW and Peter Barkworth) are in love with the same woman. Baxt created black gay detective Pharoah Love in three 1960s novels, *A Queer Kind of Death, I, Said the Demon* and *Topsy and Evil*. His last book was *The Tallulah Bankhead Murder Case* (1988) set in the McCarthy era with Dorothy Parker and Lillian Hellman as members of the cast of suspects.

Evelyn **Baxter** (Colin CAMPBELL 1954–9 R) Friskier than Mrs Christie's Christopher WREN, Evelyn Baxter in Henry REED'S THE PRIVATE LIFE OF HILDA TABLET, A VERY GREAT MAN INDEED, A HEDGE, BACKWARDS and *The Primal Scene, As It Were* was more Pan than PETER PAN. And, therefore, too open, too free, too young for BBC Radio's comfort.

Dame Hilda TABLET's teenage secretary makes it quite plain that he has the hots for Herbert Reeve. He's a SENSITIVE, Labour party supporting youth: 'I don't smoke and I don't drink, and I don't like rude stories.' But he does like a gay time. In one scene in *The Private Life*, at his mother's house, he is sewing a costume for the Chelsea Arts Ball and chattering on. In the original script, that is.

Almost all that remains is the sound of the needle and thread slipping in and out of the satin. Evelyn has been rendered practically mute. No fewer than 30 lines of his dialogue have disappeared from the play as transmitted in 1954, including 'Raymond and Billy are going in DRAG. I'm going as Tarzan.' Retained was his sparky comment to the young hero: 'Mother's always trying to marry me off ... Mind you, if you really want me to ...' But Herbert doesn't take up his offer. One of the last encounters with the divine boy comes in *The Primal Scene, As It Were* where the audience is left in no doubt that he picks up a Greek youth and enjoys himself with him in Athens.

Evelyn is the first of the new breed of gay men: confident, merry, sexually active with men his own age.

Baxter, Stanley (1928–) Scottish comedian whose rubbery features have done duty for everybody from Alan WHICKER and the Pope to Elizabeth Taylor and Queen Elizabeth II in a series of increasingly elaborate and CAMP musical-comedy shows produced first by the BBC (début *On the Bright Side* 1959–60) and then by London Weekend Television (1974–82, in partnership with producer David Bell), before returning to the BBC in 1985. His wicked mimicry and his own beaming personality failed to translate effectively to the cinema screen except in the prisoner-of-war comedy *Very Important Person* (1961). A few 'straight' roles on television: *The Confidence Course* (1965) etc.

Bayldon, Geoffrey (1924–) Tall and cadaverous of aspect with a sometimes stenching voice that usefully delineates all kinds of authority figures, some going off their chump. Best known for playing the 11th century wizard *Catzweazle* (1969 T). Gay roles include the ship's steward in *To See How Far It Is* (1968 T); chemist in *All Creatures Great and Small* 'Where Sheep May Safely Graze' (1989); and the osteopath in *Madame Sousatzka* (1988 C). Film debut as a clerk in *The Stranger Left No Card* (1952).

BBC (British Broadcasting Corporation) The mother ship of world broadcasting, satirized from the 1930s to the 1960s as a haven for long-haired Lefties (with BEARDS), fey poets, mannish women and worse. The GOONS got stuck into the Corporation in their send-up of *Nineteen-Eighty-Four* neatly called *Nineteen-Fifty-Five* (1955 R): 'Long hair and beards (and some of the men were dressed the same),' comments Neddy Seagoon about the clientele in the Grosvenor, a 'forbidden' pub.

Neddy is tortured by having to listen to MRS DALE'S DIARY in Room 101. There's worse to come – *Life with the Lyons*, and – the ultimate agony – Wilfred Pickles and *Have a Go!* Neddy eventually breaks after listening to himself singing. The BBC is finally liberated and taken over 'by a Jew who floods the country with mindless comedy shows'.

Tongues were also poked out at 'Auntie' in many comedy series (including ROUND THE HORNE) and plays like TROUPERS (1988 R). However, the idea of having ex-Mrs DALE Jessie Matthews play a character based on another ex-Mrs Dale was turned down in the early 1970S; THE KILLING OF SISTER GEORGE was eventually Readers' Digested down to an hour by the World Service in 1978.

BBC employees Featured in *Death at Broadcasting House* (ACTORS and radio director); *The Band Waggon* (two comedians living atop Broadcasting House); THE KILLING OF SISTER GEORGE (SOAP OPERA ACTRESS; TELEVISION PRODUCER; TELEVISION DIRECTOR, 1968 C and 1978 R); THE LAST ROMANTIC (TELEVISION DIRECTOR, 1978 T); TROUPERS (radio producers); *Making It Better* (BBC WORLD SERVICE STAFF, 1991 R).

BBC Enterprises Exports more than 20,000 hours of broadcasting to over 100 countries, and produces an increasingly tempting range of videos and audiocassettes of 'vintage' and recent programmes from BBC Radio and Television. Gay and lesbian material, other than in the subplots of blockbuster drama serials and sitcoms, currently very under-represented.

BBC Guidelines Published 1989. Available from the BBC or its shops.

BBC Pronunciation Unit In 1963 'homosexual' was the subject of a memo circulated to all BBC departments. It explained that the word derives from the Greek root meaning 'same' and not the Latin meaning 'man'. The directive was issued to ensure that all BBC personnel pronounced it 'homo' as in 'homage' not 'homo' as in 'Homer'. The unit admitted that it didn't really have a clue how it should be enunciated, 'but we have to be precise'. The inevitable correspondents leapt forward, including a vicar from Norfolk: 'Does it matter a tinker's cuss … why the BBC has not got the good taste to keep off this nasty subject until after the children have gone to bed' (*Sunday Telegraph*, 10.2.63).

What was forgotten in the skirmish was that the BBC was also anxious to remove the male from homosexual. 'This will bring out for the knowledgeable listener the fact that we are aware the word applies to either sex.'

BBC World Service 'Funded by the Foreign Office. A diplomatic channel really. Nothing difficult, nothing dangerous. No politics. Good lord, no. We might disturb the natives. Keep it cultural. Fill it with CAMP!' says the wife's Czech lover, Tomas (John Bluthal) in *Making It Better* (1991 R). The Service has produced little directly relevant material with the exception of solid, tried and tested plays (THE KILLING OF SISTER GEORGE; *Ross* 1980; CHARLEY'S AUNT 1987) and a handful of documentaries (*Being Gay Today* 1981; *AIDS in Africa*

1989; the impressive 6-part THE GAY AND LESBIAN WORLD 1992).

Beam me up, Scotty Catchphrase forever linked with Captain KIRK (William Shatner) in the STAR TREK series, although he never said it (except in the cartoon version). Neither did he intone 'To boldly go where no man has gone before' (that's the opening narration).

beard Arthur (Michael Hordern) in LAND OF MY DREAMS (1964 T) inveighs against 'the beardies and the weirdies and the queers'; and formidable conductor (Timothy West as *Beecham* 1979 T) rumbles on about men in the BBC whose beards stretch 'from SODOM to GOMORRAH'. A whole play, *The Man Behind the Beard* (1963 R) was devoted to the bureaucratic machinery that had to be set in grinding motion when accountant Fred Jones (Ronald Wilson) grows facial hair.

This substance is rarely found on heroes, unless they are forced to endure primitive conditions or are seeking communion with nature (and their fellow man), eg Alan Bates in WOMEN IN LOVE. Or Robert De Niro in *The Deer Hunter* (1978 C). Or the guy is a former rock singer, now grizzled (Kris Kristofferson). Occasionally, a beard will be permissible on a character who is very old and very distinguished: Raymond Burr in the PERRY MASON TV movies.

An example of a beard signalling a sexuality that could not be spoken of was Maurice Goodman (Trader FAULKNER) in *Promenade* (1959 T): a suspiciously over-zealous 'eligible bachelor' who wears a trendy haircut, has rings on his fingers and makes provocative statements.

An example of a very bearded man (prized by a select few, but generally shunned as a gay sex symbol in the era of the 'tached clone or the clean-cut preppie) is Fuzzy in LONGTIME COMPANION (1990 C). A 'now you see it, now you don't' beard plays an important role in the characterization of Eduardo (Miguel Bosé) in HIGH HEELS (1991 C).

beat generation Iconoclastic, alienated, 'un-American' arts movement in America during the 1950s, led by Jack Kerouac, Allen GINSBERG, William BURROUGHS etc. Hollywood depicted them as strung-out and pea-brained (*The Subterraneans* 1959), and later (*Heart Beat* 1979) as almost totally heterosexual. Its pretensions (and its homosexual components) were satirized in THE COMIC STRIP PRESENTS 'The Beat Generation' (1983 T).

More balanced views were in *Pull My Daisy* (1958 C); *We Dissent* (with Norman Mailer, Ginsberg and his LOVER Peter Orlovsky 1960 R); ARENA 'Burroughs' (1983 T); REBELS 'Jack Kerouac' (1986 R); ARENA *What Happened to Kerouac?* (1988 T).

Beaton, Sir Cecil (1902–80) Master of line, light, poise and glamour: photographer, stage and film designer. Now reconstituted as the 'lover' of Greta GARBO, a 'sad, disappointed snob' who 'networked furiously' (Channel 9 news bulletin about a Beaton exhibition in Melbourne, 14.9.91). His diaries were the subject (alongside those of Harold NICOLSON and Virginia WOOLF) of *Something Sensational to Read on the Train* (1970 R) and he himself was the subject of DESERT ISLAND DISCS in 1980.

C: *Kipps* (1941); *An Ideal Husband* (1948); GIGI (1958); *My Fair Lady* (1964); *On a Clear Day You Can See Forever* (1971).

T: FACE TO FACE (1962); *Initiation* (1966); *Beaton by Bailey* (1971); *This Is Noel* COWARD (1972); *Noel: The Life and Times of Sir Noel* COWARD (1976); *Rex Whistler* (1980 T); *The Beaton Image* (1984).

Gunner/Bombardier 'Gloria' **Beaumont** (Melvyn HAYES) Sometimes blushing and confused, sometimes grinning and calculating, he is the leading light of the immediately post-war concert party troupe out East in *It Ain't Half Hot, Mum* (1974–82). Mainly a cringing eunuch, 'Gloria' once rose heroically to the occasion in a tense situation with the enemy, becoming vastly virile as a result of being hit on the head by a coconut. The effect was transitory and the gluggy puddle reappeared.

beautiful friendship Mentioned in relation to men by Humphrey Bogart in *Casablanca* (1942) and by Ginger Rogers (about Fred Astaire and Hermes PAN) on *Sally Jessy Raphael* (1992 T). American poet and novelist, Conrad Aiken (1889–1973) used it about his protégé (1967 R): 'We spoke the same language, so we celebrated right off – we in fact celebrated too well, and after a few drops taken we staged a series of wrestling matches. He was a very powerful fellow – extraordinary – and I somehow fell over backwards into the fireplace and fractured my skull. That was the beginning of a beautiful friendship.'

Beauty Not usually appended to the male except in its French version Beau (regard). Exceptions were used with irony: Charles 'Beauty' Steele (Conrad Nagel) in *The Right of Way* (1932; also 1915 & 1920 C); Beauty (Paul Hunt), rough, ready and funny in *Third Alarm* (1930 C): bachelor firefighter who wants to adopt orphans; 'Beauty' Phillips (Barry Sullivan), Joan Crawford's husband in *Queen Bee* (1955 C): a bad-tempered alcoholic with a scar down one cheek.

Beckford, William (1760–1844) English author, dilettante and patron of the arts, famous for his journals and his Gothic revival country house, Fonthill Abbey: *More Best Sellers* (1967 T); *Recollections of an Excursion* [in Portugal] (1991 R).

beds As places for men to enjoy each other's warmth were first revealed, gingerly, in THE ROADS TO FREEDOM when Daniel SERENO (Daniel Massey) WRESTLES with his ROUGH TRADE. In *The Music Lovers* (1971 C) TCHAIKOVSKY's brother finds him (Richard Chamberlain) and his nobleman (Christopher Gable) languorously ensconced in the opening scene. The real stuff came in 1971 when Peter FINCH and Murray Head, in scenes one tenth as long as the

beddings Head has with Glenda Jackson, were seen horizontal, above the ground, in SUNDAY, BLOODY SUNDAY. Bedded down, discussing the events of the day, but showing 'no intimacy' (by Australia's Channel 10 dictat) were Don and Dudley in NUMBER 96 (*c* 1976 T).

Some considerable discussion took place during production of America's first homosexual television movie THAT CERTAIN SUMMER in 1972 as to whether Hal Holbrook and Martin Sheen should sleep apart during the former's son's visit. Not only did they sleep apart in the finished product but their unmade kingsize was banished from sight and the line 'But neither of them keeps my bed warm' was deleted.

During this period in Britain, it was a relative commonplace to see same-sex partners (females not males) under the sheets, though Breeze Anstey (Morag Hood) in COUNTRY MATTERS only eased Lorn (Meg Wynn Owen) between them because her room was damp and she had contracted a cold as a result. And as Breeze says, 'My bed's big enough.'

Chrissie Harvey (Myra Francis) and Jackie Smithers (Alison Steadman) literally have a bunk-up in the army hut in GIRL (1974 T). Quentin CRISP endures something akin to torture during two years of sleepless nights with the daunting Barndoor (John Rhys-Davies) in THE NAKED CIVIL SERVANT. 'The sex was all right in a domestic sort of way. But never sleep in a narrow double bed with a wide single man.' Quentin is relieved when his gravel-voiced, slow-thinking beau suggests that Quentin sleep on the floor while he takes full advantage of the mattress.

Middle-aged businessman Paul (John Stride) is kept warm during one disturbed night in the unsettling *The Ice House* (1978 T) by the blond and enigmatic Clovis (Geoffrey BURRIDGE). The prisoner and the warder's son find comfort from a harsh world in a narrow cell bed in THE CONSEQUENCE (1977 T/C). Colin and Graham have a post-coital discussion on gay age discrimination in ONLY CONNECT (1979 T). Lewis and Richie curl up like any other – shakily –

married couple in COMING OUT (1979 T).

COLETTE's nocturnal arrangements with Missy were quoted (from the short story 'Sleepless Nights') on radio in WOMEN OF WORDS (1980): 'In our house there is only one bed, too big for one, a little narrow for us both ... People who come to see us survey it calmly and do not tactfully look aside, for it is marked in the middle with but one soft valley.'

From this point on, the erotic possibilities of the bed were being more confidently explored: a beloved Alsatian bitch between lovers in WE THINK THE WORLD OF YOU (1980 T); round the world kissing while the wife's out in FACING THE SUN (1980 T); the morning after a wartime night on the town in the 'gay club' proprietress' bed in HOUSE ON THE HILL 'Something for the Boys' (1981 T); a remembrance of things past (in South Africa) in A ROOM FOR THE WINTER (1981 T); raw and uninhibited SEX on and (mostly) off the bed in TAXI ZUM KLO, a more joyful version of a cruising life than was bruited in NIGHT-HAWKS. Al Pacino was seen face down and bare-assed in a seedy hotel room in CRUISING, and you could just see Harry Hamlin and Michael Ontkean on top of the coverlet in MAKING LOVE, though the lampshade did tend to get in the way.

Because of its long tradition as a staple in pornography, the sight of women in bed together was more readily accepted by some viewers, and both LIANNA and DESERT HEARTS used the love-making as centre-pieces. There were also frank scenes in the German NOVEMBER MOON (1984 C), PERSONAL BEST and the Hungarian ANOTHER WAY.

The decadent couple André Raffalovich (Sandor Eles) and John Grey (Simon Shepherd) were seen in a suitably *outré* bedroom, mainly black with John stretched out beneath silk sheets, a kitten playing in the folds (*Aubrey* 1982 T). It was the beginning of the end for gay lovers. Censorship lurked in the wardrobe. Whereas cinema could still depict this most natural of occurrences (PRICK UP YOUR EARS, MAURICE, LAW OF DESIRE) television began to confine boys

to the sofa. A bed scene from MY BEAUTIFUL LAUNDRETTE was cut before release because 'it didn't work', though its omission may have helped the film receive a 15 certificate.

bed sharing A staple of broad comedy is the necessity of sharing a bed: LAUREL AND HARDY did it regularly, so did Morecambe and Wise. That quintessentially British pair Charters and Caldicott (Basil Radford and Naunton Wayne) in *The Lady Vanishes* (1938 C) are forced to double up at an inn. HITCHCOCK's twist on this unremarkable situation is that the men also have to share a pair of pyjamas, taking it in turns to shield the other's partial nudity.

Keith Reader observed in the book *Cultures On Celluloid* (1981) that 'The notion of bachelor or "unattached" males sharing rooms, if not sometimes beds as well is an oddly persistent one in British cinema and television comedy'. He also wrote: 'Tony Hancock was apparently worried that viewers would conclude from his sharing a bedroom with Sid James that their relationship was a homosexual one. No such qualms are reported to affect Morecambe and Wise who, like Charters and Caldicott, palm the humour of their bed-sharing off onto general good-humoured embarrassment.'

In dramas, bed sharing was usually relegated to dire emergency or to cowboys out on the range; only in LONESOME COWBOYS (1968 C) are the sexual connotations of such arrangements given an airing. Poverty sometimes entered into it, too. In the boxing exposé *Body and Soul* (1947 C) John Garfield punches the air in his sleep, which doesn't go down well with his male companion. In the first episode of UPSTAIRS, DOWNSTAIRS (1971 T, written by Fay WELDON) ROSE (Jean Marsh) snuggles up to Sarah (Pauline Collins) to keep warm.

Enforced sleeping arrangements of a more complicated sexual nature arise in SYLVIA SCARLETT, *First a Girl* (1935), QUEEN CHRISTINA and many other stories of women in male cladding.

The giggly boys-under-the-blanket mentality of Charters and Caldicott and the rest still holds sway – the English airmen in 'ALLO, 'ALLO (1984 T): 'Carstairs! Are you a grammar-school boy? Wearing your socks in bed!'

Much more uncomfortable was Stanley Roper (Norman Fell) waking up (fully clothed) next to Jack Tripper (John Ritter in vest and shorts) after a wild party in THREE'S COMPANY 'Strange Bedfellows': 'This is awful. My being in bed with you and you being a ... You've got to promise me ... this has got to be a secret between us. This never happened, right?' Jack gives him a sickly, conspiratorial smile: 'Right! And thank you for a lovely evening.'

Much more ambiguous were the nocturnal pairings of Lofty and Wicksy in EASTENDERS (1986 T) and the two brothers in ACCOUNTS.

bed wetter Terry St Marie (Patrick Cassidy) in *Bay City Blues* (1983 T), a gorgeous hunk and outstanding athlete who, for psychological reasons, still cannot control his bladder. Yet another excuse for bullying at the boys' camp in *Bless the Beasts and Children* (1972 C).

beefcake the opposite of 'cheesecake' and very 1950s. Usually relegated to the odd scene or two (Rock HUDSON in *Magnificent Obsession*, beach or bath, or atop a sarong in the South Sea Islands). Sometimes allowed to run, shirtless and muscled, through most of the action: Bill Murphy in *Fighting Coast Guard* (1951 C); Jeffrey Hunter in *Single Handed/Sailor of the King* (1953 C); supporting hunks in *Fair Wind to Java* (1953 C); Hudson in *Taza, Son of Cochise* (1954 C); William Holden in *The Bridge on the River Kwai* (1957 C) etc.

Beethoven's Fifth Background for some ultra-violence and mad driving with Alex and his friends in *A Clockwork Orange* (1971 C); and for a similarly dressed gay couple to make love to (on a couch) in 'DOCTOR MARTENS' (1991 T).

Before Stonewall (US 1984 C) Lesbian and gay history through interviews, Hollywood movies, newsreels, HOME MOVIES, snapshots and memorabilia through Depression, war, Cold War, boom and continuous oppression. We meet ordinary Jos and Joes as well as a WAAC who told off Eisenhower and Harlem's Gladys Bentley.

D: Greta Schiller and Robert Rosenberg; Research: Andrea Weiss; 87 mins.

Behind the News (UK 1953 R) Nightly BBC Home Service discussion programme which was broadcast after the 10 o'clock News. In November, Dr Jacob BRONOWSKI broke 30 years of Corporation silence by mentioning the word 'homosexuality' and initiating a (very sane) discussion of the subject and the pitiful legal situation for homosexuals.

Bell, Book and Candle (US 1958) A comedy about a witch and a warlock, and what they do to a normal man. CATS and potions notwithstanding, a group of zanies who would not be out of place at an Upper East Side dinner party. And the relationships do have a certain ambiguity.

W: Daniel Taradash from the play by John VAN DRUTEN; P: Julian Blaustein; D: Richard Quine; 103 mins.

Belle de Jour (Fr 1967 C) Middle-class housewife (Catherine Deneuve) gets paid for abasing herself in a brothel, whose proprietress (Genevieve Page) desires her. The discreet degeneration of the bourgeoisie in a film which merges illusion and reality.

W/D: Luis Buñuel from the novel by Joseph Kessel; 100 mins.

Lynn **Belvedere** Elitist character played to the hilt by Clifton WEBB in *Sitting Pretty* (1948 C): a child hater who becomes a beloved BABYSITTER. The character was considerably sweetened in the sequels, and given more of a crisp (rather than a Crisp) veneer by Christopher Hewett in the television series *Mr Belvedere* (1986–90) who was definitely not referred to by anyone as 'Lynn', and in the final episode falls in love with Ms Right.

Bend Over Backwards Johnny Mandel and Hal David composed this opening-credits song for *The Man Who Had Power Over Women* (1970 C), a would-be exposé of the British pop music world: 'The other side of the Golden Disc where they break all the top ten commandments.' The song's main thrust, only hinted at it in the plot, was the inexhaustible sexual urge of the brattish pop star and his willingness to do anything to get to, and stay at the top: 'You've got to bend/Bend over backwards.' (This phrase was repeated about 20 times.)

Bennett, Alan (1934–   ) English writer, actor and commentator on British society and the human comedy. Highly esteemed and increasingly beloved. '... fascinated by institutions, by schools, hospitals and offices: "I'm interested in their double life – the way there's an official public life going on and at the same time a quite separate underground existence which belongs to the people inside the closed worlds"' (*Radio Times* 6–12.11.82).
C: Screenplays: *A Private Function* (1984); PRICK UP YOUR EARS (1987). As writer and actor: as cottager, with John Wells in *The Secret Policeman's Other Ball* (1982). As actor: the Bishop in *Little Dorrit* (1987).
R: As actor: the young teacher Tempest in *Forty Years On* (1975); Benjamin Jowett, Victorian academic and eccentric in *The Great Jowett* (ɟo7). As reader: on his Uncle Clarence who died in Flanders (1987); *Alice Through the Looking Glass* (1988); 'Eustace and Hilda' on WOMAN'S HOUR (1991).
T: Plays: *A Day Out* (1972); *Sunset Across the Bay* (1975); *A Little Outing* (1977); *A Visit from Miss Prothero* (1978); ME! I'M AFRAID OF VIRGINIA WOOLF (1978); *Doris and Doreen* (1978); *The Old Crowd* (1978); *Afternoon Off* (1979); *All Day on the Sands* (1979); *One Fine Day* (1979); *Intensive Care* (1982); *A Woman of No Importance* (1982); *Our Winnie* (1982); *Rolling Home* (1982); *Marks* (1982); *Say Something Happened*

(1982; 1989 R); AN ENGLISHMAN ABROAD (1983); *The Insurance Man* (1986); TALKING HEADS 'A Chip in the Sugar', 'A Bed Among the Lentils', 'A Lady of Letters', 'Her Big Chance', 'Soldiering On', 'A Cream Cracker Under the Settee' (1988; 1990 R); 102 BOULEVARD HAUSSMANN (1991); A QUESTION OF ATTRIBUTION (1991). Documentaries and talks: *Canvas* 'Leeds City Art Gallery' (1970); THE SOUTH BANK SHOW 'Alan Bennett' (1979); *Byline* 'Dinner at Noon' (1988); etc. As actor: various roles in *My Father Knew Lloyd George* (1965); *The Drinking Party* (1966); Augustus Hare in *Famous Gossips* 'Augustus Hare – The Years with Mother 1834–1903' (1966); Dormouse in *Alice in Wonderland* (1966); various roles including ANTIQUE DEALER in *On the Margin* (1966–7); as Osric in *Hamlet* (1971); Stanley in *Afternoon Off* (1979); Midgley in *Intensive Care* (1982); Mr Posner in *Breaking Up* (1986); Lord Pinkrose in *Fortunes of War* (1987); Graham in *Talking Heads* 'A Chip in the Sugar' (1988); unrecognizable as Lord Dacre in *Selling Hitler* (1991); Grantley Cayper in *Ashenden* (1991); in *Julie Walters and Friends* (also co-writer, 1991). As reader: *Jackanory* (1970s); *The Wind in the Willows* (1992).

Benson, E[dward] F[rederic] (1867–1940) English novelist, creator of Mapp and Lucia: *Dead of Night* (opening story, 1945 C); *As We Were* 'A Victorian Peepshow' (1960 R); *Queen Lucia* (1984 R); *Lucia in London* (1985 R); *Mapp and Lucia* (1985–6 T); *Paying Guests* (1989 T).

bent The dual sexual/criminal associations (*Crime and the Bent Society*, Granada documentary, 1965) became apparent in David TURNER'S SUMMER, WINTER, AUTUMN, SPRING (1961 T; 1962 R). Gay son is in mid-altercation with his father:

> 'It's me. You know there's something wrong with me, don't you.'
> 'Not *wrong*. We're all of us a bit bent, one way or another. That's why I gave in when you were so keen to marry 'er. I

thought it might help to straighten you out. I'm speakin' plain now.'

In THE CONNOISSEUR, the priggish Rev. Adrian Tenterden, clergyman and teacher, is nicknamed Harpic 'because he's clear round the bend'. One of his colleagues sneers that he 'married a virgin with a pedigree and a bent offspring'. 'Is he bent? Queer? Your husband?' Michael Caine asks Giovanna Ralli about Eric PORTMAN in *Deadfall* (1968 C).

'Bent' continues to be used in a purely deviant-sexuality way: 'Sir, is it true you're bent?' a pupil asks teacher Jim in NIGHTHAWKS (1978 C); 'Not all the hair on your lip could hide from me your particular bent,' says Jackson (Tim Preece) to Frank Marsh (Allan Lander) in *The Deep Concern* (1979 T); 'He's bent in more ways than one. He's Arnie Fisher's bum boy. He leaves your bed and gets into his,' Dolly (Ann Mitchell) says to Linda (Maureen O'Farrell) about Carlos (James Lister) in episode 4 of WIDOWS (1983 T).

More ambiguously: 'bent' appears in: 'He used to take pictures from the store to impress his bank manager. If that's not bent I don't know what is' (about the art gallery swindler (Geoffrey BURRIDGE in THE GENTLE TOUCH 'Auctions' 1982 T); 'He's not bent. He's not doolalley. But is he straight?' (THE BILL 'Safe Place' 1990 T).

Bent Groundbreaking 1979 play by Martin Sherman which revealed the persecution of homosexual men in Dachau. A scene involving Ian MCKELLEN and Tom Bell was shown on *Tonight*, but a review, by Irving Wardle was not broadcast on KALEIDOSCOPE, with no explanation given. The play was performed on Broadway (with Richard Gere) and in many countries. There was another London production (with McKellen and Michael CASHMAN) in 1990. A film version was mooted in the early 1980s, to be directed first by Rainer Werner FASSBINDER and then by Costa-Gavras, but it didn't eventuate.

bereavement 'The specific pain that is experienced by gay men and lesbians after the death of a loved one, when often the straight world denies the legitimacy or even the existence of their relationship,' OUT (1991 T). 'They wouldn't let me see him. You see I'm not a relative,' Mic (David Dundas) says to Vivien in *Boy Meets Girl* 'Purposes of Love' (1968 T).

Grieving gay men include the lover (David COOK) of the married man in THE WAITING ROOM (1971 T); George in A SINGLE MAN (1972 & 1991 R), facing up to the death of Jim; PAUL (Philip Latham) haunted by the ghost of Malcolm (Robert Powell) in *Is Nellie Dead?* (1968 T); Fitz (Geoffrey BURRIDGE) in A MOMENT IN TIME (1979 T); the narrator of ME AND MR MANDEL; Gilbert (Chris Eymard) in THE CORNER HOUSE (1987 T); various characters in LONGTIME COMPANION.

Women in a similar situation include Mavis (Cicely Courtneidge) in THE L-SHAPED ROOM (1962 C); and Jean (Lois Nettleton) in THE GOLDEN GIRLS 'Isn't It Romantic' (1987 T). More untypical is Kate (Liv Ullmann) in RICHARD'S THINGS (1981 T/C), who falls in love with her just-deceased husband's mistress. Gail (Mariette Hartley) has a soothing affair with a woman when her husband dies suddenly in MY TWO LOVES. And Edith SOMERVILLE keeps in contact with her dead partner for years in ONLY GOODNIGHT (1981 R). Sarah talks about Katie, who committed suicide, in the 1980 documentary COMING OUT, while WOMEN LIKE US looked at the continuing pain of one woman's loss.

Emotional and practical problems that can occur after the death of a partner were put into strong focus during the 1980s: fictionally in AFTER HENRY and factually in documentaries like *The One Left Behind* (1987 R). However, most of these programmes were exclusively concerned with people who lost a *marriage* partner. Slowly, moved along by AIDS and by the work of Dudley Cave and the Gay Bereavement Project (featured on *Claire Rayner's Casebook* 1983 T etc), the loss of a loved one is assuming a more universal, multi-faceted form, such as Tony WHITEHEAD's talk on the death of George (*A Perspective for Living* 1992 R) and the American film *An Empty Bed* (1991).

Berlin In BBC Radio 3's celebration of the reunified Berlin, a gay man (Romy Haag) declared with salivating relish that he was very pleased with the situation because 'There's always "fresh meat" in town' (1990 R). Berlin in the 1930s has been celebrated, guardedly, in CABARET, and by people as various as Claudio Arrau, Louise BROOKS and Lotte LENYA in *Memories of Berlin – The Twilight of Weimar Culture* (1979 T) as well as by EISENSTEIN, quoted in OMNIBUS 'The Secret Life of Sergei Eisenstein': 'I was fascinated by Berlin ... every kind of sexual deviation ... this underworld of sexuality.' The city in the 1990s is no less full of flavour, contradictions, paradoxes. Daring, savage, creative, emerging. Sexually and politically. Howard WAKELING tackled this brave new world full-on fictionally in A BIT OF BERLIN (1992 R), while some of its more underprivileged homosexual citizens were spotlighted in OUT's THE BATTLE FOR TUNTENHAUS (1991 & 1992 T).

Berners, Lord [Gerald Tyrwhitt-Wilson] (1883–1950) English composer, painter, writer and eccentric, probing and exploring freedoms in elaborately airy fancies like *Count Omega* (1987 R). Timothy West played him in a 1983 radio portrait with Sir Harold ACTON, Sir Frederick ASHTON and Richard Rodney Bennett. Described as 'a sort of sub-Leonardo who wrote music, painted and concocted fantastic novels.' Mentioned by Harold NICOLSON in POR-TRAIT OF A MARRIAGE and by Robert HELPMANN in *A Knight in the Ballet* (Aust 1971 R).

Bernstein, Leonard (1918–90) Galvanic, seductive American composer, conductor and pianist who wrote *On the Town*, WEST SIDE STORY (with Stephen SONDHEIM), choral and orches-

tral works, and a musical version of *Candide*. He was a great popularizer of classical music and made many television appearances: OMNIBUS 'Leonard Bernstein's WEST SIDE STORY' (1985); OMNIBUS 'George Gershwin Remembered' (1987); etc.

best man Friend or brother or other male relative of the groom. Frequent tenderness shown between the pair on pre-nuptual night or (hungover) wedding day: *Sailor Beware!* (1956 C), *A Wedding* (1978 C), etc. Ezra Fitton not only had to have his Billy with him at the guest house after the wedding but, it is inferred, needed him to impregnate his bride (HONEYMOON POSTPONED 1961 T/THE FAMILY WAY 1966 C/*All in Good Time* 1976 R). In the final episode (1989 T) of *Life without George*, Ben (Michael Thomas) jokingly says that he will move in with Larry (Simon Cadell) if the bride doesn't show up, 'But I have to tell you one thing: I snore'.

The Best Man (US 1964 C) Will decent Henry Fonda destroy his presidential rival, nasty extremist Cliff Robertson, by going public on Robertson's affair with a fellow sailor during the war? Vidal in his element: the gore of American politics.

W: Gore VIDAL from his play; P: Stuart Millar and Lawrence Turman; D: Franklin Schaffner; 104 mins.

Best Of Friends Similar to the theme from *The Courtship of Eddie's Father* (1969–72 T), the Thrasher Brothers' country-style ditty gave a homoemotional flavour to the brothers SIMON AND SIMON (1981–2 T). Maybe somebody noticed – because the song was replaced by something less intimate, after just one season.

The Best Of Times Jerry Herman's glorious celebration of living life for today, from *La Cage aux Folles* (1983), one of those unapologetically upbeat Broadway songs that, possibly uniquely, embraced the show's gay and non-gay characters in a great burst of optimistic solidarity. It was used at much revered disc jockey Ray MOORE's memorial service, broadcast (3.3.89) from All Souls, Langham Place, performed at full throttle by the Salvation Army songsters, the BBC singers and the Syd Lawrence Orchestra. Ray Moore's favourite song, it was greeted with tumultuous applause. 'The best of times are now ... are now ... are *now*.'

The Best Way to Walk (Fr 1976 C) Group conformity at the expense of private feelings at a summer camp during the 1960s shows shifting sexuality between bully (Patrick Dewaere) and bullied (Patrick Bouchitey). A slightly braver TEA AND SYMPATHY. W/D: Claude Miller; 86 mins.

Better latent than never! An expression used by Mel Smith to Griff Rhys Jones as he discusses the wide spread of late-blooming homosexuality in a 1989 SMITH AND JONES (T). Just one of a number of outings for this natty comment.

Beverley/Beverly *See* GIRLS' NAMES FOR BOYS.

bevy/bevvy POLARI for DRINK, still used in the North of England and heard in BROOKSIDE, *Drop the Dead Donkey* (1991 T) etc.

Beyond Gravity (NZ 1988 T/C) Richard (Robert Pollock) finds out there's more to life than astronomy when the charismatic Johnny (Iain Rea) bursts into his life, to the delight of Richard's SISTER Billie (Lucy Sheehan). Johnny can't be totally trusted, though ...
W: Garth Maxwell and Graham Adams; P: James H. Wallace; D: Garth Maxwell; 65 mins.

Bhangra Jig (UK 1990 V) KHUSH ('ecstatic pleasure') is the name used by gay and lesbian South ASIANS, Indians and Pakistanis to describe themselves and their music – dance that embraces east and west.
D: Pratibha Parmar; 5 mins.

The Bible Certain sections of the King James version are regularly used to lash out at homosexuals and their sexual acts on radio and television. The whole Bible was read on BBC Radio 4 between 1991 and 1992, and the anti-homosexual injunctions can be boiled down to the following: LEVITICUS 18:22 and 20:13; Deuteronomy 23:17; I Kings 14:24; Romans 1:26–27; Corinthians 6:9–10; I Timothy 1:9–10.
The Bible as literature and as political tool was discussed by, among others, Peter Shaffer and Jeanette WINTERSON in 1988 (T), and among its supporters and critics are Joseph Campbell, Bishop John Spong and the Rev. Richard KIRKER, as well as its uncritical devotees who pop up on mainstream television and radio in very limited contexts (usually abortion and homosexuality debates).
See also EVANGELICALS; Rev. Fred NILE; St PAUL; Mary WHITEHOUSE.

The Bible [In the Beginning] (It/US 1966 C) John Huston tackled some chapters from Genesis, including Adam and Eve, the Tower of Babel, Cain and Abel, and SODOM AND GOMORRAH with Peter O'Toole as all three angels. (Orson WELLES was to have directed a version of 'Sodom and Gomorrah' as part of a 15-hour film in 1963–5).
W: Christopher Fry and others; P: Dino Di Laurentiis and Luigi Luraschi; 174 mins.

Les Biches [The Does] (Fr/It 1968 C) A graceful, glamorous tragi-comedy about a young woman Why (Jacqueline Sassard) and the older, sophisticated Frédérique (Stephane Audran), and the man (Jean-Louis Trintignant) who destroys them by love. A traditional story that develops with piquancy, but ends conventionally with blood on the carpet. W: Paul Gegauff and Claude Chabrol; D: Claude Chabrol; 99 mins.

Big Brother is watching you This doom-laden phrase came into widespread use after the 1954 BBC production of Orwell's projection into a nightmare future, NINETEEN-EIGHTY-FOUR. For some members of the British public, Big Brother's eyes were already firmly clamped upon them. In 1954, there were more men arrested and charged with 'homosexual offences' than ever before (a number unequalled until 1989–90).

Big C Popularized by John WAYNE, who was diagnosed with lung cancer in 1964. Hitherto, the disease had been spoken of in whispers and, until the coming of AIDS, it still remained *the* disease whose name many dared not speak. Judy Pile's play *Naming the Big C: Despatches from the Cancer Zone* (Aust 1991 R) maintained that 'Prejudice abounds about the causes of the malignancy, and neither orthodox nor alternative medical practice has found a way of easing the fear induced by the onset of the disease'.

Biggins, Christopher (1948–) English actor, plump and beaming, best known for his LUKEWARM in *Porridge* (1974–7 T), and for his appearances as Flub in *The Jessie James Story* (1973 T); as Nero in *I, Claudius* (1976 T); for CAMP supporting roles in *Some Mothers Do 'Ave 'Em* (1977 & 1978 T); as an effervescent Stephano in *The Tempest* (1980 C); in *Surprise Surprise* (1984 T); as an astrologer in *The Gemini Factor* (1987 T); etc.

bijou Part of POLARI, occasionally used by heterosexual characters: the bubbly wife (Julia McKenzie) in *French Fields* (1989 T), and HOOPERMAN (John Ritter) who calls his mongrel 'Bijou'. In 1991, Richard Ackland, the presenter of the Australian national morning news programme *Daybreak*, referred to 'bijou cinemaettes'.

Bill/Billie/Billy *See* BOYS' NAMES FOR GIRLS.

Bill and Ben The FLOWERPOT MEN. Used for the two gay crooks in *Bill and Ben* (1972 R), and for a married couple in *2 point 4 children* (1991–2 T): Bill (Belinda Lang) and Ben (Gary Olsen).

Billy Budd The personification of inno-

cence: the beautiful SAILOR in Herman Melville's novel and Benjamin BRITTEN's opera, destroyed by twisted desire. Terence Stamp in the 1962 film; in the opera Joseph Ward (1960 R) and Mark Tinkler (1987 R). In *Billy in the Darbies* (1980 R) Britten discusses with E. M. FORSTER and Eric Crozier how they made an opera from Melville's story. Billibud (Jason Durr) is the punk lover of Caz in YOUNG SOUL REBELS.

birds Female–female bonding of the lesser snow goose – supposedly caused by a dearth of males: reported in *Science Now* (1989 R).

Birkett, Jack [The Incredible Orlando] (194?–) English actor and dancer, long associated with Lindsay Kemp. Eyes like gobstoppers coupled with the voice of a herring in sour cream. A few, unforgettable appearances: as media baron Borgia Ginz in JUBILEE (1977 C): 'I sucked and sucked and I *sucked*'; as Caliban in *The Tempest* (1980 C); as Thersites in *Troilus and Cressida* (1981 T); as Titania in *A Midsummer Night's Dream* (1984 C); *Caravaggio* (1986 C) as the Pope; as a Berlin drag queen in OMNIBUS 'George Grosz, Enemy of the State' (1986 T).

birthdays Broadcast celebrations in honour of gay and lesbian people include: James BALDWIN; Noel COWARD; Larry GRAYSON, Peter PEARS, Erica PUNCHON; Cole PORTER; Dame Ethel SMYTH – *My Eightieth Birthday*; Michael TIPPETT. Fictional characters blowing out the candles include: Stanley (Robert Shaw) in *The Birthday Party* (1968 C); Harold (Leonard Frey) in THE BOYS IN THE BAND (1970 C); the son (Allen Rosenberg) in *Happy Birthday, Gemini* (1980 C); Steve (David Boney) at the beginning of *Night Out* (1990 C); Jamie in G.P. 'Lovers' (1990 T).

birth partner Sammy (Campbell Morrison) so describes himself in relation to Mandy (Elizabeth Estensen) at a natural childbirth group in *Life without George* (1989 T). This was basically the same idea as in A TASTE OF HONEY 30 years before: gay man easing pregnant woman through the process (COOKING, KNITTING, cajoling, comforting).

bisexual The word was first mentioned on radio in 1954 and first officially seen in practice (outside of perverse FILM NOIR like GILDA and Andy WARHOL movies) in THEOREM (1968 C); *The Lion in Winter* (1968 C); *Something for Everyone* (1970 C); SUNDAY BLOODY SUNDAY (1971 C); and CABARET (1972).

Hollywood caught on gingerly in 1968 with Terry-Thomas as a mad Hungarian producer in the Doris DAY comedy *Where Were You When the Lights Went Out?* He tells his PSYCHIATRIST that he loathes women and doesn't like the other lot any better. 'Does hatred of men *and* women make me bisexual?' In THE DETECTIVE (1968 C), a psychiatrist tells his client that there is no such thing as a bisexual, 'only a homosexual without conviction'. Some 15 years later it's a cop (hard-boiled Rod Steiger) who comes up with the definition (in *The Naked Face* 1984 C) that 'A bisexual is a FAG with a family'.

In Britain Anthony Storr, in tandem with 'SELF-CONFESSED bisexual' George MELLY, told WOMAN'S HOUR listeners in 1968 ('Dressing Up'): 'I think we are all bisexual and it's quite possible that we couldn't really relate to one another sexually if we weren't.'

Bisexuality and the West Coast American concept of 'swinging' became intertwined in the early 1970s. The abbreviation 'bi' was widely used, as was AC/DC. In the Australian soap *The Box* (1974 T) Judy Nunn played a rapacious reporter who, said her creator, 'played both sides. I think she was into anything that moved.'

'Swinging both ways' was the preferred expression, surviving the brief period of fashion bisexuality enjoyed in the mid-1970s, especially as a number of stars, usually pop, declared themselves not gay or lesbian, but bisexual. A caller to a Radio London phone-in about Gilbert HARDING in 1982 said that, as an ex-showgirl, she'd seen it all: 'I swung both ways.' In *She's Gotta Have It* (1986 C),

Opal Gilstrap (Raye Dowell) tells the heroine: 'We have the potential to be either way'; the woman (Camilla Johns) doesn't respond, though in the next scene she is shown masturbating.

Serious discussion was limited to passing mention in sex education series and the occasional brave, foolhardy or publicity-seeking celebrity confession. Yet all far-reaching surveys of human behaviour seem to agree with John Chesterman in ACCESS 'Offensive to Some' (1973 R): 'Bisexuality is the human norm, if there is one at all. It's not enough to eulogize the ancient philosophies ... The implications must be followed through in our own terms.' He went on: 'The barrage of advertising, mass circulation journals, our job and work structure and education still condition our traditional gender roles ... Man still gets the woman. The parents still own the children ... Gender polarity is deeply and totally ingrained in our culture and is completely unnatural.' But Chesterman was merely echoing what Robert Briffault had said on BBC radio in 1931, in MARRIAGE: PAST AND PRESENT.

Occasionally the word turned up in a perfectly relaxed, throwaway context: 'As someone who's bisexual, I've often wondered if his sexuality didn't make him more attractive to a lot of Europeans,' writer-producer Hallam Tennyson in the programme on Constantine CAVAFY *The Walls and the Visions* (1977 R).

'Bisexual', demoted by the end of the 1970s because of its supposed trendy dishonesty, came back into full currency with AIDS: 'The original [carrier] was a bisexual'; 'Enter the epidemic's new *bête noir*, the bisexual. Only he (in AIDS discussions bisexuals are always male) can account for and absolve the heterosexual minority of any taint of unlawful desire' (Jan Zita Grover, 'AIDS: Key Words' in *AIDS: Cultural Analysis and Cultural Activism* ed Douglas Crimp, 1989).

The presence of bisexuality within the gay/lesbian culture seems to induce disquiet. The strange, tilted camera angles regularly employed in BATMAN in the

1960s were requisitioned by OUT ON TUESDAY (1990 T) for its 'Walk On Bi' programme, presumably to indicate lack of balance or some kind of alien force at work. The show began with photographs of and quotes by various notables. These included Martina NAVRATILOVA with the legend 'I'm bisexual', followed by 'Oh really?' in parenthesis.

bisexuals Richard (Anthony Hopkins) and Philippe (Timothy Dalton) in *The Lion in Winter* (1968 C); Terence Stamp as the mysterious visitor in THEOREM (1968 C); Michael York as a beautiful con man in *Something for Everyone/Black Flowers for the Bride* (1970 C); Bob (Murray Head) in SUNDAY, BLOODY SUNDAY; Darnley (Timothy Dalton) and Rizzio (Ian HOLM), husband and secretary respectively of *Mary, Queen of Scots* (1971 C); Brian (Michael York) and the Baron (Helmut Griem) in CABARET; photographer Bruce in NUMBER 96 (1972 T); Bob (Dinsdale Landen) in *Bermondsey* (1972 T); Alan BATES as BUTLEY (1974 T/C); CALIGULA (John Hurt) in *I, Claudius*; Malcolm McDowall in *Caligula* (1980 C); tennis pro Peter (Robert Urich) in SOAP (1977 T) and Jodie's boyfriend, Dennis (Bob Seagren) in the same show (presented as a selfish, ruthless, sexist nerd); Steven CARRINGTON (Al Corley/Jack COLEMAN) in DYNASTY (1981–91 T); Gail Springer (Mariette Hartley), who describes herself as bisexual in MY TWO LOVES (1986 T) but settles for (temporary?) celibacy after a few weeks with a woman; 'I'm not gay, I'm bisexual. There's a difference,' declares Bruce (Jeff Goldblum) in *Beyond Therapy* (1986 C); nurse Rose Marie (Barbara Flynn) in A VERY PRIVATE PRACTICE (1986 T), who advances on the timid hero determined to get 'the psychodynamics' out into the open: 'My sexuality disturbs you doesn't it? ... I'm bisexual ... in common with 70 per cent of the population'; 'No job is worth having to date a woman,' says Blanche to Rose in THE GOLDEN GIRLS (1987 T) after the latter has said she needs to be 'bilingual' for a new job. Jack Carney (Hart Bochner) in *Apart-*

ment Zero (presented as a murderous, amoral psychotic – body count: 13, 1988 C); the man spreading the HIV virus (Richard Cox) in MIDNIGHT CALLER 'After It Happened' (1988 T); Brian Kerwin as Arnold's teacher lover in TORCH SONG TRILOGY (1988 C); Jamie (Michael Grandage) in *Chelworth* (1989 T) who, noticing the furrowed brow of his female bed-mate, asks: 'What is it, Miss Harper? That I am a viscount or that I am bisexual?'

bishops Cardinal Pirelli (Aubrey WOODS) in VALMOUTH; Philip Stone in *Flint* (1977 T); Bishop Charles Webster Leadbeater (Nigel Anthony) 'an incorrigible pederast', charlatan, clairvoyant, gifted seer, an Anglican curate and later a bishop in a schismatic church, one of the *The Mischief Makers*' 'five studies in talent and perversity' (1986 R).

bitch Slang term for women which POLARI extended to men ('butch or bitch?'). As a derogatory term for a woman it arrived on BBC television around about 1958 (DIXON OF DOCK GREEN) and built up a head of steam four years later, when Alf (Jon Rollason) asks, 'When will the old bitch be back?' in SUMMER, AUTUMN, WINTER, SPRING. The following year it surfaced in Z CARS and in Elaine Morgan's play *A Chance to Shine* where husband calls wife a silly bitch. This came five days before Ray Brooks referred to Kevin Stoney as a 'poor pathetic old bastard' in *The Face They See* (1962). On radio it was restricted mainly to the Third Programme ('experimental drama') or the verb form: Malcolm (Basil JONES), the hedonist in *The Boys of Summer* (1959) says, 'I'm sorry I bitched just now.'

Films reached the bitch circuitously, through sub-titles. Jean-Paul Belmondo's dying word to Jean Seberg in *Breathless/A Bout de Souffle* (1959 C) is 'bitch' ('salop'). 'What did he say?', she asks, trance-like, to a cop. 'He said you were a lousy bitch.' 'I don't understand,' she murmurs. 'You know how bitchy fags can be!' says Jennifer (Sharon Tate) to Neely (Patty Duke) in VALLEY OF THE

DOLLS, responding to scurrilous rumours about the latter's dress-designer husband.

Calling men bitches began around the time of THE DETECTIVE (1968 C): 'He was a bitch!' screams Felix Tessler (Tony Musante) when questioned about his 'ROOM-MATE'.

Its use became common in the late 1970s with the advent of strong women characters, either holding together a family or empire or manipulating its destruction. Notable among these was Joan Collins' Alexis in DYNASTY. The actress's claim to fame before gaining this role was a 1978 film called *The Bitch*. Previously 'bitch' had been spewed out by lesbian characters in a variety of fictional situations, beginning with the ALCOHOLIC journalist Mabel Warren (Anna Burden) in STAMBOUL TRAIN to her estranged girlfriend: 'You won't remember me in five years' time will you, you little bitch!'

A similarly tense relationship was indicated in JUST BEFORE MIDNIGHT 'The Worm Must Turn' (1979 R). There was the same snappish response:

> Edith: 'Stop sulking.'
> Marian: 'I'm not sulking.'
> Edith: 'Of course, you're sulking ...
> You're a hysterical little bitch.'

When George Smiley (Alec Guinness) visits Connie Sachs (Beryl REID) in *Smiley's People* (1982 T), her girlfriend Hilary (Norma West) throws a silently agitated tantrum. Connie tells Smiley to 'Go and see the mad bitch. Make sure she doesn't throw herself into the mill race.'

Men, discovering that their charms fail to ignite the expected response in a woman, sometimes catapult this word out of frustration and wounded pride. As when Warren Beatty discovers Jean Seberg and a woman (Anne Meara) together in a barn in *Lilith* (1964 C): 'You dirty bitch!' Sometimes the word has to be recharged to make the necessary impact. The sorely tried Robin (Michael Gambon) does this in THE OTHER WOMAN (1976 T) after Kim

(Jane Lapotaire) has turned away from him in bed: 'You queer bitch! No, that's the wrong word for you. You're a bastard, a bastard of a woman.' Earlier, in the 1966 film adaptation of Norman Mailer's *An American Dream* (retitled *See You in Hell, Darling* in Britain), Eleanor Parker, as the possibly bisexual wife, self-proclaims with woozy pride: 'Rich I am; bitch I am!' She is pushed off her penthouse roof to her death in the very next scene.

Cecil (Rex Harrison) calls his faithful Hawkins (Cyril Cusack) an old bitch in *The Kingfisher* (1982 T). It wounds him deeply and he hands in his notice. Next morning, sober, Hawkins grabs it back again.

'That Susan always had all the boys, the bitch!' snorts the gay brother in *Death Duties* (1987 R), while Sharon is possibly fishing for Wicksy to demur when, in EASTENDERS (1990 T), she blurts out: 'I'm a right bitch, aren't I'.

In *Boyz N the Hood* (1991 C) the young black men habitually refer to each other as 'bitch' and 'cunt'. Said director John Singleton: 'They have their manhood attacked so often they attack each other's manhood in various ways, verbally and physically' (*Sight and Sound*, August 1991).

The use of 'bitch' as prison lingo for 'passive' male sexual partner is often heard in American movies, but less frequently in those made for television. It did turn up, outside this context, in BROTHERS 'When Fools Russian' (1984 T): Lou (Brandon Maggart) is horrified when a Soviet wrestler (Peter Palmer) asks him to be 'his bitch'.

A Bit of Berlin (UK 1992 R) Vic and Barbara (James Grout and Rowena Cooper) have a lot of personal weeding to do when they visit their son Mark (Julian Rhind-Tutt), who lives in Berlin and has been bashed by neo-Nazis. Barbara copes quite well with her son's lover Dieter (Walter Van Dyk) – and the leather bar they manage – with the help of the lover's liberated mother, Anna (Maggie McCarthy). Vic remains intractable, being a prisoner of his own up-

bringing and being also trapped by a violent incident in his past – dynamically interwoven with the main events of Howard WAKELING's play. Comparatively frank (for BBC Radio 4's Monday Play slot), the plot manages to fit in a whole raft of issues, best of which is the reaction to her brother's milieu by the liberated Janet (Federay Holmes).
D: Janet Whitaker; 28.9.92; 90 mins.

black and white film Since the late 1960s all mainstream films have been made in full colour. Exceptions include *Paper Moon, The Last Picture Show, Raging Bull, Schindler's List* and IN BED WITH MADONNA. Lesbian/gay cinema – usually, but not always, for reasons of economy – often utilizes tones of black, white and grey: NOIR ET BLANC (1986); *The Long Weekend (O'Despair)* (1987); MALA NOCHE (1987); LOOKING FOR LANGSTON (1988 T); COMRADES IN ARMS (1990 T); FLAMES OF PASSION (1990 C); *Sink or Swim* (1990); *Night Out* (1990); POISON (part colour 1991); *Resonance* (1991); *Came Out, It Rained, Went Back In Again* (1991 T); NORTH OF VORTEX (1991); *The Hours and Times* (1991); SWOON (1991); TOGETHER ALONE (1991); *Amelia Rose Towers* (1992); etc.

The Black and White Minstrel Show (UK 1958–78 T) Once the most popular light entertainment show on television; taken off the air in the 1970s because of its racist dimension and, like the 1950s *Amos 'n' Andy* in America, confined to the vaults, even though it is the most requested of all BBC programmes, being fast-moving, tuneful and (happy and) gay – if middle-aged white men wearing black-face who are singing and prancing with young white women happens to be to your taste. Created by George Inns and starring the George Mitchell Singers.

Black Dyke Mills Band Now known as the John Foster Black Dyke Mills Band. Very popular in radio programmes like *Listen to the Band*, and much prized by

Afro-American lesbian visitors to Britain.

black gay men One of the prisoners in UN CHANT D'AMOUR (1950 C); Brock Peters as musician Johnny in THE L-SHAPED ROOM; and as the gangster with the white boyfriend in *The Pawnbroker* (1965 C); librarian Bernard (Reuben Greene) in THE BOYS IN THE BAND; Jo (Peter STRAKER) in *Girl Stroke Boy* (1971 C); Norman (Michael Warren) in NORMAN ... IS THAT YOU? (1976 C); prisoner (Tony Burton) in *The Moneychangers* (1976 T); Antonio Fargas as Bernstein in *Next Stop, Greenwich Village* (1976 C), and as Lindy in *Car Wash* (1977 C); PROSTITUTE 'Sugar' (Reg Tsiboe) in A HYMN FROM JIM (1977 T); Benny Luke as the 'maid' in LA CAGE AUX FOLLES (1978 C); prostitute Polo (Ben Ellison) in COMING OUT (1979 T); Felipe Rose, one of the VILLAGE PEOPLE in CAN'T STOP THE MUSIC (1980 C); the prisoner (Georg Stanford Brown) in *Stir Crazy*; Robert Christian as the victim in ... *And Justice for All* (1979 C); Nono (Gunther Kaufman) in QUERELLE; fashion designer Oliver in GEMS; Gordon Warnecke as Omar in MY BEAUTIFUL LAUNDRETTE (1985 C/T); fashion photographer (William Allen Young) in SINS (1986 T); WINSTON (Eamonn Walker) in IN SICKNESS AND IN HEALTH (1987–9 T); Hollywood Montrose (Meshach Taylor) in *Mannequin* (1987 C) and *Mannequin on the Move* (1991 C); LOOKING FOR LANGSTON; AIDS 'buddy' in LONGTIME COMPANION (1990 C); YOUNG SOUL REBELS; film critics in *In Living Color* (1990 T); Jody (Forest Whitaker) and Dil (Jaye Davidson) in *The Crying Game* (1992 C); etc.
In documentaries: *Portrait of Jason* (1966 C); WORD IS OUT (1977 C); *Rights and Reactions* (1989 T); *Eye to Eye* (1990 C) about Jack Walls, lover of Robert MAPPLETHORPE; OUT; OUT ON TUESDAY; TONGUES UNTIED (1991 C); PARIS IS BURNING (1991 C); Justin Fashnu; DONAHUE's gay wedding; etc.

black lesbians The CIA operative (Vonetta McKee) in *The Kremlin Letter*

(1970 C); Velma (Isabelle Lucas) in AGONY (1979 T); PROSTITUTE (Vikki Richards) in THE GENTLE TOUCH 'Melody' (1980 T); the maid in *Beulah Land* (1980 T); member of women's army, Adele (Jeanne Satterfield) in *Born in Flames* (1983 C); Celie (Whoopi Goldberg) and Shug (Margaret Avery) in THE COLOR PURPLE (1985 C); cock-of-the-walk prisoner 'Ernie' (C. C. H. Pounder) in *If Tomorrow Comes* (1986 T); conscience-pricking couple in *Sammy and Rosie Get Laid* (1987 C); lawyer Agatha (Sheila Dabney) in *She Must Be Seeing Things* (1987 C); Paula Kelly and Lonette McKee as two of THE WOMEN OF BREWSTER PLACE (1989 T); etc.

In documentaries: WORD IS OUT; OUT ON TUESDAY; OUT (in heavy disguise in WOMEN LIKE US/WOMEN LIKE THAT 1990–1); in the audience of *The Oprah Winfrey Show* 'Left for a Lesbian' (1991 T); DONAHUE 'She Says Her Future Groom Cheats On Her With Men' (1992 T); etc.

black leather jacket One of the great fashion icons of the 1950s (Marlon Brando wore one in *The Wild One*), which has retained its elegant, dangerous appeal for men and women. Celebrated in *Fashion Icons* 'The Black Leather Jacket' (1992 R).

blackmail It was endemic as a result of the law criminalizing male homosexual acts. The film VICTIM furnished every opportunity to say this was no longer effective or appropriate. Here was the first clarion call of indignation since André Raffalovich and his former lover John Grey co-authored *The Blackmailers*. The play was tried out at the Prince of Wales theatre, but the advent of the Oscar WILDE affair put paid to any commercial run.

Emlyn WILLIAMS brilliantly wrote and portrayed an extortionist 'William' Blake in one of the stories in *Friday the Thirteenth* (1933 C). Confronting a young man (who had been to prison) and his fiancée, Blake leers with almost orgasmic triumph at his prey, while giving

them a little biographical detail (but not too much): 'I was educated at a very nasty little school, but I have never yet been known not to behave quite beautifully ... I'm awfully *active*.'

Not until 1961 was the situation faced by gay men from all walks of life given wide exposure. The men persecuted in VICTIM are all afraid to go to the police. Lord Fullbrook (Anthony Nicholls) explains why: 'Our calm acceptance must make you surprised. But do you ever wonder about the law that makes us all victims of any cheap thug who finds out about our natural instincts? ... If we don't pay, we'll land in jail with our crimes – so called – damn near parallel with robbery with violence.'

The threat of blackmail before the change of law was indicated in *Blackmail* (1966 T), *A Coat of Varnish* (1983 R), and MAURICE (1987 C), and after in COMING OUT, *Instant Enlightenment Plus VAT* (1980 T), and *A Murder of Quality* (1991 T).

Black March Stevie Smith poem read in COMPROMISED IMMUNITY (1991 R); unconsciously(?) used by Peter to help Gerry (Michael CASHMAN) accommodate death (in a book given to Peter by another patient).

black sheep of the family The artist describes himself as one in *Donald Friend – Australian Prodigal* (1990 T); *Baa Baa Black Sheep* aka *Black Sheep Squadron* (1977–8 T) was based on a real-life situation: a squadron of misfits and rejects from other units.

The Black Sheep Of The Family A great hit in the 1930s for Fred Barnes whose career nosedived because he was publicly revealed as homosexual, after an incident in a park. It was the title of a Radio 4 biography of the singer in 1979.

Anthony Blanche (Nickolas GRACE in BRIDESHEAD REVISITED 1981 T) Divinely, unapologetically CAMP Oxford aesthete (partly based on Brian HOWARD), admirer of the wafting Sebastian. He declaims a sonnet to a young man through a beribboned megaphone to an audience of incredulous hearties. To Sebastian he coos, 'My dear, I should like to stick you full of arrows like a pincushion.' He turns up later in the story at an exhibition of Charles Ryder's paintings. The stammer, BOW-TIE, make-up and coat slung across the shoulders are unchanged. He unabashedly kisses the artist on the cheek ('Dear Charles'). Later he propels him to 'a louche little bar ... not quite your milieu, but my dear, mine I assure you'. Drawing his French ancestry about him like a fox fur he declares, in between gazing at the bar's younger patrons: 'I am not English. I cannot understand this zest to be well-bred. English snobbery is even more macabre than English morals.' There's not one wasted word or gesture in Grace's rendering of this impeccable inkspot on English society's tablecloth. Totally aware of the danger of English charm (particularly that of Sebastian), he succumbs willingly as he does to every sensation. A gem.

blasphemy Some consideration was given to the abolition of blasphemy from English common law in the wake of the GAY NEWS trial in 1977, but it was not regarded as pressing. There were few takers either for an extension of the law to cover all major religions. Wrote Alison HENNEGAN: 'Who was being protected from what? And in which men's image was God being created anew this summer down at the Old Bailey?'

Although the prosecution of the newspaper was as much an attack on its right to exist as on the poem it had printed – the prosecuting counsel sneered at its recent sex education feature: 'encouraging illegal sexual activity' – writers and producers were suddenly aware that the taking of Jesus's name in vain could be a serious matter.

This did not stop the MONTY PYTHON team, after extensive legal advice, embarking on its *Life of Brian* (1979 C), which emerged as a debunking of religious cults and political splinter groups rather than the Bible and its teachings.

The subject regained momentum in the late 1980s with the Salman Rushdie affair, and moves were afoot, not to expunge the offence, but to extend legal protection to all major religions.

A Matter of Scandal and Concern (1960 T, starring Richard Burton about an earlier case); EVERYMAN 'Blasphemy at the Old Bailey' (1977 T) and 'Blasphemy – A Law on Trial' (1978 T); *Law in Action* 'Blasphemy' (1983 R).

Isaac JULIEN set his film YOUNG SOUL REBELS in 1977. He saw it as a time when punk, the Queen's Jubilee and racism intermingle; there is no reference to the blasphemy trial by the director who says his reconstruction was influenced by punk, Gay Left, *The Leveller*, the writings of Jeffrey WEEKS and Simon WATNEY.

blonds/blondes Usually relating to female hair colour: *The Blonde Saint* (1926 C); *Platinum Blonde*; *Blonde Bombshell*, *Blondie of the Follies* and *Blondie* (Penny Singleton) married to Dagwood (Arthur Lake) in Columbia series (1938–50); Pamela Britton with Lake in TV series in the early 1950s; Patricia Harty and Will Hutchins (1968); *My Favourite Blonde*; *The Beautiful Blonde from Bashful Bend*; *Gentlemen Prefer Blondes*; *Too Many Blondes*; *Too Young to be Blonde* (Ger 1961 T); *A Blonde in Love/Loves of a Blonde*; *Moviola* 'This Year's Blonde' (1980 T, about Marilyn MONROE); *Blonde Fist* (1991 C). Characters who have 'gone blonde' include Jean Simmons in *Home Before Dark* (1958 C); actresses who dipped deep into the peroxide include Joan Bennett, Ginger Rogers, Jean Arthur, Rita Hayworth (in *The Lady from Shanghai*), Shirley Abicair and MADONNA.

Intriguingly, given Hollywood's prediliction for fair-haired people, the American version of *The Tall Blond Man with One Black Shoe* (1972 C) was retitled *The Man with One Red Shoe* in 1985. However, there is Blondy, a steel riveter (William Boyd) in *Skyscraper* (1928 C), whose buddy is called Slim. Male blonds on celluloid include Leslie Howard in *Gone with the Wind*, Danny KAYE and many, many soap opera hunks.

See also HAIR DYE.

Bloodnok, Major Denis (Peter SELLERS in THE GOON SHOW 1953–60 R) Most provocative of all the Goons: a coward, liar, thief, sexual deviate – and he's a *goodie*. Significantly in the radically altered climate of 1972, when *The Last Goon Show of All* was mounted for television and radio, Bloodnok's peccadillos could be spelt out in more detail, though to lesser comic effect: 'Time for your perversion, sir,' announced a disciplinarian mistress ('Gladys') with a deep bass voice.

In the scripts Spike Milligan published in the 1970s, he reveals his characters' supposed past histories. In the major's case, it seems he rejoined the army, after being cashiered, as one Florence Bloodnok. 'She' served one year in the ATS. A most successful disguise which gave 'her' cause to report a sailor for trying to interfere with 'her' in an air-raid shelter.

As his male self, the major is extraordinarily appreciative of male beauty, especially Neddy's:

'Why are you staring at me like that?'
'Because you are so beautiful.'
'For a moment I thought you were going to lie to me.'

Bloody Mary The opening number from *South Pacific* (1958 C), thrown away, and only half-heard as John Kerr flies into the island. Sailors are seen contentedly DANCING with one another, stripped to the waist and seemingly in seventh heaven. But the next song tells us that, however good it is to have your mates, 'There's Nothing Like A Dame'. This ditty includes a couple of men flexing biceps and five others showering in front of a screen daubed with the words 'Look, Don't Touch!' Later in the film, the nurses shower in front of a screen bearing the legend 'Slippery When Wet.'

The Bloomsbury Group A group of writers and poets in 1920s and 1930s: *Review* 'A Slightly Shocking Spectacle' has interviews with Quentin Bell and Michael Holroyd about Virginia WOOLF and Lytton STRACHEY (1972 T); David GARNETT, a member of the group, spoke about the interrelationships in THE SOUTH BANK SHOW (1977); *Nymphs and Shepherds, Come Away* (1985 R).

Blore, Eric (1887–1959) English-born actor who sailed through many a Hollywood film comedy as BUTLER/valet or other fussy factotum: most memorably in *The Gay Divorcee* (1934); *Top Hat* (1935); *Breakfast for Two* (1937); *It's Love I'm After* (1937); and the *Lone Wolf* series (1940–7). He more than held his own with the cream of Hollywood's SISSIES: PANGBORN, Grady Sutton and HORTON.

blow job The real thing was shown, not in Andy WARHOL's film of the same name but in his *Couch* (1964 C). This provoked a censorship row so that by the time MY HUSTLER appeared in 1965 only limp penises without engagement were on camera. Said Amos Vogel in *Film As a Subversive Art*: 'The erect penis (to the censor) is the most dangerous weapon in the known cinema.'

Blue, Rabbi Lionel (1930–) The first British rabbi to announce his happy homosexuality – and retain his popularity on radio and television: *Lighten Our Darkness* (1977 R); *Roger Royle: Good Morning, Sunday* (1986); *In Search of Holy England* (1993 T, especially part 2: 'Sunlight in My Soul').

The Blue Danube Waltz Rachel and Nasser (Shirley Anne Field and Saeed Jaffrey) glide around the floor of MY BEAUTIFUL LAUNDRETTE on its opening day. Neither realizes that Omar and his PARTNER Johnny are in the back room thrashing around semi-NAKED. The sweetly familiar Strauss music, the dancing couple and the young men in the throes of passion prove an irresistible combination to most people who saw this film – and millions did. No complaints about this scene, though plenty about Johnny's KISS earlier on. The scene marks a rare occasion: 'hetero and homo merged melodiously, and an audience invited to empathize and enjoy. A lilting landmark, perfectly concluded with Omar's uncle bursting in and interlocuting, 'What are you two BUGGERS up to?'

blue for a boy 'I've tied up the ladies' presents with pink ribbon and the gentlemen's with blue,' twitters one of the do-gooders at the old dears' party in THE ARCHERS (1985 R). This colour coding begins early in the life process: 'They put the blue blanket or the pink blanket on as soon as you come out. The programming starts as soon as you come out,' Frank Aquino on DONAHUE (1991 T). Incidentally, the Open University called one of the programmes in its *Raising Sons and Daughters* series 'Pink for a Girl, Blue for a Boy' (1986 R).

bluestocking Queen CHRISTINA 'rumoured' to be one as she likes Caldéron, Velasquez, Molière, arts and science over war and money. Once descriptive of any woman with a tongue in her head, an enquiring mind to go with it and no overwhelming interest in the opposite sex. She usually wears glasses. An exception was JO Stockton (Audrey Hepburn) in *Funny Face* (1956 C). She's a GREENWICH VILLAGE bookstore assistant into nihilism, existentialism and the like. In true anti-intellectual mass-market style Jo is transformed into a fashion plate, sees the error of her questioning ways (the philosophers are a bunch of phonies), and floats off down the Seine with bachelor photographer Dick Avery, a beautiful swan where once an ugly duckling was.

QUALITY STREET produced 'The Blue Stocking: Women in Revolt' for ABC radio in 1970.

Blunt, Anthony (1907–83) British art historian and keeper of the Queen's pictures who was revealed as a SPY in 1979. He was a semi-regular broadcaster from the 1930s until 1978: *Picasso in Rome* (1932 R); *Painting in Close-Up* 'Poussin's Story of Phocion: the Athenian statesman who fell into disregard for his outspokenness' (1978 R). Docu-

mentaries include: *The Profession of Intelligence* (How the Secret Services were undermined by the Cambridge 'moles' – BURGESS, MacLean and Blunt; Dr Christopher Andrew looks at the history of British intelligence since the Second World War; 1981 R); *Recruited by Blunt*: Ludovic Kennedy interviews Michael Straight (1983 T). Played by Ian RICHARDSON in *Blunt* (1987 T), and by James FOX in A QUESTION OF ATTRIBUTION (1991 T).

boarding school drama *See* ANOTHER COUNTRY; THE CONNOISSEUR; IF...; MAEDCHEN IN UNIFORM; OLIVIA.

Bob/Bobby/Rob/Robert Boys' names. Margaret Lockwood in *A Place of One's Own* (1944 C) tells Robert (Dennis PRICE) that she likes his name because 'it's manly'. They discuss unmanly names and come up with 'CECIL ... CLARENCE ... even CLAUDE'. And Bridget tells Robert Gunn (Denys Hawthorne) in *Isn't That a Girl's Locket?* (1988 R) that his is 'a nice name – a nice, solid name'. The irony is that his surname may be only too indicative of his true purpose.

Few gay Roberts traced (the very clean-cut, handsome, just a bit too smooth Robert (John Bolger) in PARTING GLANCES (1985 C) is one). As for Robs there's Rob in AGONY and Rob PENGELLY in WAGGONERS' WALK.

But a goodly number of Bobs: Bob in THE COLLECTION; Bob Elkin (Murray Head) in SUNDAY, BLOODY SUNDAY; Bob Purvis (Dinsdale Landen) in *Bermondsey*; taxi driver Bob in OUTRAGEOUS!; Bob Campbell (Jay Johnson) in SOAP; dosser Bob (Freddie Jones) in *The Mist People* (1982 R); Bob (Christopher Guest) in *Beyond Therapy* (1986 C); French Bob (Gérard Depardieu) in TENUE DE SOIREE/*Evening Dress* (1985 C); Falstaffian Bob Pigeon (William Richert) in MY PRIVATE IDAHO. And a lesbian Bob (Leila Bertrand) in *Troubled by the Scenery* (1986 R).

And lots of Bobbys. The name is popular across the board, in American media, meshing the sensitive and the sporty:

Bobby (Robert Taylor) in *Magnificent Obsession* (1935 C); self-centred racing driver *Bobby Deerfield* (Al Pacino 1977 C); Bobby Ogden (Peter Fonda) in *Outlaw Blues*: ex-con and songwriter (1977 C); Bobby Ewing in DALLAS (1978–91 T); Bobby Morrison, an ambitious, ego-maniacal jingles composer (Joe Brooks) in *If Ever I See You Again* (1978 C); Bobby Lee Burnett (Bruce Dern) who goes *Middle Age Crazy* (1980 C); Bobby Edge (Seth Wagerman), hero's son in *The Dream Merchants* (1980 T); Bobby (Jeff Conaway) in *Taxi* (1981–3 T); Bobby Chrystal (Matt Lattanzi), high-school graduate and virgin who falls for French teacher in *My Tutor* (1983 C); Dr Bobby Caldwell (Mark Harmon) in ST ELSEWHERE, spunky WOMANIZER, AIDS sufferer (1987–8 T); Bobby is the straight TWIN of gay Rick in HOOPERMAN (1989 T); Bobby Briggs (Dana Ashbrook), drug dealer in *Twin Peaks* (1989–91 T; 1992 C); Bobby Gold (Joe Mantegna), daring detective in *Homicide* (1991 C); V. I. Warshawski's police-chief sparring partner, Bobby Mallory (William Hootkins) in *Killing Orders* (1991 R) and *Deadlock* (1993).

Gay Bobbys: Bobby Walden (Ron Rickards) living with lover in AMSTERDAM in *Summer Wishes, Winter Dreams* (1973 C); Fanny's buddy, Bobby Moore (Roddy MCDOWALL) in FUNNY LADY ('Who's the PANSY?' asks Billy Rose (James Caan) 1975 C); Bobby Speed (Ray Vitte), the Zoo's manic disc jockey in *Thank God It's Friday*; Bobbi (Steven Shaw) in *A Perfect Couple* (1979 C); Bobby Hammer (Henry Gibson) in *Health* (1980 C); Bobby Shaw (Nigel HAVERS) in *Nancy Astor* (1982 T); Bobby Mills (Matt West) in A CHORUS LINE (1985 C); Bobby (Timothy Williams) in *Welcome Home, Bobby* (1986 T); Bobby in *Frankie and Johnnie* (1991 C). There was also Bobby (Ned Beatty) raped in *Deliverance* (1972 C).

In the UK, the name is seen in a much more frivolous light: Bobby Spenser (Bobby Howes), 'silly-ass secretary'; in *For the Love of Mike* (1932 C); Bobby (John Mills) pretending to be a school-boy in *Those Were the Days* (1934 C).

With the exceptions of Bobby (Dennis Waterman) in *Joe's Ark* (1974 T); Bobbo (Dennis Waterman) in *The Life and Loves of a She-Devil* (1986 T) and working-class hero Bobby Grant (Ricky Tomlinson) in BROOKSIDE (1982– T), British Bobbys tend towards the overtly gay or the black sheep of the family.

Bobby Bascombe (Jerome Wills) in *No Hiding Place* 'A Room with No View' (1964 T); Bobby Phillips (Rupert Webster) in IF ... (1968 C); Bobby (Roger Lloyd Pack) in THE ROADS TO FREEDOM, fat and on the skids; Bobby in ODD MAN OUT; fashion photographer Bobby (Ian Price) in GEMS (1987 T); Bobby (Andrew Woodall) in *Seasons of the Mist* (1987 R) sent away after family crisis; Bobby Buffet (John Sessions) in *Single Voices* 'Some Enchanted Evening' (1990 T); etc.

Bogarde, Sir Dirk [Derek Van Den Bogaerd] (1921–) English actor and writer, formerly Rank Organization glamour boy. First film *Esther Waters* (1947), most recent *Daddy Nostalgie/ These Foolish Things* (1990). His more memorable film roles include: Dr Simon Sparrow in the *Doctor* series; barrister Melville Farr in VICTIM (1961); bandit Anacleto in *The Singer Not the Song* (1961); Barrett in *The Servant* (1963); composer Von Aschenbach in DEATH IN VENICE (1971). First broadcast (auto-biographical talks) in the late 1940s; television début as Charles Granillo in ROPE (1947).

R: *I Play What I Like* (1955); DESERT ISLAND DISCS (1964 & 1989); *Sounds of a Lifetime* (1972); *The Stars* (1987); *The Forsyte Saga* (1990, narrator); *No Man's Land* (1992, as Spooner).

T: *Hallmark Hall of Fame*: as an English officer during the Irish Troubles; *Little Moon of Alban* (with George Peppard and Julie Harris 1959); narration for *The Epic That Never Was* (1965); *May We Borrow Your Husband?* (1986); *The Vision* (1987).

Also: *Russell Harty* (1981); OMNIBUS (1983); *Above the Title* (with Russell Harty 1986); *Dirk Bogarde: By Myself* (1992 T).

boggart The 'flitting boggart' was a creature from myth. Or was it? One, it was said (by Tom Norris on *The Countryman* 1960 R), occupied farmer George Chandler's home at Boggart Hole, Clyne near Blackley. He turned pictures to the wall, poured porridge on the floor and was generally vexatious. He did have good points though, cleaning the household's clogs and doing other useful chores. However, the children plagued him and eventually locked him up. He turned on them and drove out the entire Chandler family. Prunella Scales read the story of 'The Bogwoppits' by Ursula Moray Williams on *Jackanory* (1981 T): 'Bred in the marshland, these funny little creatures were fond of stealing from Aunt Daisy.' Martin Riley's 'Boggart' stories were also presented on *Jackanory*, in 1987; these included 'Boggart Sandwich', 'Nothing Else' and 'A Boggart Spotters' Guide'.

Bohemian/bohemian The very rich, very drunk and drug-sodden Una Marbury (Cherie Lunghi) straightway announces to Vanessa (Kate Burton) in *Ellis Island* (1984 T) when they meet in a swank sanitarium: 'Oh, I'm terribly Bohemian, my dear!' She elaborates, waving her cigarette holder and the silk butterfly-wing sleeves of her dress: 'My family haven't talked to me in years, thank God ... I love doing ghastly things. I love to take my clothes off in public.' She and Vanessa immediately begin a torrid affair which only ends when one shoots the other and then herself (Vanessa having realized that the babbling poseuse is only interested in her cheque book).

Musical director BOBBY Buffett (John Sessions) has fallen hook, line and sinker for a stage-hand: 'He's a bit like me in a way,' he muses, 'more than a touch of the Bohemian' (*Single Voices* 'Some Enchanted Evening' 1990 T).

Sherlock HOLMES (Clive Merrison) in *A Scandal in Bohemia* (1989 R) tells Watson that it takes two things to lead an unconventional life: 'Intelligence ... and bravery.'

Bohemianism is visible in any movie or television show made between 1920 and 1970 set in either PARIS, France, or GREENWICH VILLAGE, New York. BEARDS, long HAIR (men), short hair (women), striped or holed sweaters (men), suits (women), cigarette smoke, exaggerated posturing, effeminacy, mannishness, dominating AMAZONS with zombie-like girlfriends, pseudo-intellectual talk about Art, Music and Poetry. This is local colour, no real threat to the established order, so misguided and ridiculous does it appear.

Daniel FARSON talked about Bohemian London with some of the residents in *Bookshelf* (1987 R).

boiler suit Camille (Pam Scotcher) thinks that using the term 'FRIEND' requires a new sexual direction. 'We'll have to get a boiler suit,' she asserts. But Nicole (Primi Townsend) isn't having any: 'Oh, I'm not going *that* way' (*World's End* 1981 T).

Bolan, Marc [Mark Feld] (1947–77) British pop singer of bi-gender leanings. Some television: *The Old Grey Whistle Test*; TOP OF THE POPS; dueting with Cilla Black on her show (1972). One film: *Blame It on the Boogie* (1977).

Bolero *See* RAVEL'S BOLERO.

bona Part of POLARI, as in the Bona Guest House (ROUND THE HORNE), meaning 'good'.

bonking A dear little nursery expression that was yuppified and corrupted in the 1980s to suggest a very popular activity. After PORTRAIT OF A MARRIAGE, Vita and Violet were – non-sexistly but rather vulgarly – referred to as a couple of 'well-born bonkers' (Mark Steyn, *Evening Standard*, 24.4.91). A character in 'ALLO, 'ALLO was called Mimi La Bonk.

A Book at Bedtime (UK 1948– R) A British institution: a novel, autobiography or travel book read each night from Monday to Friday for a quarter of an hour on BBC Radio 4. First gay character noted was the villain in John Buchan's *Greenmantle* (1949). Since then, only a few relevant bedtime stories: Josephine Tey's *Brat Farrar* (read by David Spenser 1965); Morris West's *The Devil's Advocate* (1972); Radclyffe HALL's *The Well of Loneliness* (Judy Parfitt 1974); Christopher ISHERWOOD's *Mr Norris Changes Trains* (Robert Powell 1979); Jocelyn Brooke's autobiographical *The Orchid Trilogy* (David MARCH 1981); Carson MCCULLERS' *The Member of the Wedding* (Gayle Hunnicutt 1983); Georges Simenon's *Stranger in the House* (Jim Norton 1983); Patricia HIGHSMITH's *The Talented Mr Ripley* (Tom Hunsinger 1983; previously read 1963); D. H. LAWRENCE's 'The Fox' (Anna MASSEY 1984); John BOWEN's *The McGuffin* (Hugh Dickson 1985); Francis KING's *Voices in an Empty Room* (Alex Shearer 1985); Augustus Hare's *The Story of My Life* (1987); Joseph Conrad's *Victory* (John Franklyn-Robbins 1987); David COOK's *Missing Persons* (Patricia Routledge 1987); Gilbert Adair's *Love and Death on Long Island* (John Carlisle 1991); Patricia Highsmith's *Carol* (1991).

A book of verses underneath the bough,/a jug of wine, a loaf of bread – and thou/beside me singing in the wilderness Audacious, junior radical Richard (Mickey Rooney) quoting from the Rubaiyat in *Summer Holiday* (1948 C). It's his favourite book (along with Carlyle's *The French Revolution*, Swinburne's poems and THE BALLAD OF READING GAOL – 'one of the greatest poems ever written.'). What's the betting that the lad knew that Omar Khayyam wrote those words to a young man? And did MGM studio head Louis B. Mayer realize? Certainly Richard's mum frowns and mutters: 'I don't think that's the kind of reading for a young boy.'

booksellers Harold Doe (Norman Bird) runs an antiquarian bookshop off St Martin's Lane in London which, unbeknownst to him, is the contact point for blackmailed gay men in VICTIM; John TREGORRAN runs one for a time in Borchester in THE ARCHERS; Miss Cox (Susan Littler) and Miss Baker (Gay Wilde) indulge in some afternoon lovemaking in the grass where they are discovered – but not disturbed – by Alan BATES in *A Voyage Round My Father* (1982 T); Alan Cunningham (John Bull) gives fresh hope to the ballet dancer (Michael Maloney) who can no longer practise his craft because of an accident in *A New Step Every Day* (1980 R); RUSSELL is the main man in the life of Sarah in AFTER HENRY (1988–92 T): now a widow, she enjoys helping him and drawing upon his comfortable strength and lack of sexual expectations.

books The power of literature to change or retard perception is evinced by the efforts to suppress books like THE WELL OF LONELINESS and to exalt every word of THE BIBLE (itself the victim of CENSORSHIP in many countries). LIANNA wants to read about other lesbians and she is found with *The Well of Loneliness*: 'Sounds like a riot,' grunts the local lecher.

Mary Hilton (Diana Dors) finds a copy of HOUSMAN's A SHROPSHIRE LAD in her pianist/gigolo lover's flat in *Yield to the Night* (1956). The weak pretty boy (Michael Craig) explains: 'I had that when I was 15. I read all sorts of things when I was young' (WILDE? PROUST? GIDE? RIMBAUD? COCTEAU?). The same poem was also dear to mother's boy Willie Morrison (Timmy Everett) in *Ben Casey* 'A Cardinal Act of Mercy' (1963 T). Abused teenager *Sylvia* (Carroll Baker 1965 C) is turned onto Jane Austen by lesbian LIBRARIAN Viveca Lindfors and proceeds to 'give her body, but keep her mind for literature'. Marilyn MONROE (Catherine Hicks) is encouraged to explore the world's literature by her acting coach, friend and would-be lover, Natasha Lytess in *Marilyn: The Untold Story* (1980 T; Viveca Lindfors recommending a protegée's reading once again).

The temporarily besotted Lizzie is told by idol Miss Alliott (Kika Markham) that she must read *Wuthering Heights*: 'As a study of disintegration it's quite haunting ... In 20 years' time you may

thank me for lending it to you' (ALL FOR
LOVE 'Miss A. and Miss M.' 1983 T).
Pia Zadora (as Gerry in *The Lonely Lady*
1983 C) reads Gertrude STEIN, Dorothy
Parker and Hemingway as a schoolgirl;
she wins a writing prize, but how she
suffers for her art: exploited, raped, an
abortion, a nervous breakdown, seduction in a jacuzzi by a producer's wife.
Colin Fitzroy Langham Browne in
Figure with Meat (1991 R) muses: 'Melville, Flaubert, Brontë – sometimes I
pretend I'm one of the Brontë sisters –
the fourth one.'

Bookshelf (UK 1978– R) Sturdy
interviews with authors of note or
special programmes on those deceased,
such as L. P. HARTLEY. Subjects have
included: Angus WILSON (revealing how
he was blackmailed, 1984); Rosamond
LEHMANN (a very rare interview, 1982);
Mary RENAULT ('Books About Greece'
1980); Judith Krantz revealing how she
wrote the lesbian scene in *Scruples*:
'I read *The Joy of Lesbian Sex* and
split myself in two and chose the bits
that appealed to me. And I thought,
there's a lot to be said for being a
lesbian' ('Women's Romantic Fiction'
1983).

Both Sides Now Liberating Joni Mitchell song of 1972, sung that year by
Doris DAY with Perry Como (T); used
over the credits of SWITCH (1991 C)
encapsulating the hero/heroine's
insights into the male and the female:
'I've looked at life from both sides now.'

boutique/assistants/owners *See* FASH-
ION BOUTIQUE ASSISTANTS/OWNERS.

Bowie, David [David Jones] (1947–)
Chameleonic English singer/actor, who
helped to make bisexuality fashionable if
not acceptable, after 'confessing' in a
1976 *Playboy* interview. The subject of
OMNIBUS 'Cracked Actor' (1974 T).
Andy Peebles presented Bowie's BBC
recordings between 1967 and 1972 in
Bowie at the Beeb (1987 R). His Ziggy
Stardust persona was documented in

Z.S. and the Spiders from Mars, released
in 1982, a record of his 1973 'farewell'
concert.

As actor (giving a new meaning to the
word 'wooden'): *The Man Who Fell to
Earth* (as alien, 1976 C); *Just a Gigolo*
(1978 C); *Baal* (as semi-demonic,
bisexual adventurer, 1982 T); *Merry
Christmas, Mr Lawrence* (as British prisoner of war, 1982); *Yellowbeard* (cameo
as 'BUM BOY', 1983 C); THE HUNGER (as
dying vampire, 1983 C); *Absolute Beginners* (as smart-talking advertising man
David Bowie Vendice Partners, 1986
C); *Labyrinth* (as King of the Goblins,
1986 C); FBI agent Phillip Jeffries, seen
very briefly in *Twin Peaks: Fire Walk with
Me* (1992 C); etc.

bow tie 'My daddy wore a bow tie ...
because a famous statesman wore one
when he was a boy. A good reason for
using a bow tie in that it lasts four times
as long as an ordinary tie. All ordinary
ties can only be tied in one place. I can
tie this one either side of each end,'
Robin Day revealing all to a young boy
on *Jim'll Fix It* (1979 T) and again on
Aspel and Company (1989 T).
   LITTLE CAESAR (Edward G. Robinson
1930 C) struts around in bow tie and
spotted shirt telling his favourite, Joe:
'Dancin ... women ... where do they
get yer?' He was something of an exception. Bow ties were generally worn by
English gents or gentrified Americans,
often with a broad wink to the louche
and decadent: Rudolph (Ronald Colman), self-effacing Englishman with a
goatee and a droopy velvet tie who
changes places with a future king in *The
Prisoner of Zenda* (1937 C); Ronnie
Marsh (Zachary Scott), in love with
himself in *Danger Signal* (1945 C);
mean, frequently deranged Dix Steel
(Humphrey Bogart) in *In A Lonely Place*
(1950 C); feminist male Kip Kipple
(David Wayne) in ADAM'S RIB (1949 C);
fussy bachelor Cary GRANT in *Dream
Wife* (1952 C); Hamilton Burger who
wears one occasionally in 1959 episodes
of PERRY MASON 'The Case of the Garrulous Gambler', 'The Spurious Sister'
and 'The Blushing Pearls' (then it was

back to severe long-form ties); Barnett Finchley (Richard HAYDN) in THE TWILIGHT ZONE 'A Thing About Machines' (1960 T); cat-like Orson Bean as Mr Bevis (THE TWILIGHT ZONE 1960); Pee-Wee HERMAN; Geoff Hatfield (Geoffrey BAYLDON) in *All Creatures Great and Small* 'And Sheep May Safely Graze' (1989 T); Frank, retired policeman in *A Country Practice* (1992 T) with pretty pink sleeveless cardy: 'everyone wears pink these days – it's not as though it's POOFY any more.'

Bowlly, Al (*c* 1900–41) Massively popular 'English' (Lebanese) crooner of the 1930s; killed by direct hit during the London Blitz. Renewed interest after his voice heard in *Pennies from Heaven* (1978 T). Radio biographies: *Al Bowlly: What Will the Dance Do?* (1987); *They Called Me Al* (6 parts 1991, with much emphasis on his sexual exploits: he was 'a naughty boy'); rare film footage of him in *Turns* (1984 T). He can be heard singing 'This Must Be Heaven' over the Tom Berenger/Mimi Rogers tie-buying scene in *Someone to Watch Over Me* (1987 C), and 'GUILTY' in COMRADES IN ARMS (1990 C/T) as one enlisted man expresses his feelings for another. The Al Bowlly Club is one of Sydney's most exclusive gay social groups, with picnics on Anzac Day and on the Wednesday before Christmas.

Boy George [George O'Dowd] (1961–) English pop singer and sometime androgyne. Painstakingly dressed and made-up to defy gender and ethnicity, George O'Dowd created an almost doll-like persona in the 1980s that entranced audiences the world over. From his first television appearance in 1981 (*The Tube*) he was hardly off the screen, out of the newspapers or the record charts with or without his band, Culture Club. His image, if not what lay behind it, was easily mocked whether as a puppet reading the news with 'Princess Margaret' ('over made-up tart!' she snorts) and being described as a funny little creature who swings both ways by 'Tracey Ullman' in *Spitting Image* (1983 T); or

roasted by Ronnie Corbett on *The Two Ronnies* the same year.

In *The Grumbleweeds Christmas Show* (1984 T) George is played as the campest of tent rows, singing and flapping his wrists alongside impersonations of Elvis, Elton JOHN, Lennon and Rod Stewart. The young brother of *Scully* (1984 T) wants to be a model when he grows up. To this end he traipses around the house in George style, flowing garments and slap. This is fiercely revealed as just a PHASE because, in the last episode, the lad rips off his Boyish garb in a whirlwind of disgust, prior to becoming a real (little) man.

Although he fenced around the question, Boy George had become synonymous with being 'a POOF'. The totally closeted married Dave in MORE LIVES THAN ONE (1984 T) makes it clear to his friend Colin (Myles Hoyle) who's alarmed Dave might be coming out: 'I'm not Boy George. I'm not selling my personality. I'm just an ordinary man ... "With a personality defect" as they say in the Civil Service.' The image was so striking that a Boy George clone is one of the rejected applicants to become a member of the band in *The Commitments* (1991 C) – given equal time (10 seconds) and equal ridicule along with punk rockers and heavy metalists.

To the general public, at least up to George's conviction for drug possession in 1986, he was talented, sweet and non-threateningly different. The Greek widow (Billie Whitelaw) insists that the sorely tried removal men (led by Warren Mitchell) sing 'a little Boy George' as they drive off to her new home, another link in *The Chain* (1985 C).

Surviving personal and professional troubles in the mid-1980s, George has settled into being a less famous but still popular singer, putting across a spiritual message and campaigning against HOMOPHOBIA ('Clause 28') and AIDS. Early in 1993, George was one of the contributors to PINKPOP, an hour-long look at 'the gay music scene' on BBC Radio 1. He talked about the fencing over his sexuality that was deemed necessary by 'the people around' him during Culture Club's heyday (1982–5), as well as by himself and the member of the band he was having an affair with.

One thing is certain: he will never again be asked to do guest spots on US TV shows like *The A Team* 'Cowboy George' (1986).

C: Sang title track for *The Crying Game* (1992 C).

T: TOP OF THE POPS (1982–); *The Tube* (1982); *Wogan* (1983); SOUTH OF WATFORD 'Gender Benders' (1984) – are Boy George and Marilyn setting a trend or are they reflecting what's going on in the street?; *Top of the Pops Christmas Special* (1984); *Culture Club in Concert* (1984); *The Other Side of the Tracks* (with Paul GAMBACCINI 1985); *The British Connection* (including Clive Barnes saying that Americans liked Boy George because he conformed to their stereotyped views of the English, 1985); *The Montreux Rock Festival* (1987); *Wogan* (with Sue Lawley 1988); *Aspel and Company* (1991); *Pebble Mill* ('flamboyant star talks about the changes in his life and work' 1992).

The Boy Girl (US 1917 C) Jack Channing (Violet Mersereau) raised as a boy by her race-horse breeding dad, King Channing (Charles Mason) and with resulting bad manners and appalling dress sense. After dad's death, 'Jack' is taken in hand by SPINSTER aunts AGATHA and Martha, becomes a super-stenographer who foils the office snoop, saves the firm from bankruptcy, marries boss' son and has a daughter whom she saves from a shameful fate.

W: John C. Brownell; D: Edwin Stevens; *c* 60 mins.

('The Boy-Girl' was the accurate translation of the 1957 French film *La Garconne*, but it was given the title 'THE BACHELOR GIRL' for its British release.)

boyhood friends The correlation of deep intimacy and innocence suggested by boys knowing each other since they were on the potty avoids a lot of awkward questions about their abiding and often female-free time-sharing: *The Likely Lads* and THE GOODIES are two

examples. In a number of Hollywood movies of the late 1950s, this idea was extended beyond emotional frisson to include the political-yoking of a manly Hollywood star playing Gentile or Jew with an actor embodying a – then – unacceptable social or religious group. Look upon Rock HUDSON and Sidney Poitier in *Something of Value* (1957) and Charlton Heston and Stephen Boyd in BEN-HUR (1959) and, yet again, upon Paul Newman and John Derek in EXODUS (1960).

The degree of bodily touching and intense looking varies, but one element is constant: Poitier's Mau Mau terrorist, Boyd's Roman imperialist and Derek's Arab defender all meet horrible deaths: respectively, impalement in a pit; crushing and skin-flaying under chariot wheels; torture, branding and hanging. This allows their life-long friend/enemy to bid them farewell in extravagant terms; in Poitier's case, Hudson becomes the parent of his baby. Thus did homoemotionalism, homoeroticism and 'pretend FAMILIES' flit past prying eyes and meddling lips. A man may love a man he loved as a baby, but one of them must die – grotesquely and in a long-drawn-out manner – for the privilege, releasing the survivor for true love with a woman.

Even the words 'I LOVE YOU' can be used between men without questions being asked. As when Axel Foley's childhood friend Mickey (James Russo) says 'I love you' in *Beverly Hills Cop* (1984 C) . This is the reason Foley (Eddie Murphy) didn't betray him to the cops. Seconds later Mickey is dead. Once is quite enough, even from a childhood friend. Marty (Jesse Birdsall) wants Carl (Iain Glen) to say the words in *The Fear* (1988 T); to say them not just as a reflex but to mean them and express them physically beyond a kiss. Carl refuses and Marty is soon killed.

'How come you didn't tell me?'
'It's because I love you, man.'

In Britain, the boarding-school friendship/love affair has been used to underpin the adult unease of the male protagonists in *Bright Boy* (1973), *Death of an Echo* (1980 R), *The Spectre* (1983 R) and *A Man Alone* (1986) – to name four out of a score.

boy players Few of SHAKESPEARE's characters are women with physical femininity with the one exception of Cleopatra. This is very probably because the roles were all created by teenage boys: Portia by James Bryston; Lady Macbeth by Robert Goffe; Rosalind by Joseph Taylor; Juliet by Richard Robinson; Desdemona by Nathaniel Field. In the 20th century, with the exception of a handful of all-male productions of plays such as AS YOU LIKE IT, no attempt has been made to translate the qualities inherent in a teenage boy playing a young woman opposite a male actor into modern interpretations of the Shakespeare canon. The androgyny of Shakespeare's women is generally ignored, except in QUALITY STREET's 'Work for Boy Players' (written and presented by Alexander Archdale, Aust 1965 R); and Gwen FFRANGCON-DAVIES at 97 talking to her friend, Nigel Hawthorne 'about Shakespeare's ladies (some of them gentlemen – and all of them boys)' in *Still a Juliet* (1988 R).

A production of *Romeo and Juliet* with same-sex lovers was briefly shown in *Public School* (1980 T). Charles HAWTREY and George Cole played boy players in respectively *Will Shakespeare* on radio (1931) and Olivier's film of *Henry V* (1944, in the final scene, substituting for Renée Asherson as the Princess of France).

The following conversation between Tony Davenport (Gareth Johnson) and his friend Browne in CAUSE CELEBRE, although the lines were cut from the 1975 radio production:

'... to be 17 is hell. It wasn't always like that. Romeo was only 17.'
'And Juliet 13 and a ripe mess they made of things.'
'But nobody in Shakespeare's time thought they were too young, did they? If they ever played it the way it was written they'd burn the theatre down.'

a boy's best friend is his mother Popularized in song by Nellie Wallace after the First World War; mentioned by Norman BATES before he murders his guest at the motel in *Psycho* (1960 C); and it has provided the title for a number of television and radio plays.

Mrs McRobb (Sheila Law) emphasizes the truism in *A Boy's Best Friend* (1961 R) in Aberdonian dialect: 'A boy's best friend's his mither, Andy, and dinna forget it.' Her son retaliates: 'That may be, Ma, but when a man's grown up he's got ta choose.' This sends Ma into a screaming fit: 'Choose, you say? Choose ... *choose*? 'Atween *her* and me?''

A variation comes from Jane Fonda in *Stanley and Iris* (1989 C): 'A girl's best friend is her momma,' she says wistfully to her teenage daughter. 'Least, that's what it says on the greeting cards.'

The Boys In The Backroom The song that Frenchy (Marlene DIETRICH) sings in *Destry Rides Again* (1939 C). The backrooms of hotels, bars and pubs could be used for all manner of activities: after-hours drinking, illegal gambling, orgies and wife auctioning. From the 1970s onwards, gay men found comfort, relief or alienation in darkened backrooms in many parts of the world.

the boys in the band Mart CROWLEY took a line spoken by James Mason in *A Star Is Born* (1954 C) for the title of his 1968 play about one night of perdition and purgatory which became the unveiling of 'gay life' for the mass public (or the theatre-going part of it). Such was the impact that its title remains meaningful post-gay liberation and through AIDS. In a 1986 episode of HOTEL ('Passports') a wife rounds on the husband who has just informed her he is seropositive: 'You have a son. What are you going to tell him? That his father's a character from *The Boys in the Band*?'

The Boys in the Band (US 1970 C) A night of painful revelation at Harold's BIRTHDAY PARTY, catalysed by the presence of a lone heterosexual (or is he?).

W: Mart CROWLEY from his play; P: Crowley and Kenneth Utt; D: William Friedkin; 120 mins.

Gay men seen as a group for the first time in popular entertainment. One is CAMP (Cliff Gorman as EMORY); one is sweet and ineffectual (Frederick Coombs as Donald); one is BLACK (Reuben Greene as Bernard); one is JEWISH and caustic (Leonard Frey as Harold); one (the host) is CATHOLIC, nasty and self-hating (Kenneth Nelson as Michael). Then there's a couple: married Hank (Laurence Luckinbill) who lives in some kind of harmony with PROMISCUOUS Larry (Keith Prentice). There's a lot of banter, tantrums and the climactic 'Truth Game' where each of the 'boys' has to declare who he really loves. Effective, funny, uncomfortable. A classic of its kind.

boys' names for girls America seems to have had a lively tradition of using boys' names for girls and women. This used to be reflected in Hollywood productions: Katharine HEPBURN (who was the screen's first JO March) was SIDNEY in her début film *A Bill of Divorcement* (1932); Bette DAVIS was Stanley (neurotically selfish) and Olivia De Havilland her sister, Roy (sweetly enduring) in *In This Our Life* (1942); the *Seven Sweethearts* were the Van Maaster sisters: Billie (Kathryn Grayson), Regina (Marsha Hunt), Albert (Peggy Moran), Billie Victor (Cecilia Parker), Peter (Dorothy Morris), George (Frances Rafferty) and Cornelius (Frances Raeburn). Irene Dunne played a spirited young woman called Ray Schmidt in *Back Street* (1932); Margaret Sullavan was in the wartime remake, still as Ray – but Ray *Smith*. As sexual corseting loosened on the screen, naming tightened up: in the second (1961) remake with Susan Hayward, Ray becoming the more feminine 'Rae'.

But this was an exception. American women are far less restricted: Kim, Cyd, Jamie Lee and Jodie can become stars, with no adverse comment whatsoever. Screen TOMBOYS, of course, are expected to adopt BUTCH names: Anne

Baxter's Mike in *Yellow Sky* (1948 C), Jane Russell's revenge-seeking ditto in *Son of Paleface* (1952 C). Even a regular gal like Mara Corday in *Tarantula* (1955 C) can airily command the hero to 'call me Steve'. Steve was also the name of PAUL TEMPLE's wife (played on radio throughout the 1940s, 1950s and 1960s by the ageless Marjorie Westbury, in reality a plump, unpretentious woman who lived with her mother). On the air Steve was elegant, resourceful, sophisticated but always a lady.

The most insistent voice of name-reversal was Georgina KIRRIN (Michelle Gallagher) in THE FAMOUS FIVE. Her cousins thought her a bit 'peculiar' at first but soon accepted her tough demeanour, her fierce determination to be involved in every nocturnal prowl, and her need to be called 'George'. Biographers of her creator Enid Blyton say that the author was herself a rebel against all things feminine as a girl.

An adjunct of the 'male' female name is the use of initials, most famously by V. I. Warshawski (Kathleen Turner in the film and in *Killing Orders* 1991 R: 'I hate being called Victoria. My friends call me V. I.') and C. J. LAMB (Cara Jean) in L.A. LAW.

Amid the hundreds of female Adrians, Berties, Billies, Charlies, Mitches, Mickys, Mikes, Mattys, Frankies, Freddies, Leslies, Maxes, Robins and Robyns, Ronnies, Sammys, Sidneys, Sydneys, Teddys, Terrys and Terries, Theos, Tommys, Tonis and Tonys there are a few other names to which such characteristics adhere. Firstly, there are the characters named after American states, rivers and cities. These include: Alabama (Bette DAVIS) in *Parachute Jumper* (1933 C); Carol 'Kansas' Rickman (Ella Raines) in *Phantom Lady* (1944 C); Colorado Carson (Virginia Mayo) in *Colorado Territory* (1949 C); Denver (Joanne Dru) in *Wagon Master* (1950 C): she's with a medicine show and she *drinks*, 'Don't call me ma'am!' she tells Ben Johnson, but ends the picture all in white next to her man, as the Sons of the Pioneers croon 'a new little gal in the promised land'; Dallas

(Elsa Martinelli) in *Hatari!* (1962 C); Montana Wildhack (Valerie Perrine) in *Slaughterhouse 5* (1972 C); Montana Moorehead (Cathy Moriaty) who plays Nurse Nan, soap-opera star in *Soapdish* (1991 C).

The second category is made up of two surnames banged together to create independently minded women who may or may not be dangerous: woman of mystery Corey Scott (Julie London) in *The Third Voice* (1960 C); Morgan Wainwright (Joanna Cassidy), helicopter pilot in *240-Robert* (1979–80 T); Finn Gallagher (Rosie Rowell) in SOUTH OF THE BORDER (1989–90 T); Murphy Brown (Candice Bergen 1989–T), TV newsperson and daughter of Avery (Colleen Dewhurst): 'I'm a woman, I'm Murphy Brown.'

See also GIRLS' NAMES FOR BOYS.

bracelets A novelist with a penchant for the perverse, Carl Sarler (Erich von Stroheim) wears one in *As You Desire Me* (1932), as does Dick Powell in *Forty-second Street* (1933 C); rugged Artie Green (Jack Webb), wearing a bracelet, greets William Holden in *Sunset Boulevard* (1950 C) a little too effusively: 'Where have you been hiding that *gorgeous* face?'; rolling stone Michel (Jean-Paul Belmondo) in *Breathless/A Bout de Souffle* (1959 C) wears one, and a charm with two medallions; Rod SERLING's is visible in at least two of his introductions to THE TWILIGHT ZONE ('Nick of Time' 1960 and 'The Silence' 1961); KEPT MAN Jean-Louis Trintignant in *The Sleeping Car Murder* (1965 C); Charlie (Rex Harrison) in combination with his mascara and AFTER SHAVE in STAIRCASE; Elaine Stritch's attacker is identified only by a hand and a braceleted wrist for most of *Dial M for Murder* 'If You Knew Susie' (1974 T); a man throws Eric's initialled bracelet into Daniel's strawberries and cream as he dines with his friends in *Pardon, Mon Affaire* (1977 C); Robert (Hanno Proschi) in QUERELLE; etc.

Lady **Bracknell** Social dragon in THE IMPORTANCE OF BEING EARNEST, interviewing Jack WORTHING and not liking one little bit what he has to tell her about his origins. A glorious character whose forbidding presence allows actors to run the full gamut of deafening rests and pauses, dramatically dripping intakes of breath, and prohibitory silences. Played by women as different as Margaret Rutherford (1946 T), Coral Browne (1974 T), Joan Plowright (1988 T), Ruth Cracknell (Aust 1992 T) and the incomparable Edith Evans (1952 C).

breasts Parts of the western world have long had an obsession with the female mammary glands. Less so the male version, though Victor Mature, Arnold Schwarzenegger, Sylvester Stallone and others have purposely developed their chests to look alluring as well as colossal. Why do males have nipples on their breasts? *The Living World*'s Michael Clegg and Malcolm Coe attempted to answer this – and other wildlife teasers – in 1987 (R).

breeches parts Handel's Xerxes, Richard Strauss' Octavian, Mozart's Cherubino ... male roles played by female singers, an unchallenged tradition. It enabled Ken Russell to provide the first graphic depiction of 'lesbian lust' on British television, in the biography of Richard Strauss, *Dance of the Seven Veils* (1970) with Anna Sharkey as Octavian. As Ann Murray said, when interviewed on Australian National radio in 1989 about playing this 'breeches part': 'The opera starts in the bedroom and the overture graphically depicts what's going on, so you just have to get on and do it. Proper physical contact is absolutely necessary, dramatically.'

Bregonzi, Alec (1930–) English actor with lugubrious features and fussy, inquisitive air.

R: *Sam and Janet* (with David Kossoff and Joan Sims 1966); Dannie Derwent in *Rumpole and the Show Folk* (1987).

T: various roles in HANCOCK'S HALF HOUR and *Hancock* (1958–61); '2nd Young Man' at wedding reception in *You're a Long Time Dead* (1958); Sir

Arthur St John in *The Queen's Champion* (1959); 'other parts' in *The Days of Vengeance: A Bunch of Red Roses* (1960 T); *Citizen James* (1961); Captain Sergei Nikolai (Russian soldier) in *Up a Gum Tree* (by William Douglas-Home 1962); as Bill (opposite Keith Rawlings as Bert) in *Bonehead* (1962); *Frankie* HOWERD (1964); *Holiday with Strings* (Ray Galton and Alan Simpson 1975); Ken in *One of the Smart Set in a Smart Setting* (1978); steward in *The Two Ronnies* (1987); Clint Bent in *The Kenny Everett Show* (1986); Enchilada in *Pyrates* (1986); guest in *Tales of the Unexpected* 'The Boy Who Talked with Animals' (1986); waiter in *Filthy Rich and Catflap* (1987); Mr Peniket in *The Children of Dynmouth* (1987); advert for the Victoria and Albert Museum with Brian Sewell in 1989; head waiter in *Queen of Hearts* (1991 C/T).

Read extracts from literature with gay themes at the West London Group for Homosexual Equality in 1990.

Bressan, Arthur J. (1943–87) Strikingly honest American independent film director of gay subjects, notably *Abuse* and BUDDIES.

C: *Coming Out* (1972); *Passing Strangers* (1974); *Gay USA* (1977); *Forbidden Letters* (1979); *Abuse* (1983); *Daddy Dearest* (1984?); *Buddies* (1985).

T: *Thank You, Mr President* (*c* 1985).

bridegroom Ezra Fitton unable to go on his honeymoon without his mate Billy Stringfellow in HONEYMOON POSTPONED (1961 T)/THE FAMILY WAY (1966 C)/*All In Good Time* (1976 R); Jodie about to be jilted by Carol is propositioned by a former boyfriend (who tried to force him into a sex change operation before marrying a woman for the sake of his career) in SOAP (1978 T); Cliff (Paul Regina) pulling out of matrimony after answering nature's call in the first episode of BROTHERS (1984 T).

The Bride of Frankenstein (US 1935 C) Probably the greatest and grandest guignol of all time, thanks to riproaring direction and glorious performances

from Boris Karloff, Elsa Lanchester (bride) and Ernest THESIGER (co-creator).

W: John L. Balderston and William Hurlbut; P: Carl Laemmle Jr; D: James WHALE; 80 mins.

Brideshead Revisited (UK 1981 T) No expense spared (5 million pounds), very leisurely adaptation of Evelyn WAUGH's novel dealing, in the words of Edwin Muir, 'with odd Catholics who have strayed in all sorts of queer or unusual directions'. The romantic friendship between Charles (Jeremy Irons) and the Catholic aristocrat Sebastian FLYTE (Anthony Andrews) runs like a golden thread, sometimes tarnished, sometimes frayed, but never quite breaking through the stately procession of vaguely mournful people Charles encounters, with the exception of the deliciously ripe Anthony BLANCHE. The opening two episodes are justly famous for their luxuriant evocation of OXFORD and Venice during a seemingly endless between-the-wars summer. What follows is over-refined and dramatically limp in comparison.

W: John Mortimer; P: Derek GRANGER; D: Michael Lindsay-Hogg and Charles Sturridge; Granada; 13 episodes; 50 mins each.

A 1956 radio version with Robert EDDISON as Sebastian managed to condense the whole saga into under 2 hours.

Brief Encounter (UK 1946 C) An extramarital dalliance in all its achingly brave and honourable middle classness.

W: Noel COWARD from play *Still Life*; P: Anthony Havelock-Allen and Ronald Neame; D: David Lean; 86 mins.

Based on Noel COWARD's friendship with Gertie Lawrence, the dialogue abounds with decency and self-sacrifice: 'Self-respect matters ... and decency ... Do you feel guilty? ... Are you angry? ... Am I boring you? ... Will you forgive me?' At the previews in Rochester, a dock worker yelled, 'Ain't he ever goin' to 'ave it orf wiv 'er?'

Alexander Walker wrote in *Hollywood,*

England (1974): ' ... the film offered absolution for folk of Laura or Alec's age, in or out of uniform, who had "let their standards drop" and wanted to repent before peace compelled a return to respectability.'

The play was produced for radio on a regular basis from 1947 onwards, with the character of Alec's friend Stephen LYNN (Valentine DYALL in the film) shorn of lines in an entirely arbitrary manner over the decades. In the 1985 version (with Cheryl Campbell exemplary as Laura) the only hint of Stephen's jealousy is the heavily underlined 'my dear'.

briefs After years of great floppy things, men can wear black briefs every bit as skimpy and come-attable as women's. Yet men's underpants which closely resemble women's are used sparingly on the screen. One of the briefest pairs, in black, was surprisingly worn by the retiring Paul Currie (William Armstrong) in GEMS (1985 T). Tom Hanks donned them in *Big* and so did Robert Powell in *The Jigsaw Man* (1984 C) and Gérard Depardieu in TENUE DE SOIREE/ EVENING DRESS. *See also* JOCKEY SHORTS.

Brighton Sussex town with a long gay and lesbian history, only glancingly portrayed on television and radio: Andy Kershaw visits a club there in *As It Happens* (1991 T).

British Broadcasting Corporation *See* BBC.

The British Empire Driven, neurotic Empire builders include: Barttelot (Barry Foster) and Bonny (Donald Gee) in *The Rear Column* (1980 T); MERRICK in THE JEWEL IN THE CROWN; General GORDON. Histories include: *The British Seafarer* (1979 R); *The British Empire* (1985 R including Lord KITCHENER (Norman Jones)); Cecil Rhodes (William Eedle in 'Omdurman 1899 – Vereeniging 1902').

Britten, Lord Benjamin (1913–76) English composer of songs, documentary film music, operas and musical

epics such as *War Requiem*. Much of his output was written for his lover Peter PEARS.

C: 18 documentary scores, including *Night Mail* and the feature *Love from a Stranger* (1937); his setting of English folk song 'O Waly Waly' used at the end of *Distant Voices, Still Lives* (1988 C).

R: music for THE ASCENT OF F6 (1937) and *The Dark Tower* (1946); broadcasts of his operas (from PETER GRIMES in 1946 to *Death in Venice*) and orchestral/ choral works including *War Requiem* (1964); *Benjamin Britten and Peter Grimes* (1945); *In Conversation* (1960 with the Earl of Harewood); *Britten at Fifty* (1963); *Benjamin Britten: The Early Years* (1980); *Britten in America* (1988 with Andrew Branch as Britten); *Night Waves* (1992). The RICHARD SHEWIN plays (1953–9) by Henry Reed supposedly contained jabs at Britten and Pears, probably in the character of Dame Hilda TABLET.

T: productions of *Peter Grimes* (US 1952); BILLY BUDD (1966); *The Turn of the Screw; Owen Wingrave* (written for television 1971); *War Requiem* (1989 directed by Derek JARMAN). MONITOR 'Benjamin Britten: Portrait of a Composer' (1958 directed by John SCHLESINGER); *People Today*: a gallery of people in close-up (1960); *Music 625*: Benjamin Britten conducts 'Nocturne' with Peter Pears (1965); *Benjamin Britten and His Festival* (1967); OMNIBUS 'Blow the Wind Southerly' (1968 about Kathleen Ferrier); THE SOUTH BANK SHOW 'A Time There Was ...'(1980); OMNIBUS *at the Proms*: the Britten scholar Donald Mitchell talks to Jane Glover about the composer's last years (1987); *Without Walls* 'J'Accuse' (1991 with Tom Sutcliffe arguing that the composer's life and music are inseparable).

A *cordon sanitaire* of silence or obfuscation was set up around Britten by himself, Peter Pears, friends and scholars. Only very recently has a new, more rounded picture of the man begun to appear. Joanna Richardson voiced the frustration that was always present in the television and radio portraits of Britten previously constructed: 'Here, in polite conversation with the Earl of Harewood, was a modest gentlemanly character who told us surprisingly little about himself. We at least know he had been influenced by AUDEN and RIMBAUD ... [But] what was Mr Britten really like? We had no clear impression of the composer as a human being. We had spent the time on cocktail party formalities; we had not got down to essentials and we could not have picked Mr Britten out in a crowd' (*Listener*, 23.6.60.) It took 32 years for a more truthful picture of the Britten–Pears relationship to emerge, via a biography which was quoted extensively during BBC Radio 3's *A Britten Evening*.

Bronowski, Dr Jacob (1902–76) Philosopher and historian who pioneered the discussion of homosexuality on radio in his 1950 play THE FACE OF VIOLENCE and in BEHIND THE NEWS (1953). His most famous contributions were his appearances on *The Brains Trust* (R/T) during the 1950s and his ambitious series THE ASCENT OF MAN (1974–5). His personal history and intellectual life are discussed in *Life and Legacy* (1984 T).

Bronski Beat Jimi SOMERVILLE, Steve Bronski and Larry Steinbeck: probably the first openly gay group in Britain, possibly the world. They had a number of hits between 1984 and 1986, including SMALLTOWN BOY, TELL ME WHY and IT AIN'T NECESSARILY SO. Somerville quit the ensemble and formed THE COMMUNARDS.

Brontë, Charlotte (1816–55) English author of *Jane Eyre* and a few other novels, all of which have been dramatized on televison and radio. Has been portrayed by Olivia De Havilland in *Devotion* (1946) and by Julie Harris in *Brontë* (1983 T). The recent feminist rereading of her life, and especially her unexpectedly late marriage leading to her early death was only superficially explored in *After Many Cares and Bitter Sorrows* (1987 R) with Maggie

McCarthy as Charlotte and Anna MASSEY as Mrs Gaskell.

Brooke, Rupert (1887–1915) English poet. 'One of the most beautiful men in England, he had many admirers but his emotional life was far from trouble-free,' John Neville in *Apollo's Laurel Bough* (1964 R); also played by Simon Shepherd in *Sweet Wine of Youth* (1980 T); Colin Firth in *The One Before the Last* (1987 R); John Moulder-Brown in *So Great a Lover* (1989 T); Nigel HAVERS in *What Was the Matter with Rupert?* (1987 R).

Brooks, Louise (1900–85) American film actress, whose most famous work was done in German films like PANDORA'S BOX (as LULU) and *Diary of a Lost Girl* (1930), but she was especially charismatic as Nancy, dressed for most of the time as a boy, in *Beggars of Life* (1928). Interviewed in *Memories of Berlin – the Twilight of Weimar Culture* (1979 T) and *Hollywood* (1980 T).

Brooks, Romaine (1874–1970) American artist, lover of Natalie Clifford BARNEY. Possibly the inspiration behind Romaine Sage (Mary Wimbush) long exiled in Italy and fast going blind, who decides to destroy her sculptures on the eve of her 90th birthday, in Diana Bishop's *The Rest of Heaven Was Blue* (1991 R).

Brookside (UK 1982– T) Twice-weekly Channel 4 serial set on a Liverpool housing estate. Some hard-hitting plotlines which are well handled and honest. One of the families contained a gay son (Gordon COLLINS) who, for a time, lived at home with his lover Chris Duncan. Both Gordon and Chris had gone for good by 1990 and life returned to normal.

brother and sister Bruno (Anthony Corlan) and Ivich (Alison Fiske) skirt round the subject of each other's ambiguous sexuality in THE ROADS TO FREEDOM (1970); Andy (Tom Blair) and Andrée (Jane Campbell) are having a sexual relationship and she's also sleeping with his boyfriend: it's all part of *Local Color* (1978 C); gay brother, lesbian sister in *Inside Monkey Zetterland* (1992 C).

brothers Usually one likes women, the other does not – but sometimes both are gay or ambiguous: SUMMER, WINTER, AUTUMN, SPRING (1961) begins with Alf (Jon Rollason) stripping off his shirt while his brother Ted (Philip Martin) admires him. Two scenes later, Alf is telling Ted he's 'been with' a woman. Ted, half-fascinated, half-repulsed, insists that Alf does not get into the bed they share 'in yer shirt'. Alf proceeds to slowly remove his clothing, ending with the top button of his trousers before there is a rapid cutaway. The erotic potential of the relationship is explored in terms of DAVID AND JONATHAN: Alf is killed and the grieving Ted marries Alf's girlfriend who is carrying his child.

Douglas Oberon (Dennis Arundell) and sibling Francis (Richard Hurndall) seem quite content pretending to be interested in girls (*We Must Kill Toni* 1952 R); TWINS: turbulent Cal (James Dean) and gentle Aaron (Dick Davalos) in *East of Eden* (1955 C); selfless, unstinting love: from Theo (James Donald) to Vincent (Kirk Douglas) in *Lust for Life* (1956 C); Richard Anderson as Judd Steiner's (Dean Stockwell) buttoned-up brother Max calls Judd and his friend Artie 'QUEER' in COMPULSION (1959 C); two bickering brothers on a lonely fruit farm are almost married to each other in *Love Among the Wheeneys* (Aust 1966 R) with Ben Gabriel as Mort and Stewart Ginn as Jack); Donald Sutherland as a drooping aristo twin in *Start the Revolution without Me* (1969 C); TCHAIKOVSKY's half-brother Dimitri (Kenneth Colley) warns him he's becoming neglectful of his reputation in *The Music Lovers* (1971 C), though he himself lives with Alexei (Bruce Robinson); Ralph (Max Cullen), Don's OCKER sibling in NUMBER 96 (1972 T).

Cliff (Paul Regina) poses acceptance problems for bullish Lou (Brandon Maggart) as well as for his more malleable brother Joe (Robert Walden) in BROTHERS, but he receives support from them in unexpected ways. Lou tries unsuccessfully to change him, but also nearly sacrifices his sexual autonomy to save Cliff from being led astray by the supposed love of his life.

Graham (Gary Webster) wants Barry in EASTENDERS (1987) to face up to their father: 'You are going to have to stand up for what you are, if that's what you want to be', but Barry would rather go 'straight' than trust his dad's limited supply of tolerance and love. There are two unconventional brothers in LAW OF DESIRE (1987 C), one gay, one transsexual. The sibling of Ted Foster (Grant Kennedy) is 'a war hero, a bloke I've looked up to all my life ... Are you saying that it's a lie? ... I'm glad Mum and Dad aren't here' in THE FLYING DOCTORS 'Return of the Hero' (1986 T). Jeremy Irons acts as twin surgeons in DEAD RINGERS (1988 C).

Dick and Mike Stratford (Tony Carreiro and Matt Frewer) in DOCTOR, DOCTOR (1989–90 T) live in apartments on different floors in the same building: Dick is laid back and glamorous (but celibate) and Mike is frazzled, funny and always on the lookout for a woman. Dorothy's cross-dressing sibling in THE GOLDEN GIRLS (1991 T) is not seen because he is dead, while Blanche's brother (Monte Markham) is very much alive and living with a policeman. Richard Waters (James Russo) may be Mike's father rather than his elder brother (MY OWN PRIVATE IDAHO 1991 C).

Brothers (US 1984–7 T) Joe (Robert Walden) is STRAIGHT, Lou (Brandon Maggart) is very straight. Their baby brother, Cliff (Paul Regina) reveals he's gay – and a premise is born. Made for cable television, this proved to be one of the brightest comedies of the 1980s, thanks to the playing of Brandon Maggart as arch-macho man Lou WATERS and Philip Charles MacKenzie as Cliff's wall-to-wall swish friend, Donald MALTBY.

What made the situations sparkle was

the generally open-minded attitudes displayed – mainly by the stereotype QUEEN, who didn't miss a chance to show his verbal muscle and to give Cliff as much love and affection as his biological siblings. It is Donald, wrists at half nelson, tongue flapping, who fields the HOMOPHOBIA rather than Cliff who – remaining practically dormant sexually – is just a nice guy.

The episode about QUEER-BASHING 'It Only Hurts When I'm Gay' seemed to auger well for a comedy that wasn't afraid to tackle the everyday realities of urban gay life. Cliff, presumably cruising in a park, is attacked. The other brothers, together with Donald, stake out the area. They take photographs of the thugs and bring them to justice. Instead of this episode being a starting point for more serious comedy, the show spread itself to include female members of the family, played down the gay issues (no mention of AIDS), and settled in for a well-oiled series of situations in which each character exhibited an A–Z of reactions and attitudes. Precise targets, occasional bull's eyes. Easy to watch, easy to forget.
Cr: David Lloyd; P: Greg Antonacci and Gary Nardino; 13.7.84.

brotherly love Emotional and/or sexual bonding in *East of Eden* (1955 C, but the erotic scene between Cal and Aaron cut from release print); the creepy Brothers d'Amano in *The Wild Party* (1974 C); Angel (Ian CHARLESON) and Sphinx (Karl Johnson) still sleeping together in their twenties in JUBILEE (1977 C); QUERELLE (Brad DAVIS) and Robert (Hanno Poschi), both desired by Lucianne (Jeanne Moreau 1982 C); Donald (Michael McNally) and Andy (Robert Smeaton) in ACCOUNTS; Mike and Robert Gwilym in *On the Black Hill* (1987 C); *The Krays* (Gary and Martin Kemp 1990 C); Trevor (Nigel Hawthorne) who is finally able to tell his younger brother (Edward Woodward) in A ROD OF IRON (1980 T) of his true feelings for him: 'I've never put my arms around anyone. I am, if you can keep your face straight, a virgin. When I was

12 and you were 9 my heart ached for you.'

Brothers and Sisters Club A group composed of British DEAF lesbians and gays who took part in 'The All-Deaf Debate: Discrimination' on *Listening Eye* (1988 T).

William **Brown** (John Clark 1945–7 R; William Grahame 1947 C; Dennis Gilmore 1961–2 T; Adrian Dannatt 1976–7 T) Beginning as a potboiler character in 1920s magazines, the awful but spunky British schoolboy with skewed cap and baggy socks went on to vast fame in books, comics, film, radio and television. 'William is every small boy – and every small girl, too. Many women read him to this day. He is adventurous, anarchic and enquiring – the essence of childhood' (*The Woman Behind William* 1987 R). His creator, Richmal Crompton, was a classics teacher whose 60 adult books are forgotten. She never married and died in 1969.

Brown, Rita Mae (1944–) American novelist and activist, author of the classic RUBYFRUIT JUNGLE, still awaiting a film or television rendering. Co-wrote MY TWO LOVES (1986 T) and *The Long Hot Summer* (1987 T); inspired Susan (Julie Walters) to adopt her first name (*Educating Rita* 1983 C); possibly the basis for the character of Rita Sue Bliss (Cindy Williams), purveyor of 'spicy' 'pornographic' crime thrillers which Della STREET says she reads avidly in PERRY MASON 'The Case of the Poisoned Pen' (1989 T) – did Rita Sue kill her professional rival? Appeared on many American talk shows and in the documentary *Six Women*. Narrated BEFORE STONEWALL (1984 C). Her most famous heroine, the feisty Molly Bolt is '100 per cent autobiographical'.

Brummell, Beau [George Bryan Brummell] (1778–1840) The epitome of the wastrel: a fine DANDY who ended his days in an asylum, rejected by the Prince Regent and with only a faithful manservant to give a damn. Portrayed by Robert FARQUARSON in Edith Sitwell's

The Last Party (1938 R) and by Stewart Granger in *Beau Brummell* (1954 C).

bubble bath In *Naked City* 'The Well-Dressed Termite', Charles Alvis (Philip Abbott) asks his partner Sam Braden (Jack Klugman): 'What are you doing in a bubble bath?' To which Sam replies, 'What is it – against the law?' Minutes later, Charles has thrown a radio into the suds, and Sam is fried alive in them. This was an awful warning to all men who wish for over-lathered, too luxurious a bath-time. Rock HUDSON appears to have one in *Pillow Talk* (1959 C) and River Phoenix definitely does in MY OWN PRIVATE IDAHO. *See also* BATHS.

buddie movies A pillar of cinema from the earliest times – THE GAY BROTHERS (1895) – reaching its apogee with *Butch Cassidy and the Sundance Kid* (1969 C); male intimacy unencumbered by homosexuality or women. Women got into the act in the 1980s with *Times Square* (1980 C); *Little Darlings* (1980 C); CAGNEY AND LACEY; *Desperately Seeking Susan* (1985 C); *Outrageous Fortune* (1987 C); SOUTH OF THE BORDER (1989–90 T); *Bagdad Café* (1988 C); *Beaches* (1988 C); *Steel Magnolias* (1989 C); THELMA AND LOUISE (1991 C).

Buffalo Bill The character Jame Gumb (played by Ted Levine) in *The Silence of the Lambs* is obsessed with the idea of being a TRANSSEXUAL, even though he has been told by a doctor that he is not. He devotes much of his time to kidnapping and flaying women to create a female 'skin' for himself.

bugger Derived from the French *bougre*, meaning 'Bulgarian'. People from this nation fled into Europe during the 12th and 13th centuries escaping religious persecution. The men were popularly supposed to be sodomites as well as heretics.

The British Board of Film Censors resisted its use in the late 1950s when there was a loosening up of what was permissible within an 'Adults Only' certificate (although John Mills had mouthed the word in *In Which We Serve*

(1942)). The person who read the script of *Saturday Night and Sunday Morning* recommended a number of cuts, including the elimination of 'bugger' from the speech of the film's hero Arthur Seaton (Albert Finney) and his mates: 'I know that "bugger" is used in such places as the public bars of provincial pubs, but I doubt whether the average working man uses it much in his own home in front of his wife, and that ought to be the standard for us to adopt, even in films obviously designed for the factory workers section of society' (20.11.59). The film-makers tried a modification, which failed to meet with the approval of the Board's Secretary, John Trevelyan. He told the film's producer, Harry Salzman in a letter: '... we simply cannot accept the word "bogger". We have not yet accepted the use of the word "bugger" in films, and the substitution of the letter 'o' for the letter 'u' makes no significant difference ... I appreciate that words of this kind are normal in the speech of the type of people that the film is about, but I have always found, strange though it may seem, that these are the very people who most object to this kind of thing on the screen. I hope, therefore, that this script will be revised and [this word] omitted' (24.11.59). The Board was still opposed to the use of 'bugger' when John Schlesinger made the film version of *Billy Liar* in 1962. But 'bogger' was welcomed as an alternative and Wilfred Pickles used it profligately as Tom Courtenay's miserable old bogger of a dad.

'Bugger' was fully rendered to the English-speaking world three years later, in WHO'S AFRAID OF VIRGINIA WOOLF? (1966 C) and was in every other British film after *Poor Cow* in 1967.

On radio, Al Read had tried to slip in the word in his send-up of the FAIRY LIQUID advert (serene-voiced Mummy telling the inquisitive child to 'beggar-off') in *The Al Read Show* (1966 R). The following year, the *Listener* critic's ears were assailed by the word coming through on his Home Service receiver during an afternoon play, *The White Sparrow*. 'Whatever next?'

And soon it made its way through the big screen to the small. 'Another buggering dull weekend,' sighed Roy Hamill (Gawn Grainger) in the British–Danish co-production *Male Bait* in 1971. 'Bugger the bloody reindeer,' cried an un-Yuletide Frank (Harry Landis) in *Thrills Galore* (1972 T). 'You're all bad buggers. I wouldn't be here, else,' says barmaid Vera (Meg Johnson) cheerfully in WEDNESDAY LOVE (1975 T). 'I've done bugger all,' admits an old soak in A ROOM FOR THE WINTER (1981 T). Frank Harris (Leonard Rossiter) tells Oscar WILDE (Philip SAYER) that he's 'not interested in buggery and boys' in *Fearless Frank* (1978 T). The restless wife (Sharon Duce) tells the husband (Duggie Brown) that she thought she was doing him a favour by leaving him: 'Did you buggery! Since when have you done me any favours?' (in Shelagh Delaney's *The House That Jack Built* 1976 T). 'Oh buggeration!' exclaims Guy BURGESS (Anthony Hopkins) at the Reform Club in *Blunt* (1987 T).

In 1979 the BBC Radio 3 announcer was still conscious of people's sensibilities. Before Howard Brenton's *Epsom Downs* was broadcast he explained carefully that, as many working-class people went to the races, there would be 'a strong use of the vernacular'. Within the first 10 minutes there were two buggers. However, no warning went out for James Saunders' *Nothing to Declare* (1982 R) although Sophia (Zena Walker) told her husband to 'Drop dead, you silly old bugger' at least once.

Up until 1984, ITV resisted bugger or buggers. Jon Blair (fondly known as Colonel Bollocks), one of the brains behind the scandalously popular puppet show *Spitting Image*, protested about the removal by the Independent Broadcasting Authority of 'bugger' from the previous week's script. 'Arsehole' had made it to ITV that year and someone had called someone else a 'bastard' on *Minder*. 'Why,' Blair asked the IBA's Charles Denton, 'was bastard acceptable when bugger was not?' He called in Stephen Murphy, former head of the British Board of Film Censors and now part of the IBA. Murphy thought bugger was okay and took up the cudgels with the IBA Director General, John Whitney. In the North of England, where Murphy came from, bugger was a term of affection whereas bastard was questionable. In the South, of course, the situation is usually reversed. The IBA relented and 'bugger' took its place with bastard and arsehole. 'It's nice to have it sorted,' wrote Jon Blair, 'but it is not an enormous help in arriving at judgements for national network television' (quoted in Lewis Chester's book *The Inside Story of Spitting Image*, 1986).

It now can be used by nice, well-educated people like daughter-in-law Angela (Fiona Gillies) in *Mother Love* (1989 T) – four times, in fact. Or by the brother of a soldier on a fishing trip (*Resurrected* 1989 T). Or by a Pakistani entrepreneur ('What are those buggers up to?' in MY BEAUTIFUL LAUNDRETTE 1985 C/T). Or by a policeman investigating the case of JACK THE RIPPER (1989 T) 100 years ago, or by a contemporary policeman in A VERY PECULIAR PRACTICE (1988 T). A German living in Paris uses it in the documentary *Hotel Terminus: The Life and Times of Klaus Barbie* (1988 C).

Percy Topliss's adoptive Dad (Dave King) in *The Monocled Mutineer* (1986 T) exclaimed, 'I'll be buggered'; Michelle (Susan Tully) in EASTENDERS (1988 T) could tell yuppie cad Willmott-Brown (William Boyde) to 'bugger off'; the Labour Prime Minister (Ray McAnally) could take pleasure in making 'the buggers shuffle on uneasily in their shiny shoes' (the bureaucrats) in *A Very British Coup* (1988 T); a social worker in HARD CASES (1988 T) could admonish a client for 'trying to bugger his son up'; Peter Vaughan could let loose two buggers in his opening few lines in *Harry's Kingdom* (1989 T); the hooray Henry could explode 'Oh the buggers, the *buggers*' about the police who, having just played against him and the Old Boys at cricket, are now accusing him of indecency (*Old Flames* 1990 T).

On the radio, within one 8-day period

in June 1990, it was possible to hear at least seven references: to 'that long-nosed bugger' (in Allan Prior's *Nosey*, about the Duke of Wellington) and in another play, *Seven Steps to Treason* 'I don't give a bugger whether Rodjinsky goes back to Poland or not' and 'Bugger off'. That month also saw the London stage opening of Simon GRAY's *Hidden Laughter*. In the second act Natalie, the daughter, on a garden swing, rattles off 'bugger' 20 times without pausing for breath. Earlier a writer, her father's client, announces the title of his latest novel, *Bugger All*.

In Australia bugger is also well patronized. *Don's Party* (1976 C) featured it six times in various guises alongside piss off, fuckin' POOFTER, rat shit etc. In David Conway's *A Visitor Dropped By* (1989 R), set in the outback, characters say 'bugger off', 'buggery under the sun' and just plain 'bugger' within a single 5-minute period. And the Rhys Adrian play *Toytown* (UK 1987) was broadcast on ABC radio with all 25 of its buggers intact, plus 3 sods.

A programme on censorship with Sir John Johnson broadcast on BBC radio in 1988 (KALEIDOSCOPE) specifically cited 'bugger' as one of the words not allowed in any context on stage, screen, radio or television in the 1950s and early 1960s. Gordon House wrote that working for the BBC could threaten peaceful coexistence with the neighbours: 'There's a lady down our road who ever since she heard I worked for the BBC, has made a point of collecting all the naughty words she hears in plays and repeating them ... in a loud voice whenever I happen to pass. "Two buggers and a sod yesterday," she announced triumphantly as I escorted William to school this morning' (*Listener*, 15.5.88).

bull dyke Sometimes the concept is used and not the whole term. Irene Handl, roaring like a rhino, in tweeds and with a scrape of grey hair, assisted by her fly-paper thin and equally sticky sidekick (Michael WARD) in a bunch of scenes from *Doctor in Love* (1960 C). Two strippers, Dawn (Joan Sims) and Leonora (Liz Frazer) titillate her and call her, as near as dammit, a nosey old bull DYKE ('an Aberdeen Angus').

In *In Two Minds* (1987 T) the drunken Betty (Barbara Keogh) asks her boyfriend's daughter: 'Who plays the man and who plays the girl in your relationship?' Receiving no answer, the woman concludes: 'You're the cow and she's the bull! A right dollop of bull shit, your friend.' A few hours later she's found dead.

'Judges don't like *bull-dozing*, jock-busting, BUTCH lady lawyers any more than I do,' prosecution counsel to Grace (Susan Dey) in the TV movie version of L.A. LAW (1986 T).

bullying At least one in every five children in Britain suffers from bullying: 40 MINUTES 'Bullies' (1989). Specifically anti-homosexual attacks at school in ROLL ON FOUR O'CLOCK; THE TERENCE DAVIES TRILOGY 'Children' (1976); *Good and Bad at Games* (1984 T); LAND OF PROMISE. But, in real life, after James Ward appeared on BRASS TACKS 'Good as You?' in October 1988, 'Even the school bully came up to me at a bus stop and said, "Well done! I was proud of what you did."'

Probably the most extreme case was that of Private James Darkin, who killed himself in 1980 after being bullied by fellow soldiers for 18 months (and unsuccessfully asking gay organizations for help). His naked body had often been scrubbed in the bath with a hard brush, urinated on, pubic hairs shaved off or pulled out, his flesh regularly burned with cigarette ends. The army refused to admit it was bullying: it was merely 'teasing'. This was at variance with the coroner's report: the 18-year-old soldier had suffered 'a living hell'.

The WORLD IN ACTION report ('The Death of Private Darkin' 1982 T) also looked at other victims. There was Frank Cooper, a former soldier branded on the back with a hot iron and beaten when he complained. Malcolm McMichael tried to commit SUICIDE because of harassment; as soon as it was discovered he was gay, he was imprisoned for a very minor sexual offence. '... the army provides the rationale for anti-gay behaviour whilst at the same time providing no support for any young soldier who tries to accept his emerging gay identity. A chilling portrait of male tyranny and a shocking indictment of the British armed forces' (John Marshall, *Gay News* 234).

See also QUEER-BASHING.

bum boy Used by Dolly (Ann Mitchell) to Linda (Maureen O'Farrell) about Carlos (James Lister) in episode 4 of WIDOWS (1983 T): 'He's Arnie Fisher's bum boy. He leaves your bed and gets into his.' David BOWIE played a 'bum boy' (the captain's) in *Yellowbeard* (1983 C).

Bunbury/Bunburying Oscar WILDE's name for a conveniently invalid fictitious friend in THE IMPORTANCE OF BEING EARNEST. Not for nothing a cracking success in Victorian England. The basic plot rejoices in duplicity and living a partial lie. Oscar Wilde could not call the game by its real name – which for once in well-bred comedy was not heterosexual – and dubbed it 'Bunburying'. For his hero John (Jack) Worthing this means being ERNEST in town and Jack in the country. The true Bunburyist is Algernon Moncrieff: he pretends he has an invalid friend called Bunbury which excuses him from the more usual social rounds. Jack is able to come up to London ostensibly to tend to the tangled affairs and scrapes of his brother 'Ernest'; a name which Jack himself uses in London society, and probably the *demi-monde*. Wilde was not the only Victorian to make frequent use of a mythical friend whose ill health necessitates short but regular visits to a metropolis to pursue specialized interests and desires outside eye and earshot of an equally two-timing polite society. The sexual connotations of Bunburying obviously escaped the Lord Chamberlain's office then and up until 1968 when it was abolished, a year after the very law that silenced Wilde's mocking laughter.

The concept of Bunburying, so light-heartedly displayed in *The Importance ...*, was taken very seriously by many men. Francis KING, discussing E. M. FORSTER in *Aspects of the Novelist* (1979 R), on the occasion of the centenary of the birth of the novelist, said that this subterfuge necessitated by law and convention 'made him live his life in two halves. There was the life of coming up to London and those encounters, very often arranged by Joseph ACKERLEY with policemen and so on. Then there was the very circumspect life which he lived with his mother, his aunts and so on.'

Guy BURGESS had no such qualms, no loyalty save to himself; his sometime lover Anthony BLUNT (Ian RICHARDSON) announces (1987 T) that 'Today, Guy's gone Bunburying'. A 1988 MORNING STORY was called 'A Use for Bunburying'. The most recent adoptee of the practice was Gordon's sorely tried wife in *The Brittas Empire* (1990 T): she arrives back from visiting her 'sick uncle' exhausted but strangely elated.

Bunny Cousin of *Raffles* (1930 C; 1975 T; 1987 R); a traitor who comes home to die: Bunny Bingham in *The Recruiter* (Hugh BURDEN 1971 R); the blond, silent 'assistant' of Jerry in *The Love Machine* (1971 C); the practically airborne Bunny Wrigglesworth (George Hamilton) in ZORRO – THE GAY BLADE; Bunny Baynes, recalled by Maisie in COMIC'S INTERLUDE: 'he always had some fella hanging about backstage ... some unpleasantness with one of the young Chinese policemen – and the boy was only 17. That was his business.' In America, it's solely a female designation: Bunny Blake (Maggie McNamara) in THE TWILIGHT ZONE 'Ring-a Ding Girl' (1963 T); the little girl in *Bunny Lake Is Missing* (1965 C), Susan Strasberg in *Chubasco* (1967 C); Bette DAVIS as bank robber in *Bunny O'Hare* (1972 C).

Bunty Bunty Nichol (John Grieve) in THE DARK NUMBER (1967–8 T) and the first queen from SCOTLAND – 'a filthy little pig', who was one of the hero's wife's degenerate friends. Bunty is used solely as a woman's name, eg in THE VORTEX (1960 T) and *A Life of Bliss* (Bunty Blythe 1953–9 R), so the audience was primed that this man was 'different'. The name has only appeared in recent times in STRUGGLE (1983 T) for a fearsome FEMINIST (Joanna McCallum) who was taking the sexism out of the corridors of power.

Burden, Hugh (1913–85) English actor, angular and cantilevered. Creator of hapless biographer Herbert Reeve in the Richard Shewin plays. Played a number of driven gay/bisexual roles: Cocteau's *Orphée* (1962 R); Bunny Bingham in *The Recruiter* (1971 R); Evelyn WAUGH (1976 R); *Maurice Now* (1981 R); Oliver in A SUPERSTITION (1977 T).

C: *One of Our Aircraft Is Missing* (1941); *The Way Ahead* (1944); *No Love for Johnnie* (1961); *Funeral in Berlin* (1966); etc.

Burgess, Guy (1911–63) English journalist, BBC producer and spy for the Soviet Union. A man with rather individual priorities: concerned about his shares and how the dividends can be sent to Moscow tax-free for life, and desperate for a really well-made suit from his London tailor. He eats baked beans on toast with his fingers, plays trains with Donald Maclean's children, makes passes at a policeman who books him for speeding. Called 'a cheap little PANSY' by Melinda Maclean (Elizabeth Seal) in *Philby, Burgess and Maclean* (1977 T), he is nevertheless remembered as mentally razor-sharp and sexually alluring by others. Anthony BLUNT remained in love with him and he still owed the fictional Buffo (Bryan Coleman) £100: '... a lot of money in those days; probably spent it corrupting some young tart from Chelsea barracks' (COMMITMENTS 1982 T).

Burgess' florid style and endless excesses have fired thriller writers (John Le Carré), playwrights (Julian MITCHELL, Alan BENNETT) and sitcom writers (*Brass*) ever since he and Maclean flew the coop, courtesy of Blunt and

Philby in 1952. Guy Baggers (Anthony Smee) who co-opts Morris HARDACRE into espionage in *Brass*, is a clever send-up of the Anthony Blunt aesthete, rather than the garrulous, ALCOHOLIC Burgess: lower lip set in contemptuous sneer, eye on number one. 'The capitalist class in this country is unbelievably beastly to servants. It is our duty to be beastly to the working classes ... it makes them see red.'

Burgess was chosen as one of five 20th-century people 'who rebelled against society's conventions' in REBELS (1984 R). Hugh Sykes included interviews with Guy's brother, Nigel Burgess as well as university friends and BBC colleagues. *The Profession of Intelligence* (1981 R) asked some searching questions as to exactly how the Secret Services were undermined by the Cambridge 'MOLES' of Burgess, Maclean and Blunt – the three names forever entwined in notoriety and iniquity.

Burlington Bertie From Bow Sung by Ella Shields (written by her husband) in full male attire in the early part of the 20th century; reinterpreted (gamely) by Betty Grable in *Mother Wore Tights* (1948 C), (thrillingly) by Julie Andrews in the 1918 Charlot Revue number in *Star!* (1968 C), and (femininely) by Anita Harris at the Queen Mother's 90th birthday concert (1991 T). The lesbian Severine performs it in *New Anatomies* (1984 R).

Burridge, Geoffrey (1949–87) Handsome blond English actor, who appeared in many attractive gay or semi-gay roles: Clovis in *The Ice House* (1978 T); beautiful, rich and eligible but not enough to win Sonny (Lisa Harrow) in *The Look* (1978 T); pilot Fitz[roy] in A MOMENT IN TIME (1979 T); Edward Brittain's friend in TESTAMENT OF YOUTH (1979 T): 'It's lovely that Edward has got someone he can really talk to'; Ralph Partridge in THE SOUTH BANK SHOW 'No Need to Lie' (1980 T); alien Dorian in *Blake's Seven* 'Rescue' (1981 T); *Foxy Lady* (1982 T); slick and dubious Piers Roberts in THE GENTLE

TOUCH 'Auctions' (1982 T); smooth and seductive King Philippe in *The Lion in Winter* (1984 R); in drag as Pot Pourri' in *The Refuge* (1987 T). Sang 'Gigi' at the 1985 *Royal Variety Performance*.

Burroughs, William S. (1914–) American novelist, inventor of the cut-up technique that has influenced film, radio and television as well as narrative techniques. A gaunt, woman-hating, patrician figure, he has made indelible impressions in a few films (*Towers Open Fire* 1964, *Chappaqua* 1966, *Drugstore Cowboy* 1989), in readings from his works (*The Naked Lunch* on *Saturday Night Live* 1981 T), and in documentaries (ARENA *Burroughs* 1983 T, 'What Happened to Kerouac?' 1988 T).
    C: *The Discipline of D. E.* (1981); *Naked Lunch* (1992 heterosexualized by David Cronenberg); *The Wild Boys* (1993 project).

bus conductor Colin (Karl Johnson), the ex-HIPPY now gay activist (who draws the line at gay lib BADGES at work) in ONLY CONNECT (1979 T).

Butch/butch Popular name for heavy-set, slow-thinking lugs and gangsters: 'Butch' Dorgan (Jack Curtis) in *Steelheart* (1921 C); Butch (Jimmy Bradbury) in *Let It Rain* (1927 C); Butch (Reed Howes), carnival operator in *Savage Paradise* (1928 C); Butch (Wallace Beery), bullying guerrilla in *The Big House* (1930 C); Butch Clelland (Jeff Richards) in *Seagulls Over Sorrento* (1953 C); Butch (Paul Birchard), a GI frequenting a club of ill repute in ABSOLUTE HELL! (1991 T).
    You knew where you stood with butch, except for the occasional deviation like 'Butch' Hendrick (Jeff Donnell), one of the *Nine Girls* (1944 C) set in a sorority. Or Butch played by Eric BLORE in *Breakfast for Two* (1937 C) and by Grady Sutton in *Stage Door* (1938 C), who definitely weren't.
    POLARI annexed 'butch' around 1956, as a half-ridiculing, half-admiring term for overtly masculine behaviour, in or

out of bed. The burning question in days of role-playing was 'Butch or bitch?' This situation had changed by 1968: Butch (Michael Deacon) is a queeny ad man in *Nine Tales of a Cat* 'The Cat's Pyjamas' (R); Butch (Vincent Price), a frizzed HAIRDRESSER in *Theatre of Blood* (1973 C); etc. And it was, of course, *de rigueur* in front of the word 'lesbian'.
    'King Stefan asked in a gruff butch voice,' Rik Mayall reading the children's story *The Twelve Huntsmen* (1989 T).

butch hairstyle Severe, short hairstyle popularized by Doris DAY in *The Man Who Knew Too Much* (but worn with false bun, 1956 C); *Julie* (1956 C); *The Pajama Game* (1957 C); *Teacher's Pet* (1958 C); *It Happened to Jane* (femmed into a poodle cut, 1959 C). Also sported by Patricia Bright as one of the bachelorettes in *It's Always Jan* (1955–6 T); Lisa GAYE in *Rock Around the Clock* (1956); Barbara Billingsley in LEAVE IT TO BEAVER (1957); in Britain by Mary Dixon Crawford (Jeanette Hutchinson), possibly at the urging of good mate Grace MILLARD in DIXON OF DOCK GREEN (1957–8 T). One of the most recent examples of the styling was Susan Sarandon, seduced by a female vampire, in THE HUNGER (1983 C).

But he/she's a very nice person Dr Legge to Pauline in EASTENDERS (1986 T) about RUTH Lyons (Judy Wiebert), the social worker: 'She likes other women ... but she's a very nice person.' Alternatives: 'He/she's JEWISH/BLACK/DISABLED ... but he/she's a very nice person.'

But he/she's married While there have been married gay and lesbian characters on air and on screen since VICTIM (1961 C) the startled 'But he's *married*' is still a constant, as though vows and social acceptability could regulate feelings and circumstances, or even effeminacy and mannishness.
    In *Designing Woman* (1957 C) flighty, flitting hither-and-yon Randy (Jack Cole) tells an amazed Gregory Peck that

he has a 'wife and three sons'. 'Is he for real? Does he mean that?' Peck asks Lauren Bacall, who is also rather taken aback by the director-choreographer's news.

'But, Mr Farr's *married*!' detective in *Victim*.

Alan and Michael in THE BOYS IN THE BAND:

> 'But ... but ... you're *married*!'
> 'Don't you love that quaint idea – if a man is married, then he is automatically heterosexual. Alan, Hank swings both ways – with a definite preference.'

In the final ROUND THE HORNE of 1968, Julian and Sand spring a surprise: they are married ... to women. The wives enter: 'Hello, I'm Julie and this is my friend, Sandra.'

Two doctors discussing AIDS diagnosis in ST ELSEWHERE (1983 T):

> 'Is he gay?'
> 'Are you kidding ... He's got a wife and child.'

butler RiffRaff (Richard O'Brien) tells Brad and Janet that his master 'is not yet married, nor do we think he ever will be' in THE ROCKY HORROR PICTURE SHOW (1975 C); Denholm ELLIOTT does double duty as minder and nanny to the retired don and sleeping spy, Jason (Donald Pleasence) in *Blade on the Feather* (1980 T): 'He's stronger than I am.'

Dudley **Butterfield** (Chard Hayward in NUMBER 96 1974–7 T) He arrived as an assistant in the wine bar, went to live with Don, then opened a hair salon. 'He's a complete escapist. He's weak. If anything goes wrong, he'll grab a movie for support. Because Dudley is basically weak, he needs a strong person to hang on to, qualities he's more likely to find in a man than in a woman at the moment.' (Chard Hayward, quoted in *Australian TV Times*, 1974).

buttocks A spate during the silent era (*Ben Hur*) then cover-up, apart from naturist films (and the 1939 MGM film

The Spirit of Culver), until male gluteals maximus were once more revealed: Derek Bond's white bottom disappearing into the distance in *The Loves of Joanna Godden* (1947 C; his character then committed suicide); George Cole's in *Don't Panic Chaps!* (1959 C); Anthony Perkins' in *Tall Story* (US 1960 C). Female ones had long been available, silent, dubbed or sub-titled – principally in naturist films and Brigitte Bardot comedies and melodramas. In English-speaking cinema the pioneers were Julie Christie tearing off her Julie Harris-designed clothes in DARLING (1965 C), Irene Tsu losing the bottom half of her bikini in *Caprice* (1966 C), and Hayley Mills surprised in the bath in THE FAMILY WAY (1966 C).

Not much serious male buttock activity until Oliver Reed dived off a cliff into the blinding sun in *The System* (1964 C) and Alan BATES dropped his trousers for *Zorba the Greek* (1964 C). Then suddenly they were everywhere in the cinema: Bosco Hogan's in *Ulysses* (1967); followed by Robert Forster riding totally bare in REFLECTIONS IN A GOLDEN EYE (1967); Joe DALLESANDRO in FLESH (1968) and *Trash* (1970); Michael York chasing upstairs after a nymphet in *The Strange Affair* (1968); Romeo (Leonard Whiting) flitting out of the marriage bed (1968); Christopher Jones posing for his portrait in *Three in the Attic* (1968). Alan BATES and Terence Stamp were doing double shifts: respectively in *King of Hearts* (1966) and WOMEN IN LOVE (1969), and *Far from the Madding Crowd* (1967) and THEOREM (1968).

In Australia bare bottoms of both sexes were prominent features of the evening serial NUMBER 96 from 1972 onwards and British television gradually followed suit. Famous ones on the BBC were footballer Jackie Charlton's (accidentally exposed) on *Grandstand* (1963), Frank Finlay's in *Casanova* (1971), Denholm ELLIOTT's in PAST CARING (1986), and Patrick Malahide's in *The Singing Detective* (1986 T).

Matthew Collins achieved fame and notoriety in 1987 because of his hands-on report of a nudist holiday near Bordeaux for *The Travel Show*.

In British cinema, Derek JARMAN's SEBASTIANE (1976 C) had nearly all of its characters soaking up the Sardinian sun or bathing without clothes. Major Hollywood stars had been prepared to strip for their art and/or titillate their fans by a brief flash of rear view from the early 1970s: Kirk Douglas in *There Was a Crooked Man* (1970 C); Charlton Heston in *Pro* (1972 C); Doug McClure (*What Ever Happened to Charlie Farthing?* 1975 C); Rock HUDSON (*Embryo* 1976 C); Arnold Schwarzenegger in *The Terminator* (1982 C); Sylvester Stallone (*Tango and Cash* 1989 C: 'It solves the underwear problem'); Mel Gibson (*Bird on A Wire, Lethal Weapon 2* 1990 C); Jimmy Smits in SWITCH (1991 C); Keanu Reeves (with Italian woman) in MY OWN PRIVATE IDAHO; etc.

The growth of gay cinema during the 1970s and 1980s has ensured a steady supply of firmed, public-school-educated bottoms in posh productions: Charles' and Sebastian's in BRIDESHEAD REVISITED (1981 T; Richard Ingrams wrote in the *Spectator* that they should not have been shown); the woodland glade trio splashing in *A Room with a View* (1985 C); Rupert Everett wandering around his Venice hotel room in *The Comfort of Strangers* (1990 C).

The openly expressed feeling that male bums were taking over persisted – part no doubt of some gay inspired plot to rob Britain of its backbone. The following year a lady from Wisbech, Cambridgeshire drew attention to the 'repetitious and boring ... endless sight of NAKED backsides that no BBC Drama seems complete without' (*Radio Times*, 18–24.4.91). And Leslie Halliwell had already sighed apropos of *The Far Pavilions* (1984 T): 'I got weary of protracted rear views of our hero strutting here and there in his tight britches and boots' (*Halliwell's Television Companion*, 1987 edition).

Michael Parkinson complained loudly about Derek JARMAN's obsession with men's bums in CARAVAGGIO on *Film '86*. Could he have seen another film? There are 10 seconds of buttock out of 95 minutes. The biggest ratio of bums to celluloid must surely be on Yoko Ono's famous 1967 film, closely followed by *Hockney at Work* (1981 T).

Byng, Douglas (1893–1987) English revue artist and FEMALE IMPERSONATOR. Among his famous songs were 'The Pest Of Budapest', 'Sex Appeal Sarah', 'Boadicea', 'Milly The Messy Old Mermaid' and 'Blackout Bella'. An early television performer in *Cabaret* (1938), *Byng-ho* (1938) and *Queue for Song* (1938); *Pantomime in Rehearsal* 'Babes in the Wood' (SC 1938 R); *The Jubilee Show* (1955); DESERT ISLAND DISCS (1959); *A Dynasty of Dames* (1963 R); *Hotel Paradiso* (1966 C); THIS IS YOUR LIFE Danny LA RUE (1981); *Douglas Byng at 90* (1983 R); *Turns* (1984); *Billy on Byng* (1987 R with Billy MILTON). Bob Monkhouse remembered seeing Byng on television in the late 1930s 'singing something my mother said was much too rude for children to hear. For years afterwards, whenever my parents were whispering I would ask, "Are you doing a Douglas Byng?"' (*Radio Times* 25–31.10.86).

Byron, Lord George Gordon (1788–1824) English Romantic poet, traveller and libertine whose scandalous exile has made him an object of endless fascination in the 20th century. Featured at the beginning of THE BRIDE OF FRANKENSTEIN and having a high old time in Hell with Oscar in *Death of Satan* (1958 T, played by Barry Hirst). More wide-ranging portraits focus mainly on his spectacular relationships with women: Dennis PRICE as *The Bad Lord Byron* (1948 C); Jeremy Brett in *Solo* (1972 T); Keith Barron in *Biography*; Richard Chamberlain in *Lady Caroline Lamb* (1972 C), through the eyes of Frederic RAPHAEL in *Byron: A Personal Tour* (1981 T); Gabriel Byrne in *Gothic* (1986 C); Robert Powell in *Alas ... the Love of Women* (1987 R); Philip Anglim in *Haunted Summer* (1988 C).

by the end of the year 2000, the whole world will be homosexual Regarded at the time (1959/1960) as one of LA DOLCE VITA's most ringing prophesies. The subtitled line was spoken by a washed-out blond exquisite through chiffon lips as he trips and giggles alongside Marcello Mastroianni as they make their way towards the sea and the huge fish in the last scene. The latest (1990) sub-titled version translates the man-child's drugged prattling as: 'I want to retire ... But as we retire, more and more pop up. For each two who retire 10 more pop up. I bet you by 1965 it will be total depravity. It will be a real mess ... like camomile the more it is trodden, the more it will spread.'

Cabaret (US 1972 C) Sally Bowles (Liza Minnelli) slogs it out in the Kit Kat Club, falls for a penniless Englishman (Michael York), and finds that he is sharing his favours with her meal ticket, a German baron (Helmut Griem). Meanwhile, NAZISM is on the rise and Sally's Jewish friend (Marisa Berenson) is on the cutting edge. Leering over all of them is the toxic Master of Ceremonies (Joel Grey), lord of misrule, perversion and vulgarity.

W: Jay Presson Allen from the novel *Goodbye to Berlin* by Christopher ISHERWOOD; M: John Kander; L: Fred Ebb; P: Cy Feuer; D/Ch: Bob Fosse; 123 mins.

This kinetic, imaginative 'adult' musical follows the plot of John VAN DRUTEN's *I Am a Camera* rather than that of the stage version, which heterosexualized the hero. Joel Grey repeated his Broadway role to great acclaim.

Rupert Cadell A world-weary POET who rumbles his two former students' murder game in ROPE. A host of aphoristically confident actors have played this key role: Ernest MILTON (1932 R; 1939 T); Eric PORTMAN (1953 R); Dennis PRICE (1957 T); James Stewart missed by a mile in HITCHCOCK's film version (1948), but on radio the vigorously languorous Alan Rickman was just right in 1982.

Injured in the war and sickened by its waste and cruelty, Rupert affects the guise of an aesthete: 'I'm writing a little thing about doves. And a little thing about rain. Both good, very good in fact. Of course, I'm getting ahead with the big one which promises not only to be the best thing I've ever written but the best thing I've ever read.'

Originally Wyndham Brandon was planning to involve his mentor in Charles' and his perfect murder: 'He is about the only man in England who might have seen this thing from our angle, that is the artistic one ... You'll recall we contemplated at one time inviting him to share our dangers ... [but] Rupert is perhaps a little too fastidious.'

The Caesars (UK 1968 T) The whole gang from Tiberius to Claudius. Lusty, intelligent recreation of Roman honour and horror on a budget that probably wouldn't have fed a legion for a week. Caligula (Ralph Bates) is more restrained in comparison to John HURT in *I, Claudius* (1976 T); but he still presents a pluperfect image of monomania: believing himself to be a god, spiralling out of control, giving verse recitals dressed as a woman, calling his Praetorian guard by camp names, and giving them passwords like 'Lovey-kins'. This is the final straw: they plunge their swords into him.

W/P: Philip Mackie; D: Derek Bennett; Granada; 6 parts; 60 mins.

café owners Gilbert (Chris Emyard) in THE CORNER HOUSE (1987 T) in Britain; Idgie (Mary Stuart Masterson) – who can't cook – and RUTH (Mary-Louise Parker) running the café in FRIED GREEN TOMATOES AT THE WHISTLE STOP CAFE (1991 C) in America. *See also* RESTAURATEURS.

La Cage aux Folles (Birds of a Feather) (Fr/It 1978 C) The domestication of the homosexual. A Riviera FEMALE IMPERSONATOR, ALBIN (Michel Serrault) squawks and throws hysterics while his long-suffering lover, Renato (Ugo Tognazzi) ducks. Adding spice to this already savoury situation is the announcement by Renato's son that he plans to marry the daughter of the local moral rearmer and HOMOPHOBE-in-chief. How to explain Albin's presence in the household? Also involved is a dizzy 'maid' (Benny Luke) who, like Albin, is psychologically incapable of playing straight.

W: Francis Veber from the play by Jean Poiret; D: Edouard Molinaro; 110 mins. Followed by *La Cage aux Folles II* (1980) and *La Cage aux Folles III: The Wedding* (1985).

The broad theatricality of the first film, generously mixed with glitter, soft satirical targets and sentimentality, proved to be catnip to audiences all over the world. Set-pieces such as Albin trying to be a BUTCH male – 'Whatever I wear, I look

OUTRAGEOUS' – either delight or set the teeth on edge. The second film, though mired in a silly gangster plot, did contain a few very funny scenes involving Albin's disguise as a peasant woman.

Caged (US 1950 C) Naive young woman (Eleanor Parker) is corrupted by her time in PRISON, mainly by a madam (Lee Patrick) and a mountainous matron (Hope Emerson).
W: Virginia Kellogg and Bernard Schoenfeld; P: Jerry Wald; D: John Cromwell; 96 mins.
Although there had been such films before, the quality of writing, direction and acting earn *Caged* the accolade of Big Mummy of all of the 'serious' reforming women's prison films and television series. Claustrophobic and full of believable characters, censorship curtailed the depiction of sexual bonding between the women, but the situation had not really changed by the time of *Caged Heat* (1974) where Jonathan Demme has the prisoners holding hands only, or indeed in WITHIN THESE WALLS or PRISONER.

Cagney and Lacey (US 1981–7) Two New York undercover cops (Sharon Gless and Tyne Daly) confront the urban jungle, sexism, RACISM ... but not HOMOPHOBIA.
Loretta Swit played Cagney in the 1981 TV movie pilot, belatedly sparked off by *Butch Cassidy and the Sundance Kid*, but Meg Foster took over when the series began. After half-a-dozen episodes, CBS sacked Foster because, it was rumbled, the partnership between the women was 'offensive to the male audience' and Cagney was too 'strident' (Georgia Jeffries, one of the writers). The American *TV Guide* (12–18.6.82) quoted 'someone' at CBS as saying that the network had reservations because the duo was 'too tough, too hard, not feminine enough', too harshly women's lib 'and viewers perceived them as "DYKES"'. The public explanation was viewer resistance to 'inordinantly abrasive' women. This was not borne out by viewers' letters.

The series was created by Barbara Avedon and Barbara Corday, and the producer was Barney Rosenzweig.

Caiaphas 'The ecclesiastical politician, appointed like one of Hitler's bishops by a heathen government' (Dorothy L. Sayers, *The Man Born to be King*, 1941–2, 1949, 1951 & 1965). Chief priest of the conservative Jewish sect of Pharisees, often characterized as sly, vain and effeminate: Heron CARVIC in *The Man Born to be King*; Michael Deacon in *The Image of God* (1986 R). One exception was Bernard Hepton, refreshingly non-oily in *Son of Man* (1969 T).

Joel **Cairo** Kasper Gutman's memorably PERFUMED associate in *The Maltese Falcon*: Peter LORRE (1941 C); Nickolas GRACE (1984 R).

Calamity Jane [Martha Jane Canary] (1852–1903) American frontierswoman, sharp-shooter, glamorously deglamourized by Hollywood: Jean Arthur in *The Plainsman* (1936 C); Doris DAY in *Calamity Jane* (1953 C); Fay Spain in *Death Valley Days* 'A Calamity Named Jane' (*c* 1965); Abby Dalton in *The Plainsman* (1966 C); Stefanie Powers in *Bonanza* 'Calamity Over the Comstock' (1971 T).
Jane Alexander played her more realistically ('exceedingly plain Jane,' *Maltin's Movie Guide*) in the 1984 TV movie while Beth Porter sourced and grounded Ol' Calam impressively on radio in 1986, using the numerous letters she wrote to the daughter she gave away, and which were never sent. Most people prefer the Doris Day version best, riding the Deadwood Stage and singing of her SECRET LOVE.

California Suite (US 1978) One of the four stories set at the Beverly Hills Hotel concerns a British actress (Maggie Smith) and her ANTIQUE DEALER husband (Michael Caine), whose eyes are always wandering malewards, in Hollywood for the Oscars.
W: Neil Simon from his play; P: Ray Stark; D: Herbert Ross; 103 mins.
Maggie and Michael work superbly

together, especially when she, drunk and depressed, asks him to make love to her and not fantasize she's a man. He does his best to oblige.

Caligula [Gaius Caesar Germanicus] (AD 12–41) The Roman emperor whose paranoia guarantees safety for no one, and who believed he was all the gods. He ruled for four years before being killed by army officers he had 'insulted' (by calling them pet names and otherwise impugning their manhood). It's one of the great ham roles, providing a field day for actors who can be paranoid, bestial, murderous, effeminate, sexy and psychotic all at once: Emlyn WILLIAMS in the aborted 'I, Claudius' shown in *The Epic That Never Was* (1965 T); Jay Robinson in *The Robe* (1953 C) and *Demetrius and the Gladiators* (1954 C); Ralph Bates (THE CAESARS 1968 T); Tim Seely (*I, Claudius* 1970 R); John HURT (*I, Claudius* 1976 T); Malcolm McDowell (*Caligula* 1980 C); John McEnery (*A.D.* 1985 T); etc.

Call-In (UK 1973 R) One of the first phone-in programmes on homosexuality, courtesy of London Broadcasting, with Denis LEMON and Jackie FORSTER, editors of GAY NEWS and *Sappho* respectively. 'The programme did not solve anything,' decided a *Gay News* reviewer. 'It broke no new ground but it did one vital thing. It helped break through the shell of misunderstanding ... Within 15 minutes of the programme starting listeners found themselves discussing gayness with an approach so casual that they might as well have been asking for a record request.' On this occasion listeners could hear Myra with a 25-year-old gay son, Mike from London Transport and callers from organizations such as Challenge, CHE London, Friend and Parents' Enquiry. Not forgetting 'Brent of Fulham' asking Denis: 'WHAT DO YOU DO IN BED?'

Callow, Simon (1949–   ) English actor, writer and director of rich, fruity tones, powerful shaggy presence. Stage work includes GAY SWEATSHOP. Directed *The Ballad of the Sad Café* (1991 C).

C: The actor-director Emanuel Schikaneder in *Amadeus* (1984); the Rev. Beebe in *A Room with a View* (1986); Mark Varda in *The Good Father* (1986); the schoolmaster in MAURICE (1987); Otto Hunt in *Manifesto* (1988, the experience recounted in his book *Shooting the Actor or the Choreography of Chaos*); the pretentious film director in *Postcards from the Edge* (1990); Eddie Cheese, 'the world's most famous balloon-twister in *Soft Top, Hard Shoulder* (1992).

R: Sachs in *The Jail Diary of Albie Sachs* (1980); *The Wordsmiths of Gorsemere* (1982); Wolfgang Amadeus Mozart in *Amadeus* (1983, repeating his stage role); KALEIDOSCOPE 'The Actor as Director' (with Sheila Hancock 1986); *Shakespeare on His Lips* (about Charles Laughton 1987); a ballet impresario in *A Bullet in the Ballet* (1987); *Death or a Kind Gentleman* (about Micheal MACLIAMMOIR 1991); Sherlock HOLMES in *The Seven Per Cent Solution* (1993); *The Miles Kington Interview* (as Oscar WILDE 1993).

T: Max in *Instant Enlightenment Including VAT* (1980); *The Sonnets of William Shakespeare* (1984); Tom Chance in the comedy series *Chance in a Million* (1983–5); Hugo in *Dead Head* (1986); the artist Raimondi in *Cariani and the Courtesans* (1987); *Acting* in Restoration comedy (scenes from *The Relapse* 1987); Patriot Palloy in *French Revolutionary Writers* (1989); Nathaniel Quass, asthmatic recluse violinist in *Old Flames* (1990); OUT ON TUESDAY introducing 'White Flannel' (1990); SATURDAY NIGHT OUT 'To Be or Not to Be' (1991); *Without Walls* 'Dark Horses' (Shakespeare 1992); the Rev. Ronnie in *Femme Fatale* (1993).

camp Anything that was frivolous and paradoxical within a conventional framework: Oscar WILDE's epigrams; Busby Berkeley musicals like *Dames* with Dick Powell (heavily eye-shadowed and lipsticked), Ruby Keeler (plucky in tap shoes), and 50 blonde chorus girls sharing 25 beds (and thoroughly enjoying it); 'SHUFFLE OFF TO BUFFALO' sung by Una Merkel and Ginger Rogers plus a train full of chorus girls (*Forty-second Street* 1933 C). In what other Hollywood number does a man sing, 'I'll go home and get my panties ... and away we'll go!'? On television, camp could describe everybody from Katie Boyle emoting dramatically in *Golden Girl* (1960) and inconsequentially in the Eurovision Song Contest and Sarah Lawson declaiming in *The Whole Truth* (1957: 'You're mad ... mad ... mad ... mad ... mad!') to Margaret THATCHER, Keith Floyd and Julian CLARY.

Ronald Bryden discussed the meaning and implications of camp on WOMAN'S HOUR in October 1966: 'Under an affectation of bored fashion, it conceals a sharp sexual hostility, a repudiation of sexual roles ... [and] it covers itself with protective humour; it is a joke, a tease, it didn't really mean it. Or did it?'

During a *Start the Week* (1983 R) discussion, author Mark Booth was accused of historical slipshoddiness by attributing camp to the 17th-century habit of standing with the weight on the front foot and hand on hip. Brian Sewell, disputing that the word derives from Molière's *Stefan*, averred that 'camp', like 'GAY', is a distasteful word: '... by and large it seems to connote total misunderstanding of personal behaviour.' Booth thought that the very notion of a psychiatrist, an art historian, himself as the author of a book on *Camp*, the compiler of *The Penguin Book of Homosexual Verse*, and other pundits sitting around a table drinking BBC coffee, discussing camp first thing on a Monday morning was camp of the very highest order.

camp names Usually these are 'female' names such as 'Gloria' BEAUMONT, the orderly 'Sophie' in THE JEWEL IN THE CROWN, or Terri Dennis' constant exclamation of 'Jessica Christ' in PRIVATES ON PARADE. *See also* GIRLS' NAMES FOR BOYS; NAMES; NICKNAMES; SURNAMES.

Campaign for Homosexual Equality
See CHE.

Campbell, Colin (1937–) English actor, fresh, expressive creator of Evelyn BAXTER and the more troubled, introverted Reggie in *The Leather Boys* (1963 C).

 C: *Saturday Night Out* (1965); Emile, victim of the bloodshed on Cyprus in *The High Bright Sun* (1965); man listening to *Madam Butterfly* in MY BEAUTIFUL LAUNDRETTE (1985); two scenes, one as a corpse, in *Nuns on the Run* (1990).

 R: boy actor on CHILDREN'S HOUR; Leo (as a boy) in *Return to Naples* (1953); Evelyn in THE PRIVATE LIFE OF HILDA TABLET (1954) and others in the series; Jim Hanson in *Rodney Stone* (1954); hero of *The Baron's Hostage* (1958); Kit Nubbles in *The Old Curiosity Shop* (1958); Paul in *The Green Sailors* (1958); Eddie in *There's Nothing You Can't Take* (1964); etc.

 T: Bill Holiday in *Happy Holidays* (1954); Sub-Lieutenant in *Carry on Admiral* (1958); Derek in *The Harsh Word* (1960); PROBATION OFFICER; *Boyd QC*; David Ashton, charming, incompetent, incorrigible in *A Family at War* (1970); bus conductor in Stephen Frears' *Bloody Kids* (1980); Sergeant Willoughby in *The Ruth Rendell Mysteries* 'Means of Evil' (1991).

Can't Stop the Music (US 1980 C)
Cute, cute, cute gay in-jokes abound in what appears to be the story of a group of ordinary guys who become disco stars thanks to Valerie Perrine and Steve Guttenberg (playing a laundered version of VILLAGE PEOPLE's gay creator Jacques Morali).

W: Bronte Woodward and Allan Carr; P: Allan Carr and Jacques Morali; D: Nancy Walker; 124 mins.

Millions of dollars down the chute on this disco party which reached audiences months after the fad had peaked. It is honoured in the Medved brothers' *Hollywood Hall of Shame* (1984) as one of the most expensive flops in movie history. The highlight of this utterly doomed enterprise, so inherently dishonest that gays don't even figure in the final super-disco sequence is the Busby Berkeley-revisited choreography for YMCA, the first homoerotic number in post-STONEWALL cinema. And very ravishing it is. There's also a jape at the expense of Middle America called 'Milk Shake' with a child dressed *à la* Village People. With its dumb story-line and frantic acting, *Can't Stop the Music* will date and date and date until it becomes a minor but genuine delight from the bygone days of gay innocence. A big success only in Australia, it was chosen as Channel 9's new-year movie in 1993.

Can't Take My Eyes Off You The 1968 Andy Williams hit tenderly chorused by Robert De Niro, John Heard, Christopher Walken and others at Heard's stag party in *The Deer Hunter* (1978 C), half celebration, half dirge. The BRIDEGROOM-to-be is then kissed – by an older man. The overt lyricism and semi-buried eroticism of this get-together around a pool table is under-mined by what follows: an interminable wedding and reception sequence (where the song is crooned) and a hunting trip during which John Cazale calls the De Niro character a FAGGOT. In between there is a night-time conversation in a coal train wagon wherein a naked De Niro sits back to back with (a clothed) Walken.

Martin **Caplan** A symbol of degeneracy. 'He seemed to think that everybody, young, male and female, should fall in love with him.' But 'he clamoured for truth' in a murmur of lies and evasions that is known as polite society. In debt, mainly because of drug dependency, he has supposedly killed himself before J. B. Priestley's play DANGEROUS CORNER begins. He is made to take the blame for a theft and for the misspent love lives of overtly calm, respectable people. Martin is the other side of underneath, a malign influence who, nevertheless, leaves a gap in the lives of all the main characters. Priestley created one of the first BISEX-UAL characters in this 1929 time-dislo-cation play. A similar figure, Gary (Michael Pennington), who drives his fiancée to suicide and who kills himself

because of gambling debts, appears in Priestley's final play, *Anyone for Tennis?* written for television in 1968.

Capote, Truman (1924–84) American novelist and journalist with a strong Gothic sense and a need to be embraced by high society. A true exotic, an orchid who became progressively more like a wilted daisy as the 1960s became the 1970s. His rise and decline charted in THE SOUTH BANK SHOW 'Capote' (1985).

C: *Breakfast at Tiffany's* (1961); In *Cold Blood* (1966). As screenwriter: *Beat the Devil* (co-writer 1954); *Terminal Station/Indiscretion of an American Wife* (1954, two scenes only); *The Innocents* (1961). As actor: the victim of *Murder By Death* (1976).

T: *Please Murder Me* (adapted from *The Judgement of Paris* 1958); *Answered Prayers* (1961, adaptation); *The Grass Harp* (1962); *Among the Paths to Eden* (1967); THE GLASS HOUSE (1972). As actor: *Laura* (1967). Scores of appear-ances on American talk shows; a few in the UK, eg *Friday Night, Saturday Morn-ing* (1981).

The Captain's Table (UK 1958 C) Light comedy in the 'Doctor' mould set on a luxury liner, with John Gregson.
W: John Whiting, Bryan Forbes and Nicholas Phipps; P: Joseph Janni; D: Jack Lee; 89 mins.
An intermittently perky script intro-duces a sexual element missing in Richard Gordon's comic novel in the mother hen persona of the first-time captain's STEWARD, Birtweed (Reginald BECKWITH). He arrives, impeccable in blue and white, puffed and all in a bother: 'I'm sorry I'm late, Captain. My 'FRIEND' was TAKEN QUEER, on the chest. We live together, see. Mind you, strictly platonic. It's all give and take isn't it. Thinks the world of me, my friend does. I just keep myself to myself, the best thing.'

Caravaggio (UK 1986 C) Known as Il Caravaggio, he was born Michelangelo Merisi *c* 1570 and died in Tuscany

1610. Beyond a murder charge which sent him into exile, very little can be gleaned about his life. Here he is seen as the painter and lover of a rough young man, whom he eventually stabs.

W/D: Derek JARMAN; P: Sarah Radclyffe; 93 mins.

A broad trawl through the minimally documented childhood and adolescence and death of one of the masters of baroque painting (played by Nigel Terry). Superlative visuals, clever use of anachronism, usual muddy narrative patches, some pallid supporting acting. A gumbo!

In addition, JARMAN was one of the contributors to *Michele*, a 1987 radio documentary 'in seven acts on the life and work of Michelangelo Merisi da Caravaggio'.

cardigans Worn by maidenly men like Allyn Joslyn in *You Can't Run Away from It* (1956 C) and Derek Nimmo in *Go to Blazes* (1962 C), and by misogynist Henry Higgins (Rex Harrison) in *My Fair Lady* (1964 C). Cardigans jeered at by Frank Muir in *TV Heaven* (1992 T) as being garments best suited to young doctors in cough mixture commercials. Or maybe by Val Doonican who had boosted the cardigan's image for some from 1966 onwards.

career vs honesty 'We're two grown women – there's no reason to jeopardise our careers,' Marjorie to Gail in MY TWO LOVES. Ruth, the child psychology lecturer is concerned that LIANNA will blow her cover. In *Two People* (1993 R) two lesbians described their very different approaches to coming out at work.

Carlin, John (1938–) Scottish actor, whose roles often have a nervous, fey quality to them, overlaid with a disturbing, wintry dourness.

R: the King of Denmark in *Fratricide Punished* (1959); introduced *Music to Midnight* on the Light Programme in 1964.

T: *Your Verdict* 'Cause and Effect' (1961); radiologist in *Dr Finlay's Casebook* 'Cry Wolf' (1963); Simon in *Are You Ready for the Music?* (1965); Ron in

Compact 'Any Other Business' (1965); Captain Hinchcliffe in *A Question of Honour* (1968, about a 1914 court martial); as Richard Hawk in MONITOR 'Cold Comfort Farm' (1968 T); Maxime in *Père Goriot* (1968); Dr Stockoe in *Big Brother* 'There's Always a First Time' (1970); barman in *Man About the House* ('One More for the Pot' etc 1975–6); estate agent in *Down the 'Gate* with Reg Varney (1976); Hugh in *Comedy Playhouse* 'The Truth About Verity' (1978); Pierce in *The Sweeney* 'The Bigger They Are' (1978); George Briscoe in *The Foundation* 'Conclusions' (1978); casino supervisor in *George and Mildred* (1980); Charles in *Between the Covers* (1980 T); Derek in *Minder* 'Senior Citizen Caine' (1983); Ned in *Oxbridge Blues* 'Similar Triangles' (1984); Speaker of the House of Commons in *The New Statesman* (1987); the valuer in AFTER HENRY 'The Teapot' (1988); ANTIQUE DEALER in *Executive Stress* (1988); hotel manager in The Temptation of Eileen (1988); Paul Cooper in *Taggart* 'Hostile Witness' (1990, as a wife murderer, now in psychiatric hospital); etc.

Carmilla/Carmilla Karnstein known as Mircalla Lesbian VAMPIRE, dislocator of the normal, from the story by Sheridan Le Fanu, corrupting young women. Featured in films like THE VAMPIRE LOVERS (Ingrid Pitt), *Lust for a Vampire* (Yutte Stensgaard 1970) and *Twins of Evil* (Madeleine and Mary Collinson 1970) and on television in *Tales of Mystery and Imagination* (Jane Merrow 1966). Diane Le Fanu (Celeste Yarnall) was Carmilla updated in *The Velvet Vampire* (1971 C). 'The vampire is prone to ... expend inexhaustible patience and strategies for access to a particular object ... it will never desert until it has satiated with passion and drained the very life of its coveted victim' (Sheridan Le Fanu, *Carmilla* Aust 1989 R).

Carpenter, Carleton (1926–) Interesting gangly actor with pizzicato delivery, whose only starring role was in the gentle comedy about a cowboy in Las Vegas, *Sky Full of Moon* (1952). He is remembered today only for his duet-ing 'Aba Daba Honeymoon' with Deb-bie Reynolds in *Two Weeks with Love* (1950), and for his one-word appear-ance in SOME OF MY BEST FRIENDS ARE ... (1971 C). On the stage, in 1979, he was a journalist determined to secure an interview with the reclusive Barbara in 'Miss STANWYCK Is Still in Hiding'.

C: *Lost Boundaries* (1948); fleetingly seen in *Father of the Bride* (1950); blah roles in *Saddle Tramp* (1950); *Summer Stock* (1950); *Take the High Ground* (1954).

T: *Cimarron City* 'A Legacy for Ossie Harper' (1959), as a guitar player who momentarily owns Cimarron City; PERRY MASON (1963).

Carpenter, Edward (1844–1929) English writer and Utopian socialist, whose ideas influenced many socialist thinkers and homosexual reformers. In ONLY CONNECT, E. M. FORSTER (Chris-topher Banks) is seen and heard reading from Carpenter's autobiography *My Days and Dreams: How The World Looks at Seventy*: 'When I was a boy ... I [came to] the distinct conclusion that there were only two things really worth living for: the glory and beauty of nature, and the glory and beauty of human friend-ships. And today I feel the same.' But Forster, in his talk for radio, omits – accidentally? – any mention of what kind of human friendship Carpenter mainly had in mind.

In a talk in 1972, K. W. Gransden does mention Carpenter's lover, George Merrill and opines that Carpenter has been forgotten. *The Dictatorship of the Prigs* (1978 R) almost, but not com-pletely, relegates the man to the ranks of moth-eaten Victorian–Edwardian cranks and mystics, though his strong sexual attraction was eulogized by a het-erosexual former MP, Fenner Brockway (then aged 90): 'He was beautiful in an almost effeminate way ... I had no knowledge then of his sexual behaviour, but I was almost attracted to him as though I was with a woman ... He was an inspiration to my generation and *To-wards Democracy* was our bible.'

carpenters Gisela teaches delinquent boys while in hiding in London (SILENT WING); 'Andy the Furniture Maker' in SIX OF HEARTS (1986): his work includes torture furniture for prostitutes as well as 'beds to sleep on: and my beds don't creak when you're fucking'.

Carrington, Dora aka Carrington English painter who lived with both Lyt-ton STRACHEY and Ralph Partridge, and who committed suicide after the former's death. Attempts to capture her melancholy, avian spirit by Helen Blatch in *The Picture of Katherine Mansfield* (1973 T); Jill Bennett (*Lytton Strachey* 1981); Joanna David (THE SOUTH BANK SHOW 'No Need to Lie' 1980).

Steven **Carrington** (Al Corley 1981–3; Jack COLEMAN 1983–1987/91 in DYNASTY) The son of Blake and Alexis Carrington, born under the sign of Gemini, the Twins. A SENSITIVE, artistic young man unsure of what to do with his life, returning to Denver to take up some kind of role in his father's oil empire.

A latter-day saint, benumbedly smiling through whatever gay put-down is lobbed at him by his sister Fallon, his father Blake and his half-brother Adam. When he does strike some sort of spark with a man, the object of his interest dies violently (Ted and Luke) or fades away (Bart). He's none too lucky with his women either: Claudia goes berserk and dies in a hotel fire she had started. His wife, Sammy Jo is an unregenerate liar, con-artist, kidnapper, grizzler and work-ing-class trollop who turns out to be Rock HUDSON's love-child and an heir-ess. No wonder Steven spent much of the 1985–7 episodes with his young son. Only Alexis, his mainly absentee mother, can make sense of all the tan-gled knitting that is Steven: in 1983 she purred, 'I've *always* understood you, darling ... better than all of them.'

For all his painful indecision and blandness, Steven was – and remains – the first WASP gay to be prominently featured in a big, splashy successful television drama that has been seen all over the world. When last seen (*Dynasty:*

The Reunion 1991) he was happily en-sconced with Bart Fallmont, having problems with Sammy Jo over son Danny's visiting them but otherwise being an upright – and far less uptight – citizen.

'He's a sexually confused cipher through which the audience is taught that no one is ever really gay; gayness is just self-indulgent behaviour, a plot convenience that can be changed weekly to achieve a high number of sexual permutations' (Vito RUSSO, *The Celluloid Closet*, 1987).

'If you look at the media you'll learn that a gay person is like Steven Carr-ington on *Dynasty*. He has a lot of money and is white, is over 21, has blond hair and is healthy. The black community and other communities within the gay community know that's not true' (Charles Black, NY Commission on Human Rights, RIGHTS AND REACTIONS 1988 T).

Carry On series British screen com-edies made between 1958 (*Sergeant*) to 1978 (*Emmanuelle*), all heavily depen-dent upon smut and innuendo, big breasts and men (usually Kenneth WIL-LIAMS and Charles HAWTREY) dressing up as women. A comeback of sorts in 1992 with *Carry On Columbus*, minus most of the regulars (two thirds are dead) and with a clutch of 'alternative' comedians, including Julian CLARY.

car salesmen Relentlessly cheerful Phip Mortimer (Nigel STOCK) hoping to in-herit some money from the family as long as they don't find out his secret (and being willing to act as an informer on fellow gays in order to keep that secret hidden) in VICTIM (1961); Freddy (Carle Bensen) whom Connie Stevens keeps talking while Palumbo (Burt Young) searches his files, setting light to them in the process, which provokes all manner of squeals and gasps from Freddy as the pair make a getaway, in *Murder Can Hurt You* (1980 T).

Carvic, Heron (?–1980) British actor with a voice like an immaculately tai-lored gurgle, best known for his 'bram-bled' roles on radio, but chillingly memorable as the decadent ARISTO-CRAT, the Marquis De St Evremonde in *A Tale of Two Cities* on Children's Tele-vision in 1958. Carvic wrote three 'Miss Seeton' detective novels between 1968 and 1971, each one containing lesbian characters. A multitude of roles on BBC radio during the 1940s and 1950s, including CAIAPHAS in a number of pro-ductions of *The Man Born to Be King*. His later ones include:

R: Sir Andrew AGUECHEEK in *Twelfth Night* (1956); Zeus in *Prometheus Bound* (1957); Benjamin Disraeli in *The Young England Party* (1957); Mr CECIL of Christophe at Cie Couturiers in *A Knife in the Sun* (1958); Mr Scales, the lizard in *Mossy Green Theatre* (1958); CAIAPHAS in *Sparks in Judea* (1959); Cardinal Bar-berini, later Pope Urban VIII in *Hadrian VII* (1959); Anubis, Egyptian God of the Dead in *The Infernal Machine* (1960); Thomas Binder in *Break My Heart* (1961); Carl Lipscombe in *Bandaberry* (1961); the old patrician in *Caligula* (1961); Andrew Aguecheek opposite Jimmy EDWARDS' Toby Belch in *Twelfth Night* (1962); as *Mister Midnight* ('Chil-dren's Hour' 1963); Cardinal de Tour-non in *Genevan Fall* (1963): 'a victim of his own power and his ignorance about himself'; Versac in the story of a young man's entry into society and sex, *The Wayward Head and Heart* (1963); Bocca-dero, a critic in *The America Prize* (1964); Gideon Doubleday in *Man-servant and Maidservant* (1966): 'I see my life as a series of narrow-scapes'; Rod-ney Herter in *The Nose on My Face* (1966); Gandalf the Grey in *The Hobbit* (1968); Tissaphernes, a Persian satrap in *The Prisoners in the Cave* (1968); Mor-ose in *The Silent Woman* (1973): 'a gentlemen that loves not noise'; Gohux in *The Thirteen Clocks* (1973); Langrozga in *Duke Diamond* (1973).

T: *Gravelhanger* (1954); the Wizard in *The Princess and the Pea* (1961); magis-trate in *Stranger in the City* (1962).

Casement, Sir Roger (1864–1916) The Irish patriot who was shot as a traitor to

Britain in 1916. 'A lovely man,' says the patriotic Irish portrait gallery guide in *I See a Dark Stranger* (1945 C). 'The diaries contain passages which purport to show that Casement was a practising homosexual' (*Radio Times*, March 1961); this was the first time that the word 'HOMOSEXUAL' appeared in this family magazine. Peter WYNGARDE played the highly revered and despised man in *On Trial* (1960 T); the considerably less charismatic John Welsh read his transcripts in *The Verdict of the Court* 'The Trial of Roger Casement June 1916' (1961 R); and Richard Wordsworth was the lead in *On Trial* 'Roger Casement – A Question of Allegiance' (1970 T). By this time it was possible to quote from Casement's Black Diaries (often thought to be forgeries). David RUDKIN went all the way into the sexual undergrowth in CRIES FROM CASEMENT AS HIS BONES ARE BROUGHT TO DUBLIN (1973 R).

Cashman, Michael (1950–   ) English actor who won nationwide fame as Colin RUSSELL in EASTENDERS (1986–9) and as a spokesperson for gay and lesbian equality. On stage as Andy, the gay discarded lover in *Layers* (1982), and in BENT (1990) with Ian MCKELLEN.

C: Terhew in *Unman, Wittering And Zigo* (1971 C); boutique assistant Gavin in ZEE AND CO/*X, Y and Zee* (1971).

R: unsympathetic patient Gerry Grimmond in COMPROMISED IMMUNITY (1991); unsympathetic husband and father Mike in *Dirty Affairs* (1992).

T: Syd Benson in *Gideon's Way* 'The Tin God' (1964); as Billy in *You and the World* 'The Kick Off's at Three' (1970); Howard in *The Befrienders* 'The Wedding March' (1972); Mike Wallace in *The Sandbaggers* (especially 'My Name is Anna Wiseman' (1980 T); Reeves in *Bird of Prey 2* (1984); Eddie in *Season's Greetings* (1986); *Byline* 'A Kiss Is Just a Kiss' (1991); *Resonances* (1992); Malcolm Paynter in CASUALTY 'Getting Involved' (1993).

casting Homosexual/bisexual roles were, until recently, seen as the kiss of death for ACTORS and ACTRESSES. In the early 1970s, the cast from THE BOYS IN THE BAND were all severely restricted in the roles available to them; even villains were difficult to come by. In Britain, Peter FINCH said he couldn't get much work after he played Oscar WILDE despite winning two major awards; ten years later, his involvement in SUNDAY, BLOODY SUNDAY (a last-minute replacement for Ian Bannen) brought more praise, citations and no shortage of plum parts thereafter. John HURT risked a significant amount when he essayed Quentin CRISP, though he had established his reputation as a character player rather than as a star; he was probably the actor who made playing gay parts prestigious, although Alan BATES, Dirk BOGARDE and Finch had prepared the ground.

Many of the famous gay/lesbian roles were offered to – and turned down by – famous actors and actresses: offered the role Bogarde bravely took on VICTIM; Angela Lansbury passed on THE KILLING OF SISTER GEORGE; Alan BATES said no to *The Music Lovers*. Even less NEUROTIC, more heroic, sexier gay roles found few takers among star actors: the doctor Michael Ontkean eventually played in MAKING LOVE, the athlete in THE FRONT RUNNER, the main male characters in LONGTIME COMPANION. Some actors refused to play roles unless the homosexual element was removed (Charles Bronson in *The Mechanic*; Ava Gardner in *Scruples*: Gene Tierney did it because Ava wanted the role rewritten as 'motherly'). A plum role, the coach in *The Front Runner*, was turned down by every American male actor with any box office clout. Even Paul Newman, unhappy with the scripts, walked away from the project (and into *Slap Shot*) in 1977.

Those actors and actresses who repeated their stage roles include: Julie Harris in *The Member of the Wedding* (1952 C); John Kerr and Leif Erickson in TEA AND SYMPATHY (1956 C); Murray MELVIN in A TASTE OF HONEY (1961 C); Victor Henry in WHEN DID YOU LAST SEE MY MOTHER? (1967 R); Beryl REID in THE KILLING OF SISTER GEORGE (1968

C); the entire cast of THE BOYS IN THE BAND (1970 C); Ian MCKELLEN as EDWARD II; Alan Bates, Richard O'Callaghan and Michael Byrne in BUTLEY (1974 C/T); Denis QUILLEY in PRIVATES ON PARADE (1982 C); Tom Courtenay in *The Dresser* (1983 C); Miriam MARGOLYES and Natasha Morgan in GERTRUDE STEIN AND A COMPANION (1985 R); Alec MCCOWEN in A SINGLE MAN (1992 R); Stephen FRY in *Common Pursuit* (1992 T); Harvey FIERSTEIN in TORCH SONG TRILOGY (1988 C) (Matthew Broderick, who had played the role of David, Arnold's adopted son on Broadway, was Arnold's ill-fated lover in the film).

Casting that did not eventuate because of illness, change of mind or lack of financial backing includes: Dirk Bogarde as LAWRENCE OF ARABIA; Montgomery CLIFT as the major in REFLECTIONS IN A GOLDEN EYE; Rudolf NUREYEV, then Christopher Gable as NIJINSKY; Ian Bannen as Daniel Hirsch in SUNDAY, BLOODY SUNDAY; Julian Sands as MAURICE; Elton JOHN as the lesbian-converting uncle in *The Rainbow*; Sean Bean as Jesus in *The Garden*. Both Charles LAUGHTON and Noel COWARD were offered the Colonel Nicholson role that Alec Guinness played in *The Bridge on the River Kwai* (1957 C); Simon CALLOW had to turn down the role of Harry in *Heat and Dust* in 1982 (which would have been his cinema début) because of stage commitments, and Nickolas GRACE played it.

Casualty (UK 1986–93 T) Saturday night drama series set in Holby City Hospital's Accident and Emergency Department. A few of the patients are homosexual ('Blood Brothers' 1986; 'Hooked' 1987; 'Allegiance' 1991; 'The Ties That Bind' 1993), but none of the staff, save possibly for Julian Chapman (Nigel le Vaillant) who – like Ken HASTINGS in the earlier ANGELS – fought hard against degradation of the NHS and who left (on a 'Point of Principle' 1992) just as he was loosening up and becoming pregnant with possibilities.

P: Geraint Morris; BBC1; 50 mins.

caterers Jule and Sand opened BONA Caterers for one week (ROUND THE HORNE 1967 R): 'From yer Hunt Ball down to yer intimate function ... Just give us a free hand and we'll give you a do your guests will never forget.' Two fluff and gossip over the canapes at a catered affair for Jack Nicholson and Meryl Streep in *Heartburn* (1986 C).

Catholicism As Charles Bourne (John Sharp) lies dying in David Mercer's *Emma's Time* (1970 T), he is disturbed by thoughts mischievous and impure: 'Can you conceive of anything more idiotic than passing through the hands of a priest before one snuffs it? Why can't they have little boy priests? Wouldn't mind passing through a pair of hands of that sort.' Converted at the end, he decides 'to peg out in arbitrary allegiance to a great metaphor ... I mean, I decided ... that the Christ kick won on points aesthetically.'

'... it's just like going to the lavatory, only you don't have to wipe ... you aren't telling them anything they haven't heard a thousand times before – and most of them are WOOFTERS anyway.' Colin (Clive Merrison) in *Figure with Meat* (1991 R).

Cat on a Hot Tin Roof (US 1958 C) Maggie the Cat (Elizabeth Taylor) has to use every ounce of strength and sexual allure to stir her husband Brick (Paul Newman) into providing her with a son and Big Daddy (Burl Ives) an heir. Brick has taken to the bottle after rejecting his college friend, Skipper, who then committed SUICIDE.

W: Richard Brooks and James Poe from the play by Tennessee WILLIAMS; P: Lawrence Weingarten; D: Richard Brooks; 108 mins.

The glossy, vibrant, powerfully acted film version replaced Brick's lust for Skipper in the play with 'immature dependency', thereby skirting – yet scuffing – Article III, Section 6 of the Hollywood Production Code that 'Sex perversion or any inference of it is forbidden'. *Cat on a Hot Tin Roof* was the first film to be given a seal of approval in this area.

Two television versions, with Brick's homosexuality restored, were produced: with Robert Wagner, Natalie Wood and Laurence Olivier in 1976; and (more convincingly) with Jessica Lange, Tommy Lee Jones and Rip Torn in 1984.

cats Animals revered and scorned, seen as mystical or as evil; put on a pedestal or persecuted. Do they somehow act as barometers of human duality? In *Cats: Caressing the Tiger* (1991 T) Professor David McDonald, who has been studying (barnyard) cat communities for 12 years, asked: 'Why is it that people have tended to typecast cats as antisocial, as solitary creatures? ... Cat society is based on a rather subtle covert language. If you are not tuned into looking for it, you just don't see it ... the sorts of signals that pass between them ... happen very quickly and they happen very rarely. I think people have spent their lives living among cats and have formed an impression without taking into account the subtlety of relationships that occur between cats.'

Usually, pussies are portrayed as not to be trusted: Tom, perpetually thwarted hunter of Jerry; and in Disney classics, the close friend of the fox in *Pinocchio* (1940 C), the fat, lazy lump in *Cinderella* (1950 C), and the homicidal Siamese in *Lady and the Tramp* (1955 C).

There was the stalking tom in the SAUL BASS credit sequence in *Walk on the Wild Side* (1962 C) – jet black, a ruthless fighter, he walks alone, erect; *Blue Peter's* seal-point Siamese was a similarly manly little chap called Jason, who prefered drinking from a bowl marked 'Dog' and at six weeks killed his first mouse (1964 T). (The more famous Petra was a puppy at this time, but she could sit, retrieve and shake hands.)

cat-owners The appropriation of the cat to the queen, with all its supposed shiftiness and slink, extends even to some heterosexual owners. The shambling Philip Marlowe of Elliott Gould in *The*

Long Goodbye (1974 C); Inspector Mattei (Bourvil) in *Le Cercle Rouge* (1970 C, whose pets were played by director Jean-Pierre Melville's three cats: Griffaulait, Fiorello and Aufrene).

Cat-owning, when it is not linked to male homosexuality, is usually the province of the frowsy bachelor, divorcee or widower: Rigsby (Leonard Rossiter) in *Rising Damp* (1974–8 T); *Bronk* (Jack Palance 1975 T) who has a white Persian called Yankee – his wife was killed in a car crash, his daughter is brain damaged and he also plays the harmonica; honourable, thoughtful Judge Rafferty (John Woods) in *Rafferty's Rules* (Aust 1988–90) has a ginger desexed model, called Rhubarb sharing his divorced man's accommodation.

Feline companions for other men, mainly homosexual, can be found as follows: in *Seventh Heaven* (1937 C) with Chico's pal (J. Edward Bromberg) 'whose love of cats and hatred of Diane [Simone Simon] suggests some darkling thought' reckons David Shipman in his *History of Cinema*; a black kitten for extortionist Nyman in the original Swedish version of *A Woman's Face* (1938 C) but not in the American remake; the black cat in *The Third Man* (1949 C) is fond only of black-hearted Harry LIME; the snowy-haired, smooth-faced, very nicely mannered and not obviously married ALIENS in *This Island Earth* (1955 C) have an extraterrestrial puss called Neutron; Big Ears has a cat named Whiskers in *The Adventures of Noddy* (1956 T; also in NODDY 1975 T); the snow-white Persian briefly seen with Anacleto (Dirk BOGARDE), a Mexican bandit in *The Singer Not the Song* (1961 C); bumbling, accident-prone Harry Worth has his Tiddles in *Here's Harry* (1962–4 T); Ralph Richardson as smooth politician Sir Stanley Johnson has Charles (played by 'Sam') in *Heart to Heart* (1962 T); the shambolic, alcohol-soaked doctor (Peter SELLERS) in *The Wrong Box* (1966 C) lives in a house overrun by smelly, scrapping balls of fur; another white Persian for master criminal (world domination branch) Ernst Blofeld (Donald Pleasence) in *You Only*

Live Twice (1967 C) – it was retained when Telly Savalas took over the role in *On Her Majesty's Secret Service* (1969 subbing for the unavailable Robert HELPMANN) followed by Charles GRAY in DIAMONDS ARE FOREVER (1971 C); in *The Man Behind You* (1968 T) Michael Bryant's cat is the only barrier between himself and madness – when the animal is accidentally killed, he goes berserk; Jess (Christopher Sandford) in *Root of All Evil* 'West of Eden' (1968 T); Daniel SERENO (Daniel Massey) has three white Persians Scipio, Malvina and Poppaea whom he unsuccessfully tries to drown in THE ROADS TO FREEDOM (1970 T); smelly Albert Parsons (Harry ANDREWS) in *The Internecine Project* (1974 C), loves his puss to distraction; a white Persian belongs to Dicky (Derek Fowlds) in *Murder is a One Act Play*, but is mainly seen being mummied by Tony Barton (Anthony Newlands) (1974 T); Olly (Herb Edelman) in *The Yakuza* (1974 C) lives with cat, guns and samurai swords in Tokyo and teaches the Japanese American history – he is hesitant, balding, without female companionship; TEACHER Tony Kellett (Derrick Gilbert) lives in a cottage totally alone save for his moggie in STANDARD PROCEDURE (1979 R); most indulged of all gay felines is Figgie (short for Figaro), the property of flustered Alistair Proudfoot in THREE PIECE SWEET (1979 R): 'Figgie is a most discerning puss' and, to prove it, his dirt tray is lined with copies of GAY NEWS; ffolkes (Roger Moore) in *North Sea Hijack/ffolkes* (1980 C) is an 'oddball', 'eccentric' underwater saboteur who strokes his tabby.

Lorri Lee alias 'Lol, Bona Queen of Fabularity' (40 MINUTES 1981 T) has a Siamese so Lori is always 'smothered in 'airs'; a grey Persian scrabbles sensuously over the black silk sheets under which his co-master John Gray (Simon Shepherd) lies languorously naked in *Aubrey* (1982 T) while Beardsley (John Dicks) tries to make conversation; Jasper (John GIELGUD) talks to his Minkles in *Time After Time* (1986 T: 'You're a good boy, aren't you, Minkles'), provoking his sour sister May

to snarl, 'No guts ... now you're afraid of your own cat'; Siamese-besotted ASSASSIN Edward (Clive Merrison) in *Call Me Mister* 'Long Shot' (1986 T); doting Uncle Monty (Richard Griffiths) pretends he hates his grey Persian ('he's a thug') in *Withnail and I* (1986 C); the devotion of Alistair (Dominic Jephcott) to Marmalade and Pussy Galore causes a spat between himself and Nigel in *Claws* (1987 T), but it is as nothing compared to the scratching and screeching rivalries in the cat club to which Alistair belongs; the 'weak, spiteful and alcoholic' husband in *The Bill* 'The Muggers and the Gypsies' (1988 T) lending his lap to a Persian while simultaneously berating his wife for her sterility; the clairvoyant in *The Secret Identity of* JACK THE RIPPER (1988 T), has a squalling moggie; 'No one's idea of a hero' David Dunhill (Richard E. Grant) has Louis, who sits on his lap after he's beaten up in HERE IS THE NEWS (1989 T); scheming Helena (Diana Rigg) doesn't like cats but calls son Christopher (James Wilby) 'Kit' after Kitten in *Mother Love* (1989 T); chemist Geoff Hatfield (Geoffrey BAYLDON) with Alfred in 'And Sheep May Safely Graze' episode of *All Creatures Great and Small* (1989 T); cuckolded Terence Halliday (Michael Angelis) in *The Last Supper* (1990 T); an unnamed tortoiseshell one in scene with David (Bruce Davison) and Sean (Mark Lamos) in LONGTIME COMPANION (1990 C).

There are noticeably fewer cats belonging to (the noticeably fewer) lesbian characters, except for Patsy's SAPPHO (who spends more time at the vet's than did her predecessor, 'Aphra Behn') in *Is That You, Nancy?* (Aust 1991 R); and Sarah's in *The Gay Divorcee* (Aust 1991 R). And, of course, there was the one nasty SPINSTER Elvira Gulch (Margaret Hamilton), alias the WICKED WITCH OF THE WEST, has in her basket which Dorothy's dog Toto chases in *The Wizard of Oz* (1939 C), part of the cat-'n'-hag tradition.

Catwoman Spitting and snarling in her black leather jump suit (*à la* Cathy

GALE) this is a darling crypto-dyke character for the kiddies and the grown-ups, a brazen broad up to no good and loving every minute of it. She takes a tentative interest in the Caped Crusader, but he's more use to her as a claw sharpener than as a viable lover. Julie Newmar created the role in the *Batman* television series in 1966; it was then taken over by Eartha Kitt and, in the movie, by Lee Meriwether. Nearly six feet of slender muscle, super-charged and sassy. Julie Newmar was totally in control, street-wise and oddly touching. If she wasn't half-cat she'd be all Woman. Michelle Pfeiffer played her in full s/m rig in *Batman Returns* (1992 C) and its 1993 sequel.

Caught Looking (UK 1991 T) Louis Selwyn is aided by technology to indulge his sexual fantasies, over which are laid his lugubrious inner thoughts (spoken by Bloo Lips' Bette Bourne).
W: Paul Hallam; D: Constantine GIANNARIS; 25 mins.
A deliciously realized fantasy which will become reality any day now. It proved too hot for comfort in 1991, when it was shelved by CHANNEL 4 and not shown until a year later, outside its designated slot in OUT, and late at night.

Cause Célèbre (UK 1975 R) Juror Edith Davenport's son Tony (Gareth Johnson), has only had sex with boys and feels the need to try heterosexual experience. An afternoon with a prostitute is a disaster and he goes back to boys.
D: Cherry Cookson; 27.10.75; Radio 4; 90 mins.
One of Terence RATTIGAN's most autobiographical creations, part of the sub-plot which parallels the 'immorality' of the main character: Alma Rattenbury (Diana Dors, in her finest performance), on trial with her young lover for the murder of her husband. A cut version was broadcast in 1977, with some of Tony's lines (which had already been shorn from Rattigan's original) being lost. The 1987 television version,

starring Helen Mirren, dropped Tony altogether.

causes Nearly every programme 'investigating' homosexuality wants to know whether people were made or born that way. From Michael SCHOFIELD and Bryan Magee in the 1960s to GAY LIFE and Phil DONAHUE in the 1980s, and on to Dr Anthony Clare who asked Derek JARMAN in IN THE PSYCHIATRIST'S CHAIR (1990 R) if he thought it was genetic: was he 'born that way?'; Jarman thought he probably was. The father of Richard Lawson (Ray Burdis) in DREAM STUFFING (1984 T) blames it all on his wife who 'never took a fag out of her mouth' all the time she was pregnant.
Rearguard action is sometimes needed within a relationship. In MY TWO LOVES (1986 T) a widow asks her lover Marjorie: 'What makes people homosexual?' Marjorie throws the question back: 'Does anyone know why they're *heterosexual?*'

Cavafy, C[onstantine] P[eter] (1863–1935) Greek poet whose life and work were most adequately (for once) covered in a 1977 radio documentary A SLIGHT ANGLE, immediately followed by readings of his love poems in *The Walls and the Visions*. All very far away from the rectitude Cavafy's friend E. M. FORSTER brought to the subject (*In the Rue Lepsius* 1951 R). Playing with overlapping time and memory, Constantine GIANNARIS evoked the young (Rupert Cole) and the old (Cyril Epstein) Cavafy in *Trojans* (1990 C/T).

CBS Reports 'The Homosexuals' (US 1967 T) The homosexual's unhappy lot. What could be more harmful to society than ADULTERY, ABORTION or PROSTITUTION? According to a public opinion poll (from 964 people) commissioned by CBS, Americans nominated homosexuality.
One of the men interviewed said he felt no sense of guilt, and if a pill were available to help him change into a heterosexual he would not take it. But the candour and self-awareness displayed by

this man was not carried through to the rest of the programme, the main thesis of which was that many homosexuals came from homes containing over-protective mothers and detached fathers.

Professor Albert Goldman rumbled: 'Homosexuality is tending to erode our cultural stability. And when you are culturally bankrupt you fall into the hands of the receiver.'

The programme, the first produced by one of the major American networks – and still widely available on loan – maintained that homosexuality could be treated by psychological or AVERSION THERAPY. It stopped short of saying *must* be treated, but the guilt-drenched, finger-wagging presentation emphasized only the loneliness, the despair of homosexuals, displaced persons in the eyes of decent society.

Cecil A name redolent of the LISP and the hissing swan.

In the UK: Cecil Mincingham (Maurice Denham) in *Much Binding in the Marsh* (1953 R), a FASHION supremo whose every whim is reflected in his creations: 'Oh *how* d'you *do*, I'm *so* glad you were able to get along to my little show'; Cecil Davenport (Dennis PRICE), decadent POET in *Crime on Their Hands* (1954 T); the actor also played Cecil Calloway, known to his friends as Tiny in VICTIM (1961 C); fashion designer Mr Cecil (Heron CARVIC) in *A Knife in the Sun* (1958 R); Cecil reluctant to marry, clucked over by his devoted former batman in *The Kingfisher* (Rex Harrison 1982 T; Michael Hordern 1985 R); Cecil Vyse (Daniel Day Lewis), buttoned up aesthete, foolish suitor in *A Room with a View* (1986 C).

Pronounced Cee-cil in the US, and usually drifting clouds of English softness and drizzle: Cecil Lovelace (Franklyn PANGBORN) in *Exit Smiling* (1926 C); Cecil Flintridge, *maître d'hôtel* (Eric BLORE) in *Shall We Dance* (1937 C); Cecil, the seasick sea serpent in *The Beany and Cecil Show* (1962–7 T; Bob Clampett animated and voiced him); Cecil Wyntoon (John Dehner), snooty in *The Baileys of Balboa* and bickering

with Paul Ford as Sam Bailey (1964–5 T); Lord Cecil Bramwich (Harvey Jason), unscrupulous aristocrat in *The Girl from UNCLE* 'The Kooky Spook Affair' (1967 T); Sir Cecil Seabrook (Victor Buono), head of bodyguard school in *The Girl from UNCLE* 'The Phi Beta Killer Affair' (1967 T); Cecil (Severn Darden) in *They Shoot Horses Don't They?* (1970 C); Cecil (Sam Waterston) in *Rancho Deluxe* (1975 C), a drifter who rustles cattle; Cecil Colby (Lloyd Bochner) who married Alexis and promptly expired in DYNASTY (1981–3 T); Cecil (Patrick Tull), closeted, married, with tinkling English airs, working for overseas aid agency in PARTING GLANCES (1985 C).

Cedric Another high fulutin' name, associated with Cedric the Saxon in *Ivanhoe* and later with snotty Cedric Errol alias *Little Lord Fauntleroy* (Freddie Bartholemew 1936 C; Richard O'Sullivan 1957 T; Ricky Schroder 1980 T; etc). The name now has pink ribbons tied to it: Cedric Entwhistle (Alec KELLAWAY) in DAD AND DAVE COME TO TOWN (1938 C); *Dad Rudd MP* (1940 C); Cedric Malmsey (Richard Waring/ John STRATTON), one of the petulant and possibly deadly *Artists in Crime* (1953 R; 1968 T; 1990 T); Cedric (Thorley Walters), snooty and ineffectual in *Murder She Said* (1961 C); bag of wind Cedric Page (Robert Morley) in *Topkapi* (1964 C); Cedric (Frank WILLIAMS) in *Diary of a Young Man* 'Power' (1964 T); Cedric, quiet, intelligent, friendless man in *The Expert* 'Cedric' (1970 T); Cedric HAMPTON in *Love in a Cold Climate* (1980 T); a computer called CEDRIC (Chris Emmett) with a camp voice who dies singing *à la 2001*'s HAL in *There Comes a Time* (1983 T); missing brother in France shortly before the declaration of war in *Looking for Cedric* (1987 R); Cedric (Bob Moores), diminutive Salvation Army officer in *Watching* (1989 T); one of Nigel Terry's sons in *Coventry Cross* (1992 T).

The Centre Show (UK 1953 T) An innocuous BBC variety show became a *cause célèbre*, and made the establishment a laughing stock. All because Benny HILL told the audience that a football coupon had been lost in Chelsea. He requested that anyone with any information should ring the police on 'Whitehall: Home–Away, Home–Away'. Ignoring the obvious reference to 'Home and Away' games, an anonymous person from Whitehall complained to the War Office that Hill was insinuating that the civil service was riddled with homosexuality (Homo-Away, Homo-Away). The *Daily Mirror* (21.1.53) put the story on the front page – much to the amusement of its readers. However, the BBC took off the show the following week and it was never heard of again.

Chambers, Whittaker (1901–61) American journalist. Played by John Harkins in CONCEALED ENEMIES (1984 T), Chambers left the American Communist Party in the late 1930s to begin a personal crusade of exposing Communist agents in high places. (He also became a senior editor of *Time* magazine.)

He conceived a stubborn and stifling hatred for Alger Hiss. Tall, elegant, Ivy League-educated, Hiss (Edward Herrman) was poised on the brink of a brilliant career in the US State Department. Hiss' lawyers uncovered Chambers' political past, and his homosexuality but Hiss refused to use it in court. However, Chambers, discovering that the secret was out, admitted all to the FBI. The perjury case of 30 May 1949 resulted in a hung jury. At a second trial in November, Hess was convicted of perjury, receiving a 5-year sentence.

'I came to Washington as a functionary of the American Communist Party. I was connected with an underground group of which Mr Hiss was a member. I do not hate Mr Hiss. We were close friends, but we are caught in a tragedy of history. Mr Hiss represents the concealed enemy which we are all fighting and I am fighting.'

Channel 4 First mooted (as ITV2) back in 1971. In 1982 it opened, supported by all the ITV companies, promising to provide a solid alternative to the other three channels, to give opportunities to independent programme makers, and to open the new service to minorities (beautifully satirized in VIDEOSTARS a year later). By the time Jeremy Isaacs resigned as controller in early 1989, there was still no regular programming for a minority that accounted for between one in 5 and one in 10 of the British public – though there had been one-off programmes like ONE IN FIVE; a series or two like THE CORNER HOUSE and SIX OF HEARTS; plus controversial feature films; a few specially made 'Films on Four' (including MY BEAUTIFUL LAUNDRETTE); and even a season called IN THE PINK.

Jeremy Isaacs did make a rousing statement on *Right to Reply* late in 1988 (just before he handed over command to Michael Grade): 'Our neighbours, our families, our friends include gays of both genders ... They are part of us and they are entitled to see themselves on television'. But it took intensive lobbying to gain a regular (10 weeks a year) slot, first as OUT ON TUESDAY and then as OUT.

Although its audience is supposedly the more liberal, liberated part of the spectrum, a survey carried out by the company around 1988 uncovered a large disparity between preferred acceptance of gays and lesbians and what, to a significant majority of Channel 4's clientele, constituted acceptable viewing. Homosexuality was not wanted in the living room.

Un Chant d'Amour (Fr 1950 C) A voyeuristic prison warder joins in a feast of sensation among the inmates. Jean GENET scripted, directed and closely supervised the editing of this unforgettable 20-minute film, one that has not been surpassed for its erotic impact, claustrophobia, compassion and hope. It was first shown in the UK in 1971, but there has been no television screening to date.

'A convicted murderer in solitary – action occurs in the minds of inmates and a sadistic guard who spies on the masturbatory rituals. A NAKED prisoner points his genitals in the direction of the camera. A BLACK man dances with his PENIS sailing from an open zipper. It is thus, through the audience's identification with Genet's characters that the director succeeds in challenging the most rigid moralizing ... a rare and truly subversive achievement' (Jack BABUSCIO, GAY NEWS, 1976).

'... is among the most intensely lyrical [films] ever made, consisting largely of close-up faces, shoulders, crotches, phalluses all lent an almost Pauline purity by their isolation and the film's silence. Comparable in achievement to certain films of Dreyer and Bresson. Genet's short film is at least their equal' (Tony Rayns, *Monthly Film Bulletin*, November 1973).

Chapman, Graham (1941–89) English comic actor, writer, member of the MONTY PYTHON team, and former doctor. He delivered a stinging anti-traditional family values manifesto on *Opinions* 'What Will the Neighbours Say?' (1984 T), declaring that 'scandalizing and mocking decent folks has been the occupation of a lifetime' and that 'marriage and children is mind-stunting mediocrity'. He inveighed against 'the weak and the feeble amongst us who dominate the course of our lives'. Holding up a card, he revealed his philosophy of life: 'Do as you would be done by' and 'Think for yourself'.

All this was in marked contrast to another appearance, in *The Pythons* (1979 T), designed to sell the highly problematic *Monty Python's Life of Brian* to the English-speaking world. Referring obliquely to his noisy coming out in the 1970s (putting money into GAY NEWS, being interviewed and photographed with his lover David Sherlock), he agreed with the interviewer that perhaps he had been a little too outspoken and had crusaded a bit too much. 'I think the atmosphere's a lot

healthier now. I've even had doubts myself, you know, on occasions that I might perhaps be going "the other way".' That he may not have been entirely sincere in this avowal was probably lost on most viewers, especially as he was smoking his pipe with a toothsome blonde woman at his side, grinning from ear to ear.

He made up for this lapse by appearing the following year, with his lover and his adopted teenage son, on one of the first GAY LIFE programmes.

C: As actor: *Doctor in Trouble* (1970) as a swishy photographer; *The Odd Job* (1978) as husband who tries to stop the assassination of his wife he has set in motion; title role and script in *Yellowbeard* (1983); all the Monty Python films (*And Now for Something Completely Different*; *Monty Python and the Holy Grail*; *The Life of Brian* – title role; *Monty Python's Meaning of Life*; *Monty Python at the Hollywood Bowl*).

T: As writer and performer: *At Last the 1948 Show!* (1967) with John Cleese; *Marty* (1968) with Marty FELDMAN and Barry TOOK; MONTY PYTHON'S FLYING CIRCUS (1969–74); *Doctor in the House*; etc. Cut from *Just for Laughs* (CBS TV Toronto) filmed at the Comedy Festival in Montreal in 1987. As himself: GAY LIFE 'Adoption' (1980); *Only Human* (1988); etc.

Chariot of Fire (UK 1970 T) A housewife (Rosemary Leach) becomes involved with a man who has spent 20 years in prison for sexual offences against small boys. A policeman comments that a child can suffer far more from the sense of outrage of his parents and the authorities than from the event itself.

W: Tony PARKER; P: Irene Shubik; 20.5.70.

Jimmy Gardner's Stanley Wood was a pathetic, inadequate, impotent man, maimed by an obsessive love for his mother which had prevented him from maturing emotionally. It was a performance you could *smell*. This was the first – and the best – of the plays dealing with 'child molesters' as real people: victims, unable to control their desires and, to some extent, manipulated by the children they want as 'friends'. This view was disputed at the time, and it will have its opponents today, possibly some of the very people who applauded its liberal-mindedness then.

Charleson, Ian (1951–90) Scottish actor, whose first film role was playing one of the amoral TWINS in JUBILEE (1977) before being shown as the symbol of athleticism and rectitude in *Chariots of Fire* (1981). Was also seen in Drew GRIFFITHS' *Something's Got to Give* (1982 T). Most of subsequent films and television roles were mediocre and he was most acclaimed for stage work: *Cat on a Hot Tin Roof* and *Hamlet*.

Charley's Aunt Lord Fancourt Babberley just happens to be carrying a bag containing a wig, a dress and women's shoes, all the better to impersonate a South American relative of the female gender as a ruse for him and his friends to partake of tea with some pretty ladies. The classic Brandon Thomas farce has been filmed, televised and broadcast regularly in the 20th century; among those in skirt and petticoats have been: Syd Chaplin (1925 C); Charlie Ruggles (1930 C); Arthur Askey (1940 C, modern version); Jack Benny (1941 C); Ray Bolger (as *Where's Charley?* 1952); Art Carney (1957 T); Bernard Cribbins (1965 T); Danny LA RUE (1969 T); Michael COCHRANE (1987 R).

Charlie Intriguing was the placement of PAUL TEMPLE's valet/BUTLER Charlie in the scheme of things. He sounded like a former SAILOR or STEWARD, relentlessly chirpy, sometimes to the annoyance of Paul's wife. Albert Campion's Lugg but far less BUTCH, more like Angus WILSON's mimicry of a North London rent boy's accent in his novel *Hemlock and After*. Charlie worked for the Temples from 1941 (*Send for Paul Temple*) to 1963 (*The Geneva Mystery*). Among those playing him were: Frank Partington (*Call for Paul Temple* 1946; *The Gregory Affair* 1947); Kenneth MORGAN

(*The Jonathan Mystery* 1947); Billy THATCHER (*The Curzon Case* 1948); Desmond Carrington (*The Madison Mystery* 1949).

It was in the original version of *The Vandyke Affair* (1950) that Charlie (Michael Harding) is asked by Paul (Kim Peacock) to run him a bath: 'I'd like bath salts (the ones from Paris – the ones *you* like, Charlie)'. As the taps begin gushing, Paul asks him if he likes opera ('Yes, sir') and proceeds to sing excerpts from *Aida*: 'You'll be enchanted, Charlie!' This cuts directly to Charlie saying to Paul: 'Blimey, you haven't half got an appetite this morning, sir!'

James Beattie was Charlie from 1953 to 1963 (the remake of *The Jonathan Mystery*). There was vestigial evidence of sexual piquancy in his sterling playing of a role which, per serial, would probably comprise no more than 18 lines of approximately 6 words apiece. His main dialogue consisted of 'Yes, Mr Temple' or 'OKEDOKE'. There'd be the one-off complexity ('I'll pop off to bed') or a moment of high drama ('Blimey, what's going on, 'ere?').

Towards the end of the series, camp friskiness has given way to something a little more reined in. There is even talk of visiting jazz clubs with 'a girlfriend'. But whatever the written dialogue, James Beattie managed to make Charlie the quintessential male soubrette, ready for any caper. Always deferential but with that tinkly bell in his voice, he was the bridge between the smart Chelsea set and the salt-of-the-earth lower orders (criminally inclined) like 'Salty' West and Dolly Brazer and 'Snooker' Riley.

Apart from Barbara Hale as Della STREET, no actor has ever made more golden brickettes with so little straw: 'Good evening, sir, can I help you?', 'Yes, sir', 'Beryl's got the afternoon off' (*The Vandyke Affair*). His most challenging lines were 'Would you like a kipper, Mrs Temple?' and 'Would you like me to make you a nice little omelette?' He was the most pliant and pleasant of servants, a real treasure though Steve does admit to finding his merry chatter ('Did I make a bloomer?' in *The Gilbert Case* 1959) a mite irritating.

The expression 'Where's Charlie fishing?' is Paul and Steve's code for detecting whether either is in danger (the answer is 'In the Thames'). In *The Spencer Affair* a phoney Paul answers correctly, but then lets slip a 'By George' instead of 'By Timothy' – a gaffe which saves Steve from being blown up.

Charlie's Angels (US 1976–81 T) Take three young women, put them in revealing clothes and send them on an undercover mission. Occasionally one of them (usually Farrah Fawcett) would be leched by a woman. In 'Angels in Chains' (1976) prison guard Max[ine] (Mary WORONOV) tells Jill (Farrah) to take a shower, adding a lustful: 'If you need anything, just let Maxine know'. Just to make sure she gets the message and obeys her order, Max asks her: 'How long is it since you've been *sprayed*? ... Get cute in here and you can get hurt, understand?' Produced by Aaron SPELLING, the series – as dumb as dust – notched up 121 episodes.

Charming! COWARD's prima donna actress Judith Bliss used it in *Hay Fever* (1938 & 1945 T) to express exasperated disapproval of the scratching and hissing of her two children which culminates in their storming off through the French windows in different directions: '*Char-*ming!' In *Paul Temple and the Margo Mystery* (1961 R) the inspector describes a suspect: 'You should have seen him last night. The sweat was pouring off him.' Steve is revolted: '*Char-*ming!' Men did not so readily use the expression. Those that did were either Cockney rogues, or suave or would-be suave types, eg Hercules GRYTPYPE-THYNNE, HANCOCK in 'The Christmas Club' (1959).

After venting it in several CARRY ON films (Nurse 1959; Teacher 1959; Constable 1960) Kenneth WILLIAMS stored 'Char-ming!' in his verbal armoury. It has acted as shorthand for a host of

shrugging QUEENS in plays and films for three decades. And not only queens: 'Oh *char-*ming! I thought that was something only your best friend would tell you,' Tom to would-be sweetheart after she's told him he smells in *Scent* (1987 R).

Now it's quite acceptable. Young John Archer, Tony and Pat's boy, employed it when talking to Eddie Grundy (Trevor Harrison) in THE ARCHERS (1990 R); Tony Britton's son (Nigel HAVERS) in *Don't Wait Up* says, 'Charming' (1983–8); and even Alistair Cooke has used it: 'The last charming article I read [was about] the reduction in sewage system staff which would result in one million more rats' (LETTER FROM AMERICA 1991 R).

Chase me! Catchphrase of Duncan NORVELLE, who sprang up on British television in 1981. The invitation further endorsed the idea of the passive, coy, always available (to heterosexual men from 8 to 80) PETER PAN. But he had a genuine sweetness about him. Norvelle's brand of gay cheek was new, but the catchphrase wasn't. It was very popular (between boy and girl) after the First World War and had sufficient staying power for George Dixon's son-in-law Andy Crawford (Peter Byrne) to say it in a DIXON OF DOCK GREEN story, significantly entitled 'A Penn'orth of All Sorts' (1957 T). Andy has become irritated by his wife's shopping spree and her incessant talk about the dresses she has bought. So he levers up his voice, places a tea cosy on his head and minces around the room lisping 'Chase me – I'm the last bus.' His spouse hits him with her handbag.

chauffeurs All togged up in cocoa-coloured leather (tight where it matters): Mr Sloane (Peter McEnery) giving all manner of rides in ENTERTAINING MR SLOANE; a real charmer behind the wheel in *The Big Sleep* (1978 C), who ends up dead.

CHE (Campaign for Homosexual Equality) An organization, originally based in Manchester, which believes that changes for homosexual people could be better achieved through slow, steady work using traditional channels, rather than the more colourful, immediate tactics of the GAY LIBERATION FRONT and other activist groups. Many support groups were set up across England and Wales, an education kit was produced and spokespeople from CHE were regularly seen and heard from 1971 onwards: *A Measure of Conscience* 'A Taste of Freedom' (1972); WORLD IN ACTION 'Joe' (1974 T); SPEAK FOR YOURSELF (1974 T); etc. CHE Lewisham produced a short film DAVID IS A HOMOSEXUAL in 1978.

A Cheery Soul (UK 1966 T) Hazel Hughes as a converted Christian: '... a wrecker, who first of all almost destroys two private lives, then a home for old people and finally the Church.'
W: Adapted by Jonquil ANTONY from Patrick WHITE's play; 27.4.66.
Based on Alex 'Scottie' Scott, 15 stones of tough old lady who helped with White's garden, Miss Docker is full of handy hints, maxims, stray facts, anecdotes, recipes. A big bore, in mad pursuit of religious conversions and human chicks to be incubated. She cannot truly grasp why people are not as she is. And, suggests White, people like Miss Docker will seek to destroy what they cannot grasp. (Jonquil Antony believed that Miss Docker should have been played by Joan Hickson.)

Chequerboard 'This Just Happens to Be a Part of Me' (Aust 1972 T) Weekly current affairs programme produced by the ABC. Its first delve into homosexuality introduced the whole of the Australian continent to a gay couple and a lesbian one, both living in Sydney. As a result of his participation on camera, Peter Bonsall-Boone was sacked from his job in an Anglican parish, although he was not a priest and was in a secure relationship (with Peter De Waal). In 1991 the ABC's *7.30 Report* revisited the two Peters, who were still living in the same house, though as loving companions not lovers, and – another first –

transmitted the couple's 25th anniversary party, surrounded by FRIENDS.

chest hair *See* HAIR.

child custody The subject was aired in IN THE GLITTER PALACE; L.A. LAW (1991 T); *The Good Father* (1986 C); in more depth in A QUESTION OF LOVE (1978 T); CROWN COURT 'A Friend of the Family' (1979 T); the 1984 documentary *Breaking the Silence*, GAY LIFE. This thorny area is usually shown in relation to lesbians, though gay men (like Oscar WILDE) and TRANSSEXUALS (like Dick in SECOND SERVE) can also be denied access to, let alone custody, of their children. Gay men undergoing the full process of LAW, character assassination and abuse were Jodie in SOAP (1978–9, winning custody of his DAUGHTER) and Steven fighting his father for his son in DYNASTY (1984–5 T) and winning.

Childie NICKNAME for Alice in THE KILLING OF SISTER GEORGE, which encapsulates the infantile dependency of the femme STEREOTYPE; also apparent in the child-woman TEACHER Simone Simon played in OLIVIA (1950 C). One woman's reaction to seeing THE KILLING OF SISTER GEORGE was: 'It left me thinking that lesbians were women who hadn't grown up yet' (OUT 'We've Been Framed' 1991 T).

child molesters (male) 'It was all so innocent. ... Jamie was really happy with me. He'd been a right tearaway ... She couldn't look after him. Had five others. Everything was going fine until his father came home from the navy and started creating about his son living with some pervert. But I never touched them, Maisie, not if they didn't want me to. It wasn't all that important. One boy even seduced me. They always blame it on the older man. ... They came to me of their own accord.' This was George Cole telling his friend why he has been out of show business for so long in COMIC'S INTERLUDE (1981 R). A similar speech was given by Stanley Wood (Jimmy Gardner) in CHARIOT OF FIRE (1970 T).

Often the perpetrator or the threat is a lonely bachelor: *Chariot of Fire, Rafferty's Rules* (Aust 1988 T), frequently in a lowly social position (Robert De Niro in *Cape Fear* 1991 C). He may be friendly with the children's parents (*Fallen Angel* 1984 T). Sometimes he is a respected member of the community. This complex area runs over into guardianship, teaching, kidnapping, torture, rape and murder, with the child molester part of the dark family of outsiders and transgressors lumped together under the title PERVERTS.

child molesters (female) Intimated rather than shown in stories about isolated women such as *The Franchise Affair* and THE CHILDREN'S HOUR.

child psychologists Lynn Carson (Donna Pescow) in *All My Children* (1977 T): a young, attractive, personable, effective professional 'who just happened to be a lesbian'. A first for US daytime television. She didn't stay around very long, though, and her example has – to date – not been consolidated elsewhere. The self-possessed Professor Ruth Brennan who teaches child psychology can't fully join LIANNA in her euphoria because 'I have to talk parents into running psychological experiments for their children'.

children Willmouse (Richjard Williams) in *The Greengage Summer/Loss of Innocence* (1961 C); young Quentin trying on ladies' clothes and make-up in THE NAKED CIVIL SERVANT; Arnold Beckoff discovered in mum's clothes plus handbag in TORCH SONG TRILOGY (1988 C); 'model child' Arthur (Jimmy Gallagher) in *Scully* (1984 T), but it's only a phase; Steven Kaanna as *Oliver* in OLIVER BUTTON IS A SISSY (1984 T); Morris (Dermot Crowley) recalling that he was a 'gay child' in *The Mourning Thief* (1984 T); subtle hints in THE TERENCE DAVIES TRILOGY; HOME MOVIE; on talk shows and documentaries, the vivid but unformed memories of many gay and lesbian people who felt 'different' and experienced strong emotions at the ages of 4, 5, 6, 7 ...

Children's Favourites (UK 1950–65 R) A request programme whose most popular songs were (in 1959) 'Sparky's Magic Piano', 'They're Changing Guards At Buckingham Palace', 'THE TEDDY BEARS' PICNIC' and 'PINK TOOTHBRUSH/BLUE TOOTHBRUSH'. Max Bygraves it was who sang the latter: teaching children to clean their teeth, and with equal regularity, that it's neater to conform – BLUE FOR BOYS, PINK FOR GIRLS, side by side in life's bathroom.

Children's Hour (UK 1937–65 R) A cornucopia of delights for all good, non-hyperactive children to listen to, with or without mother, before they had their tea and/or got stuck into homework. *Nature Parliament, Norman and Henry Bones – Boy Detectives, Toytown, The Wind in the Willows*, fairy stories, Norse legends, *The Midnight Folk, Jennings and Derbyshire* ... Killed off by *Blue Peter, Deputy Dawg*, ROBIN HOOD, DR WHO and the rest. '*Dis*-graceful!' as Mr Growser was wont to say. *Children's Hour* was a fine pagan place where the imagination could range free, secure in the knowledge that cosy surrogate uncles and aunts would be there to rescue if the water became too deep.

The Children's Hour (US 1961 C) Entitled *The Loudest Whisper* in the UK, Lillian Hellman's indictment of unthinking prejudice: the word of a spiteful child destroys the lives of two women (Audrey Hepburn and Shirley MacLaine) running a girls' school – and, in the process, reveals one of the women's love for the other.
W: Lillian Hellman (with John Michael Hayes); P/D: William Wyler; 107 mins.
Wyler's laudable return to material he had previously tackled (as THESE THREE) with the aim of tackling its lesbian theme honestly was compromised by his unwillingness to allow either woman to fully express just what it was that held them together, a bond that endures after one of them kills herself. The omission of the central trial scene is also a grave error. What remains is a fustian confession piece, sparked into life (in the

second half) by the performances of Shirley MacLaine (as the repressed Martha) and by Fay Bainter as the lying child's grandmother. (A 1971 radio version – with Jill Bennett as Martha and Prunella Scales as Karen – was shorter and less clouded.)

Vito RUSSO noted that, out of 32 films with major gay or lesbian characters made between 1961 and 1976, 13 feature SUICIDES, of which *The Children's Hour* (with a gun on stage, hanging in the film) is one of the more distressing.

chorus boys Van Johnson, George Chakiris, James Cagney, Henry Fonda, Bob Fosse and quite a few other luminaries began by hoofing on the Broadway or London stage. Colin Clive was awarded the lead role in JOURNEY'S END after being spotted in a chorus line. Yet they are usually depicted – with the exception of their tribute musical – as being ineffectual ninnies (*Blazing Saddles*, for one) and PANSIES to a man. An exception is the character of Malcolm Reingertz (Alan Marriott) in *Figure with Meat* (1991 R).

A Chorus Line (US 1985 C) A landmark musical with nearly everything that was electric and galvanizing on stage defused in the film, including the monologue of gay Paul (Cameron English), reduced and stunted like most of the numbers.

W: Arnold Schulman; P: Cy Feuer; D: Richard Attenborough; 113 mins.

In the mid-1970s Liza Minnelli was mooted to star, with Michael Jackson as Paul, but plans fell apart.

Christians 'Are you a gay Christian? No, that's all right, I don't mind at all if homosexuality is your thing, if that's the bag you're in then that's great, fantastic ... GOD just wants you to have a rotten life. God's like that. He hates poofs,' Rowan Atkinson in *Not the Nine o'Clock News* (1981 T).

Gay Christians do soldier on: Jonathan Jeffery, a former PROSTITUTE and drug addict, now helping others, was inter-

viewed on *All Things Considered*, a Sunday morning programme from BBC Wales (1980 R). Paul Brown, a former chorister discussed his gay and Christian life in *Choices* (1982 T). Like so many 'religious' discussions, nothing was allowed to speak for itself: a neutral and an anti-viewpoint also had to be sought, creating 'an atmosphere of predetermined sinfulness and maleness of homosexuality' (*Gay News*).

See also GAY CHRISTIAN MOVEMENT.

Christina (1626–89) Queen of Sweden. Greta GARBO *is* QUEEN CHRISTINA! Theirs was the perfect mating of nationality, attitude, sexuality and soul. Others who have played this highly educated woman who ascended the throne at the age of 6 include Yvonne Mitchell in Strindberg's *Queen Christina* (1954 R); Zena Walker in 1965; Liv Ullmann in *The Abdication* (1974 C); Diana Olsson in *The Improbable Puritan* (1976 R) about Cromwell's ambassador to Sweden, Bultrose Whitelock.

Christmas Tears and self-pity as well as solidarity in a gay BAR the night before Christmas in SOME OF MY BEST FRIENDS ARE ... (1971 C); time of the year for an Englishman to pay a call on an ex-lover in Brazil in FACING THE SUN (1980 T); KISSING in a deserted bar and watched only by an envious waitress are the two women journalists in ANOTHER WAY (1982 C); braving the disapproval of uncle and aunt not to mention the open hostility of woman friend's estranged husband, Harvey (Peter John) in *That Beryl Marston* ... (1981 T). Alone, listening to Elton JOHN and 'cuddling up to his computer' Colin in EASTENDERS (1986 T). The gay cop Salardi in HOOPERMAN (1988 T) advises a young man to come out to his parents over the phone. After all, it's Christmas. The results are not encouraging. His MOTHER calls him a 'faggit'.

Christmas *can* be ghastly. Spending the occasion with parents and family even if they 'know' exposes us to the full brunt and friendly fury of heterosexuality. At best, if the celebration is pure ritual, it can be 'boring', as for Paul Currie (William Armstrong) in GEMS (1985 T); at worst it can be acrimonious and invasive, as for Rob in AGONY (1981 T): 'The usual family rows: Mike Yarwood or Morecambe and Wise, leg or breast; by the way isn't it time you settled down with a nice lass. So that's the last time my parents are going to see *me* in a long while.'

Television, in Britain at least, has become the great shrine and sanctuary at Christmas. Forget the manger, come gather round the box and worship. Usually, it's family fare but recently gay relevance has made it to the front door. CABARET was shown in 1979. Colin and Barry were uniting in 1986 (though barely speaking a year later). And, in 1987, Alf Garnett's home help WINSTON and BOOKSELLER RUSSELL in AFTER HENRY 'A Week of Sundays' (1989 T). Russell finally plucked up courage to make the break from the family: 'Bob and I shall be spending the holiday decorating and listening to the Ring cycle.'

In EASTENDERS (1987) Graham (Gary Webster) urges Barry to tell their father. But how? 'Do I drop it casual like?' 'No way', cries his BROTHER. 'Gordon Bennett, you've got to wrap it up a bit.' Barry tells his Dad, and is rejected. Gloom descends and Colin and Barry do not join in the festivities. They are the only ones not brought in from the cold: Jews, Christians, lapsed Christians, babies. Barry chokes back the tears. Colin tells him it's a different generation.

'So are we.'
'But it doesn't matter with us, does it.'

In CONSENTING ADULT (1985 T), the first breakthrough in the mother's understanding comes when she invites her son and his lover for Christmas; C. J. LAMB hugs her former (on–off) lover Maggie (Elizabeth Kemp) amid trees and tinsel after Maggie has won CUSTODY of her DAUGHTER (L.A. LAW 'The Nut Before Christmas,' 1991 T). But it is during that season of goodwill that Linda Ray Guettner loses custody of her son in A QUESTION OF LOVE.

Let Donald in BROTHERS (1984) have the last word: 'There was such joy. My parents loved each other ... they watched me open the gifts. You know. I never saw my father cry except for Christmas when he watched me opening my presents. The day I told him I was gay, Christmas died. [But] there are worse things. I could be watching *The Perry Como Christmas Special* with Mom and Dad.'

Churchett, Stephen (1947–) English actor, chunky, unassuming: creator of Pete HUNT in TOGETHER (1980–1 T).

C: Mr Mundy in *Object of Beauty* (1991 C).

T: (début) history teacher in *After the Solo*, a Play for Today (1975); John Ramsey in *The Flaxborough Chronicles* (1977); Major Reeve in *The Body in the Library* (1984); doctor in *Florence Nightingale* (1985); Energy Efficiency Year advert (1986) as man lighting cigar with £5 note; PC Lacey in *Rockcliffe's Babies* 'A Bad Few Days' (1987); Ernie Tresswell in *Gruey* (1988); Snickers sweets advert (1990 T) as shopkeeper; hotel waiter in *Minder* 'A Bird in the Hand Is Worth Two in Shepherd's Bush' (1991); regular role of book-keeper Joseph Wint in *The House of Eliott* (1992).

cigarettes/cigarette lighting Cigarettes were once regarded as deviant (unlike the manly cigar and pipe). In Oscar WILDE's view, 'They are everything you could wish for in a vice as they always leave you unsatisfied.' De Musset (Shane Briant) wants *Notorious Woman* George SAND (Rosemary Harris 1974 T) to give up 'A filthy habit. Bad enough in men, but revolting in women.' She argues that the vice is one that doesn't damage the brain or give hallucinations.'

Smoking has been more or less banished from television studio appearances, so unfashionable and unhealthful is the activity regarded. Distracting, too. Denis LEMON spent a quarter of his screen time on *The Editors* 'Sex and the

Press' (1977 T) out of camera range, shaking and stubbing out his fags. A few recent smoking gays and lesbians have, however, been noted in *Voices* 'Sexual Identity' (1987 T) and OUT ON TUESDAY (1990 T).

Cigarettes can be used, surreptitiously, to suggest all kinds of undercurrents. Edward G. Robinson lights Fred MacMurray's in the final touching confrontation in *Double Indemnity* (1944 C), a scene which critic Parker TYLER described as 'one of the great love scenes in the history of the movies'. Peter LORRE performs a similar service (for Tony Martin) in *Casbah* (1948 C), but somehow it doesn't quite have the same undertow of mute, abiding love. Paul DRAKE lights up PERRY MASON in 'The Case of the Haunted Husband' (1959 T), causing Della to give her boss a questioning look.

Earthy Alun Trevose (John Patrick) lights and passes his cigarette to Philip (Rupert Frazer) in PENMARRIC (1979 T) as a symbol of new-found intimacy. In BRIDESHEAD REVISITED (1981 T) Sebastian and Charles walk hand in hand through the botanical garden looking at the ivy; then they lie in the shade of the high elms as the smoke drifts from the young aristocrat's lips. Peter Montefiore (Peter Frechette) lights a post-coital cigarette in THIRTYSOMETHING 'Love and Sex' (1989 T).

The most erotic use of tobacco was between the two prisoners, separated by a cell wall, in UN CHANT D'AMOUR (1950 C), each blowing smoke through a straw.

Cinema (UK 1964–71 T) A smashing Friday film programme (introduced over the years by the differently alluring Bamber Gascoigne, Derek GRANGER, Mark Shivas, Michael Scott, Michael Parkinson, Brian Trueman and Clive James) which would be built around a star, a director or a subject. One week, 'peripatetic' Michael Scott would be meeting 'the less conformist inhabitants of the current cinema scene. Imperialists, NYMPHOMANIACS, athletes, tattooists, junkies, dipsomaniacs, VAM-

PIRES, nightwalkers, Indians, zombies, megalomaniacs, corrupters, necrophiliacs, kleptomaniacs.' The next, he'd be looking at the career of Rock HUDSON or Ross Hunter or Doris DAY. Or examining 'changing attitudes to sex', which was a euphemism because the films chosen for excerpting all seemed to have one thing in common: REFLECTIONS IN A GOLDEN EYE, THE FOX ... In its review of blacks in American cinema ('The Defiant Ones' 1966) Scott observed with a wall-to-wall smile: 'Often it's only the STEREOTYPES that change in Hollywood.'

cinemas For many the cinema offers darkness and invisibility. It is to a deserted one that LILITH (Jean Seberg) and her fellow psychiatric patient Yvonne (Anne Meara) go in LILITH (1964 C), but jealous Vincent (Warren Beatty) follows them there and inhibits any activity.

A place of refuge, too, for Tennessee WILLIAMS' *alter ego* Tom Wingfield in *The Glass Menagerie* (1950 C; 1976 T; 1986 C), and also, suspects his mother Amanda, a euphemism for more live-action entertainment: 'I think you have been doing things that you're ashamed of. I don't believe that you go every night to the movies. People don't go to the movies at nearly midnight and movies don't let out at 2.00 am.'

For Joe ORTON the cinema was the site of his first sexual experience. He records in his diary, as quoted by Peggy Ramsay (Vanessa REDGRAVE) in PRICK UP YOUR EARS (1987 C): 'The film was *My Favourite Brunette* ... Joe says he came all down the man's raincoat.'

Long-term relationships can begin in a cinema. Mabel Warren (Anna Burden) met Janet Pardoe (Diane Aubrey) in the dark of a Berlin kino (STAMBOUL TRAIN 1962 T); Harry Moon (Derek Thompson) and Ken Church (Denis Lawson) encountered each other in a 'rather wild cartoon cinema' (ROCK FOLLIES OF '77 1977 T); the couple in *As Is* (1987 T) met in a porno picture palace.

Sometimes cinemas can be places of business: Joe Buck (Jon Voight) meets a young student (Bob Balaban) who obviously hasn't gone there for the film either – it's about space flight and, in the circumstances, remarkably erotic – but after Joe has allowed himself to be fellated, the now frightened boy confesses he hasn't any money to pay him (MID-NIGHT COWBOY 1969 C).

In TAXI ZUM KLO (1981 C) Frank RIP-PLOH goes to a movie and comes home with the cinema manager, Bernd Broaderup, who becomes his *hausfrau* lover. In civilian life the young Scots soldier Douglas Morrison (James Telfer) in HOUSE ON THE HILL 'Something for the Boys' (1981 T) is a projectionist at the Cosmo Picture House. It is in a cinema where Philip had his first experience, age 17, and where, unbeknownst to him, his FATHER goes for relief in THE LOST LANGUAGE OF CRANES (1992 T).

Circle Line (UK 1971 T) A sexually experimental STUDENT, Tim (Michael Feast) sleeps with a 14-year-old, Tarquin (Jeffrey Baggott) – an experience both enjoy on a casual basis.
W: W. Stephen GILBERT; P: Graeme McDonald; D: Claude Whatbaam; 70 mins.

'How long can the BBC get away with this?' blared the *Sunday Post*, and used the phrase 'pernicious muck'. Gilbert says: '[Tim] was a moral blank sheet and the boy wanted experience. The relationship caused shock in the household. It was filmed in 1969 and not shown for over a year. The Festival of Light put *Circle Line* among its top ten horrors of the year, along with *Myra Breckinridge*, *Oh, Calcutta!* and Martin Cole's sex film. There was a 3-month postal strike so there was no viewer reaction. The play was 'wiped' very quickly afterwards and so never repeated.

Circuit 11 – Miami (UK 1979 T) An extraordinary series of live action court cases. 'Murder in the First Degree' involved the MURDER of an elderly gay man. 'Gay Rip-Off' concerned the robbery of a Miami man by two hustlers during an s/m 'scene'. Or, as the synop-

sis put it, 'Bruce Rowe is a homosexual ... A night's pick-up in a bar leads to SADO-MASOCHISTIC sex, then real violence, robbery and the humiliation of a court case.' As baldly enunciated in court, the events of that night seem to accurately embody the drunkenness and the debauchery of which the morals campaigners rant. Bruce Rowe is face to face with what the commentator calls the classic homosexual dilemma: 'tell the truth or shut up and let the QUEER-BASHERS get away with it'. The defence attorney, a bovine in a suit, doesn't view it as a dilemma at all: 'He wanted his cake and eat it, too.' The outcome of the trial is as bizarre as the actions which brought it about: one of the boys is acquitted and leaves Miami – *with* Bruce Rowe.

City Shorts 'Came Out, It Rained, Went Back in Again' (UK 1991 T) A joy. Disillusioned lesbian (Jane Horrocks) in London. The old coming-out dance given a new melody.
W/D: Claire Dowie; 10 mins.

'Dowie's gentle satire of our lifestyles expresses a political maturity rarely seen on TV' (Jonathan Sanders, *Gay Times*, August 1991).

civil engineers A Roman Catholic priest was quoted in Richard Davenport-Hines' book *Attitudes to Sex and Sexuality in Britain Since the Renaissance* (1990) as saying: 'You can't be a homosexual if you're a civil engineer. It's only actors and artists and people like that.' So far, after nearly a century of cinema, 70 years of radio and 50 plus of television, no civil engineer answering to the description of homosexual has been seen or heard, at least not in fiction narratives.

claiming Often a criticism lobbed by heterosexual society at gays, possibly over-anxious for ROLE MODELS, or demanding a more accurate history by claiming people as homosexual with only subtextural evidence or on hearsay. Now gay/lesbian historians are becoming very picky over who is and who isn't (Christopher MARLOWE, EDWARD II, Oscar WILDE have recently been discussed in terms of imposed, misunderstood or unsubstantiated gayness). Homosexual people are not the only group to clutch individuals to a collective bosom: recently Sir Arthur Sullivan and Johann Strauss were claimed as Jewish by some biographers and historians. Heterosexuals of all persuasions have, of course, been 'claiming' gays and lesbians as 'normal' for centuries on the bases of subtext, gossip, convention or wishful thinking.

Clarence A boy's name with something of a deviant profile, but only in the UK: Clarence Fritton (Alastair Sim), not-to-be-trusted brother of a man in a wig and dress in *The Belles of St Trinian's* (1954 C); Michael WARD as Clarence Marsh in *The Grove Family* 'Leaving Home' (1956 T); Clarance (Felix Aylmer), child molester in *Never Take Sweets from a Stranger* (1960 C); Clarence Doubleday (Lance Percival), twit in *Joey Boy* (1965 C); CLARENCE in *The Dick Emery Show* (1968–79 T); 'Clarence Rock', in I'M SORRY, I'LL READ THAT AGAIN (1968 C), considered unmasculine because he always asked for a stand-in for his love scenes and known as 'Clara' to his friends, won a best actor Oscar for his performance as Julius Caesar: 'he also received best actress for his performance as Caesar's wife'; visually handicapped *Clarence* (Ronnie Barker 1988 T): 'a lovely teddy bear of a man', a clumsy cockney removal man who sets up platonic house with ladies' maid.

US: Clarence Day (William Powell), a very difficult pater in *Life with Father* (1947 C; his wife calls him 'Clare'); Clarence 'Lumpy' Rutherford (Frank Bank), older brother Wally's schmuck friend in *Leave It to Beaver* (1957–63 T); Clarence Keller (Ben Wright), bumptious apartment supervisor, with bow tie and inquisitive boy-scout manner in PERRY MASON 'The Case of the Guilty Clients' (1961 T); Clarence Henry (Max Showalter) in *Perry Mason* 'The Case of the Legal Lazarus' (1963 T), bachelor brother, his uncle's 'protégé';

Clarence Cromwell (John Hancock) in *The Black Marble* (1980 C).

Clarence THEATRICAL DRESSER, played by Dick Emery from the late 1960s to the end of the 1970s: tightly trousered, game for anything, eternally youthful. Usually his appearances were limited to vox-pop interviews, priming for the camera, eyeing up the interviewer ('HELLO, HONKY TONKS!'). The cheapest of cheap laughs: mutton dressed as lamb, wistfully desperate. In his 1974 book *In Character* Emery wrote: 'When Clarence began life [1968] male fashions were far more subdued than they are today, and so his effeminacy had to be shown through his MAKE-UP; also he wore a wig of short blond swept-back hair. These days it is difficult to keep him ahead of fashion – what Clarence wears one week, the trendies are wearing the next, or so it seems. Now, with more emphasis on his clothes, he needs less make-up and no wig at all.' One of his more substantial contributions was as the prisoner of war who made the civilian clothes for his tunnelling mates in Emery's tribute to *The Great Escape* (1978 T). Dreaming of Errol Flynn while his fellow prisoners fantasize about Betty Grable, Clarence is the only one who doesn't get away.

Barry **Clark** (Gary Hailes in EASTENDERS 1986–9 T) After a one nighter with Colin RUSSELL, Barry, who had a record stall on the market, pursued him for a few weeks before moving in, unbidden. The more demonstrative of the two: younger, brasher, ready for anything. Spectacularly ordinary. A tendency to overweight and to moaning.

On his 21st birthday he got drunk and said playfully to a policeman: 'You can't touch me now; it's legal *I'm* legal!' 'Bet he thought I was 16. Didn't know I was gay.' In his longest speech Barry continued: 'You always said, "Oh no, Barry. We shouldn't do it, Barry. You're not 21, Barry. It's illegal, Barry" ... There was me free to put my name against a parliamentary candidate, free to fight for Queen and Country ... Stupid law. If I was a bird we could have been having it away since I was 16. Cos I'm a fella, it's 21. Sexist if you ask me.'

Nothing if not decisive, Barry wants the whole world to know and his disclosure causes Dot Cotton to warn the neighbourhood of – to her mind – the ever-present dangers of catching AIDS. Eventually the differences between him and Colin, particularly those of class and education, drive them apart. A police investigation of Colin's burglary leads to Barry's home. He is terrified of his father finding out about him, despite a pledge of support from his BROTHER. After Christmas 1987 Barry begins seeing a young woman and by February he'd moved out of Colin's flat. He then pursued his ambitions to set up as a mobile disc jockey.

The character of Barry was at times as irritating as a pair of horse-hair Y-fronts – deliberately so. His is an unresolved personality, lacking in confidence and polish and full of compensating bravado. 'I know what I want and I'm not afraid to admit it.' But when it comes to the problems of living with the staider, less emotional Colin they are not sufficiently balanced by the social acceptance – of being one of the boys – that Barry craves. When the chance to break free comes he jumps at it, rationalizing his feelings for Colin as being more like a son for his father. 'I didn't know what I wanted. But I do now.' He is probably destined to become a pudgy British barrow boy version of the sexually vacillating Steven CARRINGTON.

Clarke-Smith, D. A. (1888–1959) English stage actor who made a few films – Max in the 'Jackson, the Shipping Clerk' sequence of *Friday the Thirteenth* (1933); Phaonin in *Quo Vadis* (1951) – and portrayed Mr DULCIMER in THE GREEN BAY TREE (1946) and a thinly disguised Colonel Alfred REDL in *Colonel Judas* (1945) on radio.

Clary, Julian (1959–) English comedian. Post-Grayson Man! Courageous, disarming, with an edge of eroticism and no fear of the fey. He gave the old gay

gavotte a new insolence and chic, combining prettiness with an arrogance which confirmed and undercut the STEREOTYPE, while the loose quiz show format allowed him to play a jolly party game of 'Get the hets'. It remains to be seen if he can sustain his appeal in British slapstick films and sitcoms like TERRY AND JULIAN.

'Julian Clary is not upset by being thought of as the Larry GRAYSON of the 1980s: "he's a great comedian, but not John Inman"' (*Gay Times*, May 1989).

'There's so much to send up, but there's a danger of going right over the top' (Bobby Davro, who began impersonating Clary in 1990).

'A homosexual political sex kitten ... camp to the point whereby LIBERACE would look straight ... terribly, incredibly political just by virtue of existing.' (Fiona Scott-Walker, *Arts National*, ABC radio Australia 1991).

C: Prison governor Diego in *Carry On Columbus* (1992).

R: *Nightcap* (1988); Radio 2 Sunday afternoon phone-in (1991); INTIMATE CONTACT WITH JULIAN CLARY (1992–).

T: début as the Joan Collins Fan Club in *Cabaret at the Jongleurs* (1988); *Trick or Treat* (1989); STICKY MOMENTS (1989); impersonated by Rory Bremner (1989–) and Bobby Davro; *Sticky Moments on Tour* (1990–); *Personal File* (1990); *Star Test* (1990); *The Happening* (1991); *Hysteria III* (1991; sketch with Melvyn Bragg); *Tonight Live with Steve Vizard* (Aust 1991 & 1992); *Trading Places*, giving Cilla Black the chance to choose a *Blind Date* (1992).

Claude Boy's name with occasional gay occupants. Claude Demay (Robert H. White), fall guy, art restorer in PERRY MASON 'The Case of the Torrid Tapestry' (1961 T); Claude Crepe (Anthony GARDINER) in *Mister Ten Per Cent* (1968 C); Claud Langham (Dirk BOGARDE), switched-off married son in *Providence* (1977 C); hippy Claude (John Heard) who goes to Vietnam at the end of *Hair* (1979 C); 'that appalling twerp Claude ... an utter mediocrity, completely second-rate' in *When the Barbarians Came* (1992 R).

Clause 28 An injunction against local authorities 'promoting' homosexuality, either directly or through funding other individuals or groups to do so. Voted in as part of the Local Government Act in 1988, after unprecedented protests by gays, lesbians and others across Britain. There were scores of small items about the insurrections relating to this iniquitous piece of legislation, most famously the abseiling of a group of lesbians into the chamber of the House of Lords and the invasion by some of the same women into the BBC's 6 o'clock news broadcast in May 1988. After the Clause became a 'Section', *Brass Tacks* transmitted a programme called 'Good as You?' about the stark terror the new law was producing in teachers who were now forbidden from counselling their gay or lesbian pupils. One of the few influential voices speaking out against it was Harold PINTER (to Anna Ford): 'Clause 28 is a first example of suppression of speech or thought ... It is quite interesting that the homosexual is being seen as an ALIEN force, something to be feared and therefore rejected and repressed.'

Duffy **Clayton** (Harold SCOTT in DIXON OF DOCK GREEN 1956–62) Scrofulous, stubborn near-derelict whose physical appearance belies his intellect and breeding. His attitudes to life are basically anarchic, and it came as no surprise that he was based on a man Dixon's creator, Ted WILLIS knew as a youth. 'I gave him pennies, and in return he encouraged my reading, especially Dickens ... He was homosexual; his family had thrown him out and he ended up on the road. He was one of the great influences in my life.'

cleaners Kim (Jane Lapotaire) cleans lavatories to support her work as an ARTIST (THE OTHER WOMAN 1976 T); Agnes (Doreen Hepburn) does a little night work on the side in *Phonefun Ltd* (1982 T); the mysterious and ultimately dangerous Robert Gunn (Denys Haw-

thorne) appears in *Isn't That a Girl's Locket?* (1989 R): 'Male cleaners are supposed to be more reliable.'

Clement A rarely used first name. Society photographer Clement Clements (James Thomason) in *A Shilling for Candles* (1954 R) is prone to add the D word to his every pronouncement: 'Of course, DUCKY. The motive's obvious. Everyone knows you'd stop at nothing for a part.' Or would if the BBC's morality watchers hadn't pruned most of them, lest it be thought there was something not quite normal about this fellow. In the 1963 version he's played by Brian Haines, and a couple more duckies have been inserted to keep abreast of more liberal times: 'What was that, ducky?' he asks someone.

The other Clement is the young man, played by Nigel HAVERS, who lives with Peter (Rupert Frazer) in ALL FOR LOVE 'Combat' (1982 T) and who does a lot of sparring with Peter's MOTHER (Joyce Redman), who makes it plain that she is firmly set on a finding a wife for her boy. But there are some things that can't be regulated.

clichés Firmly held beliefs regularly parleyed are:

(1) Homosexuality is a rigidly defined category – once in, there is no escape.
(2) Homosexuality is something you acquire like a disease or a DISABILITY.
(3) Same-sex relationships do not work. Ultimately one partner will become heterosexual or asexual.
(4) There are no homosexual children, only 'SISSIES' 'TOMBOYS' or teenagers 'at risk'.
(5) In a homosexual relationship there is a seducer and a seducee. Mutual sexual attraction does not exist.
(6) Love is heterosexual. Crushes, obsessions, dark desires and unrequited passions are homosexual.
(7) Homosexual men and women exist either as singles or as couples. Homosexual people only have heterosexual friends.
(8) Homophobia does not relate to other discriminations and prejudices in society.
(9) All PROSTITUTES are female except when they are 'male prostitutes', just as

all models are female except when they are 'male models' and all STRIPPERS female save when they are 'male strippers'.

(10) Only white people are homosexual.

(11) Words like 'lover' and 'murderer' must always be preceded by the words 'homosexual', 'gay' or 'lesbian'. The same does not apply in the citing of heterosexual lovers, murderers, robbers etc.

(12) Male homosexual writers have a particular empathy with their female characters (eg Tennessee WILLIAMS, Angus WILSON, Patrick WHITE).

(13) Homosexuals have no access to organizations run for them and by them, except for (Lesbian and) GAY SWITCHBOARD.

(14) Homosexual people are not consumers; therefore they are never depicted explicitly in ADVERTISEMENTS.

(15) AIDS-related diseases and their care are the only health and political issues confronting homosexual people.

(16) Homosexual people have no history apart from Oscar WILDE and the WOLFENDEN debate.

(17) The teachings of PAUL and Old Testament males are treated as acceptable modern-day reactions to homosexuality, whereas DAVID AND JONATHAN, RUTH AND NAOMI, the social circle and domestic life of Jesus, and the lack of a commandment against same-sex love are either downplayed or ignored.

(18) The actions and needs of homosexual people, whether as individuals or in organized groups, in time of war or other crises are invisible in all news and documentary programming.

(19) Homosexual people must not be seen TOUCHING one another, KISSING, HUGGING, expressing their romantic feelings ('I LOVE YOU'), in BED together, having SEX.

(20) Homosexuality can only be 'dealt' with in ACCESS programmes, special 'magazines' or documentaries aimed at the minority, single episodes of dramatic series, plays (usually of a safe nature and only rarely commissioned works by accredited homosexual writers or adaptations of valued stage productions).

(21) A homosexual man or woman will be immediately attracted to any and every heterosexual hero or heroine – who will (aggressively or nonchalantly) rebuff them.

Clift, Montgomery (1920–66) American actor who, with Marlon Brando and James DEAN, profoundly affected male screen-acting styles. He invested even his most mediocre films with a special interior glow, a nervous intensity that repays many viewings.

Although no legend has grown up around him and he is far from being a cult figure, young actors – like Gary Oldman – still revere him. There has been one superb biography (by Patricia Bosworth), one good Italian documentary and one abysmal radio tribute called *I Had the Misery Thursday* (1986), in which the actor's 16-year career is shrunk down almost entirely to the making of one film (*Freud*).

The Clinic (Aust 1982 C) Matter-of-fact mentions of itching, discharge, sores, crabs, razor-blade pissing, tubes, sebacious glands, labia majora and minora, warts, pimples, herpes, NSU, syphilis, gonorrhoea (front and back). Some jokes – 'Here's looking up you, kid' and 'It's hard because it's not so hard' – but mainly a mosaic of the client load during one day at an STD clinic, immediately prior to the first reported cases of AIDS in Australia. Not freaks and perverts, just everyday folks with libidos and need for love and lust.

W: Greg Millin; D: David Stevens; 92 mins.

'People are often afraid of things they don't understand; and syphilis doesn't have the best reputation in the world,' says the gay venereologist. There's also talk of 'lepers' and 'a punishment for lascivious behaviour'.

'If it weren't for the obviously still taboo nature of the subject matter, the film would be an excellent TV series pilot, a medical cousin to *Barney Miller*' (*Time Out*, 1982).

The Clitheroe Kid (UK 1957–72 R) Family radio series starring Jimmy Clitheroe, who was just over 4 feet tall and who died in his early fifties.

Clive Boy's name, usually on the nice side of twit. Clive Popkiss (Tom Walls), cousin of Gerald (Ralph Lynn) in *Rookery Nook* (1930 C); Clive (Laurence Olivier), a professional divorce co-respondent in *No Funny Business* (1933 C); Clive (Ron Randell), free-spending Yank in *I Am a Camera* (a substitute, for the bisexual baron); Clive (Kenneth WILLIAMS) in *Dick and the Duchess* 'Armoured Car' (1958 T); Clive Harrington rechristened 'Philip' in the film version of *Five Finger Exercise* (1962); Clive Langham, novelist and egotist (John GIELGUD) in *Providence* (1977 C); Clive Baxter (Philip Lowrie), teacher in MAINTAINING STANDARDS (1981 R); Clive Smith (Charles Kay) in *The Spectre* (1983 R); sadistic husband Clive (John Bird) in *Oxbridge Blues* 'That Was Tory' (1984 T); perverted aristo Clive (James Warwick) in *Dead Head* (1986 T); Clive (Daniel MASSEY), HIV-positive husband in *Intimate Contact* (1987 T); Clive (Hugh Grant), nervously fence-sitting great love of MAURICE (1987 C); Clive King (George Harris), Jamaican-born staff nurse in *Casualty* (1986 T); husband Clive (Michael Kitchen) in *By a Roman Road* (1987 R).

clones Forged in New York and San Francisco in the mid-1970s, the clone look consisted of short-cropped hair, EARRING, moustache, SINGLET or plaid work shirt, jeans, keys, coloured HANDKERCHIEF (to show sexual tastes) and DOC MARTEN boots. Hyper-masculine and expressionless (particularly when sunglasses were worn), it was a boon to men over 35 with thinning hair and with time and money to work out in the gym.

The look was first noted in a character played by Neil Kennedy in ROCK FOLLIES (1976 T) and in the sequel (1977) by Ken Church (Denis Lawson) as a radicalized gay journalist. It had become entrenched as being a gay image by the time of VILLAGE PEOPLE, a manufactured group with a number of hits to their credit, working both ends against Middle America.

It prevailed. The clone was, if you lived anywhere near the centre of a large city, almost unavoidable by the early 1980s.

Gerald (Richard Pearson) complained about 'all that phoney masculinity' in COMING OUT (1979 T). When a policeman (Derek Thompson) goes undercover to find a killer of gays in THE GENTLE TOUCH 'Blade' (1980 T), he togs up in macho gear rather than silk and suedette. Similarly Al Pacino in CRUISING (1980) and Ryan O'Neal and John HURT in PARTNERS (1982). The rigid clone look was satirized, along with other even stricter dress codes by Dave Dale in his version of the First World War recruiting song 'I'll Make A Man Of [Any One Of] You' in IF THEY'D ASKED FOR A LION TAMER (1984 T). The look became visible in supporting players as a gay code in plays like *Unfair Exchanges* (1984 T, Julie Walters' ANTIQUE DEALER ex-husband) and in one of the early Taggarts *Killer!* (1983, a jogger named Bertie Scott).

Stanley Reynolds told *Punch* readers: 'If women's [*sic*] image has changed dramatically in recent times, the image of the homosexual has changed out of all recognition. If they were once stereotyped as JULIAN AND SANDY ... they are now Bif and Brad ... coming on ... like everyone's idea of the perfect, ale-swilling Outback wallah from Australia. Somehow, like most changes, I don't think this has been for the best' (April 1983).

A year later, Lucy Hughes-Hallett could assert in the *Standard*: 'Gay men these days are manlier than the straights – presumably because woman's respect for the strong, silent types is so sharply on the wane' (July 1984).

In OUT's survey of HAIR, it was said that the clone image was irrevocably consigned to the 1970s; a new clone had appeared: flat-top hairstyle and a Jimmy SOMERVILLE 'look' (1991 T). 'The British clone look, the symbolic ultra masculine thing' was, reckoned *Gay Times* scribe Richard Smith, the SKINHEAD instead of the LUMBERJACK in 'DOCTOR MARTENS' (1991 T).

close friend Euphemism for lover/ONE-NIGHT STAND: used by naval officer for a dead woman 'who knew a sailor or two' in PERRY MASON 'The Case of the Slandered Submarine' (1960 T); Reynaldo HAHN was described as the 'close friend' of Marcel PROUST in 1970 (R).

Close Relations (UK 1958 R) In this play written by Roger MacDougall, Jo (Annabel Maule) is a bad woman in the eyes of her mother-in-law. She has successfully designed a car, does not want a baby *and* has 'fancy friends', including Ernest ('Economics? What does art know of economics? ... Am I *de trop*? I feel rather *de trop*'). 'You can be as clever and as modern as you like, but a motor car isn't a substitute for a baby,' clucks mother-in-law.

Is Jo a 'hard, selfish woman'? Or a winsome wife going through a fearsome phase. Or is she an exemplar of what her father-in-law hopes will be the future human blueprint? 'We have too rigid a society here. Too rigid a form of morality. Too rigid a pattern of relationships.'

The play, hitherto calm and considered, gallops to a breathless climax, which refuses to play entirely by the rules. Careerist wife returns home from a hard day in the boardroom; hubby from a hard day on the factory floor. She falls into his arms; he falls into her arms.

> She: 'Spud! Oh, Spud!'
> He: 'Jo! Darling!'

closet By the late 1980s, the closet, and the action of COMING OUT of it was sufficiently widely known so that the concept could be loosened up a bit – by Edna EVERAGE who, in a 1989 show, announced that her son Kenny has 'just come out of the cupboard'. And reviewing *File on 4* 'CLAUSE 28', Nigel Andrew wrote that 'I fear poor old Nelson GABRIEL may have left it too late to come out of the closet' (*Listener*, February 1988).

The closet had been a dark place for skeletons and people with something to hide. In *Pinky* (1949 C) the mixed-race heroine (Jeanne Crain) is upbraided by her white lover (William Lundigan) when she declines to go back east with him. She prefers to stay in the South, with her (black) people: 'What do you expect me to do – crawl into a closet and live there?'

In GAY LIBERATION terms, the closet is the starting point. How much further they venture over that line is up to the individual gay or lesbian person. An early reference to the idea was made by Jack Nichols, later the author of *Men's Liberation*, on PBS' VD BLUES 'Hotline' (1972 T): 'We need a lot more relaxation in coming out of the closet.'

There was also reference to 'the closety type'. The previous year, the hero of *The Love Machine*, Robin Stone (John Phillip Law) was called a 'closet queen' by an angry prostitute. These were the most despised of men. Says a peeved and petulant lover of a BISEXUAL in *Scruples* (1980 T): 'Is there anything so pathetic as a closet queen trying to convince himself that he really wants to make it with a woman?' In *Dithering Heights* (1985 R), a woman novelist Jane (Joanne Zorian) takes a stallion into her bed at a literary weekend: 'I'm just proving a theory I have long cherished that every last demon lover of literature was a closet homosexual masquerading as a transcendant ram.'

The reasons why the closet is so necessary for people are usually never discussed. It is seen as a typical gay cowardice: hiding in the shadows rather than standing in the light. Those that do are, of course, accused of flaunting and militancy.

clothes The basic rig for homosexual males in drama and comedy used to be something floral, something chiffon, a wide-brimmed hat, tight trousers, worn with handbag and jewellery. For the lesbian there were two basic modes: shirt-blouse, tweeds, clompy shoes or *haute couture*, which embraced the male evening dress. A whole book could be written on the gradations of dress – and of the cross-over with heterosexual characters and real-life personalities: J. R. Ewing (Larry Hagman) is attired in safari jacket and scarf in the early episodes of DALLAS, and Princess Diana repopularized the black jacket, starched shirt and bow tie for women in the early 1980s.

There are two interesting, 'personal/political' uses of dress. In PARTNERS (1982 C) John HURT as Fred and Robyn Douglass as Julie wear almost identical pale pink (shirt and T-shirt) in a morning-after-the-night-before kitchen confrontation (where she has slept with Ryan O'Neal). In HOTEL 'Passports' (1986) a gay man and his work colleague's wife wear almost identical colours in their showdown scene.

In CROWN COURT 'A Friend of the Family' (1979 T) Diana Graham is a FEMINIST journalist. Her lover, Beth has a 13-year-old DAUGHTER. It is, therefore, of some tactical significance that Diana does not further rouse the antagonism of society as represented by judge and jury. Prosecuting counsel circulates a photograph of the defendant at a FEMINIST rally 'wearing a suit and her hair austerely short'. Why is it, the prosecutor asks snidely, 'that she is now wearing a Laura Ashley dress and her hair is long and permed?' Diana is caustic: 'I *could* have worn brogues and a tweed skirt. But I didn't.' (For her court appearance she has chosen a stylish floral frock with ruffles round the neck.)

See also CLONES; COLLAR AND TIE; SCARVES.

clubs Generally known as such in Britain as distinct from the American BARS – although Gypsy Rose Lee ran a strip club with s/m trimmings called 'The Gay and Frisky' in *Screaming Mimi* (1958 C).

Definitely not respectable was the Blue Bottom to which Anthony BLANCHE scampishly propels the staid Charles Ryder (Jeremy Irons) in BRIDESHEAD REVISITED (1981 T). In this 'louche little bar' we see men dancing together and there's a (1960s) lesbian straddling a stool. It is run by Cyril, a non-gay cockney. After giving Charles a moment or two to survey the scene (in semi-darkness) Anthony can't resist commenting that 'here you are just as conspicuous and, may I say, abnormal, my dear, as I should be at Brat's Club'. A young swish

moves in on Charles, asking Anthony if his friend would care to rhumba. He is shooed away. 'An impudent boy. A regular little gold-digger, my dear.' But the boy, Tom (Paul Clayton) refuses to retreat: 'Don't be a tease, Tony, buy me a drink.' Anthony happily complies while Charles makes his excuses and leaves.

Anthony had earlier noted with ennui that The Blue Bottom is 'a synthetic little joint' that will not last long: 'They change so fast.' More uptown is the club that Quentin CRISP is thrown out of (courteously) in THE NAKED CIVIL SERVANT (1975 T), an example of members of a minority mistreating one of their own because he dares to dress in clothes and MAKE-UP that would be unremarkable at a fancy dress party. A similar situation occurs at the 'restaurant' in the 1950s where a man dances with his young friend, kisses him and is asked to leave (*Now That It's Morning* 1992 T).

A haven for gay men, warm and cosy, that probably never existed outside the imagination of Drew GRIFFITHS (in HOUSE ON THE HILL 'Something for the Boys' 1981 T) brought together a Scottish private – a virgin – and an American GI, the nicer side of slick. Dancing to the swooning brass of Glenn Miller in Edinburgh these boys forget about the war and the restrictions on their personal lives. Immediately postwar, in London, is La Vie en Rose, a drinking establishment for GIs and marginalized men and women (ABSOLUTE HELL! 1991 T).

Very much for real was The Gateways Club which June Buckridge tells Mercy Croft is 'a fascinating little spot in Brabazon Street, just off the King's Road' (THE KILLING OF SISTER GEORGE 1968 C). There then follows a 15-minute sequence involving a talent competition and the arrival of Mrs Croft to watch – her face contorted with controlled revulsion, or is it attentive amazement? – as a basement full of DYKES disport themselves to a four-woman rock band. Cramped, smoky but infectious – except to the chillingly closeted lady from the BBC.

A billiard room was laid on for the occasion, but all the members (with the exception of four actresses) were real, card-carrying lesbians, glad of the money, although braving exposure to family, employers and friends in 35mm colour. The club itself closed in 1984 after years of loyal, if limited and cramped, service to lesbians from all over the world.

The Little Ladies (Rula Lenska, Julie Covington and Charlotte Cornwell) logically should have played a lesbian club in ROCK FOLLIES (1976 T) rather than Aladdin's Cave, a whacky joint where the barman presides in turban, bolero jacket and harem pants. No one comes to hear the 'Ladies' set. Explains the owner: 'Tonight was sheer death. Word must have gotten around about the raid last night ... they want to revoke my licence.' The Adam's Apple in STAIRCASE was the hideaway where Charlie DYER is done for importuning and wearing female attire (he touched up a man who turned out to be the fuzz).

Raids became less common in the late 1970s. The drinking/dancing places featured in shows like MINDER 'Whose Life Is It Anyway?' (1980 T) and *The Chelsea Murders* (1981 T); *A Spy at Evening* (1981 T) and *The Wilde Alliance* 'A Game for Two Players' (1978 T) were uneventful. All that was seen of a Jersey hot spot (homosexuality between consenting adults remained illegal on the island until 1990) was a poky cellar from whence Jim *Bergerac* trails a suspicious-acting Italian WAITER ('Nice People Die in Bed' 1981 T).

There was a basement joint where the erring Denny (Paul GREENHALGH) is pursued by concerned – heterosexual – neighbours in THE CREZZ 'Bent Doubles' (1976 T). Similarly low-down is the one in the suburbs of London visited by Clouseau (Peter SELLERS) in *The Pink Panther Strikes Again* (1976 C). The Earl Russell club is brought up in evidence during the CROWN COURT trial in 'Such a Charming Man' (1977 T); primarily for bridge, this gentlemen's club 'includes a number of well-heeled, eminently respectable homosexuals'.

Entertainment on offer includes drag acts (Bunny Lewis in NIGHTINGALE'S BOYS 'Flossie' (1975 T); food (a bistro upstairs 'known in the trade as the Gay Salmonella' in PLAYMATES 1978 R); music (a glum-faced, ageing four-piece band in *Simone Barbes* 1979 C).

But danger still lurked. A plain-clothes policeman cautions the punters in a search for drugs and arrests a TRANSVESTITE played by Philip SAYER in CROWN COURT 'Lola' (1976 T), while a Tory MP (Martin Shaw) is caught in a raid in *For the Greater Good* (1991 T).

Spitting Image (1984 T) dared to suggest that there was a special school which taught POLICEMEN how to be gay so they could merge as AGENTS PROVOCATEURS with the clientele before making arrests.

Clubs appeared to be relics of the past, made extinct by the arrival of the super-DISCO. But often these were open only on 'gay' nights (ie when business would otherwise have been slow) and the club, with its loosely applied membership rules, remained a necessary cocoon for some. Every city and large town had them. Like Billy's in *Playmates* (1978 R):

'It's grand is this, Nick. I never thought there was a place like this in the middle of Manchester.'
'Oh, there's places like this everywhere. With the possible exception of Salt Lake City. Advertised and all. Since we all came out.'

All so very far away from those tiny basements with the speakeasy door. Like the place where Quentin Crisp was made to feel so unwelcome: 'Quentin, DUCKY, if the police come here, *we're* normal.'

Cochrane, Michael (194?–) English radio and television actor, lively as a cricket. Well-beloved for his Cedric HAMPTON in *Love in a Cold Climate* (1980 T) and for so enthusiastically leaving no gay inference unstroked as BUNNY (1989–92) in the *Raffles* series on radio. A small sample of his work: Fredel in *The Man from Everywhere* (1973 R); Prince Richard in *The Lion in Winter*

(1981 R); Lieutenant Peter Harvey in *Time Spent in Reconnaisance* (1983 R); A BOOK AT BEDTIME 'The Stalled Ox' by SAKI (1987 R); Lord Fancourt Babberley in *Charley's Aunt* (1987 R); Richard, one of Penelope Keith's advisers in *No Job for a Lady* (1992 T).

Coco, James (1931–87) American actor who played gay roles in *Only When I Laugh* (1981) and *There Must Be a Pony* (1986 T). Appeared off-Broadway in Terrence McNally's *Next* (1968).

C: *Ensign Pulver* (1964); *Tell Me That You Love Me, Junie Moon* (1970); *A New Leaf* (1971); *The Wild Party* (1974) as a Fatty Arbuckle figure; Marcel, the café owner in *The Cheap Detective* (1978); *Murder by Death* (1976) as a Hercule POIROT clone.

T: *Calucci's Department* (1974); *Alice*; *Murder She Wrote*; ST ELSEWHERE; *The Love Boat*; Mr Van Daam in *The Diary of Anne Frank* (1980); many talk shows.

Cocteau, Jean (1899–1963) French playwright, poet, novelist, film-maker, actor and artist. Nearly all his films include strong homoeroticism: *Le Sang d'un Poète*, *La Belle et la Bête*, *Orphée*. He was instrumental in the production of UN CHANT D'AMOUR. A highly influential, multivarious figure, his life and works have been celebrated in Graeme Murphy's ballet *Poppy* (1992 T) and there are references to him in *Peter Greenaway: Anatomy of a Director* (1991 T).

R: Plays: *The Eiffel Tower* (*Les Mariés de la Tour Eiffel*), a high-brow fantasy that is amusingly 'different' (1932); *The Typewriter* (1958); *Orphée* (1962); *The Human Voice* (1966); etc. *Jean Cocteau: Poet of the Cinema* (1952); *Jean Cocteau* (1959); *Reminiscences of Marcel PROUST* (1963); *French Verse* (1964): a selection made by Jean Cocteau – including Guillaume Apollinaire, Raymond Radiguet and himself – read by Cocteau and Zena Walker; *Rimbaud and 'Les Illustrations'* (1972): Peter Porter introduced two poems in prose from *Les Illuminations* read by Cocteau.

T: *Cocteau on Film* (1989); Cocteau died before completing a script for a 'Largest Theatre in the World' project.

codpieces Mitchell LEISEN wanted them filled to overflowing in his 1948 Borgia drama *Bride of Vengeance*, but was overruled by the censors. It wasn't until ZEFFIRELLI's *Romeo and Juliet* that tights began shaping up in front. By the 1990s a reaction had set in: Kevin Costner insisted on trousers for *Robin Hood – Prince of Thieves* (1991 C), not wanting to court ridicule (a point not lost on the makers of the spoof version *Men in Tights*). Much mirth surrounds those *caches de sexe* worn by ballet dancers. Rudolf NUREYEV finally threw caution to the wind in THE SOUTH BANK SHOW biography (1991 T): 'He was allowed to unveil the contents of his ballet tights' was how the *Evening Standard* put it.

Cogan, Alma (1933–66) English 'BACHELOR GIRL' singer who rose to fame via *Take It from Here* and various bubbly, inconsequential hit songs. The only human being in the history of the world ever to broadcast from the beyond on the morning of her death (26.10.66). The *Today* radio programme began with Alma singing 'Cheek To Cheek', followed by the announcement that she had died of cancer. However, when the item was rebroadcast an hour later the song had been changed, lest reference to the afterlife in the Irving Berlin standard – 'Heaven, I'm in Heaven' – should cause offence.

R: *Gently Bentley* (1953); *Take It from Here* (1954–6) as singer and as Ma GLUM; *Midday Music Hall* (1957); *Blackpool Night* (1958) billed as 'A Laugh in Her Voice'.

T: *The Alma Cogan Show* (1958); *Juke Box Jury* (1960 etc); *Daniel FARSON Meets ...* (1962 T); scores of guest appearances.

TV biography: *The Girl with the Giggle in Her Voice* (1991); Maureen Lipman discussed her on *Start the Week* (1987); Gordon Burn, who wrote a novel called *Alma Cogan*, was interviewed about her on *Summer Strand* (1991 R).

Cohn, Roy (1927–86) American lawyer, assistant to Senator McCarthy, later *éminence grise*, social lion, orchestrator of Communist slurs and anti-gay hatred. Played by George Wyner in *Tail Gunner Joe* (1977 T), and by James Woods in *Citizen Cohn* (1992 T): 'selfish and greedy and loveless and blind.' Features prominently in Tony Kushner's two-part play *Angels in America: A Gay Fantasia on National Themes*: 'I'm a heterosexual man who fucks with men.'

Coleman, Jack (1958–) American actor who took over the role of Steven CARRINGTON in DYNASTY in 1983. Interviewed by Roger Royle on *Good Morning Sunday* (1986 R). Other roles on television include *Bridesmaids* (1989); *Nightmare Café* (1991).

Coles, Richard (1962–) English pianist, composer, broadcaster. Co-founder of THE COMMUNARDS. Prize-winning presenter of BBC Radio 5's Monday-night interview and music programme *The Mix* (1991–). Non-Communards appearance on OUT (1991) talking about his DOG.

Colette, Sidonie-Gabrielle (1873–1954) French novelist, occasional screenwriter. Colette's husband Maurice Goudeket could still say on *Late Night Live* (1972, interviewed by Sheridan Morley), at the age of 82, that she was not a lesbian 'contrary to rumour': 'I can assure you she was not a lesbian by personal experience. She was very womanly.'
C: *Claudine at School* (1938); *Gigi* (1948; and GIGI 1958); *The Cat*; *Chéri*; *L'Ingénue Libertine/Minne* (1950); OLIVIA (1950); *Ripening Seed* (1954).
R: *Claudine at School* (1977); *Claudine in Paris* (1978); WOMEN OF WORDS (1980); *Modern European Authors* (read by Maureen O'BRIEN 1986).
T: *The Gentle Libertine* (1967, banned because of 'two women kissing in bed' scene); *Chéri* (1971); *Colette* (with Macha Meril, Fr 1985).

collar and tie Shingled hair and collars with ties were all the rage in the Edwardian era and in the 1920s. GARBO, DIETRICH and Katharine HEPBURN had made it okay to wear 'slacks'.
Others parading their perversity over the years include Catherine Lacey as a suspected Nazi infiltrator in a Scottish village (*Cottage to Let* 1941 C); Lucille Ball in I LOVE LUCY ' Lucy Writes a Song' (1951 T), 'Lucy Writes a Play' (1951) and 'Lucy Writes an Operetta' (1952 T); Charlotte Rampling as one of the TWINS in *Asylum* (1973 C); Rachel Roberts as Wendy Hiller's German maid in *Murder on the Orient Express* (1974 C); Brenda (Wanda Ventham) in *The Sweeny* 'Abduction' (1975 T); Maggie Smith as Bette DAVIS' companion in *Death on the Nile* (1979 C); Quaint Irene (Cicely Hobbs), the 'gosh-golly, you chaps' painter in *Mapp and Lucia* (1985–6 T); an unnamed player in *May We Borrow Your Husband?* (1986 T); the sinister Dr Cloud (Billie Whitelaw) in *Shadey* (1986 C); Lady Caroline (Amanda Hillwood), 'the wickedest woman in London' who has one scene in the last episode of *Tender Is the Night* (1985 T); Betty Marsden as author R. B. Monody in ABSOLUTE HELL!
But it's no longer effective as a signifier of sexual taste. Ties, collars, shirts and TROUSERS are now considered very chic. Looking smart and pretty while simultaneously power dressing, courtesy of the two Di's – Keaton (*Annie Hall*) and Wales. Princess Diana led the way in Britain at a film première in 1982. DI, DI, IN HER COLLAR AND TIE took on a whole new meaning.
Collars and ties turn up fairly regularly on movie heroines (Anne Archer in *The Naked Face* 1984) without necessarily commenting on the sex-psyche of the character. Which made it all-round okay for salt of the earth Angie (Anita Dobson) to return to the Queen Vic (after a week at a health farm) wearing jacket and tie (EASTENDERS 1986 T). 'How do I look?' she nervously asks her daughter, Sharon (Leticia Dean). 'Smashing, Mum, *really smashing.*'

The Collection (UK 1961 T) Harold PINTER presented a puzzle. Did Bill

(John Ronane) sleep with Stella (Vivien Merchant)? If he did, will that radically alter his relationship with FASHION DESIGNER mentor Harry (Griffith Jones)? And does Stella's softly creeping husband James (Anthony Bate) want to kill Bill, or go to bed with him? Whatever the answer the emotional drawing together of the two men is quite spine-chilling.
P: Peter WILLES; D: Joan Kemp-Welch; Associated-Rediffusion; 11.5.61; 65 mins.

One of the first implicitly homosexual relationships on television, as well as providing strong indications of BISEXUALITY since the two men are incalculably fascinated by one another despite their rivalry. There was a second production shown by Granada on 5 December 1976; produced by Derek GRANGER and directed by Michael Apted, it starred Helen Mirren, Laurence Olivier, Alan BATES and Malcolm McDowell.

Collier, John (1901–80) English novelist: *His Monkey Wife*. Weaver of fantastic, macabre, misogynist short stories: 'The Jealous Lover' in *The Story of Three Loves* (1953); 'The Chaser' in THE TWILIGHT ZONE (1960); 'Sleeping Beauty' filmed as *Some Call It Loving* (1973). Wrote screenplays for SYLVIA SCARLETT (1936); *Her Cardboard Lover* (1942); *Deception* (1946); *Roseanna McCoy* (1949); *I Am a Camera* (1955); *The War Lord* (1965).

Gordon **Collins** Character in BROOKSIDE (1985–90), played (as a 16-year-old) by Nigel Crowley. He was packed off to France to visit his SISTER (because he had an affair with a schoolmate) after only a handful of episodes. Returned a year or so later, looking considerably older and played by another actor (Mark Burgess). Became involved with Christopher (Stifyn Parri) who came to live at his parents' house. Became a volunteer AIDS-line helper.

Collinson, Laurence (1925–86) Australian playwright and psychotherapist (transactional analysis),

involved with the Albany Trust and the gay liberation movement, especially in counter-psychiatry and counselling work. Member of original GAY NEWS collective. Wrote *Thinking Straight* for GAY SWEATSHOP (1975), a collection of poetry *Hovering Narcissus* (1977), and the television play *Loving Israel*, about the conflict between two brothers. *A Slice of Birthday Cake*, broadcast on Australian radio in 1964, centred on a mother's discovering 'the truth' about the son she believed to be naive and innocent.

Colonel Redl (East Germany/Austria/Hungary 1985 C) Impeccably produced, disturbing portrait of the web of corruption and deceit in the Austro-Hungarian Empire, and the BLACKMAILING of a gay man to serve its insatiable ends. Based on John OSBORNE'S A PATRIOT FOR ME. The performance of Karl Maria Brandauer is outstanding, a perfect counterpoint to his earlier *Mephisto* about another sensitive, intelligent man caught in a machine.
W: Istvan Szabo and Peter Dobal; D: Istvan Szabo; 150 mins.

The Color Purple (US 1985 C) A young black woman's growing up, tortuous marriage, relationship with husband's mistress and reunification with her missionary sister.
W: Menno Meyjes; P: Steven Spielberg, Kathleen Kennedy, Frank Marshall and Quincy Jones; D: Steven Spielberg; 154 mins.

Alice Walker commented that the director was simply 'too nice' to upset Middle America by going the whole distance with the relationship between Celie (Whoopi Goldberg) and Shug (Margaret Avery) as she wrote it (OMNIBUS 1985). Also lost to the film – and weakening the narrative – is the character of Celie's sister, Nettie, mostly present through letters in the book. If you accept Spielberg's rainbow vision, then it's still an engrossing, moving story.

colour symbolism *See* BLUE FOR A BOY; HANDKERCHIEVES; LAVENDER; PINK.

comedians Archie Rice (Laurence Olivier) thanked God he was normal as he capered and camped on stage in lascivious death-mask's make-up in THE ENTERTAINER. The sexual ambiguity that John OSBORNE culled in part from Max Miller is present in scores of comedians. Watching Sid Field in *London Town* (1946 C) is almost painful today, so strung out does he appear in those scenes (the majority) where he is not 'playing gay'. George Cole (as Eddie Collins) in COMIC'S INTERLUDE (1981 R) exemplified a gay, pederastic Pagliacci. The first comic to make specifically gay jokes from the inside (Peter Prince in *No Surrender* 1985 C) was jeered off the stage and left in a hurry with his boyfriend (Peter Wilson). The only consolation he has is that the conjurer who follows him doesn't even get on stage, so rough is the audience (of antagonistic Northern Irish/Scouse pensioners). There was Daisy Dolan (Carole Cooke) whose career as a top-liner suffered a dip after she came out (she was being blackmailed and decided to stop being a victim). Her self-esteem and uncorsetted view of life have never been in better shape, it would appear from her one scene and slice of her nightclub act in IN THE GLITTER PALACE (1977 T). She was based on Pat Bond, who was kicked out of the army and became a cult favourite in San Francisco (and appeared to great effect in WORD IS OUT 1977 C). *See also* Julian CLARY; Simon FANSHAWE.

The Comedians (UK (1971–4 T) Stand-up comics like Bernard Manning, Charlie Williams, Tom O'Connor and Mike Reid strutted their stuff in this Granada series. 'Their jokes are shoved home with the brutal skill of a bandilero at a bull fight, with sex, death, parrots, footballers, homosexuals – best of all, homosexual footballers – as favourite butts.' (Philip Purser, *Sunday Telegraph*, 13.6.71).

The Comedy of Errors SHAKESPEARE'S play about mixed-up twins. The THAMES television version of the National Theatre production, with Paul Brooke as Angelo, a mincing Ephesean goldsmith, stirred Peter ROBINS to pen these words in GAY NEWS (18.4.78):

> ... Trevor Nunn, you erred
> more than your players in that you preferred
> to cast your goldsmith – how could you demean
> your talents? as witless cardboard QUEEN,
> with broken wrists and hands that seemed to itch
> for every passing man, this fragile BITCH
> was some cobwebbed cartoon.
> Your mincing fop
> is not today's gay lad and it must stop.
>
> INMAN and GRAYSON we forgive, but you
> have no excuse for you know what you do.
>
> Your faulty knowledge of the current scene
> that projects gays as feeble, epicene
> negates your final curtain line:
> makes mock of brothers 'hand in hand'.
> What trendy cock ...

Comedy Playhouse 'B&B: No Son of Mine' (UK 1968 T) Bernie and Barbara Benson (Bernard Braden and Barbara Kelly) are worried because 18-year-old Johnny (Mark Griffiths) has no apparent interest in girls. Luckily *au pair* Chantal (Pauline Collins) does *le trick*. This was a pilot for a series that did not materialize. Of historical interest as the first 'comedy' about the fears of parents whose children do not appear to be setting quite right in the blancmange mould. A more recent example was *Birds of a Feather* 'Young Guns' (1991).
W: Michael Pertwee; 7.6.68; BBC1; 30 mins.

come in if you're good looking Chirruped by Gladys Plumb (Dora Bryan), reporter on the *Daily Bind* in *Much-Binding-in-the-Marsh* (1951–3 R) every time there was a knock on the door; later used by the wondrous Captain Terri Dennis (Denis QUILLEY) in PRIVATES ON PARADE (1982 C) as 'Come in, if you're pretty'.

Come Together (UK 1971 C) A short directed by 'John Shane'. Enthused Mike Coulson in GAY NEWS, just eight issues old: 'It is colourful, confused and rather appealing like G[ay] L[iberation] F[ront] itself ... By its warmth and vitality, the film should (if they ever manage to see it) convey a message of hope to timid provincials wistfully longing to escape from their CLOSETS.'

come up and see me some time Once the quintessence of suggestiveness and raunch, it remains forever Mae WEST. One of the QUEENS in her 1925 play *The Drag* gives this variant: 'Come up some time and I'll bake you a pan of biscuits.' Mae used it straight in *Sex* on Broadway, then put it on celluloid (as 'Why don't you come up some time and see me?' and 'Come up, I'll tell you your fortune') in *She Done Him Wrong* (1933 C). Craig RUSSELL, just one of the thousands of Mae West impersonators, socked it to us again with great majesty in OUTRAGE-OUS! (1977 C).

Comic's Interlude (UK 1981 R) Eddie Collins (George Cole), who had once worked with Max Miller and Josephine BAKER, makes his comeback after 20 years, refusing publicity, in a tatty variety show. He tries to become close to the theatre manager's diffident son, Steven (Michael Maloney) before the long gap in Eddie's career is exposed – a prison sentence for sexual offences against minors. He has to leave the company.
W: Stewart Permutt; D: Shaun McLoughlin; 18.2.81; Radio 4; 50 mins.
Sturdy, well-paced tears-and-tinsel drama with sterling central performance. 'Always the comic, me. There's been one or two people I've been very fond of – they just upped and left.'

The Comic Strip Presents (UK 1982–6 T) Genre parodies, the most famous being the incineration of Enid Blyton's 'FAMOUS FIVE' ('Five Go Mad in Dorset' and 'Five Go Mad on Mescalin') which has JULIAN (Peter Richardson) enjoying a romantic friendship with a boy called Toby (rejected by the others because

he's JEWISH), George (Dawn French) being called a 'DYKE' and the children's UNCLE Quentin (Ronald Allen, sex symbol veteran of both COMPACT and *Crossroads*) revealed as a master crook *and* a homosexual.

Even better were the send-ups of a rock group on the road ('Bad News Tour'), the pretensions of 'The Beat Generation' (GINSBERG, WARHOL and others), and – the pick of the crop – a back-to-the-Stone-Age 'Summer School' with Desmond (Robbie Coltrane) taken over by the phallicism of tribal religion, with Adrian Edmondson the object of his crazed desires. The Comic Strip team members proved inescapable on television during the rest of the decade – daring virtuosos all: Rik Mayall, Nigel Planer, Jennifer Saunders, plus Richardson, Edmondson and Coltrane.
W/D: various; P: 'Michael White'; 30 mins.

coming out A cornerstone of gay liberation theology. A zigzagging progress, by turns euphoric and terrifying, mined with reversals and setbacks. For most people a never-ending story. The most popular catchall title for radio and television, eg Canada's Channel 10 Toronto cable show in 1972 (half-hour prime time at 6pm); WORLD IN ACTION 'Coming Out in Newport Pagnell' (1975 T); the Southern TV documentary (1976); a BBCTV play (1979); BBC documentaries (1986 & 1989). It was also used in series: AGONY's 'Coming Out ... And Going In Again' (1980), and a short lesbian piece, 'Came Out, It Rained, Went Back in Again' (1991 T). But, in Australia, ABC radio's *The Coming Out Show* is feminist in subject matter, with only occasional specific nods to lesbian sisters.

Marjorie (Lynn REDGRAVE) in MY TWO LOVES (1986 T) spoke for many, residual British accent or no: 'Until every gay person in America has the guts to come out, I'm not going to be the sacrificial lamb.'

Coming Out (UK 1976 T) A regional programme (Southern TV), showing that gay persons are normal, ordinary TEACHERS, SOLICITORS, 'married' couples. Some of them (Alan Clarke, shown with his parents) were even political, belonging to groups such as CHE. Others, like Tony WHITEHEAD, were politicized as a result of their involvement with this film: Whitehead was sacked by British Home Stores the next day after being seen in an affectionate pose with his lover. 'The most direct and sympathetic programme yet to appear on British television' (*Sunday Times*, 28.1.76).

Coming Out (UK 1979 T) Macho WRITER Lewis Duncan (Anton Rodgers) pens a mildly pro-gay article for a non-gay magazine (under a pseudonym) and is inundated with letters from isolated, distraught men or their parents. Duncan's personal life is bumpy: his lover (Nigel HAVERS) is playing around with the ARTIST (Michael Byrne) who is painting his portrait (in hussar's uniform). The play's centrepiece is a tense DINNER PARTY staged by the painter's lover, a self-satisfied, bitchy older man, a GAY ACTIVIST, who gets on his soapbox about equality, discrimination and the need to COME OUT. Ultimately, it is the oppression faced by others (revealed in the tragic correspondence) that convinces Lewis to reveal his true self and become a crusader.
W: James Andrew HALL; P: Kenith TRODD; D: Carol Wiseman; 10.4.79; BBC1; 75 mins.

Ambitious, relatively frank (Lewis in BED with his lover and with black PROSTITUTE Polo – played by Ben Ellison), it was sunk by its totally improbable premise (an article on homosexuality causing such a tidal wave of interest in 1979) and by its negative attitude towards gay men in particular and gay political action in general. Its central theme was never fully confronted: damned if he remains untrue to himself, hopelessly compromised if he reveals he's been telling lies or leading his readers on.

The BBC crowed about this production and its showing was followed by

Valerie Singleton interviewing members of the cast on TONIGHT, carefully telling the viewers that all of them were HETEROSEXUAL. The play was popular and was repeated the following year. It received a generally favourable press, though not from me in GAY NEWS – I *hated* it. The BBC doubtless felt very pleased with itself, though a production from the Corporation a few weeks later – ONLY CONNECT, which was not ballyhooed, widely praised, or repeated – was *Coming Out*'s superior in every way. 'Given the number of limp-wristed gay STEREOTYPES which mince across our TV screens, it is not before time that the BBC is putting out a play which takes homosexuals seriously' (Sue Summers, *Evening Standard*).

Coming Out (East Germany 1989 C) A TEACHER tormented by sexual uncertainty, until he meets a young man. Gay issues as fact and metaphor in what turned out to be the dying days of the DDR with its repression of same-sex feelings. Three years in the (secret) making, it was premièred on 9 November, the night the Berlin Wall was first breached.
W: Wolfram Witt; D: Heiner Carow; 115 mins.

The coming together of the two men is a long time arriving, but this is a solid, responsible piece from a country whose cinema had completely ignored this aspect of life.

Commitments (UK 1982 T) A group of left-wing activists (including Alan Rickman and Paola Dionisetti) prepare for the 1974 British election. Their neighbour, a pompous ALCOHOLIC civil servant, Buffo (Bryan Coleman), comes to stay when his boyfriend takes a new lover.
W: Dusty Hughes; P: Ann Scott; D: Richard Wilson; 26.1.82; BBC1; 90 mins.

Despite the leftwards alignment of much gay liberation thinking, gays remain outsiders just as they were in the 1930s when some believed that Communism would provide a freer, more just and sexually sane society. People like Buffo: 'We thought they were going to liberate us, so we all joined the Party. And what did they turn out to be – QUEER-BASHERS to a man.' Buffo is the only character with traces of courage and commitment, spouting less hot air than his young 'friends' because he's learned about politics from life rather than from manifestos. 'Been hounded all my life being a queer and what did I do? I slept with the boy who slept with a girl who danced with the Prince of Wales.'

Common Threads: Stories from the Quilt (US 1989 C) The lives of five people who have died of AIDS and how their families, lovers and friends have come to terms with their losses by involvement with making QUILT panels. These people include Sara Lewinstein, who lived with, and had a DAUGHTER by, Dr Tom Waddell who was a founder of San Francisco's GAY GAMES; Sally Perry, whose husband was an intravenous drug user; Tracy Torey, a naval commander whose lover David Campbell died; Suzi and David Mandell, whose son was a haemophiliac; Vito RUSSO, who lost his lover Jeffrey Sevcik, and who would soon die himself.
W: Robert Epstein, Jeffrey Friedman and Cindy Ruskin; inspired by the NAMES Project Quilt and the Quilt Stories from the NAMES Project by Cindy Ruskin; D: Robert Epstein and Jeffrey Friedman; 75 mins.
So many lives to celebrate, so few narrated here. A sampler only of the enormous outpouring of love and grief and rage – and political activism – that the crisis slowly unleashed. Narrated by Dustin Hoffman, the film won the ACADEMY AWARD for Best Documentary 1990.

The Communards Jimmy SOMERVILLE and Richard COLES formed this group of instrumentalists after Somerville left BRONSKI BEAT. One of their first TV appearances was at the Montreux Rock Festival in 1987. The name derives from the young insurgents of the Paris Commune.

community, gay and lesbian To some, it's comforting to know that a close-knit family exists. To others, it's monolithic and unrepresentative, a ball and chain. 'It makes me very nervous, but then again most things do,' said Vito RUSSO's lover Jeffrey Sevcik when asked about his feelings about the community by a New York TV reporter in the early 1980s (the clip was shown in COMMON THREADS 1989).
The first mainstream acknowledgement came via a television news report in DOG DAY AFTERNOON (1975 C) over a picture of BRIDE and groom, Sonny and Leon who were 'married in an official ceremony. There were seven BRIDESMAIDS, all male; Sonny's mother; and 70 guests, all members of the gay community.' The phrase was incorporated into the subtitle of the EMMY-winning BEFORE STONEWALL (1984 C/T): 'The Making of a Gay and Lesbian Community'. Robert Epstein, accepting an Oscar for COMMON THREADS praised 'the gay and lesbian community' at the 62nd annual ACADEMY AWARDS, transmitted to 39 countries (1990 T).
In Britain, it was first heard in the mainstream at the start of the 1980s – disc jockey and pundit Adrian Love on *Capital Radio*'s PHONE-IN on GAY LIFE: 'The gay community created the STEREOTYPES' (25.2.80); Michael Simmons' ringing cry of 'Let the gay community spend time and energy educating us' in YOU THE JURY (1981 R). It became fully entrenched in the wake of the AIDS publicity blitz of 1987 and of the outcry over CLAUSE 28: Ross (Eric Deacon), the SOCIAL WORKER in *Hard Cases* (1988 T) who goes on a protest march, tells his secretary that 'The gay community in this country has been driven completely underground'.
It is discussed at length by 40 Sydney-based gays and lesbians in *In the Mix* 'Are You a Friend of Dorothy's?' (1992 R):
Yeasayers: 'Even those who didn't believe in it, have interesting things to

say about it'; 'An extended emotional family'; 'It's like a harness, or jockstrap or even a brassière, but it's also an emotional support'; 'Being there for each other; a functional concept, a matter of lots of little communities'; 'Social action, cultural action and, very very importantly, sexual action going on all the time; somewhere where I really belong'; 'By identifying with other people, connecting and looking for sameness'; 'Being slightly separate and building its own cultural identity'; 'Linked to the homosexual identity formed through oppression'; 'All these people here who are the same as you'; 'If I suddenly woke up and found we were all equal, I'd *still* want to spend my time with lesbians ... it informs how you see the world'; 'If you can name yourself you are constructing an identity'; 'Communities can agree to disagree'; 'It's a concept ... but if it was just a fantasy, it wouldn't have any power; and it certainly is powerful; it's out there – in a hundred different forms and places'.

And naysayers: 'Basically it's who you fuck with'; 'Probably the most over-worked word in the English language at the moment – very unspecified and undefined'; 'People I have sex with and people I haven't'; 'A social and cultural and emotional and sometimes political ghetto'; 'It does not encapsulate every gay and lesbian person'; 'It denies the richness and diversity of the group'; 'Should always be looking outwards; if we look inwards we're not a movement, we're just a club'.

Compact UK (1962–5 T) Life on a women's magazine. The BBC's first successful early evening soap was a decidedly mangy pup by the time the first explicitly effeminate characters joined the team. ELIOT Morrow (Maurice Browning) entered Compact offices in January 1965 (episode 320, 'Heart to Heart') and remained – a cascade of camp – until the series was taken off the air in July. He has a limp ('to offset the heart of gold') and was later revealed as a hero of the French [*sic*] Resistance. Completely bald, Eliot was 'difficult':

petulant and in daily need of ego massage. He could get away with his various peccadilloes because 'several million readers think of me as the kindest, the gentlest, the most sincere writer alive today'. His favourite novel was *Little Women*, he carried a small velvet cushion, and he composed his essays from a relaxed position on the *chaise longue*. Refreshingly laconic, a polite demurrer from straight society without the aristocratic protection of WILDE's male bitches, but philosophically akin: ' My life's work has been an exploration into the depths of my own subconscious.'

Now forgotten, Eliot made the dying days of *Compact* more bearable.

companion Used about Don Bachardy in relation to Christopher ISHERWOOD in AQUARIUS 'Over There on a Visit' (1977 T), and about Tony Garrett in the tribute to Angus WILSON (1991 T) – later described as 'living together' with Angus. The only other reference to their long devotion was a throwaway phrase to cover his role in Angus' illness 'doing everything he could for the now very sick novelist'. *See also* LONGTIME COMPANION.

companions Sometimes a well-bred cross-over between a lady's live-in, paid companion and a bed partner: Marian HALCOMBE (Eleanor Parker/Diana QUICK) in *The Woman in White* (1948 C; 1982 T) finding happiness in a *ménage* with her half-sister, Laura and Laura's new husband; Elizabeth Wilson hovering over *The Goddess* (Kim Stanley 1958 C) after Hollywood, drink and a couple of husbands have done their worst; Anacleto (Zorro David) whose mistress cuts off her nipples with the garden shears in REFLECTIONS IN A GOLDEN EYE (1967 C); Eve (Rachel Kempson) in love with her adulterous mistress in *Death of a Teddy Bear* (1967 T); Jennifer Wade (June Barry), business and emotional partner to an older woman in *Kate* 'A Human Weakness' (1971 T); Vivien Heilbron as Lindsay Rimmer, calculating plaything of Emma Sands in *An Unofficial Rose* (1974–5 T); Hildegarde Schmidt (Rachel Roberts), collar and tied factotum and pekinese carrier to an old princess in *Murder on the Orient Express* (1974 C); the similarly attired and similarly disposed Miss Bowers (Maggie Smith) forever trying to out-nag her querulous charge (Bette DAVIS) in *Death on the Nile* (1978 C); etc.

The Company of Strangers (Can 1990 C) Eight women lost in a wood make a home in a disused farmhouse. Most are in their seventies and include a Mohawk Indian, a nun and a bird-watching lesbian, Mary Miegs who comes out to the bemused Winnie. A documentary-style fiction, about a hastily assembled community, their harmonies and (few) disharmonies. Quiet, undemanding idyll which makes sharp, subtle sense.
W: Gloria Demers with Cynthia Scott; D: Cynthia Scott; 101 mins.

composers Very partial truth only about Stephen FOSTER in *Swanee River* (Don Ameche 1939 C) and *I Dream of Jeannie* (Ray Middleton 1952 C); George Gershwin, bachelor genius, dead well before his 40th birthday (Robert Alda in *Rhapsody in Blue* 1945 C); Cole PORTER (Cary GRANT), super-wealthy *bon vivant*, keeping up the pretence of married normality (NIGHT AND DAY 1946 C); Lorenz (Larry) HART (Mickey Rooney), ALCOHOLIC, undersized, deeply unhappy and failing to get the girl (or any girl) in MGM's recounting of his (and colleague Richard Rodgers') life, WORDS AND MUSIC (1948 C); Noel AIRMAN (Gene Kelly) in *Marjorie Morningstar* (1958 C), who fancied himself as a great Broadway composer but lacked the talent and the temperament to be anything other than a big duck (social director) in a small pond (summer camp); Von Aschenbach (Dirk Bogarde) ensnared by a boy's beauty in DEATH IN VENICE (1971 C); Nick (Steve Buscemi), leather-clad skeleton, finding strength with an old love in PARTING GLANCES (1985 C).
   In Britain: Ivor NOVELLO actor, writer and composer of Ruritanian romance was played by Laurence Payne with the

ambiguities ironed out (1956 T); Ethel SMYTH (Jean Trend) was allowed full flight in ONLY GOODNIGHT (1981 R), the story of the remarkable SOMERVILLE AND ROSS – Dame Ethel was partly the basis for the formidable Dame Hilda TABLET (Mary O'Farrell) in the 1950s series by Henry REED; Maurice Goodman (Trader FAULKNER) is all rings, CAMP chat and had no girlfriend in *Promenade* (1959 T); tormented Peter TCHAIKOVSKY is played by Richard Chamberlain in *The Music Lovers* (1971 C) and by Ronald Pickup in THE MISSING DAY (1986 R); an amateur, Peter Lester (Leonard Preston) has to provide a pop song for his boyfriend's client in THE GROUNDLING AND THE KITE (1984 T, with script and songs by Preston); Barry Black (Clive Francis) is *The Man Who Had Power Over Women* (1970 C) and also has a strong sexual hold on his manager; Jim Tayo (Christopher Guard) is a boyish teen idol with a passing interest in passing trade (A HYMN FROM JIM 1977 T); Shelley Maze (Charlotte Cornwell) lives life at 100 hours per second and is only fulfilled in the arms of her friend/lover Valerie (Vickery Turner) in *No Excuses* (1983 T).
   See also Leonard BERNSTEIN; BOY GEORGE; Benjamin BRITTEN; Jimmy SOMERVILLE; Stephen SONDHEIM.

Compromised Immunity (UK 1991 R) Spiky relationship between NURSE Peter (Phil Daniels) and AIDS patient Gerry Grimmond (Michael CASHMAN). Miscast version of an effective stage piece, written early in the struggle.
W: Andy Kirby for GAY SWEATSHOP (1986) adapted by Craig Warner; 19.9.91; BBC Radio 5; 80 mins.

Compton-Burnett, Dame Ivy (1884–1969) English novelist, eviscerator of the already decaying upper middle classes in deceptively courteous novels where there is usually arsenic in the cucumber sandwiches. Books adapted as radio plays include *A Father and His Fate; Manservant and Maidservant* (1952, 1966); *A Heritage and Its History* (1959);

The Mighty and Their Fall (1961); *Daughters and Sons* (1986); while *Elders and Betters* (1984) was adapted for television's THE SOUTH BANK SHOW. Radio biography: *Conversation* 'Ivy Compton-Burnett interviewed and discussed by her friend and LONGTIME COMPANION Margaret Jourdain' (1950); *The Family Lives Here* (1984).

Compulsion (US 1959 C) Two Chicago law students, Artie Strauss (Bradford Dillman) and his supposedly pliant partner Judd Steiner (Dean Stockwell), murder a young Jewish boy and sit back to watch the law fall on its face. But evidence points to them, and Steiner cracks under questioning.

W: Richard Murphy from the book and play by Meyer Levin; P: Richard D. Zanuck; D: Richard Fleischer; 103 mins.

A slightly fictionalized Richard Loeb and Nathan LEOPOLD who, in his 1958 autobiography, disputed the homosexuality commonly attributed to him and his friend. *Compulsion* was Hollywood's second version of the sensational 1924 Chicago trial (the first was ROPE) and had punchy direction, good performances (Orson WELLES delivering an 8-minute plea for mercy as the boys' defence attorney), and only the faintest hints of homosexuality. For a more rounded, though still mystifying, account of the murderers' motives and sexual natures the world had to wait 30 years – for SWOON.

computer sex The possibilities outlined in CAUGHT LOOKING (1991 T): tantalizing, almost real but ultimately out of reach – just like life.

Comrades in Arms (UK 1990 T) Memories of gay men and lesbians, mainly in the services, of the Second World War, including those of Dudley Cave who returns to the site of his prison camp in Thailand.

W/D: Stuart MARSHALL; P: Rebecca Dobbs; shown on OUT C4; 55 mins.

Fascinating, frequently cheering, long overdue history of tumultuous years

which helped homosexuals to meet others and to begin to find a common purpose. Adorable anecdotes – though some of the interviewees are hesitant and flat in their story-telling, but the intercut songs (Al BOWLLY, Connee Boswell) and reconstructed love scenes add texture. The use of popular music here exemplified Dennis Potter's theory (put into practice in *Pennies from Heaven* and *The Singing Detective*): 'It's a kind of yielding, a puncturing of that little hole in the heart by something that can be dismissed as *kitsch* or cheap or banal, or second-rate or popular or whatever, but it is a signpost to much more complicated feelings.'

Conan the Barbarian (US 1982 C) Arnold Schwarzenegger's 57-inch chest, 23-inch arms and 28-inch thighs embody Robert Ervin Howard's 1930s cartoon hero, who appeared in *Weird Tales*.

W/D: John Milius; 129 mins (also 115 and 123 mins).

Bondage, blood and sadism with a gayish villain (Thulsa D-om, played by James Earl Jones) and a bit of male bonding (Subotai the Mongol, played by Gerry Lopez). Robert Howard was gay and committed suicide in 1936, aged 30, after writing 21 stories. He had wanted to weave heroic fantasies of the Hyborean Age, pitting the power of brotherhood against the pitiless forces of barbarianism. That was before Hollywood's scriptwriting sledgehammer John Milius got his hands on it. Out of the hot darkness came ... Rambo. The 1984 *Conan the Destroyer*, directed by Richard Fleischer, with Grace Jones as Conan's musculatory buddy-adversary, was much flakier but fun.

Concealed Enemies (UK/US 1984 T) Alger Hiss' lawyers uncover Whittaker CHAMBERS' homosexual past, but Hess refuses to use this information in court.

W: Hugh WHITEMORE; P: Peter Cook; D: Jeff Bleckner; 22.8.84; WGBH/Goldcrest; 200 mins.

Personalized narrative rather than a temperature taking of those paranoid times and hours in America. John Harkins is chilling as the tortured, unreadable accuser who is possibly in love with Hiss.

condition Twenty years after *Male Homosexuals Talk about Their Condition* (1965 T), British Chancellor of the Exchequer, Nigel LAWSON, pontificating on *The Walden Interview* (1988 T), did not think homosexuality 'a happy condition'. Rather 'it is unfortunate and I don't think we'd want that promoted or proselytized.' Thus was CLAUSE 28 of the Local Government Act 1988 justified by a senior member of the THATCHER government.

conditioning 'They put on the PINK blanket or the blue blanket as soon as you come out. They start programming you as soon as you come out,' Frank Aquino promoting the 'choice' theory of homosexuality on DONAHUE 'Genetically Gay, Born Gay or Become Gay?' (1992 T). *See also* ARE YOU A MAN OR A MOUSE?; ARE YOU COURTIN'?; NOT MARRIED YET?

condoms In Britain, first alluded to in *A Kind of Loving* (1962), although Alan BATES comes out of the chemists with a bottle of Lucozade instead; in America, little mention until the early 1970s: Art Garfunkel in *Carnal Knowledge* and the boys in *Summer of '42*.

Gérard Depardieu offers Ornella Muti a condom whose tip is encrusted like a sea anemome – she's not interested because she's bored with his phallic brand of love-making in THE LAST WOMAN.

The first condom-fitting session was featured on *This Week* 'Sex Education' (1975 T): 'a doctor shows how to put a sheath on a penis.' But it was technically illegal, a point emphasized in *Brass Tacks* 'Too Soon to Love?' (1981 T): girls under 16 years old could not be shown how to fit a condom by their doctors.

The condom itself made its full-frontal début in 1987 with Ian Dury sheathing a statue as part of the British AIDS campaign. That same year, Ray Martin

demonstrated it on *The Midday Show* in Australia, and the lesbians and Rosie were seen slipping one on a carrot in *Sammy and Rosie Get Laid* (C).

The message had begun to get through to gays a few years earlier. By the time of *Talking Sex* (1986) one of the gay participants very chummily talked about condoms, but was more enthusiastic about 'mutual MASTURBATION – that sort of sexual activity can be very rewarding'. But for some other activities, it was the condom or nothing: 'no exchange of bodily fluids.'

The first mention of SAFE SEX as an entity occurred in A VERY PECULIAR PRACTICE 'The New Frontier' (1988), uttered by the ultra-retrogressive Bob Buzzard. The new (or perhaps it should be called the old) sexual etiquette dawdled into America's films and its television programmes: two of the girls talk about but do not display condoms in a 1989 *Beverly Hills 90210* (T); John Ritter has a luminous one in the only funny scene, unforgettable in fact, in *Skin Deep* (1989); Julia Roberts offers Richard Gere a selection in a variety of colours in *Pretty Woman* (1990 C): they're part of her safe sex stock in trade – as they are the hustlers' in MY OWN PRIVATE IDAHO (1991 C). A condom turned up, as part of the thicko truck driver's seduction kit in THELMA AND LOUISE (1991 C); not that he gets to use one in his encounter with our belligerent heroines.

conductors FOUR CORNERS 'The Big Finish: The Stuart Challender Story' (Aust 1991 T) is a tired, worn-out transcription of a human being transformed into a titan on the podium.

confidence tricksters The malicious cat and fox in *Pinocchio* (1940 C); two gay men on the fiddle, BOW TIES, deceit, antiques, paintings, 'conspiracy to defraud two old sisters – and one of them blind', in THE GENTLE TOUCH 'Auctions' (1982 T); two more in VICTIM (1961 C) diddling people out of small amounts of cash by pretending to be widows and single mothers; the pair in *The Enigma Files* 'Cook-In' (1980) sweet-talking rich widows and serving them gourmet meals, before applying the sting (for which they were not punished or apprehended by fate).

confirmed bachelor Nelson GABRIEL (Jack May) takes Clarrie (Rosalind Adams) to task in THE ARCHERS (1990 R) about her conventional, universal expectations of love and marriage. His daughter Rosemary smoothes down Clarrie's about-to-be ruffled feathers: 'Oh, don't take any notice of him. He's a confirmed old bachelor.'

The Conformist (It/Fr/West Germany 1970 C) Marcello Clerici (Jean-Louis Trintignant) is the professor in Fascist Italy whose near-seduction by the family CHAUFFEUR, Lino (Pierre Clementi) shapes his view of sex and the world, linking it to his being drawn in to the fascist net to act as ASSASSIN. Contrasted with his inner turbulence is the free-spirited but decadent Anna Quadri (Dominique Sanda), who takes public (dancing) and private (bedded) pleasure with his wife Giulia (Stefania Sandrelli). W/D: Bernardo Bertolucci from the novel by Alberto Moravia; 115 mins.

Connie (UK 1979 T) Sour, dour Connie (Marjorie Yates) lives with her mother (Gwen Nelson) and works as a machinist in a small clothing workshop where she is protective towards the younger girls, particularly Gina (Janine Duvitski), pregnant and unmarried. Connie's mother reminds her of a previous attachment to a teenager which ended in rejection.
W: Derrick Buttress; P: W. Stephen GILBERT; D: Derek Lister; 27.4.79; BBC2; 50 mins.
A seemingly wasted life which still has its occasional peaks as well as its troughs. Some wry comedy, too, in the futile attempts by her boss to woo Connie – even to raise a smile in this woman is like raising the *Titanic*. One of the very few 'gay' plays to have a (realistic) factory setting.

The Connoisseur (UK 1966 T) Derek Francis plays the cynical public school housemaster, 'a connoisseur of antiques ... and boys', willing to turn a blind eye to the 'fun and games' in the dorm (or is it rape? or organized prostitution?) in order to keep his best bats happy, especially Ballantyne (Ian Ogilvy). At the eleventh hour, just as he is about to retire, his career is threatened. The captain of the house, Christopher Tenterden (Richard O'Sullivan) exposes the nocturnal goings-on to a newspaper. Subtle and not so subtle thumbscrews are applied to this troublesome puritan, whose feelings for one of the younger boys, Harry Benson (Paul Guess) are most agonisingly confused.
W: Hugo Charteris; D: Waris HUSSEIN; 11.5.66; BBC1; 75 mins.
Made two years before IF ... and political in a different way, with few punches pulled (none of the male characters are sympathetic).
'The specific psychological reasons for homosexuality are now pretty well accepted by thinking people. Environmental reasons for it do not seem to be of such consequence, though governors of prisons obviously contend with it, as indeed most seminarists and members of monastic orders, though these last are doubtless better equipped to cope' (*Radio Times* synopsis).
'Hugo Charteris' Wednesday Play ... made his fictitious public school a concentration of the pressures of corrupt society on the individual innocent ... Tenterden discovers there are allowable vices, and unforgivable ones – such as tale-telling. And that the greatest crime is to be the odd man out. It was a brilliant play, excellently acted' (Deidre Chapman, *Scottish Daily Express*, 5.5.66).

conscientious objectors The 'conchy' during the First World War was handed a white feather (for cowardice) and if he persisted in his unpatriotic behaviour he was imprisoned and force-fed if there was further protest. In *We Will Know Them* (1981 R) Molly (Francesca Annis) tries to save her lover and so becomes involved in the pacifist movement, in which many homosexuals were allegedly active.

Probably the most famous conchy of all at this time was Lytton STRACHEY. His remark, apropos of his actions should a German soldier try to rape his sister, 'I should endeavour to interpose my body' was gleefully communicated in *Mad Jack* (1970 T) and again in *Nymphs and Shepherds, Come Away* (1985 R).

In the stage version of ANOTHER COUNTRY (1982) set in the late 1920s, the school is visited by a 'liberal apologist', fair of face, aquiline of nose, who had stood firm for his beliefs that killing people is wrong. This character, who gives Guy Bennett understanding (and his telephone number), was removed from the film version.

In America, mainstream entertainment is at pains to show that there comes a point in every pacifist's life when he (or she) will take up that right to bear (and use) arms: Private 'Conchie' Bronte (Robert Hutton) in *The Steel Helmet* (1951 C), who was going to be a priest, finally becomes a man behind a machine gun; Quaker bride Grace Kelly in *High Noon* (1952 C); Quaker paterfamilias Gary Cooper in *Friendly Persuasion* (1956 C).

In Britain, with the exception of 'half-naked savage' *Gandhi* (1982 C), the pacifist is usually a strange man who's good at sport (*Chariots of Fire* 1981 C), a priest or a homosexual: Arthur (John STRATTON) who opted out of the Second World War in WANTED: SINGLE GENTLEMAN (1967 T). 'If I'd gone into the Army, I might have enjoyed it. But the idea of their brutality horrified me ... I wasn't afraid of being kicked or bashed about ... but they'd have demanded that I did the same things ... whoring, blaspheming, defecating all over the place ... I comforted the dying ... cleaned up the dead ... helped people to safety ... I was a pariah dog.'

Ronnie (Hugh Thomas), the frisky NURSE in THE VISITING HOUR (1982 R): 'Strictly conscientious objector and pacifist, that's Ronnie-boy ... never could abide the sight of blood.' 'A hell of a boy', says his initially hostile male patient, 'once you get past the loose wrist and the diamante ... Heart of gold!'

Aidan Pratt (Greg Hicks) in *Fortunes of War* (1987 T) was a West End actor and *former* conscientious objector who joined the pay corps in Arabia after the ship he was working on (as a waiter) was torpedoed (he was one of three survivors). He blows his brains out after being spurned by the transparent, puppyish, insensitive Guy Pringle (Kenneth Branagh).

consenting adult A recurring phrase in the WOLFENDEN REPORT and consequent SEXUAL OFFENCES ACT of 1967. It has been used, mainly for wry, nudging effect, on at least three continents to mean a consensual homosexual, but the term takes in other groups of consenters as well.

VICTIM's contention, expressed by the articulate Lord Fullbrook (Anthony Nicholls), was 'consenting adults in private should not be pilloried'.

'There's one lot of consenting adults in this dump. The Masters!' Christopher Tenterden (Richard O'Sullivan) in THE CONNOISSEUR (1966 T).

Gore VIDAL trounced his ultra-right disciplinarian opponent, Sir Cyril Osborne in FROST OVER AMERICA (1967 T) with 'I'm all for bringing back the birch but only between consenting adults in private'.

In THREE'S COMPANY (1979 T) Chrissy (Suzanne Somers) asks Jack (John Ritter) what exactly happens between consulting adults. She is corrected: 'It's *consenting* adults, Chrissy.' A frown appears on her beautiful tanned Californian face. She says she was right the first time, reasoning that 'Before they can consent, they've got to consult'.

Terry (Dennis Waterman) is very jittery about acting as live-in bodyguard to a seductive young man in MINDER 'Whose Wife Is It Anyway?' His crony Arthur (George Cole) tries to reassure him: 'It's not as though you have to be a consulting adult.'

In THE GENTLE TOUCH 'Blade' (1980 T) Hugo (John Serett), the owner of a gay RESTAURANT, says he has nothing against smoking 'as long as it's done in private with consenting adults'.

'You are a consenting adult,' screams the repressed Miss Watson (Joyce James) when she is confronted by a man wearing an APRON 'and I do not want *any* part of it!' (A COUNTRY PRACTICE 1987 T.)

One of the cops in *The Bill* 'Fort Apache Sun Hill' (1989 T) says of a prisoner who's been raped in the cells: 'It was a "consenting adult job" – only *he* didn't consent.'

KALEIDOSCOPE (1990 R) examining the widespread popularity of the adultery novel found that, because '63 per cent of spouses were unfaithful', many people could identify with tales of 'adultery among consenting adults'.

Consenting Adult (US 1985 T) Twenty-year-old Jeff (Barry Tubb) comes out after thinking about it for seven years. His FATHER (Martin Sheen) is recovering from a stroke. Superficially liberal MOTHER (Marlo Thomas) consults a PSYCHIATRIST, who reassures her that homosexuality is an illness. The gay's older SISTER and husband are supportive. It's all very painful until, one Christmas, a rapprochement of sorts is made.

W: John McGreevey; P: Martin Starger, David Lavica and Ray Aghayan; D: Gilbert Cates; 2.4.85; 104 mins.

Mom manipulates, child copes and dad suffers. If anyone thinks being come out to is easy, they should see this film. For a television movie, it is quite an honest statement within its parameters. Martin Sheen is painfully real as the father. A film version was mooted for several years after the book was published in 1975, but no bankable stars could be lassoed to make the project viable. Incidentally, there was a 1978 episode of *Charlie's Angels* called 'Consenting Adults', which sniffed around heterosexual prostitution.

The Consequence (West Germany 1977 T) 'Love is being willing to die for someone.' An actor (Jurgen Prochnow) is sent to jail for loving a 15-year-old,

and falls in love with a warder's son, Thomas Manzoni (Ernst Hannawald). The boy ends up suicidal and morose in a home. His lover tries to rescue him. W: Alexander Ziegler and Wolfgang Petersen from the book by Ziegler; D: Wolfgang Petersen; 95/100 mins (made for West German TV, shown theatrically in the rest of the world).

'It would certainly be much too easy to simply dismiss it as yet another "gay suicide/breakdown and that's your only possibility" film as the sympathy lies always with the couple and opposed to the situation which oppresses them' (Scott Meek, *Gay News* 145, 1978).

' ... it is the first time I can remember seeing a film in which two actors make a gay relationship seem genuinely loving and emotional. And what a breath of fresh air that is after all those films and television plays which imply that homosexuals are by nature incapable of love' (letter from Martin Grant, *Gay News*, 199).

conservationists Donald Davis in *Joy in the Morning* (1965 C) opens up Yvette Mimieux to the joys and splendours of nature. Jed Thaxter (Ian Redford), the friend of Gideon in ARTEMIS '81 (1981 T) sees himself as a defender of the planet Earth at two minutes to midnight: 'Don't pick the flower, Gideon ... all that labour to be born ... Flowers are growing smaller in our pollution and all creatures who feed on effluent and waste are waxing large. The house fly shall weigh down the rose'.

Bart Fallmont (Kevin Conroy) challenges the Carrington plans for an oil pipeline in DYNASTY (1985 T). The nasty Adam whips up a press scandal against him, and Bart withdraws from the fight and from the life of Steven. Bart was a fairly bland character who promised much but wasn't allowed to develop politically or sexually. (He returned, played by another – younger – actor in the 1991 reunion. This time he and Steven were united in their concern for the environment.)

In *Single Voices* 'The Last Supper' (1990 T) the rejected husband, Terence

Halliday (Michael Angelis) blames his wife's defection on the people she mixes with: 'They're obsessed with the dimensions of the ozone hole and the tamperings of man with the universe.' She went off to Torremolinos and met someone. He was a VEGETARIAN. 'Acid rain, pollution, insecticide, healthy living – all that crap, I suppose.'

constant companion *See* COMPANION.

contagion *See* DIRT; DISEASE; PLAGUE.

Conversation Piece (It 1974 C) A solitary professor (Burt Lancaster) is disturbed by the presence of a countess' sexually ambiguous German lover, Konrad Hubell (Helmut Berger). Opulent, distanced chamber piece, but illuminating on the director's great love for his protégé Berger and on his own approaching death.
W: Suso Cecchi D'Amico, Lucino Visconti and Enrico Medioli; D: Luchino VISCONTI; 122 mins.

conversion In the 1977 'Roper's Niece' episode of THREE'S COMPANY Jack Tripper suffers what appears, to HOMOPHOBIC Stanley Roper, suspiciously like an 'attack of normalness' in the arms of the voluptuous Karen (Christina Hart). Stanley wonders if a miracle is taking place before his very eyes: 'I mean, my niece *is* a beautiful girl. He *could* convert. You read about it in the papers all the time – about people getting changed from women to men and vice versa.'
But Jack is a fraud: a heterosexual playing gay. Semi-real homosexuals teetering on the brink of normality or falling right over include Mr HUMPHRIES in GRACE AND FAVOUR and the snowflake (Robert Hirsch) in *Pajama Tops* (1983 T).
In Ruby Wax's chat show *Don't Miss Wax* (1987 T) a queer kind of turnabout did take place: one of the world's most famous homosexuals talked about his attraction to women and a high profile, though not 100 per cent out, lesbian, was sent on a field trip ('blind date') to dally with a man.
Much more convincing are Angie

Dickinson and her husband's driver Private Finger (Christian Vance) as they explore each other in a moonlit field in *Pearl* (1979 T). For both participants there is a moment of redemptive awe at such manifest bliss: she, a wicked woman, has seduced a pure boy; he, once quasi-queer, is now *whole* ... But not for long. Even as they exult, Japanese bombers are flying overhead on their way to wreak havoc on Pearl Harbor. The wife must return to her husband's side. Private Finger will soon die in a jeep crash and the full success of his crash course in normal sex will never be tested.

Cook, David (1940–) English novelist and playwright; created role of Trevor in *Little Boxes* (1968) written by his partner John BOWEN.
As actor: Kenneth Bradshaw in *The First Thing You Think Of* (1963 T); Private Wilson in *King and Country* (1964 C); CORONATION STREET as a teddy boy (*c* 1964); David Willoughby in *The Power Game* 'The Politician' (1964 T); Henry Laker in *Anyone for Murder?* (1967 R); James Lakin in *The Mating Machine* 'As the Bishop Said to the Actress' (1970 T); Paul in THE WAITING ROOM (1971 T); *Coronation Street* (*c* 1973) again as a Teddy Boy.
As writer: lesbian episode of *Couples* (1976 T); IF ONLY ... (1980); MARY'S WIFE (1980 T); *Walter* (1982 T); *Missing Persons* (read by Patricia Routledge, A BOOK AT BEDTIME 1987 R); etc.

cooks The simple-minded adopted brother of Richard Burton in *The Last Days of Dolwyn* (1949 C) offers to look after the soup on the stove – to the consternation of the womenfolk: 'A man cooking – I've never heard of such a thing!' But, they reason, 'with these *orphans*, you never know'.
Omar Khayyam (Cornel Wilde 1956 C) was allowed to wax lyrical about food because he was a POET and from the east (all a bit odd, those turbaned guys).
The army cook Willie Maltravers (Derek Nimmo) was conceived and played as a soppy POUF prone to tan-

trums and over-elaborate dishes in *The Amorous Prawn* (1962 C). To everyone's surprise (including his own) he becomes engaged at the end. In *Get Some In* (1976 T) Corporal Lionel Jenner (Roy Kinnear) is a windbag, a hypochondriac, a terrible chef – unhygienic, too (he has his poodle with him in the mess). LUKE-WARM (Christopher BIGGINS) is a prison trusty who helps in the kitchen in *Porridge* (1973–7 T).

Basil Fawlty's 'New Chef' Kurt (Steve Plytas) develops a passion for a young man and is so overcome with the vapours that he is unable to prepare the night's food at *Fawlty Towers* (1976 T). This impasse forces Basil into a frenzy of improvisation. Michael (Joseph Brady) cooks for his blind master while his boyfriend does the garden (in *Blind Love* 1977 T). Jack Tripper (John Ritter) reinforces his landlord's image of him by enrolling at the California Technical School as a trainee chef. He has to make a mousse pie for a competition in a 1979 episode of THREE'S COMPANY, 'The Bake Out'.

Chefs with high-pitched voices appeared in *Arch of Triumph* (1948 C), *Afternoon Off* (1978 T) with Harold INNOCENT as 'Marjory'; in *Murder She Wrote* (a pseudo-Frenchman, played by Alexander Folk in a 1986 episode); Peter WOODTHORPE in *The Man That Got Away* (1987 R). There was also the con-man (Michael Byrne) who relieved rich women of their fortunes over some skilfully prepared *foie gras* and *filet mignon* (*The Enigma Files* 'Cook-In' 1980 T).

The stigma attached to being a boy in the kitchen forces Pat Hancock (David Easter) in BROOKSIDE (1986 T) to call himself a 'food technologist' while poor young Ian Beale (Adam Woodyatt) has to brave the sneers of even right-on Kelvin in EASTENDERS (1986 T) when he elects to do a chef's course. It's the wearing of the APRON that gets up Kelvin's nose.

cooking God did not create men to cook. If they do it, it's either for money or because no little woman is around.

Heterosexual bachelors (or abandoned husbands) have to make a virtue out of a necessity in successfully preparing their own food. The cutting, stirring and kneading must be accompanied by one very important ingredient: man talk about women. Examples include:

In America: Bill (Earl Holliman) cooking up a heap of chilli while telling his colleague Pepper (Angie Dickinson) that he's hot stuff in bed (POLICE WOMAN 'Flowers of Evil' 1974 T).

In Australia: one unmarried male doctor is discovered helping another with the pasta in a 1989 episode of A COUNTRY PRACTICE. The older one (Shane Porteous) ruminates over his *sauce piquante*: 'You know, women are funny creatures, aren't they [stir, stir]. You think you're getting to know them [stir, stir] and then, wham, right between the eyes.'

In Britain: Teddy Lorimer-Smith (Michael Winn) is making breakfast after a night of clubbing in *A Flaw in the Crystal* (1964 T). Enter fellow bachelor Roger Meredith (David Buck). Without any further ado, they begin talking about 'little Maxine': 'Quite funny isn't she ... I hope she didn't ask too much.'

It was Michael Caine (as Harry Palmer) in *The Ipcress File* the following year who made cooking respectable for men. And sexy. As Palmer collects together the ingredients, whisks, pours, simmers and finally serves he is engaged in one long verbal lascivity with Sue Lloyd. This strand is still noticeable. In the first episode of *Joint Account* (1990 T), for example, househusband Peter Egan cooks energetically while simultaneously receiving two saucy and palpable propositions from women. Minutes later he is enjoying a champagne-induced night of passion with his wife. Later, peeling Brussels sprouts, the conversation turns to the prospect and feasibility of the couple having a baby.

Generally, though, males are presented as totally incompetent as soon as they pick up a saucepan or ignite the oven. Here is a selection of the many culinary disasters over the past three decades:

When Pat (Patricia Gallimore) leaves Tony (Colin Skipp) in THE ARCHERS (1978 R) and goes to Wales, Tony and lodger Mike are unable to cope with anything beyond opening a tin of pilchards. Tony invites the new barmaid at the Bull back 'for a meal' which she cooks. This was just one instance of male ineptitude in this area which the serial has described over the years. It finally prompted a letter from a woman in Clitheroe, Lancashire in *Radio Times* (28.10.89): 'Can somebody kindly tell me what is wrong with the vast majority of males in *The Archers*, who seem incapable of even the simplest of culinary activity? Is one to conclude that these wimps will all starve if their beloved wife is not available to prepare every single item of food including the many cups of tea and coffee they seem to drink.'

James Herriott (Christopher Timothy) is seen pouring boiling water into a teapot in *All Creatures Great and Small* 'The Rough and the Smooth' (1989 T), which is about the summit of his food preparation. He would probably die of starvation were it not for his partner Siegfried Farnon (Robert Hardy). But then again … In the same episode, the crusty senior vet prepares a pork pie, which Henrietta the dalmatian proceeds to eat, along with everything else. The one untouched vittle is in the oven – burnt to a cinder. Both men – the acme of competence in every other practical area of their lives – retire for cheese and pickle sandwiches at the Drovers. (Siegfried prepares a vegetarian meal with slightly more success in 'The Salt of the Earth' (1989 T).)

Tim (Stephen Garlick) burns the fish fingers in TWO PEOPLE 'The Trouble with a Kitten' (1979 T); Jack Duckworth (William Tarmey) scorches the sausages in CORONATION STREET (1984 T); a man-made *chilli con carne* explodes over walls and ceiling in *Men!* (1984 R); Bob Plackett (Ed Begley Jr) in *She-Devil* (1989 C) ruins the lasagne and gives the kids heart-shaped cookies which they loathe. If only Mom was back living with them …

The daughter of the house (who has magic powers) in *Out of This World* (1988 T) tastes one of Buzz's Seaweed Fudgies and goes 'Yeuck!' 'He must have taken a ball of dough, and rolled it across the gymnasium floor and thrown it under a horse.' She goes abracadabra and Buzz thinks he has brought forth delicious edibles.

In *Single Voices* 'The Last Supper' (1990 T) Terry (Michael Angelis) makes his estranged wife a salad with walnuts and 'her favourite', summer pudding. He has a hell of a trouble making it – 'I'm not a culinary man' – and the result, he confides, 'looked like a giant jelly-fish fallen from a great height'.

In BROOKSIDE (1990) Mick (Louis Emerick) peels the potatoes into near infinity, while (observed from a discreet distance) posher Jonathan (Steven Pinner), the estate agent shoves a suspiciously neat, prepared-in-advance casserole into the oven: 'I like things being ready before I start.'

Around the same time, Jimmy (Dean Sullivan) and Sinbad (Martin Starkie) manage to lay on a barbecue, but only after gay Gordon COLLINS has told them what to do. It is a great success and the pair wake up together on the couch next day, surrounded by debris.

Kim Tate's husband Frank (Norman Bowler) in EMMERDALE (1990 T) has barely spread marge on one piece of bread before Kim (Claire King) steps in and 'helps him out'. This is followed by a glistening close-up of a heart attack on a plate – fried eggs, fatty bacon, greasy bread prepared by Dolly Skilbeck (Jean Rogers) for her husband, who compliments her.

Ian (who's a qualified chef) gives Cindy a lavish, perfectly prepared birthday dinner in EASTENDERS while, in the same episode, Nick Cotton (John Altman) continues to serve Mum poisoned grub. In a magnificent piece of understatement, *Radio Times* informed viewers that 'Dot doesn't seem to be feeling the benefit of Nick's cooking' (1990 T). The other amateur cook in the Square is Matthew (Steven Hartley), who is preparing a salad for his wife-to-be Carmel but he only gets as far as washing one lettuce leaf (1989). The older generation doesn't even want to try: Frank (Mike Reid) tells Arthur: 'As a cook I make a very good used-car salesman' (1989).

On 'reality' television, there are any amount of breezy males, bearded and unbearded, camp and non-camp, who chop and grate, whisk and whip up dishes which are every bit the equal of those created by their female equivalent. But let an 'ordinary man' in the TV kitchen and there will always be a string of self-deprecatory remarks or snippy comments from female co-presenters. Witness Alan Titchmarsh helping Valentina Harris in a May 1990 *Daytime Live*.

He cuts up the prosciuto with perfect ease, says he'll have a go at baking, rubs the garlic into the bread. He does everything that is required. He is the model of quiet competence. Cut to female presenter: 'Well done, Valentina ... *Against all the odds*!' A few minutes later, over on *Neighbours* (episode made in 1988 T) Nick (Mark Stevens) is recalling the time he let the pressure cooker explode: all over the café. What a mess. What a chump.

Gay men, of course, know every recipe – the more involved and frou-frou the better they like it. Honorary gay Albert Steptoe (Wilfred Brambell) provides the most marvellous grub for his boy Harold: steak and kidney pie, sherry trifle and an upside-down cake (*Steptoe and Son* 'Steptoe and Sons' 1968 T). Which might explain why Harold has never married.

Nursing tutor at St Angela's, Ken HASTINGS (Michael Howarth) in ANGELS (1979–80 T) cooks for a hobby. He is as flighty in his choice of cuisines as of men. 'No more Creole. I'm into Chinese now. I bought myself a wok,' he tells a colleague.

Terry (Dennis Waterman) has to 'mind' Ronald (Alun Lewis) in MINDER 'Who's Wife Is It, Anyway?' (1980 T). 'I like to cook,' swoons Ronnie. Sigh. Pause. 'Of course, you know I'm gay.' To which Terry replies tersely: 'It had

crossed my mind.' Although freaked out, Terry does sit down to a nice bit of homo cooking before he is forced to accompany the young frippet to a club/disco.

Dainty cop Fred Kerwin (John HURT) serves up gorgeous chicken to his 'mate' (Ryan O'Neal) in PARTNERS (1982 C), helping to cement their transitory bond while working on a murder case. Bob (Gérard Depardieu) is delighted to see that the passive role he has 'encouraged' Antoine (Michel Blanc) to take in TENUE DE SOIREE/*Evening Dress* (1985 C) bedwise also extends to the kitchen: he's a great little cook for a former heterosexual, but then he is French.

An immediate source of tension between Alex (Graham Harvey) and his boyfriend's mum, who's come to stay, in G.P. 'Lovers' (Aust 1990 T) is ... the kitchen! He won't even let her into it. However, she does find his octopus salad tastier than she had expected (but how she would have preferred good old Aussie beef).

It goes against the stereotypical grain for lesbians to cook well: poor flustered Jill (Sandy Dennis) in THE FOX (1968 C) burns the muffins. Exceptions are artistic Vivienne (Camilla Sparv) in VALLEY OF THE DOLLS *'81* (1981 T): her *coquilles St Jacques* are the best, just the job for reclaiming a beautiful American from drugs and heterosexuality; and in HEARTBEAT (1989 T) nurse Marilyn (Gail Strickland) makes lasagne with her lover Patti – HUGGING as they do it (in lieu of KISSING or dancing or any other loving contact). Tee (Paula Kelly) is making a meat loaf in THE WOMEN OF BREWSTER PLACE (1989 T) when she realizes she is being spied on by the resident HOMOPHOBE. She ups and chucks most of the ingredients at the snoop.

Just as not all lesbians open a can of beans with their teeth, not all gay men cook like dreams. Three who come to mind are Quentin CRISP in THE NAKED CIVIL SERVANT; Joseph ACKERLEY (Benjamin WHITROW) in WE THINK THE WORLD OF YOU (1980 T); the harried civil servant (Pip Donnahy) in KILLING TIME (1990 T). And dinner with Joe

ORTON and Kenneth Halliwell wouldn't have been a gastronomic delight on the evidence of PRICK UP YOUR EARS (1987 C).

With the dawning of the New Age, a few American heroes (usually played by actors associated with sociopaths and psychopaths or big lugs) have unself-consciously prepared and cooked food that didn't explode or fall on the floor or get burnt or provide a dog's dinner. Al Pacino was a short-order chef in *Frankie and Johnnie* (1991 C). But Al, reported the magazine *Woman's Day*, isn't interested in cooking in his private life: 'Don't believe the movies. They lie. I'm no cook in real life. Maybe I boil water, but to get things right for the movie I had to sit around kitchens and watch cooks at work. I did a few chores to get the hang of it, but don't ask me to cook a meal.'

Tom (Nick Nolte) chops onions and fries prawns as he remembers his father being served – and thoroughly enjoying – dog food in THE PRINCE OF TIDES (1991 C). This is one of the rare films in which a Male male can and a Female female can't. 'Just because I don't know how to cook, it doesn't mean I don't know how to eat,' asserts psychiatrist Susan (Barbra STREISAND).

Robert De Niro – a chef in *Stanley and Iris* (1989 C) – cooks a thoroughly decent meal for Jane Fonda and her daughter. But the lie is still the norm: a woman's place is in the kitchen, men don't belong there unless they're not real men.

See also DRINKING; DRINKS.

Judy **Coolibah** Betty Marsden's militant Australian FEMINIST in ROUND THE HORNE (1967 R), always seeing and hearing the worst in Kenneth Horne's motives, attitudes and questions, calling him a molester and a FAIRY. Is fiercely opposed to nude calendars, particularly those *without* pictures because 'you can imagine what *might* be on them'. She's ready for any eventuality: 'I've notified the police so they know where I am.' After a brief engagement to a 'Pommie

FAGGOT' she returns home, doubtless to find her true self.

Copland, Aaron [Aaron Kaplan] (1900–90) American composer who spent his boyhood in Brooklyn and his COMING OUT in Paris and who returned home as a celebrated conjurer of America's pioneering past.

Young People's Concert (hosted by Leonard BERNSTEIN 1958 T); *Aaron Copland: A Self-Portrait* (a tribute on his 85th birthday 1986 T); *My First Dance Steps*: Aaron Copland in Paris and Hollywood 1921–38 (1987 R; adapted by Mike Steer from Copland's autobiography and read by Sam Wanamaker).

Coral Browne: Caviar to the General (UK 1990 T) The beautiful and brilliantly caustic actress is interviewed by John SCHLESINGER a few months before her death in May 1991. Those offering their recollections of working with her include Ned SHERRIN. One or two heterosexuals are allowed in for balance. Ms Browne presents a barbed recollection of filming the sex scene from THE KILLING OF SISTER GEORGE with Susannah YORK in HOLLYWOOD: eventually playing her reactions to an empty bed. Channel 4; 60 mins.

cordwangling Each week of ROUND THE HORNE's existence, the gnarled and gusseted folk performer Ramblin' Syd Rumpo (Kenneth WILLIAMS) would dip into his ganderbag for songs of lust and genitalia. These latter were only thinly disguised as 'goolies', 'cordwangles' and 'scropes'. To the tune of 'Waltzing Matilda', for example, Syd sang of someone 'toasting his splod by the faggots' gleam'. Syd asks the audience: 'Who'll come a woggling his jumbuck with me?'

A moveable feast of just 12 letters, cordwangling was used by the writers as a vehicle for Ramblin' Syd to suggest all manner of polyanthus perversity under the guise of English rustic folk songs. One of the most bare-faced of all affronts on public innocence, cordwangling went on its merry way for four years, together with bogling fork, woggle, nurk, wurdling and scroping.

In March 1967, a few months before CONSENTING ADULT, non-military males were decriminalized, Ramblin' Syd burred: 'Now, there's a lot of talk about cordwangling these days – but very few people know what it actually is. And those that practise it don't like to talk about it.' The previous month, to the tune of 'My Darling Clementine', the bard of bawd gave vent to:

There's a moral to the story: Though your
cordwangle be poor
Keep your hands off others' moulies
For it is against the law-o!

One of the most versatile of words, a true gem of long-lost English folk language: verb or noun, it could be active, passive, sweet, sour, even put out to dry:

She sneered at his cordwangle
As it hung upon the line.

Its nearest equivalent was Major Denis BLOODNOK's 'cringing naggers' on THE GOON SHOW ('The Six Ingots of Leadenhall Street' (1955) etc).

Coriolanus (UK 1984 T) Elijah Moshinsky's production for BBC Television, with Alan Howard as Coriolanus and Mike Gwilym as Tullus Aufidius, was one of the most controversial of the SHAKESPEARE series. So far it has not been released on video by BBC Enterprises. Why?

John Wain, in the *Listener*, was ecstatic up to a point:

... very intelligent ... excellent ... Then
it fell apart into self-indulgent
opinionated foolishness with the
director's frank insistence that Tullus
Aufidius has a homosexual crush on
Coriolanus. The relationship of the two
men who have given years to fighting with
each other may or may not contain a
streak of this as one ingredient – the play
does not specifically contradict it – and if
it makes the homosexual lobby happy to
have it included, I'm no killjoy. But that is
not the same as making Aufidius drool
over the text ... and finally snatching the

pen out of Shakespeare's hand, and turning the death of Coriolanus, which is specifically shown in the play as a mob lynching, into a sexually charged single combat. Rubbish like this does nothing to save the reputation of the BBC.

The Corner House (UK 1987 T) Gilbert (Christopher Emyard) is 'a screaming anti-monarchist subversive' who keeps collecting boxes on the counter for lesbian and gay and Third World causes. Sentimental and sensitive, he still keeps firm the memory of his lover of 22 years who died a decade before.

Coronation Street (UK 1960– T) Created by Tony Warren, who tells a fictionalized version of his days with GRANADA's longest running – and highest rated – programme, in his book *The Lights of Manchester* (1991). The Street has never had anything approaching a gay or lesbian character: just one or two bits of camp (a HAIRDRESSER, a WAITER) and the spectacular barmaid, then publican Bet Lynch/Gilroy who, in 1984, advised a Rover's Return customer that 'this place' is far away from reality. 'Eee, but it's grand. Acting, scripts, plots all capture the salt and vinegar of the North of England as perhaps it never was. Mark Lawson offered a minority opinion in *J'accuse* (1991 T): 'It ought to be axed.' A radio play based on a similar serial (one whose blowsy leading lady has been done in), *Who Killed Ada Tansey?*, was broadcast in 1982, with a gay actor called Dennis as one of the suspects.

corruption In THE HUMAN JUNGLE 'Conscience on a Rack' (1965 T) a headmistress (Flora Robson) receives menacing letters hinting at some dark secret. Through intensive questioning from PSYCHIATRIST Herbert Lom she confesses that she herself sent the letters. For years she has been torturing herself over one of her pupils. Had she corrupted her? If so, surely she should be hounded and punished. A tape-recorded message reassures all concerned that the pupil found the straight and narrow: husband, two children, living in New Zealand.

The same theme of corruption narrowly averted surfaced in evidence given by a stiff-backed schoolteacher in CROWN COURT 'Heart to Heart' (1979 T). Had an 18-year-old pupil corrupted a 13-year-old? Luckily not. 'She's teaching Russian literature at an excellent provincial university ... she's married ... with two children.'

The indissoluble linkage of any same-sex relationship involving a young person with the violation of their very soul was first countered by Jacob BRONOWSKI in BEHIND THE NEWS (1953 R): 'The bringing in of juniors draws a red herring across the subject. The law is perfectly well capable of punishing anyone who corrupts a young person whether that young person is a boy or a girl and it is equally a crime to corrupt them whether the corrupter is homosexual or of a more ordinary nature.'

But the equation continues to be made: for example by the Rev. Fred NILE in *Hate Crimes* (1992 T).

Corvo, [Baron] Frederick aka Fr[ederick] Rolfe (1860–1913) English novelist and self-styled head of the Roman Catholic Church. Alec MCCOWEN played him in *The Mischief Makers* (1986 R); H. C. Bainbridge discussed him in *The Riddle of Corvo* (1952 R). *Hadrian VII* (his fantasy about himself as POPE) was produced twice for radio, once with McCowen in the title role.

The Cost of Love (UK 1991 T) Procurement, soliciting and gross indecency – under the beady eye of the impending Clause 25 of the Criminal Justice Bill.
D: Richard Kwietniowski; 2 mins.

costume designers Anna GESCHWITZ who designed the exotic outfit for LULU to wear on the trapeze in PANDORA'S BOX (1928 C); a spendthrift swisher in *The Broadway Melody of 1929*; Michael WARD giving his bony all to film star

Constance Cummings in *The Intimate Stranger* (1956 C).

cottaging The inspecting of, the fondling of or having full sex with users of public toilets (usually gents though some 'powder rooms' have been known to buzz). The location offers visual excitement, anonymity, semi-privacy with the danger of getting caught and an opportunity for sexual encounter, especially for those who do not identify as gay or cannot find partners in the usual places and are looking for a fast, sordid embrace

Noel COWARD appears to be asking Alec Guinness to engage in some erotic practices in a Cuban loo in *Our Man in Havana* (1959 C), but it's all in the interest of secrecy (though the joke is repeated later in the film between Guinness and someone he is trying to recruit into espionage).

Joe ORTON, who was one of cottaging's more tireless and passionate devotees, slyly hinted at his hobby in his first play THE RUFFIAN ON THE STAIR (1964 R):

> Mick: 'I'm to be at King's Cross station at eleven ... I'm meeting a man in a toilet.'
> Joyce: 'You always go to such interesting places.'

In his final play WHAT THE BUTLER SAW (1987 T) one of the characters describes 'gentlemen's lavatories' as the 'last strongholds of male privilege'.

Just what Joe Orton saw (and did) in public loos was balletically indicated in PRICK UP YOUR EARS (1987 C); and again by John Goodall and David MacIntosh who pirouette around two toilet stalls before coming together as one in *Ten Cents a Dance* (1991 C).

The locale has also afforded comedy in such films as *High Anxiety* (1977 C, a flasher), TAXI ZUM KLO (1981 C, Frank marking the kids' essays while waiting for action), and *A Private Function* (1984 C, Michael Palin being intimidated at the urinal by Denholm ELLIOTT and his cronies). In *The Secret Policeman's Other Ball* (1982 C) Alan BENNETT (who wrote both *A Private Function* and *Prick Up Your Ears*) plays a married man explaining to John Fortune the ins and outs of cottaging etiquette.

MORE LIVES THAN ONE (1984 T) reveals the more dangerous side of the activity. David (Michael N. Harbour) is married and spends one afternoon a week watching (he says) men visiting and having sex in a public lavatory. During a police raid he hides out in the back of Steve's van. They meet a few times but drift apart. David stays married – and continues to cruise and possibly cottage. Why not? he argues. 'There's men having their secretaries in doorways, in cars, screwing them rotten.'

Not everybody sees cottaging as a harmless diversion, or as a necessary evil for those unable or unwilling to lead a more open gay life. Lewis Duncan (Anton Rodgers) in COMING OUT (1979 T) is gay, but would never countenance cottaging. He thinks it unnecessary and bad for the image: 'When a straight man goes to the gents to have a pee, do you think that he honestly enjoys being cruised by some sticky-lipped POOF? Of course, he doesn't. What's he supposed to do? Just put his hand on his heart and smile tolerantly? He's offended, for God's sake and it offends *me*!'

The likely outcome for someone who finds most of his sex in urinals is bleakly spelt out in the second of THE TERENCE DAVIES TRILOGY 'Madonna and Child' (1980 C). The erotic pleasures can be enjoyed safely – if ultimately unsatisfactorily – thanks to technology: fantasy today in CAUGHT LOOKING (1991 T); as normal as baked beans tomorrow.

An assignation sought and mostly fulfilled in women's lavatories include Ginger (Jackie Lane) indicating to Elaine (Janet Munro) that she prefers her own sex in AFTERNOON OF A NYMPH (1962 T) and Anna (Sheila Gish), a literary lioness giving the eye to Isabelle Adjani in *Quartet* (1982 C).

And what of the lavatory attendants? Do they harbour secret desires? One has pulsations which she finds difficult to keep secret: Kim (Jane Lapotaire), breaker of nearly all society's rules in THE OTHER WOMAN (1976 T). Her part-time job is most rewarding. Her friend Rose (Rosalind Adams) warns her to be careful: 'Will you never learn? What self-respecting ladies expect from their common or garden conveniences is the privacy to pass their water and check their coiffeur ... Not the likes of you pouncing on them from amongst the mops.'

counselling, radio and television
Increasingly important staples of viewing and listening. Mainly women, they include Anna Raeburn (who spun off her experiences into the sitcom AGONY), Claire RAYNER and Sally Hawkins. The last named, with a co-counsellor, answered a boy of 14 who thought he was gay in an encouraging and positive – though entirely lawful – manner, on BBC1's *Breakfast Time* (1986 T). Stinging protest letters followed.

Country (UK 1981 T) Philip Carlion (James FOX) is the youngest son of a brewing millionaire (Leo McKern). The boy writes 'salacious copy for the *Evening Standard*' and digs dirt for a satirical magazine too. He is the perfect choice to take over his father's empire on the eve of the Labour party's landslide victory in 1945. However, he does have certain handicaps: no club, no decent clothes and no wife. He didn't even serve in the war (he was declared 'unfit'). But he *did* go to Eton and OXFORD. Opting for the role of head of the family, Philip has himself nominated for Whites and the Carlton, makes an appointment with his father's tailor, and will 'enter into certain negotiations with a lady'. Trevor Griffiths' play ends with the peasants lighting bonfires outside as Clement Attlee's thin voice pours from the radio. Philip, gnomically self-contained, proposes a toast. 'The ship's sinking, gentlemen ... I give you ... the future.' Crystal glasses are raised. No doubt Philip's boyfriend Nikki ('Don't be a hussy. I'll smack your bottom for you,' he tells him over the phone) will be accommodated into the scheme of things, as will the firm's new carbonated beer.

P: Ann Scott; D: Richard Eyre; 75 mins.

country lesbians Pursuing the sylvan life, usually unsuccessfully, usually with lots of pre-lesbian tension: THE LADIES OF LLANGOLLEN; Jill and March in THE FOX; Breeze and Lorna in COUNTRY MATTERS 'Breeze Anstey'; Hilary (Norma West) and Connie (Beryl REID) in *Smiley's People* (1982 T).

Country Matters (UK 1972–3 T) Impeccably produced (by Derek GRANGER) collection of adapted stories by A. E. Coppard and H. E. Bates, including the latter's story of blighted, one-sided lesbian love 'Breeze Anstey'. It is noticeable that in the English countryside homosexuality hardly ever happens – except via townies (*A Voyage Round My Father*), aristocrats (PORTRAIT OF A MARRIAGE; BRIDESHEAD REVISITED), and the occasional aberration (Carol GREY and John TREGORRAN).

A Country Practice (Aust 1981–) The lives of a group of people in the sleepy locality of Coopers Crossing. Sleepy? No, it is rife with every commotion and concatination that can be devised by the ingenious writers.
Cr: James Davern.

A Country Practice rolled into its 909th and 910th episodes ... with the arrival of Brett Cooper, homosexual and champion cyclist. Brett's homosexuality and reaction of others to it are at the core of this fairly dramatic episode which runs over two nights. Brett is Hugo's friend and Hugo is unaware of Brett's sexual preference until Brett tells him. Hugo is shocked, as is Darcy, who fancies Brett and his earring ...' (Alison Stewart, *Sydney Morning Herald*, 20.4.92).

Five of its stories have had gay themes or characters: the above-mentioned ('Little Boy Blue'); 'Apparitions' (cricket hero returns – to die of AIDS, 1989); one about a molester of children (girls but he is a typical MOTHER'S BOY bachelor pervert, 1987); 'Secrets' (about child molestation again, 1992); 'A Kiss Before Dying', another AIDS story (the brother of a regular character,

1992). Otherwise, nothing but heterosexuality in the bush.
See also THE FLYING DOCTORS.

Coupler A matchmaker in Sir John Vanbrugh's *The Relapse*, or *Virtue in Danger*. A lusty old man who makes a play for one of the young men, and who starts the plot in motion: played by Harry Hutchinson (1947 R); Kenneth Connor aka Sidney Mincing (1954 T); Haydn Jones (1961 R). When the latter was repeated (in 1964) the *Listener*'s P. N. Furbank complained: 'It was to make the wrong [kind of] joke to present Coupler as a modern "horrible POUF". Coupler is a wit; he speaks for the purposes of the plot, the language of high intelligence, his lines aren't really manageable in a homosexual Earls Court QUEEN accent .... [And] Haydn Jones sounded young though called Old Coupler.'

Couples (UK 1975–7 T) Afternoon drama serial about a marriage guidance office. Over a period of a couple of weeks in 1976, Christine (Gay Singleton) couldn't decide whether she was gay or not. She finds the sexual relationship between her husband and their girlfriend is threatening her marriage.
W: P. J. Hammond and Tony PARKER, 26.2.76 & 16.3.76; Thames.

Couples 'What's So Different?' (UK 1982 T) Gay Search meets Mak and Mary in North Cornwall and Peter and Victor in Surrey. 'How hard was it for them to establish a stable relationship?' Thoroughly decent look at couples in very different parts of Britain, aimed at the 'God slot' audience, and part of television's noble but probably doomed attempt to normalize people who simply don't fit into little boxes by placing them in another box marked 'different'.

courtiers Osric, the gadfly in the court of Claudius and Gertrude in Hamlet (though sometimes cut); Peter Cushing (1947 C), John RYE (1960 R) and Alan BENNETT (1971 T) were among those portraying this breathless gossip. Over-made-up extras who make up the passing show in Ancient Rome (*I, Claudius*, SEBASTIANE); medieval England (EDWARD II); 17th-century France (*The Devils*); etc.

cousins Isabel Fry called *Cousins* (1954 R) a true extended family: 'Each strange yet all connected by a subtle likeness to each other ... a world of cousins, uncles and aunts.' Intriguing, sometimes sexual bondings in: AS YOU LIKE IT; characters in THE FOX based on farmer cousins; George KIRRIN and three of THE FAMOUS FIVE; *My Cousin Rachel*; Susan and Cicely in *The Cat and the Canary* (1978 C); the two young men, probably lovers, who sleep with the same prostitute in *Mandingo* (1975 C); Tony Steedman and John CARLIN's characters in *Are You Ready for the Music?* (1965 T); SOMERVILLE AND ROSS in ONLY GOODNIGHT; THE LADIES OF LLANGOLLEN.

Coward, Sir Noel (1899–1973) English playwright, short-story writer, songwriter and cabaret performer. Remembered, above all, for his clipped voice, the cigarette holder, songs dapper ('Mad Dogs And Englishmen', 'Mrs Worthington') and moving ('If Love Were All'), and his love stories: high-minded (*Brief Encounter*), perverse (DESIGN FOR LIVING) and brittle (*Private Lives*).

Played by Dennis PRICE in *The Cochran Years* (1952 T); Daniel MASSEY in *Star!* (1968 C); Francis Matthews in *Ike* (1982 T).

Cavalcade (1933 C; 1936 R; 1959 R); *Hay Fever* (1938 T); BRIEF ENCOUNTER (1947 R; 1952 R; 1958 R; 1985 R); Noel Coward introduces *Words and Music* (with Joyce Grenfell and Graham Payn 1952 R); *Nights of Gladness: The Noel Coward Story* (1954 R); *Present Laughter* (1956 R); THE VORTEX (1928 C; 1958 R; 1960 T; 1964 T; 1967 R; 1969 T); *This Happy Breed* (1962 T); DESERT ISLAND DISCS (1963 R); *Design for Living* (1964 T; 1979 T; 1991 R); *A Choice of Coward: [Present Laughter, The Vortex, Hay Fever, Design for Living]* (1964 T); *Sunday Night: Noel Coward on Acting* (1966 T); *Present Laughter* (1967

T); *Noel Coward's Birthday Party* (1969 T); OMNIBUS 'Noel Coward' (1969 T); *The First and Only Noel* (1970 R); *Noel Coward at the NFT* (1971 T); Noel Coward talks to Edgar Lustgarten (1972 R); ME AND THE GIRLS (1976); *Still Life* 'Brief Encounter' (1978 R); *A Song At Twilight* (1982 T; 1988 R); *Star Quality* (a series of adapted short stories including 'Star Quality' and 'Me and the Girls', 1985 T); *Collins Meets Coward* (six short plays all featuring Joan Collins, 1991 T).

The Songwriters (1978 T); *Side by Side by Coward* (1978 T); *I Call It Genius*: Noel Coward and Gertrude Lawrence (1980 R); *Green on Coward* (1980 R); *Noel Coward – A Private Life* (1983 T); *A Night on the Town*: Porter and Coward (1983 T); *A Talent to Amuse*: a lighthearted look at the life and music of Noel Coward (1984 R); THE SOUTH BANK SHOW (1991 T).

As actor: *Hearts of the World* (bit part, 1918 C); *The Scoundrel* (1935 C); *In Which We Serve* (1941 C); *The Astonished Heart* (1949 C); *Our Man in Havana* (1959 C); *Surprise Package* (1960 C); *Bunny Lake is Missing* (1965 C); *Boom!* (1966); *The Italian Job* (1969).

As director: *In Which We Serve* (1941 C).

'Gay? It smacks of Noel Coward.'

Cowardly Lion Played by Bert Lahr in *The Wizard of Oz*, lisping king of the jungle. He influenced LENNY THE LION and, in America, Snagglepuss ('Heavenths to Mergatroid') in *Quickdraw McGraw* (1959–62 T).

creative partnerships Some are based on traditional heterosexual marriages; others are between siblings or between a homosexual man and a heterosexual man, or between two heterosexual men, or two lesbians, or a heterosexual woman and a lesbian. Some last for decades, others drift apart or explode after a few years. Some of them, in a wide variety of arts: Woody ALLEN and Diane Keaton or Mia Farrow; Fred Astaire and Hermes PAN; Noel COWARD and Gertrude Lawrence; George CUKOR and (designer) George Hoyningen-Huene; Marlene DIETRICH and Josef Von Sternberg; Dietrich and (costume designer) Travis Banton; Francis Durbridge and Martyn C. Webster; Roger EDENS and Kay Thompson, arranger–producer team at MGM; Edens and Arthur Freed; Marty FELDMAN and Barry TOOK; Tony Hancock, Ray Galton and Alan Simpson; Greta GARBO and (cinematographer) William Daniels; Garbo and (director) Mauritz Stiller; Audrey Hepburn and Hubert De GIVENCHY; Alfred Hitchcock and Alma Reville; David HOCKNEY and Peter Schlesinger; Rock HUDSON and Douglas Sirk; James Ivory, Ismail MERCHANT and Ruth Prawer Jhabvala; Elton JOHN and Bernie Taupin; Danny KAYE and Sylvia Fine; Gene Kelly and Stanley Donen; Alfred Lunt and Lynne Fontanne; Marilyn MONROE and Natasha Lytess; Monroe and Paula Strasberg; Rudolf NUREYEV and Margot Fonteyn; Joe ORTON and Ken Halliwell; John SCHLESINGER and (editor) Jim Clark; Randolph SCOTT and Budd Boetticher; Frank Sinatra and Nelson Riddle; Lily TOMLIN and Jane Wagner; Billy WILDER and Charles Brackett; Geoffrey Webb, Godfrey Baseley and Edward J. Mason (THE ARCHERS); Stewart Main and Peter WELLS.

The Crezz (UK 1976 T) An utterly vacuous comedy-drama series set in a London crescent populated by stereotypes, this condescending, immature affair was mercifully halted after a dozen episodes. The two gays were depicted in terms of 'hubby' and wife. 'He' was Terry (Roland CURRAM), a pipe-smoking, moustached ANTIQUE DEALER; 'she' was Denny (Paul GREENHALGH) in a neck scarf and with teased thinning hair.

Both actors were interviewed by *Gay News* (107):

'They are written slightly camp but you have got to make the point ... [They have] no other friends or parents ... they're very self-contained' (Roland Curram).

'None of [the fan letters] has said, "Do you fuck?" A lot of kids say hello to me in the street now and not one single child has ever mentioned the fact that Terry and I are lovers. It probably means that *The Crezz* should have been put out at 5 o'clock as a rival to *Blue Peter*.

'... At the beginning, the producer and director got worried that what I was wearing was not everyone's idea of what a poove would wear. The wardrobe lady who took me shopping was terribly disappointed that I didn't choose brushed nylon, fur, beads and high-heeled clogs' (Paul Greenhalgh).

Their big moment came in an episode inevitably titled 'Bent Doubles'. Denny has run off with the gardener. Terry is devastated, the neighbours all pitch in to find the faithless spouse and return her/him to hearth and home. This endeavour involves the gruff doctor having to enter a gay CLUB. The reliable Alick ROWE was responsible for giving the players something to say in this episode and the more obvious obviousness was avoided. Indeed the drivelling concept of Clive Exton's concept was improved during rehearsal. The gays only said 'dear heart' and 'petal' 5 times instead of 15. A concatination of the clumsy and the careless. And Thames thought it was modern.

cricket In the glorious last episode ('Big Fish, Little Fish') of the penultimate series of *All Creatures Great And Small*, Siegfried Farnon (Robert Hardy) was forced to play cricket, SUEDE SHOES and all. 'I know how you feel about fast balls,' someone says to him. To Freddie Trueman (Bill Cashman) he concludes wistfully: 'It may well be that I took the wrong turn myself.' He is talking about cricket. Or is he? Other relevant cricketers: Guy (Rupert Everett) far more interested in gazing at his paramour than fielding in ANOTHER COUNTRY (1984 C); Maurice (James Wilby) after losing his virginity to Alec Scudder (Rupert Graves) in MAURICE (1987 C).

Cries from Casement As His Bones Are Brought to Dublin (UK 1973 R) David RUDKIN's magnificent feast of Irish history, polemic and sexual diary, with Norman Rodway as Casement. It was held together by the honesty of its protagonist, a patriot (for Ireland), traitor (against England) and sodomite (with hundreds of anonymous, mainly non-white partners). The first play to truly meld the political and personal in a gay context, darting back and forth from past to present, always alert to Casement's own evaluation of his actions. Whether or not Roger Casement was a patriot or a traitor, the fact of the matter (embellished by the contentious Black Diaries) was that he was proudly Irish and energetically sexual. His bodily needs and his spiritual idealism are presented by Rudkin in his hurtling, overwritten epic, as twin shoots from the same tree.

The sexual frankness (lists of Casement's partners and their prowess) was matched by a spellbinding ability to encapsulate centuries of Irish history into just over three hours. The sheer bulk is exhilirating, the past and its relationship with the present, the crude language of desire, memories, senses, public life, erotic adventures.

'I have voices in me no king, no cardinal would like to hear ... the voice of Empire at my beginning, the voice of Ireland at my end. The voice of the champion of Negro and Indian, the social charmer, the moral agitator, the voice of the Foreign Office, the voice of Sodom, all are Casement. All one man. Like many blood streams fuelling one discordant heart. I suffered in my dissidence but I'm thankful, thankful and joyous that I was on earth a while to suffer so.' Rudkin's 3-hour work interlaces Casement's unapologetic voice with Ireland's attempt to mould him into suitably heroic shape for his 'return' to Dublin in the 1960s.

'Was Casement queer? His childhood relationships established a classical base for homosexuality in late life – his obsessive meticulous character through almost to retardment fully accords with the Freudian anal personality. More concretely Casement's counsel at his trial, Sergeant Sullavan, was "sick to

death of hearing Casement's glory in his vice".'

The Crime at Blossoms (UK 1958 R)
The artist ADRIAN (Anthony Viccars) has a partner (John Byrning), who proclaims two lines with tart flounce but two others – 'He gave me a very queer look' and 'He was never one for being interfered with' – were cut. Radio's first gay couple, sliced in half.
W: Mordaunt Shairp; P: Audrey Cameron; 20.9.58; 90 mins.

criminal aesthetes Creatures of cunning and chintz, usually found in FILM NOIR: Kasper Gutman (Sydney Greenstreet) in *The Maltese Falcon* (1941); Ainsworth (Roy Gordon) in *Railroaded* (1947) quoting Oscar WILDE; Armitage (Albert Dekker) who has to hear TCHAIKOVSKY on a player piano before he can perform sadistic acts – helped by his opposite, Stretch Norton (Hurd HATFIELD) in *Destination Murder* (1950); right on through to Bob Pigeon (William Richert), the Falstaff of Portland's streets in MY OWN PRIVATE IDAHO (1991).

Crisp Anthony Crisp of Scotland Yard (Jim Dale) who pretends to fancy Robert Hays in *Scandalous* (1984 C) in order to put him off the scent – Crisp was Hays' wife's lover; Cullen Crisp (Richard Tyson), Los Angeles drug dealer in search of estranged wife with mother Eleanor (Carroll Baker) who is a hit woman in *Kindergarten Cop* (1990).

Crisp, Quentin (1909–) 'I am one of the stately homos of England.' From being one of the most despised of men, Quentin Crisp, on the strength of Philip Mackie's adaptation of his book, rose to become an international celebrity in his seventies. Wearing 'women's' clothes and make-up, he scored long finger nails through the veil of London hypocrisy, hetero and homo. Using an almost Eastern philosophy of fatalism alongside an unassuageable appetite for exhibitionism he risked violence daily on the streets during the period leading up to Carnaby Street and sartorial freedom.

Crisp, a hard-line traditionalist in many respects, had the double delight of seeing the youth revolt and gay liberation extol everything he practised in every area of his life.

What made Crisp so appealing, outside of his stereotypical mask, was his fathomless generosity to everyone, particularly to no-hopers. Turning the other cheek also involved listening to people as self-centred as he, but far less entertaining. He was also generous sexually and financially to the dreary and unappealing.

Marginally sneered at by gay activists for his refusal to be political and his insistence on 'personal style' above group solidarity, it is only now that Crisp's lone crusade can be fully appreciated and admired.

John HURT's portrayal of him was beyond praise: a delicate, kindly approximation of a chameleon, totally ageless, completely of his own making. A DOCTOR WHO for when the kiddies have gone to bed.

Crisp himself who introduced THE NAKED CIVIL SERVANT went on to appear in his own show (which was filmed as *An Evening with Quentin Crisp*) and to defy levity on chat shows. Now living in New York, he is a regular contributor to any programme dealing with the freaky denizens of that city. Therein lies his triumph – a true non-establishment figure tolerated but not accepted by the establishment. Only George Burns' renaissance comes close to Quentin's gerontophile achievement. His only slip-up was an ill-advised cameo as Sting's colleague in *The Bride*. Ernest THESIGER he wasn't.

The final accolade came from his home country (not THIS IS YOUR LIFE or DESERT ISLAND DISCS or an OBE) when he was entrusted with the epilogue (*Personal Choice*) on Thames TV before that station's viewers settled down for the night. It was the first time (early 1980s) when a known – if no longer practising – homosexual was trusted with the pre-dream time images of a (London only) television audience.

C: Polonius in *Hamlet* (1976); Fran-

kenstein's colleague at the start of *The Bride* (1984); *Fatal Attraction* (scene cut); Queen Elizabeth I in ORLANDO (1992).

R: LONDON CHARACTERS (1964); *Dave Freeman Phone-In* (Oxford 1981); LBC *Open Line* (1982); *The Don Durbridge Show* (Radio Medway 1982).

T: SEVEN MEN (1971); *Day by Day* 1978; *Friday Night Saturday Morning* 1980; *Paperbacks* (promoting *How to Become a Virgin*, 1981); *An Evening with Quentin Crisp* (1983); *Saturday Review: 'My Week'* (1984); *Harty Goes to New York* (1985); ARENA: 'Talk Is Cheap' with Malcolm Muggeridge on chat shows (1987); DON'T MISS WAX (1987); *Wogan* (1988); *Scoff* (1988); *Loose Ends* (1988); *Resident Alien* (1990); SATURDAY NIGHT OUT (1991).

The Critics (UK 1947–6? R) BBC radio's flagship arts programmes: five or six people expert in their own field discussing a book, a film, a television or radio programme, an art exhibition. Regarded by some as the bee's knees, by others as the pinnacle of pretentious tosh. It was certainly quite outspoken for its day (eg discussing PROUST's life), but when Elizabeth Rowley, Senior Talks Producer wanted to include a discussion of a book about lesbianism, her request was turned down flat. At that time Frank Gillard, Director of Broadcasting, told her that as lesbians 'presented no problem' the women should be allowed to 'soldier on' and left in peace. FRIGHTFULLY BBC.

Critics' Forum (UK 1974–90 R) The follow-up to *The Critics*, this time on BBC Radio 3. And still they laughed ...

'As the experts solemnly intoned their archaeological theses on the crumbling masterpieces, we felt instinctively that their criticisms were not only necessary, but somehow in a tradition of which Mr Reed would have approved (or, at least, would have written). As the eminent scholar Herbert Reeve put it so aptly (and so frequently) all those years ago: "Ye-e-es ..."' (a letter from a correspondent in St Andrews, Fife to *Radio*

Times, 11–17.7.87, dealing mainly with the repeats of Henry REED's THE PRIVATE LIFE OF HILDA TABLET and *Emily Butter*).

crossover Used about books, films, plays or music which attract a mainstream audience although originally thought to have only minority interest. *Giovanni's Room*, THE KILLING OF SISTER GEORGE, THE BOYS IN THE BAND, MY BEAUTIFUL LAUNDRETTE and LA CAGE AUX FOLLES are examples of 'gay' subjects having an appeal beyond the ghetto or constituency. David LEAVITT spoke about the phenomenon in regard to novels and short stories (*Daybreak* Aust 1991 R), relating 'crossover' to black musicians from Detroit becoming popular in the 1950s: 'It suggests that gay people and straight people are not so vastly different and I don't think they are. Finally, the similarities always strike me as more interesting than the differences.'

Crowley, Mart (1935–) American playwright, author of THE BOYS IN THE BAND. Co-produced *Hart to Hart* (1979–84 T); played Baron Adolphe De Meyer in NIJINSKY (1980 C); adapted *There Must Be a Pony* (1986 T); appeared in *The Hollywood Legends* 'Natalie Wood' (1987 T).

Crown Court (UK 1972–81 T) Beneath the rigorously factual topdressing of court procedure all sorts of prejudices are bubbling during a number of trials, fictionalized (in three 30-minute daily slices) and played to a studio jury.
GRANADA.

'On Impulse'. A schoolmaster at a comprehensive school is accused of assaulting a pupil.
25.9.74.

'Lola'. Transvestite Lola Martin (Philip Sayer) is accused of importuning and assaulting a police officer.
W: David Yallop; P: Dennis Woolf; D: Colin Bucksey; 12.4.76.

'Such a Charming Man'. Did property speculator and financial wizard Ronald

Crosby (Garrick Hagon) have a homosexual relationship with Nicholas Higgins (Derek Fowlds), or was he just leading Higgins on in order to enlist his support in his company? Found guilty.
W: Julian Roach; P: Susi Hush; D: Laurence Moody; 3.77.

'The Song Not the Singer'. Moral rearmer sues two songwriters for blasphemous libel. Dr Ruth Wilkins (Mary Peach), a member of Festival of Light and National VALA, takes out a private prosecution against two singers who wrote and performed a pop song which made sexual references to God and the Virgin Mary.
W: David A. Yallop; P: Howard Baker; 31.1.78.

'The Change'. Was Marianne Miller (Judy Loe) a man when she married? She was born Stephen Lewis and had a sex change operation two years before her wedding. She denies obtaining property by deception from her husband and from another man to whom she was engaged.
W: Judy Raines; P: June Brown; D: Brian Fortune; 14.3.78.

'The Green House Girls'. Outbreaks of hysteria and attempted suicide at home for girls 'in need of care and attention'. Social worker Johnny Jeffery (David Cardy), one of the witnesses, is gently revealed as being gay.
W: Tony Parker; 1978.

'Meeting Place'. A lonely, middle-aged bachelor Leslie Simon (Derek Smith), who was beaten up and robbed by a youth Barry Gems (Gerry Sundquist), loses his case because the jury was willing to believe Gems' defence counsel: 'Individuals have the right to physically defend themselves against homosexual advances.'
W: Kathleen Potter; 10.1.78.

'A Friend of the Family'. Diana Graham (Rachel Davies), who lives with Beth James (Dorothy White) and her daughter, is accused of causing grievous bodily harm to Beth's husband, Charles. Diana is a feminist; her defence lawyer is revealed as gay.
W: Peter King; P: Sasi Hush; D: Alan Bell; 30.1.79.

'Heart to Heart'. A radio researcher, Annette Sanderson (Judy Geeson) is sued for malicious libel by her former producer, Jean Frazer-Allardyce (Honor

Blackman). As the case proceeds the younger woman hints that she and her boss were lovers; finally Jean's old teacher reveals that she led one of her school-mates 'astray'. She loses the case.
W: Michael Robson; P: Pieter Rogers; D: Peter Ellis.

cruise/cruising Its availability to gays as a term for 'picking up talent' was obviously known to Monty WOOLLEY and Cary GRANT when they made the 'life' of Cole PORTER, NIGHT AND DAY in 1946. Woolley, playing himself, clearly relishes the line 'Cole, are you joining us on this little *cruise?*' and Grant responds with glee. The activity was not unknown to people of heterosexual persuasion. In *Brighter London* (1929 R) Raymond Postgate took listeners along the wide boulevard in Bow Road, Whitechapel in the East End of London, where young men 'and occasionally' young women would walk up and down in the hope of 'getting off'. The locale was known as Monkey's Paradise. The makers of *Carry On Cruising* may have known of what they hinted in 1962. No mistaking the clear message of a scene in that film where two young men are discovered in a compromising position in a very small cabin. *See also* COMPUTER SEX; RAPE.

Cruising (US 1980 C) Is a tour of toilet-town. It bungles every opportunity to look at shifting levels of fantasy and reality, at male sexual desire, at uniform and uniformity, at ghetto paranoia. The one 'average' gay man is butchered out of the picture before he gets too close for comfort to the hero. Of historical interest for its hard, cold stare at the SADO-MASOCHISM scene, it has one electric moment when Al Pacino's woman (Karen Allen) begins trying on his leather drag. The film introduced audiences to the gay serial killer, a potent figure throughout the 1980s and superpotent in these times of *The Silence of the Lambs*, Jeffrey Dahmer and 'American Psycho'.
W: William Friedkin from the novel by Gerald Walker; P: Jerry Weintraub; D:

William Friedkin; 106 mins (cut to 100 mins in UK).
'Should we ban a film that is bound to worsen the acceptance that gays have a right to expect? Of course not: if you demand equality, it has to be equality of obloquy as well as respectability. You have to take your chances. But it's right that public opinion be prepared in advance for the unrelieved opportunism of a film like *Cruising*' (Alexander Walker, *Evening Standard*, 10.5.80).

Crying Out Loud (UK 1982 T) Series with Anna Ford and a panel of advice gurus, who would attempt to solve the problems of one or more young people.
P: Roger Gale; D: Geoffrey Sax; Thames; 30 mins.
Vince realized he was gay when he was 14. Now, at 18, he's desperate for a lover, having recently broken up with his boyfriend and undergone the trauma of his mother discovering a love letter. The film that accompanies Vince's voice-over shows him pottering around his flat ('so used to catering for two and cleaning for two. Now's the time to look after someone, care for someone') and visiting the launderette. 'My insecurity wants a man's body just holding me … I'm not masculine enough to be able to protect a girl … I think homosexual re-lationships are more unstable than het-erosexual ones.'
In contrast to Vince, the three panel-lists are all very upbeat about Vince's future: Rose ROBERTSON from Parents' Enquiry; Phillip Hodson, a radio and magazine psychologist; 20-year-old Martin Maynard from GAY SWITCH-BOARD. They tend to talk in generalities ('He should consider who he is and where he's going') as does Vince ('I just want to be happy. I want to settle down'). The total effect veered from the wistfully pathetic to the sidesplittingly funny: Vince just wanted to be a nice, placid role-playing homosexual while his elders were aiming at another point in the compass altogether. Vince seemed even more lost and bewildered after his verbal stroking – which became more impatient as he refused to abandon the

precepts which were comfortable to him – in the studio. The message of the piece, surely unintended, was: 'For God's sake, grow up and be a [gay] man.'

Jackie Marcus in *Gay News* was as irritated by poor Vince as the panel:

> This stereotyping of everything the boy was saying about making a home, shopping, cooking and the depiction of him doing feminine domestic chores was debasing. I *know* people have to do the washing and ironing, but they have to change electric plugs and knock nails into walls. This young man was behaving like a teenage girl with nothing but marriage in mind – ammunition for any would-be queer-basher watching the programme.
>
> A panel of three were obviously as disturbed about the lad as I was. Each one exhorted him to know what he wants to do and what he wants to be.
>
> ... 'I just want to be happy and settle down,' he stated simply.

Crystal, Billy (1949–) American comedy actor and, in recent years, mainstay of the Academy Awards Ceremony. Played Jodie DALLAS, the first cuddly, warm, sympathetic gay man in the history of television.

C: *Rabbit Test* (1978) playing a pregnant man; *This Is Spinal Tap* (cameo 1984); *Running Scared* (1986); *Throw Momma from the Train* (1987); *The Princess Bride* (1987); *Memories of Me* (1988); *When Harry Met Sally* (1989); *City Slickers* (1991); *Mr Saturday Night* (1992).

T: ALL IN THE FAMILY 'New Year's Wedding' (1976); *Death Flight* (1977); SOAP (1977–81); *Human Feelings* (1978); *Breaking Up Is Hard to Do* (1979); *Enola Gay*: The Men, the Mission, the Atomic Bomb (1980); *The Billy Crystal Comedy Hour* (1982, running for only a few weeks); *Billy Crystal: A Comic's Line* (1984); *Saturday Night Live* (1984–5); HBO shows (impersonating Arnold Schwarzenegger); on DONAHUE (with Whoopi Goldberg and Robin Williams about homelessness, 1991); *Oprah Winfrey Show* (1992); etc.

cuddle A pleasant nurturing activity that needn't necessarily lead to anything more. But it is more lingering than a HUG and, therefore, not to be encouraged for male pairs. Or female: the line ... 'and you need a bit of love. A bit of cuddling ...' was scissored out of THE TINKER'S DAUGHTER on radio in 1986, an action which may have (but probably didn't) have more to do with acting logistics than with listener sensibilities. Lolly Cockrell gave away some of the intimate secrets of a radio actor (1980 R): 'Kissing and cuddling is something of a joke. When you are supposed to be in a passionate embrace with someone, you are kissing on the back of your hand and breathing hard down the mike. And if you're supposed to be hugged tightly, you hug yourself in your own arms to make it sound right.'

Cuddles are rare things, even for heterosexuals: Clarrie and Eddie Grundy in THE ARCHERS have been known to ('Oh, Eddie!'), but it's more in the line of a bit of slap and tickle. Another Eddie (Trevor Nicholls) asks Jackie (Tessa Worsley) for one in *Miss Lamb to the Slaughter* (1987 R). Most unlikely request for a cuddle came from the enamelled Sable (Stephanie Beacham) to Dex (Michael Nader) in DYNASTY (1988 T).

Cukor, George (1899–83) American film director, renowned for his stylish comedies (*The Philadelphia Story*, ADAM'S RIB) and for his adaptations of sprawling novels (*Little Women*, DAVID COPPERFIELD), but less for his more modest, bitter-sweet works like *The Marrying Kind* and *It Should Happen to You*. His masterpiece is *A Star Is Born*, but he is probably most widely discussed for the film he didn't make: *Gone with the Wind*; he was removed from the picture because Clark Gable supposedly did not want to be directed by 'a FAIRY'. He was offered CAT ON A HOT TIN ROOF, but 'turned it down because without the homosexuality it made no sense, and they wouldn't do it *with*'.

T: *Greta* GARBO: he introduced scenes from her films, including *Camille* which he directed (1955); *Forty Years in Holly-wood* (1970); *The Men Who Made the Movies* (1976); *George Cukor: Film Director* (1981); played by George Furth in *Moviola* 'The Scarlett O'Hara War' (1980).

Cullen, Anne (192?–) English radio actress who created the role of Carol GREY in THE ARCHERS (1954–); an extraordinary blend of Home Counties asperity with a warmer, more sensual sound. Taught broadcasting technique at the Royal Academy of Music. First married to Neil Turner who played opposite her in Radio Theatre's *A Blaze of Roses* (1954).

R: début in *Dick Barton* (1946), as a villainess, Henrietta; Fanny Elssler, a dancer in *L'Aiglon* (1946); Penny in *Infatuation* (1946); Nina in *Up at the Villa* (1946); Cassandra in *The Trojan Wars* (1946) with Sybil Thorndike and Margaret Leighton; in *Sometimes and Somewhere* (1946); Fiona in *The Dancing Bear* (1946); Constance Bonacieux in *The Three Musketeers* (1946); Marie in *Appointment with Fear* 'The Nutcracker Suite' (1946); Josephine in De Maupassant's *Take Life As You Find It* (1946); with Basil JONES, her *Archers* co-star-to-be, in a double bill, *Breakdown* and *The Stranger* (1946); Claudia Rivers in *Beau Geste* (1947); *Guilty Party* 'Small Hotel' (1954); Edith, Queen of Edward the Confessor in *Stories of the Saints* 'The Golden Legend of St Edward the Confessor' (1954); Kathleen Gort in *Black Magic* (1956); Esther Brodsky in *The Same Sky* (1957), with Yvonne Mitchell and Michael Crawford; Tatiana Luovna in *The Last Days of Tolstoy* (1957); Mrs Gilbert with John GIELGUD in *The Browning Version* (1957); the Woman on the Flying Mare in *The Midnight Folk* (1958); Millie in *Guilty Party* 'Camera Shy' (1958); Marilyn Roberts in 'Bomb Happy' (1958); Queen Victoria in *Golden Sovereign* (1959); Alison Trent in *Guilty Party* 'State of Anxiety' (1961); Vaux Miller, the young wife accosted by her former lover in *The Hungry Ghosts* (1961) 'her head and heart are in the right place and her surprising

manoeuvres form the substance of the play'; June Trent in *Death in the Afternoon* (1961); Meena in *Guilty Party* 'Kidnap Threat' (1962); Laura Angel in *Fallen Angel* (1962) with Basil Jones as David Jenkins; Ann Harley in *Guilty Party* 'The Curse of the Angry Actress' (1962); Holly in THE FORSYTE SAGA (1968).

T: Ruth Andrews, film continuity girl, in Donald Wilson's serial *Stand By to Shoot* in (1953) – her only television appearance.

cunnilingus Stimulation of tongue on the female genitals: outside of pornographic and semi-pornographic films (*Emmanuelle*) this is not much seen in mainstream entertainment, except for the extraordinary bout between Miguel Bose and Victoria Abril (she hanging from a rail, he half in, half out of the costume which parodies and celebrates her own mother) in HIGH HEELS. Radio has not entered this area yet, eg *Swimming and Flying* (1978):

'I'd like to lick you, Jenny.'
'Not yet, Ellie. I'm not ready yet [if I ever will be].'

In *La Muerte de Mikel/Michael's Death* (1984 C) Begona (Amaia Lasa) is asleep; her lover Mikel, after a night with the boys, drunkenly makes love to her; as she climaxes he bites savagely into her labia – and she smashes a wine bottle over his head.

cure A popular notion is that any aberrant group can be cured or brought to manageable proportions. HORIZON's 'The Fight to Be Male' brought Hitler's solution up to date. Part of the programme looked at work being carried out in East Germany. Gratifyingly, even the more conservative of television critics reacted cynically to this totally uncontexted experiment. Herbert Kretzmer, who called the overall programme 'fascinating', wrote: 'A potential homosexual may be "cured" in the womb with a simple testosterone injection. One jab, he appears to think, should do it' (*Daily Mail*, 22.5.79).

'Cures' are still sought and some people try self-administered ones. The sad Iso (Tovah Feldshuh) put her very life in danger by courting heterosexuality in THE WOMEN'S ROOM (1980 T): 'When I was in Berkeley I thought I could cure myself.' This led to attempted rape and a fear of men.

The new language of cures for homosexuality is more subtle, more reasonable in tone: 'I have no brief for HOMOPHOBIA and hostility against homosexuals,' a psychologist claimed on *Start the Week* 'Camp and Homosexual Verse' (1983 R). But with 'sympathy' she was attempting 'to overcome pathology' of 'immature, inadequate' people trapped in the 'inadequacy of parents' relationship of same sex' and a 'presupposed attempt to resume the developmental process' leading to resolution of 'same-sex ambivalence' leading to appropriate 'adult ... sexual expression'. All this could be achieved with the help of therapy and New Christian ethics. She has no objection to homosexual people, but 'as a Christian psychologist' she objects to the sexual act.

One of the quickest and simplest cures ever postulated – and proved successful – was the one recommended to the worried young wife of Miles Eastin (Timothy Bottoms) in *The Moneychangers* (1976 T). Although heterosexual, Miles was 'converted' in prison. He was forced to become the boyfriend ('BITCH') of a black prisoner. Since his release Miles has shown no interest in the marital bed whatsoever. The distressed wife confides in a neighbour, who gives her the solution. Within minutes, Miles is back on the job, in bed with his wife, accompanied by the mass strings of Henry Mancini. The recipe? 'Break something and let him fix it. Then get him to take the lids off apple sauce jars. And then make him take out the garbage. That's man's work.'

It was also fairly simple in the MARCUS WELBY MD story 'The Other Martin Loring' (1973 T). A gay husband and father, with asthma: 'with proper care he'll get better' is all the good doctor (Robert Young) can proffer.

The mother (Helen Cherry) of a young priest, takes her son on a pilgrimage to Lourdes. But he didn't recover. Now he's a happy gay man and she's an unhappy woman, she recounts to Lewis Duncan in COMING OUT (1979 T).

In SOAP (1978) Carol (Rebecca Balding) tries to convert Jodie by persuading him to sleep with her and then stimulating him. She becomes pregnant. Jodie decides to marry her. Jodie's BROTHER Danny (Ted Wass) is delighted by the news: 'I knew if I took you to enough hockey games, you'd see the light.'

Janet Pitman claimed she could cure everything – 'from hammertoes to homosexuality' – on Roger Cook's *Checkpoint* (1978 R). For some the lure of that still elusive total cure remains very strong, as evidenced by members of the ex-gay movement in HEART OF THE MATTER (1992 T).

But for others, their orientation is seen as perfectly natural, a part of them that should not be removed: 'If there was a cure to stop me doing what I'm doing, I wouldn't take it ... It's often said among ourselves that there are only two cures: death and fervent Christianity,' a TRANSVESTITE in *Sisters Under the Skin* (1990 R).

Curram, Roland (192?–) English actor who has played three major gay roles: Malcolm, the photographer in DARLING (1965 C); Terry in THE CREZZ (1976 T); FREDDIE in ELDORADO (1992–3).

C: *The Good Beginning* (1953); footman in *The Admirable Crichton* (1958); schoolboy Hamlet in *Carry On Teacher* (1959); intense medical student in *Doctor in Love* (1960); sailor in *Petticoat Pirates* (1961); mentally disturbed man giving deadly drugs to children in *The Silent Playground* (1962); etc.

T: Fred in *Flying Visitors* (1953); one of the young naval officers in *The Sky Larks* (1958); Peter Melrose in *Somerset Maugham* 'The Voice of the Turtle' (1960); *A Bride in the Morning* (1961); Roger, with Aubrey Woods as RON, in *Not At All* (1962); film director's secretary Barry Strap in *Harry Sebrof's Story*

(1973); Perkins in *Big Jim and the Figaro Club* (1981); Asreal skewered on a fence at the end of ARTEMIS '81 (1981); etc.

Curry, John (1941–) English ice-skating champion and dancer. 'His values were at odds with many of the officials he had to convince [at the 1976 Innsbruck Winter Olympic Games] ... who could not ignore his technical skills, even if they still questioned his artistic use of body movement. But the public recognized in John Curry one of the most artistic men's skaters that the world has seen' (Barry Davies 1981 T).
  T: *The John Curry Ice Spectacular* (1976); *Maestro* (1987); etc.

Curry, Tim (1946–) English actor with rich fruity voice and clown's rub-bery features. A cult hero as Frank N Furter in THE ROCKY HORROR PICTURE SHOW.
  C: *The Rocky Horror Picture Show* (1975); *Times Square* (1980); *Annie* (1981); *The Ploughman's Lunch* (1983); *Legend* (1984); *Clue* (1985); *Oscar* (1991); *Home Alone II* (1992).
  R: Lord Biro in *The Wordsmiths of Gor-semere* (1982).
  T: as *Will* SHAKESPEARE (1976); ROCK FOLLIES (1976); Teddy Wazzaz in VIDEOSTARS (1983); Spirit of Christmas Present in *A Christmas Carol* (1984); taxi driver in *Blue Money* (1984); etc.

Curtis, Jackie [John Holder Jr] (1947–85) Actor-writer in WARHOL's *Women in Revolt*; screenplays for FLESH and *Big Badge*; stage plays; last seen in *Burroughs* (1983 T).

custody cases *See* CHILD CUSTODY.

Moll **Cutpurse** 'A notorious baggage that used to go in man's apparel and challenged the field of diverse gallants', 'a very tom-rig or rumpscuttle she was'. She smoked a pipe. She lived to 75 and wrote journals: 'A sampler was to me as grievous as a winding sheet, and skirts and petticoats as hampering to my daily purpose as fetters to a man wrongly chained.' Based on Mary Frith, she stands, in Dekker and Middleton's *The Roaring Girl*, for 'honest dealing in a society based on deception' (Michael Billington, *The Guardian*).
  'I have no humour to marry – I love to lie on both sides of the bed myself. I'm man enough for a woman' (*The Roaring Girl*).

cuts Some notable cuts: at least half an hour (some of it homophobic) from *The Chelsea Murders*; 11 minutes (by British film censor) from OLIVIA; 11 minutes from American TV version of THE BOYS IN THE BAND; the blipping out of 'I love you' from *The Strange One* by US film censors and the emasculation of TEA AND SYMPATHY and CAT ON A HOT TIN ROOF; shortening of kisses on EAST-ENDERS; the removal of any mention of lesbians in a TV documentary on women and the armed forces; the removal of an erect penis for the TV showing of SEBASTIANE; the substitution of TV commercials for scenes as diverse as the rape in *The Virgin Spring* and FASSBINDER getting into bed naked in FOX AND HIS FRIENDS; alternative sex scenes shot for British TV showing of EDWARD II and US TV showing of THE LOST LANGUAGE OF CRANES; the com-plete compromising of TWO OF US by removal of kiss and alteration of one character's actions. Angus WILSON dis-cussed with Robert Robinson on *The Book Programme* that his need for friends and his closeness to two or three work-ing-class young men when he was at Oxford changed his whole political out-look; but this didn't get into the finished programme (2.3.76).

Cyril Boy's name, usually for people who do not inspire confidence: Cyril (Melvin Hayes) in *Summer Holiday* (1963 C); Cyril Kitsch (Peter Jones) in THE FAT OF THE LAND (1969 T): 'I care, surely I do. I care about *myself*'; crime boss Cyril Kinnear (John OSBORNE) in *Get Carter* (1971); loose and leaky Cyril (David Foxxe) in *The Sweeney* (1978 T); flyblown, still idealistic former hippie Cyril (Philip Davis) in *High Hopes;* Cyril Clatworthy (William Osborne) in ABSOLUTE HELL! (1991 T).

Dad and Dave Come to Town aka *The Rudd Family Come to Town* (Aust 1938 C) Australia's beloved Rudd family in their second screen outing.
W: Frank Harvey and Bert Bailey; P/D: Ken G. Hall; 97 mins.

Highly appealing folksy comedy which features an early – and sympathetic – version of Mr HUMPHRIES, here called Cedric ENTWHISTLE ('Enty') and played with brio by Alec KELLAWAY. He's the manager of the department store which Dad (Bert Bailey) inherits and he helps the Rudd family fend off the villains. 'Enty' plays a larger part in the sequel *Dad Rudd MP* (1940) when he spends some time down on the farm and lends a helping hand in Dad's election campaign. One of Australia's first screen 'sissies' and, in many ways, more human than those being proffered at the same time by America and Britain.

Dad, I think we should have a talk A preamble to many a COMING OUT speech. Just one example: Robert (Steven Vidler) in WORDS OF ONE SYLLABLE (Aust 1991 R) informing his dying father why he does not want to live in the family home. He's gay and he'd shrivel up and die if he had to live in a small country town away from his friends, not to mention his lover. *See also* FATHER–SON TALKS.

Daily at Dawn (Aust 1980) Bouncing QUEEN, Leslie (Terry Bader) shares flat with his work-mate (Paul Chubb), a burly sports writer on a daily newspaper. Lots of jokes about poofters and doileys, and some witty lines too.
W/P: Gary Reilly and Tony Sattler; D: Kevin Burston; Channel 7; 6 parts.

daisies Leigh Hunt's conceit, continued by Aubrey in *Death and the Dancing Footman* (1987 R), 'saying all one feels and thinks in clever daffodils and pinks; in puns of tulips and in phrases, charming for their truth, of daisies'.

White daisies often linked with odd couples: *Harold and Maude* (1971 C); the inscrutable child-wife (Dominique Sanda) in *A Gentle Creature* (1969 C);

the artist's illegitimate daughter (Stefanie Powers) and English gent (Timothy Dalton) in *Mistral's Daughter* (1984 T). Dick Diver (Peter Strauss) brings breakfast in bed to his wife Nicole (Mary Steenburgen), his last act of nurturing submission before he ends the marriage; on the tray, there is a small silver vase of white daisies, *Tender is the Night* (1985 T). Woody (Alan Young) in *Tom Thumb* (1958 C) has two white daisies in his hat. He also wears a shirt with filmy sleeves. 'Not even a pair for a queen?', he asks shoemaker Ian Wallace, who laughs uproariously: 'Very funny, Woody, *very* funny.' Woody must kiss the fairy he meets in the forest to make her a real woman. He finally does so, almost by accident so shy and fey is he.

The flower's primary association is with the homosexual, in relation either to milieu or to individual: Walter (Maximilian Schell) in *Five Finger Exercise* (1962 C) carries a bouquet in which white daisies predominate in his first scene with Philip (Richard Beymer) who will become obsessed with him; Simon Brunner (John Hillerman) in *Ellery Queen* (1975 T) is shown with a pot of yellow and white daisies – he's an epicene radio presenter in cravat, with red carnation; a middle-aged man, with whom he has had sex, hands José a bouquet in which daisies are paramount, as he leaves on a train in *To an Unknown God* (1975 C); noticeable in TRANSVESTITE Lounge Lizard's (very floral) living room, the place where he is about to be murdered in JUBILEE (1977 C); PSYCHIATRIST (Cliff Gorman) to Joe Gideon (Roy Scheider) in *All That Jazz* (1979 C): 'You're not gay, but you do have a lot of feminine qualities' – quick cut to Gideon in hospital with a bunch of daisies being pressed upon him by his girlfriend; a triumphant Harvey MILK carries them in the motorcade to celebrate the defeat of the Briggs amendment in THE TIMES OF HARVEY MILK (1984 C); pale daisies and an EARRING are part of the visual setting for dangerous queen, Pearl in *Santa Barbara* (1986 T); Kristian gives Patrick a present of a coffee percolator in wrapping paper covered in huge white daisies – before he knows for sure he's gay (*Friends Forever* 1987 C); in a beach house scene with the rich gay kids on the block: David (Bruce Davison) and Sean (Mark Lamos) in LONGTIME COMPANION (1990 C); these flowers predominate in the bunch ethereal Jason (Nigel Leach) carries in *Home to Roost* 'Leaving' (1990 T); Rebecca (Victoria Abril) collapses amid white daisies in the prison yard in HIGH HEELS (1991 C), to be tended by some of the butcher inmates.

Daisy/daisy James STEERFORTH called David Copperfield 'Daisy' when they were at school and thereafter: 'You are my Daisy. The daisy of the field, at sunrise, is not fresher than you are.' Dickens has Steerforth call his rejected sexual plaything Rosa Dartle 'Daisy' as well (1986 T, but not 1991R). Daisy Jane (ie daisy chain) played by M[arion] J. Marshall was a seagoing madam who was revealed as male in *Gunn* (1967 C).

Daisy (as in 'daisy chain') has anal sexual connotations, as well as penile ones. The short film made by Jack KEROUAC and other BEAT GENERATION writers, most of them homosexual or BISEXUAL, in 1958 was called *Pull My Daisy*. Its more specifically homoemotional meaning was rendered in *There Was a Crooked Man* (1970 C). Outlaw Kirk Douglas inveigles two inseparable PRISONERS (Hume Cronyn and John Randolph) into helping him dynamite his way out of the stockade. Douglas turns to a sidekick (who he is also bamboozling) and says with a dry grin that the gays will be left behind because 'you wouldn't want to run with them two old daisies, would you?'

Harry Soan on *Today* (1961) said of the common daisy: 'For the most part there can hardly be a plant in creation more downtrodden and more despised.' Which makes it a very adequate symbol for gay men.
See also DAISY BELL.

Daisy Bell (or a Bicycle Made for Two) Popularly known as 'Daisy, Daisy', it was penned in 1892 by Harry

Dacre and sung by Katie Lawrence in *I'll Be Your Sweetheart* (1948 C).

In *2001: A Space Odyssey* (1968 C) the computer HAL (voiced by Douglas Rain) seems to take a more than mechanical interest in one of the astronauts, Dave (Keir Dullea). Discovering HAL's duplicity (jealousy inspired?), Dave disconnects him. As HAL expires, he sings a melancholy 'Daisy, Daisy/Give me your answer do'. The voice begins to slow down and eventually becomes indistinct but we can discern the words 'I'm half crazy/Oh for the love of you'.

The demented husband (Michael Moriarty) who is a children's writer in *The Sound of Murder* (1982 T) uses the phrase, as if spoken by his wife asking him for a divorce: 'Daisy, Daisy, give me your answer do.'

Mrs Dale/Mary Dale Played by Ellis POWELL 1948–63; by Jessie Matthews 1963–9. Mrs Dale propelled herself through her family's upsets with hyperactive aplomb, first in MRS DALE'S DIARY, then the less cosy *The Dales*. The flat and boggy voice with its understanding and wisdom emanated as from one great hookah of homeliness. She was remarkably like everyone's vision of Queen Elizabeth, the Queen Mother with shades of her elder daughter. The only time her compassion faltered – badly – was when, in 1967, she discovered that her sister Sally's husband, Richard FULTON was homosexual. It took a lot of love from husband Jim before she could 'forgive' and 'understand' her brother-in-law.

Dall, John [John Jenner Thompson] (1918–71) An American actor comfortable in cultivated roles, mixing sly good breeding with an underlay of sweet contempt. Most famous for ROPE and *Gun Crazy*.

C: the Welsh boy, Morgan Evans encouraged by Miss Moffat (Bette DAVIS) in *The Corn Is Green* (1945); Detective Andy Cullen in *The Man Who Cheated Himself* (1951, brother of cop Lee J. Cobb); Crassus' brother-in-law Glabrus in SPARTACUS (1960); third billed as the villain Zaren in *Atlantis the Lost Continent* (1961).

T: PERRY MASON; assorted sybarites in 'The Case of the Wary Watchdog' (1962 T); 'The Case of the Reluctant Model' (1963); 'The Case of the Lonely Eloper' (1965); 'The Case of the Lonely Lady' (1965), etc.

Dallas (US 1978–91 T) Big Daddy of the American 'adult' soaps which Larry Hagman/J.R. Ewing made into his own. His *modus operandi* (snooping, smiling, then pouncing) didn't quite work when, in 1978 ('Royal Marriage'), his niece Lucy (Charlene Tilton) announces her engagement to the son of a rival oil baron. J.R. soon discovers that Kit Mainwaring (III) had recently ended a gay relationship (with a 'ROOM-MATE'), a useful future bargaining tool in J.R.'s never-ending game of inter-personal chess. But Kit (Mark Wheeler), ignoring J.R.'s blackmail, has a talk with Lucy who tearfully accepts that she is not destined to yoke her Ewing to his Mainwaring. She is distraught for at least two episodes, popping qualudes, diet pills and speed.

Two other episodes from the 1978 season had interesting undertones. In 'Fallen Idol' Richard Kelton, as a former college friend of Bobby Ewing, declares: 'I love Bobby – if a man can use that word about another man these days without it seeming dirty.' In 'Call Girl' Pam Ewing, driven beyond endurance by the intrigues of the family she has married into, goes to live platonically with a young woman (Veronica Hamel): a situation which J.R. tries to use to his advantage, setting up but failing to engineer a 'three in a bed' photograph with the flat-mate who knew J.R. in a professional sex worker–client capacity. J.R. is foiled again and Pam returns to Bobby.

Jodie **Dallas** Whimsical but practical son of Mary, step-son of Burt and nephew of Jessica in SOAP. 1977–81 T, played by Billy CRYSTAL. The show's creator, producer and writer, Susan Harris wanted somebody who was 'masculine and sensitive', who loved children, who was very much involved in family life. This, she reasoned, would enable the actor to connect with the family feuds and affection so essential to the sentimental satire. 'Someone who, as an actor and a person, is so involved that they wouldn't consider giving up their family ties.'

Jodie begins by wanting a sex change so that his football hero lover, Dennis (Bob Seagren) will feel less conspicuous with him. Jodie decides against the operation and is straightway ditched by Dennis. Soon after he is seduced by Carol (Rebecca Balding). Jodie helps produce a child and is promptly sued for custody by the mother who calls him an unfit parent. During this period he shares his apartment with a lively lesbian, Alice who helps him over the bumps. Eventually he meets a nice girl and they become engaged. In the last episodes Jodie is hypnotized and believes himself to be an old man named Julius Kassendorf.

After a tricky start Jodie, having said no to SEX CHANGE and to SUICIDE, settled in to become a sweetly sincere brotherly role-model. 'Billy's a lovely guy, a wonderful man. And he's got some of the most touching letters imaginable.' At a London lecture in 1979, Susan Harris quoted one of these letters, which said in part: 'You've shown me there is a way to be gay and to stay in touch with the family.'

In an episode of AGONY ('Problem Parents' 1980 T) the mother of Rob, on being told the truth about her boy, exclaims happily: 'I've got my *own* Jodie now!'

Dallesandro, Joe (1948–) WARHOL hero, hanging loose, mumbling, passive, yet with a distinct shining presence and no inhibitions about being natural, especially *au naturel*.

C: LONESOME COWBOYS (1968); FLESH (1968); *Trash* (1970); *Heat* (1972); *Andy Warhol's Frankenstein*(1974); *Andy Warhol's Dracula* (1974); *The Gardener* (aka *Seeds of Evil* 1974); *Je T'Aime, Moi Non Plus* (1975). There was a comeback in *The Cotton Club* (1984), and other small roles followed in *Critical Condition*

(1987); *Sunset* (1988); *Almost an Angel* (1990, last billed as 'Bank Hood Leader'); *Cry-Baby* (1990).

T: seen shaving in the bath in *Warhol* (1973); small role, as a gangster, in a *Miami Vice* episode (1985).

Dames 'In order to be a real dame you've got to kneel before a queen,' sing Charles Pierce and company (with last verse bellowed by Harvey FIERSTEIN) in one of the opening scenes of TORCH SONG TRILOGY (1988 C).

The Damned [La Caduta degli Dei] (It/West Germany 1969 C) VISCONTI takes on the Third Reich in a story of a rich German family and the viper in its breast: a paedophile called Martin.
W: Nicola Badalucco, Enrico Medioli and Luchino Visconti; P: Alfredo Levy and Ever Haggiag; 153 mins (Italian version 164 mins).
The lion's share of the close-ups go to Helmut Berger as the Nazi who rapes his mother. The massacre of Ernst ROEHM's SA troops during an orgy is effective, but the family politics of the armament manufacturing dynasty is uninvolving. Dirk BOGARDE has written that Visconti's infatuation with Berger led to large cuts in Bogarde's Macbeth-like role at the expense of comprehension and conviction.

dance halls Places of solely heterosexual pleasure: *Dance Hall* (1950 C); *The Queen of the Stardust Ballroom* (1975 T); RAY'S MALE HETEROSEXUAL DANCE HALL (1988 C) where the juke box plays 1940s big band hits and where men dance with other men in a great mercantile meat market purely to find new positions: 'No wonder no one's around lunchtime – they're all here.' But like any sexual pick-up palace, Ray's offers a constant tumble of new faces, takeovers, change of partners (leading and following), power plays and the right to dance in the spotlight with the man (employer/patron) of your dreams.

dance instructors Eric BLORE – 'he hisses like a swan' – Ginger Rogers' boss in *Swing Time* (1936 C); Ernest

(Philippe Perrotet) arriving in the closing minutes of *Our Betters* (1960 T) to instruct the Duchess; very flossy Piedi (David Kernan) in THE AVENGERS 'The Quick-Quick-Slow-Slow Death' (1966 T); Mnester (Mark Hawkins), darkly handsome flatterer of CALIGULA (Ralph Bates) in the THE CAESARS (1968 T); Les (Peter Whitford), all blondined hair and powder-blue suits in STRICTLY BALLROOM (1992 C) unselfconsciously tangoing with the hero.

Dance Little Lady Noel COWARD song, with Carroll Gibbons' orchestra, a warning to those wanton young women, the flappers: 'Syncopate your nerves/ Feel your body surge ... no rest you'll ever find' and ending with Coward's insistent, plangent refrain of 'Dance dance, dance'. It orginated in Coward's *This Year of Grace* (whose showstopper was 'A Room With A View') and was played regularly on radio from 1928. There was a period (mainly the 1960s) when BBC producers seemed inexorably drawn to use it in almost every radio play set in the brittle 1920s. Understandably, because this deceptively sweet, lace-edged ditty fairly throbs with the underlying depression and disillusion that would usher in the next decade. Hints of dissipation and sex overdrive in the lyrics give appropriate atmosphere to homosexually leaning plays like THE VORTEX (1966 version) and ROPE (1982).

Dance of the Naked Moon Ancaria (Joyzelle) – 'The most wicked and talented woman in Rome' – performs this to excite and/or degrade the captive Christian woman in *The Sign of the Cross* (1932 C): 'See what *you* can do, Ancaria'. The only extant version of the film has a whacking great cut half a minute into Anzria's erotic writhings.
Nearly twenty years later, Cecil B. De Mille asked his niece Agnes to design a dance for his *Samsom and Delilah*. He told her he wanted 'the kind of dance we had in *Sign of the Cross*: a lesbian dance'. She felt that her uncle, so publicly moral, was working out his own sexual feeling on film. 'I think he got seduced

by his own sexual dreams.' (In *Ready When You Are, Mr De Mille* 1981 T.)

dancers As Bing Crosby so gracelessly commented in *That's Entertainment* (1974 C) apropos of *Seven Brides for Seven Brothers*: 'You don't have to be a SISSY to be a dancer.'

Some movement in perception has taken place since *Brides* was released in the 1950s. An early television play of that era, *The Boxer and the Ballerina* (1952 T) presents a champ, Tony Verillo (Patric Doonan) who becomes involved with a ballet company, especially its star (Joan Greenwood). So corrupting is this brush with aesthetic sensitivity that the former pug becomes a devotee of the arts, and second cousin to Oscar Wilde. In VARIATION ON A THEME (1961 R) Ron Vale (Jon Rollason) is a second-rate dancer living with – and off – a choreographer while simultaneously playing along a rich man's mistress. In NIJINSKY (1980 C) the title character can't even be saved by marriage: he goes crazy. And in *A Bullet in the Ballet* (1987 R) the man playing Petruska in a company thick with LISPS and squeals is shot before he can take his curtain call.

Joe Massara (Douglas Fairbanks Jr) irks his admirer LITTLE CAESAR (Edward G. Robinson 1930 C) by preferring dancing (and his female partner) to him: 'I don't want no dancin'. I figure on making *other* people dance'. A few years later, Fred Astaire's puckish features and unpretentious, affable manner made it more acceptable for 'regular guy' Americans to be dancers, In *Swing Time* (1936 C) bets are hedged by making the slightly camp CHORUS BOYS in the opening number beefy jocks once they enter the dressing room (played by different performers). The replacements' masculinity makes it acceptable for one of them to joke on the phone to Astaire's prospective father-in-law: 'OK sweetheart, and a great big juicy kiss from me!'

As soon as ballet enters the picture – as distinct from 'modern dance' the barriers come up. Effeminacy is the

order of the day: Alfred Lynch in 'Big Guns' (1958 T); Oliver Reed in *The League of Gentlemen* (1960 C); Dudley Banks-Smith (Ray Fell), the ex-dancer who now runs the Celebration Club in *Ours Is a Nice House* (1970 T); the silent interloper in the life of Joanne Woodward's son in *Summer Wishes, Winter Dreams* (1973 C), doing his barre exercises in the apartment they share in AMSTERDAM; numberless comedy sketches involving lisping weeds who can't hold up the prima ballerina and have to put copious padding into their CODPIECES.

Ballroom dancing is also viewed as a no-go area for real men: Barry (Barry Howard), one half of the snotty exhibition dancing pair in *Hi-de-Hi* (1980–4 T); Gregory (Alfred Welling) in *Out of Step* (1981 T); the partners of Dot Dooly (Cheryl Murray) and Avril Vickers (Yvonne Antrobus) in *Midnight at the Starlight* (1980 T). One of them, Artie (Michael Cronin), becomes quite huffy when his masculinity is impugned: 'Just because I wear a toupee, ride a bike, like black-leather plastic gear and collect show biz pics of Judy GARLAND, it does not mean I'm a left-handed five shilling pound note'.

By 1980 no male dancer seemed to be 'that way' at all. The advent of John Travolta in *Saturday Night Fever* (1977 C) has made DISCO an accredited male mating ritual, and Mikhail Baryshnikov was obviously more than just padding in *The Turning Point* (1977 C). Emma (Anne Bancroft) explains that Wayne (Tom Skerritt) was a ballet dancer in those days (the 1950s) when that profession meant QUEER. Deedee's (Shirley MacLaine) son wants to follow both parents, but she has no worries about him: he is 'a normal baseball playing kid.' Only the choreographers in *The Turning Point* are that way inclined, and one of them, Arnold (Daniel Levans) is accused of leading 'an amoral sex life'.

The heterosexualization of dance for men, which even Astaire, Cagney and Kelly had not been able to achieve, was complete. Even though there were three gay members of *A Chorus Line* (1985 C)

(Paul, BOBBY and Greg), they were more than outweighed by the Stallone-like stud with his arm ever-draped round his wife and daring you to scream 'sissy' before he belted you. It's hyper-masculine stuff that the guys strut nowadays: Patrick Swayze in *Dirty Dancing* (1987 C), Paul Mercurio in STRICTLY BALLROOM (1992 C), and so on.

But the idea that most ballet males are not 100 per cent heterosexual persists. In 'Never Give Your Name' (a 1975 episode of *Man about the House*) Larry (Doug Fisher) attempts to persuade ROBIN's (Richard O'Sullivan) girlfriend that Robin is gay in order to allay her fears that he has made someone pregnant: 'I'm with *him*. We met at ballet school'.

During an East German production of *The Nutcracker* in *Top Secret* (1984 C) the women dancers are carried on wires because their male partners are not strong enough to bear them aloft. The prima ballerina flies by on a faulty wire, bouncing up and down on the male corp's bulging CODPIECES. Thus one of society's double-yolk fears about homosexuality is scrambled into one omelette: men who have no balls and limp cocks yet are built like stallions and ever rampant. No change from earlier decades; eg Benthoof, partner of ballerina Tumbleova, in *The World of Beachcomber* (1970 T).

A more realistic balance was struck in the 4-part drama series *Dancers* (1983 T) and in the teenagers' afternoon play 'A Proper Little Nooryeff' (*Dramarama* 1985 T). Jamie Carr (Douglas Howes) was discontented because collecting his younger sister from ballet class disrupts his social life. One day, pressed to take part, he discovers a natural affinity with dance. Should he take up ballet as a career (and pursue the lovely Anita) or stick with cricket (and the homely Sharon)?

With the greater emphasis upon health, dance has become more of an option for men. It would be madness if some ill-perceived connection between effeminacy and gayness led to potentially gifted dancers shying away from a form of expression and co-ordination requiring just as much determination and musclepower as boxing, football or athletics. That a dancer can be gay and have an identity beyond the call of art was well articulated in *A New Step Every Day* (1980 R) where, after contracting multiple sclerosis, Tom Bryceland (Michael Maloney) finds that love can make up for the thing he fears most in life: inability to dance.

dancing boys Far fewer examples than their female counterparts: grinding their pelvises towards the audience in an inviting manner in the comedy *Where the Spies Are* (1966 C); *homme fatal* (Khosrow Tabatabai), eyes rimmed with *kohl*, who takes a liking to the young American (Michael Sarrazin) in *Caravans* (1978 C) – this treacherous, lecherous teenager tries to kill heroine Jennifer O'Neill, but is himself dispatched by chieftain Anthony Quinn; very frail young terpsichoreans, each hoping for night on the cushions with Franco Nero as *The Pirate* (1979 T) who shows not a flicker of interest in their charms (which proves him to be A Real Man).

dancing together (men) Two men glide across the floor at Al Jolson's club, the *Wonder Bar* (1934 C). Jolson exclaims (pre-censorship): 'Oh, *you boys!*' accompanying the words with a coyly complicitous look.

Other males similary engaged: Mickey Rooney and Freddie Bartholemew in *The Devil Is a Sissy* (1936 C); prisoners of war at the Christmas party in *Stalag 17* (1953 C); Van Johnson and Gene Kelly in *Brigadoon* (1954 C); members of the platoon in *The Phil Silvers Show* 'Bilko's War Against Culture' (1956 T); George Raft and Jerry Lewis ('I've never done this before') in *The Ladies' Man* (1961 C); Dinsdale Landen and Derek Fowlds taught to dance by Sidney James in *We Joined the Navy* (1962 C); in STARSKY AND HUTCH 'Death in a Different Place' (1977 T) Hutch (David Soul) and Huggy Bear (Antonio Fargas) bop together during 'reconnaissance' at the Green Parrot, whereupon an 'old' gay man tries to pick up young cop; Steve teaches the uptight married David to dance after they have had sex in MORE LIVES THAN ONE (1984 T). Usually the sight of men holding each other rythmically in traditional style is held up to ridicule, going against nature. After all, who will lead? It *can* be done – enthusiastically and well: by two of THE VIRGIN SOLDIERS (1969 C), Villiers and Foster (Gregory Phillips and Wayne SLEEP), waltzing in the barrack room to 'Autumn Leaves' with only the cleaner to see them before the music changes to the Gay Gordons; by the two young Fascists at the end of SALO (1975 C); by the Scots soldier and the GI in HOUSE ON THE HILL 'Something for the Boys' (1981 T) to the music of Glenn Miller; and, impeccably performing the TANGO, by Anthony Dowell and Rudolf NUREYEV as NIJINSKY and VALENTINO (1977 C) – as do Peter Whitford and Paul Mercurio for the same brief amount of time in STRICTLY BALLROOM (1992 C). Other stylish men seen moving as one are in a smoky New York Club of the 1920S (LOOKING FOR LANGSTON 1988 C/T). In modern Manhattan at RAY'S MALE HETEROSEXUAL DANCE HALL (1988 C/T) executives ask each other onto the floor with the same go-getting, back-stabbing brio that they use in the boardrooms and washrooms.

dancing together (women) LULU and Countess GESCHWITZ in PANDORA'S BOX (1928 C); two society women moving intimately to the rhythm in *A Woman's Face* (1941 C); Dominique Sanda and Stefania Sandrell in THE CONFORMIST (1970); Carol White and Veronica Anderson (dressed as nuns) in *Some Call It Loving* (1973 C); Chrissie and Jackie in GIRL (1974 T); the young versions of Lillian Hellman and JULIA (1977 C); Cindy Pickett and partner in *Night Games* (1980 C); puffing hashish through a long cigarette holder, with seduction on her agenda, Una (Cherie Lunghi, dressed as a Tartar) with her lover (Kate Burton) in flamenco gown in *Ellis Island* (1984 T); Vita and Violet in a

French *boîte* in PORTRAIT OF A MARRIAGE (1990 T).

dandy Usually the term for a fastidious dresser, concerned with colour, line and flair: cartoonist Mark Boxer – 'self-confessed left-wing dandy' – profiled in *One Pair of Eyes* 'Half Way Mark' (1972 T); Patrick in *Obsessions* (1991 R) – 'ultraparticular about his clothes, logging every item he has worn each day over the past 23 years'. Sometimes the word has been used a the lesser of two evils: instead the pansies, Doris DAY sang 'dandies' in her 'Ten Cents A Dance' number from *Love Me or Leave Me* (1955 C), and Bert Lahr sang there was 'no denyin,' that he was 'just a dandy-lion' in *The Wizard of Oz* (1939 C).

Dangerous Corner 'Telling the truth is as dangerous as skidding round a corner at 60 miles an hour,' says a character in J. B. Priestley's 1932 play, the first to depict a homosexual character (Gordon Whitehouse) on the London stage since the matchmaker in *The Relapse*.

A man, Martin CAPLAN has apparently committed SUICIDE. He was BISEXUAL, a DRUG ADDICT and highly attractive. All the characters had reason to wish him dead, even to kill him though some of them (including Gordon) loved him. The action and dialogue reveal the damage honesty can do in a society geared to half-truths and evasion. It is the sexual outsider, who influenced many lives, who acts as the catalyst for people to face themselves. Clearly he had to die.

The was a film version in 1934. The first radio production was in 1945, while there were television productions in 1957 (with John Fraser as Gordon) and in 1983 (with Daniel Day-Lewis in the role).

Priestley's last play, *Anyone for Tennis* – written for television in 1968 – used the Martin Caplan figure (called Garry Brendon and played by Michael Pennington) in a piece of time travel. He – who had committed suicide 20 years ago because he got into debt, and faced disgrace and imprisonment – suddenly finds that he has more than one life to lead, and perhaps in Time Two he will not be 'hopelessly lazy and extravagantly foul-mouthed and foul-minded'.

Daniel Elton JOHN arguably sang the first love lyric from man to man on TOP OF THE POPS in 1972-3. A Bernie Taupin and Elton JOHN song – probably the nearest the mainstream has come to acknowledging same-sex love – played in *Alice Doesn't Live Here Any More* (1974 C) where the virile male (Kris Kristofferson) was kind, verbal, caring and sharing.

Danny Boy The words for 'Danny Boy' were written to an old Irish Air 'The Derry Air', later 'The Londonderry Air' by Fred E[dward] Weatherley and are imbued with the pain of parting. There are instructions on the 1941 sheet music that 'when sung by a man the words in italics should be used', primarily the substitution of 'Eily Dear' for 'Danny Boy'. This instruction has been conspicuously ignored even in the male/male nervous second half of the 20th century. It remains one of the few ballads addressed to a man which is still performed by a male with no explanation or special pleading.

Donald (Simon Ward) plays and sings it to the teacher he's infatuated with in SPOILED (1968 T), but stops before the line in the second verse; not so VILLAGE PEOPLE'S leather guy Glenn Hughes who gives vent to a spirited, if hoarse, rendition in CAN'T STOP THE MUSIC (1980 T), climaxing with a piercing 'Oh, Danny Boy, oh, Danny Boy, I love you *so!*' Albert Finney as Leo O'Bannion in *Miller's Crossing* (1990 C) makes one last stand and goes out, machine gun blazing, to the familiar strains, which are also heard in another gangster opus in 1990, *GoodFellas* (C). That same year, in a wartime ballroom, two members of an American bomber crew DANCED TOGETHER to 'Danny Boy' – jiving though, not smooching like the others in *Memphis Belle* (C).

R. D. Laing played 'The Londonderry Air' – soulfully – on the piano in *Didn't*

You Used to Be R. D. Laing? (1989 T), breaking off to tell us (in slurred tones) why we are not happy: 'There's a lot of people engaged in genital contact with other genitals, human and animal, that a lot of people take offence about.' Aside from the need to protect children, the controversial psychiatrist, who pretty much turned his profession upside down, felt that sexual behaviour should only concern the – consenting – participants.

Mrs **Danvers** Gaunt and gothic housekeeper of Manderley in REBECCA, deeply attached to her dead mistress. Actresses such a Sonia DRESDEL (1954 T), Enid Lorimer (1954 R), Flora Robson (1976 R) and Rosalie Crutchley (1989 R) continued Judith Anderson's tradition of playing Mrs Danvers as a tormented heavy. Anna MASSEY returned to the Daphne Du Maurier novel, as well as updating the psychology to make her slightly more human. Interviewed in *Radio Times* (13.1.79) she was forthright: 'If you want to know what I think of Mrs Danvers, then I think she was *profoundly* homosexual ... It is a mark of the changes in the times that not only do we think of Mrs Danvers now as a suppressed lesbian, but also as less of an ogre.' In the series *Devil's Advocate* (1991 R) Sue Townsend defended Rebecca's devoted slave: she was more to be viewed as a woman who was just doing her duty by her beloved mistress rather than as a spiteful meddler.

The Dark Number (UK 1967-8 T) A remorselessly cynical Scottish thriller serial, Johnny Maxen (Patrick Allen) can't stop loving his wife, Julia, even though she's a DRUG ADDICT, has killed their baby son, has had an affair with a young girl, and has now disappeared ('Just an ordinary story of mother love and devotion.') But she has paid the ultimate price: when finally discovered, she is no longer Julia but believes herself to be the Louise, the teenage who loved her and who has previously copied Julia in every respect – 'clothes, hair, everything'.

W: Eddie Boyd; P: Alan Bromly; D: Michael Ferguson; 6 parts; 25 mins.

The revelation of his wife's situation is something outside of Johnny's experience. His girlfriend Dorothy (Anne Kristen) tries to explain: 'Johnny, I do believe it's not unknown for one schoolgirl to get a crush on another.' Johnny can only murmur: 'Poor bitch.' Dorothy defends Julia/Louise (or maybe Louise/Julia): 'She's sick, Johnny!' He's not impressed. 'Sick, sick, sick. I'm fed up with that bloody word. It's been the 20th century's alibi.' A typically morose Eddie Boyd piece, with scant sympathy for any of the characters including a queen named Bunty, a friend of Johnny's decadent wife. This was a very early example of the (unpleasant) trace element of lesbianism forming part of the plot mechanism and revelation. (This serial was one of the most watched of 1968 – by over 7 million viewers.)

Dark Passions *Tales from Marquez* 'The Summer of Miss Forbes' (Sp 1988 T).
Miss Forbes (Hanna Schygulla) dreams of being abused and murdered by a man. She gets her wish. A deliciously nasty story of distended desire with an anti-heroine, a severe governess in panama hat, grey suit and boots, and an erotic gay god called Achilles, scrumptiously well defined in whispery white briefs who – unwillingly – acts as nemesis. From the director of DONA HERLINDA AND HER SON, it probably contains the greatest number of PHALLIC SYMBOLS ever gathered together in any one short television production.
D: Jaime Humberto Hermosillo; 50 mins.

Dark Secret (UK 1981 T) Strange goings-on in a Cotswold restaurant. The cook's son, Boy (Eric Deacon) is partial to Gerald, the WAITER (Paul Herzberg). He tries to seduce him with a freshly killed rabbit. And the plot thickens. One of Bowen's 'rustic chillers' in the same vein, with some of the same family members, as *Robin Redbreast* (1970) and *A Photograph* (1977).

W/P: John BOWEN; D: Christopher Hodson; LWT; 2 parts; 120 mins.

darling In Old English *deorling* meant 'beloved person or thing'; more specifically a minion, a sexually alluring young male. If 'darling' is used today by a male about another male, it is an almost automatic sign of homosexuality: gang boss Arnie Fisher (Jeffrey Chiswick) to a young man in WIDOWS (1983 T); at a chaotic wedding in *Flash, Bang, Wallop* (1981 R) a dainteous but cocky photographer (Sion Probert) tells the BEST MAN to place hand on hip because he has been referring to his friend, the bridegroom as 'darling'. Rumpole (Leo McKern) calls male colleagues '*old darling*' without raising an eyebrow.

Darling, Candy [James Slattery] (1948–74) Warhol superstar in FLESH (1968 C); *Women in Revolt*; etc.

Darling (UK 1965 C) The rise of a vapid young woman, Diana (Julie Christie), through modelling into the Italian aristocracy, helped by three men, one of whom, Malcolm (Roland CURRAM), is an actively gay photographer. Quintessential hollow 1960s film, deftly handled, but with no discernible dramatic heart, just a series of fashionable tableaux.
W: Frederic RAPHAEL; P: Joseph Janni and Victor Lyndon; D: John SCHLESINGER; 127 mins.

Darnley, Lord [Henry Stuart] BISEXUAL second husband of Mary, Queen of Scots (played by Douglas Walton in the Katherine HEPBURN version, *Mary of Scotland* 1936 C) and more explicitly by Timothy Dalton in the 1971 epic with Vanessa REDGRAVE, Nigel Lambert portrayed the syphilitic, spoilt young man in *The Killing at Kirk o'Fields* (1973 R) compiled from contemporary sources. However, it omitted the probability that Darnley was having sex with his page at the time his house was blown up by the Scottish Lords, who then stabbed him to death as they would a wild pig.

daughters Lesbian: Madge in *Piano*

Lessons: Linda Ray in A QUESTION OF LOVE (1978 T); the unseen one who's 'a very successful career woman' in *Say Something Happened* (1982 T; 1989 R); Meriel in THE TINKER'S DAUGHTER (1986 R); Cay in DESERT HEARTS (1985 C); Gail in MY TWO LOVES (1986 T); Fiona in A HORSE CALLED GERTRUDE STEIN (1991 R); Vicky (Shelley Kastner) in *My Father Is Coming* (1991 C); a lesbian who is living with a woman and who has presented her mother with a grandchild by a gay man in SALLY JESSY RAPHAEL 'Three Gays and a Baby' (1991 T).

Of gay/lesbian parent: Judy GARLAND (Andrea McArdle) in *Rainbow* (1978 T); Charlotte Crow in CROWN COURT 'A Friend of the Family' (1979 T); ROTT-INGDEAN (1980 T); Bette in FOX (1980 T); Gloria Vanderbilt (Jennifer Dundas) in *Little Gloria ... Happy at Last* (1982 T); LIANNA (1983 C); DOMESTIC BLISS (1985 T); LAW OF DESIRE (1987 C): Jenny (B. J. Jefferson) in L.A. LAW 'The Nut Before Christmas' (1991 T); gay/bisexual man's daughter who is lesbian on DONAHUE 'She Says Her Future Groom Cheats On Her With Men' (1992 T).

David and Jonathan In a religion tending to suppress the natural and idolizing the normal, this biblical story of love for one man by another has proved embarrassing: '... for he loved him as he loved his own soul ... And they kissed one another, and wept one with another until David exceeded ... Your love to me was wonderful, passing the love of women.' In *Flesh and the Devil* (1927) the pastor condemns David – though not for his possible homosexuality, but for his seduction by Bathsheba which led to his destruction by 'fire from heaven'.

In most films and television plays, David continues to be portrayed either as a fine young lad slaying Goliath or as the troubled king of Israel in adulterous union with Bathsheba: Gregory Peck (*David and Bathsheba* 1952 C); Tony Curtis (*The Stone* 1953 T); Jeff Chandler (A STORY OF DAVID 1960 C/ T); Ivo Payer (*David and Goliath* 1961

C); Timothy Bottoms (*The Story of David* 1976 T); Richard Gere (*King David* 1985 C in which Jonathan is pushed to the sidelines, killed off and brought back in a few cut-in shots of boyish innocence). Not so in Alan MEL-VILLE'S 1948 play, adapted by him for radio in 1966. JONATHAN is dead, but his memory has burrowed deep inside the king (John Justin) who surrounds himself with beautiful young men as well as dallying with Bathsheba (Elizabeth Sellars). After their son – named Jonathan – dies she realizes from David's indifference that Jonathan was closer to him than any child or any woman.

The nub of the relationship (I Samuel 20) has been much fudged by the Church. It was told – to children – by Cyril Fletcher as *The Sunday Story* (1963 T), but the language had been modernized (and de-eroticized) by the Rev. Chad Varrah. Nearly two decades on, Peter Brooks, discussing the inferred misconduct on *Thought for the Day* (1981 R), was quick to apply the whitewash: 'Of course, that's *not* a story of homosexual love. Human love can rise to such heights that it transcends sexual definition.' Without bothering to elaborate, Brooks dumped David and Jonathan and proceeded to St PAUL and his Letters to the Romans before concluding unctuously: 'Homosexuality is partly due to a world out of kilter – part of distorted human nature. So why does God have people with spina bifida or a tendency to selfishness ... flawed but still human? The BIBLE is compassionate on such things.'

There is no case of David and Jonathan being used as examples for male lovers in television drama or films, but they are occasionally cited in cases of lesbian affection – by one of the schoolteachers in *Miss Pym Disposes* (1987 R) and by Melanie to Jess in ORANGES ARE NOT THE ONLY FRUIT (1990 T): 'David and Jonathan – *they* were married and still love each other.'

See also MICHELANGELO'S DAVID.

David and Jonathan 1960s pop duo ('Lovers Of The World Unite') aka songwriters Roger Greenaway and Roger Cook whose career was discussed on *Music Makers UK II* (R 1992).

David Copperfield An orphaned boy suffers slings and arrows as well as various kinds of affection from men and women, relatives and strangers.

A whole gallery of sexual ambiguities is to be found in Dicken's masterpiece: passive, dependent David himself; fiercely independent Aunt Betsey Trotwood; Steerforth's sinister MAN-SERVANT, Littimer; the victimized schoolteacher, Mr Mell; fey Mr Dick; the mother-ridden Uriah Heep. Running through the entire book is David's need for the callous, superficial James STEERFORTH, his (and Emily's) seducer, a mother/bother/father/lover figure. The marriage of David and Dora is soon revealed as that of two children. Only in mature, balanced AGNES can give the tormented writer the solace and security he craves. How much of David is Dickens is open to surmise, but the sexual and emotional currents to be found in the book (and ignored in all the adaptations) are present in Dickens' other work, most notably *Our Mutual Friend*.

The 1935 film version is particularly lively, made with imagination by David O. Selznick and George CUKOR from a script by Hugh WALPOLE and Howard Estabrook (132 mins). The BBC has also done the story proud: notably with its 1956 and 1986 versions. The 1970 American television condensation had a evocative FLASHBACK structure in which the older David (Robin Phillips) railed against all the emotional props of his life who had splintered, principally his mother and his boyhood mentor.

Radio produced a magnificent version in 1973–4 which dramatized characters usually reduced or left out, such as Miss Mowcher and the vile Littimer who, it is strongly hinted, is Steeforth's pimp and fellow libertine. A less comprehensive version was heard in 1991 as *The Personal History of David Copperfield* (Nicholas Gatt and Gary Cady as David; Andrew Wincott as James Steerforth).

Perhaps the most overtly erotic television treatment was James Andrew HALL's in 1986 with Colin Hurley as David, Jeremy Brudenell as Steerforth, and Simon CALLOW as Micawber. Dark and bitter, with a Freudian interpretation of Mrs Steerforth's grasping need for her bad boy (presented in BYRONIC mould, smouldering, almost demonic). There is a strong inference that headmaster Creakle (John Savident) and James are having or have had a sexual relationship and that timid Mell knows all about it, which gives convincing force to Steerforth's sadistic treatment of him. This is probably the most honest version, although it lacks shading (being aimed at a teatime audience and being of relatively short duration). But there are more tender scenes that usual between the older and younger boys, and there is emphasis on the adult James' drinking and louche companions.

David Is a Homosexual (UK 1978) David makes contact with a CHE group and comes out to his parents. A 40 minute, 8mm colour film made by Lewisham Campaign for Homosexual Equality costing £450 (including £175 for the projector!). Ray McLaughlan, who came out to his parents while filming and who played some scenes while suffering German measles, is David – Mr EveryGay. (No individual credits; no television screening to date, but definitely a candidate for any British gay time capsule.)

Davies, Andrew (1936–) Welsh writer and adaptor, creator of A VERY PECULIAR PRACTICE (1986–8 T), as well as a lesbian play INAPPROPRIATE BEHAVIOUR (1987 T). A clever, open-minded wizard who manages to put spine and spirit into both his original work and his realizations of others' material. His stage work includes a number of plays with lesbian characters as well as one excellent piece for GAY SWEATSHOP in the 1970s about *Randy Robinson and his Unsuitable Relationship*.

Other T: *The Legend of King Arthur* (1979); *Fearless Frank* (1980); *Bavarian*

Night (1981); *Diana*(1983); *Mother Love* (1989); *House of Cards* (1991); *Filipina Dreamgirls* (1991); *Anglo-Saxon Attitudes* (1992). (He appeared on the 1991 TV tribute to Angus WILSON.)

Davies, Terence (1946–) English film director and former actor, cel-ebrated for his intensely personal works about family, guilt, loss and close-knit love: THE TERENCE DAVIES TRILOGY (1974–83) comprising 'Children' (1974), 'Madonna and Child' (1980) and 'Death and Transfiguration' (1983); *Distant Voices, Still Lives* (1988), *The Long Day Closes* (1992). Interviewed by Christopher Cook on *Third Ear* (1988 R); by Melvyn Bragg on the THE SOUTH BANK SHOW 'Terence Davies' (1992 T); *Screen* (Aust 1992 R); etc.

Davis, Bette [Ruth Elizabeth Davis] (1908–89) American stage and film artist, arguably the greatest star-actress of them all – a full decade of top star-dom and grade-A steak roles into which to sink her teeth: waitress/tart Mildred in *Of Human Bondage* (1934); the alco-holic actress in *Dangerous* (1935); *Jezebel* (1938); dying playgirl in *Dark Victory* (1939); 'mad' Empress Carlotta in *Juarez* (1939); the Queen of England in *The Private Lives of Elizabeth and Essex* (1939); adulterous wife in *The Letter* (1940); queen bee with sting in *The Little Foxes* (1941); spunky secretary in *The Man Who Came to Dinner* (1941); plain Jane reborn in *New Voyager* (1942); stockbroker's loveless wife in *Mr Skeff-ington* (1944); schoolmistress in *The Corn Is Green* (1945); twins in *A Stolen Life* (1946); ageing queen of Broadway in ALL ABOUT EVE (1950); former child-star, now harridan in *Whatever Happened to Baby Jane?* (1962); twins again in *Dead Ringer/Dead Image* (1964); *The Nanny* (1965); suffocating, vicious matriarch in *The Anniversary* (1967); criminal mas-termind in *Madame Sin* (1971); queru-lous passenger in *Death on the Nile* (1978); blind sister in *The Whales of August* (1987). (One of the roles she wanted to play, but didn't, was that of

Sister George in THE KILLING OF SISTER GEORGE.)

She also had a thriving, occasionally prestigious television career. There were guest roles in, eg PERRY MASON and *Wagon Train*. There were starring ones in TV movies like *Strangers* (1979); *Family Reunion* (1981); *A Piano for Mrs Cimino* (1982); the pilot of HOTEL (1983, role taken in TV series by *All About Eve* co-star Anne Baxter); *Right of Way* (1983); *As Summers Die* (1986).

Numerous – provocative – interviews on radio and television over the years, the most famous being when Dick Cavett asked her when she lost her vir-ginity (Answer: 'On my wedding night'). 1983 documentary for BBC2 entitled, some might say over-generously, *The Benevolent Volcano*.

Impersonated many times, eg by Charles Pierce in STARSKY AND HUTCH 'Death in a Different Place' (1977 T) and again in TORCH SONG TRILOGY (1988 C); by Craig RUSSELL in OUT-RAGEOUS! (1977 C); by Martha (Eliza-beth Taylor) in WHO'S AFRAID OF VIR-GINIA WOOLF? (1966 C): 'What a dump!' from *Beyond the Forest* (1949).

Bette's Margo Channing character from *All About Eve* was put into LAVENDER through the use of mische-vious cutting in *Dry Kisses Only* (1991 C/V).

Davis, Brad (1950–91) American film actor, a sensitive, hairy, virile, potent 'he-man', best known for his playing of Billy Hayes, brutalized in a Turkish prison in MIDNIGHT EXPRESS (1978); and for his address to the film industry after his death from AIDS-related causes. He starred in *The Normal Heart* on Broadway in 1984.

C: part of a *ménage à trois* in *A Small Circle of Friends* (1980 C); athlete in *Chariots of Fire* (1981 C); title role in QUERELLE (1982 C); revenge-seeking cop in *Cold Steel* (1987 C); the father of many children in *Rosalie Goes Shopping* (1989 C).

T: Elmo, an airman in *Sole Survivor* (1969 T); Brewster Crowley in *The Impatient Heart* (1971 T), young firefighter Billy Del Zell in *Firehouse* (1972 T); Peter Doyle in *Song of Myself/Beautiful Dreamer* (1976 T); racist Sonny Butts in *Chiefs* (1983 T); title role in *Robert Kennedy and His Times* (1984 T); American cousin of Mafia leader in *Blood Ties* (1986 T); Neil Travers in *The Rainbow Warrior Conspiracy* (1989 T); child psychologist in *Unspeakable Acts* (1990 T); *Habitation of Dragons*, his last appearance (1991 T).

'I make my money in an industry that professes to care very much about the fight against AIDS – that gives umpteen benefits and charity affairs with proceeds going to research and care. But in actual fact, if an actor is even rumoured to have HIV he gets no support on an individual basis. He does not work' (quoted in *Los Angeles Times*, almost immediately after his death in September 1991).

Davis, Noel (193?–) English supporting actor who, on occasions, does a nice line in pursed lips and nervous tension. Is now also casting supremo for films and television.

C: *Fahrenheit 451* (1967); the interviewer in *Young Winston* (1971); Joe's friend Philip in the art gallery scene in PRICK UP YOUR EARS (1987): 'Nice of you to come'/'Girls must stick together. I had a friend once who was in soft furnishings. The *times* I've trolled round the Ideal Home Exhibition!'

R: Gordon Whitehouse in DANGEROUS CORNER (1968).

T: Bob in *The Brown Man's Servant* (1953); motor mechanic in *Johnny You're Wanted* 'Blind Corner' (1953); Albert the footman in *Lady Frederick* (1953); Weeks in *The Dancing Bear* (1954); Redbrook in *Captain Brassbound's Conversion* (1954); Philippe, Jesuit Master in *Poor Bitos* (1964); Joyce in *Treasure Island* (1957); Squire Trelawney in *Treasure Island* (1965); receptionist in *George and the Dragon* (1966); Gilbert Paish, suspect in killing of BOUTIQUE OWNER in *No Hiding Place* 'Golden Boy' (1966); the doctor in *Lieutenant Tenant* (1967); SECRETARY in THE AVENGERS 'A Funny Thing Happened on the Way to the Station' (1967); *The Charlie Drake Show* (1968); Tupper in *The World of Woodhouse* 'Ukridge' (1968); Austrian ambassador in *Fall of Eagles* (1974); *Apartment Zero* (1988); PORTRAIT OF A MARRIAGE (1990) etc.

As casting director: THE DRESSER (1983 C); *Apartment Zero* (1988); PORTRAIT OF A MARRIAGE (1990 T); ABSOLUTE HELL! (1991 T); etc.

Davis, Roger (1884–1980) American dancer and actor, on stage in the Ziegfeld Follies, aged 17. According to *Variety* (3.3.80), he was 'longtime companion and confidant' to Fanny Brice and a 'close friend' of many 'show business greats' such as Katharine HEPBURN. Davis was often cast in bit parts by his friends simply because they wanted him around. His largest role was in *Miss Tatlock's Millions* (1948) directed by Richard HAYDN, with Monty Woolley; he was also in ADAM'S RIB and *Pat and Mike* (1952). Roddy MCDOWALL played Roger Davis (as openly gay 'Bobby Moore') in FUNNY LADY in 1975.

Dawn! (Aust 1979 C) The only person to win three consecutive medals for the same event in the Olympic Games, Dawn Fraser was the toast of Australia but her extrovert personality put her in constant strife with the authorities. The Amateur Swimming Union of Australia suspended her for 18 months after the 1960 Rome Olympics. She was then suspended for a draconian 10 years after 'borrowing' a flag from the gardens of the Emperor Hirohito's palace during the 1964 games in Tokyo. The film follows Dawn's life after her years of glory, the broken marriages, an ABORTION and an unsuccessful relationship with a journalist, Kate Hansford (Gabreille Hartley): 'When I was prepared to settle for something else, Kate's work had too big a start on me.' The film ends with Dawn at the professional and emotional crossroads.

W/P: Joy Cavill; D: Ken Hannam; 115 mins.

The wholly delightful performance

from the unknown Bronwyn Mackay-Payne produces a very different kind of heroine; gauche, powerful, vulnerable, fresh, disillusioned, but never defeated. Very underrated, probably because of the actress's lack of technique.

Day, Doris [Doris Kappelhoff] (1924–) Effervescent singer-actress, the embodiment of WASP womanhood in 1950s 'sex' comedies, but equally comfortable in TOMBOY roles or as hysterical women forced to fly planes or thwart assassination attempts at a moment's notice. Among her 'BACHELOR GIRL' characters (clinging on desperately to their virginity or asserting their independence from men) Marjorie in *On Moonlight Bay* (1951); CALAMITY JANE (1953 C); shop steward Babe in *The Pajama Game* (1957); the journalism lecturer in *Teacher's Pet* (1958); and her INTERIOR DECORATOR in *Pillow Talk* (1959). Fighter for women's rights in *The Ballad of Josie* (1968). And proclaiming her independence, even though she's the All-American wife, in *The Thrill of It All* (1963).

After her film career petered out, television made her something of a pig's breakfast in the various formats of *The Doris Day Show* (1968–72). She was seen on the cable programme *Doris Day's Best Friends* (1985), which gained worldwide attention when she filmed a segment with her physically much altered former co-star Rock HUDSON a few months before he died.

She was eulogized by Colonel Sherman Potter (Harry Morgan) on a 1978 episode of M*A*S*H (he confided he had never told his wife about their clandestine, ongoing (if one-sided) affair – in the dark), and also by Terence DAVIES in THE SOUTH BANK SHOW (1992 T). 'I wanted to *be* Doris Day ... and still do.' Harvey FIERSTEIN'S Arnold Beckoff in TORCH SONG TRILOGY was described as 'Doris Day with a dick' by Jay Scott in *Film Comment* (1989).

The star continues to attract a large lesbian following, helped by the extraordinary bipolarity of many of her roles,

the BUTCH HAIRCUT of the mid–1950s, and that song, SECRET LOVE.

She gave a rare interview for 'Doris Day: "I Don't Even Like Apple Pie"' (1989 T).

Daytime 'Gays and the GLC' (UK 1986 T) An example of British afternoon controversy television in which leader of the soon-to-be-abolished Greater London Council, Ken LIVINGSTONE attempted to explain the reasons behind the Council's manifesto, entitled 'Changing the World', and claiming equal rights for gays and lesbians in every area of life: health care, employment, education, religion and the media.

'Changing the World', a charter for gay and lesbian rights was, Ken Livingstone said, designed as an attempt to influence local councils and Parliament. The GLC spent £50 million a year to create jobs, so gays and lesbians could surely be allowed a modest £44,000 to change the world that discriminated against them, as well a £1 million over three years for a gay centre – the first in a city where so many lived and worked.

Ken Livingstone spoke in a measured way about the need to spend money on this important section of the community, ending with his belief that the GLC should act as an example to councils and service providers outside the capital city. Before these last words were out of his mouth, a journalist (from the Responsible Society, the Order of the Christian Unity, and founder of the League of Feminine Women) was leaping half out of her seat. Frothing with rage, her voice rising to a scream, she sprang: 'It says they'll withdraw civic protection from churches ... churches who denounce the sin of sodomy. We've been denouncing it for 2,000 years and we are not going to stop now.' This was the signal for general hullabaloo to break out. Mythology and prejudice from the conservatives and 'moderates', doctrinaire statements peppered with jargon from the left, the 'liberals' and sexual-political activists ...

The programme degenerated into verbal soup: 'HOMOPHOBIA', 'DISEASE',

'QUEER-BASHING', 'innocent children', 'sodomy', 'AIDS', 'rights'. A doctor maintained that homosexuality is a disease; 'a sterile product, deviant and abnormal ... so immoral it's going to deprive us of our freedom.' A concerned parent said he could see why Ken Livingstone was going to be out of a job soon: 'he's spending over a million on POUFS.' A joke was made about the GLC pushing things up people's backsides. A reverend said he was misquoted in the press: he *wouldn't* shoot his son if he found out he had AIDS. (But he wouldn't be very happy about it).

Thus was potentially valuable discussion around the huge nucleus of sexuality and freedom reduced to a chimp's tea party in a snake pit. Over 20 people spoke so that Livingstone had barely four minutes to put over dense and thoughtful ideas about, literally, 'Changing the World'. What the London charter for lesbian and gay rights said or didn't say was completely ignored; whatever benefits it might bring were left unaddressed.

'Once you start a challenge ... once you start to free people,' said Ken Livingstone in his allotted four minutes. 'Freeing people to be abnormal!' came the traditional response, dented only by the BLACK LESBIAN who said that if anything should be abolished it was that word 'NORMAL'. But this was not taken up. The discussion, such as it was, hinged almost solely on whether the GLC was 'promoting' sodomy and AIDS and practising discrimination against 'ordinary' people.

dead people Pivots of the plots, even though often unseen, except occasionally in ghostly form: lesbians in *Rebecca* DE WINTER; *The Uninvited* (Mary, 1944); HUIS CLOS (Ines 1954); THE L-SHAPED ROOM (Mavis' 'friends', 1962 C); *The Midnight Man* (Natalie Claiborn, the dead student, 1974 C); *The Happiest Women* (Madaline, 1984 R). Gay men in DANGEROUS CORNER (Martin CAPLAN, 1957 T etc); *A Streetcar Named Desire* (Blanche's husband, Alan, 1951 C etc); CAT ON A HOT TIN ROOF (Skipper, 1958

C etc); SUDDENLY LAST SUMMER (Sebastian Venable, 1959 C); VICTIM (Phil Stainer, 1961 C); *Is Nellie Dead?* (Malcolm, 1968 T); THE WAITING ROOM (1971 T); A SINGLE MAN (Jim, 1972 R etc); *A Song at Twilight* (Perry, 1982 T etc); *André's Mother* (André, 1990 T); *Tidy Endings* (1989 T); the mass return of the dead friends and acquaintances on Fire Island in the last scene of LONG-TIME COMPANION; etc.

Dead Ringers (Can 1988 C) TWIN gynaecologists Elliot and Beverly (Jeremy Irons) share every experience except one. Elliot's the sweet one, Beverly's the shit. Their narcissistic relationship ends in madness and death. W/D: David Cronenberg; 113 mins.

A bloody, hallucinationary work about men who believe their patients are monsters. Lots of sharp instruments on view, but the script is blunt, shying away – like the director's later *Naked Lunch* – from prickly issues.

deaf people One of the presenters of Sydney's weekly radio show *Gaywaves*, Tony, is partially deaf. Refreshingly, a few others who are gay or lesbian turned up to comment on matters unrelated to hearing impairment in OUT, which also presented a special programme on them called 'Actions Speak Louder' (1992 T). The discrimination gays and lesbians face within the wider deaf community formed part of a debate on sign language among an audience of over 60 deaf people, in *Listening Eye* 'The All-Deaf Debate: Discrimination' (1988 T), including members of the Brothers and Sisters Club, which was also seen on a *Link* segment in the 1980s. Very few television or cinema dramas feature deaf people: a spot of sign language in the DISCO scene in PARTING GLANCES (1985), and a young deaf man, one of the main protagonists in the French-Canadian *Straight to the Heart* (1986 C). Generally, they are marginalized into invisibility; or, in the words of the title of the famous play and film, *Children of a Lesser God*.

Dean, James Byron (1931–55) Lucifer in blue jeans, Pan in a Porsche, Rebel without a Cause. The actor who synthesized Montgomery CLIFT and Marlon Brando, and who was dead at 24 before the second of his three films was released, detonated a cult that lasts to this day.

The only non-comedic child-man the cinema has produced. His place was taken by two actors, Paul Newman and Steve McQueen, and his influence is visible in stars and near-stars like Martin Sheen, Michael Parks, Christopher Jones, Matt Dillon and Sean Penn. Dean-style attitudes and concepts have been recycled recently in characters in *Twin Peaks* and *Beverly Hills 90210*, and he noticeably influenced River Phoenix' body language in MY OWN PRIVATE IDAHO.

Dean's former room-mate, William Bast wrote a play for British television in 1958, THE MYTH MAKERS, which dealt head-on with the cult, heavily necrophiliac, that immediately grew up around the dead star. Bast called him Alan Swift, and provided him with a wife and a mother, both of whom hint at a divided, troubled psyche and secrets kept from the fans. Bast was able to deal more directly with the sexual ambiguity of his friend in the 1976 TV movie JAMES DEAN, in which Stephen McHattie played the actor as fascinated by homosexuality but using Bill Bast (Michael Brandon) to 'dabble' and report back. Other films dipping their toes in the mythology were Robert Altman's *Come Back to the Five and Dime, Jimmy Dean, Jimmy Dean* (1981) and *Wildwechsel/Jail Bait* (1972) with Harry Baer as a Dean lookalike.

Documentaries have included *The Steve Allen Show* (1956 T); *James Dean* (1956 ABC); *The James Dean Story* (1957 C, directed by Robert Altman); *The First American Teenager* (1975 C); *You're Tearing Me Apart* (1985 R); *Bye, Bye, Jimmy* (1991 T).

With Marilyn MONROE and Elvis Presley, Dean is the icon of the 1950s, exercising a strange and hypnotic appeal over people of both sexes. Movie buff Adrian (Colin Firth) is attracted to the 'James Dean *je-ne-sais-quoi*' of Jack (Hart Bochner) in *Apartment Zero* (1988 C).

James Dean calendars are best-sellers and his photographs adorn many a teenage bedroom wall – Michelle Fowler (Susan Tully) had one around the time of her marriage to Lofty in EASTENDERS (1986 T); *Shirley Valentine's* daughter (1989 C) and Pattie (Suzanna Hamilton) in *Brimstone and Treacle* (1984 C) have them in their galleries of pin-ups too; Dani (Juliette Lewis) has a moody Dean poster on her bedroom door in *Cape Fear* (1991 C); the more mature Ann Turkel has one on the office wall of her swanky bar in the pilot of HOLLYWOOD BEAT (1985 T); and there's a photograph on a (male's) school locker door in *Growing Pains* (1986 T) that piques the interest of a female student. All very mainstream and a fair way from the humble torn-out magazine picture of Dean that appeared on bikie Scorpio's wall in SCORPIO RISING (1964 C).

dear boy 'Be sure to give my love to the dear boy' says Edward Barranca (Michael WARD) in *The Richest Man in the World* (1960 T) about her sister's pretty husband, one of many examples of the thinly veiled sexual interest from one man to another (usually younger) wrapped up in those two words. Nelson GABRIEL uses it occasionally.

dear heart An extravagent appellation, favoured by a member of the *ménage à trois*, Otto in DESIGN FOR LIVING (1964 T etc); by Edward Minty (Emlyn WILLIAMS who uses it to indicate tender feelings for Victor (Denholm ELLIOTT) at the end of PAST CARING (1986 T); by the villain (Richard Hope) who calls his victims 'dear heart' in *Bellman and True* (1987 C); by public school/Oxford Red Jocelyn Coleman (John Westbrook) who teases the hero in *Castles in Spain* (1987 R) with 'What a lively imagination you have, dear boy'; by the hero's sybaritic friend (Peter Donat) in *Skin Deep*

(1989 C); and by a lot more pink-tinged men besides.

Dear John (US 1988– T) Comedy series, based on BBC version, about a man (Judd Hirsch) finding that there is life after the wife leaves you flat. But there are unforeseen dangers. Like John's new ROOM-MATE and fellow member of the 1/2 Club, Tony (Cleavon Little) who is 'romantically interested' in him, in 'Stand by Your Man' (1990). Although John repeatedly tells him that his feelings lie elsewhere, Tony won't take no for an answer. He takes the love-struck guy to a quiet restaurant and explains the situation all over again in great detail. After a temper tantrum, Tony gets the message but then John has to convince a fellow teacher – who was sitting at a nearby table – that he is not gay.

In a 1991 episode, a divorcee (Jere Burns) bumps into his ex-wife at the supermarket where she works with her female lover. 'For once the straight man comes out looking stupid and the girls are together and cool' (Kevin Dickson and Steve Gidlow, *Sydney Star Observer*, 4.10.91).

W: Peter Noah, Bob Ellison and others; D: James Burrows and others.

Dearman, Glyn (1940–) English actor, now radio director, responsible for BBC Radio 4 drama output. Has made a significant contribution to dissemination of 'gay' culture on radio: CAMP, biography, gothic, *grand guignol*, farce, drag.

As actor: Tiny Tim, 'sweetness personified' in *Scrooge* (1951 C); Arthur in *Tom Brown's Schooldays* (1951 C); Jennings (1953–6 R); the young Stephen Murray in *The Four Sided Triangle* (1953 C): one of the boys in *Billy Bunter of Greyfriars* (1954–6 T); Simon in *Return to Naples* (1953 R); Carlo Rovero in *The Dragon and the Rose* (1928); Dick Staveley in *Eustace and Hilda* (1958); Fleance in *Macbeth* (1959) with Paul Scofield; young nephew Carleton Dale who gets his hand caught in the tractor fan in *Mrs Dale's Dairy* (1959 R); various DIXON OF DOCK GREEN episodes (T); Tony in *The*

Ha-Ha (1963 R); *Jay in The Wednesday Caller* (1964 R); Stetton in *A Case of Character* (1965 R); prince in EDWARD II (1968, late role until cameo – as PROUST devotee – in *The Dead Room* 1992).

As producer: THE DALES (co-producer); WAGGONERS WALK (co-producer); *Look After Amélie* (1966); VALMOUTH (1975); *Vampirella* (1976); *Dracula* (1976); *Et Dona Ferentes* (from the Angus WILSON short story, 1976); *A Slip of the Disc* (1978); JUST BEFORE MIDNIGHT (c 1978–9); THREE PIECE SWEET (1979); *Women of Words* (about Dorothy Parker, 1980; also biography in the same series on Tallulah BANKHEAD which wasn't broadcast); *Sherlock Holmes v Dracula* (1981, also writer); *Puss in Boots* (1982); LOOK BACK IN ANGER (1982); *Douglas* BYNG *at 90* (1983 R); *Gormenghast/Titus Groan* (1984); *A Self-Made Man* (about Ronald FIRBANK, 1985); *Liberty Comes to Krahwinkel* (1985); *I'd Give My Right Arm to be Ambidextrous* (1985); PETER PAN (1987); *Miss Pym Disposes* (1987); *Death Duties* (1987); *It's the Truth!* (1987 R, also writer); *Smallbone Deceased* (1988); A SINGLE MAN (1991 R); *Hamlet* (1992 R) with Kenneth Branagh; *Paradise Lost* (1992); ALEXANDER (1993).

death The process shown in detail in A DEATH IN THE FAMILY (1986 C); Bergman's *Cries and Whispers* (1982 C – discussed by Terence DAVIES on 1990 T); *On Unbecoming* (Aust 1991 R). The last is a diary of a death from September 1987 to August 1988, by media anthropologist Eric Michaels. It uses a combination of archival recordings and readings from his journal 'On Unbecoming: An AIDS Dairy'. *See also* BEREAVEMENT; DEAD PEOPLE.

A Death in the Family (NZ 1986 C/ T) A group of friends mount a vigil around a man dying of AIDS, a situation complicated by the arrival of his parents, BROTHER and sister-in-law who are only just beginning to come to terms with his illness let alone his sexuality. A finely tuned piece, fair-minded, loving, and showing in a necessarily compressed

manner the way the 'gay family' meets the biological one in a time of need and crisis.
D: Peter WELLS and Stewart Main; *c* 60 mins.

Death in Venice (It 1971 C) A middle-aged man (Dirk BOGARDE) pursues a seemingly seductive boy (Bjorn Andresen) on the Lido as plague sweeps the city in 1911.
W: Luchino Visonti and Nicola Badalucco from the novella by Thomas Mann; P/D: Luchino Visconti; 130 mins.
A beautiful opera without songs and almost without words. The gay as frustrated hunter put out of his misery by death – to the accompaniment of Mahler's 3rd and 5th symphonies.

decadence The sense of lassitude, moral breakdown and luxury, oftentimes associated with ancient civilizations, as well as high society – especially as portrayed by Fellini – and HOLLYWOOD. It finally reached Australia when Mike says to Jenny in NEIGHBOURS (1988 T): 'We can stop in front of the television and be decadent.'

Baron **De Charlus** 'I'm a mine of experience ... an invaluable, undiscovered guide, not *only* to the past.' '[A man with] a delicate appreciation of the indelicate' (*Proust's Characters* 1957 R). Charles Swann's snobbish friend who eyes up footmen, guardsmen and students as he cruises along the boulevards in a carriage. His taste for ROUGH TRADE and bondage was more prominently explored in Harold PINTER's script for Joseph Losey's unrealized 'A la Recherche du Temps Perdu' than in the 1984 Volker Schlondorff movie, *Swann in Love*, based on *Swann's Way*, in which he was played to the hilt by Alain Delon.
Painted and increasingly desperate, De Charlus is rejected by a Jewish music student. The older man reacts angrily: 'Don't despise feelings you don't share.' He later tells Charles, equally obsessive in his pursuit of love; 'For the best of us,

the study of art and fine gardens is but a substitute. Just like Diogenes in his barrel, what we are seeking is a man.'
The baron was one of the first sexually active homosexual men to be depicted on radio: by Austin Trevor in *The Duchess at Sunset* (1952 R) and by the incomparable Max ADRIAN in *Saint Loup* (1956 R). PROUST is said to have based the character on Count Robert De Montesquiou (1855–1921), who was also the model for Duke Jean Floressas Des Esseintes in 'A Rebours' by Joris-Karl Huysmans (1991 R) and for Dorian GRAY.
Roland Petit's ballet version of Proust's *Les Intermittences du Coeur* (Aspects of Love) included De Charlus visiting a SADO-MASOCHISTIC brothel (*Dance International* 1985 T).

Odette **De Crecy** (Ornella Muti in *Swann in Love* 1984 C) A courtesan who becomes the fetish of the aristocrat Charles Swann (Jeremy Irons). Her enigmatic smile and eagerness to please entrance both sexes, and Swann is torn apart by jealousy. He demands Odette swear on the Virgin that she and Madame Verdurin did not have an affair. After much shadow boxing, Odette does admit to once being propositioned by a woman in a café who suggested that they 'go behind the rocks and look at the moonlight on the water'. A whispered conversation between Odette and a female pimp earlier has alerted the audience to the possibility that women could make up a fair percentage of Odette's clientele. Eventually, Charles and Odette marry, a circumstance that automatically bars him as well as her from the top layer of society.
Odette is PROUST's version of the *femme fatale*, a child of nature with a healthy awareness of the commercial value of her body in a materialistic society. Someone says of her: 'Would she be half so charming if she were virtuous?'

The Deep Blue Sea (UK 1954 T) Two of the original cast: Googie Withers as

Hannah and Kenneth More as Freddie, with Robert Harris as the husband. A lover's SUICIDE sparked off this story of a married woman's emotional turmoil over a charming, irresponsible young racing driver.

W: Terence RATTIGAN; P/D: Julian Aymes; 21.1.54; BBC; 85 mins.

Kenneth More played Freddie opposite Vivien Leigh in the 1955 film version.

See also Kenneth MORGAN.

Deep Night Rudy Vallee hit of the 1920s used to accompany Mike's (River Phoenix) efforts with the scouring powder, dressed in male 'maid's' attire: all the better to bring his customer to a satisfactory conclusion in MY OWN PRIVATE IDAHO (1991 C). The song is also played over the closing credits, as a reference point to Mike's narcolepsy.

M/L: Charlie Henderson.

Deep Six (UK 1984 R) Three months away from retirement at MI5, Oxford-educated, woman-hating, boy-loving secret service kingpin Sir James Simpson (Conrad Phillips) sees the old ways under threat. Fragile though his power may be, it is still power and with it he will cleanse his department of revolting elements. These include men with 'relaxed lifestyles and liberal attitudes'. Neither of which could remotely apply to the tough young lady recently arrived from the Treasury. She is 'all lacquered hair, pretty smile and blood-red fingernails'. Because she is a mere woman, Sir James pays her no attention. Yet it is she who reaps the benefits of the mayhem – which claims Sir James himself.

The hero of John Fletcher's serial (directed by Brian Miller) is an ordinary bloke who roots for good, honest folk. Needless to say, the left-wingers are portrayed in the same dreadful light as the Tories: opportunists and turn-coats depite their right-on attitudes. And the Liberals? They're sex-driven WIMPS.

One of a series of early evening Sunday thrillers from BBC Radio 4 broadcast between 1983 and 1986: all quite acerbic and all with nasty and/or weak gay or lesbian characters of whom Sir James Simpson was the most memorable.

Deep South American gothic, often spiked with madness and long buried family secrets: homosexuality – more and less – in *The Member of the Wedding*; CAT ON A HOT TIN ROOF; SUDDENLY LAST SUMMER; *Beulah Land*; REFLECTIONS IN A GOLDEN EYE; *The Heart Is a Lonely Hunter*; *Mandingo: Drum*; *Blood Kin*; *The Ballad of the Sad Café*; FRIED GREEN TOMATOES AT THE WHISTLE STOP CAFE; etc. A real-live gay man, a postman *Fighting in South West Louisiana* (1991 C/T) and a wonderfully aware, prismatic heterosexual woman doing her bit for safe-sex education in DI ANA'S HAIR EGO.

degenerate Jo SMITH calls herself and Geoff 'degenerates' in A TASTE OF HONEY: 'No design, rhythm or purpose ... The devil's own,' concurs Geoff. Gregory Peck calls Robert Mitchum one in *Cape Fear* (1962 C).

Degrassi Junior High (Can 1990–T) Very responsible, detailed school stories: a Canadian GRANGE HILL, but with slightly more queer throughput. The series is a development of *Kids of Degrassi High* in the 1980s.

In 'He Ain't Heavy' Snakes's brother, Glenn, returns home unexpectedly from medical school. An all-star basketball player, he comes out as gay, mainly so the kids can chew over the following: homosexuality, self-image, judging others, right to privacy, sibling relationships, personal values, STEREOTYPING, persistence, AIDS.

A two-parter, 'Bad Blood' has one of the boys, the heterosexual Dwayne, testing HIV positive, the revelation of which leads to BULLYING.

In 'Rumor Has It' Caitlin has disturbing dreams about Ms Avery, her favourite teacher, who is rumoured to be lesbian. Ms Avery allays 'some' of Caitlin's fears, but not before the characters have had to face homosexuality, dreams, group dynamics, attitudes, gossip and rumours.

Dehn, Paul (1912–76) English film critic, revue, radio and screenwriter. A major during the Second World War, he had also been a contemporary of Alan TURING at Bletchley Park.

C: he and collaborators won Oscar for *Seven Days to Noon* (1951); other screenplays include *Orders to Kill* (1958); *Goldfinger* (1964); *The Spy Who Came In from the Cold* (1965); *The Deadly Affair* (1966); *The Taming of the Shrew* (1967 with help from SHAKESPEARE); *The Night of the Generals* (1967); *Fragment of Fear* (1970, also producer); *Beneath the Plant of the Apes* (1970 and two sequels); *Murder on the Orient Express* (1974).

delicious debauchery Nero (Charles LAUGHTON) in *The Sign of the Cross* (1932). His other great line, which didn't catch on, was: 'Have a little consideration; would you have me late for the games?'; it was spoken to Fredric March, who is begging the emperor to spare a Christian's life.

Deliverance (US 1972 C) Four men go on an expedition and encounter primitive actions (male RAPE) and their own mixed desires and cauterized feelings.
W: James Dickey from his novel; P/D: John Boorman; 109 mins.

Joan Mellen articulates the film's thesis in her book *Big Bad Wolves: Masculinity in the American Film* (1977): 'The violence of these strangers [the mountain men who attack and rape one of the party] allows the sexuality trembling between the men to surface. The film neither applauds nor is distressed by what is revealed about men; it simply suggests that were these male friends honest enough, they would admit to such feelings for each other, accept them without shame, and feel released from the need to shoot rapids, or endlessly test their male credentials.'

Denis/Dennis Boy's name often used for leaky, callow men.
UK: Dennis Leighton (Lyndon Brook), ruthless, over-elegant crook in Gore VIDAL's *A Sense of Justice* (1958 T); Elsie Tanner's boy Dennis (Philip Low-

rie) in CORONATION STREET (1960s T); Dennis Dunstable (Peter Denyer) in *Please Sir* (1968–74 T); Dennis Cooper (Michael Palin) wide-eyed in wonderment in *Jabberwocky* (1977 C); faithful, jolly consort (John Wells) in *Anyone for Denis?* (1983 T); wilting soapie actor Dennis (Roger Phillips) in *Who Shot Ada Tansey?* (1983 R); Dennis (Royce Mills) in *Tears Before Bedtime* (1983 T); nurse Dennis (Martyn Hesford) involved in the drug operation covered up by the spiritual community in *The Black Tower* (1985 T).

US: doll-like innocent Dennis Barlow in *The Loved One* (Robert Morse 1965 C; Rupert Graves 1990 R); Dennis Jenks (Warren Stevens), THRUSH operative running boys' school in *The Man from UNCLE* 'The Children's Day Affair' (1965 T); Dennis (Bob Seagren), shallow lover of Jodie in SOAP (1977 T).

dentists BUTLEY'S is 'terribly CAMP ... one sits in that chair with one's body at his mercy' (1974 C/T); no-holds-barred sexual illumination of Spanish dentist in *What Have I Done to Deserve This?* (1985 C): he races off a young boy patient, they cohabit for a while; Jerry (Bill Young), an ex-hippy who charges patients only enough to keep himself in dope, in *Natural Causes* (Aust 1985 T).

deodorants Helena Rubinstein's ill-fated attempt to market aftershave under the name of her 'royal' husband was abandoned in the 1950s (*Beauty Queens* 1988 T).

Strong resistance was quieted gradually. First by the salt spray marketing of Old Spice and then by the unimpeachable Henry Cooper, extolling the benefits of wearing Brut. 'Henry Cooper really put the muscle into men's fragrances. And no way is Henry Cooper a poofter', said Jeni Charles about Fabergé, the makers of Brut (*Sun*, 16.9.82).
See also AFTERSHAVE LOTION; PERFUME.

Chevalier **D'Eon** (1728–1810) French diplomat who was born female. *Man or*

Woman? (1953 R); *The Secret Life of the Chevalier D'Eon* (1960 C).

De Poligny, Serge (1897–1983) French set designer. Supervised French versions of UFA films. Directed *Claudine at School* (1936); several supernatural films made during the German occupation: *La Fiancée des Ténèbres* (1944 C; a medieval religious sect is reborn in modern France) and *The Phantom Baron* (with Jean COCTEAU in creepy cameo); *La Soif des Hommes* (1949, about the 19th-century colonization of Algeria).

Desert Heart (US 1985 C) A prim East Coast lecturer (Helen Shaver) drops her inhibitions while collecting her divorce in Nevada during the 1950s. Staying at a ranch, the woman is struck all of a heap by the owner's brazenly lesbian daughter, Cay (Patrica Charbonneau), a part-time ARTIST, and discovers hidden depths can be fun – if scary to plum.
W: Natalie Cooper; P/D: Donna Deitch; Based on Jane Rule's *Desert of the Heart*; 93 mins.
A fresh, bracing love story, beautifully set, attractively played. A total vindication of Donna Deitch and the many people whom she managed to persuade (over a 4-year period) to put in small amounts of money in order to make the project a reality. It *should* have marked the beginning of a whole range of such films – but it failed to find a crossover audience, unlike movies 'not about lesbians' such as THELMA AND LOUISE and FRIED GREEN TOMATOES AT THE WHISTLE STOP CAFE.
'I wanted the film to go on and on, just to give me some pointers to my life,' one of the women filmgoers in OUT's 'We've Been Framed' (1991 T).

Desert Island Discs (UK 1942– R) A cover fantasy for personal revelation. Originated by BBC freelancer Roy Plomley over 50 years ago. From 1942 until his death in May 1985, he gently tickled his proposed castaways like trout in what was the precursor of the radio and television chat show. It remains riveting radio – and a treasure trove for future burrowers and biographers.
'I will say very little and let them get on with it. Why should I do all the work?' (Plomley on Russell *Harty* in the early 1980s).
'It is the most marvellous way of getting people ... to talk about themselves. I always felt there was something very revealing in the choice of music. Always. There was always one record which was the question I daren't ask – *This* is an affair! It was always lurking there. And there was always one.' Michael Parkinson, successor to Roy Plomley 1986–8, interviewed on *The Desert Island Discs Story* (1992 R).
A few openly gay shipwreckees have made occasional mentions of lovers, partners etc, or discussed gay rights in extremely wide, non-controversial terms.
Here is a very small selection of islanders from the over 2,000 so far set adrift, (the names have been selected because they nearly all have their own entries in this book):

1942: James Agate, critic; Ivor Novello, composer; Emlyn Williams, actor-playwright. 1943: Tom Driberg MP; 1945: Michael Redgrave, actor. 1951: Eric Portman, actor; Joan Hammond, soprano; Jimmy Edwards, comedian; Henry Kendall, actor. 1952: Gilbert Harding, broadcaster; Godfrey Winn, author; Wallace Greenslade, announcer. 1953: Robert Helpmann, dancer-choreographer-actor; Cyril Ritchard, actor. 1955: Anthony Asquith, film director; Emlyn Williams*, actor-playwright; Michael Redgrave*, actor; Beverley Nicholas, author; Anton Dolin, dancer. 1956: Nancy Spain, writer; Peter Katin, pianist; Peter Finch, actor. 1957: Peter Sellers, actor: Alan Melville, actor-playwright; Alma Cogan, vocalist. 1958: Anton Walbrook, actor, Naomi Jacob, novelist; Aaron Copland, composer. 1959: John Osborne, playwright, Frederick Ashton, choreographer; Ernest Thesiger, actor; Douglas Byng, revue artist; Frankie Howerd*, comedian; Alfred Hitchcock, film director, Benny Hill*, comedian. 1960: Liberace, pianist; Jimmy Edwards*, comedian; Kenneth Williams*, comedian. 1962: Sir John

Gielgud, actor; Gwen Ffrangcon-Davies, actress. 1963 Noel Coward, writer-actor; Ted Willis, author; Carleton Hobbs, actor. 1964: Richard Wattis, actor; Dirk Bogarde, actor; Brian Epstein, pop group manager; Tallulah Bankhead, actress. 1965 Marlene Dietrich, actress. 1966: Danny La Rue, comedian. 1967: Richard Goolden, actor; John Schlesinger*, film director; Alan Bennett, playwright. 1968: Sir Michael Tippett, composer; Marty Feldman, scriptwriter. 1969: Angus Wilson, author; Hetty King, male impersonator; Peter Pears, tenor; Sir John Wolfenden, Librarian of the British Museum; Max Adrian, actor. 1970: Joan Hammond*, soprano; James Laver, fashion writer; Ian McKellen, actor. 1972: David Hockney, artist (first openly gay castaway); Barry Humphries, entertainer. 1974: Dr Jacob Bronowski, scientist; Sir Terence Rattigan, playwright; Philip Hope-Wallace, writer. 1975: Emlyn Williams*, actor-playwright. 1977: John Curry, skater; A. L. Rowse, historian. 1978: Franco Zeffirelli, director; Margaret Thatcher MP; Anna Raeburn, writer-broadcaster; Tennessee Williams, playwright; Sir Robert Helpmann*, dancer-choreographer-actor. 1979: Alec McCowen, actor. 1980: Sir Cecil Beaton, photographer. 1981: Russell Harty, interviewer-writer; Sir Frederick Ashton, choreographer; Sir John Gielgud, actor. 1982: Frankie Howerd*, comedian; John Osborne*, writer; Sir Anton Dolin*, dancer; Carlo Curley, organist (second openly gay castaway). 1983: Sir Peter Pears*, singer; Peter Maxwell Davies, composer; Peter Bull, actor. 1984: John Hurt, actor. 1985: Sir Michael Tippett, composer*. 1986: Elton John, singer-musician-composer. 1987: Johnny Mathis, singer; Kenneth Williams*, comedian; Antony Sher, actor. 1988: Rabbi Lionel Blue; Dame Gwen Ffrangcon-Davies,* actress; Dame Edna Everage, megastar; Stephen Fry, writer-actor. 1989: Boy George, singer; Ned Sherrin, writer; Dirk Bogarde*, actor-writer. 1990: Kaffe Fassett, knitwear designer. 1992: John Schlesinger*, film director; Benny Hill*, comedian (recorded shortly before his death in April). 1993: Ken Livingstone.
* indicates two or more castings away.

Design for Living Noel Coward's seriously flippant comedy about INTER-

IOR DECORATOR Gilda's calamitous attempts to share her love with two men (who love one another) while marrying a third met a shocked reaction in 1933. It remains his most advanced and also his most intimately revealing play. In the 1979 television production (P: Louise Marks; D: Philip Saville) the moment of truth between Otto (Clive Arrindell) and Leo (John Steiner), is omitted. In the 1991 radio version Otto (Alex Jennings), in between brushing his teeth, tells Leo (Michael Kitchen): 'You've set me free from something ... The feeling that I had for you. Very deep ... I imagined it was, but it couldn't have been could it?' Leo replies: 'I said all that to you in Paris', before Otto moves into the bedroom to dress.

On television, their feelings were embodied: the two men had a SHOWER together and later cried on one another's shoulders. Verbally, their love could only be expressed in the past tense and by a third party – Gilda (Rula Lenska): 'Otto and Leo knew each other before ... I knew all about that. I came along and spoilt everything.'

desire A staple in titles and accompanying advertising of mainstream moves (*As You Desire Me; All I Desire; Desire in the Dust; Desire Me; One Desire; Desire Under the Elms*); in the gay sphere: *Desire* (Aust 1980); *Desire* (Can 1981); DESIRE (UK 1989 C/T); *L'Homme de Désir* (Fr); LAW OF DESIRE (Sp 1987 C); *Homosexual Desire in Minnesota* (US 1982 T/C).

Desire (UK 1989 C) The persecution of 'sexual perverts' in Germany and Austria by the NAZIS. The 90-minute film emphasizes the contradictory message preached by the National Socialist: same-sex bonding with copious nudity and body worship mixed with extreme prudishness and rigid sex roles. As with BENT in 1979, when the 60-minute version of *Desire* was shown as part of the 1989 OUT ON TUESDAY series on CHANNEL 4, its maker, Stuart MARSHALL was upbraided in certain quarters for 'exploiting' a tragedy. The (sparse) eyewitness accounts of concentration camp life for homosexuals were dismissed. Where was the proof?

Desperate Hours (US 1990 C) Estranged family (headed by Anthony Hopkins) reunited after being held hostage by an escaped convict (Mickey Rourke) and two confederates. Features a tough agent (Lindsay Crouse) who tries to 'turn' the thug's lawyer (Kelly Lynch) by revealing that she was once in thrall to a violent man. To give this moment a special charge, the director, Michael Cimino asked Lindsay Crouse to take Kelly Lynch's face in her hands and KISS her 'with all the passion and compassion she could manage'. This action was not included in the print as released by the studio; but it may be restored at some future date. Cimino, speaking to John Pym in *Sight and Sound* in 1990, calls it the best scene he's ever directed: 'It's a four-minute scene in one shot; there are no tricks, no cuts, it's pure performance.'
D: Michael Cimino; 105 mins.

The Detective (US 1968) The investigation of the brutal murder of a gay ANTIQUE DEALER uncovers New York's subculture and, finally – after an innocent man has been executed – the perpetrator: a man so imbued with self-hatred that he thought it better to be a murderer than a homosexual.
W: Abby Mann from the novel by Roderick Thorp; P: Aaron Rosenberg; D: Gordon Douglas; 114 mins.

A strange half-responsible, half-exploitative picture of the bad old days of self-oppression and continuous police harassment. The noticeably 'humane' attitude shown by the Frank Sinatra character is in stark contrast to the actor's flip contempt for 'them' in his two private-eye movies of the same period.

The film's gays are frightened, driven creatures herded up from the trucks by the East River where they take their furtive pleasure. The murderer is a superficially respectable married man, Colin McIver (William Windom), who has destroyed what he most hated in himself.

McIver leaves behind a tape recording in which he says that every homosexual can spot others: 'It's in the eyes.' The film doesn't allow the character to continue his train of thought as he does in Thorp's novel: 'It's in the eyes of men who don't mince or weave their hands and I was afraid it was in mine. The thought of turning, involuntarily, into one of those PANSIES sickens me.'

Rebecca **De Winter** The DEAD wife of Maxin in REBECCA (1940 C etc), loved by her maid and housekeeper, Mrs DANVERS: 'She did what she liked. I had care of her as a child ... she lived as she liked ... She had courage, too, all the courage and spunk of a boy. She cared for nothing and for no one.' A similar character, also influencing two women (one 'nice', one 'nasty') beyond the grave, was *The Uninvited* (1944 C) based on the novel *Uneasy Freehold* by Dorothy Macardle.

De Wolfe, Billy [Wiliam Andrew Jones] (1907–74) American actor and dancer; moustached FEMALE IMPERSONATOR. Well known in Britain during 1930s. Served in navy during war. On screen in kempt, soppy roles, eg as Albert the oafish family friend in *Dear Ruth* (1947), *Dear Wife* (1949) and *Dear Brat* (second billed); as Larry, producer and would-be lothario in *My Blue Heaven* (1950); as daffy Mayor Davies in *Billie* (1965); etc. Also performed monologue in semi-drag in *Blue Skies* (1946). Became well established on television after occasional guest roles (*Burke's Law* 'Who Killed the Fat Cat?' 1965); as First Officer Nelson in *The Queen and I* (1969); as ACCOUNTANT Delbert Delroy in *The Debbie Reynolds Show* (1969–70); as Willard Jarvis, Doris's perfectionist neighbour in *The Doris* DAY *Show* (1971–2).

Benjamin **Dexter** 'For a man still on the right side of 50, his passionate interest in EMBROIDERY and his habit of calming a not very tumultuous mind with tatting – a trait beloved by his disciples – certainly to others seems a little affected.' The pen name of Roly Martins, author of potboiler thrillers in Graham Greene's original *The Third Man* and based on E. M. FORSTER. In the 1949 film version, Roly became Holly and he was played, without the embroidery, by Joseph Cotten. When the character of Harry LIME was refashioned for television in the early 1960s, he was given a fussy factotum named Brad(ford) Dexter (Jonathan HARRIS).

Diaghilev, Sergei Pavlovich (1872–1929) Russian ballet impresario who brought together Satie, Massine, COCTEAU, Picasso, Stravinsky, Fokine, Rimsky-Korsakov and NIJINSKY.

Diaghilev as dramatized is usually an all-powerful creator momentarily knocked off his pedestal by the wildly talented Nijinsky. In reality, their pairing enabled works of lasting value to be created and performed. It is mirrored by many, equally traumatic CREATIVE PARTNERSHIPS between director and star, boss and employee. Although he was shaken by his young lover's sudden MARRIAGE and abandoned him to his fate, Diaghilev buried the hatchet and gave Nijinsky friendship and support in later years.

Alan BATES played him in *Nijinsky* (1980 C), Gerard Murphy in *Chinchilla* (1981 R), and Robert STEPHENS in *The False Diaghilev* (1988 R) and in *The God of Dance* (1988 R), a drama-documentary based on diaries, with Rudolf NUREYEV as Nijinsky. Stephens told *Radio Times* (23.1.88): 'I didn't want to play him as overblown and effeminate because if you're too affected the audience won't take you seriously.'

'No ordinary measure of human relations could be applied to so exceptional a man. He was a DIONYSIAN heathen. He loved all earthly things – earthly love, earthly passion, earthly beauty.' (Leonide Massine, *Diaghilev's Achievement in Ballet* 1947 R).

'He knew his power of fascination and liked to exercise it. He did not though often need his arsenal of winsomeness with his subordinates. They willingly slaved for him, hard master as he was'

(Tamara Karsavina, *Reminiscences of Diaghilev* 1952R).

'He shrieked, his voice went up, he was terrifying' (Ninette De Valois, *Homage to Diaghilev* 1964 R).

'He was a curious enigmatic thing – an artist who actually did nothing and his contribution was that rarest of abilities, to spot talent in others and prepare it for the proper exposure on the stages of the world' (*Impresario* 1971 R).

'He fell in love with Nijinsky and so he fell in love with the ballet ... Although Diaghilev was a homosexual he avoided the company of others, except for Cocteau who amused him' (OMNIBUS 'Anton DOLIN' 1982 T).

Diamonds Are Forever (UK 1971 C) James BOND in Las Vegas.
W: Richard Maibaum and Tom Mankiewicz from the novel by Ian Fleming; P: Harry Saltzman and Albert R. Broccoli; D: Guy Hamilton; 120 mins.

Sean Connery pursued by fond but very nasty couple, Wint (Bruce Glover) and Kidd (Putter Smith), whom he respectively *flambées* and drowns, symbolically buggering them in the process. There's also two female wrestlers, Bambi and Thumper (Donna Garratt and Trina Parks), whom he flattens.

Diana/Diane 'Belonging to Divia' (ie the goddess of the moon). The most recent name of Artemis, AMAZON goddess celebrated during the Iron Age. Long regarded as taboo in Britain because it was pagan, Diana Rigg and, especially, Princes Diana have been instrumental in its rehabilitation.

Lady Diana (Eleanor Boardman) in *The Squaw Man* (1931; also Ann Little 1914 & 1918); Lady Diana (Agnes Ayres) in *The Sheik* (1921) wears trousers and carries riding crop: 'What do you want with me?'/'Aren't you woman enough to know?'; Diana O'Sullivan (Louise BROOKS), 'a bobbed and understanding young sophisticate' known as Blackie, a Luna Park ticket-seller in *The Girl from Coney Island* (1926); Lady Diana (Irene Rich), brutal garrison commander's wife in *The*

Desired Woman 1927); Diana (Joan Crawford) charlestons in her undergarments in *Our Dancing Daughters* (1928); Diana Baring (Phyllis Konstam) accused of *Murder!* (1930; name changed to the 'more English' *Mary* for the German-language version which Hitchcock directed simultaneously); Michael Arlen's Iris in his novel *The Green Hat* became Diana in the film version starring Greta GARBO and renamed *A Woman of Affairs* (1929); Diana (Sally Eilers), romantic lead in Norma Shearer's *Let Us Be Gay* (1930); Diana (Lois Moran) in *The Dancers* (1930) is the kind of girl who likes a Rolls, private aeroplane and luxury liner; Lady Diana Bromford (Nora Swinburne) in *Potiphar's Wife/Her Strange Desire* (1931) falsely accuses chauffeur of assault; Diana Barry (Dorothy Mackaill), reformed keptie who falls in love with a clean boy (Joel McCrea), in *Once A Sinner* (1931): 'an ugly part' (*Variety*); Diana Merrow (Kay Francis), elegant secretary in *Strangers in Love* (1932); Diana (Myrna Loy), Americanized daughter of an Egyptian woman and a white man in *The Barbarian* (1933); Diana (Joan Crawford), an English lass in *Today We Live* (1933); Diana Harris (Carole Lombard), rich thrill-seeker in *Manhattan Love Song* (1934); Diana Wyman (Sally O'Neill), heiress who goes to the bad in *The Mother* (1934 C); Diana Carton-Curson (Juliette Compton) in *Behold My Wife* (1935) shoots her extramarital plaything: Diana Steed (Marsha Hunt) in *The Human Comedy* (1943 C).

Post-Second World War social change brought forth a few more homely, even 'common' Dianas: Diana Hopkins (Diana Dors), sexy cousin in *Here Come the Huggets* (1950 C); Diana Johnson (Jennifer Wilson) saddled with a gun-toting deserter lover in DIXON OF DOCK GREEN 'The Roaring Boy' (1958 T): 'I'm nineteen and a half. It feels like a hundred' (a re-read of the character played by Peggy Evans in *The Blue Lamp* 1950 C); Sheila Allen as Diana Looran, one of the mothers of the *Children of the Damned* (1964 C); Di (Pam ST CLE-MENT) in JUST BEFORE MIDNIGHT 'Nubile' (1980 R).

More democratic Dianas in America and Australia included: Diana Sanger (Joan Pringle), wife of Mark in *Ironside* (1974–5 T); Diana (Mariette Hartley), separated wife of architect accused of mistreating his 5-year-old daughter in *Improper Channels* (1979 T); Diana (Laura Dern) in *Mask* (1985 C); Diana Walker (Cheryl Pollack), sister of teenager who has committed suicide in *21 Jump Street* 'Best Years of Your Life' (1988 T); newly widowed Diana (Glynis McNicoll) in *Roses Bloom Twice* (Aust 1977 C); Diana (Star-Shemah Boba-toon), the sister of Booker T. Freeman in *Palmerstown USA* (1980–1 T) which is set in 1934 in a small Southern American town; Diana Bennett (Jo Anderson), heroine of *Beauty and the Beast* (1989–90 T).

In general though, postwar Dianas are still upper-class, lesbians/crypto-lesbians, women involved with bisexual men or English women in America: Dianah Buckley (Courteney Shenan) in *The Guiding Light* (1952 T); Diana Bliss (Diana Churchill), George Cole's soignée sister in *A Life of Bliss* (1953–9 R); Diana (Catherine Boyle), society wife in *The Truth About Women* (1957 C); English gentlewoman with 'foreign' lover, Diana Ashmore (Deborah Kerr) in *The Journey* (1959 C); Diana Monti (Francine Bergé) wearing black leather in *Judex* (1964 C): 'a beautiful but ruthless adventuress and mistress in disguise, who has already insinuated herself into the household as governess'; Diana Scott (Julie Christie), a moth surviving the flame in DARLING (1965 C); *Diana* (Rigg 1973–4 T) exercising English vowels in an American store, as Diana Smythe, fashion co-ordinator; Diana Prince alias *Wonder Woman* (Cathy Lee Gosby 1974 T; Linda Carter 1976–9 T); Diana, teenage temptress (Suzanne Reed) in small American town in *Gibbsville* 'Afternoon Waltz' (1976 T) with girlfriend Ivy; schoolgirl Diana who loves Val in Janet Meyers' *Getting Ready* (1977 C); Oscar-winning British actress Diana Barry (Maggie Smith) trying to stir her gay husband into sexual life in CALIFORNIA SUITE (1978 C); Diana Clark (Diane Cilento) as industrialist's feisty widow who becomes a *Tycoon* (1978 T); Jane's debby secretary Diana (Diana Weston) in AGONY (1979–81 T); Diana Harrington (Angie Dickinson) unwittingly married to a bisexual in *The Suicide's Wife* (1979 T); Diana Graham (Rachel Davies) on trial as much for her lesbian-feminism as for the crime (violence against her lover's husband) she is alleged to have committed in CROWN COURT 'A Friend of the Family (1979 T); Diana McColl (Kim Ulrich) in *As the World Turns* (*c* 1980– T); Diana Selkirk (Susan Yusen) in *Edge Of Night* (*c* 1980– T; Diana Douglas (Claudia Cron), mysterious woman in *Hit and Run* (1982 C); Diana Swanson (Lynn REDGRAVE), teacher, later guidance counsellor in *Teachers Only* (1982–3 T); Diana (Jenny Seagrove) in serial of same name (1983 T) set during the Second World War; executive's wife Diana Webber (Paula Prentiss) trying the simple life in *Packin' It In* (1983 T); Diana (Eleanor Bron), selfish neurotic with gay brother in *Quintet in October* (1985 R); Diana (Penny Nice), child welfare doctor with mounting problems on the home front in DOMESTIC BLISS (1985 T); Diana Fairgate (Claudia Lonow) in *Knots Landing* (1986 T); Diana Ferris (Pauline Letts), put-upon widow locked out of her house in *Porch Song* (1987 R); socialite hedonist Diana Broughton (Greta Scacchi) who helps create *White Mischief* (1987 C); Communist Diana Roth (Barbara Hershey), a white South African activist who neglects children (based on Ruth First), in *A World Apart* (1988 C); Diana Farrington, businessman's wife in *Dallas* (1990–1 T); Diana Avery (Sarah Berger), mistress of Maurice (Albert Finney) in *The Green Man* (1990 T) and unfazed when he suggests a threesome with his wife: 'Can't see what I'd get out of it ... I take it you want me being nice to Joyce and Joyce being nice to me ... I think it's all pretty damn schoolboyish'; Diana (Deidre Rubenstein) in *Watching Over*

Israel (1991 R), sophisticated businesswoman who takes an interest in a drug-addicted Sydney street kid because she reminds her of her daughter: 'You're not a dyke, are you?'; Diana (Stephanie Cole), one of the senior citizens in *Waiting for God* (1991– T); Diana who thinks she was burnt as a witch in *Bergerac* (1991 T); Diana Murphy (Demi Moore), the wife who sleeps with a man for US$1 million in *Indecent Proposal* (1993 C).

Di Ana's Hair Ego – Aids Information Up Front (US 1990 V) Beauty shop becomes the focus of AIDS education thanks to ebullient, sane owner. Movies, videos, oral-sex parties, SAFE-SEX darts, what to do with a CONDOM, safe-sex parties, saran-wrap panties, colouring book, sign language, role-playing, a hanging tree, songs – all over, among and amid the curlers and grips and lotions. Still no State funds, wholly dependent on donations.
P/D: Ellen Spiro; 10 mins.

Di, Di (In Her Collar And Tie) Sung by Max Pilgrim (David Allister), accompanied by the redoubtably man-hating Miss Heather Hopkins (Josie Kidd) in *A Dance to the Music of Time* 'At Lady Molly's' (1980 R). This is the ultimate celebration (via the satirical pen of Anthony Powell) of the exuberantly male-identified DYKE of the 1920s. In OUT ON TUESDAY 'DESIRE' (1989 T) a German woman sings of the charms of Hannelore, who was as dashing (and as adored) as her British counterpart.

diaries *Something Sensational to Read on the Train* (1970 R) in which Nigel Rees examines the diaries of Cecil BEATON, Harold NICOLSON, Virginia WOOLF etc; Roger CASEMENT'S Black Diaries quoted in CRIES FROM CASEMENT AS HIS BONES ARE BROUGHT TO DUBLIN (1973 R); a Welsh schoolgirl talks of her love for her music teacher in *An Apple for the Teacher* (1985 R); Alice James (Morag Hood), sister of Henry James kept a journal which Henry saw after her death – and suppressed – in *Bottled Lightning* (1987 R); *On Unbecoming* (Aust 1991 R) is a diary of a death (September 1987–August 1988) and readings from the journal of Eric Michaels.

'There's nothing about affairs or all that kind of thing in my diaries, because I'm asexual by nature and therefore don't get worked up about people in any way. I've always been frightened of love as a terrible invasion of privacy ... thank goodness that once I get into my abode, I can shut the door and the territory's mine ... mine alone' (Kenneth WIL-LIAMS 1982 R).

'I promise I won't do it again. [But then, when night came] the electric desire of their bodies ... after that, the closed carriages, the sensitive approach of body to body' (Constantine CAVAFY (David MARCH) in A SLIGHT ANGLE 1977 R).

Dick (US 1990) One hundred women on the soundtrack, 1,000 dicks (most of them attached to gay or bisexual men) on the screen.
P/D: Jo Menell; 15 mins.

Advertised by Channel 4 in April 1991, but replaced by *Jo's Dick*, in which the director discussed his film while female comments were heard about objects unseen and unseeable except in the darkness of a locked bedroom: 'It's not the size of the tractor, it's how long he's out in that field ploughing.'

Dickens, Charles (1812–70) English author. As portrayed in *Dickens' Women* (1991 R) he was a man rent and split into a thousand fissures, treating his wife with the utmost contempt and pouring a number of his more unacceptable passions into some of his female characters, as well as into James STEER-FORTH. 'To me, Steerforth has always seemed Dickens' most profound creation. He expresses more than any other character the nature of Dickens' own struggle' (Pamela Hansford Johnson in *The Betrayal of Self in Fiction* 1949 R).

dickhead Term of abuse both in America and the UK, increasing in popularity from the mid-1980s. Sally (Gami Cooper) commented about Vince Withers (Adam Bitsk) in *Meet the Apple-gates* (1991 C): 'I bagged that dickhead after he porked me'; Mike (River Phoe-nix) calls another hustler – dressed in loud finery – a dickhead in MY OWN PRIVATE IDAHO (1991 C); Berwick Kaler played the dim journalist Geoff Diquead in *The New Statesman* (1989 T): 'political correspondent with the *Sunday Sport*' whose interviewing technique is along the lines of 'How was your holiday in Monte Carlo – get your leg over much?' A classic dickhead is Gordon (Chris Barrie) in *The Brittas Empire* (1990– T), a man with limited people-skills.

Dickinson, Emily (1830–86) American poet. Played by Glenda Jackson in *The Representative of the Poem* (1967 R); Julie Harris in *The Belle of Amhurst* (1976 T); Bonnie Hurren in *Letter to the World* (1986 R). Regularly anthologized on radio, eg *Edible Gold* which was an anthology of poetry by Christopher Logue – including 'Tell All the Truth' (1983 R). Steven and Claudia discuss her in terms of their alienation in DYNASTY (1981 T); she appeared as a wraith in THIRTYSOMETHING 'I'M NOBODY! WHO ARE YOU?' (1989 T); and the two men in TOGETHER ALONE (1991 C) discuss her, particularly the line 'hope is a thing with feathers'.

diesel In POLICE WOMAN 'Flowers of Evil' (1974 T) Bill (Earl Holliman) describes a woman as being at home behind the wheel of 'a diesel truck'. *See also* DYKE.

Dietrich, Marlene (1902–92) German-born actress and singer. A ghostly icon who generously employed sexual ambiguity and gender games in many of her films, cabaret and stage performances. Her prickly, stubborn, bigoted personality was well illustrated in the documentary *Marlene* (1984 C/T) and her artistry in *The Marlene Dietrich Show* (1973 T). Dietrich was given a lesbian reading (along with her rival Greta GARBO) in *Meetings of Two Queens* (1991 V). Her only radio work was *Café Istanbul* in the early 1950s, *The Mother* (1964) and DESERT ISLAND DISCS (1965). In THE DAMNED Martin (Helmut Berger) mocks her 'Blue Angel'/Lola Lola image with a growling version of 'Falling In Love Again'. *See also* THE BOYS IN THE BACKROOM; HONEYSUCKLE ROSE; THE MAN'S IN THE NAVY.

The Different Drum (UK 1960 R)
Michael Harris (Keith White) is not playing rugby any more. He wants to spend more time practising on the organ and to be a writer. The other pupils say he's a bit peculiar, start a whispering campaign and let down the tyres of his bike – all because he was the one who scored the goals. His bachelor English teacher, Mr Bell quotes Thoreau: 'Let him step to the music when he hears a different drummer.' Bell warns him of the pain that lies in wait if he doesn't conform: 'You will keep coming across a majority that don't see things the way you do. You don't want to be like me. Non-conformists have a habit of ending up like me.'
W: Frederick Aicken; D: William Glen Doepel; 2.10.60; BBC Home Service; 60 mins.

A Different Story (US 1978 C) A highly successful real estate agent, Stella (Meg Foster) enjoys watching football, basketball and hockey. She's sloppy, she can't cook, she snores and she has recently split from her neurotic girl-friend. She marries a gay guy, Albert (Perry King) to save him from deportation. True love blossoms. Out goes sluttishness, the TV dinners and the women. In comes domesticity, mother-hood ...
W: Henry Olek; P: Alan Belkin; D: Paul Aaron; 108 mins.
The problems of gay lovers from different countries wishing to stay together have never been depicted on screen or radio. The nearest to it was the difficulties experienced by Albert, the illegal Belgian immigrant in *A Different Story*. When his American conductor lover informs on him, he escapes detection and deportation through marriage –

initially confected but which then becomes real.

A Different Way Home (UK 1988 R)
Leslie Latchmore (Bernard Cribbins) lives alone with his memories – of life, loss, love and laughter. 'It's a life he faces with a special kind of courage.' A BACHELOR'S joys and sorrows, laughter and tears. Fine writing and acting.
W: Jimmie Chinn; D: Gerry Jones; BBC Radio 4; 45 mins.

dildos Briefly discussed but not shown in *The Trials of Oz* (1991 T); shown but not discussed in *Lair of the White Worm* (1988 C): high priestess (Amanda Donohoe) advances wearing a massive gold contraption around her waist in the middle of which rises a massive gold phallus, aimed at Catherine Oxenberg who is tied to and writhing at the stake; a subject of curiosity to the brassy step-mother of a lesbian in *In Two Minds* (1987 T): 'You don't mind my asking. I've always wanted to know. Do you use one of them things?'; details of size and texture supplied by a woman in a cock-tail frock on the subway in *The Virgin Machine* (1987 C).

Dionysus The Greek god, whose Roman name was Bacchus, 'stood for deep and dangerous feelings ... comedy and tragedy derived directly from the libations and orgies and processions of men dressed as women. The first theatre was dedicated to his name – in Athens 487 BC' (*Vintage* 'Drinking the God' 1990 T). Played by Pierre Brice in *The Bacchanites* (1960 C); Robert Hardy in *The Bacchae* (1964 R).

diplomats *The Secret Life of Chevalier D'Eon* (1960 C); Daniel O'Herlihy in *The Tamarind Seed* (1974 C); Donald Maclean; Timothy Dalton in *Permission to Kill* (1975 C); Clive Smith (Charles Kay) in *The Spectre* (1983 R); Harold NICOLSON (David Haigh) in PORTRAIT OF A MARRIAGE (1991 T).

dirt/dirty Love–hate relationship with dirt: Lady Macbeth using all the perfumes of Arabia; Joan Crawford washing, washing, washing; dirty queers; dirty little affair; dirt-poor; dirt under the feet ... However, Elvis sold millions of 'Dirty, Dirty Feeling' and *Dirty Dancing* made millions of people very happy. Yet the yuppy BROTHER (Nigel) in A HORSE CALLED GERTRUDE STEIN (1990 R) reacted to the writer's name with the parrot-like 'She was a dirty lesbian!' More honestly, one of the bullies in LAND OF PROMISE (1986 R; set in the 1950s) screams at the young scapegoat: 'I hate you ... hate you ... because your kind's just dirt!' A young woman, who was told she was a dirty little lesbian as a teenager, said on *Talk About Sex* (1992 R) 'I felt dirty.' The father of Myra (Maureen O'BRIEN) said to her in *Remaining Strangers* (1986 R) that she was a 'dirty QUEER'.

disability No self-respecting homosexual will accept the worlds 'disability' and 'handicapped,' indicated TOM ROBINSON on a phone-in to the Archbishop of Canterbury (who had so dubbed homosexuals in 1981, the International Year of Disabled People). (However, Tom was complimentary to the archbishop for answering questions so fully.) Fallon tells Ted in the opening 3-hour episode of DYNASTY (1981 T): 'Steven comes from a world where culls, cripples and homosexuals are taken out behind the barn and slaughtered.'

disabled people/people with disabilities Elizabeth (Dorothea Wieck) tenderly cured of her 'lameness' by young Anna (Hertha Thiele) in *Anna and Elizabeth* (1933 C); Tom Morgan (Anthony Quinn), a gambler who loves the marshall in *Warlock* (1959 C); Paul Millicent in *Boy Meets Girl* 'The Eye of Heaven'; Harry accidentally blinded by his lover in A SUPERSTITION (1977 T); Tom (Michael Maloney), the BALLET DANCER suddenly rendered helpless in *A New Step Every Day* (1980 R); MY OWN PRIVATE IDAHO (1991 T) begins with a dictionary definition of narcolepsy, the chemical condition that makes Mike (River Phoenix) fall asleep indoors and outdoors – which causes problems in his

work as a PROSTITUTE: 'Some hustler, huh?' says his friend and colleague; a ONE-NIGHT STAND ('Your wheelchair or mine?') in OUT 'Double the Trouble, Twice the Fun' (1992 T).

Occasionally disabled homosexuals are to be found on *Link* and other regular programmes for the disabled community; also in OUT 'Gay Games' (wheelchair bound) 'Absolutely Queered' (hearing impaired) and 'We've Been Framed' (speech impediment) – all women (1991 T). On Sydney's *Gay Waves* (R) the warm and witty Tony is hearing impaired. There are probably many others in US and Europe.

See also AIDS; DEAF PEOPLE.

discos Increasingly part of the landscape for gay men and lesbians: SPEAK FOR YOURSELF (1974 T); NOW SHE LAUGHS, NOW SHE CRIES (1975 R); SILENT WING (1984 R).

Drew GRIFFITHS was given unlimited access to the chart hits of the 1970s when he wrote THE ONLY ONE SOUTH OF THE RIVER (1980 T) for Capital Radio. It was able to invest its slim story with Elton JOHN, VILLAGE PEOPLE, Rod Stewart and Boney M. 'Do you realize,' someone shouts above the hubbub on the dance floor during Olivia Newton-John's 'You're The One That I Want', 'that when we're pensioners this will be our nostalgia?' Other music threaded through the story of a gay couple and their pub disco was 'South Of The Border', 'Macho Man', 'Rivers Of Babylon', 'Last Chance For Love', 'Do You Think I'm Sexy', 'YMCA', 'AS TIME GOES BY' and 'Thank You For Being A Friend'.

Disco as a phenomenon in *Discotheque* (25 programmes, 1968 T); KALEIDOSCOPE 'Big Apple Boogie'/'Night Dancing' ('Paul GAMBACCINI investigates the British disco scene ranging from sophisticated plush clubs to the high-street dance floors; talks to disc jockeys, record promoters and dancers' with VILLAGE PEOPLE, Gary London of 'Bang' and others, 1979 R); *Disco's Revenge* (1989 T); *The Rhythm Divine* (1991 T).

diseases 'Being a lesbian was, I thought, a disease. So I got engaged to a very beautiful man' (Iso (Tovah Feldshuh) in *The Women's Room* 1980 T). Her fiancé tried to rape her, during the resistance to which she was nearly killed. She has never been near a man since.

'I fight it ... God knows I fight it. It's like being bloody crucified except you're doing it to yourself. You have to pay for what you are' (Ruby 'Mitch' Mitchell (Paola Dionisetti) in WITHIN THESE WALLS 'Mixer' 1978 T).

See also HOMOPHOBIA; RACISM; SEXUALLY TRANSMITTED DISEASES.

disgusting 'All cultures find some things disgusting, even though those things are potentially very nutritive ... Eskimos like rotted meat, but hate rotted milk. Yet *we* eat cheese. Young children, it seems, find nothing disgusting, and will put anything into their mouths. ... Somehow we learn what is disgusting. Only faeces are revolting to all people (but not young children). Why do we eat rotted milk or fermented wheat pastes?' said Jeremy Cherfas in *The Natural World* 'Why Dogs Don't Like Chilli' (1986 T) which looked at 'human learned taste aversion'. See also THE BIBLE; DIRT; DISEASE.

Diverse Reports 'What a Difference a Gay Makes' (UK 1984 T) A mythbusting exercise about homosexuals.

W/P: Denis LEMON; 5.12.84; Channel 4; 30 mins.

'Have you heard the one about the homosexual milkman? tonight's guest editor Denis Lemon – a founder of GAY-NEWS – tries to see the funny side of his life. But the unfunny thing is that, even though there are homosexual bands in the charts and gay pubs in every town, discrimination – particularly at work – is still commonplace. Most gays are still forced to lead double lives. Denis Lemon argues that part of the answer is for more gay men and lesbians to come out and face the music' (Channel 4 synopsis).

A noble, if doomed, attempt to penetrate the core of the hatred homosexuality engenders, principally by asking questions of patrons of Rugby Working Men's Club. Other interviews, with people like criminologist D. J. West ('There is even a little evidence that HETEROSEXUALS are less able to control themselves'), and playlets on various societal misconceptions and legal penalties were employed to put across a saner vision. To break down eight centuries of teeth gnashing was a very tall order in a film lasting half an hour. It ended with a rather unconvincing 'We don't want a special deal: all we want are our rights'. From those interviewed, there seemed little chance of any misconceptions being questioned. 'If they kept it to themselves there'd be no problem' seemed to be the consensus.

AIDS wasn't an issue at the time; visibility and audibility were. Gays should not be seen *or* heard. No wonder Denis Lemon, attempting an air of burly encouragement, signed off with 'it's up to us gays . . . we've got to confront the prejudice'.

Divine [Glenn Milstead] (1945–88) One of the immensities of gay underground cinema, bounteous TRANSVESTITE star of John WATERS' cult classics *Female Trouble* and *Pink Flamingos* burst fitfully upon the public via plays, disco records and 'respectable' films like *Lust in the Dust* (1985) and *Trouble in Mind* (1985; the nearest he ever came to a straight role as a Sydney Greenstreet figure called Hilly). On television he appeared in *Tales from the Darkside* 'Seymourlama' (1986) as the ambassador from the ancient kingdom of Lo-Poo.

Divine seemed set fair for stardom after the success of *Hairspray*, his reunion with Waters in 1988. He was on a publicity tour for the film when he died of a heart attack in his sleep, aged 42. His last appearance, via satellite, was on Australia's *The Midday Show*. A genuine gay icon, a huge star.

The name came via the Divine Sarah (Bernhardt), the Divine Woman (GARBO as a Bernhardt figure), and, said Divine, *before* the Divine Miss M[idler].

Dixon of Dock Green: Some Stories of a London Policeman (UK 1955–76 T) Set in the East End, Ted WILLIS drew upon a rich fount of dramatic situations and juicy eccentrics, especially the implicitly gay Duffy CLAYTON (Harold SCOTT), patrolled by chummy widower George Dixon (Jack Warner) and, from 1956 to 1961, by crisp, intelligent and unmarried Sergeant Grace MILLARD (Moria MANNION).

A Saturday night fixture, it was originally regarded as the acme of realism. As a serious, honest study of policing, some of its thunder was stolen by Z CARS, but Dixon's fans loved the idea of the boys in blue catching the wrongdoers and dispensing sage advice. Time had crusted over Dixon but the public preferred not to notice. The image of the London bobby is still that of gentle George who bids us a good New Year, '... and be careful on the roads, and mind out for those kids, regular little harum scarums. Whatever the trouble, it usually begins at home. Too much attention, perhaps, ... or too little.'

(The series was the focus of one of the Open University's *Arts Review* programmes: 'Dixon of Dock Green – Myth or Reality?' 1987 T.)

Do As I Say (UK 1977 T) The aftermath of a rape which evolves into a frightening, offputting picture of the FEMINIST unbound.

W: Charles Wood; P: Graeme McDonald; D: Barry Davis; 25.1.77; BBC1; 75 mins.

Hilary (Kate Nelligan), who once worked on a kibbutz, is now doing informal field research among the British natives: 'I can only get to understand this upper-middle-class ghetto by being in it'. Only hours after Daphne (Angela Down) has been attacked in her own home, this pushy American tries to arouse her sexually. 'Daphne I am *not* some kind of BULL DYKE, believe me.' This earns her a blunt response: 'Oh, piss off. Put your bra on properly and piss off, please.' Not to be put off, Hilary embarks upon Rowena (Gerry Cowper). 'Do you MASTURBATE?' 'None of your

business.' 'You should learn about your body. Until you know about your body and the pleasures you can give yourself.'

The play could be seen as an unusually realistic presentation of what, for many women, is a daily potential threat: intrusion into their homes and into their bodies and minds. Wood muddies the waters considerably by introducing a female menace, in the person of this insensitive Yank sociologist. Women beware women!

The Doctor (Dr Who) Time-travelling leading character from the fourth dimension in the BBC's science fiction fantasy serials *Dr Who* (1963–) – played by older actors, William Hartnell and (in two 1960s films) Peter Cushing; middle-aged actors, Jon Pertwee and Patrick Troughton; and young actors Tom Baker, Peter Davison, Colin Baker and Sylvester McCoy. Despite the Doctor's remarkable transformational powers there has not yet been a black, Asian or female manifestation.

In one of the first episodes, the Time Lord (Hartnell) gives the earthlings a thumbnail sketch of himself and his grand-daughter: 'We are not of this race. We are not of this earth. We are not of your time. We are wandering in the fourth dimension of space and time.' His successor (Troughton) played him as a Chaplinesque figure, 'a cosmic hobo', while Pertwee covered up his super-intelligence with dither and lots of comic business. Best of all was Tom Baker's wild-eyed and WILDEAN creation (1974–82): 'an anti-establishment figure, dangerous, argumentative, an exile' (to use the actor's words).

Mark Ball described this seminal television fantastic as follows: 'Part MERLIN, part jester and part reasoning scientist and part anarchic nomad, he has evolved from near villain into an unalloyed hero, embodying everything from stern omniscience to child-like helplessness' (*Listener*, 27.10.88).

Doctor, Doctor (US 1989–90 T) Theatre director Richard 'Dick' Stratford (Tony Carreiro) has a warm relationship with his medico BROTHER Mike (Matt Frewer), observing the latter's mixed-up love life with amused detachment. He himself has not had a sexual relationship since he split with Larry two years ago.

Cr: Norman Steinberg; W/D: David Frankel and others; CBS; 30 mins.

Nice, easy-going, unremarkable fare with the gay brother, a pleasant and respectable but unidimensional figure who is a passenger in, rather than a driver of, most of the plots.

In the episode 'Accentuate the Positive' one of Dick's colleagues, Deirdre, refuses to treat a patient who is HIV positive. She later reveals that she has heard from her estranged husband, who is BISEXUAL, that he is sero-positive. Mike, who has to take the test because he slept with Deirdre on one occasion, asks Dick how he copes: 'Doesn't it bother you having this spectre, this cloud, this Margaret Hamilton thing hanging over you?' Dick says that he has lost a lot of friends and will only now have sex with someone he wants to settle down with – after having a test.

Doctor Jo (UK 1958 T) The prodigal daughter (Margaret Johnston) returns from the Pasteur Institute in Dakar, after trying to vanquish mosquitoes and tsetse flies. Her sister Clare (Ane Castle) never suffered from wanderlust, but is envious of Jo all the same: 'I'm just nobody. Just a housewife ... It's all very well for some women. They've got no obligations, no loyalties.' Clare's husband once wanted to marry Jo, and still loves her. Their son seems to be being unduly influenced by this intelligent, independent 'career woman', with no evident emotional ties. The ground is set for conflict.

W: Joan Morgan from her stage play; D: John Frankau; Associated-Rediffusion; 5.9.58; 60 mins. There was a radio production with Freda Jackson in the title role, 16.9.61.

'It poses the dilemma of such a person when she has at some time in her life to come to grips with her own basic needs and individualism' (Joan Morgan, *TV*

Times). Engrossing, gripping study of sibling tangles and how they transform a perfectly logical, hard-working woman into almost a demon, a threat to hearth and home, and – so Clare believes – to the moral welfare of her young son. *Doctor Jo* can certainly be read as a 'homosexual' play: Jo as free-wheeling lesbian, Clare as heterosexual stick-in-the-mud, and the son Jim (Nicholas Chagrin) as nascent gay. Interesting that Freda Jackson, famous for her coarse, harpy roles, should be cast as Jo on radio while the more subtly commanding Margaret Johnston should embody her on television.

Doctor Martens (10 × 10 UK 1989 T) Tough working boots that 'break the barriers of class, status and sex'. Long worn by gay men, especially those 'not wanting to be seen as effeminate' and 'part of the British CLONE look'. Other comments on this, to some, rough-and-ready-footwear: 'I would say there is no one that I know on the gay scene who hasn't at least got a pair of Doc Martens', 'It's the image: leather jacket, denim jacket, jeans and Doc Martens'. 'If you want a nice, weak, effeminate man, wear Doc Martens and he'll love you.'

doctors There are gay doctors, but most do the decent thing and keep quiet about it. Dr Saunders in Somerset MAUGHAM'S *The Narrow Corner* (Garard Green 1989 R etc); Stephen LYNN (Valentine DYALL) in BRIEF ENCOUNTER (1946 C) doing his bit for heterosexuality by lending a friend his car and flat, but withdrawing the key when moral outrage (or is it jealousy?) gets the better of him; Dr Brock (Everett Sloane), a human dynamo who smashes through apathy and despair in a hospital for paraplegics in *The Men* (1950 C)), wears suspiciously ornate ties and behaves with a born outsider's reckless bravado.

It is as ROLE-MODELS that doctors were employed by the more radical mainstream writers and producers: vulnerable, intelligent, disciplined, caring Daniel Hirsch (Peter FINCH) in SUNDAY,

BLOODY SUNDAY (1971 C); in AGONY (1979–81 T) Rob (Jeremy Bulloch) was a houseman at a London hospital, and it is his appointment as registrar in the last series that tips the scales against his unemployed, chronically depressed lover Michael (Peter Denyer), who commits SUICIDE; Zack Elliot (Micahel Ontkean) was the slicked-up American version of a young, successful GP whose emotional landscape is transformed by a male patient in MAKING LOVE (1982 C); warm-hearted venereologist Eric Linden (Chris Haywood) in THE CLINIC (1982 C)'; JEWISH Dr Fadigati (Philippe Noiret) shunned and derided for loving a young man and refusing to conceal his feelings in *The Gold-Rimmed Spectacles* (1988 C); Laurie (Tony Sheldon) who, with his lover, takes his dead mum to a football cup final in *Screamers* (Aust 1992 R); Matthew Modine as the doctor who discovers he is HIV positive in AND THE BAND PLAYED ON (1993 C/T). All of these men are leading useful, solid working lives; each of them commands respect.

The pillar of the community role was affectionately guyed in DONA HERLINDA AND HER SON (1986 C). Rudolfo (Marco Antonio Trevino) is stolid and unimaginative, but his mum is proud of him because he's a physician. The only problem is that he prefers men to women and Mexican society demands that he marry.

At the other end of the stethoscope is the seedy medico: Dr Rackett (Alfred Bell) finding comfort from sexual loneliness in the whisky bottle (*The Boy in the Bush* 1983 T); real-life Dr John Polidori (portrayed as the frothing FOP and near-imbecile by Colin Spall) whose neurotic passion for BYRON sparks off all manner of psychic pyrotechnics in *Gothic* (1986 C): 'I think of myself as a general physician but I'm interested in the processes of the mind – sleepwalking and nightmares' – (Polidori wrote the novel *The Vampyre*, and was also central to the events in *Haunted Summer* 1988 C as played by Alex Winter; glamorous, drug-dealing society Doctor Woodward (Tom Chadbon) in *Floodtide* (1987 T);

osteopath Mr Cordle (Geoffrey Bayldon) in *Madame Sousatzka* (1988 C); the BLACKMAILED Richard Thorne (Kenneth Gilbert) in THE GENTLE TOUCH 'Blade' (1980 T) – he is 'permanently overworked, overtired, run-down, watching my weight, blood pressure or some damn thing' and being financially squeezed because of his affair with a former GUARDSMAN. And there is Dr Simon Radley (Felix Nobis). Although young, good-looking and popular, he ends up dead after being QUEER-BASHED in G.P. 'Tests of Conscience' (1992 T). His sex addiction, having made him act irresponsibly towards his work, leads him into personal jeopardy, too.

Most of these doctors work as general practitioners, not as members of hospital medical teams. As a conversation runs between two male doctors in *Trapper John* 'Straight and Narrow':

'Do you know of any gays on our staff? It's too difficult to tell. It's the person you least expect.'
'A gay doctor or nurse! Nonsense.'

doctors, women Sophia Jex-Blake (Sara Kestelman) tackled *The Walls of Jericho* (the male fastness that was the medical profession in the 19th century; 1981 T) and breached them. By the 1930s women practitioners couldn't be ignored, even by mainstream Hollywood: Kay Francis was *Mary Stevens MD* (1933 C) and there were women psychiatrists from the 1940s onwards in films like *Spellbound*.

Lesbian doctors are noticeable by their absence in dramas or comedies: almost alone was Diana (Penny Nice), a harassed paediatrician coping with lover, lover's daughter and an ever-expanding household of women in DOMESTIC BLISS (1985 T), while in American one caused trouble for Dr Annie Cavanero (Cynthia Sikes) in ST ELSEWHERE 'Girls Just Want to Have Fun' (1985 T).

See also NURSES; PSYCHIATRISTS.

doctors' patients Few gay patients come to TV and radio doctors with any complaint outside of HIV/AIDS and their Homosexual Problem: terminally ill Ash

(Clive Swift) making cow eyes at a teenager on his ward in *The National Health* (1973 C); *Marcus Welby MD* (1973 T) soothed a sexually psychosomatic closeted gay diabetic in 'The Other Martin Loring'; the madcap M*A*S*H medics in Korea had just one gay soldier (Richard Ely) to look after in 'George' (1974 T); a doctor falling for a patient (Harry Hamlin) in MAKING LOVE (1982 C); a victim of QUEERBASHING (himself a doctor) in G.P. 'Tests of Conscience' (1992 T) and, in the same series, two women wanting help with AID in, 'More Than Friends' (1991 T). Now, with AIDS, there is more gay traffic through TV surgeries. In 1993 CASUALTY had its first lesbian patient in 'The Ties That Bind'.

Dog Day Afternoon (US 1975 C) Sonny Wortzik (Dustin Hoffman) engineers a bank robbery that goes badly wrong in order to pay for a SEX CHANGE operation for his lover/'wife'.
W: Frank Pierson; P: Martin Bregman and Martin Elfand; D: Sidney Lumet; 130 mins.
A Vietnam veteran, living on welfare with his (female) wife and two kids. 'I had a plan, I had a plan ... I know a lot about a lot of things.' He's the Walter Mitty in us all. One who nearly does get the boy/girl of his dreams, flying to Algeria and freedom: 'Everybody's giving me shit. Everybody wants money. You wanted money for the operation and I got you money.'
The wider audience's first glimpse of the new anger and energy that was GAY LIBERATION. TRANSVESTITES and bearded men, shot in freak-show style waving banners and offering solidarity with the bungling bank robber: 'Sonny all the way.' The film also, quite wittily, indicates that all was not entirely sweetness and light within the various parties, who disagree sharply (on a news broadcast) as to the merits of Sonny's 'marriage' to Leon (Chris Sarandon).
(Holly WOODLAWN was to play Leon until 'they got all freaked out. ... Al Pacino was worried about his image and they decided that they didn't want any

real homosexuality in the script' *Gay News* 135, 1978.)

dog-owners One of the objections to Pete and Trevor living TOGETHER (1980 T) in Rutherford Court was that 'you'll have every NANCY BOY within miles running in and out wearing velvet trousers and walking poodles'.
The marriage of poof and poodle has been the most enduring in the canine world. EMORY (Cliff Gorman) had Chi-Chi in THE BOYS IN THE BAND (1970 C), which allows Michael (Kenneth Nelson) to observe that 'if one is of the male gender, a poodle is the insignia of one's deviation'.
Derek (Bryan Pringle) in *Thrills Galore* (1972 T) leads a poodle clad in a sheepskin jacket into the pub. Army chef Lionel Jenner (Roy Kinnear) is barred from the army camp kitchen after the men complain about the presence there of his poodle, in *Get Some In* (1976 T). Jack De Leon, cruising the park with his shocking pink poodle in *The Choirboys* (1977 C) discovers a bare-arsed man tied to a tree; he tells the dog that this is his 'maddest, most salacious fantasy come true'. Doubly nauseating was the consuming passion of theatre critic Miles Merridew (Robert Morley) for his 'children', two primped toy poodles. In the modern replay of Shakespeare's *Titus Andronicus*, *Theatre of Blood* (1973 C) the bloated booby's babes are served up to him in a pie.
Clement and Peter in ALL FOR LOVE 'Combat' (1982 T) had their heart set on a spaniel. Then they saw Lorna. It was love and child substitution at first sight. The two men lapse into a mixture of nursery and veterinary science whenever they talk about or to their black poodle:

'Time for din-dins.'
'Not too much ... she's on a strict diet. We take her onto the heath. It's a bit of a trek, but she does love it so.'

The breakthrough came with Rowley, Angie and Den's polite poodle in EAST-ENDERS (1986-9). Macho Den (Leslie Grantham), initially under sufferance, had to take him for walks around Albert Square. No baby talk, just unspoken respect, man to dog, dog to man. (Den and Angie should have had an Alsatian but, as no suitable animal could be found, an apricot standard poodle was substituted.)

Ageing gangster Lou (Burt Lancaster) has a shampooed and curled poodle in *Atlantic City* (1980 C); faded society ARCHITECT Miles Cooper (David Cameron) spoils his Cassandra ('Cassie') with Brie, adding so much weight that he doesn't realize she's pregnant in *Chances* 'Bite the Golden Bullet' (1991 T); serial killer D. W. Moffett has one white, one black French poodle on his San Francisco-berthed yacht in *Midnight Caller* (1990 T).

Other pooches: the sleek Afghan who accompanied the bracelet-throwing gentleman in *Pardon Mon Affaire* (1977 C). The prattling friend of Leslie, Aubrey (David Sterne) in YOU'RE NOT WATCHING ME, MUMMY (1980 T) has a sealyham terrier: 'It's the most divine little dog ... I would have brought him, but he's been away from his mummy for a week, so he's still a bit miz. He just sits with me in the shop all day. You'll love him ... white all over.'

The therapeutic role of a dog was crucial to old Tom Falconer (Maurice Denham) in *The Gate of Eden* (1980 T). Thrown out of his teaching job years before by a 'scandal', he once had a bull terrier. At the insistence of a teenage boy, Tom finally allows some affection back into his life in the form this time of a spaniel, Blake: 'It's absurd, someone of may age getting a dog, but it will be good exercise.'

The mongrel Murphy fulfils a vital emotional role for taciturn, ALCOHOLIC Nick Fawley (Kenneth Cranham) in *The Bell* (1982 T). For Victor D'Amato (John Glover) in AN EARLY FROST (1985 T) Spike is symbolic of society's indifference and of his own desperate, isolated situation: 'I may never have known how to keep a man, but I sure know how to keep a dog.' Victor found him outside a New York LEATHER BAR, the Spike one night. He took him home and straight-

way put him on a diet of 'veal and *crème brûlée*'. Before Victor dies, he bequeaths Spike's collar to the starchy head nurse: 'She'll probably look better in it than Spike ever did.'

The closest relationship yet recorded between gay man and his dog must surely be that of Joe ACKERLEY and his Alsatian Queenie in WE THINK THE WORLD OF YOU (1980 T; 1988 C). She originally belonged to a lover whose wife became jealous, not of Joe but of the dog. Says Joe (Benjamin WHITROW) in the 1980 version: 'She offered me [15 years of] single-hearted, uncomplicated mutual devotion.' There was much upset when the programme was shown. All because of a scene in which Joe and Johnny lay in bed with Queenie between them like a hot dog. It was also intimated in Paul BAILEY's script that the owner may have given the dog sexual stimulation.

dog-owners (lesbian)/doggy dykes

They have long been staples of country house thrillers for seven decades. Dogs go very well with the tweeds and the brogues, not to mention those commanding voices. Sometimes lesbian characters are found in the canine business. Hilary (Norma West) has a run-down boarding kennels and an equally delapidated lover, the dying Connie (Beryl REID) in *Smiley's People* (1983 T). Over in AMBRIDGE Mrs Marjorie Antrobus (Margot Boyd) moved into Nightingale Farm in 1985 and turned it into a haven for feminism: Portia, Bettina, Christina and other breeding Afghans.

In *In Two Minds* (1987 T) George KIRRIN has Timmy, and the young woman (Ilona Gregory) has Chico, a white terrier with a black splotch over the right eye – until he is mysteriously poisoned.

The toy fox terrier (K. D. for 'Killer Dog') sat by the side of Martina NAVRATILOVA throughout an hour of questioning on DONAHUE (1991 T).

See also CAT-OWNERS.

La Dolce Vita [The Sweet Life] (It 1960 C) DECADENCE in modern Rome, movie stars, ARISTOCRATS and hangers-

on, watched in fascinated disgust by a journalist (Marcello Mastroianni).
W: Federico Fellini, Ennio Flaiano and Tullio Pinelli; D: Federico Fellini; 180 mins.

A number of gay men – and one lesbian ARTIST (Lisa) – are participants in the climactic orgy. Marcello snarls at one, a film director played by Jacques Sernas: 'You! Half impotent as a man and as an artist.' In addition, he insinuates that Lisa paints 'just so she can make out with her female models'.

A female participant in the frolic cannot believe it when Jacques Sernas says he's never been to bed with a female. ('At least I don't remember'). She is so shocked that she asks another guest (a blondine plucked chicken) and receives the same negative response: 'Never? Never? Never?' she screams. He smiles.

A resolutely drear and unremitting piece of cinema, gorgeously set and with a few eye-catching set pieces. (Plans are afoot for Fellini to remake *La Dolce Vita* as a portrait of café society in 1993.)
See also BY THE YEAR 2000 . . .

Dolin, Anton [Patrick Healey-Kay] (1904–83) Anglo-Irish dancer, a member of DIAGHILEV'S Russian Ballet from 1923 and later of Royal Ballet. A big box-office draw during the 1930s and 1940s, he was due to play the lead in the comedy-thriller *A Bullet in the Ballet* for Ealing in 1941, but the project was cancelled because of wartime economies. (He had appeared on screen with Anna Ludmilla in the Arabian Nights sequence of *Alf's Button* (1930); and with Lydia Lopokova and George Balanchine in the Russian Ballet in *Dark Red Roses* (1930 C). Fifty years later he had a memorable speech or two as the ballet master in NIJINSKY (1980).

Appeared on television from the late 1930s in dancing roles and as himself, mainly on programmes about Diaghilev, eg OMNIBUS (1967). He was profiled on *Omnibus* (1982), coming across as an exceedingly vain and arrogant man. He was castaway on DESERT ISLAND DISCS (twice) and was a contributor to *Noel:*

The Life and Times of Sir Noel COWARD (1976 R).

dolls In the television version of Tomi De Paola's OLIVER BUTTON IS A SISSY (Aust 1984 T), the eponymous little boy no longer whiles away his time with paper dolls. Neither does he dress up in various extravagant attires. On the screen he togs up as much more acceptably boyish characters like an astronaut. His SISSYDOM is mainly confined to his love of DANCING.

To parade Lorenz HART'S real problem – without incurring the wrath of the censors – was impossible, so the makers of WORDS AND MUSIC (1948 C) filled his family living-room with dolls to indicate the extreme femininity which he was surrounded and strangled by.

The one other heretic, apart from BOY GEORGE whose fans made dolls in his image as presents during his 1982–4 heydays), was Willmouse (Richard Williams), the sweet-natured little brother of Joss (Susannah YORK) in *The Greengage Summer/Loss of Innocence* (1961 C), who spends much of his time absorbed in his 'dressage', namely designing gorgeous frocks for his dolls, Miss Dawn and Dolores.

Domestic Bliss (UK 1985 T) In the midst of chaos, Emma (Mandy More), a mother who works from home, and Diana (Penny Nice), a child welfare DOCTOR, attempt to find time and space to discuss their own problems.
W: Gillian Slovo; P: Newsreel Collective; D: Joy Chamberlain; 5.1.85; Channel 4; 55 mins.

Lesbian lovers, their children, former husbands and neighbours. The first attempt to be bright, fresh and funny about such a household on British television. Of limited impact; simply too timid and correct.

Doña Herlinda and Her Son (Mexico 1985 C) Rudolfo (Marco Antonio Trevino) is a successful (but boring) doctor in his thirties who lives with his mother and needs to be married. The problem is that he loves Ramon, known as Moncho (Arturo Meza). Mother (Guadalupe Del Toro) knows best (and Moncho is every mother's dream) and comes up with the solution. As the credits roll, Doña Herlinda sits at the christening of her grandson with son, daughter-in-law and son's lover amicably in attendance. W/D: Jaime Humberto Hermosillo; based on a story by Jaime Lopez Paez; P: Barbachano Ponce; 90 mins.

Mexico's first gay film about a wise mother who knows her own child. It blithely proves that sexual orientation, though a large problem, is not an insuperable obstacle to a life of respectability and harmony.

Donahue (US 1967– T) At least 16 programmes on cross-dressing and TRANSSEXUALISM between 1990 and 1992, plus a gay WEDDING on camera (May 1989); gay and lesbian senior citizens; JEWISH couples; arrests for gay sex in a park in Adrian, near Toledo, Ohio; lesbian transsexuals; femiphobes; gay men meeting their high-school sweethearts (female); male STRIPPERS ... they're all grist to the Donahue mill, one that has kept on grinding – and sending out sparks – for over a quarter of a century.

One of his more worthwhile shows was 'Gay Seniors' (1989). For the first time in his 22-year TV career, he was faced with an 85-year-old born-again sexual person: Buffy Dunker, who has 3 children, 19 grandchildren and 19 great grandchildren, and who is now flourishing non-monogamously with a younger woman, a softball pitcher. Other guests on the show, neither pitiable nor indomitable, were Ruby Jester, William E. Wynkoop (a retired TEACHER), Roy Strickland, Gene Harlewood and his lover Bruhs Mero (who has Alzheimer's Disease), Bob Slight and Richard Levine. However, Phil couldn't get over Buffy, and stuck with her a great deal of the time: 'Let's get this straight, Buffy, you fell in love with a *man* at 50. And you fell in love with a *woman* when you were 72?'

Cracks in Phil's liberalism become apparent when he bantered with a man in the audience who had voiced his fears about his girlfriend thinking him too soft: 'I'll ask you to be honest here – you don't have to answer any of these questions ... Maybe she'll think you, you know what I mean ... with the LIMP WRIST ... so the way you prove you're *not* ... hey, hey ... right?' I've noticed *my* wrist on some of these shows.' Buffy objected to the limp-wristed imagery that the supposedly anti-homophobic Phil was pantomiming: 'I don't like that one ... the sooner we are able to talk about this without fear, the better.' To further emphasize that there was a long way to go before the pink and lavender millenium, a woman phoned in to express her contempt: 'I think this is a hilarious show. This is a *comedy* ... I think the older you are, the worse it gets. What could they possibly *do* with each other?'

Donahue continued his interest in this area the same year with: 'Who becomes gay – and why? Are there contributing factors or are you born that way? Donahue takes an in-depth look at the origins of homosexuality.' Two years on it was 'Born Gay, Become Gay or Made Gay?'

In 'Boy Scouts vs Girls, Atheists and Homosexuals' (1991) two of his guests were Rob Schwitz and Tim Currans, SCOUTS who had been thrown out because of their honesty. They were not 'morally straight' or 'clean'. Both young men were able to boast distinguished achievements within the American scout movement. Donahue was hyperactive with his guests (the two gay ones being exemplary citizens, handsome, intelligent, every father's dream etc) and, as he is wont to do, mentioned HOMOPHOBIA without once defining or putting it into context.

Phil Donahue, for all his joshing, hyperbole and circus-style ring-mastering, has opened up homosexuality far and wide, creating some kind of forum for issues involving PAEDOPHILIA (as distinct from homosexuality), marriage and equal rights in employment. He is learning, and so is America.

Donald Friend: Australian Prodigal
(Aust 1990 C/T) A sparkling but evasive portrait of the pagan artist whose life was packed 'with amazing adventures' and 'full of good gorgeous-looking things'. Part of the King's Cross BO-HEMIAN set in Sydney during the 1930s (living with Peter FINCH), he became 'Lord Devil' in Bali where he remained for many years. The film looks briefly at his 30-year relationship with Arttilio, who got married.
W/P/D: Don Bennetts; c80 mins.

Two erotic images only: in the last minute of credits a photograph taken in Marseilles of a willowy blond youth seemingly trying to escape the camera lens; and three nude studies of another blond – 'The mango and the banana don't give nearly as much trouble as those lovely young nudes ... when you've finished painting them, you eat them.'

dong/dongler Presumably a euphemism for the penis. When BLOODNOK discovers Eccles in his Paris hotel in 'The Case of the Missing Room' (1954 R) in THE GOON SHOW, he declares: 'Dip me dongler and lower me ganjes ... you neolithic naughty boy you!' In 'The House of Teeth' (1956 R) there's a Dr Longdongler (Valentine DYALL as a sort of Baron Frankenstein) stealing teeth, directly out of people's mouths. The following year, Bloodnok exclaims 'Light my crud, flatten my dongler!' to Neddie Seagoon in 'The Mummified Priest' (1957).

Don Juan Song. A sliver of Joan Armatrading is played over photographs of movie-star Don Juans and their (female) conquests in *In Pursuit of Don Juan* (1988 T; 'One of the great archetypes ... an astonishingly promiscuous life') – although the song isn't necessarily sung by a woman to a man.

don't call me 'girlie' Radical statement by Shirley Ann Richards to smart-ass male in DAD AND DAVE COME TO TOWN (1938 C). Same idea in *Lured* (1946 C) when Lucille Ball's boss gives her this

line (but she bites her tongue and doesn't respond). Millie (Hope Lange), trying to fix her racing Maserati in *Love Is a Ball* (1962 C), asks Glenn Ford not to call her 'honey'; she pointedly returns the endearment in a later scene. When a wolf calls Abby Ewing (Donna Mills) 'cookie' in a 1984 episode of *Knots Landing* (T), she expresses her displeasure. (The actress had to plead with the producers to allow any sort of retort, *Radio Times*, 19.9.87.)

Meanwhile, back in Australia, Steve Liebmann didn't call his morning-show co-presenter Elizabeth (Liz) Hayes 'girlie' when they went to the northern New South Wales town of Orange on the *Today Express* (15.9.91): Instead he jokingly threatened to push her under a train if she wasn't a 'good girl'. Liz smiled and smiled.

Don't Call Me Girlie was the title of a 1986 documentary on the representation of women in Australian films.

don't do it, Di! Lesbian crowd members briefly encountered by TV and radio crews in the Mall , with banner, during run-up to the London wedding of the Prince of Wales and Lady Diana Spencer in July 1981. Exactly ten years later, the pair were on a second honeymoon, reportedly to 'save' the marriage. And in 1992 the pair embarked upon a second second honeymoon, before announcing a separation.

don't frighten the horses Mrs Patrick Campbell's comment on homosexuality ('I don't mind what they do as long as they don't do it in the streets and frighten the horses'), misattributed to Oscar WILDE by Harvey (Peter John) in *That Beryl Marston ...!* 'Noel-oh-Hell' (1981 T). Used in various contexts, eg actress–playwright Margaret Williams (widow of actor Hugh) told the *Sydney Morning Herald* (28.9.91) that, at the age of 77, she took longer to get ready in the morning because she didn't want to frighten the horses.

don't knock it till you've tried it Adrian Love advises a gay man, who tries to point out a few problems associated with heterosexuality in a 1980 phone-in, not to knock 'it' until he's tried 'it'. The phrase had provided the title of a *Naked City* episode in 1963.

Don't Miss Wax (UK 1987 T) How do you find a man (who is heterosexual and not 'chasing a 15-year-old bimbo')? In which Miriam MARGOLYES (as herself) goes on a blind date (with a man) and is asked about sexual attraction (for men); and Quentin CRISP (as himself) reveals the long suppressed fact that he lived a 'quasi-heterosexual life', role-modelling on women 'who said no' and, therefore, leading a no-go sex life. Adding to the mirth is Dr Glenn Wilson, dropping some pearls about hormonal changes late in pregnancy leading to homosexuality, and bringing in some white mice to show normal sexual behaviour. The musical spot has Swing Out Sister watching and listening to a big band version (sans words) of 'Break Out', and the show ends with Quentin Crisp sitting next to a blow-up man. The director was a Mr Ed Bye.

don't say 'cheese', say 'lesbian'! A larky usage, which didn't find wide public favour, by Cecil BEATON, posing in the park for David Bailey in *Beaton by Bailey* (1971 T). Instead of saying 'cheese', Beaton preferred a sibilant 'lesbian' to impart the required sickly smile. Hackney Central Library in London paid belated tribute to Mr Beaton's wheeze with a 1988 exhibition of photographs rejoicing in the title 'Don't Say "Cheese", Say "Lesbian"'.

don't tell your father 'Don't tell him. Of course you can lie.' In WORDS OF ONE SYLLABLE (Aust 1991 R) the first thing Robert's mother (Lynette Curran) asks him to do after he has told her he's gay is not to tell Dad/Frank (Max Phipps). Of course when Dad finds out, he rounds on the young man (Steven Vidler) and accuses him of causing his mother pain.

The Doors (US 1991 C) 'The Lizard King', the beautiful young man who ended up bloated and dead, becoming a neighbour of STEIN, WILDE, Balzac and Piaf in the Père Lachaise cemetery in Paris.
D: Oliver Stone; 135 mins.

Jim Morrison is made fit for teenage consumption in this loud, sanitized chronicle of his rise and fall. He becomes a fierce heterosexual, prey to drugs, alcohol and the grisly clutches of Andy WARHOL (Crispin Glover) and his freaky circus. Superficial treatment is given to Morrison's women as well as to the wilder side of his sexuality (a black HAIRDRESSER flaps by).

Dorian Name invented as man's first name by Oscar WILDE in *The Picture of Dorian Gray*: Hurd HATFIELD in the 1945 film; David PEEL on radio in 1948; Helmut Berger in the film of 1970; Peter Firth in the 1976 TV production, beauty of form masking ugliness of soul; Arthur Dorian (James Griffith), sleazy beachcomber ('I deplore idle gossip') in PERRY MASON 'The Case of the Negligent Nymph' (1957 T); Dorian (Peter Whitman), a limp mortician in *When Did You Last See Your Father?* (1979 R); Dorian (Michael Sheard) in *The Traitor* (1983 T).
Dorian Gray was also an Italian film actress (*Il Grido* 1957 etc), and a male pop singer who surfaced briefly in 1968 (*The Joe Loss Show* R etc). Lesley Joseph's character is Dorien in *Birds of a Feather* (1990– T).

Dorothy Dorothea/Dorothy derives from the Greek 'god's gift', but it tended to be used for wild gals: Dorothy Haley (Sally Eilers) who sleeps with her boyfriend in *Bad Girl* (1931 C); Lorelei's friend in GENTLEMEN PREFER BLONDES. Even after the advent of Dorothy Gale from Kansas in 1939, it mixes rough female characters in with the smooth.
  US: pregnant Dorothy Carlsson who is pushed off the roof in *A Kiss Before Dying* (Joanne Woodward 1955; Sean Young 1991 C); Dorothy Lyons (Arlene Dahl), shameless playgirl in *Slightly Scarlet* (1956 C); Dorothy (Maureen Arthur), the receptionist in *Holiday Lodge* (1961 T); wife and mother Dorothy Baxter (Whitney Blake) in *Hazel*

(1961–5 T); war bride Dorothy (Jennifer O'Neill) in *Summer of 42* (1971 C); Dorothy (Jane Alexander) in *Precinct 45: Los Angeles Police/The New Centurions* 1972 C); Dorothy, gangster's girlfriend involved in female armed robbery in POLICE WOMAN 'The Banker's Hours' (1973 T); villainess Dorothy (Tricia O'Neill) who uses a little boy as a shield in 1982 *Hart to Hart* episode; Dustin Hoffman's female persona, a TV soap actress, in *Tootsie* (1982 C); Dorothy Zbornak (Bea Arthur), the tough, good-hearted, most assertive of THE GOLDEN GIRLS (1985–92 T); Dorothy Vallens (Isabella Rossellini), perverse singer, gangster's mistress in *Blue Velvet* (1986 C); Jamie Lee Curtis (*Death of a Centerfold* 1981 T); Mariel Hemingway (*Star 80* 1983 C) playing Dorothy Stratten, the *Playboy* model and actress murdered by her jealous manager/lover. Bryant Gumbell in a March 1992 edition of *Today* asserted that 'you don't hear [the name] Dorothy now'.

UK/Australia: Peggy Cummins as the expectant mother in *To Dorothy a Son* (1955 C); Dorothy Wyld (Flora Robson), teacher with a secret in THE HUMAN JUNGLE 'Conscience on a Rack' (1965 T); Dorothy Havergal (Anne Kristen) unfazed by the offhand hero of THE DARK NUMBER (1968 T); Dorothy Bennett (Veronica Roberts) jealous of Nellie and Sally in *Tenko* (1981 T); soccer-playing Dorothy (Dee Hepburn) in *Gregory's Girl* (1981 C); Dorothy Burke (Maggie Dence), the grebe-like teacher who is revealed as a basketball champ in *Neighbours* (1990– T); the monstrous Matron Dorothy Stinking Bitch in *Let the Blood Run Free* 1990 T).

Variations include cool lesbian Dorothea Alliot (Kika Markham) in ALL FOR LOVE 'Miss A. and Miss M.' (1983 T); Theo[dora], psychic lesbian (Claire Bloom) in THE HAUNTING (1963 C); Dolly Levi (Barbra STREISAND), exhausting match-maker in *Hello, Dolly* (1970 C); Dolly (Ann Mitchell), the brains behind the heist in WIDOWS (1983 T); Dot (Rita Tushingham), frustrated wife of one of THE LEATHER BOYS (1963

C); Dot Cotton (June Brown), born-again Christian, busybody and good Samaritan, friend of the gays in EASTENDERS (1986– T).
See also FRIEND OF DOROTHY'S.

dossers Researching his book on poverty in *The Road to 1984* (1984 T) George Orwell (James FOX) is propositioned in a doss house by an inmate (Bryan Coleman): 'I'm an old Etonian myself ... I've come down in the world. We chaps who have come down ought to stick together ... May I offer you a drink?' Orwell springs to life as a hand aims for his crotch. 'I'm a writer,' he protests. '*I* haven't come down!' A real dosser, from Scotland, explained how his family had rejected him because of his homosexuality in DOSSERS (1982 T).

The Double Man (UK 1984 R) A 2-part history of one of the great croaking, fag-laden voices of the 20th century, W. H. AUDEN.
W: Ed Thomason; D: Margaret Wyndham; BBC Radio 4.

Doubletake (US 1985 T) Two decapitated corpses, a lesbian health-club owner, hookers and a weedy gay art teacher.
W: John Gay from the novel *Switch* by William Bayer; P: Thomas De Wolfe: D: Jud Taylor; 208 mins.

Amanda, the dead teacher, had 'sexually perverse tastes'. Her friend Gary (Michael Cerveris) is a total cringe-flooded individual (who, Amanda notes in her diary, is 'pathetic'): an ineffectual homosexual probably brought into the plot to make the detective (Richard Crenna) less conspicuous – what with helping the heroine (Beverley D'Angelo) with the washing and then playing the lute ('Greensleeves'). There's also a quasi-lesbian character: Hazel Carter, the head of the Fitness Salon. Very clichéd, which perfectly accords with Beverley D'Angelo's line: 'It's tabloid stuff really. Simple.'

Double Trouble (OUT series: 1991 T) Eight ABORIGINES are interviewed and discuss the two distinct yet sometimes

overlapping prejudices they face in a non-Aboriginal, heterosexual society.
P: Diane Hamer; D: Tony Ayres; 25 mins.
'One thing I noticed was an apparent reluctance to discuss acceptance within the Aboriginal community as a whole, as opposed to acceptance from individual families. I interpreted this as an understandable desire to keep any dissension within the community private. Tony agreed, saying that questions in that area didn't work, and the issue was not pursued out of respect for the interviewees' privacy ... If you just understand that there is a universality to it as well as a particularity of their experience. The particularity is their aboriginality, the universality is their homosexuality, their humanity' (Kevin Dickson interviewing Tony Ayers, *Sydney Star Observer*, 7.2.92).

Douglas, Lord Alfred (1870–1945) Anglo-Scottish writer and traveller, deeply adored, then reviled, then cherished, friend of Oscar WILDE who urged him to fight back when Douglas' father accused Wilde of sodomy. This move led to Wilde's downfall, imprisonment and exile. Douglas joined him in France for one last, mad debauch. Douglas married, embraced the Catholic faith and energetically turned his back on his youthful 'sins'. John Neville and John Fraser played this selfish, unappealing young ARISTOCRAT in the two 1960 Wilde films; Robin Lermitte gave him a BRIDESHEAD flavour in *Oscar* (1985 T) and Douglas Hodge a touch of the flower child in *Salome's Last Dance* (1988 C). Others who have briefly essayed the boy Oscar was wild about: Michael Bangerter in ON TRIAL (1960 T), Denis Lawson in *Fearless Frank* (1978 T), Simon Shepherd in *Lillie* (1978 T); Michael Hanly in *Saint Oscar* (1991).

Douglas, Bill (1937–91) Scottish film director: *My Childhood* (1972); *My Ain Folk* (1973); *My Way Home* (1978); *Comrades* (1986); *Confessions of a Justified Sinner* (1988–9, script only). 'Supported and survived by his companion, Peter Jewell' (*Sight and Sound* obituary).

Douglas, Norman (1868–1952) English novelist and travel writer. *Norman Douglas* (1949 R), a tribute by Roger Senhouse on the novelist's 80th birthday; *Norman Douglas* (1952 R) by D. M. Low; *Norman Douglas: Looking Back* (1987 R) with Timothy West as Douglas, Sir Harold ACTON and Graham Greene; in *Ciro's Boat* (1985 R), readings from *Siren Land* (1911).

Percy **Dovetonsils** Bibulously LISPING poet: one of Ernie Kovacs' characters. Can be seen in *The Best of Ernie Kovacs* (1991), five one-hour videos available from White Star Video in the US.

Do What Your Mommy Tells You Sung by Roxanne (Catherine Carlen) rubbing herself against a juke box while a man lies dead in a coffin, in *Chopper Chicks in Zombietown* (1989 C).
M/L: Richard Loring and Patrick Mitchell.

do you believe in fairies? Question asked of the audience in PETER PAN. Claude Crepe (Anthony GARDINER) in *Mister Ten Percent* (1968 C) bellows an affirming yes.

do you come here often? Married woman 'touring' a lesbian disco (Helen Atkinson Wood) trots out this icebreaker – with only the slightest trace of irony – to the impervious Gisela in SILENT WING (1984 R); perfume tycoon Sheila Thaxton (Lorraine Bracco) uses it to Amanda (Ellen Barkin) in SWITCH (1991 C) and is mildly surprised when her projected bed-mate replies: 'I used to – when I was a man.' *See also* SHALL WE DANCE?

Do You Really Want To Hurt Me? Composed by BOY GEORGE (George O'Dowd) and members of Culture Club in 1982. Played in a Cardiff gay BAR in ABOUT MEN ... AND MEN (1983 T); in pub scenes in *Resurrected*, set post-Falklands war (1989 T); in A VERY PECULIAR PRACTICE (1986 T). The song can also be heard in the American *Valley Girl* (1982 C). Regarded very much as teenage bubble-gum music, it reflected the composer–singer's problematic relationship with a member of the band.

Count Dracula 'Have you felt the Vampire's lips upon your throat? Oh my God, what have we done to have this on us!' Former civil servant Bram Stoker touched a nerve in Victorian society with his carefully researched character.

There have been over 200 incarnations of the man in black, charming, elegant, sometimes beautiful, but decadent and dead. Apart from Bela Lugosi in several Dracula films, Denholm ELLIOT (1966 T); Kenneth Haigh as *Lord Dracula* (1974 R), David MARCH as Vlad Dracula (1976 R) and, most perverse of all, Louis Jourdan as *Count Dracula* (1977 T). There was also a modern-day counterpart Prince Anton Voytek (Richard Lynch) in *Vampire* (1979 T). But the old romantic (heterosexual fantasy rapist) image was reasserting itself: Frank Langella in *Dracula* (1979 C) and George Hamilton in *Love At First Bite* (1978 C). And Gary Oldman in Francis Ford Coppola's 1992 treatment.

The Dracula phenomenon featured in KALEIDOSCOPE 'The Illusion of Immortality' (1987 R).

Dracula's Daughter (US 1936 C) Nicely spoken countess with bias towards the throats of young women.
W: Garrett Fort; D: Lambert Hillyer; 70 mins.

> 'You won't object to removing your blouse, will you?'
> 'Please don't come any closer ... Aaagh!'

draft dodging/discharge KLINGER (Jamie Farr) in M*A*S*H (1972–80 T) want a Section 8 and so dresses as a nurse, as well as in bizarre female attire, in an effort to secure release from the battle zone. A colonel sagely tells Klinger that his son tried the same thing but it didn't work. Attempts to dodge the draft also in THE GAY DECEIVERS and *Big Wednesday*.

drag Evelyn BAXTER (Colin CAMPBELL) was not allowed to say that he and his friends were preparing to go to a drag ball in THE PRIVATE LIFE OF HILDA TABLET (1954 R), but it was allowed five years later in THE GOON SHOW. Birtweed (Reginald BECKWITH), under the cover of an 'A'-certificate, could blithely babble to John Gregson in THE CAPTAIN'S TABLE (1958 C): 'The ship is like the Chelsea Arts Ball; every night . . . the full drag.' One of the sailors (Oliver McGreevy) says to his companion as Colin CAMPBELL walks into a dockside pub in the final scene of THE LEATHER BOYS (1963 C): 'Get a load of the drag' (a leather jacket with 'Dodgy' on the back).

Total enshrinement came in the poster for the Dick Lester comedy THE RITZ ('Hiding out from the Mafia can be such a drag') and the title of a 1978 *Sweeney* episode ('Drag Act'). Drag was worn by characters from CORONATION STREET and EASTENDERS like the latter's Pete and Arfur (1989) getting 'into drag', while the Queen Vic briefly had its own drag artiste (Dave Dale as John Fisher, 1986).

'Not many years ago men would have been arrested for wearing a frock in public – the drag scene was essentially underground. Today, it flourishes' (*Radio Times* blurb for *About Britain* 'One of the Girls' 1990 T).

Paul Drake Played by William Hopper in PERRY MASON (1957–66), he is Perry's personal private eye and, in Raymond Chandler's phrase, 'neither a eunuch nor a satyr'. Built like an American quarterback, he favours loud check jackets and mascara. In the more daring days of 1957, he and Perry are discovered on a fishing trip, without Della's chaperonage ('The Case of the Negligent Nymph'). Paul rescues a blonde (he looks great wet), but neither shows the slightest bit of interest in the other once on deck. He wears a pinky ring and she's the 'friend' of the murdered man's wife.

In 'The Lazy Lover' (what more appropriate description of Perry?) a year on, Paul hints at dinner together but Perry has more pressing business on the case. It is the one episode where Paul gets vamped by a glamorous suspect (in a negligée). He is looking sensational (in a stylish Alan Ladd white trench coat). She obviously can't get enough of him. She moves towards him. But he shows no interest and the camera pulls back to reveal none other than Perry by his side.

In an interview with *Radio Times* in 1964, William Hopper was asked why he never got the girl (or any girl). He did an 'aw shucks' and said it was the character's fate to fancy some wondrous blonde whom he would then find dead on the carpet. Behold a mystery! In no episode did Paul ever trip over a female corpse – he found two dead in cars and one (gay?) man shot in his living room; and on all three occasions Perry was with him. There were one or two minor attempts at seduction over the years, of a tentative nature. Every now and then he would call Della 'beautiful'. This epithet could possibly have been an attempt to rekindle an affair with Della which may have produced Paul Drake Jr as seen in some of the TV movies which turned up in the 1980s, and bearing the closest possible resemblance to Perry's pencil-sharp secretary.

There are a number of 'Paul gazing' shots in the Mason series: ostensibly all were directed at women, but they are so angled as to suggest he might be checking out a male, or admiring the women's jewellery and clothes. After all, in a 1958 episode, Perry does hand him a dress with a look that says 'This might suit *you* better'.

Paul gazes at the battleship and its hunky crew in three cut-in close-ups of extraordinary concentration, while Perry blathers on about who killed the ship's tart (female) in 'The Slandered Submarine' (1960 T). 'You know,' sighs Paul, 'I've been thinking about taking a trip.' Perry recommends that he 'join the navy and see the world'. Paul splutters bashfully while Della transmits her secret smile. During the ritual office summing-up in 'The Case of the Skeleton's Closet' (1963 T) Paul guilelessly recites the Gilbertian rhyme: 'Things are seldom what they seem/Skim milk masquerades as cream.'

In 'Paul Drake's Dilemma' (1959) the audience (and the jury) are encouraged to consider the questions: did Paul Drake kill Mrs Thatcher's husband? And what is the significance of the song played at the scene of the crime, 'I Need A Man'?

The character was played by Albert Stratton in *The New Perry Mason* (1973–4) and by William Katt (Barbara Hale's son) in some of the TV movies made between 1986 and 1988.)

dreaded lurgi An unmentionable and indescribably unspecified disease (spong was another such). Spike Milligan took the name from a Frankfurt-based company called Lurgi (from metallurgical) which won a much publicized British contract in 1952. The title of a programme dealing with the stigma of AIDS was *The Dreaded Lurgi* 'Pestilence and Punishment' (1991 T).

Dream Stuffing (UK 1984 T) Two flat-mates and their (non-platonic as well as platonic) men friends, including a handyman gay, Richard (Ray Burdis). W: Paul Hines and Su Wilkins; P: Humphrey Barclay; for Channel 4; 30 mins.

Halliwell's Television and Video Companion approved: 'Up-to-the-minute sitcom about two young girls getting by on nothing very much, with blacks . . and homosexuals (their chum) fitted in without trying to make points.'

Dresdel, Sonia [Lois Obee] (1909–76) Rock-hard surface with tiny driblets of sardonic humour. Best known for role of Ralph Richardson's coiled wife in *The Fallen Idol* (1948 C), and the murderess in *This Was a Woman* (1947 C). On television she was a malevolent Mrs DANVERS in REBECCA (1954), and the quintessential Red Queen in *The Adventures of Alice* (1961). Other films: *The World Owes Me a Living* (1942); *While I Live* (1947); *The Clouded Yellow* (1950); *Now and Forever* (1954); *The Trials of*

Oscar Wilde (1960) as Wilde's mother; *Lady Caroline Lamb* (1972).

Dressed to Kill (US 1980 C) Another murderous TRANSVESTITE born out of Norman BATES and fast forwarding to BUFFALO BILL.
W/D: Brian De Palma; Filmways; 105 mins.

The Dresser (UK 1983 C) 'Sir' (Albert Finney) and Norman (Tom Courtenay), based on Sir Donald Wolfit and author Harwood, who was the irascible, mercurial man's dresser, confidant, human football and washer of underpants.
W: Ronald Harwood from his play; P/D: Peter Yates; 118 mins.
Power-plays and petulance within a touring production of *King Lear*. Finney a perfect tyrant and Courtenay a well-worn doormat. A celebration of a kind of theatre and breed of actor that are now extinct. (Freddie Jones and Michael Palin starred in a 1993 radio version.)

Dress Gray (US 1986 T) Ray Slaight (Alec Baldwin), a third-year cadet, painstakingly discovers the truth about the death of gay David Hands, despite all attempts by the military academy to smother it.
W: Gore VIDAL from the book by Lucian K. Truscott IV; D: Glenn Jordan; 208 mins.
Career soldiers in an enclosed male world of maschismo, alcoholism, impotence and mechanical sex. Gripping thriller which elaborates on the power structures outlined in the novel at the expense of fleshing out the victim's life and sexuality.

Dressler, Marie [Leila Kerber] (1869–1934) American screen actress who changed from opera singer and tragic stage heroine into a comic, adept at slapstick, crackling repartee or warm character humour. Also organizer of the chorus girls' branch of Actors' Equity, she became an activist in the 1919 struggle between actors and management.
Achieved screen fame opposite Chaplin in *Tillie's Punctured Romance* (1914)

followed by *Tillie's Tomato Surprise* and, in 1917, by *Tillie Wakes Up* and *Tillie the Toiler*. Popular partnership with Polly Moran (wrangling, but good mates and often ending up together) in films such as *The Callahans and the Murphys* (1927), *Caught Short* (1930, as rival boarding house owners), *Reducing* (1931, partly set in women's Turkish baths), and *Prosperity* (1932).
She is best remembered as the superannuated prostitute Marthey opposite her friend and lover Greta GARBO in *Anna Christie* (1930); as Min in *Min and Bill* (1930, winning an Academy Award); as *Tugboat Annie* (1932); as the hostess Carlotta Vance in *Dinner at Eight* (1933): 'I was rather gorgeous, wasn't I? ... didn't do so bad for a little girl from Quincey, Illinois.'
The title of her autobiography is *The Life Story of an Ugly Duckling*, but the nearest Marie Dressler came to dramatization was a brief impersonation by Hermione Baddeley in *Harlow* (1965 C/T), dispensing motherly advice to Carol Lynley.

Driberg, Tom (1905–76) English journalist and MP who appeared frequently on television (*Sunday Afternoon* 1956–8; *In Search of the Truth* 1962) and radio (ANY QUESTIONS?; *A Portrait of Brian Howard* 1968). He was played by Simon Cuff in Hugh Jenkins' *Lost Tune from Rangoon* (1987 R) about the struggle for independence in Burma.
A 1990 biography revealed 'a life drenched in anonymous, sparking sensuality', which was one way of putting it.

drinking Whether as a tongue loosener or oblivion provider, alcohol is an integral part of the lives of Brick in CAT ON A HOT TIN ROOF (1958 C; 1976 & 1984 T); Mabel Warren (Anna Burden), the journalist travelling on the STAMBOUL TRAIN (1962 T) with her girlfriend; June Buckridge (Beryl REID; Sheila Hancock) in THE KILLING OF SISTER GEORGE (1968 C; 1978 R); Paul Verlaine (Ian Hogg) and Arthur RIMBAUD (Joseph Blatchely) in *Total Eclipse* (1973 T); Guy BURGESS in *Philby, Bur-*

gess and Maclean (1977 T); AN ENGLISH-MAN ABROAD (1983 T); *Blunt* (1987 T); Harry (Anthony Andrews) accidentally blinded by his lover Oliver in A SUPERSTITION (1977 T) during a drunken night; the ex-teacher returning to Ireland after years as a falling-down drunk (JIMMY 1978 R); sacked BBC producer James (Michael Jayston) with a drinking problem in THE LAST ROMANTIC (1978 T); Sebastian FLYTE permanently soused in BRIDESHEAD REVISITED (1981 T); Gerald Haxton (Barrie Dennen), Somerset MAUGHAM'S dissolute, unfaithful yet very necessary companion in WEEKEND WITH WILLIE (1981 R); Connie Sachs (Beryl Reid), the ex-MI5 clerk, drinking and dying in the country and nursed by a tense younger woman in *Smiley's People* (1982 T).

Often the drinking begins as youthful excess, as with Sebastian. 'Ought we to be drunk every night?' asks the besotted Charles. 'Yes, I think we should'. So saying, Sebastian falls into the family seat's fountain.

In the first episode of *Bergerac* (1981 T) Jim Bergerac (John Nettles) visits a branch of Alcoholics Anonymous on Jersey. A rather time-chewed man asks him if he would like a cup of tea and while pouring gives a capsule account of himself: 'I myself am a homosexual, which is why I used to booze it up. Until I met a psychiatrist with whom I now cohabit. So that's my life history.'

For gay men and for lesbians one of the problems of avoiding excessive intake is the restricted number of meeting places. Most of them offer ALCOHOL and positively discriminate in its favour. Gisela, the stolid German with a mysterious past in SILENT WING (1984 R), courts social ostracism and even physical violence when she shouts: 'Anyone who has to drink to free themselves can't ever do it. Your bloodstream is in bondage to beer.' An overbearing woman BARTENDER tells Gisela that she'd do well to change her attitude 'or it can be changed for you.'

Clearly in an alcohol-social world it takes some fortitude to control its flow. It is interesting to consider how 21-year-old Barry in EASTENDERS will cope, in later life, with the effects of the pints he was always downing. It is booze which allowed him to loosen up sufficiently for love-making with Colin in the first place. He might do well, however, to remember the fate of one of the most disturbing dramatic drunks: Don Birman (Ray Milland) in *The Lost Weekend* (1946 C). In the original novel, Birman drank to excess to suppress his feelings towards men. The film retains only hints of this in a terrifying sequence with a sadistic male nurse in a sanitarium. But whatever the motivation, Birman's question reverberates down the decades and across all persuasions: 'What *is* the difference between a drinker a drunk?'

'A lot of guys get loaded to have sex,' Larry remarks in THE BOYS IN THE BAND (1970 C). The host of the BIRTHDAY PARTY which forms the plot framework, Michael (Kenneth Nelson), is one such. He's been on the wagon for five weeks and he tells his ex-lover Donald (Frederick Combs) of the cycle of dependency, guilt and fear which being an alcoholic brings in its train. His resolve begins to waver as the evening progresses and another anxiety attack looms. The guest of honour pricks his fragile defence system and the implication is that Michael ends up in a worse state than before: hysterical and foetal, far from the wise-cracking sophisticate under which guise he lives most of his outer life. Harold, full of resonant *bons mots*, announces to the guests: 'Beware the hostile FAG. When he's sober, he's dangerous. When he drinks he's lethal.'

But the loosening-up properties of demon drink allow certain truths to be uttered by men who – even today – must be affectionate within rigid limits. An early 20th-century example is Leo in DESIGN FOR LIVING (1979 T etc). Only when he gets plastered is he allowed to rest his head on Otto's shoulder and say tremulously: 'Will you forgive me ... for ... for crying?' To which his friend Otto can only offer partial response: 'It's I who should ...'

See also ALCOHOL; ALCOHOLICS.

drinks Alan Blossom (Laurie Asprey) sips tomato juice while the other teenagers drink scotch in HIT AND RUN (1965 T), a giveaway of his extreme social deviance to be revealed later in the plot.

The alcoholic cliché for gay men is, of course, that they guzzle gin, not masculine tipples like beer or whisky. Ernest THESIGER'S crenellated Dr Praetorius in THE BRIDE OF FRANKENSTEIN (1935 C), for one. He is asked if he likes gin: 'It's my only weakness.' Refined PAUL TEMPLE likes 'Gin and It' in *the Geneva Affair* and the *Conrad Case*. Nowadays, gin figures but rarely in the gay person's liquor cabinet, Ambridge's free soul John TREGORRAN only drank dry sherry when he arrived in the village in 1953. When he bowed out in the 1980s he was onto the hard stuff: gin (with tonic).

Crème de menthe runs gin a close second. Julian likes his 'with a head on it' in ROUND THE HORNE (1967 T) and the youth (Mark Lee) who is part of THE EVERLASTING SECRET FAMILY (1988 C) drinks nothing else. A character says, apropos of Catholicism in *The Unbearable Bassington* (1965 T): 'All the same, a religion that has given us green chartreuse cannot be wholly without merit.' In Graham Green's *Cheap in August* (1987 R) a woman (Valerie Saruff) looks across a restaurant and sees a man holding a glass of *crème de menthe* between his face and his friend's – like an emerald monocle. Her 70-year-old admirer is terse: 'You're not interested in *that* type, are you?' She replies brightly: 'They're often good conversationalists.'

Precious Miles Mellough (Jack Cassidy) summons something sticky and yellow in *The Eiger Sanction* (1975 C): 'banana dyke-qari'.

Whisky: Bruno Anthony (Robert Walker) orders a double scotch in STRANGERS ON A TRAIN (1951 C): 'the only kind of doubles I play,' he tells the gorgeous tennis player he's encountered; Derek (Bryan Pringle) has scotch *and* a pint in *Thrills Galore* (1972 T); Trevor and Peter both like whisky in TOGETHER (1980–1 T). Colin headed

for large scotches *in extremis*, but generally he and Barry defied expectations in EASTENDERS (1986–9 T) by drinking pints with the other blokes at the Queen Vic.

Beer: Hank (Laurence Luckinbill) in *The Boys in the Band* was probably the first gay man to drink one, but then he was bisexual and straight acting. Emory's favourite was 'vodka martini on the rocks'.

drug addicts Nicky Lancaster (David McCallum) heavily into cocaine, alcohol, nicotine and Mummy and fast being swallowed up in THE VORTEX (1960 T); 'Sick in mind and body ... He was different. He was ill'; Martin CAPLAN, the dead libertine who is the catalyst for the emotional bloodletting in DANGEROUS CORNER (1934 R etc); Edward SHELLY (Richard Hurndall) using fluting mannerisms as a mask to hide his dope-ring connections in *Paul Temple and the Vandyke Affair* (1950 & 1959 R); Darren McGavin flexing his biceps suggestively before giving Frank Sinatra a fix in *The Man with the Golden Arm* (1955 C); Derek Farr as Kenny, seemingly benevolent BACHELOR BOY who is an integral part of *The Vicious Circle* (1957 C); Roland CURRAM, mother's pet supplying drugs to children in *The Silent Playground* (1962 C) unbeknownst to his protective mum; Rood (Lloyd Bochner) in *Tony Rome* (1967 C); Sailor (Ron Rifkin), weasel-faced barman in *Flareup* (1969 C).

Joe (Joe DALLESANDRO) peddling his body for drugs in FLESH (1968 C) and *Trash* 1870 C) as do characters in *Go Ask Alice* (1971 T); Jackie the dancer (Don De Natale) supplying the Hollywood set in *The Wild Party* (1974 C); Straker (Colin CAMPBELL) pushing smack and heading for jail at the end of *Play Things* (1976 T); Jeff Rawle, another shady gay barman in *The Wilde Alliance* 'Game for Two Players' (1978 T); drag queen pusher in *The Rose* (1979 C), *Christiane F* (1980 C) and *Woman in Flames* (1982 C); QUERELLE (Brad DAVIS), seductive, murderous supplier of opium (1982 C); LISPING black man accusing police of wrongful arrest in *Hill Street Blues* 'Of Human Garbage' (1985 T); the Greek poet Napoleon Lapathiotis had family money so he could indulge his addiction (*Meteor and Shadow* 1985 C) but Mike Nielsen (Martin Stone) has to resort to blackmail (his former MP lover) in *Inside Story* (1986 T); Adrian (Paula E. Sheppard) in *Liquid Sky* (1983 C); Mitch and Tigr in KAMIKAZE HEARTS (1987 C); Philip Middlemiss palely loitering in *Traffik* (1990 T).

Not a drug dealer in the conventional sense but sinister beneath his candy-striped veneer: Mr Bill (Aubrey WOODS) tempting the children with the sweet and sticky contents of his drug store with a song called 'The Candyman Can (Make Your Dreams Come True)' from *Willie Wonka and the Chocolate Factory* (1971 C).

And Sebastian FLYTE in BRIDESHEAD REVISITED probably needs chemical support as well as 'safe' substances and liquids to bring him to the gates of a monastery as a near derelict.

dual roles Charlie (Stephen Docherty) in *Beyond the Rainbow* (1991 R) playing the gay son of a father who ran away rather than stay 'and admit something to himself'; heroine and male drug peddler (Anne Carlisle) in *Liquid Sky* (1982 C); brother and follower (Hanno Poschi) in QUERELLE (1982 C).

duck 'Don't worry, duck,' breezy bachelor Kenny (Derek Farr) says to John Mills in *The Vicious Circle* (1957 C) – an addition to the same character's line (spoken by Francis Matthews) in the television version of Francis Durbridge's thriller (*My Friend Charles*) the year before.

'He is married and respectable on the surface, but you never know about these old ducks' says Paul Drake (William Hopper) in PERRY MASON 'The Case of the Sardonic Sergeant' (1958 T).

Jean and Jesse in Z CARS 'FRIENDS' (1974 T):

'You should care what people say, duck.'
'Well I don't, *love*.'

Maude's husband about a randy man making an assignation with a beauty queen in *Maude* (1978 T). 'He's a lucky duck.'

'Oh, Ant, my old old love. My darlingest duck. So wonderful to see you,' Guy BURGESS (Anthony Hopkins) greets his sometime lover and great friend Anthony BLUNT (Ian RICHARDSON) in *Blunt* (1987 T). Goronwy Rees calls his wife 'old duck' in the same play.

A social worker (Barry Jackson) congratulates one of his collegues in HARD CASES (1988 T), calling him 'duck'.

Ducks and Drakes (UK 1983 R) Divorced Brenda has a tightly knit circle of friends, including Joseph (Nigel Anthony) who has some hard-headed things to say about the legal state of matrimony – as it doesn't affect him and Tony (Geoffrey Collins).

W: James Brabazon; P: Jane Morgan; 28.11.83; BBC Radio 4; 90 mins.

'So if we cease to like one another there's no need for a divorce, we simply walk away. Think how easy! Think how cheap! Oh dear, if only everyone could be like Tony and me. The only justification for the state of holy Christian matrimony is that it provides for divorce lawyers – especially if they're Jewish and homosexual.'

'Do you think that Tony and I would ever have got together if we'd sat down and logically calculated the chances of it working out? I didn't even know I was gay till then ... it wasn't my head that told me I was in love with this man ... My body tells me to jump on the nearest office boy. My heart and head both tell me that would be stupid.'

But, in the last scene, Joseph goes all mimsy and recommends that Brenda tie the legal knot.

ducky 'Oliver, ducky!' gasps the engulfing Carlotta Vance (Marie DRESSLER) to an older admirer in *Dinner at Eight* (1933 C). 'Oh my ducky darling' squeaks Martita HUNT to her henpecked husband Robertson Hare in *Friday the Thirteenth* (1933 C).

A term long associated with gushing

women, it began to trickle out of the mouths of gay characters of a certain age in the 1950s. Clement Clements (James Thomason) in *A Shilling for Candles* (1954 R) was allowed one or two, and Mr Cecil (Heron CARVIC) fancies all 'those ducky policemen' coming in all directions after one of his fellow cruise passengers has been murdered in *A Knife in the Sun* (1958 R).

In the 1960s, the endearment became widely known, thanks to Julian and Sandy festooning it ROUND THE HORNE and Kenneth WILLIAMS using it extensively on the radio panel game *Just a Minute*. In *The Avengers* 'Two's a Crowd' (1986 T) Steed's deadly double is a model who says 'ducky' to distinguish him from Patrick Macnee mark 1's 'fill me up, duckie.' Director (Corin Redgrave) calls A.S.M. 'Virgin' (Lynn REDGRAVE) 'ducky' in *The Deadly Affair* (1966 C). 'You're a real killer, ducky, when you put your mind to it,' says Daniel (Daniel MASSEY) and he and a piece of ROUGH TRADE wrestle on the bed in THE ROADS TO FREEDOM (1970 T).

From the 1970s: Marvin Sprague (Ian Hendry) in *Dial M for Murder* 'Contract' (1974 T) pretends to be a hairdresser to gain access to a gangster's estate: 'And where do you think *you're* going, ducky?' says a guard. The club owner in THE NAKED CIVIL SERVANT (1975 T) makes his position clear: 'Quentin, ducky, if the police come here, we're NORMAL.'

And from the 1980s. Guy BURGESS tells Donald Maclean on the phone in (*Blunt* 1987 T): 'Not so loud, Donald, voice down, ducky.'

Although it seems as though American GI Dusty employs the word in romantic mood in HOUSE ON THE HILL 'Something for the Boys' (1981 T), which is set in 1944, he's in fact cooing: 'Duggie, Duggie.'

Frankie Diamond (Ronald LACEY) tells social worker Kevin in HARD CASES (1988 T): 'I am what I am, ducky. I do what I do. And if it doesn't fit in into your text book then you'd better go back to college and write another.'

American TV movies seem to like the word as it denotes homosexuality with-

out causing censorship ripples, especially for British aesthetes like antique dealer Brian (Jeremy Brett) in *Deceptions* (1985 T): 'We go back a long way, ducky,' he tells someone to indicate a torrid affair. (A further indication is his pink tie and pearl pin.) Similarly a chef's seemingly all-male brother emits one 'ducky' during an episode of *Jemima Shore Investigates* (1981 T).

A song in *Sesame Street* (*c* 1988) called 'Put Down The Ducky', which unmelodically combines the talents of Danny DeVito, Pee-Wee Herman, Gordon Jackson, Jean Marsh and Jeremy Irons, ends with one male Muppet exclaiming to another: 'Oh ducky, I've missed you so much!'

Dudley Dudley Leake (Edward Everett HORTON) in *It's A Boy* (1934 C); again in *Your Uncle Dudley* (1935); Cary GRANT as the ANGEL Dudley who puts David Niven and Loretta Young back together snug and warm in the matrimonial bed in *The Bishop's Wife* (1947 C); silly ass Dudley Davenport (Maurice Denham) in *Much-Binding-in-the-Marsh* (1950–3 R); Dudley Grosvenor (Peter Jones) in *In All Directions* and *We're in Business* (1950s R); Dudley (Peter Jones again) in *Schools for Scoundrels* (1960 C); Dudley Banks-Smith (Ray Fell) in *Ours Is a Nice House* (1971 T); Dudley Millington (Royce Mills) in *Starring Leslie Willey* (1987 R); Australian Dudley Butterfield (Chard Hayward) trailing clouds of gaiety in NUMBER 96 (1974–7 T).

Duffy, Maureen (1933–) English novelist, playwright and poet, author of a seminal novel about lesbians (*The Microcosm*) and someone who stood up during and after the homosexual law reform debates, most vividly in *Late Night Line-Up*, commenting on the MAN ALIVE programmes on gay men and lesbians (1967 T), and in conversation with Wilfred D'eath (1967 R). She was one of the speakers on 'The Future' in *Saturday Night Out* (1991 T). Her *Gorsaga* was (fairly freely) adapted for television in 1989 as *First Born* and she wrote two original plays; 'Josie' in *The Younger*

Generation series (1961 T) and *Only Goodnight* about SOMERVILLE AND ROSS (1981 R).

Nurse **Dugdale** 'Sporty' character created by Arthur MARSHALL (co-written with David Yates Massey) on radio during the late 1930s and the 1940s. 'A most likeable radio personality, whose line of charming spirits and astonishing background of wild life at Hornsey Hydro (there was old Mrs Muirhead out of bed and locked in a frenzied beguine with one of the Bronchials) coupled with Arthur Marshall's mimicry and his sense of the ridiculous, kindly but cruel, are a great addition to Variety' (Philip Hope-Wallace, *Listener*, 6.12.45).

Mr **Dulcimer** Frank VOSPER created the role on the London stage in 1929 and D. A. CLARKE-SMITH played him on radio in 1946: a powerful image of the homosexual as bastion of privilege. He tells his adopted son (and lover?), Julian: 'Choice is what separates the artist from the common herd ... I hope you will never forego your prerogative of choice. Never do anything that is unconsidered or take what is second best.' ADOPTED at the age of 11 by Dulcimer, Julian (Lewis Stringer) at 23 is 'a shallow bundle of sensations'.

The arrival of Leonora Yale (Sheila Burrell) in Julian's life temporarily unseats Dulcimer from his Olympian throne in the boy's universe. But the balance is restored once Julian realizes the material advantages of staying in Dulcimer's orbit. Dulcimer savours his triumph: 'I like the power of money. I have created comfort and beauty and constant change of scene out of money, and a cage for Julian's soul in which he sings to me as sweetly as in that stuffy Welsh schoolroom all those years ago.'

Shot dead by Julian's outraged father, Dulcimer's power extends beyond the grave. Julian becomes his blasé facsimile, keeping the common herd at bay: 'I am a materialist and I glory in it. But I never have to struggle to maintain my position. I know exactly what I want out of life and I get it.'

Dusty Answer (UK 1990 R) Dreamy Judith Earle (Sylvestra Le Touzel) spends summers with and loves three brothers, one of whom, Roddy (Simon Treves) is primarily gay. At university she becomes attached for a while to Jennifer (Geraldine Alexander) before having affairs of greatly differing intensity with Roddy and with his sybaritic brother Julian (Michael COCHRANE).
D: Jane Morgan; 17.9.90; BBC Radio 4; 90 mins.

Rosamond LEHMANN's novel was a sensation in 1927 because it looked in some detail at the development of womanhood and the possibility of loving people of different temperaments and of different genders. This production is heavy with period somnolence and is an irritating reminder of how little modern literary material of much greater fun and complexity reaches the airwaves.

DV8 Physical Theatre Experimental dance troupe led by Lloyd Newson which explores bonding and bondage, personal, political and spiritual. *Far Cry* 'Never Again' (1989); THE SOUTH BANK SHOW 'Dead Dreams of Monochrome Men' (1990).

Dyall, Valentine (1908–85) English actor, master of the macabre, a friendly frightener as the 'Man in Black' in the 1940s. APPOINTMENT WITH FEAR: 'Four o'clock in the morning, the hour of suicide and bad dreams.' Also made frequent guest appearances on THE GOON SHOW.
C: *Mr Satan* (1938); *Much Too Shy* (1942); German commander in *Yellow Canary* (1943); Duke of Burgundy in *Henry V* (1944); *The Life and Death of Colonel Blimp* (1943); *Caesar and Cleopatra* (1946); Stephen LYNN in BRIEF ENCOUNTER (1946); Jethrow Kean in *City of the Dead/Horror Hotel* (1960); *The Haunting; The Slipper and the Rose* (1976); *Britannia Hospital* (1982).
R: *Horatio Hornblower* (1946); Valentine Avon in *People at Sea* (1953); *Timon*

of Athens (1953); narrator of *The Black Dog* (1953, about 18th-century melancholy); Dantes in *The Count of Monte Cristo* (1956); Jonathan Brewster in *Arsenic and Old Lace* (1957); Dr Livesey in *Treasure Island* (1958 T); Pontius Pilate in *A Spark in Judea* (1959).

T: *A Show Called Fred* (1956); hypnotist in *Sykes and a ... Hypnotist* (1964); Arab chauffeur in *The Troubleshooters* 'Baptism of Fire' (1966); ADRIAN in *The Losers* 'The Naming Party' (1978); CORIOLANUS (1982); *Dr Who* 'Terminus' (1983); Lorimer in *Miss Marple* 'The Body in the Library' (1984).

Charles **Dyer** The sniping queen played by Rex Harrison in STAIRCASE (1969 C). Failed actor, reluctant father now living with fellow HAIRDRESSER Harry in an uneasy conjugal bliss. Harry had once kicked him out and to survive Charlie became an encyclopaedia salesman, living in a doss house. He is now facing a charge of GROSS INDECENCY after being found in DRAG on someone's lap in a pub. A lashing tongue and a lively turn of phrase to go with it are Charlie's mainstays in a darkening world which once promised so much. 'All I've done in 10 years is one mingy commercial for duffle coats. I only said: "Heave up the spinnaker!"' As the play progresses we begin, like Harry, to see through the cocky front: 'Ooogh, you're all intertwined, Charlie. One great big tube of *non sequitur.*'

In a note to the published version of the script, Dyer revealed: 'During the writing I began to feel that Charlie is alone. Nobody else. No Harry. Just Charlie in a grubby little barber shop.' Dyer's next play *Mother Adam* was the last of his trilogy which began with *Rattle of a Simple Man* in 1962. In this 1973 piece a bedridden, arthritic mother (Hermione Baddeley) taunts her middle-aged bachelor son (Peter WYNGARDE) about his lack of masculinity. She says she wants him to marry, but it becomes obvious that this is – and always has been – her greatest fear. Harry Leeds is an anagram of Charles Dyer (the playwright's name too). All

the other characters mentioned by Charlie are similarly anagrammatic: Archy Selder, Sherry Cade, Sherly Drace and Ed Chrysler.

dying parents *Where the Difference Begins* (1966 T); A ROD OF IRON; *The Mourning Thief* (1984 T); *Open-Ended Prescription* (1980 R); WORDS OF ONE SYLLABLE (1991).

Dyke/Dyker Used in America as first or nickname: the actor Dyke Johnson (*Ride Lonesome* 1959 C etc) and character Dyker played by David Macklin in PERRY MASON 'The Case of the Simple Simon' (1964). Sylvia Dykes (Jeff Donnell), dishrag housewife with philandering husband in *Perry Mason* 'The Case of the Angry Astronaut' (1962 T).

dyke/dike Coral Browne's crisply vicious Mercy Croft, hatchet-woman for the BBC and marauder of young girls, unnecessarily confronts Beryl REID's Sister George with the central fact of her life in THE KILLING OF SISTER GEORGE (1968 C). As heard on the soundtrack of the television version it sounds as if she's saying 'you pathetic old duck'.

In *The World of Tim Frazer* (1960 T) Vivienne Gilmore asks Tim to meet her at the Dyke coffee shop. What is the connection between the bulb catalogue, the code word 'Fantasy' and the metronome? And why is he warned off going to have coffee with Barbara Day?

Janet Leigh's henchperson role in *The Man from UNCLE* adventure *The Spy in the Green Hat* (1966 C, aka 'The Concrete Overcoat Affair' T) was given a perverse dimension (not otherwise present in script or performance) by her name: Miss Diketon.

A university lecturer known as Dykey Dora (Pearl Hackney) is described in the script of *Comedy Playhouse* 'The Importance of Being Hairy' (1972 T) as a 'stout butch type'.

Now used proudly and affectionately by many lesbians, the word finally made it onto WOMAN'S HOUR (R) in 1988 when Jill Gascoine read Sara Maitland's 'Lullaby for My Dyke and Her Cat'.

References to the joke about the Dutch boy and his finger resolutely in the hole holding back the water were made in a song at *The Wild Party* (1974 C) and by the dummy in SOAP (1979 T) when meeting Alice (Randee Heller), Jodie's roommate.

'BULL DYKE' received its first nod in *Doctor in Love* (1960 C): Irene Handl's tweedy, gruffed-voiced doctor is called an 'Aberdeen Angus' by one of the strippers (Joan Sims). The doctor fancies both of them.

'Diesel dyke' was alluded to in Noel COWARD'S 1966 play *A Song at Twilight* (1982 T; 1988 R) in which a 'Sapphist' named Liesel is a friend of Carlotta's; and, though unstressed, in Mel Brooks' *High Anxiety* (1978 C) with Cloris Leachman's Nurse Diesel.

'uppity dyke' also appears. 'I'm not sure what an uppity dyke is', says one of Bob Buzzard's (David Troughton) twins in a VERY PECULIAR PRACTICE (1986 T), having heard Daddy talk about Rose Marie. Stephen (Peter Davison) to shut him up says: 'They have lots of them in Holland.'

'Just because a woman is doing what's traditionally a man's job, she's open to be called a dyke' (*Hill Street Blues* 'Look Homeward, Ninja' 1987 C).

Among the 57 basic things 'that could go wrong with a nuclear reactor' listed in HORIZON 'The Next 1,000 Years' (1990 T) the viewer's eye is caught by 'intrusive dikes'.

See also DOG-OWNERS (LESBIAN)/ DOGGY DYKES.

Badgie **Dyke** Written and drawn by Jennie Simmons, and played by Kate Crutchley in ONE IN FIVE (1983 T), Badgie was GAY NEWS ordinary lesbian, a greatly loved strip-cartoon character. She lived in a small town called Nibley, and had hardly opened the closet door before she was expected to appear in front of the television cameras. In view of peer pressure ('I'll be labelled as closety for evermore'), she didn't dare refuse: 'I'm going on TV ... I'll stretch out a helping hand to all our poor and isolated. Demonstrate to the misin-

formed heterosexual public what being homosexual is all about. I'll be in the limelight, seen by millions ... Oh dear, I'm far too scruffy to go on TV ... I'll just have to get a new set of BADGES.'

Dressed in a shapeless roll-neck pullover, hair daggy and lank, squat, she can't back out. If she does she'll ruin her chances with Nellie Prune, Badgie's idol. 'She's now lost everything for the cause – her job, her home, her career. Even her family have disowned her. How romantic!'

The cartoon introduced a waiting world to Badgie's other friends, Hefty Smith, Doris Boot and Boobsie Prott, and even found room for 'Nibley Scene Christmas Cards', 'The 1977 Nibley Calendar' and 'The Nibley Snakes and Ladder Game'.

Dyke's Delight Actresses out to admire or to worship or to make love with fantastically: in OUT 'Out at the Movies' (1991 T) these included Meryl Streep, Jamie Lee Curtis, Vanessa REDGRAVE, Whoopi Goldberg, Marilyn MONROE, k. d. lang, Geena Davis, Madonna, Greta and Marlene.

dykes don't cry IN THE GLITTER PALACE (1977) Ellen (Barbara Hershey) is visiting her girlfriend Casey (Diana Scarwid) in prison where she is languishing unjustly accused of murder. Ellen gives her a pep talk. 'You either laugh or you cry,' she tells the frightened young woman. 'And,' Ellen adds tersely, 'dykes aren't supposed to cry.'

Dynamic Duo *See* BATMAN AND ROBIN.

Dynasty (US 1981–8/1991 T) In its heyday (1982–5), this was a close rival to DALLAS, watched on nearly 100 networks throughout the world by an audience of 100 million. Alexis (Joan Collins), Krystle (Linda Evans) and Blake (John Forsythe) were America's Olympians, leading powerful, opulent lives in 48-room mansions, country clubs and private jets. And for the ultimate fantasy family, the ultimate fantasy homosexual offspring – Steven Carrington (Al Corley). Said the series creators (and co-producers with Aaron SPELLING) Esther and Richard Shapiro: 'Steven is honest and brave and manly. And openly – if not exclusively – homosexual.' But, oh so confused. In the first episode Steven returns to Denver, angrily attacking his father's business methods (ruthless) and the oil industry's poor record on conservation. He meets the married Claudia Blaisdel (Pamela Bellwood) and they discover they have Emily DICKINSON in common. They begin an affair. This is complicated by the return of his New York former lover, Ted Dinard (Mark Withers). Steven sleeps with him again, confessing to Claudia: 'It wasn't something I wanted to happen, it just happened. We were just sitting there, talking about the old days ... You've got to know that things aren't that clear-cut in life ... I spent the night with somebody who is very ... It's not that easy for me either.'

Ted tells Steven that the latter is in 'limbo, buddy; emotional limbo. You're not in heaven and you're not in hell.' He confronts Claudia: 'I love Steven, *Mrs* Blaisdel and I'll fight for him if I have to.' A drunken Blake then discovers the two men in a (platonic) embrace and strikes Ted, who hits his head on the ground and dies.

This climaxes the first series: Blake is in the dock and Steven testifies against him. Claudia reveals details of her and Steven's sex life and Steven's long lost mother makes a dramatic appearance behind a veil.

When the serial returned, Blake is found guilty of manslaughter, Steven begins an affair with stepmother Krystle's opportunistic niece, Sammy Jo (Heather Locklear). They marry and have a child, then split up. He resumes the affair with Claudia whom he marries, but this ends because of his feelings for Luke Fuller (William Oliver Campbell), the public relations man of his mother Alexis. Somewhere along the line, Steven is involved in an oil rig explosion, undergoes plastic surgery and emerges from the bandages a new man (played by Jack COLEMAN).

In July 1985 *Mad* magazine parodied *Dynasty*. Steven became Sieve: 'I used to be gay, then I was in an oil-rig explosion. I got a new face and I went straight. I've got a wife and son and I use Brut every day.' But the explosion has changed more than his face: Sieve is now a woman and beats Renée Richards at tennis. His/her lover Luke Fuller has become Puke Buller.

Back in the plot, Luke is killed by Moldavian terrorists (the entire Carrington family miraculously survives being sprayed with bullets at very close range). After this, Steven is sued for custody of son Danny by Blake, is briefly flirted with by his lawyer Chris Deegan (Grant Goodeve), gets back with Sammy Jo, is held hostage by Claudia's ex-husband whom he kills in self-defence. Steven, now a hero, takes greater interest in the family business, is a good parent to Danny, has a flicker of sexual interest to and from Bart Fallmont (Kevin Conroy) with whom he is in litigation – on the family's behalf – over environmental degradation. He then leaves Denver for good, to reappear some years later once again played by Al Corley and now living with Bart (played now by Cameron Watson). He and Sammy Jo are still scrapping over Danny (to whom he is an excellent dad). He helps save the family fortunes from suave foreigners and, in the final scene of 'The Reunion', sits at the dinner table with the man he is committed to. The dynasty is secure. American capitalism is safe for another few years.

Each man kills the thing he loves In QUERELLE (1982 C) Lucianne (Jeanne Moreau) in black feather boa curdles Oscar Wilde's THE BALLAD OF READING GAOL by endlessly repeating 'each man kills the thing he loves' (followed by dah-de-dah, dah-de-dah), while her husband details his latest male conquest to her lover: 'When I pulled my cock out, it was covered in shit.' Lucianne then sings a portion of the poem including: 'Some do it with a bitter look,/ Some with a flattering word ...'

An Early Frost (US 1985 T) Michael (Aidan Quinn) has to confront his middle-class family with two facts: he's gay and he has AIDS.
W: Ron Cowen and Daniel Lipman; P: Perry Lafferty; D: John Erman; NBC; 96 mins.

An Early Frost was rewritten 13 times before the network censors were happy. No touching allowed, not even in the privacy of the male lovers' apartment. No shake of the hands, even though the family members can't keep *theirs* off one another. That it emerged as an honest piece is a tribute to the script, to the direction and to the fine ensemble acting of Quinn, Gena Rowlands as his mother, Ben Gazzara as his father and especially, John Glover as Victor D'Amano, the ugly physical reality of the disease.

A former chef, Victor was thrown out onto the streets by his room-mates when he told them the diagnosis. His parents also washed their hands of him. Now he is dying alone, the life and soul of the AIDS wing. 'It's the only fraternity I've ever rushed that has let me in.' His motto is: 'Laugh and the world laughs with you. Cry and you bore me to tears ... How do I cope? I put up my dukes.' Victor's feistiness is contrasted with Michael's quietly compassionate GRANDMOTHER (Sylvia Sidney), who likens Michael's situation to the fate of her beloved roses: 'I hope that an early frost doesn't come along and nip them in the bud.'

The least convincing aspect of the drama is Michael's homosexuality, more specifically his lack of physical closeness with his lover Peter (D. W. Moffett). There is an emotionally intimate moment when Peter, visiting Michael's family home for the first time, looks at photographs of Michael as a child: 'It's strange. When you see someone and they have this whole other life you know nothing about.' There is a confronting scene or two: 'When are you going to tell your parents? When are they going to have the great honour of finding out who you are – after you're *dead*?' But no TOUCHING.

Sighed the monthly gay American magazine *Christopher Street*: 'Gay-lovers-as-just-roommates is an image mid-America can swallow less painlessly than queers as affectionate husbands: too much audience hysteria would interfere with clear thinking when it comes to getting the course on AIDS across. Cross-purposes. Neither one succeeds.'

An Early Frost, for all its credible dramatics, tightly controlled statements and top-notch acting, painfully reflects the impossibility of presenting on prime-time American television the truth about AIDS as it affects gay men. The censorship of this work was but one example of what James BALDWIN, in one of his last interviews, called 'the central problem of the American condition ... the inability to love [which] masks a certain terror and that is the terror of being touched. And if you can't be touched you can't be changed. And if you can't be changed, you can't be alive.' (*Advocate*, 27.5.86).

earrings The wearing of something in an ear lobe is one of the more interesting aspects of television and film costuming: it can denote sexual allure, danger, delinquency, extroversion, deviance. First noted, outside of pirate and Arabian Nights adventures, in the lobe of Peter LORRE as the general in *The Secret Agent* (1936 C), together with greasy curled hair, make-up, satin cravat, open-neck plaid silk shirt and large rose in buttonhole. Another exotic, Gordon HEATH wore two hefty pearl droplets as

Othello, the Moor of Venice on BBC television in 1955.

The earring's association with modern urban male-male sexuality began in the 1960s: leather guys in PJ aka *New Face in Hell* (1967 C); a suspect in *The Boston Strangler* (1968 C); one of the LONESOME COWBOYS (Tom Hompertz 1968 C).

BISEXUAL musician Pablo (Pierre Clementi) wears a gold stud in *Steppenwolf* (1974 C). However, probably the first *bona fide* modern gay foreground character to wear this fashion accessory/ necessity was Neil Kennedy's Harold Shafter, manager of Ruby Slippers – 'a group with bisexual appeal' – in ROCK FOLLIES OF '77 (1977 T), accompanied by moustache and leather trousers. Kennedy wore one again as the mercenary Max in JUBILEE (1977) a very earringy film – earrings were also sported by the villainous Borgia Ginz (Jack BIRKETT) and by the gentle Sphinx (Karl Johnson).

The following year, single earrings began to sprout: probable bisexual student Skinner (Derek Thompson) emphasizes his coolness with one in ME! I'M AFRAID OF VIRGINIA WOOLF (1978 T), Jack the Lad Paul (Ian Redford) in *Born and Bred* (1978 T) arrives for his wedding carrying a bit of lobe-metal; José Ferrer's film producer in *Fedora* (1978 C) vehemently denies Wiliam Holden's suggestion that his adornment means he's QUEER; Ken HASTINGS (Michael Howarth) removes his at work for form's sake in ANGELS (1979–80 T); the sexually demonstrative, deviant delinquent (Jason Kemp) struts around in bondage trousers and 'masculine' jewellery in KIDS 'Michael and Liam' (1979 T); the sulky sultry lover (Gino Di Fulgentiis) of Alan (Michael Callan) has one in *Scruples* (1980 T); as do CLONE characters in THE GENTLE TOUCH 'Blade' (1980 T) and in CRUISING (1980 C).

The earring reached the 1980s as one of the few junctions for heterosexual and gay men; the best friends Caz (Mo Sesay) and Chris (Valentine Nonyela), from different sides of the sexual street, both decorate their ears in YOUNG SOUL REBELS (1991 C), which is set in the London of 1977, the heyday of the punk culture in which the earring was *de rigueur*.

The punkish/gay associations added to the sinister, powerful ambiguity of one of the two strangers in *Entertaining Unawares* (1981 R), who was described by the heroine thus: '... his hair was cropped close to his skull, but he was lightly BEARDED and in his left ear was a tiny earring. He seemed to be offering himself for my inspection, with something too confidently passive to be defiance. Not even his eyes evaded mine.'

In *Take Three Women* (1982 T) Sophie (Joanna Bobin), getting ready for school, counters her mother's objections to her wearing jeans: '*Some* of the girls wear earrings ... *and* some of the boys.' At the same time, she reminds her parents that the latter's lover, Kit, wears one: '*He's* not odd ... is he?'

By this time, even an apparently clueless character like Lily (Dandy Nichols) in *Marks* (1982 T) could observe to a tattooist: 'Earrings don't mean nothing. They all have earrings. *Police* have earrings.' She wasn't wrong. Suddenly, males in earrings were everywhere and not just on such obvious candidates as moody, talented DANCER Leroy Johnson (Gene Anthony Ray) in FAME (1982–3 T), or stroppy young drag artist Michael (Martyn Hesford) in *Belles* (1983 T).

Far from being something slipped on and off for social occasions, the earring had entered the work place: a SOCIAL WORKER in *Love and Marriage* 'As Man and Wife' (1982 T) displays one as does the macho black cop hero (Philip Michael Thomas) in *Miami Vice* (1984–8 T).

A headmaster voiced his concern about boys and earrings on the early morning BBC Radio 4 *Today* programme: 'What's to prevent them turning up in skirts and twinsets and pearls. It is effeminate and distasteful and it could lead to other things – boys wearing MAKE-UP' (7.3.83).

At this time male-adult penetration was limited to certain areas of Britain. In

ABOUT MEN ... AND MEN (1983 T) none of the dozen participants wears any jewellery apart from wedding rings. Two of them go to meet a couple of gays (for research purposes only), one of whom brandishes an earring.

From the mid-1980s, earrings appeared in epidemic proportions in the lobes of bad-bad or bad-good characters like Nick Cotton (John Altman) in EASTENDERS (1986–). Nick got rid of his in prison (1989), but it was back when trying to poison Mum during 1990. (When Nick went inside or on walkabout other earring-wearers moved into Albert Square – Mary's former boyfriend, Rod (Christopher McHallem) or Carmel's Matthew (Steven Hartley).) Then there was the drug-driven, BLACKMAILING boyfriend of the dead MP, Mike Nielsen (Martin Stone?) in *Inside Story* (1986 T); the slimily effeminate 'Matilda' (Trader FAULKNER), in *Call Me Mister* 'Long Shot' (1986 T); corrupt, high-born homosexual Hugo Silver (Simon CALLOW) in *Dead Head* (1986 T); viperish 'Pearl' in *Santa Barbara* (1986 T); other-worldly Echo (Bruce Payne) in THE FRUIT MACHINE (1988 C); Bernard (Stevan Rimkus), boyfriend of one of the women in *Heart of the Country* (1987 T) – he lives in a caravan and wears an ostentatiously long one; appalling psychopathic Otto (Kevin Kline) in *A Fish Called Wanda* (1988 C); TRANSVESTITE Frankie Diamond (Ronald LACEY), one of whose lobes bears a gold oak-leaf cluster in HARD CASES (1988 T); Nick (Scott Valentine) who swaps his T-shirt, camouflage pants, combat boots and earrings for a three-piece suit and a haircut to impress Mallory's parents in *Family Ties* and so become 'Mr Right' (1988 T); ECCENTRIC 'Dirty Harry' (Martin Oldfield) in a 1989 episode of *The Bill*; 'The Devil' (Bruce Payne) who has long blond locks, a banked-down British public school accent, and a diamond stud in his ear in *Switch* (1991 C); Mickey Rourke in *Harley Davidson and the Marlboro Man* (1991 C); Anthony (Gary Sauer), football player and jerk in *Trust* (1991 C).

By the late 1980s, popular culture had more or less capitulated to the idea that it was cool and sexy *and* masculine for men (usually young, nearly always problematic) to have an earring (or two) or an ear stud. 'There's more to this than meets the eye,' remarks one of the regulars about newcomer Brad Willis in NEIGHBOURS (1989 T), but a year later no such comment was passed about similarly earringed Glen Donnelly (Richard Huggett), who was allowed to teach young Toby how to 'go out with' a girl. In another Australian neck of the woods (Coopers Crossing in A COUNTRY PRACTICE) very heterosexual (and HOMOPHOBIC) abandoned-by-his-mother student nurse Luke (Matt Day 1988–91 T) is told not to wear his at work – an injunction which rouses the normally conservative busybody, Esmé (Joyce Jacobs) to blare: 'It's what's inside a person that counts ... We should show more tolerance to these young people.'

The dramatic focus on the male earring still tends to be narrow. It is the unmistakable mark of the heterosexual rebel: Johnny Depp in *21 Jump Street* (1988–90 T); Dylan (Luke Perry) in BEVERLY HILLS 90210 (1990– T); Martin Platt (Sean Wilson) in CORONATION STREET (1990 T). Or it is unapologetically homosexual: British Julian CLARY on *Trick or Treat* and STICKY MOMENTS (1989–91 T); American Eliot (Corey Parker) in THE LOST LANGUAGE OF CRANES (1992 T); Australian Brett, champion cyclist who upsets a few residents of Wandin Valley in *A Country Practice* 'Little Boy Blue' (1992 T). Or it's part of a youth culture jumble: a British Persil washing powder advert (1989 T); pop videos (New Kids On The Block's 'Call It What You Want' 1991 T); quiz contestants (one on the Australian *Sale of the Century* (1991 T) wore two curtain rings).

Although it is unlikely that a Labour party candidate would be marked down because he 'once wore an earring' (as a Liberal party agent noted to journalists during the Hillhead by-election in 1982), the accessory still carries with it that troubling echo, so that *Radio Times* could announce TOM ROBINSON'S taking over of a record request programme from a woman as 'stepping into Janice's earrings' (1987).

In many institutions, the earring, singular or plural, is not a legitimate accoutrement for the male. This was wondrously illustrated by the furore caused by a menial in *The London Embassy* who was thought to be gay and – by association – a security risk because he turned up for work wearing one of 'those' ('Charlie Hogles' Earring' 1987 T). The hero (Kristoffer Tabori), told to vet the man for any suspicious tendencies, is astonished to discover that at least three people, including the woman he sleeps with, ask him if he himself either *is* or is thinking of becoming *one* – merely because he is investigating the wearing of an earring which is probably 'a sign of being a homosexual'.

EastEnders (UK 1985– T) BBC1's twice-weekly soap set in an East London Square. It took 18 months for a gay regular character to take up residence: workaholic Colin RUSSELL (Michael CASHMAN), who was brought out of the CLOSET when he was pursued by market stall helper Barry CLARK (Gary Hailes) who, unasked, set up home with him. This led to one or two of the more moribund of the Cockney sparrers (like Pete Beale) to gripe: 'Attackers, homosexuals, winos. I don't know what the Square is coming to ...' (7.4.87).

By late 1987 the relationship was fraying, and Barry eventually did the right thing and 'became' heterosexual. Colin moped throughout most of 1988, becoming increasingly concerned about his health. Instead of being diagnosed HIV positive (which he suspected), Colin was found to be suffering from the progressive neurological disease, multiple sclerosis. He had begun living with an unassuming young man called Guido Smith (Nicholas Donovan) but, instead of remaining in Albert Square, he left London for his brother's home.

The series, created by Julia SMITH and Tony HOLLAND (both involved in the later stages of ANGELS), was honourable, progressive and – in most cases – sharply characterized. Opinion remains divided about the value of Colin to the overall dramatic life of the Square and of his political significance as a beacon and role model during a particularly nasty period for British homosexuals (the AIDS panic leading to the passing of CLAUSE 28).

Chris Stacey and Darcy Sullivan in the book *Supersoaps* (1988) commented: 'As the soap world's first permanent gay couple ... [Colin and Barry] have also drawn the spotlight. Tidy, shy Colin and beer-drinking fun fellow Barry make an odd couple, but they've also made strides towards better representation of gays on television. This hasn't always gone unchallenged: viewers launched a storm of protest after Colin kissed Barry's hand on screen. But the public has largely grown to love this duo, and a shudder passed through the nation when Barry took an AIDS test. Fortunately, it proved negative.'

The series was always surrounded by controversy, much of it whipped up by the press and relating to its actors, but some of it because of the choice of subject matter aired so early in the evening (7.30 pm and within 'family viewing time'). Colin and Barry, naturally, drew much of the fire – along with teenage pregnancy, adultery, rape, 'coarse' language and locution.

A letter-writer from London was doubtless typical of many people who felt *EastEnders* was unsuitable early evening (and Sunday afternoon) viewing: 'Ever since the first episode ... the whole gamut of crime and violence continues to be exploited against a backdrop of sleazy situations purporting to portray 'real life', taking in prostitution, and homosexuality along the way. Not that I object to some of these things in proportion to dramatic content, but when we are asked to accept such a total of criminal acts towards a handful of residents occupying an area of apparently about a quarter of a mile square, then the situation becomes ludicrously inept' (*Radio Times*, 18–24.4.87).

Also complaining about implausibility but from a different perspective, Jonathan Sanders, exasperated by the generally timid air surrounding Colin and Barry after their first full year, wrote: 'the scriptwriters cast doubts not only on the future of Colin and Barry's relationship, but also about Barry's sexuality *per se* ... how about Lofty as a strict gay leather master, or Dot as a radical lesbian feminist? It would be just as plausible' (*Gay Times*, December 1987).

East Lynne Mrs Henry Wood's 1861 novel (one of 40) has been repeatedly dramatized throughout the 20th century in Britain, with film, radio (1988 etc) and television (1978 etc) versions. Although the title is synonymous with creaking melodrama and exaggerated emotions, it remains a good yarn with a delightful ripple of physical affection between women running through it. This achieves risibility when Cornelia Carlyle, a 'snappish old maid' is most affronted when her new sister-in-law, Isabel puts her arms around her and kisses her. Cornelia exits in high dudgeon and Isabel is at a loss: 'I think your sister is a very queer person,' she tells husband Archibald. 'Do you know, I kissed her just now, and she seemed quite frightened. I don't believe she was ever kissed before.'

Eat Carpet (Aust 1988–) Short films of good quality, shown on the minority SBS network. The series is *the* conduit for challenging, innovative and (relatively) sexually explicit material, including nearly all of Peter WELLS' work from New Zealand, and important lesbian short films such as *Amelia Rose Towers* (1992).

eating Mealtime conversations, chaotic and civilized, involving gay and lesbian people featured in COMING OUT (1979 T); DOMESTIC BLISS (1985 T); PARTING GLANCES (1985 C); THE HEART EXPOSED (1986 T); EASTENDERS (1987 T); LONGTIME COMPANION (1990 C); *Byline* 'A Kiss Is Just a Kiss' (1991 T); OUT 'Guess Who's Coming to Dinner?' (1991 T); etc. Those occasions where heterosexuals discuss/decry/disparage gay and lesbian people over meals include *On the Eve of Publication* (1968 T); MORE LIVES THAN ONE (1984 T); BROOKSIDE (1987 T); A HORSE CALLED GERTRUDE STEIN (1990 R); *The Comfort of Strangers* (1990 C); etc.

Eat the Rich (UK 1987 C) The hero/heroine Alex (Lanah Pellay) is a wonderfully clapped-out creature ('I'm up to *here* in social grievance') who leads the cannibalistic insurrection against yuppies and all adherents of Thatcherism. In a gentler moment, after battles won and lost, Alex eulogizes, in misty tones that cunningly echo Mrs T herself: 'Yes, David, we *were* heroes.'
W/D: Peter Richardson; 92 mins.

Not a 'good' film in the technical sense, but one born out of the enveloping sense of desperation and impotence, and smiting targets in haphazard fashion. Crude fun though and certainly undeserving of Professor Norman Stone's diatribe in the *Sunday Times* (January 1988) as one of 'a worthless, insulting ... farrago' of 'tawdry, ragged, rancidly provincial films' (along with *The Last of England*, *Business As Usual*, *Empire State*, MY BEAUTIFUL LAUNDRETTE and *Sammy and Rosie Get Laid*). (Correspondence ran 10–12 against his views.)

eccentric 'He's just a sad eccentric,' says Chris (Simon Rouse) about his admirer Terry (Fred Gaunt) in WEDNESDAY LOVE (1975 T). It was used about Dr Frank Marsh (Allan Lander), biologist, botanist and ecologist in *The Deep Concern* (1979 T): 'he's a born stirrer ... also pretty juvenile. His muscles are as elastic as his principles.' *TV Times* described blaringly homosexual Morris (James Saxon) of *Brass* as merely 'eccentric' in June 1990.

Eddison, Robert (1908–91) Imposing English actor, on stage in SHAKESPEARE, Ibsen, Chekhov, Restoration comedy, Ionesco, Durrenmatt and WILDE. It was he who first gave life to Sebastian FLYTE, on radio in 1956. Played increasingly grand and oracular roles into his eighties.

Monologue in *Cabaret* (1938 T); John WORTHING in THE IMPORTANCE OF BEING EARNEST (1946 T); title role in *Pythias* (1947 R); the player in the prologue to *The Man Who Could Work Miracles* (1956 T); title role in *Saint-Loup* (1956 R); title role in *Mr Arcularis* (1959 R); title role in *Mr Norris Changes Trains* (1967 R); Archbishop of Canterbury in EDWARD II (1970 T); as antiquarian Anthony Wood in *Pimps and Panderers, Bawds and Buffoons, Lechery and Treachery*, 'Oxford Through the Eyes of Anthony Wood in 1667' (1974 R); Sourdust in *Gormenghast* (1984 R); Hawkins, the adoring former batman in *The Kingfisher* (1985 R); the abbot in THE ASCENT OF F6 (1988 R); Marley's ghost in *A Christmas Carol* (1988 R); chorus in *Antigone* (1986 T); Grail Knight in *Indiana Jones and the Last Crusade* (1989 C); the Keeper of the Lockets in *The Numbered* (1989 R); Robert Skinn in *Campion* 'The Case of the Late Pig' (1989 T); *Roland's After Life* (1991); etc. Read *The Memory of Troy* (1988 R).

Edens, Roger (1906–70) American pianist and composer of songs like 'It's A Great Day For The Irish', 'Pass The Peace Pipe', 'IN-BETWEEN', 'The Right Girl For Me', 'Minnie From Trinidad' and 'Dear Mr Gable (You Made Me Love You)'. An associate of Arthur Freed, he scored famous MGM musicals like *Annie Get Your Gun* and *Take Me Out to the Ball Game*, winning Oscars for *Easter Parade* and *On the Town*. At Warners he worked with Judy GARLAND on her musical numbers in *A Star Is Born*. He was associate producer on *Hello Dolly* and was to have produced the aborted big-budget *Say It with Music* in the early 1970s.

The Editors (UK 1971–8 T) September 1977 marked the beginning of the backlash that dared speak its name. Ostensibly about 'Sex and the Press', the real issue was homosexuality and blasphemy. The burning question was:

'Is the pendulum swinging back?' William Deedes, editor of the *Daily Telegraph* sitting next to Denis LEMON (now a media personality as a result of exposure at the Old Bailey and in *Newsweek*, said yes, most decidedly – and necessarily – it was. He spoke of the need to give all religions protection under the blasphemy law. Next to the convicted blasphemer (who kept dodging in and out of camera range to shake ash off or stub out his cigarettes) was Cyril Kersh of the old-established girlie magazine *Reveille*. It was he who delivered the most telling remark: 'It's not a puritan backlash, but an anti-gay backlash. Other more blasphemous things have been published.' Put another way – as Lord Ted WILLIS told GAY NEWS a month or so later: 'they're coming out of their caves. And it's you they're after.'

Edward II (1284–1327) King of England. Plantagenet ruler and the first Prince of Wales. Christopher MARLOWE's play about the 'sophister' king and his favourite, Piers Gaveston was practically the only dramatic work in the English language up until the 20th century to give more or less full vent to the same-sex passion. 'What Gaveston! Welcome? Kiss not my hand. Embrace me Gaveston as I do thee.' 'There can be no denying the painful reality of Edward's attachment to Gaveston,' wrote the *Listener*'s reviewer of the 1967 radio production (23.3.67).

C. Harmon Grisewood and Leonard Thompson played king and commoner lover in the BBC's first production in 1930; thereafter David King-Wood and Max ADRIAN 1943; Paul Scofield and Richard Hurndall 1955; Derek JACOBI and Richard Marquand 1959; Alec MCCOWEN and Ian MCKELLEN 1967; Ian McKellen and James Laurenson (complete with 'squelchy' kiss 1970 (first television production); Steven Waddington and Andrew Tiernan 1991 (first film version); David Robb in *Gaveston* (1993 R).

Edward II (UK 1991 C) Jarman's most expensive film (£850,000!): ablaze with

surly passions, venomous queens, queer activism (including a full scale OUTRAGE! demo), cruel fortune, death and destruction of the realm.
W: Derek Jarman, Stephen McBride and Ken Butler from the play by Christopher MARLOWE; P: Steve Clark-Hall and Antony Root; D: Derek Jarman; 90 mins.

Resplendent photography, dangerous electricity from Nigel Terry as Mortimer, a misogynist reading of Queen Isabella, two runty lovers, leaky personal politicking and unwieldy text (though mightily cut) add up to muckraking in a pigsty.

'It is difficult enough to be queer but to be queer in the cinema is almost impossible. Heterosexuals have fucked up the screen so completely that there's hardly any room for us to kiss there. Marlowe outs the past – why don't we out the present?' (Derek Jarman, *Queer Edward*, 1991).

'Partly recognizable as Marlowe and wholly recognizable as Jarman ... making a HETEROPHOBIC film to counter an entire history of homophobic ones seems a fair polemical strategy, the logical result of reversing the terms of reference that have often been imposed on Marlowe's play. But ...' (Jonathan Romney, *Sight and Sound*, November 1991).

Edwards, Hilton (1901–82) English actor and director, long associated with Dublin's Gate Theatre, the lover-partner of Micheal MACLIAMMOIR. He recorded fairly infrequently for the BBC in Dublin, beginning with his Algernon Moncrieff (opposite MacLiammoir's John WORTHING) in THE IMPORTANCE OF BEING EARNEST (1934). His screen work included *Call of the Blood* (1948 C); *The Road to Glannascaul* (1953 C); Cassio in Orson WELLES' *Othello* (1952 C); Micawber in DAVID COPPERFIELD (1956 T); William Scruby, BLACKMAILER and thief in *Cat and Mouse* (1958 C); King Herod in *Paul of Tarsus* (1960 T); blind con man in VICTIM; Holy Healy in *The Quare Fellow* (1962 C); a lawyer in *The Wrong Box* (1966 C).

Edwards, Jimmy (1920–88) English comic actor, sometimes known as 'Professor Jimmy Edwards' who belligerently commanded his audience to pin back its 'lugholes' and 'shut up at the back there.' He always played variants of the bluff sadist – most memorably as the 'flog 'em and beat 'em' headmaster of Chiselbury School in *Whacko!* and his irrepressibly vulgar, cunning Dad GLUM in *Take It from Here* (a role which he reprised on television two decades later, in 1978). His other TV work included *The Seven Faces of Jim/More Faces of Jim* (1961–2) scripted by TIFH's Frank Muir and Denis Norden.

For radio he created and was a regular member of the misogynist panel game *Does the Team Think?* from 1958 (belatedly transferred to TV in 1982). Publicly a rambunctious male chauvinist, he was one of the proposers of the motion 'This House Regrets That the Age of Chivalry Has Passed' in an Oxford Union Debate introduced by Norman St John Stevas and broadcast in 1958. He also played Toby Belch in TWELFTH NIGHT and Falstaff in *The Merry Wives of Windsor* (1962 R). His – mainly undistinguished – films included *Murder at the Windmill* (1949); *Treasure Hunt* (1952); *Three Men in a Boat* (1955); *Bottoms Up* (1960, screen version of *Whacko!*); *Nearly a Nasty Accident* (1961); *The Bed Sitting Room* (1969); *Rhubarb* (1970).

This extraordinarily bombastic performer, who took such pains to promote the image of a philistine country squire, was seen recalling his days at St Paul's, at Cambridge and in the RAF on *Spotlight* (1983) and heard on the *Life of Jim* (1985) taking a 'light-hearted look at his life'. He was last seen, showing off his Australian garden (but not his lover), in *Burke's Backyard* (Aust 1988 T). Also: *Radio Lives* (1993 R).

effete British Often the villain or opponent of American know-how, libertarianism and initiative, whether in Ancient Rome, Civil War America, the West or Sherwood Forest, will have a BBC/Old Vic accent and a fruity delivery: Laurence Olivier in *The Devil's Disciple*, and

Spartacus; Frank THRING in *Ben-Hur*; Alan Rickman in *Robin Hood – Prince of Thieves*; Terence Stamp in *Young Guns*. The opportunity to have non-sparkling dialogue oxygenated: beautifully enunciated with a trickle of decadence.

Eisenstein, Sergei Mihailovitch (1898–1948) Russian film director of immense human and sweeping lyrical vision who was highly influential, especially in the growth of propaganda cinema and – also through his books – of film theory. He made seven films: *Strike* (1924); *The Battleship Potemkin* (1925); *October* aka *Ten Days That Shook the World* (1972); *The General Line* (1928); *Que Viva Mexico* (1932; unfinished although sections of it were assembled under the title *Time in the Sun*); *Alexander Nevsky* (1938); *Ivan the Terrible* (1942–6). (*PRKFV*, a dramatization of the collaboration between Eisenstein (John Moffatt) and Prokofiev (Anthony Jackson) in the making of *Alexander Nevsky* was broadcast on BBC Radio 3 in 1987.)

The homoeroticism of his films has been only grudgingly appreciated in the light of more honest autobiography and the new light shed on Eisenstein's published writings. It is likely that, with greater access to all the private papers, his full stature as a film-maker and as a human being can be assessed.

Certainly the two television documentaries (one, in OMNIBUS's 'Great Directors' series (1973), was narrated by Lindsay Anderson; the other was misleadingly entitled *The Secret Life of Sergei Eisenstein* (1988) 'a life of joy, torment and excitement') failed to reveal him as a gay man, fleeing disapproval from all sides. The second documentary skipped over such fascinating areas as his time in Hollywood, Mexico, Berlin and his identification with DAVID COPPERFIELD. No mention was there of his mother's contempt for his bachelorhood; his decision, after a visit to the circus, to wear a clown's mask; his love for Grigori Alexandrov; his 'scientific investigations' into Berlin gay bars and cafés; his flight from his 'fatal weakness'; the shocking contents of his luggage opened by US

Customs; the innuendoes from bureaucrats and fellow directors; and his marriage of convenience, at the age of 39, to his secretary. The film's only real chink of light came at the end, in an extract from a letter the director wrote the day before his fatal heart attack: 'All my life, I've wanted to be accepted with affection. Yet I've felt compelled to withdraw and thus remain, forever, a spectator.'

Eldorado (UK 1992–3 T) A group of people leading an expatriate life of Riley in Spain, including Freddie MARTIN (Roland CURRAM), the initially conservative retired nurse who is trying to get over the death of his long-time lover, John. Created by Julia SMITH and Tony HOLLAND of EASTENDERS, filmed on location, receiving an almost unprecedented critical drubbing, and getting limited viewer support. BBC1; 30 mins.

electricians Not too many homosexual characters know their DC from their AC. Steve (Daniel Webb), Michael's discovery during a police swoop on a public lavatory in MORE LIVES THAN ONE (1984 T), was one; Richard (Ray Burdis) in DREAM STUFFING (1984 T) the other. Women in this profession are almost non-existent in comedy or drama although 'C. Haslett' recommended *Electrical Work for Girls* in 1929 (R): 'The type of girl who is most suitable for this work is the girl who is fond of things mechanical and of outdoor life, who can cooperate easily with both men and women and who is capable of working with her hands.'

Eliot/Elliot/Elliott/Elyot Boy's name, or surname with intimations of neurotic punctiliousness: Elliott Templeton (Clifton WEBB) in *The Razor's Edge* (1946 C); Eliot Foley (Roland Culver), BACHELOR who lives with mother in *Dead of Night's* linking story (1946 C); Eliot (Kenneth More), mystery man in *The Greengage Summer/Loss of Innocence* (1961 C); precious journalist Eliot Morrow (Maurice Browning) in COMPACT (1965 T); Eliot (Larry Casey), one of THE GAY DECEIVERS (1969 C); Elliott

Carlin (Jack Riley), paranoid member of Bob's therapy group in *The Bob Newhart Show* (1972–8 T); Elliot Garfield (Richard Dreyfuss), egocentric actor playing drag queen Richard III in *The Goodbye Girl* (1977 C); Elliot (Jeremy Irons), twin of Beverly in DEAD RINGERS (1988 C); Eliot (Corey Parker) sulky lover of Phillip in THE LOST LANGUAGE OF CRANES (1992 T).

In America it is used fairly extensively for less outré characters: federal agent Elliott Ness (Robert Stack; Kevin Costner) in *The Untouchables* (1959–63 T; 1987 C); Elliott Nash (Glenn Ford), married writer who sets out to murder his blackmailer and place him in *The Gazebo* (1960 C); Elliot Hoover (Anthony Hopkins), the scientist who exorcises the soul of his long dead daughter *Audrey Rose* (1977 C); Elliott Rosen (Bob Balaban), ruthless government inspector in *Absence of Malice* (1981 C); Elliott (Henry Thomas), 10-year-old empathetic friend of *ET: The Extra Terrestrial* (1982 C); Elliot Novak (Charles Levin) who married one of the waitresses in *Alice* (1983 T); Timothy Busfield as one of the THIRTYSOME-THING enclave (1988 T); Hank Elliott in AS THE WORLD TURNS (1988 T).

Elliott, Denholm (1922–92) English actor, renowned for discreet scene-stealing and playing a long line of slightly soused reprobates, including those with a gay tinge (or who were closely associated with gays): Abbé de Pradts in *The Land Where the King Is a Child* (1959 R); Roderick Usher in *Mystery and Imagination* 'The Fall of the House of Usher' (1966 T); DRACULA (1968 T); factotum to *Madame Sin* (1970 C/T); the PSY-CHIATRIST in *You're All Right – How Am I?* (1979 T); Geoffrey Treasure in *School Play* (1979 T); the sleeping spy's BUTLER/minder in *Blade on the Feather* (1980 T); Victor in PAST CARING (1986).

Eltinge, Julian (1882 or 1894–1941) American female impersonator and male actress. In vaudeville and theatre (*The Crinoline Girl*; *Her Grace the Vampire*). Film début in 1917, in a version of

his stage hit *The Countess Charming* with Florence Vidor, followed by another co-starring assignment with her in *The Widow's Might*. He made the all-star propaganda film *War Relief* in 1918 and *The Adventuress* (1918, supposedly VALENTINO's début). One of his last starring roles was as the mystery woman in *Madame Behave* (1924). The *Variety* obituary commented that the 'fact that he never married led to various reports, but Eltinge demonstrated his ability to take care of himself on a number of occasions'.

Elyot, Kevin (195?–) English actor and playwright, best known for the 1982 stage play *Coming Clean*, which skilfully posed the question: should gay relations be based on heterosexual mimicry? Other plays include *According to Plan* (1987 R, chance meeting of middle-aged woman and man in Italy); *The Perfect Moment* (1988 R, two women trying to celebrate an anniversary); KILL-ING TIME (1990 T; lonely man and tearaway youth). As actor: Clark in *The Imitation Game* (1980 T); Matt, investigative TV reporter's assistant in *Scandalous* (1984 C); Fritz Kolberg in *Murder East, Murder West* (1990 T); Gilbert in *The Bill* (1991 T).

embroidery Mr DULCIMER (D. A. CLARKE-SMITH is a dab hand at this in THE GREEN BAY TREE (1946 R), although his rival for young Julian, Leonora dismisses it as mere 'sewing'; Mr Peasglove (Wallas Eaton) calls himself 'the Rembrandt of the electric needle' in *Take It from Here* (1958 R); Herr Flick (Richard Gibson) hides his embroidery frame from Helga in 'ALLO, 'ALLO (1991 T). Dexterity with needle and coloured cottons is still considered a good gauge of whether a man is or isn't: 'Funny, if a boy likes COOKERY, everybody thinks he's a SISSY. Mind you, when I got my only A-level in embroidery everybody knew I was', says Richard Cawley in OUT (1991 T).

In fact embroidery is a fine art known to ancient Egyptians and Assyrians, male and female, as Mr Leigh Ashton from the Victoria and Albert Museum explained in *The Art of Embroidery* (1929 R). Actor Ernest THESIGER was proud to display his (on *Leisure and Pleasure* 1955 T, in company with Yvonne Arnaud), but Rock HUDSON (who embroidered openly during interviews with print journalists) never felt moved to reveal his work to the world.

Emerald City (Aust 1990 C) How a right-on, intellectual writer (John Hargreaves) is lacerated and maimed by the film industry. 'We get enough truth in our lives. We don't want to see it on our screens,' claims a cynical producer. A project about lesbian nuns is so compromised as to be meaningless: 'only one nun and it's got to be a tendency not consummated.' Says the producer's fresh-faced girlfriend (Nicole Kidman): 'Just occasionally I'd like to see the truth.' He is scornful. He would turn nuns into astronauts and lesbians into doughnuts if it meant the film got made.

Underlying these jokes about the film industry's philistinism is a sneer. In David Williamson's stage play (and its 1990 radio version) there was a diatribe against left-wing wankers and intellectual trendies. Adapting for the screen – and for the mass market – Williamson has dropped this speech. In its place are the hero's fears that his son will think being gay is normal, and that if he likes girls the boy will feel self-conscious and inhibited. Tacked onto this section of the film – and going completely against a similar moment in the play that shows how the stresses and strains of trying to placate Mammon have dried up the libido – is some hot foreplay between husband and wife in bed.

Emerson, Hope (1897–1960) Amazonian American actress, towering (6 feet 2 inches) and stylish, who was renowned for playing lesbians in films before lesbians were officially noted: ADAM'S RIB (1949); the salivatingly sadistic masseuse Rose in *Cry of the City* (1948); Evelyn, the terror of the cell block in CAGED (1950); Patience, one of the rolled-up sleeves, rifle-toting mail

order brides in *Westward the Women* (1951). No-nonsense, gargantuan, sometimes cruel ... but always a lady; she was also a singer. Her last role was that of 'Mother', the club owner in *Peter Gunn* (1958–9 T).

Emmerdale aka *Emmerdale Farm* (UK 1972– T) Twice-weekly serial from Yorkshire TV set in the Dales. One of its regular characters, Zoe Tate (Leah Bracknell), daughter of Frank and Kim, came out as a lesbian in June 1993.

Emmy Awards American television's best known prizes, presented from 1949 by the Academy of Television Arts and Sciences. They were first telecast in 1954, and are now very much part of the glitzy show-business landscape in many countries. Some of the relevant or piquant Emmies are:

Actors: Mary Martin for PETER PAN (1955); Raymond Burr for PERRY MASON (1958–9; 1960–1); Barbara Hale as Della STREET in *Perry Mason* (1958–9); Barbara STANWYCK in *The Barbara Stanwyck Show* (1960–1), *The Big Valley* (1965–6) and *The Thorn Birds* (1983–4); Jean Marsh as Rose in UPSTAIRS, DOWNSTAIRS (1974–5); Rosemary Harris as George Sand in *Notorious Woman* (1975–6); Powers Boothe as Rev. Jim Jones in GUYANA TRAGEDY (1979–80); Tyne Daly for CAGNEY AND LACEY (1982–3); John Glover for AN EARLY FROST (1984–5).

Writers: Rod Serling for THE TWILIGHT ZONE (1960–1); Lily TOMLIN (with others) for LILY (1973–4) and *Lily Tomlin* (1975–6), and (with Jane Wagner) for overall work on *Lily: Sold Out* (1980–1); Bob Weiskopf and Bob Schiller for ALL IN THE FAMILY 'Cousin Liz' (1977–8); Seth Freeman for LOU GRANT 'Cop' (1979–80); Ron Cowan and Daniel Lipman for AN EARLY FROST (1983–4); Terrance MCNALLY for *André's Mother* (1989–90).

Directors: James Burrows for *Taxi* 'Elaine's Strange Triangle' (1982–3).

The British version of the Emmy

Awards, the BAFTA (British Academy of Film and Television Arts) Awards, have bestowed prizes on, among others, Anthony Andrews for his Sebastian FLYTE in BRIDESHEAD REVISITED (1982); Beryl Reid as Connie Sachs in *Smiley's People* (1983); the writers of ORANGES ARE NOT THE ONLY FRUIT (1991).

Emory (Cliff Gorman in THE BOYS IN THE BAND) INTERIOR DECORATOR who has known he was gay from the age of 4. He has a poodle called 'Chi Chi', likes Mabel Mercer and knows the screenplay of ALL ABOUT EVE backwards. One of his opening lines at the party is: 'Who do you have to fuck to get a drink round here?' Emory is inseparable from Bernard, at whom he throws occasional 'nigger' insults in his never-ending, express train repartee. Emory is a queen's queen, super-swish. He delights audiences as soon as he enters, putting them offside the token straight, who takes an instant dislike to him: 'he's a bit like a butterfly on heat.' Totally unselfconscious, Emory alone plays Michael's telephone truth game, ringing a man he loved as a boy.

empathy 'We know things that heterosexuals will never know,' says Harvey FIERSTEIN, in full flight, on OUT ON TUESDAY (1989). In mainstream entertainment, homosexual life and loving is subtly or unsubtly compartmentalized. The few situations where a heterosexual audience is invited to share and identify are almost totally confined to people or characters at death's door, chirpily camping as they breathe their last. Rare exceptions are the waltz/fuck scene from MY BEAUTIFUL LAUNDRETTE, and possibly PORTRAIT OF A MARRIAGE and PRICK UP YOUR EARS (the problem of being the 'wife' of a successful writer and public personality). And RAY'S HETEROSEXUAL MALE DANCE HALL managed to cock a snook at male jockeying for power and referment, while simultaneously breaking down resistance to men DANCING, exchanging pleasantries and picking each other up in exactly the same way as men and women do every hour of the day all over the Western world.

employment discrimination Geoffrey Robertson's *Business Decisions* 'The Company Man' (1981 T) posited the question: should an excellent personnel manager be fired because he was a gay activist? The canvassed opinions supported the sacking, some unequivocally ('Homosexuality is not acceptable. I think rightly, myself ... and a lot of people would object to it'), some with ifs and buts. On the other hand, the majority of those executives assembled in the studio said that they *would* tolerate the supplying of prostitutes to clients as a business practice.

Employment discrimination legislation in Britain hasn't necessarily helped homosexuals in the work place – as DIVERSE REPORTS 'What a Difference a Gay Makes' (1984 T) attested, even though the programme featured a huge demonstration against Rugby council (who would not knowingly employ gays and lesbians) by the local government union NALGO and the Labour party. An industrial tribunal, after deliberating on the sacking of a man from a Rugby dairy, ruled that the employer was correct because 'the man's homosexuality was capable of damaging the business'. Three out of six private dairies in the city said they would not 'knowingly employ gays'.

Blinkered obduracy won the day in Rugby: 'I believe that one bad employee can do a lot of things ... in relationships with the public.' A few moments later we see the walls of an office in one of the disputations, family-orientated organizations that don't want queers on the payroll: a small gallery of totally naked female pin-ups.

The only out Member of Parliament, Chris Smith tried to be positive: 'It's the gay person ... who has to make the legislation work for them.' (This was only a year or so after Labour candidate Peter TATCHELL was vilified and hounded when he attempted to stand for Bermondsey.)

Fictional or drama-documentarized

characters who have found that skills and competency count for very little if they show their whole selves include Melville Farr (Dirk BOGARDE in VICTIM (1961 C) who knows that bringing the BLACKMAILERS to book means he cannot become a QC; Linda Ray Guettner (Gena Rowlands) who is 'stood down' as a nurse after her CHILD CUSTODY case is blazoned over the papers and airwaves in A QUESTION OF LOVE (1978 T); the highly regarded SERGEANT MATLOVICH (Brad Dourif) failing to dislodge military dogma when he put himself vs the US air force (1978 T); the radio announcer (Marcello Mastroianni) thrown out by the Fascists on A SPECIAL DAY (1977 C); Michael (Peter Denyer) identified on a radio phone-in programme about gays in AGONY 'Coming Out ... And Going In Again' (1980 T).

Encounter with Barry Jones (Aust 1968 T) The world of the homosexual, presenting interviews with a lesbian and a male homosexual. Film section includes interviews with social workers, psychiatrists and doctors who discuss the life and problems of the homosexual. The pioneer television programme for Australians. Four years later, two real gay and lesbian couples were put in the spotlight in CHEQUERBOARD.

endearments Heterosexuals Nicole (Primi Townsend) and Camille (Pam Scotcher) discuss the difficulties of usage in *World's End* (1981 T). Nicole comments: 'The word "FRIEND" is beginning to acquire funny overtones. What other word is there?' To which Camille replies: 'LOVER, PARTNER, associate, COMPANION, intimate. I guess we're stuck with "friend".' Nicole says: 'Anything is better than "wife" or "husband". They sound indecent.' Camille thinks that using 'friend' requires a new sexual direction. 'We'll have to get a boiler suit,' she asserts. But Nicole isn't having any: 'Oh, I'm not going *that* way.'

An Englishman Abroad (UK 1983 C) Droll, beautifully observed reconstruction of the visit of Coral Browne (as her

1958 self) to Guy BURGESS (Alan BATES) in his Moscow flat, and his strange, yet perfectly logical request for 'something from home'. All those involved in the film are in perfect step with their garrulous, grubby 'hero'.
W: Alan BENNETT; P: Innes LLOYD; D: John SCHLESINGER; 60 mins.

An Englishman Needs Time Eartha Kitt's meditation upon the theme of the innate and unbudgeable conservatism of the English male in all things sexual and emotional. She sang it at the Royal Variety Performance of 1962 – with firm instructions not to look up at the royal box. Used pertinently to describe the extraordinary delays in decriminalizing male homosexuality compared to France, Spain and Italy in SATURDAY NIGHT OUT 'The Rock 'n' Roll Years' (1991 T), using the 1962 rendition.

The Entertainer (UK 1960 C) John OSBORNE's *tour de force* tribute to music hall in all its tatty tartiness (and especially a celebration of the artistry of Max Miller) is perfectly matched by Laurence Olivier in what is probably his saddest and gayest role.
W: John Osborne and Nigel Kneale; P: John Croydon; D: Tony RICHARDSON; 96 mins.

Entertaining Mr Sloane (UK 1970 C) Beautiful, dangerous lodger finds himself caught in a lascivious pincer movement by a determined BROTHER and SISTER.
W: Clive Exton from the play by Joe ORTON; P: Douglas Kentish; D: Douglas Hickox; 94 mins.
Orton gothic, spring-cleaned and degutted ('They took the worst bits out,' said Beryl REID who plays Kath). What remains is gloriously rich and nasty, providing a field day for Harry ANDREWS as the creepy brother. Orton's message about the keeping up of appearances in the face of blackmail, torture and murder is successfully delivered. However, the 1968 television production by Peter WILLES is the finer because it sticks to the play and has a less absurd

Kath in Sheila Hancock. The Sloane of Clive Francis is perhaps more obviously devious than Peter McEnery's, but Edward Woodward is another blessing as (a younger, fairly attractive) Ed. A landmark play that, for once, was not totally compromised and wrecked on small or large screens.

Entre Nous (Coup de Foudre) aka *At First Sight* (Fr 1983 C) War-time and postwar relationship between the director's Jewish mother (Isabelle Huppert) and another woman (Miou Miou): 'A little more than friendship and a little less than passion.'
W/D: Diane Kurys; 111 mins.
Highly regarded by one of the women on OUT's 'We've Been Framed' segment (1991 T).

Mr (Cedric) Entwhistle ('Enty') Friendly fellow, memorably embodied, trailing clouds of pale pink, by Alec KELLAWAY in two Australian rustic comedies: DAD AND DAVE COME TO TOWN/ *The Rudd Family Goes to Town* (1938) and *Dad Rudd MP* (1940). The acceptable face of effeminacy in a man's country: very much a part of the family, and not a complete fool, though sexless and apart.

environmentalists Lieutenant Mark Templeton (Roger Torrey), Ellie's suitor says that he hopes we use our oceans intelligently and not pollute them as we have our atmosphere (*The Beverly Hillbillies* 1970 T); the film lecturer (Ian Redford) in ARTEMIS '81 (1981 T) whose concern for the planet becomes obsessive, leading – together with guilt over his gayness – to suicide; Steven CARRINGTON (Al Corley) and Bart Fallmont (Cameron Watson), coming from opposite ends of the oil pollution debate, fall in love (off-screen), resolve their differences (off-screen) and live together (on screen), in *Dynasty: The Reunion* (1991 T).

Epstein, Brian (1934–67) English manager of the Beatles, Cilla Black etc. Led on, teased, comforted and rebuked by John Lennon in *The Birth of the Beatles* (1979 T, played by Brian Jameson) and more explicitly, during a 'lost weekend' in Barcelona, in *The Hours and Times* (1991 C/T, played by David Angus); deflated by Joe ORTON in PRICK UP YOUR EARS (1987 C, played by David Cardy). He was camouflaged as Jake Braid (Keith Barron) in *The Man Who Had Power Over Women* (1970 C); and as Leggie in *The Rutles* (1978 T) who, lonely and depressed, took desperate measures and 'accepted a teaching post in Australia'. Similar managers with a very personal interest in their protégés were Alan (Harry H. Corbett) in A HYMN FROM JIM (1977 T) and Mike (Adam Faith) in *Stardust* (1974 C).

erections [phallus impudicus] Cut from the shower scene in IF...: briefly spotted (in cinema versions only) in JARMAN's SEBASTIANE and FASSBINDER's *Satan's Brew*; seen at length (Gérard Depardieu's) in THE LAST WOMAN. Otherwise, the PENIS remains flaccid – apart from pornographic material not available on national broadcasting.

Ernest Boy's name usually for drips, bores and dried-out characters, eg Phillips HOLMES as Ernest (two scenes) in *Dinner at Eight*. Some gay Ernests include the husband who has a brief but enlightening encounter with the navy (Peter SALLIS in THE OBELISK 1977 T); the young Jewish boy who makes a most interesting compromise between sexual preference and society (Martin Halm as ERNESTO (1979 C); the (unseen) 'friend' of Aubrey's (David Sterne) in YOU'RE NOT WATCHING ME, MUMMY (1980 T). The last-named sounds every bit as reprobate as the most famous Ernest, Jack's scallywag brother who needs much attention in THE IMPORTANCE OF BEING EARNEST. This phantom was made the central character (with great parallels to the decline and fall of his creator) in THE IMPORTANCE OF BEING FRANK (1990 R).

Ernesto (It 1979 C) Ernesto (Martin Halm) finds true love with someone who shares his passion for music and solves the problem of being publicly gay in Italy: he marries his boyfriend's twin sister.

W: from the book by Umberto Saba; D: Salvatore Samperi; 95 mins.

escorts *See* PROSTITUTES.

espionage *See* SPIES.

Espionage (US 1963–4 T) Filmed in Europe, mainly with British actors, and supposedly featuring a gay (spy) storyline in one of its episodes. The producer, Herbert Hirschman told *Variety* (in a 1964 story headlined 'Courageous or Desperate?': 'We speak about it openly and I believe this is the first time that the subject has been dealt with openly on American television.' *Variety* concluded that 'the homo theme' was being grafted onto shows like *Espionage* and (the equally obscure) *Room 777* because of 'flagging ratings' – noting, without elaboration, that 'the delicate subject of homosexuality has long been shunned like a plague by television producers'.

eunuchs The Roman playwright Terence acknowledged the vital importance of the castrated male in high society in *The Eunuch*, which was performed on radio in 1968. Eunuchs have been prominent background characters (usually frail and wilting or fat and wilting) in many radio and television sketches, and in films featuring harems: notably Lionel Jeffries in *The Long Ships* (1964 C) and the hundreds milling around the court of Pu Yi in *The Last Emperor* (1987 C). That they occupy a powerful (and often delinquent) role in Indian society was amply demonstrated in the documentary, *Under The Sun* 'Eunuchs – India's Third Gender' (1991 T).

Europe Britain is no longer an island. Hands across the Channel with gay or lesbian relevance have been few and far between. OUT ON TUESDAY (1990) hazarded a few guesses as to improvements in the legal status. In *Extra*, a 1989 television magazine with Janet STREET-PORTER, audiences were introduced to an Italian TRANSSEXUAL in a fish market called Peppe (with a boyfriend similarly named); a Hungarian gay CLUB; some Swedish amateur porn;

overcrowding for married and single people in Russia.

evangelical Christians Usually portrayed as quacking, prating, deprecating intolerants. Their fictional numbers include the many characters loosely based on moral rearmers: civilian and female in AGONY (1979 T) and *Figure with Meat* (1991 R); semi-military and male (Paul Hardwick) in *The Professionals* 'In the Public Interest' (1979 T) ; the relentlessly joyful, interfering, destructive Miss Docker (Hazel Hughes) in A CHEERFUL SOUL (1966 T); the stern father (Patrick Troughton) in LAND OF PROMISE (1986 R); the pretty young man (Peter Firth) using technology to clean up perversion in TICKETS FOR THE TITANIC 'The Way, the Truth, the Video' (1987 T); Jess' mother (Geraldine McEwan) and her cronies in ORANGES ARE NOT THE ONLY FRUIT (1990 T). In real life, many biblical fundamentalists appear on television denouncing, if not the homosexual, then anything pertaining to his or her emotional or sexual expression: the evangelist, whose gay son had committed suicide, determined to 'convert' homosexuals (who became 'EX-GAYS') in HEART OF THE MATTER (1992); the Manx brother and sister in THEM AND US 'Isle of Man' (1991); the strict Pentecostal parents to whom a young man had to come out in VIDEODIARIES (1991); etc.

In America they range from the obviously deranged Bible-belting mother (Piper Laurie) in *Carrie* (1976 C) to any number of attractive, plausible hell and damnation purveyors on television (a breed due to hit the United Kingdom in the next few years), not to mention members of the radical right who want gays and lesbians flushed away with other pestilence.

Australia's Rev. Fred NILE, head of the Call to Australia Party, is a regular participant in debates on everything from satanic rites to the SYDNEY GAY AND LESBIAN MARDI GRAS (both of which he is agin). The comedy show *Fast Forward* featured a fearsome figure of a man, opponent of all things gay, as the principal antagonist – bent on enslaving the minds and bodies of millions – in its version of 'Indiana Jones and the Temple of Doom' (1991 T).

Eve Adam's first wife – and, in a manner of speaking, his daughter; symbol of questing, inquisitiveness, giving into temptation. Played by women as varied as a Miss Universe (Christine Martel) in the nudist film *Adam and Eve* (1956); Mamie Van Doren in *The Private Lives of Adam and Eve* (1960 C); Swedish student Ulla Bergryd, decorously clad in long hair in THE BIBLE (1966 C); Maureen Lipman (left to the imagination in a 1987 radio play – with Miriam MARGOLYES as the other bad woman of the Creation, LILITH).

Non-biblical Eves, with distinctly Lilithian tendencies, include Barbara STANWYCK out to fleece the unwary disguised as *The Lady Eve* (1941 C); Eve Harrington (Anne Baxter) in ALL ABOUT EVE (1950 C) described, eg, as 'an assassin', 'Evil Eve', 'little Miss Evil', 'a louse' and 'a killer'; Joanne Woodward as the multiple personality (depressed, sluttish and sane) in *The Three Faces of Eve* (1957 C); Mylene Demongeot, bathing topless and driving Henri Vidal to murder his wife in *The Evil That Is Eve* (1959 C); mysterious, shifty Eve Kendall (Eve Marie Saint) in *North by Northwest* (1959 C); Jeanne Moreau as contemporary temptress *Eve* (1963 C); Eve (Geraldine Page), neurotic, house-proud mother who walks into the sea in *Interiors* (1978 C); mannish ASSASSIN Eve (Julie Newmar) in *Hart to Hart* 'A Change of Heart' (1983 T); ambiguous, manipulative Eve (Merin Canning) in GHOST TRAINS (Aust 1986 R).

Nicer Eves: Eve Gibson (Shirley Mason) in *Sin Cargo* (1926 C); brittle but kind-hearted Eve (Eve Arden) in *Stage Door* (1937 C); drama student turned sleuth Eve Gill (Jane Wyman) in *Stage Fright* (1950 C); Eve Graham (Joan Fontaine), a career woman, unable to have a child, who discovers after she goes to an adoption agency that her husband is married to another woman in *The Bigamist* (1953 C); Dr

Eve Allen (Anne Burr), TV's first woman doctor in *The Greatest Gift* (1954–5 T); Ida Lupino in *Mr Adams and Eve* (1957–8 T); Barbara Rush as the wise wife in *Strangers When We Meet* (1960 C), doing the best she can to cope with her husband's affair; Eve (Rita Tushingham), the mute bondsmaiden in *The Trap* (1966 C); Eve Gill (Jane Merrow), female *Detective* in 'End of Chapter' (1966 T), the same character as in *Stage Fright* (1950 C); Eve Mace (Rachel Kempson) in *Death of a Teddy Bear* (1967 T) in love with the blowsy woman who is infatuated with a young man; Eve Lawrence (Bibi Besch) in *Somerset* (1970–6 T), fiancée of Judge Bishop; elegant PR lady Eve Manship (Jill Melford), canny, sharp-tongued, bedding her boss in *The Organization* (1972 T); wealthy Beverly Hills widow Eve (Evelyn) Lewis (Marguerite Rae), Redd Foxx's amour in *Sanford and Son* (1980–1 T); Eve (Lesley Anne Warren), former prostitute in *Choose Me* (1983 C); Eve (Joan Severance) in *See No Evil, Hear No Evil* (1989 C); Eve Howard (Margaret Mason) in *The Young and the Restless*; Evie (Maureen Flanagan), the teenage daughter with magic powers in *Out of This World*.

Evelyn Seventeenth century boy's name now mainly used for girls.

US: Evelyn Harper (Hope Emerson), vulgar, unappealing matron in CAGED (1950 C); Evelyn (Jessica Walter) obsessed with the disc jockey – and his girlfriend whose room-mate she briefly becomes – in *Play Misty for Me* (1972 C); Evelyn Miller (Faye Dunaway) in *Chinatown* (1974 C); Evelyn Whittacher (Dinah Manoff), former lover of local heroine in *Welcome Home, Roxy Carmichael* (1991 C); Evelyn (Kathy Bates) receiving an emotional education from women, young and old, past and present in FRIED GREEN TOMATOES AT THE WHISTLE STOP CAFE (1991 C).

UK: emotionally intense and frustrated Evelyn Vining (Pamela Brown) who puts all her passion into her relationship with her young niece in *Personal Affair* (1953 C); Evelyn (Helen Morse) fleetingly seen in *Agatha* (1979 C) but originally intended as a pointer to the heroine's sexual confusion; Evelyn (Suzanna Hamilton) parting from her close friend in *Goodbye Days* (1984 T).

Male Evelyns, all British, include Evelyn BAXTER (Colin CAMPBELL), Dame Hilda TABLET's frisky secretary with the hots for the callow hero in THE PRIVATE LIFE OF HILDA TABLET etc (1950s R); Evelyn Orcham (Richard Hurndall), long widowed, very proper proprietor of the *Imperial Palace* (1959 R); nerdish Evelyn Tremble (Peter SELLERS) in *Casino Royale* (1967 C); ruthless millionaire Evelyn Rose (Ray Milland) in *River of Gold* (1971 T); Evelyn (Daniel Webb), ever ready to help the choir boys adjust their costumes in *Daughters and Sons* (1985 R).

Even Solomon (UK 1979 T)   Stephen Piper (Paul Henley) is not exactly manager material once he comes out and reports for work in a blouse and skirt. A TRANSVESTITE bank clerk braves the doctor's surgery only to be asked in a clipped, forbidding manner: 'Are you a homosexual? Do you suspect that you are a homosexual? Sore when you pee? Can't keep it up?' To which the reply is: 'My transsexualism is a relief and a reward … I want to be a woman every second of the day.'

'[The writer] is a perfectly ordinary person who is married with a child and has great sympathy for people like this,' said producer Anne Head to *Gay News* (1979).

Dame Edna Everage   Described by her manager Barry HUMPHRIES as 'a silly, bigoted, ignorant, self-satisfied Melbourne housewife'.

Edna, who fled the suburb of Moonee Ponds the year after the Queen toured Australia, worked her way up to her now unassailable position as ambassador for Australia, talk show hostie and international superstar. Her television career began in the mid-1960s as simple Mrs Edna Everage. Prime Minister Gough Whitlam made her a dame in *Barry McKenzie Holds His Own* (1974 C), and

it was in that production she began to reveal an interesting complexity. She told a black woman journalist, who enquired – with a gleam in her eye – if she'd ever 'balled a chick', that 'LESBIANISM ALWAYS LEAVES A NASTY TASTE IN MY MOUTH'.

Latterly, she has felt less inhibited about admitting her long-standing intimacy with her bridesmaid, Madge ALLSOP (*La Dame aux Gladiolas* 1979 T) and also occasionally discussing her son Kenny and his friend Cliff: 'They are supporters of Gaiety Liberation.' She is even more forthright on her album *The Sound of Edna* (1978) on which she sang 'A Woman's Woman'. On her *Edna Everage Experience* (1987 T) she danced a brief waltz with Mary WHITEHOUSE.

C: Mrs Everage in *The Naked Bunnyip*; Aunt Edna in THE ADVENTURES OF BARRY MCKENZIE (1972); *Barry McKenzie Holds His Own* (1974); Dame Edna in *Les Patterson Saves the World* (1987).

R: WOMAN'S HOUR: Guest of the Week 1987 and 1992; ad libbing with Lynda Snell (Carole Boyd) in THE ARCHERS (1988).

T: *The Late Show* (1966); *La Dame aux Gladiolas* 'The Agony and Ecstasy of Dame Edna' (1979); *An Audience with Dame Edna* (1984); *Another Audience with Dame Edna* (1984); *One More Audience with Dame Edna Everage* (1987); *Aspel and Company* (1989); *A Night on Mount Edna* (1990); *Dame Edna's Hollywood* (1991); BAFTA *Awards* (1992); *Dame Edna's Neighbourhood Watch* (1992).

She was the subject of a *Without Walls* 'J'accuse' programme (1993) in which Rory Bremner asked her if the satire of the character had been lost in the paraphernalia of genuine superstardom (a contract with Rupert Murdoch's Fox network).

Kenny Everage   Unseen son of Dame Edna. Once a member of Gaiety Liberation, Kenny got a first in Flower Arranging. Now runs Kenneth Everage Modes of Sydney, and is partly responsible for the way his mother looks. Asked about Kenny on *One More*

Audience with Dame Edna Everage (1987 T) his mother has to adjust her posture before answering the question 'Has he come to terms with his sexuality?' 'He is *red-blooded* ... my son is a *womanizer* ... in his bedroom you'll find Joan Crawford, Barbara STANWYCK, Susan Hayward, Judy GARLAND, Liza Minnelli ... He's the Australian Secretary of the Barbara Stanwyck Appreciation Society ... I said to him Kenny can't you get a live woman. He said I've got one – you. I feel for you like Anthony Perkins felt about his mother in *Psycho*.'

Everard Larry GRAYSON'S offscreen friend, into many pursuits indoor and out, such as pot-holing (SHUT THAT DOOR! 1972-4 T etc). (Everard a Norse word, also found in German, for 'strong wild boar'.)

Everett, Kenny (1944–) English disc jockey and comedian; lightly bearded, manic, highly innovative. Began on Radio Caroline, then became a cult delight on BBC Radio 1, attracting enormous media interest: *Kenny Everett Foreverette* (1968 R); *Ev* (1970 T); *Aquarius* 'Everett's London' (1971 T); *The Kenny Everett Explosion* (1970 T); *Man Alive* 'The Disc Jockeys' (1970 T); KALEIDOSCOPE 'The Kenny Everett Audio Show' (1981 R) talking to Paul GAMBACCINI. A major television star, first with Thames (*The Kenny Everett Show*) and then BBC1 (*The Kenny Everett Video Show*), during the 1970s and 1980s using provocation (female dancers), much visual wizardry, and 'naughty' characters and situations. His catchphrase was 'ALL IN THE BEST POSSIBLE TASTE.'

The Everlasting Secret Family (Aust 1988 C) Members of a clandestine homosexual society (masks and togas) are recruited from exclusive boys' schools. One inductee (Mark Lee) has been seduced by a politician, then discarded. However, he is introduced into the man's household as a BABYSITTER who, 10 years later, 'seduces' the politician's teenage son.

W: Michael Thornhill and Frank Moorhouse; based on stories in *The Everlasting Secret Family*; D: Michael Thornhill; 93 mins.

Lots of (erotic) male nudity, full-on (fun) melodrama, masks, vampiric middle-aged homosexuals, narcissistic younger homosexuals (who are really corrupted heterosexuals) never wanting to grow old; tentacles, claws, mandibles ... Like dry rot and deathwatch beetle, you never get rid of it once it catches hold. 'A great idea which deserved better treatment,' thought David Stratton. Or was it a great treatment which deserved a better idea?

Everyman 'Blasphemy at the Old Bailey' (UK 1977 T) 'Gay News Limited and Denis Lemon on a day or days unknown between the 1st day of May and 30th day of June 1976 unlawfully published or caused to be published in a newspaper called Gay News No. 96 a blasphemous libel concerning the Christian religion namely an obscene poem vilifying Christ in his life and in his crucifixion.'
P: Daniel Wolf; D: Hugh David; 18.9.77; BBC1; 75 mins.

The first trial for BLASPHEMY in Britain for over half a century. 'Was this prosecution an attack on free speech? Or was it a necessary defence of the principle that, even in a permissive society, some things must remain sacred? This dramatic documentary reconstructs the crucial moments of this historic trial, and explores the issues it raises; with Donald Eccles as Judge Alan King-Hamilton and Norman Rodway as John Mortimer QC' (*Radio Times*).

Actors impersonated Mary WHITEHOUSE and GAY NEWS editor Denis LEMON in court (neither gave evidence). Their real selves commented on the outcome: an 18-month suspended sentence for Denis Lemon and a fine for the paper. The disputed poem, 'The Love That Dares to Speak Its Name' told of a Roman centurion present at the Crucifixion, fantasizing about the body of Jesus in sexual terms. The poem ends: 'And he loved even me.'

Everyman 'The Lord Is My Shepherd And He Knows I'm Gay' (UK 1979 T) By the time the contentious Alan WHICKER title of 1973 was reused, clergymen were themselves coming out of the closet. Ian Hamilton gleefully reported the spectacle '... gay, old style they weren't. And, indeed, it must be fairly depressing to have to comb through the good book and re-examine the well-known texts of ancient queer-bashers.' (*New Statesman*, 22.5.79).

What was so irksome to the established forces of order was not the individuals themselves – 'puzzled souls' as Hamilton called them. Or the fact that some were married (to wives, brave and dutiful). The real horror was that the vow of silence had been broken. To be caught up a cassock in the vestry was pardonable. Not to be caught but to live the truth was horrid.

'Everyone knew ... that the real issue was not whether but how the Church would manage to adjust to the now glaring fact that some of its best chaps liked chaps ... disappointingly very much an outsider's view, primed with solemn stuff about "right and wrong". Everyone falls in with [Peter] France's use of the word "homosexual" ... largely to avoid gay people's chosen terminology. There isn't much to encourage the isolated gay here. The constant issue of self-oppressive views runs like an open wound ... through the film' (W. Stephen GILBERT, *Observer*, 17.5.79).

everyone's gay 'I think everyone's basically gay, don't you?' said Bob (Christopher Guest) to Prudence (Julie Hagerty), the HOMOPHOBE in *Beyond Therapy* (1986 C).

Everything I Have Is Yours Lilting ballad by Burton Lane and Harold Adamson, popularized by Joan Crawford in *Dancing Lady* (1933 C). A hymn to togetherness, melding, surrender and symbiosis, it provided ironic counterpoint to the frustrations of a lesbian's domestic bliss in *Is That You Nancy ...?* (Aust 1991 R) as well as to the mass queer 'WEDDING' in OUTRAGE: THE DOCUMENTARY (1991 R).

Everything You Always Wanted to Know About Sex * But Were Afraid to Ask (US 1972 C) One episode illustrates sodomy (with a sheep named Daisy); another TRANSVESTISM (a jolly married man). Best segment involves the terrifying journey of a sperm (Woody Allen) to an egg.
W/D: Woody ALLEN; P: Jack Rollins and Charles H. Joffe; 87 mins.

This infrequently brilliant but always diverting comedy used the title of Dr David Reuben's vexatious best-seller, which regurgitated every old saw and yoked lesbians with PROSTITUTES. Its own numbskull logic brought sodomy alongside Gene Wilder swooning over a sheep in a suspender belt ...

Every Time We Say Goodbye Rodgers and HART standard as interpreted (reedily) by Annie Lennox, first on the RED, HOT AND BLUE video (1990) with projections of all that we hold dear (including an infant Derek JARMAN), then in person in EDWARD II as the king and lover DANCE TOGETHER

Evil Under the Sun (UK 1982 C) Poirot (Peter Ustinov) on the case, sniffing out clues among the 1930s smart set on a glorious island hideaway.
W: Anthony Shaffer from the novel *Death Under the Sun* by Agatha Christie; P: Richard Goodwin and John Brabourne; D: Guy Hamilton; 117 mins.

Hollywood's most practised purveyor of torpid camp, Roddy MCDOWALL, gives it another whirl (dressing gown, cigarette holder, yachting cap, SCARF) as gossip columnist Rex Brewster, one of the suspects (he didn't do it) in the murder of a glamour goddess (Diana Rigg) on a ravishing island. McDowall was another professional gossiper in AN INCONVENIENT WOMAN (1991 T), stinging and – ultimately – stung (by a bee).

ex-gays The ex-gay movement aims to cure homosexuals, with a kinder, less violent, and *effective* alternative to AVERSION THERAPY (so its advocates say) courtesy of friendly, supportive EVAN-GELICAL CHRISTIAN 'counselling' groups. One such was played for laughs in an episode of BROTHERS (1984 T): 'Why be gay when you can be glad?' was its motto. More seriously (and soberingly) revealed in a HEART OF THE MATTER investigation called 'Fighting Against Nature' (1992 T).

Exit 19 (UK 1966 T) This 45-minute documentary, the final one in a series on love and marriage and shown on 27.7.66, was called by the popular press of the day a 'BBC Shock Sex Probe' and 'the frankest, most intimate TV programme shown in Britain'. Hundreds of viewers telephoned complaints about the ripe dialogue from some of the participants.

Its opening shot was a couple in bed, with a young woman apparently naked. For the rest of the programme, they (Maureen Safhill, a 24-year-old art student, and Jack Bond, a 28-year-old film editor) ad libbed answers to 110 questions devised by the director Philip Saville. The questions touched on homosexuality, incest, premarital relations and adultery. One question Maureen Safhill was asked was: 'Have you ever felt you would like your father to make love to you?' She was also questioned about her feelings during menstruation and intercourse, and asked when she lost her virginity and if she enjoyed the experience. The BBC said the programme was an enquiry to discover 'if in the age of the spaceship the British are still living in the steamship age when it comes to sex and ethics'.

Exodus (US 1960 C) The bloody, bitter fight to establish Israel in Palestine.
W: Dalton Trumbo from the novel by Leon Uris; P/D: Otto Preminger; 213 & 220 mins.

Paul Newman creates the state of Israel helped by Eva Marie Saint (blonde Gentile), Jill Haworth (blonde Jew, murdered), Sal Mineo (who survives rape), John Derek (boyhood friend who is a good Arab, dies horribly), and lots of healthy-looking extras. Hindering are the British (Ralph Richardson, Peter Lawford), even more effete German (Marius Goring), and bad Arabs (sodomites, child murderers, torturers etc). The relationship between Newman and Derek received no mention at the time, so successful were the film's promoters in diverting attention to the Mineo character – crying from the posters: 'They used me ... like a woman.' Unusually, for movie-soiled goods, he is not killed and the actor received an ACADEMY AWARD nomination.

The Expert (UK 1968–71 T) Marius Goring starred as a pathologist, Dr Hardy in a well-respected series, produced by Andrew Osborn for BBC2. In the episode 'The Visitor' (1969 T) the perpetrator of 11 stabbings and sexual assaults is profiled by the police as a man who is deeply afraid of women. Fitting the bill is Martin Ingram (Michael Johnson), a 25-year-old art student, brought up by his mother after his father died. His 'guilt' is endorsed in the mind of the viewer by a shot of Martin picking up a bottle of cologne immediately after Dr Hardy and his (more liberal) wife Jo (Ann Morrish) have been discussing KINSEY and homosexuality.

Does Martin hate women? 'Not hate exactly. Just fear.' Does this mean he is homosexual? Dr Hardy strokes his goatee: 'Possibly. He's certainly got the similar problems. The inability to relate with much success to a girl or woman is the classic reason for inversion.' Circumstantial evidence tightens the noose: Martin had been visiting the block of flats where the assaults took place. And his attitude towards authority is alienatingly defiant: 'I like being different and I do not want to change. You want someone to blame. You choose me ...'.

Under the influence of his wife and impressed by Martin's strong sense of self-health, 'the expert' has a blinding flash of enlightenment: 'It's not as though most of what *I* think of as criminal is even remotely illegal any more.' A last minute alibi is produced and Martin walks free. But the script offers a sting in the tail. Some things *are* still illegal.

Martin's alibi is a 17-year-old schoolboy who was with him in an intimate situation at the time of the attacks ...

explorers Probably there were many homosexual men and women who, in the heady days of empire as loyal subjects of king or queen, could, without attracting undue suspicion, exchange an inner wilderness, desert or jungle for real terrain to be subdued, opened up or simply confronted. BBC radio and television finds the lone or paired obsessive of great interest: Henry Stanley (Keith Buckley) and Richard Burton (Kenneth Haigh) in *The Search for the Nile* (1971 T); *The Explorers* (1975 T); the 1987 Radio 4 series on women striders into the wide blue yonder. Few of these portraits enquire too deeply into sexual bag and baggage; eg *Explorers* 'The Story of Alexander Von Humboldt' (1975 T) only hinted at the scientist's great love for and devastation over the death of a French colleague. In the cinema, there were sweaty, fevered looks and a few touches between Burton (Patrick Bergin) and Henry Speke (Iain Glen) in *Mountains of the Moon* (1990 C).

Expresso Bongo (UK 1959 C) A callow youth is turned into a pop poppet by an unscrupulous promoter.
W: Wolf Mankowitz from his play; P/D: Val Guest; 111 mins.

A very watered-down version of the stage musical – which was a watered-down version of what often lay in wait for young men who couldn't sing: the dedicated (and often brilliant) ministrations of a gay manager/promoter (Larry Parnes, Joe Meek, Brian EPSTEIN etc) of the kind cruelly mocked in *Absolute Beginners* (1986 C) with Harry Charms (Lionel Blair) fingering the (very young) merchandise.

The Fabulous Frump (UK 1969 T)
Swearing, dowdy, BUTCH fashion editor
Ella (Sheila Steafel) sets her sights on
mother's boy Albert (Peter Butterworth), a fashion designer, hoping that
domesticity will make her more feminine and acceptable to her publisher.
W: James Gibbens; P: Irene Shubik; D:
Peter Hammond; 8.1.69; BBC1; 75
mins.
A Wednesday Play, this muddy comedy, doubtless based on truth, aims to be
a satire on the deceit and closetry of the
fashion industry. Its only claim to fame,
apart from its theme (crassly handled),
was the one-off coming together of Jeffrey GARDINER, Arthur HOWERD, Billy
MILTON and Michael WARD, a quartet
that appears all too fleetingly as a chorus
of chattering *haute couture* minions.

The Face of Violence (UK 1950 R)
Jacob BRONOWSKI's prize-winning free-
verse radio play – 'a driving urgent
piece' about the human being's almost
limitless appetite for destruction and
hurt. Homosexuals were apparent, only
in passing, as victims of vice, exploited
by commercial venery, and incapable of
little outside triviality and excess.
Bronowski's tack would probably not
be politically acceptable today, but he
was driven by urgency, wanting to bring
the postwar world to its senses rather
than a Fascist tendency to lay waste or
impose social uniformity. He believed
that individuals making up a society
must question and change. Detectable
throughout is a compassionate intellectual's impatience with the routine and
the unchallenged that makes the play,
for all its ugliness and screeching, compelling.

Face to Face (UK 1958–60 T) One of
the most famous of television inqui-
sitions. Polite but fanged John Freeman
presented a dazzling array of (nearly all)
male celebrities: Carl Jung, Cecil BEA-
TON, Evelyn WAUGH, and most famously
Tony Hancock and Gilbert HARDING,
who, it has now been revealed, was deliberately ambushed by Freeman into
revealing his homosexuality. Harding

didn't produce the goods, but he did –
when asked about his mother – shed
tears. The Harding interview by Malcolm Muggeridge on PANORAMA in 1954
is now forgotten, but it was just as
revealing – 'I'm a dedicated phoney' –
without the tears.
P: Hugh Burnett; BBC; 30 mins.

Facing the Sun (UK 1980 T) A clean
young Englishman, Peter (David Yelland) goes to São Paulo to spend Christmas with Gilberto (Gerard Murphy), an
ARTIST with whom he had a fling in
London, and his watchful wife. After
finding more than he bargained for
(Gilberto's wife is pregnant despite
protestations of a nil sex life), Peter
returns to London to find that he has
been ditched by his girlfriend.
W: Brian Walker; P: John BOWEN; D:
Claude Whatham; 5.8.80; Thames; 60
mins.
A gorgeously designed, entertaining
piece of BISEXUAL angst: charming but
arid Brit wants, but doesn't want, sexy,
temperamental foreigner, who wants but
doesn't want him. Churning around
them is some wonderfully ripe dialogue:
'It's not easy for me', 'Do you think it's
easy for *me* . . . it's like hell', 'Perhaps we
should tell her the truth', 'She's doing
etchings to find herself again', 'It
doesn't matter. We love each other. We
are married. So these bad times will
pass.' Ultimately – despite its highly
attractive trio of actors – it is a shallow
unconvincing piece, which sticks in the
memory only because it was one of the
most homoerotic of plays the Independent Broadcasting Authority ever countenanced.
The key scene finds Peter in bed.
Enter Gilberto. His wife has gone shopping and so he has decided to renew
intimacy with his house guest. Gilberto
pulls off the bed sheet, then positions
himself on top of Peter. He kisses him
on the mouth, then moves slowly down
his body. 'I want you. I want you so
much.' The screen goes yellow, then
orange. Advertising break.
It did not go unnoticed. 'What on earth
possessed ITV to screen *Facing the Sun*

at a time when many schoolchildren are up and watching? How does one explain the sight of two men KISSING to a 14-year-old who has been taught the meaning of a heterosexual relationship?' (letter, *TV Times*, 16.8.80).

factory workers Very few homosexual ones in drama: Michael (Murray MELVIN) in PROBATION OFFICER; middle-aged machinist, dour and offputting, except where the occasional young woman is concerned in CONNIE (Marjorie Yates 1979 T); secretary Norma (Tracie Bennett) who works in an electronics factory in *Making Out* (1991 T).

fade-outs Contrary to general belief, not all screen fictions end with male and female in a securely loving embrace. Some of the surprisingly numerous exceptions: *Dinner at Eight* (1933 C; Marie DRESSLER arm-in-arm with Jean Harlow); *Casablanca* (1942 C; Humphrey Bogart walking into the mists with Claude Rains); *The Phantom of the Opera* (1943 C; Rains again but this time it is Nelson Eddy who goes off arm-in-arm with a man played by Edgar Barrier); *Cry of the City* (1948 C; a wounded (but not too badly) Victor Mature lovingly framed with a young boy in a car's rear window); *Gentlemen Prefer Blondes* (1953 C; Marilyn MONROE and Jane Russell, ostensibly giving up their freedom to marry but very much a devoted couple at the altar with their new spouses purely onlookers); SOME LIKE IT HOT (1959 C); Joe E. Brown and his husband/wife-to-be, Jack Lemmon; MY BEAUTIFUL LAUNDRETTE (1985 C; Johnny (Daniel Day-Lewis) and Omar (Gordon Warnecke) happily flicking water at one another); PRICK UP YOUR EARS (1987 C; ashes mixed); THELMA AND LOUISE (1991 C; sublimely united, even in death).

Television rarely allows its same-sex lovers to greet the closing credits in an ecstatic entwining: only the two soldiers HUGGING on the station platform in HOUSE ON THE HILL 'Something for the Boys' (1981); C. J. LAMB and her former lover Maggie Barnes in just one L.A. LAW episode 'The Nut Before Christmas' (1991). So few tender moments to satisfyingly close a story well told.

faggot (1) Applied to a fat, slatternly woman. Wayward Gwen (Jean Kent) applies the term to approved-school matron (Nora Swinburne) in *Good Time Girl* (1948 C): 'You bring my clothes or I'll knock your block off, you silly old faggot.' 'You silly old faggot,' squawks Percy the Parrot (Percy Edwards) to dotty Miss Cissie Godfrey (Nan Braunton) in *Dad's Army* 'The Battle of Godfrey's Cottage' (1977 R).

During the period 1952–4, at least four male characters (Walter, Simon, Dan and Tom) in THE ARCHERS used 'faggot' about each other and, very occasionally, about three unmarried women: (the baroness, Lady HYLBEROW and Carol GREY). Then, suddenly, the word disappeared from the serial's vocabulary and it has never been uttered in Ambridge environs again.

(2) (Also 'fag'.) To mean homosexual. 'Almost mandatory' in American films, according to Vito RUSSO in *The Celluloid Closet* (1987). First heard in *Blood Money* (1933 C) wherein a pursued George Bancroft warns a timid taxi driver ('Listen, fag . . .') not to tell the cops his destination. Thanks to the US Production Code, the word disappeared soon after, not to be heard again until 1967 when Patty Duke's booze and pill-laden screen star Neely O'Hara (partly based on Judy GARLAND) in VALLEY OF THE DOLLS confronts her fashion designer husband (Alex Davion) by the pool after his female skinny-dipping companion has scarpered into the shrubbery: 'All right, *faggot*, start explaining!' To which he, understandably bewildered, responds: 'Neely, she was hardly built like a *boy*.' 'I could have taken *that* better,' snaps the termagant. One of the more antediluvian of Frank Sinatra's police colleagues in THE DETECTIVE (1968 C) wants to see 'the faggot fry' – in electric chair, that is.

American televison copied the cinema from the mid-1970s with *Police Story* 'The Ripper' (1974) and then a whole slew of medium-salacious cop show episodes. Newt Dieter, director of the GAY AND LESBIAN MEDIA TASK FORCE, told GAY NEWS in 1980 that, such were the skew-whiff standards then prevailing, that 'crap' could not be uttered but 'faggot' could.

The word is quite popular in Britain. One of its first airings was in a radio play about two co-habiting bully boys: *Bill and Ben* (1972). It has also turned up in *The Fear* (1988 T) and in *Body Contact* (1987 T), where it was hurled at a con-man priest (Jack Shepherd) whose flock includes horned red dwarves, whip-toting nuns and androgynes in chains and collars: 'He's the biggest faggot in town.'

fag hag Originally a 19th-century term for a woman who smoked cigarettes. Now a derogatory British epithet for women who idolize certain gay men and spend most of their social life in their company. One early example, American but very cosmopolitan, was Lady Brett Ashley (Ava Gardner in *The Sun Also Rises* 1957 C), who is encountered by Jake (Tyrone Power) in a fashionable Parisian bistro into which she sweeps with four men, all wearing a touch of lavender. 'It's a *fine* crowd you're with,' he remarks cuttingly. She tosses back her head and laughs: '*Aren't* they *lovely!*' A few minutes later she and Jake leave without a word to the gay companions: they are just so much excess baggage. The inference is that Lady Brett chooses these people as friends because she can't find a real man. Her only alternatives are a drunk (Errol Flynn) and an old count (Gregory Ratoff). Jake offers her only limited solace as he is IMPOTENT. It's no wonder that much of this character's dialogue relates to her chronic unhappiness and lack of direction.

In the remake of *Farewell, My Lovely* (1975 C) Helen Gayle (Charlotte Rampling) is a frequent social partner of Lindsay Elliott (John O'Leary) because her husband, though rich, is old and not a lot of fun. After Lindsay's murder, Helen remarks with affectionate contempt: 'Lindsay was a heel . . . he accompanied me places.'

Friendship between heterosexual women and gay men is seen as a major factor in some women's empty, unhappy lives: Joan Crawford's in *Torch Song* (1953 C); Liv Ullmann's in *Face to Face* (1976 C); Maureen Lipman's in OVER THE RAINBOW (1980 R); Charlotte Cornwell's in *Only Children* (1984 T). Luckily real men are waiting in the wings for most of them. Other characters are always trying to warn these women against wasting their energy on such dead-end relationships: heiress Merle Oberon's friend (Rex Harrison) in *Over the Moon* (1937 C); Joan Crawford's mother in *Torch Song*. These associations are very much seen as character flaws: an indication of the woman's lack of self-esteem, even sex appeal.

Ageing Broadway star Helen Lawson (Susan Hayward) finds herself the object of abuse from the sloshed younger actress Neely O'Hara (Patty Duke) in the powder room during an awards ceremony in VALLEY OF THE DOLLS (1967 C). Helen tries to extricate herself by announcing that she's got a *man* waiting for her. Neely intercepts this haughty declaration with a slashing: 'It's a change from the fags you are *usually* seen with.' Which gives Helen the cue to say, in her most gloating *grande dame* manner: 'Well at least *I* didn't marry one.' This provokes a lively physical exchange during which the older woman's wig is wrenched off and flushed down the toilet.

The dynamics of a woman's friendship with a man who isn't remotely interested in her sexually has hardly ever been explored. In *My Father's House* (1981 T) Tassie (Rosemary Martin), who befriends the unhappy and periodically suicidal Ray (Steve Mann), is seen very much as a surrogate mother. But he is a necessary prop for her, too: 'They cling to each other for protection against the world'. Jill in *Only Children* (1984 T) becomes so dependent upon her waifs and strays that her only escape from their selfish, sterile influence is to become pregnant.

A pathological element is identified by the German aristocrat Von Reger (sneeringly played by Alan BADEL 1968 T) in David Mercer's THE PARACHUTE (1968 T) in relation to Anna (Jill Bennett): 'Some women need a QUEER in their life . . . it's the most harmless form of aggression they go in for.' Refreshingly, Jane Lucas (Maureen Lipman), the heroine of AGONY who seemingly has only two intimates (a gay couple), is positive about the relationship: 'You're my dearest friends. I love every gay inch of you.'

Colin uses 'fag hag' to affectionately, if inaccurately, describe his only two friends in Albert Square (Dot and Pat) in EASTENDERS (1989 T); while PSYCHIATRIST Tom Conti tells his patient Julie Hagerty that she is 'a fag hag' in *Beyond Therapy* (1986 C), which must surprise her because she identifies as a HOMOPHOBE.

The Fag Show (US 1964 T) The working title of a documentary made by WCBS-TV. Some $15,000–$20,000 was spent shooting interviews and scenes covering New York (male) homosexual nightlife. Then, according to *Variety* (24.6.64), when Al Waller took over production from James Ambandos, the footage was scrapped because 'it was not in the mainstream of current medical and scientific thought regarding homosexuality'.

A WCBS spokesman told *Variety*: 'The slant apparently was that of the various homosexual societies that they constitute a third sex that deserves equal legal and social rights without enough emphasis on the scientific opinions that consider it a mental illness provoked by environmental factors.' *Variety*'s reporter added: 'Such a slant, of course, could develop unintentionally out of the interviews filmed to date.'

fairies (1) Pagan people who, said Katherine Briggs (author of the *Dictionary of British Folk Tales*) on WOMAN'S HOUR (1974 R), are 'too good for hell and too bad for heaven. Rather they occupy another spiritual region, the netherworld. They can live in harmony with mortals, or cause tremendous friction.

Brownies are fairies that help people. BOGGARTS are brownies gone to the bad.' This complex universe was elaborated upon in *Fairies, Elves, Goblins, Hobbits and Auks: The World of Adult Fantasy* (1992 R). However, for most people, these creatures remain gossamer-winged and ethereal, with those in *A Midsummer Night's Dream* – together with Tinker Bell and magical godmothers granting wishes – probably the most prominent.

(2) A collective noun for male homosexuals often used ambiguously, eg by Billy Connolly in his title song for the 1984–5 children's serial *Supergran* (compared to this old wonder woman, Superman and other heroes were 'a bunch of fairies'), and by John INMAN prancing and giving vent to the dear old song 'Do You Believe In Fairies?' in front of a tittering, close to cackling audience in *The Good Old Days* (1983 T).

See also FAIRY; NOBODY LOVES A FAIRY WHEN SHE'S FORTY; THERE ARE FAIRIES AT THE BOTTOM OF THE GARDEN.

fairy Slang term for a homosexual, originally popular mainly in America and uttered by reporter Hildy (Pat O'Brien) to boss Walter Burns (Adolphe Menjou) in *The Front Page* (1931 C): 'Aww, Jesus, no, Walter. You make me feel like kind of fairy or something.' Censorship smothered the word for three decades, after which it quickly became established as part of a fusillade of abusive words used *about* homosexual men in American films of the late 1960s. A rare self-identified fairy was Harold, one of THE BOYS IN THE BAND (1970 C), who introduced himself, in over-deliberate, dope-induced tones as 'A 32-year-old, ugly, pock-marked Jew fairy'. One of the first mentions in Britain came from Harry Secombe in a 1955 GOON SHOW, commenting upon a man: 'There she goes . . . little fairy.' Rugged Australian Judy COOLIBAH (Betty Marsden) accused Kenneth HORNE of being a fairy in 1968. In MONTY PYTHON'S FLYING CIRCUS part of a 1972 sketch involving Biggles and his secretary contained the following exchange: 'Are you calling my fictional comrade-in-arms a fairy?'/ 'Fairy! "Poof's" not good enough for Algy, is it. He's got to be a bleedin' fairy. Mincing old RAF queen.' That same year, the word was applied to one of the two ageing nautical lovers in THE PUNCHY AND THE FAIRY (1973 T). Then *The Two Ronnies* (Corbett and Barker) got hold of it, employing it for jokes such as the gay Mafia chief who was a 'fairy godfather'. Warren Mitchell in his Alf Garnett guise called someone 'a bloomin' fairy' in a Walls sausages radio ad, but a complaint to the Independent Broacasting Authority in 1978 was not upheld because 'No discrimination was perceived'.

Fairy Liquid A washing-up solution, coloured emerald green, which was advertised throughout the 1960s on British television by a very young, very beautiful, very public school Mummy being lispingly asked by her infant daughter why her hands are so *soft*. Mummy replies that it's all due to the *soft* bubbles. This blood-curdling stuff was designed to be sent up rotten by male comedians playing both simpering participants, beginning with Benny HILL on BBC television and Al Reid on radio. The product survives today, being seen in passing – with probable ironic intent – as wicked fairy Diana Rigg (as a character who thinks of herself as a soft, mild, perfect Mummy) puts deadly poison in the marzipan animals in *Mother Love* (1989 T).

Fallen Angel (US 1981 T) Children enticed into pornography by the cuddly Ritchie who 'loves children'.
W: Lew Hunter; P: Hunter and Audrey Blaisdell; D: Robert Lewis; 96 mins.

Well-made and tense exploitation piece with fine acting from Richard Masur, the always smiling, butter-wouldn't-melt-in-his-mouth abductor, and from Melinda Dillon as the mother who fights back. But, however hard it tries, script, direction and acting all work to draw only one conclusion: homos molest children and are not to be

trusted. It is even more worrying than the more seriously ambiguous *Child's Cry*, made a few years later, where the perpetrator is the friendly, unmarried sports coach.

Bart **Fallmont** In DYNASTY Kevin Conroy played the environmentally friendly son of Blake Carrington's buddy (Richard Anderson) who falls in love with Steven (Jack COLEMAN) – even though they are antagonists in a fight over drilling rights. He appeared and disappeared during 1985, to reappear (played by another actor) as Steven's live-in six years later in *Dynasty: The Reunion*, still battling on behalf of the planet. The character, pretty much a well-intentioned blur, is best remembered for his participation in the erotic WRESTLING scene with Steven in a gym in an episode called 'The Solution'.

false accusations A good standby in drama: stir up doubts and even revulsion in an audience by pointing the finger of suspicion, then withdraw it. Did the vicar rape one of his youth club members in *Serious Charge* (1959 C)? Did the teacher corrupt, directly or indirectly, the pupil (THE CHILDREN'S HOUR 1961 C; STANDARD PROCEDURE 1979 R); MAINTAINING STANDARDS (1981 R)? Did the bachelor who lives with his mother abduct the 6-year-old boy in SOFTLY SOFTLY 'Little Boy Blue' (1974 T)? Did the pet shop owner interfere with the 9-year-old boy in JULIET BRAVO 'Lies and Liars' (1981 T)? Did the woman cop 'interfere with' one of her female suspects in POLICE WOMAN 'Trial by Prejudice (1975 T)? Did the jogger molest the black youths *he* is accusing of theft in *City of Hope* (1991 C)? The damage that a baseless accusation can do to even the strongest person was unsettlingly conveyed in the case of Irish Catholic Father Bernard Lynch, supporter of homosexual rights and AIDS activist, dragged through the courts, exonerated but left a virtual pariah (*A Priest's Trial* 1990 T).

Sir John **Falstaff** A figure of fun with

tragic dimensions, rejected and banished by the boy he lovingly nurtured but who is now a king. Played by among others George Robey in *Henry V* (1945 C); Jimmy EDWARDS in *The Merry Wives of Windsor* (1962 R); Orson WELLES in *Chimes at Midnight* (1966 C).

In the 1980 radio adaptation of Robert Nye's novel *Falstaff* (a one-man show by David Buck), the knight scornfully mentions that one of his companions, Edward Poins, was a 'POUF' who 'lived inside women's armpits'. When Henry 'robbed' Falstaff at Gadshill he knew that this wasn't a robber because he was wearing, at Poins' instigation, buckram – 'and only poufs wear buckram'.

MY OWN PRIVATE IDAHO (1991 C) includes a modernized gay version of Henry IV, Part 1 with the character of Bob Pigeon (William Richert) closely modelled on Falstaff and directly quoting from SHAKESPEARE: 'The things that we have seen . . . we have heard the chimes at midnight.'

Fame (US 1980 C) Young hopefuls at a New York academy of music and dance, where just one gay person, Montgomery McNeil (Paul McCrane), can be found: mournful and adrift, but palling up with a couple of the kids.

W: Christopher Gore; D: Alan Parker; 134 mins.

Montgomery was still a member of the team in the television version (played by P. R. Paul). However, he was so straitjacketed that he disappeared after the first (1982) season.

family A social unit that has been romanticized, decried, strengthened, weakened, destroyed, rebuilt over the 20th century. Currently the concept of the tight, nuclear family seems to be giving way to a looser, more flexible version involving single parents, two sets of parents, family friends. The tension between the two strongholds of opinion was first put across the airwaves in 1931 by Professor Bronislaw Malinowski and Dr Robert Briffault in a discussion entitled 'What Is a Family?' (part of a series called MARRIAGE: PAST AND PRESENT). The former strongly endorsed the accepted capitalist Western ideal of parents and children living closely together, while the latter instanced successful examples of one-parent, extended and lateral arrangements from all over the world. In separate talks, the men crystallized their viewpoints:

> I think we shall have to establish a single standard of morality, a greater legal and economic equality of husband and wife, much greater freedom in parental relationships ('Is the Family Doomed?').

> The assumption that there can be no other form of family, no other reproductive group than that consisting of papa, mama, baby will no doubt appear very natural to most people, but is not scientific . . . The family is unnatural . . . The family is the factory of feeble-mindedness ('The Mother').

Other talks, involving similar conservatives and iconoclasts, included those in the 1935–6 series *Family Life* (in which Dr H. A. Mess mentioned men 'who have been frightened of responsibility' developing 'feminine characteristics').

After the Second World War, the BBC took great pains to extensively promote, and discuss problems occurring in the traditional family. Its future was then giving serious cause for alarm with so many fathers sundered from their children, more women earning money outside the home, and rising divorce rates. Part of the BBC's strategy involved fictional families, following on from the war-time Robinsons: the Dales, THE ARCHERS and, finally, the Huggetts.

In America, the cosy image of husband, wife and perfect (if fractious) children reigned throughout the 1950s and 1960s. By the next decade, more single parents (usually widower or widow) were appearing: *Julia* (1968–70); *The Partridge Family* (1970–3); *The Brady Bunch* (1969–73). In the 1980s, there was more width and breadth (if not necessarily depth) in the definition of family: gay men with children (Jodie in SOAP; Steven in DYNASTY); four older women (two related, two not) cohabiting (THE GOLDEN GIRLS); etc.

Neither British nor American mainstream television is yet ready to admit other realities into the scheme of things: realities such as gays and lesbians living with heterosexuals in a family situation (as tentatively shown in films like *A Perfect Couple* (1979) and *Silkwood* (1983)); a lesbian and a gay man who have a child together (trivialized on screen in A DIFFERENT STORY (1978)); a lesbian couple with children (DOMESTIC BLISS 1985 was a one-off example); a lesbian pair, one of whom gets pregnant and has a baby.

This last situation, increasingly common, was given a calm, non-sensationalist airing in the 40 MINUTES film 'Demelza's Baby' (1984) whose editor was the new mother's sister (Jane Val Baker). Demelza, living with Judy who runs a café in Cornwall, is asked about Morgan's dad (who does not appear). 'I think he feels like he's just helped two people out.' Judy? 'She's as much part of him as I'm part of him.' Idyllically presented (walks along the shoreline, seagulls soaring), 'Demelza's Baby', though extremely well received, raised worrying questions in the minds of some reviewers: with two mums instead of a mum and a dad, is there a chance that Morgan will have two Oedipal conflicts?

By the late 1980s, the THATCHER government had hewn in rock the concept of the 'pretended family' whereby homosexual people with children (conceived 'naturally' or via AID, or achieved through adoption) live in a mockery of heterosexual norms. This distortion of real events was slightly countered by films, often but not always about the AIDS crisis, often but not always involving children: from Canada, *The Heart Exposed* (1986); from New Zealand, A DEATH IN THE FAMILY (1986); from France, *Father's Day* (1988); from the US, TORCH SONG TRILOGY (1988), LONGTIME COMPANION (1990) and *Inside Monkey Zetterland* (1992). In their different ways, solemn, sentimental, near farcical, these works place the gay person very much at the centre of one

family (with members chosen by them and who may include solely gay men, or lesbians, or heterosexuals, or a mixture) and part of (sometimes a distant, alienated part of) a biological family.

Neither is necessarily shown as being better, or more or less 'pretend' than the other. What is slowly coming across is that Peter Laslett's 'circle of loved, familiar faces, known and fondled objects' (*The World We Have Lost* 'The Sovereignty of the Family' 1960 R) is open to people who are banished from the traditional hearth and home, or who may wish to enjoy the pleasures and conflicts of two or more family circles.

Family (US 1976–80 T) Classy, relatively hard-hitting comedy series about Kate Lawrence (Sada Thompson), lawyer husband Douglas (James Broderick) and kids, living comfortably in Los Angeles. Its opening (28.9.76) posited Zeke, an old friend of one of the sons (school drop-out, hopeful writer Willie, played by Gary Frank), turning up to reveal that he is gay ('that summer when I knew I was different') to Kate, then Buddy (Kristy McNichol), then Doug, then his own father, then Willie . . . to everyone except Timmy the toddler.
Cr: Jay Presson Allen; P: Mike Nichols, Aaron SPELLING and Leonard Goldberg; ABC; 50 mins.

family drama A very popular genre, usually with much autobiography and identity crises on the part of the author. These can range from the full-on melodramatics of CAT ON A HOT TIN ROOF to the equally painful, but more reined in, *Death of a Salesman* and *The Glass Menagerie*. Plays with a family setting where homosexuality is a key irritant include THE FAMILY WAY; THE LITMUS QUESTION; A HARD GOD; *Green Street Revisited* (1982 T); *The Mourning Thief* (1984 T); WHAT A SAGA!; LAND OF PROMISE; WORDS OF ONE SYLLABLE; *Lemon Sky* (1987 T); A HORSE CALLED GERTRUDE STEIN.

family life Mary WHITEHOUSE'S war cry, never defined and used to the disadvantage of those living securely, adequately and/or usefully (never mind happily) within a different grouping. After the Second World War BBC radio pursued a policy of family restructuring through serials featuring semi-ideal middle-class and working-class families: DALES, ARCHERS, Huggetts, Lyons. Television would follow suit in the 1950s with the Groves and Appleyards, and the less traditional (widowed father, daughter and her fiancée in DIXON OF DOCK GREEN, which also admitted a probable lesbian into the fold).

During 1946, the subject of family was endlessly analysed in talks and features:

The Family Now. A case study of a particular family followed by a discussion (no. 11: 'Sex Education for the Young' concluded that such matters were 'better conveyed at school' than by parents).

Family Relationships. Included the Dean of Chichester who was concerned over falling birth rates: 'Nothing can guarantee family happiness . . . Unadventurous parents so easily become childless parents.'

Family Album. 'The true story of a professional middle-class family, whose mother and father and eight children live the sort of family life which is rapidly disappearing as the old order changes' (*Radio Times*).

Happy Families. A 'typical', usually middle-class, family talked about themselves.

The idea that family life is valuable, under threat and in need of preservation continues in broadcasting today, but perhaps with more tolerance of divergence and diversity from the old, accepted, but often mythical models.

In the late 1980s there were series like *Family – First to Last* ('A weekly examination of families, parents and children in a Britain with one in three marriages breaking up') and *Relative Values* (four portraits aimed at showing 'how shifting social and moral attitudes have affected family life). Noticeable was a shift back to the views of Robert Briffault in the 1930s: 'People talk of the family as a homogeneous entity but, in fact, it's heterogeneous to a fault' said the presenter of *Relative Values* in 1987.

But a real critique of the institution is rare and left to incendiary radicals like Donald MacRae, Professor of Sociology at the London School of Economics, who dared to say in 1962 (*What Is Wrong With Britain?* R) something which Professor BRONOWSKI had to couch in softer terms in 1974 (THE ASCENT OF MAN T) and which, even today, would raise hackles: 'We have sacred cows of all sorts . . . which we must not touch, which devour our substance, which get in the way of our reforms . . . I think . . . you can see it in terms of a new concentration on private life; on family life, turning away from any image of society to the immediate and personal life that people have.'

The Family Way (UK 1966 C) Robust North of England comedy about an unconsummated marriage shades into something more poignant when the bullying father (John Mills) and his long-suffering wife (Marjorie Rhodes) reveal the big family secret: a love both of them shared (in very different ways) for Billy Stringfellow 'a quiet, gentle lad' now dead.

W: Bill Naughton from his 1961 television play *Honeymoon Postponed* and its stage version *All in Good Time*; P: John Boulting; D: Roy Boulting; 115 mins.

A great success it is: rambunctious and tender by turns, with an unusually sensitive treatment of semi-repressed but openly expressed love – admittedly from a generally unsympathetic/pathetic character.

The Famous Five (UK 1978 T) Adults are very much also-rans in these (modernized and unremarkable) adaptations of Enid Blyton's internationally popular stories of four children (COUSINS) and dog. Parents are shadowy figures, scarcely mentioned, while nearly all the villains are BACHELORS ('now *he's* really peculiar') or stepfathers ('an odd sort'), save for one (and he's American). And an environmentalist (Ronald Fraser in

'Five Go to Smugglers' Top') is regarded as 'really peculiar' because he wants a marsh left as it is. After one or two episodes in which 'George' KIRRIN (Michelle Gallagher) is called QUEER (behind her back), she is accepted by the other three and – when not forced to look after soppy Anne – joins the boys in some of their adventures like discovering the secret of the ghost train.

famous homosexuals In an early (1977) episode of SOAP, Jessica (Katherine Helmond) has a heart-to-heart with her nephew Jodie (Billy CRYSTAL) after he has abandoned plans for a SEX CHANGE operation:

> Jessica: 'I guess you're not gay any more.'
> Jodie: 'Well, yes, Aunt Jessie, I am.'
> Jessica: 'Oh! . . . When we were younger, there were no such things as homosexuals.'
> Jodie: 'Yes there were. All through history. ALEXANDER THE GREAT . . . Plato . . .'
> Jessica: 'Mickey Mouse had a gay *dog*? First I heard of it.'
> Jodie (attempting to explain but thinking better of it): 'You didn't know? Goofy was his lover.'

In many a 'sensitive' drama about this Delicate Subject, there comes a moment when a litany of the great and good is delivered, either by a friendly heterosexual or by a homosexual person. In the former category there is the counsellor in WELCOME HOME, BOBBY (1986 T); in the latter there is Fiona, harried daughter to her hostile family in A HORSE CALLED GERTRUDE STEIN. The list always includes Alexander, Leonardo Da Vinci and MICHELANGELO.

fancy 'I've taken a fancy to you, Daisy . . . And Creakle thinks twice before touching anyone I take a fancy to,' said STEERFORTH (Barrie Justice) to DAVID COPPERFIELD (Ian MCKELLEN) in the BBC production of 1966. But by the time the BBC adapted the story again in 1974 the phrase 'taken a fancy to' was removed, as it was in the 1986 version. In the period Dickens was writing, the phrase may have meant to desire sexually rather

than, from roughly 1860 onwards, to have a high opinion of someone. It continues to have a sexual connotation in the 20th century ('fancy man', 'fancy woman', and 'fancy work' which is a man's sexual parts).

The bank manager (Peter Tilbury) says a man 'took my fancy' in THE BILL 'Safe Place' (1990 T) without his being defined as gay. Brian Blessed played PC Fancy Smith in Z CARS (1962–4 T), and one of the criminals (David Austen) in *All Coppers Are* (1972 C) was known as Fancy Boy. In TWO PEOPLE 'The Trouble with a Kitten' (1979 T) young Per (Dai Bradley) asks his older lover Ralph (Philip Sayer) about his schoolfriend who's staying in their cottage:

> Per: 'Do you fancy him?'
> Ralph: 'You'd kill me.'

Fanshawe, Simon (195?–) English radical gay comic, an ex-community worker in Brixton, who 'worships Lenny Bruce' but whose own unthreatening, friendly repartee made him one of the first openly gay comedians to penetrate mainstream television from 1985 onwards (*Cabaret*) – including a brief season with *That's Life* (1990) and chatting about 'first kisses' with Mavis Nicholson on *The Garden Party* (1990) – and (perhaps more effectively) national radio – *Fanshawe on Five* (1990– , 'serious issues in frivolous style'), *Bull!* (1992) and *Sunday Brunch* (1993 R). He chaired a couple of discussions – one on 'Love and Marriage' – in relaxed, good-humoured style for OUT (1991– T).

Farquharson, Robert (1877–1956) Chillingly extravagant English stage actor who was usually cast in flamboyant or villainous roles on film (Count Lazard in *The Man They Couldn't Arrest* (1932), and on radio (Mephistopheles in *Doctor Faustus* 1932; Beau BRUMMELL in Edith Sitwell's *The Last Party* 1938; Manner, the 'queer' caretaker in *The House on the Fens* 1942). Simon CALLOW wrote that Farquharson was the 'rumoured black magician and model for Dorian Gray' (*Charles Laughton: A Difficult Actor*, 1987).

Farson, Daniel (1930–) English journalist and television interviewer who was very popular during the late 1950s and early 1960s, investigating quirks, oddities and various familiar or forbidden facets of life (but not homosexuality) in programmes such as *Out of Step* (1958); *People in Trouble* (1958); *Farson's Guide to the British* (including 'British Men and Clothes', 'Notting Hill', 'Music Halls', 'Lorry Drivers' and 'The British as Lovers' 1960); *The Pursuit of Happiness* (interviewing, among others, Tennessee WILLIAMS, 1960); *People Apart* (1960); *Living for Kicks* (teenagers, 1960); *Meet . . .* (interviews with the likes of Alma COGAN and Lionel Bart, 1962). He wrote an episode 'The Frighteners' (about East End criminals) for the BBC's 1965 drama series *Londoners*. In the 1980s he became TV columnist for the *Mail on Sunday* and was heard on *Bookshelf* (1987 R) talking to one of his favourite groups of people: denizens of 'BOHEMIAN London'.

fashion boutique owners Arny Carnaby (Russell Hunter) fiercely defends his masculinity in THE FAT OF THE LAND (1967 T): 'Just because I'm in the fashion, I'm not like that. Quite the opposite I can assure you.' (But he is revealed to be wearing lace panties.) Very much a 1960s phenomenon: brightly coloured, tight, sexy clothes for (young) males often purveyed by men who made no secret of admiring some of the customers. They were fixtures of Swinging London films and plays (beginning with *No Hiding Place* 'Golden Boy' 1966 T), with some leftover love-lies appearing a decade or so later: Jonathan Cecil in *Rising Damp* (1980 C); Jacky Chissick in *Minder* 'A Well-Fashioned Fit-Up' (1984 T).

fashion designers In COLETTE's short story 'The Master' the arbiter of taste is described thus: '. . . will he betray his appetite for domination, claim revenge for his past as an impoverished clerk,

confess the disgusted misogyny that comes from dealing with too many females, the pleasure he takes in making them ugly, in humiliating them, in subjecting them to his half-crazed fantasies, in "branding" them?' Drama and comedy have seen this functionary as a necessary evil to be indulged or as a buffoon.

Evil ones in the UK include Arny Carnaby (Russell Hunter) in THE FAT OF THE LAND (1967 T); Oliver Lloyd (Andrew Francis) displaying a raspish tongue and a nice line in camel hair coats and cashmere scarves to set off his 6ft 2in frame and bald head in GEMS (1984–5 T); from an age of grace and elegance (the late 1950s), Henley of Mayfair (James FOX) cooing over the microphone to his titled lady clients and marrying Crepe Suzette for cover in *Absolute Beginners* (1986 C).

An evil one in the US is René AUBERJONOIS, a fashion great called Masters who is beginning to slide (in *The Rockford Files*, in a 1978 TV episode defiantly entitled 'With the French Heel Back, Can the Nehru Jacket Be Far Behind?'). He is an unpleasant, self-deluding if adventurous fashion designer. With his affected 'Briddish' accent, his op-art car-seat covers and hand on hip, he cuts a brittle, isolated figure. His latest collection – including a jade-green medical technician's gown studded with flowers plus a matching surgeon's mask which doubles as a disco bag – is derided. His fanaticism – 'a bunch of dresses, it's his whole life' – propels him to murder two women.

Buffoons in the UK include Harold LANG as Mr Louis, all blondined hair and brisk patter in *It Started in Paradise* (1952 C); Maurice Denham as designer to high society Cecil Mincingham in *Much-Binding-in-the-Marsh* (1953 R); flustered Mr Cecil (Heron CARVIC) in *A Knife in the Sun* (1958 R); twirling couturier (Peter SELLERS) in *The Wrong Arm of the Law* (1962 C); young and foolish (but sweet) Claude Crepe (Anthony Gardiner) in *Mister Ten Per Cent* (1967 C); mother's boy Albert (Peter Butterworth) set up for marriage by a hard-

boiled, unfeminine woman in THE FABU-
LOUS FRUMP (1969 T).

Buffoons in the US are asexual:
Madame Lucy in *Irene* (George K.
ARTHUR 1926 C; Arthur Treacher 1940
C); Cary GRANT subbing for 'Maurice
from Schneiders', in bow tie and with
floppy handkerchief, exclaiming over
Ginger Rogers' trousseau in *Once Upon
a Honeymoon* (1942 C); swishy Vito
Scotti cut to the quick by Joan Collins in
Warning Shot (1966 C; he exasperatedly
tells a photographer and assistant (Collins) to get away from his models and
take pictures of cows, to which Joan replies: 'In your case, it would be *bulls*' –
quick move and cut); Peter Panama
(Vincent Schiavelli) in *The Corner Bar*
(1972–3 T); one of Mae WEST's husbands (Keith Moon) in *Sextette* (1978
C).

Occasionally fashion designers are presented more substantially (but they
usually turn out to be hetero or bisexual), eg Ted Casablanca (Alex Davion)
in VALLEY OF THE DOLLS (1967 C) who
marries Neely O'Hara and sets tongues
wagging: 'You know how bitchy fags can
be'; Albert (Perry King) in A DIFFERENT
STORY (1978 C), a Belgian who marries
a lesbian to stay in the US and later
fathers a child.

Three men – one unspecified, the two
other gay – who aren't presented as
dizzy and totally impossible are Robert
Flemyng's character in *Funny Face* (1957
C; here was somebody whose artistic
flair could believably co-exist with a
gambler's recklessness and a general's
organizational cunning); Harry, the ageing designer in THE COLLECTION (Griffith Jones 1960 T; Laurence Olivier
1976 T) who is scared that his protégé
Bill is leaving him for a woman; for a
brief time on the US afternoon serial AS
THE WORLD TURNS (1988 T), a well-
built, sexy guy called Hank Elliott.

The only traceable child designer was
Susannah YORK's 11-year-old brother,
Wilmouse (Richard Williams), cutting
out patterns for his dolls in *The Greengage Summer* (1961 C).

Lesbian women have been represented
in this field, too: Claire Bloom's Mary

Quant oufitted Theo in THE HAUNTING;
Roxanne (Erica Gavin) in *Beyond the
Valley of the Dolls* (1970 C); the title
character (Margit Carstensen), obsessively in love with one of her models in
The Bitter Tears of Petra Von Kant (1972
C); Bette Green (Maggie Steed), freak-
ily dressed, with pet parrot and lesbian
mini-orgies a speciality in FOX (1980 T);
Vanessa Valerian (Barbara Bach) married to camp fellow designer and making
a pass at the nothing-doing heroine in
Princess Daisy (1983 T); Capucine as a
friendly French couturier, socializing
with editrice Joan Collins in *Sins* (1986
T). But in *Chanel Solitaire* (1981 C) the
legendary creator of the Little Black
Dress is limited to one brief liaison with
the artist Misia Sert (Catherine Alle-
gret) while on a temporary rebound
from her aristocratic true love; nasty and
cold Pamela Winter-Smith (Rowena
Wallace) appears in *Flair* (Aust 1990
T); etc.

The most unlikely fashion director was
Ilya Kuryakin (David McCallum),
whose unexpected talent for frocks came
in useful as a front while resting for 15
years after his partnership with *The Man
from UNCLE*. In *The Return of . . .* (1983
T) Napoleon Solo has little difficulty in
persuading him to return to a man's life.
'My world,' says Ilya, 'is full of weird
people.' What a treat for him to once
again mix with the villains and double-
crossers of unweird espionage.

It is interesting to note that Ingmar
Bergman used a dress designer, Ti
(Walter Schmidinger) – a melancholy
soul overly concerned with his advancing years – as his mouthpiece in a long,
often bilious monologue in his 1980 film
From the Life of the Marionettes.

fashion magazine editors Liza (Ginger Rogers), man-starved, mannishly
dressed: a candidate for psychiatry in
Lady in the Dark (1944 C); Maggie Prescott (Kay Thompson), fearsomely dictatorial ('THINK PINK!') but wise and
whacky withal in *Funny Face* (1957 C);
Ella (Sheila Steafel), the antithesis of
femininity in THE FABULOUS FRUMP
(1969 T); Jay Cee (Barbara Barrie), a

philistine closet-lesbian editor of *Ladies' Day* magazine in *The Bell Jar* (1979 C); Irene Bailey (Jessica Walter), a queen of her particular jungle, fending off all predators ('I've warned you before – stay away from my girls') in *She's Dressed to Kill/Someone Is Killing the World's Greatest Models* (1979 T); Jenny Runacre, head to toe in slinky black leather and satin in *Hussy* (1980 C); Harriet Toppingham (Gene Tierney) espies unspoiled young Melanie, promptly spoils her, and leads her on to Hollywood superstardom, drink and drugs in *Scruples* (1980 T).

fashion models An unidentified player in the fashion parade in *Over the Moon* (1937 C): a middle-aged, skeletal man dressed in olive green harem pants with blue accessories, and Rex Harrison reacting with disgust at so gross and unmanly an apparition; Monique (Andrée Debar), an unusual sort of woman in *La Garçonne* (1957 C); Karin (Hanna Schygulla) causing *The Bitter Tears of Petra Von Kant* (1972 C); *Emmanuelle* (Sylvia Kristel 1974 C); Jackie (Marcia Strassman) in *Police Story* 'The Ripper' (1974 T); Michelle and Lulu, targets for a mad killer in *Eyes of Laura Mars* (1978 C; Lisa Taylor and Darlanne Fluegel as the co-habiting beauties); hunting and shooting Kate Bedford (Cathee Sheriff), the fashion editor's pet in *She's Dressed to Kill* (1979 T): 'Football player shoulders, skier, mountain climber and big game hunter and alleged full-time skirt-chaser ... So watch yourself'; ROOM-MATE of (heterosexual) hero in *The Making of a Male Model* (1983 T; Jeff Conaway as the once beautiful, now ageing and doomed Chuck Lanyard); Margaret (Anne Carlisle) in *Liquid Sky* (1982 C) questioning the artificiality and stupidity of her world and wanting some control of a life peopled by strangers intent on destroying themselves and her; the gorgeous, tanned guys – one of whom is gay – in *Swimsuit* (1988 T).

fashion photographers 'This is the end, the absolute end,' flounces the highly strung Russell Paxton (Mischa Auer) in the final shot of *Lady in the Dark* (1944 C). For the next two decades photographers were nearly always variations upon a scream, rising to a crescendo with Sid Field in *London Town* (1946 C); Clement Clements (James Thomason 1954 R; Brian Haines 1963 R), the society photographer in *A Shilling for Candles*: 'Of course, ducky, the motive's obvious. Everyone knows you'd stop at nothing for a part'; Kenneth WILLIAMS' Hilary St Clair in HANCOCK'S HALF HOUR 'The Publicity Photograph' (1958 R): 'Snaps? I don't take snaps. I *paint* with light!'

Occasionally they were central characters: Fred Astaire as Dick Avery (ie Richard Avedon), genius of the lens in *Funny Face* (1956 C), who is happy being a bachelor in his fifties until boyish ('gamin' is the preferred word) Audrey Hepburn comes into focus. Occasionally they were female: Dora (Simone Renant), more glamorous than the model in *Quai des Orfèvres* (1947 C). Or is it that twill trousers and striped clinging jersey never date?

Generally, though, they were seedy and queer: Jessel (Donald Pleasence) in *The Shakedown* (1959). Or svelte and queer: Flagg (Dennis PRICE) in *No Love for Johnnie* (1961). Or seedily svelte and queer: Aubrey WOODS in *Portrait of a Man* (1960 T); Peter Copley as Mandrake in VICTIM (1961). The changeover came with David Hemmings in *Blow-Up* (1966 C) who is hetero potency personified. But there was a parallel strand, exemplified by Malcolm (Roland CURRAM), sexually active friend and colleague of DARLING (1965 C), and by the cheery and gay Gerry (Derek JACOBI), assistant to Baker (Robert STEPHENS) in *The Photographer* (1968 T). This braiding continued through the next decade: the flaming pink threads provided by Roddy (Graham CHAPMAN in *Doctor in Trouble* (1970 C); Donald (René AUBERJONOIS) in *Eyes of Laura Mars* (1978 C); unfaithful Bruce in NUMBER 96 (1972 T); and by a considerably less spunky David Hemmings as Jerry Nelson in *The Love Machine* (1971 C).

More grounded gay photographers were the tall, dark and handsome Larry (Keith Prentice) in THE BOYS IN THE BAND (1970 C); faithful Saul (Jonathan Hadary) who nurses a dying ex-lover in *As Is* (1986 T); Yiang who gives shelter and guidance to homeless boys in *The Outsiders* (1986 C); Jacques (William Allen Young) né Jake, BLACK American and gay in Paree in *Sins* (1986 T).

A big question mark hovers over fashion and features photographer Jeff (James Stewart) in *Rear Window* (1954 C). He fits the traditional masculine mould, but his fear of marriage borders on the pathological . . . and the original story came from the gay writer Cornell WOOLRICH.

Fassbinder, Rainer Werner (1945–82) German film director, writer and actor. He made 57 films and TV productions from 1969. First achieved success in 1972 with *The Merchant of Four Seasons* (C/T). His work, strongly influenced by the melodramas of Douglas Sirk and by Jean-Luc Godard, is formal and controlled, reckless and emotionally naked.

C: *The City Bums* and *The Small Chaos* (1965–6 shorts); *Sernes Jamaica*; *Love Is Colder Than Death* (1969); *Gods of the Plague* (1969); *Why Does Herr R. Run Amok?* (1970); *The American Soldier* (1970); *The Niklashauser Drive/Rio Das Mortes* (1971); *Recruits in Ingolstadt* (1971); *Wildwechsel/World on a Wire* (1972); *The Bitter Tears of Petra Von Kant* (1972); *Fear Eats the Soul* (1973); *Martha* (1973); *Effi Briest* (1974, box office smash); *Shadow of Angels* (1975, based on his *Trash, the City and Death*); FOX AND HIS FRIENDS (1975 C); *Mother Kusters Goes to Heaven* (1976); *Satan's Brew* (1976); *Chinese Roulette* (1976); *I Only Want You to Love Me* (1977); *Germany in Autumn* (one episode 1977); *Despair* (1978); *The Marriage of Maria Braun* (1979, his first international commercial hit); *In a Year of 13 Moons* (1979); *The Third Generation* (1979); *Lili Marleen* (1981); *Lola* (1981); *Veronika Voss* (1982); QUERELLE (1982); etc. His next films would have been *The Blue of Noon*,

adapted by Tennessee WILLIAMS from a Georges Bataille novel; *Cocaine*; *Hitman*; the life of Rosa Luxembourg; an instalment of *War and Peace* about the peace movement.

R (UK): as writer of a science fiction play, *No One Is Evil and No One Is Good* (1985).

T (West Germany): *Eight Hours Don't Make a Day* (five parts 1972); *Fear of Fear* (1975); *Frauen in New York* (1977, based on *The Women*); *Bolweiser* (two parts 1976); *Debit and Credit* (1977, but series cancelled at the last minute); *Berlin Alexanderplatz* (13 parts 1980, from the novel by Alfred Doeblin).

As actor: role in Jean-Marie Straub's *The Bridegroom, the Comedienne and the Pimp* (1968 C); title role of BISEXUAL wanderer in Volker Schlondorff's *Baal* (1969 C); silent layabout, Jorgos in *Katzelmacher* (1969 C); a porn purchaser in *Gods of the Plague* (1969 C); in Schlondorff's *The Sudden Fortune of the Poor People of Kombach* (1972 C); small-time crook, Wittokwski in Ulli Lommel's TENDERNESS OF THE WOLVES (1973, also produced); in *Shadow of Angels* (1975, also wrote and directed); starred in FOX AND HIS FRIENDS (1975 C, also wrote and directed); wrote and voiced Ed Luchman's short *The Blue Train* (1977, a version of *Shanghai Express* in which Udo Kier played all the parts); *Bourbon Street Blues* (c 1977 C); starred in Wolf Gremm's *Murder on the 31st Floor/ Kamikaze* (1978 C); etc.

English-language documentaries and biographical programmes include OMNIBUS 'Signs of Vigorous Life – The New German Cinema' (1976 T); *The Wizard of Babylon* (1982 T, including the director at work on *Querelle*); *A Man Like Eva* (1983 C, with Eva Mattes miraculously transformed into a scruffy, shambling tyrannical Fassbinder clone); *Speed: The Short, Sharp Life of Film-Maker Rainer Werner Fassbinder* (1984 R, interviews with friends/lovers/collaborators, and Fassbinder's words read by Tony Haygarth). His own biographical films include *Beware of a Holy Whore* (1969); *The Bitter Tears of Petra Von Kant* (1972); *Germany in Autumn* (one episode 1977).

'He was perhaps the only famous international director to be openly homosexual, and dealt with related themes in many of his films, often playing central roles himself' (*Variety* obituary).

Fated To Be Mated Music and lyrics by Cole PORTER, written specially for the screen version of his Broadway show *Silk Stockings* (1957) and sung by Fred Astaire, the screen's constant bachelor: a dirge on the seeming inevitability of marriage. Cyd Charisse, who also starred in this adaptation of *Ninotchka*, told Robert Ottaway in *Radio Times* (16–22.5.83) that this song expressed the writer's own feeling of entrapment: 'Cole's music and lyrics had a relevance to his life that few have realized. Many of his famous tunes like "NIGHT AND DAY" and "True Love" came directly of his experience of romance in her many moods.'

fathers Father–son conflicts were particularly prevalent in 1950s American cinema: *Fear Strikes Out*; *East of Eden*; *Last Train from Gun Hill*; and – the first where homosexuality was hovering – CAT ON A HOT TIN ROOF.

Having a gay son is usually no laughing matter, whether in drama or comedy. Examples of the latter: Redd Foxx in NORMAN, IS THAT YOU? (1976 C); Burt Campbell (Richard Mulligan), Jodie's stepfather in SOAP (1977–81 T); Ken Archer (Mark Kingston) in *Time of My Life* (1980 T); Nino Manfredi in an episode of *Heads or Tails* (1983 C) in which the son was a soccer star). In *Up the Chastity Belt* (1971 C), when Sir Cowardy Custard (Graham Crowden) arrives in Sherwood Forest in search of his son, he is horrified to find him in the camp of a LISPING ROBIN HOOD and some very merry men. 'Don't tell me you're ONE OF THEM,' hoots Lurkalot (Frankie HOWERD) to the boy. He then confides to the audience: 'If he isn't, he soon will be.'

It is especially difficult for a father who has lived and fought within institutions whose offshoots are subtle and not so subtle enforcements of sexual orthodoxy: Sergeant Matlovich's career army-officer dad (Stephen Elliott) desperately trying to do the right thing by his son and by his code of behaviour in SERGEANT MATLOVICH VS THE US AIR FORCE; vigilante-leader father (André Morell), 'a confirmed reactionary worth his weight in pure shit', confronting his disgraced son (Michael Jayston) in THE LAST ROMANTIC (1978 T); Jim JONES' father (Ed Lauter), a member of the Ku Klux Klan in GUYANA TRAGEDY: THE STORY OF JIM JONES (1980 T); Captain Magnus Von Freyer (Carl-Axel Heiknert) disgusted by his only daughter going against the family's heterosexual grain in *The Farewell* (1980 C); Thomas Murry (David Kelly), IRA activist from 1916, facing his son's supposedly English-caught pacifism and bisexuality as he lies dying in *The Mourning Thief* (1984 T): 'You broke my heart'; the father of Joe (Jason Rush) is prepared to give him money but has no interest in finding out how he is and so Joe declines the cash in EASTENDERS (1991 T).

Big business tycoons with sexually aberrant kids have included Big Daddy in *Cat on a Hot Tin Roof* (Burl Ives 1958 C; Laurence Olivier 1976 T; Rip Torn 1984 T); Loren Hardman (Laurence Olivier) in *The Betsy* (1978 C); Walker, the local Mr Big (Howard Duff) whose daughter Casey (Diana Scarwid) is on a murder charge in IN THE GLITTER PALACE (1977 T); Roger Ackerley (Freddie JONES) in SECRET ORCHARDS (1980 T) who deflects any attempt on the part of his son to come out, although he is perfectly well aware of his feelings; Blake Carrington (John Forsythe) who strikes out and kills his son's former lover in DYNASTY (1981 T) and who later tries to take custody of his grandson – in the final episode of the 1987 series he tells Steven (Jack COLEMAN): 'I want your happiness. Whatever happens I'll always love you'; Nick (Ben Gazzara) forced to acknowledge his real reasons for having children when Michael comes home sick in AN EARLY FROST (1985 T): 'I never thought the day would come when you'd be in front of me and I wouldn't know who you are.'

Terence RATTIGAN's *Man and Boy* (1971 T) had a sensational plot twist in that the ruthless oil magnate (Telly Savalas) manipulates a situation whereby he uses his son as a sexual chess-piece against a rival.

Unsympathetic and repressed dads copped the blame for the adolescent and post-adolescent difficulties of all three leading characters in MAKING LOVE, while Kim's hatred of men in THE OTHER WOMAN stemmed from paternal rape.

For the rest it's boot 'em and insult 'em: Per's father in TWO PEOPLE; Wendy/Roy's dad (Harry ANDREWS) in *I Want What I Want* (1971 C); Mr James in STANDARD PROCEDURE who is so angry when he finds out that there is even a chance that his boy may be tainted that he kicks the family cat to death; Ken Archer in *Time of My Life*: 'We never had anyone like you in the family before – Great Nance!' The ex-sports hero who hopes athletics will either sort out or tire out Wieland in *Der Sprinter* (1984 C); the icily contemptuous father Tony Lo Bianco) in WELCOME HOME, BOBBY (1986 T).

The more rigid constraints imposed upon a boy's emotional expression come kicking and screaming to the surface during most face-offs between father and transgressing son. With daughters it is sometimes shock spiked with eroticism: Alan (Leslie Phillips) who has an affair with his daughter's girlfriend in Fay Weldon's *Redundant or the Wife's Revenge* (1983 T); the brutish lout who rapes his daughter repeatedly and then, when she brings home a woman friend, calls her a 'dirty queer' in *Remaining Strangers* (1986 R); Meriel's remote papa, Lord Edgar Baigent (Richard Pasco) in THE TINKER'S DAUGHTER (1986 R), revealed to have been sleeping with his daughter's beloved Amy since she was 13: 'I'm like you. We both love, rather crave, beauty . . . landscapes, houses, books, girls. I prefer the physical act with girls of a certain age and I never saw anyone so deliciously put together as she was . . . Now you can be free . . . You can at last have happiness.'

In documentaries, some feminists/lesbians have composed complex visual and sound poems to their dads, eg about Su Friedrich's *Sink or Swim* (1990 C).

Gay/bisexual fathers include Oscar WILDE; Jodie DALLAS (Billy CRYSTAL) in SOAP wanting to do the right thing by Carol but jilted by her, then winning CHILD CUSTODY; Steven CARRINGTON (Jack COLEMAN; Al Corley); ACTOR Mathieu who has a 4-year-old son in THE HEART EXPOSED (1986 C/T); Charlie (Stephen Docherty), Judy GARLAND fan who can't give satisfaction to a woman (who is also a FRIEND OF DOROTHY) other than providing a baby; *Beyond the Rainbow* (1991 R); Owen Benjamin (Brian Cox) in THE LOST LANGUAGE OF CRANES (1992 T) who is a HOMOSEXUAL while his son (Angus MacFadyen) is *gay*. A projected UK film (1992–3) by Jeff Cole involves gay men and their fathers (gay and non-gay) and their sons (gay and non-gay).

father–son talks Any amount of these in situation comedies (usually about 'girls'), eg Michael Gross to Michael J. Fox in *Family Ties* 'Alex Doesn't Live Here Any More' (1989 T, no mention of safe sex); in drama (*Five Finger Exercise*; *Splendor in the Grass*) it's more about power plays with erotic undertones. Emotionally charged candour rejected by Joe Ackerley's father in SECRET ORCHARDS (1980 T); Scott and Dad in MY OWN PRIVATE IDAHO (1991 C); dying father in WORDS OF ONE SYLLABLE (Aust 1991 R).

The Fat of the Land (UK 1967 T) A group of thin-skinned but greedy and overweight 1960s STEREOTYPES spend Christmas at a posh health farm and spew out their boring lives.

W: Jack Russell; P: Graeme McDonald; D: Toby Robertson; 27.12.67; BBC1; 75 mins.

Bilious comedy with its nastiest barbs reserved for Cyril Kitsch (Peter Jones), gourmet RESTAURATEUR, and Arny Carnaby (Russell Hunter), FASHION BOUTIQUE supremo, revealed to be wearing women's knickers.

Arny: 'We're all too sophisticated to believe anything – the price of freedom is eternal what's-its-name . . . But I care, surely I do. I care about myself.'
Woman MP: 'Don't you believe in other people?'
Arny: 'What for? People are their own victims. Drugs release inhibitions but we must pay the price. Sex? OK. So you can do it. And if you can't there's always someone who'll do it for you. You don't even get kids any more. Who wants them?'
Mrs Suez: 'Nice normal healthy people.'
Arny: '*They* went out with the Beatles.'

Faulkner, Trader (1930–) Australian-born actor, writer and flamenco dancer who played one of the first half-way sympathetic gays, Maurice Goodman in *Promenade* (1959 T), as well as a horrible creature named 'Matilda' in *Call Me Mister* 'Long Shot' in 1986. Other roles of interest: Joseph in *A Pair of Claws* (1958 T); the artist in *The America Prize* (1964 R); a pirate in *A High Wind in Jamaica* (1965 C). For radio in 1976 he produced a notably frank and vital portrait of Federico García LORCA.

favourites Intimate court companions to kings and queens who may or may not be bed-mates. Famous examples include Piers Gaveston (to EDWARD II); Sarah Churchill (to Queen ANNE); George VILLIERS, Duke of Buckingham (to JAMES I).

Fawkes, Guy (1570–1606) English Catholic who was one of the conspirators in the plot to blow up Parliament; burnt in effigy as a homosexual Satan figure up until the late-18th century; now seen as more harmless – old clothes stuffed with straw or paper, wearing a mask. Played by Joseph O'Conor in *Gunpowder, Treason and Plot* (1953 T) and investigated by Magnus Magnusson as one of the *Living Legends* (1979 T). The 5 November commemoration of the plot is an annual celebration in England (*Once a Year in Lewes* 'Guy Fawkes Night' 1986 T) and is often used as a

setting for drama (eg the final scene of A TASTE OF HONEY 1961 C; EASTENDERS).

Fay/Faye Girl's name from the word for 'fairy', as in the cunning MORGAN LE FAY. Mainly used for fairly go-ahead, urban women, sometimes ruthless.

US: Fay (Ruth Chatterton) always crying because she has been *Unfaithful* (1931 C); Fay (Bette Davis), moll in *20,000 Years in Sing Sing* (1933 C); Fay La Rue (Glenda Farrell) in *A Man's Castle* (1934 C); Fay Edwards (Kay Sutton) in *The Saint in New York* (1938 C); Fay Lawrence (Mae WEST) in *The Heat's On* (1943 C); New York model on safari Fay Ames (Betta St John) in *Tarzan the Magnificent* (1960 C); Fay (Shelley Winters), ageing former child star in *Harper/The Moving Target* (1966 C); Fay Stuart (Lee Grant), divorce legal secretary in *Fay* (1975 T).

UK: Fé (Giovanna Ralli) in *Deadfall* (1968 T) married to a gay man who is probably also her father – 'F E with an accent,' she tells Michael Caine; Fay (Lee Remick), scheming, homicidal nurse in *Loot* (1970 C); Fay (Georgina Hale), ambitious soubrette with girlfriend in *The Boy Friend* (1971 C); glamorous prison governor Faye Boswell (Googie Withers) in WITHIN THESE WALLS (1974 T); severe Faye (Naomi Chance) who steals Regan's daughter in *The Sweeney* 'Abduction' (1975 T); palpitating amateur actress Fay (Alexandra Pigg) in *A Chorus of Disapproval* (1990 C); would-be world dominatrix Fay Morgan alias Morgan le Fay (Susie Blake) in *Wail of the Banshee* (1992 T).

feasting with panthers In *Oscar* (T) a sated Oscar WILDE (Michael Gambon) returns home after a visit to Alfred Taylor's brothel, where he has met three young men. Oscar ruminates: 'Strange and troubling personalities walking in painted pageants. It's like feasting with panthers . . . the danger is half the excitement.' The scene dissolves into that of a jeweller's shop where Oscar is requesting that a cigarette case be engraved 'Fred'. Then a shift back to the comfortable house. Oscar is reading

The Happy Prince to Cyril, his eldest son. When it is over, Cyril tells him: 'Mother cries at night.'

The Featherstonehaughs Pronounced 'Fanshawes', this British dance troupe 'takes the mickey out of stereotyped behaviour'. A few appearances on television since 1991. Their creator Lee Anderson calls them 'neither aggressively macho nor apologetically non-macho'. Rather they are 'post-gay liberation; not that any one of them would feel that all the aims of gay lib had been achieved . . . people's sexuality was their matter of choice and nothing to get excited about' (*Arts Review*, Aust 1992 R).

Feldman, Marty (1933–83) English writer and comedian, co-begetter (with Barry TOOK) of JULIAN AND SANDY and the other characters in ROUND THE HORNE (1965–7 R). A 'self-confessed paranoid neurotic maniac', he believed that 'comedy like sodomy is an unnatural act'. Had his own television series, then became a cult favourite in mainly American films. Originally worked in fairgrounds (hence his interest in POLARI). Played by Lee Cornes, he describes Judge Argyll as 'a boring old fart' in *The Trials of Oz* (1991 T).

As writer: with Barry Took: *Educating Archie* (1959 R); *Frankie's Bandbox* (1960 R); *Scott . . . on Birds* (1964 T); etc; with others: *Marty* (1968 T); *It's Marty* (1969 T); etc.

C: *Every Home Should Have One* (1969); *Young Frankenstein* (1974): 'Call me Eye-gore'; *Silent Movie* (1976); *High Anxiety* (1978); *Yellowbeard* (1983); etc.

Fellini Satyricon (It/Fr 1969 C) Petronius writ large: two boys (Martin Potter, Hiram Keller) seeking adventures and sexual partners of all kinds. A world of magic, myth, violence and cheerful amorality amidst acres of male flesh, wigs, huge sets, fiery skies, vibrant colours, raucous empty laughter.

W: Federico Fellini and Bernardino Zeppolini; D: Federico Fellini; 120 mins.

The film moves jerkily through a series of short episodes: Encolpius abusing Aclytus: 'He'll go with any boy'; Encolpius finding that his beloved (Giton) has been sold to an actor; the rescue, after which they make love; an earthquake; Trimalchio's feast; Encolpius marries a man (Lycas); a patrician husband and wife commit suicide; the reunited friends meet and flirt with a topless black maid; Encolpius battles the Minotaur.

Although the film contains a good deal of homosexual loveplay with occasional bisexual permutations, there is a central hollowness and lack of engagement that prevents surrender. The 1970 documentary about the making of the film, *Ciao, Federico*, is shorter and livelier, and contains an extraordinary scene of Fellini 'instructing' Martin and Hiram in a love scene: 'Go down, Hiram. Look at Martino. Caress him. Hiram, smile a little bit.'

female impersonators Men who dress in women's clothes either to look ridiculous, to make fun of women or to look impossibly glamorous (and yet say things that most women would not feel comfortable in saying in mixed company). Also known as 'drag' artists.

'Drag' became big business in the late 1960s, especially after the spectacular success of Danny LA RUE, and the growth of working men's clubs and 'drag' pubs (well illustrated in the 1969 documentary *What's a Girl Like You . . .?*). While certain kinds of travesty became more professional and exotic, others followed the more rancid tradition of the pantomime dame: wearing absurd or downtrodden costume and spitting out venomous wisdom or philosophical ruderies; Dame Edna Everage is, perhaps, the most unstoppable and original of these creations, which were pioneered on television and radio by Douglas BYNG, Norman Evans and MRS SHUFFLEWICK. In America, one of television's earliest and most enduring stars, Milton Berle, regularly swept across the screen in something silky, with full make-up and simper.

Sometimes club, pub and stage impersonators would appear in dramatic roles, a tradition that went back to Julian Eltinge in the First World War period and after, but in the climate after the Second World War audiences were usually made aware that the performer was a man dressed as a woman rather than as, in Eltinge's case, being made to believe otherwise.

Real-life impersonators appearing as fictional characters include Sonnie Teale in *La Poupée/He, She or It* (1962 C); Kim August in *No Way to Treat a Lady* (1968 C); Michael Rodgers and Royston Starr providing a suitably unreal frame to the story of two pathetic men in STAIRCASE; Barry Scott in *Goodbye Gemini* (1970 C); Perri St Clair (Patrick Fyffe, later known as Dame Hilda Brackett) in STEPTOE AND SON (1972 C); Ricky Renée in CABARET (1972 C); Danny La Rue in *Our Miss Fred* (1972 C); Lori SHANNON as Beverley LaSalle in three episodes of ALL IN THE FAMILY (1976–8); Bunny Lewis in the *Flossie* episode of NIGHTINGALE'S BOYS (1975 T); Charles Pierce in STARSKY AND HUTCH 'Death in a Different Place' (1977 T); Craig RUSSELL as Robin Turner in OUTRAGEOUS! (1977 C), and as Judy in *Trapper John* 'Straight and Narrow' (1982 T); Lorri Lee in 40 MINUTES 'Lol, Bona Queen of Fabularity' (1981 T); Lanah Pellay in *The Bullshitters* (1984 T), and as Alex in EAT THE RICH (1987 C); Dave Dale playing himself and various characters in IF THEY'D ASKED FOR A LION TAMER (1984 T), and the role of John Fisher who introduced the patrons of the Queen Vic pub to drag in EASTENDERS (1986 T); Lily Savage in *The Bill* (1989 T); Harvey FIERSTEIN as Arnold Beckoff in TORCH SONG TRILOGY (1988 C); Bette Bourne in *A Little Bit of Lippy* (1992 T); Regina Fong in *Now That It's Morning* (1992 T).

Female impersonators, played by actors, began to figure in films from the beginning of the 1960s, sometimes as background sleaze, but also as personages to tickle and titillate audiences as to their exact sexual orientation: Philippe Noiret as the (heterosexual?) uncle of

Zazie dans le Métro (1960 C); Paul Gilbert as Lola Diamond in *Sylvia* (1965 C); Helmut Berger 'doing' Marlene in THE DAMNED (1969 C); George Sanders as the Warlock in *The Kremlin Letter* (1970 C); Yul Brynner singing 'MAD ABOUT THE BOY' in *The Magic Christian* (1970 C); Reg Varney as Sherry Sheridan in *The Best Pair of Legs in the Business* (1969 T; 1972 C); Ken Scott (John Davidson) whose female self in his nightclub act leads him to commit murder in THE STREETS OF SAN FRANCISCO 'The Mask Of Death' (1974 T); Gunner 'Gloria' Beaumont in *It Ain't Half Hot, Mum* (1974–82 T); Paul Jabarra who vamps Donald Sutherland while singing 'Hot Voodoo' and 'I Want To Be Bad' in *The Day of the Locust* (1975 C); ALBIN (Michel Serrault) in LA CAGE AUX FOLLES (1978 etc); Captain Terri Dennis (as Marlene, Carmen and one of the Andrews Sisters, and as very much himself) in PRIVATES ON PARADE (1982 C); Michael (Martyn Hesford) turning on his audience in *Belles* (1983 T); 'Doris' (Peter Kelly) in *The Amazing Miss Stella Estelle* (1984 T); Paul San Marco (Cameron Engish), one of the dancers in A CHORUS LINE (1985 C) confessing his (adolescent) drag past; undercover Miguel Bosé having an affair with the daughter of the woman he impersonates in HIGH HEELS (1991 C); etc.

Often seen as the homosexual's disreputable half-brother, the female impersonator/drag artist/male actress can be offensive, dazzling, affectionate or frightening. As dramatic characters they have the twin advantages of shock value and a facility for cynicism and knowing ways which is always on the verge of collapsing into vulnerability. At best they have great creative energy and, even if 'untalented', they possess an instinct for survival and for creating a community among the rejected – beautifully exemplified in the documentaries PARIS IS BURNING (1991) and *Where Are We?: Our Trip Through America* (1992).

In the latter, Danny Leonard talks about himself while putting on make-up and wig to become 'Brandy', star performer in a modest BAR in the AMERICAN

SOUTH. 'I don't want to be a woman . . . I'm happy being a man. It's just that as Brandy I can get the attention that Danny can't . . . and raise thousands of dollars for AIDS in the process.' The film-makers then cut to him, out of costume, leading gays and lesbians in a warm, ceiling-raising rendering of 'UNITED WE STAND'.

The contradictions and hostilities underlying some female impersonation are most apparent in the work of Barry HUMPHRIES' Dame Edna EVERAGE; using the mask and the privileges of the female guise to demean and belittle all creatures great and small. For the man beneath the make-up, wig and gown there is often rejection: if he's straight (Sherry Sheridan in *The Best Pair of Legs in the Business*), the real life Arthur Lucan (Brian Murphy) in *On Yer Bike, Riley* (1984 T), or gay (Robin Turner played by Craig Russell in *Outrageous!* (1977 C): 'Being gay is one thing, but going in drag is something else,' his employer tells him). Dave Dale encapsulated the sexual turn-off a drag artist can expect to find in the gay world in *If They'd Asked for a Lion Tamer*:

> Potential one night stand: 'What do you do?'
> Dave: 'I'm a drag artist.'
> P.o.n.s.: 'I'll call you a taxi.'
> Dave: 'Was it something I said?'

In *Belles* Michael questions the artificial barrier between performer and audience: 'If we jump through their hoops, what does it make them? Who are the freaks?' Later he says to his partner/lover Lennie: 'Can't you hear it? Underneath the laughter. Fear. We cover it up for them.'

Femininity Sung by Deborah Whalley to Nancy (Hayley Mills) in Walt Disney's *Summer Magic* (1963 C). The advice offered is: 'Emphasize your femininity if you want to get a beau.' Hayley has been a TOMBOY prior to this Sherman Brothers ditty, designed to keep all potential baby butches firmly in line.

feminists Hard Hearted Hannahs who pour water on drowning men . . . rugged demonstrators of contorted, extreme cussedness, uncontrollable puritans waging a war against nature . . . sexual predators . . . lesbians: phoney and rapacious Hilary (Kate Nelligan) in DO AS I SAY (1977 T); overwhelming Ellie in *Swimming and Flying* (1980 R); driven Olive in *The Bostonians* (Prunella Scales 1979 R; Vanessa REDGRAVE 1984 C); stolid playwright Lena (Suzanne Bertish) in YOU'RE NOT WATCHING ME, MUMMY! (1980 T) unrequitedly in love with the leading actress: 'She doesn't go much on men . . . But then so many women don't nowadays'; barnstorming and ball-battering but foolish, superficial Bunty (Joanna McCallum) in STRUGGLE 'Manning the Barricades' (1983 T); 'fearsome' Fran (June Tobin) in *Life Skills: An Adult Education* (1985 R); self-deceiving Rebecca (Harriet Walter) living with a woman and her two boys in a partnership she believes is 'perfect in its non-sexist symbiosis' in *The Unquiet Heart* 'Rhyme or Reason' (1987 R).

More sympathetic – if downbeat – is 'strident' Margaret (Charlotte Cornwell) in *The Men's Room* (1991 T) who sleeps with the heroine's lover 'a couple of times'. She believes that as men make up half the world you might as well try to live with them, but 'we must bring up our sons to be feminists'. Shelley (Charlotte Cornwell) in *No Excuses* (1983 T) is 'the original liberated lady', 'a special case . . . a good bloke', 'a thread ever winding back onto a spool'. A famous rock singer and composer, she has been 'in charge' of her own life and has done what she wanted for over 16 years. But it didn't work out: 'I just can't handle real life. I sure fucked it up.' Even the woman who wins the fight does it with the help of magic and plastic surgery: Ruth in *The Life and Loves of a She-Devil* (Julie T. Wallace 1986 T) and *She-Devil* (Roseanne Barr 1989 C).

One of the few examples of a woman successfully – if in a fraught, tense manner – challenging the world of men, without being viewed as totally unnatural or a victim, is Candice Bergen's

Murphy Brown, currently bringing up a child with a man who is not her lover.

Joan Ferguson (Maggie Kirkpatrick in PRISONER/PRISONER: CELL BLOCK H 1982–7). Aka 'The Freak', 'Fergo', 'The Bear', 'Dickhead', 'Bitch' and 'Butch'. Disciplinarian prison officer, sometimes acting warden. Corrupt, ruthless and anti-smoking. With her bulky figure, greased back hair and gravel voice she is a SISTER GEORGE for the 1980s. Her dialogue is gloriously rudimentary ('Shut your mouth or you'll be on a charge . . . Less talk and more work') and earns her remarks like: 'The Freak is a bitch. *You* know that.' However, the actress plays this unholy terror with such wit, verve and fury that she invokes Lady Macbeth (without the conscience and trained by the Khmer Rouge).

From her very first appearance she was revealed as a woman not incompatible with the villainy inside Wentworth. But there is a tiny kernel of humanity inside her. In her last job (a jail in Queensland), she bashed up a prisoner for killing her lover: 'She was quiet, gentle, and I loved her and she loved me too.' And she loves her DOG. When this creature – her only friend in the world – is poisoned, it gives her the motivation to be even more pitiless and vengeful.

A Festival of Woman (UK 1964 R) In 411 BC, Aristophanes satirized those elements of Athenian society which he felt were corrupting that state: Agathon, a young tragic poet (Gordon Gardner) and Cleisthenes, an effeminate Athenian (Brian Haines). 'Dear ladies, I am one of you, though not in a technical sense; biologically unsound but look at my candy-soft chin. I am a woman's woman's man and I simply adore women's things.'
P: Raymond Raikes; 1.1.65; 90 mins.

Aristophanes had 'a conservative attitude towards the dandy which survives for many today . . . an element in society he felt was corrupting the state – sophistication, effeminacy and feminism' (*Radio Times*). (This was the first radio

production to intimate an erection. Gay man to hero (in drag): 'Stand up now, don't be shy. What's that you're poking down . . . like a little winkle if you ask me.')

Le Feu Follet [The Fire Within] (Fr 1963 C) Alain (Maurice Ronet) is unable to deal with life outside the clinic. After visiting old friends, including male and female lovers, he commits SUICIDE.
W/D: Louis Malle from the novel by Drieu la Rochelle; 110 mins.

What came first: a man's homosexual guilt or his alcoholism? A brilliant, painful study of a wasted life, ending with a gunshot.

Ffrangcon-Davies, Gwen (1891–1992) English stage, television and radio actress who played with style and simplicity for over 60 years.
C: Mary Tudor in *Tudor Rose* (1936): the Countess in *The Devil Rides Out* (1968); etc.
R: Desdemona in *Othello* (1933); a young nurse in *The Lady with the Lamp* (with Edith Evans as Florence NIGHTINGALE, 1933); Gwendolyn in the Gielgud–Evans recording of THE IMPORTANCE OF BEING EARNEST (1951); Lucy Amorest in *The Old Ladies* (with Edith Evans, 1968); the matriarch in *Dear Octopus* (1980); etc.
T: Emma in *The Violent Years* (1959); Lady Madeleine who lives with a companion called 'Bunker' in *The Patchwork Quilt* (1960); Mrs Nicholson, unscrupulous, possessive mother in *The Ladies of the Corridors* (1961); an emotionally draining mother again as Lilian Jason in *The Jason Grove* (1961); Mrs Ashton in *Londoners* 'The Old Man of Chelsea Reach' (1965); still appearing (in Sherlock Holmes etc) in the late 1980s and a few months before she died.

Most famous for her stage roles (Eve in *Back to Methuselah*; the mother in *The Glass Menagerie*), it is this aspect of her career that has been favoured in radio and television portraits, with a concentration on her legendary Juliet: OMNIBUS 'A Juliet Remembered' (1988 T), a master class with four Juliets; *Still a Juliet* (1988 R), talking, at 97, to her friend Nigel Hawthorne about SHAKESPEARE'S ladies (some of them gentlemen – and all of them boys).

As herself she was castaway with Roy Plomley (twice), and had her favourite poems and prose read by Anna MASSEY and Alec MCCOWEN (*With Great Pleasure* 1991 R). In 1973 she spoke disarmingly on radio about her penchant for playing queens, her partnerships with Gielgud and Evans, her lack of 'luck' in films, and the (woman) 'friend' she lived with for many years.

Fiddle About Uncle Ernie (Keith Moon) sings this John Entwhistle composition as he prepares to molest his nephew *Tommy* (1975 C). A copy of GAY NEWS is saliverously read before spontaneously combusting.

Fierstein, Harvey (1954–) American actor and playwright, with extraordinary physical presence, much of which resides in his granulous subterranean voice. The winner of two Tonys (for TORCH SONG TRILOGY and for the book of *La Cage aux Folles*), he is prized for his honesty, his affectionate humour, and for his extreme selectivity in choosing roles (usually passing on heterosexual ones): the gay on the boat to Fire Island in *Garbo Talks* (1984 C); BEREAVED and in conflict with dead lover's wife in *Tidy Endings* (1988 T, also wrote); Arnold in the 1988 film of TORCH SONG TRILOGY; Carl, Homer's secretary in *The Simpsons* 'Simpson and Delilah' (1991 T, voice only); Mark Newberger, Becky's college sweetheart, now leading a different kind of life in *Cheers* 'Rebecca's Lover . . . Not' (1992); *The Harvest* (1993 C); CBS TV series (1993 project). Talked about HOLLYWOOD timidity on a certain subject in the first series of OUT ON TUESDAY (1989 T). He appeared on *The Arsenio Hall Show* in 1992, accompanied by his lover of four years whom he had publicly thanked on the 1983 TONY AWARDS telecast.

Fifty One (UK 1958 R) An irregular outside broadcast of Wednesday night discussions by the Fifty One Society on subjects of continuing concern. During 'Examining the Family Today' a voice from the back spoke against 'the universal cult of marriage and the happy family . . . a conspiracy fed by advertisers, television and the press treatment of royalty'. David Paul in the *Listener* (11.12.58) noted this protest against 'the boosting of one kind of human relationship at the expense of every other'.

Miss **Figgis** (1) 'Mannish' SPINSTER played by Violet Gould in both radio (1949) and television presentations of Pamela Hansford Johnson's lesbian-tinged *Corinth House* (1950 & 1952 R).

(2) Senior classics mistress, possessive of one of her pupils who wants to forgo a university place and get married (Beatrix LEHMANN in *Love and Miss Figgis* 1954 T). Her opening line is: 'How I hate men. Are we never to get away from them?'

She confides in a young teacher: 'Do you think because I'm not attractive I lack every sort of feminine instinct? Of course I should like to have a child. And perhaps in the future Ideal State, it will be possible for a woman of intelligence to have one without the intolerable inconvenience of being attracted to a man for that purpose.'

By wanting her pupil to go to university, stretch her mind and then think about having husband and children, she puts herself on the side of the angels – and also the devils. Is she nature's protector or its jailer? She is described thus: 'a clumsy woman of about 50 with an unwillingness to do anything about herself. Her sandals might be worn by a man'. However, she is presented as a fundamentally wholesome, honest woman with unquenchable vitality and love of learning. As her young colleague (Joyce Heron) tells her in the staff room: 'Oh, Figs, you're the most refreshing person I know. I'm terribly fond of you.'

fighting back Until the 1970s, gays rarely answered back – let alone fought back. Jo persists in her nosey enquiries about Geoff's sex life in A TASTE OF HONEY until he tells her to mind her own business: 'I can't stand people who laugh at other people. They'd get a better laugh if they laughed at themselves.' This was a rare ripple on the dramatic pond into which the gay man's reflection was very much He Who Gets Slapped.

Small waves were generated when members of the Gay Liberation Front lashed out at a stereotyped screamer in a BBC TV play (UNDER THE AGE). The *Church Times* (30.3.72) was enraged that 'two real homosexuals were protesting that the principal characters [in a play] bore no resemblance to reality. It all seemed to be an exercise in self-indulgence by people, heterosexual or homosexual, who should be kept as far away from TV drama as possible.'

The same year, the radio version of A SINGLE MAN did not include a brief but violent speech by ISHERWOOD about the smugness of heterosexuals and how he would like to garrot some of them. The adaptation trod the acceptable path, concentrating upon an ageing gay man, alone after his lover's death, waiting for death – and warning against the innate fascism of all *minorities*.

It is from quiet, unassuming – but successful – Reg (Michael Bryne) in BUTLEY (1974 C/T) that the whiff of dragon's breath comes from a British QUEER, roundly putting the spiteful 'hero' in his place after a stream of jealousy-inspired venom has been spurted in his face. Reg points out that heterosexuals have a certain reputation for bitchiness and superficiality, too.

'They once burned witches at the stake, assuming they were depraved because they were different . . . A revolution has got to happen. And it's coming.' This assertion, in THE LITMUS QUESTION (1975 R), came not from the young gay men in the play but from the 'counsellor', a seemingly disinterested 'straight'.

From the horse's mouth: old John (Joseph O'Conor) in ONLY CONNECT (1979 T) remembering a youthful hero and lover: 'It *was* love. No matter what

they called it. When you know that, you don't give up trying to find it, and if you find it you fight to keep it. That's what I learnt from Edward.'

Most fictional homosexuals are like Marjorie (Lynn REDGRAVE), lover of newly minted lesbian Gail (Mariette Hartley) in MY TWO LOVES (1986 T). Gail asks her lover if she ever gets to screaming point with her anger at having to lead a double life. Marjorie tells her that she 'slides by', enjoys life and buries her rage.

Criticism of monolithic, rejecting heterosexuals is still very rarely voiced in mainstream broadcasting: the following examples add up to no more than 10 minutes of airtime: outbursts in the heat of the moment in SERGEANT MATLOVICH VS THE US AIR FORCE (1978 T) and A QUESTION OF LOVE (1978 T); a brief tirade from Harvey FIERSTEIN in *Tidy Endings* (1988 T); Michael (Richard Ganoung) nearly punches the taxi driver who calls him and Robert 'faggots' (his lover is embarrassed by such pugnacity) in PARTING GLANCES (1985 C); in *André's Mother* (1990) a waiter (Conan McCarthy) tells two of his customers not to be so patronizing or condescending about gays like himself. Sammy (Campbell Morrison) in *Life without George* (1989 T) won't put up with disparaging remarks about his friend Mandy bringing up a baby in a world with a queer as surrogate father. Rising to his feet in his trenchcoat, Sammy asks his attacker what it is about him that is so offending. 'Do you think I'm going to stand over the cot plucking my eyebrows in a pink kimono singing "MAD ABOUT THE BOY"?' He continues: 'Do you think that a child should be brought into a home where they never hear the sound of laughter because its parents can't stand the sight of each other?' Grimmond (Michael CASHMAN), scared of dying, isolated and with a non-gay male NURSE in COMPROMISED IMMUNITY (1991 R), does not go gently and indulges in some het-bashing, while David (Martin Kemp) lets forth a concentrated diatribe against the canoodling male–female diners in *He–She Play* 'Accentuate The Positive' (1992 T).

In real life, the fiery Frank Aqueno lambasted the (very sympathetic and gentle) 'boneheaded fundamentalist' on DONAHUE 'Born Gay, Become Gay or Made Gay?' (1992 T): 'Forty thousand babies in the world die every day. Homosexuals do not, for the most part, bring them into the world. Divorce rate is up around 50 per cent . . . wife beating, child abuse by heterosexuals . . . Get your own act together, then tell me about *my* lifestyle!' And then there's Julian CLARY roping his heterosexual contestants on STICKY MOMENTS if not branding them, and worse.

See also ACT UP; AIDS; THE BATTLE FOR TUNTENHAUS; CLAUSE 28; GAY LIBERATION; OUTING; Colin RUSSELL; STONEWALL RIOTS.

fig leaves One of these is to be found on nearly every male statue featured in American television drama and pre-liberation movies. A 10-minute prologue before the main action of *The Agony and the Ecstasy* (1965 C) manages a close-up of the crotch of MICHELANGELO's rendering of Dawn but only a cover-up (a plaster pouch) of his sublime David. The ARTIST (Charlton Heston) may have had the Front Office in mind when he complains later in the film that 'It was left to the priests to create shame'. Hollywood epics, set in 'decadent' Rome, always plaster over offending parts that would, in reality, have hung free.

The newly cleaned Sistine chapel ceiling uncovers a wealth of vibrant colour, giving new ardour to the homoerotic imagery on display and contradicting the withdrawn, grave, solitary introvert image of the artist that has been dutifully handed down the decades (OMNIBUS 'Michelangelo Revealed' (1987 T)).

film critics Usually depicted as male and disassociated from the hard masculine realities of life (ninnies almost): the fluting pretentious Sharpnose played by Victor Spinetti in Anthony Newley's satire *Can Hieronymous Merkin Ever For-*

get Mercy Humppe and Find True Happiness? (1969 C); the HITCHCOCK devotee of unsound mind (Ian Redford) in ARTEMIS '81 (1981 T); the National Film Theatre lecturer glimpsed in *Die Kinder* (1990 T). Even the semi-heroic, heterosexual Paul (Charles Dance) in *The McGuffin* (1986 T) is surrounded by sado-masochism, transvestism, murder, torture and sexual depravities of all hues before and during his visit to a rather unusual film festival.

film directors Usually portrayed in plays, films and serials as hard-driving, gruff professionals, heterosexual if in a central role – with the exception of the bisexual FASSBINDER in *A Man Like Eva* (1983 C) where the role is played by a woman.

In the as yet unreleased Orson WELLES film *The Other Side of the Wind* (1970) Hannaford (John Huston) viciously hoses down gays at every opportunity, yet can't live without them as friends and professional colleagues – which is how Huston himself is said to have behaved to people like Montgomery CLIFT. A few nonconformists did squeeze into the director's chair: Jacques Sernas, wearing a medallion and uncannily resembling Paul Newman in LA DOLCE VITA (1960 C), upbraided by the hero for being 'half impotent as a man and as an artist'; Anna (Aurore Clement) in *Les Rendez-vous d'Anna* (1978 C); Guy Jackson (Anthony HOLLAND), heroine Gerry's friend in *The Lonely Lady* (1983 C) who contributes philosophical asides like 'Hurting and being hurt, that's life' and is last seen sitting next to a bald 'friend' at the Oscar ceremony as Gerry (Pia Zadora) denounces HOLLYWOOD and all its corruption; Pablo (Eusebio Poncela), the porno director – something of a superstar himself in LAW OF DESIRE (1987 C) – who bites off more than he can chew when a ONE NIGHT STAND won't let go; real-life director George CUKOR portrayed – with discreet dignity (Cukor was still alive) – by George Furth in *Moviola* 'The Scarlett O'Hara War' (1980 T); hangdog young film-maker at the centre of events in *The Long Weekend (O'Despair)* (1988 C).

film noir Sex and violence, corrosive crisp dialogue, urban settings, alienated people, dreamlike atmosphere, betrayal, pervasive corruption, aesthetic villainy vs brute force, mean tarnished blondes – and sexual perversity: *The Maltese Falcon* (1941); *Double Indemnity* (1944); *Phantom Lady* (1944); *Raw Deal* (1948); *House of Bamboo* (1955); and one that got away in *Crossfire* (1947), which should have had a gay murder victim but censorship necessitated changing him into a Jew. Modern examples of *noir* (sometimes called *post-noir*) with bisexual/gay/lesbian elements are PERFORMANCE (1970); *Black Widow* (1986) about a pursuer emotionally if not physically seduced by her female prey; *Apartment Zero* (1988) involving a deadly relationship between two men in Buenos Aires; and perhaps most classically THE FOURTH MAN (1983 C), with its down at heel bisexual protagonist (Jeroen Krabbe) falling for a blonde spider woman and her boyfriend.

On radio and television, Eddie Boyd interwove the peculiar with the perverse with consummate ease in gaunt, unsentimental works like THE DARK NUMBER, *The Odd Man* and *Badger by Owl-Light*, a tradition possibly destined to be carried on by writers like Philip RIDLEY (OCTOBER SCARS THE SKIN) – though without the disgust for love and sexuality (particularly homosexuality) that clung to Boyd like scales.

film references Imaginative/subversive use of clips of past glories in *Myra Breckinridge* (1970 C) and *Dead Men Don't Wear Plaid* (1982 C). Verbal mentions in many films including *Apartment Zero* (1988), wherein repressed Adrian (Colin Firth) and sexual opportunist/murderer Jack (Hart Bochner) mention a dozen movies such as *The Odd Couple*, COMPULSION, *Catch 22*, *The Godfather*, *The Conversation*, *The Ten Commandments*, *Blue Velvet* and – most revealing of all – *Hangmen Also Die*. *Apartment Zero* opens with the finale of *Touch of Evil*

with the soundtrack voice of Marlene DIETRICH, whose photograph, together with those of CLIFT, DEAN and others, adorns Adrian's living room and bedroom.

In *Show Me the Way, Ugly Angels* (1990 R) the two flighty media studies teachers, one gay (Shaun Prendergast), twitter on about *One Flew Over the Cuckoo's Nest*, *Spellbound*, *Pinocchio*, *Star Wars*, LAWRENCE OF ARABIA and especially *Gone with the Wind* in between academic rivalries and thoughts on reincarnation; the film lecturer (Ian Redford) in ARTEMIS '81 (1981 T) is obsessed by the films of Alfred HITCHCOCK; nods to *The Wizard of Oz* are to be found in MY OWN PRIVATE IDAHO (1991 C); in HIGH HEELS (1991 C) there are specific comparisons to the destructive mother–daughter relationship in *Autumn Sonata*. Soap operas quite regularly recycle tried and true movie plots: the Australian NUMBER 96 raided *The Apartment*, *A Night at the Opera*, *Jaws* and REBECCA, to name just four. And Freddie (Roland CURRAM) in ELDORADO is a great film buff, especially anything with Judy G.

Films and Filming aka f&f. This monthly magazine began in 1954 and ran, with changes of ownership and emphasis, until the 1980s. Its shining period was the first decade, under the broad, brittle mind of Peter Baker. Ron PECK paid tribute to the magazine's serious discussion of cinema, so energetically and entertainingly presented, in NIGHTHAWKS 2: *Strip Jack Naked*. He also doffed his hat to f&f's admirable commitment to the naked and near-naked body, male and female, on its covers and inside pages. These images saved many from erotic starvation.

The magazine was also alert to the needs of men in need of flat-shares and hobby-shares in big cities through its personal ads page. Peter Baker wrote a crypto-gay play called 'The Golden Clown' for *No Hiding Place* in 1960, then a novel about film festivals in 1966. He occasionally surfaced as a radio interviewer through to the 1980s: a real unsung literary and social hero of the dark gay days.

films on television Hundreds and hundreds and hundreds shown since *The Student of Prague* (with Anton WAL-BROOK) was tried out by the BBC in the 1930s (followed by *La Kermesse Heroi-que/Carnival in Flanders* with its very gay courtier).

The purchase of libraries (from Alexander Korda's London Films, Selznick International and RKO) opened the floodgates and films are now a very large part of each day's programming on the four channels. The arrival of BBC2 in 1964 and of Channel 4 in 1982 has meant that the more obscure and/or controversial films have a good chance of being transmitted. Some films, beginning their life in cinemas, are made with cash from television and some – like MY BEAUTIFUL LAUNDRETTE, EDWARD II and *Truly, Madly, Deeply* – draw sizeable cinema and home audiences.

Aesthetic and censorship dictates mean that a certain number of films are turned down for home viewing. Among BBC rejects are *Straw Dogs, Death Wish, Friday the 13th, The Exorcist,* NORMAN . . . IS THAT YOU?, CRUISING and *The Devils.* Even Channel 4 – which daringly gave house room to the Derek JARMAN films and to Kenneth Anger's FIREWORKS – drew the line at *A Bigger Splash,* QUER-ELLE, all the WARHOLS save for MY HUSTLER, and some PASOLINIS such as ARABIAN NIGHTS, *The Decameron, The Canterbury Tales* and SALO.

But parameters ebb and flow, attitudes change: *Last Tango in Paris* appeared on television 20 years after its cinema screenings. Less heady brews suffer unaccountable delays: 10 years for *The Music Lovers,* NIJINSKY and YENTL to surface, and 50 years to première the innocuous sex change comedy, TURNABOUT.

Many of the films are shown in 'TV versions' with sex scenes trimmed, 'bad' language chopped or replaced with not so bad language, and violence curbed. Sometimes an uncut film will be sent out with a stern warning that it contains something indecent: most notoriously that issued for the January 1993 screening of *Edward II*, which forewarned of rude words and homosexual activity but failed to mention the film's killings and torture.

film stars Real ones with a sexuality kept secret from the public include Montgomery CLIFT; James DEAN; Marlene DIETRICH; Greta GARBO; Rock HUDSON; Danny KAYE; Rudolph VALEN-TINO. In fiction: characters in *Inside Daisy Clover* (1966 C); *The Users* (1978 T); *Scruples* (1980 T); *Celebrity* (1983 T).

Finch, Peter (1916–77) Australian-born actor who played Oscar WILDE and won a 1960 BAFTA Award for it, as well as another one for his portrayal in SUNDAY, BLOODY SUNDAY (1971 C) of the Jewish GP wishing he could have Bob (Murray Head) all, instead of some, of the time. Finch's immersion in the part is extraordinary and he is able to fill out some of the gaping holes in the scant knowledge we have of the man: his alienation from his Jewish upbringing, his exhaustion and strong love of work. Daniel Hirsch is a good man and it shines out of Finch's seamed face. The sadness is that he didn't have a more stimulating partner to play with.

'He said: "I can't play a *pouf*!" But then he got intrigued. He found it was rather a good script and I think it was about the best thing he ever did' (Olive Harding, his agent interviewed on *The British Greats* 'Peter Finch' 1979 T).

'I play a man with certain emotional problems which have nothing to do with the sex of the person he's involved with. It might just as easily be a girl, but it happens to be a boy. This is the first script I've ever seen in which homosexuality is just a fact about a character not presented at all as an issue . . . there are no revelations, no confrontations, no dramatic turns of fate. We go on living while time and circumstance settle things for us' (Peter Finch in an interview with John Russell Taylor, *Sight and Sound*, Autumn 1970).

A Fine Romance Jerome Kern music with words from Dorothy Fields to accompany Fred and Ginger's (temporary) animosity in the snow in *Swing Time* (1936 C). The lyrics cheekily pinpoint the fact that the world's top dancing duo kept most of their sexual chemistry in their smiles (and snarls) as well as in their feet (on those highly polished RKO floors).

'You won't nestle, you won't wrestle,' complains Ginger, while Fred sighs: 'A fine romance with no kisses . . . with no clinches . . . with no pinches.' This could be the theme song of most same-sex lovers on film or television: no TOUCHING sought or allowed. Unlike – thankfully – life.

fingernails A common affectation by effeminate characters, paring and buffing their nails in public: led by Samuel 'Nails' Nathan (Leslie Fenton), the 'debonair but notorious' gangster in *The Public Enemy* (1931 C) who gained his nickname from the amount of manicuring he indulged in. Later examples: high-pitched-voiced BLACKMAILER in the Swedish version of *A Woman's Face* (1938 C); Charlie (Rex Harrison) in STAIRCASE (1969 C); Hope (Greg Hicks) in TICKETS FOR THE TITANIC 'The Way, the Truth, the Video' (1987 C); Robert in *Unsub* 'And They Swam Right Over the Dam' (1990 T).

Male toenails were being painted in *Modesty Blaise* (1966 C, Arab chieftain by young women) and in a BUBBLE BATH in *Princess Daisy* (1983 T, fashion designer Ringo Starr by his wife). When a naked male corpse is found in *Floodtide* (1987 T), a detective comments grimly that the victim's nails were varnished. His colleague is incredulous that this should be of any importance in the death of a man who has been tortured and castrated. The detective admits that 'it has nothing to do with anything'.

'Never trust a man who paints his fingernails,' says the acrobat about the marquis in LULU (1975 R).

Don Finlayson (Joe Hasham in NUMBER 96 1972–7 T) The first, and the most potent role model for Australian gay men: love across that continent with fan clubs in Sydney and Melbourne. He started as a law student progressing to his own practice. His first boyfriend Bruce was a bisexual photographer. He goes off the rails when Bruce leaves him, often appearing hung-over and dishevelled the morning after. He is accused of having sex with a young boy who has, in reality, been pursuing him. Then he lives with Dudley; they split up but only temporarily. He enters into a marriage of convenience to help a lawyer colleague stay in the country.

Ian Holmes, Channel 10's programme manager, stipulated no physical contact for Don in the first year and no kissing (ever – but he and Dudley *were* seen in bed together). Creator/writer David SALE and his colleagues were, however, allowed to run the gamut with the character: long-term affairs, brief affairs, being beaten up by a sailor, being pursued by women, defending a gay client, becoming a private detective.

Don's lovers, outside of Bruce and Dudley, included an American (John McTernan) who had to leave Australia and – in the 1974 film version – John Orchik with whom he had an erotic embrace (including osculation). In the final episode, Don seems to be 'on' with a young man in a tailored leather jacket carrying a shoulder bag (Stephen O'Rourke).

Joe Hasham told *TV Times* in 1974: 'I think Don is desirable to a lot of women because he is seen to be unattainable; so many female characters in the show have tried to make him and failed. He's reliable and sympathetic, shouldering everyone's problems. I think women are attracted by his sullen nature. He's a downbeat character. But he comes forth with witty remarks.' Interviewed in 1987 for the *Sydney Morning Herald*, Hasham, now runing a film production company in Malaysia with his girlfriend, recalled his creation with the same enthusiasm: 'It proved that a person's sexuality doesn't matter. Don Finlayson was a warm and intelligent human being.'

The character was not mentioned or

shown in *35 Years of Australian TV* (1991), though in 1990 a television critic interviewed on the ABC's *Lateline* described *Number 96* and its depiction of homosexuality as the *sole* achievement of Channel 10. However, the actor Joe Hasham *was* represented in the television beanfeast: singing a pop song on a rocky shore with the waves buffeting him and bringing him down. This clip was reshown at the end, the final image in a 3-hour pantechnicon and preceding the co-sponsor's name – Omo.

Firbank, Ronald (1886–1926) English novelist and playwright, aesthete and dandy, author of *Valmouth* and *Prancing Nigger*, who pursued Arab boys and gaped at workmen. Novels adapted for radio include *The Princess Zoubaroff* (1962, with Edith Evans) and the musical VALMOUTH (1975). Angela Carter's 1985 sound 'exploration of the life and character of Ronald Firbank' – with Lewis Fiander – was entitled *A Self-Made Man.*

Fireworks (US 1947) After fondling himself, a young man goes CRUISING, is beaten up by a group of SAILORS, and ends up in bed with one of them after a stylized mutual ejaculation. *Fireworks* is Kenneth Anger's extraordinarily erotic, tightly organized yet playful 20-minute classic, one of the first American gay films. The fact that the director himself plays the young man adds to the flavour of louche delights, danger, comradeship, phallic symbolism and tinsel. CHANNEL 4 showed the film in 1987.

The First Churchills (UK 1969 T) The story of the Duke of Marlborough (John Neville) and his spunky wife (Susan Hampshire), who is the favourite of Queen ANNE (Margaret Tyzack). A scavenge through the ever-confusing period of the Jacobites, the Elector of Hanover, Monmouth, the Young Pretender, phantom pregnancies, Woodstock . . . Essentially the story of one man and three women who are jealous of each other.

W/P: Donald Wilson; D: David Giles; 27.9.69; BBC2; 13 parts; 45 mins.

Sarah meets John. She is in drag. He is being kept by King Charles' mistress. Sarah is the princess's FAVOURITE. Charles dies and James plunges the country into turmoil by making his Catholicism public. Plots and more plots. William (Alan Rowe), who likes hunting and huntsmen, marries Mary, who finds he rejects not only her body but also her mind. Churchill deserts King James for William and Mary. Mary dies. William dies. Anne becomes queen. She rejects Sarah for her poor relation Abigail Hill (Jill Balcon), who is in league with the Whigs against the Tories. Anne dies unreconciled to Sarah.

Sarah dislikes the court: 'That rout of screeching fops.' John's mistress dislikes Sarah ('a soused herring') and doesn't go for him much either ('you stinking poxy bastard'). Sarah loves John and John loves Sarah – and John's servant, Beckett loves him too. Insults are thrown hither and yon: Episode 11 is the one to watch, ending as it does with Sarah rejected, Anne distraught and Abigail triumphant. A rich tapestry, economical too – all the battles (episode 10 is particularly noisy) are achieved with 50 soldiers and tight close-ups.

Flames of Passion (UK 1990 C/T) Pocket-sized reinterpretation of BRIEF ENCOUNTER with Richard Seymour as 'Trevor' and Donald Greif as 'Celia'. W/D: Richard Kwietniowski; 18 mins.

The high-contrast black and white photography, emotive music and railway station setting are retained but essentials of plot are drastically changed in a way that Noel COWARD'S unconscious may well have approved of. While not quite attaining the resonance of its parent, the film is at least five times as affecting in its few minutes as the 1975 TV movie version with Richard Burton and Sophia Loren trying to be ordinary folks was, in nearly three times the duration.

Flaming Creatures (US 1963) Virtually structureless underground film written and directed by Jack Smith, a-swim with images of multi-gendered potential imprinted with C-A-M-P. The subject of much litigation, reissued in 1992, but unlikely to be shown on television as much for its crude 'technical quality' as for its copious male organs.

'A faggoty stag-reel, it comes as close to hardcore pornography as anything ever presented in a theatre ... Everything is shown in sickening detail, defiling both sex and cinema' (Arthur Knight, *Playboy*, October 1963). 'At once splendidly visionary and startlingly anti-illusionist, *Flaming Creatures* offered liberation from "good" technique as well as from "proper" behaviour. Everything in it is overexposed. Its aesthetic revelation is founded on the revelation of artifice: the discrepancy between sound and image, the TRANSVESTITES who flaunt their cocks, the camera that seems to participate in the orgy.' (J. Hoberman, SIGHT AND SOUND, January 1992).

flaming faggot A sharp-toothed joke in DIAMONDS ARE FOREVER (1971 C) has Mr Kidd (Putter Smith) carrying fiery shish-kebabs in the general direction of the eyes of James BOND (Sean Connery). Luckily, Tiffany Case (Jill St John) is on hand to throw brandy at the assailant, who bursts into flame (cut from TV version) and jumps into the sea. His lover, Wint, joins him moments later – blown to bits after an explosive device is inserted in his rectum.

flashbacks Marcel PROUST was one of the pioneers (if not *the* pioneer) of the technique of memory triggers in literature which film – for which it is so eminently suitable – gratefully adopted. In some stories – *The Go-Between* (1971 C) and BRIDESHEAD REVISITED (1981 T) – it is a simple framing device; in others (notably thriller) it is a narration tool which masks deceit (*Laura* 1944 C). In Proustian mode, the device involves flashbacks within flashbacks, Chinese boxes in which the past interleaves with the present in various ways, revealing or

confusing. An exemplar of this visual and verbal sleight of hand is Terence DAVIES in *Distant Voices, Still Lives* (1988 C). Other less extreme examples occurred in GIRL (1974 T); THE OTHER WOMAN (1976 T); ONLY CONNECT (1979 T); *David Roche Talks to You About Love* (1984 C); *An Empty Bed* (1990 C); FRIED GREEN TOMATOES AT THE WHISTLE STOP CAFE (1991 C).

flat-mates An English term for cohabiting people, sometimes a euphemism for a sexual arrangement, sometimes elided with 'house-mates' and the American 'ROOM-MATES'. Examples include Ian and Jimmy who may or may not be physical lovers in WHEN DID YOU LAST SEE MY MOTHER? (1967 R); the two men in *Green Julia* (1972 T), one of whom very probably desires the other; the male couple in WEDNESDAY LOVE (1975 T), both ostensibly heterosexual, but one 'passively' accepting 'favours' from men; gay man Jodie and lesbian Alice sharing in SOAP (1979 T); gay man and non-gay man sharing in *The Making of a Male Model* (1983 T) and TERRY AND JULIAN (1992 T); current male lovers – (British) Rob and Michael in AGONY (1979–81 T), (American) Michael and Peter in AN EARLY FROST (1985 T), (Australian) Simon and Robert in WORDS OF ONE SYLLABLE (1991 R). It is a very useful term to cover a multitude of unasked questions, eg Mrs Proudfoot (Margot Boyd) in THREE PIECE SWEET (1979 R) was most happy about Alistair 'sharing the flat with that *nice* man Lionel'.

flaunting it Blatant visibility and confrontational display often causes conflict. Between employer and employed such conflict can be seen in head social worker (Jack Hedley) asking Ross (Eric Deacon) who has gone on a televised anti-CLAUSE 28 demonstration in HARD CASES (1988 T): 'Was it necessary to inform the whole nation of your sexual preferences?' Between lovers, such conflict can be seen in Luke (William Oliver Campbell) not being at all happy about joining Steven at a family wedding in

DYNASTY 'Parental Consent' (1985 T): 'Flaunting our relationship that publicly, it can't do any good. We're two people who happen to care for each other.'

The concept of 'flaunting' falls most conveniently out of the mouths of those less well disposed to full homosexual equality. Geoffrey Dickens MP, for example, said: 'I believe that people like myself should stand shoulder to shoulder with the homosexual fraternity [*sic*] against the so-called QUEER-BASHERS, but you're only likely to get that support if you don't continue to flaunt your homosexuality and thrust it down other people's throats' (*Yesterday in Parliament/Today* 1990 R). (Zero Mostel brought 'flaunting' in its widest definition into the public consciousness with his frequently trumpeted 'If you've got it, flaunt it' in THE PRODUCERS (1967 C))

See also I'M GAY BUT I DON'T ...

The Flavour of Corn (Il Sapore del Grano) (It 1987 T) Twenty-two-year-old Lorenzo (Lorenzo Lena), a student teacher in a remote part of Italy, is worshipped by one of his pupils, Duilio (Marco Mestriner), who is jealous of his sister's attachment to Lorenzo. Tender, expressive story about a man and a boy who finally act out their attraction without either being punished in any way. W/D: Gianni Da Campo; based on a story by Pier Paulo PASOLINI; P: Chantal Bergamo and Enzo Porcelli; 87 mins.

Flesh (US 1968 C) Joe (Joe Dallesandro) is told to raise $200 to pay for the abortion of his wife's girlfriend. After turning a few (male) tricks and seeing his girlfriend, he returns home to find wife and lover in bed, who then proceed to taunt him for his sexual inadequacy. D: Paul Morrissey; P: Andy WARHOL; 105 mins.

Warm, itchily appealing chunk of life on and off the streets. The first picture of male PROSTITUTION, and one presented without gloom or sentimentality with the clients as rounded as he who services them: often just by paying them some attention, giving them a bit of undemanding attention.

flight attendants Formerly air stewards and stewardesses, vulgarly known as 'trolly dollies': the teenage son, John (David Edwards) in THE APPLEYARDS (1955 T) who had wanted to become one – without parental opposition (even though the job was then, and remains associated with women's work); Michel (Jean-Paul Belmondo) before he became a petty thief in *Breathless/A Bout de Souffle* (1960 C); the floppy boys in white and blue (Michael Veitch and Steve Vizard known only as 'The Stewards'), the best and brighter in QANTAS, overly concerned with fashion, gossip and quick fixes of sex and giving not a damn about anything else in *Fast Forward* (Aust 1989–92 T); steward Frank (Peter Senna) returning to Brazil to find the man who gave him the HIV virus in *Via Appia* (1990 C).

The only lesbian who walks the aisles is Jo Peters (Angélique de Moline) in *The Stewardesses* (1970 C). Jo makes a play for heroine Kathy when they arrive at their hotel after an arduous flight: 'Wouldn't it be great to go swimming in the nude? We could pretend on the bed ..., I'll pretend I'm the water.'

A Florida Enchantment (US 1914) 'A farcical fantasy in five parts' about a magic seed that turns a young woman (Edith Storey) into a man and a man into a woman. W: Archibald Clavering Gunter from his play; P/D: Sidney Drew; *c* 20 mins. '... cold and dispirited before the camera, it is only a senseless mess ... The picture should never have been put out, for there's no one with any sense of humour whatsoever, or intelligence either, who can force a smile while watching this sad "comedy"' (*Variety*, 14.8.14). Unlikely to turn up on television!

florists If male, they are one of a number of shades of pink. Impeccably attired Gibb McLaughlin is equipped with aspirant haitches in *Friday the Thirteenth*

(1933 C): 'Put a haspirin in the water or those roses won't last the weekend.' In *Deep in my Heart* (1954 C) a silver-haired man, wearing a pale LAVENDER carnation in the grey buttonhole of his grey morning suit, is seen flusteredly apologizing to composer Sigmund Romberg (José Ferrer) in a hotel boutique for confusing an order. 'If I've done anything wrong, I'll just *die*'. Ted Thorpe in the Sandra Dee–Bobby Darin comedy *If a Man Answers* (1962 C) makes, in early 1960s jive talk, a mean bouquet and has a way with a spray. Anthony Byrd (Donald Davis) loves nature, keeps his flowers fresh and himself to himself, but is still persecuted in a small college town for loving men in *Joy in the Morning* (1965 C). Stan (Richard Beckinsale), an out-of-work actor, goes to help his teasingly ambiguous Uncle Dingley (David Swift) in his shop in the comedy series *Bloomers* (1979 T). Joey Faye sweeps in briefly with a floral tribute in *The War Between Men and Women* (1974 C). John CARLIN also serves in *Shoestring* 'Looking for Mr Right' (1982 T). Bringing the florist bang up to date, in clone garb but with time-honoured wafting demeanour was Geoffrey Hutchings in *Lytton's Diary* 'The Ends and the Means' (1986 T); John Herzbergin in *The Ryan White Story* (1988 T); the eager young man encountered through a classified ad in *Six Pack* 'Loveless' (Aust 1992 T). There have been the occasional non-gay florists: the greedy, Shylock-like Mushnik (Mel Welles) in *The Little Shop of Horrors* (1960 & 1986 C).

flowers They attract and lure, often with great display, often with PERFUME, and contain male and female reproductive machinery. They usually signal an effeminate or over-polite man: Florian (Otto Gebuchr) in *The Golem* (1920 C) presented as a ridiculous fellow with willowy tight trousers, a huge feather in his hat, a gap in the teeth and a flower in the hand.

POLARI took up the word as a term of endearment or provocation in the 1950s, although people in Durham had been calling each other 'Flower', regardless of sex, for many years. Miss Mowcher (Jessie Evans) in DAVID COPPERFIELD (1974 R) calls Steerforth 'my flower'. In modern times, the Beatle-browed HAIRDRESSER (Peter Beton) in a 1973 *Bless This House* runs after Sid James, who's deliberately left his overcoat behind in the shop, crying out in a piercing hiss for the whole street to hear: 'Flower! Hi, *Flower*! It's your coat'; 'Excuse me, Flower, I couldn't help overhearing,' simpers BARMAN John CARLIN in *Man About the House* 'Never Give Your Name' (1975 T); Sammy's ex, Gerald says on the telephone in *Life without George* (1987 T): 'Hello, Flower ... Oh God, *she*'s in a mood!' Away from situation comedy, it was heard on the documentary *Sailor* (1976 T) where a bluff midshipman on the Ark Royal says to his mates: 'Arseholes to you lot – my loving flowers.'

flower names The apportioning of certain names to males and females is of great importance to tribal custom and society's mental well-being. The labelling – which has been commonplace since drama began and certainly flourished between the 16th and 18th centuries in England – can bestow qualities of masculinity or femininity, frivolity or substance in quite miraculous ways.

There is Lupin Pooter (Murray MELVIN) in *The Diary of a Nobody* (1964 T); Blossom (Orlando Martins) in *The Hasty Heart* (1949 C) threading a necklace to give to Richard Todd: 'there's no harm in him – much – !'; Alan Blossom (Laurie Asprey), the wimp who allows the boy of his dreams to take the blame for a fatal car crash in HIT AND RUN (1965 T); the liquidic Dr Flower (Michael WARD), the sidekick of the unreasoning brogues and short-back-and-sided Dr Irene Handl in *Doctor in Love* (1960 C), nearly 'raped' by two female strippers; Harry Flowers (Johnny Shannon), the boxing- (and boxer-) loving crime boss whose nickname is 'Pervert' (PERFORMANCE 1970 C); Desmond Flower (Ian Ogilvy), the impotent socialite who murders a blackmailing SHIP'S STEWARD in *Stranger in the House* (1967 C); Cutflower (David Garth), the dandified schoolmaster ("Oh la! la! la!") in *Gormenghast* (1984 R). There are also DAISY and FLOWERDEW. *See also* SURNAMES.

Flowerdew Character played by Peter SELLERS in the early GOON SHOWS – lingered on as a few languid shoulder-shrugging exclamations, or as bored officials ('Anything to declare?' in 'Beau Geste', which draws the response: 'Oh, there's *thousands* of 'em!'). Peter Sellers told Michael Parkinson on the latter's chat show in 1974: 'Flowerdew was based on two poufs. Now, I didn't mean any offence, I really didn't. One took the other to church. "Excuse me sir," one said to the priest, "Your handbag's on fire."'

No recordings exist from Flowerdew's heyday (1951–3) when his catchphrase '[Ooo] I COULD (JUST) SPIT' was greeted with waves of guffaws. However, the ether-voiced epicene does put in occasional (uncredited) appearances in later programmes, such as 'The Nasty Affair at the Burami Oasis' (1956) where he is asked by his army commander to 'run up a flag' and responds animatedly: 'I'll get the sewing machine, sir.'

Flowerpot Men (1952–8 T) Bill (high voice) and Ben (low voice) 'live in flowerpots near a shed at the bottom of a garden ... identical twins, their bodies shaped like flowerpots ... big garden gloves and magnificent but well-worn garden boots; they talk rubbish' (*Radio Times*, 13.10.52). Like ANDY PANDY and his ménage, Bill and Ben's arrangement with Little Weed has given much food for thought over the years. So too has the boys' secret language, and the fact that they are not described as 'TWINS' on the soundtrack but 'FRIENDS'.

On 3.2.84 the *Sun* reported that a retired headmistress, Mrs Hilda Brabban, claimed that the two flowerpot men were based on her brothers, Bill and Ben Wright, who ran a florist's shop in West Yorkshire. Four years later, videos

of selected episodes sold more than 120,000 copies in two months, outflanking the Royal Wedding of 1981. Among the delights were 'Bath in Hat' ('water antics with the 'rub-a-lub' song'), 'Cabbages' ('Horseplay with the naughty sprouts'), and 'Stickmen' ('Bill and Ben find a new friend in a secret place'). Another compilation was equally successful in 1990.

The voice of both Bill and Ben, Peter Hawkins (who also gave eternal life to Captain Pugwash), appeared on *Blue Peter* in 1984, which was occasioned by the miraculous return – after disappearing for over a year – of the original (and now endearingly battered) puppets. Hawkins was also present, along with a whole host of nostalgic faces and voices, in *The Trouble with the Fifties* (1992 T).

Sir Fopling **Flutter** One of the great cream puffs of Restoration comedy – and decidedly heterosexual: a character in George Ethere(d)ge's *The Man of Mode*, or *Sir Fopling Flutter*. Many comedy series of the past three decades have hacked out variations on this old (1676) theme. Unfortunately they have thrown out the Fopling and kept the Flutter. Simon CALLOW discussed this on a 1987 programme on *Acting*, and John Webb played him on radio that year.

The Flying Doctors (Aust 1985–92 T; now RFDS 1993–) All kinds of life in outback Australia from the hard-nosed to the soft-shelled. Only one gay – a Vietnam war veteran, Les Foster (Grant Kennedy) who comes home to die (of AIDS) in 1986 ('Return of the Hero'). The local priest, a bit of an OCKER, evades all the issues, which include a few not unimportant matters: the rejection of the man by his BROTHER Ted (Russell Newman) and most of the townsfolk; violence offered to his lover (Peter Fisher) when fetching medicine; the CATHOLIC CHURCH'S blanket condemnation of the man's entire sexual-emotional being. On his death-bed, the hitherto proudly atheist man asks the priest to 'do something religious'. All that's on offer from the great little bloke in the dog collar is salvation in the next life: 'God loves you. His only son died for you ... The door's open because he loves you.' Which makes a whole lot more sense than the 'gay lifestyle' back in the city. 'We can pack up and be with our friends,' says the lover after being hounded by anti-gay hooligans. '*What* friends?' The ones that don't come around any more?'

Five years passed before Coopers Crossing had to deal with anything similar: not another gay (one was enough), but with HIV/AIDS in a story called 'Being Positive' (1991). Anthropologist Jerry Davies (William McInnes), who has picked up the virus in Africa, is injured by a javelin and might have infected the staff at Coopers Crossing who had treated him. While waiting for the test results, Johnno proposes to Rowie, Jock – the bigot – has his tonsils removed, Clare has a surprise birthday party, and Jackie has a bitter sweet romance – which breaks up – with poor Jerry. The results show that the doctors and nurses are seronegative, thus dodging the central issue in the episode: should medical practitioners continue working if they are HIV positive? In the words of *Sydney Morning Herald* reviewer Alison Stewart: 'AIDS comes to Coopers Crossing this week, then goes away again.'

This series – which shares its title but not its characters with the gritty, compelling stories produced for both radio and television during the 1950s – has so far shied away from any hint of homosexuality other than in an imported character, destined to die of a SEXUALLY TRANSMITTED DISEASE. An anonymous member of the creative team drew the parallel (during an informal conversation in 1991) between ABORIGINAL characters (not exactly thick on the ground) and gays and lesbians invading the sacrosanct Australian family viewing time. 'If there is discomfort over an Aboriginal character, people watching with their children at least know that their son or daughter or husband is not going to turn black. With gay situations there may be a very real fear that something lurks in their living room, and that the person sitting next to them on the lounge might be one of *them*.'

Lord Sebastian Flyte (Robert EDDISON; Anthony Andrews 1981 T) Drowsily dignified, empty-headed younger son of the Marquis of Marchmain, in BRIDESHEAD REVISITED. He falls in love with Charles Ryder at OXFORD, but dribbles away his life in DRINK and ROUGH TRADE like the fly-blown, leeching Kurt, who is eventually taken away by the NAZIS. The only one who really understands him, apart from his TEDDY BEAR Aloysius, is his devout SISTER Cordelia. In one of his rare lucid moments, Sebastian confesses that he wishes it was 'always summer, the fruit always ripe and Aloysius always in a good temper'. He just wants to be a happy semi-heathen: 'I pray God make me good, but not yet.' Ironically he finishes his life as a blissful near-saint, ending up as a religious hanger-on in a monastery.

Rich, young and pretty, Sebastian was partly based on the Hon. Hugh Lygon, with whom Sebastian's creator, Evelyn Waugh, stayed in his (stately) home in Worcestershire. But the main model was Alistair Graham – whom Waugh described as 'the friend of my heart' – who left Oxford without a degree and went into the diplomatic service. Then, in 1933, he became a recluse in Wales. He died in 1958.

'Lord Sebastian Flyte is a dissolute homosexual, who ends up an alcoholic down-and-out living in squalor in North Africa. Anthony Andrews hopes that playing the role will kill off his image as a stiff upper-lip nice guy.' ('Low Life with a Lord' by Charles Catchpole, *Sun* 10.10.81).

footballers 'An old fogey ... teetotaller', Dr Donald Soper on *Any Questions?* (1981 R) banged on about kissing on the football pitch, now grown to epidemic proportions: 'a vital distraction between things that should be done and some things that ought not to be done'. He felt that so much passion over-excited the fans and led to violence. The Answer?

'To sign a few ugly players.' Roars of laughter and applause from the audience.

There is only one gay in the game: Justin Fashanu, transferred from Norwich to Nottingham Forest for £1 million in 1981. A committed CHRISTIAN, he came out in 1990 and fronted up to a television audience of teenagers in 1992. Later that year his (non-gay) brother John presented a lively programme, which was part of his sports series *On the Line* about gays and lesbians, black and white, playing games (including football) for pleasure not profit and about the problems they face if they try to involve themselves with heterosexually identified teams and clubs. *Out* had interviewed both professionals and amateurs for its segment, tied in with the *Gay Games* (1991 T).

In British drama there have been no gay footballers, except possibly for Jesse Alty (John Duttine) in z-CARS 'Friends' (1974 T) who is loved and cosseted by an older man. Rugby, on the other hand, was a substantial part of at least two, possibly three, gay men's lives in ACCOUNTS (1982 R; 1983 T): Donald Mawson who plays inside; his brother Andy who used to play; and the coach, James Pitney-Bowes who is described by rugby-buff author and journalist Brian Glanville as 'the archetypal rugby footballer ... a frustrated public-school homosexual who lives with his mother.' James was the lonely son of colonial parents. He mostly spent the holidays with an aunt in Tunbridge Wells. He envied the other boys he saw there because they were independent, dirty, free'. A question mark hovers over James just as much as it does over Andy. Is James simply a voyeur, happy to spend as much time as possible with young men: as a surrogate dad to Andy and Donald and as coach for the colts of Hadrian Rugby Football Club? Or is he sexually active, but never on his own threshold? His opening line has him saying how he has been 'disgracing' himself in the flesh-pots of Newcastle; a statement he immediately modifies: 'Not really disgracing myself. Wondering

whether I ought to.' Or, as a third possibility, did he and Andy have a relationship when Andy was in the colts?

In the US, football players have been used quite regularly in drama and comedy as masculine bench-marks who are revealed to be homosexual. These include Archie Bunker's drinking pal in a 1972 ALL IN THE FAMILY; Ray Church (Earl Holliman), one of the clients of PROSTITUTE *Alexander – The Other Side of Dawn* (1977 T); Jodie's lover, Dennis in SOAP (1977); sports star Adonis who becomes a (closeted) Hollywood FILM STAR and who meets a very nasty end at the hands of his son Mack Crawford (Joseph Bottoms) in *Celebrity* (1983 T); a huge bald, black player called Bubba in a 1985 episode of BROTHERS.

The most appealing of all gay footballers was Mads, Patrick's lusty lover dripping with vigour and good-humour in the Danish film *Friends Forever* (1987 C), a whopper of a role model if ever there was one.

football matches Between the Continental Baths boys (swish) and police department staff (rock solid) in *Saturday Night at the Baths* (1975 C): squeals, bum touching, screeches. *See also* CRICKET.

footmen Alfred (George Innes) serving the German baron (Von Rimmer) faithfully, in and out of bed, in UPSTAIRS DOWNSTAIRS 'A Suitable Marriage' (1971 T) and going off to live with him. Later he returns to Eaton Square, penniless and hunted by the police for murder ('Rose's Pigeon' 1973). *See also* BUTLERS; MAIDS; MANSERVANTS.

fops Men of extravagant clothing and sweeping gestures. Speaking through beribboned tongue, it is possible that the original camping exquisite – like Sir Fopling FLUTTER and Lord Foppingham – was more probably neuter, with his interest in women being confined to their decorative and ego-boosting function. From the 1970s onwards they have been rendered cast-iron homosexual: Jonathan Cecil and Vernon Dobtchef eyeing up the tender young *Joseph Andrews* (1977 T); James Hall in *Poldark* (1976 T); background chatterers in *Cyrano De Bergerac* (1985 T); nasty Lord Hampton (Richard O'Brien) and his friend Lord Darling (Paul Brooke) leading the hunt in *Revolution* (1985 C). Simon CALLOW in *Acting* (1987 T) says that Lord Foppington in *The Way of the World* is not 'merely a figure of fun but deserves to be taken seriously'. A delightful example of fopdom was the Earl of Favesham (John Papley) in THE FIRST CHURCHILLS (1969 T) forever adjusting his lace and torturing the English language: 'Now, pray, Churcheel, tell me your dis-po-sit-ion.' He is described by a disgusted English general, in goggling disbelief, as a 'Whoreson French madam'. *See also* OSRIC.

For Better or Worse: Joining Together (Ireland 1989) Four heterosexual couples, with Chris and Bill a gay couple of 10 years' standing, affirmed the importance of sex outside their relationship.
P/D: Hilary Dully and Flintan Connolly; 19.9.89; 30 mins.

For Every Man There's A Woman Music by Jule Stein, words by Leo Robin, sung by Tony Martin, and later by Yvonne De Carlo as 'For Every Woman There's A Man' in *Casbah* (1948 C). Neither rendition was entirely accurate, but HOLLYWOOD had to teach the world its sexual catechism without recourse to logic or facts (the KINSEY REPORT – showing that for some men there are other men – was published only that very same year).

Forster, E[dward] M[organ] (1879–1970) English writer, novelist, essayist and regular broadcaster whose novels have undergone an astonishing resurgence in the wake of the filming of *A Room with a View*, *A Passage to India*, *Howards End* and MAURICE, his only gay novel, written in 1914 and not published until after his death. He was connected with the BBC from 1928 (a talk on *Railway Bridges*) and in 1931 he accepted an invitation to review books on a fortnightly basis (*New Book Club*). Among his other notable broadcasts were his tribute to his friend 'Edward CARPENTER' in 1944 (reconstructed for the 1979 television play ONLY CONNECT: *In the Rue Lepsius* (about another friend, Constantine CAVAFY, 1951); *In My Library* (1949); *T. E. Lawrence and 'The Mint'* (1955); *George Crabbe and 'Billy Budd'* with Eric Crozier (1960).

All Forster's novels, with the exception of MAURICE, have been given radio and television productions. A radio literary portrait entitled *A Believer in Disbelief* was produced in 1958 and Forster appeared on television – in his rooms at Cambridge, aged 80 – on MONITOR in 1960. To mark his 90th birthday, friends and admirers mounted a television symposium on his place in literature for *Release*. His 2-volume biography (by P. N. Furbank) and his *Selected Letters* (1983) have been featured on radio arts programmes like KALEIDOSCOPE. Forster was played by Leslie French in *The Trial of Lady Chatterley* (1979 T), and by Christopher Banks in ONLY CONNECT (1979 T). The character of Roly (Holly in the film) Martins in Graham Greene's *The Third Man* (1949) was based on Forster.

'Of course, Forster was a homosexual ... there's no question about that. He wouldn't have wanted to deny it.' (K. W. Grandage 1972 R).

'One of those nice E. M. Forster films,' says Nigel PARGETTER (Graham Seed) in THE ARCHERS (1992 R).

Forster, Jackie (1928–) Scottish-born broadcaster, raconteur, journalist. One of the founders of SAPPHO and one of the few public faces of lesbianism in the 1970s. Very visible and audible in programmes like SPEAK FOR YOURSELF (1974), GAYS: SPEAKING OUT (1978) and GAY LIFE (1980), as well as many radio phone-ins. Still going strong in WOMEN LIKE US and WOMEN LIKE THAT. *See also* Jacqueline MACKENZIE.

The Forsyte Saga (UK 1967 T) Nigh on 50 turbulent years of a wealthy clan,

which includes at least one confirmed bachelor uncle.
W: Lennox Phillips and others; P: Donald Wilson; D: James Cellan Jones and David Giles; BBC2, 26 parts; 50 mins each.

Once one of Mary WHITEHOUSE's favourites, but advertised for its 1991 video release as being concerned with 'Tempestuous and scandalous affairs, smouldering scenes, repressed passion, shameless love and brutal hatred'.

fortune and men's eyes From Shakespeare's sonnet 29; one of the 15 read by Judi Dench in THE ANGELIC CONVERSATION:

> When in disgrace with fortune and men's eyes,
> I all alone beweep my outcast state,
> And trouble deaf heaven with my bootless cries,
> And look upon myself and curse my fate,
> Wishing me like to one more rich in hope...

Fortune and Men's Eyes (Can/US 1971 C) Life in a Canadian prison.
W: John Herbert from his play (and Jules Schwerin); P: Lester Persky and Lewis M. Allen; D: Harvey Hart; 102 mins. (Jules Schwerin was in charge for 31 out of 40 days; he also co-scripted and the stills are from his version. Yet he had his name taken off the film because it was so drastically compromised.)

A long, *papier mâché* version of UN CHANT D'AMOUR without the lyricism, the transgressiveness and the subtleties of the prison power game. Michael Greer shines as Queenie and Zooey Hall smoulders as the hero's 'old man'. Apart from the rape, the most provocative aspect of the project was the advertising slogan: 'What goes on in prison is a crime.'

40 Minutes (UK 1981– T) A weekly cornucopia of some known and some entirely unknown facts of life, involving institutions (prisons, the armed forces, marriage, beauty contests), groups of people (wives–mistresses–husbands, amateur actors, end-of-the-pier performers, best friends) or individuals. In the last category: 'Lol, Bona, Queen of Fabularity' (drag entertainer Lorri Lee 1981); Demelza and Judy, bringing up a child called Morgan ('Demelza's Baby' 1984); Peter, living with AIDS ('Diary of a Frontliner' 1988). Produced initially by Roger Mills and later by Edward Mirzoeff, the films, although entirely different in subject matter and style, possess a unifying understanding and refusal to judge or nudge.

Count Fosco Principal villain in the Wilkie Collins novel, *The Woman in White*, gorgeously personified by Alan BADEL (1982 T) and by Sydney Greenstreet in the 1948 film. A sharp operator masquerading as a FOP. He has a cockatoo on his shoulder – 'My pretty little smooth white rascal' – to whom he pays more attention than his wife. Whenever she tries to say anything, Fosco bolts her down with a caressing 'Thank you, my angel – have a bon-bon'. Cultivated and musical, he puffs cigar smoke over plants to kill aphids, plays with white mice and ruminates upon morality: 'Every society is as often the accomplice as well as the enemy of crime.' He deplores women selling themselves for gold to men they don't love. 'I'm a bad man, am I not?' The next minute he's back in control. 'I say what other people only think ... I'm a Jesuit, if you please; a splitter of straws, a man of scruples.' His cosmopolitan background is divertingly suggested by Badel and the costume department: check trews, cobalt-blue smock, rainbow-coloured cummerbund and hat with red ribbon band.

Foster, Jodie (1962–) American actress, expert player of TOMBOYS, teenage and adult; now also a director (*Little Man Tate*). Twice an Oscar winner (*The Accused*; *The Silence of the Lambs*). Even greater things are expected of her.
C: *Napoleon and Samantha* (1972 C); *Kansas City Bomber* (1972 C); *Tom Sawyer* (1973); *One Little Indian* (1973); *Alice Doesn't Live Here Anymore* (1974);

Echoes of a Summer (1976); prostitute Iris in *Taxi Driver* (1976); Tallulah in *Bugsy Malone* (1976); Lynn Jacobs in *The Little Girl Who Lives Down the Lane* (1976); *Freaky Friday* (1977); *Candleshoe* (1977); *Carny* (1980); *Foxes* (1980); *O'Hara's Wife* (1982); in love with Susie the Bear in *The Hotel New Hampshire* (1984); *Mesmerized* (1986), also co-producer; bisexual thrillseeker in *Siesta* (1987); *Five Corners* (1988); *Stealing Home* (1988); *The Accused* (1988); rookie cop Clarice Starling in *The Silence of the Lambs* (1991); prostitute in *Shadows and Fog* (1991); *Little Man Tate* (1991, also director); *The Silence of the Lambs II* (1993 project).

T: Joey Kelly, Eddie's schoolfriend in *The Courtship of Eddie's Father* (1970–2); title role in *The Wonderful World of Disney* 'My Sister Hank' (1970); Elizabeth, daughter of the second couple in *Bob and Carol and Ted and Alice* (1973); ABC *Afterschool Special* 'Rookie of the Year' (1973); *Smile, Jennie – You're Dead* (1974); Addie Pray in *Paper Moon* (1974–5); ABC *Afterschool Special* 'The Secret Life of T. K. Dearing' (1975); Trilby in *Svengali* (1983).

Also noteworthy for her pithy but passionate speeches at the 1990 and 1992 Academy Awards ceremonies: ... 'Violence may be human but it is never, never acceptable'; 'To all of the women who came before me: the survivors, the pioneers and the outcasts. My blood, my tradition. And I'd like to thank all the people in the business who respected my choices.'

Foster, Stephen (1826–64) American composer of 'Old Folks At Home', 'Oh! Susanna', 'Camptown Races', 'Old Black Joe', 'My Old Kentucky Home', 'Beautiful Dreamer' and 'Jeannie With The Light Brown Hair'. Eulogized by Alexander Woollcott 'relayed from New York' in 1938. Played by Don Ameche in *Swanee River* (1941 C), but no mention of the fellow composer, George Cooper ('Sweet Genevieve') he left his wife and family to live with.

Foucault, Michel (1926–84) French historian and social philosopher who died of 'a neurological disorder' (according to *Variety*) aged 57, after completing only three volumes of his history of sexuality. Hugely influential, bold and liberating, notably in his delineation of the power structures of prisons and mental hospitals, and their relation to increasingly shaky liberal democracy. His 1973 case history of Pierre Rivière, a 19th-century parricide, was adapted for the screen and directed by René Allio as *Moi Pierre Rivière, Ayant Egorgé Ma Mère, Ma Soeur et Mon Frère*. René Feret adapted Foucault's *Herculine Barbines Dite Alexina*, the memoirs of a hermaphrodite, as *The Mystery of Alexina* in 1985.

fountains Mass film entertainment isn't allowed to show orgasms so it indulges in shots of gushing fountains instead: most excessively in Kenneth Anger's *Eaux d'Artifice* (1953) and the Rome-located *Three Coins in the Fountain* (1954); LA DOLCE VITA (1960); *Two Weeks in Another Town* (1962); *Eve* (1963); etc. *See also* PHALLIC SYMBOLS.

Four Corners (Aust 1961– T) Outstanding ABC television current affairs series, most recently remembered for its 1991 tribute to one of the country's most outstanding conductors in 'The Big Finish: The Stuart Challender Story'. Made a few months before his death, a large (and much moved) Australian audience watched as a worn-out, macabre transcription of a human being transformed himself into an upright, galvanic artist on the podium. Challender, hitherto a retiring person, was so affected by the overwhelmingly positive reaction to his 'coming out' (as a 'person with AIDS') that he wanted his friend, David Marr, to produce another film in which he would talk about more personal concerns: music in Australia; the encouragement of young musicians; and the shit piled upon homosexuals and people living with AIDS. It was never made.

The Fourth Man (Neth 1983 C) A

dog-eared writer Gerard Reve (Jeroen Krabbe) is trapped in a spider's web spun by a beautiful blonde Christine (Rene Soutendijk), with a tantalizing young man Herman (Thom Hoffman) an additional sticky substance.

W: Gerard Soetman from his novel; P: Rob Houwer, D: Paul Verhoeven; 102 mins.

Down and dirty thriller with a most engaging gay anti-hero. All the traditional jolting elements of FILM NOIR, but with a special sweet flavour, that is definitely *film rosé.*

Fox, James (1939–) Pretty young actor who has become a gorgeously grizzled, solid player. Began, as William Fox, as Greer Garson's son Toby in *The Miniver Story*, then the young hero of *The Magnet*. Returned to acting in *The Loneliness of the Long Distance Runner*, prior to his big break as the spongy ARISTOCRAT so easily crumpled by *The Servant*. In astonishing contrast, but still a victim, is his East End gangster 'corrupted' by Mick Jagger in PERFORMANCE. After a long break, he made a comeback as the gay son in COUNTRY (1981 T). Other significant roles: Nancy Astor's husband and BOBBY'S father in *Nancy Astor* (1982 T); Orwell in *The Road to 1984* (1984 T); Anthony BLUNT in A QUESTION OF ATTRIBUTION (1991 T).

The Fox (Can/US 1968 C) A man (Keir Dullea) disturbs the isolated existence of Jill (Sandy Dennis) and March (Anne Heywood), provoking a change and a crisis in the *status quo* which results in Jill's death.

W: Lewis John Carlino and Howard Koch from the novella by D. H. LAWRENCE; P: Raymond Stross; D: Mark Rydell; 110 mins.

A thin story laden down with symbolism and with actors who play in wildly clashing styles: Method neuroticism (Dennis); he-man athleticism (Dullea); lady-like control (Heywood). Luckily, the film is blessed with sensational photography which milks the scenery and chilly atmosphere to the full. The last shot is of one of the dead, grinning fox

with fang-like icicles. A radio production, far less enigmatic and with the one hint of a sexual relationship between Jill and March cut, was broadcast in 1974. It was billed as: 'Two women, in search of independence, are running a farm. Bramford provides the capital. March the accounting. March does the rough work. A fox ravages the hen coop and March is fascinated by its cunning. The grandson of the farm's previous owner returns from the sea and proposes to March.' The story is based on Cecily Lambert who farmed with her cousin Violet Monk in Berkshire, and portrayed as emotionally fractured, burning with jealousy in novella and film.

Fox (UK 1980 T) The saga of a London family living on the fringes of crime. One of the sons, Joey (Larry Lamb), falls for a way-out (drinks pints, reads cards, likes boxing) FASHION DESIGNER, Bette (Maggie Steed), and is freaked out when he discovers that she's BISEXUAL – like her father.

W: Trevor Griffiths; P/D: Jim Goddard; Thames; 13 parts; 60 mins each.

An ambitious project lacking characters that stick in the mind, except for Bette, who's enormously taking with one knockout scene: 'Touching, caring, being cared for, just being … loving's not all screwing … We grow up in different ways, Joey … Billy was someone very special. So was *my* father … He was married three times, had four kids and for the last ten years of his life he lived with a man. It was tender, caring and gentle. He was just as gentle with my mother.'

Fox and His Friends (Faustrecht der Freiheit) [First Right of Freedom] (West Germany 1975 C) A carnival worker, who wins a large sum of money in the lottery, is taken up and spat out by a group of rich gay men.

W/D: Rainer Werner FASSBINDER; 123 mins.

Blunt, expertly aimed critique of a particular section of gay society – unfortunately one that is uppermost in the public's perception. Fassbinder is compelling and sympathetic in the title role. Horribly believable. 'A middle-class homosexual, pursued by the rich, cheated, abused, then thrown away. I played the character because it was about the typical homosexual relationship with heterosexual society. They control the money, the system, the power. It was a role any homosexual could play, at least the ones I know' (Fassbinder quoted in a 1982 interview in Boze Hadleigh, *Conversations with My Elders*).

Framed Youth – Revenge of the Teenage Perverts (UK 1983) Lesbian and gay eyes view Britain prior to the explosion of AIDS. Interviews, film clips, cartoons, vox pops and freeze frames with a pre-Bronski Beat Jimmy SOMERVILLE. Lesbian and Gay Youth Video Project; 50 mins.

Award-winning (British Film Institute) documentary about the needs and bad times of gay and lesbian teenagers in a Conservative Britain. Before 1 June 1988 it seemed to be the spearhead of a new kind of truth for teenagers.

freaks Dora Bryan (as Helen) did *not* call Murray MELVIN (as Geoffrey) 'a pansified little freak' in the film version of A TASTE OF HONEY (1961), as the character did on stage. However Alan's thrice-uttered imprecation against Emory – before he began punching him – was retained from the staged BOYS IN THE BAND (1970 C). Martha (Shirley MacLaine) – beside herself with fear, grief and guilt at the collapse of her life with Karen in THE CHILDREN'S HOUR (1961 C) – screams at the delivery boy who keeps staring at her: 'See, I've got 8 fingers and 2 heads. See, I'm a freak!' The prostitute Carla, who is male, is attacked in a hospital lavatory in CASUALTY 'Hooked' (1987 T) by an irate customer who thinks she may have given him HIV/AIDS; the abuser, a young travelling salesman, holds Carla down and calls her a 'Degenerate ... perverted little freak' while his friend smashes a bottle in her face.

Freddie/Freddy Version of Frederick/Frederic, often for jaunty, superficial characters: Freddy Eynsford-Hill in *Pygmalion/My Fair Lady*; Freddie Page in THE DEEP BLUE SEA (Kenneth More 1954 T & 1955 C; Michael Byrne 1982 R etc); lonely, twisted Freddie Clegg (Terence Stamp) in *The Collector* (1965 C); Freddie Calder (Ron Donachie) in *Specials* (1991 T).

Sometimes gay: camp Freddy (Tony Beckley) in *The Italian Job* (1969 C); vicious critic Freddie Lamont in YOU'RE NOT WATCHING ME, MUMMY (1980 T); Freddie MARTIN (Roland CURRAM), lonely gay man, keeping his spirits high despite onrushes of drama in ELDORADO (1992–3 T).

US: Freddy (Marlon Brando), con man in *Bedtime Story* (1964 C); Freddy Krueger (Robert Englund), the world's most famous demonic mass murderer who survived five sequels and a nasty skin condition in the *Nightmare on Elm Street* series (1984–91) and *Freddy's Nightmares* (1991 T); dopey but dishy teacher Freddy (Mark Harmon) in *Summer School* (1987 C).

Frederick II the Great (1712–86) King of Prussia. A lifelong hatred of women; Voltaire broadcast his interest in men all over Europe 'in coarse detail'. *The Emperor Frederick II* (1964 R) was a personal portrait.

French Riviera Elliott Templeton (Clifton WEBB) lives and dies a snob there in *The Razor's Edge* (1946 C); Gregory Peck encounters the dazzling but 'FRIGID' Countess Liz (Hildegarde Knef) and foolishly tries to 'change' her through marriage in *The Snows of Kilimanjaro* (1952 C); gay young things prattle in the background of *Tender Is the Night* (1985 T); 'Frank' plays a lot of golf and bridge with her two friends in THE THREE FAT WOMEN OF ANTIBES (1960 & 1968 T) only to have her idyll disrupted by her manipulative female cousin; Frédérique has a villa in St Trop in LES BICHES; booksellers Miss Baker and Miss Cox lived on the Riviera and 'met COCTEAU' in *A Voyage Round My*

Father (1969 & 1982 T); Wilf Corney (Hugh Sullivan), the dead giveaway gay in LATE CALL (1975 T), tells Sylvia (Dandy Nichols): 'It's the third year running. It's ever so gay in Cannes. Just the place for three bachelors gay'; Oliver (Hugh BURDEN) and Harry (Anthony Andrews) live a life of ease on the Riviera in A SUPERSTITION (1977 T) but not for long: 'The setting is idyllic. But one of the ironies of loving is that it rarely brings peace. Sometimes it brings hatred. It can even bring death.' The Riviera is a place of glittering success for Renato and ALBIN and their CAGE AUX FOLLES; it is a place of work, play and much bickering for Willie MAUGHAM (David MARCH) in WEEKEND WITH WIL-LIE (1981 R). Rose (Mary Peach) goes there with her mother in *Rose at Roque-brune* (1984 R). Endorsing its reputation for the outré, film director (Vito Orsini) tells rich girl from the U S of A (Lindsay Wagner) in *Scruples* (1980 T) that the blonde in the bar is a 'he' who is waiting for his lover who is a 'she'.

Freud, Sigmund (1856–1939) Austrian doctor, the founder of psychoanalysis, much quoted and misquoted. Played by Montgomery CLIFT in *Freud* (1984 C), and – with more definition of his close bond with Wilhelm Fliess (Anton Lesser) – by David Suchet in *Freud* (1984 T). His methods, with a lesbian client, were only partially explored in *1919* (1985 C).

Fried Green Tomatoes at the Whistle Stop Café (US 1991 C) Two Alabama women (Mary Stuart Masterson and Mary-Louise Parker) who battled against racism and sexism during the Depression, as remembered by an old woman (Jessica Tandy) and told to her new-found friend, Evelyn Couch (Kathy Bates).
W: Carol Sobieski and Fannie Flagg from the latter's novel; P: Jordan Kerner and Jon Avnet; D: Jon Avnet; 130 mins.
 Jon Avnet: 'People will read into it whatever they want. I wasn't interested in going into their bedroom. This is a movie about friendship.'

Mary Stuart Masterson: 'You can decide whatever you want. However you respond to it, fine. Idgie and Ruth feel more strongly about each other than the men in their lives, and how that's inter-preted is best left up to the audience.'
(This highly effective, savvy film cost US $11 million and took over $60 mil-lion at the North American box office. It was nominated for two Academy Awards. A few truths – which are in the book – got blanched in the process.)

friend The mad scientist (Leo G. Car-roll) in *Tarantula* (1956 C) lives with Eric, whom he describes as 'my closest friend'. The glorious generality that has saved many a social occasion from ter-minal embarrassment was first employed 'knowingly' in the cast list of THE CRIME AT BLOSSOMS (1958 R): a character is described as the artist Adrian's 'Friend', and he has one peki-nese yelp of dialogue. In THE GOON SHOW: 'The Tragedy of Lord Seagoon' (1958) Gladys Clutch (Peter SELLERS) is 'spelt with masculine "g" as in Gee Whiz. I'm his friend' (camp voice). In PERRY MASON 'The Case of the Scarlet Scandal' (1966 T) a character picks on Perry for using 'The coy Victorianism' 'friend' to describe 'lover'.
 The usage threaded its way through until Peggy Ramsay (Vanessa RED-GRAVE) is surprised (it's 1963), when Joe ORTON (Gary Oldman) asks if he can bring his 'friend' to their next meet-ing; she is pretty sure that this person is his lover (PRICK UP YOUR EARS). 'Friend' is used of Paul (George Peppard) who is kept by Patricia Neal in *Breakfast at Tif-fany's* (1961 C). It is also used by Gerald (Nicky Edmett) of Maurice in *The Other Side* (1967 T): 'Maurice is not my friend. He's my "friend", if you see what I mean.'
 Gay liberation failed to solve one of the greatest practical problems for male–male bondings (it was never much inter-ested in the female ones), namely what to call that special person. Colin (Karl Johnson) becomes uncharacteristically flustered over this issue in ONLY CON-NECT: 'I never know what to call him.

"Boyfriend" is coy, "lover"'s one-sided; "mate"'s too butch and just "friend" is evasive. We could do with a new word.'

Gertrude STEIN uses 'friend' regretfully when making her will in GERTRUDE STEIN AND A COMPANION (1985 R), but in reality she called Alice her Pussy, and considered herself wedded to her. Peter PEARS was still 'just' Benjamin's friend in the *Aldeburgh Master Class* (1989 T). This unshakeable ambiguity formed the crux of the Z CARS episode 'Friends': 'They're friends, that's all'; to which a police officer nods, repeating mechanically: 'Yes ... friends'.

Trying to sum up 20 years, Freddie (Roland CURRAM) in ELDORADO (1992 T) calls John, who died: 'Friend, confidant, lover. He was just perfection on legs.'

Nicole (Primi Townsend) and Camille (Pam Scotcher) discuss the difficulties of usage in *World's End* (1981 T):

Nicole: 'The word "Friend" is beginning to acquire funny overtones. What other word is there?'
Camille: 'Lover, partner, associate, companion, intimate. I guess we're stuck with "Friend".'
Nicole: 'Anything is better than "wife" or "husband". They sound indecent.'

Like all good euphemisms, penetration is never far away. The officious Mrs Smallgood in SWIZZLEWICK was quite clear where she stood: 'Friendship is all very well ... as long as it is sexually invalid.'

friend of Dorothy's Following *The Wizard of Oz*, this probably reached its zenith around the mid-1950s during Judy GARLAND's emotion-soaked expiations in various theatres, culminating in 'OVER THE RAINBOW'. It re-emerged forcefully in the late 1970s – the murderer (Richard Cox) uses 'friend of Dorothy' in his cat-and-mouse conversation with stalking cop Al Pacino in CRUISING (1980 C). Paul DRAKE calls Perry 'Dorothy' when he thinks an intruder is eavesdropping on their bedtime phone conversation in 'The Case of the Reckless Rockhound' (1964 T). It

was used as part of the title for the 1992 Australian radio programme on the gay and lesbian community *In the Mix*: 'Are You a Friend of Dorothy?'

friends What is glaringly obvious is how rarely gays are presented outside the framework of isolation or coupledom. If they do have friends, they are usually childhood pals or sympathetic straights. In MORE LIVES THAN ONE (1984 T) the ultra-closeted married David tells an old friend and business partner that the rumours are true; the friend finds this revelation doubly hard to accept, because of his liking for David's wife and because of the feelings he and David experienced at school: 'I had more boys in the bicycle shed than I've had hot dinners. But I'm not gay.'

Rob and Michael offer Jane a roof over her head when her marriage comes apart in AGONY (1980 T). Frank, the TEACHER in TAXI ZUM KLO (1981 C) has a large circle of colleague-friends. Jim in NIGHTHAWKS (1978 C) is only able to talk about himself to a new female supply teacher.

Too often the links between gays and their friends are tenuous and superficial, eg the THEATRICAL DRESSER Leslie and HAIRDRESSER Aubrey prattling on in YOU'RE NOT WATCHING ME, MUMMY. Or they flourish offscreen: Colin invites the barman from the Nightingale, Richard and Jeff, and Terry and his mates from the Warwick to his lover's surprise party, but we do not meet any of them in ONLY CONNECT. Or the circle bristles with jealousy and sexual deceit (COMING OUT).

The best example of the subtle vapour trails of affection, responsibility, sharing, compromise and shared delight that make up friendship are seen in THE NAKED CIVIL SERVANT (1975 T), WE THINK THE WORLD OF YOU (1980 T; 1988 C), PARTING GLANCES (1985 C) and DEATH IN THE FAMILY (1986 T). And real-life admiration, exasperation and understanding of fellow humanbeings shines from every frame of THE TIMES OF HARVEY MILK.

See also CLOSE FRIEND; JUST GOOD FRIENDS.

Friends (UK 1967 T) 'Cyril, a professional protester, despairs of the reactionary attitude of Frank, which threatens his intimate relationship with Tom' (*TV Times* synopsis).

W: C. P. Taylor; P: Stella Richman; D: Michael Lindsay-Hogg; 6.9.67; Rediffusion; 30 mins.

A taut playlet set entirely inside a hotel bedroom. A middle-aged British man (George Cole) and his young American Air Force Lieutenant lover (Stuart Cooper), recently returned from Vietnam and changed by the experience. HOMOPHOBIA is well personified by the hotel employee, who wants to throw them out as 'unsuitable'. A nice twist has the man retreat in a fluster upon being told by Cyril that both men are officers, fiercely anti-Communist, and fathers.

Friends Forever Sung by Tony Randall (Sidney), Swoosie Kurtz (Lori) and Kaleena Kiff (Patti) over the opening credits of LOVE, SIDNEY (1981–2 T), accompanied by clips of the three hugging each other to death. All three voices are off-key and the words are undistinguished, but they are wholly successful in blurting out the series' central idea: namely that a lonely asexual bachelor can be redeemed by the (non-sexual) love of a good woman and a cute child.

This was daring, alternative American television comedy in the first term of President Reagan: 'My life's better than before,' croaks the Sidney character. If he had remained gay, would such a song be contemplated?

friendship Between close friends sex is often only a kiss away. Devoted and passionate friendships can be found throughout drama, poetry and comedy. From Antonio and Bassanio in *The Merchant of Venice* to Morecambe and Wise.

Leo Von Harden (John Gilbert) and Ulrich Von Eltze (Lars Hanson) decide that Greta GARBO is not worth the end of their friendship: they are happier together in *Flesh and the Devil* (1927 C). Judith Traherne (Bette DAVIS and Ann King (Geraldine Fitzgerald) are devoted to each other in *Dark Victory* (1939 C). Trevor Howard as Alec uses his student chum's flat for trysts until the chum catches him at it and, crisply hurt, asks for the spare key back (BRIEF ENCOUNTER 1946 C). Charles Ryder and Sebastian FLYTE gambol through the streets and lanes of Oxford in BRIDESHEAD REVISITED. Aldo and Bruno love each other in *Death of a Friend* (1959 C, based on a Pasolini novel). Jimmy Porter cares more about Cliff than he does about his wife and his mistress in LOOK BACK IN ANGER (1959 C etc). In *The Love Machine* (1971 C) the open sexuality of the photographer Jerry (David Hemmings) threatens the career of television high-flyer Robin Stone (John Phillip Law) whose firm friend he is: 'Robin and I have always been very close. Just terribly fond of him, duckie.'

Terry and Bob (James Bolam and Rodney Bewes), friends since the cradle and known as *The Likely Lads* (1965–9 T; 1976 C). King Henry II and Thomas in *Becket* (1964 C; 1969 R). Chas and Joey (James FOX and Anthony Valentine) in PERFORMANCE, passionate enemies in London's gangland. Finny (John Heyl) and Gene (Parker Stevenson) involved in a test of strength (and sublimated sexuality) that goes very wrong in *A Separate Peace* (1972 C). Lillian Hellman (Jane Fonda) and the heroic *Julia* (Vanessa REDGRAVE 1977 C). The Irish teacher and his pupil in JIMMY: 'We're friends, Tommy and I, nothing more ... but the village decided otherwise.' John Curlew befriends the German Jewish Mark Stein: their affection is ridiculed and it leads to Mark's death in *Reach for Glory* (1962 C) and, later, in *The Custard Boys* (1976 R; 1979 C). Edward Brittain (Rupert Frazer) is home from the front with his chum Geoffrey (Geoffrey BURRIDGE) in TESTAMENT OF YOUTH (1979 T). Michael and the flamboyantly sexual Liam in KIDS 'Michael and Liam' form an uneasy bond which is ultimately damaging for the gay partner. Chris

(Nigel Lambert) and Graham (Henry Knowles) are ageing bachelors faced with a challenge after Chris' mum dies in *Running Down* (1980 R). Two successful men (Alan BATES and Dinsdale Landen) retie knots in *Two Sundays* (1975 T) and *The Best of Friends* (1980 T). Joan (Georgia Allen), off to New Zealand with her family, spends a tender last few hours with her mate Evelyn (Suzanna Hamilton) in *Goodbye Days* (1984 T).

frightening the horses Mrs Patrick Campbell coined this classic injunction at the time of the Oscar Wilde scandal: 'You can do anything as long as you don't do it in the streets and frighten the horses.' It has become a standard device for tolerating (but not empathizing with) same-sex loving for the past century. Wrongly attributed to WILDE by Georgia (Julie McKenzie) and her gay playmate Harvey in *That Beryl Marston . . . !* 'Noel-oh-Hell' (1981 T):

> Harvey: 'Two's company and three's an offence.'
> Georgie: 'Only if you do it in public and frighten the horses.'

And to a queen of England by one of the transvestite contributors to *Soundtrack* 'Sisters Under the Skin' (1991 R): 'Yes, we all get "read", that's a fact of life. But if you are presentable, you're not offending anybody. I think it was Victoria who said "as long as you don't frighten the horses". And that's the bottom line. We know what we are and the public probably knows what we are.'

Frightfully BBC The Western Brothers languidly put into song (during the 1930s) what some were whispering about. But sweet are the uses of ambiguity: it is difficult to know whether devotees of the BBC's ethos are in or out of touch, in the know or not:

> . . . We still think a PANSY
> is a kind of flower.
> (There are FAIRIES at the bottom of *our* garden.)
> We crawl to the city,
> perhaps Mincing Lane.

> Then potter to luncheon,
> And crawl home again.
> (It's all *too* tired making.)
> We know all the announcers on Greenwich (pip, pip).
> We simply *adore* the gale warnings to ships.
> We *never* shake vinegar over our chips.

frigidity Often associated with incipient lesbianism: tough aviatrix Vi (Bebe Daniels) in *Reaching for the Moon* (1931) who is called 'a cold creature . . . but underneath your frigid exterior beats a kind little heart'; REBECCA, the bad and dead first wife of Maxim DE WINTER; Christine ARCHER called 'a frigid snow queen . . . a bit of an icicle', and drawn to an older woman (Lady HYLBEROW) who 'acts very frigid' (THE ARCHERS 1952); Countess Liz (Hildegarde Knef/Neff) in *The Snows of Kilimanjaro* (1952 C); the Labour MP's frosty Communist spouse (Rosalie Crutchley) in *No Love for Johnnie* (1961 C); Carol the manicurist (Catherine Deneuve) in *Repulsion* (1964 C); psychiatrist Leslie Caron in *A Very Special Favour* (1965 C) who is led to believe that her indifference has made Rock HUDSON gay.

Two of these snow queens deserve special scrutiny: Mary Carmichael (Rhonda Fleming) is described as Miss Frozen Puss in *Spellbound* (1945 C). She is first seen playing cards with three other women and tells the players as she is led away: 'I could have beaten the *pants* off you.' Walking down the corridor she makes up to one of the nurses. Getting nowhere, she scratches his hand. Slinking into the office of her psychiatrist (Ingrid Bergman) she poses provocatively, and lies wantonly on the couch. 'Psychiatry bores the pants off me,' she says without much conviction. Enjoying being the centre of attention, and, fascinated by a female authority figure, Mary tells the doctor how she hates and loathes men. The session ends abruptly with the arrival of the doctor's colleagues, one of whom echoes the nickname 'Miss Frozen Puss'. This was an interesting development for Alfred HITCHCOCK. Here is a woman who simultaneously wants and is repelled by sex and who adopts flirtatious attitudes towards both sexes. He cunningly also suggests that the person with 'emotional problems and love difficulties' is not necessarily only Miss Carmichael.

Laura Randall (June Vincent) in PERRY MASON 'The Case of the Wintry Wife' (1961 T) is described as 'jealous', 'possessive', 'a wicked woman better off dead', 'a blackmailer' and 'a wicked woman – every life she touched she destroyed'. The other word hovering over this character is frigid, but it is not uttered. Instead, her husband calls her 'cold ... very cold' – at which Perry's eyes register understanding. But there was a reason for her problem: 'I'm never warm enough'; on her honeymoon she was caught in a blizzard and now feels the cold all the time – a circulatory problem. However, acting, direction and plot tell another story: Laura is presented as a heterosexually aloof woman with a woman secretary ('almost a nurse'), much given to bitchy politeness and GARBOESQUE poses in headscarves. She is despatched via a tablet in the milk after blowing up a factory.

frocks Began as a monk's garb, then ecclesiastical, then frock coat. Women wore frocks much later. The word was used cunningly in recent years: by FROCS (Faggots Rooting Out Closeted Sexuality) featured all over the media (as well as in OUT 'Absolutely Queered' 1991 T) and, to describe the huge interest in mixed gay/lesbian/bisexual/heterosexual dance parties in Sydney, *The Coming Out Show* called its piece 'Getting Our Frocks Off' (1992 R).

The Front Runner Patricia Nell Warren's novel about Harlan Brown, track coach, and Billy Sive, god of 10,000 metres, was a best-seller – at least in America in 1974. Everything seemed set fair for the film version, especially when Paul Newman became involved. Twenty years on, no film has appeared, no Hollywood star being

game enough to play either the younger or the older man who fall in gentle love.

Frost Over America (US 1970 T) Tennessee WILLIAMS, pinned down by David Frost, allowed, to tumultuous applause, that he had 'covered the waterfront'. America's 'greatest playwright' was, thereafter, out of the closet, and he was 75 per cent more candid in his 1975 *Memoirs*. His interviewer retained pre-liberation vocabulary on further programmes (eg 'Homosexuals: Out of Shadows' 1975) and was describing openly gay people as 'SELF-CONFESSED' as recently as 1985 (*Twenty Years On*).

Williams: 'My God, we're all victims of rape, symbolically ... society rapes, the individual ...
Frost: 'Do we all live with cannibalism in the same symbolic way? ...
Williams: 'Yes, we all devour each other in our feelings.'
Frost: 'What about things like the homosexuality and so on ... doesn't everybody live with that, too?'
Williams: 'I think everybody has some element of homosexuality in him, even the most heterosexual of us.'
Frost: 'Then no-one is all man or all woman, you mean.'
Williams: 'Oh, in my experience, no. I don't want to be involved in some sort of scandal, but I've covered the waterfront.'
(Laughter, applause.)

fruit 'You lousy fruit,' screams Zero Mostel, one of THE PRODUCERS (1967 C) at the TRANSVESTITE director (Christopher Hewett) who has upset his plans for making a mint out of a surefire Broadway flop; it is so utterly appalling that it becomes a runaway success. In the TV movie *The Woman Hunter* (1972) a party guest, short, adorned in pink, blackcurrant BOW TIE and prominent turquoise ring, leers at an approaching (young) cocktail waiter. 'Ooo, I just *love* tutti-frutti!'

Classy courtesan Daphne (Maggie Smith) suggests to the assembled 1930s glitterati that if they want to find who committed EVIL UNDER THE SUN (1982

C) they'd best 'Cherchez la fruit!' (who is dependable player of assorted sybarites Roddy MCDOWALL). As Jodie (Billy CRYSTAL) is borne aloft by extraterrestrial forces, unleashed by his stepfather, Bob the dummy exclaims: 'See the fruit fly!' (SOAP 1978 T). Sir Jarvis Fruit (Peter SELLERS), head of New Scotland Yard, is a screamer of the first water with blond wig, velvet jacket and cigarette holder in *The Case of the Mukkinese Battle Horn* (1956 C).

The Fruit Machine (UK 1988 C) Two young men (Eugene Charles and Tony Forsyth) flee gangsters, to become involved with an opera singer, his agent, (an eerie young man called Echo), and dolphins.
W: Frank Clarke; D: Philip Saville; 103 mins.

Gay lyrical script and straight, hard execution do not mesh, hence the film fails to be wholehearted on any of its levels: caper comedy; thriller with supernatural elements; male-female teenage love story; whacky fantasy.

Fry, Stephen (1957–) English writer, actor, best known for *A Bit of Fry and Laurie* and *Jeeves and Wooster*. Very imposing, droll Wildean figure with prodigious output, and with winning ways. Probably most revered for the dryly witty, informed and angry article he wrote for the *Listener* in 1988 on the passing of CLAUSE 28.
C: *The Secret Policeman's Third Ball* (1987); Peter in *Peter's Friends* (1992); screenplay of *Me and My Girl* (1993).
T: *Crystal Cube* (1983); Lord Melchett in *Blackadder II* (1986): *A Bit of Fry and Laurie* (1987–); title role in *This is David Lander* (1989); Daniel Davenport, a barrister who killed a lover's husband and who kept his Jewish background from his public school chums in *Old Flames* (1990); *Hysteria III* (1991); *Saturday Night Clive* (1991) *Wogan* (1992); poet Humphrey in *Common Pursuit* (1992 T); a languid bar steward in an advert for a beer which is 'smoother than a cashmere codpiece'.

R: *The Demon Cakestand of Beestley Chase* (1985); panellist on *I'm Sorry I Haven't a Clue* (1986); *Loose Ends* (1986); *Could Do Better* (his school report, 1987); *Delve Special* (1988; 1990); *Saturday Night Fry* (1988); *Pick of the Week*; *Just a Minute* (1992); etc.

Richard **Fulton** Character in MRS DALE'S DIARY and THE DALES (Norman Chidgey 1950–8; David MARCH 1958–67). A Wildean dandy ('I might buy myself an orchid'): an over-sensitive, malicious, hypochondriacal, grudge-bearing writer of romantic fiction and Shaftesbury Avenue plays; possessor of 16 books of press cuttings but no wife.

Mrs Dale's sister Sally is unaccountably drawn to this self-absorbed ninny. Through her, he was supplied with a manservant (Fickling) and two pekinese. After years of mild courtship, they (Sally and Richard, not Richard and Fickling) married and all seemed cosy until, in 1967, Richard suddenly upped (in his fifties or sixties) to live in Paris and 'explore his homosexuality'. The character was based on Patrick WHITE, who was a great friend of the serial's motivating force, Jonquil ANTONY.

Barry HUMPHRIES' sulphurous poem about White could have been written about Richard Fulton:

He was a typical high-minded,
interbellum, stage-struck queen.
Before the war he would have queued to
hear Bea Lillie sing.
One imagined him in private dragging
like Douggie BYNG.

Richard *could* be kind (he gives a children's party for his nephew Billy and his friends in 1954), but usually – apparently like White – he throws tantrums. A man fissured with bitterness, spite and anger far out of proportion to the merits of the case or the failings of the person. Later, when married to Sally, he was merely debonair and only occasionally on his high horse, which he was never off during his heyday in the 1950s:

To Mrs Dale: 'I'm always upset by the smell of peppermints.'

To Mrs Freeman: 'Don't shush me. I hate being shushed.'

To his secretary: 'Women should only marry for money.'

About his relatives: 'I have two nephews and three nieces, but I don't talk about them because I don't like them. I really can feel no interest in them at all. I haven't the time.'

During a dinner party, to Fickling: 'The whole evening has been ruined. I will not be dictated to by *you!*'

While looking for a country cottage: 'To live without buses! Or taxis! Under hedges with cows! And thunder and lightning and pouring rain.'

funeral directors LIBERACE cooing over the caskets in *The Loved One* (1965 C); a sinister individual in *Lady in Cement* (1968 C) and in *Diamonds Are Forever* (1971 C); the gayly abandoned Dorian and Desmond in *When Did You Last See Your Father?* (1979 R): 'We bury all the best people ... our facilities are stretched to the limit in our cold drawers.'

funny John TREGORRAN (Basil Jones) was regularly called 'a funny sort of chap' in his first year in THE ARCHERS (1953–4 R); Jean (Lois Dane) nervously sounding out her boyfriend Jesse (John Duttine) in Z-CARS 'Friends' (1974 T) about his friendship with Gordon (George Baker): 'What's all this between you and that funny fella, that Gordon fella?'; Nicole tells Camille in *World's End* (1981 T) that her mum called queers 'funny'. Madge (Pat Coombs) in EASTENDERS (1989 T) relates the story of her friend in the Women's Land Army: 'Used to lift great bales of hay with a pitchfork. Funny girl, Mavis ... joined the Navy because she wanted to be in the real war, with the fellas.' But before she quit, Mavis performed a useful service, defending Madge against the cruel advances – 'I couldn't sit down for a week' – of one Herbert Harding: 'She knocked him out with one punch.'

Funny Lady (US 1975 C) The second half of the life of a musical comedy star Fanny Brice, now pursued by a Broadway dynamo.

W: Jay Presson Allen and Arnold Schulman; P: Ray Stark; D: Herbert Ross; 138 mins.

Bricehead Revisited: Barbra STREISAND, every inch the prima donna, yet still hurting for gambler Nicky Arnstein (now married to a rich older woman), settles for a companionable but passionless marriage with composer/impresario Billy Rose (James Caan), who is jealous not of Nicky (Omar Sharif) but of Fanny's gay friend, Bobby (Roddy MCDOWALL, harmlessly washed out). There is nothing which reaches the heights of the first half of *Funny Girl*, but taken as a whole this is a lavish, atmospheric, moderately sparkling entertainment with Streisand more appealing here because she has a strong actor to respond to (Caan – who is terrifically taking).

Furse, Judith (1912–74) English actress who began with soft, sweet supporting roles before metamorphosing into the hefty, ox-shouldered battleaxe of British screen comedy. She also played her share of capable, single-minded pillars of the establishment, but the roles were usually too subsidiary to shake her fully out of type-casting.

C: as Flora, Greer Garson's friend in *Goodbye Mr Chips* (1939); Elise Batter-Jones in *English without Tears* (1944); Jane Matthews in *Johnny Frenchman* (1945); one of the relatives in *Quiet Wedding* (1946); one of the NUNS in *Black Narcissus* (1947); *Helter Skelter* (1949); *The Man in the White Suit* (1953); Dame Maud Hackshaw in *Blue Murder at St Trinians* (1957); Chief Wren in *Further up the Creek* (1958); probation officer in *Serious Charge* (1959); 'a damsel' in *Scent of Mystery/Holiday in Spain* (1960); Mrs Ayckroyd in *Live Now Pay Later* (1962); 'Battleaxe' in *Carry On Cabby* (1963); as Dr Crow in *Carry On Spying* (1964); villager in *Sky West* and *Crooked* (1965); Edna EVERAGE'S 'minder' in THE ADVENTURES OF BARRY MCKENZIE (1972).

R: debut with Peter Bull in SAKI'S *The*

Watched Pot (1937); Mrs Bathhurst in *Three Famous Mysteries* 'The Disappearance of Mr Bathhurst' (1939); lots of work on CHILDREN'S HOUR between 1949 and 1953 including singing 'Oh, Nancy was a saucy lass' in *Worzel Gummidge on the Island*; Miss Somerton in *The Avenue Goes to War* (1960).

T: Miss Hale (with Joan Lovelace as Miss Hedges) in *Little Red Monkey* (1953); 'Frank' Hickson with Anne Shelton and Joan Young in THE THREE FAT WOMEN OF ANTIBES; *The Odd Man* as Miss Croy (1960); *Hugh and I* (1962); Miss Smyth-Wilberforce in *The Secret Agent*; panellist on *Call My Bluff* (1966, with her friend Peter Bull); nurse in *The Worlds of Wooster/Ukridge* 'The Accident Syndicate' (1968).

Gabriel Patron saint of broadcasters often pictured with a lily: regarded as the left hand of GOD, he brought the news (and the seed?) to the Blessed Virgin. Dirk BOGARDE played archvillain Gabriel (blond wig, mod clothes, a mother who didn't know about his secret life) in *Modesty Blaise* (1966 C).

Nelson **Gabriel** Son of the late Walter GABRIEL and – played by Jack May – one of AMBRIDGE's most delightful and enduring dysfunctionals. He made sporadic visits to the village from 1954 onwards, casting his forbidding but polite gaze on the inhabitants. In 1967 he was reported dead in a plane crash, then re-emerged in 1968 when he was accused of being the mastermind of the Borchester mail van robbery. However, he was cleared. In 1971 he attempted to seduce Lilian Archer; she proved intractable, marrying Ralph Bellamy later that year.

For a considerable number of years he has run a wine bar/restaurant in Borchester (employing SHANE) and, with Kenton ARCHER, an antiques shop. His black bedsheets tie in well with his cynical asperity and a liking for the more urbane pleasures of life. For years he has been footloose and fancy-free, sometimes on the verge of getting involved with a woman but never quite managing it. Nelson never has and never will throw in his lot with convention. He told Christine ARCHER back in 1956. '*You* fit in. You're part of the pattern. But I'm not and I don't want to be ... I belong somewhere else ... to a different life.'

And how he enjoys his role as a courtly anachronism ('What a fascinating shade of *eau-de-Nil* you've turned, Nigel', 1992). Maybe it's a kind of revenge for the treatment he received in the village as a young man. A victim of Ambridge louts was Nelson, according to his father in 1954: 'Not very good at cricket or football ... Nobody ever got very friendly with Nelson and he took it to heart a bit. Bit slow he was. Late developing as you might say. Lots of Ambridge folks thought he was ten-a-

penny and some of 'em never took much trouble to hide what they were thinking.'

Walter **Gabriel** Venerable curmudgeon who was a hayseed mainstay of THE ARCHERS (firstly played by Robert Mawdesley, then by Chris Gittins from 1954 to 1988). With his burr-filled voice and mine of expressions and sayings (many from his 'old granny'), he was proud of being 'born naturally cantankerous ... an iggerent old country chap'. John TREGORRAN tried (in 1956) to do a Pygmalion on him ('a larynx full of hops, a voice like a corncrake'), but Walter resisted – even though he might have found himself a (second) wife if he'd spruced himself a bit. But, like his son Nelson GABRIEL, he seemed to prefer the free life, chatting with his 'ole pal, ole beauty' Simon and trying to invent excuses for Nelson's scrapes and his unmarried state.

One of Britain's most beloved radio characters. His argy-bargy, his malapropisms, his 'oh dear, oh lor', his gossiping and tittle-tattle, his chuckle are sorely missed. But much of his anarchy lives on in his only begotten son.

Mrs Cathy **Gale** Eye-catching efficient cooperative of John Steed's, played by Honor Blackman. Black leather/kinky boots-wearing judo expert, but soft and pliant with eyes only for Steed. Replaced by Mrs Emma PEEL.

'Pioneering television FEMINIST,' according to Paul Madden, director of the 1992 television tribute to THE AVENGERS (*Without Walls*). She replaced Ian Hendry's character in 1962. 'That's why it got the attention it did. If Hendry had stayed I think people would have forgotten the series. Not because he was no good, but just because it was two men together.'

Gambaccini, Paul (1949–) American-born, British-based broadcaster on many aspects of pop music. Full of ebullient enthusiasm. First worked for BBC radio in 1973 with his long-running American hits show. Among his specials have been 'The Elton John

Story' (1976), 'The Bee Gees Story', and 'Prince' (1991), 'All-American Heroes' and 'Marathon Music Quiz'. For KALEIDOSCOPE he compiled 'The Kenny Everett Audio show' and the 2-part 1979 survey of DISCO, 'Big Apple Boogie' and 'Night Dancing'.

On television, he presented three seasons of Channel 4's *The Other Side of the Tracks* (1983–5, including Culture Club, Frankie Goes To Hollywood and the Roaring Boys) as well as 'a frank interview' with Elton JOHN in 1987. He reviewed films for TV-am during the 1980s and was one of the guest hosts in the first series of OUT ON TUESDAY in 1989. He came up with the idea for *Television's Greatest Hits* (1992– T).

Ganymede Young boy, the lover of Zeus (and the assumed name of ROSALIND in AS YOU LIKE IT). Cavan Malone was Ganymede, incurring the jealousy of Zeus's wife in MARLOWE'S *The Tragedy of Dido, Queen of Carthage* (1952 R); but the part was played by a woman (Elizabeth Morgan) in the 1974 version. In a 1974 radio play, *Ganymede* (based on a Daphne Du Maurier story), Anthony Daniels was the Boy who intrigues the Man (John Le Mesurier).

Garbo, Greta (1905–90) Swedish actress, an instant legend in HOLLYWOOD, source of mystery, romance and rumour. She never married and played Queen CHRISTINA closer to the truth than was envisaged by MGM. In *As You Desire Me* (1932) she is confused as to who she is: 'Maybe I am, maybe I'm not. It's all mixed up.' She also declares: 'I WANT TO BE ALONE.' 'Naturally,' concedes Melvyn Douglas.

Her last celluloid appearance (caught unawares) was in a gay porno picture, *Adam and Yves* (1974). Yves teases Adam by dangling a bunch of grapes over his nose: 'Who does this remind you of?' Dissolve to Greta Garbo walking down First Avenue. She is alone. Commented the director Peter De Rome: 'The long stride and big sad eyes are still the same.'

The mystery of Garbo continues to fascinate. A number of Garbo figures have been at the centre of films and TV movies: Kim Novak as Elsa recreated as a film goddess in *The Legend of Lylah Clare* (1968 C); reclusive BISEXUAL Karla (Melina Mercouri) in *Once Is Not Enough* (1975 C); desiccated and games-playing Hildegarde Knef in *Fedora* (1978 C, from the Thomas Tryon novella CROWNED HEADS); Kristina Wayborn as the young Garbo in *Moviola* 'The Silent Lovers' (1980 T); Betty Comden as the old Garbo in the last scene (silent) of *Garbo Talks* (1984 C).

Although some of her films are still entertaining (*Camille*, *Anna Karenina* and *Ninotchka*), it is *Queen Christina* (1933) which provides Garbo's most satisfying dramatic statement. For the rest, look to the eyes, the unforgettable voice, the stance, the extraordinary tactility in even her most cardboard impersonation. Those films she didn't make after her 'retirement' from Hollywood (Daudet's *Sappho*; the life of George SAND, *My Cousin Rachel*, *The Duchesse De Langeais*; *Remembrance of Things Past*; *Sunset Boulevard*; and – her personal choice – THE PICTURE OF DORIAN GRAY) may contain as many of the answers as to who or what Garbo was as those she did star in during the late 1920s and on through to 1941.

The love affair that Alastair Cooke described – ignoring her wide appeal among women – in a 1933 radio broadcast retains its ardour, and its mystery, after the death of its progenitor: 'Any man who starts out to write about Garbo begins with one big advantage: he couldn't be Garbo if he wanted to ... The fame of a Greek goddess was restricted to a population something less than the population of Hampstead ... Garbo yields to no one in being the best known person in the world ... To be the most famous woman in the world is not only a social responsibility. It is at the same time, an actual social revolution ... She has become every man's harmless fantasy mistress.'

In *Meetings of Two Queens* (1991 V) celluloid is so moulded that Garbo appears to love and be loved by Marlene DIETRICH, in the 1930s the reigning queen of Paramount.

The Garden (UK 1990) A dreamscape on video and film which moves between Jarman's garden of stones (at times a Garden of Eden, at others Gethsemane) and his dreams (some evoking anti-gay persecution and AIDS). Two young lovers go through the night of the Passion. 'You are dealing with a situation in which, over the course of centuries, there has really been genocide.' W/D: Derek Jarman; E: Peter Cartwright; P: James Mackay; 92 mins.

A collage centred upon Jarman's wilderness garden in the shadow of a nuclear power station, of Christ and of two male lovers, lost in a labyrinth to which we surrender or from which we try to escape.

gardeners Peter Vernon (Nigel Greaves) seduced by Oxford don Sir Alan Tufnell and – unconvincingly – blackmailed by him in *Rumpole of the Bailey* 'The Gentle Art of Blackmail' (1980 R); Sir James Mackieson (James Drake), orchid grower and fancier of blond hunks in *The Assassination Game* (1979 T) and its sequel *The Treachery Game* (1980 T); Pete never happier than in his potting shed in TOGETHER; a don's boyfriend in *An Empty Glass* (1981 R); Chauncey Gardiner (Peter SELLERS) in *Being There* (1980 C); Denny (Paul GREENHALGH) running off with a gardener for a few passionate hours in THE CREZZ (1976 T); Vita (Janet McTeer) creating magic, first at Long Barn then at Sissinghurst Castle, in PORTRAIT OF A MARRIAGE (1990 T).

Gardeners' Club (UK 1956–1970s T) Percy Thrower, a comfortable-looking man with thinning Brylcreemed hair, was the mainstay: 'pricking winter-flowering pansies' in between dealing with meconopsis, hardy primulas and spring onions in the space of one half hour. The importance of women in horticulture was played down in this weekly series, with Frances Perry making one visit in 1958 and Sheila Macqueen flower arranging. Only in 1965 did Percy Thrower 'talk to women gardeners'.

Gardiner, Anthony (194?–) Creator of the divine FASHION DESIGNER Claude Crepe in *Mister Ten Per Cent* (1967 C). Very few sightings since: Bond Street jewellery salesperson in *Scandalous!* (1984 C).

Gardiner, Jeffrey (1928–) English actor, tall, originally curly-headed in a variety of nervy, sometimes daffy small roles across three decades of television: 'outrageous' film producer Hugo Wyncette-Twinge in *The Larkins* 'Strictly Commercial' (1958); a member of a quartet of queens in THE FABULOUS FRUMP (1969); William Bishop, the producer who wants everything light and gay in ROCK FOLLIES (1976); Mr Beauchamp who is turned down for a job in the menswear department of Grace Brothers by Mr HUMPHRIES because he is one of them and it wouldn't be good for the store's image (ARE YOU BEING SERVED? 1979).

Other TV roles include a student in *What They Say* (1956); walk-ons in *Hip-Hip Who Ray!* (with Ted Ray, 1956) and *Saturday Showtime* (with Peter SELLERS, 1956); an unsuccessful boxer who has to be hypnotized into winning in *Time Out for Peggy* (1958); Ginger Moran in *Badgers Green* (1958); one of the frequenters of Moulin Rouge in *Yvette* (1958); in the second episode of *The Strange World of Gurney Slade* (1960); the lead in *Night Call* (1961, while he was understudying Kenneth WILLIAMS in the stage revue *Pieces of Eight*); diplomat's secretary engulfed by a tidal wave in *The Andromeda Breakthrough* (1962) after exclaiming: 'God, can you hear that?'; artist in *Fantasies of the Night* (1962); Achille in *Oooh La La* 'What a Wedding!' (1964); tailor in *Père Goriot* (1965); Robin in *The Mind of the Enemy* (1965); member of the fashion house staff in THE FABULOUS FRUMP (1969); Ben in *The Silver Collection* (1971); party guest in *Man About the House* 'When the

Cat's Away' (1974); Mr Wintergreen in *Dad's Army* 'A Brush with the Law' (*c* 1976); Rupert Sutcliffe in *Small World* (1988); guest in *Tales of the Unexpected* 'The Boy Who Talked with Animals' (1986); vicar in *Life without George* (1987). On radio he was Bob Acres in *The Rivals* (1961).

Garland, Judy [Frances Gumm] (1922–69) American actress and singer: quasi-divine, who went from Child Star to Teenage Star to Adult Star to Fallen Star to Risen Star to Living Legend. As well as her films (notably *The Wizard of Oz*, *Meet Me in St Louis*, *The Clock*, *Easter Parade*, *The Pirate*, *A Star Is Born* and *I Could Go On Singing*) and television appearances (*The Judy Garland Show* 1963–4), Garland was a prodigious radio performer: on variety shows and in acting roles for *Lux Theatre* ('Morning Glory' 1942; 'A Star Is Born' 1942; 'Meet Me in St Louis' 1946; 'Alice Adams' 1950; 'The Wizard of Oz' 1950) and, as a terrorized waitress, in *Suspense* 'Drive In' (1946).

Judy Garland's special niche in male homosexual/gay culture was referred to in Alan BENNETT'S stage play *Enjoy* in 1981. The mother remarks that it wasn't the nude male photographs on her son's bedroom wall that made her realize his orientation, 'it was the picture of Judy Garland'.

Another parent – a determinedly modern mother, Dame Edna EVERAGE – described a tiff her son Kenny had with his friend Cliff 'over a Judy Garland record'. In *Not Waving* (1979 R) the heroine's landlord repeatedly plays THE MAN THAT GOT AWAY and Stanley (Peter WOODTHORPE) worships at the Garland shrine in OVER THE RAINBOW (1980 R) and wishes life were like an MGM musical. His friend Sandra (Maureen Lipman) shares his enthusiasm, but not to the point where reality disappears over a Technicolor horizon. In *Down and Out in Beverly Hills* (1987 T) Mr Whiteman (Hector Elizondo) worries about his 16-year-old son Max: 'Lately he's been listening to show tunes. I'm gonna fire his shrink if I see one picture of Judy Garland on his wall.' And a Glasgow woman falls in love during Garland's visit to the city, only to find that 'they're writing songs of love' (but not for her); the object of her affections (Stephen Docherty) is gay, besotted with Judy, but giving her a (gay) son in *Beyond the Rainbow* (1991 R).

There have been a number of articles about the sometimes excessive fan worship of the star by gay men. William R. Buckley was particularly scathing on the subject in 1968. But they were no more ridiculous than Beatles fans or a Jane Fonda workout tape or the audience at a male or female strip show. Nevertheless, the legend has it – in the deathless words of comedian Paul LYNDE – 'that the gays killed Judy Garland'.

Part of the woman's exhausting psychology can be seen in her last film, *I Could Go On Singing* (1963). There are also some glorious moments to be found in her television series, especially her work with Ethel Merman and Barbra STREISAND. Her apogee must surely be her performance as Esther Blodgett, later Vicki Lester, in *A Star Is Born* (1954). She was never more affecting, skittish and true. This is not to devalue her wondrous work in *Meet Me in St Louis* and other MGM milestones. Or to erase one second from her Dorothy Gale, twister-blown from Kansas to Oz.

A sketchy TV movie of the book *Rainbow* (1978) had Andrea McArdle as the young Frances Gumm with Don Murray as her cinema manager father, run out of town because of activities involving young men. The script was by John McGreevey who went on to adapt CONSENTING ADULT. Elaine Loudon played her as an adult in *Will the Real Judy Garland Stand Up, Please* (1983 T), and in *Beyond the Rainbow* (1991 R) she was brilliantly recreated by Mari Binnie.

Biography: OMNIBUS 'Judy: Impressions of Garland' (1972 T); Cult Heroes (1992 R): 'Years after her death, Judy Garland is revered by many – perhaps most surprisingly by the gay community. But one thing is sure – her legend will live on' (RADIO TIMES).

'Listening to Judy Garland in 1980 is

akin to a black person eating watermelon in the 1960s' wrote Vito RUSSO in GAY NEWS 205. He then proceeded to relate how a friend of his didn't move his television set out onto the balcony, as he habitually did on warm afternoons to watch *A Star Is Born* on British television. He feared that his neighbours would 'sense' he was gay.

The importance of Judy Garland to a sense of solidarity among many gay men cannot be too heavily stressed. Her unique combination of intense wonder and inner pain seemed to encapsulate the unfocused yearning of men growing up without a compass in the bleak 1950s. Her death in June 1969 coincided with the STONEWALL RIOTS. Even the lesbian comedian Robin Tyler ends her act with 'OVER THE RAINBOW'. And Freddie on ELDORADO (1992 T) is a big fan: he thinks Trish Valentine sings like Judy; but young Fizz, standing with him in the audience, asks: 'Who's Judy Garland?' In a later episode, Freddie has all Judy's albums stolen from his apartment, only to have them replaced by his fellow expatriates.

See also GET HAPPY; IN-BETWEEN.

Gascoyne, David (1916–) English writer and poet (*Roman Balcony*, 1932), translator and promoter of much French surrealist work (RIMBAUD, Dali, Breton, Buñuel). Remembered for his 1956 radio poem NIGHT THOUGHTS, 'his most ambitious work and his greatest single achievement'. He read his poems (including 'Misere') on the Third Programme/Radio 3 in 1949 and in 1968. Frank Duncan read them in *David Gascoyne in Retrospect* (1973). The poet's last work for radio was *Self-Discharged* (1987), which is the monologue of a man (John Franklyn-Robbins) listening to his fellow psychiatric hospital inmates and discovering that his own hallucinations aren't that abnormal.

The Gateways Basement club for lesbians which flourished in London during the 1960s and 1970s, immortalized by THE KILLING OF SISTER GEORGE (1968 C), and recalled (it closed in the early 1980s) in OUT 'Storm in a Teacup' (1992). The 1967 MAN ALIVE programme on lesbians extolled its virtues (and played down its modestness): 'There they can dance, drink, flirt and discuss their problems.'

Gay/Gaye A boy's name, a pet form of GAYLORD. Boyish but married New York playwright Gay Esterbrook in *No Time for Comedy* (James Stewart 1940 C; Stephen Murray 1954 C); amateur sleuth Gay Lawrence (George SANDERS) known as *The Gay Falcon* (1941 C), also seen in *The Falcon Takes Over* (1942 C) and *The Falcon's Brother* (1942 C); Clark Gable as Gay, the cowboy who is one of *The Misfits* (1961 C).

As a girl's name, it began in Britain, attained popularity in America during the 1930s, and was then readopted by the British, peaking around 1945. As a first name it became increasingly problematic in the 1960s.

UK: Dion Boucicault's Lady Gay Spanker (Ingrid Hafner) in *London Assurance* (1963 T); Gay Hardwicke (Joan Greenwood), the mute *Girl in a Million* (1946 C); Gay (Ann Todd), the porcelain wife of barrister Gregory Peck in *The Paradine Case* (1948 C); Gay Butterworth (Peggy Simpson) in *Count Your Blessings* (1953 T); Gay (Dora Bryan) soubrette in *Desert Mice* (1959 C); Gay (Peggy Cummins) in *Your Money or Your Wife* (1960 C); Gaye Stevens (Susan Travers) in *Zero One* 'The Liars' (1962 T); Gay Clifford (Veronica Hurst) in *Dead Man's Evidence* (1965 C); Gay (Rosemary McHale) in *Conception of Murder* 'Conversation Piece' (1970 T).

US: Gay Merrick (Judith Allen) in Cecil B. De Mille's *This Day and Age* (1933 C); Claire Trevor as the broken-down, alcoholic singer Gaye in *Key Largo* (1948 C); Gay Kendall (Anne James) in the Gene Autry Western *False News* (1952 C); Gay Knight (Peggy Ryan) in *All Ashore* (1952 C).

A decade later, the name had virtually disappeared from American films, except for Gaye Swinger (Barbara Nichols) in *Looking for Love* (1964 C), and Gay Erin (Susan Clark) in the Western *Valdez Is Coming* (1979 C). From the 1970s, the name was used very sparingly for female fictional characters in Britain – Lieutenant Gay Ellis (Gabrielle Drake) in *U.F.O.* (1972 T) set in the 1980s; Gay (Gail Harrison) in the Barry TOOK comedy series *A Roof Over My Head* (1977 T) – before seeming to give up the ghost.

Reviewing the series *Couples* (1981 T, which featured a gay and a lesbian couple), Peter Ackroyd remarked in *The Times* that the producer/presenter's name (Gay Search) 'sounds more like a counselling service than a young woman. It must be hard, these days, to live with a name like that.'

The last vestiges of Gay/e were to be found in Australia: Gaye (Anna Phillips), the prostitute friend of the heroine in *Tender Hooks* (Aust 1985 C). Everywhere else, alternatives had been found. There was Gail/Gayle/Gayle or, in Britain, there was Gaynor (related to Jennifer): Gaynor, a flight attendant played by Sally Osborn in a 1986 *Brush Strokes* episode, and Gaynor (Kirsty Skelhorn) in *Children's Ward* (1989–90 T).

Gail/Gale is also a diminutive for GAY-LORD from 'gai', and has been used over the centuries for boys and girls. In America there was secretary Gail Ormsby (Florence Vidor) in *The Enchanted Hill* (1925 C); then Gail Wilson (Alice Day) in *Is Everybody Happy?* (1929 C); Gail (Fay Wray) in the Western *Black Moon* (1934 C); Gail Loveless (Marion Davies), a Union spy known as *Operator 13* (1934 C); Gail Armitage (Margaret Lindsay) in *Dangerous* (1935 C); Gail Pyne (Katherine Lock) in *Straight from the Shoulder* (1936 C); Gail Dunbar (Wynne Gibson), newspaper woman in *The Crouching Bear* (1936 C); Gail Stanley (Karen Morley), a condemned man's wife in *On Such a Night* (1937 C); Rita Hayworth's title character in *Who Killed Gail Preston?* (1938 C); the film star heroine Gale Joy (Lucille Ball) in the 1943 film version of the 1941 Broadway musical *Best Foot*

Forward; Gail Mason (Joanne Dru) in *711 Ocean Drive* (1950 C).

There was a lull for a decade then a resurgence, mainly on television: Nurse Gail Lucas (Zina Bethune) in *The Nurses* (1962–8 T); Gail Armstrong (Millette Alexander), commercial artist in *Edge of Night* (1960s T); Gail Foster (Carol Lynley) in *The Night Stalker* (1971 T); Gail Stevens (Gail Strickland) in *Ellery Queen* (1975 T); Gail Goodman (Kathleen Miller), public defender in *Sirota's Court* (1976–7 T); Gail Berke (Jacqueline Bisset) in *The Deep* (1978 C); geologist Gail Weston (Anne Archer) in *Waltz Across Texas* (1982 C); Gail (Phyllis Davis), new wife of politician facing rebellious stepdaughter in *The Love Boat* 'All the Congressman's Women' (1984 T); Gail (Julie Kavner) in *Hannah and Her Sisters* (1986 C); Gail Springer (Mariette Hartley) expressing new kinds of feelings in MY TWO LOVES (1986 T); antenatal counsellor Gail (Kiki Huygellen) who has an affair with one of her clients in *Meet the Applegates* (1991 C); Gail Benson (Emma Cunningham) in *Medics* (1992 T).

UK: CORONATION STREET'S Gail Potter Tilsley (Helen Worth), married, divorced and remarried; tennis coach Gail (Prunella Scales) in *Singles* (1983 T); unstable Gail (Maureen O'BRIEN) IN *Runaway* (1992 R).

Australia: Gail Summers (Susanne Hayworth) in PRISONER (1980s T); Gail Robinson (Fiona Corke) in NEIGHBOURS (1980s T).

The first Gayle was a small girl who listens to stories by an Uncle Remus-style character in the 1949 television cartoon *Sleepy Joe* (she was played by Gayle, the daughter of animator Jimmy Scribner). The spelling 'Gayle' is moderately favoured today: Gayle O'Reagan (Amanda Muggleton), tough gal in a truck in *Queen of the Road* (1984 C); Gayle Bucannon (Wendie Malick) in *Baywatch* (1989 T); Gayle Roberts (Farrah Fawcett) in *Good Sports* (1990 T).

Gail/Gale/Gayle had been a boy's name, eg the director/stunt man veteran of 300 films, Gayle S. De Camp, who died in his eighties in 1976. However, the only male character so called was twisted Gail Wynand (Raymond Massey) in *The Fountainhead* (1949 C).

Gay/Gaye as a surname, is used for both sexes: Walter Gay, a sympathetic character in Dickens' *Dombey and Son* (Derek Seaton 1969 T etc); Steven Gaye (Herbert Marshall), middle-aged playwright pursued by young female secretary in *Accent on Youth* (1935 C; Dennis PRICE played him in the 1959 TV version called *Skyline* although when Clark Gable starred in the film remake that same year *But Not for Me*, the character was called Russell Ward); Penny Gay (Petula Clark), one of bachelor David Bliss' many girlfriends in *A Life of Bliss* (1954–5 R); M. H. L. Gay, Senior Fellow in *The Masters* (Baliol Holloway 1958 R; Harold SCOTT 1963 T); deranged Bill Gaye (Wilfred Brambell) in *In Search of the Castaways* (1962 C).

There are also other spellings of the surname: Fred Gailey (John Payne) in *Miracle on 34th Street* (1947 C); Carol Gaylee in *Down Among the Z Men* (1953 C). And after a 39-year-gap: TV news whizz Gail Gailey (Geena Davis) in *Accidental Hero* (1992 C); Herbert Gaily (John Baddeley) who turns up unannounced at a family funeral in *Gentleman and Ladies* (1993 R).

gay It was Cary GRANT who let the cat out of the bag. 'I've gone gay ... all of a sudden,' he said, leaping into the air, in an unscripted declaration to Katharine HEPBURN's creamily permed, aghast auntie (May Robson) in *Bringing Up Baby* (C 1938). In *Holiday*, made the same year, Doris Nolan recalls her first sighting of Johnny (the Grant character): 'He had a queer look on his face'. 'You're all confused, aren't you,' says Irene Dunne to her about-to-be-ex-husband Grant, who's wandering around in pyjamas in *The Awful Truth* (1937 C).

Usually 'gay' surfaced unambiguously in dialogue, eg in *Strategic Air Command* (1956 C) someone says of James Stewart and June Allyson: 'So nice to see a young couple so gay.' But there were occasions when its use was very much subcultural: Stan LAUREL (off camera) in drag in *Jitterbugs* (1943 C) trilling 'I feel so gay', while a character is introduced called 'Queen'; Johnny (Glenn Ford) observing – in the deliriously erotic, neurotic, psychotic GILDA (1946 C) – that his rescuer (from muggers) and soon-to-be-protector Munsen (George Macready) leads 'a gay life' to which the older man replies: 'I lead the life I like to lead.' Sometimes, as in THE VOICE OF THE TURTLE (1947 C), the meaning is fuzzier: Eleanor Parker wanting to put the relationship with a soldier (Ronald Reagan) on a casual but not necessarily platonic basis says: 'I thought we could keep it gay.'

Seemingly off the cuff (but deriving from a 1930s play) is Robert Morley's OSCAR WILDE (1960 C) in deep absinthe-accelerated decline. He says to the waiter: 'Ask the band to play something gay', and erupts into peals of mirthless laughter. The word also crops up in awkward places. The dead Martin in J. B. Priestley's 1932 play DANGEROUS CORNER is eulogized by his male lover thus: 'He had to be gay. When he was gay, he was gayer than anyone else in the world.'

In Britain, the word's featherlight, effervescent meaning was much in evidence on radio. Kenneth Adam's talk on the occasion of the launch of a range of colourful, geometric ties was entitled (innocently?) 'Tie Designers Go Gay' (*London Log* 1938 R). On television ITV's *The Sunday Break* was advertised in 1958 as being 'interested to show the serious side of life as well as the gay'. And Martita HUNT, possessor of the grandest vowels in British cinema, playing a baroness with a very much unmarried son in *The Brides of Dracula* (1960), recalls her castle's glorious past in a ding-dong voice: 'We had gay times ... balls.'

By the mid-1960s, censorship relaxed sufficiently for the full 'new' meaning to be communicated to a mass audience. Jason Robards Jr misunderstands Jane Fonda in *Any Wednesday* (1966 C): *she's* talking about a room full of balloons being gay, not him. But he fluffs up like a grey Persian at the mere suggestion.

The advent of gay liberation from America meant that gay was to be the accepted descriptive form for homosexuals in Britain. In the credits of the Frankie HOWERD comedy *Up the Chastity Belt*, Blondel (David Kernan) lays great emphasis when mentioning Robin Hood's Merrie Men: 'every one was gay'.

The press began to see the value of so short and increasingly recognizable a word. In 1982, both London evening newspapers used 'gay' in their headlines about the American bank robber and his transsexual lover (later the basis for the Al Pacino film). A year later, nearly all the nationals had implemented the changeover from ten letters to three, though with quotation marks.

Larry GRAYSON diffused some of the outrage with his catchphrase 'What a gay day!' in *The Larry Grayson Show* and SHUT THAT DOOR! However, some people about whom it was used were not themselves willing to adopt it; Kim in THE OTHER WOMAN says: 'When people apply that word, it's a hell of a paradox. If it's got to be a choice of the two, I think I'd prefer QUEER.' Rikki (Angus Lennie), the BARMAN in PLAYMATES thinks that 'it sounds like we're all frantically rushing around in funny hats and waving balloons and giggling'. And Linda Ray Guettner (Gena Rowlands) wonders, after her mother has roundly abused her in A QUESTION OF LOVE: 'Why do they call it "gay"?'

By the late 1970s, the word was fully fixed in TV journal consciousness (Benedict Nightingale mentions an actor who plays 'a gay teacher' (in RADIO TIMES, November 1979), but it remained interchangeable with homosexual in a way that black and negro did not. But there still had to be explanations. In 'Rumpole and the Gentle Art of Blackmail' (1980 R) Rumpole is told that a young man is not in the least bit gay and has to have it spelt out for him.

A year later, Stanley Ellis was prevailed upon (in *Enquire Within* R) to explain the 19th-century slang meaning of this now highly inflammable word. Ellis' Australian equivalent, Alan Peterson was resigned but unhappy about the situation: 'Homosexuals have captured the word "gay". Feminists have taken the more glamorous word "gender" for "sex". We could do well to teach our young to be more discriminating' (*Watch Your Language* 1992 R). He was echoing a great number of fictional and non-fictional people on television and radio who would bemoan the 'loss', eg the character played by Renée Asherson in *Love and Marriage* 'Sweet Echo' (1984 T): 'A word stolen and *abused.*'

For those directly concerned, 'gay' couldn't be adequately defined. Brash exuberance, wishful thinking, brave integrity and sound common sense. All of these and more. Like the best things in life, its verisimilitude could not be effectively communicated. However, the undertaker has been called prematurely for the other – 'nicer' – gay. In *Death of a Mean Cornet* (1992 R) Pauline Brown (Kate Binchy), talking about her daughter, says: 'She looked so beautiful and gay' (meaning that she looked beautiful and gay – there was no sexual inference whatsoever).

gay abandon 'With gay abandon' used by jolly Aussie cook Peter Russell-Clarke in his series of 5-minute bites *Come and Get It* (1987 T).

gay (and lesbian) centre A place, usually in a city, where homosexual people can come for coffee, for a discussion or to read magazines and books. One of the first was in Glasgow and was featured in OPEN DOOR (1976) and *Current Account* (1978 T).

The Gay and Lesbian World (UK 1992 R) Survey of life and politics in Britain, the Netherlands, America, India, Thailand and some other places not generally associated with openly homosexual women and men such as Africa and the Middle East.
P: David Rodgers; 6 parts; 30 mins each.

Compiled and presented by journalist and broadcaster Jim Hiley. He announced where he was coming from in the opening minute of the first programme. Each one was well organized, full of savoury interviews and crackled with a new kind of BBC World Service commitment to showing life in its diversity. As each programme made clear, being homosexual/gay/lesbian/bisexual means different things in different cultures. For too long the Western heterodoxy of gay rights, COMING OUT, a gay LIFESTYLE, anti-marriage and sexual freedom has prevailed to the exclusion of other viewpoints and shades of meaning.

gay as a ... 'gay as a daisy in May (a cliché coming true),' flutes Mitzi Gaynor in the closing moments of ME! I'M AFRAID OF VIRGINIA WOOLF from '(I'm In Love With) A WONDERFUL GUY'. The phrase also occurs in 'I Dream Of Jeannie' which was sung – unselfconsciously – by Martha Raye, aged 23, in 1939. Douglas Poole (Ronald Pickup) meets Armstrong (Andrew Branch) the boy he seduced at school, some 20 years after: 'He was camp ... gay as a Queen's hussar ... *and he was happy*' (*The Awful Insulation of Rage* 1987 R).

gay-bashing *See* QUEER-BASHING.

gay/bisexual man played by gay/bisexual man Cary GRANT as Cole PORTER (NIGHT AND DAY); Esmé PERCY as Hans ANDERSEN in *My Life is a Lovely Story* (1947 R); Danny KAYE as *Hans Christian Andersen* (1952 C); Micheal MACLIAMMOIR as Oscar WILDE in *On Trial* (1960 T), and *I Must Be Talking to My Friends*; Dennis PRICE as Tiny Calloway in VICTIM; Hilton EDWARDS as the blind con man in VICTIM; Stephen CHURCHETT as Pete in TOGETHER; Ian MCKELLEN as Piers GAVESTON in EDWARD II; Alec MCCOWEN and Ian McKellen as EDWARD II; Michael CASHMAN in EASTENDERS (1986–9 T); John SCHLESINGER as Derek in THE LOST LANGUAGE OF CRANES; John GIELGUD as

Eddie Loomis in *Quartermaine's Terms* (1987 T); etc.

gay blade Used in a double sense (for men about town who are also homosexual) in THE GENTLE TOUCH 'Blade' (1980 T) and in ZORRO – THE GAY BLADE (1981 C). Armistead Maupin, recalling the San Francisco all-night discoing, bath-housing and cruising of the 1970s: 'I was very much a gay blade in those days' (ARENA 'Armistead Maupin Is a Man I Dreamt Up' 1992 T).

Gay Bob A $14.95 plastic doll in CLONE apparel, packaged in his very own CLOSET and sold in America from Christmas 1978. The boy in *Serial* (1980 C) is given one by his PSYCHIATRIST to vent his hatred of gayness upon. *See also* BOB/BOBBY/ROB/ROBERT.

The Gay Brothers Two men, possibly not biologically related, dance together. A 5-minute film made at the Edison studio in 1895.

The Gay Sisters Long, only intermittently dramatic 1942 film about the GAYLORD girls (Barbara STANWYCK, Geraldine Fitzgerald and Nancy Coleman) who endure a long court battle over an inheritance.

gay caballero The title of one of the better Cisco Kid adventures (directed by Otto Bower in 1940) with Cesar Romero and Chris-Pin Martin as his 'fonny' sidekick. Before that, the title was used for a George O'Brien and Victor McLaglen action pic (1932). The phrase was dished up in THE BOYS IN THE BAND (1970 C).

Gay Cable Network (GCN) Formed in 1982. The menu of programmes has included: *Be My Guest*, a gay and lesbian game show; *The Right Stuff*, a political programme; the *10% Show*, arts and entertainment which in the 1990s were being aired in Atlanta, Nashville, New Orleans, Chicago and Cincinnati as well as the more well-known centres of gay population.

Gay Christian Movement Now the Lesbian and Gay Christian Movement, it first gained national exposure in *Anno Domini* (1976 T), but only after the programme had moved from 6.15 pm to 10.15 pm. A frequent antidote to Levitical views on homosexuality from some CHRISTIAN individuals and groups; EVERYMAN 'The Lord Is My Shepherd and He Knows I'm Gay' (1978 T) and HEART OF THE MATTER (1992 T).

gay community *See* COMMUNITY, GAY.

The Gay Deceivers (US 1969 C) Danny (Kevin Coughlin) and Elliot (Larry Casey) set up home together to dodge the draft. Their frisky NEIGHBOURS, Malcolm (Michael Greer) and Craig (Sebastian Brook), become suspicious when women are smuggled in.
W: Jerome Wish from an idea by Abe Polsky and Gil Lang; P: Fanfare Film; D: Bruce Kessler; 91 mins.
Splotchy comedy which fritters away a good idea and which makes no satirical points – other than ultimately revealing the ferocious army recruiting officer as having a male lover. This was the first film officially turned down by the BBC on the grounds that it was offensive to gay people. (*The Gay Deceiver* was a 1926 Metro-Goldwyn film about an actor in Paris (Lew Cody) pretending to be his rich uncle.)

Gay Diversion Retitled version of the musical *Knickerbocker Holiday* (1944 C) when it was shown on British television in 1954. Nearly 40 years later, the BBC transformed Brendan Behan's *The Quare Fellow* (1962 C) into 'Queen of Hearts'. Meanwhile, in Australia, ZORRO – THE GAY BLADE (1981 C) was rechristened *Zorro Swings Again* to make it appealing to the television audience.

The Gay Divorcee (Aust 1991 R) 'The frailty of human love and sexual attraction can be just as evident in a lesbian relationship as a heterosexual one.' The romance has gone and Gretel (Margaret Fischer) struggles to work out why Rita (Amanda Irving) has changed towards her.

W: Margaret Fischer; P: Heather Steen; ABC; 60 mins.
The ebbs and flows of love, when all about you are breaking up or breaking down. Adaptation of stage comedy which has its moments, most of them lesbian telephone gossip and political incorrectness.

Gaye, Gregory aka Gregory Gay (*c* 1900–) American supporting film actor: Count Prunier in *High Society Blues* (1930); the heroine's unpleasant neighbour in *Ninotchka* (1939); 9th billed as a comic soldier in *Charge of the Lancers* (1953); bits in *The Eddy Duchin Story* (1956) and *Auntie Mame* (1958).

Gaye, Howard (?–1955) American stage and silent film actor: General Robert E. Lee in *The Birth of a Nation* (1915); Don Livingstone, 'chum' of hero in *Diana of the Follies* (1916); Jesus in *Intolerance* (1916) and *Restitution* (1918); etc.

Gaye, Lisa [Lisa Griffin] (*c* 1935–) American film starlet and occasional TV actress, the younger sister of Debra Paget. Mainly remembered for her lively, jivey participation in *Rock Around the Clock* (1956 C). Also: *Ten Thousand Bedrooms* (as one of the Italian sisters, 1957 C); *Adventures in Paradise* 'Wild Mangoes' (1962 T); PERRY MASON; etc.

Gay Gordon A character (not obviously homosexual) played by Felix Bowness in *Porridge* 'Just Desserts' (1975 T). *See also* GORDON.

gay/lesbian marriage *See* MARRIAGE; WEDDING.

gay liberation Kept down by laws, a history denied or fogged, shackled by religious traditions, made less than equal, often less than human. Two kinds of liberation – separated by many years – were expressed in ONLY CONNECT (1979 T) set in 1974, five years after homosexual people seized the moment in the wake of the Stonewall Riots.
'If you don't know it, and you can't read it, and you're eating slop, and you're in chains then truth won't set you

free,' says John Bury (Joseph O'Conor), in his seventies, who had been one of Edward CARPENTER'S disciples and, briefly, sex partners. He now lives on his own in Manchester, his lover Alan having died. They had kept a newsagent's and tobacconist's shop after meeting in the Merchant Navy. Honest and open, very much part of the neighbourbood, the truth had set *them* free.

And Colin (Karl Johnson), who'd survived the 1960s: 'There were some of us, those of us who'd not had our brains scrambled, who did start joining things up. That's when we stopped being queer and started being gay ... Because [the STONEWALL RIOTS] happened we had the cheek to ask the landlord for a double bed. And we had the nerve to walk down Corporation Street the other night holding hands.' At the play's end Colin is making a banner in 1979, to celebrate 10 years of gay liberation.

In EDWARD II lesbian and gay demonstrators from the direct-action group, OUTRAGE!, fuse with the past waving 'Fighting Fags' and 'Pansy Power' placards, and battling with riot police.

Generally, the ethos behind the emergence of gay liberation in 1969 has been left to a handful of documentaries and discussion programmes, principally PANORAMA 'Gay Liberation Front' (1971); WHICKER WAY OUT WEST 'The Lord Is My Shepherd and He Knows I'm Gay' (1973 T); ACCESS 'Offensive to Some' (1973 R); GAY LIFE (1980 T); BEFORE STONEWALL (1984 C/T).

The Gay Liberation Follies aka *The Gay Liberation Radio Show* (US 1973–4 R) Weekly San Francisco-based radio show, produced by Len RICHMOND for KSAN. Literature, news, coming attractions, community happenings, gay music, interviews, voices from the past. Special features included 'Straight Liberation', 'Frankenstein' (about AVERSION THERAPY) and – most memorably – 'Meet the Shrinks', a TV game show where the audience applauds the best explanation of *heterosexuality*:

Bad hormones (applause).

Dominant mother. Weak father (more applause).
Improper conditioning and bad habits (ovation).
Natural expression of human emotion (disgust, horror, boos).

A few television stations followed suit, WPVI-TV of Philadelphia which produced *Out Front* with the city's Gay Media Project. Issues like HOMOPHOBIA, gays at work, the family, as well as places to go were discussed.

Gay Life (UK 1980–1 T) A series dealing with aspects of life of concern to homosexual people (mainly male) and made with an eye to whatever portion of the London area audience was up and watching near to midnight on a Sunday.

Protests (mainly by lesbians) reached into the very vitals of LONDON WEEKEND TELEVISION whose newly formed London Minorities Unit had produced this groundbreaking effort. The second series, with two presenters (Michael Attwell, producer) and Alison HENNEGAN (Literary Editor and Features Editor of GAY NEWS), was perceived as an improvement: more historical features, more balance between lesbian and gay material; more 'us', less 'them' (less 'straight' voice-overs). The reaction was more favourable. The LWT press office said that despite its late hour (still 11.30 pm) and day of the week (still Sunday) the series had been seen by between 100,000 and 400,000 people, depending on what was being offered on the other two channels.

The two series generated many calls and letters to LWT. Although its average audience rating of 350,000 viewers was not too good, its audience *appreciation* index rating was 'encouraging'. But not encouraging enough. There were no plans for a third series 'since it was such a difficult market to gauge'.

In fact, another ration of *Gay Life* wouldn't have been the answer. Shown only in the London region at an inaccessible hour (very few people had video recorders then), it seemed very modest after the American weekly series on cable and educational TV like *Glad to Be Gay* in Madison, Wisconsin and *Out Front* in Philadelphia.

The need for a regular source of information was underlined by the numbers of young gays and lesbians whose coming out was about as painful in the 1980s as it had been in the 1950s. One of the women on VERONICA 4 ROSE recounted that girls at school discovered *Gay Life*: 'Said it was disgusting to see girls kissing on telly. I said it wasn't. Wot, are you a lesbian or something? I said, yes' (1983). Some, like the young woman in Coventry (SOMETHING ELSE 1980), were optimistic: 'All the time people are becoming more aware. There are programmes, just like this one, telling people ... that homosexuality exists, that we are ordinary people.'

But the London Gay Teenagers Report Group's 'Something to Tell You' in 1984 found that TV programmes like *Gay Life* had little influence. It was the sitcoms and the cop shows that were watched by the family. 'They accept my lover but we never talk about lesbian or gay people and when I am round there and a gay person comes on the TV they call them QUEER etc. I don't think they see me as being the same sort of homosexual as the TV stereotype' (female, 20). Yet James Murray of the DAILY EXPRESS could not understand why homosexuals 'needed a whole hour'.

There were subtle and not so subtle political and structural flaws which prevented GAY LIFE from becoming the regular source of news and views that was so desperately needed across the whole country – and which would not exist for another eight years.

In GAY NEWS, John Russell Taylor summed up the dilemma with his usual clarity in relation to the first series:

The gay viewer was forced into a pattern of double-think involving such convolutions as 'If I were straight would that person on the screen seem to me to present a reasonable argument in a convincing manner?' If the decision was in the negative, the gay viewer was left little option but to feel disappointed in his

or her 'rep'; to construe the situation as a lost opportunity for convincing the great straight world that homosexuals, despite all the bad publicity, were on the whole upright citizens, apt to be unjustly persecuted.

And, a year later:

Can you afford to give an impression of disunity or internecine disputes if we are putting on our best behaviour for the straight viewers? Can you, for that matter, afford not to?

Dudley Cave, also in GAY NEWS, was more welcoming:

Gay Life reached out into the homes and the closets to places where GAY NEWS never gets, where Vulcan is known only as the God of Fire and Zipper as a fastener. From some of these homes isolated gays rang London GAY SWITCHBOARD and took the first tentative steps on the road which could lead them to gay pride.

Happily we did not get [a PR job] and equally happily, we did not get reality. Britain is not yet ready to face true reality ... Not the reality of future encounters in squalid places, the grubby beds some of us have been taken back to, of lovemaking without love and sex without satisfaction ... or the reality of a society where A Man is judged by what is between his legs and not by what is between his ears.

A noble but doomed attempt to communicate and contain the sprawling lives and interests of a few million people, *Gay Life* was the primer from which would emerge – after much lobbying and in the teeth of much greater social and political hostility – a series that was technically more inventive, larger budgeted, national, hospitably timed and made very much *for*; a series which was yet another important stage in the realization of what once seemed an impossible dream.

See also OUT ON TUESDAY.

Gaylord Boy's name which derives from the Old French 'gai' meaning 'brave'. (Gail/Gale is also a pet name for Gaylord.)

US: Gaylord Ravenal, lusty gambler on the *Showboat* (Allan Jones 1936 C; Howard Keel 1952 C); Gaylord (William Tannen) in *An Innocent Affair* (1948 C); Gaylord Grebe (Normal Fell) in *The Hanged Man* (1964 C); Gaylord Sullivan (Troy Donahue) in *Rocket to the Moon* (1967 C); Gaylord (Jonathan Terry), a bit part in *Deal of the Century* (1983), also Gilbert Gaylord (Hugh Huntley) in *Second Wife* (1930 C) as the former lover of the heroine.

UK: Gaylord (Harold Reese) in *One Man and His Dog* (1962 R); Gaylord (Dudley Sutton), easily led teenager in Z CARS 'Come On the Lads' (1963 T). 'I can't play a *Gaylord*. Bad for my image ... People see me as a butch Mary Poppins,' says Kenneth WILLIAMS in ROUND THE HORNE (1967 R). (However, the actor had previously played Gaylord fffolkes in a 1966 show, spoofing 'She'.)
See also GAY/GAYE.

Gay Music Eric Coates holds a secure place in British hearts for two reasons: he composed 'The Dam Busters March' and the signature tune for DESERT ISLAND DISCS (complete with seagulls), 'By A Sleepy Lagoon'. He died in 1957 and a special concert was held called 'Tributes to a Gay Composer'. At a supper party afterwards, a toast was drunk to the perpetuation of gay music, examples of which had been played: 'The Knightsbridge March', 'The Merrymakers Overture' and 'Dance Of The Tulips'.

It was agreed to award £1,000 to senior composition students at the Royal Academy of Music who wrote gay music. The 1963 Eric Coates Prize was won by David Lyon with his 'Divertimento for Small Orchestra', broadcast in *Saturday Comedy Hour* in 1964. RADIO TIMES accompanied the event with an article entitled 'Gay Composer', which began: 'Contemporary writing of gay music does not happen easily in these days of extreme intellectualism and "pop" ...'

Gay News 'Why don't you read GAY NEWS? There's record reviews, theatre reviews and other escapist twaddle,' says rent boy Robert to colleague Phil in RENTS, Michael WILCOX's play that was turned down for television production in the early 1980s.

GAY NEWS was a fortnightly newspaper which began in June 1972 as a collective venture. Shortly thereafter it was solely edited by Denis LEMON. Its first broadcast media mention came on *What the Papers Say* (June 1973). Then Ken Russell had the scabby Uncle Ernie leaf through an issue (which spontaneously combusts) in *Tommy* (1975 C). GAY NEWS first hit the news services in 1974 when a Bath magistrate adjudged issue 34 (with two men KISSING on the cover, a still from Yorkshire TV) not to be obscene.

The paper was later to be shredded on stage by a punk band in ROCK FOLLIES OF '77 (T); discovered under papers on a man's desk – and so leading to his coming out – in DAVID IS A HOMOSEXUAL; kept in nursing tutor Ken HASTINGS' in-tray 'just in case someone wants to talk' in ANGELS (1980 T); kept on Rob and Michael's coffee table in AGONY (1980; an issue containing an interview with the show's writers, whose photographs are visible on the cover); read by Pete HUNT in TOGETHER (1981 T).

Denis Thatcher (John Wells) fears he'll end up on the cover if he puts on one of Margaret's hats as disguise in *Anyone for Denis?* (1982 T), and it is one of the publications Channel D advertises in for programme makers in VIDEOSTARS (1983 T, shown six months after the paper folded). There's a reference to the son possibly having '16 bound volumes of GAY NEWS under the bed' in *Birds of a Feather* 'Young Guns' (1990 T).

Loved and hated, ignored and heeded in about equal quantities, the newspaper was likened to one of the 'straight' tabloids by Derek JARMAN, and was dubbed 'Grey News' by sophisticates, sexist by lesbian feminists, capitalist penis power by radical lesbian feminists. GAY NEWS achieved its own drama when it was successfully prosecuted for blasphemous libel in 1977. EVERYMAN dramatized the affair with rigorous fairness in 'Blasphemy at the Old Bailey'.

Two male rads, Graham and Colin, in ONLY CONNECT set in 1974 don't think much of it. Yet, when Graham advertises for people who had contact with early British socialists, there is no response from either the TRIBUNE or the NEW STATESMAN, only from the disparaged GN. No other gay publication has had GN's ubiquity, although Dame Edna's faithful Madge was reading HIM by the bathside in *La Dame aux Camelias* (1977 T) and CAPITAL GAY provided a clue to Marty's whereabouts in *The Fear* (1988 T).

GAY NEWS was a nine days' wonder. So fleeting was its fame that when Thames TV discussed blasphemy with Mary WHITEHOUSE in 1982 – while GN's case was still being appealed in the European Court – no representative from the paper was invited to attend. Alerted to the recording, a GN reporter was told by a Thames TV representative: 'Sorry, but it would be too expensive to change our plans.' The subject of the debate was prophetic: whether one religion should be singled out for special protection under law in 'our modern society'.

The last public appearance of GAY NEWS was on *South East at Six* (1982, its 10th birthday party).

gay nights In an EASTENDERS episode of June 1990, Sharon (Letitia Dean) tells representatives of the brewery that she and Wicksy will have gay as well as country-and-western, 1950s and 1960s nights at the Queen Vic if they are given the licence. The two-person interviewing panel makes no comment; there is no explanation of 'gay nights'. This marked the first mass-media occasion when the word 'gay' has not been qualified, condemned or ridiculed and has been listed in company that is not that of prostitutes, child molesters and drug addicts. (They *don't* get the licence.)

Gay Paree Confidently sung in VICTOR/VICTORIA (1982 C) by FEMALE IMPERSONATOR Toddy (Robert Preston, out of

drag) in a louche club called Chez Lui, packed to the rafters with the social set and TRANSVESTITES with bad teeth and appalling dress sense. The number, heavy and witless (perhaps intentionally so), repeatedly informs the audience that gay (as in Paree) also means gay (as in something else, unspecified): 'It means today/That Gay Paree is gay/They say/Paree has always been that way.' There's also a daring line or two ('There's ... bound to be/Rough trade in Paree'). Leslie Bricusse was responsible for the one-track lyrics, Henry Mancini the music. Robert Preston was nominated for a Best Supporting Oscar and won an award from the Alliance of Gay Artists. Leigh W. Rutledge in THE GAY DECADES (1992) writes that Toddy is 'probably the most relaxed and affable homosexual ever scripted into a major studio motion picture'.

Gay Pride aka Lesbian and Gay Pride. A march through some central London streets which evolved from a fairly low-key affair in 1974 into a colourful and joyous upsurge of non-violent unity and visibility. The broadcast media generally ignored it with the exception of split-second news clips of banners and bizarre costumes. An exception was *Newsnight* in 1980: Leo ABSE MP and Terry Munyard, a lawyer, discussed with ousted teacher Peter Bradley, members of GAY SWITCHBOARD and activist Jamie Dunbar the need for equal protection with blacks and women, as well as the importance of the individuals COMING OUT.

Gays: Speaking Up (UK 1978 T) Thirty lesbians and gays, including teachers Peter Bradley and John Warburton, lawyer Robert Banks, bus conductress Joanne, and train driver Alex Slater (COMING OUT in his railway cab while talking about TCHAIKOVSKY).

P: James Farrant; D: Vincent Stafford; 13.8.78; Thames (shown only in the London region – and in a part of Scotland covered by Grampian – at 11 pm).

Jackie FORSTER voices the unspoken thoughts of many when she tells presenter Llew Gardner that people must be so bored with this type of programme by now – 'the same old faces – brushed up out of hedgerows and woodwork to appear on this closet programme ... talking about being gay'.

'You begin to understand more and more. You know your gay friends so well but a programme like this shows that you don't really know them well at all,' says Vincent Stafford (who edited the programme from 1 hour 20 minutes to 52 minutes).

Gay Sweatshop A theatre company formed in 1975 by a group of homosexual men and women with a commitment to positive gay plays, and to touring these around Britain. Writers have included Edward Bond, Andrew DAVIES, Noel Greig, Drew GRIFFITHS, Martin Sherman, Carl Miller and Jill Posener. COMPROMISED IMMUNITY (1985) by Andy Kirby is the only Sweatshop play to have been broadcast (1991 R), although Greig and Griffiths produced possibly the finest of television's 'gay plays' in 1979, and Griffiths went on to create successful and entertaining gay-oriented works for commercial television and commercial radio. John OSBORNE mentions Sweatshop (from the corner of his mouth) in YOU'RE NOT WATCHING ME, MUMMY (1980 T) and also in his 1992 stage play DÉJÀ VU.

Gay Switchboard aka London Lesbian and Gay Switchboard. Invaluable lifeline for people in urban desperation or rural isolation.

In AGONY 'Coming Out ... And Going In Again' (1980 T) Michael (Peter Denyer) is recommended to ring Gay Switchboard with his problems, because he will be able to talk to other people like himself. In the original script he says: 'I don't like other gays. I just like Rob ... I tried Gay Switchboard before. It was 25 minutes before I realized I'd got a wrong number.' Because of a protest by one of the cast, this line was altered to: 'I can't ring Gay Switchboard. I *work* for them.' With a stroke of the pen, Michael went from first-time

client to Switchboard volunteer, working two nights a week. (A poster giving the telephone number was visible in many shots inside his and Rob's flat.)

In the very last episode, a young Australian (also played by Denyer) all alone in London is advised by someone who has guessed his special needs to ring up Switchboard: 'They'll only be too pleased to help.' Seven years later, Kristoffer Tabori asks his secretary to ring it in *The London Embassy* 'Charlie Hogle's Earring' (1987 T) to find a suitable venue for him to suss out a possible gay 'security risk'.

Gay Switchboard was set up in 1974 and soon became a respected and integral part of gay community life all over Britain and in many parts of the world. It 'never closed', the only 24-hour gay switchboard in the world to give out information and advice to gay people, heterosexual people with problems about gay people, the media and people undecided about their sexual orientation.

Steve, contemptuous of effeminacy, went to a Tom ROBINSON concert in the 1970s and saw a leaflet giving Switchboard's name. Through that initial contact, he joined a teenage gay support group (he was, of course, ineligible to have gay sex) and came out to his parents. He felt confident enough about his new life to appear on *Life Histories: Male Gays* for the OPEN UNIVERSITY in 1981.

T: *Inside Story* 'Coming Out' (1980); *Help!* (1984); *100%* 'I Am What I am' (1992); etc.

Similar telephone help and information services exist in many parts of Britain. Representatives appear quite regularly on regional television, eg on BBC Scotland in 1983 in *The Afternoon Show* 'John from Switchboard and Mrs Marjorie Cameron' (mother of lesbian journalist and activist Marsaili).

Gay Times Monthly magazine, a few of whose staff worked for GAY NEWS. It began in 1984 and now boasts confident writing, excellent design, an astonishing breadth of articles and reviews, and (until February 1993) a pithy, strikingly single-minded television critic in Jonathan Sanders. One of its journalists, Richard Smith is routinely asked for views on a range of topics: on 'Gay Murders' (1990 T *The London Programme*); on 'DOCTOR MARTENS' boots (1991 T *10×10*); on the gay music scene (1993 R PINKPOP); etc.

'gay' titles Films (all US unless otherwise indicated): THE GAY BROTHERS (1895); *The Great Gay Road* (UK 1920 & 1931); *The Gay Deceiver* (1926); *The Gay Old Bird* (1927); *The Gay Defender* (Richard Dix Western, 1927); *The Gay Retreat* (war comedy, 1927); *The Gay Adventurer* (Ger 1928); *In Gay Madrid* (with Ramon NOVARRO, 'much ado about a gay blade', 1930); *Let Us Be Gay* (1930); *The Gay Diplomat* (1931); *The Gay Caballero* (1932); *The Gay Buckaroo* (UK 1932); *The Gay Divorce/Divorcee* (1934); *The Gay Bride* (1934); *The Gay Deception* (1935); *The Gay Desperado* (1936); *The Gay Falcon* (1941); *The Gay Vagabond* (1941); *The Gay Caballero* (1942); *The Gay Sisters* (1942); *Gay Blades* (1942); *The Gay Mrs Trexel* (UK title for SUSAN AND GOD, 1942); *Our Hearts Were Young and Gay* (1944); *The Gay Senorita* (1945); *The Gay Cavalier* (1946, also TV series 1953); *The Gay Ranchero* (1948); *The Gay Intruders* (1948); *The Gay Lady* (US title for TROTTIE TRUE, 1949); *The Gay Adventure* (UK, 1953); *The Gay Dog* (UK 1954); *Gay Purr-ee* (1963); *Gaily, Gaily* (1969, retitled *Chicago, Chicago* in UK); THE GAY DECEIVERS (1969); ZORRO – THE GAY BLADE (1981).

Radio (all UK): *Grave and Gay* (Sandy Macpherson at the organ, 1942); *The Nights Were Gay* (Ranelagh House and Gardens, 1942); *The Bugginses Go Gay* (1942); *Gay and Sentimental* (music to suit all moods, 1943); *He Was Born Gay* (Emlyn WILLIAMS' play about Louis XV's son, with Alec Guinness, 1946); adaptation of Malcolm Saville's *The Gay Dolphin Adventure* (1946).

On television the word was often used as a subtitle; eg a gay musical, a gay comedy. It was almost never used for a main title or even a sub-title although *The Gay Cavalier* (1953) was an exception.

See also GAY DIVERSION.

Gee, Dustin (1942–86) English television actor, comedian and impersonator with manic energy and lugubrious voice. He played the DJ in ROCK FOLLIES 'The Road' (1976), and was featured in *Who Do You Do?* (1977–80) and *Russ Abbott's Madhouse* (1981–2). He had a one-off solo *Success* (1983) before teaming up with Les Dennis on *Go For It* (1984), *The Laughter Show* (1984–5) and *The Royal Variety Performance* (1984).

One of the highlights of *The Laughter Show* (which unsuccessfully tried to launch a new JULIAN AND SANDY called ROG AND RUDI) was Gee impersonating Larry GRAYSON – 'His cream horns are the talk of Lewisham' – as the 'real' one saunters on stage: 'Why do you stand like that? There's not many of us left.' 'When you're 39, you'll find yourself going limp.' The show's closing credits feature a young blonde woman on a beach watching TV. Dennis and Gee come along, grab the set and walk off – together.

Gee, Officer Krupke! Russ Tamblyn as Riff, leader of the Jets razzes psychiatry and sociology in WEST SIDE STORY (music: Leonard BERNSTEIN; Lyrics: Stephen SONDHEIM). Riff's sister apparently wears a moustache while his brother wears a dress: 'Goodness gracious, That's why I'm a mess!' The song, addressed to a neighbourhood cop, contains one of the most widely felt, if not always directly expressed, lesbian/gay sentiments inculcated after years of parenting, siblinghood, religion, education, entertainment and policing: 'Deep down inside him, he's *no good*!'

Gems (UK 1984–7 T) Set in Covent Garden, this is one of the few afternoon soaps to realistically portray a working situation (a small fashion house).
Cr: Tessa Diamond; P: Brenda Ennis and others; D: Mervyn Cumming and others.

Not much happens, and the main gay Paul Currie (William Armstrong), the brilliant, workaholic, frequently morose pattern cutter, develops only fitfully. Paul's hand-holding with his yuppie boyfriend over the dining table in 1985 provoked the wrath of Mary WHITE-HOUSE'S National Viewers' and Listeners' Association.

gender bender An expression used in the heyday of androgynous pop stars BOY GEORGE and Marilyn: SOUTH OF WATFORD (1984) wherein 'Dennis of Gravesend was seen purchasing a blouse from Top Shop' and others whom Ben Elton assured the audience were 'all heterosexuals who are simply rebelling against the strictures of role-play'.

gender polarity 'The barrage of advertising, mass circulation journals, our job and work structure and education still condition our traditional gender roles ... Man still gets the woman. The parents still own the children ... Gender polarity is deeply and totally ingrained in our culture and is completely unnatural.' But John Chesterman was merely echoing in ACCESS 'Offensive to Some' (1973 R) what Dr Robert Briffault had said on BBC radio in 1931 in MARRIAGE: PAST AND PRESENT 'The Origins of Patriarchal Marriage' and 'The Business Side of Marriage'.

gender switching Topsy-turvy gender rule in A FLORIDA ENCHANTMENT (1914 C); *Just Imagine* (1930 C); *The Warrior's Husband* (1933 C); TURNABOUT (1940 C); the number 'If Men Played Cards As Women Do' in *Star Spangled Rhythm* (1943 C); a brief flash of Judy Holliday, Jean Hagen and Tom Ewell swopping sexes in ADAM'S RIB (1949 C); a conscious attempt to walk in others' shoes in *The Lifeswappers* (1976 T); *All That Glitters* (1977 T). In the post-feminist Sweden of *Take It Like a Man, Ma'am* (1975 C) women are the workers, men the housekeepers and secretaries; it is the men who are preoccupied with clothes, cosmetics and gossip. Husband

stays home while wife takes a job in *Wait Till Your Mother Gets Home* (1983 T). Men look after babies in *Mr Mom* (1983 C); *Three Men and a Baby* (1987 C); *Three Men and a Little Lady* (1990 C); etc.

Too often the situation is merely one of laughing at people wearing clothes that 'belong' to the opposite gender: the joke soon runs out of steam. *The Two Ronnies* featured, in 1980, a serial called 'The Worm Must Turn': Betty, Janet, Susan, Cheryl and Judith are all men, whereas Brian, Jack and Cyril are women, or rather, girls. Ronnie Barker told a RADIO TIMES interviewer: 'We'll try to tread gently round the mines, of course, but they take objection to anything men do, don't they, feminists? They could pick on every line because the whole thing's "sexist". But that's true of every line in every sketch we do.'

Genet, Jean (1910–86) French novelist, playwright, poet and – once only – UN CHANT D'AMOUR (1950) – a film-maker. Seemingly coarse-grained and implacable, he starts from the bedrock of pitiless honesty and creates astonishing lyricism. His influence is palpable in such films as FORTUNE AND MEN'S EYES (1971); *Pink Narcissus* (1971); *L'Homme de Désir* (1970); *Halteroflic* (1983); *Jean Genet Is Dead* (1987); POISON (1991).

The showing of ARENA's 'Saint Genet' prompted RADIO TIMES to invite lesbian feminist Alison HENNEGAN to pen an article on Genet's significance and purpose as a man, a criminal and an artist: 'Those who determine categories – criminal, pervert, saint, sinner, alien, effeminate, traitor, insane – have power over the categorised ... Genet, implacable opponent of the bourgeois, *petit* or *gros*, is a man who believed that the two fallacious categories of masculine and feminine were innately hostile to all homosexual men and all women. And that sexism was racism's mirror image.' Filmed a year before his death, Genet is courteously mischievous, inviting the silent, faceless camera crew to revolt.

Adaptations of his works: *The Balcony* (1963 C; 1964 R); *The Maids* (1963 &

1974 R); *Deathwatch* (1966 C); QUER-ELLE (1982 C).

Biography: *Les Equilibristes* (1992 C) with Michel Piccoli as 'a Genet figure'.

genetics Robert Kelvin (Leo McKern) speaks about his louche cousin at a dinner party in David Mercer's *On the Eve of Publication* (1968 T): 'His father was a miner, lost a leg in the war. Charlie was a plump, SENSITIVE lad. At 16, he already looked like a middle-aged QUEEN. From his father's point of view, Charlie was provocative. I mean, Charlie hated their poverty ... their vulgarity ... and cultivated a passion for *art nouveau* and various other cultural quirks. You couldn't exactly say Charlie fitted in with life around there ... Charlie's bent for beautiful and delicate things must have been pretty staunch to survive the environment. Who knows how it started. The grammar school? Some sinister friend, some ageing Nottingham pouf picked up in an art gallery? For the time and the place, young Charlie was a sociological absurdity. What extraordinary genetic mutation had taken place in Charlie's mother's womb?'

EMORY (Cliff Gorman) in THE BOYS IN THE BAND (1970 C) spoke for untold millions when he said: 'I've known what I was since I was 4 years old.'

The Gentle Touch (UK 1980–4 T) Some cases of a tough woman police officer, Maggie Forbes (Jill Gascoine). A number featured (patchily developed) gay/lesbian themes, but never among Maggie's colleagues. The first series was particularly rough and ready, with three sensationalist homosexual storylines: blackmail and murder, prostitution and murder, psycho-lesbianism and grievous bodily harm. The 1982 series posited a kinder, more caring central character, and a kind, caring episode about lesbians and euthanasia. By 1984, gays were taking the law into their own hands in a particularly violent way; or they were smooth-tongued art world crims. All in all, not good community policing.

Cr: Terence Feely and Brian Finch; P:

Tony Wharmby and Jack Williams; LWT; 60 mins.

'Blade' (1980). Wrung-out doctor Richard Thorne (Kenneth Gilbert) is being held over a barrel by an ex-guardsman called Biggles who has some letters and photographs taken in a garden. A body is found on a tube train and the police investigate the sordid homosexual underworld.

'Melody' (1980). A group of prostitutes hinder the police when one of their number is murdered. Two of them, Letty (Brigitte Kahn) and Georgie (Vikki Richards), form a lesbian couple – one dressed in leather, with cuffs and LULU bangs.

'Hammer' (1980). Shirley Davies (Leslie Manville) is under the influence of the older Frances West alias 'Fancy' alias 'Hammer' (Rosalind Ayres), who robs and beats people (with a hammer) in a variety of disguises. She becomes the woman's driver, but jealousy intrudes when Maureen (Leslie Ash) wants to live with Shirley. After killing an elderly patient 'Hammer' is pushed through a plate glass window and badly injured.

'Doubt' (1981). Unbalanced by the serious injury to his young lodger – a policeman – while rescuing a woman police officer from thugs, a police physical training instructor (David Daker) kidnaps the woman's teenage son. A plot strong on pregnant silences and long, lingering looks from the older man to the younger (who is not gay).

'Solution' (1982). Clare (Sheila White), a strong-willed woman with leukaemia, demands that her lover Jean (Fiona Walker) helps end her life. Police comments on this 12-year relationship range from loosely tolerant to aggressively uncomprehending. Jean goes to the police to confess, but Clare hasn't taken the tablets.

'Auctions' (1982). Nasty Piers Roberts (Geoffrey BURRIDGE) is up to no good at the art gallery where he works; in cahoots are fellow gays Lucius Sharkey (Peter Cellier) and Nicholas Finnerman (Bernard Kay).

'Do It Yourself' (1984). Maggie's HAIRDRESSER Toby (Brian Capron) has been bashed – by AGENTS PROVOCATEURS, he says, 'safer than muggers'; a mentally retarded man is harassed by people on the housing estate (led by Dudley Sutton).

Geoffrey Boy's name, often used for rather diffuse men:

UK: Geoff (Hugh Williams), bounderish in *Bank Holiday* (1938 C); Geoffrey Levett (Donald Sinden), rather phlegmatic hero of *Tiger in the Smoke* (1956 C); Dr Geoffrey Brent (Ian Hendry), the over-idealistic *Police Surgeon* (1960 T); Geoffrey (Murray Head), Hywel Bennett's randy brother in THE FAMILY WAY (1966 C); ex-submarine commander Geoffrey (Richard Johnson) in *Twist of Sand* (1968 C); Geoffrey (Richard Beckinsale), Beryl's boyfriend anxious to have sex in *The Lovers* (1970–4 T; 1973 C); pilot Geoffrey Richter-Douglas (Michael York) in *Zeppelin* (1971 C); film star's son Geoffrey Pastmaster (John Rye) in *Send Up* (1976 R); Geoffrey (Douglas Hodge) in *Sorry!* 'Every Clown Wants to Play Hamlet' (1987 T); Geoffrey, vicar husband of Maggie Smith in TALKING HEADS 'A Bed Among the Lentils' (1988 T); Geoff Hatfield (Geoffrey BAYLDON), the comfy-cosy chemist in *All Creatures Great and Small* 'And Sheep May Safely Graze' (1989 T).

US: Mainly spelled Jeff as in Jeffrey or Jefferson (eg Jeff Colby in DYNASTY). Those with 'G' usually reprobates: Geoffrey Spaulding (Groucho Marx) in *Animal Crackers* (1930 C); or gay: Glynis Johns' companion-husband Geoffrey Harmish (John Dehner) in *The Chapman Report* (1962 C); Geoffrey Lane (René AUBERJONOIS) in THE LOST LANGUAGE OF CRANES (1992 T); or mad and bad: Geoffrey (Humphrey Bogart), the unsuccessful artist who has poisoned one wife and has plans for the second in *The Two Mrs Carrolls* (1947 C).

George (The Famous Five) *See* Georgina KIRRIN.

George, don't do that! Joyce Grenfell's admonition to one of her (unseen) charges from a 1940s monologue was frequently revived in the 1960s and 1970s on television. Julia McKenzie used it as a throwaway in a scene with

schoolchildren in *French Fields* (1990 T). No one has ever been able to discover what exactly it was George was doing, with whom or to whom – or whether one or both enjoyed it.

'Don't do that, Eccles, it's not nice,' censures Bluebottle in a 1958 GOON SHOW and, with that, topples the studio audience into near apoplexy.

Gerald Boy's name, favoured by dramatists for thin-blooded, ripply men.

US: Gerald Beresford Wicks (Errol Flynn) taken out of his feather-lined cocoon by woman reporter in *The Perfect Specimen* (1937 C); jewel thief Gerald Meldrick (Clark Gable) in *They Met in Bombay* (1941 C); secretary Gerald (Dan Tobin 1942 C; Anthony HOLLAND 1978 T); weak son Gerald Tetley (William Eythe) in *The Ox-Bow Incident* (1943 C); Dr Gerald Bayer (James Garner) in *The Thrill of It All* (1963 C); Gerald, one of the lost boys in *Bless The Beasts and Children* (1972 C); Gerald Howells (Thomas Wilson Brown), admirer of offbeat Dinky in *Welcome Home Roxy Carmichael* (1991 C).

UK: Nicky Edmett as Gerald, one half of a twosome in *The Other Side* (1967 T); Gerald Crich (Oliver Reed) in WOMEN IN LOVE (1969 C); inadequate, unmarried Gerald (Gerald Flood) in *Menace* 'Inheritance' (1970 T); grand queen Gerald Fox (Richard Pearson) in COMING OUT (1979 T); Gerald (Paul Herzberg), the available young waiter in *Dark Secret* (1981 T); Gerald (John Nettles) looking for a lost love in *Findings on a Late Afternoon* (1981 T); Gerald, unseen boyfriend of Simon, the psychiatrist in IT TAKES A WORRIED MAN (1981–4 T); Gerald Haxton (Barry Dennen) in A WEEKEND WITH WILLIE (1981 R); business whizz's dependable right-hand man Gerald URQUHART (Ivor Danvers) in HOWARDS' WAY (1986–90 T); Gerald Arbuthnot (Dominic Letts) in *A Woman of No Importance* (1991 R); Gerald Beamish (Royce Mills) in *A Glass of Blessings* (1991 R); Gerald (Malcolm Sinclair) in *Now That It's Morning* (1992 T); Julie Walters' TRANSVESTITE husband (Adrian Pasdar) in *Just Like a*

Woman (1992 C); Gerald Middleton (Richard Johnson), a scholar with a gay son in *Anglo-Saxon Attitudes* (1992 T).

Gorilla and his male human lover in *Not the Nine O'Clock News* (1981 T):

'Gerald, do you have a mate?'
'Raymond next door.'
'You didn't tell me you were friendly with Raymond.'
'Do I have to tell you everything?'

(Gerards are usually more uniformly heterosexual; eg the tall, dark and handsome hero (Sky Dumont) in *Love with a Perfect Stranger* (1990 T).)

Gertrude Stein and a Companion (UK 1985 R) Alice B. (Nastasha Morgan) and Gertrude (Miriam MARGOLYES), side by side in the Père Lachaise vault in 1967, remember how it was ... through rose-coloured spectacles.
W: Win Wells; based on the stage version by Sonia Fraser; P: Stewart Conn; 15.12.85; BBC Radio 3; 60 mins.

Neat and tidy, present and correct, rather Laura Ashley view of the constant couple. (A made for television (PBS) version appeared in 1986 with Marian Seldes and Linda Hunt as G. and A.)

Countess Anna **Geschwitz** FASHION DESIGNER who becomes enmeshed in LULU's erotic web. Her involvement leads her to being raped, becoming penniless and being killed alongside her beloved by JACK THE RIPPER.

In Frank Wedekind's original plays PANDORA'S BOX and EARTH SPIRIT (adapted by Peter Barnes as *Lulu* (1975 R)) Geschwitz (Dilys Laye) is a total loser, full of self-loathing. This characterization is also adopted in Alban Berg's opera, the third act of which (with Geschwitz openly declaring her love before she dies) was long suppressed by the composer's widow. It made its belated appearance with a 1981 Covent Garden production and was the subject of a SOUTH BANK SHOW ('Lulu's Last Act') with Jean Bailey. Other productions have included the full version in 1979 with Yvonne Minton as the unhappy noblewoman. This one

inspired Alan Blythe to write in RADIO TIMES (12.5.79): 'For all the sordid quality of the story – Lulu is also loved by the lesbian Countess Geschwitz – she is a character of consistent fascination.'

Lulu and Geschwitz are stabbed, Geschwitz inches her way across the floor towards her beloved but dies before she can touch her. Her last words are: 'Lulu, my angel. Let me see you once more. I'm near you. Always near you, in eternity.'

Jean Bailey's Geschwitz in 'Lulu's Last Act' is young, attractive, elegantly clad in a simple black dress. Her appearance is at variance with the now dishevelled Lulu, her hair turned white and hunting for clients on the streets of east London. Geschwitz decides she will go back to Germany: 'I'll go to university. I'll fight for women's rights.' But Lulu brings home a morose stranger. She introduces Geschwitz as her mad sister, but he is not fooled:'That's not your sister. She's in love with you, poor bitch.'

G. W. Pabst's silent version of Lulu's rise and fall, PANDORA'S BOX (1928 C), saw Geschwitz as 'an artist'. Her first appearance had her in trilby and tuxedo, smoking a cigar. She can't keep her eyes off the sprite Lulu and offers to design the costumes she will wear in her trapeze act. She is noticeably slimmer when she comes to the circus to congratulate Lulu: now in a satin cocktail dress, proffering a bunch of flowers.

At Lulu's wedding, Geschwitz – in stylish satin again – dances with Lulu in her bridal gown. Her new husband cuts in. A man asks Geschwitz to dance but she refuses. Geschwitz almost kisses Lulu, gives her shoulder a squeeze instead, and rushes away distraught.

Geschwitz's next and final scene comes on board a gambling ship. Now wearing a tweed coat over a COLLAR AND TIE, she performs one more generous act. She agrees to have sex with a man to give Lulu breathing space to elude her pursuers.

Alice Roberts, the Belgian actress who played Geschwitz, refused to do anything remotely approaching a love scene with Louise BROOKS, who played Lulu.

Most of her close-ups (gazing liltingly at Lulu) were wrung out of her by the director 'playing Lulu' off-camera. The total effect was that 'she looked like a very repressed lesbian who was hiding'.

Louise Brooks discussed her relationship with Alice Roberts in a BBCTV programme shortly before her death: 'Alice Roberts ... was a friend of the man who put up some of the money ... she was Belgian and she spoke just enough English to insult me.'

Get Down On It Disco number, a sort of crude version of 'RELAX', played in the empty Danish disco where Patrick works in *Friends Forever* (1987 C). He sings the refrain half hoping that his best mate Kristian will get the message. Kristian picks up other messages (from girls and women), but luckily Patrick meets a husky FOOTBALLER. Later in the film we see Patrick indeed getting down on it, with the footballer – until rudely interrupted by Kristian.

Get Happy A volcano eruption of energy from Judy GARLAND in the final number from *Summer Stock/If You Feel Like Singing* (1950 C). Clad in a man's dinner jacket, fishnet tights and black slouch hat, this is Garland (resounding to words and music by Harold Arlen) at her most exhilarating. The bisexual 'Get Happy' look has appeared in all sorts of locations since: a woman at a fancy-dress party (Bunny Brooke) in the movie version of NUMBER 96 (1974; Don, the gay character, came as Pierrot); an impersonator (Caleb Stonn) in *Saturday Night at the Baths* (1975 C); a lesbian in *May We Borrow Your Husband?* (1986 T); a man pretending to be gay (Cock, played by Philip Davis, to get out of the armed forces) in *Submariners* (1983 T). Most incongruously, Leland sings the song in *Twin Peaks* (1990 T), then collapses: 'Get ready for the judgement day.'

get you This is what Andrée Melly says to Tony Hancock as he tries to pick her up at the palais in *Hancock's Half Hour* 'The Marriage' (1955 R). 'Get you for a

Communist buttercup,' Charlie chirps to Harry in STAIRCASE (1969 C). The hero of *Badger by Owl-Light* (1975 R) baits David (John McAndrew): 'Gay Lib strikes again'; to which the palely loitering, shy young queen responds: 'Get you!' (Partridge in his *Dictionary of Slang and Unconventional English* dates this phrase back over a century, meaning 'Now I know' or 'I've guessed it'.)

When Barrett (Dirk BOGARDE) violently abuses a group of teenage girls outside a telephone kiosk in *The Servant* (1963 C), their response is a fairly light-hearted, though stunned 'Get him!'

getting into bed with A business term for a partnership of some kind; it became roaringly popular in the late 1970s. Arthur Daley (George Cole) uses it in *Minder* 'Citizen Cain' (1983 T), but qualifies it hurriedly by saying: 'in the business sense, of course.' Even ultra-conservative Queensland premier Joh Bjelke Petersen took up the phrase in 1988.

The Gulf War created many openings for the phrase. Professor Paul Wilkinson of St Andrews University, Scotland, commenting on the mortar attack on 10 Downing Street on 7 February 1991, said: 'The IRA don't want to risk their support base in the United States ... by being seen to be in bed with Saddam' (Aust, *Daybreak* R). The next day it was used about another ruthless dictator, Assad of Syria, 'who has committed just the same atrocities against his own people, but we are now in bed with him' (Aust, *Late Night Live*).

Film producer David Puttnam talks of 'climbing into the bath with' (film-makers and businessmen/corporations) three times on THE SOUTH BANK SHOW (1987 T).

getting married Psychiatrist to patient: 'You must get MARRIED. Once you get married, it's CURED' (*Open Line*, 'Gay Society', 5.4.78, Capital Radio, with the Capital Doctor and Anna Raeburn).

The Getting of Wisdom (Aust 1977 C) Girls' school life at turn of the 20th

century in Melbourne. Laura (Susannah Fowle) falls for the beautiful Isabella Shepherd (Julia Blake) in a passing phase. A fat ugly lesbian is taunted and leaves. Daughter of PICNIC AT HANGING ROCK and altogether more satisfying.
W: Eleanor Whitcombe from the novel by Henry Handel Richardson; P: Phillip Adams; D: Bruce Beresford; 101 mins.

ghosts Gerald (Nicholas Edmett) falls off a motor bike outside the garden gate of a medium (Beryl REID); she assumes he's dead and so does his boyfriend Maurice (Kenneth Farrington) in *The Other Side* (1967 T). Philip Latham is haunted by Malcolm (Robert Powell) in *Is Nellie Dead?* (1968 T). *See also* DEAD PEOPLE.

Ghost Trains (Aust 1986 R) Does Eve (Merin Canning) love Max (William Fox)? Or does Jack (Paul English) love Max? Does Max really exist? Delicious ghost story with a *Last Year in Marienbad* solemnity and series of puzzlements transferred to a Melbourne fun park.
W: Joanna Murray-Smith and Raymond Gill; P: John Hannaford; ABC; 60 mins.

Giannaris, Constantine (196?–) Greek-British film director of dry voluptuousness who appears in *Jean Genet Is Dead* (1987 T), a personal view of love; *Disco's Revenge* (1989 C), the impact of gay culture on popular music; *Trojans* (1989 C), about Constantine CAVAFY; *A Matter of Life and Death* (1990 T), the impact of AIDS and death on a gay man; *A Desperate Vitality* (1990 T), the film world of PASOLINI; NORTH OF VORTEX (1991 C); CAUGHT LOOKING (1991 T); OUT (1992 T); *Exiles of Love* (1992); etc.

Giant of Cerne A huge hill figure, 180 feet tall, carrying a 125-foot-high club and a 30-foot erect penis. He could be the Saxon god, Heil (the equivalent of the Roman Hercules), or he could be prehistoric. Protected by the National Trust, the Cerne Abbas Giant is next door to Cerne Abbey which was founded to fight the pagan religion.
Ralph Wightman in a 1946 BBC

Home Service talk was prevented from discussing the priapic figure's most obvious attribute. Instead he had to content himself with saying: 'If any couple lived within sight of him they were said to be blessed with children.' The *Listener* printed the text, together with a photograph taken at an angle which completely emasculated the giant.

Gide, André (1869–1951) French novelist, diarist and playwright (*The Immoralist* etc). His homoerotic work has still not found adequate sound or vision translation, apart from his modern satyr play *Prometheus Mismatched* (1987 R). *Tears in the Wind* from his SYMPHONIE PASTORALE with Joan Greenwood and André Morell (the first ARMCHAIR THEATRE 1956 T); *The Novels of André Gide* (1948 R) with George D. Painter; *Modern French Writers* (1982 R).

Gielgud, Sir John (1904–) English actor and director with a bony, supple frame and voice of warm pink alabaster. A genius of sensitivity and control, illuminating greatness or rubbish (of which he has had his portion).
C: 52 films including *Who Is the Man?* (1924); *The Clue of the New Pin* (1929); *Insult* (1932); *The Secret Agent* (1936); *Julius Caesar* (as Cassius, 1953; as Caesar, 1970); the Ghost in *Hamlet* (also directed, 1964); *The Loved One* (1965); *Murder on the Orient Express* (1974); *Providence* (1977); *Joseph Andrews* (1977); *The Conductor* (1980); the butler in *Arthur* (1980); blackmailing Uncle Willie in *Scandalous* (1984); *Prospero's Books* (1991); *The Power of One* (1992). Projects included 'Hamlet', 'Nijinsky' and 'The Tempest'; he was proposed for the 1930 MGM production of *Romeo and Juliet*.
R: title role in *Hamlet* (1932); title role in *Richard II* (1936 & 1961); John WORTHING in THE IMPORTANCE OF BEING EARNEST (1951, and *The 'Lost Scene'* with Rex Harrison 1954); HOLMES in *The Adventures of Sherlock Holmes* (1954) with Ralph Richardson; in the A. E. HOUSMAN biography *The Frontier of Darkness* (1954); Gary in *Present Laughter* (1956);

Crocker-Harris in *The Browning Version* (1957); title role in *Ivanov* (1967); repressed aesthete Lewis Luby in MR LUBY'S FEAR OF HEAVEN (1976); *As We Were* (1989); *The Bible* 'Genesis' (1991); the Ghost in *Hamlet* (1992); etc.

T: Crocker-Harris in *The Browning Version* (1959); *A Day by the Sea* (1959); *The Ages of Man* (1966); the Mock Turtle in *Alice* (1966); millionaire Gabriel Quantara in *The Mayfly and the Frog* (1967); the Inquisitor in *Saint Joan* (1968); the Ghost in *Hamlet* (1971); Harry in *Home* (1971); Henry Wootton in THE PICTURE OF DORIAN GRAY; Spooner in *No Man's Land* (1978); *Tales of the Unexpected* 'Neck' (1979) and 'Parson's Pleasure' (1980); *The Seven Dials Mystery* (1981); Charles Ryder's father in BRIDESHEAD REVISITED (1981); as 'himself' on *Spitting Image* (1983–6); Jasper Swift in *Time After Time* (1986); Tiresias in *The Theban Plays* 'Oedipus the King' and 'Oedipus at Colonus' (1986); Eddie Loomis in *Quartermaine's Terms* (1987); Close Up (1988); *Six Centuries of Verse* (1989); Jewish concentration camp victim in *War and Remembrance* (1989); journalist and rake Haverford Downs in *Summer's Lease* (1989); *Queen Mother's 90th Birthday* (1990); *The Best of Friends* (1991).

Biography: *Great Acting* (1966 T); *John Gielgud* (1969 R); *Gielgud and Richardson* (1976 R); *An Actor Remembers* (1977 R); reads from his autobiography *Backward Glances* (1989 R); *John Gielgud Looks Back* with students at RADA (1993 T).

Has been indefatigable in contributing to the celebration of other artists. Just a small sample: THIS IS YOUR LIFE 'Dame Sybil Thorndike' (1959 T); *This Is Noel COWARD* (1972 T); *The Faces of MAUGHAM* (1974 T); *Ingrid* [Bergman] (1984); *Death or a Kind Gentleman* (1991 R) about Micheal MACLIAMMOIR.

'I call him my fairy godfather,' commented Sir John's faithful dresser in *Mac: Memories of a Theatrical Dresser* (1971 R).

Gigi (US 1958 C) Young girl prepared for the marriage market.

W: Alan J. Lerner and Frederick Loewe from the novel by COLETTE; P: Arthur Freed; D: Vincente Minnelli; 116 mins.

Gigi lives in an unusual family – mother, grandmother and aunt all lived off immoral earnings and invested wisely. A family who 'instead of getting married at once … it sometimes happens that they get married at last'. The film's scandalous, superficial charm is topped and tailed by the character of Honoré Lachaille – introduced into Colette's screenplay for the non-musical 1949 film version – a roué permanently aroused by 'little girls who grow up in the most delightful ways'.

Minnelli and designer Cecil BEATON created a *mise en scène* of unparalleled opulence which all but crushes the slender story: the Musée Jacquemart-André, the Palais de Glace, Maxim's, the Bois de Boulogne, the beach at Trouville, the caricatures of SEM, the photographs of Henri Lartigue, the studies of parks and gardens by Eugène Atget, the paintings of Manet, Jean Beraud, Constantin Guys and Eugène Boudin, the Art Nouveau interior design of Hector Guimard. Beautiful, lush, decadent and *très, très de trop*.

gigolos Presented, from the days of silent films, as drones in spats with plastered-down hair and lavender-water eyes. The image, personified in his early pictures by Rudolph VALENTINO, has stuck. This is despite physical evidence – Richard Gere in *American Gigolo* (1980 C); 40 MINUTES 'Gigolo' (1984 T); DONAHUE (1989 T) – that men who escort women and go to bed with them for money are as unlike the lounge lizard as can be. Michel (Jean-Paul Belmondo), admiring his *jolie laide* self in the mirror in *Breathless* (1960 C), briefly considers having sex professionally. David BOWIE, down and out after the Second World War, is taken up by a Baroness and others in *Just a Gigolo* (1979 C).

From this evidence, these men are impeccably tailored, socially confident and able – they say – to divine what a woman needs. However, they are always quick to point out that they would never sleep with a man, never would, never have. As JULIAN (Richard Gere) in *American Gigolo* says: 'I don't do fags.' When Warren Beatty steps out of line in *The Roman Spring of Mrs Stone* (1961 C), his pimp (Lotte LENYA) gestures to an old ruin of an aristocrat waiting in the corridor. If the sulky boy doesn't pull up his socks, he will suffer the consequences with a new type of clientele.

There is some euphemistic linkage between a gay man and gigolo, no matter how heterosexual the practitioners of *de luxe* male prostitution insist they are. Madame Kosneyetsova certainly smelt a rat when she explained to Olga Franklin in WOMAN'S HOUR (1979 R) the terrible social problem that 'kept men' were creating for Soviet society. She began by quoting the latest census figure of '1 million gigolos'.

Against this, there are '20 million lonely hearts in the Soviet Union, mostly women between 20 and 40'. Why do these women have to pay for sex and companionship? 'Because,' said Franklin, 'there is a serious shortage of men ... the divorce rate is the highest in the world ... there are no marriage guidance councils ... there's no one to advise them.' Madame Kosneyetsova, in common with moralists of all political persuasions, would rather blame the suppliers than the buyers.

'These KEPT MEN are not men at all ... They are weaklings, slobs, spoilt by adoring mothers ... sometimes they keep a bearskin on the bed to try and look manly.' The gigolo problem has Russia beside itself. What about the future? The state needs babies. Grandmothers want babies. They quoted one gigolo as saying he didn't want to marry 'because I would get no proper sleep – I need my eight hours' sleep at night.'

More than a decade later, it would be interesting to look at the census figures to find out if some of those 'gigolos' may now be registering (law reform permitting) as gays.

See also PROSTITUTES.

Gilbert Boy's name with nerdish, inconsequential, string-vest associations.

US: Gilbert Gaylord (Hugh Huntley), the former lover in *Second Wife* (1930 C); Gilbert Gordon (Bing Crosby), playwright in *Two for Tonight* (1935 C); Gilbert Young (James Stewart) in *Ziegfeld Girl* (1941 C); Gilbert Wooley (Jerry Lewis), unsuccessful magician in *The Geisha Boy* (1958 C); 'geeky' Gilbert, 'the only guy who ever got to break his leg playing chess' in *Revenge of the Nerds – Nerds in Paradise* (1987 C).

UK: Gilbert Fordyce (John Stuart), the hero of HITCHOCK's *Number Seventeen* (1932 C); Gilbert (Michael REDGRAVE), collector of folk songs in *The Lady Vanishes* (1938 C); Gilbert Osmond (Alan WHEATLEY), profound egotist, detached in *The Portrait of a Lady* (1952 R); Ralph Michael, harried by inner voices and sexual guilt in *The Ordeal of Gilbert Pinfold* (1960 R); fussy fish shop owner Gilbert Garnish (Reginald BECKWITH) in *Wet Fish* (1961 T); Gilbert Paish (Noel DAVIS) whose partner in a BOUTIQUE has been murdered in *No Hiding Place* 'Golden Boy' (1966 T); Gilbert Cohen (Peter Welch) who never misses a first night at Covent Garden and is very fond of his mother in THE DALES (1967–9 R); Gilbert (James Culliford), sea wife to Charlie (Peter Kerrigan) in THE PUNCHY AND THE FAIRY (1973 T); Gilberto (Gerard Murphy), Brazilian bisexual artist in FACING THE SUN (1980 T); Gilbert Sage (Norman Rodway) denying love in *Death in Trieste* (1981 R): 'I don't do it. I'm afraid ... a pedagogue in the shadows'; Gilbert Chilvers (Michael Palin), impoverished chiropodist, forced into pignapping in *A Private Function* (1984 C); Gilbert (Christopher Emyard), owner of THE CORNER HOUSE (1987 T); Gilbert Colville (John HURT) who has gone bush in *White Mischief* (1988 C); Gilbert Herring (Robert Gillespie) in *Bonjour la Classe* (1993 T).

Gilbert, W. Stephen (1947–) English producer (ONLY CONNECT; CONNIE; *King of the Ghetto*), writer (the television play CIRCLE LINE; the novel SPIKED 1991) and television critic (OBSERVER, INDEPENDENT). Plans to make Ian

McEwan's *Solid Geometry* for the BBC in 1979 were derailed; worse, he was sacked for speaking out against its cancellation. Although he did work for the Corporation six years later, the resulting series did not lead to his well-deserved renaissance. He will rise again.

'Any number of vicars "who are HIV positive" performing on CASUALTY don't add up to positive images of gays and lesbians. Until we again take our place in our culture as what we are, not what we're perceived to be, we shall remain second-class citizens' (CAPITAL GAY, 7.10.88).

Gilda (US 1946 C) Ballan Mundsen (George Macready), a ruthless tungsten tycoon, runs gambling casinos in Buenos Aires. Scarred, he wants to control the world but discovers he cannot even control his private world: his ex-lover Johnny Farrell (Glenn Ford) is lusting over his wife. Comes to a bad end with a harpoon.

W: Marion Parsonnet from a story by E. A. Ellington; P: Virginia Van Upp; D: Charles Vidor; 110 mins.

Untouchable FILM NOIR, *kitsch*, camp, homoeroticism, what you will. From George Macready one of the great etchings in pure spite and ice.

See also PUT THE BLAME ON MAME.

ginger/ginger beer Cockney rhyming slang for QUEER, abbreviated to ginger in STEPTOE AND SON (1972 C) etc. Biggles (Graham CHAPMAN) convinces himself that Ginger (Terry Gilliam) is not gay even though his flying gear is accented with sequins, his face covered in silver stars, his eyes shadowed and his name suggests rhyming slang (MONTY PYTHON'S FLYING CIRCUS 1972 T). Peter Beale (Peter Dean) is irritated by the amount of time Colin and Barry spend together in the Queen Vic (EASTENDERS 1987 T); he complains to Tony (Oscar James) that 'they'll be calling it the "Ginger Beer Queen Vic" soon'.

Gingold, Hermione (1897–1989) English actress, revue artist and eccentric with whacky appearance and spectral voice.

C: *The Pickwick Papers* (1952); GIGI (1958); BELL, BOOK AND CANDLE (1958); *The Naked Edge* (1961); deprived of her one song in *A Little Night Music* (1977); reduced to a freak in *Garbo Talks* (1984).

R: Kathleen Skinner in *Before the Party* (1930); *Consider Your Verdict* (1931); schoolgirl Grizel in *The Giddiest Girl in the College* (1937); etc.

T: during the 1950s: *The Ed Sullivan Show*, *The Jack Paar Show*, *Omnibus* and *Person to Person*; *The Assassination Plot at Teheran* (1961); Major Stella, a charity worker in *The Girl from UNCLE*; *The Name of the Game* 'The Low C Affair' (1967) and 'Aquarius Descending' (1969); Peggy Revere, head of secretarial school in *Banyon* (1970, taken over by Joan Blondell in 1971 series); irresistible as a guest in HOTEL 'Charades' (1983), where the voice is described as sandpaper and cream, giving full measure to the most mundane dialogue: 'It's *Felicity* here. Can I come up?'

Ginsberg, Allen (1926–) American poet. Ignored by academic critics, seen by some as bard and holy man to the beat generation and all that came after. He is said to have strongly influenced Bob Dylan. HOWL, written in 1956, became one of the cornerstones of American dissent. Ginsberg (played by Ron Rifkin) declaimed a tiny part of the work to the outraged judge in *Conspiracy: The Trial of the Chicago Eight* (1987 T). Its length, jagged rhythms and – then – impenetrable language were regularly satirized in mass entertainment during the 1950s and 1960s, eg HANCOCK'S HALF HOUR, *The Rebel* and *A Bucket of Blood*.

The Shape of My Mind (1960 R, with Peter Orlovsky), art–anti-art; *We Dissent – A Coast to Coast Impression of America in Doubt* (1960 T); *Americans: A Portrait in Verse* (1962 T); sketches set to poems by Ginsberg, Poe, Emerson and Cummings; *Allen Ginsberg* by the American poet R. M. L. Rosenthal (1968 R); EVERYMAN 'Where Have All The

Flowers Gone?' (1978 T), seen talking, meditating and playing piano; ARENA 'Burroughs' (1983 T); REBELS 'Jack Kerouac' (1987 R); ARENA 'What Happened to Kerouac?' (1988 T, with Gregory Corso, William BURROUGHS and Kerouac); *Arena* 'Broadway – The Great White Way' (1988 T, with George Abbot and Lena Horne); *New Music American Festival* (1989 R, with Laurie Anderson and the Kronos Quartet); declaiming an ode to his 'Sphincter' in Rosa VON PRAUNHEIM's *Positive* (1990 C/T); *Allen Ginsberg and His Art* (1990 T); *Without Walls* 'The Art of Tripping' (1993 T, with Burroughs) on creativity and drugs.

As actor: Father in Bob Dylan's *Renaldo and Clara* (1977 C).

Versions of himself played by Roddy MCDOWALL in *The Subterraneans* (1960 C), and by Ray Sharkey (as Ira Streiker) in *Heart Beat* (1979 C). Also represented in THE COMIC STRIP PRESENTS ... *'The Beat Generation'* (1983) and *Naked Lunch* (1992 C).

Girl Jean (Fiona Walker) listens to Lennon and McCartney's 'Girl' at the end of THE GENTLE TOUCH 'Solution' (1982 T). Her lover Clare (Sheila White) has just died of leukaemia. The song revives, and adds lustre to, memories of the hopes and dreams they shared when they fell in love in 1967, at the time that the RUBBER SOUL album was released. This is Jean's first night alone in the bed she and Clare shared for 14 years.

Girl (Second City Firsts) (UK 1974 T) Corporal Chrissie Harvey (Myra Francis) is a snaffler-up of young talent at the barracks. She has just ditched Jackie Smithers (Alison Steadman) and is on the lookout for some new diversion. She's a career officer, much of whose love of the armed forces derives from the fact that her part of it is entirely composed of women, through whom she works like a thresher.

W: James Robson; P: Barry Hanson; D: Peter Gill; 22.2.74. BBC2.

A right, tough little piece about a thoroughly motivated, organized woman who takes a raw recruit, beds her, moulds her and tosses her aside. At least that's the theory. Myra Francis suggests that just possibly Jackie has touched her somewhere beneath the skin. Excellent atmosphere, simple spare production and full-on electricity from Steadman and Francis.

'A frank play about the powerful love between two women. Surprisingly enough, it was at least frank with few holds barred when it came to the seduction of a new recruited dolly by a WRAC resident she-wolf. Of course, it turned out that the experience, however enjoyable, was morally worthless.' (GAY NEWS 71).

'Thank you BBC2 for having the insight and the courage to show the play' (letter, RADIO TIMES).

A Girl Is A Girl Is A Girl Honouring the spirit of G. STEIN, but sung in the locker room by young male athletes in *Billie* (1965 C), the story of a top athlete (Patty Duke) who is required to become feminine.

girls' names for boys The tradition of giving 'girl' names to boys only fell into disuse after the Second World War: every Norman name could be male or female and in the 20th century Carol, PATSY, Lucy, Ann, Caroline and EVELYN can be found in Britain and/or America as men's names.

Swapping 'girl' names for 'boy' names is the most popular way of labelling deviants. Some names have official approval for use by both genders, VIVIAN, for one. In a fictional context, this is a name much sought after by parents of homosexual males to be: Clive Francis in *Villain* (1971 C); the jaunty tattooist (Roland CURRAM) in *Ooh, You are Awful* (1972 C); the eponymous and ambiguous literary agent (Harold INNOCENT) in *Vivien the Blockbuster* (1980 R). The most un-Vivianish of all was the yobbish, snot-wiping member of *The Young Ones* (1982–4) played by Adrian Edmondson: Vyvyan, paranoid about poofterism.

Other gender-confusing names include:

Beverly: Beverly Carlton (Reginald Gardiner), a one-scene Noel COWARD take-off in *The Man Who Came to Dinner* (1941 C); Beverly Niveaux (Jeremy Irons) and his TWIN Elliot cutting up and entering women for a living in *Dead Ringers* (1988 C).

Evelyn Tremble (Peter SELLERS) in *Casino Royale* (1967 C).

Hazel Motes (Brad Dourif), disturbed grandson of a preacher who sets up a church in *Wise Blood* (1979 C).

HILARY/HILLARY: father (John Barrymore) of SIDNEY (Katharine HEPBURN) in *A Bill of Divorcement* (1932 C); flamboyant actor (Peter Bowles) who's written ever such an amusing play in *Rising Damp* 'Stage Struck' (1977 T); the husband in *A Little Bit of Lippy* (1992 T).

Hyacinth Robinson (Mark Ashton) in *The Princess Casamassima* (1988 R).

Jocelyn (Jerome Cowan) in *The West Point Story* (1950 C).

Marion: intellectual (bespectacled) soldier Marion (John Lupton) bullied in *Battle Cry* (1955 C); Marion Butnick (Jimmy Boyd), a GI mistaken for a WAVE in *Broadside* (1964–5 T).

Patty/Patsy: boxers called Patsy in *Raging Bull* (1980 C) and *The Set Up* (1992 R); neighbour Patsy in *Life Is Sweet* (1990 C); Father Patty Starr, the show biz priest with an 'Honest to God' show in TALES OF THE CITY (1993 T).

Then there are, to use Vyvyan's word, the girly nicknames. 'Matilda' (after 'Waltzing') is the Australian HAIRDRESSER who fixes false passports (Trader FAULKNER) in *Call Me Mister* 'Long Shot' (1986 T). He's a long way from Chips Rafferty: German cross EARRING, dyed reddish hair, lisp, sexual provocativeness and dead eyes. And 'Dolly' (Brian Deacon), the playmate of a career woman (Charlotte Cornwell) who decides, in his mid-thirties, to have a baby (*Only Children* 1984 T). Dolly is totally dependent: he sleeps in the same bed as the woman and her lover. His own emotional life is a disaster; he is

being constantly bilked out of money and possessions by hustlers and opportunists. And 'Flossie', the schoolboy, now married (and gay) in NIGHTINGALE'S BOYS, played by David Swift. The writer, Colin SPENCER, was horrified by the changes wrought upon his script (by the producer at GRANADA). These changes included the imposition of a female nickname on the boy.

Others bearing women's names, more or less proudly, were 'Gert' (Wallas Eaton), the hotelier's sharp-tongued factotum in *A Soirée at Bossoms Hotel* (1967 T); 'Susie' (Paul Angelis), the BARMAN in UNDER THE AGE (1972 T); Mafia hit man with a liking for herbal tea, wheat-germ loaves and s&m sex (with Sheree North), Molly (Joe Don Baker) in *Charley Varrick* (1973 C) – he doesn't seem to mind jokes about his name.

Evelyn WAUGH apparently loathed his first name after a reviewer of his first novel addressed him as a female. His brother Alec advised him to become more masculine in demeanour to compensate. Evelyn simply married again and reproduced. The BBC, unworried by the male Evelyns and Beverlys in the 1920s and 1930s, debarred its local, national and international newsreaders in the 1990s from using first names that might obscure the sex of the vocalizer and worry listeners. Therefore Terry Deapp had to become Elizabeth Deapp in 1991. This does not seem to have prevented male newsreaders called Peter from retaining their names in a world of Peters and Petas.

See also BOYS' NAMES FOR GIRLS.

give me homosexuality, without any deviation! Bill Harmon, one of the producers of NUMBER 96 in 1971 after writer David SALE, asked if he could include 'two homosexuals' among the regular characters, during the initial discussion of what proved to be one of the great television landmarks. Brash, gogetting, heterosexual Harmon becomes a fierce defender of Don, resisting any effort to 'turn him': 'That's the way he is. They don't have to change like that.'

(Sing If You're) Glad To Be Gay Tom ROBINSON sang the first version during Gay Pride Week in 1976, on television in THE LONDON WEEKEND SHOW in 1977, and on film, in *The Secret Police-man's Ball*, 'You don't have to be gay to sing this chorus but it helps' (1979 C), a line which was cut from the first television showing at the end of 1979. Became *the* gay song thereafter: on GAY LIFE; on *Monty at Large* (1978 R); on the 1978 STONEWALL march in Sydney in WITCHES AND FAGGOTS, DYKES AND POOFTERS (1979 C). It's also on the soundtrack of *Public School* (followed by 'YMCA', 1980 T) and CRYING OUT LOUD 'Gay Teenagers' (1982 T). Members of the Potteries Gay Community Association requested it in *People and Places* on Radio Stoke in 1982. It was referred to obliquely, in relation to a contestant, on *Style Trial* (1990 T) as 'Sing If You're Glad To Be *Bald*'. The song is periodically revised (eg on *Talk About Sex* 1992 R).

The Glass House (US 1972 T) Alan Alda is the PhD Professor on a man-slaughter charge, Billy Dee Williams the black leader, Clu Gulager the new prison officer, while Kristoffer Tabori is the youngster, Allan Campbell. Looming over them all is Vic Morrow as Hugo Slocum who can take his pick of the talent – and does. Campbell, raped over the gym's wooden horse, kills himself.
W: Tracy Keenan Wynn from a short story by Truman CAPOTE; D: Tom Gries; 73 mins.
   The first 'exposé' of PRISON conditions – including male RAPE – on US network television, providing a field day for Vic Morrow as the sleazy Mr Big: 'There are two things Hugo Slocum can't get. One's a helicopter, the other's a woman. He gives the boy a guitar. "Just relax. Nobody's gonna hurt y'a. With me around you got no worries . . . I like you, kid".'

GLC (Greater London Council) A huge, socially radical Labour stronghold which Margaret THATCHER's Tories vowed to abolish. Despite the personal popularity and high media presence of Leader Ken LIVINGSTONE, the campaign to save the GLC failed, doubtless not helped by its commitment to equal rights for lesbians and gays, encapsulated in its manifesto 'Changing the World'. The extreme posturings of supporters and detractors, together with some half-baked and ill-advised minority projects which the tabloid press seized upon to the detriment of much that was worthwhile, made the organization a natural target for comedy, eg STRUGGLE (1983 T) and THE COMIC STRIP PRESENTS . . . GLC (1990 T).

Glen or Glenda? aka *I Led Two Lives* aka *I Changed My Sex* aka *He Or She?* (US 1953) A 67-minute 'docu-fantasy'. Its writer–director, Edward D. Wood Jr, makes a personal statement about TRANSSEXUALS and TRANSVESTITES by starring (under the name Daniel Davis) as the young man who has a yen for his girlfriend's angora jumper. The film also tells the story of Alan ('Tommy' Haynes) who is a transsexual. The haste and incompletion work in the director's favour. For all its dafty Gothic trimmings and robotic acting, the film works less as a plea for understanding of transvestism and 'sex change', and more as a quirky entertainment with a bit of a kick.
   Poured over the story of Alan is a fascinating commentary (by the director) on the sartorial restrictions imposed on men: tight hat bands, no lounging pyjamas etc. Part political manifesto, part petulant display, part misogyny: 'At home, what does the modern man have to look forward to? Little Miss Female should feel proud of the soft hats that give no obstruction to the blood flow.' It is a hoot. Adding to the general lunacy, Bela Lugosi is inexplicably on hand to mutter a few imprecations and to give some teenagers a bit of an anti-sexism lecture.
   Unique, delirious and very sincere, *Glen or Glenda?* – though frequently mad and bad – was brave for its time and still holds audiences in hysterical thrall.

The Glittering Prizes (UK 1976 T)

One of a group of 1950s Cambridge students is Denis Porson (Nigel HAVERS), an exhibitionist Footlights actor, who is later sent to prison for 'GROSS INDECENCY'. He re-emerges in the mid-1960s running a chichi restaurant in Norfolk and still whooshing it up.

W: Frederic RAPHAEL; P: Mark Shivas; D: Waris HUSSEIN and Robert Knights; BBC2; 6 parts; 75 mins each.

Much discussed serial, one of the first to excavate this particular social group (the women as well as the men). The gay character is sparingly threaded through the rich pattern of heterosexual snarings and pairings. Luckily, Nigel Havers makes the most of his every savoury line, and the terrifying power of the law to smite the most adjusted of homosexual men is at least given a nod.

The Glums (UK 1953–8 R; 1979 T) A piss-take of the over-sweet roosting of the English Family Robinson and THE DALES, as well as a slanderous depiction of the working classes as drunks, sluggards and layabouts. Dennis Norden, who with Frank Muir, reworked these priceless scripts from *Take It From Here* for television in the late 1970s said: 'What we did was send up relationships between people, family relationships, things that were sacrosanct at the time' (quoted in David Nathan, *The Laughtermakers: Quest for Comedy*, 1978).

In the original setup, Jimmy EDWARDS was overbearing Mr Glum, Dick Bentley his near gaga son, and June Whitfield the long-suffering Eth, who is a cut above her 'beloved' and his dad. The television treatment with Ian Lavender and Patricia Brake as the young ones – who never quite manage to get married – retained Edwards' gloriously grotesque patriarch: possibly an abuser of both wife and child, sentimental, raucous, bullying, cajoling.

God Bless The Child Arthur Herzog–Billie Holiday classic sung by Pearl Bailey as Ruby in *All the Fine Young Cannibals* (1960 C). Ruby's been in alcoholic seclusion, and so very reluctantly and nervously sings for the patrons of a nightclub. At first she is hesitant, the voice rough-edged. Then she belts out the words at full strength. When the film is seen on the small screen, shorn of its Metroscope, Ruby looks for all the world as if she is directing the song at a table entirely occupied by rather smartly dressed, shy young men. The words – about people on the top of the heap meting out slender charity and empathy to those on the bottom – have particular resonance for homosexuals as well as for blacks, or any other edged-out group of people.

The song was used for some very up-market Manhattan-located adverts during the 1990s.

goddess Thirty-five thousand years of goddess worship replaced by religions extolling some human beings above others and all humans above other species and genera (in the 1989 Canadian documentary *Goddess Remembered* and in *Joseph Campbell* 'Love and the Goddess' 1989 T).

God help us and Oscar Wilde Charlie's recurring expression to cope with his flabby relationship and impending morals charge in STAIRCASE (1969 C).

God made Adam and Eve, not Adam and Steve A statement coined either by Anita Bryant or by one of her supporters in her anti-gay crusade (Save Our Children) in Florida during 1977–8. Frequently used to decry and demean gay partnerships, eg in *Living with AIDS* (1987 T).

God, was I drunk last night Described as a syndrome to explain away a homosexual incident in a supposedly heterosexual's life in THE BOYS IN THE BAND (1970 C). Twenty or so years on, Tony in *Night Out* uses this as some kind of explanation to his lover Steve for his COTTAGING and being bashed up; and in TOGETHER ALONE Bryan wonders if his being drunk could be the explanation for his indulging in unprotected sex.

This excuse seems to have been around for some while. In Tennessee

WILLIAMS' autobiographical VIEUX CARRE (1985 R) set in the 1930s, a young man (based firmly on the playwright) admits that he once had sex with a man, a paratrooper: 'I turned to him and said I loved him. Of course, I was drunk.'

golden boys *Golden Boy* was the title of Clifford Odets' Broadway play about an artistic young man who gives up his music to become a boxer – shorn of homosexual references in the 1939 film version. Employed in relation to a Russian man's gay son in *The Fourth Protocol* (1987 C): 'We can't tolerate the golden boys.' Also used as a way of working round Cole PORTER's sexual inclination in YOU'RE THE TOP (1991 T): he was surrounded by 'golden boys'.

The Golden Girls (US 1985–92 T) Bright, tangy character comedy created by SOAP's Susan Harris (for CBS) about three older women sharing a Florida apartment together with the savvy mother of one of them. Searing barbs and shafts of wit and wisdom cut through any threat of sentimentality and the cutes. Any amount of 'gay sensibility' in each and every episode, but only one or two gay and lesbian people are allowed into the plots (and then only for one episode). However, when they are there – principally Dorothy's 'widowed' friend Jean (Lois Nettleton) in 'Isn't It Romantic' (1987); Blanche's brother Clayton Hollingsworth (Monte Markham) and his cop lover in 'Sister of the Bride' (1989) – they are well proportioned and a credit to the nation. The series, hugely popular with gay men, was top of CAPITAL GAY's readers' poll 1987–92.

In 'Sister of the Bride' conservative (in *some* things) Blanche is predictably appalled when her brother arrives with his 'husband-to-be', Doug, a policeman. She eventually accepts the situation, welcoming the newcomer into the family. Blanche modifies her hostile attitude amid JOKES about Bette DAVIS, FRUIT cocktails and bending over backwards: 'I don't really mind Clayton

being homosexual. I just don't like him dating men.' A quilt of clichés, perhaps, but with an ultimate emphasis upon happiness, understanding, respect and love.

(Blanche, Rose (Betty White) and Dorothy's lethal weapon of a mother, Sophia (Estelle Getty) have moved their scratchy but loving cohabitation smoothly on to another series *The Golden Palace*, upon the departure of Bea Arthur who played the towering inferno, Dorothy.)

golfers 'Lady ones depicted as stentorian Amazons' in 'The Lady Golfer' (1933 R), a sports talk by Joyce Wethered, and by 'Frank' Hickson one of THE THREE FAT WOMEN OF ANTIBES (1960 T).

The Goodies (UK 1970–81 T) Crazy children's comedy series written by its stars Bill Oddie, Graeme Garden and Tim Brooke-Taylor who play the inseparable (from infancy) unmarried friends. Lots of effeminacy gags, mainly around 'Tim'; some good satire, too.

In one episode, Clean Up TV personage Desirée Carthorse (Beryl REID) asks the Goodies to make a programme about sex which must neither show nor mention the filthy disgusting stuff. In response to the result (violence but no sex), the BBC heads for horror and every type of bone-crunching, bloodletting excess. In 'Frankenfido' Graeme Garden tries to breed bizarre dogs, but through a rather serious error ends up with a highly strung, 'sensitive' giant codfish, who is called a 'poof' by the others. Matters get out of hand, creatures multiply. Only one thing can destroy the monsters: Max Bygraves singing 'Tulips From Amsterdam'.

good in bed A very important but rather ill-defined concept of sexual adequacy veering towards Olympian heights, with a definite thumbs down for anyone who is 'bad' in the sack. 'Yes, you're good,' says Patricia (Jean Seberg) to Michel (Jean-Paul Belmondo) in *Breathless/A*

Bout de Souffle (1960 C) at his prompting.

Among those who didn't hit the mark: the scientist (Nicholas Le Prevost, playing a character based on Alan TURING) in *The Imitation Game* (1980 T). His being rendered IMPOTENT with Cathy (Harriet Walter) upsets him mightily as she recounts: 'When we went to bed, it didn't matter that he couldn't. I didn't care, I really didn't care. I liked him. He didn't have to be efficient and brilliant at everything ... I liked him more. But he couldn't bear to appear weak before me. He just couldn't stand it.'

More directly, but still evasively, Catherine (Josette Simon) tells David Dunhill (secret TRANSVESTITE, secret gay, played by Richard E. Grant) in HERE IS THE NEWS (1989 T): 'Perhaps you drank too much.' But she's obviously disappointed, and disapproving that he was the complete opposite of good in bed.

Goolden, Richard (1895–1981) English actor of small stature and uniquely melancholy voice: redolent of mothballs stuffed inside a tea cosy. Beloved as Mole in various radio, television and stage productions of *The Wind in the Willows/Toad of Toad Hall*. Also a treat in scatty or fey roles: on radio during the late 1930s and early 1940s as *Mr Penny*; Mr Dick in DAVID COPPERFIELD (1956 T); WILDE's Rev. Canon Chasuble (1958 T). He was possibly the basis for the character of the foolish old actor, played by Lockwood West, in THE DRESSER (1983 C). First broadcast as Mr Skinner in *Before the Party* (1930), and last as Zaphod Beeblebrox IV in *The Hitchhiker's Guide to the Galaxy*, whose motto is: 'Life is wasted on the Living'. Some films, beginning with *Once in a New Moon* (1938) through to *Joseph Andrews* (1977). Only starring role: *Meet Mr Penny* (1938).

The Goon Show (UK 1952–60 R; as CRAZY PEOPLE 1951–2) Brilliantly organized chaos starring Spike Milligan (who wrote or co-wrote nearly all the scripts), Peter SELLERS and Harry Secombe with valuable assistance from Max Geldray (on harmonica), Ray Ellington and His Orchestra, and announcers Andrew Timothy and later Wallace GREENSLADE. It was broadcast on the BBC Home Service with repeats on the Light Programme. Among its regular dramatis personae were two cohabiting couples (Dr Henry Crun and his 'assistant' Minnie Bannister) and archvillains (Hercules GRYTPYPE-THYNNE and his 'partner' Count Jim MORIARTY) alongside inseparable Eccles and Bluebottle and the perverse Major Denis BLOODNOK (and his probably black mistress/dominatrix Gladys – played by Ray Ellington).

Never before and possibly never since has the immateriality of radio been so cunningly and subversively mined, creating an invisible geography so gloriously off its head that all points of the compass – political, sexual, verbal, visual – mesh together with perfect illogicality.

Gordon Boy's name linked with swooning fellows in British drama, beginning with Gordon Whitehouse in DANGEROUS CORNER: 'God knows what he is, some sort of hysterical little pervert.' Gordon Zellaby (George SANDERS) in *Village of the Damned* (1960 C) is a scientist who discovers cuckoos in his own and other people's nests. Then the name took off during the 1970s. Human blancmange Gordon (John Standing), confidant of heroine in *Zee & Co/X, Y and Zee* (1971 C); Gordon Breen (Ian HOLM), a nurse set upon by elderly charges in *The Frighteners* 'The Treat' (1972 T); Gordon Glossop (George Baker), lonely football-club hanger-on who adores one of the players to death in Z CARS 'Friends' (1974 T); 'Gay Gordon' (Felix Bowness) in Porridge 'Just Desserts' (1975 T); BROOKSIDE's resident gay Gordon COLLINS (Nigel Crowley 1982–6; Mark Burgess 1987–90 T); the obnoxious Gordon Brittas (Chris Barrie) in *The Brittas Empire* (1990–3 T).

In the US most are hootingly heterosexual when they are not hootingly homosexual: Gordon (Eric BLORE) in *Swing Time* (1936 C); Gordon Reynolds

(Barry Coe), intense young actor in *But Not for Me* (1959 C); bottle-blond beach bimbo Gordon Slide (Tommy Sands) in *Love in a Goldfish Bowl* (1961 C); Gordon Kirkwood (Leon Ames), married fuss-bucket neighbour in *Mister Ed* (1964–6 T); Gordon (Lee Phillips) in PERRY MASON 'The Case of the Fatal Fortune' (1965 T), hair thick with grease, exuding virility at full throttle, would-be seducer of Julie Adams, who hints that in the fashion business men like him are hard to find; hero Gordon (Sidney Poitier) loved by a blind (white) woman in *A Patch of Blue* (1965 C); Gordon (Henry Calvert), lover of 'room-mate' George in HOT*L BALTIMORE (1975 T); a 'gay Gordon' in *No Soap, Radio* 'Miss Pelican' (1983 T); Gordon Gekko (Michael Douglas), high roller, cheat, shark but all man in *Wall Street* (1987 C); Gordon Fairchild (Roddy MCDOWALL), writer about things supernatural and spooky in *Murder She Wrote* 'Fire Burn, Cauldron Bubble' (1989 T).

Gordon, General Charles George (1833–85) English soldier, involved in the Crimean war, who then worked in China before being sent to subdue the Nile region. Finally, he was dispatched to Khartoum to assert Egyptian rule against the religious leader, the Mahdi, with fatal consequences for himself.

Played by Basil Sydney in YOU ARE THERE 'The Death of General Gordon' (1958 T); Michael Hordern in *The Last Hero* (1962 T); Alan BADEL in *Gordon of Khartoum* (1966 T); Charlton Heston in *Khartoum* (1966 C); Robert Lang in *The Death of General Gordon – A Victorian Martyrdom* (1958 R); Paul Daneman in *To Die in Africa* (1989 R). Robert Hardy did the narration in the documentary GORDON OF KHARTOUM (1982 T).

'A traumatic experience at school in Taunton aged 10. Some act of schoolboy violence ... some act of pain or cruelty or terror ... [he] was a witness to or a victim of ...? Whatever it was led to the suppression of sexual desires for the rest of his life ... [it] probably scarred his soul so he had no sexual outlets and gave him a death wish. "I wish I was a eunuch ... I remember a deep bitterness then ... I never can forget it" ... Tough though he was, he had a sensitive side ... Some pictures suggest an almost feminine delicacy, others are masculine. He loved children very much. He became an opium addict, a spiritualist, devoted to young boys "less fortunate than himself"' (*Gordon of Khartoum* 1982 T) (Spoken over shots of a little boy, standing at a window. Who is then confronted by an older boy who stands, with arms folded, wearing an expectant expression).

Gordon, Harry (1893–1957) Aberdonian comedian who portrayed pantomime dames, as well as 'wifies' (literally fishwives), in a North-East Scottish accent. He worked for BBC in Scotland during the 1920s and 1930s in sketches like 'Fish', 'The Dentist's Chair' and 'Mrs McIntyre Visits the Sick' in which she tries to cheer up Johnny: 'I would hardly have ken ye. Ae my but yer face is just like a bawbee's worth o'tea and ye're as thin as a sparrer's wind pipe.' (This tradition of relatively accurate women vocal caricatures was carried on by Al Read in England, and by Dan Agar as Mrs 'OBBS' – a woman of nature – on Australian radio during the 1950s.) Gordon appeared in Glasgow pantomimes well into the 1950s.

'Harry Gordon was never happier than when in costume for a character part, male or female,' said his biographer Iain Watson in *Leopard Magazine*, 1983.

Gorgo The companion lover of Archeanassa on Lesbos and with Andromeda and SAPPHO the most well-known teachers of the 7th century BC, whose pupils were yoked together artistically, affectionately, sexually and religiously.

In a 1960 British horror film, *Gorgo* is the 250 ft mother of a 65 ft male amphibian who is captured and exploited as a fairground attraction. She arrives from the sea to rescue him and destroys the landmarks of London in the process. A classic case of over-protectiveness.

Gosling, Ray (1936–) English journalist, broadcaster, traveller and social commentator with a phlegmatic curiosity. Possessor of a good ear and a good eye, he has built up a unique knowledge of Britain over the past two and a half decades – developmental eye-sores, Black Forest gateau classes of Blackpool, the Elite Ladies' Luncheon Club, Friends of the Inner Wheel, a wild gay CLUB in Huddersfield, Pakistani solidarity in the north etc. He published an autobiography, SUM TOTAL (1962), when he was 22.

In 1968 he wrote an article on homo-sexuality for NEW SOCIETY and, as vice-president, gave the opening address at the 1975 CHE conference in Sheffield. His highly developed sense of obser-vation makes him an instinctive, if shy and retiring, connoisseur of things national, regional, local and individual which – upon occasions and from a slight distance – brings in gay culture and politics: *Not Exactly in His Footsteps* (1983 R); *The Human Jigsaw* 'Socially Unacceptable' (1987 T).

R: *Two Town Mad* (1964–74 including Cheltenham 1968, Bournemouth 1969, Bedford 1971, Leicester, Nottingham, Aldershot, and Benidorm 1974); *A Journal by Ray Gosling*, 'a double life' (1973 R); *On the Road to Pakistan* (1980); *Not Exactly in His Footsteps* (1983); *Ray Gosling – In the House of ...* (1985); *Prophets, Charlatans and Little Gurus* (including Colin MACINNES and Homer Lane, 1986); THE ARMADA REVEALED (about Spain, 1986); *Waiting for Mrs Forbes* (about the Anglican com-munity in France, 1987); *Entertaining Mr Gosling* (1988); *Who Owns Britain?* (1988); *A Taste of ...* (on language 1991–).

T: *One Man's View* (1969); *Battle for the Skins* (1976); *Gosling on Marriage* (1986); *The Human Jigsaw* 'Socially Un-acceptable' (1987); *Speaking to Each Other* (opening of BBC Newcastle station, 1987); *Members Only* (clubs and societies, 1993); *Adultery* (1993); etc.

Got A Bran' New Suit Written by Howard Dietz and Arthur Schwartz, originally for the show AT HOME ABROAD. Sung/croaked and danced, in man's evening suit, by Eleanor Powell – backed by Tommy Dorsey and His Orchestra – in *At Home Abroad* (1935 C). It was one of five songs cut from *The Band Wagon* (1952 C). Nanette Fabray was to have sung it, in female clothes.

This would have remained one of the many still-born piquant ideas from Hollywood had it not been for Rainer Werner FASSBINDER. He has Hanna Schygulla perform the number (in Eng-lish) in *Lola* (1978 C). She is wearing (glamorous) women's clothing, and the nature of her interest in the 'bran' new girl' is unmistakabiy palpitating.

Other male-gendered songs sung with-out a hint of self-consciousness include Lena Horne's in *Two Girls and a Sailor* and Ethel Merman and Mary Martin's duet 'Tea For Two' ('We will raise a family ...') in *The Ford 50th Anniversary Show* (1953 T).

See also HONEYSUCKLE ROSE; SALLY.

Go Tell It on the Mountain (US 1984 T) John Grimes (James Bond III) is the James BALDWIN figure, son of a Baptist preacher, growing up in Harlem and forced into Bible reading. He gets an award for writing, and steals away to see OF HUMAN BONDAGE at the accursed picture theatre.

W: Gus Edwards and Leslie Lee; based on a novel by James Baldwin; P: Calvin Skaggs; D: Stan Lathan; 1.8.84; PBS; 70 mins.

Book boiled down to not much more than an hour. To date, none of Bald-win's autobiographical *adult* writing has been filmed.

Goulding, Edmund (1891–1959) English actor who became a Hollywood writer, then director, unjustifiably neg-lected today apart from his Bette DAVIS period. Director of *Sun Up* (1925); *Paris*, an early Joan Crawford Apache drama (also W/P 1926); *The Broadway Melody* (W & co-D 1929); *Devil's Holi-day* (also W 1930); *Grand Hotel* (1932); *The Old Maid* (1939); *Dark Victory* (1939); *The Great Lie* (1941); *The*

Razor's Edge (1946); *Nightmare Alley* (1947); *Teenage Rebel* (1956); *Mardi Gras* (1958); etc. Passing mention in *Hollywood* 'Valentino' (1980 T): 'Goulding was later to be ostracized for his raucous lifestyle.'

gourmets Associated with over-refined palates, greed, inconsequentiality. Their exemplar was Cyril Kitsch (Peter Jones) in THE FAT OF THE LAND (1969 T) cook (*médaillon de veau au sauce bleu*), restaurateur (L'Eglise des Escargots in King's Cross, London), presenter of a television series on taste, and author of *Variations on a Theme or 100 Different Ways with Chickens, with Notes on Stuffing* and *Fifty Ways with Ducks and How to Get the Best out of a Goose*. Kitsch goes into ecstasies at the merest whiff of food: 'The poetry of tender younger chicken sizzling on the spit ... the visual masterpiece of my *côtelettes d'agneau à la Kitsch* ... I could live forever on recipes ... I would say I compose gastronomic symphonies and concertos and the occasional little sonata.'

G.P. (Aust 1988– T) A modern medical practice in Sydney copes with all kinds of crises, physical and mental. Including gays ('Mates', 'Lovers', 'So Makes the Man', 'Tests of Conscience'), and the occasional lesbian ('More Than Friends').
Cr: Sue Masters; ABC/Roadshow/Coote/Carroll; 60 mins.

With its later time slot and a strong commitment to truthful, adult themes, *G.P.* has chipped away at one or two areas usually left alone by Australian drama series. Inevitably, there was HIV/AIDS.

In 'Mates' (1990), Mark McCarthy (Jamie Jackson) struggles to come to terms with his condition while Dr Steve Harrison (Michael O'Neill) struggles to come to terms with his friend's sexuality. He also has to overcome his initial dislike (jealousy?) of Alex (Graham Harvey) when he realizes 'just how important he is to Mark and is instrumental in getting them back together'. The press release said: '"Mates" takes us into the most intimate areas of a homosexual's life, when an AIDS victim is forced to accept the horrifying reality of his disease. We also share the varying reaction not only of people close to him, but of everyone with whom he comes in contact.'

The follow-up 'Lovers', dealing with Mark's last days and the battle between lover and 'mother-in-law', contained a very brief KISS. There were 7 calls of congratulations to the ABC – 'emotional and endearing scenes' – and 15 of protest – 'Encouraging young people to look for partners of their own sex', 'Against a moral community', 'Kissing scene not on television before, too over the top', 'I'm sick of people making excuses for homosexuals', 'Directors need a good shaking up – we don't need homosexuality thrust down our throats. They are probably poofters themselves.' That same evening (1.5.90) there were three calls to the ABC about its programme *The Investigators*, protesting because there was no mention of homosexuality in a segment on the age of consent.

The two subsequent gay episodes of *G.P.* were predicated on the homosexual man as victim of violence. In 'So Makes the Man' (1991) a teenage boy (Andrew Eikmeier) is having an affair with a teacher (John Polson) who is beaten up by the boy's father.

'Tests of Conscience' (1992) features a locum, Simon Radley (Felix Nobis) who would seem to be the ideal replacement for Dr Nicola – and to provide a gay role model into the bargain. He is young, attractive, personable and is in a steady, live-in arrangement with a teacher David Robinson (Scott Burgess). The fly in the ointment is that Simon is addicted to sex. After getting his nightly dose at a PUB called the Royal, Simon is bashed up by punk-skinheads. He doesn't mend his ways and is later beaten to death by the same youths. The penultimate image is Simon's bloody, lifeless arm held by his weeping lover in a car park.

This piece bristles with coincidences. William Sharp (Michael Craig) happens upon Simon after his first beating while David happens upon one of the attackers in the street. Livid images of sexual force-feeding (verbal only) and just desserts (closed-up eye, smashed-up car, dead body). No mention of any precautionary measures against gay bashing; no supportive gay friends. This is a sex-mad rabbit caught in his own trap, a doctor with an irresponsible attitude to his calling.

Sydney's gay community was divided over this particular episode, which Kevin Dickson and Steve Gidlow, receivers of the SYDNEY STAR OBSERVER (7.2.92), sensibly reflected:

> [gay bashing], fidelity, AIDS, prejudice, gay relationships, outing and acceptance ... There's also a subplot concerning teenage Michael's H[igher] S[chool] C[ertificate] results ... An attempt is also made to explore the basher's motivation, with repressed homosexuality hinted as the culprit. All within the first half hour of the show.
> [But] why are G.P.'s producers so reluctant to introduce a long-term gay character? The occasional appearance of gay characters and themes is fine, but the pattern that is emerging stinks of tokenism. All this episode's events would've had far greater dramatic impact if they'd been spread over an entire season, rather than neatly concluded in one hour.

Grace, Nickolas (1949–) Characterful British actor with unforgettable face and voluptuous voice.

Anthony Blanche in BRIDESHEAD REVISITED (1981 T); Harry in *Heat and Dust* (1983 C); twins in *The Comedy of Errors* (1984 T); Joel Cairo in *The Maltese Falcon* (1984 R); Sheriff of Nottingham in *Robin of Sherwood* (1984–6 T); *Max Headroom* (1986 T); Parolles in *All's Well That Ends Well* (1986 R); Oscar WILDE in *Salome's Last Dance* (1988 C); LORCA in *Lorca: Death of a Poet* (1987 C/T); Sonnenschein in *The Green Man* (1989 T); etc.

Grace and Favour (UK 1992– T) ARE YOU BEING SERVED? transplanted to a manor house. This time around, much of the humour hinges on whether Mr HUMPHRIES is or isn't (heterosexual). W: Jeremy Lloyd and David Croft; P/D: Mike Stephens; BBC1.

graffiti 'Farr is queer' splashed across the Farrs' garage door in VICTIM (1961 C); explicit drawings in the hallways of the flats in *A Clockwork Orange* (1971 C); accusations on the lavatory wall in the prison camp in TENKO (1981 T); 'Young man needs boys with big cocks' and similar wants and needs scrawled on walls of buildings in Brest in QUERELLE (1982 C); blaming him for Roberto's death, Johnny etches 'puto' on Walt's door in MALA NOCHE (1987 C); decorating a woman teacher's car in a 1990 SOUTH OF THE BORDER episode with 'lezzo', 'DYKE' etc.

Granada Television Limited Britain's most respected and oldest independent television company, which is based in the North West. At its best: wide-eyed, open and thinking. Began transmissions 3 May 1956. Alumni include Silvio NARIZZANO, Peter WILDEBLOOD, Derek GRANGER, Mike Wooller, David Plowright, Philip Mackie, Peter Nichols, John Birt, Denis Mitchell, Mike Scott, Gus MacDonald, Gordon Flemyng, Mike Newell, Russell HARTY, Kenith TRODD and Michael Apted. Doom was prophesied with the forced resignation of chairman David Plowright in February 1992. The Granada Group board decided on the action upon the recommendation of its new chief executive, an accountant.

Among the many programmes of interest, from the brilliant to the bad: *The Adventures of Sherlock* HOLMES (1984–7); *The American Dream* (1965); *Blind Love* (1977); *A Blessing or a Sin?* (1958) on AID; BRIDESHEAD REVISITED (1981); THE CAESARS (1968); *Camino Real* (1964); CAT ON A HOT TIN ROOF (1976); CINEMA; THE COLLECTION (1976); THE COMEDIANS (1971); CORONATION STREET (1960–); COUNTRY MATTERS (1972–3); CROWN COURT (1972–81) 'A Friend of the Family' (1979); *The Crucible* (1959); DANGER-

OUS CORNER (1963); *Death of a Salesman* (1957); *The Death of Bessie Smith* (1965); DESIGN FOR LIVING (1964); *D. H. Lawrence* (1966–7); *The Division* (1967); *The Glass Menagerie* (1964); *Gosling's Travels* (1974); *Granada Reports* 'Joe' (1974); *Green Julia* (1972); *Homosexuality and the Law* (1957); *It's Dark Outside* (1964); *It's Little Richard* (1964); *It's Your Right* (*c* 1980); THE JEWEL IN THE CROWN (1984); *The Knot Garden* (1984); THE LAST ROMANTIC (1978); LOOK BACK IN ANGER (1956); *Lost Empires* (1986); *The Member of the Wedding* (1960); NIGHTINGALE'S BOYS 'Flossie' (1975); *No Man's Land* (1978); *The Odd Man* (1960); ON TRIAL 'Roger CASEMENT' and 'Oscar WILDE' (1960); *Philby, Burgess and Maclean* (1978); *Prime Suspect* and *Prime Suspect II* (1991 and 1992); *Promenade* (1959); *A Raging Calm* (1974); ROLL ON FOUR O'CLOCK (1970); ROPE (1957); *The Rose Tattoo* (1964); SAKI (1962); SEVEN MEN 'Quentin CRISP' (1971); SEVEN UP (1964), and *14 Up, 21 Up, 28 Up* and *35 Up*; THE VORTEX (1964); *The War of Darkie Pilbeam* (1971); WHALE MUSIC (1983); WORLD IN ACTION 'Coming Out in Newport Pagnell' (1975), 'Conversation with a Gay Liberal' (1973), 'Gay Pride' (1979), 'In the Matter of Mr Parris' (1983), 'Private Darkin's Private War' (1982) and 'Trapped in the Wrong Body' (1978); *Youth Wants to Know* (1956); *The Zoo Story* (1961).

grandmothers A gay nannie? Nancy Reagan look-alike Chevi Coton plays her bursting with life and wholesomeness as Miriam Goodman in *Kate and Allie* 'Landlady' (1984 T); a black grandmother is in SILENT PIONEERS (1985 C/T): 'If the people in this building knew I was gay they'd probably go up in flames'; DONAHUE introduced his bucking and neighing audience to Buffy Dunker (86) in his 'Gay Seniors' show (1989 T); gay men's grans (fictional) are Sylvia Calvert (Dandy Nichols) in LATE CALL (1975 T), and the grandmother (Sylvia Sidney) in AN EARLY FROST (1985 T); a lesbian's grandmother (real)

is in THANK YOU AND GOODNIGHT (1991 C); etc.

Grange Hill (UK 1978– T) A London comprehensive school is the setting for an early evening BBC1 series, devised by Phil REDMOND (TOGETHER, BROOKSIDE) and produced initially by Susi Hush. Shoplifting, divorce, tattoos, first dates, wearing a brace, new school jitters, everything under the sun. Except ... (One of the male teachers came out as gay in early 1993.)

Granger, Derek (1921–) English television and film producer, who was also one of the presenters of CINEMA in the 1960s, as well as a Granada producer (from the later 1950s) and a LONDON WEEKEND TELEVISION executive (in 1970). Examples of his fine TV work: SEVEN UP (1964); COUNTRY MATTERS (1972–3); THE COLLECTION (1976); CAT ON A HOT TIN ROOF (1976); BRIDESHEAD REVISITED (1981). Also *A Handful of Dust* (1988 C, also co-W). Interviewed on *Outlook '70* (1970 T) when he was Literary Consultant with the National Theatre.

Grant, Cary (1904–86) English-born Hollywood star actor, equally effective as man about town in comedies, romantic comedies and comedy-thrillers, or as darker, more divided souls. His voice and persona appeared in *The Flintstones* (1963 T) as Aaron Boulder (voiced by Alan Reed), a compulsive heterosexual with cigarette holder and mauve-upholstered limo. He describes himself as 'multi-millionaire, policeman, *bon vivant* and idol of the female sex'. Some of his dialogue has a twist of pink grapefruit: 'Why don't you have a massage, Fred? ... Relax those tired muscles ... I'll see you in the steam room.'

The most famous Grant homage was Tony Curtis trying to persuade Marilyn MONROE that he is an impotent millionaire in SOME LIKE IT HOT. Taking up the rear: Frank Gorshin ('Coff-ee, coffee, coff-ee!') in *The Andy Williams Show* (1964 T); John Gavin as Cary during his love affair with Sophia Loren in the

1980 TV movie *Sophia Loren: Her Own Story*; James Read in *Poor Little Rich Girl* (about Barbara Hutton, 1987 T).

Grant, Duncan (1895–1978) English artist, part of the BLOOMSBURY GROUP, lover of Lytton STRACHEY and then of John Maynard Keynes. Contributor to *Portrait of Virginia* WOOLF (1956 R); OMNIBUS 'A Night's Darkness, A Day's Sail' (1970 T). Played by Michael Spice in *A Self-Made Man* (about Ronald FIRBANK, 1985 R).

Grant, Russell (194?–) English television astrologer and personality, spreading cheer, sunshine and a little bit of glitter. Presented DOWN YOUR WAY (1987 R) from his birthplace, the village of Harefield in Middlesex.

Gratitude/D'Habitude Kennedy Russell's song from a long forgotten British B-movie, *Judgement Deferred* (1952), occupies a unique position: the first modern love song – sweet melody, nondescript words – by a man to another man. Composed, in the film, by an old French tramp (Marcel Poncin) and called 'D'Habitude' [Forever], it is taken to music-hall star Bud Flanagan with English words under the title 'Gratitude'. The song is reminiscent of Flanagan and Allen's 'Strollin''; Bud likes it, and a recording is made.

The old man lies dying in a church crypt. His fellow derelicts gather round the record player as the sentimental words pour out. Enter a saturnine gangster, 'Frenchy' (Martin Benson). We now understand why 'The Stranger' wrote 'The Song'. 'Frenchy', alias Pierre, was in the French Resistance; the older man, with whom he had probably been living, was tortured but refused to reveal his whereabouts. The two men whisper tender words in French which echo the (now discarded and deroticized) words of the song: 'Je n'oublierai pas, mon chéri.' The man dies and Pierre explains to the small gathering of grieved men: 'You thought he was an old man. He was no more than 50. Me ... I made him look like

that ... He saved my life. The Nazis were after me ... day and night.'

Gray, Charles (1928–) English actor who appears to have swallowed George SANDERS whole and to have added a merry twinkle.

C: as a newspaper columnist in THE ENTERTAINER; Ernst Blofeld in DIAMONDS ARE FOREVER (1971); the storyteller in THE ROCKY HORROR PICTURE SHOW; dubbed Jack Hawkins' voice after the latter had his voice box removed; eg in *Shalako* and *Great Catherine*.

R: Malvolio in TWELFTH NIGHT; the father in *A Room with a View*; the psychiatrist in *The Millionairess; Lady Windermere's Fan*; Richard in *Hay Fever; The Upper Crusts*.

T: *The Big Client* (1960); Richard WATTIS' brother in *The Ant and the Grasshopper* (1960); Mazeron in *Voices from the Past* (1962); Micky in *Nine Bean Rows* 'Menace' (1970); Bertrand Asquith in *Asquith in Orbit* (1971): 'A columnist who uses his contacts and his power to get to the truth of a story'; Antonio in *The Merchant of Venice* with Christopher Gable (**1973**); Hugo in *Dial M for Murder* 'Firing Point' (1974); Harold Charles in *Across a Crowded Room* (A Play for Love, 1978); Pandarus in *Troilus and Cressida* (1981); Michael Redgrave in AN ENGLISHMAN ABROAD; Maurice Hussy in ABSOLUTE HELL (1991); Admiral De'ath in *Tales from the Poop Deck* (1992).

Dorian **Gray** Oscar WILDE's eternally youthful dilettante of cruel and perverse desires in THE PICTURE OF DORIAN GRAY based on Canon John Gray or Robert FARQUHARSON or the Comte De Montesquieu or ...?

Played by Hurd HATFIELD (1945 C); David PEEL (1948 R); Jeremy Brett (1958); Helmut Berger (1970 C); Peter Firth (1976 T); Belinda Bauer in *The Sins of Dorian Gray* (1983 T). The character also appeared in URINAL/PISSOIR (1989 C). Greta GARBO long wished to play the role, at one time hoping for Marilyn MONROE as Sybil

Vane. In 1980 a project was announced with Mia Farrow as Dorian (script by John OSBORNE).

(There is an Italian actress called Dorian Gray who appeared in *Dangerous Wife* (1958), IL GRIDO (1961) etc.)

Gray, Simon (1937–) Killer shark of British drama whose speciality is intrigue among the intellectuals, served with lashings of perversity: gay/lesbian/bisexual characters left, right and centre.
C: *A Month in the Country* (1987).
Biography: With Great Pleasure (1987 R), readings of his favourite prose and poetry by frequent collaborator Alan BATES and by Rosemary Martin.
T: SPOILED (1968); *Death of a Teddy Bear* (1967); *The Man in the Sidecar* (1971); BUTLEY (1974 C/T); *Plaintiffs and Defendants* (1975); *Two Sundays* (1975); *The Rear Column* (1980); *After Pilkington* (1987); *Quartermaine's Terms* (1987); *Common Pursuit* (1992); *Unnatural Pursuits* (1992); *Femme Fatale* (1993).

Grayson, Larry [William White] (1923–) Became a FEMALE IMPERSONATOR at 14 (as Billy Breen in RALPH READER'S GANG SHOW in the 1930s; later in JOURNEY'S END on the London stage). He went from there into variety, summer seasons, pantomime and drag shows. After 30 years, he was discovered on ITV in the early 1970s billed as 'the biggest hypochondriac in show business' on *The Leslie Crowther Show* (1971).
His camp repartee, catchphrases ('WHAT A GAY DAY!', 'SEEMS LIKE A NICE BOY') and constant hypochondria endeared him to millions in SHUT THAT DOOR! and THE LARRY GRAYSON SHOW. Not to mention his (imaginary?) friends and acquaintances, who include Slack Alice (she works behind the bar at the Cock and Trumpet); his postman Pop-it-in-Pete (when he's got something too big to put through the letterbox he knocks on the door); and EVERARD.
He was voted Show Business Personality of 1972. After SHUT THAT DOOR! (1972–3) he took over from Bruce Forsyth on *The Generation Game* (1978–81

T). He's guested on many chat and variety shows (intro music: 'THE MAN THAT GOT AWAY'), even commenting upon – and giving tips on how it could be improved – Dustin GEE's impersonation of him on *The Laughter Show* (1985 T) with his usual deprecatory flair. In 1987 he hosted a panel game called *Sweethearts* in which three couples 'have a romantic or amusing story to tell ... and only one couple is genuine'.
He is currently undergoing a small renaissance – 'one of Britain's best loved entertainers' (as he was introduced by Terry Wogan in 1984), he is now being referred to as a master of comic timing. Julian CLARY was flattered to be compared to him. To celebrate Grayson's 70th birthday, a special tribute was mounted at the Museum of the Moving Image in London as part of the 1993 gay and lesbian television season. A far cry from the days when his live shows were picketed by gay liberation groups for offensive STEREOTYPING.
Besides his regular TV shows he appeared on: *The Larry Grayson Hour of Stars* (1974), 'an affectionate look at his movie scrapbook'; *Look Who's Talking* (1974–5); *Crossroads*, playing a chauffeur at Meg's wedding; *At Home with Larry Grayson* (1983), 'a frothy mixture of studio chat and filmed inserts', a light-hearted tour of his Nuneaton home and the secret retreat in Torquay; *Wogan* with Mel Brooks and Manhattan Transfer (1984); *Blankety Blank* (1985); *A Question of Entertainment* with Ken Dodd (1988); etc.
R: *Late Night Larry* (1983): 'Larry Grayson invites you to cuddle up with your radio set for two and a half hours of music and chat.'
'Now – this is my time. My comedy was before its time. Agents were a bit afraid of me. And for television I was too camp' (*TV Times*, June 1972).

Larry **Grayson** Played by Warren Burke, he is 'sap son of a millionaire adventuress', the hero of a wild gilded youth melodrama called *Road House* (1928 C).

great dark man ' ... fetishizing that fantasy ... it's the Quentin CRISP "great dark man" scenario. It's a way for gay men to recreate themselves in *their* own image,' Richard Smith talking about 'DOCTOR MARTENS' (*10×10* 1991 T).

Greater London Council *See* GLC.

Greatest Heroes of the Bible 'Sodom and Gomorrah' (US 1979 T) Lot (Ed Ames, tired businessman with a cloth jamjar cover on his head) and Mrs Lot (Dorothy Malone playing a Florida matron worried about her daughters' marriage prospects) are tempted by the rich cities of Sodom and Gomorrah ... Will they succumb to the rich pagan life? Will they be tainted by their ways?
W: Brian Russell; D: Jack Hiveley; 'Schick Sunn Classics filmed in Page, Arizona'; 30 mins.

Part of a compendium series of history and (a lot of) myth. Included in previous productions: Joseph, Abraham, Moses (no sign of DAVID AND JONATHAN yet). This one isn't about a couple of guys called 'Sodom' and 'Gomorrah', but two cities.

The word on Sodom is not favourable. Vouchsafes one character: 'I have heard nothing good about these city people. Only that they are born thieves and murderers and they grow up even worse.' Asserts another: 'I have heard it said that they grow rich on the backs of slave labour.' Then the narrator takes over: 'Everything Lot had heard about the cities was true – and worse: kidnapping, extortion, murder for profit. The lowest form of degradation and sin ... all sense of human dignity had vanished. Sodom and Gomorrah had reached a point beyond redemption.' Which cues in Gene Barry (in long blue Muppet wig and beard) as Abraham to say with much grimacing: 'These cities are very pits of vice and sin and Bera is the arch-demon of the condemned.' The rest of the exposition is similarly emphatic. 'Patience? Hah! I'm through with patience!' says one of the Sodomites, Dagir (Rick Jason). The narrator then tells us: 'Dagir had become impatient.'

Exactly what sins set the twin cities apart, and laid them open for God's wrath is completely ignored in the story, although there is a hint. 'I have plans for him,' says King Bera (Peter Mark Richman), gazing at a captured desert chieftain's son. 'To seduce an enemy and then subdue him is much more profitable than killing him. And much less messy.' (The ruler wears the same outfit: black and white polka dots with ram's head trimmings in every scene – though months pass between whiles.)

Greek ideal Older man loving and moulding a younger one: Christopher ISHERWOOD and Don Bachardy in AQUARIUS 'Over There on a Visit' (1977 T); Angus WILSON and Tony Garrett in THE OTHER HALF (1984 T); David HOCKNEY and Peter Schlesinger in *A Bigger Splash* (1974 C); '[The Greeks] had their boyfriends and their wives. They weren't one way or the other,' Brian in TOGETHER ALONE (1991 C).

The Green Bay Tree (UK 1946 R) The heart of the plot concerns the efforts of Leonora (Sheila Burrell) to wrest vain Julian (Lewis Stringer) away from his adoptive father DULCIMER (D. A. CLARKE-SMITH). The older man is dispatched by Julian's Welsh evangelist dad, Mr Owen (Ivor Barnard) who uses Isaiah for justification: 'I myself have seen the wicked in great power and spreading himself like a green bay tree. Yet he passed away and lo, he was not; yea, I sought him, but he could not be found.'

The resolution is not as might be expected. So softened has Julian become through Dulcimer's looking-glass of grace and favour that he rejects Leonora. Sucked back into the vortex of fine wines, antiques and soft linen, he explains: 'The moment I came back here, everything began to get hold of me again. I suppose one must be as one is made. You don't know what it means to me to sleep in a comfortable bed again with decent sheets.' He is last heard arranging flowers with the valet, Trump

(Ivan Samson), his head full of unmanly pursuits. Curtain.

W: Mordaunt Shairp; Adaptor/P: Felix Felton; 5.10.46; BBC Home Service (Saturday Night Theatre); 85 mins.

Richard DYER, discussing FILM NOIR (JUMP CUT 16), describes it as 'ideological pairing of male homosexuality with luxury and decadence, with the connotation of impotence and sterility'. That definition accords perfectly with this play.

The melodrama was first produced in London in 1933: Mr Dulcimer (Frank VOSPER); Trump (Henry Hewitt); Julian (Hugh Williams). On Broadway the same year: Mr Dulcimer (James Dale); Julian (Laurence Olivier); Trump (Leo G. Carroll). In the 1950 West End revival: Mr Dulcimer (Hugh Williams); Julian (Denholm ELLIOTT). Elliott also appeared in the 1951 revival on Broadway with Joseph Schildkraut.

green carnation Oscar WILDE's emblem of defiance together with the orchid. Noel COWARD's tribute to gentlemen who wore 'Green Carnations' did *not* appear in the 1940 Hollywood version of *Bitter Sweet*. Boxer Rocky in *It's Always Fair Weather* (1955 C) incongruously wears one. The Peter FINCH film of Wilde's downfall was entitled *The Man with the Green Carnation* for its American release. A carnation is placed in a man's mouth and is picked out petal by petal by another man's teeth and lips in THE BALLAD OF READING GAOL (1988 T).

Greenhalgh, Paul (195?–   ) English actor of extreme thinness. Played Paul in *Boy Meets Girl* 'The Eye of Heaven' (1968 T); 'Thin Young Man' in *The Befrienders* 'Next Patient Please' (1972 T); in *Edward VII* (1974 T); Denny in THE CREZZ (1976 T); music shop salesman in *Tales of the Unexpected* 'Mr Botibol's First Love' (c 1978 T); QUEER-BASHED man in *Babylon* (1980 C); hospital administrator in *Shroud for a Nightingale* (1984 T); political agent in *First Among Equals* (1986 T); clerk of the court in *Cause Célèbre* (1987 T).

Greenham Common Peace protesters maintaining 24-hour vigil and dissent at American nuclear base in Britain during the 1980s: many of them were lesbian-feminists. Their extraordinary existence was shown in *Carry Greenham Home* (1984 C) and depicted with varying degrees of satire in *The Ploughman's Lunch* (1983 C); *Carrot's Lib* (c 1983 T); *The Big March* (1984 R).

Greenslade, Wallace (1914–1961) English announcer who joined THE GOON SHOW with MORIARTY and GRYT-PYPE-THYNNE in 1954 with the 5th series. His star rose with 'The Greenslade Story' (1955) in which he has to cope with massive fame (it goes to his head, of course). He's Commander Greenslade RN ('easy, old man') in 'Shifting Sands of Waziristan', and essayed the title role in 'The Phantom Head Shaver of Brighton' as a tobacconist who collects human hair and sells it as pipe tobacco. *See also* IT'S ALL IN THE MIND.

Greenwich Village Area of Manhattan popular with artists, poets and others whose differences require a sympathetic environment. Clara Bow visits a café in the Village where two waiters prance around in maids' outfits singing a song about sailors in *Call Her Savage* (1932 C). A coven of witches, most of them lesbian, meet in a bookshop to plot the destruction of a young girl in *The Seventh Victim* (1943 C). The young men out on a spree in THE BACHELOR PARTY (1957 C) try, unsuccessfully, to gatecrash a party given by Karen Norris; She is, however, most welcoming to Carolyn Jones but later, when the guys return and gain admittance, the hostess is too far gone (on something or someone) to care.

Greer, Germaine (1939–   ) Writer and broadcaster on women's issues, including art history and the menopause but forever identified with her book THE FEMALE EUNUCH (1970). Helped countless women from menstruation through masturbation and out of menses. Once known as the 'scourge of the male chauvinist pig'.

As actress: *Nice Time* (1966 T) etc.

Germaine Greer vs USA (1971 T); *It's Your Line* (1971 R) where, in answer to a phone-in caller's question about lesbians she says: 'Heaven knows what [men's] impression of lesbianism is, but if it's women who don't sleep with them on the first encounter then let's all be lesbians'; *Favourite Things* (1987 T), talking about favourite animals, plants and pleasures, authors, food: 'A surprisingly domestic glimpse of her life away from the demands of celebrity'; etc.

Grey, Antony (1928–) Lobbyist for homosexual law reform in the 1960s. Many television appearances during the period before the SEXUAL OFFENCES ACT became part of the legal framework within which gay English males must live their sexual lives. In *The Sixties* 'Swingeing' (1982 T).

Carol **Grey** (Anne CULLEN in THE ARCHERS) The market gardener who caused a stir from the moment she came to live in AMBRIDGE (she ran her own car! and had never been married! and didn't want to be!).

At one time (1957) she was considered a bit of a threat to public morals, more specifically the good conduct of part of Britain's armed forces: 'I am getting a good many complaints about the sexiness of *The Archers* these days and I hear from my son in the Regular Army in Germany that it is now eagerly listened to in the Mess to see what shape sex will rear its ugly head each night' (BBC executive, THE ARCHERS OFFICIAL COMPANION, 1985).

Her most notorious moment came that same year. A scene between Carol Grey and Tony Stobeman was faded out at a moment of surrender on her part that sounded suspiciously like an orgasm – if such things had been known about in 1957: ' ... after such scenes involving heavy breathing and what you will [they] could only lead one to suppose that Miss Grey had forgotten her mother's good advice – a supposition more than confirmed in the episode covering the following day during which Miss Grey did a good deal more sighing of a retrospective and reflective character, and again left the more worldly listener in no doubt as to what had happened on the sofa.' (THE ARCHERS OFFICIAL COMPANION, 1985).

She carried on a long and quite sexy romance with bachelor John TREGORRAN (Basil JONES). She married local squire Charles Grenville in 1961, and had a son Richard a year later. (He had insisted that his future wife have a medical as if she were a brood mare.) Widowed in 1965, she eventually married John and they later had a baby.

Unlike the blurry madcap animation of THE DALES, THE ARCHERS moved nimbly inside and outside reality. It was true to human nature with all its divergence. In Carol and John, we had the classic outsiders with voices of sensual abstraction, adapted to the contours of the permissible. Carol herself was described as 'frigid' by a number of the Ambridge men and it is now quite obvious that she and Christine Archer were created by the writers Edward J. Mason and Geoffrey Webb as quasi-lesbian characters. Of course, in the 1950s – then as now – nothing could be expressed if they wished to be retained in the 'natural' scheme of things. So Carol (and John) had to talk in code about things in their pasts: secrets, nervous breakdowns. Very naturally, the couple decided – after a long friendship and semi-flirtation – that they were made for each other. And so, to this day, they have remained.

The writers, hampered by the departure of Anne Cullen from the series in the early 1970s through her husband's illness, weren't willing or able to follow the pair through the 1980s. John made sporadic appearances, even had an affair with a younger woman, but the youthful fire had quite gone out. Of Carol there was no word. A fan even wrote to RADIO TIMES in 1988 seeking enlightenment. The reply was: 'Carol made a brief visit to Ambridge with John in 1990, but since her name is never mentioned something appalling [must have happened to her].'

Griffith, James (1915–) American actor with eerie, wiry face and deceitful manner. Début as Gary Cooper's creepy secretary in BRIGHT LEAF (1950 C). As Arthur Dorian in PERRY MASON 'The Case of the Negligent Nymph' (1958 T), and as Jack Randall in PERRY MASON 'The Case of the Fatal Fetish' (1965 T).

Griffith, Kenneth (1921–) Welsh actor and writer who played quite a number of frightened, squeaky men: *High Treason* (1950 C); Polly in *Tiger in the Smoke* (1956 C); a drunken former circus owner in *Circus of Horrors* (1960 C); *Only Two Can Play* (1961 C); *The Whisperers* (1967); Whitty in *The Wild Geese* (1978 C).

Griffiths, Drew (1950–84) English actor and writer, a founder member of GAY SWEATSHOP. Murdered, at 34, by person or persons unknown. His few plays indicate a sweet spirit, as well as a great talent for narrative and chunky humour.
SEX IN OUR TIME 'For Queer Read Gay' (1976 T, shown 1991); GRAPEVINE (1979); ONLY CONNECT (1979 T co-W); THE ONLY ONE SOUTH OF THE RIVER (1980 R); THE HOUSE ON THE HILL 'Something for the Boys' (1981 T); *Something's Got to Give* (1982 T).

Peter **Grimes** 'Neither a hero nor a villain', Grimes is 'not a nice person. He is very much of an ordinary weak person who, being at odds with the society in which he finds himself, tries to overcome it and in so doing, offends against the conventional code, is classed by society as a criminal, and destroyed as such. There are plenty of Grimeses around still, I think' (PETER PEARS in *Radio Times*, 8.3.46).
Peter Grimes in sequence of poems 'The Borough' by George Crabbe. *Benjamin Britten and Peter Grimes* (1946 R); *The Significance of Peter Grimes* (1946 R); *George Crabbe* (1960 R) in which E. M. FORSTER talks about the creator of Peter Grimes.

George **Grinsky** Played by John Matusak, ex-football player, now queen of the late night coffee/hamburger stall in HOLLYWOOD BEAT (1987 T), seen cracking two men's heads in the credits. In the pilot, he was burly and buoyant, built like a medium-sized mountain. But he fizzled into insignificance once the series began, though retaining third billing. Instead of the burgers, he was now mixing drinks at the Frolic Cocktail room. His role was stripped down to two, or one, or zero appearances each week. He was given one line in a 50-minute show; in another (about boxing) Grinsky has 2 scenes and 4 lines, the most profound of which was: 'He's a marine, Rick, just like you. Tough kid.'

grit in the eye The classic gambit for beginning a clandestine relationship: BRIEF ENCOUNTER; *Doctors' Wives* (1970 C); FLAMES OF PASSION (1989 C/T).

gross indecency Oscar WILDE was taken to Bow Street police station in chains in 1895 to be charged with 'gross indecency'. Denis Porson (Nigel HAVERS) goes down for two years in THE GLITTERING PRIZES, and Bobbie Astor (Nigel HAVERS again) for two in *Nancy Astor* (1982 T). Harry (Anthony Benson) has never recovered from the trauma of his jail sentence in MAINTAINING STANDARDS, and youth-nurturing clergyman David Sales (Neil Cunningham) is visited by the police over an incident in *Johnny Jarvis* (1983 T). As a reminder that virulent moral policing was also around in politer, more God-fearing days, a handful of headlines from the 1950s were shown in WE THINK THE WORLD OF YOU (1980 T): 'What the Signalman Saw,' 'Clergyman Fined', 'Ventriloquist Fined', 'Youths as Witnesses', 'Thirteen Punished'. WILDE's Ernest Worthing (Jack Klaff) is accused of gross indecency in the cloakroom of Victoria station in THE IMPORTANCE OF BEING FRANK (1990).

The Groundling and the Kite (UK 1984 T) Jimmy Walker (John Duttine) needs a song lyric fast: his morose lover,

Peter Lester (Leonard Preston) goes against the grain and produces one that's full of everything that he can't say to Jimmy's face.

M/L/W: Leonard Preston; P: Colin Rodgers; D: Peter Jefferies; BBC1; 75 mins.

'I spend my life looking for songs for people to sing ... but I can't actually sit down and write one.'

Jimmy, on the surface the kite, a high-flying artiste and repertoire manager for a record company. A very convincing, intelligent, ambitious man. His companion, apparently the groundling, a teacher who appears to give Jimmy no real affection or uplift (but, then, we never see them in bed or being intimate – except for a 2-second KISS on their front step, interrupted by a neighbour meaningfully banging a dustbin lid).

By turns lyrical and stodgy, the play deals unspectacularly with a neat premise: a man with faint appreciation of anything very much living with a vibrant, feeling and successful man whose urgent need for a song brings about a slight crack in the other's permafrost.

The Group (US 1966 C) Eight Vassar girls graduate, some fall in love, one with a woman: Elinor Eastlake known as LAKEY (Candice Bergen) with the Baroness (Lidia Prochnicka), briefly glimpsed in the last 10 minutes.

W: Sidney Buchman from the novel by Mary McCarthy; P: Sydney Buchman; D: Sidney Lumet; 152 mins.

Most of the film's publicity had centred on the début of Candice Bergen as a *lesbian*! She was no more than a cipher in the novel, and the adaptation faithfully followed this marginalization.

Lieutenant (Hubert) Gruber (Guy Siner in 'ALLO, 'ALLO 1984–92 T) A window dresser and then an art gallery assistant in Cologne before he was forced to join the army. Essentially a melancholy, sentimental, self-abashed, soft-hearted soul with a picture of a blond youth in a locket. Somewhat illogically he conceives a great passion (mooncalf kind)

for the café owner, René – who tries to avoid his simpering looks and cautious sexual invitations.

He is able to tell the Gestapo which of the three identical paintings of the Madonna with the Big Boobies is the real one. Gruber is then blackmailed into silence: photographed in a compromising situation with a *woman* ('My commanding officer will never speak to me again').

Guy Siner's gracious playing, coupled with doltish face, almost make Gruber into a great comic creation. He is prevented from achieving this by the limited horizons of his scripts which see him only as an Aunt Hildegarde 'Girls all look the same to me' (1984).

René is asked by a member of the Resistance if Gruber is 'one of us'. 'No,' says René dutifully, 'he is one of *them*.' Gruber pleads with the others to lower their voices: 'Please, do not tell everyone. I was very lonely on the Russian Front.'

When his colonel is about to blow out the candles on his birthday cake, René innocently counsels him that he needs 'a great pouf' to do the job. Gruber blushes and says with infinite modesty: 'No, no, it's the *Colonel's* birthday.' From the second series, Gruber was given a name (he had been billed only as Lieutenant) and a few more lines to say. In total he's progressed very little: a cowardly, morose fool who can occasionally be useful to the Resistance because of his trusting nature. 'I'm adaptable,' he says to his commanding officer who wants to bring him back into contact with 'the men' (1990).

The Grumbleweeds Leeds comedy team, popular on radio and then on television in the late 1970s and the 1980s: Albert and Carl Sutcliffe (who left in 1987), Graham Walker, Maurice Lee and Rob doing lots of characters, including two yucky-pooh male agony 'aunties'.

Hercules Grytpype-Thynne (Peter SELLERS in THE GOON SHOW 1954–60 R) Grytpype did not have a name until the 5th series. Up to then he was 'suave voice', one Peter SELLERS based on George SANDERS in ALL ABOUT EVE (1950 C). He and MORIARTY work separately until 'The Affair of the Lone Banana'. During this episode they are living high off the hog on the Riviera. By the 8th series they are domiciled in dustbins or in trees. Clothes, too, have become scarce. 'Keep still,' hisses Grytpype. 'Do you want us both out of this suit, Moriarty?'

In one remarkable encounter – during a Goonization of Orwell's *Nineteen-Eighty-Four* (here called 'Nineteen-Fifty-Five') – Grytpype (playing the interrogator) attempts to lull Neddy into confessing his treachery: against the BBC. After every increasingly anguished denial, Grytpype tells Neddy what 'a silly, twisted boy' he is. Then all is revealed. Neddy's torturer isn't from the BBC at all. He is a secret agent for commercial television (then a dangerous upstart in the Corporation's eyes). Neddy exclaims that he knew it all the time: 'by the way you smiled at me, the way you touched my hair as you passed my chair.'

Grytpype's voice of sensual abstraction, savage with polite coercion, can also be heard via Sir Percy Prunefetish in a Regency sketch (Beau Legs) in I'M SORRY I'LL READ THAT AGAIN (1968 R) played by John Cleese and in *Dead to the World* (1992 C): 'Do you love me, Jack?'

guardsmen Joe's father Roger Ackerley had possibly enjoyed a German baron while in the service: just one more of father's SECRET ORCHARDS; Joe's elderly landlord tells him that 'In those days it was one pound for footguards. Horseguards were rather more.' Bernard Saint-Harrison, alias Biggles, is a Coldstream guardsman who runs a blackmail racket in THE GENTLE TOUCH 'Blade' (1980 T): 'A sort of male good-time girl ... He was an out and out loser. Articulate, but a loser.'

Leslie (Peter SALLIS), the middle-aged dresser in YOU'RE NOT WATCHING ME, MUMMY (1980 T) cheers himself up by telling his actress boss that he's got 'a hot guardsman waiting'. Shots of guardsmen are cheekily inserted into the proceedings in *Inside Story* 'Coming Out' (1980 T).

guest house proprietors JULIAN, the sailor-fancying nephew of Dame Hilda BRACKET is first mentioned in their TV show in 1989. A gay couple (Geoffrey Palmer and Richard Pasco) with a fraying relationship take in guests as well as training (pretty young) kitchen hands/cleaners in THE HOUSEBOY (1982 T).

Guilty Two men alone in a barrack room; one, reading a newspaper on his bed, gazes at the other who is polishing his buttons. The man puts aside his newspaper, gets up and crosses to the other man, touching him on the shoulders. He then sits on the bed as this sentimental 1931 ballad plays on. AL BOWLLY with Jack Leon and his band are heard in OUT ON TUESDAY: 'COMRADES IN ARMS': 'If it's a crime then I'm guilty/Guilty of loving you ...' The song was written by Gus Kahn, Harry Akst and Richard A. Whiting.

Jame **Gumb** *See* BUFFALO BILL.

guns In *The Chase* (1966 C) much was made of a group of men standing around at a drunken party showing each other their guns. This marked the first time that Hollywood openly acknowledged how important size and speed of explosion were to so many men (not just in Texas where this film was located) and how, surreptitiously, they love to talk to each other about their sexual organs.

There are more guns than ever on display, and in constant use on television and in films. It is the badge of masculinity and must be obeyed at all times. It both saves and wastes lives. The gangster, the cop, the cowboy are all admired for their dexterity. And the soldier. As Harry Schein wrote in 'Shots in the Dark' (a chapter in EROTICA FOR THE MILLIONS 1960): 'It is firm and long and fired from the hip. It is very important how you get it out ... The hero ... gets his weapon out quickly. He shoots rarely but never misses. An upholder of society, he cannot be promiscuous.'

As with so many things (but not gay sexuality), Mae WEST had it sussed. A keen student of Freud, she sashays up to one of her lovers in *She Done Him Wrong* (1933 C) and asks, in appraising fashion: 'Is that a gun in your pocket or are you just pleased to see me?' Duke Martin (John Ireland) massages his in *Railroaded* (1947 C); Barbara STANWYCK has her own as well as *Forty Guns* (1958 C).

A man's love for his gun can sometimes come between him and a woman. The cop Eddie Egan (Robert Duvall) in *Badge 373* (1973 C) is out rowing on a lake with his girlfriend Laurie. Laying down the oars he takes out his pistol. She erupts: 'You spend more time playing with your gun than you do with me.'

See also PHALLIC SYMBOLS.

gunwomen Women in the American West, depicted as pistol-packin' but who would lay their weapon down for the right man: Gene Tierney (1941 C) and Elizabeth Montgomery (1980 T) as Belle Starr; Barbara STANWYCK (1935 C) and Betty Hutton (1950 C) as Annie Oakley; Jean Arthur (*The Plainsman* 1936 C), Yvonne De Carlo (CALAMITY JANE and Sam Bass 1949 C), Jane Russell (THE PALEFACE 1949 C), Doris DAY (CALAMITY JANE 1953 L. C), Fay Spain (*Death Valley Days* 'A Calamity Named Jane' (*c* 1965 T), Stefanie Powers (*Bonanza* 'Calamity Over the Comstock' 1971 T), Jane Alexander (1984) and Beth Porter (1986) as CALAMITY JANE; Dorothy Provine (1958) and Faye Dunaway (1967) as Bonnie Parker.

In modern times: Catherine Deneuve in *Ecoute Voir* (1978 C); Sigourney Weaver in *Alien, Aliens* and *Aliens 3*; Zoe Tamerlis in *Ms .45*; Jodie FOSTER in *The Silence of the Lambs* (1991 C); Linda Hamilton in *Terminator 2* (1991 C); Jamie Lee Curtis in *Blue Steel* (1990 C); Anne Parillaud in *Nikita*; Susan Sarandon and Geena Davies in THELMA AND LOUISE; Kathleen Turner as *V. I. Warshawski* (1991 C).

Guy From Guido. The name was apparently not used as a first name for 200 years after the Catholic plotter Guy FAWKES – a homosexual man – was burned. It became synonymous with sodomite. Guy BURGESS reawakened the gay and the traitorous connotations (Derek JACOBI in *Philby, Burgess and Maclean* 1977 T; Anthony Hopkins in BLUNT 1987 T); Guy Bennett (Rupert Everett) in ANOTHER COUNTRY; Guy Baggers (Anthony Smee) in BRASS 1982–4/1990); Guy Llewellyn (John Rowe) in *Chessgame* (1983 T).

Other sharp, less than straightforward characters with this name: Guy of Gisbourne, one of Robin Hood's foes; Guy (Patrick Waddington) in *Mr Cinders* (1939 R); Guy Haines (Farley Granger), the tennis pro with the inconvenient wife in STRANGERS ON A TRAIN (1951 C); sleazy investigator Guy Van Stratten (Robert Arden) in *Mr Arkadin/Confidential Report* (1955 C); Guy (Richard Burton), mercy-killing doctor, would-be adulterer in *The Bramble Bush* (1960 C); Guy Penrose (Tom Conway), svelte actor who is murdered in PERRY MASON 'The Case of the Simple Simon' (1964 T); suburban decadent Guy (Robin Bailey) in *Catch Us If You Can* (1965 C); John Cassavetes as Guy Woodhouse, ambitious actor–husband in *Rosemary's Baby* (1968 C); Guy Millington (Jordan Christopher), schemer in *Secrets of Midland Heights* (1980–1 T); brutal CIA operative Guy Banister (Edward Asner) in JFK (1991 C), to the right of Attila the Hun, wears rosebud, is involved in 'flip-flop' activities, and operates out of an office on the corner of Camp Street in New Orleans.

Guy Gibson was given the heroic Richard Todd treatment in *The Dam Busters* (1955 C), bouncing bombs against the Jerrys. This may have led to a more heroic strand of Guy finding its way into the consciousness of writers and producers a decade or two later. Guy Lambert (Elvis Presley) 'singer' in *Double Trouble* (1966 C); Guy Sutton (Peter Whitford), a 'down-to-earth bloke ... a glorified grease monkey' in NUMBER 96 (1974 T); Mel Gibson as ruggedly pretty Guy Hamilton, Australian broadcaster in *The Year of Living Dangerously* (1983 C); Charles Dance as Guy Perron in THE JEWEL IN THE CROWN; Guy Holden (Leonard Cottle) growing up fast in *Ceremonies of War* (1985 R); Kenneth Branagh, the captivating but irresolute Guy Pringle of *Fortunes of War* (1987 T, Jack Shepherd on radio); Guy Rogers (Paul Gregory) in *The Way Thru the Woods* (1987 R); Guy (Jeff Rawle) in *Call Me Mister* (1988 T); Dr Guy Reid (David Reyne), one of THE FLYING DOCTORS (1991– T); Guy MacFadyean (Nigel Havers) and Guy Lofthouse (Keith Barron) in *The Good Guys* (1992 T).

The name has been made safe – even for babies like Little Guy (Daniel Gregory) playing with his trucks (while Grandpa played by Anton Rogers cuddles his teddy) in *French Fields* (1989 T).

But there still are gay Guys: gangster Guy Algo (Tony Beckley) in *Revenge of the Pink Panther* (1978 C); Guy Hamilton (Aubrey WOODS) in *Tom and Jerry* (1987 R); sympathetic director (Anthony HOLLAND) and friend of the heroine in *The Lonely Lady* (1983 C); and Colin's last love, Guido SMITH (Nicholas Donovan) in EASTENDERS.

guy From Guy FAWKES and the effigy – a homosexual; used 50 years ago in Australia and now coming back; or was it Scots for gay? 'Guy' may also echo 'geezer' (a 19th-century term, used in prisons. Initially derisory against all men, not necessarily elderly – as often employed today – chiefly in Scotland and the North) and 'guiser' which meant one who goes in disguise as a masquerader or as a mummer (or possibly it derives from the Duke of Well-ington's soldiers: a Basque word 'giza', meaning 'man'). *See also* YOU GUYS.

Guyana Tragedy: The Story of Jim Jones (US 1980 T) Beginning in sweet idealism, the Rev. Jim JONES' dream of Utopia in Latin America ends in galloping paranoia, the murder of a US senator and forced mass suicide.
W: Ernest Tidyman; P: Ernest Tidyman and Sam Manners; D: William A. Graham; CBS; 208 mins.

Initially egalitarian and accepting of all manner of men and women – 'We're all the same in the eyes of God' – Jones (Powers Boothe) becomes increasingly irascible, judgemental and sexually voracious. The latter is a cue for American television's first almost-kiss between two men. Said the VILLAGE VOICE: 'When Jones seduces a male admirer ... the camera yanks away before their lips can meet ... Perhaps Jones, a drug-freaked BISEXUAL, can be depicted as an existential maniac who conceived of himself as being beyond good and evil, beyond psychology and history; but the film settles for something more banal and venial.'
Jones' own 'miasma of mortal confusion on the path of righteousness' and his relentless insistence on having to be 'all things to all men – and women' may account for the hollowness that is present in, as well as the passion that is missing from, this otherwise painstaking account which tries to make sense of what happened in Jonestown in 1978.

The 1980 radio play *Now, and at the Hour of Our Birth* (with Lee Montague as Jones) summed up the whole catastrophe in 90 minutes and included (an equally brief) seduction between the leader and a male doctor (Tim Bentinck).

H

Habanera From Bizet's *Carmen*. Impudent, arrogant, seductive: a grandly sexual assertion of Carmen's right to love 'em and leave 'em (men).

A song of power and passion perfectly in tune with the intelligent but out-of-control 'Mitch' (Sharon Mitchell), lorelei of sleaze, streetwise porno slut, adults-only movie deity in KAMIKAZE HEARTS (1987 C), whose very elastic, pragmatic view of *l'amour* perfectly mirrors the aria which plays at the start and finish of the film. It details her ultimately very sordid, empty and destructive love affair with fellow sex-film actress, later assistant producer Tigr while making a modern – X-rated – version of *Carmen*.

Hahn, Reynaldo (1875–1947) Jewish Venezuelan composer–singer. The lover of Marcel PROUST and idol of Parisian society in the 1890s. 'A man of amazingly diverse talents ... a close friend of Proust' was how the 1970 radio biography by Richard Bebb described him. He is mentioned by a character in THE VORTEX, and one of his songs introduced the readings from Sara Maitland's feminist short stories on WOMAN'S HOUR in 1987. Hahn's music was used – with that of Debussy, Fauré, Franck, Saint-Saëns, Beethoven and Wagner and with readings from REMEMBRANCE OF THINGS PAST by Jeremy Irons – for the ballet by Roland Petit *Proust Remembered* (Fr 1986 T).

Haines, William (1900–73) American actor and interior designer. Accomplished player of (increasingly ageing but babyfaced) thrusting juveniles or what VARIETY (1935) termed 'smart aleck' roles (also remarking that his voice had 'a variety of pitches'). With the possible exception of his participation in the Marion Davies inside-Hollywood comedy *Show People*, he is totally forgotten – though he was a star between 1924 and 1931.

Haines himself is the shadowy figure behind the oft-quoted removal of George CUKOR as director of *Gone with the Wind*. According to Kenneth Anger's book HOLLYWOOD BABYLON – though not documentaries like *The Making of GWTW* (1989 T) – Haines (a successful interior decorator and gossip) had had a brief fling with the leading man, about which Cukor presumably knew. Coupled with Cukor's alleged overconcentration on the female performers, this hidden 'scandal' was too much of a threat to Gable, who persuaded Selznick to fire him. At least, that's according to the Hollywood grapevine.

Haines made his film début in 1922 with *Brothers Under the Skin* after winning a 'New Faces' competition sponsored by Samuel Goldwyn. His last pictures were *The Fast Life* (1933) and *The Marines Are Coming* (1935), unsuccessful attempts to toughen up his image. He then retired to open an interior decoration studio in Beverly Hills, and was transformed into 'Billy' Haines.

hair Brings out all sorts of prickles in people, whether it is (too) long or (too) short, or there is too much (especially on certain parts of the body) or too little (especially on the head). Documentaries covering this highly charged subject include *Keep Your Hair On* (1967 T); ARENA 'Hair' (1983); and, from a queer point of view, the wide-ranging (yet omitting hairy backs and bottoms) OUT 'Talking Hairs'.

For women, short hair is often associated with derangement or anger: rape victims (Jodie FOSTER in *The Accused*); women about to be delivered of the Devil's child (*Rosemary's Baby*); irresponsible mothers (Mariette Hartley in *Silence of the Heart* 1984 T) or waifs (Leslie Caron) or elves (Audrey Hepburn) or fairies (Julia Roberts in *Hook*) or nuns (*The Sound of Music*) or aristocratic loonies (*Lady Caroline Lamb*) or kooks (*For Pete's Sake*) or artists (*Ghost*).

Sometimes, cropped hair is permissible as a symbol of liberation or free spirits: Audrey Hepburn's princess in *Roman Holiday*; Maggie McNamara in *Three Coins in the Fountain*; Jean Seberg (post-St Joan) in *Bonjour Tristesse* and *Breathless*; Ali MacGraw in *Convoy*; the sister

(Talia Balsam) in *Consenting Adult*; Joan Chen in *Twin Peaks*; etc.

Strangely enough, considering that short hair remains *à la mode* (though not *de rigueur*) in much of the real Western lesbian world, a cropped head is rarely to be found atop a fictional self-identified dyke – with the exception of some French ones: Arletty as Ines in HUIS CLOS (1954 C), Genevieve Page's Mme Anais in BELLE DE JOUR (1967 C), and Vivienne Moray (Camilla Sparv) in *Valley of the Dolls '81* (1981 T); a few British heads: Susannah York's in THE KILLING OF SISTER GEORGE (1968 C), Anne Heywood's in THE FOX (1968 C), Jane Lapotaire's Kim in THE OTHER WOMAN (1976 T), and Amanda Donohoe's C.J. in L.A. LAW (1990–2 T); two Americans: Jane Halleren's in LIANNA (1983 C) and Patricia Arquette as Grace in *Inside Monkey Zetterland* (1992 C); and one Australian: prisoner Franky DOYLE. Half and half lengths were worn by Tory Skinner (Patrice Donnelly) in PERSONAL BEST (1982) and Cay Rivvers (Patricia Charbonneau) in DESERT HEARTS (1985 C).

Occasionally, the closeness of the cut may indicate repressed or just about-to-bubble-forth sexual otherness: Jane HATHAWAY (Nancy KULP) in *The Beverly Hillbillies* (1962–71 T); Maggie (Sally Willis) in KISS AND TELL (1980 T); Bella (Eva Mottley) in WIDOWS (1983 T); Sarah (Susan Sarandon) in THE HUNGER (1983 C); Vanessa (Kate Burton) in *Ellis Island* (1984 T); Jill Layton (Kim Greist) in *Brazil* (1985 C; the character has luxuriant blonde locks in a fantasy sequence and in the sex scene); Amazon (Grace Jones) in *A View to a Kill* (1985 C); Gail (Mariette Hartley) in MY TWO LOVES (1986 T); WPC June Ackland (Trudi Godwin) in *The Bill* (1987– T); Amanda Donohoe's society wife in *Diamond Skulls* aka *Dark Obsession* (1989 C); the daughter (Claire Skinner) in LIFE IS SWEET (1990 C); k. d. lang as Kotzebue in *Salmonberries* (1992 C); Maggie (Janine Turner) in NORTHERN EXPOSURE (1991– T).

Some sort of ether-borne directive must have gone out to producers: mainstream dyke characters must wear their hair long (sometimes very long), usually tinted, and waved: Barbara Hershey and Diana Scarwid in IN THE GLITTER PALACE; Gena Rowlands and Jane Alexander in A QUESTION OF LOVE (1978); Randie Heller in SOAP (1979); Sarah Keller in KISS AND TELL (1980); Patricia Charbonneau in DESERT HEARTS (1985 C); Lynn REDGRAVE in MY TWO LOVES (1986); Gail Strickland in HEARTBEAT (1989); Maggie Barnes (Elizabeth Kemp) in *L.A. Law* 'The Nut Before Christmas' (1991).

Diana Graham (Rachel Davies) is a declared FEMINIST, yet she appears at the CROWN COURT (in 'A Friend of the Family' 1979) wearing beautifully styled long hair, make-up – and a dress. The prosecuting counsel circulates a photograph of the defendant at a feminist rally 'wearing a suit and her hair austerely short'. Why is it, he asks snidely, 'that she is now wearing a Laura Ashley dress and her hair is long and permed?' Diana is caustic: 'I *could* have worn brogues and a tweed skirt. But I didn't.' With the custody of her lover's child at stake – as well as her own guilt or innocence on the charge of beating up her lover's husband – Diana knows the tactical significance of dress so that she does not further rouse the antagonism of society as represented by judge and jury. And that dress code includes well-cut, bouncing hair.

For men, long hair remains, in many circles, a source of disapproval. In mainstream entertainment it is restricted to characters strongly indicative of the cave man or the call of the native: Robert De Niro in *Cape Fear*; Daniel Day-Lewis in *Last of the Mohicans*; Nick Nolte at the start of *Down and Out in Beverly Hills*; Michael Douglas at the start of *The War of the Roses*. It is definitely not encouraged outside of costume pictures (Marlon Brando grew his for *Mutiny on the Bounty* to indicate the foppishness of Fletcher Christian) or outside of representations of Jesus (usually wigs). Most gay male characters wear their hair cut relatively short – with the exception of the mid-1970s period, exemplified by the discreetly shoulder-length style of Don FINLAYSON in *Number 96*.

The pony tail for men is making some headway, especially in certain of the American youth-oriented television drama series. But it is still securely located in Loonyville in the public mind. Hence, Prince Charles – turned radical greenie and sent to jail – in THE QUEEN AND I (1992 R).

Admitting that men dye their hair is strictly taboo – and it is rarely referred to in a female context either on television: Lucy does tell Desi that she is going to get her hair dyed in a 1952 I LOVE LUCY. One of the jokes in THE VOICE OF THE TURTLE (1947 C) is that Eleanor Parker's admirer is a bottle blond. Chortling over this is Ronald Reagan who, years later, would be 'accused' of dipping into the colouring bottle when he was President of the United States. Reagan's press aides were still denying that his hair was dyed in 1989, even after the white stubble appeared in pictures taken after he had brain surgery. By this time Dame Edna EVERAGE was saying publicly that 'Ronnie uses Grecian 2000'. But Reagan's barber had gone on a syndicated television programme in 1983 and sworn that his client's hair colour was natural. What is more he took a lie detector to prove it.

However, some actors do dye their hair – often to blend in with the colour film as well as to make themselves look better or younger and therefore better. Some of the more glaring dye jobs include the Tarleton Twins in *Gone with the Wind*; William Powell in *Life with Father* (1947 C); Dan Dailey in *Oh Men Oh Women!* (1957 C); Dwayne Hickman (to make him look younger as *Dobie Gillis* 1959 T); George Segal in *Rollercoaster* (1977 C, the exact same colour as his screen wife Susan Strasberg's); a similar occurrence in *Trading Places* (1983 C) where Dan Aykroyd as Winthrop and Kristin Holby as Penelope blend indivisibly. Elvis Presley plus Ann-Margret and William Demarest (who dyed his hair red to match hers) were positively blinding when sharing the screen in *Viva Las Vegas* aka *Love in Las Vegas* (1964 C).

Elvis Presley had been dyeing his since 1955. EASTENDERS had two males who had recourse to artificial products: Michelle's Lofty (Tom Watt), whose hair was coloured by her with odd results in 1986; and Frank (Mike Reid), who confessed to Pat (in 1987) that he'd been doing touch-ups for quite some time.

Dyed hair is becoming much more acceptable for younger men, now that every other soap opera star and footballer is streaked and curled within an inch of his life. Hairnets, though, are still the province of the very, very weird: ANTIQUE DEALER Michael REDGRAVE in *Confidential Report* aka *Mr Arkadin* (1955 C); Poirot (Albert Finney) in *Murder on the Orient Express* (1984 C); and Schömberg (Mario Adorf) in *Devil's Paradise* (1987 C).

hairy chests John Boswell writes: 'Not all men have hairy chests, but only men have chest hair; hence chest hair is thought of as essentially masculine. Though not all heterosexual couplings are procreative, only heterosexual acts could be procreative, so heterosexuality seems essentially procreative and homosexuality essentially not' (HIDDEN HISTORY, 1990).

Chest hair has had a somewhat bumpy history in visual entertainment. A lot of actors have had to shave their torsos as any trace of hirsuteness – except under the arms – was at one time seen as unclean and crude. This attitude began to relax with the advent of the very hirsute Aldo Ray, Philip Carey, Dale Robertson, Steve Cochran, Richard Burton and Howard Keel baring their top halves in the early 1950s while, in television, Western heroes began sprouting, with Clint Walker in *Cheyenne*, Robert Fuller in *Laramie* and Robert Horton in *Wagon Train*.

Yet Hollywood was still insistent that top box-office leading men shave their chests, though sometimes the stars rebelled (stubbled chests are very unpleasant). Thus William Holden is hairy in *The Bridges of Toko-Ri* (1954), smooth in *Picnic* (1955), hairy in *The*

Proud and the Profane (1956), smooth in *The Bridge on the River Kwai* (1957). Charlton Heston was smooth in *The Ten Commandments* and *The Naked Jungle*, furry in *Ben-Hur* and *Planet of the Apes*. Marlon Brando, lightly covered in *Julius Caesar* and *Viva Zapata*, was noticeably furrier in *The Nightcomers* and *Last Tango in Paris* made 20 years later.

Hairies of the 1960s and 1970s: Sean Connery (whose James Bond was taken over by his hairless antithesis Roger Moore), Alan BATES, Ben Gazzara, Stuart Whitman, Stanley Baker, James Caan, Burt Reynolds, Robert Redford.

Hairies of the 1980s and 1990s: Brad DAVIS, Kevin Costner, John Hargreaves, Alex Baldwin, Pearce Brosnan, John James and Michael Nader in DYNASTY, Keith Allen and Peter Richardson in *The Bullshitters* (1984), Paul Mercurio.

Brian Deacon played *Jesus* hairy chested in 1979. There have been no hairy Tarzans.

The sensuality of hair is usually the province of female characters – and its appreciation is restricted to the head – hair combing: Nellie does Sally's in TENKO (1981); and washing, an erotic, spiritual, sensuous, clean way of communicating: perfect for TV movies like MY TWO LOVES (1986) in which Marjorie (Lynn REDGRAVE) gives Gail (Mariette Hartley) a shampoo before she takes her (offscreen) to bed.

hairdressers If male, they tend to be viewed as weedy and/or effeminate and/or gay: George Formby in *Keep Fit* (1937 C): 'I know I'm not athletic/And I look pathetic' ('Biceps, Muscles and Brawn' song); Donovan Winter, with lace hankie and looking very smart, preparing to doll up tramp Eddie Byrne in *Time, Gentlemen Please!* (1953 C): 'I promise you a metamorphosis'/'No, just give me a haircut'; panting Claude Stroud in PERRY MASON 'The Case of the Ominous Outcast' (1960 T); Henry (Charles Lloyd Pack), tortured by blackmail, and the blackmailer who brings on a fatal heart attack in VICTIM (1961 C); Harry (Richard Burton) and Charlie (Rex Harrison) in STAIRCASE

(1969 C); Jordan Coyle (David Robb 1977 T; Gregor Fisher 1979 R) in *Caledonian Cascade*; Robin (Craig RUSSELL) whose boss terminates his employment once he discovers he's doing drag at nights in OUTRAGEOUS! (1977 C); STARSKY AND HUTCH screaming the salon down as they work undercover in 'Dandruff' (1978 T); the demonic John Rye who gives a theatre critic's ground-down wife a Medusa hairdo in JUST BEFORE MIDNIGHT 'Getting Ahead' (1979 R); Derek (Clyde Ventura) tending Marilyn MONROE's golden locks in *Moviola* 'This Year's Blonde' (1980 T); Eric (Geoffrey Palmer) in THE HOUSE-BOY (1982 T); Roddy (Michael Kearns – 'I'm never obvious') and his friend Clarence (Barry Pearl) in *The Making of a Male Model* (1983 T); Jason (Roddy MCDOWALL) in *Hollywood Wives* (1983 T); Toby (Brian Capron) taking the law into his own hands after being QUEER-BASHED in THE GENTLE TOUCH 'Do It Yourself' (1984 T); 'Matilda' (Trader FAULKNER) who also fixes up crooks with false passports in *Call Me Mister* 'Long Shot' (1986 T); Herbie in *Split Ends* (1989 T); Bruce La Bruce (that's the *actor's* name) in *No Skin Off My Ass* (1991 C); Brent (Tate Donovan) in *Inside Monkey Zetterland* (1992 C); Tarquin (Richard Pearce) who reforms a local football club in *Totally Gutted* (1992 R); etc.

Flouncy hairdressers from the past include, under periwig and powder, Jean Claude-Briarly (who fancies fellow passenger Casanova) in *That Night at Varennes* (1982 C), and the two squealers and squeakers attacking the foot and a half high creations of Nastassia Kinski and her sisters in *Revolution* (1985 C).

The exceptions: determinedly hetero-sexual Milo (Michael Caine) in *Sleuth* (1972 C); Warren Beatty in *Shampoo* (1975 C); Victor French pretending to be a movie star's crimper in an episode of *Highway to Heaven* (1986 T); Vince (Robert STEPHENS) and Perry (John Cater) in *Unnatural Causes* 'Window, Sir' (1986 T): they have worked together 20 years, now have murderous intent; a sexy, charismatic *Shampoo*-style crimper in *Crossroads* (1976 T).

It is now generally accepted that all male hairdressers will be gay unless they look like Warren Beatty. And understanding – a shoulder for women to cry upon. The wife in *Caledonian Cascade* sees the shop as her bolt-hole: 'The most undemanding place I know.' Sometimes, though, things can go wrong: on the night of the Academy Awards, red-headed Diana Barry (Maggie Smith) looks at herself hypercritically in the mirror: 'I asked for a simple rinse, and that ditzy queen gave me crayon!' (CALIFORNIA SUITE 1978 C).

One female hairdresser who loves women: Diana Scarwid in *Silkwood* (1983 C).

HAL Born 12 January 1992; died sometime in 2001. A computer, with a rather effete voice, a first-class brain and an ability to sing old music-hall songs like 'A Bicycle Made For Two (Daisy, Daisy)'. He misbehaves rather badly, killing three of the astronauts (two in deep sleep, one outside the ship) in *2001: A Space Odyssey* (1968 C) and, as a result, has his circuits cut by the survivor, Dave Bowman (Keir Dullea). HAL, his voice turning tremulous, pleads with Dave to spare him: 'I know everything hasn't been all right with me, but I can assure you that it will be all right again.'

His one red eye with its yellow pupil is HAL's sole 'human' vestige, but his voice, mellow and bright, traces a whole lifetime of service from more conventional valets and butlers used to having the key to the pantry. Does HAL have an adolescent crush on Dave, or is it a full-blown passion after months spent gazing at him jogging round the ship? The director, Stanley Kubrick has always denied it, yet a question remains over why he substituted the voice of Douglas Rain in post-production for that of Martin Balsam, more traditionally associated with the gruffly efficient (though he would go on to play a flutter-ing ANTIQUE DEALER in *The Anderson Tapes* in 1971).

To douse any untoward future speculation about HAL, his second coming (in *2010* made in 1984 with Rain again providing the voice) gave him a female counterpart, SAL, and revealed the *real* reason for his spectacular breakdown (which had nothing whatsoever to do with undying love for Dave).

For all that HAL is – in Kubrick and Arthur C. Clarke's vision – *not* gay, the idea that such a computer *could* be wouldn't curl up and die. In *There Comes a Time* (1983 T) CEDRIC (given an epicene voice by Chris Edmett) expires while singing 'I'm half crazy/Oh for the love of you' to his master.

Marian Halcombe Character in Wilkie Collins' Victorian thriller *The Woman in White*, the half-sister of victimized Laura Fairlie – and a match for the cunning Count FOSCO. Rumoured to be based on Marian Evans (aka George Eliot). First played, in the 1928 silent by Louise Prussing, then by, among others, Eleanor Parker (1948 C) and – superbly – by Diana QUICK (1982 T). The *Radio Times* article, heralding the BBC's adaptation, read as follows: 'A woman of masculine force and intellect, with a strongly latent lesbian attraction to her half-sister, she has a graceful figure, large hands, ugly face and a faint moustache.' After thwarting the plans of Fosco, Marian settles down as COMPANION to Laura and her husband Walter Hartwright.

half a man The concept of a man robbed of his virility because of para- or quadraplegia was first discussed in *The Men* (1950 C) in relation to Marlon Brando's Ken. Barbara STANWYCK abused Edward G. Robinson for this reason in *The Violent Men/Rough Company* (1953 C). The same actress had a similarly affected spouse in *Walk on the Wild Side* (which, it is hinted, holds the key as to why she has sought out the love of women). Lana Turner strayed (with Anthony Quinn) because her screen hubby (Lloyd Nolan) couldn't satisfy her in *Portrait in Black* (1960 C); she said to her step-daughter (Sandra Dee): 'Was it because your father was only half a man that you are so eager to believe me guilty of deceit, of murder ... of every sin?'

This incapacity for full sexual intercourse is seen as casting these men into something like outer darkness as human beings. Others in similar circumstances (which was a perfect 'cover' for adultery to be 'condoned') were Clifford Chatterley (Leo Genn 1956 C; Shane Briant 1982 C; James Wilby 1993 T); and characters played by Victor Jory (*The Fugitive Kind* 1960 C) and Christopher Cazenove in *Eye of the Needle* (1981 C). Mental scarring also left Alan BATES (*The Return of the Soldier* 1981 C) and Dominic Guard (*Wilfred and Eileen* 1981 T) less than whole sexually.

Half-And-Half Sung by jolly Jessie Matthews and chorus girls (wearing black to the left, white to the right) in *First a Girl* (1935 C). At the end of this (derivatively spectacular) number, 'Victoria' doffs her hat to reveal that 'she' is a 'he' – much to the chagrin of a potential suitor, Robert (Griffith Jones). Later, seated at a bar, Robert casts aspersions on the young man's sexuality, but he (ie she) smokes cigars, downs double scotches and leers at the girls with the best of 'em. Which confuses the love-locked Robert even more.

With music by Maurice Sigler, Al Goodland and Al Hoffman, the song had lyrics by Norman Hackforth – who was the delightfully, lugubriously camp 'voice' telling the audience what the animal, vegetable or mineral objects were on *Twenty Questions* (1947–76 R).

Hall, Grayson (1928–85) Accomplished player of driven, repressed people with strikingly sharp features and 'mannish' gait, beginning with Pepe, the bistro proprietress with eyes for the heroine in *Satan in High Heels* (1962 C) and riding on through a whole crop of Gothic scientists, schoolteachers and such like: best remembered for her Judith Fellowes, the EVANGELICAL CHRISTIAN

whose lust for one of her female charges on a coach trip sends her into a frenzy of jealousy and puritanical rage in *The Night of the Iguana* (1964 C). She was toughie fashion editress in *Who Are You, Polly Magoo?* (1965 C) and a no-nonsense book critic called Jody Moore in *The Man from UNCLE* 'The Pieces of Fate Affair' (1967 T). From 1966 until 1971 she played Dr Julia Hoffman in the cult series *Dark Shadows*; she also starred in the 1971 movie version, *House of Dark Shadows*. Then came another heavy in *Gargoyles* (1972 T), and a period of time in a more traditional soap *One Life to Live* (as Euphemia Ralston).

Hall, James Andrew (1939–) English television writer and novelist (MAN IN ASPIC 1965) who created BBC Television's COMING OUT for *Play for Today* in 1979. Also of interest: ARMCHAIR THEATRE 'Harry Sebrof's Story' (1973); *Kilvert's Diary* (1977); *Broken Glass* (1982); *Love and Marriage* 'Lucifer' (1984); DAVID COPPERFIELD (1986). (He discussed *Coming Out* on *Start the Week* in 1979.)

Hall, [Marguerite] Radclyffe (1886–1943) English novelist and poet, lover of Mabel Batten and later Una, Lady Troubridge. Her openly lesbian novel THE WELL OF LONELINESS was declared obscene in 1928. Her significance for lesbians of that period and beyond was discussed briefly by Alison HENNEGAN in GAY LIFE (1981) and by Sonja Ruehl in *Introduction to Sociology* 'Sexual Identity' (1981 T). Another novel, *The Unlit Lamp* was adapted for radio in 1980.

Hall, Professor Stuart (1932–) Writer, lecturer and broadcaster on aspects of television's interrelationship with the way we live. Co-founder of University of Birmingham Centre for Contemporary Cultural Studies. *Panorama* 'Colour Prejudice' (1958 T); *Dead or Alive* (1958 R), some opinions on the state of society; *Television and Society* (1973 T); SATURDAY NIGHT OUT (1991 T); *Personal Details* (1992 T), 'the shifting realities between identity and society'; etc.

Hallatt, May (1880–1969) English actress who popped up as bustling, beaky characters (the servant in *Black Narcissus*; the char in *The Horse's Mouth*), but is most strongly etched as racing-mad, tweedy and totally nonjudgemental Miss Meacham in *Separate Tables* (1958 C), which she also played in the West End and on Broadway.

R: housekeeper in Anouilh's *The Untamed* (1953).

T: Mrs Tidmarsh in *Strictly Personal* (1953); 'An old lady' in *The Royalty* (1958); Mrs Bates in *Emma* (1960); Miss Glaser in Somerset MAUGHAM's 'The Voice of the Turtle' (1960); etc.

Hamilton, Patrick (1904–62) English novelist and playwright who had great early success with the plays *Gaslight* and ROPE. His career, which dribbled away because of alcohol and personal problems, was assessed on *Third Ear* (1992), and surviving friends recalled him in a *Late Show Special* 'Whatever Happened to?' (1988 T).

Gaslight (1939 & 1944 C etc); *Money with Menaces* (1942, 1952, 1956 & 1976 R); *Hangover Square* (1944 C); *Rope* (1949, also R/T); *Twenty Thousand Streets Under the Sky* (1993 R).

Hammond, Dame Joan (1912–) New Zealand-born soprano who sold over a million 'O My Beloved Fathers'. Proved that classical singers could be jolly good sports in television shows like *Music for You* (1958), and *A-Z* (1959 with Alan MELVILLE), and THIS IS YOUR LIFE. Interviewed by Sue MacGregor about the life she now leads in Australia, with her partner of 50-plus years, Lolita, in *Conversation Piece* (1988). That same year she filmed a number of *Master Class* programmes where her still formidable vocal power and her simple directness are well displayed. 'We all know what it's like to be in love with two men,' she tells one student in a droll throwaway, and to another (studying *Tosca*): '*I* don't sell myself to beautiful women.'

Hampstead Heath Seven hundred acres of lushness, a favoured place for fresh air, conversation, dog-walking, swimming, sunbathing, nocturnal constitutionals, and flying kites (as the couple do in THE GROUNDLING AND THE KITE 1984 T). By day lots of reclining male–female couples; by night...

There is talk of MORIARTY paying a visit in THE GOON SHOW's 'The Secret Escritoire' (1955 R): 'an eccentric lying face down on his back on Hampstead Heath.' After a spat, Rob tells Michael in AGONY 'Coming Out ... And Going In Again' (1980 T): 'If you want me, I'll be on Hampstead Heath.' Included as very much part of London's gay territory in *Public Eye* 'Age of Consent' (1992 T). However, there was no specific mention in *Down Your Way* in 1986, and the cruising scene set there was removed from NIGHTHAWKS (but was on view in *Nighthawks 2*). The Elysian Fields frolic, shot on the Heath, in *The Boy Friend*, which included a Sapphic caress or two, was cut for the cinema but reinserted for TV screenings from 1980 onwards.

Cedric **Hampton** Unbridled golddigger in *Love in a Cold Climate* (1980 T) played by Michael COCHRANE. Pink good looks in a basket of golden curls, courtesy of peroxide and tongs, devotee of peacock-blue suits – sometimes mixed with green. Cedric, from the United States, sends ripples through English society for appearing to fall for Lady Montdore: 'I do rather love her, at least love *creating* her, and she adores one.' But his true nature is always shining through: 'One's needs are very simple, but such as they are they must be satisfied – over and over again.' Among other cherishable lines, so pluperfectly rendered by the actor: 'What Trevor really specializes in is one', 'I have an acquaintance – an expert in cleaning and repairs – under my supervision', 'I have a German friend in Paris and a more frivolous creature cannot be imagined', 'You're so lucky not to be a beauty, dear. You'll never have to worry about your looks.'

Hancock's Half Hour (UK 1954–9 R; 1956–60 T) Achingly funny watershed in radio and television comedy with Alan Simpson and Ray Galton creating an alternative family for the easily wounded, bombastic Anthony Hancock: namely his waif-like friend, William Kerr, aged anywhere between 21 and 43, who has lived with (and off) him for years and is described variously as 'best friend', 'spinster of this parish', 'my Filipino houseboy' and (for tax purposes) 'dependent relative'. Later on, Grizelda Pugh (Hattie Jacques) joined the clan in Railway Cuttings, East Cheam and the disreputable Sid (James) was always popping in.

Sid would later live with Hancock (sharing a bedroom and no mention of what became of Bill). Such were the possibilities in this latter pairing that one script – 'The Italian Maid' (1959) – was rewritten on Tony Hancock's demand because the housekeeping arrangements depicted were buzzing with 'homosexual overtones'.

On radio, with the addition of Kenneth WILLIAMS ('STOP MESSIN' ABOUT'), CAMP situations were sure to arise from time to time. And did: principally in 'The Income Tax Demand' (1956, Hancock on Williams' lap); 'Cyrano De Hancock' (1956, 'proposing' to Sid but getting 'married' to Williams); 'The Male Suffragettes' (1958, Sid and Tony 'hate all women' and start men's lib); 'The Publicity Photograph' (1958, Hancock has homosexual panic when confronted by efflorescent photographer Williams); 'Bill and Father Christmas' (1958, nurturing Bill who still believes in Santa); 'The Poetry Society' (1959, pretentious queens in a send-up of the beat poets).

After leaving or being left by Tony Hancock, Sid James had his own television show, *Citizen James*, with none other than Bill Kerr. Described as 'an Australian with ambitions to be a parasite, public enemy and social evil', he was Sid's friend, factotum and foil (1960–61, scripts by Galton and Simpson). Sid's radio career continued in *It's*

a Deal (1961) with Dennis PRICE as the genteelly suffering Hancock figure.

a handbag? Shocked inquisitionary reaction by Lady BRACKNELL in THE IMPORTANCE OF BEING EARNEST to her future son-in-law's dubious nativity, usually uttered by actresses with cloth-of-gold voices: Sylvia Coleridge (1937 T); Margaret Rutherford (1946 T); Dorothy Lane (1947 R); Edith Evans (1951 R; 1952 C); Helen Haye (1957 R); Martita HUNT (1958 T); Pamela Brown (1964 T); Doris Speed (Annie Walker in CORONATION STREET (1974 T); Coral Browne (1974); Judi Dench (1977 R); Wendy Hiller (1986 T); Joan Plowright (1988 T). Probably the best known and most quoted 2-word line of any printed text in the English language, apart from 'Jesus wept'. Its currency is mostly due to Edith Evans' indelibly spellbinding rendering, all quivering, ululating pugnacity forever cradled in celluloid in one of the BBC's most regularly aired films, as well as on the 1951 recording with GIELGUD.

Commented 'Oscar Wilde' (Simon CALLOW in *The Miles Kington Interview* 1993 R): 'The measure of my success is not that everyone goes around saying "A handbag?" in a loud mezzo contralto – it is that no other British playwright has dared to mention a handbag on stage since I did. It is the only known example of the mention of a lady's accessory being proof of intent to plagiarize.'

Captain Peacock (Frank Thornton) does a passable impersonation of the society gorgon when he expostulates to Mr HUMPHRIES about the piece of ladies' equipment he is carrying in ARE YOU BEING SERVED? 'Your Figures Are Slipping' (1973 T: Mr H. was 'minding it' for Miss Brahms while she went to the Ladies).

handbags The sight or even the thought of one of these sensible carrying cases on the person of a male is enough for a heated reaction – or a sneer. In *Summer Sketch* (1938 R) John Hilton raised the pink warning flag by informing (women) listeners: 'That's what we're coming to.

We *are*. There's no other way, of course. They'll be very superior bags ... We'll either carry it like a satchel over one shoulder, or have it chained to the wrist like a bank messenger's wallet ... Then we shall be able to dress in flimsies like you.'

British-born or British-raised men continued their resistance over 40 years: '... if I have got it right the friends discovered a latent homosexuality in their relationship ... My dear, you could have knocked us out with a handbag' (review of Frederic RAPHAEL's *The Best of Friends, Listener*, 13.3.80); '... walking down the street swinging their handbags' (Patrick WHITE giving his views on gay politics in an interview on New Zealand's TV1 in 1984); 'Anyone who calls on doors in Bermondsey with a handbag deserves everything they get' (Gerry Fitt on Peter TATCHELL's campaign and harassment in Bermondsey in ANY QUESTIONS? 1983 R).

hand-holding Very rare occurrence on small or large screen: Dirk BOGARDE (dying, possibly dead) as the bandit and John Mills (wounded) as the priest in the closing scene of *The Singer Not the Song* (1961 C); Wayne SLEEP and Gregory Phillips as National Service babes, in their jammies, in *The Virgin Soldiers* (1969 C); villains Bruce Glover and Putter Smith in DIAMONDS ARE FOREVER (1971 C); John (Joseph O'Conor) and Graham (Sam Dale) in ONLY CONNECT (1979 T). Increasingly noticeable in documentaries (Colin and Terry outside the Golden Lion pub in *Public Eye* 'Age of Consent' 1992 T) and confessional shows (two women on *The Oprah Winfrey Show* 'Left for a Lesbian'; two men on DONAHUE 'Two Gay Men Get Married' (1991 T) and 'Two Gay Men Answer Questions from Teenagers' (1992 T)).

One of the first pairs of entwined hands to be seen on television belonged to Peter de Waal and Peter Bonsall-Boone in Australia's CHEQUERBOARD 'This just happens to be a part of me' (1972 T). Over a shot of the couple walking along the street bound together by palms and fingers, one of the Peters comments on the soundtrack: 'It was a very conscious act at first but, to our surprise, nobody took the slightest bit of notice – it took time to become natural.'

In THE LOCKER ROOM (1992 R) Tom ROBINSON revealed that he had been so used to the subterfuge of gay life that when he and his girlfriend were walking along a tow path with linked hands, the approach of another person automatically made him loosen his grip and separate, lest aggressive comments or actual violence ensue.

handkerchieves Indications of male–male sexual preference from the mid-1970s. Evidence of a colourful period in Western gay history and practice, partially decoded in CRUISING (1980 C). Gay sex-shop owner (Powers Boothe) explains to undercover cop Steve Burns (Al Pacino): 'light blue means you give a blow job; in the right pocket it means you take it; grey means a hustler; red ...' Burns chooses a nice yellow one. Later, in a bar, a man approaches and asks: 'Are you into water sports?' The pretend gay blinks and stammers: 'I like to watch.' The enquirer is not impressed. 'Then take that handkerchief out of your *left* pocket!'

Hanky Panky Sung by MADONNA in *Dick Tracy* (1990 C) and at the 1990 ACADEMY AWARDS in full Marilyn/*Gentlemen Prefer Blondes* rig. This was Stephen SONDHEIM at his friskiest, not to say most downmarket. It's all about S&M – apparently; certainly spanking comes into it. (The song was cut from the 1992 showing of *Dick Tracy* on Australian television. Oddly, a few weeks later, Madonna was shown – same channel, same time – singing part of the same song in IN BED WITH MADONNA.)

Happy Days Are Here Again Donny and Marie Osmond sang it on their show *Donny and Marie* (1977 T) which was watched by 15.5 million homes in the USA and seen by 10.1 million children aged 2–11. 'Howdy gay times' in

Jack Yellen and Milton Ager's 1929 song became 'Hello, *good* times'.

happy endings 'Well, my dear, let's face it, nobody's going to stand for a play on *that* subject having a happy ending. Well, I mean the sight of the two of them living happily ever after; you can't possibly suggest *that*,' says Neville Pikelet (Allan MCCLELLAND) in A HEDGE, BACKWARDS (1956 R). People like *them* are more likely to get to the final FADE-OUT fairly intact and whole, smiling even, than was the rule in the 1950s, in the 1960s and on into the 1970s. AIDS has, of course, alloyed matters – though films about illness and death *have* ended on transcendent, hopeful notes. Among the more traditional happy endings: MAKING LOVE; MY BEAUTIFUL LAUN-DRETTE; MAURICE; DESERT HEARTS; YOUNG SOUL REBELS; BEYOND GRAVITY; *Friends Forever*. Quentin CRISP marches proudly through the park at the end of THE NAKED CIVIL SERVANT and (if life after death is to be believed) the ashes of Ken and Joe make a perfect mix (though in unequal quantities) in PRICK UP YOUR EARS.

the happy homosexual Psychoanalyst Edmund Bergler was quoted in the medicine section of *Time* magazine in 1956 as saying that, in addition to a string of personality defects, 'There are no happy homosexuals'. This view was endorsed for people inside and outside America by the SHOW ME A HAPPY HOMOSEXUAL line from THE BOYS IN THE BAND.

Politicians have seized on this sickness model with enthusiasm. Nigel Lawson, Chancellor of the Exchequer when questioned about CLAUSE 28 by Brian Walden in 1988, could say, without a trace of self-doubt or shame: 'I don't think it is a happy condition and I think it is unfortunate, and I don't think we'd want that promoted or proselytized.'

But happy homosexuals there are. Twinkled Denis LEMON on LBC Radio's *Monty at Large* 'The Gay Scene in London' (1979): 'Some people in gay lib would say that to be homosexual is

one thing, to be gay is to be a happy homosexual.' Terry Sanderson, author of *How to Be a Happy Homosexual*, appeared on LBC's *The Brian Hayes Show* in 1986. He relayed how he came out 'determinedly ... not bravely' in a Yorkshire mining village. 'It's a matter of deciding whether you want to run your life or whether you want others to run it.'

Some examples of people not ashamed to admit it: 'For the first time in my life, I'm happy. I've got a life of my own' (Robert (Steven Vidler) in WORDS OF ONE SYLLABLE Aust R 1991; Robert later qualifies this by saying: 'My life is okay'); 'I've never been happier at the moment than I have in my life' (Derek JARMAN in OUT 'Love and Marriage' 1991 T); 'I'm *very* happy' (Jackie FORSTER in OUT 'Women Like That' 1991 T); 'I'm *totally* happy describing myself as a lesbian' (one of the teenagers in *100%* 'I Am What I Am' 1992 T); 'Tell them I've had a wonderful life' (WITTGENSTEIN's last words, quoted on HORIZON 'A Wonderful Life' 1989 T); 'I'm happy, sergeant ... I've learnt the secret of gracious living' (Duffy CLAYTON (Harold SCOTT) in DIXON OF DOCK GREEN 'The Salvation of Duffy' 1958 T).

Morris **Hardacre** (James Saxon in *Brass* 1982–4/1990) A primping, cowardly mine owner's son fixated by mother and TEDDY BEAR. An Oxford aesthete, with an unrequited passion for one of his father's workers – who is snaffled by his sister. Joining the church to salve his emotional wounds, Morris is recruited to spy for the Soviets by dashing Guy Baggers.

A thoroughgoing rotter: a sneaky, talentless, immoral little streak of slime. Not that his older brother is any better (just conventionally nicer looking). His only good qualities are expressed over his bear Hesketh (and in the 1990 series his gollywog) and his mother (who lets him wear her jewellery and dresses). Probably the biggest tragedy of his life was his (very nasty) father cutting his curls.

Saxon, whether in quilted dressing gown or cardinal's robes, has a field day as an *ancien régime* queen forever teetering on the edge of revisiting Brideshead. Unfortunately his lines failed to live up to the premise, being generally coarse and unadventurous: 'I've lost my friend with the beautiful hair. Do you know what it feels like when the bottom's dropped out of your world?'

In one of his last appearances (Bradley Gets On Top), Morris looks forward to the serenity of a POW camp and 'doing an all-male version of THE IMPORTANCE OF BEING EARNEST'.

Saxon was quoted in a *Daily Mirror* interview in 1984 as saying: 'My only worry in taking the part was that I didn't want it to become a stereotyped "camp" role. But it's so outrageously and completely over the top, I think I got away with it.'

Hard Cases (UK 1988–9 T) Social workers, their working lives and off-duty selves.
W: John Warren and John Singer; P: Phillip Bowman/Andrew Benson; D: Michael Brayshaw; Central; 60 mins.

Competent, unadorned drama series. Few surprises except that handsome Ross (Eric Deacon) is revealed, several episodes in, as an ordinary, hard-working, deeply caring gay man who goes on an anti-CLAUSE 28 protest march (and is hauled over the coals for bringing the SOCIAL WORK profession into jeopardy).

'How dare you judge me as a parent or a husband!' (client to Ross after finding out he's not married).

A Hard God (Aust 1980 T) Peter Kenna's classic play about displaced Irish Catholic country people living in the hard, unyielding city of Sydney involves a degree of emotional exploration: by the older generation and by the younger, solely represented by Joe Cassidy (Patrick Phillips) who can't understand why Jack (Simon Burke), who had wanted to KISS him and make love with him, rejects him as a lover and as a friend – after confessing his sin to a priest.

P: Alan Buke; D: William Fitzwater; ABC; 70 mins.

A visit to the priest convinces one of the boys that what he had thought of and experienced as pleasurable and natural was really a crime against nature. This heinous behaviour must never be repeated. Joe, the one who led Jack into temptation (though it was Jack who 'seduced' him), must be cast off as a potential lover and as friend. A hard god indeed.

> Jack: 'What do you want from me. Do you want me to lose my soul?'
> Joe: 'I'm not afraid of losing my soul. One of us has to be wrong.'
> Jack: '... I've got to take notice of the priest or I can't get absolution ... you tell me what I'm supposed to do about *that*!'

There were two radio productions: one, in 1975, had Simon Burke playing Joe instead of Jack (who was Simon Apps), and there was a BBC version (considerably cut – across all scenes – in 1976 with David Timson as Joe and Nigel Lambert as Jack). *A Hard God* is a set play for Australia's Higher School Certificate.

Peter Kenna wrote a sequel called *Furtive Love* (1978) – an altogether friskier piece than this depressingly earnest, if well-crafted warhorse: Joe is now a young artistic queen exploring sex.

Harding, Gilbert (1907–60) English panellist, quiz-master and opinionated broadcaster. 'Start speaking your mind and you're rude and offensive ... stop speaking your mind and you're namby pamby and you're slipping,' he said to Peter FINCH in *Simon and Laura* (1955 C). Began with the BBC Monitoring Service (1939–45 T) and then became a part of the fabric of British life on *Round Britain Quiz*; *The Brains Trust*; *Twenty Questions*; *We Beg to Differ*; *Purely for Pleasure*; and – his apogee – *What's My Line?* where he grumped his way onto the front pages of the newspapers and was a major talking point in a television world which was generally ultra-polite. The possibility of marriage between this confirmed bachelor and spinster Nancy

SPAIN intrigued the British no end (it came to nothing).

He described himself to Malcolm Muggeridge as 'a dedicated phoney' on PANORAMA (1954) and was reduced to tears (when asked about his mother by John Freeman) on FACE TO FACE (1960). He appeared in a dozen or so films (usually as 'himself'), opened an AMBRIDGE fête in 1952, and confessed his likes and dislikes on, eg, *Spice of Life* (personal scrapbook, 1954 R), *Harding Reads Some Lines* (from his autobiography, 1956 R), and I KNOW WHAT I LIKE. He collapsed and died just after he had recorded *Round Britain Quiz*. 'That enigmatic man ... was bad-tempered and rude, yet his friends counted him as one of the kindest, and most generous' (Owen Spencer Thomas on BBC Radio London's *Gilbert Harding* 1979).

'Every Wart and Pustule' is the title of Andy Medhurst's gay reading of the significance of Gilbert Harding in *Popular Television In Britain: Studies in Cultural History* (1991).

Hare, Augustus (1834–1903) 'A dapper little man, a snob, a confirmed bachelor, an excellent travel writer, a witty storyteller' (*Radio Times* on the occasion of A BOOK AT BEDTIME's adaptation of his autobiography, delivered by Richard Vernon, 1987 R). Two chapters had also been read, in 1968, by Robert EDDISON under the title *Touches of Delicacy*. He was included among the *Famous Gossips* 'Augustus Hare: The Years with Mother' (1966 T, played by Alan BEN-NETT).

Harris, Jonathan (1914–) American actor with crinkled, duck-like features, best known as Dr Zachary SMITH in LOST IN SPACE and as Bradford Webster in *The Third Man*. Other roles have been generally as creepy: Lysias, the sly court functionary in *The Big Fisherman* (1959 C); a doctor in THE TWILIGHT ZONE 'Twenty-Two' (1961 T) and George Alfred in 'The Silence' (1961 T); unscrupulous ANTIQUES DEALER in *Sanford and Son* 'Pot Luck' (1973 T). Also *The Grass Harp* (1962 T); *Land of the*

Giants (1969); *Night Gallery* 'Pay the Piper' (1972); *Fantasy Island*; etc.

Hart, Lorenz 'Larry' (1895–1943) American lyricist, usually in collaboration with Richard Rodgers (*On Your Toes, Pal Joey, The Boys from Syracuse* etc). Played by Mickey Rooney in WORDS AND MUSIC (1948 C).

Song by Song by Hart (1978 T); *I Call It Genius* (W/Narr: Hubert Gregg, 1980 R); *Words by Hart* (1985 R); *Saturday Review* 'For Valentine's Day an assessment of the man who wrote "My Funny Valentine"', (1987 T) with Mark Steyn discussing the qualities of some of Hart's 650 Broadway lyrics.

Hartley, L[eslie] P[oles] (1886–1972) English novelist. *Eustace and Hilda* (ie *The Shrimp and the Anemone, The Sixth Heaven* and *Eustace and Hilda*) (1958 R; 1980 T; read on WOMAN'S HOUR 1992 R); *The Go-Between* (1971 C); *Journey to the Unknown* 'The Killing Bottle' (1971 T); *The Hireling* (1973 C).

On *Bookshelf* (1979 R) it was revealed that Hilda was based on Hartley's very strong-willed mother (the anemone) who eats up Eustace (the shrimp). Francis KING spoke of Hartley's underlying ruthlessness: he had been glad that T. C. Worsley (who had given him a bad review) was dying. Frank Delaney asked why he 'sought male companions from a class into which he had not been born'. Penelope Fitzgerald likened this to Dickens and his opium dens. King thought it was a way of extending his scope as a writer: 'Leslie thought he was getting new subject matter by associating with people from the criminal classes ... He left the country and came to live in London, which is always a mistake, isn't it. I don't really know what it was. He was leading a completely different life and I think a lot of old friends felt very sad – but he knew what he was doing.'

In *Sharing the Fun* (1988 R) Norah Hartley remembers her brother: 'I very much regret not going to Venice myself. It might have helped me to understand

Leslie better.' None of the Hartley children, Leslie, Norah and Enid married.

Hartley, Marsden (1887–1943) American artist who was the basis (with another painter, Charles Demuth) for Charles Marsden, epicene novelist and brother/father figure and confidant to Nina Leeds in Eugene O'Neill's *Strange Interlude*. Marsden was played by Ralph Morgan (1932 C, with Norma Shearer); Noel Willman (1958 T, with Diane Cilento); Edward Petherbridge (1986 T, with Glenda Jackson). 'I've known many Marsdens on many different levels and it had always seemed to me that they've never been done in literature with any sympathy or real insight' (O'Neill quoted in Louis Shaeffer's *O'Neill, Son and Artist*, 1973). In the course of the play's four-plus hours, Charles Marsden is referred to as 'this ladylike soul', 'an old maid who seduces himself in his novels', 'a slacker bachelor', 'the old sissy', 'queer creature' and 'one of those poor devils who spends his life trying to discover which sex he belongs to'. However, he could be said to be far more perceptive than any of the other characters, succouring Nina. As a reviewer commented in the *Advocate* in 1985: 'He's the only one who sees all, knows all and, ultimately, heals all. O'Neill makes the man who abhors all sex with women ... the only sane, whole, rational one in the bunch.'

Harty, Russell (1934–88) English journalist, television producer, broadcaster, and very individual 1970s and 1980s television talk-show host – his 1981 interview with Dirk BOGARDE is a highlight of advance and (how to beat a quick) retreat. Also successful, just before his death, as host of *Start the Week* (1987 R). Last series on television: *Russell Harty's Grand Tour* (1988, including a meeting with actor Helmut Berger).

Biography/autobiography: *Russell Harty's Christmas Eves* (broadcast from his home for several years during the early 1980s); *Television on Trial* 'Television and Values' (1986 T); *With Great Pleasure* (1987 T, with Geraldine McEwan and Kenneth Branagh who read his favourite poems and prose pieces; ARENA 'Talk Is Cheap' (1987 T, one of the contributors on the art of the chat show); *Russell Harty* (1988 T).

'... but what was it that made total strangers like me feel diminished by his death?' (letter from a viewer in Chorley, Lancashire, *The Guardian*, May 1988).

Harvey, Ian (1914–87) Parliamentary Under-Secretary to the Foreign Office who, in 1958, was found guilty of GROSS INDECENCY. 'An ill-judged excursion into St James's Park – an indecency offence with a guardsman – had shattering implications in the 1950s when homosexuality was still a crime' (*Nationwide* 'Fighting Back').

He was the subject of one of *Nationwide*'s 'Fighting Back' programmes (1982 T). Seen frying sausages amid wild disorder in his Paddington flat, he spoke unsentimentally about his fall from grace. He had reattained a public profile – after the years in the wilderness, he came into prominence as vice president of the Campaign for Homosexual Equality (CHE) and organizer of a gay Tory group. He was also the governor of a number of schools and colleges, and in the documentary he was seen presiding over the annual general meeting of Paddington Tory Party (a picture of Maggie THATCHER by his side).

'It is said about people in our sphere that it's the danger that makes it more exciting ... you either face the world or you jump off the bridge. Once one's decided to face the battle you get on with it. I've never been ashamed of being a homosexual because that's the way I am.'

He appeared posthumously in *The Human Jigsaw* 'Socially Unacceptable' in 1987: 'I might have had a cabinet post or led the Party.'

He could have partially inspired the character of deeply conflicted Gerald Fox in COMING OUT (1979 T): as played by Richard Pearson, Gerald Fox is a smug, gourmandizing Tory, all thoughtless socializing and prickly gossip. Half annoyed, half complaisant; a gay activist, nonetheless.

Ken Hastings (Michael Howarth in ANGELS 1979–80) 'Something of a whizzkid, left-wing. Rides a motorbike (Suzuki 750). Wears an EARRING and jeans at lectures. Loathes bureaucracy. An excellent cook, wit, something of a boozer (vino). Enjoys an argument, an audience, a sauna, a disco, a jog, a Barclay James Harvest album, and continuing friendship with people he's professionally overtaken. He flaps, is over-emotional ... is dismissive about people who are not as passionately committed as he is. He is 'together' and positive. Rash, restless and unpredictable. GAY NEWS is in his office in-tray, just in case someone feels the need to talk. Holidays in California and Mykonos. Birthdate: Scorpio' (Publicity background notes for *Angels*).

Somehow this helpful, go-ahead director of nursing education at St Angela's never generated the excitement indicated in the outline. He first turns up at a nurse's party, receiving instant reaction from some of his students: 'He seems to care an awful lot ... Doesn't believe in sticking himself in his office ... Bit on the flash side, but tasty with it ... Not very popular with some of the sisters. Tells them not to overwork the students.'

Ken's disenchantment with the new Conservative government is reinforced by its attitude towards public health care. He tells his colleague and friend, Jean: 'They're going to dismantle the Health Service brick by brick ... we'll all wake up to find good hospital care's only for the rich, and the rest of us might as well go back to the leeches and the village witch.' He threatens to resign, but Jean reminds him that he's resigned at least three times before. He digs in and is one of the leaders of the patient's right to know and everybody's confidant. But what of his personal life?

All that really trickled through in the first series (it was shown very much during 'family viewing') was his over-whelming nostalgia for the 1960s ('I was

a wide-eyed lamb') and his need to change his boyfriends as regularly as he flits from Creole cooking to Indian and then on to French. He doesn't broadcast his sexuality, but he certainly doesn't hide it from those who would guess anyway (he's 32 and unmarried and 'dishy') and those in the know (he wears a lambda badge to a party) as well as his habitual jeans and earring. In the second series, he has settled down – but is never home. Rather, he's championing the cause of the NHS: trying to save St Angela's – in vain.

hated it! Perennial empty-headed, childish thumbs-down bleat of reviewers extraordinaire: 'Men on Film' Blaine (Damon Wayans) and Antoine (David Alan Grier) in *In Living Color* (1990 T). Their pet hates seem to be anything containing family life or attractive women.

Hatfield, Hurd (1918–) American actor, famous only for one role, that of Dorian GRAY in 1945. Described as the male GARBO and by Arthur Penn as 'America's least known great actor' (*Sight and Sound*, Summer 1985). A few moreish parts – mainly in the Dorian mode: drink-sodden Oliver Keane in *The Unsuspected* (1947 C); John WORTHING in THE IMPORTANCE OF BEING EARNEST (1950); *The Rivals* (1950); the besotted reporter in *The Left Handed Gun* (1957 C); Seymour Johnstone in *The Alfred Hitchcock Hour* 'None Are So Blind' (1958 T); Edmund Dantes in *The Count of Monte Cristo* with Colleen Dewhurst (1958 T); a suspect in *The Boston Strangler* (1969 C). More recently in, eg, *Crimes of the Heart* (1986 C) and *Her Alibi* (1989 C).

Jane **Hathaway** (Nancy KULP in *The Beverly Hillbillies* 1962–71 T) The conniving banker's honest secretary, a hugely capable SPINSTER who is often found in drag, eg overalls, police uniform, sailor's cap and blouson. Towards the end of the series, it seems 'Miss Jane' will be getting herself hitched – to someone called Foster

Phinney (Charles Lane). For the seduction she chooses white skirt, yellow kipper tie and tweed skirt. There's a touch more wave in the short hair but, when she imitates the call of the wild Canadian snow goose, Foster (who is only after her for her money) makes a quick exit down the fire escape ('Love Finds Jane Hathaway' 1970). She doesn't mope for long: the last few episodes find her happily living with Elly (Donna Douglas). She was her old (but older) self in *The Return of the Beverly Hillbillies* (1981).

The Haunting (UK 1963 C) A group of people drawn, privately or professionally, into a house with an unhappy past. One of them, Theo (Claire Bloom), who has psychic powers, falls in love with one of the unhappy visitors, Eleanor (Julie Harris).
W: Nelson Gidding from the novel *The Haunting of Hill House* by Shirley Jackson; P/D: Robert Wise; 112 mins.
'I'm Theodora, just "Theodora". But you can call me "Theo".' Theo, a FASHION DESIGNER has been sent to Hill House to help exorcize its demons. She is immediately attracted to Eleanor in the way that all screen homosexuals are to anyone of the same sex who walks through the door: immediately, utterly and irrevocably.
'We're going to be great friends,' Eleanor tells her. 'Like sisters?' Theo enquires optimistically. In the next scene Theo has changed into velvet waistcoat with thin chains hanging around her neck. The house begins to do strange things and it brings out Theo's vulnerability. Although she has told Eleanor that 'If you feel the least bit nervous do not hesitate to come to my room', it is she who cries out in the night and needs to be comforted: 'You big baby.' Eleanor begins to strip away Theo's coats of lacquer. 'What are you really afraid of?' The reply: 'Of knowing what I really want.'
This is the film's half-way mark; a rapid deterioration sets in thereafter. Doors pulsate and spiral staircases shake. The characters, in the face of

psychic phenomena, necessarily have little time for talk or to further develop. At the end, Eleanor drives off down the long dark drive. 'Oh, Nell, my Nell, be happy, please be happy,' whispers Theo. The car crashes ...
Claire Bloom played this role almost immediately after being an alcoholic 'NYMPHOMANIAC' in *The Chapman Report*. Kitted out in stylish (Mary Quant) black leather beret with maribou-fringed leopard skin coat, she's interesting: quizzical and enquiring (albeit in that cool screen lesbian ritualistic manner). And she doesn't die at the end. Her ESP is her curse because it denies her the protective half-truths about people's motives that most human beings have as part of their personal armoury.

Havers, Nigel (1952–) English actor who played Billy Owen, Mrs Dale's grandson aged 15 for two years in THE DALES. Because of his sensitive looks, he was given a fair number of gay roles on TV – of uneven quality – but all vividly enacted: Roger Coyne in *A Raging Calm* (1974); Denis Porson in THE GLITTERING PRIZES (1976); Richie in COMING OUT (1979); Clement in ALL FOR LOVE Combat (1982), Bobby Astor in *Nancy Astor* (1982). He excelled as the tortured Roy Calvert in *Strangers and Brothers* (1984). Now a big star thanks to *Chariots of Fire* (1982 C), *Don't Wait Up* (1983–8), *The Charmer* (1987) etc. Television début: as a member of the court in *Edward II* (1970); occasional radio including *What Was the Matter with Rupert?* (1987, about Rupert BROOKE). THIS IS YOUR LIFE (1992).

have you ever slept with a homosexual? 'No, but I've slept with somebody who has' is part of Eddie's (George Cole) patter in COMIC'S INTERLUDE. Eddie himself tends to prefer young boys who prefer girls rather than homosexuals to sleep with, though it is arguable whether they then become homosexuals after sleeping with Eddie who may himself not be homosexual because, theoretically, he has never slept with a homosexual.

have you heard the one about ...? 'Do you know the one about the Irish lesbian?' asks the Bette DAVIS drag queen in *The Rose* (1978 C). 'She went out with a *man*.' Spike Milligan told the same JOKE on *Friday Night, Saturday Morning* in 1981 – only it was about an Irish 'queer'. And trust Pete Beale in EAST-ENDERS. He is shooting his mouth off in the Queen Vic while Colin is slumped over a whisky, deeply depressed: 'Have you heard the one about the two queers? No offence' (1988). That night Colin encounters two men, has a couple of drinks with them, and is then bashed.

Miss **Havisham** Character in *Great Expectations*: once a jilted bride; now a chilling corrupter of childish innocence, a voyeur, a sadist, eaten up with rejection. In *Dickens' Women* (1991 R) Miriam MARGOLYES said that she believed that Charles Dickens *was* Miss Havisham. 'A misplaced and mismarried man, always playing hide and seek with the world' is how he described himself to his friend John Foster. Among the actresses who have inhabited this extraordinary wraith-like creature: Margaret Leighton (1974 C); Jean Simmons (1991 T), who was Estella to probably the most evocative Miss H. of all – Martita HUNT (1946 C): 'Sometimes I have sick fancies ...'

Hawtrey, Charles [George Hartree] (1914–88) Wonderful weedy-looking English comic actor who began on radio as a young boy (playing a boy actor in *Will Shakespeare* 1932) before featuring (as a schoolboy) in a number of Will Hay pictures and 1940s and 1950s British comedies (*Passport to Pimlico*; *The Galloping Major*) before becoming a fully fledged cultural icon with, first, his KNITTING Private (Professor) Hackett in *The Army Game* and, from 1958, as one of the CARRY ON team, constantly getting into stockings and wigs. One of his last roles was as an effeminate prisoner in

the radio comedy plays *Burglars' Bargain* (1979) and *The Bigger They Are* (1984).

Haydn, Richard (1905–85) British revue artist and radio comedian with gluggy adenoidal voice who went to Hollywood to make *Ball of Fire* (1941) and never came back. Films include *Please Don't Eat the Daisies* and *The Sound of Music.* Played an effete bachelor in THE TWILIGHT ZONE 'A Thing About Machines' (1960 T) and Waverly's brother-in-law in *The Man from UNCLE* in 'The Mad, Mad Tea Party Affair' (1965 T; there was talk of replacing Leo G. Carroll with him).

Bill **Haydon** The 'mole' in TINKER, TAILOR, SOLDIER, SPY (1979 T) played by Ian RICHARDSON. Sardonic, smooth, callous, brave: an embittered idealist whose betrayal of his former lover, Jim Prideaux (Ian Bannen) leads to death while he awaits trial or deportation to Russia.

Haydon seems to be an amalgam of the aristocratic and cold Anthony BLUNT and the urbane, womanizing Kim Philby: both of whom burrowed away at our vital secrets for their Russian masters whilst in positions of great power and influence. The dramatic conflict in Le Carré's story is heightened further because Bill Haydon is having an affair with George Smiley's wife.

He and Jim Prideaux – his friend from Oxford – were the 'most famous partnership' in the Secret Service: 'the velvet fist in the iron glove.' Fitting, then, that it is Prideaux, the ex-lover, who deals Haydon's death blow. Because of him, Jim had been crippled during a job which Haydon had blown the whistle on. Before killing him, Jim kisses the victim. Haydon smiles his sardonic smile: 'You haven't lost your touch, Jim.'

'I had all the traitors in mind ... Philby was a bent voluptuary. Come to think of it – yes, I gave that quality to Haydon, and perhaps I did pinch it from Philby' (John Le Carré talking about his 1974 novel, *Observer*, 1980).

Hayes, Melvyn (1935–) English actor with a particularly droopy face, trembling lower lip and quavery voice – perfect to play a sad sack (Gunner BEAUMONT) in an army concert party in *It Ain't Half Hot Mum* which he did for nearly 10 years. Was hardly off the television screens in the 1950s, often playing cringing lads in various kinds of trouble: notably as the abused, probably gay boy who likes playing Chopin in THE UNLOVED (1955). In some of the Cliff Richard musicals of the 1960s. Recently played an elf in *Santa Claus*, voiced the Skeleton in *SuperTed* (1984–5 T), and was Superbeing in *Galloping Galaxies*.

Head, Edith (1907–81) American costume designer of extraordinary flair whose own distinctive look (severe fringe and glasses) made her a sort of star in her own right, earning herself the remark that 'Edith Head gives good wardrobe'. She swathed Mae WEST for *She Done Him Wrong* (1933 C), Hedy Lamarr in *Samson and Delilah* (1949), and Elizabeth Taylor in *A Place in the Sun* (1951); designed Barbara STANWYCK's jeans for *Roustabout* (1964 C); played herself in *The Oscar* (1966 C); and popped up in *Columbo* 'Fugue for a Falling Star' (with Anne Baxter) in the early 1970s.

HeartBeat (US 1988–9 T) A medical practice specializing in women's problems. The chief NURSE, Marilyn McGrath (Gail Strickland) lives with Patti – unproblematically except for Marilyn's daughter's disapproval over her LIFESTYLE. All is resolved at the daughter's wedding.
P: Lynn Morgan and Maria Padilla for Aaron SPELLING; 60 mins.

A glossy, 'concerned' series which was only one notch above the ordinary and ran into advertising revenue problems because of the steadily more visible lesbian in its midst – in a starring role for once. Gail Strickland (dressed, fresh from DYNASTY, by Nolan Miller) looked a dream, was ultra-competent, ultra-charming, ultra-nice, but had only the most fleeting acquaintance with full

dramatic relevance and emotional breadth on a par with her team colleagues. (ABC censored her storylines, allowed her no KISSING, no DANCING, only HUGGING.)

The day of the adorable, gorgeous soap-opera dyke taking America by storm hadn't quite arrived; it is likely to be more than a *HeartBeat* away.

The Heart Exposed aka *Le Coeur Découvert* (Can 1986 C/T) Jean-Marc (Gilles Renaud) has vowed never to get involved with relationships or ONE NIGHT STANDS. Then he meets Mathieu, a handsome young ACTOR (Michel Poirier). Before they get sexually involved, Mathieu tells him he's married with a 5-year-old son, Sebastien (Olivier Chassé). Although the two men love each other, the presence of the little boy in their lives worries Jean-Marc for all sorts of reasons, (self-)accusations of PAEDOPHILIA being one of them. Basically though, the older man is frightened of change and commitment. Nervous about his ability as a lover, he feels doubly inadequate as a father. The situation is left unresolved although there is every likelihood that Jean-Marc will learn to share his affections and cope with criticisms.
W: Michel TREMBLAY from his novel *Le Coeur Découvert/Making Room*; P: Gilles Turcot; D: Jean-Yves LaForce; Société-Radio Canada; 105 mins.

A very special film. Calm, unhurried, unspectacular with a not especially exciting central character (the actor closely resembles 'ALLO, 'ALLO's René). But cumulatively it is brave in discussing subtle issues like love, courage, queer FAMILIES (Jean-Marc lives with a lesbian couple), sharing – and the whole question of gay men parenting children, the practicalities thereof.

Heart of the Matter (UK 1980–)
'Moral dilemmas, controversies and questions.' A fairly hard-hitting Sunday night religion and morality series that has tried to thrash out – among many other issues – AIDS, the anti-gay backlash, lesbians and AID, the Catholic

Church's stand on homosexuality, and the EX-GAY movement. One of the best was 'Falling Out', about the plight of lesbians and gays in the armed forces (300 had been dismissed or discharged between 1988 and 1991). Joan Bakewell related the cases of a military bandmaster and an army nurse. 'Homosexual behaviour between consenting adults is something we should support,' says former NATO Commander-in-Chief General Sir Anthony Farrar-Hockley, not unreasonably – yet unreasonably: 'But not inside the armed forces.'
P: Olga Edridge, Michael Waterhouse 1992– ; BBC1.

Heath, Gordon (1918–91) Afro-American actor of command and brio who came to London with his Broadway success *Deep Are the Roots* in the late 1940s. Much radio, some TV (title roles in *The Emperor Jones* and *Othello* directed by Tony RICHARDSON 1955); one scene as a queerish coroner ('subtle and cultured', *Variety*) in the penultimate scene in *Passionate Summer* (1958 C); the dead woman's full-of-attitude boyfriend, a lawyer, in *Sapphire* (1959 C). From the early 1960s, he lived in Paris with his lover, Lee Payant, and ran a Left Bank café called L'Abbaye for many years.

'... beautiful in cast of visage (swinging earrings as big as Lady Barnett's) grave, considerable, and delicate in the finest manner of his race ... [but] I missed ... that elemental dangerousness which should be at the heart of this character if it is to make sense ... Mr Heath remained dignified, I couldn't see him hurting a fly' (Philip HOPE-WALLACE reviewing *Othello*, *Listener*, 22.12.55).

'Perhaps if attitudes to race and sexuality were different, and memories were not so short, we might have seen more of this gifted actor in the last 30 years' (Stephen Bourne, *Gay Times*, October 1991).

Heatwave (Burning In My Heart ...)
Martha and the Vandellas' 1963 Tamla Motown hit mimed to in Michael's 'garden' – with suitably abandoned arm, leg and head movements by nearly all THE

BOYS IN THE BAND (1970 C) before Harold's birthday party turns weepy and ugly with the arrival of supposed non-gay Alan and later the birthday boy himself.

A Hedge, Backwards: A Discovery for Radio (UK 1956 R) The young biographer (Hugh BURDEN) of celebrated writer Richard Shewin learns of an unperformed play by the deceased great man which he is determined to premičre. It is about A Certain Subject and, by the time the director (Neville Pikelet, played by Allan MCCLELLAND) and the Lord Chamberlain have hacked the piece about, the young lovers have become heterosexual and only one line – the last: 'They may be against us, but ordinary people aren't' – relates at all to the position of homosexuals, not that the audience would now see it in that context.
P: Douglas Cleverdon; 29.2.56; BBC Third Programme; *c* 55 mins.

Censorship undermined but did not destroy Henry Reed's *A Hedge, Backwards*. Dialogue from Shewin's unexpurgated work between a man-about-town and his working-class lover was truncated and jokes about 'drag', 'camp' and 'butch' actors rubbed out. Enough remained for those in the know to twig that Reed was making a sly curtsey in the direction of Terence RATTIGAN, both of whose recent hits *The Deep Blue Sea* and *Separate Tables* had originated from homosexual plot springs, one directly from the author's own life.

An example of the scissored dialogue follows. In one scene the truly awful director Neville Pikelet, large of gesture, small of mind, wants husky American actor Pig Judder for his Mark Antony because he's big and lazy – and all man. He explains things to the hero:

Pikelet: 'You see, lovey, in this day and age, Mark Antony has got to be played BUTCH.'
Reeve: 'What was the word you used?'
Pikelet: 'Butch ... Antony is a big butch QUEEN. He doesn't know it, of course, but he has homosexual tendencies, you know. That's the real tie-up with Cleopatra.'

Hell is other people 'L'enfer, c'est les autres' is Jean-Paul Sartre's summation of the situation in which his characters find themselves in HUIS CLOS (1954 C; 1946 & 1963 R) (aka *No Exit* 1962 C; IN CAMERA 1964 T; *Vicious Circle* 1985 T). Ines, realizing that she, Estelle and Garcia have not been put together by chance, says: 'It's childishly simple. Obviously there are no physical torments and yet we know we are in hell. We'll stay in this room together ... the three of us, for ever and ever. Each of us will act as torturers of the others' (1963 R translation). Garcia, driven to impotent fury by Ines's tindery taunts, decides that 'Hell is other people' before strangling her.

Richard Shewin, the dead 'hero' is confronted with this truth in A VERY GREAT MAN INDEED (1953 & 1961 R). He agrees mistily, adding his own *bon mot*: 'But so is *heaven*.' Burch (Michael Bryant), puritanical and dangerously alienated, uses it as a credo in *The Man Behind You* (1968 T). It was still around in the 1990s: one of the deranged astronauts uses it to his companion and the robot in their cramped confines in the last episode of *D.A.A.S. Kapital* (1991 T).

hello, I'm Julian and this is my friend, Sandy Thus, from 1965 to 1969, would Hugh PADDICK's Jules introduce radio's first gay couple. The moiré-silk accenting of the word 'Hello' would scud through to the coy chenille of the words 'my friend', ending with the patter of chiffon as he made a meal of 'San-dee'.

Julian and Sandy lived in Chelsea with their friend Gordon, a former attendant at the local slipper baths. Julian is the soft one: he can't turn a stranger away. Gordon was down on his luck. Julian prays each night: 'Bless this lattie, strong and stout/Keeping all NAFF 'omis out.'

Each week on ROUND THE HORNE, Julian and Sandy would be engaged in some new gay pursuit. One week they would be booksellers (Bona Books), the next 'catering to the gentry'. The cadence of the opening line never altered however, alerting us to the fruity delights to come when the ultra-straight Kenneth HORNE would have a close encounter with the third kind. In Kenneth Horne's previous series, *Beyond Our Ken* (1958–64), Paddick and Williams were a prototype J. and S.: two upper-crust chinless wonders. They began their inane, double-barrelled conversations with a breathless 'Hello, Rodney!/Hello, Charles!'

hello, sailor This phrase has risen through the ranks, so to speak, and has now become an immediately recognizable signifier among both gays and non-gays. Spike Milligan claims he was responsible for its invention probably from 'A sailor is thinking of you', army and airforce frivolity for an 'itchy arse'. (However, it appears in 1940s US films like *Two Girls and a Sailor*.) Its broadcasting career began as a voice in a letter box in a 1958 GOON SHOW 'The Great Bank of England Robbery'. It was as disconnected and inconsequential as anything else in the brilliantly scripted mayhem; doubtless the BBC censors let it go that once, which set a precedent for Henry Crun's a-mouldering mistress, Minnie Bannister (Spike Milligan) to adopt it on an irregular basis. A year later, she was saying 'Merry Christmas, sailor' ('A Christmas Carol') as well as the more traditional sexual greeting/come-on ('The Tale of Men's Shirts' 1959 etc).

Spike Milligan bicycled the phrase around all his television shows of the 1960s, during which period Dudley Moore was gambolling with it on *Not Only ... But Also*. Reformed Goon Peter SELLERS employed it in a voice syrupy with suggestiveness, and with a 'queer' hat (Tyrolean with a little feather) pulled over one eye, for one of his quick-fire impersonations in the 'Look of Love' sequence from *Casino Royale* (1967 C): 'Hell-o, Sai-lor!'

By the 1980s, greater sophistication meant that it could be used as a noun, rather like 'how's your father'. Ronnie Barker (in *The Two Ronnies* 1983 T) spoke of 'a bit of hello sailor' to mean homo-hanky-panky. The next year saw the phrase heterosexualized when Bet Lynch (Julie Goodyear) greeted her policeman boyfriend with it in CORONATION STREET.

Generally, though, 'Hello, sailor' has remained true and constant to its origins. In *The Fear* (1988 T) gang boss Carl Galton (Iain Glen) uses it to denote a gay cruising area to his best mate Marty (Jesse Birdsall), little realizing his friend's own sexual foraging or the true nature of Marty's feelings for him.

Probably the finest hour of 'Hello, sailor' came at the end of THE NAKED CIVIL SERVANT (1975 T) wherein Quentin CRISP alias John HURT conjures up a fantasy of matelots, all chatting him up against a sequinned Hollywood night sky. A fitting tribute to the close ties gay men on shore have had with the men of the Fleet since time immemorial and to the countless hours (minutes?) of pleasure the one group has bestowed upon the other, and vice versa.

Eric Idle had a 1974–5 series called *Hello, Cheeky* while a 1984 *Minder* episode was entitled 'Goodbye Sailor'.

A billboard poster advertising rum with the slogan 'You don't say "Hello sailor" to a Captain Morgan drinker' was the subject of a complaint that it was anti-gay in 1975. However, the Advertising Standards Authority adjudicated in January 1976 that 'The headline employed humorousness and an idiomatic form of banter which would not reasonably be taken as insulting'.

Helpmann, Sir Robert (1909–86) Dancer, choreographer, actor and director born in South Australia on a sheep station. 'In those days, for a boy to want to be a dancer was almost incredible.' Trained by Pavlova and 'discovered' by Margaret Rawlings and her husband, Helpmann joined the Vic-Wells company, partnering and nurturing Margot Fonteyn. He was the first dancer to play in Shakespeare. He choreographed the most famous ballet film, *The Red Shoes.* In the OMNIBUS programme 'Tales of Helpmann' (1990 T, which only glancingly mentioned his

companion, director Michael Benthall), Jeremy Brett – who appeared with him on television in *The Ghost Sonata* – said he was 'an exotique and they're hard to find'. He then admitted that he was scared of him and only felt safe when he was on the set, pushing him in a wheel-chair.

C: *One of Our Aircraft Is Missing* (1942); Bishop of Ely in *Henry V* (1944); Wycroft in *Caravan* (1946); quite astonishingly CAMP – or at least the antithesis of strong, husky maledom – in *The Red Shoes* (1948, excerpted in *That's Dancing* 1985); Lindorf/Coppelius/Dapertuitto/Dr Miracle in *The Tales of Hoffman* (1953); *The Iron Petticoat* (1956); the crooked Reverend in *The Big Money* (1956, released 1958); the wily Prince in *55 Days at Peking* (1963); Weng in *The Quiller Memorandum* (1966); the Childcatcher in *Chitty Chitty Bang Bang* (1968); the Mad Hatter in *Alice's Adventures in Wonderland* (1972); title role in *Don Quixote* (1973, also co-D with NUREYEV); *The Mango Tree* (Aust 1977); Buckminster Shepherd in *Puzzle* (Aust 1978); *Patrick* (Aust 1979).

R: *How to Become a Ballet Dancer* (1949); DESERT ISLAND DISCS (1953 & 1978); *These Foolish Things* (1958); *In Conversation* (1963) with Alexander Bland and Brian Robertson; *A Knight in the Ballet* (Aust 1972).

T: *The Vic-Wells Ballet Company* (1937–9); *Two for Tea* (1953); *A Box for One* (1953); *The Ghost Sonata* (1962); *An Evening with Robert Helpmann* (1963); Fouché (opposite Kenneth WILLIAMS' Napoleon) in *Catch as Catch Can* (1964); *The Soldier's Tale* (1964, also C); *In Search of Constant Lambert* (1965); *Contrabandits* 'In for a Penny' (Aust 1968); OMNIBUS 'Helpmann' (1973); THIS IS YOUR LIFE (Aust 1975); *Second Time Lucky* (Aust 1984); A COUNTRY PRACTICE (Aust 1986); *Tales of Helpmann* (1990).

Hennegan, Alison (1948–) English journalist, author and publisher. Prominently involved with CHE and the gay and lesbian counselling organization (National) FRIEND in the 1970s, as well as being Literary and Features Editor of GAY NEWS between 1977 and 1983. Her extraordinary ability to think articulately and concisely on her feet no matter what the situation – being passionate without losing the thread of the argument – was visible and audible in many television and radio outings including GAYS SPEAKING UP; *Ladies Night* 'Lesbians' (1978 T); *Being Gay Today* (1981 R); *Not for Women Only* (1982 T); *Frank Delaney* (1984, on gay literature); *The Book Game* (1985, with Salman Rushdie, Mary McCarthy and Robert McCrum). Her presence and wit were fully showcased in the second series of GAY LIFE (1981) which she co-presented with Michael Attwell. With Jackie Forster, she was the face and voice of the British lesbian for nearly a decade.

Henszelman, Stefan Christian (1961–91) Danish film director who made only two pictures: *A Modern Woman* (1990 C) and the charming *Friends Forever* (1987 C). He died (from AIDS-related causes) while working on pre-production for *Dance On My Grave*.

Hepburn, Katharine (1907–) American film and television actress who began emancipated and stayed that way, give or take a few gooey roles: her gallery of feisty socialites, TOMBOYS, MALE IMPERSONATORS, SPINSTERS, career women, and mothers (thrice to gay sons) includes *A Bill of Divorcement*; *Morning Glory*; *Alice Adams*; *A Woman Rebels*; *Little Women*; SYLVIA SCARLETT; *Stage Door*; *Bringing Up Baby*; *Holiday*; *The Philadelphia Story*; ADAM'S RIB; *Pat and Mike*; *The African Queen*; *Summer Madness*; SUDDENLY, LAST SUMMER; *Long Day's Journey into Night*; *The Lion in Winter*; *On Golden Pond*; *Mrs Delafield Wants to Marry the Man Upstairs*. She paid tribute to director Dorothy Arzner (for whom she made *Christopher Strong*) in a 1989 documentary on women directors: 'she was a very nice person, a good director and a damn fine *cutter*.'

Here Is the News (UK 1989 T) Dr

Richard Boyle is harassed by journalist David Dunhill (Richard E. Grant) to tell all he knows about chemical warfare testing and viral experiments in Britain: 'If you come out of the closet, rather than have the [Special] Branch flush you out, the whole country will be with you.' W: G. F. Newman; P: Kenith TRODD; D: Udayan Prasad; 5.3.89; 70 mins.

David Dunhill was based on investigative journalist Duncan Campbell, who sued because Dunhill was delineated as a kleptomaniac (shoplifting), misfit (couldn't have sex with his girlfriend), and a TRANSVESTITE (frilly knickers). None of which applied to Duncan Campbell (though there were over a dozen specific resemblances to him in the play).

In May 1990 Campbell received £100,000 damages and costs in the High Court, together with a public apology from the BBC and the writer. This was the first known case where the plaintiff sued on the grounds that he himself was openly gay, and yet had been portrayed as a closet deviant, vilified as much for being gay as for the sometimes violent and unscrupulous methods Dunhill used to gain access to 'establishment cover-ups'.

here's looking at you, kid Bogie to Bergman in *Casablanca*. Used in quasi-homoemotional situation when Sam (Jonathan Pryce) says goodbye to the besotted Mr Kurtzmann (Ian HOLM), while simultaneously we hear Humphrey and Ingrid speaking the relevant dialogue on a television set outside the office in *Brazil* (1985 C). 'Here's looking up you, kid,' says venereologist to patient in THE CLINIC (1982 C).

Pee-Wee Herman Children's television (later film) character (with a coded name) played by Paul Reubens – a 9-year-old boy in a grown-up's body, engaging in some very close encounters with lipstick and men especially in his TV work: *Pee-Wee's Playhouse* (1986–7; one show had Pee-Wee getting married – to a man); *The Pee-Wee Herman Show* (1989, in which Herman frolics with

Jambi the Genie, Kap'n Karl, Mondo and other pals). Films: *Pee-Wee's Big Adventure* (1985); *Pee-Wee's Big Top* (1986).

'There's a lot of things about me that you don't know anything about; things you wouldn't understand' (Pee-Wee to Dottie in *Pee-Wee's Big Adventure*).

'A cross between NODDY and a camp hairdresser' (Victoria Mather, *Daily Telegraph*, 14.8.87).

heroes Very few and far between – and most come with qualifications and reservations: Geoff in A TASTE OF HONEY; Melville Farr in VICTIM, as well as 'Boy' Barrett (but he takes 'the coward's way out'); Sonny Wortzik (Al Pacino) in DOG DAY AFTERNOON (but he's a bank robber); Robin Turner (Craig RUSSELL) in OUTRAGEOUS! and TOO OUTRAGEOUS! (but *he*'s a drag entertainer); Michael (Aidan Quinn) in AN EARLY FROST (but he's dying); the distinguished war hero (Grant Kennedy) in an episode of THE FLYING DOCTORS (1986 T) (but he's dying too); Jodie and Steven in SOAP and DYNASTY respectively (when they're not being heterosexual); the two soldiers in HOUSE ON THE HILL 'Something for the Boys' (1981 T) (but they part the next morning); the mismatched lovers in THE GROUNDLING AND THE KITE (1984 T); two scientists in *Children of the Damned* (and one of them turns a bit nasty). Not many in a period covering over 60 years, not many for gay men to root for, BLACK and Asian gay men even fewer, with the exception of THE FRUIT MACHINE and YOUNG SOUL REBELS. However, things are beginning to change: THE MAYOR OF CASTRO STREET; AND THE BAND PLAYED ON; TALES OF THE CITY.

'The hero's prominence and one's identification with him, makes the hero the norm' (Raymond Durgnat, *A Mirror for England*, 1966).

'It is the hero who makes the fag jokes. We like the hero. When the character in question is straight, the bigots are simply proven wrong. We still like the hero. The hero is always straight and the straight guys are always our friends. The

gay character always loses' (Vito RUSSO, *The Celluloid Closet*, 1987).

heroes (lesbian women as) Countess Anna GESCHWITZ saving Lulu by sacrificing herself in PANDORA'S BOX/*Lulu*; Mischou, a militant Communist 'sort of engaged to be married' who has an affair with one of the women in the Auschwitz orchestra (*Playing for Time* 1980 T): 'She just seems so different from the others. So full of courage'; Gisela (Diana QUICK) who as Monika was a member of the Baader–Meinhof gang and withstood imprisonment and sensory deprivation in the SILENT WING (1984 R); Mme Claude Alphand (Catherine Deneuve), fearless private eye in *Ecoute Voir* (1978 C); Rachel (Josie Lawrence), righter of male wrongs in the 18th and 20th centuries in RACHEL AND THE ROARETTES (1985 T); Dawn Fraser (Bronwyn MacKay Payne), Olympic swimming champion and resister of stale convention and petty rules (DAWN! 1979 C); Miles Franklin, pseudonymous feminist from 19th-century Australia (heterosexualized in *My Brilliant Career* 1979 C); COLETTE (Clementine Amoureux), seeker after all things, loving and human (1985 T); Marian HALCOMBE (Diana Quick), fearless and razor-sharp 'companion' to her beloved Laura in *The Woman in White* (1982 T); the SUFFRAGETTES in *Shoulder to Shoulder* (1974 T); Ferial who rescues and hides her Jewish lover for most of the war (NOVEMBER MOON 1984 C); Linda Ray Guettner (Gena Rowlands) fighting for her child against a mausoleum of judgement in A QUESTION OF LOVE (1978 T); Idgie and Ruth in FRIED GREEN TOMATOES AT THE WHISTLE STOP CAFE (1991 C); THELMA AND LOUISE (1991 C); *The Terminator/Terminator* II; *The Silence of the Lambs*; *Alien/Aliens/ Alien 3*.

heroines Action heroines (Pearl White); battling heroines (Joan Crawford, Bette DAVIS, Barbara STANWYCK); suffering heroines; scheming heroines (Marlene DIETRICH); whacky heroines (Carole Lombard); intelligent heroines (Katharine HEPBURN, Ginger Rogers); etc. Now it's hero-heroines (Jodie Foster, Kathleen Turner, Linda Hamilton, Sigourney Weaver, Mary Elizabeth Mastrantonio).

heterophobia Unreasoned hatred of heterosexuals, their manner of living and their sexual acts: an expression coined in the late 1970s. 'Heterophobia is starting to rear its head: a fear of heterosexual men. If you are a white middle-class heterosexual, you have done something bad' (Kerry Davison and Robert Weir in *Australia Talks Back* 1992 R).

heterosexuality 'Heterosexuality is an ugly word,' intoned Kenneth Cope shif-tily in John Braine's 'Confession' mono-logue on THAT WAS THE WEEK THAT WAS (1963 T) and proceeded to detail the hells of living as a hetero. This was almost the first time the word had been aired – and, after this shock, it took years to catch on. There was an almost complete blackout during the rest of the 1960s and the 1970s, apart from a half-dozen major examples including Arthur Kopit's 1966 play *The Latent Hetero-sexual*, Tennessee WILLIAMS on FROST OVER AMERICA (1970 T), and Simon GRAY'S BUTLEY (1974 C/T).

Butley (Alan BATES) is desperately try-ing to prevent his young protégé and former flat-mate, Joey leaving him for another man. The rival is Reg (Michael Byrne), a successful publisher and everything Butley hates. He tries to belittle him by sneering at his working-class origins, his integrity and his sexu-ality. None of this works. Finally, Butley attacks homosexuals as a group: '... now the law, in making them safe, has made them drab. Just like the heterosexual rest of us.' Reg won't let this pass. Poli-tely but firmly: 'There's enough affec-tion and bitchiness among *heterosexuals* to be getting along with, don't you think.' His antagonist is then forced to provoke physical violence, from which he comes off second-best.

Paul BAILEY noted the word's absence, on the series *Words* (1974 R); maybe it

was because 'One doesn't automatically call a man who makes love to women "heterosexual"'.

Post-1967 the word only appears once in six years in the *Listener*, notably in Peter Black's review of the play *Moon-base 3* (20.9.73): 'The year is 2003 and Britain is among the nations that monitor lunar settlements, which are multiracial and heterosexual.'

Slowly, reluctantly, people began realizing that if 'homosexual' can be bandied around with such profligacy its opposite should also serve. Thus the radio version of *A Song at Twilight* (1988) reinstated Carlotta's question to the closeted man of letters: 'But why the implication of heterosexual ardour?' – which had been cut from the 1982 tele-vision adaptation.

A 1990 *Daytime Live* about the depic-tion of blacks and Asians on TV found Gervaise Chin Lee asserting that the medium should be open to anyone and not only to those who were 'white, male, able-bodied, heterosexual'. And a magistrate's intrusive questioning during a lesbian custody case in SOUTH OF THE BORDER (1990 T) brought forth the bitter truth from the mother's lover, Kate (Ethna Roddy) that 'they wouldn't ask heterosexuals that'.

Until the AIDS crisis, heterosexual was either not used or removed (Carlot-ta's 'We were both virgins; that is, from the heterosexual point of view' in *A Song at Twilight* 1982 T), or else defined through *homosexuality* as in 'I'm not homosexual' (*Police Story* 'The Ripper' 1974 T). This need for amplification made the 1987 television production of Joe ORTON's 20-year-old WHAT THE BUTLER SAW all the more swingeingly contemporary. Dr Prentice (Dinsdale Landen), director of a sex clinic, pro-claims loudly: 'I'm heterosexual!' At which his colleague bridles: 'I wish you wouldn't use these Chaucerian words.'

In the early stages of the AIDS epi-demic, 'heterosexual' became more valued, as a shield and as a sword. Only one of the men with AIDS in HORIZON 'Killer in the Village' (1983 T) was de-scribed as 'not a homosexual'. Over the next few years there were many more who were 'not homosexual': Joe Regalabuto says it four times in *Mama's Boy* 'Scared Straight' (1987 T); 'I'm not a TRANSVESTITE, I'm not a homosexual, I love my wife,' claims Mr Papadopoulus in PERSONAL SERVICES (1987 C).

By the late 1980s even situation comedy was daring to name the previously unnamed. Uptight businessman Donald (Peter Bowles) in the swanky sitcom *Executive Stress* (1987 T) can no longer deny he's gay with a simple 'I'm normal ... nothing funny about me'. Donald continues to reassure wifey Penelope Keith (and himself). The actual word has to be used, with massive emphasis: 'I don't want people to get the wrong idea about me. I'm 100 per cent het-ero-sex-ual.'

Large traces of evasion remain. The word didn't surface once in the WOMAN'S HOUR discussion of the 'Hite Report on Men' (1990 R), though for once 'PROMISCUITY' did, without being applied to gay men. In a 1990 programme for schools on AIDS, a man, his face hidden by a wooden beam, is asked if he is homosexual. 'No,' he replies, 'I am not homosexual ... I picked it up in Mombasa.' Similarly, in the commentary and interviews with scientists: 'What you're saying is that this is not just a homosexual disease?'

If used, there often have to be qualifications: an unmarried screen actor, interviewed in *TV Times* (1987), is '*healthily* heterosexual'; *Ken Russell's A-Z of British Music* (1988 T) presented 3 minutes of William Walton's '*normal, heterosexual Troilus and Cressida*' as distinct from 20 seconds of Benjamin BRITTEN's 'ageing pederast' opera, *Death in Venice*.

heterosexual shock *See* HOMOSEXUAL PANIC.

High Heels (Sp 1991 C) A mother and daughter, involved with the same man, are suspects in his murder. A TRANSVESTITE and a young judge play important roles in resolving the tense situation. W/D: Pedro ALMODOVAR; *c* 90 mins.

One of the brightest gems from the Almodovar jewel box: a perfectly tuned rhapsody that effortlessly mixes crazy comedy with pathos, gay sensibility with camp. Victoria Abril miraculously keeps interest and sympathy as the highly strung daughter of a self-centred movie diva whose way of dealing with problematic men in her life draws from mother her final, histrionic sacrifice. Elements of the later Joan Crawford movies vie with the Lana Turner scandal, women's prison films, gender fuck, topsy-turvy power bases and an unflagging sense of tragi-comedy. *Fatal Attraction* and *Basic Instinct* emerge as paltry puddles of piddle alongside the fluid plotting, believable characters and feelings, and various kinds of human electricity.

Highsmith, Patricia (1921–) American thriller writer, best known for STRANGERS ON A TRAIN and the Ripley books. Adaptations include *Plein Soleil* aka *Purple Noon* (1960 C, based on *The Talented Mr Ripley*); *A Suspension of Mercy* (1983 R); *The American Friend* (1977 C, based on *Ripley's Game*); A BOOK AT BEDTIME 'Carol' (1991 R, published as *The Price of Salt* 1952 by 'Claire Morgan' – her only overtly homoerotic work before *Found in the Street* 1987). Biography: THE SOUTH BANK SHOW 'A Gift for Murder' (1982 T).

Hilary/Hillary 'We ain't got many 'ilarys in the circles I move in,' says Harold Steptoe when he is told of someone (male) called Hilary in a STEPTOE AND SON episode. A name most often given to upper-bracket men and women; it has a beige with a definite fleck of pink if attached to a man (it's Greek for 'cheerful and merry').

UK: Hilary Ames (Reginald Gardiner), gay bachelor in *Cluny Brown* (1946 C); Hilary St Clair (Kenneth WILLIAMS), the photographer who 'paints with light' in HANCOCK'S HALF HOUR 'The Publicity Photograph' (1958 R); Hilary (Peter Bowles) was Rigsby's camp lodger in *Rising Damp* (1977 T), and in 'Stage Struck' he writes a romantic play with Ruth as leading lady; Hilary

(Timothy Carlton) in *Pulaski* (1986 T); Dr Hilary Jones, hunky medico on *After Nine* (1991 T); male (Mark Straker) and female (Theresa Streatfield) in *No Commitments* 'A Nice Civilized Evening' (1992 R).

US: Lieutenant Colonel Hillary Whalters (Robert Keith) in *Battle Circus* (1952 C); Hillary (Sal Mineo) drug dealer in *The Name of the Game* 'So Long, Baby and Amen' (1971 T).

Female Hil(l)arys include Deborah Kerr as the titled lady, who thinks *The Grass Is Greener* with an American tourist (1960 C); Hilary (Susannah York) who is lusted after by her brother in *Country Dance* (1969 C); Hilary (Kate Nelligan), an American FEMINIST in DO AS I SAY (1977 T) who wants to race off a woman to bed only hours after she had been raped – her incessant chatter marks a new low in sensitivity: 'I would like to get a dialogue going between you and the rapist ... How do you feel? I mean, do you feel *dirty?*'; Hillary Kramer (Barbra STREISAND), cosmetics czarina with boxer in *The Main Event* (1979 C); Hilary (Celia Imrie), the lover of Sarah B'stard in *The New Statesman* (1987 T).

Hill, Benny (1925–92) English comedian who became one of the most famous television stars in the world, but was celebrated very late in his career – and his life: OMNIBUS 'Benny Hill: Clown Imperial' (1991 T).

As well as his propensity for smutty picture-postcard humour and frolics with young women wearing very little, Hill was a satirist. In the 1960s – working for the BBC – he was a great opponent of interfering busybodies where sex and the human body were concerned. In one 1968 sketch he was a schoolboy salivating over a dirty picture. He describes it in great detail: 'There is this lady and this man. The man is touching the lady, here and here. And here. The lady is kissing him. And they have no clothes on.' A parent arrives, confiscates the book, slaps the boy. A close-up reveals the arousing object to be a photograph of Rodin's *The Kiss*. Hill's

attitudes to sexual politics, on the other hand, were pretty basic: place a rude/dirty idea in the brain, then quickly withdraw. But sometimes he made sense: 'What do you call a man who marries another man? A vicar.'

Hinge and Bracket Dr Evadne Hinge (George Logan) and Dame Hilda Bracket (Patrick Fyffe) are scatty ladies of some gentility, but no fools. Infinitely and melodiously compatible with the songs and music of 'dear Noel' and 'dear Ivor'. (They seem to know a lot of 'dear' men who have never married.) Drag for the palm court set: *What's On Next?* (1976 T); *The Enchanting World of Hinge and Bracket* (1976 R); *Dear Ladies* (1980 T); *The Random Jottings of Hinge and Bracket* (1987 R); etc.

hippies Living on the outskirts of society, especially during the 1960s, yet not necessarily empathetic to other kinds of outsiders. Colin (Karl Johnson) in ONLY CONNECT (1979 T) is less nostalgic about the 1960s because he had lived as a hippy: 'They didn't actually say they didn't like QUEERS but if I made the mistake of falling for one of them and if I ever told them that I loved them – they'd say that was "cool" man and they loved me, too. "Yeah, man, I love you too ... brother." Then they'd give a hug and run like the wind to their "old ladies" or "chicks" or "mates". Then I wouldn't see them for a couple of days. And when we did meet again, there'd be a solid brick wall of heterosexuality between us. "See you, brother".'

Daniel **Hirsch** Doctor played by Peter Finch in SUNDAY, BLOODY SUNDAY (1971 C). Serious, deeply committed to his general practice, likes opera, honours his JEWISH ancestry, in love with a young man who's also having an affair with a woman. Ends up alone, talking to himself or the cameraman or the audience about half a loaf being better than none after his lover has gone off to New York to work. Peter FINCH invests this role with great pride and self-possession in the midst of a terrible emotional crisis which the man is not able to fully express – partly because director and writer won't let him. 'Does he have to be Jewish on top of everything else?' (John SCHLESINGER's father after being told the plot, quoted on DESERT ISLAND DISCS 1992).

His and His A Broadway farce which was filmed at MGM in 1964. Before release, its title was changed to *Honeymoon Hotel* in case people thought that 'His and His' meant 'Him and Him'. The year before, another piece of froth, *Love Is a Ball* had its title made respectable in deference to British moral standards – *All This and Money Too*. Yet *Company Of Cowards?* was Anglicized (in 1964) to *Advance to the Rear*.

Hit and Run (UK 1965 T) A man is killed. A car is traced. It's a Jaguar belonging to a local businessman. But his son was driving it the night of the fatal accident – or was he? The real culprit is the son's clinging friend, Alan Blossom (Laurie Asprey), who pins the blame on the son because he rejected him.
W: Evelyn Frazer from a novel by Jeffrey Ashford; P/D: Paddy Russell; BBC2; 4 parts.

It was all *angst*, with a lying, self-denying queer breaking down in the witness box under cross-examination. His twisted desires have made him pathetically willing to send his friend to prison: 'When it came down to it ... he was just like all the others ... he made it all sound dirty ... he didn't understand.' The serial ends with the businessman and his wife agreeing to patch up their marriage (he has a mistress) and give it another go. 'It's taken a long time for us to begin to know one another, hasn't it.' As for the son: 'I'm quite NORMAL, if that's what you're worried about. I didn't realize that Alan probably isn't until just before I was arrested. As a matter of fact, until I put him straight about me. I don't think he realized certain things about himself.'

(This was BBC2's first 'modern' serial with an average young person beset by conflicts which he can't control. Unfortunately the thriller framework demanded a human sacrifice rather than a human being.)

Hitchcock, Sir Alfred (1899–1980) English film director, producer and television host. As creepy and wicked as any character in his thrillers.

In ARTEMIS '81 Jed Thaxter (Ian Redford) is a film lecturer obsessively drawn to the works of Alfred Hitchcock: 'Only a 360° shot from *Vertigo* can bring the living water to my eyes.' He has stills from the Master's later films on his wall. A source of intense and obsessive pleasure because Hitchcock's vision seems to mirror his own fears of a world in its death throes: 'Sees the world from a distance' (James Stewart in *Rear Window*); 'Refuses commitment at cost' (Stewart in *The Man Who Knew Too Much*); 'Mauled by elemental powers we ignore' (*The Birds*); 'Set our lives in an unreal direction, a hound from heaven will come' (Gary GRANT and the crop-dusting plane in *North by Northwest*); 'Our moral order must be hewn from nature, not imposed upon it' (Grant slipping off Mount Rushmore).

hitch-hikers Melville Farr sometimes used to give 'Boy' Barrett lifts on his way home in VICTIM: 'Then I stopped,' he tells his wife, '[because] I came to the conclusion that he was waiting for me. Wet or fine, he was always there ... Then he sent me letters and made phone calls' (But is Farr telling the whole truth – were his feelings becoming too hot to handle?); Mr Sloane has killed a photographer who gave him a lift and then 'befriended' him in ENTERTAINING MR SLOANE; Christopher Jones responds lethally to a French lorry driver's amorous advances in *The Looking Glass War* (1969 C); Palm Apodaca (Helena Kallionotes) and her girlfriend Terry Grouse (Toni Basil) considerably enliven part of Jack Nicholson's long journey home in *Five Easy Pieces* (1971 C); Harley McIntosh (Richard Thomas) is picked up by Cal Beamish (Stan Kamber) on his way back to army camp in *Cactus in the Snow* (1970 C), but soon realizes that Cal has another kind of ride in mind and abandons him; of all the misfits and dropouts Kowalski (Barry Newman) encounters during his cross-country flight in *Vanishing Point* (1971 C), *only* the two gays (Anthony James and Arthur Malet) prove treacherous; 'Lion' (Al Pacino) and Max (Gene Hackman) are inseparable wanderers in *Scarecrow* (1973 C); sisters (Marianne Morris and Anulka) desanguinate the (male) drivers who pick them up in *Vampyres* (1974 C); Ceil (Amy Wright), drifting through life open-mouthed in *Girlfriends* (1978 C), moves in briefly and disrupts Susan's life, not least because of her desire to 'relate' to her sexually; young male hikers are raped and murdered over the years by a farmer (Keith Carradine) in *Chiefs* (1983 T).

Hit That Perfect Beat, Boy A simple song about music, rhythm. Well, yes. But this is BRONSKI BEAT and the song is featured in the heterosexual but gay *Letter to Brezhnev* (1985 C), so there could be a semi-sublimated subtext. (The video features the group interspersed with clips from the film.)

HIV test Characters waiting for or hearing the results were included in DOCTOR, DOCTOR 'Accentuate the Positive' (1989 T); *G.P.* 'Mates' (1990 T); *Relax* (1991 C); *He–She Play* 'Accentuate the Positive' (1992 T); C. J. LAMB is asked if she has had the test in L.A. LAW 'The Nut Before Christmas': 'Yes, three years ago. It was the responsible thing to do.' *See also* AIDS.

Hobbs, Carleton (1898–1978) English actor of the thin vaselined voice, veteran of 50 years of radio acting. Best loved for Sherlock HOLMES (with Norman Shelley). Among hundreds and hundreds of gems: Ensor Doone in *Lorna Doone* (1957 R) and Pandarus in *Troilus and Cressida* (1959 R).

Hockney, David (1937–) English artist based in California. He became a successful if sporadic television person-

ality (dyed blond hair, Bradford accent, droll manner, glasses) the instant 'Pop Goes the Easel' (fellow 'pop' artists Derek Boshier, Peter Philips, Peter Blake and Pauline Boty) was shown in 1962. He could always be relied on for pithy comments on a wide range of things: the latest postage stamp (*Tonite Let's All Make Love in London* 1967 C); his ideal television service (*Review* 'Hockney's Television' 1969 T: 'there should be 39 channels, it's a great educator'); architecture (*Start the Week* 1987, complaining about the war against 'prettiness'). He was also the first openly *gay* person to be given the honour of a DESERT ISLAND DISCS castawayship (his 'book' was a pornographic work called *Route '69*). More substantially – though the result was often tedious and at a tangent – he opened himself up to a *cinéma-vérité* approach to his personal life (which included the breakup with his lover and model, Peter Schlesinger) in *A Bigger Splash* (1974 C).

Also: *Pop Art Since 1949* (1962 R): 'I paint what I like, when I like, where I like'; *Love's Presentation* (1966 C), narrating and seen illustrating erotic poems by CAVAFY; *The Shock of the New* (1980 T); *The Levin Interview* (1980 T); *Hockney at Work* (1981 T), chock-a-block with as much male NAKEDNESS as television would allow; THE SOUTH BANK SHOW (1981 T), National Gallery exhibition; *Painting with Light* (1987).

Holland, Anthony (1928–88) American actor 'known for comic portrayals of urban neurotic types' (*Variety*); writer and director collaborating with William M. Hoffman on gay comedies like *Cornboy* (1978). Roles (predominantly gay-aspected) include hotel clerk in *The Out-of-Towners* (1970 C); the pretentious prison psychiatrist in *The Anderson Tapes* (1971 C); party host in *The Sentinel* (1976 C); Gerald, the secretary in *Woman of the Year* (1978 T); fussy songwriter in *All That Jazz* (1979 C); Pia Zadora's faithful film director in *The Lonely Lady* (1983 C). Last appearance: one of the plea bargain lawyers in *The Accused* (1988 C).

Holland, Tony (194?–) English actor (Christopher WREN, gay character in *The Mousetrap*); television story editor and writer. His idea used for *The Isle Is Full of Noises* (1967, about a woman who can't stand noise); story editor for Z CARS (1973–5); *The Life and Death of Penelope* (1975); ANGELS; EASTENDERS; *The District Nurse* (1987); ELDORADO. Has enjoyed a very productive partnership with producer Julia Smith since the 1970s: together they have done much to increase gay (but not yet lesbian) visibility (and viability) during family viewing hours.

Hollywood Centre for film and television production. Two thirds heterosexual (and mostly puritanical) is one theory for its rock-hard conservatism; two thirds gay (and in the closet) is another. Surveys of 'Homophobia in Hollywood' in the wake of protests against *The Silence of the Lambs* and *Basic Instinct* on OUT (1992 T) and *The Movie Show* (Aust 1992 T). Fun with old-established movie images in *Dry Kisses Only* (1989 V) and *Rock Hudson's Home Movies* (1991 V). Scandalous tales in *Hollywood Confidential* 'Scandal' (1989 T, including Robert Mitchum's account of his penis, Charles LAUGHTON and the tomato sauce), and in *Hollywood Babylon* (1993 T). Sanitized Hollywood gay history in *The Users* (1978 T); *Moviola* (1980 T); *Rock Hudson* (1990 T).

'... a number of lesbian-themed films are in the pipeline for 1993–4. But gay men are still relegated to sniggering comedy, or AIDS stories' (OUT 'Homophobia in Hollywood').

Holm, Ian [Ian Holm Cuthbert] (1932–) English actor skilled and insightful, particularly adept at making the dogged and introverted interesting and sexy. Particularly good at being men floundering between heaven and hell. Michael Meade in *The Bell* (1982 T); the lover in *Dance with a Stranger* (1984 C); Lewis Carroll in *Dream Child* (1985 C); Mr Kurtzmann in *Brazil* (1985 C); Crocker-Harris in *The Browning Version* (1979 T); *Soft Targets* (1982 T); and –

unforgettably – James BARRIE in THE LOST BOYS (1978 T). Other roles of relevance include Granillo in ROPE (1957 T); the title role in *Becket* (1969 R, with Peter Jeffrey); nurse Gordon Breen in *The Frighteners* 'The Treat' (1972 T); Alec in BRIEF ENCOUNTER (1983 R, with Cheryl Campbell). Interviewed about working with LAUGHTON in *Shakespeare on His Lips* 'Charles Laughton in the Theatre' (1987 R).

Holmes, Phillips (1907–42) American film actor (brother-in-law of Libby Holman, son of actor Taylor Holmes) of little charisma, but was in demand for bland roles for nearly a decade. He was outed as gay in the magazine *Hollywood Fan* (1991). His most famous role: Clyde Griffiths in *An American Tragedy* (1931, played by Montgomery CLIFT in the remake *A Place in the Sun*). Also *Varsity* (1928); *The Wild Party* (1929); Captain Robert Darrington in the civil war drama *Only the Brave* (1930); an idealized farmer boy in *Devil's Holiday* (1930); Leonard St John who kills himself in *The Secret of Madame Blanche* (1933); boring Ernest in *Dinner at Eight* (1933); a millionaire who engineers his own kidnap in *Million Dollar Ransom* (1934); *Nana* (1934); Pip in *Great Expectations* (1934); *House of a Thousand Candles* (1936); as *The Housemaster* (1938).

Sherlock Holmes The world's most famous detective. 'Tall, slender, given to bouts of lethargy and depression relieved only by cocaine in a 7 per cent solution and the playing of a fiddle' (from *The Case of Sherlock Holmes* 1987 T, an investigation by Tim Pigott-Smith, who has played both the great one and his sidekick). Among other resonant interpreters: Basil Rathbone in the cinema, Carleton HOBBS and Clive Merrison on radio, and Jeremy Brett on television. Simon CALLOW – in radio's *The Seven Per Cent Solution* and *The Unopened Casebook of Sherlock Holmes* – is the most recent bringer of life to that extraordinary mind, equalled perhaps only by that other confirmed bachelor,

M. Hercule Poirot, a much more stable character but one also living mainly in his intellect.

home movies Used in *Home Movie – The Last of England*; *Sink or Swim*; THANK YOU AND GOODNIGHT; THE SILENT PIONEERS; BEFORE STONEWALL; DYNASTY: The Reunion; MALA NOCHE; *Sleep*; THE FOURTH MAN; *TV Eye* 'Multiple Murderers – And How to Catch Them'. A home movie by and of Dennis NILSEN (1985), but not in *Rock Hudson's Home Movies* (1991).

homo An abbreviation of homosexual. First bruited abroad as a reaction to Rod Steiger's over-solicitous (and murderously intentioned) wig salesman in *No Way to Treat a Lady* (1968 C). His client's sister becomes irritated by his pushiness: 'You homo!' The man counters with a hurt, pursed lipped 'That doesn't make me a nasty pers-on'. Young Luke aka Julian (Matt Day) uses it in A COUNTRY PRACTICE 'Apparitions' (1989 T). Rose (Betty White) whispers into Dorothy's (Bea Arthur) ear that Blanche's brother is a h-o-m-o. Dorothy is shocked: 'A *hobo*?' (THE GOLDEN GIRLS 'Scared Straight' 1988 T). Writer Marc Connelly in *The Ten Year Lunch* (1984 T) said some people thought Alexander Woolcott was a homo. Cary GRANT sued comedian Chevy Chase for $10 million in 1980 for referring to him as a 'homo' on a TV chat show.

homophobe Two probable homophobes: the immorality-crazed businessman in bowler and pinstripe who cries 'It's disgusting' and who wears black bra and panties on underneath, a regular character on *The Kenny Everett Video Show* (1978–80 T); J. Peasemold Gruntfuttock, evangelist and Peeping Tom in ROUND THE HORNE (1965–9, played by Kenneth WILLIAMS). Walt (Tim Streeter) introduces Roberto to (an unseen) bar acquaintance in MALA NOCHE (1987 C): 'This is Frank the Homophobe.' Sophie in THE WOMEN OF BREWSTER PLACE (1989 T) is obsessed with the two lesbians who move into the neighbourhood: 'The way they look up at each other's face. If you wallow with dogs you get up with fleas.' She is resoundingly religious (but unChristian), as is Miss Benham (Margaret Diamond), the BLACKMAILER in VICTIM (1961 C) who wants to rid the world of queers and their 'disgusting blasphemy' (and make a tidy profit at the same time). But one of the film's more chilling – because so mild and pliant on the surface – is Frank, the barman (Frank Pettitt) who pretends to like 'them', takes 'their' money and disparages them to 'normal' people.

homophobia The entertainment industry has generally steered clear of using 'homophobia' – it's too serious, too explosive. 'Homosexual panic' is much more to its liking. When John Chesterman spoke later of 'the massive social neurosis' he was unveiling something that was already dubbed in America 'homophobia' or, via THE BOYS IN THE BAND (1970 C, which had been a big bitchy popular success on Broadway and in the West End), the more accessible 'homosexual panic'.

The ungrammatical but essential word 'homophobia' was first released on US TV in *Police Story* 'The Ripper' (1974): 'Someone who convinced himself he hated homosexuals. On the other hand he could be a latent homosexual.' It wasn't heard again until DYNASTY (1981) when Brian Dennehy as the prosecution attorney asked Blake Carrington (John Forsythe), charged with murdering his son's lover, if he knew what the word 'homophobe' meant and if he was one. Blake, of course, denied so being.

Homophobia has become something of a buzz word, generally used without explanation.

Jack Davies (Struan Rodger), a university lecturer who denies he's homophobic, says to his colleague 'Pinky' in *Show Me the Way, Ugly Angels* (BBC Radio 3 1990): 'You can be a hermaphroditic Martian for all I care. It's just the way you queen around.' (However, Jack confides to the audience that he wants to know what it feels like to be penetrated by a man.)

'Despite a certain amount of homophobia in the popular press, people seem to love camp characters' (Jonathan Ross interviewing John INMAN on *Wogan* BBC1 1990).

Ken Bruce on WOMAN'S HOUR (BBC Radio 4 1990) describing why men cannot talk about sex with other men: 'Those that do seem a bit suspect ... eyes darting about ... people move back ... people joke about it, don't talk about it. A certain amount of homophobia comes into play.'

'Spike Lee confronts ... patriarchy ... and black homophobia in *She's Gotta Have It*' (*Dr Cornel West* Channel 4 1990).

'Maybe we are making some inroads into this thing called homophobia' (Phil DONAHUE 1989).

Eighty per cent of men according to the *Hite Report on Male Sexuality* have some neurosis about sex: 'A certain amount of homophobia about getting close to men, talking about sex' (WOMAN'S HOUR 1990).

But it was defined on OUTRAGE: THE DOCUMENTARY (1991 R): 'Homophobia – an irrational fear of lesbians and gays.'

Homophobia Opening credits piece for *Summer Kiss* (1988 T): very basic lyrics 'Ho-ho / Homophobia / Ho-ho / Homophobia' and Dixieland backing.

homosexual 'We don't like the word because the only letters people notice in it are the s-e-x. We are people who lead full lives and our sexual lives are part of our lives. Homosexual is a clinical medical term to describe a phenomenon, and I don't actually feel like a phenomenon. 'Gay' is our own word. It started off as an undercover word so we could talk about ourselves so we would know each other without getting social ostracism. It's our word; we prefer it,' Denis LEMON talking to Monty Modlyn on the LBC programme *Monty at Large* in June 1979.

Having been invented in 1869 by Swiss doctor Karl Karoly Maria Benkert, it was only introduced into English around 1900 – probably by John Addington SYMONDS, who referred to 'homosexual instincts' in *A Problem in Modern Ethics* (1891). Seven years later, he said that 'homosexual is a barbarously hybrid word and I claim no responsibility for it'. Compounded macaronically of a Greek prefix and Latin root, it means, literally, 'of one sex' as in homogeneous ('of one kind'). Therefore, a homosexual act means an act involving a person of one sex but to call someone a homosexual means 'of one sex'. As E. T. Scott of the *Guardian* once said of television: 'No good will come of it. The word is half Greek and half Latin' (quoted in TELEVISION: A WORLD HISTORY 1985 T).

The word was first uttered by Dr Jacob BRONOWSKI, in *Behind the News* (1953 R). It had been used in a recent House of Lords debate and Bronowski reasoned that 'what is good enough for the House of Lords is good enough for the BBC'. (He went on to espouse sexual choice but drew the line at eccentricity: 'intentional eccentricity is clearly a very bad thing.') Television undid the lock and chain on the word and the subject the following year when four gravelooking men discussed it, with seeming reluctance, on IN THE NEWS. *The Homosexual Condition* was the title of C. R. Hewitt's broadcast in 1959 where he was flanked in the Home Programme studio (at 10pm) by a psychiatrist, a prison officer, a former magistrate and 'a former homosexual'.

The word marched on through the 1960s: THIS WEEK (1964, calling its 1965 follow-up 'Lesbians') and, in America, CBS REPORTS 'The Homosexuals' (1967), and through most of the 1970s: HOMOSEXUALITY: THE YEARS OF CHANGE (1977 R).

Although undeniably useful to define a same-sex attraction, it promulgated the sham of providing fixed meanings for a tumble of behaviour, as well as encouraging the belief that homosexual meant male. The term guaranteed women almost complete invisibility. 'A Doctor' on WOMAN'S HOUR in 1964 began his talk by saying that he was only going to talk about male homosexuals and not female because they were 'lesbians'. (Consequently, lesbians were almost totally ignored by the programme until the late 1970s.)

The word was and is frequently mispronounced – even on the BBC, where Pronunciation issued a directive as far back as 1963 on correct reproduction. Activists have given up explaining that a short 'o' means 'the same' and a long 'o' 'man' and, given the derivation of the word to begin with, some thought such pedantry a waste of time anyway. Gay and lesbian became the preferred words from the late 1970s.

On a *Tuesday Call* (1982 R) the chief editor of the *Oxford English Dictionary* talked about correct pronunciation, and included 'homosexual/ity'. Misleadingly, immediately prior to this phone-in programme, Radio 4's news broadcaster had mispronounced homosexual with two long hooting Os: 'Had this been done deliberately? No one, at any rate, picked it up,' commented Christopher Reid in the *Listener* (29.7.82).

Jack Hedley as the intelligent chief social worker, Bob Sinclair, in HARD CASES (1988 T) refers to it as 'homo-sexy-ality'. Which is almost as entertaining as little Catherine Demongeot in *Zazie dans le Métro* (1960 C) calling 'someone who wears blewjeans' a 'hormosexual'. The *That's Life* team – which then included Simon FANSHAWE – invented a variation in May 1990 with an item about an amorous garden gnome with plaster women all round the world: 'At least he's not a gnomeosexual'.

As well as the confusion over the first part of the word, which encourages the exclusion of lesbians and its emphasis on the sexual to the exclusion of all else, homosexual was also thought too clinical.

Over the years the homosexual act/attraction/desire/condition became the person – which people like Father Bernard Lynch, who told of his long coming-out process in *Soul Survivor* (1990 T), regard as dangerous. However, it holds sway: 'His accent was homosexual', Nancy Banks-Smith reviewing Jack

(The Incredible Orlando) BIRKETT's performance as Thersites in *Troilus and Cressida* (1981 T).

But there is considerable divergence among lesbians and gays themselves as to what constitutes identity: 'I was a homosexual *child*. At school I longed for other boys but they wouldn't touch me,' opined Morris Murry (Dermot Crowley) in *The Mourning Thief* (1984 T).

Grandmother Buffy, on DONAHUE 'Gay Seniors' (1989 T), who had been married, strongly reacted against straitjacketing by a word: 'It is not a fixed orientation, regardless of whether it is genetic, hormonal or environmental or an interaction of all three.'

The widespread use of 'lesbian and gay' or 'gay and lesbian' has, for the foreseeable future, removed 'homosexual/ity' from the front line, although it is still used, interchangeably, with gay (and, from 1991, QUEER) when referring to males.

Homosexuality – The Years of Change (UK 1977 R) 'Linda Blandford hears from homosexuals about their lives, themselves, their feelings, about their sexuality and about society's attitudes towards them.'

In BBC Radio's last survey of the subject, in 1967, Leo ABSE said that the Act should not give homosexuals encouragement to be licentious. Neither did he, nor Lord Arran, endorse the proliferation of homosexual clubs and public meeting places. Eight years on, it came as no surprise that both men more than somewhat regretted the surging torrent of 'gay life' that had rushed through Britain since the SEXUAL OFFENCES BILL was given the royal nod. The most famous progenitor of the thrust towards law reform, Lord WOLFENDEN, was also interviewed, as was Kenneth WILLIAMS who, in his own way, had done much to bring homosexuality (certain parts thereof) 'out' to a wide public. He lambasted certain colleagues in the profession who 'exploited' homosexuals for cheap laughs – a reaction which some listeners found bewildering, if not downright hypocritical on his part.

More challengingly, the 45-minute programme invited some of 'them' to speak. Voices of gay people, all male; some still identifying as victims; others as reluctant heroes in an unending saga. It was a victory of sorts.

The Corporation's Research Department reported that listeners generally regarded the programme as 'skilfully handled, courageous and fair assessment of a difficult subject'. Disappointment was expressed that there was so little information about 'controversial aspects' like 'the psychological effects', 'the damage to young boys' and the 'apparently high failure rate of homosexual "marriage"'.

homosexual relationships don't last!
Gail's mother (Sada Thompson) is naively destructive after discovering her little girl (now in her late thirties to early forties, played by Mariette Hartley) having the bridge of her nose brushed by the lips of another woman (Lynn REDGRAVE) in MY TWO LOVES (1986 T). Lewis (Anton Rodgers) in COMING OUT (1979 T) advises his correspondents to take up sports and healthy outdoor occupations because they won't find happiness with gay people like themselves: 'And if you do it won't last – nothing does when you're QUEER.'

honeyboy Robert Taylor is called this – mockingly – by Hedy Lamarr in *Lady of the Tropics* (1939), and a theatrical agent (Vic Wise) refers to camp actor Harold Armytage (Dennis PRICE) thus in *Charley Moon* (1956 C). (Billy Murray sang of his 'Honey Boy', an absent sailor, in 1907 and Jim calls Huck 'honey' in *Huckleberry Finn*.)

Honeymoon Postponed (UK 1961 T)
Lancashire family riven by an unmentionable subject: non-consummation of marriage. Paul Rogers as Dad (who still mourns for his best mate), Patience Collier as Mum (who has her theories about her husband and said late mate), Trevor Bannister as Son (sensitive) and Lois Daine as Daughter-in-Law (bewildered and ashamed). (Became the stage

play *All in Good Time* and the film THE FAMILY WAY.)
W: Bill Naughton; D: John Knight; ABC; 90 mins.

honeymoons Athrob with expectation, virginal BRIDEGROOM Ezra Fitton takes his BEST MAN along with him for extra protection and extra affection in HONEYMOON POSTPONED aka *The Family Way* (1966 C) aka *All in Good Time* (1976 R); Charlie DYER (Rex Harrison) calls his honeymoon a holocaust in STAIRCASE (1969 C): 'one night of passion and food poisoning for 13. Maggots in the haddock, she claimed'; Phillip Castallack (Rupert Frazer) throws up and cannot proceed further in PENMARRIC: ostensibly it's because the hotel suite reminds him of the night he witnessed his father raping his mother; Charles Ryder (Jeremy Irons) goes to Venice with Sebastian in BRIDESHEAD REVISITED: 'I was drowning in honey – stingless,' he tells us, still swooning at the memory; Louis Bloom (Peter WOODTHORPE) left his wife (Prunella Scales) on the honeymoon night for the excitement of a radio transmitter – and the best man – in WHAT A SAGA! (1986 R); Phil (Lee Whitlock) and Matthew (Jason Rush) go to the coast for their 'honeymoon' but return separately in TWO OF US (at least in the version first aired in 1988 T); in *May We Borrow Your Husband?* (1986 T) a new-born bride watches helplessly as her husband is plucked from her by two shameless ANTIQUE DEALERS (Francis Matthews and David Yelland).

Honeysuckle Rose Marlene DIETRICH wore tails during the 1950s to sing love songs without substituting 'she' for 'he'. According to her daughter's biography, she believed that as men had their priorities right, only *they* could sing about love and its disenchantment with the proper authority. Yet in her final shows, the tails were nowhere in evidence. But, dressed in that shimmering, skin-tight gown, she still sang love songs to girls – and very likely *for* 'the girls' in the audience. In her slow, breathy rendition of the Fats Waller–Andy Razof classic (included in *An Evening With Marlene Dietrich* 1972 T), she repeats the word 'rose' at the end of each verse. Finally, she looks up at someone deep in the audience, possibly in a box and declaims: 'You're my honeysuckle rose ... Rose.'

Hooperman (US 1987–9 T) A glacéed but gay-friendly 'realistic' cop show, starring the very personable John Ritter as the title character, who has a dog called Bijou, a girlfriend and a lot of tolerance: 'I spent the 1960s in San Francisco. I'm open to practically anything.'
Cr: Steven Boscho, Terry Louise Fletcher and Gregory Hoblit; P: R. W. Goodwin; 30 mins.
It's mad mad San Francisco and gays positively mushroom: a TRANSVESTITE, a fey black guy at a seance, a feyer neighbour – and (on a weekly basis) Rick Salardi (Joe Gian), a handsome (desk-bound) police sergeant who 'just happens to be gay'. A few cracks at his expense naturally, but an advance nevertheless. He's young, personable, in uniform and an alive, highly evolved human being.
One Christmas (1988), Salardi advises a young man to come out to his parents over the phone. The results are negative: his mother calls him 'a faggit.' Oh well, maybe next year. Not that Salardi's own family situation doesn't have its wrinkles. In 'Reconciliation' (1989) Rick's TWIN Bobby, who's also a cop but straight (and insecure about being so), is arrested for punching a gay deputy DA, who mistook Bobby for Rick. After some considerable antipathy, the two men hug (that is to say Joe Gian embraces himself). This episode boasts a black transvestite and a possibly homicidal mother's boy as well as spunky, sweet, harmless, dramatically expendable Rick.

Hoover, J. Edgar (1895–1972) American federal agent who became head of the Federal Bureau of Investigation, who presented himself as avuncular and law-abiding while creating a vast, sticky network of blackmail – in which web he himself was caught.
Played usually as a frog-like *éminence grise* by Harris Yulin in *The FBI Story: The FBI vs Alvin Karpis, Public Enemy* (1974 T); Broderick Crawford in *The Private Files of J. Edgar Hoover* (1977 C, in which it was hinted that he and his close friend Clyde Tolson were lovers); Ernest Borgnine in *Blood Feud* (1983 T); Vincent Gardenia in *Kennedy* (1983 T); Raymond Sierra in CONCEALED ENEMIES (1984 T); Ned Beatty in *Robert Kennedy and His Times* (1985 T); Treat Williams as *J. Edgar Hoover* (1987 T).
Now fully revealed as a BLACKMAILER, TRANSVESTITE, and 'deceitful homosexual' on PBS's *Frontline* (1993 T) and the BBC's *Timewatch* 'The Secret File on J. Edgar Hoover' (1993 T).

Hope-Wallace, Philip (1911–79) English journalist who was the *Listener*'s radio and then television (CAMP and acerbic) 'Critic on the Hearth' from 1945 to 1956, taking over from Herbert Farjeon. He admitted a passion for Mrs SHUFFLEWICK and Gladys Young, was less convinced about the worth of *Take It from Here* and THE GOON SHOW, openly sneered at the middle-class values of MRS DALE'S DIARY and *The Grove Family*. Chairman of THE CRITICS and alternative chair of *Round Britain Quiz*, he produced and wrote *Oscar* WILDE (1963 R), and chose his favourite poetry and prose in *Read On from Here* (1967 R) and his favourite music (he was an opera fanatic) on DESERT ISLAND DISCS (1974 R) and *Words and Music* (1970s R). A regular contributor to *Time and Tide*, he also wrote fairly extensively on community radio in the 1970s. He spent much time at El Vino's.

Hopkins, John (1931–) British television and occasionally screen writer, best known for his *Z Cars* scripts (1962–4), his 1966 quartet *Talking to a Stranger*, and for the BBC's first 'homosexual play', HORROR OF DARKNESS (1965). Also: *Death of a Ghost* (1960); THE WEATHER IN THE STREETS (1962); *The Virgin Soldiers* (1969 C); *The Offence*

(1972); *Murder by Decree* (1978); *Smiley's People* (1983 T, with John Le Carré); etc. His play *Find Your Way Home* has never been filmed.

Horizon (UK 1964–   T) A useful, often brilliant series which clearly sets out a whole range of new scientific theories, cutting through the wire of statistics and jargon. Occasionally, it fumbled as when science and nature locked force fields in a 1979 programme (produced by Edward Goldwyn) called 'The Fight to Be Male'.

In the middle was a human tomahawk in the shape of an East German doctor who believed that anxiety in pregnant women releases too much testosterone in the womb, which results in the arrival of the Homosexual Child, passive like the white rat kept in overcrowded conditions. The programme's other sensational claim was that girl children could be successfully raised as boys, their hormonal structure changing in the process. It cited a boy who lost his penis during circumcision and was brought up as a girl, as well as Paula, a TOMBOY at 14 and rejected by her peers. According to Dr John Money, sex is biologically defined and gender is learned.

The main bone of contention for gay and lesbian people in 'The Fight to Be Male' was Dr Gerd Dörner, the East German biologist. He was allowed to posit, without any human evidence or the presence of any conflicting information, a theory which muddled homosexuality with transsexuality and which ignored lesbians and bisexuals altogether. Although he was quite definite that tension during the bombing of cities and towns contributed to the 'large numbers' of 'homosexual babies' born during and after the Second World War, his findings were based entirely on studying rats. 'Homosexual rats' were found to have female brains because of the lack of sufficient testosterone prior to birth. This change was the product of 'maternal stress'.

No apology was forthcoming from BBC2 or the Corporation to the gay community, none of whose organiz-

ations had been consulted over this section of the programme – which would have been unlikely to have been transmitted in so raw a form had it been about providing 'a solution' for a 'problem' (that of *being* homosexual rather than that of existing in an ignorant and hostile world). Especially worrying was that this claim was made by a man living and working in an authoritarian state where homosexuality was rooted out. A man, moreover, who would subsequently be described by *Time* magazine's Christine Gorman as 'notorious', a researcher motivated 'by a desire to eradicate the behaviour rather than understand, let alone celebrate, diversity' (9.9.91).

The impact of the initial criticism of the film (by conservative as well as more radical television reviewers) ripened two weeks later with well-argued letters in *Radio Times* and the *Listener*. Although there was no response from the BBC, the usual *Horizon* Sunday afternoon repeat – which was billed – did not take place.

A protest, stimulated by a couple of GAY NEWS journalists and filmed for London Weekend's *Look Here* feed-back series, had to be scrapped because of lack of cooperation from its non-commercial sister. LWT was also denied footage while the production team of 'The Fight to Be Male' was allegedly 'barred' from talking to *Look Here* because, it was argued, the issues raised were so intricate that a full programme was needed to unravel them. *Horizon* went on to address the question of sexual identity in the 1980s, and (produced by Edward Goldwyn) to (memorably) examine the roots of racism. Of Dr Dörner nothing more was said, nor has HOMOPHOBIA ever been singled out for attention as part of *Horizon*'s window on the world of mind and body.

See also GENETICS.

Horizon 'Killer in the Village' (UK 1983 T) Originally called 'Not the Gay Plague', this was the first British documentary about a disease first noted on 5 June 1981 – a rare 'cancer' which was attacking gay men in America. Ten years later, AIDS had killed 110,530 people in the US with a possible world-wide toll of 1.4 million, according to the World Health Organization.

Alex Nisbett and Jeremy Evans had filmed a gay couple for a general programme on cancer. They decided to take it out and make it one of the components of an AIDS detective story. Jeremy Evans told GAY NEWS: 'We can't get away from the fact that 94 per cent of those dead are young gay men ... relatively contained among a few high-risk groups ... the average age of the victims is 35; the average hospital bill often exceeds $100,000. Bobby Campbell, a nurse, was diagnosed at 29: he decided to tell everyone – as it is educational for them and it gave him some support. He wears a badge with an axe and the legend "I Will Survive". He has known three people who have died.'

Horizon 'Sex and Gay Men' (UK 1986 T) This was a frank and fearless discussion (involving a handful of gay and bisexual men) into what they actually did – and didn't do – in bed and in public places where sex took place. It never reached the British public, being banned outright. Fumed Christopher Dunkley of the *Financial Times*: '... what sort of daft broadcasting system have we constructed for ourselves which encourages us to watch pain being inflicted with dreadful frequency, but which flees in fear and trembling from the sight of a man daring to talk on television about homosexual practices? Practices which ... are indulged in for the mutual pleasure of the participants, often as an expression of love' (12.3.86).

At the same time, on Thames, *Someone to Talk to* 'Incest Crisis Line' was barred from its daytime slot and transmitted late at night. However, it must be said that a large group of lesbians and gays, shown 'Sex and Gay Men' at a conference on television's depiction of homosexuality, were generally quite stunned by the contents and, when asked for a show of hands, a sizeable majority was against the film being broadcast as it

would be detrimental to the perception of gay men.

Horlicks Two women rally drivers (the one with the short hair drives; the one with the wedding ring navigates) win the cup, thanks to that milky drink giving them the sleep they need. Directed by Joseph Losey at the time of THE SERVANT (1962–3).

Horne, Kenneth (1908–69) English comedian and businessman. Chortling, deliciously conservative girder for the lunacy of radio's *Much Binding in the Marsh*, *Beyond Our Ken* and ROUND THE HORNE and – less successfully – on television in *Horne a' Plenty*. He collapsed and died while hosting the Guild of Television Producers and Directors award ceremony. His irreplaceable contribution to the nation's mirth was highlighted when, in the mid-1970s, a record was issued of JULIAN AND SANDY without the puzzled, wishing to be enlightened but not really wanting to know questioning of Mr 'orne.

Horowitz, Vladimir (1904–89) Russian pianist who was long resident in America. He revisited the Soviet Union after a self-imposed exile of 61 years, which was captured in *Horowitz in Moscow* (1986). The event commenced with an announcer saying that he was still a game old gentleman who 'went dancing in discos'. What she didn't make clear was that the pianist went dancing in gay BARS and CLUBS with his lover – with his wife's full knowledge. To date, television has maintained the fiction that Horowitz lived with his watchful, discreetly organizing wife Wanda (the daughter of Toscanini) in a normal domestic arrangement, with affectionate sparring, in between playing (sublimely) Bach, Mozart, Schubert, Chopin, Liszt, Rachmaninoff and Scriabin – all in his New York apartment. (*Vladimir Horowitz, The Last Romantic* 1986). Also: *Horowitz Live!* (1978); *Horowitz in London: A Royal Concert* (1982).

Horror of Darkness (UK 1965 T) 'A highly original version of the eternal tri-

angle. A strange relationship between a commercial artist, Peter (Alfred Lynch), his girlfriend (Glenda Jackson) and an old college friend, Robin (Nicol Williamson) who comes to stay ... At first they are delighted to put him up, but after a few days, it is clear that there is a purpose behind Robin's visit. The relationship between them takes a new and disturbing meaning and Peter finds that he is not as invulnerable as he had thought to other people's emotions' *Radio Times* (25.3.65).
W: John HOPKINS; P: James MacTaggart; D: Anthony Page; BBC1; 75 mins.

The style was edgy, dialogue terse, the subject complex and compelling, with Nicol Williamson gripping as the unwanted, unlovable guest. Groundbreaking for the BBC, but very much following the path of least resistance: killing off the queer rather than seeing him resolve the situation and realize that the colourless Peter has nothing to offer him. As it is, the play ultimately has nothing very significant to say. But the young Nicol Williamson and Glenda Jackson, tight as tourniquets, are electrifying.

> Robin: 'For Christ's sake – I love you!'
> Peter: 'Friendship goes just so far and this is quite far enough!'

A Horse Called Gertrude Stein (UK 1990 R) A typically English Sunday lunch. Nigel and Pippa are cooing over the prospect of an addition to the family; Daddy is lauding the meal to the skies, and Mummy (Patricia Routledge) is talking endlessly about glazed carrots, the non-availability of broccoli spears and hormone-injected lamb. In the summer house, listening to a play about Gertrude STEIN and Alice B. TOKLAS, is Fiona (Jane Slavin). She desperately wants the family to acknowledge her relationship with Nina, to accept that she wants to be an artist, and to understand that homosexuals have included MICHELANGELO, Sappho, David HOCKNEY, Alice and Gertrude – who had a horse named after her. When Jane emerges, sits down at the table and confronts the HOMOPHOBIA she finds around it,

Mother is affronted, as much by Fiona's VEGETARIANISM as by her lesbianism; Daddy pretends nothing is happening; Nigel knocks back the drink and insults his sister; while Pippa compliments the cook on the delicious roast dinner. Fiona walks out on them – just as she has done many times before and will do again. Or will she?
W: Diana Souhami; P: David Benedictus; BBC Radio 4; 30 mins.

The formalities and trivialities of family ritual effortlessly rendered (especially by Patricia Routledge as Mummy/Georgie), offset by the daughter's attempts to be seen as herself, accepted for herself and assimilated. Difficult among a group of people that thinks homosexuals are gaining altogether too much power and that Gertrude Stein (the person not the horse) was 'a dirty lesbian' and that babies should be 'normal and healthy'.

Horton, Edward Everett (1887–1983) American light comedy actor famous for jittery uppercrust roles, sometimes coloured pinky-lilac. 'A universal favourite at women's club luncheons and ties right up to death. The only resident of Edward Everett Horton Lane; lifetime governor of San Fernando valley where he had a showplace estate. His mother acted as his hostess until her death at 101. He never married' (*Variety*).

In films from 1918, scoring a big success as *Ruggles of Red Gap* in 1923. During the 1930s, starring roles like Jeremy Dilke in *The Man in the Mirror* (confronted by apparition of his own self who promises him confidence and sex appeal) alternated with large supporting roles in films like *The Gay Divorce* and *Reaching for the Moon* (as crypto gay men).

T: *I Love Lucy*: 'Lucy Plays Cupid' (1952); *The Front Page* (1953); *The Merry Widow* (1955); *Manhattan Tower* (1956); *Dennis the Menace* 'My Uncle Ned' (1962) in which Dennis wants to write his uncle's life story but the latter refuses to have his life made public knowledge; *The Cara Williams Show*; *Burke's Law* 'Who Killed Eleanor

Davis?' (1964) and 'Who Killed Hamlet?' (1965).

Hotel (US 1981–7 T) Relatively slick package of comedy and drama, with five relevant stories: a male BABYSITTER is accused of molesting a young girl (but he's revealed as gay); two college friends have a reunion, and a stronger attachment than realized is indicated by one of the women; a man is gay-bashed and rejected by his buddy as a result; a TV sports reporter has to choose between his wife and his male lover; a married barman contracts AIDS and is helped by the gay man he has hitherto despised.

Hot*l Baltimore (US 1975 T) A sitcom based on the 1974 play by Lanford WILSON. A group of mainly endearing eccentrics – including a prostitute, two gay men, Gordon (Henry Calvert) and George (Lee Bergere, later to play butler Joseph in DYNASTY), and a 'latent lesbian' – are the residents of a once proud, now dishevelled hotel. It was cancelled after five months.
P: Norman LEAR; D: Ron Clark and Gene Maricone; ABC.

hotel managers/proprietors *Fothergill* (Robert Hardy 1981 T), former golden boy aesthete, friend of WILDE now keeping open house for eccentrics like himself; the sallow proprietor of the outback hotel (Esben Storm) in *The Coca Cola Kid* (1985 C); Harry in *Trotsky Was My Father* (1985 R).

The Houseboy (UK 1982 T) Two gay men (Richard Pasco and Geoffrey Palmer) run a guest house, with a high turnover of young male helpers. At present, it is John (Stephen Garlick).
W: Irving Wardle from his stage play; P: Pat Sandys; D: Christopher Hodson; 60 mins.
'There are more forms of marriage than the one celebrated to the strains of "Here Comes The Bride"' (*TV Times* synopsis). Well-worn domestic spats, dreams not realized – witnessed by a bewildered young outsider. A totally unremarkable play, mostly irrelevant to current concerns, made two years before, and of limited entertainment value. And yet none of the plays written for GAY SWEATSHOP got a look in on British television during the 1980s.

housekeepers Often put in a discordant note: Mrs DANVERS wedded to the memory of REBECCA (1940 C; 1979 T); the equally sinister Margaret (Judy Cornwell) in *Supernatural* 'Viktoria' (1977 T); male variety: Donald Churchill in TROUBLE FOR TWO (1958 T) and Deryck Guyler in *The Girl Who Loved Eggheads* (1960 R).

House on the Hill 'Something for the Boys' (UK 1981 T) The series was about the life of an Edinburgh house through the century. In this episode, which takes place during the Second World War, a young Scottish soldier, Duggie (James Telfer) loses his virginity to a Yank, Dusty (Raymond Thompson) after a night in an unofficial gay CLUB in Edinburgh. They part the next morning never to meet again, although the narrator – the older Duggie – says he was set up for life after the experience. The devil-may-care American soldier, who sells business equipment in civilian life, readily responds to this gaucheness of the young Scot he meets in this uncommon club. 'If you don't ask you don't get.'
W: Drew GRIFFITHS; P: Mike Vardy; D: Tina Wakerell; 3.8.81; Scottish TV; 60 mins.
A much longed-for variation on the stock GI with an eye for the main chance: good-looking, self-possessed, sexy, a regular guy.
There's a particularly nice ending. The American requests a farewell kiss at the station. Shyness gets the better of the Scot. 'How about a nice brotherly hug instead?' persists the American. They embrace, causing a male passer-by to comment favourably: 'That's what I like to see – the allies getting on together!'
A small foretaste of a talent that would have matured splendidly over the next decade had Drew Griffiths not been murdered.

housewives Two fall in love over Chopin during *Piano Lessons* (1976 T). Sally (Ann Curthoys), the pupil: 'Normal in most respects – in every respect ... I don't want babies ... the thought of it makes me sick ... every once in a while I pack a suitcase, write a little note. Once I did actually make it to the turn. But I got off at the next stop.' And Madge (Briony Hodge), the teacher: 'I'm the Lady Mayoress of Cabbageville. You can't escape your fate.' The two decide that the time is not right to live together; they'll continue as friends, wait until their husbands die and look forward to a fulfilled old age by the sea. Dame Edna EVERAGE, sharing her life with the faithful, ground-down Madge ALLSOP: two ordinary, 'perfectly normal' housewives. Celie (Whoopi Goldberg) aroused from her torpor by her husband's mistress in THE COLOR PURPLE.

housework Very few real men like to be seen to clean but, because Albert is a homosexual, he *loves* to cook and vacuum, fluff pillows and hang up Stella's clothes in A DIFFERENT STORY. WOMAN'S HOUR debated the question in 'A Man with a Mop: Is Housework a Husband's Job?' (1957 R), with Mary Gornall, Judith Chalmers and John Aldridge giving 'frank opinions'; 30 years later it returned to the knotty question in 'Boys in the Kitchen, Girls in the Workshop' (1988 R).

housing Leonard BERNSTEIN's pad was the basis for pianist Bette DAVIS' apartment in *Deception* (1946). The one belonging to the two lesbians in Jean-Pierre Melville's *Deux Hommes dans Manhattan* (1958 C) was an exact reconstruction – 'without any invention', said the director in 1971 – of a gay man's apartment seen in GREENWICH VILLAGE.

Since the beginning of the 1960s, audiences have become quite used to entering gay/lesbian domiciles, to see the habitat of the once secret commonwealth of elves, fauns, witches and fairies. Three examples:

Renato's son urges his father to change the décor in his and ALBIN's apartment before his in-laws-to-be arrive – out goes the kitsch and in come the crucifixes in LA CAGE AUX FOLLES (1978 C); when Rob's parents come to visit in AGONY (1980 T) the Tiffany glass and the Bette MIDLER poster are replaced with a picture of Geoff Boycott; Michael and Peter live in a loft in Chicago, painted white with chrome fittings and pricey objets, tastefully Spartan, in AN EARLY FROST (1985 T).

Gay men: THE COLLECTION (1961 T); VICTIM (1961 C); *Children of the Damned* (1964 C); *Point Blank* (1967 C); *Boa Constrictor* (1967); THE DETECTIVE (1968 C); *Is Nellie Dead?* (1968 T); STAIRCASE (1969); THE ROADS TO FREEDOM (1970 T); *Emma's Time* (1970 T); SUNDAY, BLOODY SUNDAY (1971 C); *The Creeper* (1971 T); NUMBER 96 (1972–7); THAT CERTAIN SUMMER (1972); *Helen – A Woman of Today* (1973 T); *A Bigger Splash* (1974 C); THE NAKED CIVIL SERVANT (1975); FOX AND HIS FRIENDS (1975); THE CREZZ (1976); *Kiss Me, Kill Me* (1976 T); A HYMN FROM JIM (1977 T); *The Rather Reassuring Programme* (1977 T); SOAP (1977–80 T); *Target* 'The Run' (1978 T); NIGHTHAWKS (1978 C); *From Here to Eternity* (1979 T); COMING OUT (1979); ONLY CONNECT (1979); MINDER 'Whose Wife Is It Anyway?' (1980 T); WE THINK THE WORLD OF YOU (1980 T); DYNASTY (1981–91 T); ALL FOR LOVE 'Conflict' (1982 T); THE GROUNDLING AND THE KITE (1984); PARTING GLANCES (1985); CONSENTING ADULT (1985); EASTENDERS (1986–9 T); PRICK UP YOUR EARS (1987); A DEATH IN THE FAMILY (1986); *Claws* (1987 T); *Floodtide* (1987 T); *Tidy Endings* (1988 T); TORCH SONG TRILOGY (1988); *Life without George* (1989 T); *Night Out* (1990 C); KILLING TIME (1990 T); *Rock Hudson* (1990 T); LONGTIME COMPANION (1990); *André's Mother* (1990 T); G.P. 'Mates' and 'Lovers' (1990 T); *Dynasty: The Reunion* (1991 T); YOUNG SOUL REBELS (1991); *Our Sons* (1991 T); G.P. 'What Makes the Man?' (1991 T); *He Play/She Play* 'Accentuate the Positive' (1992 T); G.P. 'Tests of Conscience' (1992 T); THE

LOST LANGUAGE OF CRANES (1992 T); SIX PACK 'Loveless' (1992 T).

Lesbians: THE FOX (1968); THE KILL-ING OF SISTER GEORGE; A DIFFERENT STORY (1978); A QUESTION OF LOVE (1978); DAWN! (1979 C); KISS AND TELL (1980 T); FOX (1980 T); *By Design* (1981); THE GENTLE TOUCH 'Solution' (1982 T); *Smiley's People* (1982 T); *Death of an Expert Witness* (1983 T); *Shroud for a Nightingale* (1983 T); DOMESTIC BLISS (1985); MY TWO LOVES (1986 T); *She Must Be Seeing Things* (1987 C); *Waiting for the Moon* (1987 C); PORTRAIT OF A MARRIAGE (1990 T); G.P. 'More Than Friends' (1991 T).

Gay/lesbian domiciles are also to be seen in many documentaries and series like GAY LIFE and OUT/OUT ON TUES-DAY.

Housman, A[lfred] E[dward] (1859–1936) English poet, author of A SHROP-SHIRE LAD. *A. E. Housman: The Man and the Poet* by Patric Dickinson (1945 R); *The Frontier of Darkness*, a study of Housman with Robert Harris (1954 R); *The Land of Lost Content*, William Plomer on Housman (1959 R); *The Turning World*, an Anthology by Patric Dickinson of poems by W. H. AUDEN, W. B. Yeats and Housman (1965 R).

Housman, Laurence (1865–1959) English playwright, most famous for *Victoria the Great*. Plays for radio: *The House Fairy* (1931); *Brother Elias*, a little play of St Francis (1935); *Three Victorian Plays* (1937); *Consider Your Verdict*, about a murder jury's last half hour (1938); *A Man of Words*, *Life in the Highlands*, *The Called and the Chosen* (1942); *Echo de Paris*, a group of friends meet Oscar WILDE in a Paris café in 1899 (1961). Play for television: *Moonshine* (1938). Brother of A. E. HOUSMAN.

Howard, Arthur (1910–   ) English actor, a specialist in 'old maid' roles, best known for Oliver Pettigrew in *Whacko!* (1955–9). The younger brother of Leslie Howard.

C: Dr Germont in *The Lady Is Willing* (1934 C); Anthony Ramsden in *The*

Happiest Days of Your Life (1950); soap publicity man in *Lady Godiva Rides Again*; Woodley in *The Belles of St Trinians* (1954); schoolteacher Bertram Slake in *The Intruder* (1954); Kenneth Wrath in *The Magnificent Seven Deadly Sins* (1971); doctor in *Jane Eyre* (1971 C/T); *One of Our Dinosaurs Is Missing* (1975); Deacon in *The Prisoner of Zenda* (1980); waiter in ANOTHER COUNTRY (1984).

R: Mr Inchbald in *Crime Lawyer* (1962).

T: Ernest in *The Whiteoaks Saga* (1954); Vicar in *Fool's Paradise* (1954); Oliver Pettigrew in *Whacko!* (1955–9); Harry Fairweather, a married country GP in *A Scoop for Caroline* (1956); *On a Pig's Back* (1964); THE FABULOUS FRUMP (1969).

Howard, Brian [Christian De Claiborne] (1905–58) English writer and Oxford aesthete. Sebastian Flyte partly based on him and Ambrose Silk in *Put Out More Flags* (1942). Committed suicide in Nice after accidental death of his lover. *Portrait of Brian Howard 1905–1958* with Harold ACTON, Tom DRIBERG and others (1968).

'He and (John) Minton must have suffered from the same disease (not homosexuality, though they both had that in common but the sense of bitter, humiliating failure). In the last years he fell in love with a former sailor, Sam. After Sam's sudden death he killed himself' (Maurice Richardson). (A MAN APART was a satire on Howard, and especially on Richardson's programme with its faintly mildewed collection of speakers.)

Howards' Way (UK 1985–90 T) Upmarket, fearfully smug boating and bonking serial with Polly (Patricia Shakesby) revealing – in episode 7 – to Jan (Jan Harvey) over a smoked salmon snack and a dry martini that her marriage to Gerald (Ivor Danvers) is a sham: he's gay and she thought she could handle it. In the process of not handling it, she's becoming alcoholic and shopaholic.

Cr: Gerald Glaister and Allan Prior; W:

Raymond Thompson, Jill HYEM and others; P: Gerald Glaister and D. Matthew Robinson.

'I was doing him a favour. You see, he needed a wife for business purposes ... His nights in town aren't spent with other women ... I'm a smoke screen.'

how dare you presume I'm a heterosexual! Legend on badges on sale during late 1970s. A teenage feminist-punk confronts a dispatch rider (Lenny Henry) thus, in *Lenny Henry Tonite* (1986 T), when he says he wants to marry her. She is heterosexual but even so, she shrugs, he shouldn't presume.

How Deep Is Your Love? (US 1990 T) A lavender version of the Bee Gees song from *Saturday Night Fever* (1977). D: Todd Verow and Jen Gentile; 5 mins.

Howerd, Frankie (1921–92) English comedian of gloriously flustered, ingratiating manner and fluctuating voice. Once described as having more cheek than a row of bottoms. Famed across four decades for his nervous patter and squeaks, sucked-in cheeks and wagging finger and sad expression. His catchphrases – or exclamations – were 'Ladies and Gentle-men!' and 'Ooooh!'

'I think a comedian dominates you with his weakness. Comedians represent immaturity. Their weakness is their strength' (KALEIDOSCOPE 'A Funny Thing Happened' 1987 R).

C: *The Runaway Bus* (1954); Alphonse Askett in *The Great St Trinian's Train Robbery* (1966); *Carry on Doctor* (1968); *Carry On up the Khyber* (1969); *Up Pompeii* (1970); *Up the Chastity Belt* (1971); *Up the Front* (1972); *The House in Nightmare Park* (1973).

R: *Frankie Howerd's Korean Party* (1952); *Fine Goings On* (with Hugh PADDICK, 1958); *Frankie's Bandbox* (1960); *Frankie Howerd's Forum* (as 'agony uncle' 1987).

T: *The Howerd Crowd* (1952); *Ladies and Gentle-men* (1960); *That Was the Week That Was* (1963); *Frankie Howerd*

(1964–5); *Up Pompeii* (1969–70); *Further Up Pompeii* (1971); *Francis Howerd in Concert* (1974); *The Sound of Laughter* (1976); *The Howerd Confessions* (1976); *Frankie Howerd Reveals All* (1980); *Frankie ... On Board* (1992).

Autobiography: *The Other Side of Me* (1982); DESERT ISLAND DISCS (1982 R, and also shown recording it on *Arena* 'Desert Island Discs'); KALEIDOSCOPE 'A Funny Thing Happened' (1987 R); *Aspel and Company* (1987); ARENA 'Frankie Howerd' (1990).

Howlett, Noel (1901–84) English actor, usually in roles such as solicitors or other pillars of society. He played Tom Craddock, Dirk BOGARDE's faithful (and understanding) assistant in VICTIM. Début in *A Yank at Oxford* (1937); played 'Pawnie' in THE VORTEX (1960 T).

how nice to varda your dolly old eek, Mr 'orne One of Julian's typically friendly greetings to their indefatigable customer: 'Come and have a varda.' Part of English POLARI since the 1950s; in the US much earlier (it was used in Mae WEST's 'The Drag' in the late 1920s); 'varda' had some wider currency during the 1960s, but it was looking antique when one of the suspects (Noel DAVIS) in *Who Killed Santa Claus?* (1971 T) used the word in reference to his false eyelashes: 'All the better to varda you with, my dear. D'you like them? ... It's just a bit of CAMP for Christmas.'

Hudson, Rock [Roy Fitzgerald Scherer] (1925–85) The male sex symbol of the 1950s, the male anxiety figure of the 1960s. In the 1970s: a TV cop hero. A sexual commodity produced, packaged and consumed. No wonder he was the world's top movie star for some of that period.

His characters are often seemingly autobiographical – men pretending to be what they're not: he's in drag and seemingly in need of an obstetrician in *Pillow Talk* (1959); in *Man's Favourite Sport?* (1964) he's a fishing writer who can't stand fish and makes friends with two women who appear inseparable; he's rendered impotent in *A Very Special Favour* (1965) and fakes gayness to win the frigid Leslie Caron ('Hiding in closets isn't going to cure you'), possessor of a mother's boy fiancé who is better adjusted than Rock; he reprises his impotent/gay in *Lover Come Back*: 'Now you know why I'm afraid to get married' (1962).

T: *I Love Lucy* 'In Palm Springs' (1955); *Rock Hudson's Cinema* (1969, including Judy GARLAND from *Ziegfeld Follies*); *Cinema* 'Rock Hudson' (1968); *McMillan and Wife* (1971–6); DYNASTY (1984); *Night of 100 Stars* (1985); *The Hollywood Legends* (1987 T); etc.

Eric Farr in *Rock Hudson's Home Movies* (1991 C/V) looks at the congruences between life and art in about 20 of the star's films from *The Lawless Breed* (1952) and *Taza, Son of Cochise* (1954) to *The Mirror Crack'd* (1980), bunching together: Rock CRUISING, being asked why he is not married, being taken off by (a) older women and (b) older men; the kisses (peck 'n' part); and the comedies featuring macho Rock and homo Rock.

Hudson and Halls A BBCTV series from 1987 featuring jolly New Zealand chefs (Peter and Davis) who display their culinary skills with all manner of callisthenics – hands on hip, pregnant pauses, moues, sighs and frisky banter with guests like Gorden KAYE and Sandra Dickinson.

hug A just-about acceptable form of male–male affection: father and son (in *Trapper John);* SERGEANT MATLOVICH VS THE US AIR FORCE; brothers (in BROTHERS; HOOPERMAN – twins, played by the same actor); bed partners (HOUSE ON THE HILL 'Something for the Boys'); former lovers (Tommy to Mark in the soap opera 'Other People' in LONGTIME COMPANION: 'Let me give you a hug at least'); work colleagues (Frank and Miles in *Murphy Brown* 'Male Call' (1991 T):

'Look everyone, Frank and Miles are going to hug.' (They embrace reluctantly.)

'I didn't want to hug – he made me.'

Women hugging: Marilyn and Patty in HEARTBEAT (1988–9 T); C.J. and Maggie in L.A. LAW 'The Nut Before Christmas' (1991 T); but Meriel's request to hug Amy on radio in THE TINKER'S DAUGHTER (1986) was cut!

The Human Jungle (UK 1963–5 T) 'Stories from a psychiatrist's casebook.' Including the following: 'The Flip-Side Man.' A famous pop singer, Danny Pace is constantly seeing his 'double' glaring at him. The effect is ruining his career. He is sure it is somebody out to get him. His tough manager, Laurie Winters (Annette Carrell) calls in Dr Corder to protect her investment – but her motives for doing so are mixed.
P: Julian Wintle and Leslie Parkyn; D: Sidney Hayers; 6.4.63.

'Conscience on a Rack.' Teacher Flora Robson has her fears put to rest when she receives a bouncy tape from her old love, now living in New Zealand. 'With husband and two children.' She had been so concerned that she had corrupted the girl that she has been sending blackmail demands to herself.
W: Bill MacIlwraith; P: Julian Wintle and Leslie Parkyn; D: Roy Baker; 25.3.65; 55 mins.

Humphries,   Barry   (1934–) Australian satirist, on television since 1963. Fascinated by the aesthetic movement of the late 1800s. His character, Dame Edna now has a lesbian daughter (Valmai) as well as a gay son – both glimpsed in the filmed funeral of her husband Norm ('Back with a Vengeance' stage, 1988).

C: THE ADVENTURES OF BARRY MCKENZIE (1972); *Barry McKenzie Holds His Own* (1974); *The Getting of Wisdom* (1977); *Les Patterson Saves the World* (1987).

R: *The Omar Khayyam Show* (1963) with Spike Milligan, Bill Kerr etc.

T: *The Late Show* (1966); *Canvas* 'A Corder Fan' (1970) on Charles Edward Corder; DESERT ISLAND DISCS (1973); *The Barry Humphries Show* (1975);

OMNIBUS 'A Summer Side Show' (1977); *This Is Your Lunch* (1988); *Time with Betjemin* (1983); Richard Deane, fading author in *Dr Fischer of Geneva/Bomb Surprise* (1984); *A Life in the Day of Barry Humphries* (1987); THE SOUTH BANK SHOW (1989).

'I still give offence, but I have a craving for respectability ... I'm a deeply inhibited figure. I cherish my inhibitions. I dramatize them' (*A Life in the Day of Barry Humphries*).

See also Dame Edna EVERAGE.

Mr (Wilberforce) Humphries (John INMAN in ARE YOU BEING SERVED? 1973–84 and GRACE AND FAVOUR 1992–)
In the 1972 pilot the character (who had just a handful of lines) was outlined as 'fortyish. Beginning to go thin on top and a right mixer. He comes from the North and has worked for 10 years for the store. Is second sales assistant in the gents' department.' His initial appearance is essentially that of a prattling eavesdropper. He does mention that his doctor sent him to a porno cinema 'for therapy' and he utters what was to become his catchphrase: 'I'M FREE.' The part as written was not especially camp, but costuming and John Inman's way with his bottom made it increasingly 'that way'. In the final series he throws himself upon Miss Brahms: 'It just goes to show you can't believe what you see on television.'

Brian Houghton, a gay psychiatrist related in GAY NEWS, 1977 that he and his lover didn't watch much television but enjoyed comedy programmes 'like *Are You Being Served?*' Brian was also Jewish: 'Most things are funny and from a cultural point of view many people, like the Jews, have been a source of humour for quite a long time and most of it is quite funny.'

Others took Mr Humphries much more seriously. GAY SWITCHBOARD operators reported callers beginning conversations with 'I'm gay but I'm not like John Inman' or a question such as: 'Are gay people all like they're shown on the telly?' A Switchboard worker from the West Midlands wrote to *Radio Times*

after the showing of the 1979 play COMING OUT: 'For the vast majority of gays, who have no contact with others, the images and characters provided by the media are all they know of the gay scene, and they had to take such images as truth.' But for every gay who hated the sideshow freaks, there was one (or more) who 'didn't mind' or who enthusiastically applauded them.

A look-alike of Mr Humphries turned up in *Illusions* (1983 T). Neatly white-haired, sweet but firm, he tells Karen Valentine that her husband used to slip him something under the counter (money).

See also Larry GRAYSON.

The Hunger (UK 1983 C) After seeing her male lover/brother (David Bowie) shrivel and die, a beautiful woman (Catherine Deneuve) – in reality thousands of years old – seduces a woman doctor (Susan Sarandon) and nearly succeeds in making her a partner for eternity.

W: Ivan Davis and Michael Thomas from the novel by Whitley Streiber; P: Richard Shepherd; D: Tony Scott; 96 mins.

Trendy tosh which fails to move its lesbian vampire out of the *haute couture* horror mode. The film is as much a creature in need of life blood as its protagonist, desperately seeking the same kind of quality that Susan Sarandon attempts to bring to the role of the driven doctor. Surprisingly, this film has achieved a strong cult following among lesbians despite the low level of plotting and scripting, hollow central performance and an attitude towards lesbian love-making which anticipates *Basic Instinct*.

Hunt, Martita (1900–69) 'Argentine-born English actress who specialized in later years in elegant or fading grand dames and eccentric aristocrats' (*Variety* obituary). Renowned for her Miss HAVISHAM (1946), she tended to play aristocrats and uppercrust dragons of peerless poise and rabid self-confidence. On stage, she was Diana the ageing actress 'who left a good husband for the companionship of her passionate secretary' in *Wise Tomorrow* (1937), but few of her screen roles allowed her any sexual dimension, save for eccentric display: as the forbiddingly attired and crossly expressioned woman cyclist – with her similarly uniformed but smaller companion – mistaken for Greer Garson and her friend in *Goodbye Mr Chips* (1939) and as the nursery school headmistress Ada Ford in *Bunny Lake Is Missing* (1965), living with her partner Madge and lost in recordings of children's fears and nightmares.

C: *A Rank Outsider* (1920, first film); Agnes Lightfoot in 'Mr Lightfoot in the Park' episode from *Friday the Thirteenth* (1933); Seraphina in *First a Girl* (1935); Mrs Davies, beauty parlour client in *Mr What's-His-Name* (1935); Jane's mother in *Tudor Rose* (1936); Lady Bagshott in *Good Morning, Boys!* (1937); Mme Berdi in *Trouble Brewing* (1939); Duchess of Beaumont in *Young Man's Fancy* (1939); Antoinette Dupat in *A Girl Must Live* (1939); Mme Mireille in *Quiet Wedding* (1941); Miss Finch in *Welcome Mr Washington* (1944); *The Wicked Lady* (1945); Princess in *Anna Karenina* (1948); rich client in *It Started in Paradise* (1952); Queen Eleanor in *The Story of Robin Hood*; *Melba* (1953); *King's Rhapsody* (1955); lady-in-waiting to the Grand Duchess in *Anastasia* (1956); Mrs Willis in *Three Men in a Boat* (1956); *Bonjour Tristesse* (1957); Aunt Fell ('tartly delicious,' *Monthly Film Bulletin*) in *Dangerous Exile* (1958); Baroness Meinster in *The Brides of Dracula* (1960); Lady Gore-Willoughby in *Bottoms Up!* (1960); Grand Duchess in *Song without End* (1960); Baroness *Mr Topaze/I Like Money* (1961); Queen Mother in *Becket* (1964); Grand Duchess in *The Unsinkable Molly Brown* (1964); headmistress in *The Best House in London* (1968).

R: Lady Macbeth in Val Gielgud's production of 1933; Duchess of Cheel in *The Happy Hypocrite* (1944); in Louis MacNeice's *The Careerist* (1946); Clytemnestra in *Electra* (1948); one of the four sisters in *Frolic Wind* (1948).

T: Lady Shawthorne in Ivor NOVELLO's *Fresh Fields* (1946); Mrs Julia Sharpe in *The Franchise Affair* (1955) with Gwen Watford; *The Madwoman of Chaillot* (1955); Lady BRACKNELL in *The Importance of Being Earnest* (1958); Madame Kuprin, scientist's mother in *A Call on Kuprin* (1961) with Eric Porter; Lady Bastable in *Saki* (1963); Lady Somerville in *Thriller* 'The Last of the Somervilles' (1964); Madame Desmermortes in *Ring Round the Moon* (1964); Madame Nodier in *The Happy Ones* (1964).

Pete Hunt (Stephen CHURCHETT in TOGETHER 1980–1 T) Trevor Wallace's easy-going boyfriend, never happier than when nurturing his plants in the shed: 'I'm a bit of a rolling stone; hotels, the boats, waiter, you name it.' 'One of the most down-to-earth, unselfconscious male gays yet presented on mainstream TV' (*Gay News* 188). The first sustained public introduction to the clone: unthreatening, generous, cheerful, bearded.

Hurt, John (1940–) English actor who specializes in runts of life's litter like Quentin CRISP, Timothy Evans in *10 Rillington Place* (1971), the prisoner in MIDNIGHT EXPRESS (1978), title role in *The Elephant Man*, Winston Smith in *Nineteen-Eighty-Four* etc. The first actor to give birth to a 'baby' on screen (in *Alien*). Relevant roles: Phil in *The Wild and the Willing* (1962 C); Bob Lacey in *Green Julia* (1972 T); CALIGULA in *I, Claudius* (1976 T); Fred, the cop in PARTNERS (1982 C). Recent roles include *Richard II* (1986 R) and the polymorphously perverse 'Countess' in *Even Cowgirls Get the Blues* (1993 C).

husbands Old longings revived: Gavin Maxwell in THE WORLD ABOUT US; EDWARD II; FACING THE SUN; MORE LIVES THAN ONE; MAURICE; VICTIM; etc. *See also* WIVES.

Hussein, Waris [Waris Habibullah] (1938–) Indian-born director who began with the BBC in the early 1960s with *Doctor Who*, leapt ahead with memorable drama (THE CONNOISSEUR 1966; *Death of a Teddy Bear* 1967; SPOILED 1968), tried films, then began an honourable career, jumping between TV in Britain (*Shoulder to Shoulder* 1974; *Blind Love* 1977) and bringing depth and expert workmanship to some TV movies and miniseries like *Little Gloria ... Happy at Last.* Occasional stage work: *A Single Man* (1991).

Hyem, Jill (194?–) English television, radio and stage writer, a former actress. She was responsible for much of WAG-GONERS WALK (1969–80), having also worked on its predecessor THE DALES. Two important milestones in the depiction of lesbian relationships – on radio NOW SHE LAUGHS, NOW SHE CRIES (1975 R) and on television some of the early TENKO episodes – were her creation. She was also partly responsible for mapping out the character of Gerald URQU-HART in HOWARDS' WAY. One of her most recent radio plays, *Death Drop* (1992), which was adapted from a novel, was a departure: a tale of a nasty school-boy, his affair with a teacher and what he did to keep it secret.

Lady **Hylberow** (Pauline Seville in THE ARCHERS 1952) The lavender menace of AMBRIDGE! She wanted to take Chris-tine to Ethiopia with her (as her sec-retary and companion) for two years. Christine was tempted, but Lady H.'s jealousy over her boyfriends made her think twice – much to her family's relief. Two years later, Christine discovered she has been left a sum of money in the woman's will.

A Hymn from Jim (UK 1977 T) Pop star Jim Tayo (Christopher Guard) kills ONE NIGHT STAND Sugar Abuku (Reg Tsibo) (who was going to expose him) with a golden disc. Immediately after-wards, Jim gives interview to a teeny-bopper magazine.
W: Richard O'Brien; D: Colin Bucksey; BBC2 (Première); 29.9.77; 30 mins.

A short and nasty tale about a bit of scum that lies on the top of the pop pool, with a nod towards pop stars (and their manager/lovers) who pull the wool over the eyes of the media and, in turn, the public.

> Journalist: 'What kind of girls do you like?'
> Jim: '*Your* kind.'

Iago Simon CALLOW reads and Alan Sinfield discusses 'I lay with Cassio lately' in *Without Walls* 'Dark Horses' (1992 T) with all its implications (kissing, laying a leg over Iago's thigh: 'all lurking around').

Played by D. A. CLARKE-SMITH (to Baliol Holloway as Othello 1937 T); Malcolm Keen (to Geoffrey Tearle 1937 R); Anthony Quayle (to Geoffrey Tearle 1948 R); Jack Hawkins (to John Clements 1948 R); Stephen Murray (to Alfred Drake 1955 R); Frank Duncan (to Valentine DYALL 1953 R); Micheal MACLIAMMOIR (to Orson WELLES 1952 C); Paul Rogers (to Gordon Heath 1955 T); Frank Finlay (to Laurence Olivier 1966 C); Richie Havens (to Patrick McGoohan in *Catch My Soul* 1974 C); Nicol Williamson (to Paul Scofield 1979 R); Julian Diaz (to Placido Domingo in *Otello* 1986 C); Ian MCKELLEN (to Willard White 1990 T).

'... the secret isolation of impotence under the soldier's muscles; the flabby solitude gnawing at the groin, the eye's untiring calculation' (Phillip Kemp on MacLiammoir, *Sight and Sound*, October 1992).

I Am a Camera Title of 1955 film version of Christopher ISHERWOOD's *Berlin Stories* and *Goodbye to Berlin*, spoken by Laurence Harvey.

I am one of the stately homos of England Quentin CRISP (John Hurt), resplendent and vindicated at the end of THE NAKED CIVIL SERVANT (1975 T), to a group of would-be attackers: 'You cannot touch me. I am one of the stately homos of England.' The last line in Crisp's 1968 book is: 'I stumble toward my grave confused and hurt and hungry.'

I am what I am *Mata Hari* (Greta Garbo) says it to Alexei (Ramon NOVARRO) in 1931. Peter Nuttall (Jonathan Owen) states it when his aggrieved girlfriend, Sandy (Helena Breck) in TRIANGLE (1981 T) suggests he see a psychiatrist (to 'stop' him being gay). Mario in OPEN SPACE 'Earls Court:

A Time ... A Place ... A State of Mind' (1983) says people must take him as they find him. And TRANSVESTITE Frankie Diamond (Ronald LACEY), one of the HARD CASES (1988 T), adds a bit of defiant flamboyance with 'I am what I am, DUCKIE ... I do what I do'. By this time the song 'I AM WHAT I AM' from *La Cage aux Folles* had become a second-tier *My Way*-style anthem for gays, though often depoliticized as it was mainly popular with heterosexually directed female singers.

I Am What I Am (1) Sung by Zaza alias ALBIN in the Broadway musical *La Cage aux Folles* (1982), it was delivered by its originator, George Hearn in *Julia and Company* (1986 T), and the chorus version played on a DONAHUE show about FEMALE IMPERSONATORS (1990 T). A vague derivative of this Jerry Herman song was flashed through the titles of the third LA CAGE AUX FOLLES film (*The Wedding* 1985 C), sung in English by an uncredited female singer.

Hearn sang it in drag on the 1984 grammy awards, and his version opens THE GAY AND LESBIAN WORLD (1992 R).

'I Am What I Am' was the title of the BBC2 youth programme *100%*'s 10-minute purchase on the needs of YOUNG LESBIANS AND GAYS (1992 T).

(2) A fairly glum though beaty anthem composed by Jacques Morali, Henri Belolo, Victor Willis and Beauris Whitehead. Sung by VILLAGE PEOPLE in *Thank God It's Friday* (1978 C), and heard in the 1979 Gay Pride march scenes in *Inside Story* 'Coming Out' (1980 T). The debate in *A Question of Faith* 'Homosexuality' (Capital 1979 R); between Richard Kirker of the Gay Christian Movement and Ron Gibbons of Whitely Chapel ends with the Village People rendition.

(3) 'You've got to be what you got to be' (disco song in OUTRAGEOUS! 1977 C).

I came over queer The sozzled *double entendre* of Mrs SHUFFLEWICK on *London Lights* and *Holiday Music Hall* from 1954 to 1962. In 1947 it was disallowed in

Agatha Christie's THREE BLIND MICE and changed to 'I went a bit peculiar'.

I Can't Get No Satisfaction *See* SATIS-FACTION.

I could (just) spit Expectoration has been a staple of comedy, particularly the comedy of effeminacy, eg Arthur Askey's 'Doesn't it make you want to spit' (*The Bandwaggon* 1938 R) and Mischa Auer's 'I'm so mad I could spit' (*Lady in the Dark* 1944 C). Peter SELLERS' FLOWERDEW in the first three years of THE GOON SHOW (1951-3 R), and sporadically thereafter, used the spitting line with more hair-tossing flourish coupled with a rather spongy voice. (None of the early shows survive, but Flowerdew's old identification signal can be heard in 'Ye Bandit of Sherwood Forest' 1954, denoted in the script as being said by 'camp voice'.)

Frank Muir and Denis Norden rejigged the line, now spoken by Wallas Eaton, for their *Take It from Here* (1954–9 R) as 'I'm so upset I could spit'. Muir and Norden revived the phrase in *My Word* during the 1980s. Ma Larkin (Pam Ferris) says to her baby (Oscar) in *The Darling Buds of May* (1991 T) 'Ooo I'm so mad I could spit' in response to the prejudice her young German friend (Benedict Taylor) continues to encounter from the local people, even though the war has been over for a decade or more.

A variant is the very, very upset queen voice; eg Adrian (Lockwood West) in *Unwieldy Elephant* (1962 R): 'I can't stand scenes. I'm sick of it; sick, sick, sick!'

I cover the waterfront An expression introduced in the film of the same name in 1933: a newspaper story with Ben Lyon and Claudette Colbert. The song followed. Tennessee WILLIAMS used the phrase as his America-wide COMING OUT on FROST OVER AMERICA in 1970. Less ambiguously (to some) *The Gay Book of Days* (1989) declared that Williams was 'the biggest chicken hawk of them all'.

identity *See* BADGES; COMING OUT; I AM WHAT I AM; PINK TRIANGLE.

I Didn't Know You Cared (UK 1975-8 T) Peter Tinniswood's gloriously phlegmatic Northern family whose Uncles Mort (Robin Bailey) and Staveley ('pardon?', Leslie Sarony) share a bed and where everybody else is deadpan about what goes on in their bedroom and everyone else's. The same household was seen (through a baby's eyes) in *A Touch of Daniel* (1980 R). Has a very special anarchic flavour without the raucous cruelty of alternative comedy of the 1970s and 1980s.

I don't know what it is that gives me a queer feeling when I look at you Used as the title of a lesbian and gay film festival in 1989, it was what the artist Michael Fane (Brian Aherne) said to Sylvester (really SYLVIA SCARLETT 1936 C). He can't (or says he can't) understand the hot flushes, quiverings, erections he gets everytime he sees the young fellow, all eager in his suit, trilby and short hair.

I don't shout it from the rooftops/I don't go on the streets waving a banner/I don't go flaunting it Often heard in documentaries featuring gays and lesbians during the 1970s and early 1980s, especially those living outside anonymous metropolitan areas. Shouting from the rooftops or waving banners is problematic in more exposed places, or within hidebound professions and working environs.

In mainstream broadcast drama this apologia emerged through the mouth of a Ronald Reagan supporter: a young soldier (Boyd Gaines) in HOTEL 'Hornet's Nest' (1986 T). However, he did add a rider: 'I don't shout it from the rooftops. But I'm not ashamed of it either.'

In fact, similar sentiments were being expressed many years before by gay characters, like Clem in Mae WEST's 1927 play *The Drag*: 'Now I don't give a Goddamn who knows it. Of course, I don't go flouncing my hips up and down

Broadway, picking up trade or with a sign on my back advertising it.'

Otto, the Noel COWARD surrogate in DESIGN FOR LIVING (1964 & 1979 T) has a more subtle attack/defence mechanism: 'But the whole point is it's none of their business. We're not doing any harm to anyone else. We're not peppering the world with children. The only people we could possibly mess up are ourselves. That's our lookout.'

Then Bruce (Douglas Storm) in POR-TRAIT OF A GIRL (1964 R) told Carol (Eileen Atkins): 'I don't shout it from the housetops.' But he doesn't elaborate on what 'it' is. She accuses him of lying to her: 'How *could* I know? You never said anything.' He replies: 'Why should I? It's not the kind of thing you want to shout from the housetops ... I don't have many girlfriends ... they all end up wanting the same thing ... I thought you were different. I thought we'd have fun together ... and then you go and spoil it.'

The housetops! The rooftops! How many times would variations on that theme be stated on television and radio. Bruce was probably the first person to raise his finger to his lips.

A similar but less expressive phrase is: 'I'm gay/I'm a lesbian but I don't broadcast it.' Bette Green (Maggie Steed) says in FOX (1980 T): 'I'm not ashamed of being ... I don't broadcast it, but it's not a problem with me; other people make it a problem for themselves.'

In real life, Vince, the young man in CRYING OUT LOUD (1982 T) who is seen ironing, taking his washing to the launderette and chatting to a friend feels that there's nothing different about him: 'I want the security of a man rather than a woman [but] I don't go down the road proclaiming I'm gay.'

The guppie (gay YUPPIE) version is: 'My phone machine doesn't say "Hi, I'm gay, I'm not in right now".' Which is what Russell (David Marshall Grant) says to Melissa (Melanie Mayron), who has just discovered the Truth in THIRTYSOMETHING (1989 T). But he's 'pretty open'.

'I don't go about with a great big placard "I Am a Lesbian",' says Diana in MAN ALIVE 'Consenting Adults' (1967).

I dream of a great dark man – enormously strong, enormously virile Quentin CRISP's simple recipe for happiness in THE NAKED CIVIL SERVANT (1975 T). He is destined always to be frustrated in his quest because he would not be interested in any butch homo who would find him attractive. But, then, that's all part of the delicious agony.

I Dream Of Jeannie Stephen FOSTER love song which is remembered today more for the title of the 1960s TV series than for its lyric and melody, which made it a natural title for Foster's doctored screen biography. Was 'Jeannie' really 'Jamie' or 'Johnnie'? Martha Raye retained the title when she recorded the tender-hearted piece of Americana in 1939.

I Enjoy Being A Girl A Rodgers and Hammerstein song from *Flower Drum Song* (1961 C) which is a hymn not to being *female* but about superficial *femininity*. Laurie (aka Lorri) Lee in *Black Cap Drag* (1970 C) performs his own rumbustiously irreverent version entitled 'I'm a boy being a boy'.

In its original form, performed by an unidentified female, it was the closing message in the documentary on TRANS-VESTITE men, *Sisters Under the Skin* (1991 R).

If... (UK 1968 C) Bobby Phillips (Rupert Webster with a great forelock of blond hair) is the fag who joins the three older boys and the girl in their insurrection. He and two other boys watch from the balcony as Wallace (Richard Warwick) does a 2-minute gymnastics display (in trousers and sweater). Later Bobby and Wallace are seen in bed asleep, with Wallace's arm around him. W: David Sherwin; P: Lindsay Anderson and Michael Medwin; D: Lindsay Anderson; 111 mins.

Seminal public-school-as-metaphor-for-the-establishment film, released in the year of the student riots in Paris and a few months before the breaking of the mould that was gay liberation. Refreshingly forthright, attractively cast, sexy.

I feel like a new man An unclouded personal statement of health and well-being which occasionally is given a sexual tang, eg in I'M SORRY I'LL READ THAT AGAIN (1968 R); 'What about me, DUCKY?' Used nudgingly by Maxwell Slaughter (Jackie Gleason) in *Soldier in the Rain* (1963 C). Chas (James FOX) says it urgently, to Turner and Pherber's amusement, in PERFORMANCE (1970 C): 'I feel like a new man ... all the time.'

I Feel Pretty One of Leonard BERNSTEIN and Stephen SONDHEIM's lesser songs from WEST SIDE STORY, ground into the mud by the character played by Geoffrey BURRIDGE (a putative TRANSSEXUAL) in *The Refuge* (1987 T). He sings this in the bath, repeating the line 'pretty, and witty, and gay' for the second of two cheap laughs. Elton JOHN sang it at Barbra STREISAND's AIDS benefit in 1992.

If Love Were All The character of Manon – who sings 'If Love Were All', and with whom Noel COWARD identified (spurned madame/singer) – was cut from the 1940 film version of *Bitter Sweet*, as was 'Green Carnations'.

If Only ... (UK 1982 T) Brian (George Winter) refuses to talk to anyone after the death, by drowning, of his mate Micky (Simon Chandler). A psychiatrist tells him it was just a PHASE. Only Micky himself understands how Brian feels.
P/D: Roger Tonge; BBC Schools; 25 mins.

Typically well-wrought and moving David COOK piece which tries to wrestle with both love and its loss. Brian's conversations with his dead friend help invigorate what could have been a cut to pattern sociological grey-flannel-suit-labelled BEREAVEMENT, teenage. Simple, unaffected but affecting. (Before the uncut TWO OF US was shown in 1992, this was the nearest schools broadcasting had gotten to same-sex love, but then it had the advantage of one of its

'mates' having a ghostly presence instead of being live and dangerous.)

If They'd Asked for a Lion Tamer (UK 1984 T) The life of drag entertainer Dave Dale – whose wish in this film for a regular gay character on CORONATION STREET hasn't yet come true, but he himself did land a part in EASTENDERS for a couple of months in 1986.
P: Sophie Balhetchet; D: Paul Oremland; KINESIS Films; 50 mins.

An extension but not necessarily an improvement upon 40 MINUTES 'Lol, Bona Queen of Fabularity' in 1981. Bright additional dialogue from Bernard PADDEN is a definite advantage.

If You Can Spare the Time (UK 1964 R) A dear old English village is a victim of progress invaded by vicious sniping Londoners, including silk-shirted INTERIOR DECORATOR (Gordon Gardner): 'Chelsea perverts to a man' (P. N. Furbank, *Listener*, 28.7.64).

'I blame the Government. They've got to control these people. You can't let these so-called intellectuals just go round flaunting proper authority all the time. Get 'em to work – that's the answer.'
W: Jack Russell; P: John Tydeman; 28.7.64; BBC Third Programme; 50 mins.

A typically bilious piece from Russell who went on to eviscerate other gay piranhas in *The Interior Decorator* and THE FAT OF THE LAND, before creating something more two-dimensional in his Richard I episodes of *The Devil's Crown* in 1978.

If You Knew Susie Steve (Lorrain Bertorelli), overweight and slightly slow of uptake, sings this Eddie Cantor classic (with music by Gus Kahn and words by Walter Donaldson) while menacingly stroking a brick. The words, always sung with a leer by Cantor, are given extra velocity because Steve has a lover called Mike (Gillian Rhind) whose real name is Susie. This was the first hint of full-on sex in the WITHIN THESE WALLS series ('Transfer' 1975 T): 'If you knew

Susie ... like I know Susie ... Oh, oh, oh what a girl.'

If You Think You've Got Problems (UK 1971-7 R) A Sunday BBC Radio 4 series chaired by Jean Metcalfe (ex-WOMAN'S HOUR and *Two-Way Family Favourites*; wife and mother). Very occasionally one of the Problems was That Problem. In 1975 the panel, consisting of Norman Ingram-Smith (the director of the social service unit, St Martin-in-the-Fields, London), psychologist James Hemming and Dr Wendy Greengross, chewed over – and found kindly in favour of – a letter from a young man: 'I am 22 years old and a homosexual. I find myself getting utterly depressed by society's hostility. I have recently left home because my father is not open to rational discussion. I respect his wishes not to tell my mother. I want to make my parents understand. How should I approach them?'

However, when – in 1977 – *If You Think You've Got Problems* finally dealt with lesbians, the entire programme was suppressed from on high ('not up to standard') in favour of a repeat of a tribute to the composer Sir Alan Herbert. The following week's *Problems* included a woman with a compulsion to undress in the afternoon and do her laundry the following morning. But the lesbians were never allowed to have their say. If You Think You've Got Lesbian Problems, don't call us ...

If you've got it, flaunt it! The credo of Max Biallystock (Zero Mostel) in THE PRODUCERS (1967 C). In the minds of many, homosexual people invented flaunting. Showering meteors of disapproval down on *The Well of Loneliness*, the *Sunday Express* (19.8.28) declared that 'they flaunt themselves in public places with increasing effrontery and more insolently provocative bravado.'

'If you've got it you might as well show it – and I've got it,' says Kenneth WIL-LIAMS in a *Thoroughly Modern Millie* skit on ROUND THE HORNE (1968 R).

I hate women! Rudolph VALENTINO, via title card, in the role of the bullfighter in *Blood and Sand* (1922 C). He later says to a temptress (Nita Naldi): 'Sometimes I love you, sometimes I hate you.' Audiences lapped it up as the very acme of seduction technique.

I hate yewww Archie Andrews' butler Grimble: a touchy fellow. Played first (1958) by Dick Emery and then (1959) by Warren Mitchell (*Educating Archie* R). A *Radio Times* piece in 1968 said that Emery's 'Ahhayewww' was once as famous as (the then household name) Simon Dee's 'Can't be bad'.

I have always depended on the kindness of strangers The desperately frightened Blanche Dubois in *A Streetcar Named Desire* (Vivien Leigh 1951 C; Ann-Margret 1984 T) to the doctor, clinging on to his arm: 'Whoever you are – I have always depended on the kindness of strangers.' It is the last of Blanche's lines.

Marge Simpson gives it all she's got in her acting début in THE SIMPSONS 'A Streetcar Named Marge' (1992 T). More surprising is its familiarity to HM The Queen (Miriam MARGOLYES), forcibly relocated to a housing estate, and living in greatly reduced, even desperate circumstances in THE QUEEN AND I: *A Royal Nightmare* (1992 R). Trying to get through to the man from the DSS that she is flat broke she rewords the line, but refuses to give it any of Blanche's doe-eyed pathos: 'I have been *forced* to rely on the charity of neighbours.'

Dorothy comments about Blanche in a 1991 episode of GOLDEN GIRLS: 'She's always depended on the kindness of strangers', while Quentin Crisp says: 'Like Mademoiselle Dubois I have found I can rely on the kindness of strangers.'

I have something to tell you ... Kit Mainwaring III (Mark Wheeler) to his bride-to-be Lucy Ewing (Charlene Tilton) in the only fully relevant episode of DALLAS 'Royal Marriage' (1979 T). This line has been stammered out by many gay characters over the years. It was good then to hear Lofty Holloway (Tom Watts) leading us on in EAST-ENDERS (1985 T) when he said to Michelle: 'I have something to tell you ... I'm ... I'm ... anaemic!' – by way of an explanation for his lack of sexual responsiveness to her. And Scott Howard (Michael J. Fox) tells his best buddy he is not a real man in *Teen Wolf* (1985 C): 'I'm a werewolf.' 'Better a werewolf than a FAGGOT,' says the relieved friend.

I Know What I Like (UK 1958 T) 'Caisse Noisette', a boy trumpeter, excerpts from two revues (*Cranks* and *For Amusement Only*), the song 'These Foolish Things', preparing the salad of his choice, and his pekinese Cham-Poo. These were some of Gilbert HARDING's favourite – and, given his walrus image, remarkably skittish – things in this BBC *jeu d'esprit* produced by Harry Carlisle, transmitted at 10.15pm on 6 June 1958.

I'll die! Transplanted from the big city (Sydney) to the outback in *Dad Rudd MP* (1940 C), Cedric Entwhistle (Alec KELLAWAY) has recourse to this expression more than once when he is butted by a cow and causes chaos with the local fire brigade. A passer-by, in his thirties, apologizes for bumping into Dick York in THE TWILIGHT ZONE 'A Penny for Your Thoughts' (1961 T), and a slightly fey voice says to himself: 'If he hits me, I'll *die*.'

I'll Make A Man Of You Written by Herman Fink and Arthur Wimperis in 1914 as a recruiting device (sung memorably as such by Maggie Smith in *Oh! What a Lovely War* 1969 C). David Dale, with new words by Kit and the Widow, used it to monumentally clobber gay dress codes and obsessions – which he felt were reaching ever lower depths of dictatorial absurdity – in IF THEY'D ASKED FOR A LION TAMER (1984 T).

I'll show you mine ... Julian CLARY in STICKY MOMENTS (1990 T): 'I'll show you mine if you show me your Access card.'

I Love Lucy (US 1951-7 T)/**The**

Lucy-Desi Comedy House (1957–1960) Lucy the Riveter trapped at home: wisecracking, resourceful, zany housewife resentful of not having a show business career like 'Oh, Rickee!', but happy that – at 40 – she has a baby (Little Ricky).
W: Madelyn Pugh (Davis) and Bob Carroll/Bob Schiller and Bob Weiskopf; P: Jess Oppenheimer; D: William Asher/J. V. Kern and others; CBS.

Lucille Ball and her husband Desi Arnaz decided to team up rather than split up – she was 39 going on 40, a second-grade movie star. Originally to be called 'My Favourite Husband', the series became a grand slam hit that – temporarily – saved the marriage. Spanning the 1950s, it was the most popular programme in the US between 1952 and 1954, and was voted the most popular programme of all time in viewer polls in America and Australia in 1991.

Writers Pugh and Carroll created the series *Dorothy*, set in a women's college, while Schiller and Weiskopf went on to win an EMMY for their writing of the lesbian episode 'Cousin Liz' in ALL IN THE FAMILY (1977-8).

Gale Gordon, later to be Mr Mooney, made his first appearance as the married owner of a nightclub (bow-tie wearing, bustling, over-motivated) in 'Lucy's Schedule' (1952).

Many of the shows feature veiled gay characters, such as the effete tramp who Lucy believes to be a powerful TV company representative ('Lucy and First Husband' 1952). His cover blown, the hobo sweeps out with the words 'Mother told me to expect days like this!' Friend Ethel fumes: 'Some bums have all the nerve.' Untypically for the time, 'The Ballet' presented a year earlier contains two male dancers who are depicted without a hint of ridicule.

I love you Three little words, eight little letters. The shorthand for a thousand different, sometimes conflicting feelings encapsulated – and some might say blunted with repetition and reproduction – in thousands of films, plays and books over the decades. In a certain context, of course, these three words were dynamite. They were bleeped out of *The Strange One/End as a Man* (1957 C) as 'Cockroach' (Paul Richards) confesses his feelings for the masterful Jack (Ben Gazzara). Censorship insisted that these three words be removed and replaced by an electronic hiccup (which remains in all prints circulating today).

Dirk BOGARDE insisted that 'I love you' should be written into his part of the barrister in VICTIM (1961 C). He told *The Times* in 1971: 'I said, "There's no point in half measures. We either make a film about queers or we don't."' In fact, neither he nor any other actor playing a gay character speaks the actual words (though they are twice expressed in a heterosexual context). It's a long wait until, in the final scene, Laura (Sylvia Syms) – in attempting to find out her husband Melville's true feelings about 'Boy' – goads him until he breaks down and, in a trembling voice, admits the reason he stopped seeing 'Boy' was because 'I wanted him. *Because I wanted him.*' Laura presses on: 'But was it *love?*' Suddenly, he is back in control: 'If it was love why should I want to stamp it out?' But what of the feeling of 'Boy'? presses Laura. What was that? 'Perhaps for him it *was* love,' Melville allows, adding: 'the only kind of love he could feel.' (This shallow and mean-minded back-hander is an echo of a remark made earlier in the film by the actor (Dennis PRICE) who says: 'I find love in the only way I can.') However, the scene that follows the confrontation with Laura has Melville visiting the grave of Boy.

For television audiences, the first voiced sentiments linking an outlawed kind of feeling with a legalized and widely promoted one came in 1964, in an adaptation of a 1930s play: 'I love you. You love me. You love Otto. I love Otto. Otto loves you. Otto loves me.' This was Leo (Daniel MASSEY) in COWARD'S DESIGN FOR LIVING (1964 T), British commercial television's first toe in the water of bisexual desires, needs and wants. A year later, on BBC1, Nicol Williamson loudly and clearly told

Alfred Lynch that he loved him in HORROR OF DARKNESS.

Four months earlier the 'I love him and he loves me' of one of the MALE HOMOSEXUALS broke 38 years of silence on the British airwaves.

HOLLYWOOD took a little bit longer to get around to it: EMORY (Cliff Gorman) to a boyhood friend, and Larry (Keith Prentice) to his lover Hank (Laurence Luckinbill) in THE BOYS IN THE BAND (1970 C) during Michael's cruel Truth Game wherein each guest has to ring the person he truly loves and tell him. The game ends anticlimactically because Emory's adored one is out of the house and Larry leaves his message with the answering service. But Larry does add, after putting down the phone: 'I do love him and I don't care who knows it.'

Ellen Large (Barbara Hershey) says the words to Casey Walker (Diana Scarwid), through a glass panel in the jail where Casey awaits trial for murder. This moment, in the TV movie IN THE GLITTER PALACE (1977), marked the first occasion of a woman declaring herself to another woman who is not a blood relation; one who, moreover, says: 'I love you, too.'

A TV sitcom first: Jodie's lover Dennis (Bob Seagren) in SOAP (1977 T), announcing that he is leaving Jodie to get married, even though Jodie was prepared to go through all the trauma of a sex change for him. As the nerd goes off into the arms of social acceptability, he turns to the shell-shocked Jodie and says: 'I know you'll have trouble believing this, but I love you, I really love you.' Door slam. In 1979 Jodie's ROOM-MATE Alice (Randee Heller), a lesbian, leaves for Alaska to start a new life. As she goes out the door she turns and says: 'There won't be a day that goes by that I don't think about you. You changed my life, pal. I love you.' They embrace, she leaves.

Sergeant Leonard Matlovich (Brad Dourif) and his father (Stephen Elliott) show their feelings for each other for the first time, even though the father finds his son's public stance on his sexuality hard to understand, and harder to defend to family and friends, in SER-GEANT MATLOVICH VS THE US AIR FORCE (1978 T)

Phlegmatic Britisher Michael (Peter Denyer) to repressed lover Rob in AGONY (1979 T): 'You know I love you, you berk.'

Reprobate Gerald Haxton (Barry Dennen) to equally unloveable Willie MAUGHAM (David MARCH) in WEEKEND WITH WILLIE (1981 R), to which declaration the old man replies, after a few seconds' curmudgeonly pause: 'I love you, too.'

Artist Vivienne Moray (Camilla Sparv) to Jennifer (Veronica Hamel) in VALLEY OF THE DOLLS '81 (1981 T): 'I know I haven't made you happy and that disappointed me because I love you.'

Young Lizzie (Colette Barker), besotted with the spectacular Miss Alliott (Kika Markham), shouts her passion to the rocks and trees in ALL FOR LOVE 'Miss A. and Miss M.' (1982 T).

Jo (Lois Weaver) to Agnes (Sheila Dabney), followed by peck on shoulder in *She Must Be Seeing Things* (1987 C).

Walt (Tim Streeter) says to Juan (Doug Cooneyate) in MALA NOCHE (1987 C): 'I love you.' And, in the same breath, he offers Juan $50 to sleep with him.

Ramon (Arturo Meza) to Rodolpho (Marco Antonio Trevino) in DONA HERLINDA AND HER SON (1985 C).

VEGETARIAN William to carnivore David in *The Tracey Ullman Show* 'Flesh and Desire' (1988 T) as they scrap over David eating a hamburger.

Jack (Hart Bochner) cradling the (seemingly) broken body of Adrian (Colin Firth) in *Apartment Zero* (1988 C), but he has prefaced his declaration with the words 'You're my brother, Adrian'.

Tony to the superficially unresponsive Steve at the start of *Night Out* (1990 C) during the latter's BIRTHDAY PARTY. A week later, with Tony recovering from a terrible beating and near mutilation, Steve can bring himself to say these words.

Jess (Charlotte Coleman) screams out to Melanie (Kathryn Bradshaw) 'I love

you!', while the Christian preacher loudly denounces them as degenerate daughters of Satan and his hosts in ORANGES ARE NOT THE ONLY FRUIT (1990 T).

Violet (Cathryn Harrison) and Vita (Janet McTeer) through calm and crisis in PORTRAIT OF A MARRIAGE (1990 T).

Mike (River Phoenix) to Scott (Keanu Reeves) in MY OWN PRIVATE IDAHO (1991 C) after Scott had told him that 'guys can't love each other'. River Phoenix's own words replaced writer-director Gus Van Sant's original 'Hey, I want to get laid'.

Not in so many words, but the sentiment's the same: 'I put my feet in your footsteps, moist on the bathroom mat ... I kept your comb as a souvenir ... And all this time I'd never spoken a word to you,' George (Beryl REID) recalling the months she and Childie (Susannah YORK) lived in the same bed-sit in THE KILLING OF SISTER GEORGE (1968 C).

Meriel Baigent (Deborah Makepeace) pours out her feelings to the wild and passionate servant girl (Zelah Clarke) in THE TINKER'S DAUGHTER (1986 R): 'You make me think of a seashore and birds sweeping along the water's edge.'

'I loved some women more deeply than I loved men and some women loved me more than any man,' Oprah WINFREY as Maddie in THE WOMEN OF BREWSTER PLACE (1989 T).

'I loved her,' axe murderess explaining why she did in her former girlfriend in *The Bill* (1991 T).

'I loved him,' Terence Fielding (Joss Ackland) to an unforgiving George Smiley about the pupil he was forced to bludgeon to death because the boy knew he was a murderer in *A Murder of Quality* (1991 T).

'I love him,' Steven CARRINGTON (Al Corley) about Bart Fallmont in *Dynasty: The Reunion* (1991 T) to his father Blake – who welcomes the news. (This was Steven's first such declaration – to a man – since DYNASTY began in 1981.)

And many, many more.

I love you (like a mother/sister/daughter;   father/brother/son)

There's always a pause after the word 'you'. The subsequent word is a perfect let-out for problematic feelings. Thus Kirk Douglas, having killed Tony Curtis to spare him crucifixion in SPARTACUS (1960 C), announces that he loves him '... like a son.' The dying man chokes out his reply: 'I love you ... like a father.'

I love you, too An ironic put-down to cope with a squelching, usually sweetened by a shared nonchalance. Fred MacMurray uses it to his boss Edward G. Robinson in Billy WILDER's *Double Indemnity* (1944 C). It figures again, as the very last line – this time with a deeper meaning, because we realize that the older man does love the younger one, who now lies bleeding in front of him, done in by a woman. Billy Wilder quickly devised this ending after the electrocution scene was thought to be too gruelling. In its less aggressive way, this fade-out line is as daring as was Wilder's 'NOBODY'S PERFECT' 15 years later.

Whispered by the incarcerated Casey (Diana Scarwid) when Ellen (Barbara Hershey) comes to visit in IN THE GLITTER PALACE (1977 T); in more comfortable surroundings by the about-to-get-herself-pregnant Helen (Patty Duke) to echo the verbal affection of Angie (Sara Botsford) in *By Design* (1981 C). This response was given by various characters over the 7-year period of action in LONGTIME COMPANION (1990 C), initially by the actor who rings his lover at the office to tell him about the horrifying disease attacking gay men he's read about in the newspaper.

Miles says it to Frank in *Murphy Brown* 'Male Call' (1991 T): 'I love you, too.'

Imagine John Lennon's voice and words accompany the climax of *The Killing Fields* (1984 C). The non-participation of the American hero's (former) wife in the project and her resultant absence from the plot gave the relationship between Sam Waterson and Haing Ngor a homoeroticism that was apparently not intended, although the Cambodian does jump into the American's arms and a

Warner's executive did describe the picture as Boy Meets Boy, Boy Loses Boy, Boy Finds Boy.

I Married Joan (US 1952-5 T) In 1952 Joan Davis starred with Jim Backus as the crass, clumsy childless wife of a judge in NBC's more mature, more pointed though no less madcap version of I LOVE LUCY. Unlike 'Lucy', 'Joan' is an unknown quantity to audiences today, though in many ways she was just as uproarious.

Joan Davis made over 50 films from 1935 to 1953, beginning her TV career at the age of 45 (Lucille Ball was only four years younger). The series was popular and ended only because of the star's exhaustion (she died in 1961 aged 54). The rerun rights of *I Married Joan* were – and possibly still are – tied up in wrangles over the star's estate – all her heirs having been wiped out in a fire (mother, granddaughter, and her daughter Beverley Wills who played her teenage sister in the series and who is remembered only for her 'two-legged jockey', quasi-lesbian band member in SOME LIKE IT HOT).

I'm free! Much loved and much echoed wherever ARE YOU BEING SERVED? (1973-84 T) has been shown. Perky, pixieish Mr HUMPHRIES (John INMAN), the queen of men's outfitting at Grace Bros, was free (both for legitimate business and for a bit of slap and tickle around the inside leg).

One of the *Sun* newspaper's cartoonists was grateful to Mr Humphries at the time (1987) of the Labour party's decision to put gay/lesbian rights on its agenda. The resulting cartoon had MP 'Red' Ken LIVINGSTONE prowling outside No. 10 Downing Street with a billboard advertising for a gay prime minister. Along skips Humphries/Inman in full CAMP paraphernalia carolling *his* availability in just two words.

The actor reported to Jonathan Ross (on *Wogan* 1990 T) that he continues to hear people shout at him (from kerb crawlers and pedestrians): 'Are you free?' He maintained that this recognition still pleased him.

John Inman also attempted to make 'I'm so bold' part of the national consciousness with his 1977 Thames television series ODD MAN OUT. There were no takers, probably because Kenneth WILLIAMS and Hugh PADDICK had already cornered the market with a variation a decade earlier, and partly because the series was so despised.

I'm gay! Housewife and mother (Linda Griffiths) comes out – first to her mirror: 'I'm Lianna Massey and I eat PUSSY' – then to a neighbour in the launderette – they both start laughing hysterically – in LIANNA (1983 C). Philip (Angus MacFadyen) comes out to his parents in THE LOST LANGUAGE OF CRANES (1992 T). Mother doesn't act shocked; she just has an aversion to all 'secrets' being revealed: Father says nothing; later, when his son has gone, he bursts into tears in front of his wife. *See also* I'M HOMOSEXUAL.

I'm Getting Sentimental Over You Tommy Dorsey standard (by Bussman and Washington) playing during Dianne Wiest's date with Robert Joy in *Radio Days* (1987 C). He begins weeping when he hears it because it reminds him of a departed male lover. Initially discomforted, she takes his hand and says yes, it *is* a beautiful song.

It also occupies a small but crucial place in clarifying what the script of *The Garden of the Finzi-Continis* (1971 C) and Helmut Berger's frail, retiring character couldn't say about Fabio Testi. The plangent melody is heard twice (in the same Dorsey version) during the movie.

I'm heterosexual! Very few people who are attracted to the opposite sex are prepared to come and say it in just one word, or part thereof. A rare exception was the late London-based Australian artist Sir Sydney Nolan, but this was only as an explanation as to why a homosexual (Patrick WHITE) fell out with him: 'It's jealousy, I'm fit, hetero. I produce

the goods, he couldn't stand it' (*The 7.30 Report* Aust 1992 T).

I'm homosexual! 'I'm a homosexual. Oh, Bev, I'm sorry, I thought you knew about Bruce and me.' This was DON FINLAYSON'S COMING OUT speech to Beverley (Abigail) and to the whole of AUSTRALIA (a country where such people were thought to be fit only for 'feeding to the cannibals') in NUMBER 96 (T). Not surprisingly, Bev being a nicely brought-up, all-Australian surfing carnival homecoming queen lets him have it right between the eyes: 'You filthy, filthy, DIRTY little QUEER, get out!' In subsequent episodes Bev got over it. But did *he*? *See also* I'M GAY.

I'm In Love With A Wonderful Guy *See* A WONDERFUL GUY.

I'm livid, absolutely livid When Warren Mitchell took over the role of Archie Andrews' vinegar-voiced butler in 1959 (*Educating Archie* R), censorship had relaxed sufficiently for a campier element to creep, serpent-like, into his exclamations. So, instead of Grimble merely pursing his lips and saying 'I hate yewww', he could swish a bit and be more spectacularly miffed and upset by Archie's naughtiness.

immigration John McTernan (nearly 20 years later, Robert on G.P.) played an American who has a very intimate relationship with Don FINLAYSON on NUMBER 96 (Aust 1973 T). However, he has to leave the country; he was in love with Don but couldn't stay in Australia. It wasn't until 15 April 1991 that gays and lesbians could bring in their partners as temporary residents, leading to permanent residence after two years' cohabitation.

The work of the Australian Gay and Lesbian Immigration Task Force was shown on OUT ON TUESDAY in 1989, although the segment remains untransmitted in the group's country of origin. To date, native television and radio have seemed disinclined to tackle the implications of GLITF's operations, both for immigration to other countries and for the wider definition of 'emotionally interdependent' relationships.

In A DIFFERENT STORY (1978 C) Stella, a lesbian marries a gay man (Perry King) so that he can evade the strictures of the US Immigration Department – they fall in love. More traditionally, Andie MacDowell sets about fooling the authorities to enable Gérard Depardieu to stay and get his *Green Card* (1990 C).

I'm Nobody! Who Are You? The Emily DICKINSON poem is partially recited by Claudia Blaisdel (Pamela Bellwood) to Steven CARRINGTON (Al Corley) in an early episode of DYNASTY (1981 T) to pinpoint the 'abnormality' of both of them: she with her mental problems, he with his sexual identity indecision ('Don't tell. They'd banish us, you know'). They inevitably end up together, recalling other outsiders: 'Nijinsky, Dostoevsky, Peter the Great.'

'I'm tired of being treated as if I had a social disease,' says Claudia before quoting Emily Dickinson:

> Much madness is divinest sense –
> to a discerning eye –
> Much sense – the starkest madness ...
> Assent – and you are sane –
> Demur – you're straightway dangerous –
> and handled with a chain.

Claudia then explains the words to Steven (and us). What she means is that very special people find it very difficult to survive in our society.

In THIRTYSOMETHING 'I'm Nobody! Who Are You?' (1990 T) Gary (Peter Horton) teaches the poem to his class ('You could say it was an existential exploration of egolessness'). For such pretentiousness, Gary is rewarded by a visitation (in a dream) from the poet herself.

I'm not a feminist but ... The war cry of a hundred non-militant women in the media, first heard during Vita SACK-VILLE-WEST and Harold NICOLSON's 1929 discussion on *Marriage*. This enabled her to proceed to mildly chastise the male sex. ('Men have been spoilt and flattered by women'), although Harold was given, or seized, the last word.

I'm Not At All In Love Terence DAVIES proves his devotion to Doris DAY by miming (on THE SOUTH BANK SHOW 1992 T) the introduction from this *Pajama Game* number (by Richard Adler and Jerry Ross), declaring that he/she is not in love. (Not even a bit.)

I'm not gay *See* HETEROSEXUAL.

I'm not well The catchphrase of singer–comedian George Williams who maintained a droopy, drippy MOTHER'S BOY persona. He was sometimes introduced as an 'inoffensive young man'. Formerly a ballet dancer, his enervated introduction was sometimes supported by such similarly weak admissions as 'I've gone doolalley' or 'I've had it' or 'It's getting me down'. His gloomy presentation appeared on *Variety Bandbox* (1949); *Workers Playtime* (1952); *Midday Music Hall* (1955-7); *Variety Playhouse* (1960-1).

Larry GRAYSON also says it, eg on *The Good Old Days* (1983) in response to the question 'How are you?': 'I'm not well.'

impersonal sex *See* COTTAGING; CRUISING; RAPE.

The Importance of Being Earnest (UK 1952 C; 1924, 1930, 1934, 1935, 1947, 1952, 1971 & 1977 R; 1937, 1938, 1946, (US) 1950, 1955, 1964, 1974, 1986 & 1988 T) Algy impersonates Jack's spendthrift brother Ernest – an imaginary presence who allows Jack to kick over the traces: a similar device to Algy's BUNBURY who 'lives in the country'. Full of hidden autobiography and secret symbols. Oscar WILDE's genius is perfectly aligned to his ability to tap into the universal, probably honed by his living in the shadow land, between society and fraternity.

With *The Way of the World, Hay Fever* and *Blithe Spirit, The Importance of Being Earnest* is the greatest prose comedy in the English language and far and away the most popular. Written by 'a butterfly for butterflies' specifically for Sir

George Alexander, who produced and played Jack with Allan Aynesworth as Algy, *The Importance* has received upwards of 20 productions on radio (since 1924) and television (since 1937). Excerpts (usually the 'HANDBAG' scene) have appeared in everything from CORONATION STREET in 1974 to FREDDIE AND MAX with Anne Bancroft in 1990.

When the 1952 film version of *The Importance* (directed by Anthony Asquith with Michael REDGRAVE and Edith Evans) was shown on television – for the eighth or ninth time since 1965 – in November 1987 at 2.15pm on BBC2, it garnered an audience of 2.5 million – which had reduced to 1.8 million by 3.30pm because of stronger competition from the other channels. (This showing coincided with a national survey of television viewing in which viewers compiled a diary for just one day.)

The central character of Alan Hollinghurst's novel *The Swimming-Pool Library* (1988) remarks: 'Michael REDGRAVE and Michael Denison were such bliss, so brittle and yet resilient, so utterly groomed and frivolous, dancing about whistling "La Donna è mobile" ... Afterwards James told me this theory about BUNBURY and burying buns, and how earnest was a codeword for gay, and it was really "The Importance of Being Uranist". I had heard it all before, but I could never quite remember it.'

'Twisted and yet capable of bringing forth a universal masterpiece which both exalts normalcy and subterfuge. The fact that *The Importance Of Being Earnest* has emerged as a masterpiece transcending all hatred and all objections is proof that the philosophy was not at fault' (artist Victor Passmore in a letter, *Listener*, 11.1.54).

The Importance of Being Frank 'Ernest Worthing, wit and aesthete, bearing more than a passing resemblance to Oscar WILDE, is prosecuted for indecent acts in the cloakroom of Victoria station' (*Radio Times* synopsis).
D: Paul Schlesinger; 22.10.90; BBC Radio 4; 90 mins.

Tom Holland's clever reworking of the other *Importance*, featuring John Worthing's rapscallion brother (Jack Klaff), whose downfall broadly follows that of his creator. Algernon and Gwendolyn (Alex Jennings and Jenny Howe) give questionable support; Lady BRACKNELL (Margaret Robertson) gives evidence against him; and Miss Prism – who holds the key to the whole case – is played by a man (Denys Hawthorn).

impotence Much worried about from the 1960s onwards, and usually linked with effeminacy or sexual deviance. When Marcello Mastroianni can no longer summon up the energy for his wife Sophia Loren (who has to be kept in a state of continuous pregnancy to stay out of jail), she screams at him 'You FAIRY!' in *Yesterday, Today and Tomorrow* (1964 C); and there is much speculation as to why the young man in THE FAMILY WAY (1966 C) cannot consummate his marriage. In the film version of *M*A*S*H* (1970 C) a similarly incapacitated army dentist is convinced he must be gay and plans suicide; and it is the discovery of his lack of erection with a woman that leads to the gay man killing Teresa in *Looking for Mr Goodbar* (1977 C).

Often impotence was suggested in the 1950s by a wife who was unsatisfied. This was usually displayed with lashings of NYMPHOMANIA or lip stiffening. The latter was well illustrated by Yvonne Mitchell's headmaster's wife in *Passionate Summer* (1959 C). She tells Bill Travers in that clipped, trembling British way: 'I didn't tell you that Lester is ... I can't have children.' Lester, who wears glasses and has way-out ideas about multi-culturalism and free expression, is set up as an ineffectual WIMP so this outburst is not unexpected.

The word itself first broke the surface in *The Sun Also Rises* (1957 C) when Tyrone Power, after being told the news, asks his commanding officer: 'Is it alright if I *smoke*?' The terror this state induces (including those of a liberal, environmentalist persuasion) is exemplified by Robert Redford's refusal to say 'Next time it will be better' to Barbra STREISAND after too much alcohol in *The Way We Were* (1973 C). Failure to achieve a stiffie is still regarded as curtains for most men, of whatever orientation.

This plight was graphically communicated when the promiscuous character Jack Nicholson played in *Carnal Knowledge* had to 'resort to' the ministrations of a fellating prostitute (Rita Moreno). A subtler reading of the 1971 film might indicate that it was his full love for his male buddy that put him on the slippery slope in the first place. But the film was released at a time when feminism was striking fear into the hearts and crotches of many men, and its aim was to expose villainous ball-breaking women rather than uphold love and friendship and sex between men.

Improper Conduct (Mauvaise Conduite) (Fr 1984 T/C) Interviews with Cuban refugees and French television footage reveal the imprisonment of homosexual men and women, dissidents and Jehovah's witnesses in the 1960s. Today, homosexuality is regarded as a reformable vice, alongside prostitution and drug addiction. 'Then' it meant imprisonment and torture in medieval castles, slave labour and slogans like 'Work Will Make You Men'.
P/D: Nestor Almendros and Orlando Jimenez-Leal; 114 mins.

No matter how much politics and orientation crisscrossed, sexuality was always seen as the motivating force in that person's life. Nestor Almendros' documentary about his native Cuba stirred some consciences, but hardened many other political credos. Leftwingers generally hated the correlation the film made between Castro's oppression and the suppression of gays, socialist revolution vs homophobic conservatism. The right-wing William F. Buckley demanded to know (on *First Line* 1985) why the director didn't 'talk instead about the nuns that have been persecuted'.

Improperly Dressed (Hungary 1976

C) Somewhere in Hungary during the months following the fall of the Soviet Republic in 1919, a boy (Endre Holman) disguises himself as a nurse in a sanatorium. A lonely signorina (Carla Romanelli) is attracted to 'her' and asks for some extra nursing, but copes well when 'she' is discovered to be 'he'.
W/D: Pal Sandor; 85 mins.

A rare film about sexual ambiguity from the Communist bloc. Its main strength lies, as Jack BABUSCIO said in *Gay News* 142, in 'the graceful, sensuously androgynous performance of Endre Holman, whose face and manner give this movie an extra dimension of sexual ambiguity – especially in the scene where we see him flirt, coquettishly, with several lascivious army officers'.

I'm ready for my close-up, Mr De Mille The chilling final curtain for Norma Desmond (Gloria Swanson) as she descends the staircase into total madness became a staple of drag shows and gay culture from the minute *Sunset Boulevard* first appeared in 1950. EMORY (Cliff Gorman), after being attacked in THE BOYS IN THE BAND, appraises himself in the mirror and decides: 'I am definitely not ready for my close-up, Mr De Mille.'

The staircase scene was recreated, in a baroque cinema, with Billy Wilder and Charles Brackett's original dialogue, by Frankie Diamond (Ronald LACEY) after a suicide attempt and breakdown *à la* his idol Norma/Gloria (HARD CASES 1988 T). Frankie, naturally, knows the speech off by heart; less predictably his social worker, Kevin, is word perfect, too.

The line was expressed, again to a mirror image, by Auckland TRANSSEXUAL Jewel (Georgina Beyer) in *Jewel's Darl* (1985 C). It was also the title of an L.A. LAW episode (1992 T) in which Stuart Markowitz works on the finances of an ageing movie star.

I'm Sorry I'll Read That Again (UK 1964-73 R) 'A radio custard pie' thrown by John Cleese, Graeme Garden, Bill Oddie, Tim Brooke-Taylor and Jo Kendall.

W: Simon Brett, Rolyon Baker, Graeme Garden and Jo Kendall; P: David Hatch and Peter Titheridge; BBC Light Programme.

Strainedly anarchic and fascinated by homosexuality at basement level:

Stern voice: 'I'll soon make you a man.'
Camp voice: 'Ooo, just what I want.'
Stern voice: 'All queens into the water ... Last one in's a sissy.'
Camp voice: 'So, what else is new?'

(from the *Bonnie and Clyde* farrago 'Bunny and Claude' (1968) in which, unlike the film it guys, the hero is gay).

I'm Still Here Originated by Yvonne De Carlo in the 1971 Broadway production of Stephen SONDHEIM's *Follies* as a hymn to survival, longevity and a thick skin. Shirley MacLaine, surrounded by friends – some gay – gave vent to the song in *Postcards from the Edge* (1990 C). Probably the first quality song to include the word 'camp' in its camp sense.

Inappropriate Behaviour (UK 1987 T) An educational psychologist, Jo (Jenifer Landor), who is a leading authority on behaviour modification, is drawn to an unruly pupil, 15-year-old Helen (Charlotte Coleman), who blossoms under Jo's sympathetic interest. The play ends with Helen, having killed her brutal father for his abuse of her sister, dreaming about Jo (whom she has 'seduced') living with her on the family farm. A family tragedy forces Jo to make a decision about her future direction – but Andrew DAVIES' play ends before we know whether Jo decides to live with the intelligent, tough child-woman or go back to tidy respectability.

This was one of Charlotte Coleman's major roles before appearing as Jess in ORANGES ARE NOT THE ONLY FRUIT. The character of Helen was described as 'A strong, chunky-looking girl of 15, by no means pretty'. She has a 17-year-old sister with whom her father has been sleeping. Although her IQ is in the high 130s, she detests school and will leave without a single qualification. Her behaviour becomes so bad – walking out of detention, punching a girl in the face – that Jo is called in. The latter finds a sullen, resentful person whose main interest is horses and working on the family farm: 'I can drive any bloody thing, do any job on the farm.' Helen likes women more than men but 'I don't like women either, mostly'. However, she *does* like Jo and, when the opportunity arises – Jo precariously astride a horse – she makes her move.

P: Terry Coles; D: Paul Seed; 80 mins.

In Bed with Madonna aka *Truth or Dare: On the Road and in Bed with Madonna* (US 1991 C) Madonna's 'Blonde Ambition' tour, on stage and backstage.

D: Alek Keshishian; P: Tim Clawson and Jay Roewe; EP: Madonna; 119 mins.

Fellating a mineral water bottle, gagging at Kevin Costner, talking to her (dead) mother, mothering her multiracial, sexually polarized dancers: Luis Camacho, Salim Gauwloos, Jose Guitierez, Kevin Stea, Gabriel Trupin, Carlton Wilborn and the only non-gay on the block, Oliver Crumes ... Just one happy family with Madonna as queen bee: 'I think I've unconsciously chosen people who are emotionally crippled in some way or need mothering.'

'Not only are gay men portrayed as normal healthy fun-loving people but also as being politically aware with the use of footage from a Queer Nation gay pride march. With her film, Madonna is promoting an acceptance of homosexuality to a wider audience. If she loses any fans with her positive gay attitude she does not appear unduly affected. In her own way, Madonna is trying to create a better world' (Stephen Lee, *Sydney Star Observer*, June 1991).

See also GETTING INTO BED WITH.

In-Between Just about-to-explode drag artist Michael (Martyn Hesford) mimes this to the voice of Judy GARLAND in *Belles* (1983 T). (The audience, a group of pensioners, were expecting a nice piece of family entertainment.)

Written by Mack Gordon, Harry Revel and Roger EDENS, 'In-Between' was sung by Judy Garland in *Love Finds Andy Hardy* 1938 (and rarely after that, apart from *Good News of 1939* on NBC Radio). One of the 50 songs she performed in movies.

In Camera (UK 1964 T) The first television production of Jean-Paul SARTRE's HUIS CLOS.
W: Jean-Paul Sartre adapted by Philip Saville; P: Peter Luke; D: Philip Saville; 4.11.64; BBC1.

Inez (Jane Arden) was described by *Radio Times* as 'the predatory Lesbian' who wrecked her cousin's life by seducing his wife. She is hopelessly in love with the selfish Estelle (Catherine Woodville) in a Versailles-like hotel. 'Yes, we are criminals – murderers – all three of us. We're in hell, my pets. They never make mistakes and people aren't damned for nothing.'

Incident (UK 1965 T) Two hiking TEACHERS, Molly Jones (Sheila Brennan) and Dora SMITH (Patricia England), arrive at a hotel on the moors one stormy night and find themselves embroiled in prejudice and fear. Miss Jones had booked two single rooms for herself 'and a FRIEND'. Suddenly, in the depths of the phoney beams and panelling, the snooty proprietress (Cicely Paget-Bowman) announces there are no vacancies. The women protest, but their putative hostess is adamantly evasive: 'We are always open. To anyone with absolutely no discrimination. We have a reputation for hospitality. But when the hospitality is full, what more is there to say?'

The two exhausted and bewildered women remonstrate. A booking has been made. Why has it been withdrawn? And why is Dora obviously the problem? The proprietress can hardly speak, such is her distaste for her non-guests: 'As if it weren't obvious ... She is a ... a ...'
W: David Campton; P: Anthony Comer;

D: John Davies; 27.1.65; BBC2 (Thirty Minute Theatre).

This expertly tuned piece of work successfully takes what has traditionally been a racial situation and twists it around using a sympathetic/unsympathetic lesbian couple as protagonists. The hangdog victim, Dora (whose name was changed from Jan late in rehearsals), is caught between outrage, fear and a belief that she may indeed be all the things she is accused of.

The objection of the manageress has nothing to do with sexuality or colour or class. It hinges on just one, non-negotiable factor: Dora's surname is 'Smith'. 'I don't think Smiths are allowed self-respect. They either crawl away, or sit back while others fight for them. Neither course is good for one's self-respect.'

An elderly resident, Mrs Blake (Edith Sharpe) joins in the attack: 'Everywhere one turns, one meets them. They crawl through our daily life like an unmentionable disease ... There are Smiths in the law, Smiths in medicine, Smiths in the Commons, Smiths in the Lords, Smiths in the BBC.'

The proprietress endorses her guest's view that Smiths are a menace to the British way of life. Dora protests that she is loved by her pupils – they bring her flowers on her birthday. This is twisted by the elderly woman into what amounts to an accusation of child molestation.

Molly and Dora try one last plea to common sense: 'We're both human. Two eyes, two arms, two legs, one head, one heart. What else matters?' Their judges are unimpressed. On top of her other crimes, Dora 'smells'. Totally crushed, Dora offers to leave. This backing down infuriates Molly: 'I shall spank you with my own hands. Where's your self-respect?'

The manageress, delighted by the conflict, decides to be conciliatory. Dora can sleep in the annexe. She is affronted and refuses. Molly then turns on her, callously telling her she is washing her hands of the whole business: 'Do what the hell you like!' Dora runs off into the stormy night. Molly is beside herself with guilt and worry: 'We never disagreed on anything that mattered. How could we? We are friends.'

The two assailants momentarily persuade Molly that she shouldn't fret because her friend wasn't 'one of us'. Then sanity and decency reassert themselves. Molly rounds on the pair: 'If only you could get rid of every one of 'em, you might be safe. It's pathetic. You're afraid, that's all. But who comes next? There'll always be somebody under the axe. When they're finished off whose turn will it be then? Cockneys? Schoolteachers?' Turning fiercely to Mrs Blake, she adds 'People over 60?' She grabs her bag and follows Dora out of the hotel and into the night.

An Inconvenient Woman (US 1991 T) A gay man is shot dead causing one or two ripples in the lives of the rich and famous.
W: John Pielmeier from the novel by Dominick Dunne; P: Steve Landsberg; D: Larry Elikann; NBC; 200 mins.

Hector Paradiso (Paxton Whitehead) is an *habitué* of Miss Garbo's (where elderly gentlemen 'of a certain persuasion' go) and has a pekinese called Astrid. Roddy MCDOWALL is the viperish gossip columnist Cyril Rathbone (as in Basil) who dies long and horribly in a rose bed. Gays here are all untrustworthy, whether it's poor dead Hector or Sandy Pond or a PROSTITUTE named Lonnie Edge. (Harvey FIERSTEIN turned down the chance to play Cyril.)

Indians, North American/Native Americans Brief depictions in mainstream cinema: Robert Little Star as Little Horse in *Little Big Man* (1970) who wants to be Jack's (Dustin Hoffman) 'wife'; male–male sex watched by the priest in *The Black Robe* (1991). The documentary *Honoured by the Moon* deals with what it means to be lesbian and gay for Native Americans (1989 C).

Indian and Pakistani gay and lesbian people Omar (Gordon Warnecke) in MY BEAUTIFUL LAUNDRETTE (1985 C)

not only gay but in love with a card-carrying racist; the two friends of the heroine in *Sammy and Rosie Get Laid* (1987 C) refusing to let old political sores in Pakistan go unpicked, flaunting their sexuality, taking no prisoners: self-righteous militant feminists or the only trace of conscience and decency? Documentary works on lesbian and gay Indians living in Britain include KHUSH (1991).

individualist Harold NICOLSON in *A Different World from This* (1960 R) spoke of 'the common-sense reflection of a quite sensible if pleasure-loving old man. Being an individualist by conviction, I regard individuals as responsible for their own actions.'

I never listen to gossip, duckie Sandy (Kenneth WILLIAMS) continually assures Mr 'orne of this fact whenever he dangles some scandalous titbit about your actual celebrity who may be an homi palome (*see* POLARI). In PERRY MASON 'The Case of the Negligent Nymph' (1957 T) James GRIFFITH as a campy beachcomber says: 'I *deplore* idle gossip.'

infantile names Many male gay characters have first names that end in 'ie' or 'y': Ritchie, Bobby, Kenny, Freddie etc. In THE BOYS IN THE BAND (1970 C) the party host tries to reverse the trend: 'My name is Michael, I'm not Micky.' In THE TWILIGHT ZONE 'Nervous Man in a $4 Room' (1960 T) Jackie (Joe Mantell) is rebuked by his honest, male self for being such a nail-biting wimp. The repressed side becomes dominant and a weakling stands up for himself, but now under his given name: John, not Jackie.

informers The little guy who squeals to (and possibly allows him to have his way with) Captain Munsey in *Brute Force* (1947 R); Wilson (James O'Rear) who is blowtorched to death under a press by his fellow prisoners; Luis Molina (William Hurt) reporting on his cell-mate – who eventually forgives and redeems him – in KISS OF THE SPIDER WOMAN (1985 C).

Inge, William (1913-71) American playwright whose *Picnic, Come Back Little Sheba, The Dark at the Top of the Stairs* and *A Loss of Roses* (as *The Stripper*) were all filmed. His only fully realized original script was for *Splendor in the Grass*. He used a pseudonym (Walter Gage) for *Bus Riley's Back in Town* (1965). Dissatisfied with *Picnic*, he rewrote it as *Summer Brave* which was staged shortly after his death.

Geoffrey **Ingham** Gentle 'mothering' art student in A TASTE OF HONEY who helps Jo during her pregnancy until Jo's mother shoos him away. Arguably the first modern-day gay-identified victim-hero: braving the stares at the ante-natal clinic and fending off the taunts of Jo and (less successfully) her mother. Called by Jo 'a clown', 'a big sister' and 'an old woman', and by her mother 'a nursemaid', he describes himself (and Jo) as the devil's own. John Normington played the role on radio (1961) and Ian Targett on BBC Schools TV in 1984, but it was Murray MELVIN who brought Geoffrey to shy life on stage and in the 1961 film. Thrown out by his landlady for having a man in his room, Jo's unsentimental approach to life energizes him.

'Everybody knew those characters but they hadn't been put on the stage as entertainment before that period. And interesting entertainment' (Murray Melvin in *Drama Resources* 'Bringing a Script to Life' 1985 R).

in love with the same woman A useful device to keep two males together, linked by a (worthless or teasing) woman, transcending such lustful concerns with the purity of their devotion. There are many examples including *Flesh and the Devil*; DESIGN FOR LIVING; *Rage in Heaven*; *The Life and Death of Colonel Blimp*; *Fire Down Below*; *Jules et Jim*; *Willie and Phil*; *Butch Cassidy and the Sundance Kid*; *Deux Lions au Soleil*; *Ishtar*.

Inman, John (1936–) English comedian and PANTOMIME dame with distinctive precise gait, doll-like face and figure, and a sometimes piping voice. Vilified by some, appreciated by many. Blithely exuberant (catchphrase 'I'M FREE') with much salty humour when he is playing 'himself'. Claims his hobby is sewing.

Trained as a window dresser (Austin Reed, Regent Street, London) before becoming an actor who played old men in cloth caps (influenced by Frank Randle) and then was half of a famous Ugly Sisters act with Barry Howard (later Barry STUART-HARGREAVES in *Hi-de-Hi!*). In the early 1970s, he had a long run as the queer who is converted (or is he?) in *Pajama Tops* at the Windmill Theatre before playing Mr HUMPHRIES in the *Comedy Playhouse* pilot of ARE YOU BEING SERVED?, which ran as a series from 1973 to 1984 and made him a national and partly international star. His star vehicles ODD MAN OUT (1977 T) and *Take a Letter, Mr Jones* (1981 T) were not successful. Resumed as Mr Humphries in GRACE AND FAVOUR (1992–).

C: *Are You Being Served?* (1977).

R: *Inman and Friends* (1987-8): 'Something bold, something new, something borrowed, but nothing blue.'

T: a guest on *Cilla* (1976); interviewed on *Saturday Night at the Mill* (1981); *Royal Variety Performance* (1981); *Oh Yes You Are, Oh No I'm Not* (1982, about pantomime); *The Good Old Days* (1983); *3-2-1* 'The Lilac Pimpernel' (1983); *Illusions* (1983; a look-alike appears in this US TV movie shot in London: neat, white-haired, sweet but firm, he tells heroine Karen Valentine that her husband used to give him something under the counter – money).

In 1977 Keith Howes for GAY NEWS spoke to a number of people about representations of gays on television: the name 'John Inman' came up in nearly every exchange. GAY SWITCHBOARD operators reported callers beginning conversations with 'I'm gay but I'm not like John Inman' or the question 'Are gay people all like they're shown on the telly?'

In Memoriam John Corigliano's 40-minute Symphony No. 1, played by the Chicago Symphony Orchestra conducted by Daniel Barenboim (Aust 1990 R). 'Historically, many symphonists (Berlioz, Mahler and Shostakovich, to name a few) have been inspired by important events affecting their lives, and perhaps occasionally their choice of symphonic form was dictated by extra-musical events. During the past decade I have lost many friends and colleagues to the AIDS epidemic and the cumulative effect of these losses has, naturally, deeply affected me. My first symphony was generated by feelings of loss, anger, and frustration. A few years ago, I was extremely moved when I first saw THE QUILT, an ambitious interweaving of several thousand fabric panels, each memorializing a person who had died of AIDS, and, most importantly, each designed and constructed by his or her loved ones. This made me want to memorialize in music those I have lost and reflect on those I am losing.'

Innocent, Harold (193?–93) English actor who has been adding grandeur to men of instinctive garrulity (like Mr Micawber) since the early 1960s: the Francis Bacon-esque artist in *The Avengers* 'The Medicine Men' (1963); 'Marjory' in *Afternoon Off* (1978 T); ambitious literary agent in *Vivien the Block-buster* (1980 R); Mr Gayelord-Sutton in *Diana* (1984 T); Jackson Cantelow in *Paradise Postponed* (1986 T); ANTIQUE DEALER Arnie in *Hideaway* (1986 T); bursar in *Porterhouse Blue* (1987 T); Dr Cash in *Secret Places of the Heart* (1988 R); judge in *The Brittas Empire* (1992 T); etc.

innocent victims People who had contracted the HIV virus through blood transfusion or through having sex with a bisexual person. Stuart Littlemore confronted the head of the Australian Press Council over the use of this phrase on *Mediawatch* (7.10.91) – and met something of a blank wall. 'There's no sliding scale of respectability among victims of this thing – they're just victims,' concludes one of them in THE FLYING DOCTORS 'Being Positive' (1991 T).

Inquest on a Hero (UK 1954 T) One of the great unrehearsed CAMP moments from the days of live British television occurred in this totally mundane, forgotten BBC play. On the line 'You murdered him as surely as if you'd killed him with your own hands', Trevor Howard was supposed to leave the room. Sadly the gracious mahogany door had ungraciously stuck. So the line ran: 'You [*tug*] murdered him as surely [*tug tug*] as if you'd killed him [*tug tug tug*] with your own [*tug tug tug tug*] hands.'

In Sickness and in Health (UK 1985-8 T) Alf Garnett (Warren Mitchell) was opposed to all things complex, visionary, shifting, subtle, cooperative and multi-racial. Throughout the 1960s, Johnny Speight's comic hero-villain raged against coons and wops and Micks and Harold Wilson.

When he returned in the 1980s, there had been quite significant changes in the order of things: an ultra-Conservative government (good) and an acceptance of inter-racial harmony (bad) and gender parity (bad). Alf Garnett didn't properly focus on gays until the arrival of his black home-help, WINSTON (Eamonn Walker) in 1985. Winston was a semi-stereotype, but Speight's invention flagged after one or two appearances. Winston soon retreated into repetition and supportive huddles with Alf's daughter Rita. Predictably, Rita liked Winston, but only came to his defence when Dad attacked his colour and race, not his chosen sexual expression.

In 1987 – after Winston had moved on to someone more appreciative – Alf was forced to face up to gay sex when the government sent him leaflets about AIDS through his letterbox. Again the writing fell at the hurdle. Like so many radicals, Speight and his interpreter Warren Mitchell have not properly digested rights as a civil right and gay people as individuals like any others.

The difference between a nod and a hug.

inside leg 'You're supposed to fit me, not fondle me,' says Don Alvarado (Walter Slezak) with more bluster than anger to his tailor in *The Spanish Man* (1945 C); John INMAN explores this situation at greater length with boxer Henry Cooper as his customer at the 1981 Royal Variety Performance; 'You look gorgeous – although if I had time I'd adjust your inside leg,' says Clarence (Dick Emery) to the prison camp commander in *The Dick Emery Show* (1978 T).

Inside/Outside (UK 1978 R) Blackmailed because of her sexuality, Jean, a bookkeeper embezzles money, is caught and sent to jail. Her sentence served, she returns home, is rejected by her girlfriend and becomes increasingly dependent upon her mother – who hopes she'll find Mr Right.
P: Jenny De Yong; 5.6.78; BBC Radio 4; 45 mins.
Bleakly engrossing documentary with Jean's lesbianism revealed only in the final 10 minutes of this interview with her and her mother by Jan Brookes.

Inside Story 'Coming Out' (UK 1980 T) Five people (four men and one woman), encountered first at the 1979 Gay Pride march, talk of their lives and their different stages of the coming out process. Seventy-year-old Bob, a retired civil servant, forbidden to appear by his family, told (voice-over and backview only) how his life had been changed by contact with GAY SWITCHBOARD.
D: Peter BARBER; 17.7.80; BBC2; 50 mins.
'His subjects were, in the main, pleasant but unremarkable young people with not a great deal to communicate except for the fact of their sexual bias. Fifty minutes of confession, when you've really only one thing to confess, is a long time on TV' (Richard Last, *Daily Telegraph*).
'The film shows that problems still exist for today's homosexuals, and that

in many cases their lives are far from good in the traditional sense. They tend not to be very perceptive about why they are as they are, either. A major documentary still remains to be done on this important subject' (Elizabeth Cowley, *Daily Mail*).
'While it has none of the rawness of GAY LIFE, its carefully balanced approach presents both a safe and perhaps a misleadingly simplistic picture' (Emmanuel Cooper, *Gay News* 195).

Inside Story 'George' (UK 1979 T) 'Although he is male, George Roberts' natural urge is to function as a female. His condition is defined as transexual [*sic*] ... in the first stage of his journey across the sexes, George attempts to become a national health patient and "comes out" fully by donating all his male clothing to charity and changing his name to Julia' (*Radio Times* synopsis).
P: Roger Mills; D: David Pearson; BBC2; 55 mins.
'The gay scene upset me. I eventually got a girl pregnant ... Most gay people resent TRANSSEXUALS.' George had been a prostitute and con man. He was into 'real' men. He saw a woman as someone who lay back with her legs in the air. He has internalized society's moral values, feels relaxed in women's clothes and enjoys housework only when wearing make-up and dress. The following year, another documentary appeared detailing George's progress as Julia Grant (*A Change of Sex* 'George – The Big Decision'/'Julia – My Body, My Choice').

Interior Decoration Probably the very first queer song on British television, in the days (1938) when the audience was restricted to people living in London rich enough to buy a set. This number, from the revue *Life Goes On*, was written by David Yates Massey (who went on to write a lot of material for and with Arthur MARSHALL). Three frivols – Vincent (John Baron); Francis (Lyndesay Baxter); Lord Convolvulus (Maurice

Denham) – who run Amusing Interiors Ltd guile and gambol their way through high society buying absurd *objets* and then incorporating them into their ravishing designs for rich women. They are presented as total parasites on society; with *à la mode* pretensions and inflated diction: 'Oh Francis dear, not *another* épergne', 'My dears, what heaven!', 'Just you wait a minute, poppet.'

interior decorators Among the most visible and persistent of the gay professions supposedly attracting, in the words of Jimmy PORTER, 'strutting sodomites'. Mentioned in passing by 'summer bachelor' Tom Ewell in *The Seven Year Itch* (1955 C), to emphasize his vulnerability to temptation. All wives and children have deserted Manhattan and its heat. The only people remaining in his brownstone, apart from a sweet blonde model, are 'two interior decorators'.

As Hollywood's Production Code forbade the use of any term – slang or proper – to describe 'them', writers had to rely on a combination of ingenuity (theirs) and ingenuousness (the moralists). Audiences had seen quite a number of fussy decorators in comedies (*The Jackpot*; *Father of the Bride*; *Painting the Clouds with Sunshine*) so the profession provided the ideal solution when Terence Rattigan's *Separate Tables* came to be realized as cinema. The pill-popping, ageing playgirl Anne (Rita Hayworth) comes to the Bournemouth hotel to re-establish contact with her ex-husband. They divorced because of his drinking (and consequent violence) and her 'immorality'. She remarried, but it didn't work out. John (Burt Lancaster) begins sniping when he discovers spouse number 2 was an interior decorator: 'He didn't break down the [bedroom] door to get at you?' She wipes the smirk off his face by noting: 'He didn't try to *kill* me either.'

Other mentions occur in *Surprise Package* (1960 C), in which King Noel COW-ARD mentions one of the breed semi-slightingly, in passing, at a ball, and in *The Servant* (1963 C), where Barrett

(Dirk BOGARDE) comes with good references and 'a flair' for interior decoration.

The earliest examples include Franklyn PANGBORN prattling on to his 'other half' as the stock market crashes and suicided businessmen litter the sidewalks in *Only Yesterday* (1933 C); Martin CAPLAN, the dead epicentre of DANGEROUS CORNER (1934 C; 1945 R; 1957 T; etc); an aristocrat in purple and turquoise lounging pyjamas who 'does' society matrons for a price in *Over the Moon* (Peter Haddon as 'Petzi' 1937 C).

The only half-way heroic interior decorator was Leo, one of the trio in DESIGN FOR LIVING, played by Daniel MASSEY in 1964 (T) and by John Steiner in 1979 (T). Gary Cooper couldn't play one of these in the film version (1933), so his character was made into a (butch) artist instead. But when Clark Gable had to play an ARTIST in *It Happened One Night* in 1934, it was considered too alien so they made him a reporter.

Leonora (Sheila Burrell) wonders why Mr Dulcimer doesn't design his friends' apartments. Dulcimer simply replies that he couldn't bear other people's tastes. This exchange in THE GREEN BAY TREE (1946 R) introduced the idea of the decorator as dictator, as corruptor of taste, an evil epicene influence upon the happy home. This theme was carried through in the story of the eponymous *Interior Decorator* (Barry Foster 1965 T) conspiring (with a white CAT) to take over a woman's soul as well as her swish apartment, and in the malodorous couple, Stephen and Tony (Francis Matthews and David Yelland), who ask the pointed question to the young bride in *May We Borrow Your Husband?* (1986 T).

Others who are presented with various degrees of distaste are the mascara'd and toupeed Tommy Hoskins (Martin Balsam), one of the robbers in *The Anderson Tapes* (1971 C); the unseen Gerald in IT TAKES A WORRIED MAN (1981-4 T), boyfriend of the frazzled psychiatrist; Crispin (Malcolm Stoddard) who for some reason makes husbands jealous in *Oxbridge Blues* 'That Was Tory' (1984 T).

Sometimes interior decorators will be female (and heterosexually identified): Doris DAY in *Pillow Talk* (1959 C) scorching Rock HUDSON's rampant promiscuity by transforming his pad into an automatic sex parlour; Syrie Maugham (Prunella Scales) trying to reignite her marriage in WEEKEND WITH WILLIE (1981 R); and Darryl Hannah in *Wall Street* (1987 C).

Very occasionally they will be male and not gay, eg Vincent Fish (William Nighy), the blond bombshell in AGONY 'Coming Out ... And Going In Again' (1980 T), who one of the gays mistakenly believes wants to begin an affair with him. A heftily hetero one was also spotted in a sketch on *The Tracey Ullman Show* (1989 T) with designs (sexual) upon his female client.

Even Warren Beatty didn't try to het up this profession whose practitioners – at least in Hollywood's eyes – haven't changed since the posturing ninnies of the pre-liberation decades: Pangborn and characters in *The Jackpot* (1950); *Painting the Clouds with Sunshine* (1951); *The Wheeler Dealers* (1963); *Any Wednesday* (1966); *St Elmo's Fire* (1985) which featured the ineffectual Rob (Matthew Laurence), a neighbour of Andrew McCarthy's with a penchant for pink walls and strawberry cocktails. The most memorable of the American decorators was EMORY in THE BOYS IN THE BAND (1970 C): 'I couldn't really care less if I never saw another piece of fabric or another stick of furniture as long as I live.'

The only good gay interior one was a dying one: Kendall Dobbs (Tony Goldwyn) in *Designing Women* 'Killing All the Right People' (1987 T) who wanted his friends to make sure he had a really noisy, uninhibited New Orleans funeral.

David, one of the people whose stories were told in COMMON THREADS (1989 C), wanted to be an interior decorator but, because of the stigma attached to it, became a landscape architect instead. Cut to close-up of container of yellow pansies.

The Internationale In a 1968 ROUND THE HORNE Julian is standing for the Universal Party, 'so-called because we're at it left, right *and* centre'. With Sandy as his campaign manager, Julian stands right behind the working man. His slogan is 'Keep Britain Bona'. This initiative has been taken, Julian tells Horne, because all the major parties have let 'us' down. It's up to him to get out there and put across another point of view: 'Homis and palomes, we are poised at a moment in history. The future could be NAFF. Or it could be bona. The time has come for a frank and honest varda at our awkward position. I am questing after this seat for the good of my fellow homis. Let us not mince ... words. Let us put our best lally forward and with our eeks shining with hope, troll together towards the fantabulosa futurette.'

Julian and Sandy then proceed to sing – to the tune of the Internationale – the party song:

> The party's flag is deepest puce
> With *fleur-de-lys* in pale chartreuse.
> Both working homi and *nouveaux riches*
> Will find *our* party very shish.
> We'll do our best for young and old
> Our party line is *very* bold.
> Let's mince together hand in hand.
> We'll make Great Britain *fairy*-land!

This was broadcast a few weeks after the students' revolution in Paris.

International Years Twelve months (and sometimes decades) earmarked to focus upon groups in society or on precious commodities. Thus the International Geophysical Year, the Year of the Tree, the International Women's Year, the International Year of Disabled Persons/People, the International Year of Youth and, most recently, the International Year of the World's Indigenous Peoples and the Year of the Family. Those dealing with human beings all have a word missing in their proclamations – that word is 'heterosexual'. There was the International Year of Lesbian and Gay People (1985), but it wasn't under the aegis – as were all the others – of the United Nations. Without proper funding and infrastructure, it made little or no impact.

Andrew Denton in *The Money or the Gun* (Aust 1990 T) rubbished the whole concept of putting the spotlight on a group of the underprivileged for a short amount of time. 'The International Year of the Patronising Bastard' itself went on to win a United Nations award, and was shown on Channel 4 in Britain as part of its March 1992 Disability Week.

The Interned (UK 1953 R) Canadian Captain Rickman (John Glen) becomes friendly with Second Lieutenant Grayle (Derek Hart). This upsets the former's best mate, Lieutenant Tetford (Brian Haines) and jealousy flares. Captain Conrad (Patrick Troughton) picks a quarrel and knocks Grayle to the ground. 'Leave me alone, you beast. It was a foul blow.' Tetford and Rickman are reconciled and contemplate life together in Canada. Conrad ends up on the verandah with a plant in his lap.
W: J. R. ACKERLEY; P: Wilfred Grantham; 7.5.53; BBC Third Programme; 90 mins.

THE INTERNED, whose original title was THE PRISONERS OF WAR, was based on Ackerley's own experience in a Swiss 'sanatorium' for prisoners of war in 1918. A 24-year-old virgin, he was quartered with four other officers and fell in love with a consumptive boy. The play deals – in constrained, public school fashion – with the tensions of close quarters, unnamed feelings and the central character's nervous collapse as a result of suppressed passions. What the listeners would not be aware of was the tactile responses of the men. In the stage version there is much holding of hands, playing with Grayle's curls, a hand touching a sleeve, a hand on another man's shoulder.

The Prisoners of War was the first English drama with a homosexual protagonist written for the London stage since MARLOWE's *Edward II* in 1593. Written in 1925, it was banned by the Lord Chamberlain and staged in a private theatre, not receiving another produc-

tion until 1955, and receiving a third in 1993. (A second radio production was considered in 1968, but rejected.)

In the Glitter Palace (US 1977 T) Ellen Large (Barbara Hershey) asks her former lover (Chad Everett) to defend her girlfriend Casey Walker (Diana Scarwid) on a murder charge and comes out to him at one and the same time. 'I used to go to the movies and watch Barbra STREISAND and Faye Dunaway ... bells rang and lights went on ... It didn't happen to me.'
W: Jerry Ludwig; P: Stanley Kallis; D: Robert Butler; 96 mins.

The revelation – to America's heartland and not a few other areas – that lesbian women exist was shocking enough. But this film went a couple of steps further. They exist as mothers, secretaries, actresses, judges and socialites. The foregoing are all victims of the BLACKMAILERS, the tracking down of whom provide the film-makers with the excuse to include murder and mayhem (including karate-chopping dykes and a rat-like gay BARMAN). Some telling dialogue (principally between the lawyer and his former lover, and from Carole Cooke as a former TV comedienne) is almost choked by the writer's need to inject positive uplift (some of it courtesy of the Gay and Lesbian Media Task Force) into what is essentially a very seedy, unconvincing melodrama. Because there are so many characters, you can't get bored; just confused.

In the Life (US 1991 T) A monthly show about lesbian and gay life: 'a cross between *60 Minutes* and a gay version of the Ed Sullivan show' (WNYC).

In The Middle Of A Kiss Connee Boswell number (by Sam Coslow; also sung by Johnny Downs and Arline Judge in *College Scandal* 1935), used over the romantic scenes, in stable and field, of two land girls in OUT ON TUESDAY 'COMRADES IN ARMS' (1990 T). Later on, a male singer does the honours for two bomber pilots, one in the cockpit making what may be a last fond farewell to the other.

In The Navy In 1979 *The Little and Large Show* slipped in a take-off of this big hit of VILLAGE PEOPLE (13 weeks in the US Top 40). It was a send-up of recruiting poster rhetoric. The *Daily Mirror* (7.5.79) were told: 'We've made it very camp and saucy – perhaps we'll even lose our family image.' Not a chance. The sailors were presented as simpering and the macho *double entendre* entirely eliminated. Instead, tired sema-phoring of tight buns and limp wrists. A feeble mainstream effort to use a suc-cessful attempt to ridicule orthodoxy purely as a way of mocking effeminate men in sailor suits, but the record's raf-fish undertow did not deter the Walt Disney organization from releasing a sort of homage entitled 'Macho Duck' in the following year. ('In the Navy' was briefly considered as a recruitment song for the US Navy until the subtext was pointed out.)

In the News (UK 1954 T) A Thursday night BBC television series in which (male) journalists and politicians com-mented on issues of the moment. In October 1954 the chairman, Frank Byers dropped the hitherto undiscussed and unmentioned subject of homosexu-ality into the laps of his panel. There had been no prior warning either in *Radio Times* or to viewers 'of a nervous disposition'. Byers introduced the sub-ject by saying that there had been suggestions for a Royal Commission on the subject. There were no telephone complaints, but noted Robert Carvell in the *Daily Express*: 'Four veteran debaters Sir Robert Boothby, Anthony Green-wood, W. J. Brown and A. J. P. Taylor spoke with downcast eyes.'

in the pink A catchphrase of boxer Joe (Robert Montgomery), which irritates the fastidious heavenly book-keeper (Claude Rains) who looks to be living eternally in the pink with Edward Ever-ett HORTON in *Here Comes Mr Jordan* (1941 C). Used by the daft padre in *The*

Navy Lark (1966 R) and others equally inconsequential to mean 'feeling fine' until Channel 4 enterprisingly extended its meaning by using the phrase for a lesbian and gay film season in 1986. *See also* TRIAL.

In the Pink Feminist revue aired on CHANNEL 4's opening night in 1982. Also the title of C4's 1986 gay and les-bian film season which included a dozen or so short and feature-length films and videos: classics (MAEDCHEN IN UNIFORM; SCORPIO RISING); new dramas (NOVEMBER MOON; *Buddies*; *A Window in Manhattan*; *On Guard*); histories (BEFORE STONEWALL; *Silent Pioneers*; THE TIMES OF HARVEY MILK); comedies (WHAT CAN I DO WITH A MALE NUDE?; *David Roche Talks to You About Love*); documentaries (*Breaking the Silence*); but not *17 Rooms or What Do Lesbians Do in Bed?* which was banned. A second sea-son in 1988 featured repeats plus *Chuck Solomon: Coming of Age*, PARTING GLANCES and LIANNA.

In the Psychiatrist's Chair (UK 1983–90/1993– R) Dr Anthony Clare manages to extract the most extraordi-narily open – if not necessarily always very enlightening – facets of celebrities like Spike Milligan, P. D. James, Eartha Kitt and Glenda Jackson. Lesbian and gay occupants of the chair: Pat Arrow-smith (1983); Derek JARMAN (1990); and Michael TIPPETT (1986) who said, in part:

> I once said to myself I shall never have a shoulder to cry on. I didn't want one … the crisis (in the mid–late 1930s) was brought about by extreme love experiences which were what we would now call gay. I was 18, I suppose. I saw someone, it happened, you know. I accepted, always with both hands. All right, I felt, this is what I am when it comes to a point and you discover that you are not what society thinks you should be. You play all sorts of tricks. You may do all sorts of things but it went so sharp with me that the crisis was beginning to affect my music…
> I got to a point where I accepted that it would never be right, that it would be a

matter of balance rather than absolute conviction one side or the other.

I didn't want to accept ... I was born as a much more mature artist. A genuine human being. I didn't want to hurt people but understood more clearly that I had more power over my own psychic forces to do the job whatever it was.

Intimate Contact with Julian Clary (UK 1992 R) Seven weeks of phone-in gossip, confessions and global issues wedged between Alan Freeman's *Saturday Rock Show* and *John Peel* on BBC Radio 1. This marks the spot when someone like Julian CLARY was allowed peak-time Saturday night airspace on a radio channel aimed at teenagers, the male portion of whom are under the homosexual AGE OF CONSENT. (Also 1993.)

An Introduction to Sociology 'Life Histories' (UK 1981 T) The Open University separately interviewed two gay men – Steve, a 21-year-old, and Trevor Thomas, in his late seventies – in two very satisfying programmes that were broadcast at 6.40am and 9.45am on Sundays and weekdays. That year, the OU also showed a programme about lesbian *Sexual Identity* and how it has changed over the 20th century.

inverts The word decreed by producer and director for use by everybody on the set of VICTIM (1961 C) instead of the ubiquitous 'QUEER'. In the film itself Lord Fullbrook (Anthony Nicholls), one of those paying extortion money for his natural instincts, believes that 'the invert is part of nature'. This was practically the word's only outing until it was heard, in a 1945 context, in *The Potsdam Quartet* (1981 T). Aaron (Clive Swift) uses it against two of his fellow musicians, one of whom swishes: 'Oh, he's been at the Havelock Ellis again.' Set during the same period, TROUPERS (1988 R) has its gay fighting cock, Jerry Coe, refuse to take collective blame for civilization's latest folly: 'It was *your* lot started the war. Name one invert responsible for the war.' The astonished young couple can't think of one offhand.

invisible lesbians From REBECCA to the lesbian SOCIAL WORKER in EASTENDERS and Nick's lesbian wife in BROOKSIDE and the various characters, subplots and themes in *Welcome Home, Roxy Carmichael* and FRIED GREEN TOMATOES AT THE WHISTLE STOP CAFE. Documentaries, too, sometimes sweep lesbians off the edge of the screen. Not always on purpose. In the post-CLAUSE 28 *Brass Tacks* 'Good as You?' (1988) for example. As Colin Cameron, Editor, Features and Documentaries, BBC North West explained in *Radio Times*: 'it proved difficult, and in the nature of the subject understandably so, to persuade young lesbians to appear on the screen.'

Ireland An inhospitable place for sexual experimentation, yet complex and strange with many goddess worship accretions in so Catholic a land ... And it boasted one of the first openly gay parliamentary candidates in the world: David NORRIS.

It would appear that sexual diversity is either something quickly exported (Oscar WILDE) and slowly reclaimed (posthumously) or a bad smell to be eradicated. When it raises itself about the Irish sea and cannot be ignored (Sir Roger CASEMENT) then its manifestation (the Black Diaries) are called forgeries and an English plot. In *Cries from Casement As His Bones are Brought to Dublin* (1973) the Ulster Protestant 'faced the terrifying gorgon of a split national self and chose the white lily of whose patriotism grew out of his backside'.

For many Irishmen with 'forbidden selves' like Casement the answer lies in neither North nor South but in England: JIMMY (1978 R) and *The Mourning Thief* (1984 T), both by Desmond Hogan. Unlike Jimmy, Morris Murry in the latter lives openly in a ménage with his wife and young male lover. All three come to visit Morris' dying father, an IRA man and ex-policeman whom Morris loathes. But both Jimmy and Morris are essentially broken men, emotionally sterilized by the culture they cannot erase. Suspicion and restraint are everywhere and only the aristocratic (Casement, Wilde) and the drudges (school cleaner Sadie and launderette manageress Agnes, both former prostitutes) in *Phonefun Ltd* (1982 T) can transcend the semi-attached, carefully prescribed arrangement between man and women – so powerfully displayed in A HARD GOD about Irish Catholics in Australia.

Ken Gray of the *Irish Times* rejoiced when BBC Schools broached subjects that had been taboo in Southern Ireland with the showing, in three parts, of A TASTE OF HONEY: 'Forthright plays that have something to say about the way people are and how they behave are much needed ... We are, in Ireland, a good deal less anxious to acknowledge that certain aspects of human behaviour even exist' (20.9.71).

Five years later, though, an American soap (*Executive Suite*) was yanked off in midstream because it acknowledged that two women could fall in love with one another and that another had a right to choose whether or not to terminate her pregnancy. Since the mid- to late 1970s, gay and lesbian rights have had a niche on Irish television, helped by *The Late Late Show* – which was to feature the beginnings of a coming out by an Irish priest in 1990 as well as Joni Sheerin of Liberation for Irish Lesbians (LIL) in 1980.

In Northern Ireland the first peak-time television programme on the subject in the province: *Gays in Northern Ireland* (1976) which included a gay liberation meeting and a party, as well as a vox pop ('Homosexuality – what's that?' and 'That's all right for England – but this is Ireland'). Appearing in the studio were Jeff Dudgeon of the Northern Ireland Gay Rights Association with Stella McTear from Sappho and a report on CARA Friend. Putting the 'normal' point of view was Ulster Unionist MP Rev. Robert Bradford: 'all such people need to be brought back to normal is a religious experience.' Church of England minister Rev. Jim Miller argued for full equality; James Patton, chief clinical psychologist at Belfast hospital, said homosexuality should be as normal as left-handedness...

GAY SWEATSHOP's visit to Belfast was covered in a *Grapevine* programme in 1979 (T).

Before Northern Ireland's laws on homosexuality were brought into line with Great Britain's, Ulster MP Ian Paisley was constantly 'debating' with a gay representative, eg on *Spotlight* (1977 T) with Kevin Merritt, secretary of NIGRA. This enabled Paisley to put across his one message: 'Save Ulster from Sodomy.'

Irma Girl's name, sparingly used and then for generally fairly loose and abandoned women, like Irma Gladden (Natalie Moorehead), Hollywood siren with discarded husband and a flock of *Discarded Lovers* (1932 C); dumb blonde (Marie Wilson) in *My Friend Irma* (1949) and *My Friend Irma Goes West* (1950); sharp-tongued Irma Ogden (Sandra Gough) in CORONATION STREET (1963-4 T); *Irma La Douce* (Shirley MacLaine 1964 C); scatterbrain Irma (Sue Ann Langdon) in *A Guide for the Married Man* (1967 C); four lesbian Irmas: the madam (Shelley Winters) in *The Balcony* (1963 C), the librarian (Viveca Lindfors) in *Sylvia* (1965 C); the stripper's lover (Elisabeth Fraser) in *Tony Rome* (1967 C), and the plain, plump schoolgirl (Karen Robson) who would very much like to have disappeared that sultry afternoon during the *Picnic at Hanging Rock* (1975 C).

ironing Pete (Stephen CHURCHETT) does his shirt in TOGETHER (1981 T) while he and Trevor discuss going to MYKONOS; John HURT does Ryan O' Neal's in PARTNERS (1982 C); Les (Ian Targett) in *Marks* (1982): 'Ironing's a skill,' says his mum proudly; Bobby Buffett is seen at the board at the start of *Some Enchanted Evening* (1990 T); James Hayter presses his own gown as 'The Verger', one of the Maugham stories in *Trio* (1950 C); Stanley (Robert De Niro) tells Iris (Jane Fonda) in *Stanley and Iris* (1989 C) that he'll do the ironing, he does it all the time, she must rest. She accepts but tells him not to scorch the shirts – as John Williams' strings swoop down; Charles Burrows (Joe McGann) in *The Upper Hand* (1990 T).

I shall die a bachelor Greta GARBO's declaration of intent as *Queen Christina* (1933 C) and, as it transpired, of herself. Possibly a gender reverse homage to Benedick in *Much Ado About Nothing* who declaims: 'I shall live a bachelor.'

Is He One? Mark Bunyan's jaunty number, composed around 1978 and even more friskily relevant in the post-outing era – alerting us, as it does, to all the actors, politicians, even builders' labourers who are (they or somebody else says) like that. Mark sang it live and lustily from Blackpool on A SUNDAY OUTING (1993 R).

is he or isn't he? Mr HUMPHRIES in ARE YOU BEING SERVED? (1980 T) overhears someone in the store's canteen ask: 'Is he or isn't he?' Before anyone can respond, he pipes up: 'People have been asking me that for years.' One of the few subtleties in the series was that at no time did the huge family audience ever know for sure whether he was one or not.

Fears over a son showing 'signs' have been a constant in comedy: COMEDY PLAYHOUSE 'B&B: No Son of Mine' (1968 T); *Girl Stroke Boy* (1971 C); *Afternoon Story* 'Darren's Trouble' (1980 R); *Home to Roost* (1990 T); *Birds of a Feather* (1991 T).

Isherwood, Christopher (1904-86) English novelist who spent most of his adult life in the US.
C: I AM A CAMERA (1955); CABARET (1972).
R: *Prater Violet* (1956); *Mr Norris Changes Trains* (1967 & 1984); A SINGLE MAN (1972 & 1991).
OMNIBUS 'Christopher Isherwood: A Born Foreigner' (1969 T); *Success Story* 'Cabaret' (1972 T); TONIGHT (1976 T, receiving a grilling from Ludovic Kennedy); AQUARIUS 'Over There on a Visit' (1977 T); *On the Town* (1980 R, in Los Angeles); *All About Books* (1980 T, coyly interviewed by Russell HARTY); *A Single Man: Christopher Isherwood 1904-1986*

(1986 T, Ian Hamilton and archive material); *Dear Diary* (1991 R, writing on David HOCKNEY).

I Sing The Body Electric Michael Gore's grand finale for full orchestra, singers, dancers and audiences: the graduation piece from FAME (1980 C). The title is Walt WHITMAN's, and so is the spirit of fire and uplift, but the words are someone else's. The gay character, Montgomery (Paul McCrane) sings one of the verses.

is it bigger than a breadbox? Probably the most suggestive line uttered on American television during the 1950s by Steve Allen to assorted contestants on *What's My Line?* (1951-3 T). Larry (Keith Prentice) revived it in THE BOYS IN THE BAND (1970 C) after his lover Hank has taken the token heterosexual upstairs to tend his wounds: when Hank returns, Larry zaps him with 'Is it bigger than a breadbox?' Kay Kendall as the estranged wife in *Once More with Feeling* (1960 C), determined to dislodge her conductor husband's (Yul Brynner) pomposity at a grand occasion, asks quizzically – if redundantly given their former intimacy – if 'it' is bigger than 'a breadstick'. After a long silence, Allen's once daring question returned: on a family show in Australia (*Hey! Hey! It's Saturday* 1990 T), piped by a pink puppet, Ossie Ostrich.

is this nature's way to cure the population explosion? Enquirer who says she loves gay people and wishes she knew more of them on DONAHUE 'Born Gay, Become Gay or Made Gay?' (1992 T). The panel was not game to even consider this question, receiving a chiding from the host for so doing.

it A pronoun still energetically employed to stand in for emotions and sexuality, often to dodge censorship. Elinor Glyn wrote a book and Clara Bow, via the film version, became the 'It' girl, a title which alluded to her sex appeal. Broadway songs like 'Let's Do It' and 'Do It Again' were forbidden the airwaves in the 1920s, and in the 1980s the word's potency could veil a multitude of delights in Frankie Goes To Hollywood's RELAX. The CARRY ON team regularly smirked about 'it' and Hollywood slipped it into ambiguous picture titles (*Let's Do It Again*; *You Can't Run Away from It*). The French film *La Poupée* (1962) featuring a transvestite performer (Sonne Teal) was retitled *He, She or It* for English-speaking consumption.

I think this is the beginning of a beautiful friendship Nick (Humphrey Bogart) to Captain Renault (Claude Rains) in the fog-swept climax of *Casablanca* (1942). Ingrid Bergman has flown away with her husband allowing the two men to walk off into the unknown. No sequel was made, but it would surely have been called Nick and Louis' Café. In *Burke's Backyard* (Aust 1991 T) a still of Bogart preparing to open a bottle of champagne and gazing into Bergman's eyes was offered together with Bogart intoning this line, giving entirely the wrong impression, rucking up screen history ('Here's looking at you, kid' would have been more appropriate), and heteroing one of the few male–male foggy, foggy dew endings. Ginger Rogers said that when Fred Astaire met Hermes PAN it was 'the beginning of a beautiful friendship' in *Sally Jessy Raphael* (1992 T).

I thought I was the only one (in the world) One of the Michael Schofield interviewees in MALE HOMOSEXUALS (1965 T) said he thought he was the only person in the world 'who felt like that'. Quentin CRISP (John HURT) thought he was too in THE NAKED CIVIL SERVANT (1975 T). William BURROUGHS' lover James Graverholz in ARENA 'Burroughs' (1983 T) – before, at 14, being given *The Naked Lunch* to read – 'thought I was the only person in the world who thought about sex with boys'.

Derek JARMAN told Dr Anthony Clare that 'I thought I was the only one' in IN THE PSYCHIATRIST'S CHAIR (1990 R). Bill Thorneycroft, recalling his adolescence in the 1940s, echoed the phrase in OUT ON TUESDAY 'Comrades in Arms' (1990 T). As did Tom ROBINSON in *Talk About Sex* (1992 R): 'For a long time I thought I was the only queer, not only in my class but the whole of my school, the whole of my town, the whole of my county. For all I knew I was the only 12-year-old queer in the whole of Great Britain. It was a pretty lonely feeling.'

Just six out of scores of similar expressions of total isolation in radio and television interviews with gay and lesbian people.

But the situation has changed for people born during the 1970s. Teenager James from Yorkshire was able to say on *Brass Tacks* 'Good as You?' (1988 T): 'I knew I wasn't the only one in the whole world. And it felt as though I was. I thought: I might not be the only one, but ... where's the rest?'

It Is Not the Homosexual Who Is Perverse But the Society in Which He Lives (West Germany 1970 C/T) This docu-manifesto was much reviled by gay people at the time. Now it offers a valuable record of the blissful days of liberation. Gay men and lesbians of all shapes and sizes and some very trenchant comments that still raise hackles. This was not the kind of image some gay people wanted projected.
W: Rosa Von Praunheim, Martin Dannecker and Sigurd Wurl; P: Werner Klieb; D: Rosa Von Praunheim; 65 mins.

The centrepiece of a number of (often heated) showings in America and Europe, this is a crucial piece of gay liberation in itself, one which has yet to appear on British television. Designed to pick at scabs and stir up all the contradictions that were then (and possibly still) sticking to the bottom of the sexual politics cauldron.

(Also the 30-minute *Audience Response to 'It Is Not the Homosexual'* directed by Rosa Von Praunheim, videotaped at the Gay Activist Alliance headquarters in SoHo, New York.)

it's all in the mind, you know Said

Wallace GREENSLADE reassuringly on many a GOON SHOW. His was the only voice of relative sanity, from 1953 when he took over the announcer's chores from Andrew Timothy, to the series's demise at the beginning of 1960: 'The moral is: stop thinking; because thinking is all in the mind you know. Good night' ('The Stolen Postman' 1957 R).

Occasionally, there was just a hint of something else in Wal's signings off: 'I just want you to know that you are not alone. Wallace is one of you,' he purrs in 'Six Charlies in Search of an Author' (1956 R) broadcast on Christmas Eve. In the same show, a CAMP voice erupts: 'Oh you silly BBC thing you!' And during a gender-switch wedding, the priest says: 'I leave you to discover which is which'.

it's a waste Says one cop to another about beautiful model Jacqueline Ames (Marcia Strassman) in *Police Story* 'The Ripper' (1974 T) because she prefers women. Similar cop shop exchanges can be heard in *The Laughing Policeman/ Investigation of Murder* (1973 C), and in THE GENTLE TOUCH 'Solution' (1982 T) about Jean (Fiona Walker). If only these women had met these guys *first*, then they wouldn't need to even look at another woman.

it's homophobia! Phil DONAHUE's would-be affirmative cry ('It's homophobia! It's *homo*-phobia!') on any show dealing with non-heterosexuals, whether appropriate or not: 'Gay Seniors' to 'Transvestite Prostitutes' to 'Bathroom Graffiti'. Yet he never, never says it on his shows dealing with masculinity, femininity, racism: alternative sexuality is kept firmly in the stable.

it takes all sorts to make a world The expression of the simple fact about human beings: their infinite diversity. Mysterious Ambridge-outsider John TREGORRAN, lover of things fine and beautiful, was wont to say it, but its first deliberately gay context came in *The League of Gentlemen* (1960 C) in relation to MASSEUR Kieron Moore and then by

lesbian Mavis (Cicely Courtneidge) to Leslie Caron in THE L-SHAPED ROOM (1962 C) when she shows her a photograph of her dead woman lover. (The scripts for both these films were by Bryan Forbes.)

'It takes all sorts to make a world,' says Hester (Julia McKenzie) to Chantal (Pamela Salem) who has just told her that her lover is a married man ('All the best men are married') in *French Fields* 'Who's Been Eating My Cheese?' (1989 T).

'It takes all sorts, don't it,' marvels the gas man (Mark Lambert) in *Bottom* (1991 T) when Richie (Rik Mayall) tells him that he and Eddie (Adrian Edmondson) 'make love ... but not together ... on our own'.

Nasty Brian (Brian Gwaspari) says it about David (Peter Egan) in *Joint Account* (1990 T) because David (a) looks after the house while his wife manages a bank and (b) does voluntary work at the local Citizens Advice Bureau.

It's one of Gordon's – irritating – little phrases in *The Brittas Empire* (1990-2), perhaps explaining his remarkable self-control in having two gay lovers working at his sports centre and sending young men mad with desire over their muscly legs in those shorts...

It Takes A Worried Man (UK 1981-4 T) The muddles and misadventures of a modern male: Philip (Peter Tilbury) driven to a psychiatrist, Simon (Nicholas Le Prevost), who spends all of their sessions maundering on about himself, his lack of confidence, his tax problems and his spendthrift, culinarily pretentious lover, Gerald.

W: Peter Tilbury; P: Douglas Argent; Thames for Channel 4.

An early male menopause comedy in which the addled hero's psychiatrist uses him as an emotional pincushion. Simon was built up until his absent-minded monologues took up a third of each show. 'Please don't talk to me about my mother. Love is a problematic area. Hate is much easier to define.

That's *one* thing my mother did teach me.'

Very taking 'woe is me' comedy series, but with the expected whoopee cushion jokes about psychiatrists and gay men: the only real advance is that the representatives of these groups are one and the same.

it takes one to know one No examples of its use in a gay context have been found in any broadcast media. This is surprising given the widely bruited idea that a gay person has an innate ability to 'spot' another. It does, however, crop up in Michael Carson's novel *Sucking Sherbet Lemons* (1988), set in 1962. The green hero, Benson, is picked up by a man in a library:

> 'Takes one to know one, dear.'
> 'How do you mean?' asked Benson for whom the cliché was as novel as a mango. The man shrugged. 'I mean that I knew as soon as I saw you. When I saw you having a vada in the dinge section, I said to myself, "Andrea – my name's Andy in real life actually, dear – Andrea, I said to myself, there's a gay one if ever I saw one."'

ROUND THE HORNE touched on it once – when, in the 1966 send-up of the First World War flying epic *The Blue Max*, Kenneth HORNE (as Von Richthofen) says to Von Cuckpowder (Hugh PADDICK): 'It takes a von to know a von.'

The unalloyed phrase has been relegated entirely to usage as a semi-smart put-down in heterosexual light comedy: Shirley Jones deploys it at a noisy children's party in *The Courtship of Eddie's Father* (1963 C) to break up two of the moppets; Margaret Leighton as a beady-eyed socialite impales nosey private eye Amos Burke (Gene Barry) with it in *Burke's Law* 'Who Killed Everybody?' (1964 T).

From the mid-1960s onwards, nothing was heard of it until an unaccountable revival during the mid- to late 1980s; but still in a non-gay, non-sexual context, except possibly for Prokofiev (Peter Kelly) prissily telling Shostakovich that

'It takes a poet to know a poet' in *Master Class* (1984 R).

Other users: the *nouveau riche* sister Valerie (Heather Tobias) socks it to her hippie brother Cyril (Philip Davis) in *High Hopes* (1988 C) after he's called her 'loony'; Ray McAnally ('a low-down scheming bastard' of a prime minister) in *A Very British Coup* (1988 T) acknowledges that 'It takes one to know one'; a murdered jockey's cynical widow ('What's in it for me?') to the hero of *Breaking Point* (1988 R), based on the Dick Francis novel *Nerve*.

In the 1990s it's resurfaced in Australia: 'Perhaps one shoplifter knows another,' says a perky veteran of 30 years of pilfering in *In The Mix* 'The Shoplifter's Guide' (1991 R). 'It takes one to know one,' adds the interviewer, Brent Clough. It has also resurfaced in America: Michael Douglas' good ole boy colleague on the police force, worried about his involvement with a female murder suspect in *Basic Instinct* (1992 C) tries to warn him off with 'You'll end up as crazy as she is. You know what they say, "It takes one to know one".'

(Partridge's *Dictionary of Slang* dates this phrase around mid- to late 19th century or possibly early 20th, and applying to criminals ('He's a thief. It takes one to know one.'). Partridge's contributor 'JWC' records that in America the phrase is 'almost always applied to male homosexuals', but his colleague, Robert Claborne pronounces it 'obsolescent'. However, a letter in the *Guardian Weekly* (October 1989) cites it as a current American expression.)

ITMA (It's That Man Again) (UK 1939–49 R) A Thursday night institution (especially during the war years), this was a saucy, crackingly paced convoy of gags and whacky characters which aimed to laugh at national characteristics and bureaucracy. Its postwar surrealism (transferring to Tomtopia from Foaming-at-the-Mouth) paved the way for more surreal radio comedy, culminating in THE GOON SHOW.

Ted Kavanagh was the writer, Tommy Handley the star with a whole raft of talent (Hattie Jacques, Maurice Denham – who was Mrs Lola Tickle – and Deryck Guyler). Handley himself, though adored in Britain, remains something of a mystery – one that a 1991 radio programme (*It's That Man Again* produced and presented by Phil Smith) attempted to solve, with hefty recourse to Freud and a series of asterisks. Did the bright Liverpudlian facade hide something that would not have been acceptable then – or now?

Most of those who remembered him were dead by the time this opus was compiled, but enough is said to reveal that much about Tommy Handley is unsaid. The programme was round-shouldered with question marks. What did the tight bond with his mother imply? Why was his marriage childless? What caused his wife to drink heavily? With whom were these oft-mentioned 'relationships' during the war? Why was there no mention of 'girlfriends' or 'other women'?

Former Director General of the BBC John Reith described ITMA as 'A dreadful sociological comment on the age'. He would have probably said the same about this 'exposé', which ended up neat and tidy with the remark that Tommy Handley was 'an essentially friendly and good man'. When Handley died – three days after the 310th show – it was 'the sense of a friend dying'. A phrase that would be used in 1988 when Russell HARTY died.

ITV The British commercial network which gradually from 1955 comprised 15 stations including Anglia, Central, GRANADA, Harlech, LONDON WEEKEND (ex-ATV), Scottish, THAMES. The regulatory body was the Independent Broadcasting Authority (IBA), now the Independent Television Commission (ITC).

it would be absolutely lush Dudley Davenport (Maurice Denham) paying court to Gladys (Dora Bryan) in *Much Binding in the Marsh* (1953 R), an upper-class twit with optional effeminacy.

I've Been Loving You Too Long Otis Redding song used as background to a heterosexual ballet interspersed with Lianna's reminiscence of making love with Ruth in LIANNA (1983 C).

I've gone gay – all of a sudden Unscripted remark made by Cary GRANT in *Bringing Up Baby* (1938 C). He's wearing very becoming silk night attire, fringed with feathers and, as he announces his change (to a startled old lady), he executes a small, skittish leap in the air. Possibly a jump for the sheer joy of telling the world – a few inhabitants of which *must* have got the message.

I've got *his* number The game's up ... I've seen through your disguise ... Barbara STANWYCK in *Night Nurse* (1931 C) tells the sadistic chauffeur Nick (Clark Gable): 'I've had *your* number from the minute I stepped into this house.'

Although Kenneth WILLIAMS (as Sandy and as 'himself') used it regularly about CLOSET QUEENS in ROUND THE HORNE (1965–9 R), it is more widely employed: as a veiled threat of future action possibly coupled with unconscious sexual violence, as with the drunken, unhappy policeman, Dave in THE ARCHERS (1990 R): 'I've got his number. I'll *do* him.' And one of the coppers in *The Bill* says he's got WPC Ackland's number (1990 T).

I've got something to tell you... A prelude to many a confession, which from 1970 onwards became known as coming out. Kit Mainwaring III (Mark Wheeler) uses the phrase to his fiancée Lucy Ewing in DALLAS 'Royal Marriage' (1978 T). Recently, it has been drawn into a gay red herring, for one. Lofty (Tom Watts) had EASTENDERS audiences holding their breath when he said to Michelle (who wanted to go to bed with him): 'I've got something to tell you. I'm ... I'm ... anaemic.' And James Woods, wanting to confess that he isn't all he seems, tries to tell Dolly Parton in *Straight Talk* (1992), but she won't let him finish: 'You're gay? You're married?'

I've Heard The Mermaids Singing (Can 1987 C) Polly (Sheila McCarthy) is prepared to overlook the obvious faults and inconsistencies of her boss because she fits the picture of what a goddess should be like, but she is destined to be disillusioned. Heroine-worship ends in tears and hot tea in the face. W/D: Patricia Rozema; P: Patricia Rozema and Alexandra Roffe; 81 mins.

'I'm a feminist, but I would want to distance myself from a certain brand of feminism that frightens me, the brand which seems to imply that there is less evil in the hearts of women. That's just absurd' (Interview with Patricia Rozema *Sight and Sound*, Winter 1990–1).

(The title of this slight but diverting comedy comes from a line in T. S. Eliot's 'The Love Song of J. Alfred Prufrock', about a colourless bachelor, preoccupied with social etiquette, ageing, his – (secondary) – place in the world.)

I *wanted* him! Dirk BOGARDE as Melville Farr in VICTIM (1961 C) to his wife about 'Boy' Barrett. This was the line Bogarde added to the script, insisting that the otherwise fence-sitting barrister tell the audience that he had 'loved' the young man who tried to defend him from blackmail or public exposure. (This outburst has been seen in more British cinematic compilations on television, mainstream and gay, than any other similar 'great moment' from gay cinema.)

I want to be alone First mouthed by Greta GARBO and written in an intertitle for the late (1929) silent *The Single Standard*: 'I am walking alone because I want to be alone.' The last five words which were to become her trademark were uttered by ballerina Garbo three times in *Grand Hotel* (1932 C) – and echoed by her equally weary lover, the Baron (John Barrymore). Variations turned up in her *As You Desire Me* (1932) and *Ninotchka* (1939).

When her premature retirement was announced in 1941, Garbo told reporters that 'I want to be left alone'. This was elided to fit with her screen utterances so that an indelible catch-phrase was born, together with the hand stroking the furrowed brow and the dying fall of the 'German' accented voice so that 'want' becomes 'vant'.

After the actress died in April 1990, the film clip featured on nearly every television obituary was the one from *Grand Hotel*, even though it was far from being one of her best roles or performances. It did indicate, however, the almost unheard-of stance of a public love goddess eschewing the institution of marriage or any obvious cohabitation.

Julian MITCHELL entitled a talk in the series *Writers on Themselves* 'I Want to Be Alone' (1964 R).

Jack the Ripper Unknown perpetrator of an unusually savage series of murders of women between August and November 1988 in the East End of London. His identity has been a source of speculation in countless books as well as films and documentaries. Was Jack the Ripper a satanist, Jew, homosexual or syphilitic prince?

Dramatized documentaries like *Jack the Ripper* (1973 T) and *The Secret Identity of Jack the Ripper* (1988 T) have so far not been able to answer categorically – though that the man 'disliked women' seems fairly certain.

Among the suspects are at least two homosexuals. One was Mortimer Druitt who was 'sexually insane' and belonged to a very good family most of whose members thought he was the killer. He committed suicide seven weeks after the last murder. He taught at a Blackheath boys school but was dismissed: 'Experts speculate that he had engaged in homosexual activities with the young students' (Dr David Thomas, Keeper of the Public Records Office, in *The Secret Identity*). The other suspect was the elder son of the future Edward VII, Prince Albert, who 'contracted syphilis at 26' and who died in 1892.

The programme *The Secret Identity* sought out the help of the FBI. The organization drew up a profile of the Ripper: 'a mid- to late 20s male, average intelligence, single, probably socially ill at ease with women. He had a great deal of trouble interacting with people, lived in the area, came from a broken home, and had a dominant mother who possibly sexually abused him.'

This lurking figure of the London fog has been depicted or half-depicted in a dozen or so films, notably *The Lodger* (1926, with Ivor NOVELLO) and PANDORA'S BOX (1928, killing LULU). Berg's full 3-act opera version of the latter gives more prominence to 'Jack': he murders both LULU and her lover GESCHWITZ (THE SOUTH BANK SHOW 'Lulu's Last Act' 1981 T).

Jacobi, Derek (1939–) English actor of glittering brilliance and hypnotic fascination, especially as quixotic nonconformists of all hues and nations: Hitler in *Inside the Third Reich* (1982); Frollo in *The Hunchback of Notre Dame* (1982); Guy BURGESS in *Burgess, Philby and Maclean* (1978); the bringer of death in *Tales of the Unexpected* 'Stranger in Town' (1983); etc. He has played EDWARD II (1967 R, opposite Ian MCKELLEN; Gerry in *The Photographer* (1968 T); Claudius in *I, Claudius* (1976 T); *Richard II* (1978 T); *Hamlet* (1979 T); Arthur Clenham in *Little Dorrit* (1987 C); the ANTIQUE DEALER in *Dead Again* (1991 C). Sadly, his stage performance as Alan TURING – as child and man – in *Breaking the Code* was not transferred to film or video. On DESERT ISLAND DISCS (1978).

Jacob, Naomi (1884–1964) Known as Mickie. English novelist and broadcaster who loved Ellaline Terris, Yvonne Arnaud and Simmy, a Cockney barmaid. An early supporter of women's rights, she was most famous for *The Gollancz Saga*. On her annual trips to Britain from her home on Capri, she always recorded a talk for WOMAN'S HOUR, and in 1958 she was castaway for DESERT ISLAND DISCS. Her novel *No Other Way* was serialized by *Woman's Hour* in 1984. There has been no extensive radio or television biography, but Louise Laming wrote 'Mickie: A Reminiscence' for GAY NEWS 195 in 1980.

Jailhouse Rock Leiber and Stoller's classic, performed by Elvis with a bunch of credibly life-chewed 'inmates' in the 1957 film of that title. The number, introduced by the star as the produce of 'Some of the guys and I ... horsing around', is far less erotic than legend has it. Elvis, nevertheless, *does* shin down and then up a pole; two of the 'prisoners' (octogenarians) *do* dance together, 'Spider' Murphy playing sax *does* kneel down before the star who *does* sing some very suggestive lines.

'Jailhouse' has been cleaned up since then, so much so that it could be performed by Donnie Burns and Gaynor

Fairweather on *Come Dancing* (1988 T), but on *Telethon* (1990 T) it was given a go by some real prisoners – released for the occasion to help raise £24 million.

Listening to it in the steamy 1990s of MADONNA and Cher, attention is drawn to the unavoidable fact that the word 'Rock' was but a stone's throw from a vulgar noun and verb.

Jeff Bridges in *Rock 'n Roll Heroes* (1980 T) suggested that Presley had choreographed the whole caper, but no mention appears on the credits of the film.

James I (1566–1625) King of England and as James VI, of Scotland. Fully pledged homosexual ruler who had a number of favourites, the best loved being George VILLIERS whom he made Duke of Buckingham. The note from Villiers to the king, discussed in RSVP (1992 R), is not only one of the true indications of the genuine love that passed between them after passion cooled and after George married, but also an alert to future historians that similar scraps of homosexual love must have been delivered hither and yon – and some may even still exist.

Scottish History 'The Makers of Scotland: James VI – Gentle Jamie, the Dominie King' on BBC Schools (1936); *Whom the King Delighteth to Honour* (1967 R).

Played by Duncan MacRae in *The Fortunes of Nigel* (1955 R); by Alfred Lynch in *Churchill's People* 'A Rich and Beautiful Empire' (1974) and in *The Fortunes of Nigel* (1974 T); by Bill Paterson in *Will Shakespeare* (1976 T); by James Kerry in *Walton's Lives* 'Choice Meat and Better Discourse' (1984), pages from Izaak Walton's *Short Life of Sir Henry Wotton*; and by Nigel STOCK in *The Wisest Fool* (1977 R) as the frequently hysterical, dying ruler: 'I was always pale. 'Tis luck I was born a king, for kings must paint their faces ... I love him so, because he is my sweetest dearest boy. I would love all that pleasures him. I would become part of that pleasure.'

James, Henry (1834–1916) American novelist and short story writer; sympathetic yet detached chronicler of European-American relations as well as begetter of the most enduring Victorian ghost story, *The Turn of the Screw*. In its first (1933) radio adaptation this story was described as: 'Difficult to figure out the explanation, but the idea is pretty horrible.' It was later turned into a play (*The Innocents*) and an opera, both versions of which have been translated into film and television, as have a number of his novels: *The Portrait of a Lady*; *The Aspern Papers*; *The Bostonians*; *The Europeans*; *Washington Square* (aka *The Heiress*); *What Maisie Knew*.

Hallam Tennyson's *The Spring of the Beast* (1986) is about James' friendship with Constance Fenimore-Woolson (Marian Diamond) who awakens the writer, played by John Rowe, to his true nature before she dies, probably a suicide because of her unrequited love. James acts as uncle/patron to a young sculptor, Hendrik Andersen (Nick Duning).

Other biographical broadcasts about Henry James have included: *A Call at Bly* (1954 R), the story behind *The Turn of the Screw* with Carleton HOBBS as James; *Henry James and the Young Men* (1959 R: Leonard Woolf discussing the influence James had on the young men of Cambridge in the early 1900s); *Recollections of Henry James* (1987 R), by Edith Wharton from her autobiography *A Backward Glance* (read by Faith Brook); *Bottled Lightning* (1987), about his sister Alice (Morag Hood) who kept a journal which Henry saw after her death – and suppressed.

James, M[ontague] R[hodes] (1862–1936) English linguist, palaeographer, medievalist and biblical scholar who wrote a large number of macabre and ghostly stories often about incautious bachelors, frequently set in East Anglia, the most famous of which is 'Oh, Whistle, and I'll Come to You, My Lad'.

R: David MARCH plays James who himself becomes involved in a mystery in *The Lodestone* (1989).

T: *Omnibus* 'Whistle and I'll Come to You' (1968); *The Stalls of Barchester*

Cathedral (1971); *A Warning to the Curious* (1972); *The Treasure of Abbot Thomas* (1974); *The Ash Tree* (1980); etc.

James, Sheila [later Sheila James Kuehl] (*c* 194?–) American actress, best known for being Zelda Gilroy, always in hot but hopeless pursuit of *Dobie Gillis* in the early 1960s. She left acting (apart from appearing in a Dobie Gillis TV movie) and studied law. In the 1980s, as Sheila James Kuehl, she founded the Southern California Women's Law Centre designed to change laws that affect all women. She and fellow TV actor Richard Sargent led the San Francisco Lesbian and Gay Pride parade in San Francisco in 1991.

Jackie in *The Stu Erwin Show* aka *Trouble With Father/Life with the Erwins* (1950–5 T); *Seven Brides for Seven Brothers* (1954 C); *Teenage Rebel* (1956 C); (*The Many Loves of*) *Dobie Gillis* (1959–63 T); Private Selma Kowalski, a mechanic in the WAVES in *Broadside* (1964–5 T).

She was to have had her own show, 'Zelda' in 1962, but the network cancelled it because it was decided that the character was too 'butch'. She returned to the parent show. In one episode 'Marriage Counsel' Zelda went on a business course, so desperate was she to hook Dobie. She never succeeded.

James Dean (USA 1976 T) An endlessly fascinating subject: Dean's early 1950s life through the eyes of a ROOMMATE, William Bast (Michael Brandon); answering very few questions, but with an exciting central performance by Stephen McHattie.

W: William Bast; P: William Bast and John Forbes; D: Robert Butler; 96 mins.

The only 'revealing' scene in this not especially good film comes when Dean asks Bill to help him with a script he has to prepare for class: 'It's about this guy who had a thing with his best friend and ever since it's been tearing him apart. I don't mean kid's stuff. Everybody does that.'

His friend understands Dean's drift (he's sitting on the bed dressed only in a pair of shorts) and wonders if some things aren't best left to the imagination. The charismatic Dean quotes from Stanislavski (an actor has to be prepared), tosses out a cliché ('don't knock it before you've tried it') and, before he knows what is happening, the roommate – not, we sense, unwillingly – is pushed out the door and told to 'research' Dean's role in the nearest gay BAR and report back. Shrugs Dean as the guinea pig protests: 'You've got to make certain sacrifices for your art.'

Bill dutifully trots along to a queer hangout and, although nothing supposedly happens, Dean later pumps him for every detail. Exactly why Dean didn't 'do it himself' is not analysed: such nagging questions being subsumed by the actor's air of little-boy-lost charm and appetitiveness: 'Life's too short, I want to do it all.'

'Tolerably well presented, but probably more than we wish to know' (*Halliwell's Television Companion*).

Jameson, Rex aka Jamieson (1928–84) English female impersonator, known solely for his grand, glorious and disgraceful creation, Mrs SHUFFLEWICK.

Japan From 1899 onwards there are records of Kabuki drama, including what is probably the first narrative film, *Let Us Walk Beneath the Maple Leaves* (1902). Female actresses were only allowed to take part in films from 1911: Kasuo Hasegawa was once the most popular male star and the most popular female star.

Homoerotic themes in cinema films: AN ACTOR'S REVENGE (1963); *Funeral Parade of Roses* (1970); *Merry Christmas, Mr Lawrence* (1982); *Fire Festival* (1984); *Summer Vacation 1999*; *Bushido*; MISHIMA: *A Life in Four Chapters* (1985); *Okoge* (1992), about two male lovers – one married – seen through the eyes of a woman who lets them use her bed when they have nowhere else to go.

See also Teinosuke KINUGASA.

Jarman, Derek (1942–) (Saint Derek of Dungeness of the Order of Celluloid

Knights.) English artist, film director, gardener and writer. A unique, highly visible film-maker, working on cheese-paring budgets and nearly always drawing (not always appreciative) audiences for works that are passionate, angry, frivolous, tedious, magnificent and queer.

C: As director: Super-8 works (1973–); *Sebastiane* (with Paul Humpfress 1976); *Jubilee* (1977); *The Tempest* (1980); *Caravaggio* (1986); *The Last of England* (1987); *War Requiem* (1989, also T); *The Garden* (1990); *Edward II* (1991); *Wittgenstein* (1992). As designer: *The Devils* (1971); *Savage Messiah* (1972). Brief on-camera appearances in most of his films as well as *Nighthawks* (1978) and PRICK UP YOUR EARS (as artist Patrick Proctor 1987).

R: *Michele* (1987), on life and works of Caravaggio; IN THE PSYCHIATRIST'S CHAIR (1990).

T: *Saturday Review* (1985 T); *Six of Hearts* 'Andy the Furniture Maker' (1986); *The Late Clive James* (1987, talking about being HIV positive); *Derek Jarman: 'You Know What I Mean'* (1989); *Derek Jarman: A Portrait* (1991); *The Media Show* (1991); *Banned*; *Dig* (1991), looking at his garden; OUT 'Love and Marriage' (1991); *Tonight with Jonathan Ross* (1992); *Saint Derek* (1992).

Subject of a diatribe by Alan Parker on *A Turnip Head's Guide to the British Cinema* (1986).

Jarman's *Caravaggio* aroused such ire in *Film '86* locum presenter Michael Parkinson that he felt obliged to issue what amounted to a public health warning:

> I must report that Mr Jarman seems fond of photographing bums, of the male variety. He could retort that Caravaggio was fond of painting them – in which case he should have found the perfect chronicler. But here's the point: whereas I would have enjoyed finding out a great deal about Caravaggio, I'm not the slightest bit interested in Mr Jarman's tortured soul, if that it be, and you must forgive me if I found great difficulty in separating one from the other. It won an award at the Berlin Film Festival so

someone must like it. It was funded by the BFI so you and me paid for it. I'm demanding my money back ... Now you just go upstairs and do normal things like old Biggles.

Dr Jekyll (and Mr Hyde) The divided self that has sparked the imaginations of the world for over a century. Robert Louis Stevenson was plagued by dreams of his 'duality', which sent him for medical help, which inspired the story of a good self being taken over by a monster of self-interest and spontaneous lust and cruelty.

Played by Fredric March, Spencer Tracy, Paul Massey, Jack Palance, Anthony Perkins, Paul Massie, Kirk Douglas (musical version), Michael Caine and David Hemmings, whose decadent Hyde was allowed a flutter with a boy prostitute. First radio production: 1930 with Leon M. Lion.

Jekyll, Gertrude (1845–1932) English artist and gardener. Her highly influential designs can be seen, eg, at Great Dixter in East Sussex and at Hestercombe and Tintinhull in Somerset. Celebrated in *Great Gardens* (1987 T) where the only personal revelation was that she was 'affectionately known as "Aunt Bumps" by nieces and nephews'.

Je Ne Regrette Rien This is one of Dame Edna Everage's great favourites; only she calls it 'Je ne regrette Rene', after a girlfriend of hers. The song's first and only interpreter, Edith Piaf explained in the 1988 documentary *Piaf Forever/Piaf pour Toujours* – over the song and a newsreel of her walking hand in hand with an exquisite Nordic blonde – that she had 'had every kind of experience – I've been around'. Later she elaborated: love was the only good thing in the world, the only thing worth fighting for. The mysterious blonde reappeared for a few seconds at the end. Was this the Rene about whom Edith had no regrets?

Jeremy Boy's name. In the UK, it has dandyish, wobbly connotations: Jeremy Dilke (Edward Everett Horton), *Man in* *the Mirror* (1936 C): a weed confronted by manly *alter ego* which encourages him to exude confidence and sex appeal; highwayman Jeremy Fox (Stewart Granger), ostensibly a foppish rake in *Moonfleet* (1955 C); murderous neurotic Jeremy Clay (Eric Portman) in *The Naked Edge* (1961 C); Swinging Londoner Jeremy Tove (Jeremy Lloyd) in *Smashing Time* (1967 C); prancing frog Jeremy Fisher in *Tales of Beatrix Potter* (1971 C); Jerry (Paul Eddington), Margo's henpecked husband who, in addition, has to cope with their neighbours' rustic schemes in *The Good Life* (1974–8 T); Jeremy *Poldark* (1976–7 T); uppercrust Jeremy Halsted (Timothy Carlton), barrister in *Crown Court* 'A Swinging Couple' (1978 T); a budding Noel Coward, young and 'musical' Jeremy Darwin (Dominic Savage) in *The Swish of the Curtain* (1980 T); the family of Jeremy (Stephen Garlick) worrying about the friend Trevor (John McAndrew) he's brought home in *All for Jeremy* (1981 R); Jeremy (Joe Dunlop), one half of the gay pair in *Don't Wait Up* (1986–90 T); Jeremy 'in commodities' in *Floodtide* (1987 T); Pete Beale (Peter Dean in EASTENDERS 1989) teasing Arthur (Bill Treacher), who is full of TV producer Jeremy and his smart friends whom he has met on a quiz show: 'Sounds a bit poncie to me – a geezer with a jumper round his shoulders called *Jeremy*'; wimp husband Jeremy Hardy in *At Home with the Hardys* (1989–90 R); Jeremy Ruttle (Murray MELVIN in *The Fool* (1990 C); Jeremy Coward (Nigel HAVERS), yuppie banker who is really Sergei Rublev, a Soviet agent in *Sleepers* (1991 T); Jeremy Molyneaux (Christopher Good) and Adrian Deschelles (David Foxxe) in *Lovejoy* 'Highland Fling' (1992 T), guests at a wedding in Scotland.

In the US, they are slightly more solid: Jeremy Wayne (Leslie Howard) in *Smilin' Through* (1932 C), the descendant of a jealous lover who shoots a bride on her wedding day; grizzled Jeremy Baile (Jay C. Flippen) in *Bend of the River* (1952 C); Jeremy Siddall (Patrick O'Neal), polished therapist in *Companions in*

Nightmare (1967); Jeremy Bolt (Bobby Sherman), kid brother in *Here Come the Brides* (1968–70); dogged scientist Dr Jeremy Hill (Arthur Hill) trying to find a cure for *The Andromeda Strain* (1970 C); *Jeremy* (Robby Benson), shy and sensitive cellist (1973 C); Jeremy Wendell (William Smithers) in *Dallas* (1986 T); Jeremy (Paul Roebling) in *Rage of Angels: The Story Continues* (1986 T); wily foreigner Jeremy Van Dorn (Jeroen Krabbe) in *Dynasty: The Reunion* (1991 T) who menaces the Carrington family, nearly asphyxiating Alexis.

Jesse/Jess In the Bible: David's father; Hebrew for 'God's grace'. The biggest casualty of fears about encroaching effeminization in Britain has been the biblical name of Jesse. Even though the legendary outlaw *is* one of his heroes, and he himself is an avid country-and-western music fan (and singer), Eddie Grundy (Trevor Harrison) in THE ARCHERS (1984 R) will not *hear* of his new-born son being called Jesse: 'It's a pouf's name,' he asserts. Eddie Grundy's son is called Edward. And in the vastly different world of the Carringtons in DYNASTY (1987 T) Jesse Atkinson, the husband of Adam's wife's surrogate mother, occasions the remark (from Adam-Gordon Thompson): 'What kind of a man *are* you, Jesse?'

In the UK, male Jesses are rare, and either old and traditional – Jesse Todman (Robert Sansom) in *That Yew Tree's Shade* (1958 R) – or young and fey – Jess (Christopher Sandford, flamboyant, giggly with a cat) in *The Root of All Evil* 'West of Eden' (1968 T).

In the US, usage is fairly evenly divided between Western heroes/anti-heroes: Tyrone Power as *Jesse James* (1939 C); Joseph Cotton as the kind, liberally educated son in *Duel in the Sun* (1946 C), a pacifist, and preferred over his wild brother (Gregory Peck); Quaker patriarch Jess Birdwell (Gary Cooper) in *Friendly Persuasion* (1956 C); Jess Harper (Robert Fuller) the drifter who stayed in *Laramie* (1959–62 T); Jess Remsberg (James Garner) in *Duel at Diablo* (1966 C). And modern heroes/anti-heroes, on the spunkish side: Jesse Swan (David Soul), disgraced world-class skier in *Swan Song* (1980 T); Jess Robin (Neil Diamond) in *The Jazz Singer* (1980 C); Jess (Hart Bochner), the younger of Dyan Cannon's husbands in *Having It All* (1982); Jess (Steve Inwood) in *Staying Alive* (1983 C); Jesse (Richard Gere) in *Breathless* (1983); Jesse Foley (Hector Elizondo) in *Foley Square* (1986 T); Jesse (John Stamos) in *Full House* (1988– T).

Jessica (the most popular girls' name in Australia *c*1992 and in the British top 10 in 1990) is used sporadically for female characters: Jessica (Petra Davies) in *Trespass* (1958 T); Angie Dickinson as the much visited widow *Jessica* (1962 C); Cheryl Ladd as Jessica, a chic boutique owner who is raped in *Now and Forever* (1983 T); Jessica Fletcher (Angela Lansbury) in *Murder She Wrote* (1984– T); attorney Jessica Parker (Jaclyn Smith) in *Rage of Angels* (1983 T) and *Rage of Angels: The Story Continues* (1986 T).

But Jessie has been staging a remarkable comeback since it withered in the 1930s: Jessie Bergman (Joanna Roos) in *Search for Tomorrow* (1951–82 T); Jobeth Williams in *Dogs of War* (1980 C); psychiatrist *Jessie* (Lindsay Wagner) who tracks a killer (1984 T); Jamie Lee Curtis as aerobics instructor Jessie in *Perfect* (1985 C); Sharon Stone as Jesse Huston in *Allan Quartermain* (1987 C); Nicole Eggert as Jessie Corbett, kidnapped teenage daughter in *The Omega Syndrome* (1987 C); Jessica Rabbit (Kathleen Turner), cartoon siren in *Who Framed Roger Rabbit?* (1988 C); Jessie (Kristy Swanson), figurine brought to life in *Mannequin on the Move* (1991 C).

In the UK: Jess (Emily Aston and Charlotte Coleman), the exploratory heroine of ORANGES ARE NOT THE ONLY FRUIT (1990 T). (Jess is called Jeanette in the book.)

jessie A northern English and Scottish expression for an effeminate man or KILT-lifter. Moray McLaren spoke of 'jessies' in *The Pleasure of Living in Edinburgh* (1947 R), but these were affected women of the city. However, he could have been making a coded mention because he makes a sly reference to 'the Auld Wife' often being 'a married *man* with a large family' (beating carpets while his 'real' wife looks on). BBC Radio 2's early morning radio presenter Ray Moore described it approvingly in 1984 as 'a lovely word we have in Liverpool – especially for men'.

Cleaner Mrs Mack (Madeleine Christie) thinks gentle bachelor Stanley Crumb (Deryck Guyler) is 'a real soft jessie' in *The Girl Who Loved Eggheads* (1960 R): 'Acht it makes you sick to see a man turn himself into a doormat.' But Stanley is not ashamed; an early men's libber he: 'I'm very capable. The truth is I've always liked a little housework.' The randy stage manager (Christopher Driscoll), who has an especial fondness for black men, is sneered at by suave leading man (Peter Bowles) as a 'jessie' in YOU'RE NOT WATCHING ME, MUMMY (1980 T).

The Jewel in the Crown (UK 1984 T)
Sprawling drama which interweaves the destinies of a group of people living and working in India during the British Raj, including the sadistic, class-ridden policeman, Ronald MERRICK (Tim Pigott-Smith) who finally discovers his true nature with the very people he had formerly despised.

W: Ken Taylor from *The Raj Quartet* by Paul Scott; P: Christopher Morahan; D: Morahan and Jim O'Brien; 14 parts; 52 mins each.

Merrick was hissed at by a viewership of over 500,000 million. The gargantuan serial was sold to India, China and Czechoslovakia, as well as to the whole of Europe, North America and Australasia. 'Merrick will certainly achieve new heights of hatred' said *TV Times*, commenting on the sales.

This viper is contrasted with Corporal 'Sophie' Dixon (Warren Clarke). A Cockney orderly who wins a medal for risking his neck to bring in the wounded, he looks after Ronald Merrick during his stay in hospital, assisting in his physical recovery and in his COMING OUT: 'It's a lovely stump, sir, and I've seen one or two ... I'm very good with my hands. Massage ... manipulation.'

Dixon's devil-may-care attitude to life goads Merrick to ask: 'What's the truth, Dixon: are you a hero or a bloody PANSY?' Dixon replies with muted glee: 'I don't think that's a question *you* ought to be asking, sir.'

Dixon's main function in the plot is to tell Guy Perron (Charles Dance) about a fellow orderly, PINKY, who discovers Merrick's medical records in the psychiatrist's office where he works, thereby revealing the missing piece in the puzzle.

Dixon is a bouncy bonus in the closing stages of the story: a salt of the earth Cockney sparrer with a rapid-fire tongue and an eye for the truth and bit of the other:

> Dixon: I suppose you wouldn't fancy a little 'Victory Day' celebration...
> Guy: Sorry, I've got to meet an old school friend.
> Dixon: That's what they all say!

Jewel's Darl (NZ 1985 C) Mandy (Richard Hanna), a new queen on the Auckland scene, has been taken under the wing of Jewel (Georgina Beyer). Mandy loves Jewel (but wonders if he shouldn't be in love with a man); Jewel loves Jewel (and Mandy too). They go shopping; Jewel gets bossy; Mandy protests; they make up and totter down the street in their heels in high animation. A film of glowing affection, full of loving detail and illuminated by the extraordinary features of Richard Hanna.
W: Anne Kennedy and Peter WELLS; P: Bridget Ikin and John Maynard; D: Peter Wells; 20 mins.

Jewish gay and lesbian people 'A man who has no wife is not a whole human being,' says exuberant fledgling gay Maurice Goodman (Trader FAULKNER) in *Promenade* (1959 T); Daniel HIRSCH (Peter FINCH) in SUNDAY, BLOODY SUNDAY (1971 C) living between two strong and opposing poles and cultures; young David (Dominic Guard) who is 'different' in *In Mourning* (1979 R); ERNESTO (Martin Halm 1979 C); Alice (Randee Heller), Jodie's house-mate who seems to have been programmed to be suffocating and fussy in SOAP (1979 T); respected Dr Ferugia (Philippe Noiret) in *The Gold-Rimmed Spectacles* (1988 C) facing persecution in Ferrara in the 1930s; November Messing (Gabriele Osburg) in NOVEMBER MOON (1984 C) who, put to work in a Nazi brothel, escapes and is hidden by her female lover for the rest of the war; Arnold Becker (Harvey FIERSTEIN) in TORCH SONG TRILOGY (1988 C); the heroine (who joins a Jewish lesbian group), fighting off mama's introduction (to men) service, programmed to be house-proud and suffocating in *The Gay Divorce* (Aust 1991 R); Bernie Birnbaum (John Turturro) 'seeing' Mink (Steve Buscemi) in *Miller's Crossing* (1990 C); Malcolm in *Figure with Meat* (1991 R); the son returning home to Canada for his mother's birthday in *Freud Leaving Home* (1991 C); Israeli Jonathan who befriends HIV-positive Thomas in *Amazing Grace* (1992 C); etc.

Documentary: On DONAHUE (1989 T) a Jewish lesbian couple, Connie and Ruth, who were married by a (reform) rabbi; Connie says she will not be put into the CLOSET 'as a Jew, as a woman or as the lover of a left-handed person'. Sharley McLean, refugee from Nazi Germany now a lesbian activist, interviewed as one of the *Tough Cookies* (1990 R). On OUT 'Oy Gay' (1992 T) the relationship of the Jewish community to lesbians and gay men in Britain and the similarities between Jews and members of sexual minorities, the ability to 'pass', the varying degrees of internalized self-hatred, the mordant sense of humour, the recently rekindled sense of pride and assertive identity...

'A Jew goes home to a Jewish background afterwards and sees real people, sees his family, his parents, his friends. He knows what a caricature is and knows what the difference is. A homosexual finds out that he's a homosexual in total isolation,' says John Chesterman in ACCESS 'Offensive to Some' (1973 R).

'[They] often come to see themselves through the eyes of their oppressors; they accept the attitudes of their oppressors as being at least partially true, thus incorporating a negative view of themselves as an integral part of their own self-image [like] blacks who call themselves "niggers" and Jews who refer to themselves as "kikes",' writes Lester D. Friedman in *Hollywood's Image of the Jew* (1982).

'We're just normal people ... all we want to do is to get on with our lives ... I don't want to be tolerated, I want to be accepted. I want to be understood,' speaker in EVERYMAN 'Some of My Best Friends...' (1991 T).

'That's what happens when you have a Jewish mother: you eventually become one,' says Alice in *Soap* (1979 T) who cooks and cleans and paints and straightens and *worries*.

Jex-Blake, Dr Sophia (1840–1912) One of the first women doctors in England and a pioneer of the right of women to train and practise. Played by Joan Miller in *Women in Medicine* 'Sophia Jex-Blake' (1954 R) and with engaging feistiness by Sara Kestelman in *The Walls of Jericho* (1981 T), which alludes to her long and loving relationship with Ursula du Pré (Lillian Barge), with whom she lived for many years in Edinburgh.

JFK (US 1991 C) David Ferrie (Joe Pesci) and Clay Shaw (Tommy Lee Jones) are just a few of the nasty low lifes in some way responsible for the murder of President Kennedy in Dallas, 1963. After extensive investigation, New Orleans District Attorney Jim Garrison (Kevin Costner) charges businessman Shaw with Kennedy's death. The jury threw the case out after deliberating for just one hour.

W: Oliver Stone and Zachary Sklar from the books *On the Trail of the Assassins* by Jim Garrison and *Crossfire: The Plot That Killed Kennedy* by Jim Marrs; P: A. Kit-man Ho and Oliver Stone; D: Oliver Stone.

Meticulous exposition, cardboard hero, and ravaged gay suspects, one a startling apparition with insecure wig and embrowned eyebrows. '... the message of the film is that 'they' comprise a unity ticket including the military industrial complex, the CIA (of course), the FBI and the intelligence service, anti-Communist Cubans who hated Fidel Castro, the Mafia, a New Orleans-based homosexual underground network and, wait for it, Bell Helicopters. And there is more...' (Gerard Henderson, *Sydney Morning Herald*, 14.1.92).

Jimmy (UK 1978) 'It was general knowledge in Galway that I had a bent to literature and, as such, I was respected and feared; the IRISH loving language, fearing truth ... I was 26 then. He was 17. I was a schoolmaster. He was a pupil ... I was his English teacher in a school run by Brothers ... We were friends, Tommy and I, nothing more ... But the men and women of Galway had a clear glint in their eye for scandal.'

Exiled because of a weekend away with a male pupil, a former teacher (P. G. Stephens), fallen on hard times in Britain, confronts his bitter past – including Tommy (Bosco Hogan) – by returning to his still hostile home.

W: Desmond Hogan; D: Robert Cooper; 20.8.78; BBC Radio 3; 50 mins.

Black and brooding nocturne about inescapable fate and the courage needed to confront past hurts. Very finely tuned to the experience of many gay and lesbian people.

Jo Female version of Joe, a diminutive of Josephine: often given to uninhibited characters, sometimes rebels who communicate through childlike directness. Louisa M. Alcott would surely be delighted, if amazed, at the continuing identification of her alter ego Jo (MARCH) with spirit and zest and with sporadic lesbian activity.

One of the cinema's first unashamed (though bitter and twisted) lesbians was

Jo Courtney (Barbara STANWYCK), the madame in *Walk on the Wild Side* (1962 C). Before that it had been the province of ordinary gals thrown into extraordinary situations (Rosalind Russell in *The Private Wore Skirts* 1952 C); of independently minded singers like Jo McKenna (Doris Day) severely stressed by the events in *The Man Who Knew Too Much* (1956 C); or, on radio and television in Britain, of achieving (over-achieving?) women who put personal feelings to one side to reach their goals (DOCTOR JO 1958 T, 1961 R; CLOSE RELATIONS 1958 R).

During the 1970s, Jo maintained its steady popularity in drama with occasional forays into ambiguity or bisexuality: Jo (Peter STRAKER), the *Girl Stroke Boy* (1971 C); Jo (Angélique De Moline), the FLIGHT ATTENDANT in *The Stewardesses* (1970 C).

US: Josephine Adare in *God's Country and the Women* (1916 C); Jo Bishop (Dorothy Phillips) in Elinor Glyn's *The World's a Stage* (1923), a Hollywood movie colonial wife; Jo Rossiter, third billed in *The Lady Lies* (1929 C); British Jo (Jill Esmond), one of the *Thirteen Women* (1932 C) murdered by Ursula (Myrna Loy); Jo MARCH (Katharine HEPBURN), prototype TOMBOY in *Little Women* (1933 C); Jo Barton (Beverly Roberts), lumber camp manager in *God's Country and the Woman* (1936 C); Jo (Ginger Rogers) sharing everything in an all-female household in *Tender Comrade* (1943 C); Jo March (June Allyson) in *Little Women* (1949 C): 'I'm the man of the family'; Jo McBain (Rosalind Russell) forced into uniform in *The Private Wore Skirts/Never Wave at a WAC* (1952 C); Jo March (Andrée Melly) in *Little Women* (1956 T): 'as close an autobiographical study of Louisa M. Alcott as anybody could hope to print' (*Radio Times*), followed by Annabelle Lee in *Good Wives* (1958 T) and *Jo's Boys* (1959 T); Audrey Hepburn as bluestocking Jo Stockton – ugly duckling into top model swan (with existentialist leanings) in *Funny Face* (1957 C); (Rita Hayworth), adulterous wife on murder charge in *The Story on Page One*

(1960 C); Jo Courtney (Barbara STANWYCK), lesbian madame in *Walk on the Wild Side* (1962 C); Jo Sands (Dolores Michaels), rich man's capable assistant and secret mistress, driven to murder by his three-timing in PERRY MASON 'The Case of the Playboy Pugilist' (1962 T); Jo Symington (Dodie Marshall) who lives with beatniks and artists until she discovers clean-living Elvis Presley in *Easy Come, Easy Go* (1966 C); Packer Jo (Peggy Lee), a racing car enthusiast in *The Girl from UNCLE* 'The Furnace Flats Affair' (1967 T); drug-dealing Jo Enders (Marian Morgan) who wants to have a wild affair with Pepper Anderson in *Police Woman* 'Fish' (1974 T); Jo Nelson (Ruth McDevitt), girlfriend of Bunker's friend Justin in ALL IN THE FAMILY (1972 T); Helen Shaver as Jo in OUTRAGEOUS! (1977 C); Jo Butler (Kristy McNicol), spirited teenage girl with down-at-heel dad in *My Old Man* (1979 T) based on Hemingway story (filmed as *Under My Skin* in 1950, but with a boy); Jo Keene (Elaine Monti), a lawyer in a Manhattan legal assistance bureau in *Park Place* (1980–1 T); Jo Polniazek (Nancy McKeown) in *The Facts of Life* (1980–3), a tough street kid in a young ladies' academy; Jo (Cyndy Manion), a good-time girl in *Preppies* (1983); Jo (Margarette Francis) in *Seaview* (1986 T); Jo (Joanna) Barnes (Corinne Michaels) in *Days of Our Lives* (1987 T); film-maker Jo (Lois Weaver) in her first major lesbian relationship in *She Must Be Seeing Things* (1987 C); pert teenager Jo Barlow (Cynthia Gibb) in *Malone* (1987 C); hot-shot lawyer Jo Daniels (Victoria Principal) in love with Judge Jonathan in *Naked Lie* (1989 T); Jo (Farrah Fawcett), the wife of Jeff Bridges in *See You in the Morning* (1989 C); Jo Reynolds (Daphne Zuniga) in MELROSE PLACE (1992– T).

Also: Bobby Jo (Tuesday Weld) in *Soldier in the Rain* (1963 C); Billie Jo (Meredith MacRae) in *Petticoat Junction* (1966–70 T; the series also featured a Betty Jo and a Bobbie Jo); Jo Anne Baker (Suzanne Pleshette) in *Blackbeard's Ghost* (1967 C); Jo Hudson (Carol Lynley), pretty step-daughter of

Shirley Booth in *The Smugglers* (1968 T); Jennifer Jo (J. J.) (Julie Sommars) in *The Governor and J.J.* (1969–70 T) who works in a zoo; Elly Jo Jamison (Dorothy Lyman) in *Edge of Night* (*c* 1975 T); Mama Jo (Anne Francis), the skipper of a charter boat with an all-female crew in *Riptide* (1982? T); Sammy Jo (Heather Locklear), Krystle's conniving niece and eventually Steven's wife in DYNASTY (1983–8 T); Mary Jo, one of the *Designing Women* (1986 T); Wendy Jo (Elizabeth Gorcey) in *Footloose* (1984 C).

UK: Jo Bolton (Josephine Douglas) who wants to continue studying medicine so she works in an office overtime in *It Never Rains* (1954); Jo Lewis (Annabel Maule), a brilliant designer who doesn't want children and has 'fancy' (gay) friends in CLOSE RELATIONS (1958 R); DOCTOR JO Marlowe (Margaret Johnston 1958 T; Freda Jackson 1961 R) who has sacrificed her personal life to work in Africa; coming home on a visit upsets her conventional, married sister; Nurse Jo Buckley (Barbara Clegg) in *Emergency–Ward 10* (1958 T); pregnant Rosemary Miller in *Walk on the Grass* (1959 T) who is married to an advertising agent, but wishes she'd married his less go-getting brother; Jo Halliday (Julia Lockwood) who writes a sexy exposé of her family and friends in *Please Turn Over* (1959 C); Jo(anna) Gene Anderson in *Mill of Secrets* (1961 T); Jo Lake (Liz Frazer), ruthless confidence trickster in *The Painted Smile* (1961 C); Jo Riley (Carol Maybank) turning up to school 'Incorrectly Dressed' in sweater and leopardskin pants in *Yorky* (1961 T); hard-faced, blackmailing Christian Miss Benham (Margaret Diamond) in VICTIM (1961 C), known as 'Jo' in the original script but in the film her equally ambiguous partner-in-crime calls her simply 'B' – her surname still rhymes with 'venom'; Jo SMITH (Rita Tushingham) kicking against the boundaries of society and womanhood in A TASTE OF HONEY (1961 C); Jo (Ann Murray), an actress in *The Playwright and the Star* (1963 R); Jo Craig (Eva Stuart), sympathetic sec-

retary in *A Case of Character* (1965 R); Jo Dutton (Maureen Connell), a courier in *Danger Man* 'Yesterday's Enemies' (1964 T); Jo (Anne Bancroft), a rich matron with a pathological need to be pregnant in *The Pumpkin Eater* (1964 C); Jo Davies (Beryl Calder), one of two sisters brought up as twins, but one is adopted in *Blood Test* (1965 R); Jo (Amanda Barrie), Billy Fury's zippy, horse-loving love interest in *I Gotta Horse* (1965 C); Jo Hardy (Ann Morrish), wife of THE EXPERT (1968–71 T): a doctor who expects men to treat her as an equal and who puts her career before her marriage; Wendy Gifford in *The Gold Robbers* 'The Cover Plan' (1968 T); Joanna 'Jo' Wallace (Audrey Hepburn), the wife seen across 10 years of South of France holidays in *Two for the Road* (1967 C).

Jo (Geraldine Cowper) in *Bachelor Father* (1971 T); Jo Grant (Katy Manning), the companion of DOCTOR WHO (Jon Pertwee 1972–3 T); Jo (Sally Thomsett), the bubbly flat-sharer in *Man About the House* (1973–6 T; character's name changed to Chrissy in the American version); Jo Mason (Cheryl Kennedy), sister of a gang boss with a treasure map printed on her buttock in *Ooh, You Are Awful* (1972 C); Joanna (Jo) (Fay Kelton), American-educated and eventually killed off in *Blue Hills* (Aust 1972–6 R); counsellor's daughter Jo Selby (Tina Heath), about to become too emotionally involved in *Couples* (1976 T); Nurse Jo Longhurst (Dawn Ann Cole) in *Angels* (1975–6 T), always in conflict with authority, empathizing (too much?) with the patients, who becomes a district nurse; Jo (Vicki Michelle) in *The Professionals* 'Hunter/Hunted' (1978 T); Jo (Rowena Roberts), one of those attacked in *Girls at Risk* (1980 R); Jo (and Nicky) doing duty for three pairs of lovers, heterosexual, gay and lesbian, in SOMETHING ELSE 'Intimate Confessions' (1980 T); Jo Bailey (Elizabeth Larner), an ex-alcoholic nightclub singer, befriender of gay purser in TRIANGLE (1981 T); Jo Beswick (Jan Francis) who gives cancer-stricken jockey Bob Champion such support in *Champions* (1983 C); Jo Barrett (Beverley Michaels), a 20-year-old 'pretty, laughing, teasing' Jamaican who wants to set up house with her lover in *Jury* 'Louise' (1983 T); 12-year-old Jo (Pauline Quirke) facing a future world of hate and fear with the support of Alma in *Somewhere Else* (1983 R); Jo (Irene Marat), impoverished single mother in *Intimate Strangers* (1985 C); one of the schoolgirls in SYRUP OF FIGS (1986 R); Jo (Peggy Sirr) in *The Mistress* (1986 T); Jo McLoughlin (Jenifer Landor), a psychological counsellor who becomes involved with a schoolgirl in INAPPROPRIATE BEHAVIOUR (1987 T); Jo (Juliette Grassby) in *Late Expectations* (1987 T); Jo King (Suki Armstrong) in *Knowhow* 'Hyperspace Hotel' (1988 T); the cockily defiant prisoner Jo (Lynne Fairleigh) locked away for 15 years for aiding an IRA bomber in *The Road South* (1990 R); pert teenager Jo (Anna) (Kellie Bright) in *The Upper Hand* (1990 T), jeans, pony-tail, a liking for nasty practical jokes (character is named Sam in the American version, *Who's The Boss?*); Jo Franklyn (Susannah Harker), the tycoon's daughter in *Chancer* (1990 T); Jo (Susan Devaney) in *Spatz* (1990 T); Jo (Lisa Orgolini) in *Perfect Scoundrels* 'Party Games' (1992 T); Jo Scott (Arkie Whitely), 'disturbed and mysterious' who subjects Bob Peck to 'violent harassment' and who is found dead, rolled up in a carpet, in *Natural Lies* (1992 T).

Australia: Jo Loveday (Josephine Mitchell) in A COUNTRY PRACTICE (1982–90 T); blaring, tough Jo (Joy Miller) who runs the hairdressing salon with Jan, Jess and Jackie in *Lipstick Kisses* (1993 R).

Variations include Jody/Jodie, Joey and Josie.

Jody/Jodie: the nickname of the unmarried mother (Olivia de Havilland) in *To Each His Own* (1946 C); Grayson HALL as impermeable book critic Jody Moore in *The Man from UNCLE* 'The Pieces of Fate Affair' (1967 T); Jody (Amy Irving) in POLICE WOMAN 'The Hit' (1975 T); dead yuppie drug addict in *Floodtide* (1987 T). Is occasionally

male, eg Jodie DALLAS in SOAP (1977–81 T).

Joey: Joey Drayton (Katherine Houghton), daughter of would-be liberal parents Spencer Tracy and Katharine HEPBURN, frightening the horses by wanting to marry a black man in *Guess Who's Coming to Dinner?* (1967 C); Jodie FOSTER as Joey Kelly, a schoolmate in *The Courtship of Eddie's Father* (1969–72 T); Joey (Marybeth Hurt), the youngest daughter who hates her mother in *Interiors* (1978 C); Joey (Kate O'Mara) in *Behind the Chalet School* (1983 R).

Josie: Josie Mansfield (Frances Farmer) in *The Toast of New York* (1937 C); 'Josie', teenager envious of her more independent friend in a Maureen DUFFY-scripted episode of *The Younger Generation* (1961 T); free-loving student (Samantha Eggar) in *The Wild and the Willing* (1962 C); Marianne Faithfull saying 'fuck' in *I'll Never Forget Whatshisname* (1967 C); Josie Williamson (Cherry Potter) in WITHIN THESE WALLS 'Operation Happiness' (1977 T) who has a brain operation to make her less violent and aggressive; Josie James (Amanda Redman), the mistress who proceeds to have an affair with her lover's widow in RICHARD'S THINGS (1981 C/T); Josie (Patti Love) in STEAMING (1984 C) berating the middle-class women for their hypocrisy and saving the bathhouse from demolition; short-cropped Josie Packard (Joan Chen) in *Twin Peaks* (1989–91 T); Josie (June Tobin), media man's companion in *Private Property Keep Off* (1983 R); Josie (Angela Pleasence) in *Josie* 'Family and Friends' (1987 R), prospective parliamentary candidate with home (lesbian?) problems.

Joan of Arc, St (*c* 1412–31) French national heroine who led an army against the English, was captured, tried and found guilty of heresy and blasphemy (principally for refusing to abandon wearing 'men's' clothes) by a French ecclesiastical court.

Marina Warner narrated the full history of the 'Maid of Orleans' on television in 1983. In Bernard Shaw's *Saint*

Joan dramatic portraits of the Maid include Jean Seberg on film (1957); Constance Cummings (1941 & 1947), Maria Becker (1948), Mary MORRIS (1956), Joan Plowright (1965), Judi Dench (1975) etc on radio; Joan Hart (1950), Gabrielle Lloyd (1980) etc on television. Ginger Rogers, Jane Fonda and Diane Keaton read speeches from *Saint Joan* in, respectively, *The Barkleys of Broadway* (1949), *Klute* (1971) and *The Little Drummer Girl* (1984).

Ingrid Bergman played Joan in *Joan of Arc* (1948 C); Pamela Allan in *The Servant* (1953); Hedy Lamarr in a segment of *The Story of Mankind* (1957 C); Florence Carrez in *Le Procès de Jeanne d'Arc* (1962 C); but still the most haunting is Marie Falconetti in *La Passion de Jeanne d'Arc* (1928, her only film).

Job Hunt 'Winding Up' (UK 1981 T) A discussion on getting a job in a time of high (3 million) unemployment. Alison (Janet Rawson) and Lorraine (Catherine Hall) are more interested in each other than the advice or the boys.
W: Alan Drury; 23.2.81; BBC1; 45 mins.

A tiny recognition that not all female teenagers are '*boy* mad'; some are possibly lesbian (and, on the evidence of this pair, difficult to motivate).

Jockey shorts version Otherwise known as 'gilding the willie'. Alternative shots (actors wearing underpants or jockey shorts, rarely BRIEFS) for full-frontal nude scenes; usually for the chill, suspicious latitudes of American (and Japanese) television. A recent example is THE LOST LANGUAGE OF CRANES (a BBC-WNET Boston co-production).

The Joeys Bernie Evans, Chris Eymard, Robert Llewellyn and Nigel Ordish, a group of singing comedians: 'sexist men trying not to be, and that's that.' They began in 1981, appearing in SOMETHING ELSE 'Intimate Confessions' (1982 T). After the group disbanded, Eymard and Llewellyn turned up in THE CORNER HOUSE (1987 T).

John, Elton [Reginald Kenneth Dwight]

(1947–) British pop singer and composer whose DANIEL was heard on TOP OF THE POPS in 1973. A few years later he came out as BISEXUAL. A great chat-show favourite (*Parkinson, Wogan* etc); subject of musical documentaries (*Elton John and Bernie Taupin Say ... Goodbye Norma Jean and Other Things* 1972 T; *The Dodgers and Russell Harty* 1975 T; *To Russia with Elton* 1979 C); subject of many a 'frank' interview (eg *The Best of British* 1980 T, with Paul GAMBACCINI). Biographies include *The Elton John Story* (in six parts by Paul Gambaccini, 1976 R) and *Two Rooms* (1991 T, talking with his lyricist Bernie Taupin about their often tempestuous working relationship). Elton John played the Pinball Wizard in *Tommy* (1975 C) and was set to portray the uncle in Ken Russell's version of THE RAINBOW (1989 C), but David Hemmings had to step in at the last minute. Plans for Elton and his friend Rod Stewart to star in a comedy, reminiscent of the 'Road' films with Bing and Bob, came to naught *c* 1976–7. John and Taupin's music was most recently heard on the soundtrack of MY OWN PRIVATE IDAHO (1991 C).

Johnny Go Home (UK 1975 T) In part 1, 'End of the Line' 14-year-old Tommy arrives in London, is scooped up and placed in a hostel where he is exploited and abused. Part 2 deals with the sickeningly savage events leading to 'The Murder of Billy Two Tone' involving hostel inmates and 'officers'.
P/D: John Willis; 22.7.75; Yorkshire; 100 mins.

The murky world of homeless children and teenagers, and the places that are supposed to shelter and keep them from harm. The world of Fagin and Oliver Twist a century and a quarter later. The unrelenting horror of it all led to questions in Parliament, prosecutions and an enquiry into conditions in such places. The follow-up (*What Happened to Johnny Go Home?* produced by Michael Deakin and shown on 13 January 1976) was almost equally pessimistic.

Johnny Guitar (US 1954 C) Two women – Vienna (Joan Crawford) and Emma Small (Mercedes McCambridge) – conduct a bitter personal war which ends in a gunfight on the dusty main street of an Arizona town.
W: Philip Yordan from the novel by Roy Chanslor; P/D: Nicholas Ray; 110 mins.

One of the great Hollywood follies: hate, murder, revenge, Freud, role-reversal, sublimated lesbianism (wickedly emphasized in the 'recut' scenes featured in *Dry Kisses Only* (1989–) which also 'reinterprets' ALL ABOUT EVE), and one of Joan Crawford's last stands – in Levis, with short hair, eyes and six-guns blazing.

Johnston, David (1935–90) English radio producer, much of whose work was at the edges or right of centre of queerdom: WAGGONERS' WALK; WEEKEND WITH WILLIE (1981); *The Rocking Chair* (1983); *Reputation* (1984); *The Big March* (1984); *A Study in Hatred* (1985); *La Dispute* (1987); *Death and the Dancing Footman* (1987); A BOOK AT BEDTIME 'Love Lies Bleeding' (1987); *A Song At Twilight* (1988); etc.

jokes Outlets for fears and frustrations, channels of enlightenment, reinforcement of society's values ... there are thousands of theories and millions of jokes. Trevor Griffiths' *Comedians* (1979 T) had an old hand (Bill Fraser) take a new crop of comics back to the roots of humour: Irish, Jewish, black, feminist ball-breakers and mothers-in-law. There was nothing specifically about queers: an important oversight as this section of society provides one of the richest sources of laughter.

Comedians were faced with a bit of a problem when losers looked like becoming winners with the advent of gay liberation. No matter: old STEREOTYPES were simply garnished with merry condescension and it was business as usual. Even Irish jokes were adapted for the purpose of cramming in one more mention of 'QUEER' or 'FAIRY', eg Spike Milligan (who is Irish) asked on *Friday Night,*

Saturday Morning' (1983 T) if we'd heard the one about the Irish queer: 'He went out with a woman.'

You'd think eventually that the very superficiality of the queer joke would sound its death knell. But, like the mother-in-law, the pathetic QUEEN – upon whom you mustn't at all costs turn your back – goes on with the regularity of a test cricket match played with rotten fruit. Now with the restrictions on the cruder ethnic jokes and the active support of society's institutions in the light of AIDS, the hollow laughter will continue in its persecutory way.

In ONLY CONNECT (1979 T) Colin tells his lover Graham: 'You should have heard them at the [bus] depot today. It was either "Look at the knockers on that" or queer jokes all morning. So, finally, I said, "Have you heard the one about the heterosexual man?" They looked a bit shifty and said no, they hadn't. And I said, "No, neither have I! I wonder why there aren't any." They were huffy with me the whole afternoon.'

One of the characters in Woody ALLEN's *Stardust Memories* (1980 C) argues that 'beneath a lot of comedy there's aggression, fury ... homosexual rage'. Certainly the need to distance themselves from sexual difference, while often adopting ambiguous guise, is a constant of comedians: real-life ones like Frankie HOWERD and fictional creations like Eddie in COMIC'S INTERLUDE (1981 R).

During the 1970s and 1980s, a feeling was voiced that gays and lesbians took themselves too seriously and couldn't 'laugh at themselves': an idea that was refuted by GAY NEWS news editor Harry Coen in *Bennett Bites Back* (1982 T). Now gays and lesbians have their own comics: Julian CLARY, Robin Tyler, Sandra Bernhard, Maria Esposito, Simon FANSHAWE and others who are laughing at *and* with the foibles, self-delusions, idiocies and double standards of life as it affects one minority but with applications to others. And drawing wide, non-ghetto audiences in the process.

Jonathan (UK 1966 R) King DAVID (John Justin) is still haunted by the memory of his friend as his private life collapses (he has his mistress Bathsheba's husband killed; his baby dies) and respect for him diminishes.
W: Alan MELVILLE; adapted from his (1948) comedy with serious undertones; P: Norman Wright; 1.8.66; BBC Home Service; 90 mins.

Jones, Basil (1919–) Welsh radio actor, a member of the BBC Drama Repertory Company from 1943 to 1949, who specialized in ringing-voiced heroes or hysterical neurotics – two polarities which he was able to merge to perfection in his characterization of John TREGORRAN (1953–5, 1975–6, 1990) in THE ARCHERS. Radio's Cary GRANT, his roles included a Roman soldier in *Horatius* (1943); the son in *Front Line Family* (1944); gadabout Carl Lathom in *Send for Paul Temple Again* (1945); Melville in *The Lady from the Sea* (1946); the title role in *Thomas Chatterton* by Vita SACKVILLE-WEST (1946) as the boy poet who committed suicide in a garret aged 18; the mad young man in *Displaced Persons* (1946); Faello in *The Marriage Plate* with Anne CULLEN as Christina (1946); teamed with Anne Cullen again in *House Party* (1946); Dickie in *People Like Us* (1946, with Frank Vosper); Reggie, one of the kids in *The Younger Generation* (with Denholm ELLIOTT, 1946); Brandon Wyndham in ROPE (with Donald Pleasence, 1947); Malcolm in *The Boys of Summer* (1961); Wilfred Davies, a CIA agent pretending to be backslapping Welshman in PAUL TEMPLE AND THE ALEX AFFAIR (1964): 'What is it, man? Have you seen a gh-o-st or somethin'?'; villainous Mr Jones in *Victory* (1964); Vic in *Mosaic of Loving* (1966); Thomas Parry in *Elizabeth's Admiral* (1968); etc.

Jones, Rev. Jim (1931–78) American preacher and philosopher, arguing for a new way of life for men and women based on old – but enlightened – principles. Forced to leave America, he and his followers went to Guyana and founded Jonestown. He underwent a severe personality change, becoming ever more dictatorial and sexually insatiable. After an investigating US senator was shot dead in Jonestown, Jones ordered his disciples to drink a poisoned fruit drink – which most of them did. Played on television by Powers Boothe in GUYANA TRAGEDY: THE STORY OF JIM JONES (1980), Stuart Whitman in *Crime of the Century* (1980), and Ivan Rassimov in *Eaten Alive* (1980), and on radio by Lee Montague in *Now, and At The Hour of Our Birth* (1980). Jones' actual taped speeches and conversations (growing ever more rambling and bombastic) were played in the 2-part PBS documentary *Father Cares* (US 1981 R).

Jorgensen, Christine [George] (1926–89) American man who had one of the first publicized sex changes in the early 1950s and who became an international lecturer on transgender issues. Played by John Hansen in *The Christine Jorgensen Story* (1970 C). Frequent television appearances in the US. In HBO's *America Undercover* 'What Sex Am I?' (1986 T) she was able to look back on her experiences in a country where '2,500 male and female Americans per month, in equal numbers, seek sex change operations'.

journalists Hurd HATFIELD as the reporter drawn to Billy the Kid in *The Left-Handed Gun* (1957 C); Bob (John HURT) in *Green Julia* (1971 T); Kate (Gabrielle Hartley) in DAWN! (1979 C); Larry Dawson (Robert Reed) in HOTEL 'Transitions' (1985 T); David Dunhill (Richard E. Grant) in HERE IS THE NEWS (1989 T).

Journey's End R. C. Sherriff's classic play about love, honour and death in the trenches. Passions stirring inside manly breasts, almost breaking out of tight military uniforms as the mayhem of war explodes in counterpoint.
The 1930 film version, directed by James WHALE, starred Colin Clive as Captain Stanhope and David Manners

as Lieutenant Raleigh, the man who stirs something within him. Radio productions in 1947, 1956, 1970 and 1980. Television productions include 1937 (with Reginald Tate as Stanhope), 1954 (Terence Longden), 1960 (Richard Johnson) and 1988 (Jeremy Northam).

Journey to Java (UK 1990 R) Presented with a free trip to Jakarta to study 'melancholy', 70-year-old Harold NICOLSON (Benjamin WHITROW) takes his wife Vita (Eleanor Bron) on 'the happiest journey that even we have known'. 'A necklace of uneventful days' passing through the Malacca Straits and studying the other passengers: male virgins, heavy Teutonic women (dry sticks, flabby, overfed), an Englishman 'with not even a rudimentary sense of original sin'. Harold compliments Vita on her 'odd ideas' and expresses his gratitude in such an 'enchanting companion'. Then it's back to 'daffodil-drenched' Sissinghurst.
W: Harold Nicolson; adapted by David Wheeler; P/D: Louise Purslow; 24.10.90; BBC Radio 4; 30 mins.
An antidote to the heady delights of PORTRAIT OF A MARRIAGE (which had been shown the previous month). Vita in a very minor key; stage centre is the 'senile zest' of Harold. It's a very anodyne affair, but restful.

Jubilee (UK 1977 C) A police state: the Queen has been murdered, Buckingham Palace has become a recording studio, punks roam the streets, sex-roles are reversed, love is decried (except between brothers). Punk, junk and minimalism taking in John Dee and Elizabeth I and environmental decay: an edgy pirate movie, middle-class punk trash, tightly controlled, virtuosic, a reaction to unpredictable energy and power. Offers booty for scavengers of 1970s special history.
W/D: Derek JARMAN; P: James Whalley; 104 mins.

judge ye not ... Biblical text. Used by Edward D. Wood on the opening roller of GLEN OR GLENDA? (1953 C) as his TRANSVESTITE manifesto: 'You are society ... *Judge ye not*'. Anthony Benn used it in defence of gay and lesbian people on *Any Questions?* (1981 R).

Julia (US 1977 C) Lillian Hellman's devotion to her friend over a 20-year period has a restrained, lyrical feel in the first instance and a thriller pulse in the second. The writer is played by Jane Fonda; the friend – based on Muriel Gardiner, an American psychoanalyst and resistance worker – is Vanessa REDGRAVE (she won an Oscar); and Lillian's lover – who takes up a fair bit of the story – is crusty Dashiell Hammett played by Jason Robards Jr. But ... as she loves and works (on THE CHILDREN'S HOUR) 'her memory returned again and again to Julia'.
W: Alvin Sargent from one of the stories in *Pentimento* by Lillian Hellman; P: Julien Derode; D: Fred Zinnemann; 118 mins.
In this long, sketchy and ultimately frustrating film, Lillian Hellman strikes out at the loathsome journalist when he puts her relationship with Julia in an unchaste light. Pam Rosenthal in *Jump Cut* (19, 1977) was one of the few critics to view this and similar disavowals in Fred Zinnemann's film as disturbing and damaging: 'Not only is the film's portrayal of the bar scene an offensive anti-gay gesture and a gratuitous misreading of Lillian Hellman's careful and honest comments. It is also opportunistic – loudly denying any homoerotic possibility after the earlier hazy shots of the two adolescents waltzing together, which was certainly meant as a sexual note. The point is to give us a few minutes of homoerotic material and then refute them, sublimate them, and announce this as loudly and as clearly as possible.'
Alison HENNEGAN, reviewing the film in GAY NEWS (135, 1978), disagreed quite profoundly: 'To me it seemed that its director ... has actually succeeded in presenting an intense friendship between two women which is important for its own sake and not because of the opportunities it gives them to work out

their relationships with men. It is not a sexually expressed love, though each recognizes the possibility is there, and when Lillian pushes a drunken "friend" off his chair because he has said that "everyone" knows she is having an affair with Julia, it is not the "smear" that causes her wrath. It's her fury that an all-important love between two people should become a subject for trivial and uncomprehending gossip among unthinking people. That's no cop-out.'

Julian Latin for 'soft haired, light bearded, downy'. Relating also to the family of Gaius Julius Caesar, the Julian calendar and the 'Apostate Emperor' JULIAN who tried to stem the Christian tide. The name stood at no. 41 in the British charts in 1965, but was absent from subsequent listings. Is still in 'quiet use'.

UK: Julian Rolphe, journalist in Czarist Russia in *The Yellow Ticket* (Milton Sills 1918 C; Laurence Olivier 1931 C); Julian Caird (Val Gielgud – playing a variation on himself), temperamental radio producer, with a beard in *Death at Broadcasting House* (1934 C); Julian Dulcimer (Lewis Stringer), the ward and passionate friend, surrogate son of Mr DULCIMER in THE GREEN BAY TREE (1946 R); Julian Craster (Marius Goring) in *The Red Shoes* (1948 C), besotted with Moira Shearer and heavy on the make-up; Julian Heath, the sensitive composer who loathes his drunken father in *Shadow of the Vine* (John Forrest 1953 T; Barry Warren 1958 T): 'Julian is discovered playing the piano. He is about 19, slim, good-looking, temperamental ... his brother is more virile ... in the physical sense'; suave Julian Napier (Anthony Thwaite) in *Jenny Villiers* (1954 R); theatre legend Binkie Beaumont translated into Julian De Mauncey, an agent offering Jenny Dale a hit Broadway play in MRS DALE'S DIARY (1957 R), but she gets pregnant so can't go to the US; polite warlock Dr Julian Karswell (Niall McGinnis) who unleashes the *Night of The Demon* (1957 C) but is very good to his old mum; Julian Grant (Ivan Brandt), physics

teacher who takes a close interest in a boy student's progress into university despite parental and romantic opposition in *The Boys of Summer* (1959 R); Julian Porteous (Peter Wilde) in *A Noise in the Night* (1959 R).

Julian Calvert (Brian Rix), farcical hero in *Wolf's Clothing* (1961 T); Julian Travers (Julian Glover), a tour guide in Simon RAVEN's *A Friend in Need* (1962 R), based on the author's own experiences; Julian Sloan (John Wood), personable Oxford flautist and linguist tutoring a candidate for the hand of an heiress in *Love Is a Ball/All This and Money Too* (1962 C); Julian (Barry Foster) in *A Round of Silence* (1963 R); Julian Bennett (Geoffrey Matthews) supplanting a sales executive because he is well connected in *A Kind of Strength* (1963 R); Julian Mason (Alex Scott), the fanatical organizer of a new Fascist group, tempting a young Alan Murray (Michael Crawford) in *Destiny '63* (1963 T); an obnoxious type found 100 per cent dead in *Burke's Law* 'Who Killed Julian Buck?' (1963 T); Julian (Maurice Denham), 40-year-old unselfconfident bachelor boss's son in *Any Other Business* (1964 T); Edmund Purdom as Julian, an impoverished actor who is whisked off to Hollywood in *The Comedy Man* (1964 C); soppy television director Julian Goddard (Nicholas Parsons) in *Every Day's a Holiday* (1965 C); 'bilingual' Julian (Hugh Paddick), ex-chorus boy now yer actual jack of all trades in ROUND THE HORNE (1965–9 R); actor playing cartoon hero Julian (Roy Patrick) in *The Avengers* 'The Winged Avenger' (1968 T); Julian Markham (Vincent Price) who keeps his brother prisoner in *The Oblong Box* (1969 C).

Julian (Noel Harrison), heir to a fortune who finances a Labour councillor's campaign in *Take a Girl Like You* (1970 C): will Hayley Mills take smooth-faced Noel or rough, raffish Oliver Reed?; Julian Dewar (Martin Potter) in *Goodbye, Gemini* (1970 C), corrupt or corrupted?; Julian (Nicholas Pennell) in *Mr Forbush and the Penguins* (1970? C); Julian Carter (David Wood), the son of a famous rugger star who can't stand the pressure of sporting stardom in the Welsh valleys and flees in *Sporting Scenes* 'Up and Under' (1973 T); Julian (Joseph O'Conor), fearful that he won't get promotion within British intelligence, throwing in his lot with the villains in *The Black Windmill* (1974 C); Julian (Tim Morand), one of the precious bodyguards of precious Conrad (John Savident) in *Dial M for Murder* 'Dead Connection' (1974 T); the sensitive Julian (Marcus Harris), one of THE FAMOUS FIVE (1978 T) cut into wimpsized pieces by Peter Richardson in two of THE COMIC STRIP PRESENTS ... (1982 & 1983 T); Julian Freke, a psychiatrist whom Lord Peter Wimsey consults in *Whose Body?* (1978 R).

Julian Higbee (Larry Bishop), one of the residents of the *Condominium* (1980 T); flapping television director Julian (Nigel Pegram) in *Leave It to Charlie* 'A Star Is Born' (1980 T); Julian Cake-Armitage running a guest house for armed forces in Worthing in *Dear Ladies* (1980 T): 'He has a natural bent,' says Aunt Hilda (Bracket); Julian (Frank Grimes), duplicitous bisexual in *Couples and Robbers* (1981 C); Julian (Michael COCHRANE), tennis-playing dry young stick in *Tonic Water and Ice* (1981 R); Julian (Jeff Rawle) committing suicide on video when his PhD thesis (on *Puss In Boots*) is rejected in *Crystal Gazing* (1982); Julian Spears (Charles Shaughnessy), a well-off publisher's editor, who would rather marry someone his mother would approve of than the scruffier type who's an all-round human being in *Jury* (1983 T); Julian (Nigel Planer), a student living briefly back in the Iron Age in THE COMIC STRIP PRESENTS ... 'Summer School' (1983 T); Julian Dalrymple-Sykes (Ben Aris), the second partner and swain of Yvonne, the ballroom dancer in *Hi-de-Hi!* (1984 T); Julian (Jack Carr) in need of lonely hearts' advice in *Hearts of Gold* (1984 R); Julian Tope (Paul Bown), one of the *Morons from Outer Space* (1985 C) described as a 'brainless ... thick ... dumbdumb ... twit ... a world-famous manicurist on the planet Blob'; Julius Court (Art Malik), the murderer in *The*

Black Tower (1985 T, gay in the original novel, obliquely bisexual here); Julian, owner of the hands that play the piano in the Rover's Return, finally revealed as a 29-year-old Mancunian Robert Maxwell at a stag night in CORONATION STREET (1986 T); Julian (Harry Enfield) in *Filthy Rich and Catflap* (1987 T); Captain Julian Lyndhurst, the SAS leader who helps neutralize Pearce Brosnan in *The Fourth Protocol* (1987 C); Julian (Tim McInnery), fluting television director in *Soft Soap* (1988 T); Julian, bland young suitor of Sarah's daughter in AFTER HENRY 'Intellectual Aspirations' (Jasper Jacobs 1987 R; Stephen Tomlinson 1988 T); Dr Julian Dear (David Neal), murdered just as he is about to deliver a paper on the environment in *Inspector Morse* 'The Infernal Serpent' (1989 T); a 'fairy' called Julian who catalogues Cecily's art collection in *Chelworth* (1989 T); 'the Ruperts and the Julians' is how Catherine (Josette Simon) characterizes lazy good-for-nothings in HERE IS THE NEWS (1989 T); unmarried Dr Julian Chapman (Nigel Le Vaillant) in CASUALTY (1990-2 T); Julian (Jesse Birdsall) minicab driver in *Rides* (1992 T); Julian (Michael COCHRANE), sardonic Don Juan who hates himself but loves Judith in DUSTY ANSWER (1990 R); Julian (Scott Fults), leader of a satanic cult in *She-Wolf of London* (1990 T); Julian Garrett (Simon Rouse) in *Dead Romantic* (1993 T).

Australia: Julian (Lew Luton), Jewish doctor in NUMBER 96 (1972 T); Julian (Ivor Kant), former law student now a married and dull clerk in *Silver City* (1984 C); Julian (Matt Day), a student nurse who changes his name to Luke, wears an EARRING and has the typical healthy Australian hatred for homos in A COUNTRY PRACTICE (1988– T); Julian (Simon Chilvers), police prosecutor in *Rafferty's Rules* (1988–91).

US: Julian Osborn (Conrad Nagel), the cad in *Midsummer Madness* (1920 C); Julian Marsh (Hobart Bosworth) in *The Far Cry* (1926 C); Julian Gordon (Brian Aherne) in *Shooting Stars* (1927); Julian Fields (Paul Lukas), artist who becomes rich women's plaything, pulled up when his child dies (in agony) in *Women Love Once* (1929 C); Julian (Percy Marmont), artist who goes to Paris and returns a different man in *Daddy's Gone-a-Hunting* (1929 C); Julian Marsh (Warner Baxter), neurotic stage genius in *Forty-Second Street* (1933); Julian Davis (Henry Daniell), superior, emotionally barren actor, one of the suspects in *Dressed to Kill* (1941 C); Julian Karell (Nils Asther), portrait-painting scientist who uses people's glands to retain his youth in *The Man in Half Moon Street* (1945 C); Julian Wilde (Cedric Hardwicke), the necrophiliac killer of young girls in *Lured* (1946 C), a bachelor accountant who wears glasses and looks creepy; hired killer's sidekick Julian (Robert Keith) explaining his distaste for women in *The Lineup* (1958 C): 'Crime's aggressive and so is the law. Women are not '; Julian Osborn (Fred Astaire), cynical scientist who commits suicide in a racing car in *On the Beach* (1959 C); sybaritic, friendly degenerate (all fountains, Mozart and chintz) Julian Kirk (John DALL) in PERRY MASON 'The Case of the Lonely Eloper' (1962 T); Julian Berniers (Dean Martin), an adorable failure who married a young girl for her money in *Toys in the Attic* (1963 C); Julian Wall (Karl Malden), arch-villain in *Murderer's Row* (1966 C); Julian Soshnick (Mike Kellin) in *The Boston Strangler* (1968 C); Julian, one of the LONESOME COWBOYS (1968 C) sleeping together in the sagebrush; Julian Thatcher (Troy Donahue) in *The Lonely Profession* (1969 T); aesthete Julian Hathaway (James Mitchell), a widowed English professor who's remarried in *Where the Heart Is* (1969–73).

Julian Branch (Louis Stadlen), the intellectual among the *Savages* (1972 C); Julian Kay (Richard Gere), the all-*American Gigolo* (1980 C) who doesn't 'do fags'; Julian Marty (Dan Hedaya), saloon owner, shot dead but refusing to lie down in *Blood Simple* (1983 C); Picasso-esque Julien (Stacey Keach in a bright orange wig), called either 'Julie-Ann' or 'Jewely-In' in *Mistral's Daughter* (1984 T); Lloyd Nolan as crusty millio-

naire Julian Tenley in *Murder She Wrote* 'Death in the Afternoon' (1985 T); Julian Salina (Brad DAVIS), an engineer drawn into his family's world of the Mafia in *Blood Ties* (1986 T): he knows his way around a kitchen (his mother walked out when he was a baby) and has a girlfriend called Nancy; Julian Shay (Willie Nelson), a nice preacher who becomes a homicidal maniac by the end of *Red-Headed Killer* (1987 C); Julian White (Vincent Price), a museum curator who killed his sister and is dispatched in turn by her woman friend in *The Offspring* (1987 C); Julian Wells (Robert Downey Jr), a rich kid crack addict who destroys his business, becomes a prostitute and is killed: a way out of a life that is *Less Than Zero* (1987 C); Julian (Edward Mulhare), mellifluous actor in *Murder She Wrote* 'Stage Struck' (1988 T); Julian Morrow, exquisite eccentric scholar who holds Dionysian rites in *The Secret History* (1993 C).

Julian aka Julian the Apostate (*c* 331–363) Roman emperor who, believing he was the reincarnation of ALEXANDER, ruled for only two years after attempting to bring back paganism following the death of Constantine the Great. In Henrik Ibsen's *Emperor and Galilean* (1991 R) Robert Glenister plays the man who tried to undo his uncle Constantine's work, maintaining that Christianity was effeminate and incompatible with stoicism and valour. He sought to embody a combination of the new religion with the joy of living found in the old. But Christianity was much more deeply rooted than he had thought.

Julian and Sandy Played by Kenneth WILLIAMS and Hugh PADDICK, they were former chorus boys now into anything that's going. Each week on ROUND THE HORNE, a Sunday afternoon radio gay mecca from March 1965, they would be enthusiastically promoting some new enterprise: BONA Drag, Rentachap, Bona Relations, Bona Tax Consultants, Body Bona. Their business acumen took them – and the usually nonplussed

Kenneth Horne – into catering, publishing, public relations, personal introductions, even a dude ranch ('we thought people like us should be more in the open').

Julian, who also used to be a masseur, is the more SENSITIVE and sincere, and is well bred ('a QUEEN's blood flows in his veins'). He is a sucker for lame ducks, giving a roof to Gordon, whom he met at the Slipper Baths. Shy and highly strung, he is often taken advantage of and has been involved in a number of 'misunderstandings' as when, playing football, he mistook a forward pass for something else. Or, in a steam room, with a jockey. Or getting badly stung by a Portuguese Man-of-War. Sandy seems to be the more dominant partner, though almost as generous: 'If you can't put out a hand to friends'.

For five years they minced tall, secure in the belief that it was they who were normal, the rest of the world decidedly QUEER. They weren't really suited to the 1960s any more than Mr Horne was: 'Kitchen sink isn't us, heartette. We're more yer drawing room comedy.'

(Frank Bough talked to Hugh Paddick and Kenneth Williams about their memories of Jule and Sand in *Round and Round the Horne* 1976 R; the two performers also appeared together on *Wogan* (1987 T), discussing the possibility of reviving the – now – very aged juveniles.)

Julien, Isaac (1960–) English filmmaker: *Gary's Diary* (1987); LOOKING FOR LANGSTON (1988 C); YOUNG SOUL REBELS; SATURDAY NIGHT OUT 'Some of My Best Friends' (1991 T); *Black and White in Colour* (black actors and actresses in British television from the 1930s to today, 1992 T); *The Attendant* (1992 C/T); *Daddy and the Muscle Academy* (commenting on Tom of Finland, 1992 C/T).

Juliet Bravo (UK 1980–5 T) Popular BBC1 series about a woman police inspector, Inspector Jean Darblay (Stephanie Turner) the model for whom was a married officer whose husband became the series' adviser. Anna Carteret took over, as Inspector Kate Longton from 1982.

'Kate Longton's power seems to be indicated by a lack of normal human emotions and an emphasis upon the office held ... Whenever she is shown to be wrong, it is because she has let her womanly emotions interfere with her judgement. And sexual riskiness is quite out of the question. Kate Longton is single, and this is obviously felt to be risky enough. Anna Carteret once suggested that she might be a lesbian, which was greeted by nervous laughter from the production team. The early evening slot and what is referred to as "the baked bean" audience were given as the reasons for the rather rigid moral boundaries of the series' (Gillian Skirrow, *Boxed In: Women and Television*, ed. Helen Baehr and Gillian Dyer, 1987).

June Is Bustin' Out All Over 'Fresh and alive and gay and young' is the tenor of Rodgers and Hammerstein's splendid number from *Carousel* (1956 C). The lyrics zestfully hymn fecundity and doing what comes naturally. A mob of SAILORS come ashore, but they show not one iota of interest in the orange-and-vermilion-skirted girls who try to attract their attention. The boys make an immediate bee-line for their suitors, the whalers. They strip off their shirts, tossing them indifferently to the females, and flex their tattooed muscles for the whalers' delectation. This inspires a trial of strength – a tug of war with a harpoon – which climaxes with the sailors being hurtled back into the brine.

The number that follows a while later – 'A Real Nice Clambake' – features two sailors with their arms round one another, and the climax has Billy (Gordon MacRae) walking off into the sunset with a man in a BOW TIE.

('June Is Bustin' Out All Over' fairly frequently accompanied orgasms in gay porno films of the late 1960s, according to writer Leigh W. Rutledge.)

Just Before Midnight (UK 1964–6 &

1978–80 R) Fifteen-minute tales to keep listeners awake between 11.45pm and midnight. Two had homosexual protagonists: 'Getting Ahead' (1979, a satanic hairdresser) and 'The Worm Will Turn'. In the latter the 'children' of Edith and Marion (Hermione Gregory and Amanda Murry) plot revenge on their neglectful, bickering parents. The quarrelling couple only just avoids ending up as a dog's dinner.
P: Glyn DEARMAN, Cherry Cookson, Christopher Nupen and others; BBC Radio 4.

Just Friends Michael (Kenneth Nelson) trills 'Just friends, lovers no more' to describe his arrangement with Donald (Frederick Coombs) in THE BOYS IN THE BAND (1970 C). This is the first line of a song recorded by Frank Sinatra in the 1940s and croaked by jazz trumpeter Chet Baker in the late 1950s.

just good friends The standard answer from hundreds of celebrities who were cheerfully (or not so cheerfully) committing ADULTERY or cohabiting. Of course, some (the gay/lesbian ones) were just that. It was already a huge joke in the 1950s and was a staple in THE GOON SHOW: Major BLOODNOK (Peter SELLERS) and the coal-mine voiced Gladys Throat (Ray Ellington) were j.g.f. ('The Man Who Never Was' 1956 R).
  Rob (Jeremy Bulloch) and Michael (Peter Denyer) in AGONY (1979–81 T) cohabitees for three years: 'Nice boys. Living together. Very modern. They're just good friends ... very modern.' 'Patroclus and I are just good friends – what are you insinuating?' (OPERATION LIGHTNING PEGASUS 1981 R). 'Are Phil and Matthew just good friends?' asks the BBC's publicity for TWO OF US in 1988. David NORRIS was not at all affronted by the suggestion that he and Irish president Mary Robinson had an affair in the past: 'We are just good friends,' he maintained crisply in *Late Night with Steve Vizard* (Aust 1991).

The grotesquely tasteful Whispering Glade Memorial Park in *The Loved One* (1965 C) has a special area, decorated with male Greek statuary, 'for lovers who were very close'. In Harold PINTER's THE COLLECTION, Harry (Griffith Jones 1961 T; Laurence Olivier 1976 T) allows that he and Bill (John Ronane; Malcolm McDowell) have been 'close friends' for years.

Justify My Love MTV banned this in 1990 because of 'mild sado-masochism and bisexuality'. MADONNA had included an erotic scene involving herself and a woman in male attire. At the end of her 1987 video *It's a Fools Game* she walks off with a black woman singer.

just obeying orders The centuries-old excuse for systematic torture, imprisonment and killing. Germany is seen as the well-spring of this mentality: discussed (in relation to the New Germany and anti-Communist feeling) in HEART OF THE MATTER 'Just Obeying Orders' (1992 T).

Just Sex (UK 1984 C) Seven men and seven women, aged from 24 to 84, kick around ideas on aspects of sexuality: one gay man and one lesbian are represented. One edition was entitled 'What Is Normal?': 'A look at how far we are bound by ideas of normality and how attitudes to homosexuals and lesbians have changed.'
P: Veronyka Bodnaice; D: Gina Newson; Channel 4; 40 mins.
  One of the best 'sex' series, mainly because of the way films, newsreel footage, clips from TV programmes, and blow-ups of magazine and newspaper headlines were incorporated into the discussion. Bob [Robert] Workman, former photographer for GAY NEWS, and Femi Otitoju, then with GAY SWITCHBOARD, were the representatives of the margin, showing that heterosexuals don't have an armlock on virtue or morals or ethics. For a change, the queers

were given some (not enough) time to comment on seemingly non-homosexual issues. Like MARRIAGE: 'Who's saying we *should* get married? It's the Church, it's the professions, it's people like social security ... it's the politicians, it's the state.'

Kaleidoscope (UK 1970s– R) Monday–Friday arts programme of reviews, interviews and features with increasingly relaxed gay (and even a trace of lesbian) input. Of the scores of relevant pieces, some highlights:

'An Inner Life' (1985). A rare interview with Rosamund LEHMANN.
'Charleston Revisited' (1986). A visit to the recently restored home of the BLOOMSBURY GROUP with Quentin Bell.
'Famous for 15 Minutes' (1987). How profound was Andy WARHOL's art and how great was his influence. And will he last?
'*Tumtitititumtitititumtum*' (1987). Musicians, impresarios and RAVEL himself comment on the BOLERO which has been a hit since it was first performed in 1928.
Sir Ian MCKELLEN on the success of the Stonewall Group in watering down Clause 25 (Section 31 of the Criminal Justice Act 1991) and on the importance of individual morality 'rather than the prevailing truth that surrounds you' (1991).

Kamikaze Hearts (US 1987 C) Sharon 'Mitch' Mitchell, actress in 199 X-rated films, exercises her hypnotic, destructive charm on assistant film director Tigr, who, perhaps too late, realizes that she is in love with a hollow shell.
W: Juliet Bashore, Tigr Mennett and John Khoor; P: Hein Legler, Bob Rivkin and Sharon Hennessey; D: Juliet Bashore; 77 mins.
A very unusual love story about two women who make films, are involved in live entertainment and need a lot of stimulation. They also lie a lot – especially to themselves. *The Dolly Sisters* this ain't. The boundaries between performing and being are continually – and disturbingly – crossed by the couple, who wanted the film to be called 'Truth or Fiction?'

Katharine / Katherine / Catharine / Catherine Girl's name and one of the most widely used 'heroine' names of the past 30 years (Cathy GALE etc), although its use in romantic fiction probably stems from Catherine Earnshaw in *Wuthering Heights*. The lesbian Kate/Cath contingent is relatively small but not insignificant: career-oriented Sydney journalist Kate Hannaford (Gabrielle Hartley) who provides former swimmer Dawn Fraser with an intimate experience in DAWN! (1979 C); swaggering explorer-model Kate Bedford (Cathee Shirriff) in *She's Dressed to Kill* (1979 T); suddenly widowed Kate (Liv Ullman) finding herself, with equal suddenness, in an affair with his mistress in RICHARD'S THINGS (1981 C/T); unhappy TEACHER Kate (Janet Dale) in WHALE MUSIC (1983 T) smitten with a pregnant woman, but saddled with a pupil girlfriend she doesn't love; Kath Maxwell (Kate Hook) in PRISONER (1984 T); Catherine (Elizabeth Ryder), unsatisfied SOCIAL WORKER partner of introverted Gisela in SILENT WING (1984 T); Cay (ie Cathryn Ann) Rivvers (Patricia Charbonneau) in DESERT HEARTS (1985 C); Ethna Roddy as unhappy TEACHER Kate, caught up in her lover's custody battle in SOUTH OF THE BORDER (1990 T); Lindsay Crouse as unhappy POLICEWOMAN Kathryn McBride, accused of molesting woman suspects in *Hill Street Blues* 'Look Homeward, Ninja' (1987 T); Catherine (Bridget Forsyth) whose great love in *Variations on the Snow Queen* (1980 R) is a female school friend; Katy (Tania Rodrigues) in ORANGES ARE NOT THE ONLY FRUIT (1990 T), the converted Pentecostal who gives love to Jess; Catherine Tramell (Sharon Stone) in *Basic Instinct* (1992 C), arrogant, knickerless novelist using sex to get what she wants, exploiter of men, bedder of women, possibly a serial killer.
Other ragingly popular names over the past three decades to denote 'nice' or 'naughty but nice' 'girls' are Ann/Anne/Annie; Barbara; Claire/Clare; Connie; DIANA/DIANE; Ellen; Elisabeth/Elizabeth/Lisa/Liz; Emma; Jane; Jean; Jennifer/Jennie/Jenny; Joan/Joanna/Joanne; Julia/Julie; Laura; MAGGIE; Maria/Mary; Rosie; RUTH; Sally; Samantha; Sarah; Tracey/Tracy. Interestingly enough, all these are first names that are never or almost never bestowed on lesbian characters.

Katin, Peter [Roy Katin] (1930–)
English pianist, a vice president of CHE
in the 1970s. *Henry Wood Birthday
Concert* (1953 T); *Variety Playhouse*
(1958 R); Rhapsody on Theme of Paga-
nini, Op. 43 by Rachmaninov (1958 T);
Bach Chromatic Fantasias, Brahms
Seven Fantasias, Liszt Vallée d'Ober-
mann (1986 R); Bach Charismatic
Fugue and 7 Fantasias (1987 R); Bach,
Brahms and Liszt (1987 R); played
Georges Delerue's final score, for
Memento Mori (1992 T). DESERT ISLAND
DISCS (1956 R); SPEAKING FOR OUR-
SELVES (1974 T), talking about the
negative – and positive – effects on his
career of being publicly identified with
homosexual rights.

Kaye, Danny [David Daniel Kaminsky]
(1913–87) American actor, singer and
entertainer who revelled in pantomime,
tongue-twisting lyrics, surrealism, duality and split personalities (he often
played twins or doubles), and sentimentality. At his best: mad and intense; at
his worst: blurry and sickly.

Began in two-reelers during the 1930s
before playing the swishy Russell on
Broadway in *Lady in the Dark*. Became a
big star with *Up in Arms* (1944) and
Wonder Man, but is best known for Hans
Christian ANDERSEN (1952) and *The
Court Jester* (1955). *The Secret Life of
Danny Kaye*, the 1955 documentary also
known as *Assignment Children*, was *not*
about Kaye's secret life but his work for
UNICEF. However, a more truthful
portrait emerged in *The Secret Life of
Danny Kaye* (1993 R).

T: *Danny Kaye* (variety special, with
Louis Armstrong); *The Danny Kaye
Show* (1963–7); guest on *The Judy Gar-
land Show* (1963); *Peter Pan* (1976);
Skokie (1981, as a Jew trying to prevent
an American Nazi march); *The Cosby
Show*: 'The Dentist' (1985).

Kaye, Gorden (1941–) English actor,
world famous for his role as randy café
owner René in 'ALLO, 'ALLO (1984–92
T). Also: railway guard in *Champion
House* 'Go West, Young Man' (1968 T,
as Gordon Kaye); Mervyn in *Villains*

'Sand Dancer' (1972); camp TELEVISION
DIRECTOR in ARE YOU BEING SERVED?
'Closed Circuit' (1980); Frank Broad-
hurst in *Codename Icarus* (1981 T); Fat
Henry in THE GENTLE TOUCH 'Finders
Keepers' (1984 T); Buff in *The Secret
State* (1985 T); pen pusher in *Brazil*
(1985 C); Halls and Hills' Christmas
Day programme (1991 T); DESERT
ISLAND DISCS (1991 R); Bernard in *For
Better or for Worse* (1993 R); etc.

Kearns, Michael (195?–) American
supporting actor in *Body Double*; *The
Kentucky Fried Movie*; *Murder She Wrote*;
Cheers; etc. He has played a number of
gay roles, eg *The Making of a Male Model*
(1983 T). He came out as HIV positive
in the week following Brad DAVIS's
death in September 1991. He plays a
dying immuno-suppressed man in *Life
Goes On* (1992 T) and also appears in
AND THE BAND PLAYED ON (1993 T).

Kellaway, Alec (1894–1973) South
African-born Australian-based actor,
son of actor Bryan Kellaway and brother
of Cecil. Beloved for his characterization of the flamboyant Cedric ENT-
WHISTLE in two 'Dad and Dave' comedies. Début as a conjurer in *Let George
Do It* (1938); DAD AND DAVE COME TO
TOWN (1938); a punch-drunk boxer in
Gone to the Dogs (1939); *Ants in His Pants*
(1939); *Dad Rudd MP* (1940); *Smithy*
(1946).

kemo sabe Tonto's name for THE LONE
RANGER: 'faithful friend' (or longtime
companion?).

Kennedy's Children (UK 1978 R) A
series of alternating monologues of five
'rejects, nomads, rebels, exiles and outsiders'. They comprise Wanda, a
middle-aged woman (Elaine Stritch);
Mark, a Vietnam veteran (James
Aubrey); Rona, a political activist
(Heather Pullen); Carla (Sandra Dickinson), an actress; an ALCOHOLIC actor
named Sparger (Michael Deacon).
Sparger's lover, owner of an off off-
Broadway theatre, has committed SUI-
CIDE.

W: Robert Patrick; D: Glyn DEARMAN; BBC Radio 3; 60 mins.

The first (and almost only) piece of semi-current gay theatre to be given houseroom by the BBC – radio or television. Bitter and sarcastic, Sparger exemplifies a certain type of New York gay attitude of the mid-1970s.

Kenneth/Ken/Kenny Boy's name: Kenneth and Kenny regularly associated with infantilized, inadequate adults. Sir Kenneth honest and true (and pretty) blond hero of Sir Walter Scott's *The Talisman* (Laurence Harvey *King Richard and the Crusaders* 1954 C; Patrick Ryecart 1980 T); confirmed bachelor and drugs mastermind Kenny in *My Friend Charles* (Francis Matthews 1956 T; Derek Farr 1957 C); Ken Barlow (William Roache), resident intellectual in CORONATION STREET (1960– T); Kenny (Tony Beckley) in *The Fiend*; Ken HASTINGS (Michael Howarth), trendy nursing tutor in ANGELS (1979–80 T); Ken (Mark Kingston), harassed father of a gay and a punk in *Time of My Life* (1980 T); Edna EVERAGE's son who lives with Cliff; Ken (Gary Waldhorn), the director in *The Big March* (1984 R); Ken Masters (Stephen Yardley), unscrupulous semi-villain in HOWARDS' WAY (1985–90 T); Kenny (Andrew Livingstone) who lives with his mother and has never had a girlfriend, the funniest and most dangerous of the lads in *The Ritz* (1987 T); Ken Rayner (Ian Redford) in EASTENDERS (1991 T) threatening Disa's baby; Ken Stiley (Dorian Healy) in YOUNG SOUL REBELS (1991 C), closeted killer of young gay men.

The most famous American Ken is Barbie (Doll)'s boyfriend: 'her first and only love, the man of her dreams ... a bit of a nerd ... a passive male.' No genitals these past 30 years (though a 'bump' was added later) and no marriage to Barbie either. Other US examples: Kenneth Downey (Gary Cooper) rejecting boy-meets-girl for life with day-dreaming, smothering old spinster in *Seven Days Leave* (1930 C); Kenneth Bradley (Lee Bowman) who 'keeps' Terry (a woman) in *Love Affair* (1939

C); Ken (Marlon Brando) trying to come to terms with his paraplegia – and his impotence – in *The Men* (1950 C); Ken Jorgensen (Richard Egan), long-term monogamous adulterer in *A Summer Place* (1959 C); Kenny Baird (Richard Beymer), sensitive, mother-beset boy enthralled by *The Stripper/Woman of Summer* (1962 C); Kenneth Otis (Robert Fields) in *The Incident* (1967 C); Ken Scott (John Davidson) controlled by his 'female' side in THE STREETS OF SAN FRANCISCO 'Mask of Death' (1974 T); Ken Reeves (Ken Howard), basketball coach hero in *The White Shadow* (1978–81 T); quadraplegic Ken Harrison (Richard Dreyfuss) in *Whose Life Is It Anyway?* (1980 C); Kenny (Michael Pritchard) in *Taxi* (1980 T); Ken (Charlie Sheen) in *Silence of the Heart* (1984 T), warm-hearted (reads to disabled black kids) but uncomprehending of his friend's suicidal feelings; Kenny (James Houghton) in *Knots Landing* (1986 T); maniac (Billy Zane) in *The Hillside Stranglers* (1987 T); Ken (Bernie Coulson), a pretty boy (whose student yearbook reveals an interest in 'basketball and ballet') who takes no part in Jodie FOSTER's rape in *The Accused* (1987) nor in its encouragement, phones the police and puts truth before friendship with one of the attackers; Kenny, one of nerdish twin drug dealers (the other one is called Kevin) who is killed by Johnny in *Meet the Applegates* (Philip Arthur Ross and Steven Robert Ross 1991 C).

kept man Joe Gillis (William Holden by Gloria Swanson) in *Sunset Boulevard* (1950 C); Chad (Robert Wagner by Pearl Bailey) in *All the Fine Young Cannibals* (1960 C); Paul (George Peppard by Patricia Neal) in *Breakfast at Tiffany's* (1961 C); Hermione GINGOLD's overtly gay bit of fluff (Sandor Eles) in *The Naked Edge* (1961 C); squirmy Marcel Dalio, Gladys Cooper's consort in *The List of Adrian Messenger* (1963 C); Jeff Le Vane (Paul Carr) in cahoots with lefties who kill him after he has stolen paintings from his lover to finance their activities in *The Rockford Files* 'The Empty Frame' (1978 T).

Kerouac, Jack (1922–69) American novelist, one of the heralds and exemplars of the beat generation with novels like *On the Road* (1957) and *Dharma Bums* (1958). His love for Neal Cassady was palely intimated in *Heart Beat* (1979 C). *Poetry from the Beat Generation* (1960 R); REBELS (1987 R); *Arena* 'What Happened to Kerouac?' (1987 T).

Kevin Boy's name which was very popular in Britain during the 1960s and which has, for some time, been the object of derision, eg Russell HARTY correlating Kevin with train spotting in 1988. Some Kevins fought back: 'Kevin jibes are now endemic in England (nowhere else) ... Why does the BBC alienate a section of the population on so random a basis?' asked Kevin Johnston in *Radio Times* (30.4.88) about this 'most peculiar trait'.

Kevin Topple set up the Society for the Advancement of Kevin because he felt Kevins suffered from discrimination and were presented as gormless, with girlfriends called Tracey or Sharon (eg Kevin played by Bernard PADDEN in the Tefal television adverts). 1991 was named the Year of the Kevin.

At the same time as Kevin was being appropriated by stupid or unprepossessing characters in Britain, the name became increasingly macho in America, especially after the rise of actor Kevins (Bacon, Costner, Kline etc) and is becoming popular in France.

'Pushing a pram is a *girl's* job,' Robert Scroggins as British television's first Kevin who becomes involved with a fairy at the bottom of his garden in *Pots of Money* (1955).

'The perfect picture of the homosexual – asthma, bitten nails and constipation – has been a Catholic and a Buddhist ... He won't change. He's a common type of mother-dominated homosexual,' psychiatrist about Kevin Zolotov (Clive Merrison) in LOVESICK (1967 R).

'I'm not chic and I'm not gay,' Kevin

(Andrew McCarthy) in *St Elmo's Fire* (1985 C).

Key West One of the Florida Keys, popular with gay men from the 1950s, most famously Tennessee WILLIAMS. In DYNASTY 'Parental Consent' (1985 T) Luke suggests that he and Steven fly there 'to do a little deep sea fishing'. *Entertainment USA* (1985 T) has 'Jonathan King at America's most bizarre resort, where gays, HIPPIES and free-thinking Americans indulge in outrageous carnivals and tourists cast off their inhibitions'.

Khush (UK 1991 T) Khush is the name used by South Asian and Indian lesbians and gays.
D: Pratibha Parmar; 24 mins.
'As an ASIAN lesbian filmmaker, it is crucial to me that the joy, desire and passion embodied in our lives through music, dance, images and political action are represented in all their unexplored contradictions and exciting wholeness and mysterious and erotic fantasy.'

Kids 'Michael and Liam' (UK 1979 T) Liam (Jason Kemp) ran away from his home in Liverpool when he was 10 years old, met a man and ended up on a soliciting charge a few years later. Is Liam in moral danger, or is he a danger himself to the other young people at Kingston House? Should he be allowed to develop a close friendship with Michael (Paul Easom), a melancholy 14-year-old who has attempted suicide because of increasing tension with his model middle-class adopted parents? The open-minded superintendent believes that Liam is probably a good deal better defined as a person than many other people of his age and, from the way they react, than some of the Kingston House staff as well.
W: William Corlett; 25.5.79; Thames; 60 mins.

The story's strengths lay in the manner in which the irrational and anti-gay attitudes of both young and old, liberal and illiberal, were aired and sharply elaborated. It was ground-breaking in its characterization of a young gay man, wearing an EARRING and mooning around in bondage trousers, punk shirt and mohair sweater tied provocatively around his shoulders: 'I've got a different style.'

Kiki Slang for lesbian from the 1930s to the early 1960s. Norma Talmadge as a pure girl with uncouth manners and a vicious tongue *Kiki* (1926 C; Mary Pickford in 1932 remake); Kiki Walker (Jean Brooks), a singer in *The Leopard Man* (1943 C); 'bad girl' Kiki Kelly (Binnie Barnes) in *The Dude Goes West* (1948 C); CiCi (Betty Lou Gerson), a film star's tough right-hand woman and possible lover in THE TWILIGHT ZONE 'Ring-a-Ding Girl' (1963 T); Kiki (Margaret Kirkbridge), a WASP with kids in *Condo* (1983 T); Kiki Kavanaugh (Alexa Keninin) in *Princess Daisy* (1983 T).

The Killing Of Georgie Said to be the first 'radical' gay-themed record played on television's TOP OF THE POPS (2.9.77). It's a sad tale of a boy from a small town coming to the city, where he leads the gay life and is bashed to death: just another statistic. Words and music by Rod Stewart. Played in *Rod the Mod Comes of Age* (1976 T), but the gay section was faded out.

The Killing of Sister George (US 1968 C; UK 1978 R) 'Sister George' is a much loved character in a long-running radio serial. When the show starts losing its audience, the producers decide on drastic measures. Professional and personal tensions in the life of the heavy drinking 'butch' lesbian who plays sweet, understanding Sister George surface and culminate in the loss of her job and her girlfriend leaving her for a lady from the BBC.
W: Otto Heller from the play by Frank Marcus; P/D: Robert Aldrich; 138 mins.
W: adapted by Barry Campbell; D: Gordon House; 14.12.78; BBC World Service and Radio 4; 60 mins.

The word lesbian wasn't mentioned in the original stage version. Its absence saved it from being banned or cut by the Lord Chamberlain. Passed unmolested, it was a smash hit in London and on Broadway, and played all over the world, notably with Maria Becker in Zurich. There were 40 different productions in Germany alone. It flopped only in Greece because 'In Greece, lesbianism is not yet a problem'. The playwright's wife, Jackie Marcus told GAY NEWS (1982) that 'on that night in 1965, for the first time, the British public saw two women, lovers, friends, enemies, human beings who needed no explanation and for whom no apology was made'.

'In *Sister George*, cinema has now reached a stage where it loses its self-consciousness of the fact that it is about lesbians; accepts it unquestionably, and proceeds to tell a straight story within these limits. There is no beating about the bush, no tactful innuendos ... these women do have sex with each other and what's more we see them having it. For far too long we have been expected to pick up the minutest of hints, heavily disguised at that, and to act on these in our own mind to unravel the plot where the censor forbade the narrative to do so. No longer need it be so' (Christine Smith, *Films and Filming*, April 1969).

'The representations of lesbians were really negative and unattractive and I was quite alarmed by it' (Speaker on OUT 'We've Been Framed' 1991 T).

'It is a flawed, creaky and perfunctory piece ... all architecture and no bricks and mortar ... not a comedy, albeit there are some funny lines. Nor is it serious drama – his characters don't have the necessary dimension and complexity ... He sets up a lesbian relationship ... and then retreats' (Pamela Payne reviewing a recent stage version in the *Sydney Morning Herald*, 8.10.91).

Much that was atmospheric and touching in the original play was bloated and leering by the time it reached the screen. This broad, coarse approach affected the central performance, now closer to music hall than to tragicomedy, not helped by an uneasy Susannah YORK as

CHILDIE. The film improves in its last third, thanks to the visit to the GATE-WAYS Club and Sister George's growing panic as she approaches her 'death'. History will thank Aldrich for the 10 minutes in the club if for nothing else: they grandly capture the spirit of an era. The change of viewpoint when Mercy Croft enters is ambiguous enough not to destroy the sense of women tightly packed together, free and easy with each other for a few precious hours.

The radio version (made for the World Service) had a splendid Sister George in Sheila Hancock: public school, a bit actressy, always nervous but with bright warmth and intelligence breaking through the bluster. Anna Calder-Marshall seemed stumped by Childie and Eleanor Bron was a muted Mercy, though more believable as a seemingly harmless bureaucrat in the first scene than Coral Browne (who could never be totally declawed). This production's chief disadvantage was its running time – one hour – forcing the players to gallop.

Nearly 30 years on, *The Killing of Sister George* is still performed all over the world – the only CROSSOVER lesbian play (though the word is never mentioned). To its eternal credit, *George* presents a woman of some light as well as darkness, beset with universal problems and fears – apparently based on the original Mrs DALE, Ellis POWELL ('Luggie'), with whom the author lived as a lodger for some time. Sister George is a remarkably durable creation: fearless, socially inept, fun-loving – a bit of a 'lad', lonely, proud.

Killing Time (UK 1990 T) 'Martin (Pip Donnaghay) lives alone in a cheap North London flat. He works for the DHSS, is active in gay rights. It's a long time since anyone loved him. Harry is 17, living on his wits and sleeping rough. He carries a knife. Martin invites him to stay. The boy becomes increasingly violent ... but Martin can't let go' (producer's synopsis).
W: Kevin ELYOT; D: David Attwood; P: Hilary Salmon; 9.8.90; BBC2; 75 mins.

Claustrophobic, sensitive piece which is relentlessly downbeat and chafed by a sense of not knowing whether to be a love story or a macabre melodrama. The last image, accompanied by 'WILL YOU STILL LOVE ME TOMORROW?', is indelible. 'A stunning exercise in grand Guignol, a brilliant study of the banality of evil' (Lewis Jones, *Daily Telegraph*, 10.8.90).

kilts Tony Hancock, desperate to find a wife so he can claim an inheritance, approaches someone in a tartan skirt at a *palais de dance* (HANCOCK'S HALF HOUR 1955 R). After a bit of conversation, he returns to Sid. Hancock intimates that everything would have been fine but for one thing: 'he's got a wife in Glasgow.' Nervous billows of laughter from the studio audience, but neither Tony nor Sid seem to think there was anything wrong. The man in the 'tartan skirt' was very nice; the wife in Glasgow was the stumbling block, not his gender!

Lady Caroline (Amanda Hillward), warped and cynical, dressed in full male evening rig, dances with a Scotsman in a kilt (John Sessions) in the last episode of *Tender Is the Night* (1985 T). Another turnabout using trousers and kilt occurred in *L'Armée dans les Ombres/The Army in the Shadows* (1969 C) where what seem to be the legs of a man and a woman are revealed, as the camera moves up, to be the reverse.

In *The Hasty Heart* (1949 C; 1961 T) the uptight young Scottish soldier's fellow military-hospital patients are fascinated when he appears in full Scots army uniform, complete with bagpipes and kilt. They can't wait to find out if it's true:

> Yank: 'It's indecent to be that drafty.'
> Tommy: 'Let's see if he wears anything underneath.'

One of them looks, but refuses to tell.

Kimber, Bobbie (Robert Kimberley) (1918–?) English ventriloquist and FEMALE IMPERSONATOR: the first to appear in a Royal Variety Command Performance (1947) and the first (and only?) to find a niche as a children's favourite. He had an extensive stage career – as a pantomime dame, in support of Danny KAYE at the London Palladium in 1949, with Harry GORDON in Glasgow 1952 etc.

R: *Up and Coming; Variety Bandbox* (1950); *Henry Hall's Guest Night* (1952–3); *Christmas Party* (1952); *Having a Wonderful Time* (1954).

Apart from one performance in 1939, he made his television début in *Music Hall* (from West Bromwich) which resulted in, according to the producer Richard Afton, 'literally thousands of phone calls and letters asking to know if Kimber was a man or a woman'.

His plump face, plucked eyebrows, pageboy hairstyle, dangling earrings, deep voice, warm personality and inventive guises (Brownie leader, fortune teller) made him and his dummy Augustus Peabody very popular, mainly on children's television, until the late 1950s when he opened a pub with his wife in Kentish Town, London: *Children's Variety* (1953); *Sugar and Spice* (1953–4, 'Augustus' as compère); *Nat's in the Belfry* (1956); *TV Caravan* (1956–7); *Children's Playtime* (1956); *The Eamonn Andrews Show* (1957, 'Augustus' taking over as compère); *Two's Company* (1959). For every show, he would supply detailed synopses, drawings and camera positions. Richard Afton called him 'a frustrated director'.

Retired, he made a special appearance in 'Cavalcade of Drag' at the Horseshoe Hotel in Tottenham Court Road, London in April 1969.

Kinesis Films Groundbreaking British independent company set up in the late 1970s by Paul Oremland and others to make television programmes for and about gays *and* lesbians from a non-problematic, non-sexist angle. After a controversial start with ONE IN FIVE (1983), the company went on to win praise for IF THEY'D ASKED FOR A LION-TAMER (1984); SIX OF HEARTS (1986), 'DOCTOR MARTENS' (*10×10* 1991), and the paean to disco music *The Rhythm Divine* (1991). Usually directed or co-

directed by Paul Oremland; produced by Sophie Balhetchet, Caroline Mylon etc.

King, Billie Jean (1943–) American tennis player. Wimbledon women's champion during the late 1960s and early 1970s whose private life with Marilyn Barnett was the subject of much media interest in the early 1980s. MAN ALIVE 'Billie Jean King' (1969 T): 'I hate to lose'; *Platform* (1983); *Maestro* (1987 T; Barry Davies 'talks to the woman who helped bring social change to Wimbledon'); etc.

King, Francis (1923–) English novelist, short story writer and critic: cool and lucid.

R: *A Corner of a Foreign Field* (1969); *Murder International* 'Mess' (1976); *Aspects of the Novelist* (1979); *Bookshelf* 'L. P. HARTLEY' (1980); BOOK AT BEDTIME 'Voices in an Empty Room' (1985).

T: *All for Love* 'To the Camp and Back' (1984).

King, Hetty (1883–1972) Billed in *Radio Times* as the world's greatest male impersonator (*Vaudeville* 1930); guardsman, fop, sailor, drunk and popularizer of 'All The Nice Girls Love A Sailor'. A radio regular throughout the 1930s. Also: PANORAMA (1954 T): a celebration of the Coliseum Theatre; *Lilacs in the Spring* (1955 C); *Farson's Guide to the British* 'Popularity' (1962 T); Royal Command Variety Performance (1964 T). A documentary *Hetty King – Performer* appeared a few years before her death at 89: 'I don't like knitting. I don't like sitting at home.'

Jason **King** A famous crime writer turned investigator: a character in *Department S* (1970 T) and *Jason King* (1971) played by Peter WYNGARDE (in full hot-house style: droopy moustache, long hair, flowery shirts, tight-bummed flairs). He was very popular for a while (especially with middle-aged female viewers), and an Australian series called *Catwalk* (1972) introduced a similar character called Saxon Welles.

kinky In the early 1960s it was regarded as the height of daring after Cathy GALE (Honor Blackman) in *The Avengers* introduced her judo-enabling all-leather gear, including boots. The kinky fashion look was heavily promoted, and very popular in the particularly dire winter of 1962–3 in Britain. A record, 'Kinky Boots' was released (re-released in 1990) and a pop group called The Kinks, led by Ray Davies, was formed. There was a character called Kinky (Iain Gregory) in *The Yellow Teddy Bears* (1963 C), and 'Kinks' was a gayish burglar threatening Flora Robson in *The Brighton Belle* 'In for the Night' (1966 T).

A singer (not Ray Davies) asked all the 'kinky' members of a TOP OF THE POPS audience (aged 13–14) to come to the front. That was 1968, probably the last year when the so-called permissive society could be said to have existed. The word continued in many homes and work-places to denote something unknown, terribly naughty but essentially safe. If somebody were to say or suggest anything remotely out of the ordinary they would be called a 'Kinky devil!' 'It takes me back 20 or 30 years,' a *Listener* journalist remarked in 1986.

But it lingers on ... in Australia. In EMERALD CITY (1990 C) producer J. T. Walsh (Max Cullen) changes characters in a script from two men and one woman to two women and one man because he is 'kinky for lesbians'. The male presenter of *Lunchtime* on ABC FM (1992) said: 'Vinyl is so sensual. I used to love taking the record out of the sleeve. Sounds kinky but it's not meant to be. I'm a very well-balanced person. (I can hear someone laughing in the background.)'

The Kinsey Report Dr Alfred Kinsey (1894–1956) conducted extensive studies of human sexual behaviour at the Institute for Sex Research of the University of Indiana. These studies were published as *Sexual Behavior in the Human Male* (1948, the so-called 'Kinsey Report') and *Sexual Behavior in the Human Female* (1953). There was also a specific study on homosexuality in 1978.

Kinsey, a biologist, concurred with FREUD that all human beings have the capacity to respond to either sex erotically. But they are constrained by social circumstances from so doing and generally limit themselves to one partner. Kinsey believed, as did COLETTE: 'The only unnatural sex act is that which you cannot perform' (quoted by Alistair Cooke on a LETTER FROM AMERICA 1988 R about the Bush–Dukakis election campaign).

The basic findings were that there is a sliding scale of sexual attraction from 0 to 6. Most people hover somewhere between liking men and liking women. (This concept was mentioned by the two bed partners in TOGETHER ALONE 1991 C.)

Some of the original and later research was the subject of HORIZON 'Sex and Sexuality' (1970 T) but, to date, no documentary, film or play has paid tribute to the intelligent, painstaking work of Kinsey and his team – outside of sensational cuttings like *The Chapman Report* (1962 C, not a whit interested in the sliding scale) or recent American talk shows where the findings are denigrated.

Kinugasa, Teinosuke (1896–1982) Japanese film director. A FEMALE IMPERSONATOR early in his career, he became a director in 1922 when actresses were finally allowed to play women's roles on the screen. He made 40 silent films including the intense and avant-garde *A Page of Madness/Crossways* (1928). He studied with EISENSTEIN in the USSR for two years. After the Second World War he made *Joyu/Actress* (1947); *Gate of Hell* (1953); *The White Heron* (1958); *The Little Runaway* (1967); *Before Dawn*; *Two Stone Lanterns*; *The Summer Battle of the Osaka*; *Lord for a Night*; *Symphony of Love*; etc.

Captain James Kirk (William Shatner in STAR TREK 1966–68 and 1980–   ) Commander of the star ship Enterprise. Very square-jawed but, it has been suggested, with a soft spot for Mr Spock (Leonard Nimoy), especially when the characters began their big screen career in the 1980s.

Kirker, Rev. Richard (194?-) One of the founders of the GAY CHRISTIAN MOVEMENT in Britain. Many radio and television appearances: *A Question of Faith* (Capital Radio 1979); *Day to Day* (1987 T); HEART OF THE MATTER (1992 T); etc.

Kirkup, James (1918–) English poet, the author of 'The Love That Dares to Speak Its Name' which was the subject of the GAY NEWS BLASPHEMY case in 1977.
R: *Homage to Vaslav* NIJINSKY (1950); *A Company of Fools* (1952), from his first collection *The Submerged Valley*; *A Poem on the Coronation of HM Elizabeth II* (1953, also T), declaimed at the Coronation; *The Observatory: An Adventure in Space* (1955); *Night Waves* (1992, his first reading on radio after a silence of 40 years). Also *Ritual Suicide*: 3 talks (1993 R).
T: *The Mistery of the Passion* (1960 T, adaptation).

His poems were regularly published in the *Listener* from 1949 to 1965: 'Human and Divine Love' (1949); 'Narcissus' (1949); 'The Poet and His Lice' (1952); 'The Secret Agent' (1953); 'The Dustbin' (1954); 'The Kitchen Sink' (1955): '... longed to speak, to tell them/What perhaps they knew'; 'Fever' (1960); 'The Old Trousers' (1965).

Georgina **Kirrin** aka George. Quintessential TOMBOY in THE FAMOUS FIVE.

> 'Not scared are you?'
> 'Course not.'

A scientist's daughter, dreamy, but as thirsty for adventure as her boy COUSINS and thought of as rather 'QUEER' by them, especially by 'girly' Anne. Played by Michelle Gallagher in the 1978 television series as dreamy but spunky, in love only with her dog Timmy. This fairly normal image was punctured by

Dawn French in the two COMIC STRIP PRESENTS ... spoofs: an irritatingly sporty, into everything, gawky girl who is called a DYKE to her face.

Enid Blyton claimed that she based George upon herself as a teenager. A similar character, Tik Scaliotis (Rebekah Elmaloglou), appeared as one of five friends on a remote Greek island in *Adventure on Kythera* (1991 T). As with the Famous Five, they form a secret gang and pledge never-ending allegiance.

Kiss and Tell (UK 1980 T) Young businessman sleeps with a young woman, Janey (Sarah Keller) in Paris, discovers she has an older woman lover, Maggie (Sally Willis) – who had first seduced *him* a decade and a half before – and, when he returns to Britain, learns that he has NSU.

W: Jeremy Kingston; P: Juliet Grimm and John BOWEN; D: Gareth Davies; 5.8.80; Thames; 60 mins.

Whatever the writer may have intended, the core of this play is: 'Don't sleep with a "girl" who sleeps with a woman (even if that woman is the one who first introduced *you* to sex). If you do, you will catch something very nasty between the legs and have a lot of explaining to do when you get home to the wife.'

This was *The Killing of Sister George* country: an expatriate BULLDYKE who arrives home from a hard day's work to find her girl in near *flagrante delicto* with a man. The actress has barely 30 seconds to convey exactly what (not who) she is before the adverts announce the end of the first half. Wardrobe comes to her aid: HAIR severely abbreviated, wearing a bulldog expression, a white polo-neck sweater, shapeless tweeds, and brogues. Taking in the scene, she slaps her girl's face and delivers her one and only piece of dialogue ('Whore!'). Then it's into adverts for family-sized products.

'A light, generous play, with its finger on the pulse of decent people coming to terms with the discoveries and disappointments of their lives' (Herbert Kretzmer, *Daily Mail*).

'... the nastiness is actually in the writing's attitude to a lesbian relationship. Through innuendo it manages to suggest that gay sex is distasteful, rather sad, certainly inferior and really only a desperate refuge for ageing and spurned heterosexuals' (John Wyver, *Time Out*).

Jeremy Kingston, the writer, told GAY NEWS that he had created in his mind detailed backgrounds for both women:

Initially the reason [for making the women lesbian] was structural. [Colin] goes to Paris to find his girl from long ago. He hears her voice on the other side of the door but, lo and behold, it isn't her but another girl ... Why had this girl gone with him? She's not sleeping with him strictly for pleasure, but getting her own back at a rather dominant character who she's not especially happy with ...

I know a number of girls who have, for some reason, wanted to have boys. They either find chaps who were gay or who are about to leave for South America. They then become interested in having girlfriends. There she is out in Paris and she cradle-snatches this chap; when he was 17. She may have left resonant pools of experience in this young man, but she remains unsatisfied until she meets this girl ...

There was a certain amount of discussion about whether Maggie should say anything at all or whether she should enter and stand in the doorway and stare, and slap the young man's face and not say anything at all.

I'd like to write another play about Janey. She's out there for one reason or another – just for the moment, convenience – the chance of a flat with this woman, who she perhaps works for.

No '*Kiss and Tell II*' was forthcoming. (The play was transmitted immediately after an episode of the Thames comedy *Robin's Nest*, in which Tony Britton says of his wife: 'She had a very strong masculine streak. I used to call her Wonder Woman. I used to wonder if she was a woman or not.')

kisses/kissing Uninhibited behaviour, thought shocking in public in many parts of the world. Rodin's sculpture was reviled, while the 1896 film *The Kiss* (a scene from the play *The Widow Jones*) was called 'absolutely disgusting' by *The Chap Book* and the actress involved, May Irwin, was vilified for her participation in so lewd an activity. With the acceleration of the movie-going habit and the exposure to 'daring' presentations made in Europe, kissing became acceptable in most films with only a few actors refusing to do such scenes (Fred Astaire; Pat Boone). But inter-racial osculation remained taboo until, in *Guess Who's Coming to Dinner?* (1967 C), Sidney Poitier and Katherine Houghton were allowed a momentary kiss, seen in the rear-view mirror of a taxi.

The first kiss between women occurred during Cecil B. De Mille's Babylonian orgy in *Manslaughter* (1922 C); then Marlene DIETRICH planted an unrehearsed one on a female member of her audience in *Morocco* (1930); Fraulein Von Bernberg (Dorothea Wieck) says a tender goodnight with a kiss on Manuela's (Hertha Thiele) lips (and not on the forehead as she habitually does with her pupils) in MAEDCHEN IN UNIFORM (1931); Greta GARBO encloses the lips of Elisabeth Young as Ebba Von Sparre in QUEEN CHRISTINA (1933): 'One's own life is all one has'; then a gap before OLIVIA (1950): the two teachers, Edwige Feuillère and Simone Simon; a near one from Arletty in HUIS CLOS (1954 C). Then over a decade before Anne Heywood and Sandy Dennis in THE FOX (1968); Beryl REID and Susannah YORK (as well as York and Coral Browne) in THE KILLING OF SISTER GEORGE (1968). During the 1970s they were still relatively uncommon outside of vampire films, feminist shorts and pornography, and were mainly European: Sylvia Kristel in *Emmanuelle* (1974); Catherine Deneuve in *Ecoute Voir* (1978): she would seduce Susan Sarandon in THE HUNGER (1983); Bette MIDLER and Sandra McCabe in *The Rose* (1978); Helen Mirren and Teresa Ann Savoy in *Caligula* (1979). Into the 1980s and beyond: Whoopi Goldberg and Margaret Avery in THE COLOR PURPLE

(1985); Helen Shaver and Patricia Charbonneau in DESERT HEARTS (1986); Susan Sarandon and Geena Davis at the end of THELMA AND LOUISE (1991); Sharon Stone and Leilani Sarelle in *Basic Instinct* (1992); Drew Barrymore and Sara Gilbert in *Poison Ivy* (1992); Kristin Scott-Thomas and Emmanuelle Seigner in *Bitter Moon* (1992); etc.

Lesbian vampires account for a kissing sub-genre: they began prowling around in DRACULA'S DAUGHTER (1936); became bolder in *Blood and Roses* (1960); and began planting toothy plonkers on unsuspecting virgins in *The Vampire Lovers* in 1970, followed by *Lust for a Vampire, Twins of Evil, Daughters of Darkness, The Velvet Vampire* and THE HUNGER.

British television's first lesbian kiss (the passionate scene in DANCE OF THE SEVEN VEILS was supposedly between the countess and her male lover Octavian and, therefore, squeezed past the censors – who had banned a kiss between actresses portraying COLETTE and Missy in 1967's *The Gentle Libertine*) was between Myra Francis and Alison Steadman in GIRL (1974), followed the same year by Rosemary Harris (as George SAND) and Sinead Cusack (as the actress Marie Dorval) in NOTORIOUS WOMAN. Other close engagements: Miss 'Bill' Baker and Miss Daphne Cox who believe themselves to be unobserved in the grass in *Voyage Round My Father* (1982); Gwen John (Anna MASSEY) and her woman friend in *Journey into The Shadows* (1984 T); Ursula (Imogen Stubbs) and Winifred (Kate Buffery) in THE RAINBOW (1988); Vita and Violet in PORTRAIT OF A MARRIAGE (1990); Jess (Charlotte Coleman) and her friend Melanie (Kathryn Bradshaw) in ORANGES ARE NOT THE ONLY FRUIT (1990).

On radio, the first intimacy occurred between Angela Pleasence and her lover in NOW SHE LAUGHS, NOW SHE CRIES (1975), then between Gisela and Catherine in SILENT WING (1984) and Meriel and Amy in THE TINKER'S DAUGHTER (1986). The working wife in *Swimming and Flying* (1980) *tries* to be liberated with the help of a woman she meets at a pottery evening class: 'She embraced me, she kissed me. I was terrified.'

American television has long been resistant to same-sex kissing. Unlike in Britain, the US networks have not usually discriminated between male and female in what is allowable. Some of the pretty female clients of PERRY MASON (1957–66) very noticeably do not kiss Della STREET, while they happily bestow platonic smackers on the cheeks of Perry and Paul DRAKE.

No mouth to mouth intimacy at all in IN THE GLITTER PALACE (1977) or A QUESTION OF LOVE (1978), and Lynn REDGRAVE (as Marjorie) was probably only allowed to brush her lips across the top of her lover's nose in MY TWO LOVES (1986) because Ms Redgrave is *British* and, therefore, *un-American*. So that viewers get the point, another character bursts in and accuses the American participant of 'kissing another woman'. Five years later, L.A. LAW would pick up healthy ratings in the much heralded kiss (fully and firmly on the lips) between C. J. LAMB and Abby, a pleasure that had been denied two years previously to another rare 'regular' lesbian character on television: Marilyn (Gail Strickland) in HEARTBEAT.

The idea that a man might kiss another surfaced in the accounts of Oscar WILDE's trials which, because they were part of legal and historical fact, were communicated to the public in the three 1960 tellings of the whole unpleasant business. The 'confession' marks the point where Wilde's case against Queensberry collapses, along with his composure. He falls into a self-made trap when asked by Edward Carson if he kissed a boy at Oxford: 'Oh dear, no. He was a particularly plain boy. He was unfortunately extremely ugly. I pitied him for it.'

The image of the New Testament's Judas kiss of betrayal or the decadent's tainted desire for youth dies hard.

Gay kisses were restricted to silly, meaningless ones blown to or by comedians: a fey cowboy, from a window, mouthing the words 'My hero' to Stan

Laurel in *The Soilers* (1923); Al Jolson in *Mammy* (1930); Bob Hope and Bing Crosby not meaning to kiss each other at all – they were aiming for Dorothy Lamour – in *The Road to Morocco* (1942). The absence of this particular form of physical affection became galling to some. Jean Renoir said of the couple in ROPE (1948): 'It's supposed to be about homosexuality and you don't even see the boys kiss each other. What's *that?*'

Frenchmen have, of course, been slightly freer in such matters, bussing on the cheek being a standard greeting. Georges Guetary naturally wants to give his old friend (Oscar Levant) such a greeting in *An American in Paris* (1951). Levant politely demurs: 'You'll spoil my makeup.'

That Britain didn't want any of this either was made abundantly clear by a viewer (Mr Paul Lunch from Cheadle Hulme, Cheshire – who may just have been one of Joe ORTON's hoaxes). He complained to Robert Robinson's *Points of View* programme in February 1963 of 'the nauseating spectacle of grown men kissing each other in public. It has become increasingly prevalent on television recently … may we hope that this revolting and un-British pastime may cease forthwith.' Robinson commented with splendid practicality: 'Oh! I don't know. Spontaneous displays of affection, however odd, seem to make the climate warmer.' The main source of Mr Lunch's upset was the kissing that went on between yachtsman Uffa Fox and his friends on THIS IS YOUR LIFE (a programme that was still upsetting viewers on this score in the late 1980s).

Mostly, though, male–male kissing from this period was very much seen as unpleasant subjugation and often a trigger for violence: Jean Sorel (by Raf Vallone) in *A View from the Bridge* (1961 C; 1966 & 1986 T; etc); Harry H. Corbett (by John Ronane) in *Rattle of a Simple Man* (1964 C); Roman Polanski (by Iain Quarrier) in *Dance of the Vampires/The Fearless Vampire Killers* (1967 C); John Phillip Law (by Rod Steiger) in *The Sergeant* (1968 C); Hywel Bennett (by Ian Redford) in ARTEMIS '81 (1981 T);

Michael Maloney (by Ian HOLM – who immediately apologizes) in *The Bell* (1982 T). This standard repudiation was guyed by SMITH AND JONES (1989 T): Griff Rhys Jones is repulsed by his friend and partner, Mel Smith plonking one on him – but only because Smith has been eating taramasalata.

British alternative comedy *can* take male kissing that bit further, notably the extraordinarily passionate scenes between the two daft undercover cops, Bonehead and Foyle (Peter Richardson and Keith Allen), in *The Bullshitters* (1984 T) rolling over and over on the ground, hungrily guzzling each other in preference to apprehending the villain who is holding their boss at gunpoint.

But when it's for real, an accompaniment to dialogue and tender looks, in either drama or documentary, it's double dynamite: beginning, on British television, with Ian MCKELLEN and James Laurenson in EDWARD II (1970 BBC2); Dinsdale Landen and Edward Fox in *Bermondsey* (1972 BBC2); Alfred Lynch (as King JAMES) and Richard Morant (as 'Steenie') in *Churchill's People* (1974 BBC1); Hugh Sullivan and Tim Morand in LATE CALL (1975 BBC2); the lingering one in WHICKER'S WAY OUT WEST (1973 ITV) by two men getting married, dressed in white.

By the end of the decade, such activity was still rare and circumscribed: BBC2's ONLY CONNECT had but one kiss (from Karl Johnson to Sam Dale, in bed) and BBC1 chanced its arm only twice: with kisses actually being shared (though non-saliverously) by Nigel HAVERS and Anton Rodgers in COMING OUT (1979 BBC1) and by Benjamin Whitrow's Joseph ACKERLEY and Johnny (John Blundell) in WE THINK THE WORLD OF YOU (1980 BBC1). The second provoked the *Daily Mail's* Martin Jackson to write: 'It is not yet necessary to apologize for being "straight", nor for being queasy, perhaps even offended by the spectacle of two men kissing and sharing the same bed. There are some of us who are still offended and I honestly do not understand what the BBC was attempting to prove last night.'

CHANNEL 4 showed Dov (Nigel Robson) kissing (very briefly) Faber (Tom McDonnell) in Michael TIPPETT's opera *The Knot Garden* (1984); journalist John Gill giving jazz composer Graham Collier a token of affection on the lips at the very end of the film on Collier's work, *Hoarded Talent* (1986); Daniel Day-Lewis and Gordon Warnecke enthusiastically connecting in MY BEAUTIFUL LAUNDRETTE (made for television in 1985, backed by C4, but not shown until 1987 because of its success as a cinema attraction).

Sometimes a kiss shown on television can radically affect the lives of one or both of the participants. Australians, Peter Bonsall-Boone and Peter De Waal kissed very briefly in CHEQUERBOARD (1972 T): 'This just happens to be a part of me.' But such display was a contributing factor in Bonsall-Boone's sacking the day after the programme was screened. Nineteen years later, 'Bon' repeated the action – at his and Peter's 25th anniversary party. In Britain, Tony WHITEHEAD, a trainee manager with British Home Stores, was summarily dismissed the day after he was seen on a 1976 documentary called COMING OUT, enjoying a welcome home kiss with his lover.

The furtiveness, the eternal vigilance, the need to 'peck and part' was nicely caught in the 1984 play THE GROUNDLING AND THE KITE. Jimmy (John Duttine) and Peter (Leonard Preston) are overcome by tenderness in the doorway of their flat. Their lips touch, but only for a second. A neighbour has banged a dustbin lid with great emphasis to register disapproval of such activity. In full view. On the street. In public. Says Jimmy matter-of-factly: 'That's us off the Residents' Committee.'

Family viewing guidelines have restricted both real and fictional gays to a quick hug (in BROOKSIDE 1987) or to a peck on the cheek. A situation so ridiculous that two men can kiss full on the cheek or the neck if they are brothers (in EASTENDERS 1985) or bloodsuckers (*Vampire* 1979) or if they hate every second of it (*A View from the Bridge*, acceptable for BBC Schools TV in 1986; the same service being refused access to the mutual one in TWO OF US two years later).

The most fuss was made over the kiss – lasting one and a half seconds – between Colin (Michael CASHMAN) and Guido (Nicholas Donovan) in EASTENDERS (1989). As well as giving Colin a buss on the cheek, Guido placed his hand briefly on Colin's upper abdomen and squeezed his arm (Colin's hands remained in his pockets throughout). Pauline (Wendy Richard) enters at this point to deliver the greatest overstatement of all time: 'You love birds still at it?' she sighs. 'Glad *someone's* happy.' The tabloid press created a brouhaha about 'perverted practices' in family viewing times. The BBC took note. Two years later, a kiss between two minor gay characters in EASTENDERS was cut.

A similar – but probably much more damaging storm – was avoided by the BBC through the removal of a tiny kiss between the boys in *Two of Us*, shown in distorted form on its Schools service in 1988. It wasn't until 1992 that the film could be transmitted as intended, without raging condemnation. By this time, men's lips were coming together more frequently on television: in front of a railway station poster for Family Railcards (*Byline* 'A Kiss Is Just a Kiss' 1991); on a sofa wearing denims and boots in *10×10* 'DOCTOR MARTENS' (1991); in the bedroom in THE LOST LANGUAGE OF CRANES (1992); at a party in *Anglo-Saxon Attitudes* (1992); in a library in OUT ('Actions Speak Louder Than Words' 1992) and in computerized form ('CAUGHT LOOKING' 1992).

This relatively more tolerant or desensitized atmosphere may be partly due to the not uncommon kissing in feature films shown on television, beginning in 1978 with Peter FINCH and Murray Head's clinch in SUNDAY, BLOODY SUNDAY (made in 1971). This was followed by the two Roman soldiers in SEBASTIANE (1976); the twins in JUBILEE (1977); Alan BATES saying hello to George De La Pena through a handkerchief in NIJINSKY (1980); Mel Gibson and Mark Lee bidding each other tender farewell in *Gallipoli* (1981); Daniel Day-Lewis and Gordon Warnecke in MY BEAUTIFUL LAUNDRETTE (1985); Gérard Depardieu and Michel Blanc in TENUE DE SOIREE/EVENING DRESS (1985); William Hurt and Raul Julia in KISS OF THE SPIDER WOMAN (1985); Gabriel Byrne and Julian Sands in *Gothic* (1986); Gary Oldman and Albert Molina in PRICK UP YOUR EARS (1987); Rupert Graves and James Wilby in MAURICE (1987); Gary Kemp and a teenager in *The Krays* (1990); Iain Glen and Patrick Bergin in *Mountains of the Moon* (1990); Campbell Scott and Stephen Caffrey in LONGTIME COMPANION (1990); Steven Waddington and Andrew Tiernan in EDWARD II (1991); Alec Baldwin and (71-year-old) Sydney Walker in *Prelude to a Kiss* (1992); and – the ultimate confrontation – Michael Caine and Christopher Reeve in *Deathtrap* (1982), an experience so traumatic for both men that one of them has hardly stopped talking about it (on TV chat shows) ever since.

No intimate TOUCHING, including kissing, between people of the same sex (unless they are related or it's intended as a joke), is allowed on American commercial television. Therefore a loving couple like the one portrayed in A QUESTION OF LOVE or AN EARLY FROST is allowed no tactile expression at all, no matter how extreme their circumstances: loss of children, illness or imminent death. A small but highly significant visual token of affectionate support is stripped from a minority already implanted in mass consciousness as less than human, less than caring, incapable of their kind of love.

The few that have been permitted include an almost kiss between Powers Boothe and Brad Dourif in GUYANA TRAGEDY: THE STORY OF JIM JONES (1980); Dick (Vanessa REDGRAVE – as a man) and his fiancée (Alice Krige) in SECOND SERVE (1986); one in the vicinity of her co-star's nose from Lynn Redgrave in MY TWO LOVES (1986); a very short one between Lorraine (Lonette McKee) and Tee (Paula Kelly) in THE WOMEN OF BREWSTER PLACE (1989 T);

the famous L.A. LAW collision in 1991; and – the first proper one between males – Russell Weller (David Marshall Grant) and Peter Montefiore (Peter Frechette) on THIRTYSOMETHING. Television history was made on Tuesday 7 November 1989 – and that one dry kiss (in a post-coital bed scene) lost the show's network huge amounts of advertising.

Good, juicy wet kissing is rare in mainstream cinema. If awards were given out, those for most dedication and conviction would go to Vanessa Redgrave (with Madeleine Potter) in *The Bostonians* (1984); Daniel Day-Lewis (with Gordon Warnecke) in *My Beautiful Laundrette*; Keith Allen and Peter Richardson for *The Bullshitters*. Most delightful of all were the rambunctious attempts made by hitherto mainly heterosexual Antonio (Antonio Banderas) to osculate with the very experienced Pablo (Eusebio Poncela) in LAW OF DESIRE (1987 C). After a few goes, Pablo tells the novice to relax and not to kiss 'as if you were unblocking a drain'.

kiss me, Hardy Lord Nelson (Laurence Olivier) expires on the deck in *Lady Hamilton/That Hamilton Woman* (1941 C), but not before he has had his Captain Hardy (Henry Wilcoxen) kiss him (on the forehead); in *Victory!* (1958 T) Lord Nelson (Hugh David) gasps these three words to David Langton. Later dramatizations have been more revisionist ('Kismet, Hardy!') or some long speech about doing his duty for England. Comedians, particularly Morecambe and Wise, have ignored the clean-up job and regularly satirized the great man's last, passionate words to a fellow sailor. This was referred to in *The Potsdam Quartet* (1981 T) – 'How perverted can you get' – as a joke, but Jean Rhys, interviewed by David Plante in *Paris Review* (1972), took it seriously: 'He wasn't homosexual. I don't believe it. He was bisexual as we all are.' Other Hardys given permission to be affectionate to their chief are Montague Love (to Victor Varconi) in *The Divine Lady* (1929 C); Michael Jayston in *Bequest to* *the Nation* (1973 C); Tim Pigott-Smith (to Kenneth Colley) in *I Remember Nelson* (1982).

kiss of life Artificial respiration from man to man is almost always accompanied by flailing denial of any sexual desire (Archie Bunker is horrified that the woman he has resuscitated in ALL IN THE FAMILY (1976) is a man). Richie (Rik Mayall) becomes quite excited by the thought of reviving the gas man in *Bottom!* (1991 T) after his friend Eddie (Adrian Edmondson) bawls: 'Oh, go on, you've always wanted to find out what snogging's all about.' In Australia that same year, Channel 7's *Fast Forward* had a flaming queen putting his lips to the mouth of an unconscious man by a swimming pool, while the laughter track roared its approving derision (and fear). 'Don't worry, if you have a heart attack I won't give you the kiss of life,' Rob (Jeremy Bulloch) says caustically to Laurence's anti-queer father in AGONY (1981 T).

Kiss of the Spider Woman (Brazil 1985 C) WINDOW DRESSER Luis Molina (William Hurt) is shown the political light by his fellow prisoner Valentin (Raul Julia) who gives him a brief history lesson: 'The NAZIS shoved FAGGOTS in the oven ... but then you wouldn't know reality if it was shoved up your arse.' Molina lives and dies a hero in the last few minutes of the film, after spending the previous two hours as fantasist, informer and unrequited lover of the taciturn 'real' man.
W: Leonard Schrader; based on the novel by Manuel Puig; P: David Weisman; D: Hector Babenco; 121 mins.

Fantasy-soaked, cowardly informer is redeemed – through death for a political cause and the briefly reciprocated love of a straight man. The questioning of macho and non-macho rigidity present in the novel is elbowed out in favour of cheesy movie pastiche and ghoulishly overwrought flapping from William Hurt.

In the novel Molina, who identifies with glamorous but victimized female stars, details the plots of real movies (*Casablanca*; *I Walked with a Zombie*; *Cat People*; *The Enchanted Cottage*) as well as the imaginary horror picture which gives the film its title. Valentin finds this slavish devotion to plastic creations of a capitalistic industry demeaning and destructive. But Molina, denied any other source of emotional nourishment, can't exist without them – until Valentin sheds his own inhibitions and they make love.

Copyright difficulties may account for the substitution of one imaginary plot and one resembling *Casablanca* called 'Her Real Glory'. These inventions rob the films-within-a-film element of much resonance and point, which carries through to the 'real' plot.

Kitchener, Lord Horatio (1850–1916) British soldier and statesman. Remembered now as the face on the 1914 posters: 'Your Country Needs You!' The most revealing picture – a cameo – was painted (in *Khartoum* 1966 C) by Peter ARNE as the then Major Kitchener; stripped to the waist, with vivid blond hair he cuts a fine figure, earning appreciative words from a young Egyptian about his eyes and physique. He was portrayed in a somewhat unflattering, colonialist light by Norman Jones in *The British Empire* (1985 R). An earlier, softer radio portrait of the folk hero who relieved Khartoum after GORDON's death in *K of K* (1960) included comments by Sir Harold NICOLSON.

So far, there has been no celebration, factual or dramatized, of Kitchener's very great love for Captain Oswald Fitzgerald, whom he met in 1904 and with whom he died when the ship they were travelling on struck a German mine during the First World War.

Rosa Klebb (Lotte Lenya in *From Russia with Love* 1963 C) A colonel in the KGB, she embodies in a diminutive form all the military might of the USSR: a pitiless, implacable opponent of the West and James Bond (who has bedded the beautiful agent she lusts after). In a memorable climax, Rosa hits out at Bond in a pair of stiletto-toed shoes.

Her spirit lived on in *Carry On Spying* (1964 C, Judith FURSE as Doctor Crow) and *The Saint* 'The Russian Prisoner' (1966 T), Yootha Joyce as Jolanta Milanova).

Corporal Max Klinger (Jamie Farr in *M*A*S*H* 1972-83 T) Initially, he was a married corpsman attending to the injured, who wants out of the Korean War. He attempts to persuade the authorities that he is a thoroughgoing sexual deviate. Instead of simply kissing the colonel and suggesting a date, Klinger dresses up in WAC uniform and later in all manner of women's attire (twin-sets, nurses' uniform, bobble hats and fur coats, frilly nighties) – which aids his plan not one bit.

Klinger was originally intended as a one-gag wonder, based on Lenny Bruce's donning of a WAVE uniform to obtain a naval discharge. However, the actor played the role 'straight', not in the flimsy, derogatory manner that he had been directed to do. This, said the show's creator Larry Gelbart, 'provided a colour to the show that nothing else was doing – just an absolute piece of madness every week.'

Klinger became a much loved regular character during the 1975-6 season. He stopped wearing women's clothes in 1979, remarried and was one of the gang who returned in the civilian sequel *After M*A*S*H*.

knitting Very much connected with men as well as women, with James Norbury one of the experts in a popular afternoon series *Knitting Is My Adventure* (1954 T, produced by David Attenborough) and also on WOMAN'S HOUR (until 1968). In *The Boys of Summer* (1959 R) it is intimated that the main character (a teacher who is mentor to a young male pupil), Julian (Ivan Brandt) knits. He recommends the activity to his pregnant wife: 'It calms the nerves.'

But, during the 1950s, knitting like SEWING had crossed the great divide into sissydom: Charles HAWTREY as 'Professor' who never finishes his in *The Army Game* (1957-8 T); and then to

queerdom: CIA agent FEMALE IMPERSONATOR code-named 'The Warlock' (George SANDERS) knits bed socks for his new-found Russian boyfriend in *The Kremlin Letter* (1970 C) – he uses a ball of red wool to signal danger when the KGB descend. In *Up the Chastity Belt* (1971 C) Robin Hood (Hugh PADDICK) uses the long hours of exile in Sherwood Forest to dish the dirt with his Merry Men, apply make-up, and purl and plain a few rows. LUKEWARM (Christopher BIGGINS), the plump trusty in *Porridge* (1974-7 T) is seldom seen without his needles and wool; the fractious members of *The Potsdam Quartet* (1981 T) all knit for the war effort, but queer Ronnie (Peter Eyre) can't get the hang of it: 'I keep knitting one and purling one and I've still got these enormous holes ... It's like my life: one great big woolly tangle'; the only son of the gloomy Ivy COMPTON-BURNETT's Edwardian family in THE SOUTH BANK SHOW: 'Elders and Betters' (1984 T) has an EARRING and knitting needles to identify himself as 'so'; Gary (Ashley Gunstrick) and Bernard (Jim McManus) run a knitwear store in *Casting Off* (1988 T); Sammy (Campbell Morrison) surreptitiously works on (yellow) baby clothes for Mandy's unborn child in *Life without George* (1989 T); Jeremy (Joe Dunlop), lover of Martin (Timothy Carlton) in *Don't Wait Up* (1987-9 T) knits a cardigan and bootees for neighbour Toby's (Nigel HAVERS) baby 'in white so it will do for either sex'.

'Gay men, of course, never trust each other and spend most of their leisure time quipping about lorry drivers through pursed lips or, worse still, knitting' (letter, *Radio Times*, 11.3.90).

Capital Radio's Graham Dene in 1977 was nonplussed that the world knitting record went to a man: 'I think this equal thing is going a bit far. Some people are into some really strange things ... But don't worry, this guy's not really strange. His credentials are sound – he's got a child.'

So it was with considerable courage that in 1984 CHANNEL 4, reinforcing its tradition of exploring minority areas, brought Patrick Reilly and his knitting machine onto national television in *Make the Most of* ... Patrick's contribution earned plaudits for 'bravery' from Katie Boyle in *TV Times*. This must have paved the way for American Kaffe Fassett, who became the happy, colourful and successful face of knitting, talking about his love of the art to Sue Lawley in a midsummer 1990 DESERT ISLAND DISCS and briefly referring to his PARTNER.

Korman, Harvey (1927–) American comic actor who often assumes the roles of strident, ineffectual fussbuckets, most ineradicably as Hedley ('Hedley, *not* Hedy!') Lamarr in *Blazing Saddles* (1974 C). His versatility was highly visible, though, in *The Danny Kaye Show* (1963–7) and *The Carol Burnett Show* (1967–77). Also: *The April Fools* (1968 C); *Suddenly Single* (1971 T); masochistic Dr Charles Montague in *High Anxiety* (1977 C); *First Family* (1980 C); Captain Blythe in *Herbie Goes Bananas* (1980 C); orchidaceous Count De Morne in the French Revolution section of *History of the World Part I* (1981 C); Professor Auguste Balls in *Trail of the Pink Panther* (1982 C); *The Invisible Woman* (1983 T); *The Longshot* (1986 C); manager of *The Nut House* (1989 T); etc.

Kramer, Larry (1935–) American screenwriter (*Lost Horizon*), producer (WOMEN IN LOVE), author (*Faggots*), playwright (*The Normal Heart*; *The Destiny of Me*), and activist: a man not afraid of making himself thoroughly unpopular with heterosexuals and fellow gays alike, earning himself the title of 'the angriest gay man in the whole world'. He was the subject of an ARENA programme 'Kramer vs Kramer' in 1993: '... one of the first people to take a political, active stance in bringing [the AIDS epidemic] to the attention of the world.'

The Krays East End ganglords of the 1960s, one of whom (Ronnie) is homosexual. Portrayed by (non-twin brothers) Gary Kemp (Ronnie) and Martin Kemp (Reggie) in Philip RIDLEY's *The Krays* (1990 C). The twins, though justifiably feared, almost became pop icons until they were sent to prison for life. The pederastic gangster, with or without brother, periodically features – though never directly by name – in gangland thrillers like PERFORMANCE (Johnny Shannon 1970 C); *Villain* (Richard Burton 1971 C); WIDOWS (Arnie, one of the Fisher Brothers who rearrange people's furniture 'and their features,' 1983 T). Or in comedies: *The Odd Job* (Michael Elphick 1978 C, with Richard O'Brien as a leather boy); *Body Contact* (1987 T) – Peter (Christopher Fulford), brother of Paul, says: 'I think people think I'm going soft. So I have to kill them'; MONTY PYTHON'S FLYING CIRCUS' unforgettable 'The Amazing World of the Piranha Brothers' (1971 T): Dinsdale Piranha '... takes a warm interest in boys clubs, sailors homes, chorister associations and Grenadier guards'. He also nails people's heads onto tables (but he's a very good boy to his mother).

Kulp, Nancy (1921–) American actress specializing in sour landladies or sniffy SPINSTERS until the advent of Jane HATHAWAY in *The Beverly Hillbillies* (1962–71?) who was a spinster, conservative but a good sport, well organized, gauche, dependable and almost part of the family.

C: Hazel in *The Model and the Marriage Broker* (1951); pioneer woman in *Shane* (1953); nurse captured by the Japanese in *Five Gates to Hell* (1959); a teacher (Miss Grunecker) in *The Parent Trap* (1961 C); one of Jerry Lewis' foils in *The Patsy* (1964); etc.

T: secretary in I LOVE LUCY 'Lucy Meets the Queen' (1956); the earth-bound Mrs Gann refuting a little girl's fantasies in THE TWILIGHT ZONE 'The Fugitive' (1962); Mrs Millard Gruber, the landlady in *The Brian Keith Show* (1973–4); *The Return of the Beverly Hillbillies* (1981); etc.

Lacey, Ronald (1935–91) English actor, well versed and much exercised in porcine, creepy, spotty, scungy parts, including two gays called Frankie (in *Boa Constrictor* 1967 T and HARD CASES 1988 T).

C: one of *The Boys* (1962); beatnik in *Catch Us If You Can* (1965); *The Likely Lads* (1976); *Zulu Dawn* (1979); *Raiders of the Lost Ark* (1981); *Firefox* (1982); *Red Sonja* (1985); etc.

R: Colonel Carillo in *Incident at the Devil's Gate* (about Archbishop Oscar Romero, 1987).

T: jazz-fan Len in *The Stranger* (1960); Ted in *Search Party* (1960); Terry, the office boy in *The Harsh World* (1960); Valentine in *Pig's Ear with Flowers* (1960); Ralph Nolan in *Z Cars* 'On Watch – Newtown' (1962); Maurice Pringle in *Detective* 'Death in Ecstasy' (1963); Eileen Atkins' husband in *Fable* (1965); strange young man in *The Avengers* 'The Joker' (1968); Death in *Ray Bradbury Theatre* 'There Was an Old Woman (1988); etc.

Lack, Simon (1917–80) Scottish actor who began in 'sensitive youth' roles, eg Richard in *Ah! Wilderness* (1938 T) and the boy 'seduced' by the effeminate man (revealed as a German spy) in *Sons of the Sea* (1939 C). After the war, he managed to balance his career almost equally between radio and television, playing heroes, villains, bright sparks and 'sensitive young men'. His most widely remembered role was as the German commander holding sway over some of the Channel Islands in *Enemy at the Door* (1978–80 T).

C: one of the schoolboys in *Goodbye Mr Chips* (1939); miner's son in *The Proud Valley* (1940); Scottish nobleman in *Bonnie Prince Charlie* (1948) and in *Macbeth* (1960); army officer in *On the Fiddle* (1961); etc.

R: Bob Acres in *The Rivals* (1954); member of the BBC Drama Repertory Company 1955–7; PAUL TEMPLE *and the Madison Mystery* (1955; he was in most of these from this date onwards, generally as unattached young men like 'actorish' Adrian Frost in 'The Spencer Affair' 1958); SEBASTIAN in *Twelfth Night* (1956); Tommy Rankin in *The Singing Sands* (1956); Faulkner Bellamy in *Masquerade* (1958); Herbert Pocket in *Great Expectations* (1958); Victor Prynne in *Private Lives* (1958); Alec in BRIEF ENCOUNTER (1958); Jerry Sant, a radical demagogue in *Hadrian VII* (1959); Esmé Fraser in *The Dreaming Suburb* (1959) and *The Avenue Goes to War* (1961); John WORTHING in THE IMPORTANCE OF BEING EARNEST (1959, Far East Service only); Sir Perceval Glyde in *The Woman in White* (1960); Banwell Spender, artiste at '75 Club in *Miss Dangerfield and the Irresistible Nightingale* (1963); Reggie Marchbanks in *Paul Temple and the Jonathan Mystery* (1963); starred as Robert Bristol in *La Boutique* (1967); Geoffrey Haredale in *Barnaby Rudge* (1968); Rev. James Fordyce in *Witch Wood* (1975); Ralph Manson in *The Hands* (1975); John TREGORRAN in THE ARCHERS (1975–6); etc.

T: Paris in *Troilus and Cressida* (1954); Paul Torrance from the Scientific Panel of Occult Investigation in *Trespass* (1958); archaeologist in *The Creature* (1958); Dr Roach in *The Watching Eye* (1960 T); Mr Lawrence Harper in *Emergency – Ward 10* (1960); General GORDON in *Old Man in a Hurry*, about Gladstone (1960); Prince Zadikov in *The Brockenstein Affair* (1961); Ritchie Murray in *Dr Finlay's Casebook* (1962) and again in 'Without the City' (1964) as Jock Stoddart; Dr Roper in *The Hidden Truth* (1964); Edwards Cavendish in *The Borderers* (1964); Count Maretta in *Boy Meets Girl* 'The Enchanted Shore' (1968); Andrew Seton in *Doomwatch* 'In the Dark' (1971); *South Riding* (1974); George Hesut in *The Fortunes of Nigel* (1974); *Doctor Who*; WITHIN THESE WALLS (1974); Sturmer in DIXON OF DOCK GREEN 'Domino' (1976); Major Freidel in *Enemy at the Door* (1978–80); *Telford's Change* (1979); *Love in a Cold Climate* (1980); etc.

Ladies Night (UK 1977 T) A Friday night discussion programme whose audience was made up entirely of women from the Birmingham area. Alison HENNEGAN watched the taping of the show on gay men and reported in GAY NEWS that the cameras should have been pointing towards the audience rather than at the small group of men on the platform, including GN editor Denis LEMON:

> ... for example [they] didn't capture the frenzied writhings, anguished hair-clutching and gusty sighs from the woman in pink as she learnt to her horror that a teacher in the audience did and does and will employ homosexuals – providing they can teach...
> Nor could the viewer have seen the sudden pursing lips, the indrawn breath and the shifting of backs which greeted one woman's statement that she considered homosexuality as abnormal as heterosexuality ... The studio manager didn't pick up the muttered comment of the woman behind me: 'Christ, I'd much rather have my kids taught by a gay liberal than have them picking up her ideas about class or sex.' (GN 138)

The following year, Alison Hennegan faced another similar audience from the Central Television region as a member of a small group of lesbians being asked what it was like to be attracted to the same sex.

The Ladies of Llangollen Eleanor Butler (1739–1829) and Sarah Ponsonby (1755–1831). They were rumoured to be SUFFRAGETTES or SPIES or men dressed as women, but were in fact Irish women 'of quality' who eloped to Wales in 1778 because they wished to live together 'in retirement from the world'. They were objects of considerable fascination, and visitors came from far and wide to see this apparently unique (but probably not) relationship at close quarters. The interest continues: Mari Griffith retraced 'the curious history' in WOMAN'S HOUR (1983 R) and Elizabeth Mavor visited their house and quoted from their (sometimes code-worded) diaries in *When Shall We Be Quite Alone?* (1984 R).

Lakey Elinor Eastlake, the very soignée Vassar girl, Class of '33, in Mary McCarthy's novel THE GROUP, played by Candice Bergen in the 1966 film. Fascinating and truthful, elegant and disdainful Lakey – dubbed 'the Mona Lisa of the Smoking Room' by one of her friends' husbands – goes off to Europe and returns in 1939 with her lover, a Baroness (in the book she walks off the ship in a violet suit). In her only meaty scene, the aforementioned husband, needling her with questions, turns and says with polished casualness: 'It's funny, but I never picked you for Sapphic. And yet I have a good eye.' Lakey makes no response. She has her own still centre that not even the horniest hands can invade.

According to Pauline Kael's article about the making of *The Group*, the producer Charles K. Feldman assumed that the screenplay would detail Lakey's affairs in Europe – which would have needed inventing as they are nowhere mentioned in the book: 'Instead, [screenwriter Sidney] Buchman held so close to the text that waiting for Lakey to reappear in the movie is almost like waiting for Godot.'

The United Artists publicity people ditched their original campaign which had exploited the lesbian angle because, in the event, there was none. Yet, for all that this character plays a negligible part in a 152-minute movie, it is Lakey who is the only memorable member of the Vassar eight.

(The American poet Elizabeth Benson was the likely inspiration for the character. A very muffled documentary about her appeared in 1989 T.)

Lakmé duet 'Sous le dôme épais ou le blanc jasmin...' from Léo Delibes' opera, a barcarole sung by the Brahmin princess Lakmé and her slave Mallika in Act I as they prepare to bathe in the stream. It is used by Miriam (Catherine Deneuve) when she plays the melody on the piano to soothe Sarah (Susan Sarandon) in THE HUNGER (1983 C). 'Is it a love song?' asks Sarah half excitedly. 'It *sounds like* a love song. Are you making a pass at me?' Sarah then spills red wine on her T-shirt, which necessitates her removing it. Miriam then kisses her.

Crystalline voices take over as the women are seen through gauzy curtains on a bed; these are then intermingled with queasy electronic sounds as a prelude to Miriam mingling her blood with Sarah's (a shot of it trickling down Sarah's arm is immediately followed by an oozingly rare steak which she is cutting in a restaurant).

L.A. Law (US 1986– T) Provocative drama series that bends over backwards to be politically present and correct, with every other judge a middle-aged Afro-American woman and all members of the rainbow coalition as clients. 'We don't discriminate on grounds of race, gender or sexual orientation' is the firm's motto, but it wasn't until 1988 that the handful of gays needing its ministrations stopped being transvestites or lovers of people with HIV/AIDS.

The breakthrough came in 'The Accidental Jurist' where the injured party was a spunky Olympic athlete, Matthew Leonard (Brian McNamara) who had lost a lucrative advertising contract because he had been public about his orientation. The twist in the tale was that the judge in the case (Donald Moffat) was himself gay, which may have influenced the adverse judgement against the sports star. Strongly advised (by hotshot lawyer Harry Hamlin – himself having had professional problems after playing gay in MAKING LOVE) to go for a mistrial, the young man refuses. A sportsman through and through, he does not want the judge's sexuality brought into the open.

C: Steven Bochco and Rick Wallace; P: Patricia Green; 60 mins.

See also C. J. LAMB.

C[ara] J[ean] Lamb Character played by Amanda Donohoe in *L.A. Law* (1990–2), a savvy solo practitioner with a British accent, neatly pressed short hair and a will-she? won't-she? bisexuality which finally burst asunder when she kissed fellow lawyer Abby Perkins (Michelle Greene) in a 1991 episode which centred on a man with multiple personalities, including a homicidal old lady. C.J's action was supposedly followed by a fling with Abby. Or was it?

Executive producer Patricia Green would only venture: 'I'm not sure we ever intended it to go beyond a tentativeness on Abby's part. It is possible C.J. could end up with another woman' (US *TV Guide*). Amanda Donohoe put a cheerful face on what inveterate US TV watchers knew was a token piece of ratings arousal: 'I think audiences find C.J. tantalizing. She's unpredictable. I never know what they'll write for me next.'

What came next wasn't an affair with Abby, or with anybody else. C.J. (in a December 1991 episode, 'The Nut Before Christmas') is representing her former lover, Maggie (Elisabeth Kemp) whose husband is suing her for custody of her child. A whole range of issues tumble forth: showing affection to another woman in front of the child, the likelihood of the child growing up gay, the husband's alcoholism – and her lover's promiscuity and HIV status. C.J. assures the court that she tests regularly – and is negative. The judge decrees in the mother's favour, and the episode ends with C.J. and Maggie (who is never seen again) HUGGING enthusiastically as a Christmas tree glints in the background.

C.J. bowed out of the series in a 1992 episode entitled 'Say Goodnight Gracie'. She has a new lover, David who's a client. As they cuddle up on her sofa, she feels honour-bound to tell him – a mite anxiously – about the way she is (or was): 'I don't apologize for who I am. But I've had my share of relationships with men ... and I've had my relationships with women. Does that bother you?' David, being a thinking kind of fellow (and possibly devotee of shows like *L.A. Law*) says, well ... he'll have to think about it. Continuing her confession, C.J. assures him of her undivided attention 'for as long as it's right ... I don't seem to be able to settle down for very long.'

Mortimer **Lamb** Forlorn realist played by Ronald Simpson (1954 R) and Denys Blakelock in *Manservant and Maidservant* (1967 R). He appears to be the suitor of his cousin, Lord Haslam's unhappy wife. As the play develops, it becomes apparent that his tenderly protective actions are motivated more by pity than by sexual passion. Mortimer's every entrance is accompanied by a metaphorical rustle of dry leaves on a stark and windy day. Keyed in throughout is his soul-weariness and a sense of something deeply unexpressed. 'It's a tiresome habit to look things in the face,' he maintains. The narrator talks of his 'rounded, almost deep-set eyes that held some humour and little hope'.

Mortimer's real-life counterpart was the actor Ernest THESIGER, who could be single-mindedly sinister or sweetly fey, merging both personae in his most memorable portrait: Doctor Praetorius in THE BRIDE OF FRANKENSTEIN. Thesiger married his lover, Willie Rankin's sister Janette. She in turn was in love with the poet Margaret Jourdain, who was the companion of Ivy COMPTON-BURNETT, who wrote *Manservant and Maidservant*.

Lambert, Gavin (1924–) English author (*The Slide Area*) and Hollywood screenwriter. With Karel Reisz, he had been editor of the distinguished film publication *Sequence* in the late 1940s before becoming editor of *Sight and Sound* until 1953.

C: *Bitter Victory* (1957); *Another Sky* (1959, also D); *Sons and Lovers* (1960); *Go Naked in the World* (1961); *The Roman Spring of Mrs Stone* (1961); *Inside Daisy Clover* (1966, from his 1963 novella co-W with Lewis John Carlino); *I Never Promised You a Rose Garden* (1977).

T: SECOND SERVE (co-W); *Liberace: Behind the Music* (1988). One of the interviewees in *The Hollywood Legends* 'Natalie Wood' (1987 T).

landladies/landlords Creepy Wilson (Noel COWARD) with his greasy hair, yapping dog and talks of whips in *Bunny*

Lake Is Missing (1965 C); Malcolm (Michael Greer) becoming suspicious of the number of girls coming and staying in the apartment of THE GAY DECEIVERS (1969 C); the kooky character (Paula Prentiss) disparaging her leather-dyke landlady in *Last of the Red Hot Lovers* (1971 C): 'I sleep so far away from her in the bed she'd have to take a taxi to get to me' (but is she telling the truth?); Jeremy Pease as the gabbily insolent AUSTRALIAN Ritchie in THE GENTLE TOUCH 'Blade' (1980 T); one half of a female pair in *Kate and Allie* 'Landlady' (1984 T) who is conned into believing her tenants are lesbians so that perhaps she'll not raise the rent; Frank Rammage (David Ryall), sanctimonious and grasping in *Anglo-Saxon Attitudes* (1992 T); Olympia Dukakis as the extraordinary Anna Madrigal of 28 Barbary Lane in TALES OF THE CITY (1993 T).

Land of My Dreams (UK 1964 T) One of a dying bulldog breed, Arthur Walmer (Michael Hordern) sees himself as 'just a normal Englishman with a dislike of Hebraic gentlemen and Levantine gentlemen'. He awaits the return of his son Alan who has been doing a prison term for (accidentally?) killing his mother's Jewish lover. Like father like son, or so Arthur, who runs a decimated British racist party, would like to believe. In the event, Alan rejects his father and the tottering, insular Little Englander world he represents by not coming home. To add insult to injury, he seems to have consolidated in prison the interest in the male sex towards which his father had tried to turn a blind eye, blaming his wife for making Alan too soft.

W: Clive Exton; P: John Elliott; D: William T. Kotcheff; 8.2.64; BBC1.

This splendid character study (which Hordern repeated on radio in 1967) is a flash-forward to the chilling lunacy of Alf Garnett. During the 1960s, with everything topsy-turvy, normality was a good safe place to run to. Of course, for men like Arthur the good old days were very old indeed. 'I sometimes think the whole world ended in 1915,' he tells one of his few remaining followers. 'The Empire intact. Cigarettes nine pence for twenty. A night out for two and change out of five bob. That was when England was England.' Before the Yids, before the coons, before the NANCY BOYS. In truth, Arthur's real period of contentment would have been in the days of castles and drawbridges and of witchburning.

This play, one of many left-leaning, anti-puritanism pieces which so galvanized Mary WHITEHOUSE and her associates, the National Viewers and Listeners' Association, was quick to make the – not always tenable – association between sexual and political repression: Arthur and his wife (Clare Kelly) have had separate rooms 'temporarily for 12 years'.

Land of Promise (UK 1986 R) Sixteen-year-old Simon (Paul Lockwood), struggling to find his identity in an East End school, is harassed by his mates and his EVANGELICAL CHRISTIAN father. The play, set in the 1950s, ends with Simon's SUICIDE in front of an onrushing train after a bloody fight with the school bully, Jewell (Peter Dennis) who screams at the young scapegoat: 'I hate you ... hate you ... because your kind's just dirt!'
W: John Perceval; D: Brian Miller; 10.4.86; BBC Radio 4; 60 mins.

Its historical period notwithstanding, this was a spare, effective and contemporary drama without much to say other than follow the herd if you don't have protection – otherwise the herd will trample you. The violence of the anti-gay responses – Biblical and gut – is not countered by logic or wit; only by fisticuffs and, as they have limited value, the ultimate sacrifice. A sobering 'afternoon play' but endorsing a lamb-to-the-slaughter apathy rather than the mouse that roars.

Lang, Harold (1923–69) English actor (RADA gold medallist) and drama teacher who worked in London, Chicago, Manila and Cairo (where he died). There was a queer, taunting quality

about many of his performances, usually in perfunctory roles. His sneers, surly looks, insinuating tone and tosses of his greased blond quiff are collectable. Surprising, then, to hear him tell his Central School of Speech and Drama students in the MONITOR film (directed by John Schlesinger) called 'The Class' (1960 T) that they should know 'the difference between real feeling and ham'. His showing here is spectacular: drawing out emotions through visualizations, gender-switching and risky psychodynamics. This, rather than his generally rather tawdry, predictable acting credits, is his memorial.

C: *Floodtide* (1949); spiv Stan in *Calling Bulldog Drummond* (1951); spiv Mickie in *Cloudburst* (1951); chauffeur in *The Long Memory* (1952); couturier in *It Started in Paradise* (1952); Travis, one of the gang responsible for accidentally killing Robert Preston's wife in *Blackout* (1953); Mr Bridson the pianist in *Dance Little Lady* (1954); spiv in *The Intruder* (1955); tabloid journalist in *The Quatermass Experiment* (1955); theatrical type Mervyn Wade in *It's A Wonderful World* (1956); Silent, an informer in *West 11* (1963 C); pub customer in *Paranoiac* (1964); Briggs in *The Psychopath* (1966); *Two Gentlemen Sharing* (1968, unreleased).

R: Russell in *Theatre Night* (1957); Aeschylus Aphanisis, millionaire in *The Primal Scene as It Were* (1958); the Joker in Louis MacNeice's *One Eye Wild* (1961); etc.

T: Harry the Scouse in *Tales from Soho* 'The Message' (1956); Jean-Jacques Charcot, a bitter, snarling French Communist whose sister was a collaborator in Nigel Kneale's *Mrs Wickens in the Fall* (1957): 'Je suis communist. You want a world where everybody drinks Coca Cola? So they can lick your boots better? The great American way of life! But the people know you – they're going to drive you out! Out of Europe! Out of everywhere on earth!'; the stranger in *The Lady from the Sea* (1958); ROBESPIERRE in *Danton's Death* (1959); Jenkins in *Saber of London* 'Beyond Fear' (1960); the Beast's chameleonic factotum Johnson in THE ROSE AFFAIR (1961): 'You're so dominating!'; Rheinhardt in *The Referees* (1961); crook Da Rica in *Garry Halliday* (1961); reading poetry on *Rhyme or Reason* (1962); etc.

La Rue, Danny [Daniel Carroll] (1927–) Irish FEMALE IMPERSONATOR whose brand of ultra-glamorous vulgarity proved to be catnip to the coach parties and family television audiences for a decade from the mid-1960s. He made 'drag' respectable and doused fears that there was anything odd about men who wore frocks for a living. The title of the 1966 *Tempo* special about him was called 'Don't Let the Wig Fool You, Mate'.

R: DESERT ISLAND DISCS (1966); on *Roger Royle* (1988).

T: *Secombe and His Friends* as Margot Fonteyn and with Harry Secombe as NUREYEV (1966); *The Saturday Special – A Night Out with Danny La Rue* (1968); CHARLEY'S AUNT (1970); *This Is Noel Coward* (1972); *Film '72*: Frederic RAPHAEL on location with La Rue for – his only film – *Our Miss Fred*; *Come Spy with Me* (1977); interviewed on *Wogan* (1983); *Tonight with Danny La Rue* (adding 'a touch of camp to Christmas', 1983); *Through the Keyhole* (his English house, 1990 T); with Julian CLARY wearing full leather on STICKY MOMENTS (1990); *Blankety Blank* (1991); a visit to his Australian home and garden in *Burke's Backyard* (1992). When asked if he was gay on a 1977 Monty Modlyn phone-in for LBC Radio, he replied: 'There are three things that no one ever asks me about: my salary, my bed life and my age.'

last names *See* SURNAMES.

The Last Romantic (UK 1978 T) From a converted windmill in Suffolk, retired Brigadier Gantry (André Morell) having looked at the mad world outside has decided to concentrate on the formation of a middle-class commando unit. His rigid position is undermined by the arrival of his son James (Michael Jayston) who is definitely not the man his father was or would like him to be.

W: Kerry Crabbe; P/D: Julian Aymes; 12.3.78; Granada; 85 mins.

Another Canute with a gay son. The difference between this play and LAND OF MY DREAMS (1964 T) is that the son is faint-hearted and the father, a trained soldier with a decisive personality, means business. There is a nice clash of cultures – soft and hard – and the role of the sister (Caroline Blakiston) as go-between is crucial. Poor James. Alcoholic, and blasted on both sides: by his father's pitiless bombast and by his proscenium arch London life, now in disarray (he has lost his job as a BBC producer, and his lover).

(References to the lover's walking out because James brought home 'ROUGH TRADE' were cut between preview and transmission.)

The Last Train Through the Harecastle Tunnel (UK 1969 T) A young railway fanatic (Richard O'Callaghan) meets Jackie Coulson who cooks at the guest house of his widowed dad, Adam (Joe Gladwin). Adam, who adores the lad, only wishes he'd be more interested in trains and steam engines and in brasses, like himself and his dad before him. 'I suppose he must have been a bit disappointed in me. I can remember when I was about 5 and he found I like playing with dolls. He compromised by dressing them up in railway uniforms.' But Jackie also had to walk 'every bloody mile' of the North Stratford line as far as Macclesfield and Congleton.

W: Peter Terson; P: Irene Shubik; D: Alan Clarke; 1.10.69; BBC1.

One of the jokes implicit in this sweetly sentimental but knowing play is Adam's attempt to fight nature. His boy is an obvious QUEEN, enjoying assignations in the station toilet and TROLLING the streets at night. But Adam keeps on hoping that he'll change, become a railway fanatic like him and so become a REAL MAN. It's a double joke because Jackie's grandfather, Tommy, a signalman and one of the great characters of the line, 'had a QUEER streak in him' (he wore a FLOWER in his buttonhole, which was against regulations). Of course 'they didn't have a name for it in those days'.

The Last Woman (Fr-It 1976 C) A man no longer valued for his virility or his ability to head a family. A man with his first grey pubic hair, responsible for his baby son's every need, in a relationship with a woman who wants him for sex but finds him morose and boring post-coitally. Suddenly his life as a phallocrat turns sour on him: the womanizing, the proud display of his – and his son's – cock. He takes up the electric carving knife and dismembers that once noble part of himself, howling like a wounded lion who's discovered he's a warthog.
W: Marco Ferreri and others; P/D: Marco Ferreri; 112 mins.

One of the first MEN'S LIBERATION films which makes the woman's position ambiguous but does not indulge in bashing persons of either gender or sexual preference. All praise to Gérard Depardieu in the first double role not to require trick photography: his penis, both dangling and at a right angle, plays as important a role as the rest of him.

last words Often much thought goes into the words spoken during the final seconds of a film or play. Sometimes, as in the case of THE KILLING OF SISTER GEORGE (1968 C), they're not words but sounds: of mooing. This is an indication of the heroine's next role (Clarabelle the Cow) and of her indelible despair and loneliness. For SUNDAY, BLOODY SUNDAY (1971 C) the last scene found Peter FINCH speaking to the audience, trying to make it understand why he would arrange his life around the whims of a skittish BISEXUAL: half a loaf being preferable to none at all. Compromise of another kind in THE FOX (1968 C): 'It'll be all right, I know you'll be happy' says the man (Keir Dullea) who is taking March (Anne Heywood) away to a better, a normal life. She looks blankly at him and asks rhetorically: 'Will I?'

Very few gay or lesbian films end with a ringing, upbeat phrase. LIANNA (1983 C) was typical. Sobbing on a park bench, being comforted by her friend Sandy (Jo Henderson), the heroine – having been ditched by her first woman lover – blubbers: 'So awful, I just feel so awful.' Signing off with a bang rather than a whimper, Toddy (Robert Preston), garbed in Spanish flounces and mantilla, is thrown a bouquet after his triumphant number in VICTOR/VICTORIA (1982 C). 'They're the last roses *I'll* ever see,' he remarks, before tossing the bouquet to his lover in the audience, collapsing on the stage and being kissed by a stage Spaniard.

One of the greatest challenges facing any scriptwriter was how to end a film in which half of a group of healthy young men introduced at the beginning are dead or dying at the end. Craig Lucas solved this magnificently in LONGTIME COMPANION (1990 C) by having three people on a beach imagine all their friends and acquaintances happy and well and having a huge party: a return to the hedonistic innocence of a decade earlier. Then the dream evaporates. The reality hits them again. There is no cure. But there will be one day. And says Willy (Campbell Scott), echoing the thoughts of millions of people: 'I just want to be there.'

The last last words go to the man considered to be the gay martyr elect, one of the architects of how homosexuals were perceived during the first half of the 20th century. Sozzled and alone in a Paris café, Oscar Wilde (Robert Morley) in the 1960 film downs another absinthe and asks the musician 'Will you play something ... *gay?*' before cascading into the laughter of despair.

Late Call (UK 1975 T) The Calvert family moves to a new town in the 1950s. One of the sons, Ray (Tim Morand), meets someone at the amateur dramatic society and returns to London to live with him.
W: Dennis Potter from the novel by Angus WILSON; P: Ken Riddington; D: Philip Dudley; BBC2; 5 parts; 50 mins each.

An absorbing, off-centre family saga with the gay man receiving support from

BROTHER and GRANDMOTHER but feeling trapped and drawn into the rarefied world of amateur dramatics – where he meets Terry Knowles (Nigel Winder) and escapes to London with him. Ray's fate is contrasted with that of the more flamboyant, upfront Wilf Corney (Hugh Sullivan) who, arrested on a GROSS INDECENCY charge, commits SUICIDE.

latent heterosexuals Barry HUMPHRIES on *Film '72* (T) says: 'One of the things that worries Australians in AUSTRALIA is that when English people visit Australia they describe us as latent homosexuals. It's very worrying to such a virile race. But I think Barry McKenzie proves they're not latent homosexuals but latent heterosexuals.' Dennis the quarterback (Bob Seagren) thinks he may be one in the first episode of SOAP (1977 T), but Jodie is sceptical: 'Oh, what makes you think you have these heterosexual tendencies? Just because you're not crazy about Bette MIDLER?'

Laughton, Charles (1899–1962) English actor who became one of the most enduring star-character players in Hollywood, beloved for his Henry VIII, Captain Bligh and the Hunchback of Notre Dame, and other grotesque characters packed with pathos. Simon CALLOW – influenced by his Quasimodo and author of a distinguished biography of Laughton – presented a 1987 television portrait which confronted the biased, ugly account presented by his widow Elsa Lanchester – with a halo round her as the Wronged Wife – in one of Barry Norman's *Hollywood Greats* in 1978. Callow interviewed Terry Jenkins, Laughton's last lover who helped to dispel the image of him as a kind of repulsive, male Marilyn MONROE: an overgrown, ugly child totally out of control in his work and his private life, argumentative and hyper-critical. Callow took his cue from Laughton's finely detailed, compassionate acting style rather than – as Christopher ISHERWOOD had tried to do in the Barry Norman programme – branching out into the more general self-hatred and societal oppression that bedevilled the actor.

R: repeating his film role in *They Knew What They Wanted* (1940); wartime broadcasts; etc.

T: *Love for Love* (excerpts with Elsa Lanchester, 1934); *The Ed Wynn Show* (1950); *This Is Charles Laughton* (1953); *The Ed Sullivan Show* (guest appearances from 1954 onwards, hosting the show on 28 October 1956 when Elvis Presley was top billed); *Ford Star Jubilee* 'The Day Lincoln Was Shot' (narrator, 1956); *General Electric Theatre* 'Mr Kensington's Finest Hour' (1957); *Charles Laughton: Readings* (UK 1957); *Studio 57* 'Stopover in Bombay' (1958); *General Electric Theatre* 'New York Knight' (1958); *Wagon Train* 'The Albert Farnsworth Story' (1960); *Playhouse 90* 'In the Presence of Mine Enemies' (as a rabbi with Robert Redford as a Nazi officer, 1960); *Checkmate* 'Terror from the East' (as Japanese art dealer, 1961); etc.

(Simon Callow also looked at Laughton's work in the British theatre in *Shakespeare on His Lips* 1987 R, interviewing Fabia Drake, Alec Guinness, Albert Finney and Ian HOLM.)

Laurel and Hardy Arthur Stanley Jefferson (1890–1965) and Oliver Hardy (1892–1957) were the screen's unrepeatable comedy team who displayed a fluid approach to gender : raising a baby in THEIR FIRST MISTAKE (1932); playing their own wives in *Twice Two* (1933); indulging in 30 minutes of boot fetishism in *Be Big* (1930). One could say it was a more innocent age wherein such harmless, childish playacting held no 'darker' side. But this fails to explain why so much scripted and filmed sexual (especially homosexual) innuendo was cut from so many of their two-handers.

Laurents, Arthur (1918–) American playwright (*Time of the Cuckoo*; *Home of the Brave*) and screenwriter (ROPE (1948); *Caught* (1948); *Bonjour Tristesse* (1957); WEST SIDE STORY (co-W); *The Way We Were* (1973); *The Turning Point* (1977); etc.)

lavender In PETER PAN, Wendy observes that 'The mauve fairies are boys and the white ones are girls – there are some colours who don't know what they are'.

When the new commander (John Gregson) takes over his ship in THE CAPTAIN'S TABLE (1958 C), he has to borrow his steward's garters at the last minute. He is horrified to see the colour – though he should have known as the steward is the dotingly droopy Birtweed (Reginald BECKWITH). The blackmailing Alfred Taylor (James Booth) in *The Trials of Oscar Wilde* (1960 C) seems like a regular bloke until attention is drawn to the tell-tale coloured handkerchief in his top pocket. The tie and brocade waistcoat also alert the audience that family lawyer Keith Michell is BENT in more ways than one in *House of Cards* (1967 C) and viewers are therefore not surprised when he is revealed as a woman-hating neo-Nazi.

Archvillain GABRIEL (Dirk BOGARDE) quaffs violet wine from a goblet containing a live goldfish in *Modesty Blaise* (1966 C). Charlie Drake chooses lavender of the deepest hue when he imitates Oscar Wilde in *Mister Ten Per Cent* (1967) while, in the same film, Derek Nimmo's shirt is light mauve and Anthony GARDINER (as Claude Crepe) is lavender all over. Peter FINCH in SUNDAY, BLOODY SUNDAY (1971 C) restrains his colour coding as a successful GP, but lashes out with a lavender neckerchief at a party.

Now that all men are free to wear all the colours of the rainbow, lavender is no longer totally restricted to gay characters: Ernie Wise's lavender shirt and handkerchief with André Previn and the Royal Philharmonic Orchestra (1973 T); lavender and pink shirts for the young detective who helps Adam Dalgliesh in *Death of an Expert Witness* (1983 T); BROOKSIDE's Billy Corkhill (Dean Sullivan) wearing a lavender shirt as he discusses marriage to Sheila – it matches Tracey's tracksuit; a button-down lilac shirt for tough Senior Detective Inspector Frank Burnside (Christopher Ellison) in *The Bill* 'Action Book' (1990 T).

Seven times out of ten, though, the hue is used to semaphore deviation: Cedric HAMPTON in *Love in a Cold Climate* (1980 T) giving his distinctly coloured shirts to soldiers in Spain; the arty talk show host (tie and hankie) in *Wood and Walters* (1982 T); the estate agent in *Down and Out in Beverly Hills* (1986 T); violet robes for charismatic bishop, purple tie, lavender handkerchief and five rings in *UNSUB* 'And the Dead Shall Rise to Condemn Thee' (1989 T); Kate (Ethna Roddy) in the 1990 lesbian episode of SOUTH OF THE BORDER wearing a lavender sweater and pictured with a crucial envelope, which exactly matches the garment; while in the children's cartoon *The New Adventures of Mighty Mouse* (1988 T) the hero is cruised by a mauve-haired fellow convict: 'Hey pretty boy, *you* don't look the criminal type.'

And, of course, Quentin CRISP can still be seen forcing grey out and lavender in.

Laver, James (1899–1975) English writer of novels, short stories, essays, and books on period costumes. Head of the Department of Engravings, Illustrations and Design at the Victoria and Albert Museum, London. A tireless campaigner for male dress reform who was a regular broadcaster from the early 1930s. His last address to the nation was in the appropriately titled *Larger Than Life* (1970 R) in which he reminisced about 'the more flamboyant figures of the last 50 years'.

'I don't think men will ever be as gorgeous as they were at the end of the 18th century ... Why should those who have the courage to dress comfortably be ridiculed? Why should they be stared at? Why can't we wear open-neck shirts if we want to or discard our jackets in restaurants as women do?' (*Clothes – Taboo and Convention* 1932 R).

'As soon as women began to go about the streets in large numbers, men retired ... The party was over. The world was suddenly a serious and rather anxious place' (*Men's Dress Reform* 1937 T).

law 'Attitudes don't change because the law changes ... neither the law nor the Church has the right to tell another human being who he or she can or can't love,' said James BALDWIN to Mavis Nicholson in *Mavis on 4* (1987 T). For most homosexual people, at some time in their lives, depending upon circumstance, desire or location, the law is liable to intrude with brutal and immutable force into their most personal and private space. In many countries, the eternal watchfulness of a NINETEEN-EIGHTY-FOUR state of emergency is a painfully ubiquitous reality.

In DIVERSE REPORTS 'What a Difference a Gay Makes' (1984 T) Denis LEMON didn't have to poke around in the more outlandishly discriminatory backwaters of English law to provide examples of potential danger in his superficially light-hearted mini-'Guide to Staying Out of Trouble'. Among the findings: two women KISSING in public could be done for 'a breach of the peace'; two men kissing is potentially 'insulting behaviour'; a threesome between men in the city, the suburbs, a village or a country estate is illegal; men and women in the armed forces can be dishonourably discharged if there is any provable allegation of a sexual relationship with a colleague or civilian of the same sex; jobs can be lost simply because the person is discovered to be gay, as in the case of a man whose sexuality was deemed by an industrial tribunal to make him unfit as a swimming-pool attendant even though he 'has not shown any tendencies towards young children'; gay or lesbian people applying for custody of their children are probably going to be refused.

Other implications of a whole skein of legal constraints on behaviour have been discussed in programmes dealing with such recent manifestations as CLAUSE 28 and the Spanner case involving SADO-MASOCHISTIC activities in private. The experiences of lesbian and gay people under the law has been dramatized in such series as CROWN COURT and L.A. LAW.

See also POLICE; PRISONS; TRIALS.

Law of Desire (Sp 1987 C) A trendy sex-film director (Eusebio Poncela) takes home a male fan (Antonio Banderas) for the night, but the disturbed young man refuses to leave his life. The director's sister (formerly his brother) becomes involved, and murder and mayhem ensue.

W/D: Pedro ALMODOVAR; P: Miguel A. Perez Campos; 100 mins.

Almodovar's satire on Spanish melodrama, pornography, bisexual closets, ONE-NIGHT STANDS and gender confusion. Not to mention lithe, tanned men in white underwear; the devoutly religious daughter of a lesbian model living with her mother's ex-lover; cocaine-sniffing cops; and the tantalizingly autobiographical-seeming filmmaker juggling two men, one who loves him not enough in one way and one who loves him – fixedly – too well in another. A sort of gay *Play Misty for Me* or *Fatal Attraction*. Humour, amorality and superb technique.

'Almodovar's treatment of homosexual passion and love is intense and exciting, and the relationship he presents could be a model for heterosexual love as well' (National Film Theatre programme note, August 1991).

Lawrence, D[avid] H[erbert] (1885–1930) English novelist whose life continues to provide speculation as to the exact nature of his feelings towards women and men: from *D. H. Lawrence: The Man* (1945 R) to Howard SCHUMAN's 'D. H. Lawrence, High Priest of Love' in *Without Walls* 'Dark Horses' (1992 T), which revealed his strong and possibly physically expressed homosexuality and quoted from some of his works, especially 'The Prussian Officer' and the suppressed prologue to *Women in Love*.

Also: Geoffrey Hutchings as Lawrence in MONITOR 'Death of My Mother' (1964 T); Tom Courtenay in *Solo* (1972 T); Ian MCKELLEN in *Priest of Love* (1981 C); Barry Foster in *Adventuring Together* 'The Story of a Friendship' about Lawrence and W[illiam] E. Hopkin (Garard Green) (1985 R); Richard

Pasco in *The Tarnished Phoenix* (1985 R): 'A portrait of D. H. Lawrence as revealed in his poems and letters and in his wife's memoirs.'

Novels and novellas: *Lady Chatterley's Lover* (1956 & 1981 C; 1993 T); *Sons and Lovers* (1960 C; 1981 T); THE FOX (1968 C; 1974 R); WOMEN IN LOVE (1969 C; 1980 R); *The Virgin and the Gypsy* (1970). Short stories: *D. H. Lawrence* (1966–7 T); Plays: *The Daughter-in-Law* (1986 T); etc.

Lawrence, T[homas] E[dward] (1888–1935) English soldier and folk hero whose legend has been burnished by his victories in Palestine, his 'rape' at D'era, his attempt to find anonymity as Shaw and Ross, and his early death. Guesses as to the exact nature of his sexuality were hazarded in LAWRENCE OF ARABIA, *Ross*, *A Dangerous Man* and, most explicitly, in *Castle of the Star* (1992 R) where his love for Salim Ahmed (whom he called Dahoum) was most tenderly caught. The Lawrence persona was depicted in such plays as THE ASCENT OF F6 and George Bernard Shaw's *Too True to Be Good*.

Played by Peter O'Toole (1962 C; Dirk BOGARDE was scheduled to star in a 1958 version by Terence RATTIGAN, which later became *Ross*, while Marlon Brando and Albert Finney were also considered by David Lean); Paul Daneman (1965 R), Ian MCKELLEN (1970 T) and Michael Williams (1981 R) in *Ross*; Ralph Fiennes in *A Dangerous Man* (1992 T); Simon Chandler *Castle of the Star* (1992 R).

Biography: *T. E. Lawrence – The Man* (1940 R): '[He was] not a woman hater ... [but he had] no team spirit'; *The Spell of Arabia* (1947 R); *As I Knew Him – T. E. Lawrence* by Major-General Ronald Storrs (1951 R); *Lawrence of Arabia* (1955 R): Storrs roundly criticized the book by Richard Aldington, producing 'evidence which discounts the accusation of abnormality'; *Lawrence of Clouds Hill*, a study of Lawrence in his later years (as Shaw) living near Bovington in Dorset (1958 R); *The Amazing AC2*, Group Captain Charles Findlay on

Lawrence (1958 R); *T. E. Lawrence* (1962 T); *Mighty Myths* 'Lawrence of Arabia: Says Whom?' (1984 R); OMNIBUS: *Lawrence and Arabia* (his words read by Michael Pennington, 1986 T). 'Visually every scene between Feisal and Lawrence seemed charged with homoerotic tension' (Jonathan Sanders reviewing *A Dangerous Man*, *Gay Times*, April 1992).

Lawrence of Arabia (UK 1962 C) The story of T. E. LAWRENCE: his fascination with the desert and the Arab culture, his almost mythic status among warring factions, and the irritation he caused in the British military mind.

W: Robert Bolt; P: Sam Spiegel; D: David Lean; 222 mins.

A massive logistical exercise with a cold and enigmatic man at its core is transmuted into a dazzling, churning epic which is satisfying on all levels. The restored version begins with Lawrence wearing mascara and behaving for all the world like Noel COWARD. The ambiguity of his relationships with King Feisal and with the Omar Sharif character are astonishingly direct, certainly as far as looks, vocal tone, body and camera placement are concerned.

'The whole story, and certainly Lawrence, was very, if not entirely, gay. We thought we were being very daring at the time. Lawrence and Omar, Lawrence and the Arab boys ' (David Lean interviewed by Jonathan Yardley, *Guardian*, 28.4.91).

lawyers 'Some men are heterosexual, some men are bisexual and some men think they don't want sex at all. They become lawyers,' Woody ALLEN musing in *Love and Death* (1975 C).

Some of the homosexuals who slipped through the net: Duncan (Wallace Ford) in *The Breaking Point* (1950 C); Bannister (Everett Sloane) in *Lady from Shanghai* (1948 C); Melville Farr (Dirk BOGARDE in VICTIM 1961 C), a successful barrister about to become a QC faced with an impossible choice: pay blackmail or expose the racket and lose marriage and career; Keith Kossett

(John Bonney) who sets up the plot in *Paranoiac* (1964 C); Don FINLAYSON in NUMBER 96; Joseph (Nigel Anthony), a divorce lawyer with some sharp points to make in favour of gay relationships, his own among them, as against legalized heterosexual ones in DUCKS AND DRAKES (1983 R); Steve Rideaux (Patrick Malahide) in VIDEOSTARS (1983 T): backer of Cable Concern, with a strong line in conservative moralizing, imperishable public-school *sang froid* and legal nous, not to mention his ability to lie through his teeth; Agatha (Sheila Dabney) in *She Must Be Seeing Things* (1987 C); Alan (aka 'Fuzzy'), an entertainment contracts lawyer who becomes a gay activist in LONGTIME COMPANION (1990 C).

In *First Tuesday* 'Called to the Bar' (1992 T) Paul Higham talks about all the jobs he should have got since he had the right qualifications: 'If I want to be called to the bar, I have decisions to make whether I am out about my sexuality.'

See also Roy COHN; C. J. LAMB.

Lear, Norman (1928–) American writer and producer who blew a few holes in the walls of America's commercial television Jericho in 1971 with ALL IN THE FAMILY, followed by *Maude, Sanford and Son, Mary Hartman*, HOT*L BALTIMORE, *The Nancy Walker Show* etc.

leather bars first surfaced on television in LOU GRANT 'Cop' (1979 T) when the Coronet is burnt down, killing one member. Lou prints the names of some of those rescued: a minister, an army captain, a lawyer and a philanthropist's son. In CRUISING the undercover cop is surprised to see fellow officers when he visits the Ramrod. He rubs his eyes and discovers it's Precinct Night and everyone is dressed for the occasion. The advent of *Cruising* even tempted critic Alexander Walker to walk on the wild side: 'I checked them out to a timid extent ... in New York ... Unlike some critics, I do believe that the thrill of danger is an intrinsic part of a homosexual community's make-up. And where

there's danger there's violence. I must add that in some heterosexual bars, I've felt much worse vibrations' (*Evening Standard*, 10.4.80). From this time onwards, leather BARS were always featured in films about gays and/or the underworld: PARTNERS (1982); *Police Academy* (1984–90). Claire Bloom, as the wife of an HIV-positive man, follows two gay men into a leather BAR in *Intimate Contact* (1987 T). The lovers in A BIT OF BERLIN (1992 R) run one.

The Leather Boys (UK 1963 C) The strains on Reggie (Colin CAMPBELL) after an ill-considered marriage to Dot (Rita Tushingham) lead him to seek comfort with his mate Pete (Dudley Sutton), but he backs away from a sexual relationship with him.

W: Gillian Freeman from the novel by 'Elliot George'; P: Raymond Stross; D: Sidney J. Furie; 108 mins.

Interestingly dated, mildly sensationalist story given great pathos by the performance of Dudley Sutton as the boy wanting to make the kind of home for Reggie that (screaming harpy) Dot is incapable of providing. The final scene (dockside queer PUB leading to Reggie's total rejection of Pete) is a severe letdown to what has preceded (quite persuasively if lacking in total emotional honesty).

leather jackets Symbol of rebellion, originally intended for military use. *The Wild One*'s Brando popularized them for men – and for male-acting women (Mercedes McCambridge as the vicious biker-dyker in *Touch of Evil* 1958 C; Rita Tushingham as the rackety Dot in THE LEATHER BOYS). The guys in SCORPIO RISING fetishize them. Now acceptable to lend decadent fashion ambience for semi-lesbians like C. J. LAMB in L.A. LAW, Finn in SOUTH OF THE BORDER (1988–91 T), Paula (Francesca Annis) in *Inside Story* (1986 T), and Kim (Jane Lapotaire) in THE OTHER WOMAN (1976 T).

leather men Used as comic characters in films as diverse as *Police Academy* and

THE PRINCE OF TIDES (1991) wherein Nick Searchy as 'Man at party' asks Tom (Nick Nolte) to dance. Queen's Freddie Mercury prancing in black leather on TOP OF THE POPS. Leather dyke Roxy (Leliani Sarelle) in *Basic Instinct* (1992 C).

Leave It to Beaver (US 1957–63 T)

The Cleaver family of Mayfield: patient, all-wise Dad, everything under control, dazzlingly well-groomed Mum, all-American kid brother and the runt, Theodore or the Beaver who is always getting into strife. A Norman Rockwell-style American TV family popular in the late 1950s and 1960s; revived by the Disney network in 1984. 'I thought it was going to be like *Leave It to Beaver*,' opined 'Anthony', whose marriage broke up after two days (DONAHUE 1989 T).
C/W/P: Joe Connelly and Bob Mosher.
  A very lively family, with a kid hero who announces that he is never going to get married, 'especially to a girl' ('BLACK EYE' 1957). Unfortunately he disregards his own inner voice and, in the 1984 series, is overweight and divorced.

left-handedness Often equated with homosexuality – though rarely by homosexual people themselves: 'No one should no more deplore homosexuality than left-handedness,' a speaker on 'Towards a Quaker View of Sex' in *Thoughts from the Air* (1963 T); James Patton, chief clinical psychologist at a Belfast hospital who said on BBC Radio Northern Ireland in 1976 that 'homosexuality should be as normal as left-handedness'.

Lehmann, Beatrix (1898–1979) English actress, sister of John and Rosamond LEHMANN, whom the *Listener*'s J. C. Trewin, apropos her contribution to *The Dance of Death* (1953 T), called 'an expert in theatrical acid tossing'. Philip HOPE-WALLACE praised her Miss Figgis in LOVE AND MISS FIGGIS (1954 T): 'a slightly oversized but wonderfully compounded study in exasperated feminism.' Her Aunt Matty in *A Family and a Fortune* (1952) was, decided Trewin, 'a

self-pitying scorpion ... she talks throughout in verminous italics.' Today, she is remembered by a devout few as a craggy face and a voice redolent of guttering candles, lead-light windows and blue-grey slate: always old, even when young. She probably played more mothers of gay men than any other artist, beginning on stage with her Mrs Venable in *Suddenly Last Summer*.
  C: *The Passing of the Third Floor Back* (1935); villainous cousin Elfrida in *Strangers on a Honeymoon* (1936); Marguerite in *The Rat* (1937): 'a sinister housekeeper ... a female killer as sinister as the most menacing on the screen' (*Variety*); *Candles at Nine* (1944); Rex Harrison's slurping, screaming, senile mum in STAIRCASE.
  R: Carrie Craik, a faded spinster in *Pleasant Portion* (1935); Ines in HUIS CLOS (1946); the unloved wife in *Manservant and Maidservant* (1954); the dowager in *The Repair of Heaven* (1957); Lorna in *Pillars of Society* (1962); *Nathan and Tabileh* (1962); Lady Ottoline Morrell in *A Dialogue on Pacifism* (1964); Agave, Pentheus' mother in *The Bacchae* (1964); an ancient in *Back to Methuselah* (1965); Freda Borgman waiting for the death of her husband in *Walk in the Dark* (1968); title role in *Hecuba* (1976, winning an Imperial Tobacco award for best radio performance in this play by David RUDKIN).
  T: Lady Anne in *Richard III* (1937); La Cachirra in *Somerset Maugham Hour* 'The Mother' (1961); the mummy in *The Ghost Sonata* (1962); *The Aspern Papers* (1962); Volumnia in *The Spread of the Eagle* (1963); Mrs Touchett in *The Portrait of a Lady* (1965); Mrs Fennel, mother of gay man in *Is Nellie Dead?* (1968); Mrs Millicent in *Boy Meets Girl* 'The Eye of Heaven' (1968); dying mother of probably gay son in *Menace* 'Inheritance' (1970); dotty aunt in *Love for Lydia* (1977).

Lehmann, John (1907–87) English writer, founder and editor of *New Writing* in 1936. Brother of Beatrix and Rosamond LEHMANN. He broadcast regularly on the Home and Overseas services, and compiled and wrote for the radio magazine *New Soundings*. He was particularly interested in the interlocking mythology and symbolism of the pagan and Christian worlds (*Christ the Hunter* 1964 etc).

Also: *Portrait of Virginia Woolf* (1956 R); *Favourite Characters* 'James STEERFORTH' (1959 R); *Radicalism Then and Now* (1962 R); *Writers' World* 'In the Shadow of Cain' (First World War poets, 1964 T); *The Faces of* MAUGHAM (1974 R); KALEIDOSCOPE 'An Inner Life' (on Rosamond Lehmann, 1985 R); etc.

Lehmann, Rosamond (1901–90) English author, sister of Beatrix and John Lehmann, whose novels DUSTY ANSWER (1990 R) and THE WEATHER IN THE STREETS (1962 & 1984 T) both included male and female homosexuality in the subplots. Occasional radio talks; first TV interview on *Bookmark* (1985).

Leisen, Mitchell (1898–1972) American film and television director, formerly a production and set designer (the 1922 ROBIN HOOD and some De Mille epics). Mainly cherished for his flawlessly designed, cynical 1930s comedies and 1940s period pieces, but he also helmed a couple of classic TWILIGHT ZONES.

C: *Cradle Song* (directorial début, 1933); *Death Takes a Holiday* (1934); *Murder at the Vanities* (1934); *Hands Across the Table* (1935); *Easy Living* (1937); *Midnight* (1938); *Hold Back the Dawn* (1941); *Lady in the Dark* (1944); *Frenchman's Creek* (1944); *Kitty* (1945); *Bride of Vengeance* (1949); *Captain Carey USA* (1950); *The Girl Most Likely* (1957).

T: *Shirley Temple's Story Book* (1958); *The Twilight Zone* 'The Sixteen Millimetre Shrine' and 'Escape Clause' (1959); *Adventures in Paradise* (1959); *Markham* (1960); *The Twilight Zone* 'People are the Same All Over' (1960); *Thriller* 'Worse Than Murder' and 'Girl with a Secret' (1960); *Wagon Train* 'The Prairie Story' (1960); *Follow the Sun*

(1961); *Empire* (1961); *The Girl from UNCLE* 'The Doublegate Affair' and 'The Petit Prix Affair' (1967).

Leisure and Pleasure (UK 1953–5 T) The BBC's early afternoon miscellany of personalities (photographer Jane Bown, writer Vera Brittain, Richard WATTIS dancing the TANGO with Marjorie Stewart, actors Ursula Jeans and Roger Livesey, and a 16-year-old Corin Redgrave), hobbies, music, fashion. It was a programme with more than a touch of rococo, full of poseurs and posturers in aquamarine, bouteille and eau-de-Nil decorated and inlaid with over 18,000 Majorcan pearls. All this brought a touch of what later became identified as camp to BBC programmes 'for women'. These were sedate affairs far removed from the tawdry discussions (demystifying schizophrenia) that assault women today. In this setting, blow waves and SUEDE SHOES were acceptable because these men were harmless eccentrics. Moreover, they were 'experts' and television, then as now, was hungry for expertise. It was, therefore, a safe harbour where Ernest THESIGER could show off his embroidery (in 1955), fashion emperors could gush about gowns, and a travel agent called Merlin could discuss these new-fangled things called 'package holidays'.

Lemon, Denis (1945–) English gay activist, editor of GAY NEWS (1972–82). He was played (without dialogue) by Peter Machin in EVERYMAN 'Blasphemy at the Old Bailey' (1977 T).

Became a powerful voice on gay issues and related matters, especially after he was successfully prosecuted by Mary WHITEHOUSE: *Call-In* (1972 R); 100th edition of GN (1976 LBC R); *Newsbreak* (1976 R); *After Lunch Special* (1977 LBC R); THE EDITORS 'Sex and the Press' (1977 T); *The World at One* (1977 R); LADIES NIGHT 'Homosexuals' (1977 T); *The Heart of the Nation* (1978 BBC Radio Birmingham); *Monty [Modlyn] at Large* (1979 R); *Theatre Call* (1979 R, about BENT); *Brass Tacks* 'Some of the Nicest People I Know' (1981 T, about

SEXUALLY TRANSMITTED DISEASES); *Late Night from Two* (1982 T Granada area; he said his greatest ambition was 'to be a castaway on DESERT ISLAND DISCS). He presented and produced DIVERSE REPORTS 'What a Difference a Gay Makes' (1984 T).

Lenny the Lion Children's television character, given movement and voice by Terry Hall who got the idea in 1954 when an old lion yawned at him in a zoo. Instead of being King of the Jungle, Lenny was its Queen, a combination dummy and puppet (known as a 'vent') who combed his hair, blew his nose, fluttered his eyelashes and LISPED 'Don't embawass me!'

Beginning with *Variety Parade* at the start of 1955, Lenny appeared on many variety shows and ended his days very usefully – helping British literacy in *Reading with Lenny* (1978 T). At his peak, he was sold in shops along with soap, slippers and balloons bearing his image. His fan club included more than 20,000 children from Dr Barnardo's Homes and he was Mascot of Millwall Football Club, which Lenny regarded as 'vewy exciting'. He slept beneath a pink coverlet and relied heavily on a little girl fwend (Judy Horn), even though he re-alized that 'It is a bit SISSY to wely on a girl to get me out of my twubbles'.

Lent (UK 1985 T) A young boy, Paul (Graham McGrath) is stuck over the holidays in a prep school run by his uncle. He is befriended by the mainten-ance man, Maitland known as Matey (Harry ANDREWS). He was married in 1919 and divorced two years later ('It didn't suit us'). The head questions Paul as to whether he was in Matey's room or not and, if so, what were they doing?

W: Michael Wilcox; P: Tom Kinni-mont; D: Peter Barber-Fleming; 10.2.85; BBC2 Scotland (Screen Two); 60 mins.

Michael Wilcox's play set in the 1950s is slight, but contains one classic scene in which 'beef tea' becomes an issue of deafening significance. The boy has

some nice, busting-out-all-over things to say on the growing up other people want to force him into: 'Looks as if I'm going to be a man whether I like it or not...'

Lenya, Lotte [Caroline Blamauer] (1899–1981) German singer and actress, wife of Kurt Weill and friend and collaborator of Bertolt Brecht. Linked with the Berlin of the 1920s and 1930s, which she evoked in an OMNIBUS interview recorded shortly before her death, spiced with performances of 'Mack The Knife', 'Pirate Jenny' and 'Surabaya Johnny'. She made only a few films: the 1931 *Threepenny Opera* (Die Dreigroschenoper), followed after a gap of 30 years by her Academy Award-nominated pimp in *The Roman Spring of Mrs Stone*. She was a gloriously stone-faced lavender menace (name of Rosa KLEBB) in *From Russia with Love* (1963) and, again after a hiatus, as Clara Pelf, chiropractor and guru in *Semi-Tough* (1977).

Leonard Boy's name, sometimes used for characters with a tendency towards concealment.

UK: theatrical Leonard Pirry (Dennis PRICE) in *The Intruder* (1954 C); Leo-nard Vole in *Witness for the Prosecution* (Tyrone Power 1957 C: Beau Bridges 1982 T); *Leonard Marjoribanks (Kenneth WILLIAMS) in *Carry On Cruising* (1962 C); Leonard Brazil (Tim CURRY), powerful local radio DJ in *City Sugar* (1978 T); Leonard (Mark Burns) in *The Bitch* (1980 C); FEMALE IMPERSONATOR Lenny (Robert Gary) in *Belles* (1983 T); Leonard Meopham (Stephen Dillane), poet in *Heading Home* (1990 T); Leo-nard Gray (Ronald Pickup) in *Gray Clay Dolls* (1991 R).

US: Leonard St John (Phillips HOLMES), who kills himself in *The Secret of Madam Blanche* (1931 C); Leonard Arlen (Hardie Albright) in *Red Salute* (1935 C): 'perverts the minds of the younger generation ... an immigrant'; crusty Dr Leonard Gillespie in *Dr Kil-dare* (Lionel Barrymore 1942 & 1943 C; Raymond Massey 1961–6 T); Wally

Cox in the title role in *Fireside Theater* 'Leonard Sillman's New Face' (1949 T); Leonard Borland (Paul Douglas), wrecking contractor with undiscovered baritone voice in *Everybody Does It!* (1951 C); Leonard (Martin Landau), jealous secretary of James Mason in *North by Northwest* (1959 C); Leonard (Elliott Reid) in *The Wheeler Dealers* (1963 C); Dr Leonard 'Bones' McCoy (DeForest Kelley), the medical officer in STAR TREK (1966–9 T; 1980– C), jealous of Captain Kirk and Spock?; Leonard Zelig (Woody ALLEN), a human chameleon in *Zelig* (1983 C); Leonard Gluck, first-class nerd and reject in *The Love Boat* 'Julie's Blind Date' (1983 T); Leonard Lowe (Robert De Niro) brought back to life by the drug Aldopa and by Robin Williams in *Awakenings* (1991 C).

'Lens' tend to be heterosexual, but wayward and stroppy when roused, eg Len Fairclough (Peter Adamson) in *Coronation Street* and Len (Tom Bell) who is having an affair with a teenage girl in *All the Right Noises* (1971 C).

Leon Morin, Priest (Fr 1961 C) An unfulfilled love affair during the Occupation between a priest (Jean-Paul Belmondo) and Barny (Emmanuelle Riva), a woman on her own but in an ambiguous relationship with the Amazonesque Sabine Levy (Nicole Mirel).
W/D: Jean-Pierre Melville, based on an autobiographical novel by Beatrix Beck; P: Carlo Ponti and Georges De Beauregard; 128 mins (originally the film ran for 3 hours 13 minutes).

'A priest is always frustrated. Look at how the only people asking to be allowed to marry at the moment are the priests. No one wants to get married any more except them. In any case, Leon Morin is a man, and men need to make themselves suffer ... being a priest is a way of making oneself suffer'. He is Don Juan, driving the women wild. She is a Communist, a feminist, who converts to get him into bed. 'She has come close to the priest, to his thoughts, but suddenly this isn't enough; she must make love with the agent of God.' (Jean-Pierre Melville

quoted in Rui Nogueira, *Melville on Melville*, 1971).

Leonardo Da Vinci (1452–1519) Italian scientist, artist and engineer, renowned for the *Last Supper* fresco, the *Virgin of the Rocks* and the *Mona Lisa*. Ralph Steadman, the artist and cartoonist who has a passionate fascination for the life and work of the artist, passionately declares in his documentary *Don't Tell Leonardo* (1984 T) that the man wasn't gay. No proof either way, just a categorical statement.

Leopold and Loeb Nathan Leopold (1906–71) and Richard Loeb (1907–36) were American law students who murdered a young boy in 1924; they escaped the death penalty, receiving life plus 99 years. ROPE (1948 C etc); COMPULSION (1959 C); Warren Stanhope and Marvin Kane in *The Sentence of the Court* (compiled by Edgar Lustgarten, 1964 R); Martin McDougall and Alexis Denisof in *Never the Sinner* (1990 T); Craig Chester and Daniel Schlachet in SWOON (1991 C).

lesbian First heard in the cinema in THE GROUP (1966 C) and in WARHOL's *The Chelsea Girls* (1966): 'You're not even a vegetable – but you *are* a lesbian. When did you develop these lesbianic tendencies?' On British television: as an 'ism' by John WOLFENDEN in 1957; as 'ian' in THIS WEEK (1965). On British radio, apart from brief mentions, in the play LOVESICK (1967): 'What do you mean I'm not really a lesbian. I love her. I've never been so happy.'

The stage version of *The Killing of Sister George* (1965) received the blessing of the Lord Chamberlain's office only because the word 'lesbian' was not uttered. But in Lukas Heller's screen adaptation (1968) CHILDIE (Susannah YORK), furious at George's (Beryl REID) consistently delinquent public behaviour (ie flaunting her sexuality), turns on her pell-mell: 'Not all girls are raving, bloody lesbians, you know.' To which George replies grandiloquently: 'That is a misfortune of which I am perfectly well aware.'

A year later, the word turned up in a comedy, THE VIRGIN SOLDIERS (C). The RSM (Nigel Patrick) accuses his wall-flower daughter (Lynn REDGRAVE) of being FRIGID and 'a lesbian'. The inclusion of the latter was the cause of many letters and telegrams to and from the producers making the film in Singapore and Columbia Pictures in Hollywood. Would this word spoil the picture's chances of television sales? Was it necessary to the plot? Finally, Columbia relented and 'lesbian' was uttered three times; each time in a negative context.

These two films were successful, as were LES BICHES and THE FOX. Lesbian and its -ism were now okayed for television. The ethereally wild Ivich (Alison Fiske) could drag her brother's mistress (Georgia Brown) on to the dance floor and remain there, hip to hip, in THE ROADS TO FREEDOM (1970 T). Afterwards, Ivich asks Boris (Anthony Corlan) if he is 'basically QUEER'. To which, quite reasonably, he rejoins: 'Are you basically lesbian?' Neither of them answers the other's question.

The word occasionally could be heard WITHIN THESE WALLS (1974–8 T) but almost never in the Australian cousin PRISONER/PRISONER: CELL BLOCK H. A producer of *Within These Walls* has commented that every single episode should have included sex and desire instead of only 5 out of 65 or so.

'Lesbian' bounced back and forth during the 1970s. It was described by the maker of THE IMPORTANT THING IS LOVE (1971 T) as 'an ugly word'. Many of the women who went on camera in the film preferred to be called 'gay'.

'I got these weird impressions from television that lesbians have muscles and thick eyebrows,' commented Rose as she plays bar billiards in the documentary VERONICA 4 ROSE. Lesbian, if used, was usually turned into a negative with a negative: 'I'm not a lesbian ... They just say that 'cos they're jealous of me and Mike. And I'm not mental,' said Chrissie Mead (Lillian Rostakowska) in WITHIN THESE WALLS 'Transfer' (1975

T); 'I'm not really a lesbian after all,' said Felicity (Veronica Quilligan) in *The History Man* (1981 T).

There were mentions in passing like Henry Fonda's of his FUNNY neighbour in *On Golden Pond* (1981 C), and fleeting glimpses like Nick Black's wife in BROOKSIDE (1986 T) and the social worker ('She's a lesbian but she's a very nice person') in EASTENDERS (1986 T). And there were a few jokes: fingers in ... and The Dick Van ... Show.

'Heaven knows what [men's] impression of lesbianism is, but if it's women who don't sleep with them on the first encounter then let's all be lesbians' – this was Germaine GREER's answer to a woman caller's question during a phone-in on *It's Your Line* (1971 R).

Lesbians were also gay, at least they used to be. Before disenchantment with their brothers and their growing invisibility brought about a separate identity in the late 1970s. Dusty SPRINGFIELD was described as being 'at the top of the gay girls' hit parade' in GIRL (1974 T). And the 1930s song, which Breeze (Morag Hood) in COUNTRY MATTERS 'Breeze Anstey' (1972 T) turns to for the bitter-sweet ecstasy also present in her day-to-day existence with Lorna (Meg Wynn Owen), was chosen for its double meaning:

> There's no reason why
> I should conceal
> Why I'm feeling far from gay.

'Lesbian' could hardly ever be said without some qualification or distortion to heighten its scurrilous, shady appeal: thespian (*The Wild Party*; *The Ray Moore Show* 1984 R) etc.

In the 1980s it could be occasionally found served up as a statement of regrettable fact: 'Do you think she was a lesbian? Most nannies are, you know. Subconsciously, of course,' Phyllis Calvert in *Tales of the Unexpected* 'The Reunion' (1983 T). Or as a trendy declaration: 'I'm a bald, black lesbian mother,' Velma (Isabelle Lucas) in AGONY 'Too Much Agony, Too Little Ecstasy' (1979

T); 'She's a black Jewish lesbian,' an introduction to Linda Bellos on ANY QUESTIONS? (1988 R). Or as a blooper: 'Lesbian forces moved into the Sinai Desert: I'm sorry, Lebanese forces moved into the Sinai desert,' Max Ambrose, ABC Radio National, Australia, *c* 1984. Or as guilt by association: 'It's not that she's *butch* or *lesbian*, but she's the greatest man-hater I've ever met,' Clive Arrindell in *Cover* 'What Are You Doing, My Little Men?' (1981 T). Or as titillation: in PERSONAL SERVICES (1986 C) Shirley (Shirley Stelfox) and Christine (Julie Walters) meet the needs of a barrister who fantasizes about being a schoolgirl; as they flick through 'Sex on Lesbos', Shirley turns and tells her friends, that, gosh, she's come over 'all lesbian'; with the same robust determination a child would give to a lollipop, Shirley gushes: 'I love being a lesbian, don't you.'

A larky usage, which didn't find wide public favour, was that of Cecil BEATON, posing in the park for David Bailey in *Beaton by Bailey* (1971 T). Instead of saying 'cheese', Beaton preferred a sibilant 'lesbian' to impart the required sickly smile. Hackney Central Library in London paid belated tribute to Beaton's wheeze with a 1988 exhibition of photographs rejoicing in the title 'Don't Say "Cheese", Say "Lesbian"'.

'I don't like being called a lesbian ... I didn't know I'd done wrong ... It sounds all right when you're with me. But when I'm away ... I've got to know where I am,' says Amy (Zelah Clarke) in THE TINKER'S DAUGHTER (1986 T).

Lesbian and Gay Broadcasting Project *See* ARE WE BEING SERVED?

lesbian erotica Includes Barbara Hammer's *Women I Love, Dyketactics* and *Multiple Orgasm* as well as *Compartment* (1980), *Mano Destra* (1986), and *Nicotine Porn* (1990). The first to reach national British audiences was the very restrained – but erotic – *Rosebud* in 1992.

lesbianism always leaves a nasty taste in my mouth Dame Edna EVERAGE (Barry HUMPHRIES) upon being asked by a trendy journalist if she's ever 'balled a chick' in *Barry McKenzie Holds His Own* (1974 C). In *The Dame Edna Experience* (1988 T) she was leering at Nana Mouskouri and Zsa Zsa Gabor 'communicating with our juices, our drives ... our little electric vibrators'. When this is correctly interpreted, the Dame becomes untypically abashed: 'You're not suggesting playing hospitals with a person of your own sex, are you?'

lesbians Lots of them in the GATEWAYS scene in THE KILLING OF SISTER GEORGE (1968 C), all seemingly having a good time; four different kinds of lesbian in one shot in *Ecoute Voir* (1978 C): butch collar and tie, butch/femme in a bun, femme/butch in a trilby and trench coat, and femme ordinaire – a young woman; more dancing around in LIANNA (1983 C) and *Simone Barbes* (1979 C); and a cross-section in IN THE GLITTER PALACE (1977 T). Making a grand gesture on behalf of her sisters, Brigitte Kahn's black leather-garbed Letty says in THE GENTLE TOUCH 'Melody' (1980 T): 'The point is, darling, we've always been around and we always will be. You can't fight Mother Nature, so why not accept it?'

Leslie Boy's name which is used, with this spelling, as a girl's name in America but as 'Lesley' in the UK. Very much yoked with gay or effeminate characters in Britain.

UK: Leslie Benn (Sonnie Hale) in *Evergreen* (1934 C); Lieutenant Leslie Phillips (Leslie Phillips), silly ass, left-hand-down-a-bit navigator on HMS Troutbridge in *The Navy Lark* (1958–77 R; 1959 C); Leslie (Malcolm Hayes) in *The Day After Tomorrow* (1960 R) living in one room in Primrose Hill; Leslie Darkin (Roger Davenport) in SOFTLY SOFTLY 'Murder Reported' (1974 T); Leslie Simons (Derek Smith) in CROWN COURT 'Meeting Place' (1978 T), self-proclaimed asexual, living with his sister, accused of forcing his attentions upon a lad, gnawingly unsympathetic, a frightened rabbit; Lesley Burrows

('Spelt with a "Y": you see Mum wanted a girl' (Hugh PADDICK) in SHARE AND SHARE ALIKE (1978 R); the simpering dresser (Peter SALLIS) in YOU'RE NOT WATCHING ME, MUMMY (1980 T); Leslie (Terry Bader), newspaper-office token poofter *Daily at Dawn* (Aust 1980 T); Leslie (David Banks), WINDOW DRESSER in *Keep It in the Family* 'The Mouthtrap' (1980 T): is he or isn't he?; domesticated son (Ian Targett) who lashes out and gets tattooed in *Marks* (1982 T) and who finds out that the 14-year-old girl he mildly fancies is called Lesley (Traclynn Stephens): 'It put me right off' (his mum thinks it's a nice name: '*In a boy*'); Les Foster (Grant Kennedy) in THE FLYING DOCTORS 'Return of the Hero' (Aust 1986 T); Leslie Titmuss (David Threlfall), unscrupulous local boy makes good Tory in *Paradise Postponed* (1986 T) and *Titmuss Regained* (1991 T); Leslie Willey (Leslie Phillips) in *Starring Leslie Willey* (1988 R); Leslie Latchmoor (Bernard Cribbins) rising above lonely bachelorhood in *A Different Way Home* (1988 R); Leslie from Shepherds Bush (Mark Hadigan) visiting his Uncle Reg in Melbourne in *The Boys from the Bush* (1991 T); Leslie (Frank Windsor) expressing serious sorrow after his lover's death in CASUALTY 'Allegiance' (1991 T).

US: Leslie (George K. ARTHUR) in *Wickedness Preferred* (1928); Leslie Trotter (Charles Drake), the sailor who awakens repressed Charlotte in *Now, Voyager* (1942 C); Leslie Wiggins (Stephen Crane) in *Tonight and Every Night* (1945 C); interior decorator Leslie (Alan Mowbray) in *The Jackpot* (1950 C); Deputy Sheriff Les Martin (Cornel Wilde), the hero of *Edge of Eternity* (1959 C); Leslie Hall (Edward Kemmer), blackmailer and murder victim in PERRY MASON 'The Case of the Pathetic Patient' (1961 T); the Great Leslie (Tony Curtis), all aglow in white, hero of *The Great Race* (1965 C); Leslie Harrington (Paul Langton) in *Peyton Place* (1964–9 T); Leslie Whitlock (Kevin McCarthy) in *If He Hollers, Let Him Go* (1968 C), jealous of his wife's money, blaming her death on a black

man; Captain Leslie Anders (Jim Brown) in *Ice Station Zebra* (1968 C); Leslie Washburn (Hari Rhodes) in *The Protectors* (1969–70 T, black DA first seen in *Deadlock* 1969); Leslie 'Buddy' Krebs (Brian Dennehy) in *Star of the Family* (1982 T); Leslie Slote (David Dukes), American diplomat officer in *The Winds of War* (1983 T); Leslie Huben (John Lithgow), unpleasant head missionary in *At Play in the Fields of the Lord* (1991 C).

Letter from America (UK/US* 1946– R) The venerable, venerated Alistair Cooke has been delivering these sound missives for nearly 50 years with nary a break. An outsider-insider's look at our American cousins from Roosevelt to Clinton, through the Depression, the New Deal, the Second World War, McCarthyism, Korea, the Bay of Pigs, Vietnam, women's liberation, Watergate, Reaganomics, AIDS. Calm, considered, syntactically superb, Cooke's observations are conservative, considered and informed – save in one or two areas. Cooke had virtually ignored gay rights until forced – in an extraordinary 'apology and correction' on 7 February 1993 – to acknowledge the parallels between the opposition to blacks being integrated into the American armed forces and that now being mounted against President Clinton's proposals for 'public' recognition of homosexual personnel. The only other time Cooke had deigned to recognize gays as a force – albeit a violent one – was at the time of the San Francisco rioting when the murderer of Harvey MILK was given a 2-year prison sentence. In the February 1993 'letter' Cooke described himself as 'a pundit and codger'. In fairness to this remarkable broadcaster, when he does turn his mind to these matters he is even-handed and measured but refuses to engage fully with the subject, seeing it as a 'Pandora's Box'.

*Began as *The American Half Hour* in 1935, dealing with such subjects as 'The Negro'.

letters Usually expressing feelings of desire and/or tenderness, these are dramatically useful in bringing together characters who are geographically apart, or to serve as revelations to the audience or to other characters of the sexual natures of one or both correspondents. EDWARD II opens with Gaveston reading a letter from the King; letters between women weaving fantasy romances are basic to the plots of SYRUP OF FIGS (1986 R) and *Heavenly Creatures* (1993 C); letters written but not received are at the core of THE COLOR PURPLE (1985 C) and *Calamity Jane* (1986 R); *The Kremlin Letter* (1970 C) is a secret agreement between Russia and China forged and fought over by a group of top Soviets, most of them homosexual; more conventional same-sex love letters in POR-TRAIT OF A MARRIAGE (1990 T) and LAW OF DESIRE (1987 C), but less so in THE LOST BOYS (1978 T) where they are written by an older man to male children and youths. Lorraine (Lonette McKee), one of THE WOMEN OF BREWSTER PLACE (1989 T), was thrown out of her home at 16 because of a communication discovered which said things women are not supposed to say to one another. Letters used for BLACKMAIL purposes in VICTIM (1961 C), *A Song at Twilight* (1982 T; 1988 R) etc and they helped seal the fate of Oscar WILDE. A loving note from Buckingham to 'Dear Dad and husband' JAMES I was the basis for an RSVP programme (1992 R): '[the equivalent of] a silly notelet' [but] 'The most extraordinary letter ever made public by an English king.'

Let Yourself Go Irving Berlin number from *Follow the Fleet* (1936 C), sung first by Ginger Rogers, then by Fred Astaire and a group of fellow sailors. He is teaching them to dance – together. They are enjoying it greatly until three (envious?) marines break it up. Fred remains totally unfazed by whole thing.

Leviticus A book of laws in the BIBLE which has been used by a number of religions to illegitimate homosexuality, and often to talk about it in plague-laden terms.

'Thou shalt not lie with mankind, as with womankind: it is abomination. Neither shalt thou lie with any beast to defile thyself therewith.' Like most things divinely inspired, it all lies in the interpretation. Young Fowler (Tristram Oliver) reads from Leviticus to the school assembly in ANOTHER COUNTRY (1984 C). The older boys shift uncomfortably in their seats, recalling their own delicious misdeeds in this direction and knowing that Fowler has supped well of what he decries, at least in his power-dominated imagination. The scene is intercut with Guy Bennett's (Rupert Everett) half-playful, half-diligent attempts to get Tommy Judd (Colin Firth) into bed after lights out.

When Michael Meade (Ian HOLM) plucks up courage to take the hand of Toby Gashe (Michael Maloney) in *The Bell* (1982 T), the adaptor cuts to a sermon both men are listening to. It has as its theme adulterers and sodomites: 'They in themselves are not disgusting, they are simply forbidden ... Truth is what counts.' But in the 1950s this truth could land both men in prison.

See also SODOM AND GOMORRAH.

lezzos 'They say that half of prison warders are lezzos and the other half are frustrated,' says Bea Smith (Val Lehman) about Vera Bennett (Fiona Spence) in PRISONER/PRISONER: CELL BLOCK H (1979 T). This abusive term for lesbians is also scrawled on Kate's (Ethna Roddy) car in SOUTH OF THE BORDER (1990 T).

Lianna (US 1983 C) The far from smooth coming out of an American wife and mother (Linda Griffiths).
W/D: John Sayles; P: Jeffrey Nelson and Maggi Renzi; 115 mins.

A little tale told with a good light touch, and blessed with a striking performance from Jane Hallaren as the self-possessed Professor Ruth Brennan who carries Lianna on a lavender cloud, but cools considerably when commitment threatens. She explains crisply that she – who teaches child psychology – can't fully join Lianna in her onrush of public sexual freedom because she has 'to talk parents into running psychological experiments for their children'. Another source of pleasure in the film is the cameos: friends, neighbours, local lech, a lesbian army officer encountered in a bar. And Lianna's diligently cool and unruffled 13-year-old son who appears to be a bit ahead of mom in his personal politics:

> Mother: 'Sometimes people get to be good friends and live together.'
> Son: 'You mean "homos".'
> Mother: 'And when it happens between women.'
> Son: 'They're called "lesbians".'
> Mother: 'I'd rather not use that word.'

Liberace [Wladziu Valentino] (1919–87) American pianist and showman who weathered the jokes, the slurs and the massive shifts in musical fashion. He was one of the very few consistent artists in this field to have spanned 40 years without actually wearing women's clothes – although he was never far away in his feathered cloaks and jewel-encrusted jump suits. Violinist Nigel Kennedy said in 1991 that he was very honoured to be compared to Liberace. Elton JOHN has also been put into this league.

C: *South Sea Sinner/East of Java* (as a pianist, 1950); *Sincerely Yours* (a remake of *The Man Who Played God* with Liberace as a deaf pianist, 1955 C); *The Loved One* (showing off funeral caskets, 1965 C).

T: *You Bet Your Life* (with Groucho Marx, 1955); *The Liberace Show* (1960); DESERT ISLAND DISCS (1966 R); Chandell in *Batman* (1966 T); *Here's Lucy* (1970); *The World of Liberace* (1973); playing 'Chopsticks', boogie-woogie and a Chopin nocturne on *The Muppets* (1978); at New York's Radio City Music Hall in *Friday People* (1985); etc.

Biography: *The World of Liberace* (1973 T); *Old Stagers* (1988 R); *Liberace* (with Andrew Robinson) (1988 T); *Liberace:*

Behind the Music (with Victor Garber, 1988 T).

'This is not glistening eyeballs and tripping around as though it was one big lark. He was a very talented man and probably could have been a concert pianist' (Andrew Robinson interviewed about *Liberace*).

'We didn't want to make a nasty business out of it. The sum of his life's work shouldn't be that terrible, unfortunate thing that happened to him. This man brought joy to a lot of people' (Peter Locke, associate producer of *Liberace: Behind the Music*, in *Sun-Herald TV Guide*, Australia, November 1988).

Liberace and the Press (UK 1956 T)
Liberace had sued *Confidential* for $25 million. He said he was fighting for the reputation 'of every entertainer and good American'. He settled out of court for $40,000. He then sued – again successfully – Britain's *Daily Mirror* for an article by 'Cassandra' (William Connor) which again impugned his masculinity.
D: P. Jones; 8.10.56; Granada; 30 mins.

This programme, holding its hand over its mouth at certain points, doggedly covered the proceedings which publicly nailed the lie that Liberace was 'less than a man' and led to the *Daily Mirror* forking out a small fortune to repair the damage to his self-esteem and public standing. The star 'laughed all the way to the bank' and how.

The pianist was still maintaining, a year before he died, that he was holding himself in readiness for 'Miss Right'. This man's bare-faced cheek was truly remarkable. For four decades, he led his fans and the media a merry dance. Teased and teasing, he wooed the right-wing Daughters of the American Revolution, putting Mom and popped-up classics on the map amid candelabra and sequins. While men scoffed, their womenfolk stoutly defended him. No HOMO he. Rather, this was someone to be admired: a great entertainer, good to his mother and poignantly denied every American male's right – Miss Right.

'Contrary to gossip, he is not lonely or obsessed by his mother. His taste is controlled, even demure ... He is not homosexual' (Tony Palmer, director of *The World of Liberace* (1973 T, quoted in the *Observer*, 1973).

Liberation VILLAGE PEOPLE number sung very quietly in a scene from CAN'T STOP THE MUSIC. Composed by Jacques Morali, Henri Belolo, Phil Hurtt and Beuris Whitehead.

librarians One of the most maligned professions, presented as washed-out creatures, obsessed by rules (especially the one bidding 'Silence'). A few relevant custodians of stores of knowledge: Bertha Anderson (Georgia Backus) in *Citizen Kane* (1941 C), fearsome wardress of the Thatcher Library in Philadelphia ('You will be required to leave this room at 4.30 prompt-ly') and described in the shooting script as 'an elderly mannish spinster'; Irma (Viveca Lindfors) guiding young *Sylvia* (Carroll Baker 1965 C) to Jane Austen and the like; Philip Johnson (Barry McCarthy), woman-shy in THE EXPERT 'True Confessions' (1970 T); Bernard (Reuben Greene) in THE BOYS IN THE BAND (1970 C) shown behind the New York Public Library counter during the opening credits; the school librarian (Les Lye), protective, blondined, dripping in lavender and jewellery in *You Can't Do That on Television* (Can 1983 T); Liz (Helen Atkinson Wood) now running an alternative theatre company in *Blood and Bruises* (1988 R).

Life Goes On: A Revue for Television (UK 1938 T) One of a half-dozen or so slick and knowing concoctions of song and sketch which were then so popular in the West End. The numerous sly allusions to things forbidden (including 'GAY', 'FRUIT' and 'QUEEN' in the song 'INTERIOR DECORATION', and 'ball fringe' and 'busts' elsewhere) must have either bewildered or captivated the two persons and their dog who made up the television audience (London area only, and sets were pricey).
W: Nicholas Phipps (and David Yates

Massey); M: Geoffrey Wright; P: Reginald Smith; 21.7.38; 30 mins.

A Life Is for Ever (UK 1972 T) The routines, the hopelessness, the petty fights and the problems faced by a heterosexual man, Johnson, pursued by his cell-mate, young McCallister (Tony Meyer) who makes clear his intentions by jumping out of his bed – bum naked – and staring him down. 'If there was someone who really liked me and told me he didn't want anyone else to ... and I loved him and he knew it and he let me prove it, then there was nothing I wouldn't do for him ... would you pass my shirt, please?' In toilet recess, McCallister asks Johnson to love him. Johnson beats him up. In the final scene, McCallister, working in the library, is abused by another prisoner. To McCallister's surprise, Johnson punches the man and appears to be staking a claim as his protector.
W: Tony PARKER; P: Irene Shubik; D: James Ferman; 75 mins.
Very much up to Tony Parker's standard: fine on prison details, good dramatic punch, but depressing and oppressive. The gay man is presented as physically attractive but sly and neurotic, giving sexual favours to screws and 'hardmen' prisoners alike. There are echoes of the much later KISS OF THE SPIDER WOMAN, but without even that film's superficial character building. The producer was quoted as saying how pleased she was to have been involved in a production which, possibly for the first time, showed homosexual 'sex' in an honest light.

Life Is Sweet (UK 1990 C) Mum and Dad (Alison Steadman and Jim Broadbent) are still happy together, but one of their twin daughters, Nicola (Jane Horrocks), is a mess: anorexic and a gobbledegook FEMINIST. On the other hand, her sister, Nat (Claire Skinner) is in great shape: a plumber with no fixed attachments ('single and carefree, thanks') aged 22. Not quite what the girly girl Mum – who works in a children's clothes shop – had intended, but not to worry...

W/D: Mike Leigh; P: Lorraine Goodman; 109 mins.

Of interest solely because of the friendly, natural way that Nat is introduced into the flimsy story. She's no bother, gets on with life, is her own person. Maybe she doesn't have a need for a social life; maybe she's a secret raver. All options left open, but the impression remains a clear one: she's a dyke, now or in the future; the sort of person anyone would value and trust.

lifestyle Ubiquitous jargon word used to express the whole manner and matter of an individual's life, but tending towards the commercial and materialistic and sexual. Very apparent in good gay-fearing American talk shows as well as gay-flattering dramatic jobs as in HOOPER-MAN and HEARTBEAT.

Derived from a German word, it became very popular in the 1970s to cover a multitude of material ambitions and comforts as well as the exotic and the taboo. Quentin CRISP, who had been a proponent of 'style' at all costs in one's 'life', was one of the prompters for dissenters and conformists alike to begin seriously discussing the intricacies of their 'lifestyles'. Advertisers neatly packaged it, no questions were asked. Which made it the perfect smokescreen for the English presenter travelling out East for a radio series. He encounters curious natives who ask him about wife and children. He 'explains his lifestyle' to them. They ask him if he's happy. Emphatically he says, yes, he is. The details obviously disturb his listeners (but not us, as we are not privy to them) because they exclaim in horror: 'But, we want you to go to Paradise' (*On the Train to New Zealand* 'Pakistan' 1980).

'If it were a *girl*, the jury might naturally think you were trying to indoctrinate her into a lesbian lifestyle,' prosecution counsel to a mother fighting for the custody of her young son in A QUESTION OF LOVE (1978 T).

'Your new lifestyle is damaging to your child,' prosecuting counsel to Maggie in

L.A. LAW 'The Nut Before Christmas' (1991 T).

'Does the blame lie in pursuing a gay lifestyle? You might as well blame the road because you had a car crash on it,' speaker on THE GAY AND LESBIAN WORLD programme dealing with the spread of HIV/AIDS (1992 R).

light/light on his feet Soft footfalls bespeak soft minds and twisted motives: Rock HUDSON's nimble Irish patriot *Captain Lightfoot* (1954 C) may be a hero, but Gary Cooper's secretary (James GRIFFITH) irritates the hell out of him the way he floats around his tobacco-financed mansion in *Bright Leaf* (1950 C). The term also describes someone apparently predisposed to unmanly pursuits (with other men): the prize fighter disparaged to Tom Selleck in *Lassiter* (1984 C); and possibly Clint Eastwood's younger partner Jeff Bridges in the second half of *Thunderbolt and Lightfoot* (1974 C). The soap opera star in LONGTIME COMPANION is worried about doing a gay role on TV in case future employers say that 'he's a little light'.

lilies In a 1987 episode of COUNTRY PRACTICE the middle-aged bachelor Maxwell Laurence (Frank Lloyd), who works in the bank, is obsessed by his dead mother and attracted to young *girls*. He is presented as a pathetic, prissy, cravat-wearing wimp surrounded by pictures of himself as a baby, and with a pot of lilies very visible in a number of his scenes. Lilies are also well to the fore in the house of ladylike vampire Miriam (Catherine Deneuve) in THE HUNGER (1983 C).

Lilith The demonic first wife of Adam, from the non-canonical part of the Bible called the Apocrypha. She was the first woman, created at the same time as Adam, out of the same clay. She saw herself as equal and was driven out of Eden for refusing to be second class. In Isaiah 34:14 Lilith is a 'night monster' or 'screech owl', and in the Jewish tradition she is an ugly demon. As Lilith

Arthur (Jean Seberg) says of her biblical namesake (*Lilith* 1964 C): 'She wants to leave the mark of her desire on every living creature in the world.'

In *Lilith and Ly* (1919 C); she (Elga Beck) is a statue brought to life: 'the menacing incarnation of female desire'; in *The Tree of Knowledge* (1920 C) she (Yvonne Gardelle) attempts to seduce Adam in the Garden. More recently, she was played by Marianne Faithfull in *Lucifer Rising* (1981 C), and incarnated as Lilia, a white bisexual vampire who meets a black lesbian researcher in *The Mark of Lilith* (1986 C). Miriam MARGOLYES as Lilith took tea with the Lord in *Gardens of Eden: Poems for Eve and Lilith* (1987 R), while Lilith (Gabrielle Heht) spoke an unintelligible ancient language, ate a lot of apples and seduced housewife Susan in *Scrumping* (1992 R).

Non-biblical versions include the cold, calculating psychologist Lilith Ritter (Helen Walker) who helps drag Tyrone Power further down the *Nightmare Alley* (1947 C); sweet pioneer gal Carroll Baker in *How the West Was Won* (1962 C); Dr Lilith Sternin-Crane (Bebe Neuwirth), 'eccentric' humourless psychiatrist with an alphabet soup of qualifications in *Cheers* (1988–92 T).

(Radio Lilith was the name of a pioneering feminist station in Rome.)

lily of the valley Prominent in the buttonhole of *Oscar* WILDE (Robert Morley 1960 C) during the first part of the trial of Lord Queensberry. The bouncing flower (sometimes known as 'fairy bells') mirrors Oscar's confident, aphorism-spouting mood. After he stumbles badly over the matter of not kissing a boy because he was ugly, his mood and his decoration changes dramatically. A starkly triangular top-pocket handkerchief replaces the sprig of lily of the valley.

Alex Walker's new bride in THE TWILIGHT ZONE 'Young Man's Fancy' (1960 T) has a spray of lily of the valley, as does he. He looks at a photograph of his dead mother and there's a flash of lily of the valley. When he finally makes her

spirit rise, the woman is wearing a dress entirely covered with these FLOWERS.

Harry Lime Character played by Orson WELLES in *The Third Man* (1949 C) and by Michael Rennie in the 1959 TV series. A black marketeer of swivelling loyalties in the original, he became – through television mastication – an international art dealer with a lugubrious 'secretary', Bradford Webster (Jonathan HARRIS). Only the zither music stayed the same.

Carol Reed, the director of the film, was said to have based Lime on the character and demeanour of Jimmy, played by Cary GRANT in SYLVIA SCARLETT (1935 C). Superficially 'a little friend to all the world', he is pretty much a rotter through and through, dividing the world into 'sparrers' and ''awks', totally immoral, taking the path of greatest profit no matter what the human cost. The casting of Welles (Reed's original choice was Noel COWARD) brings out Lime's ebullience and sexual power, enhanced by the tight black coat and slouch hat. He reminds Holly Martins (Joseph Cotten) about the days when they meant a great deal to each other: Lime was the schoolfriend who 'stopped him feeling lonely'. 'I loved him,' Holly tells the heroine. '... We did everything together.'

limp wrists Buckling, flapping, unflexing: this is the primary indication that a gay man is in the vicinity in plays and comedies. Usually the man himself will downturn his feeble appendage, often with a purse of the lips, a flick of the lashes and a turn of the foot. On occasion the het character will adopt the pose either to make a silent comment about someone or to reflexively deny that he is any way that way inclined.

In THE ENTERTAINER (1960 C) Archie Rice (Laurence Olivier) ends his act with carefully couched contempt at his (sparse) audience. As he leaves the stage, he gives them not a two-fingered salute but a limp wrist.

In *Dancers* 'The Benefit' Mark (Charles Kearney) massages the heroine's foot, while he talks of his new male lover: 'My athlete's doing all right. He was full of the usual prejudices. You know, male dancers are wilting lilies' (he turns his hand into a wilting lily to emphasize the point).

The World About Us 'The Manwatcher' (1977 T) showed some results of field studies carried out in 25 European countries and in Tunisia to look at the interpretation, distribution and variation of 20 key gestures. These included the balled fist, the cheek screw and the temple screw. The limp wrist was not among them.

Lindsay / Lyndsay / Lyndsey / Lyn / Lynn

Boy's name until the late 1950s. Popular in Britain during the 1960s, but only for girls.

US: Lindsay Atwell (Conrad Nagel) in *Ann Vickers*; Lindsay Marriott in *Farewell, My Lovely* (Douglas Walton 1944 C; John O'Leary 1975 C): 'he was a heel but nobody deserves to die like that'; Lyn BELVEDERE (Clifton WEBB), prissy bachelor babysitter in *Sitting Pretty* (1948 C); etc.

UK: Stephen LYNN (Valentine DYALL etc), the sardonic friend of Alec in BRIEF ENCOUNTER whose overreaction to finding him and Laura at the flat smacks of red-hot jealousy; 'confirmed bachelor' Lyndsay (Robert Stephens) who has turned his house and grounds into a paradisial recording venue in *Studio* (1983 T); Henry Lindsay (Trevor Bowen), bachelor leader of the Tories in *First Among Equals* (1986 T): the smile on the face of a grey pussy cat.

Australia: teenager Lindsay Seymour (Ben Mendelsohn), sensitive boy whose parents worry when they discover that his friend is gay (and opposed to the Vietnam war) in *All the Way* (1987 T).

The name is only rarely in use for female characters. US: Lynn (Bette Davis) in *Fashions of 1934*; Lynn Ashton (Wynne Gibson) in *The Crosby Case* (1934 C); Lynn Markham (Joan Crawford) as the threatened *Female on the Beach* (1955 C); child psychologist Lynn Carson (Donna Pescow) in ALL MY CHILDREN (1977).

UK: Lindsay Rimmer (Lorna Heilbron) in *An Unofficial Rose* (1974–5 T): companion to and lover of a prickly woman novelist); Lynn Palmer, the warden of the flats in TOGETHER (1980–1 T); Lynn (Georgina Hale), fashion queen in *Gems* (1987 T).

lisp/lisping It gives an added squelch to anti-gay put-downs like Dennis Waterman's Terry surveying the queen-sized bed in MINDER 'Whose Life Is It Anyway?' (1980 T) with 'Oh, it's thooper!', or FLOWERDEW's (Peter SELLERS) 'I'm so mad, I could spit' in early GOON SHOWS. Peter Jones as Cyril Kitsch in THE FAT OF THE LAND (1969 T) has a speech impediment which makes him even more ridiculous and childlike. The narrator of *The Wild Party* (1974 C) regards the lisps of the gay brothers D'Amano as a further proof of their unnaturalness. One of THE VIRGIN SOLDIERS (1969 C), Roy Holder, wants to get out of the army: 'Do you think I'd get a discharge if I said I was queer?' He then proceeds to lisp.

Listen with Mother (UK 1950–82 R)
A 15-minute pool of sticky sweetness: stories, songs and rhymes for children under 5. The regular readers were Daphne Oxenford and Julia Lang, who, during the 1950s, told of 'Noel and the Yule Log Fairies' (1954); 'Tom's Grown-Up Trousers' and 'Buster the Bus' (both 1956); 'Tom Tabby Goes Adventuring', 'Elizabeth Helps Mother' and 'Tommy's Morning Out' (all 1958). In the next decade it was 'My Naughty Little Sister and the Big Girl's Bed' and 'Marmaduke and the Sailors' (1966); 'Gusty Jim and the Very Naughty Boy', 'Margaret Ellen and the French Lady' and 'Jonathan Buys the Bread' (all 1968). Among the programme's many adult fans were groups of stewards on luxury liners; one bunch wrote to *Radio Times* in 1964 vowing that they daily switched over from the pop music on Radio Luxembourg to listen *with Mother*. Its successor, *Listening Corner*

has slightly bolder, more realistic stories; 'The Little Car Feels Peculiar' (1986); 'OLIVER BUTTON IS A SISSY' and 'Mrs Plug the Plumber' (both 1987).

The Litmus Question (UK 1975 R)
Paul Smith (Steve Hodson), a bishop's son who is falsely accused of COTTAGING, is in a relationship that he's happy with and proud of. But his father Richard (Alan Rowe) cannot accept his son's chosen path, despite the sermons he preaches. It is only when another minister, Charles Holt (Richard Hurndall), who has inside knowledge, takes the older man through his learned reactions to the real meaning of the Christian message that some degree of rapprochement can begin.
W: Leonard Barnett; BBC Radio 4.

The Litmus Question was the first post-gay liberation radio play and the first to mount a mild criticism of the majority's abuse of its power. It showed a gay man who has fully accepted his own difference and has effectively created a whole new way for living based on a few political assumptions. 'It's true. I'm not ashamed of it any more … It's no more sordid or dangerous to us than your loving mother was to you. It's a good and beautiful thing.'

The vicar Charles Holt puts the need for gay liberation succinctly: 'They once burned witches at the stake, assuming they were depraved because they were different. A revolution has got to happen. And it's coming.'

The author was vicar of Ballards Lane Church, Finchley in North London. He had regular spots on BBC's *Thought for the Day* and Radio London's *Platform*. His specific interest in gay people found focus in his involvement in Parents' Enquiry (a counselling service for families of gay sons), in his book *Homosexuality: Time to Tell the Truth*, and this play, broadcast on a Thursday afternoon in May and never repeated. The Rev. Barnett was not a supporter of the gay liberation movement, especially its radical (and by then defunct) activist wing, the Gay Liberation Front. To him, the banners, the chanting and the zaps on the straight world were 'negative and counter-productive'.

The problem in the play is not sparked off by Paul who lives with and loves his boyfriend and is happy with things as they are. He says to his lover Ian (John RYE): 'I feel I've come alive somehow – I'm living a real life. Nobody's trying to fit me into a pattern. I'm not a phoney anymore.' The fly in the ointment is the wicked gay libber, Paul's former lover. This loathsome creature (Duncan, hissingly played by Michael Deacon) is a social security scrounger, 'a rather unsavoury type of person': a thoroughgoing bad lot, in fact. In a scene of limited conviction, the villain lures Paul into a public lavatory. The vice squad pounce and Paul is charged with GROSS INDECENCY.

The meat of the play lies in the dialogue not between father and son, but between the former and an old friend, also a priest. This character helps at a counselling service for gay men. It is likely that this interest and commitment has a more personal basis than he is willing to admit to his prickly friend. There is much thundering about SODOM, the rape and pillage of the word GAY, the true love of parent for child, and other issues too rarely discussed after WOMAN'S HOUR, let alone *on* it.

The almost complete absence of plays addressing issues fundamental to the full integration of gay children in the family makes *The Litmus Question* possibly of more consequence than it would otherwise be. And given the play's stance on the gay movement, GAY NEWS (74) was kind: 'This sketch is just the right sort of medicine to give a society sick with HOMOPHOBIA. It deals with the religious roots of the difficulty some heterosexuals have in accepting young gays … Being a methodist minister himself who has had to work through the usual prejudices himself has given Dr Barnett the insight necessary to bring off a significant homophile public relations exercise.'

Little Caesar (US 1930 C) Glorifying the American gangster – or does it? The fast rise and nasty fall ('... is this the end of Rico?') of a strutting, snarling bully who is not interested in dames, dotes on his protégé (Douglas Fairbanks Jr), wears snazzy clothes and gets too big for his tailor-made shoes.

W: Francis Faragoh from the novel by W. R. Burnett; D: Mervyn LeRoy; Warner; 80 mins.

Piercing, relentless gangster opus, the template for a whole host of such throughout the decade, given an extra something by the performance of Edward G. Robinson, who, with Peter LORRE, was probably the most physically disconcerting leading actor in Hollywood. The not-so-submerged feelings Rico has for his Joe are put across in jagged, flame-throwing manner by Robinson – but not in any way returned by Fairbanks Jr.

little girls' room A euphemism which falls naturally from the ever-so slightly pursed lips of Mercy Croft in THE KILLING OF SISTER GEORGE; in the 1978 radio version a genteelly pulled chain is clearly audible. Hollywood has been a long time coming to terms with the intestinal tracts of women, not to mention their ovaries: it's still a shock when women talk about such things in a fictional or even a documentary setting.

From the late 1980s things seemed to be changing: Shelley Long says 'I'm getting my period' in *Outrageous Fortune* (1987 C); Mimi Rodgers announced that she wanted 'a pee' in *Someone to Watch Over Me* (1987 C) and she is seen in a crouching position (before she's attacked – by a man) in a public toilet. Superficially sedate, well-groomed Henrietta (Edwina Day), harassing her unfaithful husband in HARD CASES (1988 T), has ears flapping when she growls: 'If my husband was on fire I wouldn't piss on him.' Probably the most natural of natural functionaries were Margi Clarke and Alexandra Pigg, chatting the while in *Letter to Brezhnev* (1985 C).

Little Queen (NZ 1988 C/T) Growing up gay in the 1950s: fantasies about

Queen Elizabeth II and the reactionary attitude to 'queens'.

W/P/D: Peter WELLS and Stewart Main; 15 mins.

Little Richard [Richard Wayne Penniman] (1932–   ) American rock singer and evangelist who has been gay, not been gay, returned to being gay, ceased being gay – very publicly for quite a few years (THE SOUTH BANK SHOW; *Ebony*; etc). He recently had a guest spot as 'Himself' on *Guys Next Door* (1990 T) giving one of the boys advice on rhythm, or in Little Richard-speak: 'A-wop-bom-aloo-mop-a-lop-bam-boom.' His parting shot was: 'I love you guys. I mean, I really love you.'

C: *The Girl Can't Help It* ('Ready Teddy', 'She's Got It', 'The Girl Can't Help It' 1956); *Don't Knock the Rock* ('Tutti Frutti', 'Long Tall Sally' 1957); *Mr Rock 'n' Roll* ('Lucille', 'Keep a-Knockin'' 1947); *Catalina Caper/Never Steal Anything Wet* ('Scuba Party' 1967); *Keep on Rockin' (Sweet Toronto)* from Toronto Pop Festival ('Good Golly Miss Molly' etc 1969); *Let The Good Times Roll* ('Lucille', 'Good Golly Miss Molly', 'Rip It Up' 1973); *Down and Out in Beverly Hills* (as a preacher, 1986).

T: *It's Little Richard* (with the Shirelles and Sounds Incorporated, 1964); *The London Rock 'n' roll Show* (from 1972 Wembley Pop Festival, London – 'Lucille' etc 1974); *Diana Ross – Red, Hot Rhythm and Blues* (1987); impersonated on *In Living Color* (1990); etc.

live and let live Frank Sinatra used it in THE DETECTIVE (1968 C), surrounded by sneering colleagues, in relation to homosexual men having sex in the backs of trucks on the dockside. Simpering old silly Ernest (Arthur HOWARD) says it – about his gay nephew Finch – in *The Whiteoaks Chronicles* 'Jalna' (1954), and Barry's brother in EASTENDERS (1987 T) accepts his homosexuality with a cheery, resigned 'You're my kid brother and that's all there is to it. Live and let live. That's my motto!'

A year earlier in Albert Square, Angie (Anita Dobson) is the first person to suss out Colin RUSSELL. She knows that the quiet graphic designer hasn't been dumped by a girlfriend as he shakily claims. 'I know what you mean,' she reassures him over a gin. 'We used to have a couple of gay blokes come in. Some people think they're off another planet but ... live and let live, that's my motto. Your secret's safe with me.' And it is Colin's motto, too. When Donna (Matilda Ziegler) derogates Colin after he's left the Square, Dot (June Brown) defends him: 'I don't 'old with it meself, but live and let live, I say.'

The Living End (US 1992 C) Two young men, one on the run, both immuno-suppressed, hit the road. Sex on a deserted beach, a couple of ice-pick murdering lesbians, a loaded gun held (to his own mouth) by a man reaching orgasm ...

W/D: Gregg Araki; P: Jan Gerrans; 86 mins.

The flowering of the talent first visible in the late 1980s with films such as *The Long Weekend (O'Depair)*. Araki's budget for this feature? A mere $20,000.

'Intriguing premise has malleable young gay writer John (Craig Gilmore) taking up with a callow, volatile, hard-boiled drifter Luke (Mike Dytri) shortly after both learn they are HIV positive. 'Till death do us part' is their motto when they're forced to hit the road after the drifter shoots a cop ... Shot with economy and verve ... pic is not without its sterling moments' (Amy Dawes, *Variety*).

'Pay attention. Something important is happening on the screen and it has everything to do with what is happening in the world at large. Araki's Californian wasteland is not the sanitized lotus-land traditionally served up by Hollywood. It's a stale and barren landscape whose desolation serves as the canvas for a desperate love affair of depth and complexity' (Robert Julian, *Bay Area Reporter*, 27.8.92).

Livingstone, Ken (1946?-) English politician (MP for Brent East), former Leader of the GLC. His relaxed, jokey style has made him a regular on nearly every kind of chat, current affairs, news quiz, record request and miscellaneous show: *Question Time* (1986 T); *Pick of the Week* (1987 R); OPEN SPACE 'The Page Three Debate' (1987 T); DESERT ISLAND DISCS (1993); etc. During the mid-1980s, under the GLC umbrella, he attempted to promote a manifesto for full lesbian and gay equality in every sphere of life on a number of programmes. The title of the document: 'Changing the World'. He gave it his best shot, but ...

Lloyd, Innes (1925–91) British producer (with the BBC until 1980) linked with Alan BENNETT: *A Day Out* (1972); *Sunset Across the Bay* (1974); *Objects of Affection* (1982); AN ENGLISHMAN ABROAD; TALKING HEADS; A QUESTION OF ATTRIBUTION. Also: *Standing by for Santa Claus* (1968); *The Snow Goose* (1971); *Orde Wingate* (1976); *Fothergill* (1981); *How Many Miles to Babylon?* (1981); *Reith* (1983).

The Locomotion The zestful pleasures of this 1963 Gerry Goffin–Carole King hit sung by Little Eva provide the musical key that finally unlocks Jess (Charlotte Coleman) as she rides the dodgems and enjoys the other fairground attractions in company with the free spirited Katy (Tania Rodriques) in ORANGES ARE NOT THE ONLY FRUIT (1990 T); 'I know you'll get to like it if you give it a chance ... Come on, come on/Do the Locomotion with me ...' It was also sung – and danced, more or less in synchronicity – by upward of a hundred lesbians and gays in a segment of OUT's piece of olde tyme gaye world (*c* 1950s and 1960s) in 'Storm in a Teacup' (1992 T).

Lola Song by Ray Davies about a man's attraction to TRANSSEXUAL Lola. The Kinks performed this piece of pop pioneering on TOP OF THE POPS and *The Kenny Everett Explosion* (1970 T). It was still being used in the 1980s to denote homosexuality, rather than transsexualism – accompanying the gay Italian

BARTENDER as he cycles along narrow Jersey roads in *Bergerac* 'Nice People Die in Bed' (1981 T).

London Characters (UK 1964 R) Compiled by Phillip O'Connor, this was a BBC Home Service series of half-a-dozen 'testimonies' from people who had let their personal idiosyncracies sprout and blossom without pruning. One was a 'self-made beauty' whose advice to housewives was not to bother about the dusting: 'after the first four years your dust doesn't grow any more.'

This heresy and the man's languid delivery of a total preoccupation with gilding the self to the exclusion of dull, routine existence upset Arthur Calder-Marshall no end: 'The imperception necessary to the practice of exhibitionism, produces an obliviousness to the outside world which is pitiable ... The price of privacy has been affectation and the price of affectation is that nobody will believe anything which he says sincerely' (*Listener*, 5.3.64).

But to the speaker, one Quentin CRISP, 10 years away from international fame espousing the very same philosophy, sincerity and insincerity were interlocking, relative bodies floating in the space between nature and artifice.

London Lesbian and Gay Switchboard *See* GAY SWITCHBOARD.

The London Weekend Show (UK 1977–8 T) A Sunday lunchtime slot aimed at young people, produced and presented by Janet STREET-PORTER. Her take-it-or-leave-it cockney accent, ever-changing hair colour, confronting teeth and spectacles became symbols of the new brooms that were at work in television, soon to become more visible – and at times even more whacky than Janet – in the series produced by London Weekend Television's Minorities Unit, by the BBC (16 UP; *Something Else*) and, later, under the aegis of CHANNEL 4.

For the first time, young gays and lesbians were included in the mix of post-pubescent London, albeit in one-off

packages called 'Teenage Gays' (which introduced Tom ROBINSON and brought him to the attention of a record company); 'Young Lesbians' (bus conductress Joanne and student Claire – who KISSED at the end: a first for Sunday lunchtime); and more gingerly (shown on a Saturday night) 'RENT BOYS'. A year later, the Show followed up some of the participants. Claire and Joanne reported no ill effects on their lives as a result of talking about themselves on camera. And Tom Robinson and his band had notched up two hit records.

The London Minorities Unit was formed which begat GAY LIFE, and Janet Street-Porter moved on to *Twentieth Century Box* which would deal with sex, ballroom dancing and incest.

London Weekend Television *See* LWT.

loneliness Miles Cooper (David Cameron) is 'just alone': an ageing gay man, once the toast of society, now given succour by a non-gay woman and female poodle in *Chances* 'Bite the Golden Bullet' (1991 T).

A favourite image of the 1960s – the lonely gay and lesbian – gave way to one of isolated gays or lesbians: a twosome with, if they were lucky, a decent heterosexual friend to give them a pet. Sometimes these were labelled 'boyfriend' or 'girlfriend' (Eileen Atkins in WANTED: SINGLE GENTLEMAN (1967 T), or they were neighbours (the prostitute who gives Sister George a place to shed a tear: she was a clairvoyant in the stage version). The homosexual friends on offer were usually far from supportive (FOX AND HIS FRIENDS 1975 C; COMING OUT 1979 T). With a few exceptions (the wounding but essentially comforting, stimulating and funny BOYS IN THE BAND 1970 C; the unseen but named people invited to Graham's party in ONLY CONNECT 1979 T; the woman who organizes the farewell bash for Robert in PARTING GLANCES 1985 C; the alternative families that surround sick and dying men in A DEATH IN THE FAMILY 1986 C/T and LONGTIME COMPANION 1990 C), gays and lesbians are seen as essentially anti-social, though perhaps not by choice. It is that good and patient straight person who, ultimately, is seen as the one who cares: in THE L-SHAPED ROOM (1962 C); NIGHTHAWKS (1978 C); AGONY (1979–81 T); *My Father's House* (1981 T); LIANNA (1983 C); THE GROUNDLING AND THE KITE (1984 T); etc.

Only in THE NAKED CIVIL SERVANT and DESERT HEARTS (1985 C) is the homosexual person seen as the lynchpin of a whole network of relatives, friends, lovers, former lovers and acquaintances; criss-crossing gender, age and sexuality, a full player in life, rather than a reserve. In the main, the lesbian is Dolly (Cher) in *Silkwood* (1983 C) succoured by her straight surrogate mother and father and the homosexual is the man on the ferry (Harvey Fierstein) to Fire Island in *Garbo Talks* (1984 C): 'I'm not looking for sex, just someone to talk to.'

Persistent imagery across three decades. In 1980 Sir Geoffrey Jackson of British Telecom, one of the guests on *Midweek* (R), laughingly said that, for him, the typical television play was one in which 'two elderly gays sat and looked melancholy at one another'.

Loneliness (UK 1957 T) Gilchrist Calder's documentary touched, for the first time, on male homosexuality in Britain. Disguised, of course, as single men – twice as many were living on their own compared to 25 years previously.

The Lone Ranger He and his faithful Indian friend, Tonto were the targets of innuendo on *Rowan and Martin's Laugh-in* (1968 T) with Sammy Davis Jr as the man on the white horse and Dan Rowan as his lisping, swishing sidekick. Kenny EVERETT revamped the concept each week on his show (1983) with similarly limited ambitions: handbag swinging, make-up and much tossing of the hair. Funniest by a hoof was Kenneth WILLIAMS as the Palone Ranger on ROUND THE HORNE (1967 R).

In 1977 Rupert Hine composed a song for his group Quantum Jump called 'The Lone Ranger' which presented the

masked man as a drug-smoking homosexual man. 'I came to wondering why we always saw him and Tonto riding off together and never with a woman.' The BBC removed the song from its playlist in 1977. Kenny EVERETT broke the ban on his radio programme, and in 1979 a new version was recorded which reached no. 4 in the charts.

Lonesome Cowboys (US 1968 C) A band of 'brothers' – Julian, Micky-Lou, Eric and Little Joe – rides into a sleepy (and very underpopulated) town, and engages in some chat with the sheriff (who enjoys slipping into a corset and wig) and a gal named Ramona who does/doesn't want to be treated rough by one or two of the boys simultaneously.

This 100-minute film blips and hiccups, the dialogue is desultory and frequently inaudible, the plot (surprisingly moral and 'family' centred) keeps getting lost, as do the actors' trains of thought, so doped up do they seem to be. In other words, it's Andy WARHOL and the factory (Joe DALLESANDRO, Viva, Taylor Mead, Louis Waldron) way out West. As daft and irritating as much of it is, *Cowboys* probably paints a truer picture of the dreamers and drifters in the Old West as most oaters. None of the Hollywood variety ever suggested, as this film so unselfconsciously does, that men on the range peed together, dressed and undressed in front of each other, gossiped and had sex (either with the few available women or with each other).

Long Alone The eerily evocative song playing on the juke box in the Washington gay bar in ADVISE AND CONSENT (1962 C). The lyrics by Ned Washington are interpreted by Frank Sinatra, and mark the first ever written for a Hollywood film that consciously set out to express same-sex yearnings.

The melody by Jerry Fielding is also the film's theme, thereby linking a subculture to the mainstream of the élitist world of Washington politics. Why then was it never issued commercially? The words are a trifle downbeat but as nothing compared to Sinatra's 'One For My Baby'. The scoring is lush and commercial. Sinatra is in fine voice. The clue to why there was no release of the soundtrack lies in the latter half of the recording. Without warning a strange electronic hum cuts across the strings and brass. This displacement of what has been melodious and piquant may indicate a genuine concern on producer-director Otto Preminger's part to convey, through distortion, the acute alienation of the men socializing together before facing the real world. More likely, the slurry of strange vibrations on the record was intended to convey queerness as an accompaniment to the sublime despair of the words as delivered by Sinatra. (Deterioration of sound to convey ominous, unnerving shadings was probably first employed by Sergei EISENSTEIN with Prokofiev's 'Battle on the Ice' music in *Alexander Nevsky*.)

longtime companion This phrase became noticeable outside America in the early 1980s, historian Jeffrey WEEKS using it to refer to George Merrill in relation to Edward CARPENTER in a *Journal of Homosexuality* paper called 'Inverts, Perverts and Mary-Annes' (Fall–Winter 1980–1).

Before this period, it had been seen in obituaries, eg the actress Marjorie Rambeau's 'longtime companion' is mentioned in *Variety* in 1970. The single word COMPANION tended to be used solely for women. In Omnibus' 'Portrait of Mary RENAULT' (1981 T) the writer was shown on a South African beach with 'her COMPANION ... friend and adviser' Julie Mullard, who had begun living with her in the 1930s.

Peter PEARS, in a spousal relationship with Benjamin BRITTEN for five decades, was described as his 'longtime companion' in THE SOUTH BANK SHOW 'A Time There Was' (1980 T), which was billed as 'a unique insight into Britten's life and loves'. The phrase 'lifelong friend' was applied to Pears in the introduction to PETER GRIMES when the 1981

production was shown in Australia in 1989.

The Australian television networks desribed Manoly Lascaris as 'long-time friend' (Channel 9), 'lifelong partner' (ABC) and 'longtime companion' (Channel 7) of novelist Patrick WHITE when the latter died, aged 78, in 1990. SBS, the minority ethnic channel, dealt with the matter by ignoring Manoly's existence – as one half of a 49-year partnership, which White described as 'the central mandala in my life's hitherto messy design' and his 'sweet reason'.

An expatriate Australian, dancer, choreographer and actor Robert HELPMANN was given the biographical treatment in 'Tales of Helpmann' (1990 T): his 'lifelong relationship' with Michael Benthall meriting a couple of minutes, securely anchored in matters artistic. In the tribute to British novelist Angus WILSON (1991 T) Tony Garrett was called his 'constant companion', with one mention of their 'living together'.

The personal–political implications of the word for which longtime companion is most often a more acceptable replacement were briefly alluded to in the 1990 film of the same name in a scene where a gay man's obituary is being written: 'Some people don't like "lover", do they?' Out goes the single word, in come two.

Longtime Companion (US 1990 C) A group of friends are left reeling, helplessly at first when a number of them contract the 'gay cancer' which becomes known as AIDS and then HIV/AIDS.
W: Craig Lucas; P: Stan Wlodkowski; D: Norman Rene; 96 mins.
Soft-pedalling but rigorously constructed mainstream story spanning virtually a decade from the first reports of the disease to the devastating fact of a million infections and no cure in sight – a disaster which the film's only female character likens to the Second World War. Of the mainly young cast, Bruce Davison contributes one wrenching scene as he helps his lover, Sean (Mark Lamos), physically and mentally ravaged by the disease, let go and die. (The film

was made for the PBS's AMERICAN PLAYHOUSE but given a theatrical release beforehand.)

Look Back in Anger John OSBORNE's 1956 play which challenged much West End orthodoxy and introduced the character of the 'angry young man', Jimmy PORTER, who hits out in all directions – though mainly at his wife – against what he sees as a country paralysed by the fearful and the second rate. His only sources of comfort seem to be his friend Cliff (who lives with the Porters) and his TEDDY BEAR. When she hears about the latter, the wife's friend exclaims acidly: 'I didn't realize he was fey on top of everything.' A sequel, *Déjà Vu* (1992) found the incorrigible, rampantly misanthropic Jimmy divorced with a daughter, still with Cliff (exchanging CAMP badinage), and carrying on alarmingly about FEMINISTS, trendies and – continually – queers.

Look Back in Anger was originally televised late in 1956, directed by Tony RICHARDSON for Granada, with the London cast, including Kenneth Haigh as Jimmy and Alan BATES as Cliff. Jimmy was later played by Richard Burton (1959 C), Nicholas Gecks (1982 R, a production which hinted that friend Helena was sexually attracted to wife Alison), and Kenneth Branagh (1989 T).

Looking for Langston (UK 1988 C/T) A monochrome dream of desire set in the Harlem of the 1920s, blending the poetry of Langston Hughes with the words of contemporary black gay writer Essex Hemphill. With Ben Ellison and Matthew Baidoo (as 'Beauty').
W/D: Isaac JULIEN; P: Sankofa Films; 45 mins.
Smoky clubs with entwined male couples in tuxedos, walks along beaches, fear in alleyways, languorously sated passion in bedrooms. Lush images of a legendary, lost gay world mingle with sharper realities in a meandering piece that either bewitches or bores, sometimes at one and the same time.

The Look of Love Sung by Dusty SPRINGFIELD, this dreamy Burt Bacharach–Hal David love song was composed for *Casino Royale* (1967 C) where it is languorously laid over a scene in which Peter SELLERS and Ursula Andress make capricious love under rose petals. The orchestral version by Herb Alpert and the Tijuana Brass provided the music three years on for the smoochy dance under paper lanterns in THE BOYS IN THE BAND. Nothing like this had ever been seen before; never had heterosexual love music been used in this way. It suggested that men's feelings for each other could be and very likely were the same as some men's for some women.
Sandra Bernhard performs the song in *Without You, I'm Nothing* (1990 C).

Loony Left A term coined by the British tabloid press to describe various 'out of control', POLITICALLY CORRECT socialist local councils (mainly in the North and inner London) who spent big and wide during the 1980s on all manner of adventurous organizations and projects, some probably gimcrack, some possibly magnificent – with a lot of merely useful things in between. Laughed at in STRUGGLE (1983 T); *The Stanley Baxter Christmas Show* (1985); *And There Were in the Same Country* (1987 R); *Blood and Bruises* (1988 R); THE COMIC STRIP PRESENTS . . . GLC (1990 T). The branding of people and policies in this way was analysed by Goldsmiths' College Media Research Group, London in OPEN SPACE 'The Media and the Loony Left' (1988), arguing that 'the press, using half truths and lies, have helped undermine local democracy and supported the government proposals to reduce the power of councils'.

Lorca, Federico García (1898–1936) Spanish poet and playwright whose life and legend – though not always his sexuality – have been explored through poetry, dance and documentary: most vividly in Trader FAULKNER's *Lorca: The Anguish of a Poet* (1976 R); ARENA 'The Spirit of Lorca' (1987 T) with Ian Gibson; Gibson's *How a City Sings* (1992 R, 'in search of the voice of Granada and of Lorca').

Also: David Richards' dramatic poem *Death and the Poet* (1964 R); *Garcia Lorca: Black Sound, Deep Sound* (1968 T, Andalusian poetry); *The Arts World* 'Lorca' (1978 R); *Cruel Garden* (1982 T, a ballet about 'a man apart ... a poet in conflict with a bull'); *Lorca: Death of a Poet* (Sp 1987 T, with Nickolas GRACE as Lorca); *Bookshelf* with neighbour of the Lorca family in the Andalusian countryside; *Federico's Ghost* (1988 R, a monologue read by Kenneth Haigh). Lorca's life and poetry suffuse the Spanish film *To an Unknown God* (1975).

His plays have been dramatized for film, radio and television; eg *The House of Bernarda Alba* (UK 1960 T; US 1962 T; Sp 1986 C; UK 1991 T) and *Yerma* (UK 1950 & 1988 R). However, his explicitly gay *The Public*, performed for the first time in the 1980s, awaits adaptation for the mass media.

'I have to present to the eyes of idiots who look at me, a blood red rose with the sexual tint of an April peony, which doesn't correspond at all to the truth of my feelings' (Lorca quoted in *Lorca: The Anguish of a Poet*).

'His works show that Lorca was a man with a secret, a secret that had to be kept hidden at all costs ... Awareness of ... his predicament as a homosexual in a hostile environment, gives us a deeper insight into everything he wrote ... [His concerns were] death, unhappy love, identification with gypsies ... characters desperately aware of a central menace to their existence' (*Lorca: The Anguish of a Poet*).

Lorre, Peter [Laszlo Loewenstein] (1904–64) Hungarian actor, typed as mad genius, slimy villain or feline, philosophical policeman. His bulging eyes set in a pasty spherical face coupled with his spider-silk voice gave Lorre's persona wide-ranging prominence in spoofs and in cartoons like *Bugs Bunny*'s 'Hare-Raising Hare' (voiced by Mel Blanc). The Lorre intonation can also be detected in Jeff Bridges' performance as the murderer in *The Vanishing* (1993 C).

He began his film career in Germany in 1929, making a huge impact as the child murderer in *M* (1931). He travelled to England to play a supporting (QUEER) villain in HITCHCOCK's first *The Man Who Knew Too Much* in 1934, before going to Hollywood for *Mad Love* and *Crime and Punishment* (1935), then back to Hitchcock for *The Secret Agent* (1936) before settling in the movie capital: *Mr Moto* series (1937–9); *The Face Behind the Mask* (1941); *The Maltese Falcon* (1941, as Joel CAIRO); *Casablanca* (1942); *The Mask of Dimitrios* (1944); *Arsenic and Old Lace* (1944); *The Chase* (1946); *The Verdict* (1946); *The Beast with Five Fingers* (1946); *Casbah* (1948); *Beat the Devil* (1953); *20,000 Leagues Under the Sea* (1954); *Silk Stockings* (1957); *The Story of Mankind* (1957, as Nero); *Tales of Terror* (1962); *The Raven* (1963); *The Comedy of Terrors* (1963); *The Patsy* (1964); etc. He returned to Germany in 1950 to direct and star in *Der Verlorene* [The Lost One].

T: *Lux Video Theatre* 'The Taste' (1952); *Alfred Hitchcock Presents* 'The Diplomatic Corpse' (1958, as a pederastic policeman) and 'Man from the South' (1960).

The Lost Boys (UK 1978 T) J. M. BAR-RIE's deep and complex relationship with the Llewellyn-Davies family, especially with two of the boys, George and Michael. A knotty situation: about childhood dominion and adult power with their potentially terrifying overlap. Yet at its root, the internationally beloved 'innocence' of PETER PAN.

W: Andrew Birkin from his book; P: Louis Marks; D: Rodney Bennett; BBC2; 3 parts; 90 mins each.

An extraordinarily concentrated biography which dealt wholeheartedly, and as explicitly as it could, given the existing documentation (much correspondence had been burnt), with Barrie's overriding love for 'his' boys.

Using letters and voice-overs, the serial managed to cover ground previously studiously avoided: Barrie's desire to be kicked by George, his wish that George was a girl ('to say the things I want to say to you'), his throbbing excitement at removing the 8-year-old's boots and blouse (but stopping at his trousers), taking him to bed and reading him a story. The visual language was less intense (a hand on a young arm, a motor bike jaunt), but Barrie's desire to get 'closer and closer' to two of the boys was strongly to the fore. His possessiveness was seen as worthy of criticism, but not his unresolved sexuality.

The adolescent Michael's lover, Roger Senhouse wants him to choose between 'Uncle Jim' and himself: 'He only cares about himself. If he really loved you, he'd let you go instead of suffocating you ... I for one think he's a morbid little man and the sooner you break away from him the better. It's an unhealthy relationship and I'm not the only one who thinks so.' Michael asks him to define 'unhealthy'. Roger stumbles: 'I don't know, but it goes beyond the bounds of ordinary affection.' Not like Roger's with Michael, of course. Angered by Roger's hypocrisy, Michael agrees that Uncle Jim's love for him does break the bounds of normal affection: 'And so does mine for him.'

The Lost Boys, anchored by Ian HOLM's supremely confident, managing yet hopelessly besotted Barrie, is nagging and disturbing in its implications. Not solely because of the main taboo area it occupies. It also begs the question: why is the all-consuming physical and emotional adoration shown by Barrie any less admirable (or unpleasant) than that displayed by a biological father to a son or daughter?

Lost in Space (US 1965–8 T) Jolly comedy-adventure series about an American 'Family Robinson' marooned on a planet. Their lives are considerably buoyed (as is the audience's pleasure) by the presence of a sophisticated robot and the extraordinarily taking 'villain', stowaway Dr Zachary SMITH (Jonathan HARRIS), a would-be Queen of Outer Space.

Occasionally, what was intended as a children's show dived into deeper waters, eg in a 1967 episode 'The Colonists'. A tribe of women led by man-hating Queen Neolani (Francine Stewart) comes to Jupiter looking for male sperm, all the men on their planet being impotent slaves wearing grey track suits. She is a magnificent specimen, resplendent in black with a red cloak and spangled headgear. She needs 'male animal strength' and rather unexpectedly decides upon Dr Smith as her mate. His interest in women is rudimentary, but then her emotional vocabulary is rather limited too, not to mention the spoken kind ('Hearken to me,' she keeps on saying). Mom (June Lockhart) disparages the visitor: 'That woman (or *whatever* she is).' However, after a few days sequestered together, Mom emerges radiant and smiling, with the Queen advising her enigmatically that 'You will now fulfil your *true* destiny.'

W: Peter Packer; P: Irwin Allen; D: Ezra Stone; 60 mins.

The Lost Language of Cranes (UK 1992 T) Philip (Angus MacFadyen) comes out to his father Owen (Brian Cox) who has a secret life of his own. David Leavitt's American novel transferred to Maida Vale, North West London.

W: Sean Mathias; P: Ruth Caleb; D: Nigel Finch; 9.2.92; BBC2 (Screen Two); 90 mins.

A mudslide of bad writing and worse psychology.

'Some people will dislike the film because of their prejudices against gay people and their general anxiety about sex, but I hope people can see beyond that' (Brian Cox, *Radio Times*).

'A knockout adaptation of David Leavitt's gay outing novel ... looks set to stir up controversy in whatever medium it's shown ... Sean Mathias' neatly paced, humour-flecked script takes the conventions of Brit living room drama and turns them on their head with the gay subject matter ... Pic's other strength is the off-handedness of the male bonding sequences. Bedroom scenes are shot and played with the ease of hetero equivalents and nudity is unblinking but natural in the context' (Derek Elley, *Variety*, 18.11.91).

Lot in Sodom (US 1933 C) The city is governed by wondrous queens, who take a great liking to the beautiful young man who comes to lead Lot and his family away from the coming destruction.
D: Melville Webber and James Sibley Watson; *c* 20 mins.

Spartan, cheeseparing version (although hypnotic and very imaginative, particularly in its use of miniatures and dissolves) of the biblical story which cleverly condemns the inhabitants of SODOM while encouraging the audience to lap up the gorgeous Angel under his hood and eyeliner. It was voted one of the top 10 films of 1934 (with *The Lost Patrol* and *The Thin Man*) in the D. W. Griffith Awards.

Loud, Lance (1955–) American journalist and (bit part) actor (psychiatrist in *Inside Monkey Zetterland* 1992) who became a national celebrity when he came out in AN AMERICAN FAMILY (1973). 'A very theatrical individual, also entertaining. Out of the blue, on this highly watched show, here you saw this real person coping – humorously – with being a homosexual in a real family,' Frank Rich in THE GAY AND LESBIAN WORLD (1992 R).

Lou Grant 'Cop' (US 1979 T) Dave Lambert (Joe Penny) is about to testify against drug racketeers when their leader rings him up. 'I had a little talk with your brother-in-law. He really spilled the beans. Names, places, dates. He doesn't even think you're fit to be a cop because you're a homosexual.' Liberal newspaper editor Lou (Ed Asner) tries to rationalize the man's fears. 'But if a married man has a mistress, she calls his employers.' Lambert throws Lou a heavy look. 'Do you really think it would be half as bad?' Lou knows full well that the heterosexual and homosexual situations are not analogous. Same actions, but for guys like Lambert different penalties.

W: Seth Freeman; P: Seth Freeman and Gene Reynolds; D: Roger Young; 60 mins.

One of the best of the large crop of Gay POLICEMEN Fighting the System (and losing) stories of the period, deservedly winning Emmys for writer and director.

> I once busted a guy for drink driving. Turns out he owned a pizza parlour – he offered free pizza. My sergeant and the other guys wanted to fix the case in return for the pizza. I said no, I made a good bust and I won't change it. The next day I was in a very intense crowd-control situation. I called for back-up. I never got it. I could have been killed. How much back-up do you think I'd get if all the other officers knew I was gay? ... [gay cop]
> Do you know what it's like to be let down by someone you thought you could trust? ... How does a cop know he can count on a partner in a crisis if he's a FAIRY ... I've met a lot of gays and they're unstable people. [straight cop]

love Sublime ecstasy or a punch in the stomach. Or both. Gay love first broadcast in 1930: in a play nearly four centuries old, and in verse.

Marlowe's EDWARD II was allowed to lyricize:

> Sometimes a lovely boy in DIANA's shape,
> With hair that gilds the water as it glides,
> Crownets of pearl about his naked arms,
> And in his sportful hands an olive tree
> To hide those parts that men delight to see.

The King's beloved, Piers Gaveston appears to return the sentiments, swooningly, upon his recall from exile:

> Sweet prince, I come; these, these thy amorous lines
> Might have enforced me to have swum from France
> And, like Leander, gasped upon the sand,
> So thou wouldst smile and take me in thy arms.

Another English king, who died not violently but in his bed, was also extensively affectionate in the 1977 radio play, *The*

Wisest Fool (played by Nigel STOCK) about his darling 'Steenie', George VILLIERS: 'Each night, often near dawn, I fall asleep with some thought of you playing round and round in my head. Where am I to look for happiness if not to you? I care not a jot for England. I care for nothing in the world if I lose your love.'

Intense love by one for another was also expressed in poetry, more resistant to erasure perhaps than other forms of art, beginning on radio with *A Shropshire Lad* in the 1930s.

With the exceptions of THE IMPORTANT THING IS LOVE (1971 C) and ONLY CONNECT (1979 T) it wasn't until the 1980s that homosexual love, rather than sex, was allowed to show its face, as well as speak its name, fully, mutually and successfully (without murder and suicide intervening); THIS THING CALLED LOVE (1983 R); Angus and Tony in THE OTHER HALF (1984); MY BEAUTIFUL LAUNDRETTE (1985 C/T); THE TINKER'S DAUGHTER (1986 R) which has Meriel Baigent (Deborah Makepeace) conjugating the verb 'aimer' before she discovers, pleasurably and painfully, what it truly means with Amy (Zelah Clark).

Falling in love for the first time was documented, probably for the first time in a homosexual context, in WORD IS OUT (1977) which was full of people tenderly reminiscing about the hows and whys of the irrational and sometimes inexplicable.

The question of how much is too much love was somewhat alarmingly raised in *Love Talk* 'Linda and Rachel: Love Crazy' (1991 T), which focused on a couple who simply couldn't get enough of each other and whose lives were intricately and overwhelmingly bound together.

'I've discovered love since we parted, George ... It addles the hormones, rots the teeth. Grab yourself a bit of love, George, and wait for Armageddon' says Connie Sachs (Beryl REID) to George Smiley (Alec Guinness) about Hilary (Norma West) in *Smiley's People* (1982 T).

See also I LOVE YOU; THE LOVE THAT DARE NOT SPEAK ITS NAME.

Love And Affection A rapturous, contemplative Joan Armatrading song featured in the women's disco in SILENT WING (1984 R) and on the Queen Vic's jukebox in EASTENDERS (1986 T). It is briefly heard in the 'raunchy' sex scene between lesbian and new lesbian (housewife with kids) in *Sex Now* (1991 T).

Love and Miss Figgis (UK 1954 T) Senior classics mistress (Beatrix LEHMANN) at a provincial school – educationalist and FEMINIST – deplores human things like love and marriage. Her best student, Meg Day falls in love with an electrician and wants to sacrifice her place at Oxford to marry and settle down. Miss Figgis mounts a rearguard action to make the girl see sense before she's 30, 'old, with backaches, headaches, corns and [her] brilliance buried in a pram ... All I'm concerned about is that she should have the chance of doing something else besides marrying. And when she does marry, she must marry a man who can share her interests.' Meg has second thoughts, although she recognizes the problems ahead: 'It's all right for a man to be cleverer than a woman, but the other way round doesn't seem to work.'

W: Stella Martin Currey adapted by Alwyne Whatsley and Tatiana Lieven; P: Tatiana Lieven; 22.8.54; BBCTV; 90 mins.

A feminist play (probably the first to be produced on television by women) and with a leading character who is unfeminine, uncompromising, and passionately devoted to knowledge and women realizing their full potential – not necessarily in tandem with men. Although she does mention that she would have liked to have had a baby, Miss Figgis is a proud child of SAPPHO (a few of whose words are uttered, again for the first – and, to date, only – time on British television).

'A few melodramatic rough edges, but ... generally carried a good deal of conviction ... hard-faced school-marm ... As Miss Figgis, Beatrix Lehmann gave us a slightly oversized but wonderfully compounded study in exasperated feminism, and although remaining convincing somehow backed the argument [that this is an] important event for a girl, perhaps more so than a first infatuation, in such a way that the value of it was seen' (Philip HOPE-WALLACE, *Listener*).

Stella Martin Currey, the writer, was the wife of the poet R[alph] N. Currey. She was a contributor to *Good Housekeeping* and *Woman's Journal* in 1947, and gave radio talks the following year on *How Not to Renovate a Lawn* and *On the Impossibility of Boiling an Egg*. She read her 'Private View' as a 1949 *Mid-Morning Story*, spoke on *One Woman's Year* in 1953, and wrote a biblical radio play in the late 1950s.

Almost the same plot as that in *Love and Miss Figgis* was used nearly 40 years later in *Roseanne* (1991 T): Becky (Lecy Goranson) is torn between college and marriage to boyfriend Mark (Glenn Quinn) whom Roseanne (Roseanne Arnold) hates. This time around it was the working-class *mother* who was saying many of the things Miss Figgis counselled.

Love For Sale Bellowed gaily by Elsa Maxwell (an uncredited actress looking not unlike Miriam MARGOLYES), waving a champagne glass, dressed in white suit, atop a matching piano during a 1930s Riviera garden party in *Poor Little Rich Girl* (1987 T); the song runs only a couple of half verses at either end of a love scene because the title is sufficient to tell the audience that Prince Alexis Mdivani's (Nicholas Clay) intentions to Barbara Hutton/Farrah Fawcett are not entirely romantic. Roland Gift did it on RED, HOT AND BLUE, but it was cut from showings on World AIDS Day 1 December 1990. The song is said to have been inspired by Cole PORTER's encounter with a 12-year-old boy prostitute in Paris.

love letters *See* LETTERS.

lovely boy A phrase of Sergeant Major Windsor Davies in *It Ain't Half Hot Mum* (1973–82 T). His fatherly affection for one of the soldiers is milked for the most obvious innuendo in 'My Lovely Boy' and 'It's a Wise Child' (1974). This is allowed because the older man is fearsomely masculine, sentimentally Welsh – and the boy is, unknown to him, his illegitimate offspring. 'Your feelings are purely paternal ... you have no other feelings for this boy. What a thing, not to be able to hug him to your chest and kiss him,' says Ranjee to the Warrant Officer Christopher Mitchell in 1986.

Joan Crawford told Peter Haigh on *Picture Parade* (1957) that it's not possible to call a man 'lovely': 'It's not nice.' Blossom Dearie's rendition of 'I Won't Dance' changes the 'lovely' to 'You know what, you're handsome', although it disrupts the rhythm and sounds wrong.

lovers 'What are you two – *lovers?*' Margo (Bette DAVIS) asks half seriously in ALL ABOUT EVE (1950 C), after her screenwriter lover (Gary Merrill) has been hymning the praises of 20th Century Fox studio head Darryl F. ZANUCK for whom he is working; the clatter this word made in a male–male context was silenced for another two decades until Gay Liberation spread it around. Matthew (Jason Rush) spells it out in TWO OF US (1988 T): 'We're not just mates. Phil and me are lovers. We *do* it. We sleep together. We KISS. We hold hands. We touch. It's not a laugh. It's not just a bit of a giggle. We mean it.'

Lovesick (UK 1967 R) 'Psychiatrist falls in love with a patient – the man's brother, himself happily incestuous with his own mother, switches the treatment (ie to make patient fall in love with him) so that the girl comes out lesbian and the man a queer with designs on the psychiatrist. Really a very moral tale ... when you think about it' (David Wade, *Listener*, 8.4.86).
W: Caryl Churchill; P: John Tydeman; BBC Third Programme.

Thirty minutes of Freudian foolishness that kicks psychiatry in the teeth for its human rights abuses – including the use of AVERSION THERAPY.

Love, Sidney (US 1981–3 T) A lonely New York bachelor commercial artist (Tony RANDALL) befriends a single mother soap-opera actress (Swoosie Kurtz) and her little daughter (Kaleena Kiff).
W: Oliver Hailey, Hal Daffan and others; based on a story by Marilyn Cantor Baker; P: April Kelly; D: Jay Sandrich; 30 mins.
Sidney's failed life as a gay man was sketched in SIDNEY SHORR: A GIRL'S BEST FRIEND (1981 T). When the series was mooted, the Rabid Right was in full cry. Under no circumstances could a sympathetic character be gay, not even lugubriously and celibately. So he was just a lonely old single with an overnight family. 'Well-written comedy series that has lost something of the original TV movie's bite in playing down the gayness of Sidney' (*Standard*, 31.8.84).

Love Story (UK 1964–9 T) A collection of single plays on all aspects of *l'amour (propre* and *fou)* with women increasingly presented as the arbiters of their fate. Its producer (for ATV) Pieter Rogers commented: 'As a confirmed bachelor I believe in the equality of the sexes.' The scope of the series was confined solely to heterosexuality – though the heroine of 'Pinkie' (Patsy Rowlands 1966) lived with two 'boys', Walter (Tony Bateman) and Billy (Peter MacKriel), and 'Spilt Champagne' (1968) featured a THEATRICAL DRESSER (Reg Pritchard).

the love that dare not speak its name
The line, from the poem 'Two Loves' by Lord Alfred DOUGLAS published in *The Chameleon* in 1894, was brought into the limelight by the prosecution during WILDE's first trial. He defined this unspoken love – which makes its appearance in a fantasy garden – as: 'the great affection of an elder for a younger man, as there was between DAVID AND

JONATHAN; such as Plato made the very basis of his philosophy; such as you find in the sonnets of SHAKESPEARE. It is that deep spiritual affection that is as beautiful as it is perfect. It is beautiful. It is fine. It is the noblest form of affection. There is nothing unnatural about it. That it should be so is [because] the world doesn't understand. The world mocks at it and sometimes puts one in the pillory for it.' Wilde's speech (quoted verbatim in *The Trials of Oscar Wilde* 1960 C, *Oscar Wilde* 1960 C, *On Trial* 'Oscar Wilde' 1960 T and *Oscar* 1985 T) is applauded by the gallery, which is then reprimanded by the judge for its unseemly behaviour.

Heterosexuality's outriders were quick to pounce on the love that had been in enforced silence for at least five centuries. One of the lines cut from the 1961 release print of THE CHILDREN'S HOUR/THE LOUDEST WHISPER was spoken by Martha (Shirley MacLaine): 'I couldn't call it by name before, but I know now.'

Time magazine's anonymous book critic tore into David Storey's novel *Radcliffe* in 1964: 'the love that dare not speak its name has become the neurosis that does not know when to shut up.'

In a 1968 book *Sex in the Movies* Alexander Walker was moved to comment that the recently ungagged love 'hardly seems to shut its mouth these days'. This glib putdown (never heard in relation to heterosexual expression) became a commonplace during the following decade. In the Australian sex-in-Sydney soap NUMBER 96 (1972 T) Maggie Cameron (Bettina Welch) discovers that Don (Joe Hasham) and Bruce are 'on together'; this moment of truth inspires her to snarl: 'So *this* is the love that dare not speak its name!' The leeringly insinuating civil servant Jackson (Tim Preece) in *The Deep Concern* (1979 T) tries to bait the hunky environmentalist Frank Marsh (Allan Lander) by saying: 'There's something about you ... in the face. Not the mark of Cain, dear boy, but of something gayer, something Wilde ... but you dare not speak its name.'

At the end of the decade, *Time*, like a dog with a bone, couldn't resist another go in 1979: 'The love that once dared not speak its name now can't seem to keep its mouth shut.' Its rival, *Newsweek* employed the phrase in the 1980s. A propos of *The Potsdam Quartet*'s gay couple (1981 T) Jack Tinker felt honour-bound to comment: 'Two of them were going through one of those homosexual bust-ups which make one fervently wish their love still did not dare to speak its name' (*Daily Mail*, 14.3.81).

A Greek proverb says that 'There are some things so dangerous they must not be spoken'. However, danger must be confronted, as the macho writer Lewis Duncan (Anton Rodgers) eventually concedes during his preparation for his COMING OUT (1979 T). But not without much pain and anguish, and some venom, mainly directed at the one representative of gay rights: a spiteful middle-aged, upper-middle-class queen (Richard Pearson): 'Why can't men like you just sit down and shut up? Why can't you exercise a little dignity once in a while?'

The ultra-dignified and very closeted great man of letters in *A Song at Twilight*, Hugo Latymer (Paul Scofield 1982 T; Michael Denison 1988 R), excused his non-involvement in pre-1967 gay rights thus: 'Even when the actual law ceases to exist there will still be a stigma attached to the love that dare not speak its name in the minds of millions of people for generations to come.' Lewis' disgust and Hugo's pessimism are really directed at themselves for their double lives.

In 1977 a poem published in GAY NEWS was totally banned because of its BLAS-PHEMY. Its title was 'The Love that Dares to Speak Its Name'. (EVERYMAN: 'Blasphemy at the Old Bailey' 1977 T.)

This finger in front of the lips mentality was perfectly symbolized by the Sexual Offences Act, Section 28 of the Local Government Act and, in the light of the latter, Quentin CRISP's complete version of Lord Alfred Douglas' poem in THE BALLAD OF READING GAOL.

Lowes Dickinson, Goldsworthy (1862–1932) English historian and philosopher whose ideas helped institute the League of Nations. He was at the centre of the Cambridge Apostles and was classics tutor to E. M. FORSTER, Bertrand Russell, Lytton STRACHEY and Leonard Woolf. He gave a number of BBC talks on Goethe between 1930 and 1932. The 1960 radio portrait stimulated a letter to the *Listener* saying that 'It was incorrect to stress that he was not interested in women'.

The L-Shaped Room (UK 1962 C) Elderly Mavis (Cicely Courtneidge), the ex-soubrette/MALE IMPERSONATOR, and John (Brock Peters), who has to listen to the man he loves having sex with a woman through his bedroom wall, are two of the residents of a seedy London boarding house.

W: Bryan Forbes from the novel by Lynn Reid Banks; P: James Woolf and Richard Attenborough; D: Bryan Forbes; 142 mins.

Not a very happy affair. Spongy where it should be springy, po-faced when it should be lyrical, too pat, too pallid. But Cicely gives her part some warmth and oomph: the first characterization of an 'ordinary' lesbian in British cinema.

lubricant *Last Tango in Paris* (1972 C) first brought this sexual aid to general notice, a very upmarket version: best butter. One shot of Brando sliding the packet across the floor so that he can use it on Maria SCHNEIDER was excised from the British print. Regarding same-sex couplings, Frank Sinatra makes mention of lubricant stains on the dead man's sheets in THE DETECTIVE (1968 C) and JUBILEE (1977 C) contains a memorable injunction spoken by Angel (Ian CHARLESON) to Mad (Toyah Willcox) after she jumps on the bed he is occupying with his brother/lover: 'You clumsy slag! You've put your fat arse on the KY!' In THE COMIC STRIP PRESENTS ... 'Five Go Mad In Dorset' (1982 T) a huge can of Vaseline is one of the clues to the whereabouts of Toby, while Walt takes Vaseline from the cupboard during his first night with Robert but still gets a 'sore ass' in MALA NOCHE (1987 C).

Ludwig II (1845–86) King of Bavaria. In VISCONTI's *Ludwig II* (1972 C) he was impersonated by Helmut Berger as totally neurotic and obsessed with opera (Wagner's), pretty young men and building fairy-tale castles – which, omitting the second interest, is pretty much how the world has been taught to see him. Other versions of him as a mad recluse or over-demanding sybarite in *Ludwig – Requiem for a Virgin King* (Harry Baer 1972 C) and *Wagner* (Laszlo Galffi 1983 T). Slightly more balanced portraits in the documentary *Footprints* 'The Swan King' (1964 T) and Douglas Young's *Ludwig (Fragments from a Mystery)* (1987 R), a 65-minute music and dance piece showing, in addition to his abiding fascination with Wagner's music, with beautiful young men and with architecture, his alienation because of his homosexuality, culminating in his mysterious death.

Lukewarm Character played by Christopher BIGGINS in a handful of episodes of *Porridge* (1974–7 T). The token gay prisoner, he is sweetly benign and ineffectual in his bespectacled plumpness. His boyfriend is seen on the bus bringing 'wives and sweethearts' in the episode 'Men without Women'.

Lulu The mistress of a powerful newspaper editor; dancer and prostitute: the anti-heroine of Frank Wedekind's two plays, made into a film with Asta Nielsen and more lastingly with Louise BROOKS. A complete hedonist, she plays with the emotions of men and women. Previously ignoring the besotted Countess GESCHWITZ, she is happy to pretend love if it secures her money, a passport and escape from the law: 'Only you can save me! Throw yourself at him ... to please you, he'll do anything you like ... he's going to tell the police about me.' The fascination of Lulu is all-important to the conviction Geschwitz carries. The power exercised by Louise Brooks makes it entirely reasonable that this woman would sacrifice money, self-respect, sexual autonomy, possibly her life for this child-woman.

Danny Peary writes in *Cult Movies* (1981): 'Lulu is a passive character, but Brooks has the intelligence to realize that that passivity does not rule out a character having substance ... Brooks is Wedekind's conception of Lulu: a young, vivacious innocent with animal beauty and no moral sense. She doesn't want to harm anyone, but her very existence causes the weak men around her to self-destruct ... Brooks plays Lulu as if she were a spoiled but not malicious schoolgirl who forgets she is no longer 10 years old when she sits in men's laps ... very likeable, a very warmhearted free spirit without worries or inhibitions, that rare bird without jealousy. She only asks to be loved and cannot bear rejection.'

The 'Lulu' hairstyle has remained remarkably potent. It can be seen adorning a Lyons prostitute in *The Kiss* (1929 C) and vampish Cyd Charisse in the Broadway Ballet from *Singin' in the Rain* (1952 C). Miss Benton (Martita HUNT) has a nude portrait of her lover Madge – *à la* Lulu – above their bed at the top of the nursery school they run in *Bunny Lake is Missing* (1965 C). 'Dreadful painting of Madge,' she says with ostentatious dismissal.

Lulu/Louise's helmet of sleek black hair turns up on Melanie Griffith's out of control head in *Something Wild* (1986 C); on Elizabeth (Lyndsey Baxter) in *Starlings* (1988 T; she goes as Lulu to a fancy dress party and has photographs from the film on her bedroom wall); on the female lawyer who has a touch of the androgynous in *Without Her Consent* (1990 T); on Syd (Cyndi Lauper) in *Off and Running* (1991 C).

lumberjack A Kumano lumberjack, Tatsuo (Kanya Kitaoji) in *Fire Festival* (1984 C) is caught between old superstitions and changing community in 1959. The 'Blade' episode of THE GENTLE TOUCH (1980 T) laughed at the gay dress code, while finding humour in the heterosexual response to it. A young policeman (Derek Thompson) preparing for heavy plainclothes duty in Earls Court is appraised by his boss Maggie Forbes (Jill Gascoine). 'I like the macho look,' she purrs. He grunts. 'Basic street gay, they call it. They look like well-dressed lumberjacks.'

The Lumberjack Song With words by Eric Idle, this is sung by Michael Palin and a hearty Royal Canadian Mounted Police chorus, the Fred Tomlinson Singers, in MONTY PYTHON'S FLYING CIRCUS (1969 T) and in *And Now for Something Completely Different* (1972 C). A hymn to all that was straight and masculine:

> I cut down trees, I eat my lunch.
> I go to the lavatory...
> I cut down trees, I skip and jump,
> I like to press wild flowers.
> I put on women's clothing
> And hang around in bars.

The singing Mounties begin to look uncomfortable, but carry on as heartily as they can. Their coping mechanisms break down with the next verse, however:

> I cut down trees, I wear high heels,
> Suspenders and a bra.
> I wish I'd been a girlie
> Just like my dear Mama.

The choir starts throwing rotten fruit at 'Bevis' and there is a strong complaint registered by a brigadier whose best friends are 'mainly lumberjacks' (the rest are TRANSVESTITES).

luv One gangster (Harry) calls another (Joe) 'luv' and asks him to join in a 'knees up' on an East End pub dance floor in *Londoners* 'The Frighteners' (1966 T). Accountant Noel (Gary Marshall) calls Marlo Thomas 'luv' in *That Girl* 'He, She and He' (1968 T); he's Briddish and wears a lavender tie. Rugger-hearty Jerry in TINKER, TAILOR, SOLDIER, SPY (1988 R) calls George Smiley 'old love' and 'old boy'. We are alerted that there is something 'different' about Alistair (Dominic Jephcott) in *Claws* (1987 T) when he calls the heroine (and

her husband) 'luv' and 'dears'. Marty FELDMAN called fellow writer Johnny Speight 'luv' repeatedly on *Late Night Live* (c 1967).

LWT (London Weekend Television) The ITV company which has held the franchise for the London region since 1968. Among its more relevant work: *Aquarius*; UPSTAIRS, DOWNSTAIRS; WITHIN THESE WALLS; *The Stanley Baxter Show*; *Lillie*; *Helen – Woman of Today*; AGONY; *By Bennett* (including ME! I'M AFRAID OF VIRGINIA WOOLF); THE LONDON WEEKEND SHOW; TWO PEOPLE; THE SOUTH BANK SHOW; GAY LIFE; THE GENTLE TOUCH.

Waldo **Lydecker** Acidulous radio critic who lives in a magnificently exotic apartment, types in his bath and – in the words of John OSBORNE (1992 T) – 'has a bad word for everybody': Clifton WEBB in *Laura* (1945 C); Truman CAPOTE (1966 T). Lydecker is also the surname of the bullied soldier on *On the Yankee Stadium* (1985 R).

Lynde, Paul (1926–82) American film and television comedian of manic appearance and flapping energy. He generally played well-meaning but highly strung fusspots, married and single. His most memorable moment came in *Bye Bye Birdie* (1960 stage, 1963 C) when, as the driven to distraction father, he lets rip about all the frustration of having 'kids'.

T: début on *The Ed Sullivan Show*; *The Colgate Comedy Hour*; *The Golddiggers*; *Stanley* (1956–7, with Buddy Hackett and Carol Burnett); guest on *The Perry Como Show*, *The Martha Raye Show*, *The Red Buttons Show* etc; Uncle Arthur in *Bewitched* (1965–7 T); *Hey Landlord* (1966–7); married lawyer Paul Simms in *The Paul Lynde Show* (1972–3); hospital administrator Dr Paul Mercy in *The [New] Temperatures Rising Show* (1973–4). He occupied centre square on *Hollywood Squares* for 13 years from 1968 until it ended in 1981.

C: *New Faces* (1954); *Son of Flubber* (1962); *Under the Yum Yum Tree* (1963);

Send Me No Flowers (1964); secret service agent, in drag for one scene in *The Glass Bottom Boat* (1966); *How Sweet It Is* (1968); *Rabbit Test* (1978); Nervous Elk in *Cactus Jack* (1979); etc.

Stephen **Lynn** Character in BRIEF ENCOUNTER (1945 C), played by Valentine DYALL. A bachelor DOCTOR of refined sensibility who becomes very chill when he discovers Alec entertaining a woman in his flat one afternoon. After making a few stilettoed comments he asks for his key back. No more than a smattering of dialogue, but the manner is Cowardian, the feelings behind it ambiguous. Is he envious of Alec? Is he envious of the woman? Were he and Alec lovers at medical school? Each radio production has trimmed Stephen's little speech of outraged morality – this is the only scene not filtered through Laura's eyes and feelings. In the most recent, Crawford Logan's 'my dear' to Alec speaks volumes.

Billy WILDER said he based Jack Lemmon's put-upon executive – who lends his bosses his home for assignations in *The Apartment* (1960 C) – on 'that guy in *Brief Encounter*'.

M

McClelland, Allan (1917–89) Irish actor of the lulling, feathery voice and the sharply lived-in features. He created the role of Christopher WREN in Agatha Christie's THREE BLIND MICE (1947 R) and on stage in THE MOUSETRAP (1952). He was the hugely deplorable Neville Pikelet in A HEDGE, BACKWARDS (1956 R), the flowing thespian Lauriston Squire in *A Poor Player* (1960 R), and Leopold Bloom in his own adaptation of *Bloomsday* (1960 R). He was the narrator of Ken Russell's MONITOR film on the Scottish painters Robert McBryde and Robert Colquhoun (1959).

C: *The Damned* (1963); Control in *The Spy Who Came in from the Cold* (1966); etc.

R: Aramis in *The Three Musketeers* (1946); Orsino in TWELFTH NIGHT (1947); Fabian in TWELFTH NIGHT (1956); Jonathan to Peter WYNGARDE'S David in *Also Among the Prophets* (1956); Pride in *The Tragical History of Doctor Faustus* (1956); starred as *The Celebrated Mr Bangston* (1958); as *Coningsby* (1958); starred in *Night of the Gods* (1959); Captain Barnes in *Green for Danger* (1959); Edward Laurence in *The Mechanical* (1966); *Dear Mr Shaw* (1981) and again as G. B. Shaw in *Stalin vs Wells* (1985); Mick in Rose TREMAIN'S *Will and Lou's Boy* (1986); Control in *Smiley's People* (1986); James Douglas, a father who bequeaths a legacy of hate to his son and daughter in *Cross Words* (1987 R).

T: *Phineas Finn* (1953); Sidcombe in *Charlesworth at Large* (1958); Inspector Docherty in *Three Days in the Year* (1958); James Wilson, the *Private Investigator* (1959); journalist in *Quatermass and the Pit* (1959); Duncan, café proprietor in *The Referees* (1961); *Maigret* 'The Reluctant Witness' (1962); John Andrews in *Z Cars* 'Hit and Run' (1963); *Z Cars* 'Stray Cat' (1973); etc.

McCowen, Alec (1925–) English actor who has had a quietly spectacular career playing off-centre men, beginning with young men on the edge, currently mousy men who sometimes roar.

C: début in *the Cruel Sea* (1953);

murder suspect in *Town on Trial* (1957); man due to be hanged in *Time without Pity* (1957); Brown in *The Loneliness of the Long Distance Runner* (1962); Bottom (voice only) in *A Midsummer Night's Dream* (1961); priest in *The Witches* (1966); Nephew in *Travels with My Aunt* (1972); police inspector who is forced to eat rich gourmet food by his wife night after night in *Frenzy* (1972); 'Young man' in *Stevie* (1978); client in PERSONAL SERVICES (1987): 'Since my retirement I have devoted myself to transvestism and sexual perversion. What's the point of being old if you can't be dirty?'; etc.

R: Plato Cartwright in *Boys in Brown* (1954); Sir Fopling Flutter in *The Man of Mode* (1961); *The Flies* (1966); as EDWARD II (1967); as *Ivanov* (1967); title role in *The Tragical History of Doctor Faustus* (1970); as *The American* (1975); as Hadrian VII (1979); title role in *Bimbashi McPherson: A Life in Egypt* (1983); Baron Corvo aka Fr William Rolfe in THE MISCHIEF MAKERS (1985); Edmund Wye in *Broad Daylight* (1986); J. M. BARRIE in *Peter Pan* (1987); dean in *Dandy Dick* (1987); Archbishop Romero in *Incident at the Devil's Gate* (1987); George in A SINGLE MAN (1991); etc.

T: Major Richard Weston in *No Man's Land* (1956); Pierre Gobert in CHANGE OF HEART (1956); Wyndham Brandon (to Ian HOLM's Charles Granillo) in ROPE (1957); *Angel Pavement* (1958); Bill in THE VOICE OF THE TURTLE (1958); Sammy Noles in *Call Me a Liar* (1958); Mack Heath in *The Little Beggars* (1958); Maurice Bouillet in *The Model Marriage* (1959, with Mai Zetterling); Private Secretary in *Sir Jocelyn, the Minister Would Like a Word* (1965); as *Alexander Graham Bell* (1965); as T. S. Eliot in OMNIBUS 'The Mysterious Mr Eliot' (1971); Vincent Van Gogh in *Solo* (1972); *The Gospel According to St Mark* (1979); Malvolio in *Twelfth Night* (1980); Ralph Bonner in *The Reason of Things* (1981); *Mr Palfrey of Westminster* (1984–5); THE SOUTH BANK SHOW 'Kipling' (1984); David Hume in *Dialogue in the Dark* (1988, with James Boswell); Canon Chasuble in THE IMPORT-

ANCE OF BEING EARNEST (1988); Mr Tooth in *The Messenger* (1988); Aeneas Simpson, head of an insurance firm with wicked designs in the Dickens' story *The Hunted* (1989); retired Scotland Yard man in *Bergerac* 'Trenchard's Last Case' (1989); etc.

Autobiography: WOMAN'S HOUR 'Guest of the Week' (1968 R); *Release* 'Birth of a New Star' (1968 T): 'This actor of long promise who has just come into his own (in *Hadrian VII*), discusses his career with Peter Lewis' (1968); reading from his autobiography *Young Gemini* (1980 R); DESERT ISLAND DISCS (1979 R); THIS IS YOUR LIFE (1991 T): he refused to allow the programme to be transmitted unless some acknowledgement was made of the existence and importance in his life of the late Geoffrey BURRIDGE.

McDonald, Graeme (1931–) Joined the BBC from Granada in 1966 and produced 110 WEDNESDAY PLAYS and PLAYS FOR TODAY. Head of BBC Serials from 1977, then of BBC Drama. Creator of *All Creatures Great and Small*.

McDowall, Roddy (1928–) English-born actor who became a Hollywood child star (*How Green Was My Valley*; *My Friend Flicka*) and stayed the course through scores of (mainly fey) supporting roles (FUNNY LADY; EVIL UNDER THE SUN) and a few leads (*Lord Love a Duck* 1965; *The Poseidon Adventure* 1972). Also very active on television (*Planet of the Apes* 1974; *Hollywood Wives* 1985; AN INCONVENIENT WOMAN; a writer on the occult in an episode of *Murder, She Wrote* 1989). A rare appearance as himself on *The Hollywood Legends* 'Natalie Wood' (1987 T); he also narrated *Hollywood's Children* in 1982.

MacInnes, Colin (1914–76) English novelist (*City of Spades*; *Absolute Beginners*), journalist and commentator upon subcultures, especially Soho and West Indian immigrant communities in London during the 1950s.

C: *Absolute Beginners* (1986).

R: *Imaginary Journeys: Encounter with the Bunyip* (1954), meeting with ABORIGINES; *Coast and Country* 'Upstream to Isis'. (1958), journey by river steamer to Oxford and people encountered on the way; *A Cruel Soil for Talent* (1961), interviewing Norman Mailer about psychiatry, religion and pornography.

T: interviewed Tommy Steele for *Release* (1967).

Autobiography: SOUTH OF WATFORD (1986 T); *Prophets, Charlatans and Little Gurus* (1986 R); *Bookshelf* (1986 R).

Biography: *Authors in Focus* (1954 R), interviewed by D. J. West.

McKellen, Sir Ian (1935–) English actor of commanding presence equally adept at kingly or meek roles. Latterly gay activist.

C: outlaw in *Alfred the Great* (1969); Sandy Dennis' lover in *A Touch of Love* (1969); D. H. LAWRENCE in *The Priest of Love* (1981); diplomat in *Plenty* (1985); John Profumo in *Scandal!* (1989); AND THE BAND PLAYED ON (1993 C/T); RICHARD III; etc.

R: Orestes in *Electra* and *The Flies* (1966); the son in *A Lily in Little India* (1966); Gaveston, with Alec MCCOWEN as EDWARD II (1967): 'there can be no denying the painful reality of Edward's attachment to Gaveston' (*Listener*); piano teacher in *Related Variations* (1990); etc.

T: as DAVID COPPERFIELD (1966); Simon Bliss in *Hay Fever* (1968); as EDWARD II (1970); *Solo* 'John Keats' (1970); T. E. LAWRENCE in *Ross* (1970); George Tesman in *Hedda Gabler* (1972); Captain Plume in *The Recruiting Officer* (1973); *Macbeth* (1979, opposite Judi Dench); Soviet dissident in *Every Good Boy Deserves Favour* (1979); Paul Chauvelin in *The Scarlet Pimpernel* (1982); *Acting Shakespeare* (1982); as *Walter* (1982); *Walter and June* (1983); IAGO in *Othello* (1990); *D'Art* (1992, on theatre access for deaf actors and audiences); George Bernard Shaw in *Without Walls* 'Mister Shaw's Missing Millions' (1993 T); etc.

Autobiography: THE SOUTH BANK SHOW (1981 & 1985 T); DESERT ISLAND

DISCS; *Words, Words, Words* (1983 R), a personal choice of poetry and prose; etc.

In his activist role: *Wogan* (1988 T); OUT ON TUESDAY (1989 T); KALEIDOSCOPE (1991 T); THEM AND US (1991 T); SATURDAY NIGHT OUT 'To Be or Not to Be' (1991 T); talking about the 'gay community' in A SUNDAY OUTING (1993 R); etc.

MacKenzie, Jacqueline (1928–   ) Scottish-born actress and raconteur with stylish, crisp delivery. A great sensation in the mid-1950s for her innovative straight-to-camera reporting with witty observations, vocal impersonations and zany facial expressions. The *TV Mirror* put her on its cover in 1957, and in 1958 she was able to tell readers that 'I'm getting married on Saturday'. She married Peter Forster in 1958 (they were divorced in the early 1960s) and sometimes acted under her real name. As Jackie Forster, she edited *Sappho* in the 1970s and appeared on many phone-ins and documentaries like *Gays: Speaking Out* (1978 T), continuing to express herself with originality and vigour.

C: *You're Only Young Once* (1952); *The Dam Busters* (1955); *Lilacs in the Spring* (1955).

R: *The Gay Galliard* (1951, as Valerie Hobson's sister); *The Man Born to Be King* (1951); *The Younger Generation* (1953); WOMAN'S HOUR 'Matters of Tact' (1956); *A Scot in Drury Lane* (1957); *These Foolish Things* (1957); *Small Talk* (Overseas Service 1958, on Wimbledon, fashions etc); *Dateline* (1957); *Does the Team Think?* (1957, guest); *A Brains Trust from Cheltenham* (1957); *Woman's Hour* 'About Your Wedding' (1958); *How to Handle Men* (1958, 'Chairman'); daughter of the Duchess of St Neots who meets a seditious socialist in *Christmas Pudding* (1959): 'When I grow up, I'm going to be either a duchess like mummy or a tart like Annabelle. Nothing in between for me'; Titania in *Titania Has a Mother* (1959); *The Amazing Dr Clitterhouse* (1959); *An Hour of Charm* (1959); *Kippers* (Overseas Service 1962); *Rounda-*

bout 'Six Tales' (1962); *Woman's Hour* 'How They Proposed' (1962); etc.

T: began in BBC television as stage manager and bit part player in *The Triumphant* (1951); nurse in *To Save a Life* (1952); Sarah, the canteen girl in *Pilgrim Street* (1952); student in *Love and Mr Lewisham* (1952); prostitute in *Crime and Punishment* (1953); Molly in *Under Their Skilled Hands* 'Dangerous Drugs' (1953); Fanny O'Dowda in *Fanny's First Play* (1956, extract from Edinburgh Festival production). Her solo career began with *Highlight* (1956–7, doing all the voices, visiting Berlin, Amsterdam etc); then [GILBERT] *Harding Finds Out* (1956); *Mad About Each Other* (1956, sitcom with Peter Jones); *Place the Face* (1957); *Hotfoot* (underwater fishing in Cannes, attending an eisteddfod, investigating a Bedouin encampment, commenting upon holy and unholy aspects of Rome, sightseeing in Clacton); PANORAMA (item on tattooing scrubbed because of the Suez crisis); bubble bath adverts on ITV; appearances on ITN 1957; visiting *Chipperfield's Circus* (1957); *State Your Case* (1957); TROUBLE FOR TWO (1958, about two women – with a male 'daily' – sharing a flat, but taken off after four weeks); *Late Extra* (1958, events around London); *Discovering America/Jacqueline MacKenzie in America* 'You're Welcome', 'The Most' and 'We Do It for Kicks' (1960); Brenda in *Probation Officer* (1960); *Wednesday Magazine* 'Let's Imagine' and 'The Perfect Holiday' (1962); etc. (A clip from a BBC appearance was featured in *The Gate of Eden* (1980 T, set 1956) along with pictures of Tony Curtis and Elvis.)

McKuen, Rod (1933–   ) American poet, composer, and actor of shaggy introspection whose songs include 'Jean', 'Come to Me in Silence' (1973), 'Love's Been Good to Me' (1979) and 'Looking for a Friend' (1980).

C: film scores for *Joanna: Travels with Charley* (1968); *The Prime of Miss Jean Brodie* (1969); *Scandalous John* (1971); *The Borrowers* (1973); *Emily* (1976); etc.

T: *McKuen* (1971 T); *The Loner*

(1974); *Portrait of Rod McKuen* (1982 T).

MacLiammoir, Micheal [Albert Willmore] (1899–1978) English actor who assumed an Irish name, accent, persona and family history. Ran the Gate Theatre in Dublin with his lover Hilton EDWARDS. With his dark probing voice he could be deathly demonic or disarmingly sophisticated: perfectly cast as WILDE in ON TRIAL (1960 T), *I Must Be Talking to My Friends* (1963 T), Jonathan Swift in *Farewell to Greatness* (1957 R), and *Richard Brinsley Sheridan* (1957 R), but equally memorable as IAGO in *Othello* (1952 C) and sinister Judge Brack in *Hedda Gabler* (1957 R).

Also: Algy in THE IMPORTANCE OF BEING EARNEST (Gate Theatre production with Hilton Edwards, 1934 R); charmingly adulterous husband Etienne Enface in *A Holiday Abroad* (1960 T); another unfaithful husband in *Think of the Day* (1960 T); *Compass* 'The Importance of Being Oscar' (1961 T); *Oscar Wilde* (1963 R); narrator of *Tom Jones* (1963); *Best Sellers* 'Oscar Wilde' (1967 T); narrator of *30 is a Dangerous Age, Cynthia* (1968 C); ham actor in *What's the Matter with Helen?* (1971 C); etc.

Autobiography: with Michael Ayrton in after-dinner conversation (1960 R); *Frankly Speaking* (talking to H. A. L. Craig and Lionel Hale, 1961 R); *Micheal MacLiammoir Remembers* (reminiscing with Patrick Garland, 1972 T); reading from his autobiography *All for Hecuba* (1972).

Biography: *Death or a Kind Gentleman* (1991), compiled and presented by Simon CALLOW: 'confirming and exploring his sexuality, which was strongly, passionately directed towards his own sex'.

Montgomery **McNeil** Character in *Fame* (1980 C) played by Paul McCrane and in the television series by the remarkably similar P. R. Paul. A lonely music student, with a dancer mother, he is presented as very much not of the fold – a couple of friends, but no one special person. As Vito RUSSO pointed out, the only remarkable thing about him is that he is the only acknowledged gay in the class.

machismo No emotion, no passion, no complications. Best exemplified in QUERELLE (1982 C), in the hilariously po-faced posturings of the 'hero' ('I'll just give my ass, that's all ... I've got my jewels but I don't show them off ...') and his fellow sailors ('If he asks you, would you do it?', 'Why not, if I felt like it. Too bad you're not a girl. Nono agreed to fuck me more or less to be nice', 'You're a pal. All the others are assholes, but you're a pal').

Another man who declared himself mainly heterosexual ('I don't usually sleep with men') but became passionately, eventually dementedly involved with a man was Antonio (Antonio Banderas) in LAW OF DESIRE (1987 C).

VILLAGE PEOPLE played with the whole concept of full-on machismo in their 1978 hit song 'Macho Man', and American comedy shows have sometimes created (usually one-off) gay characters who are in unassailably 'masculine' professions: the football players (ALL IN THE FAMILY; *Alice* 1976; SOAP 1977; BROTHERS 1985); former footballers (HOLLYWOOD BEAT 1985); POLICEMEN (LOU GRANT 'Cop' 1979; THE STREETS OF SAN FRANCISCO 1977). In an orgy of overcompensation, the macho gay will often be seen lifting weights, coaching a soccer team and drinking beer – frequently all at once – during the first 10 minutes.

Machismo has bestowed some wonderfully pungent names upon its practitioners – usually strong silent types: William Bendix's Biff Koraski in *Abroad with Two Yanks* (1944 C); Gregory Peck's Stretch in *Yellow Sky* (1948 C); John WAYNE's Sergeant John M. Stryker in *Sands of Iwo Jima* (1949 C); Gary Cooper's Blayde Hollister in *Dallas* (1950 C); *Biff Baker USA* (Alan Hale Jr 1952–3 T); Randolph SCOTT's Stride in *Seven Men from Now* (1956 C); Jack Pickard's Captain Shank Adams in *Boots and Saddles* (1957–9 T). Occasionally, there's irony: Brick in CAT ON A HOT TIN

ROOF; John Travolta as muscly but sensitive Strip in *Moment by Moment* (1978).

Mad About The Boy Typically clipped, airless song from Noel COWARD (WORDS AND MUSIC 1932) said to have been dedicated to Cary GRANT. Sung by Yul Brynner (in drag) to Roman Polanski in *The Magic Christian* (1969 C).

Madonna [Madonna Ciccone] (1959–) American singer, dancer, actress and performer who has saturated pop music, films, video and print: next stop visual reality. Is part of a line of notorious women people either love or hate: Nell Gwynn, George SAND, Isadora Duncan, Mae WEST, Marlene DIETRICH, Marilyn MONROE, Brigitte Bardot, Elizabeth Taylor, Jane Fonda, Germaine GREER. She has inherited some of Dietrich's cautionary ambivalence despite the raunchy poses and fetishistic accessories and the very public espousal of the gay (and lesbian) subculture. Film career began in earnest as the punk floozette in *Desperately Seeking Susan* (1985), with various kooky or hard-boiled dames leading to *A League of Their Own*. Extraordinary videos (mostly directed by Mary Lambert) with LIKE A VIRGIN and JUSTIFY MY LOVE.

Maedchen in Uniform (Ger 1931 C) Manuela (Hertha Thiele) falls in love with her teacher, Fraulein Von Bernberg (Dorothea Wieck) in a rigidly run school for daughters of the military where loving feelings are banished. She is saved from suicide by the other girls. D: Leontine Sagan; 89 mins.

An extraordinarily beautiful film rediscovered at the end of the 1970s, written as *Yesterday and Today* (aka *The Child Manuela*) by Christa Winsloe, the poet and lover of Dorothy Thompson, murdered in Vichy France.

A lavish colour version with Romy Schneider as the schoolgirl enchanted by her teacher (Lili Palmer) was directed by Geza Von Radvanyi in 1957. The first radio version (with Lydia Sherwood as Von Bernberg) was pro-

duced (as *Children in Uniform*) in 1946, followed by Mai Zetterling as Manuela in the early 1950s and another in the mid-1960s. Rudolph Cartier's 1968 television version (*Girls in Uniform*) featured a memorably glowing Virginia McKenna and an ardent Francesca Annis as Manuela.

'In this school, tradition is more sacred than life. Our sacred duty is to rear Spartan women, not weaklings. The revolution, thank God, has passed us by,' Gladys Young as the headmistress in the 1946 production.

Maggie Girl's name, a derivative of Margaret, often denoting a tough, no-nonsense businesswoman, secretary or wife: fashion supremos Maggie Prescott (Kay Thompson) in *Funny Face* (1956 C) and Nina Foch in *Mr Broadway* 'Maggie, Queen of the Jungle' (1958 T); Maggie the Cat in CAT ON A HOT TIN ROOF; Mag Wildwood (Dorothy Whitney), Holly Golightly's flat-mate (lesbian in the Truman CAPOTE original) in *Breakfast at Tiffany's* (1961 C); Maggie (Sonia Graham), perfect secretary who has baby out of wedlock in *Compact* (1962 T); Maggie, owner of circus (Barbara STANWYCK) in *Roustabout* (1964 C); Maggie Cameron (Bettina Welch), fashion boss, lover of bisexual Bruce in NUMBER 96 (1972 T); lesbian Maggie (Sally Willis) in KISS AND TELL (1980 T); Maggie (Stefanie Powers), French model in *Mistral's Daughter* (1984 T); Maggie Barnes (Elizabeth Kemp), former lover of C. J. LAMB in L.A. LAW (1991 T); pilot Maggie (Janine Turner) in NORTHERN EXPOSURE; etc. The model (Anne Carlisle) in *Liquid Sky* (1983 C) is a rare example of the use of Margaret.

Ma, He's Making Eyes At Me A man goes soggy and coy because another man is trying to pick him up. This rates as probably the first homoerotic (though very light-hearted) song ever set on celluloid. Performed by an unidentified singer (carrying a duck), this early 1900s sound piece was disinterred and played at the 1991 ACADEMY AWARDS ceremony. It was adopted by Eddie Cantor, who delivered it on the soundtrack of his 1952 film biography while Keefe Brasselle mouthed the words, all rolling eyes and shy body language from a more 'innocent' age.

maidservants ROSE (Jean Marsh) devoted to Miss Elizabeth in UPSTAIRS, DOWNSTAIRS (1971–5 T), cuddling up with Sarah (Pauline Collins) to keep warm in the attic, and turning down a marriage proposal; Joanna David trying to replace her mistress's late lamented bulwark (emotional and possibly sexual) against her husband in *The Lady's Maid's Bell* (1983 T); Pauline (Jean Renée Foster), Selma's maid in *Beulah Land* (1980 T) who becomes her lover and co-founder of a school: strong, silent, supportive.

Maintaining Standards (UK 1981 R) Clive Baxter (Philip Lowrie), a popular and experienced history TEACHER in a secondary school, takes some boys to a football match. The reserve is left with him in the coach while the team get changed. During tea at home, the reserve David Mosley, a third former, tells his parents that he has been sexually assaulted. Clive is investigated and exonerated, but emerges bruised from the experience, determined to keep out of any areas which would draw attention to himself, refusing even to sign a petition to reinstate a teacher who has been unfairly dismissed. No more politics. He's after a quiet life and promotion.
W: Peter Whalley; D: Roger Fine; 21.1.81; BBC Radio 4; 50 mins.
Clive is a schoolteacher and Harry (Anthony Benson) a tax collector. What could be more respectable and responsible than this couple? But neither can afford to be complaisant. Harry says he has to be more honest and more polite because he's gay: 'more anything you care to mention to make up for the fact that I'm gay.' He takes a jaundiced view of the new openness, having himself been pilloried and imprisoned in the 1960s for having sex with a man 'in public', committing 'GROSS INDECENCY'. He doesn't think anything has changed: 'People outside of London trendies still hate queers.' By the end of this highly charged and compact play Clive is forced to agree with his lover. The same conditions prevail as in the 1950s. He was 'innocent', he didn't lose his job, but he'll have to be vigilant for the rest of his career. 'A play rooted in the reality – and fears – of many gay teachers' lives' (*Gay News*).

make-up All actors wear cosmetics to enhance their appearance in front of the footlights or on camera. Sometimes it is overdone: purposely (Marius Goring in *A Matter of Life and Death*; Akim Tamiroff in *Touch of Evil*); sometimes seemingly unconsciously (Marius Goring again, in the first scene of *The Red Shoes*; Sean Connery in *Marnie*; Michael Caine in *Alfie*, Charles Bronson in *Once Upon a Time in the West*, Ryan O'Neal in *The Big Bounce* etc).
Quentin CRISP brought make-up to the streets of London in THE NAKED CIVIL SERVANT; one of the prisoners (Michael Gough) in *Standing by for Santa Claus* (1968 T) pats soot on his eyes to make himself feel gorgeous; Pherber (Anita Pallenberg) paints the lips and eyes of Chas (James FOX) in PERFORMANCE (1970 C); Von Aschenbach (Dirk BOGARDE) wore it to give himself a more youthfully appealing look as his fever took hold in DEATH IN VENICE (1971 C); a character in *Taggart* 'The Run' (1978 T) wears make-up while doing the cooking; Gilberto (Gerald Murphy) seems to be dipping into his wife's mascara in FACING THE SUN (1980 C); The Japanese soldier (Ryuichi Sakamoto) is a stickler for the rules of war while dripping in blue eyeshadow (*Merry Christmas, Mr Lawrence* 1982 C); 'Cock' Roach (Philip Davis), a messhand, daubs his face in an effort to be given a discharge in *Submariners* (1983 T); Kenneth Halliwell (Alfred Molina) never goes outside the front door *au naturel* in PRICK UP YOUR EARS (1987 C).
The very word can have a double meaning. Alan BENNETT, lampooning

T. E. LAWRENCE in *Forty Years On* (1975 R), had the headmaster (John GIELGUD) mellifluously recall the school hero who had 'something feminine in his make-up. But his make-up was *always* discreet'.

The old image sticks. Francis BACON shocks a garrulous hanger-on in an after-hours drinking club by trilling, semi-comically: 'I'm not one of those poufs who wear makeup' (THE SOUTH BANK SHOW 1985 T).

A trendy mother (Pam Scotcher) discovers her young son Tim (Daniel Holender) putting on her lipstick and eyeshadow in *World's End* (1981 T). Trying not to show her hysteria, the mother reasons: 'You've got lovely clear skin. You shouldn't spoil your skin with make-up.' Tim rejoinders: '*You* do.' To which she replies: 'Yes, but I'm a woman. You're a boy. Boys don't wear make-up.'

Sometimes it is manly to wear face paint. Arnold Schwarzenegger does in both *Commando* (1985) and *Predator* (1987) – and very fetching it looks too. In the former, he kills perhaps 50 people, burns houses, throws a knife into someone's guts ('Stick around'), and dispatches a homosexual (but he doesn't kill a woman).

The whole issue of make-up for men was turned into a flimsy joke – involving a fireman – on THE SIX O'CLOCK SHOW (1983 T).

make-up artists Joe (Aubrey Morris) in AFTERNOON OF A NYMPH (1962 T): 'I'd love to be made a fuss of. I suppose that's why I went into this business in the first place. I do it to them because I'd like them to do it for me. That's psychological, isn't it'; Ray Lacey (Noel DAVIS), all camp chatter in *Who Killed Santa Claus?* (1971 T); Wayne Rouge (Ronnie Corbett) in *The Corbett Follies* (1971 T); the flighty number in *The Making of a Male Model* (1983 T); gregarious Bud in *The Lonely Lady* (1983 C); Newdell (Charles Robinson), sturdy, introspective black guy presented without fluttering mannerisms in *Buffalo Bill* (1983–4 T).

making it compulsory With the passing of legislation in Britain and the testing of the waters in some American states, there was some feeling of panic among certain sections of the majority culture. The new mood of assertiveness was countered by remarks such as Bob Hope's 'Homosexuality is legal in California. I'm getting out before they make it compulsory.'

The thought (which Hope had expressed first on a late 1960s television special) made its way into the film version of Paul Theroux's *Saint Jack* (1979). One of the odious colonialists says: 'The last time I returned to England they made it legal. I used to say to my wife, "Let's get out of here before they make it compulsory".' A year later, the London *Daily Mail*'s critic Martin Jackson (reviewing WE THINK THE WORLD OF YOU) theorized that 'we' were not content with it being legal, and 'now wanted to make it compulsory'.

In the mock general election in part 4 of the documentary *Public School* (1980 T) one of the students, standing as a gay liberation candidate, uses a loud hailer to tell the boys: 'In 1880 homosexuality was punished by whipping; in 1980 it may be compulsory.'

Bob Hope continued to make anti-gay remarks throughout the 1970s and 1980s. After protests in 1989 from homosexual groups, he publicly apologized in a specially filmed advert condemning QUEER-BASHING. He said JOKES help create an atmosphere whereby gay people are persecuted.

Making Love (US 1982 C) Nice successful DOCTOR (Michael Ontkean) leaves nice successful wife (Kate Jackson) – not for handsome unsuccessful WRITER (Harry Hamlin: he prefers promiscuity and watching old movies on video) but for (unseen) rich architect. His wife has remarried too (legally). Roberta Flack sings us out with the title song as the gay hero drives along a long empty road back to the city, leaving the heroine a secure and glowing part of a nuclear family breathing fresh country air.

P: Sherry Lansing; 113 mins.

'Boy meets boy, leaves wife' story with three fairly charismatic actors adrift in a sea of blandness. Directed by *Love Story*'s Arthur Hiller with a script by Barry SANDLER, openly gay but previously responsible for such raucous fare as *Gable and Lombard* and *The Duchess and the Dirtwater Fox*. His task on this occasion: to make an entertaining, true and honest film about two gay men for the Middle American couple in Milwaukee.

Making Love A first! A thoroughly gooey, unremarkable title song written by top talent (Carol Bayer Sager and Burt Bacharach) and hoisted aloft by Roberta Flack. It should have been in the great Hollywood heterosexual tradition of 'Love Is A Many Splendored Thing', 'A Certain Smile', 'Three Coins In The Fountain', 'The Shadow Of Your Smile', the theme from 'Love Story' and 'The Way We Were', But, like the film it accompanied, it didn't quite make it; audiences didn't come out humming, bathed in a golden glow of universal togetherness, understanding and tolerance.

Making Out (UK 1989–91) Life at the Shangri-La Electronics Factory with Queenie (Margi Clarke), Pauline (Rachel Davies), Carol May (Shirley Stelfox) and others.
W: Debbie Horsfield; P: John Chapman 1989; Carol Wilks; D: Chris Bernard, Bren Simson and others; BBC1; 55 mins.

This highly regarded, rambunctious comedy drama about female bonding and brawling in a factory fixed up secretary Norma with a woman partner in the penultimate episode of the last series.

making plans for the future As the American dream cannot yet accommodate successful homosexual relationships, mainstream entertainment can only allow gays and lesbians a few minutes of happiness before the figurative guillotine blade slides down. If a same-sex couple begin to lay plans for cohabitation, travel, honeymoon, anniversary or any of the milestones common to a heterosexual duo's life, the audience is being subtly cued that something terrible is about to happen – because as homosexual relationships can't/don't work, they have no future.

In *Strange Cargo* (1940 C) big fascist lug Moll (Albert Dekker) almost proposes marriage to pretty young Dufond (John Aldrege): 'I thought you and me might sling along together ... I've gotten to like you quite a lot, kid – like a guy does his kid brother. How does that strike you?' The kid isn't too sure at first, but comes round after his dewy-eyed admirer says: 'We'll travel far, we'll travel fast.' In the very next scene, a shark attacks one of their fellow driftees. Dufond attempts to save the man only to be restrained – with a punch – by Moll. The kid then falls to the floor and promptly dies. Saved from a fate worse than death? Later, Moll drinks seawater as a form of redemptive ritual suicide.

In DYNASTY (1985 T) Steven (Jack COLEMAN) and Luke (William Oliver Campbell) have a conversation ornamented with (totally atypical) loving commitment, mutual need and a feeling that they may – in the years to come – have something true and sustaining. But this is big-time American television. In the next episode, attending a royal wedding, machine-gun terrorists burst into the cathedral. Mayhem and massacre. Yet the only male character to be killed is Luke, leaving Steven to mourn a second male lover.

These are two of the more radical examples of the ingenuity that is poured into making homosexuality invalid as a day-to-day commitment. Other obstacles include SUICIDE, disease and death, MURDER, chronic promiscuity, warfare or one partner's resurfacing heterosexuality.

Mala Noche [Bad Night] (US 1987 C) Portland, Oregon. Walt Curtis (Tim Streeter) loves Mexican migrant Johnny (Doug Cooneyate) and doesn't keep quiet about it, least of all to Johnny –

who leads him by the nose in a strange courtship ritual which erotically leads only to his bovine friend Roberto (Ray Monge).

W/D: Gus Van Sant from a novella by Walt Curtis; P: Edison Manfred Salzgerber; 78 mins.

Enormously appealing, no frills telling of cheerfully unrequited love in a small, scrungy town. This is made all the more refreshing by the narration of an openly gay hero, the hangdog indifference of his object of desire, and an absolute refusal to see the characters purely in terms of loser, victim, exploiter, exploited.

Male Homosexuals (UK 1965 R) The first full-frontal foray of BBC Radio (Home Service: 5 & 12.1.65) into the day-to-day feelings of gay men: hopes, fears, emotions. Of course, psychiatrists and sociologists were in attendance but, under the careful direction of Michael SCHOFIELD, a much truer picture emerged than hitherto. There was mention of certain CLUBS, of people falling – and remaining – in love, and of AVERSION THERAPY: 'I think the biggest thing of all is the sheer relief of the unpleasant shock fading away.'

> Schofield: 'I think ... we must accept that homosexuals are going to be with us for a long time yet and we have got to accept them in the society.'
> Psychiatrist: 'I think that all this pop art and advertising project an ideal of heterosexuality which very few people will ever reach.'
> Schofield: 'All the propaganda from art to film to advertising shows how wonderful heterosexual life is.'

male impersonators Vesta TILLEY who did it all on the time of stage (and made films between 1900 and 1916) as did the comparable Hetty KING. The piquancy of the weaker sex playing the stronger proved a popular theme in films, as it had been in plays like A FLORIDA ENCHANTMENT (filmed in 1914). In the 1910 *Behind a Mask* a woman dresses as a man to fight a duel to save her honour.

Mary Pickford would quite frequently tog up in trousers and cap (*Poor Little Peppina* 1915; *The Hoodlum* 1919), not to mention velvet knickerbockers and long curls as *Little Lord Fauntleroy* (1921).

Asta Nielsen played *Hamlet* as a woman raised as man in the 1920 film (she also played LULU around this time); Douglas Fairbanks couldn't find an actor to play the rotund Persian Prince in *The Thief of Bagdad* (1925 C) so he filled the role with Mathilde Comont; Molly Burns (Clara Bow) does a 'boy' impersonation in *The Lawful Cheater* (1926 C); Louise BROOKS dresses as a hobo in *Beggars of Life* (1928 C), as does Veronica Lake for much of *Sullivan's Travels* (1941 C); the centenarian played by 'John' Dudgeon in *The Old Dark House* (1932 C) was actually Elspeth; *Viktor and Viktoria* (1933 C) were one and the same (Renate Mueller), remade in England as *First a Girl* (1935 C) with Jessie Matthews and five decades later as VICTOR/VICTORIA (1982 C) with Julie Andrews: a woman 'forced by circumstances' (starving to death) to become a FEMALE IMPERSONATOR; Katharine HEPBURN was SYLVIA SCARLETT (1935 C), but it was her guise as pretty Sylvester Scarlett which caused momentary problems for one of the male characters; Elizabeth Taylor as Velvet Brown rode to victory in the Grand National in male silks (*National Velvet* 1944 C); the master spy Mr Christopher was a woman in drag, Elsa Gebhardt (Signe Hasso) in *The House on 92nd Street* (1946 C); Hana-gi (Miko Taka) was the male lead in a Takarazuka revue in *Sayonara* (1957 C); the Chevalier D'Eon (Andrée Debar) in *The Secret of Chevalier D'Eon* (1960 C) kept up a disguise as a man for years, as did *Monsieur Hawarden* (1968 C); Ethel Le Neve (Samantha Eggar) was dressed as a boy to escape detection when she and her lover fled to America in *Dr Crippen* (1963 C); George and CHILDIE entertain the patronnes of the Gateways with their impersonations of LAUREL AND HARDY in THE KILLING OF SISTER GEORGE (1968 C); Diana Rigg appeared as a walrus-moustached policeman and an Afro-wigged hairdresser in *Theatre of Blood* (1973 C); Maria SCHNEIDER was a sailor in love with a crew member in *White Journey* (1980 C); Eva Mattes played an in-all-but-name version of director FASSBINDER in *A Man Like Eva* (1983 C); Brooke Shields donned a moustache in *Sahara* (1983 C); Linda Hunt won an ACADEMY AWARD for her flawless playing of Billy Kwan in *The Year of Living Dangerously* (1983 C). Recently Tilda Swinton played equally convincingly in *Man to Man* (1992 T) and ORLANDO (1992 C).

Television has tried female to male transvestism only a few times: Lucille Ball in I LOVE LUCY; Jane HATHAWAY (Nancy KULP) in 1970 episodes of *The Beverly Hillbillies* 'forced' by her boss to dress as security guard, sailor etc; *The Virgin Fellas* (1972); *Perfect Gentlemen* (1979 C) as a means of robbing a bank); in *Her Life As a Man* (1984) Carly Perkins (Robyn Douglass) becomes Carl Parsons to improve her job prospects; Dyan Cannon in *Jenny's War* (1985) eschewing glamour to help her son escape from a concentration camp.

See also ACTRESSES PLAYING MALE CHARACTERS; TRANSVESTITES.

male nurses *See* NURSES.

male rape *See* RAPE.

male strippers *See* STRIPPERS.

Donald **Maltby** (Philip Charles MacKenzie in BROTHERS (1984–7 T) Cliff's platonic friend who dispenses wisdom and camp repartee in about-equal amounts. A book editor, he briefly has an (unseen) friend called Gary ('he's a very nice guy, dumb as a truck, but he's not sending up SkyLab'). Donald's all-time high was having sex on Mr Toad's Wild Ride at Disneyland. Taken to task over one of his outfits (silk shirt, tight trousers, turquoise jacket and scarf) he lets fly: 'It takes a real man to wear this ... You think I'm effeminate, don't you ... You think I'm a trifle swishy ... Well, let me tell you ... I'm a fella ... I shave and I swear and I pee

standing up (though I don't like to do that on weekends because I have to stand there with my gown over my head).'

Donald is the acceptable, though not necessarily reassuring, face of homosexuality on the show. Never at a loss for words, bouncing back from life's adversities and always ready to give troglodyte 'brother' Lou (Brandon Maggert) as good as – usually much better than – he gets: 'a man isn't measured by the tobacco he chews.'

The other brother Joe likes Cliff having such a fairy as a friend because (despite a few references to sex) he is not a fully potent being: 'He's the man who walks with a lisp.' Joe finds it difficult to cope on the few occasions when Cliff has a lover: 'I've accepted he's homosexual ... but this is the first time he's had a homosexual to be one with.'

Perhaps it is indicative of the thinking behind *Brothers* that Donald is the only character with any real grounding in sexual politics, the one who (occasionally) alludes to the unmentionable, and who doesn't give a damn about convention. He has all the chutzpah of a drag queen without wearing a dress. But as Lou said in 1986: 'Donald is a WIMP. Even if he was straight, he'd still be a wimp.'

mama's boys The American euphemism for an effeminate, immature male who may or may not be homosexual. Used for the title of an *M Squad* episode in 1960, still going strong 30 years later: *Sally Jessy Raphael*'s guests each tell why 'I Hate Being Married to a Mama's Boy' (1991 T). *See also* MOTHER'S BOYS.

Man Alive (UK 1965–75 T) Provocative, entertaining rambles down life's lesser travelled roads: its under- and overachievers, its taboos. Fearlessly dealing with wife swapping, SKINHEADS, singles' weekends, nudism and sex education, it quite naturally tackled homosexuals, male and female, in 'Consenting Adults', shown during the month when homosexual acts between (most) males over 21 were made legal. No experts were present: each person spoke for themselves.

E: Tom Conway, Bill Morton and Desmond Wilcox; 5 & 14.6.67; BBC2; 2 parts; 50 mins each.

'Desperately lonely men, scared of discovery ... Most are backs to the camera but a couple of middle-aged men don't hide ... [Among the women] were Steve who is only happy dressed as a man ... a married woman with two children ... and ... what seemed a very happy, very settled couple of women talking as matter of factly as any couple does about their relationship' (Francis KING, *Listener*, 22.6.67).

A Man Apart: A Sound Portrait of an Enigma of the Twenties (UK 1968 R) The long road to anonymity and obscurity of Basil Vacuum, 'Bore? Drunk? Layabout? Dilettante and degenerate? An untalented parasite? Was he anything more?' Decides the narrator: 'The answer must inevitably be no.'

W: John Wells and Richard Ingrams; BBC Radio 3; 30 mins.

Mainly a catty rejoinder to a recent radio documentary on OXFORD aesthete Brian HOWARD, the targets were a first eleven of homosexual British novelists, journalists and musicians, including W. Somerset MAUGHAM, Beverley NICHOLS, Godfrey WINN, Robin MAUGHAM and Benjamin BRITTEN. The programme was gimcrack in its assemblage of cheap snipings (the hero was expelled from school, where he was known to masters and boys alike as Tarte), but it did shine a spotlight on the carefully arranged whitewash jobs it mocked: like those on Howard, T. E. LAWRENCE and Norman DOUGLAS. Such programmes would feature various cultured people (usually male) discussing in the most élitist tones villas and parties, and a stream of vague, ungendered friends or acquaintances from many walks of life (namely the forces or labour exchange).

Basil Vacuum and Conrad Plume and Godfrey Wheen were itinerant aesthetes, out for whatever they could pick up – 'Hallo ducky, how's tricks?' –

whether animal, vegetable or mineral. Their camping grounds were mainly Piccadilly or the South of France (the Villa dei Puovi). There was much talk of Osbert, Evelyn, Harold, Maurice and Johnny, and occasional references to the Mauve Carnation Club and green trouser snakes. And PANSIES were everywhere stewn.

Appearing some 10 months after the passing of the SEXUAL OFFENCES BILL, this was very much *Private Eye* (which Richard Ingrams edited) going for the Public Ear – eviscerating easy targets: etiolated, enamelled men who lived their lives constrained by all kinds of personal guilts and criminal laws.

Mr X: 'No fairy cakes, thank you, I'm trying to give them up.'

man-hating 'I detest all men. Curse them!' cries Consuelo (Dorothy Mackaill) via title card in *The Dancer of Paris* (1926 C); Estella was brought up to loathe yet exploit men by Miss HAVISHAM in *Great Expectations* (1946 C etc); *Rebecca* DE WINTER (1940 C; 1979 T; etc) 'despised all men'; the Anti-Sex League in NINETEEN-EIGHTY-FOUR (1954 T; 1956 C; 1965 R; 1984 C) seemed to be made up entirely of thrusting well-muscled women who seek to deprive all men of their simple pleasures; Ines in HUIS CLOS makes it quite clear she has no need of the other sex; Esther (Ingrid Thulin) in THE SILENCE (1963 C) is revolted by the 'fishy odour of SEMEN'; Carol (Catherine Deneuve) cannot abide a male's touch (*Repulsion* 1964 C) and her women clients in the beauty salon confirm her in her feeling: 'Men! Why are they so bloody filthy? ... Keep them on their knees, they love it'; *Marnie* (Tippi Hedren 1964 C) is horrified by any masculine closeness after seeing her mother with sailors; Colin McIver (William Windom), the murderer in THE DETECTIVE (1968 C), was raised by a mother who found both men and sex distasteful; June Allyson is a marauding, murdering bulldozer in *They Only Kill*

Their Masters (1973 C); housewife Madge (Briony Hodge) suggests all-out attack on the husbands of herself and of her pupil – and would-be lover – (Ann Curthoys) in *Piano Lessons* (1976 T): 'Let's wear them out. Let's taunt them and tease them and drive them to drink. Never give them a moment's peace. Let's nag them both to an early grave.'

Another wife is told that she's being used: 'He just sees you as an object, Jennie. That's what men are like,' says Elspeth ('Ellie') in *Swimming and Flying* (1980 R).

Janet Mayer (Linda Darrow) saw her mother beaten and molested by her father: she now hates all men and ill-treats her young son in STARSKY AND HUTCH 'The Crying Child' (1977 T); Ruby 'Mitch' Mitchell (Paola Dionisetti) encourages two of her girlfriends to waylay and beat up men in WITHIN THESE WALLS 'Mixer' (1978 T); Olive Chancellor (Prunella Scales 1979 R; Vanessa REDGRAVE 1984 C) dislikes and distrusts men, particularly her cousin Basil who woos and wins her protégée in *The Bostonians*; Diana Graham (Rachel Davies) agrees that, yes, it would be fair to say that she doesn't like men: 'It's war ... If you want to exist as an equal' in CROWN COURT 'A Friend of the Family' (1979 T); mute Thana (Zoe Tamerlis) wastes men with a .45 in New York City (*Ms .45* 1980 C); Elizabeth Morrison (Wendy Hiller) is said only to like men if 'they carry a bell like a leper' in *Miss Morrison's Ghosts* (1981 T); Garp's mother Jenny (Glenn Close) writes a bestseller which attracts a cult of fanatic man-hating women who have cut out their tongues to commemorate a celebrated rape victim in *The World According to Garp* (1982 C); a group of women murder a man just for being a man in *A Question of Silence* (1982 C); Sonia (Jacqueline Tongue) plans a fiery range for the men who did her and her friends wrong in *Heart of the Country* (1987 T), haranguing a carnival crowd about 'the wickedness of men and the wretchedness of women': she likens her aversion as being akin to the hatred of women by men; Sister Hilda Rolfe (Andrée Evans)

in *Shroud for a Nightingale* (1984 T) refers to a father who didn't believe in education for girls: 'You have got to respect a sex that has brought selfishness to such an art.'

See also FEMINISTS.

Manila: In the Claws of Darkness aka *Manila: In the Claws of Neon* (Philippines 1975 C) Everything and anything goes in this city of easy money, quick-fix sex and technicolor dreams. A country boy (Rafael Roca Jr), searching for his girl, falls briefly into prostitution: a mirror image of the fate that has befallen her.
W/D: Lino Brocka from a story by Edgardo Reyes; 125 mins.

A sometimes blinding insight into the seductive charms of a superficially bustling city and the ooze that lies beneath. The handful of scenes involving male PROSTITUTES (led by Tommy Abuel) are as cold and businesslike as the transactions themselves, save for some moments of silliness involving a customer who insists on his peke Bullett being on the bed throughout the session: 'Wait till Mama is finished.'

The Man I Love Mimed, accompanied by (American) sign language, by a deaf man to the Bessie SMITH version of the Gershwin song in a film about choreographer Pina Bausch (*One Day Pina Asked ...* 1987 T) and her 26 dancers. Daniella (Ruti Goldberg) sings it to herself constantly in *It's That Age* (1990 C), but she ends up in bed – and later in love – with a 32-year-old sculptress, Michal (Idit Terperson).

The Man in Black *See* APPOINTMENT WITH FEAR.

Manley Hopkins, Gerard (1844–89) English poet and Jesuit priest whose conflict between sainthood and emotional activity led to bouts of 'nervous prostration'. Hugh Ross played him in a piece about the writing of *Felix Randal* (1987 R), and Edward Petherbridge showed the poet at other stages of his creative and spiritual life in *The Uncreated Light* (1989 R).

Mannion, Moira (*c* 1920–1964) South African-born actress, with reposeful yet purposeful manner, who played Sergeant Grace MILLARD for five years in DIXON OF DOCK GREEN.

R: Violet Miller in *Presumed Dead* (1946); Mary Turner in *Birds of a Feather* (1947; as *Jadwiga, Queen of Poland* (1947); *Words and Music* (with Turner Layton, 1948); Miss Thorpe, a ladylike potential pick-up for Bob in MRS DALE'S DIARY (1948); replaced as Peggy the Policewoman before transmission of the first episode of *The Huggets* (1953); *Return to South Africa* (1961); *The Narrow Search* (1963); member of BBC Drama Repertory Company 1964.

T: *The Ends of the Earth* (1949); Mary, Queen of Scots in *The Lady from Denmark* (1951); modiste in *King's Rhapsody* (1959); canon's wife in *The Cathedral* (1959); Miss Verney, slave-driving head of the secretarial pool, very protective of at least one of her girls, in *A Young Affair* (1958).

manservants Among those who always aimed to please: Roger (Edward Everett HORTON) in *Reaching for the Moon* (1931 C); adviser in affairs of the heart and sock-darner-in-chief Eric BLORE (for Robert Montgomery) in *Piccadilly Jim* (1936 C); Jameson (Blore again) in *The Lone Wolf* series (1940s C); Passepartout (Cantinflas) in *Around the World in 80 Days* (1956 C); Fickling (Robert Webber) in MRS DALE'S DIARY (1950s R); Thomas (John Alderton) in UPSTAIRS, DOWNSTAIRS (1972 T); the retired Edward Minty (Emlyn WILLIAMS) in PAST CARING (1986 T). The more devilish ones included STEERFORTH's Littimer in DAVID COPPERFIELD (Brian Haines 1974 R; Norman Jones 1991 R); Peter Quint in *The Turn of the Screw/The Innocents* (Peter WYNGARDE 1961 C etc); Barrett (Dirk BOGARDE) in *The Servant* (1963 C); Conrad Ludwig (Michael York) in *Something for Everyone* aka *Black Flowers for the Bride* (1970 C).

Mansfield, Katherine [Kathleen Mansfield Beauchamp] (1888–1923) New Zealand-born short story writer. Played by Vanessa Redgrave in *A Picture of Katherine Mansfield* (1973 T); Anna MASSEY in *A Child of the Sun* (1979 R); Moir Leslie in *The Voyage* (1985 R); Jane Birkin in *Leave All Fair* (1987 C). A number of stories read on WOMAN'S HOUR and *The Daughters of the Late Colonel*, about two women forced to face life after the death of their father, dramatized in 1945 and 1983 (R).

The Man's In The Navy As a café singer deported from a number of South Sea islands, Marlene DIETRICH plys her seductive trade at the *Café of the Seven Sinners* (which was the British title of the 1940 *Seven Sinners*). With an audience of naval officers (including John WAYNE), she cocks a snook at authority by dressing in dress whites with braided cap and epaulettes in order to render – ambiguously as always – this Frank Loesser–Frederick Hollander ditty. Is she saying that no man is safe because 'she's' in the navy, or that wives have no need to fear for their husbands offshore if she is really a he? Or is it something else: 'Mister, watch your wife/The man's in the navy.' Most disarming whichever way it is perceived: jaunty, insolent, wicked.

According to her daughter Maria Riva, Marlene always wanted Noel COWARD to sing this song in cabaret, 'which he never did, because he hadn't written it, but mostly because that tasteless a homosexual he was not!'

a man's man In MINDER 'Whose Wife Is It Anyway?' (1980) Arthur (George Cole) enthusiastically tells Terry (Dennis Waterman) about a mate of his whose shop needs protection. 'A real hard case in his time,' he says, 'A real man's man.' Never a truer word was spoken (at least by Arthur). Terry soon learns that the mate is a young man's man.

When Colin RUSSELL (Michael CASHMAN) comes to look over the upstairs flat, Tony (Oscar James) takes an immediate liking to him in EASTENDERS (1986 T). Just a feeling, he tells his wife.

'A real man's man. You can always tell when someone is STRAIGHT.'

Alun Trevose (John Patrick), the superficially rough-hewn miner in PEN-MARRIC (1979 T), is one of the rare fully gay, traditional men's men: 'A man to respect, a man to trust ... a man to play darts with.'

man's name for a woman See BOYS' NAMES FOR GIRLS.

The Man That Got Away Ira Gersh-win–Harold Arlen torch song belted out by Judy GARLAND in the smoky after-hours club, watched by James Mason in *A Star Is Born* (1954 C). It was repro-duced, with almost exactly the same set-ting and orchestration, on *The Judy Gar-land Show* in 1962. In two unusual – and daring – pieces of gender confusion Jerry Van Dyke (on *The Judy Garland Show* 1963) and David McCallum (on *The Andy Williams Show* 1965) lip synched to the (live) Garland voice. The classic rendition turned up in *Not Wav-ing* (1979 R) where the elderly landlord (Philip Voss) trembles over each and every word that Judy tears from her throat: 'That anguish!' he cries. A saloon singer serenades *Liberace* (Andy Robinson) with the song (20 years before it was written) in the 1988 TV movie. It serves – majestically and not a little boldly – as Larry GRAYSON's theme music.

man to man A conjunction that some-times has intimations of shared feelings or can be a cue to remind someone of their effeminacy: 'The one man I could talk to as man to man, the one I could talk to about everything,' says Stanhope (Colin Clive) to Raleigh (David Man-ners) in JOURNEY'S END (1930 C); when Leslie (Hugh PADDICK) asks Jack (Michael Robbins) if he can talk to him man to man, Jack immediately rejoins: 'Well, I'm not sure *you're* properly quali-fied' (SHARE AND SHARE ALIKE 'Age of Consent' 1978 R).

Mapplethorpe, Robert (1947–89) American artist and photographer who first achieved attention by being the sub-ject of *Robert Having His Nipple Pierced* (1971 C). His career was discussed on ARENA 'Robert Mapplethorpe' (1988 T), and the Cincinnati *cause célèbre* over some of the explicit (mainly sado-maso-chistic) photographs was explored in *Damned in the USA* (1991 C/T). His lover Jack Walls talked about his personal and professional relationship with Mapplethorpe in *Eye to Eye* (1990 T). (A fictional artist was involved with sado-masochistic images and a resulting court case in *Law and Order* 'Prisoner of Love' 1990 T.)

Marbury, Elisabeth (1856–1933) American theatrical figure, described by *Variety* as 'one of the leading play agents of the '90s and early part of this century ... a leader in theatrical, political and fashion worlds ... sharing her home (the old Washington Irving homestead in Irving Place) with Elsie De Wolfe, now Lady Mendl ... With Miss De Wolfe she engaged in the interior decorating business for a time, did war work and became an adviser and member of the National Democratic cause ... She never married.' Portrayed – after a fashion – by Edna May Oliver as a jolly, bustling SPINSTER in *The Story of Irene and Vernon Castle* (1938 C), and by Cherie Lunghi as a rampant money-grabbing fraud called Una Marbury – who seduces Richard Burton's daughter and is eventually shot dead by her – in *Ellis Island* (1984 T).

March, David (1925–   ) English radio actor of deep vocal resonance who did a roaring trade in all manner of colourful, flowing gentlemen from the early 1950s to the late 1980s, including Patroclus in *Nine Days Wonder* (1953 R); Richard FULTON in MRS DALE'S DIARY and THE DALES; Raoul De Ravigne in *Death in Ecstasy* (1969); Somerset MAUGHAM in WEEKEND WITH WILLIE (1981 R); Count DRACULA in *Vampirella* (1976); Mr Nor-ris in *Mr Norris Changes Trains* (1984 R). He can also comfortably play sympath-etic parts such as the vicar in the popular *The Dog Collar* series (1958–9).

Other work includes: Maxim De Camp

in *A Man Apart* (about Flaubert, 1981); Latimer Honiton in *Who Wrote Horse-back Hall?* (1985); MORNING STORY 'The Funny Side' (1986), 'The Hounds of Fate' (1986) and 'Wrappers' (1987) about Geoffrey, a second-hand book-seller taking a train to see a friend; Sbirro, restaurateur with human flesh on the menu in *Fear on 4* 'The Speciality of the House' (1988); Lucullus in *Timon of Athens* (1989); M. R. JAMES in *The Lodestone* (1989); *Alexander* (1993).

Jo March   Character in *Little Women* who gets over her (wholesome) TOMBOY phase and settles down with a male mate in *Good Wives* and *Jo's Boys*. The second daughter of the family, as was Jo's crea-tor, Louisa May Alcott – who did not marry. Katharine HEPBURN played her in 1933; June Allyson in 1949; Meredith Baxter Birney in 1978 (TV movie); Andrée Melly was one of a number of British TV Jos (1957); and the most recent, on radio, was Buffy Davis (1992).

March Of The Women   Composed by Dame Ethel SMYTH for the SUFFRA-GETTE movement. When she and her fellow protesters were arrested, Dame Ethel conducted and sang this feminist anthem from her prison cell, keeping time with her toothbrush; a scene enacted by Maureen Pryor in *Shoulder to Shoulder* (1974 T). Violet (Kathleen Helme) sings it from the vantage point of 1977 in *House Wives* (1981 R) and Ken Russell includes it, sung by Rita Cullis, under 'G for Girls' in his *ABC of British Music* (1988 T).

Marcus Welby MD   'The Outrage' (US 1975 T)   A young boy has been attacked but he refuses to reveal the name of his abuser – who is the boy's psychotic teacher.

   Forewarned by American gay media organizations (who had picketed ABC television), in Britain CHE Chairwoman Glenys Parry requested a showing and afterwards asked that a statement be made before transmission that gays were not all CHILD MOLESTERS. This was not granted. Thames' Programme Co-ordi-nation Chief said no to an announce-ment and no to a cancellation. All that diluted the false generalities was the inserted line of dialogue from the police sergeant to the boy's father: 'There's nothing homosexual about this. It's a case of violent child molestation.'

   The following is an extract from an interview with Gore VIDAL by Steven Abbott and Thom Willenbecker in *Gay Sunshine* 26–7 (1975–6):

> Vidal: 'The fag show about a 14-year-old who loses his manhood because he gets seduced and he wasn't even buggered, was he? I think he was just drained of his seminal juices.'
> Interviewer: 'The opening scene featured a boy standing before a mirror, with either hickeys or bruises all over his torso ... Raped by the science teacher as the story goes.'
> Vidal: 'Indeed. I suppose the heteros think that the back of his head will now fall off. Or he will wear eye liner in the gym.'
> Interviewer: 'The show lent itself to the myth of the child molester homosexual: an atavistic dread.'

Mardi Gras   *See* SYDNEY GAY AND LES-BIAN MARDI GRAS.

Margolyes, Miriam (1941–)   English actress whose vocal lyricism and voluptuous, small physical frame often find her in widely varying roles in sound as opposed to vision. After supplying hundreds of voice-overs for television and radio adverts, she achieved nation-wide fame with the Telecom series also featuring Maureen Lipman (1988–90 T) and became the definitive 'Her Maj' (and her daughter, not to mention the rest of the family) in THE QUEEN AND I (1992 R).

   C: warder in *Scrubbers* (1982); 'Lady Scientist' in *Morons from Outer Space* (1985); 'BULL DYKE' receptionist in *The Little Shop of Horrors* (1986); Flora Finching in *Little Dorrit* (1986); *The Fool* (1989); Realtor in *Pacific Heights* (1990); Audrey in *As You Like It* (1992).

   R: hotel proprietor in *Defeating Mrs*

Dresden (1963); Emilia Carter in *Inspector Scott Investigates* 'The Mail Van Robbery' (1963); second porpoise in *The Dark Ages* (1964); one of the women of Thesmophona in A FESTIVAL OF WOMEN (1965); Mollie in *Escapade* (1965); Margery Ripe in *Cavalcade in Cowdray* (1965); the murdered man's girlfriend in ROPE (1966); MORNING STORY 'Penny Ledigo's Quiet Life' (1968); Elspeth in *Salute to Adventure* (1970); read *Bhowani Junction* (1974); tailor's wife in *Following Suit* (1975); starred in *Harvey's Festival* (1975); *Get On with It* (with Kenneth WILLIAMS and Lance Percival, 1975); Stinking Iris in *The Wordsmiths of Gorsemere* (1984); Vera Panova in *Leningrad Speaks* (1983); Nadia Ebony in *Unman Wittering and Zigo* (1984); Marie David, lover of Siri Von Essen in THE ROAD FROM KYMMENDO BAY (1985); Miss Stein in GERTRUDE STEIN AND A COMPANION (1985); LILITH IN *Gardens of Eden: Poems for Eve and Lilith* (1987); Mimi in *The Bohemians* (1987); *Mary of Magdala* (by Sara Maitland, 1988); *Short Stories for Holy Week* 'Mary of Magdala' (1988); Mary Garden, the opera singer in *Garden Notes* (1989); *Dickens' Women* (1991, also discussed it on KALEIDOSCOPE); reading THE QUEEN AND I (1992).

T: *At the Eleventh Hour* (with Richard Neville, 1967–8); Miss Baberton/Miriam in *The Lifeswappers* (1976); CROWN COURT 'Auld Lang Syne' (1978); Jane Wright, the 'fat girl with brains' in *The Girls of Slender Means* (1979); rehearsing THE SOUTH BANK SHOW 'Cloud Nine' (1979); Italian maid in an episode of *Take a Letter, Mr Jones* (1981); *Freud* (1984); narrated *The Living Body* (1984); Princess Marie in *Blackadder II* 'The Queen of Spain's Beard' (1985); Mrs Corney in *Oliver Twist* (1985); Nurse Hopkins in *The Life and Loves of a She-Devil* (1986); Tony's mama in *Body Contact* (1987); randy witch in *Mr Majeica* (1988); Nellie Quass, doting sister (of Simon CALLOW) in *Old Flames* (1990); stars in a Norman LEAR series about a woman surviving divorce (1993).

'What about my private life? Well, you can say I am deliberately unmarried.

Then you could add, "An evil leer played about her lips and there was a twinkle in her eye" ' (the actress to Jane Ellison, *Evening Standard*, 2.12.79).

'Although she does not parade with Gay Lib banners, she allows that she is "deliberately unmarried" ' (Michele Field, *The Bulletin* (Australia), 24–31.12.91).

Marian / Marianne / Marion Girl's name, mainly for heroines (some transgressors) in America, and mainly for lesbian-slanted characters in Britain.

US: Marion Dorsey (Hope Hampton), faithful wife of man with gambling debt in *Lawful Larceny* (1923 C); Marion (Ann Harding), 'pert, cute and determined' in *Biography of a Bachelor Girl* (1935 C); Marion Crane (Janet Leigh) having an affair with a married man, who absconds with her firm's cash and meets death in a shower in *Psycho* (1960 C); Marian the Librarian (Shirley Jones) in *The Music Man* (1962 C); Marian (Elaine Stritch) in *Who Killed Teddy Bear?* (1965 C); Marian Crane (Mala Powers), secretary to the mayor (Anthony Quinn) in *The Man and the City* (1971–2 T); Marianne (Goldie Hawn) in *Bird on a Wire* (1990 C).

UK: Marian HALCOMBE, burly protector of her half-sister Laura in *The Woman in White* (Joan Carol 1943 R; Eleanor Parker 1948 C; Diana QUICK 1982 T; etc); Marion Sharpe, spinster accused of abducting teenage girl in *The Franchise Affair* (Dulcie Gray 1952 C; Rosalie Crutchley 1962 T; Joanna McCallum 1988 T; etc); spunky (Maid) Marian (Bernadette O'Farrell and Patricia Driscoll) in *The Adventures of Robin Hood* (1955–9 T; played by Audrey Hepburn as a middle-aged nun in *Robin and Marian* (1976 C); Marian Snow (Fanny Rowe) in love with her younger business partner in *Kate* 'A Human Weakness' (1971); Marian Robertson (Caroline Mortimer) in love with Carol in WITHIN THESE WALLS 'Transfer' 1975; the sex-changed Marianne Miller (Judy Loe) in CROWN COURT 'The Change' (1978 T); Marian (Amanda Murry), nearly eaten, with her lover, by a dog in JUST BEFORE MID-NIGHT 'The Worm Will Turn' (1979 R); civil servant with young lover in *Left-Handed Sleeper* (1982 R); Marian Owen (Margaret John) in *Crossroads* (1985 T).

Marlowe, Christopher (1564–93) English playwright whose mysterious life and death have been the subject of much discourse on radio and television, beginning with a talk by Leslie Hotson in 1925 – which was forbidden any mention of the possible sexual dynamics behind his supposed stabbing at an inn by 'a bawdy serving man, a rival of his in his lewde love'. What had been left to 'informed listeners' imaginations' was spelt out a little more clearly by Hotson in *The Death of Christopher Marlowe* in 1964. Speculation about the exact nature and circumstances of his death have led to television programmes such as *Tempo* 'The Marlowe Murder Mystery' (1964 T) and *The Marlowe Inquest* (1986 T).

Hotson discussed the official report of the coroner's inquest on Marlowe's death. He may have been an agent provocateur to trap free-thinkers into indiscretions ... Was he killed or did he stab himself? Or was it a cover-up? Was he the second greatest writer in Elizabethan England or did he not write any of the plays attributed to him?

The man himself has been portrayed in *Will* SHAKESPEARE (by Leslie Perrins 1931 R; Sebastian SHAW 1947 R; Esmond Knight 1938 T; John Colicos 1953 T); by Laurence Payne in *The Prodigal* (1953 R); by Ian McShane in *Will Shakespeare* (1976 T); by Ronald Herdman in *The Gloriana Murder Mystery* (1992 R); etc. The fragmentary aspects of his character were pieced together in QUALITY STREET 'Brief Glory' (Aust 1964 R), but even these are in doubt in the light of some 1992 evidence about his double-dealing.

Marlowe's handful of works – notable for cynicism and cruelty – (including *Doctor Faustus, The Tragedy of Dido Queen of Carthage* and *Tamburlaine the Great*) have received radio productions, with EDWARD II in 1930 marking the first

overt love scene between two men on any 'stage' for a few centuries.

'What we know of him is mostly bad, and what we do not know is probably worse ... But it is as well to remember that there is nothing too vile for those who kick against established dogma and morality; and unfortunately none of his friends have left their account of this remarkable man' (G. B. Harrison in the series *Queen Elizabeth's Subjects* 1934 R).

Miss Marple A small, orderly soul living on a fixed income in St Mary Mead: a village which, for 40 years, was a hotbed of murders, robberies and assaults – most of them solved by this suspicious, beetling busybody. Lots of SPINSTERS and interesting BACHELORS either live there or cross Miss M.'s path. Played by Margaret Rutherford (in four 1960s films), by Helen Hayes (in some 1970s and 1980s US TV movies), and – definitively – by Joan Hickson (1984–92). In *Nemesis* (1986 T) the sleuth receives a tiny bit of help from Miss Cooke (Jane Booker) and Miss Barrow (Alison Skilbeck) gruff and attired as for a duck shoot.

marriage Generally taken to be a legal and emotional bond between two people of the opposite sex, but increasingly being discussed as an option for lesbians or gay men. Many programmes have dealt with this subject, few with the rigour of MARRIAGE: PAST AND PRESENT (1931 R) or *Pictures of Women* 'Who Do You Love?' (1984) – both in their different ways saying that the prevailing model is an artifice: 'Most people support it because it seems to fulfil emotional needs. The Royal Wedding and the whole panoply of marriage [encourage this] ... It became channelled into "normal" after a long process.'

The feminist view was put into the mainstream in the 1970s, but within certain, tight parameters. In a courtroom interrogation of a woman 'on the edge' of society, Diana Graham (Rachel Davis) in CROWN COURT 'A Friend of the Family' (1979 T) responds to the comment that she doesn't approve of marriage. 'No ... because men have all the rights in marriage; in exchange for financial security a woman gives up her rights to her money, her possessions.'

Soundings (1985 R) and ANALYSIS 'The Matrimonial State' (1992 R) were content to see marriage as an institution which remained popular despite all the pitfalls. Although there is 'more diversity in relationships', the 'moral, stable institution of marriage' is still a requirement for many people. The more recent programme questioned why lesbian and gay people were increasingly opting for the 'shackles' of real or quasi *de facto* or married states.

Marriage (UK 1929 R) Harold NICOLSON and Vita SACKVILLE-WEST believed not in common interests but 'common values effortlessly accommodating'. According to their son Nigel Nicolson (in the 1973 book *Portrait of a Marriage*), both thought marriage unnatural but couldn't say so as it was 'not for a BBC audience'. (This talk, like a number of others they gave singly or together, was produced by Hilda Matheson, who was for a time Vita's lover.)

marriage (gay/lesbian) Spoofed or turned into grotesque spectacle in SOME LIKE IT HOT (1959 C); *Loving Couples* (1964 C). ENTERTAINING MR SLOANE (1968 T; 1970 C); FELLINI SATYRICON (1969 C); SALO (1975 C); *Scum* (1978 C); DOG DAY AFTERNOON (1975 C); *History of the World, Part 1* (1981 C); *City of Women* (1980 C); LA CAGE AUX FOLLES; THE WEDDING (1985 C); Pee-Wee HERMAN. Played out for real on television in WHICKER WAY OUT WEST (1973); gay lesbian marriage Rod and Bob Jackson-Paris on DONAHUE (1992); etc.

The whole concept of queer legalized coupledom was discussed in OUT 'Love and Marriage: Sacred Institution or Con Trick?' (1991 T). The programme was introduced by Frank Sinatra singing from the song: 'Love and Marriage/ They go together like a horse and carriage.'

marriage of convenience (involving lesbian or gay man) THE ROADS TO FREEDOM (1970 T, Daniel and Marcelle); NUMBER 96 (1977 T, Don and fellow lawyer, briefly); CALIFORNIA SUITE (1978 C, Sidney and Diana); A DIFFERENT STORY (1978 C, lesbian Stella and gay illegal immigrant Albert); HOWARDS' WAY (1985–90 T, Gerald and Polly); *Pardon Mon Affair Too* (1978 C, Daniel); *Forbidden* (1984 C/T, the countess and a friend); THE TINKER'S DAUGHTER (1986 R, Meriel and rich man); *Heretics* (1992 R, gay Gavin to a woman priest). Proposed by gay man (but rejected): A TASTE OF HONEY (1961 C); *Pete 'n' Tillie* (1972 C); *Only When I Laugh* (1981 C).

Marriage: Past and Present (UK 1931 R) A series of talks by Professor Bronislaw Malinowski (representing traditional matrimony, the nuclear family and the mother at home) and Dr Robert Briffault (espousing extended families, wider choices and more clear-headed view of the past):

> Civilized man is essentially lonely. To be released from that necessity of being on our guard, to be able to trust another human being, in other words to be loved, is in those circumstances one of the deepest cravings of human nature.
> ... science teaches that marriage and the family are rooted in the deepest needs of human nature ... A bee hive is a family, but it is not patriarchal.

The previous year, Desmond MacCarthy had been advising a wider vision: 'Other equally stable societies have been founded on quite different marriage laws. The point is to discover what kind of relationships of the sexes are really condusive to human happiness.

marriage troubled by the presence of a man CAT ON A HOT TIN ROOF (1958 C; 1976 T); *Oscar Wilde* (1960 C); *The Trials of Oscar Wilde* (1960 C); VICTIM (1961 C); ADVISE AND CONSENT (1962 C); REFLECTIONS IN A GOLDEN EYE (1967 C); *Total Eclipse* (1973 T); *Gold* (1974 C); *The Tamarind Seed* (1974 C);

DOG DAY AFTERNOON (1975 C); PEN-MARRIC (1979 T); THE GENTLE TOUCH 'Blade' (1980 T); FACING THE SUN (1980 T); *Bergerac* 'Nice People Die in Bed' (1981 T); MORE LIVES THAN ONE (1984 T); HOTEL 'Transitions' (1985 T); *Oscar* (1985 T); *May We Borrow Your Husband?* (1986 T); etc.

marriage troubled by the presence of a woman *10.30 P.M. Summer* (1966); *Wednesday's Child* (1971 T); *The Golden Road* (1973 T); *Executive Suite* (1975–6 T); *Play Things* (1976 T); CROWN COURT 'A Friend of the Family' (1979 T); ANOTHER WAY (1982 C); ENTRE NOUS (1983 C); *Oxbridge Blues* 'The Muse' (1984 T); *The Berlin Affair* (1985 C); THE ROAD FROM KYMMENDO BAY (1985 R); PORTRAIT OF A MARRIAGE (1990 T); etc.

marriage with a gay or lesbian or bisexual partner producing children *Oscar* WILDE (1960 C); *The Trials of Oscar Wilde* (1960); STAIRCASE (1969 C); THAT CERTAIN SUMMER (1972 T); BERMONDSEY (1972 T); *Total Eclipse* (1973 T); *The Tamarind Seed* (1974 C); DOG DAY AFTERNOON (1975 C); *Nightingale's Boys* 'Flossie' (1975 T); A QUESTION OF LOVE (1978 T); *Rainbow* (1978 T); LA CAGE AUX FOLLES (1978 C); *The Suicide's Wife* (1979 T); MARY'S WIFE (1980 T); DYNASTY (1981–91 T; *Celebrity* (1983 T); MORE LIVES THAN ONE (1984 T); *Hotel* 'Transitions' (1985 T); *Oscar* (1985 T); DOMESTIC BLISS (1985 T); THE HEART EXPOSED (1986 C/T); THE LOST LANGUAGE OF CRANES (1992 T); etc.

the marrying kind *See* NOT THE MARRYING KIND.

Marshall, Arthur [Charles A. Barker] (1910–89) On radio from 1934 as various female characters: Miss Plaintain, games mistress at St Berthas in *The Giddiest Girl in the College* (1937) and *Midland Marionettes* (1939); Nurse DUGDALE in *Nurse Dugdale Has a Clue* (1946); etc. Later became a raconteur (*Home on Saturday* 'Female of the Species' 1960 R; WOMAN'S HOUR (1964

R) on modelling; etc) and a regular on panel games like *Call My Bluff* (1980–88). Was the subject of THIS IS YOUR LIFE (1983 R); read from his autobiography *I'll Let You Know* in 1981. Contributor to *The Faces of Maugham* (1974 R) and *You're a Brick Angela!* (on schoolgirl fiction, 1976 R, also co-W).

Marshall, Stuart (1949–93) English film-maker who unearthed much gay and lesbian history on large and small canvases: *Bright Eyes* (1984, W only); OUT ON TUESDAY 'DESIRE' (1989) and 'COMRADES IN ARMS' (1990); OUT 'OVER OUR DEAD BODIES' (1991) and 'Blue Boys' (1992).

Freddie Martin (Roland CURRAM in ELDORADO 1992–3) Surprisingly elastic, with interesting developments promised after his few months grappling with a bashing or two, a robbery and the appearance of his DAUGHTER ...

'It's a great part. Freddie is a retired NURSE who came to live in the South of Spain, but his partner died. Freddie is now a lonely man ... He isn't a political gay and he hates the overtones of the gay community' (Roland Curram quoted in the *Pink Paper*, 19.7.92).

'On the surface, a glaring gay stereotype: a lonely, slightly camp repressed homosexual. Even his name has an archetypal ring (I remember being called "a Fred" at school)' (Jonathan Sanders, *Gay Times*, October 1992).

(I Went To) A Marvellous Party Languid Noel COWARD song with assorted gay references: 'Good old CECIL and I in armour and feathers'; BOBBY who 'did a stunt at the bar with a lot of extraordinary men'; Elise (in a fisherman's vest) making an entrance with Meg, 'frightfully gay, nobody cares'. But the party is something of a let-down for the two gay blades: 'we went as we were and we stayed as we were (which was hell)'. This sharp-toothed, sharp-tongued piece of frippery is often rendered in musical 'tributes' to its composer or to the 1920s and 1930s. Its most downmarket outing was in PRIS-

ONER/PRISONER: CELL BLOCK H, sung in would-be 'posh' tones by Amanda Muggleton during a rehearsal for a concert while an escape plan is being hatched in the background.

Mary's Wife (UK 1980 T) Alec's wife and teenage son cope with his TRANS-VESTISM, but at a party one of the wives' outbursts triggers off resentment – and Alec (Robert Gillespie) announces his intention to seek a sex change. A subplot involves working-class Kevin/Angela (Ray Burdis) and Tina (Helena Breck), who organizes lingerie-selling parties (*à la* Tupperware). They discover their parents live streets away in Bermondsey. He buys something from her. He's wearing ill-fitting mail-order clothes. She thinks that Angela is an unsuitable name for someone from the East End. She suggests he let his hair grow instead of wearing a wig. She makes up his eyes. He likes kids and keeping the house neat. They fall in love, marry and consider themselves lucky to have so much in common.

W: David COOK, P: Peter Ansorge; D: Peter Jeffries; 2.5.80; BBC2; 55 mins.

Very honest, fast-moving, lively exposition with the subplot equal to and certainly more immediately appealing than the necessarily unresolved dilemma of Alec, his wife and his son. A perfect example of empathetic tragicomedy rather than a sentimental freak show. (Commissioned as a BBC 'Play for Today', it was turned down (too jokey) and picked up by ATV in 1976. BBC then bought it and showed it.)

masculinity A seemingly fixed property which, if analysed, seems to be as much culturally as genetically based. Ronald Reagan disagreed with his director (Edmund GOULDING) as to how his part in *Dark Victory* (1939 C) should be played: he didn't think it was masculine-inflected enough. The Young General (Sabu) wears a perfume called *Black Narcissus* (1947 C) and dresses fit to bust in brocades, silks and jewels; this drives one of the nuns – frustrated Sister Ruth (Kathleen Byron) – to urge

him to be a real man. Spencer Tracy has to sleep in his daughter's frilly four-poster bed, the tulle distracts him from reading in bed and outrages his sense of masculine bedtime decorum in *Father's Little Dividend* (1951 C). Tom Lee (John Kerr) disrupts the women and the men by his feminine ways of doing things in TEA AND SYMPATHY (1956 C). Gigi's husband Clive (John Bird) in *Oxbridge Blues* 'That Was Tory' (1984 T) makes a snide remark about her and gay Crispin showing 'feminine solidarity', but is stopped in his tracks by his wife reminding him that 'selling wine to Hooray Henrys and Wino Wendys isn't exactly virile'. George (Brian Murphy) bucks against staying at home while Mildred (Yootha Joyce) works in *George and Mildred* (1978 T): 'The milkman's winked at me *twice*,' he says, gathering his ambushed masculinity about him.

In *Tea and Sympathy* Tom Lee's father (Edward Andrews) is disgusted at his offspring's lack of interest in humping baseballs and his wanting to sing folk songs; he is delighted to hear he has been with a prostitute (even though he went berserk with a pair of scissors). In THE FAMILY WAY (1966 C) curmudgeonly Ezra Fitton (John Mills) is horrified that his son is not fulfilling his husbandly role; he forgets that on his own honeymoon he elected to go and walk on the sand with his best man. Old Kemp (Alan Webb) in ENTERTAINING MR SLOANE (1970 C) hasn't spoken to his son in 20 years ('One day, shortly after his seventeenth birthday I had cause to return home unexpected and found him committing some kind of felony in the bedroom'), but the greater menace of Sloane brings a (brief) reconciliation. In Joe ORTON's other filmed play *Loot* (1970 C) Hal's dad, McLeavy (Milo O'Shea) asks: 'WHERE DID I GO WRONG? ... Even the sex you were born into isn't safe from you.'

From Wimps to Warriors (1991) seeks to explode the myth that masculinity is fixed and natural.

masochists *See* SADO-MASOCHISM.

Mason, Michael (1947–) English journalist and publisher, former news editor with GAY NEWS, now editor of *Capital Gay*. Admirably clear-voiced and clear-headed on many subjects from the general (WORLD IN ACTION 'Gay Pride' 1979 T) to the specific (CHE's education kit on LBC's *Open Line* 1976 R; the legalization of 'homosexual acts' in Scotland on *Today* 1980 R; the resignation of the Queen's bodyguard on *London Rush Hour* 1982 R; the 'pink economy' on A SUNDAY OUTING 1993 R). He was also seen to effect talking about his relationship on *Take Two* (1975 T) and, as part of a large congregation, in GAYS: SPEAKING UP (1978 T).

masquerade Pretending to be queer: Rock HUDSON in *Pillow Talk* (1959 C), *Lover Come Back* (1961 C) and *A Very Special Favour* (1964 C); THE GAY DECEIVERS (1969 C, dodging the draft); George (Warren Beatty) in *Shampoo* (1975 C); Jack Tripper (John Ritter) fooling the landlord in THREE'S COMPANY (1977–83 T); Reginald Perrin (Leonard Rossiter) playing gay (1977 T); STARSKY AND HUTCH taking up the dryer as two temperamental *artistes de coiffeur* in 'Dandruff' (1978 T); Al Pacino in CRUISING (1980 C) and Ryan O'Neal in PARTNERS (1982 C) playing gay to catch murderers; Stephen Rea answering an advert for a feminist male to share driving in Europe and wearing a gay badge as a disguise in *Loose Connections* (1983 C); David Hasselhof, an ex-con securing a secretarial job with a soap opera queen (Joan Collins) he plans to rob in *The Cartier Affair* (1984 T).

The Masquerade Richard Carpenter song used ambiguously in *Superstar: The Karen Carpenter Story* (1987 C): Karen marries but soon realizes that she is 'lost in the masquerade'.

masseurs/masseuses They can provide pain and pleasure; sometimes with a strong erotic charge. Useful for film-makers and drama producers when wanting to suggest more than they can show – the intake of breath, the look of satisfaction . . . the changes of position, the kneading of the flesh, the pressing down on the upper thighs: Charlotte Greenwood, lankily lapping up the pulchritude in *Palmy Days* (1932 C; mountainous Rose Given (Hope EMERSON) in *Cry of the City* (1948 C); rugged Lieutenant Stevens (Kieron Moore) in *The League of Gentlemen* (1960 T) who runs a health club after leaving the army; porcine and lascivious Cyril (David Foxxe) in an episode of *The Sweeney* 'Bad Apple' (1976 T); Randy Brent (Tony Curtis) says 'so long, handsome' to one in *The Users* (1978 T); Nick (Bill Nighy) gives Harley (Norman Eshley) a mutually appreciated rub in *Fat* (1980 T); Rev. JONES (Powers Boothe) is getting very close to one of his disciples, David (Brad Dourif), in GUYANA TRAGEDY: THE STORY OF JIM JONES (1980 T); part of the MEN'S GROUP (1983 R) involves sensuous (but not sensual) massage; a black masseur goes beyond regular massage into (requested) pain, agony and beyond in NOIR ET BLANC (1986 C); the hero (Charles Dance) given the once over by libidinous Italian who is revealed as a practitioner of ultra-violence in *The McGuffin* (1986 T); 'I'm a qualified osteopath' Winifred (Kate Buffery 1988 T; Amanda Donohoe 1989 C) nurtures Ursula (Imogen Stubbs 1988 T; Sammi Davis 1989 C) after their swim in *The Rainbow*.

On a more informal basis: Jill gives March a 'rub' in THE FOX (1968 C) while reading about the eponymous carnivore; Rufus (Jeremy Northam) rubs oil on Adam (Douglas Hodge) in *A Fatal Inversion* (1992 T).

Massey, Anna (1937–) English actress whose heroine days were short (*Gideon's Day* 1958 C; *Peeping Tom* 1960 C) but who soon firmly established herself as a character player with the ability to essay warm or chilling roles with equal insight and authority. Stand-outs are her MRS DANVERS in REBECCA (1979 T); the self-centred actress in YOU'RE NOT WATCHING ME, MUMMY (1980 T); Gwen John in *Journey into the Shadows* (1984 T); Virginia WOOLF in *Mrs Woolf* *and a Room* (1984 T); Guy's mother in ANOTHER COUNTRY (1984 C); Mother Superior in *Sacred Hearts* (1985 C); the heroine of *Hotel du Lac* (1986 T); the lonely French woman in *The Darling Buds of May* (1991 T). Also has a thriving radio career, playing Katherine MANSFIELD (in *A Child of the Sun* 1979); Victorian explorer Amelia Edwards in *With Passport and Parasol* 'Mere Mortals and Englishwomen', (1988); the socialite in *The Reluctant Debutante*; etc. Sister of Daniel MASSEY.

Massey, Daniel (1933–) Always interesting, sometimes brilliant English actor who made his debut, aged 9, in *In Which We Serve* (1942 C). His glinting, plummy delivery and spare frame effectively used as Leo in DESIGN FOR LIVING (1964 T); Noel COWARD (his godfather) in STAR! (1968 C); Daniel in THE ROADS TO FREEDOM (1970 T); Nicholas Black in *The Devil's Advocate* (1978 C); Lytton STRACHEY (1980 R); the husband who contracts the HIV virus from a female in *Intimate Contact* (1987 T); Debussy in *Moonlight and the Black Cat* (1989 R); etc. Brother of Anna MASSEY.

Mastermind (UK 1982– T) A hypnotic BBC1 quiz in which four people answer general knowledge questions before being grilled on a specialist subject. Exquisite agony, chaired by Magnus Magnusson. Relevant subjects have included the life and films/novels/ works/music/poetry/reign of Greta GARBO, Lord BYRON, Paul Scott, Benjamin BRITTEN, ALEXANDER THE GREAT, Edward Lear, Federico García LORCA, Gwen John, Aaron COPLAND, Oscar WILDE, Iris MURDOCH, Maurice RAVEL, LUDWIG II of Bavaria, Lillian Hellman.

masters of ceremonies Joel Grey bids the audience 'Wilkomen, bienvenue, welcome' in CABARET (1972 C) from inside a doll's mask face; camp innuendoes skitter from the throat of the ballroom dancing competition MC (Gerald Flood) in *Midnight at the Starlight* (1980 T) who 'hangs around the toilets at Stockwell underground' and fancies Fred, one of the entrants; Andrew Logan is dressed in gown and tights down one side of his body and male evening attire down the other in THE ALTERNATIVE MISS WORLD (1980 C); David Calder baits one of the drag queens, while secretly trying on his clobber in *Belles* (1983 T); Tony Randall as Putzi is a Joel Grey look-alike but less satanic in *Hitler's SS: Portrait of Evil* (1985 T).

masturbation A subject about which most programmes are oversqueamish, although it clearly enters many lives. First seen (at first by a very limited number of people) in UN CHANT D'AMOUR (1950 C) in which a prisoner, clothed, caresses his penis through his trouser pocket). The word was probably first mentioned by Norman St John Stevas in 1957, in *Paper Talk* (for ATV Birmingham).

Other mentions until the 1970s – when Robert Hughes could talk of 'a masturbatory fantasy' when describing the Mona Lisa in FIRST ELEVEN (1970 T) – were indirect: 'I don't know how the little rascal keeps it up . . . with a towel or flannel . . . a boy will gaily bounce the hours away till nightfall' (Robert Harris as A. E. HOUSMAN in *The Frontier of Darkness* 1954 R); 'I usually hold it in my landlady's bathroom . . . I find it the best place to have a practice' (Mr Gruntfuttock in ROUND THE HORNE 1967 R).

The repressed Ester (Ingrid Thulin) seeks comfort from her own hands in THE SILENCE (1963 C) as do Adele (Gunnel Lindblom) who marries beneath her in *Loving Couples* (1964 C) and Ellen March (Anne Heywood) in a steamy bathroom in THE FOX (1968 C) looking at herself in the mirror. The first British woman to talk about these actions was Emma (Michelle Dotrice): she tells a bed partner that she hasn't been able to masturbate since her lover died (*Emma's Time* 1970 T). The first mention in a US film was also by a British actress, Diana Rigg, in *The Hospital* (1971 C) – her character had lived among the Hopi Indians: 'I masturbated a great deal ... and ate a great deal of rabbit.'

More explicitly: the lesbian couple (Sylvia Miles and Beverly D'Angelo) stimulate themselves in *The Sentinel* (1976 C) and rodents appear from inside their vaginas; Hilary (Kate Nelligan) asks a young woman if she masturbates in DO AS I SAY (1977 T) and, if not, why she doesn't; Lindsay Duncan has a session in *The Reflecting Skin* (1991 C); and the great masturbation demystifyer, MADONNA runs into trouble in Toronto with her song 'Like A Virgin': she goes ahead and performs it – with writhings and moans – regardless (IN BED WITH MADONNA 1991 C).

It took longer for mass entertainment to come to terms with the fact that men did masturbate – alone or with a partner. It was first shown – on stage – in Frank Wedekind's *Spring Awakening* during the early part of the 20th century: a young prisoner joins four others, who make a circle and race each other to ejaculation. This is followed by a fight. In *Night Games* (1966 C) a huge pop-eyed, pot-bellied man wearing only a periwig masturbates during an orgy. This was cut from British versions as was the poolside masturbation of the two brothers in *Heat* (1972).

That same year in A LIFE IS FOR EVER (1972 T) Charles Johnson (Maurice O'Connell), resisting the attentions of a younger prisoner, explodes: 'You nasty little ... sooner toss meself off.' The BBC had cut a masturbation scene from the script of CIRCLE LINE in 1969 (two years before it was transmitted). The subject was broached, though not depicted, in *Too Hot to Handle* (1974 T) wherein a husband rejects his wife for porno magazines. Much bolder was THE LAST WOMAN (1976 C) in which Gérard (Gérard Depardieu) tells Valerie (Ornella Muti) that he's going to jerk off and promptly stands in front of bathroom sink with a magazine propped against the mirror.

Woody ALLEN in *Stardust Memories* (1980 C) says: 'Art and masturbation – two areas where I'm an expert'; Lieutenant Sablon, Querelle and Robert enjoy it – separately – in QUERELLE (1982 C); Stella's father, out of work for months, regularly pleases himself with the curtains closed at lunchtime in *The Amazing Miss Stella Estelle* (1984 T); Juan (Antonio Banderas), masturbates after seeing a sexy gay film at the start of LAW OF DESIRE (1987 C).

The relationship between Joe ORTON (Gary Oldman) and Kenneth Halliwell (Alfred Molina) has deteriorated so badly that Joe no longer wants sex with him (PRICK UP YOUR EARS 1987 C):

Joe: 'Lay off. Have a wank!'
Ken: 'Have a wank? Have a wank? I need three days' notice to have a wank. You can't just stand there and do it. Me, it's like organizing D-Day. Forces have to be assembled, magazines bought, the past dredged for some suitably unsavoury episode, the dog-eared thought of which can still produce a faint flicker of desire. "Have a wank!" It would be easier to raise the *Titanic*.'

In a comic context, the subject is allowable – as in *Have I Got News for You* (1992 T): 'A driver who had a close erotic relationship with his Austin Metro, masturbated inside it ... which must have made overtaking rather dangerous.'

But even late at night, this is a performance that television prefers to keep private. All signs of film-maker Jon Jost's penis (flaccid to erect) were removed in one of his short films transmitted after midnight in 1983 on Channel 4. A black square was used as a block-out, changing size subtly to cope with engorgement of blood cells in Mr Jost's member while he intoned: 'Of these things I know, just as you know. My hand rests on my penis and your hand rests on your penis or vagina. And yet of these things we cannot speak.' The sequence which followed was altogether too much. 'For this television screening,' said the printed announcement, 'a close-up of masturbation has been blanked out.'

On American television, the word and the deed are still *verboten*, except in the most frolicsome, depilated way – as in this exchange in *Equal Justice* (1991 T):

Male lawyer: 'I always practice safe sex.'
Female lawyer: 'How dangerous can it be when you're on your own!'

For the rest, the message – loudly in America, more mutedly in Britain – is that if you do it yourself 'You'll go blind' (*Bless the Beasts and Children* 1972 C).

mates 'Best mate a man ever had was Billy. Wherever he is, God bless him,' says Ezra Fitton (John Mills) as he remembers his bosom pal in THE FAMILY WAY (1966 C). 'Sounds like a handy boy, this Billy,' laughs Barry Foster as Jack, with a secret of his own. Two best friends or *Mates* (1978 T) cause their wives perturbations with their closeness; while two school friends go off on holiday together to discover whether that friendship needs a physical expression in TWO OF US (originally entitled 'Mates' 1988 T). Confronting a prying – and sexually aggressive – girl, Matthew (Jason Rush) politely but impassionedly tells her not to interfere between him and Phil (Lee Whitlock): 'We're not mates. Phil and me are lovers. We do it. We sleep together. We kiss. We hold hands. We touch. It's not a laugh. It's not just a bit of a giggle. We mean it. That's why we're here. We've dumped the other lot.'

This remains a very grey area, beautifully and melodically encapsulated in that song from *Casablanca*: 'Woman needs man and man must have his mate/That no one can deny.'

mateship Men who devote much time to being masculine at the top of their voices. This is an area of psychological precariousness discussed in *The Locker Room* (1992 R). It is a peculiarly Australian cultural tradition, which is crystallized in *Gallipoli* (1981 C) and in the films of Chips Rafferty (*The Rats of Tobruk* etc). John Singleton, discussing the phenomenon on television in 1987, said it was homosexuality 'without the brown sauce'. *Whicker's Walkabout* in 1971 explained the then (and, in some areas, still) prevailing attitude with the title to episode number 5: 'This is the problem – women are not people.' Said *TV Times*: 'Today's *Whicker's Walkabout* is unsuitable for women – if they're thinking of going to Australia.'

Mathis, Johnny (1935–) American singer whose renditions of (mainly) ballads are a strange marriage of pain and celebration. Became popular from the mid-1950s, partly through a string of hits, including film title songs like *A Certain Smile* (1957, singing it in a nightclub scene), *The Best of Everything* (1959) and *Tender is the Night* (1962), as well as singing 'It's Not For Me To Say' and 'Warm And Tender' in *Lizzie* (1957). However, it was Erroll Garner's version of 'Misty' that so excited the female psychopath in *Play Misty for Me* (1971 C). Mathis came out as gay in the 1980s without too much damage to his record sales, although he seems to have increased the number of duets (with women singers like Deniece Williams, eg 'WITHOUT US' played over the closing credits of *Family Ties* 1988–90 T).

T: *The Perry Como Show* (1958); *The Record Years* (1959); *Juke Box Jury* (1959, slagging off British recording artists in a 'bitchy' manner); *The Johnny Mathis Show* (1961 & 1962); *Personal Appearance* (1961); *Presenting Johnny Mathis* (1965); *Johnny Mathis* (1975); *The Kenneth Williams Show* (1976); *The Muppets Go to Hollywood* (1979 T); *A Musical Tribute to Nat 'King' Cole* (1983); etc. Was interviewed in *The Mathis Magic* (1982 T), and came out in a June 1982 interview published in *Us* magazine: 'Homosexuality is a way of life that I've grown accustomed to.'

A Matter of Sex (UK 1992 R) Abigail (Diane Bull) meets James (Anna Savva), little realizing that he is a she. Harried and ridiculed, James falls in with a gay man, Peter Mistieres (Sylvester Morand) and another TRANSVESTITE, Job (Colin McFarlane) and is taught a modicum of self-respect. The strains of a double life prove too much and James kills himself, leaving Abigail to face the mob when the truth is revealed on the mortician's slab.

W: Nick Stratford 'based on true events'; D: Claire Grove; 9.1.92; BBC Radio 4; 60 mins.

With its copious sexual and blasphemous euphemisms ('bewattle it!', 'scratch doodlies', 'the crack in his windy', 'smubble', 'dubbing her', 'jigs', 'going right to the fubsy', 'a pluker of the first order'), this piece fairly crackles and jumps, reaching its most satisfying point with the nascent queer community of James, Abigail, Peter and Job. Ironic that Patricia Hayes, veteran of so many gutsy little boy roles on BBC radio since the 1940s, should play the older self of a woman who married a man who wasn't.

Maugham, Robin [Viscount Robert Maugham] (1916–81) English writer whose novels and novellas *The Black Tent, The Rough and the Smooth, The Intruder* (aka *Line on Ginger*) and *The Servant* have been filmed. For television: *The Two Wise Virgins of Hove* (1960); *Gordon of Khartoum* (adapted by David Benedictus, 1966); *Enemy* (1976). Also spoke about his uncle W. Somerset MAUGHAM on *Maugham* (1981 T).

Maugham, W[illiam] Somerset (1874–1965) English novelist and playwright. Well observed, witty, stingingly wise regarded as equal with Thackeray, Dickens, Trollope and Kipling. Over 40 films made from his novels and plays.

Plays: *Lady Frederick* [1907] as *The Divorcee* (1919 C); *The Land of Promise* [1913] (1917 C) and as *The Canadian* (1926 C); *Our Betters* [1917] (1933 C; 1960 T); *Sheppey* [1933] (1939 & 1959 T); *Home and Beauty* as *Too Many Husbands* (1940 C) and as *Three for the Show* (1955 C); *Caesar's Wife* [1919] as *Infatuation* (1925 C and 1951 T); *The Circle* [1921] as *Strictly Unconventional* (1925 & 1930 C); *The Constant Wife* [1926] as *Charming Sinners* (1929 C); *The Sacred Flame* [1928] as *The Right to Live* (1929 & 1935 C and 1989 R); *The Beachcomber* as *Vessel of Wrath* (1938 C) and as *The Beachcomber* 1955 (C).

Novels: *The Magician* [1908] (1926 C);

Of Human Bondage [1915] (1934, 1946 & 1964 C; 1954 R); *The Moon and Sixpence* [1919] (1942 C; 1960 & 1967 T); *The Painted Veil* [1925] (1934 C) and *The Seventh Sin* (1957 C); *Ashenden* [1928] as *The Secret Agent* (1937 C and 1991 T); *The Narrow Corner* [1932] (1933 C), as *The Isle of Fury* (1936 C), as *Three in Eden* (1936 C) and as *The Narrow Corner* (1947 & 1989 R; 1951 T); *Theatre* [1937] as *Adorable Julia* (1963 C); *Christmas Holiday* [1939] (1944 C); *Up at the Villa* [1941] (1968 T); *The Hour Before Dawn* [1942] (1944 C); *The Razor's Edge* [1944] (1946 C; 1984 C/T).

Short stories: *The Fall of Edward Barnard* [1921] (1969 T); *Before the Party* [1922] (1969 T); *P & O* [1923] (1969 T); *Rain* [1923] as *Sadie Thompson* (1928 C), *Rain* (1932 C), *Miss Sadie Thompson* (1954 C) and *Rain* (1960 T); *The Letter* [1924] (1929 & 1940 C; 1969 & 1982 T) and as *The Unfaithful* (1947 C); *East of Elephant Rock* (1977 C); *Change of Destiny* (USSR 1989 C); *The Force of Circumstance* [1924] (1970 T); *Louise* [1925] (1969 T); *The Creative Impulse* [1926] (1969 T); *Footprints in the Jungle* [1927] (1970 T); *Virtue* [1931] (1970 T); *The Door of Opportunity* [1931] (1970 T); *The Vessel of Wrath* [1931] (1938 C) and as *The Beachcomber* (1955 C; 1970 T); *The Back of Beyond* [1933] (1969 T); THE THREE FAT WOMEN OF ANTIBES [1933] (1953 & 1964 R; 1960? & 1969 T); *The Book Bag* [1933] (1970 T); *A Casual Affair* [1935] (1969 T); *A Man with a Conscience* [1940] (1969 T); *Lord Mountdrago* [1940] as one of the *Three Cases of Murder* (1955 T) and separately (1969 T); *The Facts of Life* [1940] in *Quartet* (1948 C with *The Alien Corn* [1931], *The Kit* [1947] and *The Colonel's Lady* [1947] and as a single play in *Tales of the Unexpected* 1980 T); *Sanitarium* [1947] filmed as part of *Trio* (1950 C) with *The Verger* [1924] and *Mr Know-All* [1925]; *The Ant and the Grasshopper* [1924] filmed with *Winter Cruise* [1947] and *Gigolo and Gigolette* [1935] in *Encore* (1951 C); *A Woman of Fifty* [1946] as *Mother Love* (1969 T); *Episode* [1947] (1969 T); *Flotsam and Jetsam* [1947]

(1970 T); *The Unconquered* [1947] (1970 T).

Autobiography: as Guest of the Week on WOMAN'S HOUR (1954 R); *Should Every Picture Tell a Story?* (1958 T) with Maugham and Graham Sutherland who painted his portrait.

Biography: played by Herbert Marshall in *The Moon and Sixpence* (1943 C) and *The Razor's Edge* (1946 C); by David MARCH in WEEKEND WITH WILLIE (1981 R); by Paul Scofield in *A Song at Twilight* (1982 T); by Michael Denison (1988 R); *Memories of Maugham* (by his neighbour, 1954 R); *Memories of Maugham* (1967 T), the auction of the contents of the Villa Mauresque with Alan Searle, his secretary and companion for 40 years; *Maugham* (1981 T), 'An account of his uneasy life and complicated times' by his nephew Robin MAUGHAM, Alan Searle and others who 'recall a victim Of Human Bondage'; *Woman's Hour* 'The Day I Met Somerset Maugham' by Godfrey WINN (1959 R); etc.

Maurice (UK 1987 C) Bursting with gauche vitality, Maurice Hall (James Wilby) falls in love with Clive (Hugh Grant) but loses him to the dictates of society. Visiting Clive and his wife, Maurice is visited one night by the gamekeeper, Alec Scudder (Rupert Graves). After a number of vicissitudes, the two men settle down together in the glow of a happy ending.
W: Kit Hesketh-Hervey and James Ivory from the novel by E. M. FORSTER; P: Ismail MERCHANT; D: James Ivory; 140 mins.

Beginning as an amiable duffer, Maurice attains stature as he consciously rejects compromise. Not the conventional hero, and initially disconcerting for this reason (the more willowy Julian Sands was originally cast).

Forster's thesis is succinctly put across by an American – the PSYCHIATRIST Lasker-Jones (Ben Kingsley) to whose couch Maurice flees with his sexual 'problems': 'England has always been disinclined to accept human nature.'

The doctor tells Maurice to give vent to his feelings discreetly.

The film springs into life with the belated appearance of assistant gamekeeper Alec Scudder (Rupert Graves), who seduces his elder and better, plays a mercenary game for a while, leaves for Australia but ends up in Maurice's arms instead. For once, in gay films, an unalloyed – if far-fetched – happy ending.

Peter Kemp wrote in the Australian FILM NEWS (November 1988):

> ... a bit like moving from Shakespeare's *Romeo and Juliet* to one of the more ambivalently confessional sonnets ... one of the resounding strengths of *Maurice*, on page and screen, is its calmly concentrated, quietly savage critique of how insidiously Church, state and culture continue conspiring to stop chaps getting off with other chaps.
> ... in the AIDS-addled late 1980s, during these pink and black plague years, perhaps what gay cinema might sorely need ... are a few more tweely improbable fairy tales.
> ... what grants ... the film its very discernible oomph and potential significance is its completely unapologetic, unashamed presentation of a joyous homosexuality, the strong suggestion that there might be some (deeply satisfying) fun to be had when one consenting male human being lies down with another. In our recent memory of British Cinema, only these two *Beautiful Laundrette* lads are actually seen (and felt) to take authentic pleasure in the engaging caress of each others' bodies.

a mauve one! Originally a riotous exclamation over a boiled sweet on *Take It from Here* (*c* 1952 R) which was then applied to every other object on the show. No discernible 'lavender' context, however.

The Mavis Bramston Show (Aust 1965–8 T) A Wednesday night must for sophisticated viewers. A comedy show in a revue format with a strong political kick, which dealt with subjects hitherto the province of documentary. Fast-paced, laced with CAMP and men dressing up as women. Starred June

Salter, Barbara Angel, John Bluthal, Carol Raye, Barry Creyton and Gordon Chater, who left after the first six months to be replaced by Ronnie Stevens. Taboo subjects tackled included prime ministers Robert Menzies and Harold Holt (and wife Zara), politicians of all hues, society leaders, Australia's involvement in Vietnam, the Queen and her mother: 'I have this nasty daughter who makes me walk two steps behind and wouldn't let me buy ostrich feathers at Harrods.'

W: David SALE and Ken Shadie; P: David Sale (1966–7) and Johnny Whyte (1967–8); D: Hugh Taylor; Channel 7.

'When *Mavis* started you couldn't say pregnant on the ABC. By making fun of serious subjects *Mavis* actually opened the way for subjects to be treated seriously in depth. We never thought about doing anything gay; what was there to do? It was 1966. What would you do? The only thing to do would be to send it up with wrist-flapping stereotypes. It was just not a big issue, not a popular issue, or contentious. Because nobody had seen that there could be a better way' (David Sale 1992).

Maxwell, Gavin (1914–69) English naturalist and writer. In THE WORLD ABOUT US documentary ('Gavin Maxwell and the Ring of Bright Water' 1979 T), he (Nicholas Jones) is viewed as a violent man who runs out on his wife after a year of marriage. Their rows were dramatized but not explained. 'How depressing it is that a programme produced in 1979 actually manages to be less honest than Maxwell's own far-from-open book written 20 years ago,' said Alison HENNEGAN in GAY NEWS.

Maxwell Davies, Sir Peter (1934–) English composer with relatively high visibility: *Problems of a British Composer Today* (1959 R); *Two Composers, Two Worlds* (1961 T, with Dudley Moore); opera *The Mines of Sulphur* (1966 T); score for *The Devils* (1971 C); arranged music for *The Boy Friend* (1971 C); DESERT ISLAND DISCS (1983 R); *Peter Maxwell Davies at Large* (1985 R), at

concerts, in rehearsals, giving lectures and at home in the Orkneys; *Symphonies and Silence* (1983 R); KALEIDOSCOPE 'Works in Progress' (1987 R); THE SOUTH BANK SHOW; etc.

medical theories *See* CAUSE.

Meeting Point 'The Complexity of Love' (UK 1963 T) The BBC's Sunday evening 'God slot' devoted an early evening half hour to *Towards a Quaker View of Sex*. This was based on a report – the first of its kind by any long-established religious body – into all aspects of the prickly subject, including one of its main taboo areas. The programme was probably the first to use the word 'affection' in the context of homosexuality and to emphasize the quality of the relationships rather than specific sexual acts. Said the report's compilers: 'Homosexual affection can be as selfless as heterosexual affection and therefore we cannot see that it is in some way morally worse'. The emphasis was the quality of the relationship rather than the action.

There were not a few protests at the invasion of such views into the BBC's religious haven: 'I used to look forward to seeing *Sunday Break* and *Meeting Point*, but now I hesitate to turn these programmes on for fear of what the children may hear' (letter, *Nottingham Evening News*).

Me! I'm Afraid of Virginia Woolf (UK 1978 T) Trevor Hopkins (Neville Smith), a college lecturer with a dominating mother (Thora Hird) and a blood-curdlingly caring and sharing girlfriend, falls in love with a male student (Derek Thompson).

W: Alan BENNETT; D: Stephen Frears; London Weekend; 2.12.78; 60 mins.

Gentle and beguiling – and semi-autobiographical (it was later revealed on THE SOUTH BANK SHOW) – with underdrawn males and overdrawn females, and an ending which lifts the heart (and makes it yearn for an act 2). '... a secret homosexual finally owns up, at least to himself, and Bennett suggests the love of one man for another can be as gentle and comforting and innocent as that of Daphnis and Chloe' (Philip Purser in *Halliwell's Television Companion*).

Melly, George (1926–) English jazz singer, writer, critic, surrealist art expert and former homosexual who came out in his 1966 *Owning Up*, followed by *Rum, Bum and Concertina*. He was impersonated – for a couple of minutes – by Alfred Molina in *The Trials of Oz* (1991 T).

He has been a very bright and loud presence in television and radio arts programmes, quizzes and documentaries for four decades: WOMAN'S HOUR 'Dressing Up' (1968 R); *The Secret Life of Edward James* (1978 T); *Call My Bluff; Whatever Happened to Bill Brunskill?* (1984 T) about the jazz musician; *Gallery* (1984–6 T); *Don't Fuss* (1985 R), a portrait of Edward Burra 'watercolour artist and eccentric'; *Quote, Unquote* (1988 R) with Katharine Whitehorn and Julian MITCHELL.

Radio Times said of him when he took part in *My Heroes* (1988): ' "Good-time George." Entertainer, high-liver, collector, lover of shocking suits, raunchy ties and broad hats, teetotal "except for wine, port, sherry and champagne", the dean of decadence, he is also much admired as a blues historian, modern-art expert, book critic, film critic and celebrated autobiographer.' Among the people who influenced him – his 'heroes' – Picasso, Léger and COCTEAU.

Melville, Alan (1910–83) English stage, radio and television writer, best known for *Simon and Laura* and his 1950s series *A–Z* and *Merely Melville*. He created, produced and wrote a great deal of *Front Line Family* for the BBC Overseas Service from 1941: Home Front life in wartime London with Dulcie Gray as one of the stars, with guest artists like Malcolm Sargent and Michael Denison. This developed into *The Robinson Family* on the BBC Light Programme.

Among his plays which were adapted for radio: *Jonathan* (1966) about DAVID'S

overriding love for his friend and his unmoveable sadness after his death. Also: *Before the Fringe* (1967–8 T); *Comedy Playhouse* 'Haven of Rest' (1970 T); *The World of Ivor Novello* (1976 R); *Blithe Thou Never Wert?* (1989). Last appearance: as the skinflint husband in *Puss in Boots* (1982 R).

Melvin, Murray (1932–) English actor with extraordinarily Gothic face and puddly voice. Played the British stage's first 'ordinary' queer, Geoffrey INGHAM, in *A Taste of Honey* (also in the 1961 film) and has enjoyed a very solid career as a supporting player ever since.

Michael Lawson in PROBATION OFFICER (1960 T); prisoner in *The Criminal* (1960 C); sailor in *Petticoat Pirates* (1961 C); Tosh in *Somewhere for the Night* (1962 R); Ted Collis in *Paradise Walk* (1962 T); *Sparrows Can't Sing* (1963 C); *The Ceremony* (1963 C); Lupin Pooter in *Diary of a Nobody* (1966 T); KALEIDOSCOPE (1966 C); the hero's friend in *Alfie* (1966 C); Turgis in *Angel Pavement* (1967 T); 1st Exquisite in A SMASHING TIME (1967 C); Thumb in *The Memorandum* (1967 T); the Dauphin in *Saint Joan* (with Janet Suzman, 1968 T); Luther Jezreal in *The Flaxton Boys* (1970 R); Mignon in *The Devils* (1971 C); *The Boyfriend* (1971 C); doctor in *The Adventures of Don Quixote* (1973 T); courtier in *Gawain and the Green Knight* (1973 C); *Ghost Story* (1974 C); fop in *Barry Lyndon* (1975 C); *The Bawdy Adventures of Tom Jones* (1976); *Shout at the Devil*; Hans ANDERSEN in *Scenes from a Flying Trunk* (1979 C); secretary Leopold in *Nutcracker* (1982 C); the Devil in *The Soldier's Tale* (1982 T), in various disguises with Wayne SLEEP; *Sacred Hearts* (1985 C); one of the convicts in *Comrades* (1986 C); censor in *Testimony* (1989 C/T); *Mistress of Suspense* (1990 T); teacher in *Let Him Have It!* (1991 C); cameo as Palm Court tearoom waiter in *Sunday Pursuit* (1992 T, starring his *Taste of Honey* partner Rita Tushingham).

He discussed *A Taste of Honey* and its groundbreaking depiction of taboo subjects (but not his role as Geoffrey) on the BBC Schools radio series *Drama Resources* 'Bringing a Script to Life' (1985).

men having babies John Hubbard pregnant at the end of TURNABOUT (1940 C); Ox Bentley (Rod MCKUEN in *Summer Love* (1957 C); Rock HUDSON – false alarm – in *Pillow Talk* (1959 C) and again in *Strange Bedfellows* (1964 C); Marcello Mastroianni as *The Slightly Pregnant Man* (1973 C) who doesn't give birth; Billy CRYSTAL who takes his to full term in *Rabbit Test* (1978 C); Nigel Planer, victim of a woman scientist, having *Frankenstein's Baby* (1990 T); the men in *Alien Nation* (1990 T). Documentaries looking at the subject as a possible probability: *Bodymatters* 'Male Mothers' (1986 T); *DEF II* '21st-Century Sex' (1992 T).

men nurturing babies Seriously in THE LAST WOMAN (1975 C) with Gérard Depardieu bathing, feeding, cuddling and playing with Petey (David Biffani); humorously in *Three Men and a Baby* (1987 C) and gay couple Dante and Frank in *AIDS Babies* (1991 T).

men's liberation In the 1970s groups of men met together to explore what it meant to be a man, how they could relate better to woman, children and other men. These bondings featured in two plays *Men's Group* (1983 R) and *Men!* (1984 R) and, over-intense and ingenuous, they bring little comfort or growth to their participants.

In the first play, Jock (Bill Leadbiter) is very much into everyone taking off all their clothes and dispensing with 'gender stereotypes, whether gay or straight'. He warms to his theme: 'If we could think of each other as sexual beings instead of breeding partners that have formed tight little nuclear units, maybe we could all feel less enslaved ... I would like contact first before we discuss anything else. Could we enhance our flagging solidarity by just holding hands for a minute?'

'It's the HUGGING – I can't stand the hugging. It gets to you, and it goes on for hours. Like you've just returned from crossing Antarctica on foot,' complains Miles Henderson (Denis Lawson) to his wife in *Love After Lunch* (1987 T). An American Miles is one of three of *Murphy Brown*'s colleagues who go off on a special weekend in 'Male Call' (1991 T). This is men's liberation Mark II which aims to put men back in touch with their *maleness*: banging drums, chanting the 'Indian word "ho"' and communing with their masculine selves. As a result, inhibited Miles can just about put his arms round Frank – for a few seconds before relieved withdrawal.

Although very much associated with late 1960s and early 1970s, G. M. Carstairs in one of his *This Island Now* Reith lectures 'The Changing Role of Women' (1963 R) talked about men's liberation before it was described as such: '... the abandonment of the old, rather rigid definition of male and female roles has made it possible for us to recommend and give expression to the feminine aspect of man's nature and the masculine element in women.' Carstairs, like a number of people who confront this subject, was quick to distance these more feminine men from those 'so constituted, or so biased by their early experience that they can only feel strengthened in a homosexual relationship'.

As with any new pathway, denial and ridicule have been used to undermine the very real benefits exploring different aspects of the self might bring to some people. In *Encounter* 'Landscape of the Soul' (Aust 1989 R) Andrew Harvey was unusual in expressing his gratitude to the enlightenment he has found through meeting men who were open and genuinely loving:

Most of the men I'd known in my life, whether as lovers or as my father, were cold and hard and trapped in the Western macho masculine nonsense. To see a man liberated and tender and awake and very sweet as he was ... was a revolution because it showed me that the real state, not just of masculinity and femininity, but of human beings was this state of being awake ... what has been lost perhaps in this vast argument is that there is something that transcends sexuality, an awakeness, a state of love in which males and females are fused perfectly . . . to create the androgyne, the person who has the deepest and best of both genders. I've never met any man who [transcended sexuality] without going through a spiritual revolution.

men's names for women *See* BOYS' NAMES FOR GIRLS.

men who wear glasses They are either fools or intellectuals, or both: Cary GRANT in *Monkey Business*; Tony Curtis impersonating Cary Grant in SOME LIKE IT HOT; bribe-taking murderer Lawrence Kent (Philip Terry) in a 1960 PERRY MASON; TV's Mr Grouser, Gilbert Harding. Even the excited delight that greeted Michael Caine's Harry Palmer in 1965 did not lead to hero figures looking owlish. You wouldn't catch James Bond in bifocals. Woody ALLEN's nebbish persona perfectly accords with the man with four eyes, and Britain loved Larry GRAYSON's pair dangling on a chain around his neck. Dark or tinted glasses are another matter entirely. It's the *clear* glass indication that they have been overstraining their eyes and not doing enough manual work that is the probable turn-off. Now, with contact lenses, men can hide their shame and their weak eyes behind plastic.

Intellectuals, nerds, weeds, male virgins only (eg Arnold Feather in NUMBER 96 1972–7 T) with a few major exceptions: Michael Caine's Harry Palmer (though he does like to c-o-o-k: *The Ipcress File, Funeral in Berlin* and *Billion Dollar Brain*); William Hurt's Darryl Deever in *Eyewitness/The Janitor* (1981 C) who is handsome, sexy but a bit of a sad sack: 'dogs and children love me'; Nick Nolte in *Cape Fear*; Bryan (Todd Stites) in TOGETHER ALONE (1991 T); Mark (Bill Nighy) in *The Men's Room* (1991 T); Peter Balliol MP (Martin Shaw) in *For the Greater Good* (1991 T); Peter (Robin Williams) in *Hook* (1991 C).

Merchant–Ivory Ismail Merchant (1936–) and James Ivory (1928–) are the extraordinarily prolific and artistically as well as financially rich filmmaking team who – with writer Ruth Prawer Jhabvala – have created solid but softly textured films, many of them based on the works of writers like Henry JAMES and E. M. FORSTER. All three live in the same New York apartment building. Their inseparable creative styles and personal relationships were superficially plumbed in *The Wandering Company* (1983 T). Ivory and Merchant were DESERT ISLAND DISCS castaways in, respectively, 1983 and 1986.

Merlin The first great magician. A shaman who symbolizes the fight between paganism and Christianity. His mystical and spiritual significance often fuzzed over in films and plays, where he is represented as a crusty old man with a flowing beard rather than the dual sides, dark and light, of human nature as conjured up by T. H. White, Anthony Burgess and other writers.

Played by Mitchell Harris in *A Conecticut Yankee* (1931 C); Felix Aylmer in *Knights of the Round Table* (1954 C); Cyril Smith in *The Adventures of Sir Lancelot* (1956 T); Karl Swenson (voice only) in *The Sword in the Stone* (1963 C); Mark Dignam in *Lancelot and Guinevere* (1963 C); Laurence Naismith in *Camelot* (1967 C); Robert EDDISON in *The Legend of King Arthur* (1979 T); Nicol Williamson in *Excalibur* (1981 C); George Winter as a younger man in *Merlin of the Crystal Cave* (1991 T); Michael Angelis in *Wail of the Banshee* (1992 T); etc.

Major Ronald Merrick (Tim Pigott-Smith in THE JEWEL IN THE CROWN 1984 T) 'A frosty sort of bugger', who is an uptight, overregulated man with a terrific fear of the raw sexuality that India represents.

Enters the army from the Indian police, where he had a reputation for rule-book severity and lack of compassion. He had sexually interfered with one of the prisoners, Hari Kumar, and his violation of a holy place earns him the enmity of a group of devotees. He loses an arm in an explosion, marries a friend's widow and is murdered after a bout of SADO-MASO-CHISTIC sex with a local boy.

A lonely, almost Ortonesque figure, he is rendered an outsider by his upbringing (grammar school) and his sexuality. His sense of racial superiority coupled with a need to control and be controlled by Indians makes him a perfect symbol of colonial rule, the less benign face thereof.

'I'm a ruler and you're one of the ruled,' he tells the naked Kumar. 'Contempt on my side, fear on yours. We need to live with it and act it through – this relationship between us – so we can have no doubt it is contempt and fear ... There is no true love between human beings, only power and fear.'

Me ... Tarzan ... You ... Jane!

Written by gay Ivor NOVELLO for MGM's *Tarzan the Ape Man* (1932 C). Endlessly paraphrased by movie buffs, professional and non-professional comics and 130-pound weaklings thereafter as the quintessential male–female exchange. The original dialogue is as follows:

'Tarzan ... Jane ... Jane ... Tarzan.'
'Tarzan–Jane! Jane–Tarzan!'

Jane (Maureen O'Sullivan) runs out of patience. 'Listen,' she tells the big lug. 'I can't stand this. Please let me go.'

'Me Tarzan, You Jane!' was the title of a 1978 *Man Alive Report* on traditional and progressive ways of bringing up children. A car mechanics class for girls at Manchester, mixed classes, sewing, cookery and dancing for boys, women steelworkers, women refereeing rugby and men doing housework. . .

Michelangelo Buonarroti (1475–1564)

Italian artist, architect and poet, one of the cornerstones of the Italian Renaissance. He was trapped in 'a conflict between his passionate nature and strict moral scruples' (*Without Walls* 'Dark Horses: Michelangelo – Bound by Beauty' (1992 T).

Also: *The Age of Conflict* in which Dr Tancred Borenius believed that Michelangelo, 20 years younger than LEONARDO, was one of the most purely subjective artists that ever lived (1929 R); MONITOR 'An interview with Michelangelo' by Francis of Holland (1960 T); *Michelangelo Buonarroti* 'Sonnets' (1962 R); *Contours of Genius* 'Michelangelo the Divine' (1966 T); *The Secret of Michelangelo* 'Every Man's Dream' ABC art documentary with Christopher Plummer (US 1968 T); OMNIBUS 'Michelangelo Revealed' (1987 T): 'Obscured by over four-and-a-half centuries of soot and grime, Michelangelo's masterpiece now emerges resplendent'; *Art of the Western World* '7, Heroic Ambition, Michelangelo' (1989 T).

Michelangelo's David

Nude marble statue, housed in Florence but reproduced in its millions. Explored in more homoerotic detail than usual in *Without Walls* 'Dark Horses: Michelangelo – Bound by Beauty' (1992 T): a bridge between Christian sanctity and classical paganism. Featured in many plays involving gay characters: the lieutenant (Franco Nero) flicks through photographs of Michelangelo sculptures, including David, in QUERELLE (1982 C). *See also* STATUES.

Midler, Bette (1944–)

American singer and actress who must have assumed that the audience on *The Oprah Winfrey Show* (1991 T) knew who her early audiences were: 'They just loved me and they supported me and they bought my records and they carried on ... When I stood in front of them – a couple of thousand men in towels ... I thought it was completely natural ... you know, I must be a pretty odd person. They kicked me into the mainstream.'

Ol' Redhair Is Back (1977); *Divine Madness* (1980); *Bette Midler Art or Bust!* (1988); *Pink Cadillacs and Pretty Boys and Great Big Knockers* (1992). After her film début in *The Rose* (1979) she has had flops (*Jinxed* 1982; *For the Boys* 1992) and hits (*Down and Out in Beverly Hills* 1986; *Outrageous Fortune* 1987; *Big Busi-*

ness 1988; *Beaches* 1988) as well as medium-sized successes (*Stella* 1990; *Scenes from a Mall* 1991).

Midnight Caller 'After It Happened' (US 1988 T) Mike Barnes (Richard Cox) knows he has the HIV virus, yet he has an affair with the hero's former lover (female). Barnes is not shot at the end by one of his female victims, but saved by a cop. 'Even your life is worth something.'
W: Stephen Zito; D: Mimi Leder; 60 mins.

The BISEXUAL as infector and vampire. Only belching fire and raining brimstone were missing from this medieval morality playlet. Protests were mounted and a more positive episode about AIDS went out the following year.

There is a sympathetic gay man in the story: Ross Parker (J. D. Lewis) who is Barnes' abandoned and dying lover. But he is presented as totally without community support, desperate, rootless. 'It's just nice to talk to somebody,' he tells the hero, Killian. 'I don't get a lot of company these days.' When Ross says that he didn't deserve this, Killian replies, 'No, you don't. Nobody does.'

Midnight Cowboy (US 1969 C) Joe Buck (Jon Voight) hopes to take Manhattan by storm, but nobody wants to know him – just his body. His friendship with the semi-vagrant Ratso Rizzo (Dustin Hoffman) – his 'manager' – ends with the latter's death on a Florida-bound bus.
W: Waldo Salt from the novel by James Leo Herlihy; P: Jerome Hellman; D: John SCHLESINGER; 113 mins.

Romantic and cynical by turns, this is a very potent piece of movie-making, brilliantly realized in every department. The relationship between Joe and Ratso begins in mutual disgust but convincingly grows into friendship and genuine concern. Ratso, hobbling, con artist, full of nervous tics and foul-mouthed, homophobic street argot, lovingly cooks for Joe. He provides the semblance of a home, while the idealistic Joe becomes increasingly desperate and violent in his search for money so that the two of them can make a new life together in Florida.

The film doesn't in any way depict Joe and Ratso as homosexual and, like MY OWN PRIVATE IDAHO, Joe's gay clients – like Towny (Barnard Hughes) – are shown as pathetic, dismissable creatures, as are his women customers. Still, this was the first Hollywood film to look squarely at male prostitution and the underbelly of New York life. It was popular, it won Oscars – the first X-certificate film to do so.

Midnight Express (UK 1978 C) Billy Hayes (Brad DAVIS) is locked in a hellish Turkish prison with sadistic guards and seemingly has no hope of getting on the mythical train of the title.
W: Oliver Stone; P: David Puttnam; D: Alan Parker; 121 mins.

Notable for its almost love scene between two men (which drew horrified gasps from audiences) and the tearing off of a Turkish ear (loud cheers from audiences). The film attracted huge audiences and gained an Oscar. Based on memoirs (later revealed as less than accurate) of a bisexual American incarcerated for drug smuggling.

Miles/Myles Boy's name often materializing in cultivated, artificial men.
US: Sam Spade's murdered partner Miles Archer (Jerome Cowan) in *The Maltese Falcon* (1941 C); Miles Fischer (Severn Darden) in *Dead Heat on a Merry Go Round* (1968 C); Miles Mellough (Jack Cassidy) in *The Eiger Sanction* (1975 C); 1930s private investigator Miles Banyon (Robert Forster) in *Banyon* (1971–3 T); Miles Colby (Maxwell Caulfield), young spunk with poor attitude in *The Colbys* (1986–8 T); Miles (David Clennon) in THIRTYSOMETHING (1987–91 T); Miles (Grant Shaud) in *Murphy Brown* (1989– T); young Miles (Macauley Culkin) in *Uncle Buck* (1989 C); etc.
UK: Miles (Martin Stephens) in *The Innocents* (1961 C); Miles Becket (Peter Sallis) whose meeting with a young man leads him into trouble in *Blackmail* 'The Set Up' (1966 T); Miles Merridew

(Robert Morley), 'daddy' to two poodles in *Theatre of Blood* (1973 C); Miles Henderson (Denis Lawson), whose marriage is crumbling around him, sniffing around the outskirts of men's LIBERATION in *Love After Lunch* (1987 T); etc.

Australia: Miles Cooper (David Cameron) in *Chances* 'Bite the Golden Bullet' (1991 T).

militant homosexuals Usually a hostile description for gay and lesbian activists used by the press. When one of FROCS's spokespersons was asked in OUT (1991 T) if he was a militant homosexual, he bridled: '[I'm a] radical queer with fierce attitude. *Please* – this is the 1990s.' The bad odour that 'militant' is held in goes back to the faction of the Left first given an airing on WORLD IN ACTION 'The Militants' in 1967, and before that to the SUFFRAGETTES.

Milk, Harvey (1930–78) American politician who was assassinated, with the Mayor of San Francisco in 1978. The subject of an ACADEMY AWARD-winning documentary THE TIMES OF HARVEY MILK (1984 C), and due to be portrayed by a Hollywood star in *The Mayor of Castro Street* (1993 C).

Sergeant Grace **Millard** Character in DIXON OF DOCK GREEN played by Moira MANNION from 1956 to 1961. Calm and organized, warm but never sentimental, Grace was unmarried and – to the eternal credit of the writer, Ted WILLIS – she was never forced into a heterosexual pigeon-hole. (The character was based on a POLICEWOMAN who lived 'happily' with a headmistress – a dramatic development which no television network was – or is – ready for.)

She is presented as an essentially quiet, self-sufficient person, although lonely. PC Dixon and his daughter Mary make her very much part of the family. 'Thanks for everything. For having me here ... putting up with me. Maybe you don't know what it's like living in a flat on your own. It can get damned lonely. If it hadn't been for you and Andy and

old George, well, you know.' ('A Penn'orth of All Sorts' 1957).

The only inkling of any 'past' (apart from mention of a brother and a woman schoolfriend) is a brisk remark ('I've been near [to getting married] a couple of times but never took the plunge – you know') in Mary and Andy's wedding episode, 'Father-In-Law' (1958).

Grace didn't survive far into the 1960s. She was replaced by a younger, more feminine WPC who soon married one of the regulars. Maybe something had been said about Grace. Comments that she seemed a bit too happy in her silver-buttoned jacket, tie and cap. And too settled into her unmarried state. It could have been that the Police Federation demanded a real woman to help recruitment. Or perhaps it was simply time for Grace to move on and climb the promotion ladder.

Many a lesbian never felt quite the same about Dock Green again. The series itself soldiered on until 1976, despite competition from the grittier, more violent Z CARS and American cop shows.

Milton, Billy (1905–) English singer and actor, mainly in musical and light comedy roles who was very popular on stage and films during the 1930s. He made a comeback in the 1950s and 1960s as a supporting player, and in the 1980s performed on stage with Douglas BYNG.

C: *The Flag Lieutenant* (1926); *Young Woodley* (1930); *Three Men in a Boat* (1933); *Along Came Sally* (1934); *Aren't Men Beasts?* (1937); *Yes Madam* (1938); *The Key Man* (1957); *Heavens Above!* (1963); *Monster of Terror* (1965); *Hot Millions* (1968); *The Black Windmill* (1974); *Sweet William* (1979); etc.

R: *I Found Romance in London*: 'Billy Milton reminisces with records' (BBC Forces Radio 1942); *Overture and Beginners*: 'Music from ballet, opera and musical comedy' (1987); *Billy on Byng* (1987).

T: *After The Show* (1959); THE FABULOUS FRUMP (1967 T); *Special Branch* 'You Won't Remember Me' (1974); etc.

Milton, Ernest (1890–1974) English actor of willowy aspect and, when called for, flowing mannerisms. Best remembered for CAMP role of the impresario Archie Raymond in *It's Love Again* (1936), one of only a handful of film roles: *The Scarlet Pimpernel* (1935); stationmaster in *The Foreman Went to France* (1941); Ancient Roman in *Fiddlers Three* (1944); college dean in *Alice in Wonderland* (1951, and as the King of Hearts in *The Adventures of Alice* 1961 T); scientist in *Cat Girl* (1957). He was Dauphin to Constance Cummings' *Saint Joan* (1947 R).

The Milton Berle Show (US 1948–59/ 1966–7 T) The first – and most successful – American television variety show. 'Uncle Miltie' used sight gags, crazy characters (including Arnold Stang as the creepy stage manager), and outlandish costumes (he would frequently wear drag) to punch across a new style of entertainment: cleaned-up vaudeville, with a heart, for the entire family.

Minder 'Whose Wife Is It Anyway? (UK 1980 T) Terry has to 'mind' the antique shop of Arthur's old friend Alex Brompton (David Daker) while Alex is in hospital. Terry also has to look after the man's lover – Ronald (Alun Lewis). Terry is cooked for and taken to a gay disco but manages to preserve his honour. He does, however, have a fling with Alex's estranged wife – who is the brains, together with the dissembling Ronald, behind the plot to steal from Alex's shop.
W: Tony Hoare; P: Lloyd Shirley; D: Roy Ward Baker; 18.9.80; Thames; 60 mins.
A good idea ruined by the predictable responses of the Terry character – who would, in reality, probably have a quick fling with Ronnie as part of the perks of the job. 'It's the usual "wind-up" for Terry and Arthur who are asked to mind an antique shop run by a gay couple. The show's a riot but apparently *Gay News* is not amused' (Baz Bamigboye, *Evening Standard*, 18.9.80).

mini-series A form of story-telling which was coined in America for serializations of big fat books like *Roots* and *Rich Man, Poor Man*. Sometimes these monsters would be shown across consecutive days or weeks. Some – *Beulah Land*; GUYANA TRAGEDY; THE WOMEN OF BREWSTER PLACE – did allow for a little more depth in homosexual plot threads than was usual in TV movies, but others like *Hollywood Wives* and AN INCONVENIENT WOMAN were the usual schlock writ large and long.

misbehaviourists A euphemism, possibly first uttered on radio by Professor Bronislaw Malinowski in MARRIAGE: PAST AND PRESENT (1931): 'The misbehaviourist is bent on destroying the home since that is to him the symbol of boredom and repression ... The misbehaviourist also believes that sex is for recreation and not for procreation.'

The Mischief Makers (UK 1986 R) 'Five studies in talent and perversity' including Fr Rolfe who loved the 'rosy-brown sinuosities of youth' and Bishop Charles Webster Leadbeater, 'incorrigible pederast,' charlatan, clairvoyant, gifted seer, an Anglican curate and later a bishop in a schismatic church'.

Mishima, Yukio (1925–70) Japanese writer and right-wing militarist who committed suicide by ritual hara-kiri. His life and work variously celebrated: on radio (*Death at Midday* 1983); on television (ARENA 'The Strange Case of Yukio Mishima' 1985); in film (*Mishima: A Life in Four Chapters* 1985, including three dramatizations of his stories). Mishima's widow forbade any explication of his homosexuality (most of it apparently violent, self-punishing and closeted) in the last. Mishima was one of the homosexual icons portrayed in URINAL/PISSOIR (1989 C).
Adaptations of his stories and novels also include: *The Sailor Who Fell from Grace with the Sea* (1972 C); *The Damask Drum* (1986 R); *Primary Colours* (1991 R).

Miss Celie's Blues Quincy Jones composition, sung by Shug Avery (a dubbed Margaret Avery) in THE COLOR PURPLE (1985 C) and supposedly written by her while convalescing and being cared for by her lover's wife, Celie (Whoopi Goldberg). The song appears at a crucial juncture in the plot, preceding the two women's love scene in which Celie discovers the pleasures of her own body.

It is repeated when Celie's sister returns after years as a missionary in Africa. A very direct method of bringing lesbian sisterhood to a mass audience film, making female eroticism palatable, palpable and possible to Middle America: 'Sister! You've been on my mind ...'

The Missing Day (UK 1986 R) Victim of a civilized murder plot. TCHAIKOVSKY (Ronald Pickup) is advised to seek an honourable solution to the problem of his uncovered sexuality revealed in a letter submitted by Count Fermor Steenbock.
W: Derek Kartun; D: David JOHNSTON; BBC Radio 4; 90 mins.

A horror story – a squalid, indefensible procedure – equal to Dreyfus or St Joan (though its factual basis has been much disputed). Tchaikovsky is told that, by his association with a young man, he has brought down disgrace on his own head. Death before dishonour. The reputation of a school above the life and work of a great artist. The public will not miss tunes they will never hear.

Mitchell, Julian (1935–) English writer. Successful television adaptor: *Persuasion* (1971); *Jennie, Lady Randolph Churchill* (1975); *Staying On* (1980); THE WEATHER IN THE STREETS (1984); *Inspector Morse* 'The Ghost in the Machine' (1988); etc. He wrote the final *Inspector Morse* episode, 'Twilight of the Gods' (1993 T), which contained a small but unpleasant amount of homosexual stereotyping. Another of his fortes is black comedy: *Black and Blue* 'Rust' (1973 T); *Abide With Me* (1976 T); *Survival of the Fittest* (1990 R). For the cinema he adapted his 1982 stage play ANOTHER COUNTRY (1984) and

wrote the script for Robert Altman's Van Gogh film *Vincent and Theo* (1990).

He is a fairly frequent broadcaster (*Start the Week* 1982; *Quote, Unquote* 1988) and was interviewed about generalized public school passions in OUT ON TUESDAY 'White Flannel' (1990 T). In more personal mode: *I Want to Be Alone* (1964 R); *The Novelist's Voice* (1976 R); *All the Waters of Wye* (1991 T), a recreation of an 18-century rowing boat trip down the River Wye.

models *See* ARTIST'S MODELS; FASHION MODELS.

Moffat, Roger (192?–87) English radio and television announcer and music presenter. Sallow of features, lugubrious of manner, with hair and face not unlike the about-to-be-introduced crinkle-cut chip, Moffatt was a modest master and mistress of light entertainment programmes, notably *Make Way for Music* (1959–60 T). His cardigans were seen as daring, even though Rex Harrison had brought them a certain hunkiness in MY FAIR LADY. Protected by public unawareness, Roger Moffat was too much himself once homosexuality became identified and rigidly defined to survive the next decade. He ended his career in local radio in Sheffield in 1983. When he died, a friend, Brian Watson, wrote in *Radio Times*: 'What then was considered OUTRAGEOUS is now quite normal.'

Moll (Albert Dekker in *Strange Cargo* 1940 C) Despite the lavishly applied cockney accent, this 'gorilla' of a man is supposed to be French, and consequently Moll is most likely a surname rather than a nickname based on his lust-love for a young fellow convict.

A man unused to articulating his feelings except through his fists. Tragically, he finds the voice of his heart too late – asking a young man to live with him, gaining his assent and then killing him in an attempt to save him from becoming a shark's dinner.

Mollie/Molly A name used for gay men in the 18th century, it is a girl's name which has shown remarkable longevity as a name for resolute or spunky or just plain nice heroines throughout the 20th century, along with NANCY and RUTH. The most famous lesbian with this name, Molly Bolt, heroine of RUBYFRUIT JUNGLE still awaits characterization on film, television or radio.

US: Molly Bolt (Mae Marsh) in *The Marriage of Molly-O* (1916 C); Molly Burns (Clara Bow) who impersonates a 'boy' in *The Lawful Cheater* (1926 C); Molly (Josephine Dunn) in *The Singing Fool* (1928 C); Molly Carr (Janet Gaynor) in *Sunny Side Up* (1929 C); Molly Prescott (Rose Hobart) in *Chances* (1931 C) loved by two soldiers during war; *The Front Page* (1931 C), condemned man's girl (Mae Clark 1931 C; Carol Burnett 1974 C); Molly Beaumont (Maureen O'Sullivan) in *A Yank at Oxford* (1937 C); Molly Sullivan (Sally Eilers), nice girl who converts criminal in *Full Confession* (1939 C); Barbara STANWYCK, the stalwart 'Oirish' postmistress and Jill of all trades in *Union Pacific* (1939 C); Molly (Donna Reed) in *Shadow of the Thin Man*; Molly Moran (Betty Grable) in *My Blue Heaven* (1950 C); Molly (Debra Paget), Louis Jourdan's wife in *Anne of the Indies* (1951 C); Mollie (Kim Novak) in *The Man with the Golden Arm* (1955 C); Molly Jorgensen (Sandra Dee), pregnant and unmarried in *A Summer Place* (1959 C; the actress was also Mollie in *Take Her, She's Mine* 1963 C); Molly Wood (Pippa Scott), newspaper editor in *The Virginian* (1962–4 T); Wall Street whizz Molly Thatcher (Lee Remick) in *The Wheeler-Dealers/ Separate Beds* (1963 C); Debbie Reynolds hoydenish in *The Unsinkable Molly Brown* (1964 C); Mollie (Jean Simmons) in *Rough Night in Jericho* (1967 C); a woman (Blythe Danner) harmoniously accommodating two men over the years in *Lovin' Molly* (1973 C); Nurse Molly Gibbons (Dena Dietrich) in *The Practice* (1976 T); Molly (Molly Ringwald) in *The Facts of Life* (1979–80 T); Molly Bell (Lucie Arnaz) in *The Jazz Singer* (1980 C); Blair Brown in *The Days and Nights of Molly Dodd* (*c* 1986 T); Molly (Kyndra Joy Casper) in *Working It Out* (1990 T); Molly (Demi Moore), the potter wife of the *Ghost* (1990 C); etc.

UK: *Molly Capers and Prodger* (the story of a burly Welsh woman and her dog, 1937 R); Gracie Fields, the bombastic housekeeper in *Molly and Me* (1945 C); Molly (Barbara White) in *Mine Own Executioner* (1947 C); Molly (Jane Hylton) in *Passport to Pimlico* (1949 C); Moll CUTPURSE, *The Roaring Girl* (Fay Compton 1956 R); Molly Jones (Sheila Brennan) in INCIDENT (1965 T); Moll Flanders (Kim Novak 1965 C; Julia Foster 1975 T); Molly Bloom (Barbara Jefford) in *Ulysses* (1967 C); Molly Prior (Jenny Agutter) in *The Eagle Has Landed* (1977 C); Lady Molly, a social lioness in *A Dance to the Music of Time* (1978–82 R); Molly (Francesca Annis) involved with the pacifists in the First World War in *We Shall Know Them* (1981 R); Molly (Pat Heywood) in *Rolling Home* (1982 T); Molly (Pauline Letts), a former opera star who lives with and over-controls her son in *The Fishkeeper* (1987 R); Molly (Jaye Griffiths) in *The Persian Lesson* (1987 R); Molly (Alison Steadman) tormented by voices of family and friends while facing an Oxford viva examination in *Viva* (1986 R); etc.

molly Slang term for homosexuals: 'You think I'm trying to tell if a man wears a salmon pink shift at home, he's not necessarily a molly', says Abigail (Diane Bull) in A MATTER OF SEX (1992 R).

molly-coddle Arthur (Michael Hordern) accuses his wife (Clare Kelly) of molly-coddling his son and probably 'making him' gay in LAND OF MY DREAMS (1964 T). Phrase dates from *c* 1849.

A Moment in Time (UK 1979 T) 'Is Fitz what you call "queer"?' asks the incredulous heroine. 'Yes, but what does that matter in the true loving of somebody?' But shortly afterwards (fellow pilot) 'Mac' O'Conor (Neil McCaul) is killed and Fitz (Geoffrey BURRIDGE) is rigidly grief-stricken ('I loved *him*'). There is equality in death as well because, a few months later, Fitz has to tell the heroine that she has also lost her lover to the Luftwaffe.

W: Robin Chapman from the novel by H. E. Bates; P: Colin Tucker; D: Renny Rye; 4.9.79; BBC1; 4 parts.

Gay love was awarded equal honours, if not screen time. (There was also a production on BBC Radio 4 in 1983, starring Daniel Day-Lewis with Gary Cady as Fitz and Peter Wickham as Mac.)

MOMI (Museum of the Moving Image) Two visits confirm the total wondrousness of this treasure trove of film and television on the South Bank in London. Bias totally heterosexual with Kylie/ Charlene's wedding dress near the exit and not a whiff of Nancy SPAIN, Sergeant Grace MILLARD, or even INMAN and GRAYSON. It is the venue of the lesbian and gay television season, 'OUT OF THE ARCHIVES', which Stephen Bourne began curating in 1992.

Mona Lisa Ned Washington song first vocalized by Nat 'King' Cole in *Captain Carey USA* (1950 C, Oscar winner). This classic version was heard in *Raging Bull* (1980 C); *Deadly Lessons* (1983 T), a vital clue as to the whereabouts of a kidnapped schoolgirl; *Mona Lisa* (1986 C), to hint at the more-than-meets-the-eye nature of Simone (Cathy Tyson). Is it only because you're lonely they have blamed you for that Mona Lisa strangeness in your smile?

Monitor (UK 1957–65 T) BBC arts series, introduced by Huw Wheldon and giving early employment to directors like Ken Russell and John SCHLESINGER. Among the scores of imaginative films: 'Death of My Mother' (about D. H. LAWRENCE, 1964); 'Benjamin BRITTEN' (1958); Scottish painters Robert McBryde and Robert Colquhoun (1959); 'The Class' (Harold LANG, 1960); 'Elgar' (1962); 'Pop Goes the Easel' (David HOCKNEY, 1962); 'Evelyn WAUGH' (1964); 'People in Rather Odd Circumstances' (Stevie SMITH, 1965).

Monroe, Marilyn [Norma Jean Baker]

(1926–63) American film actress. According to the religious fundamentalist group Exodus South Pacific (at its 7th conference in 1991), 'gay men suffer from the Marilyn Monroe syndrome: poverty; child abuse; riches; fame; success; sex addiction; depression; suicide.'

There have been over 50 book biographies and a dozen television documentaries.

Portrayed, directly or obliquely, by Kim Stanley in *The Goddess*; Jayne Mansfield in *Will Success Spoil Rock Hunter?/Oh! For a Man* (1957 C); Carroll Baker in *The Paradise Suite* (1963 T); Connie Stevens in *The Sex Symbol* (1974 T); as a plaster icon that heals the sick in *Tommy* (1975 C); Misty Rowe in *Goodbye Norma Jean*; Constance Forslund in *Moviola* 'This Year's Blonde'; Catherine Hicks in *Marilyn: The Untold Story* (1980 T); Theresa Russell in *Insignificance* (1985 C); Hetty Baynes in *Anyone Can See I Love You* (1985 R); Madonna in MATERIAL GIRL; Rebecca De Mornay in AN INCONVENIENT WOMAN (1991 T).

Monroe was to have made her TV debut as Sadie Thompson in *Rain* in 1962. She was also lined up for the role Joanne Woodward played in *The Stripper/Woman of Summer*, and also for *Irma La Douce*.

Monty Python's Flying Circus (UK 1969–74 T) Unhinged comedy, often brilliantly inventive. But, such was the pandemonium style and the aggressive heterosexuality of its overall vision – openly gay Python Graham CHAPMAN notwithstanding – that its message didn't seem all that different to that of Ernie and Eric and Dick Emery. Graham Chapman defended the show's stance in GAY NEWS (1972), one of whose early backers he was: 'All we were doing ... is just using the word, not making any reference to it, whether it's good or bad or anything. We don't care ... any of us, anyway.' *Gay News* raved: 'All of which comes across in the nicest possible way. Instead of relying on the usual stereotyped images of "limp-wristed FAGGOTS".'

A fair number of the sketches contained gay references, often reversing the stereotypes and genders by involving authority figures such as bishops and generals, and icons like ALGY, Biggles and Ginger. Women, young and old, were almost always ridiculed.

'Some of the attitudes now make me cringe. Especially towards women and homosexuals. There was some pretty crude stuff. We were six men who found it difficult to write for women. We didn't really think a lot about homosexuality. We weren't anti, just very CAMP. Which I don't think we would do now' (Terry Jones, *Sydney Morning Herald*, 30.3.91).

The Goon Show writ small.

The Morecambe and Wise Show (UK 1964–82 T) In a 1966 show (ITV) the two comedians appear in sequinned sheath dresses with bouffant hair-dos. This was a jokey homage to one half of their singing duo guests, Pearl Carr and Teddy Johnson. Eric looks askance at Ernie who was supposed to be playing Teddy. Why is he dressed as Pearl? 'Teddy Johnson doesn't wear a dress like that.' 'Not on stage he doesn't,' avers Ernie. 'But I've seen him walking around Piccadilly looking in shop windows and waving – to all his fans.'

At this point Teddy Johnson wanders on. He is dressed in a tutu-styled evening gown. Mild badinage follows, and the trio are joined by the show's writers Sid Hills and Dick Vosburgh who are also dressed *à la* Pearl Carr. She plays no part in these proceedings, though comically logically she should have entered wearing a man's suit. The sketch instead peters out. Eric now turns to Ernie and says he's got a 'confession' to make. Ernie looks at the camera for a moment or two before commenting, through thinly disapproving lips: 'I'm not saying a word.' This is followed by a joke about a famous dancer which intimates that he is a woman. 'We asked his permission to use that gag', says Ernie to the by now hysterical audience. 'Unfortunately he didn't give permission.'

More Lives Than One (UK 1984 T) Troubled family man (Michael N. Harbour) spends Wednesday afternoons chasing sex with men in public toilets. A police raid propels him into the safety of an electrician's van – and into the bed of the electrician (Steve, played by Daniel Webb). A neighbour sees them together and tells David's wife. She asks him to leave. The situation resolves itself. 'I'm not saying I prefer anything. I just wanted to find out.' However, David continues to gaze at men from inside his car.

W: John Peacock; P: Alan Shallcross; D: Michael Darlow; 18.12.84; BBC1; 75 mins.

A picture of an unimaginative, bovine man whose gay awakening has hitherto been totally at crotch level. His few liaisons with the liberated Steve show him that same-sex love operates in a much more sustaining way. The play suggests that one day he may be able to fulfil that side of his personality, making him a far more giving and interesting man. 'You haven't read a book since you stopped reading the BEANO,' says his sorrowing wife. David is probably the last of television's pre-AIDS no-man's-land gays, searching, searching and almost finding.

'... a play about homosexuality, sails against the tide because, in an era when sexual aberration increasingly gains respectability through acts of public confession, John Peacock's play harks back to the days of closed minds and hopelessness ... This play, short on prurience and long on anguish, is scornful of the tactics of police snoopers who drill holes in the ceilings of public conveniences. It does, in these violent times, seem an awful waste of manpower and surveillance equipment. But until the law is changed, it is a highly effective way of preventing a private indulgence from degenerating into a public nuisance' (Peter Davalle, *The Times*).

Morgan, Kenneth (1918–49) British actor who was the lover of Terence RATTIGAN from 1946 to 1949. He appeared as Babe Lake in the 1939 screen version of Rattigan's *French without Tears* and went to live with the playwright after meeting him again at the end of the war. Morgan wrote and acted in a radio play called 'A Mind in Shadow' for the AP-POINTMENT WITH FEAR series in 1946. He played a young writer living with another in a country cottage. One goes mad and murder ensues. Among Morgan's other roles were a schoolboy (Morgan) in *Goodbye Mr Chips* (1939 C) and as CHARLIE in a 1946 PAUL TEMPLE serial. He committed suicide, partly because of an unhappy post-Rattigan love affair. His death, apart from being the trigger for THE DEEP BLUE SEA, was said to have affected Rattigan for the rest of his life, influencing all his subsequent relationships.

Morgan le Fay King Arthur's sorceress half-sister. Played by Myrna Loy in *A Connecticut Yankee* (1931); Anne Crawford (in *Knights of the Round Table* (1954); *Sword in the Stone*; Helen Mirren (in *Excalibur*); Moyra Frazer in *Camelot*; Patsy Kensit/Maureen O'BRIEN in *The Legend of King Arthur*; Susie Blake as Fay Morgan in *Wail of the Banshee* (1992 T).

Count Jim 'Thighs' **Moriarty** aka Comte Toulouse-Moriarty of the House of Roland. Played by Spike Milligan, the confederate and lover of GRYTPYPE-THYNNE in THE GOON SHOW (1952–60 R). 'A French schemer ... a French scrag and lackey.' 'He has played the male lead in over 50 postcards.' War correspondent of *Health and Strength*. A 'feathered SHIRT LIFTER' and champion barbed wire hurdler (until his tragic accident).

He and Moriarty begin working in tandem in 'The Affair of the Lone Banana' (1954) when they are discovered living high off the hog on the Riviera. By the 8th series they are domiciled in dustbins ('Now, which of all these fish-bones is you, Moriarty?') or in trees. Clothes, too, have become scarce. 'Keep still,' hisses Grytpype. 'Do you want us both out of this suit, Moriarty?'

Moriarty is motivated purely by greed. As he characteristically puts it:

'Owwwwwww, owwwww, sapristi, nadgers, if it works we'll get rich beyond the dreams of Olwen – owwww, the money, the moolah, the grisbee. Owwwwww, owwwww, owwwww.'

In *The Last Goon Show of All* (1972 R/T) censorship had loosened sufficiently for someone to say of the Count: 'Thanks to him, there's a government health warning on every sailor's shirt.'

Morning Story (UK 1949–91 R) A daily 15-minute short story by new writers as well as established practitioners of the craft. 'The only regular radio outlet for unpublished short stories in this country ... We are in a prime position to inspire and mould a generation of new writers and to set trends in the art of short story writing,' said Sheila Fox, producer in the 1980s.

Homosexual themes were as rare as hen's teeth: 'A Gay Little Story' by Doris Rust (read by Gordon Gow in 1952) certainly did not qualify.

However, in 1979 gay activist Eric Presland produced a nice tale of love and loss, 'Me and Mr Mandel'. A Jewish tailor, who was NOT THE MARRYING KIND, 'adopts' a younger man as more than a paying guest and more than a friend. He dies and his 'son' grieves alone in a hostile, uncomprehending world. Michael wasn't allowed to see him as he lay dying because he wasn't next of kin, though they had lived together for 15 years. There's no money for a rabbi, funeral or a stone. Mr Mandel lies in the freezer. Some of Presland's innocuous language was toned down because of its mid-morning slot, directly after the *Morning Service*. 'I loved that man, loved him. It was comfortable ... I rubbed Vic on his chest ... I do miss him. He was a wonderful man.'

In 'Gobbo and Son' by Patrick O'Sullivan (1986) two bachelors play out a paternal–filial relationship until a woman appears on the scene. It is quite clearly stated that the pair are not sexually inclined towards each other in any way, shape or form.

Others of interest included: 'Aunt Lil

Goes to Hollywood' by Richard Rowe, read by George Layton (1987); 'A Cigarette with Bette DAVIS' by Tom Wakefield, read by David Horovitch (1991): 'You can't eat popcorn during a Bette Davis film. Colin says you have to smoke – even if you don't know how'; 'Gravity' by David LEAVITT, read by Garrick Hagon (1991).
See also SHORT STORY.

Morris, Jan [James] (1926–) British travel writer and broadcaster whose personal account of a sex change (*Conundrum* in 1974) was accorded huge coverage. Sporadic television appearances: *On the Matter of Wales* (1982); *When I Get To Heaven* (1987); 'What happens to us after we die?'. Also radio: *Bookshelf* (1987); etc.

Morris, Mary (1915–88) English-based actress who imparted savage grace and distinctive clipped diction to dozens of meaty roles on radio and television for four decades, retaining a clearly defined lesbian persona. She was also an artist. Born in the Fiji Islands, she made her first stage appearance in Barbados. She ran her own repertory company at 21, before signing a contract with MGM and going to Hollywood.
  Because of confusion with a stage actress, she was asked to change her name, which she refused to do. No parts materialized and the agreement was rescinded – by mutual consent – and her subsequent film career, apart from her (much cut) role as the sorcerer's henchwoman in *The Thief of Bagdad* (1940), was patchy and modest, and entirely based in England.
  C: princess in *Victoria the Great* (1937); gamin in *Prison without Bars* (1938); Edwards, the chauffeuse who helps kidnap a young woman in one scene in *The Spy in Black* (1939); Ludmilla Koslowski in *Pimpernel Smith* (opposite Leslie Howard, 1941); *Major Barbara* (1941); Yugoslavian peasant Anna Petrovich in *Undercover* (1943); Sarah Dubois in *The Man from Morocco* (with Anton Walbrook, 1945); Peter FINCH's unsympathetic wife whom he murders in *Train of*

Events (1949); Communist saboteur Anna Braun in *High Treason* (1951); *The White Wedding Dress* (1955); then nothing until her old lady with a secret in *The Haunting of Julia/Full Circle* (1977).
  R: Marie Bashkirtseff in *Leaves from a Journal* (1948); title role in Anouilh's *Medea* (1948): 'found as she too seldom does ... a part to sink her teeth in and chew with relish'; title role in Anouilh's *Antigone* (1949) with Alec Guinness and Peter Ustinov; Epifania in *The Millionairess* (1952); the Angel in Yeats' *The Hour Glass* (1954); *Heloise and Abelard* (1954); *Saint Joan* (with John WYSE as the Dauphin, 1956); *Antigone* (with Robert Harris, 1957); Goneril to Stephen Murray's *King Lear* (1960) with June Tobin and Rosalie Crutchley as her sisters; 'an unusually strong' *Lady Macbeth* (1960); with Brenda Bruce in *The Maids* (1963); as Inez in *Huis Clos* (1963); brothel madame Irma in *The Balcony* (1964); Atossa the Dowager Empress in Aeschlyus' *The Persians* with Donald Wolfit (1965); *The Erasers* (1965); Agatha in *The Family Reunion* (1966); Queen Clytemnestra with Ian McKellen and Eileen Atkins in *Electra* (1966) and the same character in *The Flies* (1966) with Ian MCKELLEN as Orestes and Michael Hordern as Zeus; Miss Madrigal in *The Chalk Garden* (1968) opposite Edith Evans and Angela Pleasence: giving 'a different dimension to the part made famous by Peggy Ashcroft' (*Radio Times*); 'carved out of warm marble,' said the *Listener* about her performance in *The Marriage* (1968); Margaret of Parma, daughter of the Emperor Charles V, regent of the Netherlands whose secretary was Machiavelli in *Egmont* (1970); Abbess of Argenteuil in *Abelard and Heloise* (1975); Dowager Marquise de Bellegarde in Henry JAMES' *The American* (1975); *City of the Horizon: The Dream/The Reality* (1976) set in Egypt 3,000 years ago; Naomi in THE THRESHING FLOOR (1982); Marjorie Dennis in *The Happiest Women* (1984); the voracious Empress Livia in *I, Claudius* (1985); the devouring mother in *The Watched Pot* (1988).

T: Cressida, a Trojan widow in *The Face of Love* (1954); 'dazzling' as the daughter in *Six Characters in Search of an Author* (1954) with 'a laugh that long echoes in the memory'; Aurore (George SAND) in *Nom-de-Plume* 'Child of Her Time' (1956); frightened Bella in *Gaslight* (1957) with Peter Cushing and Billie Whitelaw; Lettie Quincey, the incestuously inclined sister of Peter Cushing in *Uncle Harry* (1958); Ingrid Hoffman, international blackmailer in *International Detective* 'White Blackmail' (1960); Margaret, Queen of England in *An Age of Kings* 'The Sun in Splendour' etc (1960); Lady Macbeth in *Macbeth* (BBC Schools, 1960); Professor Madeleine Dawnay in *A for Andromeda* (1961) and *The Andromeda Breakthrough* (1962): with this portrayal – originally written for a man – she established what was to become her established image for the next 27 years – strong, uncompromising, ironic; Fraulein Doktor Mathilde Von Zahnd who runs the asylum in *The Physicists* (1964): 'the redoubtable hunchbacked would-be mistress of the world'; Cleopatra opposite Keith Michell in *The Spread of the Eagle* (1963); Number Two, dressed as PETER PAN in *The Prisoner* 'Day of the Dead' (1968); detective story writer Emma Sands in *An Unofficial Rose* (1974/5); the Dame, head of a touring ballet company in *Village Hall* 'Dancing in the Dark' (1975); Madame Fidolia, another dance martinet, in *Ballet Shoes* (1975); dowager in *Everard and Eloise* (1976); Aunt Tatty in *Ten from the 20s* (1977); grande dame in *Anna Karenina* (1978); Queen Mother in *Richard II* (1979); *Victoria the Great* (1979); *Seaton's Aunt* (1984); Mrs Browning-Browning, a cat breeder in *Claws* (1987); trying to cheat Death in *Ray Bradbury Theatre* 'There Was an Old Woman' (1988); Caroline Faraday in *Campion* 'Police at the Funeral' (1989); Mrs Wan in *Sometime in August* (1990).

She appears, in a blue denim suit, for two electrifying minutes in *The Golden Years of Alexander Korda* (1970 T), every bit as charismatic as the other more conventionally dressed former Korda actresses (Merle Oberon, Ann Todd,

Elisabeth Bergner). Her words are not minced: 'A God-like figure, like Zeus. I think I hated him.'

morris dancing Eddie Grundy insinuates it's effeminate, while Shula says it's manly – deriving as it does from Moorish dancing (THE ARCHERS 1990). 'The morris is a traditional male dance for men sworn to manhood, fiery ecstasy, ale, magic and fertility. For woman to dance the morris is a contradiction in terms' (letter, *Radio Times*, 26.5.1990).

Morrison, Jim (1943–71) American rock singer, now cult hero. Flirted with and usually indulged in everything before dying young. His songs heard in movies such as *Apocalypse Now*, *Neighbors* and *Taps*. Given the Hollywood treatment, played by Val Kilmer, in THE DOORS (1990 C). Morrison's dictum 'Live fast, die young and leave a beautiful corpse' was quoted by Jon (Craig Gilmore) in THE LIVING END (1992 C).

Mossman, James (1926–71) English international roving reporter for PANORAMA in the 1960s, then presenter of the BBC2 arts programme *Review*. A very sleek, incisive personality with more than a touch of glamour and mystery. 'A James Bond of current affairs,' Philip Purser called him in *Halliwell's Television Companion* (1986). One of his most unusual assignments came in a television series called *Free for All* in 1969 in which he encountered SKINHEADS, Hell's Angels, hippies and other nonconformist young people. In the last programme ('Those Concerned') he discussed issues arising from the previous ones (principally what should be the limits of personal freedom) with a group of 'STRAIGHTS'.

most child molesters are heterosexual Spoken by Kate Nelligan in *Without a Trace* (1983 C) – almost a throwaway line, and probably not processed by most audience members as Philippe (Keith McDermott) is presented as a man who easily could have molested/killed her child, even though his past charge for sodomizing a minor was (he says) confected by the boy's Mormon parents.

Mother Used for Henry Silva's vicious drug peddler (not gay in the film as on the stage) in *A Hatful of Rain* (1957 C); Steed's boss (Patrick Newell) in the Tara King *Avengers* (1969–71); a 1960s paranoid (Dan Ackroyd), always espousing theories about conspiracies to defraud people in *Sneakers* (1992 C).

mothers Many are presented as burying their boy children at least in fallopian darkness, keeping or trying to keep them dependent by fair means or foul:
Hannah Jessop (Henrietta Crossman) in John Ford's *Sacrifice* (1933 C) who sends her boy to his death in the First World War rather than lose him to the girl he loves; Mrs Hart (Jeanette Nolan) in WORDS AND MUSIC (1948 C); the feral 'Ma' Garrett (Margaret Wycherley), defender and accomplice of Cody (James Cagney) in *White Heat* (1949 C); Amanda Wingfield (Gertrude Lawrence) in *The Glass Menagerie* (1950 C); the burbling Mrs Anthony (Marion Lorne) in STRANGERS ON A TRAIN (1951 C); Mrs Venable (Katharine HEPBURN) in SUDDENLY LAST SUMMER (1959 C); Mrs Bates, the stuffed figure in the cellar who lives only by courtesy of son Norman in *Psycho* (1960 C); Mrs Morel (Wendy Hiller) in *Sons and Lovers* (1960 C); Nicky Lancaster's mama in THE VORTEX (1960, 1964 etc); the woman who appears to want to draw her just married son Alex back into childhood in THE TWILIGHT ZONE 'Young Man's Fancy' (1960 T); apron-string-tying Ruth White, mother of Eli Wallach in *Sunday Night Theatre* 'Lullaby' (1962 T) who nearly smothers his young bride as well; Korean war hero's brainwashing, ball-breaking parent (Angela Lansbury) in *The Manchurian Candidate* (1962 C); Mrs Flagg (Marjorie Bennett) incessantly nagging at her idle, monstrously piping son, Edwin in *Whatever Happened to Baby Jane?* (1962 C); the devouring snob in *Five Finger Exercise* (Rosalind Russell 1962 C; Margaret Lockwood 1970 T); Dick Van Dyke's cross to bear,

forever threatening to drop down dead: Maureen Stapleton in *Bye Bye Birdie* (1963 C); Glenda Farrell mugged by her own son (Timothy Everett) in *Ben Casey* 'A Cardinal Act of Mercy' (1963 T); Mrs Hilyard (Olivia De Havilland) driving her over-sensitive son Malcolm out of the house, an event which turns her into a *Lady in a Cage* (1964 C); Jessica (Margaret Robertson) bringing up 'a typical homosexual' in LOVESICK (1967 R); pushy, shrill Jewish Eileen Heckart, mother of detective George Segal who is almost as demented by her ministrations as the murderer he is out to catch in *No Way to Treat a Lady* (1968 C); senile and screaming Beatrix LEHMANN, the mother of Charles DYER in STAIRCASE (1969 C).
Mrs Hobday in *Mrs Mouse Are You Within?* (1970 T); Cathleen Nesbitt as gangster Vic Dakin's sweet white-haired, bedridden mother in *Villain* (1971 C); in her dotage and a total tie: Paul's mother (Beatrix LEHMANN) in *Is Nellie Dead?* (1968 T); Bobby Walden escapes to Amsterdam to escape America and mother (Joanne Woodward) in *Summer Wishes, Winter Dreams* (1973 C); Mrs Byatt moving from place to place with her son who is still considered a criminal because of past offences involving children in *Softly Softly* 'Little Boy Blue' (1974 T); the mother of Sonny Wortzik coming to the bank he's robbing to plead with him to give himself up in DOG DAY AFTERNOON (1975 C); Mrs Morgenweiss (Anita Dangler) for whom her baby (a stage producer) can do no wrong, even when he's creating flatulent rubbish in *The Goodbye Girl* (1977 C); Mrs Hopkins (Thora Hird) who has brought up Trevor single-handed and never lets him forget it in ME, I'M AFRAID OF VIRGINIA WOOLF (1978 T); Alistair's overpowering parent (Margot Boyd) in THREE PIECE SWEET (1979 R); John INMAN as Mr HUMPHRIES played his own mother in ARE YOU BEING SERVED? 'Heir Apparent' (1981); Mrs Fox whose devoted boy Sidney is on trial for murder in *Lady Killers* 'A Boy's Best Friend' (1981 T); Morris HARDACRE (James Saxon) in

Brass (1982–4/1990); Mrs Bennett (Anna MASSEY) in ANOTHER COUNTRY (1984 C); the rigid, proud widow (Monserrat Salvador) who very probably kills her son to avoid scandal in LA MUERTE DE MIKAEL (1984 C); Mrs Vyse (Maria Britneva) in *A Room with a View* (1985 C) with a tight grip on Cecil who is afraid of women, most of whom his mother thinks aren't classy enough for so rarified a nature; obsessively loving, forsaking all others Mother (Margaret Courtenay) of Son in *La Comptime* (1986 R); the much too much Mrs Beckoff (Anne Bancroft) in TORCH SONG TRILOGY (1981 C); Rosemary Daley (Patricia Routledge) whose 40 years of life with her son Terence is under threat in *Trouble Sleeping* (1990 R); the tightly controlled Katharine (Sada Thompson) who is also *André's Mother* (1990 T); Eleanor (Jane Lapotaire) in *The Devil's Crown* (1978 T): 'Sleep with your wife. If you can't stand her sleep with someone else's wife.'

mothers who are happy for their sons to be gay or indifferent to it Mrs Loud in AN AMERICAN FAMILY (1973 T); Mrs Piper (Sylvia Kaye) in EVEN SOLOMON (1979 T); Maggie Cunningham (Jill Balcon) in *A New Step Every Day* (1980 R); Alexis Carrington (Joan Collins) in DYNASTY (1981–9); Mary Campbell (Cathryn Damon) in SOAP (1977–80); the glue-sniffing mother (Carmen Maura) in *What Have I Done to Deserve This?* (1985 C) whose 13-year-old son goes off to live with a dentist to help with the family bills; Doña Herlinda (Guadalupe De Torro) who determinedly marries off her son but is happy that his male lover lives with them in DONA HERLINDA AND HER SON (1986 C); Lady Carlion (Wendy Hiller) in COUNTRY (1981 T) not too concerned as long as no horses are frightened; Doreen Mantle, marauding, fantasizing mother of an opera buff who lives with a chap in *Trotsky Was My Father* (1985 R); Anna (Maggie McCarthy) in A BIT OF BERLIN (1992 R); etc.

mothers who resign themselves to the fact that their sons are gay *Nancy Astor* (Lisa Harrow 1982 T); Mrs Cowley (Pearl Hackney) in MORE LIVES THAN ONE (1984 T); Mrs Delafield (Katharine HEPBURN) in *Mrs Delafield Wants to Marry* (1986 T); Mrs Pearson (Gena Rowlands) in AN EARLY FROST (1985 T); Laura Hobson (Marlo Thomas) in CONSENTING ADULT (1986 T); Julie Andrews in *Our Sons* (1991 T); etc.

mother's boys Those men who have never untied the apron strings, severed the umbilical cord or pulled away from the teat. Used in a (hostile) sexual context in *Spellbound* (1946 C) in regard to Lieutenant Cooley, a detective. 'Mama's Boy' has been used quite frequently as an episode title on American crime shows (*M Squad* 1960 through to *The Equaliser* 1990), and as a theme in *Ben Casey* 'A Cardinal Act of Mercy' (1963 T, with Timmy Everett) and many more. At the climax of *Maigret and the Burglar's Wife* (1962 T) the mother (Fay Compton) of the dentist Guillaume (Hugh BURDEN) is revealed as the killer of his second wife. She doesn't want any woman to be close to him but herself. Her last line is: 'Now be a good boy and Mama may have a chocolate in her bag.'

Alistair Proudfoot (Christopher Good) in THREE PIECE SWEET (1979 R) is upbraided by his landlady for being 'an overgrown mother's boy. It's unnatural.' In 1980 Suzy Quatro performed 'Mama's Boy' on *Top Of The Pops*; after lyrically laying into her guy, she assured us that 'Under all the feathers and lace/ Beats the heart of a real man'. Dick (Michael Pennington) is called this by his wife Jan (Francesca Annis) because of the tight emotional embrace he is held in by his mother (Avril Elgar) in *Tonic Water and Ice* (1981? R); he resolves the impossible choice between the two women by committing suicide.

Other examples: Manners (John Barrymore Jr) in *While the City Sleeps* (1956 C) who kills blondes and reads comics; Roger Thornhill (Cary GRANT in *North by Northwest* (1959 C) devoted to Jessie Royce Landis; William Shatner torn between mother Jessie Royce Landis and bride-to-be Gia Scala in *Alfred Hitchcock Presents* 'Mother, May I Go for a Swim?' (1962 T); Percy Windrush (Harry H. Corbett), 35 and still living with Mum (Thora Hird) in *Rattle of a Simple Man* (1964 C); Schact (Lionel Hamilton), Nazi stalwart and still close to Mutter: he climbs into her bed and commits SUICIDE (THE PARACHUTE 1968 T); FASHION DESIGNER Peter Butterworth finally plucks up courage to wriggle out of mother's clutches to marry a 'masculine' woman in THE FABULOUS FRUMP (1967 T); Michael (Kenneth Nelson), a baby at 35 in THE BOYS IN THE BAND (1970 C); Stanley Wood (Jimmy Gardner) who can't shake off the memory of mother in CHARIOT OF FIRE (1970 T) and can only relate emotionally to young boys; Denzil Davies (John Thaw) shut away with his reclusive actress mother (Brenda Bruce) in *Budgie* 'Sunset Mansions' (1971 T); Montgomery MCNEIL in FAME (1980 C; 1982 T) whose dancer Mom is a big part of his life; Chris (Nigel Lambert) trying to come to terms with life after Mum's death in *Running Down* (1980 R); Sidney Shorr (Tony RANDALL) downcast and dejected on the anniversary of his mother's death in a 1982 episode of LOVE, SIDNEY; Maxwell Laurence (Frank Lloyd) who is obsessed by his mother and kills himself with a piece of glass from a smashed frame containing her picture in A COUNTRY PRACTICE (1987 T); milksop Norman (Christopher Strauli) in *Only When I Laugh* (1979–84 T); Ronnie Corbett still struggling to escape maternal dictatorship in *Sorry!* (1982–6 T); Graham (Alan BENNETT) in TALKING HEADS 'A Chip in the Sugar' (1988 T) whose mother, thought senile, suddenly kicks over the traces, leaving her son abandoned and adrift.

'Daddy's girl' has been used very rarely: once, certainly by Michelle (in relation to Arthur) in EASTENDERS (1987 T).

'mothers-in-law' Naomi, a pillar of strength in *The Story of Ruth* (Peggy Wood 1960 C) and THE THRESHING FLOOR (Mary MORRIS 1982 R); Peggy Pope as the brash Texan who gives Jodie the once-over in SOAP (1978 T); acid Joyce Redman in ALL FOR LOVE 'Combat' (1982 T); sophisticated Zizi (Genevieve Page) in *Beyond Therapy* (1986 C) who takes pains to scotch her son Bruce's romance with a *woman*; Mark's mother reluctantly obeying his lover's ground rules in the kitchen when she comes to stay in G.P. 'Lovers' (1990 T).

mothers of lesbians (most of whom can't cope with the fact) Sally's mum (Lala Lloyd) in *Piano Lessons* (1976 T); Linda Ray Guettner's in A QUESTION OF LOVE (1978 T); Gwen Nelson as the mother of CONNIE (1979 T); Thora Hird, mum of the unseen Margaret in *Say Something Happened* (1982 T; 1989 R); Lady Baigent (Barbara Leigh Hunt) in THE TINKER'S DAUGHTER (1986 R); Dorothea (Sada Thompson) in MY TWO LOVES (1986 T): 'Why were you kissing that woman?'; Jess' adoptive mother (Geraldine McEwan) in ORANGES ARE NOT THE ONLY FRUIT (1990 T); Lady Sackville (Diana Fairfax) in PORTRAIT OF A MARRIAGE (1990 T).

mothers who are themselves lesbian Sybille (Françoise Brion) in *Nea* aka *A Young Emanuelle* (1976 C); Andra Akers in *Rafferty* (1977 T); Diana Graham (Rachel Davies) and Beth James (Dorothy White) in CROWN COURT 'A Friend of the Family' (1979 T); Jill Davis (Meryl Streep) in *Manhattan* (1979 C); Linda Ray Guettner (Gena Rowlands) in A QUESTION OF LOVE (1978 T); Gloria Vanderbilt (Lucy Gutteridge) in *Little Gloria ... Happy At Last* (1982 T); Vanessa (Kate Burton) in *Ellis Island* (1984 T); LIANNA (Linda Griffiths 1983 C); Marilyn (Gail Strickland) in HEARTBEAT (1988–9 T); Vita SACKVILLE-WEST (Janet McTeer) in PORTRAIT OF A MARRIAGE (1990 T); C.J.'s former lover, Maggie Barnes (Elizabeth Kemp) in L.A. LAW (1991 T). Also: 40 MINUTES 'Demelza's Baby' (1984 T).

mountaineers Passions and rivalries

exposed during THE ASCENT OF F6 (1938 R etc); mention of the all-gay Everest climb in TOGETHER (1981 T); *K2* (1991 C).

The Mousetrap The thriller by Agatha Christie (1952) based on her radio play THREE BLIND MICE. Now in its forty-something year in the West End.

Move Over, Darling Swoony title song from a long forgotten Doris DAY comedy of 1964 in which Doris was given an up-tempo, funky sound which made the record a popular hit. It was wickedly used in *Clause 28* (1988 T/V) for a lesbian coming out anthem. The lyrics gush about trying to resist (but giving in), of being too weak to fight, and of waving Doris' conscience 'bye-bye'.

Movie-Go-Round (UK 1956–69 R) Sunday afternoon BBC Light Programme film magazine, containing studio roundups, interviews and 'pocket editions' of two new films. It broke new ground (for that timeslot) by condensing (into a quarter of an hour) the plots of *The Trials of Oscar* WILDE and *Oscar Wilde* in 1960 and VICTIM the following year. (But 'homosexuality' as such was not mentioned.)

Mozart Mozart is playing in the bedroom during the honeymoon night of (intellectual) Arthur (Hywel Bennett) and (nice ordinary) Jenny (Hayley Mills) in THE FAMILY WAY (1966 C), however, the bed collapses, she laughs and he can't sustain an erection thereafter – his family blames it on his reading books and listening to classical music. A trio from a Mozart opera is Daniel's (Peter Finch) lifeline in SUNDAY BLOODY SUNDAY (1971 C). Colin RUSSELL (Michael CASHMAN) in EASTENDERS (1989 T) knows his Wolfgang Amadeus; his friend/lover Guido (Nicholas Donovan) tells Carmel and Matthew: 'Play him any bit of Mozart and he'll give you the K number.'

Mr Luby's Fear of Heaven (UK 1975 R) Louis Luby (John GIELGUD) is a Byronophile. He has read and written

reams about the poet. His mellifluous voice summons up his idol's libertine verses on the slightest pretext. Imagine then his disgust when he finds, at Heaven's Gate, his partner through eternity is to be a grossly philistine Northern English businessman, Tommy Fletcher (Peter WOODTHORPE). The latter, contrary to appearance and expectation, leads a rampantly full sex life. He may vote Tory, but he has managed to retain wife, boyfriend and sister as lovers throughout his adult years – and without inflicting the damage Lord BYRON did on his ménages.

W: John Mortimer; P: John Tydeman; BBC Radio 4; 60 mins.

This is Mortimer in fine form and high immoral spirits. Twitting the noses of straights is fun, but twitting those of people who feel superior to straights is even more delightful.

Mrs Dale's Diary (UK 1948–63 R) This daily 15-minute serial was listened to by millions during the 1950s. By the time it ended in 1969 as THE DALES, there had been 5,500 episodes, 70,000 pages of script and 16¼-million words spoken by more than 1,000 characters.

Created by Jonquil ANTONY and 'John Bishop' (ie Ted WILLIS) with Ellis POWELL in the title role, Thelma Hughes as her sister Sally, and Courtney Hope (later Dorothy Lane) as their feisty mother Mrs Freeman. Billy THATCHER, he of the 'light voice', was replaced as son Bob after just four weeks – but returned in 1957 to write the scripts. In 1963 Ellis Powell was sacked and Jessie Matthews took over.

The serial was regularly spoofed: particularly in 'Mrs Doom's Diary' (on *Home at Eight* 1952) with Hermione GINGOLD and Alfred Marks:

'Tea, Edmond?'
'Yes, Drusilla.'
'Millock?'

The original setting was Parkwood Hill (really Pinner) and, although she fussed over everybody and was always worried about husband Jim (who had a history of colds and a tendency to get overtired), life wasn't that arduous. (Bos'n the cat spilling tea on Mrs Freeman's skirt was a highlight of 1950; a kitten strewing parts of a grandfather clock over the carpet was a fairly big event in 1951.) Eventually, in the 1960s – with a gradually diminishing audience – pressures built up to make the serial more relevant. The family moved to Exton New Town (in East Anglia) and daily confronted some social issue or other: abortion, young widowhood, spastic children, unmarried mothers and – in 1967 – the joint number one taboo (with incest and cancer): Richard FULTON changed from being a happy queer to an exiled homosexual, leaving Mrs Dale in a bother. For all her gurgling, practical tolerance, she couldn't accept that her brother-in-law – whom she had known as a gentleman of obviously aesthetic temperament and taste for nearly 20 years – was ONE OF THEM.

Once a national institution, known by its glissando harp theme and the perennial 'I'm worried about Jim', *The Dales* had only 4 million listeners (9 out of 10 of them women over 50) by the late 1960s. It was replaced by younger, trendier, London-based WAGGONERS' WALK.

Mrs Delafield Wants to Marry (US 1986 T) Mother, well into her sixties, is wooed and won – much to the upturned noses of her children (except gay Chipper) because she is Catholic and husband-to-be is Jewish.
W: James Prideaux; P/D: George Schaefer; 100 mins.

Manages to include favourable mentions and depictions of Jews, blacks, women priests and – with reservations – homosexuals. Chipper (Charles Frank) is a WINDOW DRESSER – fresh-faced, handsome, blond – who eventually gives his mother (Katharine HEPBURN) away at a half-Jewish, half-Catholic ceremony in an 'alternative' church.

Mrs D. is presented as a bit of a relic, but a game one – and quite willing to wish Chipper the best of luck when, sometime in the past, he brought a 'leather guy who worked in a flower shop' called Orville to her home and sat with his 'greasy jeans on the sofa . . . and you said you were going to set up housekeeping . . . and what did I tell you at the time? . . . I said to you "I love you" and "Good luck"' (the relationship didn't mature).

La Muerte de Mikel [Michael's Death] (Sp 1984 C) Basque activist (Imanol Arias) cannot survive his personal crisis (catalysed by a proudly charismatic TRANSVESTITE singer) and is destroyed by the police, his political colleagues and his rigid mother (Monserrat Salvador), who is no Doña Herlinda.
W: Jose Angelo Rebolledo and Imanol Uribe; P: Jose Cuxarti; D: Imanol Uribe; 85 mins.

Mikel is doomed from the moment he crosses the great divide – symbolized by his driving into oncoming traffic on a motorway. The film flinches from a more positive set of actions for him – embodied by lover Fama, the priest and the PSYCHIATRIST – and sadly shows him capitulating to the forces of unthinking authority. That's how it appears – but the long-held freeze frame of mother on the balcony at the end tells us that perhaps Mikel did not commit suicide. Would he have transcended his society and braved the new world of sexual rather than ethnic politics? 'Man falls for drag queen and is murdered by his own mother' (Vito RUSSO, *The Celluloid Closet*, 1987).

murderers Enrico Bandillo (Edward G. Robinson) in LITTLE CAESAR (1930 C); students killing golden youth in ROPE (1931 R etc); cat-like husband (Anton WALBROOK) tormenting his young bride (Diana Wynyard) in *Gaslight* (1939 C); Joseph Cotten as the beautifully mannered uncle in *Shadow of a Doubt* (1943 C) slowly unfolding himself as a cold-blooded killer to his adoring niece; the eternally handsome man-about-town strangling the man who painted him in THE PICTURE OF DORIAN GRAY (1945 C etc); aesthete Waldo LYDECKER (Clifton WEBB) in *Laura* (1946 C); Bruno

Anthony (Robert Walker) killing Guy's unfaithful wife in STRANGERS ON A TRAIN (1951 C); Sandy (Robert Ryan), head of crime syndicate in *House of Bamboo* (1955 C) despatching his lover (Cameron Mitchell) in a bath house; Manners (John Barrymore Jr), 'MAMA'S BOY' in *While the City Sleeps* (1956 C) killing blondes and reading comics; Kenny (Derek Farr), not the uncomplicated 'CONFIRMED BACHELOR' after all but part of *The Vicious Circle* (1957 C); Artie Strauss (Bradford Dillman) and Judd Steiner (Dean Stockwell) killing a young boy 'for kicks' in COMPULSION (1959 C), a true story fictionalized in ROPE; Norman BATES (Anthony Perkins) protecting his dear mother from prying eyes in *Psycho* (1960 C) and only superficially cured in *Psycho II* and *Psycho III* (Norman gave birth to many other disturbed, sensitive and heterosexually unattached males for the next three decades); Eleanor (Françoise Prevost) killing *The Girl with the Golden Eyes* (1961 C); Carol (Catherine Deneuve) lashing out at the hated touch of men in *Repulsion* (1965 C); Mr Sloane killing a photographer who loved him and an old man who knows he did it in ENTERTAINING MR SLOANE (Clive Francis 1968 T; Peter McEnery 1970 C); Colin McIver (William Windom) taking out all his pent-up self-hatred on the man who picked him up in THE DETECTIVE (1968 C); Why (Jacqueline Sassard) stabbing her girlfriend in LES BICHES (1968 C) after being rejected for a man; Harry (Leonard Rossiter) shooting his two paying guests in *Harry-Kari and Sally* (1971 T); McCallister (Tony Meyer) doing time for killing his father in A LIFE IS FOREVER (1972 T); Barry Foster, a chirpy barrow boy who most definitely doesn't like women in *Frenzy* (1972 C); June Allyson as a homicidal butch lesbian housewife in *They Only Kill Their Masters* (1972 C); footman Alfred (George Innes) repaying his elderly patron/lover with treachery and death in UPSTAIRS, DOWNSTAIRS 'Rose's Pigeon' (1973 T); mass-murdering cannibal Kurt Raab in TENDERNESS OF THE WOLVES (1973 C); businessman (Albert Paulson) shooting at and killing passengers aboard a San Francisco bus in *The Laughing Policeman/Investigation of Murder* (1973 C); knife-wielding TRANSVESTITE (Christopher Morley) spitting out defiance in *Freebie and the Bean* (1974 C); withdrawn young woman, Helen (Angela Pleasence) who keeps her girlfriends in chilling perpetuity in *Symptoms* aka *The Blood Virgin* (1974 C); Ken Scott (John Davidson) who kills when inhabiting his female self, Carol, in THE STREETS OF SAN FRANCISCO 'Mask of Death' (1974 T); three women slaying little old ladies entrusted to their care in POLICE WOMAN 'Flowers of Evil' (1974 T); Thelma Baker (Christina Gretorex) in WITHIN THESE WALLS 'For Life' (1975 T); Jean Trevelyan (Patricia Garwood) in *Within These Walls*: 'The Animals Came in Two by Two' (1975 T); a real killer – but shrouded in mystery in *The Legend of Lizzie Borden* (1975 T, with Elizabeth Montgomery); Oliver (Hugh BURDEN) ridding himself of the obsessed ex-lover Curtis (John Stratton) in A SUPERSTITION (1977 T); the blackmailed judge (Salome Jens) in IN THE GLITTER PALACE (1977 T); Andrea (Talia Shire), pathologically jealous in *Windows* (1980 C); the remorseless serial killer in CRUISING (1980 C); the blank psychotics in *The First Deadly Sin* (1981 C) and *The Fan* (1982 C); bisexual QUERELLE (Brad DAVIS 1982 C) slitting a man's throat for no obvious reason; John Charles Turner (Shannon Presby) who stabs a young woman because he couldn't keep an erection in *Trackdown: Finding the Goodbar Killer* (1983 T) – a real-life character who inspired Doug (Bruce Boxleitner) in *Kiss Me ... Kill Me* (1976 T) and Gary (Tom Berenger) in *Looking for Mr Goodbar* (1977 C).

The punk (Maxwell Caulfield) who pulls a girl off his best friend and kills her in *The Boys Next Door* (1985 C); Wayne Williams (Calvin Levels), the accused disc jockey in *The Atlanta Child Killings* (1985 T); Julius Court (Art Malik) coldly bumping off two old people (suffocation by polythene bag) and a younger woman (getting her drunk then hanging her) in order to cover up his drug-smuggling operation in and around *The Black Tower* (1985 T); Wang Kei-Lung who killed his lover and is now involved with a young man who closely resembles the dead one in *The Outsiders* (1986 C); the artist CARAVAGGIO (Nigel Terry 1986 C) stabbing his lover Ranuccio and fleeing into exile; 'The Tooth Fairy' (Tom Noonan) in *Manhunter* (1986 T, a variation on *The Silence of the Lambs*); fractured Iluned Jones in *In Two Minds* (1987 T); young fan Antonio (Antonio Banderas) in LAW OF DESIRE (1987 C) removing the competition from his lover's life; the initially silent 'Billy' in *The Interrogation of John* (1987 T); Jack Carney aka Michael Weller (Hart Bochner) in *Apartment Zero* (1988 C) who helps clean up for right-wing forces in Argentina; Terence Fielding (Joss Ackland), public school teacher battering two people to death, one the boy he loves, in *A Murder of Quality* (1991 T); 'BUFFALO BILL' (Ted Levine) all jumbled gender with a poodle named 'Precious' in *The Silence of the Lambs* (1991 C); 'evil' Ken (Dorian Healy) in YOUNG SOUL REBELS (1991 C), a closeted white man who kills a young black guy during preliminaries to sex and tries to kill one of the heroes at a 'Rock Against Racism' concert; the assassin of EDWARD II (1991 C); real-life mass murderer John Wayne Gacy (Brian Dennehy) in *To Catch a Killer* (1991 T); from an earlier era, Richard Loeb (Daniel Schlachet) and Nathan Leopold Jr (Craig Chester) in *Swoon* (1992 C); Catherine (Sharon Stone), bisexual prime suspect in a series of grisly sex killings in *Basic Instinct* (1992 C) – other suspects include lesbian killers: Roxanne Hardy (Leilani Sarelle) and Hazel Dobkin (Dorothy Malone); Luke (Mike Dytri) who dispatched two queer-bashing punks in THE LIVING END (1992 C); teenager Stephen Durrant (Marc Murphy) who kills the boy who saw him with a male lover in *Death Drop* (1992 R); Julian Sands as the bringer of simultaneous sexual climax and death during same-sex coitus in *Naked Lunch* (1992 C).

murder victims Homosexuals in fiction meet all kinds of sad, lonely and gruesome ends.

Gay men: Piers Gaveston (beheaded) and Edward (tortured and then killed by red-hot poker up his rectum) in EDWARD II; Basil Hallward in THE PICTURE OF DORIAN GRAY; Lindsay Marriott in *Farewell, My Lovely*; Mr DULCIMER in THE GREEN BAY TREE; the informer in *Brute Force*; Plato in REBEL WITHOUT A CAUSE; Sandy in *House of Bamboo*; Sebastian in SUDDENLY LAST SUMMER; the hairdresser in VICTIM; SOFTLY, SOFTLY 'Murder Reported'; transvestite in *No Way to Treat a Lady*; Teddy in THE DETECTIVE, head smashed in with STATUE and penis cut off; Toto dispatched with a hat pin in his jugular in *Justine*; amorous lorry driver in *The Looking Glass War*; Ernst ROEHM and SA members in THE DAMNED; decadent aesthete shot by an arrow in *The Creeper*; the Warlock thrown out of a window in *The Kremlin Letter*; Ludwig II; a number of corpses in *Police Story* 'The Ripper'; film director in *The Last of Sheila*; ANTIQUE DEALERS in *Blacula*; elderly man in Brighton in UPSTAIRS DOWNSTAIRS 'Rose's Pigeon'; man in steam bath in *The Day of the Jackal*; old man bludgeoned in *The Internecine Project*; Miles Mellough in *The Eiger Sanction*; diplomat in *Permission to Kill*; butler in *The Pink Panther Strikes Again* (1976 C); SEBASTIANE tortured and pincushioned with arrows; accountant and lover in *The Man Who Fell to Earth* thrown out of window and crushed under barbells respectively; governor in *Swashbuckler/ The Scarlet Buccaneer* stabbed; reverend decapitated in A SUPERSTITION; the twins in JUBILEE; policeman in STARSKY AND HUTCH 'Death in a Different Place'; chauffeur in *The Big Sleep*; the mole in TINKER, TAILOR, SOLDIER, SPY; guardsman in THE GENTLE TOUCH 'Blade'; gangster in *The Long Good Friday*; various men in CRUISING and PARTNERS; Winckelmann killed by a cook in the 18th century – an event which haunts a man of the 20th century in *Death in Trieste*; Steven's lovers, Ted Dinard and Luke Fuller, in DYNASTY;

film star Mack Crawford shot by his son in *Celebrity* (1983 T); Michael probably fatally drugged by his own mother in LA MUERTE DE MIKEL (1984 C); Ronald MERRICK ritually murdered in THE JEWEL IN THE CROWN; Molina shot by police in KISS OF THE SPIDER WOMAN; Rannucio, model and sometime lover of CARAVAGGIO, stabbed; TCHAIKOVSKY forced to take poison – according to THE MISSING DAY; Pablo's lover thrown over a cliff in LAW OF DESIRE; pick-up stabbed many times in *The Fourth Protocol* (1987 C); drug peddler's lover Aubrey mutilated, possibly sodomized with weapon in *Floodtide* while his lover is given a massive heroin overdose; Joe ORTON battered by lover in PRICK UP YOUR EARS; drag queen in THE FRUIT MACHINE; Arnold's lover, Alan QUEER-BASHED in TORCH-SONG TRILOGY; poet killed by firing squad in *Lorca: Death of a Poet*; Vincent queer-bashed in OCTOBER SCARS THE SKIN; man on the heath in YOUNG SOUL REBELS; Cyril, gossip columnist stung by a bee and left to die in AN INCONVENIENT WOMAN (1991 T); Simon in *G.P.* 'Tests of Conscience' (1992 T) bashed to death with iron bar; Chris shot with his own gun by two pick-ups in *The Boys Next Door* (1984 C); etc. (Real-life murders of gay men discussed in *The London Show* 'Gay Murders' 1990 T and on news programmes in 1993.)

Lesbian victims: schoolgirl in *Miss Pym Disposes*; *The Girl with the Golden Eyes*; heroine's friend in *Who Killed Teddy Bear?*; scientist in *Fraulein Doktor*; Why in LES BICHES; Lori in *Doctors' Wives*; Roxanne in *Beyond the Valley of the Dolls*; prostitute in *Hands of the Ripper*; prostitute and one wife in *Bluebeard*; student in *The Midnight Man*; Frances Amthor, madam in *Farewell, My Lovely* (1975); LULU and GESCHWITZ in *Lulu* and THE SOUTH BANK SHOW 'Lulu's Last Act'; blackmailed woman in IN THE GLITTER PALACE; models in *Eyes of Laura Mars*; one of the relatives in *The Cat and the Canary*; Judy Morris in *Skyways* (found in shower with 57 stab wounds); television director's assistant in *Someone's Watching Me*; novelist in *Lovekill*; secretary's lover in *The Left-*

Handed Sleeper (1982 R); one of the lovers in *Death of an Expert Witness*; spinster strangled while putting out washing in *Miss Marple* 'A Murder Has Been Announced'; lover in *In Two Minds*; Cije in *Knots Landing*; etc.

Murdoch, Iris (1919–) English novelist, most of whose books contain wonderfully complex characters and situations reaching out across a wide spectrum of desire. Those filmed or dramatized for television: *A Severed Head*; *An Unofficial Rose*; *The Bell*. She appeared on THE SOUTH BANK SHOW (1989 T) and on *Bookmark* (1987 T) where three excerpts from *An Unofficial Rose* and *The Bell* featuring gay characters (but no lesbian ones) were shown, uncontexted and used without any seeming relevance to the foregoing discussion.

music Loaded with emotion; its connotations, subtle and persuasive, embracing a whole range of drives and desires. As Duffy CLAYTON says in DIXON OF DOCK GREEN (1956 T): 'That's the amazing thing. It's abstract, my dear fellow and you can make it mean whatever you want to ... Music doesn't tie you down like books.'

Classical music used in a homosexual context includes THE BLUE DANUBE WALTZ in MY BEAUTIFUL LAUNDRETTE (1985 C/T); the Prelude to Act 1 of *Lohengrin* for the education of Verena (Madeleine Potter) by Olive (Vanessa REDGRAVE) in *The Bostonians* (1984 C); and, from Mahler's 5th Symphony, the adagio for harp and strings composed in 1902 and taken at a lugubrious pace in DEATH IN VENICE (1971 C) – which rekindled interest in Mahler's whole repertoire.

Dennis Potter's television trilogy – *Pennies from Heaven* (1978), *The Singing Detective* (1986) and *Lipstick on Your Collar* (1993) – is probably the best known example of the use of (1930s, 1940s and 1950s respectively) popular music to reveal deep longings. But gay film-makers like Kenneth Anger (*Scorpio Rising* 1963), Stuart MARSHALL

(COMRADES IN ARMS) and Terence DAVIES (*Distant Voices, Still Lives*) have shown that this method of filling in gaps or telling a whole story through popular song can be just as effective in a full or oblique homosexual context.

Drew GRIFFITHS' THE ONLY ONE SOUTH OF THE RIVER (Capital Radio 1980) had a legitimate reason to feature pop music as the play was set in and around a pub disco during 1978. 'Macho Man' introduced the yobbo who will eventually bring about the closure of 'the only one south of the river'. The opening night appears to be a disaster ('Boogie No More'), but a flood of people arrive after 10 pm and the night ends with a smoochy 'Last Chance For Love'. Months pass ('As Time Goes By'). There is a misunderstanding, during which the publican's wife stands by the gay DJ John ('Thank You For Being A Friend'). The disco, nonetheless, goes from strength to strength ('YMCA'). John is asked to be the DJ for the yobbo son's 18th birthday party which, unlike the gay nights, is drunken and aggressive ('Do You Think I'm Sexy?'; 'Hit Me With Your Rhythm Stick'). There is a fight; John is blamed and told never to come near the pub again. The play ends with John ringing his lover and says he's bringing home a new record. It's called 'I Will Survive'.

Noticeable is the almost complete absence of 'love themes', lyrical pieces specifically written for gay or lesbian lovers. In *Brideshead Revisited* (1981 T) the nearest Geoffrey Burgon gets to it is 'Sebastian's Summer' which adds harp and a few sublime passages to the sonorously elegiac main theme as Sebastian and Charles enjoy each other's company in the Oxfordshire countryside. Almost the only other example is Stanley Myers' charming theme from PRICK UP YOUR EARS (1987 C), but it comes only during the end credits when both men are dead and turned to ash.

musical Winston Churchill, asked for a description of sex with Noel COWARD, allegedly proffered but one word: 'musical'.

'Well you always were musical,' GRYT-PYPE-THYNNE murmurs to MORIARTY in THE GOON SHOW 'The Jet-Propelled Guided NAAFI' (1956 R); the latter later hides in the elastic of Grytpype's underpants. EASTENDERS (1985 T) had the dedicated heterosexual Wicksy (Nick Berry) say 'I'm musical' for a doubly meant in-joke. The young boy Laszlo (Corrin Helliwell) in *A Room in Budapest* (1990 R) speaks of the 'charmingly musical captain' he has met. Noting that the only nice men are gay, Kay McLennan introduced some 'very nice and very musical men' – the New York Gay Men's Chorus giving voice to Michael Praetorius's 'Lo How Air Rose Ablooming' on *Sacred Music* (Aust 1991 R).

Music and the G word were almost inseparable during the 1950s. This is but a small sample: 'A gay Scottish musical' (Robert Kemp's *The Highland Fair* 1953 T); six concerts of gay music in *Light Music Festival* (1956 R); 'The gay and exciting rhythm of the Van Wood Quartet' (1958 R); 'Eurovision takes you to Paris for a gay Bank Holiday show' (*Paris by Night* 1958 T); 'The gay eventful career of the star whom millions remember with affection' (Ivor NOVELLO 1958 R); 'A frank glorious gaiety' (the Brahms–Simon musical *Titania Had a Mother* 1959 R).

musicians Pepe (Eli Wallach), saxophonist and casino robber in *Seven Thieves* (1960 C); John (Brock Peters) in THE L-SHAPED ROOM (1962 C); sleek, seductive Pablo (Pierre Clementi) in *Steppenwolf* (1974 C); *The Potsdam Quartet* (1981 T) including a squabbling gay couple, playing Mozart and Bartok to generals and politicians who own part of the world and are engaged in carving it up. *See also* PIANISTS.

My Beautiful Laundrette (UK 1985 T) A young Anglo-Pakistani and his racist former schoolfriend become partners – in business and in bed – to make a go of a run-down launderette. W: Hanif Kureishi; P: Sarah Radclyffe and Tim Bevan; D: Stephen Frears; 94 mins.

Racism falls victim to the hormone fairy. Made for Channel 4 but shown – to great acclaim – in cinemas first, yet still gaining large audiences (2–4 millions) for five television showings between 1987 and 1993. Witty, observant script combine with a fascinating blend of issues and a totally convincing performance from Daniel Day-Lewis as tearaway, former Paki-basher Johnny to make this one of British television's finest hours (and a half). A small rainbow arching over a confused and grimy cityscape. But not everyone liked it.

A letter to *TV Times* on the occasion of the film's first home screening indicated that it had everything (racism, violence, bad language, extra-marital relations, homosexuality) but the humour the viewer had been led to expect from the high repute in which it was held. When shown on Australian television, there were 10 complaints to the switchboard of the ABC (8.6.90). These included: 'We will never watch ABC TV again' 'Not fit for people to watch' and 'Seeing two POOFTERS kissing is degrading. Please ask the presenter to announce the disgusting scenes like this when the film is shown.'

My Buddy The elegiac 1922 ballad of a soldier reminiscing about 'gay times' with his pal. One of the most tender love songs sung by a man to another, it was popularized by Al Jolson and later by Bing Crosby and especially Frank Sinatra in the 1940s. It provided the perfect accompaniment to shots of men in arms, and in each other's arms, during the Second World and Korean wars in BEFORE STONEWALL (1984 C/T). Doris DAY sang it (to Danny Thomas playing her screen husband Gus Kahn, who wrote the lyrics to Walter Donaldson's melody) in *I'll See You in My Dreams* (1951 C).

my dear/my dears A favourite device to indicate a certain propensity in male characters of a certain age; eg Stephen LYNN (Valentine DYALL) in BRIEF ENCOUNTER (1945 C); Adrian Lee (Alan WHEATLEY) in *Simon and Laura* (1955 C): 'My dears, what a divine room ... she's *absolute* heaven'; Uncle Willie (John GIELGUD) in *Scandalous* (1984 C); Henry Cawardine (John Franklyn-Robbins) in *The Black Tower* (1985 T).

My Forgotten Man The heartstopping finale of *Gold Diggers of 1933* (1933 C). An unsurpassed combination of social criticism and schmaltz (lyrics by Al Dubin, music by Harry Warren) with Joan Blondell reminding the audience of the men who, having fought in the First World War, returned to face disillusionment, unemployment and near-starvation. It contains the line 'Ever since the world began, a woman's *got* to have a man', and this may be the reason why the music is so strongly featured in *Female* (1933 C) about a woman (Ruth Chatterton) who uses men like tissues. 'Mannish' and with a gay secretary but deep down is looking for a big strong man to pamper her.

My Friend Charles (UK 1956 T) Many of Francis Durbridge's serials feature unmarried men of hinted depravity and no visible means of support. Kenny (Francis Matthews), friend of the hero Dr Howard Latimer (Stephen Murray), says he has lots of girlfriends, but he mentions no names and there is not so much as a stray stocking in his chi-chi flat. A policeman is not fooled by Kenny's bluster. He tells the hero: 'Your friend has some strange tastes if I may say so, sir'.
P: Alan Bromly; 8.7.–16.8.56; BBC.

My Hustler (US 1965 C) Andy WARHOL's 70-minute comedy about four people, a beach and a beach house on Fire Island. Ed (Ed Hood) is a great upmarket queen – vowels drawled, head bald, glasses dark, manner that of a Roman emperor (and looking not unlike Roy COHN). With his friend Genevieve (Genevieve Charbon), he watches the beach deserted except for his holiday purchase, Paul (Paul America). Topics discussed mainly involve the length and colour of Paul's hair, his chest hair (but not the little clumps at the top of his shoulder blades).

Ed guesses correctly that Genevieve wants to bed Paul – she's a FAG HAG after all. Then new competition arrives in the squat shape of the Sugar Plum Fairy (Joseph Campbell). Genevieve and Paul frolic in the waves as Ed and Joey elaborate on the actual and likely charms of Paul. Ed languidly wagers that neither Genevieve nor Joey will get their man. Quick cut to Ed's guest bathroom. Joey gets into the shower as Paul steps out. Slowly Joey gets the conversation round to hustling and a kind of seduction ensues. To those used to Warhol's previous films, *My Hustler* was a surprise. Gone was the burpy cutting, the stoned repartee, the 'white outs'. Here was a fully fledged gay social comedy that COWARD or WILDE would have felt quite at home in. (This was the first Warhol film to be shown – in the late 1980s – on British television.)

My Love Is Like A Red, Red Rose Robert Burns' words sung by Pat Boone to Diane Baker in *Journey to the Centre of the Earth* (1959 C), but cut from many release prints. They were also sung by Angel (Ian CHARLESON, with genuine Scottish intonation although the character is a Londoner) while in bed with his brother/lover Sphinx, and Sphinx's new-found love Viv, in JUBILEE (1977 C). In the film's Britain, rapidly dying from media manipulation, street violence, high-rise alienation and pollution, the simple sentiments of the song as a defence against a loveless universe are all the more poignant.

My Man (Mon Homme) Mistinguett dedicated 'arguably the very first torch song' to her bisexual American dancer lover, Harry Picer. The American version was popularized by Fanny Brice, and Barbra STREISAND climaxed *Funny Girl* (1968 C) with a blazing rendition. Craig RUSSELL also full-throated it (dressed as Barbra) in *Outrageous Too/ Too Outrageous* (1987 C).

My Own Private Idaho (USA 1991 C) Outcast Mike Waters (River Phoenix) who suffers from narcolepsy and his friend, from the right side of the tracks, Scott Favor (Keanu Reeves) sell their bodies in Seattle. Includes interviews with real working boys and updates HENRY IV PART I.
W/D: Gus Van Sant; P: Laurie Parker; 102 mins.

Sex is little seen and the preferences of Mike and Scott unclear in a film uncomfortably displaying a range of stylistic skills. Burdens of the past, sweetened by dreams, attempt to create a world of comfort and communion, passing relationships, entering other people's lives and yet making no impact. One character is self-contained and purposeful, a member of the world's oldest profession possibly en route for the world's second oldest; the other anxious, apprehensive, on the highway to nowhere. Both boys are locked in the same defeat; death in life, the life of quiet desperation.

My Own Way Home (UK 1978 C) In the third part of the trilogy by Bill Douglas, Jamie wants to study art but, after running away from his foster home and living rough, he returns to his Scottish mining village to find his father's home deserted. He meets the educated Robert while doing his national service in Egypt. On their return to England, Robert invites Jamie to come and stay with him.
W/D: Bill Douglas; 78 mins.

'. . . there is a scene of Jamie and Robert in a rare moment of pleasure in the nonsense routines of National Service, which ends with an abrupt cut at the point at which Jamie has put his head against his friend's shoulders. Almost subliminal, I had to replay to make sure that this moment of physical affection had taken place. The almost obsessive reticence which underplays these moments is not prurient, it is simply uncertain: a fragility within the films around the possibility of sustaining relationships. And yet these glimpsed moments ground the films emotionally, opening them to complex possibilities rather than burying them in easy despair' (John Caughie, *Sight and Sound*, November 1991).

The Myth Makers (UK 1958 T) Alan Swift, a restless young film star, is worshipped after his death. His widow (Pat English) wants to tell the truth: she loved him when they first married but couldn't give him 'the kind of love he needed'. His mother (Kate Reid) believes that the cult surrounding her son is 'wrong and dangerous'. She astonishes the crowd, during a hyped-up tribute, by attempting to reveal feet of clay: 'Hail the misfit! That's what he was – or didn't they tell you.'
W: William Bast; D: Silvio NARIZZANO; 16.4.58; Granada; 90 mins.

'The basic theme of this play appears to be that he who digs a pit for others usually falls into it himself. Jerry Ross, a man of 40, confident, sharp, helped to place Alan Swift on a pedestal. Alan was a fine actor but Jerry could not leave it at that. He concocted a legend and, when Alan died in a fire in his Malibu Beach home, Jerry sent out the story that he had tried to save his wife from the flames. "They think what they're told to think," he says of the star's fans. "If I'd told them he was trapped because he passed out dead drunk, they'd believe that instead. But this way he is a nice guy. He gets a hero's tribute and Falcon Pictures gets some sensational publicity"' (*TV Times* synopsis).

My Two Loves (US 1986 T) Mother and daughter (Sada Thompson and Mariette Hartley) come to blows because of the direction the former's life has taken after widowhood. Lynn REDGRAVE is the lesbian threat who says all the right things, looks great, holds down a good job, exercises etc. Having come across a little unexpected complexity, the heroine moves on (whither we know not) to become a better heterosexual/bisexual in the process.
W: Rita Mae BROWN and Reginald Rose; D: Noel Black; 100 mins.

An earnest approximation of the truth, with a cheerful Lynn Redgrave adding the only lustre to predictable proceedings. But this was lesbianism on primetime US television which didn't involve (1) murder, (2) BLACKMAIL and (3) a CHILD CUSTODY case.

naff/naph Now widely used after Princess Anne told intrusive cameramen to naff off at the Badminton Horse Trials in 1983. But JULIAN AND SANDY – dipping into their ganderbag of POLARI (where it means 'bad') – were in royalty's vanguard or, to use yer actual French, in its *avant-garde*: 'I had a naff experience in Bognor,' says Jule tremulously, 'and when I've been on the gin, it wells up' (*Round the Horne* 'Bona Caterers' 1967 R).

Boosted by the princess, 'naff' marched on into the far reaches of family viewing, finally becoming part of the fun and games (a 'naff' quiz) in the 1990 British *Telethon*, the final accolade to a word which combined with 'off' could be taken to mean something very rude indeed.

'It's naff ... meganaff,' says THE DOCTOR's assistant, Ace (Sophie Aldred) in *Doctor Who* 'Dragonfire' (1987 T) (Ace describes herself as 'a 16-year-old yompy sort of person').

'I'm an honourable man,' says the lecturer (Struan Rodger) in *Show Me the Way, Ugly Angels* (1990 R). 'I don't mess around with students. Naff, eh?' (But the female student proves irresistible and he allows her to have her way with him half a minute later.)

Den (Leslie Grantham) didn't use the word at all until he goes to prison in EASTENDERS (1989 T). Then he tells queer Queenie (John Labanowski) and Nick Cotton (John Altman) singly and together to 'naff off' or to get out of his 'naffing' way. Gerry (Buki Armstrong) is the most recent exclaimer (to Dieter in ELDORADO 1992 T).

The exact meaning of the word is unclear. It could have come from NAAFI or from the backwards spelling of fan/fanny (after FANNY HILL) or from *naf*, the French word for NAVEL. Partridge in *A Dictionary of Slang* hazards a guess that it may derive from 'not available for a fun/fucking'.

When asked by the Australian *Sixty Minutes* programme in 1984 what it means, BOY GEORGE didn't mince words: 'Naff is "stupid". I don't want people to say, "He looks like a poof but he can sing." Up yours, man! I don't *want* your approval.'

nail filing *See* FINGERNAIL FILING.

The Naked Civil Servant (UK 1975 T) The story of Quentin CRISP, sometime artist's model, sometime PROSTITUTE, full-time exhibitionist and focus for people's fears and frustrations.
W: Philip Mackie from the book by Quentin Crisp; P: Verity Lambert; D: Jack Gold; Thames; 100 mins; also shown 1976, 1984, 1989 (as part of Thames' 21st anniversary celebration) and 1991 (on BBC2 as part of SATURDAY NIGHT OUT).

John HURT won every award going for his performance in this film, which Thames TV had adopted after the BBC had given it the thumbs down. Its success set Quentin himself down the starry slide from which, unlike others, he has gratefully never jumped off.

It was a quantum leap. It made at least one man's life (involving sex with men, tireless devotion and Christian charity) acceptable and appropriate to the British public. According to a survey by the Independent Broadcasting Authority, only 18 out of a sample 475 viewers switched off because of the content. And 85 per cent said that the production was 'not shocking'. Few felt that Crisp's story 'encouraged' homosexuality. (No survey has ever asked if, for example, CORONATION STREET encourages heterosexuality.)

Writing in the DAILY MAIL in the late 1970s, Martin Jackson, primarily concerned about the IBA's banning of the sex education primer SEX IN OUR TIME (one of whose segments was entitled 'For "Queer" Read Gay'), asked whether the Crisp story succeeded 'because public taste had moved on to be ready for it, or was acceptability extended overnight by *The Naked Civil Servant?*'

The historical setting (1930s and 1940s Soho and environs), the brazen effeminacy of Crisp and the saintliness of his actions may all have contributed to the public's benign acceptance. The

IBA, in allowing the programme to be screened in its entirety (save the MAS-TURBATION in the bath), conjectured that 'Attitudes ... towards homosexual behaviour [sic] will be conditioned to a large extent by the way in which the subject is presented'.

John Hurt saw it another way. 'Many people said don't do it. Don't do it, career-wise. And I must confess that it wasn't an immediate decision. There's been a history of unfortunate events when people have played homosexuals. But there's nothing like playing a HERO and he is a hero.' He went on: 'If I could deliver that line [of Quentin's] about never closing my hand, not even to the unloveable, then I would pat myself on the back. I've too often turned my back ... I'm not trying to sanctify him ... He was a man who wanted to love other men. And he did bring it to the surface ... He did' (*Gay News* 89, 1976).

'A man who stands against all the others ... He has more love than any church could offer, more tenderness than any corporate body of charity' (writer Robert Bolt quoted in a letter to John Hurt).

'It had incredible impact. I watched it while my parents were at a works dinner. I knew they would be back at midnight and it didn't finish until 12.30. I sat near to the on–off switch in case they came back. By the third showing I had come out, so we watched it together. It was tense-making because I wanted them to like it' (writer and media lecturer Andy Medhurst, interviewed by Keith Howes, July 1992).

nakedness Women have been everywhere unclothed: in the museums and art galleries, on posters and in the cinema almost from its beginning, the Italian *Idolo Infranto* in 1913 being the first extant example. It was followed by 'The Naked Truth' in Lois Weber's *The Hypocrites* (1915); Audrey Munson in George Foster Platt's *Inspiration* 1915 (she played an artist's model in this and again in *Purity* 1916); swimmer Annette Kellerman in *Daughter of the Gods*; Ira Rina in Gustav Machaty's *Eroticon*

(1929); then Hedy Lamarr in *Extase* (1933) and films from (Nazi) Germany and Scandinavia. Brigitte Bardot became an international sensation after baring her bottom just once in *God Created Woman* (1956). Her American counterpart, Marilyn Monroe would have been the first Hollywood star to be seen without clothes had she not died before *Something's Got to Give* (1962) could be completed. The deluge began with Anne Heywood in THE FOX and Jane Fonda in *Barbarella* in the late 1960s, and involved starlets, glamour stars as well as actresses like Glenda Jackson, Katherine Schofield and Helen Mirren.

For men, it was a slower, more underground business, though the first full front male was thought to have been seen in *Dante's Inferno*, from Italy in 1912. Then a long gap until exposure by one of the prisoners in UN CHANT D'AMOUR (1950) of the lower part of his body. Some complete nudity in the very early Andy WARHOL films, as well as the more widely released MY HUSTLER (1965) where Joseph Campbell chats in the shower after Paul America has stepped out of it. The first major male star to bare himself was intended to be Rock HUDSON in the wine-treading sequence in *Seconds* (1966 C), but the scene was reshot. Terence Stamp undressed completely in THEOREM (1968), but the shower scene involving Malcolm McDowell, Richard Warwick and David Wood in IF (1968) was cut after the press show (it reportedly contained an erection); Joe DALLESANDRO, playing a hustler, was naked for whole sections of FLESH (1968) and *Trash* (1970); Robert Forster removed his underpants in *Medium Cool* (1969, after being seen from afar in REFLECTIONS IN A GOLDEN EYE two years before); then Alan BATES and Oliver Reed wrestled in WOMEN IN LOVE (1969; Bates also strides through long and not-so-long grass near the beginning) and Mick Jagger lay between two women in PERFORMANCE (1970, but scene cut).

By this time, male nudity had become international: Don Johnson in *The Magic*

Garden of Stanley Sweetheart (1970); *Woodstock* (bathing in river, walking through grass, 1970); Norman Manzon in *What Do You Say to a Naked Lady?* (1970); John Karlen in *Daughters of Darkness/Le Rouge aux Lèvres* (1971); Robert Walker Jr in *The Road to Salina* (1971); *The Canterbury Tales* (1972); Alain Delon in *Traitment de Choc/The Doctor in the Nude* (1972); John Moulder-Brown in *King Queen Knave* (1972); Martin Kove in *Women in Revolt* (1972); Rutger Hauer in *Danish Blue* (1973) and also in *Spetters* (1980); Jack Thompson as *Petersen* (1974); Graeme Blundell as *Alvin Purple* (1974) and in *Alvin Purple Rides Again* (1975); Peter Schlesinger and David HOCKNEY in *A Bigger Splash* (1974); *Arabian Nights* (1974); Jan-Michael Vincent in *Buster and Billie* (1974 C); Helmut Berger in CONVERSATION PIECE (1975) and *Salon Kitty* (1976 C, wearing only a Nazi armband in a sauna scene); Perry King in *Mandingo* (1975); Robert Aberdeen and Don Scotti in *Saturday Night at the Baths* (1975); Robert De Niro and Gérard Depardieu in *1900* (1975); most young cast members of SALO: THE 120 DAYS OF SODOM (1975); the cast of SEBASTIANE (1976) save for Barney James (who also covered up as the Special Branch cop in JUBILEE); Gérard Depardieu in THE LAST WOMAN (1975); Rip Torn in *The Man Who Fell to Earth* (1976); Anthony Meyer in *Hamlet* (1976); John HURT in *East of Elephant Rock* (1977); Ian CHARLESON and Karl Johnson in JUBILEE (1977); Peter Firth in *Equus* (1977); Franco Nero and Patrick Dewaere in *Victory March* (1978); most of the young members of the cast of *Private Vices, Public Virtues* (1978); Serge Avedikian in WE WERE ONE MAN (1979); Treat Williams in *Hair* (1979); Tom Berenger in *In Praise of Older Women* (1978); Bill Adler in *Van Nuys Boulevard* (1979); Richard Gere in *American Gigolo* (1980); Peter Fonda in *Outlaw Blues* (1980); Christopher Atkins in *The Blue Lagoon* (1980); David Meyer in *The Tempest* (1980); Malcolm McDowall in *Caligula* (1980); John GIELGUD in *The Conductor* (1980); Frank Ripploh in TAXI

ZUM KLO (1981); Bruno Ganz in *Circle of Deceit* (1981); Nicholas Clay in *Lady Chatterley's Lover* (1981); Ian MCKELLEN in *Priest of Love* (1981); Malcolm McDowall in *Britannia Hospital* (1982); Peter Gallagher in *Summer Lovers* (1982); Michael Feast in *The Draughtsman's Contract* (1982); Richard Gere in *Breathless* (1983); Gene Davis in *Ten to Midnight* (1983); Tom Cruise in *All the Right Moves* (1983, possibly a body double-insert shot); Christopher Atkins in *A Night in Heaven* (1983 C); Charlie Martin Smith in *Never Cry Wolf* (1983); Albert Finney in *Under the Volcano* (1984); John HURT in *1984* (1984); Gérard Depardieu in TENUE DE SOIREE/EVENING DRESS (1984); Eric and Brian Deacon as twins Oliver and Oswald in *A Zed & Two Noughts* (1983, in at least four scenes); David Keith in *Gulag* (1985); Rupert Graves, Julian Sands and Simon CALLOW in *A Room with a View* (1985); Julian Sands in *Gothic* (1986); Rupert Graves in MAURICE (1987); Tim Streeter in MALA NOCHE (1987); Eusebio Poncela in LAW OF DESIRE (1987); LOOKING FOR LANGSTON (1988); Willem Dafoe in *The Last Temptation of Christ* (1988); Viggo Mortensen in *The Indian Runner* (1991); Michael Clarke, John GIELGUD and others in *Prospero's Books* (1991); Robin Williams as Parry communing with nature in New York's Central Park in *The Fisher King* (1991); NORTH OF VORTEX (1991); Marco Hofschneider in *Europa, Europa* (1991); two sailors in EDWARD II (1991); a group of mystical men (and women) in *House of Angels* (1991); Clive Owen in *Close My Eyes* (1991); Michael Douglas in BASIC INSTINCT (1992, back view, with testicles only; also features a corpse's penis); character in *The Crying Game* (1992 C).

Mainstream American television continues to protect its viewers from the full impact of the male form. In a shower scene in *Thirtysomething* 'I'm Nobody Who Are You' (1990 T) a man asks the first part of a question 'naked' and, courtesy of sharp cut, finishes off asking the question wearing trousers and a shirt.

In Britain male nudity is accepted, if fleetingly. Usually it comprises a shower sequence or a strategically obscured (by leaves or murky water) dip in rivers or lakes. Kenneth Cranham and Paul GREENHALGH bathing in a lake would have been the first completely uncovered scene in *Boy Meets Girl* 'The Eye of Heaven' (1968), but it was cut. The BBC finally took the plunge in 1970. Complaints (by guess who) predictably greeted the frontals of actors in *The Lie* and one of the *Somerset* MAUGHAM stories and, apart from Tony Meyer jumping out of bed without pyjamas in A LIFE IS FOREVER (1972), very few males have been seen fully naked outside of feature films – though wishful thinking and possibly poor reception have led many people to imagine that such sights have been authorized for national consumption.

Excellent eyesight was needed to check whether Michael Maloney (in *The Bell* 1982) and Daniel Day-Lewis (in *How Many Miles To Babylon?* 1982) were wearing microscopic black pouches or not in their bathing scenes. Back views only of Michael Maloney again in *Sharma and Beyond* (1983), of Stuart Wilson and Art Malik in THE JEWEL IN THE CROWN (1984), and of Anthony Andrews and Jeremy Irons sunbathing in BRIDESHEAD REVISITED (1981). The only honestly revealing scenes took place in ACCOUNTS (Michael McNally doing pressups in the showers) and John Duttine in *Psy-Warriors* (1981), both involving coercion, with elements of sadism. There was also a fairly slow disrobing (by Nick Reding) in a flashback (complete with vaselined lens) in *Oscar* (1985). Alan Howard fell downstairs dead and starkers in *A Better Class of Person* (1983) and Anthony Andrews cleansed himself under a waterfall in the post-nuclear holocaust drama, *Z For Zachariah* (1984). Compare these with the fairly relaxed stroll out of bed without a stitch on of John Moulder-Brown in the German production, *The Confessions of Felix Krull* (1983).

The only recent completely-and-utterly-naked-as-nature-intended males have been Rudolf NUREYEV in the final credits sequence (bathing off his private island) in *Nureyev* (1991); Alistair Mac-Fadyen in THE LOST LANGUAGE OF CRANES (1992); Tony Poli in the Australian police series *Phoenix* (1992). And, of course, the NATURISTS enjoying swimming, sauna and chatting at the bar in *Open Space* 'Full Frontal' (1992).

While female actors are expected to be fully or semi-naked in sex scenes, their male counterparts can be wearing anything from baggy shorts to a track suit without their partner raising the slightest question of its inaptness for the business at hand. And if there is a suggestion of all-out nudity, long shots will reveal miraculous quick change artistry – as when, in *Secret Weapon* (Aust 1991 T), the hero is lying apparently naked in bed waiting for his girlfriend to emerge from the bathroom. Three men burst in, restrain him and chain him to the bed. In these few seconds, he has somehow managed to grab a pair of boxer shorts and pull them on.

If the male actor is older than his female partner, it is almost certain that he will be barricaded by voluminous shorts or sheets held up to the chin or clavicle while she will be stitchless (Marlon Brando in *Last Tango in Paris* 1972 C; Oliver Reed in *Castaway* 1986 C; Alan BATES – once so free-spirited – in *Unnatural Pursuits* 1992 T). Even if the actor is young (eg Paul McGann in *The Monocled Mutineer*), he may be fully clothed while his partner exposes everything or her torso. The man will carefully cover himself as he rises from the sheets. There may be a whisper of pubic hair (*Tender Is the Night* (1985) or a flash (*Cause Célèbre* 1987; *The Men's Room* 1991).

When Gus MacDonald announced (on *Right to Reply* 1985 T) that 'We've got round the problem of nudity by showing a scene where most of the cast are lying face down', he was talking about the 'problem' of male genitalia, not female. The film was SEBASTIANE (1976 C), the showing of which (fairly late at night) had provoked some upset among Channel 4 viewers.

A discussion between Clive James and Oliver Reed in 1987 on 'blokes stripping off on screen' was quickly drawn to a conclusion by Mr Reed (18 years on from *Women in Love*): 'I find the subject matter of a woman's body more interesting than a man's.' Audience laughter. On to the next topic ...

Strange that, as inheritors of a visual art tradition where at certain periods the male nude reigned supreme, there is a virtual taboo imposed with no sign of the fig leaf being removed. The ARENA programme on Robert MAPPLETHORPE was coyness incarnate while telling viewers that it was celebrating an artist who 'has been instrumental in the restoration of the male nude to a primary place in mainstream art'. Virtually the only 1992 programmes where the camera was free to stop and stare at male flesh, muscle and hair were the first part of Ian Gibson's portrait of Spain, *Fire in the Blood*, and John Byrne's exploration of MICHELANGELO in *Without Walls* 'Dark Horses'. In both cases the object of the intense scrutiny – David – was inanimate, and a universally acclaimed work of art, crafted by someone who lived hundreds of years ago. (The Spanish one was an exact replica used – and then burnt – in a festival.)

'[With all the female nudity] (beginning with *Black Eyes* in 1989, continuing with *The Men's Room*, *The Camomile Lawn*, *A Sense of Guilt*, *A Fatal Inversion*, *A Time to Dance*, *Anglo-Saxon Attitudes* and *Friday on My Mind*) should there be more naked men to even up the score? Or do women really prefer to look at women's bodies?' (Jennifer Selway, *Observer Magazine*, 21.6.92; she estimated that the average age of the male in British television sex scenes was 49 and of the female 23.5).

See also BUTTOCKS; JOCKEY SHORTS VERSION; MICHELANGELO'S DAVID; NATURISM; PENISES.

names *See* BOYS' NAMES FOR GIRLS; FIRST NAMES; GIRLS' NAMES FOR BOYS; NICKNAMES; SURNAMES.

Nancy Girl's name (a pet form of Ann/ Anne) which has proved remarkably resilient for tarts (in *Oliver Twist* Kay Walsh 1948 C, Carmel McSharry 1962 T and Cherie Lunghi 1984 T; Shani Wallis in *Oliver!* 1968 C); tomboys (Louise BROOKS in *Beggars of Life* 1928 C – 'looks attractive even in men's clothes,' said *Variety*; virgins (Rita Tushingham in *The Knack* 1965 C; Lori Martin, the daughter in *Cape Fear* 1962 C – she was 'Danni' in the 1992 remake); yuppies (Melinda Dillon in *Harry and the Hendersons* 1987 C and *Bigfoot and the Hendersons* 1988 T; Patricia Wettig in *Thirtysomething* 1988–91 T); chummy lesbians (Sandra Bernhard in *Roseanne* 1992– T).

nancy/nancy boy Used about 'Victor' (Jessie Matthews) by Robert (Griffith Jones) in FIRST A GIRL (1935 C); about Ray Calvert (Tim Morand) in the 1950s-set LATE CALL; about a close relative of a US president in a 1981 *Not the Nine O'Clock News* sketch ('When he spoke of Nancy he was, of course, referring to his wife and not to his son'); by Cyril (Ronald Baddiley) to his fellow tramp (Freddie Jones) about the latter's young boyfriend in *The Mist People* (1982 R): 'An old man like you and a nancy boy. It's disgusting!' The taciturn Peter (Leonard Preston), having been chided for his disparaging remarks about an older man and a much younger one enjoying a trip on the Thames in THE GROUNDLING AND THE KITE (1984 T), turns to his lover Jimmy and grunts: 'What's it to you what I say about a couple of nancy boys?' One of the contributors to the THE SOUTH BANK SHOW's portrait of 'Ray Cooney' in 1986 said that the producer of successful West end farces gave the public what it wanted: 'nancy boys and bare bums.'

nancy girls In a street survey (broadcast on Radio London's breakfast programme in February 1981) the habit of men interlocking arms as they walk together was dismissed by some passersby as definitely un-British ('You see it on the Continent, but we know about these Continentals'). A woman comments that 'in the old days women who did it used to be called nancy girls – now they're lesbians'. She adds resolutely: '*I* wouldn't do it with another woman.'

Naomi Girl's name which in Hebrew means 'beautiful, pleasant, delightful' and is linked with the Moabitess who converted to Judaism and who, unbowed by famine and the deaths of husband and sons, gave support to and was in turn supported by her daughter-in-law Ruth. Dr Robert Briffault in *Family Life* 'The Mother' (1935 R) called Naomi the originator of the maternal clan: 'she is the personification of life giving, an agricultural figure, one of the great mothers-in-law'.

The name is generally given to three types of women. Firstly, simple, trusting creatures, often handmaidens or children of nature: Naomi (Vera Doria) in *Salome* (1918 C); Naomi (Gertrude Howard) in *The Prodigal* with Lawrence Tippett (1931 C); Naomi Hoktor (Felicia Farr), daughter of Shem who puts credo before libido in *Jubal* (1955 C); Naomi (Chana Eden), a Cajun girl in *Wind Across the Everglades* (1958 C); Naomi (Vickery Turner) in *The Mind of Mr Soames* (1969 C); Brenda Sykes as a slave in *Skin Game* (1971 C); Naomi (Derin Altay), teenage daughter with various problems in *The Baxters* (1979 T) – reborn as Allison when the show shifted producers and countries (US to Canada) in 1980; undead Naomi, damsel in distress in *Dark Shadows* (1990 T); one of the women in *Eating* (1991 C) and the only one not to have a monologue, just bursts of chit-chat.

Secondly, put-upon wives and/or mothers usually abandoned or mothers who abandon their children: Naomi (Norma Talmadge) left by husband with a child in *Fifty-Fifty* (1916 C); Naomi Kellogg, unmarried mother who marries religious bigot and tries to guide her daughter from afar in *Right to Love* (1931 C); Naomi Murdoch (Barbara STANWYCK), mother who deserts her family to go on the stage in *All I Desire* (1953 C) but redeems herself; long-

suffering Naomi (Connie Booth), the British MP's American wife in *For the Greater Good* (1991 T) pushed out by his homosexual needs – although he accuses her of spending too much time 'dining out with your queer dress designer'. (These are based to some extent on one interpretation of the biblical character, played by Peggy Wood (of 'Climb Every Mountain' fame) gently indominatable, sweetly long-suffering in *The Story of Ruth* 1960 C.)

Thirdly, sinners of various kinds.

US: 'NYMPHOMANIAC' Naomi Shields (Claire Bloom) who tries to seduce her interviewer in *The Chapman Report* (1962 C), is raped and commits suicide; a saloon girl (Constance Ford) who shows courage in *Frontier Circus* 'Champagne' (1962 T); Naomi Sutherland (Lysa D'Arblay) who tries to throw a little girl off a parapet because the child knows she killed a man in PERRY MASON 'The Case of the Missing Button' (1964 T); Naomi (Jane Birkin), a fanatical anti-Czarist in *Romance of a Horse Thief* (1971 C); Naomi Oakes (Dorothy Lyman), called the 'queen of tarts' by her mother-in-law in *Mama's Family* (1983–9 T); Naomi (Barbara Beckley), a prostitute in an episode of DALLAS (1989 T).

UK: Naomi (Caroline Munro), Bond villainess with a couple of scenes in *The Spy Who Loved Me* (1976 C); Naomi Dare (Rosalind Knight), bisexual novelist, 'ground-sheet for the Home Counties', who has a liaison with her female secretary and (accidentally) manipulates her own murder in *Lovekill* (1983 R); Naomi Leichman, a suspected Soviet agent in *Seven Steps to Treason* (1990 R); Naomi (Moya O'Shea), treacherous young journalist in *The Flight of Fellowship* (1991 R); Naomi (Elizabeth Kelly) in *Understanding Women* (1992 R) who poisoned three members of her family.

A few fictional Naomis (and they are on the increase, as they are in the 'real' world) take their cue from the way Mary MORRIS interpreted the biblical one in her love of Ruth in THE THRESHING FLOOR (1982 R) – sturdy, somewhat blunt, supportive, womanly: Naomi

(Andra Akers), confidante of Lily TOM-LIN in *Moment by Moment* (1978 C); Naomi David (Margot Boyd), jolly clair-voyant who helps the repressed gay man in *Running Down* (1980 R); Naomi (Moir Leslie), niece investigating a complicated ménage in *Dead Reckonings* (1988 R); one of the four sisters (others are Ruth, Rachel and Phoebe) in *The Exiles* (1992 R, a serialized book for young people by Hilary McKay, read by Su Pollard).

Narizzano, Silvio (1927–) Canadian director who has achieved a remarkable body of drama and documentary work in British television, especially during his years with Granada (1956–64). His cinema career produced only three suc-cesses: *Georgy Girl* (1966); *Loot* (1970); *Who Will Shoot the Teacher?* (1977); he was originally to have directed *Women in Love*. He introduced his ON TRIAL 'Oscar WILDE' at the 1992 'OUT OF THE ARCHIVES' lesbian and gay television season at the Museum of the Moving Image (MOMI) in London.

T: *The Lion's Share* (1956); *Appoint-ment with Fire* (Outside Broadcast on the fire service 1956); *Guest in the House* (1957); *An Enemy of the People* (1957); *Home of the Brave* (1957); *Death of a Salesman* (1957); *Mary Broome* (1957/8); *Thou Shalt Not Kill?* (should mercy killing be legalized? 1957); *Homosexu-ality and the Law* (a prologue to the WOL-FENDEN REPORT, 1957); *Thunder on Sycamore Street* (1957); *The Trouble Makers* (1958); *A Blessing or a Sin?* (arti-ficial insemination, 1958); *Doomsday for Dyson* (1958); THE MYTH MAKERS (about the cult surrounding a James DEAN-type figure, 1958); *Ebb Tide* (1959); *Sugar in the Morning* (1959); *The Shrike* (1960); *On Trial* 'Oscar Wilde' (1960); *The Boy Next Door* (1960); *Shadow of Ignorance* (1960); *Paris 1900* (1963); *War and Peace* (1963); *The Glass Menagerie* (1964); *The Changeling* (1964); *Women Beware Women* (1965); *The Old Boys* (1965); COUNTRY MATTERS 'The Simple Life' (1973); *Staying On* (1980); *Miss Marple* 'The Body in the Library' (1984); *Young Shoulders* (1984); etc.

narrators Instead of homosexuals being talked about by experts, the first person narrative – knowing or naive – invites identification with and closer proximity to lesbians and gays, helping the audience to get inside the skin of another person, beginning with THE NAKED CIVIL SERVANT (spoken by John HURT). Other examples: MALA NOCHE (spoken by Tim Streeter); CAUGHT LOOKING (spoken by Bette Bourne); THANK YOU AND GOODNIGHT (spoken by Jan OXENBURG). A third person example is NORTH OF VORTEX (spoken by Kevin Graal).

natural and unnatural An old puzzle: moulded by the environment or written in the genes? Sir William Beveridge dis-cussed the conundrum as part of the *Changes in Family Life* in 1932 as did J. B. S. Haldane, more extensively, in *Nature and Nurture* (1947 R) and the world was no nearer the solution. Many years later, in 1992, Phil DONAHUE was asking: 'Born Gay, Became Gay or Made Gay?' The panel bringing its intelligence to bear on the issue was composed entirely of gay men: Simon Le Vay PhD ('His research indicates that gay men are born that way'); John DeCecco PhD ('Feels people choose to be gay'); Jim Weinrich PhD ('Feels homosexuality is genetic'); Frank Aqueno ('Feels he wasn't born gay'); Dotson Rader ('Feels he was born gay'). No firm conclusions were reached, nor were they on the British equivalent, *Equinox*. However, with the advent of programmes like *Brain Sex* (1992 T, fea-turing 'the homosexual brain'), the puz-zle may be solved in next to no time. *See also* GENETICS.

The Nature of Prejudice (UK 1968 T) Using vox pop interviews, film clips and studio discussions, an attempt to look at individually and group held negative beliefs about sections of the community.

Prejudice was here defined as an atti-tude 'always irrational, deeply emotional and deeply held, impervious to argu-ment or reason'. Like so much in mass entertainment, this subject is shot through with moral judgements and evasions of uncomfortable reality. And so is liberalism. This was one of the very few series to go to the heart of the matter. Produced by Stuart HOOD and shown on ATV on Sunday afternoons during March and April 1968, it included, for the first time, homosexuals – as part of one of the seven segments – with other minorities which attract suspicion, ire and violence: black people, teenagers, gypsies, feminists.

What cut into the noble aim of the series was the lack of balance between victims of prejudice and those harbouring it. Totally absent from this second under-represented group were any extremists. Another more unavoidable problem was the lack of film material on manifestations of hatred, other than against Jews (by the Fascist party) and black and Asian immigrants (by the Nationalist and neo-Nazi groups). The use of feature film excerpts, illustrating stereotyping, was a partially effective substitute for these gaps.

Originally planned as a 13-week adult education series, it would be instructive to make a similar series in a Britain whose prejudice is now more diverse, far less clear-cut: a cat's cradle of classism, sexism, racism, ableism, ageism, heterosexism, HETEROPHOBIA . . .

naturism The belief by some people that clothes inhibit freedom of movement and personality – and their practical solution of spending much of their free time naked – has fascinated programme-makers for many years. Radio in the 1930s approached the subject gingerly: 'To Strip or not to Strip?', meaning the wearing of swimming costumes; but the medium's comedy shows were always making sniggering remarks about 'nudists' with the unspoken inference that orgies and suchlike were the real motive behind the doffing of clothes.

Naturists themselves, when they were finally given a chance to express themselves (in programmes like Daniel FARSON's *Out of Step* in the late 1950s), were always quick to point out that their clubs weeded out 'undesirable elements' and that a 'family atmosphere' was encouraged in which sex was the last thing on anybody's mind. The barely suppressed puritanism of the subjects and their interviewers made them a perfect target for comedians like Marty Feldman who presented a defence of 'Clothism': 'We believe that clothes are perfectly natural' (*It's Marty* 1969).

The growth of 'clothing optional beaches' has defused the issue to some extent and there is a discernible difference in the tone of *Man Alive* 'Let's Go Naked' (1979 T) and OPEN SPACE 'Full Frontal' (1992 T, made by the British Naturist Association itself). There's less defensiveness – although naturism, as the 1987 BBC Radio North East programme (broadcast nationally in *The Local Network*) showed, is 'Barely Acceptable'. The subject contains within it the shock ('Is naturism decent exposure, or an offence against public morals?') and the smirk ('Is it taking off in Britain?') so dear to the culture.

See also NAKEDNESS.

The Naughty Lady Of Shady Lane
Sung by Ray Ellington and his Quartet on THE GOON SHOW 'Under Two Floorboards – A Story of the Legion' (1955). This was as suggestive a piece as the BBC ever broadcast before the loosening up/lowering of standards in the late 1960s. Pruriently describing the forbidden delights of the 'Lady', it appears to be a hymn to casual sex and prostitution. Until the final line of 'She's *only* nine days old' – which in a trice turns a man's desire for a woman of easy virtue into a father's sweet, uncomplicated delight after the birth of a daughter.

navels In most pre-production code films made in America or Britain, the navel – female *or* male (eg Gary Cooper getting dressed in front of a man in *A Farewell to Arms* 1932 and Jon Hall diving off a boat in *The Hurricane* 1937) – was always neatly hidden. The only major Hollywood star allowed – or determined – to show his navel was William Holden. It's there for all to see in a few shots in *Sunset Boulevard* and *Picnic*.

Nearly all the 'beefcake' still photographs of the 1940s and 1950s featured bare male midriffs, but in moving pictures they were inadmissible. Even in action scenes – like the fight between Richards Denning and Carlson in *The Creature from the Black Lagoon* (1954 C) – the actors' swimming trunks or trousers are firmly secured so that they cannot slide down by even a fraction. Later, grappling underwater with the monster, their navels remain out of sight.

In *Green Fire* (1954 C) Stewart Granger is tossing and turning in bed, stripped to the waist and possibly beyond, mad with jungle fever. However, as he writhes and groans, he is careful to keep the top of the sheet decorously level with his navel. One that got away was Mickey Rooney's in *The Human Comedy* (1943 C). It is clearly visible in one scene in which the actor, wearing only pyjama bottoms, does press-ups watched by his enthralled younger brother. Then comes a change of camera angle and the navel has disappeared: the pyjama trousers are tied firmly and obviously tight around his waist. Robert Mitchum spends the last quarter of CAPE FEAR (1962 C) stripped to the waist, a hunter in pursuit of his human prey. Yet his navel is disclosed once only.

With the full flowering of the 1960s the navel came out – for women (in a succession of bikinis) and, more cautiously, for the opposite sex, beginning with, eg, Steve McQueen in *Soldier in the Rain* (1963 C), then Charlton Heston was becomingly clad in a loin cloth (briefer than the one he wore for a few scenes in *Ben-Hur* 1959 C) on *Planet of the Apes* (1967 C) and Angie Dickinson's fingers (followed by the camera) glided over Lee Marvin's belly towards his indent in *Point Blank* (1967 C). A decade later and audiences could marvel at the once secret place: William Hurt's, Richard Gere's and Nick Nolte's were all on view.

Recently, a cover-up seems to have been taking place so that in *Pretty Woman* (1990 C), when Richard Gere showers, he is seen above the nipples only. Later, in a bath, his navel is seen, then promptly obscured when he crosses his legs.

American television does not like navels. Its rule books forbid their exposure wherever possible, sometimes straining dramatic credibility, sometimes adding to the visual richness. In a 1978 episode of DALLAS Bobby Ewing (Patrick Duffy) emerges from his swimming pool in skimpy orange shorts, but his arm and then body angle prevent a view of the top of the abdomen. Later, his wife Pam (Victoria Principal) rings him in the middle of the night (they're estranged). He's in bed, unclothed. The conversation is troubled and involves considerable involuntary movement and expressions. But, throughout the entire conversation, Bobby's bedsheet remains neatly folded across the stomach at the base of the breastbone. And when it threatens to change position, Bobby/ Duffy pulls it up (this action is seen in at least five shots). In the same episode, he has to – as a married, if estranged, man – fend off the vamp Kristin (Mary Crosby) who encounters him just as he walks out of the shower in long shot. He puts on his shirt in record time. In a further scene, he turns his body sharply as he comes through a door to answer the phone so that no trace of the secret inside his shorts will be visible. (Remarkably, in a series known for its raunchy scenes, the female characters all wear low-cut but one-piece bathing suits – around their private pools.)

Such was the timorousness in the 1970s that even married actors Natalie Wood and Robert Wagner kept their navels covered in a TV movie called – and all about – *The Affair* (1974). In *Hart to Hart* (1980) Wagner and his co-star Stefanie Powers – playing a very demonstrative, free-spirited married couple – had to obey the same credo in 1980.

Now it's a hit and miss thing. HOTEL had male characters in towels naturally displaced, yet during the same period

(1985–6) in DYNASTY (made by the same producer) Jeff Colby (John James) tosses and turns in bed dreaming of his missing wife Fallon (Emma Samms), his unconscious brain somehow signalling to his hands to put the sheets over his stomach while in deep if troubled slumber. Six years later, in *Dynasty: The Reunion*, Miles Colby (Maxwell Caulfield) emerges, dripping and magnificent, from the sea in shorts, but immediately dives behind Fallon while talking to Jeff so that his rippling body will not ripple in an unacceptable way. The biggest – and longest – cover-up of all has been that of Tarzan, the Ape Man. Supposedly a creature at one with nature, his loincloth (abbreviated in the very early Johnny Weismuller pictures) was always generously cut, giving his navel complete protection. This convention has remained: the child and adolescent lollop around naked in the early scenes of *Greystoke: The Legend of Tarzan, Lord of the Apes* (1984 C), although in a curious triangular fashion so that no genitalia are visible despite their caperings. Suddenly, the adult version (Christopher Lambert) hoves into view wearing a custom-made, navel-obliterating loincloth. *Haute couture* for the noblest of savages.

Navratilova, Martina (1956–) Czechoslovakian-born, American-naturalized tennis champion who is probably the most widely transmitted lesbian in the world, still participating in Wimbledon, the Virginia Slims and other international competitions. Her personal problems involving a broken relationship received commensurate coverage in the early 1990s.

Her non-playing appearances (not especially 'sympathetic') include DONAHUE (in March 1984 with friend, rival and colleague Chris Evert: blonde for the first time and also for the first time wearing – too much – make-up); an 11-line role as 'herself' in a *Hart to Hart* episode (1984 T); *Nirvana* (1987 T); and, talking about HOMOPHOBIA in sport and life, with Phil Donahue again (1992 T). The Martina cult was alluded to in

Who Dares Wins ... Martina Navratilova's Sweat Band (1984 T) and, via interviews with besotted or just tennis-crazy dykes, in 'Suddenly Last Summer' (1991 T) which was part SATURDAY NIGHT OUT. Jokes about her directly, or about 'certain women tennis players', are made in *Top Secret* (1984 C); *Dame Edna's Hollywood* (1992 T); THE GOLDEN GIRLS (1992 T) final episode which has Sophia walking in and finding Rose and Blanche in an embrace: 'What *is* this – *Wimbledon?*'

'I now urge all of you who are still in the closet to throw away your excuses. Instead, find all those wonderful reasons why you should be out' – Navratilova addressing the crowd at the Gay and Lesbian March on Washington (25.4.93).

Nazimova, Alla (1879–1945) Russian-born actress who made an almost all-gay version of *Salome* in 1923. She also starred in *A Doll's House* (1922, directed by her husband Charles Bryant) and, with Rudolph VALENTINO, in *Camille* (1921). She was still playing a gamin (in Montmartre among the Apache) in *The Redeeming Sin* (1924). After *My Son* (1925) she didn't film again until *Escape* (1940), with her last appearance just before her death in *Since You Went Away*. She was depicted as a flamboyant lesbian in Ken Russell's *Valentino* (played by Leslie Caron with Michelle Phillips as her lover Natacha Rambova, 1977 C).

Nazism From 1933 onwards, the National Socialists systematically destroyed the German homosexual rights movement begun in 1897. It was squashed flat. All records were destroyed. German and Austrian homosexuals who were detected and caught were sterilized, imprisoned or killed.

Until Martin Sherman's BENT in 1979, dramatists were only interested in highlighting gay or lesbian characters within the Nazi ranks or those who were informers or quislings. These include Captain Bergman (Harry Feist) and Ingrid in ROME: OPEN CITY (1945 C), the schoolteacher Henning in *Germany Year Zero* (1947 C), and Schact (Lionel Hamilton) in THE PARACHUTE (1968 T).

Ernst ROEHM, leader of the SA, was pictured as the personification of perverse Hitlerism in THE DAMNED (1969 C) and in *Hitler's SS: Portrait of Evil* (1985 T). Vile women, depraved and rapacious in uniforms, inclined to slaver over younger ones, were also a staple of the 1970s s&m movies which came out of Italy in the wake of *The Night Porter* (1974). In an unusual reverse, the ghastly crew of lesbian concentration camp guards in Fania Fenelon's *The Musicians of Auschwitz* were reduced to one (Viveca Lindfors) when the book was adapted by Arthur Miller as *Playing for Time* (1980 T).

The reality was that Heinrich Himmler put on record that 'the homosexuals must be entirely eliminated'. Gay men were placed in Level 3 camps under triple discipline. Their work was harder, they had less food and received no medical treatment. Although they died in droves, Rudolf Hoess remarked in his diary: 'It was often not easy to drive them to the gas chambers.' Hoess reckoned that there were nearly as many gays in Dachau as Jews. And he should have known: he was the commandant. He was something of an expert, as he personally supervised the extermination of 2 million Jews, Gypsies, Communists, religionists and 'sexual deviants'.

For the past 20 years, television has rightly kept Jewish suffering and pride in the public consciousness. Apart from one line in *Holocaust* and one scene in the German film about Rudolf Hoess (*Death Is My Trade* 1978), gays play no part in this vast tragedy. (This is similarly true in programmes dealing with the Stalin terror and the gulags in the Soviet Union.)

Without *Bent*, based on one or two first-hand accounts of the camps, the wider world would probably never have known. Prior to this work, recently revived, there had been only the most fleeting references to any systematic crack down on sexual nonconformity. Wagner's daughter-in-law said (in *The*

Confessions of Winifred Wagner 1974 T) that she had intervened personally with Hitler to save some gay friends. Unity Mitford (Lesley Anne Down) is also asked to help an Englishman's German soldier-boy lover in *Unity* (1981 T). There is passing reference to the fate of Sebastian's feckless lover Kurt (Jonathan Coy) in BRIDESHEAD REVISITED (1981 T).

The furore which *Bent* caused among certain individuals and groups – inside and outside the homosexual world – was repeated, to a lesser degree, with the showing – on OUT ON TUESDAY and in a longer cinema version – of Stuart Marshall's DESIRE (1989). *Desire* mixed a few personal stories with a cultural history of Germany before and during the Hitler period: a mix of physical well-being and psychological dictatorship fuelled by scapegoating.

Modern-day Nazis are just as hell bent on destroying the limited gains of gay rights as were their predecessors. Bernd watches a TV programme in TAXI ZUM KLO (1981 C) where a neo-Nazi calls for all homosexuals to be put in work camps. Flashing forward five years to a time when QUEER-BASHING had become justified by illness and death, William F. Buckley was demanding in the *New York Times* (18.3.86) and on screen that all AIDS carriers be tattooed on the upper forearm. One of the leaders of the new German extreme right was totally unemotional when he stated (in *Hitler's Legacy* 1992 T) that when he and his Nazis take power 'gays will be put in concentration camps'.

See also THE BATTLE FOR TUNTENHAUS; CABARET; THE DAMNED; MY BEAUTIFUL LAUNDRETTE; NOVEMBER MOON; SALO; A SPECIAL DAY; WE WERE ONE MAN.

neighbours Gay ones (usually supportive): sparky Malcolm (Michael Greer) in THE GAY DECEIVERS (1969 C); honourable Don FINLAYSON in NUMBER 96 (1972–7 T); diverting Rikki (Angus Lennie) in PLAYMATES (1978 R); Mike's ever-present, ever-cheerful but fearsomely fussy Raymond (Robert Gaus) from next door in *Fat Angels* (1980 C);

open Pete HUNT and Trevor Wallace in TOGETHER (1980–1); delicate (Frank WILLIAMS) in *Tears Before Bedtime* (1983 T); prissy (Joe Dunlop and Timothy Carlton) in *Don't Wait Up* (1986–7 T); reliable Colin RUSSELL in EASTENDERS (1986–9 T); nice Tim (Nathan Lane) in *Frankie and Johnny* (1991 C); warmly witty Graham (Peter Friedman) who lives with Bobby and who is the heroine's friend and protector until he is MURDERED in *Single White Female* (1992 C). Lesbians: motherly Mavis (Cicely Courtneidge) in THE L-SHAPED ROOM (1962 C); very nasty (Beverly D'Angelo and Sylvia Miles) in *The Sentinel* (1977 C).

Neighbours (Aust 1986–   T) Laminexed Australian families doing lots of perky or pathos-ridden things in a fictional street.
Cr: Reg Watson; Channel 10.
Wildly popular soap which became BBC1's surprise hit. Kenny EVERETT sent its genre up regularly from December 1987 in a marvellous excuse to fill the screen with handsome, tanned, muscular young men wearing either briefs or brief towels (*The Kenny Everett Television Show*).
Although the inhabitants of Ramsay street project a thoroughly heterosexual WASP image and the plots don't rely too heavily on social texture, literacy or wit, there is always a redeeming bit of social consciousness (be nice to people, do the right thing, give others a fair go) to lift the spirits. Occasionally, it even goes a bit transcendental: a male stripper was sighted in July 1991 while in the same episode Harold spoke of his near-death experience to Dorothy.

Ne Me Quitte Pas [If You Go Away] Jacques Brel song of torment sung by Maisa Matarazzo in LAW OF DESIRE (1987 C). Firstly when Pepe's boyfriend (Miguel Molina) spends the night with him before leaving for the country; then on stage where the sister (Carmen Maura) is performing COCTEAU's *The Human Voice*; and finally as Pepe cradles

the dead youth (Antonio Banderas) in his lap after he has shot himself.

neurotic In 1932 used by *Radio Times* to describe the two young men in ROPE, the first play to deal semi-directly with homosexual relations (though veering towards the homicidal): 'a curious play dealing with two neurotic young men who ... strangle a perfectly harmless friend, purely for the excitement of the thing ... it is strong meat'.
Despite being ostensibly heterosexual, David Linden (Robert Young) is dubbed 'neurotic' and 'funny' in *The Shining Hour* (1938 C) and Melville Farr (Dirk BOGARDE) in VICTIM (1961 C) employs it vehemently about the dead Phil Stainer: 'a neurotic and an hysteric' (a line not in the original script but inserted during filming). Dennis Hopper as the would-be Führer in THE TWILIGHT ZONE 'He Lives' (1963 T) has no interest in women, is surrounded by men and, though a Nazi, loves an elderly Jew – who calls him 'sick, sad, neurotic'.
Yet only one of the MALE HOMOSEXUALS (1965 R) saw himself as in any way neurotic solely on the basis of sexual choice: 'At 26, things haven't worked out. I think there is a degree of neurosis to all this.' The linkage was not challenged in Britain until the early 1970s, but earlier in America (on KPFA–FM's *The Homosexual in Our Society* 1958 R) psychiatrist Blanche Baker denied that homosexuality was a neurosis: 'Now that doesn't mean that homosexuals may not become neurotic and I think they often do, because society is so hostile to them ... they are subject to a great many pressures and a great deal of unhappiness.'

Nevertheless (I'm In Love With You) Bert Kalmar and Harry Ruby song from the 1920s used – in a voice, guitar and violin version – at various points along the road in the coming out of LIANNA (Linda Griffiths 1983 C). It cleverly symbolizes erotic love, wistful romance, giddy elation, political awakening and sweet resignation. In one scene, it accompanies Lianna cruising women on doorsteps, at bus stops and gazing out of car windows. The song acts as the perfect bridge between her euphoria (after a night in a bar) and life as it is actually lived (her lover tells her that they cannot hold hands in the street: 'This is the real world'.

The song – sung by Jeanne Freed – is played in full during the end credits which finish abruptly on the word 'breaking' (as in a 'heart that is breaking').

news programmes Live broadcasts which generally attract large audiences. In America, during the 1970s, some programmes emanating from New York and Los Angeles were occasionally zapped by gay liberationists, who would handcuff themselves to cameras and protest about anti-gay prejudice in the seconds before transmission would be cut. More recently, national anchorman Dan Rather had his equilibrium upset on CBS Evening News by ACT UP demonstrators in 1991 (the confrontation shown in VOICES FROM THE FRONT). In Britain, in May 1988, Sue Lawley and her colleague managed to carry on reading the six o'clock news despite a small posse of lesbians protesting against CLAUSE 28 (1988 T, incident shown on SATURDAY NIGHT OUT 'The Gay Rock 'n' Roll Years' 1991).

New Zealand Two islands, a large indigenous minority, increased biculturalism, long-entrenched Conservative government followed by a more socially quick-witted, broader-based Labour administration (now fallen). A small but exciting film industry, producing relevant works since the early 1980s: *The Squeeze* (1980); *Among the Cinders* (1983, white New Zealander and Maori friend); *Sylvia* (1984, based on the teaching experiences of Sylvia Ashton-Warner); *The Navigator: A Medieval Odyssey* (1988, fusion of the 14th-century Black Death with the present); A DEATH IN THE FAMILY; BEYOND GRAVITY; A TASTE OF KIWI; JEWEL'S DARL; *Heavenly Creatures* and *Desperate Remedies* (both 1993).

nice boy *See* SEEMS LIKE A NICE BOY.

Nicholas/Nick/Nicky/Niki/Nikki
Boy's name with devilish attachments: Nicky and Nicholas are quite often bestowed upon gay and fey or neurotic characters as well as heterosexuals who have a flirtation with villainy.

UK: Nicky Lancaster, dope addict, mother fixated in THE VORTEX (1928 C etc); Nicky Blake (William Young), enticing and mildly dangerous student in *Promenade* (1959 T); etc.

US: Nickie Elkins (Richard Barthelmess), father killer in *The Noose* (1928 C); Nicky Solomon (Chester Morris), 'cheap stick-up guy with a sheik pan, a tux that fits, a roadster with a trick horn and money to go with' in *Playing Around* (1930 C); Nickie Ferrante (Cary GRANT), playboy and – at 53 – still an eligible bachelor in *An Affair to Remember* (1957 C); pert warlock Nicky (Jack Lemmon) in BELL, BOOK AND CANDLE (1958 C); Nicky Arnstein (Omar Sharif), gambler and kept man in *Funny Girl* and FUNNY LADY: 'Nicky Arnstein, Nicky Arnstein! He has polish on his nails!'; Nicky (Mandy Patinkin), librarian husband in *Maxie* (1985 C); etc.

Also: the Italian Nicky (Erland Josephson), wanting always to be young and carefree in TO FORGET VENICE (1979 C).

US: Nick Hunter (Gregory Rozakis), hustler involved in the killing of a gay cop in STARSKY AND HUTCH 'Death in a Different Place' (1977 T); Nick Lobo (Richard Masur) with a talent for wrecking things in *Rhoda* 'Kiss Your Epaulets Goodbye' and 'The Love Song of J. Nicholas Lobo' (1977 T); Nick Handris (Ron Rifkin) in *One Day at a Time* (1980 T), thief, liar, doper, dope pusher, murderer and born-again Christian; Nick Pearson (Ben Gazzara), uptight father in AN EARLY FROST (1985 T); rock musician with HIV/AIDS: Nick (Steve Buscemi) in PARTING GLANCES (1985 C); Nick (Jan Michael Vincent) in HOTEL 'Hornet's Nest' (1986 T) faced with the problem of a gay army buddy; top photographer Nick Donato (Lee Horsley), one-night-stand husband in *Infidelity* (1987 T); etc.

UK: Nick Moffat (Ian Redford), hero of *A Raging Calm* (1974 T); loosely married Nick (Bill Nighy) massaging a man he fancies in *Fat* (1980 T); Nick Hawley (Kenneth Cranham), Michael's alcoholic former lover in *The Bell* (1982 T); scrapegrace who becomes increasingly sociopathic and dangerous: Nick Cotton (John Altman) in EASTENDERS (1986–T); Nick, Paul's lover who leaves the City and opens Nick's diner in GEMS (1987 T); etc.

US: charming Dr Nicholas Agi (Louis Jourdan) in *The Swan* (1956 C); husband whose first wife, reported dead, turns up: Nicholas (James Garner) in *Move Over Darling* (1964 C); rich businessman Nicholas (Joseph Cotten) in *Airport 77* (1977 C); etc.

UK: Nicholas (James Mason) in *The Seventh Veil* (1945 C); Nicholas Whiteoak (Richard Caldicott), sottish middle-aged bachelor in *Jalna* and *Whiteoaks* (1954 T); Nicholas Higgins (Derek Fowlds) in CROWN COURT 'Such a Charming Man' (1977 T): did he go to bed with Crosby in exchange for investment information?; Nicholas Black (Daniel MASSEY), reprobate gay painter in *The Devil's Advocate* (1977 C); Nicholas Finnerman (Bernard Kay), trendy junk dealer with Gunther in THE GENTLE TOUCH 'Auctions' (1982 T): 'Dabble, dear, dabble. Just for fun. Bye-ee!'; etc.

Nichols, Beverley (1898–1983) English playwright, journalist, gardening writer and broadcaster, briefly an actor (eg the Hon. Richard Wells in *Glamour* 1931 C). He had a male 'companion' for more than 40 years and was relatively open in public lectures he gave – though not noticeably on radio or television.

A Day in a Journalist's Life (1926 R); *Personal Diary* (gardening talks for amateurs, 1932 R); *The Flower Show* (1934 R); *Seven Years Hard* (1934 R), three reasons for going to church: 'the Church has produced much excellent matter'; *Down the Garden Path* (describing his garden in Huntingdonshire, 1937 R); *Picture Page* (singing songs from his revue *Floodlight*, 1937 T);

WOMAN'S HOUR 1950s etc; *Friends and Contemporaries* (with Edith Evans, Robert Boothby and Constance Spry, 1970 R); talking about his life in March 1983 to celebrate his 85th birthday in the following September in *Not Only Down the Garden Path* (3 parts, R).

nicknames A vast floating pool of affection, flirtatiousness and frivolity between good friends, lovers and 'married' partners; sometimes contemptuous: JAMES I called George VILLIERS 'Boy George' and 'Steenie' ('Now close the shutters, Steenie. It's too bright in here. The sun is up', says the dying man in *The Wisest Fool* 1977 R and the monarch also uses 'Boy George' in *Churchill's People* 'A Rich and Beautiful Empire' 1975 T); Lord Alfred DOUGLAS was 'Bosie' (coined by his family, not Oscar Wilde); Alice B. TOKLAS called Gertrude STEIN 'Lovey' (she was 'Pussy'); Richard Loeb refers to Nathan LEOPOLD as 'Babe' in SWOON (1991 C) and they also call each other 'Kitten' and 'Pussy'; Lord Petcliff, lighter-than-air interior decorator known by his middle-aged women clients and certain men as 'Petzi' in *Over the Moon* (1937 C); Vladimir and Estragon are 'Gogo' and 'Didi' respectively in WAITING FOR GODOT (1960 R etc); Elinor Eastlake is always known as 'LAKEY' by THE GROUP (1966 C); Alice McNaught is 'Childie' in THE KILLING OF SISTER GEORGE (1968 C etc); 'Per' chose his own nickname as a way of proclaiming the perversion which was the source of so much bullying at school in TWO PEOPLE (1979 T); in PORTRAIT OF A MARRIAGE (1990 T) 'Nouschka' alias Violet TREFUSIS, 'Haji' alias Harold NICOLSON and 'Mitya' alias Vita SACKVILLE-WEST; Alan, known as 'Fuzzy' in LONGTIME COMPANION (1990 C); because of her hirsutism Kotzebue (k. d. lang) is 'Boo-boo' while her friend Roswitha is 'Sweeta' in *Salmonberries* (1991 C); Abigail and 'James' in A MATTER OF SEX (1992 R) refer to each other by terms denoting their most appreciated sexual speciality, respectively 'Touchbun' and 'Flabber'; in *Death Drop* (1992 R) the teacher Brian Innis is referred to privately as 'Bruin' by his pupil lover; behind his back the head of the US Federal Bureau of Investigation was known as J. 'Edna' HOOVER according to TIMEWATCH (1993 T).

Nicolson, Sir Harold (1886–1968) English diplomat, politician, novelist, biographer, journalist and broadcaster, husband of Vita SACKVILLE-WEST. He was involved in the Treaty of Versailles, spoke against the Munich agreement between Hitler and Chamberlain, was at the Ministry of Information during the Blitz, was involved in the birth of the State of Israel, and was present at the Nuremberg trials. He was also a director of the BBC.

A regular broadcaster from 1928, emphasizing the individual and his [*sic*] responsibility for his own actions: MARRIAGE (with Vita, 1929); *Utility vs Beauty* (1929); *Parents and Children* (1929): 'There is a danger that the broadmindedness of the present parent may lead to slack-mindedness in the present child'; *Happiness* (with Vita, 1930); *How YOU Affect Modern Writers* (1931); *Address to a Low Brow* (1932), 'certain to sparkle'; *As Others See Us* 'How the English Appear to the Foreign Mind' (1935); contributor to *Do You Remember?* the BBC's 25th Birthday Programme (1947 R); *A Different World from This* (1960); *K of K* (about Lord KITCHENER, 1960 R); etc.

Autobiography: *Frankly Speaking* (1958 R); *Friends and Contemporaries* (1962 R): 'the common-sense reflections of a quite sensible if pleasure-loving old man'; *Something Sensational to Read on the Train* (his DIARIES discussed by his son Nigel, 1970 R).

Played by Brett Usher in *A Self-Made Man* (about Ronald FIRBANK, 1985 R); by David Haigh in PORTRAIT OF A MARRIAGE (1990 T); by Benjamin WHITROW in JOURNEY TO JAVA (1990 R); by Christopher Cazenove in *The New Party* (about his friendship with Oswald Mosley, 1992 R).

'As with all the best broadcasters you had a feeling that he was talking directly to you, and more, that he knew you were listening. This is, and always will be, the acid test of achievement on the air' (John Pringle, *Listener*, 27.9.62).

Nigel Boy's name popular in Britain from the 1940s (tying with Stuart at no. 37 in 1950) and peaking in the 1960s (reaching no. 23) but fading fast from the 1970s onwards. (It is Anglo-Saxon for 'night', or possibly a short form of nightingale, ie to sing at night.)

Almost entirely restricted to British characters, with heroic ones very thin on the ground: Anthony Andrews in Sir Walter Scott's *The Adventures of Nigel* (1974 T, trying to reclaim his lands from villains during the reign of JAMES I) is one of the few; the doctor played by George Baker in *No Time for Tears* (1957 C) is another. Ridiculed by *The Two Ronnies* ('the nice Nigels') and other comedians, and mainly allotted to wet, public school types personified by Nigel PARGETTER in THE ARCHERS: 'Oh *goody*, I love presents!' A Nigel was one of the finalists in the Upper Class Twit of the Year competition alongside Gervaise, Oliver and VIVIAN in MONTY PYTHON'S FLYING CIRCUS (1972 T).

Rev. Nigel Hartley (Ralph Richardson) in *The Ghoul* (1933 C); ornamented aesthete Nigel, sentimental friend of the hero in UNDERGRADUATE SUMMER (Frith Banbury 1939 R; Elwyn BROOK-JONES in 1951 R); Nigel (Derek Bond), nice young sailor in *The Weaker Sex* (1948 C); Nigel Lorraine (Robert Flemyng), dashing teacher in *The Guinea Pig* (1948 C); prisoner-of-war Nigel (Peter Burton) in *The Wooden Horse* (1950); Nigel, the Silkworm (Maurice Denham) in *Much-Binding-in-the-Marsh* (1954 R); Nigel Bowser-Smyth (Graham Stark) in *Archie's the Boy* (1954 R); smooth BLACKMAILER Nigel Dennis (Dennis PRICE) in *The Naked Truth/Your Past Is Showing* (1958 C); Nigel Miller-Watford (Francis Matthews), chum of Lords Ambrose and Timothy in an episode of PROBATION OFFICER (1960 T); suave Anglo-out-East Nigel Costairs (Michael Wilding) in *A Girl Named Tamiko* (1963 C); clumsy, naive political candidate (Keith Barron) in *Stand Up, Nigel Barton* and *Vote, Vote, Vote for Nigel*

Barton (1965 T); Nigel French (John Williams), a very proper Englishman in *Family Affair* (1966–71 T); Nigel (Roy Marsden), a boyfriend of one of *The Liver Birds* (1968 T); a dizzy photographer in *The Touchables* (1969 C) called Nigel BENT (Simon Williams), gay 1960s swinger, tight white trousers, jaunty cap; in the same mould Nigel Garfield (Terry Scully) in *Goodbye Gemini* (1970 C); Nigel (Melvyn HAYES) in *Man About the House* (1974 C); Nigel who wants to be a stage designer in *The Swish of the Curtain* (1980 T); Nigel PARGETTER (Nigel Carrington) who tried to jump into Shula's bed in THE ARCHERS (1980s–   R); Harvey's departed in *That Beryl Marston ... !* (1981 T); Nigel Smallfoot (Rowan Atkinson), twit of a British government representative in the Bahamas in *Never Say Never Again* (1983 C); used as a 'gay name' in *The Grumbleweeds Radio Show* (1984 T); villain Nigel Steen (Richard Morant) in *Cast in Order of Disappearance* (1984 R); Nigel (Christopher Villiers) in *Top Secret* (1984 C) fellated by a calf and sodomized by a bull; Nigel (Julian Fellowes) simpering in *Baby: Secret of the Lost Legend* (1985 C); Nigel (Gerard Logan), exasperated lover of cat-besotted Alasdair in *Claws* (1987 T); Nigel (Don Warrington) in *CATS Eyes* (1988 T); Nigel (Peter Sands) in *A Perfect Spy* (1987 T); Nigel (Charles Simpson, homophobic, wine-guzzling, 'sprog'-producing brother in A HORSE CALLED GERTRUDE STEIN (1990 R); Nigel (Sion Probert), a Welsh cook who works with his lover (James Bolam) in preparing a banquet for a visiting industrialist in *Sticky Wickets* (1990 T); yuppie burglary victim Nigel Cape (Gregory Floyd) nagging *The Bill* to 'Beat Crime' (1990 T); detective Nigel STRANGEWAYS (Glyn Houston 1964 T; Richard Hurndall 1966 R; Simon Cadell 1986 R); Nigel Crimmond (Michael COCHRANE), former mental hospital patient who abducts a young hitchiker in *The Chief* (1991 R); Nigel Dobson (Hugh Grant), a prim, dull young man who encounters two decadents on a trip to Paris with his wife in *Bitter Moon* (1992 C); 'Nervous

Nigel' (Bob Moody), a cringing Northern Larry GRAYSON look-alike with a whippet in *Bunch of Five* 'Blue Heaven' (1992 T); Nigel (Paul Bradley) in EASTENDERS (1992–   T).

In 1991 Carol Johnson and Helen Petrie of Sussex University surveyed 255 people, asking them to assess the masculinity and femininity of 86 first names. The most problematic was Nigel: respondents had some difficulty deciding whether Nigel was a macho name or a name with wimpish associations.

Night and Day (US 1946 C) 'Inspired by' the life and work of Cole PORTER (Cary GRANT) who is given a helping hand through his student days and over some of the bumps in his marriage by Monty Woolley (playing 'himself').

W: Charles Hoffman, Leo Townsend and William Bowers; D: Michael Curtiz; P: Arthur Schwarz; 132 mins.

Shamelessly packaged, it offered Monty and Cary a field day in innuendo: 'Cole, are you joining us for this little cruise?', 'Let's you and I have a little drink together and you can lay your head on Uncle Monty's shoulder', 'Love can be a delight, a disease or a disaster', 'The only marriage I ever approved of was that of my mother and father', 'I never realized there were so many bars', 'Your wife told me to take care of you.' All these lines are delivered with orotundity and a twinkle. Between the two actors and the scriptwriters the truth seems to be kicking and screaming to be heard. A delicious piece of double-dipping.

Much emphasis is laid – by Monty Woolley – upon Porter's inadequacy as a husband, reason unspecified: 'You shouldn't have gotten married in the first place. And in the second place, you should have tried to act more like a husband than a guy who shouldn't have gotten married in the first place.'

(Cary Grant had wanted to play George Gershwin and, according to the biography *The Lonely Heart*, was hypercritical and difficult throughout the making of the Porter film, knowing that he was playing a total lie.)

Night and Day Cole PORTER's ravishingly sinuous and full-blooded classic, evidencing his own sexual outpourings; you can almost smell them.

Originally sung by Fred to Ginger in *The Gay Divorce/Divorcee* (1934 C) and then by Deanna Durbin in *Lady on a Train* (1945 C). It was used – with much poetic licence – in the film biography of the same name.

Nighthawks (UK 1978 C) The quite terrifying fight to finance this film – the first by and about the London gay community – would have made a more exciting story than the one that fitfully emerges on the screen. The central character, Jim (Ken Robertson), TEACHER by day, cruiser by night, doesn't warrant too much analysis and even less EMPATHY. His various bed partners are moderately sympathetic but, ironically, it's the hets who have the best lines: the sympathetic woman friend and a schoolroom of kids asking 'sir' to justify his life. The cramped budget must be blamed for the feeling of tiredness in many scenes, but the script is sketchy and provides frustratingly few opportunities for characterization, visual effects or blazing drama.

Ron PECK and Paul Hallam's film does pick up considerably from the midway point, and it is of no little historical significance, coming from that period of the growing marketability and commercially based tolerance for gays in London. Men like Jim could still feel just as lonely and alienated as their counterparts did before the law was changed. It was in stark contrast to Dutch TV's *Hoera Ten Homo* [Hooray, a Homo] in three parts about a teacher in a suburban school.

W/P/D: Ron Peck and Paul Hallam; 113 mins.

Nighthawks 2: Strip Jack Naked (UK 1991 C/T) Out-takes from NIGHTHAWKS together with the director's own navigations through the coming out

maze and his call for unity and acceptance of gays and lesbians by gay and lesbian people.

W: Ron Peck and Paul Hallam; D: Ron Peck; 91 mins.

A biography of a London-based filmmaker who poured much of his 1970s life into the film *Nighthawks*. He explores his personal conflicts and the compromises these, and gay ghetto solidarity, imposed upon the final version. Mark Finch describes it in the San Francisco lesbian and gay film festival programme (1990) as 'a farewell note to England's last three decades – inked with humour, politics and a penchant for posing pouches'.

Nightingale, Florence (1820–1910) English pioneer of nursing. Played by Edith Evans in *The Lady with a Lamp* (1933 R, also Gladys Young 1946 R and Anna Neagle 1951 C); Kay Francis in *The White Angel* (1936 C); Joyce Bland in *Sixty Glorious Years* (1938 C); Madoline Thomas in *Never, Miss Nightingale* (1948 R); Barbara Couper in *The Spinster of South Street* (1950 T); Jayne Meadows in *Meeting of Minds* (1978 T); Jaclyn Smith in *Florence Nightingale* (1985 T).

She was one of the *Pioneers of a Humaner World* (along with Mary Wollstonecraft Godwin, Elizabeth Fry, Robert Owen and Lord Shaftesbury) in 1933. Margery Fry called her 'a young Englishwoman of genius ... efficient and masterful ... with a sharp tongue so well hung on her humour ... She wasn't always popular with the authorities'.

'A couple of English gentlemen cast affectionate glances Florence's way, but realize immediately that she is not for the service of any one household but of all humanity' (from a 1936 radio talk).

Nightingale's Boys 'Flossie' (UK 1975 T) David Fryer (David Swift) was the gentle, sensitive member of Bill Nightingale's class of 1965. Now, seemingly happily married with two children, his routine is upset by two events: a chance meeting with the debonair Giles (Robert Swann) from schooldays and a visit to

Manchester to see his father, who is seriously ill.

W: Colin SPENCER; P: Brian Armstrong; D: Richard Everitt; 4.2.75; Granada.

Within the framework of a teacher reconnecting with some of the lads in his class of 1965, Spencer focused on the school queer, now married but re-exploring his feelings towards men after meeting a friend who had taken the opposite path. Granada insisted that the boy's nickname be 'Flossie', thereby immediately imposing a sissy classification.

Spencer said in GAY NEWS (1977):

> The script I tried to write was about a man who had suppressed his gayness, got married, had kids, then released his tensions by having one-night stands ... I was away when the script was filmed. A mistake, as it happened, but television companies do not pay authors rehearsal money, do not ask for their advice and obviously fear an author's warming to his theme. I was horrified to discover that dialogue had been changed, characters had been thrown out and most important of all: the positive gay message had been toned down to insignificance. However, a few members of the public wrote to me and thanked me for its refreshing honesty.
>
> So maybe more got through than I had thought. I had the impression that Granada thought they were being very controversial in showing the play at all.

Night Out (Aust 1990 C/T) The ramifications of bashing in the wake of a few minutes of infidelity in the relationship of Tony (Colin Batrouney) and Steve (David Bonney). Because of the guilt associated with it, the love bite on Tony's neck gives him more pain than his broken ribs.

W/D: Lawrence Johnston; 50 mins.

A morality tale speckled with greys. Motivations believable, consequences of actions disturbing, conclusions drawn sensible. It lacks the spontaneous combustion in the acting of the lovers to give it lasting power, but at its core is directing talent of quality.

a night out with the boys Ma (Peggy Mount) is horrified in *The Larkins* 'Come Cleaner' (1960 T) when her neighbour (Barbara Mitchell) reads into her son's night at the pub something deviantly dissolute. On WOMAN'S HOUR (1963) a wife again opened up the throwaway line to scrutiny: 'I only pray they will never find out how near they are to the mark when [friends] make their cheery little jokes about his having a night out with the boys.' Dinah Sheridan uses it about her husband and her son in *Don't Wait Up* (1983–7 T).

The Night They Took Miss Beautiful (US 1977 T) Five beauty contest contestants are held hostage.

W: George Lefferts; P: George Lefferts and Don Kirshner; D: Robert Michael Lewis; 96 mins.

Another serving of TV junk food made chewable only by the performance of Sheree North as Layla Burden, a strung-out, dangerously trigger-happy TERRORIST whose pleasant job it is to guard the beauty queens. When one of them tells Layla to go to hell, she lets out a dry laugh: 'I've already been there, honey.'

Bored with the long wait before money and a plane are made available by the US government, Layla decides to stage her own beauty contest with the frightened girls. She openly desires one of them: 'I had a friend like you in prison. She was a real nice black girl. She double-crossed me and that's made me real *bigoted*.' Almost immediately after this, she machine-guns a man to death. The sleepy eyes, regimental sergeant major bark and provocative clothing (midriff-revealing shirt, shorts and cap) make Layla one of the most frighteningly alluring villains of the recent past.

Sheree North invests a nothing role of predictable responses with a manic power that is funny, chilling and impossible to ignore. The visible evidence of her past drug-taking and the knowledge that she is a convicted killer ('Thirteen years for killing the Devil. He was my husband') give her every half-crazed line and threatening or non-threatening movement a compulsion that most cold, fanatical terrorist lesbians simply do not have. As so many hostages have found, the captive viewer ends up rather admiring a woman like Layla ('I kicked the junk in Rayford Penitentiary') and almost willing her to survive (she does, though captured).

An example of American television's total myopia in its vision of lesbians during the 1970s, and how an actress can take a deflated balloon, pump some air into it, paint it, tie a ribbon round it and keep the audience in a modicum of suspense as to when it will explode.

Night Thoughts: A Radiophonic Poem for Voices and Orchestra (UK 1956 R) A man (Robert Harris as the Solitary) walks on Primrose Hill in London pondering the fathomless, pitiable, frightening loneliness of human beings, as voices speak of their anxiety and fear of the unknown.
W: David GASCOYNE, M: Humphrey Searle; P: Douglas Cleverdon; 7.12.55; BBC Third Programme; 60 mins.

From the sizeable extracts that remain, this is a grating, sometimes electrifying closet gay confessional. Even though the man 'returns to his wife', the sense of a search for pleasures transient in dark places is palpable:

> Greetings to the solitary ... you are not strangers to me.
> We are closer to one another than we realize.
> Let us remember one another at night, even though we do not know each other's name.

Lots of chunky observations on the rush and senselessness of urban living (called Meglametropolis and Beelzebub), and a good drown in a vat of despair every now and again from a Soul in Anguish (David William) and Voice of the Mortal Soul (Hugh David), as well as getters and spenders (all male: Frank Duncan, Alan Reid, Leonard Sachs, Peter Claughton and Norman Shelley). This is quintessential Third Programme queer poetry-drama: spellbinding in its way, but exasperating because

the truths Gascoyne was able to describe in his poems could not be uttered on Britain's only national broadcasting network.

'I realize that I never in my life had any genuine, unmistakable feelings about a woman, whereas I know by long experience that I can be physically attracted by men, that to make love with a man can give me great physical pleasure and emotional release' (David Gascoyne, *Paris Journal 1937–1939*, 1978).

Nijinsky (US 1980 C) The final stages in the nurturing of a rare talent: that of the dancer Vaslav Nijinsky (George De La Pena) by Sergei DIAGHILEV (Alan BATES) amid the artistic and psychological turmoil of the Ballets Russes and his wooing by an ambitious young woman.
W: Hugh Wheeler; P/D: Herbert Ross; 125 mins (some versions 129 mins).

De-luxe production and a myriad of extraordinary performers (including Anton DOLIN, Alan BADEL, Jeremy Irons and Leslie Browne – as Romola who is determined to marry Nijinsky no matter what the cost to him or to her) contribute to a confident Hollywood biography of a (dying) love that is barely able – still – to speak its name but, boy, did it produce some spectacular dancing. Bates pours himself fully into the role of divine bully, cheat, cajoler, daemon, charmer, but it is depressing that no progress has been made since the Oscar WILDE films: his rejection by Nijinsky turns him into a traditionally thwarted woman, giving no consideration to the fact that, like Wilde and Bosie, the relationship did continue – after a cooling-off period – on a new footing.

Vito RUSSO found the film cowardly and homophobic, rooted in the concept of 'a sissy marries a woman to prove he wasn't queer and it drives him crazy' and with Nijinsky implying that he wouldn't be homosexual if he hadn't met Diaghilev (GAY NEWS 194).

Nijinsky, Vaslav (1890–1950) Premier Russian choreographer and dancer who stopped performing in 1919. Played by George De La Pena in NIJINSKY (1980

C). Also: Anthony Dowell in *Valentino* (1977 C); John HURT reading his words in *Nijinsky: God of the Dance* (1978 T); Peter Craze in *The False Diaghilev* (1988 R). His life and talent also influenced the plots of *The Mad Genius* (with Donald Cook, 1931 C) and *The Red Shoes* (with Moira Shearer, 1948 C). Rudolf NUREYEV and then Christopher Gable were mentioned for the role in the proposed Melvyn Bragg–Ken Russell Nijinsky film between 1966 and 1970, which would have suggested parallels between the puppet Petrushka and the puppeteer who brings the doll to life. Alexander Korda had also planned a film in 1933 with John GIELGUD, based on the book by Romola Nijinsky.

A 1950 radio talk on *Vaslav Nijinsky* contained not one mention of DIAGHILEV! 'Nijinsky was a pretty good dancer, but who remembers her last movie?' says a philistine television writer in THE TWILIGHT ZONE 'The Bard' (1962 T). In the first episode of DYNASTY (1981 T) Nijinsky is mentioned by Claudia Blaisdel (Pamela Bellwood) in a list of the great and famous thought to be mad.

Nile, Rev. Fred (1934–) Australian Christian evangelist, leader of the Call to Australia party. He has helped link and galvanize the gay and lesbian community in New South Wales, especially with his annual opposition to the SYDNEY GAY AND LESBIAN MARDI GRAS. Strong fundamentalist views on prostitution, black magic, abortion, teenage literature and AIDS. Countless radio and television appearances since the mid-1970s when he was an organizer of the Festival of Light. He had his own Sunday night programme on Sydney's 2GB radio station during the 1980s. Recent appearances include *Encounter* 'Sect or Religion?' (the sectarian character of religion in Australia, 1991 R); *The Dead Sea Scrolls* (1991 T); *Sixty Minutes*; *The Midday Show*; *The 7.30 Report*; *Hate Crimes* (1992 T); *Feed Them to the Cannibals* (1993 T).

In a 1991 *Fast Forward* television pastiche of *Indiana Jones and the Temple of Doom*, the high priest (Michael Veitch)

yearns for a world 'where everyone is free and innocent, and there are no homosexuals and it rains on every Gay Mardi Gras'. He believes that the only true light is the Festival of Light and is heartily sick of having 'other people's genitals rammed down my throat'. His helper is a Mrs Bland whose method of killing opponents is to bash them over the head with a Bible. The appearance of a pontificating radio talk show host puts paid to both priest and disciple: Mrs Bland expiring while wailing 'I'm melting ... melting'.

Nile was glancingly mentioned (by Gertrude STEIN) in *Is That You, Nancy?* (1991 R): 'An Australian man ... with the name of an Egyptian river.'

Nilsen, Dennis (1945–) The MURDERER and butcher of 15 mostly gay men over a period of five years. A superficial enquiry into why he did what he did (schizoid personality disorder? malice? abdication of the will?) was included in the 1988 series on *Evil*, which included excerpts from a HOME MOVIE of Nilsen taken by a lover (previously shown in a 1985 *TV Eye* 'Multiple Murderers and How to Catch Them'). The image of the lonely, alienated gay man who killed without remorse, dismembered his victims and finally stuffed body parts into a drain was evoked in *The Interrogation of John* (1987 T, also in sequels *A Wanted Man* and *The Secret Shoreland* 1990 T: implacable evil behind a pretty baby face, played by Michael Fitzgerald); *10 × 10* 'The Monochrome Murderer' (1990 T); and less ferociously in KILLING TIME (1990 T). His true story was told on *TV Eye* ('a home movie by and of Dennis Nilsen' promised the synopsis, 1985); *Evil* (1988 T); *Bookmark* 'Monochrome Man' (1991 T). There has been as yet no adaptation of the fascinating book about Nilsen's family background, childhood and adult life, *Killing for Company* by Brian Masters (1985).

Nineteen-Eighty-Four George Orwell's terrifying flash forward to a totalitarian state where expressions of love are banned, language is devalued and changed, war is perpetual and informers are everywhere. The 1954 television production by Rudolph Cartier, with Peter Cushing as Winston Smith and André Morell as a caressingly seductive O'Brien, scared Britain half to death. The film versions (1955 and 1984) were more elaborate depictions of this physically and psychologically bruising world of having to watch what you say and looking over your shoulder lest the slightest hint of deviation be evident: a world which gay men and lesbians knew – and know – only too well.

nipples *See* BREASTS.

Nobody Loves A Fairy When She's Forty A 1940s comic piece originally sung by Tessie O'Shea. It was given an extra special plaintiveness and croak – 'Nobody loves a fairy when she's *old*' – by announcer Douglas Smith who, said Kenneth HORNE, 'wishes it to be known ... (but from the way he's been acting it's not surprising)' with a dainty, tinkly arrangement by Max Harris on ROUND THE HORNE in 1966.

nobody's perfect! One of the most famous last lines of all time: spoken with pixillated finality – 'Well, nobody's perfect!' – by millionaire Joe E. Brown in SOME LIKE IT HOT (1959 C) when it is revealed that his lady love and intended ninth wife (Jack Lemmon) is a 'he'. Alex (Alyson Reed) counteracts her husband's (John Ritter) verbal bloodletting against his – just deceased – gay friend (Peter Donat – 'an egotistical, uncharitable, narcissistic scoundrel' etc) in *Skin Deep* (1989 T) with a staunching '*Nobody's* perfect'. Edouardo (Miguel Bose) justifies his extraordinary masquerading (as junkie and drag queen) to Rebecca (Victoria Abril) in HIGH HEELS with a throwaway 'Nobody's perfect'. And time-chewed, New York-soiled Jack (Sydney Pollack) in *Husbands and Wives* (1992 C), begging for a reconciliation with spouse Judy Davis (having just had an affair with a much younger woman), can only say in his defence:

'Everybody screws up – nobody's perfect!'

Noddy aka Little Noddy. Enid Blyton's cheeky, naughty little fellow, whose best chum is Big Ears, was created in 1949 and clocked up 100 adventures which earned her over £100 million. Rex Firkin and A. D. Peters' *The Adventures of Noddy* (1956–7 T) gave children the unadulterated version – including the wicked gollies, the spanking schoolmistress and a young lad's unquestioning (and reciprocated) love for a gentleman with a white beard. A toned-down version appeared in 1975 (but Big Ears and NODDY did spend a night in a tent), but it was nothing like as POLITICALLY CORRECT as the third version in 1992: positive black characters (including Dinah Doll) and gremlins rather than golliwogs.

'Everything is different when you're camping ... I'd like to stay here for ever and ever ... Is camping always such fun?' This comes from 'Noddy at the Seaside' (1975) in which he and Big Ears retire for the night in pink and blue sleeping bags. The audience is not shown the pair huddled together in the tent as the wind buffets the canvas. However, a long-held shot of the tent flap is pregnant with meaning.

Noel Seasonal boy's name (though sometimes given to a girl, more usually spelt Noele or Noelle). Has become increasingly less grounded, more grand jetté since the 1930s.
US: hero Noel Anson (Conway Tearle) in *The Dancer of Paris* (1926 C); Noel Blake (Ken Maynard), hero in *North Star* (1926 C) with Clark Gable and Strongheart the dog; Noel Adams (Clive Brook) in *Scandal Sheet* (1931 C), a no-good, about-to-snaffle Kay Francis from lawfully wedded George Bancroft; bland serviceman Noel Wheaton (Lee Bowman) in *Cover Girl* (1944 C); Noel AIRMAN (Gene Kelly), butterfly lover of *Marjorie Morningstar* (1958 C); Noel Johnson (Barry Sullivan), brusque and unsympathetic in *The Light in the Piazza* (1962 C); very Briddish Noel (Gary

Marshall), all togged up in mod gear in *That Girl* 'He, She and He' (1967 T).

UK: Noel Bastable, a poet and the most 'delicate' of *The Treasure Seekers* (and its sequel *Five Children and It* 1950s R & T, also 1989 T); debonair Noel Snaith (Alan WHEATLEY) in *Murder without Crime* (1950 C); Noel Goddard (Ronald Howard), renegade colonial sahib in a 1960 *Danger Man* episode; Noel Holcroft (Michael Caine) in *The Holcroft Covenant* (1984 C); Noel (Edwin Richfield) in *Marjorie and the Preacherman* (1987 T).

Australia: Noel (Terry Norris) in *Homicide*: 'The Set Up' (1972 T).

Used for a female character: Noel Varner (Judith Ivey) in *The Long Hot Summer* (1985 T); Noel (Deborah Makepeace) in *the One Before Last* (1987 R).

Noel! Possibly the shortest line of dialogue spoken by a supporting (as distinct from bit) player in a gay role. This was one-time MGM yearling Carleton CARPENTER in SOME OF MY BEST FRIENDS ARE ... (1971 C) as a frail 'FAIRY' at Christmastide. (The shortest line spoken by a lesbian character occurs in KISS AND TELL 1980 T.)

Noir et Blanc (Fr 1986 C) Shy ACCOUNTANT Antoine becomes addicted to the pummelling of black masseur Dominique.
W/D: Claire Devers; adapted from the short story 'Desire and the Black Masseur' by Tennessee WILLIAMS; 80 mins.

'I never know where your hands will go. Each blow hurts ... my muscles are on fire. My bones break. But I'm not afraid of physical violence. I'm afraid only of death.' Claire Devers slowly and horribly reveals that both men are involved in a ritual of pain which both enjoy but know will soon end. The two actors (Francis Frappat and Jacques Martial) presumably used pseudonyms to emphasize the gladiatorial nature of their combat of flesh and muscle.

no need to lie Larry (Keith Prentice) wants a relationship with Hank (Laurence Luckinbill) in THE BOYS IN THE BAND (1970 C) which will allow space for them to grow and where there will be 'no need to lie or pretend'. THE SOUTH BANK SHOW's depiction of the Lytton STRACHEY – Dora CARRINGTON – Ralph Partridge household was called 'No Need to Lie' (1980 T). Marjorie (Lynn Redgrave) and Gail (Mariette Hartley) cursorily discuss the possibility of a time where subterfuge will be neither necessary nor acceptable in MY TWO LOVES (1986 T).

normal Like a drumbeat, the word became more insistent as more difference was uncovered. Manley (Rupert Davies), the head of a school for emotionally disturbed teenage boys, puts a new colleague on the spot by asking 'Normal? ... Who is normal? Are you? Am I?' in THE UNLOVED (1955 T). But such sentiments – and programmes such as *What Is Normal?* (by 'A Doctor' 1932 R) and *No Such Thing As Normal* (1962 R) – made little dent in the shifting but essentially static force field of 'normality' that is daily trotted out literally or by implication in nearly every area of broadcasting.

The 1960s were supposed to be a time of revolutionary change, but many see the period in hindsight as having qualities embodied at the time in characters written by Jack Russell in THE FAT OF THE LAND (1969 T). The embodiment of moral rectitude and exploitative entrepreneurism, Mrs Suez (Joan Greenwood) speaks wistfully of 'nice normal healthy people', only to be dismissed with a ferocious '*They* went out with the Beatles' from one of her self-indulging clients, teenage-fashion czar, Arnie Carnaby (Russell Hunter).

Lapping up its 'live now, pay later' philosophy but despising its more idealistic, experimental trappings, gangster Chas (James FOX) claims defensively in PERFORMANCE (1970 C) that 'There's nothing wrong with me, I'm *normal*', while tired pop lion Turner (Mick Jagger) and his household prove, with the help of drugs, that Chas was anything but.

Proving that abnormality and its mirror image are relative, a decade after the Beatles brought forth the wrath of the short-back-and-sides establishment because of their long hair, Sid James was able to say to his shoulder-length-styled and conditioned-haired son (Robin Stewart) in *Bless This House* 'Two for Tea, Four for Tea' (1973 T) with some relief (and no irony): 'At least you *look* normal.'

Irony comes from those outside looking in: Barbara (Dolores Fuller) extolling the promise of the normal life she and Glen (Daniel Davis) will lead together in GLEN OR GLENDA?/I LED TWO LIVES (1953 C) before the cat, or rather the angora sweater, is let out of the bag and he tells her – what the audience already knows – that he is a TRANSVESTITE.

Larry (Keith Prentice) defines normality in THE BOYS IN THE BAND (1970 C) as 'a wife and mistress', while Mike (River Phoenix) in MY OWN PRIVATE IDAHO (1991 C) sees it as 'Normal husband, wife and dog. Normal, normal ...'

Many regard normality as heaven-sent. John OSBORNE was presumably serious when he revealed (in *A Full Life* 1984 T) that he had been given two of God's greatest gifts: 'to be born English and heterosexual. You can't really go much further than that.' This statement was accepted without comment. Jocelyn Coleman (John Westbrook) meets a similarly smug attitude from the hero in *Castles in Spain* (1987 R) with regard to the former's enduring love for a boyhood friend: 'You obviously don't consider that there is any love other than a heterosexual one.'

Wieland (Wieland Samolak) in *Der Sprinter* (1984 C) decides to give up being gay and become a real man to please his father. Out go his symbols of deviancy: cigarettes, alcohol, friends. Down from the bedroom wall comes his near naked poster-sized Christopher Atkins from *The Blue Lagoon*. 'Yes, dearie,' he tells a mate, 'I've become normal.'

Just what normal is has been put under the microscope in a few programmes during the 1980s, mainly from CHANNEL 4 which was prepared to prod a few sacred cows, at least during its early years, and question the inevitability of what is natural and normal, indeed the very meaning of the words themselves (eg *Pictures on Pink Paper* 1985; *Am I Normal?* 1992 R).

Maybe it's the women who will lead the way out of the normal straitjacket. Women like Opal (Raye Dowell) in *She's Gotta Have It* (1986 C) who 'hates the word normal', and Josie (Suzanne Packer) in BROOKSIDE (1990 T) who tells Billy: 'I had kids because I was told it was fun ... like normal people with normal husbands. How normal are *you*, Billy Corkhill?'

In American television, only bigots like Archie Bunker and cartoon characters like Homer Simpson can throw the idea of blind, bullish obedience into stark relief. 'Never say anything unless you know it is what everybody else thinks,' Homer tells Marge in THE SIMPSONS (1991 T).

'What is normal?' asks a transvestite on DONAHUE 'People Who Hate Being Referred to as Sexual Oddities' (1992 T).

Norman ... Is That You? (US 1976 C) Father (Redd Foxx), betrayed by his wife (Pearl Bailey), discovers that his son Norman (Michael Warren) is not only gay but living with a (camp) white man (Dennis Dugan). He brings in a (female) prostitute to unbend his baby boy. But ...

W: Ron Clark and Sam Bobrick from their play; P/D: George Schlatter: 92 mins.

Cheerfully low-rent, dirtyminded farce which attempted to move America into macro-homosexuality within a framework of a bickering, blaring black family comedy. The most daring thing about the film version, adapted from an unsuccessful Broadway play which became a hit on the dinner theatre circuit, is that all of the main protagonists, save for the boyfriend, are black.

Norris, Senator David (1944–) Chairman of the Irish Gay Rights Movement, Senior Lecturer in Modern English at Trinity College, Dublin, civil libertarian and Joycean scholar. Senator from 1987. Profiled on OUT ON TUESDAY (1990 T). A frequent – merry, flippant, wholehearted – broadcaster in Ireland, and in Britain (on gay literature, *Frank Delaney* 1984 T).

Northern Exposure (US 1990–   T) Life and the eccentrics who live it in the Alaskan town of Cicely, which was named after one half of a lesbian couple who helped found it.
Cr: Joshua Brand and John Falsey; P: Cheryl Bloch and Matthew Nodella; 60 mins.
An Emmy award-winning series, neither comedy nor drama, soap nor alternative, but one that manages to be popular and a cult at the same time. Two of its main characters are an exiled young doctor, Joel (Rob Morrow) and a pilot, Maggie (Janine Turner). John Fisk, Professor of Media Studies at the University of Wisconsin told *Screen* (Aust R 1993): 'It very quickly established itself as part of the American culture ... This has quite clearly something to do with its taking place on the margin ... the margin is much looser, there's much more freedom there; life is lived according to quite different rules ... There's a sense of gay or lesbian subtext in Maggie and Joel's sense of self-sufficiency and their total inability to have a sexual relationship.'

Northern Ireland *See* IRELAND.

North of Vortex (UK 1991 C/T) Poet, sailor and waitress hit the roads of Nevada.
W/D: Constantine GIANNARIS; P: Rebecca Dobbs; 55 mins.
Rich in (BLACK AND WHITE) pictorial effects, with appealing motifs and rhythms, a limpid jazz score by John Eacott, and a convincing bout of sexual shadow boxing from Stavros Zalman and Howard Napper.
'My film isn't just a gay or bisexual variation on the ROAD MOVIE. It's about

sexuality, jealousy, the confusion of DESIRE and our inability to capture that "obscure object of desire" ... I think a very strong element of anybody's desire is that it can never be 100 per cent fulfilled. Or even 50 per cent. And that's what keeps us going ... People who have the money to buy their desires are intensely unhappy' (Constantine Giannaris interviewed by David Melville, *Gay Community News* (Ireland), February 1992).

Norvelle, Duncan (1958–) Nicely presented, pinky and perky comedian and impressionist with a flossy, come-hither yet non-threatening gay persona. His catchphrase 'CHASE ME' further endorses the idea of the passive, coy, always available (to heterosexual men from 8 to 80) PETER PAN. But he has a genuine sweetness about him and, like Julian CLARY, is definitely not neuter: 'Now, what are you going to do with me now you've caught me?'
Appeared on *The Main Attraction* (1984 T, billed in *TV Times* as 'The outrageous humour of "Chase me, chase me"'; *3–2–1* (1985 T): 'The doctor said I've got some bad news and some good news: The bad news is you're 90 per cent the other way. The good news is I love you'; *Laugh Attack* (1986 T); *Celebrity Squares* (1993 T); etc. Was one of the players on *Blankety Blank* (1985 & 1987 T). In 1985 he presented the pilot of a dating game show called 'It's a Hoot' which went on to be a big hit – but without him – as *Blind Date*. (Bobby Davro impersonated him in *Live From Her Majesty's* 1985 T.)

Nostradamus [Michel De Nostredame] (1503–66) French astrologer and physician, a prophet of ambiguous impenetrability. In *Nostradamus: The Final Chapter* (Aust 1989 T) one of the verses is translated as: 'Heaven weeps too much over the birth of the androgyne.' The inference is that this refers to gay people: 'Androgyne is ... quite appropriate when we consider that the AIDS disease was initially associated with homosexuals.'

not as other men Used frequently in the ROUND THE HORNE send-ups of films and plays, particularly those involving master villain Chou-En Ginsberg (Kenneth WILLIAMS). Nicole (Primi Townsend) in *World's End* (1981 T) recalls her father using it, which causes her friend Camille (Pam Scotcher) to scoff: 'Not as other men! How discreet can you get!'

not married yet? One of Michael Schofield's gay men in MALE HOMOSEXUALS (1965 R) spoke for millions of homosexual people the world over, now as then: 'I dread the question "Are you married?" because I think they will eventually ask, "Why aren't you married?"'

Heterosexuals are far from immune. In one of his 1980 shows, Kelly Monteith confided:

If you aren't married by a certain age people are suspicious. At a school reunion a typical jock says, 'Hey, where's your wife?'
'I haven't got one.'
'I should have known. You're in show business. I expect you've been divorced three times.'
'I'm not married.'
'You mean you've never gotten married? Well, I'll be damned ... My God, I used to dress next to him in the gym.'

not the marrying kind The phrase is usually a disparagement, as in Steve Temple's (Marjorie Westbury) 'he's not the marrying kind' to Carl Lathom (Simon LACK) in *Paul Temple and the Alex Affair* (1964 R). It goes back a long way – to the early part of this century: 'You're like me. You're not the marrying kind,' says Alun Trevose to Philip in PENMARRIC. And further: The young MORGAN LE FAY (Patsy Kensit) tells MERLIN in *The Legend of King Arthur* (1979 T): 'I have no wish to marry.'

It's been a staple in drama since the 1960s as it neatly tells those who wish to know that something queer is going on: 'Somehow I never thought of you as the marrying sort,' says Ian Carmichael to Derek Nimmo in *The Amorous Prawn* (1962 C). 'Neither did I, sir,' he

simpers. Nimmo, this time as Jago Peters in THE DALES (1967), told *au pair* Gunnel that, much as he'd like to, he couldn't because he just wasn't ...

Sandra is angry that her sister Gwen (Margaret Ward) is pouring cold water on her daughter's future plans in *A Bowl Full of Sixpences* (1964 R): 'Jane's the marrying kind. What you want for her is all right for some women but not all women. Some prefer being SPINSTERS all their lives. They're made that way I guess. Jane isn't ...'

Kathy Roache (Maureen Kershaw) in BROOKSIDE (1990 T) tries to cool down the wedding fever which is enveloping everyone by saying simply and clearly: 'Some of us are the marrying kind and some aren't.'

The phrase is mainly used to clue in the audience that the hero knows there is something queer going on: the villain of *Royal Flash* (1975 C), Alan BATES says of Florinda Bolkan's fiery Lola Montès: 'If I was the marrying kind, she'd be the last woman on earth.' But the audience, having seen the way he ogles Malcolm McDowell's Flashman, knows these are empty words.

Or to make someone even more miserable than they were previously: 'We never saw our headmaster as the marrying kind,' giggles Tony, one of the boys, to the nervous young bride (Victoria Carling) in *Mortal Term* (1990 R).

Or as saving polite characters from having to use blunt terminology: 'She's not the marrying sort,' says Mother (Thora Hird) bitterly about her career woman daughter who hardly ever visits in *Say Something Happened* (1989 R). 'But she's happy.' (This passage was not included in the 1982 television production: '[Margaret] could have been married. Married three or four times over if she'd wanted.')

Deeply hurt that René is getting married in 'ALLO, 'ALLO (1987 T) the hangdog Lieutenant GRUBER (Guy Siner) dabs his eyes with a piece of toilet paper in the church. Choking back his rejection, Gruber says: 'I had the distinct impression that you were not the marrying kind.'

Ultimately, it helps people cope with the daunting truth that not everybody follows the same path in life, for whatever reason. When a caller, a woman in her forties, tells Phil DONAHUE (1990 T) and his audience how happy she is, she is pressed for information on her husband, boyfriend or lover. Of these she has none. Donahue, fumbling, tries to neatly wrap her up: 'Perhaps you're not the marrying sort of person.'

Young Anthony Moore (Benedict Taylor) in *A Man Alone* (1986 R) rationalizes: 'I don't know whether I shall get married. I'm not sure I'm the marrying sort. It may be fun to have a mistress. Or just a very close friend.'

Novarro, Ramon [Ramon Samaniegoes] (1899–1968) Mexican-born Hollywood star of the silent period, a rival of Rudolph VALENTINO: dashing, light-hearted lover (although his only durable role was as the increasingly ruthless Messala in *Ben Hur* in 1927). Of his talkie roles, only his partnering Greta GARBO in *Mata Hari* (as a young soldier who goes blind) created a ripple down the years. He is now only mentioned – on programmes about Hollywood's 'seamier side' – with regard to his death: a particularly brutal slaying, apparently by two young men he brought home to have sex with. He was bashed with a bronze dildo said to have been a gift from and modelled by Valentino.

C: began as an extra; *The Prisoner of Zenda* (1922); *Scaramouche* (1922); *The Midshipman* (1925); *The Student Prince* (1927); Lord Gerald Brinsley in *A Certain Young Man* (1928 – made in 1926, refilmed – as a roué); *Across to Singapore* (1928); *Forbidden Hours* (1928); *The Pagan* (1929); *In Gay Madrid* (1930): 'much ado about a gay BLADE'; *Call of the Flesh* (1930); *Son of India* (1931); *The Son–Daughter* (1932); *The Barbarian* (1933); *The Sheik Steps Out* (1937); *We Were Strangers* (1948); *The Big Steal* (1949); *Crisis* (1950); the villain De Leon in *Heller in Pink Tights* (1960); etc.

Novello, Ivor [Ivor Davies] (1893–

1951) Welsh actor, playwright (*The Rat*) and creator of musical romances (*Glamorous Night*; *The Dancing Years*). An untrained musician, he wrote evergreens like 'Keep The Home Fires Burning' and 'We'll Gather Lilacs' (from *Perchance to Dream*). His memory is kept throbbing by occasional revivals of his Ruritanian musical romances, by BBC Radio 2 orchestral galas and by HINGE AND BRACKET.

C: *Carnival* (1922); *The Bohemian Girl* (1922); *Bonnie Prince Charlie* (1923 C); *The White Rose* (1923); *The Man without Desire* (1923); *The Rat* (1925); *The Lodger* (1926): probably his best known role, directed by HITCHCOCK; *The Triumph of the Rat* (1927); *Downhill* (1927); treasure hunter Vernon Winslowe in *A South Sea Bubble* (1928); Lewis Dodd in *The Constant Nymph* (1928); Nicky in THE VORTEX (1928); *The Lodger* (1932); the railway conductor hero in *Sleeping Car* (1933); *I Lived with You* (1934); Tyrolean in *Autumn Crocus* (1934); etc. He wrote several screenplays in Hollywood in 1931, contributing to *Tarzan, the Ape Man*.

R: Anthony Allen in *Glamorous Nights* (1939); DESERT ISLAND DISCS (1942); Charles I opposite Yvonne Arnaud in *Charles, the King* (1946); Max Clement, a penniless composer in THE TRUTH GAME (1950); etc.

T: *Starlight* (1937) etc.

Biography: *The Man Behind the Mask* (1938 R); *The Ivor Novello Story* (1958 R): 'The gay eventful career of the star whom millions remember with affection'; *Ivor Novello* (1964 R); *Story Time* 'Ivor' (1971 R) read by John Palmer; *Ivor: The Life and Times of Ivor Novello* (1973 R, award-winning 7-part series); *Ivor Novello: Celebration* (1974 R); *The World of Ivor Novello* (1976 R); *The Songwriters* (1978 T); *Song by Song by British Lyricists* (1982 T).

November Moon (West Germany–France 1984 C) Jewish woman November Messing (Gabriele Osburg) is loved and protected during the Second World War by a Gentile, Ferial (Christiane Millet) in Paris.

W/D: Alexandra Von Grote: 107 mins.

A love-in-war story that is told with enormous flair and enacted with great passion. Perhaps one of thousands of stories involving homosexuals in time of enormous chaos, hardship and fear – but how many ever make it onto the big screen. This one did, and it deserves to be better known.

Now She Laughs, Now She Cries (UK 1975 R) Married Carol Martin (Angela Pleasence) gives up life in Kensington to live with Leah Sutcliffe (Penelope Lee) in Belsize Park. She experiences joy, disillusionment and pain, not to mention seeing lesbian friends pilloried and one driven to suicide.

W: Jill HYEM; D: Jane Graham; 14.4.75; BBC Radio 4 (The Monday Play); 90 mins.

Mainstream BBC Radio's first modern play about lesbians: ambitious in scope, intelligent – and praised at the time in the pages of *Sappho*. The Sunday afternoon repeat did not go ahead as it was deemed 'unsuitable'. The play blends love scenes, classical and pop music ('BOTH SIDES NOW'), the heady atmosphere of all-women spaces, brushes with the law (CHILD CUSTODY) and the glassy 'understanding' of straight friends.

'Society's attitudes towards homosexuals have become more tolerant over the last few years, at any rate so far as men are concerned. But with women it's a different matter. It seems that most of us find the idea of relationships between two women totally unacceptable' (*Radio Times* synopsis).

Now That It's Morning Title song of the Neil BARTLETT short (1992 T) with lyrics by Bartlett and music by Nicholas Bloomfield, a dirge sung (on a café juke-box) by Sonia Jones, as Gerald (Malcolm Sinclair), Ian (Nicholas Pickard) and their drag queen companion, Regina Fong greet the dawn. 'Now that it's morning, put out that last cigarette ...'

nowt so queer as folk A Yorkshire expression that travelled South, without direct relevance to same-sex activity. The philosophy fell regularly from the lips of Bernard Miles' Mummerset/Hertfordshire countryperson *Nathaniel Titlark* (1956–7 T) who delivered salty monologues about the goings-on of the people in his village, from vicar to milkman. Pam Tickell partly used the expression as the title of her play (*Nowt So Queer* 1972 R) about a village so secluded it is unable to receive television and so has to find its entertainment in other (dangerously medieval) ways.

Now, Voyager Walt WHITMAN's poem used for the Bette DAVIS film of the same name, and at the end of the gay brief encounter in FLAMES OF PASSION (1989 C):

Now, voyager
Sail thou forth
To seek and find.

nudge, nudge, wink, wink Eric Idle as a grotesquely salacious (but not coarse) salesman in MONTY PYTHON'S FLYING CIRCUS (1969 T). Used widely thereafter to cover the many, many things that people cannot say. *See also* OUTING.

nudism *See* NATURISM.

nudity *See* NAKEDNESS.

Number 96 (Aust 1972–7 T) The lives of people living in a block of flats in Sydney.

W: David SALE, Michael Boddy, Eleanor Whitcomb, Bob Caswell and Tim Purcell; P: Don Cash and Bill Harmon for Cash-Harmon Productions and Channel 10; D: Peter Bernardos, Brian Phillis and Johnny Whyte.

Number 96 was the first of its kind: a provocative daily serio-comedy with copious nudity and a broad-brush approach to sexuality including homosexuality. It was a trigger for change, which made viewers feel that prejudice against homosexual men was beyond a joke.

Set in Sydney's Paddington (modelled

on a block of flats at 83 Moncur Street, Woollahra), this runaway success was shown five nights a week (winning top ratings on each one) to an adoring and amazed audience that couldn't get enough of its lively characters (Jews, Greeks, Indians, Aborigines, gays), inventive situations, humour, sex and nudity. There was abortion, Nazism (a war criminal exposed), a lesbian witch (played for laughs; 'a very stereotyped dyke,' wrote Dennis ALTMAN) and, says its creator David Sale (who wrote the pilot in four days), 'all the girls were raped, including the Aboriginal hairdresser'.

Its plots became wilder as invention flagged – bits of *Jaws* and REBECCA; the Pantyhose murderer (a woman); the knicker-snipper; the hooded rapist; and an explosion which claimed the lives of five regular characters. Through it all, solicitor Don FINLAYSON (Joe Hasham) maintained his gay life with dignity and was a popular hero, not only with Australian gays but with housewives and old folk. The writers ran the gamut with Don: long-term affairs, brief affairs, beaten up by a sailor, defending a gay man who had lost his job, marrying for convenience, solving a murder case.

Number 96 restored the fortunes of Channel 10 and became the first series anywhere in the world to have across the board top ratings every weekday night. It won 9 Logie awards, including 4 for best drama series. *The Box*, set in the steamy world of Australian television, soon appeared on a rival channel and, although far less popular, managed to survive for 4 years, ending 3 months before its competition.

David Sale says:

Americans were fascinated by *Number 96*. They kept on wanting to do it, but they said we have to Americanize it. They kept on trying to do something with it. It became *Number 96, Sunset Boulevard*. It became a condominium inhabited by young actors and actresses. It had nothing to do with *Number 96*. The minute they started fiddling about with the characters, it ceased to have any viability. But they are fascinated with success ... They

wanted it, but couldn't take it in the form we had it here ... With its black elements, nudity, sex and homosexuality it would have contravened 'The American Black Book of Television', with its rules and regulations, vetoes and embargoes this thick. They could never network something like *Number 96*. They couldn't have shown it in the Deep South or the Bible Belt.

'In 2–3 years it has moved from an almost total boycott ... to guarded expressions of liberal tolerance in about half the big city press and much of radio and television. ... But ... basically it is a thing apart' (Dennis Altman, *New Journalist* (Sydney) 8, 1973 discussing the influence *Number 96* had on Australian-wide 'acceptance' of homosexuals).

nuns Sister Luke/Gabrielle (Audrey Hepburn) in *The Nun's Story* (1959 C) was based on Marie-Louise Habets, who, subsequent to leaving the religious life after the Second World War, lived with the book's author Kathryn C. Hulme from 1945 until 1981 when Ms Hulme died. After the scandal of *La Religieuse* (1966 C) with its openly lesbian abbess, many films of the 1970s (*The Nun of Monza*; *The Devils*) harped on the repressed sexuality of nuns: orgies, self-mutilation and lesbian passion; while Debbie Reynolds, trying to emulate Julie Andrews, played 'THE SINGING NUN' in 1966 as a dewy-eyed do-gooder. The real 'Soeur Sourire', Jeanne Deckers ended up poverty-stricken and committing suicide with her female lover in the 1980s. There were no takers for the movie rights of the sequel, but Australian radio produced a docu-drama in 1990 about the whole sad story. Reversing the usual situation, Sister Juana, the poet Juna Ines De La Cruz (Assumpta Serna), dresses as a nun because she is not allowed to dress as a man, and falls in love with the vice-reine (Dominique Sanda) in *I, the Worst of All* (1991 C). The fascination the nun exercises was interestingly narrated in *Damned If You Don't* (1990 C), a short which spliced in scenes from the great nun film *Black Narcissus*.

Nureyev, Rudolf (1938–93) One of the greatest male dancers of the 20th century and a natural successor to NIJINSKY. He journeyed from being, in his first teacher's words, 'an obstinate little idiot, who knows nothing of dancing' to adulation as a god of dance, and a sex symbol. He was still projecting the latter when he was no longer the former. His very last television appearance, swimming off his private island in the documentary *Nureyev* (1991 T), revealed him to have a fair old dangler. He was a natural television and film performer (although his few acting roles were stilted and lacking in charm), bringing dance and the male dancer into cracks and crevices of resistance all over the world.

C: *A Leap by the Soul* (USSR 1959); *Romeo and Juliet* (choreographed by Kenneth MacMillan, 1966); Don Basilio in *Don Quixote* (with Australian Ballet, 1973, co-D); title role in VALENTINO (1977); a terrorist in *Exposed* (1983). Also: projected Nijinsky film (1966–70).

R: NIJINSKY in *Nijinsky: The God of Dance* (based on his diaries, 1988).

T: *The Bell Telephone Hour* (Ger 1962); *An Evening with the Royal Ballet* (1963); *The Hollywood Palace* (with Fred Astaire, 1965); *Le Jeune Homme et la Mort* (choreographed by Roland Petit, Fr 1966); *The Burt Bacharach Special* 'Big Bertha' (choreographed by Paul Taylor, 1966); *Petrushka* (1966); *Swan Lake* (with State Opera of Vienna, 1966); *Sleeping Beauty* (with National Ballet of Canada, 1972); *Parkinson* (1974); *The Morecambe and Wise Christmas Show* (c 1975); *The Muppet Show* (partnering Miss Piggy, 1978); *Video Sera* (with Vittora Ottolenghi, It 1978); *Tim Tam* (with Vittora Ottolenghi, 1980); *Julie Andrews' Invitation to the Dance* (1980); *Giselle* (with Carla Fracci, 1980); *Romeo and Juliet* (choreographed by Nureyev with La Scala Ballet, 1982); *Dedicated to* DIAGHILEV (1982); *Dancer* (1983); *Raymonda* (with Paris Opera, 1983); *L'Altro* (by Paolo Calvetti, It 1983); *Nureyev–Dupond: The*

Meeting of Two Stars (by Paolo Calvetti, It 1984); *Inauguration of the Five* 'Washington Square', suite (1986); *The Dame Edna Everage Experience* (1987); *Cendrillon* (with Paris Opera, 1987); OMNIBUS 'Sir Fred: A Celebration' (1988); *Schiaccianoci* (with Paris Opera, 1988); *Margot Fonteyn* (1990).

Autobiography: *I Am a Dancer* (1972 C); interviewed by Lindsay Anderson (1974 T); *The Eloquent Masochist: Rudolf Nureyev* (1978 R); *Nureyev* (interviewed by Mavis Nicholson, 1981); *Nureyev* (1991 T).

Adulated – and satirized (in THAT WAS THE WEEK THAT WAS 1963, in the farce *Not Now Comrade*, and by comedians as unalike as Danny LA RUE 1965 T and Harry Secombe 1966 T). His influence on the shape of male dancing was acknowledged in the series *Dancer*. He remained very much a household name three decades on; eg the children's play *A Proper Little Nooreyev* (1987 T). (A film biography is being prepared by Franco ZEFFIRELLI for which Patrick Swayze has been mentioned as a possibility to fill the leading role.)

nurses Enshrined, usually as selfless, young and female in a number of films and TV series. UK: *Nurse Edith Cavell* (1939 C); *The Lamp Still Burns* (1943 C); *White Corridors* (1951 C); *The Lady with a Lamp* (1951 C); *The Feminine Touch* (1955 C); *No Time for Tears* (1957 C); *Carry On Nurse* (1959 C); *Twice Round the Daffodils* (1962 C); *Nurse on Wheels* (1963 C); ANGELS (1976–82 T); *The District Nurse* (1984 T). US: *Night Nurse* (1931 C, Barbara STANWYCK and Joan Blondell as two hard-bitten students, sharing a room and – at one point – a bed); *Sister Kenny* (1946); *Janet Dean, Registered Nurse* (1953 T); *The Nun's Story* (1959 C); *The Nurses* (1962–4 T); *Nurse* (1980 T); *Florence Nightingale* (1985 T); *Nightingales* (1988 T); *Nurses* (1991– T).

The only lesbian-identified, relatively sane nurse was Marilyn (Gail Strickland), a regular shining light in HEART BEAT (1988–9 T). All the others, with the exception of the briefly encountered 'happily married dyke' in *The Laughing Policeman/An Investigation of Murder* (1973 C), were usually women on the verge of a nervous breakdown: Alma (Bibi Andersson) transferring some of her own *Persona* (1966 C) to her patient Elisabeth (Liv Ullmann); Shirley Marlowe (Prunella Ransome) helping a wife through convalescence, falling in love with her and then taking an overdose in *Wednesday's Child* (1970 C); three lesbians (Laraine Stephens, Fay Spain, Lyn Loring) bilking elderly women in their care and then killing them in POLICE WOMAN 'Flowers of Evil' (1974 T); Linda Rae Guettner (Gena Rowlands) asked to hand in her badge while her custody case is in process in A QUESTION OF LOVE (1978 T); Australian Nellie Keene (Jeananne Crowley) in TENKO (1981 T) falling in love with the pregnant Sally; Nurse Diesel (Cloris Leachman) in *High Anxiety* (1978 C), a nasty piece of work; Opal (Mary Regan), the district nurse in love with teacher *Sylvia* (1984 C); Hilda Rolfe (Andrée Evans) and Ethel Brumfett (Thelma Whitely) in *Shroud for a Nightingale* (1984 T), the latter sharing her life with the charismatic Sister Mary (Sheila Allen) and being killed by her because she knows too much.

Men now account for 10 per cent of the profession and are now no longer necessarily described in television series as 'Male Nurse' – as was a walk-on played by Ron Kennedy in PERRY MASON 'The Case of the Murderous Mermaid' (1965 T) in the credits.

Are there any heterosexual (male) nurses? Most assuredly – and television has taken great pains (in CASUALTY especially) to celebrate this fact. One episode of this series contained a walk-on described in the cast list as 'Gay Male Nurse' (1987 T), just to point the difference between such a person and male 'Male Nurse' Charlie (Derek Thompson). ('Male' is also put in front of other hitherto unmanly professions: model, prostitute, stripper – but not florist. And 'homosexual' rarely has male (or female) in front of it even though the discussion relates to one sex only. 'Woman' is

usually added to doctor and there has been the odd 'Lady Librarian', eg in *Perry Mason* 'The Case of the Nervous Client' 1957 T.)

Nurses are portrayed in comedy as sexy blondes in skimpy uniforms or monstrous (older) women. Men hardly ever figure. THE GOODIES (1973 T) gave the (ailing) National Health service a drubbing featuring a 6ft 6ins, burly, bearded man in uniform. 'He's a male nurse' asserted one of the trio. 'No, he's *not*.' End of joke.

Gay nurses include Gordon Breen (Ian HOLM) terrorized on a picnic by his elderly charges in *The Frighteners* 'The Treat' (1972 T); Ken HASTINGS (Michael Howarth), chief student-nurse training officer in ANGELS (1979–80 T) with a copy of GAY NEWS in his in-tray and a crusading spirit; a couple in giggly attendance in *The Nation's Health* (1983 T); Ronnie (Hugh Thomas) tucking in the men after THE VISITING HOUR (1982 R); Dennis Learner (Martyn Hesford) involved in dirty doings in and around *The Black Tower* (1985 T); Deirdre's former husband, now HIV positive in DOCTOR, DOCTOR 'Accentuate the Positive' (1989 T) and a nurse who was always 'going off with men', Freddie MARTIN (Roland CURRAM) who retired to Spain in ELDORADO (1992 T).

Medical orderlies: Maturette (Robert Deman) helping Steve McQueen and Dustin Hoffman escape in *Papillon* (1973 C); Whitty (Kenneth GRIFFITH) in *The Wild Geese* (1978 C) giving up his job to be dropped behind enemy lines in Africa to be with his 'boys'; 'Sophie' (Warren Clarke) who has MERRICK's measure in THE JEWEL IN THE CROWN (1984 T).

Others: George Woodbridge in *The Black Sheep of Whitehall* (1941 C); Cuddles in *A Star Is Born* (1937 & 1954 C); Alan Welbeck (Tim Preece) in *The Funny Farm* (1975) with wife and two kids; Kevin Buckley (Michael Troughton) who plays football in the lunch break and dies of a haemorrhage in *Angels* (1978); Peter Dennis (Phil Daniels) in COMPROMISED IMMUNITY (1991 R); Dennis Taylor (Peter

Phelps), nurse and counsellor in *RFDS* (1993– T).

nymphomaniacs Laced with FRIGIDITY and sapphism, these creatures go back to Greek temples which were staffed by 'colleges' of unmarried priestesses, nubile young women independent of men called nymphs. The word later came to mean a bride, as in 'bride of God', but during the Middle Ages it became synonymous with FAIRIES. The overweening sexual urge is connoted because of legendary fertility rites associated with these women. Hence nymphomania, which has become a staple of entertainment: Myrna Loy in *Love Me Tonight* (1932 C) is asked: 'Don't you think about *anything* but men?' 'Yes,' she replies with a rapacious glint: '*Schoolboys.*'

When Hollywood flirted with psychoanalysis in the mid-1940s, the nymphomania was an obvious excuse to portray sexually abandoned women laced with frigidy and sapphism: Miss Carmichael (Rhonda Fleming) in *Spellbound* (1945 C); homicidal Emmy Baudine (Siobahn McKenna) in *Daughter of Darkness* (1948) from the 1938 Max Catto play *They Walk Alone*; Margaret Hayes as Emily in *Violent Saturday* (1955 C): 'You're an alcoholic and *I'm* a tramp,' she tells husband Richard Egan; Clara (Françoise Arnoul), a canteen worker in *La Rage au Corps* (1954 C) who was 'a tainted gal'; Ava Gardner as Lady Brett Ashley in *The Sun Also Rises* (1957 C); Claire Bloom as NAOMI Shields in *The Chapman Report* (1962 C). Nymphomania became a staple of television drama from 1959 onwards with *The Torrents of Spring* and *Through a Glass Darkly*.

In 1960s cinema 'the disease' began to be used for laughs: Alan BATES crept by his landlady's door in *Nothing But the Best* (1964): 'All quiet on the nympho front,' he asided to the audience in voice-over. Melina Mercouri played the first self-identified example in American cinema (*Topkapi* 1964), followed by a whole caravan of over-sexed harpies – most famously Glenda Jackson in *The Music Lovers* (1971), which Ken Russell sold on a one-line synopsis: 'The story of a homosexual and a nymphomaniac.'

In the 1980s Christine Baranski was fourth billed as 'The Nymphomaniac' in *Lovesick* (1980 C); Emily Morgan trapped a policeman in her flat in an effort to make him some sort of love slave in *The Bill* 'That Old Malarkey' (1989 T); Judi Dench 'shocked' her fans and amazed her critics by playing 'alcoholic nymphomaniac' Christine Foskett in ABSOLUTE HELL! (1991 T, which is how she was made up to look) – her last line, croaked amid the ruins of her club La Vie En Rose, is: 'Don't let me be alone!'; Tracy Camila Johns, the heroine of *She's Gotta Have It* (1986 C), had a large appetite, though the film's politics stopped short of presenting her as a 'nympho'.

Recently, one or two male characters have begun wondering if they too should not be considered pathological sex maniacs: Walter Matthau in *House Calls* (1976 C) and the neighbour in *Empty Nest* (1989 T) who describes himself to Charlie (Richard Mulligan) as 'a male tramp'. And Jack Carney (Hart Bochner) in *Apartment Zero* (1988 C) spends the night with a woman, explaining somewhat defensively to Adrian (Colin Firth) the morning after: 'I didn't *plan* to be a slut.'

Mrs **'Obbs** Character in an Australian commercial radio comedy (sponsored by a cold-remedy firm) which ran for well over a thousand episodes during the 1950s. Dan Agar was Liz 'Obbs and Leslie Lofton her husband Alfie.

'It was like folksy humour: tragic, sad, nostalgic, funny ... Basic local humour. If you listen to all of them you will not find any double meaning, any dirt, any dirty four letter words or what I call public lavatory wall writing. Liz 'Obbs, [was] played by Dan Agar (who was a shortish, roundish, nice benevolent young bloke) ... to me and to the rest of the cast [he] *was* Liz 'Obbs. Although he'd be dressed in male attire (normal everyday suit), he was the very embodiment of Liz 'Obbs. He *was* a woman, in fact. And during the tender scenes when Alfie would be kidding to him, I'd put my arms round Dan, and he or she would lay her head on my shoulder and it was husband and wife. And there was nothing unhealthy about it,' Leslie Lofton, interviewed in the 1970s, heard on *Tony Baldwin's Radiogram* (Aust 1992 R).

The Obelisk (UK 1977 T) A dowdy couple on a day's outing and their encounter with two sailors, one of whom, Tiny (Nick Ellsworth), 'won't say no to anything' and has a brief fling with the snobbish little schoolteacher husband, Ernest (Peter SALLIS) – while his wife (Rosemary Martin) is well satisfied with the second tar. Nice one!
W: Pauline Macauley from the story by E. M. FORSTER; P: Graham Benson; D: Giles Foster; 13.10.77; BBC2 (Première); 30 mins.

Oberon, King of the Fairies. Character in *A Midsummer Night's Dream*. Accompanied by his servant PUCK, he is involved in some dirty work with his estranged wife whose changeling boy he craves. Oberon presents a glorious opportunity for malevolent seductiveness, power-hungry manipulation and shadowy sexuality. Played in the cinema by Victor Jory (1935, with Kenneth Anger as his desired prize); David Warner (1968); Michael Matou (1984, with his consort Titania incarnated by Jack 'The Incredible Orlando' BIRKETT). Played on radio by Laurence Payne (1953); Robert Harris (1959); Gabriel Woolf (1964); Malcolm Hayes (1979); Nigel Hawthorne (1983); Hakeem Kae-Kazim (1991); (also by Patrick Waddington in *Depression Over Fairyland* 1933). Played on television by John Justin (1958); Robert STEPHENS (hissing fit to bust, 1971); Peter WYNGARDE (1964); Peter McEnery (1984).

A frisky character played by Ronnie Stevens in the Norman Wisdom comedy *On the Beat* (1962 C) was called Oberon, and there were also the soppy unmarried Oberon brothers in *We Must Kill Toni* (David Markham and Andrew Osborn 1951 T; Richard Hurndall and Dennis Arundel 1952 R; Bob Monkhouse and Alfred Marks – as 'cousins' – in 1962 film version *She'll Have to Go!*).

O'Brien, Maureen (1943–) British actress whose performances always make instinctive sense whether she's essaying sinewy tragic heroines, foolish wives or virgins, sprites and sylphs, raging neurotics or women of strong, practical beliefs. With the less prolific Cheryl Campbell and Diana QUICK, she is British radio's premier woman player of her generation, a talent that can confidently handle much of the huge range of roles this medium can offer.

She began her career on television: she was one of the DOCTOR's companions, eg *Dr Who* 'The Time Meddler' (1965). More recently she was James BARRIE's wife Mary in THE LOST BOYS (1978), MORGAN LE FAY in *The Legend of King Arthur* (1979), and Elizabeth Straker in *Casualty* (1987).

On radio she won the 1978 Best Actress award for *By Grand Central Station I Sat Down and Wept*; she was Allie, threatened by her sister's 'uninhibited' approach to sex in *The Elephant and the Panda* (1978); Verena Tarrant, beloved protégé of Olive Chancellor in *The Bostonians* (1979); Mary whose vision of the Virgin Mary pursues her from childhood in *Down to Earth* (1980);

the feminist artist in *The Bracelet* (1980); Titania (opposite Nigel Hawthorne) in *A Midsummer Night's Dream* (1983); Lou Andreas Salome in *Dissonance* (1984); Iphigenia in *Iphigenia at Tauris*, priestess of Diana's temple and sister of Orestes (1986); *Mrs Dalloway* (1986), the politician's wife preparing for a party; Myra Lacey who conceives a passion for a woman she meets on a train in *Remaining Strangers* (1986); Helena in *All's Well That Ends Well* (1986); Imogen Gresham in *The Tortoise and the Hare* (1986); reading stories by COLETTE (1986); Octavia in *All for Love* (1987); Egle in *La Dispute* (1987); Elizabeth Fry in *Prisoners* (1987); Rachel liberated in Venice in *The Third Mask* (1991); the haunted Christine in *Ghosts from the Past* 'Blue Stockings and Broken Mirrors' (1992); unstable but valiant Gail in *Runaway* (1992); reading A BOOK AT BEDTIME 'The South' (1992); etc.

Ocker/Ockerism The most extreme version of that unique species of AUSTRALIAN male, who feels uncomfortable in the presence of women, wears stubbies (shorts), SINGLETS and thongs (recently replaced by Reeboks and socks), drinks 'tubes' of beer, talks of cricket and the footie, is mocking, knocking and loud-mouthed ... Personified by Barry McKenzie and Sir Les Patterson (Barry HUMPRHIES), and is to be given a wide berth. Very much the image of Australians overseas, and everything many Australians hate – although Ockers are revered in some quarters for their humour, playfulness and stout hearts.

Paul O'Grady, the openly gay New South Wales MP, commented on this phenomenon (apparently named after a character called Oscar in a 1960s TV series) in *Life Matters* (1993 R): 'getting stuck into the poofters or the lezzos is quite acceptable. Ockerism goes with sexism and HOMOPHOBIA.'

October Scars the Skin (UK 1989 R) Ashley (Dominic Rickhards) discovers the body of Vincent October (Richard Pearce) who has been QUEER-BASHED.

He goes to see the dead man's long estranged mother Stella (Carole Boyd) and draws close to her, as also he does to Gideon, Vincent's lover (Ian Targett). Ashley finally confesses to Stella that he could have saved Vincent's life, but had long entertained fantasies of discovering a corpse so he made no attempt to prevent Vincent's death.

W: Philip RIDLEY; D: Gerry Jones; 16.1.89; BBC Radio 4; 90 mins.

Radio noir with a quiverful of juicy characters, especially the mother and Ashley's Aunt Sally (Eva Stuart). A number of side issues are brought into the plot, such as Ashley's unconventional relationship with Kit (John McAndrew), his sexual attraction to Gideon via the memory of Vincent ('We kissed each other like *this*. Does it feel wrong?'), and Gideon losing his job because the police came to his work asking him about Vincent. Overlaying the central mystery is the alienation of children by parents. Ashley solaces the mother who rejected her son for same reason Ashley's father turns away from him.

Stella tells Ashley: 'I felt he was alien to me ... a creature from another planet, a monster almost. It's true he was my own flesh and blood and I could barely believe him human. Does that shock you?'

Ashley asks his father: 'How can your love for me depend on who I fell in love with. I don't understand. I just don't understand. It's not rational, it's not.'

Through one gay man's needless death, another achieves full existence, but it's a blighted one as the title suggests.

Odd Man Out (UK 1977 T) Neville Sutcliffe owns a fish and chip shop which he runs with his (unseen) friend Bobby. His life changes drastically when he inherits half of a rock factory with his prudish half-sister (Josephine Tewson).

John INMAN's breakaway series was a headbutt to ARE YOU BEING SERVED?'s kick in the groin. It had hand-me-down scripts and archaic situations not sighted since Old Mother Riley.

The uneventful, quasi-romantic relationship between 'brother and sister' plus seaside postcard jokes about effeminate men and girls with big breasts has to provide the sole source of humour. There are no other gay characters, save for the hapless Bobby on the other end of the phone, carrying on at the chippie. The hoped-for merriment hinges on sylph-like Neville (in some most becoming suits: his favourite colour is pink) pressed against the chests of large women.

Produced by Carry On expert Gerald Thomas for Thames, *Odd Man Out* nearly capsized Inman's career at its zenith. The only memorable aspect is the uncanny ability of its creator to weave seven identically bad episodes, with nothing to choose between them.

Alan Coren, writing in *The Times*, couldn't understand why Inman 'wishes to do no more than camp around around a cheap set, limping heavily on both wrists. Merely being gay may have done for a cheap laugh in the last series, but should he not now build upon that single characteristic? ... In my view, Mr Inman is getting dangerously close to being an Auntie Tom.

'Be not afraid of effeminacy. Some men are born effeminate, some achieve effeminacy, and some have effeminacy thrust upon them. And if you are lucky enough to ring all three bells, chances are you could end up with your own series.'

Ode to Billy Joe Bobbie Gentry's song is silent on the matter, but the 1976 film version reveals why Billy Joe McAllister jumped off the Tallahatchie bridge. It seems that he (Robby Benson) was unable to make love to his girlfriend, because he had 'allowed himself' to be seduced by his male boss, couldn't deal with the tumultuous emotions unleashed, and ended it all. Which left his girlfriend to pretend she was pregnant by him, and leave town in order to 'save' Billy Joe's good name.

Ode to Walt Whitman By Federico García LORCA, written in New York, full of 'agony, agony' and ending with the thought that 'life is not noble or wholesome or holy'. The poem brings comfort to the troubled inner life of José (Hector Alterio) in *To an Unknown God*. (1975 C). He plays a tape of it before he goes to sleep in his purple-covered bed surrounded by identical-shaded walls, haunted by the memory of Pedro, the beautiful young boy in the house where his mother was a servant in Granada in the 1930s.

Towards the end of the film, a meek pianist (José Pagan) suddenly reveals to José – before fellating him – that he was the secret older lover of the dead Pedro. The next morning, as José leaves for Madrid on the train, the man brings him a bunch of FLOWERS which he shyly hides from other passengers. José accepts them with joy.

The film indicates that José may have moved on, freed from the memory of unrequited love and able to see his fellow gay men as something other than the creatures depicted in the poem: 'On rooftops or huddled in bars ... catlike and serpentine perverts – all of them perverts, grimy with tears, meat for the whiplash, the boot or the bite of the animal tamers.'

oh, get on with it! A piece of fierce Kenneth WILLIAMS pique begun on ROUND THE HORNE (1965) and taken on board in *Just a Minute* (1967–87 R). The phrase then became the title of Williams' unsuccessful 1976 radio show.

okedoke/okey-dokey A popular distortion of 'okay' which was popular in America from the mid-1930s and indicated many an idle female prattler in Britain from the late 1940s, eg the dizzy babysitter Gladys (Vera Day) who accidentally sets Mai Zetterling's flat on fire in *Dance Little Lady* (1954 C).

Dizzy males used it too: like Paul and Steve Temple's live-in factotum: CHARLIE, a cheery, gay chappie, and a man of few words (mainly 'okedoke'). It was in full usage by the mid-1950s when the addled Fairy (Violet Gould) disdainfully uses it in *Pots of Money* (1955 T) to show how up to date with the modern lingo she is.

Although Burt Reynolds' character uses the expression in the opening episode of *Evening Shade* (1990 T), it is now rarely heard: Fiona (Pamela Stephenson), masquerading as American bimbo, chirps it in *Scandalous* (1984 C) and Lady Mary Fairfax uses it in answer to her secretary in FOUR CORNERS 'Bad Blood' (1991 T).

older homosexual/gay men Characters grappling with various physical or psychological problems of ageing: played by Charles Lloyd Pack and Hilton EDWARDS in VICTIM (1961 C); Eric PORTMAN in *Deadfall* (1968 C); Lloyd Pack again in THE ROADS TO FREEDOM (1970 T) and *An Unofficial Rose* (1974–5 T); Maurice Denham in *The Gate of Eden* (1980 T); David MARCH in WEEKEND WITH WILLIE (1980 R); Bryan Coleman in COMMITMENTS (1984 T); John GIELGUD in QUARTERMAINE'S TERMS (1987 T); Joss Ackland in *A Murder of Quality* (1991 T); etc.

Those finding that life is richer for being older and wiser: John HURT in the last scene of THE NAKED CIVIL SERVANT (1975 T); Joseph O'Conor in ONLY CONNECT (UK 1979); Emlyn WILLIAMS in *Past Caring* (1986 T); Werner Dissel in COMING OUT (1989 C); characters in *Adieu Victor*.

Documentaries: *Aquarius* 'Over There on a Visit' (1977 T); John Burnside and Harry Hay in WORD IS OUT (1977 T); THE SOUTH BANK SHOW 'A Time There Was' (1980 T) and 'Sir Angus WILSON' (1980 T); *Inside Story* 'Coming Out' (1980 T); Gifford Skinner in GAY LIFE 'Gay Life in the 1930s' (1981 T); AN INTRODUCTION TO SOCIOLOGY 'Life Histories' (1981 T); *Nationwide* on Ian HARVEY (1982 T); *Claire Rayner Casebook* 'Bereavement' (1983 T); *An Evening with Quentin Crisp* (1983 T); *Silent Pioneers* (1984 C); THE OTHER HALF 'Angus and Tony' (1984 T); OPEN SPACE 'It's Called Jo-Anne' (1986 T); OUT ON TUESDAY (1989–90); DESIRE (1989 T); COMRADES IN ARMS (1990 T);

DONAHUE 'Gay Seniors' (1989 T); *Resident Alien* (1990 T); OUT 'Storm in a Teacup' (1992 T); etc. (Gay men are almost never seen or heard on TV/radio programmes by and about or for and about older people.)

'First rule of survival. Get there under your own steam or if you can't manage it, hang on until they reach you with the bedpan. Otherwise, as you rightly put it, off to gas chambers,' says Edward Minty (Emlyn Williams) in PAST CARING (1986 T).

older homosexual/gay women/lesbians Nancy Price in *Mandy* (1952 C); Mary O'Farrell in A VERY GREAT MAN INDEED (1953 R), THE PRIVATE LIFE OF HILDA TABLET (1954 R) etc; Cicely Courtneidge in THE L-SHAPED ROOM (1962 C); Beryl REID in *Smiley's People* (1982 T); Mary MORRIS in *An Unofficial Rose* and *The Happiest Women* (1984 R); Chevi Colton in *Kate and Allie* 'Landlady' (1984 T); TINY AND RUBY – HELL DIVIN' WOMEN (1988 C/T); Idgie (Jessica Tandy) in FRIED GREEN TOMATOES AT THE WHISTLE STOP CAFE (1991 C).

Documentaries: Elsa Gitlow, a 77-year-old poet in WORD IS OUT (1977 C); GAY LIFE (1981 T); SILENT PIONEERS (1984 C); Erica PUNCHON (Monty) on *The Midday Show* (Aust 1987 T); Buffy Dunker in DONAHUE 'Gay Seniors' (1989 T); Mary Miegs in THE COMPANY OF STRANGERS (1990 C); DESIRE (1989 T); COMRADES IN ARMS (1990 T); WOMEN LIKE US (1990 T); *Women Like That* (1991 T); occasionally on TV/radio programmes by and about or for and about older people.

Old-fashioned Girl aka I'm Just An Old-fashioned Girl. Deceptively sweet melody with tinkly orchestration coupled with cynical words about woman acquiring man and, more importantly, his bank account. A direct relative of 'Diamonds Are A Girl's Best Friend', being all about soaking rich men for the sparklers.

Eartha Kitt made it her own on record, while also delivering the lyrics with clawing impropriety, purring and projecting languorous looks on a chaise longue and a mocking cackle on television – principally *The Nat 'King' Cole Show* (1958), her solo *Kaskad* (1961) and *The Royal Variety Performance* (1962), where she was barred from directing the song at Prince Philip. Thirty years later she was on the chaise with the same growl and those long fingernails, proclaiming that she was still the same 'old-fashioned' person of the female gender in *The Happening*.

The composer Michael TIPPETT requested 'Old-fashioned Girl' ('it has this lyric that cheers me') for his desert island stay in 1985 explaining that he 'identified' with the lyrics – which are definitely more than first meets the ear. Ms Kitt declares that VIOLETS are her favourite flowers, and one of the acquisitions her rich 'husband' could provide her with is two apartment buildings 'labelled "Hers" and "Hers"'.

The Old Ladies A bullying woman destroys the tranquillity of another, driver her to death. Hugh WALPOLE's terrifying story of the power of the strong over the weak was adapted as a play by Rodney ACKLAND, providing meaty roles for actresses like Edith Evans, (as the juggernaut Agatha, and Gwen FFRANCGON-DAVIES, as the meek Jane who dies with the name of the woman she had loved on her lips (1968 R; also 1975 & 1984). Katina Paxinou was chilling in the 1967 television version.

Oliver Boy's name sometimes used for floppy or slippery characters and general misfits.

US: Edward Everett HORTON as Oliver the butler in *Once a Gentleman* (1930 C); Oliver (Robert Young), a marginal who falls in love with another in *The Enchanted Cottage* (1945 C); Oliver Niles (Charles Bickford), stern but fair studio head in *A Star Is Born* (1954 C); Theodore Bikel as Oliver Krangle, overbearing busybody, snoop and moral crusader, 'a dealer in petulance and poison' in THE TWILIGHT ZONE 'Four O'Clock' (1962 T); Oliver Pope (Edward Andrews), purse-lipped bureaucrat responsible for child's death in THE

TWILIGHT ZONE 'You Drive' (1964 T), Oliver Douglas (Eddie Albert) in *Green Acres* (1965–71 T); rich boy transformed by love and grief (Ryan O'Neal) in *Love Story* (1970 C) and *Oliver's Story* (1978 C); Oliver Franklin (Brad Savage), judge's son in *The Tony Randall Show* (1976–9 T); Beaver's son in *The New Leave It to Beaver Show* (1984–5 T); initially arty Oliver Rose (Michael Douglas) who becomes a vicious warrior in *The War of the Roses* (1989 C).

UK: Oliver Twist; Oliver (Reginald BECKWITH), 'touchy ballet master' in *Murder without Crime* (1950 C); Oliver Pettigrew (Arthur HOWARD) in *Whacko!*; Oliver Bramwell (Jack Hawkins), insurance assessor who falls for arsonist in *Fortune Is a Woman/She Played With Fire* (1957 C); Oliver (Hugh BURDEN) pursued by guilts involving two male lovers in A SUPERSTITION (1977 T); Oliver Lloyd (Andrew Francis) in GEMS (1984–5 T).

Oliver Button Is a Sissy (Aust 1984 T) Little Oliver (Steve Kaanna) enjoys dressing up and dancing. Ridiculed by his schoolmates, he enters a dancing competition, wins and finds he is the toast of his class, and is seen as an asset in playground football because of his lightning movements and kicks.

Adapted and directed by Margot Phillipson from the book by Tomie De Paola; ABC; 15 mins.

The triumph of a SISSY – except that his dressing up has been considerably modified (astronauts and pirates) in this retelling, and his acceptance by the other kids seems to happen literally overnight. An interesting bit of social engineering all the same: real boys can dance (and put on costumes) and still be an asset all the time. (The story was read on *Listening Corner* BBC Radio 4 1987 10 mins.)

Olivia Girl's name: the noble lady in *Twelfth Night* who is attracted to the woman dressed as a boy (Thea Holme to Beatrix LEHMANN's Viola 1937 T); Olivia (Joan Crawford) in *The Shining Hour* 1938: 'I didn't like any of the things I did and the people I did them with'); English schoolgirl OLIVIA (Marie-Claire Olivia 1950 C). It was the name of the American feminist record company set up in the 1970s.

Olivia aka *The Pit of Loneliness* (Fr 1950 C) English girl (Marie-Claire Olivia) caught up in passionate feelings for headmistress Julie (Edwige Feuillère) and her companion Cara (Simone Simon) at a French boarding school.
W: COLETTE from the novel by Dorothy Bussy; D: Jacqueline Audry; 96 mins.
'In Jacqueline Audry's hands *Olivia* becomes an almost overpoweringly erotic piece of work. Warmingly intimate lighting bathes sets which are opulent without vulgarity and which proved the perfect background for the subtle and very potent ardour of Julie and Olivia. It's astonishing that a film intended for the commercial market should deal so uncompromisingly and so powerfully with emotions which are almost universally derided in popular literature and film' (Alison Hennegan, *Gay News*, 1979).

omipaloni/hommes paloni Meaning – in POLARI – homosexual (omi = man, paloni = woman). In a 1966 ROUND THE HORNE gangster Baby Face Homi-Palome (Kenneth WILLIAMS) has to choose between a sawn-off Shirley Bassey and a Dusty SPRINGFIELD rifle.

Omnibus (UK 1967– T) BBC1's resplendent arts series which now comprises some 500 biographies and interviews with most of the major people in arts and entertainment over the past quarter of a century: Franco ZEFFIRELLI, Dirk BOGARDE, Mary RENAULT, David BOWIE, Graham Greene, MORECAMBE AND WISE, Lotte LENYA, Lillian Hellman, Frederick ASHTON, Edmund WHITE and Benny HILL. The series also enabled Barry HUMPHRIES to seek 'the ghosts of long dead pederasts in Dieppe', recalling the Uranian heaven of Oscar WILDE, Bosie, John Addington SYMONDS, Aubrey Beardsley and refugees from the Cleveland Street scandal

in 'A Summer Side-Show' (1977). Other memorable portraits of those departed include 'Judy: Impressions of GARLAND'; 'A Night's Darkness, A Day's Sail' (Virginia WOOLF); DIAGHILEV; 'In Search of Lost Time' (Proust); 'Dance of the Seven Veils' (Richard Strauss, with the BBC's first 'lesbian KISS').

One in Five (UK 1983 T) A miscellany of dykedom and gaydom, based in London's Heaven super-disco.
P: Caroline Mylon; D: Paul Oremland; 1.1.83; KINESIS Films for Channel 4; 60 mins.
Homosexuals having a night out on their (super-glossy, whizz-bang) home turf. Fighting for attention were disco diva Grace Jones, film critic Jack BABUSCIO, COMEDIANS Wendy Wattage and Bernard PADDEN, drag act the Trollettes (David Raven and Jimmy Court), actor Stuart Turton, actor–interviewer Stephanie Pughsley, Badgie DYKE alias Kate Crutchley plus nearly a dozen more. It was a mish-mash, on the loud, confused and whispy side but darkly funny at times. There were 100 phoned-in reactions to Channel 4 (on New Year's Day): 60 to 40 in favour. GAY NEWS readers had their say, across 3 pages, over 2 editions (257–8). In summary it was felt that *One in Five* 'did nothing to help', made us 'ashamed to be gay', was 'fundamentally boring' and an 'unrelieved disaster', and 'put the clock back'.
Henry from West Sussex wrote: 'I'm angry, very very angry that this gay world apparently shrieks ghastly musak, lives in discos, dressed in a ludicrous bizarre fashion, 'butch' chains, Nazi caps, heavy beards or shaved heads, all looking as if they had fallen out of a cheap box of crackers.'
He went on: 'Me? I'm just a poor gay boob who for 27 years paid a mortgage, looked after an invalid sister for 30 years – [and worked as] a landscape gardener.'
Jeff from West London said: '[I] had told so many straight friends to watch the programme and my sense of shame that such a terrible programme should

have been produced by gay people was truly bad. Where were all the beautiful men, where were all the beautiful boys one sees in clubs, pubs, parties? Are all gay people left-wing? God, I could have hurled the television set out of the window at the misrepresentation of the programme.'

H. I. Karilo and R. P. Blows commented: 'There is no reason why a programme about gays should automatically be better than any other programme on television, but it is sad that ... the makers of *One in Five* should have produced such an unrelieved disaster ... The film showed only a tiny London-based eccentric fragment of life among homosexuals. The self-regarding attitudes displayed by those lucky or confident enough to face the cameras can have evoked little sympathy:'

N. R. King said: 'Small wonder gays receive such a biased press when producers of these kinds of programmes see fit to portray them in this way ... Where did the producer find them? ... They [gays] were shown to be rather sad parodies of seemingly unhappy misguided human beings. *One in Five* may certainly be like that, but how about the other four?'

A Cheshire reader reckoned: 'It's put the "gay" clock back 150 years ... With certain respectful exceptions, all we saw was a mass of utterly bizarre, crude, inarticulate, ludicrous people mainly between the ages of 18 and 30.'

However, reviewer Jackie Marcus felt the programme exuded 'an atmosphere of love and laughter and sheer enjoyment at being gay and it not being any kind of heavy scene ... ask for more'.

One of the few correspondents who agreed with her, Tony Cafferata, said he was 'convinced that all the letters ... were written by members of the ordinary – 100 per cent Straight-Looking-Average-Everyday-Gay Liberation Group. How sad it is they're appalled and so apologetic to heterosexual friends watching all these types they disown: clones, limp wristers, effeminates ... moustaches'. Which prompted more letters from 'the ordinary 100 per cent

etc who just blend in with the grey featureless landscape of Straightsville'.

Not since GAY LIFE had there been such reaction: mostly umbrage taken at the mix of people on display (noticeably almost as many lesbians as gay men) and its free-floating style.

one night stands First heard in PERRY MASON 'The Case of the Sardonic Sergeant' (1958 T): club hostess Nikki (Barbara Luna) tells Paul Drake that "it wasn't a one night stand'; reiterated by uptight business whizz Molly Thatcher (Lee Remick) in *The Wheeler Dealers/Separate Beds* (1963 C).

In DYNASTY (1988 T) Alexis (Joan Collins), aghast that former husband Dex (Michael Nader) has slept with her most hated rival Sable (Stephanie Beacham), screams: 'Tell me it didn't mean anything! Tell me it was just a one night fling!'

Although one-nighters are not usually recommended for women in plays, a BBC memo – concerned about the lack of (defined) sexuality in SOUTH OF THE BORDER (1988–90) – allegedly ordered one written into the character of Finn (Rose Rowell). Other heterosexuals who indulged have included Philip (Ronald Pickup) in *A Man Alone* (1986 R) who tells his wife Jennifer: 'It was a one night stand, for Christ's sake. I did it because I wanted to feel wanted.' (Jennifer promptly commits suicide.)

Married man (Michael Douglas) has what he thinks is a quickie with a woman he meets at a party, but all hell breaks loose (*Fatal Attraction* 1987 C). More laid back was the nightclub photographer (Andrea Cunningham) who defines herself matter-of-factly as 'a one-night stand' after a few hours in bed with the hero (Gary Sweet) in POLICE RESCUE 'Reason to Live' (Aust 1992 T).

Gay one-nighters, usually ending in either disillusionment or murder, surfaced in THE DETECTIVE; A HYMN FROM JIM; NIGHTHAWKS; CRUISING; LAW OF DESIRE; TOGETHER ALONE. In LA CAGE AUX FOLLES a night's gambol leads to a gay man having a son.

Lesbian examples are scarce: LIANNA

(1983 C) and army officer Cindi (Betsy Julia Robinson) end up in bed (pleasurably and with no strings attached) after meeting in a bar.

Sally Jessy Raphael presented a programme in 1992 entitled 'One Night Stand That Ruined My Life' about a young woman who contracted HIV/ AIDS after sex with a man (and died four months after the interview went on air).

one of them Used by Cliff Richard's worried screen dad (Percy Herbert) about the vicar in *Serious Charge* (1959 C). In *The Dick Emery Show* (1971 T) the roving VOX-POP interviewer asks CLARENCE if he believes in class distinction. Clarence has to be prompted. 'Like "Us" and "Them".' Clarence ponders for a few seconds, then gushes that it doesn't bother him either way 'because I'm one of them.'

'Is he one of them?' asks Jo (Katy Manning) when faced by the rather extravagant time-lord (Patrick Troughton). His successor (Jon Pertwee) reassures her: 'He's not so much one of them as one of us ... we are two parts of the same person' (*Dr Who* 1970 T).

Horrified by her daughter's insinuation that she and her friend are lesbians, rigid Mum (Patricia Routledge) outbursts in THREE PIECE SWEET (1979 R): 'As if anyone could take *me* for one of *them*.' Gail's mother (Sada Thompson) tries to dissociate her daughter from 'one of those people' in MY TWO LOVES (1986 T).

René (Gorden KAYE) is asked by a member of the Resistance whether Lieutenant Gruber (Guy Siner) is 'one of us' in 'ALLO, 'ALLO (1984 T). 'No,' hisses René, 'he's one of them.' Gruber begs René to keep his voice down. 'Please do not tell everybody. I was very lonely on the Russian front.'

THE FLYING DOCTORS 'Being Positive' (1991 T) has one of the audience-identification figures say of an HIV-positive man. 'He's one of them.' But he isn't. Two of the townspeople in *Salem's Lot* (1980 T) discussing writer David Soul say:

'What's his book about?'
'His latest is about two men.'
'Not one of *those?*'

Only Connect (UK 1979 T) In 1974 Graham (Sam Dale), writing a thesis about Edward CARPENTER and the socialist movement, goes to visit John Bury (Joseph O'Conor), who knew Carpenter when he was a youth. What begins as a routine interview ends surprisingly, putting Graham more closely in touch with gay history and himself. The past and future are represented by E. M. FORSTER (Christopher Banks) giving a talk to celebrate Carpenter's centenary (removing any indecorous mention of Carpenter's preachment and practice on homosexuality), and Graham and his lover Colin (Karl Johnson) preparing for a gay pride march in 1979. W: Noel Greig and Drew GRIFFITHS; P: W. Stephen GILBERT; D: Richard Stroud; 18.5.79; BBC2 (The Other Side).

> The political becomes personal as Graham's insufferably liberated, politely contemptuous façade crumbles – along with the viewer's – into fascinated awe and a kind of love. Age limits become meaningless as do other kinds of fetters. The circle is completed but there is a bitterly ironic ending. It is a sensational work in the truest sense: changing our perceptions, stimulating our minds, stretching us. Why doesn't Graham catch the train (back to Birmingham and to his lover)? Why does the faceless windbag become, at Graham's request, the co-occupant of a double bed? Why does the title of his thesis change from 'The Roots of Socialism' to 'The Life and Works of Edward Carpenter'? And why is it never completed? (*Gay News*)

Shown around the same time as the full but empty COMING OUT, the play marked the 100th anniversary of E. M. Forster's birth, the 50th anniversary of Edward Carpenter's death, and the 10th anniversary of Stonewall and the birth of gay liberation. Through its use of time past, time present and time future, *Only Connect* was history informed by Carpenter's utopian socialist vision, by the gay movement and by inter-generational tensions – none of which had ever been dramatized on television before (or since).

'I think it's the first time gays have been presented without quotes and on their own terms,' said its producer W. Stephen Gilbert.

Forster's injunction which gives the play its title was used by Gillian Reynolds in the *Second Edition* programme (1987 R) on links between people, living and dead. Alistair Mant, a psychologist interviewed on *Life Matters* (Aust 1993 R) said that Margaret THATCHER, brilliant strategist though she was, had one Achilles' heel. 'The civil service said she couldn't make connections, could not see the effects that a set of actions would have. As E. M. Forster said, "Only connect" and the problem is that many people in power don't.'

The Only One South of the River (UK 1980 R) In 1978 John (Philip Davis) negotiates with a Clapham publican, Mr Moore (George A. Cooper) and his wife Eileen (Irene Sutcliffe) to use their upstairs room for a Sunday night gay disco. Moore is initially resistant, but his wife urges him to give the venture a chance: 'It's 1978; things have changed.' Moore comments: 'Not in my back yard they haven't.' To which she replies: 'Then it's time you did some weeding.' All goes well until their son Terry's 18th birthday, when heterosexual horseplay gets out of hand. John is blamed and barred from the pub. He is determined to try again somewhere else and the publican's wife loses a good friend.
W: Drew GRIFFITHS; Capital Radio; 60 mins.

Very pleasing, if diagrammatic, moral tale which successfully uses lashings of MUSIC to set the scene, outline some of the characters and change pace. The writer's strengths are most visible in the character of the publican's wife taking her exposure to gay life (including a 'back room') in her stride and perhaps wishing that John were her son in preference to the ungracious lout she seems

to have raised. The play was voted Best Drama Production in the Rediffusion/ Radio Month Local Radio Awards in 1981. Said Drew Griffiths: 'It's particularly nice because it's so rare to hear anything gay on the radio.'

'The bitter ending, based on misunderstanding and predetermined ideas, is a more than accurate reflection on many people's experiences. Yet despite its crusading message, I would have liked more than just a plot and a statement of position; some attempt to create characters which are more than just cut-outs would have suggested the complexity of the emotions and the feelings ... Drew Griffiths' play suggested but did not confront the intricacies of "gay LIFE-STYLE"; it would be marvellous to see how he dealt with and developed the themes he only touched on ... in a much longer piece' (Emmanuel Cooper, GAY NEWS 210).

the only person in the world *See* I THOUGHT I WAS THE ONLY PERSON IN THE WORLD.

On Trial 'Oscar Wilde' (UK 1960 T) WILDE (Micheal MACLIAMMOIR) in the dock at the Old Bailey with flashbacks to the previous case when the Marquess of Queensberry was the defendant.

The disgust the case engendered lay not only in the nature of the sexual acts themselves, but also in the enjoyment Wilde had with young men, exclusively from 'the lower classes'. The boys had sex willingly, receiving small presents and, sometimes, friendship from their partner. For these liaisons Wilde's career, family structure, fatherhood, physical and mental health, fortune and reputation were utterly destroyed.

A loosely Christian society – which J. B. Priestley lambasts at the end – sanctioned the mammoth over-reaction by police and judiciary to cases involving gay men, of which the Wilde trial is the most famous. In his summing up Judge Willis said: 'I would rather be engaged in the most shocking murder case than this ... the worst case I have ever tried ... [the prisoner] was at the centre of a circle of corruption of the most hideous kind ... His sentence is totally inadequate for a crime such as this.'

All in the name of 'protecting the public'.

This hypnotic production, lit by Mac-Liammoir as the no longer brazen Wilde, was the first to present male prostitutes or 'good-time' boys on the screen. (Neither of the Wilde cinema films emphasized the sexual partners, save for Bosie, in any way.)

'We pretended it was all about Famous Trials, rather than just the Wilde. I was very straight; married at the time – I wondered why they gave me this one to direct ... I'd like to say there was a kind of liberal thing from Granada, but there really wasn't,' said Silvio NARIZZANO at 'OUT OF THE ARCHIVES' (21.7.92).

Also in the series: Roger CASEMENT. Other trials involving homosexual people or situations include *The Portsmouth Defence* (1966 T); CRIES FROM CASEMENT (1973 R); SERGEANT MATLOVICH VS THE US AIR FORCE (1978 T); A QUESTION OF LOVE (1978 T); CROWN COURT (1972–84 T); *Ladykillers* 'Murder at the Savoy' (1980 T); CIRCUIT II – MIAMI (1979 T); L.A. LAW (1986– T).

ooo! aka oooh! Frankie HOWERD exclamation from the days of *Variety Bandbox* (1952 T) through *Up Pompeii!* (1969–71 T) to 1990s adverts for crisps and tea ('putting the "ooo" in Typhoo!'). It most resembled the gargling sound of satisfied innocence that a baby might make – a rather *salacious* baby.

ooo in'e bold! A hooting expression which found immediate favour with the general public after Sandy/Kenneth WILLIAMS first browbeat Kenneth HORNE with it in ROUND THE HORNE (1965–9 R). Mr 'Orne would only have to express the mildest interest in Jule and Sand's personal doings, or gingerly place his toe in a sea of *double entendre* for his boldness in so doing to be shriekingly pointed out to Julian by his ever-watchful partner: 'Oooowh, inny bowwld!' *See also* I'M FREE!

ooo, stop messin' about *See* STOP MESSIN' ABOUT.

Open Space (UK 1973– T) BBC2 ACCESS series in which groups and individuals put across ideas and activities with the help of the BBC's Community Programme Unit. Among those availing themselves of this doorway into Britain's living rooms: residents of Earls Courts (including one or two gay ones) in 'A Time ... A Place ... A State of Mind' (1983); Peter TATCHELL in 'Peter Tatchell and the Battle for Bermondsey' (1983); Magor Ladies' Rugby Team in 'Ungentlemanly Conduct?' (1985); the Gay Media Group in 'A Plague on You' (1985): 'tackling the lurid and misleading reporting of AIDS in the press'; a male-to-female TRANSSEXUAL in 'It's Called Jo-Anne' (1985); parents falsely accused of child abuse in 'Innocents at Risk' (1986); witches and satanists in 'Lucifer Over Lancashire' (1987); Stephen Burn in 'Straight and Narrow-Minded' (1988); Goldsmiths' College Media Research Group in 'The Media and the Loony Left (1988); a social worker living with AIDS in 'Dealing with the Beast' (1990 T); British Naturist Association in 'Full Frontal' (1992); the Metropolitan Community Church (1992); Frances Allam in 'Unspeakable Acts' (1993): about female rape, child abuse by women and lesbian domestic violence.

Open to Question (UK 1984– T) Among those facing 'a studio audience's tough questioning' in this BBC series: singer Cliff Richard (1985); actor Michael CASHMAN (with the Rev. David Holloway, 1988); footballer Justin Fashanu (1992).

Open University *See* OU.

Operation Lightning Pegasus (UK 1981 R) A very free version of the Trojan Wars and how the horse got into the city.

W: Alick ROWE; D: Shaun McLoughlin; 14.11.81; BBC Radio 4; 90 mins.

A sort of Carry on Trojans for radio ('We need someone who is tight at the back'), with ACHILLES (Henry Stamper) presented as a Glaswegian who is having severe problems with his machismo, his penis size and his closetry: 'Patroclus [Nicholas Courteney] and I are just good friends.' Then, in the heat of the battle, he decides to come out: 'All the years I lived in illusion ... All my life I've been suppressing my feelings ... Now I'm free. I'm out of the CLOSET. Gay is good.' But it's no good. His fate is sealed – a wound in the heel:

> 'Achilles, it's only a little prick.'
> 'Even *that* you knew!' (Dies.)
> 'Poor Achilles. The first victim of gay liberation!'

oranges are not the only fruit Nell Gwynn said it first, but it is not actually spoken in the 1990 television production of Jeanette WINTERSON's novel. Instead, the mother is shown doggedly bringing the same kind of fruit each day when she visits Jess in hospital: clamped to routine in shopping as in the spiritual side of her life.

Oranges Are Not the Only Fruit (UK 1990 T) Young Jess (Emily Aston) grows up among Pentecostal Christian adults (Geraldine McEwan, Kenneth Cranham etc) who have no room for doubt or ambiguity. As an adult, she (Charlotte Coleman) becomes a charismatic preacher and is then banished from the fold when she falls in love with women (Kathryn Bradshaw, Katy Rodrigues).
W: Jeanette WINTERSON; P: Philippa Giles; D: Beeban Kidron; BBC2; 3 parts; 50 mins each.
A joyous saga of shackled childhood and youth, played with great finesse and simplicity. It's a horror comic of child abuse, but the author's forgive and forget attitude carries all before her. The evangelicals are given their due as single-minded folk carrying out the word of the Lord – to the letter; some being better at it than others. This was the first modern lesbian novel to be adapted for television, and its high good spirits were garlanded with British Academy of Film and Television Awards.

Orchard, Julian (1930–79) English television and occasional film actor of splendidly lugubrious, ineffably comic manner combined with the face and voice of an unturned pancake. Some dramatic roles (the man whose child is killed underneath the wheels of an aristocrat's carriage in *A Tale of Two Cities* 1958), but usually in comedy: the head waiter in *It's All Lovely* (1963); one of the residents, 'an old maid', in *Comedy Playhouse* 'Haven or Rest' (1970); Snout in *A Midsummer Night's Dream* (1971); the prissy journalist in *Grubstreet* (1974); and – taking over from Arthur-HOWARD – as Oliver Pettigrew in *Whacko!* (1971). He was toothy and gushing in *On the Beat* (1962) and *Revenge of the Pink Panther* (1978), but mingled his mannerisms with genuine warmth as the Lord Chamberlain in *The Slipper and the Rose* (1976). Also: *Show of the Week* (1972 T).

orgasms The knotted fists, head- and bed-banging, panting, gasping, clutching, groaning, moaning, roaring, and complete capitulation to ecstasy are becoming more familiar on radio and on television as a way of neatly denoting sexual intercourse. A close-up of a face caught between pain and pleasure obviates the need for nude bodies and lots of actorly writhing.
Among the more noticeable orgasms in the cinema: Ava Gardner's in *Bhowani Junction* (with Bill Travers, but it was cut, 1956); Jeanne Moreau's in *Les Amants* (with Jean-Marc Bory, 1958); Bernadette Lafont's in *Les Bonne Femmes* (in a wood and synchronized with the cry of a bird, 1960); the noisy male one (dubbed, it transpires) at the beginning of LAW OF DESIRE (1987); Meg Ryan's in the restaurant scene with Billy CRYSTAL in *When Harry Met Sally* (1989); Pauline Collins' in *Shirley Valentine* (partnered by Tom Conti off a Greek island on a boat's sunlit deck); River Phoenix's symbolic one (a house falling from the sky) in MY OWN PRIVATE IDAHO (1991);

Iggy's drawing forth dripping honey from the bee's nest to give to Ruth in FRIED GREEN TOMATOES AT THE WHISTLE STOP CAFE (1991); and there was Paco (Jorge Sanz) screaming out in acute exultation as he climaxes with Lucia (Victoria Abril) in *Lovers* (1991): she has maximized his pleasure by inserting a silk handkerchief into his anal passage, which she slowly withdraws at the moment of ejaculation.

On television Mark (Bill Nighy) was heard loud and clear (partnered by Harriet Walter as Charity) in *The Men's Room* (1991). He was one of a number of men making his pleasure manifest in this way in television serials of the early 1990s.

On radio the most famous, if erroneous, orgasm was that of Carol GREY (Anne CULLEN) in a 1957 episode of THE ARCHERS. Her 'surrender' on the sofa – to a man – was completed by the sound of vigorous exhalations which were revealed to be ... Aunt Laura's bicycle pump in the succeeding scene. Radio's longest delayed orgasm was that of Lesley Manville and male partner in Mike Leigh's play *Too Much of a Good Thing*, which was recorded in 1979 but not transmitted until 1991 because of its sexual indiscretion. Marvelled Robert Hanks in the *Independent* (21.7.92): 'Sex on radio is nothing novel, and this was done in much the usual way – a sequence of rustling and panting, punctuated by occasional embarrassed negotiations over positions and clothes. But it was remarkable for its length and the precise choreography of breathing, gasping and sighs – so that the exact moment of penetration was obvious. All the same this doesn't seem enough by itself to make the play unbroadcastable.'

orgies Absolutely standard issue in every Hollywood and Italian biblical epic. Tables groaning with grapes and wild boar, dancing girls gyrating, salivating men pawing at cleavages, lots of ribaldry and overflowing goblets of wine. The first to indicate that some orgies involved more than heterosexual activity was Cecil B. De Mille's *Manslaughter* in 1928 (two women were briefly seen embracing).

When the Hollywood epic declined, liberated Europe took over the orgy: *Les Cousins* (1959 C); LA DOLCE VITA (1960 C); THE CAESARS (1968 T); FELLINI SATYRICON (1969 C); *I, Claudius*, (1976 T); *Anno Domini* (1985 T); *Scandal!* (1989 C); etc. There are bisexual orgies in *The Servant* (1963 C); DARLING (1965 C); *Night Games* (1966 C); *Beyond the Valley of the Dolls* (1970); *The Wild Party* (1974 C); SALO: THE 120 DAYS OF SODOM (1975 C); *Private Vices and Public Virtues* (1976 C); *Caligula* (1980 C); etc. The most abiding image of a male homosexual orgy (drunken young men in various states of male and female undress slumped over their similarly inebriated older admirers) is that of the stormtroopers' revels in THE DAMNED (1969 C).

Orlando Boy's name used for the hero who falls in love with Ganymede/Rosalind in AS YOU LIKE IT (Laurence Olivier 1936 C etc). Also for the lone outsider (Jennie Stoller 1984 R; Tilda Swinton 1992 C) wandering through the centuries in Virginia WOOLF's eponymous novel based on Vita SACKVILLE-WEST: 'a man till the age of 30, when he becomes a woman.'

Orton, Joe [John Kingsley Orton] (1933– 67) English playwright. Brave, bold, self-centred iconoclast of the 1960s, relentless attacker of good taste. Remembered almost equally for his black farces, his sex-charged life and his death at the hands of his lover and mentor, Kenneth Halliwell. In PRICK UP YOUR EARS (1987 C) Gary Oldman presents Orton as a runty satyr, bursting with energy and bravado and unabashed cockiness. 'When I die,' he says to the artist who is painting him in the nude (save for his socks), 'I want people to say "He was the most perfectly developed playwright of his day".' Not an admirable character by any stretch of the imagination or loveable. But alive, alive-o.

'Every good play expresses something of the time in which it was written and at the moment we're living in a sick one' (from Orton's introduction to *The Ruffian on the Stair* in *Radio Times*).

C: *Entertaining Mr Sloane* (1970); *Loot* (1970).

R: *The Ruffian on the Stair* (1964).

T: *The Erpingham Camp* (The Seven Deadly Sins, 1967); *The Good and Faithful Servant* (The Seven Deadly Virtues, 1967); *Funeral Games* (1968); ENTERTAINING MR SLOANE (1968); *The Ruffian on the Stair* (*c* 1970); *What the Butler Saw* (1987).

Appeared as a panellist on *Call My Bluff* (with Gordon Jackson, Maxine Audley and Patrick Campbell, 1967 T).

Osborne, John (1930–) English playwright. Brilliant, daring iconoclast, despiser of pretension and woolly thinking; or small-minded, male chauvinist with fragile ego and obsessively hard on soft targets? His furious body of work contains a number of gay characters, usually whiners or unheroic victims. In one television play, almost the entire cast was revealed – Proust-like – to be homo or bi.

C: *Look Back in Anger* (1959); *The Entertainer* (1960); *Tom Jones* (1963); *Inadmissible Evidence* (1968); *The Charge of the Light Brigade* (1968).

R: A PATRIOT FOR ME (1981); *Look Back in Anger* (1982).

T: LOOK BACK IN ANGER (1956, 1958, 1976 & 1989); *A Matter of Scandal and Concern* (1960); *The Right Prospectus* (1970); *Ms, or Jack and Jill* (1972); *A Gift of Friendship* (1974); *Almost a Vision* (1976); THE PICTURE OF DORIAN GRAY; *The Hotel in Amsterdam* (1971); YOU'RE NOT WATCHING ME, MUMMY; *Very Like a Whale* (1980); *A Better Class of Person* (1985); *God Rot Tunbridge Wells!* (1985).

Autobiography: THE SOUTH BANK SHOW (1981 & 1992 T); DESERT ISLAND DISCS (1982 R); *A Full Life* (1984 T); A BOOK AT BEDTIME (1993 R) reading from his autobiography *A Better Class of Person*.

As actor: THE PARACHUTE (1968 T); *Get Carter* (1971 C); Alfred REDL in a short scene from the 1965 stage production of *A Patriot for Me* shown on THE SOUTH BANK SHOW (1992 T).

Oscars *See* ACADEMY AWARDS.

The Other Half 'Angus and Tony' (UK 1984 T) One of 'Six love stories about six very different couples. People in the public eye and the partners who share their lives.'

P: Edward Mirzoeff; 29.2.84; BBC1; 30 mins.

Radio Times daringly featured a photograph of Angus WILSON and Tony Garnett almost holding hands, the picture cropped off in mid-arms. They met on 31 December 1945, at the British Museum where both worked (Wilson was deputy superintendent of the Reading Room). We see them in the garden, at work (correcting a manuscript), at a preview of a television serialization of *The Old Men at the Zoo*, and at a dinner party with 'heterosexual friends' (as they don't always want to fraternize with gays).

The pair talked blithely about their years together as they busied themselves with preparations for a book launch. They were allowed one small dig at the 'other half'. While dining in Covent Garden, Angus and Tony observe a young man and young woman necking strenuously. 'I don't want to be unkind,' shimmers Angus, 'but there is an element of exhibitionism ... We do seem to attract oddballs, don't we.'

'Sir Angus Wilson and his companion Tony Garnett looked back over their 32 years together. Of the ménages so far ... this seemed to be the calmest and the happiest and, though I suppose it had the highest curiosity value, this episode also turned out to be the most dignified into others' lives' (Philip Purser, *Sunday Telegraph*, 4.3.84).

'This in itself is something of a breakthrough in the depiction of homosexuality on television. By their brave agreement to participate in this series, Sir Angus and Tony Garrett have probably done more for the acceptance and toleration of homosexuals than all the banner-waving militants put together. A

historic film. There's never been anything quite like it' (Herbert Kretzmer,
Daily Mail, 30.2.84).

The Other Other Woman (UK 1985
T) An American, Harriet (Diana
QUICK) living in Britain for 10 years who
teaches English in the 'C' stream:
'extra-mural, extra-curricular, expatriate – I'm becoming more ex- by the
minute.' She is repeatedly told by her
gay/transvestite colleague, Richard
(Michael Graham Cox), and by a heterosexual woman friend, Jill (Anne Carroll) that she's her own worst enemy.
Neither an affair with the married Stella
(Joanna McCallum) nor attendance at
women-only events gives her succour: 'I
don't know anything, I'm confused.'
W: Aileen La Tourette; D: Jane Morgan; 18.2.85; BBC Radio 4; 80 mins.

Many people will have identified with
the heroine: an insider's outsider –
having learned the hard way what she
doesn't want (unfulfilling relationships,
empty dogma), she's clueless about how
to go about getting what it is she does
want.

She thought the lesbian group would
be the answer. It wasn't. 'I've stopped
going. I could be some of myself all of
the time and all of myself some of the
time. But I'm greedy. I want to be all of
myself all of the time. Anyway I never
intended to leave behind one set of
social dogmas and formulas only to pick
up another . . . The patriarchy supports
its own and the radical lesbian feminists
support each other beautifully. And if
you're cut off from both sides you float
on your own. I could use that support, I
really could.'

And on and on she goes, irking the
Listener critic (28.2.85) in the process:
'sadly she came across as tactless,
demanding, self-pitying and an utter
pain in the neck as well as a good candidate for Sir Keith Joseph's purge of
unsuitable teachers'.

However, it was supposed to be a comedy.

The Other Woman (UK 1976 T) Kim
(Jane Lapotaire), an ARTIST, disrupts

the lives of Robin (Michael Gambon)
her married lover, and Nikki (Lynne
Frederick) an uncomplicated young
person for whom Kim is the other
woman.
W: Watson Gould; P: David Rose; D:
Michael Simpson; 6.1.76; BBC1; 70
mins.

An extraordinary farrago of the lucid
and the lurid. Kim operates purely in
the realms of art and emotion. She has
no interest in pleasing, or being polite or
particularly civilized. She is an amoral
character in a moral/immoral world. But
her views on life and religion are challenging and high-principled. The writer
claimed that her play was not about lesbianism directly but was 'a denunciation
of the patriarchal system and an analysis
of its continuing success'. Or was,
before it went into rehearsal.

At the time Kim was very much the
unacceptable face of lesbianism, and
much scorn was poured on the play after
its one and only transmission. Its angry,
disturbed nature rings on in the brain.

GAY NEWS 86 commented: 'The pressures of being a gay woman thrown out
of her lodgings and then her job (for
making heavy passes) were seen by Ms
Gould as less important than the pressures of being an (unrecognized) artist
and a militant feminist. And a difficult,
uncompromising human being.'

Watson Gould described the production as 'slimy' and agreed with the
women who wrote in anger that 'the
BBC had to make it a sex play, *as usual*':
'Kim, a composite character (directly
based on myself – weirdo or not), lost
half her personality in production. Her
inner fight to overcome her masculine
vices with her womanly virtues – a
personification of the world's need to do
likewise and the whole point of my play
– was destroyed.'

Her experiences with *The Other Woman*
would make a play in itself. Originally a
book (unpublished and much more violent: Kim 'hammered the hell out of the
kid'), the play diluted her views about
the existence of a third sex: 'To get my
views across I had to compromise myself
. . . I wrote a play with sex and violence

to carry my views: they cut my views and left in the sex and violence.' Particularly galling to her was the removal of any true friendship between Kim and Robin. The effect was to make a harpy out of Kim and a piece of toilet paper out of Robin, whose attraction to her was inexplicable.

Despite the author's disaffection with the finished product, the cuts and the emphasis on the violent sexual aspects of Kim's personality, the character still comes across as a powerful and passionate woman who acts on her instincts. But, for many, she remained a Scorpiorising, hard-drinking, raped-by-herfather flaming STEREOTYPE.

She – and *The Other Woman* – inspired the poem 'lesbian play on t.v.' by Caroline Gilfillan which was included in *One Foot on the Mountain. An Anthology of British Feminist Poetry 1969–1979* edited by Lillian Hohin (1979).

> ... she is ... potsmoking christian artist
> lavatory cleaner workingclass
> rapedbyherfatherat theageof11.

Other more immediate responses united mainstream television critics, conservative-minded viewers and feminists:

'Television is always getting it in the neck for depicting homosexuality as comic figures. But it would be hard to imagine anything more unsympathetic than the brutal realism of last night's serious portrayal of a lesbian' (Richard Last, *Daily Telegraph*, 7.1.76).

'I have just sat through *The Other Woman* and I feel quite ill with disgust at this evil parody of lesbianism. I wanted to turn if off but I wanted to see how it ended. I felt quite defiled and filthy for hours afterwards' (letter to *Radio Times* calling for censorship of such plays).

'As it stood, the play violated lesbians, made mockery by using stereotyped images, jumped onto the Women's Liberation bandwagon, with semi-contradictions of using a man in order to have a place to work, and hashed out immature ideas about Jesus' (Emma Read, *Gay News* 87).

OU (Open University) Home study leading to a recognized university degree, using a mixture of specially made radio and television programmes on a wide range of subjects, together with 'personal' tutoring, summer schools and other group activities. Among the relevant programmes: Radclyffe Hall *(Sexual Identity* (1981 T); interviews with two gay men *(An Introduction to Sociology* 1981 T); *Morality* (1980 R); *Modern French Writers* (André GIDE, 1982 R); *American Authors* (Gertrude STEIN, Tennessee WILLIAMS etc 1987 R).

Our Sons (US 1991 T) The coming together of two very different women: wealthy and sophisticated (Julie Andrews) and a rough-hewn barmaid (Ann-Margret) because the latter's estranged son (Zeljko Ivanek) is dying of AIDS and the former's son (Hugh Grant) is his lover.

W: Micki Dickoff; D: John Erman; 100 mins.

Regardless of the actual content (sincere; miscast – except for Hugh Grant, fairly predictable), this deserves attention, being the very first occasion American mainstream television had used the word 'our' in relation to gay people. This message could be seen as a rather crumpled one to Middle America (it was only *two* gay people, and one was dying), but even so, it acknowledged the fact that if gay people have parents then some of 'them' people must be 'ours'. It had taken over three decades for such a title to be chosen for such a project: from *The Homosexuals* (CBS REPORTS) to *Our Sons*, via A QUESTION OF LOVE, MAKING LOVE, PERSONAL BEST and MY TWO LOVES (all four of which involved a heterosexual apex to a triangle).

Out (UK 1991–2 T) OUT ON TUESDAY Mark II, with a new production company and transmitted on Wednesdays for a couple of months over two summers at 9pm.

P: Rebecca Dobbs and Cheryl Farthing (Alfalfa Entertainment); Channel 4; 60 mins.

Out's most immediately noticeable difference – apart from being shown on a different day – was the virtual disappearance of its predecessor's guest presenters like Lily SAVAGE, Pat Arrowsmith, Simon CALLOW, Beatrix Campbell, Paul GAMBACCINI and Julian CLARY. Otherwise it was more of the 'the latest in lesbian and gay issues' whizzed in the blender to produce sometimes spicy, occasionally bland or indigestible purees: good nourishing stuff on the whole, especially the first series which offered country and western music, a follow-up to WOMEN LIKE US, THE BATTLE FOR TUNTENHAUS, pet-owners and the politics of body HAIR.

The second series, though it contained the commendable 'Oy Gay' (lesbian and gay Jews) and 'Actions Speak Louder Than Words' (deaf lesbians and gays), didn't seem to work as wholeheartedly – or maybe it was raising issues that were too prickly or too complex for a 20-minute once-over: the sometimes great divisions between the men and the women; the dangerous allure of skinhead culture; class conflicts between women ('Working Class Dykes from Hell'); 'HOMOPHOBIA in Hollywood' in the wake of *Basic Instinct*; the 'gay brain' controversy; etc. There seemed to be a flattening off if not an actual decline; but, to some, *Out* seemed to have veered off course. A rethink was due, as indicated by the 'Pink Think' comment in the *Pink Paper* (10.7.92): 'Is the *Out* team's professionalism too streamlined? The complaint before was that the features were too bitty. The problem, now that the series is no longer new or innovative, is that it doesn't have any bounce at all ... The rest of television has changed in the last few years and *Out* should have changed, too. It should be reflecting our world – punchier and more interesting than the straight world that is ELDORADO. We can take our negative images, too. Perhaps *Out* has just drifted too far out.'

Although the average audience stayed around the 1.3 million mark (it had dipped from 1 million in 1989 to 0.9 million in 1990, but fully recovered the following year), CHANNEL 4 decided to rest the series for at least a year.

outing A concept briefly introduced by the US gay magazine *OutWeek*, involving the revelation of a person's homosexuality under certain circumstances (the person was rich, dead and homophobic; the person was rich and homophobic; the person was a movie star). The term itself – according to *OutWeek*'s Michelangelo Signorile in THE GAY AND LESBIAN WORLD (1992 R) – was coined by the magazine *Time* and 'given the same sinister significance as "wilding"' [the indiscriminate attack by a group of youths on a woman jogger].

In the wake of the *OutWeek*-inspired de-closeting of a number of men and women in America, a British group promised the media more of the same – only, having watched the slavering, to reveal that it was a hoax. The imbroglio – '200 queers will be named' – was enthusiastically recalled by Peter TATCHELL (who acted as telephone contact for the group FROCS and received hundreds of calls from all over the world) and the two instigators, Lofty Loughery and Shane Broomhall. The programme posed – but didn't completely answer – the question: cowardly fiasco or cunning exposure of mass hypocrisy?

The word stayed behind long after the strategy was found seriously wanting and abandoned. Writer William Goldman raised it as a matter of grave concern with Ian MCKELLEN nearly six months later in *Chain Reaction* (1992 R) and, around the same time in Australia, a fictional gay character, David Robinson (Scott Burgess) in G.P. 'Tests of Conscience' (1992 T) declared that he was not *totally* against it.

Almost a year after the furore, Noel COWARD's current biographer Philip Hoare spoke of the tendency to disapproval he had encountered among the theatrical establishment and media (in *Visiting Lives* 1992 R): 'They thought I was going round doing this terrible outing job ... prodding them about what Noel was like in the sack ... they thought that this homosexual thing is going to dominate the book, and quite right that it does ... a lot of people he worked with shared his sexual preference: a lot of his work and his life was defined by sexuality.'

At the time Hoare spoke, others were extending the concept, taking it out of the homosexual arena. In America former television talk-show host Dick Cavett told *Sally Jessy Raphael* (while discussing depressive illness on 'The Secret Life of Patty Duke' 1992) that he had 'outed' another talk show supremo, Mike Wallace (as a depressive) on his show. In Britain John Wilson on KALEI- DOSCOPE (1992 R) reported that 'several galleries were outed for not showing works by women in the last year'.

Although the press, television and radio united to condemn outing, all the media had been condoning the practice, in lots of subtle and not so subtle ways, for years. There were the thinly veiled references to Godfrey WINN in A MAN APART (1968 R); the visibility of 'Rock HUDSON Is Gay' on a wall during a 1968 *Laugh-In* sketch; the puppet on *Breakfast Time* (1983 T) loudly demanding that a (very embarrassed) fellow guest 'come out'; an elderly actor squirming on an Australian late night show (broadcast only a month before 'outing' was attempted – disastrously – in that country) because the host had mentioned (with a smirk) that he cruised bathhouses; numerous remarks about a member of the royal family; the author of a book about another of the royals being given the pink nod on *Have We Got News for You* in December 1992.

There was a call – by entrepreneur and philanthropist Dick Smith – for tobacco company executives to be 'outed by having their photographs and names on the front of cigarette packets' in *The 7.30 Report* 'Teenagers and Smoking' (Aust 1993 T).

Out of the Archives: Lesbians and Gays on TV Title of a collection of gay/lesbian British television pro- grammes screened by the British Film Institute's Television and Projects Unit,

curated by Stephen Bourne, under the umbrella of Television on the South Bank. The screenings took place on four Tuesdays at the Museum of the Moving Image in 1992 encompassing the extra- ordinary ENTERTAINING MR SLOANE, ON TRIAL and ONLY CONNECT, with the more problematic GIRL and COUNTRY MATTERS, together with some choice documentary extracts as well as the EVERYMAN programme on the GAY NEWS trial. Following a season on the rep- resentation of black people on British television, this was the first recognition of a significant body of work in the five years of MOMI's existence. 'Out of the Archives' later toured regional film theatres.

The second season (July 1993) included the plays THE OBELISK, HORROR OF DARKNESS, WITHIN THESE WALLS 'One Step Forward, Two Steps Back', THE OTHER WOMAN, *The Picture of Dorian Gray*, A HYMN FROM JIM, COMING OUT and, by popular demand a repeat screening of GIRL. In addition there were two documentaries: MAN ALIVE 'Consenting Adults: The Women' and WORLD IN ACTION 'Coming Out in Newport Pagnell'. To celebrate Larry Grayson's 70th birthday, there were showings of SHUT THAT DOOR!, *The Generation Game* and *At Home with Larry Grayson*.

Out on Tuesday (UK 1989–90 T) Nationally networked series of docu- mentaries, short features, video letters and news items for lesbians and gays by lesbians and gays. There was also a sub- sequent series entitled OUT. P: Abseil Productions (Susan Ardill and Clare Beavan); EP: Christopher Herd; D: Phil Woodward (1989), Richard Kwietniowski (1990); Channel 4.

This long-awaited and much appre- ciated series employed a great deal of surface sheen to project the diverse, tra- gic-funny-surreal lesbian and gay world, still reeling from CLAUSE 28. Sometimes the programmes were sandwiches: a piece on opera queens between others on gay Tories and death in the era of AIDS. Other subjects covered were the implications for gay and lesbian rights of Britain's full entry into the EC; HOLLYWOOD's stereotyping; AMNESTY INTERNATIONAL's turmoil over homosexual prisoners; political and living conditions in Poland and the emerging Russia – all pretty heavy stuff but rubbing shoulders with disco music, dyke detectives, public school film romances and a top advertising company being stumped on a successful method of 'promoting' homosexuality.

A grand aspect of the format was that it also allowed the showcasing of hour-long documentaries such as the invaluable DESIRE. Like GAY LIFE nearly a decade before, *Out on Tuesday* and its successor provided a much needed sourcing and ordering of queer history: covering (in *Out on Tuesday*) the war years (COMRADES IN ARMS), gay liberation ('After Stonewall') and lesbian life (*Women Like Us*), and (in *Out*) London from the 1940s to the 1970s ('Storm in a Teacup'), anti-fascism in the reunified BERLIN (THE BATTLE FOR TUNTENHAUS and its sequel), and aspects of gay erotica (CAUGHT LOOKING).

'[It shows that] homosexuality is healthy, spontaneous and individual and in no way impairs functioning (unlike misogyny) [but] for a series with its title it suffered from a claustrophobic lack of fresh air. The interviews were seldom more searching than for a school magazine' (Jonathan Sanders, *Gay Times*, May 1989).

(Australia's Special Broadcasting Service (SBS) showed *Out on Tuesday* and *Out*, usually six months later and sometimes substituting other lesbian and gay material for items that were either out of date or involved copyright problems.)

outrageous A cover-all term for anyone who does or says anything the least bit eyebrow-raising, which is why it is commonly applied to anything or anybody gay. It is now extremely non-enraging or outraging, except in its unthinking ubiquity. In the 1950s and 1960s there was another word that meant more or less the same – 'audacious': 'Some confessions of an audacious young man of the twenties' (*Young But Not Angry* 1958 R).

Among those regularly labelled outrageous: DIVINE (who really was); Dame Edna EVERAGE (who really is); LIBERACE (who was up to a point); Kenny EVERETT (who only became really outrageous when he campaigned for Mrs THATCHER); Elton JOHN (until he married); Julian CLARY (it's his middle name); 'The outrageous humour of "Chase me, chase me"' Duncan NORVELLE on *The Main Attraction* (1984 T).

A Prince of the Realm (in 1990) thought it was 'just outrageous to suggest this sort of thing', while at the same time Caroline (Sara Coward) was urging the menopausal Nelson GABRIEL (Jack May) in THE ARCHERS (1990 R) to go out and 'do something outrageous and get it out of your system. Like racing.'

Outrageous! (Can 1977 C) Toronto HAIRDRESSER Robin Turner (Craig RUSSELL) who eventually finds fame and a full-time career as a FEMALE IMPERSONATOR in New York in between acting as life-belt to the sinking Liza (Hollis McLaren), his schizophrenic roommate.

W/D: Richard Benner; based on the short story from *Making It* by Margaret Gibson; P: William Marshall and Henk Van Der Kolk; 96 mins.

A showcase for Robin/Craig: histrionically as he tries to cope with the roller-coaster moods of his best friend, survive disappointing relationships with gay men, and fight against anti-drag prejudice; and musically as he impersonates BANKHEAD, DAVIS, WEST, STREISAND, GARLAND and Carol Channing.

Many people found this film enormously uplifting (it drew crowds for some weeks after it opened in the New York cinema which had just shown *Rocky*). However, it is dramatically tepid, wearing its heart on its sleeve with the organ barely beating.

Russell himself, bright, willing, openly gay and playing a relatively uncloseted man (although we don't see his biological family), is an acquired taste, and of the characters only David McIlwraith's New York gay taxi driver Bob has any dimension. In the sequel *Outrageous Too/Too Outrageous* (1987) also directed by Richard Benner, there is more of the same with an excruciatingly bad out-of-drag number by Russell which is supposed to be a triumph. In this opus also McIlwraith is a tower of strength.

'... a film in which nobody ever seems to stop screaming, unwittingly enforces stereotypes as dangerous as those favoured by Anita Bryant' (Vincent Canby, *New York Times*, 1.8.77.)

'... noteworthy for being a commercial film with a relationship between a young man and a young woman that is based on friendship rather than romance ... the characters care for and look after each one another ... [Russell's] Robin has great range: he is kind-hearted, angry, witty, philosophical, moody, weak to criticism, strong when he has to be, even heroic, extremely sarcastic and harmlessly bitchy ... And when Robin does his impersonations ... he is dazzling ... Perhaps the film's title shouldn't be *Outrageous!* but *Courageous!* (Danny Peary, *Cult Movies*, 1982).

OutRage!: The Documentary (UK 1991 R) OutRage! was defined by one of its members as 'A bunch of media-oriented stroppy queens getting up your noses ... an organization committed to direct action and civil disobedience to defend the human rights of lesbians and gay men'. With the voices of Jimmy SOMERVILLE, Michael CASHMAN, Derek JARMAN, John Stokes MP, JULIAN AND SANDY, and OutRage! members Martin Harrington, Malcolm McDonald, Megan Radclyffe, John Jackson, Graham Knight, Patrick McCann, Lynn Sutcliffe and Peter TATCHELL.
P: Turan Ali; 20.12.91; BBC Radio 5; 30 mins.
A jog through the previous 16 months of OutRage! UK which was set up in May 1990, largely in response to the fate of actor Michael Boothe who was kicked to death. Among the educational entertainments the group laid on are the mock burning at the stake during the

enthronement of the Archbishop of Canterbury; the Bow Street police station turn-in; the queer WEDDING; the lesbian and gay family Christmas; the Piccadilly Circus kiss-in: 'What if heterosexuals went up there and KISSED ... what's the point of advertising it?'; as well as a lot of talking back to the majority: 'It's the heterosexuals who are CHILD MOLESTERS'.

Over Our Dead Bodies (UK 1991 T) Contrasting AIDS activism and gay politics in Britain and the US: ACT UP, Queer Nation and OUTRAGE!.
P: Rebecca Dobbs; D: Stuart MARSHALL; *c* 60 mins (also 90 mins).
A bleeding chunk of film which – while stepping back from the less clear-cut aspects of 'acting up' – melds footage of demonstrations and ingenious methods of waking up, sometimes blasting the establishment, through confronting interviews with a whole range of people who have become involved in this extraordinary civil rights movement prompted by a disease. The British and American contributors (including Michael Callen and Simon WATNEY) are all fighting for better health care, dignity for those who are sick and dying, decent housing – and a cure. Grief and anger are there on both sides of the Atlantic, but the ways of dealing with them are markedly different.

'It explores the constructive expression of anger and frustration by this new breed of activist, the burn-out and exhaustion associated with queer activism, and the reclamation of the word "QUEER" as a self-empowering, self-identifying term' (Karl Knapper, San Francisco International Lesbian and Gay Film Festival programme, 1991).

overpopulation Is the world's human population excess to requirements and, if so, will it lead to a pitiless obsolescence for civilization? This has been a subject of debate, both scaring and complacent, for almost the whole of broadcasting's history. For a couple of decades the worry had been a population decline (especially after the two world wars), but during the 1950s and 1960s fearsome statistics began to rend the airwaves: 'Twenty-five million people in 35 years' time and 20 million motor cars' (*Towards 2000* 1964 R). According to more recent reports *Ockham's Razor* (Aust 1991 R) 250,000 babies are being born per day contributing to a world population of 5.2 billion.

It is salutary to note that there were a few blunt warnings about an imbalance between food production and distribution and human needs over the past 40 years beginning with Dudley Baker's *Britain Has Too Many People* in 1948: 'The evident over-population of Britain (above 50 million) is [a] serious threat to our survival and undoubtedly to our liberty.' However such broadcasts were usually confined to a 10-minute burst on the BBC Third Programme and were often drowned out by the conflicting statistics of talks such as *The Reluctant Stork* 1946: 'Dramatic presentation of the dangers and opportunities that attend a falling birthrate'; *Fair Play for Parents* (1949), Sir Hubert Henderson on the Royal Commission On Population; *Was Malthus Right?* (1949), John Green on 'World Population and Food Supplies'; *Limiting the Population* (1952) and *Population and Family* (1953) by David Glass; the Emmy award-winning television documentary *The Population Explosion* (US 1958); *World Population* (1958): 'The whole human race could stand shoulder to shoulder on the Isle of Wight and still leave the beach free for bathing. This does not mean that there is no population problem. Ninety million babies are born every year. At this rate, the world population will double by the end of the decade.'

Many of these talks piloted around a great many issues: homelessness, unemployment, cultural traditions, improved birth control methods without making any connections, and almost always avoiding issues such as religion and pressures to marry and procreate.

Apart from *Is Population Growth a Menace to Britain?* (a debate between David Eversely, Reader in Population Studies at the University of Sussex and Swedish economist Goran Ohlin, in 1978), the subject almost disappeared from radio (and continued to be under-represented on television). Colin Tudge noted in *Lost in the Crowd* (1987 R) that 'in the 1970s the notion of the Population Explosion became unfashionable'; and four years later, in *Bye Bye Baby* (1991 R), Neil Walker and David Clayton talked to groups who were concerned that none of the major political parties had a policy on population, including those who say that 'Britain has 20 million people it can't afford'.

Over the years, a few individuals have made comments on what for many people is a taboo area: the interference in a natural process, for whose results there is always a place. In *We British* (1978 T) the writer Elaine Morgan said if fewer children were produced they might be more valued, while Dora Russell disputed the notion that a woman has to have a child to fulfil herself. 'A couple who don't want children would be well advised not to have them.'

In drama, comments are usually limited to doom-laden science fiction prophesies. 'André' (Susan Hampshire) and Dr Fleming (Peter Halliday) in *The Andromeda Breakthrough* (1962 T):

> 'In about 150 years from now there will be a war in which the whole of your city will be destroyed. It will come when the number of people in the world has at last grown too great. ...'
> 'We can only live as we are, within the limits of what we understand ... the world must be free to make its own mistakes – or save itself.'

Or they are misanthropic/misogynistic remarks from men who have a vested interest in ridiculing procreation: 'popping from wombs, swarming indiscriminately with the single aim of popping back again,' says RICHARD I (Michael Byrne) in *The Devil's Crown* 'When Cage Bird Sings' (1978 T).

Every now and again, on a television talk show usually, someone will get up and say: 'Maybe homosexuality is nature's way of curbing the population' (*The Oprah Winfrey Show* (1992 T etc)).

With the current PERCENTAGE of lesbians and gays to heterosexuals being hotly contested, and the option to bear and raise children being taken up by a not insignificant number of lesbians, this neat idea seems not to augur any very potent solution.

What did perhaps merit some exploration – but didn't secure any – was a doctor's remark, not elaborated upon, in a 1963 WOMAN'S HOUR talk on (male) homosexuality. He was concerned that the fear of being thought homosexual by relatives and friends was driving many young men to marry in their teenage years or to father children, in or out of wedlock, so that tongues would be silenced.

See also MARRIAGE.

Over the Rainbow (UK 1980 R) Stanley (Peter WOODTHORPE) manages a menswear shop in Willesden, in North West London. He's bored, 'but think of the fun I have in the fitting room. If you try everyone you're sure to find someone.' He had a boyfriend, Sebastian, 'but that was three fellas ago. In the last game of musical chairs I was left standing.' Stanley's off men – 'they should all be shot ... Men are horrible' – and spends most of his free time with his friend Sandra (Maureen Lipman). They're both heavily into fantasy, the Hollywood variety. Stanley worships Judy GARLAND and knows every line of *The Wizard of Oz* and *A Star Is Born*. 'There's only one man who's any good and he's no good for me. Oh, poor Judy.' When Sandra gets herself a boyfriend, Stanley has visions of cruel abandonment: 'Don't change. What would happen to us? How would I survive?'

W: Bernard Kops; P: Cherry Cookson; 11.10.80; BBC Radio 4; 90 mins.

No grisly cliché of lonely gaydom is unturned in this inattentive, uneasy blend of character and caricature which wastes two excellent players and a savoury idea.

Over The Rainbow Sung by Judy GARLAND as Dorothy, just before the 'twister' hits in *The Wizard of Oz* (1939 C). Removed three times during post-production, 'Over The Rainbow' became the film's hit song, Judy's anthem and a pick-me-up for many gay men during the 1950s and 1960s when the star gave concerts at which they were a noticeable portion of the audience.

Harold Arlen and Yip Harburg's ballad has a soulful yearning quality; its lyrics pointing towards a place 'where there isn't any trouble'. This is obviously appealing to most people, in many countries (it is sung in Finnish over the closing credits of *Ariel* 1988 C). It has been requested by a diverse bunch of DESERT ISLAND DISCS castaways over the years: comedian Dick Bentley (1951); composer Vivian Ellis (1951); actress–singer Jean Carson (1953); composer Lionel Bart (1960); actor Michael Wilding (1961); footballer Danny Blanchflower (1961); comedian Bob Hope (1961); racing driver Graham Hill (1963); female impersonator Danny LA RUE (1966); car designer Raymond Mays (1969); novelist Fay WELDON (1980); etc. But for homosexual people, the words hold a special meaning, particularly in a time when being gay was a criminal offence in most countries.

Apart from *the* version, the song was warbled by James Stewart in *The Philadelphia Story* (1940 C) and 'played' by him in *The Glenn Miller Story* (1954 C). Eileen Farrell sings it lustily on the soundtrack of *Interrupted Melody* (1955 C), while Eleanor Parker (playing Australian soprano Marjorie Lawrence, who contracted polio) mimes and performs the first wheelchair-choreographed number (executed in one extraordinary continuous take) in the course of entertaining wounded soldiers. 'Over The Rainbow' was the finale of the 62nd Academy Awards: chorused by people in five capital cities linked by satellite and Diana Ross.

It provided the musical trajectory for the triumphant finale of RAY'S MALE HETEROSEXUAL DANCE HALL (1987 C): to its strains, the young hopeful finally gets to dance with *the* man, Mr Big, the man of his (professional) dreams *in the* spotlight, and have Glenn Miller and his orchestra take him to where happy little bluebirds – or corporation men – fly. As a soaring anthem it was also featured in BEFORE STONEWALL (1984 C/T) and at the end of a 1992 televised British concert for those who died from AIDS-related illnesses.

While fully appreciating that heterosexuals need their flights of fantasy too, a couple of generations of gay men – and, increasingly, lesbians – now regard 'Over The Rainbow' as 'theirs'.

Stanley (Peter WOODTHORPE), one of Judy's biggest fans, regards this and other Hollywood milestones as a shelter from a cruel world in OVER THE RAINBOW (1980 R). Much earlier, in the BBC's first 'homosexual play' HORROR OF DARKNESS (1965 T), the song is employed by Robin (Nicol Williamson) in an attempt to prod Peter (Alfred Lynch) into expressing his feelings for him: 'Why then, oh why can't I?' sings Robin.

The ballad's merits for all romantic people and its demerits for Judy Garland herself were voiced in *Beyond the Rainbow* (1991 R) which tentatively explored the Garland fascination for gay males. As a soaring anthem it was also featured at the end of a 1992 televised British concert for those who died from AIDS-related illnesses: '... There's a land that I've heard of/Once in a lullaby ...'

Owen, Wilfred (1893–1918) English war poet, only five of whose poems were published in his lifetime. A selection was set to music by Benjamin BRITTEN in 1964 as *War Requiem*, filmed by Derek JARMAN in 1989. His relationship with Siegfried SASSOON – when they were both invalided out of the war – was detailed in Stephen MacDonald's *Not About Heroes* (1983 R, played by the author). Other interpreters: Stephen Murray in *The Shadow of the Moon* (1963 R); Michael Jayston in *Solo* (1970 T); David Sibley in *The Fatal Spring* (1980 R); etc. The deep, exultant anguish and

pained sense of regeneration in his poems were well caught by Jocelyn Brooke, John Betjeman and John LEHMANN in *Writers' World* 'First World War Poets' (1965 T), and especially by Michael REDGRAVE in his narration for *The Great War* (1964 T).

Oxenburg, Jan (194?–) American film-maker, one of the first women to humorously interweave present perceptions (lesbian–feminist) with past concerns (Jewish suburban) in *Home Movie* (1973 C); *I'm Not One of Them* (1973 C); *A Comedy in Six Unnatural Acts* (1975 C, on the absurdity of stereotypes); THANK YOU AND GOODNIGHT (1990 C).

Oxford and Cambridge Gleaming spires, clean-limbed chaps, lofty ideals about the masses, and some pretty rum behaviour: first celebrated in UNDERGRADUATE SUMMER (1939 R, just before the insulated world would be breached by wider concerns). The homosexual side of college life mainly represented by Dennis (Nigel HAVERS) in THE GLITTERING PRIZES (1976 T); the legendary partnership of Jim Prideaux (Ian Bannen) and Bill HAYDON (Ian RICHARDSON) which began at Oxford, passionate at first and eventually fatal in TINKER, TAILOR, SOLDIER, SPY (1979 T); Charles and Sebastian in BRIDESHEAD REVISITED (1981 T). That Cambridge was a seed-bed of treachery was indicated in *Philby, Burgess and Maclean* (1978 T), *Blunt* (1987 T), *Blade on the Feather* (1980 T) and ANOTHER COUNTRY (1984 C).

Penelope Keith and her television husband in *No Place for a Lady* (1989 T) say:

'He's not a fruit drop. Just because he went to Oxford.'
'He's a wine gum then.'

Intrigue and sublimated passions in the women's colleges are less well known: *Miss Morrison's Ghosts* (1981 T); *Gaudy Night* (1986 T); DUSTY ANSWER (1990 R).

P

pacifists *See* CONSCIENTIOUS OBJECTORS.

Padden, Bernard (195?–) English television actor and writer (ONE IN FIVE; IF THEY'D ASKED FOR A LION TAMER), doe-eyed, with a mop of black curly hair, best known as clumsy newly-wed Kevin in the Tefal non-stick saucepan adverts (1983–4). He told the DAILY MIRROR: 'Kevin's a bit of a wally and so am I. But, honestly, if I was married to him I would have strangled him by now.' He also told the newspaper: 'Yes, I'm gay. I don't think I'll ever get married. But that's what Elton JOHN said.'

A former child actor, his adult credits include John in *It's Your Choice* 'Options and Consequences' (BBC Schools 1979 T); Midge who poses as a photographer to defeat a terrorist group in *Dempsey and Makepeace* 'Nowhere to Run' (1983 T); average gay man in a disco in *One in Five* (1983); a servant in *The Bride* (with one delicious moment, eyeing up a male guest, 1984 C); henchperson Bernardo in *Zastrozzi: A Romance* (1986 T). He did a brief stint as a TV-am gossip columnist in 1984.

Paddick, Hugh (*c*1924–) English comic actor of the imposingly rounded vowels and homely iridescence, comfortable as infinitely superior salespersons, fruitily enthusiastic fellows or wan creatures like his immortal Julian in ROUND THE HORNE.

C: instructor in *School for Scoundrels* (1960); excellent as Freddie, the TV soap director in THE KILLING OF SISTER GEORGE; ROBIN HOOD in *Up the Chastity Belt* (1971); a WINDOW DRESSER in *That's Your Funeral* (1973); etc.

R: *The Trouble with Toby* (1957); *Fine Goings-On* (with Frankie HOWERD, 1958); Mr Niggle in *Floggits* (1958); *Beyond Our Ken* (1958–64); *We're in Business* (with Peter Jones, Harry Worth, Dick Emery and Irene Handl, 1960); *Play It Cool* (Eric Merriman scripts with Ian Carmichael and Joan Sims, 1963); *Round the Horne* (1965–9); *Round and Round the Horne* (1976); Lesley in SHARE AND SHARE ALIKE (1978); *Wise on the*

Wireless (as Ernie Wise's secretary, 1987); *On the Air* (panelist on a nostalgia quiz covering 60 years of radio history, 1988); Ben Gunn in *Treasure Island* (1989); etc.

T: *Cymbeline* (1937); Bernard Braden series (1958); toy shop assistant in *Lance at Large* (1964): 'Are you sure I can't tempt you to take the turquoise, sir? It's such a delicious colour'; an infuriating supervisor in *The Tommy Steele Show* (1965); *Before the Fringe* (1967–8); *Beryl Reid says 'Good Evening'* (1968); *Comedy Playhouse* 'View by Appointment' (as Sid Jelliott, 1968; also in the series *Wink to Me Only* 1969); *The Marty Feldman Comedy Machine* (1971); *The Morecambe and Wise Show* (1982); interviewed on *Breakfast Time* (1985); *Wogan* (with Kenneth WILLIAMS, 1987); *Alas Smith and Jones* (1987); Keanrick in *Blackadder the Third* (1987); etc.

paedophiles Technically people who are sexually attracted to pre-pubertal children, but in society's mind confused with those who are attracted to young adolescents. They were usually depicted as mentally retarded: Kingsway Jenkins (Peter Butterworth) in *A Menace to Decent People* (1964 T); or as pathetic men with a mother fixation: Stanley Wood (Jimmy Gardner) in CHARIOT OF FIRE (1970 T); Thomas Byatt (Ellis Dale) in SOFTLY, SOFTLY 'Little Boy Blue' (1974 T). Sometimes, like pet shop owner (Jeff Rawle) in JULIET BRAVO 'Lies and Liars' (1981 T), they were falsely accused. Only rarely were they appealing characters who made no secret of their delight in the barely post-pubertal, eg ageing Teddy Boy (and pill pusher) Straker (Colin CAMPBELL), a constant visitor to the adventure playground in *Play Things* (1976 T): 'Sorry about that. My little weakness ... No harm done, is there?'

Two famous men of letters who had much involvement with children were Charles Dodgson/Lewis Carroll (Ian HOLM in *Dreamchild* 1985 C) and James BARRIE (Ian Holm), author of PETER PAN in THE LOST BOYS (1978 T). Elements of paedophilia are sometimes embodied by characters in children's films such as *Pinocchio* (1940: the fox, the cat and the coachman); *Chitty Chitty Bang Bang* (1968: the Child Catcher); *Willie Wonka and the Chocolate Factory* (1971: the drug store proprietor Mr Bill).

In American televisions movies, the paedophile is presented as the friendly guy, unmarried, often involved with local families through sports or entertainments, luring children away to service groups of men or to appear in pornography (*Fallen Angel* 1981; *Child's Cry* 1986; *When the Bough Breaks* 1986).

Increasingly, such stories involve Catholic priests, young and personable, in dramas like *Lamb* 1985 and *Judgement* 1990 or, depicted as an evil force, the subject of cover-up in WORLD IN ACTION 'Sins of the Fathers' (1992).

Frank RIPPLOH took pains to show that not all gay TEACHERS are out to seduce one half of their pupils in TAXI ZUM KLO (1981 C), but sometimes the media have seemed to suggest otherwise. Which was why it was a considerable breakthrough to have Dr Philip Pallister MD (GP, geneticist, father of 15 children) stand up and say on *The Oprah Winfrey Show* 'Town's Dirty Secret' (1992 T): 'I was not as cognizant of the concept of paedophilia in the late 1950s. We're talking about homosexuality as another thing, separate and apart from paedophilia. But in those days it was lumped together – at least in my mind and in the people I knew, other psychiatrists.' Dr Pallister went on to say that, had he and other professionals been able to separate the two, the repercussions of a child rape case in 1959 might not have had the widespread and scarring effects on a number of the people of his town 33 years later.

palari *See* POLARI.

Pan, Hermes [Hermes Panagiotopulous] (1905–90) American dancer and choreographer who 'was' Ginger Rogers and Rita Hayworth in all rehearsals with Fred Astaire. 'Hermes played "Ginger" often enough for some waggish writers to call him "Fred's favourite dancing partner,"' wrote Ginger Rogers in her 1991 autobiography. She introduced Pan to Astaire, calling it 'the beginning of a beautiful relationship'. He was to be Astaire's assistant on 19 films and 4 TV specials. The only time the two men danced together – jitterbugging and being mock-flirtatious – was in a five and a half minute comedy number ('Me And the Ghost Upstairs') which was cut from the final print of *Second Chorus* (1941).

Apart from the Astaire–Rogers and solo Astaire vehicles, Pan's other credits include *My Gal Sal* (1942); *Diamond Horseshoe* (1945); *Lovely to Look at* (1952); *Can-Can* (1960); *Cleopatra* (1963); *My Fair Lady* (1964); and his unfortunate swan song, *Lost Horizon* (1973). He appeared as 'speciality dancer' in *A Life of Her Own* (1950) and was one of Betty Grable's rare dancing partners apart from Dan Dailey in *Moon Over Miami* etc).

Pan won an Academy Award for the 'Stiff Upper Lip (Stout Fella)' routine, set inside a fun house in *A Damsel in Distress* (1937). He was also nominated for *Top Hat* ('The Piccolino', 1935) and *Swing Time* ('Bojangles', 1936).

His few non-dancing, on-camera appearances included *The RKO Story-Tales from Hollywood* 'Let's Face the Music and Dance' (1986); *The Golden Years of Hollywood* (1987); *Rita Hayworth: Dancing into the Dream* (1990); and, for a few seconds, in YOU'RE THE TOP: THE STORY OF COLE PORTER (1991). For BBC Radio he spoke briefly about his partnership with Astaire in *Singers at the Movies* (*c* 1989).

Ginger Rogers, interviewed on *Sally Jessy Raphael* a year after his death, cursorily gave Pan his due by saying: 'I was frequently unavailable. In those instances, Hermes would step in and dance my part with Fred. When I arrived, Hermes would teach me the routines.' Referring to him as an 'Italian', she added: 'He was a darling man, and I miss him.'

Pandora's Box (Ger 1928 C) A child of nature brings about the ruin of all who

cross her path, including the designer Countess Anna GESCHWITZ.
W/D: G. W. Pabst from two plays by Frank Wedekind; 110 mins.

The workings of fate, the effortless allure of seeming innocence, the moth edging ever nearer to the flame. The time-honoured story of temptress and tempter receives a bolt of reviving lightning in the form of Louise BROOKS. As pure as a nymph, as deadly as nightshade, she creates a thoroughly credible figure, not quite human but always sympathetic. Her performance is ageless, but it has to do battle with the lumpen storyline and indifferent co-performances. Alice Roberts as 'the screen's first lesbian' was apparently unhappy with her role, and played the scenes of passion while looking at the director off-camera rather than at her female *amour*. It is symptomatic of the domination of LULU over film and characters that Geschwitz – who makes half a dozen appearances – is given only one line (on a title card): 'I've brought the designs'.

"What's all this fuss about Louise Brooks?" said George CUKOR. "I remember her. She was a nothing."

'But in the two films she made for Pabst she is one of the great icons of the silent screen, with a unique beauty and an erotic presence second to none. This version of Wedekind's play, LULU, finds her delightedly wandering the primrose path, playing havoc with the men who desire her and even pausing for a caress with a lesbian countess' (National Film Theatre monthly programme, February 1991).

Pangborn, Franklin (1893–1958) American character actor, lavish with extroversion and affronted looks. Luxuriously, uproariously queer, with bells and drums, he enjoyed a 30-year film career as gawking clerks, bank tellers, milliners, hotel managers, pet shop owners, floorwalkers, flunkeys, modistes, secretaries, playwrights and theatricals. A horse face with the voice of pungent, pulverized lavender: once seen and heard never forgotten. No one was more crimson, more violet, more

puce, but he always retained a shred of dignity – even when bested by the equally peculiar Shirley Temple in *Just Around the Corner* (1938).

From the hundred or so films he made, a handful of Pangborn personages: Cecil Lovelace, the *jeune premier* of the rundown acting troupe in *Exit Smiling* (1926); the modiste who helps Marie Prevost get even with husband by providing her with a wig in *Blonde for a Night* (1928); the 'PANSY script writer' Leach in *Not So Dumb* (1930); Sport in *Her Man* (1930); the hotel manager in *International House* (1933); Tom Franklyn in *Only Yesterday* (1933); the secretary to George Barbier in the Burns and Allen comedy *Many Happy Returns* (1934); another hotel manager in *Mad About Music* (1938); bank examiner J. Pinkerton Snoopington in *The Bank Dick* (1940); the manager in *My Dream Is Yours* (1949); one of Marie Antoinette's courtiers in *The Story of Mankind* (1957). He also appeared in some of the Astaire and Rogers musicals (*The Gay Divorcee/Divorce* (1934; *Carefree* 1937); in screwball comedies (*My Man Godfrey* 1936; *Bluebeard's Eighth Wife* 1938); in romantic dramas (*Now, Voyager* 1942); in the works of Preston Sturges (*Hail the Conquering Hero* 1940, *The Palm Beach Story* 1942). He appeared on radio, eg opposite Barbara STANWYCK and Robert Taylor in 'My Favourite Wife' for *Screen Guild Theatre* (1942). His only television work was in *Myrt and Marge* (1953).

Panorama (UK 1954–   T) The BBC's current affairs juggernaut, a Monday night fixture, forever identified with the Dimbleby family (Richard and David), although it was originally presented by Pat Murphy, followed by Malcolm Muggeridge. Forthright and well researched, the programme has consistently sold the long march of homosexual rights short. One item (featuring men dancing in an AMSTERDAM club and upbeat interviews with openly gay men) was scrapped when a new editor was appointed in 1964. An 18-minute piece on the Gay Liberation Front was favourably received in 1971. Since then

– apart from 'AIDS – The Race for a Cure' (1986), 'AIDS – The Fight for Control' (1987) and 'Heterosexual AIDS, the Myths and the Menace' (1992) – nothing has been forthcoming. An anticipated special on the continuing inequality over the AGE OF CONSENT did not materialize in mid-1992: instead there was a piece on dentists and the NHS – which was no doubt equally timely.

Pansy A girl's name, from the Greek for 'fragrant' and also from the French *pensée* ('thought'). A relatively popular name for proletarian screen characters: Pansy O'Donnell (Bebe Daniels) beginning as salesgirl in *2 Weeks with Pay* (1921); Pansy (Polly Moran) in *Way out West* (1930); Pansy Gray (Ruth Chatterton) in *Anybody's Woman* (1930); tough chorus girl Pansy (Charlotte Greenwood) in *Flying High* (1931); Mrs Pansy Jones (Margaret Hamilton) in *Hat, Coat and Gloves* (1934); etc. The heroine was called Pansy O'Hara in the first draft of Margaret Mitchell's GONE WITH THE WIND, but the author was persuaded by her editor to change the name to Scarlett.

Since the mid-1930s, it has been used parsimoniously: Debbie Reynolds as Pansy Hammer, the very studious student in *The Affairs of Dobie Gillis* (1952 C, but no such character turned up in the television series); Pansy Osmond, daughter of Gilbert in Henry JAMES' *The Portrait of a Lady* (Pamela Stirling 1952 R; Suzanne Neve 1968 T); Lana Morris as Pansy Bolton in Somerset MAUGHAM's *Britannia of Billingsgate* (1953 T); Pansy Skinner, an artist who runs an arts supply shop with her husband in WAGGONERS' WALK (1969 R); Shelley Duvall, the gay young thing in the 1920s sequence of *Time Bandits* (1981 C); Pansy Morgan (Julianne Allen), sister of Sissie in *We Are Seven* (1989 T).

Pansy Thomson (Kerry Shale) was the black boxer on the skids who refuses to take a fall in Joseph Moncure March's narrative poem *The Set-Up* (1992 R):

Mean as a panther
Crafty as a fox
He could kick like a mule
And he knew how to box ...

In the 1949 film version the boxer, as played by Robert Ryan, was white, married and renamed 'Stoker'.

pansy A constant in plays and films of the 1960s and 1970s; prevalent also in the early talkies such as Eddie Cantor's comedy *Palmy Days* (1931) in which a man ordering a birthday cake lisps: 'And no pansies!' Asked by a rival gangster what flowers he would like at his funeral in *Night After Night* (1932), George Raft snarls: 'Anything you like, except *pansies*.'

Rodgers and HART's 'Ten Cents A Dance', written for the 1930 show SIMPLE SIMON, contains the line 'Pansies and tough guys'. By the time its singer, Ruth Etting, had her screen biography mounted, censorship forbad mention of the former. So, in *Love Me or Leave Me* (1955), Doris DAY sang of 'Dandies and tough guys'.

The word has carried much venom in the 20th century. One abuser told Quentin CRISP that he was 'an effing pansy' and 'ought to be locked up' (THE NAKED CIVIL SERVANT 1975 T). Australia's Prime Minister, Paul Keating, an alleged master of invective, thought so badly of the members of the Senate that on 5 November 1992 he sweepingly called them all, in front of the television cameras, 'pansies', regardless of gender. The day after, he revised his opinion – whether upwards or downwards is not recorded – referring to them as 'swill'.

An Australian fictional character, Robert Darryl (Bill Kerr) in *Baked Avocado* (Aust 1991 R) made it quite clear to his son that, if he was one, then he better look elsewhere for parenting: 'What are you – a pansy or something? Well, don't come whining home to me with your tail between your legs.'

The late Australian artist Sir Sidney Nolan sugared the pill by referring to Patrick WHITE and his kind as 'so-called pansies' on *The 7.30 Report* (Aust 1992 T).

The terrible reverberations pertain in Britain, too. Eric Morecambe did a double double-take when his screen wife seemed to be suggesting that they name their (unborn) son 'Pansy' in THE MORECAMBE AND WISE SHOW (1982 T). And Tony Archer (Colin Skipp) flatly refused to wear the sexy shorts his wife Pat bought him to war on holiday (THE ARCHERS 1984 R) because 'they make me look like a pansy'.

All this fuss over the name of what Geoffrey Smith called a 'friendly little FLOWER' in a programme devoted to it and the viola (*The World of Flowers* 1984 T). Three decades before, in the WOMAN'S HOUR talk 'How to Grow Pansies' (1954 R), the splendidly named Professor K. de B. Codrington had a few tips 'for the breeder': give them soot water, beware slugs and 'fresh manure is fatal'.

In COMMON THREADS: STORIES FROM THE QUILT (1989 C) an American man records how his lover became a landscape artist instead of an INTERIOR DECORATOR because of the stigma attached to the latter profession and consequent fear of exposure. At this point, the camera, roaming around the man's own spectacularly designed garden, suddenly alights upon these most culturally inflammatory volubles of tiny plants, bobbing away gently and merrily in the sun.

Pansy A projected film by Derek JARMAN using some of the more intemperate remarks about homosexuality by politicians, religious representatives and media pundits – spoken by the very people these righteous mouthpieces claim to be protecting: children. Briefly discussed on *At Home with Derek Jarman* (1991 R), but at the time of writing still embryonic.

pantomime These seasonal (Christmas and New Year) entertainments remain very popular in Britain and practically nowhere else. Gaudy, bawdy and sometimes magical, they began as classic

examples of double standards: pantomime was acceptable to the middle classes, music hall wasn't. Sexual ambiguity and cross-dressing, taboo in life, are regarded as almost sacrosanct in panto.

Sir John Irvine complimented 'Miss Fay Compton' in 1933 (*Pantomime and Plays* R) on her 'boyish gaiety which is irresistible in a woman'. Adding to 'her beauty and her accomplishment and her distinction' is 'a gay and genial and easy spirit'.

'Sex is almost absent in pantomime. There mere idea of a principal boy played by a girl destroys that,' asserted producer Julian Wylie during a discussion with Hollywood comedy producer Mack Sennett (*Pantomime vs Film* 1934). (This was Mr Wylie's last word on the subject as he dropped dead soon after recording his contribution.)

In fact, pantomime as the exclusive domain of the transvestite female in doublet and hose, slapping her thighs and paying court to the heroine (also played by a woman), is of relatively recent origin. In the late 19th and early 20th centuries, many of the 'boys' were 'real men', including George Lashwood ('The Beau Brummel of Variety'), Mark Sheridan, Whit Cunliff, Harry Welchman and gay Fred Barnes.

When television started mounting its own pantomimes in the 1960s, the female boy tradition was maintained: Yvonne Marsh as Dick Whittington in 1963; Anita Harris as Prince Charming in 1970. A cross-current of casting male pop idols as Dick or the Prince weakened the thread and now the principal girl/boy seems to be under threat.

Not so the dame, whose role is to be as raucous and as vulgar as possible within the confines of family entertainment. This early introduction of British children to DRAG – in the guise of Widow Twanky, Mother Goose, the Ugly Sisters and Dame Trot – has led to some concern, as when Sheila Steafel (playing Cinderella in her 1988 radio show (*Presenting Sheila Steafel*) felt obliged to seek professional advice: 'Dear Anna Raeburn. I've met this boy who has been taking my shoe around with him. My sisters are TRANSSEXUALS, my father's a bankrupt and now I've found out that my boyfriend is a TRANSVESTITE.'

The pantomime achieved some sort of apotheosis on television in 1986 when Danny LA RUE played the Wicked Stepmother in *Cinderella* as full-on glamorous, sexy, alluring: almost the real thing. This was acceptable because the Ugly Sisters were played – grotesquely – by men and the principal boy did not have breasts, hairy legs and a moustache.

More traditional dames on radio and television have included Rex Land as Widow Twanky in *Aladdin* (1938 R); Tommy Fields (brother of Gracie) also as the Widow (1939 R); Douglas BYNG in 'Babes in the Wood' from the King's Theatre, Edinburgh (*Pantomime in Rehearsal* 1942 R); Wilfred Pickles as the Trouper in *The Story of a Pantomime Dame* (1954 R): 'Don't you do that to me again, you saucy thing you. Oh, hello children!'); Terry Scott as Daphne the cook in *Dick Whittington* (1963 T); Scott again as one of the Ugly Sisters whose striptease in *Cinderella* (1967) elicited the categorical 'I have never laughed so much at a pantomime dame' from Peter Black in the *Listener*; Labour politician Denis Healey dressed in full dame décor in 1980 (*Nationwide*); Ronnie Coyles as the Queen of Hearts wired for sound during 'Humpty Dumpty' in *The Frock and the Falsie* (1988 R).

Documentaries: DESERT ISLAND DISCS with Clarkson Rose, (1962 R); *A Dynasty of Dames* (with Shaun Glenville, Clarkson Rose, George Lacy and Douglas BYNG, 1963 R); *Pantomime Dames* (with Terri Gardener and Billy Dainty, 1967 T only Wales and West); *Oh Yes I Am, Oh No You're Not* (with John INMAN, Terry Scott, Windsor Davies, George Lacy, Nat Jackley and Cyril Fletcher, 1982 T); *Getting On* (with Billy Dainty and Billy Whittaker, 1984 T); *Oh, Yes It Is!* (a history of pantomime in 7 parts, 1986 R); etc.

'... the comic repellence of pantomime dames – a male caricature of the ugliness and sexual desperation of elderly women ... a homosexual joke [which] would be unsympathetic to an ordinary, heterosexual audience, if it were not in on [the joke] ... it knows ... the dame is a comedian in skirts. It is only a tease, we didn't really mean it', said Ronald Bryden on WOMAN'S HOUR (1966 R).

See also FEMALE IMPERSONATORS; MALE IMPERSONATORS.

pantywaists Horned unreconstituted straight male Brian (Brian Gaspawri) in *Joint Account* (1990 T) looks askance at househusband David (Peter Egan). Trying hard to adopt a tone of light banter, but noticeably spitting fire at such an abuse of the male role, Brian has an excuse to draw upon the transatlantic section of his vocabulary: 'The Yanks – they've got a good word: pantywaists. No room for pantywaists in my world (not that *you're* one).'

The Parachute (UK) German pilot Werner Von Reger travels back in time to try and reconcile the conflicts with his father. These conflicts are exacerbated by his involvement with his father's mistress, Anna, who is involved in a plot to kill Lieutenant Schacht, like Werner a MOTHER'S BOY, who is about to take up an appointment as commandant of one of the first concentration camps.

W: David Mercer; P: Tony Garnett; D: Anthony Page; 1968; BBC1; 90 mins. Werner (John OSBORNE); Baron Von Reger (Alan BADEL); Anna (Jill Bennett); Schacht (Lionel Hamilton).

W: David Mercer adapted by Denys Hawthorne; D: Jane Morgan; 1986; BBC Radio 4; 90 mins. Werner (Kenneth Branagh); Baron Von Reger (Jack May); Anna (Tessa Boychuk); Schacht (Adrian Egan).

An enervated aristocracy, a vacillating intelligentsia, a childlike military, a rash and romantic left-wing: these elements which led to the rise of Hitler are embodied by the characters in Mercer's ambitious but empty fable. The television and radio productions, separated by 20 years, seem to be grappling with thin air. What make both of interest is Mercer's awakening fascination with homosexuality (the homoerotic military academy; the pathetic, sketchily-drawn Schacht; Anna's attraction to the fastidious, ambiguous Werner whilst also sleeping with his father, who despises her because she likes 'QUEERS'). The playwright would take this remarkable combination of sympathetic insight and blind disgust further in *Emma's Time* (1970), A SUPERSTITION (1977) and A ROD OF IRON (1980), parading rather than resolving any conflicts.

Paradjanov, Sergei (1924–90) Soviet film director, writer, musician and painter. An Armenian raised in Georgia with strong Ukrainian nationalist beliefs, he spent most of the 1970s in labour camps 'for incitement to suicide, homosexuality and currency offences'. After his release he was blacklisted. Between *Shadows of Our Forgotten Ancestors* (1964) and his death he managed to make only three films: *Sayat Nova* (1969, retitled *The Colour of Pomegranates* and released in 1974); *The Legend of the Suram Fortress/The Fortress of Suram* (1985, co-D); *Ashik Kerib* (1988). One of his stories formed the basis of *Swan Lake, the Zone*, directed by his friend and collaborator Yuri Ilyenko in 1990.

Sergei Paradjanov: A Portrait (1990) took the form of an interview on the set of *Ashik Kerib* in which the director discussed his love for the people and the culture of the Caucasus, PASOLINI and Italian cinema, his difficulties working under the Soviet system, and his years in prison (he served two prison terms, one under Stalin, one under Brezhnev and Andropov).

Coursing through the words are extraordinarily vibrant images: beautiful faces, gorgeous silks, dazzling pottery, things and people picked up from here and there to make his moving collage. *Ashik Kerib* is about a wandering minstrel who journeys through Georgia, Armenia and Azerbaijan encountering all manner of human deceit, usually at the hands of despots and philistines. But his travels also enrich him because of the kindness he receives and the wonder and magic he experiences. The parallels between the real and celluloid artist,

both without bitterness at the treatment they have received for worshipping beauty and freedom of expression, are inescapable. What is lacking in the film about the film is any attempt to examine one of the primary reasons for the Soviet authorities' successful attempt to silence him.

'But why such cruelty? And why, specifically, did Paradjanov ... suffer such ferocious political persecution? Why was it suddenly so urgent to "discover" his long-known homosexuality and to use it as a pretext for a punishment unusually atrocious even for those harsh times? What exactly was so dangerous about Paradjanov that of the three most uncompromising and most suppressed directors of the time – Andrei Tarkovsky, Kira Muratova and himself – he was dealt the deadliest blow? What outrageous transgression had to be neutralized and according to what logic? Or was there none?' (Leonid Alekseychuk, in SIGHT AND SOUND, Winter 1990–1).

Nigel **Pargetter** Character played by Nigel Caliburn, Nigel Carrington and, currently, Graham Seed in THE ARCHERS. A romantic, frightfully well-meaning fellow, who uses 'sweet' and 'mama' a lot. Brought up by a nanny, he is scared of Mummy: 'I'm almost allowing myself to get excited as long as I don't think about Mummy.' But he is relatively snug with Elizabeth Archer (Alison Dowling): 'He tries to flirt a bit but it doesn't mean anything: we're just friends.' Expect wedding bells any day. Nigel is very much an asexual clown figure which no long-running radio serial would be without: Richard FULTON in MRS DALE'S DIARY, Jago Peters in THE DALES etc. Occasionally they are allowed to be Pagliacci.

Paris Hotbed of style, jazz and experimentation: George Gershwin (Robert Alda) discovered a possible soul mate in (the fictional) Christine Gilbert (Alexis Smith) in *Rhapsody in Blue* (1945 C); Oscar Levant as the other *American in Paris* (1951 C) was nearly kissed there by Georges Guetary; Gregory Peck found his way into a café populated by strange men and women in *The Snows of Kilimanjaro* (1952 C) and his companion Ava Gardner was later discovered (in *The Sun Also Rises* 1957 C) to be in the thick of a forest of gay men. Yet another American, Jennifer (Veronica Hamel) was rescued from drugs and degradation by artist Vivienne (Camilla Sparv) in VALLEY OF THE DOLLS '81 (1981 T) who did expect something in return, which was reciprocated for a while. In *Private Benjamin* (1980 C) Goldie Hawn finds the man of her dreams while her ferocious ex-commanding officer (Eileen Brennan) finds the perfect (disciplinarian/German) woman (Sally Kirkland). The British also have bitter-sweet experiences in this city: it was the place where Richard FULTON sequestered himself when, aged sixtysomething, he decided it was time to lead a gay life to the full (THE DALES 1967 R); and it was the location for a young businessman's return visit to the scene of his first sexual experience where history repeats itself with an unpleasant difference (KISS AND TELL 1980 T). The city has also been the backdrop to the society so caressingly described by PROUST (*Swann in Love* 1984 C) as well as by COLETTE (1985 T), George SAND (Rosemary Harris in NOTORIOUS WOMAN 1974 T) and Sartre (THE ROADS TO FREEDOM 1970 T).

That Paris is frivolous and pleasure-seeking goes without saying. That it may be gay in another way is a possibility which English-speaking culture is always ready to exploit, although the 'Gay paree' joke in the 1973 *Morecambe and Wise Christmas Show* (spoken by Eric Morecambe as Napoleon) had its punchline removed. Drag artiste Robert Preston sings 'GAY PAREE' in VICTOR/VICTORIA (1982 C) and draws from it every dilapidated innuendo. Sometimes the phrase is employed without a built-in snigger, eg by Angela Down (as Avril) in *Take Three Women* (1982 T): 'I spent three years in gay Paree learning how to be an artist. Three years padding around the Louvre.'

Paris Is Burning (US 1991 C) The vogueing balls of Harlem and the Bronx. Prizes are awarded for 'realness': the ability to pass as a military man, a business executive, a socialite, a woman, a HETEROSEXUAL. 'Realness can be a matter of survival. If you can pass for STRAIGHT, you may avoid getting beaten up by the "phobes".'
D: Jennie Livingston; P: Jennie Livingston and Barry Swimar; 87 mins.

A real spectacular, cut down from 70 hours of footage shot in 1987, giving prominence to a whole strata of the gay community normally shut out of the action: Pepper Labeija, Dorian Corey, Venus Xtravaganza, Willi Ninja, Freddie and Kim Pendavis, Octavia Saint Laurent, Carmen and Brooke, and Angie Xtravaganza. A headlong dive into a pool with some very strange fish, a minority within a minority splashing around in the mainstream. American dreams percolated through TV soaps, glossy magazines, Hollywood and Vine. What penetrates most strongly is a sense of community, of family, of shared struggle and of making whoopee once in a while until the real thing comes along.

Parker, Tony (1923–   ) English writer, most at home in tightly-enclosed, single-sex communities where tensions run high, notably prisons and other places of detention: A LIFE IS FOREVER (1972 T); *Couples* (1976 T); CROWN COURT 'The Green House Girls' (1978 T); *Associated Residents* (1980 R); THE GENTLE TOUCH 'Hammer' (1980 T); *Visitors for Anderson* (1980 T); *The Sin Bin* (1981); *Responses* (1984 R); WALRUS 'What Should I do?' (Endings, 1985 T).

parlari *See* POLARI.

Parry, Ken (1930–   ) British actor, effectively apoplectic as a variety of bloated, jumpy fellows, often with little to say and what little there is coming out very fast and high-pitched.

T: Stanley Timpkins in *A Run for the Money* (1960); waiter in *Knight Errant '60* 'Eve and the Serpent' (1960); Mr Spink in *My Representative* (1960); *Arth-*

ur's Treasured Volumes 'A Blow in Anger' (1960); Mr Potter in *Ask Mr Pastry* 'Vote for Children' (1961); customer in *Maigret* 'Unscheduled Departure' (1961); Tubby Tidmarsh in DIXON OF DOCK GREEN 'The Vanishing Bummaree' (1961); the Sultan in *Dick Whittington* (1963); tailor in *Z Cars* 'The Kiter' (1963); football club member Neville Turner in *Comedy Playhouse* 'The Mascot' (1964); barman in *The Big Toe* (1964); only starring role (4th billed) in *Comedy Playhouse* 'Current Affairs' (set in a power station, 1968); Sister Ringstead in *Never Say Die* 'The New Sister' (1970); Starveling in *A Midsummer Night's Dream* (1971); Harold's friend in *Two Days That Shook the Branch* (1978); fat guard in *The Devil's Crown* 'Bolt from the Blue' (1978); film producer Luigi Lugosi in *Hazell and the Big Sleep* (1979); chef in *Blott on the Landscape* (1985); Jack in *Children's Ward* (1992); etc.

parties A group of men, some of them pederasts, getting together in Ancient Greece to celebrate the success of one of their number, and discussing the joys and pains of Eros the night long: in Plato's *The Symposium* (1990 R) modernized as 'The Drinking Party' (*Sunday Night* 1965 T). Similar social occasions are rare outside of BIRTHDAY PARTIES: the occasional golden 'wedding' anniversary (fictionally in *The Rather Reassuring Programme* 'Has Family Life As We Know It Gone Forever?' 1977 T; for real in *The 7.30 Report* 1991 T about Peters Bonsall-Boone and De Waal who had lived together for 25 years), and one or two intimate gatherings – for a dozen or so men in BROTHERS 'The Gang That Could Shoot Straight' (1986 T), a dinner party for four (COMING OUT 1979 T), or a small mixed straight, gay and/or lesbian gathering (*Goodbye Gemini* 1970 C; DAWN! 1979 C). For the rest, it is homosexual people, singly or in couples, at the centre of wild and decadent festivities, often in the 1920s: *The Making of a Male Model* (1983 T); THE WEATHER IN THE STREETS (1984); *Ellis Island* (1984 T); etc. A leaving party for a gay

man (given by a woman friend) formed the focus of the last third of PARTING GLANCES (1985 C). Gay men – often spectacularly clad and exclaiming trivialities or sexual innuendoes – as guests at parties given by heterosexual people are a familiar feature on television (THE CREZZ 1976; *The Two Ronnies* 1980; *Goodbye, Darling* 1981) and in films (SUNDAY, BLOODY SUNDAY 1971; THE PRINCE OF TIDES 1991). Colin RUSSELL was an invitee to a stag night in EASTENDERS (1988 T) at which he was a catalyst for views, pro and con, on marriage and the single state (but, in his cups, describing himself as a lonely middle-aged man).

Parting Glances (US 1985 C) Twenty-four hours in the lives of three gay men: Robert (John Bolger), who is preparing to leave New York to work in Africa, his partner Michael (Richard Ganoung) and Michael's ex-lover Nick (Steve Buscemi), a rock musician–composer who is dying. At Robert's farewell party, Michael overhears a conversation which pains and confuses him, Nick is lusted after by the young Peter (Adam Nathan), and a heterosexual artist is fascinated by the dance of death which AIDS represents. Robert's overseas trip is cancelled, but it is the two former lovers who greet the dawn on Fire Island.

W/D: Bill Sherwood; P: Yoram Mandel and Arthur Silverman; 90 mins.

A day perfectly captured in the lives – and, in one case, imminent death – of a group of people, mainly gay, in Manhattan. Bill Sherwood's only film (he died of AIDS-related causes in 1990) is an almost totally successful amalgam of gay yuppiedom, gentle bohemian satire, tender love story and some stark realities. The film's real triumph – apart from its general air of affirmation and relaxed intimacy – is the character of Nick, intelligent, deadpan and ballsy: no victim he.

A landmark movie made at a time when the Big Apple was feeling particularly apprehensive and defeatist and when Hollywood, through television movies like AN EARLY FROST, was tentatively tackling AIDS through the respectable face of male homosexuality (high-income professionals, motivated, young and attractive); a face which *Parting Glances* shows – via the character of Robert – to be somewhat pockmarked.

partners First used with the full double meaning in the 1960 radio play *The Partnership*, which describes the nefarious doings of Sid and Bert (Jon Rollason and John Dearth) who live together and bicker a lot – and assassinate people. Other business partners who enjoy or who once enjoyed a sexual relationship include schoolteachers Mlle Julie (Edwige Feuillère) and Cara (Simone Simon) in OLIVIA (1950 C); hoteliers Mlle Zizi (Danielle Darrieux) and Madame Claudette (Claude Nollier) in *The Greengage Summer/Loss of Innocence* (1961 C); Madame Irma (Shelley Winters) and Carmen, her bookkeeper (Lee Grant) in *The Balcony* (1963 C); Charlie (Rex Harrison) and Harry (Richard Burton) in STAIRCASE (1969 C); newsagents and tobacconists John (Joseph O'Conor) and the now deceased Alan in ONLY CONNECT (1979 T); the guest house proprietors (Richard Pasco and Geoffrey Palmer) in THE HOUSEBOY (1982 T); junior entrepreneurs Omar (Gordon Warnecke) and Johnny (Daniel Day-Lewis) in MY BEAUTIFUL LAUNDRETTE (1985 C); ANTIQUE DEALERS Francis Matthews and David Yelland always on the lookout for an *objet d'art* in *May We Borrow Your Husband?* (1986 T); language school head Eddie (John GIELGUD) and his ailing co-owner in *Quartermaine's Terms* (1987 T); wine bar owners Sammy (Campbell Morrison) and (the mainly unseen) Gerald in *Life without George* (1987 T); Dan (Peter Copley) and Leslie (Frank Windsor) running an office equipment firm in CASUALTY 'Allegiance' (1991 T).

Simon CALLOW, in his radio biography of Micheal MACLIAMMOIR entitled *Death or a Kind Gentleman* (1991), said with flowing simplicity: 'In June 1927 he met Hilton EDWARDS. Almost immediately

they became partners in love and in work.'

By the 1990s this word, divorced from its business connotation, has become widely accepted as a synonym for LOVER and LONGTIME COMPANION. Guido (Nicholas Donovan) pioneered it by referring thus to the unseen Des in EASTENDERS (1988 T), while in a 1991 episode Joe (Jason Rush) called Michael (Leonard Preston) his. Leslie in the *Casualty* episode doesn't know quite how to react when he is asked by one of the nurses if Dan is his 'partner', but in G.P. 'Tests of Conscience' (1992 T) David Robinson (Scott Burgess) thanks stick-in-the-mud doctor William Sharp (Michael Craig) for acknowledging his significance in the private life of William's colleague by describing him, without embarrassed hesitation, as David's 'partner'.

The wider implications of the word 'partnership' (rights as next of kin, as inheritors of insurance and pension rights, as tax payers) were discussed in a 1991 OUT segment on the pros and cons of legal recognition of gay and lesbian partnerships.

See also CREATIVE PARTNERSHIPS.

Partners (US 1982 C) Womanizing cop (Ryan O'Neal) and reined-in gay colleague (John HURT) pose as lovers to trap a killer who is working his/her way through Los Angeles' gay ghetto.

W: Francis Veber; P: Aaron Russo; D: James Burrows; 98 mins (cut to 92 in the UK).

The hetero's handsome and desirable, the queer's a closeted blob. What unadulterated bliss to pen them up together in the middle of Gayland! The gay loves the straight, the straight remains impervious. The gay cooks and cleans (happily), the straight becomes an (unwilling) sex object for homosexual men. The gay becomes a real man (by using a gun) and dies, only to be resurrected by the straight's (false) declaration of love.

Essentially a one-hour episode of any old TV police show, for all its nods in the direction of peaceful co-existence, sexual stereotyping and the growing 'brotherhood' between Chalk and Cheese. O'Neal, WASPish and smug, appears to be having a good time, but Hurt (seemingly squirming with some intestinal complaint) is totally at sea in this stagnant hogwash (which was pumped out of the bilges by one of the collaborators on LA CAGE AUX FOLLES).

'Picture this: a lot of Jews have been murdered and a Gentile cop is teamed up with a Jewish cop who's fixed his nose and changed his name. They go into this mysterious Jewish community and every Jew they find is pushy, foul-mouthed, vulgar, greasy, aggressive and a gold digger' (Stephen Harvey, INQUIRY (US), March 1982).

'The cinema seems to be having an even tougher time coming to terms with homosexuality than the society whose attitudes it's supposed to reflect' (Margaret Hinxman, *Daily Mail*, June 1982).

Pasolini, Pier Paolo (1922–75) Italian film-maker, poet, novelist, screenwriter and polemical essayist who made one of the most highly regarded 'Christian' films (*The Gospel According to St Matthew* 1964) and one of the most spat-upon 'godless' ones (SALO: THE 120 DAYS OF SODOM 1975). In between, he hymned Rome's street people (*Accatone* 1961; *Mama Roma* 1962), laughed at religious epics (*RoGoPaG* 1963), made mock of ancient and modern cannibalism (*Pigsty* 1969), had a Christ figure seduce all members of an upper-middle-class family (THEOREM 1968), and had his idiosyncratic way with *Oedipus Rex* (1967), *Medea* (1969), *The Decameron* (1971), *The Canterbury Tales* (1971) and *The Arabian Nights* (1974). Nearly all of them present sexuality, in all its forms, as mysterious and liberating, imaginative and thirsty. Which may explain why so few have been shown on British television.

His poetry was read by Jack Klaff in *A Voice on the Margin* (1991 R). Pasolini was played by Alfred Molina (with Dexter Fletcher as Giuseppi Pelosi, the teenager who allegedly murdered him after a sexual encounter) in *The Life and Death of Pier Paolo Pasolini* (1990 R). The manner of his life and the reasons for its violent end were debated in the Dutch *Whoever Says the Truth Must Die* (1981 T). Two of Pier Paolo Pasolini's friends insist that his death was 'execution by dark forces', committed by more than one person. Said one friend: 'Violence *was* endemic in Pasolini's sexual attractions. He liked young boys from street gangs. But torture? A car driven over him? A whole body broken and shattered?'

Even death wasn't a suitable punishment. Both the radio and television accounts marvelled at the posthumous lynching of Pasolini by the Italian press: for his immoral ways and for corrupting youths (most of whom 'were well along the path, at least in the arts of stealing and violence').

Those of his friends and colleagues who favoured a conspiracy theory leading to his death cite Pasolini's denunciation of the Christian Democrats, which was published a few months before the event. It accused them of collusion with oil companies, with the CIA, of murder, of destruction of the landscape, of the despoliation of schools, hospitals and public offices.

Now firmly embedded in myth, Pasolini is a potent subject for a full-scale film biography. So far none has been forthcoming. His enormous body of work and his wildly contradictory life were summed up in a 1988 programme in the radio series REBELS: 'He was a Roman Catholic, a Communist, a defender of traditional standards, a PROMISCUOUS homosexual, a stern moralist and a rebel against bourgeois values ... He had two souls: one mad, damned, riotous; the other mild, tranquil, charitable, full of compassion.' The work and the life were also summed up in the subtitle of a 1990 reflection (which included writers Alberto Moravia and Umberto Eco, director Bernardo Bertolucci and *Theorem*'s leading actor Terence Stamp): *A Desperate Vitality*.

passing (1) Passing as in Afro-Americans, Hispanics and Asians hiding their racial heritage: Fredi Washington in *Imitation of Life* (1934 C, Susan Kohner in 1959 remake); Jeanne Crain as *Pinky* (1949 C); Sonya Wilde self-explanatorily in *I Passed for White* (1960 C). There is mention of 'passing' during the degredation and attempted rape of Anita (Rita Moreno) in WEST SIDE STORY (1961 C).

The situation in reverse: James Whitmore as a white investigative journalist in the American South in *Black Like Me* (1964 C); a miraculously bleached Lenny Henry in *True Identity* (1991 C); and the WASP bigot (played by black Godfrey Cambridge) who wakes up one morning to find himself transformed into his worst nightmare in *Watermelon Man* (1970 C).

The once common occurrence of Jews pretending to be Gentile (or keeping quiet about their family backgrounds) was highlighted in the 1947 *Gentleman's Agreement* (Gregory Peck as a journalist taking on a JEWISH cultural colouration for an anti-Semitism exposé). Three decades later, in some parts of American society, the situation appears unchanged. Business executive George Segal hasn't told his colleagues that he's Jewish for fear of losing status in *Carbon Copy* (1981 C). They therefore receive a double shock when he reveals this fact and introduces them to his recently-discovered son – who happens to be BLACK.

(2) Passing as heterosexual is a common situation for homosexual men and women, especially those brought up in the days of blanket prohibition or those strongly influenced by fundamentalist religious beliefs. It was a way of life endemic to the men in VICTIM and also to characters who feared loss of family respect (SUNDAY BLOODY SUNDAY 1971 C) or blackmail (STARSKY AND HUTCH 'Death in a Different Place' 1977 T; IN THE GLITTER PALACE 1977 T) or loss of career (SERGEANT MATLOVICH VS THE US AIR FORCE 1978 T; *Rock* HUDSON 1990 T). Sometimes the need to hide 'in the CLOSET' and adopt 'straight' mannerisms was the subject for comedy (LA CAGE AUX FOLLES 1978 C; AGONY 'Problem Parents' 1980 T). However, the predicament of a heterosexually-

oriented person MASQUERADING as a homosexual is much more prevalent, eg CRUISING (1980 C) and PARTNERS (1982 C). The deeply damaging results of pretended NORMALITY for many homosexual people has been confronted in plays like COMING OUT (1979 T) and MORE LIVES THAN ONE (1984 T).

(3) Passing or achieving 'realness'. This is the aim of many participants in the voguing balls which were celebrated in PARIS IS BURNING (1991 C). Most of the people involved are Afro-American, Asian and Hispanic gays and TRANSSEXUALS and, for the duration of the ball, they take on the exact physical and emotional likenesses of representatives of certain admired groups in American society: high-flying business executives, supermodels, military officers, assorted glitterati. For some of the gay men involved, their goal is to pass ... as HETEROSEXUAL.

passing phase *See* JUST A PHASE; PHASE.

Past Caring (UK 1986 T) The tepid, watery soup of Edward Minty's (Emlyn WILLIAMS) life in an old peoples' home is heated and spiced up considerably by the arrival of Victor (Denholm ELLIOTT), who also takes a shine to superficially liberal, tolerant, kindly, caring matron Linda (Connie Booth). When things get a mite out of control Victor and Edward (having abandoned his walking frame and ready for anything) take off together for pastures new.

W: Tom Clarke; P: Kenith Trodd; D: Richard Eyre; 2.1.86; BBC1; 80 mins.

Although Denholm Elliott is as wickedly appealing as ever as the dirty (not so) old man, the play belongs to Emlyn Williams as the former valet 'with a whinnying laugh, a fluting voice and an over-elegant mode of speech which he picked up in the 1920s from some ageing patron, some relic of *fin de siècle* days' (author's description from 'stage' directions on the shooting script).

With his insolently superior air and peacock appearance (polka dot BOW TIE, velvet jacket, neatly pressed trousers and ancient but highly polished shoes), Edward is a thorn in matron's side: 'I hang on to my life to annoy them, you know,' he tells the newly arrived Victor, his one and only soul-mate. A true conservative, Edward finds Victor's outspokenness on matters sexual delightfully daunting. He is even encouraged to remove the chiffon scarf from his gilded past. He was, as if anyone would be particularly surprised to learn, a gentlemen's gentleman who went to bed with gentlemen (and a few who were not so gentle): 'In my day it was a matter not of creed but of taste. One had merely to be discreet and a member of the proper class.'

This is one of the few television plays with a virtually unclouded happy ending for its queer protagonist, although there is a distinct possibility that the equally eccentric Victor is simply taking Edward on a spree which will end when Edward's money runs out. No matter. Victor's exact motivations are irrelevant. He has lifted Edward's spirits, halted his invalidism and possibly resurrected his libido. There should be one Victor per gay inmate in all hidebound, hetero-centric 'old folks' dumping grounds, and a 'Victoria' for the lesbians.

Pathétique Symphony (Symphonie Pathétique) The closing passages have been used twice by Ken Russell: in the Swiss chalet sex fantasy between Glenda Jackson (as 'TCHAIKOVSKY's wife' and Vladek Sheybal as 'the composer' in WOMEN IN LOVE 1969 C), and in the final scene in *The Music Lovers* (Glenda Jackson playing the wife for real, in a madhouse being groped through a grating by male and possibly female incarcerates); as fade-out music to THE MISSING DAY (1986 T), a fitting conclusion to this fictionalized story of Tchaikovsky's final hours.

The work, written in 1893, his sixth and last symphony, was dedicated to the composer's beloved nephew, Bob Davydov. Warren Johansson calls the Pathétique (in *The Encyclopaedia of Homosexuality*, 1990) 'the fullest outpouring of the emotions he had felt during a lifetime', encapsulating David Brown's view (in *The New Grove Dictionary of Music and Musicians*, 1980) that the finale is a 'mixture of anguish, brooding and sorrow'.

It is ironic then that the music that Tchaikovsky described as his most 'sincere' was spooned like dream-topping over the end titles of *The National Health* (1973 C), as a comment upon the saccharine mythology of television hospital romances, with all their emotional secret drawers, long-buried scandals, intimate revelations – and rigid sexual orthodoxy.

A Patriot for Me (UK 1981 R) The Hapsburg Empire held together with all kinds of alliances, public and private, dependent upon a vast spy network. Colonel Alfred REDL (Gary Bond) is a brilliant soldier who has fought his way out of the pack rather than ascending through aristocratic privilege. With his rank goes money, prestige and access to sensitive information. He also has an ACHILLES' heel which makes him the perfect SPY. His dilemma is that his guilty secret opens him up to BLACKMAIL, forcing him to become a double agent. When the game is up, he has no other choice but to shoot himself.

W: John OSBORNE; P: John Tydeman and Anton Gill; 15.3.81; BBC Radio 3; 165 mins.

Rats in the cellar, mould in the cheese, rust on the medals. Osborne is himself a double agent in this play (first performed in the mid-1960s). One half delights in charting a vivid course of greed and heartlessness. The other pities Colonel Redl, the classic outsider, hopelessly compromised by his sexual desires and his obedience to empire. While – at the outset at least – Redl is portrayed as a man of backbone, his public and private worlds are populated by people who appear to have stepped out of a PAUL TEMPLE serial: from the higher orders, Baron Von Epp (John Moffatt) and, from the lower, Viktor (Richard Gibson) and Paul (Martyn Read).

Osborne's theatrical finery is somewhat squashed on radio, leaving too many empty spaces. Written when the homosexual as tragic victim, helpless in an uncharitable world, was very much to the liking of a rebel conservative, there's a self-satisfaction which mirrors the empire that was to crumble rather than an angry call for radical change which was being sounded in Germany by Magnus Hirschfeld and others at the time this play is set.

Patsy (1) Girl's name, pet form of Patricia (Joanna Lumley as the darling, sweetie, bibulous friend of Jennifer Saunders in *Absolutely Fabulous* 1992 T etc).
(2) Irish and English pet form of Patrick: bristling James Cagney in *Mayor of Hell* (1933 C) as racketeer Patsy who, much to his surprise, becomes superintendent of a boys' reform school; a less socially responsible gangster, Patsy (Dink Templeton) in *Night After Night* (1932C); an amiable alcoholic lawyer (Bryan Pringle) whose real name is Trumper in *The Portsmouth Defence* (1966 T); Patsy, a neighbour of Jim Broadbent and Alison Steadman in LIFE IS SWEET (1990 C).
(3) An American expression for fool (Jerry Lewis as *The Patsy* 1964 C) or fall guy: 'I'm just the patsy,' says Lee Harvey Oswald (Gary Oldman) upon his arrest in *JFK* (1991 C).

In Australia 'patsy' can mean homosexual, but there are no traceable examples of this usage in broadcasting. But PANSY is still going strong.

The Pattern of Marriage (UK 1953 T) A dramatized documentary about two young people, Peggy (Billie Whitelaw) and David (Peter Byrne), trying to keep their heads in an 'age of shattered belief and upset values'.
W: Caryl Doncaster and Ted WILLIS; P/ D: Caryl Doncaster; 11–30.3.43; BBC; 4 parts.
In 1950 there were 60,000 divorces. The BBC decided that the nation needed to know why so many marriages were crumbling. Following the early months of a 'typical' lower-middle-class marriage, the major source of blame was found to be the wife's fear of sex and the

husband's temptation to stray because of her inhibitions. Equally inhibiting to writers and actors was the BBC's own refusal to allow mention of the subject except in the most oblique terms: 'I can't explain,' Peggy says to her mum. 'I want to love David, but I can't. He's patient with me or was.' Mum finds the whole subject most upsetting: 'David will have to learn to keep himself in check ... There are some things that you can't discuss, even with your own daughter.' It is David who, decent – if slobbish – man that he is, gives up his potential mistress (named Blanche) and undergoes a rapid maturation process: 'We'll work things out ... It's my fault ... I'm such an amateur. I wish I had loads of affairs before I married you.'

This was remarkably daring for its day. A doctor (male) talking about the need for more education for marriage; a social worker (female) hinting at a whole cat's cradle of problems; the nibbling round the question of adultery (trips to the pub and cinema with Blanche); a mother (David's) recalling that her (dead) husband did *all* the COOKING on Sundays 'and cleaned most of the house'; the young husband rolling up his sleeves and drying the dishes as part of a new spirit of co-operation in their ménage; the wife stopping 'letting herself go' and becoming more alluring ...

Billie Whitelaw won enormous praise for her performance (unforced and with a slight Northern accent, the latter a great rarity outside comedy) as did Peter Byrne. They were chosen by Ted Willis as the youthful focus of his 1955 DIXON OF DOCK GREEN (she left after the first series, but he stayed on until 1976 as Mary Dixon's fiancée and subsequent husband). They did the WASHING UP together in *Dixon*, too.

'... based on the notion of the family as the basic unit of social organization ... [and represented] the family as a secure unit which, although not without its internal differences, must be upheld' (Jane Booth, 'Watching the Family' in the Women and Media issue of *Women's Studies International Quarterly* vol. 3 no. 1, 1980).

'The erotic, the daringly passionate and the realistically sadistic are types of story which TV very properly usually avoids' (BBC YEARBOOK, 1953).

Paul Boy's name, prominent in novels from the 1910s to the late 1950s which featured SENSITIVE, often mother-dominated hero–victims (eg Paul Morel in SONS AND LOVERS). This preponderence of Pauls was noted in Henry REED's A HEDGE, BACKWARDS (1956 R), which includes one so named in a mildly erotic fantasy sequence at the beginning.

The first homosexually identified man was called Paul Korner (Conrad VEIDT) in the German film *Different from All the Others* (1919). In sound and vision, it was and remains, at least in Britain, fairly popular for those men who are different.

UK, France and Ireland: Griffith Jones (Paul Beaumont) in *A Yank at Oxford* (1937 C); Paul TEMPLE, suave detective (1938–68 R; 1968–70 T); Paul (Anton WALBROOK), the murdered woman's nephew and sadistic husband in *Gaslight* (1939 C); aesthete living in a fantasy world Paul Mangin (Eric PORTMAN) in *Corridor of Mirrors* (1948 C); Paul (Edouard Dhermitte) in *Les Enfants Terribles* (1949 C); a naked bathe between ('brothers') Peter and Paul *à la* D. H. LAWRENCE opening the satire on HOMOPHOBIA and censorship in A HEDGE, BACKWARDS (1956 R); Sir Paul Deverill (Keith Michell), reckless Regency rake in *The Gypsy and the Gentleman* (1958) who marries for money to keep his mistress in funds; Paul Torrance (Simon LACK) from the scientific Panel of Occult Investigation who dresses in Savile Row suits in *Trespass* (1958 T); Paul Slade (Gordon HEATH), the epicinely mocking, sports-car-driving boyfriend of *Sapphire* (1959 C); decadent, beautifully turned out, probably bisexual Paul (Jean Claude Briarly) in *Les Cousins* (1959 C): 'Am I not living proof of the futility of working? ... Eat, drink and smash everything'; artistic Paul Morel (Dean Stockwell) in *Sons and Lovers* (1960 C); tired businessman Paul Andros (Richard Burton) in *The VIPs*

(1963 C); Paul (Michael Johnson) in *It's a Woman's World* 'Julie' (1964 T); mastermind Paul (Stanley Baker) in *Robbery* (1967 C); blind Paul Millicent (Paul GEENHALGH) who is happy with Tom until a female turns up in *Boy Meets Girl* 'The Eye of Heaven' (1968 T); Paul Fennel (Philip Latham), obsessed by dead lover Malcolm in *Is Nellie Dead?* (1968 C/T); playboy Paul Maurice Ronet) in *The Champagne Murders* (1967 C); Paul Hatcher (David COOK), lover of dead man who meets his widow in THE WAITING ROOM (1971 T); Paul SMITH (Steve Hodson), a bishop's son falsely accused of cottaging in THE LITMUS QUESTION (1975 R); Paul (John Nettles) in *The Liver Birds* (1970s T); Paul (John Stride), emotionally lost businessman succoured by beautiful young man in *The Ice House* (1978 T); Paul (Ian Redford), devil-may-care bridegroom in *Born and Bred* (1978 T); Paul (Michael Troughton), briefly-seen lover of Ken HASTINGS in *Angels* (1980 T); Paul Currie (William Armstrong), workaholic cutter at the small dress factory in GEMS (1984–7 T); Paul Deedman (Nicholas Day) in *The Citadel* (1986 T); Paul Hatcher (Charles Dance), film critic embroiled in murder and gay s&m in *The McGuffin* (1986 T); Paul Robinson (Stefan Dennis) in NEIGHBOURS (1986– T); Paul Ryman (Peter Egan), thorn in Martin's side in *Ever Decreasing Circles* (1986–7 T); Paul Young (Stuart Organ) in *Proof* (1987 R); Paul (Douglas Hodge), the teenage son in *The Glass Extension* (1987 R); wifekiller Paul Cooper (John CARLIN) in *Taggart* 'Hostile Witness' (1988 T); Paul (Stuart Organ/Hugh Jenkins), young diplomat in Burma who becomes distinguished statesman in *Lost Tune from Rangoon* (1987 R); Paul Collins (Jim Wiggins) in BROOKSIDE (1988 T); Paul McCabe (Richard Harris), egocentric and selfish man who hasn't spoken to his wife for 18 years in *The Field* (1990 C); etc.

US: Paul (Tom Mix) in *The Yankee Señor* (1926 C); Paul Jones (Creighton Hale) in *The Cat and the Canary* (1927 C); Paul Bergot (Harry Langdon) in *The*

Strong Man (1926 C); Paul Lockridge (Frederic March) in *Laughter* (1930 C); Paul Brandt (Reginald Denny) in *A Lady's Morals* (1930), young composer in love with Jenny Lind who becomes blind; young Belgian soldier Paul Baumer (Lew Ayres) in *All Quiet on the Western Front* (1930 C); Paul (Conrad Nagel), the other man in *Ex-Wife* (1930 C); Paul (John Barrymore), libertine and possibly paedophile in *Rasputin and the Empress* (1932 C); Paul DRAKE, very unmarried private eye in PERRY MASON series on film, radio and television; penniless singer Paul Allison (Nelson Eddy) in *Maytime* (1937 C); Paul Van Tyre, an ARTIST with a terrible secret who suicides in *Children of Loneliness* (1939 C); Paul Lundy (Lee Bowman), hero of *Tonight and Every Night* (1945 C); violinist Paul Boray (John Garfield) in *Humoresque* (1947 C); intellectual Paul Verrall (William Holden), Washington correspondent in *Born Yesterday* (1950 C); sybaritic Broadway songwriter Paul Merrick (Bing Crosby) aka *Mr Music* (1950 C); Paul Blake (John Howard) in *Ford Theatre* 'Deception' (*c* 1953/4 T) as the son supposedly missing in Korea who returns home to his mother; Paul Kedes (Jason Robards Jr), refugee lover of milady Deborah Kerr in *The Journey* (1958 C); Paul Hodges (Tony Curtis), finagling corporal in *The Perfect Furlough/Strictly for Pleasure* (1959 C); Paul Baxter (George Nader), alcoholic reporter in *Appointment with a Shadow* (1959 C); Paul Biegler (James Stewart) in *Anatomy of a Murder* (1959 C) loved by Parnell McCarthy (Arthur O'Connell); casino robber Paul (Rod Steiger) in *Seven Thieves* (1960 C), deeply attached to mentor Edward G. Robinson; Paul Raine (Bradford Dillman) in *Circle of Deception* (1960 C) who is chosen for an experiment because of his wimpishness but proves resilient; Paul Varjak (George Peppard), the Truman CAPOTE inspired KEPT MAN in *Breakfast at Tiffany's* (1961 C); Paul Strand (George Hamilton), evangelist living with woman twice his age in *Angel Baby* (1961 C); Paul Martin (Dick Powell), married man having non-sexual affair in

The June Allyson Theatre 'Summer Lovers' (1961 T); Paul Saxon (John Gavin), called Walter in original, now heir to department store in 1961 remake of *Back Street*; Dr Paul Graham (Jack Ging), assistant clinical psychologist in *The Eleventh Hour* (1962–4 T); ranch hand Paul Moreno (Charles Bronson) in *Empire* (1963–4 T); Captain Paul Slater (Jim Hutton) in *The Hallelujah Trail* (1965 C); Paul America in MY HUSTLER (1965 C); Paul in *Barefoot in the Park* (Robert Redford 1966 C; Scooey Mitchell 1970 T); TV commercial director Paul (Peter Fonda), who experiments with LSD in *The Trip* (1967 C); Paul (Keir Dullea), intruder, symbol of the male, despoiler of lesbian closeness in THE FOX (1968 C); Paul Montgomery (James Caan), living off his wife in *Games* (1968 C); Paul Ryan (Robert Conrad), deputy district attorney in *The DA: Conspiracy to Kill* (1971 T); expatriate burnt-out case Paul (Marlon Brando) in *Last Tango in Paris* (1972 C); Paul (Charles Bronson), family man turned into vigilante in *Death Wish* (1974 C and sequels); convict Paul Crewe (Burt Reynolds) in *The Longest Yard/The Mean Machine* (1974 C); Paul Jensen (Leslie Nielsen) in *The Day of the Animals*; submarine commander Paul Blanchard (Charlton Heston) in *Gray Lady Down* (1978 C); Dr Paul Holliston (Rock Hudson) in *Embryo* (1976 C) who injects a 3-month-old foetus with growth hormone; Dr Paul Bradley (Sean Connery), America's leading astrophysicist in *Meteor* (1979 C); Paul Rossini (James Booth) in *The Jazz Singer* (1980 C); Paul Jones (Michael Callan) in *The Cat and the Canary* (1978 C); Paul (Stanley Knap), a rich married junkie in *Liquid Sky* (1983 C); Paul (Cameron English), former transvestite dancer in A CHORUS LINE (1985 C); Paul (Brad Dourif), vampire in *I, Desire* (1989 T).

St Paul Jewish name Saul. Christian missionary and fundamentalist who was beheaded in Rome *c* 65. Generally accepted as the author of 14 epistles to churches and individuals which form part of the BIBLE's New Testament and were first read on BBC radio 3.45–4.30pm each Sunday in 1929 and, most recently, 10.15–10.30am, from Mondays to Fridays in 1992. Some of these letters contain prohibitions against homosexuality.

This highly controversial, fascinating figure – a devout Jew who was an enthusiastic persecutor and suppressor of Christianity until he was converted on the road to Damascus – has been played by Anthony Hopkins in *Peter and Paul* (1981 T), by Philip SAYER in *Anno Domini* (1985 T) and, with torrents of anger, self-hatred and fierce single-mindedness, by Patrick Troughton (later to become the second interplanetary DOCTOR) in the BBC children's serial *Paul of Tarsus* (1960 T).

Paul is usually parlayed in documentaries about the birth of Christianity as a man who stood for range and inclusion rather than proscription and prohibition: 'there is no longer Greek or Jew, circumcised or un-, slave or free.' The picture painted is very much that of a tortured, divided soul who, nevertheless, was opposed to slavery and was dedicated to breaking down barriers. To many gay and lesbian people he is seen as an exemplar of Christian rigorism, impregnated with fear of women and of effeminacy.

'When Paul told the women of Corinth to cover their heads he meant their *entire* heads, shutting them up.' RSVP 'St Paul's letter to the Corinthians' (1992 R).

Paul Temple (UK 1938–68 R) One of the first radio serials, beginning with *Send for Paul Temple*, starring Hugh Morton. There were about a dozen stories, some produced twice, over a period of 30 years, all written by Francis Durbridge and produced by Martyn C. Webster. Accompanying the debonair thriller writer and amateur sleuth on most of his adventures (called 'Affairs', 'Cases' or 'Mysteries') were wife Steve (Bernadette Hodgson; from the second series until the end, Marjorie Westbury) and the heart-pounding signature tune by Vivian Ellis, 'Coronation Scot'. All

the plots were hugely convoluted, usually set in and around shady night-clubs and studded with murders and attempted murders, halting deathbed revelations, breathtaking escapes from gunfire, flooded mills or burning boats, a final episode gathering of the suspects among whose number would be at least one artistic, SENSITIVE piece of English manhood. And in 'The Vandyke Affair' (1950 & 1959) the criminal mastermind (involved, as always, in drug smuggling and extortion) hid behind a queer veneer. Temple, in the shape of Francis Matthews (with Ros Drinkwater as Steve, but without CHARLIE) moved to television in 1968 for a 2-year run.

PBS (Public Broadcasting System) Partially funded by the US government (between 40 and 50 per cent) and by corporate sponsorships and pledge drives. Among its most highly-regarded series are AMERICAN PLAYHOUSE and *The Civil War* (1991). Many British drama series (including THE FIRST CHURCHILLS, NOTORIOUS WOMAN and the vastly popular UPSTAIRS, DOWNSTAIRS) have been shown under the title *Masterpiece Theatre*. Among the relevant programmes PBS has aired: *The War Widow* (1976); *Waiting for the Moon* (1988); LONGTIME COMPANION (1990) and YOU'RE THE TOP (1991).

Pearl (US 1979 T) The effect of the bombing of Pearl Harbor on a group of civilians and military personnel.
W: Stirling Silliphant; P: Sam Manners and Gayne Rescher; D: Hy Averback and Alex Singer; 288 mins.

Angie Dickinson is lying in a sugar cane field (in a sapphire evening gown, her hair anachronistically streaked and 'feeling things I never thought I could feel again') atop Christian Vance (as hitherto gay Private Finger) as John Addison's music rhapsodizes. The camera soars up to the moon and there is a nifty cut to Japanese pilots readying for the attack on Pearl Harbor. End of Part 1.

The line 'She was trying to regain her youth ... that's why she liked being around virgins and homosexuals' (referring to Angie Dickinson's character) failed to make it out of Katherine Helmond's mouth in the final print.

Pears, Sir Peter (1910–86) English tenor and co-creator of the Aldeburgh Festival. He was variously regarded as a rich and rare talent or the modestly gifted possessor of a shrill-disconsolate voice. However, he was indispensable to the private life of Benjamin BRITTEN. He was his muse, the interpreter of his settings of poems, sonnets and folk songs as well as of his operas.

Among the solo roles created for Pears were PETER GRIMES, Captain Vere in *Billy Budd*, *Albert Herring*, OBERON in *A Midsummer Night's Dream*, Von Aschenbach in *Death in Venice*, and the General in *Owen Wingrave* (composed especially for television, 1971). Aside from his lover's works, he took roles such as Boaz, Naomi's kinsman in Eric Crozier and Lennox Berkeley's opera *Ruth* (1968 R).

Pears spoke with moderate frankness about his life with Britten in THE SOUTH BANK SHOW 'A Time There Was' in 1980 and presented himself as an individual in *An Evening with Peter Pears* ('A personal choice of poetry and prose', 1970 T); *A Voice Is a Person* (1978 R); DESERT ISLAND DISCS (1983 R); *With Great Pleasure* (recorded in January and broadcast on 29 November after his death, 1986 R).

Other appearances include: *The Significance of Peter Grimes* (1946 R); MONITOR 'Benjamin Britten' (1958 T); OMNIBUS 'Blow the Wind Southerly' (a tribute to singer Kathleen Ferrier, 1968 T); *Peter Pears* (1969 T); reading MICHELANGELO's Sonnets during the intervals of a broadcast of Britten's *A Midsummer Night's Dream* (1974 R).

Biography: *The Instrument of His Soul* is a profile of 'an artist who divided audiences by the individual timbre of his voice. As the life-long companion of Benjamin Britten, as a festival director, as a teacher and enthusiastic commissioner of new music, he had a unique effect on postwar musical life in this country' (with Eric Crozier, the Earl of Harewood, Sir Michael TIPPETT, Julian Bream and Mstislav Rostropovich, 1988 R). Pears' and Britten's first meeting, their slow-blooming love, professional and emotional symbiosis, their time in America as 'accidental refugees' from 1939 to 1942, and the full flowering of their talents with *Peter Grimes* in 1945 made up the content of Paul Godfrey's play *Once in a While ... the Odd Thing Happens* (Aust 1993 R), with Paul Goddard as Pears and Richard Roxburgh as his lover and co-venturer.

Pears, accompanied by Britten, can be heard over the closing scene and end credits of *Distant Voices, Still Lives* (1988 C) singing, in extraordinarily haunting, bi-gender fashion, the traditional English ballad 'O Waly Waly' with its intimations of solitude and death as well of a lover deceived, support not given and a ship carrying jewels possibly sunk. The darker, more fleshly aspects of the Britten–Pears nexus was brought into focus a few years later with the publication of a biography which occasioned BBC Radio 3 to create *A Britten Evening*, which included fact and speculation about this indissoluble partnership.

Peel, David (1920–) British actor, one of the most beautiful ever to spend a large proportion of his career unseen – behind the microphone. He blended stylish clarity with a warm decadence (he played Dorian GRAY in 1948 and again in 1956, and one of ROPE's killers on both radio 1952 and television 1953).

He began his radio career in 1938 (*L'Aiglon*; *Macbeth*; *A Midsummer Night's Dream*). After the war he played gushing Bentley Summerhayes in *Candida* (1946); Captain Stanhope in JOURNEY'S END (1947); the young nephew, Peter in *The Bachelor* (1950); Christopher in the second production of UNDERGRADUATE SUMMER (1951); Bertram in *All's Well That Ends Well* (1952); the title role in *Martin Chuzzlewit* (1954); Simon Ashby in *Brat Farrar* (1959); etc. On television in 1958, he played the decadent Duke in *Rigoletto*. His last role was in *Please Stand By* in 1972.

Among only a handful of film appearances: a pilot in *Squadron Leader X* (1942); an intellectual nicknamed 'Oxford' in the submarine drama *We Dive at Dawn* (1943); a British soldier in *They Who Dare* (1953). He has become something of a cult among horror buffs for his Dorianesque interpretation of Baron Meister (a perfect face concealing a twisted interior) in *The Brides of Dracula* (1960 C), a portrayal given much prominence in the documentary *Heartstoppers: Horror at the Movies* (1988, wherein narrator Anthony Perkins refers to him as 'David Peek').

Mrs Emma Peel Character played by Diana Rigg, with probing insouciance, in *The Avengers* (1965–7 T). A sexy, irresistible strong woman (with Man Appeal), who was not a trained secret agent but the widow of a test pilot (who turned up alive in 'The Forget-Me-Knot', and whisked her off and out of John Steed's life). Her relationship with Steed was never fully explained, which added to her Dyke Appeal. Villain Kenneth J. Warren in 'The Destruction of Emma Peel' (1967) said that she was 'A woman who fights back yet remains feminine.'

pekinese *See* DOG OWNERS.

Rob Pengelly Character played first by Mike Grady (1979–80) and then by Michael Mundell (1980) in WAGGONERS' WALK (R). Described in the serial's bible as: 'Illegitimate, mother dead, father unknown ... Homosexual, no stable relationships.' He was in his early twenties, originally from the West Country. He shared a flat with local reporter Dickon Fish (whom he fancied but there was nothing doing) and initially worked as assistant manager of a local restaurant. His main function in the plot was to become great mates with 8-year-old Jeremy Tyson. (This association – purely platonic: he taught him to ski – is used by Mr Tyson in a bitter custody battle with Jeremy's mother.)

Apart from a muffled involvement with one 'Rocky' Rowlands, Mike didn't have any lovers (he had had an unhappy love affair in the past). According to one of the chief writers on the series, Jill HYEM, this situation was set to change. She told GAY NEWS that a stable relationship was waiting in the wings – with a fashion designer: 'a jet setter, slightly camp.' They had already met at this juncture, but nothing had transpired: it would be 'a fairly slow burner'. Too slow as it turned out. At the end of 1980, after 11 years, WAGGONERS' WALK was cancelled.

penises Very few of the most noticeable sections of the human male's sexual organs are shown on television, while many of those in feature films (see NAKEDNESS) are clipped out before they reach the home circuit. Until the 1970s, they were visible only – usually wrapped in a gourd – in anthropological documentaries about remote native peoples who cannot speak English. On sound radio one was 'seen' in a 1957 GOON SHOW when GRYTPYPE-THYNNE stands up in the bath, provoking Eccles to exclaim: 'Owww!' Says Harry Secombe in an aside to the audience: 'Now you know why this show can never go on television.'

The bundle of hot-wired blood cells and nerve endings was eulogized in the 15-minute documentary called DICK, scheduled, advertised but yanked from CHANNEL 4's schedules in 1991. Women only were given the chance by the film-makers to describe their feelings and reactions to what was variously called 'pee-wee', 'worm', 'wang', 'that little chocolate stick', 'white meat', 'one-eyed trouser trout', 'hooker', 'sword', 'big guy', 'winkle', 'my better half', 'hot rod', 'gigglestick', 'wick', 'dead meat', 'the snake', 'zinger', 'junior', 'hood', 'poker', 'sexy piece', 'turkey-neck', 'willywhacker', 'Uncle Wiggly', 'heat-seeking moisture missile', 'a Spitfire with two bombs', 'purple and veiny and throbbing and angry', 'a cluster of bananas', 'a vacuum cleaner hose', 'this big thing coming at me', and 'cutie'. Most of the commentators observed men's enormous pride in the (usually) dangling object hanging between their legs:

'They're totally obsessed with it', 'They're always fondling it, touching it, making sure it's still there' and 'I'll bet that even business executives will go and pull their pants down after a meeting and talk to their penis: "So how was I? Was it good for you?"'

Despite the serial's reputation for nudity and much heavy-breathing, the penis was barred from Australia's NUMBER 96 (1972–7 T). Even the word could not be uttered. However, one did appear, in clear outline, during episode 7. It belonged to Chard Hayward, very fetchingly clad in skimpy, straining underpants as an unnamed hippy, washing his clothes in the launderette with his similarly attired female companion. (In 1974 the actor was to materialize as waiter–then hairdresser–then disco owner Dudley BUTTERFIELD, Don FINLAYSON's lover.)

Whether on cinema or television, it is the blood-engorged penis that is most closely monitored – and kept from sight, except in scenes featuring 'joke' erections in, eg, *Fireworks* (1947); *Meatballs III* (1987); *Sex, Lies and Videotape* (1989); *Skin Deep* (1989).

The two most famous erections on British television, both courtesy of Channel 4, were almost surreal in their visible invisibility. The first, belonging to Ken Hicks, had been snipped out of SEBASTIANE before it was okayed for its home viewing première in 1985. On its second showing, in 1991, the love scene between the two soldiers was similarly emasculated. Soon afterwards, in *Sex and the Censors*, one of a group of programmes under the collective title of *Banned*, Derek JARMAN described the editing of his film for television: why it was necessary and how it was achieved. Meanwhile, behind him in the studio, the cut portions were displayed. Scotland Yard received a complaint about the presence of 'an aroused member' in one of the clips, and the threat of prosecution (under the Obscene Publications Act, from which broadcast material had been exempt until 1988) briefly hung over the fourth channel. Such a reaction to half a minute's stiffness must have made the network thankful that they had taken evasive action with their other problem penis back in 1983. Shown after midnight, Jon Jost's 'personal and political autobiography', *Speaking Directly: Some American Notes* contained a contemplation of his penis, flaccid (with a litany of slang names read – by a woman – on the soundtrack) and erect (stimulated, presumably to orgasm, by the director). A large – and enlarging – black square was superimposed over these scenes, with mesmerizing, comedic results.

The hundreds of penises on view in *Dick* were all limp, all in monochrome and none was moving. But the film proved, at the last minute, unshowable. Recently, the only programme declaring an interest in this area of the male body was *The Phallus and Its Function* which featured sculpture by Joy Toma (1992 T).

(American television may be edging its way up or down the shaft. The words 'penis' and 'pubic hair' were repeated constantly in the televised US Senate Judiciary Committee hearing into charges of sexual harassment against Judge Clarence Thomas in October 1991.)

See also PHALLIC SYMBOLS.

penis names In A VERY PECULIAR PRACTICE (1988 T) the FEMINIST Rose Marie (Barbara Flynn) holds a male sexuality workshop at the university. She is delighted with the result, summing up with a mixture of nannyish bustle and lubricious sadism: 'James has shared his feelings about his "willy" in a very open way and we've heard from Albert's "dick" and from Gregory's "little man" and Peter's "winkle", Ian's "Jimmy Riddle" and Winston's "teapot". I think what's emerging – and I find this very moving – is shared group perception of male sexuality as something very delicate and fragile … and fraught with fears and anxieties.'

Some examples from the small, but resilient subgenre of characters with penile names:

Ivor **Biggun** (Geoffrey McGivern) in *Blackadder the Third* (1987 T).

Cutthroat Jake (Peter Hawkins), the rival of *Captain Pugwash* (1957–75 T). His name allegedly had something to do with circumcision. Apart from Pugwash himself, the crew included Pirate Willie (who had a great appetite for bananas), and Seaman Staines.

Dong Suck, a Chinese violinist mentioned along with German baritone Wilhelm Von Dangler Schlapper on *The Miles and Milner Show* (1992 R at 6.30pm, with other jokes featuring Andrew Lloyd Webber, singer Kylie Minogue and THE SATANIC VERSES).

Tom **Goodwillie**, the woman-hating BACHELOR in J. M. BARRIE's autobiographical *The Professor's Love Story* (1960 T): 'A sad case.'

Captain Hugh **Jampton**, a bumbling, ineffectual captain in the British army played by Spike Milligan in THE GOON SHOW 'The Man Who Never Was' (1956 R) and in 'Scragje' (1956 R). Peter SELLERS resurrected the name, this time as a famous BBC commentator, during his last interview (July 1980) with Peter McDonagh for the British Forces Broadcasting Service. His audience presumably still got the joke: Hampton Wick was Forces' rhyming slang for 'dick'.

Elmer **Prettywillie** (W. C. Fields) in *It's the Old Army Game* (1926 C).

Cyril **Smallpiece** (Peter SALLIS), a not noticeably hardy theatrical dresser in *Across a Crowded Room* ('Play for Love' 1978 T).

Ivor **Whopper** (Gareth Hale) in *Filthy Rich and Catflap* (1987 T).

Private James **Widdle** (Charles HAWTREY) in *Carry On up The Kyber* (1968 C).

Doctor **Tinkle** (Kenneth Williams) in *Carry On Doctor* (1968 C). The film also has Winkle and Biddle.

penis titles These *double entendres* are examples of good, healthy British/Australian bad taste, none of the films showing what their titles desire to invoke: *What a Whopper!* (1961); *Percy* (1971) and *Percy's Progress* (1972); *Up the Front*

(1973); *Carry on Dick* (1974); *Barry McKenzie Holds His Own* (1974); *Stand Up Virgin Soldiers* (1977); PRIVATES ON PARADE (1982 C); *Me and Him* (1989). The last-named centred on Griffin Dunne's 'special friend' voiced by Mark Linn-Baker. Television has so far only contributed the more indirect STICKY MOMENTS (1989–91).

The title (PRICK UP YOUR EARS) of John Lahr's biography of Joe ORTON, and of the 1987 film adaptation, is a triple pun – as 'ears' is an anagram. This was probably the one and only time that a basic description of a sexual act has been proclaimed in cinemas and later on national television. Orton's lover, Kenneth HALLIWELL originally suggested it for the abortive Beatles project.

Penmarric (UK 1979 T) In episodes 9–11 unhappily married and morose Philip Castallack (Rupert Frazer) falls in love with mining engineer Alun Trevose (John Patrick), even though he is about to marry. Philip tries psychiatric help to overcome his lack of interest in his wife – he believes this is linked to seeing his father rape his mother. The affair with Alun intensifies, but he is killed when the mine caves in. After self-exile in Canada to exorcise his grief, Philip returns to face hostility from within the family of which he is the theoretical head. He is accused of assaulting his young nephew and commits SUICIDE.
W: John Prebble from the novel by Susan Howatch; P: Ron Craddock; D: Tina Wakerell; BBC1; 12 parts; 55 mins each.

A departure for family sagas: a relatively sympathetic homosexual hero. Philip, who is likened to RICHARD I in this updated (late 19th and early 20th century) version of the Plantagenets, narrates part of the 1971 epic novel, which enables the reader to better understand his melancholy personality. On television Philip comes across as fairly soulless and Alun as a mini-Oliver Mellors, surly and taciturn. Neither actor is given enough time or scope to kindle the kind of passion that makes Philip's departure credible.

In the novel Philip says: 'We thought alike, felt alike, acted alike. For he was a born miner, just as I was … I knew soon after I met him that this was the best friend I would ever have, anywhere at anytime … He was half Welsh, half Cornish, totally Celt … He had been married but it hadn't worked out … After a time, people forgot his strangeness and learned to live with his eccentricities because he was a good man to have around and kind, too, for all his roughness and coarse speech.'

A few scraps of the book's intense feeling remain: Alun angrily telling Philip not to expect him at the wedding; Alun picking up a young man in a pub in an effort to elicit some kind of commitment from Philip; a candlelit dinner; a tryst in the Cornish hills (Alun lighting a CIGARETTE and putting it in Philip's mouth); Philip, on his return from Canada, telling one of his brothers that he'll never love anyone like he loved Alun.

(The serial, extensively promoted and initially considered a natural successor to *Poldark*, failed to draw an audience and was not seen again until 1992, when it turned up on UK Gold.)

People in Conflict (UK 1968 T) A BBC1 series in which Colin Morris, writer of THE UNLOVED (1954), *The Newcomers* (1965) and other socially aware dramas, talked to individuals with difficulties: blind, agorophobic, widowed, imprisoned, overweight, in debt etc. Morris, a former social worker, continued in this vein for nearly two decades, in sporadic series about the troubled. Significantly, by the time he focused on a gay man (Jonathan Walters in *Heart to Heart* 1977), Jonathan's 'problems' all clearly stemmed from society's bird-brained ideas about sexuality. Ideas only too well symbolized by the interviewer – who, just possibly, may have been playing devil's advocate, though it is unlikely because a confrontation with a lesbian (mother-to-be) a few years later (on *My Life*) was equally condescending and determinedly problem-seeking.

people with disabilities *See* DISABLED GAY AND LESBIAN PEOPLE.

percentages How many homosexual people are there? What percentage of the total population do they constitute? Dr Alfred KINSEY and his team's research findings in the late 1940s laid down a conclusion that a third of the adult male population in the US had participated in a 'homosexual act'. In Britain, after the WOLFENDEN Committee reported in 1957, the public became increasingly familiar with the more conservative estimate of ONE IN TWENTY, which was the title of Bryan Magee's best-selling book based on research and interviews for his 1964 THIS WEEK programme. This percentage was still being accepted by the time male homosexual acts were partially decriminalized in 1967, although Michael Schofield said on *Late Night Line Up* that year: 'The popular estimate is one in every twenty people. We don't know whether or not it is higher.'

By the early 1970s, on programmes featuring members of the Campaign for Homosexual Equality (CHE) and the Gay Liberation Front, the percentage jumped to one in ten, taking into account the Kinsey findings – representing adult males who said they were predominantly homosexual for at least three years – and the seemingly wide prevalence of bisexual men and women and a social climate which now discouraged 'PASSING for STRAIGHT'.

For the next two decades, one in ten was adopted by most commentators on sexual minorities, although some groups and individuals have stated otherwise. The crusty cop (Darren McGavin) was told by his pregnant girlfriend in *Police Story* 'The Ripper' (1974 T) not to worry: 'Two per cent of the population is homosexual.' She therefore argues (with an assumption that the child will be male) that the odds on having a queer baby are fifty to one. In the opinion of THE LONDON WEEKEND SHOW (1977 T) the likely British homosexual tally was 'one in fifty across the country, with one in ten in London'. Colin Morris was told on *Heart to Heart* the same year that the number was probably 'one in seven'. Channel 4's New Year and gay lesbian celebration was boldly entitled ONE IN FIVE (1983).

Now it seems to be a more or less clear contest between supporters of 5 per cent – eg Johnnie Walker's *The AM Alternative* (1992 R); *Public Eye* 'Age of Consent' (1992 T) – and 10 per cent – eg *Day by Day* (1987 T): 'As many as one in ten of us'; *Family Matters* 'Accepting the Unacceptable' (1990 T): 'One in ten of us is homosexual'; *Soul Survivor* (1990 T): 'Ten per cent, maybe 20 per cent; some would say more'; THE GAY AND LESBIAN WORLD (1992 R): 'One in ten according to some estimates'; PUBLIC EYE 'Age of Consent' (1992 T): the representative from the Stonewall Group doubled the commentator's 5 per cent. However, the 1992 Anglo-French questionnaire elicited a 2–3 per cent homosexual response.

American homosexuals have also been wedded to 10 per cent, which has been communicated through the media in a variety of ways: on chat shows and documentaries, by gay activists and anchor men and women; via Thelma Houston's credit title song of 'One in Ten' from NORMAN ... IS THAT YOU? (1976 C); the Gay Cable Network's *The 10% Show* (received in Atlanta, Nashville, New Orleans, San Francisco, Los Angeles, Chicago and Cincinnati); *2 in 20* aka *Two in Twenty*, the late 1980s Sapphic soap cabled from Boston.

Most recent studies – notably the National Opinion Research Center (NORC) at the University of Chicago between 1989 and 1992 – suggest that the correct figure is somewhere over 2 per cent, although a 1991 survey suggests a figure of 6 per cent homosexual or bisexual, concluding that 4 per cent of the US male population and 2 per cent of the female is primarily and predominately homosexual in terms of sexual response. On this basis, with a population of 200 million, there are a possible 12 million men and women who are exclusively homosexual.

Tom ROBINSON (1992 R) said:

'There's no way round it. You have to be aware that at least one in twenty of your classmates and friends are feeling exactly the same way and keeping dead schtumm about it.' Part of a conversation between schoolfriends in WELCOME HOME, BOBBY (1986 T) runs:

'Gays are only 10 per cent of the population – how are they going to take over?'.
'By recruiting.'

Philip Hodson in DIVERSE REPORTS 'What a Difference a Gay Makes' (1984 T) comments: 'Homosexuality has been experienced in all periods of history in roughly equal proportions. It's not as though it's a group of people that you can get rid of, like a disease.'

Percy, Esmé (1887–1957) English actor who, whatever the occasion or the part, seemed to have *eau-de-Cologne* running through his veins.

C: the homicidal TRANSVESTITE 'half-caste' trapeze artist in HITCHCOCK'S *Murder!* (1930); *Nell Gwynne* (1934); *The Amateur Gentleman* (1936); *The Invaders* (1936); *The Frog* (1936); Robinson, valet to Douglas Fairbanks Jr in *Jump for Glory* (1937); Colonel Pickering in *Pygmalion* (1938); Napoleon in *Invitation to the Waltz* (1938); the rebel leader in *Our Fighting Navy* (1938); Richard Brinsley Sheridan in *The Return of the Scarlet Pimpernel* (1938); *Twenty-One Days* (1939); *The Young Mr Pitt* (1942); Major Domo in *Caesar and Cleopatra* (1945); the doll-like ANTIQUE DEALER Mr Rutherford in 'The Haunted Mirror' story from DEAD OF NIGHT (1945 C); one of *The Ghosts of Berkeley Square* (1946); *Death in the Hand* (1948); etc.

R: Alexander, the brother-in-law, in *Uncle Vanya* (1935); Cosmo Vaughan in *Death in the Hand* (1939); Uncle Nicholas in *The Reluctant Stork* about the falling birthrate (1946); music hall artist Roscoe in *Evening Primrose* (1946); Jonathan West in *Farewell to the Pegasus* (1946); 'a sinister surgeon of souls' in *The Puppet Master* (1946); *My Life Is a Lovely Story* (Hans ANDERSEN, 1947);

Osric in *Hamlet* (1948); Pandarus in *Troilus and Cressida* (1952); title role in *Disraeli* (1953); Vivaldi in *The Battle of the Masks* (1953); Count Shabelsky, uncle of *Ivanov* (with John GIELGUD, 1954); the Ladies' Tailor in *The Banquet* (1954); Devil in *Don Juan in Hell* (1954); Heron Lloyd in *The Singing Sands* (1956). (He talked about working with Sarah Bernhardt in 1953 and Bernard Shaw in 1955.)

T: an exquisite murder suspect in the Val Gielgud serial *Gravelhanger* (1954); etc.

Esmé Percy is discussed – negatively – in David Holbrook's book *A Play of Passion* (1978).

Performance (UK 1970 C) Ruthless gangster Chas (James FOX), forced to hide out from the big boys, finds perverse companionship and – through magic mushrooms – parts of his identity which he never dreamed existed. In the final sequence, Chas appears to transcend death, taking on the form of his alter ego.
W/D: Donald Cammell and Nicolas Roeg; P: Donald Cammell; 106 mins.

Ambiguous and permeable alienation and disintegration fantasy, centring on two kinds of performers: a pop star who has lost his daemon (Mick Jagger) and a bully boy whose big mistake is killing a man (Anthony Valentine) who wants him to admit what he really is.

By turns irritating and magnificent, empty and provocative. The contrasting ambiences of the criminal and pop music worlds are successfully captured, and the influence of Francis BACON is unmistakable in Jagger's one song in which he portrays the homosexual gang boss and appears to order his men to strip and adopt humiliating poses.

The film shrieks sexual ambiguity from every frame. Not one single character is straight. However, its exploration of sexuality remains skin-deep: Jagger in bath and bed with two androgynous women, Fox in long wig and make-up, Jagger applying make-up, but never Jagger and Fox *together*. Severely compromised because of cuts in the first half

(and the loss of Jagger and Fox writhing naked on a bed with one of the women), *Performance* would, for all its brilliant editing and photography, be a frustrating, almost pointless exercise were it not for James Fox, as an increasingly unconfident man clinging onto his presumed normalcy in the terrifying but ultimately reassuring face of choice and option.

This was the first major film to indicate the strong homoeroticism of Britain's gangland which would be further trekked in *Villain* (1971 C), *The Long Good Friday* (1980 C), WIDOWS (1983 T), *The Fear* (1988 T) and *The Krays* (1990 C).

Peter Webb wrote in *The Erotic Arts* (1975): 'The mutilation of *Performance* is a perfect example of the short-sightedness and destructiveness of film censorship.'

perfume Before the mid-1960s, perfume, if worn by a man, was an automatic branding.

UK: too too divine Nigel in UNDERGRADUATE SUMMER (Frith Banbury 1939; Elwyn BROOK-JONES 1951) likes Rose du Bellay which is 'not a soap but a purificant'; old maidish Pawnie, as well as Florence, gives himself daily dabs of Narcisse Noir in THE VORTEX (Noel HOWLETT 1960 T etc); Sir Edward Carson (Ralph Richardson) lays particular silken emphasis upon the perfume – 'not incense' – in the house frequented by *Oscar Wilde* (1960 C); club owner Nick (Andreas Malandros) uses a 'masculine' perfume (made by his brother-in-law) called Off-Drive in *Crime on Their Hands* (1954 C), but is still regarded as odd by the hero; Belgian *Poirot* (David Suchet 1990– T), solving crimes all over the world but principally in Britain, couldn't do without his lavender water: 'very good for the little grey cells'); soon-to-be debauched Tony (James FOX) has a large bottle of cologne in his bathroom in *The Servant* (1963 C).

US: Roger (Edward Everett HORTON) sprays Embrassez-moi! onto his employer (Douglas Fairbanks) who backs away, giving Roger the excuse to blast himself with it (in *Reaching for the*

Moon (1931 C); always heavy on the make-up Dick Powell sang of his perfume being borrowed by a girlfriend ('Lulu's Back In Town' from *Broadway Gondolier* 1935 C); Cornel Wilde as a SENSITIVE writer quotes from his novel about the bliss of perfume in *Leave Her to Heaven* (1945 C); rather too smooth suspect Tracey Walcott (Robert Brown) spills his cologne provoking a snide comment from Paul DRAKE in PERRY MASON 'The Case of the Sleepy Slayer' (1964 T); it is the talk of the prison that Warden LeGoff uses cologne in *There Was a Crooked Man* (1970 C); Walter Matthau is caustic about FLORIST Jimmy Twitchell (René AUBERJONOIS) in *Pete 'n' Tillie* (1972 C): 'You smell better than your flowers'; Richie (Mitchell Lichtenstein) in *Streamers* (1983 C) further either inflames or fascinates his bound-for-Vietnam buddies by his ostentatious toilette which includes generous splashes of cologne.

Essentially, men smelling of something other than natural body odour or coal tar soap was viewed by the British, Germans and Americans as Southern European or Asian or Arabic and, therefore, soft and unmasculine, and redolent of all manner of vice.

The DANCER, drug dealer and pimp Jackie (Don De Natale) in the 1930s poem 'The Wild Party' (filmed in 1974) was summed up with congealed contempt by the narrator:

Perfect of form and face
In his veins flowed the blood of more
than one race,
He left a subtle trail of scent
Floating behind him as he went.

The title of the classic *Black Narcissus* (1947 C) refers not to the flower but to the perfume worn by the Young General (Sabu). This causes great perturbation to the most neurotic and rigid of the nuns (Kathleen Byron); she sees it – and the jewels and pretty clothes the youth wears – as conduct unbecoming.

The German actor Hendrik Hofgen (Klaus Maria Brandauer) – only half-seriously predicting public opinion – says he must be suspect because of his limp handshake and lavender perfume: 'shocking behaviour in a man,' he says, feigning distaste in *Mephisto* (1980 C).

Perfume was an effective signifier of depravity in American thrillers of the 1930s and 1940s. In *Farewell, My Lovely/Murder, My Sweet* (1944 C which the now toughened-up, unrouged Dick Powell starred in), Lindsay Marriott (Douglas Walton) carries a strong whiff of it as did, more outstandingly, Joel CAIRO (Peter LORRE) in *The Maltese Falcon* (1941 C). The censors would allow no mention of Cairo's penchant, but he was given leave to present Spade with a visiting card impregnated with the scent of gardenia. The 1984 radio *Falcon* restored Dashiell Hammett's original characterization, aided by the heady performance of Nickolas GRACE. After Cairo hands his card to Spade's secretary Effie, she gives it to her boss: 'There's a "man" wants to see you'. He reads it and is simultaneously assailed by the scent of chypre. Effie joins up the dots for him and the audience: 'The guy is QUEER.'

In Neil Simon's mockery (spliced with chunks of *Casablanca*) *The Cheap Detective* (1974 C), Cairo has become Damascus (Dom De Luise). He is a great gluggy puddle of a man. He tells Sam Spade (Peter Falk): 'I hope my disgustingly cheap perfume doesn't offend you. I purposely stink to stop my enemies getting too close.' Sam advises him to bathe in turpentine.

The first hint of a revolt against smelliness came at the end of the 1950s when John OSBORNE (in 1959) chose perfume as his DESERT ISLAND DISCS luxury. (It had previously only been selected by a woman – Cleo Laine. It would later be chosen by Franco ZEFFIRELLI for his sojourn.) That the state of male armpits (and other areas) might become a source of contention to the resistant British was first indicated in *The Servant* when Susan (Wendy Craig) figuratively crinkling up her nose asks Barrett (Dirk BOGARDE) if he wears a DEODORANT in an effort to destabilize him.

In the 1990 series *Magic Moments* (R),

Nigel Fountain traced the history of Britain's capitulation to 'personal hygiene' through the development of AFTERSHAVE lotion. 'The Fragrance Aspirant' gleefully scanned the Englishman's suspicion and terror of the effete, and his complete indifference to putrid body odour: 'It makes them effeminate. A man's got to be a man. If he isn't he's sissy or effeminate' (a Northern man interviewed in 1965).

The advertising agency promoting Old Spice in 1957 was told: 'Englishmen aren't like that ... you're wasting your time.' Unable to sell Old Spice as scent or perfume, the advertisements went for freshness. Images of men splashing themselves with sea water and a female voice-over: 'Men with adventure in their hearts. Men who go in for the feel of cold fresh spray on their faces. Men who go for masculine freshness. The masculine freshness of Old Spice'. Old Spice was a huge success from the beginning, promising the ultimate in virility: 'You'll find success ... Old Spice ... The classic fragrance ... The mark of a man.'

The next stage came when the Mark Vardy Group advertised 'men's toiletries' on British television in 1961, resulting in 'meagre' sales. Then, Brut co-opted machismo in the reassuringly battered shape of boxer Henry Cooper: 'Lovely way to freshen up.' 'Enry took away those nagging male doubts: 'After shave, after shower, after ...'

Thirty years later, the deodorant business is worth £65 million, and, according to *Magic Moments*, 'more men than women use it'. Fountain deduced that 'changing notions of sexuality and greater affluence' as well as heartfelt compliments and thanks from lovers, colleagues and family ensured that British men who did not take care of personal hygiene were the exceptions.

Even though the second generation of fragrances for men are 'sweeter and softer', the selling of them still has to be caked in mud and rough textures: Pub ('virile, vital, potent ... a social necessity for men who mix') and Denim ('it does encourage a feeling of freshness').

For some people, perfume and the male body still equate with homosexuality. In A HYMN FROM JIM (1977 T) a detective discusses a corpse: 'the body had been drenched in a highly expensive aftershave – known to be used predominantly by homosexuals.' Petty thief Eddie (Denis Lawson) is put on the alert about police inspector (George Baker) in *Dead Head* (1986 T) when he gets a whiff of him: 'Definitely a cream puff.' These are probably the kind of men who still use Brut: unpretentious and straight (although in the early 1960s it was one of the giveaway smells of the dedicated deviate). Dear old Brut, advertised in the 1990s as being 'for men who get rubbed up for a living'.

Perry Mason (US 1957–66 T) Two hundred and seventy-one prosecutions, all successfully defended by the increasingly Mikado-like defence lawyer, aided by his beautiful, super-efficient first-class secretary (and would-be lover) Della STREET (Barbara Hale), his rugged leg-man (and possible lover) Paul DRAKE (William Hopper), and viewed with suspicion, awe and amazement by police lieutenant Tragg (Ray Collins) and (the world's most undiscouraged loser) district attorney and public prosecutor Hamilton Burger (William Talman). Made to a rigid formula (circumstances leading to a murder; the trial; the uncovering of fresh evidence or a surprise witness; court confession of the real killer; debriefing with Perry, Della and Paul, ending with a cute curtain line followed by the crashing chords of Fred Steiner's theme).

The producer was Ben Brady (for Paisano Productions, ie Cornwall Jackson, Gail Patrick Jackson and Erle Stanley Gardner). The first case was 'The Restless Redhead' (21.9.57), and the last was 'The Final Fade-Out' (22.5.66). *The New Perry Mason* (with Monte Markham, Sharon Acker, Albert Stratton, Harry Guardino and Dane Clark) lasted 14 episodes (1973–4). After a 19-year hiatus, Raymond Burr and Barbara Hale made the TV movie *Perry Mason*

Returns in 1985, followed by a further 20, including 'The Case of the Lost Love' (1987) which rustled up a previously unmentioned 'old flame' (Jean Simmons).

Perry Mason was created in 1933 by Erle Stanley Gardner whose novels ushered in a short film series with Warren William as a rather GAY DOG, who married Della (Claire Dodd) in 'The Case of the Curious Bride'. He was succeeded by Ricardo Cortez and Donald Woods. A radio version ran from 1943 to 1955.

The television series finds Perry and Della as boss and secretary, but also – with Paul Drake very much the third man – great pals. During the first couple of seasons, Della tries desperately to interest Perry in matters other than the case in hand, but he prefers weekend fishing expeditions with Paul ('The Case of the Negligent Nymph' 1957). She seems to accept the situation and some kind of non-cohabitational ménage à trois seems on the cards (especially in 'The Case of the Borrowed Baby' 1962).

With its rigid formula, grimly sustained pace, the all-consuming sobriety of Perry and the histrionic predictability of the 'guest' casts, the only real pleasures of this series lie in the few clues dropped as to the exact nature of Perry and Della's (and Paul's) relationship. The game of peek-a-boo played by the deductive male and the highly intelligent, if far less long-winded, female continues to this day with most of the TV movies including at least one barbed or ironic reference to the couple's extraordinary lack of sexual or emotional commitment. It's all part of the 'mystique', although Perry's orientation may have been revealed – appropriately enough – in the very last shot of the very last episode in the series.

There were only two overtly gay stories, both shown in 1959. The first is 'The Case of the Jaded Joker', which hinges on the murder of a dishonest impresario. It contains a peculiar dive called the Purple Wall – 'no liquor, no laughter – just sitting around hating

each other' – and three unrelated men in their thirties living together, two in a very tight bond, the third (Bobby Troup) with a deep hatred of 'square' society. No dames in sight. A streak of rare dramatic lightning runs through this episode, intensified by Bobby Troup's music – defiant, desolate, like the character Troup himself plays.

Following very closely behind came 'The Case of the Bedevilled Doctor'. Who murdered nasty, neurotic Mark Douglas (Barry McGuire) who was in cahoots with his friend Ronnie to blackmail a psychiatrist over a patient's revelations? Who did it: The psychiatrist? The patient? The patient's alcoholic wife? The dead man's partner? His sister?

'You know, sometimes it's best to leave some questions unanswered,' Perry tells a client in 'The Case of the Watery Witness' (1959).

'It is frustrating not to be able to get at an itch to scratch it,' Perry to Della (he's hurt his arm) in 'The Case of the Fatal Fetish' (1965).

'I'm holding out for a sulky *boy*,' Perry's closing line in 'The Case of the Sulky Girl' (1966).

'We're missing something, I don't know what it is, but there's something missing,' Perry to Della in 'The Case of the Lethal Lesson' (1989), followed by an immediate cut to Della whose expression is a priceless mixture of blank disbelief and worn indulgence.

Personal Best (US 1982 T) Love on the athletics track which takes a permanent detour when one of the two women falls in love with a male runner.

W/D: Robert Towne; P: (David) Geffen Company; 127 mins (some versions 122 mins).

Lots of movement but little vitality in this broken-backed story of athletics and two kinds of love. More successful in its later (heterosexual) stages with Chris Cahill (Mariel Hemingway) forsaking lover/rival Tory Skinner (Patrice Donnelly) for bland athlete Denny Stiles (Kenny Moore) whom she inducts into kinky sex (watching him while he pees).

Soundtrack features – in pointed succession – Boz Scaggs' 'It's Over', Kenny Loggs' 'You Don't Know Me' and Fletcher Man's 'You Make Loving Fun'.

'I honestly never thought of it as a lesbian relationship when I read the script. That word, lesbian, sounds so perverse, so wrong. What I saw in the script were two people, both innocent in some ways. It was a very shaky time for them emotionally. And the relationship between them seemed natural. It didn't seem morbid or sordid. It just seemed innocent and honest' (Mariel Hemingway discussing playing Chris, *Rolling Stone*, 1982).

In a 1988 episode of NEIGHBOURS, a teenage boy and girl decide not to watch 'girls in shorts' in *Gregory's Girl* and *Personal Best* and settle for something 'mushy and romantic'.)

Personal Best (UK 1991 T) The interaction of sport and sexuality evidenced by lesbian footballers and Gay London Swimmers along with all manner of greased, sweat-drenched bodies selling sportswear and deodorants.
D: Richard Kwietniowski; 20 mins.

Personal Services (UK 1987 C) The life and sometimes great times of suburban brothel owner (or giver of parties) Christine Paynter (Julie Walters), a thinly disguised Cynthia Payne.
W: David Leland; P: Tim Bevan; D: Terry Jones; 105 mins.

Some beautiful swipes at British hypocrisy and energetic supporting performances set off the star to perfection. Highlights include two very different parties: a wedding reception at which home truths are loudly and fractiously voiced, and a wonderful revel for men with all manner of sexual tastes, including Alec MCCOWEN's dedicatedly 'dirty old man' and a football team of 'fathers and grandfathers, fornicators all'.

The film's ethos is very straightforward (and simplistic): nobody is NORMAL. Desires should be fulfilled as long as they don't hurt anybody else (who doesn't wish to be hurt). And the only

way to have a sensible conversation with a man is to despunk him first: 'When the balls are full, the brain is empty ... If she gives him sex, he might give her a three piece suite.' When all is said and done (and by the time the film ends, Christine has done pretty much everything in her line of personal service), 'Most men don't like sex very much; they *want* it'.

pervert The word had cropped up sporadically during the 1950s. The headteacher (Rupert Davies) in THE UNLOVED (1955 T) tells a newcomer: 'We get three kinds of people who want to work here ... Idealists, NEUROTICS and perverts.'

Inspired by advertising blandishments promoting passionate relationships between owners and automobiles, Millicent Martin has an erotically verbal car in a 1963 THAT WAS THE WEEK THAT WAS sketch. She energetically pursues some of its more *outré* demands, but balks when the vehicle suggests reversing: 'Pervert!'

The 1960s permissiveness in the cinema encouraged Barbara STANWYCK's Jo Courtney to upbraid her less than responsive would-be girlfriend (Capucine) in *Walk on the Wild Side* (1962): 'You're being perverse!'; while Stuart Whitman's Norman Mailer surrogate in *An American Dream/See You In Hell Darling* (1966) condemns his estranged wife's 'sick parties and perverted friends – and everything that goes with it ... sex in 57 varieties'.

From an earlier, more dignified age, ballet progenitor DIAGHILEV (Ronald Pickup) observes wearily after receiving a tongue-lashing from NIJINSKY's soon-to-be wife in *Chinchilla* (1981 R): 'Why is it that whenever anyone gets angry, the only thing they can think of is to call me a pervert?'

'The film struck me as dreary and dull. It showed the sort of people, perverts and homosexuals whom he portrays in his works ... Taken as a whole, however, it is not offensive, 'commented Judge (later Lord) Denning as he summed up the case brought against the showing of the WARHOL documentary in 1973.

To the public, homosexuals were perverts and perverts homosexuals. The 16-year-old (Dai Bradley) in TWO PEOPLE (1979 T) makes a virtue out of an obscenity. The kids at school say he's a pervert because he loves men so he renames himself 'Per'. Refusing to accept society's definition, the German director who had renamed himself Rosa VON PRAUNHEIM siphoned his anger off into a film manifesto called concisely IT IS NOT THE HOMOSEXUAL WHO IS PERVERSE BUT THE SOCIETY IN WHICH HE LIVES (1970 C/T).

perverted practices! 'Perverted practices during family viewing ... It's absolutely disgusting that this revolting scene goes out at 7.30pm.' Virgins being deflowered? Animals being tortured? Children bashed and brutalized? No: merely a few seconds of an exchange of affection on the mouth from Guido to Colin on EASTENDERS in February 1989. But the SUN newspaper was determined that British families be protected, never mind the length, from the sexually cosmopolitan, the love universal. Very much the same thing was written in 1896 when, in *The Kiss*, May Erwin and Jonas C. Rice behaved in a similarly loose manner, bringing corruption in its wake.

petal Terry (Roland CURRAM) and Denny (Paul Greenhalgh) simper this to straight men in THE CREZZ (1976 T); supposedly straight Harry Essendorf (Hywel Bennett) dubs a gay man thus in COMING OUT (1979 T); Barnaby Blake (David Simeon) calls Nicola Freeman this in *Crossroads* (1985 T): 'You must never, never lose your aura of mystery, petal.'

Peter Pan Character created by J. M. BARRIE and based on the Llewellyn-Davies boys, principally George and Michael. The latter, who was the model for the statue in Kensington Gardens (which featured prominently in Ray GOSLING's *The Human Jigsaw* 'Socially Unacceptable' 1987 T), drowned, aged 21, in a possible suicide pact with a male lover.

Androgyny's child with the stated ambition never to mature or to conform: 'Nobody is going to catch me, lady, and make me a man,' he tells Wendy in the play (first filmed in 1924, with Betty Bronson, and performed on radio in 1941, with Patricia Hayes) which is subtitled *The Boy Who Wouldn't Grow Up*. Later Peters have included Mia Farrow (1976 T); Mark Rylance (1987 R); Robin Williams (portraying him as an adult, with children of his own, but still battling his fairy nature and his arch enemy Captain *Hook* 1991 C).

In a specifically gay context: Peter Pan is the name of the club frequented by the drag queens and their friends in *The Drag* (1927 stage); Claire Trevor as the rock-hard mother of *Marjorie Morningstar* (1958 C) suggests to Noel AIRMAN (Gene Kelly) that he is a fly-by-night rather than a suitable life-mate for her girl: 'Like Peter Pan?' he grins – to which she replies with icy force: 'Peter Pan was a *fairy* story'; the producer William Bishop (Jeffrey GARDINER) in ROCK FOLLIES OF '77 (T) sees himself as being 'light and gay'; his dictum is 'Think Peter Pan'.

Also: Rumpole of the Bailey (Leo McKern) calls bachelor Mordred (Derek Farr) 'the Peter Pan of the pulpit' in 'Rumpole and the Man of God' (1979 T). The writer Tom Vermeer (Peter WHITMAN) uses it as part of self-evaluation in *Slipping Away* (1984 R): 'Like Peter Pan, I'll never grow up.' The equally desperately decaying Smithy (Charles Kay) in *The Spectre* (1983 R) worships at Peter's statue in Kensington Gardens, after a long time overseas in the diplomatic service. He sees it as a fountain of his lost youth and innocence. The patrons of the Blue Jay bar chant the traditional cry to revive Tinkerbell to cheer up a waiter, who's unlucky in love on Christmas Eve: 'We believe in fairies,' they cry in SOME OF MY BEST FRIENDS ... (1971 C); as does Claude Crepe (Anthony Gardiner) in *Mister Ten*

Per Cent (1967 C): 'Yesssssss!' he bellows, knowing that he's legal at last.

When one of the *Tough Guys* (1986 C), Kirk Douglas, returns to Los Angeles after many years in jail, he looks in at the BAR he had frequented in his salad days. A man begins talking to him; no, not talking to him, chatting him up. This would seem to be an accurate reflection of the bar's changed clientele (if not 1980s gay pick-up lines): 'I'm Peter Pan and I've come to take you to Never-Never Land.'

'ANDERSEN was a Peter Pan ... he never grew up. I cannot rid myself of the feeling that he is faintly sinister and this film did not help me do so,' commented Lady Southorn on the Danish television documentary *Hans Andersen and the Ugly Duckling* (1955), quoted in the *Listener* (31.3.55).

'I haven't got the equipment, DUCKIE ... I'm the perennial Peter Pan,' said Kenneth WILLIAMS on ROUND THE HORNE (1966 R).

John INMAN was introduced by Jonathan Ross on WOGAN (1990 T) as 'that wayward Peter Pan from men's outfitters'.

It applies to people who grew up in the 1960s too. On DONAHUE 'Forty and Female' in 1990, a former model, now a successful businessperson, said proudly: 'We are of the Peter Pan generation. We never grew up.'

The name Tinker Bell, after Peter Pan's fairy companion, is now a form of mild abuse for gay men, mainly in America. Stanley Roper (Norman Fell) habitually baits Jack Tripper (John Ritter) in THREE'S COMPANY (1978–81 T) with it; and the admirer of Georgie (Julia McKenzie) refers to her gay friend Harvey (Peter John) by this handle in *That Beryl Marston ...*! 'Noel-Oh-Hell' (1981 T): 'Have you ever seen Peter Pan?'

pet names *See* NICKNAMES.

pets OUT (1991 T) on lesbians and gays and their pets. *See also* CAT OWNERS; DOG OWNERS.

phallic symbols Any number of these: Sigismund, the fetishist caressing Kurbisky's sword in *Ivan the Terrible* (1943 C); Gary Cooper's drill in *The Fountainhead* (1949 C, itself a phallic symbol; Kenneth Anger's *Eaux d'Artifice* (1953) and Joseph Losey's gushing outlets in *Eve* (1963); Richard Anderson stroking what looks like a large plastic sausage shortly before he is torn to bits by Walter Pigeon's id in *Forbidden Planet* (1956 C); Pancho (Eli Wallach) playing his saxophone on his knees while Joan Collins gyrates in front of him in *Seven Thieves* (1960 C); the old (twisted and gnarled) tree that ends up between Jill's legs in THE FOX (1968 C); sausages and BANANAS vie with the Depardieu member swinging free and holy or ramrod straight in at least ten scenes in THE LAST WOMAN (1976 C); lots of trees and axes in *Fire Festival* (1984 C); Schwarzenegger's opponent Bennett (Vernon Wells) impaled on a pipe which emits little puffs of steam in *Commando* (1985 C); the multi-dentured, dripping, pulsating *Aliens* that pursue and eventually impregnate RIPLEY (1986 C); bananas again and other edible items in *Dark Passions* 'The Summer of Miss Forbes' (1988 T); Ronnie's snakes in *The Krays* (1990 C); etc. 'DYNASTY aficionados have never doubted that bisexual Steven would turn straight in the end since his accompanying symbol (in the credits) is a phallic oil derrick' (Celia Brayfield, *Evening Standard*, 7.2.85). *See also* GUNS; PENISES.

phase According to psychiatric orthodoxy before the Second World War, all adolescents go through a same-sex attraction phase. Then the curtain falls and rises for the final act. Except, that is, for a few retards. This theory is now pretty much disproved – sexual development is parallel, not sequential – but not dislodged in the public mind.

Ma Larkin (Peggy Mount), possibly seeing grandmotherhood passing her by, hotly denies there is anything 'like that' about her son in *The Larkins* (1960 T): 'He is just going through a phase,' she tells her noxious neighbour (Barbara

Mitchell). Terry Priestley (Fred Peart), confiding to the barman in WEDNESDAY LOVE (1975 T), thinks he may grow out of it 'like stamp collecting'.

Eric Archer (Nigel Hughes) *Time of My Life* (1980 T) says: 'He's 22. He's been going through this phase since he was 16'; Libby Purves writes of Gerald's gay phase in HOWARDS' WAY (1990 T) in *Radio Times* (24.11.90); mum hopes son will grow out of in BIRDS OF A FEATHER 'Young Guns' (1991 T); Barry CLARK (Garry Hailes) in EASTENDERS (1988 T) blows out his relationship with his Colin in the neat certainty that 'It was just a phase I was going through.'

In *Brass Tacks* 'Good As You?' (1988 T) James' father's reaction to his declaration was memorably British: 'I think I'll go and make a cup of tea' – he had hoped it was 'just another of the phases a teenage boy goes through because he's a *very* enthusiastic lad'. Mary (Cathryn Damon) on her son Jodie's impending sex change in SOAP (1977 T) says: 'I just get used to you being homosexual ... I thought [this] was just a phase'; one of the Spaniards tells his mother not to worry about 'one of those phases teenagers go through' in ELDORADO (1992 T).

Guy and Tommy converse as follows in ANOTHER COUNTRY (1984 C):

> 'It's all just a passing phase'
> 'Exactly. Just like you being a Communist.'

phase, heterosexual 'I had a very happy heterosexual phase out of which I've grown, mercifully, into a thoroughly adjusted lesbian' says Jackie FORSTER, who had her first relationship with a woman at 32, to Monty Modlyn in *Monty at Large* 'The Gay Scene in London' (1979 R).

'Yes, I was heterosexual once. But it was just a phase I was going through,' says Simon FANSHAWE in *The Garden Party* (1990 T).

Tony and Pat Archer (Colin Skipp and Patricia Gallimore) are worried about their 14-year-old son, John having a

crush on a woman and spending 'hours' in the bathroom. 'It's just a phase', reckons Pat (who reads the GUARDIAN), 'He'll grow out of it.'

Philip/Phillip Boy's name, often descriptive of the sensitive outsider, the unbalanced, the nervy ones.

UK: Philip Weeks (Anthony Bushell) in *Five Star Final* (1931 C); sensitive doctor Philip Carey in *Of Human Bondage* based on his creator Somerset MAUGHAM (Leslie Howard 1934 C; Paul Henreid 1946 C; Laurence Harvey 1964 C); Philip Hyde (Simon LACK), cadet son carried away by mysterious stranger in *Sons of the Sea* (1939 C); Philip Trottwood (Geoffrey Banks) who has a sentimental friend, Nigel, during his UNDERGRADUATE SUMMER (1939 R); Pip born Philip Pirrip (John Mills) in *Great Expectations* (1946 C); Philip 'Phil' Archer (Norman Painting), young blood who became stick-in-the-mud farmer in THE ARCHERS (1951–   R); Philip Ashley (Richard Burton) whose beloved cousin Ambrose may have been poisoned by his newly wed Rachel – he ends up causing her death in *My Cousin Rachel* (1952 C); Philip Wayne (Jack Hawkins), sturdy pioneer in New Zealand in *Land of Fury/The Seekers* (1954 C); stiff upper lipped Philip Truscott (Laurence Payne) in *The Trollenberg Terror/The Crawling Eye* (1958 C); Philip Main (John Paul) as the PROBATION OFFICER (1959–60 T); Phil Stainer, the man who loved Melville Farr at university and killed himself over him in VICTIM (1961 C); Phil Corbett (John HURT), lonely, hero-worshipping student in *The Wild and the Willing* (1962 C; Nigel Anthony in radio version entitled *The Tinker* 1961); Philip Moss (Wallas Eaton), lover of Robin in HORROR OF DARKNESS (1965 T); Philip Cooper (Jeremy Bulloch), spunky, freckled son in *The Newcomers* (1966–8 T) briefly suspected of being less than a man; taciturn Phillip Scott (Stephen Boyd) in *Assignment K* (1967 C); schoolboy Philip Dreaper (Clive Endersby) in *Walk a Crooked Path* (1969 C); Philip Johnson (Barry McCarthy), librarian in

THE EXPERT 'True Confession' (1970 T); Philip Nuttall (Brian Cox) in *The Master and the Mask* (1970 R); Philip Calvert (Anthony Hopkins), disagreeable hero of *When Eight Bells Toll* (1971 C); Pip (Edward Fox), longtime lover of Bob in *Bermondsey* (1972 T); Philippe (Patrick Bouchity) is neither homosexual nor transvestite but *sensitif* in THE BEST WAY TO WALK (1976 C); brother Philip in *Just Before Midnight* 'Tick Tock, Tick Tock' (1978 R): 'He was the cry baby. But that was sissy, wasn't it. Boys never cry. Only little girls, who learn to use tears as a weapon. Even when they're old'; Philip Castallack (Rupert Frazer), gay son and heir in PENMARRIC (1979 T).

Philip Carlion (James FOX), son and (unmarried) heir in COUNTRY (1981 T); Philip Roach (Peter Tilbury) seeking solace with distractedly gay psychiatrist in IT TAKES A WORRIED MAN (1981–5 T); confirmed bachelor – or is he? – Philip (William Gaunt) in *Love and Marriage* 'Lucifer' (1984 T); Philip (Timothy Hyam/Garard Green), rector's son haunted by childhood prank that ended in death in *The Trumpet* (1986 R); Phillip Frank (Lewis Collins) who puts few restraints on his desires for power and young men in *Robin of Sherwood* 'The New Sheriff'(1986 T); Philip (James Saxon) in *Brush Strokes* (1986 T); Philip Marlowe (Michael Gambon) in *The Singing Detective* (1986 T); Philip Roy (James Goode), a dangerous young scientific genius who plots in his garden shed in *One of the Beautiful Offspring* (1987 R): 'My name is Philip Roy ... with the power to destroy'; Philip (Mick Ford), boyfriend and possible attacker in *The Fiend* (1987 R); Philip Hughes (Peter Acre), childhood sweetheart revisited in *The Three Trees* (1987 R); Philip (Noel DAVIS), mutual friend of Orton and Halliwell who urges Ken to leave Joe in PRICK UP YOUR EARS (1987 C): 'Girls must stick together. I had a friend once who was in soft furnishings. The times I've trolled round the Ideal Home Exhibition'; Phil (Lee Whitlock), bisexual/gay in the unexpurgated TWO OF US (1988 T), turned het-

erosexual in the broadcast version; Philip Tremayne (Ronald Pickup), *A Man Alone*, writer/TV producer obsessed with love for Anthony at prep school (1988 R); Philip known as Pinky (Shaun Prendergast) in *Show Me the Way, Ugly Angels* (1990 R); Philip Benjamin (Angus MacFadyen), hero of THE LOST LANGUAGE OF CRANES (1992 T); ineffectual, long-haired Philip (Jimmy Mulville) in *GBH* (1991 T); Philip Chagrin, all-purpose theatrical queen based on Noel COWARD in *Curtain* (1993 T project); etc.

US: Philip Durban (Lionel Barrymore), business magnate in *A Man of Iron* (1925 C); Philip Collett (Lloyd Hughes), wealthy sportsman and Mary Astor's lover in *The Scarlet Sinner* (1926 C); Philip Homer (Jack Mulhall), struggling GREENWICH VILLAGE artist in *The Golden Calf* (1930 C); Philip Marlowe (James Kirkwood), pilot and painter in *Hired Information* (1934 C), Philip Monrell (Robert Montgomery) with stubborn passion for his best friend (or is it mental imbalance?) in *Rage in Heaven* (1941 C); ice-cold gunman Phillip Raven (Alan Ladd) in *This Gun for Hire* (1942 C); Philip Marlowe (Dick Powell), hardboiled private eye in *Murder, My Sweet/Farewell My Lovely* (1944 C); Robert Mitchum appeared in the 1975 remake and also in the 1978 version of *The Big Sleep* (1946 C) which had starred Humphrey Bogart; Elliot Gould was a shaggier, more ramshackle version in *The Long Goodbye* (1974 C) and Phil(ip) Carey essayed Raymond Chandler's creation in *Philip Marlowe* (1959–60) on television as did Powers Boothe in 1983; Phil Green (John Garfield), nice Jewish boy, good to his mother in *Gentleman's Agreement* (1947 C); one half of homosexual killing duet Philip Morgan (Farley Granger) in ROPE (1949 C), changed from the play's Charles Granillo; Philip Ainley (Ray Milland) in *Night into Morning* (1951 C), a college professor whose wife's death leads him to drink and morbid thoughts; Philip (John Ericson) in *Teresa* (1951 C), simple sensitive GI, lonely and shy; Lieutenant Commander Philip Francis

Queeg (Humphrey Bogart) in *The Caine Mutiny* (1954 C): increasingly unbalanced or merely operating by the book?; Phillip Hannon (Van Johnson), blind playwright who overhears a murder plot in *23 Paces to Baker Street* (1956 C); Philip Warren, hero of Gore VIDAL's novel THE JUDGEMENT OF PARIS: 'his speaking voice was manly but marred by a lisp', although he was lispless in the TV version *Please Murder Me* (1958); Philip Adams (Cary GRANT), charming American diplomat who is *Indiscreet* with Ingrid Bergman (1958 C); Philip Vandamm (James Mason), smooth villain in *North by Northwest* (1959 C); Philip Wrayner (Jeremy Slate), framed nephew in PERRY MASON 'The Case of the Captain's Coin' (1961 T); Phil Edwards (Joe Di Reda) in *Perry Mason* 'The Case of the Devious Detour' (1961 T), a sweating coward, blackmailed, frightened of his wife and a murderer; Philip Harrington (Richard Beymer), sensitive, hero-worshipping son in *Five Finger Exercise* (1962 C, called 'Clive' in the stage version); suave bachelor business tycoon Philip Shayne (Cary Grant) in *That Touch of Mink* (1962 C) colliding with virgin Doris DAY; smoothie Philip (James Mason) in *The Last of Sheila* (1972 C) who unravels the mystery and ends the murder game; millionaire Philip Stevens (James Stewart) in *Airport 77* (1977 C); Phillip Payne (David Warner) in *Nightwing* (1979 C), eccentric killer of vampire bats; faded football star Philip Elliot (Nick Nolte) in *North Dallas Forty* (1979 C); bosom buddies who love movies and the same woman in *Willie and Phil* (1980 C); Sergeant Philip 'Phil' Esterhaus (Michael Conrad) in *Hill Street Blues* (–1983 T): 'Let's be careful out there'; Philippe (Keith McDermott) in *Without a Trace* (1983 C): gay but is he also a CHILD MOLESTER?; Felipe Cruz (Esai Morales) in *Miami Vice* 'God's Work' (1986 T), Mafia scion with a secret; Phillip Colby (Michael Parks), rival to Jason in *The Colbys* (1987 T); Philip Gills (Robin Thomas), two-faced headteacher with appalling taste in sports jackets, mis-taken for gay by Freddy (Mark Harmon) in *Summer School* (1987 C); etc.

phone-ins From the early 1970s, radio phone-ins raged across Britain. Cheap, grass roots and sure-fire controversial. Anna Raeburn became noted as dispenser of advice and reassurance. She rejected blandness. If she was shocked or angry or tearful, she shared her state with listeners and callers. She funnelled her experience into a 1979 TV series, AGONY (co-written with Len RICHMOND), set in a woman's magazine and a radio station.

In the second series, written by others, the Raeburn surrogate Jane Lucas (Maureen Lipman) interviews a gay friend on air about the problems of gay relationships ('Coming Out ... And Going In Again'). The interview generates good ratings. Her boss demands 'six minorities by the end of the year'. Meanwhile, the friend, promised but not granted anonymity, is recognized by his pupils and loses his teaching job.

The other kind of radio phone-in selects a subject, strange or familiar, heart-warming or bloodboiling, and lets waggling, concerned listeners assail the airwaves. Here is a handful of nationwide and London-based examples: *It's Your Line*: Germaine GREER on LESBIANS (1971); CALL-IN 'HOMOSEXUALITY' (1972); *The Jimmy Young Show* (1973); *Platform* (Radio London 1972); *The Marsha Hunt Show* (Capital 1973); *Nightline* (LBC 1974); *Speakeasy* (1975); *Talkabout*: Jonathan King (1977 & 1979); *Capital Phone-In*: 'Lesbians' (1978), 'GAY LIFE' (1980) and 'Teenage Gays' (1981); *It's Your Call* (complaints about programmes on homosexuality and drug addiction 1985 R): viewers call in to Phil DONAHUE's TV show while it is on the air.

'Phone-ins, in general, give the illusion of participation in and access to mass hysteria, though in effect the level of participation is strictly controlled, and by giving the studio expert or host the final word, they reinforce the unimportance and impotence of the caller' (Anne Karpf, 'Women and Radio' in the

Women and Media issue of *Women's Studies International Quarterly* vol. 3, no. 1, 1980).

photographic models John Brown in WHAT CAN I DO WITH A MALE NUDE? (1985 C/T) turns out to be a member of the vice squad, and proceeds to run in the photographer; two hunky fellows are salivated over by the virtual reality sampler in the 1950s sequence of CAUGHT LOOKING (1991 T). *See also* ARTIST'S MODELS.

photographs A compromising one of Melville Farr (Dirk BOGARDE) and 'Boy' (Peter McEnery) in VICTIM (1961 C) described, but never shown and burnt in the last scene. Others in *A Photograph* (1977 T) and *Judgement* (1990 T). A strip of film showing a Cabinet Minister enjoying flagellation and bondage with a RENT BOY as *The McGuffin* (1986 T). Photographs showing lovers together, without guilt or fear of discovery: Chrissie (Myra Francis) and Jackie (Alison Steadman) in GIRL (1974 T): Edward CARPENTER and George Merrill in ONLY CONNECT (1979 T); etc. The loving brothers (Jon Rollason and Philip Martin), pictured in a frame, was the very first image in SUMMER, AUTUMN, WINTER, SPRING (1961 T).

In his first scene, Farr in *Victim* is sitting at his desk with his wife's picture massively visible: as assertion of his normality – and one which features in a hundred films and plays, as well as television documentaries: prominent photographs of the 'wife', the 'husband', the 'children'. A typical establishing shot appeared in JFK (1991 C): hero, desk, wife's picture. Such barometers of acceptability, love of family and home, special feelings are almost entirely absent from plays about homosexuals or from documentary interviews because they are usually not filmed at work (even if they are out of the closet) and, if filmed at home, photographs of loved ones may be removed from sight because of other people's sensitivities, or because there is *no need* to display in this manner the people with whom daily lives are spent.

Physical Olivia Newton-John song (by Steve Kipner and Terry Shadick), a 1981 hit. The video, set in a health hydro, had a lot of fun with six fat men who are transformed into mountains of young, rippling muscle. This jolly jape was trimmed after its initial showing on TOP OF THE POPS, because the two young men in the final scene left the gym in a state of vibrant, sexually expectant togetherness, leaving Olivia wide-eyed – but not censorious. Featured in full in the singer's showcase *Physical* (1981 T), but shown in its abbreviated form on *The Chart Show Video Vault* (1992 T).

pianists/accompanists Classically trained piano-playing men often signal sexual perfidy or suspicious over-refinement: Nicky Lancaster (Ivor NOVELLO) in THE VORTEX (1928 C etc); David Linden (Robert Young), a 'spoiled neurotic' rattles off Chopin in *The Shining Hour* (1938 C); Dorian GRAY plays a Chopin étude prior to a seduction in THE PICTURE OF DORIAN GRAY (1945 C); Finch Whiteoak (Lyndon Brook) in *Whiteoaks* (1949 T); Kip Kipple (David Wayne) in ADAM'S RIB (1949 C); John TREGORRAN (and Phil Archer) occasionally caressed the ivories in THE ARCHERS during the 1950s; young concert pianist Julian in *Shadow of the Vine* (John Forrest 1953 T; Barry Warren 1958 T); Mr Bridson (Harold LANG), the keeps-himself-to-himself little man who is ballerina Mai Zetterling's accompanist in *Dance, Little Lady* (1954 C); Victor Buono as Edwin Flagg is forced to enter a nightmare world when he helps an ex-child star with her comeback in *Whatever Happened to Baby Jane?* (1962 C); Richard Pryor as Billie Holiday's jangled pianist in *Lady Sings the Blues* (1972 C); Paul Winter (Edward Hardwicke), one of the people whose murderous childhood game results in Mia Farrow's nightmares in *The Haunting of Julia/Full Circle* (1977 C); Elaine Loudon's Judy GARLAND has a gay accompanist in *Will*

the Real Judy Garland Stand Up, Please?
(1982 T), possibly based on Roger
EDENS; Michael (Robert Aberdeen) getting more than he bargained for when he
takes a job in a gay establishment in
Saturday Night at the Baths (1975 C);
Richie (Nigel HAVERS) teaches snotty-
nosed, homophobic child in COMING
OUT (1979 T); Chris (Nigel Lambert),
lonely piano teacher in *Running Down*
(1980 R); John Wheatley as Maurice
then and Hugh BURDEN as *Maurice Now*
(1981 R); Michael (Aidan Quinn) and
his mother play a duet in AN EARLY
FROST (1985 T); Max (Peter Kelly) in
10 × 10 'Secret Friends' (1990 T).

Only a smattering of lesbians at the
keyboard: Madge (Briony Hodge),
trained in Vienna, now giving *Piano
Lessons* (1976 T) to neighbour Sally
(Ann Curthoys) and falling in love with
her; Heather Hopkins (José Kidd)
accompanying 'that old QUEEN Max Pilgrim' at the Merry Thought in *A Dance
to the Music of Time* 'At Lady Molly's'
(1980 R); Belle (Capucine) joining her
ex-husband on his island in the company of her girlfriend in *Murder She
Wrote* 'Paint Me a Murder' (1986 T).

The Picture of Dorian Gray (US 1945
C) The most famous of all literary oil
paintings (seen in brief Technicolor
inserts) growing ever more misshapen
and torpid over the decades – while its
subject remains young and flawless,
although he is continuing to lead a life of
unmentionable and unshowable vice,
which involves a lot of late nights.
W/D: Albert Lewin from the novel by
Oscar WILDE; 110 mins.

Topped and tailed by a quotation from
THE RUBAIYAT OF OMAR KHAYYÁM, this
film, boxed in by censorship, is more
interesting for its side dishes (George
SANDERS overcome by monstrous *ennui*
as Lord Henry WOTTON; Angela Lansbury's affecting Sybil whom Dorian
Gray picks up and casts aside) than for
its main course: the evil odyssey of Dorian himself (an expressionless, waxen
Hurd HATFIELD). Not a story which fitted very snugly within MGM's safe
family entertainment ethos of the time,

but the sets and period atmosphere do
much to suggest Wilde's sunlit, sweet-
smelling conservatories and dark byways
of foppish extroversion, private recognition and ironies, mannered dress and
behaviour, and obsessive *amours*. Or as
VARIETY put it: 'Lewin has very subtly
but unmistakably pegged Gray for what
he was.'

Other versions of the story, with its
echoes of the Faust legend, were produced for radio (1948 and 1956) and for
television (1957, 1973 and, most faithfully, 1976). There was also a modernized female version in the US TV movie
The Sins of Dorian Gray (1983).

Georgie **Pillson** Character in E. F. BEN-
SON's novels: Lucia's prim, soft and
over-civilized confidant done to a
boobyish turn by both Nigel Hawthorne
in *Mapp and Lucia* (1985–6 T) and
Jonathan Cecil in *Queen Lucia* (1984 R)
and *Lucia in London* (1985 R). A
painted, bewigged, puffing culture-
vulture, all pampered, candied artifice.

pilots PUSSY Galore and her gals in
Goldfinger (1964 C); Virgil Tracy, one of
the brothers in the puppet film *Thunder-
birds Six* (1968 C) and International
Rescue pilot of Thunderbird 2, is handsome, seductively voiced, pink-shirt
wearing – and he paints; Captain Oveur
(Peter Graves) who loves showing
young boys all the knobs and dials in
AIRPLANE! (1980 C); Mac and Fitz, two
of the Few in A MOMENT IN TIME (1979
T; 1983 R); COMRADES IN ARMS (1990
T); David Ferrie (Joe Pesci) in JFK
(1991 C), hot-shot pilot 'canned after an
alleged homosexual incident', hysterical,
bewigged, made-up: was he a getaway
pilot for Lee Harvey Oswald?

pink is for girls A cultural construction:
before the First World War it was blue
that was considered soft and dainty, and
pink and/or red colours that belonged
on boys. At present, the situation is
reversed, and still rigidly maintained.
After years of resistance, men of all
backgrounds can at least entertain the
idea of going out in a pink shirt: Hamp-

stead lefties (Jim Hacker) in *Yes, Minister* (1980 T); Mancunian publican Alec Gilroy (Roy Barraclough) in *Coronation Street* (1990 T); Philip (Angus MacFadyen) in THE LOST LANGUAGE OF CRANES (1992 T); etc.

In America the shift began slightly earlier with cop Bill (Earl Holliman) in POLICE WOMAN 'Night of the Full Moon' (1974 T), followed by someone in the same line of business, Captain *Barney Miller* (Hal Linden 1980 T, and James Gregory as his boss in 1982). Trendy lawyers like Jonathan (Brent Underwood) in L.A. LAW (1990– T) would occasionally dip into the pink.

But certain parts of Australia found pink on men unacceptable, whether on their backs – or in the case of Western Australian Premier Don Dunstan in the 1970s – around his waist and half-way down his legs. 'I didn't think the people of South Australia would be so cretinous as think that pink was for girls and blue was for boys. But I was wrong,' talking to Philip Adams about wearing (neat, well-tailored, but pink) shorts in the State Parliament (Aust *Late Night Live* 1991 R).

Pinkpop (UK 1993 R) Presented by Laurie Pike, this Mandy Wheeler Sound Production is a breathless 60-minute sprint through gay pop music over the past two decades, sandwiched between Adrian Juste and Johnnie Walker on a Saturday afternoon in January on BBC Radio 1. As notable for the absentees (no current big-name stars and no women) as for those who did speak, including Tom ROBINSON and BOY GEORGE, with comments from guru John Peel and GAY TIMES' Richard Smith. Among those nostalgically recalled: VILLAGE PEOPLE, Elton JOHN, Pet Shop Boys, punk, glitter rock, house, disco ...

pink triangle A triangular piece of pink cloth, it was one of the symbols of male homosexuals in German and Austrian concentration camps.

In *Death Is My Trade/From a German Life* (1978) the man who arranges

FLOWERS in the house of Franz Lang (Gotz George as a thinly disguised Rudolf Hoess) wears one, and in a later scene they are prominently displayed on the uniforms of a labour gang. 'No sleeping here, you lazy bastard,' shouts a guard as one of the men collapses in sub-zero temperatures.

The producers of the 1983 remake of *To Be or Not to Be* had seen Martin Sherman's BENT. They courted history by including a character, Anne Bancroft's dresser Sasha (James Haake), who tried to save Jews. He was forced to wear the pink triangle, a mark of Cain even more contemptible in some eyes than the yellow star: 'I hate it. It clashes with everything.' Jewish organizations in America were outraged by the film's equation of pink triangle with yellow star, according to Mel Brooks, one of the few Hollywood names to protest against the long silence (on a BBC Radio 2 late night chat show).

BRONSKI BEAT's album cover for THE AGE OF CONSENT was a pink triangle which inevitably dominated the ads on Channel 4.

Tom ROBINSON wore one in *The Secret Policeman's Ball* (1978 C); the following year, *Bent* agonizingly explained why the inverted pink triangle must not be forgotten; and Dame Edna EVERAGE wore triangular glasses on a chat show at the time of the 1979 gay pride celebrations: 'I think there might be a little minority out there who may know what this means.' In *Peter Cook & Co* (1980 T) a sketch called 'Are You Gay?' was set in a railway carriage. In place of the usual 'No Smoking' sign there was a pink triangle. A dinner guest in MORE LIVES THAN ONE (1984 T) hopes that gays will soon be taught a lesson as they were in Nazi Germany, pink triangles and all.

Since the late 1970s, the pink triangle has been worn and displayed on books, posters, banners and record albums as a reminder of the Nazi oppression and the continuing attacks on homosexual people by many governments, of different hues, all over the word; eg in OUT 'Sex and the Sandinistas' (1991 T) pink triangle BADGES were well to the fore on the clothing of gay and lesbian activists in Nicaragua.

Pinky Nickname which often conveys a sexual statement, eg Richard Cromwell as the prettiest of the sponge divers in *Fifty Fathoms Deep* (1934 C); Pinky (Edward Everett HORTON) in *The Gay Divorce/The Gay Divorcee* (1934 C); Eddie Pink (Eddie Cantor) in *Strike Me Pink* (a thimbleful of masculinity increased to eggcup size after reading MAN OR MOUSE – WHAT ARE YOU?, 1936 C); scarfaced thug Pinky (Richard Attenborough) in *Brighton Rock* (1947 C); gay Pinky alias Lance Corporal Pinker (Richard Tolan) in THE JEWEL IN THE CROWN (1984 T) who discovers MERRICK's secret; Pinky (Shaun Prendergast), robustly camp media lecturer in *Show Me the Way, Ugly Angels* (1990 R).

But sometimes it supplies confusing, feminizing colour to hulking bears like Pinky Peters (William Bendix) in *Woman of the Year* (1940 C); Pinky Grayson, the belligerent, buttoned-up artist and jealous husband in *Love Crazy* (1941 C); Adam Bonner (Spencer Tracy), hard-nosed but open-minded lawyer in ADAM'S RIB (1949 C) who is dubbed 'Pinky' by his resolutely FEMINIST wife Amanda (Katharine HEPBURN) whom he calls 'Pinkie'.

Occasionally it turns up as a surname: Pink (Peter O'Toole) in *Country Dance/Brotherly Love* (1971), a wilful Scottish misfit in love with his sister.

Pinter, Harold (1930–) English playwright, best known for his malevolent, elliptical, crackling 'comedies of menace' *Night Out* (1959 R; 1960 T); *The Lover* (1963 T); *The Caretaker* (1964 C; 1966 T); *No Man's Land* (1978 T; 1992 R); etc. Is also a masterful adaptor of others' novels: *The Servant* (1963 C; 1970 R); *Accident* (1967 C); *The Go-Between* (1971 C); *The Comfort of Strangers* (1990 C); his unfilmed REMEMBRANCE OF THINGS PAST. As a director he reprised his stage version of BUTLEY for cinema and television showings in 1974. A few of his plays – THE BIRTHDAY PARTY (1968 C; 1987 T); THE DUMB WAITER; THE HOT HOUSE (1981 T); MOUNTAIN LANGUAGE – are explicitly political, dealing with successful efforts to smash and or silence nonconformists. On OMNIBUS (1988 T) he talked about his 'lifelong concern for the plight of the individual in a Britain choked with censorship like poison gas in the first World War'. .

pipe An indication of strength and reliability, once a vital element in the ritual and display of what the culture decides is masculine – poor but honest, muscular and desired by all: Fabio Testi in *The Garden of the Finzi-Continis* (1971 C); good ole dependable lawyer Jim Garrison (Kevin Costner) in JFK (1991 C) vs cigarette chain-smoking queers Clay Shaw and David Ferrie.

Phil (Nigel STOCK) in VICTIM (1961 C) appears to be a back-slapping hearty, calling people 'sport' and full of racy patter. However, in his very first scene, the agitated twisting and turning of an unlit pipe in his hand shows that he is not all he seems. As the film progresses, he's unmasked as a frightened homosexual who is secretly exposing his friends to a gang of blackmailers. The pipe is one of the tools he uses for his protective camouflage, a symbol of his bluff duplicity.

Only two major gay characters have smoked a pipe, with the possible exception of Sherlock HOLMES. Roland CURRAM explained his decision to play Terry in THE CREZZ (1976 T) as a stem-chugger: 'After DARLING I had quite a lot of that "Oooh, deah, get you!" and "Weren't you *outrageous!*" But, in fact, if you look at that film, I wasn't outrageous at *all*. I mean, I just played it like *me*. In a way with *The Crezz*, I was trying to get my revenge on the people who'd said, "Ooo, whoops!" I thought, right, this time I shall play it with a *pipe*! I know several people who are heavy on the pooves and heavy on the pipe as well' (GAY NEWS 107).

Mr HUMPHRIES takes one up as part of his gentrified Country Life change of life (complete with female bed-mate) in GRACE AND FAVOUR (1992–   T).

pirates Conducting buccaneering forays into plunder and swordplay: Mary Read (June Holden) and Ann(e) Bonn(e)y (Flora Robson), transvestite terrors of the Caribbean in *Mary Read* (1950 R): 'Brought up as a boy, passing as a man' whose lover is an effeminate youth; Wanda Ventham played Read in *The Pirates* (1986 T) and Jean Peters was Bonny in *Anne of the Indies* (1951 C); Gianna Maria Canale was Captain POOF in *Queen of the Pirates* (1960 C, followed by *Tiger of the Seven Seas*); Connie Blackheart (Helen Atkinson Wood) in *Tales from the Poop Deck* (1992 T, played as a sort of MADONNA amidships: she has a lover called Captain Stallion).

Gay ones include Jean-Claude Drouot (who starts flaring his nostrils and acting very strange when his gang discover Kirk Douglas in *The Light at the Edge of the World* (1971 C) and possibly Captain Hook (Dustin Hoffman 1991 C etc).

Pitt, William, the Younger (1759–1806) Bachelor Tory Prime Minister (1783–1801 and 1804–6) who failed to anticipate the full import of the French revolution, became embroiled with Napoleon but 'solved' the Irish question. Played by Robert Donat in *The Young Mr Pitt* (1942 C) and by Jeremy Brett in *Number 10* (1983 T).

'I felt it was a dull picture ... It think that with such a long, intricate, rather distorted version of historical events it would have been very difficult to keep the entertainment going around that sort of person. After all Pitt was known as a cold fish in his day. Though nobody knows how cold he really was or what his private life was really like' (Frank Launder, co-writer of *The Young Mr Pitt*, quoted in Geoff Brown, LAUNDER AND GILLIAT, 1977. The film contained a fanciful love affair between the politician and Eleanor Eden played by Phyllis Calvert.)

plague Films about outbreaks of disease often link them to things effeminate

and/or sinister (*Panic in the Streets* 1950 C) or feline and female (*The Mad Death* 1983 T). Sometimes homosexual characters are likened to a viral contamination: Karen and Martha in THE CHILDREN'S HOUR/THE LOUDEST WHISPER (1961 C), and Nicholas Black (Daniel MASSEY) in *The Devil's Advocate* (1977 C). Having had his sexuality compared (by Catholic priest John Mills) to 'a plague – famine, misery and sorrow. It's like an earthquake, hurricane – a baby with two heads', Nicky responds with equal fervour: 'What *I* do is what I want and what I want is done according to the nature that God gave me.'

The original title of the HORIZON documentary on the then (1983) new and rapidly spreading 'cancer' was 'Not the Gay Plague' – by which name the popular press was referring to AIDS. It's a phrase that has remained – increasingly unvoiced – in the public perception despite thousands of disavowals. Said Nick Partridge in THE GAY AND LESBIAN WORLD 4 'AIDS' (1992 R): 'As everyone should know by now, AIDS certainly isn't the gay plague it was described in the press.'

Play for Today Umbrella for BBC1's original plays, after THE WEDNESDAY PLAY, beginning in 1970. They included A LIFE IS FOR EVER (1972); THE OTHER WOMAN (1976); COMING OUT (1979); and, one of the last, MORE LIVES THAN ONE (1984).

A discussion between father and son about *Play for Today* in an episode of I DIDN'T KNOW YOU CARED (*c* 1978 T):

'How many lesbian women?'
'The usual.'
'How many transvestite traffic wardens and perverts?'
'The usual. Seven.'
'What about bent detectives?'
'None. Must be their night off this week.'
'Dear, or dear. All this violence and squalor and obsession with sex. Why do we 'ave to 'ave it rammed down our throats every night on the telly?'
'Good God, we see enough of it in our homes.'

Playmates (UK 1978 R) Rikki (Angus Lennie) is the nextdoor NEIGHBOUR of the play's central character Lena (Carole Hayman). She works in a club whose punters buy their pleasure in the same way as Rikki buys his. But Rikki is looking as much for pain as pleasure: he dreams of being the doormat for a young leather-clad Taurus. He finds him – and ends the play with a ruptured spleen after being bashed up by the ROUGH TRADE.
W: Gilly Fraser; D: Kay Patrick; 7.8.78; BBC Radio 4; 90 mins.

Despite the Scottish accent, Rikki is conceived along fairly standard lines. A plain, ageing man who judges people on their looks and their star signs: 'Aries? I'm Virgo. We should get along – we've got nothing in common.' His import-ance lies in his role as exemplar of the kind of gay male aspirations and atti-tudes that some gay liberationists hoped would disappear: poor self-image, female-identification, political indiffer-ence, eternal passivity. But Rikki didn't want to change. He works as a barman in a gay club and is singularly unim-pressed by new developments including the twin ethos of COMING OUT and being glad. He belongs to the 'Pick Yourself Up and Start All Over Again' school and cannot see any advantages in going back to college to take a higher degree in being himself. He's made his bed and he'll be beaten up on it – which he is.

'I think you preferred it when it was underground. Secret and definitely sordid.'
'*Too right!*'

(A bitterly intelligent writer, Gilly Fraser has contributed mightily to the scripts of EASTENDERS and, more recently, ELDOR-ADO. Probably her finest single tele-vision play is the 1980 *Not for the Likes of Us* starring Pam ST CLEMENT.)

playwrights *See* WRITERS.

poetry Often hovers on the curve of deviant behaviour. ZORRO adopts the foppish disguise of a poet; young and innocent Sophie (Anne Baxter) is fed Keats by the hero (Tyrone Power) of *The Razor's Edge* (1946 C): before long, she becomes a slobbering drunk, hawked around the inmates of an opium den; Michael Craig as the shallow bar crawler in tow with older women who keep him in *Yield to the Night* (1956 C) reads A. E. HOUSMAN; *Sylvia* (Carroll Baker 1965 C) is showered with verse and good books by a lesbian librarian: rape and prostitution follow, but she survives to grow roses and write poetry; Walter Burns (Walter Matthau) equates poetry with PANSIES in *The Front Page* (1974 C); the magician (Hector Altiero) goes to bed listening to LORCA's 'ODE TO WALT WHITMAN' in *To an Unknown God* (1975 C); a poem by James KIRKUP, 'The Love That Dares to Speak Its Name', is arraigned at the Old Bailey (1977 C); *Stevie* (Smith) played by Glenda Jackson (1978 C) lives the archetypal SPINSTER's life in the suburbs with her elderly aunt; Steven CARR-INGTON (Al Corley) and Claudia Blais-del (Pamela Bellwood) salve their injured psyches by reading Emily DICK-INSON together in DYNASTY (1981 T): 'What she means is that very special people find it very difficult to survive in our society'; Skip (Chad Lowe) is read-ing Sylvia Plath's collected works on the day he drives his car over a cliff in *The Silence of the Heart* (1984 T).

Poets as peculiar beings, spouting forth pretentious and precious nonsense, have long been a foundation of comedy: in HANCOCK'S HALF HOUR 'The Poetry Society' (1959 R) all the men are frantic poseurs, blush-makingly untalented. This is the image that dogs the real practitioners. A group of male poets (and actors) agreed wholeheartedly with one of their number who, during a dis-cussion on the role of poetry in society on *Helicon* (Aust 1987 R, said: 'I was thought to be peculiar [writing poetry]; I had to be very careful how I presented myself.' It was, therefore, gratifying to find in ACCOUNTS (1983 T) that the more rambunctious (and more diligently heterosexual) of the two farming brothers was as much at home with poetry as was his more permeable sibling.

The role of poetry in giving a voice to same-sex love, long accepted by students of Greek and Latin, burst out of its ancient coating in 1983 with the publication of *The Penguin Book of Homosexual Verse*, which was discussed – in combination with a book on CAMP – a memorably whacky free-for-all (involving at least two HOMOPHOBES as well as a caricature South African matron called Mitzi Wildebeeste) on *Start the Week* (R).

poets Generally, poets are presented as palely loitering, ineffectual and incompetent. In an episode of *The Two Ronnies* (1977 T) Ronnie Barker said: 'We'll be looking at the works of three distinguished poets: Gerard MANLEY HOPKINS, Gerard Not So Manly Hopkins and Gerard Out and Out Fairy Hopkins.' Occasionally, the essential function of the poet is elaborated, eg (heterosexual) Jean Louis, in *Temporary Shelter* (1984 C): 'I won't be rich and famous. I write about the soul and this is unfashionable. I write about change from within a man ... change from within a person will change society, not political parties.'

Included among homosexual poets: the Ancient Greek Agathon (Gordon Gardner) in A FESTIVAL OF WOMEN (1965 R); Julian Jebb in *The Drinking Party* (1965 R; Robert Dawsin in *The Symposium* 1989 R); Tom Wingfield, Tennessee WILLIAMS' alter ego in *The Glass Menagerie* (Arthur Kennedy 1950 C; John Malkovitch 1987 C; etc) working in a warehouse by day, dreaming of and cruising men by night; Cecil Davenport (Dennis PRICE) in *Crime on Their Hands* (1954 T); Sebastian Venable torn apart by urchins on a blinding white beach in SUDDENLY LAST SUMMER (1959 C); Byron (Jeremy Brett) in *Solo* (1970 T); aesthete Lawrence Kirkbridge (Ian Ogilvy) in UPSTAIRS, DOWNSTAIRS (1972 T) leading his young wife into an élitist, inaccessible world and a sexless bed; Arthur RIMBAUD (Joseph Blatchley), 16 when he met and moved in with Paul Verlaine (Ian Hogg) and his wife (Jane Asher) in *Total Eclipse* (1973

T); Walter Kranz (Kurt Raab) in *Satan's Brew* (1976 C) who thinks he is a reincarnation of Stefan George – and in an effort to get under the poet's skin, he goes to a public loo and tries to pick up a young man; Emily DICKINSON (Julie Harris) in *The Belle of Amhurst* (1976 T); Ira Streiker (Ray Sharkey), a pale shadow of Allen GINSBERG who loved both Jack Kerouac and Neal Cassady (*Heart Beat* 1979 C); the Greek poet Napoleon Lapathiotis influenced by Wilde and seeking caresses from various young men while lapsing into a twilight of drugs in *Meteor and Shadow* (1985 C); BYRON (Gabriel Byrne) adoring Shelley (Julian Sands) and treating Dr Polidori (Colin Spall) with sensual contempt in *Gothic* (1986 C); the poet (Stavros Zalman) in NORTH OF VORTEX (1991 T); Savannah Wingo (Melinda Dillon) in THE PRINCE OF TIDES (1991 C); Humphrey (Stephen FRY) in *Common Pursuit* (1992 T); etc.
See also WRITERS.

Poison (US 1990 C) Three interwoven stories of 'transgression and punishment': 'Hero', 'Horror' and 'Homo'. The final one, inspired by GENET's writings, is a story of long-term, violent prisoners in love.
W/D: Todd Haynes; P: Christine Vachon; 85 mins.

Shot in different styles (1950s sci-fi, TV documentary, erotica), each story deals with social outcasts: a scientist who becomes a leprous murderer; a solitary, eventually patricidal, boy; and two men (James Lyons and Scott Renderer) who can only express love through violence. As an exercise it's impressive (especially the 'Homo' sections); as a concept it's muddled, and its execution often vexing.

polari aka palari/parlari. The language of showmen and actors, gypsies and tramps (18th–19th centuries). The word derives either from PARLARE ('to speak') or PARLIAMO ('let's speak'), and was originally known as 'parlyaree'. It was an underground lingo, and a parallel version passed from ships to dockside pubs to fairgrounds, race tracks, the East End of London and gay meeting places. It provided a safe outlet for knowing, secret provocation, systematic insolence and impudence, not to mention sexual explicitness. Under its cover, gay men were able to communicate with and support one another, as well as feel some kind of empowerment against a hostile, uncomprehending world. 'A complex language ... is a defence against the clichés of the other world,' said Richard Kwietniowski in *Alfalfa* (1988 C), rewriting Anthony Burgess's quote from his novel EARTHLY POWERS.

Barry TOOK, who had appeared in West End REVUES, and Marty FELDMAN, who had worked in fairgrounds, funnelled polari into the mainstream through JULIAN AND SANDY in ROUND THE HORNE in the mid-1960s: 'CAMP', 'NAFF', 'bi', 'BIJOU', 'BONA', 'CRUISING', 'SEND-UP', 'ONE NIGHT STAND', 'ROUGH TRADE', 'slap', 'varda', 'omee', 'barnet', 'riah', 'COTTAGING' and 'DRAG' were suddenly lifted out of a secret world of gypsies, tramps, thieves and chorus boys and served up with the Sunday roast. By the second series, Jule and Sand's screams of 'OOO, IN'E BOLD!' were being aired in pubs, factories and living rooms all over Britain – and overseas. Like Kenneth HORNE himself – 'Oh, he's got the polari off!' – the world was quick to learn the QUEEN's English, courtesy of the BBC Light Programme.

Discoloured and untidy, what had been an effective lingua franca for generations of omipaloni, as sleek as a sealion or as fluffed out as an angry cat, accompanied by a quizzical lift of half-closed eyes, or a nudging aside, was now out in the open, in the hands of friends and enemies alike, terms of abuse as well as amusement.

'In London, parlari has established itself even among the youngest generation which did not know *Round the Horne*' (David Rowan, *Guardian Weekly*, 29.7.90).

See also DYKE/DYKER; FAG HAG; GET YOU!; NANCY.

policemen American gay cops in *Spell-*

bound (1945 C); Peter LORRE in *Alfred Hitchcock Presents* 'The Diplomatic Corpse' (1957 T); Clare Quilty (Peter SELLERS) in police uniform 'pretending' to seduce Humbert Humbert (James Mason) in *Lolita* (1962 C); a quartet of quasi-fascist vigilantes, led by a pre-Hutch David Soul, knocked down by Dirty Harry in *Magnum Force* (1974 C); Allen Feinstein in an episode of *Bronc* (1978 T; a TRANSVESTITE); a respected member of the force (Art Fleming) found dead in a gay hotel in STARSKY AND HUTCH 'Death in a Different Place' (1977 T); Barry Primus being BLACKMAILED or coerced in THE STREETS OF SAN FRANCISCO 'A Good Cop, But ...' (1977 T); Joe Penny in LOU GRANT 'COP' (1979 T); the head of the FBI obsessed with the sex lives of others, though himself frightened of women and in a long-term relationship (non-cohabitational) with a man, in *The Private Files of J. Edgar* HOOVER (Broderick Crawford, 1978 C); Al Pacino sent undercover to solve a series of gay murders in CRUISING (1980 C) and adopting Christopher Street colouration; John HURT as sad-sack police clerk, Fred Kerwin, forced to live with a gorgeous straight partner (Ryan O'Neal) to catch a murderer specializing in gays in PARTNERS (1982 C); Joseph Cali as Joey Santori, victim of an assassination attempt because of his sexuality in *Trapper John* 'Straight and Narrow' (1982 T); friend of the child psychologist hero (Richard Masur) in *When the Bough Breaks* (1986 T); Rick Salardi (Joe Gian) in HOOPERMAN (1987–9 T); the lover of Blanche's brother in THE GOLDEN GIRLS; gay cop hero in *Layers of Skin* (1993 C project). The issue of queer cops was looked at – with typically wry, alleged detachment – by Alan WHICKER in 1980.

In Britain very few gay policemen have emerged, in comedy, drama or documentary: a rare exception was one who teams up romantically with a gay ex-con in *Inside Out* (1985 T). Which isn't to say that they haven't been prominent in broadcasting. They have, or at least they were. Among the very first members of the Metropolitan Police Force to show the 'human face' of the British bobby on radio was PC Harry Daley whose first talk was part of a Tuesday evening series called *My Day's Work* (1929). This was a 15-minute view of London from a copper on the beat, told in a relaxed, sometimes whimsical style: 'Lunatics ... suicides ... drunks ... thieves ... poor people ... lost children ... people out on the streets at nights because of bed bugs ... those who missed the last train home or couldn't afford a taxi ... Quite a little kingdom, in fact, and I am responsible for it all ... On my beat is a green surrounded by seats. A well-known retreat for down and outs. Runs along beside a river. I like this silence. It gives a chap a chance to think.'

Here and in subsequent 'chats' by Daley (1930 and 1932) and a few years later by Bob Buckingham (the great love of E. M. FORSTER – who was also a friend of Daley) were laid the groundwork for what would become 'basic bobby', achieving its greatest impact and penetration with the 1950 film *The Blue Lamp* and its television spinoff DIXON OF DOCK GREEN (1955–76). What, of course, the public didn't know was that PC Daley was a more or less openly homosexual man, engaging in unlawful acts whilst upholding the law. The full story would be told in his posthumous autobiography THIS SMALL CLOUD (1986). This presented a much less rosy picture of fellow police officers (some of whom ridiculed and mocked him as well as telling how they acted as AGENTS PROVOCATEURS against gays).

The hounding by police of gay men (and sometimes lesbians) has been documented fictionally in *The Professionals* 'In the Public Interest' (1979 T), which brought Bodie and Doyle (Lewis Collins and Martin Shaw) face to face with a Christian fundamentalist chief of police (Paul Hardwick) who was 'cleansing' his city of undesirable elements, using tactics of extreme force and ruthlessness. Police proceeding beyond the call of duty in their dealings with gays can be seen in SOFTLY, SOFTLY 'Murder Reported' (1966 T); THE

NAKED CIVIL SERVANT (1975 T); CROWN COURT 'Lola' (1975 T); THE GENTLE TOUCH 'Melody' (1980 T) and 'Blade' (1980 T); *One Summer* (1983 T); WHAT CAN I DO WITH A MALE NUDE? (1985 C); EASTENDERS (1987 T): 'All I know, Barry, is that the police suddenly seem less interested in the burglary and more interested in my relationship with you.'

In America, police harassment and knee-jerk revulsion shown in, eg, *The New Centurions* (1972 C), in *Freebie and the Bean* (1973 C), and in this conversation from THE DETECTIVE (Frank Sinatra 1968 C):

> Police pathologist: 'Twenty years, but they still disturb the hell out of me.'
> Detective: 'That's a very interesting comment.'

See also PRIVATE DETECTIVES.

policewomen As uniformed professionals, they first came into prominence in the stage and radio productions (but not the original film) of *The Blue Lamp*, 1953 film *Street Corner* and DIXON OF DOCK GREEN's Grace MILLARD (1956–61 T) – although the pioneer was PW Joan Kelly (Dorothy Allison) in *Pilgrim Street* (1952). British radio's first woman bobby was 'Peggy the Policewoman' (Mary McKenzie) in *Meet the Huggets* (1953).

Since the 1960s, policewomen have been regular characters in TV series such as THE GENTLE TOUCH (1980–4), JULIET BRAVO (1980–5), *The Bill* and – played as a grotesque – WPC Rene (pronounced 'Reen') in TERRY AND JULIAN (1992). In the US there were any amount of undercover, plain-clothes 'lady' cops in films and television series from the 1930s. Barbara STANWYCK was due to follow her two appearances as Lieutenant Agatha Stewart in *The Untouchables* (1963) with a regular series, but it didn't eventuate. Probably the first prominent women in this line of work were the colleagues of *Ironside* in the late 1960s. The doors were opened for the much higher profiles of Raquel Welch in *Fuzz* and Angie Dickinson's Lieutenant Pepper Anderson in the

1970s, CAGNEY AND LACEY in the early 1980s, Jamie Lee Curtis in *Blue Steel* (1990 C), Jodie FOSTER in *The Silence of the Lambs* (1991 C), and Jackie (Laurie Metcalf), Roseanne's younger sister in the first couple of ROSEANNE series (1989–90 T).

Lesbian cops have included Marlene Simpson (Patricia Crowley), the former room-mate and now ex-cop who helps 'prove' that Pepper is straight in POLICE WOMAN 'Trial by Prejudice' (1975 T); the character played by Lindsay Crouse in *Hill Street Blues* 'Look Homeward Ninja' (1987 T), accused – like Pepper – of 'molesting' two female suspects; Amy Wallace (Laurie Metcalf) shot, probably fatally, by fellow cop Richard Gere in *Internal Affairs* (1990 C).

See also PRIVATE DETECTIVES.

Police Woman (US 1974–8 T) Angie Dickinson starred as Lieutenant Pepper Anderson, often going undercover so as to wear the most plunging of halter tops and the shortest of skirts. If the show was dipped into during channel switching, the viewer might well have gained the impression that the series was about a prostitute or a stripper. Pepper had no lover, but her colleague (Earl Holliman) was mighty smitten by her. Gays appeared only as Norman BATES-style murderers, flashy heads of phoney model agencies and drug dealers. As for lesbians, they were frequently inserted (eg in 'Fish', set in prison) so that Pepper could be placed against them in heterosexual relief: tough she might be, a gay lady she was not.

In the episode 'Flowers of Evil' (1974) three lesbians systematically kill old ladies in their care. One was a feral, conscienceless creature, Mame Doran (an almost unrecognizable Fay Spain: in a ratty, close-cropped wig with what looked like concrete on her face); another, a sleek and calculating Gladys Conway (Laraine Stephens), Mame's lover and brains behind the operation; and the third, naive young Janet Richards (Lyn Loring) who loves her. (W: John W. Bloch from a story by

Joshua Hanke; P: Douglas Benton; D: Alex(ander) Singer; 60 mins.)

There was protest to ABC television from the Gay Media Task Force, but MCA–TV refused to take the episode out of circulation (it was still being shown in 1989). The producer David Gerber argued at the time: 'If, as you indicate, there are 20 million homosexuals in America, then there must be at least 180 million heterosexuals. To our knowledge, not one heterosexual has ever pressurized us or attempted to dictate programme content.' His view had not changed several years later: 'That was a tough-minded show about homicidal maniacs who happened to be homosexual. That's honest. That's realistic' (*US TV Guide*, 30.5.81).

In a 1975 episode ('Trial by Prejudice') Pepper was accused of sexually assaulting two female suspects. She was saved by her ex-police colleague and ex-ROOM-MATE (Patricia Crowley) who risks her job (as a business executive) by revealing her homosexuality on the witness stand and claiming that Pepper was not that way inclined (W: Sean Baine; P: Douglas Benton; D: Barry Shear; 60 mins.).

political activists Toni (Gina Lollobrigida) is hell bent on 'saving' unmarried mothers in *Strange Bedfellows* (1964 C). Her first appearance comes when she's daubing slogans on walls. And that's not all: her fanaticism extends to fertility control in 'backward' nations and to gypsies. Husband Rock HUDSON says she'd 'join a bus queue and start a picket'. In her spare time she's a fashion editor and knows some very strange people, including a gay man and a lesbian. In *Malibu* (1983 T) Eva Marie Saint neglects her husband (James Coburn) and tries suicide all because of her ecological obsession: 'Save the whale and the penguin, but you don't care about human beings.' In SILENT WING (1984 R) Gisela (Diana QUICK), formerly Monika, works on the fringes of German urban terrorism, for which involvement she pays with imprisonment, psychological torture, exile and loss of peace of mind. Of the men, Cyril (George Cole) is having an affair with an American soldier at the height of the Vietnam war protests in FRIENDS (1967 T); James Van Santen (Jack Shepherd), a former activist in South Africa, is now reduced to eating cat food in a London bedsit in A ROOM FOR THE WINTER (1981 T).

politically correct (1) A term coined for a concept promoted with rigour by some FEMINISTS, gays and other civil rights groups as a challenge to false and often damaging certainties in language and imagery, especially as applied to women, racial and sexual minorities, resulting in widespread disputes within the establishment – and within the groups themselves – as to 'correct' forms of address, behaviour and contents of materials, usually to combat racism and sexism (including HOMOPHOBIA).

(2) From the late 1980s, a half-serious, half-ironic description – circulated by supporters of social and sexual equality – of people who are corseted in ideology (usually feminist or anti-racist) and who take themselves too seriously, being blind to ambiguity or believing themselves more liberated, more sophisticated, more progressive than their fellow humans. Discussing his production of PYGMALION on KALEIDOSCOPE (1992 R), Simon CALLOW commented: 'God knows, I would rather die than do something politically correct.'

This gentle mockery was picked up by American and British politicians, academics and the media (eg *Newsweek*, *Time*, an Oxford Union debate televised on OPEN SPACE) from the beginning of 1991 as Orwellian thought control, indicative of a new moral order putting involuntary restraints on free speech, and raising serious doubts about 'positive discrimination'.

For all that it annoys and irritates with its pedantry, and allows words like 'racist', 'sexist' and 'homophobe' to be hurled at opponents without definition or allowing for further debate, political correctness does make people think about the language they glibly use and the concepts words and images embody. It is certainly not a new phenomenon and has been instrumental in, eg, removing Jew-baiting from most productions of *The Merchant of Venice* and the more racist-jingoistic-snobbish observations from the works of Kipling and Enid Blyton.

politicians Senator Brigham Anderson (Don Murray) driven to SUICIDE when a former lover emerges from the past and threatens scandal in ADVISE AND CONSENT (1962 C); Senator Joe Cantwell (Cliff Robertson) faced with a gay indiscretion in the navy in THE BEST MAN (1964 C); Laurence Luckinbill as a presidential hopeful who kills those able to reveal his non-vote-catching sexual orientation, namely his lover and his sister in *Dan August* 'Dead Witness to a Killing' (1971 T); anti-fascist Congressman Roberto Orbea (José Sacristan) in *El Diputado/The Deputy* (1978 C) who is caught in a trap laid by his opponents involving an adolescent; a senator (George Lazenby) caught, on film, making love to a teenage boy in *Saint Jack* (1979 C); a candidate's agent explains in *House Wives* (1981 R) that his sexual tastes would still preclude selection for Labour candidacy; successful politician (Michael Brandon) who is headed for glory but is derailed when he is diagnosed as having AIDS in a 1984 episode of ST ELSEWHERE; would-be candidate dropped for selection because of his involvement with a drag artist in LA MUERTE DE MIKEL (1984 C); the unmarried status of a Tory Prime Minister (Trevor Bowen) raises questions, quickly dismissed, in *First Among Equals* (1986 T); Australian politician (Arthur Dignam) marries but keeps on his young male lover as CHAUFFEUR and BABYSITTER in THE EVERLASTING SECRET FAMILY (1988 C); a cabinet minister involved with RENT BOYS in *The McGuffin* (1986 T); an MP being blackmailed by his young lover in *Inside Story* (1986 T); Tory backbencher (Martin Shaw) arrested during police raid on GAY club in *For the Greater Good* (1991 T); San Francisco legend Harvey

MILK in *The Mayor of Castro Street* (1993/4 C).

Documentaries: WORLD IN ACTION 'Confessions of a Gay Liberal' (1973 T) and 'In the Matter of Mr [Matthew] Parris' (1983 T); OPEN SPACE 'Peter TATCHELL and the Battle for Bermondsey' (1983 T); THE TIMES OF HARVEY MILK (1984 C); OUT ON TUESDAY 'Gays on the Right' (1990 T); OUT 'Senator David NORRIS' (1991 T); etc.

ponce A person who lives off a PROSTITUTE's earnings; extended to cover or to link in with gay men.

A NAZI supporter in THE PARACHUTE (1968 T; 1986 R) describes 'the authentic voice of Germany' as being that of 'jackals ... lice ... ponces ... pederasts'. Briggs (Terence Rigby) calls his former lover Foster (Michael Kitchen) a 'neurotic POUF and ... an unspeakable ponce' in *No Man's Land* (1978 T). A terrorist (Stephen Yardley) challenges public school-educated Charles Vyvyan (Cavan Kendall) to an arm-wrestling match in *Blood Money* (1981 T): 'If you beat me, I'll know you're not a ponce'; Charles is then called a 'POOFTER' when he declines the tournament.

Chaotic, cheesy PSYCHIATRIST Simon (Nicholas Le Prevost) in IT TAKES A WORRIED MAN (1983 T) is contemptuous of his unseen lover Gerald's obsession with macramé – which to Simon is 'poncing around with his knots'. Pete Beale (Peter Dean) warns Arthur (Bill Treacher) not to be taken in by the flash types he met at the TV quiz show in EASTENDERS (1989 T): 'Sounds a bit poncie to me – geezers in jumpers round their shoulders, called Jeremy.' In one of the few gay MORNING STORY productions, 'Me and Mr Mandel' (1979 R), 'that kid' was changed to 'that young ponce'.

poodle *See* DOG OWNERS.

poof/pouf First heard on British television in the WEDNESDAY PLAYS. In one, *The Portsmouth Defence* (1966 T) about a milkman wrongly accused of homosexual assault, the word and its variations fell from the lips of a policeman (patrolling the streets in a car rounding up men for an identity parade: 'There's a blond with poofy lips'); a lawyer ('No one's going to believe a story like that. He's got a conviction for poofin' already'); and the accused's wife ('We've got two little babies – what are they going to say when they read in the papers that their father's a poof?').

The word's lighter-than-air quality has made it a great favourite on British television for knee-jerk talk-show hosts, game-show contestants and news-quiz pundits. Peter FINCH was supposed to have said, according to his agent in *The British Greats* (1980 T), when offered the part of the doctor in SUNDAY, BLOODY SUNDAY: 'I'm not playing a poof ... I can't play a poof' (thereby cancelling out Oscar WILDE's claim to poofdom). To date, poof – unlike QUEER – has not become a prideful, defiant term, being mainly used by semi-discreet, often tremulous people like Freddie in ELDORADO (1992–3 T): 'Me being a poof is neither here nor there.'

See also PUFF.

poofter/pooftah Apparently imported from Britain to AUSTRALIA at the turn of the 20th century and then retransported in the late 1960s as part of OCKER Bazza McKenzie's swill of terminology. The 1972 film *The Adventures of Barry McKenzie* was classified as NPA (No Poofters Allowed), a manifestation of an ideology which MONTY PYTHON had aired two years before in its sketch about a group of Aussies (all called Bruce) selecting members for their 'club'. Rules one, three and seven were identical: 'No Poofters.' The word is not quite as HOMOPHOBIC as it may at first appear, generously including – alongside pillow-biters – artists, poets, writers, dancers, singers, people who go to the Sydney Opera House, people who don't spend their lives talking about sport, non-drinkers, left-wing politicians, right-wing politicians, intellectuals of any kind, environmentalists etc.

It took a decade for the British to fully readopt the word, within its narrowest definition. In the banned *Scum* (1978 T) Carlin (Ray Winstone) takes a fellow Borstal inmate as his 'missus'. However, he tells him: 'I'm no poofter. I want that understood from the start. Nothing BENT.'

Alistair Proudfoot (Christopher Good) strikes his landlady (Patricia Routledge) as a 'nasty little poofter' because he was seen in a shop with a man in a pink suit (THREE PIECE SWEET 1979 R). The ventriloquist's dummy, Wilf, on the *Ark Royal* (in the *Sailor* update 1984 T) was surprised to receive a fan letter from a poofter: 'Didn't answer it though', says the polystyrene man with saucy inflection.

The Australian connection was made in THE GENTLE TOUCH 'Blade' (1980 T). Ritchie (Jeremy Pease) with a broad 'Strine' accent reveals to a police inspector (Brian Gwaspari) that his murdered tenant was gay: 'As in Paree. Pommie poofter, that's what they'd call him on Sydney Hill. SHIRT LIFTER.' At which point the cop asks: 'Are you one too, Bruce?'

popes Joan (Liv Ullmann), a 9th-century preacher's daughter, sickened by the excesses of the Holy Roman Empire, was elevated to the papal throne in *travesti* (or so the legend went) as *Pope Joan* (1972 C); *Hadrian VII* alias George Arthur Rose (Max ADRIAN 1959 R; Alec MCCOWEN 1979 R); lubricious Paul V (Jack BIRKETT), patron of CARAVAGGIO (1986 C); some less than holy ones in *The Borgias* (1981 T), but, thus far, none of the more blatant and/or infamous gay incumbents – John XII, Benedict IX, Paul II, Sixtus IV, Leo X, Julius III and, possibly, Pius XXII – have been characterized as such.

pop singer/pop group managers Johnnie (Laurence Harvey) taking a brotherly/sharkish interest in the earnings if not the sexual capacity of naive Bongo Herbert (Cliff Richard) in *Expresso Bongo* (1959 C); Jake Braid (Keith Barron), a Brian EPSTEIN figure humiliated and discarded by his protégé in a toilet in *The Man Who Had Power*

Over Women (1970 C); Alan (Harry H. Corbett), friend and possibly long-term lover of his money-making protégé in A HYMN FROM JIM (1977 T); Webster Jones (David Doyle) smoothing Jack Jones' path to *The Comeback* (1977 C) and revealed as a shock-horror TRANSVESTITE; the Rev. David Sales (Neil Cunningham) guiding a pop group after he's been booted out of the Church for sexual offences; in *Johnny Jarvis* (1983 T); Harry Charms (Lionel Blair), 1950s promoter of barely post-pubescent, willing, possibly available, in *Absolute Beginners* (1986 C).

pornography In the gay sexual variety: male genitals that do more than flop, real ejaculations, body contact. An almost totally no-go area for British television: softly sexual explicit, 'respectable' films like TAXI ZUM KLO (1981) and *A Bigger Splash* (1974) are unlikely to receive a screening in an uncut form, let alone any of the hundreds of masturbatory fantasies – the most famous and enduring being *The Boys in the Sand* (1971), clips of which (minus genitalia) were allowed to penetrate one sequence of ARENA '[Larry] KRAMER vs Kramer' (1993 T). Similarly trimmed scenes also turned up in OUT 'Blue Boys' (1992 T, on the Obscene Publications Squad) and 'Skin Complex' (1992 T).

CAUGHT LOOKING (1991), a speculation on the contribution of virtual reality to gay men's lives, was suppressed by Channel 4 (via the Broadcasting Standards Council), then unleashed the following year, very late at night. However, the BBC documentary *Every Conceivable Position* 'Inside Gay and Lesbian Pornography' made for SATURDAY NIGHT OUT in 1991 remains shut in the vaults. The nearest the BBC has come to the real thing was in its specially shot porn scenes for the TV films *The McGuffin* (1986) and THE LOST LANGUAGE OF CRANES (1992).

Pornography involving lesbianism (whether glossies like *Emmanuelle* or grotties like *Anybodys, Anyway*) is also taboo, although it is debatable whether some of the 'lesbian scenes' in upmarket produce like THE RAINBOW and PORTRAIT OF A MARRIAGE are really any less tasteless or more relevant to the stories. Or, indeed, whether films made by men about women loving women should be labelled pornographic and exploitational while those made by women should be given more house room (as well as showing on television) as LESBIAN EROTICA.

Porter, Cole (1891–1964) American composer and lyricist who produced a mother-lode of 20th-century popular music: skin-prickling tunes and lyrics, often highly sensual, sometimes explicitly (homo)sexual. One gay man's life set to music the world continues to adore.

HOLLYWOOD turned him in for psychosexual remodelling in NIGHT AND DAY, but at least he was played by Cary GRANT. A television celebration in 1991 was almost as closeted about Porter's emotional and sexual drives as that notorious 1946 movie. Ned SHERRIN cut through the wire elegantly in *Song by Song by Porter* (1980 T): 'Sometimes, like his well-manicured public married life, the songs are glossy and brittle and bullet-proof, somehow a sense of frustration and hopelessness creeps in which better accords with contemporary accounts of the more unorthodox side of that marriage which surfaced when he was tempted by the hedonistic delights or surface pleasures of Hollywood or the Lido.'

He wrote songs for the following films and adaptations of his stage musicals: *The Battle of Paris* (1929); *The Gay Divorce/Divorcee* (1934); *Born to Dance* (1936); *Anything Goes* (1936 & 1955); *Break the News* (1937); *Rosalie* (1937); *The Broadway Melody of 1940* (1939); *You'll Never Get Rich* (1941); *Panama Hattie* (1942); *Dubarry Was a Lady* (1943); *Let's Face It* (1943); *Something to Shout About* (1943); *Hollywood Canteen* (1944); *Something for the Boys* (1944); *The Pirate* (1947); ADAM'S RIB (1949); *Kiss Me Kate* (1953, also 1964 T); *High*

Society (1956); *Les Girls* (1957); *Silk Stockings* (1957); *Can-Can* (1960).

Among Porter classics featured outside their original show or film context: 'You Do Something To Me' (*The Sun Also Rises*, 1957 C); 'Anything Goes' (sung by Harpers Bizarre in THE BOYS IN THE BAND, 1970 C; sung by Kate Capshaw in *Indiana Jones and the Temple of Doom*, 1984 C); 'You're The Top' sung by Barbra STREISAND in *What's Up Doc?* 1972 C); 'Love For Sale' (*Cause Célèbre*, 1987 T); 'Begin The Beguine' (RAY'S MALE HETEROSEXUAL DANCE HALL, 1987 C); 'Night and Day' (ABSOLUTE HELL! 1991 T); 'Wunderbar' and 'I'm Always True To You In My Fashion' (played during an investiture in *Elizabeth R*, 1991 T); 'At Long Last Love' (sung by Frank Sinatra in *First Love*, 1992 R); 'Let's Do It' (sung by Eartha Kitt in Halifax Building Society advert, 1992 T).

Selections of his works included in such films as *At Long Last Love* (1974 C); EVIL UNDER THE SUN (1982 C); *Skin Deep* (1989 C); as well as in tributes such as *Young King Cole* (1946 R); *Song by Song by Porter* (1980 T); RED HOT AND BLUE (1980 T); YOU'RE THE TOP: THE COLE PORTER STORY (1991 T).

Jimmy **Porter** Leading character in LOOK BACK IN ANGER who returned in 1992 with more fury from the edge in *Déjà Vu*. 'A spokesman for none but myself', he remains close to Cliff (calling each other 'duck', 'dear' and 'dreamboat'. 'He always was very CAMP,' says Cliff, 'when no one knew what that meant'). He now lives in a village 'full of lesbians' with his TEDDY BEAR (male) and his dog (male). From his cottage he can inveigh against futurologists, people called KEVIN and Sharon, FEMINISTS, gays and anti-smokers. (His daughter says he's got fags – of both sorts – on the brain.) Occupying his second division of pet peeves are God, VEGETARIANS, trendy vicars, theatrical types, foreigners, AIDS benefits and AUSTRALIANS. Part of his time is spent making up limericks about BLACK feminist

DYKES and NANCY BOYS. 'Frankly I stink,' he admits.

Portman, Eric (1903–69) English actor who could be equally convincing projecting warmth and vulnerability, cold implacability or pink and amber aestheticism. On stage he created the roles of Andrew Crocker-Harris in *The Browning Version* and the disgraced Major Pollock in *Separate Tables*. On screen the foundation for his continued popularity lay in *49th Parallel* (1941), *One of Our Aircraft Is Missing* (1942), *We Dive at Dawn* (1943), *Millions Like Us* (1943) and *Dear Murderer* (1947).

His misanthropic/misogynist persona was most famously displayed as Thomas Colpeper ('Life is full of disappointments') in *A Canterbury Tale* (1944): magistrate, gentleman farmer and the man who pours glue on young women's heads; as the haunted woman-killer in *Wanted for Murder* (1946); as the daydreaming narcissist in *Corridor of Mirrors* (1948); and – on radio, in the role of his choice – as Rupert CADELL in ROPE (1953). His last major role was that of a BISEXUAL man who was married to his own daughter in *Deadfall* (1968 C). He was the subject of DESERT ISLAND DISCS in 1953.

Other credits include:

C: *The Girl from Maxim's* (1933); *Maria Marten* (1935); Giuliano De Medici in *The Cardinal* (1936); 'slightly reminiscent of Cary GRANT' in *Uncensored* (as a cabaret performer in a script by Rodney ACKLAND and Terence RATTIGAN, 1942); the district commissioner in *Men of Two Worlds* (1946); the husband in *The Deep Blue Sea* (1955); plain-spoken Yorkshireman Jess Oldroyd in *The Good Companions* (1957); Jeremy, the murderer in *The Naked Edge* (1961); a secret agent in *The Spy with the Cold Nose* (1966); a cameo as a notary in *Assignment to Kill* (1968).

R: Sydney Carton in *A Tale of Two Cities* (1950); defending counsel in *The Case of Private Hamp* (1956); reading *A Boring Story* (1967).

T: Arthur Collings in *The Whip* (1952); Arthur Gosport in *Harlequinade* (1953,

which he also played on stage); opposite Barbara Mullen in *Jeannie* (1954); the actor playing Othello who can't separate fact from fiction in *A Double Life* (1957); Fagin in *Oliver Twist* (US 1959); Jones, the queer villain in *Victory* (1960); *Naked City* 'The Pedigree Sheet' (1960); *The Elder Statesman* (1960); *A Call on Kuprin* (1961); *The Different Drum* (1964); *The Habit of Loving* (1964); one of Patrick McGoohan's adversaries in *The Prisoner* 'Free for All' (1968).

Portrait of a Marriage (UK 1990 T) Childhood friends and later passionate lovers Vita SACKVILLE-WEST (Janet McTeer) and Violet TREFUSIS (Cathryn Harrison) run away, disguised as a married couple – with their crestfallen and angry husbands (David Haigh and Peter Birch) in pursuit.

W: Penelope Mortimer from the book by Nigel Nicolson; P: Colin Tucker; D: Stephen Whittaker; BBC2; 4 parts; 50 mins each.

A central event in the lives of Vita, Violet and Harold, yet told very much in summary despite the 200-minute running time. Rather than creating a multi-layered fabric, this emerges as vapidly handsome upmarket melodrama, raking over a scandal involving a bland man and two tyrannically forceful women rather than a three-way relationship, in which the most extraordinary marriage of minds is cradled.

'As played in this overlong and reverent BBC mini-series, Violet is a simpering twit. So quite why the studiedly literary, darkly tempestuous and boyishly handsome Vita would harbour a lifelong passion for such a giggly if scrumptious popsy is a mystery. Piquantly and unsatisfactorily, the production inadvertently solves the puzzle in love scenes between the two (when Violet's mouth is otherwise occupied) which are steamily convincing and played absolutely straight – as it were' (Diana Simmonds, *Bulletin* (Australia), 10.3.92).

Janet McTeer in her wide-brimmed hats, wide coats, trousers and boots created as much of a fashion flurry as a dramatic one – at least for the readers of the *Daily Express* which, for the first time, devoted a double-page spread to lesbian love, in the gorgeously attired persons of 'Vita' and 'Violet', languorously framed by greensward and stately home: the country dyke look under the sedate heading of 'Portrait of an Era'.

positive vetting A semi-regular weeding process of undesirables and/or people at risk of BLACKMAIL carried out by the British government, civil service and especially the secret service to ensure the minimum threat to national security and the minimum leaking or stealing of 'sensitive' information. Homosexual men were, until very recently, prime targets in these purges, especially in the backwash of spy scandals such as the defection of BURGESS and Maclean, and the Vassall case in 1962. THAT WAS THE WEEK THAT WAS seized upon the establishment jitters with great glee after it was found that a government minister had written to John Vassall in over-effusive terms, which could have been a tool of coercion by Britain's enemies.

Peter Shaffer wrote a sketch which had a senior civil servant (Lance Percival) carpeting a junior (David Kernan) because of an allegedly compromising letter he sent to a Member of Parliament and a Minister. He points out that phrases such as 'my dear', 'pursuant to' ('it has an erotic penumbra'), 'favour' and 'thanking you in anticipation' and 'yours faithfully' ('even "yours" is dangerous because it 'suggests a willingness to surrender') are open to misconstrual. ' "Your obedient servant" can *ipso facto* smack of sexual deviancy. And that, as we all know, is *ipso facto* a confession of treason.'

The older man also feels the need to gratuitously expatiate on the then (1962–3) current debate about making 'queers legal': 'I think you secretly believe that the way to stop homosexuals being blackmailed is to change the law so that they can't be ... Nonsense! ... The only way to stop a homosexual being blackmailed is to stop him being a homosexual. And the only way you can

do that is to lock him up in a building with 500 other men. That way he can see how unattractive they are.' He asks the junior secretary's name. When told it is 'FAIRY', he comments that he should have a very successful career in the civil service.

(The British Foreign Office, prompted by an announcement by Prime Minister John Major which spoke of 'new social attitudes', issued a confidential memo ('Homosexuality and Security Vetting') in July 1991. Lesbian and gay diplomats were encouraged not to veil their private lives because, said the memo, 'the extent to which an officer is open about his or her sexuality, LIFESTYLE and relationships' is relevant to his or her susceptibility to blackmail. This was a belated recognition – one month before the official fall of Communism in the USSR – that homosexual diplomats are (1) male and female and (2) neither more nor less prone to blackmail than their heterosexually biased counterparts.)

See also SPIES; TRAITORS.

Powell, Ellis (1909–63) English radio actress and the prototype for SISTER GEORGE. Daughter of the editor of the *Financial Times*, she acted in *Jew Süss* on Broadway during the 1930s. Apart from her 14-year stint as Mrs DALE, she was Mrs Williams in *The English Family Robinson* (1946), Vi Waters in *Troubled Waters* (1946, with Miriam Karlin as her daughter), and Calypso in *The Sixth Canto* (1957). She spoofed her radio role with Peter SELLERS and Harry Secombe in a GOON SHOW entitled 'Where Does Santa Claus Go in the Summer?' (1952). She died only a few weeks after her sacking from THE DALES – 'of a broken heart,' said the *Daily Mirror*.

practising homosexual The most ubiquitous response to such a question was the one Jodie (Billy CRYSTAL) made when asked in a 1979 SOAP if he was practising: 'I don't have to practise, I'm very good at it.'

Deployed in Rod SERLING's introduction to 'A Thing About Machines' in

THE TWILIGHT ZONE (1960 T) to deride the over-neat, insufferably precious Bartlett Finchley (Richard HAYDN). But as Serling was not allowed to use the second word or anything like it, Mr Finchley became 'a practising *sophisticate* who writes very special and very precious things for gourmet magazines and the like'.

For US immigration purposes, applicants for residence, according to Quentin CRISP on *Friday Night, Saturday Morning* (1980 T), had to state if they were practising homosexuals. Quentin said he wasn't because he no longer was.

predatory homosexuals/gays/lesbians Any amount of these: from the cat and the fox in *Pinocchio* (1940 C), agents of the evil owner of Whale Island, to Wolf (Bruce M. Fischer) who sucks on strands of spaghetti and holds a lit match between his fingers in an effort to make himself desirable to new inmate (Clint Eastwood) in *Escape from Alcatraz* (1979 C). Less evil but just as persistent is Guy Bennett (Rupert Everett) in ANOTHER COUNTRY (1984 C): 'I'll get you one day. Everyone gives in in the end. It's Bennett's law'; and while there's a hard core to the insouciance of the two ANTIQUE DEALERS (Francis Matthews and David Yelland) as they stalk the BRIDEGROOM (Simon Shepherd) with well-bred rapacity while priding themselves on their self-restraint in *May We Borrow Your Husband?* (1986 T).

Here are three examples of predatory non-gays: Howard Kirk (Antony SHER), the sociology lecturer in *The History Man* (1981 T), battens on to every student and wife in sight. The speciality of Jerry (John Sayles) in LIANNA (1983 C) is picking at the flesh of women who have recently left – or been left by – their husbands. He comes to call on the recently separated college wife: 'I figure it's been a while … you're a healthy woman … I thought I'd come over … sorry if I came on strong … technique must be getting a little rusty.' In TWO OF US (1988 T) the free-wheeling Suzie (Zoe Nathenson) can't see what the boys are running away from: 'Why choose? The same. The opposite. Both sexes. Hetero. Homo. Bi. Designer sex. We're all mixed up. It's all labels. It's all part of the con.' Then, in the same breath, she's propositioning one of them, using society's oldest technique: 'You *really* don't think you could do it with a girl?' – a ploy which, when brandished by a man over a man, is called coercion and proselytizing.

Some lavender menaces stalking their prey include DRACULA'S DAUGHTER (Gloria Holden 1936 C) and other VAMPIRES; devil worshipper Mrs Redi (Mary Newton) in *The Seventh Victim* (1943 C); Lady HYLBEROW (Pauline Seville) in THE ARCHERS (1952 R); Ines in HUIS CLOS; Mrs Mercy Croft, transparent blood dripping from her fangs as she eats into CHILDIE and into the girl's long-term home-making with George in THE KILLING OF SISTER GEORGE (Coral Browne 1968 C; Eleanor Bron 1978 R); Genevieve Page as the brothel keeper Mme Anaïs in BELLE DE JOUR (1967 C); Chrissie (Myra Francis) in GIRL (1974 T) from whom no army recruit is safe: 'Can you understand that,' one of her cast-offs says to the new apple of Chrissie's eye, 'you're looking at a bloody she-wolf? … If there's the faintest sign of something in the wind, she'll track it down – she's got a nose for it'; Kim (Jane Lapotaire) who makes it quite clear to young Nikki (Lynne Frederick) that it's her body she's after following their first meeting in THE OTHER WOMAN (1976 T); 'Aunt' Lucy inveigles young Valerie to be her maid and begins to corrupt her with dirty books in WITHIN THESE WALLS 'Invasion of Privacy' (1977 T); Diana Graham (Rachel Davies) seen by her lover's husband as a 'sexual predator' in CROWN COURT 'A Friend of the Family' (1979 T); the cornered Miss WADE (Sonia Fraser), the abductor of young Tattycoram in *Little Dorrit* (1980 R): 'I don't know what you are, but what you can't hide is what a dark spirit you have within in you'; Carla Romanelli (Carla Maria Peroni) seduces *The Lonely Lady* (1983 C) while her male producer lover views each move appreciatively; at the feminist DISCO in SILENT WING (1984 R) the serpentine Jane (Helen Atkinson Wood) tries it on Gisela (Diana QUICK) with the most famous predatory question of all: 'Do you come here often?'; Amanda (Ellen Barkin) is warned to 'be careful' of Sheila (Lorraine Bracco) (in SWITCH 1991 C): 'she can be dangerous.'

pregnancy, male *See* MEN HAVING BABIES.

pretty *Pretty Woman*, yes; *Pretty Man*, never! VARIETY, reviewing THE PICTURE OF DORIAN GRAY (1945 C), described the hero/villain as 'pretty' while commending the director's subtlety in revealing 'what he was'. When Kay Kendall compliments Peter FINCH in *Simon and Laura* (1955 C) as he titivates himself in the mirror, her 'very pretty' is not intended as a wifely compliment or reassurance but as a slur on his potency.

In *Raging Bull* (1980 C) Jake LaMotta (Robert De Niro) says of 'pretty boy Genero': 'I don't know whether to fuck him or to fight him'. After the bout in which Jake had badly mauled him, the winner can say with satisfaction – and relief: 'He ain't so pretty no more.'

The 1987 television production of *Vanity Fair* had crusty Osborne (Robert Lang) telling 'orff' his son George (Benedict Taylor) for his wild ways: 'A pretty boy indeed. I know of your doings, sir, with Captain Crawley. Have a care, sir, *have a care.*' Having rebuked, he relents: 'Well ... you're only young once.'

David HOCKNEY spoke out hotly in defence of pretty on THE SOUTH BANK SHOW (1988 T): 'I do know that people who think they are very serious hate the word. They think that pretty can't be serious and, frankly, I've never understood that. I think architects have forgotten about the word "pretty".' (This arose from a disagreement with the Royal Institute of British Architects' president Maxwell Hutchinson – who argued for beauty against prettiness – immediately prior to their taking part in radio's *Start the Week*, a few days before

Hockney recorded his Melvyn Bragg piece.)

Price, Dennis [Dennistoun Rose-Price] (1915–73) English actor, a star in the 1940s who became a tireless toiler in supporting roles (in nearly 90 films), usually of tarnished suavity or genteel shadiness. He was practically the only 'name' actor to play gay roles – at least five of them before it was 'safe' to do so (*Crime on Their Hands*; *Charley Moon*; *Oscar Wilde*; *No Love for Johnnie*; VICTIM). Prancing along beside these were a whole raft of BACHELORS, DANDIES and aesthetes, including Lord BYRON. Apart from his exquisitely dry mass murderer (of six Alec Guinnesses) in *Kind Hearts and Coronets*, Price was most widely known as Jeeves, the perfect butler which formed part of an extremely satisfying (star parts all) television career.

C: *A Canterbury Tale* (1944) as Peter Gibbs ('once an organist always an organist'); the victim in *Dear Murderer* (1947); the homicidal Squadron Leader Hardwicke in *Holiday Camp*; Louis Mazzini in *Kind Hearts and Coronets* (1949); *Murder without Crime* (1950 C): 'exquisitely sadistic ... a deadly dandy ... Dorian GRAY all over again' (NEW YORK TIMES); actor Leonard Pirry in *The Intruder* (1953); ham actor and pantomime dame Harold Armytage in *Charley Moon* (1956); ineffectual husband Tracey Moreton in *Fortune Is a Woman* (1957); BLACKMAILER Nigel Dennis in *The Naked Truth/Your Past Is Showing* (1957); Bertram Tracepurcel in *I'm All Right Jack* (1959); possible German informer Rupert Callender in *Danger Within/Breakout* (1959); Dunstan in *School for Scoundrels* (1960); Robbie Ross in *Oscar Wilde* (1960); French artist 'Jim Smith' in *The Rebel* (1960); Flagg, a society photographer in *No Love for Johnnie* (1961); matinée idol 'Tiny' Calloway in VICTIM (1961); the headmaster in *Tamahine* (1963, one of his most praised later roles); Mr Soul, a flamboyant mortician in *That's Your Funeral* (1972 C); an example of the typical British upper-class pervert in *The*

Adventures of Barry McKenzie (1972); the King of Hearts in *Alice's Adventures in Wonderland* (1972); a Lewis Carroll-spouting dandy in *Pulp* (1972); Mr Pollack, estate agent in *Horror Hospital* (1973); critic Hector Snipe in *Theatre of Blood* (1973); DRACULA (a couple of shoddy Spanish quickies); etc.

R: *Top of the Town* (Twyford, Berkshire, his home town, 1954); Major Denzil Pierce in *Happy Holiday* (with Dick Emery and Peter SELLERS, 1954); Prince John in THE GOON SHOW 'Robin Hood and His Merry Men' (1956); *Desert Island Discs* (1956); Commander Price in *The Navy Lark* (1957–8); himself in *Holiday Playhouse* (1958); *Alfred Marks Time* (1960); property developer's smooth assistant in *It's A Deal* (with Sidney James, 1961); *Variety Playhouse* (1962); etc.

T: Noel COWARD in *The Passing Show* 'Charles B. Cochran Presents' (1953); Cecil Davenport, poet in *Crime on Their Hands* (1954); the husband in a De Maupassant tale, *The Jewels* (1954); Rupert CADELL in ROPE (1957); Constantine Chase in *Myself When Young* (1958); Roger Storer in *Lover's Leap* (1958); actor Martyn Coleman in *The Witching Hour* (1958); *Design for Murder* as director Rex Berkeley (1958); Charles Appleby in *Eden's End* (1958); hosted *On with the Show* (1958); the lawyer in *Somerset Maugham Hour* 'The Letter' (1960); *Ladies and Gentle-men* (with Frankie HOWERD, 1960); Captain Robert Forestier in Somerset MAUGHAM's *The Lion's Skin* (1960); Henry WOTTON in THE PICTURE OF DORIAN GRAY (1961); Victor Frey, fashion boss in *The Secret Agent* 'The Height of Fashion' (1963); an unsympathetic doctor in *Hancock* 'The Girl' (1963); Harry Debrett, suave Hollywood lover returning home after deserting his wife, in *Love Story* 'Spare the Tears for Happiness' (1964); De Varelle in *The Lady of the Camelias* (with Billie Whitelaw, 1964); the leader of *The Confidence Course* (with Stanley BAXTER, 1965); Reginald Jeeves in *The World of Wooster* (1966); David Bliss in *Hay Fever* (with Celia Johnson, 1968); retired Edward

Wilkin in *Comedy Playhouse* 'The Gold Watch Club' (1968); etc.

He was OUTED after his death in THE UNSINKABLE HERMIONE BADDELEY (1984). The actress, who was having simultaneous affairs with Price and Laurence Harvey in the 1950s, wrote that one day Price noticed her bruises. ' "Some of my boyfriends knock me about, too." Then he winked. "I quite enjoy it." I did not wink back.' Discussing the making of *Victim* in *By Myself* (1992 T), Dirk BOGARDE said: 'The people who were in the film were all straight, I think, except for Dennis Price who was at that time a homosexual but didn't mind a bit – nobody else had the courage to do it.'

Prick Up Your Ears (UK 1987 C) A male wife, driven beyond endurance, frenziedly kills and then commits SUICIDE. Flashbacks, in the form of diary entries and interviews, reveal the roots of the relationship between Joe ORTON (Gary Oldman) and Kenneth Halliwell (Alfred Molina), its influence on the playwright's work, and its deterioration in the light of Joe's growing celebrity.

W: Alan BENNETT; based on the book by John Lahr; P: Andrew Brown; D: Stephen Frears; 110 mins.

Sex – Passion – Homos – Homicide! It could have been a grisly, depressing melodrama; instead it's wittily confronting, sexy, black and breezy. It is also one of the few films to balleticize one of the most confined – and disparaged – of sexual pleasures, and to have the problems of its gay couple glancingly reflect those of Orton's biographer and his wife.

The central character is a monster but, with his guiltless queer spirit, an attractive one. Bad, a bit mad and dangerous to live with, he nevertheless illuminated the dark places of the English psyche while using all the tricks of the trade: farce, *double entendres*, picture postcard stereotypes, brazen self-advertisement.

As Orton's star ascends, Halliwell, who had been mentor and muse as well as lover, becomes a pill-popping drudge, prey to his neuroses and sense of worthlessness. 'I caught up on a big backlog of dusting,' he tells Joe with splenetic fury. 'Then I slipped out to the end of the road to replenish our stock of cornflakes. When I got back I rinsed a selection of your soiled underclothes by which time it was four o'clock, the hour of your scheduled return.' For some reason, the director has seen fit to make of Ken some kind of ALIEN creature: bald, twitchy and sexless; a bat out of hell. His crucial importance in the making of Orton is cancelled out by the strange visual apparition he presents.

Surrounding the odd couple is a small constellation of pungent characters: the literary agent Peggy Ramsay (a gloriously unfettered Vanessa REDGRAVE), the dogged biographer John Lahr (Wallace Shawn), Orton's termagant mother (Julie Walters), the sister who keeps the flame (Frances Barber), a twitchily puritanical Brian EPSTEIN (David Cady) as well as a charivari of sex partners from street, park, lavatory and (Tunisian) hotel.

priests Anthony Quayle accused of sexual assault on a teenager, a *Serious Charge* (1959 C) later proved groundless; a Catholic priest (John Mills), the unlikely love object of ruthless bandido Dirk BOGARDE in *The Singer Not the Song* (1961 C); defrocked Paul Curtis (John STRATTON) who died 'to all intents and purposes' the day he entered Belsen with the liberation forces in A SUPERSTITION (1977 C): now he's obsessed with his former lover, tracking him remorselessly; Don Trajella (François Simon) deposited in a barren Italian town after certain irregularities at the seminary in *Christ Stopped at Eboli* (1979 C/T): he's just given up until the arrival of a political exile; Jamie Cooper, not guilty about being gay, yet his mother (Helen Cherry) takes him to Lourdes for a CURE – as she sadly recalls in COMING OUT; John Gray (Simon Shepherd) from libertine to pillar of the Catholic Church in *Aubrey* (1982 T); the Rev. David Sales (Neil Cunningham), a port in the storm for young boys before he is slung out of his living in *Johnny Jarvis*

(1983 T); Morris HARDACRE intoxicated by the clerical purple and red in *Brass*, but an irredeemable sybarite underneath the drag; Mark Dolson (Zeljko Ivanek) finding the kindling of social conscience almost impossible to reconcile with the roots and branches of the Mother Church in *Mass Appeal* (1984 C); Brother Sebastian aka Michael Lamb (Liam Neeson) in *Lamb* (1985 C) who takes an interest in a 10-year-old boy, which is misconstrued when the two run away together; bachelor Rev. Charles Holt (Richard Hurndall) helps a fellow priest over the hurdles of prejudice when his son comes out as gay in THE LITMUS QUESTION (1975); Father Chaisson (Mathieu Carrière) in *The Bay Boy* (1984 C) attracted to Donald (Kiefer Sutherland); Andrew (Geoff Cartwright), who 'fell from grace', is now running a refuge for street kids in G.P. 'A Question of Survival' (1992 T); etc.

Documentaries include the quite extraordinary trilogy about Catholic Father Bernard Lynch, Irish but working for a long time in New York. He was accused of crimes he didn't commit, marginalized and shut out for espousing unpopular minorities and finally, agonizingly, came to respect and identify himself as a gay man in *A Priest's Testament* (1987), *A Priest on Trial* (1990 T) and *Soul Survivor* (1990 T). Father Robert L. Arpin appeared on DONAHUE 'A Catholic Priest Who Has AIDS' (1992 T).

The Prince of Tides (US 1991 C) A man (Nick Nolte) confronts a horrific incident in childhood with the help of the psychiatrist (Barbra STREISAND) who is also treating his twin sister (Melinda Dillon), and through coaching her son (Jason Gould) in football.

W: Pat Conroy and Becky Johnston from the book by Pat Conroy; P: Barbra Streisand and Andrew Karsch; D: Barbra Streisand; 120 mins.

A story of TWINS: and one of them is a lesbian and she's INVISIBLE. At least in the film. Tom Wingo and his gifted but unstable sister Savannah were both important in the book; here she's pretty much a basket case, occasionally seen and talked of but with no real existence, and certainly no sexual identity. Her role in Tom's recall to life is practically zero.

With its emphasis upon cutting through the tentacles of the past (a very nasty one for Tom and Savannah who had a sadistic father and were both raped by escaped convicts) and being whole and not co-dependent, it is particularly unpleasant to find a star straddling the story like a cowboy on a goldfish, digging in those spurs at every opportunity to make it go *her* way. There's a quite unnecessary flitting gay character, an underwritten part for Blythe Danner as Tom's wife, an overwritten one for Kate Nelligan as the selfish mother, and a basic belief that going to bed with your PSYCHIATRIST cures everything (as long as you're male and she's female).

The only sections of the film which have genuine spirit and dimension are those involving the psychiatrist's son Bernard (played by Barbra Streisand's own son). Daringly pegged as neither heterosexual nor gay (though he is seen looking through a book on Ancient Greek art for a couple of seconds), Bernard has a natural life that the other characters have lost on the long journey from page to celluloid.

Prisoner aka *Prisoner: Cell Block H* (Aust 1979–87 T) Life in Wentworth Detention Centre.
Cr: Reg Watson; P: Ian Bradley; Channel 10; 60 mins.

Now screened in 40 countries and in 12 languages, PRISONER's characters are the stuff that many a lesbian's dreams are made of (not to mention many a gay man's and heterosexual's). Haven't we all, at one time or another, wanted to be down and dirty like Frieda 'Franky' DOYLE (Carol Burns: sadly killed by the police a few months after the show began, leaving her only friend Doreen (Colette Mann) to grieve)? Calm and capable like Judy Bryant (Betty Bobbitt), lover of deceased Sharon Gilmour (Margot Knight)? Tense and tight, just

waiting to be elasticated like warder Vera 'Vinegar Tits' Bennett (Fiona Spence)? Cool and elegant like governor Erica Davidson (Patsy King)? Intuitive and crafty like 'Queen' Bea Smith (Val Lehman)? Just plain nice like warder Meg (Elspeth Ballantyne)? Just plain nasty (and cruel and powerful) like warder Joan 'the Freak' FERGUSON (Maggie Kirkpatrick)? And they are just a few of the scores of characters who have passed through those clanging doors in the 692 episodes of a series planned to run for just 14.

The lesbian aspects of prison existence are more understood than stated, there is hardly any physical contact and the love play is rudimentary ('Want to have it off?'). But, in comparison with the earlier and very British WITHIN THESE WALLS (1974–8 T), it's a hive of activity, especially in the episodes relating to Franky and Doreen, Judy and Sharon, and Lynn Warner (Kerry Armstrong) and her former lover Karen Travers (Peta Toppano). And, of course, there's always the lowering – but never depressing – presence of Joan Ferguson, one of the great villains of television: implacable, barely human and almost invincible.

Shown in various ITV regions from 1987, PRISONER has never been fully networked in Britain, although it attracts good (late night) audiences (shown three nights a week in the Midlands) and has a fanatical core following (possibly with lesbians predominating). In Australia the serial is on its third rerun, daily at 4am.

Packed with intrigue and incident, spiced with (a little, mainly hetero) sex and (a little, mainly incipient) violence, it is primarily an arena for various loose cannon to fire off in different directions, and for one very sharp blade to strike at every opportunity she gets. Strong stuff.

'I don't want any fighting in here unless I start it myself,' Bea Smith.

'This place is as much fun as a leakin' dunny,' Doreen.

'The prisoners are the same all over and it's only the faces that change,' Joan Ferguson.

'I suppose she does look like the girl-next-door – if you happen to live on Cell Block H,' Frank Skinner in *Bunch of Fives* 'Blue Heaven' (1992 T).

A video called *'Prisoner – On the Outside … ' Tour 1990 'The Great Escape'*, which contains scenes of Bea, Lizzy, Chrissie and (a resurrected) Franky receiving a triumphal welcome in Derby (home of the Prisoner Fan Club), as well as performing on stage and celebrating National Prisoner Day (1 September 1990), was released by the Fan Club in 1991.

Prisoner (Theme from) aka 'On The Outside' With words and music by Allan Caswell, it is sung by Lynne Hamilton, once over a (1979) scene of a young woman dreaming of the outside world where her lover (male) waits for her, and used regularly as a wistful accompaniment to the closing credits. The song reflects the many tender and touching moments among the women inside, as well as their paybacks, rivalries and plotting. An anthem for many lesbians and for all those people who feel enclosed and trapped, under lock and key.

prisons There was a silence about sexual desire in men's prisons – apart from the German *Sex in Chains* (1928 C) and *Brute Force* (1947 C) and the poetry of sexual fantasy gushing forth in UN CHANT D'AMOUR (1950 C). Slowly from the early 1960s, the full import of enclosed spaces and lack of women began to trickle through: usually a pretty first-time offender being lined up for protective cohabitation (*The Pot Carriers* 1962 C; FORTUNE AND MEN'S EYES 1971 C; THE GLASS HOUSE 1972 C), or the would-be seductive prisoner trying it on a heterosexual (a hysterical manipulator also entangled with at least one warder) in A LIFE IS FOREVER (1972 C).

Gay prisoners are also part of the supporting babble of most prison stories: bitter and twisted in *Standing By for Santa Claus* (1968 T); 'two old DAISIES' in *There Was a Crooked Man* (1970 C); the owlish LUKEWARM endlessly KNIT-

TING in *Porridge* (1974–7 T); the prison rapist in *Scarecrow* (1973 C); the bulking menace who tries to seduce Clint Eastwood in *Escape from Alcatraz* (1979 C).

There are a few gay governors of men's prisons (eg *There Was a Crooked Man*) as well as warders (eg *Brute Force*). But it is the custody of women that provokes the most excitement: sexual dominance goes hand in hand with authority, beginning in the 1940s, reaching a peak with CAGED, chugging through the 1950s and on into the 1970s with *Caged Heat* (1974 C).

Few stories adequately show the effect of prison on gay prisoners. The exceptions are the dramatized histories of Oscar WILDE and THE CONSEQUENCE (1977 C).

The presumed effectiveness of incarceration in 'turning' somebody gay has been depicted in *The Moneychangers* (1976 T), THE NIGHT THEY TOOK MISS BEAUTIFUL (1977 T), FORTUNE AND MEN'S EYES (1971 C) and MINDER 'Whose Wife Is It Anyway?' (1980 T). In *Visitors for Anderson* (1980 T) it is the wife of one prisoner who arrives to announce she is carrying another man's child, but not that she is preparing to set up home with a woman.

The adjustment to life under a long sentence (sometimes for relations with somebody under age) was detailed in CHARIOT OF FIRE (1970 T), COMIC'S INTERLUDE and *Keep It Dark* (1982 R). The only female examples thus far are Jacki Holborough's *Wednesday Is Yoga Day* (1982 R) and *The Road South* (1990 R) – the writer also plays the leading role in the former. 'What do you need an old lady for? She's out there and you're in here.'

US: *Sex in Chains* (1928 C); *Brute Force* (1947 C); *Deathwatch* (1966 C); *There Was a Crooked Man* (1970 C); FORTUNE AND MEN'S EYES (1971 C); THE GLASS HOUSE (1972 T); *The Moneychangers* (1976 T); *Attica* (1979 T); *Escape from Alcatraz* (1979 C); *Stir Crazy* (1981 C); *Nancy Astor* (1982 T); *Gaskin* (1983 T); *The Bigger They Are* (1984 R); *Oscar* (1985 T); *Wings and Landings* (John

Williams' prison journals, (1992 R); *Alien 3* (1992 C).

UK: *The Pot Carriers* (1960 T; 1962 C); *Blackmail* 'The Man Who Could See' (1966); *Standing By for Santa Claus* (1968 T); A LIFE IS FOREVER (1972 T); *Porridge* (1974–7 T; 1980 C); *Scum* (1978 T; 1980 C); *The Hardman* (1979 R); *The Sin Bin* (1981 T); POISON (1990 C); SWOON (1991 C).

Documentaries: MAN ALIVE 'Here We Go Round the Mulberry Tree' (1979 T); *Jailhouse Shock* (Rahway in New Jersey, 1979 T); *Prison Portraits* (three ex-prisoners, 1975 T); *Inside Story* 'Prison/Parole' (1979); *Secret Hospital* (1979 T); *Strangeways* (1980 T); 40 MINUTES 'Jail Within a Jail' (Thanet wing of Maidstone Prison 1983 T); *First Tuesday* 'Life in San Quentin' (1983 T); *Turning the Screws* (Wandsworth, 1993 T).

Incarcerated women have been the source of much melodrama from the 1930s, with peak performance in the 1950s, the 1970s and the 1980s. Mostly the films were cheap and nasty, but with all the scratching and hair pulling, humiliation and lust, titillation in the showers, cruel uncompromising guards and sweaty, big-breasted bodies in torn clothing they turned in tidy profits for their makers. There are some people who feel that a little more of this grossness and eroticism wouldn't have gone amiss in the two main women's prison series, WITHIN THESE WALLS and PRISONER/PRISONER: CELL BLOCK H, both of which tended to concentrate on relatively intricate human situations, the disappointments and the fast-fading elation, and the boredom, loneliness and fear of being locked away from familiar things and people.

US: *Girls in Chains* (1943 C); CAGED (1950 C); *Women's Prison* (1955 C); *Women in Chains* (1972 T); *Born Innocent* (1974 T); *Caged Heat* (1974 C); POLICE WOMAN 'Fish' (1975 T); *Cage without a Key* (1975 T); CHARLIE'S ANGELS 'Angels in Chains' (1976 T); *If Tomorrow Comes* (1986 T); *Prison Stories: Women on the Inside* (1991 T).

UK: *Prison without Bars* (1939 C, remake of *Prison sans Barreux* 1937 C);

Girl in a Birdcage (1960 T); *The Quare Fellow* (1962 C); PORTRAIT OF A GIRL (1964 R); WITHIN THESE WALLS (1974–8 T): 'The Animals Came in Two by Two', 'For Life', 'Invasion of Privacy', 'Transfer' and 'Mixer'; *Scrubbers* (1982 C); *Wednesday Is Yoga Day* (1982 R); SILENT WING (1984 R); *The Road South* (1990 R); prisoner's bisexual wife in *Visitors for Anderson* (1980 T).

Australia: PRISONER/PRISONER: CELL BLOCK H (1979–87 T).

Documentaries: *Women, Women, Women* 'My Sister's Keeper' (Styal, 1966 T); MAN ALIVE 'Women in Prison' (Holloway, 1971 T); *The Man Alive Report* 'Girls Behind Bars' (Bullwood Hall, 1978 T); INSIDE/OUTSIDE (1978 R); *Living in Styal* (1982 T); *Sex and Violence in a Women's Prison* (Holloway Project Workshop, 1984 T); *Ten Days in Holloway* (1986 T); *First Tuesday* 'Locking Up Women' (Holloway, (1992 T).

private detectives Mostly they don't care much for FAGGOTS, but will treat them well if they are paying for their services. Famous MACHO ones include Sam Spade, Philip Marlowe and Magnum. More at ease with himself was Perry Mason's favourite gumshoe, Paul DRAKE.

Most versatile member of the profession: Neil McVane (Paul Burke) in DYNASTY (1985 T) who manages – convincingly, it would appear, though we don't see him up close – to disguise himself as Alexis (Joan Collins). Comedically, Richard Briers as Gannett meets a glamorous woman on a case and she introduces him to the explosive joys of heterosexuality in *Rentadick* (1971 C).

Three women PIs: Meg Hammer (Joyce Hazzard) in *Murder in a Mist* (1983 T) and Claude Alphand (Catherine Deneuve) equally at home, out of her trilby and trenchcoat, with male or female; Pearl (Buki Armstrong) and Finn (Rosie Rowell) in SOUTH OF THE BORDER (1988–90 T); Kathleen Turner as *V. I. Warshawski* (1991 C; 1991 & 1993 R).

The Private Files of J. Edgar Hoover

(US 1978 C) FBI Director (Broderick Crawford), obsessed with sexuality and sexual deviance, lives neatly and chastely, spending most evenings with his beloved Clyde Tolson (Dan Dailey). An icy-dark world where anything can be uncovered – or covered up.
W/D: Larry Cohen 112 mins.

Thought to be quite daring at the time, but now very pale in the light of the 1993 HOOVER revelations of rampant blackmail, seduction of young men at orgies, and dressing up in clothing not pertaining to his gender.

The Private Life of Hilda Tablet (UK 1954 R) 'A parenthesis for radio.' Was composeress Dame Hilda (Mary O'Farrell) the inspiration for one of Richard Shewin's great romantic heroines? Will Herbert Reeve (Hugh BURDEN) ever finish the Shewin biography or will it be hijacked by the grandiose literary plans and beastly beatitudes of Hilda?
W: Henry REED; D: Douglas Cleverdon; 24.5.54; BBC Third Programme; *c* 55 mins.

Another grand concatenation of mickey-take and affectionate parody of early 1950s English highbrowism. Mary O'Farrell plays Dame Hilda up to the hilt and beyond. The woman is all unbridled ego and bellicose heartiness, but she is also radio's first and practically only lusty, talented (if a trifle wayward) and FEMINIST lesbian who favours swallow tails and white shirt front and won't use verbs like 'manhandle'. In this, the second of the Shewin series, fresh-cheeked, gullible Herbert enters the deep shallows of Hilda's ménage (including her protégée, the anxiety-prone soprano Elsa Strauss whom he – perhaps diplomatically – mistakes for Hilda's 'daughter', and her secretary Evelyn BAXTER, a gay young spark). He is the perfect foil for this whip-cracking dynamo, full of dash and vitality, still with an eye for a pretty filly (or two, or three) and playing along with Herbert's vision of her and Richard as great but forbidden lovers. As an aged – and surly – family retainer remarks: 'Miss 'Ilda always wuz a bit of a TOMBOY.'

Privates on Parade (UK 1982 C) Captain Terri Dennis (Denis QUILLEY), head of a theatrical troupe in Malaya, emulator of dear Noel, wearer of DRAG and much make-up, off-stage as well. Considerably given to camp phraseology which throws the military mind (represented by John Cleese) into a spin.
W: Peter Nichols from his play; D: Michael Blakemore; 95 mins.

A somewhat misconceived comedy-drama, which is enlivened by the presence of Terri Dennis and his refusal to give one inch to authority and the rule-book. Heterosexual orthodoxy quakes and quivers when he's around. A creation based on Barrie Chatt, who was in the same army unit as Peter Nichols (and Kenneth WILLIAMS), and here immortalized, along with renditions of 'Marlene' and 'Carmen' by the impeccable Quilley, who reworked the role from his 1978 stage performance. A stereotype with a brain and heart, not to mention occasionally stirring guts. (The title was used by Captain Mainwaring (Arthur Lowe) in a *Dad's Army* episode: 'You're not putting my privates on parade.')

private tutors *See* TEACHERS.

Probation Officer (UK 1959–60 T) A landmark series from ATV, produced by Antony Keary: factually based and popular. A group of probation officers, led by John Paul and Honor Blackman, got to grips with basic problems besetting people in trouble with the law. One episode, written by Tessa Diamond and transmitted at 9.35pm on 30 November 1959), is said to have featured one of British television's first male couples: Dr Portway (Sebastian SHAW) and John Forbes (Ralph Michael). Another episode, written by Julian Bond and transmitted on 18 January 1960, centred on an effeminate factory hand, Michael Lawson (Murray MELVIN), driven to crime because of persecution at work.

probation officers Judith FURSE as the thoroughly professional, solid, supportive, very probably unmarried and possibly lesbian woman in *Serious Charge* (1959 C). Linda Thorne (Susan Clark) in *The Midnight Man* (1974 C) is glamorous and competent, but she was once married to a gangster; she's also a killer: 'That's what happens when they put a broad in a man's job. She was having an affair with her woman victim, who was also her client.' Much less complicated is Ross Kennedy (Brian Deacon) in HARD CASES (1988–9 T): he's revealed, several episodes in, as an ordinary, hard-working, deeply caring gay man.

The Producers (US 1967 C) Nervous nellie (Gene Wilder) and overbearing bully (Zero Mostel) hit on a scheme to make a huge profit on an oversubscribed certain-flop Broadway show. Called 'Springtime for Hitler', it contains something to offend the theatre-going public (in other words it's anti-Semitic and HOMOPHOBIC). Directed by a TRANSVESTITE (Christopher Hewett), written by a NAZI (Kenneth Mars) and starring a stoned HIPPY (Dick Shawn), its tasteless excesses are accorded CAMP status, and it becomes a hit, ruining the boys' scam and landing them in jail where they mount ... a gay musical called 'Prisoners of Love'.
W/D: Mel Brooks; P: Sidney Glazier; 88 mins.

According to taste, a much loved – or much despised – epic of gross insensitivity and bad taste. Full of stereotypes and with a central relationship that recalls LAUREL AND HARDY, their love for one another and their intense frustration.

promiscuous A rare example of the word used in a non-sexual sense came in the 'Black Eye' episode of LEAVE IT TO BEAVER (1957 T). Ward Cleaver (Hugh Beaumont) teaches his son Beaver (Jerry Mathers) to box, but counsels the boy not to use his knowledge promiscuously: 'I don't want you to go round picking fights.'

Usually the word is used in the sense of having more than one – usually a lot more than one – sexual partner. The promiscuity, usually called randiness, or

sowing wild oats, or playboyishness of heterosexual men has been a constant, highly welcomed theme in popular entertainment. From the early 1950s, there were swathes of films and television series about 'swinging' bachelors or married man let off the leash: from *The Moon Is Blue* (1953 C), *The Tender Trap* (1955 C), *A Hole in the Head* (1959 C) and *Come Blow Your Horn* (1963 C) – all starring Frank Sinatra – right through to the 1970s and early 1980s with *Ten* (1980 C) and *The Man Who Loved Women* (1981 C).

Guy De Maupassant was described as *A Glutton for Life* in the title of the 1946 radio biography; John F. Kennedy was 'carefree' in *Kennedy* (1983 T) even though he was married and Catholic; Gary Cooper (also married and Catholic) had a 'lusty healthy sexuality' (Barry Norman in THE HOLLYWOOD GREATS 1978 T). Dedicated pagan Errol Flynn's multiple-multiple couplings were just his *Wicked, Wicked Ways* (1984 T). Frank Sinatra, Georges Simenon (who claimed over 10,000 sex partners), Anthony Quinn, Kirk Douglas, Elia Kazan ... they were all at it with droves of women.

Without any prompting, singer Rudy Vallee told the interviewer on *The Golden Years of Hollywood* (1987): 'I have had sex with 184 women.' And the singer Al BOWLLY in *They Called Me Al* (1991 R) 'kept late hours and dodgy company', 'fell victim to every redhead, blonde and brunette', 'kept a list of runners and riders' and enjoyed 'his flirting and beyond'.

None of these men is described as promiscuous and, in *Who's Had Who* (1987), the word doesn't appear until page 358 (and only then in relation to a famous British call girl).

Some characters did meet sticky ends as a result of some of their sticky moments: Don Juan/Don Giovanni dragged down to the ultimate basement; the cad in *Goodbye Charlie* (1964 C, returning as – the ultimate insult – a woman; a theme reworked in SWITCH 1991 C); and the sleek Pete (Victor Varconi) in *Safe in Hell* (1931) gunned down (by Dorothy Mackaill) after delivering the line: 'I've known a million women; some of them were plenty nifty, but I forget 'em as soon as I leave 'em.'

In the main, lusty men, though 'tamed' by marriage, in the end are never rebuked or punished for their tom-catting. Even the married boss (Fred MacMurray) who causes Shirley MacLaine's suicide attempt in *The Apartment* (1960 C) fails to meet a sinner's end.

For women, it is a different script altogether. Katherine HEPBURN's question in ADAM'S RIB (1949 C) reverberates down the decades: 'Why not nice if she does and nice if he does it? ... a boy sows a wild oat or two the whole world winks; a girl does it – scandal!'

Sally (Elvi Hale) in THE VOICE OF THE TURTLE (1958 T) deduced that there's nothing men hate so much as talking about sex. Bragging, yes; talking, no. This is borne out when her soldier pickup (Alec MCCOWEN) anxiously asks her if she's promiscuous. She bounces the question back and he ducks: 'I've never counted. And if I had, I wouldn't tell you.' Sally remonstrates: 'I told *you* ... You think it's different for a man?' To which he replies: 'I think the *permissible* number's different for a man.'

In the 1991 *Cape Fear* Max Cady's female victim 'slept with at least three guys in one week'. It is the suppression of a report to this effect that sets in train Cady's 14-year revenge plan that causes another rape (which includes cheek-gouging), the death of a dog, the intimidation of a family and the deaths of two people.

Ken Bruce used the word, once, of men on a WOMAN'S HOUR discussion of the Hite Report (1990 R): 'Men who marry, lose interest in their wives and find ... wish-fulfillment in promiscuity.' The host of *The Late Clive James* (1991 T) told Shere Hite herself that most men want to impregnate all the women they see.

Typically, promiscuity was not mentioned at all in *Style Trial* (1990 T), one of whose protagonists more than fitted the definition: 'Trev's the name/Making love's my game.' And 'former gigolo'

(Frank Cooper) on DONAHUE (1989 T) described his move into intensive professional sex as being prompted by his 'seeing a lot of women, to support my insecurity'. Laurie on EASTENDERS (1989 T) saw himself as a 'bit of a Jack the Lad with the girls'. Rory on NEIGHBOURS (1991 T) is described by the (jealous) Paul as a 'lech'.

When the series REBELS dedicated a programme to the writer 'Albert Camus' (1988 R), it found a whole new way to say promiscuous: 'His many, many affairs can be seen far more as being fun than a series of empty conquests. Camus' good looks ensured him a steady success with women and quite endearingly he was rather proud of it.'

Yet promiscuous *is* a widely heard word on television and radio, beginning in 1957 with the first post-WOLFENDEN REPORT programmes. Not in connection with the hundreds of thousands of men who are acquainted with female prostitutes (which was also part of the committee's brief), but almost solely with men who have sex with men. As was pointed out by a PSYCHIATRIST on MALE HOMOSEXUALS in 1965: 'Most homosexuals will go through a period of promiscuity at some time of life ... It is a mistake to assume that homosexuals and promiscuity go together.' This was followed by a gay man saying: 'My friend and I have been together for a long time.'

After GAY LIBERATION, it was the pros rather than the cons of multiple partners that received most attention. Films made by gays like TAXI ZUM KLO (1981) hymned multiple choice; others, like NIGHTHAWKS (1978 C), showed a constant turnover to be an empty and unsatisfying experience. With the grip AIDS continues to have on most gay men – and increasingly on lesbians – the arguments have taken on a more medical tone, with sex being viewed as a potentially overdosable, dangerous drug. Exceptions to this rule are people like Derek JARMAN, who continued to say (in programmes like OUT 'Love and Marriage' (1991 T) that he felt his promiscuity had been valuable.

The most powerful counter-argument against gay liberation's espousal of almost spontaneous sexual arousal and satisfaction came from Larry KRAMER in the early 1980s after AIDS became a recognizable and ever-spreading reality. A decade later (ARENA 'Kramer vs Kramer'), and now HIV positive himself, he maintained his position: 'I guess I sound like a prude when I say it, but STRAIGHTS don't do it – most of them. Of all the fights we have to fight, this fight for the right to unlimited public sex seems very far down on the list.' He went on to say that most of those who promulgated multivarious sex are now dead.

In many debates where gay men are hammered for their sexual lives, the word 'monogamy' is prominently used as an antidote to all problems, a cure-all. It is often presented as a natural state for human beings and its transgression being a sign of disorder and ultimate destruction. It is refreshing then to have Professor Robert Stoller, from the University of California, assert (on *Trading with the Enemy* 1990 R) that most people 'need a considerable number of partners.' Not, he underlined, *all* people. 'But if you are talking about most people, God it certainly looks like it.'

See also NYMPHOMANIACS; ONE NIGHT STANDS.

pronunciation In 1953 a memo from the BBC Pronunciation Unit explained that the word 'homosexual' derives from the Greek root meaning 'same' and not the Latin meaning 'man'. The directive was issued to ensure that all BBC personnel pronounced it 'homo' as in 'homage' not 'homo' as in 'Homer'. The unit admitted that it didn't really have a clue how it should be enunciated, 'but we have to be precise'.

The inevitable correspondents leapt forward. This one from a vicar in Norfolk: 'Does it matter a tinker's cuss ... why the BBC has not got the good taste to keep off this nasty subject until after the children have gone to bed' (*Sunday Telegraph*, 10.2.63).

What was forgotten in the skirmish was that the BBC was also anxious to remove the male from homosexual: 'This will bring out for the knowledgeable listener the fact that we are aware the word applies to either sex.'

prostate Without the prostate, the gland surrounding the urethra between the bladder and the PENIS, no ejaculation can take place. Brian in TOGETHER ALONE (1991 C) thinks that this could be the secret that gays keep from straight people: the inexpressible pleasure of prostate stimulation by another man.

This part of a man's body has become a joke (like housemaid's knee and gout), principally because of Dame Edna EVERAGE's persistent laugh-milking remarks about her husband Norm's discomfort, transplant and eventual death (the life support machine was switched off in 1989). Yet prostate cancer is one of the biggest killers of middle-aged and older men.

prostitutes Charles Parker, Fred Atkins, Edward Shelley etc; the boys who had relationships with Oscar WILDE (ON TRIAL 1960 T; *Oscar Wilde* 1960 C; *The Trials of Oscar Wilde* (1960 C; *Oscar* 1985 T); Gloria (Adrian Shergold), Liz (Roger Lloyd Pack) and Norma (Shane Bryant) trilbyed, suited and made-up friends of Quentin CRISP in THE NAKED CIVIL SERVANT (1975 T): 'No roughs in tonight, thank heaven. They get on my tits.' Quentin observes that 'Courtship in such cases consists of the words, "'Ow much?" "Seven and six pence".'

Ralph (Myles Reithermann) in THE ROADS TO FREEDOM (1970 T) is a haggard 25-year-old 'boxer' who specializes in sado-masochism for rich Parisians. Daniel (Daniel MASSEY) is one of his clients. But he's not fooled: 'A typical butch queer with his strong man act ... worse than the female queen with her tatting and her housework. It's all acting.' Daniel gets the better of Ralph as they wrestle on the BED: 'You're a real killer, DUCKIE, when you put your mind to it.' Ralph's appearance (in episode 5) is described in David TURNER's script: '... short pants and vest. His attic walls are decorated with a few photographs cut from magazines of male film stars and wrestlers.' He is a 'professional homosexual prostitute who plays excessively masculine roles of coarseness, aggression, muscularity and obscenity for clients who seek humiliation, degredation, feminine abasement and servitude'.

In America: William Holden as Joe Gillis in *Sunset Boulevard* (1950 C) supplements his income as a script writer (director Billy WILDER was allegedly a gigolo in Vienna during the 1920s). Paul Newman as Chance Wayne in *Sweet Bird of Youth* (1962 C) is back in his home town with his latest acquisition: an ageing Hollywood star. In Tennessee WILLIAMS' 1960 play Chance alludes to sex with men and the climax has him castrated rather than, as in MGM's film version, 'scarred for life'. Joe (Joe DALLESANDRO), ordered to raise $200 to pay for his wife's girlfriend's abortion, returns home to find both in bed; the women then proceed to taunt him for his inadequacy in FLESH (1968 T). Joe again in *Trash* (1970 C) stands naked and shoots up heroin while a husband and wife who were planning a threesome bicker loudly.

Still in America: Jon Voight as Joe Buck in MIDNIGHT COWBOY (1969 C) thinks the women of New York will flock to him: they don't; he is forced to go to a news CINEMA where a young student sucks him off, and then admits he has no money to pay him. Cowboy (Robert La Tourneaux) in THE BOYS IN THE BAND (1970 C) has Harold's birthday present: a midnight cowboy of sweet disposition but limited time to spend. Sex-for-hire can be seen with Mike Waters (River Phoenix) and Scott Favor (Keanu Reeves) in MY OWN PRIVATE IDAHO (1991 C), which also includes a scene in a Seattle café where hustlers talk about why they're where they are.

In Canada: Yves (Roy Dupuis) in *Being at Home with Claude* (1992 C).

In Italy: Warren Beatty in *The Roman Spring of Mrs Stone* (1961 C) making lira from rich women and being kept in line by the threat of also having to accommodate paying male customers. Simone (Renato Salvatori), the boxer who sleeps with female clients but repels the advances of a man in *Rocco and His Brothers* (1960 C).

In Britain: Leslie Darkin (Roger Davenport) in SOFTLY, SOFTLY 'Murder Reported' (1966 T); Mr Sloane open to anything and everything in ENTERTAINING MR SLOANE (Clive Francis 1968 T; Peter McEnery 1970 C); Eddie (Emile Charles) in THE FRUIT MACHINE (1988 C), a Liverpool rent boy on the run in Brighton; *Young Man Seeks Part-Time Work* (1973 T) is the small ad placed in a tobacconist's window which an American tourist misconstrues. In the Philippines: Bobby Reyes in MANILA: IN THE CLAWS OF DARKNESS (1975 C) reveals to his new friend the source of his comfortable lifestyle: 'Don't worry, I'm not gay. It's my job. I'm a call boy. There's nothing wrong with being a call boy. Our clients are human beings. And how could I eat like this without them? I'm not pressurizing you into it, but ... You'll need guts but I'm sure you have, after working in construction.'

In Russia: Patrick O'Neal as a CIA operative who pretends to be a Russian prostitute called Jorgy in *The Kremlin Letter* (1970 C). His client asks him if he has slept with men. No: 'That's for others. I specialize in women.' She then navigates him into a sado-masochistic situation: 'Help to destroy me,' she slavers, 'and I'll love you for it.' He pushes her away. He doesn't do *that* either.

In Brazil: the young *Pixote* (1980 C) goes around with a gang of boys, some of whom are involved in prostitution.

In Germany: Detlef (Thomas Haustein), the boyfriend of *Christiane F* (1981 C), finally confesses he is a prostitute. He then becomes involved with one of her clients and she leaves him. He is last seen trying to get off heroin but still hustling. Detlef earlier insists that he only jerks off 'the SISSIES', but soon admits to sleeping with them and not being averse to being penetrated. Christiane says: 'Do you think I like it when your "John" pushes his prick up your arse?' Detlev insists that the very thought repels him, but this is contradicted later.

American commercial television faced up to the fact that men walk the streets as women do in the gorgeous Californian blond shape of Leigh McCloskey, who played Alex Duvall, an artist forced onto the sidewalks in *Dawn: Portrait of a Teenage Runaway* (1976 T). That the wages of sin were death and decay was spelt out in the sequel *Alexander: The Other Side of Dawn* (1977 T).

Black Polo (Ben Ellison) in COMING OUT (1979 T) reckons he makes about £500 a week, tax free. 'It's overheads, see. Laundry and things like that. And I charge extra for dressing up. Boots. Breeches. Guardsman. Sailor boy. Drag. Cops. Got to pay for the clobber; comes expensive ... Forty-two guys I went with last week – and all of them dogs.'

prostitutes, female Usually portrayed as brassy and insensitive, coarse and materialistic, or passive victims.

In Harold Greenwald MD's study *The Call Girl* (1958, filmed as *Girl of the Night* in 1961) the vast majority of his (limited) survey respondents said that they as prostitutes detested men and that they were lesbian out of working hours. The updated version, *The Elegant Prostitute*, with '25–50 per cent of new material' (1970) showed that the sexual revolution of the 1960s had increased that number. Films and plays were quick to reflect the situation, usually for titillation purposes.

Prostitutes in love with each other include Billa (Sylvia Syms) and Ginnie (June Ritchie) who lie on the bed laughing at the end of *The World Ten Times Over* (1963 C; most of this aspect of the script was lost to censorship); the very young Poppy (Sissy Spacek) and Violet (Janit Baldwin) in *Prime Cut* (1972 C); Letty (Birgitte Kahn) and Georgie (Vikki Richards) in THE GENTLE TOUCH 'Melody' (1980 T): 'The point is, darling, we've always been around and we always will be. You can't fight

Mother Nature so why not accept it?'; Simone (Cathy Tyson) and the new recruit (Kate Hardie) in *Mona Lisa* (1986 C); and, though retired from active service, Catholic Agnes (Doreen Hepburn) and Protestant Sadie (Leila Webster) living under one affectionate, industrious Belfast roof in *Phonefun Ltd* (1982 T).

Mixing business with pleasure: Hallie (Capucine), the special favourite of brothel madam Jo (Barbara STANWYCK) in *Walk on the Wild Side* (1962 C). Other so favoured were Jane Seymour as Kate in *East of Eden* (by Anne Baxter as Fay, 1980 T), Catherine Deneuve as BELLE DE JOUR (by Genevieve Page as Madame Anaïs, 1968 C) and Lee Grant as Carmen in *The Balcony* (by Shelley Winters as Madame Irma, 1963 C).

Proust, Marcel (1871–1922) French novelist who created a tradition of homosexual writing which was carried on by André Gide and Jean GENET. Proust developed a fluid style of allusion and memory which influenced both writers and film-makers (most recently Terence DAVIES in *Distant Voices, Still Lives* and *The Long Day Closes*).

Alan BATES played Proust in *102 Boulevard Haussmann* (1991 T). A hypochondriac, he is protected from the outside world (and the First World War) by his money, his cork-lined, soundproof room and his housekeeper. For stimulation – literary, spiritual and sexual – he employs a string quartet (which includes an attractive viola player) for nocturnal recitals of César Franck.

Documentaries: OMNIBUS 'In Search of Lost Time' (1971 T); *Proust Now* with A. S. Byatt, J. B. Priestley, Malcolm Bradbury, Roger Shattock, Nathalie Sarraute, Harold PINTER and Michael Butor (1980 R); *Proust Remembered* (Fr 1986 T); *The Modern World* 'The Great Writers' (words read by Roger Rees, 1988 R). Says George Stoupe (Derek Francis) in THE CONNOISSEUR (1966 T): 'Ever since your son became captain of my house I have felt as though I'm living in a novel by Marcel Proust.'

See also REMEMBRANCE OF THINGS PAST.

psychiatrists Psychiatrists were part and parcel of radio and television programmes 'about homosexuality' from 1957 to 1967. Some of them were strikingly sane and reasonable, portraying the subject as part of the human continuum. Others ignored facts and mouthed platitudes; a few spoke highly of AVERSION THERAPY ...

With the arrival of gay liberation, psychiatry was seen as a *bête noire*, at best condescending with its generalized talk of incomplete development, incomplete severance from the parent of the opposite sex etc. Suddenly, gays and lesbians were 'the experts'; psychiatrists were no longer automatically summoned when homosexuality was debated.

The mainstream media have been grossly stereotyping psychiatrists since the 1940s, making out many of these professionals to be crazier than the people they undertake to support or cure. Out of legions, a small selection: was Denholm ELLIOTT doctor or patient in *You're All Right – How Am I?* (1979 T)?; Dr Robert Elliott (Michael Caine), far from giving succour to frightened Angie Dickinson, was actually trailing her in a blonde wig and STILETTO HEELS, eventually stabbing her in DRESSED TO KILL (1980 C); *A Severed Head*'s Honor Klein (Claire Bloom) was at least as frightening in aspect: a female samurai, ferociously intense (1970 C).

This escalating nuttiness reached its pinnacle with the character of Simon (Nicholas Le Prevost) in IT TAKES A WORRIED MAN (1981–4 T). Absentminded, utterly depressed and confused, this man is far more concerned to steer each interview towards his own problems (with his patients, the tax man, his lover Gerald) than he is to deal with the mid-life crisis of Roach (Peter Tilbury). Roach knows Simon's useless, but can't give him up. Dependency? No. As he explains to his girlfriend: 'He's going through a bad patch. If I left him now, he'd go to pieces.' So he's stuck with a totally out of control, self-centred

man who charges extortionately for therapy which consists solely of saying 'look on the bright side'.

Saner examples include Jill Clayburgh's in *An Unmarried Woman* (1978 C): Penelope Russianoff was intended to have more of a lesbian psychology in the original script); Martin Dysart (Richard Burton 1977 C; Peter Barkworth 1980 R) trying to break through Alan Strang's troubled psyche in *Equus*; Dr Jenny Isaksson (Liv Ullmann) in *Face to Face* (1977 C/T), one of whose female patients exposes her breasts to her and strokes her face. But Jenny herself is slowly falling to pieces and is only saved from the abyss by a friend (Erland Josephson) who reveals himself as gay.

In ARE YOU BEING SERVED? 'Is It Catching?' (1981 T) Mr HUMPHRIES (John Inman) felt the need of one, but as always roles were reversed:

'Did he find out what your problem was?'
'No, but we found out what his was and we're discussing it tonight – over dinner.'

Documentaries: WORD IS OUT (1977 C); BEFORE STONEWALL (1984 C), THE TIMES OF HARVEY MILK (1984 C); *Silent Pioneers* (1985 C); *Changing Our Minds* (1992 C) about Dr Evelyn Hooker, the psychologist whose research led to the removal of homosexuality in 1974 from the list of official mental disorders. But some members of the jargoning chorus have remained obdurate: there are constant reminders of how much progress needs to be made in, eg *Start the Week* (1983, on *The Penguin Book of Homosexual Verse*), THE GAY AND LESBIAN WORLD (1992 R) and *Equinox* (1992 T).

'The quote of the year ... Speaking of a man before the court at Basildon, Essex charged with two serious offences against young girls, a psychiatrist told the court that "previously this man had been before us with offences that indicated a somewhat homosexual nature. These latest offences are an indication of a step in the right direction,"' David Frost in *That Was the Year That Was* (1962 T).

'I might have persuaded him to have

treatment. He loved me enough to do anything for me. More than anyone else has ever done. But I was too disheartened to start again at once and he killed himself before I got down to it ... no one could blame me for not loving him. I've got homosexual tendencies like anyone else, but well suppressed ... and suicide clearly runs in the family,' psychiatrist in Caryl Churchill's play LOVESICK (1967 R).

See also IN THE PSYCHIATRIST'S CHAIR.

psychologists One of the few discernible gay ones: Dr Tom Llewellyn (Ian Hendry) putting the human dimension before the purely scientific and logical one postulated by his lover, biologist David Neville (Alan BADEL) in solving the problem of the *Children of the Damned* (1964 C). (Radio and television psychologists tackling all manner of personal problems include Anna Raeburn, Philip Hodson and Claire RAYNER.)

Public Broadcasting Service *See* PBS.

public displays of homosexual affection In HOUSE ON THE HILL 'Something for the Boys' (1981 T); ANOTHER WAY (1982 C); OUTRAGE: THE DOCUMENTARY (1991 R); *Oprah Winfrey Show* 'Left for a Lesbian' (1991 T); *Accentuate the Positive* (1992 T). *See also* KISS; MARRIAGE (GAY/LESBIAN).

public houses Meeting places in Britain and Australia, often with FEMALE IMPERSONATORS: VICTIM (1961 C, filmed in the Salisbury off Leicester Square in London but called the Chequers); THE LEATHER BOYS (1963 C, a dockside pub where Reggie discovers 'the truth' about Pete); SOFTLY SOFTLY 'Murder Reported' (1966 T, a Liverpool one where intended victim meets his murderer); WHAT'S A GIRL LIKE YOU ...? (1969 T, the Vauxhall Tavern and other drag pubs); NIGHTHAWKS (1978 C); *Fothergill* (1981 T, an inn/hotel called the Spread Eagle, run by the flamboyant John Fothergill); G.P. 'Tests of Conscience' (1992 T, Sydney's the Royal outside which a

man is attacked by QUEER-BASHERS); etc.

Non-gay pubs also featured as meeting places or bolt holes for homosexual characters in THE KILLING OF SISTER GEORGE (1968 C, the Marquis of Granby); *Thrills Galore* (1972 T); WEDNESDAY LOVE (1975 T); *The Night Nurse Slept in the Day Room* (1976 R); EASTENDERS (the Queen Vic); etc.

See also BARS; CLUBS; RESTAURANTS.

public lavatories *See* COTTAGING.

public schools Bastions of privilege and repression, often downright sadism, from *Tom Brown's Schooldays* onwards. Those involving 'crushes' or love affairs between boys (usually younger and older) and/or masters include THE CONNOISSEUR (1966 T); IF ... (1968 C); *Two Sundays* (1975 T); *School Play* (1979 T); *Death of an Echo* (1980 R); *The Spectre* (1983 R); *Good and Bad at Games* (1983 T); ANOTHER COUNTRY (1984 C); *A Man Alone* (1986 R); MAURICE (1987 C); *A Murder of Quality* (1991 T); *The Life and Times of Henry Prott* (1992 T); *Death Drop* (1992 R). Documentaries include *The Public School: An Enquiry* (Harrow, Mill Hill etc, 1961 T); *Public School* (Radley, 1980 T); *The Rapture and the Wretchedness* (1982 R); OUT ON TUESDAY 'White Flannel' (1990 T).

Aroused passions in girls' schools (usually convents or ladies' colleges) are to be found in MAEDCHEN IN UNIFORM (1931 C etc); OLIVIA (1950 C); *Picnic at Hanging Rock* (1975 C); *The Getting of Wisdom* (1977 C); *Frost in May* (1980 T); *Sacred Hearts* (1984 T); SYRUP OF FIGS (1986 R). Documentaries include *An Apple for the Teacher* (a girl's wartime diary about her love for the music teacher, 1985 R); *You're a Brick, Angela!* (schoolgirl fiction, 1985 R); *Blood Sports for Girls* (power relationships, bullying and manipulation, 1992 R).

See also STUDENTS; TEACHERS.

publishers Jule and Sand brought their business acumen to the book trade, explaining to Kenneth HORNE in 1966:

Sandy: 'We're Bona books. We're just filling in ... Normally (if you'll pardon the expression) we're actors by trade.'
Julian: 'Trade's been a bit rough lately. We had to take whatever we could get.'

Mr 'Orne has brought them his tome 'The Life Cycle of the Water Vole'. By the time the enthusiastic pair have worked their magic, the title has been changed (to 'Vole Flanders') and the content considerably spiced up: 'Dorian's hot muzzle pressed against her furry cheek.'

Reg Nuttall (Michael Byrne) is able to put his rival's nose out of joint by offering the man's worst enemy a book contract (BUTLEY 1974 C/T). In retaliation, Butley (Alan BATES) pours anti-gay scorn over Reg. In another Simon GRAY piece *Two Sundays* (1975 T) Bates played a teacher whose boyhood friend (Dinsdale Landen), now a successful publisher, couldn't shake off his 'crush' on him.

In *The Woman Next Door* (1981 C) Roland (Roger Van Hool) is 'uninterested in women', always being seen in the company of a silent youth; and, although married, Robert (Ben Kingsley) seems to have more in mind than simple jealousy when he discovers that his friend (Jeremy Irons) is spending afternoons with his wife in *Betrayal* (1982 C).

Puck Or Robin Goodfellow Puck, a merry figure linked to the old religion. OBERON's helper in *A Midsummer Night's Dream* and, like SHAKESPEARE's other sprite Ariel, sometimes played by a woman: Gillian Lynne (1964 T); Judi Dench (1968 C); Emma Fielding (1991 R); but mostly by adolescent males: Mickey Rooney (1935 C); Sean Barrett (1959 R); Bunny May (1971 T); Ethan Hawke in *Dead Poets Society* (1989 C, the boy whose cruelly dashed acting dreams result in his SUICIDE). Other Pucks have included Frank Duncan (1953 & 1964 R); Sean Arnold (1970 R); Peter STRAKER (1983 R); Reginald BECKWITH (in *Winter Witchcraft* 1946 R). Lindsay Kemp made Puck a satyr in the 1984 film version of *A Midsummer Night's Dream*, and Kenneth Anger used Puck as the name of and symbol for his film company during the 1960s.

puff An observation during a buccaneering sketch ('We haven't had a puff for weeks' in reference to lack of wind at sea) inspires petulant protest from Tim Brooke-Taylor in I'M SORRY I'LL READ THAT AGAIN (1968 R) – just one of the sporadic examples of relating a puff and puffs to inconsequential or effeminate males. The most famous was Rudolph VALENTINO (Rudolf NUREYEV) taking on a reporter in a boxing match because he had called the star 'a powder puff', in *Valentino* (1977 C); the clip from this film in which the actor denies he is a puff was used in a number of radio obituaries for Nureyev in 1993.

Characters with this name include Mr Puff in Sheridan's *The Critic* and Puff Randolph, a flapper played by Ginger Rogers in her 1930 début feature movie *Young Man of Manhattan*, who sings 'I Got It, But It Don't Do Me No Good' and whose catchphrase is 'Cigarette me, big boy!'

See also POOF; POOFTER.

punk Uttered in exasperation by RICHARD I (Michael Byrne) about the boy who eludes his lustful grasp in *The Devil's Crown* (1978 T) ('Punk! Ploughboy!'), this word sometimes means homosexual (especially in prison or crime movies like *The Maltese Falcon* 1941 and *The Street with No Name* 1948) and sometimes a delinquent (Leif Erickson calls Elvis Presley a 'fresh punk' in *Roustabout* 1964 C; Gacy played by Brian Dennehy about his murder accomplice in *To Catch a Killer* 1991 T).

Sometimes its meaning will straddle the queer and the antisocial as with teenaged and SENSITIVE Timmy who is described in the title of a PERRY MASON as the 'The Case of the Devious Deviate' (1963 T) but called a punk in the script, and neo-Nazi Dennis Hopper in THE TWILIGHT ZONE 'He's Alive' (1963 T) to whom a policeman says: 'What's the matter, punk, no more big speeches?'

In the mid-1970s, punk rock and its adherents, wearing all manner of fierce haircuts, bondage clothing, nose-rings and spectacular MAKE-UP, disturbed the popular music landscape. First depicted in ROCK FOLLIES OF '77 (1977 T), a few punks were defined as both sexually and socially deviant: the twins in JUBILEE (1977 C); 'D' (Sara Sugarman) in WHALE MUSIC (1983 T); Billibud (Jason Durr) in YOUNG SOUL REBELS (1991 C); and – diluted for the screen – *Sid and Nancy* (1986 C).

Nicholas Cage, attacked by a bunch of punks in *Wild at Heart* 1990 C, calls them 'FAGGOTS' though no clue is given as to their sexuality.

Punchon, Erica [Ethel May] (1882–1989) Australian writer and translator. Known as Monty, she had given a 'coming out' interview to an Australian gay magazine, an action which upset the organizers of the Queensland International Expo, of which she was an ambassador, being one of the few people alive who could remember a similar event nearly 100 years before. Monty, who joined Mensa at the age of 93, talked of her deep and abiding (though long ago sundered) relationship with a woman called Debbie in the article (and also in the book *Australian Centenarians*), but was encouraged to speak in generalities on Channel 9's *The Midday Show* where she celebrated her 105th birthday, alongside her companion. All she would say about her sexuality to presenter Ray Martin was: 'I like being with women because I feel more confident – men are different – it's like cat and dog ... I think women are nice, don't you? ... And even at my age, it doesn't drop off, you know.'

pussy Miss Galore, rendered relatively harmless in the transition from Ian Fleming's pumping descriptions on the printed page to the 1964 film of *Goldfinger*. However, Sean Connery with his Glaswegian accent made a meal of the word: 'Poosy, Poosy,' he cooed to Honor Blackman, who forgot all about her girl pilots after a tussle in the barn with 007. The true circulator of 'pussy' (meaning the female sexual organs) to the mass audience was Mrs Slocombe (Mollie Sugden) in ARE YOU BEING SERVED? (1973–84 T). LIANNA (Linda Griffiths 1983 C) makes an announcement that she likes pussy as part of her COMING OUT.

Put The Blame On Mame Rita Hayworth's apogee: sashaying in a strapless gown while slowly taking off her long gloves in GILDA (1946 C). Still a mesmerizing achievement, with a stinging erotic charge, though the words harp on the theme of woman as a dangerous force of nature, responsible for disasters such as the Chicago fire and the San Francisco earthquake. Vivian Ellis pastiched it with great success (as 'Lady Spiv', sung by Greta Gynt) in the British *Easy Money* (1948 C) and Peggy Lee – whose 'Fever' slightly resembles 'Mame' – changed the title to 'Put The Blame On Me' for a visually witty as well as slinky production number on *The Andy Williams Show* (1965 T).

Patsy Kensit (as Rebecca) went back to the original in *Prince of Shadows* (1991 C), delivering the Doris Fisher and Allan Roberts number in an exact replica of *that* dress in a seedy Madrid nightclub. Most piquant of all was its materialization in SECOND SERVE (1986 T). A confused Richard Radley (Vanessa REDGRAVE) watches a singer in a bar perform 'Mame' with all the Rita/Gilda trademarks. However, on the last line, the voice drops a few octaves and the voluptuous redheaded woman is thus revealed as a man. In the next scene, Dick, his dilemma resolved, is taking active steps to change his gender.

Pygmalion The play by George Bernard Shaw, filmed in 1938 with Leslie Howard and Wendy Hiller as the flower girl turned into a lady, televised with Robert Powell and Twiggy, and on radio with Simon Cadell and Imelda Staunton. Because of the musical adaptation *My Fair Lady*, it is regarded as a love story in which the confirmed bachelor Henry Higgins is thawed by Eliza Dolittle. This reading was disputed by Simon CALLOW in KALEIDOSCOPE (1992 R) who was told by Alan J. Lerner's widow, Liz Robertson, that he [Lerner] and Frederick Loewe had wanted to reflect Shaw's original intention, which was to produce 'one of the most succinct and deeply felt accounts of the inherent tensions between men and women in our society, the more so because it isn't in the framework of a love story'.

Quality Street (Aust 1946–73 R) Originally produced by John Thompson and concentrating mainly on poetry and prose (first reader: Peter FINCH), under Norman Gear's 15-year stewardship this Sunday night half-hour became much more ambitious, combining in-house productions with those from the BBC. At a time when censorship was extraordinarily tight, this sound panorama offered an opening into other times, different attitudes.

Among the scores of presentations during the still repressed 1960s were Oscar WILDE (1964; Walt WHITMAN (included in 'Three Poets of Personal Voice', 1964); 'Homage to DIAGHILEV' (1964); Christopher MARLOWE ('Brief Glory', 1964); 'Lord BYRON' (1964); Rupert BROOKE ('Apollo's Laurel Bough', 1964); William SHAKESPEARE ('Work for Boy Players', 1965); Samuel Butler ('The Man Who Said No', 1965); 'Evelyn WAUGH' (1966); 'Herman Melville' (1967); Sir Francis BACON ('A Wise, Sinuous, Dangerous Creature', 1967); 'A Portrait of Siegfried SASSOON' (c 1968); 'J. B. Priestley' (1968); 'The Wit of Oscar Wilde' (1969); 'The Blue Stocking: Women in Revolt' (1970); Noel COWARD ('The First and Only Noel', 1970).

queen Vernacular term for an effeminate homosexual, who is often affected and piss-elegant, used affectionately or aggressively. It is now regarded by many a gay person as an affectionate amalgam of grit and gaiety.

Introduced from the underground by JULIAN AND SANDY in ROUND THE HORNE and fully operational by the late 1960s; the weakling central character of ROLL ON FOUR O'CLOCK (1970 T) was described as an 'embryo queen' and a remark on *Better Late* 'ABC of Britain' ('Q is for Queen, the royal sort we hope', 1970 R) had the *Listener*'s critic grinding his teeth (3.9.70).

In his shallow bow to UPSTAIRS, DOWNSTAIRS, Stanley BAXTER's Mrs Britches says she hasn't cried so much 'since the old queen died', which prompts 'Rose' (also played by Baxter) to say indignantly: 'Oh, Mrs Britches, you mustn't talk about Mr 'Udson like that' (*The Stanley Baxter Moving Picture Show* 1974 T). Lorri Lee gave a full run-down on the queen scene in 40 MINUTES 'Lol, Bona Queen of Fabularity': 'Drag queen ... Camp queen ... Black market queen (one who jumps up on people) ... Blob-type queen ... Clone queen (one spits, they all spit).'

See also WICKED QUEEN.

The Queen (US 1968 C) Backstage and onstage at the national finals of a drag beauty contest in New York. Which dazzling creature will win the trophy: Harlow (Richard Finochio) or Miss Manhattan (Crystal)?

P: Si Litvinoff and Don Herbert; D: Frank Simon; 68 mins.

Vital and engaging *cinéma vérité* charting the escalating tensions between a gaggle of drag queens, narrated by one of them – Flawless Sabrina alias Jack Doroshow. Well photographed, intimate (cleavage pencilling, leg shaving, hair plucking, sexual chit-chat), supportive-competitive, and with shamelessly heart-tugging tears amid the tinsel climax as Miss Manhattan stages a tantrum and the winner takes the crown. One of the first gay documentaries where the 'freaks' were behind as well as in front of the camera.

The Queen and I: A Royal Nightmare (UK 1992 R) Miriam MARGOLYES gives the spectacular life to the whole Windsor Family and their new proletarian friends and neighbours in Sue Townsend's wicked satire. Charles, now a dedicated Greenie, is sent to prison; Prince Edward is married off to the Emperor of Japan's daughter; the Queen has to deal with the intricacies of the Department of Social Security; and Princess Anne learns plumbing and has an affair with her teacher. (*The Queen and I* was used as the title of a 1968 American comedy series set aboard a pleasure cruiser, starring Billy DE WOLFE.)

P: John Tydeman; BBC Radio 4; 8 parts; 15 mins each.

Queen Christina (US 1933 C) Greta GARBO's Swedish ruler strides about with easy grace in large brimmed hats, suede jerkins, breeches and pigskin boots. Love thaws her (or so HOLLY-WOOD insisted) and she lights up like a Christmas tree. Glitter from head to foot and a hairstyle that predates the one concocted for the COWARDLY LION.

Racing to exile in the penultimate scene, Christina/Garbo once again adopts male dress. It is in cloak and doublet, with hair unpermed that we last see her, in one of cinema's most abiding images.

W: Salka Viertel, H. M. Harwood and S. N. Behrman; P: Walter Wanger; D: Rouben Mamoulian; 97 mins.

Queen Christina didn't have an encounter at an inn with a handsome Spanish nobleman anymore than MICHELANGELO necessarily had a liaison with a principessa (*The Agony and the Ecstasy* 1965 C) or Charlotte and Emily Brontë fought over the same man (*Devotion* 1946 C) or Hans Christian ANDERSEN loved a ballerina. But this does not reduce the potency of this ravishing swoon through a part of Swedish history filtered through the psyches of both MGM and its most prestigious female star.

Queenie The affectionate nickname of Queen (which derives from *Cwen* or *Cwene* meaning 'woman'). Used mainly for proletarian characters, tough, broad and lusty: Queenie Gibbons (Kay Walsh) in *The Happy Breed* (1944 C): 'It's sometimes said that all I think about is having a good time'; Queenie Shears (Hilda Schroder) in MRS DALE'S DIARY (1950s R); Queenie Edwards, murdered old soak in PAUL TEMPLE *and the Vandyke Affair* (1950 & 1959 R); North Country matriarch played by Diana Dors in *Queenie's Castle* (1970-2 T); *Queenie* (1987 T) alias film-star Merle Oberon played by Mia Sara: 'the rise of Queenie O'Brien from the slums of Calcutta'; her majesty of the shop floor – 'sooner lose her knickers than her lipstick' – Margi Clarke as Queenie in *Making Out* (1989–91 T); Queenie (Sasha), Joe

Ackerley's Alsatian in WE THINK THE WORLD OF YOU (1980 T).

Male Queenies include American Michael Greer in FORTUNE AND MEN'S EYES (1971 C) and another incarcerated camp man: Queenie (John Labanowski), pony-tailed, moustached in powder-blue SINGLET, doing aerobics in a cell, one of whose walls was adorned with (tasteful) male pin-ups, in EAST-ENDERS (1988 T).

The Queen's Christmas Message aka *HM The Queen*. The shortest (barely five minutes) and most watched (80 million worldwide) annual monologue of all time. HM's curiously strained manner has hardly changed since the 1950s. All subjects are anodyne with an emphasis upon the family. No mention that homosexuals fit anywhere in her Commonwealth, although she did talk about accepting 'difference' during her commemoration of the United Nations International Year of Disabled People in 1981.

queer Popular as anti-homosexual scorn in America and Britain, variously relating to the word's meaning as counterfeit coin or banknote, or as feeling ill, or as peculiar and ALIEN. 'The word's declining popularity may ... reflect today's greater visibility and acceptance of gay men and lesbians and the growing knowledge that most of them are in fact quite harmless, ordinary people' (Wayne R. Dynes, *Encyclopaedia of Homosexuality*, 1990). The Q word travelled up from the underground to become a form of abuse, which it remained until 1990–1. It is now clawing back its proudly exotic connotation.

It was, far more than gay, a 'useful' word, cropping up in all kinds of situations where something untoward was taking place: 'I set myself to discover when this queer taboo asserted itself,' Gerald Heard in *Among the Islanders* 'Nation in Uniform' (1935 R); 'A sort of a face and a handle and a queer little body – sort of pixie thing,' Chris ARCHER (Pamela Mant) describing a toby jug in THE ARCHERS (1951 R). It occurred in the serial two years later when Dan's farmhand Simon – supposedly in relation to 'the Peeping Tom of Penny Hasset', but possibly also referring to another topic of AMBRIDGE gossip (Chris' lack of interest in men) – said 'Very queer behaviour all round if you ask me.' However, queer never took the villagers' fancy in the same way as FAGGOT.

BBC Radio had a curious love-hate relationship with the Q word. From the 1930s to the early 1970s, it bobbed up and down on the airwaves: in titles (Algernon Blackwood's *Queer Stories* which included 'Homicidal Dream' 1934; *Queer Names and Queer Trades* 1935; *The Queer Affair at Kettering* 1946) and in plays like ROPE (1932 etc) and DANGEROUS CORNER (1945 etc), both of which consciously use the word to mean 'odd', 'disturbing', 'unnatural' ... and 'homosexual':

'This is very queer, dark and incomprehensible'/'We do quarrel about queer things, don't we'/'I've always thought it queer that Martin should have done such a thing'/'Queer how it works out, isn't it'/'That's a queer thing to say.'

In I'M SORRY I'LL READ THAT AGAIN (1964–73 R) certain words would merit long pauses so that John Cleese and others could announce 'I thought I noticed a queer ...', which would allow Tim Brooke-Taylor to slide in a vapidly frisky 'Hel-lo!' Yet three homosexual characters – Christopher WREN (Allan MCCLELLAND) in THREE BLIND MICE (1947 R), Finch (David Enders) in WHITEOAKS (1948 R), and the artist (Anthony Jacobs) in THE CRIME AT BLOSSOMS (1958 R) – were prevented by the censors from being described as 'queer' or giving someone a 'queer look', and 'peculiar' or 'odd' were substituted. The 'you're a queer boy' scene from *Whiteoaks* was similarly nobbled in its television production in 1949 and again in 1954.

In the cinema, the word in its homosexual sense was first spoken in two 1961 films: *No Love for Johnnie* (by a guest at a Chelsea party) and A TASTE OF HONEY (about Geoffrey played by Murray MELVIN). The same year, it appeared scrawled on a garage door in VICTIM. According to Dirk BOGARDE (1980, 1983 & 1992 T), audiences in the North of England were totally perplexed by this scene. They didn't understand why the writing of 'Farr is queer' should have such a devastating effect on the hero: 'They thought it meant being taken poorly.' Strange then that in Bolton, the setting for HONEYMOON POSTPONED (1961 T) which later became the stage play ALL IN GOOD TIME and the film THE FAMILY WAY, the word is employed as a means of exposing a man's abiding love for his dead mate – the same man who berates his son for not being a 'proper' husband and having queer tastes.

Unquestionably, though, by the late 1960s a good laugh across the nation could be guaranteed. Gurgled Benny HILL in 'Much Ado About Bo Peep' on one of his 1968 BBC1 shows:

One queer sheep,
Though sad, was gay.
But if approached
Would turn the other way.

Two decades on, it could still raise a titter – even on Channel 4's *Chance in a Million* (1984 T). Prospective tenant Tom (Simon CALLOW) asks prospective landlady Josephine Tewson if she has 'any queries?' Quick as a flash she responds with: 'Yes, two nice boys who live across the road.'

That same year, in the BBC1 *Play for Today* MORE LIVES THAN ONE, a man swallows hard and contorts his features after learning of his best friend's true sexual feelings. 'So you think you're queer?' he says, before trying to persuade him that he'd better have another think. Small wonder that the title of one of the segments of the banned SEX IN OUR TIME in 1976 was 'For "Queer" Read "Gay"' and Colin (Karl Johnson) in ONLY CONNECT (1979 T) could declare with relief that the early 1970s were 'when we stopped being queer and started being gay'.

It was obvious that 'queer' (meaning

one of *them*) had achieved a foothold in America's consciousness when an entire song, 'YOU'RE A QUEER ONE, JULIE JORDAN', could be cut from both television showings and cinema revivals of Rodgers and Hammerstein's *Carousel* (1956 C). The word, needing no explanation, bowed in, along with similar terms of abuse, spoken by Jennifer (Sharon Tate) in VALLEY OF THE DOLLS (1967 C).

On national television the following year, imperturbable conservative William F. Buckley – during a memorable altercation at the time of the Democratic Convention riots in Chicago – attempted to dislodge the urbane Gore VIDAL from his Democratic perch by lashing out at him with: 'Now listen, you *queer*, stop calling me a crypto-Nazi or I'll smash you in the goddamn face.' Vidal commented later: 'Buckley wanted to smear me as a FAG, hoping that my figures on poverty, say, would be disbelieved. These people are like that.'

In the era of AIDS and religious fervour, America's conservatives could throw the word around like a grenade with complete equanimity. And not all were wearing nicely tailored suits and dresses: 'Queers like you, spreading your sickness around!' says a street thug to Roger Gage (Boyd Gaines) in HOTEL 'Hornet's Nest' (1986 T).

Generally, the word is applied to men, although the fey kindergarten head (Martita HUNT) in *Bunny Lake Is Missing* (1965 C) identifies herself as 'a queer old party' and Robin (Michael Gambon), sexually frustrated, hurls 'You queer bitch!' at his lover Kim (Jane Lapotaire) in THE OTHER WOMAN (1976 T). The brutal, sexually abusing father of Myra (Maureen O'BRIEN) in REMAINING STRANGERS (1986 R, a distaff reworking of STRANGERS ON A TRAIN) rains down 'queer' upon her head because of her adoration of another woman.

'Queer' continues to savage and rend many individuals, bestowing upon most of its targets an unwonted and unjustified stigma of unnaturalness. Recently – especially after the formation of Queer Nation groups in America – there has been a move by some gays and lesbians to square up to this disease-ridden and detested application. This process had begun in Britain rather earlier with the video pastiche of the police instruction manual on the correct procedures for sexual subversives in *Watch Out, There's a Queer About*.

The third lesbian and gay film festival in London (1988) was titled 'A Queer Feeling When I Look at You' in celebration of the ingenuous (or was it?) remark made by the artist Michael Fane (Brian Aherne) to Katharine HEPBURN, disguised so erotically in Eton crop and suit, in SYLVIA SCARLETT (1936 C). He thinks she (Sylvia) is a he (Sylvester). But something stirs within his manly loins: 'I don't know what it is that gives me a queer feeling when I look at you.' Feelings of the queer kind had hitherto been limited to man and maid as with Orson WELLES' Rochester in *Jane Eyre* (1944 C): 'I sometimes have a queer feeling with regard to you – especially when you are near me, as now' (a direct quote from Chapter 23 of the novel).

Smartly deflecting rather than deflating his female colleague's pushily amorous interest in him, SOCIAL WORKER Ross (Eric Deacon) in HARD CASES (1988 T) simply tells her: 'If I ever think of turning queer, I'll let you know.'

Whether queer's liberation will be a permanent one remains to be seen. Post-1990 its use by queers themselves is very much about the politics of recognition and validation as well as cheekily confronting a strongly pejorative word. To other people – 'gay', 'lesbian', even 'homosexual' – are preferable to bringing back 'queer' into everyday use. At present, the boundary lines between self-definition and common abuse and a description of diversity are sometimes difficult to see.

'This queer don,' Kingsley Amis on his 1978 novel *Jake's Thing* to Paul Vaughan on KALEIDOSCOPE (1991 R).

'The 1990s are going to be a queer decade – and I'm not talking about sexuality,' Harold, one of the contributors to *Men Talk* (1992 T).

'You get some queer people here,' Frances Ashford (Valerie Hunkins) can say (to her brother) as they sit in CASUALTY 'Facing Up' 1991 T).

While NORMALITY is idolized there may be little chance of 'queer' shedding its pariah meaning, as a noun or adjective, despite the best efforts of queer people themselves, including Julian CLARY ('Uncanny and Unnatural/That's what I am').

queer as a . . . Usually it's a coot which, according to Partridge's *Dictionary of Slang*, derives from the 18th century: 'a silly person' or a 'man of inferior quality'. The phrase is applied to Stephen Piper (Paul Henley) by a colleague at the bank in EVEN SOLOMON (1979 T): 'He's as queer as a coot, BENT and a perfect POOFTER. What gets me is that they should have PUBS and CLUBS and that . . .'

Variations have included queer as 'as a bun' from railway fanatic (John Le Mesurier) about deceased signalman Tommy Coulson in LAST TRAIN THROUGH THE HARECASTLE TUNNEL 1969 T); 'as a cloth hammer . . . and doesn't care who knows it' about Ray Lacey (Noel DAVIS), a TELEVISION MAKE-UP MAN who's 'great fun' in *Who Killed Santa Claus?* (1971 T); 'as . . . a 10-groat piece' from one of the Knights of the Round Table about Sir Galahad the Gay in an Arthurian spoof on *The Dick Emery Show* (1979 T); 'as . . . a left-handed 5-shilling pound note' from ballroom dancer Fred (Michael Cronin) denying that he's like that in *Midnight at the Starlight* (1980 T); 'as a cat's fart' from Franny (Jodie FOSTER) about lonely brother Frank (Paul McCrane) in *The Hotel New Hampshire* (1984 C).

queer: feeling queer/being taken queer Phyllis Monckton sings 'District Nurse' in A TUNE TO TAKE AWAY: A REVIEW OF REVIEWS (1938 T): 'So if you're feeling queer/Just have the district nurse'; while worried housewife (Hilda Fenemore) says about her little daughter in *Quatermass II* 'The Food' (1955 T): 'She was taken queer.'

The sly double meaning of being taken queer was utilized by THE CAPTAIN'S TABLE (1958 C). Steward Birtweed (Reginald BECKWITH) arrives late and breathless to met his new captain (John Gregson). Birtweed explains his unpunctuality by saying: 'my FRIEND got took queer . . . on the chest.' This source of humour was being mined 15 years on in NUMBER 96 (Aust 1972 T). One of Don FINLAYSON's neighbours is mightily perplexed on hearing a would-be girl-friend scream out: 'You're queer! You're queer! You PERVERT!' She turns to her husband and mutters: 'It was something about Don being queer. But he looked all right the last time I saw him.'

Alan Bates as BUTLEY (1974 C/T), in an effort to wear down conservatively gay Reg (Michael Byrne), harps on about being rejected for National Service on account of his being taken queer. This develops into an elegantly barbed litany of SLANG TERMS which is punctuated at regular intervals by the word 'queer':

> Butley: 'Does it offend you?'
> Reg: 'It's beginning to . . .'

The large and flowing college bed-maker (Paula Jacobs) momentarily unsettles a callow young don (John Sessions) when she enquires in *Porterhouse Blue* (1987 T): 'Have you been taken queer?'

queer-bashing aka gay-bashing. Attacks on gay men have been quite frequently illustrated, though hardly ever analysed. In pop songs: Rod Stewart's 'THE KILLING OF GEORGIE' and BRONSKI BEAT's 'SMALLTOWN BOY'. In films: *Young Torless* (1968); *L'Homme de Desir* (1970); *Babylon* (Paul GREENHALGH as a helpless victim in London's West End, 1980); *The Boys Next Door* (Chris, played by Paul C. Dancer, murdered in his apartment, 1985); *9½ Weeks* (Mickey Rourke and Kim Basinger, who is dressed in a 'man's suit', are chased through the streets by men yelling 'queers', 1986); TORCH SONG TRILOGY

(Alan played by Matthew Broderick, 1988 C); Steve in *Night Out* (1990); *Resonance* (1991); *City of Hope* (a teacher out jogging accused of trying to molest the two youths who mugged him, 1991); THE LIVING END (three men with baseball bats are shot dead by their intended victim, 1992). On television: *A Raging Calm* (Roger Coyne, played by Nigel HAVERS, set upon in a car park, 1974); THE NAKED CIVIL SERVANT ('Some roughs are really queer and of course some queers are really rough,' reports Quentin CRISP/John HURT, 1975); NUMBER 96 (Don FINLAYSON beaten up by a sailor, 1975); *The Birth of the Beatles* (Brian EPSTEIN roughed up outside a Liverpool club, 1979); THE GENTLE TOUCH 'Do It Yourself' (HAIRDRESSER Toby played by Brian Capron, 1984); HOTEL 'Hornet's Nest' (soldier Roger Gage played by Boyd Gaines, 1986); CASUALTY 'Hooked' (transvestite Carla, 1987); EASTENDERS (Colin RUSSELL played by Michael CASHMAN, 1988); L.A. LAW 'Do the Spike Thing' (1991); A COUNTRY PRACTICE 'Little Boy Blue' (cycling champion Brett, 1992); G.P. 'Tests of Conscience' (Dr Simon Radley played by Felix Nobis, 1992); MELROSE PLACE (social worker Matt Fielding played by Doug Savant, 1992). On radio: *Men's Group* ('heterosexual' Mike played by Spencer Banks, 1983); OCTOBER SCARS THE SKIN (Vincent October whose brutal death is the catalyst for the play, 1989); A BIT OF BERLIN (Mark, played by Julian Rhind-Tutt, whose beating by neo-Nazis brings his parents to Berlin, 1992).

One of the members of the *Men's Group* (1983 R) who identifies as heterosexual relates an experience while on holiday in the Isle of Wight: 'I was wearing this shirt, sort of transparent with embroidery on it. I was walking by the sea feeling really good, really happy and these guys came up to me. I didn't really see them until they were right in front of me. They started to call me names – "bleeding HOMO", stuff like that. I thought I could reason with them. They ripped my shirt. It was like the fights at school when somebody's on the ground

and nobody tries to break it up ... I went crazy. I started to bite and kick. I ran for my life.' This sort of attack, motivated by fears of 'otherness' or of something unexpressed and frightening within the attackers themselves, causes physical and psychological injury, sometimes permanent paralysis, sometimes death. Among queer-bashing's victims are gay men, lesbians, TRANSVESTITES, TRANSSEXUALS, BISEXUALS and HETEROSEXUALS – anyone who appears to fit a stereotype.

Sometimes the law itself colludes in making the victim the villain. In CROWN COURT 'Meeting Place' (1978 T) a 19-year-old (Gerry Sundquist), accused of inflicting grievous bodily harm upon a middle-aged man, Leslie Simons (Derek Smith), claims that he had been fending off the man's unwelcome advances. The defence submits that 'individuals have the right to physically defend themselves against homosexual advances', and some of the witnesses display a willingness to condone violence as long as it is directed at 'queers'. The studio jury, after hearing the prosecution case which contended that the accused was looking for someone to bash that night and used the man's sexuality as an excuse, found the defendant guilty. He was sentenced to three months in a detention centre.

Sometimes the so-called Portsmouth Defence benefits the criminal greatly, as in the eponymous 1966 black comedy by lawyer Nemone Lethbridge. It all too convincingly followed the downward spiral of a mild-mannered milkman who has to undergo the humiliation of being falsely accused of homosexual assault by the villain who bashed him in the street. Through the indifference and incompetency of his lawyers and the prejudice that the Portsmouth Defence itself embodies, the victim is gradually transformed into a molesting monster. His job is lost, his children reject him, his neighbours jeer, while his attacker walks away free.

Generally queer-bashing is discussed in relation to violence against homosexuals (and people who 'look like' homosexuals) as it occurs on the streets, in parks or in people's homes, eg OPEN TO QUESTION (with Michael CASHMAN, 1988 T) and *Hate Crimes* (Aust 1992 T). However, it is also extremely prevalent in institutions like schools (*Truth or Dare* Aust 1992 V; *Attitude* 'Homophobia in Schools' Aust 1993 T) and prisons (*Wings and Landings* 1992 R).

Actor Felix Nobis, interviewed in the *Sydney Morning Herald Television Guide* (Aust 10–16.2.92), commented about his role as the doctor in G.P. 'Tests of Conscience' who is bashed twice, the second time fatally: 'When people read about a gay bashing, they inevitably feel distanced from it. Hopefully, through this episode, they will have a connection.'

Former prisoner John Williams in *Wings and Landings* (1992 R) said: 'The guy Robbie killed was gay. So many of the boys I've met have killed what threatened them most and thrown years of their own life down the drain.'

See also BULLYING; MURDERERS; MURDER VICTIMS; RAPE.

queer cinema 'American queer cinema has achieved critical mass. Encouraged by 25 years of gay activism made urgent by the AIDS crisis and a right-wing homophobic backlash, queer filmmakers have fought back through the production of images' (Amy Taubin, *Sight and Sound*, September 1992).

A manifestation on celluloid of the new queer consciousness, not closeted or apologetic, responding with energy and imagination to a changed social, sexual and political landscape two and a half decades on from gay liberation. Usually male, *avant garde*, violent and macho, with a tendency to put two fingers up to the POLITICALLY CORRECT, these films often deal with HIV/AIDS, murder and death, and involve people on the fringes of a minority culture.

Perhaps Gregg Araki's THE LIVING END (1992) best summarizes the ethos: beginning with a scrawled "Fuck the world" (the film's original title), its two HIV-positive heroes go on the road determined to grab life 'by the balls' in a world 'spiralling out of control'. Says its writer–director: 'The film has a real-in-your-face attitude ... it's not asking for acceptance ... it's about taking your life in your hands ... and [having] lots of great, interesting and unusual sex.'

Among the cornerstones of queer cinema are (from the US) MY OWN PRIVATE IDAHO, POISON, PARIS IS BURNING, TONGUES UNTIED, SWOON, the works of Sadie Benning; (from the UK) EDWARD II, *The Hours and the Times*, RELAX, NORTH OF VORTEX, CAUGHT LOOKING; (from New Zealand) A TASTE OF KIWI; (from Australia) NIGHT OUT, Resonance.

Among the influences are Jean COCTEAU, Kenneth Anger, Jack Smith, Andy WARHOL, rap music, Morrissey of the SMITHS, FASSBINDER – and Rosa VON PRAUNHEIM, who describes himself as 'very anti-academic, anti-theoretical' and has no time for 'sentimental shit about gays as poor little victims'.

Another mentor – and practitioner – of 'in your face' cinema, Derek JARMAN, greeted the new dawning during his introduction to a 1992 Channel 4 screening of *Relax* and *North of Vortex*: 'We've been led down the garden path of either/or ... The new queer cinema blurs the edges. For me, it's thrilling that a new generation of film-makers can be so matter of fact about their sexuality.'

Quentin Boy's name, principally associated with dumbclucks and those of perverse disposition redolent of daffodil buds and – post-1975 – of Quentin CRISP (born Dennis Pratt).

UK and France: Pauncefort Quentin (Noel HOWLETT 1960 T; Tony Bateman 1964 T; Alan MELVILLE 1969 T); Quentin Savory (Robert Sansom), author in STAMBOUL EXPRESS (1962 T); Uncle Quentin (Ronald Allen) in THE COMIC STRIP PRESENTS ... 'Five Go Mad in Dorset' and 'Five Go Mad on Mescalin' (1982–3); public school hero who never quite adjusted to the adult world: Quentin Niles (Martyn Stanbridge) in *Good and Bad at Games* (1983 T); Quentin (Jean-François Pichette),

DEAF mute in love with photo journalist Pierre Kurwenal in *Straight to the Heart* (1987 C); Quentin (Roger Lloyd Pack) in *Archer's Goon* (1992 T). There was a brief period in 1976 (after the second showing of THE NAKED CIVIL SERVANT) when children called each other Crisps or Quentins. There were occasional references on radio and TV to the symbol of all who are 'self-evident, self-professed effeminate homosexuals for all the world to see'.

US: A soldier called Texas (Robert Mitchum) is gently ribbed by his mates in *The Human Comedy* (1943 C) when he reveals his real first name: 'Bring up the rear, *Quentin*'; Quentin Barnaby (Chad Everett), pretty American fire investigator in *The Firefighters* (1970? C); Quentin Collins (David Selby) in *Dark Shadows* (1966–70 T); industrialist villain Quentin Hapsburg (Robert Goulet) in *The Naked Gun 2: The Smell of Fear* (1991 C).

The only female Quentin was the callow and restless sister (Joanne Woodward) in *The Sound and the Fury* (1959 C).

Querelle (West Germany 1982 C) A SAILOR variously brings sexual frustration, erotic fulfilment and death to various men (and one woman) while on shore leave, as well as facing up to his true nature.

W/D: Werner Rainer FASSBINDER from the novel *Querelle of Brest* by Jean GENET; 120 mins.

Is this, the director's final film, a deadly serious metaphor for oppression, repression and depression in Western society? Or is it a beautifully managed, artificial display of out-and-out lunacy? Best to opt for bad, mad, neurotically self-torturing, degrading, glutinously unreal. A bit like *Blind Date*. Buried somewhere underneath its tawdry grandiloquence and alienating MACHO posturing is a parable about a man whose life has been obsessed with having and getting, learning about being and becoming.

There is a distinct possibility that Fassbinder was inviting his audience to gaze upon a relatively lavish, semi-satiric 2-hour version of Tom of Finland and find amusement in the whole concept of hyper-masculinity with its grunted terms of affections, its zomboid romanticism, unfulfilled desires, quick bursts of violence, attraction to dominance–submission, and total anal–phallocentricity (which leaves Jeanne Moreau very much out in the cold). Then again ...

'Might have been called "A Guy in Every Port" ... gamy but slickly produced ... manages to induce boredom and giggles in equal measure' (*Leonard Maltin's Movie and Video Guide*).

Que Sera, Sera (Whatever Will Be, Will Be) This great jammy pastry (written by Jay Livingstone and Ray Evans) hinges on the whole question of whether the destinies of little boys and little girls are programmed genetically (or in the lap of the gods) or whether ambition, talent and environment play vital, contributing factors. All very light and frothy (girls hope to be 'pretty', boys 'handsome') especially in the ACADEMY AWARD-winning version sung by Doris DAY in *The Man Who Knew Too Much* (1956 C) which became the most requested record on *Housewives' Choice* (R) that year.

Regarded as kitsch at the time, 'Que Sera, Sera' is now charming balderdash and, therefore, perfect for the three queens of terror, the *Heathers* (1989 C). Sung over the opening scene by Syd Straw in an echo-chambered, tinkly version and over the end credits by Sly and the Family Stone with gospel soul accretions, the sentiments expressed have never sounded so hollow.

Looked at another way – through the ears of a little boy fascinated by his mother's clothes and make-up – the song becomes quite a profound nursery rhyme about dreams and expectations, leaving gender divisions undrawn. It was used in this spirit over the credits (boy watching mother in front of her mirror) in *Just Like a Woman* (1992 C) and in OUT's look at whether homosexuality is inherent or environmental in 'Gay Sera, Sera' (1992 T).

Question de Temps (Fr 1979 T) A social and geographical cross-section of French homosexuals of all ages, with shots of gay gatherings in Paris and Marseilles. A groundbreaker from France's 'minority' television channel: the kind of document that had become a staple on British screens.

D: Dominique Fernandez and Jean Le Bitou for Antenne 2; 20.8.79; 60 mins.

A Question of Attribution (UK 1991 T) The months leading up to Anthony BLUNT's public exposure, disgrace and exile.

W: Alan BENNETT; P: Innes LLOYD; D: John SCHLESINGER; 20.10.91; BBC2; 70 mins.

The subtle structure, encapsulated in the title, deals with the simultaneous uncovering of one or even two figures in the murky depths, underneath varnishes and overlays, of a famous painting and the revelation that the art historian and administrator of the Queen's art collection had been one of the most senior spies for the Soviet Union. Painstaking, skilful but rather cold and prissy – like its subject. Prunella Scales dominates in her 10-minute turn as Her Maj, all seeing, all knowing under the twittering, stagey exterior.

A Question of Love (US 1978 T) The ex-husband of nurse Linda Ray Guettner (Gena Rowlands) sues for custody of their youngest SON. With difficulty she finds a lawyer, risks losing her job and faces leering questions in court. Her lover Barbara Moreland (Jane Alexander) sticks by her.

W: William Blinn; P: William Blinn and Jerry Thorpe; D: Jerry Thorpe; 26.11.78; ABC; 100 mins.

Based on the real-life ordeal of Mary Jo Risher, Rowlands plays her with blazing sincerity (matched by Alexander), but her carefree glamour and seeming absence of any physicality in her relationship with her lover raise a question of credibility. Her problem is too soaped up to be dramatically satisfying.

'There are several strong reasons for thinking adults to watch ... it is power-ful. It is suspenseful, it is sensitive. It is thought provoking. Smartly cast, splendidly acted and slickly directed' (*Denver Post*).

quiche eaters A 1980s version of milksops. Real men don't eat quiche according to Bruce Feirstein's 1982 book. Richard Hawley in OUT 'Guess Who's Coming to Dinner?' (1991 T) confirmed its popularity though *he* didn't serve it to his guests. Quiche eaters were linked to SHIRT LIFTERS by H. G. Nelson (Aust 1991 R).

Quick, Diana (1946–) English actress, vividly beautiful with delicate but impassioned quality which has been seen (and increasingly simply heard) to great effect as Sebastian's sister whom Charles also loves in BRIDESHEAD REVISITED (1981 T); Marian HALCOMBE in *The Woman in White* (1982 T); Monica/Gisela in SILENT WING (1984 R); Harriet in THE OTHER OTHER WOMAN (1985 T); Anna in *Nineteen Nineteen* (1985 C), the socialist free thinker whose rejection of Sophie causes her to attempt SUICIDE. Some of her other work is listed below.

R: Helena in *A Midsummer Night's Dream* (1983); country wife Pamela in *Secrets, Beautiful Lies* (1986); Rosa (after Rosa Luxemburg), the *avant-garde* flautist who is having a baby as a statement that there is a future in *The Awful Insulation of Rage* (1987); Princess Aouda in *Around the World in 80 Days* (1991); Augusta in *Gondal* (1992); reader of *The Proper Respect* by Isabel Allende (1992).

T: Lenio in *Christ Recrucified* (1969); the heroine in *The Three Hostages* (1978); the soprano who is murdered in *The Phantom of the Opera* (1983); aviatrix, horsetrainer and writer Beryl Markham in *World without Walls* (1985, narration only); the poet Tullia in *Cariani and the Courtesans* (1987); panellist on the odd *Call My Bluff* (1987); a lady of fashion in *Clarissa* (1991); Madam in *The Orchid House* (1991).

The gracefully controlled intensity of her radio and television work has so far not been matched by her film career which began with *Nicholas and Alexandra* (1971) and includes *A Private Enterprise* (1971); *The Odd Job* (1978, as the target of Graham CHAPMAN's assassination plot); *The Duellists* (1978); *The Big Sleep* (1978); *Ordeal by Innocence* (1985); *Wilt* (1990).

Quilley, Denis (1927–   ) English actor with resonant voice and aquiline nose who can be the determined square-jawed symbol of law (*The Desperate People* 1963 T; *The Interrogation of John* 1987 T) or muted civility (*Murder on the Orient Express* 1974 C; EVIL UNDER THE SUN 1982 C) or dashing heroism (*Cage Me a Peacock* 1954 R; Bassanio in *The Merchant of Venice* 1955 R) or different kinds of gayness (one of the Shewin teenagers in A VERY GREAT MAN INDEED 1953 R; Walt WHITMAN in THE WOUND DRESSER 1986 R; the thunderously camp Teri Dennis in PRIVATES ON PARADE 1982 C).

The Quilt aka the AIDS Memorial Project Quilt. Woven, stencilled, appliquéd, embroidered, painted panels, a tribute to the thousands who have died from AIDS-related causes created by lovers, friends, relatives. Inaugurated on 11 October 1987 in Washington and toured round the US. Originally the size of two football fields, it is now many times larger – while continuing to represent only a small proportion of the people who have succumbed to AIDS. A similar creation exists in Australia but, so far, not in the UK.

Said Tony WHITEHEAD in OUT ON TUESDAY 'A Matter of Life and Death' (1990 T): 'A homage to the past and also a foundation for the future. We haven't found ways in this country of working out in real tangible terms what is happening and what is going to get worse in the coming years.'

Also: *The Inaugural Display of the Names Project Quilt* (1988 C/V); *International AIDS Day* (1988 T); COMMON THREADS: STORIES FROM THE QUILT (1989 C/T); IN MEMORIAM (John Corigliano's Symphony No. 1, 1991 R).

quota Armistead Maupin was told not to exceed one third of gay characters in his TALES OF THE CITY newspaper articles (ARENA 1992 T). When Warners bought the movie rights, he was repeatedly advised to play down the gays until, prior to filming, he was instructed to remove them altogether. Most films and plays containing more than a couple of main characters combine homos and heteros in usually unequal proportions. Very few fully enter into a world which, at various times and to different degrees, is almost entirely composed of people with compatible sexualities.

Mainstream works which exceeded the invisible quota of one or two homosexuals to nine or ten heterosexuals include *Echo de Paris* (1960 R, about Oscar WILDE and his friends); VICTIM (1961 C, 7 hetero characters vs 14 queers); LONESOME COWBOYS (1968 C, except for Viva); FLESH (1968 C, except for Joe's girlfriend), THE KILLING OF SISTER GEORGE (1968 C, with the possible exception of the bondage prostitute); possibly PERFORMANCE (1970 C) before it was cut; THE BOYS IN THE BAND (1970 C, except the surprise guest); SOME OF MY BEST FRIENDS ARE ... (1971 C, except for a number of female characters and some of the bar's staff and owners); NOW SHE LAUGHS, NOW SHE CRIES (1975 R, except the heroine's supposedly liberal friend); FOX AND HIS FRIENDS (1975 C, except for the hero's friend and his lover's father); OUTRAGEOUS! (1977 C, except Robin's friend and flatmate and her boyfriend); NIGHTHAWKS (1978 C, except the woman teacher); ONLY CONNECT (1979 T); COMING OUT (1979 T, except the magazine editor, the secretary and the priest's mother); YOU'RE NOT WATCHING ME, MUMMY (1980 T, except the central character and her fellow actress); TAXI ZUM KLO (1981 C, except a couple of friends); QUERELLE (1982 C, except the café owner's wife); THE HEART EXPOSED (1986 C/T, except the wife and her lover); A DEATH IN THE FAMILY (1986 C, except the dying man's parents, brother and sister-in-law); LAW OF DESIRE (1987

C, except the mother and the two policemen); TORCH SONG TRILOGY (1988 C, except the mother and the lover's wife); LONGTIME COMPANION (1990 C, except the sister); ABSOLUTE HELL! (1991 T, except the drinking club manageress and one or two of her clients); THE LOST LANGUAGE OF CRANES (1992 T, except the mother, and the flatmate – who was lesbian in the book).

When reviewing the early drafts of the script for *Victim*, the British Board of Film Censors, in addition to unease over the violence and one 'vindictive outburst against homosexuals', complained about the over-prevalence of homosexuals.

Rachel and the Roarettes (UK 1985 T) Rachel Roaring Girl (Josie Lawrence), bestriding three centuries with her band of women, confronting love and danger'. In the 18th she's a dashing, iron-nerved highwaywoman – in love with a corrupt judge's daughter; in the 20th she's a 'biker Boadicea' – teaching a bride-to-be the language of liberation (and how to ride a Harley Davidson 125).

W: Jude Alderson; P: Roger Gregory; D: Rob Walker; BBC1; 65 mins.

The first lesbian musical, a colourful and bustling attempt to 'remove women from the cramped deceiving pages of history', is an unhappy misfire. Arch and self-conscious, plagued with tinny songs, it is, however, deeply blessed with a splendid authoritative lead performance. Awaiting the noose, the 18th-century Rachel upbraids her persecutor, a corrupt judge, in fine style: 'I have freedom that you envy. Strength that you despise. And love that you deny. Why, sir, you would have women estranged from their true feelings and force them to play out some stale and shallow seesaw of a marriage?'

racism/racists A hellishly difficult area within whose parameters lie personal ignorance, institutionalized prejudice, legal bumbling, jealousy, envy, economic paralysis, greed, sexual mythology. Among the films which have tackled the subject: *Imitation of Life* (1934 & 1959); *Home of the Brave* (1949); *Intruder in the Dust* (1949); *Pinky* (1949); *Sayonara* (1957); *The Defiant Ones* (1958); *Sapphire* (1959); *I Passed for White* (1960); *Flame in the Streets* (1961, based on the 1959 TV play *Hot Summer Night*); WEST SIDE STORY (1961); *Black Like Me* (1964); *Guess Who's Coming to Dinner?* (1967); *Roots* (1977) and *Roots II* (1979); *The Sailor's Return* (1978); THE COLOR PURPLE (1985); *Do the Right Thing* (1989).

Among the UK television documentaries that have confronted this issue: PANORAMA 'Colour Prejudice' (1958: in the wake of the Notting Hill riots); MEETING POINT 'I Was a Stranger' (1958: 'What really governs our attitudes towards the coloured man? How can prejudice be overcome?' – synopsis); THE NATURE OF PREJUDICE (1968); *Not All Black and White* (1986: Jill Cochrane on the nature of racism); HORIZON 'Are You a Racist?' (1987); WITHOUT WALLS 'I Want Your Sex' (1991: sexual stereo typing of black men and women); *Black and White in Colour* (1992: Afro-Caribbean actors on television since the 1930s to the present). Among US TV documentaries: DONAHUE 'Parents Who Bring Up Their Children to be Racists' (1990); *The Oprah* WINFREY *Show* 'Racism in the 1990s' (including 'Too Little, Too Late' 1992 – the treatment of NORTH AMERICAN INDIANS since the 18th century and their continuing fight for equality, and 'Are We All Racist? Blue Eyes v Brown Eyes' – an experiment involving the studio audience, which was segregated into 'superior' brown eyes and 'inferior' blue eyes, with parallels briefly drawn between racial discrimination and HOMOPHOBIA).

The most prominent fictional gay racist was Johnny (Daniel Day-Lewis) in MY BEAUTIFUL LAUNDRETTE (1985 C/T) who discovers that love can drill through the hardest of preconceptions.

'In good old homophobic and racist America ... there are Republican gays and there are Southern Baptist gays ... and, yes, there are racist gays' (Phil Donahue on DONAHUE 'Interracial Gay Couples' 1992 T).

'This is the '90s and we should stop picking on the gays and lesbians, and the blacks and the whites. It's about time everyone started treating everyone equally. We should think of people equally': Young woman in the audience of DONAHUE 'Boycott Battles: Group Fighting for Their Rights in Colorado' (1993 T).

See also ABORIGINALS; BLACK GAY MEN; BLACK LESBIANS; DISABLED PEOPLE; JEWS; SKINHEADS.

radical queer *See* MILITANT HOMOSEXUAL.

radio The subject of homosexuality

raised in WOMAN'S HOUR (1946–); ANY QUESTIONS? (1948–); ROUND THE HORNE (1965–9); THE DALES (1967); WAGGONERS' WALK (1969–80); *File on 4* (1977–); WEEK ENDING (1972–); *The Locker Room* (1992–); A SUNDAY OUTING (1993). Also in plays like EDWARD II (1930); ROPE (1932); DANGEROUS CORNER (1945); CHILDREN IN UNIFORM (1946); THE GREEN BAY TREE (1946); HUIS CLOS (1946); THE INTERNED (1953); A HEDGE, BACKWARDS (1956); *The Waste Disposal Unit* (1964); THE RUFFIAN ON THE STAIR (1964); CRIES FROM CASEMENT (1973); MR LUBY'S FEAR OF HEAVEN (1976); SILENT WING (1984); TROUPERS (1988); OCTOBER SCARS THE SKIN (1989); A BIT OF BERLIN (1992).

The glories of radio have been briefly summoned up in Terence DAVIES' *Distant Voices, Still Lives* (*Beyond Our Ken* etc) and *The Long Day Closes* (*Ray's a Laugh*), *Lift Up Your Hearts*); and the intricacies (and absurdities) of radio production have played a major role in the plots of:

UK: *Death at Broadcasting House* (1934 C); HANCOCK'S HALF HOUR 'The Bowmans' (1961 T); *Ecoute Voir* (1978 C); ONLY CONNECT (1979 T); AGONY (1979–81), *Shoestring* (1979–80 T); *City Sugar* (1980 T); *Who Shot Ada Tansey?* (1983 R); *Radio Pictures* (1985 T); *Static* (1987 R); A HORSE CALLED GERTRUDE STEIN (1990 R); YOUNG SOUL REBELS (1991 C); *Open Mike* (1992 R).

US: *Letter to Three Wives* (1949 C); THE TWILIGHT ZONE 'Static' (1963); *Play Misty for Me* (1972 C); *Citizens Band/Handle with Care* (1977 C); *Radio Days* (1987 C); *Do the Right Thing* (1989 C); NORTH OF VORTEX (1991 T); *RSVP* (1991 T).

The Rainbow (UK 1988 T; 1989 C)
An uncompromising young woman's journey through narrow corridors of class, religion and sexuality. Ursula Brangwen's outer restlessness and inner turmoil lead her to the brink of madness.
T: W: Anne Devlin; P: Chris Parr; D:

Stuart Burge; 4.12.88; BBC1; 3 parts; 60 mins each.
C: W/P/D: Ken Russell; 112 mins.

Two adaptations of D. H. LAWRENCE's saga of three women across 50 years which necessarily cut large sections and – in the television version – employed memory shifts, dream sequences, the supernatural and stylized colour to convey the Brangwen generations, and the complexity of an England moving fully into an industrial society. The main focus fell upon Ursula Brangwen (Sammi Davis C; Imogen Stubbs T) and her relationships with her teacher Winifred Inger (Amanda Donohoe C; Kate Buffery T) and with the young army officer Anton Skrebensky (Paul McGann C; Martin Wenner T).

Originally written as the first part of the later novel WOMEN IN LOVE and suppressed shortly after its publication in 1915, Anne Devlin's vision is truer to the 1980s than to Lawrence's ambiguous view of women, especially in the 2nd episode ('Widening the Circle') which deals with Ursula and Winifred (the relevant chapter in the book is called 'Shame'). 'I don't regard lesbianism as shameful,' the adaptor told *Radio Times* (3–9.12.86), and I've treated the relationship as something joyful.' Anne Devlin went on to say: 'The present society has its roots in the 19th century and there's been a return to some of its narrower values. In an age of new puritanism there are severe and serious consequences for a country which tries to legislate for the emotional life of its community. I see *The Rainbow* as a timely reminder of how much we need that freedom.'

Lawrence's bold and evocative novel also gives Ken Russell the slip, and he settles for a period romance which in some ways is preferable to Devlin's – which often threatens to plunge into parody of both Lawrentian *angst* and television North Country family saga (an attention to detail that becomes cloying, a certain feeling of constraint and artificiality, everything too pressed and dry-cleaned). The result is richly coloured but dramatically pallid with Ursula cutting a frequently absurd figure. The outcome of the attraction between Ursula and Winifred is particularly unconvincing in a story in which too many things remain hidden and unconfronted.

'I came into your bed last night because that was where I wanted to be. And that is where I want to be because my desire for you and your company is greater than my desire for any living thing on this planet. But I know these things are limited,' said Winifred in the television version.

Randall, Tony [Leonard Rosenberg] (1920–) American actor, a specialist in manic wrigglers whose passive demeanours become grimmer, nervous tics more pronounced and voices more arching as the plots progress. Though often married, his characters are sometimes crypto-gay as was brilliantly demonstrated in *Rock Hudson's Home Movies* (1991 V). His Sidney Shorr was desexed between TV movie and TV series, but he was allowed to get his teeth into a juicy cameo as a gay entertainer tortured by the NAZIS in *Hitler's SS: Portrait in Evil* (1985 C/T).

C: *Oh Men! Oh Women!* (1957); title role in *Will Success Spoil Rock Hunter?/Oh! for a Man* (1957); Rock HUDSON's best buddy in *Pillow Talk* (1959; also in *Lover Come Back* 1961 and *Send Me No Flowers* 1964); billionaire's aide in *Let's Make Love* (1960); title role in *Seven Faces of Dr Lao* (1965); Poirot in *The Alphabet Murders* (1966); *King of Comedy* (1983); etc.

T: Mac in *One Man's Family* (1949–52); English teacher Harvey Weskitt in *Mr Peepers* (1952–5); starred in *Philco Television Playhouse* 'A Little Something in Reserve' (1953); guest villain in *Captain Video* (*c* 1955); *Holiday in Las Vegas* (1957); *Four for Tonight* (with Beatrice Lillie, Tammy Grimes and Cyril RITCHARD, 1960); guest host *Hippodrome* (1966); Felix Unger in *The Odd Couple* 1970–4); Rudi in *Here's Lucy* 'The Mountaineer' (1971); *The Sonny and Cher Comedy Hour* (1972); widowed judge Walter Franklin in *The Tony Ran-*

dall Show (1976–8); SIDNEY SHORR: A GIRL'S BEST FRIEND (1981 and in *Love, Sidney* 1981–3); Putzi in *Hitler's SS: Portrait in Evil* (1985 C/T); etc.

rape Still very much regarded as part of women's oppression and, until quite recently (BROOKSIDE 1987 T and EAST-ENDERS 1988 T) presented as a single action (often titilatingly so) with little examination of the after-effects: in mainly American films like *Anatomy of a Murder* (1959); *Town without Pity* (1961); *Two Women* (1961); *The Chapman Report* (1962); *Cape Fear* (1962); TELL ME THAT YOU LOVE ME, JUNIE MOON (1970); *A Clockwork Orange* (1971); *Straw Dogs* (1971).

The situation affecting men is now only beginning to surface. Until recently its depiction had been limited to attacks within all-male institutions or by male authority figures or uncivilized peoples, and called 'forcible sodomy', or 'child molestation' or 'homosexual rape': EXODUS (1960 C); LAWRENCE OF ARABIA (1962 C); THE CONNOISSEUR (1966 T); FORTUNE AND MEN'S EYES (1971 C); DELIVERANCE (1972 C); THE GLASS HOUSE (1972 T); MARCUS WELBY 'The Outrage' (1975 T); *The Moneychangers* (1976 T); *Scum* (1980 C); *Walter* (1982 T); THE RAPE OF RICHARD BECK (1985 T); THE PRINCE OF TIDES (1991 C); *Castle of the Star* (1992 R), about T. E. Lawrence); CASUALTY 'Child's Play' (1993 T). Most of these acts of violence involved the humiliation of heterosexual men and boys by implicitly or explicitly gay ones. A much more widespread difficult and complex situation began to emerge in the mid-1980s, reflected in the programmes like OPEN SPACE '*Rape*' (1984 T) and *Breaking the Silence: The Untold Story of Male Rape* (1986 T).

In *Male Rape* (1991 T) a boy speaks of being repeatedly assaulted by his stepfather; a teenager relives the experience of being raped on his way home; a prisoner describes the almost daily occurrence of being sexually used by fellow inmates. The documentary revealed that rape was 'probably the easiest crime to get away with in Britain because the victim won't report the crime'. (Rape of a male person is not technically a crime under British law.) A woman PSYCHIATRIST bluntly stated what had been obliterated or distorted for years: 'The truth is that ... very many of the men who attack the victims are heterosexual and the victims can be homosexual or heterosexual ... this is a violent, brutal attack ... [expressing] anger, aggression and power.'

Taking part were Richie McMullen and Martin Dockrell, who in 1986 had set up Survivors, a male rape victim self-help group, after a 2-part feature in *Capital Gay* first aired the subject. (In 1990 an estimated 60,000 sexual assaults on males took place in the London area alone.) They and other speakers emphasized the shame and humiliation of the act itself and its reliving in the mind for years afterwards: 'The fact that you have been used as a sexual object by another man demeans your male conditioning. It puts you on the level of a vessel, of a done to rather than a doer' and 'Much of the problem is how we see ourselves as men.'

The spectacle of a woman raping another woman is rarely seen outside of steamy prison sagas (eg a pack rape with a broom handle in *Born Innocent* 1974 T), but did occur in *Windows* (1980 C) where Andrea (Elizabeth Ashley) got her kicks by employing a man to assault the woman she desired, and in PORTRAIT OF A MARRIAGE (1990 T) with an out-of-control Vita SACKVILLE-WEST (Janet McTeer) savaging Violet TREFUSIS (Cathryn Harrison). The rape of a man by a woman has been postulated only for its more erotic elements: warder Steve Faulkner attacked (offscreen) in PRISONER/PRISONER: CELL BLOCK H (1982 T) and Hildy (Jennifer Jason Leigh) had her way with the boyfriend of the woman she yearns to be in *Single White Female* (1992 C).

The Rape of Richard Beck (US 1985 T) Divorced, insensitive policeman (Richard Crenna) is raped by cop-hating PUNK (Nicholas Worth), which changes his cut and dried, hard-hearted view of (female) victims of such crimes. 'It takes a brutal rape to make a decent man of Richard Beck' (publicity).

W: James G. Hirsch; P: Robert Papazian; D: Karen Arthur; ABC; 104 mins.

'He kept screaming at me and yankin' my hair .. he kept telling me to say how much I wanted it.' In the movie's most eviscerating scene Beck, watched by two embarrassed young cops, clutches at his shoes, whimpers and hunches up under a blanket. Once the bruises fade, the trauma remains fairly superficial, squaring off in a fight between Beck and a FEMINIST (Meredith Baxter Birney) rather than Beck confronting other men with his experience. In this respect, the story was not so much about the effects of rape on a human being but how a man comes to better understand what a woman undergoes in such circumstances. Richard Crenna won an Emmy for his performance: 'the most demanding, yet rewarding, I've ever played.'

Raphael, Frederic (1931–) English writer of wit and precision who has a special knack for portraying the boorish and self-centred, but his depiction of homosexuality is often heavy-handed: *Nothing But the Best* (1964 C); DARLING (1965 C); *Two for the Road* (1967 C); THE GLITTERING PRIZES (1976 T); *School Play* (1979 T); *The Best of Friends* (1980 T); *Byron: A Personal Tour* (1981 T); *Death in Trieste* (1981 R); RICHARD'S THINGS (1981 C/T); *Oxbridge Blues* (1984 T). Among his adaptations: CAPOTE's *Answered Prayers* (1961 T); Iris MURDOCH's *A Severed Head* (1971 C); Geoffrey Household's *Rogue Male*. On DESERT ISLAND DISCS (1981 R).

Rat A water-rat, known as 'Ratty', the LONGTIME COMPANION of Mole in *The Wind in the Willows*, based (according to *The Oxford Companion to Children's Literature*, 1984) partly on its author Kenneth Grahame ('his fondness for male company, good food and country rambles') and partly on his friends Frederick Furnivall and Edward Atkinson. The 1931 edition ends with an E. H. Shepard illustration of Mole and Ratty going off to bed in nightshirt and pyjamas respectively. Ratty was played by Andrew Osborn (1949 T), by David MARCH (1961 R) and by Peter SALLIS in the puppet series *Oh, Mr Toad* aka *The Wind in the Willows* (1988 T).

Rat's partner is Mole 'the sleek, sinuous, full-bodied' dressed in a black velvet smoking jacket, a trifle pettish ... looking for 'a bijou riverside residence ... remote from noise and dust'. Theirs is probably the fastest, most ecstatic courtship and cohabitation of two adult male mammals in the history of literature. Who could resist Rat's 'coldtongue-coldhamcoldbeefpickledgherkins-saladfrenchrollscresssandwigespotted-meatgingerbeerlemonadesodawater–'?

Ratty's much quoted saying is even more languorous in its original form: 'Believe me, my young friend, there is nothing – absolutely nothing – half so much worth doing as simply messing about in boats.' He went on dreamily: 'Simply messing, messing – about in boats, messing –' This was a pastime other same-sex couples have enjoyed: Charles (Jeremy Irons) and Sebastian (Anthony Andrews) in BRIDESHEAD REVISITED (1981 T); Guy (Rupert Everett) and James (Cary Elwes) in ANOTHER COUNTRY (1984 C); Vera (Cheryl Campbell) and Winifred (Joanna McCallum) in TESTAMENT OF YOUTH (1979 T); Sophia (Sara Kestelman) and Ursula (Gillian Barge) in *The Walls of Jericho* (1981 T); Ursula (Imogen Stubbs) and Winifred (Kate Buffery) in THE RAINBOW (1988 T).

rats Heterosexual ones irrevocably turned queer, according to Dr Dörner in HORIZON 'The Fight to Be Male' (1979 T) and, in 'light-hearted vein', Dr Glenn Wilson used some white mice to show normal sexual behaviour in DON'T MISS WAX (1989 T), dropping some pearls about hormonal changes late in pregnancy leading to homosexuality. Love between man and rat: in *Willard* (1972) and *Ben* (1973, which gave rise to Michael Jackson's serenade to a rodent).

Rattigan, Sir Terence (1911–77) English playwright and screenwriter whose scrupulous craftsmanship led him to become one of the pre-eminent men of the theatre during the 1940s and 1950s; the only one, apart from Noel COWARD, to be knighted. A humanistic realist, he dealt with people looking life in the face but beset by sexual drives and frustrations, often caused by emotional concealment. His reputation sank badly during the later 1950s and the 1960s – 'Oh ducky, it's pure Rattigan,' squeals Sandy in ROUND THE HORNE 'Rentachap' in 1965 – but he is now viewed both as a superb technician and as a true voice, quietly raging against human frailty and society's pigheadedness. His confronting *After the Dance*, unperformed since 1939, was produced on television in 1992.

C: uncredited scripts pre-1938; *French without Tears* (1939); *Quiet Wedding* (1940); *The Day Will Dawn* (1942); *Uncensored* (with Wolfgang Wilhelm and Rodney ACKLAND, 1942); *English without Tears* (1944); *Journey Together* (1945); *The Way to the Stars* (1945); *Brighton Rock* (with Graham Greene, 1947); *While the Sun Shines* (with Anatole De Grunwald, 1947); *Bond Street* (with De Grunwald and Ackland, 1948); *The Winslow Boy* (with De Grunwald, 1948); *The Sound Barrier* (1953); *The Final Test* (1953); *The Man Who Loved Redheads* (from *Who is Sylvia?* 1955); *The Deep Blue Sea* (1955); *The Prince and the Showgirl* (from *The Sleeping Prince*, 1957); *Separate Tables* (1958); 'Lawrence of Arabia' (project only 1958); *The VIPs* (1963); *The Yellow Rolls Royce* (1964); *Goodbye Mr Chips* (1969); *Bequest to the Nation* (1973).

R: *Flare Path* (1944); *The Deep Blue Sea* (1957); *The Browning Version* (1957 & 1982); VARIATION ON A THEME (1961 & 1969); *Separate Tables* (1965); *Ross* (1965 & 1981); etc. There was a season of his plays in 1957.

T: *The Final Test* (1951); *Harlequinade* (1953); *The Deep Blue Sea* (1954); *The Browning Version* (1958 & 1985); *Adventure Story* (1960); *The Winslow Boy* (1961, 1976 & 1989); *Ninety Years On*

(1962 & 1964); *Heart to Heart* (1962); *Nelson – A Portrait in Miniature* (1966); *All on Her Own* (1968); *Ross* (1970); *Man and Boy* (1971); *High Summer* (1972); 'NIJINSKY' (project only, 1973); *In Praise of Love* 1976); *Separate Tables* (1983); etc.

Rattigan's Theatre, 'Portrait of a playwright' (1976 R, in which David RUDKIN praised his 'existential bleakness and irresolvable carnal solitude'); *Sir Terence Rattigan* (1977 T).

Ravel, Maurice (1975–1937) French composer, pianist and conductor whose very secret sexual life was hinted at in the documentary *Ravel* aka *Maurice Ravel* (1988 T) and, more explicitly, in the play *An Afternoon with Ravel* (John Church 1987 R). He was also played by Andy Rashleigh in *Memoirs of an Amnesiac Remembered* (about Eric Satie, 1989 R) and he was also seen briefly in NIGHT AND DAY (1946 C). His *Rhapsodie Espagnole* was heard in the closing minutes of *Fire in the Blood* (1992 T) over shots of two men with their arms round each other against a burning MICHELANGELO'S DAVID and his String Quartet in F minor was the basis of the music for *The Camomile Lawn* (1992 T).

'There is too little evidence for an adequate picture of his sexual relationships to be formed, although one cannot doubt that their nature would be relatable to, and hence liable to shed light on, other instances of self-expression: the music. However, where an overzealous commentator has been compelled to eke out the slender direct evidence with assumptions deduced from the works, these deductions, in themselves incapable of fresh illumination of the music, fail to be of interest' (G. W. Hopkins in *The New Grove Dictionary of Music and Musicians*, 1980, probably alluding to rumours that Ravel was involved in ménage à trois with composer Manuel De Falla and pianist Ricardo Viñes).

Ravel's Bolero One of the most popular classical 'bon-bons', greatly boosted by the Dudley Moore movie, always appropriated by heterosexuals – although it was more likely a paean to wild, writhing, climactic male–male sex.

A joyful celebration of the present tense, a mixture of music, dance and erotica. Wave after wave of the same theme repeated 80 times, inducing a trance-like state in common with Mike Oldfield's *Tubular Bells* and Henryk Gorecki's Symphony No. 3 ('Symphony of Sorrowful Songs'). Written for a ballet in 1928, it provided the exciting and sensual climax to a 1934 film of the same name: played as accompaniment to a speciality dance by George Raft and Carole Lombard, ending with Raft's death by stabbing. It was one of the first modern works to be transmitted in Britain (by the BBC Television Orchestra in 1937); was interpreted by a 14-minute Australian film, *Bolero* (1967); was played, danced and sung in front of the Eiffel Tower in *Les Uns et les Autres* (aka *The Ins and the Outs/Bolero* 1981); was used in an attempt to make mainstream porn by Bo and John Derek post-10 in *Bolero* (1984 C); helped Torvill and Dean rejuvenate ice skating at the 1984 Winter Olympics; was used as background music to the story of Jesus Christ's second coming in *The Return* (1992 C); etc.

It wasn't until 1991 that the work returned to what was most likely its true wellspring – as a rousing anthem of love, laughter and 'Pride' on the march through parts of central London in OUT (T), an extraordinary explosion of power and passion involving thousands and thousands and *thousands* of laughing, smiling, affectionate, peaceable lesbians and gay men enjoying a Saturday afternoon in the sun.

The work was dissected by members of an orchestra in KALEIDOSCOPE 'Tom-ticketatom' (1987 R) and in *Workshop* 'Mirrors: Reflections on Maurice Ravel' (1987 T) by pianist Paul Crossley who 'digs beneath the brilliant surface of Ravel's music to reveal one of this century's most troubled and haunting musical personalities ... a sophisticated artist with a child's heart' (*Radio Times*).

Raven, Simon (1927–) English novelist and playwright, master of the beguil-
ingly picaresque. He is most celebrated
for *Alms for Oblivion*, a 10-novel
sequence beginning with *The Rich Pay
Late* (1964) and completed by *The Survivors* (1976), with an autobiographical
gay main character. Many of his original
television plays were set within men-
only enclaves (school, army, college).
Since the 1970s he has limited himself
to adaptations.

R: *A Present from Venice* (about dugs,
1961); *A Friend in Need* (1962); *Panther
Larkin* (1964); *Salvation Island* (1972).

T: *Royal Foundation* (début, 1961);
Loser Pays All (1961); *the Move Up
Country* (1961); *The Scapegoat* (1964);
*Sir Jocelyn, the Minister Would Like a
Word* (1965); *The Pallisers* (1975);
Edward and Mrs Simpson (1978); *Love in
a Cold Climate* (1980); *The Blackheath
Poisonings* (1992); etc.

Profile (Aust 1968 R); *Line Up* (talking
to Tony Bilbow, 1970 T); *Boys Will Be
Boys* (a 60th birthday appreciation, 1987
R); *Bookshelf* (on his autobiography
Memoirs of a Private Nuisance to Nigel
Forde, 1991 R).

Ray, Johnnie (1927–90) American
singer renowned for his 'Cry', and similar outbursts of unmanly emotion,
during the 1950s. Spoofed in A VERY
GREAT MAN INDEED (1953 & 1961 R;
with Denis QUILLEY as Owen Shewin
singing 'Baby, Don't Hurt My Heart,
Baby', ending with 'Am I wet or am I
wet?') and in *As Long as They're Happy*
(1955 C, with Jerry Wayne as Bobby).
Some television appearances, as well as
playing Steve, the priest son of Ethel
Merman and Dan Dailey, in *There's No
Business Like Show Business* (1954 C).

Rayner, Claire (1936–) Capacious
radio and television counsellor, a former
nurse, also a successful novelist. An
embodiment of enthusiastic tolerance
and liberalism: *Claire Rayner's Casebook*
(1983–5 T) looked at BEREAVEMENT,
TRANSVESTITES and TRANSSEXUALS;
Crossing Over (1979 R); *Living with ...
Homosexuality* (1991 & 1992 R)
considers the different problems faced
by gay people and their families, and
Rayner talks to parents of lesbian and
gay children and to homosexuals themselves. Interviewed as one of *Sob Sisters*
(1972 R, when she was an 'agony aunt'
on *Petticoat* magazine, and was IN THE
PSYCHIATRIST'S CHAIR (1988 R).

Ray's Male Heterosexual Dance Hall
(US 1987 C) Sam Logan (Boyd
Gaines) gets to meet the right people in
this all-male mercantile meat market
that is 100 per cent heterosexual. Top
executives invite one another onto the
floor in the same way as they manipulate
a boardroom or sales pitch, shamelessly
currying favour as they whirl around to
the strains of 'OVER THE RAINBOW',
'September Song', 'It Happened In
Monterey' and 'Ramona'.

W/D: Bryan Gordon; 25 mins.

The discomfort, the euphoria, the fast
footwork, the jockeying for attention,
equally relevant to men in a sexual setting as to those comingling for business
purposes. They're all here: the wall-
flowers, the bores, the prick teasers and
the guy everybody wants to share the
smoochiest dance with under the spotlight – in this case Dick Tratten (Lyman
Ward). A film like no other: mellow,
surefooted, satirically lyrical and –
though first impressions might suggest
differently – absolutely heterosexual.

read my lips George Bush's mouthed
whisper promising 'No new taxes' prior
to his election as US President in 1988.
This phrase appears on Fuzzy's T-shirt
(also decorated with two men kissing)
worn in the beach reunion scene of
LONGTIME COMPANION (1990 C), as an
ironic comment on Bush's indifference
to AIDS. However, Bush didn't origi-
nate it: 'Read my lips,' hisses Richard
Gere with cocky assurance to the car
salesman in *Breathless* (1983 C). To
which the man replies: 'Read *my* lips, fat
arse. I could have sold that car to 50
other guys.'

Read My Lips was the title of Jimmy
SOMERVILLE'S 1990 album which

included a song of the same name sub-titled 'Enough is Enough':

> Read my lips
> Money is what we need not complacency
> ...'

Performed by him in Berlin in *Red Hot + Dance* (1991 T), it was played over the credits of VOICES FROM THE FRONT (1991 C/T).

Most recently used by Caroline (Sara Coward) in THE ARCHERS (1992 R), and by Jon (Craig Gilmore) to Luke (Mike Dytil) after he has beaten a man over the head with a transistor radio – 'Read my lips, *dude*: get the fuck out of here' – in THE LIVING END (1992 C), which has a number of anti-Bush references.

'real' man This elusive concept, the ab-solutely 100 per cent male: 'I've seen lots of men but I've never seen a real one,' declares male-identified business-woman Alison Drake (Ruth Chatterton) as she searches for those strong arms which will enfold her in *Female* (1933 C); Mother (Jessie Royce Landis) in *To Catch a Thief* (1955 C) encourages Francie (Grace Kelly) to see more of John (Cary GRANT), unaware that he is a notorious cat burglar: 'he's a real man; not one of those milksops you usually take up with ... the first man who wouldn't roll over for you', Helen (Susan Hayward) proudly tells Neely (Patty Duke) in VALLEY OF THE DOLLS (1967 C) that she has a 'real man' wait-ing for her but, quick as a whip, Neely delivers an undercut: 'Well, that makes a change from the fags you're usually seen with.'

During the next two decades, this often mythical being was highly prized. On *Jack DeManio This Afternoon* (1976 R) a woman doctor qualified 'a real man' as being 'a HETEROSEXUAL man', a state-ment reiterated during a very serious panel discussion (including Jilly Cooper) on what makes a man a man on *The Six O'Clock Show* (1982 T).

Sometimes the concept was mocked as in the pre-credits scene of *The Living Daylights* (1987 C) when a bikini-clad woman on a yacht sighs that she needs 'a real man' just before James Bond/ Timothy Dalton paraglides onto the deck ready and able to satisfy her every wish. 'I'm a real man,' brags Michael Gill (Brad Dourif) in *Miami Vice* 'Evan' (1985 T). Crockett (Don Johnson) refutes this by saying: 'A real man uses his brain.'

Quentin CRISP long ago in SEVEN MEN (1971 T) outlined his desire for a great dark man whose rampant maleness would naturally disqualify Crisp from being honoured by his favours, Gifford Skinner recalled the absolute taboo in the 1930s on having sex with his 'sis-ters': 'Only real men would do' (GAY LIFE 1981 T).

Rebecca (US 1940 C) A shy young woman (Joan Fontaine) becomes the wife of a sophisticated man (Laurence Olivier) and mistress of a large house over which hovers the spirit of the first wife, Rebecca DE WINTER and the earthly presence of the HOUSEKEEPER, Mrs DANVERS (Judith Anderson).

W: Robert E. Sherwood and Joan Har-rison from the novel by Daphne Du Maurier; P: David O. Selznick; D: Alfred HITCHCOCK 130 mins.

A lushly melancholic rendering of a Gothic romance, given power and inten-sity by the violently contrasting person-alities of the two female leads, as well as the glowering presence of the title character – with a 'Jewish' name – who never appears.

Despite its theme (husband is revealed to have murdered his cold, heartless wife), the LADIES HOME JOURNAL saw fit to reprint what immediately became one of the most popular novels of the late 1930s – and David O. Selznick chose *Rebecca* (with a changed ending) as his next production after *Gone with the Wind*. Alla NAZIMOVA was the first choice to play Mrs Danvers. Orson WELLES (starring with Agnes Moore-head) garnered one of the largest US radio audiences with his version – vir-tually a dramatized reading – in 1938.

Other productions include a memor-able televised one by Rudolph Cartier in

1954 with Sonia DRESDEL as Mrs Danvers, Jeanette Sterke as the girl and Patricia Laffan as Beatrice, and a serialized televised version in 1979 with an explicitly lesbian Mrs Danvers played by Anna MASSEY subtly terrorizing Joanne David (W: Hugh WHITEMORE; P: Richard Beynon; D: Simon Langon). On radio: 1947 (with Dulcie Gray, Nancy Price and Reginald Tate); 1954 (Enid Lorimer as Mrs Danvers in *The Stars in Their Choices*); 1976 (Flora Robson and Jane Asher); 1989 (Rosalie Crutchley, Janet Maw and Christopher Cazenove). The novel was serialized on WOMAN'S HOUR (1993 R) read by Harriet Walter.

Stories with similarly dominating women (dead and alive) were *The Uninvited* (with Cornelia Otis Skinner and Gail Russell, 1944); *While I Live* (re-titled *The Dream of Olwen* 1946 C with Sonia Dresdel); *The Second Woman* (with Betsy Drake and Florence Bates, 1951 C; also R).

Margaret Forster's biography reveals – in the words of the synopsis for *Celebration* 'Daphne Du Maurier – The Loving Spirit' (1993 T) – how she 'struggled with her sexuality', had 'an illicit wartime relationship', and maintained 'her love for Gertrude Lawrence'.

On *Books and Writing* (Aust 1993 R) Margaret Forster said that, when Du Maurier was involved in a relationship with a woman, her male characters became weak and unfocused and her women passionate, violent and sometimes malevolent: 'She had a conflict inside her about what she called her Venetian tendencies ... she never missed an opportunity to deny that she was a lesbian ... and when her children were adults, she went out of her way to denigrate homosexuals ... even though she had homosexual friends.'

Rebels (UK 1986–8 R) Twentieth-century people, rich, bold or foolish enough to venture outside accepted norms written and presented by Hugh Sykes, who 'considers the price they had to pay for their acts of rebellion'. 'They'

included Guy BURGESS, Albert Camus, Jack Kerouac, Henry Miller, Joe ORTON, Pier Paolo PASOLINI, Wilhelm Reich and – just two women – Bessie Braddock MP and Vita SACKVILLE-WEST. Well-drawn portraits, not especially revealing but searching out unusual interviewees such as Burgess' brother.

P: Gaynor Shutte; BBC Radio 4; 30 mins.

Rebel without a Cause (US 1955 C) James DEAN defends the weakling, defeats the bullies, confronts his squabbling parents and sets up a 'pretended' family.

W: Stewart Stern; P: David Weisbart; D: Nicholas Ray; 111 mins.

A great bleeding smear of Cinemascope and Warnercolor with the *Sturm und Drang* of Leonard Rosenman's blowsy score. A love story between three people encased in a now-it-can-be-told exposé of a nation's out-of-control youth. Evocative locations, much tenderness as well as violence, swags of homoerotic markers and at its core the mocking, challenging presence of post-Brando, post-Clift, post-Garfield American man/boyhood.

Reviewing THE LIVING END (1992 C) Robert Julian wrote: 'This time around, the two male anti-heroes do to each other on screen all those things Sal Mineo and James Dean were rumoured to have done in private ... When the history of QUEER CINEMA is written, it may prove to be as important to this current gay generation as ... *Rebel* was to the alienated teens of the 1950s' (*Bay Area Reporter*, 27.8.92).

receptionists When male often played by Michael WARD or Reginald BECKWITH, putting on either a superior or an effusively chummy front. Also memorable were Noel DAVIS, simpering behind the desk in *George and the Dragon* (1966 T), and in *Frenzy* (1972 C) Jimmy Gardner asking Jon Finch (booking in under a false name – 'O Wilde' – with his mistress) if he 'would like anything from the pharmacy' and then telling the pursuing police that 'the lusts of men make me want to heave'.

Redgrave, Lynn (1943–) English actress, now almost entirely based in America: a bright, positive personality known mainly for *Georgy Girl* (1966 C), being dropped from an American series for breast-feeding her baby on the set and for her dietary advice for Weight Watchers. She proved herself a bright and open-minded television interviewer in *Fighting Back* (1992). She was the first famous person to talk about having a gay/bisexual parent within the pages of *Radio Times* (20–6.6.92).

C: Rita Tushingham's friend in *Girl with the Green Eyes* (1964); a cameo as gushing assistant stage manager at the Royal Shakespeare Company in *The Deadly Affair* (1966); the near-spinster frightened of accusations of lesbianism in THE VIRGIN SOLDIERS (1969); a Tennessee WILLIAMS heroine in *Blood Kin/ Last of the Mobile Hot Shots* (1969); a medieval queen with a chastity belt in EVERYTHING YOU ALWAYS WANTED TO KNOW ABOUT SEX (1972); a romantically inclined nurse in *The National Health* (1973); as *The Happy Hooker* (1975); a fashion designer aboard *The Big Bus* (1976); world-weary woman who is looking for love in *Getting It Right* (1989); etc.

T: as COWARD's *Pretty Polly* (1967); the governess in *The Turn of the Screw* (1974); the artist's abandoned wife in *Gaughin the Savage* (1981); assistant hospital administrator Ann Anderson in *House Calls* (1979–81); as *The Faint Hearted Feminist* (1984); the mother in *The Bad Seed* (1985); intelligent, sane, non-homicidal glamma-lesbian in MY TWO LOVES (1986); politically ambitious mother in *Morgan Stewart's Coming Home* (1987); ex-child star turned sister's keeper in *Whatever Happened to Baby Jane?* (1991 T); etc.

Redgrave, Sir Michael (1908–85) English actor of tremulous voice and haunted look, effective as coiled and jittery ventriloquist Maxwell Frere in *Dead of Night* (1945 C); the sad, defeated schoolmaster in *The Browning Version* (1951 C); the hairnetted ANTIQUE DEALER in *Confidential Report/Mr Arkadin* (1955 C); the icy inquisitor in NINE-TEEN-EIGHTY-FOUR (1956 C); the cynical, opium-smoking journalist in *The Quiet American* (1958 C): 'I wish there existed someone to whom I could say that I was sorry'; and (in his final performance, on radio) as the dying, raging Tolstoy in *The Power of Dawn* (1983). His quavering voice perfectly projected the growing horrors of the Great War documentary series in 1964. He discussed his craft in *Great Acting* (1966 T) and was recalled in more intimate circumstances by Corin Redgrave in *Fathers by Sons* (1985 T).

C: the hero helping to solve the mystery in *The Lady Vanishes* (1938); schoolteacher son from mining family in *The Stars Look Down* (1939); title role in *Kipps* (1941); blunt Yorkshireman in *Jeannie* (1941); haunted lighthouse keeper on *Thunder Rock* (1942); one of the RAF officers in *The Way to the Stars* (1945); the Czech prisoner of war impersonating a British officer in *The Captive Heart* (1946); idealistic MP in *Fame Is the Spur* (1947); John WORTHING in THE IMPORTANCE OF BEING EARNEST (1952); Barnes Wallis, inventor of the Bouncing Bomb in *The Dam Busters* (1955); the uncle of *The Innocents* (1961); the prison governor in *The Loneliness of the Long Distance Runner* (1962); a drunken medical officer in *The Hill* (1965); the young boy as an old man in *The Go-Between* (1971); etc. In his later years he tended to play mainly supporting roles in beards: dawdling or exasperated fathers, uncles and grandfathers. Of his starring parts the less said the better (they included an MP tempted by a nymphet in *Goodbye Gemini* 1970, and a teacher sacked for a (homo)sexual indiscretion while working as a janitor in the school where he taught in *Connecting Rooms* 1971).

T: the butler in *Ruggles of Red Gap* (1957); Tesman in *Hedda Gabler* (1962); General Cavendish in *Return to the Regiment* (1963); as *Uncle Vanya* (1963 C); the Blue Caterpillar in *Alice in Wonder-*

land (1966); Dickens in *Charles Dickens of London* (1967); *Gaughin in Tahiti: The Search for Paradise* (a 'CBS News Special', reading from the journals, 1967); *The World of Beachcomber* (1967); Prospero in *The Tempest* (1968); the ghost in *The Canterville Ghost* (1968); grandfather in *Heidi* (1968); as *Monsieur Barnett* (1968); Dan Peggotty in *David Copperfield* (1970); Polonius in *Hamlet* (1971); *Dr Jekyll and Mr Hyde* (1973); etc.

Charles GRAY played an unnamed actor who was Redgrave in AN ENGLISHMAN ABROAD (1983 T).

Redgrave, Vanessa (1937–) English actress. A light switched on around the time she played ROSALIND in AS YOU LIKE IT (1963 T) is still burning at full power. Among her extraordinarily varied roles: an ordinary housewife in *Maggie* (1964 T); the nurse in *A Farewell to Arms* (1965 T); the wife of a demented man in *Morgan – A Suitable Case for Treatment* (1966 C); woman of mystery in *Blow-Up* (1966 C); Queen Guinevere in *Camelot* (1967 C); a Victorian English rose in *The Charge of the Light Brigade* (1968 C); as Isadora Duncan in *Isadora* (1968 C); Nina in *The Seagull* (1969); Mrs Pankhurst in *Oh, What a Lovely War* (1969 C); a possessed nun in *The Devils* (1971 C); *Mary, Queen of Scots* (1972 C); Katherine MANSFIELD in *The Picture of Katherine Mansfield* (1973 T); suspected of *Murder on the Orient Express* (1974 C); Lillian Hellman's adored JULIA (1977 C); the wartime wife in *Yanks* (1979 C); as Agatha Christie in *Agatha* (1979 C); a concentration camp musician in *Playing for Time* (1980 T); wicked queen in *Snow White and the Seven Dwarves* (1983 T); FEMINIST Olive Chancellor in *The Bostonians* (1984 C); an upper-crust woman in STEAMING (1985 C); a suspected witch in *Three Sovereigns for Sarah* (1968 T); Richard who becomes Renée in SECOND SERVE (1986 T); literary agent Peggy Ramsay in PRICK UP YOUR EARS (1987 C); Thomas More's wife in *A Man for All Seasons* (1988 T); a Tennessee WILLIAMS heroine in *Orpheus Descending* (1990 T); the persecuted sis-

ter in *Whatever Happened To Baby Jane?* (1991 T); the boxer Amelia in *The Ballad of the Sad Café* (1991 C); the ailing wife who is the lynchpin of *Howards End* (1992 C); etc.

Documentaries: *Tonite Let's All Make Love in London* (1967 C); *The Palestinian* (1974 C).

Red Hot and Blue (UK 1990) Cole PORTER dragged half out of the closet for a good cause: an all-star record and video for International AIDS day 1990 in which a dozen or so of his classics were battered into near insensibility by pop stars. Shown in over 30 countries and selling over 1 million 'units' (video and album) worldwide between November 1990 and October 1991.

Avril MacRory, Channel 4 commissioning editor for music, deleted a shot of two men embracing on a bed from Jimmy SOMERVILLE's 'From This Moment On' because, she explained on *The Media Show* (1990 T), the sighting was 'a touch of the shock-horror syndrome'. As for Roland Gift's 'LOVE FOR SALE', this segment had a woman's voice overlaid which transformed him from selling love to men into a more acceptable GIGOLO. But at least the whole song wasn't cut in its entirety as it was in Australia where a few intimate seconds from k.d. lang's thrilling version of 'SO IN LOVE' were also lopped off.

A follow-up, *Red, Hot + Dance*, for World AIDS Day 1991 consisted of intercut pop footage in the MTV style.

Redl, Colonel Alfred (*c* 1864–1913) Austrian soldier and spy; commander of the Eighth Army and later head of Military Intelligence at the Vienna War Ministry who became a double agent for the Russians, before he was appointed as head of Counter-Intelligence. His access to all military information may well have brought about Austria's defeat in the First World War. He himself was used as an example of traitorous homosexuals both in Germany during the rise of that country's homosexual equality movement, and after the Second World War in America, his name being mentioned in a Senate subcommittee investigating the red menace. Four films were made in Germany (1925, 1930, 1955 & 1984); D. A. CLARKE-SMITH played him as Major Sergei Zoubaroff in *Colonel Judas* in 1945 (R), but the most famous portrait was that in John OSBORNE'S A PATRIOT FOR ME (1981 R Gary Bond).

Redmond, Phil (1949–) English writer and producer who worked on a number of outward-looking television programmes, including TOGETHER (1980), *What Now?* and *Going Out* before, in 1982, devising BROOKSIDE, which for a while (1986–9) offered at least one young, self-assured gay man.

red ribbons An initiative of the fashion industry to raise money for and awareness of the AIDS crisis, inspired by the piece of yellow ribbon folded in two and worn for the troops coming home from the Gulf war. They were first seen – without explanation – at the 1991 ACADEMY AWARDS, but the following year Richard Gere made a short speech about pouring money into AIDS research rather than the military. Jamie Lee Curtis and Ron Silver made brief speeches about the ribbons at the 1991 Emmys and the 1992 Tonys respectively.

They were still being worn as silent statements at most entertainment awards ceremonies in Australia and the US. At the 1993 Academy Awards Clint Eastwood wore a red bow-tie instead.

One of the first individuals to wear a red ribbon on national television, apart from people directly affected by HIV/AIDS, was presidential-hopeful Jerry Brown (he can be seen with one on his lapel in the documentary *Feed* 1992 T).

Reed, Henry (1914–86) English translator, poet (*Naming of Parts*) and ingenious radio dramatist whose plays formed the basis of a cult in the 1950s, especially the Richard Shewin series lampooning the arts establishment. These were linked by Herbert Reeve (Hugh BURDEN), Reed's kid-gloved bookish alter ego who is desired by both male and female characters. Reed appeared regularly on THE CRITICS during the 1950s.

Reflections in a Golden Eye (US 1967 C) Major Weldon Templeton (Marlon Brando) is attracted to one of his men (Robert Forster), while his frustrated wife (Elizabeth Taylor, for whom the young soldier has an unexpressed passion) has an affair with a neighbour, another officer (Brian Keith), whose wife (Julie Harris) consoles herself with a frisky houseboy (Zorro David).
W: Chapman Mortimer and Gladys Hill from the novel by Carson McCullers; P: Ray Stark; D: John Huston; 108 mins.

'There is a fort in the South where a few years ago a murder was committed.' This simple quote from the novel opens and closes the film which is less a whodunit but a who-will-do-it (and to whom)?

A coalescence of tragedy and comedy which at times seems like a mickey take of every Deep Southern cinematic stew. However, a great director is in charge, swivelling from tragedy to comedy, bringing up all manner of strange things and lots of symbols (a white stallion, a whip). Entertaining, atmospheric, stimulating, realistic and unrealistic; a genuine mainstream oddity which may have been even better had Montgomery CLIFT played the major (he was offered the brooding central role which Brando had turned down, but died before production began).

regular gay/lesbian characters Those who have appeared in more than one season of a series on radio and television include the following:
R: CHARLIE (1946–64); FLOWERDEW (1950–4); Richard FULTON (1951–67); Nelson GABRIEL (1953–); Carol GREY (1954–); Hercules GRYTPYPE-THYNNE (1954–60); JULIAN AND SANDY (1965–9); Count Jim MORIARTY (1952–60); Rob PENGELLY (1979–80); John TREGORRAN (1953–); SHANE (1986–); RUSSELL (1985–92).

T: Gunner 'Gloria' BEAUMONT (1973–82); Dudley BUTTERFIELD (1974–7);

Steven CARRINGTON (1981–91); CLARENCE (1968–78); Barry CLARK (1986–8); Duffy CLAYTON (1956–62); Gordon COLLINS (1984/1986–90); Paul Currie (1984–6) in GEMS; Jodie DALLAS (1977–81); CHRIS DUNCAN (1986–9) in BROOKSIDE; Joan 'the freak' FERGUSON (1980–7); Don FINLAYSON (1972–7); Lieutenant GRUBER (1984–92); Morris HARDACRE (1982–5); Ken HASTINGS (1979–80); Mr HUMPHRIES (1972–84); Pete HUNT and Trevor Wallace (1980–1); Donald MALTBY (1984–7); Freddie MARTIN (1992–3); Michael and Rob (1979–81) in AGONY; Sergeant Grace MILLARD (1956–61); Colin RUSSELL (1986–9); Sammy (in *Life without Marge* 1987–8); Barry STUART-HARGEAVES (1980–3); Zoe Tate in *Emmerdale*; Gerald URQUHART (1985–90); Lee WHITEHOUSE (1974–7); WINSTON Churchill (1985–97).

Reid, Beryl (1918–) English actress, a star of revue and music hall since 1936, a radio personality during the 1950s (*Educating Archie*) and, after playing SISTER GEORGE in the West End, on Broadway and in Hollywood during the 1960s, a much respected film and television player (Kath in ENTERTAINING MR SLOANE: Connie Sachs in TINKER, TAILOR, SOLDIER, SPY and *Smiley's People*).

C: a soprano in *Spare a Copper* (1940); monocled, tweedy, jolly hockey stick schoolteacher in *The Belles of St Trinians* (1954); dreamy film fan in *The Extra Day* (1956); the wife who drives Richard Attenborough to murder in *The Dock Brief* (1962); a music hall artiste in STAR! (1968); Kath in ENTERTAINING MR SLOANE (1970); Flora Robson's sister Mrs Slipslop in *The Beast in the Cellar* 1971); Lady Booby's maid in *Joseph Andrews* (1977); reprising her Sister George role with Susannah YORK in *Late Flowering Love* (1981); alcoholic victim of the body-snatchers in *The Doctor and the Devils* (186); etc.

R: *Children's Hour* (doing impressions, Manchester 1936–8); *A Quarter of an Hour with Beryl Reid* (Manchester, 1937–9); *Workers' Playtime* (1942–52); *Variety Bandbox* 1943–52); *Music Hall*

(1951); *Starlight Hour* (1951–2); *Educating Archie* (as Monica and Marlene, 1952–6); Maria in *Twelfth Night* (1962); Mistress Quickly in *The Merry Wives of Windsor* (1962); *Petticoat Line* (1965–72); Madge in *Fault on the Line* (1966, and in the series *The Trouble with You, Lillian* 1969); title role in *Miss Lambert's Last Dance* (Capital Radio 1981); a soliloquy in *The Studio* (1982); *Start the Week* (1984); etc.

T: *Diversion* (a revue with Turner and Layton, 1951); THE CENTRE SHOW (1952); *Garrison Theatre* (1952); *The Benny Hill Show* (1955); *Musical Cheers* (with Noele Gordon, 1955); *Tea with Noele Gordon* (1956); Alice, the maid in *Mr Bowling Buys a Newspaper* (1957); *Lunch Box* (1957); Arethusa Wilderspin in *The Most Likely Girl* (1957); Marlene in M&B beer commercials (1958); *The Good Old Days* (1964, 1965 & 1973); *Not So Much a Programme, More a Way of Life* (1965); *BBC 3* (1965); Kate Reilly in LOVE STORY 'Duggie' (1966); Tony Awards Show (winning Best Actress for *Sister George*, US 1967); Ugly Sister Marlene in *Cinderella* (1970); Mrs Malaprop in *The Rivals* (1971); Amelia in *Will Amelia Quint Continue Writing 'A Gnome Called Shorthouse'?* (1971); reading the nativity story on *Stars on Sunday* (1971); Mrs Désirée Carthorse in THE GOODIES (1971); Queen Victoria and Monica in *Patrick, Dear Patrick* (an evening with Patrick Cargill, 1971); *Good Afternoon* (interviewed by Mavis Nicholson, 1975); singing 'BURLINGTON BERTIE FROM BOW' in *Night of 100 Stars* (1977); *Beryl Reid* (including a scene from stage version of *Entertaining Mr Sloane*, 1977; another collection of scenes and monologues, 1979); Connie Sachs in *Tinker, Tailor, Soldier, Spy* (1979) and *Smiley's People* (1982); Marty, opposite Susannah YORK, in a John Betjeman poem in *Betjeman's Britain* aka *Late Flowering Love* (1980); antenatal clinic lecturer in AGONY 'Arrivals and Departures' (1981); Beryl, the landlady in *Get Up and Go!* (1981, 1982 & 1983); Captain Briggs in *Dr Who* 'Earthshock' (1982); Mrs Knox in *The Irish RM* (1983); British Academy

Awards (receiving Best Actress for *Smiley's People*, 1983); Matron in *Cuffy* 'Cuffy and a Holiday' (1983); Ruby Todd in *Minder* 'Second Time Around' (1984); Grandmother Mole in *The Secret Diary of Adrian Mole Aged 13 and three quarters* (1985); Miss Broome in *Bergerac* 'Low Profile' (1985); *Aspel & Company* (1985); etc.

Autobiography: DESERT ISLAND DISCS (1963 & 1983 R); *Movie-Go-Round* (interviewed about Sister George, 1968 & 1969 R); WOMAN'S HOUR (Guest of the Week, 1970 & 1980 R); *Parkinson* (1973 T); *Good Afternoon* (1975 T); THIS IS YOUR LIFE (1976 T); *Be My Guest* (1979 R); *Nationwide* (1980 T); *Private Lives* (1983 T); *The Time of Your Life* (flashback to September 1952, 1984 T); *Wogan* 1984 T); *Favourite Things* (1985 T); etc.

Relax (UK 1990 T) Philip Rosch plays a man waiting for his HIV TEST results while recalling a sexual encounter which may or may not have been 'safe'. We also see his less uptight friend (Grant Oatley). The film does not utilize the Frankie Goes To Hollywood song.
W/D: Chris Newby; 20 mins.

Relax A pop blockbuster written and performed by Frankie Goes To Hollywood (Holly Johnson, Mark O'Toole and Peter 'Ped' Gill), released at the end of 1983. The song's openly suggestive lyrics and the gayness of some of Frankie's personnel ensured this a *succès de scandale*. The accompanying video was directed by Bernard Rose (who went on to make *Body Contact* 1987 T), and set in a bordello with heavily sleazy images of an s&m orgy 'with loads and loads of sex' and with Nero feeding people to lions and tigers. (It was shown in uncut form only once: on *The Midsummer Night's Tube* around 1 am on Channel 4.)

On 11 January 1984 disc jockey Mike Read declared that 'The lyrics are obviously obscene' on his *Wednesday Breakfast Show* chart rundown. A few days later, BBC Radio 1 withdrew 'Relax' – which had already been played nearly 90 times from its playlist. Within a fortnight of being effectively banned from Britain's airwaves, the record became no. 1. It spent 37 weeks in the British charts (from November 1983 to June 1984) and is one of the most successful singles ever released, along with Paul Anka's 'Diana' and Wings' 'Mull Of Kintyre'.

Despite – or perhaps because of – its (very basic) lyrics, 'Relax' became oft-heard background music in plays, series episodes and documentaries. These included the DISCO scene at the beginning of DIVERSE REPORTS 'What a Difference a Gay Makes' (1984); the afternoon serial GEMS (a scene in which an unmarried character tells her workmates she is going to have a baby, 1985); HOLLYWOOD BEAT (background to a car chase and fight, 1985); *Mother Love* (distracting the babysitter so that she gives away a vital clue to the malevolent woman played by Diana Rigg, 1989). Usually its raunchier lyrics ('Relax/don't do it/When you want to come') were cut or muffled when used in the mainstream, with ultimate desexing occurring in the 1990–2 Ambre Solaire sun cream commercial ('When you have to get to it').

'The record was a huge success, because it captured exactly (and failed to challenge) the contradiction inherent in the glittering marriage of pleasure to consumerism ... The music is forgotten, a new product is offered us, and the doctrine of endlessly repeated, endlessly elusive pleasure as the only solution to our poverty goes unchallenged' (Neil BARTLETT, *Who Was That Man? A Present for Mr Oscar Wilde*, 1988).

'The subversive power of Frankie's transgression against heterosexual propriety becomes mood music for one commonplace male heterosexual narrative of titillation' (O.N.C. Wong discussing the song's appropriation by the makers of *Miami Vice* in 'Sex and Drugs and Rock 'n' Roll in the TV Market', *Jump Cut*, no. 33, 1988).

religion *See* THE BIBLE; BLASPHEMY.

Remaining Strangers (UK 1986 R) Repressed Myra Lacey (Maureen O'Brien) meets sophisticated, rich but dull Helen (Marian Diamond). Myra decides to help Helen by murdering her husband (John Hollis).

W: Barbara Ann Villiers; D: Richard Wortley; 12.7.86; BBC Radio 4; 90 mins.

Intriguing idea with two women from completely different social backgrounds accelerating, colliding and interlinking. Stock characters and tired plot development ensure that this doesn't transpire. Maureen O'BRIEN effectively pathetic and wheedling as the 'Bruno' character in this borrowing from STRANGERS ON A TRAIN with changed genders.

Remembrance of Things Past Marcel PROUST's *A La Recherche du Temps Perdu* is a skein of memory and time centring upon relationships – false, treacherous, deceitful, exciting – in the brilliant but vapid society of the Faubourg Saint Germain. With Darwin's *Origin of Species*, Freud's *Essays on Psychoanalysis and Sexuality*, Mao's *Little Red Book*, Marx and Engels' *Communist Manifesto* and Tolstoy's *War and Peace*, Proust's books make up one of those fearful unread modern masterpieces.

The multi-volume, plotless work with its recurring themes and characters (nearly all revealed as homosexual) was partially adapted for radio on BBC's Third Programme in a chronology by Pamela Hanford Johnson (though without her planned 'Cities of the Plain', which would have presented attitudes towards homosexuality). They included *The Duchess at Sunset* (1952); *Swann in Love* (1953); *Baron De Charlus* (1954); *Albertine Regained* (1955); *Saint-Loup* (1956). They were all produced by Rayner Heppenstall.

Harold PINTER, with Joseph Losey and Barbara Bray, rendered the whole work down into 455 shots for a 1975–6 film version that was never made (though the screenplay was published (in 1978), with hardly any Odette and Swann or Rachel and Saint-Loup but including the baron chained and naked, being beaten in a male brothel. It had been planned to have an all-start cast (DIRK BOGARDE; Brigitte Bardot).

The work was requested by a number of DESERT ISLAND DISCS castaways including pantomime dame Clarkson Rose in 1963.

Renault, Mary [Mary Challans] (1905–83) English author who brought Ancient Crete and Greece – and especially ALEXANDER THE GREAT – to life. Although her contemporary (elliptically homoerotic) novel *The Charioteer* is highly regarded for its skill and sanity, she is celebrated for her recreations of ancient civilizations, beginning with *The Last of the Wine* followed by her two Theseus books *The King Must Die* and *The Bull from the Sea*, and the Alexander novels.

A very private person, she did give a few radio and television interviews just before she died, from her home in South Africa which she shared with Julie Mullard, whom she had met during the 1930s when she was nursing. She displayed her 'liberal attitude' towards homosexuality in these together with her 'lack of sympathy' with the gay liberation movement. In 1993 a comprehensive biography appeared, written by David Sweetman with the full support of Julie Mullard, and revealing what Mary Renault felt she could not reveal during her lifetime.

Her 1939 novel *Purposes of Love*, about a young man who falls in love with the sister of his beloved dead friend, was used as the basis for one of the *Boy Meets Girl* plays (1968 T) but without its lesbian subplot. *The King Must Die* and *The Bull from the Sea* were serialized on radio on 1963 and 1983, and *The Last of the Wine* was considered for production by BBC Radio 4 during 1985–6. Her Alexander trilogy remains undramatized, although Arthur Seidelman had plans to film *Fire from Heaven* and *The Persian Boy* in the mid-1970s.

'I think I was trying to get across the message that homosexuals in Greece were exposed to social standards. I mean, they had to behave themselves.

They didn't have to make fools of themselves and get together in gangs in a defensive sort of way. You know, they were people like any other people – but most of them were BISEXUAL anyway and I think it is much healthier that all this should be given free play' (Mary Renault talks to Sue MacGregor on KALEIDOSCOPE 1980 R).

rent boys Generally regarded as living lives of despair and aimlessness. The British concept of 'rent boy' was slow to develop in common knowledge and parlance, although one was interviewed in a radio documentary about homeless youth in London in 1968 (*Focus on the Lost Generation*), and there were also hints that Mr Sloane might have been on the game at one time or another in ENTERTAINING MR SLOANE (1968 T; 1970 C).

On television the first characters to be associated with the trade – apart from Oscar WILDE's cohorts in ON TRIAL (1960) – were Ralph (Myles Reitherman) in THE ROADS TO FREEDOM (1970) and Leslie Darkin in SOFTLY, SOFTLY 'Little Blue Blue' (1974): 'Obviously a male PROSTITUTE,' says a script note. Quentin CRISP's dad (Lloyd Lamble) calls his son a 'male whore' in THE NAKED CIVIL SERVANT (1975) because of his MAKE-UP, but he is probably unaware that Quentin is part of a quinquereme of queens doing noisy business on certain streets and in certain cafés in London.

The very young end of the profession was represented by 14-year-old Liam (Jason Kemp) in KIDS 'Michael and Liam'; (1979 T): 'He was soliciting for money, for security.' His new mate Michael can't cope with this at all: 'Did you really go with men? That's sick, that is.' To which Liam replies: 'It's only mucking around. The same as couples.'

The term 'rent boy' was unveiled, in the capital city area only, in THE LONDON WEEKEND SHOW 'Rent Boys' (1977 T). Ashley Knight was cited in the cast of *Dr Jekyll and Mr Hyde* as 'Boy prostitute' in 1980 (T). That same year, in MAN ALIVE 'Young and Drifting',

'John' was introduced as a '17-year-old male prostitute'. A more comprehensive view of the scene (in Birmingham) was provided by 40 MINUTES 'Rent Boys' (1984).

The rent boy is now so well-established in the British imagination (thanks mainly to the tabloid press) that he can supply an episode title for the comedy series *Men Behaving Badly* (1992). Julian CLARY's first sitcom was allegedly going to be called 'Meet the Rent Boy' – it had formerly been 'The Man from Uranus' and finally emerged as TERRY AND JULIAN.

'Fucking tedious work ... getting an erection to order' (Andy in SIX OF HEARTS 'Andy the Furniture Maker', 1986 T).

restaurants/cafés Only stills survive of the BERLIN restaurant catering to a special clientele in the 1927 remake of *Different from all the Others* entitled *Laws of Love*: men and women are dancing (though not together). The American *Call Her Savage* (1932) shows a GREENWICH VILLAGE café where a mainly deviant clientele imbibes happily as two waiters in frilly caps and aprons entertain. For the next three decades, censorship shut the door on such places, although in *The Snows of Kilimanjaro* (1952 C) sharp-eyed viewers can discern women wearing discreet bow-ties and an eunuchoid man with an elderly lover in the Montmartre boîte to which Gregory Peck repairs.

Slowly, after censorship was partially lifted, gays and lesbians made their way, as patrons and owners, into eating establishments: lesbians and vicars lunch (at separate tables) in *The Servant* (1963 C); Laure's is 'a place for women in the Rue des Martyrs ... a fraternity [*sic*] of shared perversions' in *Nana* (1968 & 1982 T) where lesbians can eat a 3-franc dinner (*vol-au-vent à la financière*, chicken and rice, *crème caramel*); 'gay people welcome here' is the message given by the waiter to the four lesbians in NOW SHE LAUGHS, NOW SHE CRIES (1975 R); Bumpkins – 'with the emphasis on the 'Bum' – is a simple country pub in Norfolk turned chi-chi by Denis Porson (Nigel HAVERS) in THE GLITTERING PRIZES (1976 T): the food is 'served slightly underdone with a tossed green salad and just a tincture of whoops-dearie'; Chez Hugo in Earls Court in THE GENTLE TOUCH 'Blade' (1980 T) is where the murdered man worked as a waiter: 'Ask for the menu and you get a big kiss. Ask for the wine list and who knows what you get,' says Inspector Croft (Brian Gaspawri); Nuts in May is a health food establishment run by Harvey (Peter John) in *That Beryl Martson …!* (1981 T); Peter (Rupert Frazer) and Clement (Nigel HAVERS) PLAN TO OPEN A PLACE IN BATH IN ALL FOR LOVE 'Combat' (1982 T).

On one of the 1982 (Michael) *Parkinson* shows, Michael Caine talked not too unkindly about cramped establishments run by two men 'of the kind my father thought I was. One in a pink APRON in the kitchen, the other in a BOW-TIE in the restaurant.'

revues aka reviews. Early British television was created by those in the theatre and music hall and watched by people in the London area. Therefore, sophisticated revues (mixtures of show-biz and slightly precious contemporaneity) formed part of the fare – in 1937: *Rush Hour; They're Off; Pasquerade; Cameo: A Little Show*; in 1938: A TUNE TO TAKEAWAY: A REVIEW OF REVIEWS, *Rococo*; in 1939: *Oleograph*. Usually frivolous and scornful of social comment, revue continued after the war in more elaborate guise (*A–Z; On the Bright Side*) until it merged with satire in THAT WAS THE WEEK THAT WAS and THE MAVIS BRAMSTON SHOW.

Theatre revues themselves died at the beginning of the 1960s, eulogized in two series of *Before the Fringe* (1967–8) presented by Alan MELVILLE. The early television ones were notable for the use of the words 'QUEEN', 'FAIRY' and 'QUEER' in certain of the musical numbers such as Phyllis Monckton's 'District Nurse' and the trio 'INTERIOR DECORATION'.

Richard I the Lionheart (1157–99) King of England. Poet and Crusader, second son of Henry II and Eleanor of Aquitaine; more in legend than in fact brave and chivalrous, though he very likely was the passionate friend of the King of France. Uninterested in women, he married Berengaria of Navarre but produced no heirs, and they parted after a year. He fought first and foremost for the booty, and in the process bankrupted England's exchequer, ravaged lands, put hundreds to the sword. Yet he remains a pivotal romantic figure, usually portrayed as dignified or lusty (sometimes gay).

Wallace Beery in *Robin Hood* (1992 C) and *Richard the Lion-Hearted* (1923 C); Henry Wilcoxon in *The Crusades* (1935 C); Patrick Barr in *The Story of Robin Hood and His Merrie Men* (1952 C); Norman Wooland in *Ivanhoe* (1952 C); William Devlin in *The Talisman* (1952 R); George SANDERS in *King Richard and the Crusaders* (1954 C); Bruce Seton in *Ivanhoe* (1957 T); Dermot Walsh in *Richard the Lion Heart* (1962 T); John Castle (1968 C) and Michael COCHRANE (1981 R) in *The Lion in Winter*; Clinton Greyn in *Churchill's People* 'Silver Giant, Wooden Dwarf' (1975 T); Richard Harris in *Robin and Marian* (1975 C); Michael-John Jackson in *The Legend of Robin Hood* (1977 T); Michael Byrne in *The Devil's Crown* (1967 T); Stephan Chase in *The Talisman* (1980–1 T); Julian Glover in *Ivanhoe* (1982 T); Robert Hardy in *The Zany Adventures of Robin Hood* (1984 T); Neil Dixon (very briefly) in *Lionheart* (1987 C); Sean Connery in *Robin Hood, Prince of Thieves* (1991 C); etc. He was updated – as Philip Castallack (Rupert Frazer), the sensitive son – in PENMARRIC (1979 T).

'… you were the truest lover that never loved a woman. You were the most generous man that ever killed his enemy. You were the prettiest poet that ever couched lance. And you were the most faithful of unbelievers that ever asked God for mercy … Don't think what he did but what he might have done' (Bertram De Born (Freddie Jones) eulogizing the dead king in *The*

Devil's Crown 'Richard – Yea and Nay', 1978 T).

When the verger is caught drinking in a gay BAR in *Hell's Bells* 'Big Boys Don't Cry' (1986 T), the bishop (Robert STEPHENS) can only invoke the shining example of such ordinary everyday chaps as MICHELANGELO, TCHAIKOVSKY and Richard the Lionheart. 'But,' splutters the terrified verger, who lives with his mum and who has always kept his head down, 'Richard the Lionheart doesn't live down *our* street.'

Richardson, Ian (1934–   ) English actor whose every word, expression and change of posture impart pedigree, pride, active stillness and intelligence: in a word – civilization. Among a gallery of extraordinary performances: the son in *A Voyage Round My Father* (1971 T); Richard Young in *Hire a Shroud* (1973 T); the advocate in *The Winslow Boy* (1989 T); Nehru in *Mountbatten*; Bill HAYDON in TINKER, TAILOR, SOLDIER, SPY (1979 T); Ray in *Star Quality* (1985); Francis in *House of Cards* (1991 T).

Richardson, Tony [Cecil Antonio] (1928–91) English director who began as a producer for BBC in 1953 (*Othello* 1955 etc). With George Devine, he created the English Stage Company in 1955, and directed his first film *Momma Don't Allow* (a short) in 1955. Scenes from *The Loneliness of the Long Distance Runner* (1962 C) and the eating scene from *Tom Jones* (1963 C) featured in *Naked Hollywood* (1991 T). Other films included *Look Back in Anger* (1959); A TASTE OF HONEY (1961); *The Loved One* (1965); *Mademoiselle* (1966); *The Charge of the Light Brigade* (1968); *Ned Kelly* (1970); *A Delicate Balance* (1973, also T); *Joseph Andrews* (1977); *The Hotel New Hampshire* (1984); *Blue Skies* (1992). For television he directed *A Death in Canaan* (1978).

Richard's Things (UK 1981 CT) Suddenly widowed Kate (Liv Ullmann) finds herself having an affair with the husband's young mistress, Josie (Amanda Redman).

W: Frederic RAPHAEL based on his novel; P: Mark Shivas; D: Anthony Harvey; 16.6.81; Southern; 104 mins.

Lesbianism as expiation, as love–hate, as hole-in-the corner. A very private place unrelated to everyday life. Josie is a free spirit with a streak of ruthlessness; Kate is repressed and depressed; her admirer Peter (Tim Pigott-Smith) is nice but boring; Richard, the husband, was a REAL MAN and the lynchpin of the whole plot. An interesting but unbelievable concept, a hapless leading performance and Georges Delerue's twee music all but suffocate the expert photography of Freddie Young and the glowing, energetic performance of Amanda Redman.

'The feeling is mutual and irresistible and the ensuing relationship is persuasively developed in Frederic Raphael's script. Amanda Redman plays Josie with the radiant concentration of a child pulling wings off a fly: an effective contrast with Ullmann's dogged tenderness' (Jennifer Selway, *Observer*, 16.8.81).

'I cannot imagine myself turning to a woman sexually. For my understanding of the part I used the fact that the woman lost a daughter in infancy to explain the fondness for the girl of a similar generation, who at once reawakens her feelings of maternity and guilt' (Liv Ullmann, *Sunday Times*, 29.6.81).

Richmond, Len (194?–   ) American television writer, one of the guiding lights behind THE GAY LIBERATION SHOW in the mid-1970s. In the UK, with Anna Raeburn, he created and co-wrote the first series of AGONY. Also *Three's Company* 'Handcuffed' (1980); *The Lucie Arnaz Show* (the US version of *Agony*, without the gay characters); *Split Ends* (1989); etc.

Ride of the Valkyrie aka Valkyrs. Enormously stirring, almost frenzied, certainly furious theme to accompany the entrance – upon winged steeds, in battle dress with drawn swords – of the eight wild gals from Valhalla crying out

'Ho-yo-to-ho' in the opening of act III of Wagner's *Die Walküre*. It is also heard in *Siegfried* and *Götterdämmerung*.

One of the most sublimely rousing popular classical themes, it has been heard countless times in drama and comedy, often to usher in powerful, threatening women or to mock the conventions of opera. It has also done duty in a BLACK AND WHITE MINSTREL SHOW skit in THAT WAS THE WEEK THAT WAS (1963 T); in the dreamscape whipping of wives and mistresses by Marcello Mastroianni in *Fellini Eight and a Half* (1963 C); in THE CONNOISSEUR (1966 T) as background to a public school caning; in *Apocalypse Now* (1979 C) when Robert Duvall's Colonel Kilgore and his helicopters swooped into view to its strains; in *Selling Hitler* (1991 T) as a CAMP production number.

It was one of the pieces of music requested on the very first DESERT ISLAND DISCS in 1942 (by comedian and violinist Vic Oliver who asked for it again in 1955). Other castaways who thrilled to its pulsating motion include actress Margaret Lockwood (1951); actor Richard Todd (1953); broadcaster Richard Dimbleby (1958); comedian Charlie Drake (1958); comedy actress and novelist Irene Handl (1962); interior designer David Hicks (1966); theatre historians Mander and Mitchenson (1978(.

Probably the nearest equivalent in today's mythology of the Valkyrie would be the Dykes on Bikes contingents which proudly ride in various lesbian and gay parades in the US and Australia, dressed in all manner of exotic attire. In Australia, Sydney's DOB also work with the police, patrolling the streets and sounding the alarm in the event of QUEER-BASHING attacks.

Ridley, Philip (1960–) English writer and film-maker of force and imagination who has almost exclusively dealt with gay themes. For the television: a memorably quirky 'The Universe of Dermot Finn' in the *Short and Curlies* series (1990); for radio: the arresting OCTOBER SCARS THE SKIN (1989) and

Shambolic Rainbow (1991); for cinema: the powerful *The Krays* (1990) and the atmospheric *The Reflecting Skin* (1991).

Rights and Reactions (US 1988 T) The city of New York passed a gay rights bill in 1986.
P: Phil Zwickler and Jane Lippman; D: Phil Zwickler; 60 mins.

Lesbians and gays vs the Rest? Not quite, although at times it seems like it in this red-hot battle to uphold a basic right of citizenship, vehemently opposed by representatives from various religions (some of whose adherents also make up the bill's supporters). Very exciting grassroots politics, a signpost of many battles to be fought all over the world in the years to come. Ian MCKELLEN introduced the film on Channel 4 in June 1989, setting the events in the context of the previous year's noisy and spectacular but ultimately doomed attempt to prevent local councils being gagged or at least restrained by CLAUSE 28.

Rimbaud, Arthur (1854–91) French poet whose explosive relationship with Paul Verlaine was well captured in *Total Eclipse* (Kenneth Cranham 1969 T; Joseph Blatchely 1973 T; River Phoenix 1993/4). *Honouring a prophet* (1954 R) has John Russell on Rimbaud but no mention of Verlaine; *Rimbaud and 'Les Illustrations'* (1972 R) is read by Jean COCTEAU; *Incredible Floridas* (1972 C/T) has no mention of Verlaine, although his sketches of his lover are included.

Ellen **Ripley** A member of the crew of an American space ship, a character played by Sigourney Weaver, first in *Alien* (1979), then in *Aliens* (1986), and with a much changed appearance in *Aliens 3* (1991). Cited as a rare example of a female character portrayed in a large-budget movie as intelligent, attractive, supercompetent, resourceful and brave (let alone not noticeably heterosexual) she needed to be, pitted as she was against some of the most cunning, endlessly metamorphosing creatures from Out There. In the second film she has been deep in hyperspace for 57 years. Although very much the TOMBOY in appearance and with no obvious attachments, Ripley is revealed to have a daughter who dies at 76 (while her mother remains young). Impregnated by one of the *Aliens*, she exits from the third film in spectacular fashion, accompanied by much hissing (though not from her).

Ripploh, Frank (1948–) German writer, film-maker and actor, a former teacher whose mainly autobiographical TAXI ZUM KLO (1981) brought a certain kind of urban gay life into sharper focus for large and generally appreciative audiences in more broad-minded countries. He belatedly followed it with the bland and perversely mainstream *Taxi to Cairo* (1988 C) while in between making *Kamikaze '89* (1982 C) and *Miko: From the Gutter to the Stars* (1986 C also playing the central character's friend and manager). As well as exposing general audiences to a wide variety of gay sex, Frank Ripploh will be principally remembered as the scruffy guy with smelly socks who begins each morning with a bowel movement – and who also happens to be gay (and how).

Ritchard, Cyril (1896–1977) Australian actor of spidery, gleaming propensities who became a family favourite in America after a career as musical comedy actor in Britain.

C: *On with the Dance* (1927); the ARTIST who is stabbed by Anny Ondra in *Blackmail* (1929); Victor Smiles in *Piccadilly* (1929); *I See Ice* (1938); *Half a Sixpence* (1967); *Can Hieronymus Merkin Ever Forget Mercy Humppe and Find True Happiness?* (1969).

R: DESERT ISLAND DISCS (1953).

T: *Cameo: A Little Show* (1937); *Pasquerade* (1937); *Ruggles of Red Gap* (1951); *Mrs Dane's Defence* (1951); *Treasure Chest* (1952); *Pontius Pilate* (1952); *Two for One* (1953); *Here's Father* (1954); *The King and Mrs Candle* (1954); *The Merry Widow* (1954); PETER PAN (1955); *Visit to a Small Planet* (1955); *The Spongers* (1955); *Dearest Enemy* (1955); *The Good Fairy* (1956); *Jack and the Bean Stalk* (1956); *Caesar and Cleopatra* (1956); *Aladdin* (1958); *HMS Pinafore* (1959); *Peter Pan* (1960); *Four for Tonight* (1960, with Beatrice Lillie, Tony RANDALL, Tammy Grimes); *The Man Who Brought Paradise* (1965); Lone T. Wolf in *The Dangerous Christmas of Red Riding Hood* (1965, with Liza Minnelli); *Hans Brinker* (1969); *Foul* (1970); *Danny Kaye's Enchanted World* 'The Emperor's New Clothes' (1972); *Love, Life, Liberty and Lunch* (1976); *The Hobbit* (1977).

(In an on-set 'home movie' clip shown in OMNIBUS 'Alfred Hitchcock' (1986 T), HITCHCOCK makes a playful (and unusually energetic) lunge for Ritchard's genitals during the shooting of *Blackmail*.)

The Ritz (UK 1976 C) Very straight businessman (Jack Weston), on the run from the Mafia, finds himself in a gay bath house where he is the object of attention from a 'chubby chaser', an undercover detective with a high-pitched voice, and a female singer whose talent is more in her mind than in her larynx. After a series of misadventures, the man's wife and violent brother-in-law arrive for a showdown.

W: Terrence McNally from his play; D: Richard Lester; P: Denis O'Dell; 90 mins.

A cut above most comedies of this kind because of its robust sense of gay politics, its deliriously CAMP setting and a clutch of good players. It is noticeable that this is yet another tour of the sexual undergrowth, but the straights are as ridiculous as their gay brothers. Jack Weston is the piggy in the middle; Rita Moreno twists her words something chronic as Googie; Treat Williams flexes his muscles and talks in a squeak as the undercover dick; F. Murray Abraham looks ghoulish in a towel; Kaye Ballard (dressed as a man) arrives late as the wife to whom an explanation is owed. A series of squibs rather than true fireworks, but very lively.

That such films were needed – in unstoppable quantities – was evidenced by the reaction of the show business bible: 'To have a tolerance, even an acceptance of homosexuality doesn't rule out having an underlying physical distaste for it ... There are simply too many male gay stomachs, arms and faces at too short a range. It spoiled the picture' (Richard Eder, *Variety*, 13.8.76).

The Road from Kymmendo Bay (UK 1985 R)

Playwright August Strindberg (Ian Hogg) becomes insanely jealous when his wife Siri (Lorna Heilbron) meets and falls in love with a socialist lesbian, Marie David (Miriam MARGOLYES).

W: Michael Stirling; D: Michael Heffernan; 10.4.85; BBC Radio 3; 90 mins.

Strindberg, marinating in narcissistic self-pity, presents himself always as the injured party during his marital jujitsu, all aggrieved innocence and battered male pride, with fascinating, repellent lesbianism as his friction factor.

A particularly bruising look at the animus and animosity that brought forth *The Dance of Death* and *The Father*: misogyny: 'Women suck men; they feed greedily on his penis and his brain'; jealousy: 'She's mine. She belongs to me'; latent homosexuality: 'A woman's body is a boy's with breasts'; masochism: 'Humiliate me ... tread on me'. Ian Hogg successfully reserves a small drop of sympathy for this astonishingly selfish man, while from Lorna Heilbron there is a strange kind of yearning eroticism. Miriam Margolyes is in the middle as verbal punching bag and referee.

road movies A car, a couple of guys and a gal or a mixture of same, on the run or just drifting. The road they're travelling on is sometimes dead straight, sometimes long and winding. A staple of American cinema since *Easy Rider* in 1969 (and occasionally on television, eg ROUTE 66): mainly an excuse for buddy activities, but THELMA AND LOUISE (1991 C) may lead to more women on wheels.

Gay ones include the British short *Dream A40* (1965); the British-made, American-located NORTH OF VORTEX (1991 T); THE LIVING END (1992 C): 'a queer couple on the run' movie in the tradition of *They Live by Night* (1949), *Bonnie and Clyde* (1967) and *Badlands* (1973). The road as the symbol of adventure, infinity, challenge and hopelessness played a small but crucial role in MY OWN PRIVATE IDAHO (1991 C).

The Roads to Freedom (UK 1970 T)

PARIS 1938–40, a time of false hopes, self-doubt and disillusionment, all reflected in one of the three central characters: a dispassionate, reluctant homosexual, Daniel SERENO (Daniel MASSEY) with a liking for ROUGH TRADE, but who marries Marcelle (Rosemary Leach) to spite his friend, her lover, Mathieu (Michael Bryant). Other deviationists in the cast include an elderly cruiser (Charles Lloyd Pack), Bruno (Anthony Corlan) and his sister Ivich (Alison Fiske).

W: David TURNER from *The Roads to Freedom* (comprising the novels *The Age of Reason*, *The Reprieve* and *Iron in the Soul*) by Jean-Paul SARTRE; P: David Conroy; D: James Cellan Jones; BBC2; 11 parts; 50 mins each.

An extraordinary epic, memorable as much for its lacerating interior monologues (dealing mainly with human worth and moral responsibility) as for its concentrated sense of impending doom and blending in the manoeuvrings of Hitler, Daladier, Chamberlain and Halifix with the fictional domestic drama. For the first time, a gay man was seen having sex (with a PROSTITUTE), railing at God, pretending unalloyed friendship to a man whose girlfriend he doesn't want but takes in a MARRIAGE of convenience. Thanks to the truth of writing and playing, this was exhilirating rather than simply depressing and reprehensible. As W. Stephen GILBERT told GAY NEWS in 1977: 'It showed the ecstasy as well as the agony of being gay.'

Robby the Robot The machine who looks after Alta and Morbius 'like a mother' and who thinks nothing of carrying sheets of 10-ton steel or building a house, but gives equal care to designing and making Alta's clothes and arranging flowers. 'The question of [my] sex is irrelevant,' he/she tells the spaceship commander. Later, apologizing for his tardiness in answering his bell, Robby tells the captain he was giving himself 'an oil job'. This robot is more than a servant – he can create life: fruit, vegetables, whisky ... babies?

Other relevant robots include Dr SMITH's source of perturbation in LOST IN SPACE (1965–6 T); Hymie (Dick Gautier) in *Get Smart!* (1965–79 T): one episode has Hymie and Maxwell Smart declaring their love for one another; and one belonging to a futuristic – but very old-fashioned – gay couple: taking mincing steps, dangling a limp wrist and wearing an APRON in *Sleeper* (1973 C).

Robertson, Rose (19?–) A former social worker; she set up Parents' Enquiry to help young gay people and their parents in 1968. She presented a dignified, commonsensical and surprising face of gay liberation on such programmes as *The London Programme* 'Gays and the Police' (1978 T); WOMAN'S HOUR 'Teenage Gays' (1979 R); CRYING OUT LOUD 'Teenage Gays' (1983 T); and *Talkabout* 'Gay Teenagers' (giving Leo ABSE a piece of her mind, 1980 R).

Robespierre, Maximilien François Marie Isidore De (1758–94) French revolutionary, leader of the Jacobins, incorruptible; ousted and guillotined. Usually presented as a cold, thin-lipped, unfeeling ascetic with effeminacy bubbling under the surface: Richard Basehart in *Reign of Terror* (1949 C); Harold LANG in *Danton's Death* (1958 T); Richard Morant in *The Scarlet Pimpernel* 1982 T). Kenneth WILLIAMS donned white wig, breeches and frock coat as 'Camembert' in *Don't Lose Your Head* (1967 C).

Robin Boy's name (a pet form of Robert) which is sometimes, especially in Britain, reserved for characters who go

bob, bob, bobbin' through life: immature, frightened, dependent, sexually questionable ...

UK: Robin [né Robert] (Ronald Simpson) in *The Bachelors* (1950 R) who acts as wife and mother to his younger brother; Robin Carter (Leslie Phillips), soppy solicitor in *The Smallest Show on Earth* (1957 C); Nicol Williamson as the pathetic college chum of Alfred Lynch, wanting to start an affair or break up his relationship with Glenda Jackson in HORROR OF DARKNESS (1965 T): he commits suicide; Robin (Jeffrey GARDINER), First Private Secretary in *The Mind of the Enemy* (1965 T) who throws a party; Robin (Clive-Colin Bowler), polo-necked assassin in a 1967 *Avengers*; Robin Tripp (Richard O'Sullivan) who is a trainee chef in *Man About the House* (1972–6 T) and a chef and later restaurateur in *Robin's Nest* (1977–81 T) (in the American version, THREE'S COMPANY, he was renamed Jack Tripper); the sorely tried man who loves/adores artist Kim in THE OTHER WOMAN (1976 T); Robin (Peter Neville), boyfriend of Peter (David Swift) in *Breakaway Girls* 'Sarah Carter' (1978 T); a New Man (Neville Smith), not averse to the idea of non-sexism and of men wearing make-up in *World's End* (1981 T); dress designer Robin Valerian (Ringo Starr) who wouldn't go out the door without make-up and painted nails in *Princess Daisy* (1983 T); Robin (Peter Machin) as non-sexist, non-racist, non-person in STRUGGLE (1983 T); Robin (Mark Greenstreet) in *Freddie and Max* (1990 T); Robin Stokes (Tim Meats), flexible, resolutely unstuffy non-stipendiary vicar who doubles as a vet and who sets female hearts aflutter in THE ARCHERS (1991– R); Robin Tatian (Steve Hodson) in *A Fatal Inversion* (1991 R); Robin Bradley (Ben Daniels), a college friend whom Philip meets again, this time behind a gay bar, in THE LOST LANGUAGE OF CRANES (1992 T): they eventually throw caution to the winds; Robin Middleton (Nicholas Jones), John's brother in *Anglo-Saxon Attitudes* (1992 T).

US: Robin (the Boy Wonder), the

secret identity of Dick Grayson, the teenage companion (and 'ward') of the Caped Crusader (Burt Ward in the TV series 1965–7, film 1966, cartoon series *The New Adventures of Batman* 1977 etc) – there was no Robin to be explained away or heterosexualized in the 1989 and 1992 film extravaganzas; Robbin Elcott (Wendell Corey), unhappy brother-in-law (of Alexis Smith) in *Any Number Can Play* (1949 C); insurance investigator hero Robin Scott (Rick Jason) in PERRY MASON 'The Case of the Dangerous Robin' (1961 T); ruthless, somewhat unbalanced Robin Stone (John Phillip Law), TV executive, a ratings whizzkid, known as *The Love Machine* (1971 C), who stimulates serious gossip because of his closeness to his gay friend Jerry; psychokinetic Robin (Andrew Stevens) taken over by thoroughly evil, misogynist forces in *The Fury* (1978 C); doctor hero fights off what looks like a giant salami in Robin (Robert Foxworth) in *Prophecy* (1979 C); Robbin (Bubba Smith), the store's night manager in *Open All Night* (1981–2 T); Robin Prince (Mark Harmon), pool cleaner who also attends to housewives in *Prince of Bel-Air* (1988 T) (Will Smith, who took over in the sitcom spin-off *Fresh Prince of Bel-Air* (1990 T), was called 'Will Smith'); slick, deceitful Robin Colcord (Roger Rees) in *Cheers* (1989–91 T) who uses Rebecca for business purposes.

See also BOBBY.

Robin Hood Mythical character, partly based on Sir Robert Locksley who lived during the reigns of Kings RICHARD I and John. He and his Merrie Men have long been the subject of frisky comment. The title card says that Douglas Fairbanks' silent Robin of 1922 is 'afeard of women and prefers revelling with male companions', But, as most heroes must, he marries. On the wedding night, King Richard (Wallace Beery) insists that he join Robin in the bedchamber. But Robin ignores his royal friend's insistent pounding on the door – on that night at least.

With greater censorship, Robin had to bring up the drawbridge on such activities, and the only hints in recent years have been King Richard's dependency upon him and Maid Marian's jealously of Little John in *Robin and Marian* (1975 C): 'You've had years [with Robin] and I'll lose him.' For laughs there was Hugh PADDICK's sibilant version, all eye shadow, knitting and worrying about putting on weight in *Up the Chastity Belt* (1971 C). But the homoerotic dimensions were not entirely absent from one of the more recent incarnations: prettified and teenaged *Robin of Sherwood* (1984–6) T). Here, Robin was a willowy young spunk, half man, half myth: first Michael Praed, who was dark-haired, and then Jason Connery, who was cool and blond with an intriguing *décolleté*, handy bow and smoochy eyes. A real 14th-century pin-up who, in 'The New Sheriff' (1986) had to battle against a gay Sheriff of Nottingham, Phillip Frank, played – in black leather – by former 'Professional' Lewis Collins.

Despite the presence of Maid Marian, all the screen Robins – whether played by Errol Flynn or Hugh Paddick – are essentially men in tights who spend most of their time holed up in a deep forest with a motley band of men sharpening their weapons and waiting for the call to arms. He's very much a merrie man's man – a fact which the latest version, *Men in Tights* (1993 C), is sure to exploit (a spoof on Kevin Costner's *Robin Hood – Prince of Thieves* (1991 C), whose star insisted on wearing trousers and possibly on his followers being supplemented by a number of wenches).

Robins, Peter (193?–) English short story writer, journalist and radio producer, a former PT instructor and Congo war correspondent. Worked as a reporter for *Radio Newsreel* (1960–3), produced the *Today* programme, *The Week in Westminster, Profile* etc in the 1960s and 1970s before moving from the BBC to commercial radio (LBC). Long a promoter of gay literature, editor of a number of anthologies. His 'An Exorcism', first published in GAY NEWS in 1976, was adapted as a MORNING STORY in 1982 (read by Jeff Rawle).

Robinson, Tom (1952–) The first openly gay – and successful – British pop singer. His most famous song – ('SING IF YOU'RE) GLAD TO BE GAY' – was first heard on THE LONDON WEEKEND programme 'Teenage Gays' in July 1977. This appearance led to a contract for the Tom Robinson Band (himself, Danny Kustow, Ian 'Quince' Parker and Preston Heyman) with EMI, which produced the hit '1-2-3 Motorway'.

He had been a gay activist since the early 1970s. One of his first radio appearances came on a 1976 Radio Merseyside phone-in when he asked the Rev. David Sheppard, Anglican Bishop of Liverpool, if the time had come for the Church to climb off the fence and be much more open and welcoming towards homosexuals. His work for London GAY SWITCHBOARD was included as part of Granada's 1979 documentary TOO GOOD TO BE TRUE? Even before this (on *The London Weekend Show* 1978) the question was being asked: had he sold out? He turned to the camera and asked: 'What have *you* done?'

Until the late 1980s, Tom Robinson was one of the great gay ROLE-MODELS: chunkily affable yet palpably sincere and vocal about lesbian and gay rights as well as strongly anti-racist. He was the subject of a BBC Radio 4 *Profile* in 1979; talked about gay records on *LBC Reports* (1978 R); sang 'Glad To Be Gay' at the AMNESTY benefit, *The Secret Policeman's Ball* (1979 C); played his favourite songs and chatted about his boyfriend on *Personal Call* (1979 R); surfaced on the *Oxford Road Show* (1981 T) and *Revolver* (1982 T); extolled his car in 40 MINUTES 'Ford Cortina' (1982 T); revealed *My Top Ten* (1983 R); talked about teenagers and anti-gay oppression on *Claire Rayner's Casebook* (1983); went with *Whistle Test on the Road* (1983); discussed his favourite year (1977) on *The Colour Supplement* (1984 R); was guest presenter on *ORS 85* (1985 T); sang 'Motorway' and 'Jobsworth' on *Cue to Music* (1987); wrote the lyrics for the drama series HARD CASES (1988 T). His first hit was included in THE ROCK 'N' ROLL YEARS (1991 T) along with Kate Bush, Blondie, the Jam, the Boomtown Rats and Police.

Just when predictability seemed to be settling in – 'Tom Robinson has "come out" so many times on television, he might pull off a major feat of public relations by going back inside again' (Peter Ackroyd in the *Spectator* 1983) – a considerable change occurred in his private life which jolted some of his many admirers. As he explained on *Talk About Sex* (1992 R): 'To my great surprise, I find myself now at the age of 42 a settled family man, a father and very happy. I still fancy other men but in a way I prefer to call myself gay because BISEXUAL seems such a cop-out. In a way all these kinds of labels ... are really pointless and restricting. In the way that if you are walking down the street you become a pedestrian and as soon as you get in a car you're a motorist. For me, I've taking up driving but I'm still the same pedestrian that used to walk down the street. So in the same way, for me, I'm still the same gay man that I ever was; it's just that I happen to live with and be in love with a woman.'

As well as appearing on OUT ON TUESDAY 'Walk On by' (1990 T, identifying as 'gay' in this segment on bisexuality) and PINKPOP (1993 R, on gay music), Tom Robinson presented BBC Radio's first regular programme about and for men – 'that women can't afford to miss' – *The Locker Room* (1992–), which had similarities with Channel 4's *Men Talk*, although the former tended to move into thornier areas like violence, the military and gay culture.

TRB's music lives on: 'Glad To Be Gay', still being updated, remains one of the British gay movement's few immediately recognizable icons, and 'Up Against The Wall' was played during a *Gaywaves* report on anti-gay violence (Aust 1992 R).

Rock Name given to Roy Scherer by agent Henry Willson in the late 1940s.

Coupled with 'HUDSON', it was thought to impart the kind of rugged masculinity that made men envious and women swoon – and warded off any untoward questions. Other Hollywood hunks given these masculine monikers over the next few years were Tab Hunter (born Arthur Gelien), Troy Donahue (originally Merle Johnson) and Rip (formerly Elmore) Torn. ('Clint Eastwood' was not a made-up name.)

Rock Follies/Rock Follies of '77 (UK 1976–7 T) The triumphs and travails of an all-female rock group who, in the second series, employ the services of a cocky but sensitive gay man, Harry Moon (Derek Thompson), who met his lover, 'alternative' journalist Ken Church (Denis Lawson), in a 'rather wild cartoon CINEMA'. Harry has a brief but enjoyable affair with one of the 'Little Ladies', Q (Rula Lenska).

W: Howard SCHUMAN; M: Andy Mackay (formerly of Roxy music); L: Schuman; P: Andrew Brown; D: Jon Scoffield; Thames; 60 mins.

A swipe at punk rock, teenage exploitation, commercials, pop journalism, Americanization, the backlash, pretentiousness of all kinds. *Rock Follies*, innovatively written and produced with what were then new visual techniques, was a highly peppered ragout and not to all tastes. Packed with well-observed caricatures (agents, producers, journalists, club owners), both series were overweighted with half-digested details and decorations. Their audacity and high spirits kept them aloft – even during the truncated showing of the second series, the last few episodes of which were delayed, for many weeks, by a strike.

'When we were working on *Rock Follies* it seemed quite barbarous, but seeing it on the screen, although it hadn't been censored, the show hasn't got the guts to say the things it should about political and social issues. It's been put through the media mincer' (Derek Thompson, *Gay News*, 1977).

The Rock 'n' Roll Years aka *The Gay Rock 'n' Roll Years* (UK 1991 T) Homosexual British history from the early 1950s to the present: from Doris DAY singing of her 'SECRET LOVE' to the British press in a feeding frenzy over OUTING. The times that were a-changing (but nowhere near quickly – or securely – enough) were jollied along by frequent lilts from the likes of Elton JOHN, BOY GEORGE and Culture Club, Gloria Gaynor, Donna Summer, Dusty SPRINGFIELD, Sandie Shaw, Marc Almond, Gene Pitney and Elvis Presley. They accompanied many news clips and film stills of the bad good old days. (This was the opening presentation of BBC2's SATURDAY NIGHT OUT – and generally regarded as the highlight of the evening.)

The Rocky Horror Picture Show (UK 1975 C) Brad and Janet, lost in a storm, knock at a castle door. Inside, a man wearing high heels, make-up and suspender belt is preparing to create a sexy young man, Rocky. Events conspire to thwart his plans.

W: Jim Sharman and Richard O'Brien from the stage musical; P: Michael White; D: Jim Sharman; 100 mins.

An overstretched spoof of low-budget horror films pepped up with sexual diversity personified by the sweet TRANSVESTITE from Transylvania played right up to the hilt by Tim CURRY, and NORMALITY pilloried by Barry Bostwick and Susan Sarandon as the terminally wet Brad and Janet. A loud and clear message about variety in all things and a few subversive moments (Frank seducing Janet as Brad and vice versa, the cross-dressed climax).

Not outstandingly successful when first released, this film is more famous for the cult which grew around it, leading to late-night showings before audiences who dress as the characters and recite chunks of dialogue. These act-alongs and their devotees have been seen as background dressing in FAME (1980 C), *Willie and Phil* (1980 C) and *Brick is Beautiful* (Ian Mercer, a Rocky Horror fanatic who is of 'dubious sexuality', 1986 T). (A sequel is promised called

'The Revenge of the Old Queen' 1993–4 C.)

Roderigo Character in *Othello*, described as a Gentleman of Venice. A DANDY who becomes Iago's tool in the destruction of Cassio, he is often presented as crossing over from dandyism into queendom, as with Heron CARVIC'S interpretation (1948 R) and James Maxwell (1955 T; Iago plays with his BEARD: '*Now* I see the mettle in thee, be bold, take thy stand'). In his 1952 film Orson WELLES dubbed his own voice (with accents effetely English) over Robert Coote's performance in that role. Peter Egan played him (opposite Paul Scofield, 1979 T) and Michael Grandage the plaything of Ian MCKELLEN (1990 T).

Rodg and Rudi Owners of a videoshop: 'You name it, we've got it.' Played in *The Laughter Show* (1985 T) by Dustin GEE and Les Dennis in a vain attempt to update JULIAN AND SANDY. They imitate film stars, male and female, to stimulate sales, but, as they have none of the videos one young couple ask for, they accompany them home: 'We CAMP everywhere.'

A Rod of Iron (UK 1980 T) The death of a mother brings two sons home again. W: David Mercer; 29.4.90; Yorkshire; 60 mins.

Trevor (Nigel Hawthorne) is an intelligence officer – 'a glorified clerk really, all very routine really, – who is planning early retirement in a small cottage on the West Coast. He's stopped eating meat – 'nothing doctrinaire' – and he's on tonic water. He's come to visit his dying mother and see his father. His younger brother (Edward Woodward) offers him what emotional support he can. Trevor has never come to terms with his sexuality: 'I saw a programme in which it said it was something to do with mother fixation, but I don't hold with prejudice,' says the other brother unhelpfully. Trevor doesn't think his mother ever had any idea: 'She would have thought it was a privilege of the upper classes.' He admits that 'I've never put my arms around anyone. I am, if you can keep your face straight, a virgin. When I was 12 and you were 9 my heart ached for you.'

This is a glum reworking of an earlier play, *Where the Difference Begins* (1961 & 1966 T), in which both brothers were heterosexual. The play's dramatic 'rod of iron' is the finely judged performance of Nigel Hawthorne, who also played two very different – though equally doleful – gay roles in *Mapp and Lucia* (1985–6 T) and *The Shawl* (1988 T).

Roehm, Ernst (1897–1934) German soldier and politician, leader of the SA (*Sturm-abteilung* or Brownshirts) which was instrumental in the rise to power of the NAZI party. Despised by Hitler as an uncouth soldier of fortune and a notorious homosexual with his harem of good-looking young Brownshirts; 'a homosexual clique,' said Hugh Greene in his documentary about Roehm's downfall, *The Night of the Humming Bird – Hitler's 1934 Massacre* (1981 T). The raid against Roehm and his men while they were relaxing with lovers at the Hanselbauer Pension, Bad Wiessee, near Munich was vividly depicted in THE DAMNED (1969 C) and *Hitler's SS: Portrait in Evil* (1985 C/T with Michael Elphick as Roehm). The dawn attack on the SA's mountain chalet and the discovery of men in bed with blond youths created the belief that homosexual bias and NAZISM go together. In fact, most of the party leaders were energetically heterosexual.

The Night of the Humming Bird revealed a letter Roehm had written to a German doctor in 1929 while he was living in Bolivia. In it he said he'd had affairs with women, but now women revolted him. His German friend had refused him any sexual relationship and Bolivians, though they might walk hand in hand, were not homosexual. 'What was he to do? It is a cry for help in a very strange letter.' In 1931 he was recalled by Hitler as Chief of Staff for the SA, which he expanded from 300,000 to 4 million.

Hitler, who had previously tolerated the openly expressed sexuality of his most valued and earliest supporter, was apparently suspicious of a coup attempt and used homosexuality as the excuse to strike against his former friend. A story was put out that the bloody action – some of the stormtroopers were shot on the spot, others (including Roehm himself) executed a couple of days later – was necessary to protect Germany's male youth from people of 'a special disposition'. On the same day Hitler made an order to purge all gays from the army.

Roger Boy's name more often given to saps and sillies rather than to stouthearted men.

UK: Roger SHELLY (Richard Hurndall) who runs a mother's help agency and displaces much air in *Paul Temple and the Vandyke Affair* (1950 & 1959 R); slimy British politician Roger Renfrew (Donald Pleasence) in *No Love for Johnnie* (1961 C); Roger (Richard Briers) in *Brothers-in-Law* (1963 T); smooth, unattached psychiatrist Dr Roger Corder (Herbert Lom) in THE HUMAN JUNGLE (1963–5 T); Roger (*John Fraser*), dreamy, long-suffering secretary to *Isadora* (Vanessa REDGRAVE 1968 C); two Rogers – one a young man (Scott Jacoby) with a speech impediment, the other a Frenchman (Jean-Pierre Cassel) whose girlfriend has died – forming a close bond in *Baxter!* (1973 C); Roger Coyne (Nigel HAVERS), rich student in love with the wrong (i.e. heterosexual) guy in *A Raging Calm* (1974 T); Roger Ackerley (Freddie Jones), happily at play in his SECRET ORCHARDS (1980 T) that may have included being kept by a man; Roger Flower (Jonathan Pryce) caught in the tentacles of separation, divorce and new love affair in *Roger Doesn't Live Here Any More* (1981 T); sour, frustrated Wildean queen Roger Monk (David McAlister) in *An Empty Glass* (1981 R); RODG (AND RUDI) in *The Laughter Show* (1985 T); Roger (John Standing) in *A Touch of Love* (1990 T); Roger Fabian (Tyler Butterworth) in *Rumpole of the Bailey* 'Rumpole for the Prosecution' (1991 T); sad sap Roger

Smith (Tony Robinson) in *Virtual Murder* 'A Bone to Pick' (1992 T).

US: Roger Van Horn (George K. ARTHUR) in *Pretty Ladies* (1925 C); excitable valet Roger (Edward Everett HORTON) in *Reaching for the Moon* (1931 C); *Roger* (Eric BLORE) in *I Dream Too Much* (1935 C); bandleader Roger Grant (Tyrone Power) in *Alexander's Ragtime Band* (1938 C); Roger Bradley (Donald O'Connor), a dope in *The Milkman* (1950 C); Roger Evans (Reginald Gardiner), harassed godfather in *Elopement* (1951 C); Roger Shulman (Robert Stack), barnstorming pilot in *The Tarnished Angels* (1958 C); Roger Thornhill (Cary GRANT), much divorced man whose best friend is mother in *North by Northwest* (1959 C); Roger Shackleforth (George Grizzard) finding that a woman's adoration can be suffocating in THE TWILIGHT ZONE 'The Chaser' (1960 T); Roger Altar (Ernie Kovacs), disenchanted best-selling macho novelist in *Strangers When We Meet* (1960 C); clean, neat, unobjectionable Roger Henderson (Tab Hunter), beau of Debbie Reynolds in *The Pleasure of His Company* (1961 C); prey to every disaster Roger Hobbs (James Stewart) in *Mr Hobbs Takes a Vacation* (1962 C); wrongly thought to be homosexual Roger (Gig Young) in *That Touch of Mink* (1962 C); Roger Willoughby (Rock HUDSON) in *Man's Favourite Sport?* (1964 C), fishing expert exposed as an 'amiable phoney' at the Lake Wakapoogee competition; Roger Berry (Alex Davion), suspicious half-brother of Peter Murphy in *The Man Who Never Was* (1966–7 T); Roger Buell (Richard Deacon), flustered TV writer in *The Mothers-in-Law* (1967–8 T); Dr Roger Cabe (Lloyd Bochner) in *Terraces* (1977 T) packing his bags to leave wife for a young man; Roger (Steve Guttenberg), the spunky hotel manager in *No Soap, Radio* (1982 T); woman inside a man's body Roger Cobb (Steve Martin) in *All of Me* (1984 C); Roger Gage (*Boyd Gaines*), all-American boy soldier and Reagan supporter who is QUEER-BASHED in HOTEL 'Hornet's Nest' (1986 T); Chief Roger Kendrick (Ronny Cox) in

Cop Rock (1990–1 T); Roger Ferrant (Martin Shaw) who catches V. I. Warshawski's eye in *Killing Orders* (1991 R).

role models Everyday gays, daily dykes. Still very much a pipe-dream on television as most halfway honourable and attractive homosexual characters either fade away – like Chris (Stifyn Parri) in BROOKSIDE and Colin in EASTENDERS – or vacillate and oscillate wildly (Steven in DYNASTY and Matt Fielding in MELROSE PLACE).

Like heterosexuals, homosexual people may at certain times need fictional characters to look up to, take comfort from, empathize with. After all, daily romantic serials perform this function for part of the majority. In the past, it was only a happy accident that enabled a young gay man to be influenced by another's actions and philosophy, as was John Bury (Joseph O'Conor) in ONLY CONNECT (1979 T). He gratefully recalled the influence Edward CARPENTER had on him as the first openly gay man he had met: 'I didn't know anything about his politics ... It's just that he was the only other person like me I'd ever heard of and he didn't give a damn who knew ... That was the reason I went down to Guildford to see him.'

Among those writers who consciously set out to provide characters who were more than a collection of mannerisms are Susan Harris, creator of Jodie and Alice in SOAP (1977–81 T), and Howard SCHUMAN who told GAY NEWS in December 1977: 'The only thing I'm sorry about is that it didn't show Harry and Ken in BED together. I thought that it was important to have an unforced physical scene between them and I actually wrote it, but we didn't feel it worked so it was scrapped. But if anything has been successful in ROCK FOLLIES '77, I'd like to think it is the character of Harry. If kids, for example, like Harry and really respond to him ... it should make them less afraid or uptight about being gay. But it's an opening volley. It's only useful in the larger context of different strands which

are picked up and developed by other people.'

Gay teenager Steve in INTRODUCTION TO SOCIOLOGY (1981 T) was contemptuous of effeminacy and did not want to be associated with POUFS. Then he went to a Tom ROBINSON concert, whose star was an openly gay person he could relate to; and he 'never looked back', COMING OUT to his parents and friends, and fully accepting himself.

'Larry GRAYSON and John INMAN were not my ideals ... I was like – ohmigod – is that what I'm going to be? I'd rather not have sex than turn into a screaming queen' (Michael Clark on growing up gay in Aberdeen without a single positive role model, to Lynn Barber, *Independent Magazine*, 7.6.92).

See also Jodie DALLAS; Colin RUSSELL.

Roll On Four O'Clock (UK 1970 T) St Josephs' School, Manchester. Fourteen-year-old Peter Latimer (Frank Heaton) earns the wrath of pupils and teachers because he's no good at the tug of war, likes art and English, and he's thick and colourless. He is therefore an ideal candidate for being picked on. Mr Tate is a single man, bullying and fiercely anti-queer: 'He's a POOF, an embryo QUEEN ... he needs putting away', 'In every school you have one or two ... every school the same, they're there', 'We don't cater for poofs', 'My job is to make sure that the lads know how to hold their own', 'A lad like him, what chance has he got around here ... he'll have to hide.'

Max Fielder (Clive Swift) tells Peter he understands: 'As you get older you'll find other boys and men ... The kids at school don't understand, just as you don't understand them.' Max then says: 'As you get more mature you'll find other boys and men who'll be a great comfort. You're not alone ... you will learn to live with it.' However, the boy steals a motorcycle and is badly injured in a crash.

W: Colin Welland; P: Kenith TRODD; D: Roy Battersby; 20.12.70; Granada; 60 mins.

The Romans in Britain A play by
Howard Brenton which was prosecuted
by Mary WHITEHOUSE for allowing an
act of sodomy (Roman soldier upon a
Briton) to be performed in a public
place (the National Theatre). This was
Mrs Whitehouse's first foray into the
law since the GAY NEWS trial for BLAS-
PHEMY.

In *Till Death* ... (1981 T) Alf Garnett
(Warren Mitchell) wants to know what
they were doing on that National
Theatre stage to so offend the good lady
Whitehouse. His lugubrious sister-in-
law (Patricia Hayes) is happy to tell him
it was 'men ... NAKED ... doing things
... to other men'.

'Wot, PANSY boys was they?'
'No! Romans!'
'And they were doing it in the theatre ...
on the stage. Cheeky devils. Ain't art is it.
Buggery.'
'Anyway, it's legal now.'
'It's not legal to do it in public.'
'Most of the sex you see in the theatre and
films, it's done by actors. [Wistful pause.] I
sometimes wish my Bert had gone to
drama school. Once a month if I was
lucky.'

Rome Open City (It 1945 C) The first
part of Rossellini's war trilogy, filmed
almost like a newsreel, largely on the
actual locations only weeks after liberation. The Germans are presented as
sadists, the collaborators (including a
lesbian) as scum. The film that set in
motion the link between NAZISM, Fascism and homosexuality which was to be
mined so extensively in later decades.
W: Sergio Armidei and Federico Fellini;
P/D: Roberto Rossellini; 102 mins.

A Room for the Winter (UK 1981 T)
James Van Santen (Jack Shepherd), a
white South African writer facing arrest
for sabotage, escapes to England. He
leaves behind him his lover Stephen
(Michael Kitchen). With little money
and a disinclination to work, he fights a
battle of wills with his Jamaican landlady
and is forced to assess his invidious position when Stephen offers him a pardon
(bought with sexual favours) and his
British lover Robert (Paul Copley) is

beaten up. The play ends with James
alone: he's writing a letter. He turns on
his black landlady: 'You hate white
people, you despise them.' She rounds
on him: 'You don't try at nothin'.'
W: Rose TREMAIN; P: June Roberts; D:
Jim Goddard; 3.11.81; BBC1; 65 mins.

room-mates *Variety* lists the actors
playing the gay couple in *Point Blank*
(1967 C) as 'Room-mates', In THE BOYS
IN THE BAND (1970 C) Larry says if two
men are living together they're lovers
not room-mates, so why pretend? But
this is the term Hank uses to describe
Larry and himself to Alan.

Kit Mainwaring (Mark Wheeler) has
an 'ex-room-mate' in DALLAS 'Royal
Marriage' (1979 T). Peter (D. W. Moffett) in AN EARLY FROST (1985 T) is
known to Michael's family only as a
room-mate; he has not even spoken to
them on the phone. When Jeff (Barry
Tubb) comes out to his room-mate in
CONSENTING ADULT (1985 T) after
much anguished preparation, the friend
only shows concern for himself: 'I don't
believe this is happening to me.'

Other examples of close proximity: Ian
(Victor Henry) and Jimmy (Simon
Ward) in WHEN DID YOU LAST SEE MY
MOTHER? (1967 R); Bob (John Hurt)
and Jake (Michael Jayston) in *Green
Julia* (1971 T); John Eric Hexum and
Jeff Conaway in *The Making of a Male
Model* (1983 T); Judd Hirsch and Clea-
von Little in an episode of DEAR JOHN
(1991 T).

Lesbians and heterosexual women who
'roomed' together, usually at college,
include Martha and Karen in THE CHIL-
DREN'S HOUR/THE LOUDEST WHISPER
(1961 C); Pepper and Marlene (Patricia
Crowley) in POLICE WOMAN 'Trial by
Prejudice' (1975 T); Dorothy and Jean
(Lois Nettleton) in GOLDEN GIRLS 'Isn't
It Romantic' (1987 T).

A rare example of a gay man and a
lesbian sharing the rent: Jodie and Alice
(Randee Heller) in SOAP (1979 T).

Rope (US 1948 C) Two young men,
Shaw Brandon (John DALL) and Philip
Granillo (Farley Granger), murder

another. After hiding his body in a trunk, they prepare for a cocktail party to which the dead man's father and fiancée have been invited. Another guest – the killers' mentor, Rupert Adell (James Stewart) – becomes suspicious, and returns and challenges his hosts, who confess.

W: Arthur LAURENTS and Hume Cronyn from the play by Patrick HAMILTON; P: Sidney Bernstein and Alfred Hitchcock; D: Alfred HITCHCOCK; 81 mins.

Hitchcock at his most suffocatingly claustrophobic with a miscast James Stewart and a problematic '10-minute take' technique. Not all is lost: John Dall is repellently Nietzschean and the early dialogue between the 'boys' remarkably suggestive. The shock opening alone – the strangulation – lives on in the mind's eyes.

'... there is no hero as such in *Rope* – James Stewart is the murderers' nemesis, but he is also (as their erstwhile teacher) the spiritual author of their crime. The audience's surrogate here is in the trunk – or gathered around it in the other party guests whom Brandon clearly lumps with his victim as ordinary mortals who "merely occupy space"' (Richard Combs, 'Hitchcock × 2: Just Enough Rope', *Monthly Film Bulletin*, February 1984).

The film of *Rope* was based on Patrick HAMILTON's 1929 stage play *Rope's End*. Set in fashionable Mayfair, it was unusual in that it dealt fairly explicitly with a gay relationship. When it was first broadcast by the BBC, in February 1932, the Corporation issued copious warnings about the thriller's likely effect upon those of a nervous and delicate disposition. *Radio Times* in its billing described *Rope* as 'A curious play dealing with two NEUROTIC young men ... who strangle a perfectly harmless friend, purely for the excitement of the thing. It is strong meat.'

Meat that proved tasty to the British public. *Rope* became a staple of repertory companies and of radio and television, and among those playing the murderous lovers, Wyndham Brandon and Charles Granillo, have been Basil C. Langton

and Oliver Burt (1939 T); David Markham and Dirk BOGARDE (1947 T); Basil JONES and Donald Pleasence (1948 R); David Markham and Peter WYNGARDE (1950 T); David PEEL and Roger Delgardo (1953 R); Alec MCCOWEN and Ian HOLM (1957 T); Michael Kilgariff and Tim Seely (1966 R); Adam Bareham and Andrew Branch (1982 R).

Rosalind Character in AS YOU LIKE IT who pretends to be a youth called Ganymede – after the boy kidnapped as a sex slave by Zeus. Played by Elisabeth Bergner (1936 C); Barbara Jefford (1953 R); Margaret Leighton (1953 T); Claire Bloom (1955 T); Vanessa REDGRAVE (1963); Helen Mirren (1980 T); Emma Croft (1992 C).

Rose The head parlourmaid in UPSTAIRS, DOWNSTAIRS (1970–5 T), the audience identification figure, the bridge over central events, including the gay ones. Writing and acting (Jean Marsh was co-creator with Eileen Atkins) ensure that Rose develops credibly. Her sexuality remains enigmatic, but she does always come to the aid of underdog, even when, in the case of footman Alfred (George Innes), he's a jackal. The first episode has a winning scene where Rose and Sarah (Pauline Collins) hug each other in bed, for two kinds of warmth in their narrow garret bed. 'Rose a lesbian. What next at Eaton Place?' (Gerald Clarke, *Time*, 15.1.79, who includes Sarah saying of Rose's current room-mate 'I'll bet she's not as warm to snuggle up to as I was').

The Rose Affair (UK 1961 T) An updating of Beauty and the Beast with Harold LANG as Johnson, lonely, disfigured millionaire Anthony Quayle's 'man', all *entrechat* and attitude: 'Oh, you're so dominating!' he says to the stiff corporate lawyer (Joseph O'Conor).

W: Alun Owen; P: Sydney Newman; D: Charles Jarrott; 8.10.61; ABC; 60 mins.

Lang's performance was described as 'all-out hamming' (*The Times*); 'delightfully daffy' (*Northern Daily Mirror*); 'hammed up' (*Daily Worker*); 'picaresque' (*Observer*); 'madly overplayed' (*Stage and Television Today*); 'supercilious' (*Glasgow Herald*). A few years on, the character's fey demeanour and frequent changes of costume and persona would be neatly summed up in just one word: CAMP.

Roseanne (US 1989– T) A gutsy, no-shit wife and mother (Roseanne Arnold) understands only too well why certain animals eat their young.
Cr: Matt Williams; P: Roseanne Arnold (formerly Barr) and Tom Arnold (with Al Lowenstein, Jeff Abugov and others); ABC; 30 mins.
A return to the smeared window on the world television comedy last opened by the Bunkers in ALL IN THE FAMILY, *Maude* and *Mary Hartman, Mary Hartman* in the 1970s. Roseanne is totally comfortable dealing with PMT, pregnancy testing or the price of bread and the high cost of a college education. The star, in the tradition of Lucille Ball, Joan Davis and Mary Tyler Moore, calls the shots and has full artistic control. She signalled boat-rocking developments for the 1992–3 season of the series and beyond.
So far, Roseanne's boss at the department store diner, Leon Carp (Martin Mull), has been revealed as gay and her friend Nancy (Sandra Bernhard) came out as lesbian. Plans for Leon and his lover Jerry (Michael Des Barres) to adopt a child did not materialize, however, as the relationship split asunder. Two other characters, Roseanne's daughter Darlene (Sara Gilbert) and her sister Jackie (Laurie Metcalf), have the potential to develop along unconventional lines.
This is a great, galumphing show, raw and straight to the point, like its central character. She's not afraid to show warmth to her husband and daughters, nor to be extremely scathing, and at times rejecting, in a way that hitherto would have been unthinkable for an American television mother-figure, role-model: 'I've always wanted to have a family. Maybe not the one I've got ...'

a rose is a rose is a rose The writer (Miriam MARGOLYES) in GERTRUDE STEIN AND A COMPANION (1985 R) tries to explain her famous line to Alice: 'The rose is red for the first time in 600 years. Just read the words on the page. Be simple, then you'll understand.'
Used, naturally enough, as the title of a 3-part series on the rose by writer and garden designer Jane Fearnley-Whittingstall (1991 R). Used many times to denote high literary endeavour; eg in the elocution song 'Moses' sung by Donald O'Connor and Gene Kelly in *Singin' in the Rain* (1952 C): 'A rose is a rose/A nose is a nose.' An episode of *The Donna Reed Show* (1962 T) was entitled 'A Rose Is a Rose' (Mom helps Son with his grammar).
Examples of other similar expressions: 'A child is a child is a child' (Audrey Hepburn on DONAHUE 1990 T); 'A cat is a cat is a cat' (*Cats: Caressing The Tiger* 1991 T).

Rottingdean (UK 1980 T) A family is moving – to Rottingdean in Sussex. Husband Frank (Trevor Peacock) – 'I just like things to be lovely' – is having an affair with the cleaner Daryl (Max Hafler). Wife Joan (Pat Heywood) is a dishrag, desperate for a woman like Margaret THATCHER to lead her out of the darkness.
W: Richard Crane; P: Anne Head; D: Mark Cullingham; 22.3.80; BBC2; 60 mins.
An effective piece about the fraying and tattering of a family unable to communicate:

Daughter (Sarah Neville): 'There's nothing remotely natural about this family.'
Mother: 'It's all because we were never honest. We never spoke face to face. We never sat down as a family to iron things out.'

rough trade Usually unknown sexual partners who may offer violence before, during or after a sexual encounter.
'Ruff Trayde and the Cruisers' were mentioned on ROUND THE HORNE (1966 R). Daniel (Daniel MASSEY) patronized rough trade in THE ROADS TO FREEDOM

(1970 T) and was full of admiration for the NAZI soldier boys as they arrived to occupy Paris. But it's not only a homosexual fascination. The unkempt, ferociously sexual Kim (Jane Lapotaire) in THE OTHER WOMAN (1976 T) is able to gather up teenage secretary Nicola (Lynne Frederick) and get her into bed precisely *because of* her direct gaze and crude manners. Robert Preston mentions it in his song 'GAY PAREE' from VICTOR/VICTORIA (1982 C).

'Picking up a bit of rough were you?' says the insinuating Lucy, the sister of Gordon COLLINS (Mark Burgess) in BROOKSIDE (1990 T); he's spent the night with a young guy who, to Gordon's horror, asked for money. Dolly (Ann Mitchell) tells Linda (Maureen O'Farrell): 'Go back to the rough trade you're so fond of' (WIDOWS 1983 T). 'You could do with a bit of rough,' Pinky (Shaun Prendergast) says to the hero of *Show Me the Way Ugly Angels* (1990 R).

A probation officer arrives at work bruised in HARD CASES (1988 T), which prompts a colleague's remark about 'a bit of rough last night'. When one of the senior police officers, Burnside (Christopher Ellison), in *The Bill* 'One of the Boys' (1989 T) intimates that WPC Martella's interest in a crook is based on his being her bit of rough, she explodes and tells him that he has overstepped the boundary: 'Don't you ever speak to me like that again, *sir*.' And Angie (Anita Dobson) surmises that the main appeal her husband Den (Leslie Grantham) has for sleek executive Jan (Jane How) in EASTENDERS (1986 T) is that he is her 'bit of rough'.

It was mentioned in AFTER HENRY 'Intellectual Aspirations' (1987 T), and Vince Withers was so described in the US film *Meet The Applegates* (1991): daughter Sally likes them rough and to prove it she grabs Vin and has sex with him in an open grave. 'I'm the bit of rough/She wanted to lay,' sings Dennis Waterman over the closing credits of *On the Up* (1990 T).

Round the Horne (UK 1965–9 R) A rainbow bridge between the 'harmless'

lunacy of ITMA and THE GOON SHOW and the blunter new comedy of I'M SORRY I'LL READ THAT AGAIN and MONTY PYTHON, it quickly became a Sunday lunchtime mecca, probably the last radio comedy to have a large popular following. The accent was on smut and innuendo, the pace lively and the performers choice: 'swarthy beauty' Betty Marsden, 'dusty tigress' Hugh PADDICK and 'Bill Pertwee of the apple-cheeked and pear-shaped body' as well as the Kenneths (HORNE and WILLIAMS) and announcer Douglas SMITH.

Regulars in the show, which became curiouser and curiouser and bolder and bolder (despite complaints), were archvillain Chou En Ginsberg (and his baritone-voiced houri Lotus Blossom); straight-as-a-die Sir Gladys Harbinger; Dame Celia Molestrangler and ageing juvenile Binkie Huckaback (as breathless screen lovers Fiona and Charles); prickly, sex-phobic Australian backpacker Judy COLIBAH; mucky folk singer Rambling Syd Rumpo, devotee of CORDWANGLING; cookery commando Daphne Whitethigh; and gay not-so-young things JULIAN AND SANDY.

Galloping through the imaginations of Marty FELDMAN and Barry TOOK (later Johnnie Mortimer, Brian Cooke and Donald Webster) were streams of weird and wonderful names: Ruff Trayde and the Cruisers; Raving Jim Grunt and the Pubes; Peg-Leg Loombucket; Puberty Griswold, the Boxing Rabbi, Fazackerly and Pubes (cross-talk comedians); Yeti Rosencrantz; Chiswick Flo; Sherpa Gutbucket and the Electric Druids; and the Reverend Peeping Tom Codpiece, the jogging theosophist.

The series opened up wondrous vistas of English traditional activities such as 'Knock a Rabbi Out of Bed' at Battersea Fun Fair; 'Hip Throbbing' at Whipsnade Zoo; 'Finger Bogling' at the Spotted Dick Memorial Hall; 'Festoon a Goose with Bacon Day'; a Chicken Trembling exhibition by the Ladbrooke Grove Buddhist Girl Pipers; the Washroom Attendants' Annual Flannel Dance; the Posing Brief Collectors' Journal Splod Toasting; and the ever-popular Over Eighties' Nudist Glee Club Bring and Buy Sale.

Double entendres were thick on the ground: 'I'm trying to get something up and I'd like you to put your name on it', 'I find the bathroom is the best place to have a practice,' and 'Instructions on how to look up your friend.'

Round the Horne crossed over into a hitherto forbidden zone: open and practising homosexuality. 'We felt that people like us ought to get into the open,' exclaimed Jule and Sand, those walking dictionaries of the secret language, POLARI. Each week, Kenneth Horne sought out the services the boys provided, such as full relief at the Bona Nature Clinic (1966): 'We're your actual homeopathic practitioners – we're not recommended by doctors, but we're well known up all the all-night chemists ... we're on the fringe.'

Bona Drag, Rentachap, Bona Relations, Bona Tax Consultants, Body Bona ... For five years they minced tall, secure in the belief it was they who were NORMAL, the rest of the world decidely QUEER. Enterprising, to say the least, and in their own way philanthropic: 'Well, if you can't put out a hand to friends ...'

More than one gay man used to listen to the show on HAMPSTEAD HEATH surrounded by many others, all splitting their sides with laughter. (Gays were also present in sizeable numbers as part of the raucous audiences during recordings.)

Blue Murder 'grandly but with a lot of nudging' was gotten away with on those BBC Light Programme Sundays at 2.30 pm before *The Billy Cotton Band Show* ... 'Wakey-wakey' indeed.

The series – and its guiding light – was fondly remembered in *Round and Round the Horne* (1976 R).

Route 66 (US 1960–4 T) Todd Stiles (Martin Milner) and Buzz Murdock (George Maharis) zip across America in a Corvette. Each week they encountered people like Keir Dullea, Bruce Dern, Lee Marvin, Walter Matthau, Peter LORRE, Martita HUNT, Robert Redford and Ethel Waters. Their perfect relationship – a sanitized, Disneyfied version of beats Jack Kerouac and Neal Cassady – ended when Buzz decamped, to be replaced by the equally cute Lincoln Case (Glenn Corbett) in the autumn of 1962.

W: Stirling Silliphant etc; P: Herbert B. Leonard; CBS; 50 mins.

The utterly captivating strings, brass and electric guitar theme music, lush and lithe, provided Nelson Riddle with a modest hit in 1962, and is probably the first such to encapsulate a gay fantasy: a fast car, a cute companion, no strings and no barriers, just get in and go.

The series was a barely concealed appropriation of beat culture (principally Kerouac's ON THE ROAD), most apparent in its wonderfully pretentious titles, a few of which aptly describe the subtext: 'Only by Cunning Glimpses', 'There I am – There I Always Am', 'Suppose I Said I Was the Queen of Spain?' 'Come Out, Come Out Wherever You Are', 'Hey, Moth, Come Eat the Flame', 'A Long Piece of Mischief', 'Kiss the Monster, Make Him Sleep', 'Cries of Persons Close to One', 'This Is Going to Hurt Me More Than It Hurts You', 'Who in His Right Mind Needs a Nice Girl?'

'Their attachments to women were resolved with a "kiss them goodbye" attitude; their permanent constructions were moments spent together probing their male relationship on-the-move' (Gordon Johnston, *Which Way Out of the Men's Room? Options for the Male Homosexual*, 1979).

The music filled in the gaps necessitated by 1960s censorship on touching – realizable only partially later in *Easy Rider* and STARSKY AND HUTCH, and signposting to series which may be possible in the 21st century and which have been developed in one-off ways in a few road movies. David HOCKNEY chose as his DESERT ISLAND DISCS book a pornographic novel entitled *Route 69* in 1972.

Rowan and Martin's Laugh-In aka *Laugh-In* (US 1968–73 T) Sight gags, impudent one-liners, brief skits, catchphrases ('Sock it to me!'), political barbs. Fast and irreverent, it went where no other American comedy show (or NBC) had gone before – even into a men's lavatory where 'Rock HUDSON is gay' was scrawled on the wall (bottom right hand of screen; in a sketch involving Arte Johnson). 'We were big enough to get away with anything,' said the show's co-producer George Schlatter in TELEVISION: A WORLD HISTORY (1988 T). No subject was taboo. Lily TOMLIN, Henry Gibson and Goldie Hawn were among the regular funsters, and guests like Richard Nixon and John WAYNE (dressed as the Easter Bunny) added to the hilarity.

P: George Schlatter and Ed Friendly (succeeded by Paul Keyes in 1971): NBC; 50 mins.

Rowe, Alick (194?–) English radio and television writer of larky gayish versions of mythology (OPERATION LIGHTNING PEGASUS; *Odysseus on an Iceberg*) and of plays about confused and turbulent young emotions including *Up School* (1970 T); *Apples and Tea* (1972 R); TWO PEOPLE (1979 T, with Julian Bond); *Morgan's Boy* (1984 T); *A Sort of Innocence* (1987 T). He's also been responsible for more basic fare: THE CREZZ 'Bent Doubles' (1976 T) etc; *The Great Balloon Debate* (1979 R); *Totally Gutted* (1992 R); *Friday on My Mind* (1992 T); etc.

Rowse, Dr A[lfred] L[eslie] (1904–) English historian, Shakespearean scholar, poet and broadcaster who looked back on his working-class Cornish childhood and tutoring at All Souls College, Oxford in such programmes as *On the Sea Front at Hornsea* ('my 55th birthday', 1960 R), and *The Time of My Life* (1970 R). Also featured in *Speaking Personally* (1952 R); *Robinson Country* (1984 T); and *The Media Show* (discoursing on EDWARD II, 1991 T).

RSVP (UK 1992– R) A very special series of cameos: letters to or from famous people to which there is no known reply. Among the correspondents

Vincent Van Gogh (to his brother Theo), George VILLIERS (to King JAMES I) and St PAUL (to the Corinthians). What gives the idea added zest are the comments and quizzing (of 'experts') by Matthew Parris, former Tory MP, now out and about in broadcasting.

P: Julia Gillett; BBC Radio 4; 15 mins.

Rubyfruit Jungle A 1973 best-selling American novel by Rita Mae BROWN. Dedicated to Hollywood star Alexis Smith (NIGHT AND DAY etc), its central character, Molly Bolt, is a Southern girl who lost her virginity to her girlfriend. 'An all-American, true-blue gay – and proud of it,' read the front cover blurb. The filming of this novel remains a HOLLYWOOD pipe dream in the tradition of *The Catcher in the Rye* or THE FRONT RUNNER. Sadie Benning celebrates Molly in her 4-minute *Me and Rubyfruit* (1989 V): 'I had read *Rubyfruit Jungle* for the first time when I was 13 or 14 – [I] started reading it and I was like "I'm just like this character".'

Rudkin, David (1936–) English playwright (*Afore Night Come*) who melds a pagan past with a guilty, shifty present in such eruptive, disturbing, sometimes overstuffed works as *The Stone Dance*, *Children Playing* (1967 T); CRIES FROM CASEMENT AS HIS BONES ARE BROUGHT TO DUBLIN (1973 R); *Penda's Fen* (1974 T); *Churchill's People* 'The Coming of the Cross' and 'The Great Alfred' (1974 & 1975); ARTEMIS '81 (1981 T); *Across the Water* (1983 T); *The Lovesong of J. Alfred* HITCHCOCK (1993 R).

The Ruffian on the Stair (UK 1964 R) The lives of a middle-aged couple, Joyce (Avis Bunnage) and Mike (Dermot Kelly), are disrupted by the intrusion of Billy Wilson (Kenneth Cranham), who is a disaffected youth; a little murder and a suicide (but not incest – that was written afterwards, for the TV version)

W: Joe ORTON; P: John Tydeman; 31.8.64; BBC Third Programme; 60 mins.

Orton's début. A three-hander containing elements that would be buffed up in *Loot* and ENTERTAINING MR SLOANE. His aim was contexted in a RADIO TIMES article which appeared at the time of the play's first broadcast: 'In a world run by fools, the writer can only chronicle the doings of fools or their victims. And because the world is a cruel and heartless place, he will be accused of not taking his subject seriously ... But laughter is a serious business, and comedy a weapon more dangerous than tragedy. Which is why tyrants treat it with caution.'

The version of *Ruffian* now available is one that Orton revised for the television production in 1967, sans BBC blue pencilling and with a more explicitly sexual feeling between Billy Wilson and his dead brother: 'Wilson's relationship ... had developed ... into a full-blown passion' (Orton's Diary, 25.4.67). Even so, the loving closeness the two had shared was at least open to a 1964 listener's interpretation. As was the opening dialogue about important private transactions in public conveniences.

Rupert Boy's name often carrying dash and flash and a hint or two of degeneracy.

UK/US: Rupert Endon (Ian Keith) in *Prince of Diamonds* (1930 C); Rupert (Paul Lukas), wounded German husband of Ann Harding in *The Fountain* (1934 C); Prince Rupert of the Rhine (Nigel Bruce) giving enthusiastic support to a Canadian trading company in *Hudson's Bay* (1940 C); Rupert of Hentzau, permed hair, thoroughly amoral in *The Prisoner of Zenda* (Ramon NOVARRO 1992 C; Douglas Fairbanks Jr 1939 C; James Mason 1952 C); unwitting accomplice to murder Rupert CADELL in ROPE (1948 C etc); a philanthropic-minded squirrel in *The Great Rupert* (1950 C); Rupert Ward (Derek Aylward), the over-neat public relations man who is covered in black ammoniac slime in *Quatermass II* (1955) and dies horribly; Rupert Dreisler, impresario, drug boss in *Paul Temple and the Spencer Affair* (1957 R); Rupert (Warren Mitchell), prattish member (reading 'Blank

Detail') of HANCOCK's 'Poetry Society' (1959 R); Rupert Callender (Dennis PRICE), suspected traitor in *Danger Within/Breakout* (1959 C); Rupert (Terence Alexander) in *The League of Gentleman* (1960 C); Rupert (Robert Hutton), wicked stepbrother of *Cinderfella* (ie Jerry Lewis 1960 C); Peter WYNGARDE in *Rupert of Hentzau* (1964 T); Rupert Rowbotham (*Richard* HAYDN) in *Zebra in the Kitchen* (1965 C); Rupert Street (Dudley Moore), pianist who has six weeks to get married in *30 Is a Dangerous Age, Cynthia* (1968 C); Rupert (John Cleese), wet blanket pseudo in I'M SORRY I'LL READ THAT AGAIN (1968 R); Rupert Vaughan (Nigel Anthony, Derek Seaton, Nicholas Edmett and Mark Cooper) in WAGGONERS' WALK (1969–72 R), an art student who hates his name and is called Rusty because of his red hair; Rupert Harcourt (John Normington) in *England, Their England* 'The Cricket Match' (1971 T); Rupert (Horst Janson), murdered German prisoner in *The McKenzie Break* (1970 C); Rupert Wilde (John Stride) suave crime-buster in *The Wilde Alliance* (1978 T); Rupert Purvis in *The Dog It Was That Died* (Dinsdale Landen 1982 R; Alan Howard 1989 T), a counter-counter spy who cracks; Rupert Jackson (William Boyde) in THE GENTLE TOUCH 'The Good, the Bad and the Rest' (1983 T), a very blond, smoothie lawyer who uses phrases like 'nigger in the woodpile' (to Maggie's disgust); Rupert Darley (Julian Glover) in *Only Yesterday* (1986 T); Rupert Imison (Jerome Willis) in *Bergerac* 'Low Profile' (1986 T); the dissolute brother Rupert Seymour (Pavel Douglas) – 'Thank God you'll never produce an heir' – in *First Among Equals* (1986 T); Rupert alias 'Pot Pourri' (Geoffrey BURRIDGE) deciding not to have a sex change in *The Refuge* (1987 T); Rupert (Anthony Daniels) in *Three Up, Two Down* (1987); Rupert Sutcliffe (Jeffrey GARDINER) in *Small World* (1988 T); Rupert (Gene Hackman), the FBI man in *Mississippi Burning* (1988 C); Rupert Draper (Simon Williams), married ANTIQUE DEALER in *Bergerac* 'All for Love' (1988 T); Rupert

Sethley, headless corpse in *The Mystery of the Butcher's Shop* (1991 R); Rupert Bright (Geoff Kelso), disturbed young man put into psychiatric care in A COUNTRY PRACTICE (1992 T); Rupert Campbell-Black (Marcus Lilbert), the degenerate anti-hero of *Riding* (1993 T); etc.

Russell Boy's name used for men superficially not built for competition: Russell (Harold LANG) in *Olive Ogilvie* (1957 R); Russell Weller (David Marshall Grant) in bed with Peter Montefiore (Peter Frechette) in THIRTYSOMETHING 'Love and Sex' (1989 T).

Russell The only regularly encountered male in AFTER HENRY, he is a civilized gay gentleman (cohabiting with the unseen, unheard Bob) who runs Bygone Books where Sarah (Prunella Scales) works. Played by Benjamin WHITROW (1985–9 R) and Jonathan Newth (1988–92 T), Russell has no surname, no customers and barely a lover. The TV version gave him the short-back-and-sides LOVE SIDNEY treatment. Even his mild remarks about diverging from traditional family pathways have been eliminated in the transfer from sound to sight. GAY TIMES' Jonathan Sanders said in 1988: 'References are rare and enigmatic: "I'm always scratching when Bob's away".'

Colin **Russell** Character played by Michael CASHMAN in EASTENDERS (1986–9 T), the only gay character to be featured regularly in a popular serial for two and a half years. Generally quiet, humourless and totally law-abiding – except for his having sex and cohabiting with a 20-year-old male, Barry CLARK (Gary Hailes). However, he's always ready to talk to people about their problems, canvasses for the Labour Party, at the 1987 election, refuses to take Pete Beale's put-downs, and rails against the THATCHER government's excesses, including the situations into which gays are forced and the unstoppable slide downwards marked by the imposition of CLAUSE 28.

Barry encourages Colin to go drinking and to discos. Eventually it is Barry who breaks off the year-long affair. He decides to leave Colin and get himself a girlfriend for the sake of family harmony. Colin finds it difficult but necessary to keep Barry's friendship, although the geographical proximity and the loneliness are punishing. One night, he starts talking to two young men in the Queen Vic. They all leave together, but the pair beat up Colin for his money. Later, his flat is done over.

He meets Guido (Nicholas Donovan) at a dinner party and has one or two months of happiness before, *Dark Victory*-style, Colin is diagnosed with multiple sclerosis and leaves Albert Square to go and live with his brother; he leaves with a couple of kisses to send him on his way. This disappearing act, without *éclat*, was altogether typical of the soap opera ethos. Steven in DYNASTY, social worker Ruth in EASTENDERS, and Christopher and Gordon in BROOKSIDE all left by the back door.

'I'm thankful for Colin and Barry. They may not kiss, they may not cuddle but at least, twice a week, I know that more than a third of the British population will see a positive image of homosexuality. Five, or even two years ago, that would have been unthinkable. In the face of so much hostility, it is important that we do not lose sight of important advances like this' (Paul Davies, *Capital Gay*, 20.11.87).

'... about as dreary an image for gay men to look to as could be imagined. Not only did he never really find a niche in Albert Square because he was gay, he also stuck out like a sore thumb because he was middle class ... Colin will fade out ... and none of us will be any the wiser about gay life in the East End' (W. Stephen GILBERT, *Capital Gay*, October 1988).

'In EASTENDERS you can lie, cheat, steal and do anything else that can be frowned upon, without being condemned in the narrative by becoming a one-dimensional villain (Nick Cotton is the possible exception). But one thing seems to be a greater sin than all the crises and missteps soap narrative can conceive, and that is to be a homosexual. Colin Russell is paying for being a homosexual, he is being nice. He is condemned to a lifestyle of being nice, helpful, considerate and caring' (John Marshall, 'Colin: Soapsuds and Tears – A Negative Image', *Gay Times*, April 1989).

'... for all the criticisms, I think Colin will be seen as a step forward and at a time when we as a community were being forced to take steps back by the government and the media' (Jonathan Sanders, *Gay Times*, May 1989).

'A fully fledged member of the Albert Square community,' commented Pauline (Wendy Richard) approvingly about Colin in 1987.

'No matter how much I love someone it will never be hang out the flags, have a celebration ... Don't take any notice of me. I'm just a middle-aged old POUF who always wants what he can't have,' Colin said at Matthew's stag night in 1988.

Russell, Craig (1948–90) Canadian FEMALE IMPERSONATOR whose career and relationships were folded into two comedy-dramas, OUTRAGEOUS! (1977, for which he won the Best Actor award at the Berlin Film Festival) and *Outrageous Too/Too Outrageous* (1987). Other roles included 'Judy' in *Trapper John* 'Straight and Narrow' (1982 T).

Russo, Vito (1946–91) American writer and gay activist whose invaluable history *The Celluloid Closet: Homosexuality in the Movies* was published in 1981. He was described as 'one of the five most important gay people' in OVER OUR DEAD BODIES (1992 T), and VOICES FROM THE FRONT (1991 T) ends with a freeze frame of him. He spoke about his deceased lover in COMMON THREADS: STORIES FROM THE QUILT (1989 C).

Ruth Girl's name (Hebrew for 'friend'). Like NAOMI, a favourite with Puritans in the 17th century, but unlike Naomi it is still quite popular.

US: Ruth Wonderly, dissembling murderess in *The Maltese Falcon* (Bebe Daniels 1931 C; Mary Astor 1941 C); escaped convict Ida Lupino in *The Sea Wolf* (1941 C); Ruth Holland (Margaret Sullavan) in *So Ends Our Night* (1941 C); good twin Olivia De Havilland accused of a murder her sister committed in *The Dark Mirror* (1946 C); nice girl (Joan Caulfield) impersonated by brattish kid sister in *Dear Ruth* (1947 C); Ruth Benton (Agnes Moorehead) in CAGED (1950 C); the 'plain' one (Betty Garrett) in *My Sister Eileen* (1955 C); *This Island Earth* (1955 C); unhappy wife accused of murdering nasty husband in PERRY MASON 'The Case of the Lame Canary' (1959 T); Ruth Latimer (Patch McKenzie) in *Goodbye Norma Jean* (1976 C); the cool and controlled teacher from out of town (Jane Hallaran) in LIANNA (1983 C); Ruth (Mary Stuart Masterson) in FRIED GREEN TOMATOES AT THE WHISTLE STOP CAFE (1991 C); etc.

UK: Sister Ruth (Kathleen Byron), the nun whose sexual frustration sends her over the edge in *Black Narcissus* (1946 C); Ruth Madden (Lana Morris) in *Solo for Canary* (1958 T); Dr Ruth Coliton (Elizabeth Weaver) in *The Hidden Truth* (1964 T); lesbian social worker Ruth Lyons (Judy Liebert) in EASTENDERS (1986 T); the wife who becomes a force for power and (limited) destruction: Julie T. Wallace in *The Life and Loves of a She-Devil* (1986 T) and Roseanne Barr in *She-Devil* (1989 C); Isla Blair as the photographer wife suffocated to death in a directly indirect way by Diana Rigg in *Mother Love* (1989 T); etc.

Ruth and Naomi In the Book of Ruth in THE BIBLE, two women from different cultures, a widowed daughter-in-law and her MOTHER-IN-LAW, give each other support in time of direst emotional and spiritual need. Ruth pledges her eternal devotion in words which Peter Brooks in a *Thought for the Day* in the early 1980s said almost sounded like a heightened form of the marriage contract:

... whither thou goest, I will go; and

where thou lodgest, I will lodge: thy
people shall be my people, and thy God
my God:
Where thou diest, will I die, and there
will I be buried ...

'Whither thou goest, I will go' was used
on the gravestone of a recently deceased
woman whose lover is planning to have
her own name incorporated when she
dies (one of the WOMEN LIKE US 1990
T). The passage (from Ruth 1:16–17)
is used in a number of lesbian marriage
ceremonies, blessings and funerals.

Ruth and Naomi were played by Elana
Eden and Peggy Wood in *The Story of
Ruth* (1960 C), and by Wendy Murry
and Mary MORRIS in *The Threshing Floor*
(1982 R).

Rye, John (193?–) English radio actor
with a knack of extracting juice from the
driest bones: flighty Osric in *Hamlet*
(1960); an 'Irritable Young Man' in *The
Girl Who Loved Eggheads* (1960); *Romeo
and Juliet* opposite Mary Miller (1965);
Jonadab in JONATHAN (1966); Algernon
Moncrieff in THE IMPORTANCE OF BEING
EARNEST (1971); Paul's lover in THE
LITMUS QUESTION (1975); Geoffrey
Pastmaster, a film star's ageing son in
Send Up (1976); satanic hairdresser in
JUST BEFORE MIDNIGHT 'Getting Ahead'
(1979); ACHILLES IN *Troilus and Cressida*
(1980); perverse husband Alex in *A
Murder of Quality* (1983); Charles in *The
Rocking Chair* (1983); read THE PICTURE
OF DORIAN GRAY (*Story Time* 1983); as
both Warder Plunkett and his lover
Geoffrey Peters in *The Bigger They Are*
(1984); caustic critic in *Tuesday Follies*
'Sticks and Stones' (1988); etc.

Sackville-West, Vita [Victoria] (1892–1962) English novelist, poet, playwright, biographer, travel writer, broadcaster and gardener, wife of Harold NICOLSON.

In 1918 she embarked upon an affair with Violet Keppel whom she had known as a child. Violet married Denys Trefusis a year later, but the two women continued to meet in secret. In 1922 Vita met Virginia WOOLF with whom she had an intermittent love afair throughout the decade. He love affair with Violet TREFUSIS formed the basis of POR- TRAIT OF A MARRIAGE (1988 T) in which she was played by Janet McTeer. She was portrayed at other stages in her life by Kate Buffery in *The New Party* (1992 R) and by Eleanor Bron in JOURNEY TO JAVA (1988 R). Vita was also the basis for the character of ORLANDO (Jennie Stoller 1984 R; Tilda Swinton 1992 C).

Radio broadcasts: a regular contributor to BBC Talks (45-minute reviews of *New Books/New Novels* on Mondays at 6.50pm until Miss E. M. Delafield took over in 1935); MARRIAGE (with Harold Nicolson, 1929), followed by *Happiness* (1930); *In Other Gardens* ('She has been described by Hugh WALPOLE as "a woman with every sort of talent"', 1938); *The Changing English Garden* (1948); *The Personality of Walter De La Mare* (1953); *Famous Women* 'Gertrude Bell' (1954); *Portrait of Virginia* WOOLF (1956); *Dame Ethel* [SMYTH] *Remembered* (1958); *The World of Books* (on rejected novels, 1961); etc.

Novels, plays, short stories: *Thomas Chatterton* (on the boy poet who committed suicide in a garret, 1946); *The Heir* read by Walter Fitzgerald on WOMAN'S HOUR (1969 R); *The Edwardians* (1964 R and *Woman's Hour* story 1987 R); *All Passion Spent* (1986 T); etc.

Biography: *Vita Sackville-West Called Victoria* by her neighbour Richard Church (1962 R); *Friends and Contemporaries* by Father Martin D'Arcy (1978? T); *Friday Night, Saturday Morning* (Nigel Nicolson and Vita's biographer Victoria Glendinning, 1981 T); *The English Garden*, an anthology compiled and read by Jill Balcon and John Rowe with John Westbrook: 'from Andrew Marvell to Vita Sackville-West' (1986 R); REBELS (R): 'She resembled a blend of both sexes, Lady Chatterley and her lover rolled into one ... Her marriage to Harold Nicolson survived despite her intense love affair with Violet Trefusis and the knowledge that her husband was a homosexual.'

'I don't mind whom you sleep with, as long as I may keep your heart' (Vita to Harold in a letter).

sado-masochism aka s&m. Pleasure as pain, pain as pleasure. The implicitly or explicitly consensual giving or receiving of pain for erotic gratification including bondage, verbal abuse, humiliation, piercing, toys, waste products, dressing up, fantasy, smacking, tickling, torture. The roles of sadist and masochist are often interchangeable. Theories and practices principally developed through the writings of the Marquis De Sade in the 18th century and of Leopold Ritter Von Sacher-Masoch and Richard Von Krafft-Ebing in the 19th. A fine line divides roughplay and s&m.

The British courts did not view sado-masochism lightly or as a matter of informed consent. A bit of slap and tickle that may be more slap than tickle, the very heart of human darkness, secret desires that should remain suppressed, its iconography is now in full blood with *The Terminator*, *The Silence of the Lambs*, *The Naked Lunch*, Julian CLARY and MADONNA.

Always on the periphery of films of such directors as Luis Buñuel, Alfred HITCHCOCK and Orson WELLES, it is also noticeable in some of the Johnny Weismuller and Lex Barker Tarzan movies, in GILDA (1946 C), the films of Erich Von Stronheim in the 1920s (particularly *Queen Kelly* 1929 C), and of those of Cecil B. De Mille, based on the Bible. Von Stroheim the actor seemed locked into some kind of strange sexual power play (as Carl Sarler) with Zaza (Greta GARBO) in *As You Desire Me* (1932 C); Beaumont (Alan Ladd) and Jeff (William Bendix) in *The Glass Key* (1942 C; in the Dashiell Hammett novel

Jeff as well as enjoying bouncing Ned 'off the walls' calls him his 'SWEET-HEART'); BLOODNOK ties up women in THE GOON SHOW 'The Secret Escritoire' (1955 R); elements in some of the 'Freudian Westerns' like JOHNNY GUI-TAR (1954 C), *The Man from Laramie* (1955 C), *Last Train from Gun Hill* (1959 C) and *One-Eyed Jacks* (1961 C) – whippings, eye-gouging, hand-smashing etc; the uncle in *Viridiana* (1961 C); *Whatever Happened to Baby Jane?* (1962 C with Davis and Crawford; 1991 T with the REDGRAVE sisters), criminal and her loving captor; Tippi Hedren and Sean Connery in *Marnie* (1964 C); greasy landlord Noel COWARD with the yapping dog and collection of whips in *Bunny Lake Is Missing* (1965 C); Peter O'Toole as LAWRENCE OF ARABIA strangely stirred by his beating/rape at D'era (1962 C); Miss Diketon (Janet Leigh) has a taste for pain in *The Man from UNCLE* 'The Concrete Overcoat Affair' (1966 T) and *The Spy in the Green Hat* (1966 C); Catherine Deneuve enthusiastically responding to her new job – and dreaming of bondage – in BELLE DE JOUR (1967 C); the two women in THE KILLING OF SISTER GEORGE play games of a disciplinary/submissive nature – juxtaposed with 'Miss Whiplash' who performs the same services for profit; the Black Queen (Anita Pallenberg) dresses in black leather with knives on each finger in *Barbarella* (1968 C); Basil (Alan Rowe) doesn't need much encouragement to humilate and beat up Arthur (John Stratton) in WANTED: SINGLE GENTLE-MAN (1967 T): 'He's too good a target, always asking for it'; public school flogging, whipping, maceration of the soul were well covered in IF ... (1968 C) and ANOTHER COUNTRY (1984 C).

CIA agent (Patrick O'Neal), posing as a PROSTITUTE, is horrified when a client (Bibi Andersson) implores him to rough her up in *The Kremlin Letter* (1970 C); Vanessa REDGRAVE in *The Devils* (1971 C); gardener (Marlon Brando) and governess (Stephanie Beacham) in *The Nightcomers* (1972 C); Joe Don Baker slapping Sheree North around in *Char-*

ley Varrick (1973 C), seemingly with her full consent; *The Maids* (Susannah YORK and Glenda Jackson 1975 C/T); the four judges in SALO: THE 120 DAYS OF SODOM (1975 C) force their prisoners through every kind of rarefied degradation before having them butchered; men are led through a Swedish park on leashes attached to their necks and genitals in *Taboo* (1977 C); the obsessed priest is ritualistically killed in his former lover's swimming pool in A SUPERSTITION (1977 T) – a fitting end after the years the man has spent following him only to be rejected: 'I was six weeks in hospital after that last beating you gave me'; Bulle Ogier is a dominatrix, the *Maitresse* (1978 C); a policeman is caught by a colleague in a prostitute's dungeon in *The Choirboys* (1977 C); policeman Al Pacino has to learn the rules of New York's gays and s&m scene in order to trap the killer in CRUISING (1980 C), but can't put the accoutrements to one side after the case is closed; the protagonist of TAXI ZUM KLO (1981 C) is urinated upon by his friendly service station attendant after work; policeman Harvey Keitel ties up John Lydon in the bath in *Order of Death* (1983 C); there were forty-eight written complaints about the German night club scene in *Smiley's People* (1982 T); British colonial rule unrestrained with very un-public school Ronald MERRICK beating a young boy in THE JEWEL IN THE CROWN (1984 T), then trying bondage with Indian youths; Jason Connery manacled to a wall in classic bondage pose in DR WHO 'Vengeance on Varros' (1985 T); the villain's abiding interest in *Commando* (1985 C), Arnold Schwarzenegger seems to betoken extensive painful eroticism: 'Think of sticking your knife into my flesh ... and twisting it. You don't want to deny yourself that pleasure,' he (Vernon Wells) croons before being killed; Augst Strindberg (Ian Hogg) in THE ROAD FROM KYMMENDO BAY (1985 R): 'Humiliate me ... tread on me'; George Cole tied up in *Blott on the Landscape* (1985 T); the subject of scandal and concern when the sadist beating RENT BOYS is a government minister in *The McGuffin* (1986 T); Julie Walters forgetting to let a client out of his box in PERSONAL SERVICES (1987 C); clean-cut hero (Kyle McLachlan) and older woman (Isabella Rossellini) in *Blue Velvet* (1986 C); repressed ACCOUNTANT (Francis Frappat) and MASSEUR (Jacques Martial) locked into increasingly satisfying but ultimately fatal sessions of love and pain in NOIR ET BLANC (1986 C); kidnap victim (Victoria Abril) denying her jailer (Antonio Banderas) his ultimate satisfaction during love-making in *Tie Me Up, Tie Me Down* (1990 C); the sybarite (Julian Sands) who kills his young lover during sex in *Naked Lunch* (1992 C); Alex Taylor (Jeremy Sims) having his jaded sexual tastebuds stimulated by twin sisters who bind his wrists with leather thongs in *Chances* 'Breaststrokes' (Aust 1992 T); Catherine (Sharon Stone) tying up Nick (Michael Douglas) in *Basic Instinct* (1992 C); Willem Dafoe having hot wax dripped over him by MADONNA in *Body of Evidence* (1992 C); CATWOMAN (Michelle Pfeiffer) and BATMAN (Michael Keaton) in *Batman Returns* (1992 C) which Kim Newman described (in *Sight and Sound* August 1992) as 'the strangest s&m relationship in mainsteam cinema'; a German gay man attempts to explain to a horrified Englishwoman in A BIT OF BERLIN (1992 R) why he and others find controlled pain and fetishistic clothing satisfying and liberating.

The subject has appeared in a number of documentary contexts ranging from the highly sensational (*Gay Power, Gay Politics* 1980 T; CIRCUIT 11 – MIAMI 1979 T) through the artistic (ARENA 'Robert MAPPLETHORPE' 1988 T) to the witty and well-argued *Free for All* 'A Legal Beating' (1992 T) presented by Derek Cohen ('Hello, I'm a sado-masochist!') which was triggered by the imprisonment of a number of gay men involved in consensual activities in this area of SEXUALITY.

safe sex/safer sex A wide variety of pleasurable sexual activities which have been recommended as involving no risk or a low risk or transmitting HIV/AIDS. These practices range from various forms of fantasy to full physical contact without intimate exchange of bodily fluids.

'Safe sex' was publicized by AIDS organizations within months of the discovery of the HIV virus in April 1984, but its specific details, even its emphasis upon the wearing of CONDOMS, have been conspicuously absent from plays and films dealing in any way with homo- or heterosexual acts. Precautions were discussed though not taken in *Show Me the Way, Ugly Angels* (1990 R), *The Men's Room* (1991 T), TOGETHER ALONE (1991 C) and *Husbands and Wives* (1992 C). Barbara (Lindsay Duncan) asks Michael (Robert Lindsay) *not* to wear a condom before they have sex in episode 5 of *GBH* (1991 T).

Notable trailblazers in the promotion of safe sex to the mass audience have been Julia Roberts as Vivian, the 'bargain basement hooker' in *Pretty Woman* (1990 C); the makers of EASTENDERS (T, a packet of condoms is mandatory 'set dressing' for every bedroom scene), and Sharon Stone who insisted that condoms be prominently displayed in her scenes with William Baldwin in *Sliver* (1993 C) and who was widely quoted in the popular press as saying 'Hollywood is in the public eye and we have a responsibility to promote safe sex'.

After nearly a decade of health education about the many and various ways of decreasing the risk of contracting HIV/AIDS, the safe-sex message continues to be unheeded by mainstream media, except for token mentions (MELROSE PLACE 1992 T) or jokes.

'I don't think all this safe sex is all it's cracked up to be. My husband and I had it in bed. And I was usually asleep. I don't think you can get any safer than that!' an elderly woman in *Designing Women* 'Killing the Right People' (1987 T).

sailors In *Fireworks* (1947 C) a group of sailors beat up a young man, but one ends up going to bed with him; 'I'm a very good friend to sailors,' explains Jacky aka Frenchy (Martin Benson) in *Judgement Deferred* (1952 C) – he has recently brought 'three little boys' ashore; CAMP sailor (Murray MELVIN) and cook (Angus Lennie) in *Petticoat Pirates* (1961 C); in BILLY BUDD (1962 C) Billy (Terence Stamp) is innocence unprotected, desired by the repressed Claggart (Robert Ryan); the two presidential candidates with a gay secret had both been in the US Navy: Don Murray in ADVISE AND CONSENT (1962 C) and Cliff Robertson in THE BEST MAN (1964 C); the rich old man (Orson WELLES) is obsessed with the sailor with the golden locks (Norman Eshley) in *The Immortal Story* (1968 C); similarly in *Malpertuis* (Welles with Mathieu Carriere 1971 C); a couple of tars who are also a 'couple' in *The Punchy and the Fairy* (1973 T); Tiny (Nick Ellsworth) in THE OBELISK (1977 T) 'won't say no to anything'; a bunch of the lads have lascivious designs on THE GOODIES (1976 T); Quentin CRISP's idea of heaven is a night under the stars in Portsmouth with the fleet in THE NAKED CIVIL SERVANT (1975 T); John Bury (Joseph O'Conor), ex-merchant navy in ONLY CONNECT (1979 T); any amount of jokey reference to gay men and sailors – Morris HARDACRE in *Brass* (1982 T) is advised by his father not to join the navy: 'Pity,' he murmurs, 'I've sometimes thought I might make a sailor'; QUERELLE (1982 C) is lusted after by the captain and by the café owner, and his mates discuss the outcome of a game of dice: 'When you win you get to have your pick; when you lose you have to let him fuck you'; Spider (Philip Davis) tries it on to get out of his contract aboard a nuclear submarine in *Submariners* (1983 T); taciturn, skinheaded companion on the road (Howard Napper) in NORTH OF VORTEX (1991 C).

'When the sailor changes from his bell-bottoms to his flared jeans, his psyche changes too. Gone is the rover, to be replaced by domesticated men. Only those without families do not change. They carry on the enduring and endearing traditions and pursuits of sailors of all generations' (*Radio Times* on *Sailor* 'Back Home' 1976 T).

St Clement, Pam (1942–) English actress with vibrance and control. Her most famous role is that of Pat Butcher (née Wicks) in EASTENDERS (1986–) who began as a semi-prostitute and all-round trouble-maker, then married Frank Butcher, faced problems with stepchildren and mother-in-law and, in 1992, accidentally killed a child when driving while drunk. Her only other starring role of similar sweep was as the fantasizing, Junoesque housewife in *Not for the Likes of Us* (1980 T).

She was interviewed in GAY NEWS in April 1980 by which time she was known as a player of brazen women like Doll Tripe in Vanbrugh's *A Journey to London* (1975 R) and Willard's wife in *One of the Boys* (1978 T). Later she was Di in *Nubile* (1980 R); Jean Bainbridge in *Angels* (1981 T); Noreen Mullin (with Irish accent) in TOGETHER (1981 T); a warder in *Scrubbers* (1982 C); a washerwoman in *Nineteen-Eighty-Four* (1984 C); Mother Superior in *Biggles* (1986 C); Ann Scott who is found dead in a caravan in *Indelible Evidence* 'Gaslight' (1987 T); etc. In *Partnerships* (1993 R) she discussed her professional relationship with Mike Reid who plays her husband in EASTENDERS.

St Elsewhere (US 1982–9 T) Set in St Eligius, a Boston public hospital known as a dumping ground, hence the title.
C: Joshua Brand and John Falsey; 60 mins.

Another show in the *Hill Street Blues* mould from MTM Enterprises, with Cynthia Sikes as Dr Annie Cavenero (whose 'secret' friendship with a lesbian doctor causes adverse comment in 'Girls Just Want to Have Fun' 1985) and Mark Harmon as dedicated, libidinous and HOMOPHOBIC surgeon Bob Caldwell, who has to come to terms with being HIV positive (or as the script had it: 'exposed to AIDS'). Wrote Jonathan Sanders in *Gay Times* in 1989: '[Caldwell says:] "I'm not too thrilled there are homosexuals but, when you get down to it, all we really want is to connect with someone." I'm not too thrilled about stories where gays are always the charges of hettie professionals to whom the emotional and oral focus is invariably shifted, enabling them to deliver a magnanimous message about homosexuals to the viewers.'

Other associated stories were 'AIDS and Comfort' (1984) and 'Split Decision' (1989). A sex change operation (on the friend of one of the senior surgeons) and gay-bashing (outside the hospital) also figured in this generally attractive, energetic series in which CAGNEY AND LACEY writer Georgia Jeffries was substantially involved.

Saint Laurent, Yves (1936–) French *haut couturier* responsible for many daring and extraordinary 'looks' for women and men since the early 1960s. He dressed Catherine Deneuve in many films, outstandingly in BELLE DE JOUR (1967 C) – leather coats, tennis togs, pink dressing gown, and a 'military' dress which inspires the lesbian madam to exclaim: 'What a cut, look at the detail!'

Biography: *The Look* (1992 T): 'an in-depth probe of the undisputed king of *couture*, an intensely private man, ridden by self-doubt'.

St Valentine's Day This rural tradition, a remnant of Roman Lupercalia, on 15 February of choosing a partner or a friend goes back to the 15th century at least and is mentioned in *A Midsummer Night's Dream*. Neither of the saints Valentine, whose special days both fall on 14 February, has any link to lovers or a wooing ceremony, or with women.

In THE GOLDEN GIRLS 'Valentine's Day' (1988 T) Blanche (Rue McClanahan) talks to a young man in a bar who is nervously waiting for his lover. He thanks Blanche for giving him the confidence to reveal his true feelings. The friend arrives and, to Blanche's controlled consternation, he's male. The young man tells him he loves him and they go off in close harmony. Blanche turns to the camera: 'Some things don't

change. Love is forever.' Then she pauses. 'No. Some things *do* change.'

Colin makes a Valentine's Day card for Barry in EASTENDERS (1987 T) which tips off Nick Cotton to the secret relationship.

To celebrate St Valentine's Day in 1993, BBC2 presented a whole weekend of 'romantic' fare, none of which related to same-sex love. However, over on BBC Radio 4, two hours were allotted to lesbians and gays in a special called A SUNDAY OUTING.

Saki [H(ector) H(ugo) Munro] (1870–1916) English writer, mainly known for his short stories; cruel, witty and iconoclastic, often about gentlemen who suffer from too much repose. Adaptations of his works include *The Watched Pot* (1938 & 1988 R); *Alfred Hitchcock Presents* 'The Schartz-Metterklume Method' (1959 T); *Great Ghost Tales* 'Sredni Vashtar' (with Richard Thomas, 1961 T); *The Unbearable Bassington* (1965 T); *The Liars* (1966 T); *Clovis in the Country* (1976 R); *The Unrest Cure* (1981 R); MORNING STORY 'The Hounds of Fate' (1986 R); *Hyacinth* (1987 R); *Short Story* 'The Lumber Room' read by John Moffatt (1992 R).

Played by John RYE in *Who Wrote 'Horseback Hall'?* (1985 R, about the anarchic detective novel he wrote in the trenches in the First World War), and by Charles Kaye in *Saki: The Storyteller* (1982 R): 'Munro wore a mask – behind it he hid his ... homosexuality. He shared bachelor rooms ['chumming'] with a young man ... A sense of brooding ... hovers over all his writing, a prevailing sense of loneliness.'

Sale, David (194?–) Australian novelist (*Twisted Echoes*), television scriptwriter (creator of NUMBER 96), producer and former actor whose last role, in a television commercial (with Peter Whitford in 1965), was a frozen pea: 'Ooo, it's cold in here.'

Scripts for THE MAVIS BRAMSTON SHOW (he later became executive producer); nine episodes of *The Group* (1971–2, 'three girls and three guys sharing a flat'); *Jill* (musical special starring Jill Perryman, 1974 T); *Gloria* (musical special starring Gloria Dawn, 1975 T); *Arcade* (1980 T); A COUNTRY PRACTICE; etc.

Film projects included a camp version of 'Ned Kelly' and 'Carnage', 'an Australian *Texas Chain Saw Massacre* with intimations of *Friday the 13th* and *Hallowe'en*'. One of his novels, *Come To Mother*, was made into a 1974 TV movie by Universal with a changed title (*Live Again, Die Again*), plot and characters.

'They can show all the bare bums they want to, but they'll never capture what we had in NUMBER 96: character and fun.'

salespersons If male, usually overly fussy and grand. Apart from those played in British productions by Brian Oulton and Michael WARD and in American ones by Franklin PANGBORN and James Millholin, examples include plotting Louis Manzini (Dennis PRICE) in *Kind Hearts and Coronets* (1949 C); loquacious Paul LYNDE in *Burke's Law* 'Who Killed Mr Colby in Ladies Lingerie?' (1965 T); Mr Martin (Frank WILLIAMS) who thinks Eddie and Bill are a couple in *Love Thy Neighbour* (1972 T); Peter McKriel, also heavily into bedding in an episode of *Cuckoo Waltz* (1976 T); MR HUMPHRIES, mine host of menswear in ARE YOU BEING SERVED? (1973–84 T).

Sallis, Peter (1921–) English actor, good as fusspots or slightly askew colourless people: Mr Milroy, the lodger in *The Stranger* (by Angus WILSON, 1960 T); the victim in *Blackmail* 'The Man Who Could See' (1966 T); THEATRICAL DRESSER in *Across a Crowded Room* 1978 T) and YOU'RE NOT WATCHING ME, MUMMY (1980 T); husband who has a fling with a sailor in THE OBELISK (1977 T); the very velouté television cookery expert in *Who Is Killing the Great Chefs of Europe?* (1978 C).

Also: *The War of the Peasants* (1948 T); Feste in (scenes from) *Twelfth Night* (1948 T); Wallace Porter, hero of *Whistling in the Dark* (1954 T); *Child's*

Play (1954 T); *Anastasia* (1956 C); *The Trial of Dr Fancy* (1964 T); *Inadmissable Evidence* (1968 C); *Last of the Summer Wine* (1974–86 T); *The Pallisers* (1975 T); *Strangers and Brothers* (1984); *Uncle of the Bride* (1985 T); *The Bretts* (1987 T); Rat in *Oh! Mr Toad* (1988 T); etc.

Sally Sung by Gracie Fields in *Sally in Our Alley* (1931 C), supposedly a lament by a soldier for his girl with whom he pleads 'Don't ever wander' (away from the alley and him). It was Gracie's signature tune and the preamble about the soldier was dropped. On *Daytime Live* (1990 T) Karen Lynne sang it, complete with final verse ('Marry me, Sally'). As 'Our Gracie' she asked the studio audience, and the one 'at 'ome', to join in. There were no sniggers. Granny (Paula Tilbrook) sang it in *Over the Rainbow* (1992 R) but without the 'marry me' section.

Karen Lynne said that Gracie Fields couldn't abide 'Sally': 'She would have liked to have strangled Sally with her bloody aspidistra.' One of the reasons the words stuck in her throat was that her husband's mistress (who lived with them for eight years) composed the final 'Marry me, Sally/And happy forever we'll be' couplet.

(Other paens to women sung by women include Raquel Welch's 'Singapore Sally' in *The Wild Party* 1974 C and Rita Hayworth's 'PUT THE BLAME ON MAME' in GILDA 1946 C.)

Salo: The 120 Days of Sodom (It 1975 C) A group of young people are herded into a sumptuous villa for the sole use of imperious pillars of (Fascist, *c* 1944) Italian society (Paolo Bonicelli, Giorgio Cataldi and Umberto P. Quintavalle).
W: Pier Paolo PASOLINI and Sergio Citti; based on *The 120 Days of Sodom* by the Marquis De Sade; P: Franco Cristaldi; D: Pier Paolo Pasolini; 117 mins.

Pasolini does not ask for involvement in the escalating horrors, only that his audience become as numbed as his unnerved and disoriented victims by the crisp tedium of the pornographic stories narrated by a series of CAMP ladies, the abrupt and immediate sexual release demanded by the impassive captors, the hideous 'WEDDING' of man and boy, and the senseless torture. Only in the final scene does any sense of human decency or hope penetrate: two boys DANCE TOGETHER.

This is a truly awe-inspiring film, made with an exact and unerring sense of the medium: a gripping, unblinking catalogue of humankind's capacity for inflicting pain and its ability to create a 'moral' framework (here Fascist, but it could just as easily be Communist, anarchist or religious) within which to wield total power. A masterpiece which has to be seen whole and uncut to appreciate the full force of the director's black vision.

'A summary of all Pasolini's interests, passions and vices: his love for the countryside, his feelings of mixed repulsion and attraction for physical suffering, his contempt for all kinds of prostitution linked to the exercise of political power (and for the art that serves it), and his faith in the Third World, Communist youth and the consolation of the transcendental' (Tulli Kezich, *La Repubblica*, 11.3.77).

'It's very hard to sit through and offers no insights whatsoever into power, politics, history or sexuality' (Geoff Andrew, *The Time Out Film Guide*, 1989).

Sand, George [Amandine-Aurore Lucille Dupin] (1804–76) French novelist who wore both men's clothes and a man's first name. The lover of actress Marie Dorval as well as Chopin, Mérimée and De Musset, but who, despite her bravado, was not openly lesbian and did not write about this area of sexuality.

Played by Merle Oberon (in top hat and waistcoat) in *A Song to Remember* (1945 C); Mary MORRIS in *Nom-de-Plume* 'A Child of Her Time' (1956 T); Patricia Morrison in *Song without End* (1960 C); Rosemary Harris in *Notorious Woman* (1974 T); Rosemary Leach in *Dialogue Between Friends* (corresponding with Gustave Flaubert played by Michael Byrne, 1981 R); Eleanor Bron in *A Winter in Majorca* (1987 R); Judy Davis in *Impromptu* (1991 C). (Greta GARBO also considered playing the role for George CUKOR in 1946.)

Biography: *The Good Lady of Nohant: The Story of George Sand* (1976 R, 'called a NYMPHOMANIAC, a lesbian, writer of genius and the Muse of the 1848 revolution').

Sanders, George (1906–72) English actor based in Hollywood who is prized for his portraits of cads, bounders, dilettantes, scoundrels and criminals in such films as REBECCA (1940); THE PICTURE OF DORIAN GRAY (1945); *Lady Windermere's Fan* aka *The Fan* (1949); *Samson and Delilah* (1949); ALL ABOUT EVE (1950, as Addison De Witt); *Moonfleet* (1955); *Solomon and Sheba* (1959, as King David's 'other' son); *Bluebeard's Ten Honeymoons* (1960); *A Shot in the Dark* (1964). On television, he reprised Clifton WEBB's Waldo LYDECKER in *Laura* (1966).

But, on occasion, he could cast off his aching *ennui* to be sympathetic, heroic even: *The Falcon* series (1940–2); *Rage in Heaven* (1941); *The Moon and Sixpence* (1942); *Uncle Harry* (1945); *Forever Amber* (1947); *Call Me Madam* (1953); *King Richard and the Crusaders* (1954, in the title role); *Village of the Damned* (1960, saving the world by killing the evil children and himself); and – seen first in long blonde wig and feather boa playing piano and singing in a San Francisco gay bar – in *The Kremlin Letter* (1970, as the Warlock).

Sandler, Barry (194?–) American screenwriter who, in 1982, wrote the first mainstream, major studio gay film, MAKING LOVE.

Also: *Kansas City Bomber* (1972); *Gable and Lombard* (1976); *The Duchess and the Dirtwater Fox* (1976); *The Mirror Crack'd* (1980); *All American Murder* (1992); *Family Values* (about a journalist with a gay BROTHER, 1993).

Sapphist In *A Song at Twilight* (1982 T; 1988 R) Noel COWARD had an unseen character called Liesel, whom his central character dismissed as a 'leather-skinned old Sapphist'.

Sappho (*c* 612–*c* 560 BC) One of the most famous and celebrated women in the ancient world, regarded as the 'tenth muse' in Hellenic and Mediterranean civilizations, whose lyric poetry was inspired by the attachment of the teacher for the protégée. Only 200 or so fragments of her nine books remain, telling of love and its rejection – an inspiration to classical and modern writers and bequeathing the word 'lesbian' to the 19th century.

'She was one of the world's greatest poets; she was Greek; she was married; she was a mother; she was a widow. She set up a college of culture on Lesbos for women to learn, to love and to explore together. We felt that covered all the aspects of women,' said Jackie FORSTER (who co-edited the magazine *Sappho*) on *Monty at Large* 'The Gay Scene in London' (1979 R). She continued: 'Lesbianism ... means you can be married, you can be a mother, you can be living in a couple with children or in a couple without children, or you can live alone.'

'Suddenly, there was a lady poet. It was unprecedented because all of the famous writers and poets thought that Sappho was the top and there it is. She was finally exiled for her political thoughts and so on and so forth, but she must have been a remarkable person,' Peggy Glanville-Hicks in *P.G.-H: A Modern Odyssey* (1991 T) about *Sappho*, the opera she composed. This film ends with a fragment by the poet:

Am I to be no more found in this Fair World
For all the search of the revolving Moon
And patient shine of Everlasting Stars?

This and all Sappho's other existing words was read, in both Greek and English, on the BBC Third Programme in January 1953, a 'tribute' lasting just 20 minutes. In 1982 a radio documentary, WHO IS SAPPHO? was produced (by former singer Susan Denny) in which poet Judith Kazantzis gave 'a brief but spirited account of Sappho's love of women': 'Of course she went to bed with women ... it was a pre-Christian society without guilt ... just this wonderful world of women.' This was in opposition to Professor Mary Lefkowitz and Dr Angus Bowie who maintained that there was no homosexual element in Sappho's writings.

Jackie Marcus in GAY NEWS made up her own mind on the basis of the evidence: 'Sappho's writing, according to these scholars, becomes a sort of sophisticated advertising of feminine virtues for would-be husbands to scan ... Listening to her marvellous poems read to the accompaniment of lyre music, moved by their intelligence, passion and wit, I was certainly prepared to believe, whether or not it's romantic, that of course they came out of honest love and passion for other women.'

References to Sappho in mainstream entertainment: Dame Hilda TABLET (Mary O'Farrell) has knowledge of her in THE PRIVATE LIFE OF HILDA TABLET (1954 R) and one of her fragments was quoted (by Joyce Heron) in LOVE AND MISS FIGGIS (1954 T). She appeared in tableau for a quarter of a minute in *Circus of Horrors* (1960 C: 'the incomparable Sappho surrounded by her gorgeous handmaidens!') and was the subject of a 1960 Italian epic, *Saffo, Venere di Lesbo*, with Tina Louise as a poetess and Aphrodite worshipper who relinquishes her religion for the love of a man (Kerwin Matthews). It was sold to the English-speaking world as *The Warrior Empress* in 1962. Marina Vlady played a modern *Sappho* (1970 C) who admits, very softly, in one scene that she 'likes women, too'. Gounod's – heterosexual – version of the poet's life, *Sapho*, was broadcast on BBC Radio 3 with Katherine Cienski in the title role. Burt Lancaster speaks scornfully of Sappho and her Lesbians 'doing their thing' in *The Midnight Man* (1974 C), and a disco named after her was the setting for Helen Mirren's attempted pick-up by a fashion editor (Jenny Runacre) in *Hussy* (1980 C). (A MORNING STORY 'The Sappho Lectures' (1986 R) had no relevance, save for its title.)

Sappho has been used once as the name of a fictional character – a male – Sappho Holyrood (Felix Felton) in *The Man in Armour* (1954 T). The only female was Sappho Henderson, wife of the pilot who flew the wreckage of the alien space ship in the 1940s after the crash in Roswell, Ohio (interviewed in the documentary *UFOs: Mystery of the Unknown* 1990 T).

Sartre, Jean-Paul (1905–80) French philosopher, novelist, playwright, essayist and political activist with an increasingly thoughtful, if grim attitude towards homosexuals, heterosexual men uncertain of their masculinity, exploited women, prisoners and other minorities, encouraged by his lover Simone De Beauvoir.
   HUIS CLOS (1946 R etc); *Crime Passionnel* (1960 T); *The Respectful Prostitute* (1964 C); THE ROADS TO FREEDOM (1970 T).
   Biography: *Modern European Writers 3* with Michael Bryant as Sartre and Jill Balcon as De Beauvoir (1986 R).

Sassoon, Siegfried (1886–1967) English poet and novelist. Celebrated in *Writers' World* 'First World War Poets' (by Jocelyn Brooke, John Betjeman and John LEHMANN, 1966 T); *The Story of the Young Soldier Poet* (compiled and performed by Peter Barkworth, 1987 R); *War Requiem* (1989 C/T). He was played by Stephen MacDonald in *Not About Heroes* (1983 R) who also read *Memoirs of a Fox-hunting Man* (1986 R). Interviewed in *A Portrait of Siegfried Sassoon* (by Vernon Scannell, 1968 R).

(I Can't Get No) Satisfaction The 1965 Rolling Stones song (written by Mick Jagger and Keith Richard) which is effectively used to indicate what cannot be shown in THE CONNOISSEUR (1966 T): the erotically sinister nocturnal happenings at a PUBLIC SCHOOL. The captain of CRICKET, Ballantyne (Ian Ogilvy) sings it unaccompanied to indicate his ruthless pursuit of nubile flesh. The lyrics irresistibly conjure up a powerful system of restrictions and re-

straints pulling against burgeoning sexuality. In another scene, Ballantyne and his cohorts try to break down the will of the repressed Christopher Tenterten (Richard O'Sullivan) by singing another song: 'Just lean towards me ... relax, let yourself go ... lean towards me and let me do it again.' 'Satisfaction' was also heard in *Melvin and Howard* (1980 C) and *Young Einstein* (1988 C) and accompanying the Voyager II space-probe footage in the opening scene of *Starman* (1984).

Saturday Night Out (UK 1991) Six hours of specially made programmes (with one big exception). The largest undertaking of its kind on behalf of lesbian and gay people by any national television company (BBC2), it was regarded by some as a damp squib, reshowing THE NAKED CIVIL SERVANT (an ITV production, which the BBC had turned down in the 1970s) in place of a documentary on PORNOGRAPHY, and becoming noticeably windier and less engrossing as the evening progressed. Among the entertaining items were THE ROCK 'N' ROLL YEARS, *To Be or Not to Be* (homosexuals working in the theatre), and *The Martina Factor* (lesbian Navratilova fans at the international womens' tennis tournament in Eastbourne).

Saturday Night Theatre A 90-minute BBC Home Service (later Radio 4) drama slot. It celebrated its 50th anniversary in April 1993 with Agatha Christie's *The Pale Horse*, with veterans Mary Wimbush and Hilda Schroder. Among its more daring productions: DANGEROUS CORNER (1945); THE GREEN BAY TREE (1946); *Children in Uniform* (ie MAEDCHEN IN UNIFORM, 1946 & 1949); *Corinth House* (1949); *Miss Pym Disposes* (1952); *The Girl Who Loved Eggheads* (1960); THE MISSING DAY (1986).
   Monday Night Theatre began in 1947 and provided among others: A TASTE OF HONEY (1961); THE CHILDREN'S HOUR (1971); A SINGLE MAN (1972); NOW SHE LAUGHS, NOW SHE CRIES (1975). It is now known as *The Monday Play*, a title that has embraced a few strong homo-

sexual plays: SILENT WING (1984); THE TINKER'S DAUGHTER (1986); A BIT OF BERLIN (1992); etc.

saunas/Turkish baths Places of seduction leading to death: a murder amid the steam in *Othello* (1952 C); a meeting that leads to murder in *The Day of the Jackal* (1973 C) when the assassin (Edward Fox) allows Anton Rodgers to pick him up so that he can use the pick-up's flat as a hiding place; a sauna owner (Rosa VON PRAUNHEIM) refusing to institute safe-sex regulations until he is diagnosed as HIV positive and meets rejection and oppression in *A Virus Has No Morals* (1986 C). A less violent – lyrical even – seduction between Barbara Carrera and Merete Van Kamp in DALLAS (1986 T) was scripted but not filmed – at the insistence of one of the actresses. *See also* BATHS; MASSEURS; SHOWERS.

Savage, Lily [Paul O'Grady] (195?–)
English FEMALE IMPERSONATOR, a former social worker whose glamorous creation of baleful eye and puckered lips, not unlike Vlad the Impaler, has 'a bit of a mean mouth on 'er an' all'. Married, 'Lily' lives in Liverpool with a whippet called Queenie and two Persian cats, shoplifts to survive and talks matter of factly of the pill, the coil, PMT and hormone replacement therapy. Appeared in *The Bill* (1988 T), OUT ON TUESDAY (1990 T) and OUT (1991 T). Best known as the box office woman, ice cream saleslady and usherette in *Out*'s 'night at the pictures' header, used by SBS for its gay movie *Special Features* (1993).

Sayer, Philip (1947–89) English actor, tall and impressively medieval of face. Achieved greatest fame as Marcel Leibovici, the lover of Miss *Bluebell* (1986 T), and the revenge-driven Ramsey in *Floodtide* (1986–7) after playing less traditional leading-man parts: TRANSVESTITE 'Lola' in CROWN COURT (1976 T); a gay orgy participant in SEBASTIANE (1976 C); Oscar WILDE in *Fearless Frank* (1978 T); gay activist Dennis Church in

The British Situation: A Comedy (shown at the 1978 Edinburgh Television Festival and at the 1992 OUT OF THE ARCHIVES lesbian and gay television season); lover of a teenage boy in TWO PEOPLE (1979 T); St PAUL in *Anno Domini* aka *A.D.* (1985 T); Basil Underwood, black magic exponent in *Star Trap* (1988 T). Final appearance: *Edens Lost* (1989 T).

SBS (Special Broadcasting Services) Semi-national Australian television and radio service, which began in 1980, whose brief is to supply programmes which relate to AUSTRALIA's multicultural society. Peter Barrett, Director of Programming, said in *Capital Q* (18.12.92):

We see our responsibility to push the boundaries of public taste and explore what are acceptable issues in the public mind. We do that because you cannot talk about cultural diversity and pluralism in society unless you accept that implicit in that [ethos] are a range of value systems at work ... [We] treat gays and lesbians naturally in the same way as other programming. If it's something important and contributing to the debate about society and leading to a better society, then we will proceed with it. Equality is not now an issue. What is at issue are the [broadcasting of] more extreme manifestations of a gay and lesbian LIFESTYLE. We've taken the view that we have got to be balanced, responsible, cautious but not cowardly.

Among its more notable 'in-house' productions: *Vox Populi*, EAT CARPET and *Face the Press*. Imports include OUT/OUT ON TUESDAY, films from the HORIZON series, *Drop the Dead Donkey*, *Lenny Henry and The American Civil War*. Its mega-diversity may be under threat because, in 1992, SBS had to accept advertising and sponsorship to survive.

scarves Silk for preference, pastel in shade and wafting in texture – essential garb for the 1960s queer: Dick Emery's CLARENCE, the Italian boyfriend of Charles in *Emma's Time* (1970 T), and DENNY AND TERRY in THE CREZZ (1976

T). The flying foulard could also be seen around the throats of (dandyish) heterosexual characters: Patrick Cargill's in *Father, Dear Father* (1968–73 T), and Tony Curtis and Roger Moore in *The Persuaders!* (1971). Even J. R. Ewing (Larry Hagman) wore a modified version in the first series of DALLAS (1978–9 T).

The scarf as ritual wear for the gay man began to lose its grip in the late 1970s: it was not included as standard issue for Jodie in SOAP or Harry in ROCK FOLLIES. The article's last gasp came in *Fort Apache: The Bronx* (1981 C): the would-be suicide was swathed in a foot and a half strip of pink silk.

Scene (UK 1968–) A lively, intelligent and occasionally controversial series of plays, interviews and documentaries about issues facing young people, produced for BBC Schools Television by Roger Tonge. Writers have included David COOK (IF ONLY), Leslie Stewart (TWO OF US) and Andrew DAVIES, but the veracity they are more than capable of bringing to their less acceptable subjects is hamstrung by restraints imposed as much by legislation as by the standards required by the BBC. In 1987 *Scene* produced a special on HIV/AIDS using playlets, interviews and practical advice.

Schlesinger, John (1926–) Incisive, sympathetic English film director, a former actor. Equally at home with characters from top and lower rungs of the social ladder, and with a sympathy for dashed hopes and self-delusion. Some of his more commercial projects like *Honky Tonk Freeway* (1981) have been depressingly noisy and hysterical.

Made his first film at the age of 9 (about his grandmother), followed by a more ambitious experimental work, *Star Fighter*, while he was in the army (his fellow soldiers included Kenneth WILLIAMS and playwright Peter Nichols). His documentary *Sunday in the Park* was shown on BBCTV in 1956, leading to numerous short-film assignments for TONIGHT, followed by MONITOR (his

subjects included Benjamin BRITTEN, a drama school class and children painting with teenagers commenting in *The Innocent Eye* 1959).

He was in charge of the second unit on *The Four Just Men* (1959 T) and *The Valiant Years* (1960 T) before achieving a big breakthrough with a 35-min documentary, *Terminus* (about Waterloo Station) which led to a generally illustrious film career: *A Kind of Loving* (1962); *Billy Liar* (1963); DARLING (1965); *Far from the Madding Crowd* (1967); MIDNIGHT COWBOY (1969); SUNDAY, BLOODY SUNDAY (1971); *Visions of Eight* (segment on the 1972 Berlin Olympics marathon, 1973); *The Day of the Locust* (1976); *Marathon Man* (1976); *Yanks* (1979); *The Falcon and the Snowman* (1985); *The Believers* (1987); *Madame Sousatzka* (1988); *Pacific Heights* (1990); *The Innocent* (1993).

For television he has made AN ENGLISHMAN ABROAD (1983), *Separate Tables* (1983) and A QUESTION OF ATTRIBUTION (1991) as well as copious amounts of commercials (including Fry's Turkish Delight and Polo mints). He acted as narrator and interviewer in CORAL BROWNE: CAVIAR TO THE GENERAL (1990).

As actor: 'Player/Singer' in *Will Shakespeare* (1950 T); *Yerma* (1950); Fabius Maximus in *The Road to Rome* (1952 T); Amiens in *As You Like It* (1953 T); *Oh Rosalinda!* (1955 C); sailor in *The Battle of the River Plate* (1956 C); lawyer in *Brothers-in-Law* (1957 C); Mr Gribble in THE GROVE FAMILY 'Business as Usual' (1957 T); Charles Reade in *A Woman of Property* (1957 C); Derek, half of a gay couple in THE LOST LANGUAGE OF CRANES (1992 T).

Biography/autobiography: *Movie Men* (1970 T, with Jon Voight and Alexander Walker); *Man of Action* (1972 R); DESERT ISLAND DISCS (1967 & 1991 R); etc.

Schneider, Maria (1952–) German actress who was one of the first to lead a high-profile lesbian/bisexual life. Her film career has been sporadic and modest since her sensational début opposite Marlon Brando in *Last Tango in Paris* (1972, replacing Dominique Sanda), followed by *Reigen* (1974); Michelangelo Antonioni's *The Passenger* (1975, opposite Jack Nicholson); *The Babysitter* (1975); *A Woman Like Eve* (1979); *Mama Dracula* (1980); etc. She was David Suchet's wife in *A Song for Europe* (1986 T) and a long-time prisoner given her freedom in *Au Pays de Juliette* (1992 C). She was interviewed for the French series *Cinema Cinema* (shown on Channel 4's *Visions* in 1984) discussing her mainly traumatic experiences while making *Last Tango*.

schools *See* PUBLIC SCHOOLS; STUDENTS; TEACHERS.

Schuman, Howard (1942–) American, British-based writer whose work has been almost exclusively for television. A very original talent with a sparkish, kinetic feel for storytelling, a love of pop culture and a nose for trends and current pretensions. Best known for ROCK FOLLIES, his other TV work include: *Vérité* (1973); *Censored Scenes from King Kong* (1974); *Churchill's People* 'The Liberty Tree' (about the Boston Tea Party, 1975); *Red Letter Day* 'Amazing Stories' (1976); *Up Line* (1987); *Small World* (adaptation of David Lodge's novel, 1988); *Soldiers* (1991); *Selling Hitler* (1991).

Appeared on GAYS: SPEAKING UP (1978); GAY LIFE 'Gays in the Media' (1980); OUT ON TUESDAY 'Lesbians and Gays in Film and Television' (1989); 'D. H. Lawrence, High Priest of Love' in *Without Walls* 'Dark Horses' (1992); etc. He was script consultant for the history of London gay club and pub life in OUT 'Storm in a Teacup' (1992). He has recently become an occasional radio interviewer and reviewer on arts programmes such as *Third Ear*, *Writers Talking*, *First Night* and *Night Waves*.

science fiction A remarkably wide genre within whose sometimes fantastic, sometimes realizable purlieus can be found all manner of role reversal and gender bending, not to mention acceptance of more fluid sexual rules: woman into man in A FLORIDA ENCHANTMENT (1914 C); husband and wife switching places in TURNABOUT (1940 C); ROBBY THE ROBOT in *Forbidden Planet* (1956 C); episodes of THE TWILIGHT ZONE (1957– 64 T); THE ROCKY HORROR PICTURE SHOW (1975 C); *Red Letter Day* 'Amazing Stories' (1976 T); *Logan's Run* (1976 C; 1977 T); Spock and Kirk in the STAR TREK movies (1979–); *Alien/Aliens/ Alien 3* (1979–92 C); *Alien Nation* (1988 C; 1989 T); *Quantum Leap* (1989– T); *Fair Exchange* (1992 R); etc.

scientists Dr Praetorius (Ernest THESIGER) in THE BRIDE OF FRANKENSTEIN (1935 C), creator of homunculi ('Science, like love, has her little surprises') and provider of a mate for the monster, who was 'booted out' of academia for knowing too much of the mysteries of life and death; 'You think I'm mad ... Perhaps I am'; the humourless head of the Cold Research Centre (Irene Handl) in *Doctor in Love* (1960 C) referred to as an 'Aberdeen Angus' by the two young women she lusts after; Madeleine Dawnay (Mary MORRIS), intense, skull-like professor creating (female) life in *A for Andromeda* (1961 T) and destroying whole cities in her determination to push the boundaries of science in *The Andromeda Breakthrough* (1962 T); biologist Tom (Ian Hendry) and psychologist David Neville (Alan BADEL), uneasy colleagues and scratchy 'flatmates' in *Children of the Damned* (1964 C); Dr Saforet (Capucine) inventor of poison gas in *Fraulein Doktor* (1968 C); Ray Walston as the chemist involved in industrial espionage, murder and transvestism in *Caprice* (1967 C); Dr Frank Marsh (Allan Lander) in *The Deep Concern* (1979 T), a bronzed and bearded AUSTRALIAN who calls everyone 'Cobber' and is 'a born stirrer' and 'like a lot of so-called scientists he's also pretty juvenile ... And like a lot of gays, he chatters a lot'; Dr Alan TURING, inspired, slightly eccentric co-inventor of the computer, Enigma code smasher and unashamed homosexual brought to television – under another name – as a mother-weighted prig in *The Imitation Game* (Nicholas Le Prevost 1980) and in HORIZON 'The Strange Life and Death of Dr Turing' (1992 T); biologist Boris (Gary Waldhorn), easy-going, socializing, murdered by Miranda Richardson in *After Pilkington* (1987 T).

Scorpio Rising (US 1963 C) The allure of chrome and black leather, jeans and T-shirt, Jesus, PUCK and James DEAN set down next to 'innocent' songs by Rick Nelson ('Fools Rush In'); The Ron-Dells ('Wind-Up Doll'); Bobby Vinton ('Blue Velvet'); Elvis Presley ('Devil In Disguise'); Ray Charles ('Hit The Road Jack'); Martha and the Vandellas ('HEATWAVE'); the Crystals ('He's A Rebel'); Claudine Clark ('Party Lights'); Kris Jensen ('Torture'); Gene McDaniels ('Point Of No Return'); Little Peggy March ('I Will Follow Him'); the Surfaris ('Wipe Out').
W/P/D: Kenneth Anger; 25 mins.

A film of dark forces and rough magic, both pure and dangerous. The camera approvingly lingers over men in biker's uniforms, male pin-ups, chains, oiled flesh, an orgiastic party where someone's genitals are smeared with mustard, a skull with a cigarette between its teeth.

'If I'm in the right mood, the intensity and brilliance of [Anger's] films convey a feeling for gay desire as part of an elemental system of powers that defies and disrupts strait-laced conventional views of the world. At other times, it just seems like a lot of silly people getting dressed up in silly clothes and playing at evil, with little grasp of what cruelty and wickedness really are. But then perhaps this is the point – the 'silly', giggly, *naughty* quality of Anger's films is a spirit which at times feels irritating, unhelpful to the cause of gay rights, but at others is a tonic refusal to grow up into the drab oppressiveness of normal straightness' (Richard Dyer, *Now You See It. Studies on Lesbian and Gay Film*, 1990).

Scotland Usually doused in much cosy folkloric of burring voices, KILTS and heterosexual conformity. Some of its more divergent citizens – a few living over the Border – include Bonnie Prince Charlie (David Niven 1948 C; Russ Abbot in *Russ Abbot's Madhouse* 1982 T, etc); the painters Robert McBryde and Robert Colquhoun (MONITOR 1959); ship's cook who is not very proud of his spotted dick (Angus Lennie) in *Petticoat Pirates* (1961 C); Bunny (John Grieve) in THE DARK NUMBER (1967/8 T); tough army officer (Ellen McIntosh) in GIRL (1974 T) who calls her former lover 'a right piece of Sassenach shite'; BARTENDER Rikki (Angus Lennie) in PLAYMATES (1978 R); Sir James Mackieson (James Drake) in *The Treachery Game* (1979) and *The Assassination Run* (1980); Duggie (James Telfer) in HOUSE ON THE HILL 'Something for the Boys' (1981 T); Jack (Ewan Stewart) in *Green Street Revisited* (1982 T) telling his parents that he is opening a restaurant with a Spanish lover: 'José and I love each other. We want to grow old together'; Jock (Bill Leadbiter) one of the principal stirrers in the *Men's Group* (1983 R); Billy in the documentary *Dossers* (1984 T) who explains how his family's violent response to his homosexuality led him to uproot and live on the streets; Sammy (Kenny Ireland, then Campbell Morrison), wine bar manager, friend of the heroine in *Life without George* (1987–88 T); drag entertainer Annabelle (Robbie Coltrane) at THE FRUIT MACHINE (1988 C) where he is abruptly terminated with a cutthroat razor; Annie (Colette O'Neill), the surprising and sensuous MOTHER-IN-LAW in WILD FLOWERS (1990 T); the young man who worships Judy GARLAND and, miraculously, gets to spend an afternoon with her, which leads to the birth of another gay man in *Beyond the Rainbow* (1991 R); Jimmy SOMERVILLE; etc.

The first local television programme to single out homosexual Scots as a distinct minority was *This Is the Day* 'Disease, Disposition or Deviation?' in 1967.

In 1976 the Scottish Minorities Group, which had begun in 1969, produced *Open Door* 'Glad to Be Gay?' which *Radio Times* described in SMG's own words: 'Gay people often hide from society, fearing ridicule. We are finding other solutions.' Broadcast nationwide at 11.10pm, it was not given the honour of the usual Saturday afternoon repeat.

Two years later, *Current Account* talked to gay and lesbian couples and to married gays as well as visiting the flourishing Glasgow Gay Centre and the Edinburgh Gay Advisory Centre. At the core of the programme was discussion of the Bill to legalize homosexuality in Scotland – which was finally allowed a few years later.

Scotland's GAY SWITCHBOARD was represented on *The Afternoon Show* 'Gays' (1983 T) which also interviewed Marjorie Cameron about being the mother of lesbian activist, writer and former GAY NEWS contributor Marsaili Cameron.

The 1992 video *Step We Gaily*, through the medium of Scottish dancing, is a depiction of Scotland's generally low-lying, fairly close-knit lesbian and gay population.

Scott, Harold (1891–1964) English actor, singer, pianist, author and historian of the music hall, one of the founders of the Players Theatre, and the Dauphin opposite Sybil Thorndike's Joan in *Saint Joan*. Very much the Bloomsbury and Chelsea erudite BOHEMIAN, his friends included E. M. FORSTER, Sir Osbort Sitwell, Ramsay MacDonald, the first Zionists, VEGETARIANS, mystics, progressives, Quakers, POETS, *avant gardists*, while his next-door neighbours were critic James AGATE, actor–singer Paul Robeson, economist John Maynard Keynes, actor–writer Miles Malleson and sculptor Jacob Epstein. Twice married (to Raymonde Collignon and Audrey Lucas, daughter of E. V.), a lover of Elsa Lanchester (with whom he founded the theatre-cabaret Cave of Harmony, patronized by H. G. Wells, Evelyn WAUGH, Aldous Huxley and James WHALE).

In the second series of DIXON OF DOCK GREEN (1956 T) Ted WILLIS created for Harold Scott his most famous role: louche, erudite, very likely homosexual Duffy CLAYTON who transcended his grotty living circumstances with lofty idealism, creative solitude, a sharp tongue (especially against the police), and a love of Beethoven.

C: *The Water Gypsies* (1932); *Disraeli* (1933); *The Man in Grey* (1943); the heroine's music hall-loving father in *Trottie True* (1949); *The Woman with No Name* (1950); *The Spanish Gardener* (1956); *The Brides of Dracula* (1960); *The Young Ones* (1961); the judge in *The Boys* (1962); *The Yellow Rolls-Royce* (1964); etc.

R: *The Trees Are Not for You to Pick* (1933); Thomas Telford, road and bridge maker in *The Road to Ireland* 'London to Holyhead' (1934); *Thieves Kitchen* (1936); *The Dialogues of Plato* (1947); Pompey in *Measure for Measure* (1948); Sicinius Velutus in *Coriolanus* (1950); etc.

T: *Songs* (1934); *Cabaret* (1936–7, singing 'The Sentimental Starfish' and 'Take Me In Your Arms, Love' but not ''Arold' or ''Orace Up The River' – both considered unsuitable for television); Tony in *Two Gentlemen of Soho* (1937); *Rococco* (1938); *Oleograph* (1939, with Patricia Hayes, Freda Bamford and Richard GOOLDEN); Babberley alias CHARLEY'S AUNT (1938); title role in *Sheppey* (1939); Don Victorio in *Fortunato* (1947); Dr Manette in *The Only Way* (1948); Joel O'Brien in *The Front Page* (1948); White King in *Alice in Wonderland* (1948); Delius Handle in *Mr Bowling Buys a Newspaper* (1950); singing 'unusual songs' on *Children's Hour*; the magician in *The Bookworm of Brookland* (1951); the father of *The Children of the New Forest* (1955); the judge in *The Seddons* (1956); DIXON OF DOCK GREEN (1956 episode 7, thereafter at least one annual appearance until 1962); Mr Lamb in *Charles and Mary* (1958); Guillaume Dubarry in YOU ARE THERE 'The Death of ROBESPIERRE' (1958); in *The Naked Lady* (1959); Justice Charles in ON TRIAL (in the Queensberry libel case, 1960); Aquilla in *Paul of Tarsus* (1960); starred as Matheson in *The Matheson Story*; Bobbie Lambert in *The Affair* (1962); in an episode of *The Mar-*

riage Lines (1962); Maigret 'The Revolver' (1962); etc.

Autobiography: *I Remember* 'Harold Scott' (1960 R). He also narrated and helped compile radio documentaries during the 1940s on the clown *Grimaldi, Old Pleasure Resorts, Night Clubs* and *The Cave of Harmony*. One of his radio projects, 'Achilles and the Boarding School', was vetoed partly because the central character spends much of his time in drag.

Scott, [George] Randolph (1898–1987)
American actor, durable star of nearly 100 films spanning comedies, musicals and Westerns. A second banana and light leading man, he was Margaret Mitchell's original choice to play Ashley in *Gone with the Wind*. In 1949 he became a fully-fledged Western star, totally convincing as the leathery, taciturn, not-over-fond-of-women solitary doing what he has to do in critically admired works like *Ride Lonesome* (1959) and *Comanche Station* (1960). His swan song, playing an appealing bad man after years of understated heroism, was Sam Peckinpah's classic *Ride the High Country/ Guns in the Afternoon* (1962).

Born wealthy, he became super-wealthy through marriage after living – openly – with Cary GRANT (at the self-styled 'Bachelor Hall' between 1932 and 1935).

He began in 1928 as an extra, gaining a bit role four years later in *Sharp Shooter*. His first starring role was with Cary Grant in *Hot Saturday*. The two men appeared together again in *My Favourite Wife*, with Irene Dunne, in 1940: a comedy which includes a scene where Grant drinks in Scott's physique.

Also: *Island of Lost Souls* (1933, with Charles LAUGHTON); *Roberta* (1935) and *Follow the Fleet* (1936, both with Fred Astaire); *She* (1935); *Go West, Young Man* (with Mae WEST, 1936); *Rebecca of Sunnybrook Farm* (1938, with Shirley Temple); *Jesse James* (1939); *Virginia City* (1940); *The Spoilers* (1942, with Marlene DIETRICH); *A Lawless Street* (1955); *Seven Men from Now* (1956); *Decision at Sundown* (1957); etc.

He was one of the very few Hollywood stars who never made a television appearance of any kind.

'Ya look like a fat Randolph Scott,' Tuesday Weld to Jackie Gleason in *Soldier in the Rain* (1963 C).

scouts 'You've got to believe in God and you've gotta be straight' was how Phil DONAHUE summed up the ethos in 'Boy Scouts vs Girls, Atheists and Homosexuals' (1991 T). This programme, in part, devoted itself to fine, upstanding, well-respected ROLE MODELS Rob Schwitz and Tim Curran turfed out of the scout movement for being gay, but fighting back through the courts.

Scouts and especially scoutmasters have been sources of humour, if not downright ridicule for years, beginning with high-pitched John Tilley, the immature booby commanding his boys through the woods, who was a great favourite on radio during the 1930s; prissy TV star Clifton WEBB is thawed by his involvement with young boys in uniform in *Mister Scoutmaster* (1953 C), even though initially he can't tell a toggle from a woggle or a dub dub from a dib dib or a reef knot from a reefer; victimized Arthur (John STRATTON) in WANTED: SINGLE GENTLEMAN (1967 T) looks back on his days in the Scouts with watering eyes: 'You didn't have to prove your manhood by the number of women you'd knocked around with. Just with your capacity for service and your ability to get on with the other chap. It was healthy too ... And safe. I've never known such safety'; similarly nostalgic is Harry Leeds (Richard Burton) in STAIRCASE (1969 C): 'Suppose I felt important ... manly. Putting on a bit of style, I suppose'; Ash (Clive Swift) entertains romantic thoughts in hospital with a young lad while basketweaving and reminiscing about scouting days in *The National Health* (1973 C); Sebastian (Anthony Andrews) reads a newspaper report of 'another naughty scoutmaster' as he and Charles (Jeremy Irons) sun themselves on the lawn in BRIDESHEAD REVISITED 'Home and Abroad' (1981 T); Tiger Timms (Nigel STOCK), a devotee of Robert Baden-Powell's teachings in *Scouting for Boys* (1983 R: 'I'm glad 'e learned me Scouting. Given a lot o' pleasure to a lot of lads') and fast friend of the much younger Coop (Alex Jennings) 'the best sort o' lad a man could wish for'; Commander Abigail (John Bird) in *The Children of Dynmouth* (1986 T): a bit of a lad with the littler lads given half an opportunity; a scout-master is among those suspects inter-viewed about a molested boy in *Indelible Evidence* (1987 T).

sculptors Countess Liz (Hildegarde Neff) in *The Snows of Kilimanjaro* (1952 C) saving her fire for her young female model rather than for husband Gregory Peck; MICHELANGELO (Charlton Heston) tied by relentless deadlines and a truculent nature (and possibly some-thing else) from falling in love with an aristocratic woman in *The Agony and the Ecstasy* (1965 C); Hallie Ross (Capucine) in *Walk on the Wild Side* (1962 C), quoting T. S. Eliot and spending the money she earns in the brothel on a few Brancusis; Bob Elkin 'whose neon-lit pieces resemble his own limited nature' (Alexander Walker) in SUNDAY, BLOODY SUNDAY (1971 C); Gertrude Vanderbilt Whitney (Angela Lansbury) leading a double life as a society gorgon and as GREENWICH VILLAGE sculptress in *Little Gloria ... Happy at Last* (1982 T); Cay Rivvers (Patricia Charbonneau), sculptor and potter, supplementing her limited income as a casino croupier in Reno in DESERT HEARTS (1985 C); Mical (Idit Tersperson), at 32 ready to fall in love (with a woman) in *It's That Age* (1990 C). *See also* ARTISTS; STATUES.

Seabrook, Jeremy (1939–) English playwright, sometimes in tandem with Michael O'Neill; a former social worker and author of a book of interviews with gay men (and a few lesbians) *A Lasting Relationship: Homosexuals and Society* (1976). He opened himself up with some courage to detail his agonizing dependence upon his mother in *The Light of Experience* 'Mother and Son' (1980 T) and, in slightly fictionalized

form, *Melancholy: Memoir of a Man in Middle Age* (1980 R, with Micheal Spice). With Michael O'Neill he wrote: *Deep* (1971 T); *Black and Blue* 'Soap Opera in Stockwell' (in which all the – middle-aged – women's roles were taken by men, 1973 T); *Children of the Sun* (1975 T); CROWN COURT 'Beyond the Call of Duty' (1976 T); *Living Private* (1978 R); *Life Skills: An Adult Education* (1985 R); etc. He was one of the conversationalists (the others were Fay WELDON and Rabbi Jonathan Sacks) in *A Word in Edgeways* (1987 R).

Sebastian (1) Boy's name frequently allotted to over-civilized, pampered, leisured men.

UK/France: Sebastian (Hugh Sinclair), heroic soldier in *Farewell Again* (1937 C); Sebastian Giro (Bobby Henry), chubby piano prodigy in *The Wonder Kid*; games-playing aesthete Sebastien in *Castle in Sweden* (Alan WHEATLEY 1962 R; Curt Jurgens 1963 C); boorish Marxist journalist Sebastian Cruttwell (Kenneth More) in *In Praise of Love* (1976 T); Sebastian (Michael Howe) in *Solo* (1981 T); Sebastian FLYTE (Anthony Andrews) drowsily car-ousing and frittering his life away in BRIDESHEAD REVISITED (1981 T); Sebastian (Michael Jenner) who plea-surably 'accosted' the writer Tom Ver-meer (Peter WHITMAN) on a plane in *Slipping Away* (1984 R); Lamb aka Brother Sebastian (Liam Neeson), a Catholic priest who flees to London with a 10-year-old epileptic boy and meets much pain and misery in *Lamb* (1985 C); Sebastian Pearce (Jeremy Brudenell) in *The House of Eliott* (1991 T), charming but unscrupulous half-brother; Sebastian Groom (Benedict Taylor) coifed, blondined, up himself and energetically het in *An Actor's Life for Me* 'A Kiss Is Just a Kiss' (1991 T); one of the exiled Duke's courtiers Sebastian (Kenneth Cranham) in *Prospero's Books* (1991 C) based on *The Tempest*; etc.

US/Canada: Sebastian Mauré (Lewis Stone), author with a past in *The Blonde Saint* (1926 C); Sebastian (Irving

Pichel), a sauve scoundrel in *House of 1,000 Candles* (1936 C); crooked businessman Alex Sebastian (Claude Rains) tighly bonded with his stone-faced mother in *Notorious* (1946 C); secret agent Victor Sebastian (David Hedison) in *Five Fingers* (1959–60 T); the cannibalized POET Sebastian VENABALE in SUDDENLY LAST SUMMER (1959 C); Luther Sebastian (Bradford Dillman), leader of a cult called the Third Way in *The Man From UNCLE* 'The Prince of Darkness Affaire' (1967 T, aka *The Helicopter Spies* C); Sebastian Stromboli (Hans Conried), violin virtuoso in *The Beverly Hillbillies* (1971 T) unabashedly decked out in black hat, scarf and cloak; Sebastian, the vampire's servant (Cleavon Little) in *Once Bitten* (1985 C); Mathieu's little son (Olivier Chassé) in THE HEART EXPOSED/LE COEUR DÉCOUVERT (1986 C/T): 'I have three daddies and one mummy'; Sebastian, fussy and fey Caribbean crab: a crustacean Franklyn PANGBORN, voiced by Samuel E. Wright in *The Little Mermaid* (1989 C); Sebastian Timms (Mark Bringleson) in *The Lawnmower Man* (1992 C); etc.

(2) Twin brother of Viola, doting on and seemingly infatuated by the Duke, sometimes regarded as homosexual and somewhat unconvincingly married off to Olivia at the end of TWELFTH NIGHT: Simon LACK (1956 R); Ian HOLM (1958 R); Hugh Dickson (1962 R); Michael Thomas (1980 R); etc. Sometimes doubled by the actress playing Viola: Margaretta Scott (1934 R); Mary Hinton (1936 R); Peggy Ashcroft (1939 T); etc.

St Sebastian His arrow-pierced body is a recurring motif in Catholic art: a statue of him in *I Walked with a Zombie* (1943) and a painting on Sebastian Venable's studio wall in SUDDENLY LAST SUMMER (1959 C). His mythical martyrdom is recreated for dramatic effect in *The Debussy Film* (1965 T) and URINAL/PISSOIR (1989 C: 'Dorian GRAY', played by Lana Eng, is seductively posed on a bed with arrows stuck in him); and for 'real' in SEBASTIANE (1976 C). Antonio Piero Del Pollaiuolo's *The Martyrdom of Saint Sebastian* was the subject of a BBC Third Programme art critique by L. D. Ettlinger in 1960.

Sebastiane (UK 1976) Emperor Diocletian's favourite Sebastian (Leonardo Treviglio) is banished to an isolated outpost because of his heretical beliefs. Refusing to relinquish his devotion to one loving God, he is reviled, tortured and eventually slain by his fellow soldiers.

W: Derek JARMAN; P: Howard Malin and James Walley; D: Derek Jarman and Paul Humfress; 86 mins.

A superb melding of poetic myth with savage contemporary reality. The Latin dialogue adds piquant vigour to the sun-drenched, languorous images of men living uneasily together, subtly taunted and exposed by the gentle young man they unthinkingly scapegoat or frustratedly desire.

second-class citizens A phrase that became increasingly noticeable from the late 1950s onwards: 'Are women second-class citizens?' was the question posed to Geoffrey Gorer and Marghanita Laski (who both denied it) on *Mainly for Women* (1959 T); a month earlier, on WOMAN'S HOUR (R), journalists Henry Fairlie, lawyer Fenton Bresler and two women MPs were asked the same thing (two agreed). Carol (Angela Pleasance) in NOW SHE LAUGHS, NOW SHE CRIES (1975 R), regardless of all the obstacles in her path, refuses to go back to her husband after having opted for a new life as a lesbian: 'Sink back to second-class citizenship with a resigned sigh? No thank you!' Michael CASHMAN decried the passing of CLAUSE 28 on OPEN TO QUESTION (1988 T) because 'it suggests that homosexual relationships are unacceptable ... it makes us second-class citizens'.

Second Serve (US 1986 T) Dick Radley, ophthalmologist, husband, father and weekend tennis player into Renée Richards, tennis star and coach of, among others, Martina NAVRATILOVA.

W: Stephanie Liss and Gavin LAMBERT from the book *The Renée Richards Story: Second Serve* by Renée Richards and John Adam; P: Lorimar/CBS; D: Anthony Page; 104 mins.

Vanessa REDGRAVE (brilliantly made up by Peter Owen) adds another extraordinary performance to her curriculum vitae as a former male (called Richard Raskins) who overcame much inner doubt and outer opposition (including that of his mother, a PSYCHIATRIST) to change sex and to continue both as a medical practitioner, and playing and coaching international tennis. The script slides over many crucial areas, concentrating overmuch on 'Dick Radley's' long process of agonizing, readjusting to norms rather than on life lived home and free. There's also a total lack of even the most rudimentary period markers so that the whole story seems to take place in a cold limboland called Case Study. But then that's American TV drama: struggle, struggle, kiss and cuddle.

secretaries Female: acting as nurse and surrogate mother (Elizabeth Wilson) in *The Goddess* (1958 C): 'I'll take good care of her ... I kind of love her'; CHILDIE (Susannah YORK), mini-skirted typist and dictation-taker somewhere in London's rag trade in THE KILLING OF SISTER GEORGE (1968 C); dripping forbidden sex, Pherber (Anita Pallenberg) and taking a shower with a boyish girl in PERFORMANCE (1970 C); Jean MARSH simmering with jealousy over the visits of the estranged husband to her boss (Barbara Leigh-Hunt) in *Frenzy* (1972 C); Lorna Heilbron as Lindsay Rimmer administering to the querulous but passionate writer of detective fiction, Emma Sands (Mary MORRIS) in *An Unofficial Rose* (1974/5 T); Valerie, the young girl who becomes secretary – and more – to Aunt Lucy in WITHIN THESE WALLS 'Invasion of Privacy' (1976 T); Nikki (Lynne Frederick) swept off her feet by force-of-nature Kim in THE OTHER WOMAN (1976 T); Annette Sanderson (Judy Geeson), 'a girl Friday, Saturday and every day' to radio producer Jean (Honor Blackman) in CROWN COURT 'Heart to Heart' (1979 T); etc.

Male: Pettigrew ('Pet') played by Ferdinand Gottschalk, secretary to the fearsomely powerful *Female* (1933 C) played by Ruth Chatterton, where his fluttery presence and comments about attractive men serve to highlight the 'unnaturalness' of women being dominant and men submissive – three quarters through the film, she melts into the right mould and he starts taking an interest in one of his (middle-aged, female), typists; the obedient Italian David Rizzio (John Carradine) in *Mary of Scotland* (1936 C), and a quivering BISEXUAL in *Prisoners of Power* (Sean Barrett 1970 R) and *Mary Queen of Scots* (Ian HOLM 1972 C); Dan Tobin works for Katharine HEPBURN – and betrays her trust – in *Woman of the Year* (1942 C; Anthony HOLLAND in the 1976 TV movie version and subsequent series); James GRIFFITH creeping around in almost silent shoes much to his employer Gary Cooper's extreme irritation in *Bright Leaf* (1950 C); theatrical agent Miss Waterbury (Agnes Moorehead) has a young man called Graham to take her dictation in *Main Street to Broadway* (1953 C); Richard Deacon is Jack Lemmon's tactful treasure in *My Sister Eileen* (1955 C); Bradford Webster (Jonathan HARRIS), all watchful maternalism and pop eyes in *The Third Man* (1959–62 T); Leonard (Martin Landau), jealous of Philip Van Damm's (James Mason) interest in Eva Marie Saint (or is it in Cary GRANT?) in *North by Northwest* (1959 C); Roger (John Fraser) trying to keep the wayward attention of *Isadora* (Vanessa REDGRAVE 1968 C); Barry Strap (Roland CURRAM) in *Harry Sebrof's Story* (1973 T); Anthony Perkins interrogated by Hercule Poirot about his murdered master in *Murder on the Orient Express* (1974 C); Ken Olfson as the aspiring actor who takes care of the Hollywood agent in *The Nancy Walker Show* (1976 T); Ernani (Lewis Fiander), the 'slimy toad' in *Ladykillers* 'Murder at the Savoy' (1980 T); Sean Mathias catering to a film star in *Priest of Love* (1981 C);

bright as a button, nicely groomed, intuitive Graham Jones (John INMAN) ministering unto Rula Lenska in *Take a Letter, Miss Jones* (1981 T); Martin Johnson (Michael COCHRANE) trying to keep the peace between Somerset MAUGHAM, Syrie and Gerald Haxton in WEEKEND WITH WILLIE (1981 R); treacherous Gary Murdoch (Stuart Margolin) as Julie Andrews' factotum in *SOB* (1981 C); Peter Cassell (Richard Morant) covering up the real reason his boss/lover died in *Bergerac* 'Nice People Die in Bed' (1981 T); Mark Steiner (Henry Polic II) in *Scruples II* (1981 T), the heroine Billy Ikehorn's (Lindsay Wagner) secretary, variously described as 'all brains, no guts', 'a snake', 'that tame parrot', 'the only person who can make "hello" sound menacing' – it is Steiner who, with the help of a boy-friend, is stealing gowns from Billy's department store; Roddy MCDOWALL bitching happily with his Great Actress employee (Elizabeth Taylor) in HOTEL 'Intimate Strangers' (1984 T).

Secret Love Doris DAY as rough and ready CALAMITY JANE (1953 C), having been done over and femmed up, gives vent to her true feelings about big-headed Bill Hickock (Howard Keel): 'Now I shout it from the highest hill ... my secret love's no secret anymore.' It was a big hit then (winning that year's Oscar too) and Kathy Kirby took it into the (British) charts again in 1964. The combination of the words, the dam-burst of emotions and two cult women singers have made 'Secret Love' a very special anthem for British and American lesbians, its finer nuances being pointed up by its insertion in BEFORE STONE-WALL (1984 C) and in the '1953' section of THE ROCK 'N' ROLL YEARS (1991 T).

Secret Orchards (UK 1980 T) Joe ACKERLEY (Joseph Blatchley) slowly learns that his father Roger (Freddie Jones) has been keeping two families, practically next door to each other. Father won't discuss the matter, nor will he allow Joe to unburden his own secret

life. After Roger's death, Joe uncovers another mystery: Roger, as a young GUARDSMAN, would appear to have been 'kept' by a German baron.

W: William Trevor from *My Father and Myself* by J. R. Ackerley and *The Secret Orchards of Roger Ackerley* by Diana Petrie; P: James Brabazon; D: Richard Loncraine; Granada; 104 mins.

William Trevor does this muted piece proud with a performance of sly bravado from Freddie Jones and some of his mannerisms reflected by Joseph Blatchley. Two scenes clarify Joe's sexuality with disarming brevity: his ogling FOOT-BALLERS and his having it away with a WAITER in a (moving) train's WC.

'Obscurely narrated family saga,' wrote Leslie Halliwell in his *Television Companion.* His co-editor Philip Purser disagreed. Linking it with the other Ackerley outing of the year, WE THINK THE WORLD OF YOU on OMNIBUS, Purser wrote in the *Sunday Telegraph*: 'On these two utterly disparate productions ... you could see all that is true and fine and gently stated in British television still thriving in 1980.'

seems like a nice boy! Coyly roguish comment from Larry GRAYSON in relation to certain of the (younger, usually well-muscled) male contestants who appeared during his tenure as host of *The Generation Game* (1978–81 T). 'Nice boy' had long been used as a semi-abusive euphemism for mother-domi-nated/fixated homosexual and/or suburban epicene, but Grayson rang the changes by seeming to make this 'nice-ness' as tasty and crotch-centred in the same way that other quiz hosts verbally and physically eye up certain parts of certain women contestants.

The phrase was current in America, featuring in STARSKY AND HUTCH 'Gillian' (1977 T). Massage parlour mana-geress Sylvia Sidney 'mistakes' the two cops for a gay couple: 'They seem like nice boys,' she comments with a trace of over-sweet condescension.

'Nice' still carries a particularly empty, coy and prissy charge when applied to men: Frank Butcher (Mike Reid) sneered that someone was 'a nyth boy' on EASTENDERS (1989 T).

See What The Boys In The Backroom Will Have See 'THE BOYS IN THE BACKROOM'.

Seinfeld (US 1991– T) The story of a BACHELOR (Jerry Seinfeld) coping with life in the 1990s. NBC demanded 'a girl, a broad, a woman' after viewing the all-male pilot in 1991. Such a figure was inserted and the series is still running.

self-confessed 'Many of bass guitarist Tom ROBINSON's songs ... reflect his strong political convictions. And as a self-confessed homosexual, Robinson has produced his most recent, entitled "GLAD TO BE GAY",' said Norman Moss in *Profile* (1979 R). Naturalist and writer Gavin Maxwell was, the narrator said in THE WORLD ABOUT US biography 'Gavin Maxwell and Ring of Bright Water' (1979 T), 'a self-confessed homosexual'.

With more people coming to terms with their sexuality in their adolescence and earlier, the use of this epithet to describe someone living honestly and openly is becoming increasingly archaic: insulting, dripping with guilt and rebuke. One of the last 'enlightened' people to use it was David Frost – persistently – in *Twenty Years On* (1985 T).

Sellers, Peter (1925–80) English comic actor, a vocal and visual sponge whose career falls into five distinct categories: Rise: (through THE GOON SHOW and other radio series, such as *Ray's a Laugh* in which he played a coyly provocative Crystal – 'Oh you saucy thing!' – Jollibottom, and supporting roles in films like *The Ladykillers* 1955 and *The Smallest Show on Earth* 1957); Ascendency: (huge critical and popular success in films like *I'm All Right Jack* 1959, *The Pink Panther* 1964 and *Dr Strangelove* 1964); Decline: (idling in increasingly desperate productions such as *I Love You, Alice B. Toklas* 1968, *The Magic Christian* 1969 and *Soft Beds and Hard Battles* 1973); Renaissance: (a return to

his role as Inspector Clouseau); Twilight: (more poor vehicles save for his penultimate film *Being There* 1980).

Among Sellers' many roles there were the inevitable queers. In his hands, they seemed swaggeringly furtive, almost demonic: FLOWERDEW (1951–4), GRYTPYPE-THYNNE (1954–60) and the doiley-voiced Captain of the Guards in *The Goon Show* 'The Stolen Postman', eg: 'Not another dancing girl, dear. You haven't touched the old ones yet,' he tells the Sultan (Ray Ellington).

Other predacious homosexuals dipped in the Sellers' acid bath were his spinsterish Richard III as played by Laurence Olivier (declaiming, on a 1965 record, 'A Hard Day's Night' rather than 'Now is the winter of our discontent'); his ridiculing of the THE CRITICS on an earlier recording; a brief spasm of HELLO, SAILOR! (while trying on a natty Tyrolean hat) in *Casino Royale* (1967 C); his extraordinary Clare Quilty, supercilious voyeur and connoisseur of teenage girls in *Lolita* (1962 C); his multiple roles in the film act as comments on the sick actions of himself and Humbert Humbert (James Mason). Quilty is the film's true face of perversion (overfed, debauched, above the law) playfully mimicking the voice of authority to scare his rival, sad sympathetic Humbert: firstly as a gay police officer ('Me being lonely and NORMAL ... perhaps we could do something normal together') and then as child psychiatrist Dr Zempf ('Do you mind if I am putting to you the blunt question?').

His star status possibly prevented Sellers from flouting more conventions in his choice of roles (his President of the United States in *Dr Strangelove* was originally intended to be homosexual), but he did cross the gender barrier (playing female cameos in *The Mouse That Roared* and *The Great McGonagall* and the chillingly asexual Chauncey in *Being There*). He didn't, however, take the role Kenneth WILLIAMS had played on stage in *My Fat Friend* as announced and his cameo of 'the Homosexual' in *A Day at the Beach* never materialized because the 1971 film has never been publicly shown.

semen The word first heard during the rape trial in *Anatomy of Murder* (1959 C), then in THE SILENCE (1963 C) where the lesbian sister says it smells of fish. Outside of pornography – and one brief encounter (with a garage attendant) in TAXI ZUM KLO (1981 C) – this important substance, 40 gallons of which are produced by each man during an average lifetime, is relegated solely to symbolic representation: waterfalls (THE RAINBOW 1989 C); white paint (Carol White lies in a pool of it after she has sex in *I'll Never Forget Whatshisname*, 1967 C); Lindsay Kemp is squirted with it during his orgiastic dance with a fake phallus in SEBASTIANE (1976 C); etc.

A semen-like substance lands on Ellen RIPLEY's face at the end of *Aliens* (which causes her to carry a child in *Alien 3*), and explorers Speke (Iain Glen) and Burton (Patrick Bergin) have to spew a white viscious fluid into each other's face and those of their companions as a part of a tribal greeting in *Mountains of the Moon* (1990 C).

See also SAFE SEX.

semiotics *See* SIGNS AND SIGNALS.

Send In The Clowns Sophia (Estelle Getty) in THE GOLDEN GIRLS 'Scared Straight' (1987 T) maintained that if a man knew all the words to the Stephen SONDHEIM song (from the 1973 musical *A Little Night Music*) he was definitely gay. Such is the widespread popularity of this bitter-sweet ballad that Sophia had to revise her claim: 'If a man knows the entire score from GIGI then he is ...' she rasped in a 1991 episode.

'Clowns', which deals with the impossibility of two people sharing exactly the same tender feelings at exactly the same time, has been recorded by Judy Collins, Frank Sinatra and Barbra STREISAND as well as by Glynis Johns and Elizabeth Taylor who delivered it on stage and in the film respectively. It was requested as one of the songs to be cast away with on DESERT ISLAND DISCS by Cleo Laine and Robert HELPMANN (1978), Tom Lehrer (1980), Morris West (1981) and Frankie HOWERD (1982): 'I sing it in my bath ... sometimes I can't remember the words, though.'

send-up A part of POLARI: gentle or not so gentle ribbing of an individual, a genre or a piece of work popular or obscure. Elizabeth Troop used it as the title of her 1976 radio play about Geoffrey Pastmaster (John RYE), a film star's ageing bachelor son, and it turned up in a Melbourne women's prison: 'We're only sending up a bit,' says a giggly Doreen (Colette Mann) to Judy (Betty Bobbit) who is sharing her cell with an attractive younger woman (in reality, she is Judy's long-lost daughter) in PRISONER/PRISONER: CELL BLOCK H (1980 T). More recently, Russell (Jonathan Newth) was moved to ask his friend and helpmate in AFTER HENRY 'Poor Relations' (1992 T): 'You're not sending me up, are you, Sarah?'

sensitive/sensitivity Problematic – for a man. 'I think I've made you sensitive,' frets Mr DULCIMER (D. A. CLARKE-SMITH) to his 'son' Julian (Lewis Stringer) in THE GREEN BAY TREE (1946 R). 'So sen-sit-ive and highly strung' is agent Agnes MOOREHEAD's thumbnail sketch to star Tallulah BANKHEAD of playwright Anthony Monoco (Tom Morton) in *Main Street to Broadway* (1953 C); Tallulah understands perfectly, dah-ling.

In the MGM teen romance *Joy in the Morning* (1965) newly-weds Yvette Mimieux and Richard Chamberlain fight over the former's friendship with the town's FLORIST, Anthony Byrd (Donald Davis). 'Can't you see he's sensitive', she says defensively. Her husband is confused: 'Like a woman is sensitive! It's not that I'm jealous ... but I am. He's a man. Isn't he?'

James BARRIE (Ian HOLM) tells the parents of Michael (Charles Tatnall/William Relton) in THE LOST BOYS (1978 T): 'He's sensitive ... Great care should be taken ... Be careful and watch him'; Philippe (Patrick Bouchity) is neither homosexual nor transvestite in THE BEST WAY TO WALK (1975 C) but 'sensitive', as is Steven CARRINGTON in DYNASTY (1981–91 T). Angie Dickinson's deceased – and very closeted – husband Wayne Harrington (Peter Donat) in *The Suicide's Wife* (1979 T) was 'sensitive and vulnerable'.

Ballroom dancer Barry (Barry Howard) goes into a decline after his partner Yvonne (Diane Holland) glides around the floor with a temporary replacement in *Hi-de-Hi* (1983 T). One of the staff at Maplin's Holiday Camp counsels that Barry's depression must be carefully monitored because he's 'highly strung and sensitive'.

The unsympathetic barman, Frank Jessup (Ken Kercheval) in HOTEL 'Passports' (1986 T) objects to working with Joey (Leigh McCloskey) because he's gay. Asked to elaborate, Frank can only bluster: 'He's over-sensitive. It must be in the genes.' To which his enquirer sweetly but firmly rejoinders: 'We all have the same genes. We all feel pain.'

'Alistair's just a little bit sensitive. He needs the right woman to take him out of himself,' says his mother (Margot Boyd) none too convincingly in THREE PIECE SWEET (1979 R).

sequels DANGEROUS CORNER's Martin CAPLAN was reincarnated under a different name and through different time stations by J. B. Priestley in *Anyone for Tennis?* (1968 T); CHEQUERBOARD, the 1972 interview with an Australian gay couple, Peter Bonsall-Boone and Peter De Waal, was supplemented in 1991 by a *7.30 Report* showing them still together but not in quite the conventional way; EVERYMAN 'Blasphemy At the Old Bailey' (1977 T) was followed some months later by a programme on the appeal against Mary WHITEHOUSE's successful prosecution of GAY NEWS; *A Change of Sex* (1980 T) followed George/Julia's operation and its aftermath which had been discussed the year before in INSIDE STORY; *The Interrogation of John* (1987 T) begat two more plays ending with the gay murderer's suicide; 'After It Hap-

pened', a 1988 episode of MIDNIGHT CALLER involving the bisexual man spreading the HIV virus, was followed up a year later, after protests about gross misrepresentation, with something less hysterical and meretricious; *Remembering Terry* (1987) detailed the last months of Terry Madeley who had caught Britain's attention in an HIV/AIDS documentary earlier that year; *Resident Alien* (1990) caught up with Quentin CRISP 15 years after THE NAKED CIVIL SERVANT, including a meeting between Crisp and John HURT; NIGHTHAWKS 2: STRIP JACK NAKED contained unusued footage from NIGHTHAWKS overlaid with a 1990s perspective from the director; in WOMEN LIKE THAT some older gay women revisited one year on after WOMEN LIKE US (1990 T); tying up loose ends with the Carringtons, DYNASTY: *The Reunion* (1991 T) finds that Steven loves Bart True.

Hanif Kureishi had intended MY BEAUTIFUL LAUNDRETTE as the final part of a *Godfather*-like study of some Pakistani men and women in Britain. The prequel (involving Omar's father and uncle during the 1960s) has so far eluded production.

Daniel **Sereno** One of the main characters, played by Daniel MASSEY, in THE ROADS TO FREEDOM (1970 T) and called Daniel Lalique in Jean-Paul SARTRE's novels. A crawling mass of society's ingested maggots: crazed, furtive, omnipotent, pathetic – one of the great self-lacerators, spewing out gobbets of honesty amid almost drenching unhappiness. He begins in pre-war Paris and ends gazing down on some German soldiery, doubtless his next stop on the road to self-debasement. Compulsively loathsome – and all too human, though he regards himself as the very devil because of his sexual direction.

In David TURNER's adaptation this swirling torrent of guilt and self-disgust almost shares a surname with Sartre's other unhappy homosexual: Ines Serrano in HUIS CLOS. Ennobled by her intelligence and a certain serrated humour that the other two damned characters in the play do not possess, Ines mirrors Daniel's ironic honesty and less than benign laconicism. Both are in a state of impure being with no future.

'As a child, one of the few books he read over and over again was Sartre's *The Age of Reason* with its depressing portrait of a homosexual, deeply ashamed of his sexuality' (Dancer Michael Clark, *Independent Magazine*, 7.6.92).

Sergeant Matlovich vs the US Air Force (US 1978 T) A blind adherent of bigoted beliefs, Sergeant Leonard Matlovich (Brad Dourif) used to pray before each date with a girl that he wouldn't be tempted to 'go all the way'. He went through several thousand torments – hating queers, Jews and niggers – before he discovered his true sexual direction. He declared himself to be gay and receives a less than honourable discharge. This sober account of a fascinating case ends with a voice-over: 'The time has come to reappraise the problems homosexuals present.'

W: John McGreevey; P/D: Paul Leaf; NBC; 104 mins.

A Vietnam veteran with an impeccable 12-year military record. One Purple Heart, teetotal, redeemed racist and anti-Semite, the perfect soldier, and dedicatedly anti-gay. Then came the extraordinary about-turn and the military's kneejerk reactions. The film follows the court records, but intersperses the disengaging process with fairly basic yet effective dramatizations of Matlovich's relations with his parents (Stephen Elliott and Rue McClanahan) and his only friend (Marc Singer) who rejects him. Honesty did not pay, but the courage of Sergeant Matlovich, who died in 1988 of AIDS-related causes, spurred on others in the military to successfully fight for their rights.

'I was a racist, an anti-Semite. I was raised a a Catholic in Georgia and later became a Mormon. I got full marks for everything. My conduct was impeccable. My private life was non-existent. I was still a virgin at 29. There was all this tension coming out of me. Thirty years

of foreplay and then the climax,' Matlovich told GAY NEWS in 1977.

serial killers   *See* MURDERERS.

Serling, Rod (1924–75) American writer, director, poet, administrator, and creator of THE TWILIGHT ZONE (1959–64 T). He was – like Mendelssohn – master of his chosen medium, ridiculously successful, acclaimed in his lifetime, happily married and without obvious traumas. Intelligent, humorous, extrovert and creative, he had extraordinary insight into the feelings of shy, sensitive people, as well as superficially strong people in situations of danger and power relations between a younger and older man.

He explored homoemotional situations in a number of his television plays (Playhouse '90's *A Long Time Till Dawn* – 'tumultuous conflict in a young poet' – with James DEAN, 1953), in his Hollywood Western *Saddle the Wind*, and in the war film *Between Heaven and Hell* for which he wrote the first draft. But it was in *The Twilight Zone* that Serling's human and political concerns were allowed almost free rein, veiled as they were through a layer of fantasy and wild imagining: 'Sometimes the situations were clichéd, the characterizations two-dimensional, but always there was at least some search for emotional truth, some attempt to make a statement about the human condition' (Marc Scott Zicree, *The Twilight Zone Companion*, 1982).

Seven Men (UK 1971 T) Quentin Crisp's first television outing. He was introduced in *TV Times* as having written a book which deals with his problems as a 'pathological homosexual'.

P/D: Denis Mitchell; Granada; 26.3.71; 30 mins.

When he spoke as one of the LONDON CHARACTERS on radio, Crisp was billed simply as 'a London artist's model'. By 1971 he was one of *Seven Men*; the other six were Michael Burn, René Cutforth, Douglas Glass, Ivor Montague, Frank Shaw and Commander Charles Drage.

Presented as living in a tiny Soho room almost untouched by cleaning, the viewer was encouraged to gawp at this eccentric, ageing old QUEEN, filmed in TV-pathetic style. His speech was electrifying, it's true. But didn't the *bons mots* sound a mite defiant, the product of a lonely empty life? Now, thanks to the removal of the filters, these 'drawbacks' endemic in the man's life are seen as virtues. All part of the LIFESTYLE Crisp half-mockingly advocates in his books and one-man shows.

Seven Up (UK 1964 T) Among British television's most magic moments: a group of 7-year-olds (only upper- and working-class children were selected, with only 4 girls out of the 20) talk about their lives, hopes, fears, ambitions and aspirations. They have been revisited every seven years, a formula which has now been put in place in America, Germany, Russia, Japan and South Africa.
P: Derek GRANGER; D: Michel Apted; Granada; 5.5.64; 25 mins. Also: *14 Up*, *21 Up*, *28 Up* and *35 Up*.
Full of wisdom about marriage, aspirations, personality changes, class distinction. Some unexpected attitudes and one or two lives that didn't turn out as their 7-year-old selves would suggest. In *35 Up* (1991) most of the subjects are happily married with kids or happily unmarried with kids. No gay or lesbian people have yet shown themselves in the series although Michael Apted, who asks the questions, is perhaps not the person best attuned to subtleties: he always takes the traditional tack. In *35 Up* he was still asking ostensibly uncoupled men about their search for the right 'woman'. Expect more of the same in *42 Up*, *49 Up*, *56 Up*, *63 Up*, *70 Up*, *77 Up*, *84 Up*, *91 Up*, *98 Up* and so on.
'I love *him*!' (as distinct from her), one 7-year-old boy says to another, as they embrace (jokingly?) before three smitten girls in *Seven Up*. Neither of these boys appeared in any other segments.

sewing Very few men are allowed to be useful with a needle and thread: Jock and Gus (the mice) volunteer to help the women finish off the ball gown in Disney's *Cinderella* (1950 C), but they are soon shoved away: 'Leave the sewing to the *women!*' In *My Sister Eileen* (1955 C) Wreck (Dick York), a whizz at housework, draws the line at sewing: 'No sewing. That's WOMAN'S WORK.'
Some practitioners of this minority activity for men: ageing Broadway dancer Tony (Fred Astaire) tells Cyd Charisse (who makes no comment) in *The Band Wagon* (1953 C) that 'I can still thread a needle without my glass eye'; Tom Lee (John Kerr) was taught to sew by the family maid and has no inhibitions about doing it publicly in TEA AND SYMPATHY (1956 C) although it leads to accusations, as it does with Rudolpho (Jean Sorel) who can cut a dress pattern and sing tenor in *A View from the Bridge* (1961 C); Geoffrey (Murray MELVIN) makes Jo's baby clothes in A TASTE OF HONEY (1961 C); Trevis (Kevin Lloyd) stitches his wife's ballroom dress in *Midnight at the Starlight* (1980 T); Ryan O'Neal is domesticated by John HURT in PARTNERS (1982 C) and is glimpsed with a needle and thread; Georgie PILLSON (Nigel Hawthorne) does it in *Mapp and Lucia* (1985–6 T), a complement to his piano duetting and his sketching; the older brother in the family nannied by Mr BELVEDERE (1986 T) makes his brother's costume for the school play, but only because he needs to gain a credit for his degree; Leo (Edward Highmore) is given a job as a machinist in the sail loft in HOWARDS' WAY (1986 T), which causes his girlfriend Abby (Cindy Shelly) to react in a resolutely old-fashioned way: 'Maybe they'll teach you to cook as well. Then you'd make someone a beautiful wife'; MI5's David Valentine (Ronald LACEY) sews as he watches a television news broadcast about him which mentions 'probable mental instability' in *Blind Justice* 1988 T; Sammy (Campbell Morrison) tells Larry in *Life without George* (1989 T): 'I'm a wizard with a Singer.'
See also EMBROIDERY; KNITTING.

Sex and the Censors (UK 1991 T)

Part of Channel 4's *Banned* season which explored the reasons behind the censorship of television programmes on various grounds including sexual taboo. In this section, Derek JARMAN discussed how he edited SEBASTIANE for television, while the offending scenes were played on a screen in the background. Scotland Yard received a complaint about the presence of 'an aroused member' in the film's lovemaking between two Roman soldiers. The complaint was not upheld (unlike the member), but the action only served to highlight the tightrope television companies walk: broadcast material, exempt from the Obscene Publications Act until 1988, was now well within its remit and could be jumped upon with the full force of the law. Both fools and angels would be well advised to tread carefully.

sex change *See* TRANSSEXUALS.

Sex in Our Time 'For "Queer" Read "Gay"' (UK 1976 T) Intended as part of an unblushing THAMES series to be transmitted on Monday night between eleven and midnight, the contents proved too strong for the Independent Broadcasting Authority (IBA), especially those episodes dealing with female sexuality (containing close-ups of the labia and female anus) and homosexuality, which included this declaration from a male couple: 'We are planning for a life relationship. Some people call it a parody of a heterosexual marriage ... the monogamous role is the right one for us. [Sex for us is] touching, licking, caressing. The basis of lovemaking is to reach arousal together, if possible, mutual masturbation, oral masturbation, anal intercourse – the latter is perhaps not as frequent as thought.'

'For "Queer" Read "Gay"' (itself a fairly confronting statement) attempted to cover a vast amount of territory: a Black Country CHE group meeting in Walsall, gay relationships in Birmingham, a patronizing TV interview (with Tony Bilbow and actors from GAY SWEATSHOP's production *Mister X*); aspects of lesbian-feminism with Sweat-

shop's Jill Posener and actresses Nancy Diuguid and Daria; Drew GRIFFITHS' personal experience of being gay; Patric Farrell on AVERSION THERAPY.

In November 1976 a letter appeard in *The Times* signed by 50 programme makers, headed by Jonathan Dimbleby, which said in part that the decision to ban the 7-part series should 'profoundly disturb all those who are concerned to preserve the freedom of communication in Britain'.

This episode only finally saw transmission as part of Channel 4's *Banned* season in April 1991, when Mark Steyn of the *Evening Standard* viewed it as 'an elegy for a lost age of quaint courtly customs like open marriages and ONE NIGHT STANDS, blessed by the all-powerful magic of the Pill. Fifteen years ago, you couldn't talk freely about sex on TV, but you could do it with reasonably carefree abandon. Today, it's the other way round' (24.4.91).

sexuality 'Sex is the producer of diversity and sex is the propeller of evolution ... the dazzling divergence and differences within species,' said Dr Jacob BRONOWSKI in THE ASCENT OF MAN (1973/4 T). National forests have been used up for books and magazines solely devoted to the subject. Millions of feet of celluloid and millions more of videotape have been devoured to produce hours of sexually informative or misinformative entertainment and education whose sole reason for being is erotic stimulation.

BBC radio, long the nation's reticule of rectitude on things sexual, did occasionally admit that attitudes had changed since the First World War. In a 1932 talk, Dr C. De Lisle Burns was approving: 'There is much more frankness in the discussion of sexual relations, both between married couples and otherwise ... we are beginning to see that a wife who is only a wife is a bore, as a husband who is only a husband is generally a beast.'

At the same time, films were fairly dripping with suggestiveness – both in Britain (almost all the HITCHCOCK thrillers and comedies of the period) and in America (shameless, satirizing Mae WEST, bra-less, creamy Jean Harlow). 'Let's forget sex ... *no sex*,' insists Gilda (Miriam Hopkins) in DESIGN FOR LIVING (1933 C). But Gary Cooper only has to roll his eyes and she's on the couch beckoning. Earlier in the film, it is Cooper and his chum (Frederic March) who appear to have been, at the very least, cuddling up (on a train), thereby intimating Noel COWARD's original intention – nearly all of which had been jettisoned for the screen version (only one line of the play's dialogue had been retained).

Hints were one thing, spelling it out was quite another. In *Ex-Wife* (1933 C) Bette DAVIS was required to describe what she had on her mind (throughout most of the running time) only as 'dash dash asterisk'. At least she was allowed to go to bed with a man (her husband) in the film. The following year, with the strict enforcement of the Hollywood Production Code (the antics of Mae West were probably its main impetus, though there had been considerable disquiet from church groups for years), beds had to be separate and two people of the opposite sex could not be shown in or on one unless the feet of one or both were visibly on the ground.

A BBC talk had summed up the anti-libertarian view which was to hold sway from the mid-1930s until the late 1950s: 'Men have always been afraid of their sex instincts ... In so far as opinions down the ages can be read by institutions and morals, it shows an instinctive fear that unless this dangerous stirring sex instinct is controlled it will destroy much that makes life worth living, and censorship, at bottom, is based on this age-old fear'.

Unlike America, where fire and brimstone were regular occurrences (from evangelical preachers on local and national radio stations), the Church of England, which held sway over Britain's airwaves until the 1950s, was altogether gentler in its moral teaching. Said one churchman in 1930: 'We have to fight and control the lower propensities, the trials and temptations of life.' He then quoted not the Bible but Browning: 'Evil is null, is nought, is silence implying sound.'

The influence of the Church remained strong until the end of the Second World War. Society was in a state of flux: social trends, particularly those regarding the rising divorce rate, could not be ignored. Sex had to be confronted – but in a delicate way so that only those who had experienced it would know it was being discussed.

'Peggy, darling, I want you, I need you, I can't go on like this, having you so near and yet so far...' was how David Mason (Peter Byrne) put it to his recent bride Peggy (Billie Whitelaw) in THE PATTERN OF MARRIAGE, a 1953 dramatized television documentary which was regarded as the height of daring. (The mere fact that one or two characters in the dramatization of the WHITEOAKS novels the following year had sex lives outside marriage caused an uproar, with demands that the repeat performance be cancelled.) In the Ambridge of THE ARCHERS, where a relative frankness on matters reproductive could be thought acceptable, the country folk had to watch their ps and qs. A dialogue on the merits of spanking was removed as were lines such as 'my missus ... she was iggerant' and 'spud pickers called a spade a spade if you know what I mean'.

By the mid-1950s, HOLLYWOOD – with massively declining audiences as a result of the onslaught of television and now competing with sexually explicit films from Europe – gradually began testing the waters. Anne Francis in *The Blackboard Jungle* (1955) was now allowed to say 'sex' to her husband (Glenn Ford) over the breakfast table in the presence of their son because she spelled out the letters rather than joined them together. The following year – after months of negotiation – the first American film about homosexuality was released by a major company (MGM). At least TEA AND SYMPATHY *had* been about that subject when it was a stage play. The film version went as far as effeminacy and no further. The same company also had to fight the Production Code authorities over CAT ON A HOT TIN ROOF which was allowed general exhibition only with the removal of any direct references to homosexuality – which had been the whole crux of the stage version.

British theatrical censorship (under the control of the Lord Chamberlain) forbad the production of *Cat on a Hot Tin Roof* without cuts. It was presented under theatre club membership conditions and its 1958 first night covered in a special programme by the BBC. In it, director Peter Hall and Gore VIDAL extolled the virtues of Tennessee WILLIAMS, especially his 'humanity', but without any mention of the play's subject matter which had led to it being performed in such restricted conditions.

By the late 1950s, British television, like Hollywood, had capitulated to a degree: sex outside marriage was a fact of life, as was sex inside marriage. Beds were still strictly for sleeping – and people always wore pyjamas – but, within certain strict guidelines, sexuality could be indicated. In the 1960 play *The Offshore Island*, Ann Todd was seen doing up her blouse, an action which told more perceptive viewers that she had enjoyed relations with a man. Not enjoyed, exactly. There had been a nuclear explosion on the mainland. She and the man, on an isolated island, were survivors. The human race had to be carried on.

Philip Larkin maintained that 'Sexual intercourse began/In 1963', but the waters had begun breaking a while earlier with the wide spread of barely disguised carnality in rock 'n' roll lyrics (not to mention 'the beat' itself); the greater publicity given to 'immoral' but popular people (Marilyn MONROE, Elizabeth Taylor); the pressing need for sex education (in the face of rising numbers of unmarried mothers, marriage breakdown and vastly increased cases of venereal disease); and the litigation over books such as *Lady Chatterley's Lover* and *Lolita* and magazines like *Playboy*.

The cry that had gone up as early as 1958 – mainly from television critics –

became louder by 1963: 'too much sex on television'. Coupling their concern with the issue of violence in programmes like Z CARS and a serialization of *Oliver Twist*, a small but well-connected group of citizens organized themselves as the National Viewers' and Listeners' Association (National VALA) whose leader, Mrs Mary WHITEHOUSE, soon became a television celebrity in her own right: a symbol of beseiged family values or of outdated, interfering morality?

Barriers that had once been thought impregnable were daily smashed throughout the 1960s. BED scenes, semi-NAKEDNESS, RAPE scenes, ABORTIONS. Not a week went by without complaints in the British press about visual or aural excesses on *Till Death Us Do Part* or THE WEDNESDAY PLAY.

Concurrent with staged depictions of sex (mainly heterosexual) were increasing numbers of documentaries: *The Young Adults* (1965 T); EXIT 19 (1966 T); *Young World* 'The Two Sexes' (1967 T); MAN ALIVE 'The Facts of Life' (1968 T); *What Shall We Tell the Children? Sex Education in Britain Today* (1968 T). These led, in the early 1970s, to sex education series on BBC Schools and then ITV Schools television.

During this turbulence, sex had become inextricably linked with violence, partly because of increasingly complicated censorship debates over films like *A Clockwork Orange* and *Straw Dogs* ('Sex and Violence' was the title of a 1972 *Doomwatch* episode which the BBC gated because its subject matter was considered 'unsuitable'. It was finally shown nearly 20 years later at London's National Film Theatre.)

Sexuality remains a battleground and its depiction outside of private, enclosed places a never-ending war. What had seemed clear-cut when public sexual outlets were so few, now has a jagged edge. The expression of pleasure is now clouded with issues of mutual consent, domestic violence, rape and abuse of nature. Where once it was old fogies who wanted less sex or none at all, now some younger people are beginning to ask – as did *Evening Standard* critic Mark

Steyn (24.4.91) – if there isn't a bit too much of it: '"Not tonight, dear, I've got a headache," you sigh, as another swatch of pubic hair moves into view hotly pursued by a studio discussion.'

If heterosexuality continues to work people up into a lather of shocked excitement about the abnormal and the disquieting, its cousin homosexuality, still constrained in comprison, is even more problematic. Before the onrush of HIV/AIDS programmes, watchdogs had ensured that the discussion and depiction of same-sex activities remained alien and disconnected from the heights of joy and excitement. Penned and padlocked, it was allowed out only within certain hours or within distinct parameters. It was, to borrow the title of a 1989 series about the 'bad old days' of sexual ignorance and 'sin', *A Secret World of Sex*.

Even though viewers and listeners now know more about the nuts and bolts of 'homosexual intercourse' as a result of AIDS education, its connection with heterosexuality remains remote and isolate, a thing of acts rather than enjoyment and identity. As one of the young men in the series *Public School* (1980 T), seemingly playful in his assumption of gayness for a mock general election (he stood for the Gay Party), comments: 'You're bound to have a sexuality. It's a sexuality, not a homosexuality.'

Television is making inroads on the desert that is sexual ignorance. Since the 1980s, a number of series have at least included lesbians and gays (nearly always in separate segments) in their reckonings. These include 16 UP 'Happy Loving Couples' (1982); TWENTIETH CENTURY BOX (1982); SOMETHING ELSE 'Intimate Contact' (1982); JUST SEX 'What Is Normal?' (1984); *Sex* (Aust 1992–); *Well Being* 'Teenagers Talk Sex' (1986). On radio, there was, eg, *20th Century Sex* (1987).

For most people, sex remains a maze, full of excitements and dead ends, a sense of completion and frustration. Its subtleties and challenges have only begun to be scaled by the broadcast media, restricted as much by their own ignorance and timidity as by the growlings of secular and religious censors. What remains remarkable is firstly that sexuality – for all its daily familiarity from billboards, books and screens – retains its appetizing taste for most people (according to the World Health Organization (WHO) in 1991 there are more than 100 million acts of sexual intercourse worldwide every day), and secondly that some writers, directors and actors are able to communicate even a fraction of its delights and diversions to audiences supposedly jaded and thirst-slaked in a sexual universe where disease and death threaten.

Ecstatic, joyful gyrations and otherwise realistically pleasurable contributions to the expression of same-sex sexuality have been few and far between. Exceptions include:

Male: *UNCHANT D'AMOUR (1950 C); SUNDAY, BLOODY SUNDAY (1971 C); *ARABIAN NIGHTS (1974 C); *A Bigger Splash* (1975 C); THE ROCKY HORROR PICTURE SHOW (1975 C); SEBASTIANE (1976 C); THE CONSEQUENCE (1977 C/T); *WE WERE ONE MAN (1979 C); *TAXI ZUM KLO (1981 C); FACING THE SUN (1980 T); MAKING LOVE (1982 C); MY BEAUTIFUL LAUNDRETTE (1985 C); PARTING GLANCES (1985 C); DONA HERLINDA AND HER SON (1986 C); PRICK UP YOUR EARS (1987); MAURICE (1987 C); LAW OF DESIRE (1987 C); LOOKING FOR LANGSTON (1988 C); *MALA NOCHE (1987 C); *The Long Weekend (O'Despair)* (1988 C); BEYOND GRAVITY (1988 C/T); THIRTYSOMETHING 'Love and Sex' (1989 T); POISON (1991 C); SWOON (1991 C); *A TASTE OF KIWI (1991 C); TOGETHER ALONE (1991 C); YOUNG SOUL REBELS (1991 C); CAUGHT LOOKING (1991 C/T); THE LOST LANGUAGE OF CRANES (1992 T); *THE LIVING END (1992 C); TALES OF THE CITY (1993 T).

Female: GIRL (1974 T); *Je ... Tu ... Il ... Elle/I ... You ... He ... She (1974 C); *Once Is Not Enough* (1975 C); PERSONAL BEST (1982 C); ANOTHER WAY (1982 C); LIANNA (1983 C); NOVEMBER MOON (1984 C); THE COLOR PURPLE (1985 C); DESERT HEARTS (1985 C);

*KAMIKAZE HEARTS (1987 C); THE
RAINBOW (1989 C); PORTRAIT OF A MAR-
RIAGE (1990 T); ORANGES ARE NOT THE
ONLY FRUIT (1990 T); *Rosebud* (1992
T).

See also BEDS; KISSING; LOVE; MASSAGE;
ORGASMS; ORGIES; SADO-MASOCHISM;
SAFE SEX; TOUCHING.

* Indicates cinema films which to date have not received
national television showings in Britain, the US or Australia.

sexually transmitted diseases aka
venereal diseases. A taboo subject first
mooted in a number of productions of
Ibsen's *Ghosts* during the 1950s
(Andrew Osborn as Oswald whose
mother played by Cathleen Nesbitt has
keep a family secret from him, 1951 T)
and of the sensationalist *Pick-Up Girl*
(1953 R; 1957 T; *Too Young to Love*
1960 C). HOLLYWOOD swept the subject
under the carpet and the only information available came through medical
textbooks, military health films and
poverty-row films like *Damaged Lives*
and *Damaged Goods* (both 1936).

British television and radio began to
tackle the alarming rise in syphilis and
gonorrhoea at the beginning of the
1960s with one-off documentaries
(instead of a co-ordinated public awareness campaign) which included –
usually with backs to the camera – a
number of homosexual men who had
become infected. But as Millicent
Martin sang in an anxiously cheeful
roundelay on THAT WAS THE WEEK THAT
WAS (1963 T): 'Carol gave it to Tony
and Tony gave it to Claire...'

By 1972 a BBC Radio 4 report, *Shadow Over Venus*, was asking 'Is disease
the price of sexual liberation?' and, in
America the same year, Public Broadcasting System (PBS) devoted much of
one night to a revue-style television
show called VD BLUES followed by a
nation-wide phone-in designed to shed
light on what lay behind the alarming
statistics. Two openly gay men were on
camera – only during the call-in – answering questions from the host about
sexual practices, the bath house culture
and the generally responsible attitude of
gays towards getting tested and treated.

One of the men, Jack Nichols (who was
to write the first book on *Men's Liberation*), asked one of the doctors in the
studio if you could contract VD through
mutual masturbation ('Possible for
syphilis, I doubt it for gonorrhea') and
through fellatio ('Absolutely').

Denis LEMON, editor of GAY NEWS was
one of those interviewed on *Brass Tacks*
'Some of the Nicest People I Know
Have STD' (1981). He was the only
openly gay person on the programme,
even though homosexuals were singled
out (along with businessmen who travel
abroad, engineers and young people)
because they 'tend to change partners
quite frequently, and some of the sexual
activities they engaged in make them
vulnerable ... they have sex with
strangers and that is one of the certain
ways of contacting STD'. However, one
of the venereologists made it quite clear
that 'homosexual men are often very
responsible about [coming for check-
ups]'.

The programme took careful aim not
to present STD as 'the most dreadful
disease you could get', but two years
later (1983) PANORAMA devoted an
entire programme to 'Love's Pestilence',
making much of 'new strains' that may
be resistant to penicilin. Around the
same time, HORIZON was readying its
special report on a disease that was attacking Haitians and gay men...

Sexually transmitted diseases prior to
and during the early years of the AIDS
epidemic were hardly ever mentioned in
a fictional context. A young husband
finds he has syphilis after sex with a
bisexual woman in KISS AND TELL (1980
T); Frank contacts hepatitis from a
pick-up in TAXI ZUM KLO (1980 C);
there's a matey CLONE and a TRANSVES-
TITE among the patients as well as a gay
venereologist working at THE CLINIC
(1982 C); male and female flat-sharers
in *Hard Feelings* (1984 T) each get 'a
dose' after co-mingling; in *Beverly Hills
Cop* (1984 C) Eddie Murphy declares he
has herpes simplex 10 as a way of causing consternation and thereby slipping
into a club; Antonio asks Pablo if he 'has
anything', but this is *after* they have

uninhibitedly enjoyed each other's bodies in LAW OF DESIRE (1987 C). Regular announcements of a check-up service once a week are heard over the loudspeaker at the bath house known as THE RITZ (1976 C). 'You can catch athlete's foot in a place like this,' says one customer. 'You're lucky if that's all you catch,' quips one of the attendants.

See also SAFE SEX.

Sexual Offences Act 1967 After a 10-year campaign, the laws which treated all homosexual acts between males as crimes in England and Wales were altered on 3 July 1967, receiving the royal assent on 27 July. However, homosexuality was decrimilalized rather than made legal and then only within a rigidly patrolled definition of 'in private' for consenting men over 21 who were not in the armed forces and didn't 'practise' in Scotland or Northern Ireland, not to mention the Channel Islands.

The first programme to look at the likely changes in the lives of homosexual men (and lesbians – who were not directly criminalized but stigmatized all the same) was a 2-part MAN ALIVE, the second slice of which was discussed by a group of people – including some who are openly homosexual today – on *Late Night Live*.

In 1977 Linda Blandford interviewed people who were involved in the Bill's passing (HOMOSEXUALITY – THE YEARS OF CHANGE R), and its importance and inadequacies have been mulled over on GAY LIFE (1980 T) and *The Sixties* 'Swinging' (1982 T).

Noel COWARD, who had not supported law reform although he had been canvassed, used the character of closet gay Hugo Latymer (played by himself) as a mouthpiece in his 1966 stage play *A Song at Twilight* (1982 T; 1988 R): 'Even when the actual law ceases to exist there will still be a stigma attached to the LOVE THAT DARE NOT SPEAK ITS NAME in the minds of millions of people for years to come.'

See also Leo ABSE; Antony GREY; WOLFENDEN REPORT.

Shakespeare, William (1564–1616) English poet and playwright, nearly all of whose works have been regularly produced for cinema, radio and televison. BBC television's interpretations of the canon appeared at regular intervals from the late 1970s to the mid-1980s. The 1992 radio production of *Hamlet* (starring Kenneth Branagh) was so successful (selling large quantities of audio cassettes) that plans are afoot to record each and every play, beginning with *Romeo and Juliet* and what was radio's very first full-length drama, TWELFTH NIGHT.

Shakespeare was fascinated by humanity in all its shades and by sexuality in all its forms. Although none of his plays deals directly with homo- or bisexuality, a number deal with two males set apart by a female as well as the comedies of gender reversal, which would have been spiced by the performances of men and boys in all the women's roles, young or old. Certain whiffs of homoeroticism can also be taught in some of the tragedies: *The Merchant of Venice*, *Coriolanus*, *Othello* and *Romeo and Juliet*.

Though facts are scarce, John Mortimer decided that his *Will Shakespeare* (Tim CURRY 1978 T) was a man for all sexual seasons and did love the Earl of Southampton (Nicholas Clay) and did address some of his 154 sonnets to him.

Well-seasoned arguments about Shakespeare's sexuality occurred in a number of the 15-part *The Sonnets of William Shakespeare* series (1984 T, with comments by John Mortimer, A. L. ROWSE, Stephen Spender and Gore VIDAL) and in *Without Walls* 'Dark Horses' (1992 T presented by Simon CALLOW). There is also the visualization of 14 sonnets (read by Judi Dench) as a love story involving two young men in THE ANGELIC CONVERSATION (1985 C).

The sequence of lyric poems, the first 126 being homoerotic, are dedicated to Mr W. H. For all that they are disputed, they form one of the most comprehensive friezes of bisexual, if not homosexual passion, lust, tenderness, regret and loss written to a Mistress/Master. They include Sonnet 53 'What is your substance, whereof are you made' (on the theme of hero worship), Sonnet 121 (declaring 'I am that I am'), and Sonnet 18 *'Shall I compare thee to a summer's day?'

This famous love poem – traditionally and currently supposed to be addressed to a woman by a man – was, said Professor Leslie Fiedler in *The Sonnets of William Shakespeare*, in fact written to a man by a man. Simon Callow in *Without Walls* commented with restrained glee: 'Not a lot of people, as Mr Caine would say, know that.' He continued: 'Shakespeare was deeply interested in sexuality and [the Sonnets offer] a chance to examine from the inside ... desires that you, the reader, may not directly feel yourself ... The result is bound to be a happier world to love in.'

'William Shakespeare was a homosexual. It doesn't make him a bad person, for God's sake!' Gail (Maureen O'BRIEN) to her father in *Runaway* (1992 R).

'"Shall I compare thee to a summer's day?" he asked politely' (the first line of Robert Nye, *Mrs Shakespeare – The Complete Works* 1992, Anne Hathaway's 'memoirs').

* One of the most consistently requested pieces of recorded prose by DESERT ISLAND DISCS participants, including writer Clemence Dane (1951, author of the play *Will Shakespeare*); actress Sybil Thorndike (1952); actress Coral Browne and film producer Sir Michael Balcon (1961); Noel COWARD (1963); writer Stephen Grenfell (1964); writer Mary Stewart (1969); singer Cleo Laine and writer Dan Jacobson (1977).

shall we dance? Jimmy PORTER requests the pleasure of his best mate Cliff in LOOK BACK IN ANGER (Kenneth Haigh and Alan BATES 1956 T etc), but Jimmy becomes aggravated when Cliff won't let go as they waltz round their tiny Midlands flat, watched numbly by Jimmy's wife Alison.

The sleazy Anthony Goodwin (Michael Coles), up on a charge of attacking and robbing a milkman, refuses to play ball with an interrogating detective in *The Portsmouth Defence* (1966 T): 'You break my heart. Shall we dance?'

This twist on the standard heterosexual invitation, whether for strangers or lovers, was probably a nod to THE GOON SHOW, some of whose male characters were wont to subtly proposition each other thus, in 'Lurgi Strikes Britain' (1954 R):

Neddy Seagoon: 'I love you. Shall we dance?'
Moriarty: 'I don't wish to know that.'

In 'Rommel's Treasure' (1955) MORIARTY demands that Neddy and Hercules GRYTPYPE-THYNNE stop that 'sinful dancing'. They obey, but the show ends with them smooching. The image of these two men quick-quick-slow-ing together was suitably outrageous, for Spike Milligan to redeploy it in other shows, along with another dance-floor conversational ploy 'Do you come here often?' This was a question asked of Neddy by Major Denis BLOODNOK or Moriarty (in 'The Choking Horror' in 1956 etc), or by Grytpype-Thynne who in 'The Fireball of Milton Street' calls him 'DARLING' before asking if he comes here often, to which Neddy pertly replies: 'Only in the mating season.'

Shall We Dance? This sweeping, dazzling waltz is both the zenith and the sunset of the governess's relationship with her Siamese employer in *The King and I*. This is also true for Matthew and Phil in the TWO OF US, at least in the first (cut) version shown on television in 1988. Simultaneously whooping with joy and letting fly with society's verbal slings and arrows ('NANCY BOY ... BENT ... dangerous deviants!'), the lovers begin whirling around in each other's arms on a beach, as the old favourite thunders forth. The pair's happy delirium is watched, from a cliff-top, by a man, his arm protectively around his young son.

The use of familiar show tunes is especially effective for jogging rigid minds into a new gear, as the surprising last-minute burst of Mitzi Gaynor and Rodgers and Hammerstein proved in ME! I'M AFRAID OF VIRGINIA WOOLF (1978 T). Severely weakening the euphoria of the scene in *Two of Us* is the particular recording chosen. It is not the film soundtrack rendering by Deborah

Kerr (with high notes dubbed by Marni Nixon) and Yul Brynner, but a grossly inferior Muzak sing-along. The homogenized, jarring sound robs these few moments of their intended *frisson*.

shamans In the third part of the series on comarative religions and mythologies *Joseph Campbell: The Power of Myth* (1989 T), Campbell outlines the difference between a shaman and a priest: while the latter is a functionary carrying out ritual, a shaman's power is as an interpreter of mythological life for the tribe. He expresses the power not from established lore or teachings but directly from his own ecstatic experience. This derives from an overwhelming psychological upheaval in the adolescence of shamans 'that turns them totally inwards ... they experience dying and resurrectioning ... have deep dreams, mystical encounters ... they are drawn from the normal world to the world of the gifted'.

Unfortunately, having summoned up these men who take unto themselves a wholeness which embraces both sexes – and whose adolescent turmoil could be said to resemble some people's 'COMING OUT' – Campbell (or the producer of the series) dissolves them by embarking upon yet another description of courtship.

The role of the shaman in many diverse cultures is shrouded in mystery. They are usually portrayed as inscrutably malevolent, eg John Hoyt who is called 'the Shaman' in the Genghis Khan epic *The Conqueror* (1956 C), or as old and without sexual dimension, eg MERLIN.

Shane Waiter at Nelson GABRIEL's wine bar, with a boyfriend who is a flight attendant with the Australian airline QANTAS. He has never opened his mouth, but his presence has been felt on THE ARCHERS for a number of years as the only gay person in the Borchester–Ambridge area: 'he's having one of his tantrums'.

Shane was first referred to on 3 March 1986 and is one of a baker's dozen of silent characters including Madge Piggott (who was 'gone on' Reg Fiddler), Baggy, Snatch, Barry Simmonds, Higgs the chauffeur, Alf, Trudie, Sammie Whipple, Graham Pollard the cowman, Freda and the legendary Prue. When pressed by *Gay Times* in 1992 as to when Shane would speak and generally take a more activist role in proceedings, the series' editor, Vanessa Whitburn, was not at all sure that he would make a good spokesman for or personification of gay life.

His most significant contribution to life in Britain so far has been his recipe – squeezed out of him by Nelson for *Radio Times* readers – for tomato, orange and tarragon soup. Caroline Bone, restaurant manageress at Grey Gables, pronounced the dish 'excellent, and a good way to use up the glut of tomatoes we often get in September'. (For more details of Shane's soup, which involves tomatoes, potatoes and onions pushed through a sieve or liquidizer with stock, garlic and tarragon, orange juice and zest, see *Radio Times*, 23–9.8.86.)

Shannon, Lori [Don McLean] (1941–84) American FEMALE IMPERSONATOR, actor–producer and director–writer based mainly in San Francisco. Played Beverley La Salle in three episodes of ALL IN THE FAMILY (1975–7) and also appeared in the telemovie *For the Love of It* (1980). One of the top attractions at Finnochio's bar–nightclub between 1977 and 1983, he was also entertainment critic for the *Sentinel* gay newspaper.

Share and Share Alike (UK 1978 R) Lesley (Hugh PADDICK) lives in Edgware, his brother Jack (Michael Robbins) in Chelsea. Lesley [*sic*] does *The Times* crosswords, watches nature documentaries and is a VEGETARIAN anti-smoking virgin. Jack is a meat-eating, hard-drinking and wenching chauvinist slob. Then their mother dies, specifying in her will that they will only gain their inheritance if they live together for three years.

W: Harold Snoad and Michael

Knowles; P: John Dyas; 24.7.–11.9.78; BBC Radio 4; 30 mins each.

Crude culture-clash comedy, most of whose laughs are wrung out of Lesley's neuter sexuality and prissy habits. Highlight of the series – which has about it the smell of a dead cat – are a strike at the factory (where both brothers work: Lesley in management, Jack on the shop floor), a seance, an evening class and middle-aged Lesley's search for his first woman. There's also a queer FILM DIRECTOR (Frank Thornton) who wants to make a documentary 'starring' the brothers whom he momentarily mistakes for a couple. Gay listeners who regarded this as the nadir of 1970s comedy had to revise their opinion of *Share and Share Alike* in the light of the even more lamentable THREE PIECE SWEET a year later.

Shaw, Sebastian (1903–) English writer and actor, thick-set; cast from a relatively early age as dignified, substantial professional men, which made his role as a homosexual DOCTOR in a PROBATION OFFICER episode in 1959 all the more startling. Was that way inclined again in *Dead of Night* 'Death Cancels All Debts' (1972 T) as Powys Jubb, a dying world-famous writer whose wife struggles to come to terms with his rejection of her for a man.

Other roles include *Caste* (1930 C); Jimmy in *The Lady* (1935 C); Edmond Davy in *Men Are Not Gods* (1936 C); Captain Reed in *Farewell Again* (1937 C); hero in *The Spy in Black* (1939); Kit [Christopher] MARLOWE in *Will Shakespeare* (1947 R); Hugh Marvell MP in *Laxdale Hall* (1947 C); as Horatio opposite GIELGUD in *Hamlet* (1948); as *Corialanus* (1950 R); *The Glass Mountain* 1949 C); Priam in *The Tragedy of Dido, Queen of Carthage* (1952 R); *Libel* (1953 R); Sammy Rice in *The Small Back Room* (1954 R); a writer in *Cul de Sac* (1960 T); the doctor in *It Happened Here* (1966 C); Quince in *A Midsummer Night's Dream* (1968 C); Luke Skywalker's father in *The Empire Strikes Back* (1980 C); *Fothergill* (1981 T); *Return of the Jedi* (1983 C); Dr Percy Thurson in *The*

Nation's Health (1983 T); *Reith* (1984 T); Lord Tolle in *Chelworth* (1989 T); etc.

Edward **Shelly** Richard Hurndall in PAUL TEMPLE *and the Vandyke Affair* (1950, 1959 R): 'a rather flamboyant individual' who runs a Hampstead Mothers' Help Bureau providing sitters-in, nursemaids and ladies' companions and is 'not the reticent type'. He is revealed to be the brain behind a Paris drugs syndicate, the mysterious Vandyke, who was using his 'precious act' as an obliging cover. He falls to his death from a train. He is the most extreme example of the 'spoilt' youngish men who populate the Temple adventures, full of hysteria and coyness: 'It's very naughty of me to call round at this time, but I had to see you, Temple.'

Sher, Antony (1949–) South African, British-based multi-faceted actor and writer with guts and *brio*, who first appeared on *2nd House* (in an excerpt from the West End musical *John, Paul, George, Ringo and Bert* 1974 T). He worked in one of GAY SWEATSHOP's plays in the 1970s and took the role of Arnold in the London production of *Torch Song Trilogy*. He played a man with prophetic powers who wants to change his gender in his first substantial film fole, *Shadey* (1986). He was one of the participants in SATURDAY NIGHT OUT's look at being openly gay in the theatre in 'To Be or Not to Be'.

C: one of the *Yanks* (1979); badly post-synched as a gum chewing Niagara Falls hotel bellboy ('have a happy whatever') in *Superman II* (1980); etc.

R: WOMAN'S HOUR 'Guest of the Week' (1985); DESERT ISLAND DISCS (1987); *Third Ear* (1991), talking to Paul Allen about his novel *The Indoor Boy*; Pete Singer in *Singer* (1992), partly based on 1960s slum landlord Peter Rachman; etc.

T: Morris in *Cold Harbour* (1978); Howard in *The History Man* (1981); *Newsnight* (1985), excerpts from *Torch Song Trilogy*; *Tartuffe* (1985); *The Miser*

(1987); OMNIBUS 'Caryl Churchill' (1992); etc.

Sherriff, R[obert] C[edric] (1896–1975) English playwright whose greatest success was his 1927 drama of the trenches, JOURNEY'S END (1930 C etc), which was staged in 20 countries and originally written fro the Kingston upon Thames Rowing Club. Other plays include the 1930 *Badger's Green* and the 1950 *Home at Seven* (1953 C etc). A literary adviser to producer Alexander Korda during the 1930s, he became a successful and prodigious scriptwriter (*The Invisible Man* 1933; *Goodbye Mr Chips* 1939; *Lady Hamilton* 1941; *Odd Man Out* 1947; *The Dam Busters* 1955; televisions *Suspense* series; etc). His 1969 autobiography was entitled (regretfully? resignedly? matter of factly? triumphantly?) *No Leading Lady.*

Sherrin, Ned (1931–) English writer, producer, presenter, quiz master, raconteur and wit, known for his invigorating ennui and quicksilver tongue. A former barrister, he produced TONIGHT from 1957 to 1959 before moving on, via *Laugh Line* (1960) and radio and television scripts (usually with Caryl Brahms), to THAT WAS THE WEEK THAT WAS (1962–3), *Not So Much a Programme . . . More a Way of Life* (1964–5) and *BBC3* (1965–6). He then became an enterprising and initially very successful film producer: *The Virgin Soldiers* (1969); *Every Home Should Have One* (1969); *Up Pompeii* (1970); *Up the Chastity Belt* (1971); *Girl Stroke Boy* (1971); *Rentadick* (1972); *The Alf Garnett Saga* (1972); *The National Health* (1973); *Up the Front* (1973).

He took to the stage as narrator of *Side by Side by Sondheim* in 1976, extending the concept to other popular composers in *Song by Song* (1978–80) and (with Caryl Brahms) to the conductor Sir Thomas *Beecham* (1979 & 1983 T). He produced one of the 1970s oddest television series, *The Rather Reassuring Programme,* and started to become urbanely ubiquitous at awards ceremonies. His radio career blossomed in the 1980s

with *And So to Ned* (1982); the Saturday morning chat show *Loose Ends* (1985–); the musical quiz *Counterpoint* (1987–). He celebrated his late writing partner in *Too Dirty for the Windmill* (1987) and was one of the men come to praise CORAL BROWNE (and 'out' himself that bit further) in *Caviar to the General* (1990 T). He was on hand to talk about another sacred monster in *Without Walls* 'J'Accuse Dame Edna EVERAGE' (1993 T) and to remember the extraordinarily heady Saturday nights of *TW3* in *Carry On up the Zeitgeist* (1992 R). He appeared in the small but juicy role of Addison in ORLANDO (1992 C).

He returned to his old school, Sexey's, with actor Robin Phillips to read some of his favourite poetry and prose in *With Great Pleasure* (1971 R).

Richard **Shewin** *See* A HEDGE, BACKWARDS; THE PRIVATE LIFE OF HILDA TABLET; A VERY GREAT MAN INDEED.

ship's stewards Howard Marion-Crawford proves a goldmine of sexual experience – 'golden days!' – for Roland in *The Dark Tower* (1946 R): the steward was modelled on an Oxford scout of playwright Louis MacNeice's acquaintance; Birtweed (Reginald BECKWITH) giving his newly arrived 'sir' all the little homely touches, regardless of whether 'sir' wants them in THE CAPTAIN'S TABLE (1958 C); senior steward Dawson (John Turner), sharing his cabin with young Cliff (Haywood Morse), becomes jealous of Cliff's dalliance with a woman passenger and throws himself overboard in *Trapped* 'Journey into Nowhere' (1968 T); Palmer (Geoffrey BAYLDON) seemingly benign, maternally managing in *To See How Far It Is* (1968 T); the snooty Scottish purser (John Grieve) forever poking his nose into the heteros' fun and games in *Doctor at Sea* (1971 T); Alec BREGONZI in *The Two Ronnies'* miniseries 'Caribbean Nights' (1984 T).

shirt lifters First used on radio in THE GOON SHOW occasionally (1957: 'feathered shirt lifters; 1959: 'a box of feathered shirt lifters' mentioned by

'Scrooge' in the pastiche of 'A Christmas Carol'). By the time of *The Last Goon Show of All* (1972 R/T) censorship had loosened sufficiently for someone to say of Count MORIARTY: 'Thanks to him, there's a government health warning on every sailor's shirt.'

The term has also been heard in THE GENTLE TOUCH 'Blade' (1980 T); PRICK UP YOUR EARS (1987 C); and in Australia on *This Sporting Life* (1990–   R/T) whose rampaging sports and current affairs commentators (rough of tongue, at least partly satirical in intent), Dr H. G. Nelson and Roy Slaven, yoke shirt lifters with 'NANCY BOYS and quiche eaters'.

Sidney Shorr Middle-aged New York JEWISH man, played by Tony RANDALL. The first gay fictional character to give his name to a (1981) TV movie. It was qualified by a sly subtitle: *A Girl's Best Friend.* He would also have been the first gay man to have his forename in the title of a TV comedy series. But by the time LOVE, SIDNEY was unveiled to the public (also in 1981) the character, though remaining in the hands of Tony Randall, had lost his balls. He was simply a 'lonely' bachelor, who eventually adopts dear little Patti...

Short Story (UK 1978–   R) A regular 15-minute weekday afternoon spot on BBC Radio 4 which has found room for a small wad of telling tales by among others Michael Carson and Philip RIDLEY – and some enthralling false alarms like 'Darren's Trouble' (1980: son is not a transvestite); 'Maid in Heaven' (1992: proud spinster is not a lesbian); 'Pagans' (1992: two gay men chatter briefly on the sidelines before wafting away). *See also* MORNING STORY.

showers Private places for gentle reflection or vigorous wash-downs; also an excuse to show more of the bodies of actresses and (less often) actors. Before the crackdown by the Hollywood Production Code (1933–4) a movie star like George Raft could be seen showering with the strong suggestion of total NA-KEDNESS (eg *Night After Night*). The same actor had to be more decorous in the same situation in later films, although in *Invisible Stripes* (1940) he shared a shower stall with Humphrey Bogart. The Code was so strict about the camera straying to the NAVEL and beyond that some producers, rather than have their male characters unwashed, filmed them through the thickest frosted glass or clad them in jockey shorts (Robert Cummings in *Marry Me Again* 1953). As if in rebellion against this sorry spectacle, *Charade* (1963 C) included a scene where Cary GRANT takes a shower fully clothed.

Group showers were almost unheard of (the most famous one, in *The Spirit of Culver* with Jackie Cooper and Freddie Bartholomew, was astonishingly – it was 1939 – allowed to let slip more than was intended). However, Ben Gazzara and his acolytes were seen baring shoulders and most of their chests in another military school drama (*The Strange One/End as a Man* in 1957 C), and Warren Beatty and his fellow football jocks were allowed to be seen (cut off mid-abdomen) lathering themselves and making bawdy inferences in *Splendour in the Grass* (1961 C).

On British television, one of the first men seen having a shower – in itself a daring innovation in a country wedded to the bath – was a languorous young man, Nicky Blake (William Young), 'slow of speech and movement' who chats to his sister Tricia (Susannah YORK) wet and naked to the waist in *Promenade* (1960 T).

The erotic–sadistic possibilities of the shower for women having been made manifest for women in *The Seventh Victim* (1943 C) and *Psycho* (1960 C) were extended to man in *The Servant* (1963 C, James FOX hiding from the seeking Dirk BOGARDE), but only if they were fully clothed.

From the late 1960s, wide-angled shots of communal showers became acceptable in American movies, though few of those featuring males went beyond dorsal views (*Number One* 1969; *The Strawberry Statement* 1970; *Slap Shot*

1977; *North Dallas Forty* 1979). Situations where all the boys together were shown in their natural state comprise only a handful: from America, *Revenge of the Cheerleaders* (1976 C) and *Losin' It* (1982 C); from Britain, *Kes* (1969 C), ACCOUNTS (1983 T) and *Good and Bad at Games* (1984 T); from Australia an episode of *Phoenix* (1992 T).

American television permits showerers only if they are photographed carefully, sometimes above the breastbone (the TV remake of *Splendour in the Grass* was even more coy than the film 20 years before), sometimes below (ST ELSEWHERE; THIRTYSOMETHING; etc).

Occasionally the shower is used to suggest sexual congress of the worst kind: Randy Brent (Tony Curtis) and a male friend emerge from one – to the horror of Randy's wife – in *The Users* (1978 T); Robert Reed and Granville Van Dusen are in an identical situation in HOTEL 'Transitions' (1985 T); without intrusion and with more obvious lust-slaked connotations are Otto (John Steiner) and Leo (Clive Arrindell) in DESIGN FOR LIVING (1979 T), and Robert (John Bolger) and Michael (Richard Ganoung) in PARTING GLANCES (1985 C).

Sex in the shower was most unconvincingly (at the behest of the film company) refused by Brad DAVIS after being so sweetly offered by a fellow prisoner (Norbert Weisser) in MIDNIGHT EXPRESS (1978 C), and offered to Colin (Paul Freeman) by Pierce Brosnan in what proves to be a fatal come-on, at the swimming baths in *The Long Good Friday* (1980 C).

Examples of people, fully and also unashamedly naked, enjoying a relaxing spray and soak, singly or partnered, for no other reason than to cool off and/or get clean include Anita Pallenberg and Michele Breton in PERFORMANCE (1970 C); David HOCKNEY in *A Bigger Splash* (1974 C); Nicholas Clay in *Lady Chatterley's Lover* (1981 C); Jimmy McNichol in *Night Warning* (1982 C); Terry Jostrow in *Waltz Across Texas* (1982 C); Albert Finney in *Under the Volcano* (1984 C); David Keith in *Gulag* (1985 C);

Julie Walters in *She'll Be Wearing Pink Pyjamas* (1985 C/T) who insisted that if she and her fellow female actors took off all their clothes for a shower scene, then members of the crew (mostly male) should be similarly exposed.

See also BATHS; SAUNAS.

show me a happy homosexual and I'll show you a gay corpse Michael (Kenneth Nelson) quoting 'someone' to Donald (Frederick Coombs) during the former's *crise* at the end of THE BOYS IN THE BAND (1970 C). It was the most quoted line of the picture – mostly by heterosexually identified reviewers and commentators.

show me one straight guy and I'll show you a hundred grateful women A cry from the heart of many a woman (usually urban American). Widowed Gail (Mariette Hartley) utters these words in MY TWO LOVES (1986 T). Just a little while before she rolls into bed with a woman. Similar sentiments were expressed by thirtysomething characters played by Donna Mills in *Knots Landing* 'Night' (1982 T); Mary Kay Place in *The Big Chill* (1983 C); Judy Davis in *Husbands and Wives* (1992 C): 'single ... and not gay!' she marvels after meeting Michael (Liam Neeson).

A Shropshire Lad A very thinly disguised homoerotic poem written by A. E. HOUSMAN in 1896, inspired by his love for his undergraduate friends Moses and Adalbert Jackson with whom he lived. Moses couldn't respond to him sexually; his brother did but died soon after.

A series of 63 verses, nostalgically evoking a 'land of lost content', addressed to or spoken by a farm-boy or a soldier, it was first read on radio in 1938 (by Mary Tully and Godfrey Baseley – who later created THE ARCHERS). Patric Dickinsoin (in *A. E. Housman: The Man and the Poet* 1945 R) described Housman as 'an ascetic bachelor don' and *A Shropshire Lad* – one of the most enduring poems from its period, hugely popular during the First World War and after – as having been 'written in a few months of intense disturbance.'

> Oh when I was in love with you
> Then I was clean and brave ...

> Because I liked you better.
> Than suits a man to say,
> It irked you and I promised
> To throw the thought away.

In 1954 another reading of the poem was prefaced by a brief biography of its creator: 'He was an enigmatic man and one cannot resolve the enigma.' This resulted in a letter to *Radio Times* from a clergyman: 'Who could suspect that *A Shropshire Lad* was, as [Housman] admitted, the result of physical upheaval, due to a temporary lapse from a strict asceticism'.

Kingsley Amis discussed the poem (which was given a reading on BBC Radio 4 in 1986) in some (conservative heterosexually sieved) detail in 1990.

The fictionalized playboy (played by Michael Craig and based on the racing driver shot by Ruth Ellis in the early 1950s) keeps a copy of the poem by his bed in *Yield to the Night* (1956 C). 'I used to read a lot of things when I was young,' he acknowledges sadly to Mary Hilton (Diana Dors) who will later shoot him for his fecklessness and betrayal of her with a rich, older woman who keeps him.

Shuffle Off To Buffalo One of Busby Berkeley's less geometric but nonetheless stimulating extravaganzas (music and lyrics by Al Dubin and Harry Warren) from *Forty-second Street* (1933 C). Set in a Pullman carriage populated almost entirely by scantily dressed women happily sharing sleeping berths, the rhythm of the wheels, the bumpity-bump motion of the music, the crystalline sound of the women's chorus, their tissue-thin lingerie and the saucily drawn silk curtains create an extraordinarily Sapphic backdrop to a number which is ostensibly about a pair of honeymooners. The scene is awash with billing and cooing frm everyone except two of the women, Una Merkel and Ginger Rogers, who – one peeling a

BANANA, the other biting deep into an apple – cynically comment on the likely outcome for the two heterosexuals: divorce.

In what other song does a man (Clarence Nordstrom) croon to a woman (Ruby Keeler):

> I'll go home and get my panties
> You go home and get your scanties
> And away we'll go.

Performed and directed for maximum salacity, complete with a bit of ambiguous fumbling behind a curtain from which emerges a pair of women's shoes.

Other Berkeley choreographies – full of dizzying, dazzling Sapphism – during his relatively brief Warner Brothers period are 'The Shadow Waltz' from *Gold Diggers of 1933* (ecstatically playing neon-edged violins); from DAMES, the title number (scores of women in bed together) and 'Petting In The Park' (women silhouetted in a shower); from *Gold Diggers of 1937*, the breathtakingly pseudo-feminist 'All's Fair In Love And War' (an army of marching women easily overcoming the enemy – with perfume – in 'No Man's Land' and tirelessly parading in single-sex triumph).

Mrs **Shufflewick** Character created by Rex JAMIESON aka Jameson. A radio original, this bibulously ribald woman – 'broadminded to the point of obscenity ... weak-willed and easily led' – was partly based on an aunt with an equal liking for men and pints of stout (with gin chasers). This red-nosed, moth-eaten, time-chewed battler also became briefly popular on television – 'her' photograph appearing on the cover of *TV Mirror* in 1955. After television and radio variety outlets became scarcer in the early 1960s, Mrs Shufflewick, already a favourite in seaside shows and pantomime (25 appearances as the Dame), found her natural habitat: working men's clubs and drag pubs. Pickled, sour and dangerous, freed from broadcasting and family entertainment's clamp, 'Shuff', a one-off, was able to be as down and dirty as he/she pleased – and had always amply signposted. She was one of those rare creations – conceived in variety, born on radio, graduating on television and maturing in live entertainment – whose decline in material circumstances added more lustre to the characterization.

It could also be argued that Rex Jamieson's sturdy, if often stuporous, sense of himself (as a gay man, living with David Buckley) gave his act a depth and ironic honesty it might not otherwise have had. Gay sensibility? Most definitely, meeting as it did Vito RUSSO's criterion of 'not taking the heterosexual world into account when creating an idea ... a blindness to sexual divisions, an inability to perceive that people are different because of sexuality, a natural conviction that there is no such thing as normal even when the majority of people think so' (*The Celluloid Closet: Homosexuality in the Movies*, 1987). At the same time, Mrs Shufflewick also seems to be the pinnacle of what Barry TOOK objected to in general about female impersonation: '... the point they make is that women are vulgar and obnoxious, stupid, dirty-minded, sexually aggressive or antisocial' (*Listener*, 27.1.83).

R: *Variety Bandbox* (1950 etc); *Midday Music Hall* (1954–9); *Blackpool Night* (1956); *Variety Playhouse* (1956); *London Lights* (1961–2); *Holiday Music Hall* (1961–3); etc.

T: *Evans Abode* (with Norman Evans, 1954); *It's a Great LIfe* (1955–6); etc.

Mrs Shufflewick's last incumbency was as resident star of the Nashville Room in West Kensington, London, on Sundays from 1979, coupled with 'the Amazing Maurey Richards'.

shut that door! Uttered in Larry GRAYSON's wannest tones, with a tired flip of the wrist, this regular effort on his part – presumably to protect himself from the draughts that gave rise to his backache and some of his many other ailments, real and imagined – creased up sections of the British nation from 1972 until Larry left ITV for the BBC in 1977. His first three series were entitled *Shut That Door!* rather than the more appropriate – if equally (at that time) opaque, but

possibly also too radical – 'What a Gay Day!'

The 1973 series of *Shut That Door!*, produced and directed for ATV by Colin Clews and shown on Friday nights between 8.30 and 9pm, garnered 7,500,000 viewers, tieing in popularity with the BBC's *The Dick Emery Show* with its gallery of the afflicted including CLARENCE. A letter to *TV Times* (June 1973 said: 'Larry is the best thing that has happened to television since colour. So hurry back, Larry and open that friendly door because it just won't be a gay day until you do.'

Apart from semi-regular outings by Larry Grayson himself or by his numerous impersonators, the expression 'shut that door!' enjoyed its last hurrah (as anti-gay abuse) in MAINTAINING STANDARDS (1981 R), and turned inside out, from Angela Carter in her reworking of *Puss in Boots* (1982 R). Here the cat (Andrew Sachs) perfectly replicates the blocked adenoids, flaccid larynx and resultant dying vocal fall to miaow: 'Open that door!'

See also SEEMS LIKE A NICE BOY!; WHAT A GAY DAY!

Sidney/Sydney Boy's name often stuck to rather flaccid, pale pink characters.

UK: Sydney Carton in *A Tale of Two Cities*, sottish lawyer who redeems himself by doing that far, far better thing (William Farnum 1917 C; Ronald Colman 1935 C; Dirk BOGARDE 1958 C; Peter WYNGARDE 1958 T; John Wood 1965 T; Chris Sarandon 1980 T; etc); simultaneously stodgy and soggy Sid Mincing (Kenneth Connor) in *Ray's a Laugh* (1954–61 R); irrefutably crooked but credible at least to Hancock) 'Sid' (Sidney James) in HANCOCK'S HALF HOUR (1954–9 R; 1956–60 T; also *Hancock* 1960–1 T); Sidney (Bryan Murray), the shy and lonely projectionist in *Poor Sidney* (1960 T); Sidney (Ken PARRY), pop-eyed member of a darts team in Z CARS 'On Watch – Newtown' (1962 T); Sydney (Hugh PADDICK) in *Wink to Me Only* (1969 T); homicidal MOTHERS' BOY Sydney (Dudley Sutton) in *Conception of Murder* 'Mother and

Child' (1970 T); Sidney Larkin – 'Larkin by name, Larkin by nature' (David Jason) in *The Darling Buds of May* (1990–2 T); etc.

US: Sidney (Ernest Cossart), flighty choreographer in *The Great Ziegfeld* (1936 C); Sid Jeffers (Oscar Levant) in *Humouresque* (1947 C): 'Leave your hair mussed,' he tells his friend (John Garfield), 'you look pretty that way'; Sid Rafferty (Patrick McGoohan), crusty doctor of faint eccentricity in *Rafferty* (1977 T); Sidney SHORR (Tony RANDALL), lonely gay man in SIDNEY SHORR: A GIRL'S BEST FRIEND (1981 T), no longer gay in LOVE, SIDNEY (1981–3 T) but not heterosexual either, just 'happy to have someone to talk to'; astute country bumpkin Sidney Dean (Wesley Snipes) in *White Men Can't Jump* (1992 C); etc.

As a female name it was first used – for the forthright character played by Katharine HEPBURN and spelled as 'Sidney' in the credits – in *A Bill of Divorcement* (1932 C) and sporadically thereafter, most recently being given to Lisa Hartman's character (spelt 'Sydney'), a clever lawyer beached on a desert island in *Bare Essentials* (1990 T and the lawyer (Mariel Hemingway) in *Civil Wars* (1991– T).

(A young dancer, born Tula Ellice Finklea, was called Sid – aka Sidonie – Charisse by the time she arrived at MGM in the early 1940s. She revealed in a 1990 documentary, *Cyd Charisse*, that the studio decreed that her first name was 'too masculine'. As she had changed her name at least twice before during her time as a ballerina, she refused to budge. A more feminine compromise was quickly agreed upon.)

Sidney Shorr: A Girl's Best Friend (US 1981 T) An isolated, shy New York bachelor (Tony RANDALL) befriends single mother Laurie (Lorna Patterson) and her daughter (Kaleena Kiff). Having problems paying the rent and in need of someone to talk to, Sidney is only too delighted to have the pair move in with him, although they

seriously disrupt his rigidly systematic way of living.

W: Oliver Hailey; based on a story by Marily Cantor Baker (daughter of Eddie Cantor); D: Russ Mayberry; 104 mins.

The unhappy homosexual, a graphic artist, without a single friend, gay or heterosexual, given a reason to live (those hours spent in the dark watching GARBO weepies were doing him no good whatsoever). Heartwarming stuff just about kept above freezing point by its central performance, but patronizing just the same and totally inadequate given the representation of gay people on American television at that time.

When a series was mooted, the Radical Right was in full cry. Under no circumstances could a sympathetic character be gay, not even lugubriously and celibately. So in LOVE, SIDNEY (1981–3 T) he was just an ageing solitary with an overnight, ready-made family. Sidney Shorr: The Gay Who Never Was. His homosexuality denied by everybody who worked on the series, except the writers...

Signed: Lino Brocka (US 1987 C/T) A free-ranging documentary about the Filipino film-maker who locked horns with the Marcos government (and more specifically with Imelda Marcos) and who attempted to honestly depict life in the Philippines, especially the situation of slum-dwellers and young people forced into prostitution (MANILA: IN THE CLAWS OF DARKNESS). In the virtual stream-of-consciousness *Signed*, he comes out as gay, shows scenes from his long-thought lost *Gold-Plated* (which has a gay theme), and is pictured rehearsing actors for what was to be his penultimate film, *Macho Dancer*. But mostly he talks about his life and the radical politics forged by that life: his turbulent childhood; working as a monk among lepers in Hawaii; his emerging sexuality; fighting to make films of artistic and social truth in the lightweight Filipino industry; his growing disgust with the corrupt governments and resulting activism.

W/D: Christian Blackwood; 83 mins.

A passionate, candid piece of self-expression from a courageous man whose bumpy but sometimes brilliant film career was prematurely ended by his death in a road accident.

'Film for me recaptures the spontaneous, pure, nonsensical relationship I had with the world as a child. This is why later, when I learned what was happening to my countrymen, I decided I also wanted to be part of those who tell the truth – I wanted to cry and I wanted to disturb.'

sign language Increasingly seen at lesbian and gay conferences and meetings but still rare (one of the women discussing OUTING in OUT 'Absolutely Queered' 1991) on television. *Out* 'Actions Speak Louder Than Words' (1992 T) included a mountingly sensual demonstration of some (British) signs used among DEAF and partially deaf homosexual people for 'gay', 'lesbian', 'bisexual', 'straight', 'deaf', 'partially deaf', 'hearing', 'coming out' (two of these), 'queen', 'drag', 'butch', 'clone', 'femme', 'horny', 'mincing', 'eyeing up', 'cruising', 'attraction', 'lust' (five different signs), 'a lot of lust', 'condom' (two signs), 'kiss', 'French kiss' and '69'.

signs and signals aka semiotics A symbolic visual and verbal language, secret or open, sometimes a light camouflage of innuendo, circumlocution and allusion, sometimes unveiled and provocative: either invented and employed by homosexual people themselves (POLARI; BADGES; the PINK TRIANGLE; keys worn left or right; HANDKERCHIEVES; SONGS; HAIRSTYLES; clothing; diction; humour; choice of friends; conversations about lovers who have no gender); or part of an endless landscape of objects, names and actions thought appropriate or inappropriate at different times in history – and energetically employed as shorthand by television, radio and film productions biased in favour or against a more fluid definition of gender (APRONS; BOYS' NAMES FOR GIRLS; BRACELETS; CAT OWNERS; DOG OWNERS; GIRLS' NAMES FOR BOYS; LIMP WRISTS; SCARVES; SUEDE SHOES; STRIPED SHIRTS; SURNAMES; WASHING UP; etc).

The Silence (Sw 1963 C) A lesbian (Ingrid Thulin), intelligent and strong, is attracted to her younger sister (Gunnel Lindblom) who seeks comfort from male strangers. Lustful Anna and repressed, dominant Ester play various power games until Anna leaves her dying sister alone in the oppressive foreign town in the care of an old man whose language she doesn't understand. W/P/D: Ingmar Bergman; 96 mins.

Completing the trilogy on faith and the silence of God begun with *Through a Glass Darkly* and *Winter Light*, Bergman tries to come to grips with basic passions felt and expressed by women, diametrically opposite but linked by blood and familiarity. In 1972 he would return to this theme, more wholeheartedly, in *Cries and Whispers* (a film discussed lovingly by Terence DAVIES in a Channel 4 series in 1990).

In *The Silence* the natures of both woman remain diagrammatic and the suffocating situation never quite resolves itself dramatically. Bergman is again unlocking the door into his own psyche with this cold preachment against two clearly damned women stuck in an empty hotel in an oppressive town, unable to communicate with anyone except through sex – one with a male pick-up, the other through self-stimulation.

The film was a milestone in the battle to extend the boundaries of what could be shown on the screen to adults, but inevitably it furthers the understanding of lesbianism not one jot. Ingrid Thulin is a pulsating death's head, antagonistic, MAN-HATING, unappealing, coughing her last. Her family ties are stretched to breaking point as she attempts to wear down Anna, who is presented as a sweating bitch on heat.

This great director, who was shackled to a limited number of unrelenting and ultimately alienating themes during the 1960s and 1970s, would only obliquely – and without great originality – tackle male homosexuality (in *Hour of the Wolf*

1968, *Face to Face* 1976 and *From the Life of the Marionettes* 1980).

Silence = Death Accompanied by a PINK TRIANGLE, this legend was on posters and stickers as well as BADGES and T-shirts from 1988 onwards, as part of the ACT UP campaign to arouse public awareness, particularly on drug-testing and care facilities for people with AIDS. Displayed in the Gay Men's Health Crisis office scene in LONGTIME COMPANION; and – unofficially stuck – on the record bins at the HMV shop in Oxford Street when Harry 'picks up' Martin in KILLING TIME (1990 T). Posters and badges bearing this sign have also been featured in DI ANA'S HAIR EGO (1990 V); DONAHUE 'Bereavement' (1990 T, worn by a bereaved gay man on the top half of his immaculately tailored suit); OVER OUR DEAD BODIES (1991 C/T, Keith Haring shown painting 'Silence = Death Ignorance = Fear'); *RSVP* (1991 T); VOICES FROM THE FRONT (1991 C/T); *Hate Crimes* (Aust 1992 T); *Sally Jessy Raphael* 'One-Night Stand Ruined Her Life' (1992 T); etc.

Silence = Death (US/Ger 1988 C) A film by Rosa VON PRAUNHEIM about both the responsiveness and the non-responsiveness of groups and individuals in the face of HIV/AIDS.

Silent Wing (UK 1984 R) The slow reorientation and evolution of Monika, formerly associated with a gang of urban terrorists, into a relatively normal world after she has escaped from prison and makes a new life, as Gisela, in Britain. Among the more than cosmetic changes Monika makes are sexual relationships with women instead of men. For three years Gisela remains undetected, teaching carpentry to young offenders. Then one of them gets into trouble with the law, she goes to court to speak in his defence. Recogized as Monika, she is arrested and awaits deportation back to Germany where she must complete her sentence.
W: David Zane Mairowitz; D: Jane Morgan; 15.6.84; BBC Radio 4; 90 mins.

Diana QUICK manages the prickly abrasive personality of this woman, based on Astrid Proll, with consummate ease and manages to make all thoughts and actions totally convincing. Monika's fugitive status, self-exile, and false name and identity enable her to clearly identify with the underdogs in British society, to react angrily to injustice and to criticize what she sees as wrong and limiting within the lesbian/feminist social scene.

The play is more than a monologue between divided selves, one on fire, one packed in ice. The writer brilliantly paces the to-ing and fro-ing between the incarcerated Monika and the freer, yet haunted Gisela while allowing the outside world (flat-mates, supermarkets, lovers, discos, work) to impinge to just the right degree.

There's a tingling quality about the writing indivisible from the central performance that burrows beneath the surface drama of a woman whose rigid principles are bent under pressure, making her a different, possibly a 'better' person. Yet Monika/Gisela's ultimate belief in truth – as it affects individuals – drives her to sacrifice hard-won freedom for incarceration. However, as the final scene shows, her spirit, now far less dogma-driven, and her newly freed imagination will triumph over her captors with their incessant fluorescent lighting that denies sleep, and the ever-vigilant eye of the surveillance camera.

'Diana Quick managed to convey something very unpleasant indeed about the nature of a certain kind of solitary confinement akin to sensory deprivation. The play said little, though perhaps implied enough, about the mark left by urban terrorism' (David Wade, *The Times*, 16.6.84).

silhouettes These used to be the rule rather than the exception in British television programmes about homosexuality before the law changed in 1967. During the 1970s and early 1980s, they became increasingly redundant since appearing on television without barriers to recognition became part and parcel of some people's COMING OUT journey.

Now, with the need to speak out about HIV/AIDS but, for many reasons, to sometimes preserve anonymity, the masking process has begun anew. Silhouettes are regarded as too sinister and slightly ridiculous, and other techniques are now in place such as obliterating most of the features with 'mosaic', blurring or a black square. Sometimes the camera itself performs the defacing by cunning angles – such as the extraordinary lengths on OUT ON TUESDAY that WOMEN LIKE US (1990 T) and the follow-up WOMEN LIKE THAT went to in order to honour a couple of the participants' requests not to go 'on camera' (hands clasping and unclasping in laps, booted feet walking through snow, the back of the head etc). In a 1990 ITV schools programme about AIDS, 'Steve' is 'headless' as he is interviewed by doctors and remains so when, later, he inserts his drip: 'It's not an easy life, there's no cure.'

However irritating some of these blotting out devices – sometimes extending to electronically distorting the voice – can sometimes be to the viewer, the beneficial power of television to increase awareness must also be balanced by an awareness of its power to blight individual lives if they are unfairly victimized or find themselves unable to cope with public attention as a result of one brief appearance in millions of homes.

Sometimes, a gay man may be endorsing an illegal act by speaking on television. This explained why *Public Eye* 'Age of Consent' (1992 T) only showed parts (hands, an eye, the back of the head) of a man who was under 21 and in a homosexual relationship with someone older.

Silhouetting of any kind will perhaps no longer be necessary as a shield against misunderstanding and family sensitivities, but the new techniques, though obtrusive, do act as a reminder of the enormous restraints on personal freedom of expression which the majority of people have to endure. The current techniques are certainly no more risible than the gay man who, on CBS REPORTS 'The Homosexuals' in 1967, was photographed throughout behind a potted palm.

Simon & Simon (US 1981–5 T) Two San Diego-based brothers – chalk and cheese as played by Jameson Parker (college graduate) and Gerald McRaney (Vietnam veteran) – work as private eyes.
P: Philip DeGuere; CBS; 50 mins.

This light-hearted crime series was no more homoerotic than others of its mindless ilk, though viewers could spend an entertaining minute or so in each episode pumping pink into lines like 'Feel me, go ahead, touch me' or 'I want to talk about a little trade' (Peter Kastner in 'The Hottest Ticket in Town' 1982) before switching channels in the hope of something more productive.

However, Maureen Paton, TV critic of the *Star* was alerted in 1984 to the hidden message of *Simon & Simon* by its title song, 'Best Of Friends': '...More than brothers/We're just good friends.' (Composed and sung by the Thrasher Brothers, this country-styled ditty was in fact replaced in the second season by an instrumental theme.) Ms Paton, doing a bit of detective work herself on behalf of her readers, nailed the boys as secret homos rather than brothers because 'each throws terrible fits of jealous pique every time the other so much as looks at a woman ... Every week there's a new female for one of the brothers to fall for, but I'm not persuaded they're interested in anything more than borrowing the girl's dress for the night.'

The series became progressively duller as the years rolled by with nary a hint of the moustached Simon putting on drag or the clean-cut one wearing his keys on his belt and, as a result, retained its place, just behind *Magnum PI*, as one of the top shows in America.

The Simpsons (US 1989– T) On the bottom rung of the middle-class ladder,

Homer Simpson and his wife Marge live in Springfield (a tribute to *Father Knows Best*) with their rackety son Bart, shy-sweet daughter and a baby. They're just an ordinary, insensitive family of American battlers (though with 4 fingers instead of 5) in a peaceful town (whose main features are a tyre dump and a nuclear power plant, where Homer works).

C: Matt Groening; Ed: James L. Brooks (for 20th Century Television); Fox; 30 mins.

The Simpsons grew from a 5-minute cartoon spot on *The Tracey Ullman Show* in 1987–8 and fitted perfecly into the half-hour sitcom format. The animation is always dazzling and the targets for satire range far beyond the usual domestic concerns. The characters are always poking their animated noses into everything the Reagans told Americans to hate or ignore.

Even Marge, who appears to be the standard-issue wife, nevertheless has a hairstyle closely based on Elsa Lanchester's in THE BRIDE OF FRANKENSTEIN and does a good job of keeping Homer from strangling Bart, and Bart – whose biggest fear is being normal – from doing permanent injury to talented, sensitive saxophone virtuoso Lisa and his other sister, the until recently silent Maggie who doesn't miss a trick.

The message given out by this series through the misadventures of its charmless but sympathetic and basically honest central characters is: Don't cheer up, things *are* as bad as you think.

Like its live-action and working-class counterpart, ROSEANNE, this show declares war on glamour and slickness. It's spiky and sloppy, full of bounce and inquisitiveness. Harvey FIERSTEIN is just one of a number of guest voices who has fitted in perfectly with the anti-authoritarian style: he played Carl, Homer's gay SECRETARY at the power plant in the 1990 episode 'Simpson and Delilah'. He takes the blame for one of Homer's actions but later returns to help his boss write a speech. Carl KISSES Homer after telling him: 'My mother taught me never to kiss a fool.'

Cartoon figures had never been used in such a penetrating way on American television before, getting away with behaviour and subjects that would very likely have been forbidden to flesh and blood characters. Ironically produced by a network controlled by Rupert Murdoch, it was one of the few counterblasts to the packaging of politics and social issues, and the continuing encouragement of individuals to be swallowed up in the mass.

(Mike, played by River Phoenix, watches a segment where the Simpsons are visited by alien beings while his client potters around the kitchen after sex in MY OWN PRIVATE IDAHO 1991 C.)

sin Genesis 2 and 3 burden human beings with a responsibility for sin and evil that can, if dwelt upon, hobble some people's lives from infancy to the grave. Although homosexuality is not specifically apportioned to either Adam or Eve (or the serpent) and is not one of the behaviours abjured in the Ten Commandments, its linkage to SODOM AND GOMORRAH and other mixed messages in Leviticus and in PAUL's letters allows some people, believers and non-believers alike, to freely use the words 'sin' and 'sinners' when publicly or privately discussing any homosexual manifestation. Often during radio or television discussions, sin colours the most rational, disinterested arguments and creates rowdy, spiteful conflicts between the seemingly righteous (who hate the sin but love the sinner) and everyone else.

The loyal black maid played by Juanita Moore in *Imitation of Life* (1959 C), very much a God-fearing woman who suffered many cruel rejections from her daughter (who wishes to pass for white), put sinfulness in its place very simply and in a way many homosexual people could identify with: 'It's a sin to be ashamed of what you are.'

The Singing Nun The popular name of Soeur Sourire, a Belgian nun who recorded a simple song called 'Dominique' which became a no. 1 hit in America and was enormously popular all over Europe. A totally imaginary film, starring Debbie Reynolds – in full natural make-up – was released in 1966, the same year that the real Singing Nun, Jeanine Deckers, left her order after seven years to live with her female lover in Wavre. Plagued by debts and tax demands linked to royalties (with which the Catholic Church had refused to assist owing in part, it was claimed, to the former nun's intransigence and total inability to manage her financial affairs), she, aged 52, and her lover Annie Pêcher committed suicide in March 1985. The pathetic story was related by composer Moya Henderson in a part-spoken work called *Meditation and Distractions on the Theme of the Singing Nun* (Aust 1990 R).

A Single Man (UK 1972 R) George (David MARCH) is an English teacher at San Tomas State College, California. Known for his wit and irony, he has layers stripped off him when he has to face up to the death of his young lover Jim. He is helped through the tunnel by his intellect and by colleagues like Charley (Mary Wimbush) and Kenny (Geoffrey Beevers) with whom he is encouraged to frolic.

W: Eric Ewens from the novel by Christopher ISHERWOOD; P: Richard Wortley; 22.5.72; BBC Radio 4; 90 mins.

A very moving account of a man passing through much pain into something like peace and acceptance. For once, the 'problem' wasn't homosexuality but the loss of a loved one – who happened to be homosexual.

In the novel, Isherwood's alter ego had some brief but violent comments to make on heterosexuals (he would like to 'garrot' some of them) which were not included in the radio version. What did cross over from printed page to air were George's equally scathing remarks – written pre-STONEWALL and gay liberation – about the inherent fascism of all underdogs, especially those into whose paws a little power drops: 'A minority has its own kind of aggression. It also dares the majority to attack it. It hates the majority – not without cause, I grant you. It even hates the other minorities – because all minorities are in competition.'

George, lecturing on Aldous Huxley, warms to his theme: 'A minority is only thought of as a minority when it constitutes one kind of a threat to the majority. Then we run into liberal heresy. Because the persecuting majority is vile, says the liberal, therefore the persecuted minority must be stainlessly pure. Can't you see what nonsense that is? What's to prevent the bad from being persecuted by the worse? Did all the Christian victims in the arena have to be saints?'

A second version of the novel, based on a stage adaptation, was broadcast in 1991 on BBC Radio 4 with Alec MCCOWEN as George. (*A Single Man* was also the title of an appreciation of Christopher Isherwood by Ian Hamilton using archive interviews on Radio 4, 19.1.86.)

singlet A form-fitting garment now no longer confined to labourers, truck drivers or businessmen who may or may not wish to display part of their breasts and all of their arms. Part of gay erotic iconography as worn by Brad DAVIS in QUERELLE (1982 C); Matt Dillon in *Rumble Fish* (1983 C); Daniel Webb in MORE LIVES THAN ONE (1984 T); Steven Waddington in EDWARD II (1991 C). Brought into the mainstream by Don Johnson in *The Long Hot Summer* (1985 T) and *The Hot Spot* (1990 C), and Bruce Willis in *Die Hard* (1988 C).

The singlet, usually white, is currently being marketed for men and women as inner and outer wear having been hugely popularized by Paul Mercurio in STRICTLY BALLROOM (1992 C). This film has made a fortune for Chesty Bonds, created in 1938 as part of the bronzed, sweaty, beer-swilling OCKER image, now best known for being worn by a dancer with long hair.

Sins (US 1986 T) Jacques aka Jake (William Allen Young), a BLACK American in Paris, befriends the young heroine Helen. His photographs of her lead to her fame and fortune (and the chance to be played in early middle age by Joan Collins). Jacques spends part of the story in bad odour having caused Helene's husband's death by inciting an impotent Count to attempt rape, the spectacle of which causes the husband's heart to give out.

W: Laurence Heath from the novel by Judith Krantz; P: Steve Krantz; D: Douglas Hicox; 200 mins.

The usual hokey rags to riches plot is enhanced by some really entrancing photography (by Jean Tournier) and an easy on the ear score (partly by Francis Lai). Jacques, who has a slight Southern American accent, is bright, breezy, a good friend to the heroine (offered a lot of money to defect to another couturier, he refuses) at least until his unfortunate lapse, but all is forgiven at the end. Although no more than a glorified stage-hand to set the heroine's career in motion (he is absent for huge amounts of the middle section), it is rare for a black gay character – 'escaping from a number of prejudices' – to be presented in such a debonair, positive way. He has his own theme music and even an (off-screen) sex life (with various of his laboratory staff and possibly with his sexy assistant, played by Timothy Wood).

The Sir Roger De Coverley Merry dance involving multiple partners: a favourite in practically every Hollywood film set in 18th-century England (*Wuthering Heights* 1939; *Devotion* 1946). Sir Roger was regularly mentioned in Joseph Addison's *Spectator* pieces between 1711 and 1714 and may have been extracted from his friend, the bachelor poet and MP William Walsh (1663–1708) who lived at Abberley Lodge, Abberley, Wiltshire.

Sissy Girl's name, a pet form of Cecilia, Cecil(e)y or Cecile. Fictional ones can be shy or retiring, dithery or forceful. They include Sissy Jupe (Michelle Dibnah), innocent daughter of a circus clown in Dickens' *Hard Times* (1977 T); Sissy Davis (Debra Winger) in *Urban*

Cowboy (1982 C); Sissy Morgan (Ellen Jones), sister of Pansy in *We Are Seven* (1989 R); Dr Sissy Wetheral (Elaine Smith), member of the *RFDS* [*Royal Flying Doctor Service*] (Aust 1993 T).

sissy/sissies The male equivalent of TOMBOY, but much more disapproving and often an incitement to attack the boy or man so called, verbally or physically. A diminutive of 'sister', originating in the 19th century, it became associated with young boys like over-pampered, effeminately dressed Cedric Errol in the novel and subsequent plays and films of *Little Lord Fauntleroy*. (A newer – less corrosive – word popular during the 1980s is WIMP.)

Occasionally 'sissy' will be used about over-dainty or cowardly young women. The nasty bullying schoolgirl in THE CHILDREN'S HOUR/THE LOUDEST WHISPER (1961 C) calls her friend one, and one of the pilots in *The Last Flight* (1931) played by John Mack Brown tells Helen Chandler she's 'a sissy drinker' as she sips champagne through a straw. (In the same film, another grounded flyer tells his best friend that he's a 'sissy'.)

Boys and young men are liable to be called one of these if:

They like classical music: 'The silvery tinkle boys – Chopin and Debussy – that's sissy stuff,' teacher to young Rolfe (Melvyn HAYES) in THE UNLOVED (1955 T).

Or kiss girls: 'Ugh, no, it's sissy,' deaf children talking about growing up (1972 T).

Or appreciate nature: 'He loved the trees and the flowers. You thought he was a sissy. He was just a boy trying to grow up in his own way. He needed to be understood.' Mother to Father during a discussion on their son who left home in *Seasons of the Mist* (1987 R).

Or ride a horse: 'That's sissy,' school bad boy (Tony Bywater) in *Me, Sir? Who, Sir?* (1987 T).

Or live without a father but with two mothers: 'Because I live with a bunch of women, the other kids say I'm a sissy,' Allie's son Chip (Frederick Koehler) in *Kate and Allie* 'Odd Boy Out' (1984 T).

Or have an interest in botany: 'He used to press flowers in an album until he decided it was sissy – then he returned to bulbs in jars instead,' father (Kenneth Cranham) of 12-year-old son David (Gary King) in *Death Drop* (1992 R).

Or kiss Christopher Reeve: 'Supercissy!' (1982 headline in the *Sun* newspaper over Michael Caine kissing the actor who played Superman in *Deathtrap*).

Some actors have made entire careers out of playing fluttery feminine-seeming men. In Britain the prime example is Michael WARD. Other include Murray MELVYN who began by forging a strong 'big sister' image in A TASTE OF HONEY (1961 C), before descending all too quickly into portraying supporting simperers (*Petticoat Pirates* 1961 to *Nutcracker* 1984); Reginald BECKWITH flapping and hissing in scores of films and television plays, but specifically homosexual in only a few like THE CAPTAIN'S TABLE (1958 C) and DOCTOR IN LOVE (1960 C); Larry GRAYSON who added hypochondria to the mix during the 1970s and 1980s; John INMAN's Mr HUMPHRIES and variations upon this theme; Julian CLARY who has almost single-handedly reinvented the sissy for the 1990s to acclaim from the home team and the away players; and probably the leading sissy of his generation, Kenneth WILLIAMS.

In America their equivalents reached cult status either within their lifetimes or because of the early 1980s' gay liberationists' greater tolerance for those who communicated what had hitherto seemed (and remain) such poor role models to the world at large prior to the 1960s. '... The characters created by [Franklin] PANGBORN, [Grady] Sutton, [Edward Everett] HORTON, [Clifton] WEBB and dozens of others brought a brief electric contact with the quicksilver truth and wrought a comic chaos that the social order suppressed' (Vito RUSSO, *The Celluloid Closet: Homosexuality in the Movies*, 1987).

Gay News critic Jack BABUSCIO divided them into three main categories. Firstly, prim snobs: Arthur Treacher in *Thank You Jeeves* (1936 etc); Alan Mowbray (*My Man Godfrey* 1936 etc); Eric BLORE (*Gentleman's Gentleman* 1939 etc); Robert Greig (THE PICTURE OF DORIAN GRAY 1945 etc). Secondly, flustered effetes: Edward Everett Horton in *Your Uncle Dudley* (1935 etc); Franklyn Pangborn in everything. Thirdly, sinister sissies: Noel COWARD in *The Scoundrel* (1935 etc); Clifton Webb (*Sitting Pretty/ The Razor's Edge* 1947 etc).

In one-off but long-running roles, the following actors gave their services to sissydom: Tim Brooke-Taylor in THE GOODIES (1971–80 T); Melvyn HAYES as 'Gloria' in *It Ain't Half Hot Mum* (1973–82 T); Michael Crawford's heterosexually identified but totally sissified Frank Spencer in *Some Mothers Do Have 'Em* (1973–8 T); Morris HARDACRE as James Saxon, an exaggerated version of *Brideshead Revisited*'s Sebastian FLYTE, in *Brass* (1982–4/90 T); and, the most recent American leader of the field, Philip Charles Mackenzie's Donald in BROTHER (1984–7 T).

There can be young sissies. Like Jeremy Darwin (Dominic Savage), musician, composer, director and embryonic Noel COWARD in *The Swish of the Curtain* (1980 T); Susannah YORK's doll-dressing brother Willmouse (Richard Williams) in *The Greengage Summer* (1961 C); and in OLIVER BUTTON IS A SISSY (1984 T) a little Australian boy who prefers tap dancing to football is rejected by his schoolmates but, having triumphed on the dance floor, becomes the star of the school, his friendship and participation in playground games eagerly sought. These young people prove that it is possible to be a happy sissy, secure in the knowledge that they are forging ahead towards creativity and self-fulfilment while the other mule-heads bang a ball around a field and say stupid things to girls.

Sometimes boys start out as sissies and become REAL MEN. General Douglas MacArthur was, according to the documentary *American Caesar* (1984 T), 'a sissy who became a legend of war'. His mother had dressed him in skirts until he was 8 years old.

American evangelicals like Jerry Falwell took great pains on their radio and television shows during the 1980s to diassociate Christianity from the taint of effeminacy because it, partially, preaches love, tolerance and peace. Falwell used to say that Jesus, being a carpenter by trade, was 'no sissy'; in fact he was a muscular he-man, 'a Rambo'. Another inspired Christian, Branch Davidian cult-leader David Koresh, who claimed to be the incarnation of Jesus, was quick to defend his use of arms against his enemies (the FBI and dissenting members of his sect) by telling a reporter on *A Current Affair* 'The Madman of Waco' (Aust 1993 T) that 'My friends aren't sissies'. In April 1993, after a 51-day armed stand-off against the FBI, he and over 80 of his followers – including his 'wives' and children – were incinerated in their compound in Waco, Texas.

sister boy The nickname given to Tom Lee (John Kerr) by his fellow college students in TEA AND SYMPATHY (1956 C). Because the 'real' smear words like 'FAG' and 'FAIRY' were off limits by decree of the Hollywood Production Code, a word stronger than 'sissy' had to be invented. (In the British A TASTE OF HONEY (1961 C) Jo (Rita Tushingham) tells Geoff (Murray MELVIN): 'You're just like a big sister to me.')

Sister George The character played in the ARCHERS-style serial in the stage and (1978) radio versions of THE KILLING OF SISTER GEORGE (turned into a broadly satirized television soap with Mummerset accents in the 1968 film).

The lovable district nurse, a maiden lady beloved by the entire village, is in direct contrast to the woman who acts her: June Buckridge, hard-drinking, stroppy, tweedy – and fairly openly lesbian. As played by Beryl REID, with some subtlety on stage but far less on film, June/George seemed to be the first crystallization of the public's image of the clompy, stomping DYKE. A BUTCH woman living with a daffy, feminine lover who was considerably younger and emotionally in thrall to her commanding, disciplinarian patroness.

For many lesbians, Sister George became the first identifiable lesbian in a world where role models of any kind were hard to come by. In fact, she – and her partner CHILDIE – had been around, in almost identical form, for years. As the butch–femme couple they were represented by Dorothy Burgess as Mabel Warren (bull) and Irene Ware as Janet Pardoe (calf) in *Orient Express* (the film version of Graham Greene's STAMBOUL TRAIN 1934); Mary O'Farrell as Dame Hilda TABLET (living with her 'protégée' Elsa Strauss, played to put-upon perfection by Marjorie Westbury) in the Richard Shewin radio plays of the 1950s; Miss Hale (Judith FURSE), the woman described as a 'bulldozer' in *Little Red Monkey* (1953 T, with Joan Lovelace as fluffily adoring Miss Hedges); 'Frank' Hickson (Judith Furse again), one of THE THREE FAT WOMEN OF ANTIBES (1960 T); two women, one in her fifties, the other much younger, affectionately talking on a train to Cheltenham in *Unwieldy Elephant* (1962 R); the two hiking schoolteachers (Sheila Brennan and Patricia England) in INCIDENT (1965 T); etc.

What gave Sister George that added twist – apart from her being the centrepiece of an enormously acclaimed and popular play – was the spark of eroticism (some of it SADO-MASOCHISTIC gamesplaying) that occasionally ignited George and Childie's relationship. Set in concrete, they became *the* lesbian couple.

Diana Jeffery of the support group Icebreakers told Adrian Love on Capitol Radio's *Open Line* in 1977: 'It frightened the life out of me when I saw Sister George because I knew I wasn't like that at all and I think that must have been the same for many other lesbians.' (This led Adrian Love to ask rhetorically: 'Is it better to have a Sister George than a Larry GRAYSON?')

Sister George still has her fans. She's a serio-comic figure with the courage to be who she is. In the space of a few weeks she has to face up the staleness of her life with Childie, the artistic and personal restrictions placed upon her by incarnating a character she has come to detest, her sacking, and – finally – the rejection of her by the only stable thing in her life, Childie. For all her rapaciousness (in the film) and streaks of morose self-pity, she is recognizably human under the STEREOTYPICAL trappings.

'I have *no intention* of restraining myself,' she announces at her otherwise sedate BBC leaving party. These few words encapsulate why Sister George has endeared herself to, as well as alienated, so many people over three decades.

Sister George was also the name of a go-ahead young nun played by Stella Stevens in *Where Angels Go, Trouble Follows* 1968 – which was the same year the 'other' Sister George was released by Hollywood.

Sister Moon Blues–soul number sung by Salome Bey to the music of Chico Hamilton in *By Design* (1981 C). It accompanies a constrained awkwardly dance between Helen (Patty Duke) and Angie (Sara Botsford) after the latter has enjoyed herself a bit too much for Helen's liking at a heterosexual disco. The setting, Sister Moon's, is a gold-brocaded, candelabra-ed lesbian club where the clientele is very select, very formal – and somewhat unconvincing.

sisters The blood ties between two women do not necessarily mean that a sisterly relationship is one without all the emotions which in non-biological pairings would be called passionate desire. Marian HALCOMBE in *The Woman in White* (1948 C; 1966 – 1982 T) is Laura Fairlie's half-sister, a fact which adds both respectability and piquancy to the depth of her love for Laura; Martha (Ginger Rogers) visits Lucy (Doris DAY) in *Storm Warning* (1950 C) and seems unnaturally possessive, though it could be – and clearly passed the censors as – protectiveness in the face of her unvoiced knowledge that Lucy's husband is a member of the Ku Klux Klan;

Dorothy and June Lyons (Arlene Dahl and Rhonda Fleming) were incestuously involved in the book upon which the crime thriller *Slightly Scarlet* (1956 C) was based (and which was once – *c* 1982 – set to be remade with Catherine Deneuve and Brigitte Bardot); in *The Maids* (1963 R; 1974 T), Clare and Solange bring their interwoven psyches to bear on the destruction of their hated mistress; Ester (Ingrid Thulin) and Anna (Gunnel Lindblom), one agonizingly drawn to the other – who can't respond – in THE SILENCE (1963 C); Marianne Morris and Anulka as hitch-hiking *Vampyres* (1974 C) killing men, lusting after each other; Lee Grant and Carol Kane, equally captive and captor in *The Mafu Cage* aka *My Sister, My Love* (1978 C); etc.

One of the few lesbians not incestuously drawn to her female sibling was teacher Sarah (Kathleen Byron) in WITHIN THESE WALLS 'Invasion of Privacy' (1976 T) who reveals that she was in love with one of her pupils when she visits her sister, prison governor Helen (Katharine Blake).

Sisters have played a fairly significant role – as shoulders to cry on, someone to talk to, arbiters in family disputes – for gay fictional, and at least two real-life, men. In two cases (*Goodbye Gemini* 1970 C and *Local Color* (1978 C) a character is involved with his female twin and with a male lover.

Kath enters into an arrangement with her BROTHER Ed over a matter of mutual interest, namely the bedroom logistics of how they will continue ENTERTAINING MR SLOANE (1968 T; 1970 C); TCHAIKOVSKY's (Richard Chamberlain) sister was the only woman he is attracted to, according to *The Music Lovers* (1971 C); the widowed and dying opera star Marta (Hella Petri) gives maternal/sororial affection to her brother Nicky (Erland Josephson) in TO FORGET VENICE (1979 C); Cordelia (Phoebe Nichols), grave and religious, is the only member of the Marchmain family to understand Sebastian in BRIDESHEAD REVISITED (1981 T); Leonie (Frances Barber), phlegmatic, capable sister of Joe ORTON – and keeper of the flame – in PRICK UP YOUR EARS (1987 C); Billie (Lucie Sheehan), bubbly almost to the point of overkill, sharing a flat with brother Richard in BEYOND GRAVITY (1988 C/T); Lisa (Mary-Louise Parker), rock-solid friend of brother Fuzzy (Stephen Caffrey) in LONGTIME COMPANION (1990 C); Jonesey (J. B. Jones), punk sister of Bruce in *No Skin off My Ass* (1989 C); coping sister of Max Blair (who is AIDS affected and in need of a friend in the family) in A COUNTRY PRACTICE 'A Kiss Before Dying' (1992 T), etc.

A few sisters do not always perform on cue the role of nurturer, counsellor, go-between or love object: Fallon Carrington (Pamela Sue Martin) is initially very cutting about Steven's need for men and testifies on her father's behalf when he is accused of killing Steven's former lover – but the rift heals (DYNASTY 1981–91 T); Michael's pregnant sister (Sydney Walsh) refuses to come near or let her son visit him when she discovers he has AIDS in AN EARLY FROST (1985 T); Janey is FEMINIST and makes all the right noises in the direction of sexual liberation, but finds herself condemning activities in the leather bar which brother Mark (Julian Rhind-Tutt) runs with his lover in A BIT OF BERLIN (1992 R).

On occasion, sisterly concern is misplaced and fiercely rejected: Marjorie Clayton (Mary Hinton) wants to save Duffy (Harold SCOTT) from himself and restore him to the bosom of the family in DIXON OF DOCK GREEN 'The Salvation of Duffy' (1958 T), but he has no wish – and no need – to be 'normal'.

Sometimes a gay man is attracted to a woman because she reminds him of her brother: Mic (David Dundas) pairing with Jan's sister (Vivien Heilbron) after his death in *Boy Meets Girl* 'Purposes of Love' (1968 T); Charles (Jeremy Irons) with Julia (Diana QUICK) who, physically at least, closely resembles Sebastian and, in her own way, is just as restless and unfulfilled in *Brideshead Revisited* (1981 T); Ernesto (Martin Halm) is sufficiently motivated by family pressures and by the physical near-exactness

to see his marriage to his male lover's twin sister (both played by Lara Wendel) as an almost perfect match in ERNESTO (1979 C).

A rare case in which a sister who is lesbian plays a pivotal role in a heterosexual story was Savannah Wingo in THE PRINCE OF TIDES. Such are the vagaries of adaptation or, more likely, the demands of box office success that in the 1991 film her character (played by Melinda Dillon) was reduced to a whisper, and her whole sexuality to not even a sigh.

Sisters Are Doing It For Themselves

A résumé of women's significant, though still limited, successes in the face of continuing worldwide struggle for freedom of movement, expression and sexuality. Written by Annie Lennox and Dave Stuart, performed by them (as the Eurythmics) with Aretha Franklin. The 1989 video has the two women performing in front of a cheering, all-female crowd while the political message behind the triumphant, romping-stomping song is pressed home with film clips of suffragette rallies broken up by the police, women working in factories, Women's Liberation marches, women wearing the veil, women protesting against racism, women of many races ... Noticeable by their absence are two unavoidable (it would seem) pillars of women's fight for self-determination: the issue of ABORTION and the presence all over the world of lesbians. This particular history lesson, so invigoratingly staged, does not present the full picture, in common with so many non-musical ones that do not have such wide exposure. ('Sisters' was heard in *Just Like A Woman* (1992 C), the story of a woman and a man who is a TRANSVESTITE.)

Sisters of Perpetual Indulgence
Male nuns (now supplemented by female 'brothers') who first became visible, often heavily moustached and bearded, wearing sunglasses, in American gay rallies in the 1970s. They attained a much firmer place in the community – in the

US as well as in Britain and Australia – in the following decade through public blessings (and exorcisms of places tainted by HOMOPHOBIA), AIDS activism and confronting those who are religious and inflexible. Highly picturesque, vocal, mobile and ubiquitous, the Sisters – who are God's gift to the television cameras on news flashes of marches and demonstrations – would seem to be perfect for a comedy series (starring Sister Armageddon To Be A Habit With You?) with spiritual overtones.

situation comedies Usually family or romantic situations with wise-cracks, farce and slapstick added to zap them along. Stuart HALL discussing TERRY AND JUNE in an OPEN UNIVERSITY programme on television and society in 1981 summed up the predominant ethos: 'They don't try to contest our view of the world, they play around with it ... but in resolution [the situation] returns to normality ... So a strong and capable woman will be told at the end that "forcefulness isn't everything". These shows play on and reinforce conventional social roles.'

BBC producer John Howard Davies, speaking in the same programme, felt that popular television can and does probe 'the limits of taboos'. Which is why, during the 1980s, gays and lesbians could not be contained comfortably with the confines of family comedy or family drama. They either left (BROOKSIDE; EASTENDERS) or they adapted (SOAP; DYNASTY). The programme concluded, with the help of clips from *Terry and June*, that sitcoms 'showed the resilience of the family to outside pressures and threats. Older women, moving, mothers-in-law, gays, lesbians ... these were no more than disruptions.'

It remains to be seen whether the influence of alternative comedy like *The Young Ones* and TERRY AND JULIAN or off-centre mass audience fare like AGONY (1979–81), BROTHERS (1984–7), THE GOLDEN GIRLS (1985–92) and ROSEANNE (1989–) will enable otherness to be more than a sometime thing

in television comedy. Radio, apart from severely constrained series about husbandless families such as THREE PIECE SWEET and AFTER HENRY, seems to be trying not at all.

See also SOAP OPERAS.

The Six O'Clock Show 'Make-up for Men' (UK 1983 T) A segment of the early (Friday) evening show asked, in the words of the lightly dusted Michael Aspel: 'Will face-packs for fellas catch on?' Not if this programme had anything to do with it, they wouldn't.

Having set the sniggering tone, the producers sent out intrepid Andy Price (in heavy slap) to reveal how a group of 'fellas' (male chauvinists) reacted to some newly available lotions and the paints. With revulsion, according to Andy Price. With blissful abandon and sensuous vanity according to the pictures accompanying his commentary.

As well as shots of the make-up session, men in the street were asked for their comments on the finished articles:

'And what would you do, sir, if your son came home wearing make-up?'
'I'd slap him right round the ear hole.'
(Enormous audience laughter.)
'And what do you think about it?'
'Well, wearing heavy make-up, people would naturally think you was a WOOFTER.' (More audience laughter.)
'Would you repeat that?'
'A woofter.' (Even more laughter.)
'Thank you.'

The 'victims' (all London firemen) were not given any help in applying the mascara, rouge and lipstick. Consequently the results were patchy, if not entirely unpleasing. Their new appearance inspired one to ask his colleague – jokingly – if he'd like to come out with him on a date ('Shame, he's going out with his old woman tonight').

In case viewers were in any way admiring the men's new look and the male section of the audience was tempted to follow suit, the programme was quick to staunch any implication that it was endorsing such behaviour. Said Andy: 'If this is what happens when you let a bunch of grown men loose on a make-up bag, then perhaps we'd *all* be better off sticking to plain old soap and water.'

If this wasn't chastening enough for any intrigued dad, husband, brother or son watching the programme, Michael Aspel was heard to comment with a shudder: 'Makes your blood curdle, doesn't it?'

To ensure maximum impact, and to retain the subject for another dose of ridicule in a few years' time, a panel of 'three ladies' was asked for its views. Their reactions were as expected – reactionary: 'It's all right as long as they keep away from me', 'Cleansing lotion's fine but not make-up', 'They probably won't be able to apply it properly and it will look awful.'

Thus was an amusing but viable subject turned into a family viewing freakshow, heavily HOMOPHOBIC. 'Strangely, one touch of this and they were anybody's.' As GAY NEWS said: 'a questioning of accepted behaviour successfully smothered.'

P: Maeve Haran and Tony Cohen; 6–7pm; LWT.

Six of Hearts (UK 1986 T) A sextet of films about lesbians and gays leading lives, successfully working, striking out in new directions, surviving, having sex ... Among those featured were a holiday representative ('Paola's Secret Life'); singer–comedian Carol Prior ('Waiting for the Green Light'); journalist Kris Kirk ('A Boy Called Mary'); a former tearaway, RENT BOY, now the toast of the arts world 'Andy the Furniture Maker'; a group of men who enjoyed cruising ('Tall Dark Stranger').

P: Paul Oremland for KINESIS FILMS; 11.45pm–12.45am; Channel 4; 60 mins.

Real-live human beings, unshackled from having to talk about issues, seen in a variety of locations interacting with all kinds of people. A bit like life, and long overdue. The acknowledged star of the series was Andy whose language, past history and outlook caused upset among moralists like Mary WHITEHOUSE.

Six Pack 'Loveless' (Aust 1992 T) Tom (Simon Burke) makes a film about a father and his gay son.

W: Tony Ayers; D: Rodney Fisher: SBS; 60 mins.

Still waters stirred when a film-maker's professional and personal lives intermingle. Troubled, too, is the young heterosexual who finds that playing gay awakens all kinds of fears and insecurities. The atmosphere of creating a fictional drama while real-life dramas swirl around the cameras and microphones is well captured, but the convoluted method of storytelling obscures more than it reveals.

'A rare and sensitive exploration of male-to-male relationships in all their permutations, deftly weaving several separate but interlinked strands ... a rich mixture of ideas, images, poignancy, humour and universal human possibilities to savour and digest. There might be those who will not bother to watch – rather like not bothering with Shakespeare because it's costume drama' (Diana Simmonds, *Bulletin* (Australia), 5.5.92).

16 Up (UK 1982 T) '... in which young people give their views on love, sex and marriage.' One of the three programmes included gay and lesbian people as part of 'Happy Loving Couples' – rather than apart as hitherto on late-night sex and relationship spots like this (it was shown 11.40pm–12.05am).

W: John Cooper Clarke; P: Tony Matthews; D: Patrick Titley: BBC1; 25 mins.

What are the rules in the game of relationship? Why should the male always make the first move? Do you have to sleep together on the first night? Instead of the usual ghettoized exchange of pre-set opinions, this was an entertaining, non-judgemental look at the similarities rather than the differences between people in certain situations – in this case making eye contact, chatting up, dancing, escorting home and the personal freedoms involved in sleeping with a stranger. One of the first series to look at the person rather than the gender ... and to *connect*.

skinheads This group of people, linked with motorbikes, RACISM, QUEER-BASH-ING and neo-Nazism in the public mind throughout the 1970s, are part of a newspaper and television demonology which was long thought to preclude identification with or inclusion by gay people. One of the OUT series' most controversial programmes, 'Skins Complex' (1992 T), talked to gay skinheads, racist and anti-racist, violent and non-violent. Were these people 'who want to indulge their sexuality or disguise it?'

A skinhead (played by Klaus Von Brede) was the very responsive object of the love and desire of a hairdresser (Bruce La Bruce) in *No Skin off My Ass* (1989 C). Toyah Wilcox made an indelible impression as a lesbian skin (called Mad) in JUBILEE (1977 C).

See also SADO-MASOCHISM.

slang words for homosexual Usually coined by or for the majority (many deriving from 17th- or 19th-century underworld parlance), but sometimes they are minority words given widespread virulence by the mass. Many words from POLARI intersect with anti-homosexual slang and abuse. Television and radio concentrate on just a small number from a vast supply of words which mainly mock any sign of effeminacy or men who find sexual pleasure everywhere but from the vagina. *See also* AUNTIE/AUNT/AUNTY/AUNTY-MAN; BATTIE/BATTY MAN/BATTIE/BATTY BOY; BENT; BITCH; BUGGER; BULL DYKE; BUM BOY; CAMP; CLONES; CLOSET; DEGENER-ATE; DIESEL/DIESEL DYKE/DIKE; DIRT/DIRTY DYKE/DIKE; EUNUCHS; FAGGOT; FAIRY; FLAMING FAGGOT; FOPS; FREAKS; FRUIT; FUNNY; GAY; GENDER BENDER; HOMO; HONEYBOY; INVERTS; JESSIE; KINKY; LEZZOS; LIGHT/LIGHT ON HIS FEET; LIMP WRISTS; MAMA'S BOYS; MOLLY; MOLLY-CODDLE; MOTHER'S BOYS; NANCY/NANCY BOYS; NANCY GIRLS; ONE OF THEM; PAEDOPHILES; PANSY; PANTYWAIST; PERVERT; PHASE; PONCE; POOF; POOFTER; PRACTISING HOMOSEXUAL; PUFF; QUEEN; QUEER; QUEER AS A...; SHIRT LIFTERS; SISSY; SISTER BOY; SOD; UNCLE; WOOFTERS.

Sleep, Wayne (1948–) English classical and jazz dancer. As an actor he was one of the two gay VIRGIN SOLDIERS (1969 C) as well as the hero of *The Soldier's Tale* (1982 T) fending off the devil in the shape of Murray MELVIN. According to *Down Your Way* (1987 R), he gave up a promising rugby career in Hartlepool to be a ballet dancer. He is best known for Andrew Lloyd Webber's *Song and Dance* and for his 1980s television series *The Soft Shoe Show*. Also memorable was his reaction to being the subject of THIS IS YOUR LIFE (T) in the early 1980s.

A Slight Angle (UK 1977 R) The world of the poet Constantine CAVAFY (David MARCH) who only had to work in the morning thanks to an extremely generous allowance from his parents. The personal was at the centre of his work, much of it instinctive and sexual (though driven), and, according to some of the people in this programme, futile: 'All his poems are, in a sense, middle-aged ... there's a sense of sterility and sorrow' and 'He knew his life to be sterile and that it will end in failure and rejection, but the handsome young man of the theatre in the poem doesn't feel ashamed.'

Yet *A Slight Angle* does not take the usual well-trodden road of assuming that all homosexuals face middle age with cynicism, marshalling living artists like David HOCKNEY and dead ones to endorse what the poet himself wrote about his life: 'What needless futile regret ... [for] in the loose living of my early years ... the boundaries of my art were formed.' W. H. AUDEN was quoted as saying: 'The erotic world he depicts is one of casual pick-ups and short-lived affairs ... But he refused to pretend that his memories of moments of sensual pleasure are unhappy or spoiled by feelings of guilt'; while E. M. FORSTER was quoted as commenting: 'He was at a slight angle to the universe ... an exquisite balance of irony and tenderness'.

W: Colin Nears; D: John Theocharis; BBC Radio 3; 60 mins.

This was among the most cherishable radio feature documentaries of its period on a gay man. Clear-sighted, crisply narrated, bold in its spirit of enquiry, wide-ranging in its sources. Even more astute was the programme of Cavafy's poems which followed immediately afterwards. Called *The Walls and the Visions*, it made no attempt to erase any of the works' homoeroticism even though the poet 'avoided adjectives ... verbs, thank goodness, avoid the gender.'

In between the poetry, producer and writer Hallam Tennyson chatted with John Theocharis who had made *A Slight Angle*. Although they agreed that 'Love in Cafavy is rarely more than physical passion, causal pick-ups and short-lived affairs', both men felt that this was irrelevant in terms of mood and depth of feeling. Auden was quoted once more, as saying that Cavafy was 'interested in failure rather than in victory'.

This was possibly the first discussion which in any way approached the question of a gay sensibility as well as gay experiences communicating themselves to a wider readership.

In a memorable exchange, Hallam Tennyson remarked: 'As someone who's bisexual, I've often wondered if his sexuality didn't make him more attractive to a lot of Europeans. As a heterosexual, John, do you think it expresses a moment of truth?' To which John Theocharis replied: 'It acquires universal appeal ... one doesn't have to be homosexual to appreciate SAPPHO or Roman Catholic to appreciate Gerard MANLEY HOPKINS.'

Smalltown Boy BRONSKI BEAT song about isolation, QUEER-BASHING and COMING OUT from the group's 1984 début album, *The Age of Consent*, which also included the now equally seminal 'I Feel Love' and 'It Ain't Necessarily So'. With its PINK TRIANGLE cover and television advertising (on Channel 4,

notably during the screening of the lesbian telemovie A QUESTION OF LOVE), the album launched the group's singer and co-composer Jimmy (then Jimi) Somerville. The dance track 'Tell Me Why' and 'Smalltown Boy' were included on the soundtrack of the film PARTING GLANCES the following year.

In the atmospheric video the 'Smalltown Boy' (Somerville) is beaten up because he's gay and escapes to the big city: 'Always the lonely boy/You were the one that they'd talk about/Around town as they put you down ...' His meeting with a sympathetic young man on the train will lead, it is hinted, to the 'boy' taking an active and vital part in the life of the metropolis. '... the answers you seek could never be found at home.../Run away, turn away, run away.'

Jimmy Somerville talked to GAY TIMES about the song in December 1990:

> ... we presented this idea to people: 'You are not alone. We are everywhere.' I don't think music ever really does convert people, but it can influence them and start them thinking.
> Our reaction was that everyday heterosexuality is rammed down our throats ... People do come up and say things like '"Smalltown Boy" helped me get through this terrible period' [and] '"Smalltown Boy" helped me come out. Thanks for what you've done' ... It might be only one person a month, but they're so important to me, those people.

Bea **Smith** Character played by Rubensesque Val Lehman in PRISONER/PRISONER: CELL BLOCK H. Top dog at Wentworth Prison from 1979 to the mid-1980s. One of the icons of lesbian television: the ultimate pragmatist, cunning, ruthless, intelligent, sensual, a survivor. Afraid of no one, except perhaps Officer FERGUSON, she is rightly named Queen Bea.

Smith, Bessie (1894–1937) American jazz singer and composer who is represented entirely by brief film footage and musical shorts: no biography of her has been mounted for cinema or television unlike her near-contemporaries

Billie Holiday and Josephine BAKER. Vincente Minnelli's plans for a film starring Tina Turner came to naught in the early 1970s.

She was enacted on radio, zestfully, by Carmen Munroe in *If I Ever Get on My Feet Again* (1986) giving a young fan (Frances Barber) some lessons about the blues and life (though not 'the life' of which Bessie knew a lot) from the ethereal plane. She was also featured (without her lesbian lyrics) in the documentary *Bessie* (1963 C); *The Devil's Music* 'Crazy Blues' (1976 T); and as part of a history of black women singers, *Brown Sugar* (1988 T). She was rather more accurately shown in *Wild Women Don't Have the Blues* (about Bessie, Alberta Hunter, Ma Rainey, Ida Cox and others, 1988 C).

(She does not appear in Edward ALBEE's *The Death of Bessie Smith* (1963 T), which deals with the RACISM that sanctioned her being driven miles to a hospital for 'niggers' when she was critically ill rather than being treated at a whites-only establishment close by.)

Dora Smith Character played by Patricia England in David Campton's play INCIDENT (1965 T) which is specifically about RACISM but also relates directly and equally to HOMOPHOBIA. With her lover Molly, Dora arrives at a hotel on the moors to discover that the booking she has made is invalid. All the rooms are full, the women are told, although they know this to be a lie. The true reason for their shunning soon emerges. It is not Dora and Molly who are unacceptable but solely Dora, and only because of her surname. One of the commonest names in the English-speaking world has become in the eyes of the woman running the hotel unutterably tainted. Smiths are responsible for most of the troubles in the world, are taking over the country, are everywhere. Finally Dora, hitherto unaware that she bore the mark of the pariah owing to an accident of birth, is driven away, followed – after momentarily entertaining anti-Smithism herself – by the half-outraged, half-fearful Molly. Molly may

be next. Her last name is Jones. (In a play of which the fulcrum is a name, it is curious to note that Dora was originally called Jan and underwent a change – feminization? – only during the final stages of rehearsal.)

Smith, Douglas (192?–72) English announcer who joined the European Service of the BBC in 1946, then worked in national radio and television as a newsreader. A perfect bubble to be burst, his fastidious combination of wafty hauteur and priggish lost boyishness was first exploited on *Beyond Our Ken* (1958–64) and more intensively in ROUND THE HORNE (1965–9) along the same lines as THE GOON SHOW audience was made to laugh with and at Wallace GREENSLADE. The cast members regularly made him a target of innuendo ('We all know about *him*'; 'Douglas Smith – a suitable case for treatment – is there a vet in the house?'), while each and every week he was forced – in the spirit of the theatre of cruelty – to make a game attempt to play – in the film spoofs – something either animal, vegetable or mineral. Among his more memorably portrayals were a boat ('chug chug'), a cow ('moo moo'), a sheep ('baa baa'), a First World War biplane ('It's time to turn me over') and a volcano ('I've got lava flowing down my sides'). His greatest moment came when he sang, tremulously and with feeling, 'NOBODY LOVES A FAIRY WHEN SHE'S FORTY'.

Guido Smith Happy-go-lucky character, played coolly and confidently by Nicholas Donovan, who briefly became Colin's low-key but sympathetic friend and lover in EASTENDERS. When they met – at a dinner party in October 1988 – Guido was living in Islington with his PARTNER. He worked in a furniture factory and had gone to the function to meet a prospective client. After a second encounter, in the wine bar, the pair begin a fairly loose-knit relationship which is put on a permanent basis a few weeks later when Guido moves in. Sexual and affectionate, Guido was essentially a make-weight during the period when Colin was worrying that he might be HIV positive. After he was told he had multiple sclerosis, Colin quickly made plans to leave Albert Square and live with his brother in the North. Guido stayed on for a few episodes to take part in dialogue relevant to Colin's departure and then simply disappeared.

Guido Smith was the second of the serial's pleasant but undeveloped gay characters (the first being Colin's ex-lover Richard who came to give him a bit of support in the summer of 1988), and very much the 'ordinary' gay men on the street ROLE MODEL much sought after but rarely fleshed out in discussion programmes on television representations of homosexuals. As with Joe a few years later, Guido came, was sympathetic and then he was gone...

Jo Smith Fictional character closely based on Shelagh Delaney whose central focus she was in A TASTE OF HONEY: a taciturn schoolgirl dreaming of escape from her mother and their sordid surroundings, pregnant by a black seaman, befriended by a gay man, striking out angrily in all directions, detesting being pregnant and the prospect of motherhood. Played by Jacqueiline Lane (1961 R), Rita Tushingham (1961 C), Rosalind Elliott (1971 T), Annette Robertson (1977 R) and Sara Sugarman (1984 T), Jo was the antithesis of other romantic but troubled TOMBOYS of the time. Unruly, wistful, sometimes spiky, she was a fighter for some kind of hazy new tomorrow which would give her more scope than her sex was allowed. In this she is beautifully contrasted with the gentle, maternal and accepting Geoff INGHAM.

Smith, Julia (*c* 1940–) English television director and producer who has worked for the BBC since 1963 (*Dr Finlay's Casebook*; *Dr Who*; *The Newcomers*; *The Railway Children*; *Spytrap*; etc). She began working with writer Tony HOLLAND in the 1970s (Z CARS; ANGELS). In 1985 the pair launched

EASTENDERS. Another collaboration, ELDORADO (1992), proved less durable.

Leslie **Smith** Character played by Frank Windsor, he is the grieving business and domestic partner of Dan in CASUALTY 'Allegiance' (1991 T), coping with Dan's daughter's refusal to accept the fact of her father's 20-year love for Leslie as well as with Dan's sudden illness and impending death. Another 'ordinary', 'colourless' homosexual man forced into an extraordinary situation, made more painful by family prejudice – which may well have been similarly manifested if he had been a stepmother.

Paul **Smith** Character played by Steve Hodson in THE LITMUS QUESTION (1975 R). An ordinary gay man, in a settled relationship, whose life is suddenly split asunder when he is falsely accused of impropriety in a public lavatory. Telling his father is not easy: he's a bishop. Luckily he has support from his lover, GRANDMOTHER and a friend of the family who manages to make the father see, if not reason, then some kind of connection between Paul's feelings for another man and the feelings he had for his late wife.

Smith, Stevie [Florence Margaret] (1902–71) English poet and novelist, witty and scarifying, whose best known poem is 'Not Waving But Drowning' (1957). She lived most of her life with her aunt in the London suburb of Palmers Green, casting a cold eye on life and death and occasionally being disturbed by a film crew, eg for MONITOR 'People in Rather Odd Circumstances' (1965 T). She was played by Glenda Jackson in *Stevie* (1978 C). *See also* BLACK MARCH.

Dr Zachary Smith Character played by Jonathan HARRIS in LOST IN SPACE (1965–8 T), a conceited, waspish agent of an enemy power. He was to have sabotaged the spacecraft; instead he ended up marooned on a planet in troublesome proximity to his foes, a nice all-American family whose son doesn't mind the silly fool too much.

Dr Smith is the chief delight of *Lost in Space*, regularly employing all manner of CAMP gesticulations and dipping into a colourful set of denigrations for his major irritant, the Robot, most of which are a case of pot calling the kettle: 'Bubble-Headed Booby', 'Floundering Flunky', 'Foolish Fop', 'Frightful Fractious Frump', 'Lily-Livered', 'Lead-Lined Lump', 'Monochrome Misfit', 'Nattering Ninny', 'Preening Popinjay', 'Plated Tattle-Tale', 'Weakling' and 'Worry Wart'.

'I am deliciously wicked. I am selfish, self-pitying, pompous, pretentious, peremptory, conniving, unctuous, scornful, greedy, unscrupulous, cruel, cowardly, egotistical, and it is absolutely delightful' (Jonathan Harris, *TV Guide*, June 1966).

'A merciless and deceitful man changed into a self-important coward and buffoon ... an irritant, the grit in the oyster. He is the "in-house villain"' (Paul Monroe, *The Lost in Space Handbook*, 1989).

Smith and Jones (UK 1989–) The opening programme (shown on 16 November 1989) had Griff Rhys Jones forced to endure so-called liberation from his heterosexual male hang-ups through the physical encroachments of Mel Smith, culminating in a sink-plunger kiss from which Rhys Jones retreats, beetroot-coloured, squirming and furiously wiping his lips. Smith, it seems, has been eating ... taramasalata! This radical sketch – watched aghast by at least a portion of the nation – is immediately followed by a CAMP little musical number about bicycle messenger boys who wiggle their bums in lycra shorts and make phallic gestures.

W: Griff Rhys Jones and others; P: Jamie Rix; D: John Kilby; BBC1; 30 mins.

(On BBC2 at the same time that evening 40 MINUTES presented a programme about 'Best Friends': 'What is a best friend and the special quality that makes the relationship tick? Is it true that only women have really close friendships?')

The Smiths British pop punk band of the early 1980s, whose moody lyrics – by leader and singer (Steven) Morrissey – could be interpreted in a number of ways. 'My whole generation came out to the Smiths,' film-maker Gregg Araki (THE LIVING END) told the *Bay Area Reporter* (27.8.92). 'What was HOLLYWOOD or even independent cinema doing of comparable power at the time?'

Smyth, Dame Ethel (1858–1944) English mountaineer, bicyclist, golfer, chain-smoker, suffragist, best-selling author (of memoirs in which she was open about her lesbianism) as well as composer of six operas (which she also produced), a choral mass, orchestral works, much chamber music and songs including 'THE MARCH OF THE WOMEN'. The main inspiration for the rugged, tenacious, feminist, eccentric and talented Dame Hilda TABLET, she died – in true BBC Third Programme satirical style – after a fall occasioned by a chamber pot in the dark.

Dame Ethel Smyth made occasional radio broadcasts – *Two Meetings with the Kaiser Before the War* (1937: she thought him much maligned) and *My Eightieth Birthday* (1938) – and appeared on television in 1937 – *Speaking Personally* (a 13-minute talk on dogs at 9am). Programmes commemorating her included *Ethel Smyth 1858–1944* narrated by Denis QUILLEY (1958 R); WOMAN'S HOUR 'Dame Ethel Smyth Remembered' (by among others Vita SACKVILLE-WEST, 1958 R); *Bicycling Days* (1961 R) in which Sir Compton Mackenzie recalled that she 'insisted on wearing knickerbockers and had to change into evening dress in the shrubbery'.

Most of her music has fallen into obscurity. The overture to *The Boatswain's Mate* formed part of *A Concert of Music by Women Composers* in 1930, and Act 1 of *The Wreckers*, an opera about smugglers in Cornwall, was broadcast in September 1932, conducted by John Barbirolli. Her Mass in D was performed by the BBC Symphony Chorus and soloists in 1987 (R), and early risers on Good Friday 1993 could hear her *Wreckers* overture on BBC Radio 3 at 7.05am.

Recently her work has claimed the attention of FEMINIST scholars, one of whom told listeners to *Arts National* (Aust 1991 R), in respect of *The Wreckers* and other operas: 'She inscribed her sexuality in the juxtaposition of tenor and alto voice, converging and going up into counter-tenor, creating a oneness.'

Played – as slightly batty – by Maureen Pryor in *Shoulder to Shoulder* (1974 T) and by Jean Trend in *Only Goodnight* (1981 R, about SOMERVILLE AND ROSS whose friend she was). Anna MASSEY read from her musical memoirs *Streaks of Life* (1988 R).

The most recent reference to this much loved public figure – 'I am the most interesting person I know and I don't care if anyone else thinks so,' she said in 1935 – occurred in the correspondence between Vita SACKVILLE-WEST and Harold NICOLSON: 'a huge deaf octogenarian roaring drunk on sherry, blowing her nose on her muffler' (*Vita and Harold's Letters*, 1992).

snips and snails and puppy dogs' tails Americanized English nursery rhyme sexism, very anti-male: girls are 'all things nice', whereas the boys are all squashy or associated with dirt and fundament. The rhyme features prominently and effectively in GLEN OR GLENDA?/*I Led Two Lives* (1953 C). A nightmare sequence finds the confused Glen (Daniel Davis aka director Edward Wood Jr) in a classroom where all his friends and teachers are forcing him against the blackboard upon which is written the rhyme. Bela Lugosi, in an otherwise unintelligible performance, intones as though it were part of the Black Mass.

so A companion to 'musical' in 1930s argot. Bermondsey Liz (Adrian Shergold) asks if newcomer to the game Quentin CRISP is 'so' in THE NAKED CIVIL SERVANT (1975 T).

Soap (US (1977–81 T) Mad and merry doings between two opposed Connecticut families joined only by two sisters: feet on the ground Mary Campbell (Cathryn Damon) whose son (by a former husband) Jodie DALLAS (Billy CRYSTAL) is gay, and dizzy, easily led Jessica Tate (Katherine Helmond). The Mafia, people from outer space, murder, suicide attempts and Jodie's successful fight for custody of his baby daughter are all in the mix, viewed from a subtly judgemental, magisterial distance by Benson, the black butler (Robert Guillaume) who went on to his own series.
Cr/P: Susan Harris; D: Jay Sandrich; ABC; 30 mins.

A soap opera send-up, more safely whacky than its inspiration *Mary Hartman, Mary Hartman*, with engaging ensemble playing and the gay Trojan horse in the shape of an inseparable gay couple who don't know they are one (and half of which is a dummy): Chuck and his loquacious friend, room-mate and possible bed partner (both played by Jay Johnson).

Heavily breathed upon by network censors and special interest groups, the plotlines veered from the charmingly surreal and the zany to the downright stupid. Jodie broadened out from a would-be trans-gender patient (all for love of a self-serving BISEXUAL) to being cruelly treated by the woman who seduced him into bringing up his daughter as a single parent (with some help from a lesbian called Alice) to meeting Ms Right and then being overtaken by the spirit of an elderly Jewish man. Too much already. What Jodie never achieved in three and a half years was a gay male lover – which could have been part of the madcap humour, but really wasn't.

soap operas Mercilessly pilloried as inane, superficial, an insult to the intelligence, sexist, selective, these morning, afternoon and evening serials are popular the world over. Pioneered on radio during the 1930s, usually grounded by the presence of a narrator (doctor, wife and mother, grandmother, reverend), television refined them, then made them more seductive through larger budgets, glossier actors, prettier clothes. The stories, bogglingly complex, contain a great many points of view, concurrent, interwoven plot strands which allow for any number of social issues. However, each saga operates from the same narrow focus: boy meets girl, marries, has baby, divorces, remarries (often to each other). Abortion, incest, homosexuality, child abuse, serial killers come and go: marriages are forever (until they break up). Anything that threatens the status quo is apportioned to one character, usually unconnected with the regulars, who can be quickly moved out of the picture once the issue has been raised, defused and then disposed of.

The conventions of 'soapies' have been the subject of mirth for decades beginning in Britain with *Simon and Laura* (1955 C), which took a warring show business couple and plonked them in the middle of a cosy domestic setting in which they were supposed to be as lovey-dovey as newly-weds. On radio CORONATION STREET was invoked in *Who Shot Ada Tansey?* (1983), a comic murder mystery set among the scrapping stars of a cosy clogs and beer Northern serial. THE KILLING OF SISTER GEORGE managed to kill two birds with one stone: recalling the 'brutal sacking' of the mainstay of MRS DALE'S DIARY in 1963 as well as putting the boot in THE ARCHERS which was invoked in the country life programme the central character worked on, 'Applehurst'. The 1991 film *Soapdish* made mock of American daytime soaps like *All My Children* and *Days of Our Lives*, as well as slugging the behind the scenes jealousies and indiscretions.

A number of lesbian and gay soap operas have surfaced on public television (*Two in Twenty* in the US and *Buck House* in Australia), but an idea that remains strictly in the realms of fantasy was the leather men's soap called 'Left Side, Right Side'. This was one of the ideas submitted to the minority television network in the play VIDEOSTARS (1983 T). To be produced and directed by Raymond (David Quilter) and Platt (Phil Smeeton), it told of a redundant steel apprentice from Corby 'who comes to London and enjoys something no other teleplay about homosexuals has ever had – *really fabulous* sex!'

See also BROOKSIDE; DALLAS; DYNASTY; EASTENDERS; ELDORADO; GEMS; HOWARDS' WAY; WAGGONERS WALK.

soap opera stars SISTER GEORGE alias June Buckridge in THE KILLING OF SISTER GEORGE (1968 C; 1978 R); Dorothy Richards (Dustin Hoffman) who is really a male actor who had to change his gender to get a job in *Tootsie* (1982 C); a group of gay men who each week dress as and play their favourite soap opera divas in *Exclusive Yarns* (1987 T); 'Nurse Nan' alias actress Montana Moorehead (Cathy Moriarty). who turns out to be not all she seems in *Soapdish* (1991 C); Howard (Patrick Cassidy) whose character becomes involved in a gay storyline which stops well short of the bedroom door in LONGTIME COMPANION (1990 C).

Soave sia il vento The Act 1 trio from the Mozart–Da Ponte opera *Cosi fan tutte* which prays 'May the wind be gentle, the sea be calm ...' Played repeatedly over the traumatic weekend by Daniel (Peter FINCH) in SUNDAY, BLOODY SUNDAY (1971 C).

'There's a homosexual doctor who's having a love affair with this boy who is also having an affair with a girl and he's very remote and lonely because he's a homosexual, but every time you see him in his flat he's playing this trio from Mozart which is a superbly beautiful piece of music. It just lifts you whenever you see him. You see him through rose-coloured spectacles and you end up seeing this queer, fucked-up doctor like some sort of Marilyn MONROE figure, you know what I mean' (singer–composer Pete Townsend interviewed by Richard Barnes in *The Story of 'Tommy'*, 1977).

social workers Helping people who are economically disadvantaged and socially maladjusted but not able to cope with riotously gay Liam (Jason Kemp) in the children's home in KIDS 'Michael and Liam' (1979 T); Johnny Jeffery (David Cardy) seems a nice young man at the start of a court case in CROWN COURT 'The Green House Girls' (1978 T): by the end he is revealed as a nice young man who is also gay; Ralph (Philip SAYER) needs to be circumspect because he's having an affair with a 15-year-old boy in TWO PEOPLE (1979 T); Louise (Kate Crutchley) has casual sex with a man but she is more emotionally drawn to her client in *Prostitute* (1989 C); Tom is not fazed by a client's expectation that a woman would better help her sort out problems with social security in *Love and Marriage* 'As Man and Wife' (1982 T): 'That can be arranged. But my mother put pink sheets on the bed till I was 15,' says he, blithely displaying an EARRING and a complicitous smile; Catherine (Elizabeth Proud), the infinitely understanding lover of the prickly, puritanical Gisela in SILENT WING (1984 R); WINSTON (Eamonn Walker) used to be called a home help: today he defines himself as a social worker, doing Alf Garnett's housework and acting as a bouncing ball for the curmudgeon's prejudices against blacks and gays in IN SICKNESS AND IN HEALTH (1985–7 T); Matt Fielding (Doug Savant), who lives in the apartment block MELROSE PLACE (1992–   T), is fired from the half-way house for teenagers where he works because he's gay.

Socrates (469–399 BC) Ancient Greek philosopher and teacher, proponent of the Socratic ideal or what, in the Middle Ages, became known as platonic love: pure and idealistic feeling between a man and a boy, found through a person rather than in a person. Although he left no writings, his trial and death (found guilty of 'introducing strange gods and corrupting the youth', he was sentenced to die by drinking a cup of hemlock) have reverberated through the centuries. This event has been the subject of a number of reconstructions and reflections: YOU ARE THERE 'The Trial of Soc-

rates' with Liam Redmond (1958 T); *The Trial and Death of Socrates* with Donald Davis (1961 T); *The Last Days of Socrates* with Leo McKern (1986 R); *The Trial of Socrates* with Enoch Powell looking at 'the implications for democracy then and now' (1988 R). Max ADRIAN played the philosopher in *Triad*, a series of three radio plays set during the Peloponnesian war (1965, 1967 & 1968).

sod This derivative from sodomite was first spoken on television by blond psychopath Sloane (Clive Francis) in ENTERTAINING MR SLOANE in 1968 ('I don't give a sod what's for supper') but possibly used surreptitiously earlier: 'One of my pew-sod-o-nims is Benjamin BRITTEN,' says Sam Costa to Kenneth HORNE in *Much-Binding-in-the-Marsh* (1953 R).

'. . . dirty, mangy, sod-buster!' explodes Nella (Jane Russell) in *The Tall Men* (1956 C), recalling – with heavy emphasis upon the first part of the third word – her father who 'destroyed my mother's dreams'.

The word has now become acceptable as generalized abuse (though aimed only at males) increasingly within family viewing hours. A rough character (played by Dudley Sutton) in THE GENTLE TOUCH 'Do It Yourself' (1984) tells the police to 'sod off' while his daughter (Elaine Lordon) says that 'he doesn't give a sod for me'; Dad Mole (Stephen Moore) refers to Adrian as 'you stupid sod' in *The Secret Diary of Adrian Mole* (1985); Trish Valentine (Polly Perkins) calls her TOY BOY an 'arrogant little sod' in ELDORADO (1992). On radio, 'sod' was used five times in 30 minutes by all five characters in Rhys Adrian's afternoon play *Toytown* (1987). There were, however, 25 BUGGERS.

Sodom and Gomorrah Twin cities destroyed, with three others, by God's wrath and buried under or near the Dead Sea (according to *Ancient Secrets of the Bible* 1992 T). Alternatively: a myth to explain the barrenness and salinization of the shores of the Dead Sea.

The first City of the Plain gave its name to sodomy in the 12th century, a wide-ranging term to cover a number of 'crimes against nature' including anal intercourse (involving the opposite or the same sex) and bestiality; linked to the biblical story of why God vented his anger so comprehensively.

The exact nature and relevance of the cities' sins were fiercely debated in the play THE LITMUS QUESTION (1975 R) by clerics Richard Smith (Alan Rowe) – 'The men of Sodom were destroyed not supported' – and Charles Holt (Richard Hurndall) – 'Witchcraft ... the Bible doesn't condemn ... Rape, prostitution and sensuality – heterosexual or homosexual – that's what the Bible condemns.'

References to these supposedly iniquitous places have included full-scale epics like *Sodom and Gomorrah* ('Twin cities of sin', one ruled by a lesbian queen, but with no male–male activities in sight, possibly owing to British censor cuts before release); low-budget tracts like the oddly titled GREATEST HEROES OF THE BIBLE 'SODOM AND GOMORRAH' (1978 T); an episode of THE BIBLE (1966 T) which featured a number of men wearing glitter and eye shadow shouting (a dubbed) 'Bring them out that we may know them' to George C. Scott who was protecting three hooded ANGELS, all played by Peter O'Toole.

The Man from UNCLE team was doubtless strongly encouraged by the network to change the title of a 1966 episode from 'The Sodom and Gomorrah Affair' to something a little more prime-time ('The Super Colossal Affair'). However, the following year Julie Andrews was allowed to rhyme 'adorable' with 'Sodom and Gomorrahable' during the title song from *Thoroughly Modern Millie* (her last successful starring film for 15 years).

Apart from frequent mentions on discussions involving Levitical Christians on the breakdown of modern society and John GIELGUD resonating the tale in readings from Genesis – after the Daily Service and before WOMAN'S HOUR in September 1991 – Sodom and Gomor-

rah is viewed with some jocularity in popular culture, being used to cover any kind of potentially or actually riotous or erotic behaviour. 'We can't all just kip down [together] like Sodom and Gomorrah,' exclaims a horrified Mrs Slocombe (Molly Sugden) in ARE YOU BEING SERVED? 'Camping In' (1977 T); 'Or like Swann and Edgar,' chirrups Mr HUMPHRIES. 'By the time we get back the place will be like Sodom and Gomorrah,' Tony (Oscar James) says to his wife in EASTENDERS (1987 T); he is worried about the mess that his son Kelvin's friends will most likely leave in their wake at his 18th birthday party.

In 1991 THEM AND US (T) investigated reports of Britain's newest Sodom and Gomorrah: Llanelli in Wales. A pit of violence and vice, according to a vicar. Not true, said nearly all the other interviewees. In the same programme, Ian MCKELLEN faced ultra-conservative religionists on the Isle of Man, who see gay rights as leading beyond ordinary sodomy to bestiality and the end of civilization.

(In 1981 Robert Fox visited the *Cities of the Plain* (R), but these were northern Italian cities, including two threatened with catastrophe: Venice and Ravenna.)

sodomy As performed in SODOM AND GOMORRAH and many other places. Before the coming of AIDS (when it was more likely to be called 'anal intercourse' or 'ANAL SEX') the word was used sparingly, mainly about certain British institutions: 'A hotbed of sodomy' was how the navy (of old) was dismissed in *The British Seafarer* (1979 R). A Russian in *The Fourth Protocol* (1987 C) talks disparagingly of his son who 'practises sodomy'.

Softly, Softly (UK 1966–76 T) A spin-off from Z CARS, which moved Inspector Barlow (Stratford Johns) away from Liverpool to a less gutsy but no less crime-ridden area in the Midlands. There were almost no homosexual men and certainly no lesbians to be found – they had probably been scared off by Barlow's evil reputation. A few sad souls did turn up in a 1966 episode called 'Murder Reported', which was opaquely described in the synopsis thus: 'Barlow works in the background adjusting reactions to suit the situation as it twists and changes in a thoroughly delicate case.' Translated is means that a man is found murdered in a notorious cruising area. He is married and was involved with an unsavoury character whom he met in a PUB called the Angel.

This was British television's first entry into a queer pub. Its aged landlady, 'Aunty May', describes the plight of her clientele to a copper: 'Some of them don't make much. They get found out and don't stay in the same job long enough ... They often are [hunted] ... Not persecuted, I don't mean that ... They are usually polite. And nice to an old lady. I don't think there's an ordinary pub I could run at my age.' She concludes this speech with: 'Some of them fight against it. It's the worst for them.'

At complete variance to her few words are the homosexuals characterized in this piece, to wit a vicious QUEEN (whom the dead man had 'chased') and an even more vicious queen ('as nasty and unpleasant a piece of work as ever crawled out from under') who flirts with the policeman (carrying on a tradition that began with THREE BLIND MICE in 1947). The episode ends with the killer (the even more vicious queen) apprehended and the dead man's wife deciding to testify in court.

W: Elwyn Jones; D: Philip Dudley; 23.11.66; BBC1; 50 mins.

(The series returned to homosexuality in a 1974 story entitled 'Little Boy Blue' about the disappearance of a 6-year-old. One man, with a record of offences against boys (and who lives with his mother), is strongly suspected of the supposed assault and murder. However, he has an alibi: a male with whom he spent the day and night in question. The child is found – accidentally drowned.)

So In Love k. d. lang's galvanic rendition of Cole PORTER's (originally satirical) obsessive outpouring from *Kiss Me Kate* (1953 C, 1964 T etc) was almost the sole justification for the pop world's insensitive ransack of his repertoire in RED, HOT AND BLUE (1990 T). The segment begins with lang visiting a hospital, presumably to see her dying girlfriend, and continues with her washing clothes back home, their odours and textures evoking poignant memories. This quite flawless piece, so movingly performed and crisply directed by *Bagdad Cafe*'s Percy Adlon, was trimmed when it was shown on Channel 10 in Australia and banned outright in America.

The Canadian singer, who was to make her acting debut as the androgynous Kotzebue in Adlon's *Salmonberries* in 1992, did not feel able to be open about her sexuality until recently. Hence she fuzzed the emotional specificity of 'So In Love' in interviews, such as the one to give to *Elle* in June 1992 (just before she became officially 'out'): 'It could be a lover, or a daughter or a mother or a grandmother. The message was women get AIDS.' When Percy Adlon was interviewed (in *Screen Aust* 1992 R), he said it was always intended as being the lament of a lesbian remembering her lover.

Whether it is about one woman or all women, 'So In Love', as interpreted with hollowed-out passion by k. d. lang, says much that is deep and unsayable.

soldiers During the London blackout in the Second World War Quentin CRISP encounters a hillbilly US soldier of whom dreams are made and stories embellished. Quentin feels obliged to tell him that, despite appearances to the contrary, he's not a woman. The soldier doesn't care and, afterwards, suggests they have another piece of chewing gum 'and do it again' (THE NAKED CIVIL SERVANT (1975 T).

Men (and occasionally women) in the ranks who felt powerful forbidden attachments include the captain nobly expressing and yet repressing love in the trenches in JOURNEY'S END (1930 C; 1938 T; etc); 'The Lily-white Boys', lovers who fought and died side by side mentioned *In Parenthesis* (1948 R); two prisoners of war planning a life together in Canada, jealously watched by another (Patrick Troughton) whose frustrated desires mentally unbalance him in THE INTERNED (1953 R); Captain 'Waco' Grimes (Broderick Crawford) surrounded by pretty blond guards in *Between Heaven and Hell* (1956 C); Captain Dann (Ian Bannen) obliquely propositioning Private Saul (David Andrews) in *The Tent* (1960 R); *Private Potter* (Tom Courtenay 1963 C) who says he's seen God: perhaps he could be a QUEER – damned clever those queers'; Willie Maltravers (Derek Nimmo), oh so temperamental army cook in *The Amorous Prawn* (1962 C); General George GORDON in *Khartoum* (Charlton Heston 1966 C) and *Gordon of Khartoum* (Alan BADEL 1966 T) etc; a major (Marlon Brando) obsessed with an enlisted man who goes riding naked in REFLECTIONS IN A GOLDEN EYE (1967 C); Tom (Stuart Cooper), 'a blond effeminate American Air Force Lieutenant recently returned from Vietnam' in FRIENDS (1967 T); *The Sergeant* (Rod Steiger 1968 C), in love with one of his men, is rejected and kills himself; Ed, ex-soldier in ENTERTAINING MR SLOANE (Edward Woodward 1968 T; Harry Andrews 1970 C); target of an assassin: Schacht in THE PARACHUTE (Lionel Hamilton 1968 T; Adrian Egan 1986 R); jumpy, soft as butter Bombardier 'Gloria' Beaumont (Melvyn HAYES) in *It Ain't Half Hot Mum* (1973–82 T); Chrissie (Myra Francis) snaffling all the prette new recruits in GIRL (1974 T); a sensitive injured private (Richard Ely) in *M*A*S*H* 'George' (1974 T); German (Horst Janson) and Englishman (Michael Kitchen) have a brief liaison in the Western Desert in *Enemy* (1976 T); Prewitt (Steve Railsbeck) and Maggio in *From Here to Eternity* (1979 T) supplementing their pay with a little hustling; Yank and Scot (Raymond Thompson and Douglas Telfer) meeting in an improvised gay club and given overnight accommodation by the 'manageress' in HOUSE ON THE HILL 'Something for the Boys' (1981 T); Alfred Redl BLACKMAILED into spying and driven to SUI-

CIDE in A PATRIOT FOR ME (Gary Bond 1981 R) and in COLONEL REDL (Klaus Maria Brandauer 1984 C); Richie (Mitchell Lichtenstein), flamboyantly queer, attracting the more repressed attentions of at least one fellow soldier headed for Vietnam in *Streamers* (1983 C); Tom Birkin (Colin Firth) and Moon (Kenneth Branagh) trying to forget the Western front during *A Month in the Country* (1987 C).

Real-life stories of same-sex relationships in barracks and off-limits – and the penalties and persecutions for those suspected or found out – were told in COMRADES IN ARMS (1990 C/T); HEART OF THE MATTER 'Falling Out' (1991 T); *Where Are We? Our Trip Through America* (1992 C/T). Physical beatings for people who didn't fit into the macho ideology were described and shown in WORLD IN ACTION 'The Death of Private Darkin' (1982 T) and G.P. 'Get a Life' (1993 T).

solicitors Useful citizens, sometimes presented as crooked but hardly ever as bent: Keith Kossett (John Bonney) in *Paranoiac* (1964 C) and Terry Priestley (Fred Peart), 'a sad eccentric' in WEDNESDAY LOVE (1975 T) were the exceptions.

Some Like It Hot (US 1959 C) Two musicians, witnesses of the St Valentine's Day massacre, hide out as members of an all-female band in Florida. One, Jerry/Daphne (Jack Lemmon), is wooed by a lusty, much married millionaire (Joe E. Brown), in whose disguise his pal Joe/Josephine (Tony Curtis) seduces the band's singer Sugar (Marilyn MONROE) by playing 'impotent' (aka gay).
W: Billy WILDER and I. A. L. Diamond; P/D: Billy Wilder; 122 mins.

The blithest of spirits in a comedy that never stales, thanks to lean writing, convincing (if belief is suspended) situations, attractive period detail (including three knockout songs), and a Cary GRANT impersonation which manages to be both tribute and in-joke. The film's ending – with Daphne bound for marriage with her millionaire even though he now knows she's a he – is one of the most offhandedly groundbreaking ever committed to mainstream celluloid.

The basic situation spawned a number of parodies (by Dick Martin, Steve Lawrence and Carol Burnett on one of her 1970 shows) and imitations, chiefest among them being *Nuns on the Run* (1990 C, which in turn inspired *Sister Act* 1992 C) and *Bosom Buddies* (1980–2 T). *Bosom Buddies* finds artist Kip (Tom Hanks) and copywriter Jack (Peter Scolari) dressing as women in order to secure accommodation in a women-only hotel.

some of my best friends are... A symbol of everything that is racially patronizing and phonily liberal. Its first mention came in *Gentleman's Agreement* (1947 C) when a man in a bar says it to reassure a journalist (Gregory Peck) that he personally feels no animosity just because he's a JEW. The superficiality of that tolerance is brilliantly underscored later in the film when the heroine Kathy (Dorothy McGuire) rounds on the entire JEWISH population after her support for one Jew's rights is tested beyond endurance: 'They always make trouble for everyone, even for their friends. They force people to take sides against them.' It later occurred, in relation to mental illness, in *Autumn Leaves* (1956 C) where the nurse (Maxine Cooper), who is chatting to a patient, says with a cynical shrug: 'Some of my best friends are in joints like this.'

Apart from a 1971 movie in which all the 'best friends' of the title were gay, this expression became more and more discredited, odiferous and irony-laden when applied to minorities from the late 1960s onwards. It is impossible to tell whether Laurence Olivier was being patronizing, satirical or simply honest when he said – after discussing being regarded as a SISSY at school – on a 1983 SOUTH BANK SHOW: 'Some of my best friends are QUEER.'

More transparently, Paul BAILEY quipped (in *Words* 1974 R) that 'some of my best friends are only averagely witty

homosexuals'. And one of the lesbians on DONAHUE (1988 T) had no qualms about saying that some of her best friends were gay and that it was 'absolutely great'. Ditto Gail (Mariette Hartley) in MY TWO LOVES (1986 T) – though none is shown.

The phrase was most recently used in the title of a 1991 television documentary about the resurgence of prejudice and hate crimes against Jews in Britain. It could just as easily have been applied to one shown during the same January week on attacks against Jews and gay people in Europe.

Although the dreaded words are never spoken, Frankie and Johnny (Ronald LACEY and Philip Locke), who are discussing their heterosexual friends in *Boa Constrictor* (1967 T), reveal the ethos (owners to pets) behind them:

> Johnny: 'They like us.'
> Frankie: 'They patronize us.'
> Johnny: 'They think we're witty and clever.'
> Frankie: 'They indulge us.'
> Johnny: 'They think we're absolutely super.'
> Frankie: 'They pity us.'

Some of My Best Friends Are ... (US 1971 C) A GREENWICH VILLAGE gay BAR (run by heterosexuals and with Mafia associations) on Christmas Eve offers alcohol, the chance of sex, a whiff of romance, succour, heartbreak, violence and the stirrings of community support under the Christmas tree.

W/D: Mervyn Nelson; 109 mins.

Filmed at a real Manhattan bar (the Zodiac), this sweet valentine to gay love (individual and group) takes a while to get going (as do the night's festivities) and contains some groaningly obvious homilies and dizzy dialogue. But straining to get out is a very true, touching portrait of the bar scene in New York just after gay liberation. Glimmerings of pride almost but not quite sunk under oceans of dissembling and self-pity. Rue McClanahan is excellent as the demon queen alias 'fruit fly' (she's also referred to as a 'FAG HAG'), and Sylvia Syms (the

American singer not the British actress) had a beautiful moment when she thanks her 'boys' for being there for her during her illness. Candy DARLING, a WARHOL discovery, has to bear the brunt of the melodramatic violence (consciously identified as HOMOPHOBIA) as a young TRANSSEXUAL. The gay characters tend to be less memorable, more mouthpieces than individuals in a film that too consciously sets out to be an antidote to THE BOYS IN THE BAND. But it does have a heart and the enclosed setting gives the fragmented dialogue and action some soapy cohesion. (The film's songs – including 'Where Do I Go?' played over the last scene as the remaining patrons wander home – fit Noel COWARD's definition of 'cheap music', namely 'potent'.)

'This ghetto melodrama resembles the little theatre production that the patrons of a gay bar might put on for their friends: a plea from the inside for the understanding and tolerance of ghettoized and exploited people' (Vito RUSSO, *The Celluloid Closet: Homosexuality in the Movies*, 1987).

Someone To Watch Over Me
Gershwin classic particularly affecting in the version by Julie Andrews (as Gertrude Lawrence, who originated this yearning-to-be-protected song in *Oh, Kay!* on Broadway) in STAR! (1968 C). Robert Altman chose it as the theme of *Beyond Therapy* (1986 C) to cover his heterosexual lovers (in recordings by Linda Ronstadt and Yves Montand) and his gay pair (sung by Lena Horne: 'He may not be the kind of guy you think of as handsome/But to my heart he carries the key...').

some people! With a toss of the locks and a tut-tut in the voice, emphasizing the sheer exasperation of having to deal with insensitive, rude, unappreciative and unattractive oicks, Oliver Reed first let this loose as a miffed chorus boy in *The League of Gentlemen* (1960 C). There was also a straighter version used by equally testy people like Inspector Barlow (Stratford Johns) who favoured it as part of his dour exclamatory repertoire in SOFTLY SOFTLY (1966–76 T).

some people would say... A favourite ploy of radio and television presenters to introduce an unpleasant element into an interview with which they would prefer not to be associated, or to inject the all-important voice of consensus into debate. Examples of this devil's advocacy, often possibly expressing the very real prejudices of the speaker, are: 'Some people would say that AIDS is a punishment from God', 'Some people would say that gay/lesbian relationships are basically unstable', 'Some people would say that gay teachers will interfere with boy pupils', 'Some people would say that homosexuality is a result of bad parenting', and 'Some people would say that as lesbians you are bringing up your child to hate men.'

Somerville, Jimmy (1961–) Scottish pop singer and composer with the voice of an ANGEL, which is the role he played in ORLANDO (1992 C). Originally part of BRONSKI BEAT then, with Richard COLES and others, as the Communards; now solo.

T: FRAMED OR REVENGE OF THE TEENAGE PERVERTS (singing 'Screaming', 1983 V/T; he was also one of the editors); TOP OF THE POPS (1984–); *The British Record Industry Awards* (1985); *People to People* 'Giro – Is This the Modern World?' (chatting with unemployed young people, 1985); *French Radio* (1989); *Eggs 'n' Baker* (on Christmas Day 1989 in between *A Flintstone Christmas* and *Roy Castle's Christmas Celebration*); OUT ON TUESDAY (1990); RED, HOT AND BLUE (singing 'From This Moment On', 1990); *Red, Hot + Dance* (singing 'Read My Lips', 1991); *Tonight with Jonathan Ross* (1992 T).

His vocal presence was almost *de rigueur* in gay or semi-gay films, plays and documentaries from the mid-1980s: *Letter to Brezhnev* (1985 C); PARTING GLANCES (1985 C); COMPROMISED IMMUNITY (1991 R); etc.

Somerville and Ross Edith Somerville (1858–1949) and Violet Martin (1862–1915) were Irish writers whose relationship – which endured even after the death of Violet – was etched in Maureen DUFFY's play *Only Goodnight* (with Mary Wimbush as Edith and Rosalind Adams as Violet, 1981 R) and in *The Irish Cousins: On the Hunt for Somerville and Ross* ('a remarkable friendship that lasted beyond death' with Kate Binchy as Edith, Sorcha Cusack as Violet, 1986 R). Their most famous work – stories of a resident magistrate in Ireland prior to the Free State (*Some Experiences of an Irish RM* and two sequels) was adapted for television in 1983–4 as *The Irish RM*, staring Peter Bowles. (Edith Somerville made at least one radio appearance: reading poetry in 1926.)

something The Glaswegian mother, recalling her long-flown boyfriend in *Beyond the Rainbow* (1991 R), believes that if he had stayed with her he would have had to admit 'something' to himself 'and he wouldna' have bin' able to cope with that something'.

Something Else: Intimate Confessions (UK 1982 T) Sketches and interviews, songs, poems, montage and interviews (with Hugh Warren and Rose Collis) on areas not customarily tackled, eg: 'What if you fancy the opposite sex, but you can't do anything about it? What if the opposite sex fancies you, but you don't fancy the opposite sex? ... What happens if you want to be the opposite sex, and fancy someone of the same sex who turns out to be the opposite sex, but fancies you because they don't know you want to be the opposite sex?' (*Radio Times*).

P: 'made with the help of the BBC Community Programme Unit'; 23.10.82; BBC2 ; 45 mins.

A much raunchier relative to 16 UP made the same year. This programme (in a series which began in 1980) very much says and lesbians and gays are here to stay, get used to them. Its brilliant centrepiece was a teen romance in which three separate couples – male–female, male–male and female–female (all called 'Jo and Nicky') – meet at a disco, chat and go home together.

The banal words on the dance floor, the hesitant fumblings for conversation on the way home 'for coffee', and the ultimate let-down are shown to be common to all three couples. The action is overlaid with exterior and interior dialogue, the one unconnected with the other. It was a witty exercise, and the sexual communalty – though not news to most lesbians and gays – must have been a revelation to its teenage target audience and others (watching between 10 and 10.45pm) reared on screen and print romances.

It had taken 15 years for BBC2 to follow up William Bast's THIRTY MINUTE THEATRE piece *Boa Constrictor* (which looked at three couples – white heterosexual, black heterosexual and white male homosexual, all called 'Frankie and Johnny') and show that relationships follow very similar patterns. Three years later came MY BEAUTIFUL LAUNDRETTE.

something to tell you These words mark the deathless moment in a film or play where the lesbian or gay character fronts up to father, mother, sister, brother or best friend, readying themselves for a negative reaction if not outright rejection. Often the person being 'COME OUT' to intercepts with a 'I know – you're gay' or 'If it's what I think it is...' Examples include Jamie (Michael Grandage) to his father in *Chelworth* (1989 T: but the parent doesn't want to know); Philip (Angus MacFadyen) to both parents in THE LOST LANGUAGE OF CRANES (1992 T: mother copes, father – who's secretly gay – breaks down in tears); Leonard (Brad Dourif) to room-mate in SERGEANT MATLOVICH VS THE US AIR FORCE (1978 T: room-mate can't cope, becomes violent, then confused, blames his friend for lying to him); Gisela (Diana QUICK) in SILENT WING (1984 R) to a flat-mate, who becomes abusive, accusatory, can't cope. Tony (Nick Stock) doesn't need to come out to his friend Michael (Brian Rooney) in G.P. 'Get a Life' (1993 T); Michael uses instinct, connects a few facts, lets Tony himself manoeuvre the subject into position, then says 'You're gay', thinks about it for a few minutes, integrates it into his consciousness as one aspect of his mate, and continues more or less as before. *See also* DAD, I'VE GOT SOMETHING TO TELL YOU.

Somewhere 'There's a place for us...' But 'US' is remarkably selective in Barbra STREISAND's video of her hit version of the Stephen SONDHEIM–Leonard BERNSTEIN love song from WEST SIDE STORY, which she recorded for her 1986 *The Broadway Album*. As with 'People' in *Barbra Streisand: A Happening in Central Park* 20 years earlier, so too with the more ethereal but equally all-encompassing 'Somewhere'. Lesbians and gays are still not ready to be included in the gathering in of humanity's sheaves. Yet the omission is equivalent to taking a song written by Afro-American people, making a video which includes people from all over the world – except those who are black.

Somewhere Over The Rainbow *See* 'OVER THE RAINBOW'.

Sondheim, [Joshua] Stephen (1939–) American composer and lyricist whose musicals include WEST SIDE STORY (with Leonard BERNSTEIN, 1961 C); *Gypsy* (with Jule Styne, 1962 C); *A Little Night Music* (1978 C); *Company* (the show album recording filmed, 1971 C); *Sweeney Todd* (rehearsals shown on THE SOUTH BANK SHOW; also filmed for television, 1981); *Follies: Four Days in New York* (1985 T); *Into the Woods* (filmed for television, 1990); etc.

He has also written film scores (*Stravsky* 1974) and songs for films ('I Never Do Anything Twice' for *The Seven Per Cent Solution* 1977; 'Sooner Or Later' and 'Hanky Panky' for *Dick Tracy* 1990). He wrote, with Anthony Perkins, the screenplay for *The Last of Sheila* (1973) and, for British television, a play in the 1960 *Rendezvous* series, 'In

an Early Winter', about a young bride who discovers frightening things about her husband's parents.

Among the extraordinary cavalcade of Sondheim's songs can be found many calls for individual freedom, cries of rage against society's manacles, promises of saner tomorrows, calls for patience and understanding in adversity. These include 'Everybody Says Don't'; 'Nothing's Gonna Harm You'; 'Being Alive'; 'Every Day A Little Death'; 'Something's Coming'; 'Cool'; 'I'm Still Here'; 'Everything's Coming Up Roses'. His songs with gay references include 'You Could Drive A Person Crazy' and 'We're Gonna Be All Right'; together with overtly sexually perverse numbers like 'I Never Do Anything Twice' and 'Hanky Panky'.

The murderers in both CRUISING (1980 C) and *The Fan* (1982 C) have the Broadway album of *Gypsy* (for which Sondheim wrote the lyrics) clearly visible in their apartments; Sophia (Estelle Getty) has Blanche's brother (Monte Markham) taped after she hears – in THE GOLDEN GIRLS 'Scared Straight' (1987 T) – his word-perfect rendition of Sondheim's most famous song, 'SEND IN THE CLOWNS'; Russell (David Marshall Grant) tells Melissa (Melanie Mayron) in THIRTYSOMETHING 'Love and Sex' (1989 T) that he is a bit concerned that the guy he has just met and plans to see that evening may not be quite what he's looking for as a bed partner and possibly a friend: 'Secretly I think he is [queeny]. I can tell. He's probably going to show up with a tape of *Sweeney Todd*.'

In addition to appearances at gala evenings devoted to his repertoire, Stephen Sondheim has been frequently interviewed on radio (by Sheridan Morley: *Song by Song by Sondheim* 1986) and television (by Bernard Levin: *The Levin Interview* 1980).

Song For Guy Elton JOHN, but without Bernie Taupin. An appealing instrumental which was dribbled in to a few scenes in order to solace Colin when he was having problems with Barry in

EASTENDERS (1986–7 T). It was also prominently featured in the OPEN SPACE film 'Dealing with the Beast' (1990 T) made by a young SOCIAL WORKER living with AIDS.

songs Original ones or popular standards or resurrected neglected ones are useful shorthand in documentary or drama, combining atmosphere with a rhythmic form of language that people can immediately respond to, and which helps to create mood and to get a message across without interfering with other aspects of the information-giving or story-telling. Probably the first film to consciously use mainstream songs 'I Will Follow Him'; 'Blue Velvet') for sexually subversive purposes was Kenneth Anger's SCORPIO RISING (1963). Songs which were specially written to impart a sexually ambiguous or directly homosexual flavour include 'LONG ALONE' from ADVISE AND CONSENT (1962 C) and 'ALL GONE' from *The Servant* (1963 C). The works of gay composers like Cole PORTER who wrote for a heterosexual audience are being radically reinterpreted in productions such as RED, HOT AND BLUE (1990 T) and EDWARD II (1991 C).

'They're playing our song' has long been a cliché in heterosexual romances (it was rendered lesbian for the first time by Lueen Willoughby in NOW SHE LAUGHS, NOW SHE CRIES 1975 R), evoking all manner of joyful or bitter-sweet memories. Now lesbians and gays are profligately playing their own songs, and other people's, sometimes regardless of personal pronouns.

See also 'AN ACTOR'S LIFE FOR ME'; 'AFTER YOU – WHO?'; 'AIN'T NOTHING BAD ABOUT FEELIN' GOOD'; 'ALFIE'; 'ALL THINGS BRIGHT AND BEAUTIFUL'; 'ANYONE CAN FALL IN LOVE'; 'ANYONE HERE FOR LOVE?'; 'ANYTHING GOES'; 'AS TIME GOES BY'; 'BACHELOR BOY'; 'A BACHELOR GAY AM I'; 'BEND OVER BACKWARDS'; 'BEST OF FRIENDS'; 'THE BEST OF TIMES'; 'THE BLACK SHEEP OF THE FAMILY'; 'BLOODY MARY'; 'BOTH SIDES NOW'; 'THE BOYS IN THE BACKROOM'; 'BURLINGTON BERTIE FROM BOW';

'CAN'T TAKE MY EYES OFF OF YOU'; 'DAISY BELL (OR A BICYCLE BUILT FOR TWO)'; 'DAMES'; 'DANCE LITTLE LADY'; 'DANIEL'; 'DANNY BOY'; 'DEEP NIGHT'; 'DI, DI (IN HER COLLAR AND TIE)'; 'DON JUAN'; 'DO WHAT YOUR MOMMY TELLS YOU'; 'DO YOU REALLY WANT TO HURT ME?'; 'EACH MAN KILLS THE THING HE LOVES'; 'EVERY TIME WE SAY GOODBYE'; 'FATED TO BE MATED'; 'FEMINITY'; 'FIDDLE ABOUT'; 'A FINE ROMANCE'; 'FOR EVERY MAN THERE'S A WOMAN'; 'FRIENDS FOREVER'; 'FRIGHTFULLY BBC'; 'GAY PAREE'; 'GEE, OFFICER KRUPKE!'; 'GET DOWN ON IT'; 'GET HAPPY'; 'GIRL'; 'A GIRL IS A GIRL IS A GIRL'; 'GLAD TO BE GAY'; 'GOD BLESS THE CHILD'; 'GOT A BRAN' NEW SUIT'; 'GRATITUDE/D'HABITUDE'; 'GUILTY'; 'HABANERA'; 'HALF-AND-HALF'; 'HANKY PANKY'; 'HEATWAVE'; 'HIT THAT PERFECT BEAT'; 'HONEYSUCKLE ROSE'; 'HOW DEEP IS YOUR LOVE?'; 'I AM WHAT I AM'; 'I DREAM OF JEANNIE'; 'I ENJOY BEING A GIRL'; 'I FEEL PRETTY'; 'IF LOVE WERE ALL'; 'IMAGINE'; 'I'M GETTING SENTIMENTAL OVER YOU'; 'I'M LEANING ON A LAMPPOST'; 'I'M STILL HERE'; 'IN BETWEEN'; 'THE INTERNATIONALE'; 'IN THE MIDDLE OF A KISS'; 'IN THE NAVY'; 'IT AIN'T NECESSARILY SO'; 'IT'S FINE TO HAVE A FRIEND'; 'I'VE BEEN LOVING YOU TOO LONG'; 'JAILHOUSE ROCK'; 'JE NE REGRETTE RIEN'; 'JUNE IS BUSTIN' OUT ALL OVER'; 'JUST FRIENDS'; 'JUSTIFY MY LOVE'; 'THE KILLING OF GEORGIE'; 'LET'S PUT OUT THE LIGHTS AND GO TO SLEEP'; 'LET YOURSELF GO'; 'LIBERATION'; 'THE LOCOMOTION'; 'LOLA'; 'THE LONE RANGER'; 'THE LOOK OF LOVE'; 'LOVE AND AFFECTION'; 'LOVE AND MARRIAGE'; 'LOVE FOR SALE'; 'THE LUMBERJACK SONG'; 'MAD ABOUT THE BOY'; 'MA, HE'S MAKING EYES AT ME'; 'MAKING LOVE'; 'THE MAN I LOVE'; 'THE MAN'S IN THE NAVY'; 'THE MAN THAT GOT AWAY'; 'MARCH OF THE WOMEN'; '(I WENT TO) A MARVELLOUS PARTY'; 'THE MASQUERADE'; 'MISS CELIE'S BLUES'; 'MONA LISA'; 'MOVE OVER DARLING'; 'MY BUDDY'; 'MY LOVE IS LIKE A RED, RED ROSE'; 'MY FORGOTTEN MAN'; 'MY MAN'; 'THE NAUGHTY LADY OF SHADY LANE'; 'NE ME QUITTE PAS'; 'NEVERTHELESS

(I'M IN LOVE WITH YOU)'; 'NIGHT AND DAY'; 'NOBODY LOVES A FAIRY WHEN SHE'S FORTY'; 'ODE TO BILLY JOE'; 'OLD-FASHIONED GIRL'; 'OVER THE RAINBOW'; 'PHYSICAL'; 'PRISONER (THEME FROM)'; 'PUT THE BLAME ON MAME'; 'QUE SERA, SERA (WHATEVER WILL BE, WILL BE)'; 'READ MY LIPS'; RED HOT AND BLUE'; 'RELAX'; 'SALLY'; 'SATISFACTION'; 'SECRET LOVE'; 'SHALL WE DANCE?'; 'SHUFFLE OFF TO BUFFALO'; 'SISTER MOON'; 'SISTERS ARE DOING IT FOR THEMSELVES'; 'SMALLTOWN BOY'; 'SOAVE SIA IL VENTO'; 'SO IN LOVE'; 'SOME ENCHANTED EVENING'; 'SOMEONE TO WATCH OVER ME'; 'SOMEWHERE'; 'LE SPECTRE DE LA ROSE'; 'STAIRCASE'; 'STAND BY ME'; 'SUICIDE IS PAINLESS'; 'TAKE OFF WITH US'; 'THE TEDDY PEARS' PICNIC'; 'TEN CENTS A DANCE'; 'THAT OLE DEVIL CALLED LOVE'; 'TOGETHER'; 'TOO DARN HOT'; 'TWENTIETH CENTURY BLUES'; '21 TODAY'; 'TWO LADIES'; 'UNITED WE STAND, DIVIDED WE FALL'; 'WANDRIN' STAR'; 'WE KISS IN A SHADOW'; 'WE LOVE YOU'; 'WHAT A WONDERFUL WORLD'; 'WHAT IS THIS THING CALLED LOVE?'; 'WHO?'; 'WILL YOU STILL LOVE ME TOMORROW?'; 'THE WIND BENEATH MY WINGS'; 'WITHOUT US'; 'A WONDERFUL GUY'; 'YMCA'; 'YOU CAN FOOL ALL OF THE PEOPLE'; 'YOU COULD DRIVE A PERSON CRAZY'; 'YOU LIED'; 'YOUNG AND BEAUTIFUL'; 'YOU'RE A QUEER ONE, JULIE JORDAN'; 'ZIP'.

songs, banned Among those deemed unsuitable by the BBC over the years (and consequently removed from its bible called 'the playlist'): Cole PORTER's 'The Physician' and 'Love For Sale'; 'If Everything Was Upside Down' ('... pansies would flower again'); the 1950 spiritual 'He's Got the Whole World in His Hands'; 'Something About A Sailor'; 'RELAX'.

One that escaped notice was the deeply disturbing 'I'd Like To Dunk You In My Coffee' recorded by Chick Endor's orchestra with Eddie Polo on vocals in 1933. The singer quite openly admits that he wants to do some rather unusual, not to say startling things to his (lady?) love. His desires include spreading her

('on bread'), smothering her ('with mushrooms') and finally eating her ('up').

The Sonnets of William Shakespeare *See* William SHAKESPEARE.

sons Whether their parents' pride and joy or neglected and despised, gay sons nearly always provide problems in comedy or drama, although mothers tend to be more accepting than fathers. Among those more or less accepted into the fold are Jodie (Billy CRYSTAL) in SOAP (1977–81 T); Rob (Jeremy Bulloch) in AGONY 'Problem Parents' (1981 T); another doctor in DONA HERLINDA AND HER SON (1986 C).

For the rest, it's a bumpy road: Norman (Michael Warren) in NORMAN ... IS THAT YOU? (1976 C); Brick in CAT ON A HOT TIN ROOF; (Robert Wagner 1976 T; Tommy Lee Jones 1984 T); Paul SMITH (Steve Hodson) in THE LITMUS QUESTION (1975 R); James (Michael Jayston) in THE LAST ROMANTIC (1978 T); Steven in DYNASTY (1981–91 T); Michael (Aidan Quinn) in AN EARLY FROST (1985 T); Gordon Collins (Mark BURGESS) in BROOKSIDE (1985–90 T); Barry (Gary Hailes) in EASTENDERS (1986–8 T); the deceased son in *André's Mother* (1990 T); Ann-Margret's boy (Zeljko Ivanek) in OUR SONS (1991 T); Michael Tolliver (Marcus D'Amico) in TALES OF THE CITY (1993 T); etc.

And not much easier when gay men have sons of their own. These include Nick (Scott Jacoby) in THAT CERTAIN SUMMER (1972 T); (very possibly) Joe Ackerley (Joseph Blatchley) in SECRET ORCHARDS (1990 T); Kevin (River Phoenix) in HOTEL 'Transitions' (1985 T); 6-year-old Sebastien (Olivier Chassé) in THE HEART EXPOSED (1986 C/T); Philip (Angus MacFadyen) in THE LOST LANGUAGE OF CRANES (1992 T); etc.

Sometimes sons appear to be gay, which sends mother and/or father into a frenzy, although it is always a false alarm: John (Mark Griffiths) in COMEDY PLAYHOUSE's *B&B* 'No Son of Mine' (1968 T) saved from taking the wrong step by a sexy au pair; the son of one of the *Birds of a Feather* ('Young Guns' 1991 T) not up to something with his (public) school mate as first feared; etc.

The South Bank Show (UK 1978–   )
The successor to *Aquarius* and probably the most high-profile arts panorama (though not the best) since MONITOR.
P: Nick Elliott and others; LWT; 60 mins.

Passengers in Melvyn Bragg's purring stretch limo of a series have included Laurence Olivier, Ray Cooney, Ian MCKELLEN, Alan BENNETT, Claudio Arrau, Barry HUMPHRIES, John OSBORNE, Bob Fosse, David HOCKNEY and LITTLE RICHARD. Highlights have included gay artist Philip Core with boxers (1982), the long-lost third act of *Lulu* (1981), and the extraordinary dance group DV8 in 'Dead Dreams of Monochrome Men' (1990). Major disappointments have been the 1980 interview with Angus WILSON (which avoided any mention of his personal life between the ages of 20 and 70) and Tony Palmer's film about Benjamin BRITTEN with the slack questioning of Peter PEARS ('A Time There Was ...' 1980).

The South Bank Show tends to play safe, loving gigantism and celebrity, and is less interested in artistic flashpoints and those who break the rules. Its tone is inevitably that of its mentor and anchor, a fair-minded son of the media who refuses to rock any boats (or go in for cheap sensationalism). Among some of its many programmes of interest (not always up to expectation): 'Beryl Cook' (scenes in a Plymouth gay pub which seemed to have no gays in it, 1979); 'Joint Stock's "Cloud Nine"' (rehearsing Carryl Churchill's sexually challenging play, 1979); 'No Need to Lie' (about Lytton STRACHEY's ménage à trois, 1980); 'David Garnett and the BLOOMSBURY Set' (1981); 'Noel COWARD' (1991).

South of the Border (UK 1988–90 T)
Two private eyes, Pearl Parker (Buki Armstrong) and Finn Gallagher (Rosie Rowell), right wrongs, best men and have noticeably few lesbian friends or clients. One only: in a 1990 story about an architect, Anna Tarrant (Joanne Stoner) threatened with losing her child in a custody case and generally harassed because she loves a woman, Kate (Ethna Roddy).
Cr: Susan Wilkins; P: Caroline Oulton and others; D: Suri Krishnamma and others; BBC1.

A polished, intelligent series with two excellently contrasted central players, lots of punchy dialogue, jazzy characters, believable actions. Finn, with her leather jacket, cropped hair and face free of make-up, was a dyke on a bike looking for permission to be one and, to nobody's surprise, permission was not forthcoming. Instead there were orders from on high to heterosex her up a bit (with a one night stand or two). (Buki Armstrong moved on to become Gerry, Freddie's hand-holder and perker-upper in ELDORADO.)

South of Watford (UK 1984–6 T)
Alternative Friday-night delve into the more *outré* areas of popular culture: Colin MACINNES; Gilbert and George; Steven Berkoff and 'Gender Benders'. The last – investigating the trend begun by BOY GEORGE and Marilyn – tracked down 'Dennis of Gravesend' to a Top Shop where was seen purchasing a blouse. To show it's lack of bias, another episode on the changing image of masculine beauty declared: 'Exit the WIMP, enter the hunky he-man.'
Presented by Ben Elton; networked by Channel 4; 11.30–12pm; 30 mins.

Trail-blazing, street-credible culture vulturing, indicative – said critics of Channel 4 – of the perverse byways down which young people were being led. More likely it was the young people leading everyone else. One or two shows were denied airtime, most notoriously one about lovers of leather, rubber, plastic and other textures next to their skin.

Spain, Nancy (1918–64) English writer and broadcaster of rare wit and a 'safe' but 'unmistakable' lesbian mien: short hair, sweaters, cravat, trousers, no make-up. She successfully inched her way along the fine line between practical show business flippancy and an equally practical jolly hockey stick brand of feminism. She was a bit player in local radio at 17, before entering the WRENS and acting on Forces radio (*The Brown Family*; *The Brown Family Goes North*).

A bright and able all-weathers features journalist and fashion writer, as well as a light thriller writer, she became, on radio, a welcome semi-regular on WOMAN'S HOUR (1954–63) and ANY QUESTIONS? (1958–63) and a fixture on *These Foolish Things* ('based on an idea by Nancy Spain', 1956–8); *My Word* (1957–64); *Roundabout* (1960–3). Among her one-offs: *My Favourite Villain* 'The Tart with a Heart' (about Marlene DIETRICH, 1955) and *Where Do I Live?* (1963). She was also popular on television, being seen as comfortably intelligent and a 'bit of a lad': *Mainly for Women* (1959); *Laugh Line* (1960); *Juke Box Jury* (1962–4); etc.

Among those – hand-picked – people she interviewed on *Home for the Day* (R) were Arthur MARSHALL, Jean-Louis Barrault, Noel COWARD, Sophie Tucker, Mr Waddilove (private secretary to the Duke of Windsor), Elsa Maxwell, Antonio and Gilbert HARDING (with whom she was 'romantically linked' – by the press). The one *Woman's Hour* she was allowed to compile (5.10.55) caused something of a riot for its 'daring' choice of subjects and Rodean hoydenishness.

'Everyone knew Nancy was a lesbian, but at that time no one talked about it. The atmosphere somehow forbade it' (Jackie FORSTER interviewed for 'The Reign of Spain' in *Gay News*, 1978). 'She loved champagne, stars and other women', *Radio Lives* (1993 R).

Spartacus (US 1960 C) A slaves' revolt (led by all-American Kirk Douglas) savagely crushed by the might of Imperial Rome (Laurence Olivier with a languorously clipped British accent and a yen for male as well as female slaves). W: Dalton Trumbo from the novel by Howard Fast; P: Kirk Douglas; D: Stanley Kubrick; 184 mins.

Now fully restored after televison and censorship depredations over the years (including the erotically inclined conversation between Olivier and Tony Curtis about a liking for oysters or snails), this is a hugely impressive epic, full of expected gore and superbly martialled battle scenes. What makes it special are the personalities involved, especially Charles LAUGHTON and Peter Ustinov as two very different embodiments of cunning and survival. Alex North's music score, the photography, the sets and John Gavin in a toga and bath towel add to the overall tapestry of primitive battles for freedom smote by the might of empire.

Speak for Yourself 'Homosexual Equality' (UK 1974 T) This enterprising and pioneering piece was shot on a Thames river boat disco. Roger Baker spoke to two couples, Maureen and Yolande and Eddie and Chris. The mother of a gay man, Michael Launder, also joined in. Mention was made of media stereotyping, via stills of LIBERACE, Kenneth WILLIAMS, Frankie HOWERD and Dick Emery.

Shown in the London Weekend TV region, and at 11.20pm, LWT reported that, despite the late hour, the audience was 'five or six times the capacity of Wembley Stadium'. The film was topped by Jackie FORSTER (her first TV appearance in her new persona) and others at Speakers' Corner and tailed by an interview with Peter KATIN, whose piano recital had been cancelled because he was revealed as one of the vice presidents of the Campaign for Homosexual Equality.

Speak for Yourself tried to blend the ordinariness of gay lives with the savage realities (crowd reaction at Speakers' Corner; Katin's loss of employment). The river disco provided an unusual and lively background to the personal statements and to the unavoidable political reality that 'gays are indistinguisable in society but are discriminated against socially'.

The show did not please GAY NEWS columnist Leo Madigan: 'A coy, corny pathetic piece of film. I wanted to hiss. It left a sticky taste in my mouth and a childish whine in my ears. I feel we should be above excuses and explanations; indeed I thought we were' (*Gay News* 53).

Special Broadcasting Services *See* SBS.

A Special Day (It 1977 C) Housewife Antoinetta (Sophia Loren) understands slightly more about Fascism after a brief encounter with Gabriele (Marcello Mastroianni), a lonely radio announcer recently sacked for being homosexual and soon to be taken into exile.
W: Ruggiero Maccari and Maurizio Constanzo; P: Carlo Ponti; D: Ettore Scola; 106 mins.

Notable for its exquisite period 'look' (late 1930s, shot in a desaturated colour process), this provides fat juicy parts for the stars and was well received by critics and public. Noble in its intention to show homosexuals as particularly threatening to a totalitarian state, it neatly turns on a double seduction: her sexual one of him and his political one of her.

'Weaving personal relationships and political overtones, this absorbing film concerns the historic occasion when Adolf Hitler arrived in Rome for a series of propaganda meetings and parades with Il Duce. The day is also special because ... housewife ... and radio announcer find themselves drawn together despite their contrasting views on Mussolini' (*Movies on TV and Videocassette*, ed Steven H. Scheuer, 1992–3).

Le Spectre de la Rose Sung (twice) by Jessye Norman over the radio as Andrew's request in *RSVP* (1991 T). The aria comes from the opera by Berlioz, *Les Nuits d'Eté*. *RSVP* is a series of reactions by people who knew Andrew – his lover, his friends, his parents – as the music (which Andrew had requested some months before his death) is played first in Toronto and then, an hour or so later, in Winnipeg.

Spectrum (UK 1988 R) One of radio's intermittent attempts to popularize science. To kick off the first programme, Michael Ruse speculated on the 'CAUSES' or homosexuality in a 15-minute piece called 'The Straight Facts'. Refreshingly, Ruse quickly abandoned the usual headbanging of genetics vs upbringing and looked towards the important role homosexuals did and could increasingly play in society – as providers and carers. 'There's more to reproduction than having offspring' and homosexuals, generaly without childrearing responsibilities, are 'freed to look after members of their families, often financially'. Other investigations in the BBC Radio 3 initiative included farting cattle and the build-up of greenhouse gases, sexual selection of females, and organic electronics.

speedos Male SWIMWEAR, developed firstly for Australian lifesavers. Thin bands of material acting as pouchettes for the genitals with a very short distance from waistband to pouch. Shown off to their best advantage in the 1984 film *The Coolangatta Gold* (principally by Josh McWilliam and Colin Friels).

Speedos, which eroticize parts of the male body in much the same wet and clinging way that women's swimming costumes have been doing for much of the 20th century, were featured in a 1992 exhibition in Sydney 'Success in Innovation'. They were proudly displayed alongside other great Australian inventions such as robotic sheep shears, cochlea implants and computer-made socks that never fall down.

Spelling, Aaron (1928–) American television producer, a former actor (*Crime in the Streets* etc), who operates a conveyor belt of entertainment with big budgets, glamorous people, up to the minute social issues, and lots of sugar and spice (*Beverly Hills 90210* being currently the most successful). He has long been an enterprising and energetic packager of homosexuality for Middle America: in episodes of STARSKY AND HUTCH (1975–9); CHARLIE'S ANGELS

(1976–81) and HOTEL (1983–6); in television movies like *The Users* (1978), *The Making of a Male Model* (1983) and AND THE BAND PLAYED ON (1993); and intermittently through regular characters in DYNASTY (1981–91), HEARTBEAT (1988–9) and MELROSE PLACE (1991–).

Spencer, Colin (1933–) English playwright, novelist and vegetarian cookery writer who was celebrated in the radio series *Culinary Characters* (1986) as having 'lifted the nut cutlet to the level of gourmet cuisine' (Marjorie Lofthouse). Both his daring and delicious comedies (*Splitting Image*; *Keep It in the Family*) and deeply felt books (about being denied access to his son because of his bisexuality and, most recently, about an early love affair) have been ignored by television, radio and cinema – to the detriment of all three mediums. His only television work was the 'Flossie' episode of NIGHTINGALE'S BOYS (1975) about the resurrection of a married man's long-buried homosexual feelings.

spies Working against the dastardly French revolutionaries on behalf of aristocratic émigrés and in the interests of his government (which was based on his – frightened – fellow landed gentry) was Sir Percy Blakeney, alias *The Scarlet Pimpernel*, pretending to foppishness and *ennui* while really being a demon with a rapier, a master of disguise and the acme of cunning: incarnated by, among others, Leslie Howard (1935 C), Marius Goring (1954–5 T), Anthony Andrews (1982 T) and, for a sketch on *3, 2, 1* (1983 T), John INMAN as 'The Lilac Pimpernel'; Commander James Bond, who married but once (his bride was almost immediately gunned down – by a lesbian named Bunt – in *On Her Majesty's Secret Service* 1969 C), had a string of ONE NIGHT STANDS (mainly with enemy agents) and had fastidious taste (among his opponents was the merciless Rosa KLEBB, connoisseur of the KGB's young female operatives); *Fraulein Doktor* (Suzy Kendall 1969 C)

who has to be sexually flexible in pursuit of information necessary to her work as a First World War double agent (including sleeping with a woman scientist); *Mata Hari* (Sylvia Kristel 1985 C) similarly has to make sacrifices for her craft: enduring the ogling, and more, of a German agent (Gaye Brown); George SANDERS, laying low as a female impersonator in a gay bar before being summoned to do undercover work in Moscow, on behalf of the Americans, to learn the secret of *The Kremlin Letter* (1970 C) and using that city's gay network to achieve his ends. *See also* POSITIVE VETTING; TRAITORS.

spinsters Also known as 'old maids'. Women living without a male mate are viewed by popular culture as frustrated, lonely, kindly, courageous, inspiring and stoical. For example, Bette DAVIS played the single mother whose child grows up ignoring her in *The Old Maid* (1939 C); the dowdy Charlotte in *Now, Voyager* (1942 C); the doughty teacher Miss Moffat in *The Corn is Green* (1945 C); the anti book-burning librarian in *Storm Center* (1955 C); the street musician in *Connecting Rooms* (1971 C).

Other examples of the more positive side of spinsterhood include Florence NIGHTINGALE; Marian HALCOMBE in *The Woman in White* (Eleanor Parker 1948 C; Diana QUICK 1982 T); Rose Allnutt (Katharine HEPBURN) based on Eleanor Roosevelt in *The African Queen* (1952 C) – other Hepburn spinsters are the tourist in *Summer Madness/Summertime* (1955 C), Lizzie, the victim of *The Rainmaker* (1957 C), and Miss Moffat (1979 T); glamorous, persevering and still (in her thirties) unmarried market gardener Carol GREY (Anne CULLEN) in THE ARCHERS (1954–61); single-minded, stern, but revered and forward-thinking feminist teacher (Beatrix LEHMANN) in LOVE AND MISS FIGGIS (1954 T); Sergeant Grace MILLARD (Moira MANNION) in DIXON OF DOCK GREEN (1956–61), intelligent companionable woman police officer, close friend of the Dixon family; Sybil Railton-Bell drawn to the phoney major against the iron-clad dictates of her mother in *Separate Tables* (Deborah Kerr 1958 C; Julie Christie 1983 T); Gladys Aylward (Ingrid Bergman) in *The Inn of the Sixth Happiness* (1958 C); sketch artist Hannah Jelks (Deborah Kerr) looking after her dying grandfather in *The Night of the Iguana* (1964 C); Joanne Woodward as the teacher in *Rachel, Rachel* (1968 C); dependable ROSE (Jean Marsh) in UPSTAIRS, DOWNSTAIRS (1970–5 T); Maggie Smith in *The Lonely Passion of Judith Hearne* (1987 C); the much respected Welsh villager who marries purely and simply to give her foster child a father in SHORT STORY 'Maid in Heaven' (1992 R); etc.

On the other side of the spinster fence are those women whose unmanned state has turned them inwards, making them neurotic, complaining, eccentric, prone to delusions or writing nasty letters – generally causing trouble. Among these, almost by popular cultural definition, can be found one or two suppressed or overt lesbians: superficially composed vicar's sister, Mary Rider (Flora Robson) sending the letters of the title in *Poison Pen* (1937 C); witch-like Elvira Gulch (Margaret Hamilton) who hates children and little dogs in *The Wizard of Oz* (1939 C); reclusive, jilted Miss HAVISHAM relentlessly tutoring a young girl in the fine art of male heart-breaking in *Great Expectations* (Martita HUNT 1946 C; Margaret Leighton 1974 C; Jean Simmons 1989 T); acid Miss Cornelia (Joan Young) in *East Lynne* (1964 T), jealous of her brother's recent happy marriage; *The Daughters of the Late Colonel* (1945 & 1983 R) still sharing a bed and with no interests or outlets save each other; jilted Evelyn (Pamela Brown) possessively and – it is hinted – lustfully drawn to her teenage niece in *Personal Affair* (1953 C); Shirley MacLaine plagued by frustration and two strongly contrasting suitors in *Spinster/ Two Loves* (1961 C); Deborah Kerr as the governess prone to strange and kinky fancies – or are they frighteningly real? – in *The Innocents* (1961 C); missionary Agatha Andrews (Margaret Leighton), one of the *Seven Women* (1966 C), a

viper's nest of religious fervour and anti-Levitical passions; Edna Shaft (Jessica Tandy) whose book on BYRON is her only comfort once the woman she loved got married in BUTLEY (1974 C/T); poet *Stevie* (SMITH) who lives comfortably (but with inner turmoil) with her maiden aunt (Glenda Jackson and Mona Washbourne 1978 C); the warped Miss WADE (Sonia Fraser) in *Little Dorrit* (1980 R) who takes a young girl to live with her in Venice; the two academics (Hannah Gordon and Wendy Hiller) who see strange things at Versailles in *Miss Morrison's Ghosts* (1981 T); purse-lipped Miss Banner (Pauline Letts), one of whose hobbies is cutting up photographs of men – across the genitals – in *The Outsider* (1983 T); the increasingly out of control 'Lady of Letters' of the TALKING HEADS series (played by Patricia Routledge, 1988 T), whose controlling, contrary personality undergoes a significant and sympathetic change when she is forced into an all-female environment.

Spinsters do not have the social cachet of BACHELORS, being viewed essentially as failures because, in the words of that *Gold Diggers of 1933* song 'MY FORGOTTEN MAN', 'Ever since the world began/ A woman's *got* to have a man'. WOMAN'S HOUR took spinsterdom fully on board once only, in a 1955 special edition entitled 'Single Woman's Hour' which included a long-awaited item: 'On Being a Happy Spinster'. The previous year, one of the programme's most popular – if occasionally too riotous – contributors, Nancy SPAIN, confessed that she used to be 'a child-hating spinster', but having spent time looking after her friend's baby she was a changed woman. And all due to 'That Tiny Helpless Bundle' who – and one or two listeners must have thought this curious – was living with Nancy and her friend in 'our' flat.

Spoiled (UK 1968 T) Angelic-looking Donald Clenham (Simon Ward) has left school but is retaking some O-levels. In the week before his maths examination, he stays at his tutor's home. Richard

(Michael Craig) is attractive; his wife (Elizabeth Shepherd) is pregnant; the boy, while hysterical and demanding, has charms. Relationships become, said the synopsis, 'tense and complicated'. Hearing Donald crying, Richard goes into his room. What happens next is not shown, but its import is suitably dramatic for his frazzled wife to ask point-blank: 'Well, did you in the end or didn't you? And do you do this to all your pupils?'

The next morning, Richard and Donald have a heart-to-heart: 'What happened, Donald, it was one of those, well, the kind of thing we talked about once. It caught us both, me, um, forget what happened but remember me as a ... teacher. And a friend. In the end it won't matter, nothing will matter except that we got on together ... That's how I'll remember it. And, Donald, if, well, you won't tell anyone about it, will you?' W: Simon GRAY; P: Graeme McDonald; D: Waris HUSSEIN; 22.8.68; BBC1; 75 mins.

A variation of the theme of cuckoo in the nest which is orchestrated with only some of the stinging verve for which Simon Gray would become deservedly famous in the following decades. Aside from witty observations from the minor characters (including two of Donald's work-mates who are more or less openly homosexual), this is a mainly depressing drama whose elliptical nature (doubtless encouraged by censorship) ensures minimum engagement with its three protagonists.

Spoiled (which was popular enough to be repeated the following year – and presented in a stage version in the early 1970s) found favour with Mary WHITE-HOUSE, who, in a letter to BBC executive Michael Swann, wrote that she admired the play – which 'gave us all cause to examine ourselves and to understand others more fully' – because 'you did not glamourize, normalize or justify deviation, but showed it for the tragedy it is'.

spotted dick A traditional English dessert whose name ensures a hearty laugh. The ship's cook (Angus Lennie) has a brief but spirited conversation about his spotted dick with equally effete sailor (Murray MELVIN) in *Petticoat Pirates* (1961 C): 'Your spotted dick gives me a stomach ache'/'My spotted dick *always* tastes funny.'

There was more innocent phallic hilarity, this time around a family dinner table in LATE CALL (1975 T) which was set in the 1950s. Arthur (Leslie Dwyer) tells his new granddaughter-in-law that he could show her 'a good spotted dick'. Deeply embarrassed on the young woman's behalf, his wife Sylvia (Dandy Nichols) quickly – if needlessly – translates: 'It's a sort is a light suet pudding with raisins.' But Arthur won't be denied his bit of bawdy fun. Turning to his son he says, giggling: 'I'll *bet* my spotted dick is as good as yours anyday.'

The diametrically opposed brothers, Lesley (Hugh PADDICK) and Jack (Michael Robbins), in SHARE AND SHARE ALIKE 'The Strike' (1978 R) find themselves at daggers drawn after an industrial dispute at the factory where both work (one in management, the other a a lowly labourer). After the strike is over, Lesley, as a peace offering, serves his favourite meal of 'eggs, bacon, sausages and beans and' [pausing for maximum queeny effect] 'I've made a lovely spotted dick ... with custard'.

Springfield, Dusty [Mary Catherine O'Brien] (1939–) English pop singer – shy, vulnerable, powerful, dazzling, spectacular – who made scores of television appearances in her heyday (1964–8). Beginning as one of the Lana Sisters, she began to fully establish herself as a member of the Springfields trio which was regularly heard and seen on radio and television from 1961 onwards. As a solo performer she had a string of hits ('You Don't Have To Say You Love Me'; 'I Only Want To Be With You'), and appeared on the very first TOP OF THE POPS (New Year's Day 1964, with Cliff Richard, the Swinging Blue Jeans and the Hollies). She had a number of series of her own including *Dusty* (guests Woody ALLEN, José Feliciano,

Peter Cook, Dudley Moore etc, 1966–8 T); *It Must Be Dusty* (with brother Tom Springfield etc, 1968 T); *Decidedly Dusty* (1969).

With her glorious blonde beehive hair-dos, yards of false eyelash and full-throated voice, she was *the* 'girl singer' of her era, and a guest on every conceivable pop music and light entertainment show: *Juke Box Jury* (and, on the same night on the same channel – BBC1 – an hour later turning up on *The Billy Cotton Band Show* 1965); *Tarbuck at the Prince of Wales* (1966); *Thank Your Lucky Stars* (1966); *Tom Jones!* (1966); *The Liberace Show* (1969); *It's Lulu* (1970). Of late, her appearances have been mainly restricted to talk-shows linked to sporadic come-backs: *Parkinson* (1976 T); *Afternoon Plus* 1983 T); *Wogan* 1987 T); etc.

Among the film and television themes she has recorded are:

C: 'The Corrupt Ones' (*The Corrupt Ones/The Peking Medallion* 1967); THE LOOK OF LOVE (*Casino Royale* 1967); 'Sea And Sky' (*Time for Loving/Paris Was Made for Lovers* 1971); 'Give Me The Night' (*Corvette Summer/The Hot One* 1978); 'Bits And Pieces' (*The Stunt Man* 1980); 'Nothing Has Been Proved' (*Scandal!* 1989); 'Getting It Right' (*Getting It Right* 1989).

T: 'Learn To Say Goodbye' (*Say Goodbye, Maggie Cole* 1972); 'Six Million Dollar Man' (*The Six Million Dollar Man* 1972); 'As Long As We've Got Each Other' (*Growing Pains* 1985); 'I Just Don't Know What To Do With Myself' (played over the end credits of the serial *Take Me Home* 1989). A number of her songs gave erotic counterpoint to the sedate images in *17 Rooms or What Do Lesbians Do in Bed?* (1984).

Staircase (UK/US/Fr 1969 C) Two small-time, back-street barbers, one sentimental and flabby (Harry, played by Richard Burton), the other hysterical and routinely camp (Charlie, played by Rex Harrison), play love and hate in a needling match, which Harry easily wins, despite his being completely bald and sexually rejected. For Charlie, vicious tongue and young pick-ups not withstanding, is a very worried, frightened man with loneliness never quite held at bay, a deranged mother in a home and a court case (importuning a policeman) on the horizon.

W: Charles DYER from his play; P/D: Stanley Donen; 101 mins.

When the mid-slinging palls, there's the plain, plucky truth of Richard Burton's performance to compensate for the unconvincing sets (it was mainly filmed in France though set in London) and for Rex Harrison's posturings and off-key, sing-song delivery of what were originally funny lines. The inclusion of a few other characters (one of them a gormless bit of 'TRADE') does nothing for what started out as – and remains – a tart and pathetic double act.

Staircase Rodgers and Starr open the film version of Charles Dyer's play with a relatively stylish drag number, which deliberately echoes the Monroe–Russell pre-credits 'Two Little Girls From Little Rock' in *Gentlemen Prefer Blondes* (1953 C).

The lyrics capture what is to follow only too accurately: 'We'll build a staircase up to the sky/We'll not be lonely flying so high.' Then the blonde member of the duo confides in best brimstone and treacle drag-queen voice to the (unseen) audience: 'Wait till *you're* lonely, dear. Try calling them then, *dear*. You're the back entrance.' This purging is immediately followed by Dudley Moore's sepulchral electric organ version of the song – which is later reprised in a pub scene – over Maurice Binder's staircase credits. Then into children singing 'ALL THINGS BRIGHT AND BEAUTIFUL'.

Stamboul Train (UK 1962 T) Based on Graham Greene's novel, the story finds booze-soaked, muck-raking journalist Mabel Warren (Anna Burden) on the track of political intrigue in Czechoslovakia. Her girlfriend Janet Pardoe (Diane Aubrey) is with her on the eponymous train, but Mabel is much more interested in a young dancer, Coral Musker (Susan Burnet). Eventually Janet gives up Mabel's fierce – if sometimes fickle and often drunken – devotion for marriage to a rich business-man.

W: John HOPKINS; P: Prudence Fitzgerald; 11.9.62; BBC; 50 mins.

The first BBC television play to clearly signpost female homosexuality. The *Listener* critic wrote that the reporter and her companion were probably en route 'for Lesbos', while remarking of the clapped-out plot that 'Spike Milligan would have been hard-pressed to produce a better parody of adventure melodrama'. (The 1934 film version of Greene's novel, *Orient Express*, which was co-written by Oscar Levant, featured Dorothy Burgess as Mabel, Irene Ware as Janet and Heather Angel as Coral.)

Standard Procedure (UK 1979 R)
Teacher Tony Kellet (Derrick Gilbert) provides a refuge for a runaway pupil and suffers the almost inevitable reaction from the law, even though nothing untoward has happened.

W: Michael WILCOX; D: Alfred Bradley; 1.8.79; BBC Radio 4; 55 mins.

A workmanlike piece in which Tony is the victim of what begins as simple human kindness towards a lost soul, then escalates into the faint glimmerings of a friendship which is immediately jumped upon by the law and Johnny's parents. (Michael Wilcox wrote of the real-life situation upon which the play was based in *Outlaw of the Hills: A Writer's Year* 1991.)

Stand By Me Sung by Ben E. King at the end of the 1986 film of the same name to enable the viewer to ponder Wil Wheaton/Richard Dreyfuss' true feelings ('Darlin' darlin', stand by me ...') for his recently deceased childhood friend, Chris (played as a boy by River Phoenix), after it has been established that Gordie (the character Dreyfuss plays briefly as an adult), through his fathering of a son, is heterosexual. This emotional outburst (by Elmo Glick – ie Jerry Leiber and Mike Stoller – and Benjamin Earl Nelson – ie Ben E. King)

offers the film-makers a chance to uncork what has been stoppered. (Meatloaf, BOY GEORGE and Elton JOHN joined forces to sing 'Stand By Me', on AIDS Day 1987, in *Cue the Music* 1988 T.)

Stand on Your Man (UK 1991 T)
Orginally shown as part of the OUT series, this is a campfire special on lesbians and country music with television clips of Patsy Cline and other gals in check shirts, jeans and some calico dresses, coming bang up to date with k. d. lang. Interviews with dyke country-music lovers, fans and fanatics add to the brew.

P/D: Susan Ardill; 25 mins.

Why do lesbians like these often senti-mental and usually hetero ballads and choruses? Love and sex are universal ... the female singers are scrummy ... the lyrics are often witty as well as poignant ... And why should the 'boys' have a monopoly on CAMP?

Stanwyck, Barbara [Ruby Stevens] (1907–90) American actress. At ease in skirts or trousers, she fought, she tongue-lashed, she was gentle, she rode, she sang, she loved (and on a number of occasions asked for sex), she cuckolded, she killed, she danced the hoochie-coo-chie, she was slangy and she was ladylike ... And she was the first Hollywood star to play a practising lesbian (in *Walk on the Wild Side* 1962). (She herself was described as 'the great American les-bian' in *Dry Kisses Only* 1989 V/C.)

Wrote Homer Dickens in *The Films of Barbara Stanwyck* (1984): 'Her ladies have included every conceivable female: con artist, chorine, jewel thief, reporter, stripper, moll, society lady, killer, taxi dancer, eyewitness, rancher, dizzy débutante, nurse, evangelist, concert pianist, gambler, imposter, wife, mother, daughter, the other woman, white squaw, lesbian, madam, matriarch.'

She made 84 films, all in starring roles, of which the most remembered are *Baby Face* (1933: sleeping her way up from bottom to top of a corporation); *Annie Oakley* (1935: sharpshooter); *Stella Dal-*

las (1937: sacrificing everything for a daughter who rejects her); *The Lady Eve* (1941: masquerading as English aristocrat); *Ball of Fire* (1941: raunchy burlesque dancer); *Double Indemnity* (1944: ruthless co-murderer of her husband); *The Strange Love of Martha Ivers* (1946); *Sorry, Wrong Number* (1948: querulous rich invalid targeted for death); *Forty Guns* (1957: land baron); *Roustabout* (1964: running a carnival with Elvis Presley).

The film roles she was lined up for but didn't play include Josephine to Edward G. Robinson's Napoleon (*c* 1936); Linda in *Holiday* (Katharine HEPBURN played it in 1938); lead in *Hollywood Cavalcade* (Alice Faye played it in 1939); lead in an Ayn Rand thriller, *The Night of January 16th* (Ellen Drew played it in 1941); nightclub performer Texas Guinan (Betty Hutton played it in *Incendiary Blonde* 1944); lead in *Road Show* (Carole Landis played it in 1941); 'The Life of Sophie Tucker' 1952; librarian in 'Circle of Fire' (Bette DAVIS did it as *Storm Center* 1955); loyal secretary to Clifton WEBB in *Three Coins in the Fountain* (Dorothy McGuire played it); the wife in *We're No Angels* (Joan Bennett did it); the 'good' sister in 'Love's Lonely Counterfeit' (Rhonda Fleming did it as *Slightly Scarlet* 1956); Vera in *Pal Joey* with Kirk Douglas (Rita Hayworth played it opposite Frank Sinatra); Judy GARLAND's mother in the life of Elsie Janis (1957); as a rich, bored woman in LA DOLCE VITA ('seriously considered' by Federico Fellini, part reshaped, played by Nadia Gray); Rock HUDSON's mother in *This Earth Is Mine* (Dorothy McGuire did it); lead in 'The Possessors' (for William Castle, based on a novel by John Christopher, 1965).

Her television work comprised *The Jack Benny Show* (1952, in a spoof of *Gaslight*); *Ford Theatre* 'Sudden Silence' as a marshall's wife (1956); Reagan Moore, hiring man to kill her husband in Dick Powell's *Zane Grey Theatre* 'Hang The Heart High' (1956); ex-prisoner Midge Varney in *Turn of Fate* 'Three Years Dark' (1957); Julie Holmes in *Zane Grey Theatre* 'Trail to Nowhere' (1958); *The Real McCoys* 'The Real McCoys Visit Hollywood' (1959, as herself); *Zane Grey Theatre* 'Lone Woman' (1959); *The Barbara Stanwyck Show* (starring in 32 stories out of 36 beginning with 'The Mink Coat', 1960–1); Dora Dunphy in *The Joey Bishop Show* 'A Windfall for Mom' (1961); a wagonmistress in *Wagon Train* 'The Maud Frazer Story' (1961); Lili Parrish in *General Electric Theatre* 'Star Witness' (1961); 'The Captain's Wife' in *Rawhide* (1962); alcoholic Irene Phillips in *The Dick Powell Theatre* 'Special Assignment' (1962); captured by Indians in *Wagon Train* 'The Caroline Casteel Story' (1962); *The Untouchables* as Lieutenant Agatha Stewart in 'Elegy' (1963); *Wagon Train* 'The Molly Kincaid Story' (1963) and 'The Kate Crawley Story' as Captain Hale's love interest (1963); *Calhoun Country Agent* opposite Jackie Cooper (1963); Victoria Barkeley in *The Big Valley* (111 episodes in four years, 1965–9); *The House That Wouldn't Die* (1969); *A Taste of Evil* (1971); Geraldine Parkington in *The Letters* (three scenes cut from her episode 'Dear Penelope'); Toni in CHARLIE'S ANGELS 'Toni's Boys' (1980); Mary Carson in *The Thorn Birds* 1983); Constance in *The Colbys* 'Dynasty II' (1985–6).

There were also unrealized plans for her to star as Josephine Little, an importer–exporter in Hong Kong, in a series based on a pilot film, *The Miraculous Journey of Tadpole Chan* (1961). Also unrealized were plans for her to play cop Agatha Stewart on a regular basis in *The Untouchables* (1963), a pilot in *Calhoun: County Agent* (1963), and a fight trainer in *Ringside* (1963). A regular role in a male version of *Charlie's Angels* also came to nought after one story was screened in 1980.

Barbara Stanwyck's radio career began in 1936, mainly in shortened versions of film scripts: *The Rudy Vallee Hour; Hollywood Hotel; The Chase and Sanborn Show* (with Edgar Bergen and Charlie McCarthy: she performed an extract from *Anna Christie*); *Camel Caravan* ('Just Imagine' with Ray Milland); *Screen Guild Theatre* 'Allergic to Love' and 'My Favourite Wife' (with Robert Taylor and Franklyn PANGBORN); *Lux Radio Theatre* 'Main Street' (1936, one of the most popular plays in US radio history); 'Stella Dallas', 'Holiday' and 'These Three' (with Mary Astor and Errol Flynn (all 1937); Judith Traherne in 'Dark Victory' (with Melvyn Douglas, 1938); Eva Lovelace in 'Morning Glory'; Cathy in 'Wuthering Heights', (opposite Brian Aherne, 1940); 'Only Yesterday' (with George Brent); 'Smilin' Through' (with Robert Taylor); 'The Lady Eve', 'Penny Serenade', 'Ball of Fire', 'This Above All' and 'The Gay Sisters (all 1942–3); 'My Reputation' and 'The Other Love' (1947); 'Sorry, Wrong Number' (1950); 'Goodbye My Fancy' (1951); etc.

In 1981, having won two EMMY awards (for *The Barbara Stanwyck Show* and *The Big Valley*), she was presented with a special ACADEMY AWARD. She was again honoured with an Emmy in 1983 (for *The Thorn Birds*) and was the subject of an American Film Industry tribute in 1987 which was filmed for television.

'You must be a master, not a slave; be strong, be brave, be determined and you will be a success,' advice given to – and taken by – Barbara Stanwyck's character Lily Powers in *Baby Face* (1933).

'Can I do something for you, honey?' black cook Chico (Theresa Harris) who later goes to New York with her in the same film.

'Kiss me on the lips – like a lover!' Stanwyck to Richard Chamberlain in *The Thorn Birds* (1983 C).

Star! (US 1968 C) The fictionalized biography of Gertrude Lawrence (Julie Andrews), star of West End and Broadway plays and musicals (*Private Lives*; *The King and I*) and a few films (*Rembrandt*), and the stage partner of Noel COWARD (Daniel MASSEY).

W: William Fairchild; P: Saul Chaplin; D: Robert Wise; 175 mins (some prints 194 mins).

Taken as a mammoth Julie Andrews special (with long yawning passages involving a string of dull lovers, all male) with splendid songs, costumes and witty

interruptions from Massey, this has many pleasing moments. These include Andrews' 'BURLINGTON BERTIE FROM BOW' (pregnant and in drag), 'Parisian Pierrot' and 'Jenny'. She's in great crystalline voice, is superbly coiffeured and dressed, and even gets away with going 'Oriental' in the 'Limehouse Blues' number. If the film were made today would MADONNA play Gertie with Meryl Streep as Daphne Du Maurier?

Starsky and Hutch (US 1975–9 T) 'Tough and rough – but likeable and friendly police patrolmen Starsky and Hutch make a good team. They work together, they like each other – and manage to keep a sense of humour.'

A weekly dollop of buddy-up (produced by Aaron SPELLING) between a pair of lads in dark blue, given a packaging (especially the opening credits) which looks like a serious attempt to attract the (almost fully emergent) gay market. There's a lot of manly hugging, sulks (when one has a girlfriend, as in 'Gillian' 1977), and teasing. In a 1978 episode 'Dandruff' the guy go undercover as HAIRDRESSERS (of the more extrovert kind), and in the 1977 'Death in a Different Place' (W: Tom Bagen; P: Joseph T. Naar; D: Sutton Roley) they even have to confront serious homosexuality when a closeted colleague, John Blane (Art Fleming) is killed.

Amid a plethora of sleazy characters in matching settings, Hutch (David Soul) and Starsky (Paul Michael Glaser) engage in a half-hearted bout of CLOSET cleaning. Hutch complains that Starsky, with whom he spends 75 per cent of his life, is 'not even a good kisser'. Starsky is mock-aggrieved at this slight. 'How do you *know* that?' he yelps. But before anything can be confirmed or denied, the scene ends in a freeze frame and the closing credits roll. As Mirna Risk wrote in her review in GAY NEWS 212: 'The function of this episode has been to confirm the ambiguity, winking with one eye at its gay and the other at its straight audience.'

Star Trek (US 1966–9 T) Extraordinary adventures and encounters from the log of the starship *Enterprise* as interpreted by 22nd-century man: Captain James Kirk (William Shatner). Cr: Gene Roddenberry; P: Gene Coon, later John Meredyth Lucas and Fred Freiberger; NBC; 60 mins.

This adult science fiction series, brought back in the 1980s firstly in a series of big budget cinema films and then (with a completely new 'crew') returning to television, has attracted a world-wide cult whose devotees are known as 'Trekkies'. Despite its idealistic new world order futurism, the sexual politics have remained firmly grounded in convention. At least until 1992 when the producers of *Star Trek: The Next Generation* promised that heterosexual hegemony was due to end with the arrival of 'gay and lesbian' characters. Up to that point, the show had fronted only one gay man – a predatory aesthete wishing aloud to see a male crew member's member or, as the 1990 script had it: 'Personally, I'd be delighted to see you go around *naked.*'

There are those who have perceived hidden desires between Kirk and his colleague, Science Officer (Dr) Spock (Leonard Nimoy), a part alien, part earthling with pointed ears and arched eyebrows. A 1992 edition of *In the Mix* (Aust R) devoted 10 minutes to the efforts of a group of (mainly female) fans in America who believe Kirk and Spock to be the perfect male couple: 'two heterosexual men who just happen to love and have sex with each other; other men who were equal, who could share, love and work.' These pioneers in the cause of heterosexual gay bonding are seen in action in a number of episodes which the fans have 'rewritten' (by recutting, known as 'slash culture') with new music tracks, pointing up the homerotic feeling. Parallel with this belief that the two men are lovers (thought *not* homosexual) is the feeling that *Star Trek* represented a homosexual triangle with Dr Leonard 'Bones' McCoy (DeForest Kelley) as the jealous, rejected third party.

Journalist John Gill, leaving Spock out

of the equation, told GAY NEWS readers (in a COMING OUT piece published in 1975 when he was 19) that it was Kirk and McCoy who filled his early adolescent fantasies: 'Lieutenant Uhuru was a good-looking woman, but Dr McCoy and Captain Kirk seemed to hold the greater sex-fantasy potential. So they became my bed-partners, only with a multitude of other vogue symbols of machismo. It had all begun with vaguely masochistic hero-worship but, as my sexual awareness increased, so did their night-time activity.'

In the 22nd century anything is possible.

statues An easily grasped form of erotic identification and typing for homosexual men and women. Life-size or miniature, they are effortlessly redolent of pagan times when gymnasia meant a place of naked men, when nymphs were not NYMPHOMANIACS and when muscles did not mean steroids. Occasionally heterosexual characters will decorate their rooms with them, but they are usually BOW-TIE wearing neurotics like Humphrey Bogart in *In A Lonely Place* (1950 C: a Venus De Milo, wearing a bra) or accredited eccentrics like Rumpole (Leo McKern) in *Rumpole of the Bailey* (1978– T: MICHAELANGELO'S DAVID on the mantelpiece) or clownish leches (a large one in a helmet carrying a spear in *How to Succeed in Business without Really Trying* 1966 C).

Male examples of significant naked or near-naked sculptures include two Roman busts at either end of the mantelpiece in Ricardo's (Gilbert Roland) hacienda in *The Last Train from Madrid* (1937 C), which are lit and positioned so as to be very noticeable immediately following a scene which features a close-up of Eduardo (Anthony Quinn) and Ricardo holding hands in a car; Hermes, Adonis and ephebic youths in the domiciles of both Basil (Lowell Gilmore) and Dorian (Hurd HATFIELD) in THE PICTURE OF DORIAN GRAY (1945 C), and a bronze athlete very noticeable at the Two Turtles tavern scene where one is shifted in and out of focus during Dorian's first meeting with Sybil; muscle flexers in the bookshop Katharine HEPBURN visits in *Undercurrent* (1946 C); BLACKMAILER Sandy (Derren Nesbitt) in VICTIM (1961 C) has a PHOTOGRAPH of a discus thrower on his wall which, combined with his appreciation of classical music, makes him even more suspect and reprehensible in the eyes of the makers; one (glimpsed on top of a cupboard) is included as part of Barrett's interior decoration of Tony's house in *The Servant* (1963 C); there is a special park of male-nude statuary 'for lovers who were very close' in *The Loved One* (1965 C); Marlon Brando is obsessed with a photograph of one in REFLECTIONS IN A GOLDEN EYE (1967 C); antique dealer is bashed and killed with one of his statues before being castrated in THE DETECTIVE (1968 C); Richard Moreau (Eric PORTMAN) has a pair of silver filigree wrestlers on his drinks table in *Deadfall* (1968 C); a small plaster discus thrower can be espied in just one shot in Charlie's 'bedroom' in STAIRCASE (1969 C); the prison warden's boudoir comes equipped with one in *There Was a Crooked Man* (1970 C); master/mistress of overkill Frank N Furter (Tim CURRY) in THE ROCKY HORROR PICTURE SHOW (1975 C) has two 6-foot Davids in his castle.

Female characters are more likely to be surrounded by ornaments in flowing drapery showing discreet body contours. Sometimes, for women who dissent from orthodoxy, they are the subject of sharp focus in early character-establishing scenes. These include the voluptuous pieces of marbled womanhood in the living rooms of two very liberated women: business mogul Alison (Ruth Chatterton) in *Female* (1933 C) and graphic artist Helen (Bette DAVIS) in *Ex-Lady* (1933 C: 'Nobody has any rights over me except me'); the Aphrodite in the apartment of sisters June and Dorothy (Rhonda Fleming and Arlene Dahl) in *Slightly Scarlet* (1956 C) is the only indication of the eroticism of their relationship as strongly indicated in the original novel, where they are also NYM-PHOMANIACS; the heroine of THE L-SHAPED ROOM (1962 C) shouldn't have been surprised when Mavis (Cicely Courtneidge) reveals she is a lesbian because she has a lamp whose base is a very lightly clad nymph; the Black Queen (Anita Pallenberg) sleeps on a bed sculpted into the shape of a sensuously reclining woman in *Barbarella* (1968 C).

Statues and all they suggested about certain men and women began to be phased out by set directors in the 1970s. None were to be found, for example, in the murdered young man's apartment in *Police Story* 'The Ripper' (1974 T), or in the domiciles of Michael (Peter Denyer) and Rob (Jeremy Bulloch) in AGONY (1979–81 T) or of Steven CARRINGTON in DYNASTY (1981–91 T). Paul GREENHALGH who played one half of a couple in THE CREZZ (1976 T) told GAY NEWS: 'The director said he didn't want a lot of male nude statues.'

But because of their rapidly conveyed odours of eroticism, closetry and decadence, these atmosphric objects continue to feature as standard issue in much fictional queer décor: a large, crudely formed Grecian-style female statue dominates the disco in the 1977 TV movie IN THE GLITTER PALACE; a piece of fig-leafed Greek manhood, artfully placed near to a photograph of Judy GARLAND, gives the viewer early warning, in the very first scene of *The Users* (1978 T), of the sexual varieties of film star Randy Brent (Tony Curtis), assisted further by a shot of him being sensuously worked on by a MASSEUR; the assured journalist Kate (Gabrielle Hartley) has two Sapphic pieces in her Sydney harbour-front apartment in DAWN! (1979 C) and, therefore, it comes as no real surprise when she leads the heroine into an affair after the party; when Brian EPSTEIN (Brian Jameson) signs up the four musicians in *The Birth of the Beatles* (1979 T), John Lennon (Stephen MacKenna) picks up the semi-naked David in the otherwise starkly functional office and, brimming over with knowingness, begins playing with the young Liverpool businessman's carefully groomed hair; the lavish mews flat of Alex (David Daker) and Ronald (Alun Lewis) in MINDER 'Whose Wife Is It, Anyway?' (1980 T) boasts a revelatory *objet* in a cabinet and another in their black marble bathroom with yet another in the all-pink bedroom; there is a comically obvious one in the rented apartment (owned by a middle-aged man of flowing gesture) where John HURT and Ryan O'Neal set up house to catch the murderer in PARTNERS (1982 C); strategically placed for humour, too, is the huge white one on the stair of the house Bob (Gérard Depardieu) and Antoine (Michel Blanc) come to 'rob' in TENUE DE SOIREE/EVENING DRESS (1985 C); another discus thrower appears on the landing of the house of TRAITOR Sir Adrian Chapple (John GIELGUD) in *The Whistle Blower* (1987 C); there's a respectably erotic Greek statue in the bedroom of Dr Woodward and Aubrey's Derbyshire cottage in *Floodtide* (1987 T), next to a portrait of Vivien Leigh as Scarlett O'Hara; there's a tiny one on the stair alcove of the house of faded TV star Dale Davenport (Terence Morgan) in *King and Castle* 'Friends' (1986 T); Uncle (Richard Griffiths) is a proud possessor in *Withnail and I* (1986 C); Ceri (Iola Gregory) is battered to death with one by her female lover in *In Two Minds* (1987 T); etc.

Steaming (UK 1985 C) Support and solidarity between working- and upper-middle-class women when their one source of assured relaxation and pleasure is threatened with the chop.
W: Patricia Losey from the play by Nell Dunn; P: Paul Mills; D: Joseph Losey; 95 mins.

Flaccid adaptation of what had been an earthy and appealing eavesdrop on some women in a public bath house. Two minor characters have been expanded and at least one damagingly undercast. The growing solidarity between the women in the face of the baths' closure is perfunctorily handled.

A disastrous mismatching of material, and director Joseph Losey, terminally ill, was publicly unsympathetic to the ideology behind the story: 'Why do they say these terrible things about men?' The dismissal of Georgina Hale – who had so memorably created the role of the dependent, foul-mouthed Josie – during the first week of filming (through 'artistic differences') lost the production its essential heart and soul.

When finally released over a year after it was made, the publicity machine was anxious to disassociate *Steaming* from the droplets of eroticism present in the original and now virtually wiped away except for streaks in some scenes involving Sarah Miles and Vanessa REDGAVE. Said the press kit reassuringly: 'Despite the implications, there is no lesbianism in the film.'

James **Steerforth** The headstrong, seductive benefactor of young DAVID COPPERFIELD who reappears later in the story to bring tragedy to some of the other people David loves. The writer is unspecific as to whether the relationship progressed into bed, but Dickens/Copperfield's simple romantic feelings for his school idol appear to become more muddied later on. These almost find voice when, after a bout of drinking and uproar with Steerforth and 'two very gay and lively fellows', the adult David (or DAISY as Steerforth calls him) wakes up the next morning scared that he has 'committed a thousand offences I had forgotten and which nothing could ever expiate'.

No adaptor has been game to fully take on Steerforth's strong sexual attraction for Davy, nor the implications of Dickens' statement that Emily – whom Steerforth seduces, 'ruins' and then casts aside – is David's alter ego. James Andrew HALL's adaptation for BBC1 in 1986 probably came closest by putting the man-boy (Jeremy Brudenell) securely in the Byronic mould: sensuous and cruel, possibly giving sexual favours to the repulsive headmaster Creakle in return for free rein over the staff and boys.

Other interpretations have included those of Hugh Williams in the 1935 film (the actor had some years before played the part of the seriously corrupted and then corrupting Julian in the London stage version of THE GREEN BAY TREE); Richard Bebb (1951 R); Anthony Tancred (1956 T); Barry Justice (1966 T); James Faulkner (1970 C/T); Nigel Anthony (1973/4 R); Anthony Andrews (1974 T); Andrew Wincott (1991 R).

Hesketh Pearson made no mention of Steerforth or Emily when he discussed the book in 1949 (R). Neither did Sir K. J. Fielding in his radio talk, *The Making of 'David Copperfield'*, two years later. However, two writers saw much significance in David's dark friend.

Said Pamela HANSFORD JOHNSON in *The Betrayal of Self in Fiction* (1949 R): 'To me, Steerforth has always seemed Dickens' most profound creation. He expresses more than any other character the nature of Dickens' own struggle. In the imaginative world of his novels, Dickens found release by worrying, by pitying, at last by idealizing the anti-bourgeois outlook, the irresponsible drifter, the alien DANDY – a figure his society rejected and with whom Dickens had nothing in common, save unspoken thoughts.'

John LEHMANN chose 'James Steerforth' as one of his *Favourite Characters* (1959 R), remarking that: 'He pursues any means of excitement that presents itself boldly to him ... consorts with sailors, lies dead with his head upon his arm.' The latter image, noted Lehmann, transports David back to his first ecstatic reverie, gazing at Steerforth in the moonlit dormitory: 'How often had I seen him in bed at school.'

Stein, Gertrude (1874–1946) American author who lived in Europe for many years, mostly with – in the words of *Variety*'s obituary – 'her secretary and constant companion, Alice B. TOKLAS'. Physically squat and bullish, she was portrayed as alert, quite droll, pampered and comfortable with her sexuality by Miriam MARGOLYES in GERTRUDE STEIN AND A COMPANION (1985 R); by Jan Mines on the television version (1986); by Linda Bassett in the deliberately non-factual *Waiting for the Moon* (1987

C/T); by Bernard Cribbens in *The Adventures of Picasso* (1978 C, opposite Wilfred Brambell).

She also featured, directly or in spirit, in *Is That You, Nancy?* (Aust 1991 R) in which she gives a dinner party for stateswomen who have fallen from power, and in A HORSE CALLED GERTRUDE STEIN (1990 R). In the latter, a radio programme about her and Alice provides the tinder for a family explosion when one of the diners calls Gertrude 'a dirty lesbian': 'So am I!' proclaims the daughter as her family proceed to talk louder and faster and clatter the cutlery.

Radio programmes about her life and work include *American Point of View* (1934: one of her rare broadcasts); *Gertrude Stein's Gertrude Stein* (1969); *Options* 'American Authors' (1987); KALEIDOSCOPE (1992) where her recent biographer, Diana Souhami, described the 40-year-long relationship with Alice as 'for all practical purposes, a marriage ... bonds of steel forged by sex ... A *very* sexual relationship bonded by food, sex and Alice's belief in Gertrude's genius'.

'When they came into a room everyone stared. But despite that, they loved each other. They were themselves, true to themselves,' Fiona (Jane Slavin) in *A Horse Called Gertrude Stein*.

Stephen/Steven Boy's name used by Radclyffe HALL in *The Well of Loneliness*, and doing duty for a variety of men-loving men since then: Steve Hagen (George Macready), the very personal business associate of Charles LAUGHTON in *The Big Clock* (1948 C); Stephen (Spencer Leigh), the adolescent simultaneously experiencing feelings for men and exploring pagan beliefs in *Penda's Fen* (1974 T); Stephen Piper (Paul Henley) coming to work in women's clothes in EVEN SOLOMON (1979 T); artist Stephen Grain (Ian Hogg) in *Very Like a Whale* (1980 T); white South African liberal Stephen (Michael Kitchen) coerced into sleeping with a member of the homophobic police force in A ROOM FOR THE WINTER (1981 T); Steven CARRINGTON (Al Corley/Jack

COLEMAN) in DYNASTY (1981–91 T); rascally ACCOUNTANT with a minority television company Steve Rideaux (Patrick Malahide) in VIDEOSTARS (1983 T); cottager Steve (Daniel Webb) in MORE LIVES THAN ONE (1984 T) encountered by the hero during a raid; snooty ANTIQUE DEALER Stephen (Francis Matthews) in *May We Borrow Your Husband?* (1986 T); handsome, sexy Steven (Joe Spano) all too soon murdered in *The Pride, the Passion* (Aust 1989 T); Steve (David Bonney) who is bashed on the beach and has to live with the repercussions, physical and emotional, after just one NIGHT OUT (1990 C/T); Stephen Durrant (Marc Murphy), unbalanced schoolboy whose affair with a master has to be kept quiet, no matter what the cost, in *Death Drop* (1992 R).

Quite frequently encountered non-gay men of this name include gullible, far to the Left Steve (Tim Pigott-Smith) in STRUGGLE (1983 T); Stephen Daker (Peter Davison), bewildered young university doctor in A VERY PECULIAR PRACTICE (1986 & 1988 T); Stephen Crowe (David Hayman) in *Underbelly* (1992 T); and the most comprehensive case of male cosmetic surgery in the world: Steve Austin (Lee Majors), the American astronaut who is rebuilt from top to toe after a training accident, equipped with bionic arm, eye and legs, at a cost of $6 million (*The Six Million Dollar Man* 1973–8 T).

Three female ones: Steve (Mara Corday) a scientist on the track of the giant marauding *Tarantula* (1955 C); bouncy, almost flying nun Sister Steve in *The Father Dowling Mysteries* (1989–90 T); Steve Temple, wife, helpmate and exemplar of 'women's intuition', mainly played by Marjorie Westbury throughout the PAUL TEMPLE radio series, and by Ros Drinkwater on television (1969–71).

Stephens, Robert (1931–) English actor, not afraid to tackle roles of dissipation and decadence: the vulgarian boyfriend and Jo's potential stepfather in A TASTE OF HONEY (1961 C); the detective, suspected of unnatural vice with Dr Watson in *The Private Life of Sherlock* HOLMES (1970 C); 'The Confirmed Bachelor' in *Vienna 1900* (1975 T); Jasper Bentwick in *Eustace and Hilda* (1977 T); 'CONFIRMED BACHELOR' Lindsay in *Studio* (1983 T); wizard Abner Brown in *Box of Delights* (1984 T); The trendy bishop in *Hell's Bells* (1986 T); as *The False* DIAGHILEV (1988 R); Vincent – 'a dried-up old QUEEN ... a vampire' – in THE FRUIT MACHINE (1988 C); etc.

Steptoe and Son (UK 1964–73 T)
Mainly duologues between rag and bone men, father and son (Wilfred Brambell and Harry H. Corbett), lots of snarling, sulking, protestations of devotion, hasty quarrels, jealousy, envy, misunderstandings, revelry, conniving, support – in a word love or in two: mutual dependence. Among the more obviously queer episodes: 'Come Dancing' (1970) where the milkman catches Albert teaching Harold the TANGO. The first of two film versions (1972) found Dad briefly entranced by a drag artist (Perri St Clair).
W: Ray Galton and Alan Simpson; D: Duncan Wood; BBC1; 30 mins. (Also BBC Radio 4 versions of the scripts during the mid- to late 1970s.)

Alert and witty intimacy perfectly suited to television and radio, but broadened and diluted on the big screen. 'Arold never did leave his old dad.

stereotypes A cluster of archetypal characters, composed of a few very crude characteristics, which have successfully penetrated and saturated much public thinking about homosexuality. These include the frustrated, immature and sexually indiscriminate QUEEN; the hard, bellicose, cropped-haired woman who dresses in tweeds or BOILER SUITS; the lonely young man unsure of his sexuality, cured by the right girl; the sophisticated, glamorous predatory lesbian. The word 'stereotype' was first noted in this context in the Michael Schofield discussion on MALE HOMOSEXUALS in 1965: 'Not all of them are like the stereotype of a homosexual ... the PANSY.'

During the 1970s (when SISTER GEORGE and MR HUMPHRIES were seen as representatives of lesbians and gays by many people) some attempts were made to challenge the lazy assumption of a LISP, a jutting bottom or a strutting gait to personify homosexuals. John Chesterman and a colleague from the Gay Liberation Front deplored (on *Late Night Lineup*) the swishing of a BARMAN in a 1972 BBC2 play called UNDER THE AGE. However, the *Church Times* (30.3.72) was enraged that 'two real homosexuals were protesting that the principal characters [in a play] bore no resemblance to reality. It all seemed to be an exercise in self-indulgence by people, heterosexual or homosexual, who should be kept as far away from TV drama as possible.'

Great efforts were made both in 1970s documentaries and in drama to 'avoid' stereotypes, to show 'ordinary', 'normal' gay people. But there were writers who felt that stereotypes had their place. Jeremy SEABROOK, who had presented one – Howard (James Laurenson) – as a squeaking, sex-mad tourist holed up in an African airport while terrorist bullets fly around and about (in a 1975 play *Children of the Sun*) told *Gay News* in 1976: 'To be able to satirize and caricature, then we've also got to be able to satirize and caricature gays. We can't be reverential about being gay because, you know, part of integration is being able to accept as many pictures of people as possible.'

Howard SCHUMAN, who definitely included caricature and satire in his two ROCK FOLLIES series, took pains to create fully textured leading characters, including the three women rock musicians and the gay couple. In a 1977 *Gay News* interview he said: 'I find the treatment of gay people in British situation comedy a true obscenity. It's one of the things I most hate – John INMAN and that school. Even Kenneth WILLIAMS whom I think is a genius. I simply don't know why it's tolerated. Gay resistance is really overdue on a whole

host of levels. How can one sit there and listen to this litany of anti-gay JOKES?'

The end of the 1970s saw a number of complaints registered by lesbians and gays against cinema, television and radio's continued use of shop-worn CLICHÉS that were doing nothing to enlighten people about a persecuted and mainly hidden group of people. Usually, the protests were seen as humourless and an interference with traditional family fun or dramatic licence. 'I'm surprised that you take Steve Wright's jokey characters so seriously as you suggest, homosexuals come in all sorts of shapes and sizes and are surely all fair game for the odd harmless humourous send-up – like fat women, mothers-in-law etc,' said Derek Chinnery, Controller of BBC Radio 1, to Richard Desmond of CHE about *Steve Wright in the Afternoon* (who regularly impersonated a lisping HAIRDRESSER), quoted in *Gay News* 258.

The steady stream of cut-outs induced strong antipathy in many lesbians and gay people, especially those in the process of establishing a self- and group identity.

Chris told Roger Baker in SPEAK FOR YOURSELF (1974 T): 'When you're young and discovering that you're gay, you see homosexuals portrayed as swishy, handbang-swinging individuals who adopt a caricatured effeminate manner.'

'I got these weird impressions from television that lesbians have muscles and thick eyebrows,' said Rose as she plays bar billiards in the documentary VERONICA 4 ROSE (1983 T).

Hanif Kureishi (in his essay 'The Rainbow Sign' which prefaced the published script of MY BEAUTIFUL LAUNDRETTE, 1986) expressed many of the same frustrations and revulsions from another perspective: 'Television comics used Pakistanis as the butt of their humour. Their jokes were highly political: they contributed a way of seeing the whole. The ... reduction of racial hatred to a joke did two things: it expressed a collective view which was sanctioned by its being on the BBC, and it was a celebration of contempt in millions of living rooms in England. I was afraid to watch TV because it was too embarrassing, too degrading.'

The relative increase in more varied homosexual representations during the 1980s has led to a more lighthearted tolerance of stereotypes among some people, and a round of applause for those like Julian CLARY who take the expected attitudes and mannerisms and make of them something challenging and elegant. However, others still regard stereotypes as damaging, trivializing and inciting sources of misinformation. Rose Marie (Barbara Flynn) is one. Her male colleague in A VERY PECULIAR PRACTICE (1986 T) can't work out whether she, an avowed lesbian FEMINIST, is making a pass or not, and becomes very flustered. She has no patience with his confusion: 'You can't reconcile me with the stereotype of a lesbian, can you?'

(The BBC's latest charter of 1989 specifically states that 'Stereotypes must be avoided'.)

Sticky Moments/Sticky Moments on Tour with Julian Clary (UK 1989–91 T) A quiz master who causes heterosexuals to quake, is 'not fussy about the answers' and forces contestants to paint in 60 seconds, make paper Concordes, act in *Madame Butterfly*, cram prawn crackers, cake or popcorn into their mouths – all in the cause of gay liberation, sorry, entertainment. P: Toni Yardley; D: John Henderson; Channel 4; 45 mins.

Sample exchange:

> Julian CLARY: 'What sticky substance do all American girls have stuck to their teeth?'
> Contestant: 'Chewing gum.'
> J.C.: '*Wrong.* Condoms!'

Adam Fulton wrote in the *Sydney Morning Herald* (28.8.92):

> Julian Clary is a must-see. Watching this brutally sharp wit belittle and verbally maul players ... is immeasurably amusing and, in spots, hilarious. Clary looks harmless enough, prettily preserved face with lipstick, striking camp attitudes, effeminate English brogue, total

composure. But once his sardonic tongue is loosed, faces redden and squirming embarrassment ensues...

The barrage of swipes and quips continues as Clary unorthodoxly runs the show, awarding points at whim while the sitting duck players (six start, one wins) answer silly or sometimes libertine questions, and [are] subject to laughable tests of dexterity like bouncing big balls to imitate kangaroos.

(The idea of a tacky, overblown, invasive and stupid game show was taken a couple of steps further by Barry HUMPHRIES in *Dame Edna's Neighbourhood Watch* in 1992.)

stiletto heels Dominatrices and drag queens give their expert opinions on these shoes for women that taper off into near infinity in *Dressed to Thrill* (1990 T): 'They make you taller, your bum sticks out and you look far more voluptuous and sexy.' Supposedly first created by Salvatore Ferragamo for his 1958 court shoes at a 45 per cent angle (with 13-cm heels) for Marilyn MONROE (and worn in SOME LIKE IT HOT), but noted earlier showing off the ankles of Zizi Jeanmaire in *Anything Goes* (1955 C), Jayne Mansfield in *The Girl Can't Help It* (1956 C), and Lauren Bacall in *Designing Woman* (1957 C). On British television they were worn for deliberately erotic effect by the seemingly unfaithful wife (Vivien Merchant) in *The Lover* (1963 T). More recent examples of these spine misaligning creations: the TRANSVESTITE stalker in DRESSED TO KILL (1980 C); Shannen Doherty in *Heathers* (1989 C); Connie Booth in *For the Greater Good* (1991 T); Barbra STREISAND as Susan Lowenstein in THE PRINCE OF TIDES (1992 C); and, of course, Victoria Abril in HIGH HEELS (1991 C).

Stiller, Mauritz (1883–1928) Finnish-born director who worked mostly in Sweden, discoverer of Greta GARBO (in *Gosta Berling's Saga* 1922), maker of sexy comedies (*Love and Journalism* 1916; *Erotikon* 1920), historical dramas (*Sir Arne's Treasure* 1919), and what is now regarded as the 'first gay film', the long-lost *The Wings* from 1916. His ill-fated trip to Hollywood with Garbo was fancifully related in MOVIOLA 'The Silent Lovers' (1980 T).

Stock, Nigel (1919–1986) English actor who played the blackmailers' go-between in VICTIM (1961 C). He successful managed to mix weasels with lions throughout a career that began as a naval cadet with one line in *Sons of the Sea* (1939 C) and included a crook in *Brighton Rock* (1947 C); one of *The Dam Busters* (1955 C); a stuffy businessman in DANGEROUS CORNER (1957 T); the husband bewildered by his wife's soul-bonding with a young man in THE UNQUIET SPIRIT (1960 T); Edgar, the self-pitying son in *Where the Difference Begins* (1961 T); a Truman CAPOTE hero in *Answered Prayers* (1961 T); a suburban father trying a fling with Wendy Craig in *Late Summer Affair* (1962 T); Vladimir in WAITING FOR GODOT (1962 R); Dr Watson in *Sherlock* HOLMES (1965 & 1968 T); Owens in the medical soap *The Doctors* (1970s T); Roddy Martindale, a possible 'mole' in TINKER, TAILOR, SOLDIER, SPY (1979 T); Pandarus in *Troilus and Cressida* (1980 R); Winston Churchill in *The Wilderness Years* (1981 T); 'Tiger' Timms in *Scouting for Boys* (1984 R); Pilate in *The Image of God* (1986 R); a member of the Chorus in *Oedipus the King* (1986 T); Iwakichi, an old man obsessed with his beautiful wife in MISHIMA's *The Damask Drum* (1986 R).

Stonewall Rebellion The 3-day battle waged between TRANSVESTITES, gays, lesbians and street people against the police around the Stonewall Inn, a drag BAR off Sheridan Square in Greenwich Village in June 1969. After the victory (the police withdrew and stopped harassing people in the bar), 'gay liberation' groups began organizing, marching, shouting and zapping.

Stonewall was the lighting of the blue touch paper for an international homosexual rights movement after many long years of uncoordinated – and generally unpublicized – campaigns, lobbying, publishing and social/support groupings. No film footage of the event appears to have been taken, only still photographs – which are regularly featured in documentaries about the birth of the new consciousness and demand for equality.

'On June 27, 1969, a chorus line of drag queens can-canned into New York's Sheridan Square, high-kicking their way into a two-day battle with police. The Stonewall Riots marked the beginning of the Gay Decades, an astonishing twenty-plus-year flowering of gay culture that would change America forever' (back cover blurb for Leigh W. Rutledge, *The Gay Decades*, 1992).

'For your information, if it wasn't for those militant drag queens, we wouldn't have been able to *be* ourselves in that bar last night. Don't forget, they are the ones that started the Stonewall Riots back in 1969, and the entire gay rights movement. Many a press-on nail and spiked heel were broken so that you can have the freedoms that you are taking for granted,' Bryan (Todd Tites) upbraiding Brian (Terry Curry) who is criticizing militant drag queens who demand 'that we all come out of the closet and force ourselves on society' in TOGETHER ALONE (1991 C).

stop messin' about Downtrodden, soppy, daft, daffy, flirtatious: Kenneth WILLIAMS' voice could subtly vary this 3-word catchphrase to suit whatever degree of idiotic 'pest' he was playing in HANCOCK'S HALF HOUR (1954–8 R). In 'The Tax Demand' (1958) he's an Inland Revenue officer whose gormless manner leads Hancock to become too familiar, even sitting on his lap. At this point, with studio audience hysteria rising, Williams looses his famous injunction.

When Kenneth HORNE died suddenly in 1969, the remaining scripts were broadcast, with announcer Douglas SMITH replacing Kenneth Horne as straight man, under the title *Stop Messin' About*. Kenneth Williams retained the phrase, with increasing intimations of illicit sex, in his repertoire, together with his tics, squeals, shrieks and ferociously enunciated roars. In 1987, only months before the actor's death, Peter Cook appeared on *Saturday Night Clive* (T) mocking the government's 'SAFE SEX' campaign. Cook thought the televison ads would have no effect whatsoever on people's sexual behaviour: 'You might as well have Ken Williams saying "stop messin' about".'

Stop the Church (US 1990 V) The 16 December 1989 protest against Cardinal O'Connor and the precepts of the Catholic Church as they affect lesbians and gays and inhibit the flow of information about SAFE SEX. Members of the public, members of the congregation at St Patrick's Cathedral, New York, and members of ACT UP say their pieces on the day the cathedral was 'stormed'. A pin to prise open a walnut; a controversial action which tried – in a bullish way – to get to the heart of matters of concern.
P/D: Robert Hilfery; P: A Robert Hilfery Inquisition; Altar Ego Productions; 24 mins.

Story of a Girl (UK 1965 R) 'If your father wants you to be a boy and you don't like it much, you may find your life is extremely complicated.' Carol Burns (Eileen Atkins), brought up as a boy, is attracted to a gay man, Bruce (Douglas Storm), whom she beats up when he rejects her sexually.
W: Pauline Spender; P: R. D. Smith; 13.7.64; BBC Home Service; 45 mins.

It was a mishmash: reminiscent of A TASTE OF HONEY, without the humour. Bruce would appear to be the perfect partner for Carol who can't bear being 'mauled about and messed up' by men. But her feelings get the better of her and he can't respond: 'It makes me sick ... being slobbered over by a soppy girl ... You make me sick.' He is attracted to her because of her boyishness. When she comes on to him as a woman, he shouts: 'Why did you have to be a girl?'

Stout-Hearted Men Rousing male chorus from 1928 operetta *The New*

Moon (lyrics by Oscar Hammerstein II, music by Sigmund Romberg). Sung by Nelson Eddy and pals in the 1940 film, it was resurrected to mock a Tory Prime Minister (who appeard to sing it falsetto on THE MORECAMBE AND WISE SHOW in the early 1970s), and by the San Francisco Gay Men's Chorus who gave its words added force on ARENA 'Armistead Maupin Is a Name I Dreamt Up' (1992 T).

Strachey, [Giles] Lytton (1880–1932) English biographer and member of the BLOOMSBURY GROUP. His obsessive relationship with Dora CARRINGTON and their joint infatuation with Ralph Partridge were detailed in THE SOUTH BANK SHOW 'No Need to Lie' (1980 T, with Edward Petherbridge) and *Nymphs and Shepherds, Come Away* (1985 R, with Jack Shepherd). Jonathan Cecil played him in a piping cameo in *Mad Jack* (about Siegfried SASSOON, 1970 T). Michael Holroyd assessed Strachey's contribution to the art of biography (having written Strachey's) and partially described the personal dynamics of the man (played by Daniel MASSEY) in *Lytton Strachey* (1980 R).

straight The opposite of BENT, and used in the context of fine, upstanding and true, until its drug-free and then heterosexual flavouring in the 1960s and 1970s. However, it may have had gay connotations previous to this time. The unmarried, fortysomething 'J. Davidson' described as *A Man in Domestic Service* told listeners (in 1936): 'Let men come in. It's a good life, but show manliness. Be calm, be firm, be straight.'

'Is he straight, Inspector?' Paul TEMPLE grimly asks in relation to a suspect in *The Vandyke Affair* (1950 R); 'If by that you mean what I think you mean,' replies the policeman with moustache-twiddling gravity, 'then the answer is...' PC George Dixon described Duffy CLAYTON (Harold SCOTT) as 'pretty straight' in DIXON OF DOCK GREEN 'The Salvation of Duffy' (1958 T).

Alan WHICKER'S 1973 investigation into American (really Californian) gay life gave 'straight' (as in heterosexual) its first mass audience airing. Then came a *Police Story* episode 'The Ripper' (1974 T) which brought two meanings into alignment: 'He's a straight upstanding heterosexual.' Almost simultaneously, in an English prison context, Fletcher (Ronnie Barker) tells LUKEWARM (Christopher Biggins) that he wishes he'd had a mother like him: 'I might have gone straight'; 'Or bent,' simpers his companion, plonking a flabby hand on the older man's knee (*Porridge* 'The Hustler' 1974 T). After having his faults and self-satisfactions catalogued in WEDNESDAY LOVE (1975 T) Gordon (Nikolas Simmonds) turns round and tells his flatmate Chris (Simon Rouse): 'At least *I'm* straight.' A young openly gay man living in a commune (John McAndrew) tells the hero of *Badger by Owl-Light* (1975 R) rather regretfully and somewhat ambiguously: 'They're all straight here. No matter how hard they try.' Rock singer Q (Rula Lenska) compliments her gay manager Harry (Derek Thompson) in ROCK FOLLIES OF '77 (1977 T): 'Three years [in a relationship] is a lot longer than most straight people manage'; they then go to bed together.

The word is now quite commonly used in the titles of gay-themed plays and series such as *Play It Straight* (1983 R), 'Straight and Narrow' (*Trapper John* 1982 T) and 'Scared Straight' (THE GOLDEN GIRLS 1988 T; *Mama's Boy* 1987 T). The host of *Tonight with Jonathan Ross* described a male guest as being 'as straight as they come' in February 1992, while Charles (Jim Carter), father of Gail in the *Runaway* (1992 R), is cognizant of the three major meanings of the word as it applies to people: 'I mean "straight" as in honest.'

Straker, Peter (194?–) British-based actor, dancer and singer who appeared on stage in *Hair* and – billed simply as 'Straker' – as the androgynous 'Jo' in *Girl Stroke Boy* (1971 C). His striking face and sensual voice have made his parts few and far between: BALLET DANCER Adrian in *Village Hall* 'Dancing

in the Dark' (1974 T); a flamboyante in *Censored Scenes from King Kong* (1974 T, which was banned by the BBC); PUCK in *A Midsummer Night's Dream* (1983 R); a rag trade type in *Connie* (1984 T); singing and dancing in *Blues in the Night* (1987 T); a drug dealer in *The Orchid House* (1991 T); etc. The nearest Peter Straker has ever come to a television showcase was *If This Was the Last Song* (1970) in which for 10 minutes (after midnight in the Thames area only) he commented on songs 'that reflect aspects of today's modern outlook on life, love, self-fulfillment, personal relationships and "LIVE AND LET LIVE".'

strange bedfellows A description frequently used in television comedy series like THREE'S COMPANY (1977) and THE GOLDEN GIRLS (1988), sometimes to indicate plots in which one man ends up ('innocently') under the sheets with another. In the Rock HUDSON–Gina Lollobrigida comedy, *Strange Bedfellows* (1964 C), Rock is in bed ('innocently') with Edward Judd. Morris HARDACRE (James Saxon) begins to think war can't be so bad when he finds himself in the back of a German truck, prison camp bound with his long-unrequited love, Matthew Fairchild, in *Brass* 'Their Finest Half Hour' (1990 T): 'War makes strange bedfellows, Matt'; unfortunately for Morris, they are rescued by the resistance.

Strangers on a Train (US 1951 C) A criss-cross murder (wife for father) is planned by the increasingly deranged Bruno (Robert Walker). He kills for Guy (Farley Granger), but the latter refuses to complete his part of the 'bargain'.
W: Raymond Chandler and Czenzi Ormonde from the novel by Patricia HIGHSMITH; P/D: Alfred HITCHCOCK; 101 mins.

One of the postwar screen's first queers ('But Guy, I *like* you'), Bruno was an especially sinister threat because he and Guy are similar in age, social backgrounds and physical features. And it is the gay who does what the heterosexual has been longing to do: rid himself of his wife.

Hitchcock's psychologically acute direction is at one with Robert Walker's bristling delivery of the wittily ingratiating dialogue. Walker provides the perfect portrait of infantilism and megalomania, given an extra depth by the sexual nuances and perceptive dressing of the man who has no doubt about the double meaning of the yacht he and his mother vacationed on, the *Fairy Princess*. Bruno Anthony is, in his own estimation, 'a very clever fellow'.

'Walker was excellent,' said Patricia Highsmith in *Sight and Sound* (Autumn 1988). 'He had elegance and humour and the proper fondness for his mother.' She felt the actor would have made a good Tom Ripley, her amoral drifter later played by Alain Delon.

The story was remade heterosexually as *Once You Kiss a Stranger* (1969 T) with Carol Lynley as the psychopath, and homosexually with Maureen O'-BRIEN as a father-abused, pathologically clinging young woman in REMAINING STRANGERS (1986 R). *Throw Momma from the Train* (1987 C) was the comedy version with Danny DeVito and Billy CRYSTAL.

(In the 1950 novel, Guy *does* kill Bruno's hated father and Bruno – Charles Anthony Bruno – dies by throwing himself off a boat rather than being crushed by an out-of-control carousel. Only the opening scene aboard the train follows Highsmith's narrative.)

Stratton, John (1925–) English actor adept at playing mousey men. Hardly off televison in the 1950s, he contributed two arresting studies in gay masochism: Arthur in WANTED: SINGLE GENTLEMEN (1967 T) and Paul Curtis in A SUPERSTITION (1977 T).

C: a scientist in *The Small Back Room* (1948); a saboteur in *Seven Days to Noon* (1950); naval officer in *The Cruel Sea* (1953); policeman in *The Long Arm* (1956); survivor of an ocean liner sinking in *Seven Waves Away* (1957); a member of Jayne Mansfield's gang in *The Challenge* (1960); etc.

T: Roman spy in *Coriolanus* (1948); one of the sons in *Death of a Salesman* (1957); a meek Welsh shopkeeper who is a medium in *Trespass* (1958); a villain in *The Frog* (1958); creepy as Paul in *Julie's Gone* (1966); *The Pallisers* (1975); *The Good Companions* (1980); *The Tale of Beatrix Potter* (1981); *My Cousin Rachel* (1985); etc.

Della **Street** Perry Mason's ever-diligent, ever-fond secretary played in the cinema (1934–6) by Margaret Lindsay, and on television (on and off since 1957) with cool precision by Barbara Hale. Back in the 1930s, the film Della married Perry (in *The Case of the Curious Bride*). On television it's been quite a different story: the longest non-courtship, non-consummation, non-romance between BACHELOR and SPINSTER in the history of popular culture. The question the world is still asking is: why have they remained 'just friends' for seven decades? Neither Raymond Burr nor Barbara Hale will hazard a guess, merely making teasing remarks in interviews and pointing out that Perry and Della were not sweethearts in the Erle Stanley Gardner novels (but omitting to say that the writer, a lawyer, *did* marry the secretary upon whom Della was based).

When the PERRY MASON series first began, Della hardly bothered to bank her sexual fires, at least within the tight restrictions then in place. Lying across her boss's desk, offering to make him dinner, working extra late at the office, massaging him, nursing him when he has a cold: 'I'm a *very* handy girl to have around,' she intones with a meaningful look. No matter what she did, Perry, always appreciative and always the gentleman, seemed impervious. On the few occasions when his guard did drop and he waxed lyrical it was because he was thinking about his favourite subject after the law: his stomach. In one 1958 episode he deflected his secretary's ardour by rhapsodizing about 'rack of lamb ... Lyonnaise potatoes ... and crêpes Suzette'.

The reason for Perry's indifference to

the more abandoned side of his utterly faultless secretary may possibly be found in *The Case of the Caretaker's Cat*. In this 1959 story he and his private detective colleague and friend, Paul DRAKE (William Hopper), are discovered dining together. Smoochy music is playing and the other diners are noticeably male. 'All we need is a rumour to get things going,' teases Perry in his murmurous voice.

By 1961 Della has become a cross between a cipher and a mannequin. Perry's casual attitude is now paralleled by the scriptwriters'. 'Right away, Perry' is her sole contribution to *The Case of the Roving River*, and in *The Case of the Bizarre Bequest* she again has but one line. A few episodes later, she is rendered totally speechless and functions only by getting up from her seat and walking in front of the camera and, in one cherishable scene coming slightly out of character, shooting a scathing look at the director beyond. The actress was still receiving second billing for what had become a walk-on.

She was slightly more stretched the following year. The gods seem to be smiling on her in *The Case of the Borrowed Baby* when she and Perry (working late as always) discover a baby in their office. Della takes it home and Paul helps her care for it, while Perry looks on with a smirk. For a while it appears that all four will live together, but the real mother comes forward. Paul and Perry and Della return to their separate homes. Always civilized, always companionable and always socializing together (with no romantic involvement suggested with each other or with anybody else), this has to be one of the most unusual of television's adult 'families'.

There are a few hints that Della may be equally interested in women. The only friends she has (accused of murder usually) are women at least 10 years younger than herself. And, with that sandpapery voice and 'I've seen it all' air, she could well be giving out vibrations to the young heiress, cleared – thanks to the peerless Perry – of murder in *The Case of the Lonely Eloper* (1962 T). The client proceeds to give tactile

thanks to 'the people who helped me' – namely Perry, Paul and Della. A kiss for Perry on the cheek, one for Paul in the same area. Saving the best up for last, she is about to give Della one too. But she – or the watchful censor – thinks better of it and removes herself from Della's expectant gaze.

(Barbara Hale won a best supporting actress EMMY for her work during the 1958–9 season, and she continued with her good-natured, cool and collected self-effacement until 1966, returning 19 years later for the *Perry Mason* specials which average two a year. These films usually include at least one reference to the leading pair's unmarried states. At a conservative reckoning, Perry Mason is now in his mid-seventies while Della Street is some five years his junior.)

See also THINGS ARE SELDOM WHAT THEY SEEM.

Street-Porter, Janet [Bull] (1946–)
English journalist, pundit and garrulous, irritating, daring and effective presenter–producer of innovative and imaginative television (THE LONDON WEEKEND SHOW 1977–8; *Twentieth Century Box* 1980–2). From 1988 she has been the provider of intelligent and relevant programmes for young people of all kinds (eg *Def II, 100%, Reportage* and *Extra*) in her role as editor of the BBC's Youth Programming Unit.

Seemingly always in an ecstasy of enthusiasm and overdrive, she has been consistently portrayed, with a braying Cockney accent, as a shrieking trendoid on *Spitting Image* and other satirical shows. Among her other appearances: THE SIX O'CLOCK SHOW (1983 T, making adverse comments about men wearing make-up); *After Midnight* (1983–4 T, with Auberon WAUGH); *Start the Week* (1985 R); *The Look* (1992 T). She was given the third degree by teenagers in OPEN TO QUESTION (1991 T) and had to face an old school report in *Could Do Better* (1987 R). She was the producer of the alternative chat show *The Full Wax* (1990–1 T).

The Streets of San Francisco 'A Good

Cop, But...' (US 1977 T) 'A police-man, is shot dead. The killing is wit-nessed by another officer, Dave Lam-bert (Barry Primus), but he has already lied about being homosexual. Could be lying bout the murder as well?' (Syn-opsis).

W: Charles Larson; P: William Robert Yates; D: Harry Falk; ABC; 60 mins.

This episode of the long-running (1972–7) series starring Michael Doug-las and Karl Malden effectively, if too patly, portrays the dilemma of the clos-eted as against the openly gay cop: the unhelpful attitude of his colleagues, the day-to-day sexism (ogling women, making dirty jokes), and the vulner-ability to BLACKMAIL. Robert Walden (later to play one of the BROTHERS) con-tributes an effective performance as Lambert's partner who feels especially betrayed by his revelation because he had hoped Lambert would marry his sister.

(The series, remarkable for one shot on location in one of the world's most teemingly gay cities, managed to encounter no substantial homosexual characters, good or bad, in five years, save for a psychotic drag queen (John Davidson) – being driven to murder by his hated female side – in 'Mask of Death' in 1974.)

Streisand, Barbra [Barbara] (1942–   )
American actress, singer, producer and director who began her career perform-ing in Manhattan gay BARS. A woman of sensational talent, she can be arresting and affecting (*Funny Girl*; FUNNY LADY; YENTL; her 1960s TV specials) or over-arching and offputting (*The Way We Were*; *A Star is Born*; THE PRINCE OF TIDES). After a lot of thought (first optioning the work in 1986) she is plan-ning to direct and star in Larry KRAMER's *The Normal Heart* (1993–4 C).

'Very popular among the Jews and homosexuals. In fact, Jewish homosex-uals, when the combination arises, are said to faint at the mention of her name,' one of the inquisitors during a fantasy sequence from Craig Warner's play

Figure with Meat (1991 R). She is accused of 'blasphemy, Jewry and taking breaths in all the wrong places'.

Strictly Ballroom (Aust 1992 C) A young dancer (Paul Mercurio) listens to his own heart rather than to the dictates of tradition or vested interest when he prepares for a competition with a shy, frumpy new partner (Tara Morrice).

W: Andrew Bovell, Baz Luhrmann and Craig Pearce; P: Tristan Miall; D: Baz Luhrmann; 94 mins.

Full of larger-than-life characters (including one gay-seeming STEREO-TYPE played with grace and favour by Peter Whitford), this is an entertain-ment of beauty, spirit and pulsating rhythm, whose message is that individ-uals can – and should – dance their own steps. The secret is not to live in fear because 'a life lived in fear is a life half lived'. This transcendence of human trepidation, prejudice and conservatism – without threatening those in the com-munity who wish to move in ensemble – through the magic of love and dance made *Strictly Ballroom* vastly popular all over the world. Like *Ghost* (1990) it's a modern fairy tale: moral but non-judge-mental, decent but not twee, black and white but with myriad other colours, and comfortingly ambiguous. Like *Ghost*, *Ballroom* struck an immediate chord with gays: *Capital Gay* readers voted it their film of 1992.

striped shirts Indicative of shading dealing, selfishness, loose living and often effeminacy.

US: Edward G. Robinson as gangster Rico known as LITTLE CAESAR (1930 C) wears a silk one while declaring that there's 'nothing soft about me, nothing yellow', and of his 'boys' he says proudly that 'They're 100 per cent all right' but the camera reveals that two of them are wearing shirts almost identical to his; the odiously unfeeling Bruno (Ralf Har-olde), prison commandant and hangman in *Safe in Hell* (1931 C), is attired in EARRING and striped shirt; someone in *Casbah* (1948 C) remarks that Carlo (Douglas Dick) cannot be trusted because he wears 'a *striped* silk shirt'; William Bendix as the vulgar American in London in *The Rough and the Smooth* (with check tie and matching waistcoat, 1959 C); the very tall, beefy but noticeably unaffianced Paul DRAKE (William Hopper) fetchingly wore one at the end of a 1961 PERRY MASON episode without prompting a slighting remark, but one was never again part of his wardrobe; one of the satire merchants in the Stateside THAT WAS THE WEEK THAT WAS, Elliott Reed, was a noticeable devotee of vertical stripes; gruff cop Jake (Walter Matthau) was similarly togged up in a couple of scenes in *The Laughing Policeman/Investigation of a Murder* (1974 C). With such a 'craggy' actor fronting up in stripes, the 'effete' taboo was broken and now these garments can be seen in all manner of (usually urban) situations: L.A. LAW (Becker played by Corbin Bersen, 1986– T); *Kojak* 'Ariana' (Telly Savalas, 1989 T); daytime soaps like *The Bold and the Beautiful*; *The Equalizer* (Edward Woodward, 1986–7 T); *Tucker: The Man and His Dream* (Jeff Brides, 1988 C); NORTHERN EXPOSURE (Rob Morrow, 1990– T); THE PRINCE OF TIDES (Nick Nolte, 1991 C); *The Player* (Tim Robbins as Griffin Mill, 1992 C); and by 'anchor men' like Bryant Grumbel. A long way from queer gangsters and the casbah.

UK: set in the early 1990s, *Carnival* (1946 C) had as its romantic hero an ARTIST, Maurice Avery (Michael Wilding) who parallels the reckless, feckless ways of the heroine's father (though not his alcoholism). Should she (Ginny Pearl, played by Sally Gray) marry the 'selfish pampered weakling' with the soft face and the striped shirting or the nice, dull Christian man (Bernard Miles) who wears plain white next to his vest? In *Once a Jolly Swagman* (1948 C, but partly set in the 1930s) arrogant and ambitious speedway star Bill Fox (Dirk BOGARDE) is shown mellowing and maturing. This is mainly due to some hard knocks and the love of a good woman, and partly perhaps due to his abandonment of shirts with stripes (the expanding width of which gives notice to

his increasing sexual abandon). This cleansing process ends with marriage and the steady wearing of white shirts.

First sighted in postwar Britain on the backs of 'spivs' and 'wide boys' and queer eccentrics like George Crumb (Charles HAWTREY) who goes off to live with Kenneth More at the end of *Brandy for the Parson* (1952 C), striped shirts began to creep in for the fashion-conscious male at the beginning of the 1960s. In VICTIM (1961 C) barrister Melville Farr's (Dirk Bogarde) link with homosexuality is clearly signalled from his first appearance: the pinky ring and the narrowly striped shirt cuff, endorsed in a subsequent scene in a car with firmer attention paid to the shirt front, connecting with but not corresponding to those worn by the gay couple, P.H. (Hilton EDWARDS) and Mickey (David Evans), in the PUB scenes. Alan BADEL as David Neville also wears one in his first scene in *Children of the Damned* (1964 C) though his (BISEXUAL?) lover (Ian Hendry) does not. By this time these articles of clothing were fast moving into the (upper-middle-class) mainstream after they had been modelled almost nightly by sophisticated television presenter Kenneth Allsop on TONIGHT from 1961 (raffishly but elegantly setting off his razor-cur hairstyle) and by dandified sleuth John Steed (Patrick Macnee) in *The Avengers* (1960–8 T). Their ultimate acceptability for intellectuals of all hues came 12 years later when Dr Jacob BRONOWSKI made them comfy when worn with a black leather jacket in THE ASCENT OF MAN.

Striped shirts are now worn by a wide range of middle-class characters in their thirties and forties: recently the attractive cad (and rapist) Willmott-Brown (William Boye), leader of the YUPPIE invasion in EASTENDERS (1987–9 T); Peter Balliol (Martin Shaw), the MP involved in a raid on a gay BAR in *For the Greater Good* (1991 T); James FOX as a top wartime plastic surgeon (with glasses and BOW-TIE) in *A Fine Hero* (1991 T); NURSE Charlie Fairhead (Derek Thompson) in CASUALTY (1993 T); Laurence (Nigel Planer), the web-footed but well meaning French teacher in *Bonjour la Classe* (1993 T).

Strip Jack Naked (1) The novel by John Hampson about the love of two brothers, freely adapted by David TURNER as *Now More Than Ever* (1961 R) and then SUMMER, AUTUMN, WINTER, SPRING (1961 T; 1962 R).
(2) The 1974 radio play by Susan Hill about an ailing recluse (Ian RICHARDSON) looked after by Randall (Dinsdale Landen) and shaken out of his automatic existence by a visit from his estranged wife Diana (Siân Phillips) who acquaints him with the fact that Randall loves him.
(3) The subtitle of Ron PECK's NIGHTHAWKS 2 (1990 C).

strippers/striptease artists The male variety is now as popular as the female, being much sought after by gay BARS and 'hen parties', as well as drawing crowds to theatres where they perform in lavishly choreographed and (un)dressed shows.

In the UK the earliest example (chastely restricted to radio and rather corpulent) was Neddy Seagoon (Harry Secombe) in the title role of THE GOON SHOW 'I Was a Male Fan Dancer' (1952). Then a long gap until a nicely brought up young man of good breeding, Carlton Campbell alia 'The Sultan of Desire' (Joseph Blatchley), was prevailed upon by at least four young women in his audience in *A Passage to Inverness* (1977 T) to 'Get them off!' In America: hard-up actor (Gregory Harrison) in *For Ladies Only* (1981 T); student Rich (Christopher Atkins) in *A Night in Heaven* (1983 C); Larry (Ken Olandt), a schoolboy who moonlights – until his mother, come to see the saucy show, finds him out – in *Summer School* (1987 C); undercover cop (Thomas Calabro) provided with 'little cover and maximum exposure' in *Ladykillers* (1988 T); etc. Real-life ones, bursting with brawn, and not a hair out of place, were shown in action on DONAHUE (1990/1 etc T) and *Sex Talk* 'Male for Sale' (1990 T).

Female strippers are portrayed as either brainless or hard and brassy, illused by life (unlike the men who are bursting with health and vitality). A few lesbian ones: in *Screaming Mimi* (1958 C, involved with the owner of 'the Gay and Frisky'); Sally (Virginia Vincent) in *Tony Rome* (1967 C): 'a sexy stripper who is interested only in the physical attentions of her ugly lesbian ROOMMATE (Joan Shawlee)' (*Monthly Film Bulletin*); Jackie (Carol-Jean Thomson) making a play for her colleague (Raquel Welch) in *Flareup* (1969 C) and put charitably but firmly in her place.

Worship of the male body has long been confined to Greek statuary and one or two magazines. The advent of the male stripper introduces men to the prospect of being full sex objects. With many pairs of eyes appraising the body, still and moving, expectations demand some kind of revelatory climax. Although most shows are Women Only, men are confused. Should they be flattered or feel used?

Struggle (UK 1983 T) A frequently guffawable piece of artillery aimed at the GLC, then undergoing its long pre-death agonies. Tim Pigott-Smith was the hopelessly naive, abundantly caring Steve, leader of the ultra-left-wing council spending rate monies on crèches, anti-violence campaigns and services for lesbians and gays. These services were kept well in the background, except possibly for rabid FEMINIST Bunty (Joanna McCallum) in the episode 'Manning the Barricades': 'history' and 'herstory', she corrects Steve. She wants men emptying pots, wiping bums ... the usual.
W: Peter Jenkins; P/D: Graham Evans; LWT for Channel 4; 6 parts; 30 mins each.

Barry **Stuart-Hargreaves** Character played by Barry Howard in *Hi-de-Hi!* (1980–3 T). Rigidly elegant in deportment, with a voice like a damp sand, he is Yvonne's husband and equally toffeenosed dancing partner at Maplin's Holiday Camp.

He seems to have had some kind of brush with the law in the past (loitering with intent), but is now the soul of maidenly respectability with his Mantovani records and dry sherry. One of the highlights of his time in the series was the cocktail party he and Yvonne organized in 'Nice People with Nice Manners' (1983) which is gatecrashed by the *hoi polloi*. His lowest ebb is reached when he and the equally SENSITIVE Yvonne are dragooned into entering a 'That's Your Bum' competition.

The soggy STEREOTYPE is given a new twist by being 'married' to the throbbingly snooty Yvonne, to whom he always defers: 'You know best, dear.' (He was replaced by Julian Dalrymple-Sykes, played by Ben Aris, after he 'put his back out', disappearing from the camp and from his marital partnership.)

students Manuela (Hertha Thiele) in MAEDCHEN IN UNIFORM (1931 C etc); the killing boys in ROPE (1983 R etc); Tom (John Kerr) in TEA AND SYMPATHY (1956 C) who is more attracted to 'feminine' hobbies than rough group sports; dandy Maurice Goodman (Trader FAULKNER), everybody's friend in *Promenade* (1959 T); the undergraduates who each had a motive for wishing one of their number dead in *The Truth About Alan* (1964 T); Phil Corbett (Nigel Anthony) risking his life in a Rag Day prank because of 'hero worship' in *The Tinker* (1961 R; John HURT in the 1962 film version *The Wild and the Willing*); torn between outrage at the sexual depravity he sees around him and his own repressed love, Christopher Tenterden (Richard O'Sullivan) in THE CONNOISSEUR (1966 T); Jimmy and Ian (Simon Ward and Victor Henry) living in uneasy proximity in WHEN DID YOU LAST SEE MY MOTHER? (1967 R); Simon Ward cramming for A-level maths but being diverted by feelings for his TEACHER in SPOILED (1968 T); Joe Buck (Jon Voight) picked up in a cinema by sex-starved, inepcunious NYU student (Bob Balaban) in MIDNIGHT COWBOY (1969 C); Tim (Michael Feast), the living embodiment of nihilism in CIRCLE LINE (1971 T); Joey Keyston (Richard O'Callaghan), the former student, flatmate and possibly lover of Ben BUTLEY (Alan BATES 1974 C/T); Chris (Simon Rouse), a postgraduate who possibly knows more about men than he cares to tell his new girlfriend in WEDNESDAY LOVE (1975 T); night-school student Skinner (Derek Thompson) belatedly responding to the clumsy signallings of his lecturer in ME! I'M AFRAID OF VIRGINIA WOOLF (1978 T); Graham (Sam Dale), researching the early Labour movement in ONLY CONNECT (1979 T), learns that sexual politics are more than didactics and slogans; Felicity Phee (Veronica Quilligan), full of confusion after the heterosexual charisma and bull-shit of her sociology lecturer has been turned upon her in *The History Man* (1981 T); Sebastian and Charles (Anthony Andrews and Jeremy Irons), carefree and in love in BRIDESHEAD REVISITED (1981 T); mature student LIANA (Linda Griffiths 1983 C) falls for her teacher, a woman of the world; theology student (Rolf Saxon) in *Brontosaurus* (1983 R); D. (Sara Sugarman) grumpily in tow with the woman teacher who is also her lover in WHALE MUSIC (1983 T); trainee priest (Mark Zeljko) wrestling with his gay past and the dictates of the Catholic Church in *Mass Appeal* (1984 C); Ah-ching (Sun Yueh) thrown out of his home for being gay is befriended by a paternal photographer, becoming part of his family of strays in *The Outsiders* (1986 C); the dangerously protective schoolboy who kills to protect his affair with a master in *Death Drop* (1992 R); etc.

suck my dick! Increasingly threatening drunk in car park indicates his desires thus to Thelma (Geena Davis) and Louise (Susan Sarandon) before being shot dead through the heart by the latter in THELMA AND LOUISE (1991 C). Doris (Sandra Cathcart), the very male-identified American army officer, bawls this at an abusive Nicaraguan male in *Walking on Sticks* (Aust 1991 R).

Suddenly Last Summer (UK 1959 C)

A neurosurgeon (Montgomery CLIFT) probes into the deeply troubled psyche of a young woman (Elizabeth Taylor) to find what really happened on the holiday she took with her late cousin, the POET Sebastian Venable – a truth his rich and influential mother (Katharine HEPBURN) is most anxious to obliterate (permanently, through a lobotomy).

W: Gore VIDAL from the play by Tennessee WILLIAMS; P: Sam Spiegel; D: Joseph L. Mankiewicz; 114 mins.

Yet another evil, invisible, dead (raped, murdered, possibly eaten) gay man as the source of mystery, pleasure, fear, corruption, revelation and destruction, ruining the lives of two women, one of whom, Mrs Venable, is presciently Thatcheresque in the hands of Katharine Hepburn. The sets by Oliver Messel are particularly taking.

'... the only movie that has ever offered the paying public for a single admission, a practising homosexual, a psychotic heroine, a procuress-mother, a cannibalistic orgy and a sadistic nun ... Says Sam Spiegel: "It's a theme the masses can identify with." ' (*Time*, 11.1.60).

suede shoes 'I was known as the man who wore suede shoes ... It was known if you wore suede shoes and a Liberty tie you were ...,' said Trevor THOMAS in INTRODUCTION TO SOCIOLOGY 'Sexual Identity' (1981 T). This was endorsed the same year by Gifford Skinner in GAYLIFE 'Gays in the Thirties': 'You were a homosexual or an effeminate man if you wore them.'

A *blue* suede pair was okay, thanks to Gene Vincent but, in the 1950s and early 1960s, brown ones continued to be a marker for Them. Among their defiant wearers: a male member of Gene Kelly's acting/dance troupe during the evangelical number from *Summer Stock/If You Feel Like Singing* (1950 C); Adrian Lee (Alan WHEATLEY) with matching jacket and, in a second scene, with tomato-red shirt in *Simon and Laura* (1955 C); Max Bygraves as *Charley Moon* (1956 C) who takes a curiously long time to show the remotest interest in his childhood girlfriend; John Steed in *The Avengers* 'The

Medicine Men' (1963 T) worn with a striped shirt (he has dove grey ones in the 1967 series: 'Lucky for you I'm a devious fellow,' he tells Mrs PEEL); Andy (Terence Alexander), the cad who deflowers Jenny (Janet Munro) while she's intoxicated in *Bitter Harvest* (1963 C); Michael Billington as the man who picks up a sexy HITCHHIKER in *Dream A40* (1965 C); Siegfried Farnon (Robert Hardy) who is dragooned into playing cricket in his in *All Creatures Great and Small* 'Big Fish, Little Fish' (1989 T), set in the early 1950s. Ben Butley (Alan BATES) tells Reg (Michael Byrne) in BUTLEY (1974 C/T): 'You make me want to throw up, all over your characteristically suede shoes.'

The threat of ridicule by extreme prejudice has diminished now that gay men have supposedly given up glovelike, soft but durable suede footwear for construction workers' boots. Yet only a few heterosexual characters slip into them: William Hurt as a teacher took a fully clothed dip in a swimming pool wearing them in *Children of a Lesser God* (1986 C) and Michael Palin, as another teacher, Jim Nelson, owned at least one pair in *GBH* (1991 T). A close-up of John OSBORNE's feet as he sits listening to 'A BACHELOR GAY AM I' after a discussion on his CAMP affectations of yesteryear on THE SOUTH BANK SHOW (1991 T) reveal him to be suede shod.

Michael Aspel remarks upon Keith Floyd's 'ginger shoes'. In the past, he says, they were only worn by 'consenting adults in private' in *Aspel and Company* (1988 T). This was followed by Yoko Ono defending John Lennon's name after his being posthumously called a vicious homosexual drug addict by a biographer. 'These appalling accusations,' Aspel calls them in a show which he proudly calls 'sexually balanced: boy-girl-boy-girl' (average age = 45).

(Brad Pitt wears his black suede shoes with pride in *Johnny Suede* 1992 C.)

suffragettes The struggle for voting rights in Britain and America has usually been represented by spinsterly, misguided women who come to sticky ends or are disabused of their notions by a strong man: Loretta Young played a representative of the movement in Wyoming in *Lady from Cheyenne* (1941 C); Alec Guinness was all too briefly Lady Agatha in *Kind Hearts and Coronets* (1949 C), fatally plummeting to the ground after a well-aimed arrow pierces her balloon if not her *sang froid* over Berkeley Square; Margaret Hamilton, hatchet faced and hatched voiced in an episode of *Laramie* (1960 T); Glynis Johns, silly absentee mother, singing 'Sister Suffragette' in *Mary Poppins* (1964 C); Natalie Wood in *The Great Race* (1965 C); Vanessa REDGRAVE as Christabel Pankhurst in *Oh! What a Lovely War* (1969 C); ROSE (Jean Marsh) and Miss Elizabeth (Nicola Padget) are attracted to the movement briefly because of the charisma of one of its adherents (Georgia Brown) in UPSTAIRS, DOWNSTAIRS 'Votes for Women' (1973 T); Mrs Pankhurst (Siân Phillips) and her two daughters, Christabel (Angela Down) and Sylvia (Pamela Quinn), in *Shoulder to Shoulder* (1974 T); Marie David (Miriam MAR-GOLYES) coming between man and wife in THE ROAD FROM KYMMENDO BAY (1985 R); Violet (Kathleen Helme), once a suffragette, now a woman Labour candidate's grandmother in *House Wives* (1981 R); Vicky (Elizabeth Hurley), a fiery young woman 'active in the suffragette movement' in *The Young Indiana Jones Chronicles* (1991 T); etc.

The history of women's emancipation and the winning of the vote has been documented on radio and television in programmes such as *Queen Victoria Was Furious* (a 3-part series about Emily Davies, founder of Girton College, Elizabeth Garrett Anderson, pioneer of women's medicine, and Millicent Fawcett, a leader of women's suffrage, 1946 R); YOU ARE THERE 'The Ordeal of Christabel Pankhurst' (with Sarah Lawson, 1958 T); WOMAN'S HOUR (an interview with Mrs Aileen Graham-Jones – 'the first woman to apply for the RAC certificate to become a driver and who chauffeured Mrs Pankhurst to and from meetings, rallies and court appearances', 1962 R); *Fanatics* ('The mad, wicked followers of women's rights', 1962 T); *Votes for Women* 'The Story of the Suffragettes' (survivors 'recall the battle', 1968 R); etc. *Shoulder to Shoulder* (1974 T) was a lavish 6-part dramatization of the lives of six suffragist leaders (including Siân Phillips as Emmeline Pankhurst) with the lesbian input left unsung save for a few jolly bursts of support from Dame Ethyl SMYTHE (Maureen Pryor).

An admirer (David Cavendish) told Carol GREY (Anne CULLEN) in THE ARCHERS (1954 R) that she would

> 'make a good suffragette.'
> 'Definitely!' she agreed, 'One of the militant ones.'

Sixty-one years since British women won the vote, an unimpressed and ungrateful Ethel Skinner (Gretchen Franklin) in EASTENDERS (1989 T): 'Mrs Pankhust and her suffering jets.'

Suicide Is Painless Song by Johnny Mandel and Robert Altman to accompany the last supper of the army dentist before he takes the fatal overdose in *M*A*S*H* (1970 C). He is brought to this pass by his not being able to 'get it up'. Ergo he must be 'a FAIRY'. Ergo he must commit SUICIDE. The medical unit play up to this and give him a raucous farewell, complete with this song whose music became the theme of the subsequent long-running TV series.

The song resurfaced dramatically during 1991 in programmes dealing with 'America's obsession with euthanasia and assisted suicide ... or self-deliverance.'

suicides In VICTIM (1961 C) the arrival of Laura in Melville Farr's life disturbed the relationship between him and Phil Stainer at university – leading, via Farr's savage rejection of him, to death by his own hands. Taxed for his part in the tragedy, Farr drops his barrister's mask: 'He was a NEUROTIC and a hysteric. "Deny me, I'll kill myself!" He was always crying wolf ... When we were up at Cambridge together he was clever and amusing but corrupt, unstable and possessive. One night he rang me and said he was going to kill himself ... He'd said it before.'

This device of a dead queer haunting a not so normal pillar of the community had been used before in drama: Martin CAPLAN in DANGEROUS CORNER (1934 C) – who, in fact, did not end his own life but was accidentally killed by the woman he was trying to rape – and, around the same time, Martha in THE CHILDREN'S HOUR. John HOPKINS expanded the theme slightly in HORROR OF DARKNESS (1965 T) with Peter (Alfred Lynch) losing his lover (Glenda Jackson) and having his house defiled by his college friend Robin's (Nicol Williamson) particularly messy last exit, slashing his wrists and then his throat – the latter method also chosen by Brig Anderson (Don Murray) in ADVISE AND CONSENT (1962 C).

Suicide or deliberately seeking life-threatening situations used to be a constant in the depiction of homosexual individuals in or out of relationships. Examples – some bloodier than others – appear in *Anders als die Anderen* [Different from the Others] (1919 C); MAEDCHEN IN UNIFORM (not the 1931 film but the radio and television adaptation of 1946, 1965 and 1968); HUIS CLOS (1946 etc, by gas); *A Streetcar Named Desire* (1951 C & 1984 T, by drowning); CAT ON A HOT TIN ROOF (1958 C; 1976 & 1984 T); *Victim* (1961 C, by hanging); *The Sergeant* (1968 C, by gunshot); *Boy Meets Girl* 'The Eye of Heaven' (1968 T, by drowning); *Deadfall* (1968 C, by shooting); FORTUNE AND MEN'S EYES (1971 C, by razor); *Play It As It Lays* (1972 C, by pills); NOW SHE LAUGHS, NOW SHE CRIES (1975 R, by pills); LATE CALL (1975 T, by gas); THE CONSEQUENCE (1977 C/T, by drowning); *The Betsy* (1978 C, by jumping out of a window); KENNEDY'S CHILDREN (1978 R, by cutting off one hand and hacking away at the neck with the other); *The Suicide's Wife* (1979 T, by gunshot); ...*And Justice for All* (1979 C, by hanging); PENMARRIC (1979 T, by walking

into the sea); AGONY 'Arrivals and Departures' (1981 T, by pills); *The Making of a Male Model* (1983 T, by pills); ANOTHER COUNTRY (1984 C, by hanging); *A Man Alone* (1986 R, by gunshot); PRICK UP YOUR EARS (1987 C, by pills after battering lover with hammer); *The Gold Rimmed Spectacles* (1988 C; by shooting); *The Reflecting Skin* (1991 C, by drinking and dousing in petrol before striking a match); *Still Life* 'The Virgin in the Garden' (1992 R, by slashing with knife at body then covering it with flowers); *Children of the Dragon* (1992 T, method unknown).

There are attempted suicides in *A Raging Calm* (1974 T); SOAP (1977 T); *My Father's House* (1981 T); *The Potsdam Quartet* (1981 T); etc. There is also murder made to look like suicide: Stella (Fiona Walker) in *Death of an Expert Witness* (1983 T).

The only fictional gay suicide that received any kind of analysis (a 3-minute section on a television feedback programme called *Look Here* 1981) was that of Michael, the young man who had lost his teaching job because he had accidentally been identified on a radio phone-in on COMING OUT in AGONY. His death had brought letters of concentrated outrage which prompted this London Weekend Television slot to probe its company's action.

Said one correspondent to GAY NEWS: 'All my friends as well as I myself were horrified at Michael's death and felt that a reasonable cause for depression had been trivialized to the point of vacuity. Are we now into comedy *noir* or was Michael's position too much for the scriptwriters and producers to cope with? Michael's success at the one thing he was surely not meant to achieve – suicide – compounded the "failure" syndrome of homosexuality as a disease, sickness ...*Agony* had gone over the top and dodged one of the major challenges it had set up for itself.'

In the event, the gay criticism received less than a minute's airtime while the company was given double that, citing the actor's prior commitment and his request to leave. Emmanuel Cooper called it 'a feeble reply [which] did nothing to justify the bad decision. Neither was there any discussion or any questioning. Nevertheless, it was good to have, however truncated, some acknowledgement that our feelings mattered' (*Gay News* 211).

A Samaritans' report in 1990 found that between two and three hundred lesbian and gay YOUNG PEOPLE are believed to commit suicide every year because of their sexuality. This issue has rarely been tackled: only in *100%* 'Teenage Suicide' (1992 T, where a member of a lesbian and gay counselling service was interviewed but not identified as such) and *Attitude* 'Homophobia at School' (Aust 1993 T).

In HEART OF THE MATTER 'Against Nature?' (1992 T) part of a suicide note from a young man was shown and read out (by his father, prompted by the tragedy to stop hating gays and start helping them – by turning them into heterosexuals): 'I die now as one who found love and let it go. But can anyone live without love?'

Summer, Autumn, Winter, Spring (UK 1961 T) Ted Borlay (Philip Martin) loves his BROTHER Alf (Jon Rollason). They share the same bed, and Ted cooks and cleans for him and his contemptuous widowed FATHER, Saul (Geoffrey BAYLDON). Alf is killed in an accident a few weeks before marrying Laura (Ellen Dryden) who is expecting a baby. Ted decides to marry her, despite the scoffing of Saul, and Laura helps him to come to terms with Alf's loss and (it is suggested) his lack of sexual interest in women.
W: David TURNER; based on the novel *Strip Jack Naked* by John Hampson; P/D: Don Taylor; 11.9.61; BBC; 75 mins.
A modern version of DAVID AND JONATHAN in which Ted's motives are cloudy. Is he marrying Laura simply to give the baby a name? Is it to keep his brother's standing high in the neighbourhood? Or is it to attach himself to someone his brother also loved? David Turner, in adapting and updating the novel, filled out what had been only

hinted at: a very real desire for one brother by another, of which Saul is only too aware: 'I loved Alf as well, you know. But not like you ... not like *you*. It was wrong.'
(David Turner had originally prepared a radio adaptation called 'Unfair Enemy' in 1959. This was produced and broadcast (in the Midlands only and cut by 20 minutes) two years later as *Now More Than Ever*. After its full-length television showing between 9.10 and 10.25pm, it was nationally networked for radio – as *Summer, Autumn, Winter, Spring* – in 1962 with Jon Rollason playing the role of Ted instead of Alf.)

Sunday, Bloody Sunday (UK 1971 C)
A DOCTOR Daniel (Peter FINCH) and a personnel executive Alex (Glenda Jackson) are in love with the same man, Bob (Murray Head). During one weekend the situation, which is increasingly unsatisfactory for at least two of the participants, is resolved.
W: Penelope Gilliatt (and John SCHLESINGER); P: Joseph Janni; D: John Schlesinger; 110 mins.
A seismic shift had taken place between 1965 (the year of DARLING) and 1971 which allowed this film to receive both a relatively large budget and a wide showing. A winner of numerous awards, it appears tentative and under-developed today, the KISS and BED scene notwithstanding, though the everyday details of the Finch and Jackson characters' lives are well integrated into the simple plot.
The film is weakened by making the object of desire so lacking in affect, so bland and accommodating. This central vacuum, together with overlength and a skeletal story, deals a death blow to full involvement in the characters' dilemmas. Finch and Jackson (the latter especially in a scene with a retrenched businessman) are, however, excellent and it's to be regreted that they have only one (oblique) scene together.
(The showing of *Sunday, Bloody Sunday* on BBC2 in 1978 provoked an outcry because of the scene at the beginning when Peter Finch and Murray

Head tenderly kiss. Its most recent screening was the only example of homosexuality/bisexuality in the BBC's special ST VALENTINE's inspired (long) weekend of LOVE in 1993, being shown very late on the *Tuesday* night on BBC1. However, see the next entry.)

A Sunday Outing (UK 1993) Seventy years since BBC radio began, an affirmative programme made by and for lesbian and gay people which ran for two hours (between 8 and 10pm) on ST VALENTINE'S DAY, 14 February 1993. It was made by the independent gay and lesbian company, Outcast, for the BBC, and broadcast immediately after *Bookshelf* (on true romances) and was followed by the news and *The Memoirs of Sherlock* HOLMES.

A Sunday Outing was a compote of razzle-dazzle, news items, flippancy and serious discussion. A number of plums especially the songs, comic patter and fun and games direct from the Flamingo Club in Blackpool) and a few sour apples (a far too superficial rumination on 'the pink pound' and some sluggish readings). In general, though, it was a good curtain-raiser for a hoped-for weekly series, crisply guided by Matthew Parris and rather less comfortably by Beatrix (aka Bea) Campbell, with items on coming out, queer love, holidays, long-term relationships, funerals, religion and the drag scene, as well as lesbian and gay fiction readings.

Matthew Parris, a former Tory MP, had achieved television prominence in 1984 when he lived on £26.80 supplementary benefit for a week in Scotswood, Newcastle and reported his progress on camera (in WORLD IN ACTION: 'For The Benefit Of Mr Parris'). After he left Parliament he became a columnist for *The Times*, presented a current affairs programme for LWT, turned up in OUT ON TUESDAY ('Gays on the Right' 1990 T), and devised and presented RSVP (1992 R) in which letters from Van Gogh, George VILLIERS and ST PAUL were among those analysed. Beatrix Campbell is an experienced journalist and broadcaster (WOMAN'S HOUR; OUT ON TUESDAY) on all manner of subjects from child abuse to lesbian feminist thrillers.

supermarket managers One only: young Alan Loader (Gary Love) who becomes a pawn of investigative journalist David Dunhill (Richard E. Grant) in HERE IS THE NEWS (1989 T).

A Superstition (UK 1977 T) Harry (Anthony Andrews), accidentally blinded by his much older lover Oliver (Hugh BURDEN), lives with him in a villa in the South of France. Ex-spy Oliver, drenched in guilt, is at war with his puritanism, as well as being pursued by a wild-eyed ex-lover. Life is a dip in the pool, baccarat in Cannes, candlelit suppers on the terrace. It ends with a machete and blood – and at least one body in the pool.

W: David Mercer; D: David Cunliffe; Yorkshire 60 mins.

Growing fat and lazy, never having to measure themselves by normal standards – 'We recoil at the idea that life could be profound' – Oliver and Harry have their protective layers stripped away by the arrival of Oliver's crazy ex-lover, a former priest (John STRATTON). Death to all weak decadent Westerners, skewered by natural forces unleased by sick passions!

Designer Eileen Diss (glistening spider's web; a lizard squashed under a beautiful paperweight) is the real star of this fevered postcard from the edge which featured a group of unpleasant people who have done and will do exceedingly unpleasant things to one another. It's full of epigrams, guilt and hate, and ends in a ritual murder. This is an elegant, GREEN BAY TREE version of *The Texas Chainsaw Massacre.* Maybe a bit of an exaggeration, but you would definitely not ask any of these men to babysit your child.

'You emanate a reproving stench, Harry. I squirm in it, I'm corrupted by it,' says Oliver.

surnames Like first names, these have

an intricate life of their own, announcing or concealing. They have been used to proclaim characteristics and immediate energies since drama began.

Classical Greek comedies abounded in effeminate characters. Their names betrayed their animus: Aristophanes' Sostrate (instead of Sostratos) and Cleonyme (instead of Cleonymos, for *Clouds*). This playwright, of whose works only 11 comedies survive, would also employ NICKNAMES which allude to 'swishy' gestures and walk as well as clothes.

There was Ben Jonson's Sir Diaphanous Silkworm (John Moffatt) in *The Magnetic Lady* (1987 R); Mr Puff in Sheridan's *The Critic*; Horace Femm (Ernest THESIGER) in *The Old Dark House* (1932 C); Jasper Bentwick (Robert STEPHENS) in *Eustace and Hilda* (1977 T). The names of these men usually bespeak softness and luxury as do more recent examples like Keith Kossett (John Bonney) in *Paranoiac* (1964 C) and Claude Crepe (Anthony Gardiner) in *Mister Ten Per Cent* (1967 C).

Frederic RAPHAEL is probably the best-known dramatist who, with particular relish, comments upon the degree of masculinity in some of his creations, despite Albert Finney saying to Audrey HEPBURN in his *Two for the Road* (1967 C): 'The only thing that fits into a pigeon hole is a pigeon.' One of the heroes of *The Best of Friends* (1980 T) is called Michael Stayman (Keith Barron) and he does indeed remain intact, even after a playful invitation to bed by a male friend. Another character, an inconsequential capon with an acid-tipped beak, is named Vivian Malleson (Aubrey WOODS). An exceedingly badly developed character, Vivian simply disappears from the story after Raphael has paraded him in a couple of scenes for viewer disapproval. This friend of the trendy couple is all tiffs and put-downs. His equally ne'er-do-well friend, George (Gerard Murphy) is described by Vivian as 'pig ignorant from Cardiff'. In the same play is a character called Crispin Le Coq; and there's another

Crispin in Raphael's 'That Was Tory' in the *Oxbridge Blues* series (1984 T): a bearded, floppy INTERIOR DESIGNER, Crispin Maycock (Malcolm Stoddard).

Some gay characters have first names only, like a child. Only the heterosexual Alan has a surname in THE BOYS IN THE BAND (1970 C). Toby (Brian Capron), the HAIRDRESSER who was being harassed by bashers, was the only character not to have a last name in THE GENTLE TOUCH 'Do It Yourself' (1984 T). Roland CURRAM has played three characters, Malcolm No Surname in DARLING (1965 C), Terry No Surname in THE CREZZ (1976 T), and Freddie No Surname in ELDORADO (1992 T); Freddie was the only character, with the exception of his friend Gerry (Buki Armstrong), not to have a full name, but this situation was rectified four months into the serial's run.

Some examples of surnames as signifiers of effeminancy or gayness or heterosexuality (or, occasionally, priapism and sexual insatiability):

Brunette, slimy gambling ship boss played by Anthony Zerbe in *Farewell, My Lovely* (1975 C). The name – which is in the original novel – had been changed to Burnett in one of its film versions, *The Falcon Takes Over* (1942 C).

Arthur **Caresse** (Kevin McCarthy), THRUSH agent running cosmetic company in *The Man from UNCLE* 'The Moonglow Affair' (1966 T).

Percy **Dovetonsils**: Ernie Kovacs' precious, lisping poet on his television show (1951–6). Other characters included Irving Wong, a Chinese songwriter and Walter Puppybreath.

Mr **Dulcimer** (Dulcie) (D. A. CLARKE-SMITH) in THE GREEN BAY TREE (194 R); fond of beautiful things including his adopted son Julian.

Feather: Theodore Feather (Richard WATTIS) in *Park Plaza 605* (1953 C), friend of detective Norman Conquest (Tom Conway); the paterfamilias Laban Feather (Rod Steiger) in *The Lolly Madonna War* (1972 C); Arnold Feather (Geoff Keveney) in NUMBER 96 (1974 T) took himself off to cookery classes and, unwittingly(?), almost(?) went to bed with young woman called Robyn, who was a man. A reluctant virgin, he marries, but his wife is soon a victim of the pantihose strangler. He described himself as 'an unwanted child who had no friends before I came to *Number 96*. Pompous and impossible.' Most recently: Gavin Featherley (Tim Marriott), one of the two gay staff working in *The Brittas Empire* (1990– T).

Featherbrain: Walter Brennan who would like to shack up with the toothless old hag even though he knows that 'she' is really Bob Hope in drag in *The Princess and the Pirate* (1944 C).

Finch: Lena Finch (Olga Gwynne 1960 T; Elizabeth Sellars 1969 T) who disrupts the comfortably gluttonous life of THE THREE FAT WOMEN OF ANTIBES; Humphrey Finch (Charles Lloyd Pack), writer living in comfortable 'arrangement' with his wife in *An Unofficial Rose* (1974/5 T); Eric Finch (Ellis Rabb), eccentric customer in a 1982 episode of *Cheers* (T); Alastair Finch (Dominic Jephcott), 'macho in a way men just can't afford to be these days' but tempered by his love of cat Marmalade and, less passionately, Nigel in *Claws* (1987 T); the inexorable Pastor Finch (Kenneth Cranham) who drives a Godmobile with a collapsible cross in ORANGES ARE NOT THE ONLY FRUIT (1990 T) and energetically attempts to deliver Jess from evil; Oscar Finch (Patrick McGoohan), a brilliant attorney in *New Columbo* 'Agenda for Murder' (1991 T).

Flower: Buddy Flower (Frank Aletter), bachelor nephew of unmarried sisters Violet and Iris Flower (Enid Markey and Doro Merande) in *Bringing Up Buddy* (1960–1 T); Roger Flower (Jonathan Pryce) in *Roger Doesn't Live Here Any More* (1981 T) told by a Divorce Court official (Doug Fisher): 'People like you ought to be castrated'.

Jason **Flowerdew**: Frank Duncan as the actor who plays big sister and brother to the heroine of *Deal with Murder* (1964 R) and yet is the person behind attempts to scare her to death.

Flowers: Leslie Dwyer as an old lag who sells button holes, and acts as go-between in a drugs racket. The flower-seller's real name is George Hardman [*sic*], but he is called 'my old dandelion' by his mates in *Judgement Deferred* (1952 C). Other characters called Flowers – none of them gay identified – appeared in *They Came to a City* (1962 T), DIXON OF DOCK GREEN (1961 T), and *Saint Jack* (1979 C) whose

shabby hero is Jack Flowers (Ben Gazzara).

Torquil **Flute** (George Howe), a translator of Horace and pioneer advocate of Greek dancing in working men's clubs in *Sir Jocelyn, The Minister Would Like a Word* (1965 T). He has lived with Baroness Cleethorpe for many years and suddenly asks her to marry him. He tells her that he is a born-again (as of last week) Christian.

Sir Flopling **Flutter** (Geoffrey BAYLDON) in *The Man of Mode or Sir Fopling Flutter* (1960 T).

Martin **Foxglove** (Noel HOWLETT) in *Eye Witness* (1950 C).

Sir Jarvis **Fruit** (Peter SELLERS), exotically epicene as the head of Scotland Yard in *The Case of the Mukkinese Battle Horn* (1956 C).

Gaily: Fred Gailey (John Payne), the lawyer who defends Kris Kringle/Santa Claus in *Miracle on 34th Street* (1947 C; a name change was essential for the 1973 TV remake); Carole Gaylee (singer Carole Carr) in *Down Among the Z Men* (1951 C); Gail Gailey (Geena Davis) in *Hero/Accidental Hero* (1992 C); Herbert Gaily (John Baddeley) who turns up unannounced at Faith Lavender's funeral in *Gentleman and Ladies* (1993 R).

Gay (female): Mrs Gaye (Thora Hird) in *The Weaker Sex* (1948 C); Binky Gay (Shelley Winters) in *Phone Call from a Stranger* (1952 C) nightclub entertainer; conventional daughter Sally Gay (Shirley King) in *The Gay Dog* (1953 T; Petula Clark in the 1954 film); Penny Gay played by Petula Clark as one of George Cole's more patient girlfriends in *A Life of Bliss* (1954–7 R; Moira Lister was her worldly older sister, Sally during 1955); Vicki Gaye (Cyd Charisse), dancer and *Party Girl* (1958 C); Logan Gay (Shelley Hack), a teacher of deaf children, in *Trackdown: Finding the Goodbar Killer* (1983 T).

Gay (male): Peter Gay played by Hugh McDermott as the nice American man who doesn't smash Ann Todd's hands in *The Seventh Veil* (1946 C but she doesn't love him); Gee Gee Gay (Terence Alexander) in *Only When I Larf* (1968 C).

Gaylord: siblings (Barbara STANWYCK, Geraldine Fitzgerald and Nancy Coleman) involved in prolonged litigation, known as *The Gay Sisters* (1942 C); Mr Gayelorde-Sutton (Harold INNOCENT) in *Diana* (1984 T).

Eunice **Gaysmile**, daffy TV panellist played by Betty MARSDEN on *Beyond Our Ken* (1958–9 R). Based on a number of glamorous stars and starlets, including Eunice Gayson who appeared on *I've Got a Secret* (1958 T).

Mervyn **Glue**, film critic in *The World of Beachcomber* (1970 T).

Peter **Golightly** (Kenneth WILLIAMS) in *Carry on Sergeant* (1958 C), and in the opposite bed: Horace Strong (Kenneth Connor).

Sheridan **Honeydew** (Brian Fairman), a TV presenter in *The Rise and Fall of Reginald Perrin* (1977 T) whose guests are Peregrine Trembley (Neville Barker) and Colin Pillock (Timothy Carlton).

Chloris **Jakeman** (Mossie Smith), harpy feminist-lesbian who complains that she and her friend Jo Lentill (JoJo Cole) have been verbally raped by Jock McCannon (Graham Crowden) during lectures in A VERY PECULIAR PRACTICE 'Values of the Family'/'The Big Squeeze' (1988 T).

Lacey: often used to 'soften' male and female characters: Captain Algernon Lacy, aka Algy, a friend of *Biggles* (1960 T); Vyvyan Lacey, thespian patient in *Emergency – Ward 10* (1960 T); Ray Lacey (Noel DAVIS), the TV make-up man who isn't ashamed to openly appreciate men in *Who Killed Santa Claus?* (1971 T); lonely Robert Lacey (John HURT) in *Green Julia* (1972 T) abandoned by flat-mate/unrequited lover Jacob; Tony Lacey (Paul Simon) as the very Californian singer–composer in *Annie Hall* (1977 C); touch-talking, active but tender-hearted policewoman Mary Beth Lacey (Tyne Daly) in CAGNEY AND LACEY (1981–7 T); misfit Myra Lacey (Maureen O'BRIEN) besotted with a married woman in *Remaining Strangers* (1986 R); chunky, avuncular PC Lacey (Stephen CHURCHETT) in *Rockcliff's Babies* 'A Bad Few Days' (1987 T); and John Lacey (Judd Hirsch) faced with new ways of living after his wife leaves him in DEAR JOHN (1988–91 T).

Jo **Lentill** (JoJo Cole), a lesbian-feminist student at Lowlands University in A VERY PECULIAR PRACTICE 'Values of the Family'/'The Big Squeeze' (1988 T). According to René-James Herail and Edwin A. Lovatt's *The Dictionary of Modern Colloquial French* (1985), a *trieuse de lentilles* is a lesbian (or dyke or 'les'). It refers to 'the finger-flicking action of someone sorting lentils prior to cooking'.

Sonia (Jacqueline Tongue) stirs lentils in a pan before declaring her feelings for her house-mate in *Heart of the Country* (1987 T).

Light/Lightfoot: soft footfalls bespeak soft minds and twisted motives: Rock HUDSON's nimble Irish patriot *Captain Lightfoot* (1954 C) may be a hero, but the term describes someone apparently predisposed to unmanly pursuits (with other men): the prize fighter disparaged to Tom Selleck in *Lassiter* (1984 C), and possibly Clint Eastwood's younger partner Jeff Bridges, as the second half of *Thunderbolt and Lightfoot* (1974 C). The hero of OCTOBER SCARS THE SKIN (1989 R) is called Ashley Light (Dominic Rickhards); he is a strange boy, obsessed with cleanliness, who finds a dead body.

Lovelace: Lovelace (Sean Bean), the rake in *Clarissa* (1991 T); spindly Cecil Lovelace (Franklyn PANGBORN) in *Exit Smiling* (1926 C).

Manley: H. R. Manley (Steve Cochran), hysterical scandal magazine publisher in *Slander!* (1956 C).

Manners (John Barrymore Jr), fastidious, over-mothered killer of women in *While the City Sleeps* (1956 C).

Roland **Milk**, poet in *The World of Beachcomber* (1968 T) as in Milksop. The real-life San Francisco politician, Harvey MILK in the late 1970s gave the name vigour, pride and poignancy.

Mr **Mince** (Robert Gillespie) who is saving up for a sex change in AGONY (1979 T).

Sidney **Mincing**, a miserable catarrhal creature played by Kenneth Connor in *Ray's a Laugh* (1953–9? R).

Cecil **Mincingham** (Maurice Denham) in *Much Binding in the Marsh* (1953 R); imperator of Britain's *haute couture*. Based on a British dress designer, with whom listeners had become acquainted in the weeks leading up to the Queen's coronation in June (broadcast August).

Clare **Quilty**: Peter SELLERS as the extravagant aesthete; Humbert Humbert's rival for *Lolita* (1962 C) with a penchant for the sexually precocious and for disguising himself (as a German child psychiatrist and a gay policeman). The surname was first used for the wonder-filled, spunky heroine Bridie (Deborah Kerr) in *I See A Dark Stranger/ The Adventuress* (1946 C).

Rimmer: Von Rimmer (Horst Janson), the gay baron in UPSTAIRS, DOWNSTAIRS

'A Suitable Marriage' (1971 T); Lindsay Rimmer (Vivien Heilbron), the inscrutable, calculating secretary/lover of a woman novelist in *An Unoffical Rose* (1974/5 T); Lord Henry Rimmer (Christopher Strauli) in *Lytton's Diary* 'Come Uppance' (1985 T), head of the British Patriots' Party, a beacon for disaffected youths, especially SKINHEADS.

St Clair: Hilary St Clair (Kenneth Williams), photographer who 'paints with light' and who scares Tony Hancock to death in HANCOCK'S HALF HOUR 'The Publicity Photograph' (1958 R); John St Clair (Richard Seff) whose lover, a secret member of a terrorist group, cheated and betrayed him in *The Rockford Files* 'The Empty Frame' (1978 T); theatre director Llewellyn St Clair in THE SIMPSONS 'A Streetcar Named Marge' (1992 T): 'I've had three heart attacks; let's try for a fourth' ('That's how much he cares about his theatrical craft,' marvels someone).

Humphrey **Silk** (Derek Benfield) in *Emergency – Ward 10* (1960 T).

Nigel **Strangeways**: the detective hero of Nicholas Blake, alias C(ecil) Day-Lewis, based on his friend W. H. AUDEN. Played by Glyn Houston in *Detective* 'End of Chapter' (1964 T), by Richard Hurndall in *I am Lucy Wragby* (1966 R), and by Simon Cadell in *The Smiler with the Knife* (1986 R).

Poll **Sweedlepipe** (Michael Graham-Cox) in *Martin Chuzzlewit* (1987 R).

Eustace **Tewksbury** (Geogre K. ARTHUR) in *Spring Fever* (1927 C).

Jerome **Thisby** (Richard HAYDN), stage supremo in *Mr Music* (1950 C).

Mervyn **Trellis** (James COCO) in *There Must Be a Pony* (1986 T), gay friend of faded Hollywood movie star (E. Taylor); wears pink shirt, cooks, gossips.

Simon **Willow** (Charles HAWTREY), 'blithe, friendly but lonely' boarder in the 1960 comedy series *Our House*.

See also BOYS' NAMES FOR GIRLS; FIRST NAMES; GIRLS' NAMES FOR BOYS; NICK-NAMES.

The Sweeney 'On the Run' (UK 1976 T) Convicted armed robber Tim Cook (George Sweeney) hides out at the country home of a gay JP, 'Uncle' (John Sharp), who is badly beaten by Cook when a demand for money is refused.

The JP's boyfriend, Pinder (Brendan Price) helps Tim get away.

W: Roger Marshall; P: Ted Childs; D: David Wicks; 20.12.76; Thames; 60 mins.

The scene in the wood between the boys is silent and lyrical, and Sweeney and Sharp contribute brilliantly jarring portraits of self-absorption from completely opposite sides of the bench. 'Oh the ignominy of it ... and the humiliation ... If you spoil things for that boy, for him and me, I'll have you hunted like a rabid dog.' At which the expressionless youth roughs up the man and pushes him through a (closed) glass door. It's very nasty indeed, but convincing behaviour all round.

sweetheart/sweetie Clark Gable nudges the audience towards a recognition of MOLL's (Albert Dekker) sexuality in *Strange Cargo* (1940 C) by calling him 'sweetheart'. Oscar Levant (as Sid Jeffers) tells Paul (John Garfield) not to be stupid, 'sweetheart', and to leave his hair all mussed because 'you look pretty that way' (*Humoresque* 1947 C). Humphrey Bogart calls frightened BAR-MAN Louis (George Chandler) a sweetheart in *Dead Reckoning* (1947 C), as does Lloyd Gough to his client William Holden on the golf course in *Sunset Boulevard* (1950 C): 'Sweetheart, you may need another agent.' Liberal, tolerant widowed father Stan Rivkin (Ron Liebman) calls his young son 'sweetheart' in *Rivkin: Bunty Hunter* (1981 T) – a rare aberration in the annals of American television. Former lover, and now friend, Richard (Chris Matthews) addresses Colin as 'sweetoe' in EAST-ENDERS (1988 T) and Stephen FRY similarly referred to the chairman of *Just a Minute* in 1989 on radio.

Other forms of endearment more common to women but occasionally diverted to the opposite sex include: 'Baby' – Adolphe Menjou's special name to his beloved played by Gary Cooper in *A Farewell to Arms* (1932 C); 'Lady' – the jazz musician (Dexter Gordon) addresses his male friends thus in *'Round Midnight* (1986 C); 'Sugar' –

Humphrey Bogart as the brash film producer calls the *maître d'* 'sugar' in *Stand-In* (1937 C), and the similarly rough and ready Willie Stark (Broderick Crawford) uses the same word to a male aide during a political campaign in *All the King's Men* (1949 C).

swimwear Part of male/female display with a definite increase in exposure of flesh from the 1930s, culminating in almost unisex creations on certain beaches where men and women wear next to nothing against their skin.

In AMBRIDGE, when Tony Archer (Colin Skipp) is packing for a holiday in Greece, he vetoes a pair of (presumably brief) swimming trunks. Not because he doesn't like them. Not because he hasn't got the figure to show them off. No, it's simply 'because they make me look like a PANSY' (THE ARCHERS 1984 R).

See also SPEEDOS.

Switch (US 1991 C) Steve is shot dead but returns as the beautiful Eve (Ellen Barkin), much to the bewilderment of his/her buddy Walter (Jimmy Smits) and would-be lover Sheila (Lorraine Bracco).

W/D: Blake Edwards; P: Tony Adams; 114 mins. C

For all those men who long to bear children, to marry a best mate, to exist in a polymorphous world – if drunk, castrated or dead. Edwards gets stuck in his habitual bottleneck – HOMOPHOBIA. The footling scenes involving the lesbian attraction are particularly offensive, given that Ellen Barkin could have handled such a theme with aplomb. She's superbly sassy and in control, and it's a crying shame she couldn't have been blessed with a more roadworthy vehicle than this clapped-out variation of *Goodbye Charlie* (1964 C), itself no limousine.

Swizzlewick (UK 1964 T) A satire on all that is underhand and small-minded in local government. Mrs Felicity Smallgood (Margot Boyd), cleaning up the town of Swizzlewick, advocates anti-sex lessons in schools. Her aide Kenneth

(Patrick Mower) tells her not to bother: 'I think we can leave that to the teachers ... they're trained for that sort of thing.'

Swizzlewick was written by David TURNER who, it was widely reported at the time, was ordered to dilute certain aspects of his characters (including Mrs Smallgood's bigotry) because of complaints from individuals and from the council – notoriously dilitory and corrupt – upon which this ill-fated early evening BBC1 serial was based.

Swoon (US 1991 C) Why did two well-educated, well-dressed, well-fed Chicago teenagers go on a crime spree which led to an emotionless, methodical killing of a little boy?

W/D: Tom Kalin; P: Christine Vachon; 94 mins.

Tom Kalin mixes in Sacher-Masoch, the jazz age, surrealism, anti-Semitism and HOMOPHOBIA to shine a little more light on a couple who had 'no way to be gay'. Resplendently stylish, always fascinating, it lacks a cogent philosophy and obfuscates just as much as did COMPULSION by becoming progressively nihilistic, drawing out rather than drawing in. Loeb (Daniel Schlachet) and Leopold (Craig Chester), learned, ironic, disturbing, calculating, are an extremely erotic pair of lovers, and there is a gem of a scene where a courtroom is cleared of women because the word 'PENIS' is uttered.

Sydney Elsa Chauvel in *Australian Walkabout* (1958 T) enthuses about the 'gay life of our cities' at the moment a shot appears of Sydney's raffish King's Cross area. But Alan WHICKER refuses to say the word 'gay' when he visited the same territory in *Waltzing with Matilda?* (1988 T). Rather he enunciates: 'Sydney has become the ho-moh-sexual capital of the Southern hemisphere.' Yet not one of the people he speaks to uses the word.

Sydney Gay and Lesbian Mardi Gras
From a 1,000-strong demo – which led to 160 arrests in 1978 when homosexuality was still illegal in New South Wales

– it has metamorphosed into the highly regarded annual festivity of the 1980s and 1990s which draws crowds of 450,000 and is called by Sydney's police 'the best organized community event ... a textbook for running such an operation'. The biggest gay event in the South Pacific region (and entirely run by volunteers with no outside funding), it is the culmination of a month of festivities. Said its 1992 organizer Susan Harben (*In the Mix* Aust R): 'It walks the line between mainstream and margin – as homosexuals do every day.'

The event has been featured in WITCHES, FAGGOTS, DYKES AND POOFTERS (1979 C); *We Will Dance If We Want To!* (Aust 1984 T); *Where There's Life* (1986 T); *Celebration!* (Aust 1988 T); radio serial *Murder at the Mardi Gras* (Aust 1988 R); OUT 'Double Trouble' (1991 T); *Talking History* 'Sydney Gay and Lesbian Mardi Gras' (Aust 1992 R); *Helicon* 'Fat Tuesday' (Aust 1992 R); *Sex* (Aust 1992 R); *Fed Them to the Cannibals* (1993 T); *Face the Press* with Susan Harben (Aust 1993 T); *The Pink Patrol* (Aust 1993 R); etc.

Sylvania Waters (Aust 1992 T) An ordinary Australian family living in a well-off if not necessarily salubrious suburb of Sydney.
P: Paul Watson; EP: Paul Watson; D: Brian Hill and Kate Woods; August–September 1992; ABC; 60 mins. (Also: UK; April–July 1993; 30 mins.)

Unmarrieds Noeline and Laurie and their kids in an endless replay of Us against Them (and each other). Crass? Materialistic? Bigoted? Unruly, mostly depressing reality heightened by the presence of a television crew for weeks on end. The producer called it living soap opera.

Noeline, with her blunt methods of expression, her smoking and drinking and general what-the-hell attitude, became an icon of sorts. Her future son-in-law managed to be simultaneously liberated (he sews) and hidebound (making grindingly obvious remarks about the participants in the SYDNEY GAY AND LESBIAN MARDI GRAS and POOFTERS in general from the comfort of his chair in front of the television).

Symonds, John Addington (1840–93) English writer, scholar, historian, poet, reviewer, essayist and pioneer of homosexual rights. Author of *A Problem in Greek Ethics* (1833) and *A Problem in Modern Ethics* (1891) among other works. His memoirs were published only in 1984 and formed the basis for *Speaking Out: Confessions of a Victorian Man of Letters* with Michael Bryant (1984 R). Its compiler and producer Brian Gear said: 'There's no doubt in my mind that English literature is enriched by the publication of his memoirs. The frankness in some passages is astounding, good reason for their suppression in his lifetime or that of his immediate family ... They're undoubtedly Symonds' best writing, containing what he alone could have given the world – his own extraordinary story. They're a moving picture of a man forced to lead a double life very much against his natural honesty, because of his persistent passion for the male sex.'

Syrup of Figs (UK 1986 R) Set in a girls' day school during the late 1950s, Anne Baker (Susie Brann) has a crush on English mistress Helen West (Emma Piper). They read Robert Browning's 'Perfidious Lover' together. Sister Catherine warns that 'such intimacy can lead to all kinds of ... difficulties'. In parallel with her love for an adult, Anne dyes her hair and has a relationship, via letters, with Fiona (Elaine Claxton) who pretends to be an English air force officer. A dour, lacklustre piece which is noted only because of its faint echoes of MAEDCHEN IN UNIFORM, ending with a girl's SUICIDE.
W: Jo Heaton; D: Patrick Rayner; 30.6.86; BBC Radio 4; 90 mins.

Dame Hilda **Tablet** Character played by Mary O'Farrell in the plays of Henry REED, the inspiration for Madeleine in Richard Shewin's novel 'The Head and the Heart'. An exacting and temperamental composer, a battler for women's rights, Dame Hilda lives with her protégée/lover/drudge Elsa Strauss (Marjorie Westbury) whom she refers to as 'You silly little dotty'. She also has a secretary, Evelyn BAXTER (Colin CAMPBELL) who has an affectionate, effusive nature, especially towards young men. Her favourite informal mode of address is 'Old cock' and she likes to wear chiffon ties which she runs up herself to go with her suits. She asks Stephen Shewin (Carleton HOBBS) if they look a bit SISSY: 'Nothing could look sissy on you,' he mockingly reassures her.

Herbert Reeve (Hugh BURDEN), interviewing Dame Hilda for his biography of Richard Shewin in A VERY GREAT MAN INDEED (1953 R), assumes that the young singer Elsa Strauss is her daughter. 'That's a good one. She's been taken for my niece before now by a few nice-minded people, but 'daughter', that's a new one to me'. Her family retainer puts it another way to the conscientiously naive Reeve: 'For 'ee mus' unnerstand, sir, as *Miss Ilda were hallways a bit of a tomboy.*'

Richard Shewin loved Hilda, but she told him straight: 'I'm just NOT THE MARRYING SORT of girl, that's all ... I don't mind the odd kiss ... now and then.' But when it comes to young women it's a different matter. Surrounded by excited 6th form autograph hunters during a visit to her old school, she is more than happy to sign *and* to give out her telephone number 'in case any of you want to ring me up anytime'.

Her massive ego demands that Reeve temporarily abandon his masterwork on Shewin and write her biography 'in not more than 12 volumes ... It was good enough for Gibbon, it was good enough for PROUST'.

Among her musical works are the all-female opera *Emily Butter* (1954 R), 'The Shewin Sonata' (composed in A VERY GREAT MAN INDEED) and 'Nocturne' which is composed of bits from the Book of Isaiah, Emily DICKINSON, St John of the Cross, Cyril Connolly and Kingsley Amis. It was her unrealized ambition to adapt GIDE'S LES FAUX MONNAYEURS for operatic performance.

Dame Hilda also appears in THE PRIVATE LIFE OF HILDA TABLET (1954), *Emily Butter: An Occasion Recalled* (1954), A HEDGE, BACKWARDS (1956), *The Primal Scene, As It Were ...*: NINE STUDIES IN DISLOYALTY (1958), and *Musique Discrète*: A REQUEST PROGRAMME OF MUSIC BY DAME HILDA TABLET (1959).

Roger Savage wrote in 'The Radio Plays of Henry Reed' (a contribution to BRITISH RADIO DRAMA, ed John Drakakis, 1981):

> The plays are farcical and satiric, but the satire is not harsh or dismissive. Take the redoubtable composeress herself. Miss Tablet is certainly something of a monster of egotism and imposition ... her music comes over as parodying everything from TCHAIKOVSKY to Webern; and *à clef* she seems to be a blend of Dame Ethel SMYTH (the mannish dress, boisterous FEMINISM, gentrified parents, and fondness for soldiers), Elisabeth Lutyens (the BOHEMIAN life-style and the pioneering of English serialism) and Benjamin BRITTEN (the love life and fondness for single-sex opera). But she is evidently a genuine creator (and so a *sacred* monster); her parodic music is simply the equivalent of Richard Shewin's novels; Reed's script describes her significantly as having a warm and jolly voice; and we have no reason to assume that Reed disapproved of her 'models', if such they be.

tailors 'You're measuring me for a suit, not trying to make love to me,' hisses villain Walter Slezak to his over-solicitous fitter in *The Spanish Main* (1946 C); CLARENCE, the former tailor now a POW, gazing at a pin-up of Tyrone Power before he goes to sleep in *The Dick Emery Show's* dishevelment of *The Great Escape* (1978 T); the elderly Jewish man who cared for a younger one in MORNING STORY 'Me and Mr Mandel' (1979 R: 'He never got married or anything like that ... He wasn't the marrying kind, if you know what I mean'); the grebe-like Pole (Jean-François Wacek) lovingly attending to the hero (John Moulder Brown) in *The Confessions of Felix Krull* (1982 T): 'I'm working for Mr Krull because he's a handsome man, that's why ... What a first-class *garçon*, far too beautiful to be a waiter'); Paul Currie (William Armstrong), a brilliant cutter, self-effacing, diligent, only slightly temperamental and keeping his private life sewn up in GEMS (1984–7 T) until one of the young women in the workshop falls for him.

Take Off With Us A deliberately snaky, insinuating song and dance routine involving sexual permutations among pilots and flight attendants, this was a pastiche of airline soft-sell sex, by Fred Tobias and Stanley Lewbowsky, written for *All That Jazz* (1979 C). Director Joe Gideon (Roy Scheider) stages the number for the backers of his projected Broadway show. As the erotica unwind, one worried producer says to the other: 'We've just lost the family audience.'

The brief instant when two of the dancers, Gary Flannery and Bruce Davis, briefly fondle each other appeared to mark the breaking of the waters on same-sex passion in the Hollywood musical. In positive terms it meant very little: the gay and lesbian caresses were merely the hot sauce on the side.

The film's director – and its very thinly disguised central character – Bob Fosse discussed this scene with Melvyn Bragg on THE SOUTH BANK SHOW (1981 T): 'It's a *double entendre*. One is an ad for an airline, the other is sexual innuendo. I put in my own feelings about sexual perversion.'

taking a fancy to... An expression which has undergone several changes of emotional temperature between the 18th and 20th centuries. STEERFORTH could say that he'd taken a fancy to Davy/Daisy in the 1964 TV adaptation of DAVID COPPERFIELD, but not in subsequent versions. The only available

example in a female context is Eva (Joan Crawford) in *Queen Bee* (1955 C) remarking to the pretty young woman (Lucy Marlow) that the near-demented and at least 20 years older Sue McKinnon (Fay Wray) has 'taken a fancy to you'. *See also* FANCY.

Tales of the City aka *Armistead Maupin's Tales of the City* (UK 1993 T) San Francisco *c* 1976. The interconnected lives and hedonistic times of single, gay, bisexual, heterosexual, transvestite and transsexual, all drawn to the apartment house at 28 Barbary Lane and the extraordinary landlady, Anna Madrigal (Olympia Dukakis).

W/P: Richard Kramer; based on the book by Armistead Maupin (based on a series of daily columns in the SAN FRANCISCO CHRONICLE); P: Richard Kramer with Working Title; D: Alastair Reid; Channel 4; 6 parts; 55 mins each.

Described as 'the Charles Dickens of San Francisco', Armistead Maupin managed to scale the walls of prejudice and rancour with his interlocking stories of jet-setters of all persuasions, living in 'Bagdad-by-the-Sea' in the far-off days of flares, platform shoes and freely available and obviously safe sex. 'It was a time of joy, a time of great affection and of great promise. That is what we are celebrating ... and celebrating it without judgement, without trying to taint it with this horrible hindsight' (co-producer Alan Poul, *New York Times*, 28.2.93).

Tales was originally optioned by Warners in 1979. The company wanted 'not a gay movie but a movie that happens to be gay'. However, just before production began in earnest they asked that the gay characters be removed or made heterosexual. 'What sticks in my mind,' Maupin told Betsy Sharkey of the NEW YORK TIMES (28.2.93), 'was a dinner I had with a potential screenwriter who heaped praise on the property but concluded that the gay gynaecologist should be a serial killer.'

Throughout the 1980s Hollywood studios wanted to do it BUT ... The sticking point was either that there were too many lesbians and gays in the story (and with not a serial killer among them) or that there were *any* at all. Finally, THIRTYSOMETHING's producer, Working Title (which had made MY BEAUTIFUL LAUNDRETTE), and Channel 4 collaborated on an adaptation which Maupin claims will be the most faithful to its source material since BRIDESHEAD REVISITED.

The genesis of the series was explored in ARENA 'Armistead Maupin Was a Name I Dreamt Up' (1992 T). The first book was published in 1978, followed by MORE TALES OF THE CITY (1980), FURTHER TALES OF THE CITY (1982), BABYCAKES (1984), SIGNIFICANT OTHERS (1987) and SURE OF YOU (1989).

Talking Heads (UK 1988 T) Monologues by a series of entertainingly befuddled, self-deluding or freedom-seeking souls: vicar's wife (Maggie Smith); colonial widow on hard times (Stephanie Cole); aspiring actress (Julie Walters) trying to make something artistic out of a part in a pornographic film; senior citizen (Thora Hird) seeing her independence shrivel before her eyes; a busybody (Patricia Routledge) who interferes once too often and is put out of harm's way; the simple-minded, middle-aged son (Alan Bennett) whose mother's new-found romance threatens to leave him stranded.
W: Alan BENNETT; P: Innes LLOYD; D: Stuart Burge and Giles Foster; BBC1; 30 mins. (Also presented on BBC Radio 4 with the same actors, 1991.)
Minimalist drama: each week one actor, a few simple sets, a camera, lighting and words. The results are spellbinding, with the Smith and Hird stories being particularly savage (and sad and funny). Minimal, too, are the homosexual references, but when they come (in relation to hidden magazines, group therapy, church flower arrangers and prison) they effortlessly help to join up the dots in a beautifully ugly and unfinished picture called Human Life (As We Know It).

Talking Hets (Aust 1991 C/V/T) A brief investigation of what has been called one of the greatest social problems facing Australia today.
W/D: Dianna Carr; P: Queer-ie Productions/UTS Melbourne; 6 mins.
Have you ever worked with anyone who was ...? Do you socialize with one? Are children safe with them? Should they be allowed to adopt? What causes it? What would you do if your child was one? Is there a cure?

These are just some of the pressing questions which more or less receive answers in this short but impressive encounter with heterosexuals (some disguised) and (of course) those who strongly disagree with their way of life. Some of the interviewees are pathetic (one man 'tried to be normal' – joining the boy scouts and the football club – but 'it didn't work'); others militant ('Straight Rights Now!').

Television comes in for much of the blame for the prevailing fog of ignorance and narrow-mindedness: 'I'd just like to see a bit more acceptance of straights on TV ... like you never see them. Why don't we have a few straights on *Perfect Match*? Why don't we see straights presented as normal? ... It's awful to walk down the street without people staring at you and abusing you.'

The report's conclusion is an upbeat one, if rather difficult to put into practice: 'The world's full of different people and you'll just have to accept it.'

talk shows Talk is cheap. Talk is bland. Talk can also be stimulating and controversial. Talk can open minds.

One of the staples of American television from the mid-1950s onwards, these programmes developed out of late-night variety shows in which a host would 'chat' to one or more 'guests'. With Steve Allen, Jack Paar, Johnny Carson, Dick Cavett, Merv Griffin and others at the helm, they often allowed 'alternative' voices such as Truman CAPOTE, Gore VIDAL, Jack Kerouac, and Orson WELLES to be heard, sometimes at great length. In Britain, during the 1960s, *The Eamonn Andrews Show* (1964–6) and *Not So Much a Programme ... More a Way of Life* (1964–5) were popular, but only Ireland's *The Late Late Show* with Gay Byrne stayed the course. The format didn't completely catch fire until the stewardship of people like Russell HARTY, Terry Wogan, Michael Parkinson, Michael Aspel, Jonathan Ross and Mavis Nicholson.

The approved format – blending and refereeing sometimes fractious celebrities who have books, films, series, plays or causes to publicize – has been satirized for its obsequious triviality or determined sensationalism by Australians Norman Gunston (alias Gary McDonald) and Edna EVERAGE, and by American Ruby Wax (*The Full Wax*).

On radio, talkfests have also proved audience pleasers: *A Word in Edgeways, Stop the Week, Start the Week* and *Loose Ends* have all had long runs.

In tandem with these generally rather sedate shows are evangelical-style but secular confessionals developed in the late 1960s by Phil DONAHUE and swamping the airwaves in the mid- to late 1980s: in America Sally Jessy Raphael, Oprah Winfrey and Whoopi Goldberg and in Britain Robert Kilroy-Silk. These platforms have provided outlets for more openly gay and lesbian people to say their piece, both on the stage and from the audience.

tango This dance's exaggerated precision and erotic positionings make it a natural for films and plays: from Rudolph VALENTINO in *The Four Horseman of the Apocalypse* (1921) to Al Pacino in *Scent of a Woman* (1992).

But the participants are not always the conventional male-female couple. Countess GESCHWITZ and LULU were under the tango's spell in PANDORA'S BOX (1928 C); Joe E. Brown and Jack Lemmon swung into one before a blindfolded gypsy orchestra in SOME LIKE IT HOT (1959 C); George Raft swept Jerry Lewis off his feet in *The Ladies' Man* (1961 C); Dominique Sanda and Stefania Sandrelli danced it divinely in THE CONFORMIST (1969 C); Rudolf NUREYEV and Anthony Dowell performed it erotically and perfectly in *Valentino* (the 1977 film's single scene of quality and one

which disapproved the notion that men cannot dance together as elegantly as men and women or women and women).

Other same-sex (though not necessarily homosexual) tangoing couples (usually to 'La Composita' by Rodriguez) include STEPTOE AND SON (in 'Come Dancing' – watched in rigid amazement by the milkman, 1970 T); two women in *Rabbit Test* (1978 C); Cindy Pickett and female friend in *Night Games* (1980 C); leather guys in *Police Academies 1 & 2* (1984 & 1985 C); two businessmen in RAY'S MALE HETEROSEXUAL DANCE HALL (1987 C); Catherine Deneuve and Linh Dan Pham (as her adopted daughter) in *Indochine* (1992 C); Peter Whitford and Paul Mercurio in STRICTLY BALLROOM (1992 C).

The ruthlessly driving rhythm, gliding, swooping, dipping movements within a locked embrace and its dignified air of carnality, submission and penetration were there in spirit if not in actuality in the thriller *Apartment Zero* (1988 C). Set in Buenos Aires, one of the cradles of the tango, the musical score, voluptuously tight like the squeeze of a boa constrictor, perfectly complemented the story of two very different men (Colin Firth and Hart Bochner) connecting and then being glued into a perilous power game.

Generally, radio and television histories (such as *Hooked on Tango* 1991 R) glide over or ignore completely the male homosexuality inherent in the music and motions of the Argentinian tango, which has its roots in Africa, Spain and Cuba. Very few accounts go beyond its founding in the riverfront bars and bordellos to confront the facts that many of its main, early dancers were men joined at the hip, with proud looks and jutting chins, spines exquisitely curved, moving to the 2–4 rhythm of flute, violin and guitar.

One of the rare programmes to even hint that some of the amalgamations may have been unconventional was *Tony Baldwin's Radiogram* (Aust 1991 R). It ventured that the Moorish-Spanish-African-influenced sound and movement was brought to Buenos Aires, Montevideo and the poor cities of the River Plate by 'disaffected immigrants who went to the clandestinos, decadent, dirty meeting places for social outcasts and small-time crooks. Here the tango found its instrumentation, social function and emotional basis.' Apparently shunned by the Argentine middle class, the tango travelled to Europe around 1915 where its combination of aggression, eroticism and melancholy perfectly suited the 'here today; gone tomorrow' mood of the First World War.

When VALENTINO (with Alice Terry) made it popular at the beginning of the postwar decade, 'smart middle-class suburbs of North America' who had previously rejected it as decadent and sleazy took it up with gusto. And, concluded Tony Baldwin sadly, the tango became 'Trivialized into cafés and family gatherings, and quitted the world of brothels, scarring (emotional and physical) and steamy underworlds'. The music of the poor and alienated, danced to express forbidden passion, was 'gentrified' by the very Argentinian suburbs who had formerly despised it.

A Taste of Honey Geoffrey INGHAM, an art student, moves in to cook and housekeep and look after Jo SMITH while her baby – conceived during a brief fling with a black sailor – is born. The alternating big sister/little brother relationship is broken up, possibly only temporarily, by the re-emergence of Jo's unpleasantly controlling mother, Helen.

Shelagh Delaney's durable comedy-drama-romance is one of the few plays containing a homosexual character to be allowed into Britain's schools. It has received two (1971 and 1984) BBC Schools Television productions as well as being discussed on its radio equivalent in *Drama Resources* (1985).

Geof appears to fit the bill as the quintessential queer: passive, homeless, effeminate – a SISSY Buttons to Jo's tart-tongued TOMBOY Cinderella. But Delaney's work (which was considerably reshaped by her director Joan Little-

wood) is so truthful in its melancholy-camp way that even the most insensitive and hostile audience cannot fail to see Geof's practical strengths and courageous tenderness, and Jo's less than attractive qualities, including her unpleasant prurience when it comes to her friend's sexual activities.

Jo is portrayed as being at the crossroads between childhood and maturity: a rebellious, sulky, dissatisfied adolescent who is totally unprepared for the results of her actions. An outsider like Geof, she can be read as a future lesbian or at least as a woman who will not have a 100 per cent heterosexual life; having no special interest in boys, feeling revulsion for certain aspects of being female, and remaining throughout a defiantly unconventional female.

The play makes the point quietly but resonantly that Jo, unlike Geof, is unformed and has not come to terms with who she is. Yet, because the boy is shy and persecuted, she feels able to adopt a sometimes proprietorial, sometimes dictatorial manner towards him, pecking away at his insecurities while postponing the confrontation of her own. In the main, Geof gives as good as he gets, which gives the central section of the play so much flavour and charm.

The play was first performed on BBC radio early in 1961, the same year as Tony RICHARDSON'S film version. As well as the television productions (both presented in three episodes), there were two other radio treatments in 1966 and 1977. (Shelagh Delaney's 1983 radio play *Don't Worry About Matilda* centred on the relationship of an unmarried, middle-aged actress, living in wild disorder, who is visited by her fastidious married brother. Elements of the actress, revealed as working exclusively in pornography, were reminiscent of Jo.)

A Taste of Honey (UK 1961 C) 'A poignant exploration of interracial love' was how the SAN FRANCISCO CHRONICLE described this classic film in the obituary of the film's director Tony RICHARDSON (15.11.91). The handful of scenes between Jo (Rita Tushingham) and the

sailor (Paul Danquah) are delightful – and crucial to the plot – but the film's heart lies with Jo and Geof (Murray MELVIN) as they form an alliance against a drab, hostile world represented by Jo's ghastly mother (Dora Bryan) and her perfect mate (Robert STEPHENS).
W: Shelagh Delaney and Tony Richardson; P: Tony Richardson; 100 mins.

The grittily poetic treatment of director Richardson and cameraman Walter Lassally is in total accord with the affecting but unsentimental playing of Tushingham and Melvin, which is complemented at every turn by a plaintive but buoyant score by John Addison. A gem.

A Taste of Kiwi (NZ 1990 C) Anal intercourse and fellatio with hulking, sweaty rugby players – in two minutes flat, courtesy of some cunningly intercut footage of the All Blacks rugby team (in a beer commercial) and a gay sex film. Unlikely to be shown on television despite the fact that the advert is almost as raunchy with its powerful thighs, sweating bodies, upraised bottoms and spurting liquid as the undraped body parts with which it competes.
P/D: Stewart Main and Peter WELLS; 2 mins.

All Blacks (courtesy of Stein Lager) meet gay porn with arse upwards poses common to both games. Wells pushes against the crush barriers to ask: when does an all-man's game become sex and when does sex become a couple of guys (or more) in a tackle and scrum?

Tatchell, Peter (1952–) British-born, Australian-reared and educated, now British-based activist and writer whose Labour Party candidacy and its aftermath were another nail in democracy's coffin. In OPEN SPACE 'Peter Tatchell and the Battle for Bermondsey' (1983 T) he told his side of the story, with contributions from Tory MP Matthew Parris and Labour's Tony Benn. They had been among his defenders during 15 months of common abuse, vilification and threats – from Fleet Street, individ-

uals within his own party, political opponents and constituents – when he was pilloried as a Communist, a foreigner ('an upstart invader from Down Under'), a draft-dodger, traitor, homosexual ('Red Aussie pouf') and nigger-lover. He is now a fairly frequent broadcaster outing Fleet Street's hypocrisy in OUT 'Absolutely Queered' (1991 T), discussing OutRage! in OUTRAGE!: THE DOCUMENTARY (1991 R), and 'OUTING lots of dead generals' on *Midweek* (1992 R).

tattoos Semi-permanent body decorations usually assigned to the arms and occasionally the chests of raffish, sexually adventurous male characters like little Joe (Dallesandro) in FLESH (1968 C) and *Trash* (1970 C); Mike (Ringo Starr) in *That'll Be The Day* (1973 C: located on one buttock); Bob (Gérard Depardieu) in TENUE DE SOIREE/EVENING DRESS (1985 C); PROSTITUTE Willie O'Keefe (Kevin Bacon) in JFK (1991 C); volatile former convict Frankie (Viggo Mortensen) in *The Indian Runner* (1991 C: birds, skull, Jesus and question mark on the right shoulder); the SAILOR (Howard Napper) in NORTH OF VORTEX (1991 C); Luke (Mike Dytil) in THE LIVING END (1992 C: a 'handprint' on his left shoulder blade); and the daddy of them all, Max Cady (Robert De Niro) in *Cape Fear* (1991 C) of whom Robert Mitchum says: 'I don't know whether to look at him or read him' (both sides of his torso are covered with the crucifixion, biblical texts and the scales of justice). There is a tattooed lesbian in *Rosebud* (1992 C/T: a rose).

'Tattoos always turn me on,' says an unseen male lover stroking the one on the arm of Les (Ian Targett) in the final scene of Alan BENNETT's *Marks* (1982 T), which centres on the desire of Les to be tattooed, against the wishes of his mother (Marjorie Yates).

The artistic and sensual elements of the process – so regularly viewed with wonderment in anthropological documentaries about 'natives' – were fully reported in a Western European context, along with much practical detail, in *Ero-*

tic Tattooing and Body Piercing (1991 & 1992 C) with all manner of piercings and cutting from San Francisco, New York and Amsterdam including 'clit and cock stretching'. (A television showing is unlikely.)

taxi drivers Bob (David McIlwraith) in OUTRAGEOUS! (1977 C), a sexy leather guy who becomes Robin's agent: 'By "hanging out with a star" he gets to score with a lot of gay customers' (Danny Peary, CULT MOVIES, 1981); in *Taxi* 'Elaine's Strange Triangle' (1982 T) Alex Reiger (Judd Hirsch) somehow ends up in a gay BAR dancing on a table with a man, Kirk Muldaur (John David Carson); there were no lesbians or gays on the payroll of the firm in this series but, in Britain, a lesbian minicab driver was made unwelcome in *Rides* (1992 T).

Taxi to Cairo (West Germany 1987 C) Frank (RIPPLOH) is told to get married or lose the inheritance. His friend Klara (Christine Neubauer) comes to the rescue, but complications occur when they both fall in love with the same man – their NEIGHBOUR Eugen (Udo Schenk), a BISEXUAL computer-media freak.
W: Frank Ripploh and Tamara Kafka; P/D: Frank Ripploh; 90 mins.
   Sleepy, thoroughly obvious comedy that could have been made by anybody: anybody, that is, except the maker of TAXI ZUM KLO. A fairly major disappointment.

Taxi Zum Klo (Taxi to the Toilet) (West Germany 1981 C) Frank RIPPLOH strips naked, physically and emotionally, as a footloose and fancy-free gay man: TEACHER, cruiser of parks, toilets and service station forecourts, client of STD clinics and eventual activist. In contrast to Frank's sexual ever-readiness, his boyfriend Bernd (Bernd Broaderup) is happy with Frank and domesticity.
W/D: Frank Ripploh; P: Frank Ripploh, Horst Schier and Laurens Straub; 92 mins (3 mins 20 secs were removed from the British release print; yet the film won a German award for the best comedy of its year).
   A ripe and explicit look at a scruffy German schoolteacher (closely based on Ripploh) who, dressed in leather, does every beat with great dedication (and still manages to do his job – and have a permanent lover). Only the ending – Frank facing his shocked class in drag – is misconceived. Mostly it's courageous, frothy and engagingly personal.
   The film was glowingly received by the majority of critics in Britain and America, of which these comments from BBC Radio 3's *Critics' Forum* (1981), although perhaps more explicit, are fairly typical:

> Paul Bailey: 'It's revolutionary because it shows a male homosexual … enjoying the thrill of the chase … As a homosexual myself … I found it refreshing that here was a film that shows homosexual life as neither heroic nor despairing'. He went on to say that it dares to describe four men 'examining each other's persons in a cottage'.
> George Melly: 'It could be a heterosexual comedy.' He explained that he was, for a long period of his life, homosexual. 'I am worried that many people may be physically sickened by some of the scenes … I admire Ripploh for not using Albinoni and soft focus [but it] will appal a lot of sexual liberals without homosexual leanings.'
> Richard Cork: 'I wasn't at all offended … hard sex treated in such a humane way … a lack of shame, pimples on the buttocks … explicit yet not pornographic.'

Tchaikovsky, Peter Ilych [Piotr Ilich] (1840–93) Russian composer whose semi-open homosexuality, marriage of convenience, musical emotionalism, long-distance relationship with his patroness Nadezhda Von Meck, and whose curious death have made him an invaluable addition to the gallery of tortured geniuses, no more so than in Ken Russell's *The Music Lovers* (1971 C) where he was portrayed by Richard Chamberlain. Other interpreters include Innokenti Smoktunovsky in *Tchaikovsky* (1971 C: without a hint of homosexuality); Mike Gwilym in

Tchaikovsky: A Fateful Gift (1984 R); Ronald Pickup in THE MISSING DAY (1986 C); Edward De Souza in *The Mask of Music* (1987 R).

Tea and Sympathy (US 1956 C)
Archetypal shy, SENSITIVE college student Tom (John Kerr) prefers 'womanly' pursuits like SEWING and tennis and acting to the aggressive quasi-homosexual activities of the guys, egged on by the housemaster (Leif Erickson). His father (Edward Andrews) is disgusted with him: 'This boy would rather sit around and listen to music, read POETRY and strum his guitar ... he wants to be ... a *folk singer*!' After a disastrous night with a local prostitute, his housemaster's wife, Laura (Deborah Kerr), who has befriended him, takes him to a wood where they make love. Some years later he returns to the college, as a successful married WRITER, and learns of the sacrifice Laura made for his sake (and for the sake of the status quo).
W: Robert Anderson from his play; P: Pandro S. Berman; D: Vincente Minnelli; 122 minutes.

A well-mannered assault on the forces in society that make useful lives wretched. Under the film's glossy surface calm bubble all sorts of tensions about men and women that would be voiced, though not always talked through, in the 1970s and 1980s.

Perhaps the miscasting of John Kerr as Tom, too long in the tooth by then to play his stage role with total conviction, and the presence of Deborah Kerr have given this film an undeserved reputation for rectitude and for pushing homosexuality under the rug. Hollywood's censorship mills ground for a whole year before allowing the production to go ahead, albeit with a revised ending obliterating any thought of homosexuality in the boy and emphasizing the wife's guilt, Tom's success as a writer and his 'adjustment' to heterosexual life (married, with a ring).

Seen 30 years on, the piece rings with a truthful clarity, partly because of Minnelli and his cast's skill and partly because

the housemaster, rough-housing with his boys and totally at sea with his new wife's individualism, is presented with considerable understanding and subtlety. There are contradictions in his character which the last scene, though foisted on the makers, does indicate more clearly than in the play.

In the wife, the playwright invests all that is vital and good in the human spirit: a refusal to stand by in the face of BULLYING just because it is deemed normal; an ability to share feelings; a reaching out; a natural grace. Director and actress are perfectly in tune with Anderson's conception. That a commercial film – from MGM no less – should be allowed to feature such straying from the norm of American society is moderately breathtaking.

The censorship of Tom's sexuality serves in a strange way to make *Tea and Sympathy* more potent because the 'problem' is no longer his, but that of the people who persecute him. Despite the compromises, the film does nothing to suggest that Tom's being heterosexual won't change his neatness, good taste, liking for knitting and sewing, and enjoyment of reading George Bernard Shaw on the beach.

Needless to say, Minnelli's shaping of each scene, his impeccable sense of colour and décor, the blending of interiors and exteriors, and his supple guiding of the actors and the resulting underplaying serve the text magnificently.

'... adultery is okay – impotence is okay, but perversion is their *bête noire*. But ... it really is a play about persecution of the individual and compassion and pity and love of one human being for another. And as such can stand alone, I think, without the additional problems of homosexuality (letter written to the director by Deborah Kerr, quoted in Vincente Minnelli with Hector Arce, I REMEMBER IT WELL, 1974).
'He is not like [you], therefore he is capable of all possible crimes. He is not one of us, a member of the tribe. So the tribe has to find a scapegoat, to reaffirm

your shaky position,' Laura to her husband.

teachers Homosexual men and women in positions of authority and trust, surrogate parents; mostly just doing their jobs but sometimes mixing structured guidance in a classroom with the intensely personal and private (*Germany Year Zero*; THE HUMAN JUNGLE; *Walk a Crooked Path*; WITHIN THESE WALLS; BUTLEY; JIMMY; LIANNA; WHALE MUSIC; INAPPROPRIATE BEHAVIOUR; *Miss Pym Disposes*; THE RAINBOW; G.P.; *Death Drop*; *Still Life*).

(1) Teachers in infant/junior and senior schools Men: the gross sadist in *Zéro de Conduite* (1933 C); Henning (Erich Guhnme), a sleazy NAZI sympathizer who barely disguises his interest in some of his pupils in *Germany Year Zero* (1947 C); John Hemming (Tenniel Evans) accused by a boy pupil of making untoward advances in *Walk a Crooked Path* (1968 C); flamboyant bachelor Max Fielder (Clive Swift) who gives the bullied boy advice on future survival in ROLL ON FOUR O'CLOCK (1970 T); in CROWN COURT a teacher (Keith Drinkel) went 'Beyond the Call of Duty' (1976 T) with his disciplining; the science teacher who rapes a boy in MARCUS WELBY MD 'The Outrage' (1975 T); Ernest (Peter SALLIS) enjoying the siren song of the navy while on holiday with his unsuspecting – and anyway fully occupied – wife in THE OBELISK (1977 T); gay activist Peter Whitelaw (Colby Chester) in STARSKY AND HUTCH 'Death in a Different Place' (1977 T); Ken (Ken Robertson) finally opening himself up to questioning – and abuse – from his class in NIGHTHAWKS (1978 C); an Irishman (P. G. Stephens) made an outcast for 20 years because of one weekend spent with a 17-year-old boy, JIMMY (1978 R); Tony Kellett (Derrick Gilbert) accused of abducting a 15-year-old boy in STANDARD PROCEDURE (1979 R); Frank RIPPLOH – who marks his pupil's work while waiting for action in a public toilet – comes out to his class at the end of TAXI ZUM KLO (1981 C);

Michael (Peter Denyer) in AGONY 'Coming Out ... And Going In Again' (1980 T) sacked for taking part in a radio discussion about COMING OUT and answering back to the heckles of his class the next day; the central hurt in the life of Tom Falconer (Maurice Denham), namely his dismissal after a scandal involving one of his boys, is temporarily salved through his gentle friendship with a young boy in *The Gate of Eden* (1980 T); the teacher of severely subnormal young people, Paul (Michael Troughton), the lover of Ken HASTINGS, seen briefly in a couple of episodes of ANGELS (1980 T); Kidder (James Hazeldene) beaten up by the police in *One Summer* (1983 T) for suspected sexual assault on a runaway boy; Peter Lester (Leonard Preston) composing love songs in his head while listlessly teaching his equally apathetic class to appreciate ROMEO AND JULIET in THE GROUNDLING AND THE KITE (1984 T); art teacher Morris Murry (Dermot Crowley) reluctantly back in Ireland to pay his last respects to his prickly former terrorist father in *The Mourning Thief* (1984 T) with wife and boyfriend in tow; Richard Wilson (Michael Graham-Cox), the school 'POUF', target of abuse for all the (SUN newspaper-reading) kids in THE OTHER OTHER WOMAN (1985 R); Jean-Marc (Gilles Renaud) who suddenly has to become a parent to his new lover's 6-year-old son in THE HEART EXPOSED/LE COEUR DECOUVERT (1986 C/T); student teacher Lorenzo (Lorenzo Lena) tempted by, but deciding not to respond to, one of his pupils in THE FLAVOUR OF CORN (1987 T); bisexual Ed (Brian Kerwin) in TORCH SONG TRILOGY (1988 C); Terence Fielding (Joss Ackland) responsible for *A Murder of Quality* (1991 T); Robert (Steven Vidler) in WORDS OF ONE SYLLABLE (1991 R); Brendan (John Polson), having an affair with a 17-year-old pupil, incurring the violent wrath of his lover's father in G.P. 'So Makes the Man' (1991 T); Lucas Simmonds (Mark Straker), a biology teacher who involves a pupil – his lover – in dangerous psychological experiments in *Still*

Life 'The Virgin in the Garden' (1992 R); PE teacher Brian Innis (David Learner) involved in what turns out to be deadly intimacy with a boy in *Death Drop* (1992 R); one of the male teachers coming out in GRANGE HILL (1993 T).

Women: Fraulein Von Bernberg, the idol of Manuela and the other girls who wait longingly for her goodnight kisses in MAEDCHEN IN UNIFORM (Dorothea Wieck (1931 C) and in *Girls in Uniform* (Virginia McKenna 1967 T); pathetic Miss Gilchrist (Eve March) on the fringes of a satanist cult in *The Seventh Victim* (1943 C); Mlle Cara (Simone Simon), coquettish and hypochondriacal, who runs a school with Mlle Julie (Edwige Feuillère) in OLIVIA (1950 C) where joy unconfined and petty jealousies abound in more or less equal proportions; cropped-haired, resolutely unfeminine Jane Ellis (Nancy Price), hearing-impaired assistant head of the school for DEAF children she founded in *Mandy* (1952 C); Miss Wilson (Beryl REID), monocled, tweedy science mistress in *The Belles of St Trinians* (1954 C); keeper of the flame for university education for her brighter girls, Miss FIGGIS (Beatrix LEHMANN) in LOVE AND MISS FIGGIS (1954 T); Karen Wright (Audrey Hepburn) and Martha Dobie (Shirley MacLaine) watching their life's work destroyed by a child's lie in THE CHILDREN'S HOUR/THE LOUDEST WHISPER (1961 C); the schoolmistress excitedly hosing down Angela (Gio Petre) after a sauna in *Loving Couples* (1964 C) but being rejected by her – which leaves her literally clawing at the ground; Miss Benton (Martita HUNT) who ran the kindergarten with her friend Maud in *Bunny Lake Is Missing* (1965 C) and now fills her days in their attic flat above the school listening to tapes of children's nightmares and fantasies; Miss Jones (Sheila Brennan) torn between her love for Miss SMITH (Patricia England) and her need to conform in INCIDENT (1965 T); Dorothy (Flora Robson) haunted by a fear that she may have 'ruined' one of her girls for life in THE HUMAN JUNGLE 'Conscience on a Rack' (1965 T); Calla (Estelle Parsons)

in *Rachel, Rachel* (1968 C), a recently born-again Christian, which only increases her guilt over her love for a colleague; Sarah Westmore (Kathleen Byron) bitterly envious of her more successful married sister and confessing to crossing the dividing line between encouraging a pupil and loving her in WITHIN THESE WALLS 'Invasion of Privacy' (1976 T); Mrs Appleyard (Rachel Roberts) taking to drink in *Picnic at Hanging Rock* (1975 C) after the disappearance of three of the girls and a teacher she was fond of; Ruby Mitchell (Paola Dionisotti) in *Within These Walls* 'Mixer' (1978 T) booted out for 'corrupting some of the girls'; Claudia (Eleanora Gorgi) in TO FORGET VENICE (1979 C); Selma (Madeleine Stowe) and her former maid, now lover and colleague, Pauline (Jean Renée Smith) in *Beulah Land* (1980 T), integrating black and white children during the Civil War; 'Miss A. and Miss M.' played by Kika Markham and Jennifer Hilary in ALL FOR LOVE (1983 T), fractious and superior, splitting asunder in their holiday cottage, watched at close quarters and from afar by a lovesick young girl; Kate in WHALE MUSIC (Janet Dale 1983 T; Alison Steadman 1984 R) on the rebound from her heterosexual flatmate, now having an uneasy affair with one of her pupils, 'D'; Harriet (Diana QUICK) finding it easier to be brave and confront sexism in the classroom than undiluted HOMOPHOBIA, of which she has personal knowledge in THE OTHER OTHER WOMAN (1985 R); Helen West (Emma Piper) driven to despair because of a pupil in SYRUP OF FIGS (1986 R); child psychologist Jo (Jenifer Landor) becoming steadily closer to a 15-year-old girl in INAPPROPRIATE BEHAVIOUR (1987 T); Winifred Inger in *The Rainbow* (Kate Buffery 1988 T; Amanda Donohoe 1989 C) spending pleasurable time with Ursula; Lorraine (Lonette McKee), one of THE WOMEN OF BREWSTER PLACE (1989 T), lost her job in Detroit because of her sexuality; Kate (Ethna Roddy), the victim of anonymous abuse by pupils and/or colleagues in SOUTH OF THE BORDER (1990 T).

(2) Private tutors Men: Walter, the German tutor who captivates a mother, a daughter and especially a teenage son in *Five Finger Exercise* (Maximilian Schell 1962 C; Gary Bond 1970 T); Richard (Michael Craig) is led down an unexpected path when he tutors 19-year-old Donald for his maths O-level in SPOILED (1968 T); Richie (Nigel HAVERS (teaching scales to nasty boys and girls, at least one with a rabidly homophobic father in COMING OUT (1979 T).

Women: Miss HAVISHAM, guardian and instructress of Estella in the arts of coquetry and heart-breaking in *Great Expectations* (Martita HUNT 1946 C; etc); Annie Sullivan dragging blind and deaf Helen Keller out of her pit of darkness, silence and rage with a mixture of coercion, persuasion and passion in *The Miracle Worker* (Anne Bancroft 1962 C; Patty Duke 1979 T) – and continuing by her side at college in *Helen Keller: The Miracle Continues* (Blythe Danner 1984 T); Madge (Briony Hodge) gives a neighbour *Piano Lessons* (1976 T), and soon they are planning how to rid themselves of their boring husbands so they can be together; Elizabeth Rodney (Caroline Mortimer) wants Joan to 'elope' with her and so free herself from her mother's handcuffs in *The Unlit Lamp* (1980 R); Miss WADE (Sonia Fraser), taciturn governess in *Little Dorrit* (1980 R) spiriting away a young girl to live with her in Venice.

(3) Teachers in further education, colleges and universities Men: Rupert CADELL appalled that his aesthetic philosophies have been turned into calculated, cold-blooded murder in ROPE (Ernest MILTON 1932 R; James Stewart 1948 C; etc); George, the English teacher at a Californian college, facing up to a lover's death in A SINGLE MAN (David MARCH 1972 R; ALEC MCCOWEN 1991 R); bisexual Ben (Alan BATES), gay Joey Keyston (Richard O'Callaghan) and lesbian Edna Shaft (Jessica Tandy), uneasy English department colleagues in BUTLEY (1974 C/T); Wayne Harrington (Peter Donat) killing

himself in *The Suicide's Wife* (1979 T), maybe because he couldn't cope with the academic rat race rather than because he was (very probably) bisexual; Sir Alan Tufnell, pillar of Oxbridge and renowned TV pundit drawn to seducing young heterosexual men, giving them presents and then claiming they stole from or tried to BLACKMAIL him in *Rumpole of the Bailey* 'The Gentle Art of Blackmail' (1980 R); the late Professor Little's arrangement with his wife allowed him occasional affairs with young men in *An Empty Glass* (1981 R); Humphrey (Stephen FRY), POET and Senior Moral Tutor at a Cambridge college in *Common Pursuit* (1992 T).

Women: 'Dykey Dora' (Pearl Hackney) chatting up the female college body in *Comedy Playhouse* 'The Importance of Being Hairy' (1972 T); Professor Ruth Brennan (Jane Hallaren), right-thinking lesbian-feminist somewhat ruffled by the exuberant COMING OUT of her student/lover LIANNA (1983 C); Gisela (Diana QUICK) hiding from the authorities, teaching carpentry to boys on probation in SILENT WING (1984 R); Vivian Bell (Helen Shaver), professor of English at Columbia University finds love with a woman in Reno in DESERT HEARTS (1985 C); Miss Hodge (Joan Sims), very noticeably prone to 'favouritism' herself, turning a blind eye to the passionate friendships at the physical education teachers training college in *Miss Pym Disposes* (1987 R).

'I'd rather you didn't call me Ruth in class ... I need to keep a certain amount of distance,' Professor Ruth Brennan in *Lianna*.

'... it's a chance to talk. Schools aren't the best places to talk,' a teenage pupil explaining to a male teacher why he has come to see him in his remote cottage in *Standard Procedure*.

'I started off teaching her English; now I'm teaching her this,' Kate, indicating her pupil 'D' – lying apparently asleep (but taking in every word) – in bed beside her in *Whale Music*.

'You don't know what it's like ... I just stare at the phone.' Irritating, affectionate, exuberant Calla (Estelle Parsons) unrequitedly loving her colleague (Joanne Woodward) who tries to comfort her in *Rachel, Rachel* (1968 C): 'I hope you find what you want.' To which Calla replies: 'Not to worry ... I'll survive.'

In *Maintaining Standards* (1981 R) Clive Baxter (Philip Lowrie), falsely accused of taking advantage of a young boy, analyses his reasons for choosing his career to his lover Harry (Anthony Benson):

'Why am I – a queer – in teaching? ... This case has made me face the fact that I am getting my kicks from teaching *boys*.'
'Don't heterosexual men get their kicks from teaching girls?'*
'It's different for them. It doesn't make them think any less of themselves.'

* Male heterosexual teachers do also fall in love with their pupils (like Ronnie, played by Nigel HAVERS, in a 1980s *Rumpole of the Bailey* episode: 'The Course of True Love'). They can also be dismissed for innocently taking too much interest in a pupil (*Tonight is Friday* 1962 R etc). But in drama, homosexuals outnumber them 10 to 1.

See also CLAUSE 28; STUDENTS.

tears Homosexual men, perennially viewed as big soft nellies, are piled so high with sorrows, guilts and vices (named and unnamed) that they can't help but gush forth. Oversensitive Finch Whiteoak in WHITEOAKS (Lyndon Brook 1949 T; Andrew Ray/John Charlesworth 1954 T) was one early example, and Gordon Whitehouse in DANGEROUS CORNER (John Fraser 1957 T) another. This shedding of tears was especially noticeable in the 1960s when breaking up or being rejected was *de rigueur* for deviants. Edward Shelley (Michael Carridia), one of Oscar's boys, breaks under cross-examination in ON TRIAL 'Oscar WILDE' (1960 T); 'Boy' Barrett's tearfulness in a photograph with an 'acquaintance' is used to BLACKMAIL him in VICTIM (1961 C); Frank Wells (Ben Cooper), bespectacled, unmarried baby brother with 'an insatiable appetite for money', blubbers and splutters as he

confesses all in PERRY MASON 'The Case of the Impatient Investor' (1961 T; two other 'unmanly' men – played by James Milhollin and Denver Pyle in other 'Cases' that same year – betrayed trembling lower lips and watery eyes under pressure); Arthur (John STRATTON) cries 'like a baby' after one of his frequent rows with Basil (Alan Rowe) in WANTED: SINGLE GENTLEMAN (1967 T); Ian (Victor Henry) breaks down into angry tears when lukewarm Jimmy (Simon Ward) walks out after struggling free from Ian's drunken embrace in WHEN DID YOU LAST SEE MY MOTHER? (1967 R): 'You bastard. You knew. You knew!'; murder suspect Felix Tesler (Tony Musante) bawls his eyes out in THE DETECTIVE (1968 C); Michael (Kenneth Nelson) casts off his acid-soaked confidence to reveal chronic insecurity and self-laceration at the end of the party in THE BOYS IN THE BAND (1970 C); Doug Salter (Hal Holbrook) is last seen in THAT CERTAIN SUMMER (1972 T) with tears splashing down his face (unscripted ones, but retained by the director); Albin (Michel Serrault) blubbers in the street when Renato asks him to go away for a few days while he entertains his son's soon-to-be in-laws in LA CAGE AUX FOLLES (1978 C); in FACING THE SUN (1980 T) arrogant Gilberto (Gerard Murphy) gives full vent to his emotions after his British lover goes off for a night with someone else 'You've succeeded – *I'm jealous*'; the verger Wilfred (Milton Johns), caught in a gay club in *Hell's Bells* 'Big Boys Don't Cry' (1986 T), is told to stop crying by his bishop: 'We have enough trouble with rising damp as it is. Gay? It's nothing to cry about'; Bryan (Todd Stites) in TOGETHER ALONE (1991 C/T) when he is suddenly informed by his bed partner that he is married with a child; Leslie SMITH (Frank Windsor) in CASUALTY 'Allegiance' (1991 T) when his lover dies; closeted Owen (Brian Cox) in THE LOST LANGUAGE OF CRANES (1992 T) when his son tells him he's one, too; Freddie (Roland CURRAM) about two dead lovers in ELDORADO (1992 and 1993 T).

Some gay men do cry. Quentin CRISP, indomitable, taking whatever life has to throw at him. And Peter Lester (Leonard Preston) in THE GROUNDLING AND THE KITE (1984 T) whose problem lay not in his sexuality but in his inability to express his feelings or offload powerfully buried emotions. He *couldn't* cry (only write rather painful love songs).

'Dykes don't cry,' declared Ellen (Barbara Hershey) in IN THE GLITTER PALACE (1977 T). But at least one did (in secret), nipping round to a neighbour for a chat and a weep. But June Buckridge (Beryl REID) finally opens the floodgates when she realizes the full extent of her betrayal in THE KILLING OF SISTER GEORGE (1968 C).

The sight of REAL MEN crying used to be limited to occasional bursts by accredited he-men: Clark Gable – very reluctantly – in *Gone with the Wind* (1939 C); Spencer Tracy – just fooling – in ADAM'S RIB (1949 C). Or by self-pitying alcoholics: Richard Egan in *Violent Saturday* (1955 C): 'Go away please. I don't want you to see me cry'; the superficially well-slicked executive, played by Michael Craig, crumbling in a police station in *A Case of Character* (1963 T). Or callow teenagers: Lew Ayres snivelling over GARBO on the tennis court in *The Kiss* (1929 C); James DEAN railing against father and mother in *East of Eden* (1955 C); Sal Mineo – with his face turned away from the camera – in EXODUS (1960 C); Peter Fonda in *Easy Rider* (1969 C).

In the 1980s, tears began to be seen in Britain and America as a legitimate form of letting go of tension, of expressing joy, anger, pain or exasperation rather than loss of control only displayed by men who were not completely male. Writers and directors began to get this message across that tears were not solely the province of the weak and the wicked. Michael Parkinson presented a programme in 1985 called *A Crying Shame* in which this four-square Yorkshireman defended sportsmen (and others) who wept publicly, talking with stiff-upper-lipped public schoolboys and with psychologists about the 'naturalness' of let-ting tears flow regardless of gender. WOMAN'S HOUR had looked at the area a year before in 'Men Don't Communicate with Each Other at That Kind of Level'. Schoolboys had been asked to 'research their feelings' the better to understand and feel for others, particularly future lovers.

Male tears are nevertheless rare and still mainly confined to characters pushed to the limit of endurance such as Arthur (Bill Treacher) having a nervous breakdown in EASTENDERS (1986–7 T); deposed underworld king Carl Galton (Iain Glenn) over the death of the only man who loved him in *The Fear* (1988 T); the son (Dean Williams), uncontrollably, at his wedding reception in *Distant Voices, Still Lives* (1988 C); Pete Beale (Peter Dean) over his estrangement from his wife Kathy in EASTENDERS (1989 T); LA cop Nick (Andy Garcia) in *Internal Affairs* (1990 C); abused and harried teacher Jim (Michael Palin) in GBH (1991 T, but not until episode 6); Pascoe (David Ryall) after admitting embezzlement in *The Men's Room* (1991 T); Tom (Nick Nolte) crying in his psychiatrist's lap after having described his own and his family's rape and its even more horrifying aftermath in THE PRINCE OF TIDES (1991 C); iron-souled businessman (Anthony Hopkins) in *Howards End* (1991 C).

'That's something you must stop. A grown man crying. You're a grown man, now,' Mrs Hicks to her son Ralph in *At Cousin Harry's* (1964 R).

See also MEN'S LIBERATION.

Teddy Boy's name, a diminutive of Edward. Given to silly ass Teddy Deakin (Richard Murdoch) in *The Ghost Train* (1941 C); the botanist Teddy Lamp in THE ASCENT OF F6 (David Learner 1988 R etc) who is in love with the leader of the climbing expedition and is the only member to die (losing his balance while grasping for a flower); the murdered ANTIQUE DEALER in THE DETECTIVE (1968 C); FASHION DESIGNER Teddi Casablanca (Steve Inwood) in *Valley of the Dolls '81* (1981 T).

teddy bear owners Originally called bear dolls or bear toys prior to 1903, toy bears took the name of Teddy from President Theodore Roosevelt. The Western world – its female and especially its male citizens – can't seem to get enough of them. In addition to millions of fluffy toys of all sizes, there are Winnie the Pooh, Rupert Bear, Sooty and Teddy (not forgetting Soo), Paddington Bear and so on.

Among the male devotees who are inseparable from their furry dolls: Jimmy PORTER who communicates with his wife (who has a toy squirrel) almost entirely through his in LOOK BACK IN ANGER (Kenneth Haigh 1956 T; etc): 'Is he fey – on top of everything?' someone asks; Artie Strauss (Bradford Dillman), one of the two child murderers in COMPULSION (1959 C); millionaire Mr Howell (Jim Backus) who sleeps with one on *Gilligan's Island* (1964–7 T); Albert Gill (Peter Butterworth) who is close to his mother and to Perry, his teddy, in THE FABULOUS FRUMP (1969 T); Julian (Martin Potter) who asks his beloved Agamemnon if it's all right to have sex with a man in *Goodbye Gemini* (1970 C); Bobby (Bobby Kendall), pretty young hero of *Pink Narcissus* (1971 C); Pike (Ian Lavender) who can't get to sleep without 'Mr Snugley' in *Dad's Army* (1968–77 T); racing driver Donald Campbell, each of whose three wives had to learn to love 'Mr Woppit', his longtime companion (Neil Nisbet in *Speed King* 1979 T; Dexter Fletcher/Anthony Hopkins in *Across the Lake* 1987 T); Corporal 'Radar' O'Reilly (Gary Burghoff) in *M*A*S*H* (1972–83 T); fluff-headed Sebastian (Anthony Andrews) totally bonded with 'Aloysius' in BRIDESHEAD REVISITED (1981 T); Morris (James Saxon) in *Brass* (1982–4 T) similarly loves his 'Hesketh' to distraction and is devastated when he 'dies' (bravely) in the Spanish civil war after 'sleeping' with Robert Graves – as a replacement Morris gets not another bear but 'a little black friend': 'Armstrong', a golliwog (*Brass* 'Bradley Gets On Top' etc 1990 T); Lofty (Tom Watts) has one called Basil in EAST-ENDERS (1985 T); varsity man carries bear with him in *Crown House* (1988 R); Barry (Gary Hailes) leaves a battered bear as a token of affection (and remorse?) after he quits Colin's flat in *EastEnders* (1988 T); decadent Kingsley (Michael Gough) in *Blackeyes* (1989 T); cynical soap opera scriptwriter Sean (Mark Lamos) who has a small white one with him in hospital in LONGTIME COMPANION (1990 C); Sebastian Rich, brave and resourceful ITN cameraman, told CNN on the day after the bombing of Bagdad which began the Gulf war in January 1991 that he goes nowhere without his teddy 'T.B.'; Mr HUMPHRIES (John INMAN) uses his as a comfort against his marauding female bedmate in GRACE AND FAVOUR (1992–   T).

Women who revere their stuffed Bruins have included amoral Patricia (Jean Seberg) who has one in her bedroom in *Breathless/A Bout de Souffle* (1960 C); still innocent Rose (Betty White) in THE GOLDEN GIRLS 'Old Friends' (1988 T) who is distraught when her teddy, one of her emotional bedrocks, is 'kidnapped' by a little girl; the young wife runs to hers for comfort after a (mother-in-law engineered) death in the family in *Mother Love* (1989 T); Vivian's fellow prostitute friend (Laura San Giacomo) sleeps with one in *Pretty Woman* (1990 C).

See also CAT OWNERS; DOG OWNERS; DOLLS.

The Teddy Bears' Picnic 'If you go down in the woods today you're sure of a big surprise ...'

Mindless, feathery song (by John Bratton and Jimmy Kennedy) which has been a children's favourite in Britain since the early 1930s when it was recorded by Henry Hall and the BBC Dance Orchestra. Sung by a ferociously demure (unidentified) male, it opens delicious possibilities of what teddies might do if left to their own devices: enjoy a picnic in the woods, thoroughly exhaust themselves having a good time, and be taken home by their mummies and daddies for an early bedtime. In other words, a very subtle piece of mind control for children who are difficult to get to bed.

The song's most unusual outing came in the last scene of *A Zed & Two Noughts* (1985 C) when twin brothers, widowed zoologists Oswald and Oliver Deuce (Brian and Eric Deacon), remove all their clothes, inject themselves with a drug overdose, and lie down – in front of a stop action camera (to record their decomposition) – to die. Their posthumous plans are thwarted when thousands of slurpy snails march over and around them, chomping through the power cable and so prematurely terminating their last home movie. So ends, too, the silly song ('See them gaily gad about') and the voice of its nannyish vocalist, not to mention one of the most extended visions of male NAKEDNESS in recent memory.

teenagers *See* YOUNG GAY AND LESBIAN PEOPLE.

teensy weensy A babyish expression for tiny or small, heard most often from the lips of precious, overly well-bred women – or those trying to ape them like screechy-voiced Lina Lamont (Jean Hagen) in *Singin' in the Rain* 1952 C: 'Aren't you just the teensiest bit in love with me?' A few men have employed the expression: spoilt rich alcoholic Boyd Fairchild (Richard Egan) in *Violent Saturday* (1955 C) who describes, disgustedly, smashing a glass into 'teensy weensy pieces ... and you count every single one'; preening Simon Templar (Roger Moore) alias *The Saint*: 'Don't you think this is being the teensiest weensiest bit odd?' he says with quizzical sarcasm to a police inspector in 'The Art Crowd' (1967 T); the selfish bachelor ANTIQUE DEALER Kenton ARCHER (Graeme Kirk) in THE ARCHERS (1992 R) regarding the price of a set of tin soldiers as being 'just a teensy weensy bit over the odds'.

television One of the most powerful mediums of communication so far developed, achieving worldwide penetration from the 1970s onwards. A purveyor of millions of hours of sport, news, drama, comedy, documentary, music, health information, hobbies, sex education and religion plus a whole host of advertising and propaganda messages. Television's representations and lack of representations of homosexuality have been only cursorily discussed on the medium itself in GAY LIFE 'Gays in the Media' (1980); *Right to Reply* 'Gays and Broadcasting' (1986, portrayed as 'an early evening sinner or late night deviate'); OUT ON TUESDAY (1989).

'Keeping Faith? Channel Four and Its Audience' (1987), a C4 survey of its viewers, found that the reaction of gay men was generally one of 'cautious gratitude' rather than a strong call for more gay programmes: 'Most were not interested in the politics of the gay movement and had many other cultural resources within the gay community where they would rather spend their time – television was peripheral to their lives and their attitudes reflected this.'

See also OUT OF THE ARCHIVES.

Television: A World History (UK 1985 & US 1986 T) A 13–part series, the first to tackle the medium as a worldwide phenomenon, developing shakily in the 1920s to become, in the 1980s, the foremost conduit of news and entertainment.

P: Michael Murphy and Norman Swallow; P/D: Michael Beckham, Brian Blake, Philip Casson, Stephen Peet and Leslie Woodhead; GRANADA and PBS; 13 parts; 55 mins each.

The American version includes gay-oriented scenes from BRIDESHEAD REVISITED, THAT CERTAIN SUMMER and AN EARLY FROST, but not lesbian works such as *The War Widow* (1976), IN THE GLITTER PALACE or A QUESTION OF LOVE.

Among its plethora of heartstopping moments (from 'Hi honey, I'm home' to the Apollo moon landing) is a hilarious 1953 mickey-take of THIS IS YOUR LIFE from Sid Caesar's *Your Show of Shows* (the subject endlessly clasping, hugging, embracing and squeezing a male friend).

Equally priceless is a promotional film showing a 'typical' American family watching TV in the very early 1950s. Mom, Dad, two or three kids and ... another man. In his early thirties and dressed in a smart shiny suit, this decidedly untypical person has his arm round the back of the sofa. Upon closer inspection the limb could be construed as being around the back of Dad sitting *on* the sofa in close proximity. *Who was that man?* A brother? A lodger? A neighbour? A friend? An ex-army buddy? A significant other?

Francis Wheen's book 'Television: A World History' (1985) which accompanied the British series includes one full-colour photograph of *Brideshead*'s Charles and Sebastian (the latter in his decline). There is also a postage stamp-sized photograph of the very first television production of ROPE (1939) ... But that is as far as it goes in tracing this particular minority's representation by, and contribution to, the once bulky and blurry television machine which is now entering the 'Third Age of Broadcasting' with satellite and cable hi-technology.

television cookery experts Many men have appeared over a hot stove from Philip Harben (*The Man in the Kitchen*: beard and blue striped butcher's APRON) in the 1940s to Keith Floyd in the 1990s, with demeanours ranging from the bluff and hearty to the velouté and soufflé. In television and film fiction they are presented as vain and ruthless – Martin Landau in *Columbo* 'Short Fuse' (1971 T); Simon (Dennis Lipscomb) whose boyfriend Alastair ties up Maddie and David in an episode of *Moonlighting* (1985 T) and who is later found murdered – when they are not sudsy and silly like Mr St Claire (Peter SALLIS) in *Who Is Killing the Great Chefs of Europe?* (1978 C) whose Bombe Surprise is, unbeknownst to him, one of the deadly kind.

Female video chefs have also been soft targets for satire – impossibly glamorous ones like Fanny Craddock (ROUND THE HORNE's Daphne Whitethigh: 'Hippo in

its shell is a must!') or homely examples like Julia Child who once, during the making of 'Monkey Bread' in the 1960s, told her viewers to add the herb dill to their dough, and then to 'thoroughly knead the dill-dough'.

television directors/producers Fictionalized as frazzled, pettish creatures: perpetually pacing David Prentice (Ian Carmichael) – 'Do you mind if I wander around a bit?' – in BOW TIE and powder-blue CARDIGAN in *Simon and Laura* (1955 C); Victor Spinetti, highly strung and arty-farty, having his pink bubble pricked by the Beatles in *A Hard Day's Night* (1964 C); Julian Goddard (Nicholas Parsons) stressed and worn to an absolute shadow in *Every Day's a Holiday* (1965 C); Freddy (Hugh PADDICK) – 'That was wonderful, children. A thing of beauty' – comfortable with his campery in THE KILLING OF SISTER GEORGE (1968 C); one proposes a bisexual threesome in the studio canteen in *The Box* (1974 T); James (Michael Jayston) sacked from the BBC Drama Department for his alcoholism and returning to his unwelcoming home after splitting up with his boyfriend in THE LAST ROMANTIC (1978 T); 'John' in *Quatermass: The Conclusion* (1979 T), a churner-out of pornography as mass entertainment, noisily pouty because his studio is being disrupted by irritating people trying to save the human race from alien harvesting; TV commercials' director Jerry Sperling (Robert Donnison), blazer draped across shoulders, shades on top of head, butch-effete in a 1979 episode of *Hart to Hart* (T); more camp at the controls in *Leave It to Charlie* 'A Star Is Born' (1980 T), *A Slip of the Disc* (1978 R, Jocelyn Knight played by Andrew Branch); and *Soft Soap* (1988 T, Julian played by Tim McInnery); etc.

Ken (Gary Waldhorn) seems more interested in sizing up the male talent in the pop festival crowd than in broadcasting it for television in *The Big March* (1984 R): 'Why do handsome men have slags as girlfriends? ... It's been worrying me for years,' he mutters testily. His knowledge of pop music is equally pathetic: 'You haven't heard of Eric Clapton?' The reply: 'Darling, I've only just heard of Gene *Krupa*.'

On the other hand, George Caldwell (Barry Creyton) in *Image of Death* (1978 C), although camp and cynical, calling his colleagues 'sweetie' to a man and obviously fancying one of them, *is* a professional: 'I have this absolutely *horrendous* programme to do ... It's being done with absolute honesty. After all, isn't that what television is all about?'

Top-flight sports programme director Biff (Granville Van Dusen) has been having a 2-year relationship with his sports presenter (Robert Reed) in HOTEL 'Transitions' (1985 T), although the only intimacy shown behind the cameras is the pair emerging from the shower, midriffs chastely wrapped.

television personalities David Dane (James Villiers), the toast of TV, far more scared that police investigations will reveal his involvement with drugs rather than his homosexuality – though both are illegal in *Girl in the Headlines* (1963 C); religious show host Tom Dobrey (Lewis Stringer) opening a village fête with his biker boyfriend lurking in the background in *A Game of Tombola* (1972 R); husky sports personality Larry Dawson (Robert Reed) in HOTEL 'Transitions' (1985 T); way past his salad days is Dale Davenport, wilted and broke, living with a lover in *King and Castle* 'Friends' (1986 T, played with relish by former *Sir Francis Drake*, Terence Morgan); Percy Eliot alias Uncle Ralph (Peter Carroll) charged with behaviour in the swimming pool showers that does not sit well with his image as a children's TV favourite in *Rafferty's Rules* (Aust 1988 T); homeless Channel 4 celebrity Julian CLARY nesting with his antithesis in TERRY AND JULIAN (1992 T). *See also* SOAP OPERA STARS.

television versions (of cinema films)
Films which contain potentially offensive language, nudity or sexual situations are just as likely to be 'specially edited' for the 'captive' home audience as those containing 'excessive violence'. In

Britain much depends on the time of transmission, although with children having widespread access to video-recorders, some films are off limits for television showing altogether. At the time of writing, the forbidden ones of gay interest include *A Bigger Splash*, FLESH, *Trash*, SALO: THE 120 DAYS OF SODOM and TAXI ZUM KLO.

Probably the most significant omission from the schedules has been THE BOYS IN THE BAND. The American television version contains at least 40 excisions totalling 11 minutes. These include the word 'FAG'; the phrase 'Jew FAIRY' (though not 'frozen fruit' and 'AFRICAN QUEEN'); the question 'IS IT BIGGER THAN A BREADSTICK?'; the comment 'You have just eaten Sebastian VENABLE'; the boys' DANCING; the KISS from Cowboy to Harold after wishing him 'Happy birthday'; mention of EMORY encountering a vice cop in the baths; Donald's joke about his parents being gay; and the famous line about rimming a snowman. The film's expertly controlled pacing and the crackling tension as the evening unwinds have been pretty much destroyed. The soundtrack bleeps and burps, and characters are made to appear truly fairylike, whizzing from one side of a room to the other, usually in mid-sentence, their feet often not touching the ground.

Since the mid-1980s, British television has been regularly showing doctored works – though not the butchered *Boys* – with viewers treated to war films in which all the soldiers use the word 'friggin'', sex scenes with parts of bodies shadowed over, genitals cut out (SEBASTIANE being the prime example) or commercial breaks arriving at crucial points to hide the fact that frames have been removed (FOX AND HIS FRIENDS). In most cases, however, the work has already been carried out by the filmmakers who, in many instances, will shoot 'cover' material which will be substituted for contentious dialogue or actions in what is known as 'the television version'. Even Derek JARMAN provided two versions of a couple of scenes for EDWARD II, most likely at the direct behest of the BBC which was putting up the money and needed to be able to present the film 'uncut' after its cinema release.

It would be a gross misrepresentation of television's policy regarding cinema films to see it purely in terms of denying an audience a work as originally conceived. Television has resurrected countless films, providing access to treasures of the past as well as small or large 'cult' movies. In addition, Channel 4 and the BBC have financed films like MY BEAUTIFUL LAUNDRETTE, *Truly, Madly, Deeply, Howards End, Distant Voices, Still Lives* and PRICK UP YOUR EARS.

In the midst of sometimes crudely performed surgery on certain films before they are allowed to be screened, there is also the valuable salvage work on pictures which were insensitively cut for the cinema and, thanks to television, are shown in their longer versions or in the 'director's cut'.

Tell Me That You Love Me, Junie Moon (US 1970 C) Three variously DISABLED people rent a house together: Junie (Liza Minnelli), disfigured during a rape; Arthur (Ken Howard), an epileptic; Warren (Robert Moore), shot during a hunting trip by the boy he loved.

W: Marjorie Kellogg from her novel; P/D: Otto Preminger; 112 mins.

A wholesome but undercooked narrative meets an overblown director with foreseeably tragic results: sluggish drama, forced comedy. The idea of showing an outcast 'family' making a go of their lives is considerably undercut by the miraculous conversion of Warren by two young women, under the supervision of a radiant black man (Fred Williamson). After his breakthrough into heterosexuality, Warren casts off his APRON. No more making brownies for *him!*

The film is of interest if only for the buzzing presence of Robert Moore as Warren, whose sexuality is a bit of a problem for the other male member of the household ('He winks at me'. 'Well,

you don't have to wink back'). Moore managed to successfully juggle Broadway (directing THE BOYS IN THE BAND 1968), television (THURSDAY'S GAME) and film (*Murder by Death* 1976) with occasional acting parts (*Diana* 1973–4 T, where he again played basic, though not stupid, dizzy gay). He has one or two good scenes in *Junie Moon* before he is dispatched to that place of no return: Heterosexual Conversion.

Leonard Frey (Harold in THE BOYS IN THE BAND) has a couple of silly flashback scenes as Warren's gay adoptive father (the film manages to link homosexuality with upbringing, paraplegia and manic bouts of COOKING). For its time, though, a 'brave' film, and one not dismissed lightly by everyone. 'Moments of comedy, melodrama, compassion expertly blended' (*Leonard Maltin's Movie and Video Guide*, 1992–3).

Paul Temple Fictional crime writer and amateur sleuth now almost entirely identified with the voice of Peter Coke who played him in a number of radio serials from 1954 to 1968. The personable man of the world embodied by Coke was very far from the ascetic gentleman with long fingers, cigarette in holder, thin top lip, BOW TIE and aquiline nose pictured in the RADIO TIMES on the occasion of his first 'case' in 1938. He was, listeners of *Send for Paul Temple* were told, born in Ontario but educated at Rugby and at Oxford where he 'had a certain reputation as one of the best dressed undergraduates'.

Based on a man his creator Francis Durbridge met on a London–Birmingham train, Temple sniffed out clues, charmed the innocent and guilty alike, survived all manner of ambushes, and always successfully exposed criminal masterminds at little soirées to which the malefactor unaccountably always turned up.

Publishing his first detective novel at 22, he later employed an assistant, a resourceful and charming journalist called Steve Trent, whose real name was Louise Harvey. They married and Steve, with her much commented upon (to the point of screaming tedium) 'woman's intuition', rescued them from some rather nasty scrapes over the years in a series of 'affairs', 'cases' and 'mysteries' usually set in Kensington flats, Chelsea nightclubs, Mayfair hotels or boutiques – with detours to an eerily deserted mill or a motor repair shop full of gorblimey cockneys. Between them, Paul and Steve had to sift through clues such as a horse's head swizzle-stick, a glove, a shoe, a coat, a blood-stained doll and a gramophone record (with a male vocalist) called 'My Heart And Harry'.

Steve was a gem and, for most of her radio life, was played by Marjorie Westbury who made her utterly feminine, despite the name, and game for pretty much anything. She was Nora Charles without the dog and the heavy drinking. The perfect companion for a cheery yet cerebral soul like Paul. Steve did reveal, enigmatically, in the last of the line (*The Alex Affair*) that she had spent 'many years in Cairo before I was married'. This probably explains her remarkable tolerance of the frisky CHARLIE, who back in the 1940s would be in her husband's vicinity while he took a bath. A perfect marriage? It always seemed so, although Steve would occasionally exclaim: 'I can't understand you at all, I really can't!'

There was no reason to believe that Steve was anything but perfectly satisfied with her hard life (being shot at, nearly run over, trapped in a burning mill, left to drown, bombed). An amateur singer, she would sometimes be encouraged to reveal her talent. Once, obviously mainly as a token of appreciation to Paul, she sang Rodgers and HART's 'I Didn't Know What Time It Was (Till I Met You)'.

Bernadette Morgan originally played Steve (opposite Hugh Morton), but Marjorie Westbury took over from the second serial onwards: partnering Morton (1938–9), Carl Bernard (1942), Barry Morse (1945), Howard Marion Crawford (1946) and Kim Peacock (1946–51) before finally being joined to Peter Coke for 14 years. (John Bentley played Paul in four films between 1946 and 1952, and Francis Matthews took him to his final resting place in two television series 1968–70.)

Ten Cents A Dance The film biography of Ruth Etting, *Love Me or Leave Me* (1955) quite naturally contained this hardbitten Rodgers and HART Broadway number (it was one with which she was closely associated). But when Doris DAY belted it out as a dance hall hostess on the screen, one tiny phrase had been altered. Instead of the 'PANSIES and rough guys/Tough guys...', it was 'DANDIES and rough guys/Tough guys who tear my gown'. Yet the lines 'Sometimes I think I've found my hero/But it's a queer romance' stayed put.

Tenderness of the Wolves (West Germany 1973 C) CRUISING's older, nastier German cousin, this is a full-on depiction of a homosexual rapist and murderer, Fritz Haarman (Kurt Raab) who drained his adolescent victims' blood after sex, boiled their bones for soup and sold their flesh to a black market butcher. As well as being a MURDERER and a VAMPIRE, he was also a BLACKMAILER, thief, forger and fence. It was upon Haarman that Fritz Lang based his (girl) child killer in *M*.

W: Kurt Raab; P: Rainer Werner FASSBINDER and Michael Fengler; D: Ulli Lommel; 87 mins (cut to 83 mins in the UK).

Equal in repellence to *The Silence of the Lambs* and, like that film, ghoulishly droll in parts with a similarly macabre yet human central performance from the actor-author. This hairless, blood-crazed monster is surrounded by 'wolves' from both the upper and the under-worlds (the latter including Fassbinder himself). All the while the 'lambs' are being readied for the slaughter, providing both sexual excitement and a means of survival during the years before Hitler came to power.

'What I am after is an open realism, one which allows for an emotional identification with characters which society has taught us to despise' (Fassbinder commenting some years later on the fierce protests against the film by Germany's Homosexual Law Reform Group).

Tenko (UK 1981–4 T) Based on the reminiscences of women interned by the Japanese in Singapore: constant hardships, grime, heat, sweat, bickering, the ever-present threat of violence and a strange harmony.
Cr: Lavinia Warner; P: Ken Riddington; D: Pennant Roberts; BBC1; 31 episodes: 50 mins.

In the first series, one of the nine prisoners, Nurse Nellie Keene (Jeananne Crowley), has feelings for another, Sally, who is about to have a baby, which begin to develop in episode 6 when she combs Sally's hair. In episodes 9 and 10 (by Jill HYEM and Anne Valery) she moves into Sally's hut to help her convalesce when the baby is stillborn. Her growing friendship with Nellie enables Sally to overcome the loss. However, Dorothy (Emily Bolton) becomes jealous and spreads rumours. Then GRAFFITI is scrawled on the wash-hut: 'Sally and Nellie are filthy perverts.'

Sally finds the very idea of lesbianism disgusting and the blunt declaration of what, on Nellie's part at least, is very likely more than friendship destroys the easy trust between the couple. Nellie moves back to her own hut. When the women are marched to another camp, Nellie does not go with them.

In episode three of the second series (by Jill Hyem 1982), Sally, shattered by the loss of her child and by the terrible conditions, purposely disrupts the inspection of the camp by a Japanese general by cutting her wrists.

Jill Hyem suggested during the planning stage that two of the younger women should be lesbian. As she related some years after (in 'Entering the Arena: Writing for Television', a contribution to BOXED-IN: WOMEN'S TELEVISION eds Helen Baehr and Gillian Dyer, 1987), ex-prisoners told her and the other writers of women who were 'special friends'. 'The idea was rejected out of hand ... "turn-off time" and that

the characters concerned would lose audience sympathy ... compromise ... could not use the word "lesbian" ... It was probably one of the best episodes I wrote. The audience figures did not plummet, nor did the characters lose popularity. This was an important breakthrough. In the subsequent series we were allowed to deal with such controversial subjects as abortion, euthanasia and suicide. But Nellie Keene never appeared as a regular character.' She is left behind with Beatrice, the doctor, as the others march off to their unknown fate. There was no final scene between Nellie and Sally.

Tenue de Soirée aka *Evening Dress* (Fr 1985 C) Macho Bob (Gérard Depardieu) enlists Antoine (Michel Blanc) and Monique (Miou Miou) as accomplices in his burglary business. To Monique's surprise – but not horror – the *ménage à trois* which also ensues takes a strange new direction when Bob strenuously woos her mousy husband. Eventually worn down, Antoine gives in, goes off with the hulking Bob and becomes a downtrodden *petite femme*. It all ends with both men in drag whoring and Bob quipping: 'Catherine Deneuve is the man I've always wanted to be.'
W/D: Bertrand Blier; P: Philippe Dussart; 84 mins.

A shaggy dog story about a lovable lug with an incurable itch for an unprepossessing little man. The unsubtle wooing ('Resistance is what I'm after ... Your asshole will quiver with joy') and panicky demurrals ('Take your hand off my fly ... hands off') are a splendid slant on the heterosexual caveman approach to romance. Once Antoine capitulates, Bob stops trying, takes his partner for granted – even the scallops in tarragon sauce he serves so perfectly.

The casting of France's top male star as a dedicated homosexual makes the film a good deal more disarming than it deserves to be. Bob, after all, 'picked up' his singular connoisseurship of the male anal passage (he's not 'into balls') in jail. The choice of occupation ('locksmith') is also made inseparable from his sexual interests (like a hole, a lock needs lubrication). Antoine is another convert to homosexuality (he comes to prefer men because women 'haven't got any balls') and, although Bob insists that they're made for each other 'like the sky and the sea', the amalgamation is so preposterous, and the sexual dynamics so muffled, that sympathy drains away and laughter ceases three quarters of the way through.

For all that *Tenue de Soirée* does not live up to its promise, and its anti-sexism, which is remarkably superficial, Depardieu and his two partners fill in the holes (so to speak) with commendable dexterity and – until the misjudged final scene – balance on the rough edges with great poise.

The Terence Davies Trilogy (UK 1974–83 C) Short, black and white films about one man's inexorably gloomy life: young Robert Tucker (Philip Maudesley), child of his beloved mother and of the Catholic Church, bullied at school, angel in the nativity (*Children* 1974); middle-aged Robert (Terry O'Sullivan), haunted by religion and sexual guilt, trapped in his double role of socially accepted son and worker, and furtive cottager (*Madonna and Child* 1980); old Robert (Wilfred Brambell) facing *Death and Transfiguration* (1983) in a hospital ward.

W/D: Terence DAVIES; 85 mins.

Robert is the epitome of the 1950s-reared, tortured, self-hating homosexual. A trapped but not unimaginative man, existing on a diet of dreams and anonymous encounters with other men in public private places, he dies as he has lived: humble, cowed, unheard and unloved. John Russell Taylor, writing of the second part in GAY NEWS, saw Robert's 'homosexuality, guilt and repression' as the 'fearful products of a violent, "sick" society'. A bleak life amid mean streets with unsympathetic people. A study in suffocating greys, shot through with memorable images, salty wit and the promise of things (*Distant Voices, Still Lives*) to come.

Breaking into colour with his later films has not altered Davies' clearly defined inscape, nor his tremendous validation of his family (or rather the female members of it). With *The Long Day Closes* (1992) Davies appears to expiate the cruel bewilderment of much of his childhood and beyond, ending with the stirrings of sexual self-realization and love beyond the confines of biology.

Not so. 'It has not been [a cathartic experience]. It just sharpens up your sense of loss and your sense of futility at the suffering of people. It doesn't change anything. It just makes things bearable.' (*HQ*, Summer 1992–3)

Terraces (US 1977 T) A classy apartment complex with elderly couple, unhappy marrieds, innocent single, gold-digging dancer (Julie Newmar) and sweet gay actor, Alex Brinkston (James Phipps). Will Alex's stuffy doctor lover, Roger Cabe (Lloyd Bochner) sever his bonds with wife Dorothea (Lola Albright) and move in with him where 'the neighbours aren't nosey – just nosey enough in case of burglars'?

W/P/D: Lila Garrett; Ex P: Charles Fries; 78 mins.

Very peppy, very Californian, but resolutely formulaic pilot for a series which did not come to pass. There's a pretty score from Peter Matz to while away the time before periodically returning to Alex's problem. He is presented as a sprite with an unhappy past (drugs and sex), who is recalled to life by the love and respect of Dr Roger but who cannot complete that important lifestyle change on his own. America had to wait another four years before it was deemed ready for a regular, young and attractive gay on what it considers is weekly adult drama.

terrorists Fanatics, often without recognizable human feelings. Contemporary Valkyrie Sybil Danning bitingly in command of the hijacked plane in *Victory at Entebbe* (1978 C); Leyla Burden (Sheree North) with a voice like a sergeant major keeps a number of young women prisoner in THE NIGHT THEY TOOK MISS

BEAUTIFUL (1977 T); a gay couple of surly aspect in an episode of *Paris* 'Burnout' (1979 T); a bossy-boots of bullish mien (Antonia Ellis) inducting sweet and refined Olivia Hussey into the PLO in *The Pirate* (1978 T); Jeff Le Vane (Richard Seff) supplementing a violent organization by arranging for his lover's paintings to be stolen in *The Rockford Files* 'The Empty Frame' (1978 T); Charles Vivian (Cavan Kendall) has to arm wrestle with one of his collaborators in a kidnap plot to 'prove' he's not 'a ponce' in *Blood Money* (1981 T); Monika (Diana QUICK) robs a bank and is accused of wounding two policemen during her time with the Baader-Meinhof gang in SILENT WING (1984 R); over-polite, extremely cold young men, George Sharp alias Valchik (Anthony Daniels), Daines (Jonathon Scott) and Simon (Peter Acre), who kidnap Britain's Labour Prime Minister and his wife in *Death May Surprise Us* (1984 R).

Terry and Denny Characters in THE CREZZ (1976 T) without SURNAMES, much given to fluttering forms of address ('dear heart', 'angel'), flowing SCARVES and pert comments about any man who crosses their path. Of the very grand Nigerian who arrives at the party held in the Crezz's communal garden, Terry (Roland CURRAM) observes skittishly to his 'wife' Denny (Paul Greenhalgh): 'Ooo, a chocolate soldier!' To which Denny responds, proprietorially: '*I* saw him first!'

The pair continues its quaint existence until, one day, Denny absconds with the gardener (Nicholas), which sends the neighbours into a spin: they don't want to see their favourite (and only) queer couple split up, nor do they want to lose a perfectly good gardener. Denny is tracked down to a (basement) CLUB, given a bit of a talking to and all is NORMAL again.

Terry and Julian (UK 1992 T) A glamorous but homeless television celebrity (Julian CLARY) and a Streatham nerd (Lee Simpson) find themselves locked in incongruity.

W: Julian Clary, Paul Merton and John Henderson; P: Toni Yardley; D: Liddy Oldroyd for Channel 4; 6 parts; 30 mins each.

A cautionary live-action strip telling of what can befall a young South London lad when he takes a gay one as his lodger. Marriage, to each other, for one thing. Death, of Terry's girlfriend Policewoman Rene, for another. Not to mention cannibalism, bestiality and a visit to the local supermarket by MADONNA and Frank Sinatra.

Sets and costumes pleasingly garish, plots pleasantly exaggerated, scant avoidance of the puerile and the smutty, little truck with sophistication or the finer nuances of role-modelling, social cosmetics or gay politics. Above all floats the superior offhandedness of the king of queens, who pulls off the trick of being just the kind of rapacious homosexual many a person would be only too happy to take home to meet the family.

Gleefully eclectic, unrepentantly one-track, plundering Punch and Judy, pantomime, farce and STICKY MOMENTS, it's an itsy-bitsy star vehicle that fails to resist the tendency to veer towards the ditch, yet holds the road for Julian until something better comes along.

The highlight of the series was Julian's miraculous transformation into a heterosexual – rivalling in reverse John HURT in THE NAKED CIVIL SERVANT and Denis QUILLEY in PRIVATES ON PARADE, and certainly outdistancing William Hurt's Oscar-winning role in KISS OF THE SPIDER WOMAN. In 'The Other Side of Julian' Terry's mate turns out to be the spitting image of Julian whose place he hurriedly and coarsely takes as host of the Royal Variety Performance. Julian's own royal performance shows remarkable powers of observation, having got a particular type of promiscuous heterosexual's mannerisms off pat: the braggadocio, the beer swilling, the burping, the uncontrollable sexual urges, the bad manners.

'... it's a worthwhile show and Julian Clary is one of the funniest funny men around – and let's face it, there are a few around who are as funny as a limp fish

... Just don't expect a masterpiece and you just might find yourself tuning back in every week' (Michael Idato, *Daily Telegraph Mirror* (Sydney), 22.3.92).

Some samples: 'Get Thee Behind Me': 'Ooh, what a big banana', 'Time for a quick one, vicar' and 'Can I interest you in one of my cheesy balls?' ('No thanks, I've just had one').

Terry and June (UK 1979–87 T) A sublime SITCOM, closely patterned on *Happy Ever After* (1974–8) which also paired Terry Scott and June Whitfield. It provided the perfect model for Julian Clary and Paul Merton not to base their own version upon (TERRY AND JULIAN 1992) – although June Whitfield made a guest appearance (as wife of the Governor of the Bank of England who lusts after the superstar in 'Julian's Private Deposit').

Testament of Youth (UK 1979 T) The early life of Vera Brittain (Cheryl Campbell) whose brother Edward (Rupert Frazer) as well as his romantic friend Geoffrey (Geoffrey BURRIDGE: 'someone he can really talk to') perish in the First World War. Providing much solace from her grief and pain is a fellow STUDENT at Oxford, Winifred Holtby (Joanna McCallum), described in the script thus: 'She is like a young goddess. Very tall, delicately bronzed complexion, golden haired, glowing with youth and vitality, with strong features and eager, shining, very blue eyes.'

W: Elaine Morgan from book by Vera Brittain; P: Jonathan Powell; D: Moira Armstrong; BBC1; 5 parts.

Against a background of legitimized mass murder and a gradual erosion of accepted beliefs and standards, Vera fights her own battles against constraints imposed upon her by sex and tradition, reinforced by her father (who also forbids his son an 'artistic' career), and challenged by her continuing education, personified by Winifred. From her, Vera learns about clothes and poise; together they discuss the crucial place of education in every woman's life, and the need for truth as against censorship. Just

what passed between the two women otherwise – with the exception of a romantic punt down the river in 1921 – is hazy in the extreme.

testicles/testes Along with the beard, the penis and the Adam's apple, one of the indisputable signs of maleness and as an external body part even more vulnerable than the eye, which has a lid. Very much a part of the language in slang form ('a lot of balls', 'ballsy', 'in the balls'), but hardly ever discussed except in relation to cancer (first mention on TV-am's *Good Morning* (1985); young Michael who has to have one removed in G.P. (1992 T) but can still have sex) or violence: James BOND kneed in the groin by one of the female wrestlers in DIAMONDS ARE FOREVER (1971 C); Len Fairclough punched in that region in CORONATION STREET (1970s T); George Jackson as well in BROOKSIDE (1990s T); the testicle-kicking scene in *Blood Simple* (1984 C); Robert of Locksley (Kevin Costner) attacked below the belt by Maid Marian in *Robin Hood – Prince of Thieves* (1991 C). Although, for men, testicles are an everyday reality, viewed proudly, indifferently, protectively, erotically, they are hardly ever referred to as such: 'A man was injured in a delicate part of his anatomy after he was attacked by a policeman with a machete in Toxteth, Liverpool' (BBC Radio 4 news broadcast, 9am, 2.8.81). *See also* PENISES.

Thames British independent television company which operated the weekday broadcasting for the London area from 1968 to 1992. Among its undertakings were THIS WEEK (1968–78/1986–   ); *Do Not Adjust Your Set* (1968); *Man About the House* (1973–6); *The Sweeney* (1974–8); THE NAKED CIVIL SERVANT (1975); *The World at War* (1975); SEX IN OUR TIME (1976); ROCK FOLLIES (1976–7); ODD MAN OUT (1977); *Out* (1978, crime series); MINDER (1979–92); *Fox* (1989); *Hollywood* (1989); IT TAKES A WORRIED MAN (1981–4); *Death on the Rock* (1988); AFTER HENRY (1988–92). It was the first television company – under the leadership of Jeremy Isaacs – to allow time to a group of lesbians and gays without opposing forces being present in GAYS SPEAKING OUT (1978 T).

Thank You and Goodnight (US 1991 C) Musings by and on a glum, fatalistic GRANDMOTHER by her questioning and openly lesbian granddaughter. Should the older woman stop feeling guilty when she obviously enjoys it so much? Was her life really as rotten as she makes out or did she tip the scales? P/D: Jan Oxenburg; *c* 55 mins.

Another chapter in the director's public family album which, while concentrating on a mournful gran, brings in other members who appear to be enthusiastically maintaining the clan's tradition of holding on 'to every shred of misery'. A quietly hilarious rumination upon family dynamics, Jewish culture, and three generations of women greatly embellished by Paula De Koenigsberg's life-sized cut-out of the old lady in her youth (still slow to smile or feel optimism) ... There is one mystery, however: why are there gay men but no lesbians seen accompanying grandma and others down the tunnel to Heaven?

That Certain Summer (US 1972 T) 'Nick Salter (Scott Jacoby) lives with his divorced mother in Los Angeles, and each summer flies to San Francisco to spend a week or two with his father. This particular summer, Doug Salter (Hal Holbrook) is living with a lover and, although Gary McClain (Martin Sheen) obligingly moves out before Nick's arrival, the boy begins to sense, though not quite understand that his father's relationship with this good-looking and personable "friend" is strange and somehow threatening. Gary tries to win his approval, but Nick grows increasingly hostile ... Doug is not yet willing to tell him the truth ... Nick finally realizes and runs away ... The wife confronts the two men. Doug tells Nick and is rejected. He goes back to Los Angeles with his mother' (synopsis).

W: Richard Levinson and William Link; P: Harve Bennett; D: Lamont Johnson; 74 mins. (First UK showing, in the LWT area only, 27.9.74.)

Carefully written, sincerely acted (especially by Sheen) showcase for the idea that gay men are attractive, responsible, sober, non-effeminate, married, reproducing, contributing members of white middle-class society. There are no villains in this piece except, by inference, a society that funnels so much ignorance about difference into young (Nick) and old (Gary's superficially liberal brother-in-law) alike.

The movie, the first of its kind on American television, attracted an audience of around 20 million and provoked no public outcry, except from gay groups. Why no KISSING or TOUCHING between the two men? Why did Doug cry at the end? Why did his son reject him for being gay? Why did Doug say that, given a choice, he would not be gay?

Maverick author John Rechy, in a *Gay Sunshine* interview (no. 23, November–December 1974), predictably gave it the thumbs down: '... it was crumbs ... It was safe. They chose the safest types: they didn't take a marvellous queen, a radical queen, a promiscuous homosexual. They chose the closest thing they could come to in middle-class America.'

In Britain GAY NEWS (October 1974) turned up its nose: 'The whole impression the film gave was negative. The gay father was full of self-pity. The only likeable character was the up-front lover.' John Russell Taylor in *Sight and Sound* (Spring 1975) called it a 'Solemnly silly homosexual drama ... which is the gay equivalent of the sort of black film in which Sidney Poitier lends Dignity'.

However, the American mainstream critics raved, the *Boston Evening Globe*'s reviewer hailing *That Certain Summer* as a major achievement, partly for the fact of its 'just being on the air'. Charles Champlin, film critic of the *Los Angeles Times*, graciously reviewing a TV movie (a despised breed), was laudatory: 'A landmark in the emergence of television as a dramatic medium.' EMMY nominations and one award (for Scott Jacoby as the son) followed. A few years later, this landmark – which electrified and pleased many non-activist gay people, according to the producers – was shown at the Museum of Modern Art in New York.

In their book *Stay Tuned* (1981) Levinson and Link illuminatingly describe the genesis of the project (which inspired piles of hate mail when it was announced) and the considerable compromises made to please the network censors. Not only could Doug and Gary not be seen being physically affectionate towards one another, even their (carefully made, unrumpled) bed was declared unsuitable for the viewers of America. And this for a couple which, after much thought, had been rendered exemplary: non-promiscuous, domesticated, devoted.

'We felt it was essential that [Doug and Gary] should be members of the upper middle class. Most plays and works of fiction dealing with the subject tended to view homosexuals as exotics and frequently pathetic denizens of an underground subculture. But since our film would be seen in the homes of 20-odd million people, we wanted our two men to reflect the values and living standards of middle-income America. In this way we hoped to minimize any protective distancing on the part of the viewer ... the nice men next door, or down the block with "respectable", occupations and traditional lifestyles could not be so casually dismissed.'

Doug Salter was placed in the construction business, solely because the two writers were having work done to their homes at the time of fashioning the story. They wanted Gary to be a 'more modern homosexual ... reflecting the growing awareness of the younger generation of gays' – and he wound up in a recording studio, in front of massive consoles, supervising a symphony orchestra album.

The caution inherent in dipping the first toe in the torpid waters of the mass-viewing public with regard to people they had been taught to hate is apparent in the finished film. It's rather prim, episodic, and the ending seems to side with the very prejudice it has been supposedly combating. Two decades later, it is impossible to recapture the enormous public impact of this modest but well-made and intelligent film. Even so, when viewed today, it is crisp, efficient and, at times, surprisingly moving. Given the tenor of American television in the early 1970s (ALL IN THE FAMILY was only a year old; *M*A*S*H* had only just begun), its virtues more than outweigh its vices.

Thatcher, Billy (1921–64) English radio actor, later scriptwriter. A former child player whose voice remained interestingly light and weightless. He was cast as Bob Dale (a male heterosexual role-model) in MRS DALE'S DIARY in 1948, but after one month he was replaced in the daily serial for which he was later (1956–7) to write. His roles included that of the adolescent members of *Front-Line Family* (later *The Robinson Family* 1942); a dancer in *A Bullet in the Ballet* (1944); Percy in *Flarepath* (1944); CHARLIE in *Paul* TEMPLE *and the Gregory Affair* (1946); the sailor in *This Happy Breed* (1949). With the exception of *The Gay Lord Quex* in 1954, he worked almost exclusively for BBC CHILDREN'S HOUR during the 1950s (*Flint of the Flying Squad*; *Hullo There*; *Tai Lu Talking*; *Goodbye Mr Chips*; *Charter Pilot* in which he played a regular role between 1957 and 1961). He committed suicide three years later.

Thatcher, Baroness Margaret (1925–) English politician, formerly leader of the British Conservative Party and Prime Minister (1979–90), voted 'Woman of the Year' by the listeners to *The World at One* from 1982 to 1990. Loved, loathed, feared and jeered at, Mrs Thatcher is an economic rationalist, a defender of traditional family values (CLAUSE 28 etc), a social iconoclast, and no supporter of gay equality (though she did vote for decriminalization in 1967). Humour is not outstanding in her character, which has made her the perfect target for satirists. One of her first television appearances was as a member of the panel discussing *The Trouble with Men* in 1962 (alongside Barbara Cartland, Penelope Mortimer and Fanny Craddock).

Among those who have mimicked the increasingly deepening voice, lacquered hair, steely gaze and impeccable suits have been:

> In the cinema: Faith Brook in *North Sea Hijack/ffolkes* (1980); Janet Brown in *For Your Eyes Only* (1981, in the final scene, with John Wells); Nigel Pegram [*sic*] in *Riders of the Storm/The American Way* (1986, planeload of Vietnam veterans kidnap a 'conservative female politician'). (She played 'herself', presiding over a Tory party conference in *The Ploughman's Lunch* 1983.)
>
> On radio: Madeleine Cemm as a very ambitious civil servant called Linda who alone survives all the plots and carnage in her department in DEEP SIX (1984); WEEK ENDING (David Tate [*sic*] 1975–7); Sheila Steafel 1977–82); Tracey Ullman 1982–3); Sally Grace 1983–). (*Ten Years with Maggie*, a compilation of *Week Ending* sketches, was issued by BBC Enterprises in 1991.)
>
> On television: Paula Scott (1975–7); Faith Brown (1977–); Janet Brown (*Ted on the Spot* 1979 etc); Angela Thorne in *Anyone for Denis?* (1982, with John Wells as Denis); Steve Nallon [*sic*] (on *Spitting Image* 1984–); Sylvia Syms (1991, play about her downfall); Maureen Lipman in *About Face* (1991, with Wells).

She was a DESERT ISLAND DISCS castaway in 1978, choosing Bob Newhart's 'Introduction Of Tobacco To America' monologue and Jerome Kern's 'Smoke Gets In Your Eyes' among her eight gramophone records.

Her non-political television highlights include playing the PM opposite Nigel Hawthorne and Paul Eddington in a special charity performance of *Yes Minister* (glowingly watched by Mary WHITEHOUSE and others, and shown on *Nationwide*); *Woman to Woman* (1985, with Dr Miriam Stoppard); as a 'typical' housewife (voiced by Steve Nallon) in the Australian 'Mr Muscle Floor Cleaner' advert of 1991; alarmingly

unkempt and distraught as a *Spitting Image* puppet on *The Amnesty 30 Show* (1992).

Certain film and television characters possess, with hindsight, Thatcheresque qualities and may, indeed, have – through some miraculous ethereal process – been influenced by the younger Margaret or, more likely, contributed in some way to her later persona as the Iron Lady. They include Jackie (Cyd Charisse), the television producer in *It's Always Fair Weather* (1955 C); landowner Barbara STANWYCK always accompanied by her *Forty Guns* (1957 C); Judith Thatcher (Jennifer Howard), freezing cold blonde in *Perry Mason* 'The Case of Paul Drake's Dilemma' (1959 T); Violet Venable (Katharine HEPBURN) in SUDDENLY LAST SUMMER (1959 C); Margaret Johnston as one of the members of a coven in *Night of the Eagle/Burn Witch, Burn* (1961 C); Molly Thatcher (Lee Remick), highly successful stockbroker with pink bows and cute hairdos in *The Wheeler Dealers/Separate Beds* (1963 C).

That Ole Devil Called Love A surprise hit for Alison Moyet who recorded this Billie Holiday blues number in 1985. Colin (Michael CASHMAN), alone at Christmas, plays it as he thinks of Barry (Gary Hailes) at home with his parents (EASTENDERS 1986 T). A few months later, Colin and Barry are now living together. Colin tells Dot (June Brown) he's worried about Barry's health. On the pub juke box is the caressive, resigned, tingly sound of 'That Ole Devil Called Love'.

That's What Friends Are For Burt Bacharach and Carol Bayer Sager wrote this song which Rod Stewart sang in the Henry Winkler–Michael Keaton comedy *Night Shift* in 1982. It later achieved wide popularity as a fund-raiser for AIDS research and care, sung by Elton JOHN, Stevie Wonder, Dionne Warwick and others. It featured on International AIDS Day 1988 (*That's What Friends Are For* T) and over the credits of the AIDS TV movie *Just a Regular Kid . . .*

Neil BARTLETT performed a great hiss-ing, spitting, trenchant monologue – about his gay lovers and friends, about their pride and their worth, about gay life in the midst of death – under this title on *Alter Image* in the same year.

That Was the Week That Was (UK 1962–3 T) A group of young satirists (including one woman, at least one Jew, one American and, who knows, possibly one gay), an unadorned and messy tele-vision studio (with cameras and cables made part of the décor) and, in charge, a grinning relentless 22-year-old David Frost. The aim of the programme: to mercilessly pummel the dozy establish-ment, complacent Tory politicians, the beastly *nouveau riche*, crooks of all kinds, the formerly safe and secure. Its specific targets: corruption, hanging, unavailabi-lity of safe and legal abortions, the persecution of homosexuals, lack of knowledge about venereal diseases, the incompetence of nationalized industries ... and the doings of a certain model called Christine Keeler. And it was all happening – until it was yanked off for good in the middle of a series in December 1963 – on Auntie BBC, the bastion of impartiality and consensus. P: Ned SHERRIN (supported by Donald Baverstock); BBC; 60 mins (but would often overrun past midnight).

Informative and entertaining Saturday night saturnalia which made vicious lampooning of national symbols accept-able for mass consumption. Its knives were out for bigots and fogeys of all kinds and all races: in the Church, in the press, in both houses of Parliament. A genuinely shocking spectacle whose credibility was enormously heightened by the revelations that gushed from the Profumo scandal (which, to everyone's surprise, led to the downfall of the Conservative government after 13 years).

TW3, patchy and messy though it sometimes was, has never been replaced as genuine *TV à clef* ... Thirteen million people stayed up way past their bedtime or came back from the pub early to hear all manner of gossip and previously

inside information. As one of the pro-gramme's devotees said in a segment of *Carry On up the Zeitgeist* (1992 R), apathy began to diminish and was re-placed by a healthy sense of mistrust. Politics became exciting and challenging again. And wasn't that what democracy was supposed to be all about?

(A 1992 series, *A Stab in the Dark*, brought back a whiff of the old *TW3* brimstone and grapeshot.)

theatre critics Pompous, disdainful fel-lows, ice in their veins, words of discouragement and animosity flowing out of their critiques. Some of these gentlemen are bachelors: Addison De Witt (George SANDERS) in ALL ABOUT EVE (1950 C) is 'nobody's fool' and is on to Eve's game: '[In our] inability to love and be loved we belong to each other'; Meredith Merridew (Robert Morley), a pink-hued bag of wind who is served his pet pooches in a pie by the actor whose career he helped destroy in *Theatre of Blood* (1973 C); Freddie Lamont (John Gill), the cherubic knave who can de-stroy the work of years with a few ill-chosen words – 'I'm just off to write my vicious piece' – in YOU'RE NOT WATCH-ING ME, MUMMY (1980 T).

theatre directors Usually presented as demons of masculine drive (Warner Baxter in *Forty-Second Street* 1933 C; Michael Douglas in A CHORUS LINE 1985 C) or barely masculine monsters of ego and pretension: Jack Buchanan in *The Band Wagon* (1953 C); Christopher Hewett squealing and dragged up as Roger De Bris, Broadway's worst in THE PRODUCERS (1967 C); Mark Morgen-weiss (Paul Benedict), mother-girt, wildly *avant garde* in *The Goodbye Girl* (1977 C), forcing Richard Dreyfuss to play Richard III as a queen; Ray Mal-colm (Ian RICHARDSON) in *Star Quality* (1985 T) effortlessly soothing the ego of his prima donna with the invaluable help of his ex-pro boyfriend; Dick Stratford (Tony Carreiro) staging a punk version of *King Lear* in DOCTOR, DOCTOR 'Accentuate the Positive' (1989 T); go-getting, stinking rich Hector (Richard

Wilson) in *Unnatural Pursuits* (1992 T) involved in every fashionable liberal cause going, including membership of Poets Against Bigotry; etc.

theatre dressers Fusspots, mother hens and usually totally asexual, though often deeply in love with the person they serve night after night: in *It's Love I'm After* (1937 C) Leslie Howard has the indispensable services of Eric BLORE who is quite embarrassingly open about his feelings for 'sir'; Reg Pritchard swished in *Spilt Champagne* (1968 T); Bobby (Roddy MCDOWALL) endures the wisecracks of Billy Rose as he tends to Fanny Brice in FUNNY LADY (1974 C); CLARENCE (Dick Emery) in a POW camp, dreaming of Errol Flynn and sewing for dear life so that the real men can do a great escape in *The Dick Emery Show* (1978 T); Cyril Smallpiece (Peter SALLIS) in *Across a Crowded Room* (1978 T); Leslie (Peter Sallis again) rules his star's roost in YOU'RE NOT WATCHING ME, MUMMY (1980 T): 'My friends may be just a pack of old queens, but some of them do have quite good taste, believe it or not'; Norman waits on 'sir' with nannying diligence in THE DRESSER (Tom Courtenay, 1983 C; Michael Palin, 1993 R); Malcolm (John CARLIN) continues to live, as an almost silent partner, with his beloved stage darlings (Ralph Michael and Renée Asherson) after retirement in *Love and Marriage* 'Sweet Echo' (1984 T); etc.

theatrical A state of mindlessness, a string of affected words, a form of abandoned body language, a sense of playfulness, an air of calculated audience pleasing ... It's nearly always abroad in the comedies of Noel COWARD, and in the tragi-comedies of three other former actors, John OSBORNE, Harold PINTER and Charles Dyer.

Charley [DYER] (Rex Harrison) in Charles Dyer's STAIRCASE (1969 C) is always reminding his friend of his triumphs in the theatre: ''Course I was a big time in those days ... Played all the Number Ones. Don't think you realize how big I was.' Harry (Richard Burton)

loathes this side of his lover: 'Blast you – you and your whole cruel West End sardonic bunch. You balance your own failures by insulting others.'

Others with a theatrical air: JULES AND SAND (Hugh PADDICK and Kenneth WILLIAMS), ex-chorus boys and firm advocates of do-it-yourself in ROUND THE HORNE (1965–9 R); almost the entire cast of characters in *The Boy Friend* (1971 C) whose blazing bitchery, one-upping, limelight-stealing, conniving and bed-swapping is viewed as part and parcel of a crummy English provincial theatre; Denis Porson (Nigel HAVERS) uses his flair and projection from university acting days for his RESTAURANT after he's come out of jail for sex with the wrong gender in THE GLITTERING PRIZES (1976 T); William Bishop (Jeffrey GARDINER) putting on a show in ROCK FOLLIES OF '77 (1977 T): 'Think PETER PAN. Light and gay', which doesn't impress a younger, less repressed gay man: 'Tits for the husband and queer gags for the wife ... the chorus are stoned and half the boys have gonorrhea'; no longer young but eternally hopeful *jeune premier* who hasn't quite made it, George Banks in *Me and the Girls* (Peter WOODTHORPE 1976 R; Tom Courtenay 1985 T); etc.

Their First Mistake (US 1932 C) Having been so advised by Stan (LAUREL), Ollie (HARDY) adopts a baby boy so that his wife (Mae Busch) will be kept occupied and therefore less irritated by her husband's going out at night (with Stan). But when he arrives home with the little mite, his wife has departed and is beginning divorce proceedings which include suing Stan for alienation of affection. Left holding the baby, the pair settle down into cosy domesticity. P: Hal Roach; D: George Marshall; 20 mins.

> Ollie: 'She says I think more of you than I do of her.'
> Stan: 'Well, you do, don't you.'
> Ollie: 'We won't go into *that*.'

This was *way* ahead of its time, managing to air some of the difficulties of the married gay plus offering a practical guide to male–male child rearing. There's a mesmerizing scene where Ollie, in bed with Stan and baby, sleepily puts the bottle in his friend's mouth by mistake. The prolonged ecstatic sucking that ensues is worthy of COCTEAU or Buñuel.

Thelma and Louise (US 1991 C) Mostly about two women (Geena Davis and Susan Sarandon), push-button housewife and life chewed waitress, who get to do, in Geena Davis' words, 'guy kinda things – shooting and driving, blowing up kinda stuff'. Also killing a man, locking another in a car boot in the desert, having unsafe sex, driving while drunk, smoking intensively, causing whiplash and possible paraplegia to a number of cops in cars – then driving off into the middle of Grand Canyon, after a big KISS on the lips.
W: Callie Khouri; P: Ridley Scott and Mimi Polk; D: Ridley Scott; 129 mins.

This film's title became shorthand for female bonding and power. Or three words that sum up female violence and mayhem. Although the chase ended with the women's zooming off into the infinite depths of one of America's natural wonders, the stars indicated at the 1992 Oscar ceremony that there might be a sequel.

'Next time a woman passes an 18-wheeler and points her finger like a pistol at the tyres, the driver might just put his tongue back in his mouth where it belongs' (Margaret Carlson, *Time*).

Them and Us A weekly 30-minute series of three short films showing members of a community fighting back against injustice, stupidity or outrage. As HOMOPHOBIA embraces all three, law reform on the Isle of Man was a natural inclusion. The subject needed the full might and majesty of Britain's first out gay knight to pull it off. Which Ian MCKELLEN did, with the necessary gravitas, establishing gay men not only as a legally battered group (a status emphasized by the concentration camp garb of the IoM's sole openly gay person) but as

an 'US' instead of a 'Them'. And it was broadcast at 7.30pm on BBC1.

Theorem aka *Teorema* (It 1968 C) An apparently angelic young man (Terence Stamp) satisfies the immediate desires and inner needs of an unhappy rich family: father (Massimo Girotti), mother (Sylvana Mangano), daughter (Anne Wiazemsky), son (Andras José Cruz) – and maid (Laura Betti) who levitates spectacularly.
W/D: Pier Paolo PASOLINI; P: Franco Rossellini and Mario Bolognini; 98 mins.

Marx meets Jesus (or is he the Devil?). The fascination of the seduction gives way to considerable mirth with the maid floating upwards and the family's wild carryings-on when the stranger suddenly departs. As a gay wish-fulfulment and an antidote to the restraints of the usual family ties, it is full of delights. As a parable for our times (the son who becomes the stranger's bedmate and disciple is called 'Pietro'), it's creaky.

There Are Fairies At The Bottom Of The Garden Made famous first by Liza Lehman in 1917 (she sang it on radio in 1925) and then with careless innuendo in the 1940s by Beatrice Lillie who sang it, inferences intact, on *The Eamonn Andrews Show* in 1964.

When Barry HUMPHRIES was the subject of DESERT ISLAND DISCS in 1973, he chose the 'Faery Song' as one of the records he wished to have with him in case he was shipwrecked. 'Who knows,' he said puckishly, 'there might be FAIRIES at the bottom of my island.' Presenter Roy Plomley capped this by saying that there were quite a few people they *both* knew who would fit that description.

Terry Wogan in a 1984 edition of his breakfast radio show told listeners that Larry GRAYSON was at the bottom of *his* garden.

there goes the neighbourhood! An expression originally applied to black families moving into white neighbourhoods in America. Phil DONAHUE employed it tongue-in-cheek, with clicking tongue, over the Boy Scouts Association's barring of gay men in a 1991 discussion: 'You let gay people in and there goes the neighbourhood!'

there's a lot of it about If BBC Radio 2 presenter Ray Moore (*The Morning Show* 1979–86) sniffed anything sexually ambiguous (such as a record request for 'a woman called Peta'), he would candidly proffer his opinion that this was just the tip of the iceberg: 'There's a lot of it about.' Steve (Daniel Webb) says it with artless irony to the terrified David (Michael N. Harbour) in MORE LIVES THAN ONE (1984 T) as they hide from the police raiding a COTTAGE; David regularly visits to see – but until this moment never to talk with – other men like him. *See also* PERCENTAGES; THEY'RE EVERYWHERE.

There's One in Every Family (US 1952–3 T) Not an early COMING OUT, but merely a kind of variety show which introduced 'ordinary' people with 'unusual abilities'.
P: Richard Levine for CBS.

These Three (US 1936 C) Lillian Hellman's THE CHILDREN'S HOUR deliberately concealed with a juicier title and changing what the nasty little girl saw into one of the schoolteachers sleeping with her friend's fiancée.
W: Hellman; P: Samuel Goldwyn; D: William Wyler; 93 mins.

A strong performance from Miriam Hopkins puts some meat on the bones of a play picked clean by Hollywood's cleansing brigade. And its original theme is *still* not talked about in front of the kids.

In *Hollywood's Children* (1982 T) the film was discussed, in relation to Bonita Granville who played the lie-spreading child, as being based on a play about 'a touchy subject'. The actress is then interviewed – not about *These Three*, but about 'the disintegration of family life'.

Thesiger, Ernest (1879–1961) English actor of wasted appearance, dithery cunning, reedy voice and look of tottering

hauteur, most prominent in *The Old Dark House* (as Horace Femm, 1932 C) and evil genius Dr Ludovic Praetorius in THE BRIDE OF FRANKENSTEIN (1935 C).

He was the inspiration for the maidenly realist, Mortimer LAMB in Ivy COMPTON-BURNETT's *Manservant and Maidservant* (played on radio by Ronald Simpson in 1952 and by Denys Blakelock in 1966). He wrote his autobiography *Practically True* in 1927, followed by *Adventures in Embroidery* in 1941. He appeared on television with his embroidery and tapestry on LEISURE AND PLEASURE in 1954, but he did not wear his more outlandish garb (he was a founder of the Men's Dress Reform Society), which sometimes comprised strings of pearls, green-painted toenails and blue velvet shorts with matching blouse.

C: *The Real Thing at Last* (unfinished, 1916); *Number Thirteen* (HITCHCOCK film uncompleted, 1922); Bertram in *Week-End Wives* (1928); Laing in *The Ghoul* (1934); a neurotic novelist who kills a millionaire newspaper man in *The Night of the Party* (1934); Duke of Berri in *Henry V* (1944); Theodotus in *Caesar and Cleopatra* (1945); one of *The Ghosts of Berkeley Square* (1946); Sir Edgar Follesmark in *Jassy* (1947); an undertaker in *Scrooge* (1951); Endicott in *Laughter in Paradise* (1951); Sir Trevor Lampington in *Last Holiday* (1951); the skeletal industrialist in *The Man in the White Suit* (1951); an earl in *The Magic Box* (1951); Mr McDonald in *Meet Mr Lucifer* (1952); Emperor Tiberius in *The Robe* (1953); French aristocrat in *Father Brown* (1954); Kay Kendall's husband in *Quentin Durward* (1955); judge in *The Truth About Women* (1957); Hickson in *The Horse's Mouth* (1958); Paul Morel's patron in *Sons and Lovers* (1960); head of the firm in *The Battle of the Sexes* (1960); an Italian count in *The Roman Spring of Mrs Stone* (1961); etc.

R: Mr Poland in *Money with Menaces* (1941); Ctesiphon in *Pythias* (1947); WOMAN'S HOUR 'Guest of the Week' (1956); etc.

T: First Witch in *Macbeth* (1949, warning Stephen Murray); Mr Skaife in

Joyous Errand (1957); Colonel Gyll in *Do As I Do* (1958); Mr Justice Finston in *Result of an Accident* (1959); Professor Galton in *Suspicious Mind* (1959); eccentric millionaire Andrade in *Invitation to Murder* (1959); Dean of Paddington in *Lord Arthur Savile's Crime* with Terry-Thomas (1960); *The Happy Couple* (1960); Calvin Broderick in *Night Train to the West* (1960); His Lordship in *Somerset Maugham* 'The Verger' (1960); etc.

thespians Usually pronounced 'thesbian', this term covers actors ('damned thespian gypsies' in Arthur Gower's overbearing father's opinion in *Trelawny of the 'Wells'*); gays (inhabitants of Los Angeles were all described as having 'a thespian tendency' in *Rough Guide to the World* (1990 T) and one of the murder suspects, played by Glyn DEARMAN, in *The Dead Room* (1992 R) – who liked PROUST – was so called); and lesbians (it was a favourite expression of Ray Moore in his early morning radio show (1979–86).

they all look alike to me A favourite blanket expression for any race, political group or minority that seems upon superficial acquaintance to be undifferentiated in physiognomy, clothing, attitudes. 'All faggots look exactly alike,' reckons unquenchably macho cop Ryan O'Neal in PARTNERS (1982 C) at the outset of his brief sojourn among Los Angeles' gays, sharing an apartment with the living disproof of his statement: non-sexy, non-muscular, non-clonish John HURT.

they're either married or gay *See* SHOW ME ONE STRAIGHT GUY ...

They're Either Too Young Or Too Old The Arthur Schwartz–Frank Loesser comic lament was sung by Jane Froman (mimed by Susan Hayward) in *With a Song in My Heart* (1952 C), but it was rendered more famously by non-vocalist Bette DAVIS ruefully reassuring the troops in *Thank Your Lucky Stars* (1943 C) that she and the other wives are not playing up while they are over-

seas fighting for democracy and the American Way. How could there be, she insists, any hanky panky when the only men available are either boy scouts or old men? Bette doesn't include gays in her song – which includes one whirlwind jive display with Conrad Widell – because most were fighting, too; but there are a couple of men in the background who could very likely be friends of Dorothy – they certainly appear to be fans of Bette.

they're everywhere! This encapsulates the belief that homosexual people represent some inexorable force, growing in numbers (possibly by recruiting the impressionable), and because of their ability to look normal could be the person you least suspect. Miss Benham (Margaret Diamond), the BLACKMAILER in VICTIM (1961 C), certainly believed in the queer invasion theory, and so do a lot of callers to the DONAHUE shows which deal with things deviant. On 'She Says Her Future Groom Cheats On Her with Men' (1992 T) a woman from Kentucky rang in to say: 'They're everywhere. They even approach me at work.' *See also* SHOW ME ONE STRAIGHT GUY ..., THEY SHOULD ALL BE PUT ON AN ISLAND.

Lewis Duncan (Anton Rodgers) decides to really frighten one person ill-disposed to his future existence in COMING OUT (1979 T) by announcing that gays are spreading 'like greenfly'.

they should all be put on an island 'Homosexuals and bisexuals should be rounded up and put on an island and there they'd sit,' said a caller to Phil DONAHUE on the subject of 'She Says Her Future Groom Cheats On Her with Men' (1992 T) (*see* THEY'RE EVERYWHERE). She had no 'final solution' in mind for them, nothing inhumane, just perpetual banishment.

In *100% 'I Am What I Am'* (1992 T) young Tony's mother also posited this solution (to the homosexual 'problem') when he told her how he wished to live his personal life. She had hoped that by making all gays quit NORMAL society their influence (on people like Tony) would cease. But this was before she met his friends, and started going out to PUBS and CLUBS with him. After this exposure, she was no longer seeking restrictions for people like Tony but equality with the rest of society.

Things Are Seldom What They Seem During the ritual office summing-up of another PERRY MASON triumph in 'The Case of the Skeleton's Closet' (1963 T), Paul DRAKE (William Hopper) guilelessly recites a little rhyme: 'Things are seldom what they seem/Skim milk masquerades as cream.'

These words – by W. S. Gilbert from *HMS Pinafore* – provoke an interesting reaction from Della STREET (Barbara Hale). Adopting her most scythingly ironic tone – after shooting a meaningful look at Perry and another at his friend and colleague – she says: 'Right, Paul! Things *are* seldom what they *seem*.' This has the effect of practically bringing about a seizure in the chunky Mr Drake. Della has made other ambiguous comments before about the state of affairs, specifically Paul's remarkable lack of success in even getting women to go on a date with him ('And that explains that'). On this occasion, however, she has decided to blow the gaffe; discreetly, of course, as a good legal secretary should.

Think Pink A breezy bit of George Gershwin, extolling the colour between red and white as the last word in chic, blasted out *con brio* by Kay Thompson as the Diana Vreeland-styled fashion dragon in *Funny Face* (1957 C). In THE GARDEN (1990 C) Derek JARMAN draped the number but not, regrettably, the Thompson version over shots of the 1989 Lesbian and Gay Pride march with the film's heroes, superimposed and looking acutely embarrassed in pink suits, earning the director some censure from gay critics for 'trivializing' such an occasion. In truth, any complaint should have hinged on the damage done to this utterly trivial but classy song.

third sex 'There are men ... There are women ... There is the third sex,' screamed the poster for the German film *Different from You and Me/The Third Sex* (1957). However, it never caught on as a phrase. Bolshie artist Kim (Jane Lapotaire) in THE OTHER WOMAN (1975 T) believed passionately in the concept of three genders: 'It doesn't show in bodies. Sexuality is controlled by the brain, not by the genitals.' The documentary about the extraordinary community of eunuchs was subtitled *India's Third Gender* (1991 T).

Thirty Minute Theatre A mainly invigorating collection of plays from BBC2 including INCIDENT (1965); *Boa Constrictor* (1967); *The Other Side* (1967); THE WAITING ROOM (1971).

Thirtysomething (US 1987–91 T) A group of men and women, mostly married, coming to terms with their various pre-mid-life crises. One single person is Melissa (Melanie Mayron) who is trying to meet the right man. In one episode 'Love and Sex' her friend Russell Weller (David Russell Grant), an advertising art director, thinks he may have met the answer to his prayers in Peter (Peter Frechette). In a later episode he has to come to terms with the fact that he is HIV positive.

W: Richard Kramer, Paul Monette and others; P: Richard Kramer and Marshall Herskovitz; ABC; 60 mins.

A handsome example of the less android face of American television. Slick presentation of brow-wrinkling issues by quite subtle characters. A shame, then, that Russell appeared so sporadically. When his big moments came (his being seen in bed with his new lover provoked advertiser withdrawal on a huge scale in November 1989), they were lessened because he seemed like a stranger within the tightly bound group of questing, interrelating people born in the late 1950s when life seemed so simple.

This Girl's In Love With You The 1968 Hal David–Burt Bacharach song is used nostalgically in GIRL (1974 T) to recapture a once rapturous love affair between Jackie (Alison Steadman) and Chrissie (Myra Francis) that began when it was 'top of the gay girls' hit parade'. This is the Dionne Warwick version which the women dance and sing along with in the army hut, holding on to each other tightly and, at the crescendo, kissing. Dusty SPRINGFIELD croons it over the closing credits.

This Is Your Life (US 1952–61/1970/ 1983; UK 1955–64/1969– ; also Aust T) One of television's most popular shows, loved and loathed for its overbearing sentimentality, unctuous trivializing and heterosexual bias. Many worthy people have had their achievements extolled by acclamatory friends, relatives and business associates – many of them not seen for years – after being pounced on by the various hosts (including Ralph Edwards, Eamonn Andrews and Michael Aspel) in all manner of ingenious ambushes and ruses. Spouses are very much in evidence, but life partners of homosexual subjects either cease to exist for the duration or are introduced to the audience as a friend, a manager or a personal assistant. Alec MCCOWEN has possibly helped break this mould when he refused to let his programme go on air unless there was at least one mention of the late Geoffrey BURRIDGE.

This Is Your Life has been sent up fairly consistently over the years for its all-enveloping niceness, and the determination with which it preserves the myth that the whole world is either heterosexual or asexual. In Sid Caesar's *Your Show of Shows* (1953), much is made of the inordinate amount of time two men spend hugging and squeezing one another in exuberant greeting. One of the tracks on the early 1970s album *God Save the Queens* relates the squirming embarrassment of a Hollywood star ('Stone Missouri') when faced with his past: friends from boy scout days, army buddies, young acquaintances, every one of whom seems all too eager to spill some of his carefully guarded beans.

This situation was relocated to Britain, featuring an ordinary closeted gay man, in the play *Kenny Hyding: This Is Your Life* (1978).

'I hope you're not going to tell everything,' a famous male dancer said when faced by Eamonn Andrews in an early 1980s programme.

This Week 'Homosexuals' and 'Lesbians' (UK 1964 and 1965 T) Bryan Magee, one of the reporters on this highly respected current affairs show (which had begun in 1956), drew back the veil on yet another semi-hidden aspect of British life in 'Homosexuals'. He had been working his way through a number of top taboos (abortion, suicide, drug addiction, sex) and it was now homosexuality's turn for a 27-minute, well-researched treatment (with many of his interviewees provided by the Albany Trust).

It was the first time the subject had been dealt with in a non-judgemental way. A geneticist was interviewed about the 'CAUSES', but the report was mainly composed of gay men, some in SILHOUETTE, some very bravely – considering the legal implications – facing the camera.

Nothing was cut. The programme, which was aired in October, drew high ratings and much praise. The Rediffusion postbags bulged for weeks with hundreds and hundreds of letters, from both heterosexuals and homosexuals. The biggest shock for audiences came, not so much from the scene of men KISSING and DANCING together in Amsterdam, but from the two shop assistants who were lovers. They revealed that they had met in church!

Six weeks later the women journalists from three important newspapers – Monica Furlong of the *Daily Mail*, Anne Sharpley of the *Evening Standard* and vastly influential Marjorie Proops of the socialist *Daily Mirror* – began to prepare ringing pieces for their readers about the crucial need for a change in the law.

In all Magee interviewed over 200 people and many of their experiences found their way into a book *One in*

Twenty (1966). It was translated into eight languages and continued to sell well into the 1970s.

A sour note was struck by Magee's criticism of lesbians. He had given no thought to female homosexuals while researching his programme. But he told viewers that lesbians were lacking in courage and should reveal themselves as they weren't under threat from the law. Many lesbians wrote to him saying (presumably among other things): 'What about us?'

Magee got to work and lesbians faced British households in a *This Week* programme shown at the beginning of 1965. The *Daily Express* fulminated in its leader: 'You still have time to stop this filth entering your living room.' But this filth entered and Magee reckoned the *Express* had helped supply at least another million viewers. This time all the participants were shown out of the shadows including a couple (two schoolteachers) and one of their MOTHERS (delighted that her daughter had found happiness at last). There was also a married woman who had left her husband.

'We didn't know we were lesbians. We didn't know the word,' Diana Chapman recalling this period in WOMEN LIKE US (1990 T).

Three Blind Mice (UK 1947 R) A snowbound hotel at Christmas. A murderer on the loose. A group of peculiar guests. A long-buried secret.
W: Agatha Christie; P: Martyn C. Webster; 30.4.47; BBC Light Programme; 30 mins.

The queen of crime's present to Queen Mary, widow of George V, who had expressly asked for a radio thriller as part of her 80th birthday homage. Agatha Christie may or may not have known the royal predilection for gay men of a certain stripe and lustre, but her majesty must have been delighted with the presence of Christopher WREN (Allan MCCLELLAND) who found the policeman much to his liking and gave the straight-backed husband the willies (but appealed greatly to his wife).

Among the other murder weekend stereotypes were a gruff former magistrate (Gladys Young) and a crazy/sinister foreigner (Raf De La Torre).

A few years later, considerably fattened up but retaining McClelland, the play was produced on the London stage as *The Mousetrap* and is still packing them in.

The Three Fat Women of Antibes (UK 1960 T) Frank (Judith FURSE) is the mannish member of a trio, completed by Beatrice (Joan Young) and Arrow (Anne Shelton), which is doing very nicely on the Riviera until the arrival of the managing Lena Finch (Olga Gwynne). Diets and exercise become the order of the day and their indulgent existence is imperilled.
W: W. Somerset MAUGHAM adapted by Basil Dawson; P: Norman Marshall; Associated-Rediffusion; 50 mins.

This production was part of a series called SMS (ie Somerset Maugham Stories), and another version of this delectable tale of women's solidarity in the pursuit of hedonism was produced by the BBC in 1969 with Renée Houston as the golf-mad Frank Hickson, Elspeth March as Beatrice, June Ellis as Arrow, and Elizabeth Sellars as the fly in their gin fizz.

(Maugham himself read the story – in the most succulent manner possible – on radio in 1954. It is one of the few to delineate an obviously lesbian character.)

Three Piece Sweet (UK 1979 R) An unmarried woman (Paula Wilcox) lives with her sour mother (Patricia Routledge) and lets out a room to a mother's boy, Alistair (Christopher Godwin) who, unbeknownst to them, has recently quit sharing a flat with a man called Trevor.
W: Jill HYEM and Jennifer Phillips; P: Glyn DEARMAN; BBC Radio 4; 6 parts; 30 mins.

A few noble sentiments, quite a bit of anti-queer abuse from the horrendous mother, and almost no laughter. The camp man's CAT (whose litter tray was lined with copies of GAY NEWS) received the best notices. (Originally designed for television as a comedy with serious overtones, with much more subtle relationships and with a quite differently conceived mother and daughter.)

Three's Company (US 1977–84 T) Janet (Joyce DeWitt) and Chrissy (Suzanne Somers) share an apartment with Jack (John Ritter), a situation which is allowed by their puritanical landlord Stanley Roper (Norman Fell) because he believes Jack to be a 'TINKERBELL'.

Cr: Don Nicholl, Michael Ross and Bernie West; W: Paul Wayne, George Burditt and others; D: Bill Hobbin; ABC; 30 mins.

Based on the British *A Man About the House* – but with considerably more gay innuendo, including Jack and the HOMOPHOBE waking up in bed together ('Strange Bedfellows' 1978):

Roper: 'This is awful. My being in bed with you and you being ... You've got to promise me ... this has got to be a secret between us. This never happened, right?'
Jack: 'Right! And thank you for a *lovely* evening.'

Also, there is some confusion over Jack's exact orientation when 'Roper's Niece' (1978) comes on a visit. 'Dating him is as safe as sending her out in an armoured truck,' Roper tells his wife, but then he catches the pair necking furiously. 'Do you think some trickle of normalness might be possible for Jack?'

The Threshing Floor (UK 1982 R) The story of Ruth-Obed (Wendy Murry) the Moabite whose destiny is linked with that of her widowed mother-in-law Naomi (Mary MORRIS), an Ephraimite who provides her with a second husband, Boaz (John Turner). The union will lead eventually to David (and thence to Jesus).

W: James Forsythe; P: Ian Cotterill; BBC Radio 4; 90 mins.

One of the few plays to explore the extraordinary bond of love between the two women from different cultures, RUTH AND NAOMI.

Mary Morris, with her voice of shivered steel, makes no secret of her attraction to the younger woman. Yet a scene strongly reminiscent of one between Estelle and Ines (which the actress played in 1963) in HUIS CLOS was cut:

Naomi: 'For looking, my lovely, at your lovely eyes – always clear so that I seem to be looking into a crystal.'
Ruth: 'Oh, Naomi.'
Naomi: 'No, don't veil them from me.'

The most famous passage is beautifully rendered with Naomi, worn down by hardship and the death of a husband and two sons (one, Mahlon, bringing Ruth no heirs, because she hints he couldn't make love to her), lonely and poverty-stricken, begging Ruth to leave her. It is not good for someone with all her life before her to cling to 'a woman wasting her life away'. Which causes her daughter-in-law to say, reassuringly: 'All I understand is that wherever you go, there I will go.'

Thring, Frank (1926–) Australian actor, mesmerizingly taut and lubricious player of various florid and greasy citizens, some patrician, others feral. But he's probably most widely known as Dr Alexander Stack in *Skippy, The Bush Kangaroo* (1969 T).

C: a lawyer in *A Question of Adultery* (1958); King Aello in *The Vikings* (1958); Pontius Pilate in *Ben-Hur* (1959); Herod Antipas in *King of Kings* (1961; he had played the same role in *Salome* on the London stage); an Emir in *El Cid* (1961); Godfrey, the art dealer in *Age of Consent* (1969); a judge in *Ned Kelly* (1970); *Alvin Rides Again* (1975); *The Man from Hong Kong* (1975); *Mad Dog Morgan* (1976); *Mad Max III* (as 'the Collector', 1985); *Bullamanka* (1985); Jack Citron, HITCHCOCK-like film director in *The Howling II: The Marsupials* (1987); etc.

T: Judge Atkins (with Leo McKern as Captain Bligh) in *The Man Who Shot the Albatross* (1972); etc. Interviewed by

Steve Vizard on *Tonight Live* (Aust 1991).

Tickets for the Titanic 'The Way, the Truth, the Video' (UK 1987 T) The EVANGELICAL CHRISTIANS are on the march across Britain led by a triumvirate of slickly packaged young messiah (Peter Firth), a sin-sniffing chief of police (George Baker), and the God-sanctioned housewife Mrs Pollard (Annette Crosbie) of the National Association of Socially Concerned Individuals (NASCI). This National Purity Alliance brandishes computer lists of subversives, a filth map of the whole country, plans for firearms for the constable on the beat, and an Anti-Permissive Bill to save the public from unbridled decadence.

W: Alistair Beaton; P: William G. Stewart; D: Barbara Derkow; Channel 4; 50 mins.

TRADITIONAL FAMILY VALUES enforced by draconian laws become 'an increasingly viable grass-roots option' in a Britain echoing to war cries such as 'Better a dead deviant than a corrupted child', 'Armageddon Days Are Here (Again)', 'If you recognize a sinner send a postcard with his name' and 'Let yourself be mugged by the word of God'.

Prescient satire (CLAUSE 28 would be enacted the following year) which spends rather too much time knocking off soft targets (sexually repressed and out-of-touch moral rearmer: 'So-called gay clubs – what a sad misuse of a lovely word'; diabolical born-again Christian in a penthouse) instead of tilting at the mechanisms (tabloid press, parliamentarians and constituents, television and radio, puritanical left-wingers) that enable freedoms to be swept away. The 'killing off' of one opponent is also a sign of the production's lack of rigour, if not imagination.

till death us do part From the Christian wedding oath, scrawled in mirror-writing on the phone booth window by Luke (Mike Dytil) for Jon's benefit in THE LIVING END (1992 C).

Till Death Us Do Part (UK 1964–74 T) Tirading Alf Garnett (Warren Mitchell) lays down his lore on race, welfare state, teenagers, sex, Scouse gits, Harold Wilson and his beloved Queen. Attempting to make him see reason are his daughter and son-in-law (Una Stubbs and Anthony Booth) and – through pursed lips – his wife Elsie (Dandy Nichols).

W: Johnny Speight; BBC1; 30 mins.

This was a truly spooky love affair – a beloved bigot loudly and unself-consciously expressing dark fears and ignorance: hostile, harsh, unbending. Millions watched and his every outburst was a national talking point. NANCY BOYS were, of course, ever-present in the Garnett demonology.

An American Alf, less grotesque but just as much of a Godzilla of liberalism, appeared as Archie Bunker in 1971. Alf returned in *Till Death* (in 1981) and was back on the BBC for IN SICKNESS AND IN HEALTH in 1985 (a nancy boy had penetrated his inner sanctum, black to boot).

Tilley, Vesta [Matilda Alice Powers] (1864–1952) English MALE IMPERSONATOR who first wore drag aged 5. A more decorous 'male' than her American lesbian counterparts Annie Hindle and Ella Wesner and the English Bessie Bonecliffe, she delighted music hall audiences as soldier, sailor, policeman or 'masher' with 'Strolling Along With Nancy', 'Burlington Bertie' and 'Jolly Good Luck To The Girl Who Loves A Sailor' before retiring as Lady De Freece. 'I concluded that female costume was rather a drag. I felt that I could express myself better if I was dressed as a boy,' she wrote in *The Recollections of Vesta Tilley* (1934).

She was returned to public notice via a number of nostalgic cavalcades and dramas in the years immediately after her death, principally those starring Pat Kirkwood (*The Great Little Tilley* 1956 T and *After the Ball* 1957 C).

'Does Tilley earn this much time on the telly? Her story was treated as if it had great cultural and almost national

being coached by Dad in woman-hand-ling) in *Make Room for Daddy/The Danny Thomas Show* 'Rusty and the Tomboy' (1961 T); wild Eddie who is very much the butch – until she dons a party frock in *Dobie Gillis* 'Girls Will Be Boys' (1963 T); Debbie Reynolds, a carrot-headed wildcat before love and money feminize her, at least on the surface, in *The Unsinkable Molly Brown* (1964 C); Carol Burns (Eileen Atkins) brought up as a boy and attracted to a gay man whom she beats up when he rejects her sexually in STORY OF A GIRL (1964 R); top school athlete *Billie* (Patty Duke 1965 C) who sings soulfully of being a 'Lonely Little In-Between'; Spring Tyler (Hayley Mills) who looks wistfully at a blue dress before stowing it away and continuing to wear jeans and shirt in *The Truth About Spring* (1965 C); Bus-bee (Marilyn Rickards) in *The Touch-ables* (1969 C) who wears trousers, drives fast cars, loads guns and has 'a slightly Amazon quality'; Sybilla Melvyn (Judy Davis) knows there's more to life than frills and marriage, eg becoming a successful author, in *My Brilliant Career* (1979 C); Valerie Von Freyer (Sanna Hutlman) has always tried to be the boy her martinet father hoped for in *The Farewell* (1980 C); the heroine of *The Journey of Natty Gann* (Meredith Salenger 1985 C) fighting the elements to find her father; *Vera* (Ana Beatriz Nogueira) using her physical strength to browbeat the other girls in the orphan-age (1986 C); Fred Smith (Leslie Ash) one of the three women operatives in *CATS Eyes* (1985–7 T): 'I see Fred as a tomboy. I know what it's like to be a Fred. I've been brought up with a man's name. When I was a kid I was a real tomboy ... playing Cowboys and Indians' (Leslie Ash, *TV Times*, 25.4.87); Jo[anna] (Kellie Bright) in *The Upper Hand* (1990– T); younger daughter Darlene (Sara Gilbert) in ROSEANNE (1989– T); Idgie Thread-goode (Mary Stuart Masterson) in love with Ruth Jamison (Mary-Louise Parker) in FRIED GREEN TOMATOES AT THE WHISTLE STOP CAFE (1991 C).

Tomlin, Lily (1939–) American actress who became famous playing a number of roles (including Ernestine, the vinegary telephonist) in ROWAN AND MARTIN'S LAUGH-IN (1968–73 T). Among her televised one-woman shows: *Lily* (1973); *Lily Tomlin* (1975); *Lily: Sold Out* (1980), part written and di-rected by her friend Jane Wagner, who was also at the helm of the 1978 romance which co-starred her – in an awesome feat of traditional role reversal – with John Travolta. Far happier was her participation in *Nashville* (1975: as the seduced housewife); *The Late Show* (1977: as a private eye's uncalled for assistant); *9 to 5* (1980: as a secretary); *The Incredible Shrinking Woman* (1981: title role plus two smaller parts). Recently she played two cameos: a pros-titute in *Shadows and Fog* (1992 C) and public health official Selma Dritz in AND THE BAND PLAYED ON (1993 C/T). She was one of the participants in GAY LIB-ERATION FOLLIES (1974 R).

Tongues Untied (US 1989 C/T) Poetry, personal testimony, rap, per-formance, Eddie Murphy, the Church, the gay scene and protest marches. The black gay experience in America.
W: Joseph Bream, Craig Harris, Regi-nald Jackson, Steve Langley, Alan Miller and Donald Woods; P/D: Mar-lon T. Riggs; 55 mins.
Jill Forbes wrote in *Sight and Sound* (Winter 1990–1):

Unidentified African, Caribbean and Afro-American gay men proclaim their lives, some through KISSING and caressing, some through mime, some through poems, some through 'Snap/thology' (communication through snapping fingers). There's also a choir of vilifiers, a restaurant discussion of gay activism and a series of obituaries and photographs of black men felled by AIDS. There is no formal narrative but running through are landmarks of humiliation, abuse and rejection. The film ends with a call to brotherhood and identity.

Riggs takes black singers, actors and performers of all kinds and intercuts snatches of their poetry with shots of encounters between black gay men, mixing video footage, freeze frames and location-shot scenes with voice-over commentary, interior monologue and performances.

tonguing and grooving La Stupenda of suburban Sapphism, Dame Edna EVER-AGE, has mentioned this several times as an activity engaged in by herself and former bridesmaid Madge ALLSOP, presumably relating to carpentry (*A Night on Mount Edna* 1990 T etc). Somewhat more specifically, the Dame has made a play for some of her female guests in front of millions: advising Zsa Zsa Gabor that she could gobble her up (1987), wanting to play 'hospidales' with Gina Lollobrigida (1990), and almost being unable to keep her hands off 'Little Kim Basinger' (1991).

Tonight (UK 1957–65 T) Remarkably inventive and casual-seeming compendium of interviews, vox pops and all manner of quirky film reports (by Fyfe Robertson, Alan WHICKER, Jacqueline MACKENZIE and others) anchored more or less imperturbably by Cliff Michelmore, Derek Hart and Kenneth Allsop, and initially produced by Ned SHERRIN. It was all very jolly and remarkably sophisticated for an early evening show, featuring controversial items such as the WOLFENDEN REPORT ('There's no knowing where it will end. We may even have husbands running away from their wives,' declared Jean Mann MP). All the studio pieces were live, which is why an interviewee in 1959 managed to let slip that he had spent 'all night' with a young man in blue jeans (there were protests).

A late night current affairs series, with the same title but without its illustrious predecessor's variety and fun (and archness), took up residence on BBC1 in the mid-1970s. Subjects undertaken included AID for lesbian couples and the play COMING OUT (1979 T), with Valerie Singleton making sure it was known that the leading players were all married with children. There was also the occasion in 1977 when an extraordinarily bellicose Ludovic Kennedy

accused Christopher ISHERWOOD of seducing innocent German boys in the 1930s.

Tony Awards Broadway's premier celebration of excellence (named after Antoinette Perry), telecast in many parts of the world. After years of voluntary and later enforced silence about the private joys of the Great White Way's many homosexual nominees and winners – in contrast to the copious hosannas to spouses, mistresses, lovers, sweethearts from the heterosexual part of the family – one of the producers of *Torch Song Trilogy*, John Glines, publicly thanked his male lover while accepting his award on 5 June 1983. The following year, on 3 June 1984, after being specifically asked not to, *Torch Song*'s author and star thanked *his* lover when collecting a statuette – his third – for writing the 'book' of *La Cage aux Folles*.

In 1993 Tony Kushner, creator of the 3½-hour epic *Angels in America: Millennium Approaches*, said he was accepting the award for Best Playwright 'on behalf of all my gay and lesbian brothers and sisters'. The play garnered three other awards, and the musical *Kiss of the Spider Woman* was the recipient of seven Tonys during the same ceremony.

Too Darn Hot A hoochie-coochie-style number from *Kiss Me Kate* transformed by Erasure (and directors Adelle Lutz and Sandy McLeod) in RED, HOT AND BLUE (1990 T) into a witty and skilful big parade of statistics, ACT UP demos, SAFE SEX messages and images of complacent America (a blindfolded family watching television, a man and woman slow dancing, hamburgers in a pan, a conga line). This version includes mention of the 'marine with his queen' (as well as the 'GI with his cutie pie') cut from MGM's 1953 film of the Cole PORTER masterpiece (although a sailor and his boyfriend – in drag – *did* flit across the screen in the same studio's *An American in Paris* two years earlier).

Too Good to Be True? (UK 1979 T) The Tom ROBINSON Band in performance during a nationwide tour interleaved with its leader's autobiography (stormy adolescence, COMING OUT, performing 'GLAD TO BE GAY' at the CHE conference, working as a volunteer on GAY SWITCHBOARD, being the first openly gay performer with a hit record). Or as *TV Times* described it: 'A film profile of rock star Tom Robinson whose band had a hit single last year with '2–4–6–8 Motorway' and the LP *Power in the Darkness* also made a big impact on the British charts ... Many of bass guitarist Tom Robinson's songs reflect his strong political convictions. And as a SELF-CONFESSED homosexual, Robinson produced his recent single ... a scathing condemnation of what he regards as the general attitude towards homosexuals.' P: Chris Pye; D: Mick Gold; Granada; 20.2.79; 60 mins.

Portrait of a young gay ROLE-MODEL on the crest of a wave encapsulated in a title some may see these days as presciently ironic now that Tom is glad to be living with a woman and the father of a child. But the beliefs and commitments expressed here have remained essentially the same: pride in one's self, solidarity with those individuals and groups who are pushed to the margins, a love of rock/rhythm and blues, a vigilance against erosions of hard-won rights and freedoms.

Took, Barry (1928–) English comedy writer, biographer (of Frankie HOWERD and Benny HILL), radio and television presenter, quiz chairman, briefly in charge of light entertainment at London Weekend Television.

R: As performer: *The Carrol Levis Show* (1954, one of Levis' 'Discoveries'); chairman of *Sounds Familiar* (1974); presenter of *Points of View*; member of panel on *Top Secret* (1982–3); etc. As writer: *Take It from Here* (with Eric Merriman); *Frankie's Bandbox* (1960, for Howerd); *Beyond Our Ken* (*c* 1961–4, with Marty FELDMAN); ROUND THE HORNE (writing 50 scripts with Marty Feldman, 20 others with David Webster and Brian Cooke); etc.

T: As writer: *The Army Game* (*c* 1959);

Bootsie and Snudge (1960–4, with Feldman); *Scott on ...* (1964–5, with Feldman); *The World of Beachcomber* (1967); *Horne a 'Plenty* (1968); *Marty* (1968–9, with Feldman); *Grubstreet* (1978); etc.

Top of the Pops (UK 1964– T) An all-sorts pop music mixture which has featured nearly everyone who has made a hit record, either in live or mimed performance or through videos. This was the BBC promoting the idea of teenagers (a new batch in the studio each week) having fun and the financial wherewithal to purchase lots of vinyl. Critics either scoffed at its 'ancient' disc jockeys grooving with the kids or screamed that it was encouraging widespread indulgence in sex outside marriage or, as Wayne Fontana and the Mindbenders put it in November 1964, encouraging a lot of 'um, um, um, um, um'.

In its time *Top of the Pops* has featured a lot of gay music, covert and overt: VILLAGE PEOPLE, the Kinks, Frankie Goes To Hollywood (though RELAX was banned after its first appearance), Marc Almond, the Buzzcocks, BOY GEORGE, Erasure, the Smiths and Rod Stewart, whose 'The Killing Of Georgie' – about a friend who was QUEER-BASHED and killed – in 1976 added fuel to the idea that the show was a consistently corrupting influence on Britain's teenagers. A worried parent wrote to *Melody Maker* to protest: 'I have children who listen to the radio and are of an age when they could question the meaning of certain phrases. I think young children should be protected from this sort of thing. Don't get it wrong. I'm not a puritan or a square.' But, at the same time Rod was singing about George, the Rubettes were immortalizing two men who lived and loved 'Under One Roof'.

Torch Song Trilogy (US 1988 C) Drag performer Virginia Hamm is loud and blowsy; inside he is Arnold Beckoff (Harvey FIERSTEIN), still strident but looking for love and the chance to daily shower affection like confetti upon Another. He adores life, rabbits and –

with many reservations – his mother (Anne Bancroft). Like many gay New Yorkers he has few answers but a lot of questions. He meets Ed (Brian Kerwin) who prefers being heterosexual but maintains a friendship which later encompasses – after the murder of Arnold's lover Alan (Matthew Broderick) – Arnold, his mother and Arnold's adopted gay son (Eddie Castrodad).

W/P: Harvey Fierstein based on his plays *The International Stud* (1978); *Fugue in a Nursery* (1981) and *Widows and Children First* (1981); P: Howard Gottfried; D: Paul Bogart; 117 mins.

Gays can be monogamous, nurturing, domestic, practical and coping, too.

The writer-star is the film's strength and its liability. His director allows him to tilt Arnold towards parody. Seen at such close quarters, the constant need for approval, acceptance, recognition and gratitude is sometimes grating. Anne Bancroft, with one too many tirades, also teeters on the grotesque, but sheer technique and some brilliant writing see her through. Matthew Broderick, on the other hand, underplays to perfection as the thoroughly level-headed lover whose life is cut off in a gungy New York street.

The film comes fully alive after Alan's death. The idea of a gay FAMILY is appealingly demonstrated and the chemistry between all the actors is a joy to behold. Everything finally comes together to present an earthshaking, tearjerking, wisecracking challenge to heterosexuality's assumed Divine Right. Fierstein has so much to say and so much to give that it is a source of regret that a better way of bringing the trilogy to a mass audience wasn't found than squeezing it into a 2-hour entertainment (with the first half-hour perversely padded with drag routines and shtick). With a first-class film, as distinct from television, director in control this could have had the pace and the pathos that made it so special on stage.

touching Lots of manly HUGGING between men, and loving embraces between women, as well as DANCING and KISSING. But sometimes – between characters of the same sex – it is more than friendship. The question is 'when?' Rare touching scenes have included: Duncan (Wallace Ford), the shady lawyer putting his hand on John Garfield's shoulder in *The Breaking Point* (1950 C) and letting it remain there (he continues to touch him through subsequent encounters); Eve Harrington (Anne Baxter) seeming to touch nearly all the female characters in ALL ABOUT EVE (1950 C) while hardly laying a finger on the men; the pianist Chummy (Harry Morgan) going over to the bachelor impresario (George Tobias) in *The Glen Miller Story* (1954 C) and comforting him instead of his leader's widow as they listen to the final broadcast; March (Anne Heywood) and Jill (Sandy Dennis) caressing in THE FOX (1968 C) and, just as briefly, Sister George (Beryl REID) and Childie (Susannah YORK) in THE KILLING OF SISTER GEORGE (1968 C); Perrin (Leonard Rossiter) disguised as a gay man panicking when the male employee he is chatting up begins returning the interest via touch in *The Fall and Rise of Reginald Perrin* (1977 T); Anton Rodgers, marked for death, resting a hand on assassin Edward Fox's shoulder in a sauna in *The Day of the Jackal* (1973 C); Leo's hands falling on Otto's BARE BUTTOCKS in DESIGN FOR LIVING (1979 T); Alun Trevose (John Patrick) resting his head in the lap of Philip Castallack (Rupert Frazer) in PENMARRIC (1979 T); black maid Pauline (Jean Renée Foster) and white mistress Selma (Madeleine Stowe) holding each other's hand and later being provocatively painted in this posture in *Beulah Land* (1980 T); Gilberto (Gerald Murphy) taking the hand of Peter (David Yelland) while his wife makes coffee in FACING THE SUN (1980 T); Pete (Stephen CHURCHETT) and his lover Trevor (Paul Hastings) in the very last episode of TOGETHER (1981 T), seen from afar, the former's arm encircling the other's shoulder; Sebastian (Anthony Andrews) and Charles (Jeremy Irons) drape their arms round each other in Venice – not London or Oxford – in BRIDESHEAD REVISITED (1981 T).

English frigidity in matters tactile is commented upon in *Men's Group* (1983 R): 'Our chilly Anglo-Saxon blood. Italians will do this naturally. And Greeks. I've seen Turkish men holding hands in Camden Town.' But it also extends to American men (outside of team sports).

Of the Jon Voight and Dustin Hoffman characters in MIDNIGHT COWBOY (1969 C) Joan Mellen (in *Big Bad Wolves*, 1977) commented: 'The men seem to reach out for each other but are not allowed to touch ... in avoiding the depiction of homosexuality to escape an X-rating or to save the reputation of male stars not wishing to be so characterized, [John] SCHLESINGER sets the tone for many buddy films to come.'

In one of his final interviews (*Advocate*, 27.5.86) James BALDWIN theorized that 'The inability to love is the central problem of the American condition because that inability masks a certain terror and that is the terror of being touched. And if you can't be touched you can't be changed. And if you can't be changed, you can't be alive ...'

Arms round shoulders, handshakes, even hugs are acceptable to a degree – and can even be employed by gay characters to one another. Other kinds of tactile proximity are likely to be banished from the screen if they involve two attractive men of approximately the same age or a younger with an older man. Thus all verbal or visual references to Doug (Hal Holbrook) and Gary (Martin Sheen) holding hands, sharing a bed or otherwise enjoying loving contact were shaved from the script of THAT CERTAIN SUMMER (1972 T), while scenes showing Hank (Laurence Luckinbill) and Larry (Keith Prentice) in THE BOYS IN THE BAND (1970 C), and Sonny (Al Pacino) and Leon (Chris Sarandon) in DOG DAY AFTERNOON (1975 C), lying on or in beds did not reach the screen although they were filmed.

It is not only two men in or on a bed that causes so much perturbation, but any meaningful physical contact between male lovers or between a gay male and a heterosexual one. In A CHORUS LINE (1985 C) the director (Michael Douglas) lays his hand fleetingly on Paul's (Cameron English) left shoulder blade to comfort him after he breaks down, instead of – as in the stage version – wholeheartedly embracing him.

Peter (D. W. Moffett) does touch Michael's (Aidan Quinn) ear in AN EARLY FROST (1985 T) and there's a joke involving the frightened SISTER (Sydney Walsh) who is pregnant and, therefore, won't go near her HIV-infected brother – until she sees the error of her ways: 'Mom, Susie's touching me!' Somehow it didn't seem enough in a film that was supposedly about people reaching out to each other in a time of terrible crisis. Among the family members there is plenteous touching, squeezing, kissing and hugging; only the two lovers are affected by the embargo, even though the drama hinges partly on their love for one another *in extremis*.

The terror also extends to women. Totally acceptable was the tender touching between blind and deaf Helen Keller (Mare Winningham) and her devoted friend Annie Sullivan (Blythe Danner) in *Helen Keller – The Miracle Continues* (1984 T). However, the pairs in A QUESTION OF LOVE (1978 T) and MY TWO LOVES (1986 T) behave as if only the most superficial intimacy has even taken place between them.

'You're not taking this *personally*, are you?' says Debra Winger's character apologetically to Theresa Russell the *Black Widow* (1986 C) while practising her artificial respiration technique on her. Obviously this strictly above-board intimacy did make an impact because, at the end, Russell tells Winger that 'Of all the relationships I'll look back on in 50 years' time, I'll always remember this one.'

In Britain, EASTENDERS Colin and Barry – whether at the beginning of, during or towards the end of a supposedly full sexual relationship – contented themselves with the occasional hug (though Colin *did* rest an arm on his amour's recumbent flu-bound form in one scene in 1987). BROOKSIDE was more daring: Gordon (Mark Burgess) put his arm around Christopher (Stifyn Parri) on the family sofa and, at Christmas 1987, the latter gave Gordon a peck on the cheek.

toy boys When Mortimer in MARLOWE's *Edward II* talked of needing to wean his monarch from 'such toys', it was a man (Piers Gaveston) of whom he spoke. Today such contemptuously dismissed creatures are adolescent to early-twenties males, usually blond, with wide inviting smiles and butterfly brains, who are the playthings of middle-aged women.

In the early part of the 20th century Florence Lancaster dallied with Tom Verryan who was the same age as her son in *The Vortex*; Greta GARBO played women surrounded by very young men in *The Kiss* (1929 C) and *As You Desire Me* (1932 C) while 24-year-old Robert Montgomery was her *Inspiration* (1931 C); industrial empress Alison Drake (Ruth Chatterton) picked a different young man every night from her factory in *Female* (1933 C), plied them with vodka and then had her way on silken cushions (except with one very handsome homosexual who kept it charmingly platonic).

Television's first toy boy was one Adam Shaw whom Vera (Elaine Lee) appraises (while lying next to him in bed) as 'far too young but quite delicious' in NUMBER 96 (1974 T).

Although widow Ellen Grant (Georgann Johnson) enjoyed Dale Robinson (Jameson Parker) in *Somerset* (1976 T) and Mrs Manson (Sheila Allen) took advantage of her grieving son-in-law (James Aubrey) in *Another Bouquet* 1977 T), the major breakthrough in making male 'bits of fluff' acceptable for women as well as for men came with Peter (Christopher Atkins), the student counsellor who had an affair with Sue Ellen (Linda Gray) in DALLAS (1981 T). There was considerable sneering about Peter's too PRETTY (for a man) face and figure and, together with similar scoffing in newspaper gossip columns about

mature actresses and their 'handbags', toy boys for a while were assumed to be gay.

The record was well and truly put straight when a fortysomething businesswoman (played by Penelope Keith) involved herself with an architect (Christopher Villiers) 16 years her junior in *Sweet Sixteen* (1983 T). There was heavy condemnation at the time of such 'offensive' material. Yet within just a few years toy boys have become saucy cultural icons, and not only for saucy (read 'brassy') women (Alison Steadman's gossip columnist Jackie Johns in *News Hounds* 1991 T; Polly Perkins' singer Trish Valentine in ELDORADO 1992 T; Vera Duckworth (Elizabeth Dawn) in CORONATION STREET (1987 T) who was asked apropos of a party: 'Are you taking your toy boy with you?') Now these junior studs can be affixed, usually only in jest, to nice, respectable types like Gail Tilsley (Helen Worth) who married hers in 1990 and Peggy (June Spencer) in THE ARCHERS (1992 R) whose husband Jack pampered her by serving her breakfast in bed 'just in case you run off with a toy boy'.

Hitching his wagon to another syndrome, Phil DONAHUE talked to women who like 'boys' and to 'boys' who prefer older women in a 1989 show called 'She Was 53 ... He Was 17 ... It's Called a "toyboy" Affair'.

trade Derived from POLARI and signifying a sexual partner (usually penetrative and heterosexually oriented) of brief acquaintance. First mentioned in THE CAPTAIN'S TABLE (1958 C) by Birtweed (Reginald BECKWITH: 'Oh, we know how to look after the tools of our trade, sir'), but it was put into full operation by Julian (Hugh PADDICK) in ROUND THE HORNE) (1965–9 R: 'Trade's been a bit rough lately. We've had to take whatever we could get'). A decade later it resurfaced in the vocabulary of Pete HUNT (Stephen CHURCHETT) in TOGETHER (1981 T) who, although devoted to Trevor, probably wasn't averse to 'a bit of passing trade'. Julian CLARY asked a young male contestant on STICKY

MOMENTS (1989 T): 'Did you pick up any trade on your way here?' *See also* ROUGH TRADE.

traditional family values A very loose and ill-defined term for a rigidly over-centralized concept shaped by the old order of things, and increasingly verbalized in various moral panics such as those arising in 1987, 1988 and 1993 in Britain and during the US presidential election campaign in 1992. According to Anne Summers on *Foreign Correspondent* (Aust 1992 T) the phrase is 'a code word for heterosexuality'. The term is highly popular with moral rightists such as those on DONAHUE 'Towns Legally Forcing Gays Back into the Closet' (1992 T), but it is becoming common parlance for people looking for an easy answer to the problems of the world without pondering *which* tradition, *what* families and *whose* values. It is to be hoped that the United Nations International Year of the Family in 1994 will shed much needed light on this volatile and complex area.

train movies A hardy perennial of mass entertainment from *The Great Train Robbery* to *Caught on a Train* and back again via *The Railway Children*. Gays, lesbians and transvestites are sometimes passengers: an ornithologist (Michael WARD) exquisitely uninterested in women on the *Sleeping Car to Trieste* (1948 C); Bruno (Robert Walker) picking up a young man in STRANGERS ON A TRAIN (1951 C); Daphne and Josephine (Jack Lemmon and Tony Curtis) joining the girls in SOME LIKE IT HOT (1959 C); Mabel (Anna Burden) and Janet (Diane Aubrey) with different agendas in STAMBOUL TRAIN (1962 T); one of the terrorized passengers in *The Incident* (1967 C); 'the Homosexual' (Gary Bolling) riding the subways during *The Taking of Pelham One, Two, Three* (1974 C); millionaire's secretary (Anthony Perkins) and a countess's companion (Rachel Roberts) involved in the *Murder on the Orient Express* (1974 C); Joe ACKERLEY (Joseph Blatchley) slipping into a toilet with a rail steward in SECRET

ORCHARDS (1980 T); the mysterious woman in *Blue Distance* (1983 C); Lady Windermere (Delphine Seyrig) in *Joan of Arc of Mongolia/Johanna D'Arc of Mongolia* (1989 C); the two briefly encountered lovers in FLAMES OF PASSION (1989 C); etc. A well-regarded deceased signalman was 'queer as a bun' according to a character in LAST TRAIN THROUGH THE HARECASTLE TUNNEL (1969 T) and real-life engine driver (Alex) used TCHAIKOVSKY to come out to his mate, as he related on GAYS: SPEAKING UP (1978 T).

traitors Portrayed as craven greedy people, usually homosexual men, betraying their country by revealing closely guarded military secrets and putting single lives or thousands at risk. Or sometimes as idealistic dupes who, once hooked, couldn't wriggle free.

Real spies include Anthony BLUNT; Guy BURGESS; Sir Roger CASEMENT; Guy FAWKES; Alfred REDL; John Vassall. Among their fictional selves: Redl in *Colonel Judas* (1945 R); Burgess in ANOTHER COUNTRY; Blunt – with lots of Kim Philby – as Bill HAYDON etc; 'Adrian Harris' (John Le Mesurier), a conglomerate of Burgess, Maclean and Philby in *Traitor* (1971 T); Burgess again as Bunny Bingham (Hugh BURDEN) returning to Britain from exile in Moscow in the last weeks of his life in *The Recruiter* (1971 R); Burgess and Maclean alias *Smith and Jones* (1968 R Aust) with Robert X (John Ewart) and Mark Y (Don Pascoe).

Others of dangerous persuasions: Jimmy Ellis (Kenneth GRIFFITH) with his CAT and his hysteria, a Soviet sympathizer involved in *High Treason* (1951 C); a pair of Communist-inclined intellectuals, SISSY male (Ronnie Stevens) and butch female (Eleanor Summerfield), involved in an artistic conciliation behind the Iron Curtain in *Top Secret* (1952 C); Robert Walker as the Communist agent who is cold, superior, contemptuous in *My Son John* (1952 C), burrowing into the very foundations of American family life; Alexei Bresnavitch (Orson WELLES) doing the dirty on his fellow Communists and gays in *The Kremlin Letter* (1970 C); Ambassador Stephenson (Dan O'Herlihy) in *The Tamarind Seed* (1974 C); Jason (Donald Pleasence), a 'sleeper' in *Blade on the Feather* (1980 T); Ian Stevens (Christopher Benjamin), frequenter of gay clubs in *A Spy at Evening* (1981 T), etc.

See also POSITIVE VETTING; SPIES.

transsexuals People who wish to reverse their biological gender because they come to regard themselves as being born in the wrong body. The word 'transsexual' was first heard in 1953 (in GLEN OR GLENDA?/I LIVED TWO LIVES), the same year as it appeared in an article published in the *International Journal of Sexology*. The idea of sexual metamorphosis, of men being fitted with a neovagina and acquiring female breasts, and of women gaining a penis continues to fascinate the media.

The 'sex change' operation first came to prominence at the beginning of the 1950s, especially publicized by Christine JORGENSEN, whose story was told after a fashion in a 1970 film with John Hansen. By 1959–60 the operation was well into the mainstream as totally freakish, but within the realms of possibility. A newspaper headline referring to 'the operation' appears at the beginning of LOOK BACK IN ANGER (1959 C), while in *Doctor in Love* (1960 C) GP Michael Craig angrily refutes a confusion over his gender: 'When I'm changing my sex I'll send you a postcard.' To which the response is a jocularly restraining 'Keep your hair on.'

By the 1970s there had been sufficient publicity – including a very dignified personal account by Jan (formerly James) MORRIS entitled *Conundrum* (1974) – for audiences to pick up immediately on the report of a scene in the 1976 film version of *The Likely Lads*. Bob (Rodney Bewes) visits Terry (James Bolam) and, when faced with bra and panties in the bathroom, asks: 'Have you got something to tell me? Do you want me to lend you the fare to Denmark?'

Although there had been a number of

fantasy film comedies about switching gender (TURNABOUT 1940; *Goodbye Charlie* 1964; *Myra Breckinridge* 1970; *All of Me* 1984; etc) as well as television and radio plays (*The Lifeswappers* 1976; *Fair Exchange* 1992), the first mainstream series to include a character who is contemplating the big step was SOAP in 1977.

The male to female transsexual had become during the 1970s a staple of drama, effective as a figure of pathos and also of titillation: John LaZar as the rock music producer in *Beyond the Valley of the Dolls* (1970 C); Roy/Wendy (Anne Heywood) in *I Want What I Want* (1971 C); Candy DARLING in SOME OF MY BEST FRIENDS ARE ... (1971 C); Leon Schermer (Chris Sarandon) in DOG DAY AFTERNOON (1975 C); Marianne Miller (Judy Loe) in CROWN COURT 'The Change' (1976 T); José Maria/Maria José (Victoria Abril) in *Cambio de Sexo/ Sex Change* (1976 C); Erwin/Elvira Weishaupt (Volker Spengler) in *In a Year with 13 Moons* (1978 C); Stephen Piper (Paul Henley) in EVEN SOLOMON (1979 T); Mr Mince (Robert Gillespie) in AGONY (1979 T): 'The doctor wouldn't let me pay for the sex change on my Access card.' The same actor played a family man cross-dressing and wanting to fully become a woman in MARY'S WIFE (1980 T).

The first post-operative transsexuals to appear on British television talking about their lives without judgemental or salivating intermediaries were members of the Transsexual Liberation Group in one of the OPEN DOOR programmes (1973 T). Michelle Calleghan, the first man to have a sex change in Ulster, was interviewed on *Good Morning Ulster* (1976 R) and Jan Morris was the subject of a 1978 radio *Profile*. On WOMAN'S HOUR (R) the following year Dr Wendy Greengross spoke to 'the wife of a transsexual'.

In the widely seen *Inside Story* (1979 T) Julia Grant was shown being created out of George Roberts, a process even more extensively – and surgically – documented a year later with a repeat showing followed by the operation and living as Julia.

There was a similar interest in the 1980s in one-off stories about men who felt that their masculinity was alien to them. There have been TV movies (SECOND SERVE 1986), and cinema films (*The Woman Inside* 1981, with Gloria Manon as a Vietnam veteran; *The Mystery of Alexina* 1985, the true story of Adelaide Barbin; *Shadey* 1985, with Antony SHER).

Among the more outstanding characters have been Georgine Beyer who is a law unto herself and the object of a young queen's devotion in JEWEL'S DARL (1985 C/T); Tina (Carmen Maura), formerly the film director's brother and now his sister in LAW OF DESIRE (1987 C); Marje in THE CORNER HOUSE (1987 T); Maurice (Griff Rhys Jones), who was once Monica, meeting his former husband Giles (Mel Smith) for the first time in years in SMITH AND JONES: *In Small Doses* 'The Whole Hog' (1989 T): 'Fifteen separate operations, major tissue redistribution and some hydraulic installations'; Denise (David Duchovny) in *Twin Peaks* (1991 T); Carl/Carol (Nicola Cowper) in CASUALTY 'Cherish' (1992 T); Toni (Anthony Wong) saving for a sex change and helping his brother in his dangerous political activities in *Sex Diary of an Infidel* (Aust 1992 R).

The flow of documentaries continues: *Phantom Ladies* (1984 T); OPEN SPACE 'It's Called Jo-Anne' (1986 T); 40 MINUTES 'Stop the Wedding' (1987 T); *Under the Sun* 'Eunuchs: India's Third Gender' (1991 T); *Soundtrack* 'The Making of Christine' (1993 R); etc.

One of the recent advocates for a change in the British law regarding passports and the right to legally marry has been model Tula who, as Caroline Cossey, has spoken on trans-gender and gender reassignment issues on programmes such as HEART OF THE MATTER (1990) in Britain and *Sixty Minutes* (1991) in Australia.

Despite increased visibility and volubility, male to female transsexuals are usually heard at the beginning of any programme disassociating themselves from homosexual men or TRANSVESTITES (a confusion still widespread in the community). Some homosexual men used to appear in television documentaries – like the man with his back to the camera who said during a TONIGHT report in 1957: 'What I would most like in life is to be a woman.' During the 1980s, Quentin CRISP was continuing to regret that he hadn't had 'the change'. One of the 1992 *Video Diaries* which was kept by a pre-operative transsexual was entitled 'Not a Transvestite'.

Women who change their sex are much more rarely documented. Exceptions have been Ben in WORLD IN ACTION 'Trapped in the Wrong Body' (1978 T); Jasper Laybutt formerly Francine in *F2M* (1992 V); *Max* (American Blackfoot Indian Anita Valerio 1992 C). Karen Black played a female to male transsexual in *Come Back to the Five and Dime, Jimmy Dean, Jimmy Dean* (1982 C), and one of the central protagonists in *My Father Is Coming* (1991 C) turned out to have been originally female.

Transsexuals in fictional roles have included Holly WOODLAWN in *Trash* (1970 C) and Jayne County who develops 'lesbian tendencies' in *City of Lost Souls* (1982 C).

See also TRAPPED IN THE WRONG BODY.

transvestites Individuals who feel comfortable all or some of the time in clothing regarded as inappropriate for their sex. As with TRANSSEXUALS, cross-dressing will usually involve a long process of self-understanding, which may lead to the discovery of many vital layers within.

Transvestism is a term introduced by Magnus Hirschfeld in 1910, which was followed a year later by Edward CARPENTER's proposal of cross-dressing. The word 'transvestite' was first mentioned by a psychiatrist to a policeman in GLEN OR GLENDA?/I LIVED TWO LIVES (1953 C). The cop gives it the thumbs up: 'If that's the word you men of science use for a man who dresses up in women's clothes ... It's not an unfriendly word, nor is it vicious when you get to know the people involved.'

Male to female transvestites – as distinct from FEMALE IMPERSONATORS or drag queens – began to appear in the American cinema in the works of Andy WARHOL and Jack Smith in the early 1960s. In the mainstream, men who spend most of their lives (or a secret part) dressed as women have included prisoner 'Mary' Sheldon (Clifford David) in *Riot* (1967 C); stage director Roger (Christopher Hewett) in THE PRODUCERS (1967 C); Ray Walston as the industrial chemist in *Caprice* (1967 C); Michael Greer as Queenie in FORTUNE AND MEN'S EYES (1971 C); Barry Scott in *Goodbye Gemini* (1970 C); Lou Jacobi as the mild married man in the 'Are Transvestites Homosexual?' segment from EVERYTHING YOU ALWAYS WANTED TO KNOW ABOUT SEX (1972 C); Gloria (Mittie Lawrence) in *Precinct 45: Los Angeles Police/The New Centurions* (1972 C); Jamie Farr as Max KLINGER in *M*A*S*H* (1972–83 T); Snowflake in the cartoon *Coonskin* (1973 C); Robyn Ross (Carlotta) whom Arnold Feather meets and falls in love with – until he discovers her secret – in NUMBER 96 (1973 T); Helen Brown (Bert Remsen) in *California Split* (1974 C) dresses the way she does 'because I never had any balls'; Frank N Furter (Tim CURRY) singing 'I'm a sweet transvestite from transsexual Transylvania' and dressed in corset and net stockings in THE ROCKY HORROR PICTURE SHOW (1975 C); CALIGULA (John HURT) in *I, Claudius* (1976 T); Philip SAYER as Lola Martin in CROWN COURT 'Lola' (1976 T); singer's agent (David Doyle) in *The Comeback* (1977 C); the husband in *The Brute* (1978 C); three villains in *Blazing Magnum* (1978 T); Robert Christian in *...And Justice for All* (1979 C); the psychiatrist (Michael Caine) in DRESSED TO KILL (1980 C); Kevin (Ray Burdis) and Alex (Robert Gillespie) who want to be MARY'S WIFE (1980 T) as well as her husband; Fama (Fama), elegant tall, intelligent, proud singer in a rowdy Bilbao club in LA MUERTE DE MIKEL (1984 C); son Max (Evan Richards) in *Down and Out in Beverly Hills* (1986 C); suburban devotees of a TV soap opera dress

up as their favourites in *Exclusive Yarns* (1987 T); Sandra (Matt Zimmerman) empowered by *Sainte Carmen of the Main* (1987 R); Vanessa (James Telfer) in *Apartment Zero* (1988 C); judge (Jeffrey Tambor) in an episode of *Hill Street Blues* (1989 T); BUFFALO BILL (Ted Levine) who wants to be a woman but is not considered a transsexual by doctors in *The Silence of the Lambs* (1991 C); the young husbands in *A Little Bit of Lippy* (1992 T): Danny Cunningham as Rick Fairley) and *Just Like a Woman* (1992 C); Ipanja Bent (Rose Leaf) who gets beaten up and takes off with a heterosexual man in *Buck House* (Aust 1993 T); *M Butterfly* living with a man who was unaware of the true situation (1993 C); the character played by Jaye Davidson in *The Crying Game* (1992 C).

Female to male transvestites form a small select group as far as entertainment is concerned: George SAND; Queen CHRISTINA; the Ingrid Thulin character in *The Magician/The Face* (1958 C); the diplomat Chevalier D'Eon De Beaumont (Andrée Debar) in *The Secret of Chevalier D'Eon* (1960 C); *Monsieur Hawarden* (1968 C) was really a woman (Ellen Vogel) who kept up the disguise for 15 years; Kathleen Widdoes in *Savages* (1972 C); Rachel Roaring Girl (Josie Lawrence) in RACHEL AND THE ROARETTES (1985 T); COLETTE (Clementine Amoureux) in *Colette* (1985 T); *La Monja Alferez/The Lieutenant Nun* (1987 C); *Mlle de Maupin* (Nichola McAuliffe 1987 R); Kotzebue (k. d. lang) in *Salmonberries* (1991 C); James Allen (Anna Savva) in A MATTER OF SEX (1992 R); Pat Quinlan in *The Story of Doctor Barry* (1992 R).

Documentaries on the subject have included a discussion between George MELLY and Anthony Storr in WOMAN'S HOUR (1968 R): 'Far from producing homosexuals, I think it's more likely to produce people who are not homosexual, but who might have been before on account of having to suppress their effeminacy'; *Problems* (Cherry and Bill 1977 T); *Crossing Over* (1979 R: Claire RAYNER talks to transvestite men and their wives); *Claire Rayner's Casebook*

(1983 T: 'Most are at pains to point out that they are now homosexual or transsexual'); *Sisters Under the Skin* (1991 R: transvestites at a weekend conference talk about themselves); *Lady Boys* (1992 T: about Thai tranvestites); DONAHUE 'Living Next Door to a Transvestite' (1992 T) and 'People Who Hate to be Referred to as Sexual Oddities' (1992 T); *I Am My Own Woman* (1992 C/T: the story of the best known transvestite in east Germany, Charlotte Von Mahlsdorf).

Girl Talk (1980 T) reversed the idea of male transvestism by having three men, dressed in women's clothes, arrive at one of their homes and surreptitiously try on plain sweaters, pairs of trousers and Hush Puppies shoes. As they swagger around, one of the wives (Frances Cuka) comes home unexpectedly with her mother. They are dumbfounded by what they see. The husband (Robert Swales) tries to explain: 'It's just the clothes, Mavis: just something I can't help. Do you think you can ever accept me like this?' Mavis can't accept and demands he get medical treatment for his aberration. However, Marion Fairley (Alison Swann) in *A Little Bit of Lippy* (1992 T) takes her husband's need for suspender belt and make-up in her stride: 'Underpants or ladies' briefs – what's the difference? It's what's underneath that counts.'

trapped in the wrong body The most common phrase about people who are transsexual, deriving from Karl Heinrich Ulrich's idea of 'a female soul trapped in a male body'. Used about Glen (Daniel Davis) in GLEN OR GLENDA?/I LIVED TWO LIVES (1953 C); about Leon Schermer (Chris Sarandon) in DOG DAY AFTERNOON (1975 C); by both Ben and Penny in the eponymous WORLD IN ACTION report in 1978; by Alec (Robert Gillespie) in MARY'S WIFE (1980 T); by Jo-Anne in OPEN SPACE 'It's Called Jo-Anne' (1986 T); by an unnamed man (Paul Gist) before he punches the hero (John Ritter) in a 1988 episode of HOOPERMAN; about 'Christine' in *Soundtrack* 'The Making

of Christine' 'married with two children but trapped in the wrong body' (1993 R).

Trefusis, Violet (1894–1962) English novelist and love of Vita SACKVILLE-WEST. After 20 years of separation, she could still write that her love for Vita 'always burns in my heart whenever I think of you'. Played by Cathryn Harrison as an emotional sponge in PORTRAIT OF A MARRIAGE (1990 T) and, lightly disguised, as Sasha in ORLANDO (Amanda Murry 1984 R; Charlotte Valandrey 1992 C).

John **Tregorran** Character in THE ARCHERS (R) played by Basil JONES (1953–65 and 1976–7), Philip Morant (1965–74), Simon LACK (1975–6), Roger Hume (1979–81) and John Bott (1981).

An ex-university lecturer who, having won the pools, arrived in AMBRIDGE driving a gypsy caravan. He is knocked off his scooter by Carol GREY (Anne CULLEN) and they are immediately attracted. He takes her to look at a rare flower and she is bitten by an adder. The pair have an on-off romance until Carol marries Charles Grenville. John later marries a nurse who is killed in a car crash. He and Carol eventually marry after she, too, is bereaved. He then lectures on antique furniture, opens a bookshop in Borchester and, with Jennifer Aldridge, writes a history of Ambridge. Carol forgave him for his brief romance with Jennifer and the pair left the area in 1981. Their most recent visit was in 1990.

On the surface – and as far as *Archers'* historians are concerned – the statutory airy bachelor, smitten by an equally sophisticated woman, watching her marry another, then, having both lost partners, marrying the girl of his dreams. However, as written and played for over 10 years, John Tregorran was anything but conventional. With his cheerful conceitedness, bantering tone and outgoing personality he could fool a lot of people. But he didn't fool Carol. She recognized a fellow spirit. Someone who sat on the sidelines of life, watching and meditating. In his own words he was a man looking for 'some little place' where he might fit in. To Carol he was 'a lily of the field'; to the squire he was 'a drifter'. Women flocked to him, but his relationships always involved him in being 'useful', 'an escort and adviser' and 'the best of friends'. Before he arrived in the village he had done a lot of 'comforting' of the diddicoys and gypsies ('Well, we won't go into that').

For quite some months, John was regarded with great suspicion by Ambridge men. A glib stranger who never confided in anyone, fobbing off personal questions with a jest. Hunting and shooting he loathed; for 'the great god football' he had no time. He was much more interested in finding out about others, providing a shoulder to cry on, riding around on his motor scooter, encouraging local handicrafts, reading books and doing his own interior decorating at Blossom Hill Cottage.

He becomes Carol's gay cavalier, extravagantly proposing to her at every opportunity, pushing her to reveal the 'truth' about herself when she refuses. He regards her as 'someone who must be tamed and kept under control ... a disturbing influence'. To her he is initially no more than a man who fills his time with 'rather precious things'. For three or four years they fence with one another, always threatening to tell each other some 'home truths', but always pulling back. Carol even admits at one point (in 1957) that there are some things she could say to him but she'd be 'out of my depth'. But John has opened up, to Jack Archer (Denis Folwell) who in 1954 had a nervous breakdown. John tells him that he went through a very bad period at university. He lost confidence (a girl 'dropped' him). He was on the verge of a breakdown and had to go into hospital. After 'treatment' he emerged 'a new man'.

John married Carol, fathered children, had an extra-marital affair and, (save for a brief period in the 1970s) shorn of his originator's captivating sad-bright voice, lost most of his intriguing dimensions.

He entered the serial (episode 740, 23.11.53) as a voice off in the bushes (he was suspected of poaching by Tom Forrest). What will be his final contribution is as mysterious as his past: the *Archers'* production office said in mid-1992 that 'No one knows if he is still alive'.

'He's kind, makes me laugh and a gentleman ... most considerate and very charming,' Ann Trentham to Carol (23.3.57).

'You're rather a nice man, John. People would understand you much better if you didn't keep yourself to yourself,' Carol (29.5.57).

Tremain, Rose (1943–) English novelist and playwright with a beguiling bleakness and insight, an ability to write sour and trenchant male characters, to evoke loving memory and to subtly reverse domination and weakness. Gay characters have been prominent in *The Wisest Fool* (1977 R: about JAMES I and Buckingham); A ROOM FOR THE WINTER (1980 T); *Findings on a Late Afternoon* (1981 T); and one of her best works, *Temporary Shelter* (1984 R).

Tremblay, Michel (1942–) French-Canadian playwright and novelist whose novel *Le Coeur Découvert/Making Room* was turned into a 1986 film THE HEART EXPOSED/LE COEUR DECOUVERT. Quebec's most revered dramatist, a national icon, he writes mostly in *joual*, a Montreal dialect which contains a large quantity of English words. TRANSVESTITES and homosexuals feature in many of his plays from *Les Belles-soeurs* in 1968 to *Johnny Mangano and His Astonishing Dogs* and *Sainte Carmen of the Main* (1987 R). Autobiography: *Kaleidoscope* (1988 R); *The Politics of Song* (1988 R).

Treut, Monika (1954–) German film-maker who crashes through all sorts of sexual barriers in black comedies like *Seduction: The Cruel Woman* (1985 C) and *My Father Is Coming* (1991 C), biographical works like *Max* (1992

C/T), and the futuristic *The Virility Factor* (1993 C).

Trevor Boy's name that sometimes carries with it a prissy, inactive odour: the boyfriend of Lukewarm in *Porridge* 'Men without Women' (1975 T); Trevor (Peter Egan), man who becomes a woman (Mrs Trevor) in *The Lifeswappers* (1976 T); Trevor (Rick Riccardo), lover of Oliver Farnsworth in *The Man Who Fell to Earth* (1976 C); Trevor (Nigel Hawthorne) in A ROD OF IRON (1980 T); Trevor Wallace (Paul Hastings) in TOGETHER (1980–1 T); Cedric's lover in *Love in a Cold Climate* (1980 T); Trevor (Vas Blackwood) drummer in *You Start, I'll Join In* (1987 R); Trevor Botting (Michael Sharvell-Martin) in *No Place Like Home* (1987 R); Trevor, jealous of his mother's new boyfriend in HOOPERMAN (1988 T); son of *The Watched Pot* (1988 R); Barry's new friend in EASTENDERS (1988 T); Trevor Coghlan (Glyn Grinstead) in *The Manageress* (1990 T); Trevor (Tim Brooke-Taylor) in *The Upper Hand* 'Blind Date' (1992 T); Trevor (William Hurt) in *Until the End of the World* (1992 C); Trevor Jordache (Bryan Murray) in BROOKSIDE (1993–); etc.

trials Public airings of private matters that offend public morality, the status quo or special interests. For some lesbians and gays, justice becomes a question of doer and did, surrounded by jargon, sophistry, perjury, prejudice and cavalier distortions: YOU ARE THERE 'The Trial of Socrates' (1958 T); ON TRIAL 'Oscar WILDE' (1960 T); *Oscar Wilde* (1960 C); *The Trials of Oscar Wilde* (1960 C); *The Marlowe Murder Case* (1964 T); *The Portsmouth Defence* (1966 T); *Owen Marshall: Counsellor at Law* 'Words of Summer' (1972 T); POLICE WOMAN 'Trial by Prejudice' (1975 T); CROWN COURT (T); THE NAKED CIVIL SERVANT (1975 T); EVERYMAN 'Blasphemy at the Old Bailey' (1977 T); A QUESTION OF LOVE (1978 T); SERGEANT MATLOVICH VS THE US AIR FORCE (1978 T); CIRCUIT ELEVEN – MIAMI 'Gay Rip-Off' (1979 T); *Shine On Harvey Moon*

'Mud Sticks' (1985 T); THE MISSING DAY (1986 R); L.A. LAW 'The Accidental Jurist' (1988 T) and 'The Nut Before Christmas' (1991 T); *Rafferty's Rules* (Aust 1988 T); *The Trials of Rosie O'Brien* (1991 T); SWOON (1991 C); etc.

Triangle (UK 1981–4 T) In the first series of this early evening serial set aboard a North Sea ferry, the cornered ship's purser Peter Nuttall (Jonathan Owen) reveals he's gay to his fiancée Sandy (Helena Breck), who then tries to kill herself.

Cr: Luyansha Greer; P: Bill Seller; D: Marc Miller and John Bird; BBC1; 25 mins.

It was usually shown between 6.55 and 7.20pm on Mondays and Wednesdays. Out of the 26 episodes, the relevant ones are nos. 15–17.

Bleak, wintry setting for uninspiring characters in confined spaces:

> Peter: 'Some people say it's just a matter of choosing a LIFESTYLE. I wouldn't want to speak for everyone but, in my case, that's not true. The only choice I have is to be what I am or live a lie.'
> Sandy: 'But you never acted like you were. You made love to me. How could you ...'
> Peter: '... Why don't you ask me how I feel about it? You think it's easy. I'm told it's a sin against God. Some people say it's a mental illness. You think I got up this morning and said, "Hey, I think I'll become a homosexual today." It certainly doesn't enhance my career potential.'

Peter's final appearance has him tell his friend Jo (Elisabeth Larner), the ship's singer: 'I don't know what I want. But I know what I need. I need gays.'

Trodd, Kenith (194?-) English television producer, vigorous and intelligent, connected with one very good gay play, ROLL ON FOUR O'CLOCK (1970), and one not so good, COMING OUT (1979). Long associated with the plays of Dennis Potter: *Moonlight on the Highway* (1969); *Son of Man* (1969); *Brimstone and Treacle* (1976); *Pennies from Heaven* (1978); *Blue Remembered Hills*

(1979); *Blade on the Feather* (1980); *The Singing Detective* (1986). Also: *Banglestein's Boys* (1969); *Shadows on Our Skin* (1980); *Caught on a Train* (1980); *United Kingdom* (1981); *The Aerodrome* (1983); *Unfair Exchanges* (1985); *Unnatural Pursuits* (1992); etc.

troll From POLARI meaning to 'walk' or 'cruise' as in Sandy (Kenneth WILLIAM)'s perennial question after Julian (Hugh PADDICK) had introduced him in ROUND THE HORNE (1965–9 R): 'What brings you trollin' in 'ere?' Its popularity derived from its slangy rhythm, and for making the previously unthinkable correlation between upright family/business man Kenneth HORNE and wet nights on HAMPSTEAD HEATH or trawls up and down tow paths. The show preferred the British 'troll' to 'cruise', although there was mention of a pop group called Ruff Trayde and the Cruisers in 1966.

'Why don't you troll over to the local and I'll join you in 10 minutes,' Colin (Roger Hammond) to his shop assistant Barbara and his lover Kit in WAGGONERS' WALK (1970 T).

'I bumped into that 'nephew' of yours you used to troll around with. He's working in a bar – balding head and pot belly – married with children,' colleague to Eddie (George Cole) in COMIC'S INTERLUDE (1981 R), and to which the latter replies: 'On the straight and narrow now ...'

'I don't go trolling down the aisle with a man for the fun of it,' Joan Collins on *Aspel and Company* (1988 T).

Trouble for Two (UK 1958 T) Two women involved in show business – Jacqueline MACKENZIE and Lorrae Desmond – live together, and employ a cleaner called Humphrey (Donald Churchill).
W: Jacqueline Mackenzie, Johnny Whyte and others; P: Ronnie Marsh; BBC; 30 mins.

A wildly before its time comedy series which was taken off two weeks early (by the producer) because the 'BACHELOR GIRL' repartee, the songs, the physical comedy (including wrestling), the impressions, the near-the-knuckle jokes (one about Godfrey WINN), and the occasional guest appearance (one by Nancy SPAIN) never cohered.

Troupers (UK 1988 R) A group of variety entertainers stage a strike during an outside broadcast from a factory in the Second World War. This unheard-of insurrection is led by novelty instrumentalist Jerry Coe (Terry Molloy) whose lover, comedy VENTRILOQUIST Larry (Alton Douglas), is dying of TB. Jerry stands firm against having to perform with amateurs. Bob Blacker (Tim Brierley) is sent to Crewe to quell the rebellion. He fails, and Jerry and his colleague retain their professional status.
W: Ron Hutchinson; D: Philip Martin; BBC Radio 3; 120 mins.

Some of the less than honourable motives behind radio production, including HOMOPHOBIA. There are some interesting sidelights on BBC policy and 1940s attitudes. The heterosexuals pity yet admire the homos ('... all that daily courage they needed just to go about the life they'd chosen. All that fight and undefeatedness in them'). Jerry, a great fighter and protector of his lover and his profession, takes a dim view of certain heteros who can't behave themselves: 'Always the way. Invite normal people into your digs and violence breaks out.'

trousers Katharine HEPBURN, Marlene DIETRICH and Greta GARBO helped popularize – and feminize – them as 'leisure-wear' for women during the 1930s. In the previous decade they had been ascribed to lesbians (Hepburn called them dungarees in *RKO: The Golden Years of Hollywood* 1988 T). On screen Garbo's were figure-hugging worn with boat-necked top and flyaway blonde wig in the 'Zaza' opening scene from *As You Desire Me* (1932 C) and Ginger Rogers' were satin in *Follow the Fleet* (1936 C). Made acceptable by the war, Gene Tierney, as the embodiment of the evil that women do, spends most of *Leave Her to Heaven* (1945) in them, although they are technically 'lounging pajamas'.

On television Lucille Ball wore them regularly in 1951–2 episodes of I LOVE LUCY, thereafter on fairly rare occasions ('The Puppy' 1956 T; etc). In the 1960s Mary Tyler Moore made 'ski pants' *à la mode* in America, and Cathy GALE and Emma PEEL slipped into tight leather and pvc in Britain. (However, trousers were still called slacks in THE DALES up until its demise in 1969.)

Acceptable now for young and old, and not at all mannish. All the little girls in the American version of *Seven-Up* wore trousers on their day out with the boys (1992 T) and all THE GOLDEN GIRLS wore them in the last episode (1992 T).

Interestingly Barbara (Mariette Hartley) is never seen without a pair (usually accompanied by a shirt tied round the midriff) in *The Silence of the Heart* (1984 T). She is presented as an emotionally absentee mother whose teenage son commits suicide. Her only concession to the feminine is the black jacket and black short skirt at the funeral.

Wearing the trousers is a warning that the woman is ruling the roost and upsetting nature's plan: 'I think the main trouble is that Peg's wearing the trousers now ... she's the boss of the Bull,' Jack (Denis Folwell) tells his mother-in-law Mrs Perkins (Pauline Seville) in THE ARCHERS (1954 R); Arthur (Bill Treacher) is told that his wife Pauline (Wendy Richard) is wearing what only he should wear in EASTENDERS (1987 T).

A Tune to Take Away: A Review of Revues (UK 1938 T) Queenie Leonard, Edward Cooper, Wendy Toye, Maurice Denham, Graham Payn, Lindesay Baxter joke about schools, fortune tellers, folk music and FAIRIES as they go 'all Peter Panish' so that 'thy cares' they will 'banish'.
W: Nicholas Phipps and Geoffrey Wright with additional songs and scenes by David Yates Massey and Michael Treford; P: Reginald Smith; BBC; 40 mins.

Turing, Alan (1912–54) English scientist who was a designer of early computers and a pioneer of computer programming and artificial intelligence (author of the classic paper 'Computer Machinery and Intelligence'). He was also the breaker of the code used by the German Enigma machines during the Second World War.

The HORIZON documentary 'The Strange Life and Death of Dr Turing' (1992 T) calls him one of the great minds of the 20th century: '... a brilliant mathematician and a scientist of great originality ... A visionary genius.' He was found guilty of an 'offence against morals' in 1952 and underwent a year's treatment during which he was injected with female hormones to smite his sex drive. In 1954 he killed himself by eating an apple he had injected with cyanide. As the documentary's synopsis put it: 'He had helped the Allies win World War II and invented the computer. But he ended his life as a social pariah, under surveillance by the very government he worked for.'

Played – under another name – by Nicholas Le Prevost in *The Imitation Game* (1980 T). Hugh WHITEMORE's play about Turing's life, *Breaking the Code*, still awaits transfer to cinema, television and/or radio. *The Touring Machine* [*sic*], a 1991 Australian radio play, obliquely celebrated the mathematician's early article on computable numbers which was known as 'the Turing machine', predecessor of the automatic electronic digital computer with internal programme storage.

Turnabout (US 1940 C) A husband and wife are granted their oft-repeated wish: to be in each other's shoes – he at the office all day, she wafting around her boudoir or going on shopping trips. Suddenly he's speaking in a falsetto and she's a baritone. His mannerisms become loose and expressive, hers stocky and contained. He finds out about her fiddling of her dress allowance; she discovers that he's been doing a little pimping for agency clients. With relief, they manage to have the spell lifted but there has been a slight slip-up ...

W: Mickell Novak, Berne Giler, John McLain and Rian James from the novel by Thorne Smith; P/D: Hal Roach; 83 mins.

Splendidly anarchic satire, taking off from where Hal Roach left the scramble of the sexes in THEIR FIRST MISTAKE. As their normal selves Carole Landis and John Hubbard are dull, trivial people; as each other they fairly glide through their new roles, perfectly replicating the other's mannerisms, raising a whole raft of ticklish misunderstandings for friends (especially Mary Astor, a queen WASP), work colleagues (Verree Teasdale as a very commanding secretary), and boss (Adolphe Menjou, never funnier).

The script is astonishingly gamey for its period (mentions of 'QUEER' and 'BULL'), the situations savoury and the punchline almost as daring as that in SOME LIKE IT HOT. Franklin PANGBORN has three scenes as Mr Pingboom who finds the newly feminized Tim very much to his liking. Subtly paralleling their sex-change employers are Marjorie Main as the imperturbable, roaring bull cook and Donald Meek as the flustered, flossy-voiced butler.

'Many of the situations, from today's viewpoint, remained unexplored, but it was quite bold for its time' (Ronald Bergan, *The United Artists Story*, 1986).

(A television version came and went in 1979 with John Schuck and Sharon Gless. A 1992 radio play *Fair Exchange* employed the same idea.)

Turner, David (1927–90) English writer and adaptor, tough minded with a feel for bitter irony: *Works Outing* (1955 R); *The Knights of the Shadows* (*Children's Hour* 1956); *Fresh as Paint* (1956); *Skeins of Birmingham Life* (3 short radio plays: 'Me, Me Dad, His 'n''1956; 'A Change of Plan' 1957; 'Mind Your Own Business' 1958); 'Unfair Enemy' (1959; first version of STRIP JACK NAKED, cut from 70 to 60 minutes and not broadcast on radio); *The Train Set* (1961 R/T); *Any Other Business* (1961 R); *Choirboys*

Unite (1961 T); *The Wall* (1961 T); *Now More Than Ever* (1961 R; second version of *Strip Jack Naked*, Northern BBC Region only); SUMMER, AUTUMN, WINTER, SPRING (1961 T; 1962 R; third version of *Strip Jack Naked*); *Semi-Detached* (1963 R); SWIZZLEWICK (1965 T); *Père Goriot* (1968 T); THE ROADS TO FREEDOM (1970 T); *Helen – Woman of Today* ('Harold', 'Father' etc, 1973); *Fall of Eagles* 'Requiem for a Crown Prince' (1974); *Germinal*; etc.

Twelfth Night Or What You Will. One of Shakespeare's most famous comedies involves Viola dressing as a page while Olivia's steward Malvolio and the flimsy Sir Andrew AGUECHEEK are quite often played with effete inflections. This was the first full-length Shakespearean play presented on radio (in 1923). Subsequent radio productions have been in 1947, 1952, 1956, 1958, 1962, 1982 and 1993, and on television 1939, 1956, 1970 etc.

Twentieth Century Blues The nightclub number from Noel COWARD's *Cavalcade* (1933 C) preceded by a tumultuous montage of terrible events: financial collapse, suicides, murders, fears of war, divorces, unemployment ... Just before Ursula Jeans – dressed in satin and feathers – begins her dirge, male and female homosexual couples are glimpsed (looking debauched) at little tables. The singer's voice – backed by an all-black band – quivers with morbid trepidation. All around is 'chaos and confusion' where 'people seem to lose their way'; God (if he exists) has stopped grinning and there are few who can escape those 'dreary 20th-century blues'.

24-Hour Call 'Cry for Help' (UK 1963 T) Young Tim Gregory (Brian Smith) goes to his GP, Dr Bennett (Godfrey Quigley) with a problem.

W: N. J. Crisp; D: Philip Barker; 10.35–11.20pm; 17.3.63; ATV; 50 mins.

An unusual problem, at least for TV doctors 30 years ago. The advice given is without frills, but also without judgement or blame: 'Understand this. There's no pill, no injection, no course of medical treatment that's going to solve your problem.' The doctor didn't direct him to the nearest gay club, but it was a step forward.

Inevitably it didn't please some. The *Sunday Mirror*'s television critic Bernard McIlwane thought it a terrible waste of a busy doctor's time. The National Health service didn't exist for people like Tim. 'A young lad with a homosexual history was pressurized by a thug into falling back into the clutches of an unseen old degenerate. The boy didn't phone the police. Instead he contacted helpful do-gooder Dr Bennett. If this gets around, doctors will be pestered to help with anything from leaking taps to parking the car.'

This little scene did indicate a shift to-wards a greater reality. Tim wasn't a dress designer or somebody who was anxious to be a woman. He was a 'decent' person looking for reassurance and a way out of his present threatening situation. The doctor – who was cer-tainly not speaking for the mass of the population at the time* – provided him with at least some basis upon which to live his life, no matter what the law or society said. Unlike an earlier character, 'Boy' Barrett (Peter McEnery) in VICTIM (1961 C) who was driven to take desperate measures, stealing to pay BLACKMAIL demands and finally hanging himself in a prison cell.

*In a National Opinon Poll taken the same year 93 per cent of people surveyed saw homosexuality as a disease requir-ing treatment and 65 per cent were opposed to decriminal-ization (with 16 per cent in favour).

21 Today Barry (Gary Hailes) cele-brates his (homosexual) AGE OF CON-SENT by tipsily serenading Colin (Michael CASHMAN) in Ali's cafe in EASTENDERS (1987 T): 'I've got the key of the door/Never been really legal before.' This song is increasingly irrel-evant as most young British men mark their reception into adulthood at 18 when they are allowed to vote. For Barry and Colin it's absolutely crucial because it means that they can now fully enjoy

each other's bodies without feeling guilty about it or exposing themselves to BLACKMAIL or to legal penalties for the older partner. Beyond this, the tiny scene indicated that there is a need for equality under law (heterosexual males being free to have sex with consenting females if all parties involved are over 16) when it comes to private lives.

TW3 *See* THAT WAS THE WEEK THAT WAS.

twilight area The concept of a shadowy Bohemia or perhaps something more insidious and enveloping.

A creation of the press during the 1950s witch hunts and carried on by such programmes as THIS WEEK 'Homo-sexuals' (1965 T) through to MAN ALIVE 'A Public Disgrace' (1976 T). Even Stanley BAXTER was described by Stan-ley Reynolds in *The Times* (1973) as being an exponent of a CAMP humour where 'sex's twilight area is always just around the corner'. THAT WAS THE WEEK THAT WAS alone exposed the con-cept to humour: Kenneth Cope's token heterosexual spoke – in a nicotined monotone – of the 'strange twilight world I live in' (1963 T).

'The average lesbian will always want to live in the shadows because that is where she wants to be' was the con-clusion of a BBC Home Service pro-gramme back in 1965. This came di-rectly after a psychologist had said that 'the average lesbian gets more satisfac-tion than the average wife in the average marriage'.

Ray Morby, a Conservative MP, de-scribed a programme on homosexuality on *Late Night Line Up* in 1967 as 'deal-ing with a twilight area of abnormal people and not suitable for public dis-cussion'. It proceeded into the next decade: 'In a really astounding report at 10.30pm, Alan WHICKER examines the not-so-twilight world of the homosex-ual' (*TV Times*, 1973). However, more recently other forms of deviance have taken over the soubriquet, eg 'the twi-light world of the unemployed' (*Giro* 1985 T) and 'the twilight world of international drug smuggling' (*Traffik* 1990 T).

The Twilight Zone (US 1959–64 T) A weekly 30-minute (later 60) anthology of science fiction and fantasy stories. The framework allowed a number of taboo themes to be tackled: death, RACISM, mass hysteria, NAZISM, love of different kinds, role reversal, dualism. 'There is a fifth dimension beyond that which is known to men. It is a dimension as vast as space and as timeless as infinity. It is the middle ground between light and shadow, between science and superstition, and it lies between the pit of man's fears and the summit of his knowledge. This is the dimension of imagination. It is an area we call the twilight zone' (the show's perennial opening lines).

W: Rod SERLING and others; P: Buck Houghton (1959–63); Herbert Hirschman (1963–4), Rod Serling; CBS. (The series began on 2 October 1959; two other series, not involving any of the original team, were transmitted in 1985 and 1988.)

At its best, rich and rare television which attracted an average weekly audience of 18 million and some of whose stories were bolder than most in examining the role of the individual and the most obstinate problem of civilization: the human condition. The scripts often exhibit a supple concept of sex roles, acknowledging complexity and variety: women fleeing accusations of spinsterdom, men in thrall to convention. 'Sometimes the situations were clichéd, the characters two-dimensional, but always there was at least some search for an emotional truth, some attempt to make a statement on the human condition' (Marc Scott Zicree, *The Twilight Zone Companion*, 1982).

Rod Serling wrote 92 out of 156 episodes. His fury – most brilliantly exemplified in 'The Monsters Are Due on Maple Street' (1960) – was directed at ugly group identity, moral cowardice and unthinking prejudice. But he was also angry at television itself, and wished to use the vehicle of science fiction to

challenge 'A cheapness of mind, a cheapness of taste ... a dark-room squint at a world whose sunlight has never gotten through' (from his spoken introduction to 'The Four of Us Are Dying' 1960).

Among the relevant productions: 'Walking Distance' (1959: a bachelor returns to his younger self in a small town where it is always summertime); 'Mirror Image' (1960: two young people discover their other selves at a night-time bus station); 'A Thing About Machines' (1960: a prissily pretentious bachelor, played by Richard HAYDN, is targeted for destruction by his hated electronic appliances); 'The After Hours' (1960: a department store mannequin is allowed to 'come out' as a human being and doesn't want to return to 'normal'); 'The Big Tall Wish' (1960: a small black boy helps the man he loves – a boxer – overcome his physical failings); 'The Midnight Sun' (1961: two women cling together emotionally as the earth fries up); 'Young Man's Fancy' (1961: a young bride unsuccessfully tries to wean her new husband off his dead mama); 'Person or Persons Unknown' (1962: a man wakes up to find all evidence of his identity has disappeared); 'The Fugitive' (1962: a TOMBOY befriends a king from outer space); 'The Little People' (1962: a queeny astronaut rules a microscopic civilization); 'Miniature' (1963: a sensitive bachelor finds true happiness in a doll's house); 'He's Alive' (1963: an American Nazi is destroyed by his love for an elderly Jewish man); 'Ring-a-Ding Girl' (1963: a possibly lesbian film star saves her home town from certain disaster); 'Number Twelve Looks Just Like You' (1964: a world where ugliness is banished and everyone can look like the 1960s equivalent of Mel Gibson and Princess Diana).

Probably the most apposite of all the tales was 'It's a Good Life' (1961) from the short story by Jerome Bixby. A cute little boy (Billy Mumy) ruthlessly rules over his family and their friends. He will brook no dissent and those who thwart him end up as petrified scarecrows in the cornfield. One man alone rebels when the child refuses to let him play a Perry Como record he has been given as a birthday present. However, no one will support him against this conscienceless monster and he is dispatched to the field. Eventually his friends' inaction destroys them all.

Homosexual people in many cultures will be able to relate to this bland group of adults: always smiling, always placatory, acting in order to survive – yet nurturing, through paralysis of will, their own destruction. In return for 'safety' they have fear and constriction, all because a sweet-faced little boy stamps his foot and tells them at whim how they will think and behave. Scared to overthrow the dictator as a group, they live their lives repeating endlessly with as much conviction as they can muster: 'It's a *good* life'.

(This episode was remade as part of *Twilight Zone – The Movie* in 1983, but with its whole essence sucked out in order to make the boy wholly sympathetic – (just a mite disturbed) – and to introduce all manner of special effects, including cartoon characters come to life.)

twins A number of studies have been carried out on fraternal and identical twins with as yet inconclusive results as to whether homosexuality has a genetic component. In *The Oprah Winfrey Show* 'Gay Twin/Straight Twin' (1991) five sets of identical twins described 'how they felt' when they discovered one of them was gay and one of them wasn't – and what it is like to have a double who is different in one very important way. Also present were Simon LeVay, neuroscientist at the Salk Institute (who believes that homosexuality is genetic), and John De Cecco, Professor of Psychology at San Francisco State University (who doesn't think sexual preference can – or should – be located and homed in on).

Fictional identical twins who show markedly different, if superficial, sexual characteristics include feminine Cicely and athletic Bertha (both played by Cecily Courtneidge) in *Things Are Looking Up* (1933 C); the epicene aristocrat and his revolution-minded brother (Donald Sutherland) in *Start the Revolution without Me* (1970 C); Bobby and Rick Salardi, both cops but with very different sexual interests in HOOPERMAN (1987–9 T).

More compatible, but suffocatingly so were Beverly and Eliot Mantle (Jeremy Irons) in DEAD RINGERS (1988 C), and Benjamin and Lewis Jones (Mike and Robert Gwilym) in *On the Black Hill* (1987 C): 'I look at Lewis and I see me. If one of us dies before the other ... we should love to go together somehow.'

ERNESTO (Martin Halm 1979 C) loves a young man (Lara Wendell) but, as he can't be openly gay, he marries his twin sister (also played by Lara Wendell) instead and carries on pretty much as before.

A small mystery worth investigating is the Gayer-Anderson twins who were profiled in *The Eye Witness* by Kay Batchelor (1960 R). Nicknamed 'The Pasha and the Colonel', they left the army early and retired, unmarried, to renovate their cottage in the medieval style 'being interested in art and collecting beautiful things'.

See also BROTHERS; SISTERS.

Two in Twenty (US 1990 T) Lee is a Jewish blue-collar worker and union activist, with a young daughter, Charlene. Her lover Miki is a therapist. Also sharing the house are Sharon, a black medical student, and Luna Birdsong, a separatist astrologer. Friends include M.J., a rock musician, and her roommate Helene. Lee's ex-hubby is fighting for custody of Charlene. Miki is pondering having an affair. Helene is trying to come out. Sharon is working at the hospital with a man living with AIDS.
P: Laurie Chiles for Cable TV WCLT; 5 parts.

The first steps towards a lesbian soap or a soap with lots of lesbians in it. The series reached a potential audience of 1.5 million people per week on two Los Angeles stations.

Two Ladies Joel Grey's Master of Ceremonies croons this as obscenely as possible in CABARET (1972 C). The Kander and Ebb number about a threesome leads directly into an intimate scene between the Baron and Brian and the beginnings of what could have been a song called 'Two Gentlemen'.

The MC was one of the more skilful representations of the NAZI threat in popular entertainment: the painted face of a devil doll, the slurping smile and the twinkling eyes that miss nothing. Christopher ISHERWOOD praised the performance and the concept ('uncannily like Daumier come to life') in an interview with GAY NEWS in 1977, but he had seen the character very differently when the musical was first being planned: 'I wanted to make him a lodger in the house, Jewish and beaten up by the Nazis.' (Tony RANDALL brought this idea brilliantly to life in his cameo role as 'Putzi' in *Hitler's SS: Portrait in Evil* 1985 C/T.)

Two of Us (UK 1988 T) Two 17-year-olds – Matthew (Jason Rush) who believes that he's gay and Phil (Lee Whitlock) who's not at all sure – go on a kind of honeymoon to see if their relationship can be more than friendship. An already ticklish situation is made impossible by the presence of police, a runaway and Phil's jealous girlfriend.
W: Leslie Stewart; P/D: Roger Tonge; 25.3.88; BBC1; 55 mins.

This compact and thoughtful film was made – under the title 'Mates' – for BBC Schools Broadcasting in 1986 for showing as part of its SCENE series the following year. By the time it was actually screened (on BBC1 very late at night in 1988), the ending – the boys together and in love – had been removed and a heterosexual denouement indicated. A very brief KISS in a tent had also been eliminated.

The hold-up was due to a changed British moral climate, with media and government whipping up public fears about homosexuality being 'promoted' in the classroom. By making the production available to adults first (over 2 million of them watched), much criticism was defused and *Two of Us* was seen by large numbers of British schoolchildren early the following year. The uncut version, which had been transmitted without any fuss in Australia, finally made it into the country of origin's schools in 1991, and is now available on video.

Radio Times published a number of very moving letters a few weeks after the March 1988 screening; here are just two extracts: 'For the first time in my life I feel clean about myself' and 'I've tried suicide twice. After seeing this, I don't think I'll try again.' The film continues to generate hope and joy for many young and not so young people. In May 1993 it was shown as an adult feature movie on Australia's SBS television.

Two People (UK 1979 T) Per (Dai Bradley) and his much older lover Ralph, a SOCIAL WORKER (Philip SAYER), offer 15-year-old schoolfriends (Stephen Garlick and Nicola Cowper) a place to be together when they run away.
W: Julian Bond and Alick ROWE; D: John Reardon; P: Paul Knight; LWT; 6 parts.

Like TWO OF US, this production was shelved for over a year because of its under-age lovers, homosexual and heterosexual. Per (a self-chosen name, short for 'PERVERT') is a bruised teenager whose strong sexual identity allows him to cope with BULLYING at school and the tests of an unlawful relationship with an older man. The episode 'The Trouble with a Kitten' beautifully illustrates how homosexuals can provide ROLE MODELS for straights in difficult situations. For once, it is the queers who provide sanctuary for the normal – while themselves being outlaws.

What makes this episode so special is the conviction of Dai Bradley and Philip Sayer, and the layered nature of their words and mannerisms. Said GAY NEWS 150: 'There was love there, certainly. But underneath the careful lack of role-playing and the good-humoured physicality there were needs and wants which neither could ever fulfil for the other ... All four were struggling – against social forces and forces within themselves, to conform and throw in the towel ... Verbal, visual, sexual and non-sexual clues were given about each of the four people. Truisms about gender and "natural" behaviour were unselfconsciously but unequivocally rebutted. Above all, links were made and parallels drawn.'

Tim to Per in 'The Trouble with a Kitten':

'It never worries you? I don't mean the gay thing. I mean love.'
'The loving and being in love – that was easy. No, not easy, simple.'

Two Weeks with the Queen (UK 1993 T) Colin comes to Britain to see if the Queen can help him save his brother's life but Her Majesty is not the only person who can assist. In episode 4 Colin finds support in an unlikely place and from a person not usually encountered.
W: Morris Gleitzman; read by Kristian

Schmid; 4.45–5pm 15–19.3.93; BBC1; 5 parts.

Death, AIDS and homosexuality in a sensitive and humorous serving – the first for BBC's younger viewers, who would have encountered this just before *Dizzy Heights* and *Newsround*. (A film version with a script by the author and produced by Verity Lambert is due 1993–4.)

Tyler, [Harrison] Parker (1904–74) American novelist (*The Young and the Evil* with Charles Henri Ford), biographer (GARBO; *Chaplin – Last of the Clowns*), and trailblazing film critic. A tenacious grasp on the American underground, gay cinema and Hollywood CAMP, contextualizing, refocusing and reclaiming in the great tradition of Pauline Kael, Andrew Sarris and Jim Hoberman, and seeking the emotional core, psychological truth, aesthetic dynamics and social criticism which others (like Vito RUSSO and Jack BABUSCIO) have deepened and broadened. The larger body of his work remains unpublished.

The Ugliest Girl in Town (US 1968 T) 'What if Twiggy is really a boy?' Hollywood talent agent Timothy Blair (Peter Kastner) poses as hippie girl to be with his girlfriend in London. Once there 'Timmy' is turned into a fashion model by David Courtenay (Nicholas Parsons). In the last episode 'The Track Star' a Russian athlete (Bill Maynard) falls for Timmy and defects to the West. Cr: Robert Kaufman; P: Harry Ackerman; D: George McCowen, Lindsay Shonteff, E. W. Swackhamer, and Peter Duffel; ABC; 30 mins.

A talented young actor (*Nobody Waved Goodbye; You're a Big Boy Now*) in a lamebrained series that may have nostalgic interest. Typically, his female self was made as deliberately ridiculous as possible so that any erotic comic tension inherent in the idea was immediately detonated.

an ugly word 'Heterosexuality is an ugly word,' said the shamefaced Kenneth Cope in the television John Braine sketch of 1963 (THAT WAS THE WEEK THAT WAS). Many of the women in THE IMPORTANT THING IS LOVE (1971 T) called themselves gay because, said the voice-over, 'Lesbian' is an ugly word – a view endorsed by Edna EVERAGE in *Barry McKenzie Holds His Own* (1974 C) and by Gail's mum (Sada Thompson) in MY TWO LOVES (1986 T): 'Lesbian – what an ugly word!'

Unchained Melody A big hit by Al Hibbler (lyrics by Hy Zaret with music by Alex North), this rich, bleeding chunk of sob and heartbreak was the theme for the now forgotten 1955 prison film, *Unchained*. A cover version was recorded by Goons Bluebottle and Eccles on the Parlophone label, but the record was not released – possibly because two men (even adult babies) crooning 'Oh my love, my darling, I've hungered for your touch a long, lonely time' was considered a bit iffy, especially as the B-side was 'Dance With Me Henry'. Restored to rude, haunting heterosexual health, 'Unchained Melody' was heard (prominently and effectively)

in *Ghost* (1990 C) and *The Naked Gun 2 and a Half: The Smell of Fear* (1991 C).

Uncle Unlike real life, gay characters are very rarely to be found in this role in its strictly biological definition: Uncle Staveley (Leslie Sarony) still carrying a torch for his friend who was killed in the First World War in I DIDN'T KNOW YOU CARED (1976–8 T); Richard Griffiths in *Withnail and I* (1986 C) trying to seduce his nephew's friend. The title is more likely to be used by an overly doting guardian: 'Uncle' (Laurence Naismith) finally shot by the man he loves – Anacleto (Dirk BOGARDE) – in *The Singer Not the Song* (1961 C); J. M. BARRIE alias Uncle Jim in THE LOST BOYS (1978 T). Or by a pederastic man in a position of economic authority: the former magistrate (John Sharp) in THE SWEENEY 'On The Run' (1976 T); 'Uncle Val the junkie's pal' (Gabriel Byrne), the malevolent, highly sexual drug boss in *The Courier* (1987 C) who makes some not so subtle passes at the hero ('The further up you go, the better it gets').

Ray GOSLING meets an Indian boy in *On the Train to Pakistan* (1980 R) who shows him a hundred or so airmail letters from his Dutch friend Henk: 'You and Henk have a homosexual relationship?' 'Henk is uncle to me. No sex.'

The boy, Gosling discovers, has many more uncles.

John TREGORRAN (Basil JONES) in THE ARCHERS (R) uses the word about himself when talking with Carol Grey (Anne CULLEN), perhaps as a euphemism for the female equivalent:

> 'What's your problem? Tell Uncle John all about 'em. He'll answer 'em in a plain, sealed envelope' (1956).
> '. . . craftspeople look on me as a brother, as an uncle, as a . . .' 'A sugar daddy?' (1955).

Undergraduate Summer (UK 1939 R) An impression of a term at an OXFORD college through the dewy eyes of Philip Trottwood (Geoffrey Banks) who is captivated by all manner of sights and sounds as well as by the ravishingly unmanly Nigel (Frith Banbury), with whom he enjoys – rather to Trottwood *père's* disapproval – a bit of a sentimental friendship.

W/P: Stephen Potter; 8.15–9pm; 10.8.39; BBC; 45 mins.

Using professional and amateur actors recorded on location in Merton and Balliol colleges, at the Oxford University Dramatic Society and at the Union (debating Society), the scripted passages are interwoven with T. S. Eliot and Evelyn WAUGH lecturing, the Student Christian Society, actor Leslie French directing the OUDS in *The Tempest*, and Robert HELPMANN instructing rugger hearties how to be lovely in a ballet sketch for the student revue

A sometimes delectable, always fascinating evocation of a tight little island caught slumbering at a crucial time in world affairs. The comforting sounds of church bells and bustling coffee shops, superficial debates about far-off places full of foreigners, and the idle chatter of sweetly silly Nigel – jabbering on about Cromwell and Aristotle and his *objets* and his PERFUME – are as buzzing bees just about to be attacked by a swarm of wasps. All is blissful ignorance of other people's lives and living conditions; the fate of Poland and the ambitions of Hitler simply couldn't happen here. Within a month of *Undergraduate Summer*'s broadcast, Britain was at war with Germany.

(A second radio production, with Elwyn BROOK-JONES as the swooning air-head Nigel, was broadcast in 1951.)

underpants *See* BRIEFS; JOCKEY SHORTS VERSION.

undertakers *See* FUNERAL DIRECTORS.

Under the Age (UK 1972 T) BARTENDER 'Susie' (Michael Angelis) chews the cud with a bunch of unruly teenagers who are contravening the licensing laws – and possibly, in the case of one or two, the age of sexual consent. W: E. A. Whitehead; D: Alan Clarke; BBC2 (THIRTY MINUTE THEATRE).

'Susie' was the first gay STEREOTYPE

(flamboyant, cynical, shoulder-shrugging, superficial) to be the subject of debate. John Chesterman of the Gay Liberation Front appeared on a discussion programme *Line-Up* immediately following the play to protest against television's strait-jacketing: 'A typical homosexual never goes into bars of any sort at all. They live out lives of misery and of suppression of all their natural life forces and instincts.' He intimated that plays like this one wouldn't encourage such people to be more outgoing. *The Church Times* commented that television ought to be protected from homosexual characters and from gay libbers.

United We Stand, Divided We Fall A group called the Brotherhood of Man had a hit with this in Britain and America in the late 1960s. It was given additional power when chorused (in WHICKER WAY OUT WEST 'The Lord Is My Shepherd and He Knows I'm Gay' 1973 T) by the Rev. Troy Perry and his congregation as a memorial for those who had died in an arson attack on a New Orleans BAR. The customers had been singing it minutes before the disaster. The programme made such an impact that the song was reissued in Britain the following week.

Nineteen years later it was sung with great fervour by FEMALE IMPERSONATOR (aka Danny Leonard) as a gay anthem in a small but lively bar in America's South in the documentary *Where Are We?* (1992 C/T).

University Challenge (UK 1962–87 T) Oxbridge, redbrick, gowns, beards, very long hair, very short hair, single earrings, mascots ... Across three decades strode the intellectual cream of Britain's youth under the firm but fair hand of questionmaster Bamber Gascoigne in this game for eggheads which all the family could play. One of Granada's cheapest but most durable series, Bamber's 'Your starter for ten' and his boyish bespectacled face became part of Britain's culture, guyed by Benny HILL, Stanley BAXTER, Mike Yarwood and others. The programme itself was roasted alive on *The Young Ones* (1984 T) with upper-class twits Griff Rhys Jones, Emma Thompson and Stephen FRY (as Lord Snot) ranged against Richie, Vyvyan and Neal.

Go for It (1984 T) mounted a spectacular contest between Queens Hospital and Queens College with 'Bamber' asking the College team (comprising impersonations of John INMAN, Danny LA RUE and Larry GRAYSON by Les Dennis, Allan Stewart and Dustin GEE) such questions as: 'What is the capital of France?' ('Gay Paree.'); 'Who said "A man's a man for all that"?' ('We don't know, but we certainly agree with him.'); 'What did Nelson say before he died?' ('"KISS ME, HARDY", ... Lucky Hardy.')

This profoundly wretched sketch was peppered with another familiar Gascoigne exclamation, 'Well remembered, Queens!', in conjunction with 'Fingers on buzzers' ('Oooh!'), 'Only on buzzers, Queens' ('Oooh!'), 'Come on, Queens, you're dragging badly' ('Oooh!'), and 'Queens, can you take it?' ('Oooh, yes!').

On *University Challenge* Luke Fitzgerald, captain of the winning Lancaster University team in the early 1970s, wore a gay BADGE and, although he was shot in a tighter close-up than the others, it was still noticeable. Other relevant participants included future media writer and lecturer Andy Medhurst (Sussex, 1984), and writer–actor Stephen Fry (Queens College, Cambridge, 1980), who was invited back in 1992 to captain a valedictory pro-celebrity *University Challenge* as part of the BBC's salute to *Granadaland*.

university lecturers *See* TEACHERS.

The Unloved (UK 1955 T) Jimmy Rolfe (Melvyn HAYES) arrives at a school for maladjusted boys run by Mr Manley (Rupert Davies). Jimmy says little, daydreams, is interested in music (Chopin) and thinks of himself as irredeemably ugly. Regarded as a SISSY, he begins to show interest in a woman teacher, which is surprising since 'for the past years his thoughts have been in quite another direction'. Another pupil, Todd (Robert

Sandford: 'Pre-psychotic 15-year-old, can't cry. IQ 142') keeps a diary and draws pictures of what he'd like to do to the man (his stepfather) who sexually abused him.

W: Colin Morris; D: Gilchrist Calder; 7.6.55; BBC; 60 mins.

A studio-bound dramatized documentary which efficiently pits a steadfast authority figure (Manley!) against the effects on young minds of bad homes and negligent parents. It only hinted at Jimmy's likely orientation ('your private affairs'), but Melvyn Hayes' performance, all juddering feral hysteria buttressed by grim determination to appear indifferent, reverberates in the mind's eye down the years.

'You don't get difficult children without difficult parents. We get three kinds of people who want to work here apart from the few who could. Idealists, NEUROTICS and PERVERTS' Manley to new teacher Harris (Philip Levene).

unnatural Supposedly relating to sexual acts which run contrary to nature. 'Friendship between women, yes,' screams the actress–aunt (Miriam Hopkins) in *The Children's Hour* (1961 C). 'But not this insane devotion. Why, it's unnatural. Just as unnatural as can be!'

The companion word is abnormal, and is far more apposite, homo- and heterosexualities being so much the constructs of various societies at different periods of their history. Gail (Mariette Hartley) in MY TWO LOVES (1986 T) is momentarily caught off guard by her mother's discovery of her with a new lover (who is not male) and the abusive knee-jerk reaction that follows. But within seconds, Gail, having registered the main word in the tirade, responds with poise: 'Well, it seemed perfectly normal to me!'

Julian CLARY was unbowed on the subject in one of his 1989 STICKY MOMENTS:

Uncanny and unnatural
That's what I am ...
Call me a TRANSVESTITE
And I'll lend you a frock.

The Unquiet Spirit (UK 1939 T)

Marceline (Catherine Lacey), married and restless, keeps on meeting Antoine (Percy Marmont) who is increasingly dissatisfied with his wife. What is the force that brings these two together over a decade? Desire? Curiosity? Attraction of equals? Or something so deeply buried that only a third party (Marceline's brother) can explain it?

W: Jean-Jacques Bernard, translated by J. Leslie Finch; P: Royston Morley; 3.3.39; BBC; 65 mins.

Written in 1928, the concept of a split soul allowed a discreet discussion of thoughts and feelings more appropriate to psychodrama with Marceline and Antoine crossing into the taboo area of masculine and feminine respectively. The play was updated and its language similarly modernized by commercial television (directed by Peter Potter; shown 3.6.60). Barbara Jefford ('married to' Nigel STOCK, and David Knight (to Mahri Russell) were the sister/ brother/lover/soul mates with David McCallum contributing another of his fascinating 'neurotics' of the period as the brother who outlines the concept of the perfect partner.

Uppity Dykes *See* DYKES.

Upstairs Downstairs (UK 1970–75 T) The fortunes of the Bellamy family and its servants, living in Eaton Square in the early part of the 20th century.

Cr: Jean Marsh and Eileen Atkins; P: John Hawkesworth; 75 parts; 60 mins each.

Careful period detail, robust characters (Mr 'Udson, Mrs Bridges, Thomas and Sarah), and canny linkage of them with historical events was cemented by ROSE (Jean Marsh). Devoted, dependable, a bit stick-in-the-mud, she was the maid who loved her Miss Elizabeth – seeing her through brief encounters with both women's rights and a homosexual husband – and refusing a marriage proposal from a nice Australian in order to stay with the family. She was involved – steadily growing in understanding – in all the series' gay episodes including 'A Suitable Marriage', 'Rose's Pigeon' and

'The New Man'. Her relationship with an under-maid (Pauline Collins), with whom she shared a room and often a bed, was only sketched in (from episode 1) but was obviously sustaining while the arrangement lasted.

Uranians A cohesive group of late 19th-century writers and poets whose philosophy was broadly that of a classical, 'heavenly' love for adolescent males. (Uranism – derived from Aphrodite's father URANUS – was used as a term for homosexuality as a naturally occurring phenomenon in some late 19th and early 20th century writings.) Barry HUMPHRIES paid somewhat mockingly awed homage to the 'Uranian heaven' in OMNIBUS 'A Summer Side-Show' (1977 T) 'seeking the ghosts of long-dead pederasts' in Dieppe where some of them fled after the Cleveland Street scandal. Among those recalled: Oscar WILDE, Lord Alfred DOUGLAS, John Addington SYMONDS and Aubrey Beardsley.

urinal A useful place for male characters to stand and talk while relieving themselves – a part of the masculine culture from which women are by definition excluded.

The more ridiculous deadpan aspect of standing semi-exposed with other men looking at a wall and not elsewhere was first critiqued by the wife (Marjorie Rhodes) in THE FAMILY WAY (1966 C) and later treated with levity in *A Private Function* (1984 C: Michael Palin and the local mafia); in *The Crying Game* (1992 C: Forest Whitaker given a hand by Stephen Rea – in a rural setting); in *The Distinguished Gentleman* (1993 C: Eddie Murphy and acquaintance).

As a locale for cryptic dialogue the urinal is becoming increasingly familiar: *Pennies from Heaven* (1978 T); *The Commitments* (1991 C); *GBH* (1991 T). In fact, complaints began to surface (one in a 1988 letter to *TV Times*) about the 'obligatory urinal scene ... two men ... talking while performing nature's function'.

Sometimes a simple action provokes

violent reaction. In G.P. 'Get a Life' Tony (Nick Stock) is urinating in a pub loo when two of his army mates come in, stand beside him and begin making all kinds of provocative remarks (how big is it? can we feel it?). They then proceed to beat him up until interrupted.

See also COTTAGING.

Urinal aka *Pissoir* (Can 1989 C) Recalled to life to impact upon the modern gay world: Sergei EISENSTEIN (Paul Bettis), Langston Hughes (George Spelvin), Frida Kahlo (Olivia Rojas), Yukio MISHIMA (David Gonzales) and Dorian GRAY (Lana Eng). W/P/D: John Greyson; 100 mins.

As a concept magnificent; some homosexual and bisexual icons communicate with one another and contribute to the present. In execution it lacks the words to match the images and is overlong. Yet the entertainment more than bears out Neil BARTLETT's view that lesbians and gays have a duty to reinvent their history, twist their idols out of shape, melt them down and start again if necessary. This series of interlinked cameos is part of the process.

Gerald **Urquhart** Character in HOW-ARDS' WAY (1985–90 T) played by Ivor Danvers, a lawyer, solicitor and chartered accountant, representing a syndicate headed by Charles Frere. As Frere's hatchet man, he's responsible for hirings and firings. Not really a part of the yachting and boatbuilding world, he can talk rather more fluently about achieving expansion objectives and the need to cross-fertilize.

In episode 6 of the first series his marriage to Polly (Patricia Shakesby), who had been a fellow student at Cambridge, is in name only. She knew he was gay from the outset, but believed that a shop window arrangement would be good for his business standing and comforting for her. However, the convenience has become a prison. They have a daughter, but it is later revealed that Gerald was not the father. Polly has become a shopaholic in an effort to fill her life with some meaning. She either has had or

has fantasized having young male bed partners. Gerald takes his lovers to a London *pied à terre* and they remain a distant hum in the background until, in the third series, one of them, an artist James Gittings (seen only briefly), dies of an AIDS-related illness. Gerald turns to Polly in his grief and they decide to make a fresh start: 'If we are going to make a go of our marriage, we have got to forget about what happened in the past – and look to the future'.

Ivor Danvers, interviewed in the book of the series by Gerard Glaister and Ray Evans (1988), revealed that 'At the beginning, Gerald was rather a sketched-in character and I couldn't see how to play it. When I asked the director who'd cast me he said, "Play him enigmatically, for the moment!" They certainly hadn't conceived the character as a homosexual ... and it was quite a handful to cope with that and the fact that I wasn't Abby's real father after all.'

Ursula A girl's name most commonly tied to relentlessly questing, crazy or overwhelming women characters: crazed 'half-caste' Ursula (Myrna Loy) one of the *13 Women* (1932 C) and the murderer of some of them; 'Ursula' played by William Powell in drag who tells Susan (Myrna Loy) that if she feels lonely during the night 'don't hesitate to come to me' (in *Love Crazy* 1941 C), but Susan's mother decides to stay the night in order to make sure there is no hanky panky; Ursula Suddlechop, 'a bonny lass' in *The Fortunes of Nigel* (June Watson 1974 T; Elizabeth Ashley 1955 R); Ursula Prune (Pat Coombs) unrequitedly in love with Ted in *Ray's a Laugh* (*c*1956–8 R); chilly murderess Ursula Somerville (Phyllis Thaxter) in *Thriller* 'Last of the Somervilles' (1961 T); Ursula Poe (Juliet Prowse) seduced and abandoned (by Frankie Vaughan) in *The Right Approach* 1961 C); Ursula, one of the lesbians on the train in *Unwieldy Elephant* (1962 R); Ursula Brangwen in *Women in Love* (Jennie Linden 1969 C) and as her younger, more experimental self in *The Rainbow* (Imogen Stubbs 1988 T; Sammi Davis 1989 C); the unseen woman loved in perpetuity by Edna (Jessica Tandy) in BUTLEY (1974 C/T); Ursula Gatsby (Gilly Flower), one of two spinsters, in *Fawlty Towers* 'The Builders' (1974 T); Ursula (Jessica Walter), sophisticated schemer in *Wheels* (1978 T); Ursa (Sarah Douglas), the black leather-clad, thoroughly evil cohort of Zod in *Superman/Superman II* (1978/1980 C), described as a threat to children; Ursula Du Pré, the lover and supporter of Sophia Jex-Blake in *The Walls of Jericho* (1981 T, played by Gillian Barge); Ursula (Elizabeth Morton) in *Brookside* (1983 T) removing Barry Grant from the straight and narrow; Ursula (Pat Carroll), monstrous queen of the deep, with voice to match in *The Little Mermaid* (1989 C); Ursula (Constance Chapman), the unwelcome visitor who threatens the relationship between mother and son in *Trouble Sleeping* (1990 R); etc.

us A word which implies belonging, community, communality and empathy – unlike 'them'. Its use in titles of lesbian- and gay-related projects has been rare: the last episode of *The Walls of Jericho* described the future of Sophia Jex-Blake (Sara Kestelman) with Ursula Du Pré (Gillian Barge) in 'Not Me, But Us' (1981 T). The OUT ON TUESDAY documentary reclaiming and proclaiming lesbian lives was called 'WOMEN LIKE US' (1990 T) and Ian MCKELLEN went fossicking for homophobes on the Isle of Man (finding one or two) in the series THEM AND US (1991 T) – with the anti-gays definitely in the former category for once. From 'us' to 'our' is only a short step cognitively, but a huge one in practical terms for an entertainment industry mired in whiskery prejudices. Therefore, the mere fact that the 1991 TV movie starring Julie Andrews and Ann-Margret used the word in a gay context was something to marvel at. Its linkage with another majority-precious word was near-miraculous: OUR SONS.

vaginas The passageway from the vulva to the uterus, rarely seen or mentioned, outside of sex education (and satires on same, as in Simon CALLOW's beach oration at the beginning of MAURICE 1987 C).

It has appeared in symbolic form: described by the thumbs and forefingers of Jo (Rita Tushingham) outstretched in a rough triangle across which is a thin skin of a soap bubble (during the opening credits of A TASTE OF HONEY 1961 C). This information was given wider and more explicit currency as the cover illustration of Rita Mae BROWN'S novel *Rubyfruit Jungle*. By then the hand sign – and the phrase from which the title comes – had become well known among feminists to denote the vagina.

Evelyn (Kathy Bates) and fellow members of the consciousness-raising group are exhorted to examine their private parts in front of each other in FRIED GREEN TOMATOES AT THE WHISTLE STOP CAFE (1991 C). The first close-up vagina (known in the film business as a 'gratuitous beaver shot') seen in a mainstream movie (but not in the US version) belonged to Catherine (Sharon Stone) in *Basic Instinct* (1992 C), a talking point scene (lasting all of three seconds) which was deservedly trashed in *Loaded Weapon* (1993 C).

Valentine's Day *See* ST VALENTINE'S DAY.

Valentino, Rudolph [Rudolfo Alfonzo Raffaelo Pierre Filbert Gugliemi Di Valentina D'Antonguolla] (1895–1926) Italian–American screen idol who danced the TANGO indelibly in *The Four Horsemen of the Apocalypse* (1921), manhandled Agnes Ayres in a tent in *The Sheik* (1921), fought bulls in *Blood and Sand* (1922), wore satins and beads (but not much of either) in *The Young Rajah* (1922), and put on powdered wigs and lots of make-up in *Monsieur Beaucaire* (1924). A cult grew up immediately after his death that was not equalled until those surrounding James DEAN and Marilyn MONROE.

Valentino has been played by Anthony Dexter (1952 C); Franco Nero (1974 T); Rudolf NUREYEV (1977). Documentaries include *The Legend of Rudolph Valentino* (1962 T) and *Hollywood 'Valentino and Swanson'* (1980 T). (A 1993–4 'Valentino' project is set to star Antonio Banderas under the direction of Nagisa Oshima.)

The actor and his sultry sheik image have been lampooned or gently mocked by cross-eyed comedian Ben Turpin, Bebe Daniels who has Richard Arlen brought to her tent in *She's a Sheik* (1927 C); Alberto Sordi as *The White Sheik* (1951 C: about the hero of a photo-strip story); Cliff Richard in *Wonderful Life* (1964 C); Gene Wilder in *The World's Greatest Lover* (1977 C); Ron Leibman in *Won Ton, the Dog Who Saved Hollywood* (1976 C: called Rudy Montague, he goes to see his movies in female attire and enthusiastically applauds every scene he appears in).

valets *See* MANSERVANTS.

Valley of the Dolls (US 1967 C) Three women take various paths to perdition in the SODOM AND GOMORRAH that is HOLLYWOOD. Neely O'Hara(!) (Patty Duke) drinks, takes pills ('dolls') and picks up men. Jennifer (Sharon Tate) is wanted only for her body and commits suicide after breast cancer is diagnosed. Anne (Barbara Parkins) is a country girl who becomes a model, starts to slide into the valley but is pulled out by a strong man. Other characters include a *Tyrannosaurus Rex* of a Broadway star (Susan Hayward), a dress designer (Alex Davion) whom everybody thinks is 'a FAG' but isn't, and various hangers-on and victims.

W: Helen Deutsch and Dorothy Kingsley from the novel by Jacqueline Susann; P: David Weisbart; D: Mark Robson; 123 mins.

One of the first films to be described by critics as CAMP and a possible SEND-UP of every alleged exposé of the tawdry world behind the showbiz glitter. Drawing deeply from the well of recent Hollywood/Broadway mythology (with characters supposedly based on Marilyn

MONROE, Judy GARLAND, Grace Kelly and Ethel Merman – and Jacqueline Susann herself), it is rankest garbage yet eminently siftable. Among its daft pleasures are a vulgarly effective *tour de force* from Patty Duke, stunning production design and shamelessly banal direction allied to an unflaggingly rhapsodic musical score. Feisty as Susan Hayward is, it's difficult not to superimpose Judy Garland (who withdrew from the production after a few days), especially during her two (hideous) numbers. Hard, too, not to luxuriate in the possibilities inherent in the author's own casting: Bette DAVIS as Broadway's most sacred monster; Liza Minnelli as the out-of-control Neely; Mia Farrow as the unworldly New Englander; Elvis Presley as the immature singing idol; and Linda Lovelace as the sex-film actress Jennifer.

In the 1981 television mini-series version (W: Leslie Stevens, and Laurence Heath; P: Renée Valente; D: Walter Grauman; 196 mins) Jennifer (Veronica Hamel) is down and out in PARIS. Heavily into drugs, deserted by her man, jobless, friendless. And ripe for seduction of the third kind. Enter a glamorous painter, Vivienne Moray (Camilla Sparv) who has a nicely appointed apartment, a comfortable bed and a winning way with Coquilles St Jacques. Within a trice they become lovers and Jennifer's wardrobe undergoes something of a change: white blouson-shirts and hacking jackets.

Vivienne paints Jennifer and takes her to fashionable places. As quickly as the affair began, it ends. A chance meeting with a male friend fills the exile with thoughts of home and normality. Not wishing to seem callous, but not wanting to upset Middle America either, the script has Jennifer deliver a homily: 'Vivienne's an incredible woman. She was very kind to me, straightened me out. We were very close for a while.'

This is lesbian love as a glamorous retreat, a cleansing, a halfway house, a necessary but temporary stopping-off point before returning to the basics of everyday living.

Valmouth (UK 1975 R) A succulently over-ripe masseuse (Elisabeth Welch) works her magic fingers on the residents of, and visitors to, a geriatric paradise on the banks of the Val which becomes a veritable SODOM and is appropriately destroyed by thunder and lightning. Among the saints and sinners: a lascivious widow, a TRANSVESTITE pederastic cardinal, a gay shepherd, a doggily adoring lieutenant and his more heterosexually inclined friend, a nun who breaks her vow of silence once a year, and an anti-vice Irish priest. Among their preoccupations: erotomania, religious mania, sodomy, BLASPHEMY, miscegenation, transvestism and satanism.

W: Sandy Wilson adapted from his stage musical which was based on the novel by Ronald FIRBANK; D: Glyn DEARMAN; 26.12.75; BBC Radio 3; 90 mins.

No cause for alarm. What may at first appear as an Edwardian retelling of SODOM AND GOMORRAH is a captivating musical for innocents of all ages set amid paradisal cherry and peach blossom, frangipane trees and custard apple orchards where characters do what comes naturally, if not strictly within the bounds of convention.

This production with a cast that boasts Fenella Fielding, Peter Gilmore, Elaine Delmar and Aubrey WOODS – as well as Ms Welch – is well within the sublimely queer tradition of a certain kind of BBC Third Programme–Radio 3 entertainment. Genteel innuendo, perfect diction and, despite the carryings-on, containing absolutely nothing to frighten the horses.

The attractive songs include 'I've Got Magic Fingers'; 'Big Best Shoes'; 'When All The Girls Were Pretty And All The Men Were Strong'; 'What Do I Want With Love?'; and the far too brief 'David and Jonathan' duet, 'It's Fine to Have A Friend'.

Most listeners can only concur with the producer's (1992) reminiscence: 'We had an absolute ball. We received nothing but praise. You can get away with more in a musical. The fact that Cardinal Pirelli sings about the things he does takes the curse off it. The only thing that was cut was "Harehutch Hall' but only because of length.'

The Vampire Lovers (UK 1970 C) A young woman (Ingrid Pitt) insinuates herself into a household and vampirizes its women.
W: Tudor Gates, Harry Fine and Michael Style from the novel CARMILLA by Sheridan Le Fanu; P: Harry Fine and Michael Style; D: Roy Ward Baker; 91 mins.
More like dentistry than Gothic fantasy: a painfully drawn-out affair, especially in the American television version which cuts out all the sex between the women and, as a result, nearly all of the vampirism as well. A particularly pallid cast is illuminated only by Kate O'Mara as a governess who becomes another of Carmilla's drained disciples. Hammer Films struck box office gold with this one and there erupted a brief 'lesbian' cycle: of the films, *Lust of a Vampire* and *Twins of Evil* are, like their progenitor, markedly lacking in imagination and effect, unlike the potent *Daughters of Darkness* and *The Velvet Vampire*, made during the same period (in Belgium and the US respectively). However, the last in the cycle, *Countess Dracula* (1972: with Ingrid Pitt), is made with some awareness of vampire mythology and a lush pictorial sense, not to mention a powerful erotic flow.

vampires Creatures of the night, sucking the sexual will and the very life-force out of healthy young men and women. From *Dracula* (1930) onwards these undead possessors have tickled the cinema-going public's imagination, being the perfect vehicle for expressing fears about sexuality and death, decadence and desire, plague and contamination. Lesbian vampires have stalked their prey in DRACULA'S DAUGHTER (1936 C); *Blood and Roses* (1960 C); *The Vampire Lovers* (1970 C); THE HUNGER (1983 C) and others, while male heroes had to watch out for same-sex desanguination in *Dance of the Vampires* aka *The Fearless Vampire Killers* (1967 C), *Once*

Bitten (1985 C) and *Vampire* (1979) which was made for television. Jason Miller (who took on the devil in *The Exorcist*) is no match for the single-minded count (Richard Lynch). What happens is not shown but is narrated after the event: 'He leaned over me and made me look into his eyes ... I tried to fight it with everything I had in me but it was impossible. I wanted him for that instant. The eyes were so hypnotic, I felt I belonged to him and I wanted to ...'
A famous real-life vampire was portrayed – as everything degenerate and slug-like, yet not totally unsympathetic – by Kurt Raab in TENDERNESS OF THE WOLVES (1973 C).
With sexually transmitted deadly disease now a cultural constant for more than a decade, the vampire is once again a major object of fear and fascination, with Gary Oldman in *Bram Stoker's* 'DRACULA' (1992 C) proving that the walking dead are very much alive.

Van Damm, Sheila (1923–87) English rally driver and theatre manager who worked for her father at the Windmill Theatre ('We never close') from the age of 17. During wartime service (in the air force) she ran tours of the Windmill Girls through British and American bases. The winner of 27 major car rallies, she also took over the running of the Windmill from 1960 until its closure in 1964. She recalled the hairbreadth escapes from censorship as well as the many famous comedians and actors who began their careers on its stage in PANORAMA 'The Windmill' (1964 T); *The Windmill Story* (presented by Jack De Manio, 1964 R) and *If It Moves, It's Rude* (1970 T).
With her short hair, jumpers, tweeds and trousers it looked at one stage as if she might fill the void left on television by the death of Nancy SPAIN. Instead she made occasional, rather tentative forays into the medium, becoming better known on radio as a sometime member of the all-women *Petticoat Line* (in February 1972 swapping opinions and life experiences with Mary WHITEHOUSE).

Van Druten, John (1901–57) English playwright and screenwriter. He had a huge early success with *Young Woodley* (filmed 1930) and maintained his popularity with *Old Acquaintance* (1943 C), *I Remember Mama* (1948 C), THE VOICE OF THE TURTLE (1949 C; 1958 T) and BELL, BOOK AND CANDLE (1958 C). He adapted Christopher ISHERWOOD's Berlin stories for the stage and screen as *I Am A Camera* (1955 C).

His other work included *Unfaithful* (1931 C); *After Office Hours* (1932, filmed by HITCHCOCK from the stage play *London Wall*); *Night Must Fall* (1937 C); *Johnny Come Lately* (1943 C); *My Life with Caroline* (1959 T); *The Druid Circle* (1960 T). Jeffrey WEEKS relates in *Coming Out* (1977) how Van Druten spoke at the World Congress of the World League for Sexual Reform in 1929, castigating the theatre for its one-sided portrayal of homosexuals as ineffectual and irrelevant.

vanilla Recently used for a bland, possibly feminine role-playing lesbian. Calla (Estelle Parsons) upbraids Rachel (Joanne Woodward) for not striking out in life, comparing her timidity to her stubborn preference for one kind of ice cream: '[Vanilla's] not the only kind. There are 30 other flavours as well as Flavour of the Month. There are more people on the earth than just you.' 'I'll take vanilla' was a determinedly inconsequential saying, popular in the 1930s (Helen Chandler as a bubble-headed American in Paris included it among her box of conversational tricks in *The Last Flight* 1931 C).

Van Sant, Gus (1952 –) American film director tipped for greatness: *Alice in Hollywood* (a 'featurette' 'screwball comedy', unreleased 1978); *The Discipline of D.E.* (from William BURROUGHS' short story, *c* 1981 C); *Five Ways to Kill Yourself* (1984 C); MALA NOCHE (1985, released 1987); *Drugstore Cowboy* (1989); MY OWN PRIVATE IDAHO (1991); *Even Cowgirls Get the Blues* (1993); 'Andy Warhol' (project, 1993–4); 'The Mayor of Castro Street' (Van Sant quit the project in April 1993); 'The Wild Boys' (project 1993–4).

Variation on a Theme (UK 1961 R) Rich, much-married Rose Fish (Mary Wimbush) falls for a second-rate BALLET DANCER, Anton Valov né Ron Vale (Jon Rollason) who is being kept by choreographer Sam Duveen (Brian Haines). Rose, a consumptive, loses her German banker lover and her life because of her passion for this vain, self-centred young man.

W: Terence RATTIGAN; P: Norman Wright; 8.12.61; BBC Home Service (*The Monday Play*); 90 mins. (A second production starred Margaret Lockwood and Geoffrey Collins, with John Pullen, *Saturday Night Theatre*, 17.11.69.)

The playwright's source materials were drawn from *La Dame aux Camélias*, from his own love affairs, and from Margaret Leighton (who played Rose Fish on stage) and Laurence Harvey who was her lover, while simultaneously living with and being moulded into a star by film producer James Woolf. He eventually left his patron to marry the actress.

T. C. Worsley was one of the few critics to champion the work when it was staged in 1958, calling it 'passionate, raw and truthful ... [about] a half-cocky, half-cringing stripling who preys by flattery on lonely women'. Unlike some of Rattigan's other plays, *Variation on a Theme* has not been rediscovered and is known now only as a footnote to British theatre history. Shelagh Delaney was so incensed by what she regarded as its artificiality and beating around the bush on matters sexual, that she straightway sat down to write A TASTE OF HONEY, which was completed inside a fortnight and was both a critical and a popular success (at the Theatre Royal, Stratford East) before *Variation* closed after a disappointing West End run.

Michael Darlow and Gillian Hodson wrote in *Terence Rattigan: The Man and His Work* (1979):

'When he tried to move with the times, he failed. The removal of theatrical taboos coincided with an increased preoccupation in his play with sex, rather than sex subsumed in love. When he tried to write openly about sex, he found he could not. This was not so much from fear or lingering doubts about the acceptability of homosexuality on the stage, but because his whole personality and quality as a writer was geared to the oblique and the implicit. In any case a lifetime of concealment and regret of one's own homosexuality is hardly the best preparation for successful uninhibited writing about it. The result was plays which, in the atmosphere of exuberant taboo-smashing that characterized the decade after *Look Back in Anger*, seemed evasive. *Variation on a Theme* in particular seemed to be downright dishonest and the audience felt short-changed.'

vaseline *See* LUBRICANT.

Vautrin Character in Honoré De Balzac's *Comédie Humaine* series of novels, played in *Père Goriot* by Andrew Keir (1968 T) and David Ross (1992 R). An arch criminal who loved a handsome young man so greatly and all-consumingly that he took the blame for a crime the young man committed.

VD Blues (US 1972 T) A PBS special: songs and sketches about SEXUALLY TRANSMITTED DISEASES, followed by a nationwide VD hotline.
D: Don Fouser and Sidney Smith; 60 mins (plus the off-air phone-in).
  Probably for the first time on nationwide (non-commercial) American television, a specific invitation – from Geraldo Rivera to a previously unaddressed group of individuals: 'If you have a call or if you happen to be gay and you want to talk to someone who is also gay, give us a call. Whatever hang-ups they have outside the studio, hopefully, we don't have them in here.'

vegetables Their erotic potential is mostly limited to jokes about marrows and cucumbers, or to SAFE-SEX demonstrations involving carrots ('more attractive than ding-dongs,' says one of the lesbians in *Sammy and Rosie Get Laid* 1987 C) and cucumbers (*Female Parts* 1992 T). Barbara Hammer is one of the

artists and film-makers to examine them from inside and outside as vaginal iconography (cabbages, artichokes, lettuce, broccoli, onions, corn on the cob and cauliflowers in *Women I Love* 1977 C). The nearest mainstream American television has come to making the connection between the veined leaves and luscious folds of such vegetables is a shopping scene in MY TWO LOVES (1986 T) where Mariette Hartley and Lynn REDGRAVE tentatively discuss their shape, texture, colour and seed-filled interiors from a sexual point of view. *See also* FRUITS.

vegetarians As rare as hen's teeth until the late 1960s when a number of celebrities (including Paul McCartney and Jon Pertwee) declared that they didn't eat meat. There had been occasional programmes in the preceding decades as when 'Christa' made suggestions on a vegetarian-balanced diet; this was in March 1929 and broadcast at a time when most listeners were asleep (10.45–11pm).
  British culture decreed that vegetables were for boiling and then for eating with meat. Those who chose to forgo the latter were regarded as very odd. A talk on WOMAN'S HOUR (1963 R) resulted in a letter which was read out on air. The writer was incensed by the strong inference that she and her fellow vegetarians were cranks: 'We are no more cranks than nudists!' The following year, one of its Christmas-time items featured Jessica Davies (wife of actor Rupert) explaining how she and her family celebrated the festival without meat (a nut roast topped with mushrooms).
  In comedy and drama of the period – and extending to the present day – vegetarians were depicted as being of six often interconnecting types:
(1) Females of repellent aspect, including severe, joyless, tight-lipped Mavis (Eileen Way) in HANCOCK'S HALF HOUR 'The Reunion Party' (1959 T) who has turned Hancock's old wartime comrade (Hugh Lloyd) into a miserable moralizing blob. Also on *Hancock's Half Hour* there is frumpish, pretentious 'beatnik'

Veronica Stillwell (June Whitfield), a possible candidate for wedlock in 'The Succession – Son and Heir' (1961 T), but she wants only a free and voluntary contract, regarding marriage as barbaric and primitive. She therefore rejects Tony – *and* his frozen TV dinner (meat and two veg).

(2) Male virgins of repellent aspect, including Arty (Charles HAWTREY), the intellectual snob of a nephew disdainfully watching the Coronation with his family in *All on a Summer's Day* (1953 T); Rudy (Tony RANDALL) in *Here's Lucy* 'The Mountaineer' (1971 T), 'all alfalfa sprouts and yoghurt', disgustingly fit, exhaustingly extrovert; Tolstoy disparages his friend Vladimir Chertkov (named as his lover by his jealous wife) as 'a skinny vegetarian' in *The Power of Dawn* (Emlyn WILLIAMS (1977 T; Michael REDGRAVE 1983 R); Lesley (Hugh PADDICK, non-smoking, tofu- and seaweed-eating snob and weed in SHARE AND SHARE ALIKE (1978 T); Trevor (Nigel Hawthorne), an intelligence officer in A ROD OF IRON (1980 T) who's still a virgin (and gay), has stopped eating meat ('nothing doctrinaire'), and drinks only tonic water.

(3) Teenage girls who are going through a phase, including Lucille Hewitt (Jennifer Moss) in CORONATION STREET (1964 T); Melissa in NEIGHBOURS (1990 T); Fiona (Jane Slavin) in A HORSE CALLED GERTRUDE STEIN (1990 R): 'I don't want to eat anything with a face ... I don't want to eat anything that's been killed'; Lucy Perks (Tracy Jane White) in THE ARCHERS (1992 R): Elizabeth Archer tells her mother Jill that they shouldn't pander to 'them', shouldn't 'put themselves out', shouldn't have to cook 'brown rice'.

(4) Animal liberationists and (left-wing) political activists, including Sandra (Nerys Hughes) who becomes a vegetarian and an animal rights campaigner in *The Liver Birds* (1976–8 T); investigative reporter David Dunhill (Richard E. Grant) in HERE IS THE NEWS (1989 T), a secret TRANSVESTITE *and* a shoplifter and very likely a closet homosexual; the wife of Terence Halliday

(Michael Angelis) in *Single Voices* 'The Last Supper' (1990 T) who has gone to live with a vegetarian: 'Acid rain, pollution, insecticide, healthy living – all that crap, I suppose ... they're obsessed with the dimensions of the ozone hole and the tamperings of man with the universe'; militant vegetarians in *Delicatessen* (1991 C); Mary Shelley (Gerda Stevenson) in *Blood and Ice* (1992 R).

(5) Health freaks, including Larry (Simon Cadell), who ridicules his wife's pre-birth vegetarianism ('mountains of tofu, lentilburgers and raw broccoli') in *Life without George* (1989 T), referring to the members of the natural childbirth group – which includes at least one (very soppy) vegetarian mother-to-be – as 'wallies ... all horn-rimmed glasses and dungarees'; aerobics teacher Sam (Lysette Anthony), dogmatic and babbling, into tofu and crystals in *Husbands and Wives* (1992 C): 'I flip over couscous!'

(6) Homosexuals and bisexuals; including *Culinary Characters* 'Colin SPENCER' (1986 R); Walt (Tim Streeter) in MALA NOCHE (1987 C): 'It's not bad to eat food without meat anymore,' he tells one of his young Mexican friends; Jo McLoughlin (Jenifer Landor in INAPPROPRIATE BEHAVIOUR (1987 T); one of the lovers (Joe Malone in a *Tracey Ullman Show* sketch (1987 T) whose partner (Dan Castellaneta) cannot give up meat: 'Now you want me to give up red meat. I love it. I like it barbecued, braised, burnt to a crisp, blood rare but still mooing'/'I love you and if it makes you happy go ahead, have it'; Madonna in IN BED WITH MADONNA (1991 C): mostly confined to a large, closed plastic container and near-empty bottle of Tamari sauce.

'Are most lesbians veggie?' was one of the questions posed during a meal cooked by Richard Hawley in OUT 'Guess Who's Coming to Dinner?' (1991 T). One guest found that her relationships with women didn't last 'if they were only into lentils and rice – and many were, so they didn't'.

'Don't want vitamins. Want a good dinner,' PC George Dixon (Jack

Warner) turning down a salad in a 1956 episode of DIXON OF DOCK GREEN (T).

'Foie gras and champagne instead of dandelions and such like': James BOND (Sean Connery) craftily smuggling provisions into the health farm he's been sent to for toning up by his boss in *Never Say Never Again* (1983 C).

Veidt, Conrad (1893–1943) German film actor who made a solid career in Britain as a leading man, becoming a British citizen in 1939. In the last few years of his life, he was a star character actor in Hollywood, sending a large portion of his salary back to his adopted country.

A riveting, enigmatic personality with finely chiselled features and a moody reserve who is mainly remembered for four shadowy, glinting portraits: the mime-murderer in *The Cabinet of Doctor Caligari* (1920); the spinechilling yet plausible Grand Vizier in *The Thief of Bagdad* (1940), the perverse nobleman in *A Woman's Face* (1941); Colonel Strasser, the Gestapo chief in *Casablanca* (1942). His last role in *Above Suspicion* (1943), was as another representative of a regime which he had fled and which was dedicated to cleansing itself of Jews (like his – third – wife), of 'sexual deviates' (like himself) and of 'immoral' films like *Anders also die Anderen* aka *Different from the Others* (1919) in which he starred as the hounded gay violinist.

C: début in *Der Spion* (1917); Schubert in *Das Dreimmaderlhaus* (1918); Chopin in *Nocturno der Liebe* (1919); Phileas Fogg in *Around the World in 80 Days* (1919); the rich and ruthless *Prinz Kuckuck* (1920); Death in *Unheimliche Geschichten* (1920); a blackmailer in *Der Reigen* (1920); a variation of Dr Jekyll and Mr Hyde in *Der Januskopf* (1920); the Devil in *Kurfurstendamm* (1920); Nelson in *Lady Hamilton* (1921); Cesare Borgia in *Lucrezia Borgia* (1922); *Paganini* (1923); Ivan the Terrible in WAXWORKS (1924); as *The Student of Prague* (1926); the haunted pianist in *The Hands of Orlac* (1926); Louis XI in *The Beloved Rogue* (1927); as *The Man Who Laughs*

(1928); a stage magician in *The Last Performance* aka *Erik the Great* (1929); as *Rasputin* (1931); Metternich in *Congress Dances* (1931); Captain Stanhope in *Die Andere Seite* (ie JOURNEY'S END 1931); nasty German commandant in *I Was a Spy* (1933); as *The Wandering Jew* (1933); as *Jew Süss* (1934); the Christlike stranger in *The Passing of the Third Floor Back* (1935); Cardinal Richelieu's henchman in *Under the Red Robe* (1936); the mysterious sea captain in *Dark Journey* (1937); a German captain in *The Spy in Black* (1939); a Danish captain in *Contraband* (1940); a Nazi in *Escape* (1940); as the *Nazi Agent* (1942) and his meek twin; the dancing master in *The Men in Her Life* (1942); another Nazi agent (foiled by Humphrey Bogart) in *All Through the Night* (1942); etc.

'Veidt's friends regarded him as heterosexual when sober, homosexual when drunk,' David Shipman in *The Great Movie Stars: The Golden Years*.

venereal diseases *See* SEXUALLY TRANSMITTED DISEASES.

ventriloquists The duality of human nature and the ambiguity of sexuality can be effectively dramatized by flesh and blood men being possessed by inanimate DOLLS, into which they alone breathe life. The dummy is the dominant self, the ego. Painted, dandyish with a high-pitched voice and lascivious grin: the perfect paradigm for a divided, restless soul spilling over into mental disorder. The relationship between man and dummy can be as binding as a marriage, with the same potential for possessiveness, jealousy and destruction.

In the most famous episode of *Dead of Night* (1945 C) Michael REDGRAVE plays Maxwell Frere whose other half Hugo 'flirts' with another man, 'seduces' him, rejects his 'lover' and goes to 'live with' the other man, driving Maxwell to violence and finally to murder. But is the surviving partner Maxwell or Hugo? The same theme was elongated (without acknowledgement) and heterosexualized in *Magic* (1978 C) with Anthony Hopkins.

Claude Rains activated a female doll in *Alfred Hitchcock Presents* 'And So Died Riabouchinska' (1956 T) with chilling results; Cliff Robertson was in danger of complete submission to his all-too-human Willy in *The Twilight Zone* 'The Dummy' (1962 T); Jackie Cooper in the same series is framed by his wooden tyrant in 'Caesar and Me' (1964 T); Larry (Alton Douglas) was a gay ventriloquist dying of tuberculosis in TROUPERS (1988 R).

The comedy *Knock On Wood* (1954 C) has a psychiatrist (Mai Zetterling) elicit all sorts of Freudian motives from Danny KAYE to explain his ventriloquism. SOAP (1977–81 T) featured Chuck Campbell (Jay Johnson) who slept with, went to the toilet with and enjoyed as near as feasible a full relationship with the brash, randy Bob.

The first voice-manipulator on British television was Bobbie KIMBER brawnily dressed in various female get-ups to engage in banter with Augustus Peabody in *Music Hall* (1952 T). Saveen's famous schoolgirl dummy Daisy Mae started out as a schoolboy and was effortlessly adapted. One of the most famous dummies of recent years was 'Wilf', the irrepressible puppet dressed in a sailor suit in the documentary series about life on the *Ark Royal* in *Sailor* (1976 T) and in *Sailor* 'Eight Years on' (1984 T): '... had a lot of letters didn't we? Even got one from a POOFTER. Didn't answer it though.'

Vernon Boy's name, as like as not signifying a wobbly masculinity.

UK: treasure hunter Vernon Winslowe (Ivor NOVELLO) in *A South Sea Bubble* (1928 C); Vernon, the snooty psychology student who works as a holiday camp kitchen hand in A WEEK IN CHALET LAND (1948 R) and is not interested in girls; Vernon (Max ADRIAN), the circus performer crook in *Pool of London* (1951 C); ageing bachelor singing star Vernon Carew (Jerry Desmonde) in *Follow a Star* (1959 C); Vernon Mycroft (Christopher Benjamin) seeking heart-to-heart advice in *Dear Miss Hope* (1969 R); Vernon Bentley (Bernard Archard), the

lover of one of the two herb-farming women, patronizingly aware of the other's 'sexual problem' in *Country Matters* 'Breeze Anstey' (1972 T); Vernon Standish (Frank Thornton), a documentary film director, very intense and very SENSITIVE, who mistakes Jack and Lesley for lovers in SHARE AND SHARE ALIKE (1978 R); Vernon Bayliss (Denholm ELLIOTT), perennially inebriated journalist in *Defence of the Realm* (1986 C); artistic, theatrical Verne (Aubrey WOODS) in *The Random Jottings of Hinge and Bracket* (1987 R); etc.

US: Fred Astaire, one half of a real-life dance partnership in *The Story of Irene and Vernon Castle* (1939 C); Vernon Simpson (Ray Milland), an introverted college professor who becomes a baseball player in *It Happens Every Spring* (1949 C); Vernon (Charles Farrell), the father in *My Little Margie* (1952–55 T); Vernon Hightower (Jeff Bridges) estranged husband of *Nadine* (1987 C); etc.

Veronica 4 Rose (UK 1983 T) Lesbians single, lesbians in partnership, lesbians in friendship, lesbians feminist, lesbians solely.
D: Melanie Chait for Lusia Films; 11–12pm; Channel 4; 60 mins.

A persuasive double-decker documentary. The young women are filmed, recorded, edited and screened talking about 'what it's like' being a dyke. Then, after having seen that part-finished programme, the subjects are shown reacting to what they have said, how it has been presented by the director, and the bits that were cut out.

'What a joy to watch and listen to a film which is a film made by a team of women, in which young lesbians watched a film about themselves and their lifestyle and [then] discuss what the film meant to them and what their parents would say' (Jackie Marcus, *Gay News* 258).

A Very Great Man Indeed (UK 1953 R) Desperately earnest, infinitely gullible Herbert Reeve (Hugh BURDEN) goes in search of the real Richard Shewin, poet and Great English Novelist, recently deceased. With every fumbling step he takes, the hapless biographer totters through fraudulent facts, secret alliances, unabashed monomania, dissolving reputations and dusty answers in a cultural scrambling of impeccable venomosity. Exactly what Richard Shewin was into ('everything' according to his brother Stephen) remains just out of reach.

W: Henry REED; P: Douglas Cleverdon; 7.9.53; BBC Third Programme; 70 mins. (A second production, with almost the same cast, went on air in June 1961.)

This was the first of a series* of radio plays full of mockery but no malice. Their author confidently treads the fine line between surface levity and underlying respect for his monsters, though surely delighting in slowly but surely tearing down Shewin (whose titles include 'The Hot and the Cold', 'The Floor and the Ceiling' and 'The Arse and the Elbow') from the Olympian heights to the plateau of mediocrity.

'The aspects of himself that he presented to the world were but a simulacrum. My brother's interests and habits were very far-ranging, Mr Reeve. They were not simply confined to seduction, adultery and rape,' said Stephen Shewin.

* THE PRIVATE LIFE OF HILDA TABLET (1957); *Emily Butter: An Occasion Recalled* (1954); A HEDGE, BACKWARDS (1956); *The Primal Scene, As It Were ...: Nine Studies in Disloyalty* (1958); *Not a Drum was Heard: The War Memoirs of General Gland* (1959); *Musique Discrete: A Request Programme of Music by Dame Hilda Tablet* (1959).

A Very Peculiar Practice (UK 1986/1988 T)

Closely observed urban lunatics, misfits, POLITICALLY CORRECT but totally self-serving lesbian-bisexuals, malingerers, Tory terrors, American bloodsuckers, potty professors, capering nuns, gay Olympic hopefuls and other funny folk caught on the treadmill of fashionable education theory.

W: Andrew DAVIES; P: Ken Riddington; D: David Tucker; BBC2; 50 mins.

Into any self-respecting time-capsule should go this broadly targeted look at a red-brick university in the blood-red sunset of Thatcher's England. It's an inglorious age of invasive computerization, sexism, anti-sexism, AIDS, born-again Christians and the commercialization of academia. Yet there is love to be found.

In the episode 'Values of the Family' (1988) Bob Buzzard (David Troughton), the hide-bound Tory doctor, becomes the unwilling object of a young man's fancy. Not just any young man but Britain's best new prospect on the running track, the next Steve Cram, Glenn Oates (James Noble). Love disables him. He can't run, can't train, can't sleep and can't work, so crazy about the right-wing prat is he. Bob is torn in three directions. He abhors 'them', hates being the apple of another man's eye yet, despite himself, he does love his suitor. But not enough to submit to even a little KISS. 'Put all that sort of thing behind you, so to speak,' he counsels his moonstruck friend.

Thoroughly chewed up, Bob has to break off the relationship, later telling his colleague Jock (Graham Crowden) what happened. 'The worst of it was he was a *really nice* bloke.' Jock is shocked. 'My dear man, why should he not be? These men you call POOFTERS, they are just like you and me. We all need love, Bob.' As he speaks, Jock's hand flops onto Bob's. More homophobic apoplexy. 'Not *you* as well!' But Jock only wants Bob for his spare room as he's been made homeless.

Meanwhile, on another branchline of the plot, the frighteningly right-on FEMINIST Rose Marie (Barbara Flynn) is helping some of the male students come to terms with their PENISES, encouraging two lesbian students to sue Jock for sexual harassment, and more than encouraging the attentions of a big bucks American who has taken over the establishment with a view to maximizing its efficiency.

Holding the various plots together is the bewildered Dr Stephen Daker (Peter Davison), so desperate to do the right thing in a world where around every corner is a toe to be trodden on, an open mouth into which to put your foot.

vests *See* SINGLETS.

veterinarians In the 1961 film comedy *In the Doghouse* Miss Enid Ritter (Freda Bamford) is interviewed for the part of vet Leslie Phillips' assistant. She is highly qualified, massively competent and is licensed to drive a lorry as well as a car. Leslie Phillips takes one aghast look at her and chooses instead the voluptuously peroxided candidate of trance-like vacuity. Better a know-nothing sex-pot than a know-all dyke is the scene's loud and clear message.

Another lesbian in this profession which requires every possible medical speciality within the one person is the prickly, red-cheeked woman (Ann Morrish) who takes care of Queenie, the adored Alsatian of Joe ACKERLEY (Benjamin WHITROW) in WE THINK THE WORLD OF YOU (1980 T).

Of the males there is Siegfried (Robert Hardy), gruffly insouciant, SUEDE SHOE wearing and for a long time bachelor gay in the dales looking after *All Creatures Great and Small* (1977–90 T).

vicars Usually portrayed as doddery remnants of a God-fearing age (Kenneth Williams in HANCOCK'S HALF HOUR 1954–9 R) or trendily whistling in the dark (Maggie Smith's unseen husband in TALKING HEADS 'A Bed Among the Lentils' 1988 T). The very name 'vicar' is guaranteed to provoke guffaws – as Julian CLARY was very aware in TERRY AND JULIAN (1992 T).

Unlike PRIESTS, few fictional ones seem lustily drawn to their fellow men: only David (Neil Cunningham) in *Johnny Jarvis* (1983 T: who becomes a pop group manager after being arrested for GROSS INDECENCY) and Sonnenschein (Nickolas GRACE) in *The Green Man* (1990 T).

There was also the vicar (Frank WILLIAMS) IN *Dad's Army* (1968–77 T) of whom the ARP warden (Bill Pertwee) in the 1972 'Time on My Hands' episode (which includes the simulated anal pen-etration of Clive Dunn with a sword by a small person in a cloak) says with great emphasis: 'I've heard you're an expert on *fairies*.' Which the vicar doesn't attempt to deny.

Victim (UK 1961 C) Melville Farr (Dirk BOGARDE), the reluctant hero of Britain's first film about 'inverts', was a self-confessed non-practising homosexual. He tells three well-heeled men: 'I may share your instincts, but I've resisted them.' For two men, loving Farr has led to death: his university lover Phil Stainer and 'Boy' Barrett (Peter McEnery) who sacrifices himself so that the barrister's career and home life will not be harmed. His wife (Sylvia Syms) is not convinced: 'The rot's still there: you haven't changed, in spite of our marriage.' The blackmailers couldn't be more dissimilar. There is Sandy (Derren Nesbitt), a peroxided, running to seed leather boy with pictures of Ancient Greek athletes on his wall. His partner, who works in a bookshop, has neatly permed hair, horn-rimmed spectacles, flat shoes and shapeless clothes. They have different reasons for doing what they do. Sandy's are mostly related to money although he does enjoy making 'fine, upstanding bastards jump'. The woman, Miss Benham (Margaret Diamond) hides cold avarice behind religious clichés. Her task is a moral one: to hose down the Augean stables of every last piece of dung.

W: Janet Green and John McCormick (additional dialogue by Lukas Heller); P: Michael Relph; D: Basil Dearden; 100 mins.

One of the most significant propaganda films, *Victim* quite consciously set out to change a law. There is no doubt that, in the nine years it took to implement the recommendations of the WOLFENDEN Committee, the film – both in its successful cinema release and on (commercial) television in 1966 – did help to change public perceptions. Among its, for some still, radical contentions were that not all gays were 'posh', effeminate or attracted to young boys. It also introduced the idea that married men can be gay, too.

What is timeless about *Victim* is its presentation of the smothering influence of establishment gays on the struggle for full equality, and of the 'sheep to the slaughter' mentality of gay men, even when blatant discrimination threatens their jobs, families, inner tranquillity, even their very lives.

The blackmailers themselves are characterized quite clearly as being repressed – a gay man and a lesbian respectively; an evil system turning like against like. The main victim of their ruthless strategy, 'Boy' Barrett, most closely approximates to the gay man of the 1990s. He is the one who, were he not so anxious to protect the man he loves, would have stood up to them and refused to play their never-ending game.

That such a film was made in a notoriously conservative industry and distributed by the Rank Organization shows the depth of feeling for the situation gays found themselves in – not seen since the 1890s. That Dirk Bogarde agreed to be in the direct line of fire on the screen and in interviews shows a courage that none of the equivalent 'glamour boy' stars in the American cinema, with the exception of Al Pacino and William Hurt, have felt able to match.

The most chilling aspect of *Victim* resides in one short scene where the hale and hearty licensee of the 'queers' pub' (Fred Pettitt) casually spills out his hatred of his clientele. The very suddenness of the outburst from such a mild and underplayed character – salt of the earth, slice of roast beef – says more about the undergrowth of conditioning and the inability to make connections than the rest of the film put together.

victims After 1967 most gay men could no longer be legitimately called victims of blackmailers, although many still fell foul of the stricter legal enforcements on behaviour not condoned by the new law. With HIV/AIDS the gay victim was once more paraded in television documentaries: 'Bill – the first victim of AIDS to be interviewed – caught the disease through homosexual intercourse (*TV Eye* 1985). Within a very short time, the concept of the 'innocent victim' was born: a person who contracted the HIV virus through a blood transfusion or a needle stick. Before the decade was out it would also be applied to people who became infected through heterosexual intercourse.

Victor/Victoria (UK 1982 C) Under the tutelage of an ageing FEMALE IMPERSONATOR (Robert Preston), a waif (Julie Andrews) becomes a gay Polish count who delights Parisian audiences (and James Garner as an American gangster) as a beautiful woman.

W/D: Blake Edwards from *Viktor und Viktoria* (1933 C); P: Tony Adams; 134 mins.

Leigh W. Rutledge in *The Gay Decades* (1992) reckoned that 'in some ways' the film achieved more than 13 years of gay liberation: making 'an impression on the general public's consciousness of homosexuals as compassionate and likeable people who should be left alone to live and love as they please'.

Were it not for the abundant good humour of Robert Preston as Toddy – who ends up in bed with a gangster's muscle-bound, middle-aged bodyguard – it's unlikely that this character would have garnered so much praise, not to mention an Oscar nomination. Toddy's not a total freak, that's true. Nor is he merely incidental to the plot. But he dislodges not one preconception. Obvious and unoriginal, like his song 'GAY PAREE'.

Vidal, Gore (1925–) American novelist, essayist, playwright, political and social commentator, actor, creator of Myra Breckinridge and one of the most public bisexual/homosexual celebrities in the US since the late 1960s. He has produced 23 novels, 6 plays, 8 volumes of essays and many original television scripts including *The Death of Billy the Kid* (1955, filmed in 1957 as *The Left-Handed Gun*) and *Summer Pavilion* (1959 UK, about a woman who wants to escape her dull marriage when she meets a younger man).

His film screenplays include *The Catered Affair* aka *Wedding Breakfast* (1956); *Ben-Hur* (1959, co-W); THE BEST MAN (1964, from his stage play); *Caligula* (1980); *Kalki* (1993). For television he has done DRESS GRAY (1986). He played upright and decent Liberal Senator Brickley Paiste in *Bob Roberts* (1992 C).

Documentaries: many US talk shows; KALEIDOSCOPE (1978 R); *Vidal in Venice* (1985 T); *90 Years at the ICA* 'No Place Quite Like It: Writers at the ICA' (1987 T); *The Clive James Interview* (1991 T).

Autobiography: *Gore Vidal – The Man Who Said No* (1983 T).

video diaries A new art form beginning in the late 1980s: a video camera loaded with tape is given to an individual to record – without the intervention of a film crew or interviewer – their thoughts and impressions, conversations, confrontations. Relevant ones include 40 MINUTES 'Diary of a Frontliner' (a man living with AIDS, 1987 T); *Video Diaries* 'Off the Rails' (20-year-old Stephen Hawthorne comes out to his parents, 1991 T) and 'Not a Transvestite' (1992 T). In America, Paul Wynne broadcast a weekly diary about his life, his health and his impending death on KGOP, the San Francisco ABC affiliate, for nearly seven months in 1990. *See also* DIARIES.

Videostars (UK 1983 T) Teddy Whazz (TIM CURRY) is the link person for Channel D, a new television outlet aiming at the marginalized, banalized, ostracized and despised. Teddy himself is fresh out of jail where he had a severe case of homosexual panic. He is terrified at the approach of any male: 'They all want to enter me.' His on-air patter is aptly described as 'blasphemous, puerile and incomprehensible'. While hitherto ignored potential screen stars beat a path to Channel D's doors with pro-gramme ideas (including a leathermen soap opera), blackmail and intimidation are going on behind the scenes as a young Australian, Eric Dancer (Tim

Potter) attempts to pressurize an ex-lover, the station's crooked lawyer Steve Rideaux (Patrick Malahide), by broadcasting his sexual indiscretions.

W: Howard SCHUMAN; P: Kenith TRODD; D: Colin Bucksey; 8.12.83; BBC1; 75 mins.

As ever with his finger on the pulse of today's society, Howard Schuman produces another goofy-spoofy special which lacerates the trendy, deep-fries the laid-back and accessorizes the smallest character with revealing dialogue. And, in the middle, the extraordinary Tim CURRY, even more demented than in THE ROCKY HORROR PICTURE SHOW, attempting to take tele-history at the flood but leading only to misfortune.

Vieux Carré (UK 1985 R) A group of yearning romantics of various sexual outlooks in a wormy rooming house in the French Quarter of New Orleans.

W: Tennessee WILLIAMS from his stage play; D: Martin Jenkins; 20.6.85; BBC Radio 3; 125 mins.

The dying poet Nightingale (James Maxwell) seeks love from the callow writer (Mark Rolston, based on Williams who had no consummated homosexual affair till he was 28). The young man hesitantly tells of sex with a paratrooper when he was 'drunk'. This forms one of the very rare male-love scenes in this dramatist's work:

'I told him that I ... loved ... him. I'd been drinking ... He laughed and said, "Forget it. I'm flying out tomorrow for training base".'
'He said to you "forget it" but you didn't forget it.'
'No ... I don't even have his address and I've forgotten his name.'
'Still, I think you loved him.'

This crucial dialogue was cut just before the play's West End opening in 1978.

Village People Jacques Morali created a disco singing group dressed as various American macho stereotypes (and one racist stereotype): Ray, policeman (Ray Simpson: originally a motorcycle man played by Victor Willis); David, construction worker (David Hodo); Felipe,

American Indian (Felipe Rose); Randy, cowboy (Randy Jones); Glenn, leatherman (Glenn Hughes); Alexander, a GI (Alexander Briley: originally a sailor).

In 1977 they appeared on Dick Clark's *Bandstand* singing 'SODOM AND GOMORRAH'. At that time they were more or less openly gay: 'I'm gay and I wanted to make a top star gay group,' said Morali. It worked. Hits like 'Macho Man' (six weeks in the Top 40) and 'IN THE NAVY' led Allan Carr to build a multi-million dollar musical around them. Then came the disaster of CAN'T STOP THE MUSIC, their film début in 1980: too much and too late.

The Village People went under with it, save for a few days' duty on *The Love Boat*. They broke up in 1981, reformed with a slick new image that didn't catch on. Returning as their lovable old selves in the mid-1980s, they now delight mainly heterosexual audiences with their old hits, rousing anthems to all that is clean, vigorous, manly (and mechanistic) in American life. One of their rare television appearances was on *20/20* 'Whatever Happened to the Village People?' (1990).

Billy CRYSTAL, remarking on his friend's cowboy drag in *City Slickers* (1991 C), scoffs: 'You look like one of the Village People.' In *Step by Step* 'Frank and Son' (1991 T) Suzanne Somers says the same thing about Frank's (Patrick Duffy) young son – dressed in a hard hat and check shirt.

Village People are especially popular in Australia (the only country in the world where *Can't Stop the Music* was a big hit). They provided the entertainment at the big Rugby League match in September 1991 and sang all their hits including 'Macho Man'. Exulted gravel-voiced commentator Dr H. G. Nelson on radio just before the game began: 'This is what the League's all about: big blokes bouncing up and down!'

villains Gay men and lesbians up to no good include the burly Eric Campbell mistaking Edna Purviance for a boy and preparing his bottom accordingly in the Chaplin comedy *Behind the Screen* (1916

C); the rat-like Mr Jones (Philippe Hessat) and his catamite Ricardo (Pierre Sergeol) in *Dans une Ile Perdue* (1931 C: based on Joseph Conrad's *Victory*); Kasper Gutman (Dudley Digges) searching for *The Maltese Falcon* (1931 C: 'I'm a man who likes to talk to a man who likes to talk') and feeling towards young Wilmer Cook (Dwight Frye) like a father does to a son – yet the lad is described as his 'boyfriend' by Sam Spade (Sydney Greenstreet and Elisha Cook played the parts in the 1941 remake); Sandy (Robert Ryan) who runs a crime syndicate in Japan in *House of Bamboo* (1955 C); Arnie Fisher (Jeffrey Chiswick), one of the KRAY-like brothers in WIDOWS (1983 T). *See also* Joel CAIRO; CALIGULA; CATWOMAN; Joan FERGUSON; Count FOSCO; Hercules GRYTPYPE-THYNNE; Rosa KLEBB; Harry LIME; Waldo LYDECKER; Ronald MERRICK; Count Jim MORIARTY; MURDERERS; *Querelle*; Ernst ROEHM; Edward SHELLY; SPIES; James STEERFORTH; TRAITORS; VAUTRIN; Miss WADE.

Villiers, George (1592–1628) 1st Duke of Buckingham. English courtier who replaced JAMES I's favourite, the Earl of Somerset, after having been dolled up and pushed in front of the King's nose by the Archbishop of Canterbury and the Lord Chamberlain in 1614. By 1618 Villiers was a marquess and by 1623, now married, the first non-royal duke for almost a century. He became one of the richest men in England. When he was assassinated James described himself as a 'sorrowful widow' and Villiers was given a royal tomb in Westminster Abbey.

'Was he a man on the make or did he genuinely love James?' asked Matthew Parris in *RSVP* (1992 R). Said Jenny Wormold: 'He was a very highly sexed young man – I would be very surprised if something didn't happen.'

The story of the remarkable relationship was told, through contemporary documents, in *Whom the King Delighteth to Honour* (1967 R), and in dramatized form with Nigel STOCK as the King and Nigel Anthony as Buckingham in *The*

Wisest Fool (1977). Richard Morant played the royal favourite, nicknamed 'Steenie' and 'Boy George', in *Churchill's People* 'A Rich and Beautiful Empire' (1975). Simon Ward played him – without James – in *The Three Musketeers* and *The Four Musketeers* (1973 and 1975 C).

Viola Twin sister of SEBASTIAN who transforms herself for plot purposes into the page Cesario to become the confidant of Duke Orsino in TWELFTH NIGHT. Players on television include Beatrix LEHMANN (1937); Greer Garson (1937); Peggy Ashcroft (1939); Joan Plowright (1970); Felicity Kendall (1980). On radio: Margaretta Scott (1934); Gwen Cherrell (1956); Dorothy Tutin (1958); June Tobin (1962); Wendy Murry (1982); Eve Matheson (1993). Jenny Quayle discussed how she prepared for the part (neuter body language etc) on WOMAN'S HOUR (1992 R) with Jenni Murray who tried, in vain, to discover if the role had changed her perceptions. (Joseph L. Mankiewicz wanted to film the play with Audrey Hepburn as both twins and with Danny KAYE as Sir Andrew AGUECHEEK. The 1958 project stagnated because neither performer was free at the same time.)

violence *See* MURDER VICTIMS; QUEER-BASHING; RAPE; SUICIDES.

Violet Girl's name, once very popular, now almost entirely associated with proletarian women.
US: Violet Carson (Jewel Carmen) in *The Kingdom Of Love* (1918 C); Violet (Beatrice Lillie), big-hearted drudge in *Exit Smiling* (1926 C); Violet Gilbert (Dorothy Revier), Mrs Newly-wed in *When Husbands Flirt* (1926 C); Violet Morgan (Corinne Griffith) in *Infatuation* (from Somerset Maugham's *Caesar's Wife*, 1926 C); Violet Barton (Vera Ralston) in *Surrender* (1950 C); Violet Venable (Katherine HEPBURN), tenacious mother of wayward son who used her to procure young men until she got too old in SUDDENLY LAST SUMMER (1959 C); Violet Ryder (Barbara

Stuart), former hat-check girl, now a brassy, neglected pilot's wife with a good motive to kill him – but she didn't – in PERRY MASON 'The Case of the Guilty Clients' (1961 T); Violet McKisco (Bea Benderet), boorish American at large on the Riviera in *Tender Is the Night* (1962 C); commanding Violet Jordan (Geraldine Fitzgerald) in *The Best of Everything* (1970 T); Violet (Cassie Yates) in *Convoy* (1976 C); Violet Newstead (Lily TOMLIN), one of the office workers who decides enough is enough in *9 to 5* (1980 C); etc.
UK: lisping schoolgirl Violet Elizabeth Bott in *Just William* (Jacqueline Boyer 1954 R; Bonnie Langford 1976–7 T); Violet (Barbara Ferris), Janet Munro's conventional friend in *Bitter Harvest* (1963 C); young Violet Beauregarde (Denise Nickerson) in *Willie Wonka and the Chocolate Factory* (1971 C); young Violet (Susan Tebbs) in *Escape from Darkness* aka *The Littlest Horse Thieves* (1975 C); bathhouse manager Violet (Diana Dors) in STEAMING (1985 C); etc.

violets Emblems of homosexuality, originally used as a token for 'the other love' by the poet Stefan George (lavender for love, violet for sex). A bunch was worn by Marlene DIETRICH between her – knickerless – legs at the opening of *The Blue Angel* in 1930, and earlier as a corsage in a Berlin revue *It's in the Air* with Margo Lion (who also wore a large bunch). Another marker appeared in the 1926 play *La Prisonnière*: the wife's female lover has a whole box of the FLOWERS delivered – which made the violet problematic as an adornment in parts of America in the wake of the play's scandalous reputation when it was performed in New York as *The Captive*. Violets are seen on reposeful characters like Melanie (Olivia De Havilland) in *Gone with the Wind* (1939 C) and on flighty creatures like the heroine's girlfriend Francie (Lana Morris) in *Trottie True* (1949 C). LILITH (Marianne Faithfull) crushes and smells a posy and throws it to the high priest in *Lucifer Rising* (1981 C).

virginity Currently held in low esteem for both young men and young women. Philippa Raskin (Lynn REDGRAVE) goes to bed with the first man who asks her in THE VIRGIN SOLDIERS (1969 C) to prove she's not a lesbian. Kristy McNicol and Tatum O'Neal allow liberties to be taken in *Little Darlings* (1980 C) to prove they're not like that. Phil DONAHUE interviewed four or five men in their twenties and thirties who are 'Male Virgins' (1992 T) and who are determined to remain that way until the right woman comes along.

The Virgin Soldiers (UK 1969 C) Experiences funny, sexy and tragic of a group of National Servicemen in 1960 Singapore.
W: John HOPKINS from the novel by Leslie Thomas; P: Leslie Gilliat and Ned SHERRIN; D: John Dexter; 96 mins.
Very smooth production of what is familiar British fare of the nudge and wink variety. An original touch for the time was the inclusion of two lovers (Wayne SLEEP and Gregory Phillips) whose periods of service overlap so they have to keep signing on for another six months in order to be together. 'That is definitely love!' laughs a mate.

Visconti, Luchino (1906–76) Italian stage and film director, screenwriter and former art director who began with FILM NOIR (*Ossessione* 1942) and neorealism (*La Terra Trema* 1948) then glided into grand historical frescos like *Senso* (1953), *The Leopard* (1963), THE DAMNED (1969) and *Ludwig II* (1972). His smaller films, also exquisitely set and designed, include DEATH IN VENICE (1971), CONVERSATION PIECE (1974) and *The Innocent* (1976). Autobiography: *Visconti: A Film Profile* (in conversation in his villa, 1961 T); *Man of Three Worlds* (1966 T).

The Visiting Hour (UK 1982 R) NURSE and patient face each other across the bed. One is gay, the other doggedly and proudly straight. Both are Welsh. Tensions rise, resentments surface, but Ronnie (Hugh Thomas) always has the upper hand and never lets Thomas (Gerald James) forget it. 'All that fuss about nothing. Put it under the pillow and smoke it in the morning.' Thomas survives his ordeal: 'A hell of a boy ... once you get past the loose wrist and diamanté ... a heart of gold'.
W: William Ingram; D: Enyd Williams; BBC Radio 4 (*The Monday Play*); 75 mins.
CAMP chat and HOMOPHOBIA shaken and stirred together with much vigour but with no very long-lasting effect. Thomas' panic at the thought of Ronnie touching him when his defences are down is amusingly caught: 'I had my fists at the ready in case things started getting out of hand. But when it was all over and yours truly safe and intact in his 'jamas again, do you know what that BUGGER said? "It's for me to decide time and place ... Don't sulk." ' Ronnie is an unflappable professional throughout, tossing off a few personal tidbits ('Strictly CONSCIENTIOUS OBJECTOR and pacifist, that's Ronnie-boy ... never could abide the sight of blood') as he goes about his business with his truculent patient. Florence NIGHTINGALE would be proud.

Vivian/Vivien/Vyvyan Boy's name (from the Latin for 'alive') which since the 1940s has been almost exclusively reserved for girls, having been popularized by the actress Vivien Leigh (christened *Vivian* Mary Hartley). Female versions include:
UK: sleek assistant woman's magazine editor Vivien (Patricia Haines) on *Compact* (1963–4 T); perfect wife and mother Vivienne Cooper (Maggie Fitzgibbon) in *The Newcomers* (1966–8 T); punk artist Viv (Linda Spurrier) in JUBILEE (1977 C) whose studio's walls are black and bare; WPC Viv Martella (Nula Cornwell) in *The Bill* (1987– T).
US: Vivian Trent (Constance Talmadge) in *Uncle Bill* (1914 C); Vivian Truffle (Anita Page), Marie DRESSLER'S daughter in *Reducing* (1931 C); 'cold ... frigid' aviatrix Vivian Banton (Bebe Daniels) known as Vi in *Reaching for the Moon* (1931 C); Vivian Deverse (Ann

Dvorak) in *Three on a Match* (1932 C) who slips down the social scale and lands with a heavy thud; the witch-like Vivian Darkbloom (Marianne Stone), the familiar of creepy Clare Quilty (Peter SELLERS) in *Lolita* (1962 C); Vivian Harmon (Rue McClanahan) in *Maude* (1973–8 T); the lesbian ARTIST Vivienne Moray (Camilla Sparv) in VALLEY OF THE DOLLS (1981 T); newly divorced Vivian Bell (Helen Shaver) who finds the real thing with a young woman in Nevada in DESERT HEARTS (1985 C); Vivian (Julia Roberts), the hooker who is moulded into a 'lady' in *Pretty Woman* (1990 C).

Fictional males with this name have a tendency towards the flyaway and efflorescent:

UK: Vivian Kenway (Rex Harrison) using wealthy women in *The Rake's Progress* (1945 C) and brought to heel by Rikki (Lilli Palmer) ('Vivian' was based on an 'amoral' friend of writer–directors Frank Launder and Sidney Gilliat); Vivian Kennedy, one of Chris ARCHER'S beaux in THE ARCHERS (1953 R); Vyvyan Lacey (Henry Vidon), grand old thespian with grand manners who is a patient in *Emergency – Ward 10* (1960 T); a man sharing a flat with someone called Vivian starts behaving 'a little que-er' in *No, That's Me Over There* (1970 T);Vivian (Clive Francis), aristocratic gangsters' groupie in *Villain* (1971 C): 'Stop flicking ash on my rug!'; Vivian Carson (Michael Gwynn), a topclass interrogator with a devious mind in *Spy Trap* 'Who Among Us?' (1972 T); Harold INNOCENT as the hermaphroditic literary agent in *Vivien the Blockbuster* (1980 R); Vivian Malleson (Aubrey WOODS) supremely spiteful in *The Best of Friends* (1980 T); Charles Vivian (Cavan Kendall), public school-educated TERRORIST, accused of being a 'PONCE' by a colleague in *Blood Money* (1981 T); the grotty, uncontrollable punk Vyvyan (Adrian Edmondson) in *The Young Ones* (1982–4 T) who is agin anything and everything, particularly if it's 'girly'; Viv, the partner of 'Trix', the male agony aunties in *The Grumbleweeds Radio Show* (1985–8 T); five times married Great

Actor Vivian Bancroft (Tony Britton) in *Don't Tell Father* (1992 T), described in the *Radio Times* synopsis as 'conceited, vain, egocentric, insensitive towards others, over-sensitive about his own feelings, and he fancies himself like mad'.

US: Viv Donovan (William Boyd), West Point cadet in *Dress Parade* (1927 C).

The Voice of the Turtle aka *One for the Book* (US 1947 C) Actress Sally (Eleanor Parker) picks up a soldier, Bill (Ronald Reagan), presumably for a ONE NIGHT STAND. They engage in some frisky by-play about the double standards which apply to the male of the species. Commenting from the sidelines is Sally's greatly more experienced friend (Eve Arden).

W: John VAN DRUTEN from his stage play; P: Charles Hoffman; D: Irving Rapper; 103 mins.

Much diluted 1940s sex comedy with some serious things to say about the restrictions imposed on women and how, in wartime situations, the bonds can be loosened somewhat. Eleanor Parker, fey but spunky, is well partnered by Eve Arden as her human razor blade friend. Ronald Reagan does his best to be a bit of a devil (he has had 'lots' of girl-friends), a sensitive soul (he learned to cook 'in Paris') and a fine upstanding all-American soldier-on-leave within the censored confines then prevailing.

Among the overlong film's periodic charms is Bill insisting on cooking scrambled eggs for Sally:

'You shouldn't do that ... It's not a man's thing to do.'
'You'd be surprised how many men are doing it'.

A tea towel round his waist, Bill collects eggs, milk, pepper and salt. 'Now come and learn how to make it properly,' he tells her. They start kissing and the scene cuts as he begins beating the eggs.

The British television version (P/D: Stuart Burge; 8.30–10pm; 27.2.58; BBC; 90 mins) was more or less faithful to the stage piece with Elvi Hale and

Alec MCCOWEN enjoying a brief encounter which can be interpreted as crypto-gay. In the morning, Bill expresses a hope (almost a command) that Sally isn't the kind of girl who has affairs 'promiscuously'. She parries by asking him to define PROMISCUITY, in numerical terms. She herself doesn't think of herself as promiscuous 'yet' (she's had one previous affair). Bill repays Sally's honesty by refusing to discuss his past in any way. She presses on: 'You think it's different for a man?' Bill won't be drawn other than to say that he thinks 'the permissible number' *is* different for a man.

Voices from the Front (US 1991 T) Moving testimony from activists and people living with AIDS, combined with alarming statistics of the accelerating number of deaths. Scenes involving angry protesters storming the National Institute of Health, the American Medical Association, pharmaceutical companies and HIV/AIDS conferences convey the frustrated urgency of the fight.
P/D: Robyn Hutt, Sandra Elgear and David Meieran; 88 mins.
  Fire in the belly, hope in the heart and time running out: human ingenuity in the face of bureaucracy, commerce, public indifference, media manipulation, personal exhaustion and the Reagan–Bush administrations.

Von Praunheim, Rosa [Holger Mischwitzki] (1942–) Described by *Variety* as 'Germany's most commercial underground film-maker', he has remained very much outside the mainstream both of commercial cinema and – until recently – correct gay politics. Intensely personal, fearlessly political, he has directed over 40 films, including shorts in the 1970s, television 'fictions' and a trilogy of AIDS activist films. He took the name 'Rosa' in commemoration of the PINK TRIANGLES worn in Nazi concentration camps by homosexual prisoners.
  Beginning his career in 1967, then becoming assistant to Gregory Markopoulos, Von Praunheim first achieved

prominence – and notoriety – with his scalding documentary IT IS NOT THE HOMOSEXUAL WHO IS PERVERSE BUT THE SOCIETY IN WHICH HE LIVES (1970 C/ T). He remains one of the rawest and most confronting of directors, lighting fires under gay audiences by criticizing their inaction and their complicity in maintaining 'the system'. His 'softer' side is exemplified in two personal portraits of two extraordinary women friends: the actress Lotti Huber in *Affengeil: Life Is Like a Cucumber* (1991) and Charlotte Von Mahlsdorf (Lothar Barfelde), the best known TRANSVESTITE in East Germany in *I Am My Own Wife* (1992).
  C/T: *Army of Lovers or Revolt of the Perverts* (1978); *City of Lost Souls* (1983); *A Virus Has No Morals* (1986: in which he also plays the lead role of an irresponsible sauna owner who contracts HIV/AIDS); *Anita: Dances of Vice* (1989); SILENCE=DEATH (1990); *Positive* (1990: about a group of artists and poets involved in AIDS activism. German television cut the opening scene – a man shooting himself in the anal passage – and one half of Allen GINSBERG'S poem 'Sphincter' which describes the joy and pleasure he receives from being fucked); etc.
  Mark Nash calls Von Praunheim 'an ethnographer of sexual life' (in *Monthly Film Bulletin*, September 1990). In the same article Von Praunheim himself said: 'My films provoke extreme reactions, and I'm rather proud of that. I still feel I have a responsibility to be provocative in my films. It's what I did for the gay movement in the 1970s and I need to remind people now that we can keep on fighting even if the odds seem hopeless ... Most gays are very conservative. They vote for governments that will protect the status quo. To push gays into action you have to confront them. When they saw my films, many gays felt anger and hatred for the first time, though it was directed at me, myself and at the films. But that's the reaction I wanted.'

The Vortex (UK 1960 T) Florence Lancaster (Ann Todd), an ageing beauty with a young lover has to confront her jealousy when her son Nicky (David McCallum) brings his 'boyish' fiancée down for the weekend. A concert pianist, Nicky exhibits all kinds of irrationality until he confesses to his mother that he is a drug addict. The play ends with the two frightened people trying to climb out of the vortex.

W: Noel COWARD from his stage play; P: Harold Clayton; BBCTV; 90 mins.

One of the first plays on British television to deal – from the vantage point of a 1920s Oedipal crisis – with drug addiction. David McCallum, all long blond hair and cadaverous features, took the role Coward had acted on stage (followed by John GIELGUD) and Ivor NOVELLO had played in the 1928 film. Very much a coded homosexual character, Nicky was offset by Pauncefort Quentin known as 'Pawnie' (Noel HOWLETT), 'an elderly maiden gentleman'.

A second production appeared on commercial television four years later (with Margaret Johnston and Nicholas Pennell, with Tony Bateman as Pawnie) and the BBC remounted the play in 1969 with Margaret Leighton, Richard Warwick and Alan MELVILLE. There was a particularly good radio production in 1966 with ravishing performances by Joan Greenwood (raddled mother) and Richard Briers (desperate, almost babbling son), and another (with Elizabeth Sellars and Martin Jarvis) in 1975.

Vosper, Frank (1899–1937) English actor and playwright, originator of Mr DULCIMER on stage: a marbled, resonating presence.

C: début in *Blinkeyes* (1926); head of the French Sûreté in *Rome Express* (1932); the *Prince of Waltzes in Vienna* (1933); the main villain, Ramon Levine in *The Man Who Knew Too Much* (1934);

and nasty again in *Jew Süss* (1934). His final role was in *The Secret of Stamboul* (1936).

vox pop Interviews aiming to broadcast 'the voice of the people' were first regularly carried out in public places on issues, serious and trivial on TONIGHT (1957–64 T). Knee-jerk reactions, waggish off-the-cuff quips, outlandish often rabidly bigoted statements from passers-by became one of television's mainstays (*That's Life* 1975 – ; THE SIX O'CLOCK SHOW 1982–4) etc. The tongue-tied or garrulous interviewees were also the stuff of comedy: *It's a Square World* (1963 T); *The Dick Emery Show* (1968–79 T) with CLARENCE dizzily trying to think of something to say that didn't relate to the male interviewer's body parts.

Homosexuality was confined to the safety of the studio until GAY LIFE dug into the hearts and minds of men and women in the street on the subject of those invisible creatures called lesbians in 1981. The makers of FRAMED YOUTH (1983 V/T) quizzed people on their perceptions of homosexuals, as did the OUT team (1991 T) who ambushed men and women around Piccadilly Circus (in general, the public image was male and effeminate) and also to ask if homosexuals were fit to be parents or guardians of children (in general, this idea was not viewed as a threat or a problem). *Free for All* 'A Legal Beating' (1992 T) asked members of the public: 'Are you a SADOMASOCHIST? A bit of slap and tickle perhaps?'

Irish vox pop (2.11.76):

'Homosexuality – what's that?'
'That's all right for England – but this is IRELAND.'

See also PHONE-INS.

Miss **Wade** Character in Charles Dickens' *Little Dorrit*, played by Sonia Fraser in the 1980 radio production. A misanthropic governess who takes the young girl Tattycoram (Shona Morris) to live with her in Venice, possibly attracted to her because she, too, is illegitimate: 'She had no name as I have no name.' She is very much presented as a stronger older person battening onto a younger, weaker one. A perverse creature who hates people who treat her well or who are deferential to her.

In *Dickens' Women* (1991 R) Miriam MARGOLYES calls Miss Wade 'a lesbian', a person of 'startling modernity' and 'a self-tormenter'. She notes that the novel was written while Dickens was going through the break-up of his marriage, during which process he is revealed as every bit as frozen-hearted and implacable as this character. Miriam Margolyes read a passage in which Miss Wade bitterly recalls her love for a schoolfriend: 'I have the misfortune of not being a fool ... I loved that stupid mite in a passionate way ... I loved her faithfully and one time I went home with her for the holidays ... She tormented my love beyond endurance ... When we were alone in our bedroom at night, I would reproach her with perfect knowledge of her baseness ... I would hold her in my arms till morning, loving her so ... I wanted to hold her in my arms and plunge to the bottom of the river and hold her until after we both were dead.'

(Miss Wade is usually cut from adaptations of *Little Dorrit*, including an earlier radio version in 1959 and the 1987 2-part film.)

Waggoners' Walk (UK 1969–80 R) Three young women living in Belsize Park, near Hampstead, come into contact with people from different age groups, social classes and ethnic backgrounds.
Cr: Richard Imison, Keith Williams, Jill HYEM and others; W: Jill Hyem, Barbara Clegg, Alan Dowson, Johnny Whyte and others; P: Glyn DEARMAN, Anton Gill

and others; weekdays; BBC Radio 2; 15 mins.

The successor to THE DALES – and based on a 1969 radio play called THE ROPEWALK – began partly as a crime story, partly as a belated dip into the Swinging Sixties, only minus sex. It was a disaster. Radically rethought, it metamorphosed into a worthy saga of the travails of modern urban living. Its heroines had to deal, directly or through others, with rape, epilepsy, racism, vasectomy and – between October 1971 and January 1972 – with homosexuality.

One of the subsidiary characters, Colin Bartley (Roger Hammond), was a resting actor in whose antique shop Barbara Watling (Patricia Gallimore) works. Colin meets a sexy young pianist, Kit (Roy North) who goes to live with him. Charming, unscrupulous Kit is BISEXUAL and blithely pays court to Barbara, assuring her that Colin means nothing to him. A game of musical flats ensues with Kit trotting back and forth, finally decamping to the Riviera and leaving Colin presumably more cynical than before – and of no further use to the day-to-day happenings. He was never heard of again.

Although the serial was set in an area where many young single people lived, no other gay male character raised his head for eight years, and the only lesbian was somebody's sister's flatmate in Sussex, mentioned but not characterized. When somebody stopped visiting Sussex, the lesbian like Colin dematerialized.

In 1979 Rob PENGELLY (Mike Grady, later Michael Mundell) arrived. He was a nice guy who worked in a local restaurant. He loved – unrequitedly – his flatmate Dickon, a local reporter. He then became friendly with a young boy, Jeremy Tyson. This association (platonic) was used by Jeremy's father in a nasty custody battle with his wife.

Interviewed by GAY NEWS early in 1980, Jill Hyem – one of the serial's writers and its script editor – said that Rob's character would develop further. A 'stable' relationship was in the works.

With a 'fashion designer'. Who was 'a jet setter, slightly camp'. They had already met but nothing had happened. The relationship was 'a fairly slow burner'. A bit too slow because, at the end of 1980, to the surprise of its production team *Waggoners' Walk* was cancelled. Although it had chalked up 2,824 episodes, it had failed to attract the envisaged 4 million listeners. Rob never did get his stable relationship, or sex of any kind, with anybody.

waiters Serving food and drink with a special sparkle is the alluring Spaniard in DARLING (1965 C) as he shares his favours between heroine and her male photographer friend; Allan Warren letting out a few saucy squeaks in *Catch Me a Spy!* (1971 C); John Bull making the lesbians feel very welcome in NOW SHE LAUGHS, NOW SHE CRIES (1975 R); a Tunisian man is shared by Fox and his lover while on holiday in FOX AND HIS FRIENDS (1975 C); Fred (Dino Schofield), a regular at *Archie Bunker's Place* (1979–83 T); Bernard Harrison, the dead man in THE GENTLE TOUCH 'Blade' (1980 T), worked at a gay restaurant, Chez Hugo; two ageing gossips (Michael Medwin and Fulton Mackay) in *Sleepwalker* (1984 C); SHANE, the unheard but discussed mainstay of Nelson's winebar in THE ARCHERS (1986– R); Janviet (Jacques Lussier) caught up in a security van robbery with his lover in *Pouvoir Intime* (1986 C); Conan McCarthy who squares up to homophobic customers in *André's Mother* (1990 T); the moustached, pony-tailed cruiser in LONGTIME COMPANION (1990 C); Vin Salad (Paul Firth) in *Anglo-Saxon Attitudes* (1992 T); etc.

Waiting for Godot Samuel Beckett's funny, elegant, melancholic, despairing homoemotional odyssey of two tramps. A profound anatomy of marriage, of exploitation, of nihilism and of the human condition. Like so many people Vladimir and Estragon are frightened of protest or commitment, bored with each other yet lost apart:

Estragon: 'Don't touch me. Don't question me. Don't speak to me. Stay with me.'
Vladimir: 'I missed you ... and at the same time I was happy. Isn't that a queer thing?'

This work, one of the greatest in 20th-century theatre, is open to Christian, atheistic, Communist and absurdist interpretations. The two men can be viewed as holy fools, lovers, representatives of sheeplike conformity, Christ and a disciple. And Godot as any number of mystical beings, distant promises of a better future or God Almighty. The genius of Beckett ensures that the motivations and explanations remain murky and contradictory while casting erratic and fascinating light on the follies of human existence. Two separate radio productions were transmitted within two years (1960 and 1962; Peter WOODTHORPE was a memorable Estragon in the latter) and it was performed on television in 1961. There was a Canadian television version in 1987 and a Cuban film interpretation called *Sirs* in 1991.

The Waiting Room (UK 1971 T) A man (David COOK) and a woman (Barbara Leigh-Hunt) sit in a hospital waiting-room. He has lost his lover. She has lost her husband. They talk and gradually discover that the man they mourn was common to both.
W: John BOWEN; P: Innes LLOYD; D: Robert Knights; BBC2; 29.3.71; (THIRTY MINUTE THEATRE).
The nature of love seen from two very different but interlinked points of view. A typically astute, stinging piece of work from John Bowen. No palliatives here. No sentimentality. Instead, bleakness and poignancy mixed with salty observation.
The young man didn't love but *liked* the dead man. He felt comfortable in his company, enjoyed talking to him, appreciated his attention and generosity. The dead man's attraction to him was equal to the feeling he had for his wife: 'both failures which he liked'. There's a crisp speech about the melting away of supposedly mutual friends after a death or the

end of an affair: 'They weren't rude but they were always busy. Except for one or two of the older ones and all they wanted was ...'

On neutral ground, linked by loss, the couple can give each other some kind of support. The ending is intriguingly inconclusive. After jointly identifying the body, they walk away, possibly separately, possibly not.

Wakeling, Howard (194?–) English television and radio playwright, one of the founders of the Gay Liberation Front's street theatre troupe in the early 1970s. *The Disappearance of Harry* (1981 T); *Sand* (1982 R); *Men!* (1984 R); *Troubled by the Scenery* (1986 R); *My Generation* (of 1964 ... and what happened to them, 1988 R); A BIT OF BERLIN (1992 R); etc.

In an interview in *Gay Times* (September 1992) Wakeling said: 'The days of having piss-pots emptied over my head may be over, but the point about street theatre was that we performed on the streets, or the tube, outside law courts ... behind enemy lines. In a much subtler way, I suppose, I'm still doing that – trying to stir up Joe Public's grey matter. I'm not into entertaining the troops or preaching to the converted which is what most gay theatre seems to be about these days.'

Walbrook, Anton [Adolf Wohlbruck] (1900–68) Austrian – later naturalized British – film actor of polish, arrogance, charm and occasional venom who became a popular star in Britain after *Victoria the Great* and gained a new lustre in the 1950s following his performance as the worldly master of ceremonies in *La Ronde* (his song 'La Ronde de l'Amour' reaching the hit parade).

Among his showier roles: the suspicious admirer in *Viktor und Viktoria* (1933: also in the French version *Georges et Georgette*); *The Student of Prague* (1935 C); Prince Albert in *Victoria the Great and Sixty Glorious Years* (1937/8); the sadistic jewels-obsessed husband in the British version of *Gaslight* (1940); the Polish flyer and pianist

in *Dangerous Moonlight* (1941); the religious sect leader in *49th Parallel* (1941); Theo Kretschmar-Sculdorff, the gentle German in *The Life and Death of Colonel Blimp* (1943); the ballet impresario Lermontev based on DIAGHILEV in *The Red Shoes* (1948); the ruthless guardsman in *The Queen of Spades* (1949); Johann Strauss the Elder in *Wien Tanz* (1951); a nobleman in *Lola Montes* (1955); Bishop Cauchon in *Saint Joan* (1957); Esterhazy in *I Accuse* (1958).

'We've got to play for maturity and experience ... Just think of yourself as Anton Walbrook and you'll be alright,' Sid JAMES to Tony Hancock in HANCOCK'S HALF HOUR 'The Inheritance' (1955 R).

Wales Homosexual life seen only fitfully: homicidal, immature Danny in *Night Must Fall* (1937 C; 1964 C etc); the young brother in *The Last Days of Dolwyn* (1949 C); *The Bachelor Brothers* (1960 T) who adopt a son; Vivian's lover (Gerard Murphy) in *The Best of Friends* (1980 T); the nurse (Hugh Thomas) in THE VISITING HOUR (1982 R); the LADIES OF LLANGOLLEN in *When Shall We Be Quite Alone?* (1984 R); the two women in *In Two Minds* (1987 T); the twins in *On the Black Hill* (1987 R; 1987 C); the lover of the dying man in *Two Weeks with the Queen* (1993 T). The importance of gay and lesbian support during the 1984 miners' strike was revealed in *Dancing in Dulais* (1985 V), and a Welsh gay man, Stephen Burn forcefully took bigotry to task in OPEN SPACE 'Straight and Narrow-Minded' (1988 T).

walk Tom (John Kerr) is instructed by his room-mate (Darryl Hickman) to walk 'properly' (like a man) in TEA AND SYMPATHY (1956 C). But Tom decides it is too late to change his high instepping. A similar situation occurred in a French summer camp in which the bully (Patrick Dewaere) teaches a young TRANSVESTITE (Patrick Bauchitey) THE BEST WAY TO WALK (1975 C) and turns him towards heterosexual yuppiedom.

Renato (Ugo Tognazzi) gives up on ALBIN (Michael (Serrault) in LA CAGE AUX FOLLES (1978 C): his John WAYNE walk is camper than his normal small-steps gracefulness. The only effect his swaying swagger has is to rouse a passer-by to brusquely call out: 'Hey, pedé!'

The taking of tiny steps and the prominence of the buttocks in the locomotion is favoured by Mr HUMPHRIES (John INMAN) in ARE YOU BEING SERVED? (1973–84 T). Difficult then for him to be a macho Aussie, but he gives it a go in 'Undesirable Alien' (1980).

Diagrammatic mincing can also be a rebuke to racists. Bill (Rudolph Walker) starts flouncing and fluttering in retaliation when Eddie (Jack Smethurst) abuses him in *Love Thy Neighbour* (1973 C).

The idea that gays 'give themselves away' by their walk was given credence in THE DETECTIVE (1968 C): 'There was something about the way he walked' is how the murderer knew that Teddy was gay.

Walk On The Wild Side A deadpan homage to transvestism and prostitution dedicated by its composer–interpreter Lou Reed – semi-ironically – to various members of Andy WARHOL's band of players including Holly Woodlawn, Jackie Curtis, Candy Darling and Joe DALLESANDRO. It entered the US Top 40 in March 1973 and rose to no. 16. In Britain, it marked the first time the BBC had – presumably unconsciously – given airplay to a song which included the line 'She never lost her head when giving head'.

Marky Mark and the Funky Bunch performed 'Walk' on *Red Hot + Dance* (1991 T). It was one of the hits chosen to represent its year in a celebration of the 1970s, *From Loon Pants to Safety Pins* 'All the Boys and Girls' (1992 R: segueing into an organ and trumpet fanfare for the wedding of Princess Anne), while it was the subject of an ARENA 'Tales of Rock 'n' Roll' special (1993 T).

The title may have originated with Nelson Algren's 1950s novel A WALK ON THE WILD SIDE, which was filmed in 1962. The raunchy invitation to 'take a walk on the wild side' was issued to Tom (Nick Nolte) by a male party guest in THE PRINCE OF TIDES (1991 C).

Walpole, Sir Hugh (1884–1941) New Zealand-born novelist (*The Herries Chronicles*) and Hollywood screenwriter (DAVID COPPERFIELD 1935) whose plots sometimes involved passionate jealous relationships between a younger and an older man – or between women – ending in violence.

C: *Vanessa: Her Love Story* (1935: from his novel 'Vanessa'); *Mr Perrin and Mr Trail* (1948). The son of a bishop, he played the vicar in *David Copperfield* as well as adapting the novel.

R: *What's Wrong with the Theatre* (1930: talk); *The Bachelors* (1950); THE OLD LADIES (1975).

T: *Thriller 'Flowers of Evil'* (1961); *The Liars* (1966: anthology series of short stories by Oscar WILDE, SAKI and Walpole); *The Old Ladies* (1967).

Biography: *On Meeting Hugh Walpole* (1958 R: talk by Sewell Stokes).

Wandrin' Star Lovers of Alan J. Lerner and Frederic Loewe musical *Paint Your Wagon* doubtless thought that no more harm could befall this homespun Western ballad after Lee Marvin had his gruff way with it in the 1970 film. But they hadn't reckoned with tenderfoot Julian CLARY who, in May 1990, unleashed his even slower, more out of tune regurgitation. For diehard Clary fans there was some typical innuendo sandwiched between lyrics: 'I wish I hadn't started this low down (but I'm always saying that)' and 'I'll just clear my passages.' However, played on BBC Radio 1 on a Sunday afternoon in June, it was no more shocking – except to lovers of melody and the human voice – than what was playing at almost the same time on Radio 2: the Cliff Adams Singers' rendition of 'In The Strawberry Patch With Sally'.

Julian unburdened himself of 'Wandrin' Star' in front of a 'live' audience in

British Satellite Broadcasting (BSB)'s *The Happening* in 1990 which, owing to that network's demise, eventually surfaced a year later on Channel 4. (Time had not improved it.)

Wanted: Single Gentleman (UK 1967 T) Arthur (John STRATTON) and Basil (Alan Rowe) live in an attic flat in Notting Hill Gate. Theirs is a tense household: good-natured Arthur is a doormat upon which sadistic Basil continually wipes his feet. Both are in their thirties and show little sign of maturing, although marriage is always on the cards in the shape of the motherly 'girlfriend' they share, Mabel (Eileen Atkins). Answering the boys' advert for a lodger is a suave character (Edward Fox) who is gradually revealed as the cuckoo who fouls their nest with some much needed reality.
W: James Broom Lynne from his stage play *The Trigon*; P: Irene Shubik; D: John Gorrie; 18.10.67; BBC1 THE WEDNESDAY PLAY; 75 mins.

All is scratchy boredom and impotence between grouch 'hubby' and dishrag 'wife', umpired by their chattering female friend (and hopeful spouse) until the shattering arrival of the 'single gentleman.' A classic plot, skilfully negotiated by the four actors – especially John Stratton, plumply dreaming of the good old days in the scouts. No one mentions the word 'QUEER', but it is apt for every aspect of the production.

war The two world wars have thrown up numerous stories of manly devotion in battle, loving courage in captivity, tender comradeship on the home front, sexual frolics during leave and other situations during those extraordinary periods which were seen by many as the best and the worst of times. Male bondings of different levels of intensity in JOURNEY'S END (1930 C; 1938 T; etc: officers and men keeping their pride and some passion under constant fire); THE INTERNED (1953 R: love and frustration among 'privileged' prisoners of war); *The Tent* (1960 R: a senior officer tries to seduce a private); *King and Country*

(1964 C: pity grows into a kind of love during a court martial in the trenches); *Enemy* (1974 T: German and British soldiers transcend hatred and fall in love); THE NAKED CIVIL SERVANT (1975 T: Quentin CRISP finding all manner of willing partners during the blackout); *From Here to Eternity* (1978 T: a soldier makes extra money by 'rolling queers'); PEARL (1979 T: a sensitive soldier and his mate during Pearl Harbour); A MOMENT IN TIME (1979 T: death claims a pilot's lover during the Battle of Britain); WE WERE ONE MAN (1979 C: French man and German deserter form an alliance); HOUSE ON THE HILL 'Something for the Boys' (1981 T: Anglo-American ties strengthened on the dance floor and in bed); NOT ABOUT HEROES (1983 R: Wilfred OWEN and Siegfried SASSOON discovering mutual interests in a military hospital); NOVEMBER MOON (1984 C: a woman hides her Jewish lover throughout the Second World War); SWING SHIFT (1984 C: mutual support and – in the director's cut but not the released 'Goldie Hawn version' – a clearly defined affection between two of the women working on the armament factory floor).
Personal testaments of men and women rounded up during the pre-war period in Nazi Germany in DESIRE (1989 C/T); women working for victory in *The Life and Times of Rosie the Riveter* (1980 C); British and American Second World War tales in BEFORE STONEWALL (1984 C/T) and COMRADES IN ARMS (1990 C/T).

Ward, Michael (1915–) English actor. Very tall, very thin player of gossamer-accented minor functionaries, conceited and servile ('Madam has such excellent taste!'), and sundry boneless morsels in scores of films of the 1950s and 1960s, including a number of CARRY ONS and Norman Wisdom comedies. On television he managed to play one or two slightly more substantial parts such as the queer son whose inheritance goes to a simple country girl (Susannah YORK) who enchants his father in *The Richest Man in the World* (1960).

C: Tommy Trafford in *An Ideal Husband* (1947: cut from most existing prints); the tour guide in *Send for Paul Temple* (1947); Elvin in *Sleeping Car to Trieste* (1948 C: almost his only 'straight' role – as an ornithologist, or is he?); a couturier in *Saraband for Dead Lovers* (1948); a servant in *The First Gentleman* (1948: he had played Prince William in the stage version); an ARTIST in *Once a Jolly Swagman* (1948: 'darling, the times are turning out to be deliciously devastating,' he says to a fellow party guest while eyeing up Dirk BOGARDE); the pianist in *Trottie True* (1949); a valet in *High Jinks in Society* (1949); BBC announcer in *Helter Skelter* (1949); Armand in *The Queen of Spades* (1949); Pierre in *Stop Press Girl* (1950); *Seven Days to Noon* (1950); the British consul's private secretary (moustached with sloping walk) in *So Long at the Fair* (1950); a photographer in *Tony Draws a Horse* (1950); the lead role as Lord Gerald in a B picture *What the Butler Saw* (1950); a bank clerk in *Trio* 'The Verger' (1950 C); a salesman in *No Trace* (1950); a diplomat in *High Treason* (1950); *Street Corner* (1953); a floorwalker in *Trouble in Store* (1953); *Private's Progress* (1955); a 'BOHEMIAN' in *Josephine and Men* (1955); Maurice in *Up in the World* (1956); film star's dress designer in *The Intimate Stranger* (1956); a photographer in *Brothers-In-Law* (1957); Cranley, jewellery salesman in *Just My Luck* (1957); head waiter in *The Rough and the Smooth* (1959): sent up by William Bendix, 'Maybe you're not his type,' he chortles to the hero; *I'm All Right Jack* (1959 C); Dr Flower, a nervous cohort of Irene Handl in *Doctor in Love* (1960); *Carry On Regardless* (1961); James Robertson Justice's clerk in *A Pair of Briefs* (1962); *Carry On Cabby* (1963); *Father Came Too* (1963); *Doctor in Distress* (1963); *Carry On Spying* (1964); *Carry On Cleo* (1964); *Carry On Screaming* (1966); aristocrat Henri in *Don't Lose Your Head* (1967); *Man About the House* (1973: with Melvyn HAYES as his boyfriend); *Revenge of the Pink Panther* (1978); a photographer in *Ouch!* (1978); etc.

R: Cowardian playwright Beverly Carlton in *The Man Who Came to Dinner* (repeating his stage role); *Death of Angels* (1942); *Silence in Heaven* (1949); etc.

T: courtiers in *Henry IV* and *The Queen's Maria* (1948); Gallant in *Vestreen* (1949); Regency dandy Ned Pym in *Milestones* (1951); Mr Willett in DIXON OF DOCK GREEN (1956, episode 5: a bespectacled youth worker in a sports coat and flannels, cravenly ineffectual and by inference responsible for juvenile crime – 'I've shouted at them till I'm blue in the face. I've been giving them play readings and discussions and quizzes ... Boxing? Dear me!'); Clarence Marsh in *The Grove Family* 'Leaving Home' (1956); shop assistant in *Dick and the Duchess* 'The Bank Robbery' (1958); third billed as Mr Cobb in *Please Murder Me* (1958: from Gore VIDAL's *The Judgement of Paris*); a man eating lunch in *Hancock's Half Hour* 'The Economy Drive' (1959); Edward Barranca in *The Richest Man in the World* (1960); Dominic Boyd in *My Representative* (1960); on the same day, an unnamed role in *Our House* 'To Please Louise' (1960); *Saki* (1962); *Zero One* (1962); in *Lord Raingo* (1966); one of a quartet of chatterbox queens in THE FABULOUS FRUMP (1969); Adrian in *The Morecambe and Wise Show* (1970); etc.

Warhol, Andy [Andrew Warhola Jr] (1930–87) American artist, filmmaker, entrepreneur, social commentator and cultural icon. Revered as a genius, bridging surrealism and pop art and bearing an extraordinary gift for commercial self-mockery and sharp realism. Reviled as empty and overhyped, an exploiter of beautiful 'nobodies' involved in the pop and drug culture, a mediocre miniaturist.

As a film-maker he ploughed profits from sales of his art works into an extraordinary string of seemingly unstructured, sexually adventurous movies (some barely moving) such as *Blow Job* (1963), *Vinyl* (1965), the two-screen *The Chelsea Girls* (1966), and the relatively more sophisticated and narratively coherent MY HUSTLER (1965). He then 'collaborated' with Paul Morrissey on more mainstream efforts such as LONE-SOME COWBOYS (1968) and FLESH (1968). Warhol's influence has been noted in the works of such dissimilar people as Wim Wenders, Chantal Aker-man, Jacques Rivette, Rainer Werner FASSBINDER, Barbet Schroeder and John WATERS. Warhol himself drew on the rough techniques and camp references of Kenneth Anger and Jack Smith.

C: 1963–4: *Haircut*; *Blow Job*; *Couch*; *Harlot*; *Empire State*; *Sleep*; *13 Most Beautiful Boys*; *Taylor Mead's Ass*; *Bitch*; *Camp*; *The Closet*; *Andy Warhol Films Jack Smith Filming 'Normal Love'*; *Tarzan and Jane's Regained, Sort Of*; 1964–6: *Bike Boy*; *Kitchen*; *50 Fantasies and 50 Personalities*; etc; *Trash* (1970); *Andy Warhol's Bad* (1971); *Heat* (1972); *Andy Warhol's Dracula* (1974); *Andy Warhol's Frankenstein* (1974); etc. He played him-self in *The Driver's Seat* (1974) and was portrayed by an actor in *The Doors* (1991). (River Phoenix has been sug-gested to play Warhol in a biography due to be directed by Gus Van Sant, 1993–4.)

T: MONITOR 'Susan Sontag' (1964: she visits 'The Factory' to interview him but he's not there); *Painters Painting* (1972); *Warhol* (1973): initially the subject of a British court injunction, it was watched by over 7 million viewers); OMNIBUS 'Andy Warhol – But the People Are Beautiful' (1973: a Warhol exhibition with comments from 'the beautiful people'); ARENA 'The Chelsea Hotel' (1981); *Songs for Drella* (1990); ARENA 'Tales of Rock 'n' Roll: "Walk on the Wild Side"' (1993); *The Late Show* 'The War over Warhol' (1993: the fight over the inheritance). He played himself in a 1983 episode of *The Love Boat*.

R: KALEIDOSCOPE 'Famous for 15 Minutes' (1987: 'How profound was his art? How great was his influence? How long will his reputation endure?' – syn-opsis); *Review* 'Andy Warhol – At Home' (1988: the auction of his pos-sessions by Sothebys in New York).

warnings When ROPE was broadcast in 1932, not only did the announcer make

it clear beforehand that the events about to unfold could be disturbing to people of a nervous disposition, but two weeks earlier there was a special talk about the play and its contents.

BBC television regularly put out spoken and written warnings during the 1950s to alert viewers to subject matter that was violent or of an 'adult' nature, eg *The Quatermass* serials. In the 1960s and 1970s these red alerts were regu-larly broadcast before British documen-taries, feature films and plays revolving around homosexual 'acts'. John Ches-terman in his ACCESS programme 'Offensive to Some' (1973 R) described these written and spoken notifications of 'material likely to cause offense to some viewers' as being deeply insulting to gays and lesbians in the audience.

In America ALL IN THE FAMILY went out for six weeks with a warning from a nervous CBS: 'The programme you are about to see is *All in the Family* ... it seeks to throw a humorous spotlight on our frailties, prejudices and concerns. By making this a source of comedy, we hope to show ... just how absurd they are.' Commented producer Norman LEAR on the 21st anniversary pro-gramme: 'They needn't have worried – nobody watched. It was only discovered in summer reruns.' 'Due to subject matter, parental discretion is advised' was flashed repeatedly by ABC after advertising breaks during the screening of the lesbian courtroom drama A QUESTION OF LOVE in 1978.

In Britain THAMES worded its moral directive more plainly before the bisex-ual drama FACING THE SUN went on air (at 9pm) in 1980: 'The play deals with relationships between men and women and men and men.'

When the BBC Schools play TWO OF US was issued to teachers for classroom showing and discussion in 1988, the videotape was accompanied by four tight ribbons of moral red tape: a child psy-chologist's introduction, an outline of the law in relation to homosexuality, the Judaeo-Christian point of view, and this proviso: 'The 1986 Education Act makes the governors of each school responsible for its sex education policy. It is therefore necessary to consult your headteacher before using this programme with pupils.'

For its late-night viewers in January 1993, BBC2 provided EDWARD II with a forewarning that Derek JARMAN's film contained 'Strong language and the depiction of male homosexuality'. However, there was no mention of the stabbings and extremely realistic piercing of someone's jugular vein.

A month later, the BBC's equivalent in Australia showed the lesbian and gay documentary *Feed Them to the Cannibals* at 8.30pm with simulations of fellatio and cunnilingus without any warning; unlike the programme that followed at 9.30pm: part 3 of the all-heterosexual *The Camomile Lawn*, which was preceded by a stern mention of 'Strong sex scenes ... Adult viewing only'.

With the prevalence of videotaping and the distinct possibility that children will be exposed to material transmitted after they are in bed, the BBC pastes warning notices over a wide assortment of its programmes, including the 1992 OPEN SPACE programme 'Bi' made by the London Bisexual Group 'whose members openly discuss their sexuality'. The documentary went out at 11.20pm.

washing up A rarity: a man with his arms in soapy water or wielding a tea towel. In America: Andy Hardy (Mickey Rooney) and Dad (Lewis Stone) in *Judge Hardy's Son* (1939 C) and Franklin PANGBORN washing up while Johnny Weismuller dries in *Stage Door Canteen* (1943 C). A hint that one of the delinquent boys in *The Lawless* aka *The Dividing Line* (1949 C) may help with the washing-up (he has 'dishrag hands') is viewed as an insult and a call to arms.

When the American captain (Charles Drake) offers to help Barbara (Jean Simmons) with the dishes in the wartime romantic drama *Until They Sail* (1957 C), she is horrified: 'That's woman's work!' He retaliates: 'Is it some sort of crime for a man to wash dishes?' But she remains firm on the subject: 'Father would never have done it.' The

soldier has, it seems, ulterior motives for standing by the sink. He wants to get to know Barbara's sister Joan Fontaine – who does allow him near a tea towel. Later, she becomes pregnant and he is killed in action.

Ted WILLIS took pains to show men doing some women's work, whenever possible. Peter Byrne helped his screen wife Billie Whitelaw in THE PATTERN OF MARRIAGE (1954 T) and again, when they were cast as Andy Crawford and Mary Dixon, in the first series of DIXON OF DOCK GREEN a year later. Philip HOPE-WALLACE commented in the *Listener* (14.7.55): 'Mary, being a sensible girl, clearly means to begin as she intends to go on. The males are made to help with the washing-up. On this vital subject alone, Ted Willis, the co-author, no less than the producer Douglas Moodie who kept us hard at it at the sink – with roller towel well to the fore – obviously knows the way round the great heart of the viewing public.'

As a male–female ritual it remains unusual, even in today's equal opportunity television households. One sighting was William (Anton Rodgers) sloshing around in the suds as his wife Hester (Julia McKenzie) dries in *French Fields* (1989 T), but he is wearing SUEDE SHOES. Another sighting was Danny (Sam Jephcott) drying while Michelle (Susan Tully) washes in EASTENDERS (1990 T) during a discussion on the true identity of baby Stephen's father; a few weeks later – prior to telling family and friends that they are leaving Albert Square – it is she who is holding the towel while he's doing the messy part of the operation.

Benito Alessi (George Spartels) and his son Rick (Dan Falzon) do their chores together while discussing Rick's date with someone called Debbie and Bennie's new car business in NEIGHBOURS (1992 T: a thoroughly natural and pleasing scene, although immediately before the father has been shown listening to Beethoven).

The teenage son in the FAIRY LIQUID advert (1990) is forced to wash up because Dad's asleep and Mum's out. A chunky lad, he wears no apron or gloves and describes work as 'recycling dishes', and quotes his mother: 'It's kind to hands.'

Among same-sex couples: Karen (Audrey Hepburn) and Martha (Shirley MacLaine) in THE CHILDREN'S HOUR/ THE LOUDEST WHISPER (1961 C); Harry Moon (Derek Thompson) in ROCK FOL- LIES OF '77 (1977 T) tells someone that his relationship with Ken Church (Denis Lawson) works all right: 'I wash, he dries'; Per (Dai Bradley) and Ralph (Philip SAYER) wash up happily and noisily together in TWO PEOPLE 'The Trouble with a Kitten' (1979 T) while thrashing out the problem of the runaway boy and girl to whom they have given sanctuary; Jean and Mathieu discuss the latter's young son over the kitchen sink in THE HEART EXPOSED (1986 C/T); BARRY'S dirty dishes cause a rift between him and Colin in a 1987 episode of *EastEnders*; Ruby Lucas, the partner of Tiny Davis in TINY AND RUBY – HELL DIVIN' WOMEN (1988 C/T), is very particular about her dishes and launches into an impassioned speech about 'washing up as I go'.

'What do you mean "the kind of man who does the dishes"? You won't find any of *them* on Albert Square,' Pat (Pam ST CLEMENT to Cindy (Michelle Collins) in *EastEnders* (1988).

'I've always done it,' Nelson GABRIEL (Jack May) in THE ARCHERS (1990 R).

See also COOKING; IRONING.

Waters, John (1946–) American film-maker, for many years dedicated to the uproariously seamy side of suburban living in films mostly starring DIVINE: *Roman Candles* (1964); *Mondo Trasho* (1969); *Multiple Maniacs* (1970); *Pink Flamingos* (1972); *Female Trouble* (1974); *Polyester* (1981); etc. Now in the teen mainstream with *Hairspray* (1988); *Cry-Baby* (1990); *Serial Mom* (1993). Appeared in *Something Wild* (1986 C); *Homer and Eddie* (1990 C). Autobiography: *The Incredibly Strange Film Show* 'The Pope of Trash' (1988 T).

Lou **Waters** Character played by Bran-

don Maggart in BROTHERS (1984–7 T). A card-carrying HOMOPHOBE who has to cope with the deviant sexuality of his younger brother, Cliff (Paul Regina). A loud-mouthed construction site fore-man 'with the sensibility of a landfill', Lou goes through all the stages of grieving for the 'loss' of his baby brother. Anger, disbelief, denial, rage, more rage, despair and total bewilderment.

He tries to help Cliff by taking him to an organization which 'helps normal guys like himself to stop messing around like sissified grasshoppers.' He even leads on a Russian who is using Cliff to gain political asylum. The experience is devastating: 'The Commie is a HOMO. He tries to go where no man has ever gone before ... He asked me to be his *bitch* ... it's like my whole manhood has been cast in doubt.'

Lou's greatest torture is being bested by Cliff's effulgent friend, Donald MALTBY (Philip Charles Mackenzie). The latter's blithe indifference to Lou's revolting misconceptions and offensive language, and Donald's enjoyment of being himself, cause Lou many a sleep-less night. Negativity is always more fun than wholesomeness in sitcoms. One of the ironies in Lou's character – so obsessed with other people's sex lives – is his own absence of bedroom excite-ments. He's been married (to Flo) for years and is 'great at faking orgasms'.

Watney, Simon (194?–) English art historian, journalist, AIDS activist, author of *Policing Desire* etc. Numerous television appearances: GAY LIFE (1981); OUT ON TUESDAY; OUT; WITHOUT WALLS 'Dark Horses: D. H. LAWRENCE' (1992) and 'Dark Horses: Michelangelo – Bound by Beauty' (1992); etc.

Watson, Bobby aka 'Bobby' Watson and Bobbie Watson [Robert Watson Knucher] (1888–1965) American actor who began as a Shubert juvenile in Broadway shows, then played flouncy roles in films until the early 1940s when he achieved his greatest fame: impersonating Adolf Hitler.

C: Hofer in *That Royle Girl* (1926);

second billed as Benny, the male half of a ballroom adagio team in *Syncopation* (1929); *Moonlight and Pretzels* (1933); a hotel valet in *The Countess of Monte Carlo* (1934); Lawrence in *Wine, Women and Song* (1934); *Mary of Scotland* (1936); Mugsy in *Adventurous Blonde* (1937); *The Awful Truth* (1937); *In Old Chicago* (1938); *Boys Town* (1938); *That Nazi Nuisance* (1942); *The Devil with Hitler* (1942); *Hitler – Dead or Alive* (1943); *The Hitler Gang* (1944); *The Big Clock* (1948); *The Paleface* (1948); *Singin' in the Rain* (1952); THEATRE DRESSER in *The Band Wagon* (1953); Hitler in *The Story of Mankind* (1957).

Wattis, Richard (1912–75) English actor. Bald, owlish, steely-eyed, condescending bastion of neurotic authority who, although prominent in over 100 films, was best known as Eric and Hattie's snooty overseeing next-door neighbour in *Sykes* ... One of his few meaty 'straight' roles was that of the sympathetic embassy official, Peter Northbrook in *The Prince and the Showgirl* (1957: he had also played it on stage four years earlier). His last television appearance – as one of a ménage (the others were Mona Washbourne and Freddie Jones) in Rhys Adrian's *Tea at Four* – was transmitted on 4 February 1975, three days after his death, aged 62, as a result of suffering a heart attack while dining with friends in a restaurant.

C: tutor in *A Yank at Oxford* (1938); teacher Arnold Billings in *The Happiest Days of Our Lives* (1950); film casting director in *Lady Godiva Rides Again* (1951); Seton in THE IMPORTANCE OF BEING EARNEST (1952); schoolmaster in *The Intruder* (1953); one of the sons-in-law in *Hobson's Choice* (1954); as the Department of Education's harassed Manton-Bassett in *The Belles of St Trinians* (1954; also played role in *Blue Murder at St Trinians* and *The Great St Trinians Train Robbery*); one of the escapees in *The Colditz Story* (1954); *I am a Camera* (1955); Controller of (BBC) Television in *Simon and Laura* (1955); an anaesthetist in *Eyewitness* (1955); Harold in *It's a Wonderful World* (1956);

manager of the London Palladium in *The Man Who Knew Too Much* (1956); Mr Christopher in *The Crowded Day* (1956); *A Touch of the Sun* (1956); lingerie clerk in *The Iron Petticoat* (1956); 4th billed as Peter Fox in *The Abominable Snowman* (1957); doctor in *The Green Man* (1957); travel agent in *The Inn of the Sixth Happiness* (1958); Dr Chatterway in *Follow a Star* (1959); Harding-Pratt, Ian Carmichael's political agent in *Left, Right and Centre*; *Follow That Horse* (1960); Wagstaff in *Nearly a Nasty Accident* (1961); *Play It Cool* (1962); director of Heathrow VIP liaison in *The VIPs* (1963); Cobley in *Carry On Spying* (1964); *The Amorous Adventures of Moll Flanders* (1965); *Up Jumped a Swagman* (1965); scientist's assistant in *Wonderwall* (1968); the wine shop owner in *Games That People Play* (1971); *Coppers End* (1971); 'rancid old queen' (*Films and Filming*) Elroy, secretary to a witch (Ava Gardner) in *The Devil's Widow* (made 1971, released 1977); *Diamonds on Wheels* (1973); *Hot Property* (1973); *That's Your Funeral* (1973); *Take Me High* (1974); *Confessions of a Window Cleaner* (1975).

R: Simon Paul in *Double Bedlam* (1946); DESERT ISLAND DISCS (1964).

T: dancing the TANGO with Marjorie Stewart on LEISURE AND PLEASURE (1953); hotel manager in HANCOCK'S HALF HOUR 'The Alpine Holiday' (1957); Peter Jamison in *Dick and the Duchess* (1958–9); Old Vic Theatre manager in *Hancock* 'The Knighthood' (1959); Hardy in *Danger Man* 'The Sisters' with Mai Zetterling and Barbara Murray (1960) and 'The Lonely Chair' (1960); diplomat Richard Greatham in *Hay Fever* with Edith Evans (1960); George Ramsay, one of two bachelor brothers (the other was Charles GRAY) in *The Ant and the Grasshopper* (1960); Mr Brown in *Sykes* ... (1960); *Ladies and Gentle-men* (1960); panellist (with Katie Boyle) on *Juke Box Jury* (1965); *The Prisoner* 'The Chimes of Big Ben' (1968); *The Liberace Show* (1969: as the great man's valet).

'I suppose I do have an understanding of this particular sort of personality. I really don't think it's me. At least I hope not. I find very conventional people rather boring and lifeless.' (Wattis commenting on playing 'uptight neurotics' in a TV TIMES interview, May 1960).

'He's been a godfather five times. He's never wanted to get married himself: "It would probably take eight psychiatrists to sort out why"' (RADIO TIMES interview, 27.1.72).

Waugh, Auberon (1939–) English satirical novelist (*The Foxglove Saga*), broadcaster and journalist (long-time contributor to *Private Eye*). Quite contrary, fearless harrier of things sensitive and POLITICALLY CORRECT, prodder and kicker of sacred cows. Fairly even-handed in that he sneers at everything some of the time, but has consistently mounted aggravating assaults on most aspects of homosexual equality.

R: DESERT ISLAND DISCS (1986); *Man's Hour* (presenter of the 1987 turnabout version of the popular daily programme); etc.

T: *This Is Waugh* (1976); *A Personal Report* (on critics, 1977); *After Midnight* (1983–4); *The Waugh Trilogy* (1987); etc.

Waugh, Evelyn (1903–66) English satirical novelist, travel writer, journalist and occasional broadcaster. Among his adapted works: BRIDESHEAD REVISITED (1956 R; 1981 T); *The Ordeal of Gilbert Pinfold* (1960 R); *The Loved One* (1965 C); *Sword of Honour* (1967 T); *Decline and Fall* (1968 C); *Vile Bodies* (1970 T; 1984 R); *Scoop* (1986 T); *A Handful of Dust* (1988 C).

Talks: *To an Unmarried Listener* (1932 R); 'Up to London' ('events and personalities that have interested him on his last month's trip to London' 1938); etc.

Autobiography: FACE TO FACE (1960 T); *The Ordeal of Gilbert Pinfold* (Ralph Michael as a man beset by hallucinations and paranoid feelings, tortured by accusations of being homosexual, alcoholic, Jewish, Fascist and a social butterfly, 1960 R); *Evelyn Waugh* (a radio portrait, 1965).

Biography: *Waugh* (1967 R); *Evelyn*

Waugh (played by Hugh BURDEN, 1976 R); *A Sense of Loss* (1978 T); *The Waugh Trilogy* (1987 T).

The Way He Makes Me Feel A luscious rhapsody of feeling from Barbra STREISAND, in suit with hair boyishly cut, fully expressing her love for big and bearded Mandy Patinkin in the sanctuary of her room. They embrace, they kiss, they laugh as she croons the Alan and Marilyn Bergman song from *Yentl* (1983 C). It remains unclear whether this is dream or illusion. If real, then both characters are committing a heinous sin – because they are Jewish, students of the Talmud and (as far as anyone outside the audience knows) male.

Wayne, John [Marion Michael Morrison] (1907–79) American film actor who, in the words of *Variety* in 1992, 'gave the world an image of maleness to live by'. His relentlessly gung-ho, steely-eyed image bloated with hawkish sentiments about Communism, civil rights and the Vietnam war belied the affection and sensitivity as well as stubborn inhumanity he brought to films like *Red River* (1948), *She Wore a Yellow Ribbon* (1949), *The Searchers* (1956), *True Grit* (1969) and his swan song, *The Shootist* (1976).

T: I LOVE LUCY (1955: guest); *Screen Directors' Playhouse* 'Rookie of the Year' (1955); *Rowan and Martin's Laugh-In* (1969: as the Easter Bunny); *Raquel:* (1970: guest); *The American West of John Ford* (1971); *The Last American Picture Star* (1976).

A 1987 HORIZON television programme on 'Police Stress' was subtitled 'The John Wayne Syndrome'. This referred to the bottling-up of emotions by police officers in pursuit of some mythical male stoicism, no matter how much stress or physical pain they are experiencing. The 'Syndrome' was causing many officers to suffer delayed reactions, often in the form of full-scale nervous collapse. Concluded the programme: 'The remedy seems to be to forget John Wayne – or risk losing health and relationships, and even life.' (As a boy,

Wayne/Morrison was persistently harassed at school – partly for having a girl's first name. Later, he was refused entry to a naval college for undisclosed reasons.)

'From my people to your people!' 'Roy Scherer' (as narrator of his own story in *Rock Hudson's Home Movies* 1991 V/C) adding extra colour (pink) and bite (sharp) to a scene from *The Undefeated* (1969) where the acting Rock Hudson knocks the acting John Wayne to the ground with a deft right hook. (Wayne – who used the 'my people' expression in a number of his cowboys vs Indians movies – was said to be fearsomely anti-gay, although he supposedly became friendly with Hudson.)

we are everywhere Jackie FORSTER ended GAYS: SPEAKING UP (1978 T) with this challenging statement which was reiterated, as GRAFFITI on a wall, in GREENWICH VILLAGE in CRUISING (1980 C) – though with considerably more calculatedly chilling and paranoia-inducing effect. *See also* I THOUGHT I WAS THE ONLY ONE (IN THE WORLD); THEY'RE EVERYWHERE.

The Weather in the Streets (UK 1984 T) A poignant love story in which the married man's sister, Marigold Spencer (Holly Palance) confides in her schoolfriend Olivia (Lisa Eichhorn) that she thought having babies would 'cure her'. She puts her arms around her friend's waist, commenting 'How thin you are – like a boy' before abruptly asking if Olivia knows any QUEER people. This leads into a brief discussion about lesbianism. Other subsidiary characters include a 'queer' couple, Colin (Sylvester Morand) and Simon (Jonathan Newth), and the handsome German one of them sleeps with.
W: Julian MITCHELL from the novel by Rosalind LEHMANN; P: Alan Shallcross; D: Gavin Millar; 13.2.84; BBC1; 125 mins.

Glossy, functional 1930s potboiler from a once-daring book. The character of the bisexual hedonist had been diluted into a docile decadent in John

HOPKINS' 1962 television adaptation (where she was played by Jill Melford) and also – for less reason (it was nearly 20 years later) – in the 1979 radio version (with Valerie Sarruf).

'The story was considered a shocker in its time, and it's still pretty racy stuff today, with hints of lesbianism and all manner of loose-living eccentrics and deviants on view ... It's what is still called "A woman's picture" and I'll thank feminist readers not to bother me with questions about my use of that useful, misunderstood phrase' (Herbert Kretzmer, *Daily Mail*).

Webb, Clifton [Webb Parmelee Hollenbeck] (1889–1966) American stage and film actor, a former opera singer and dancer, of clipped speech and barely concealed pomposity. At his best, a welcome jet of asperity and élitism in thrillers or family comedies. He was also capable of fine dramatic work, eg as the noble father in *Titanic* (1953). Apparently kept off the screen during the 1930s and early 1940s because of his acknowledged and 'obvious' homosexuality, he became an overnight middle-aged star after playing Waldo LYDECKER in *Laura* (1944).

Memorable in *The Dark Corner* (1946: as the villain); *The Razor's Edge* (1946: as Elliott Templeton); *Sitting Pretty* (1948: as babyminder Mr BELVEDERE); *Cheaper by the Dozen* (1950: as prolific papa); *Dreamboat* (1952: as a silent movie star making a comeback); *Woman's World* (1954: as the appraising boss); *The Remarkable Mr Pennypacker* (1958: more mass reproduction); etc. His only television appearance was as Roderick Usher in *The Fall of the House of Usher* (1949).

'... a man who is Marlon Brando and Clifton Webb combined? Thanks a lot, but no thanks!' Dolores Gray listing all the things she can do without, in a number from *It's Always Fair Weather* (1955 C).

weddings The lawful state of matrimony is only possible for gays and lesbians in Scandinavia at the time of writing. A

ceremony in a church involving a blessing for two men was shown on Danish
television in 1973, as part of a series
called *Prejudices*. It was followed by a
debate during which two political parties
pledged support for legalized gay marriages. A wedding between two women,
one of whom was previously male, was
shown on Finnish television (and
around the world) in 1987.

The idea of two people of the same sex
'getting married' has provided great
fodder for mass entertainment: whether
in the farcical LA CAGE AUX FOLLES III:
THE WEDDING (1985 C) or the documentary WHICKER WAY OUT WEST: 'THE
LORD IS MY SHEPHERD AND HE KNOWS
I'M GAY' (1973 T). The latter had Alan
WHICKER as a fly-on-the-wall during the
nuptials of Ed Brenden, a US Navy
petty officer aged 17, and Joseph Brown,
a hotel clerk aged 20, in the Metropolitan Community Church of San Diego.

DOG DAY AFTERNOON (1975 C) made
great play of a television news report
about Sonny (Al Pacino) and Leon
(Chris Sarandon) being 'married in an
official ceremony'. Over a picture of the
'bride and groom', the newscaster
relates that 'There were 7 bridesmaids,
all male; Sonny's mother; and 70 guests,
all members of the gay COMMUNITY'.
The pay-off line is that the priest who
performed the service 'has now been
defrocked'.

Kate and George were in the middle of
their ceremony when the telephone rang
and the registrar stopped the wedding
because Kate was born male. They were
one of four couples who didn't get married for various reasons and whose
stories were told in 40 MINUTES 'Stop
the Wedding!' (1985 T).

Other unconventional weddings – all
fictional – occurred in *Our Wife* (1931
C: LAUREL accidentally being married to
HARDY); *Loving Couples* (1964 C: artist
Stallen played by Jan Malmsjo and
friend parody the marriage service);
FELLINI SATYRICON (1969 C: old ruin
and pretty young boy); in SALO: THE 120
DAYS OF SODOM (1975 C: bearded judge
in tasteful female attire with young male
captive); *Scum* (1978 C/T 1980: inter-

racial Borstal boys); *City of Women* (1980
C); *History of the World Part I* (1981 C:
the first gay marriage, caveman style);
Pee-Wee HERMAN and friend in *Pee-
Wee's Playhouse* (1987 T).

Love 'The Ultimate Triumph' (1982
T) included a segment which asked 'if
the Christian Church should bless the
unions of homosexuals in church'.

Homosexuals also turn up at traditional
matrimonial solemnities: As the BRIDE-
GROOM: Cliff in BROTHERS (1984 T),
but he couldn't go through with it; Jodie
in SOAP (T), but his bride didn't turn up.
As the 'father' of the bride: Chipper
(Charles Frank) escorting his mother
(Katherine HEPBURN) up the aisle for
her second wedding in *Mrs Delafield
Wants to Marry* (1986 T).
As the mother of the bride: Marilyn
(Gail Strickland) in off-white satin sup-
ports her daughter Alison (Hallie
Todd), though not without initial friction – in the church and afterwards – in
HEARTBEAT (1989 T).
As the BEST MAN: Billy Stringfellow in
THE FAMILY WAY (1966 C) standing firm
even on the honeymoon; the friend of
Louis Bloom (Peter WOODTHORPE) in
WHAT A SAGA! (1986 R) sharing his
interest in ham radio so Louis climbed
out of his new wife's bed and went to
play with his best man on the honeymoon.
As the photographer: Sion Probert calling the bridegroom 'darling' and telling
the best man to place his hand on his hip
(to cheers and whistles from the guests)
in *Flash, Bang, Wallop!* (1981 R).
As the wedding organizer: Geraldine
Chaplin in *A Wedding* (1977 C); Martin
Short in *Father of the Bride* (1991 C).
'... those stupid bitches who dress up
and get a ring and get splashed over the
Sunday papers', Chrissie (Myra Francis) to Jackie (Alison Steadman) in GIRL
(1974 T). 'It's the one reason I wish she
was a fella. So we could be official,' Sorcha (Patricia Leventon) in NOW SHE
LAUGHS, NOW SHE CRIES (1975 R).

Wednesday Love (UK 1975 T) Weak
and shifting sands of an alcoholic postgraduate student (Simon Rouse) flirting

with a married gay, Terry Priestley (Fred Gaunt) in a seedy drinking club, but having sex with a weary housewife. W: Arthur Hopcraft; P: Graeme McDonald; D: Michael Apted; 8.5.75; BBC1 (PLAY FOR TODAY); 70 mins.

An amalgam of SUNDAY, BLOODY SUNDAY and ACKLAND'S 'The Pink Room' aka ABSOLUTE HELL!, with the central character a sexual question mark, awash in alcohol and passivity. A young man who is quite content for assumptions to be made, and who enjoys the sexual tensions he stirs up. Whether he satisfies those engendered lusts is left only one-half (the heterosexual half) answered.

'I don't respond; not easily. I hold people off. It leads to disappointment ... I suppose I've encouraged it, or anyway not discouraged it. There's some excitement in it ... also some pathos ... [it's a] painful conflict that I can't resolve and probably will never be able to. They're nearly always married men ... I'm a bit attracted by pathos.'

The Wednesday Play BBC1's prime spot for original drama began in 1964. Writers included Tony Garnett and Kenneth Loach, David Mercer, Peter Nichols, James Hanley, Dennis Potter, John HOPKINS, Simon GRAY, Jim Allen and one or two women (Nemone Lethbridge; Brigid Brophy). Among the relevant works: IN CAMERA (1964); *Up the Junction* (1965); *The Interior Decorator* (1965); HORROR OF DARKNESS (1965); THE CONNOISSEUR (1966); *The Portsmouth Defence*; WANTED: SINGLE GENTLEMAN (1967); SPOILED (1968); THE PARACHUTE (1968); LAST TRAIN THROUGH THE HARECASTLE TUNNEL (1969). The name was changed to *Play for Today* in the early 1970s.

Week Ending (UK 1972– R) BBC Radio 4's satirical news magazine which, since the late 1970s, has maintained a consistently fair-minded approach to matters gay (if not so much lesbian) as they relate to the national and international stage: law reform, politicians caught in strange places, OUTING, CLAUSE 28, President Clinton and les-

bians and gays in the US military. One of the most consistently lustrous comedy jewels in the BBC's crown and one of the least valued.

Weekend with Willie (UK 1981 R) An unsophisticated couple dine at the Villa Mauresque with Somerset MAUGHAM (David MARCH), his brother (Richard Huggett), his lover Gerald Haxton (Barry Dennen), and ex-wife Syrie (Prunella Scales). They fail to pick up the hate-tinged atmosphere relating to battles won, lost and drawn. W: Richard Huggett; D: David JOHNSTON; 26.9.81; BBC Radio 4 (*Saturday Night Theatre*); 90 mins.

Sometimes works rejected by television companies would surface in sound. This is one of the most famous examples, unproduced for 10 years. A reconstruction overlaid with drawing-room comedy, the seemingly wretched passion of Willie Maugham for the dynamic, feckless Gerald Haxton is subservient to the brittle clamour of ill-assorted people. Compromise is in the air: Gerald will be allowed back in Britain if Maugham agrees to certain conditions.

Overhanging the proceedings was a languor that even David March couldn't penetrate. Ultimately, these were tiresome, unpleasant people squabbling. Director David Johnston had himself visited Maugham at the Villa Mauresque and defended his decision (in the *Daily Mail*) to remove certain passages: 'I don't believe in offending people and I took out words which might be offensive to some listeners and which weren't absolutely essential to the plot.'

A Week in Chalet Land (UK 1948 R) Life for visitors and staff at a British holiday camp told in a dramatized documentary style. W/P: Jennifer Rayner; BBC Home Service; 45 mins.

All the fun of organized frivolity: beauty contests, knobbly knees, glamorous grannies, mass dining, free rides, children very much welcomed (and cared for in the evenings). Told from a variety of perspectives (and narrated by the magisterial Mary O'Farrell), this is a fascinating step back into a post-war mirror when holiday camps were seen as the answer to austerity and the stranglehold of seaside landladies and bleak days huddled on a pier or jammed on a pebbly beach.

One of those who sneer at the innocent fun and games is a fragile psychology student called Vernon (dressed in green corduroys and wearing glasses) who is working as a kitchen hand during his holidays. He's a frightful little snob and not stirred by all the pretty girls wandering around and making themselves available at dances and, so it is said, in their chalets. (The camps are collectively described as 'the biggest marriage market in the country'.) Queer Vernon is contrasted with a nice Scots lad (Alec) who is looking for a girl to dance with and sharing his chalet with two 'boyfriends', who are engineers like Alec.

Weeks, Professor Jeffrey (1945–   ) Welsh social and sexual historian (*Sexuality and its Discontents*, 1985), and one of the most valued in the British lesbian and gay community as a result of his 1977 book *Coming Out* and *Between the Acts: Lives of Homosexual Men 1885–1967* which he co-edited. He has been a welcome sight on television, communicating with unforced intelligence and perfect pitch all manner of fascinating finds and ideas about homosexual politics from the 19th century to the present day. His only disaster was as part of a discussion on the comedy film *Tootsie* in 1983 (*Visions*): he was so po-faced and earnestly dogmatic that it almost became a textbook definition of what was wrong with Channel 4 in its first year.

R: *Being Gay Today* (1981); THE GAY AND LESBIAN WORLD (1992).

T: *Sexual Identity*: Radclyffe HALL (1982); GAY LIFE (1981); *Voices* 'Sexuality and Identity' (1983); OUT ON TUESDAY (1990); *Sex Now* 'Same Sex, Better Sex?' (1991).

We Kiss In A Shadow Rodgers and Hammerstein's cry from the heart: dedicated to all prohibited love, but sung in *The King and I* by the Burmese captive and her lover. It is danced briefly by Frankie and Johnny (Ronald LACEY and Philip Locke) in *Boa Constrictor* (1967 T) prior to leaving for a party, at which they, as a queer couple and as a couple of queers, are the unofficial, unpaid entertainment.

Welcome Home, Bobby (US 1986 T) Is Bobby (Timothy Williams) gay or not? His parents (Tony Lo Bianco and Gisela Caldwell) are worried. He had a relationship with an older man and as a result is treated like a leper in his home town.

W: Conrad Bromberg; P: Thomas DeWolfe and Cyma Rubin; D: Herbert Wise; CBS; 100 mins.

Fuddled and fugged up by commercial dictates, only a blurred outline of the original intention remains. So careful is the screenplay that the boy's sexuality is never fully focused. His older lover is a cipher, and there is, as usual, nary a hint that anything approaching a gay community or a small group of understanding individuals could be there for Bobby to help him sort through his muddled feelings. However, there are some sharp scenes between Bobby and his heterosexual friends, and a powerful one in which a school counsellor reveals that he is gay but must be careful not to show it.

Weldon, Fay (1932–   ) English novelist and writer, responsible for some superbly engrossing feminist 'good viewing' from her Jane Austen adaptations to those from her own books such as *The Life and Loves of a She-Devil* (1986), *Heart of the Country* (1987) and *The Cloning of Joanna May* (1992 T). She also wrote some of the early UPSTAIRS DOWNSTAIRS including the first with the glimmerings of expedient romance between ROSE and Sarah.

R: *The Spider* (1972); *Housebreaker* (1974); *Mr Fox and Mr First* (1974); *The Doctor's Wife* (1975); *Polaris* (1978); etc.

T: *The Fat Woman's Tale* (1966); *A Catching Complaint* (1966); *Smokescreen* (1968); *Happy Ending* (1969: contributor); *Kate* 'Say It with Flowers' (1970) and 'The Female Rebellion' (1971); *Splinter of Ice* (1972); *Life for Christine* (1980); *Pride and Prejudice* (1980); *Out of the Undertow* (1984: contributor); *Without Walls* 'J'Accuse England's Jane [Austen]' (1991); etc.

Biography: THE SOUTH BANK SHOW 'Fay Weldon' (1980 T); DESERT ISLAND DISCS (1980 R: memorably ruffling the generally unrufflable Roy Plomley); etc.

Welles, Orson (1915–85) American actor and bracingly original film-maker whose 1941 *Citizen Kane* topped *Sight and Sound*'s 1992 poll as the best film of all time. His increasing bulk, hasting, quizzical intelligence and growling purr of a voice made him the most instantly recognizable underemployed genius of his generation.

As well as *Kane* and *The Magnificent Ambersons* (1942 C) Welles gripped the popular imagination by marrying Rita Hayworth, by playing Harry LIME (through the zither) in *The Third Man*, by selling Domecq sherry and by scaring America half to death in 1938 with his radio adaptation of *The War of the Worlds*.

Gay resonances and shivers can be heard and felt in *The Lady from Shanghai* (1948 D); *Othello* (1952 D); *Confidential Report* aka *Mr Arkadin* (1955 D); *Touch of Evil* (1958 D); *The Immortal Story* (1968 D); *Oedipus the King* (1968: as TIRESIAS); *The Kremlin Letter* (1970); *F for Fake* (1973 D); *The Other Side of the Wind* (1976: unreleased); *Filming Othello* (1978); *Someone to Love* (1987).

R: *Rebecca* (1938); reading from 'A Song of Myself' by Walt WHITMAN (1953); *Black Museum* (C 1955).

T: *King Lear* (1953); *Orson Welles' Sketchbook* (1956); I LOVE LUCY (1956: guest); *Round the World with Orson Welles* (1955); *Twentieth Century* (1956); *Colgate Theatre* 'Fountain of Youth' (1958 D); *The Method* (1958); *The Man Who Came to Dinner* (1972); *The ABC Comedy Hour* (1972: guest host); *Great Mysteries* (1977); *The Name of the Game* 'The Enemy Before Us' (1980: with Katina Paxinou); *Night of 100 Stars*

(1982); *Tales of the Klondike* (1983: as narrator); etc.

Biography: *The Orson Welles Story* (1982 T); *The Big O* (1990 C); *The Real Citizen Kane* (1991 T); *Without Walls* 'J'Accuse: "Citizen Kane"' (1991 T).

The Well of Loneliness Banned in 1928 after a legal case that sent its author Radclyffe HALL into exile. In *Sexual Identity* 'Radclyffe Hall' (1982 T) author and former headmistress Rosemary Manning related how she was affected by '*The Well*'. She was a prefect at the time of the trial and involved with two girls at school who were in a lesbian relationship. Rosemary was told off for merely discussing *The Well* with them. Nearly 50 years later, after it had been deemed fit for wide public circulation, it became A BOOK AT BEDTIME (read by Judy Parfitt, 1974).

Wells, Peter (1953–) New Zealand novelist (*Dangerous Desires*) and film-maker (*Little Queen*: A TASTE OF KIWI; JEWEL'S DARL; A DEATH IN THE FAMILY). Apart from his special gifts of emotional honesty and delectable eccentricity of observation, he made a stir when he yelled at John INMAN during an awards ceremony in the mid 1980s: 'Fuck off, you horrible sexist deadshit.' The actor asked him to repeat it and Wells complied. First full-length feature *Desperate Remedies* (1993 C).

well what if I am? One of Max Miller's bold-faced catchphrases which referred to his flowery suits and made-up face. The comedian, who was part inspiration for John OSBORNE'S THE ENTERTAINER (1960 C), was recently commemorated in *The Cheeky Chappie* (with Joe Melia, 1989 R).

We Love You One of the earliest (1967) pop videos; by the Rolling Stones in the wake of Mick Jagger's trial for marijuana possession. Jagger, in the dock of the Old Bailey, is dressed as Oscar WILDE with Marianne Faithfull as Bosie. The white-faced, lipsticked pop idol immediately creates resonances between the pillorying of the writer and the image carried in *The Times* editorial about himself as being a butterfly broken on a wheel to set an example to the youth of Britain. (The song was included, by Ken Russell, in the history of pop videos 1986 T.)

we're here; we're queer; we're not going shopping! 1990s battle cry heard in OUTRAGE!: THE DOCUMENTARY (1991 R) and IN THE MIX 'Are You a Friend of Dorothy's?' (Aust 1992 R).

West, Mae (1892–1980) American actress, singer and writer, an irreverent sender-upper of sex; named by Christine Cremen in *Screen* (Aust 1991 R) as MADONNA's grandmother. Ann Jillian played her bright and sassy, not plump and satirical, in a well-shaped but deeply bland TV biography in 1982, which made no mention of her homosexual play THE DRAG which was raided and closed after only a couple of performances. Her first film role – as Maudie Triplett with whom goodness had nothing to do in *Night After Night* (1932) – finds her somewhat swarthy and waking up in bed with Alison Skipworth after a heavy evening. She was then subjected to Paramount's glamour refinery for her starring vehicles – which accelerated the call for much tighter censorship; *She Done Him Wrong* (1933) and *I'm No Angel* (1933). After *The Heat's On* in 1943, she was not seen again until a guest spot on television's *Mister Ed* in the mid-1950s. With much fanfare she made a proper comeback in *Myra Breckinridge* (1970) and finally, in 1977, filmed her long cherished *Sextet* which provided her with six husbands, including a shrieking gay. Both films showed that the world had caught up, and her attitude to sex seemed sleazy and sad.

West Side Story (US 1961 C) Gang warfare on New York streets between Jets and Riffs. Maria (Natalie Wood) dances with the 'wrong' boy (Richard Beymer) and unleashes violence.
W: Ernest Lehman from the play by Arthur Laurents after SHAKESPEARE; M: Leonard BERNSTEIN; L: Stephen SOND-

HEIM; P: Robert Wise; D: Robert Wise and Jerome Robbins; 155 mins.
Three strong women characters (Wood's Maria, Rita Moreno's Anita and Susan Oates's 'TOMBOY' Anybodys, described as 'an American tragedy') versus three essentially passive males (played by Beymer, Russ Tamblyn and George Chakiris) in the first Hollywood musical to have intimations of mortality, racism, homosexuality (Anybodys and 'Baby John'), transsexuality in (GEE OFFICER KRUPKE), drug taking – and a bed scene. Some weak casting aside, the experience is thrillingly dramatic, angry and moving. Standout numbers are the opening, 'America', the 'Tonight' quintet, 'Cool' and the 'Rumble' Ballet.

We Think the World of You (UK 1980 T) A gay man, Joe ACKERLEY (Benjamin WHITROW) and his DOG Queenie (Sasha). The dog originally belonged to a lover, Johnny whose wife became jealous – not of Joe but of the dog.
W: Paul BAILEY from the autobiographical novel by J. R. Ackerley; D: Tristram Powell; 15.5.80; BBC1; 55 mins.
There was much upset that the programme was shown because of a scene in which Joe and Johnny lay in bed with Queenie between them like a hot dog. It was also intimated that the owner may have given the dog sexual stimulation. In a letter to the *Listener* (12.6.80) Mary Whitehouse referred to 'The homosexual – and worse – relationships in *We Think the World of You*'.

We Think the World of You (UK 1988 C) In 1950s London, bisexual Johnny (Gary Oldman) is befriended by cultured civil servant Frank (Alan BATES) who then becomes involved with the lad's family and his dog Evie. 'A must for animal lovers ... romantics' (*Leonard Maltin's Movie and Video Guide*, 1992–3). W: Hugh Stoddart; based on the book by J. R. Ackerley; D: Colin Gregg; 94 mins.

We Were One Man (Fr 1978 C) A French simpleton, Guy who collects sap (Serge Avedikian) and a runaway German soldier (Piotr Stanislas) embark upon a very physical mutual development programme. After realizing that he can love a man as deeply as a woman, Serge sees his lover taken away by the authorities. Grabbing a gun, he runs blindly into the village, shoots the German before he can be executed, and takes the body away on a cart. He pulls the body into a makeshift grave, gets in and begins to cover himself with leaves. W/D: Philippe Vallois; 90 mins.

A pastoral romance between the childlike Frenchman and the reserved German which is genuinely touching and, for once, doesn't shy away from the sexual dynamics – including a surprising piece of role reversal. Starting out as a conventional village idiot, Serge triumphs over all his limitations but cannot transcend the barriers created by war. The scenes of the two men fishing, eating, shitting and spending time with Guy's girlfriend (who will 'betray' them) are lilting and fresh, brilliantly contrasting with the small handful of full-on dramatic scenes: the fate of Serge's dog; Serge's willingness – at last – to have the German make love to him 'as if I was a woman'; the hysterical ending.

Whale, James (1889–1957) English film director, a former actor (J. R. ACKERLEY'S *The Prisoners of War*), who went to Hollywood to make *Journey's End* in 1930 and stayed to film some of the most enduring horror-fantasies: *Frankenstein* (1931); *The Old Dark House* (1932); *The Invisible Man* (1933); THE BRIDE OF FRANKENSTEIN (1935). Also effective was his handling of the musical *Show Boat* (1936), *Remember Last Night* (1935) and *The Man in the Iron Mask* (1939). After a gap of nearly a decade, he made a 40-minute version of William Saroyan's *Hello Out There* with Henry Morgan and Marjorie Steele, finally shown at the New York Gallery of Modern Art in 1967, 10 years after he was found dead at the bottom of the swimming pool of the house he shared with his lover, producer David Lewis. Boris Karloff discussed him briefly in *Birth of a Monster* (1977 R). (*The James*

Whale Radio Show was an unrelated 1989 late-night television talk haven.)

Whale Music (UK 1983 T) Friends, including a lesbian teacher, gather round Carolyn in a seaside town as she enters her last month of pregnancy.
W: Anthony Minghella; P: Howard Baker; D: Pedr James; Granada; 60 mins.

A dour, meandering play smacked into life by the character of the teacher's lover – her pupil. Calling herself 'D', dressed in a black leather jacket crackling with badges of every colour and cause, she is no oil painting. In fact, as Sara Sugarman plays her, D's surly iconoclasm makes her a close spiritual sister to A TASTE OF HONEY'S Jo SMITH. A tough-tongued, sensitive-souled diesel dyke in the making and a political activist from the cradle, she keeps herself busy on the holiday defacing sexist posters.

The possibilities of the piece peter out as Carolyn decides to leave the seaside town and have the baby elsewhere. The teacher, Kate (Janet Dale) confesses that she doesn't love D; she is just a replacement for her one true love – Carolyn – who is heterosexual.

(A radio production with Alison Steadman as Kate followed in 1984.)

what a gay day! Larry GRAYSON's second most famous exclamation: an airy observation on his show SHUT THAT DOOR! (1972–4 T). This was the point of entry into the mainstream of the recently redefined nice, innocent, unassuming, useful word. Grayson eased its path by robbing it of any revolutionary intent or fervour. Hence TV TIMES could exhort its readers to 'Shut that door ... And make yourself at home for a GAY evening'.

What a Saga! (UK 1986 R) Louis Bloom (Peter WOODTHORPE) left his wife (Prunella Scales) on their honeymoon night for a transmitter and the BEST MAN. Now he lives in a shed on the allotment. An amazing sight with orange curly whiskers ('like shredded wheat') in vest and underpants and earphones, he spends his days surrounded by wires and being nuzzled – in between radio messages – by a Hebridean boat builder called Garth ('We're doing some intricate receiving,' Louis explains). But that's the least of Mrs Bloom's problems. She will have to cope alone with a pregnant daughter and the 'male' cat who appears to be in the same condition. W: Diana Souhami; D: Clive Brill; 1.7.86; BBC Radio 4.

Mrs Bloom just about keeps her head above water as domestic crisis follows domestic crisis. A companion piece to the writer's A HORSE CALLED GERTRUDE STEIN (1990 R); suburban anxieties nobly contained by the woman of the house. Prunella Scales and Peter Woodthorpe cleverly adapt the same, whiney, scratchy accents as the ill-matched pair.

What A Wonderful World The song by John Barry and Don Black from *On Her Majesty's Secret Service* (1969 C) is played by an army band in Regent's Park while former bandsman Robert F., dismissed for being gay, looks on forlornly. In what had been his wonderful world, Robert lived for the army and music. His dismissal was preceded by days of detention and questioning which included being asked if he had sex with his two brothers and with his dog. This was Britain in the late 1980s. (HEART OF THE MATTER 'Falling Out' 1991 T.)

What Can I Do with a Male Nude? (UK 1985 C/T) Set in a modern Britain, the narrating voyeur (John Levitt) warns that 'Times have started to change. There have been seizures, raids, fines, imprisonments. There are soon to be erasures. It is no longer safe to keep SARTRE on the shelves'. His paranoia is proved to be justified in the closing minutes of his photographic session with a naked model (John Brown).
W/D: Ron PECK; P: James Mackay; 25 mins.

A funny–chilling vignette perfectly attuned to the pre-CLAUSE 28 mood of a *Sun*-soaked, THATCHER-governed

country. The lugubrious photographer rails against 'A history of aesthetic monomania, in which extraordinary photographic ingenuity and acrobatic skills have been employed to draw attention to that which cannot be revealed'. It is perfectly fitting that, in a film devoted to the naked male body, the camera keeps a discreet distance until just before the Body Beautiful is revealed as PC Plod of the Obscene Publications squad.

what does g.a.y. stand for? Answer: 'Got AIDS yet?' First voiced in the 1984 short *Sleepwalker* by Michael Medwin to Fulton McKay; more recently by a villain to Ian in relation to Joe (Jason Rush in EASTENDERS 1991 T) and referred to in SATURDAY NIGHT OUT's THE ROCK 'N' ROLL YEARS (1991 T).

what do you do in bed? A source of fascination for some people is the sexual activities of lesbian and gay people. Jo SMITH (Rita Tushingham) in A TASTE OF HONEY (1961 C) says that Geof (Murray MELVIN) can stay with her on one condition – he must tell her what he 'does' with men: '*Go on!* I've always wanted to know about people like you. I want to know what you do. I want to know why you do it. Tell me or get out.' He won't divulge a thing but she lets him stay anyway.

The following year a character in STAMBOUL TRAIN (1962 T) asked what lesbians did in bed. He didn't receive a reply either. Members of the public had to wait six years – for the penultimate scene in THE KILLING OF SISTER GEORGE (1968 C) – to find out at least part of a likely sequence of moves.

The women at *Don's Party* (1976 C) are just about to discuss lesbian positions and particularities when they are interrupted by a man. The police chief in ANOTHER WAY (1982 C) enquires eagerly of one of the women 'Tell me, how do you *do* it?' while interviewing her about a quite unrelated matter. Caroline Sheldon's short *17 Rooms: What Do Lesbians Do in Bed?* was 'banished' from Channel 4 in 1984 for trying to elucidate the matter. (The film found that among the favoured activities were drinking tea, playing Scrabble, watching television and listening to Dusty SPRINGFIELD records.)

One phone-in caller to the London Broadcasting Company (LBC) programme in 1973 insisted that the two speakers on homosexuality tell him – identified only as Brent of Fulham, aged 35 – 'what they do in private'. In return for this information, he would magnanimously 'agree with homosexuality'. Denis LEMON offered to tell him, but Jackie FORSTER intercepted: 'What do *you* do in bed with your wife?' 'I go to sleep' came the proud reply.

It remains a common belief that homosexual love-making is entirely lust-driven, involves a small range of 'acts', and is ultimately sterile and unsatisfying. Diana Graham (Rachel Davies) appealing to the jury in CROWN COURT 'A Friend of the Family' (1979 T) tried to set her sexuality in some kind of recognizable perspective: 'I don't want you to think I'm being patronizing, but you are mostly straight men and women here. You live in the accepted world, the normal world, with normal relationships, whereas I am a lesbian. Therefore I'm a threat to men. People don't think we exist outside of our sexuality. Because of what I do in bed, people no longer see me as a person. Because of what I do in bed, I shall probably lose my job. Because of what I am, I have already lost my two children whom I love very dearly. And because of what I am, my lover may lose her child. But what I am is important to me. And like any straight, I'm a person first with a personality.'

whatever turns you on A throwaway expression from the late 1960s which implies total acceptance of an individual's path towards satisfaction and pleasure (with the optional proviso that it harms no one). Its air of *laissez-faire* is sometimes accompanied by an ironic, mocking undertow as when Sid Perks (Alan Devereux) uses it in an episode of THE ARCHERS (1992 R) after Kathy

(Hedli Niklaus) has told him she's been rearing battery hens. Jon (Craig Gilmore) employs it half in amazement half in horror in THE LIVING END (1992 C) when Luke (Mike Dytil) makes him promise to have sex with him at the point of death – 'the ultimate orgasm'.

what have I done to deserve this? A much heard plaint from parents of gay sons and daughters, which can be traced back to self-pitying Mrs Rolfe (Hilda Fenemore) in THE UNLOVED (1955 T) about her Jimmy (Melvyn HAYES). Other examples are Dad (Milo O'Shea) about scallywag Hal (Hywel Bennett) in *Loot* (1970 C); Janna Castallack (Annabel Leventon) about non-reproducing Philip (Rupert Frazer) in PENMARRIC (1979 T); Australian outback mother (Lorraine Bayly) about cricketing ace son Stewart (David McCubbin) in A COUNTRY PRACTICE 'Apparitions' (1989 T); George Light (John Baddeley), the father of Ashley (Dominic Rickhards) in OCTOBER SCARS THE SKIN (1989 R): 'You're my only child. Your mother spoils you,' he cries after finding a gay magazine in his son's room; Bishop Smith (Alan Rowe) in THE LITMUS QUESTION (1975 R). Bishop Smith is particularly inconsolable when he finds out that his only son Paul (Steve Hodson) is gay and also on a 'gross indecency' charge (later proved to be false). Only a friend of the family, involved in gay counselling, can provide balm: 'You didn't go wrong ... there's no need for self-reproach. Homosexuality is unusual, but not unnatural.'

what if she/he turned out to be gay? Usually the first question when the subject of lesbian/gay parenting (actual or desired) is raised on television or radio. The child psychologist confronts the lesbian mother (Gena Rowlands) with it in A QUESTION OF LOVE (1978 T). So does Gail's mother (Sada Thompson) in MY TWO LOVES (1986 T), despite being oblivious to the fact that her granddaughter at 15 is vivacious and intelligent, without obvious hang-ups about males or females.

It is a constant on all discussion programmes related to this issue. Underlying the concerned question is not a desire for the child to be fulfilled, wholehearted, loving, exploratory; rather it is a matter of whether this child is going to be scarred for life, no longer marketable as a human being, difficult to pigeon-hole, an individual.

What Is This Thing Called Love?

Cole PORTER song which tries to work out the whole crazy business, eventually appealing to 'the Lord in Heaven above' so contrary and shifting are the emotions involved. It provided the perfect comment on the 'one crazy year' enjoyed by *Willie and Phil* (Michael Ontkean and Ray Sharkey 1980 C) and Jeanette (Margot Kidder). The threesome carol the song after their first meeting and it's played when Jeanette – having married Willie – ups and goes to live with Phil. During a sequence of the trio horsing around on the beach and in the jacuzzi, Billie Holiday is heard singing it soulfully. It's finally improvised by a motley group of jazz musicians in the last scene where the two men go to see their favourite film *Jules et Jim*. The narrator rather ambiguously informs the viewers that 'Willie and Phil eventually got married and had children'.

Other performers who were serenaded by this song include Woody ALLEN, Mia Farrow, Sydney Pollack and Judy Davis in *Husbands and Wives* (1992 C: a jazz version played over opening and closing credits) and two women who met in prison in Professor Laurie Taylor's 1983 radio valentine *This Thing Called Love* (which also slipped in a male couple for good measure).

What Makes A Man A Man? (Comme Ils Disent)

Charles AZNAVOUR composition about a lonely, abused FEMALE IMPERSONATOR – 'Je suis un homo ... comme ils disent' – who lives with his mother. Aznavour sang it with mournful defiance – in the slightly toned-down English version – on a number of the more open-minded television variety shows during 1973. Aznavour, who began his career as a drag singer, ends the song with a passionate assault on the society that points the finger as well as on his own self-pity: 'Nobody has the right to be the judge of what is right for me.'

Marc Almond recorded the song in 1993 with a dedication to 'all those who have the conviction to be different in the face of adversity'.

What the Butler Saw (UK 1987 T)

A series of thwacks at arrogantly omniscient medical practitioners – as personified by Dr Prentice (Dinsdale Landen) – amid the farcical chaos of cross-dressing, mistaken identities and switched genders, the madness of the sane and the sanity of the mad. Winston Churchill's 'missing part' is in there as well. W: Joe ORTON; P: Shaun Sutton; D: Barry Davis; 24.5.87; BBC2; 90 mins

Orton portrays the very essence of despotic authority in the rampaging figure of Dr Rance, who manipulates facts to fit his own crackpot notions. Apt in the late 1960s, apter in the 1980s with state interference in personal matters gathering momentum. There were complaints that it was unsuitable early evening viewing (8.30pm), what with comments about the doctor's wife having been born 'with her legs open', references to every sexual permutation and semi-nude cast members.

The director told RADIO TIMES: 'Now we have the fierce backlash of puritanism and a crackdown by authority on those who do not conform – developments which would have attracted Orton's attack. It may not have the power to shock now, but it still provokes thoughtful laughter.'

what will the neighbours say?

One of the most effective and concentrated verbal mechanisms for social control. Graham CHAPMAN in *Opinions* (1984 T) vented his spleen on this cliché: 'Why should the weak and the feeble amongst us dominate the course of our lives?' His maxims were 'To thine own self be true' and 'Do unto others as you would have them do unto you'.

In WOMAN'S HOUR (1992 R) the sister of a gay man said that his AIDS-related illness and his life were denied by the rest of the family at the funeral and afterwards because of what people would say. Another voice, that of the wife of a man who died, talked of covering tracks with the family: 'It's very much about what the neighbours will say.'

A priest's mistress in *Priests of Passion* (1992 T) lived in daily fear of exposure: 'What would people in the neighbourhood say?'

Wheatley, Alan (1907–91) English actor, an industrial psychologist and BBC wartime news reader. Most of his roles were careful studies in domineering refinement, often played as if with ice at the base of his spine. Remembered as the Sheriff of Nottingham in *The Adventures of Robin Hood* (1955–9 T).

Other credits include: John WORTHING in THE IMPORTANCE OF BEING EARNEST (1938 T); the dandified crook who is hunted and killed in *Brighton Rock* (1947 C); Humphrey Rhodes, affected exquisite in *Promise of Tomorrow* (1950 T); Gilbert Osmond, egotist husband of Isabel in *The Portrait of a Lady* (1952 R); Rupert CADELL in ROPE (1953 T); King Arthur in *Sir Gawaine and the Green Knight* (1953 R); Mr Dash in *A Recluse* (1954 T); James Blenkinsop in *Mrs Dot* (1954 T); Adrian Lee, the designer in *Simon and Laura* (1955 C); reader of T. S. Eliot's *The Love Song of J. Alfred Prufrock* (1957 R); title role in YOU ARE THERE 'The Trial of Charles I' (1958 T); Mr Murdstone in *Young Davy* (1959 T); a don in *A Jolly Bad Fellow* (1964 C); Francis BACON in *Sweet England's Pride* (1968 R); Soames in *The Forsyte Saga* (1967–8 R); Abbé Faria in *The Count of Monte Cristo* (1987 R); Major Liconda in *The Sacred Flame* (1989 R).

When Did You Last See My Mother (UK 1967 R) Ian (Victor Henry) and Jimmy (Simon Ward), two students sharing a flat, are involved in a loose sexual relationship, complicated by the presence of a young man and a young woman. In a fit of jealous rage, Ian alienates Jimmy, then, cold-bloodedly, Ian sets out to seduce his friend's mother (Gwen Watford), who – upon learning the truth – drives off into the night and is killed.

W: Christopher Hampton from his stage play; D: Archie Campbell; BBC Third Programme; 90 mins.

Superficially a wooden, unappealing melodrama, it has life and a brazen honesty breathed into it by Victor Henry's performance as the spiky, desperately lonely – and fairly openly gay – despoiler of the nest. This was one of the first plays to insinuate a full sexual relationship between two men of the same age outside a school setting. There's an edgy, erotic undertow throughout.

Where Do I Go? The closing credits song from SOME OF MY BEST FRIENDS ARE (1971 C) which illustrates, in Vito RUSSO'S words from *The Celluloid Closet* (1981), 'the predicament of people allowed to congregate safely only on someone else's terms and for a price'. M/L: Gordon Rose.

Where Is Love? Plaintive Lionel Bart song from *Oliver!* (1968 C). Phil DONAHUE suggested this as an anthem for gay and lesbian people, harried at every turn, during his 'Interracial Gay Couples' show in 1992. He didn't elaborate save to say that it's sung by poor Oliver, working in a blacking factory, gazing out through the bars at the bleak, unfriendly world which gobbles up innocent little children and spits them out. In a piping voice Oliver (Mark Lester) asks: 'Where-ere-ere-ere, where-ere-ere-ere is love?'

which one are you – husband or wife? A frequent question stated and unstated in relation to same-sex couples. It was asked – in a roundabout way – of the two Peters in CHEQUERBOARD (Aust T 1972) – 'Which one is the active partner? Do you have fixed roles?' – and directly of Wayne and Michael on DONAHUE 'Whatever Happened to Love

Relationships After [the] Donahue [Show]' (1992 T).

Whicker, Alan (*c* 1923–) English roving reporter, purveyor of barbed television portraits of people and places. Always impeccably dressed, unruffled, gently amused by obsessions and foibles of others. One of Britain's most successful performers from his days on TONIGHT (1956–61) through series like *Whicker's World* (1963–), *Whicker's Walkabout* (1971), WHICKER WAY OUT WEST (1973) and *Living with Uncle Sam* (1985). His output has been phenomenal, his *savoir faire* prodigious, his couth undented. No matter where he is or with whom – in the Australian bush, chatting to a billionaire, investigating gay and lesbian cops or at the Sydney Sleaze Ball – he remains uncreased, quizzical and always just on the verge of smirking. Inevitably he has provided much fodder for Stanley BAXTER, Mike Yarwood and the MONTY PYTHON team.

Whicker Way Out West 'The Lord Is My Shepherd and He Knows I'm Gay' (UK 1973 T) Alan WHICKER's flying visit to parts of California's nascent gay communities. The always sardonic Whicker talked to happily 'married' carpet layer and his lover, as well as to the Rev. Troy Perry and members of his church, one of whose buildings would later be burned to the ground.

The producer/director, Michael Deacon had to fight Yorkshire Television firstly for permission to film these sexual nonconformists and then, having done so, to title the results as above. 'The film isn't pro-gay lib,' Deacon told GAY NEWS in October, 'but simply a sane adult reflection of the gay situation based on the theory that all men are brothers, and homosexuality is no different from having red rather than black hair.'

The newspaper, while welcoming a programme which gave nearly 60 minutes of airtime to many radical ways of being homosexual – 'No longer will we allow you to tell us what we are,' one participant told a bemused Whicker –

noted that it 'failed to say anything at all about the problems facing the American homosexual, the nature of their oppression, their history and progress of gay action, the work of the gay community, the position of the homosexual at the present moment and their chances for the immediate future. Nor did it attempt to depict the life-styles – professional or private ... These are serious omissions ... It was real Evelyn Home stuff, right down to the couple who couldn't afford the rings, but managed to get married in white.'

However, the *Oldham Evening Chronicle* critic liked it: 'It was a powerful documentary that could only have set people thinking about all those "queer" jokes that they themselves cracked or laughed at many times. As one of the liberationists pointed out, "It's no sickness, it's a preference".'

But the *Newcastle Evening Journal* reviewer didn't: '... watching and listening you felt foreign as though you had strayed on to an inhabited star a million light years away. It was, of course, a profound example of how tolerant we've suddenly become because nobody squealed about corruption and nobody with a closed mind and false air of rectitude lashed out with their platitudes about the sanctity of family life. I don't think my father, bless his dear dead fundamentalist heart, could have sat through the last passionate kiss as the wedding concluded.'

whistling There was a persistent legend that the true test of whether a man was a hopeless degenerate or a regular guy was to ask the individual to whistle. If he couldn't, then there was a good chance he was queer, would never produce offspring or lead a virtuous life. Typically, Christopher WREN (and the equally immature murderer) hums rather than whistles the nursery rhyme clue in THREE BLIND MICE (1947 R).

Tony HOLLAND paid a tribute of sorts to this quaint notion in a 1986 Christmas episode of EASTENDERS. Dot Cotton (June Brown) is shown the key-ring with the built-in whistle that Barry has given Colin. As if to reassure herself that Colin is not one of them, she asks him to whistle spontaneously. He passes the test. Maybe it is a sign that there is hope for him.

White, Edmund (1940–) American novelist (*A Boy's Own Story*), biographer (Jean COCTEAU; Jean GENET) and co-founder of Gay Men's Health Crisis with Larry KRAMER. A sincere talent at full stretch, he has appeared effectively on radio and television talking about Jean GENET (*Books and Writing* Aust 1991 R; THE SOUTH BANK SHOW 1992 T), gay literature (*Frank Delaney* 1985 T), Robert MAPPLETHORPE (ARENA 1988 T), and 'My Most Difficult Book' (OMNIBUS 1989 T).

White, Patrick (1912–91) English-born Australian novelist, playwright and latterly defender of the environment and ABORIGINALS, opponent of nuclear armaments and greed-driven development. The first Australian writer to win the Nobel Prize, and to live openly with his lover, Manoly Lascaris in Sydney. A deft unmasker of the pretentious and self-deluding, angry at injustice, cant and the second-rate, he had scant respect for gay liberation. He called himself a 'homosexual' and a 'POOFTER', but never 'gay'.

Some of his novels and plays have coded queer characters, eg the brothers Aldo and Waldo in *The Solid Mandala* and 'aunt' Theodora in *The Aunt's Story*. He came out publicly in his autobiography *Flaws in the Glass* (1981), but so far none of the broadcast celebrations has fully explored his sexuality in relation to his art.

C: *The Night the Prowler* (1978: a screenplay based on his short story).

Biography: *Now Read On* 'The Art of Patrick White' (1970 R: by Peter Porter); *Patrick White* (Aust 1987 R); *Patrick White: Part Dragonfly, Part Shark* (1987 R: with A. S. Byatt, David Malouf and George Steiner); *Encounter* 'Patrick White and a Difficult God' (1991 R: 'He was able to speak what was not

spoken'); *The Burning Piano: A Portrait of Patrick White* (Aust 1993 T).

'... regarded by many Australians as some curmudgeonly, affected old queer,' speaker on *Books and Writing* (Aust 1991 R).

(Huw Wheldon turned down the idea of a programme on him for MONITOR 1962–3.)

See also Richard FULTON.

Whitehead, Tony (*c* 1953–) English HIV/AIDS activist, one of the founders of the Terrence Higgins Trust and one of its chairpersons. First seen on television in *Coming Out* (1976) wherein a shot of him kissing his lover lost him his job as a trainee manager at British Home Stores. Other appearances: an extra in NIGHTHAWKS (1978 C); *Bright Eyes* (1984 T); OUT ON TUESDAY 'A Matter of Life and Death' (1990 T); *A Perspective for Living* (1992 R: remembering his deceased partner, George); etc.

Lee **Whitehouse** Character in *The Box* (Aust 1974–7 T); a television company employee played by Paul Karo. The actor told the *Australian TV Times* (29.6.74): 'I'd originally intended him to be more of the knowledgeable sophisticate who loves Shirley Bassey, stays up all night to watch old movies and is mad on horse racing, that sort of thing. I think it would have been more authentic, but the role calls for me to play it CAMP and that's the way it is. Homosexuals may resent this STEREOTYPE but I think it's one that many homosexuals seem to want to conform to.'

Whitehouse, Mary (1910–) English moral rearmer and Christian absolutist who, in 1964, helped launch the Clean Up TV campaign, which soon after became the National Viewers' and Listeners' Association (NVALA). She prosecuted successfully GAY NEWS in 1977 and, a few years later, less successfully, the National Theatre for showing simulated rape by Roman invaders on Druid men in Howard Brenton's THE ROMANS IN BRITAIN.

As one of *The Controversialists* (1980 T) she warned of the creeping gay influence (through openly gay teachers, 'biased' class discussions, books and the CHE Education Kit) in some British schools. Vito RUSSO reviewing this programme for GAY NEWS said 'What she fails to realize is that the same spirit that made early Christians refuse to shut up is exactly the same spirit that urges gay people on to assert their equal rights with heterosexual males and females.' Neither did she realize, he continued, 'that some of us will never consent to hide simply to make them more comfortable with their illusions that everyone is heterosexual'.

One of the few women immediately identifiable solely by her last name, Mary Whitehouse has been a British media celebrity for nearly 30 years. Among her credits: *Petticoat Line* (1972 R); *The Lively Arts* 'Mary Whitehouse Down Under' (1976 T); *Politics of Pressure* 'Using the Media' (1987 T); *The Dame Edna Experience* (1987 T: seen happily waltzing with Dame Edna during the closing moments); *The Robbie Vincent Telephone Programme* (1988: as a one-off co-presenter); and *House Style* (1993 T).

A contributor to hundreds of public and studio debates on sex and violence on television, child pornography, adult pornography, prostitution, sex education and BLASPHEMY, her personal religious beliefs, which she pursues zealously in the public arena, were explored in *Thought for the Day* (1978 R); *Person to Person* (1979 T); *A Voice Crying in the Wilderness* 'Jeremiah' (1985 R: the prophet 'with undimmed courage' finding strength to march forth).

Portrayed (by an unidentified actress) as a spectral figure, smiling softly through joyless lips in EVERYMAN 'Blasphemy at the Old Bailey' (1977 T), this sinister killjoy image was belied by the 'real' Mrs Whitehouse's contributions to the programme. Bouncy, almost coquettish, sincere, smiling, she came across as a woman with a burning passion to change the world through the word of God, a world in which gay and lesbian life and love have no part.

Mary Whitehouse has been regularly 'taken off' on television, usually crudely as a vehement moral proselytizer with a prurient interest in other people's sex lives. Among these likenesses: Desirée Carthorse (Beryl REID) hysterically on the rampage in THE GOODIES (1971); Dr Ruth Wilkins (Mary Peach), a GP suing a folk singing duo for blasphemous libel in CROWN COURT 'The Song Not the Singer' (1978 T); Emily (Sheila Keith), a sour, puritanical problem-page writer in AGONY (1979 T) of chilly aspect and ferocious Northern vowels involved in the 'Hear No Evil/See No Evil' campaign; Mrs Pollard (Annette Crosbie) of Mothers and Housewives for Purity in TICKETS FOR THE TITANIC 'The Way, the Truth, the Video' (1987 T); the Older Woman (Judy Parfitt), convinced that Britain is taking a downward spiral into Hell, having an art exhibition closed on grounds of blasphemy in *Figure with Meat* (1991 R).

'Oh, so reasonable, with just the odd hint of an ingenuousness so great as to be entirely unconvincing' (Alison HENNEGAN reviewing EVERYMAN 'Blasphemy at the Old Bailey', GAY NEWS 127).

Whitemore, Hugh (1936–) English author, playwright and television scriptwriter, former actor. Very prolific as an adaptor (COUNTRY MATTERS 'Breeze Anstey' 1972; DAVID COPPERFIELD 1974; REBECCA 1979; *The Boy in the Bush* 1984) and originator of quietly polished, psychologically acute character studies (*Dan, Dan the Charity Man* 1966 T; *Dummy* 1977 T; *Stevie* 1978 C). He wrote *Breaking the Code* – the stage play about Alan TURING. He revisited some of his drama-school colleagues (including Susannah YORK) in *Twenty Years On* (1979 T).

Whiteoaks A play, adapted from her own family saga novel by Mazo De La Roche which opened in London in 1936 and in New York two years later. Nancy Price repeated her role as the matriarch Adeline Whiteoak in the radio and television versions in 1948 and 1949 respectively, with Jean Cadell taking the role in 1954 (the 2-part *The Whiteoaks Chronicles* T) and Kate Read in 1972 (in a 13-part series *The Whiteoaks of Jalna* T). Her grandson Finch Whiteoak was played by David Enders 1948, Lyndon Brook 1949 T and John Charlesworth 1954 T.

The original play contains a scene – which was performed on television in 1937 – where Adeline more or less directly tells the sensitive Finch that, although she knows he may not marry and produce children, she is going to leave him her money:

'I like boys about me. And you're a nice boy. You are, aren't you?'
'No, I'm not ... Not nice ...'
'I say you're very nice.'
'You're wonderful, Gran. You're twice the man I'll ever be.'

She tells him to stand up for himself, but reinforces that, although she knows him to be a 'queer boy' (this was changed to 'odd' for broadcasting), she still likes him 'very much'.

Finch's brother, the poet Renny, is a reprobate, and it was this aspect of the production – not Finch's 'oddness' or 'queerness' that provoked controversy in 1954. Philip HOPE-WALLACE in the *Listener* applauded 'the efforts of the good Mazo De La Roche to indicate that even Whiteoaks have sexual union (otherwise there would be no series) ... There is much agitation today about what is and what is not obscene. Evidently the notion that anyone is free to inflict his own phobias on the public dies hard ... It was *Young Renny* which led to the Grundys ringing up Lime Grove in horror and demanding expurgations which were granted, it was said, in the interests of "art" – not a yielding to criticism.'

Whitman, Peter (1946–) American-born, British-based actor: fragile but resilient and full of kinetic energy.

C: cop Dwayne ('holy skunk sweat!') in *Superman II* (1980): 'I can't eat beans because I come out in a rash if I eat beans'; the radio producer in *Dream Child* (1985); the hysterical air controller who witnesses the alien craft landing in *Morons from Outer Space* (1985); etc.

R: Rick Barlow in *Pretty Polly Barlow* (1975); Tony Orford in *Star Quality* (1975); funeral director Dorian in *When Did You Last See Your Father?* (1979); Roddy, author with writer's block in *Vivien the Blockbuster* (1980); Tom, the gay writer in *Slipping Away* (1984); Hector Malone in *Man and Superman* (1984); starring as Lydecker, the bullied American soldier in Vietnam in *On the Yankee Stadium* (1987); *Short Story*: reading 'The Smile' and 'The Gift' by Ray Bradbury (1991); Claude 'Buck' Eatherly, ex-509th Squadron, USAF in *Thin Boy* (1991); George in *Of Mice and Men* (1992); etc.

T: the rabbi, who arrives at Jane and Laurence's son's circumcision with a pair of garden shears in AGONY (1981); Buzz, one of *The Brylcreem Boys* (1981); gangster Spats in *Raspberry Ripple* (1988); etc.

Whitman, Walt (1819–1892) American poet and prose writer, passionate and penetrating, whose 'Calamus' section of *Leaves of Grass* (1855) influenced sexual revolutionaries Edward CARPENTER, Havelock Ellis and John Addington SYMONDS. Some sections of *A Song of Myself* (which Orson WELLES read on the BBC Third Programme in 1953) are also homoerotic. Whitman's overwhelming sense of loving brotherhood was evoked in MY OWN PRIVATE IDAHO (1991 C).

Biography: *How to Enjoy Life at 80* (1948 R: Alys Russell remembers her friend – 'Old and poor and half paralysed, he looked forward to the future'); QUALITY STREET 'Three Poets of Personal Voice' (1964 R); *A Celebration of Walt Whitman: A Child of Adam* (1976 R); *Song of Myself* aka *Beautiful Dreamers* (1976 T: with Rip Torn as the poet, and Brad DAVIS as Peter Doyle, the streetcar conductor he fell in love with); THE WOUND DRESSER (1986 R: played by Denis QUILLEY).

Vincent Price requested *Leaves of Grass* as his DESERT ISLAND DISCS book in 1969. This poem sequence, set to the music of Delius [Sea Drift], Roy Harris [Symphony for Voices], Vaughan Williams [Three Poems by Walt Whitman], William Schuman [Carols of Death] and Hamilton Harty [The Mystic Trumpeter], was heard on BBC Radio 3 in 1991.

Whitrow, Benjamin (193?–) English actor of great depth and wry feeling. Was a perfect Joe ACKERLEY in WE THINK THE WORLD OF YOU (1980 T) and, as Russell in AFTER HENRY (1985–9 R), made the most of his limited opportunities to create a rounded gay man.

Other credits include: the priest in *Londoners* 'The Old Man of Chelsea Reach' (1965 T); Edward Reynolds, the husband with the poodle in *A Dog's Ransom* (1978 T); *Tales of the Unexpected* 'What Have You Been up to Lately?' (1981 T); man in street in *Brimstone and Treacle* (1982 C); dictator's right-hand man Neville Tyldsley in *Beloved Latitudes* (1985 R); *Sharma and Beyond* (1985 T); Mr Marsden, one of the clients in PERSONAL SERVICES (1987 C); tin-pot tyrant Arkwright in *On the Black Hill* (1987 C); Alistair in *Blood and Bruises* (1988 R); Robert Douglas in *Chancer* (1990 T); Dr Fenton in *No Commitments* (1992 R); James in *Ghosts from the Past* 'A Warden for All Saints' (1992 R).

Who? First sung by Jack Donahue in the Oscar Hammerstein–Jerome Kern Broadway musical *Sunny* (1925), then by Jack Buchanan on the London stage. It is the latter's recording that is so adored by Guy Bennett (Rupert Everett) in ANOTHER COUNTRY (1984 C). He sings it softly, lying on the floor of the moonlit study after a rendezvous with James Harcourt (Cary Elwes) who has stolen his 'heart away', pausing on the line 'dreaming dreams that will never come true'.

The real Bennett, Guy BURGESS, plays the song endlessly in his Moscow flat in AN ENGLISHMAN ABROAD (1983 T), pro-

viding a strong link with his visitor, CORAL BROWNE who was the lover of Jack Buchanan during the 1940s. The song provides the poignant climax of the documentary about the actress, *Caviar to the General* (1990 T). 'Who?' was crime writer Edgar Lustgarten's favourite song – he played it at Oxford in the 1920s according to the 1992 radio biography *The Murder Man*.

Who Are We? The original title of WORD IS OUT (1977 C).

Who's Afraid of Virginia Woolf? (US 1966 C) Anatomy of a marriage: Martha (Elizabeth Taylor) and George (Richard Burton) who can't live with, can't live without. Horrified onlookers: George Segal and Sandy Dennis.
W/P: Ernest Lehmann from the play by Edward ALBEE; D: Mike Nichols; 129 mins.

Swingeing psychodrama about blighted hopes and dreams, rituals, vendettas, rants, skirmishes, retreats, charges, and – temporary? – cease-fire and surrender. A radio version was produced by Glyn DEARMAN in 1975 with Elaine Stritch and Ray McAnally, Blain Fairman and Pinkie Johnstone (17.2.75; BBC Radio 3; *c* 100 mins). (Albee has consistently denied that George and Martha were, in reality, a homosexual couple.)

why do people hate gays? Ian MCKELLEN answered screenwriter William Goldman's question thus in *Chain Reaction* (1992 R): 'Most women don't have a problem with gays; it's heterosexual men who have the problem ... If they meet a man who defines himself in different terms, [that man] challenges something basic in what they think about themselves.'

why tarnish his memory? In ONLY CONNECT (1979 T) E. M. FORSTER (Christopher Banks) finishes recording his talk on the life and work of Edward CARPENTER for the BBC. He then says to his producer: 'I never said he was ...' The man doesn't quite catch Forster's drift. 'I didn't say he was homosexual.' There is a long pause before his producer dismisses the omission. No need to re-record.

A question, voiced and unvoiced by countless radio, television and film producers/directors when making tributes to famous men (and women). Instead of viewing them in their totality, the acceptable is magnified (wives/husbands, children, heterosexual excess) and the problematic ignored or downplayed into insignificance. Just a handful of examples: MICHELANGELO in *The Agony and the Ecstasy* (1965 C); Angus WILSON on THE SOUTH BANK SHOW (1980 T); *Florence* NIGHTINGALE (1985 T); MISHIMA *A Life in Four Chapters* (1985 C).

Drawing up a code in 1989 (the first since 1945), the British Broadcasting Corporation pledged itself to 'accuracy, impartiality and responsibility'. These 'are at the heart of the BBC's contract with its audience,' said Director General Michael Checkland in March of that year.

wicked queen Grasping, opulent women often with sapphic accoutrements in the shape of handy handmaidens, or thirsty looks in the direction of the heroines: mad, whip-wielding Queen Regina (Seena Owen) in *Queen Kelly* (1929); the stepmother in *Snow White* (1938 C); Queen Bera (Anouk Aimée) in SODOM AND GOMORRAH (1962 C); the Black Queen (Anita Pallenberg) in *Barbarella* (1968 C); Queen Taramis (Sarah Douglas) in *Conan the Destroyer* (1984 C); Queen Bavmorda (Jean Marsh), all-purpose sorceress in *Willow* (1988 C; the actress had graduated to wicked queendom after playing another dabbler in dark arts, Princess Mombi, in *Return to Oz* 1985 C); Queen Isabella (Tilda Swinton) in EDWARD II (1991 C); Queen Gedren (Sandahl Bergman) in *Red Sonja* (1985), about which Nigel Floyd wrote in *Monthly Film Bulletin* (November 1985): 'Since there are suggestive hints in the way in which Gedren looks at Sonja, the heroine's quest for vengeance is also an exorcism of latent lesbian desire – a symbolic rejection of what might be thought of as the corollary of her man-

hating stance. The despatch of Gedren, and hence the removal of the spectre of "abnormal" desire, becomes a necessary precondition of Sonja's regaining her ability to relate normally to men.'

Male wicked queens who come and go in puffs of pink and lavender smoke spewing out all manner of nasty, cutting remarks are a feature of many a film or television play, notably Michael (Kenneth Nelson) in THE BOYS IN THE BAND (1970 C) and Gerald (Richard Pearson) in COMING OUT (1979 T).

See also QUEEN.

The Wicked Witch of the West The antithesis of the fubsy, warm and affectionate folks in *The Wizard of Oz* (1939 C), unforgettably characterized – with pointy hat, black cloak and emerald green face and cackle – by Margaret Hamilton. The character's most famous line – 'I'll get you, my pretty' – was used as a synonym for AIDS in DOCTOR, DOCTOR 'Accentuate the Positive' (1989 T).

widows Kate (Liv Ullmann) propelled by loneliness, fascination and fury into an affair with her dead husband's mistress in RICHARD'S THINGS (1981 C/T); Gail (Mariette Hartley) finding emotional commitment impossible with either her late husband's friend or a pushy, attractive female in MY TWO LOVES (1986 T); Theresa Russell bumping off spouses but dangerously enthralled by a suspicious insurance investigator (Debra Winger) in *Black Widow* (1987 C).

Widows (UK 1983 T) Three women (Ann Mitchell, Maureen O'Farrell and Fiona Hendley) team up to carry out a heist after their men are killed when a job goes wrong. The 'widows' are joined by a sullen black woman of ambiguous sexuality, Bella (Eva Mottley), and are hindered by police and by the powerful Fisher brothers, one of whom Arnie (Jeffrey Chiswick) tenderly calls his boyfriend 'darling'.

W: Lynda La Plante; P: Linda Agran;

D: Ian Toynton; Thames; 6 parts; 60 mins each.

A novel idea, studded with strong characters muttering or spitting pithy dialogue. Bella – 'I wouldn't touch her anyway. She looks too much like a fella,' says leader Dolly (Ann Mitchell) to Shirley (Fiona Hendley) – is all aggressive attitude and wistful looks. (The actress died before the second series went into production: another character, played by Debby Bishop, was substituted.)

Wilcox, Michael (1943–) English stage and television writer, especially fine on the subtle awakenings of adolescence. One of his best works, *Rents*, about two male prostitutes in Glasgow, staged in the late 1970s, is long overdue for filming.

R: STANDARD PROCEDURE (1979); *Accounts* (1982); *Marriage* (1986); etc.

T: *Clean Sweep* (1981); *Cricket* (1982); *Midnight Feast* (1982); ACCOUNTS (1983); LENT (1985); *A Case for Justice* 'A Party to Crime' (1985, apparently not transmitted); *Inspector Morse* 'Last Bus to Woodstock' (1988); etc.

Wilde, Constance (1858–98) Delicately indomitable, she stands in the margins of the Oscar WILDE tragedy: the loving wife, the society hostess, the shattered woman, the supporter and then the rejector of her husband, denying Wilde access to his sons and forbidding contact with Bosie after his release from prison. Played by Phyllis Calvert (*Oscar Wilde* 1960 C); Yvonne Mitchell (*The Trials of Oscar Wilde* 1960 C); Amanda Boxer (*Lillie* 'America' 1978 T); Emily Richard (*Oscar* 1985 T). However, what is lacking in these portraits is the reality of Constance Wilde as very much a 'New Woman': editing *Rational Dress* (an attack on bustles), sending one of her sons to an experimental school (Bedales), and maintaining friendships with strong-minded, eccentric women like the Ranee of Sarawak, Princess Alice of Monaco and Lady Mount Temple.

Wilde, Oscar [Oscar Fingal O'Flahertie Wills Wilde] (1856–1900) Irish wit, poet, novelist, dramatist, political essayist, writer of fairy tales and short stories, convicted criminal, exile, bankrupt, decadent aesthete, dandy. Inimitable, incomparable and irrefutable, his supreme talent for decoration and colourization, together with his crossing of the class and sexual divides, provided the rope for his own lynching.

Played by Paul Whitsun-Jones in *Death of Satan* (1958 T: the inhabitants of Hell – including Oscar – are enjoying themselves too much so the Devil has come down to take back some unhappy souls); Robert Morley, flabby, a bit of a windbag but warm and compassionate beneath the superior pose in *Oscar Wilde* (1960 C); Peter FINCH, all muscular, dry grandeur, withdrawn and reflective in *The Trials of Oscar Wilde* (1960 C); Max ADRIAN coruscating in exile (*Echo de Paris* 1961); Micheal MACLIAMMOIR, a florid Irish aesthete, wrenching melancholy soon replacing the jaunty amorality in ON TRIAL (1960 T), *The Importance of Being Oscar* (1961 T) and *Oscar Wilde* (1963 R); Alan BADEL as the prematurely aged pariah, rechristened 'Monsieur Sebastien Melmoth' (*Famous Gossips* 1965 T); Freddie Jones rheumily arch in *A Bruisèd Daffodil of Last Night's Sin* (1971 T); Micheal MacLiammoir again in *Best Sellers* (1967 T); *I Must Be Talking to My Friends* (1968 R), and another round of *The Importance of Being Oscar* (1971 T); Michael Deacon glintingly irresponsible in *Oscar Wilde in America* (1971 R); Philip SAYER in the Frank Harris saga *Fearless Frank* (1978 T: two scenes in the Café Royal blowing kisses and deciding to fight Queensberry against Harris' advice); Peter Egan as the young dandy wooing Lillie Langtry in *Lillie* (1978 T); jauntily aestheticizing America in *Nothing to Declare But My Genius* (1982 R, played by Martin Jarvis who also read some of the short stories in character in 1984 T); Michael Gambon, crisp and soldierly at the start, baffled and beaten at the end in *Oscar* (1985 T); Nickolas GRACE puckishly libidinous in *Salome's Last Dance* (1988 C);

Stephen Rea gravely gay and socialist in *Saint Oscar* (1991 T); Simon CALLOW pronouncedly Irish, triumphant and – although dead – dying for a fag in *The Miles Kington Interview* (1993 R).

There have been scores of other portrayals, lampoons and guest appearances. He was one of the personalities in *The Balloon Game: A Question of Survival* (who should be thrown out – BYRON, Chaucer or Wilde? 1976 T); OMNIBUS 'A Summer Side-Show' (1977 T) found him 'scribbling beseeching notes to his titled paramour even after his rejection and betrayal by him'; he was part of the glittering coterie in the Ronald FIRBANK biography *A Self-Made Man* (1985 R: played by James Kerry); made into a bit of a buffoon as the lily-carrying poet Reginald Bunthorne (Derek Hammond-Stroud) in *Patience* (1982 R etc), the Gilbert and Sullivan jest at the expense of the aesthetic movement; on the cover of the Beatles' *Sergeant Pepper's Lonely Hearts Club Band* (next to Hopalong Cassidy); the inspiration for the Rolling Stones' song and short film WE LOVE YOU in 1967 (Jagger in the dock, Marianne Faithfull as Bosie); woven into the mystery of *The Blackheath Poisonings* (1992 T: played by Richard Strange).

His name, life, downfall, wit and wisdom have been evoked or invoked in a variety of contexts: quoted by the larcenous 'Captain' (Geoffrey King) in a 1956 episode of DIXON OF DOCK GREEN ('You should study Oscar Wilde ... He pointed out that education only makes some rogues cleverer than others'; included in Charlie's oath in STAIRCASE ('God help us all and Oscar Wilde'); used as subterfuge in HITCHCOCK's 1972 *Frenzy* – a couple check into a hotel for love in the afternoon, registering as Mr and Mrs O. Wilde); demonized by John OSBORNE's grandfather who spoke of him and Lord Alfred DOUGLAS in disparaging terms while John was growing up (*A Better Class of Person* 1985 T); inspiring the Greek poet Napoleon Lapathiotis who found the reports of the Wilde scandal – as well as the man's works – of great comfort during his tor-tured youth in the 1920s (*Meteor and Shadow* 1985 C); by the name of the sapphic train passenger Lady Windermere (Delphine Seyrig) in *Johanna D'Arc of Mongolia* (1987 C).

Documentary accounts and literary appraisals include *The Genius of Oscar Wilde* (1946 R); *Wisdom Under a Jester's Mask* (1954 R: talk by Lionel Hale); *The Good Life* 'What Lies Ahead?' (1953 R: '[Wilde's] sense seems to have been at the mercy of sensuality,' commented Alan Pryce-Jones); *Compass* 'Oscar Wilde: The Man and the Writer' (1961 T); *Oscar Wilde* (1963 R: with Micheal MacLiammoir, Tyrone Guthrie, Jacques Brunius, Andrew Salkey, Arthur Calder-Marshall and Philip HOPE-WAL-LACE – who also produced); *Lady Wilde's Tea Party* (1969 R: Patience Collier as his mother); QUALITY STREET 'The Wit of Oscar Wilde' (Aust 1969 R); *Chronicle* 'The Alexandrians' (1970 T); *The Name is Oscar Wilde* (1975 R); *Makers* 'Joyce, Yeats and Wilde' (Ireland 1983 T: Seamus Heaney and Professor Richard Ellman 'explore the unique qualities of these writers' imaginations and their enduring meaning for us' – synopsis); *Oscar Wilde: Spendthrift or Genius?* (1987 T); *New Light on Oscar* (1985 R: Rupert Hart-Davis' *More Letters of Oscar Wilde*); *Bookmark* (1987 T: Victoria Glendinning, Jack Klaff and Kenneth WILLIAMS discuss the Richard Ellman biography); 'The Making of An Aesthete' (1988 R: from Ellman's book, read by John RYE to accompany the broadcast of Act 2 of *Patience*); one of the four contestants in a 1989 MASTER-MIND bout chose to answer questions on 'The Life and Works of Oscar Wilde' (the other special subjects were 'the History of Ireland', 'Boys' Public Schools of England' and 'World Heavyweight Championship Fights').

Plays: THE IMPORTANCE OF BEING EARNEST (1924 R; 1937 T; 1952 C; etc); *An Ideal Husband* (1947 C; 1954 R; etc); *Lady Windermere's Fan* (1926 & 1948 C; 1968 R; etc); *A Woman of No Importance* (1949 & 1960 T; 1990 R; etc); *Salome* (1958 R; and excerpts in *Salome's Last Dance* 1988 C).

Novel: THE PICTURE OF DORIAN GRAY (1945 C; 1948 R; 1957 T; etc).

Short stories: 'Lord Arthur Savile's Crime' (in *Flesh and Fantasy* 1943 C; 1960 T; in *The Liars* series 1966 T; etc); *The Canterville Ghost* (1944 C; 1962 T; etc); *Stories by Oscar Wilde* (read by Martin Jarvis, 1984); 'The Nightingale and the Rose', 'The Happy Prince' and other stories for children (read by Philip Schofield, 1992 R etc and these works requested as their books by Phyllis Calvert and CORAL BROWNE on DESERT ISLAND DISCS 1951 and 1961 respectively).

Poetry and essays: THE BALLAD OF READING GAOL (1963 R etc); *In The Gold Room* (read by Keith Michell, 1984 R).

'Oscar Wilde said that the one duty we owe to history is to rewrite it ... We articulate a challenge which Wilde could not. We suggest that a gay culture is something to be struggled for, not dreamt or bought. At this point, our rewriting of history becomes a truly dangerous activity' (NEIL BARTLETT, *Who Was That Man? A Present for Mr Oscar Wilde*, 1988).

See also BUNBURYING; EACH MAN KILLS THE THING HE LOVES.

Wildeblood, Peter (1923–91?) English journalist who was sent to prison for two years in the early 1950s for 'GROSS INDECENCY', later becoming a campaigner for homosexual law reform – in books and articles and in a number of television plays he produced and sometimes wrote: *The Younger Generation* (11 plays; as P 1961); *The Duke Ellington Show* (1963 P); *Victoria Regina* (1964 P); *It Only Seems Like Yesterday* (1965 P); *Six Shades of Black* (1965 W/P); *Blackmail* (1966 P, including 'The Man Who Could See' W); *Rogues Gallery* (1968–9 P, including 'The Curious Adventures of Miss Jane Rawley Who, by Forsaking Her Sex, ...' 1968 W); *Conception of Murder* (Exec P, including 'Conversation Piece' 1970 W); *Stables Theatre* 'The People's Jack' (1970 W); *Confession* 'Death of a Ladies' Man' (1970

W); *Victorian Scandals* (1976 P); *Tales of the Klondike* (1983 story ed); etc.

Wilder, Billy [Samuel Wilder] (1906–   ) Austro-Hungarian writer-director, renowned for his mordant wit, bilious outlook on life and love of the perverse. Among his screenplays (always written in collaboration): *Midnight* (1939); *Ninotchka* (1939); *Ball of Fire* (1941); *The Major and the Minor* (1942 also D); *Double Indemnity* (1944 also D); *The Lost Weekend* (1945 also D); *Sunset Boulevard* (1950 also D); *The Seven Year Itch* (1955 also D); *Witness for the Prosecution* (1958 also D); SOME LIKE IT HOT (1959 also D); *The Apartment* (1960 D); *The Fortune Cookie* aka *Meet Whiplash Willie* (1966 also D); *The Private Life of Sherlock Holmes* (1970 also D); *Fedora* (1978 also D); *Buddy Buddy* (1981 also D).

Autobiography: *Billy, How Do You Do It? The Billy Wilder Story* (3 parts, 1991 T).

Wild Flowers (UK 1990 C/T) Sadie (Beatie Edney), who is travelling down from Glasgow to Gourock to attend her mother-in-law Annie's funeral, reminisces about their first meeting and how they fell in love.

W: Sharman MacDonald; D: Robert Smith; 75 mins.

Love of the unconventional kind blossoms on the west coast of Scotland. Colette O'Neill communicates what the script does not as the comfortable siren daring to be generous with her feelings in a tight little community.

Willes, Peter (1913–91) English television producer, former Hollywood actor (*The Dawn Patrol* 1930; *Idiot's Delight* 1939; etc). A great champion of Joe ORTON's works on television. He left Rediffusion in 1971 after a decade as head of light entertainment and then drama, to supervise Yorkshire's drama output. He is mentioned extensively in *The Orton Diaries*, ed John Lahr, 1986.

The Seven Deadly Virtues (including Orton's *Funeral Games* and *The Erpingham Camp*, 1966); *The Seven Deadly Sins* (including Orton's *The Good and*

Faithful Servant, 1967); *The Root of All Evil* (1968); ENTERTAINING MR SLOANE (1968); *The Ten Commandments* (including *The Ruffian on the Stair*, 1969); *Young Man Seeks Part-Time Work* (1973); etc.

Williams, Emlyn [George Williams] (1905–87) Welsh actor, playwright and screenwriter of great wit and *brio*. Although passionately concerned with social and personal-political issues in his fiction, he never wrote anything dealing directly with bisexuality, except for the second part of his autobiography (*Emlyn*, 1973) in which he discusses an affair with 'an actor'.

Screenplays: contributed to *Friday the Thirteenth* (1933), *The Man Who Knew Too Much* (1934) and *Evergreen* (1934); wrote *The Last Days of Dolwyn* (1949, also D); and *Time without Pity* (1957), based on his play *Someone Waiting*.

Plays: *Night Must Fall* (1937 & 1964 C; 1938, 1954 & 1985 R; etc); *The Corn Is Green* (1945 C; 1979 T; etc); *He Was Born Gay* (about Louis XVI's son, 1946 R); *Someone Waiting* (1955 R); ACCOLADE (1957 T); *The Power of Dawn* (1977 T); *Slowly Does It* (about a bachelor who has to get married or lose his farm, Wales 1985 T also D); *Cuckoo* (1987 R); etc.

C: As actor: Lord Lebanon in *The Case of the Frightened Lady* (1932); the blackmailer in the 'Blake, Gentleman of Fortune' segment of *Friday the Thirteenth* (1933); Chen in *Broken Blossoms* (1936); CALIGULA in *I, Claudius* (1937, abandoned); *The Citadel* (1938); *Dead Men Tell No Tales* (1938); *They Drive by Night* (1938); *The Stars Look Down* (1939); Harry the Pedlar in *Jamaica Inn* (1939); Tracy in *This Girl Is News* (1940); *Major Barbara* (1940); *Hatter's Castle* (1941); *The Last Days of Dolwyn* aka *Woman of Dolwyn* (1949); *Another Man's Poison* (1951); a bank manager in *The Magic Box* (1951); Maxwell Bard, an urbane San Francisco bachelor and friend of the three wives and the *Three Husbands* (1951); David Dunbar in *The Scarf* (1951); Wamba in *Ivanhoe* (1952); *The Deep Blue Sea* (1955); Emile Zola in *I Accuse* (1958); *Beyond This Place* (1959);

the abortionist in THE L-SHAPED ROOM (1962); Alain De Montfauçon in *Eye of the Devil* (1967); art dealer Jack Foil in *The Walking Stick* (1970); Mr Dick in DAVID COPPERFIELD (1970 also T).

R: As actor: title role in *Will Shakespeare* (1931); *The Corn Is Green* (excerpts, 1938); *He Was Born Gay* (1946); Danny in *Stars in Their Choices* 'Night Must Fall' (1954); *Someone Waiting* (1955); fortune teller Gerald Lowen accused of murder in *Mind Over Murder* (1963); etc. (He was played by Joe Dunlop in *View to a Death* 1989 which chronicled Actors' Equity's 1950s witch-hunt to root out Communists and subversives.)

T: As actor: the QC in *The Winslow Boy* (1959); Tolstoy in *The Power of Dawn* (1977); a retired lawyer in *The Deadly Game* (1982); Horace Brittling, an artist accused of forgery in *Rumpole of the Bailey* 'Rumpole and the Genuine Article' (1983); Edward Minty in PAST CARING (1986).

Autobiography: DESERT ISLAND DISCS (1942 & 1956); *For St David's Day* (1954 T: a talk about 'a brief encounter in the hills'); *This Is Your Life* 'Sybil Thorndike' (1959); *The Epic That Never Was* (1965 T: about *I, Claudius*); *The World of One Man Shows* (1967 T: about his Dickens' readings).

Williams, Frank (193?–) English television and stage actor, over 6 feet tall, usually resident inside the pale skins of twittery, harmless men. Played Captain Pocket in about 70 episodes of *The Army Game* (1958–60 T); and the Vicar of Walmington-on-Sea in *Dad's Army* (1968–77 T). He is also a playwright (*Murder by Appointment*; *Alibi for Murder*; *The TV Murders*; etc).

C: Nuttall in *A Stitch in Time* (1964); Second Witch in *The Deadly Affair* (1966).

T: Mr Meiklejohn in *Abigail and Roger* (1956); waiter in *The Frog* (1958); Cedric in *Diary of a Young Man* 'Power' (1964); John De La Poeur Whiting in *Sir Jocelyn, the Minister Would Like a Word* (1965); the good-natured and flirtatious bedding salesman in a 1973 episode of *Love Thy Neighbour*; one half of a male couple in *Tears Before Bedtime* (1983); etc.

Williams, Kenneth (1926–88) English comic actor, purveyor of nostril-flaring camp in *Carry On* films, radio shows (HANCOCK'S HALF HOUR; ROUND THE HORNE), quiz games (*Just a Minute*), variety (*International Cabaret*) and talk shows (*Parkinson; Wogan*) for four decades.

C: *Trent's Last Case* (1952); *The Beggars' Opera* (1952); an early New Zealand colonist in *The Seekers* aka *Land of Fury* (1954); *Moby Dick* (1956); *Carry On Sergeant* (1958) and a dozen other *Carry Ons* and offshoots until *Carry On Emmanuelle* (1978); *The Hound of the Baskervilles* (1978).

R: *Hancock's Half Hour* (1955–8, including Hilary St Clair in 'The Publicity Photograph' (1958); *Good Evening Each* (with Beryl REID, 1958); *Beyond Our Ken* (1958–63); *The Private World of Kenneth Williams* (1961); *Diary of a Madman* (1963, broadcast 1991); *Round the Horne* (1965–9); STOP MESSIN' ABOUT (with Hugh PADDICK, 1969); *Oh, Get On with It!* (1969–70); *Just a Minute* (1967–87); *Unique Hancock* (1973); *The Secret Life of Kenneth Williams* (with Josephine Tewson as his wife, 1973) and *More Secret Life* (minus wife, 1973); *Get On with It* (1975); *Kenneth Williams' Cabaret* (1986); etc.

T: the angel in *The Wonderful Visit* (1952); Bentley Summerhayes in *Misalliance* (1954); the Rev. Silas Maydig in *Cold Comfort Farm* (1956); *The Man Who Could Work Miracles* (1956); *Hancock's Half Hour* (all 1957): the Yodeller of Dulwich in 'The Alpine Holiday', repertory company producer in 'Lady Chatterley's Revenge', policeman in 'The New Neighbour', Prince Paul in 'The Pianist' and old man in 'The Auction'; Clive, a silly young playboy who gets a job with a bank which is then robbed in *Dick and the Duchess* 'The Armoured Car' (1959); Napoleon in *Catch As Catch Can* (1964); *International Cabaret* (series compère, 1966–8); *The Kenneth Williams Show* (1976); *The Light*

Princess (1978); *Will o' the Wisp* (children's series, 1980s); etc.

Autobiography: DESERT ISLAND DISCS (1961 & 1987 R); *The Time of My Life* (in the army, 1973 R); HOMOSEXUALITY – THE YEARS OF CHANGE (1977 R); *Man of Action* (1976 R); *Round and Round the Horne* (1976 R); ARENA 'A Genius Like Us' (on his friends Joe ORTON and Kenneth Halliwell, 1982 T); *Comic Roots* 'The Cromer Estate, St Pancras' (1983 T); *Revelations* (1983 T); *An Audience with Kenneth Williams* (1984 T); *Wogan* (reunited with Hugh Paddick, 1986 T); *Arena* 'Talk Is Cheap' (his views on TV chat shows, 1987 T); *Cover to Cover* (discussing Richard ELLMAN's *Oscar Wilde*, 1987 T); *Could Do Better* (summer 1941 school report, 1987 R); etc.

'When he lifts an eyebrow, the public become eagerly consenting adults. He smiles vivaciously at them, calls them "duckie" and flirtatiously urges them to "stop messin' about"' (Patrick Skene Catling, *Sunday Times Magazine*, December 1967).

'The fact is that his talent is anarchic – he is the force that deflates the structures of pomposity' (Simon Brett, producer of *Oh, Get On with It!*, quoted in Wilfred D'Ath, *The Rise of the Campanologist*, *Listener*, 24.10.76).

'His hallmark, an outrageously campy delivery, with a high nasal English twang, early established him as a master of social snobbery and sexual innuendo' (*Variety* obituary, 20.4.88).

Williams, Tennessee [Thomas Lanier Williams] (1911–83) American writer, many of whose works have been filmed with variable success and who became – with Arthur Miller and Jack Kerouac – a popular literary icon of the 1950s, even being mentioned on I LOVE LUCY ('What are you ... a Tennessee *knocker*?' Lucy screams accusingly at a philistine in 'Lucy Writes a Play' 1951 T). Although many of his 70 plays deal with isolated individuals seeking a kinder, more accepting world, he wrote very few rounded, sympathetic gay or lesbian characters. His true sexual feelings are more apparent in his short stories.

Plays: *The Glass Menagerie* (1950 & 1987 C; 1964, 1966 & 1973 T; 1980 R); *A Streetcar Named Desire* (1951 C; 1984 T); *The Rose Tattoo* (1955 C; 1964 T); *Baby Doll* (1956 C); CAT ON A HOT TIN ROOF (1958 C; 1976 & 1984 T); SUDDENLY LAST SUMMER (1959 C); *Sweet Bird of Youth* (1961 C; 1991 T); *Summer and Smoke* (1962 C); *Camino Real* (1964 T); *The Night of the Iguana* (1964 C); *This Property Is Condemned* (1966 C); *Boom!* (adapted from 'The Milk Train Doesn't Stop Here Anymore', 1968 C); *Last of the Mobile Hotshots* aka *Blood Kin* (from 'The Seven Descents of Myrtle', 1970 C); VIEUX CARRÉ (1985 R); *Orpheus Descending* (1990 T, and as *The Fugitive Kind* 1960 C); etc.

Screenplays: 'The Blue of Noon' (adapted from a George Bataille novel, due to be filmed by Rainer Werner FASSBINDER and abandoned after his death in 1982); *Secret Places of the Heart* (unproduced, broadcast in a radio version 1988).

Novels: *The Roman Spring of Mrs Stone* (1961 C); *The Migrants* (adapted by Lanford WILSON, 1974 T).

Short stories: *Talk to Me Like the Rain* (a short made by Douglas Sirk in the 1970s, C); *One Arm* (1985 R); 'Death and the Black Masseur' (filmed as NOIR ET BLANC 1986 C); *Something by Tolstoi* (read by Tom Hunsinger, 1986 R: 'There's a great danger when love for one person becomes the core of one's life. For when the love is lost, the life is lost').

Autobiography: *Frankly Speaking* (to John BOWEN, Peter Duval-Smith and John Freeman, 1959 R); *The Pursuit of Happiness* 'The Secret' (1960 T); *Hollywood and the Stars* 'The Making of "The Night of the Iguana"' (1964 T); *The Method* (1964 T); *In Town Today* (1968 R); FROST OVER AMERICA (1970 T); *The Lively Arts* 'Tennessee Williams' (with Melvyn Bragg, 1976 T).

Biography: MONITOR (reporting direct from the London first night of *Cat on a Hot Tin Roof* in 1958 with director Peter Hall and Gore VIDAL both insisting that, despite the choice of subject matter and the Lord Chamberlain's ban, Williams was a highly moral writer); *Options* 'American Authors' (1987 R).

willie/willy Slang word for the penis. 'Fifty-three per cent of the population of Belfast's got a willy, so what's wrong with it?' maintained Billy Connolly in *Big Banana Feet* (1976 C). One of the running jokes in EASTENDERS (T) for the first four or five years was Ethel's 'Willy' (her pug dog), as in 'Where's my Willy?'

the willies 'He gives me the willies,' says Liz Garrison (Sissy Spacek) to her husband (Kevin Costner) when she sees Lee Harvey Oswald on the television in *JFK* (1991 C).

Willis, Baron Ted (1918–92) English writer who pioneered TV realism in plays like THE PATTERN OF MARRIAGE (1954), *Woman in a Dressing Gown* (1956) and *Hot Summer Night* (1959). *The Guinness Book of Records* cites him as the most prolific television scriptwriter in the world – 41 television serials including DIXON OF DOCK GREEN (1955–62), *Mrs Thursday* (1966) and *Hunters Walk* (1973–4) – as well as 37 stage plays and 39 film scripts – including *Good Time Girl* (1948), the first Norman Wisdom comedy *Trouble in Store* (1953), and *Bitter Harvest* (1963). He adapted two of his novels for radio: *The Left-Handed Sleeper* (1982) and *Death May Surprise Us* (1984). The novel he had finished just before his death has a strong homosexual subplot.

Will You Still Love Me Tomorrow?

Dusty SPRINGFIELD's version of the Carole King–Gerry Goffin 1961 Shirelles classic is sung, in *Killing Time* (1990 T), over a tableau of two men in bed together. One is gently rocking the other, who is dead. Another – uncredited – version is given a brief hearing in THE WOMEN OF BREWSTER PLACE (1989 T), prior to one of the lesbians slamming out of the apartment after a fierce argument with her lover. It is also the accompaniment to Patrick Swayze and Jennifer Gray going to bed together in *Dirty Dancing* (1987 C).

Wilson, Sir Angus (1913–91) English satirical writer with his finger on the button of human and inhuman affairs. A member of the Homosexual Law Reform Committee in the 1960s and vice-president of the Campaign for Homosexual Equality (CHE) in the following decade.

Novels and short stories: *After the Show* (from *A Bit off the Map*, 1959 T); LATE CALL (1969 R; 1975 T); *Crazy Crowd* (1976 R); *The Little Companion* (1976 R); *Et Dona Ferentes* (1976 R); *The Old Men at the Zoo* (1984 T); *Anglo-Saxon Attitudes* (1992 T); SHORT STORY 'Higher Standards' (1992 R); *The Middle Age of Mrs Eliot* (1993 T).

R: 'Left in the Middle' (the adventures of Norman Spondee, a political innocent in the 1930s, 1956); *The Memoirs of Mrs Cramp* (play, 1956); *Political Metaphors* 'The Politics of the Family' (1974 R: he refers to gay liberation, along with women's liberation, as 'instant antics').

T: *The Stranger* (play, 1960); *Writer's World* 'The Incestuous Muse' (can a writer enter the mind of another artist? 1964); *Contrasts* 'Angus Wilson on the Sex War' (1968); *Charles Dickens 1812–1870: A Celebration* (1970); *The Book Programme* (the predicament of women in English literature, 1976).

Autobiography: DESERT ISLAND DISCS (1969 R); *The Book Programme* 'Angus Wilson' (his discussion with Robert Robinson on the change in his political outlook as a result of the relationships he'd had with three working-class men while at Oxford was cut before the programme went on air in 1976); THE SOUTH BANK SHOW 'Sir Angus Wilson' (restricted to childhood, adolescence and the present, 1980 T); *Bookshelf* (he described being blackmailed by a cockney butcher, *c* 1982 R); THE OTHER HALF 'Angus and Tony' (his relationship with Tony Garrett, 1984 T); *Bookmark* 'Home Thoughts from Abroad' (1987 T); *Bookmark* 'Angus Wilson – Skating on Thin Ice' (1991 T).

Wilson, Ian (1902–) English actor; small and fiercely bespectacled, described by David Quinlan in his 1985 dictionary of supporting players as 'the archetypal fussy little man of the British cinema'. Two of his most noticeable roles were the man who had become mute and agoraphobic as a result of being blown up by his own explosives (in *Mrs Wickens in the Fall* 1957 T), and the nightwatchman gobbled by a giant vegetable (in *The Day of the Triffids* 1962 C).

C: *The Master of Craft* (1922); *The Cavern Spider* (1924); bandsman in *Would You Believe It?* (1929); Theodore in *Bed and Breakfast* (1930); theatre callboy in *Facing the Music* (1933); schoolboy in *Those Were the Days* (1934); *Quiet Wedding* (1943); *Seven Days to Noon* (1950); many Boulting Brothers films of the 1950s and *Carry Ons* (*Cruising, Cowboy, Jack* and *Cleo*); Dwarf in *The Phantom of the Opera* (1962); villager in *The Wicker Man* (1973); etc.

T: Ernie in *Quatermass II* (as a worker who raids the food plant, lifting a bazooka, in his usual 1950s garb of hat, glasses, undersized jacket and grey shirt); registrar in *Judge for Yourself* (1956); prisoner in *Arrow to the Heart* (1956); walk-on in *Whirligig* (1956); Philby in *New Hope for Old* (1956); customer in *Potts in Poravia* (1956); walk-on in *The Queen and the Rebels* (1957); *Arsenic and Old Lace* (1957); postman in *Onion Boys* (1958); Goebbels in YOU ARE THERE 'The Death of Hitler' (1958); journalist in episode 4 and a shop customer in episode 6 of *Quatermass and the Pit* (1959); *The Alan King Show* (1959); *The Jimmy Logan Show* (1959); a clerk in *Garry Halliday* (1960); *The Song of a March Hare* (1960); left-luggage attendant in *Sykes ...* (1961); etc.

Wilson, Lanford (1937–) American playwright of incisive observation and slow-building plots. Pulitzer Prize for *Talley's Folly* in 1980.

R: *Brontosaurus* (1983); *Talley's Folly* (1985).

T: *Stables Theatre* 'The Gingham Dog' (1970); *The Migrants* (1974: adapted from Tennessee WILLIAMS' story); HOT*L BALTIMORE (1975); *Telling Tales* 'Lemon Sky' (1987).

wimp A term for a soft, cowardly male (or female), not as provocative or actionable as SISSY. Opera singer Nadina (Elizabeth Taylor) refers to *Young Toscanini* (Thomas Howell 1988 C) as 'a *wimp*-ering boy'. John Archer hates wearing his crash helmet in THE ARCHERS (1992 R) because it makes him look like 'a wimp', while Elizabeth calls Nigel PARGETTER one because he won't stand up to his mother: 'I don't know how you could be such a wimp, Nigel' (1992).

Marty McFly calls his son one in *Back to the Future II* (1989 C), and Charity (Harriet Walter) in *The Men's Room* (1991 T) asks Mark (Bill Nighy) 'What kind of wimp are you?' after he returns home, sheepishly, following being caught out having an affair.

US President George Bush – whatever else he may have been – was not, according to a DONAHUE programme on the eve of the 1991 Gulf war, 'a wimp'. But, according to Lou WATERS in BROTHERS (T), Donald MALTBY was the quintessence of American wimpishness.

The crossover point may have been reached between the idea of the cowering male and the allegedly sexually passive one: 'If you're a wimp, you must be gay – so let's pinch your bottom!' says Phil Donahue rhetorically after a teenage boy has told how he was bullied and sexually harassed in a 1992 show.

The Wind Beneath My Wings A 1981 Larry Henley–Jeff Silbar song which Bette MIDLER delivered at full lung power over the closing credits of *Beaches* (1988 C) to epitomize her relationship with long-time friend Hilary (Barbara Hershey). Far from being the weak partner, it is quiet Hilary, content to stay on the sidelines, who has made it possible for the extrovert to soar.

This also encapsulates the not noticeably sensitive Bart's feelings for his father in a 1991 episode of THE SIMPSONS (T).

window dressers Eddie Hatch (Robert Walker) who falls in love with a sculpture in *One Touch of Venus* (1948 C); the pompous drip (Michael WARD) whom

Norman Wisdom bests before a crowd of passers-by in *Trouble in Store* (1953 C); Hugh PADDICK strutting his stuff in *That's Your Funeral* (1972 C); Mervyn (Gorden KAYE) who gives the escaped convict an ill-judged lift in *Villains* 'Sand Dancer' (1972 T); Marshall Tyler (Robert Moore), the shiny public face of Buckley Department Store in *Diana* (1973–4 T); *Rhoda* (Valerie Harper 1974–7 T), one of the rare (at any rate, in comedy) female exponents of the craft; Norman (Michael Warren), a window designer who is eventually drafted in NORMAN ... IS THAT YOU? (1976 C); Leslie (David Banks), tall, tough and definitely not gay (though everyone expects him so to be, especially as he is wearing a dress when Dad walks in) in *Keep It in the Family* 'The Mousetrap' (1980 T); Lieutenant GRUBER (Guy Siner) in 'ALLO, 'ALLO (1984–92 T) who cultivated his artistic leanings before the war by dressing plaster mannequins; Luis Molina (William Hurt) in KISS OF THE SPIDER WOMAN (1985 C); Chipper (Charles Frank), the younger son of Katharine HEPBURN in MRS DELAFIELD WANTS TO MARRY (1986 T) who's happy doing the window dressing for New York's Fifth and Sixth Avenue stores; Diane Lane as a window dresser pursued in *Lady Beware* (1987 C); Hollywood Montrose (Meshach Taylor) in *Mannequin* (1987 C) and *Mannequin on the Move* (1991 C), head of visual display – and quite a display in himself – at the Prince and Co department store.

The following conversation is heard in *Mrs Delafield Wants to Marry*:

> Disapproving elder brother: 'It doesn't seem manly to me.'
> Chipper Delafield: 'What am I supposed to do, go into meat packing?'

Winfrey, Oprah (1954–) American actress, producer and host of a daily television talk show from 1984. She has dealt matter-of-factly with a range of lesbian and gay issues, often making a direct linkage between HOMOPHOBIA and RACISM. As an actress she has appeared – most impressively – in THE

COLOR PURPLE (1985 C) and THE WOMEN OF BREWSTER PLACE (1989 T).

Winn, Godfrey (1910–71) English human-interest columnist at the *Daily Mirror* and then the *Daily Express*; a former actor (*Blighty* 1927 C etc). Satirized as 'Godfrey Wheems' in A MAN APART (1968 R) and as 'Eliot Morrow' in COMPACT (1965 T). (He was known as 'Winifred God' on Fleet Street.)

C: Guest appearances: *Very Important Person* (1961); Truelove in *The Great St Trinians Train Robbery* (1966); the bishop in *Up the Chastity Belt* (1971).

R: WOMAN'S HOUR 'My Week' (he confides that he loves to go out for breakfast and have kippers, 1950; also 1960); DESERT ISLAND DISCS (1952); *Housewives Choice* (as disc jockey, September–October 1958 etc); *Woman's Hour* 'My Annual Fast' and 'The Day I Met Somerset MAUGHAM' (1960); *Frankly Speaking* (in which he says he gets letters from women although he does not consider himself 'particularly successful' with them, 1960); *That Reminds Me* (1964).

T: *Picture Page* (with his dog Mr Sponge, 1937); *As Others See Us* (a series where he suggests a solution for family, social and domestic problems, 1955–9); *This Is Your Life* 'Kenneth More' (1959 T); *Birthday Honours* (interviewing Cliff Richard, 1960); *Living Writers* (interviewing H. E. Bates, 1971); etc.

Winston Character played by Eamonn Walker in IN SICKNESS AND IN HEALTH (1985–7 T). Alf Garnett's worst nightmare: black, called Winston (last name: Churchill), gay (with a white lover) and, although he's the home help, he parries all the racist thrusts (but not the gay ones such as being nicknamed 'Marigold' and continually being sneered at). To Alf, Winston is an uppity coon whose rational arguments can always be staunched by calling him a 'big girl'. Nevertheless, a kind of wary trust grows between them after Else Garnett's death and Winston moves in as Alf's lodger. Winston never misses an opportunity to

ridicule the ageing Little Englander who still thinks the Empire is something more than a cinema in Leicester Square ('Yes, b'wana!' and 'I'm British with a *gorgeous* tan so eat your heart out').

Winterson, Jeanette (1959–) English novelist (*Writing on the Body*) and short story writer. In 1990 with the dramatization of her novel ORANGES ARE NOT THE ONLY FRUIT she became a literary star, the subject of articles in *Newsweek* ('Britain's most talked about feminist writer').

Her adoptive parents were strict Pentecostal evangelicals. She herself became a preacher at 12, and at 16 fell in love with someone at Bible study. When it was revealed, she was tied up for hours while members of the church tried to drive the demons of lust out of her. Feigning a complete cure, she eventually escaped. After driving an ice cream van and making up corpses in a funeral parlour, she went to Oxford.

R: *Static* (play, 1988); WOMAN'S HOUR 'O'Brien's First Christmas' (Christmas Eve short story, 1991); etc.

T: *Mavis on 4* 'Comparing Notes' (life as a lesbian 'now' compared to 'then', with Rosemary Manning, 1987); *Bookmark* 'The Bible' (1988); *The Late Clive James* (1990); OMNIBUS 'Signs of the City [London]' (1992); etc.

Winwood, Estelle [Estelle Goodwin] (1882–1984) English actress strongly reminiscent of Quentin CRISP on speed. Married four times, her best friend was Tallulah BANKHEAD, and she herself attained notoriety by being apparently the first person to wear lipstick off the stage. After a long career on the London and New York stage she became a familiar presence in Hollywood films of the 1950s: flaky, whimsical with a quavering voice and poached-egg eyes. At 96, playing Elsa Lanchester's 'nurse' in *Murder by Death* (1976), she was the oldest working film actress in the English-speaking world.

C: *The House of Trent* (1934); one of a trio of gossips in *Quality Street* (1937); a long gap then she materialized as a gabbling, off the planet fairy godmother (Mrs Toquet) in *The Glass Slipper* (1955); royalty in *The Swan* (1956); a barmaid in *23 Paces to Baker Street* (1956); spunky Mabel in *Alive and Kicking* (1958); Sheelah, Michael's (Sean Connery) mum with choppy Irish brogue in *Darby O'Gill and the Little People* (1959); a Salvation Army woman in *The Misfits* (1961); Mrs Dunhill in *The Notorious Landlady*; Ruth, a psychiatric patient in *The Cabinet of Doctor Caligari* (1962); a desiccated relative of Bette DAVIS in *Dead Ringer* (1964); Guinevere's lady-in-waiting in *Camelot* (1967); Miss Beattie in *Games* (1967); a woman with a violent passion for Zero Mostel in THE PRODUCERS (1967); etc.

T: appearances in *Alfred Hitchcock Presents* 'Bull in a China Shop' (1958) and 'There Was an Old Woman' (1958); Aunt Felicia, the hero's aunt who is being diddled out of money in *The Adventures of Seahawk* 'Bread upon the Waters' (1959); Laurette Bowen, the abandoned wife who shoots her 'younger' (by scores of years) husband in THE TWILIGHT ZONE 'Long Live Walter Jameson' (1960); *Thriller* 'Welcome Home' (1961, with Boris Karloff); headmistress Hester Partridge who is really a THRUSH operative in *The Man from UNCLE* 'The Her Master's Voice Affair' (1966); Winifred Glover, faded but still temperamental movie star accused of murdering her director in PERRY MASON 'The Case of the Final Fade-Out' (1966); Lady Bramwich in *The Girl from UNCLE* 'The Kooky Spook Affair' (1967); etc.

witches Cackling hags (*The Wizard of Oz*; *Snow White and the Seven Dwarves*; *Hansel and Gretel*; *Into the Woods*) or glamorous sorceresses (*Willow*; *Supergirl*; *Bewitched*) – these stereotypes seriously compromise reality of centuries of torture and killings of 'wise' women who were accused, interrogated, drowned or burnt in many European and Scandinavian countries as well as in America: *Witchcraft Through the Ages* (1922 C); *Day of Wrath* (1943 C); *The Crucible* aka

The Witches of Salem (1956 C; 1960 T; etc).

The full story of the destruction of women who may have practised 'the old religion' (but in many cases were simply arrested and tried on hearsay) has been told only recently. Before the women's movement, broadcasters like C. J. Pennethorne Hughes (West of England BBC Home Service 1948) referred to witches only in the present tense as 'a peasant custom' or as the activity 'of a few freaks and social irreconcilables'.

Recent programmes which have explored and explained the killing of 9 million women (and probably a large number of men) between 1350 and 1750 include *Burning Embers* 'Witches and Women' (1990 T: Juliet Mitchell, Penny Mitchell, Wilmette Brown and Suzanne Fageol make links between the witchcraft trials and the relationship of women with the Church and medicine, women's ordination, IVF, abortion and 'the fight for women to gain real power in the world'); *The Burning Times* (Can 1989 T: 'the largest mass killing of human beings by other human beings not caused by warfare'); *Witchcraft in the Channel Islands* (1989 R); WOMAN'S HOUR (1992 R: one report was of a woman and her two daughters being burnt alive – they should have been strangled first).

'They used to burn witches,' liberal policeman (John Barrie) to his puritanical, hard-line colleague (John Cairney) who believes queers deserve imprisonment (and probably worse) in VICTIM (1961 C).

Witches, Faggots, Dykes and Poofters (Aust 1980 V) Beginning with an expertly illustrated history of HOMOPHOBIA, this video from the One In Seven Collective opens out into Sydney's first STONEWALL celebration march (in June 1979) which is violently disrupted by the police with many arrests. There follows a rowdy meeting to organize a protest against the police action and interviews with some of those held in custody overnight at the notorious Darlinghurst Police Station. Also speaking out are

some of those fighting other related forms of oppression – child custody and expulsion from university.
P: Digby Duncan; 44 mins.

A first-rate exposition of the state of 'gay rights' in New South Wales (and virtually for the whole of AUSTRALIA) in the backward late 1970s. The march – which was so overreacted to – went on to become one of the city's most popular events: the SYDNEY GAY AND LESBIAN MARDI GRAS. Some of the big thoughts on changing the world expressed by some of the participants may take a while longer to come to pass.

Within These Walls (UK 1974–8 T)
Some stories of life and occasionally love within Stone Park Prison under Governors Googie Withers (1974), Katharine Blake (1975–7) and Sarah Lawson (1978).
W: Tony PARKER, David Butler, Tony Hoare and others; P: Kim Mills and others; D: Philip Casson and others; London Weekend; 60 mins.

A pseudocommunity (based on Holloway Women's Prison) which daily battles against painful realities of hopelessness, separation from family and friends, and all kinds of provocative behaviour from prisoners and warders. Highly charged emotional relationships abound between the inmates (sexually motivated only in the episodes 'For Life' 1975, 'The Animals Came in Two by Two' 1976, 'Transfer' 1976 and 'Mixer' 1978). On at least two occasions ('One Step Forward, Two Steps Back' 1974 and 'Deception' 1975) passionate feelings crackle between prisoners and officers.

Unlike its Australian cousin PRISONER aka PRISONER: CELL BLOCK H, this series changed most of its inmates from episode to episode, seriously hampering the creation of a realistic living environment. However, the setting provided ample opportunity for all kinds of dramatic behaviour, from the cheerfully gregarious to the spectacularly anti-social.

Less full-on and blowsy than *Prisoner*, *Within These Walls* at its best was thoughtful and subtle, graced by some intelligent and moving performances in individual stories by, among others, Caroline Mortimer (as a manipulative political activist in 'Transfer'), Christina Greatorex (as Thelma Baker, serving a sentence 'For Life'), and Paola Dionisotti (as bitter, violent lesbian Mitch in 'Mixer'). Governor Helen Forrester (Katharine Blake) had to confront the fact of lesbianism in her own cosy, well-appointed flat when her unhappy sister (Kathleen Byron) came to stay in 'Invasion of Privacy' (1976).

The series was not averse to sensationalism in matters lesbian as GAY NEWS (135, 1978) attested in a review of 'Mixer':

> The writing had all the sensitivity of *Knitting Pattern Weekly* ('I exchanged one prison for another,' decides the new governor Sarah Lawson as she recalls her broken marriage); and the acting (perplexed frowns, wounded nostril-flaring, perceptive eyebrow-raising and eyes rolling around like fried eggs on a greasy plate) complements it perfectly. And, just in case a whiff of reality should creep in, there is Dennis King's emetic theme music, the art department's pretty pastel *Homes and Gardens* sets and the tender ministrations of the hairdressing department, shellacking all the female prison officers into Mrs Thatcher-casual hairdos that threatened to knock over some of the ornaments, as well as other actors in their inexorable path.
>
> All this might have been diverting in a hellish kind of way if the producer and director hadn't seen fit to wallow in the photogenic violence and cheapen a potentially intelligent and gritty performance by Miss Dionisotti by the smeary 'Killing of Convict George' melodrama. Watching this was hard labour.

Without Us A duet by Johnny MATHIS and Deniece Williams over the opening credits of *Family Ties* (1988 T) proving that an out-of-the-closet singer is acceptable on prime-time American television – as long as he sings about the joys of family life with a female partner. The lyrics by Jeff Barry (to Tom Scott's music) drip fudge, and lesbian and gay viewers may feel the urge to retain the title but insert new words.

Wittgenstein, Ludwig (1889–1951) Austrian-born aeronautical engineer, soldier, schoolmaster, gardener, hospital porter, architect, recluse and Cambridge Professor of Philosophy. A thinker of baffling density, one of the most original of the 20th century. Like Descartes, Newton, Locke, Pascal, Spinoza, Kant, Leibnitz, Schopenhauer, Nietzsche and Kierkegaard, he did not marry or produce children and mostly lived alone.

His coded diaries of 1914–16 were deciphered and published in *L'Espresso* in 1986. They reveal suicidal depression and 'bestial' feelings. In a later period of his life (1928) he went looking in public places for sex with men. The 1989 television documentary *A Wonderful Life* stayed silent on the matter and its relationship to his dictum, variously cited as 'Whereof one cannot speak, thereof one must remain silent' and 'What we cannot talk about must be passed over in silence'.

Drama has allowed a more multifaceted view of the man who published only one work (*Tractatus Logico-philosophicus*) during his lifetime: Keith Barron was *A Thinking Man as Hero* (1973 T); David Suchet was the philosopher dying in Cambridge, his mind *On the Edge of Certainty* (1987 R), ablaze with philosophy and Carmen Miranda movies; Karl Johnson was a queer *Wittgenstein* in Derek JARMAN's minimalist portrait (1992 C).

wives (1) Displaying many degrees of acceptance, rejection, accommodation and suspicion: women who knowingly or unwittingly find themselves married to men who have been or are currently sexually attracted to other men, or wish to live as women or in women's clothes. Sometimes the female spouse is presented as a harpy, sometimes as a saint. Some hit out blindly, others appear to come to terms with the situation, although they may wonder if they haven't merely been used as fig-leaves of respectability.

The depiction of the 'homosexual's wife' in drama offers a whole landscape of disillusionment as well as of renewal. Not all of the wives take it as a mark of failure on their part. Some, having gradually abandoned romantic notions of love, may settle for something more relaxed and realistic.

Among those confronted with a gay or transvestite spouse: Queen Isabella (Catherine Salkeld 1947 R; Pamela Brown 1955 R; Freda Dowie 1959 R; Marjorie Westbury 1967 R; Diane Keen 1970 T; Tilda Swinton 1991 C) in EDWARD II, plotting the overthrow of the King and his male lover; Laura Farr (Sylvia Syms) who married Mel knowing everything about him in VICTIM (1961 C): 'I loved him then and in spite of everything I still love him'; the young American senator's fraught wife (Inga Swenson) in ADVISE AND CONSENT (1962 C: 'Who was that creature on the phone, and why was he saying those terrible things about you?'); Dot (Rita Tushingham), a peroxided virago riding pillion in THE LEATHER BOYS (1963 C: 'I thought he was safe ... I didn't realize he had zips up both sides of his trousers,' she says to Reggie about Pete); Tom Byatt's widow, preparing to give evidence against his killer and in the process revealing the dead man's sexuality in SOFTLY, SOFTLY 'Murder Reported' (1966 T); Lucy Fitton (Marjorie Rhodes) resigned to her husband Ezra's cantankerousness, knowing that it hides a deep insecurity: he insisted that his best friend accompany them on their honeymoon in THE FAMILY WAY (1966 C); Lenora Pendleton (Elizabeth Taylor) saddled with a repressed, stiff-backed husband (Marlon Brando) and stuck on an army post in REFLECTIONS IN A GOLDEN EYE (1967 C); Harriet (Barbara Leigh-Hunt) meeting her late husband's boyfriend in THE WAITING ROOM (1971 T); Matilde Verlaine (Jane Asher) coping with a moody husband (Ian Hogg), three children and his moody neurotic young lover in *Total Eclipse* (1973 T); Margaret Stephenson

(Sylvia Syms) spewing out her venom to her ambassador husband (Daniel O'Herlihy) after a few gins in *The Tamarind Seed* (1974 C: 'You pervert! ... your sordid little boyfriends, your Cambridge affairs ... I just hope to hell [our son] doesn't turn out to be bent!'; a young woman (Joanne Woodward) treated with callous indifference by her husband James Devereaux (Richard Derr) in *The Drowning Pool* (1975 C); Carolyn Cassady (Sissy Spacek) finding Neal (Nick Nolte) in bed with a man (and a woman) in *Heart Beat* (1979 C); Helena trying to play down the disappointment of the wedding night to Philip Castallack (Rupert Frazer) in PENMAR-RIC (1979 T: 'We've all the time in the world as long as we're patient with each other'; Beverly (Joanne Woodward) visiting her dying husband Brian (Christopher Plummer) and meeting his lover Mark in *The Shadow Box* (1980 T); Romola Pulasky (Leslie Browne) determined to have NIJINSKY (1980 C) at any cost – to her, to him and to DIAGHILEV; Diana Scarwid forced to watch the reverend (Powers Boothe) seduce her husband (Brad Dourif) in GUYANA TRA-GEDY: THE STORY OF JIM JONES (1980 T); the reunion of David with his old schoolfriend Chris (David MARCH) isolates wife from husband in *Death of an Echo* (1980 R); Ken Archer's (Mark Kingston) wife having an affair with her gay son's friend to the howling outrage of hubby in *Time of His Life* (1980 T); Vera (Victoria Fairbrother) is not unduly worried that her husband Gilberto (Gerald Murphy) is having sex with house guest Peter (David Yelland) in FACING THE SUN (1980 T: 'He's a child. He really believes I do not know. I've been through these situations before. Don't worry, I don't mean to belittle those feelings ... Now I know it will pass – I've seen you together'; Claire (Barbara Leigh-Hunt) reaches the end of her tether with her transvestite husband (Robert Gillespie) in MARY'S HUSBAND (1980 T: 'I married a man not a woman! ... I don't want my clothes examined, discussed and possibly even worn by somebody else – it's a

quirk of mine'); charitable and philosophical Emily Little (Avril Elgar) who loved her late husband wholeheartedly and was, therefore, better able to accept his occasional affairs with young men, usually his students, in *An Empty Glass* (1981 R); Claire Elliott (Kate Jackson) well able to deal with the craziness of network television production but momentarily going to pieces when her husband Zack (Michael Ontkean) tells her he's in love with a man as well as her in MAKING LOVE (1982 C); the young politician's wife (Caroline Smith) has to come to terms with her husband's bisexuality and his AIDS seropositivity in the same instant in ST ELSEWHERE (1983 T); Constance WILDE stands by her husband and gives him an allowance on condition that he never sees their two sons again (Yvonne Mitchell in *The Trials of Oscar Wilde* 1960 C; Phyllis Calvert in *Oscar Wilde* 1960 C; Emily Richard 1985 T); Poopy Travis (Charlotte Attenborough), the naive bride whose mate (Simon Shepherd) is catnip to two men in *May We Borrow Your Husband?* (1986 T); Anne Durham (Phoebe Nichols) propelled into an ideal marriage with Clive (Hugh Grant) – but is it? – in MAURICE (1987 C); Claudia Blaisdel (Pamela Bellwood) drawn to Steven CARRING-TON (Al Corley/Jack COLEMAN) by his outcast status, introspection, sensitivity and good looks in DYNASTY (1981–6 T); Sammy Jo (Heather Locklear) initially attracted to Steven by his future prospects ($$$) as heir apparent of the Carrington millions and his easily exploited vulnerability in *Dynasty* (1982–8 T); etc.

'She's got to be something of a saint to put up with me ... I'm an odd animal, I know damn well I am,' Terry Priestley (Fred Gaunt), a married Manchester solicitor who spends much of his spare time eyeing up young men in a drinking club in WEDNESDAY LOVE (1975 T).

Documentaries which focused on wives who discover their partners to be gay, bisexual or transvestite have included items on WOMAN'S HOUR (1963 R: 'Six years later, I go on loving him. He goes on being a homosexual. Life is one long pretence ... He is not a vicious man. He is just a man who can't stand women'); GAY LIFE (1980 T: Penny Edwards of the SIGMA support group); and Claire RAYNER's meeting with transvestites in *Crossing Over* (1979 R).

(2) Women who are lesbian or bisexual who knew or didn't know their orientation when they married: Amy North (Lauren Bacall), socialite patron of young women artists in *Young Man with a Horn* aka *Young Man of Music* (1950 C: 'You're a sick girl, Amy. You'd better see a doctor'); Susan Hayward as the game-hunting wife (based on Ernest Hemingway's Pauline) in *The Snows of Kilimanjaro* (1952 C) and in the same film Countess Liz (Hildegarde Knef) whom the hero unwisely weds; Florence in HUIS CLOS (aka *Vicious Circle* etc 1946 R; 1954 C; 1964 & 1985 T) seduced by her husband's cousin Ines, who alone dies in a bungled suicide pact, going straight to Hell and being haunted by visions of Florence continuing to lead her life; Jo Courtney (Barbara STANWYCK) despising her paraplegic husband and forcing her attentions on one of her 'girls' in *Walk on the Wild Side* (1962 C); Amy (Ann Lynn) reassuring orphan Luci (Linda Hayden) in the bath and in the bed in *Baby Love* (1969 C); Della Rogan (Rachel Roberts) and Lori (Dyan Cannon) having a fling that ends in one woman killing the other in *Doctors' Wives* (1970 C); Zee (Elizabeth Taylor) using a past schooldays' passion to compromise her husband's mistress Stella (Susannah YORK) and destroy the liaison in ZEE AND CO aka X, Y AND ZEE (1971 C); Dominique Sanda as the decadent Anna who seduces another married woman in THE CONFORMIST (1969 C); Celine (Bernadette Lafont) and Julia (Bulle Ogier) in *Les Stances A Sophie* (1979 C), their boredom leading to solidarity and later to love; diplomat's wife *Emmanuelle* (Sylvia Kristel 1974 C) having satisfying affair with archaeologist Bee (Marika Green); Melissa Hampton (Mona Kristensen) teaches the art of love to *Bilitis* (Patti D'Arbanville 1976 C) and gets carried away; Katharine Blake in *Wednesday's Child* (1970 T) in love with her nurse (Pru-

nella Ransome); Christine (Gay Singleton), confused about her attraction to another woman, goes for professional help in *Couples* (1976 T); the growing intimacy between Sally (Ann Curthoys) and Madge (Briony Hodge) during *Piano Lessons* (1976 T) leads Sally to question her marriage to a hypocritical man with whom she does not want children; Madame Dejoie (Genevieve Page) and Madame Volet (Zouzou) have a romantic lunch under the appraising eye of a man who misreads the situation in *Shades of Greene* 'Chagrin in Three Parts' (1976 T); basketball player's wife Melinda Dillon appeals to Paul Newman partly because he believes he can cure her in *Slap Shot* (1977 C); the unhappy wife of a businessman pairing up with another: Leona Galt (Patricia Smith) in *Executive Suite* (1976–7 T), Florence Carlin in an episode of *Paris* (1979 T) and, in a story in the first episode *Rafferty* series, Andrea Akers as a socialite who neglects her child (1977); Beth James (Dorothy White) living with a FEMINIST in CROWN COURT 'A Friend of the Family' (1979 T); Linda Ray Guettner (Gena Rowlands) fighting for the right to bring up her son in a lesbian household in A QUESTION OF LOVE (1978 T); Jennie Reilly (Sarah Badel) not prepared to go all the way in her break for freedom in *Swimming and Flying* (1980 R); ballroom dancing wives run off together after the last waltz in *Midnight at the Starlight* (1980 T); Steph Anderson (Gabrielle Lloyd) doesn't tell her husband that she's living with a woman when she goes to see him in prison in *Visitors for Anderson* (1980 T); LIANNA (Linda Griffiths), wife of a university lecturer, falls in love with her child psychology professor (1983 C); Livia (Grazyna Szapolowska) is shot in the neck by her jealous husband because of her affair with Eva in ANOTHER WAY (1982 C); August Strindberg can't bear his wife's close attachment to an actress and tries to kill his rival in THE ROAD FROM KYMMENDO BAY (1985 R); Samantha Hellier (Isobel Black) dangerously attracted to a lesbian feminist peacenik in *The Brief* (1984 T); two friends who are able to express their love in non-sexual terms (according to the daughter of one of them): Miou-Miou and Isabelle Huppert in ENTRE NOUS aka *Coup de Foudre* (1983 C); Ellen (Carol Royale) presenting her unfaithful husband with a surprise in *Oxbridge Blues* 'The Muse' (1984 T); the unseen and now dead REBECCA (1940 C; 1979 T); Alice (Sandy Ratcliff) tells her husband that she has met, fallen in love with and will now leave him for an American photographer, Portia in *Play Things* (1976 T); Jill (Meryl Streep) lives in close harmony with her son and lover in *Manhattan* (1978 C), but upsets her husband by publishing a no-holds-barred story of her married life; Yola (Michal Bat-Adam) married with a child, but besotted with a woman in *Moments* (1979 C); the husband of COL-ETTE (1985 T) asks his mistress to show his young wife (Clementine Amoreux) some other aspects of love-making: she leaves him soon after and forms a cheerful bond with a woman known as Missy; two women in their forties – Min (Ann Bell) and Julia (Rosemary Martin) – put their deepest feelings to the test when they share an isolated farmhouse in Devon in *A Pebble's Rattle* (1986 R); lonely empress Wan Jung (Joan Chen) is easy prey for a bisexual spy for the Japanese in *The Last Emperor* (1987 C); Celie (Whoopi Goldberg) given sensuality and confidence by her husband's mistress in THE COLOR PURPLE (1985 C); Capucine as Belle, the ex-wife of Stewart Granger melding into his weekend party with her girlfriend Anne (Judy Geeson) in *Murder She Wrote* 'Paint Me a Murder' (1986 T); the ex-wife in DEAR JOHN (1991 T) is slagged off by her ex-husband in the supermarket where she works with her lover – but, retaining her composure, wins on points; Maggie Barnes (Elizabeth Kemp) in L.A. LAW 'The Nut Before Christmas' (1991 T); Connie Wakefield (Mossie Smith) who left Luke for an Australian panel beater in *Mr Wakefield's Crusade* (1992 T).

'My friendship and love for Diana ... it's beautiful, it's warm, it's gentle and yet I shuddered with guilt ... Diana came along [after the baby arrived] and understood and demanded nothing and eventually I fell in love with her because I trusted her ... She opened up the other side of my sexuality,' Beth James (Dorothy White) in *Crown Court* 'A Friend of the Family'.

Wolfenden, Baron John (1906–85) English educationalist (at one time headmaster of Uppingham and Shrewsbury schools before becoming Vice-Chancellor of Reading University in 1950). Later Director of the British Museum. In 1954 he was appointed Chairman of what became known as the Wolfenden Committee (see next entry).

An occasional panellist on radio's ANY QUESTIONS? (1956, with Tom DRIBERG; 1966, with Lady Barnett, Lady Bonham Carter and Ralph Wightman; 1973, with Lord Soper and Jean Rook; etc), he spoke frequently and moderately on behalf of homosexual law reform on current affairs programmes and in public debates during the 1960s, but was critical of the use made of the freedom in the 1970s (*Profile* 1971 R; HOMOSEXUALITY – THE YEARS OF CHANGE 1977 R).

The Wolfenden Report (The Report of the Departmental Committee on Homosexual Offences and Prostitution) A British government publication, based on three years of research, submissions and widespread debate, which led to the only significant positive legislation for homosexuals in England and Wales in the 20th century, and the first radical break in the chain of prohibition from Henry VIII's edict in 1533. Its recommendations to decriminalize 'male homosexual acts' between 'CONSENTING ADULTS' within very strict limits were given prominence by television news programmes (including TONIGHT) and radio programmes like WOMAN'S HOUR immediately prior to or on the day of publication (3.9.57). The Report sold 5,000 copies within hours and went into a second printing the next day.

Wolff, Dr Charlotte (1904–86) German-born writer, psychiatrist, sexologist and psychologist (who correlated hand traits and personality). She escaped from Germany in the 1930s and lived the rest of her life in Britain. Her circle of friends and acquaintances included Aldous Huxley, Virginia WOOLF, Bernard Shaw, Osbert Sitwell, T. S. Eliot, Thomas Mann and surrealists André Breton, Antoine De Saint-Exupéry and Paul Eluard. Among her publications: her autobiography *On the Way to Myself* (1964); *Love Between Women* (1971); a biography of Magnus Hirschfeld (1986); an autobiographical lesbian novel *An Older Love* (1976).

She appeared on television in 1937 with Peter the chimpanzee (talking about the correlations and divergences between human and chimpanzee palm figurations) in a series called *Experiments in Science*. Although well respected within her field, she did not, as far as can be ascertained, appear before the cameras again until 1980, when Russell HARTY interviewed her about her second volume of autobiography *Hindsight* on *All About Books*.

Woman's Hour (UK 1946– R) One of BBC Radio's institutions which originally went out each weekday at 2pm on the Home Service, being first presented by a man. When this proved unacceptable ('pompous, patronizing and dull,' said one journalist), Joan Griffiths took over (in January 1947). By the early 1950s, there was an audience (now Light Programme) of over 30 million for this pioneer of consumer affairs and sexual candour. By 1988 this number was down to 3 million, 20 per cent of which was made up of men. Now with Jenni Murray as frequent presenter, and broadcast in the morning on Radio 4, the programme is relatively popular and influential, bringing forth ire for its 'feminist, left-wing bias' but across-the-board praise for its recent breast cancer campaign.

Introduced mainly from London, Bristol, Birmingham and Manchester, a typical week's topics will include sharply edited, intelligently angled items on subjects such as attitudes of families towards people with HIV/AIDS, redheads, persecution of witches, lesbian publishing, bridge and how to kiss effectively. Each hour-long programme always culminates in the reading of a short story or an episode from a novel, autobiography or travel book.

Gays and lesbians were regular contributors in the 1950s: Godfrey WINN ('My annual fast') and Nancy SPAIN ('on launching a crane') were especial favourites. (But, of course, nothing was said.) John WOLFENDEN was interviewed about homosexuals and the law in 1957, and homosexual men and their wives, along with (very positive) psychiatrists and doctors, made contributions in 1963 and 1965. In the 1970s there was a piece about young gays and, in the following decade, the situation of lesbians in Northern Ireland was featured.

In *The Woman's Hour Book* (1981) former producer Wyn Knowles claimed that the series 'has no desire to take risks'. This seems less true today: 'Dear Woman's Hour, I really must protest at the attitudes expressed in your programme. They are outspoken, dangerous and immoral' (quoted in programme publicity in *Radio Times* 18.11.87).

'I have given up hope of even the most platonic kiss. Occasionally he stays out all night,' wife on *Woman's Hour* 1963.

'I suggest that those homosexuals who have withstood this pressure and have opted to remain single rather than being a liability to a marriage partner are more worthy of our admiration than our contempt,' doctor on *Woman's Hour* 1965.

Women at Arms (UK 1979 T) A 4-part documentary from which interviews with lesbians in the British armed forces were removed during the late editing stages. Commented a producer: 'It wasn't appropriate ... We were making a documentary about women in the army and like every other subject, a lot of stuff had to be cut out.'
BBC1; 4 parts; 50 mins each.

women cohabiting Sometimes happily:

Tender Comrade (1943 C); *How to Marry a Millionaire* (1953 C); THE CHILDREN'S HOUR (1961 C); THE GOLDEN GIRLS (1985–92 T); *The Golden Palace* (1992– T); but mostly scratchily: *Stage Door* (1938 C); *Seven Brides for Seven Brothers* (1954 C); *Les Girls* (1957 C); *The Nun's Story* (1959 C); *Designing Women* (1986– T). Sometimes there's lesbian involvement: OLIVIA (1950 C); *The Beguiled* (1979 C); JUBILEE (1977 C). Sometimes not all the women *are* women: SOME LIKE IT HOT (1959 C); *Bosom Buddies* (1980–2 T).

women in comfortable shoes 'We can't even use the word "DYKE", you can't even say the word "LESBIAN". It's women in comfortable shoes.' So believes manic army disc jockey Adrian Cronauer (Robin Williams) in *Good Morning, Vietnam* (1987 C).

Women in Love (UK 1969 C) Two sisters, Gudrun (Glenda Jackson) and Ursula (Jennie Linden), involved in intense affairs with close friends Gerald (Oliver Reed) and Rupert (Alan BATES). Rupert believes in absolute sexual honesty – although this stops short of admitting lust for Gerald (it is, rather, blood brotherhood). Gudrun also becomes fascinated by a queer artist (Vladek Sheybal) at a ski resort, a liaison which proves too much for her husband who walks off into the snowy wastes.
W: Larry KRAMER from the novel by D. H. Lawrence; P: Larry Kramer; D: Ken Russell; 129 mins.

The director is given every encouragement by his source material to charge head-on into every kind of sensual situation, notably Gudrun dancing in a field of cows and the two men wrestling naked by firelight in a locked room. Larry KRAMER talked about the adaptation in ARENA 'Kramer versus Kramer' (1993 T) and the long-suppressed homoerotic introduction to the novel was excerpted in *Without Walls* 'Dark Horses' (1992 T). The wrestling bout was re-enacted, together with scenes from another, far less well-known, Law-

rence work which pulsates with a desire to rub manly flesh against manly flesh.

A 1980 radio version was recorded on location with Peter McEnery and Clive Francis as Rupert and Gerald, and Penelope Wilton and Sarah Badel as Gudrun and Ursula. George Pravda was a very sedate Loerke, played so spectacularly, unquenchably, mischievously gay in the film (D: Trevor Hill; BBC Radio 4; 6 parts).
See also THE RAINBOW.

Women Like Us (UK 1990 T) A number of older women talk about their lives: family, working and emotional–sexual. Included are Jackie FORSTER; Vick Robson, a wiry, independent spirit; Nina Miller, a former nurse grieving for her partner; Rachel Pinney, a doctor in her eighties and Sally Maxwell, her much younger lover; Diana Chapman, the co-founder (in 1965) of the support group for lesbians, Arena Three (also the title of a magazine).

Part of the OUT ON TUESDAY series, this is one from the heart, even more rich and illuminating when viewed with its companion piece, *Women Like That* (1991) in which nearly all the participants – including the most closeted – meet up, chat, laugh, stroll along a beach and dance.

The Women of Brewster Place (US 1989 T) The shifting social positions, tumultuous interactions and sexual intensities of a group of black ghetto women in the 1960s (Oprah WINFREY, Jackee, Olivia Cole, Robin Givens and Cicely Tyson, with Paula Kelly and Lonette McKee as lovers).
W: Karen Hall from the novel by Gloria Naylor; P: Oprah Winfrey; D: Donna Deitch; 192 mins.

A satisfying chronicle of the intertwined lives of seven women, the sassy lesbian couple arriving only in the second half (causing much perturbation among certain elements). All about closeness, respect, love, personal autonomy, breaking ties with men, the importance of tradition and community and fighting racism. The film, fluidly directed, throws up some meaty performances, good-looking production design, much interesting detail – and a terrible fate for one of the dykes.

Described in *Steven Scheuer's Movies on TV* as 'melodramatic male-bashing that provides many talented black actresses with juicy roles' and in *Leonard Maltin's Movie and Video Guide* as 'well-acted ensemble drama ... [with] a multi-dimensional script'.

(*Women* inspired a short-lived weekly television series called *Brewster Place* featuring a few of the original characters, but not the surviving lesbian, T.)

Women of Words 'Colette' (UK 1980 R) The story of the French novelist (Ursula Hanray) COLETTE: her love for her mother, her unhappy first marriage, her scandalous love affair with 'Missy', her happy second marriage to a much younger man ...
W/P: Roger Snowden; 8.2.80; BBC Radio 4; 30 mins.

'There just didn't seem any other way to do it – her lesbianism was an essential factor in her view of life' (the producer quoted in *Gay News*).

'Are you asleep? No, as I put my cheek against yours, I feel your eyelashes flutter as the wings of a captive fly. You are not asleep, you are spying upon my excitement' (Colette).

'The relationship with Missy was traced through to its ends with a regard for detail often lacking in the portrayal of gay couples. Missy's later history was traced to her suicide, alone and penniless in 1939. And the biographer's sympathy stayed with her' (*Gay News*).

women's bands Fictional ones in *Victory* (1919 & 1940 C); SOME LIKE IT HOT (1959 C); ROCK FOLLIES (1976–7 T); *Studio* (1983 T); *Beyond the Valley of the Dolls* (1970 C). Mention of the International Sweethearts of Rhythm in TINY AND RUBY – HELL DIVIN' WOMEN (1988 C/T); Rosemary Schonfeld and Jana Runnah of the lesbian-feminist Ova in *Inside London* (1984 R).

women's names for men *See* GIRLS' NAMES FOR BOYS.

The Women's Room (US 1980 T) A middle-class mother (Lee Remick) takes a deep breath and launches herself into a world of study, paid-employment and WOMEN'S LIBERATION. Among her friends are a lesbian couple, Iso (Tovah Feldshuh) and Kyla (Lisa Pelikan). Kyla quickly returns to her husband leaving Iso, a graduate student, even more negative, neurotic and miserable than before she came out. Comments the group's earth mother (Colleen Dewhurst): 'Pain is her payment. If it hurts enough she has permission to be a lesbian ... Strange is ordinary these days.'
W: Carol Sobieski from the novel by Marilyn French; P: Kip Gowans and Anna Kottle; D: Glenn Jordan; ABC; 140 mins.

The shiny surface and the breezy heroine are contrasted with the burdens put on womankind: captives of the home, prone to alcoholism, diminution of sexual attractiveness, threats of violence and rape. The solution appears to be: get a pretty young lover (male) and pay a lot of money for clothes and coiffeurs. The total effect is one of creeping inertia, probably because it's directed and photographed like a Mitzi Gaynor musical of the early 1950s without Mitzi and without any songs.

women's work Something apart, related to the hearth and home; domestic chores with which no man should get involved. Acting as gatekeepers: Jane (Brenda Joyce) ticking off her mate for sweeping up in *Tarzan and the Amazons* (1945 C); the wise mother (Anne Revere) in *Gentleman's Agreement* (1947 C) who nearly has heart failure when John Garfield offers to help her with the cooking ('Not while I'm conscious you won't!'); the proprietorial lady mice in Disney's *Cinderella* (1950 C) refuse to let the gay one loose with a needle and thread; Lucy Marlowe's cohabiting (but platonic) boyfriend (Dick York) in *My Sister Eileen* (1955 C) drawing the line at ironing ('That's women's work'); Jean Simmons as a New Zealand war widow in *Until They Sail* (1957 C) is adamant that the American captain (Charles Drake) will not get his hands on her tea towel: ('This is *my* job ... that's woman's work').

'There's men's work and women's work,' explodes Saul (Geoffrey BAYLDON) at his son Ted (Philip Martin) in SUMMER, AUTUMN, WINTER, SPRING (1961 T), 'That ain't men's work.' The 'that' in question is arranging some flowers. Retorts the lad: 'I arrange the shop window, don't I. *What's the difference?*' His dad has no answer.

A Wonderful Guy 'I'm not ashamed to reveal/The world-famous feeling I feel,' exults Mitzi Gaynor on the soundtrack of *South Pacific* (1958 C). The Rodgers and Hammerstein hit was captivatingly used for quite another kind of revelation, at 11.30pm on UK television, during the closing moments of ME! I'M AFRAID OF VIRGINIA WOOLF (1978 T). The mousy hero, Trevor Hopkins has just had his affectionate interest in one of his male students reciprocated (in the form of an agreement to meet 'for a drink'). This extraordinary event brings about a rush of blood to Trevor's head. The only way his ecstasy can be adequately communicated is for Trevor to borrow the voice of Nellie Forbush, the homely nurse who is wooed by a mysterious, sexy older man. This was gay love in borrowed but rainbow-coloured clothes. Suddenly, on a Saturday night, a gay character was asserting his right to be as 'corny as Kansas in August' and 'as normal as blueberry pie' and, with a blush, 'as trite and as gay as a daisy in May'. Said Alan BENNETT over the swirling orchestration: 'He was to look back on this as a happy day.' It was official: gay men were partakers of that 'world-famous feeling' and were not 'ashamed to reveal' it.

Wood, Edward D., Jr (1923–78) American writer and film director of GLEN OR GLENDA aka *I Changed My Sex* (1953, also acted, as Daniel Davis);

Bride of the Monster (1953); *Jail Bait* (1954); *Night of the Ghouls* (1960). His 1956 *Plan 9 from Outer Space* was voted 'The Worst Film of All Time' in a readers' poll conducted by the Medved brothers in the early 1980s. (Michael and Harry had already acclaimed him as 'The Worst Director of All Time'.) His own story was told in *The Incredibly Strange Picture Show* (1989 T).

Woodlawn, Holly (1947–) American personality, best known as an Andy WARHOL superstar (brilliantly mercurial and mucky in *Women in Revolt* and *Trash*) and now a survivor of those speedy times. She was most recently seen – reclining on cushions in soft focus – in *Tales of Rock 'n' Roll* (1993 T) hazily staggering down memory lane, recalling the days of the Factory and being immortalized by Lou Reed in 'WALK ON THE WILD SIDE'.

Woods, Aubrey (1928–) British actor of great facial and vocal angularity and singularity, perfect for reedy characters. Began playing pathetic or beguiled boys and young men (Smike in *Nicholas Nickleby* 1947 C; Roderick Usher in *The Fall of the House of Usher* 1949 T). More recently known for his radio adaptations of E. F. Benson's *Queen Lucia* (1984), *Lucia in London* (1985) and *Secret Lives* (1989). Among his original plays for the medium: *Spook and the General* (1988).

C: *The Queen of Spades* (1948); teacher in *Spare the Rod* (1961); *Just Like a Woman* (1966); Mr Bill in *Willie Wonka and the Chocolate Factory* (singing 'The Candy Man', 1970); *The Abominable Dr Phibes* (1971); *Zero Population Growth* (1971); *The Spy Who Loved Me* (1976); etc.

R: John Cromartie in *A Man in the Zoo* (1959); Philippe in *Murder in Montmartre* (1960); David Dane in *The Nose on My Face* (1966); Alan Wakefield in WAGGONERS' WALK (1970); Player King in *Hamlet* (1971); Cardinal Pirelli who goes to a ball in Rome dressed as SAPPHO in VALMOUTH (1975); *Story Time* 'Lucia's Progress' (1979); *Make Way for Lucia!* (documentary on E. F. Benson's novels, 1980); Jimmy Trotter, down-on-his-luck impresario in *Dithering Heights* (1985); Verne in *The Random Jottings of* HINGE AND BRACKET (1987); Meercraft in *The Devil Is an Ass* (1987).

T: Lieutenant the Hon. Wily Aughton in *The Sky Larks* (1958); photographer in *Portrait of a Man* (1960); the Lord Chamberlain in *The Princess and the Pea* (1961); Johnson in *Captain Brassbound's Conversion* (1962); *What the Public Wants* (pre-TW3 satire, 1962); *Clochemerle* (1973); *Witness for the Prosecution* (1982); *Auf Wiedersehen Pet* (1985); theatre director in *Star Quality* (1985); *I'll Take Manhattan* (1987); Squiffy in *T. Bag and the Pearls of Wisdom* (1990); etc.

the woods are full of them Originally a nondescript line spoken by Bill (Gary Merrill) in ALL ABOUT EVE (1950 C: 'The woods are full of one-scene wonders'), it was occasionally incorporated into Hercules GRYTPYPE-THYNNE'S slimy patter in THE GOON SHOW (1954–5 R), possibly as an ad lib from Peter SELLERS who was a great admirer of *Eve*. The 'them' in the woods varied each week, although the main implication was that these were the people your parents warned you about. (In 'The Hastings Flyer', G.-T. says that the woods are full of people who are 'MUSICAL'.)

Woodthorpe, Peter (1931–) English actor, highly effective as outsized bluff or aggressive characters but can also be superlatively pathetic, wheedling or creepy. Played Smeagol aka Gollum ('Nice hobbit … nice master') in the 1978 cartoon film of *The Lord of the Rings*, repeating the role on radio in *The Hobbit* (1980) and again in *The Lord of the Rings* (1981).

C: *Hysteria* (1964); the villainous hypnotist in *The Evil of Frankenstein* (1964); German flyer in *The Blue Max* (1966); soldier in *The Charge of the Light Brigade* (1968); scoutmaster in *The Mirror Crack'd* (1980); *Eleni* (1985); *A Christmas Carol* (1985); etc.

R: *Blind Tom* (1960); Estragon in WAITING FOR GODOT (1962); Scratcher in *A Man Talking to Seagulls* (1962); the judge in *The Balcony* (1964); Corporal Hill in *Chips with Everything* (1968); one of the Seven Deadly Sins in *The Tragical History of Doctor Faustus* (1970); psychiatric patient Tom in *The Night Nurse Slept in the Day Room* (1976); Tommy Fletcher in MR LUBY'S FEAR OF HEAVEN (1976); perennially hopeful musical comedy performer George Banks in *Me and the Girls* (1976); Stanley, Judy GARLAND'S biggest fan in OVER THE RAINBOW (1980); Greene in ORLANDO (1984); Louis Boom in WHAT A SAGA! (1986); chef in *The Man That Got Away* (1987); etc.

T: Valdes in *Dr Faustus* (BBC Schools 1960); Garth Britten in *The Big Eat* (1962); Alex Docherty in *Odds on Johnny* (1963); Quasimodo in *The Hunchback of Notre Dame* (1968); Samuel Johnson in *The Highland Jaunt* (1968); Max in *Inspector Morse* (1987–93); Count Pumpernickel in *T. Bag's Christmas Ding-Dong* (1990 T); etc.

woofters Lofty (Tom Watts) in EASTENDERS (1987 T) tells Wicksy (Nick Berry) that Michelle has given him a bouquet of flowers (via Interflora) as a kiss-and-make-up gift. Wicksy relays this to his dad Pete (Peter Dean) who responds as per Pavlov's dog 'I thought only woofters gave each other flowers.' Lofty stammers: 'Oh, Michelle likes to be different.' Fiona's ghastly 'hooray Henry' brother (Nigel) also uses it in reference to gay men in A HORSE CALLED GERTRUDE STEIN (1990 R).

(News reports in Australia in December 1992 described the practice of 'woofing'. A few members of the country's army had been putting vacuum cleaner attachments onto the ends of their mates' penises and then switching on the machine. A judge, when fining the men, called their conduct 'immature'.)

See also POOFTERS.

Woolf, Virginia (1882–1941) English novelist of pellucid prose and a rheumy eye for the shallows and eddies of upper-middle-class life. An occasional broadcaster: *Miniature Biographies* 'Beau BRUMMELL' (1929 R).

Adaptations of her novels include *The Waves* (read by Jill Bennett, 1957 R); *To the Lighthouse* (1983 T); ORLANDO (1984 R; 1992 C); *Mrs Dalloway* (with Maureen O'BRIEN, 1986); *Between the Acts* (1992 R).

Autobiography: *Something Sensational to Read on the Train* (the DIARIES of Cecil BEATON, Harold NICOLSON and Virginia discussed with Nigel Nicolson, Quentin Bell etc, 1970 R); *Mrs Woolf's Room* (with Anna MASSEY, 1983 T); *A Room of One's Own* (a television adaptation of Eileen Atkins' stage version of a 50-minute lecture given in 1928 by Virginia at Girton College, Cambridge, on the subject of liberty, literature and the role of women, 1990).

Biography: *Seven Days in March* (a portrait and a chronicle of the seven last days of her life, 1946); *Portrait of Virginia Woolf* (compiled and introduced by George Rylands with Margery Fry, David Garnett, Duncan Grant, John LEHMANN and Vita SACKVILLE-WEST, 1956 R); *Virginia Woolf and 'Orlando'* (a 1955 talk by Vita who said that the novel was 'inspired by her own strange concepts of myself, my family and Knole, my family home'; Virginia wrote in a letter to Vita: 'It's all about you and the lure of your mind – heart you have none'); *Virginia Woolf* (a portrait of the 'writer and personality' with Leonard Woolf, 1964 R); *Leonard Woolf: An Undeceived Intellectual* (1967 R); *Look Back* 'Remembering Virginia' (with Leonard Woolf, 1967 T); OMNIBUS 'A Night's Darkness, a Day's Sail' (1971 T); *A Child of the Sun* (about Katherine MANSFIELD with Elizabeth Bell as Virginia, 1979 R); *Dearest Mongoose* (Leonard and Virginia, 1980 R); narrator (played by Tessa Worsley) in *Nymphs and Shepherds Come Away* (about Lytton STRACHEY, 1985 R); *The Modern World: Ten Great Writers* (Virginia's *Mrs Dalloway* read by Eileen Atkins, 1988 T); the commander of the South East Asian army discusses Virginia Woolf with Francis Ford Coppola's wife during the filming of *Apocalypse Now* (recorded in the documentary *Hearts of Darkness* 1991 C/T).

'Seems pretty morbid to me,' Vernon (Bernard Archard) witheringly about Breeze's choice of *The Waves* as reading matter in COUNTRY MATTERS 'Breeze Anstey' (1972 T).

'If you had to choose between sleeping with Virginia Woolf and George Eliot which would you choose?' Rose (Frances Barber) to Sammy (Ayub Khan) in *Sammy and Rosie Get Laid* (1987 C); he opts for the former whose photograph adorns a wall in their flat.

(Edward Albee's WHO'S AFRAID OF VIRGINIA WOOLF? makes no direct mention of the writer or any of her works.)

Woolrich, Cornell (1903–68) American crime and mystery novelist who also wrote under the name William Irish. Best remembered for *Rear Window* (1954 C) where the hero's fears about marriage could be standing in for homosexual feelings common to his creator. Adaptations of his novels, novelettes and short stories: *Street of Chance* (from *The Black Curtain*, 1942 C); *The Leopard Man* (from 'Black Alibi', 1943 C); *Phantom Lady* (1944 C); *Suspense* 'The Black Curtain' (with Cary GRANT as a near psychotic, 1945 R); *Black Angel* (1946 C); *Deadline at Dawn* (1946 C); *The Guilty* (based on 'Two Men in a Furnished Room', 1947 C); *Fear in the Night* (1947 C); *Night Has A Thousand Eyes* (1948 C); *The Window* (1949 C: remade as *The Child Who Cried Murder* 1962 C); *No Man of Her Own* (from *I Married a Dead Man*, 1950 C; remade as *I Married a Shadow* 1982 C); *Rear Window* (1954 C); *Nightmare* (1956 C); *Alfred Hitchcock Presents* 'Four O'Clock' (1957 T); *Thriller* 'Papa Benjamin', 'Guillotine' and 'Late Date' (1960–1 T); *The Bride Wore Black* (1967 C); *Union City* (1979 C); etc.

Word Is Out (Stories of Some of Our Lives) (US 1977 C) Shared experience. The discovery of being different, passing for straight (Part 1 'The Early Years'); struggling towards definition (Part 2 'From Now On'); options for the

future (Part 3 'Growing Up'). The lives of Whitey, Rick, Pat, George, Nadine, Harry and John, Dennis, Sally, Betty, Cynthia, David, Pam and Rusty, Freddy, and Linda plus 10 other lesbians and gays (out of 200 interviewed) who all get six minutes' screen time each. A 78-year-old poetess; once-married lesbians with children; former army woman; two women who were introduced by their local Avon lady; an Asian American; a woman who had repeated sessions of aversion therapy; two pioneers of homosexual rights ...
P: Peter Adair; D: Mariposa Film Corporation (Peter Adair, Nancy Adair, Veronica Selver, Andrew Brown, Robert Epstein and Lucy Massie Phenix); 128 mins.

A landmark project. Talking heads but hardly a dull moment. Originally intended as a film of 20–30 minutes, called 'Who Are We?' designed to provide positive ROLE-MODELS for young people, it ballooned into a feature which took six years to research, shoot and assemble, on a budget of a quarter of a million dollars. Fifty hours of material had to be cut down to two and a bit.

Newsweek called it 'extraordinary ... informed by the spirit of gay liberation, it never stoops to sloganeering or sensationalism.'

Variety told its readers: 'Even filmgoers who imagine they'd rather sit through root-canal work than find out what it's like to be homosexual may find themselves unexpectedly captivated by the film's friendly, even-handed approach to a potentially diverse subject.'

Nicholas De Jongh in the *Guardian* (December 1977) was less enthusiastic: 'The camerawork is inept – perhaps intentionally so, as if in homage to early Warhol. Since faces are the film's *raison d'être* it seems not only perverse but silly to keep losing focus and allowing important lips to slip out of view ... The film's structure is also haphazard and, with some exceptions, poorly arranged ... The fact that the director Peter Adair has achieved a film so fundamentally flawed does not diminish the force of the insights and perspectives it provides, particularly from the older members of the cast.'

GAY NEWS (157) said simply: '... what is most remarkable about the film is the way in which it involves us with its people – all of whom are seen as proud and self-accepting.'

Words and Music (US 1948 C) The musical partnership of Richard Rodgers (Tom Drake) and Lorenz 'Larry' HART (Mickey Rooney) with some fanciful romantic detours.
W: Fred Finkelhoffe; P: Arthur Freed; D: Norman Taurog; 120 mins.

A big, overstuffed MGM biopic with Mickey Rooney acting up a storm as the lyricist who never quite seems to get the girl, loves his mom perhaps a bit too much and *drinks* ... He is cigar-chomping and hyper-active (while reading *Vanity Fair* he gets a sudden inspiration and scribbles 'Manhattan' on the back of the magazine). He lives, according to the film, in an all-female household composed of maid, sister and Mrs Hart (Jeanette Nolan). Her apple cake is second to none and there are many jolly musical get-togethers in the DOLL-filled living room. Desperate for love, he seeks counsel from a young woman, Peggy Lorgan McNeil (Betty Garrett): 'You're a woman so maybe you can tell me why there's something about me.' She can't – or rather isn't allowed to – put her finger on what that SOMETHING might be. Burning the candle at both ends, Larry obligingly dies to the pertinent strains of 'My Heart Stood Still' and 'With A Song In My Heart'. Somebody says of him, pityingly: 'The little guy who thought he was all alone.'

'Biog ... sticks to truth about as closely as can be presented on the screen ... The yarn is strikingly sound from a psychological view, catching Hart's zest for life and its gradual change to a tragic chase after a happiness he couldn't achieve – a chase that led to his death' (*Variety*, 8.12.48).

Words of One Syllable (Aust 1991 R) 'Frank (Max Phipps) is a dying man who is confronting the knowledge that his son Robert (Steven Vidler) is a homosexual who would rather live in another town with his lover than take over the family home after Frank's death and care for his mother Kath (Lynette Curran). This is a play which charts the dynamics of family life in all its tensions, love and humour' (synopsis in ABC Radio's *24 Hours*).

W: Richard Barrett from his stage play; P: Anny Wynter and Stephen Tilley; D: Robert Kingson; 8.10.91; 70 mins.

A highly praised stage piece which seems drained of its vital juices in this production. Honourable, dogged and undeniably true to life in its pauses, hesitations and evasions yet lacking in personality and rootedness.

The World About Us 'Ring of Bright Water. Gavin Maxwell 1914–1969' (UK 1979 T) A dramatized documentary about the naturalist (played by Nicholas Jones) who was internationally known for his book about otters, *Ring of Bright Water*. Here he is seen as a violent man who left his wife after a year of marriage. The feelings Maxwell had for his teenage boy assistants are completely unacknowledged in the script, an empty space which renders inexplicable the intensity of the rows between husband and wife.

W: Alan Cormack; P: David Cobham; BBC2; 9.9.79; 60 mins.

'How depressing it is that a programme produced in 1979 actually manages to be less honest than Maxwell's own far from open book written 20 years ago' (Alison HENNEGAN in *Gay News*).

World in Action 'The Death of Private Darkin' (UK 1982 T) 'Rookie kills himself over fear of bullies' read the front page report in the *Daily Mirror* in April 1980. Granada's long-running punchy tabloid-style documentary series belatedly followed up the story having discovered a horrifying tale of systematic brutality over a period of 18 months.

James Darkin, because of his sensitivity and emerging homosexual identity, had his body regularly scrubbed in the bath with a hard brush, his pubic hairs shaved off or pulled out, cigarette ends stubbed out on his flesh. He had been regularly urinated upon. He had unsuccessfully approached gay organizations for help. Even after his death, and the coroner's report which said he had suffered 'a living hell', the army refused to admit he had been subjected to BULLYING: it was 'teasing'.

The programme also looked at the experiences of Frank Cooper, a former soldier (branded on the back with a hot iron and beaten when he complained) and Malcolm McMichael who tried to commit suicide because of the harassment.

'... the army provides the rationale for anti-gay behaviour whilst at the same time providing no support for any young soldier who tries to accept his emerging gay identity. A chilling portrait of male tyranny and a shocking indictment of the British armed forces' (John Marshall, *Gay News* 234).

(Other relevant *World in Action* programmes include 'Coming Out in Newport Pagnell' 1975; 'Gay Pride' 1979; 'For the Benefit of Mr Parris' 1984: gay Tory MP living on unemployment benefit for a week in a suburb of Newcastle.)

World Service *See* BBC WORLD SERVICE.

Worlds of Sound A multi-media show presented in the Concert Hall at Broadcasting House in London 'celebrating 70 years of BBC radio 1922–92'. Among the events, individuals and productions represented, interspersed with the music of Bliss, BRITTEN, Coates, Walton and Elgar were the Blitz, D-Day, the Coronation, test matches, THE ARCHERS, Robert EDDISON, DESERT ISLAND DISCS, Tony Hancock, Frankie HOWERD, THE GOON SHOW, ROUND THE HORNE and MR LUBY'S FEAR OF HEAVEN.

Woronov, Mary (1946–) American actress, a cult star of horror, sci-fi, action, sexploitation and teen films. A supporting actress in more mainstream fare, she invests the most unrewarding of roles with violent intensity, a steely gaze, raspy voice and winning world-weariness. A regular interpreter of the kind of lesbian nobody would want to take home to meet mother.

C: *The Chelsea Girls* (1966); *Seizure* (1974); 'Calamity Jane' in *Death Race 2000* (1975); *Hollywood Boulevard* (1976); *Jackson County Jail* (1976); Miss Evelyn Togar, the beady principal in *Rock 'n' Roll High School* (1979); *Eating Raoul* (1982); diving instructor in *Black Widow* (1986); *Nomads* (1986); *Scenes from the Class Struggle in Beverly Hills* (1989); half of a murderous dyke duo in THE LIVING END (1992: 'I just love it when she gets jealous').

T: Maxine aka Max in CHARLIE'S ANGELS 'Angels in Chains' (1976); bartender in IN THE GLITTER PALACE (1977); etc.

John 'Jack' **Worthing** JP. Character in THE IMPORTANCE OF BEING EARNEST. A slightly confused BUNBURYIST whose birth is shrouded in mystery. In London a great deal to supposedly sort out the tangled affairs of his wayward brother Ernest (who bore a strong resemblance to Oscar WILDE when finally tracked down, portrayed by Jack Klaff, and accused of GROSS INDECENCY in the cloakroom of Victoria station in THE IMPORTANCE OF BEING FRANK 1990 R).

C: Michael REDGRAVE (1952).

R: Cyril Estcourt (1924); Harman Grisewood (1930); Hilton EDWARDS (1934); Ivan Samson (1935); William Fox (1947); John GIELGUD (1951, and on stage 1930, 1939, 1942 & 1947); Robert EDDISON (1958); Simon LACK in an excerpt in *English Talk for Asia* (1959); Peter Tuddenham (1971); Richard Pasco (1977); etc.

T: John Abbott (1937); John WYSE (1938); Hurd HATFIELD (1950); Michael Denison (1958); Ian Carmichael (1964); Michael Jayston (1974); Gary Bond (1986); Paul McGann (1988); etc.

Lord Henry **Wotton** Supercynical character in THE PICTURE OF DORIAN GRAY based on Lord Ronald Gower, sculptor and art critic, trustee of the National Portrait Gallery and MP for Sutherland. Lord Henry suited George SANDERS' air of inactivity and torpor to a tee in the 1945 film ('Marriage is a habit, a very bad habit' and 'I like the person rather than the principle and persons without principles even more'). Also played by Hugh Miler (1948 R); Anthony Jacobs (1956 R); Dennis PRICE (1957 T); Richard Todd (1970 C); John GIELGUD (1976 T); etc.

The Wound Dresser (UK 1986 R) Six years after *Leaves of Grass* (which he published himself), Walt WHITMAN was displaying extraordinary devotion to the soldier boys of both sides during the American civil war. Arriving in Washington in 1862 to look for his brother, the revolutionary poet spent 10 years as a volunteer visitor in the military hospitals, supporting himself as a government clerk. He nursed them, sat with them, held their hands, wrote letters for them, comforted them when they were dying. He continued his visits after the war until he had a stroke. He was disabled for 20 years until his death.

W: Barry Carman; P: John Knight; Narr: Brian Gear; BBC Radio 4; 12.4.84; 45 mins.

The man who was, 20 years later, revered as the nation's bard, is seen here tenderly overseeing gashed and broken boys and young men. All the horrors of a soldier's life without the euphoria: 'I see America already brought to hospital in their fair youth.' Denis QUILLEY's Whitman resonates with deep feeling blended with practicality and outrage in the face of the enveloping carnage. A rare situation: man as nurse/confessor/buddy. But there was no hint of the strong sexual motivation behind Whitman's obsessive devotion.

Christopher **Wren** Character in THREE BLIND MICE (1947 R). Agatha Christie gave instructions that Christopher, who claims to be an architect then admits 'I'm just a nothing', be played (by Allan MCCLELLAND) in 'a shrill rather PANSY voice'. His only pertinence to the plot, outside of being a murder suspect, is to puff out six or seven inconsequentially silly-sinister lines and make saucy remarks about the saturnine police inspector: 'He's very handsome, isn't he. I do so adore the police.'

There's no overt gay-baiting in the radio script (unlike the much longer stage presentation, *The Mousetrap*). The husband (Barry Morse) vents his dislike by grunting only that Wren is 'NEUROTIC'. Neurosis, in this context, is confined to being edgy (he's trapped in a snow-bound guest house), fancying policemen (just being law-abiding) and humming a nursery rhyme (but not WHISTLING because people like him can't).

The BBC censors removed or cleaned up a few of Mrs Christie's lines. These included: 'It's the QUEER way the Italian turned up' (changed to 'funny way') and 'I went a bit queer' (becoming 'I went a bit peculiar'). They retained Christopher's rudimentary CAMP patter (consisting of 'It's too thrilling' and 'MY DEARS!').

wrestling Rupert (Alan BATES) says to Gerald (Oliver Reed): 'You know I've got the feeling that if I don't watch myself I shall do something silly.' Replies Gerald: 'Why not do it?' This leads in Ken Russell and Larry KRAMER's version of WOMEN IN LOVE (1969 C) to the locking of the door, the taking off of all clothes and then into some Japanese-style wrestling: 'You come at me any way you want,' says Rupert, 'and I'll try to get out of it.' There follow neck holds, kicks, squeezes, flailing, grappling, throwing, rolling, arms twisted behind backs and spinning over accompanied by cries, gasps, bangs and slaps. Finally, panting and sweaty the friends lie together on the carpet staring up at the ceiling.

'Was it too much for you?' asks Gerald. 'No,' replies Rupert. 'One *ought* to struggle, wrestle and be physically close. It makes one sane ... We were meant to be spiritually close. We should be physically close ... the German knights swore oaths in blood. To swear to love each other, perfectly.'

But Gerald holds back: 'We'll wait until I understand it better. Shall we have a bath?'

Ken Russell related (in his autobiography *A British Picture*, in A BOOK AT BEDTIME 1992 R) that after the film was released he received many propositions, face to face or by letter: 'The men who wanted to wrestle nude with me were legion.'

This scene was recreated, without nudity and in a gym rather than a private house, by Steven CARRINGTON (Jack COLEMAN) and Bart Fallmont (Kevin Conroy) in a 1985 DYNASTY episode – the nearest the series came in eight years to same-sex sex. Other wrestling couples were to be found – on beds – in THE ROAD TO FREEDOM (1970 C), in TOGETHER ALONE (1991 C) and in another realization of Gerald and Rupert's bout in 'D. H. Lawrence: High Priest of Love' in *Without Walls* 'Dark Horses' (1992 T).

American poet and novelist Conrad Aiken (1889–1973) talked about his wrestling bout with a young man, his protégé, in a BBC Third Programme talk in 1967: 'We spoke the same language, so we celebrated right off – we in fact celebrated too well, and after a few drops taken we staged a series of wrestling matches. He was a very powerful fellow – extraordinary – and I somehow fell over backwards into the fireplace and fractured my skull. That was the beginning of a beautiful friendship.'

writers Christopher MARLOWE (Ian McShane) and his mate *Will Shakespeare* (Tim CURRY 1978 T); *The Bad Lord BYRON* (Dennis PRICE 1948 C); *Hans Christian Andersen* (Danny KAYE 1952 C), weaver of fairy tales; Arthur RIMBAUD (Joseph Blatchley) and Paul Verlaine (Ian Hogg) tearing each other apart and then falling into bed in *Total Eclipse* (1973 T); Oscar WILDE; SAKI alias Hector Munro (John RYE) creating an anarchic detective novel in the trenches in *Who Wrote 'Horseback Hall'?* (1985 R); Somerset MAUGHAM (David

MARCH) in WEEKEND WITH WILLIE (1981 R); Vita SACKVILLE-WEST in PORTRAIT OF A MARRIAGE (1990 T); Edith Somerville (Mary Wimbush) in *Only Goodnight* (1981 R); COLETTE (Clementine Amoreaux and Macha Meril) in *Colette* (1984 T); Noel COWARD (Daniel MASSEY) in STAR! (1968 C); Gertrude STEIN (Miriam MARGOLYES 1985 R; Jan Miner 1986 T) in GERTRUDE STEIN AND A COMPANION; etc.

In fiction, writing is one of the most oversubscribed queer professions: Charles Marsden in *Strange Interlude* (Ralph Morgan 1932 C; Noel Willman 1958 T; Edward Petherbridge 1986 T); the epicene friend of Nina (Diane Cilento/Glenda Jackson), a 'queer fellow', 'MOTHER'S BOY' and 'old SISSY', 'one of those poor devils who spends his life trying to decide which sex to belong to'; Beverley Carlton (Reginald Gardiner 1941 C; Michael WARD 1941 R; Philip Garston Jones 1960 R), Cowardian exquisite in *The Man Who Came to Dinner*; Don Birman (Ray Milland) drowning his sorrows and his (subtextual) sexual longings in *The Lost Weekend* (1945 C); Richard FULTON (Norman Chidgey/David MARCH) in MRS DALE'S DIARY/THE DALES (1950–67 R); the deceased Richard Shewin in A VERY GREAT MAN INDEED (1953 R); Ronald Simpson as the prissy author of 'My Lady Obleeges' in *The Memoirs of Mrs Cramp* (1956 R); Tom (John Kerr) returning as a successful novelist to his college and its bitter-sweet memories in TEA AND SYMPATHY (1956 C); Quentin Savory (Robert Sansom) in STAMBOUL TRAIN (1962 T); Claire Quilty (Peter SELLERS) playing cat and mouse with James Mason in *Lolita* (1962 C); Robin Fletcher (Nicol Williamson) who pretends to be a best-selling writer in HORROR OF DARKNESS (1965 T); crime novelist Emma Sands (Mary MORRIS) in *An Unofficial Rose* (1974/5 T); James Devereaux (Richard Derr) 'writes unproduced plays' in *The Drowning Pool* (1975 C); Alan Alanson (David Burke), macho Australian in *Rooms* 'Alan and Peter' (1975 T); Michael Otway (John Stride) in *A Photograph* (1977 T: a man

of letters, who gives talks on BBC Radio 3 and appears on television; his life is elegant, his tastes sophisticated; nothing can disturb his poise until one day ...); Yola (Michal Bat-Adam) in *Moments* (1978 C); Andrew Lyon (Douglas Werner) who meets Randy Brent in a Hollywood disco in *The Users* (1978 T) and settles in for a night of mutual using; Jill Davis (Meryl Streep), now living with a woman, savaging her ex-husband in print in *Manhattan* (1979 C); Lewis Duncan (Anton Rodgers) who wants to be known as a good novelist – 'not a good gay novelist' – in COMING OUT (1979 T); Harley David (Norman Eshley), a poseur with a pen in *Fat* (1980 T); Michael Spice as the writer in *Melancholy: Memoirs of a Man in Middle Age* (1980 R); Hugo Latymer, a mixture of Noel COWARD and Somerset MAUGHAM in *A Song at Twilight* (Paul Scofield 1982 T; Michael Denison 1988 R); Zack (Harry Hamlin) in MAKING LOVE (1982 C); Gerard (Jeroen Krabbe) in THE FOURTH MAN (1983 C) involved in a mystery far more fascinating than anything he could pen; Marjorie Dennis (Mary MORRIS) writing as Dennis Contra in *The Happiest Women* (1984 T); Rich (Robert Carradine) in *As Is* (1987 T); 'the Writer' (Mark Rolston) who is Tennessee WILLIAMS as a young man in VIEUX CARRÉ (1985 R); Tom Vermeer (Peter WHITMAN) given a second chance in *Slipping Away* (1984 R); Henry (John Woodvine) in *Eating Words* (1989 R); David Dunhill (Richard E. Grant), thorn in the establishment's side in HERE IS THE NEWS (1989 T: 'You're terribly held back. Some people think you're gay'; journalist Cal Porter (Richard Thomas) in *André's Mother* (1990 T); Catherine (Sharon Stone) weaving life into her successful fictions in *Basic Instinct* (1992 C); etc.

'I can't do the pseudo-political stuff that's rife now. When I did appeal, it was to the middle of the road people and you know what happens to people who stand in the middle of the road ... My suppressed sexual hysteria made [my plays] seem more *avant garde* than they were. Can I pick myself up is the big question.

Does anyone care?' Tom Vermeer (Peter WHITMAN) in *Slipping Away* (1984 R).

Phyllis (Bridget Turner) quizzes Clive Morris (Shaun Scott) in Alan Ayckbourn's *Season's Greetings* (1986 T):

'Are you a homosexual, for instance? A lot of them are, aren't they? If you were a homosexual, do you think it would make any difference to the way you write?'
'Well, I might hold my pen differently.'

See also POETS.

Wyngarde, Peter (19?–) South African-born actor, long resident in Britain. An incomparable player of dashing, juicy rakehells, men on the edge, pagan creatures. A star actor in the grand style, with the ability to lengthen his vowels and pierce with his eyes, never afraid to add touches of the absurd and the surreal. Remembered now not for his extraordinary range and charisma during the 1950s, but for his campy thriller-writer sleuth Jason KING in the early 1970s (*Department S*; *Jason King*).

C: *Alexander the Great* (1956); a Russian anarchist in *The Siege of Sidney Street* (1960); schoolteacher hero in *Night of the Eagle* aka *Burn, Witch, Burn!* (1961); Peter Quint in *The Innocents* (1961); a masked baddie in *Flash Gordon* (1980); etc.

R: ORLANDO in *As You Like It* (1955, with Claire Bloom); *Coriolanus* (1959); chief of police in *The Balcony* (1964); etc.

T: Wyndham Brandon in ROPE (1950); *Will Shakespeare* (1953); John the Baptist in *Jesus of Nazareth* (1956); Anthony Cavendish in *The Royal Family of Broadway* (1958); John Silver in *The Adventures of Ben Gunn* (1958); Sydney Carton in *A Tale of Two Cities* (1958); Jan Wicziewsky, a handsome and dangerous soldier in *South* (1959); Roger CASE-MENT in ON TRIAL (1960); Garry Essendine in *Present Laughter* (1964); as *Rupert of Hentzau* (1964); OBERON in *A Midsummer Night's Dream* (1964); Paul Panacek in *The Men in Room 17* 'First Steal Six Eggs' (1966); an ageing ringleted vampire movie star in LOVE STORY 'It's a Long Way to Transylvania' (1967); *Miss TV Europe* (1968: kissing the winner Sylvia Kristel); Sir Guy in *The Two Ronnies Christmas Special* 'The Ballad of Snivelling and Grude' (1984); *And the Wall Came Tumbling Down* (1985); etc.

Wyse, John (1904–) English actor, slim and towering (over 6 feet) who was usually cast in eccentric or sinister parts. For the stage in 1948 he directed one of the first post-war homosexual plays, Travers Otway's *The Hidden Years*. On television in the early 1950s he played Hamlet in *For Children*, wearing tights, toupee and ballet shirt. Interviewed in 1985 for David Marr's 1991 biography of Patrick WHITE, he related having sex with White in 1940, both men wearing identical silk pyjamas *under* the bed as bombs fell outside the London flat: 'It was very pleasant.' With Patrick White, he may have been the inspiration for Richard FULTON in MRS DALE'S DIARY. His former wife, Jonquil ANTONY, wrote the scripts.

R: the Dauphin in *Henry V* (1953); same role in *Saint Joan* (1956, with Mary MORRIS); the rector in *The Banana Song* (1958); etc.

T: supporting role in *Cyrano De Bergerac* (1937); Mercutio in *Romeo and Juliet* (1937); Rafi in *Hassan* (1937); John WORTHING in THE IMPORTANCE OF BEING EARNEST (1938); the judge in *The Black Cap* (1954); *The Fourpenny Box* (1956); a Spanish waiter in *They Met in a City* (1960); Sir Anthony Absolute in *The Rivals* (1962); etc.

Yentl (US 1983 C) A young Jewish girl living in Eastern Europe at the turn of the 20th century dresses as a boy in order to receive an education. She loves her fellow student (Mandy Patinkin), but he desires another (Amy Irving) whom she has to marry and bluff her way through the wedding night and quite a few nights thereafter.

Co-W/P/D: Barbra Streisand; 133 mins.

Much love and care went into this production and it's all there on the screen – and so is its star, Barbra STREISAND, who also produced, directed and co-wrote the script (from the short story by Isaac Bashevis Singer). It says a lot for her basic plausibility in all departments that the mystical and colourful intensity of the story is so winningly conveyed, despite the length of its running time. Some of the 12 soliloquies (by Alan and Marilyn Bergman and Michel Legrand) are very beautiful as are the two co-stars (neither of whom get to sing). For once a woman is following in the footsteps of Charlie Chaplin, Orson WELLES and Woody ALLEN. If you've got it, then flaunt it (and produce, write and direct it, too; and sing all the songs, why not). (The documentary *Yentl: A Film is Born* (1983 T) has a short sequence about the nerves felt by both Barbra Streisand and Amy Irving with regard to having to KISS one another.)

YMCA VILLAGE PEOPLE'S most popular song – and last American hit. A cheeky 1979 number (by Jacques Morali, Henri Belolo and Victor Willis) about the various uplifting activities to be found in certain of the Young Men's Christian Association hostels dotted around America's cities. The group's film CAN'T STOP THE MUSIC (1980 C) gave it the full Busby Berkeley treatment. The difference is that it's the male form divine being geometrically choreographed, rhapsodized over by the music and saluted by the camera.

This exhilarating DISCO classic (which stayed in the American dance charts for 40 weeks) was given a satirically alternative treatment in LONGTIME COMPANION (1990 C): an apparently highbrow chamber music trio turn the familiar bouncy melody and 'feel good' lyrics into a mournful dirge at a 'Living with AIDS' benefit night. In its more traditional form, it was played by the pro-gay 'but we've all got girlfriends' boys at a *Public School* (1980 T).

yoo-hoo! A gauche and often irritating way of gaining attention. The snobbish Mrs Rothwell (Thora Hird) discreetly hollars it out of the bedroom window to the returning honeymooners in *A Kind of Loving* (1962 C). Generally considered 'unmanly', Danny (Tony Curtis) nevertheless uses it occasionally to greet his friend Brett (Roger Moore) in *The Persuaders!* ('Nuisance Value' 1971 etc). But then Danny also cooks and wears tight funky threads, and his last name is Wilde.

York, Susannah [Susannah Fletcher] (1941–) British actress who did much excellent work on television upon leaving drama school: *Promenade* (1959: as pre-Swinging Sixties student); *The Crucible* (1959: as malicious Abigail); *The Richest Man in the World* (1960: as a sweet country girl of seeming guilelessness); *The Prince Regent* (1962: as Princess Charlotte); *The Importance of Being Earnest* (1964: as Cecily).

She rapidly graduated to international stardom in the cinema via THE GREENGAGE SUMMER aka *Loss of Innocence* (1961), *Tom Jones* (1963) and THE KILLING OF SISTER GEORGE (1968). In *Sister George* the role she played was the archetypal wide-eyed, dizzy, dependent femme lesbian, going over some of the same ground in ZEE AND CO aka *X, Y and Zee* (1971 C) *The Maids* (1974 C/T) and *Late Flowering Love* (1980 C/T).

After a series of increasingly flimsy roles in the 1970s (including playing Superman's mother) she returned to television with *We'll Meet Again* (1981: as an adulterous wife in wartime), *Star Quality* (1985: as a temperamental actress), *Devices and Desires* (1991: a murder suspect) and *Trainer* (1991: as Rachel Wade). She appeared in *Twenty*

Years On (1979 T) reminiscing with Hugh WHITEMORE about their drama-school days.

You Are There (US 1953–7 and 1971–2 T; UK 1958 T) Reporters in modern dress, led by Walter Cronkite, question participants in or witnesses of a famous historical event. The engrossing but short-lived British version featured 'The Murder of Gustavus III' 'The Trial of SOCRATES', 'The Death of General GORDON', 'The Fall of ROBESPIERRE', 'The Ordeal of Christabel Pankhurst' etc.
W: Robert Barr and others; P: Michael Mills; BBC; 40 mins.

You Bet Your Life (US 1947 & 1950–61) A precursor of *Sticky Moments*. Groucho Marx ad libbing disgracefully, and mocking unknown contestants and guest stars with equal callousness. The latter group included LIBERACE, Rodgers and Hammerstein, Phyllis Diller and a very young Candice Bergen.
P: John Guedel; NBC; 30 mins. (The British version *Groucho* was seen in the early 1960s).

you can always tell Colin (Michael CASHMAN) buys the upstairs flat from Tony Carpenter (Oscar James) in mid-1986. Tony takes an immediate liking to him: 'It's a feeling – man-to-man. You can always tell when someone is straight' (EASTENDERS T). The hero of IN THE GLITTER PALACE (1977 T) reckons he can always spot a lesbian. They stand out a mile. Or do they? His former girl-friend (Barbara Hershey) has some news for him. She's one, too. He gulps and stammers. 'See,' she says in quiet triumph, 'you can't always tell.'

You Can Fool All Of The People Plaintive ballad by Julian More written specially for the film version of *Expresso Bongo* (1959). The singer is a middle-aged American film-star (Yolande Don-lan) who has embarked upon an affair with a very young pop singer (a very young Cliff Richard). Looking in her mirror as he lies sunbathing on the terrace, she can no longer deceive her-self even though the glossy surface might dazzle her public. The song could also be said to fill in what the film leaves out: the closetry of the British pop industry of that period, with so many of its leading lights, artists and managers, preferring intimacy with their own sex yet relentlessly selling 'Boy meets Girl'.

you can't tell the men (boys) from the women (girls) these days A dogmatic blanket statement which began to be extensively voiced in the early 1960s when Beatle-fired unisex spread out beyond a small group of eccentrics, peaking with the Small Faces, Twiggy, the Rolling Stones, David BOWIE and Alice Cooper, then bubbling up in the 1980s with BOY GEORGE, Marilyn, k. d. lang and Phranc.
'You're a woman, aren't you ... You've got to be careful these days,' Neddy to Eccles in an episode of THE GOON SHOW (1955 R).
'The way young people look, you can't tell a boy from a girl,' Senator Long (Walter Matthau) in JFK (1991 C: scene set in 1966).
'Time's up, gentlemen – or is it ladies? Can't tell these days,' the brigadier (Anthony Sharp) upon encountering two hard-to-define birdwatchers in an episode of *To the Manor Born* (1981 T).

You Could Drive a Person Crazy Sung by Bobby's three girlfriends/one night stands in the documentary about the album recording of Stephen SOND-HEIM'S *Company* (1970 C/T). The trio question why their lover is so emotionally unresponsive. A light seems to dawn. Could he be a 'FAG'? Does that explain his wham-bang-thank-you-ma'am kind of loving?
The boo-boo-be-doop-style song was frizzed and curled up even further by Millicent Martin, Julia McKenzie and David Kernan (dressed as the Andrews Sisters) in *The John Curry Spectacular* (1976 T) and included the line 'That person is a fag'. But when Cleo Laine recorded the song she deleted this por-tion (1988 T).

you guys Quite commonly used for more than one man in the 1920s and

1930s. 'You guys watch me if you want,' says shady lawyer Peter (Victor Varconi) in *Safe in Hell* (1931 C). 'You guys think you're so *damn smart!*' says the rotter to his fellow pilots in *The Last Flight* (1931 C). 'What are you guys running, a school for PANSIES?' says Butch (Pat O'Brien) in *Bureau of Missing Persons* (1933 C). Although Bebe Daniels as Vi is heard to say 'Hello there, guys' in an ironic but very likely sisterly greeting to two lesbians (stylish and intimate in lounging pyjamas) in *Reaching for the Moon* (1931), 'guys' doesn't appear to have been used for 'normal' American women until the 1950s when teenager Wally in *Leave It to Beaver* refers to Mom and Dad as 'you guys' at the breakfast table ('Black Eye' 1958 T).

Thirty years later the expression is *de rigueur* on American television, regurgitated with somnambulistic efficiency. In *The New Leave It to Beaver* (1984 T) little Kelly (Kaleena Kiff) refers to a brother and sister bullying team thus and, in the very next scene, applies it to her two girlfriends. It was Alex's (Michael J. Fox) final line in the last episode of *Family Ties* ('Goodbye you guys' to his father, mother, brother and two sisters). Melissa (Melanie Mayron) dubs her female friends 'you guys' in THIRTY-SOMETHING 'Love and Sex' (1989 T). A little girl says it to an even littler girl and a dog in *Full House* 'The Volunteer' (1991 T). Cecillia Peck calls both grandparents (Lauren Bacall and Gregory Peck) 'you guys' in *The Portrait* (1993 T).

Other examples of this blanket masculinization occurred in HOOPERMAN (1987 T: 'You guys don't get along,' says the hero (John Ritter) to his lover about her and her mother); in a 1989 episode of ROSEANNE (T) the leading character, who is trying to get a moment's peace from her daughters, says to them: 'Why don't you guys get out?'; in *Chopper Chicks in Zombietown* (1989 C) heavy-duty lesbian Roxanne (Catherine Carlen) tells her women cohorts: 'You guys are all I got': in IN BED WITH MADONNA (1991 C) the star refers at various times to her father and stepmother, to her

female backing singers and to her male dancers as 'you guys'; in the HIV-test episode of THE GOLDEN GIRLS (1991 T) 'you guys' falls from the lips of Rose (Betty White) when addressing Dorothy and Blanche. In L.A. LAW 'The Nut Before Christmas' (1991 T) Corbin Bernsen calls his male and female colleagues plain, unadorned 'guys'. Within the first 10 minutes of Woody ALLEN'S *Husbands and Wives* (1992 C), the main male–female couples have called each other 'you guys' at least twice.

You Lied Fragment sung by (uncredited) black woman pianist in nightclub scene in *Pillow Talk* (1959 C). Rock HUDSON is putting the flim-flam on Doris DAY by pretending to be a harmless Texan. In this guise, he lulls her into a false sense of security by drawling on about his beloved mother and his favourite recipes. The singer aims the lyrics right between the wolf's eyes: 'You lied, you *rat*, and you'll be sorry'. Yet another example of the double-double twist involved in the Hudson screen persona: pretending to be a heterosexual who is pretending to be a homosexual.

you'll grow out of it A variation on 'It's just a PHASE'. Cheryl Crane told a questioner on the DONAHUE show in 1989 that when she was 13 she told her mother Lana Turner that she was in love with a girl. Mother didn't seem duly alarmed. 'She just said, "You'll grow out of it".' With a beaming smile, Cheryl added: 'But I never did'. 'It's a thing you grow out of, boy, and believe me, with me behind you you'll grow out of it.' Ed (Edward Woodward) tells the very wayward young man in ENTERTAINING MR SLOANE (1968 T).

you'll make someone a wonderful wife An opinion expressed by Jo SMITH (Rita Tushingham) with a mixture of admiration and castigation when Geoffrey (Murray MELVIN) proves to be a much better expectant mother than she does in A TASTE OF HONEY (1961 C).

When Robin (Richard O'Sullivan) tells

Jo (Sally Thomsett) that he plans one day to open a restaurant in the first episode of *Man About the House* 'Three's a Crowd' (1972 T), she simpers that he'll make someone a wonderful wife.

Abby (Cindy Shelly) sarcastically tells Leo (Edward Highmore) that he'll make a 'beautiful' wife in HOWARDS' WAY (1986 T) after he's exhibited his SEWING and COOKING capabilities (and communicated his non-traditional ideas on what a wife's role should be). They eventually married but later parted – Leo having changed from a caring environmentalist to a polluting yuppie wet bike salesman, bitterly fighting a custody battle over his young son (1990).

Glasgow's junior Al Capone, Johnny (Bill Paterson), mutters mirthlessly 'Someday I'll make someone a good wife, I don't think' as he resists marriage and family in *The Hardman* (1979 R). A few scenes later he has stabbed a man through the eye and carved up his girlfriend Carol's face.

Freddie (Roland CURRAM) tells Gerry (Buki Armstrong) that someday she'll make someone a wonderful wife in ELDORADO (1992 T), but she's not interested, only enquiring: 'Is this a proposal?'

you'll regret it in your old age Attempt to dissuade women from asserting too much independence: 'Mum keeps asking me about getting a proper job. Getting married. Or I'll regret it in my old age', says pop star Shelly Maze (Charlotte Cornwell) in *No Excuses* (1983 T).

Or living as lesbians. Some of the older participants in OUT 'Women Like That' (1991 T) said they had been told – sometimes by mothers – that they would regret their choice, but all of them were glad that they had disregarded this particular piece of advice.

You Make Me Feel (Mighty Real) Late 1970s disco hit composed by Sylvester (who also performed it), Tip Wirrick and Tim McKenna. Used on the soundtrack of THE TIMES OF HARVEY MILK (1984 C) and for well over a decade an American gay anthem.

you never see a black on *The Honeymooners* A rap song from the documentary about composer and arranger Quincy Jones *Listen Up* (1990 C). *The Honeymooners* was a legendary US comedy series starring Jackie Gleason (1951–6.) It is a salutary experience to look at the almost totally white personnel involved in both television comedy and television drama during the 1950s and most of the 1960s in America. A search for Afro-American and Asian characters in the 9-year PERRY MASON series yielded 6 Asians (in leading roles), 3 black men (as porters and shoeshines). (There were 6 crypto-gay and 2 crypto-lesbian characters, making 10 if you include Perry and Paul DRAKE.)

Young and Beautiful Elvis Presley (as Vince) unselfconsciously plays and sings the slow and tender Leiber and Stoller ballad ('It was taught to me by my uncle') to his cell-mate (and father-figure) in *Jailhouse Rock* (1957 C). His crooning earns him an enthusiastic if sleepy response from fellow prisoners. He next performs the song after his release in a swanky bar where customer indifference causes him to smash his guitar. 'Do you always bust guitars on talking customers?' the heroine asks him. 'I guess I *do* get a lot of wrist action into it', he modestly concedes.

Young and Gay (US 1950 T) A short-lived series based on the lives of real-life 'girlfriends' Cornelia Otis Skinner and Emily Kimbrough (played by Bethel Leslie and Mary Malone) whose stories had been told in the films, set in the 1920s, *Our Hearts Were Young and Gay* (1944) and *Our Hearts Were Growing Up* (1946).
P: Carol Irwin; D: David Rich; CBS; 30 mins.

young gay and lesbian people Gay and lesbian teenagers face loneliness and ostracism and guilt. They may also find themselves homeless and/or clinically depressed. Yet they live within the same political system, possess the same range of potential, house the same impulse systems, the same instincts, the same fears as their heterosexual counterparts.

Among the documentary programmes that have dealt with what used to be an invisible minority within a minority:

R: WOMAN'S HOUR 'Talking Point: Teenage Homosexuals' (1979: John Sketchley from Friend and Rose ROBERTSON from Parents' Enquiry discuss 'the problems' and how they and their parents cope with them; in the second programme three teenagers talked about being homosexual); *Talkabout* 'Gay Teenagers' (1980: 'Adrian Love talks to a group of gay teenagers and discovers the problems facing them in a society that, as they see it, casts them in a stereotyped mould and denies them the freedom to be themselves'); Claire RAYNER on 'Young Gays and Lesbians' (1991); *Call Nick Ross* 'Age of Consent' (1992).

T: THE LONDON WEEKEND SHOW 'Young Lesbians' (1977: the programme focused on the lives of Joanne, 21, a bus conductress, and Claire, 19, a student, and dealt mainly with the problems they had experienced in coming out; workmates and fellow students also gave their reactions to the revelation); *The London Weekend Show* 'Gay Teenagers' (1977: with Nigel Hart, Tom ROBINSON, Rose ROBERTSON, a Tory MP, a representative from the Gay Teenagers' Group, and a psychiatrist); *The London Weekend Show* 'Teenage Prostitutes' (1978); *The London Weekend Show* 'Special Report: Rent Boys' (1978); GAY LIFE 'Young Lesbians' (1980 T); *Something Else* (1980: 'Coventry'); SOMETHING ELSE (1982: 'Intimate Confessions'); INTRODUCTION TO SOCIOLOGY 'Life Histories: Male Gays: Steve' (1981); 16 UP 'Happy Loving Couples' (1982); *Twentieth Century Box* 'Teenage Sexual Attitudes' (1982: for a boy to be called 'QUEER' is 'the ultimate insult', for a girl, the fearsome words are 'lesbian' and 'FRIGID', but 'slag' is worse); CRYING OUT LOUD 'Teenage Gays' (1982); VERONICA 4 ROSE (1983); FRAMED YOUTH OR

REVENGE OF THE TEENAGE PERVERTS (1983, shown 1987); *Extra* (1988?); *Brass Tacks* 'Good as You?' (1988: the effects of Section 28 on young people); *Video Diaries* (1991); *100%* 'Teenage Suicide: Young Lesbians and Gay Men' (1992); *100%* 'Insight: I Am What I Am: Young Lesbians and Gay Men' (1992); *Attitude* 'Homophobia in Schools' (Aust 1993).

Among the fictional works:

C: Young gay men: A TASTE OF HONEY (1961); THE LEATHER BOYS (1963); THE TERENCE DAVIES TRILOGY (1976–83); THE CONSEQUENCE (1977); EVEN SOLOMON (1979); ONLY CONNECT (1979); FAME (1980); ANOTHER COUNTRY (1984); MAURICE (1987); THE FRUIT MACHINE (1988); YOUNG SOUL REBELS (1991); *The Crying Game* (1992). Young lesbians: MAEDCHEN IN UNIFORM (1931 & 1958); OLIVIA (1950); *Amelia Rose Towers* (1992).

R: Young gay men: LAND OF PROMISE (1976); STANDARD PROCEDURE (1979); OCTOBER SCARS THE SKIN (1989). Young lesbians: THE TINKER'S DAUGHTER (1986).

T: Young gay men: ROLL ON FOUR O'CLOCK (1970); *Penda's Fen* (1974); *Scum* (1978); TWO PEOPLE (1979); KIDS 'MICHAEL AND LIAM' (1979); ERNESTO (1979); ACCOUNTS (1983); FAME 'Best Buddies' (1984); LENT (1985); WELCOME HOME, BOBBY (1986); EASTENDERS (1986–91); BROOKSIDE (1986–90); *Forever Friends* (1987); TWO OF US (1988); EASTENDERS (1991: Joe Jason Rush); POISON (1991); *The Long Day Closes* (1992: Bud). Young lesbians: WHALE MUSIC (1983); ORANGES ARE NOT THE ONLY FRUIT (1990); *Nocturne* (1990).

'If people go around hiding in their closets only relating to other gay people in crowded pubs and clubs we're only repressing ourselves and believing what society tells us: we're sick, we're absurd and we oughtn't to exist openly just in case we offend or shock society,' one of the speakers in *Crying Out Loud* 'Teenage Gays' (1982 T).

Young Soul Rebels (UK 1991 C)

Childhood friends Chas (Valentine Nonyela) and gay Caz (Mo Sesay), who operate a private radio station, stumble on evidence relating to a gay man's murder in the Queen's Jubilee summer of 1977.

W: Isaac JULIEN, Paul Hallam and Derek Saldaan McClintock; P: Nadine Marsh-Edwards: D: Isaac Julien; 103 mins.

Miniaturist Isaac Julien runs the gauntlet of punk, funk, skinheads, a murder, a heterosexual romance and a full-length narrative. The main interest lies in its recreation of the tensions between PUNKS and SKINHEADS, gay and straight, black and white, black and not so black. The main characters are outsiders in both white and black society, one having a white mother, the other being gay. In this film the detail is more interesting than the character, the few jokes are milked for all they're worth, and the gay MURDERER seems to have stepped out of another, lesser film.

your actual Brought to the mass public's attention simultaneously by Peter Cook in *Not Only ... But Also* (1965 T), Alf Garnett in TILL DEATH US DO PART (1965 T) and JULIAN AND SANDY, in ROUND THE HORNE (1966 R): 'Nouvelle Vague. That's your actual French, that is.'

You're a brick Upper-crust English expression of deep approval, eternal support and possibly even abiding love and affection. Bunny (Michael COCHRANE) is always having cause to say it to *Raffles* (Jeremy Clyde 1987–92 R). Phil (Norman Painting) bestows this accolade on a girl called Marjorie in a 1956 episode of THE ARCHERS (R), while Mary Dixon (Jeanette Hutchinson) commends Grace MILLARD (Moira MANNION) in this fashion in DIXON OF DOCK GREEN 'The Magic Eye' (1959 T: Grace has taken over the running of the house while Mary is having a baby).

But 'bricks' are most regularly found in boys' and girls' public schools, as when Anthony Moore (Benedict Taylor) vents his reined-in feelings to his idol Philip

(Ronald Pickup) in *A Man Alone* (1986 R): 'You've been a brick these last weeks, I don't know what I'd have done without you. You can love a fellow, you know, without it being sinister.'

You're A Queer One, Julie Jordan Sung by two mill girls, Julie (Shirley Jones) and Carrie (Barbara Ruick), at the beginning of Rodgers and Hammerstein's *Carousel* (1956 C). Carrie upbraids her friend for being so self-contained: 'You're quieter and deeper than a well. And you never tell me nothin'.' 'That's because,' interjects Julie peevishly, 'there's nothin' that I care to choose to tell.'

On the Capitol soundtrack recording this little interchange segues into '(When I Marry) Mr Snow', a hymn to marriage and fertility by Carrie. However, the print of *Carousel* now in circulation to television stations goes clumsily from the end of one scene into the beginning of 'Mr Snow'. Into a black hole has gone 'Julie Jordan', possibly on account of her being 'queer' or possibly because of one line which makes it clear that the girls sleep together; definitely in the same room – and given the conditions of the time – probably in the same bed.

The song, short but integral to the understanding of Julie's contrary nature, first went missing when the film was reissued in the late 1950s. As shown, Gordon MacRae bids a temporary farewell in daylight to Julie and Carrie. In the next moment, it's dusk and the closing bars of 'Julie Jordan' are just discernible before Carrie says that now Julie has a man of her own *she* can sing of her Mr Snow – which she proceeds to do. All the complexity has gone from Julie's character with the elimination of the little duet.

you're never alone with a Strand One of the most memorable slogans from a British television advert. Appearing in March 1960, it featured a boyish, under-nourished man (Terence Brook) in a white Cecil Gee overcoat and pull-down trilby photographed at night, alone in Sinatra mode outside Australia House (in the Strand, London) with suitably plaintive background music (by Cliff Adams).

The commercial – and its 'Lonely Man Theme' – attracted immense publicity and interest. Other similarly smouldering vignettes followed over the next 18 months. These were shot in Blooms-bury, on the seafront in Brighton, inside a Baker Street coffee bar and – most memorably – on the Thames embank-ment. While the lonely man became a household favourite, the product he was selling – Strand cigarettes from W. H. and D. O. Wills – failed to catch on with the smoking public and eventually ceased manufacture in 1961.

It remains a mystery why such a potent image was not matched in product sales terms. Was it because the cigarettes were no good? Or because loneliness is a frightening prospect for most viewers? Or because the man was minus the usual commercial accoutrement – the dazzling young woman? Was he a lonely man or a man alone cruising London's darkened streets until his eyes met those of an interested party?

You're Not Watching Me, Mummy (UK 1980 T) Into the dressing room of a selfish, shallow West End actress, Jemima (Anna MASSEY), crowd a group of hangers-on. They include her dresser Leslie (Peter SALLIS), an alternative American playwright Stanley Klob (Ronald Whelan), a vitriolic critic Fred-die (John Gill), a lesbian-feminist Lena (Suzanne Bertish), an ambitious would-be actress Shirley (Karen Mayo-Chandler), and a gigolo René (Douglas Heard).

W: John OSBORNE; D: James Ormerod; 20.1.80; Yorkshire; 50 mins.

Almost all the characters are gay, les-bian, bisexual, eunuchoid or ready to sleep with anything for the right price or 'lucky' break. Spider woman Jemima is heterosexual, but 'cold-hearted, mean-spirited with her queer minions and various EUNUCHS because she's incapable of anything real or difficult or not self-promoting'.

Master of Ceremonies is managing, gossiping Leslie, existing only in the golden glow of the successful. Lurking in the shadows is poor Lena, desperate for the slightest token of affection from the actress who speaks her words. Says the unimpressed Leslie: 'She's in your bleeding dressing room nearly every night ... She doesn't go much on men ... But then so many women don't now-adays.' Reinforcing the ALL ABOUT EVE ambience is the pink-cheeked new-comer who, looking coyly inviting at Lena, purrs: 'I'll do anything, absolutely anything, to get a start.'

This is slimepit comedy: an Osborne psychodrama concerned with the depredations on normal folk inflicted by women, gays (who would like to be women) and lesbians (women who like women). Fruitily acted by all, savagely written and disgustingly enjoyable.

You're the Top: The Cole Porter Story (USA 1991 T) Reminiscences of those whose lives he influenced.
PBS; 60 mins.

A 'tribute' that presents the talent, but jettisons the inner core. A string of cel-ebrated people (including a mute Cyd Charisse and an almost so Hermes PAN) are wheeled on and off, making it a gala occasion. None of the songs are placed within the context of his inner life or deep feelings. It's all top soil.

'*You're the Top* was singled out by *TV Guide* for its "sheer frankness". In other words, the word "homosexuality" was actually used, once – in one of two refer-ences to Porter's gayness; the other was the "golden boys" lying around his Hollywood pool ... Narrated by Bobby Short and featuring Michael Feinstein, Saint Subber etc, the programme was steeped in references to the Marriage and the Wife. "The Cole Porter we never knew" gushed one reviewer. And still don't' (Boze Hadleigh, *The Vinyl Closet: Gays in the Music World*, 1991).

your wheelchair or mine? A slant on the more usual sexual invitation 'Your place or mine?' marking the first mutual gay assignation between men with disabilities: Tim (Nabil Shaban) and Peter (Mark Beer) in OUT 'Double the Trouble' (1992 T).

you silly, twisted boy, you The half-seductive, half-threatening GRYTPYPE-THYNNE'S regular exclamation to Neddy Seagoon inveigled into yet another of G.-T. and Moriarty's 'get rich/rule the world'-quick schemes: 'You silly, twisted boy, you' in THE GOON SHOW 'Lurgi Strikes Britain' (1954 R) and 'Yehti' (1955 R).

you spend more time with him than you do with me! A man's love for his mate can sometimes come between him and a woman, be it the affection between college buddies (Jack Nicholson and Art Garfunkel) in *Carnal Knowledge* 1971 C); comrades in arms ('You'd rather be with him than me,' says Joan Fontaine to Douglas Fairbanks Jr about Victor McLaglen in *Gunga Din* 1939 C); overgrown babies ('She says I care more about you than her,' Oliver Hardy indirectly quotes his wife to Stan Laurel in THEIR FIRST MISTAKE (1933 C); or just *Mates* (Peter Denyer and Nicholas Clay 1978 T). Variations or extensions on the theme are 'Why don't you go to bed with him?' and 'You're always kissing his ass.'
A man's love for his gun can also become a barrier to affection. The cop Eddie Egan (Robert Duvall) in *Badge 373* (1973 C) is rowing with his girlfriend. Laying down the oars, he takes out his pistol. She erupts: 'You spend more time playing with your gun than you do with me.'

You the Jury 'Discrimination on the Grounds of Homosexuality Should Be Made Illegal' (UK 1981 R) Chaired by Peter Jay, Lord Beaumont of Whitley spoke for the motion with evidence from activists Barry Protheroe and Susan Shell. Speaking against was Michael Simmons, supported by journalist Gillian Tindall and David Asrat of the CRO.
P: Maggie Redfern; 18.12.81; BBC Radio 4; 25 mins.
Lord Beaumont tried in vain to persuade 'the jury' that 'It's not a gay lib case, it's a human lib case'. The motion was defeated 51 per cent to 33 per cent (pre-debate it had been 35 per cent in support and 26 per cent opposed, with 39 per cent of the studio audience abstaining). It had been said that the great majority of those who abstained appeared to have swung against the motion, believing that anti-discrimination laws would be 'counter-productive and ineffectual'. Said Michael Simmons: 'Let the gay community spend time and energy educating us'.

yuppies Young upwardly mobile people, very much a feature of the 1980s. Lesbian ones were featured in one of the OUT segments (1990 T). Males included Robert (John Bolger) in PARTING GLANCES (1985 C) and Colin RUSSELL (Michael CASHMAN) with his computer, his classical music, his dinner parties and his inseparable Filofax in EASTENDERS (1986–9 T). Colin is redeemed though by his leadership of a playgroup, his editing of the Neighbourhood Watch newsletter and his all-round humility.

Zanuck, Darryl F. (1902–79) American movie mogul: head of 20th Century Fox and producer of some of Hollywood's more 'adult' films (*The Grapes of Wrath* 1940; *Gentleman's Agreement* 1947; ALL ABOUT EVE 1950; *Viva Zapata* 1952; *The Longest Day* 1962).

Margo Channing (Bette DAVIS), during an argument with her playwright lover Bill (Gary Merrill), vents her spleen over the latter spending so much time away in Hollywood working on a project for Darryl F.: 'Zanuck, Zanuck, Zanuck! What are you two – *lovers?*' 'Only in some ways' comes the unfazed reply.

This is a unique example of a celebrated figure of the American cinema being linked with homosexuality, even in so mild and unproven a way. Zanuck himself was a capaciously PROMISCUOUS heterosexual man who enjoyed the company of the unashamedly gay Clifton WEBB, mainly because of the latter's witty chat and good taste.

Z Cars (UK 1962–78 T) The influential drama series set in Liverpool which portrayed policemen as less than saintly. Three years into the run, one of the regular writers, John HOPKINS, introduced the BLACKMAIL of a gay man into the plot of 'Somebody ... Help' (P: David E. Rose; D: Robin Midgley; 3.6.64; BBC1; 50 mins). The episode seems not to exist in any form, even being missing from the microfilmed scripts of the entire *Z Cars* output. This is how it was introduced in *Radio Times*:

A man attempts to blackmail Frank Wood. Wood has only to go to the police to tell them, and they will make every possible effort to catch the man. Given normal circumstances, Wood's course of action is plain but Wood is a homosexual, a man outside the law and unable to go to the police without incriminating himself. If he reveals the attempt to blackmail him he will also reveal why he is being blackmailed. Then he faces trial, prison, probation anyway, the certainty of local scandal, even the end of his business career. The man who preys on anyone like Wood can count on his reluctance to go to the police, in 9 cases out of 10, and 'screw' money out of him until there is no money left and then

pass on to the next victim. In 9 cases out of 10 he can practise safely and secretly until the tenth man stands up and says no.

In 1974 there was a story entitled *Friends* (W: Allan Prior; P: Roderick Graham; D: Fiona Cumming; 14.10.74; BBC1; 30 mins) which involved a young car thief, Jesse Alty (John Duttine) who is also a good centre forward. He and one of the police officers, Quilley, play for the same team – and are trained by the same man, Gordon Glossop (George Baker). Gordon is 40-plus and single, living on milk and fish fingers, his room a shrine to football – with a picture of Jesse on the wall. A figure of fun, whose only official function at the club is to gather up the sponges. He takes a suffocating interest in Jesse, who rebels but depends on the older man. Deadlock is reached because Gordon cannot withdraw the deep feelings and Jesse is unable to respond (to Gordon anyway), and the story ends with the younger man being killed, with Gordon – in Lover's Lane.

Zee and Co aka *X, Y and Zee* (UK 1971 C) A wife, Zee (Elizabeth Taylor) moves in the heavy emotional artillery to rescue her man Robert (Michael Caine) from the clutches of a milk-and-water rival, Stella (Susannah YORK). She is helped by a flighty gay friend (John Standing) and by Stella's long-dormant lesbian tendencies.
W: Edna O'Brien; P: Elliot Kastner, Alan Ladd Jr and Hal Kanter; 109 mins.

A loud and raucous star vehicle with all the familiar early 1970s trappings: party scenes, copious drinking, a lesbian encounter, a shrill queen, suicide attempts and wave after wave of four letter words. There's a glimpse of Michael CASHMAN as a boutique assistant called Gavin.

Zeffirelli, Franco (1922–) Italian theatre, opera and film director who had spectacular early success. His eye for detail, talent for daring innovation and thirst for passion have been best exemplified on screen in his Shakespearean adaptations (including *Hamlet* with Mel

Gibson), his sweeping opera films (*La Traviata*; *Otello*), and the made-for-television *Jesus of Nazareth*. A future project is the screen biography of Rudolf NUREYEV.

Autobiography: *Tempo* 'A Wind of Change' (1964 T: The art of *Zeffirelli*, staging *Hamlet*); *The Movies* 'Shakespeare on Film' (1967 T); *Our World* (1967 T: appearing on the first live worldwide broadcast 1967 T); *Film Night* (1970 T); *Man of Action* (1976 T); DESERT ISLAND DISCS (1982 R); OMNIBUS 'Franco Zeffirelli' (1983 T); *Zeffirelli* (1987 R); *The Making of 'Hamlet'* (1991 T); etc.

He has not so far talked with great candour about his personal life on radio or television; however, he did come out in an interview with the *Advocate* (9.6.83): 'I'm gay ... it happens that people who have to go through this particular sexual syndrome are forced to refine certain receptive instruments in the mind and soul: they become much more sensitive, more ready to talk and to deal with things of the spirit. They suffer more than the normal person. I think it is not easy to be gay. I know this. You have to go through a very, very anguishing time.'

Zip A ladylike and very intellectual striptease number by Rodgers and Hart, sending up Gypsy Rose Lee in their 1940 Broadway show *Pal Joey*. Performed by Rita Hayworth (dubbed by Jo Ann Greer) in the very belated (1957) film version, the line 'Zip, I'm a heterosexual' was cut for the screen. Retained from the original, however, was the dropping of the name of Arthur Schopenhauer, the misanthropic German philosopher who showed that homosexuality is part of nature across all periods of history and all peoples.

Zorro The cloaked and masked avenger of Old California who, in reality, is the studiedly foppish Don Diego De Vega. The character began in a strip cartoon in 1919 and was then made flesh and blood by Douglas Fairbanks in 1920 and 1925. Tyrone Power (1940 C) and Guy Williams (1957–8 T) also had fun with the double-sided nature of the role. George Hamilton went a step further in ZORRO – THE GAY BLADE.

Zorro – The Gay Blade (US 1981 C) Bunny Wigglesworth (né Ramon Vega) steps daintily into the breach when his twin brother is temporarily indisposed and cannot engage in the righting of wrongs.
W: Hal Dresner; P: George Hamilton and C. O. Erickson; D: Peter Medak; 93 mins.

Muted slapstick and farce with George Hamilton flashing his teeth, acting a little strange, getting into drag and harbouring the most strangulated Spanish–English accent since Manuel's in *Fawlty Towers*.